NASB

NEW AMERICAN STANDARD BIBLE

NASB 2020 Outreach Bible
Published in 2021 by The Lockman Foundation
La Habra, California, 90631

New American Standard Bible, NASB
Copyright © 1960, 1962, 1963, 1968, 1971, 1972, 1973, 1975, 1977, 1995, 2020
by The Lockman Foundation
A Corporation Not for Profit
La Habra, CA. All Rights Reserved.
www.lockman.org

The "NASB," "NAS," "New American Standard Bible," and "New American Standard," and the
Eightpoint Logo, are registered trademarks of The United States Patent and Trademark Office
by The Lockman Foundation. Use of these trademarks requires the permission of The
Lockman Foundation.

For information concerning the use of the NASB, please visit
www.lockman.org

Printed in the U.S.A.
20 09 05 07 06 05 04 03 02 01

NASB 2020 Outreach Bible
Published in 2021 by The Lockman Foundation
La Habra, California, 90631

New American Standard Bible - NASB
Copyright © 1960, 1963, 1971, 1977, 1995, 2020
by The Lockman Foundation
A Corporation Not for Profit
La Habra, CA. All Rights Reserved.
www.lockman.org

The "NASB", "NAS", "New American Standard Bible", "New American Standard", and lighthouse logo are trademarks registered in the United States Patent and Trademark Office by The Lockman Foundation. Use of these trademarks requires the permission of The Lockman Foundation.

For information or to request permission to quote the NASB, please visit www.lockman.org

Printed in the U.S.A.
10 09 08 07 06 05 04 03 02 01

Jesus Saves: A Simple Solution to Our Problem

Everyone is destined to die, but life does not end with death. The Bible says that after death there will be a judgment where each person will give an account of his life to God (Hebrews 9:27). When God created Adam and Eve in His own image in the Garden of Eden, He gave them an abundant life, and the freedom to choose between good and evil. They chose to disobey God and go their own way. As a consequence, death was introduced into the human race, not only physical death, but also spiritual death. For this reason, all people are separated from God. "For all have sinned and fall short of the glory of God." Romans 3:23

We have tried to overcome this separation in many ways: by doing good, through religion or philosophy, or by attempting to live morally and justly. However, none of these things is enough to cross the barrier of separation between God and humanity, because God is holy and people are sinful.

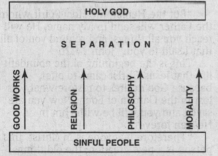

This spiritual separation has become our natural and normal condition, and because of this we are condemned: "The one who believes in Him is not judged; the one who does not believe has been judged already, because he has not believed in the name of the only Son of God." John 3:18

There is only one solution to our problem: Jesus responded and said to him, "Truly, truly, I say to you, unless someone is born again he cannot see the kingdom of God." (John 3:3); that is, it is necessary to be born again in the spiritual sense. God Himself has provided the means that makes it possible for anyone to be born again, and this is the plan that He has for us because He loves us.

God's Plan: Salvation

"For God so loved the world, that He gave His only Son, so that everyone who believes in Him will not perish, but have eternal life." John 3:16

(Jesus said)... "I came so that they would have life, and have it abundantly." (A full and meaningful life.) John 10:10

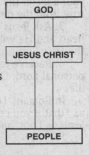

"The one who believes in the Son has eternal life; but the one who does not obey the Son will not see life, but the wrath of God remains on him." John 3:36

(Jesus said)... "I am the way, and the truth, and the life; no one comes to the Father except through Me." John 14:6

"And there is salvation in no one else; for there is no other name under heaven that has been given among mankind by which we must be saved." Acts 4:12

When Jesus Christ died on the cross, He substituted Himself for our sins and bridged the separation of people from God. Because of this sacrifice, every person who is born again can have true fellowship with God.

Jesus Christ is alive today

After Jesus Christ died on the cross at Calvary, where He received the punishment that we deserved, the Bible says that He was buried in a tomb. But He did not remain there: He resurrected! For all those who believe in Jesus Christ, the resurrection is a guarantee that they will also be resurrected to eternal life in the presence of God. This is very good news! (Gospel of Salvation!)

"Now I make known to you, brothers and sisters, the gospel which I preached to you, which you also received, in which you also stand, by which you also are saved, if you hold firmly to the word which I preached to you, unless you believed in vain.

For I handed down to you as of first importance what I also received, that Christ died for our sins according to the Scriptures, and that He was buried, and that He was raised on the third day according to the Scriptures, and that He appeared to Cephas, then to the twelve." 1 Corinthians 15:1-5

How to receive God's love and plan

In His mercy, God has determined

that salvation is free. To receive it, you need to only do this:

1. Admit your problem: being separated from God by sin. Recognize that you have sinned, need God's solution, and repent.

2. Believe that Jesus Christ died for your sins on the cross, was buried, and rose from the dead.

3. Ask Jesus Christ to come into your heart and He will give you salvation and the Holy Spirit to guide your life.

4. Receive Jesus Christ now as your personal Lord, God, and Savior of your life.

In Romans 10:9 and 13 the Bible tells us "that if you confess with your mouth Jesus as Lord, and believe in your heart that God raised Him from the dead, you will be saved...Everyone who calls on the name of the Lord will be saved."

A Suggested prayer to receive Jesus Christ

Dear Lord Jesus, I know that I have sinned against You and that I am not living within your plan. For this I repent and ask You to forgive me. I believe that You died and rose again for me and in doing so, You paid the penalty for my sins. I am willing to turn from my sins, and now I ask You to come into my heart and life as my personal Lord, God, and Savior. Send Your Holy Spirit and Help me now to change, to follow and obey You and to find Your perfect will for my life. Amen.

My personal decision

On (date) _____, I, _____ repented of my sins, believed, confessed, and received Jesus Christ as my personal Lord, God, and Savior. Amen.

You Have Eternal Life

When you called upon the Lord, He listened. Your sins have all been forgiven (Colossians 1:14), you became a child of God (John 1:12), you are born again (John 3:3) you will not be judged (John 5:24), you now have eternal life (John 3:16).

Do not be concerned with your feelings, for they may change sometimes under the pressure of daily life. Place your trust in your Heavenly Father "having cast all your anxiety on Him, because He cares about you." 1 Peter 5:7

"If we confess our sins, He is faithful and righteous, so that He will forgive us our sins and cleanse us from all unrighteousness." 1 John 1:9

His Promise Fulfilled

(Jesus said)... "If you continue in My word, then you are truly My disciples; and you will know the truth, and the truth will set you free. ...So if the Son sets you free, you really will be free." John 8:31-32, 36

"The one who has the Son has the life; the one who does not have the Son of God does not have the life. These things I have written to you who believe in the name of the Son of God, so that you may know that you have eternal life." 1 John 5:12-13

"But the Helper, the Holy Spirit whom the Father will send in My name, He will teach you all things, and remind you of all that I said to you." John 14:26

This is the beginning of the abundant life that Jesus Christ came to offer, because God desires to restore what was lost in the Garden of Eden. Now you are saved and you will be with Him in Heaven forever!

"Therefore if anyone is in Christ, this person is a new creation; the old things passed away; behold, new things have come." 2 Corinthians 5:17

What Should I do Now?

Pray and read the Bible daily to stay in contact with the Lord, starting with the Gospel of John in this New Testament. Attend a Bible preaching and teaching Christian church, get involved with a Bible study, fellowship with Christian friends so that you may strengthen one another, and witness to others about Jesus Christ.

"They were continually devoting themselves to the apostles' teaching and to fellowship, to the breaking of bread and to prayer. ...Praising God and having favor with all the people. And the Lord was adding to their number day by day those who were being saved." Acts 2:42, 47

FOREWORD

SCRIPTURAL PROMISE

"The grass withers, the flower fades,
but the word of our God stands forever."
Isaiah 40:8

The New American Standard Bible has
been produced with the conviction that the
words of Scripture as originally penned in
the Hebrew, Aramaic, and Greek were
inspired by God. Since they are the eternal
Word of God, the Holy Scriptures speak with
fresh power to each generation, to give wisdom that leads to salvation, that people may
serve Christ to the glory of God.

The NASB strives to adhere as closely as
possible to the original languages of the Holy
Scriptures and to make the translation in a
fluent and readable style according to current English usage.

THE FOURFOLD AIM OF
THE LOCKMAN FOUNDATION

1. These publications shall be true to the
   original Hebrew, Aramaic, and Greek.
2. They shall be grammatically correct.
3. They shall be understandable.
4. They shall give the Lord Jesus Christ His
   proper place, the place which the Word
   gives Him; therefore, no work will ever
   be personalized.

PREFACE TO THE
NEW AMERICAN STANDARD BIBLE

In the history of English Bible translations, the King James Version is the most
prestigious. This time-honored version of
1611, itself a revision of the Bishops' Bible
of 1568, became the basis for the English
Revised Version appearing in 1881 (New
Testament) and 1885 (Old Testament). The
American counterpart of this last work was
published in 1901 as the American Standard
Version. The ASV, a product of both British
and American scholarship, has been highly
regarded for its scholarship and accuracy.
Recognizing the values of the American
Standard Version, The Lockman Foundation
felt an urgency to preserve these and other
lasting values of the ASV by incorporating
recent discoveries of Hebrew and Greek tex-
tual sources and by rendering it into current
English. Therefore, in 1959 a new and original translation project was launched, based
on the time-honored principles of translation
used for the ASV and KJV to produce an
accurate and readable English text. The
result is the New American Standard Bible.

This edition of the NASB represents
updates according to modern English
usage and refinements recommended over
the last several years as well as updates
based on current research of the ancient
manuscripts.

PRINCIPLES OF TRANSLATION

MODERN ENGLISH USAGE: The goal is
to render the grammar and terminology in
contemporary English. When it was felt that
the word-for-word literalness was unaccept-
able to the modern reader, a change was
made in the direction of a more current English idiom. In editions that include the full
set of translator's notes, in the instances
where this has been done, a more literal
rendering is indicated by "Lit" notes when
necessary. These notes provide the "literal"
meaning of the word or phrase in question,
or as more technically known, its formal
equivalent in the immediate context. Almost
all words have a range of meanings, and a
"Lit" note supplies the literal or formal
meaning for that particular context. There
are a few exceptions to this procedure.
Punctuation is a relatively modern invention, and ancient writers often linked most
of their sentences with "and" or other con-
nectives, which are sometimes omitted at
the beginning of sentences for better English.

GENDER ACCURACY: In past editions
it was common practice to translate the
Greek word *anthropoi* as "men," as well as
all pluralistic uses of *ish* and similar words.
The same was true for singulars, as mascu-
line. This was never intended to be gender-
exclusive when the context indicated that
women were included; it was assumed at
that time that readers inferred the inclusion
of women. Gender accuracy is important,
however, so in this edition Greek words that
are not actually exclusive in gender as they
are used in a given context are rendered by
inclusive terms, such as "people." Just as
important, when the words in the original
languages are in fact referring only to males
or females, the distinction is maintained in
English.

THE WORD BRETHREN: This word was
used in past editions of the NASB as the
plural of the Greek "brothers" (*adelphoi*)
because it can still be used in a formal setting to address members of a profession,

society, or church, regardless of gender. However, most people today would seldom use "brethren" informally and not often in most churches. This created the challenge of choosing a replacement that would have the same meaning that led to the original usage of "brethren," and only "brothers" was deemed adequate. To be gender-accurate, when it is clear that the author or speaker is referring to women as well as men, "*and sisters*" is added in italic for accuracy and clarity. The italic is necessary to indicate that the addition is implied in the meaning of *adelphoi* for the context, and the addition is not in the Greek text itself.

LET'S FOR ACTION: In most places the phrase "let us" has been replaced with "let's" when a proposal is being made by one or more persons within a group to engage in an action. Such a proposal is common not only in English, but also in the ancient languages of the Bible; however, it is expressed in the ancient languages grammatically rather than by using an auxiliary, "helping" verb such as "let." It is common today for readers to understand "let us" to mean "allow us," so in effect, "let us" has become unintentionally misleading to most readers. Therefore, the simple contraction "let's" has emerged as the clearest expression because this form reflects the nuance of meaning in the original languages–that is, a proposal to do something. However, in some situations "Let Us" is retained for intimate discourse within the Godhead, as in Gen 1:26. "Let us" is also kept when there is a request for permission, and in some other select cases.

ALTERNATIVE READINGS: In addition to the more literal renderings explained under MODERN ENGLISH USAGE, notations have been made to include alternate translations, readings of variant manuscripts, and explanatory equivalents of the text. Only such notations have been used as have been felt justified in assisting the reader's comprehension of the terms used by the original author.

HEBREW TEXT: In the present translation BIBLIA HEBRAICA STUTTGARTENSIA and, where available, BIBLIA HEBRAICA QUINTA have been employed, together with the LXX, the Dead Sea Scrolls, ancient versions, and the most recent scholarship from lexicography.

HEBREW TENSES: The timing of tenses in Hebrew can be a challenging element of translation and careful attention has been given to the requirements of accurate translation, the sequence of tenses, and the immediate and broad contexts.

THE PROPER NAME OF GOD IN THE OLD TESTAMENT: In the Scriptures, the name of God is most significant. It is inconceivable to think of spiritual matters without a proper designation for the Supreme Deity. The most common name for the Deity is "God," a translation of the original Elohim. One of the titles for God is "Lord," a translation of Adonai. There is another name which is understood as God's special or proper name, that is, the four Hebrew letters equivalent to the English letters YHWH (Exodus 3:14 and Isaiah 42:8). This name has not been pronounced by the Jewish people because of reverence for the great sacredness of the divine name. This edition consistently translates this name as LORD. The only exception to this translation of "YHWH" is when it occurs in immediate proximity to the word "Lord," that is, Adonai. In that case it is regularly translated "GOD" in order to avoid confusion.

For many years YHWH has been transliterated as Yahweh, however there is no complete certainty about this pronunciation. While "Yah" can be verified separately, the rest of the name cannot.

NAMES IN THE NEW TESTAMENT: The Greek versions of Hebrew names found in the New Testament, such as "Zacharias," are usually given in their original Hebrew forms, as in "Zechariah" for "Zacharias." Exceptions occur when the person is very commonly known by another name in English versions of the Bible. One of the most notable of such names is "James." An accurate translation would render this name "Jacob." Unfortunately, many would find it confusing to suddenly change the name "James" to "Jacob." There are other special cases where we do not follow the pattern outlined above, and these are often noted. The name "Jesus" itself is a special case, based on the Greek, from an abbreviated form of "Joshua." In fact, in two cases in the New Testament the Greek name refers instead to the famous Joshua of the Old Testament (Acts 7:45; Heb 4:8).

GREEK TEXT: Consideration was given to the latest available manuscripts with a view to determining the best Greek text. In most instances the 28th edition of the

Nestle-Aland NOVUM TESTAMENTUM GRAECE was followed. For Acts and the General Epistles, the Editio Critica Maior (ECM) was followed in most instances. However, the apparatuses provided by both editions are intended to enable scholars to make informed decisions about readings, and sometimes alternate readings with better support to those chosen by the editors were preferred.

GREEK TENSES: A careful distinction has been made in the treatment of the Greek aorist tense (usually translated as the English past, "He did") and the Greek imperfect tense (normally rendered either as English past progressive, "He was doing"; or, if inceptive, as "He began to do" or "He started to do"; or else if customary past, as "He used to do"). "Began" is italicized if it is added to translate an imperfect tense, in order to distinguish it from the Greek verb for "begin." In some contexts the difference between the Greek imperfect and the English past is conveyed better by the choice of vocabulary or by other words in the context, and in such cases the Greek imperfect may be rendered as a simple past tense (e.g., "had an illness for many years" would be preferable to "was having an illness for many years" and the first option would be common in English).

Not all aorist tenses have been rendered as English pasts ("He did"), because some of them are clearly to be rendered as English perfects ("He has done"), or even as past perfects ("He had done"), judging from the context in which they occur. Such aorists have been rendered as perfects or past perfects in this translation.

As for the distinction between aorist and present imperatives, these have usually been rendered as imperatives in the customary way, rather than attempting any fine distinction such as "Begin to do!" (for the aorist imperative), or, "Continually do!" (for the present imperative).

As for the sequence of tenses, care was taken to follow English rules rather than Greek in translating Greek presents, imperfects, and aorists. For example where English says, "We knew that he was doing," Greek puts it, "We knew that he does"; similarly, "We knew that he had done" is the English for "We knew that he did." Likewise, the English, "When he had come, they met him," is represented in Greek by, "When he came, they met him." In all cases a consistent transition has been made from the Greek tense in the subordinate clause to the appropriate tense in English. In the rendering of negative questions introduced by the Greek particle *me* (which always expects the answer "No") the wording has been altered from a mere, "Will he not do this?" to a more accurate, "He will not do this, will he?"

EXPLANATION OF GENERAL FORMAT

FOOTNOTES are listed by the chapter and verse numbers to which they refer. This edition contains a smaller set of footnotes.

PARAGRAPHS are designated by indentation in prose text and the paragraph symbol (¶) in poetry.

CAPITALIZED WORDS are used to provide helpful information. Personal pronouns are capitalized when pertaining to Deity. The word "Law" is capitalized when pertaining to Mosaic Law.

ITALICS are used in the text to indicate words that are not found in the original Hebrew, Aramaic, or Greek but are implied by it, or are sometimes necessary for correct English. Italics are used in the marginal notes to signify alternate readings for the text. Roman text in these marginal alternate readings is the same as italics in the Bible text. There are also special cases of italics referring to words that actually are in the original text. Italic "began" mentioned in GREEK TENSES is one example, where "began" communicates the grammatical tense of a verb. Another is italic possessive pronouns for Greek articles ("the" in Greek) used as possessive pronouns, a common feature in the Greek language. "*His* good pleasure," literally: "the good pleasure" in Phil 2:13 is an example. The purpose of the italic in this case is to inform the reader that the expected Greek word (the Greek possessive pronoun) is not found in the original text, but is represented by another word (the article) in the original text.

SMALL CAPS in the New Testament are used in the text to indicate Old Testament quotations or references to Old Testament texts. Variations of Old Testament wording are found in New Testament citations depending on whether the New Testament writer translated from a Hebrew text, used existing Greek or Aramaic translations, or paraphrased the material. It should be noted that modern rules for the indication of direct quotation were not used in biblical times,

and the ancient writer would use exact quotations or references to quotation without any specific indication of them.

ASTERISKS are used to mark verbs that are historical presents in the Greek grammar and have been translated with an English past tense in order to conform to modern usage. The translators recognized that in some contexts the present tense seems more unexpected and unjustified to the English reader than a past tense would have been. But Greek authors frequently used the present tense for the sake of heightened vividness, thereby transporting their readers in imagination to the actual scene at the time of occurrence. However, the translators felt that it would be wise to change these historical presents to English past tenses.

ABBREVIATIONS AND SPECIAL MARKINGS:

Aram = Aramaic
DSS = Dead Sea Scrolls
Gr = Greek
Heb = Hebrew
Lat = Latin
LXX = Greek translation of O.T. (Septuagint)
MT = Masoretic Text
Lit = A literal translation (formal equivalent)
Or = An alternate translation justified by the original language
Ancient versions = O.T. manuscripts that are not Hebrew
[[ ]] = In text, double brackets indicate words very likely not in the original manuscripts
[ ] = In text, brackets indicate words probably not in the original manuscripts
[ ] = In notes, brackets indicate references to a name, place, or thing similar to, but not identical with that in the text
ch = chapter
cf. = compare
ff = following verses
ms, mss = manuscript(s)
v, vv = verse(s)

THE BOOKS OF THE BIBLE

In the Back:
Introductions to the Books of the Bible
Read Through the Bible in a Year
The Parables of Jesus
The Miracles of Jesus

THE OLD TESTAMENT

GENESIS

The Creation

1 In the beginning God created the heavens and the earth. 2 And the earth was a ¹formless and desolate emptiness, and darkness was over the surface of the deep, and the Spirit of God was hovering over the surface of the waters. 3 Then God said, "¹Let there be light"; and there was light. 4 God saw that the light was good; and God separated the light from the darkness. 5 God called the light "day," and the darkness He called "night." And there was evening and there was morning, one day.

6 Then God said, "Let there be an expanse in the midst of the waters, and let it separate the waters from the waters." 7 God made the ¹expanse, and separated the waters that were below the expanse from the waters that were above the expanse; and it was so. 8 God called the expanse "heaven." And there was evening and there was morning, a second day.

9 Then God said, "Let the waters below the heavens be gathered into one place, and let the dry land appear"; and it was so. 10 And God called the dry land "earth," and the gathering of the waters He called "seas"; and God saw that it was good. 11 Then God said, "Let the earth sprout vegetation, plants yielding seed, *and* fruit trees on the earth bearing fruit according to their kind with seed in them"; and it was so. 12 The earth produced vegetation, plants yielding seed according to their kind, and trees bearing fruit with seed in them, according to their kind; and God saw that it was good. 13 And there was evening and there was morning, a third day.

14 Then God said, "Let there be lights in the expanse of the heavens to separate the day from the night, and they shall serve as signs and for seasons, and for days and years; 15 and they shall serve as lights in the expanse of the heavens to give light on the earth"; and it was so. 16 God made the two great lights, the greater light to govern the day, and the lesser light to govern the night; *He made* the stars also. 17 God placed them in the expanse of the heavens to give light on the earth, 18 and to govern the day and the night, and to separate the light from the darkness; and God saw that it was good. 19 And there was evening and there was morning, a fourth day.

20 Then God said, "Let the waters teem with swarms of living creatures, and let birds fly above the earth in the open expanse of the heavens." 21 And God created the great sea creatures and every living creature that moves, with which the waters swarmed, according to their kind, and every winged bird according to its kind; and God saw that it was good. 22 God blessed them, saying, "Be fruitful and multiply, and fill the waters in the seas, and let birds multiply on the earth." 23 And there was evening and there was morning, a fifth day.

24 Then God said, "Let the earth produce living creatures according to their kind: livestock and crawling things and animals of the earth according to their kind"; and it was so. 25 God made the animals of the earth according to their kind, and the livestock according to their kind, and everything that crawls on the ground according to its kind; and God saw that it was good. 26 Then God said, "¹Let Us make mankind in Our image, according to Our likeness; and ²let them rule over the fish of the sea and over the birds of the sky and over the livestock and over all the earth, and over every crawling thing that crawls on the earth." 27 So God created man in His own image, in the image of God He created him; male and female He created them. 28 God blessed them; and God said to them, "Be fruitful and multiply, and fill the earth, and subdue it; and rule over the fish of the sea and over the birds of the sky and over every living thing that moves on the earth." 29 Then God said, "Behold, I have given you every plant yielding seed that is on the surface of all the earth, and every tree which has fruit yielding seed; it shall be food for you; ³⁰ and to every animal of the earth and to every bird of the sky and to everything that moves on the earth which has life, *I have given* every green plant for food"; and it was so. 31 And God saw all that He had made, and behold, it was very good. And there was evening and there was morning, the sixth day.

2 And so the heavens and the earth were completed, and all their heavenly ¹lights. 2 By the seventh day God completed His work which He had done, and He rested on the seventh day from all His work which He had done. 3 Then God blessed the seventh day and sanctified it, because on it He rested from all His work which God had created and made.

The Creation of Man and Woman

4 This is the account of the heavens and the earth when they were created, in the day that the LORD God made earth and heaven. 5 Now no shrub of the field was yet on the earth, and no plant of the field had yet sprouted, for the LORD God had not sent rain upon the earth, and there was no man to cultivate the ground. 6 But a mist used to rise from the earth and water the whole surface of the ground. 7 Then the LORD God formed the man of dust from the ground, and breathed into his nostrils the breath of life; and the man became a living ¹person. 8 The LORD God planted a garden toward the east, in Eden; and there He placed the man whom He had formed. 9 Out of the ground the LORD God caused every tree to grow that is pleasing to the sight and good for food; the tree of life *was* also in the midst of

---

1:2 ¹Or *waste*   **1:3** ¹I.e., a command, not a request; and so throughout the ch   **1:7** ¹Or *firmament*
1:26 ¹I.e., indicating united action, not a request   ²I.e., have them rule   **2:1** ¹Lit *host* i.e., sun, stars, etc.
2:7 ¹Or *soul*

the garden, and the tree of the knowledge of good and evil. 10 Now a river flowed out of Eden to water the garden; and from there it divided and became four rivers. 11 The name of the first is Pishon; it flows around the whole land of Havilah, where there is gold. 12 The gold of that land is good; the bdellium and the onyx stone are there *as well.* 13 The name of the second river is Gihon; it flows around the whole land of Cush. 14 The name of the third river is Tigris; it flows east of Assyria. And the fourth river is the Euphrates.

15 Then the LORD God took the man and put him in the Garden of Eden to cultivate it and tend it. 16 The LORD God commanded the man, saying, "From any tree of the garden you may freely eat; 17 but from the tree of the knowledge of good and evil you shall not eat, for on the day that you eat from it you will certainly die."

18 Then the LORD God said, "It is not good for the man to be alone; I will make him a helper suitable for him." 19 And out of the ground the LORD God formed every animal of the field and every bird of the sky, and brought *them* to the man to see what he would call them; and whatever the man called a living creature, that was its name. 20 The man gave names to all the livestock, and to the birds of the sky, and to every animal of the field, but for ¹Adam there was not found a helper suitable for him. 21 So the LORD God caused a deep sleep to fall upon the man, and he slept; then He took one of his ribs and closed up the flesh at that place. 22 And the LORD God ¹fashioned into a woman the rib which He had taken from the man, and brought her to the man. 23 Then the man said,

"At last this is bone of my bones,
    And flesh of my flesh;
    She shall be called 'woman,'
    Because she was taken out of man."

24 For this reason a man shall leave his father and his mother, and be joined to his wife; and they shall become one flesh. 25 And the man and his wife were both naked, but they were not ashamed.

The Fall of Mankind

3 Now the serpent was more cunning than any animal of the field which the LORD God had made. And he said to the woman, "Has God really said, 'You shall not eat from any tree of the garden'?" 2 The woman said to the serpent, "From the fruit of the trees of the garden we may eat; 3 but from the fruit of the tree which is in the middle of the garden, God has said, 'You shall not eat from it or touch it, or you will die.'" 4 The serpent said to the woman, "You certainly will not die! 5 For God knows that on the day you eat from it your eyes will be opened, and you will become like God, knowing good and evil." 6 When the woman saw that the tree was good for food, and that it was a delight to the eyes, and that the tree was desirable to make *one* wise, she took some of its fruit and ate; and she also gave *some* to her husband with her, and he ate.

7 Then the eyes of both of them were opened, and they knew that they were naked; and they sewed fig leaves together and made themselves waist coverings.

8 Now they heard the sound of the LORD God walking in the garden in the cool of the day, and the man and his wife hid themselves from the presence of the LORD God among the trees of the garden. 9 Then the LORD God called to the man, and said to him, "Where are you?" 10 He said, "I heard the sound of You in the garden, and I was afraid because I was naked; so I hid myself." 11 And He said, "Who told you that you were naked? Have you eaten from the tree from which I commanded you not to eat?" 12 The man said, "The woman whom You gave *to be* with me, she gave me some of *the fruit of* the tree, and I ate." 13 Then the LORD God said to the woman, "What is this *that* you have done?" And the woman said, "The serpent deceived me, and I ate." 14 Then the LORD God said to the serpent,

"Because you have done this,
    Cursed are you more than all the live-
       stock,
    And more than any animal of the field;
    On your belly you shall go,
    And dust you shall eat
    All the days of your life;
15   And I will make enemies
    Of you and the woman,
    And of your ¹offspring and her
       ²Descendant;
    He shall bruise you on the head,
    And you shall bruise Him on the heel."
16 To the woman He said,
"I will greatly multiply
    Your pain in childbirth,
    In pain you shall deliver children;
    Yet your desire will be for your husband,
    And he shall rule over you."

17 Then to Adam He said, "Because you have listened to the voice of your wife, and have eaten from the tree about which I commanded you, saying, 'You shall not eat from it';

Cursed is the ground because of you;
    With hard labor you shall eat *from* it
    All the days of your life.
18   "Both thorns and thistles it shall grow for
       you;
    Yet you shall eat the plants of the field;
19   By the sweat of your face
    You shall eat bread,
    Until you return to the ground,
    Because from it you were taken;
    For you are dust,
    And to dust you shall return."

20 Now the man named his wife ¹Eve, because she was the mother of all *the* living. 21 And the LORD God made garments of skin for Adam and his wife, and clothed them.

22 Then the LORD God said, "Behold, the man has become like one of Us, knowing good and evil; and now, he might reach out with his hand, and take *fruit* also from the tree of life, and eat, and live forever"—23 therefore the LORD God sent him out of the Garden of Eden, to cultivate the ground from which he was

---

2:20 ¹Or *man*   2:22 ¹Lit *built*   3:15 ¹Lit *seed*   ²Lit *Seed;* i.e., a prophetic reference to Christ
3:20 ¹I.e., living; or life

taken. 24 So He drove the man out; and at the east of the Garden of Eden He stationed the cherubim and the flaming sword which turned every direction to guard the way to the tree of life.

Cain and Abel

4 Now the man had relations with his wife Eve, and she conceived and gave birth to Cain, and she said, "I have obtained a male *child* with *the help of* the LORD." 2 And again, she gave birth to his brother Abel. Now Abel was a keeper of flocks, but Cain was a cultivator of the ground. 3 So it came about in the course of time that Cain brought an offering to the LORD from the fruit of the ground. 4 Abel, on his part also brought *an offering,* from the firstborn of his flock and from their fat portions. And the LORD had regard for Abel and his offering; 5 but for Cain and his offering He had no regard. So Cain became very angry and his face was gloomy. 6 Then the LORD said to Cain, "Why are you angry? And why is your face gloomy? 7 If you do well, will *your face* not be cheerful? And if you do not do well, sin is lurking at the door; and its desire is for you, but you must master it." 8 Cain talked to his brother Abel; and it happened that when they were in the field Cain rose up against his brother Abel and killed him.

9 Then the LORD said to Cain, "Where is Abel your brother?" And he said, "I do not know. Am I my brother's keeper?" 10 Then He said, "What have you done? The voice of your brother's blood is crying out to Me from the ground. 11 Now you are cursed from the ground, which has opened its mouth to receive your brother's blood from your hand. 12 When you cultivate the ground, it will no longer yield its strength to you; you will be a wanderer and a drifter on the earth." 13 Cain said to the LORD, "My punishment is too great to endure! 14 Behold, You have driven me this day from the face of the ground; and I will be hidden from Your face, and I will be a wanderer and a drifter on the earth, and whoever finds me will kill me." 15 So the LORD said to him, "Therefore whoever kills Cain, vengeance will be taken on him seven times *as much.*" And the LORD placed a mark on Cain, so that no one finding him would kill him.

16 Then Cain left the presence of the LORD, and settled in the land of Nod, east of Eden.

17 Cain had relations with his wife and she conceived, and gave birth to Enoch; and *Cain* built a city, and named the city Enoch, after the name of his son. 18 Now to Enoch was born Irad, and Irad fathered Mehujael, and Mehujael fathered Methushael, and Methushael fathered Lamech. 19 Lamech took two wives for himself: the name of the one was Adah, and the name of the other, Zillah. 20 Adah gave birth to Jabal; he was the father of those who live in tents and *have* livestock. 21 His brother's name was Jubal; he was the father of all those who play the lyre and flute. 22 As for Zillah, she also gave birth to Tubal-cain, the forger of all implements

of bronze and iron; and the sister of Tubal-cain was Naamah.

23 Lamech said to his wives,
"Adah and Zillah,
Listen to my voice,
You wives of Lamech,
Pay attention to my words,
For I have killed a man for wounding me;
And a boy for striking me!
24 "If Cain is avenged seven times,
Then Lamech seventy-seven times!"

25 Adam had relations with his wife again; and she gave birth to a son, and named him Seth, for, *she said,* "God has appointed me another child in place of Abel, because Cain killed him." 26 To Seth also a son was born; and he named him Enosh. Then *people* began to call upon the name of the LORD.

Descendants of Adam

5 This is the book of the generations of Adam. On the day when God created man, He made him in the likeness of God. 2 He created them male and female, and He blessed them and named them "mankind" on the day when they were created.

3 When Adam had lived 130 years, he fathered *a son* in his own likeness, according to his image, and named him Seth. 4 Then the days of Adam after he fathered Seth were eight hundred years, and he fathered *other* sons and daughters. 5 So all the days that Adam lived were 930 years, and he died.

6 Now Seth lived 105 years, and fathered Enosh. 7 Then Seth lived 807 years after he fathered Enosh, and he fathered *other* sons and daughters. 8 So all the days of Seth were 912 years, and he died.

9 Now Enosh lived ninety years, and fathered Kenan. 10 Then Enosh lived 815 years after he fathered Kenan, and he fathered *other* sons and daughters. 11 So all the days of Enosh were 905 years, and he died.

12 Now Kenan lived seventy years, and fathered Mahalalel. 13 Then Kenan lived 840 years after he fathered Mahalalel, and he fathered *other* sons and daughters. 14 So all the days of Kenan were 910 years, and he died.

15 Now Mahalalel lived sixty-five years, and fathered Jared. 16 Then Mahalalel lived 830 years after he fathered Jared, and he fathered *other* sons and daughters. 17 So all the days of Mahalalel were 895 years, and he died.

18 Now Jared lived 162 years, and fathered Enoch. 19 Then Jared lived eight hundred years after he fathered Enoch, and he fathered *other* sons and daughters. 20 So all the days of Jared were 962 years, and he died.

21 Now Enoch lived sixty-five years, and fathered Methuselah. 22 Then Enoch walked with God three hundred years after he fathered Methuselah, and he fathered *other* sons and daughters. 23 So all the days of Enoch were 365 years. 24 Enoch walked with God; and he was 1not, for God took him.

25 Now Methuselah lived 187 years, and fathered Lamech. 26 Then Methuselah lived 782 years after he fathered Lamech, and he fathered *other* sons and daughters. 27 So all the

days of Methuselah were 969 years, and he died. ²⁸Now Lamech lived 182 years, and fathered a son. ²⁹And he named him Noah, saying, "This one will give us comfort from our work and from the hard labor of our hands *caused* by the ground which the LORD has cursed." ³⁰Then Lamech lived 595 years after he fathered Noah, and he fathered *other* sons and daughters. ³¹So all the days of Lamech were 777 years, and he died.

³²Now after Noah was five hundred years old, Noah fathered Shem, Ham, and Japheth.

The Corruption of Mankind

6 Now it came about, when mankind began to multiply on the face of the land, and daughters were born to them, ²that the sons of God saw that the daughters of mankind were beautiful; and they took wives for themselves, whomever they chose. ³Then the LORD said, "My Spirit will not remain with man forever, because he is also flesh; nevertheless his days shall be 120 years." ⁴The ¹Nephilim were on the earth in those days, and also afterward, when the sons of God came in to the daughters of mankind; and they bore children to them. Those were the mighty men who *were* of old, men of renown.

⁵Then the LORD saw that the wickedness of mankind was great on the earth, and that every intent of the thoughts of their hearts was only evil continually. ⁶So the LORD was sorry that He had made mankind on the earth, and He was grieved in His heart. ⁷Then the LORD said, "I will wipe out mankind whom I have created from the face of the land; mankind, and animals as well, and crawling things, and the birds of the sky. For I am sorry that I have made them." ⁸But Noah found favor in the eyes of the LORD.

⁹These are *the records of* the generations of Noah. Noah was a righteous man, blameless in his generation. Noah walked with God. ¹⁰And Noah fathered three sons: Shem, Ham, and Japheth.

¹¹Now the earth was corrupt in the sight of God, and the earth was filled with violence. ¹²And God looked on the earth, and behold, it was corrupt; for humanity had corrupted its way upon the earth. ¹³Then God said to Noah, "The end of humanity has come before Me; for the earth is filled with violence because of people; and behold, I am about to destroy them with the earth. ¹⁴Make for yourself an ark of gopher wood; you shall make the ark with compartments, and cover it inside and out with pitch. ¹⁵This is how you shall make it: the length of the ark *shall be* ¹three hundred cubits, its width fifty cubits, and its height thirty cubits. ¹⁶You shall make a window for the ark, and finish it to a ¹cubit from the top; and put the door of the ark on the side; you shall make it with lower, second, and third decks. ¹⁷Now behold, I Myself am bringing the flood of water upon the earth, to destroy all flesh in which there is the breath of life, from under heaven;

everything that is on the earth shall perish. ¹⁸But I will establish My covenant with you; and you shall enter the ark—you, your sons, your wife, and your sons' wives with you. ¹⁹And of every living thing of all flesh, you shall bring two of every *kind* into the ark, to keep *them* alive with you; they shall be male and female. ²⁰Of the birds according to their kind, and of the animals according to their kind, of every crawling thing of the ground according to its kind, two of every *kind* will come to you to keep *them* alive. ²¹As for you, take for yourself some of every food that is edible, and gather *it* to yourself; and it shall be food for you and them." ²²So Noah did *these things;* according to everything that God had commanded him, so he did.

The Flood

7 Then the LORD said to Noah, "Enter the ark, you and all your household, for you *alone* I have seen *to be* righteous before Me in this generation. ²You shall take with you seven pairs of every clean animal, a male and his female; and two of the animals that are not clean, a male and his female; ³also of the birds of the sky, seven pairs, male and female, to keep *their* offspring alive on the face of all the earth. ⁴For after seven more days, I will send rain on the earth for forty days and forty nights; and I will wipe out from the face of the land every living thing that I have made." ⁵So Noah acted in accordance with everything that the LORD had commanded him.

⁶Now Noah was six hundred years old when the flood of water came upon the earth. ⁷Then Noah and his sons, his wife, and his sons' wives with him entered the ark because of the waters of the flood. ⁸Of clean animals and animals that are not clean and birds and everything that crawls on the ground, ⁹they *all* went into the ark to Noah by twos, male and female, as God had commanded Noah. ¹⁰Now it came about after the seven days, that the waters of the flood came upon the earth. ¹¹In the six hundredth year of Noah's life, in the second month, on the seventeenth day of the month, on that day all the fountains of the great deep burst open, and the floodgates of the sky were opened. ¹²The rain fell upon the earth for forty days and forty nights.

¹³On this very same day Noah, Shem, Ham, and Japheth, the sons of Noah, and Noah's wife and the three wives of his sons with them, entered the ark, ¹⁴they and every animal according to its kind, and all the livestock according to their kind, and every crawling thing that crawls on the earth according to its kind, and every bird according to its kind, all sorts of birds. ¹⁵So they went into the ark to Noah, by twos of all flesh in which there was the breath of life. ¹⁶Those that entered, male and female of all flesh, entered as God had commanded him; and the LORD closed *the door* behind him.

¹⁷Then the flood came upon the earth for forty days, and the water increased and lifted up the ark, so that it rose above the earth.

6:4 ¹Lit *fallen ones;* LXX *giants*   **6:15** ¹About 450 ft. long, 75 ft. wide, and 45 ft. high or 135 m, 23 m, and 14 m   **6:16** ¹One cubit is about 18 in. or 45 cm

18 The water prevailed and increased greatly upon the earth, and the ark floated on the surface of the water. 19 And the water prevailed more and more upon the earth, so that all the high mountains everywhere under the heavens were covered. 20 The water prevailed †fifteen cubits higher, and the mountains were covered. 21 So all creatures that moved on the earth perished: birds, livestock, animals, and every swarming thing that swarms upon the earth, and all mankind; 22 of all that was on the dry land, all in whose nostrils was the breath of the spirit of life, died. 23 So He wiped out every living thing that was upon the face of the land, from mankind to animals, to crawling things, and the birds of the sky, and they were wiped out from the earth; and only Noah was left, together with those that were with him in the ark. 24 The water prevailed upon the earth for 150 days.

The Flood Subsides

8 But God remembered Noah and all the animals and all the livestock that were with him in the ark; and God caused a wind to pass over the earth, and the water subsided. 2 Also the fountains of the deep and the floodgates of the sky were closed, and the rain from the sky was restrained; 3 and the water receded steadily from the earth, and at the end of 150 days the water decreased. 4 Then in the seventh month, on the seventeenth day of the month, the ark rested upon the mountains of Ararat. 5 And the water decreased steadily until the tenth month; in the tenth month, on the first day of the month, the tops of the mountains became visible.

6 Then it came about at the end of forty days, that Noah opened the window of the ark which he had made; 7 and he sent out a raven, and it flew here and there until the water was dried up from the earth. 8 Then he sent out a dove, to see if the water was low on the surface of the land; 9 but the dove found no resting place for the sole of its foot, so it returned to him in the ark, for the water was on the surface of all the earth. Then he put out his hand and took it, and brought it into the ark to himself. 10 So he waited another seven days longer; and again he sent out the dove from the ark. 11 And the dove came to him in the evening, and behold, in its beak was a fresh olive leaf. So Noah knew that the water was low on the earth. 12 Then he waited another seven days longer, and sent out the dove; but it did not return to him again.

13 Now it came about in the six hundred and first year, in the first *month,* on the first of the month, *that* the water was dried up from the earth. Then Noah removed the covering of the ark, and looked, and behold, the surface of the ground had dried up. 14 And in the second month, on the twenty-seventh day of the month, the earth was dry. 15 Then God spoke to Noah, saying, 16 "Go out of the ark, you and your wife and your sons and your sons' wives with you. 17 Bring out with you every living thing of all flesh that is with you, birds and animals and every crawling thing that crawls on the earth, that they may breed abundantly on the earth, and be fruitful and multiply on the earth." 18 So Noah went out, and his sons and his wife, and his sons' wives with him. 19 Every animal, every crawling thing, and every bird, everything that moves on the earth, went out by their families from the ark.

20 Then Noah built an altar to the LORD, and took some of every *kind of* clean animal and some of every clean bird and offered burnt offerings on the altar. 21 The LORD smelled the soothing aroma, and the LORD said to Himself, "I will never again curse the ground on account of man, for the intent of man's heart is evil from his youth; and I will never again destroy every living thing, as I have done. 22 "While the earth remains,
Seedtime and harvest,
Cold and heat,
Summer and winter,
And day and night
Shall not cease."

Covenant of the Rainbow

9 Then God blessed Noah and his sons, and said to them, "Be fruitful and multiply, and fill the earth. 2 The fear of you and the terror of you will be on every animal of the earth and on every bird of the sky; on everything that crawls on the ground, and on all the fish of the sea. They are handed over to you. 3 Every moving thing that is alive shall be food for you; I have given everything to you, as *I gave* the green plant. 4 But you shall not eat flesh with its life, *that is,* its blood. 5 I certainly will require your lifeblood; from every animal I will require it. And from *every* person, from every man *as* his brother I will require the life of a person.
6 "Whoever sheds human blood,
By man his blood shall be shed,
For in the image of God
He made mankind.
7 "As for you, be fruitful and multiply;
Populate the earth abundantly and
multiply in it."

8 Then God spoke to Noah and to his sons with him, saying, 9 "Now behold, I Myself am establishing My covenant with you, and with your descendants after you; 10 and with every living creature that is with you: the birds, the livestock, and every animal of the earth with you; of all that comes out of the ark, every animal of the earth. 11 I establish My covenant with you; and all flesh shall never again be eliminated by the waters of a flood, nor shall there again be a flood to destroy the earth." 12 God said, "This is the sign of the covenant which I am making between Me and you and every living creature that is with you, for all future generations; 13 I have set My rainbow in the cloud, and it shall serve as a sign of a covenant between Me and the earth. 14 It shall come about, when I make a cloud appear over the earth, that the rainbow will be seen in the cloud, 15 and I will remember My covenant, which is between Me and you and every living creature of all flesh; and never again shall the water become a flood to destroy all flesh. 16 When the rainbow is in the cloud, then I will look at it, to remember the everlasting

covenant between God and every living creature of all flesh that is on the earth." [17] And God said to Noah, "This is the sign of the covenant which I have established between Me and all flesh that is on the earth."

[18] Now the sons of Noah who came out of the ark were Shem, Ham, and Japheth; and Ham was the father of Canaan. [19] These three were the sons of Noah, and from these the whole earth was populated.

[20] Then Noah began farming and planted a vineyard. [21] He drank some of the wine and became drunk, and uncovered himself inside his tent. [22] Ham, the father of Canaan, saw the nakedness of his father, and told his two brothers outside. [23] But Shem and Japheth took a garment and laid it on both their shoulders and walked backward and covered the nakedness of their father; and their faces were turned away, so that they did not see their father's nakedness. [24] When Noah awoke from his wine, he knew what his youngest son had done to him. [25] So he said,

"Cursed be Canaan;
¹A servant of servants
He shall be to his brothers."

[26] He also said,

"Blessed be the LORD,
The God of Shem;
And may Canaan be his servant.
[27] "May God enlarge Japheth,
And may he live in the tents of Shem;
And may Canaan be his servant."

[28] Noah lived 350 years after the flood. [29] So all the days of Noah were 950 years, and he died.

Descendants of Noah

10 Now these are the records of the generations of the sons of Noah: Shem, Ham, and Japheth; and sons were born to them after the flood.

[2] The sons of Japheth were Gomer, Magog, Madai, Javan, Tubal, Meshech, and Tiras. [3] The sons of Gomer were Ashkenaz, Riphath, and Togarmah. [4] The sons of Javan were Elishah, Tarshish, Kittim, and Dodanim. [5] From these the people of the coastlands of the nations were separated into their lands, every one according to his language, according to their families, into their nations.

[6] The sons of Ham were Cush, Mizraim, Put, and Canaan. [7] The sons of Cush were Seba, Havilah, Sabtah, Raamah, and Sabteca; and the sons of Raamah were Sheba and Dedan. [8] Now Cush fathered Nimrod; he became a mighty one on the earth. [9] He was a mighty hunter before the LORD; therefore it is said, "Like Nimrod a mighty hunter before the LORD." [10] And the beginning of his kingdom was ¹Babel, Erech, Accad, and Calneh, in the land of Shinar. [11] From that land he went to Assyria, and built Nineveh, Rehoboth-Ir, Calah, [12] and Resen between Nineveh and Calah; that is the great city. [13] Mizraim fathered Ludim, Anamim, Lehabim, Naphtuhim, [14] Pathrusim, Casluhim (from whom came the Philistines), and Caphtorim.

[15] Canaan fathered Sidon, his firstborn, and Heth, [16] the Jebusite, the Amorite, the Girgashite, [17] the Hivite, the Arkite, the Sinite, [18] the Arvadite, the Zemarite, and the Hamathite; and afterward the families of the Canaanite were spread abroad. [19] The territory of the Canaanite extended from Sidon going toward Gerar, as far as Gaza; and going toward Sodom and Gomorrah, Admah, and Zeboiim, as far as Lasha. [20] These are the sons of Ham, according to their families, according to their languages, by their lands, and by their nations.

[21] Also to Shem, the father of all the children of Eber, and the older brother of Japheth, children were born. [22] The sons of Shem were Elam, Asshur, Arpachshad, Lud, and Aram. [23] The sons of Aram were Uz, Hul, Gether, and Mash. [24] Arpachshad fathered Shelah; and Shelah fathered Eber. [25] Two sons were born to Eber; the name of the one was Peleg, for in his days the earth was divided; and his brother's name was Joktan. [26] Joktan fathered Almodad, Sheleph, Hazarmaveth, Jerah, [27] Hadoram, Uzal, Diklah, [28] Obal, Abimael, Sheba, [29] Ophir, Havilah, and Jobab; all of these were the sons of Joktan. [30] Now their settlement extended from Mesha going toward Sephar, the hill country of the east. [31] These are the sons of Shem, according to their families, according to their languages, by their lands, and according to their nations.

[32] These are the families of the sons of Noah, according to their descendants, by their nations; and out of these the nations were separated on the earth after the flood.

The Tower of Babel

11 Now all the earth used the same language and the same words. [2] And it came about, as they journeyed east, that they found a plain in the land of Shinar and settled there. [3] Then they said to one another, "Come, let's make bricks and ¹fire them thoroughly." And they used brick for stone, and they used tar for mortar. [4] And they said, "Come, let's build ourselves a city, and a tower whose top will reach into heaven, and let's make a name for ourselves; otherwise we will be scattered abroad over the face of all the earth." [5] Now the LORD came down to see the city and the tower which the men had built. [6] And the LORD said, "Behold, they are one people, and they all have the same language. And this is what they have started to do, and now nothing which they plan to do will be impossible for them. [7] Come, ¹let Us go down and there confuse their language, so that they will not understand one another's speech." [8] So the LORD scattered them abroad from there over the face of all the earth; and they stopped building the city. [9] Therefore it was named ¹Babel, because there the LORD confused the language of all the earth; and from there the LORD scattered them abroad over the face of all the earth.

Descendants of Shem

[10] These are the records of the generations of Shem. Shem was a hundred years old when

---

he fathered Arpachshad, two years after the flood; 11 and Shem lived five hundred years after he fathered Arpachshad, and he fathered *other* sons and daughters.

12 Arpachshad lived thirty-five years, and fathered Shelah; 13 and Arpachshad lived 403 years after he fathered Shelah, and he fathered *other* sons and daughters.

14 Shelah lived thirty years, and fathered Eber; 15 and Shelah lived 403 years after he fathered Eber, and he fathered *other* sons and daughters.

16 Eber lived thirty-four years, and fathered Peleg; 17 and Eber lived 430 years after he fathered Peleg, and he fathered *other* sons and daughters.

18 Peleg lived thirty years, and fathered Reu; 19 and Peleg lived 209 years after he fathered Reu, and he fathered *other* sons and daughters.

20 Reu lived thirty-two years, and fathered Serug; 21 and Reu lived 207 years after he fathered Serug, and he fathered *other* sons and daughters.

22 Serug lived thirty years, and fathered Nahor; 23 and Serug lived two hundred years after he fathered Nahor, and he fathered *other* sons and daughters.

24 Nahor lived twenty-nine years, and fathered Terah; 25 and Nahor lived 119 years after he fathered Terah, and he fathered *other* sons and daughters.

26 Terah lived seventy years, and fathered Abram, Nahor, and Haran.

27 Now these are *the records of* the generations of Terah. Terah fathered Abram, Nahor, and Haran; and Haran fathered Lot. 28 Haran died during the lifetime of his father Terah in the land of his birth, in Ur of the Chaldeans. 29 Abram and Nahor took wives for themselves. The name of Abram's wife was Sarai, and the name of Nahor's wife was Milcah, the daughter of Haran, the father of Milcah and Iscah. 30 Sarai was unable to conceive; she did not have a child.

31 Now Terah took his son Abram, and Lot the son of Haran, his grandson, and his daughter-in-law Sarai, his son Abram's wife, and they departed together from Ur of the Chaldeans to go to the land of Canaan; and they went as far as Haran and settled there. 32 The days of Terah were 205 years; and Terah died in Haran.

Abram Journeys to Egypt

12 Now the LORD said to Abram,
"Go from your country,
And from your relatives
And from your father's house,
To the land which I will show you;
2 And I will make you into a great nation,
And I will bless you,
And make your name great;
And *you shall* be a blessing;
3 And I will bless those who bless you,
And the one who curses you I will
curse.
And in you all the families of the earth
will be blessed."
4 So Abram went *away* as the LORD had

spoken to him; and Lot went with him. Now Abram was seventy-five years old when he departed from Haran. 5 Abram took his wife Sarai and his nephew Lot, and all their possessions which they had accumulated, and the people which they had acquired in Haran, and they set out for the land of Canaan; so they came to the land of Canaan. 6 Abram passed through the land as far as the site of Shechem, to the oak of Moreh. Now the Canaanites *were* in the land at that time. 7 And the LORD appeared to Abram and said, "To your descendants I will give this land." So he built an altar there to the LORD who had appeared to him. 8 Then he proceeded from there to the mountain on the east of Bethel, and pitched his tent with Bethel on the west and Ai on the east; and there he built an altar to the LORD and called upon the name of the LORD. 9 Then Abram journeyed on, continuing toward the ¹Negev.

10 Now there was a famine in the land; so Abram went down to Egypt to live there for a time, because the famine was severe in the land. 11 It came about, when he was approaching Egypt, that he said to his wife Sarai, "See now, I know that you are a beautiful woman; 12 and when the Egyptians see you, they will say, 'This is his wife'; and they will kill me, but they will let you live. 13 Please say that you are my sister so that it may go well for me because of you, and that I may live on account of you." 14 Now it came about, when Abram entered Egypt, that the Egyptians saw that the woman was very beautiful. 15 Pharaoh's officials saw her and praised her to Pharaoh; and the woman was taken into Pharaoh's house. 16 Therefore he treated Abram well for her sake; and he gave him sheep, oxen, male donkeys, male servants and female servants, female donkeys, and camels.

17 But the LORD struck Pharaoh and his house with great plagues because of Sarai, Abram's wife. 18 Then Pharaoh called Abram and said, "What is this *that* you have done to me? Why did you not tell me that she was your wife? 19 Why did you say, 'She is my sister,' so that I took her for myself as a wife? Now then, here is your wife, take her and go!" 20 And Pharaoh commanded *his* men concerning him; and they escorted him away, with his wife and all that belonged to him.

Abram and Lot

13 So Abram went up from Egypt to the ¹Negev, he and his wife and all that belonged to him, and Lot with him.
2 Now Abram was very rich in livestock, silver, and gold. 3 And he went on his journeys from the ¹Negev as far as Bethel, to the place where his tent had been at the beginning, between Bethel and Ai, 4 to the place of the altar which he had made there previously; and there Abram called on the name of the LORD. 5 Now Lot, who went with Abram, also had flocks, herds, and tents. 6 And the land could not support *both of* them while living together, for their possessions were so great that they were not able to remain together. 7 And there

was strife between the herdsmen of Abram's livestock and the herdsmen of Lot's livestock. Now the Canaanites and the Perizzites were living in the land at that time.

8 So Abram said to Lot, "Please let there be no strife between you and me, nor between my herdsmen and your herdsmen, for we are relatives! 9 Is the entire land not before you? Please separate from me; if *you choose* the left, then I will go to the right; or if *you choose* the right, then I will go to the left." 10 Lot raised his eyes and saw all the vicinity of the Jordan, that it was well watered everywhere—*this was* before the LORD destroyed Sodom and Gomorrah—like the garden of the LORD, like the land of Egypt going toward Zoar. 11 So Lot chose for himself all the vicinity of the Jordan, and Lot journeyed eastward. So they separated from each other. 12 Abram settled in the land of Canaan, while Lot settled in the cities of the vicinity of the *Jordan,* and moved his tents as far as Sodom. 13 Now the men of Sodom were exceedingly wicked sinners against the LORD.

14 The LORD said to Abram, after Lot had separated from him, "Now raise your eyes and look from the place where you are, northward and southward, and eastward and westward; 15 for all the land which you see I will give to you and to your descendants forever. 16 I will make your descendants as *plentiful as* the dust of the earth, so that if anyone can count the dust of the earth, then your descendants could also be counted. 17 Arise, walk about in the land through its length and width; for I will give it to you." 18 Then Abram moved his tent and came and lived by the oaks of Mamre, which are in Hebron; and there he built an altar to the LORD.

War of the Kings

14 And it came about in the days of Amraphel king of Shinar, Arioch king of Ellasar, Chedorlaomer king of Elam, and Tidal king of Goiim, 2 *that* they made war with Bera king of Sodom, and with Birsha king of Gomorrah, Shinab king of Admah, and Shemeber king of Zeboiim, and the king of Bela (that is, Zoar). 3 All these *kings* came as allies to the Valley of Siddim (that is, the Salt Sea). 4 For twelve years they had served Chedorlaomer, but *in* the thirteenth year they rebelled. 5 And in the fourteenth year Chedorlaomer and the kings who were with him came and defeated the Rephaim in Ashteroth-karnaim, and the Zuzim in Ham, and the Emim in Shaveh-kiriathaim, 6 and the Horites on their Mount Seir, as far as El-paran, which is by the wilderness. 7 Then they turned back and came to En-mishpat (that is, Kadesh), and conquered all the country of the Amalekites, and also the Amorites, who lived in Hazazon-tamar. 8 And the king of Sodom and the king of Gomorrah, the king of Admah and the king of Zeboiim, and the king of Bela (that is, Zoar) came out; and they lined up for battle against them in the Valley of Siddim, 9 against Chedorlaomer king of Elam, Tidal king of Goiim, Amraphel king of Shinar, and Arioch king of Ellasar—four kings against five. 10 Now the Valley of Siddim was full of tar pits; and the kings of Sodom and

Gomorrah fled, and they fell into them. But those who survived fled to the hill country. 11 Then they took all the possessions of Sodom and Gomorrah and all their food supply, and departed. 12 They also took Lot, Abram's nephew, and his possessions and departed, for he was living in Sodom.

13 Then a survivor came and told Abram the Hebrew. Now he was residing by the oaks of Mamre the Amorite, brother of Eshcol and brother of Aner, and they were allies with Abram. 14 When Abram heard that his relative had been taken captive, he led out his trained men, born in his house, *numbering* 318, and went in pursuit as far as Dan. 15 Then he divided his forces against them by night, he and his servants, and defeated them, and pursued them as far as Hobah, which is north of Damascus. 16 He brought back all the possessions, and also brought back his relative Lot with his possessions, and also the women, and the *other* people.

God's Promise to Abram

17 Then after his return from the defeat of Chedorlaomer and the kings who were with him, the king of Sodom went out to meet him at the Valley of Shaveh (that is, the King's Valley). 18 And Melchizedek the king of Salem brought out bread and wine; now he was a priest of God Most High. 19 And he blessed him and said,

"Blessed be Abram of God Most High,
Possessor of heaven and earth;
20   And blessed be God Most High,
Who has handed over your enemies to you."

And he gave him a tenth of everything. 21 Then the king of Sodom said to Abram, "Give the people to me and take the possessions for yourself." 22 But Abram said to the king of Sodom, "I have sworn to the LORD God Most High, Possessor of heaven and earth, 23 that I will not take a thread or a sandal strap or anything that is yours, so that you do not say, 'I have made Abram rich.' 24 I will take nothing except what the young men have eaten, and the share of the men who went with me, Aner, Eshcol, and Mamre; let them take their share."

Abram Promised a Son

15 After these things the word of the LORD came to Abram in a vision, saying,
"Do not fear, Abram,
I am a shield to you;
Your reward shall be very great."

2 But Abram said, "Lord GOD, what will You give me, since I am childless, and the heir of my house is Eliezer of Damascus?" 3 Abram also said, "Since You have given me no son, one who has been born in my house is my heir." 4 Then behold, the word of the LORD came to him, saying, "This man will not be your heir; but one who will come from your own body shall be your heir." 5 And He took him outside and said, "Now look toward the heavens and count the stars, if you are able to count them." And He said to him, "So shall your descendants be." 6 Then he believed in the LORD; and He credited it to him as righteousness. 7 And He

said to him, "I am the LORD who brought you out of Ur of the Chaldeans, to give you this land to possess it." 8 But he said, "Lord GOD, how may I know that I will possess it?" 9 So He said to him, "Bring Me a three-year-old heifer, a three-year-old female goat, a three-year-old ram, a turtledove, and a young pigeon." 10 Then he brought all these to Him and cut them in two, and laid each half opposite the other; but he did not cut the birds. 11 And birds of prey came down upon the carcasses, and Abram drove them away.

12 Now when the sun was going down, a deep sleep fell upon Abram; and behold, terror *and* great darkness fell upon him. 13 Then *God* said to Abram, "Know for certain that your descendants will be strangers in a land that is not theirs, where they will be enslaved and oppressed for four hundred years. 14 But I will also judge the nation whom they will serve, and afterward they will come out with many possessions. 15 As for you, you shall go to your fathers in peace; you will be buried at a good old age. 16 Then in the fourth generation they will return here, for the wrongdoing of the Amorite is not yet complete."

17 Now it came about, when the sun had set, that it was very dark, and behold, a smoking oven and a flaming torch *appeared* which passed between these pieces. 18 On that day the LORD made a covenant with Abram, saying,

"To your descendants I have given this land,
From the river of Egypt as far as the great river, the river Euphrates:
19 the *land of the* Kenite, the Kenizzite, the Kadmonite, 20 the Hittite, the Perizzite, the Rephaim, 21 the Amorite, the Canaanite, the Girgashite, and the Jebusite."

Sarai and Hagar

16 Now Sarai, Abram's wife, had not borne him a child, but she had an Egyptian slave woman whose name was Hagar. 2 So Sarai said to Abram, "See now, the LORD has prevented me from bearing *children.* Please have relations with my slave woman; perhaps I will obtain children through her." And Abram listened to the voice of Sarai. 3 And *so* after Abram had lived ten years in the land of Canaan, Abram's wife Sarai took Hagar the Egyptian, her slave woman, and gave her to her husband Abram as his wife. 4 Then he had relations with Hagar, and she conceived; and when *Hagar* became aware that she had conceived, her mistress was insignificant in her sight. 5 So Sarai said to Abram, "May the wrong done to me be upon you! I put my slave woman into your arms, but when she saw that she had conceived, I was insignificant in her sight. May the LORD judge between you and me." 6 But Abram said to Sarai, "Look, your slave woman is in your power; do to her what is good in your sight." So Sarai treated her harshly, and she fled from her presence.

7 Now the angel of the LORD found her by a spring of water in the wilderness, by the spring on the way to Shur. 8 He said, "Hagar, Sarai's slave woman, from where have you come, and where are you going?" And she said, "I am fleeing from the presence of my mistress Sarai." 9 So the angel of the LORD said to her, "Return to your mistress, and submit to her authority." 10 The angel of the LORD also said to her, "I will greatly multiply your descendants so that they will be too many to count." 11 The angel of the LORD said to her further,

"Behold, you are pregnant,
And you will give birth to a son;
And you shall name him 1 Ishmael,
Because the LORD has heard your affliction.
12 "But he will be a wild donkey of a man;
His hand *will be* against everyone,
And everyone's hand *will be* against him;
And he will live in defiance of all his brothers."

13 Then she called the name of the LORD who spoke to her, "You are a God who sees me"; for she said, "Have I even seen *Him* here *and lived* after He saw me?" 14 Therefore the well was called 1 Beer-lahai-roi; behold, it is between Kadesh and Bered.

15 So Hagar bore a son to Abram; and Abram named his son, to whom Hagar gave birth, Ishmael. 16 Abram was eighty-six years old when Hagar bore Ishmael to him.

Abraham and the Covenant of Circumcision

17 Now when Abram was ninety-nine years old, the LORD appeared to Abram and said to him,

"I am God Almighty;
Walk before Me, and be blameless.
2 "I will make My covenant between Me and you,
And I will multiply you exceedingly."
3 Abram fell on his face, and God talked with him, saying,
4 "As for Me, behold, My covenant is with you,
And you will be the father of a multitude of nations.
5 "No longer shall you be named 1 Abram,
But your name shall be 2 Abraham;
For I have made you the father of a multitude of nations.
6 I will make you exceedingly fruitful, and I will make nations of you, and kings will come from you. 7 I will establish My covenant between Me and you and your descendants after you throughout their generations as an everlasting covenant, to be God to you and to your descendants after you. 8 And I will give to you and to your descendants after you the land where you live as a stranger, all the land of Canaan, as an everlasting possession; and I will be their God."

9 God said further to Abraham, "Now as for you, you shall keep My covenant, you and your descendants after you throughout their generations. 10 This is My covenant, which you shall keep, between Me and you and your descendants after you: every male among you shall be circumcised. 11 And you shall be circumcised in the flesh of your foreskin, and it

---

16:11 1 I.e., God hears　16:14 1 I.e., the well of the living one who sees me　17:5 1 I.e., exalted father 2 I.e., father of a multitude

shall be the sign of the covenant between Me and you. [12] And every male among you who is eight days old shall be circumcised throughout your generations, *including* a slave who is born in the house or who is bought with money from any foreigner, who is not of your descendants. [13] A slave who is born in your house or who is bought with your money shall certainly be circumcised; so My covenant shall be in your flesh as an everlasting covenant. [14] But *as for* an uncircumcised male, one who is not circumcised in the flesh of his foreskin, that person shall be cut off from his people; he has broken My covenant."

[15] Then God said to Abraham, "As for your wife Sarai, you shall not call her *by* the name [1]Sarai, but [2]Sarah *shall be* her name. [16] I will bless her, and indeed I will give you a son by her. Then I will bless her, and she shall be *a mother of* nations; kings of peoples will come from her." [17] Then Abraham fell on his face and laughed, and said in his heart, "Will a child be born to a man a hundred years old? And will Sarah, who is ninety years old, give birth *to a child?*" [18] And Abraham said to God, "Oh that Ishmael might live before You!" [19] But God said, "No, but your wife Sarah will bear you a son, and you shall name him [1]Isaac; and I will establish My covenant with him as an everlasting covenant for his descendants after him. [20] As for Ishmael, I have heard you; behold, I will bless him, and make him fruitful and multiply him exceedingly. He shall father twelve princes, and I will make him into a great nation. [21] But I will establish My covenant with Isaac, whom Sarah will bear to you at this season next year." [22] When He finished talking with him, God went up from Abraham.

[23] Then Abraham took his son Ishmael, and all *the slaves* who were born in his house and all who were bought with his money, every male among the men of Abraham's household, and circumcised the flesh of their foreskin on this very same day, as God had said to him. [24] Now Abraham was ninety-nine years old when he was circumcised in the flesh of his foreskin. [25] And his son Ishmael was thirteen years old when he was circumcised in the flesh of his foreskin. [26] On this very same day Abraham was circumcised, as well as his son Ishmael. [27] And all the men of his household, those who were born in the house or bought with money from a foreigner, were circumcised with him.

Birth of Isaac Promised

18 Now the LORD appeared to Abraham by the oaks of Mamre, while he was sitting at the tent door in the heat of the day. [2] When he raised his eyes and looked, behold, three men were standing opposite him; and when he saw *them,* he ran from the tent door to meet them and bowed down to the ground, [3] and said, "My Lord, if now I have found favor in Your sight, please do not pass Your servant by. [4] Please let a little water be brought and wash [1]your feet, and make yourselves comfortable under the tree; [5] and I will bring a piece of bread, so that you may refresh yourselves; after that you may go on, since you have visited your servant." And they said, "So do as you have said." [6] So Abraham hurried into the tent to Sarah, and said, "Quickly, prepare three measures of fine flour, knead *it,* and make bread cakes." [7] Abraham also ran to the herd, and took a tender and choice calf and gave *it* to the servant, and he hurried to prepare it. [8] He took curds and milk and the calf which he had prepared, and set *it* before them; and he was standing by them under the tree as they ate.

[9] Then they said to him, "Where is your wife Sarah?" And he said, "There, in the tent." [10] He said, "I will certainly return to you at this time next year; and behold, your wife Sarah will have a son." And Sarah was listening at the tent door, which was behind him. [11] Now Abraham and Sarah were old, advanced in age; Sarah was past childbearing. [12] So Sarah laughed to herself, saying, "After I have become old, am I to have pleasure, my lord being old also?" [13] But the LORD said to Abraham, "Why did Sarah laugh, saying, 'Shall I actually give birth *to a child,* when I am *so* old?' [14] Is anything too difficult for the LORD? At the appointed time I will return to you, at this time next year, and Sarah will have a son." [15] Sarah denied *it,* however, saying, "I did not laugh"; for she was afraid. And He said, "No, but you did laugh."

[16] Then the men rose up from there, and looked down toward Sodom; and Abraham was walking with them to send them off. [17] The LORD said, "Shall I hide from Abraham what I am about to do, [18] since Abraham will certainly become a great and mighty nation, and in him all the nations of the earth will be blessed? [19] For I have chosen him, so that he may command his children and his household after him to keep the way of the LORD by doing righteousness and justice, so that the LORD may bring upon Abraham what He has spoken about him." [20] And the LORD said, "The outcry of Sodom and Gomorrah is indeed great, and their sin is exceedingly grave. [21] I will go down now and see whether they have done entirely as the outcry, which has come to Me *indicates;* and if not, I will know."

Abraham Appeals for Sodom

[22] Then the men turned away from there and went toward Sodom, while Abraham was still standing before the LORD. [23] Abraham approached and said, "Will You indeed sweep away the righteous with the wicked? [24] Suppose there are fifty righteous people within the city; will You indeed sweep *it* away and not spare the place for the sake of the fifty righteous who are in it? [25] Far be it from You to do such a thing, to kill the righteous with the wicked, so that the righteous and the wicked are *treated* alike. Far be it from You! Shall not the Judge of all the earth deal justly?" [26] So the LORD said, "If I find in Sodom fifty righteous within the city, then I will spare the entire place on their account." [27] And Abraham replied, "Now behold, I have ventured to speak

---

to the Lord, although I am *only* dust and ashes. 28 Suppose the fifty righteous are lacking five, will You destroy the entire city because of five?" And He said, "I will not destroy *it* if I find forty-five there." 29 And he spoke to Him yet again and said, "Suppose forty are found there?" And He said, "I will not do *it* on account of the forty." 30 Then he said, "Oh may the Lord not be angry, and I shall speak; suppose thirty are found there?" And He said, "I will not do *it* if I find thirty there." 31 And he said, "Now behold, I have ventured to speak to the Lord; suppose twenty are found there?" And He said, "I will not destroy *it* on account of the twenty." 32 Then he said, "Oh may the Lord not be angry, and I shall speak only this once: suppose ten are found there?" And He said, "I will not destroy *it* on account of the ten." 33 As soon as He had finished speaking to Abraham the LORD departed, and Abraham returned to his place.

The Doom of Sodom

19 Now the two angels came to Sodom in the evening as Lot was sitting at the gate of Sodom. When Lot saw *them,* he stood up to meet them and bowed down *with his* face to the ground. 2 And he said, "Now behold, my lords, please turn aside into your servant's house, and spend the night, and wash your feet; then you may rise early and go on your way." They said, "No, but we shall spend the night in the public square." 3 Yet he strongly urged them, so they turned aside to him and entered his house; and he prepared a feast for them and baked unleavened bread, and they ate. 4 Before they lay down, the men of the city—the men of Sodom—surrounded the house, both young and old, all the people from every quarter; 5 and they called to Lot and said to him, "Where are the men who came to you tonight? Bring them out to us that we may †have relations with them." 6 But Lot went out to them at the doorway, and shut the door behind him, 7 and said, "Please, my brothers, do not act wickedly. 8 Now look, I have two daughters who have not had relations with *any* man; please let me bring them out to you, and do to them whatever you like; only do not do anything to these men, because they have come under the shelter of my roof." 9 But they said, "Get out of the way!" They also said, "This one came in as a foreigner, and already he is acting like a judge; now we will treat you worse than them!" So they pressed hard against Lot and moved forward to break the door. 10 But the men reached out their hands and brought Lot into the house with them, and shut the door. 11 Then they struck the men who were at the doorway of the house with blindness, from the small to the great, so that they became weary of *trying* to find the doorway.

12 Then the *two* men said to Lot, "Whom else do you have here? A son-in-law and your sons and daughters, and whomever you have in the city, bring *them* out of the place; 13 for we are about to destroy this place, because their outcry has become so great before the

LORD that the LORD has sent us to destroy it." 14 So Lot went out and spoke to his sons-in-law, who were to marry his daughters, and said, "Up, get out of this place, for the LORD is destroying the city." But he appeared to his sons-in-law to be joking.

15 When morning dawned, the angels urged Lot, saying, "Up, take your wife and your two daughters who are here, or you will be swept away in the punishment of the city." 16 But he hesitated. So the men grasped his hand and the hand of his wife and the hands of his two daughters, because the compassion of the LORD *was* upon him; and they brought him out and put him outside the city. 17 When they had brought them outside, one said, "Escape for your life! Do not look behind you, and do not stay anywhere in the surrounding area; escape to the mountains, or you will be swept away." 18 But Lot said to them, "Oh no, my lords! 19 Now behold, your servant has found favor in your sight, and you have magnified your compassion, which you have shown me by saving my life; but I cannot escape to the mountains, for the disaster will overtake me and I will die; 20 now behold, this town is near *enough* to flee to, and it is small. Please, let me escape there (is it not small?) so that my life may be saved." 21 And he said to him, "Behold, I grant you this request also, not to overthrow the town of which you have spoken. 22 Hurry, escape there, for I cannot do anything until you arrive there." Therefore the town was named †Zoar.

23 The sun had risen over the earth when Lot came to Zoar. 24 Then the LORD rained brimstone and fire on Sodom and Gomorrah from the LORD out of heaven, 25 and He overthrew those cities, and all the surrounding area, and all the inhabitants of the cities, and what grew on the ground. 26 But Lot's wife, from behind him, looked *back,* and she became a pillar of salt.

27 Now Abraham got up early in the morning *and went* to the place where he had stood before the LORD; 28 and he looked down toward Sodom and Gomorrah, and toward all the land of the surrounding area; and behold, he saw the smoke of the land ascended like the smoke of a furnace.

29 So it came about, when God destroyed the cities of the surrounding area, that God remembered Abraham, and sent Lot out of the midst of the destruction, when He overthrew the cities in which Lot had lived.

Lot and His Daughters

30 Now Lot went up from Zoar with his two daughters and stayed in the mountains, because he was afraid to stay in Zoar; and he stayed in a cave, he and his two daughters. 31 Then the firstborn said to the younger, "Our father is old, and there is not a man on earth to have relations with us according to the custom of all the earth. 32 Come, let's make our father drink wine, and let's sleep with him so that we may keep our family alive through our father." 33 So they made their father drink wine that night, and the firstborn went in and slept with

her father; and he did not know when she lay down or got up. 34 On the following day, the firstborn said to the younger, "Look, I slept last night with my father; let's make him drink wine tonight too, then you go in and sleep with him, so that we may keep our family alive through our father." 35 So they had their father drink wine that night too, and the younger got up and slept with him; and he did not know when she lay down or got up. 36 And *so* both of the daughters of Lot conceived by their father. 37 The firstborn gave birth to a son, and named him Moab; he is the father of the Moabites to this day. 38 As for the younger, she also gave birth to a son, and named him Ben-ammi; he is the father of the sons of Ammon to this day.

Abraham's Treachery

20 Now Abraham journeyed from there toward the land of the ᶦNegev, and settled between Kadesh and Shur; then he lived for a time in Gerar. 2 And Abraham said of his wife Sarah, "She is my sister." So Abimelech king of Gerar sent *men* and took Sarah. 3 But God came to Abimelech in a dream of the night, and said to him, "Behold, you are a dead man because of the woman whom you have taken, for she is married." 4 Now Abimelech had not come near her; and he said, "Lord, will You kill a nation, even *though* blameless? 5 Did he himself not say to me, 'She is my sister'? And she herself said, 'He is my brother.' In the integrity of my heart and the innocence of my hands I have done this." 6 Then God said to him in the dream, "Yes, I know that in the integrity of your heart you have done this, and I also kept you from sinning against Me; therefore I did not let you touch her. 7 Now then, return the man's wife, for he is a prophet, and he will pray for you and you will live. But if you do not return *her,* know that you will certainly die, you and all who are yours."

8 So Abimelech got up early in the morning and called all his servants, and told all these things in their presence; and the people were greatly frightened. 9 Then Abimelech called Abraham and said to him, "What have you done to us? And how have I sinned against you, that you have brought on me and on my kingdom a great sin? You have done to me things that ought not to be done." 10 And Abimelech said to Abraham, "What have you encountered, that you have done this thing?" 11 Abraham said, "Because I thought, surely there is no fear of God in this place, and they will kill me because of my wife. 12 Besides, she actually is my sister, the daughter of my father, but not the daughter of my mother; and she became my wife; 13 and it came about, when God caused me to wander from my father's house, that I said to her, 'This is the kindness which you will show to me: everywhere we go, say of me, "He is my brother." ' " 14 Abimelech then took sheep and oxen and male and female servants, and gave them to Abraham, and returned his wife Sarah to him. 15 Abimelech said, "Behold, my land is before you; settle wherever you please." 16 To Sarah he said, "Look, I have given your brother a thousand

pieces of silver. It is your vindication before all who are with you, and before everyone you are cleared." 17 Then Abraham prayed to God, and God healed Abimelech and his wife and his female slaves, so that they gave birth *to children.* 18 For the LORD had completely closed all the wombs of the household of Abimelech because of Sarah, Abraham's wife.

Isaac Is Born

21 Then the LORD took note of Sarah as He had said, and the LORD did for Sarah as He had promised. 2 So Sarah conceived and bore a son to Abraham in his old age, at the appointed time of which God had spoken to him. 3 Abraham named his son who was born to him, the son whom Sarah bore to him, Isaac. 4 Then Abraham circumcised his son Isaac when he was eight days old, as God had commanded him. 5 Now Abraham was a hundred years old when his son Isaac was born to him. 6 Sarah said, "God has made laughter for me; everyone who hears will laugh with me." 7 And she said, "Who would have said to Abraham that Sarah would nurse children? Yet I have given birth to a son in his old age."

8 And the child grew and was weaned, and Abraham held a great feast on the day that Isaac was weaned.

Sarah Turns against Hagar

9 Now Sarah saw the son of Hagar the Egyptian, whom she had borne to Abraham, mocking *Isaac.* 10 Therefore she said to Abraham, "Drive out this slave woman and her son, for the son of this slave woman shall not be an heir with my son Isaac!" 11 The matter distressed Abraham greatly because of his son *Ishmael.* 12 But God said to Abraham, "Do not be distressed because of the boy and your slave woman; whatever Sarah tells you, listen to her, for through Isaac your descendants shall be named. 13 And of the son of the slave woman I will make a nation also, because he is your descendant." 14 So Abraham got up early in the morning and took bread and a skin of water, and gave *them* to Hagar, putting *them* on her shoulder, and *gave her* the boy, and sent her away. And she departed and wandered about in the wilderness of Beersheba.

15 When the water in the skin was used up, she left the boy under one of the bushes. 16 Then she went and sat down opposite him, about a bowshot away, for she said, "May I not see the boy die!" And she sat opposite him, and raised her voice and wept. 17 God heard the boy crying; and the angel of God called to Hagar from heaven and said to her, "What is the matter with you, Hagar? Do not fear, for God has heard the voice of the boy where he is. 18 Get up, lift up the boy, and hold him by the hand, for I will make a great nation of him." 19 Then God opened her eyes, and she saw a well of water; and she went and filled the skin with water and gave the boy a drink.

20 And God was with the boy, and he grew; and he lived in the wilderness and became an archer. 21 He lived in the wilderness of Paran,

---

and his mother took a wife for him from the land of Egypt.

Covenant with Abimelech
22 Now it came about at that time that Abimelech and Phicol, the commander of his army, spoke to Abraham, saying, "God is with you in all that you do; 23 so now, swear to me here by God that you will not deal falsely with me or with my offspring or with my descendants, but according to the kindness that I have shown to you, you shall show to me and to the land in which you have resided." 24 Abraham said, "I swear it." 25 But Abraham complained to Abimelech because of the well of water which the servants of Abimelech had seized. 26 And Abimelech said, "I do not know who has done this thing; you did not tell me, nor did I hear of it until today."

27 So Abraham took sheep and oxen and gave them to Abimelech, and the two of them made a covenant. 28 But Abraham set seven ewe lambs of the flock by themselves. 29 Then Abimelech said to Abraham, "What do these seven ewe lambs mean, which you have set by themselves?" 30 He said, "You shall take these seven ewe lambs from my hand so that it may be a witness for me, that I dug this well." 31 Therefore he called that place Beersheba, because there the two of them took an oath. 32 So they made a covenant at Beersheba; and Abimelech and Phicol, the commander of his army, got up and returned to the land of the Philistines. 33 Abraham planted a tamarisk tree at Beersheba, and there he called on the name of the LORD, the Everlasting God. 34 And Abraham resided in the land of the Philistines for many days.

The Offering of Isaac
22 Now it came about after these things, that God tested Abraham, and said to him, "Abraham!" And he said, "Here I am." 2 Then He said, "Take now your son, your only son, whom you love, Isaac, and go to the land of Moriah, and offer him there as a burnt offering on one of the mountains of which I will tell you." 3 So Abraham got up early in the morning and saddled his donkey, and took two of his young men with him and his son Isaac; and he split wood for the burnt offering, and set out and went to the place of which God had told him. 4 On the third day Abraham raised his eyes and saw the place from a distance. 5 Then Abraham said to his young men, "Stay here with the donkey, and I and the boy will go over there; and we will worship and return to you." 6 And Abraham took the wood for the burnt offering and laid it on his son Isaac, and he took in his hand the fire and the knife. So the two of them walked on together. 7 Isaac spoke to his father Abraham and said, "My father!" And he said, "Here I am, my son." And he said, "Look, the fire and the wood, but where is the lamb for the burnt offering?" 8 Abraham said, "God will provide for Himself the lamb for the burnt offering, my son." So the two of them walked on together.

9 Then they came to the place of which God had told him; and Abraham built the altar there and arranged the wood, and bound his son Isaac and laid him on the altar, on top of the wood. 10 And Abraham reached out with his hand and took the knife to slaughter his son. 11 But the angel of the LORD called to him from heaven and said, "Abraham, Abraham!" And he said, "Here I am." 12 He said, "Do not reach out your hand against the boy, and do not do anything to him; for now I know that you fear God, since you have not withheld your son, your only son, from Me." 13 Then Abraham raised his eyes and looked, and behold, behind *him was* a ram caught in the thicket by its horns; and Abraham went and took the ram and offered it up as a burnt offering in the place of his son. 14 And Abraham named that place The LORD Will Provide, as it is said to this day, "On the mountain of the LORD it will be provided."

15 Then the angel of the LORD called to Abraham a second time from heaven, 16 and said, "By Myself I have sworn, declares the LORD, because you have done this thing and have not withheld your son, your only son, 17 indeed I will greatly bless you, and I will greatly multiply your ¹seed as the stars of the heavens and as the sand, which is on the seashore; and your ²seed shall possess the gate of their enemies. 18 And in your ¹seed all the nations of the earth shall be blessed, because you have obeyed My voice." 19 So Abraham returned to his young men, and they got up and went together to Beersheba; and Abraham lived in Beersheba.

20 Now it came about after these things, that Abraham was told, saying, "Behold, Milcah also has borne children to your brother Nahor: 21 Uz his firstborn, Buz his brother, Kemuel (the father of Aram), 22 Chesed, Hazo, Pildash, Jidlaph, and Bethuel"—23 and *it was* Bethuel *who* fathered Rebekah. These eight Milcah bore to Nahor, Abraham's brother. 24 His concubine, whose name was Reumah, also gave birth to Tebah, Gaham, Tahash, and Maacah.

Death and Burial of Sarah
23 Now Sarah lived 127 years; *these were* the years of the life of Sarah. 2 Sarah died in Kiriath-arba (that is, Hebron) in the land of Canaan; and Abraham came in to mourn for Sarah and to weep for her. 3 Then Abraham arose from *mourning* before his dead, and spoke to the sons of Heth, saying, 4 "I am a stranger and a foreign resident among you; give me a burial site among you so that I may bury my dead out of my sight." 5 The sons of Heth answered Abraham, saying to him, 6 "Hear us, my lord: you are a mighty prince among us; bury your dead in the choicest of our graves; none of us will refuse you his grave for burying your dead." 7 So Abraham stood up and bowed to the people of the land, the sons of Heth. 8 And he spoke with them, saying, "If you are willing to *let me* bury my dead out of my sight, listen to me, and plead with Ephron the son of Zohar for me, 9 that he may give me the cave of Machpelah which he owns, which is at the end of his field; for the full price let him give it to

---

22:17 ¹Or descendants   2 Or descendants   22:18 ¹Or descendants

me in your presence for a burial site." 10 Now Ephron was sitting among the sons of Heth; and Ephron the Hittite answered Abraham so that the sons of Heth heard, that is, all who entered the gate of his city, saying, 11 "No, my lord, listen to me; I give you the field, and I give you the cave that is in it. In the presence of the sons of my people I give it to you; bury your dead." 12 And Abraham bowed before the people of the land. 13 But he spoke to Ephron so that the people of the land heard, saying, "If you will only please listen to me; I will give the price of the field, accept it from me so that I may bury my dead there." 14 Then Ephron answered Abraham, saying to him, 15 "My lord, listen to me: a plot of land worth 1four hundred shekels of silver—what is that between me and you? So bury your dead." 16 Abraham listened to Ephron; and Abraham weighed out for Ephron the silver which he had named in the presence of the sons of Heth, four hundred shekels of silver, currency acceptable to a merchant.

17 So Ephron's field, which was in Machpelah, which faced Mamre, the field and the cave which was in it, and all the trees which were in the field, that were within all the confines of its border, were deeded over 18 to Abraham as a possession in the presence of the sons of Heth, before all who entered the gate of his city. 19 After this, Abraham buried his wife Sarah in the cave of the field of Machpelah facing Mamre (that is, Hebron), in the land of Canaan. 20 So the field and the cave that was in it were deeded over to Abraham for a burial site by the sons of Heth.

A Bride for Isaac

24 Now Abraham was old, advanced in age; and the LORD had blessed Abraham in every way. 2 Abraham said to his servant, the oldest of his household who was in charge of all that he owned, "Please place your hand under my thigh, 3 and I will make you swear by the LORD, the God of heaven and the God of earth, that you shall not take a wife for my son from the daughters of the Canaanites, among whom I live; 4 but you will go to my country and to my relatives, and take a wife for my son Isaac." 5 The servant said to him, "Suppose the woman is not willing to follow me to this land; should I take your son back to the land from where you came?" 6 Then Abraham said to him, "Beware that you do not take my son back there! 7 The LORD, the God of heaven, who took me from my father's house and from the land of my birth, and who spoke to me and who swore to me, saying, 'To your descendants I will give this land'—He will send His angel ahead of you, and you will take a wife for my son from there. 8 But if the woman is not willing to follow you, then you will be free of this oath of mine; only do not take my son back there." 9 So the servant placed his hand under the thigh of his master Abraham, and swore to him concerning this matter.

10 Then the servant took ten camels from the camels of his master, and went out with a variety of good things of his master's in his hand; so he set out and went to Mesopotamia, to the city of Nahor. 11 He made the camels kneel down outside the city by the well of water when it was evening, the time when women go out to draw water. 12 And he said, "LORD, God of my master Abraham, please grant me success today, and show kindness to my master Abraham. 13 Behold, I am standing by the spring, and the daughters of the men of the city are coming out to draw water; 14 now may it be that the young woman to whom I say, 'Please let down your jar so that I may drink,' and who answers, 'Drink, and I will water your camels also'—may she be the one whom You have appointed for Your servant Isaac; and by this I will know that You have shown kindness to my master."

Rebekah Is Chosen

15 And it came about, before he had finished speaking, that behold, Rebekah, who was born to Bethuel the son of Milcah, the wife of Abraham's brother Nahor, came out with her jar on her shoulder. 16 The young woman was very beautiful, a virgin; no man had had relations with her. She went down to the spring, filled her jar, and came up. 17 Then the servant ran to meet her, and said, "Please let me drink a little water from your jar." 18 And she said, "Drink, my lord"; then she quickly lowered her jar to her hand, and gave him a drink. 19 Now when she had finished giving him a drink, she said, "I will also draw water for your camels until they have finished drinking." 20 So she quickly emptied her jar into the trough, and ran back to the well to draw, and she drew for all his camels. 21 Meanwhile, the man was taking a close look at her in silence, to find out whether the LORD had made his journey successful or not.

22 When the camels had finished drinking, the man took a gold ring weighing a 1half-shekel, and two bracelets for her wrists weighing ten shekels in gold, 23 and he said, "Whose daughter are you? Please tell me, is there room for us to stay overnight at your father's house?" 24 She said to him, "I am the daughter of Bethuel, Milcah's son, whom she bore to Nahor." 25 Again she said to him, "We have plenty of both straw and feed, and room to stay overnight." 26 Then the man bowed low and worshiped the LORD. 27 And he said, "Blessed be the LORD, the God of my master Abraham, who has not abandoned His kindness and His trustworthiness toward my master; as for me, the LORD has guided me in the way to the house of my master's brothers."

28 Then the young woman ran and told her mother's household about these things. 29 Now Rebekah had a brother whose name was Laban; and Laban ran outside to the man at the spring. 30 When he saw the ring and the bracelets on his sister's wrists, and when he heard the words of his sister Rebekah, saying, "This is what the man said to me," he went to the man; and behold, he was standing by the camels at the spring. 31 And he said, "Come in, blessed of the LORD! Why do you stand outside, since I have prepared the house, and a place

---

23:15 1About 12.5 lb. or 5.7 kg **24:22** 1A shekel was about 0.5 oz. or 14 gm

for the camels?" ³²So the man entered the house. Then Laban unloaded the camels, and he gave straw and feed to the camels, and water to wash his feet and the feet of the men who were with him. ³³But when *food* was set before him to eat, he said, "I will not eat until I have stated my business." And he said, "Speak on." ³⁴So he said, "I am Abraham's servant. ³⁵The LORD has greatly blessed my master, so that he has become rich; and He has given him flocks and herds, and silver and gold, and servants and slave women, and camels and donkeys. ³⁶Now my master's wife Sarah bore a son to my master in her old age, and he has given him all that he has. ³⁷My master made me swear, saying, 'You shall not take a wife for my son from the daughters of the Canaanites, in whose land I live; ³⁸but you shall go to my father's house and to my relatives, and take a wife for my son.' ³⁹Then I said to my master, 'Suppose the woman does not follow me.' ⁴⁰And he said to me, 'The LORD, before whom I have walked, will send His angel with you to make your journey successful, and you will take a wife for my son from my relatives and from my father's house; ⁴¹then you will be free from my oath, when you come to my relatives; and if they do not give her to you, you will be free from my oath.'

⁴²"So I came today to the spring, and said, 'LORD, God of my master Abraham, if now You will make my journey on which I have been going successful; ⁴³behold, I am standing by the spring, and may it be that the young unmarried woman who comes out to draw *water,* and to whom I say, "Please let me drink a little water from your jar"; ⁴⁴and she says to me, "You drink, and I will draw for your camels also"—let her be the woman whom the LORD has appointed for my master's son.'

⁴⁵"Before I had finished speaking in my heart, behold, Rebekah came out with her jar on her shoulder, and went down to the spring and drew *water,* and I said to her, 'Please let me drink.' ⁴⁶She quickly lowered her jar from her *shoulder,* and said, 'Drink, and I will water your camels also'; so I drank, and she watered the camels also. ⁴⁷Then I asked her, and said, 'Whose daughter are you?' And she said, 'The daughter of Bethuel, Nahor's son, whom Milcah bore to him'; and I put the ring on her nose, and the bracelets on her wrists. ⁴⁸And I bowed low and worshiped the LORD, and blessed the LORD, the God of my master Abraham, who had guided me in the right way to take the daughter of my master's brother for his son. ⁴⁹So now if you are going to deal kindly and truthfully with my master, tell me; and if not, tell me now, so that I may turn to the right or the left."

⁵⁰Then Laban and Bethuel replied, "The matter has come from the LORD; *so* we cannot speak to you bad or good. ⁵¹Here is Rebekah before you, take *her* and go, and let her be the wife of your master's son, as the LORD has spoken."

⁵²When Abraham's servant heard their words, he bowed himself to the ground before the LORD. ⁵³And the servant brought out articles of silver and articles of gold, and

garments, and gave them to Rebekah; he also gave precious things to her brother and to her mother. ⁵⁴Then he and the men who were with him ate and drank and spent the night. When they got up in the morning, he said, "Send me away to my master." ⁵⁵But her brother and her mother said, "Let the young woman stay with us *a few* days, say ten; afterward she may go." ⁵⁶However, he said to them, "Do not delay me, since the LORD has prospered my way. Send me away so that I may go to my master." ⁵⁷And they said, "We will call the young woman and ask her." ⁵⁸Then they called Rebekah and said to her, "Will you go with this man?" And she said, "I will go." ⁵⁹So they sent away their sister Rebekah and her nurse with Abraham's servant and his men. ⁶⁰And they blessed Rebekah and said to her,

"May you, our sister,
Become thousands of ten thousands,
And may your descendants possess
The gate of those who hate them."

⁶¹Then Rebekah got up with her female attendants, and they mounted the camels and followed the man. So the servant took Rebekah and departed.

Isaac Marries Rebekah

⁶²Now Isaac had come *back* from a journey to Beer-lahai-roi; for he was living in the Negev. ⁶³Isaac went out to meditate in the field toward evening; and he raised his eyes and looked, and behold, camels were coming. ⁶⁴Rebekah raised her eyes, and when she saw Isaac, she dismounted from the camel. ⁶⁵She said to the servant, "Who is that man walking in the field to meet us?" And the servant said, "He is my master." Then she took her veil and covered herself. ⁶⁶The servant told Isaac all the things that he had done. ⁶⁷Then Isaac brought her into his mother Sarah's tent, and he took Rebekah, and she became his wife, and he loved her; so Isaac was comforted after his mother's death.

Abraham's Death

25 Now Abraham took another wife, whose name was Keturah. ²She bore to him Zimran, Jokshan, Medan, Midian, Ishbak, and Shuah. ³Jokshan fathered Sheba and Dedan. And the sons of Dedan were Asshurim, Letushim, and Leummim. ⁴The sons of Midian *were* Ephah, Epher, Hanoch, Abida, and Eldaah. All of these *were* the sons of Keturah. ⁵Now Abraham gave all that he had to Isaac; ⁶but to the sons of his concubines, Abraham gave gifts while he was still living, and sent them away from his son Isaac eastward, to the land of the east.

⁷These are all the years of Abraham's life that he lived, 175 years. ⁸Abraham breathed his last and died at a good old age, an old man and satisfied *with life;* and he was gathered to his people. ⁹Then his sons Isaac and Ishmael buried him in the cave of Machpelah, in the field of Ephron the son of Zohar the Hittite, facing Mamre, ¹⁰the field which Abraham purchased from the sons of Heth; there Abraham was buried with his wife Sarah. ¹¹It came about after the death of Abraham, that

God blessed his son Isaac; and Isaac lived by Beer-lahai-roi.

Descendants of Ishmael

12 Now these are *the records of* the generations of Ishmael, Abraham's son, whom Hagar the Egyptian, Sarah's slave woman, bore to Abraham; **13** and these are the names of the sons of Ishmael, by their names, in the order of their birth: Nebaioth, the firstborn of Ishmael, Kedar, Adbeel, Mibsam, **14** Mishma, Dumah, Massa, **15** Hadad, Tema, Jetur, Naphish, and Kedemah. **16** These are the sons of Ishmael and these are their names, by their villages, and by their camps; twelve princes according to their tribes. **17** These are the years of the life of Ishmael, 137 years; and he breathed his last and died, and was gathered to his people. **18** They settled from Havilah to Shur which is east of Egypt going toward Assyria; he settled in defiance of all his relatives.

Isaac's Sons

19 Now these are *the records of* the generations of Isaac, Abraham's son: Abraham fathered Isaac; **20** and Isaac was forty years old when he took Rebekah, the daughter of Bethuel the Aramean of Paddan-aram, the sister of Laban the Aramean, to be his wife. **21** Isaac prayed to the Lord on behalf of his wife, because she was unable to have children; and the Lord answered him, and his wife Rebekah conceived. **22** But the children struggled together within her; and she said, "If it is so, why am I *in* this *condition?*" So she went to inquire of the Lord. **23** And the Lord said to her,

"Two nations are in your womb;
And two peoples will be separated from your body;
And one people will be stronger than the other;
And the older will serve the younger."

24 When her days *leading* to the delivery were at an end, behold, there were twins in her womb. **25** Now the first came out red, all over like a hairy garment; and they named him Esau. **26** Afterward his brother came out with his hand holding on to Esau's heel, so he was named *'*Jacob; and Isaac was sixty years old when she gave birth to them.

27 When the boys grew up, Esau became a skillful hunter, a man of the field; but Jacob was a civilized man, living in tents. **28** Now Isaac loved Esau because he had a taste for game; but Rebekah loved Jacob. **29** When Jacob had cooked a stew *one day,* Esau came in from the field and he was exhausted; **30** and Esau said to Jacob, "Please let me have a mouthful of that red stuff there, for I am exhausted." Therefore he was called *'*Edom *by* name. **31** But Jacob said, "First sell me your birthright." **32** Esau said, "Look, I am about to die; so of what *use* then is the birthright to me?" **33** And Jacob said, "First swear to me"; so he swore *an oath* to him, and sold his birthright to Jacob. **34** Then Jacob gave Esau bread and lentil stew; and he ate and drank, and got up and went on his way. So Esau despised his birthright.

Isaac Settles in Gerar

26 Now there was a famine in the land, besides the previous famine that had occurred in the days of Abraham. So Isaac went to Gerar, to Abimelech king of the Philistines. **2** And the Lord appeared to him and said, "Do not go down to Egypt; stay in the land of which I shall tell you. **3** Live for a time in this land and I will be with you and bless you, for to you and to your descendants I will give all these lands, and I will establish the oath which I swore to your father Abraham. **4** I will multiply your descendants as the stars of heaven, and will give your descendants all these lands; and by your descendants all the nations of the earth shall be blessed, **5** because Abraham obeyed Me and fulfilled *his* duty to Me, *and kept* My commandments, My statutes, and My laws."

6 So Isaac lived in Gerar. **7** When the men of the place asked about his wife, he said, "She is my sister," for he was afraid to say, "my wife," *thinking,* "the men of the place might kill me on account of Rebekah, since she is beautiful." **8** Now it came about, when he had been there a long time, that Abimelech king of the Philistines looked down through a window, and saw *them,* and behold, Isaac was caressing his wife Rebekah. **9** Then Abimelech called Isaac and said, "Behold, she certainly is your wife! So how *is it that* you said, 'She is my sister'?" And Isaac said to him, "Because I thought, 'otherwise I might be killed on account of her.'" **10** And Abimelech said, "What is this *that* you have done to us? One of the people might easily have slept with your wife, and you would have brought guilt upon us." **11** So Abimelech commanded all the people, saying, "He who touches this man or his wife will certainly be put to death."

12 Now Isaac sowed in that land and reaped in the same year a hundred times *as much.* And the Lord blessed him, **13** and the man became rich, and continued to grow richer until he became very wealthy; **14** for he had possessions of flocks and herds, and a great household, so that the Philistines envied him. **15** Now all the wells which his father's servants had dug in the days of his father Abraham, the Philistines stopped up by filling them with dirt. **16** Then Abimelech said to Isaac, "Go away from us, for you are too powerful for us." **17** So Isaac departed from there and camped in the Valley of Gerar, and settled there.

Argument over the Wells

18 Then Isaac dug again the wells of water which had been dug in the days of his father Abraham, for the Philistines had stopped them up after the death of Abraham; and he gave them the same names which his father had given them. **19** But when Isaac's servants dug in the valley and found there a well of flowing water, **20** the herdsmen of Gerar quarreled with the herdsmen of Isaac, saying, "The water is ours!" So he named the well Esek, because they argued with him. **21** Then they dug another well, and they quarreled over it too, so he named it Sitnah. **22** Then he moved away from there and dug another well, and they did

not quarrel over it; so he named it Rehoboth, for he said, "At last the Lord has made room for us, and we will be fruitful in the land." **23** And he went up from there to Beersheba. **24** And the Lord appeared to him the same night and said,

"I am the God of your father Abraham;
Do not fear, for I am with you.
I will bless you and multiply your
    descendants,
For the sake of My servant Abraham."

25 So he built an altar there and called upon the name of the Lord, and pitched his tent there; and there Isaac's servants dug a well.

Covenant with Abimelech

26 Then Abimelech came to him from Gerar with his adviser Ahuzzath, and Phicol the commander of his army. **27** Isaac said to them, "Why have you come to me, since you hate me and have sent me away from you?" **28** They said, "We have seen plainly that the Lord has been with you; so we said, 'An oath must now be *taken* by us,' *that is,* by you and us. So let us make a covenant with you, **29** that you will do us no harm, just as we have not touched you and have done to you nothing but good, and have sent you away in peace. You are now the blessed of the Lord." **30** Then he made them a feast, and they ate and drank. **31** In the morning they got up early and exchanged oaths; then Isaac sent them away, and they left him in peace. **32** Now it came about on the same day, that Isaac's servants came in and told him about the well which they had dug, and said to him, "We have found water." **33** So he called it *Shibah; therefore the name of the city is Beersheba to this day.

34 When Esau was forty years old he married Judith the daughter of Beeri the Hittite, and Basemath the daughter of Elon the Hittite; **35** and they brought grief to Isaac and Rebekah.

Jacob's Deception

27 Now it came about, when Isaac was old and his eyes were too dim to see, that he called his older son Esau and said to him, "My son." And he said to him, "Here I am." **2** Then Isaac said, "Behold now, I am old *and* I do not know the day of my death. **3** Now then, please take your gear, your quiver and your bow, and go out to the field and hunt game for me; **4** and prepare a delicious meal for me such as I love, and bring it to me that I may eat, so that my soul may bless you before I die."

5 Now Rebekah was listening while Isaac spoke to his son Esau. So when Esau went to the field to hunt for game to bring *home,* **6** Rebekah said to her son Jacob, "Behold, I heard your father speak to your brother Esau, saying, **7** 'Bring me *some* game and prepare a delicious meal for me, so that I may eat, and bless you in the presence of the Lord before my death.' **8** So now, my son, listen to me as I command you. **9** Go now to the flock and bring me two choice young goats from there, so that I may prepare them *as* a delicious meal for your father, such as he loves. **10** Then you shall bring *it* to your father, that he may eat, so that

he may bless you before his death." **11** But Jacob said to his mother Rebekah, "Behold, my brother Esau is a hairy man and I am a smooth man. **12** Perhaps my father will touch me, then I will be like a deceiver in his sight, and I will bring upon myself a curse and not a blessing." **13** But his mother said to him, "Your curse be on me, my son; only obey my voice, and go, get *the goats* for me." **14** So he went and got *them,* and brought *them* to his mother; and his mother made a delicious meal such as his father loved. **15** Then Rebekah took the best garments of her elder son Esau, which were with her in the house, and put them on her younger son Jacob. **16** And she put the skins of the young goats on his hands and on the smooth part of his neck. **17** She also gave the delicious meal and the bread which she had made to her son Jacob.

18 Then he came to his father and said, "My father." And he said, "Here I am. Who are you, my son?" **19** Jacob said to his father, "I am Esau your firstborn; I have done as you told me. Come now, sit and eat of my game, so that you may bless me." **20** Isaac said to his son, "How is it that you have *it* so quickly, my son?" And he said, "Because the Lord your God made *it* come to me." **21** Then Isaac said to Jacob, "Please come close, so that I may feel you, my son, whether you are really my son Esau or not." **22** So Jacob came close to his father Isaac, and he touched him and said, "The voice is the voice of Jacob, but the hands are the hands of Esau." **23** And he did not recognize him, because his hands were hairy like his brother Esau's hands; so he blessed him. **24** And he said, "Are you really my son Esau?" And he said, "I am." **25** So he said, "Bring *it* to me, and I will eat of my son's game, that I may bless you." And he brought *it* to him, and he ate; he also brought him wine and he drank. **26** Then his father Isaac said to him, "Please come close and kiss me, my son." **27** So he came close and kissed him; and when he smelled the smell of his garments, he blessed him and said,

"See, the smell of my son
Is like the smell of a field which the Lord
    has blessed;
28   Now may God give you of the dew of
        heaven,
    And of the fatness of the earth,
    And an abundance of grain and new wine;
29   May peoples serve you,
    And nations bow down to you;
    Be master of your brothers,
    And may your mother's sons bow down to
        you.
    Cursed be those who curse you,
    And blessed be those who bless you."

The Stolen Blessing

30 Now it came about, as soon as Isaac had finished blessing Jacob, and Jacob had hardly gone out from the presence of his father Isaac, that his brother Esau came in from his hunting. **31** Then he also made a delicious meal, and brought it to his father; and he said to his father, "Let my father arise and eat of his son's game, that you may bless me." **32** His father

---

26:33 ¹Meaning uncertain, perhaps *oath*

Isaac said to him, "Who are you?" And he said, "I am your son, your firstborn, Esau." ³³ Then Isaac trembled violently, and said, "Who then was he who hunted game and brought *it* to me, so that I ate from all *of it* before you came, and blessed him? Yes, *and* he shall be blessed." ³⁴ When Esau heard the words of his father, he cried out with an exceedingly great and bitter cry, and said to his father, "Bless me, me as well, my father!" ³⁵ And he said, "Your brother came deceitfully and has taken away your blessing." ³⁶ Then *Esau* said, "Is he not rightly named Jacob, for he has betrayed me these two times? He took away my birthright, and behold, now he has taken away my blessing." And he said, "Have you not reserved a blessing for me?" ³⁷ But Isaac replied to Esau, "Behold, I have made him your master, and I have given to him all his relatives as servants; and with grain and new wine I have sustained him. What then can I do for you, my son?" ³⁸ Esau said to his father, "Do you have only one blessing, my father? Bless me, me as well, my father." So Esau raised his voice and wept.

³⁹ Then his father Isaac answered and said to him,

"Behold, away from the fertility of the earth shall be your dwelling,
And away from the dew of heaven from above.
⁴⁰ "And by your sword you shall live,
And you shall serve your brother;
But it shall come about when you become restless,
That you will break his yoke from your neck."

⁴¹ So Esau held a grudge against Jacob because of the blessing with which his father had blessed him; and Esau said to himself, "The days of mourning for my father are near; then I will kill my brother Jacob." ⁴² Now when the words of her elder son Esau were reported to Rebekah, she sent *word* and called her younger son Jacob, and said to him, "Behold your brother Esau is consoling himself concerning you *by planning* to kill you. ⁴³ Now then, my son, obey my voice, and arise, flee to Haran, to my brother Laban! ⁴⁴ Stay with him a few days, until your brother's fury subsides, ⁴⁵ until your brother's anger against you subsides and he forgets what you did to him. Then I will send *word* and get you from there. Why should I lose you both in one day?"

⁴⁶ And Rebekah said to Isaac, "I am tired of living because of the daughters of Heth; if Jacob takes a wife from the daughters of Heth like these from the daughters of the land, what good will my life be to me?"

Jacob Is Sent Away

28 So Isaac called Jacob and blessed him and commanded him, saying to him, "You shall not take a wife from the daughters of Canaan. ² Arise, go to Paddan-aram, to the house of Bethuel your mother's father; and from there take to yourself a wife from the daughters of Laban, your mother's brother. ³ May God Almighty bless you and make you fruitful and multiply you, so that you may

become a multitude of peoples. ⁴ May He also give you the blessing of Abraham, to you and to your descendants with you, so that you may possess the land where you live as a stranger, which God gave to Abraham." ⁵ Then Isaac sent Jacob away, and he went to Paddan-aram to Laban, son of Bethuel the Aramean, the brother of Rebekah, the mother of Jacob and Esau.

⁶ Now Esau saw that Isaac had blessed Jacob and sent him away to Paddan-aram to take to himself a wife from there, *and that* when he blessed him he commanded him, saying, "You shall not take a wife from the daughters of Canaan," ⁷ and that Jacob had obeyed his father and his mother and had gone to Paddan-aram. ⁸ So Esau saw that the daughters of Canaan displeased his father Isaac; ⁹ and Esau went to Ishmael, and married, besides the wives that he had, Mahalath the daughter of Ishmael, Abraham's son, the sister of Nebaioth.

Jacob's Dream

¹⁰ Then Jacob departed from Beersheba and went toward Haran. ¹¹ And he happened upon a particular place and spent the night there, because the sun had set; and he took one of the stones of the place and made it a support for his head, and lay down in that place. ¹² And he had a dream, and behold, a ladder was set up on the earth with its top reaching to heaven; and behold, the angels of God were ascending and descending on it. ¹³ Then behold, the Lord was standing above it and said, "I am the Lord, the God of your father Abraham and the God of Isaac; the land on which you lie I will give to you and to your descendants. ¹⁴ Your descendants will also be like the dust of the earth, and you will spread out to the west and to the east, and to the north and to the south; and in you and in your descendants shall all the families of the earth be blessed. ¹⁵ Behold, I am with you and will keep you wherever you go, and will bring you back to this land; for I will not leave you until I have done what I have promised you." ¹⁶ Then Jacob awoke from his sleep and said, "The Lord is certainly in this place, and I did not know it!" ¹⁷ And he was afraid and said, "How awesome is this place! This is none other than the house of God, and this is the gate of heaven!"

¹⁸ So Jacob got up early in the morning, and took the stone that he had placed as a support for his head, and set it up as a memorial stone, and poured oil on its top. ¹⁹ Then he named that place ¹Bethel; but previously the name of the city had been Luz. ²⁰ Jacob also made a vow, saying, "If God will be with me and will keep me on this journey that I take, and give me food to eat and garments to wear, ²¹ and I return to my father's house in safety, then the Lord will be my God. ²² And this stone, which I have set up as a memorial stone, will be God's house, and of everything that You give me I will assuredly give a tenth to You."

Jacob Meets Rachel

29 Then Jacob set out on his journey, and went to the land of the people of the

---

28:19 ¹ I.e., the house of God

east. 2 He looked, and saw a well in the field, and behold, three flocks of sheep were lying there beside it, because they watered the flocks from that well. Now the stone on the mouth of the well was large. 3 When all the flocks were gathered there, they would roll the stone from the mouth of the well and water the sheep. Then they would put the stone back in its place on the mouth of the well.

4 Jacob said to them, "My brothers, where are you from?" And they said, "We are from Haran." 5 So he said to them, "Do you know Laban the son of Nahor?" And they said, "We know *him*." 6 And he said to them, "Is it well with him?" And they said, "It is well, and here is his daughter Rachel coming with the sheep." 7 Then he said, "Look, it is still high day; it is not time for the livestock to be gathered. Water the sheep, and go, pasture them." 8 But they said, "We cannot, until all the flocks are gathered, and they roll the stone from the mouth of the well; then we water the sheep."

9 While he was still speaking with them, Rachel came with her father's sheep, for she was a shepherdess. 10 When Jacob saw Rachel the daughter of his mother's brother Laban, and the sheep of his mother's brother Laban, Jacob went up and rolled the stone from the mouth of the well, and watered the flock of his mother's brother Laban. 11 Then Jacob kissed Rachel, and raised his voice and wept. 12 Jacob told Rachel that he was a relative of her father and that he was Rebekah's son, and she ran and told her father.

13 So when Laban heard the news about Jacob, his sister's son, he ran to meet him, and embraced him and kissed him, and brought him to his house. Then he told Laban all these things. 14 And Laban said to him, "You certainly are my bone and my flesh." And he stayed with him a month.

15 Then Laban said to Jacob, "Because you are my relative, should you therefore serve me for nothing? Tell me, what shall your wages be?" 16 Now Laban had two daughters; the name of the older was Leah, and the name of the younger was Rachel. 17 And Leah's eyes were weak, but Rachel was beautiful in figure and appearance. 18 Now Jacob loved Rachel, so he said, "I will serve you seven years for your younger daughter Rachel." 19 Laban said, "It is better that I give her to you than to give her to another man; stay with me." 20 So Jacob served seven years for Rachel, and they seemed to him like *only* a few days because of his love for her.

Laban's Treachery

21 Then Jacob said to Laban, "Give *me* my wife, for my time is completed, that I may have relations with her." 22 So Laban gathered all the people of the place and held a feast. 23 Now in the evening he took his daughter Leah and brought her to him; and *Jacob* had relations with her. 24 Laban also gave his female slave Zilpah to his daughter Leah as a slave. 25 So it came about in the morning that, behold, it was Leah! And he said to Laban, "What is this *that* you have done to me? Was it not for Rachel

that I served with you? Why then have you deceived me?" 26 But Laban said, "It is not the practice in our place to marry off the younger before the firstborn. 27 Complete the week of this one, and we will give you the other also for the service which you shall serve with me, for another seven years." 28 Jacob did so and completed her week, and he gave him his daughter Rachel as his wife. 29 Laban also gave his female slave Bilhah to his daughter Rachel as her slave. 30 So *Jacob* had relations with Rachel also, and indeed he loved Rachel more than Leah, and he served with Laban for another seven years.

31 Now the LORD saw that Leah was unloved, and He opened her womb; but Rachel was unable to have children. 32 Leah conceived and gave birth to a son, and named him Reuben, for she said, "Because the LORD has seen my affliction; surely now my husband will love me." 33 Then she conceived again and gave birth to a son, and said, "Because the LORD has heard that I am unloved, He has therefore given me this *son* also." So she named him Simeon. 34 And she conceived again and gave birth to a son, and said, "Now this time my husband will become attached to me, because I have borne him three sons." Therefore he was named Levi. 35 And she conceived again and gave birth to a son, and said, "This time I will praise the LORD." Therefore she named him Judah. Then she stopped having children.

The Sons of Jacob

30 Now when Rachel saw that she had not borne Jacob *any* children, she became jealous of her sister; and she said to Jacob, "Give me children, or else I am going to die." 2 Then Jacob's anger burned against Rachel, and he said, "Am I in the place of God, who has withheld from you the fruit of the womb?" 3 Then she said, "Here is my female slave Bilhah: have relations with her that she may give birth [1] on my knees, so that by her I too may obtain a child." 4 So she gave him her slave Bilhah as a wife, and Jacob had relations with her. 5 Bilhah conceived and bore Jacob a son. 6 Then Rachel said, "God has vindicated me, and has indeed heard my voice and has given me a son." Therefore she named him Dan. 7 And Rachel's slave Bilhah conceived again and bore Jacob a second son. 8 So Rachel said, "*With* mighty wrestling I have wrestled with my sister, *and* I have indeed prevailed." And she named him Naphtali.

9 When Leah saw that she had stopped having children, she took her slave Zilpah and gave her to Jacob as a wife. 10 And Leah's slave Zilpah bore Jacob a son. 11 Then Leah said, "How fortunate!" So she named him Gad. 12 And Leah's slave Zilpah bore Jacob a second son. 13 Then Leah said, "Happy am I! For women will call me happy." So she named him Asher.

14 Now in the days of wheat harvest Reuben went and found mandrake fruits in the field, and brought them to his mother Leah. Then Rachel said to Leah, "Please give me some of your son's mandrakes." 15 But she said to her,

---
30:3 [1] I.e., Prob. referring to a ritual of adoption

"Is it a small matter for you to take my husband? And would you take my son's mandrakes also?" So Rachel said, "Therefore he may sleep with you tonight in return for your son's mandrakes." 16 When Jacob came in from the field in the evening, Leah went out to meet him and said, "You must have relations with me, for I have indeed hired you with my son's mandrakes." So he slept with her that night. 17 God listened to Leah, and she conceived and bore Jacob a fifth son. 18 Then Leah said, "God has given me my reward, because I gave my slave to my husband." So she named him Issachar. 19 And Leah conceived again and bore a sixth son to Jacob. 20 Then Leah said, "God has endowed me with a good gift; finally my husband will acknowledge me *as his wife,* because I have borne him six sons." So she named him Zebulun. 21 Afterward she gave birth to a daughter, and named her Dinah.

22 Then God remembered Rachel, and God listened to her and opened her womb. 23 So she conceived and gave birth to a son, and said, "God has taken away my disgrace." 24 And she named him Joseph, saying, "May the LORD give me another son."

Jacob Prospers

25 Now it came about, when Rachel had given birth to Joseph, that Jacob said to Laban, "Send me away, so that I may go to my own place and to my own country. 26 Give *me* my wives and my children for whom I have served you, and let me go; for you yourself know my service which I have rendered you." 27 But Laban said to him, "If it pleases you at all, *stay with me;* I have determined by divination that the LORD has blessed me on your account." 28 He continued, "Name me your wages, and I will give them." 29 But *Jacob* said to him, "You yourself know how I have served you and how your livestock have fared with me. 30 For you had little before I came, and it has increased to a multitude, and the LORD has blessed you wherever I turned. But now, when shall I provide for my own household also?" 31 So he said, "What shall I give you?" And Jacob said, "You shall not give me anything. If you will do this *one* thing for me, I will again pasture *and* keep your flock: 32 let me pass through your entire flock today, removing from there every speckled or spotted sheep and every black sheep among the lambs, and the spotted or speckled among the goats; and *those* shall be my wages. 33 So my honesty will answer for me later, when you come concerning my wages. Every one that is not speckled or spotted among the goats, or black among the lambs, *if found* with me, will be considered stolen." 34 Laban said, "Good, let it be according to your word." 35 So he removed on that day the striped or spotted male goats, and all the speckled or spotted female goats, every one with white on it, and all the black ones among the sheep, and put them in the care of his sons. 36 And he put *a distance of* three days' journey between himself and Jacob, and Jacob fed the rest of Laban's flocks.

37 Then Jacob took fresh rods of poplar, almond, and plane trees, and peeled white stripes in them, exposing the white that *was* in the rods. 38 He set the rods which he had peeled in front of the flocks in the drinking troughs, *that is,* in the watering channels where the flocks came to drink; and they mated when they came to drink. 39 So the flocks mated by the rods, and the flocks delivered striped, speckled, and spotted *offspring.* 40 Then Jacob separated the lambs, and made the flocks face toward the striped and all the black in the flock of Laban; and he put his own herds apart, and did not put them with Laban's flock. 41 Moreover, whenever the stronger of the flock were mating, Jacob would place the rods in the sight of the flock in the drinking troughs, so that they would mate by the rods; 42 but when the flock was sickly, he did not put *them* in; so the sickly were Laban's, and the stronger *were* Jacob's. 43 So the man became exceedingly prosperous, and had large flocks, and female and male servants, and camels and donkeys.

Jacob Leaves Secretly for Canaan

31 Now Jacob heard the words of Laban's sons, saying, "Jacob has taken away all that was our father's, and from what belonged to our father he has made all this wealth." 2 And Jacob saw the 1attitude of Laban, and behold, it was not *friendly* toward him as *it had been* before. 3 Then the LORD said to Jacob, "Return to the land of your fathers and to your relatives, and I will be with you." 4 So Jacob sent *word* and called Rachel and Leah to his flock in the field, 5 and said to them, "I see your father's attitude, that it is not *friendly* toward me as *it was* before, but the God of my father has been with me. 6 You know that I have served your father with all my strength. 7 Yet your father has cheated me and changed my wages ten times; however, God did not allow him to do me harm. 8 If he said this: 'The speckled shall be your wages,' then all the flock delivered speckled; and if he said this: 'The striped shall be your wages,' then all the flock delivered striped. 9 So God has taken away your father's livestock and given *them* to me. 10 And it came about at the time when the flock was breeding that I raised my eyes and saw in a dream—and behold—the male goats that were mating *were* striped, speckled, or mottled. 11 Then the angel of God said to me in the dream, 'Jacob'; and I said, 'Here I am.' 12 He said, 'Now raise your eyes and see *that* all the male goats that are mating are striped, speckled, or mottled; for I have seen everything that Laban has been doing to you. 13 I am the God *of* Bethel, where you anointed a memorial stone, where you made a vow to Me; now arise, leave this land, and return to the land of your birth.'" 14 Rachel and Leah said to him, "Do we still have any share or inheritance in our father's house? 15 Are we not regarded by him as foreigners? For he has sold us, and has also entirely consumed our purchase price. 16 Surely all the wealth which God has taken away from our father belongs to

---

31:2 1 Lit *face*

us and our children; now then, do whatever God has told you."

17 Then Jacob stood up and put his children and his wives on camels; 18 and he drove away all his livestock and all his property which he had acquired, the livestock he possessed which he had acquired in Paddan-aram, to go to the land of Canaan to his father Isaac. 19 Laban had gone to shear his flock, and Rachel stole the household idols that were her father's. 20 And Jacob deceived Laban the Aramean by not telling him that he was fleeing. 21 So he fled with all that he had; and he got up and crossed the *Euphrates* River, and set out for the hill country of Gilead.

Laban Pursues Jacob

22 When Laban was informed on the third day that Jacob had fled, 23 he took his kinsmen with him and pursued him *a distance of* seven days' journey, and he overtook him in the hill country of Gilead. 24 However, God came to Laban the Aramean in a dream of the night and said to him, "Be careful that you do not speak to Jacob either good or bad."

25 And Laban caught up with Jacob. Now Jacob had pitched his tent in the hill country, and Laban with his kinsmen camped in the hill country of Gilead. 26 Then Laban said to Jacob, "What have you done by deceiving me and carrying away my daughters like captives of the sword? 27 Why did you flee secretly and deceive me, and did not tell me, so that I might have sent you away with joy and with songs, with tambourine and with lyre; 28 and did not allow me to kiss my ¹grandchildren and my daughters? Now you have done foolishly. 29 It is in my power to do you harm, but the God of your father spoke to me last night, saying, 'Be careful not to speak either good or bad to Jacob.' 30 Now you have indeed gone away because you longed greatly for your father's house; *but* why did you steal my gods?" 31 Then Jacob replied to Laban, "Because I was afraid, for I thought that you would take your daughters from me by force. 32 The one with whom you find your gods shall not live; in the presence of our relatives point out what is yours among my belongings and take *it* for yourself." Now Jacob did not know that Rachel had stolen them.

33 So Laban went into Jacob's tent, and into Leah's tent, and into the tent of the two slave women, but he did not find *them*. Then he went out of Leah's tent and entered Rachel's tent. 34 Now Rachel had taken the household idols and put them in the camel's saddlebag, and she sat on them. So Laban searched through all the tent, but did not find *them*. 35 And she said to her father, "May my lord not be angry that I cannot stand in your presence, because the ¹way of women is upon me." So he searched but did not find the household idols.

36 Then Jacob became angry and argued with Laban; and Jacob said to Laban, "What is my offense? What is my sin that you have hotly pursued me? 37 Though you have searched

through all my property, what have you found of all your household property? Set *it* here in front of my relatives and your relatives, so that they may decide between the two of us. 38 For these twenty years I *have been* with you; your ewes and your female goats have not miscarried, nor have I eaten the rams of your flocks. 39 I did not *even* bring to you that which was torn *by wild animals;* I took the loss myself. You demanded it of my hand *whether* stolen by day or stolen by night. 40 *This is how* I was: by day the heat consumed me and the frost by night, and my sleep fled from my eyes. 41 For these twenty years I have been in your house; I served you fourteen years for your two daughters, and six years for your flock, and you changed my wages ten times. 42 If the God of my father, the God of Abraham and the fear of Isaac, had not been for me, surely now you would have sent me away empty-handed. God has seen my affliction and the labor of my hands, so He rendered judgment last night."

The Covenant of Mizpah

43 Then Laban replied to Jacob, "The daughters are my daughters, the ¹children are my ²grandchildren, the flocks are my flocks, and everything that you see is mine. But what can I do this day to these daughters of mine or to their children to whom they have given birth? 44 So now come, let's make a covenant, you and I, and it shall be a witness between you and me." 45 Then Jacob took a stone and set it up *as* a memorial stone. 46 Jacob said to his relatives, "Gather stones." So they took stones and made a heap, and they ate there by the heap. 47 Now Laban called it ¹Jegar sahadutha, but Jacob called it ²Galeed. 48 Laban said, "This heap is a witness between you and me this day." Therefore it was named Galeed, 49 and ¹Mizpah, for he said, "May the LORD keep watch between you and me when we are absent one from the other. 50 If you mistreat my daughters, or if you take wives besides my daughters, *although* no one is with us, see, God is witness between you and me." 51 Laban also said to Jacob, "Behold this heap and behold the memorial stone which I have set between you and me. 52 This heap is a witness, and the memorial stone is a witness, that I will not pass by this heap to you for harm, and you will not pass by this heap and this memorial stone to me, for harm." 53 The God of Abraham and the God of Nahor, the God of their father, judge between us." So Jacob swore by the fear of his father Isaac. 54 Then Jacob offered a sacrifice on the mountain, and called his relatives to the meal; and they ate the meal and spent the night on the mountain. 55 Then early in the morning Laban got up, and kissed his ¹grandchildren and his daughters and blessed them. Then Laban departed and returned to his place.

Jacob's Fear of Esau

32 Now as Jacob went on his way, the angels of God met him. 2 And when he

---

saw them, Jacob said, "This is God's camp." So he named that place [1]Mahanaim.

3 Then Jacob sent messengers ahead of himself to his brother Esau in the land of Seir, the country of Edom. 4 He commanded them, saying, "This is what you shall say to my lord Esau: 'Your servant Jacob says the following: "I have resided with Laban, and stayed until now; 5 and I have oxen, donkeys, flocks, and male and female servants; and I have sent *messengers* to tell my lord, so that I may find favor in your sight." ' "

6 And the messengers returned to Jacob, saying, "We came to your brother Esau, and furthermore he is coming to meet you, and four hundred men are with him." 7 Then Jacob was greatly afraid and distressed; and he divided the people who were with him, and the flocks, the herds, and the camels, into two companies; 8 for he said, "If Esau comes to the one company and attacks it, then the company which is left will escape."

9 Then Jacob said, "God of my father Abraham and God of my father Isaac, LORD, who said to me, 'Return to your country and to your relatives, and I will make you prosper,' 10 I am unworthy of all the favor and of all the faithfulness, which You have shown to Your servant; for with *only* my staff I crossed this Jordan, and now I have become two companies. 11 Save me, please, from the hand of my brother, from the hand of Esau; for I fear him, that he will come and attack me *and* the mothers with the children. 12 For You said, 'I will assuredly make you prosper and make your descendants as the sand of the sea, which is too great to be counted.' "

13 So he spent the night there. Then he selected from what he had with him a gift for his brother Esau: 14 two hundred female goats and twenty male goats, two hundred ewes and twenty rams, 15 thirty milking camels and their colts, forty cows and ten bulls, *and* twenty female donkeys and ten male donkeys. 16 Then he placed *them* in the care of his servants, every flock by itself, and said to his servants, "Pass on ahead of me, and put a space between flocks." 17 And he commanded the one in front, saying, "When my brother Esau meets you and asks you, saying, 'To whom do you belong, and where are you going, and to whom do these *animals* in front of you belong?' 18 then you shall say, '*These* belong to your servant Jacob; it is a gift sent to my lord Esau. And behold, he also is behind us.' " 19 Then he commanded also the second and the third, and all those who followed the flocks, saying, "In this way you shall speak to Esau when you find him; 20 and you shall say, 'Behold, your servant Jacob also is behind us.' " For he said, "I will appease him with the gift that goes ahead of me. Then afterward I will see his face; perhaps he will accept me." 21 So the gift passed on ahead of him, while he himself spent that night in the camp.

22 Now he got up that same night and took his two wives, his two female slaves, and his eleven children, and crossed the shallow place of the Jabbok. 23 He took them and sent them across the stream. And he sent across whatever he had.

Jacob Wrestles

24 Then Jacob was left alone, and a man wrestled with him until daybreak. 25 When *the man* saw that he had not prevailed against him, he touched the socket of Jacob's hip; and the socket of Jacob's hip was dislocated while he wrestled with him. 26 Then he said, "Let me go, for the dawn is breaking." But he said, "I will not let you go unless you bless me." 27 So he said to him, "What is your name?" And he said, "Jacob." 28 Then he said, "Your name shall no longer be Jacob, but [1]Israel; for you have contended with God and with men, and have prevailed." 29 And Jacob asked him and said, "Please tell me your name." But he said, "Why is it that you ask my name?" And he blessed him there. 30 So Jacob named the place [1]Peniel, for *he said,* "I have seen God face to face, yet my life has been spared." 31 Now the sun rose upon him just as he crossed over Penuel, and he was limping on his hip. 32 Therefore, to this day the sons of Israel do not eat the tendon of the hip which is on the socket of the hip, because he touched the socket of Jacob's hip in the tendon of the hip.

Jacob Meets Esau

33 Then Jacob raised his eyes and looked, and behold, Esau was coming, and four hundred men with him. So he divided the children among Leah and Rachel, and the two slave women. 2 He put the slave women and their children in front, and Leah and her children next, and Rachel and Joseph last. 3 But he himself passed on ahead of them and bowed down to the ground seven times, until he came near to his brother.

4 Then Esau ran to meet him and embraced him, and fell on his neck and kissed him, and they wept. 5 He raised his eyes and saw the women and the children, and said, "Who are these with you?" So he said, "The children whom God has graciously given your servant." 6 Then the slave women came forward with their children, and they bowed down. 7 And Leah likewise came forward with her children, and they bowed down; and afterward Joseph came forward with Rachel, and they bowed down. 8 And he said, "What do you mean by all this company which I have met?" And he said, "To find favor in the sight of my lord." 9 But Esau said, "I have plenty, my brother; let what you have be your own." 10 Jacob said, "No, please, if now I have found favor in your sight, then accept my gift from my hand, for I see your face as one sees the face of God, and you have received me favorably. 11 Please accept my gift which has been brought to you, because God has dealt graciously with me and because I have plenty." So he urged him, and he accepted *it.*

12 Then Esau said, "Let's journey on and go, and I will go ahead of you." 13 But he said to him, "My lord knows that the children are frail

and that the flocks and herds that are nursing are a matter of concern to me. And if they are driven hard *just* one day, all the flocks will die. **14** Please let my lord pass on ahead of his servant, and I will proceed at my leisure, at the pace of the cattle that are ahead of me and at the pace of the children, until I come to my lord at Seir."

15 Then Esau said, "Please let me leave with you some of the people who are with me." But he said, "What need is there? Let me find favor in the sight of my lord." **16** So Esau returned that day on his way to Seir. **17** But Jacob journeyed to ¹Succoth, and built for himself a house and made booths for his livestock; therefore the place is named Succoth.

Jacob Settles in Shechem

18 Now Jacob came safely to the city of Shechem, which is in the land of Canaan, when he came from Paddan-aram, and camped before the city. **19** He bought the plot of land where he had pitched his tent from the hand of the sons of Hamor, Shechem's father, for a hundred pieces of money. **20** Then he erected there an altar and called it ¹El-Elohe-Israel.

The Treachery of Jacob's Sons

34 Now Dinah the daughter of Leah, whom she had borne to Jacob, went out to visit the daughters of the land. **2** When Shechem the son of Hamor the Hivite, the prince of the land, saw her, he took her and lay with her and raped her. **3** But he was deeply attracted to Dinah the daughter of Jacob, and he loved the girl and spoke tenderly to her. **4** So Shechem spoke to his father Hamor, saying, "Get me this young woman as a wife." **5** Now Jacob heard that he had defiled his daughter Dinah; but his sons were with his livestock in the field, so Jacob said nothing until they came in. **6** Then Hamor the father of Shechem went out to Jacob to speak with him. **7** Now the sons of Jacob came in from the field when they heard *about it;* and the men were grieved, and they were very angry because he had done a disgraceful thing in Israel by ¹sleeping with Jacob's daughter, for such a thing ought not to be done.

8 But Hamor spoke with them, saying, "The soul of my son Shechem longs for your daughter; please give her to him in marriage. **9** And intermarry with us; give your daughters to us and take our daughters for yourselves. **10** So you will live with us, and the land shall be open to you; live and trade in it and acquire property in it." **11** Shechem also said to her father and to her brothers, "Let me find favor in your sight, and I will give whatever you tell me. **12** Demand of me ever so much bridal payment and gift, and I will give whatever you tell me; but give me the girl in marriage." **13** But Jacob's sons answered Shechem and his father Hamor with deceit, because he had defiled their sister Dinah. **14** They said to them, "We cannot do this thing, *that is,* give our sister to a man who is uncircumcised, for that would be a disgrace to us. **15** Only on this *condition* will we consent to you: if you will

become like us, in that every male of you will be circumcised, **16** then we will give our daughters to you, and we will take your daughters for ourselves, and we will live with you and become one people. **17** But if you do not listen to us to be circumcised, then we will take our daughter and go."

18 Now their words seemed reasonable to Hamor and Shechem, Hamor's son. **19** The young man did not delay to do this, because he was delighted with Jacob's daughter. Now he was more respected than all the household of his father. **20** So Hamor and his son Shechem came to the gate of their city and spoke to the people of their city, saying, **21** "These men are friendly to us; therefore let them live in the land and trade in it, for behold, the land is large enough for them. We will take their daughters in marriage, and give our daughters to them. **22** Only on this *condition* will the men consent to us to live with us, to become one people: that every male among us be circumcised just as they are circumcised. **23** Will their livestock and their property and all their animals not be ours? Let's just consent to them, and they will live with us." **24** All who went out of the gate of his city listened to Hamor and to his son Shechem, and every male was circumcised, all who went out of the gate of his city.

25 Now it came about on the third day, when they were in pain, that two of Jacob's sons Simeon and Levi, Dinah's brothers—each took his sword and came upon the city undetected, and killed every male. **26** They killed Hamor and his son Shechem with the edge of the sword, and took Dinah from Shechem's house, and left. **27** Jacob's sons came upon those killed and looted the city, because they had defiled their sister. **28** They took their flocks, their herds, and their donkeys, and that which was in the city and that which was in the field; **29** and they captured and looted all their wealth and all their little ones and their wives, even everything that *was* in the houses. **30** Then Jacob said to Simeon and Levi, "You have brought trouble on me by making me repulsive among the inhabitants of the land, among the Canaanites and the Perizzites; and since my men are few in number, they will band together against me and attack me, and I will be destroyed, I and my household!" **31** But they said, "Should he treat our sister like a prostitute?"

Jacob Moves to Bethel

35 Then God said to Jacob, "Arise, go up to Bethel and live there, and make an altar there to God, who appeared to you when you fled from your brother Esau." **2** So Jacob said to his household and to all who were with him, "Remove the foreign gods which are among you, and purify yourselves and change your garments; **3** and let's arise and go up to Bethel, and I will make an altar there to God, who answered me on the day of my distress and has been with me wherever I have gone." **4** So they gave Jacob all the foreign gods which they had and the rings which were in their ears, and

---

33:17 ¹ I.e., booths   **33:20** ¹ I.e., God, the God of Israel   **34:7** ¹ I.e., violating her

Jacob hid them under the oak which was near Shechem.

5 As they journeyed, there was a great terror upon the cities which were around them, and they did not pursue the sons of Jacob. 6 So Jacob came to Luz (that is, Bethel), which is in the land of Canaan, he and all the people who were with him. 7 Then he built an altar there, and called the place El-bethel, because there God had revealed Himself to him when he fled from his brother. 8 Now Deborah, Rebekah's nurse, died, and she was buried below Bethel under the oak; and it was named 1Allon-bacuth.

Jacob Is Named Israel

9 Then God appeared to Jacob again when he came from Paddan-aram, and He blessed him. 10 God said to him,

"Your name is Jacob;
You shall no longer be called Jacob,
But Israel shall be your name."

So He called him Israel. 11 God also said to him,

"I am God Almighty;
Be fruitful and multiply;
A nation and a multitude of nations shall
come from you,
And kings shall come from you.

12 "And the land which I gave to Abraham
and Isaac,
I will give to you,
And I will give the land to your
descendants after you."

13 Then God went up from him at the place where He had spoken with him. 14 So Jacob set up a memorial stone in the place where He had spoken with him, a memorial of stone, and he poured out a drink offering on it; he also poured oil on it. 15 And Jacob named the place where God had spoken with him, 1Bethel.

16 Then they journeyed on from Bethel; but when there was still some distance to go to Ephrath, Rachel began to give birth and she suffered severe difficulties in her labor. 17 And when she was suffering severe difficulties in her labor, the midwife said to her, "Do not fear, for you have another son!" 18 And it came about, as her soul was departing (for she died), that she named him 1Ben-oni; but his father called him 2Benjamin. 19 So Rachel died and was buried on the way to Ephrath (that is, Bethlehem). 20 And Jacob set up a memorial stone over her grave; that is the memorial stone of Rachel's grave to this day. 21 Then Israel journeyed on and pitched his tent beyond the tower of Eder.

The Sons of Israel

22 And it came about, while Israel was living in that land, that Reuben went and slept with his father's concubine Bilhah, and Israel heard about it.

Now there were twelve sons of Jacob— 23 the sons of Leah were Reuben, Jacob's first-born, then Simeon, Levi, Judah, Issachar, and Zebulun; 24 the sons of Rachel were Joseph and Benjamin; 25 and the sons of Bilhah, Rachel's female slave, were Dan and Naphtali; 26 and the sons of Zilpah, Leah's female slave, were Gad

and Asher. These were the sons of Jacob who were born to him in Paddan-aram.

27 Jacob came to his father Isaac at Mamre of Kiriath-arba (that is, Hebron), where Abraham and Isaac had resided.

28 Now the days of Isaac were 180 years. 29 Then Isaac breathed his last and died, and was gathered to his people, an old man of ripe age; and his sons Esau and Jacob buried him.

Esau Moves

36 Now these are *the records of* the generations of Esau (that is, Edom).

2 Esau took his wives from the daughters of Canaan: Adah the daughter of Elon the Hittite, and Oholibamah the daughter of Anah, the granddaughter of Zibeon the Hivite; 3 also Basemath, Ishmael's daughter, the sister of Nebaioth. 4 Adah bore Eliphaz to Esau, and Basemath gave birth to Reuel, 5 and Oholibamah gave birth to Jeush, Jalam, and Korah. These are the sons of Esau who were born to him in the land of Canaan.

6 Then Esau took his wives, his sons, his daughters, and all his household, and his livestock and all his cattle, and all his property which he had acquired in the land of Canaan, and went to *another* land away from his brother Jacob. 7 For their possessions had become too great for them to live together, and the land where they resided could not support them because of their livestock. 8 So Esau lived in the hill country of Seir; Esau is Edom.

Descendants of Esau

9 These then are *the records of* the generations of Esau the father of the Edomites in the hill country of Seir. 10 These are the names of Esau's sons: Eliphaz the son of Esau's wife Adah, *and* Reuel the son of Esau's wife Basemath. 11 The sons of Eliphaz were Teman, Omar, Zepho, Gatam, and Kenaz. 12 Timna was a concubine of Esau's son Eliphaz, and she bore Amalek to Eliphaz. These are the sons of Esau's wife Adah. 13 And these are the sons of Reuel: Nahath, Zerah, Shammah, and Mizzah. These were the sons of Esau's wife Basemath. 14 And these were the sons of Esau's wife Oholibamah, the daughter of Anah, the granddaughter of Zibeon: she bore to Esau Jeush, Jalam, and Korah.

15 These are the chiefs of the sons of Esau. The sons of Eliphaz, the firstborn of Esau, are chief Teman, chief Omar, chief Zepho, chief Kenaz, 16 chief Korah, chief Gatam, *and* chief Amalek. These are the chiefs descended from Eliphaz in the land of Edom; these are the sons of Adah. 17 And these are the sons of Reuel, Esau's son: chief Nahath, chief Zerah, chief Shammah, *and* chief Mizzah. These are the chiefs descended from Reuel in the land of Edom; these are the sons of Esau's wife Basemath. 18 And these are the sons of Esau's wife Oholibamah: chief Jeush, chief Jalam, *and* chief Korah. These are the chiefs descended from Esau's wife Oholibamah, the daughter of Anah. 19 These are the sons of Esau (that is, Edom), and these are their chiefs.

35:8 1 I.e., oak of weeping   35:15 1 I.e., house of God   35:18 1 I.e., the son of my sorrow   2 I.e., the son of the right hand

20 These are the sons of Seir the Horite, the inhabitants of the land: Lotan, Shobal, Zibeon, Anah, 21 Dishon, Ezer, and Dishan. These are the chiefs descended from the Horites, the sons of Seir in the land of Edom. 22 And the sons of Lotan were Hori and Hemam; and Lotan's sister was Timna. 23 And these are the sons of Shobal: Alvan, Manahath, Ebal, Shepho, and Onam. 24 And these are the sons of Zibeon: Aiah and Anah—he is the Anah who found the hot springs in the wilderness when he was pasturing the donkeys of his father Zibeon. 25 And these are the children of Anah: Dishon, and Oholibamah, the daughter of Anah. 26 And these are the sons of Dishon: Hemdan, Eshban, Ithran, and Cheran. 27 These are the sons of Ezer: Bilhan, Zaavan, and Akan. 28 These are the sons of Dishan: Uz and Aran. 29 These are the chiefs descended from the Horites: chief Lotan, chief Shobal, chief Zibeon, chief Anah, 30 chief Dishon, chief Ezer, and chief Dishan. These are the chiefs descended from the Horites, according to their various chiefs in the land of Seir.

31 Now these are the kings who reigned in the land of Edom before any king reigned over the sons of Israel. 32 Bela the son of Beor reigned in Edom, and the name of his city was Dinhabah. 33 Then Bela died, and Jobab the son of Zerah of Bozrah became king in his place. 34 Then Jobab died, and Husham of the land of the Temanites became king in his place. 35 Then Husham died, and Hadad the son of Bedad, who defeated Midian in the field of Moab, became king in his place; and the name of his city was Avith. 36 Then Hadad died, and Samlah of Masrekah became king in his place. 37 Then Samlah died, and Shaul of Rehoboth on the Euphrates River became king in his place. 38 Then Shaul died, and Baal-hanan the son of Achbor became king in his place. 39 Then Baal-hanan the son of Achbor died, and Hadar became king in his place; and the name of his city was Pau; and his wife's name was Mehetabel, the daughter of Matred, daughter of Mezahab.

40 Now these are the names of the chiefs descended from Esau, according to their families and their localities, by their names: chief Timna, chief Alvah, chief Jetheth, 41 chief Oholibamah, chief Elah, chief Pinon, 42 chief Kenaz, chief Teman, chief Mibzar, 43 chief Magdiel, and chief Iram. These are the chiefs of Edom (that is, Esau, the father of the Edomites), according to their settlements in the land of their possession.

Joseph's Dreams

37 Now Jacob lived in the land where his father had lived as a stranger, in the land of Canaan. 2 These are the records of the generations of Jacob.

Joseph, when he was seventeen years of age, was pasturing the flock with his brothers, while he was still a youth, along with the sons of Bilhah and the sons of Zilpah, his father's wives. And Joseph brought back a bad report about them to their father. 3 Now Israel loved Joseph more than all his other sons, because he was the son of his old age; and he made him a multicolored tunic. 4 And his brothers saw that their father loved him more than all his brothers; and so they hated him and could not speak to him on friendly terms.

5 Then Joseph had a dream, and when he told it to his brothers, they hated him even more. 6 He said to them, "Please listen to this dream which I have had; 7 for behold, we were binding sheaves in the field, and behold, my sheaf stood up and also remained standing; and behold, your sheaves gathered around and bowed down to my sheaf." 8 Then his brothers said to him, "Are you actually going to reign over us? Or are you really going to rule over us?" So they hated him even more for his dreams and for his words.

9 Then he had yet another dream, and informed his brothers of it, and said, "Behold, I have had yet another dream; and behold, the sun and the moon, and eleven stars were bowing down to me." 10 He also told it to his father as well as to his brothers; and his father rebuked him and said to him, "What is this dream that you have had? Am I and your mother and your brothers actually going to come to bow down to the ground before you?" 11 And his brothers were jealous of him, but his father kept the matter in mind.

12 Then his brothers went to pasture their father's flock in Shechem. 13 And Israel said to Joseph, "Are your brothers not pasturing the flock in Shechem? Come, and I will send you to them." And he said to him, "I will go." 14 Then he said to him, "Go now and see about the welfare of your brothers and the welfare of the flock, and bring word back to me." So he sent him from the Valley of Hebron, and he came to Shechem.

15 A man found him, and behold, he was wandering in the field; and the man asked him, "What are you looking for?" 16 He said, "I am looking for my brothers; please tell me where they are pasturing the flock." 17 Then the man said, "They have moved from here; for I heard them say, 'Let's go to Dothan.'" So Joseph went after his brothers and found them at Dothan.

The Plot against Joseph

18 When they saw him from a distance, and before he came closer to them, they plotted against him to put him to death. 19 They said to one another, "Here comes this dreamer! 20 Now then, come and let's kill him, and throw him into one of the pits; and we will say, 'A vicious animal devoured him.' Then we will see what will become of his dreams!" 21 But Reuben heard this and rescued him out of their hands by saying, "Let's not take his life." 22 Then Reuben said to them, "Shed no blood. Throw him into this pit that is in the wilderness, but do not lay a hand on him"—so that later he might rescue him out of their hands, to return him to his father. 23 So it came about, when Joseph reached his brothers, that they stripped Joseph of his tunic, the multicolored tunic that was on him; 24 and they took him and threw him into the pit. Now the pit was empty, without any water in it.

25 Then they sat down to eat a meal. But as they raised their eyes and looked, behold, a

caravan of Ishmaelites was coming from Gilead, with their camels carrying labdanum resin, balsam, and myrrh, on their way to bring *them* down to Egypt. 26 And Judah said to his brothers, "What profit is it for us to kill our brother and cover up his blood? 27 Come, and let's sell him to the Ishmaelites and not lay our hands on him, for he is our brother, our *own* flesh." And his brothers listened *to him.* 28 Then some Midianite traders passed by, so they pulled *him* out and lifted Joseph out of the pit, and sold him to the Ishmaelites for 'twenty *shekels* of silver. So they brought Joseph into Egypt.

29 Now Reuben returned to the pit, and behold, Joseph was not in the pit; so he tore his garments. 30 He returned to his brothers and said, "The boy is not *there;* as for me, where am I to go?" 31 So they took Joseph's tunic, and slaughtered a male goat, and dipped the tunic in the blood; 32 and they sent the multicolored tunic and brought it to their father and said, "We found this; please examine *it to see whether* it is your son's tunic or not." 33 Then he examined it and said, "*It is* my son's tunic. A vicious animal has devoured him; Joseph has surely been torn to pieces!" 34 So Jacob tore his clothes, and put on a sackcloth *undergarment* over his waist, and mourned for his son many days. 35 Then all his sons and all his daughters got up to comfort him, but he refused to be comforted. And he said, "Surely I will go down to Sheol in mourning for my son." So his father wept for him. 36 Meanwhile, the Midianites sold him in Egypt to Potiphar, Pharaoh's officer, the captain of the bodyguard.

Judah and Tamar

38 And it came about at that time, that Judah departed from his brothers and visited a certain Adullamite, whose name was Hirah. 2 Judah saw there a daughter of a certain Canaanite whose name was Shua; and he took her *as a wife* and had relations with her. 3 And she conceived and gave birth to a son, and he named him Er. 4 Then she conceived again and gave birth to a son, and she named him Onan. 5 She gave birth to yet another son and named him Shelah; and it was at Chezib that she gave birth to him.

6 Now Judah took a wife for Er his firstborn, and her name *was* Tamar. 7 But Er, Judah's firstborn, was evil in the sight of the LORD, so the LORD took his life. 8 Then Judah said to Onan, "Have relations with your brother's wife and perform your duty as a brother-in-law to her, and raise up a child for your brother." 9 Now Onan knew that the child would not be his; so when he had relations with his brother's wife, he wasted his seed on the ground so that he would not give a child to his brother. 10 But what he did was displeasing in the sight of the LORD; so He took his life also. 11 Then Judah said to his daughter-in-law Tamar, "Remain a widow in your father's house until my son Shelah grows up"; for he thought, "*I am afraid* that he too may die like his brothers." So Tamar went and lived in her father's house.

12 Now after a considerable time Shua's daughter, the wife of Judah, died; and when the time of mourning was ended, Judah went up to his sheepshearers at Timnah, he and his friend Hirah the Adullamite. 13 And Tamar was told, "Behold, your father-in-law is going up to Timnah to shear his sheep." 14 So she removed her widow's garments and covered *herself* with a veil, and wrapped herself, and sat in the gateway of Enaim, which is on the road to Timnah; for she saw that Shelah had grown up, and she had not been given to him as a wife. 15 When Judah saw her, he assumed she *was* a prostitute, for she had covered her face. 16 So he turned aside to her by the road, and said, "Here now, let me have relations with you"; for he did not know that she was his daughter-in-law. And she said, "What will you give me, that you may have relations with me?" 17 He said, therefore, "I will send you a young goat from the flock." She then said, "Will you give a pledge until you send *it?*" 18 He said, "What pledge shall I give you?" And she said, "Your seal and your cord, and your staff that is in your hand." So he gave *them* to her and had relations with her, and she conceived by him. 19 Then she got up and departed, and removed her veil and put on her widow's garments.

20 When Judah sent the young goat by his friend the Adullamite, to receive the pledge from the woman's hand, he did not find her. 21 He asked the people of her place, saying, "Where is the temple prostitute who was by the road at Enaim?" But they said, "There has been no temple prostitute here." 22 So he returned to Judah, and said, "I did not find her; and furthermore, the people of the place said, 'There has been no temple prostitute here.'" 23 Then Judah said, "Let her keep them, otherwise we will become a laughingstock. After all, I sent this young goat, but you did not find her."

24 Now it was about three months later that Judah was informed, "Your daughter-in-law Tamar has prostituted herself, and behold, she is also pregnant by prostitution." Then Judah said, "Bring her out and have her burned!" 25 It was while she was being brought out that she sent *word* to her father-in-law, saying, "I am pregnant by the man to whom these things belong." She also said, "Please examine and see, whose signet ring and cords and staff are these?" 26 And Judah recognized *them,* and said, "She is more righteous than I, since I did not give her to my son Shelah." And he did not have relations with her again.

27 It came about at the time she was giving birth, that behold, there were twins in her womb. 28 Moreover, it took place while she was giving birth, that one *baby* put out a hand, and the midwife took and tied a scarlet *thread* on his hand, saying, "This one came out first." 29 But it came about as he drew back his hand that behold, his brother came out. Then she said, "What a breach you have made for yourself!" So he was named 'Perez. 30 Afterward his brother came out who had the scarlet *thread* on his hand; and he was named 'Zerah.

37:28 1 About 10 oz. or 280 gm   **38:29** 1 I.e., a breach   **38:30** 1 I.e., a dawning or brightness

Joseph's Success in Egypt

39 Now Joseph had been taken down to Egypt; and Potiphar, an Egyptian officer of Pharaoh, the captain of the bodyguard, bought him from the Ishmaelites, who had taken him down there. 2 And the LORD was with Joseph, so he became a successful man. And he was in the house of his master, the Egyptian. 3 Now his master saw that the LORD was with him and *that* the LORD made all that he did prosper in his hand. 4 So Joseph found favor in his sight and became his personal servant; and he made him overseer over his house, and put him in charge of all that he owned. 5 It came about that from the time he made him overseer in his house and over all that he owned, the LORD blessed the Egyptian's house on account of Joseph; so the LORD's blessing was upon all that he owned, in the house and in the field. 6 So he left Joseph in charge of everything that he owned; and with him *there* he did not concern himself with anything except the food which he ate.

Now Joseph was handsome in form and appearance. 7 And it came about after these events that his master's wife had her eyes on Joseph, and she said, "Sleep with me." 8 But he refused and said to his master's wife, "Look, with me *here*, my master does not concern himself with anything in the house, and he has put me in charge of all that he owns. 9 There is no one greater in this house than I, and he has withheld nothing from me except you, because you are his wife. How then could I do this great evil, and sin against God?" 10 Though she spoke to Joseph day after day, he did not listen to her to lie beside her *or* be with her. 11 Now it happened one day that he went into the house to do his work, and none of the people of the household was there inside. 12 So she grabbed him by his garment, saying, "Sleep with me!" But he left his garment in her hand and fled, and went outside. 13 When she saw that he had left his garment in her hand and had fled outside, 14 she called to the men of her household and said to them, "See, he has brought in a Hebrew to us to make fun of us; he came in to me to sleep with me, and I screamed. 15 When he heard that I raised my voice and screamed, he left his garment beside me and fled and went outside." 16 So she left his garment beside her until his master came home. 17 Then she spoke to him with these words: "The Hebrew slave, whom you brought to us, came in to me to make fun of me; 18 but when I raised my voice and screamed, he left his garment beside me and fled outside."

Joseph Imprisoned

19 Now when his master heard the words of his wife which she spoke to him, saying, "This is what your slave did to me," his anger burned. 20 So Joseph's master took him and put him into the prison, the place where the king's prisoners were confined; and he was there in the prison. 21 But the LORD was with Joseph and extended kindness to him, and gave him favor in the sight of the warden of the prison. 22 And the warden of the prison put Joseph in charge of all the prisoners who were in the prison; so that whatever was done there, he was responsible *for it.* 23 The warden of the prison did not supervise anything under Joseph's authority, because the LORD was with him; and, the LORD made whatever he did prosper.

Joseph Interprets Dreams

40 Then it came about after these things, *that* the cupbearer and the baker for the king of Egypt offended their lord, the king of Egypt. 2 And Pharaoh was furious with his two officials, the chief cupbearer and the chief baker. 3 So he put them in confinement in the house of the captain of the bodyguard, in the prison, the *same* place where Joseph was imprisoned. 4 And the captain of the bodyguard put Joseph in charge of them, and he took care of them; and they were in confinement for some time. 5 Then the cupbearer and the baker for the king of Egypt, who were confined in the prison, both had a dream the same night, each man with his *own* dream *and* each dream with its *own* interpretation. 6 When Joseph came to them in the morning and saw them, behold, they were dejected. 7 So he asked Pharaoh's officials who were with him in confinement in his master's house, "Why are your faces so sad today?" 8 And they said to him, "We have had a dream, and there is no one to interpret it." Then Joseph said to them, "Do interpretations not belong to God? Tell *it* to me, please."

9 So the chief cupbearer told his dream to Joseph, saying to him, "In my dream, behold, *there was* a vine in front of me; 10 and on the vine *were* three branches. And as it was budding, its blossoms came out, *and* its clusters produced ripe grapes. 11 Now Pharaoh's cup was in my hand; so I took the grapes and squeezed them into Pharaoh's cup, and I put the cup into Pharaoh's hand." 12 Then Joseph said to him, "This is the interpretation of it: the three branches are three days; 13 within three more days Pharaoh will [1]lift up your head and restore you to your office; and you will put Pharaoh's cup into his hand as in your former practice when you were his cupbearer. 14 Only keep me in mind when it goes well for you, and please do me a kindness by mentioning me to Pharaoh, and get me out of this prison. 15 For I was in fact kidnapped from the land of the Hebrews, and even here I have done nothing that they should have put me into the dungeon."

16 When the chief baker saw that he had interpreted favorably, he said to Joseph, "I also *saw* in my dream, and behold, *there were* three baskets of white bread on my head; 17 and in the top basket *there were* some of all kinds of baked food for Pharaoh, and the birds were eating them out of the basket on my head." 18 Then Joseph answered and said, "This is its interpretation: the three baskets are three days; 19 within three more days Pharaoh will lift up your head from you and will hang you on a wooden *post,* and the birds will eat your flesh off you."

20 So it came about on the third day, *which was* Pharaoh's birthday, that he held a feast for

---

40:13 [1] I.e., a royal gesture of forgiveness

all his servants; and he lifted up the head of the chief cupbearer and the head of the chief baker among his servants. 21 He restored the chief cupbearer to his office, and he put the cup into Pharaoh's hand; 22 but he hanged the chief baker, just as Joseph had interpreted to them. 23 Yet the chief cupbearer did not remember Joseph, but forgot him.

Pharaoh's Dream

41 Now it happened at the end of two full years that Pharaoh had a dream, and behold, he was standing by the Nile. 2 And behold, from the Nile seven cows came up, fine-looking and fat; and they grazed in the marsh grass. 3 Then behold, seven other cows came up after them from the Nile, ugly and thin, and they stood by the *other* cows on the bank of the Nile. 4 Then the ugly and thin cows ate the seven fine-looking and fat cows. Then Pharaoh awoke. 5 But he fell asleep and dreamed a second time; and behold, seven ears of grain came up on a single stalk, plump and good. 6 Then behold, seven ears, thin and scorched by the east wind, sprouted up after them. 7 And the thin ears swallowed the seven plump and full ears. Then Pharaoh awoke, and behold, *it was* a dream. 8 Now in the morning his spirit was troubled, so he sent *messengers* and called for all the soothsayer priests of Egypt, and all its wise men. And Pharaoh told them his dreams, but there was no one who could interpret them for Pharaoh.

9 Then the chief cupbearer spoke to Pharaoh, saying, "I would make mention today of my *own* offenses. 10 Pharaoh was furious with his servants, and he put me in confinement in the house of the captain of the bodyguard, *both* me and the chief baker. 11 Then we had a dream one night, he and I; each of us dreamed according to the interpretation of his *own* dream. 12 Now a Hebrew youth *was* there with us, a servant of the captain of the bodyguard, and we told him *the dreams,* and he interpreted our dreams for us. For each man he interpreted according to his *own* dream. 13 And just as he interpreted for us, so it happened; *Pharaoh* restored me in my office, but he hanged the chief baker."

Joseph Interprets

14 Then Pharaoh sent *word* and called for Joseph, and they hurriedly brought him out of the dungeon; and when he had shaved himself and changed his clothes, he came to Pharaoh. 15 Pharaoh said to Joseph, "I have had a dream, but no one can interpret it; and I have heard it said about you, that when you hear a dream you can interpret it." 16 Joseph then answered Pharaoh, saying, "It has nothing to do with me; God will give Pharaoh an answer for his own good." 17 So Pharaoh said to Joseph, "In my dream, there I was, standing on the bank of the Nile; 18 and behold, seven cows, fat and fine-looking came up out of the Nile, and they grazed in the marsh grass. 19 Then behold, seven other cows came up after them, poor and very ugly and thin, such as I had never seen for ugliness in all the land of Egypt; 20 and the thin and ugly cows ate the first seven fat cows. 21 Yet when they had devoured them, it could not be detected that they had devoured them, for they were just as ugly as before. Then I awoke. 22 I saw also in my dream, and behold, seven ears of grain, full and good, came up on a single stalk; 23 and behold, seven ears, withered, thin, *and* scorched by the east wind sprouted up after them; 24 and the thin ears swallowed the seven good ears. Then I told it to the soothsayer priests, but there was no one who could explain it to me."

25 And Joseph said to Pharaoh, "Pharaoh's dreams are one *and the same;* God has told to Pharaoh what He is about to do. 26 The seven good cows are seven years; and the seven good ears are seven years; the dreams are one *and the same.* 27 The seven thin and ugly cows that came up after them are seven years, and the seven thin ears scorched by the east wind will be seven years of famine. 28 It is as I have spoken to Pharaoh: God has shown Pharaoh what He is about to do. 29 Behold, seven years of great abundance are coming in all the land of Egypt; 30 and after them seven years of famine will come, and all the abundance will be forgotten in the land of Egypt, and the famine will ravage the land. 31 So the abundance will be unknown in the land because of that subsequent famine; for it *will be* very severe. 32 Now as for the repeating of the dream to Pharaoh twice, *it means* that the matter is confirmed by God, and God will quickly bring it about. 33 So now let Pharaoh look for a man discerning and wise, and appoint him over the land of Egypt. 34 Let Pharaoh take action to appoint overseers in charge of the land, and let him take a fifth *of the produce* of the land of Egypt *as a tax* in the seven years of abundance. 35 Then have them collect all the food of these good years that are coming, and store up the grain for food in the cities under Pharaoh's authority, and have them guard *it.* 36 Let the food be *used* as a reserve for the land for the seven years of famine which will occur in the land of Egypt, so that the land will not perish during the famine."

37 Now the proposal seemed good to Pharaoh and to all his servants.

Joseph Is Made a Ruler of Egypt

38 Then Pharaoh said to his servants, "Can we find a man like this, in whom there is a divine spirit?" 39 So Pharaoh said to Joseph, "Since God has informed you of all this, there is no one as discerning and wise as you are. 40 You shall be in charge of my house, and all my people shall be obedient to you; only *regarding* the throne will I be greater than you." 41 Pharaoh also said to Joseph, "See, I have placed you over all the land of Egypt." 42 Then Pharaoh took off his signet ring from his hand and put it on Joseph's hand, and clothed him in garments of fine linen, and put the gold necklace around his neck. 43 And he had him ride in his second chariot; and they proclaimed ahead of him, "Bow the knee!" And he placed him over all the land of Egypt. 44 Moreover, Pharaoh said to Joseph, "*Though* I am Pharaoh, yet without your permission no one shall raise his

hand or foot in all the land of Egypt." **45** Then Pharaoh named Joseph [7]Zaphenath-paneah; and he gave him Asenath, the daughter of Potiphera priest of On, to *be his* wife. And Joseph went out over the land of Egypt.

46 Now Joseph was thirty years old when he stood in the presence of Pharaoh, king of Egypt. And Joseph went out from the presence of Pharaoh and went through all the land of Egypt. **47** During the seven years of plenty the land produced abundantly. **48** So he collected all the food of *these* seven years which occurred in the land of Egypt and put the food in the cities; he put in every city the food from its own surrounding fields. **49** Joseph stored up grain in great abundance like the sand of the sea, until he stopped measuring *it,* for it was beyond measure.

The Sons of Joseph

50 Now before the year of famine came, two sons were born to Joseph, whom Asenath, the daughter of Potiphera, priest of On, bore to him. **51** Joseph named the firstborn [7]Manasseh; "For," *he said,* "God has made me forget all my trouble and all of my father's household." **52** And he named the second [7]Ephraim; "For," *he said,* "God has made me fruitful in the land of my affliction."

53 When the seven years of plenty which had taken place in the land of Egypt came to an end, **54** and the seven years of famine began to come, just as Joseph had said, then there was famine in all the lands; but in all the land of Egypt there was bread. **55** So when all the land of Egypt suffered famine, the people cried out to Pharaoh for bread; and Pharaoh said to all the Egyptians, "Go to Joseph; whatever he says to you, you shall do." **56** When the famine was *spread* over the entire face of the earth, then Joseph opened all the storehouses and sold grain to the Egyptians; and the famine was severe in the land of Egypt. **57** Then *the people of* all the earth came to Egypt to buy grain from Joseph, because the famine was severe in all the earth.

Joseph's Brothers Sent to Egypt

42 Now Jacob saw that there was grain in Egypt, and Jacob said to his sons, "Why are you staring at one another?" **2** Then he said, "Look, I have heard that there is grain in Egypt; go down there and buy *some* for us from that place, so that we may live and not die." **3** So ten of Joseph's brothers went down to buy grain from Egypt. **4** But Jacob did not send Joseph's brother Benjamin with his brothers, for he said, "I am afraid that harm may happen to him." **5** So the sons of Israel came to buy grain among those who were coming, because the famine was *also* in the land of Canaan.

6 Now Joseph was the ruler over the land; he was the one who sold grain to all the people of the land. And Joseph's brothers came and bowed down to him *with their* faces to the ground. **7** When Joseph saw his brothers, he recognized them, but he disguised himself to them and spoke to them harshly. He said to them, "Where have you come from?" And they said, "From the land of Canaan, to buy food."

8 But Joseph had recognized his brothers, although they did not recognize him. **9** And Joseph remembered the dreams which he had about them, and he said to them, "You are spies; you have come to look at the undefended parts of our land." **10** And they said to him, "No, my lord, but your servants have come to buy food. **11** We are all sons of one man; we are honest men, your servants are not spies." **12** Yet he said to them, "No, but you have come to look at the undefended parts of our land!" **13** But they said, "Your servants are twelve brothers *in all,* the sons of one man in the land of Canaan; and behold, the youngest is with our father today, and one is no longer alive."

14 Yet Joseph said to them, "It is as I said to you, you are spies; **15** by this you will be tested: by the life of Pharaoh, you shall not leave this place unless your youngest brother comes here! **16** Send one of you and have him get your brother, while you remain confined, so that your words may be tested, whether there is truth in you. But if not, by the life of Pharaoh, you are certainly spies!" **17** So he put them all together in prison for three days.

18 Now Joseph said to them on the third day, "Do this and live, for I fear God: **19** if you are honest men, let one of your brothers be confined in your prison; but as for *the rest of* you, go, carry grain for the famine of your households, **20** and bring your youngest brother to me, so that your words may be verified, and you will not die." And they did so. **21** Then they said to one another, "Truly we are guilty concerning our brother, because we saw the distress of his soul when he pleaded with us, yet we would not listen; for that reason this distress has happened to us." **22** Reuben answered them, saying, "Did I not tell you, 'Do not sin against the boy'; and you would not listen? Now *justice for* his blood is required." **23** They did not know, however, that Joseph understood, for there was an interpreter between them. **24** Then he turned away from them and wept. But when he returned to them and spoke to them, he took Simeon from them and bound him before their eyes. **25** Then Joseph gave orders to fill their bags with grain, but *also* to return every man's money in his sack, and to give them provisions for the journey. And that is what was done for them.

26 So they loaded their donkeys with their grain and departed from there. **27** But when one *of them* opened his sack to give his donkey feed at the overnight campsite, he saw his money; and behold, it was in the opening of his sack! **28** So he said to his brothers, "My money has been returned, and look, it is right in my sack!" Then their hearts sank, and they *turned* trembling to one another, saying, "What is this that God has done to us?"

Simeon Is Held Hostage

29 When they came to their father Jacob in the land of Canaan, they told him everything that had happened to them, saying, **30** "The man, the lord of the land, spoke harshly with

us, and took us for spies of the country. 31 But we said to him, 'We are honest men; we are not spies. 32 We are twelve brothers, sons of our father; one is no longer alive, and the youngest is with our father today in the land of Canaan.' 33 But the man, the lord of the land, said to us, 'By this I will know that you are honest men: leave one of your brothers with me and take *grain for* the famine of your households, and go. 34 But bring your youngest brother to me so that I may know that you are not spies, but honest men. I will give your brother to you, and you may trade in the land.' "

35 Now it came about, as they were emptying their sacks, that behold, every man's bag of money *was* in his sack; and when they and their father saw their bags of money, they were afraid. 36 And their father Jacob said to them, "You have deprived me of my sons: Joseph is gone, and Simeon is gone, and *now* you would take Benjamin; all these things are against me." 37 Then Reuben spoke to his father, saying, "You may put my two sons to death if I do not bring him *back* to you; put him in my care, and I will return him to you." 38 But Jacob said, "My son shall not go down with you; for his brother is dead, and he alone is left. If harm should happen to him on the journey you are taking, then you will bring my gray hair down to Sheol in sorrow."

The Return to Egypt

43 Now the famine was severe in the land. 2 So it came about, when they had finished eating the grain which they had brought from Egypt, that their father said to them, "Go back, buy us a little food." 3 Judah spoke to him, however, saying, "The man sternly warned us, 'You shall not see my face unless your brother is with you.' 4 If you send our brother with us, we will go down and buy you food. 5 But if you do not send *him,* we will not go down; for the man said to us, 'You will not see my face unless your brother is with you.' " 6 Then Israel said, "Why did you treat me so badly, by telling the man whether you still had *another* brother?" 7 But they said, "The man specifically asked about us and our relatives, saying, 'Is your father still alive? Have you *another* brother?' So we answered his questions. Could we possibly know that he would say, 'Bring your brother down'?" 8 So Judah said to his father Israel, "Send the boy with me and we will arise and go, so that we may live and not die, we as well as you and our little ones. 9 I myself will take responsibility for him! You may demand him back from me. If I do not bring him *back* to you and present him to you, then you can let me take the blame forever. 10 For if we had not delayed, surely by now we could have returned twice."

11 Then their father Israel said to them, "If *it must be* so, then do this: take some of the best products of the land in your bags, and carry down to the man as a gift, a little balsam and a little honey, labdanum resin and myrrh, pistachio nuts and almonds. 12 And take double *the* money in your hand, and take back in your

hand the money that was returned in the opening of your sacks; perhaps it was a mistake. 13 Take your brother also, and arise, return to the man; 14 and may God Almighty grant you compassion in the sight of the man, so that he will release to you your other brother and Benjamin. And as for me, if I am bereaved of my sons, I am bereaved!" 15 So the men took this gift, and they took double *the* money in their hand, and Benjamin; then they set out and went down to Egypt, and stood before Joseph.

Joseph Sees Benjamin

16 When Joseph saw Benjamin with them, he said to his house steward, "Bring the men into the house, and slaughter an animal and make preparations; for the men are to dine with me at noon." 17 So the man did as Joseph said, and brought the men to Joseph's house. 18 Now the men were afraid, because they were brought to Joseph's house; and they said, "*It is* because of the money that was returned in our sacks the first time that we are being brought in, so that he may attack us and over-power us, and take us as slaves with our donkeys." 19 So they approached Joseph's house steward, and spoke to him at the entrance of the house, 20 and said, "Oh, my lord, we indeed came down the first time to buy food, 21 and it happened when we came to the campsite, that we opened our sacks, and behold, each man's money was in the opening of his sack, our money in full. So we have brought it back in our hand. 22 We have also brought down other money in our hand to buy food; we do not know who put our money in our sacks." 23 But he said, "Peace be to you, do not be afraid. Your God and the God of your father has given you treasure in your sacks; your money was in my possession." Then he brought Simeon out to them. 24 Then the man brought the men into Joseph's house and gave them water, and they washed their feet; and he gave their donkeys feed. 25 So they prepared the gift for Joseph's arrival at noon; for they had heard that they were to eat a meal there.

26 When Joseph came home, they brought into the house to him the gift which was in their hand, and they bowed down to the ground before him. 27 Then he asked them about their welfare, and said, "Is your old father well, of whom you spoke? Is he still alive?" 28 And they said, "Your servant our father is well; he is still alive." Then they bowed down *again* [1] in homage. 29 And as he raised his eyes and saw his brother Benjamin, his mother's son, he said, "Is this your youngest brother, of whom you spoke to me?" Then he said, "May God be gracious to you, my son." 30 Joseph then hurried *out,* for he was deeply stirred over his brother, and he looked *for a place* to weep; so he entered his chamber and wept there. 31 Then he washed his face and came out; and he controlled himself and said, "Serve the meal." 32 Then they served him by himself, and Joseph's brothers by themselves, and the Egyptians who ate with him by themselves; because the Egyptians could not

---

43:28 1 I.e., great respect and honor to a superior

eat bread with the Hebrews, for that is an abomination to the Egyptians. 33 Now they were seated before him, from the firstborn according to his birthright to the youngest according to his youth, and the men looked at one another in astonishment. 34 Then he took portions to them from his own table, but Benjamin's portion was five times as much as any of theirs. So they drank freely with him.

The Brothers Are Brought Back

44 Then he commanded his house steward, saying, "Fill the men's sacks with food, as much as they can carry, and put each man's money in the opening of his sack. 2 And put my cup, the silver cup, in the opening of the sack of the youngest, and his money for the grain." And he did as Joseph had told *him.* 3 As soon as it was light, the men were sent away, they with their donkeys. 4 They had *just* left the city, *and* were not far away, when Joseph said to his house steward, "Up, follow the men; and when you overtake them, say to them, 'Why have you repaid evil for good? 5 Is this not *that* from which my lord drinks, and which he indeed uses for divination? You have done wrong in doing this!' "

6 So he overtook them and spoke these words to them. 7 And they said to him, "Why does my lord say such words as these? Far be it from your servants to do such a thing! 8 Behold, the money which we found in the opening of our sacks we have brought back to you from the land of Canaan. How then could we steal silver or gold from your lord's house? 9 With whomever of your servants it is found, he shall die, and we also shall be my lord's slaves." 10 So he said, "Now let it indeed be according to your words; he with whom it is found shall be my slave, but the rest of you shall be *considered* innocent." 11 Then they hurried, each man lowered his sack to the ground, and each man opened his sack. 12 And he searched, beginning with the oldest and ending with the youngest; and the cup was found in Benjamin's sack. 13 Then they tore their clothes *in grief,* and when each man had loaded his donkey, they returned to the city.

14 When Judah and his brothers came to Joseph's house, he was still there, and they fell down to the ground before him. 15 Joseph said to them, "What is this thing that you have done? Do you not know that a man who is like me can indeed practice divination?" 16 So Judah said, "What can we say to my lord? What *words* can we speak? And how can we justify ourselves? God has found out the guilt of your servants; behold, we are my lord's slaves, both we and the one in whose possession the cup has been found." 17 But he said, "Far be it from me to do this. The man in whose possession the cup has been found, he shall be my slave; but as for you, go up in peace to your father."

18 Then Judah approached him and said, "Oh my lord, may your servant please speak a word in my lord's ears, and do not be angry with your servant; for you are equal to Pharaoh. 19 My lord asked his servants, saying, 'Have you a father or a brother?' 20 And we said

to my lord, 'We have an old father and a little boy *born in our father's* old age. Now his brother is dead, so he alone is left of his mother, and his father loves him.' 21 Then you said to your servants, 'Bring him down to me so that I may set my eyes on him.' 22 But we said to my lord, 'The boy cannot leave his father, for if he should leave his father, his father would die.' 23 You said to your servants, however, 'Unless your youngest brother comes down with you, you will not see my face again.' 24 So it came about when we went up to your servant my father, we told him the words of my lord. 25 And our father said, 'Go back, buy us a little food.' 26 But we said, 'We cannot go down. If our youngest brother is with us, then we will go down; for we cannot see the man's face unless our youngest brother is with us.' 27 Then your servant my father said to us, 'You know that my wife bore me two sons; 28 and the one left me, and I said, "Surely he is torn to pieces," and I have not seen him since. 29 If you also take this one from me, and harm happens to him, you will bring my gray hair down to Sheol in sorrow.' 30 So now, when I come to your servant, my father, and the boy is not with us—since our father's life is so attached to the boy's life— 31 when he sees that the boy is not *with us,* he will die. So your servants will bring the gray hair of your servant, our father, down to Sheol in sorrow. 32 For your servant accepted responsibility for the boy from my father, saying, 'If I do not bring him *back* to you, then my father can let me take the blame forever.' 33 So now, please let your servant remain as a slave to my lord instead of the boy, and let the boy go up with his brothers. 34 For how shall I go up to my father if the boy is not with me? *I fear* that I may see the evil that would overtake my father."

Joseph Deals Kindly with His Brothers

45 Then Joseph could not control himself in front of everyone standing before him, and he shouted, "Have everyone leave me!" So there was no one with him when Joseph made himself known to his brothers. 2 Then he wept so loudly that the Egyptians heard *it,* and the household of Pharaoh heard *about it.* 3 And Joseph said to his brothers, "I am Joseph! Is my father still alive?" But his brothers could not answer him, for they were terrified in his presence.

4 Then Joseph said to his brothers, "Please come closer to me." And they came closer. And he said, "I am your brother Joseph, whom you sold to Egypt. 5 Now do not be grieved or angry with yourselves because you sold me here, for God sent me ahead of you to save lives. 6 For the famine *has been* in the land these two years, and there are still five years in which there will be neither plowing nor harvesting. 7 So God sent me ahead of you to ensure for you a remnant on the earth, and to keep you alive by a great deliverance. 8 Now, therefore, it was not you who sent me here, but God; and He has made me a father to Pharaoh and lord of all his household, and ruler over all the land

---

44:6 1 I.e., the steward

of Egypt. 9 Hurry and go up to my father, and say to him, 'This is what your son Joseph says: "God has made me lord of all Egypt; come down to me, do not delay. 10 For you shall live in the land of Goshen, and you shall be near me, you and your children and your grandchildren, and your flocks and your herds and all that you have. 11 There I will also provide for you, for there are still five years of famine *to come,* and you and your household and all that you have would be impoverished." ' 12 Behold, your eyes see, and the eyes of my brother Benjamin *see,* that it is my mouth which is speaking to you. 13 Now you must tell my father of all my splendor in Egypt, and all that you have seen; and you must hurry and bring my father down here." 14 Then he fell on his brother Benjamin's neck and wept, and Benjamin wept on his neck. 15 And he kissed all his brothers and wept on them, and afterward his brothers talked with him.

16 Now when the news was heard in Pharaoh's house that Joseph's brothers had come, it pleased Pharaoh and his servants. 17 Then Pharaoh said to Joseph, "Say to your brothers, 'Do this: load your livestock and go to the land of Canaan, 18 and take your father and your households and come to me; and I will give you the best of the land of Egypt, and you will eat the fat of the land.' 19 Now you are ordered, 'Do this: take wagons from the land of Egypt for your little ones and for your wives, and bring your father and come. 20 And do not concern yourselves with your property, for the best of all the land of Egypt is yours.' "

21 Then the sons of Israel did so; and Joseph gave them wagons according to the command of Pharaoh, and gave them provisions for the journey. 22 To each of them he gave changes of garments, but to Benjamin he gave three hundred *pieces of* silver and five changes of garments. 23 And to his father he sent the following: ten male donkeys loaded with the best things of Egypt, ten female donkeys loaded with grain, bread, and sustenance for his father on the journey.

24 So he sent his brothers away, and as they departed, he said to them, "Do not quarrel on the journey." 25 Then they went up from Egypt, and came to the land of Canaan, to their father Jacob. 26 And they told him, saying, "Joseph is still alive, and indeed he is ruler over all the land of Egypt." But he was stunned, for he did not believe them. 27 When they told him all the words of Joseph that he had spoken to them, and when he saw the wagons that Joseph had sent to carry him, then the spirit of their father Jacob revived. 28 Then Israel said, "It is enough; my son Joseph is still alive. I will go and see him before I die."

Jacob Moves to Egypt

46 So Israel set out with all that he had, and came to Beersheba, and offered sacrifices to the God of his father Isaac. 2 And God spoke to Israel in visions of the night and said, "Jacob, Jacob." And he said, "Here I am." 3 Then He said, "I am God, the God of your father; do not be afraid to go down to Egypt, for I will make you into a great nation

there. 4 I will go down with you to Egypt, and I will also assuredly bring you up again; and Joseph will close your eyes."

5 Then Jacob left Beersheba, and the sons of Israel carried their father Jacob and their little ones and their wives in the wagons which Pharaoh had sent to carry him. 6 They also took their livestock and their possessions, which they had acquired in the land of Canaan, and came to Egypt, Jacob and all his descendants with him: 7 his sons and his grandsons with him, his daughters and his granddaughters, and all his descendants he brought with him to Egypt.

Those Who Came to Egypt

8 Now these are the names of the sons of Israel who went to Egypt, Jacob and his sons: Reuben, Jacob's firstborn. 9 And the sons of Reuben: Hanoch, Pallu, Hezron, and Carmi. 10 And the sons of Simeon: Jemuel, Jamin, Ohad, Jachin, Zohar, and Shaul the son of a Canaanite woman. 11 And the sons of Levi: Gershon, Kohath, and Merari. 12 And the sons of Judah: Er, Onan, Shelah, Perez, and Zerah (but Er and Onan died in the land of Canaan). And the sons of Perez were Hezron and Hamul. 13 And the sons of Issachar: Tola, Puvvah, Iob, and Shimron. 14 And the sons of Zebulun: Sered, Elon, and Jahleel. 15 These are the sons of Leah, whom she bore to Jacob in Paddan-aram, with his daughter Dinah; all his sons and his daughters *numbered* thirty-three. 16 And the sons of Gad: Ziphion, Haggi, Shuni, Ezbon, Eri, Arodi, and Areli. 17 And the sons of Asher: Imnah, Ishvah, Ishvi, Beriah, and their sister Serah. And the sons of Beriah: Heber and Malchiel. 18 These are the sons of Zilpah, whom Laban gave to his daughter Leah; and she bore to Jacob these sixteen persons. 19 The sons of Jacob's wife Rachel: Joseph and Benjamin. 20 Now to Joseph in the land of Egypt were born Manasseh and Ephraim, whom Asenath, the daughter of Potiphera, priest of On, bore to him. 21 And the sons of Benjamin: Bela, Becher, Ashbel, Gera, Naaman, Ehi, Rosh, Muppim, Huppim, and Ard. 22 These are the sons of Rachel, who were born to Jacob; *there were* fourteen persons in all. 23 And the sons of Dan: Hushim. 24 And the sons of Naphtali: Jahzeel, Guni, Jezer, and Shillem. 25 These are the sons of Bilhah, whom Laban gave to his daughter Rachel, and she bore these to Jacob; *there were* seven persons in all. 26 All the people belonging to Jacob, who came to Egypt, his direct descendants, not including the wives of Jacob's sons, *were* sixty-six persons in all, 27 and the sons of Joseph, who were born to him in Egypt, were two; all the people of the house of Jacob, who came to Egypt, *were* seventy.

28 Now *Jacob* sent Judah ahead of him to Joseph, to guide him to Goshen; and they came into the land of Goshen. 29 And Joseph prepared his chariot and went up to Goshen to meet his father Israel; as soon as he appeared to him, *Joseph* threw himself on his neck and wept on his neck a long time. 30 Then Israel said to Joseph, "Now let me die, since I have seen your face, that you are still alive." 31 But Joseph said to his brothers and to his father's

household, "I will go up and tell Pharaoh, and will say to him, 'My brothers and my father's household, who *were* in the land of Canaan, have come to me; 32 and the men are shepherds, for they have been keepers of livestock; and they have brought their flocks and their herds and all that they have.' 33 When Pharaoh calls for you and says, 'What is your occupation?' 34 you shall say, 'Your servants have been keepers of livestock since our youth even until now, both we and our fathers,' so that you may live in the land of Goshen; for every shepherd is an abomination to the Egyptians."

Jacob's Family Settles in Goshen

47 Then Joseph went in and told Pharaoh, and said, "My father and my brothers and their flocks and their herds and all that they have, have come out of the land of Canaan; and behold, they are in the land of Goshen." 2 And he took five men from among his brothers and presented them to Pharaoh. 3 Then Pharaoh said to his brothers, "What is your occupation?" So they said to Pharaoh, "Your servants are shepherds, both we and our fathers." 4 They also said to Pharaoh, "We have come to reside in the land, for there is no pasture for your servants' flocks, for the famine is severe in the land of Canaan. Now, therefore, please let your servants live in the land of Goshen." 5 Then Pharaoh said to Joseph, "Your father and your brothers have come to you. 6 The land of Egypt is at your disposal; settle your father and your brothers in the best of the land, let them live in the land of Goshen; and if you know any capable men among them, then put them in charge of my livestock."

7 Then Joseph brought his father Jacob and presented him to Pharaoh; and Jacob blessed Pharaoh. 8 And Pharaoh said to Jacob, "How many years have you lived?" 9 So Jacob said to Pharaoh, "The years of my living abroad are 130; few and unpleasant have been the years of my life, nor have they attained the years that my fathers lived during the days of their living abroad." 10 So Jacob blessed Pharaoh, and went out from his presence. 11 Now Joseph settled his father and his brothers and gave them property in the land of Egypt, in the best of the land, in the land of Rameses, as Pharaoh had ordered. 12 Joseph also provided his father and his brothers and all his father's household with food, according to the number of their little ones.

13 Now there was no food in all the land, because the famine was very severe, so that the land of Egypt and the land of Canaan languished because of the famine. 14 And Joseph collected all the money that was found in the land of Egypt and in the land of Canaan *in payment* for the grain which they bought, and Joseph brought the money into Pharaoh's house. 15 When the money was all spent in the land of Egypt and in the land of Canaan, all the Egyptians came to Joseph saying, "Give us food, for why should we die in your presence? For *our* money is gone." 16 Then Joseph said, "Give up your livestock, and I will give you

food for your livestock, since *your* money is gone." 17 So they brought their livestock to Joseph, and Joseph gave them food in exchange for the horses and the flocks and the herds and the donkeys; and he fed them with food in exchange for all their livestock that year. 18 But when that year ended, they came to him the next year and said to him, "We will not hide from my lord the fact that our money is all spent, and the livestock are my lord's. There is nothing left for my lord except our bodies and our lands. 19 Why should we die before your eyes, both we and our land? Buy us and our land for food, and we and our land will be slaves to Pharaoh. So give us seed, so that we may live and not die, and that the land may not be desolate."

Result of the Famine

20 So Joseph bought all the land of Egypt for Pharaoh, for every Egyptian sold his field, because the famine was severe upon them. So the land became Pharaoh's. 21 As for the people, he relocated them to the cities from one end of Egypt's border to the other. 22 Only the land of the priests he did not buy, because the priests had an allotment from Pharaoh, and they lived off the allotment which Pharaoh gave them. Therefore, they did not sell their land. 23 Then Joseph said to the people, "Behold, today I have purchased you and your land for Pharaoh; now, *here is* seed for you, and you may sow the land. 24 At the harvest you shall give a fifth to Pharaoh, and four-fifths shall be your own for seed of the field and for your food, and for those of your households and as food for your little ones." 25 So they said, "You have saved our lives! Let us find favor in the sight of my lord, and we will be Pharaoh's slaves." 26 Joseph made it a statute concerning the land of Egypt, *valid* to this day, that Pharaoh was to have the fifth; only the land of the priests did not become Pharaoh's.

27 Now Israel lived in the land of Egypt, in Goshen, and they acquired property in it and were fruitful and became very numerous. 28 And Jacob lived in the land of Egypt for seventeen years; so the length of Jacob's life was 147 years.

29 When the time for Israel to die drew near, he called his son Joseph and said to him, "Please, if I have found favor in your sight, place your hand under my thigh now and deal with me in kindness and faithfulness: please do not bury me in Egypt, 30 but when I 1lie down with my fathers, you shall carry me out of Egypt and bury me in their burial place." And he said, "I will do as you have said." 31 And he said, "Swear to me." So he swore to him. Then Israel bowed *in worship* at the head of the bed.

Israel's Last Days

48 Now it came about after these things that Joseph was told, "Behold, your father is sick." So he took his two sons Manasseh and Ephraim with him. 2 When it was told to Jacob, "Behold, your son Joseph has come to you," Israel collected his strength and

sat up in the bed. [3] Then Jacob said to Joseph, "God Almighty appeared to me at Luz in the land of Canaan and blessed me, [4] and He said to me, 'Behold, I will make you fruitful and numerous, and I will make you a multitude of peoples, and will give this land to your descendants after you as an everlasting possession.' [5] Now your two sons, who were born to you in the land of Egypt before I came to you in Egypt, are mine; Ephraim and Manasseh shall be mine, as Reuben and Simeon are. [6] But your children that you have fathered after them shall be yours; they shall be called by the names of their brothers in their inheritance. [7] Now as for me, when I came from Paddan, Rachel died, to my sorrow, in the land of Canaan on the journey, when there was still some distance to go to Ephrath. I buried her there on the way to Ephrath (that is, Bethlehem)."

[8] When Israel saw Joseph's sons, he said, "Who are these?" [9] And Joseph said to his father, "They are my sons, whom God has given me here." So he said, "Bring them to me, please, so that I may bless them." [10] Now the eyes of Israel were *so* dim from age *that* he could not see. And Joseph brought them close to him, and he kissed them and embraced them. [11] And Israel said to Joseph, "I never expected to see your face, and behold, God has let me see your children as well!" [12] Then Joseph took them from his knees, and bowed with his face to the ground. [13] And Joseph took them both, Ephraim with his right hand toward Israel's left, and Manasseh with his left hand toward Israel's right, and brought them close to him. [14] And Israel reached out his right hand and placed it on the head of Ephraim, who was the younger, and his left hand on Manasseh's head, crossing his hands, although Manasseh was the firstborn. [15] And he blessed Joseph, and said,

"The God before whom my fathers
　　Abraham and Isaac walked,
The God who has been my shepherd all
　　my life to this day,
16　The angel who has redeemed me from all
　　　evil,
　　Bless the boys;
And may my name live on in them,
And the names of my fathers Abraham
　　and Isaac;
And may they grow into a multitude in
　　the midst of the earth."

[17] When Joseph saw that his father placed his right hand on Ephraim's head, it displeased him; and he grasped his father's hand to move it from Ephraim's head to Manasseh's head. [18] And Joseph said to his father, "Not so, my father, for this one is the firstborn. Place your right hand on his head." [19] But his father refused and said, "I know, my son, I know; he also will become a people and he also will be great. However, his younger brother shall be greater than he, and his descendants shall become a multitude of nations." [20] So he blessed that day, saying,

"By you Israel will pronounce blessing,
　　saying,

'May God make you like Ephraim and
　　Manasseh!'"
And *so* he put Ephraim before Manasseh. [21] Then Israel said to Joseph, "Behold, I am about to die, but God will be with you, and bring you back to the land of your fathers. [22] And I give you one portion more than your brothers, which I took from the hand of the Amorite with my sword and my bow."

Jacob's Prophecy concerning His Sons

49 Then Jacob summoned his sons and said, "Assemble yourselves, so that I may tell you what will happen to you in the days to come.

2　"Gather together and listen, sons of Jacob;
　　Yes, listen to Israel your father.
3¶　"Reuben, you are my firstborn,
　　My might and the beginning of my
　　　strength,
　　Preeminent in dignity and preeminent in
　　　power.
4　"Uncontrollable as water, you shall not
　　　have preeminence,
　　Because you went up to your father's bed;
　　Then you defiled *it*—he went up to my
　　　couch.
5¶　"Simeon and Levi are brothers;
　　Their [1]swords are implements of violence.
6　"May my soul not enter into their council;
　　May my glory not be united with their
　　　assembly;
　　For in their anger they killed men,
　　And in their self-will they lamed oxen.
7　"Cursed be their anger, for it is fierce;
　　And their wrath, for it is cruel.
　　I will scatter them in Jacob,
　　And disperse them among Israel.
8¶　"As for you, Judah, your brothers shall
　　　praise you;
　　Your hand shall be on the neck of your
　　　enemies;
　　Your father's sons shall bow down to you.
9　"Judah is a lion's cub;
　　From the prey, my son, you have gone up.
　　He crouches, he lies down as a lion,
　　And as a lion, who dares to stir him up?
10　"The scepter will not depart from Judah,
　　Nor the ruler's staff from between his
　　　feet,
　　Until Shiloh comes,
　　And to him *shall be* the obedience of the
　　　peoples.
11　"He ties *his* foal to the vine,
　　And his donkey's colt to the choice vine;
　　He washes his garments in wine,
　　And his robes in the blood of grapes.
12　"His eyes are dull from wine,
　　And his teeth white from milk.
13¶　"Zebulun will reside at the seashore;
　　And he *shall be* a harbor for ships,
　　And his flank *shall be* toward Sidon.
14¶　"Issachar is a strong donkey,
　　Lying down between the sheepfolds.
15　"When he saw that a resting place was
　　　good
　　And that the land was pleasant,
　　He bowed his shoulder to carry *burdens,*
　　And became a slave at forced labor.

49:5 [1] Or *plans;* meaning uncertain

16¶ "Dan shall judge his people,
   As one of the tribes of Israel.
17 "Dan shall be a serpent in the way,
   A horned viper in the path,
   That bites the horse's heels,
   So that its rider falls backward.
18 "For Your salvation I wait, LORD.
19¶ "As for Gad, a band of raiders shall attack
   him,
   But he will attack *at* their heels.
20¶ "As for Asher, his food shall be rich,
   And he will yield royal delicacies.
21¶ "Naphtali is a doe let loose;
   He utters beautiful words.
22¶ "Joseph is a fruitful branch,
   A fruitful branch by a spring;
   Its branches hang over a wall.
23 "The archers provoked him,
   And shot *at him* and were hostile toward
   him;
24 But his bow remained firm,
   And his arms were agile,
   From the hands of the Mighty One of
   Jacob
   (From there is the Shepherd, the Stone of
   Israel),
25 From the God of your father who helps
   you,
   And by the Almighty who blesses you
   With blessings of heaven above,
   Blessings of the deep that lies beneath,
   Blessings of the breasts and of the womb.
26 "The blessings of your father
   Have surpassed the blessings of my
   ancestors
   Up to the furthest boundary of the
   everlasting hills;
   May they be on the head of Joseph,
   And on the top of the head of the one dis-
   tinguished among his brothers.
27¶ "Benjamin is a ravenous wolf;
   In the morning he devours the prey,
   And in the evening he divides the
   spoils."
28 All these are the twelve tribes of Israel, and this is what their father said to them when he blessed them. He blessed them, every one with the blessing appropriate to him.

Jacob Dies

29 Then he commanded them and said to them, "I am about to be gathered to my people; bury me with my fathers in the cave that is in the field of Ephron the Hittite, 30 in the cave that is in the field of Machpelah, which is opposite Mamre, in the land of Canaan, which Abraham bought along with the field from Ephron the Hittite as a burial site. 31 There they buried Abraham and his wife Sarah, there they buried Isaac and his wife Rebekah, and there I buried Leah— 32 the field and the cave that is in it, purchased from the sons of Heth." 33 When Jacob finished commanding his sons, he drew his feet into the bed and breathed his last, and was gathered to his people.

Jacob Is Buried

50 Then Joseph fell on his father's face, and wept over him and kissed him. 2 Joseph commanded his servants the physicians to embalm his father. So the physicians embalmed Israel. 3 Now forty days were required for it, for such is the period required for embalming. And the Egyptians wept for him seventy days.

4 When the days of mourning for him were past, Joseph spoke to the household of Pharaoh, saying, "If now I have found favor in your sight, please speak to Pharaoh, saying, 5 'My father made me swear, saying, "Behold, I am about to die; in my grave which I dug for myself in the land of Canaan, there you shall bury me." Now then, please let me go up and bury my father; then I will return.' " 6 Pharaoh said, "Go up and bury your father, as he made you swear."

7 So Joseph went up to bury his father, and with him went up all the servants of Pharaoh, the elders of his household and all the elders of the land of Egypt, 8 and all the household of Joseph and his brothers and his father's household; they left only their little ones and their flocks and their herds in the land of Goshen. 9 Chariots with teams of horses also went up with him; and it was a very great company. 10 When they came to the threshing floor of Atad, which is beyond the Jordan, they mourned there with a very great and sorrowful lamentation; and he observed seven days of mourning for his father. 11 Now when the inhabitants of the land, the Canaanites, saw the mourning at the threshing floor of Atad, they said, "This is a grievous mourning for the Egyptians." Therefore it was named Abel-mizraim, which is beyond the Jordan.

Burial at Machpelah

12 And *so* his sons did for him as he had commanded them; 13 for his sons carried him to the land of Canaan and buried him in the cave of the field of Machpelah opposite Mamre, which Abraham had bought along with the field as a burial site from Ephron the Hittite. 14 And after he had buried his father, Joseph returned to Egypt, he and his brothers, and all who had gone up with him to bury his father.

15 When Joseph's brothers had seen that their father was dead, they said, "What if Joseph holds a grudge against us and pays us back in full for all the wrong which we did to him!" 16 So they sent instructions to Joseph, saying, "Your father commanded *us* before he died, saying, 17 'This is what you shall say to Joseph: "Please forgive, I beg you, the offense of your brothers and their sin, for they did you wrong." ' And now, please forgive the offense of the servants of the God of your father." And Joseph wept when they spoke to him. 18 Then his brothers also came and fell down before him and said, "Behold, we are your servants." 19 But Joseph said to them, "Do not be afraid, for am I in God's place? 20 As for you, you meant evil against me, *but* God meant it for good in order to bring about this present result, to keep many people alive. 21 So therefore, do not be afraid; I will provide for you and your little ones." So he comforted them and spoke kindly to them.

Death of Joseph

22 Now Joseph stayed in Egypt, he and his

father's household, and Joseph lived 110 years. 23 Joseph saw the third generation of Ephraim's sons; also the sons of Machir, the son of Manasseh, were born on Joseph's knees. 24 Joseph said to his brothers, "I am about to die, but God will assuredly take care of you and bring you up from this land to the land which

He promised on oath to Abraham, to Isaac, and to Jacob." 25 Then Joseph made the sons of Israel swear, saying, "God will assuredly take care of you, and you shall carry my bones up from here." 26 So Joseph died at the age of 110 years; and they embalmed him and placed him in a coffin in Egypt.

EXODUS

Israel Multiplies in Egypt

1 Now these are the names of the sons of Israel who came to Egypt with Jacob; they came, each one with his household: 2 Reuben, Simeon, Levi, and Judah; 3 Issachar, Zebulun, and Benjamin; 4 Dan and Naphtali, Gad and Asher. 5 All the people who descended from Jacob were seventy people, but Joseph was *already* in Egypt. 6 And Joseph died, and all his brothers and all that generation. 7 But the sons of Israel were fruitful and increased greatly, and multiplied, and became exceedingly mighty, so that the land was filled with them.

8 Now a new king arose over Egypt, who did not know Joseph. 9 And he said to his people, "Behold, the people of the sons of Israel are too many and too mighty for us. 10 Come, let us deal shrewdly with them, otherwise they will multiply, and in the event of war, they will also join those who hate us, and fight against us and depart from the land." 11 So they appointed taskmasters over them to oppress them with hard labor. And they built for Pharaoh storage cities, Pithom and Raamses. 12 But the more they oppressed them, the more they multiplied and the more they spread out, so that they dreaded the sons of Israel. 13 The Egyptians used violence to compel the sons of Israel to labor; 14 and they made their lives bitter with hard labor in mortar and bricks and at all *kinds of* labor in the field, all their labors which they violently had them perform as slaves.

15 Then the king of Egypt spoke to the Hebrew midwives, one of whom was named Shiphrah, and the other was named Puah; 16 and he said, "When you are helping the Hebrew women to give birth and see *them* upon the birthstool, if it is a son, then you shall put him to death; but if it is a daughter, then she shall live." 17 But the midwives feared God, and did not do as the king of Egypt had commanded them, but let the boys live. 18 So the king of Egypt called for the midwives and said to them, "Why have you done this thing, and let the boys live?" 19 The midwives said to Pharaoh, "Because the Hebrew women are not like the Egyptian women; for they are vigorous and give birth before the midwife can get to them." 20 So God was good to the midwives, and the people multiplied, and became very mighty. 21 And because the midwives feared God, He established households for them. 22 Then Pharaoh commanded all his people, saying, "Every son who is born, ¹you are to throw into the Nile, but every daughter, you are to keep alive."

The Birth of Moses

2 Now a man from the house of Levi went and married a daughter of Levi. 2 And the woman conceived and gave birth to a son; and when she saw that he was beautiful, she hid him for three months. 3 But when she could no longer hide him, she got him a papyrus basket and covered it with tar and pitch. Then she put the child in it and set *it* among the reeds by the bank of the Nile. 4 And his sister stood at a distance to find out what would happen to him.

5 Now the daughter of Pharaoh came down to bathe at the Nile, with her female attendants walking alongside the Nile; and she saw the basket among the reeds and sent her slave woman, and she brought it *to her.* 6 When she opened *it,* she saw the child, and behold, *the* boy was crying. And she had pity on him and said, "This is one of the Hebrews' children." 7 Then his sister said to Pharaoh's daughter, "Shall I go and call a woman for you who is nursing from the Hebrew women, so that she may nurse the child for you?" 8 Pharaoh's daughter said to her, "Go *ahead.*" So the girl went and called the child's mother. 9 Then Pharaoh's daughter said to her, "Take this child away and nurse him for me, and I will give *you* your wages." So the woman took the child and nursed him. 10 And the child grew, and she brought him to Pharaoh's daughter and he became her son. And she named him Moses, and said, "Because I drew him out of the water."

11 Now it came about in those days, when Moses had grown up, that he went out to his fellow Hebrews and looked at their hard labors; and he saw an Egyptian beating a Hebrew, one of his fellow Hebrews. 12 So he looked this way and that, and when he saw that there was no one *around,* he struck and killed the Egyptian, and hid his body in the sand. 13 Now he went out the next day, and behold, two Hebrews were fighting with each other; and he said to the offender, "Why are you striking your companion?" 14 But he said, "Who made you a ruler and a judge over us? Do you intend to kill me as you killed the Egyptian?" Then Moses was afraid and said, "Surely the matter has become known!"

Moses Escapes to Midian

15 When Pharaoh heard about this matter, he tried to kill Moses. But Moses fled from the presence of Pharaoh and settled in the land of Midian, and he sat down by a well.

16 Now the priest of Midian had seven daughters; and they came to draw water and filled the troughs to water their father's flock. 17 Then the shepherds came and drove them away, but Moses stood up and helped them and watered their flock. 18 When they came to their father Reuel, he said, "Why have you come *back* so soon today?" 19 They said, "An Egyptian saved us from the shepherds, and what is more, he even drew water for us and watered the flock." 20 So he said to his daughters, "Where is he then? Why is it that you have left the man behind? Invite him to have something to eat." 21 And Moses was willing to live with the man. And he gave his daughter Zipporah to Moses. 22 Then she gave

---

1:22 ¹Some ancient versions insert *to the Hebrews*

birth to a son, and he named him Gershom, for he said, "I have been a stranger in a foreign land."

23 Now it came about in *the course of* those many days that the king of Egypt died. And the sons of Israel groaned because of the bondage, and they cried out; and their cry for help because of *their* bondage ascended to God. 24 So God heard their groaning; and God remembered His covenant with Abraham, Isaac, and Jacob. 25 And God saw the sons of Israel, and God took notice *of them.*

The Burning Bush

3 Now Moses was pasturing the flock of his father-in-law Jethro, the priest of Midian; and he led the flock to the west side of the wilderness and came to Horeb, the mountain of God. 2 Then the angel of the LORD appeared to him in a blazing fire from the midst of a bush; and he looked, and behold, the bush was burning with fire, yet the bush was not being consumed. 3 So Moses said, "I must turn aside and see this marvelous sight, why the bush is not burning up!" 4 When the LORD saw that he turned aside to look, God called to him from the midst of the bush and said, "Moses, Moses!" And he said, "Here I am." 5 Then He said, "Do not come near here; remove your sandals from your feet, for the place on which you are standing is holy ground." 6 And He said, "I am the God of your father—the God of Abraham, the God of Isaac, and the God of Jacob." Then Moses hid his face, for he was afraid to look at God.

7 And the LORD said, "I have certainly seen the oppression of My people who are in Egypt, and have heard their outcry because of their taskmasters, for I am aware of their sufferings. 8 So I have come down to rescue them from the power of the Egyptians, and to bring them up from that land to a good and spacious land, to a land flowing with milk and honey, to the place of the Canaanite, the Hittite, the Amorite, the Perizzite, the Hivite, and the Jebusite. 9 And now, behold, the cry of the sons of Israel has come to Me; furthermore, I have seen the oppression with which the Egyptians are oppressing them.

The Mission of Moses

10 And now come, and I will send you to Pharaoh, so that you may bring My people, the sons of Israel, out of Egypt." 11 But Moses said to God, "Who am I, that I should go to Pharaoh, and that I should bring the sons of Israel out of Egypt?" 12 And He said, "Assuredly I will be with you, and this shall be the sign to you that it is I who have sent you: when you have brought the people out of Egypt, you shall worship God at this mountain."

13 Then Moses said to God, "Behold, I am going to the sons of Israel, and I will say to them, 'The God of your fathers has sent me to you.' Now they may say to me, 'What is His name?' What shall I say to them?" 14 And God said to Moses, "'I AM WHO I AM"; and He said, "This is what you shall say to the sons of

Israel: 'I AM has sent me to you.'" 15 God furthermore said to Moses, "This is what you shall say to the sons of Israel: 'The LORD, the God of your fathers, the God of Abraham, the God of Isaac, and the God of Jacob, has sent me to you.' This is My name forever, and this is the 'name for all generations *to use* to call upon Me. 16 Go and gather the elders of Israel together and say to them, 'The LORD, the God of your fathers, the God of Abraham, Isaac, and Jacob has appeared to me, saying, "I am indeed concerned about you and what has been done to you in Egypt. 17 So I said, I will bring you up out of the oppression of Egypt to the land of the Canaanite, the Hittite, the Amorite, the Perizzite, the Hivite, and the Jebusite, to a land flowing with milk and honey."' 18 Then they will pay attention to what you say; and you with the elders of Israel will come to the king of Egypt, and you will say to him, 'The LORD, the God of the Hebrews, has met with us. So now, please let us go a three days' journey into the wilderness, so that we may sacrifice to the LORD our God.' 19 But I know that the king of Egypt will not permit you to go, except under compulsion. 20 So I will reach out with My hand and strike Egypt with all My miracles which I shall do in the midst of it; and after that he will let you go. 21 I will grant this people favor in the sight of the Egyptians; and it shall be that when you go, you will not go empty-handed. 22 But every woman shall ask her neighbor and the woman who lives in her house for articles of silver and articles of gold, and clothing; and you will put them on your sons and daughters. So you will plunder the Egyptians."

Moses Given Signs

4 Then Moses said, "What if they will not believe me or listen to what I say? For they may say, 'The LORD has not appeared to you.'" 2 The LORD said to him, "What is that in your hand?" And he said, "A staff." 3 Then He said, "Throw it on the ground." So he threw it on the ground, and it turned into a serpent; and Moses fled from it. 4 But the LORD said to Moses, "Reach out with your hand and grasp *it* by its tail"—so he reached out with his hand and caught it, and it turned into a staff in his hand— 5 "so that they may believe that the LORD, the God of their fathers, the God of Abraham, the God of Isaac, and the God of Jacob, has appeared to you."

6 The LORD furthermore said to him, "Now put your hand inside the fold of your robe." So he put his hand inside the fold, and when he took it out, behold, his hand was leprous like snow. 7 Then He said, "Put your hand inside the fold of your robe again." So he put his hand into the fold again, and when he took it out of the fold, behold, it was restored like *the rest of* his flesh. 8 "So if they will not believe you nor pay attention to the evidence of the first sign, they may believe the evidence of the last sign. 9 But if they will not believe even these two signs nor pay attention to what you say, then you shall take some water from the Nile and

---

3:14 1 Related to the name of God, *YHWH,* rendered *LORD,* which is derived from the verb *HAYAH,* to be
3:15 1 I.e., name used in prayer, vows, and ceremony

pour it on the dry ground; and the water which you take from the Nile will turn into blood on the dry ground."

10 Then Moses said to the LORD, "Please, Lord, I have never been eloquent, neither recently nor in time past, nor since You have spoken to Your servant; for I am slow of speech and slow of tongue." 11 But the LORD said to him, "Who has made the human mouth? Or who makes *anyone* unable to speak or deaf, or able to see or blind? Is it not I, the LORD? 12 Now then go, and I Myself will be with your mouth, and instruct you in what you are to say." 13 But he said, "Please, Lord, now send *the message* by whomever You will."

Aaron to Be Moses' Mouthpiece

14 Then the anger of the LORD burned against Moses, and He said, "Is there not your brother Aaron the Levite? I know that he speaks fluently. And moreover, behold, he is coming out to meet you; when he sees you, he will be overjoyed. 15 So you are to speak to him and put the words in his mouth; and I Myself will be with your mouth and his mouth, and I will instruct you in what you are to do. 16 He shall speak for you to the people; and he will be as a mouth for you and you will be as God to him. 17 And you shall take in your hand this staff, with which you shall perform the signs."

18 Then Moses departed and returned to his father-in-law Jethro, and said to him, "Please, let me go, that I may return to my brothers who are in Egypt, and see if they are still alive." And Jethro said to Moses, "Go in peace." 19 Now the LORD said to Moses in Midian, "Go back to Egypt, for all the men who were seeking your life are dead." 20 So Moses took his wife and his sons and mounted them on a donkey, and returned to the land of Egypt. Moses also took the staff of God in his hand.

21 And the LORD said to Moses, "When you go back to Egypt, see that you perform before Pharaoh all the wonders which I have put in your power; but I will harden his heart so that he will not let the people go. 22 Then you shall say to Pharaoh, 'This is what the LORD says: "Israel is My son, My firstborn. 23 So I said to you, 'Let My son go so that he may serve Me'; but you have refused to let him go. Behold, I am going to kill your son, your firstborn." ' "

24 But it came about at the overnight encampment on the way, that the LORD met Moses, and sought to put him to death. 25 So Zipporah took a flint and cut off her son's fore-skin and threw it at Moses' feet; and she said, "You are indeed a groom of blood to me!" 26 So He left him alone. At that time she said, "*You are* a groom of blood"—because of the circumcision.

27 Now the LORD said to Aaron, "Go to meet Moses in the wilderness." So he went and met him at the mountain of God and kissed him. 28 Moses told Aaron all the words of the LORD with which He had sent him, and all the signs that He had commanded him *to do.* 29 Then Moses and Aaron went and assembled all the elders of the sons of Israel; 30 and Aaron spoke all the words which the LORD had spoken to Moses. He then performed the signs in the

sight of the people. 31 So the people believed; and when they heard that the LORD was concerned about the sons of Israel and that He had seen their affliction, they bowed low and worshiped.

Israel's Labor Increased

5 And afterward Moses and Aaron came and said to Pharaoh, "This is what the LORD, the God of Israel says: 'Let My people go so that they may celebrate a feast to Me in the wilderness.' " 2 But Pharaoh said, "Who is the LORD that I should obey His voice to let Israel go? I do not know the LORD, and besides, I will not let Israel go." 3 Then they said, "The God of the Hebrews has met with us. Please, let us go a three days' journey into the wilderness so that we may sacrifice to the LORD our God, otherwise He will strike us with plague or with the sword." 4 But the king of Egypt said to them, "Moses and Aaron, why do you let the people neglect their work? Get *back* to your labors!" 5 Again Pharaoh said, "Look, the people of the land are now many, and you would have them cease from their labors!" 6 So the same day Pharaoh commanded the taskmasters over the people and their foremen, saying, 7 "You are no longer to give the people straw to make bricks as previously; have them go and gather straw for themselves. 8 But you shall impose on them the quota of bricks which they were making before; you are not to reduce any of it. Because they are lazy, for that reason they cry out, 'Let us go and sacrifice to our God.' 9 Let the labor be heavier on the men, and have them work at it so that they will pay no attention to false words."

10 So the taskmasters of the people and their foremen went out and spoke to the people, saying, "This is what Pharaoh says: 'I am not going to give you *any* straw. 11 You go, get straw for yourselves wherever you can find *it;* but none of your labor will be reduced.' " 12 So the people scattered through all the land of Egypt to gather stubble for straw. 13 And the taskmasters pressed them, saying, "Complete your work quota, *your* daily amount, just as when you had straw." 14 Moreover, the foremen of the sons of Israel, whom Pharaoh's taskmasters had set over them, were beaten and asked, "Why have you not completed your required task of making bricks either yesterday or today, as before?"

15 Then the foremen of the sons of Israel came and cried out to Pharaoh, saying, "Why do you deal this way with your servants? 16 There is no straw given to your servants, yet they keep saying to us, 'Make bricks!' And behold, your servants are being beaten; but it is the fault of your *own* people." 17 But he said, "You are lazy, *very* lazy; for that reason you say, 'Let us go *and* sacrifice to the LORD.' 18 So go now *and* work; for you will be given no straw, but you must deliver the quota of bricks." 19 The foremen of the sons of Israel saw that they were in trouble, since they were told, "You must not reduce your daily amount of bricks." 20 When they left Pharaoh's presence, they met Moses and Aaron as they were waiting for them. 21 And they said to them,

"May the LORD look upon you and judge *you,* because you have made us repulsive in Pharaoh's sight and in the sight of his servants, to put a sword in their hand to kill us!"

22 Then Moses returned to the LORD and said, "Lord, why have You brought harm to this people? Why did You ever send me? 23 Ever since I came to Pharaoh to speak in Your name, he has done harm to this people, and You have not rescued Your people at all."

God Promises Action

6 Then the LORD said to Moses, "Now you shall see what I will do to Pharaoh; for under compulsion he will let them go, and under compulsion he will drive them out of his land."

2 God spoke further to Moses and said to him, "I am the LORD; 3 and I appeared to Abraham, Isaac, and Jacob as God Almighty, but *by* My name, [1]LORD, I did not make Myself known to them. 4 I also established My covenant with them, to give them the land of Canaan, the land in which they lived as strangers. 5 Furthermore I have heard the groaning of the sons of Israel, because the Egyptians are holding them in bondage, and I have remembered My covenant. 6 Say, therefore, to the sons of Israel, 'I am the LORD, and I will bring you out from under the labors of the Egyptians, and I will rescue you from their bondage. I will also redeem you with an outstretched arm, and with great judgments. 7 Then I will take you as My people, and I will be your God; and you shall know that I am the LORD your God, who brought you out from under the labors of the Egyptians. 8 I will bring you to the land which I swore to give to Abraham, Isaac, and Jacob, and I will give it to you *as* a possession; I am the LORD.' " 9 So Moses said this to the sons of Israel, but they did not listen to Moses on account of *their* [1]despondency and cruel bondage.

10 Now the LORD spoke to Moses, saying, 11 "Go, tell Pharaoh king of Egypt to let the sons of Israel go out of his land." 12 But Moses spoke before the LORD, saying, "Behold, the sons of Israel have not listened to me; how then will Pharaoh listen to me, as I am unskilled in speech?" 13 Nevertheless, the LORD spoke to Moses and to Aaron and gave them a command concerning the sons of Israel and Pharaoh king of Egypt, to bring the sons of Israel out of the land of Egypt.

The Heads of Israel

14 These are the heads of their fathers' households. The sons of Reuben, Israel's firstborn: Hanoch and Pallu, Hezron and Carmi; these are the families of Reuben. 15 And the sons of Simeon: Jemuel, Jamin, Ohad, Jachin, Zohar, and Shaul the son of a Canaanite woman; these are the families of Simeon. 16 And these are the names of the sons of Levi according to their generations: Gershon, Kohath, and Merari; and the length of Levi's life was 137 years. 17 The sons of Gershon: Libni and Shimei, according to their families. 18 And the sons of Kohath: Amram, Izhar,

Hebron, and Uzziel; and the length of Kohath's life was 133 years. 19 And the sons of Merari: Mahli and Mushi. These are the families of the Levites according to their generations. 20 Now Amram married his father's sister Jochebed, and she bore him Aaron and Moses; and the length of Amram's life was 137 years. 21 And the sons of Izhar: Korah, Nepheg, and Zichri. 22 And the sons of Uzziel: Mishael, Elzaphan, and Sithri. 23 Aaron married Elisheba, the daughter of Amminadab, the sister of Nahshon, and she bore him Nadab and Abihu, Eleazar and Ithamar. 24 And the sons of Korah: Assir, Elkanah, and Abiasaph; these are the families of the Korahites. 25 Now Aaron's son Eleazar married one of the daughters of Putiel, and she bore him Phinehas. These are the heads of the fathers' *households* of the Levites according to their families. 26 It was *the same* Aaron and Moses to whom the LORD said, "Bring out the sons of Israel from the land of Egypt according to their multitudes." 27 They were the ones who spoke to Pharaoh king of Egypt about bringing out the sons of Israel from Egypt; it was *the same* Moses and Aaron.

28 Now it came about on the day when the LORD spoke to Moses in the land of Egypt, 29 that the LORD spoke to Moses, saying, "I am the LORD; say to Pharaoh king of Egypt all that I say to you." 30 But Moses said before the LORD, "Behold, I am unskilled in speech; how then will Pharaoh listen to me?"

I Will Extend My Hand

7 Then the LORD said to Moses, "See, I have made you *as* God to Pharaoh, and your brother Aaron shall be your prophet. 2 As for you, you shall speak all that I command you, and your brother Aaron shall speak to Pharaoh that he let the sons of Israel go out of his land. 3 But I will harden Pharaoh's heart, so that I may multiply My signs and My wonders in the land of Egypt. 4 When Pharaoh does not listen to you, I will lay My hand on Egypt and bring out My armies, My people the sons of Israel, from the land of Egypt by great judgments. 5 Then the Egyptians shall know that I am the LORD, when I extend My hand over Egypt and bring out the sons of Israel from their midst." 6 So Moses and Aaron did *this;* as the LORD commanded them, so they did. 7 And Moses was eighty years old and Aaron eighty-three, when they spoke to Pharaoh.

Aaron's Staff Turns into a Serpent

8 Now the LORD spoke to Moses and Aaron, saying, 9 "When Pharaoh speaks to you, saying, 'Work a miracle,' then you shall say to Aaron, 'Take your staff and throw *it* down before Pharaoh, *so that* it may turn into a serpent.' " 10 So Moses and Aaron came to Pharaoh, and so they did, just as the LORD had commanded; and Aaron threw his staff down before Pharaoh and his servants, and it turned into a serpent. 11 Then Pharaoh also called for *the* wise men and *the* sorcerers, and they too, *the* soothsayer priests of Egypt, did the same with their secret arts. 12 For each one threw down his staff, and they turned into serpents. But Aaron's staff

swallowed their staffs. **13** Yet Pharaoh's heart was hardened, and he did not listen to them, just as the LORD had said.

Water Turned into Blood

14 Then the LORD said to Moses, "Pharaoh's heart is stubborn; he refuses to let the people go. **15** Go to Pharaoh in the morning just as he is going out to the water, and position yourself to meet him on the bank of the Nile; and you shall take in your hand the staff that was turned into a serpent. **16** And you shall say to him, 'The LORD, the God of the Hebrews, sent me to you, saying, "Let My people go, so that they may serve Me in the wilderness. But behold, you have not listened up to now." **17** This is what the LORD says: "By this you shall know that I am the LORD: behold, I am going to strike the water that is in the Nile with the staff that is in my hand, and it will be turned into blood. **18** Then the fish that are in the Nile will die, the Nile will stink, and the Egyptians will no longer be able to drink water from the Nile." ' " **19** Then the LORD said to Moses, "Say to Aaron, 'Take your staff and extend your hand over the waters of Egypt, over their rivers, over their streams, over their pools, and over all their reservoirs of water, so that they may become blood; and there will be blood through all the land of Egypt, both in *containers of* wood and in *containers of* stone.' "

20 So Moses and Aaron did just as the LORD had commanded. And he lifted up the staff and struck the water that *was* in the Nile in the sight of Pharaoh and in the sight of his servants; and all the water that *was* in the Nile was turned into blood. **21** Then the fish that *were* in the Nile died, and the Nile stank, so that the Egyptians could not drink water from the Nile. And the blood was through all the land of Egypt. **22** But the soothsayer priests of Egypt did the same with their secret arts; and Pharaoh's heart was hardened, and he did not listen to them, just as the LORD had said. **23** Then Pharaoh turned and went into his house with no concern even for this. **24** So all the Egyptians dug around the Nile for water to drink, because they could not drink from the water of the Nile. **25** Seven days passed after the LORD had struck the Nile.

Frogs over the Land

8 Then the LORD said to Moses, "Go to Pharaoh and say to him, 'This is what the LORD says: "Let My people go, so that they may serve Me. **2** But if you refuse to let *them* go, behold, I am going to strike your entire territory with frogs. **3** The Nile will swarm with frogs, which will come up and go into your house, and into your bedroom and on your bed, and into the houses of your servants, and on your people, and into your ovens and kneading bowls. **4** So the frogs will come up on you, your people, and on all your servants." ' " **5** Then the LORD said to Moses, "Say to Aaron, 'Extend your hand with your staff over the rivers, over the streams, and over the pools, and make frogs come up on the land of Egypt.' " **6** So Aaron extended his hand over the waters of Egypt, and the frogs came up and covered the land of Egypt. **7** However, the soothsayer priests did the same with their secret arts, making frogs come up on the land of Egypt.

8 Then Pharaoh called for Moses and Aaron and said, "Plead with the LORD to remove the frogs from me and from my people; and I will let the people go, so that they may sacrifice to the LORD." **9** And Moses said to Pharaoh, "The honor is yours to tell me: when shall I plead for you and your servants and your people, that the frogs be destroyed from you and your houses, *that* they be left only in the Nile?" **10** Then he said, "Tomorrow." So he said, "*May it be* according to your word, so that you may know that there is no one like the LORD our God. **11** The frogs will depart from you and your houses, and from your servants and your people; they will be left only in the Nile." **12** Then Moses and Aaron went out from Pharaoh, and Moses cried out to the LORD concerning the frogs which He had inflicted upon Pharaoh. **13** The LORD did according to the word of Moses, and the frogs died out of the houses, the courtyards, and the fields. **14** So they piled them in heaps, and the land stank. **15** But when Pharaoh saw that there was relief, he hardened his heart and did not listen to them, just as the LORD had said.

The Plague of Insects

16 Then the LORD said to Moses, "Say to Aaron, 'Extend your staff and strike the dust of the earth, so that it may turn into gnats through all the land of Egypt.' " **17** They did so; and Aaron extended his hand with his staff and struck the dust of the earth, and there were gnats on *every* [1] person and animal. All the dust of the earth turned into gnats through all the land of Egypt. **18** The soothsayer priests tried with their secret arts to produce gnats, but they could not; so there were gnats on *every* person and animal. **19** Then the soothsayer priests said to Pharaoh, "This is the finger of God." But Pharaoh's heart was hardened, and he did not listen to them, just as the LORD had said.

20 Then the LORD said to Moses, "Rise early in the morning and present yourself before Pharaoh, as he comes out to the water; and say to him, 'This is what the LORD says: "Let My people go, so that they may serve Me. **21** For if you are not going to let My people go, behold, I will send swarms of flies on you and on your servants and on your people, and into your houses; and the houses of the Egyptians will be full of swarms of flies, and also the ground on which they *live*. **22** But on that day I will set apart the land of Goshen, where My people are living, so that no swarms of flies will be there, in order that you may know that I, the LORD, am in the midst of the land. **23** I will put a division between My people and your people. Tomorrow this sign will occur." ' " **24** Then the LORD did so. And thick swarms of flies entered the house of Pharaoh and the houses of his servants, and the land was laid waste because of the swarms of flies in all the land of Egypt.

8:17 [1] I.e., Egyptians and their livestock

25 Then Pharaoh called for Moses and Aaron and said, "Go, sacrifice to your God within the land." 26 But Moses said, "It is not permissible *for us* to do so, because we will sacrifice to the LORD our God that which is an abomination to the Egyptians. If we sacrifice that which is an abomination to the Egyptians before their eyes, will they not stone us? 27 We must go a three days' journey into the wilderness and sacrifice to the LORD our God, just as He commands us." 28 Pharaoh said, "I will let you go, so that you may sacrifice to the LORD your God in the wilderness; only you shall not go very far away. Plead for me." 29 Then Moses said, "Behold, I am going to leave you, and I will plead with the LORD that the swarms of flies may depart from Pharaoh, from his servants, and from his people tomorrow; only do not let Pharaoh deal deceitfully again in not letting the people go to sacrifice to the LORD."

30 So Moses left Pharaoh and pleaded with the LORD. 31 The LORD did as Moses asked, and removed the swarms of flies from Pharaoh, from his servants, and from his people; not one remained. 32 But Pharaoh hardened his heart this time also, and he did not let the people go.

Egyptian Livestock Die

9 Then the LORD said to Moses, "Go to Pharaoh and speak to him, 'This is what the LORD, the God of the Hebrews says: "Let My people go, so that they may serve Me. 2 For if you refuse to let *them* go and continue to hold them, 3 behold, the hand of the LORD will come *with* a very severe plague on your livestock which are in the field, on the horses, on the donkeys, on the camels, on the herds, and on the flocks. 4 But the LORD will make a distinction between the livestock of Israel and the livestock of Egypt, so that nothing will die of all that belongs to the sons of Israel."'"
5 And the LORD set a definite time, saying, "Tomorrow the LORD will do this thing in the land." 6 So the LORD did this thing on the next day, and all the livestock of Egypt died; but not one of the livestock of the sons of Israel died. 7 And Pharaoh sent *men,* and *they learned that,* behold, not even one of the livestock of Israel was dead. But the heart of Pharaoh was hardened, and he did not let the people go.

The Plague of Boils

8 Then the LORD said to Moses and Aaron, "Take for yourselves handfuls of soot from a kiln, and Moses shall toss it toward the sky in the sight of Pharaoh. 9 Then it will become fine dust over all the land of Egypt, and will turn into boils breaking out with sores on *every* person and animal through all the land of Egypt." 10 So they took soot from a kiln, and stood before Pharaoh; and Moses tossed it toward the sky, and it became boils breaking out with sores on *every* person and animal. 11 The soothsayer priests could not stand before Moses because of the boils, for the boils were on the soothsayer priests as well as on all the Egyptians. 12 But the LORD hardened Pharaoh's heart, and he did not listen to them, just as the LORD had spoken to Moses.

13 Then the LORD said to Moses, "Rise up early in the morning and stand before Pharaoh and say to him, 'This is what the LORD, the God of the Hebrews says: "Let My people go, so that they may serve Me. 14 For this time I am going to send all My plagues on you and your servants and your people, so that you may know that there is no one like Me in all the earth. 15 For had I now put out My hand and struck you and your people with plague, you would then have been eliminated from the earth. 16 But indeed, for this reason I have allowed you to remain, in order to show you My power and in order to proclaim My name throughout the earth. 17 Still you exalt yourself against My people by not letting them go.

The Plague of Hail

18 Behold, about this time tomorrow, I will send a very heavy hail, such as has not been *seen* in Egypt from the day it was founded until now. 19 So now, send *word,* bring your livestock and whatever you have in the field to safety. Every person and animal that is found in the field and is not brought home, when the hail comes down on them, will die."' " 20 *Everyone* among the servants of Pharaoh who feared the word of the LORD hurried to bring his servants and his livestock into the houses; 21 but *every-one* who did not pay regard to the word of the LORD left his servants and his livestock in the field.

22 Now the LORD said to Moses, "Reach out with your hand toward the sky, so that hail may fall on all the land of Egypt, on *every* person and animal, and on every plant of the field, throughout the land of Egypt." 23 So Moses reached out with his staff toward the sky, and the LORD sent thunder and hail, and fire ran *down* to the earth. And the LORD rained hail on the land of Egypt. 24 So there was hail, and fire flashing intermittently in the midst of the hail, *which was* very heavy, such as had not occurred in all the land of Egypt since it became a nation. 25 The hail struck everything that was in the field through all the land of Egypt, from people to animals; the hail also struck every plant of the field, and shattered every tree of the field. 26 Only in the land of Goshen, where the sons of Israel *were,* was there no hail.

27 Then Pharaoh sent for Moses and Aaron, and said to them, "I have sinned this time; the LORD is the righteous one, and I and my people are the wicked ones. 28 Plead with the LORD, for there has been enough of God's thunder and hail; and I will let you go, and you shall stay no longer." 29 Moses said to him, "As soon as I go out of the city, I will spread out my hands to the LORD; the thunder will cease and there will no longer be hail, so that you may know that the earth is the LORD's. 30 But as for you and your servants, I know that you do not yet fear the LORD God." 31 (Now the flax and the barley were ruined, for the barley was in the ear and the flax was in bud. 32 But the wheat and the spelt were not ruined, for they *ripen* late.) 33 So Moses left the city from *his meeting* with Pharaoh, and spread out his hands to the LORD; and the thunder and the hail stopped, and rain no longer poured on the earth. 34 But when

Pharaoh saw that the rain and the hail and the thunder had stopped, he sinned again and hardened his heart, he and his servants. **35** So Pharaoh's heart was hardened, and he did not let the sons of Israel go, just as the LORD had spoken through Moses.

The Plague of Locusts

10 Then the LORD said to Moses, "Go to Pharaoh, for I have hardened his heart and the heart of his servants, so that I may perform these signs of Mine among them, **2** and that you may tell in the presence of your son, and of your grandson, how I made a mockery of the Egyptians and how I performed My signs among them, so that you may know that I am the LORD."

3 So Moses and Aaron went to Pharaoh and said to him, "This is what the LORD, the God of the Hebrews says: 'How long will you refuse to humble yourself before Me? Let My people go, so that they may serve Me. **4** For if you refuse to let My people go, behold, tomorrow I will bring locusts into your territory. **5** And they will cover the surface of the land, so that no one will be able to see the land. They will also eat the rest of what has survived—what is left to you from the hail—and they will eat every tree of yours which grows in the field. **6** Then your houses will be filled *with them,* together with the houses of all your servants and the houses of all the Egyptians, *something* which neither your fathers nor your grandfathers have seen, from the day that they came upon the earth until this day.' " And he turned and left Pharaoh. **7** Then Pharaoh's servants said to him, "How long shall this man be a snare to us? Let the people go, so that they may serve the LORD their God. Do you not yet realize that Egypt is destroyed?" **8** So Moses and Aaron were brought back to Pharaoh, and he said to them, "Go, serve the LORD your God! Who specifically are the ones who are going?" **9** Moses said, "We shall go with our young and our old; with our sons and our daughters, with our flocks and our herds we shall go, for we must hold a feast to the LORD." **10** Then he said to them, "So may the LORD be with you, when I let you and your little ones go! Watch out, for evil is on your mind! **11** Not so! Go now, *but only* the men *among you,* and serve the LORD, since that is what you desire." So they were driven out from Pharaoh's presence.

12 Then the LORD said to Moses, "Reach out with your hand over the land of Egypt for the locusts, so that they may come up on the land of Egypt and eat every plant of the land, everything that the hail has left." **13** So Moses reached out with his staff over the land of Egypt, and the LORD directed an east wind on the land all that day and all that night; and when it was morning, the east wind brought the locusts. **14** The locusts came up over all the land of Egypt and settled in all the territory of Egypt; *they were* very numerous. There had never been so *many* locusts, nor would there be so *many* again. **15** For they covered the surface of the whole land, so that the land was darkened; and they ate every plant of the land and all the fruit of the trees that the hail had left. Therefore nothing green was left on tree or plant of the field throughout the land of Egypt. **16** Then Pharaoh hurriedly called for Moses and Aaron, and he said, "I have sinned against the LORD your God and against you. **17** So now, please forgive my sin only this once, and plead with the LORD your God, that He would only remove this death from me." **18** Then he left Pharaoh and pleaded with the LORD. **19** So the LORD shifted *the wind* to a very strong west wind, which picked up the locusts and drove them into the Red Sea; not one locust was left in all the territory of Egypt. **20** But the LORD hardened Pharaoh's heart, and he did not let the sons of Israel go.

Darkness over the Land

21 Then the LORD said to Moses, "Reach out with your hand toward the sky, so that there may be darkness over the land of Egypt, even a darkness which may be felt." **22** So Moses reached out with his hand toward the sky, and there was thick darkness in all the land of Egypt for three days. **23** They did not see one another, nor did anyone rise from his place for three days, but all the sons of Israel had light in their dwellings. **24** Then Pharaoh called for Moses, and said, "Go, serve the LORD; only let your flocks and your herds be left behind. Even your little ones may go with you." **25** But Moses said, "You must also let us have sacrifices and burnt offerings, so that we may sacrifice *them* to the LORD our God. **26** Therefore, our livestock too shall go with us; not a hoof shall be left behind, for we shall take some of them to serve the LORD our God. And until we arrive there, we ourselves do not know with what we shall serve the LORD." **27** But the LORD hardened Pharaoh's heart, and he was not willing to let them go. **28** Then Pharaoh said to him, "Get away from me! Be careful, do not see my face again, for on the day you see my face, you shall die!" **29** Moses said, "You have spoken correctly; I shall never see your face again!"

The Last Plague

11 Now the LORD said to Moses, "One more plague I will bring on Pharaoh and on Egypt; after that he will let you go from here. When he lets you go, he will assuredly drive you out from here completely. **2** Speak now so that the people hear, that each man is to ask of his neighbor, and each woman of her neighbor, articles of silver and articles of gold." **3** And the LORD gave the people favor in the sight of the Egyptians. Furthermore, the man Moses *himself* was greatly esteemed in the land of Egypt, *both* in the sight of Pharaoh's servants and in the sight of the people.

4 Then Moses said, "This is what the LORD says: 'About midnight I am going out into the midst of Egypt, **5** and all the firstborn in the land of Egypt shall die, from the firstborn of the Pharaoh who sits on his throne, to the firstborn of the slave girl who is behind the millstones; all the firstborn of the cattle as well. **6** So there shall be a great cry in all the land of Egypt, such as there has not been *before* and such as shall never be again. **7** But not *even* a dog will threaten any of the sons of Israel, *nor anything*

from person to animal, so that you may learn how the LORD distinguishes between Egypt and Israel.' 8 And all these servants of yours will come down to me and bow themselves before me, saying, 'Go out, you and all the people who follow you,' and after that I will go out." And he left Pharaoh in the heat of anger.

9 Then the LORD said to Moses, "Pharaoh will not listen to you, so that My wonders will be multiplied in the land of Egypt." 10 So Moses and Aaron performed all these wonders before Pharaoh; yet the LORD hardened Pharaoh's heart, and he did not let the sons of Israel go out of his land.

The Passover Lamb

12 Now the LORD said to Moses and Aaron in the land of Egypt, 2 "This month shall be the beginning of months for you; it is to be the first month of the year for you. 3 Speak to all the congregation of Israel, saying, 'On the tenth of this month they are, each one, to take a lamb for themselves, according to the fathers' households, a lamb for each household. 4 Now if the household is too small for a lamb, then he and his neighbor nearest to his house are to take one according to the number of persons *in them;* in proportion to what each one should eat, you are to divide the lamb. 5 Your lamb shall be an unblemished male a year old; you may take it from the sheep or from the goats. 6 You shall keep it until the fourteenth day of the same month, then the whole assembly of the congregation of Israel is to slaughter it at twilight. 7 Moreover, they shall take some of the blood and put it on the two doorposts and on the lintel of the houses in which they eat it. 8 They shall eat the flesh that *same* night, roasted with fire, and they shall eat it with unleavened bread and bitter herbs. 9 Do not eat any of it raw or boiled at all with water, but rather roasted with fire, *both* its head and its legs along with its entrails. 10 And you shall not leave any of it over until morning, but whatever is left of it until morning, you shall completely burn with fire. 11 Now you shall eat it in this way: *with your garment* belted around your waist, your sandals on your feet, and your staff in your hand; and you shall eat it in a hurry—it is the LORD's Passover. 12 For I will go through the land of Egypt on that night, and fatally strike all the firstborn in the land of Egypt, from the human *firstborn* to animals; and against all the gods of Egypt I will execute judgments—I am the LORD. 13 The blood shall be a sign for you on the houses where you live; and when I see the blood I will pass over you, and no plague will come upon you to destroy *you* when I strike the land of Egypt.

Feast of Unleavened Bread

14 'Now this day shall be a memorial to you, and you shall celebrate it *as* a feast to the LORD; throughout your generations you are to celebrate it *as* a permanent ordinance. 15 For seven days you shall eat unleavened bread, but on the first day you shall remove dough with yeast from your houses; for whoever eats anything with yeast from the first day until the seventh day, that person shall be cut off from

Israel. 16 And on the first day you shall have a holy assembly, and *another* holy assembly on the seventh day; no work at all shall be done on them, except for what must be eaten by every person—that alone may be prepared by you. 17 You shall also keep the *Feast of Unleavened Bread,* for on this very day I brought your multitudes out of the land of Egypt; therefore you shall keep this day throughout your generations as a permanent ordinance. 18 In the first *month,* on the fourteenth day of the month at evening, you shall eat unleavened bread, until the twenty-first day of the month at evening. 19 For seven days there shall be no dough with yeast found in your houses; for whoever eats anything with yeast, that person shall be cut off from the congregation of Israel, whether *he is* a stranger or a native of the land. 20 You shall not eat anything with yeast; in all your dwellings you shall eat unleavened bread.' "

21 Then Moses called for all the elders of Israel and said to them, "Go and take for yourselves lambs according to your families, and slaughter the Passover *lamb.* 22 And you shall take a bunch of hyssop and dip it in the blood which is in the basin, and apply some of the blood that is in the basin to the lintel and the two doorposts; and none of you shall go outside the door of his house until morning.

A Memorial of Redemption

23 For the LORD will pass through to strike the Egyptians; but when He sees the blood on the lintel and on the two doorposts, the LORD will pass over the door and will not allow the destroyer to come 'in to your houses to strike *you.* 24 And you shall keep this event as an ordinance for you and your children forever. 25 When you enter the land which the LORD will give you, as He has promised, you shall keep this rite. 26 And when your children say to you, 'What does this rite mean to you?' 27 then you shall say, 'It is a Passover sacrifice to the LORD because He passed over the houses of the sons of Israel in Egypt when He struck the Egyptians, but spared our homes.' " And the people bowed low and worshiped.

28 Then the sons of Israel went and did *so;* just as the LORD had commanded Moses and Aaron, so they did.

29 Now it came about at midnight that the LORD struck all the firstborn in the land of Egypt, from the firstborn of Pharaoh who sat on his throne to the firstborn of the captive who was in the dungeon, and all the firstborn of cattle. 30 And Pharaoh got up in the night, he and all his servants and all the Egyptians, and there was a great cry in Egypt, for there was no home where there was not someone dead. 31 Then he called for Moses and Aaron at night and said, "Rise up, get out from among my people, both you and the sons of Israel; and go, worship the LORD, as you have said. 32 Take both your flocks and your herds, as you have said, and go, and bless me also."

Exodus of Israel

33 The Egyptians urged the people, to send

them out of the land in a hurry, for they said, "We will all be dead." 34 So the people took their dough before it was leavened, *with* their kneading bowls bound up in the clothes on their shoulders.

35 Now the sons of Israel had done according to the word of Moses, for they had requested from the Egyptians articles of silver and articles of gold, and clothing; 36 and the LORD had given the people favor in the sight of the Egyptians, so that they let them have their request. Therefore they plundered the Egyptians.

37 Now the sons of Israel journeyed from Rameses to Succoth, about six hundred thousand men on foot, aside from children. 38 A mixed multitude also went up with them, along with flocks and herds, a very large number of livestock. 39 And they baked the dough which they had brought out of Egypt into cakes of unleavened bread. For it had no yeast, since they were driven out of Egypt and could not delay, nor had they prepared any provisions for themselves.

40 Now the time that the sons of Israel had lived in Egypt was 430 years. 41 And at the end of 430 years, on this very day, all the multitudes of the LORD departed from the land of Egypt.

Ordinance of the Passover

42 It is a night to be observed for the LORD, for having brought them out of the land of Egypt; this night is for the LORD, to be observed by all the sons of Israel throughout their generations.

43 And the LORD said to Moses and Aaron, "This is the ordinance of the Passover: no foreigner is to eat it; 44 but *as for* every slave that someone has purchased with money, after you have circumcised him, then he may eat it. 45 A stranger or a hired worker shall not eat it. 46 It is to be eaten in a single house; you are not to bring any of the meat outside of the house, nor are you to break any bone of it. 47 All the congregation of Israel are to celebrate this. 48 But if a stranger resides with you and celebrates the Passover to the LORD, all of his males are to be circumcised, and then he shall come near to celebrate it; and he shall be like a native of the land. But no uncircumcised male may eat it. 49 The same law shall apply to the native as to the stranger who resides among you."

50 Then all the sons of Israel did *so;* they did just as the LORD had commanded Moses and Aaron. 51 And on that very day the LORD brought the sons of Israel out of the land of Egypt according to their multitudes.

13 Then the LORD spoke to Moses, saying, 2 "Sanctify to Me every firstborn, the firstborn of every womb among the sons of Israel, among people and animals *alike;* it belongs to Me."

3 And Moses said to the people, "Remember this day in which you departed from Egypt, from the house of slavery; for by a powerful hand the LORD brought you out from this place. And nothing with yeast shall be eaten. 4 On this day in the month of Abib, you are about to go out *from here.* 5 And it shall be when the LORD brings you to the land of the Canaanite, the Hittite, the Amorite, the Hivite, and the Jebusite, which He swore to your fathers to give you, a land flowing with milk and honey, that you shall perform this rite in this month. 6 For seven days you shall eat unleavened bread, and on the seventh day there shall be a feast to the LORD. 7 Unleavened bread shall be eaten throughout the seven days; and nothing with yeast shall be seen among you, nor shall any dough with yeast be seen among you in all your borders. 8 And you shall tell your son on that day, saying, '*It is* because of what the LORD did for me when I came out of Egypt.' 9 And it shall serve as a sign to you on your hand, and as a reminder on your forehead, that the law of the LORD may be in your mouth; for with a powerful hand the LORD brought you out of Egypt. 10 Therefore, you shall keep this ordinance at its appointed time from year to year.

11 "Now when the LORD brings you to the land of the Canaanite, as He swore to you and to your fathers, and gives it to you, 12 you shall devote to the LORD every firstborn of a womb, and every firstborn offspring of an animal that you own; the males belong to the LORD. 13 But every firstborn of a donkey you shall redeem with a lamb, but if you do not redeem *it,* then you shall break its neck; and every firstborn among your sons you shall redeem. 14 And it shall be when your son asks you in time to come, saying, 'What is this?' then you shall say to him, 'With a powerful hand the LORD brought us out of Egypt, from the house of slavery. 15 And it came about, when Pharaoh was stubborn about letting us go, that the LORD put to death every firstborn in the land of Egypt, from human firstborns to animal firstborns. Therefore, I sacrifice to the LORD the males, every firstborn of a womb, but every firstborn of my sons I redeem.' 16 So it shall serve as a sign on your hand and as phylacteries on your forehead, for with a powerful hand the LORD brought us out of Egypt."

God Leads the People

17 Now when Pharaoh had let the people go, God did not lead them by the way of the land of the Philistines, even though it was near; for God said, "The people might change their minds when they see war, and return to Egypt." 18 Therefore God led the people around by way of the wilderness to the Red Sea; and the sons of Israel went up in battle formation from the land of Egypt. 19 And Moses took the bones of Joseph with him, for he had made the sons of Israel solemnly swear, saying, "God will certainly take care of you, and you shall carry my bones from here with you." 20 Then they set out from Succoth and camped in Etham, on the edge of the wilderness. 21 And the LORD was going before them in a pillar of cloud by day to lead them on the way, and in a pillar of fire by night to give them light, so that they might travel by day and by night. 22 He did not take away the pillar of cloud by day, nor the pillar of fire by night, from the presence of the people.

Pharaoh in Pursuit

14 Now the LORD spoke to Moses, saying, 2 "Tell the sons of Israel to turn back and camp in front of Pi-hahiroth, between Migdol and the sea; you shall camp in front of Baal-zephon, opposite it, by the sea. 3 For Pharaoh will say of the sons of Israel, 'They are wandering aimlessly in the land; the wilderness has shut them in.' 4 And I will harden Pharaoh's heart, and he will chase after them; and I will be honored through Pharaoh and all his army, and the Egyptians will know that I am the LORD." And they did so.

5 When the king of Egypt was told that the people had fled, Pharaoh and his servants had a change of heart toward the people, and they said, "What is this *that* we have done, that we have let Israel go from serving us?" 6 So he had *horses* harnessed *to* his chariot and took his people with him; 7 and he took six hundred select chariots, and all the *other* chariots of Egypt with officers over all of them. 8 So the LORD hardened the heart of Pharaoh, king of Egypt, and he chased after the sons of Israel as the sons of Israel were going out boldly. 9 Then the Egyptians chased after them *with* all the horses *and* chariots of Pharaoh, his horsemen and his army, and they overtook them camping by the sea, beside Pi-hahiroth, in front of Baal-zephon.

10 As Pharaoh approached, the sons of Israel looked, and behold, the Egyptians were coming after them, and they became very frightened; so the sons of Israel cried out to the LORD. 11 Then they said to Moses, "Is it because there were no graves in Egypt that you have taken us away to die in the wilderness? Why have you dealt with us in this way, bringing us out of Egypt? 12 Is this not the word that we spoke to you in Egypt, saying, 'Leave us alone so that we may serve the Egyptians'? For it would have been better for us to serve the Egyptians than to die in the wilderness!"

The Sea Is Divided

13 But Moses said to the people, "Do not fear! Stand by and see the salvation of the LORD, which He will perform for you today; for the Egyptians whom you have seen today, you will never see them again, ever. 14 The LORD will fight for you, while you keep silent."

15 Then the LORD said to Moses, "Why are you crying out to Me? Tell the sons of Israel to go forward. 16 As for you, lift up your staff and reach out with your hand over the sea and divide it, and the sons of Israel shall go through the midst of the sea on dry land. 17 And as for Me, behold, I will harden the hearts of the Egyptians so that they will go in after them; and I will be honored through Pharaoh and all his army, through his chariots and his horsemen. 18 Then the Egyptians will know that I am the LORD, when I am honored through Pharaoh, through his chariots, and through his horsemen."

19 Then the angel of God, who had been going before the camp of Israel, moved and went behind them; and the pillar of cloud moved from before them and stood behind them. 20 So it came between the camp of Egypt and the camp of Israel; and there was the cloud along with the darkness, yet it gave light at night. Therefore the one did not approach the other all night.

21 Then Moses reached out with his hand over the sea; and the LORD swept the sea *back* by a strong east wind all night, and turned the sea into dry land, and the waters were divided. 22 So the sons of Israel went through the midst of the sea on the dry land, and the waters *were like* a wall to them on their right and on their left. 23 Then the Egyptians took up the pursuit, and all Pharaoh's horses, his chariots, and his horsemen went in after them into the midst of the sea. 24 But at the morning watch, the LORD looked down on the army of the Egyptians through the pillar of fire and cloud, and brought the army of the Egyptians into confusion. 25 He caused their chariot wheels to swerve, and He made them drive with difficulty; so the Egyptians *each* said, "Let me flee from Israel, for the LORD is fighting for them against the Egyptians."

26 Then the LORD said to Moses, "Reach out with your hand over the sea so that the waters may come back over the Egyptians, over their chariots and their horsemen." 27 So Moses reached out with his hand over the sea, and the sea returned to its normal state at daybreak, while the Egyptians were fleeing right into it; then the LORD overthrew the Egyptians in the midst of the sea. 28 The waters returned and covered the chariots and the horsemen, Pharaoh's entire army that had gone into the sea after them; not even one of them remained. 29 But the sons of Israel walked on dry land through the midst of the sea, and the waters *were like* a wall to them on their right and on their left.

30 So the LORD saved Israel that day from the hand of the Egyptians, and Israel saw the Egyptians dead on the seashore. 31 When Israel saw the great power which the LORD had used against the Egyptians, the people feared the LORD, and they believed in the LORD and in His servant Moses.

The Song of Moses and Israel

15 Then Moses and the sons of Israel sang this song to the LORD, saying:

"I will sing to the LORD, for He is highly exalted;
The horse and its rider He has hurled into the sea.

2 "The LORD is my strength and song,
And He has become my salvation;
This is my God, and I will praise Him;
My father's God, and I will exalt Him.

3 "The LORD is a warrior;
The LORD is His name.

4 "Pharaoh's chariots and his army He has thrown into the sea;
And the choicest of his officers are drowned in the Red Sea.

5 "The waters cover them;
They went down into the depths like a stone.

6 "Your right hand, LORD, is majestic in power;

Your right hand, LORD, destroys the
enemy.
7 "And in the greatness of Your excellence
You overthrow those who rise up
against You;
You send out Your burning anger, *and* it
consumes them like chaff.
8 "At the blast of Your nostrils the waters
were piled up,
The flowing waters stood up like a heap;
The depths were congealed in the heart of
the sea.
9 "The enemy said, 'I will pursue, I will
overtake, I will divide the spoils;
I shall be satisfied against them;
I will draw my sword, my hand will
destroy them.'
10 "You blew with Your wind, the sea covered
them;
They sank like lead in the mighty
waters.
11 "Who is like You among the gods, LORD?
Who is like You, majestic in holiness,
Awesome in praises, working wonders?
12 "You reached out with Your right hand,
The earth swallowed them.
13 "In Your faithfulness You have led the
people whom You have redeemed;
In Your strength You have guided *them* to
Your holy habitation.
14 "The peoples have heard, they tremble,
Anguish has gripped the inhabitants of
Philistia.
15 "Then the chiefs of Edom were terrified;
The leaders of Moab, trembling grips
them;
All the inhabitants of Canaan have
despaired.
16 "Terror and dread fall upon them;
By the greatness of Your arm they are
motionless as stone,
Until Your people pass over, LORD,
Until the people pass over whom You
have purchased.
17 "You will bring them and plant them in the
mountain of Your inheritance,
The place, LORD, which You have made as
Your dwelling,
The sanctuary, Lord, which Your hands
have established.
18 "The LORD shall reign forever and ever."
19 For the horses of Pharaoh with his chariots and his horsemen went into the sea, and
the LORD brought back the waters of the sea on
them, but the sons of Israel walked on dry land
through the midst of the sea.
20 Miriam the prophetess, Aaron's sister,
took the tambourine in her hand, and all the
women went out after her with tambourines
and with dancing. 21 And Miriam answered
them,
"Sing to the LORD, for He is highly exalted;
The horse and his rider He has hurled
into the sea."

The LORD Provides Water
22 Then Moses led Israel from the Red Sea,
and they went out into the wilderness of Shur;
and they went three days in the wilderness and
found no water. 23 When they came to Marah,
they could not drink the waters of Marah,
because they were bitter; for that reason it was
named ⁷Marah. 24 So the people grumbled at
Moses, saying, "What are we to drink?" 25 Then
he cried out to the LORD, and the LORD showed
him a tree; and he threw *it* into the waters,
and the waters became sweet.

There He made for them a statute and
regulation, and there He tested them. 26 And
He said, "If you will listen carefully to the voice
of the LORD your God, and do what is right in
His sight, and listen to His commandments,
and keep all His statutes, I will put none of the
diseases on you which I have put on the
Egyptians; for I, the LORD, am your healer."
27 Then they came to Elim where there *were*
twelve springs of water and seventy date
palms, and they camped there beside the
waters.

The LORD Provides Manna

16 Then they set out from Elim, and all the
congregation of the sons of Israel came
to the wilderness of Sin, which is between
Elim and Sinai, on the fifteenth day of the
second month after their departure from the
land of Egypt. 2 But the whole congregation of
the sons of Israel grumbled against Moses and
Aaron in the wilderness. 3 The sons of Israel
said to them, "If only we had died by the
LORD's hand in the land of Egypt, when we sat
by the pots of meat, when we ate bread until
we were full; for you have brought us out into
this wilderness to kill this entire assembly with
hunger!"

4 Then the LORD said to Moses, "Behold, I
will rain bread from heaven for you; and the
people shall go out and gather a day's portion
every day, so that I may test them, whether or
not they will walk in My ⁷instruction. 5 On the
sixth day, when they prepare what they bring
in, it will be twice as much as they gather
daily." 6 So Moses and Aaron said to all the sons
of Israel, "At evening you will know that the
LORD has brought you out of the land of Egypt;
7 and in the morning you will see the glory of
the LORD, for He hears your grumblings against
the LORD; and what are we, that you grumble
against us?"

The LORD Provides Meat
8 And Moses said, "*This will happen* when the
LORD gives you meat to eat in the evening, and
bread to the full in the morning; for the LORD
hears your grumblings which you grumble
against Him. And what are we? Your grumblings are not against us but against the LORD."
9 Then Moses said to Aaron, "Say to all
the congregation of the sons of Israel, 'Come
forward before the LORD, for He has heard your
grumblings.'" 10 And it came about, as Aaron
spoke to the entire congregation of the sons of
Israel, that they looked toward the wilderness,
and behold, the glory of the LORD appeared in
the cloud. 11 And the LORD spoke to Moses,
saying, 12 "I have heard the grumblings of
the sons of Israel; speak to them, saying, 'At
twilight you shall eat meat, and in the morning

---

you shall be filled with bread; and you shall know that I am the LORD your God.'"

13 So it came about at evening that the quails came up and covered the camp, and in the morning there was a layer of dew around the camp. 14 When the layer of dew evaporated, behold, on the surface of the wilderness there was a fine flake-like thing, fine as the frost on the ground. 15 When the sons of Israel saw *it*, they said to one another, "What is it?" For they did not know what it was. And Moses said to them, "It is the bread which the LORD has given you to eat. 16 This is what the LORD has commanded: 'Everyone gather as much as he will eat; you shall take *¹an omer apiece according to the number of people each of you has in his tent.'" 17 The sons of Israel did so, and *some* gathered much and *some* little. 18 When they measured it by the *¹omer*, the one who had gathered much did not have too much, and the one who had gathered little did not have too little; everyone gathered as much as he would eat. 19 Moses said to them, "No one is to leave any of it until morning." 20 But they did not listen to Moses, and some left part of it until morning, and it bred worms and stank; and Moses was angry with them. 21 They gathered it morning by morning, everyone as much as he would eat; but when the sun became hot, it would melt.

The Sabbath

22 Now on the sixth day they gathered twice as much bread, *¹two omers for each one. When all the leaders of the congregation came and told Moses, 23 then he said to them, "This is what the LORD meant: Tomorrow is a Sabbath observance, a holy Sabbath to the LORD. Bake what you will bake and boil what you will boil, and all that is left over put aside to be kept until morning." 24 So they put it aside until morning, as Moses had ordered, and it did not stink nor was there a maggot in it. 25 Then Moses said, "Eat it today, for today is a Sabbath to the LORD; today you will not find it in the field. 26 Six days you shall gather it, but on the seventh day, *the* Sabbath, there will be none."

27 Yet it came about on the seventh day that some of the people went out to gather, but they found none. 28 Then the LORD said to Moses, "How long do you refuse to keep My commandments and My *¹instructions? 29 See, the LORD has given you the Sabbath; for that reason He gives you bread for two days on the sixth day. Remain, everyone, in his place; no one is to leave his place on the seventh day." 30 So the people rested on the seventh day.

31 And the house of Israel named *the bread* manna, and it was like coriander seed, white, and its taste was like wafers with honey. 32 Then Moses said, "This is what the LORD has commanded: 'A *¹full omer of it is to be kept safe throughout your generations, so that they may see the bread that I fed you in the wilderness, when I brought you out of the land of Egypt.'" 33 And Moses said to Aaron, "Take a jar and put a *¹full omer of manna in it, and place it before the LORD to be kept safe throughout your generations." 34 As the LORD commanded Moses, so Aaron placed it before the Testimony, to be kept. 35 And the sons of Israel ate the manna for forty years, until they came to an inhabited land; they ate the manna until they came to the border of the land of Canaan. 36 (Now an *¹omer is a tenth of an ephah.)

Water in the Rock

17 Then all the congregation of the sons of Israel journeyed by stages from the wilderness of Sin, according to the command of the LORD, and camped at Rephidim, and there was no water for the people to drink. 2 So the people quarreled with Moses and said, "Give us water so that we may drink!" And Moses said to them, "Why do you quarrel with me? Why do you test the LORD?" 3 But the people were thirsty for water there; and they grumbled against Moses and said, "Why is it that you have brought us up from Egypt, to kill us and our children and our livestock with thirst?" 4 So Moses cried out to the LORD, saying, "What am I to do with this people? A little more and they will stone me!" 5 Then the LORD said to Moses, "Pass before the people and take with you some of the elders of Israel; and take in your hand your staff with which you struck the Nile, and go. 6 Behold, I will stand before you there on the rock at Horeb; and you shall strike the rock, and water will come out of it, so that the people may drink." And Moses did so in the sight of the elders of Israel. 7 Then he named the place *¹Massah and *²Meribah because of the quarrel of the sons of Israel, and because they tested the LORD, saying, "Is the LORD among us, or not?"

Miraculous Battle against Amalek

8 Then Amalek came and fought against Israel at Rephidim. 9 So Moses said to Joshua, "Choose men for us and go out, fight against Amalek. Tomorrow I will station myself on the top of the hill with the staff of God in my hand." 10 Joshua did just as Moses told him, and fought against Amalek; and Moses, Aaron, and Hur went up to the top of the hill. 11 So it came about, when Moses held his hand up, that Israel prevailed; but when he let his hand down, Amalek prevailed. 12 And Moses' hands were heavy. So they took a stone and put it under him, and he sat on it; and Aaron and Hur supported his hands, one on one side and one on the other. So his hands were steady until the sun set. 13 And Joshua defeated Amalek and his people with the edge of the sword.

14 Then the LORD said to Moses, "Write this in a book as a memorial and recite it to Joshua, that I will utterly wipe out the memory of Amalek from under heaven." 15 And Moses built an altar and named it The LORD is My Banner; 16 and he said, "Because the LORD has sworn, the LORD will have war against Amalek from generation to generation."

16:16 ¹Lit *an omer for a head;* about 3 qt. or 2.8 liters   16:18 ¹About 3 qt. or 2.8 liters   16:22 ¹About 6 qt. or 5.6 liters   16:28 ¹Or *laws*   16:32 ¹About 3 qt. or 2.8 liters   16:33 ¹About 3 qt. or 2.8 liters   16:36 ¹About 3 qt. or 2.8 liters   17:7 ¹I.e., test   ²I.e., quarrel

Jethro, Moses' Father-in-law

18 Now Jethro, the priest of Midian, Moses' father-in-law, heard about everything that God had done for Moses and for Israel His people, how the LORD had brought Israel out of Egypt. 2 And Jethro, Moses' father-in-law, took *in* Moses' wife Zipporah, after he had sent her away, 3 and her two sons, one of whom was named Gershom, for Moses said, "I have been a stranger in a foreign land." 4 And the other was named Eliezer, for *he said,* "The God of my father was my help, and saved me from the sword of Pharaoh."

5 Then Jethro, Moses' father-in-law, came with his sons and his wife to Moses in the wilderness where he was camped, at the mountain of God. 6 And he sent word to Moses: "I, your father-in-law Jethro, am coming to you with your wife and her two sons with her." 7 Then Moses went out to meet his father-in-law, and he bowed down and kissed him; and they asked each other about their welfare, and went into the tent. 8 Moses told his father-in-law everything that the LORD had done to Pharaoh and to the Egyptians for Israel's sake, all the hardship that had confronted them on the journey, and *how* the LORD had rescued them. 9 And Jethro rejoiced over all the goodness which the LORD had done for Israel, in rescuing them from the hand of the Egyptians. 10 So Jethro said, "Blessed be the LORD who rescued you from the hand of the Egyptians and from the hand of Pharaoh, *and* who rescued the people from under the hand of the Egyptians. 11 Now I know that the LORD is greater than all the gods; indeed, it was proven when they acted insolently against the people." 12 Then Jethro, Moses' father-in-law, took a burnt offering and sacrifices for God, and Aaron came with all the elders of Israel to eat a meal with Moses' father-in-law before God.

Jethro Counsels Moses

13 And it came about the next day, that Moses sat to judge the people, and the people stood before Moses from the morning until the evening. 14 Now when Moses' father-in-law saw all that he was doing for the people, he said, "What is this thing that you are doing for the people? Why do you alone sit *as judge* and all the people stand before you from morning until evening?" 15 Moses said to his father-in-law, "Because the people come to me to inquire of God. 16 When they have a dispute, it comes to me, and I judge between someone and his neighbor and make known the statutes of God and His laws." 17 Moses' father-in-law then said to him, "The thing that you are doing is not good. 18 You will surely wear out, both yourself and these people who are with you, because the task is too heavy for you; you cannot do it alone. 19 Now listen to me: I will give you counsel, and God be with you. You be the people's representative before God, and you bring the disputes to God, 20 then admonish them about the statutes and the laws, and make known to them the way in which they are to walk and the work they are to do. 21 Furthermore, you shall select out of all the people

able men who fear God, men of truth, those who hate dishonest gain; and you shall place *these* over them as leaders of thousands, of hundreds, of fifties, and of tens. 22 Let them judge the people at all times; and let it be that they will bring to you every major matter, but they will judge every minor matter themselves. So it will be easier for you, and they will carry *the burden* with you. 23 If you do this thing and God *so* commands you, then you will be able to endure, and all these people also will go to their places in peace."

24 So Moses listened to his father-in-law and did everything that he had said. 25 Moses chose able men out of all Israel and made them heads over the people, leaders of thousands, of hundreds, of fifties, and of tens. 26 Then they judged the people at all times; they would bring the difficult matter to Moses, but they would judge every minor matter themselves. 27 Then Moses said goodbye to his father-in-law, and Jethro went his way to his own land.

Moses on Sinai

19 In the third month after the sons of Israel had gone out of the land of Egypt, on that very day they came into the wilderness of Sinai. 2 When they set out from Rephidim, they came to the wilderness of Sinai and camped in the wilderness; and there Israel camped in front of the mountain. 3 And Moses went up to God, and the LORD called to him from the mountain, saying, "This is what you shall say to the house of Jacob and tell the sons of Israel: 4 'You yourselves have seen what I did to the Egyptians, and *how* I carried you on eagles' wings, and brought you to Myself. 5 Now then, if you will indeed obey My voice and keep My covenant, then you shall be My own possession among all the peoples, for all the earth is Mine; 6 and you shall be to Me a kingdom of priests and a holy nation.' These are the words that you shall speak to the sons of Israel."

7 So Moses came and called the elders of the people, and set before them all these words which the LORD had commanded him. 8 Then all the people answered together and said, "All that the LORD has spoken we will do!" And Moses brought back the words of the people to the LORD. 9 Then the LORD said to Moses, "Behold, I will come to you in a thick cloud, so that the people may hear when I speak with you and may also trust in you forever." Then Moses told the words of the people to the LORD.

10 The LORD also said to Moses, "Go to the people and consecrate them today and tomorrow, and have them wash their garments; 11 and have them ready for the third day, for on the third day the LORD will come down on Mount Sinai in the sight of all the people. 12 But you shall set boundaries for the people all around, saying, 'Beware that you do not go up on the mountain or touch the border of it; whoever touches the mountain shall certainly be put to death. 13 No hand shall touch him, but he shall certainly be stoned or 'shot through; whether animal or person, *the*

19:13 1 I.e., with arrows

violator shall not live.' When the ram's horn sounds a long blast, they shall come up to the mountain." ¹⁴So Moses went down from the mountain to the people and consecrated the people, and they washed their garments. ¹⁵He also said to the people, "Be ready for the third day; do not go near a woman."

¹⁶So it came about on the third day, when it was morning, that there were thunder and lightning flashes and a thick cloud over the mountain and a very loud trumpet sound, so that all the people who *were* in the camp trembled. ¹⁷And Moses brought the people out of the camp to meet God, and they stood at the foot of the mountain.

The LORD Visits Sinai

¹⁸Now Mount Sinai *was* all in smoke because the LORD descended upon it in fire; and its smoke ascended like the smoke of a furnace, and the entire mountain quaked violently. ¹⁹When the sound of the trumpet grew louder and louder, Moses spoke, and God answered him with thunder. ²⁰Then the LORD came down on Mount Sinai, to the top of the mountain; and the LORD called Moses to the top of the mountain, and Moses went up. ²¹Then the LORD spoke to Moses: "Go down, warn the people, so that they do not break through to the LORD to stare, and many of them perish. ²²Also have the priests who approach the LORD consecrate themselves, or else the LORD will break out against them." ²³And Moses said to the LORD, "The people cannot come up to Mount Sinai, for You warned us, saying, 'Set boundaries around the mountain and consecrate it.'" ²⁴Then the LORD said to him, "Go down and come up *again,* you and Aaron with you; but do not let the priests and the people break through to come up to the LORD, or He will break out against them." ²⁵So Moses went down to the people and told them.

The Ten Commandments

20Then God spoke all these words, saying,

²"I am the LORD your God, who brought you out of the land of Egypt, out of the house of slavery.

³"You shall have no other gods before Me.

⁴"You shall not make for yourself an idol, or any likeness of what is in heaven above or on the earth beneath, or in the water under the earth. ⁵You shall not worship them nor serve them; for I, the LORD your God, am a jealous God, inflicting the ᶠpunishment of the fathers on the children, on the third and the fourth generations of those who hate Me, ⁶but showing favor to thousands, to those who love Me and keep My commandments.

⁷"You shall not take the name of the LORD your God in vain, for the LORD will not leave him unpunished who takes His name in vain.

⁸"Remember the Sabbath day, to keep it holy. ⁹For six days you shall labor and do all your work, ¹⁰but the seventh day is a Sabbath of the LORD your God; *on it* you shall not do any work, you, or your son, or your daughter, your male slave or your female slave, or your

cattle, or your resident who stays with you. ¹¹For in six days the LORD made the heavens and the earth, the sea and everything that is in them, and He rested on the seventh day; for that reason the LORD blessed the Sabbath day and made it holy.

¹²"Honor your father and your mother, so that your days may be prolonged on the land which the LORD your God gives you.

¹³"You shall not murder.

¹⁴"You shall not commit adultery.

¹⁵"You shall not steal.

¹⁶"You shall not give false testimony against your neighbor.

¹⁷"You shall not covet your neighbor's house; you shall not covet your neighbor's wife, or his male slave, or his female slave, or his ox, or his donkey, or anything that belongs to your neighbor."

¹⁸And all the people were watching *and hearing* the thunder and the lightning flashes, and the sound of the trumpet, and the mountain smoking; and when the people saw *it all,* they trembled and stood at a distance. ¹⁹Then they said to Moses, "Speak to us yourself and we will listen; but do not have God speak to us, or we will die!" ²⁰However, Moses said to the people, "Do not be afraid; for God has come in order to test you, and in order that the fear of Him may remain with you, so that you will not sin." ²¹So the people stood at a distance, while Moses approached the thick darkness where God *was.*

²²Then the LORD said to Moses, "This is what you shall say to the sons of Israel: 'You yourselves have seen that I have spoken to you from heaven. ²³You shall not make *other gods* besides Me; gods of silver or gods of gold, you shall not make for yourselves. ²⁴You shall make an altar of earth for Me, and you shall sacrifice on it your burnt offerings and your peace offerings, your sheep and your oxen; in every place where I cause My name to be remembered, I will come to you and bless you. ²⁵And if you make an altar of stone for Me, you shall not build it of cut stones, for if you wield your chisel on it, you will profane it. ²⁶And you shall not go up by steps to My altar, so that your nakedness will not be exposed on it.'

Ordinances for the People

21"Now these are the ordinances which you are to set before them:

²"If you buy a Hebrew slave, he shall serve for six years; but on the seventh he shall leave as a free man without a payment *to you.* ³If he comes alone, he shall leave alone; if he is the husband of a wife, then his wife shall leave with him. ⁴If his master gives him a wife, and she bears him sons or daughters, the wife and her children shall belong to her master, and he shall leave alone. ⁵But if the slave plainly says, 'I love my master, my wife, and my children; I will not leave as a free man,' ⁶then his master shall bring him to God, then he shall bring him to the door or the doorpost. And his master shall pierce his ear with an ᶠawl; and he shall serve him permanently.

20:5 ¹I.e., punishment for the wrongdoing   **21:6** ¹I.e., a pointed tool

7 "Now if a man sells his daughter as a female slave, she is not to go free as the male slaves do. 8 If she is displeasing in the eyes of her master who designated her for himself, then he shall let her be redeemed. He does not have authority to sell her to a foreign people, because of his unfairness to her. 9 And if he designates her for his son, he shall deal with her according to the custom of daughters. 10 If he takes to himself another woman, he may not reduce her food, her clothing, or her conjugal rights. 11 But if he will not do these three *things* for her, then she shall go free for nothing, without *payment of* money.

Personal Injuries

12 "He who strikes someone so that he dies shall certainly be put to death. 13 Yet if he did not lie in wait *for him,* but God caused *him* to fall into his hand, then I will appoint you a place to which he may flee. 14 If, however, someone is enraged against his neighbor, so as to kill him in a cunning way, you are to take him *even* from My altar, to be put to death.

15 "And one who strikes his father or his mother shall certainly be put to death.

16 "Now one who kidnaps someone, whether he sells him or he is found in his possession, shall certainly be put to death.

17 "And one who curses his father or his mother shall certainly be put to death.

18 "Now if people have a quarrel and one strikes the other with a stone or with a fist, and he does not die but is confined to bed, 19 if he gets up and walks around outside on his staff, then he who struck him shall go unpunished; he shall only pay for his loss of time, and shall pay for his care until he is completely healed.

20 "And if someone strikes his male or female slave with a rod and *the slave* dies at his hand, he shall be punished. 21 If, however, *the slave* survives a day or two, no vengeance shall be taken; for *the slave* is his property.

22 "Now if people struggle with each other and strike a pregnant woman so that she gives birth prematurely, but there is no injury, *the guilty person* shall certainly be fined as the woman's husband may demand of him, and he shall pay as the judges *decide.* 23 But if there is *any further* injury, then you shall appoint *as a penalty* life for life, 24 eye for eye, tooth for tooth, hand for hand, foot for foot, 25 burn for burn, wound for wound, bruise for bruise.

26 "And if someone strikes the eye of his male or female slave and destroys it, he shall let the slave go free on account of the eye. 27 And if he knocks out a tooth of his male or female slave, he shall let the slave go free on account of the tooth.

28 "Now if an ox gores a man or a woman to death, the ox shall certainly be stoned and its flesh shall not be eaten; but the owner of the ox shall go unpunished. 29 If, however, an ox was previously in the habit of goring and its owner has been warned, yet he does not confine it and it kills a man or a woman, the ox shall be stoned and its owner also shall be put to death. 30 If a ransom is demanded of him,

then he shall give for the redemption of his life whatever is demanded of him. 31 Whether it gores a son or a daughter, it shall be done to him according to the same rule. 32 If the ox gores a male or female slave, the owner shall give his *or her* master ¹thirty shekels of silver, and the ox shall be stoned.

Property Rights

33 "Now if someone opens a pit, or digs a pit and does not cover it, and an ox or a donkey falls into it, 34 the owner of the pit shall make restitution; he shall give money to its owner, and the dead *animal* shall become his.

35 "And if someone's ox injures another's ox so that it dies, then they shall sell the live ox and divide its proceeds equally; and they shall also divide the dead *ox.* 36 Or *if* it is known that the ox was previously in the habit of goring, yet its owner has not confined it, he must make restitution of ox for ox, and the dead *animal* shall become his.

Property Rights

22 "If someone steals an ox or a sheep and slaughters it or sells it, he shall pay five oxen for the ox and four sheep for the sheep— 2 If the thief is caught while breaking in and is struck so that he dies, there will be no guilt for bloodshed on his account. 3 If the sun has risen on him, *there will be* guilt for bloodshed on his account—*A thief* shall certainly make restitution; if he owns nothing, then he shall be sold for his theft. 4 If what he stole is actually found alive in his possession, whether an ox or a donkey or a sheep, he shall pay double.

5 "If someone lets a field or vineyard be grazed *bare* and lets his animal loose so that it grazes in another person's field, he shall make restitution from the best of his own field and the best of his own vineyard.

6 "If a fire breaks out and spreads to thorn bushes, and stacked grain or the standing grain or the field *itself* is consumed, the one who started the fire must make restitution.

7 "If someone gives his neighbor money or goods to keep *for him* and it is stolen from the neighbor's house, if the thief is caught, *then* the thief shall pay double. 8 If the thief is not caught, then the owner of the house shall appear before the judges, *to determine* whether he laid his hands on his neighbor's property. 9 For every breach of trust, *whether it is* for ox, for donkey, for sheep, for clothing, *or* for any lost thing about which one says, 'This is it,' the case of both parties shall come before the judges; he whom the judges condemn shall pay double to his neighbor.

10 "If someone gives his neighbor a donkey, an ox, a sheep, or any animal to keep *for him,* and it dies or is injured or is driven away while no one is looking, 11 an oath before the LORD shall be taken by the two of them that he has not laid a hand on his neighbor's property; and its owner shall accept *it,* and he shall not *be* compelled to make restitution. 12 But if it is actually stolen from him, he shall make restitution to its owner. 13 If it is all torn to

---

pieces, have him bring it as evidence; he shall not *be compelled to* make restitution for what has been torn to pieces.

14 "And if someone borrows *an animal* from his neighbor, and it is injured or dies while its owner is not with it, he shall make full restitution. 15 If its owner is with it, *the borrower* shall not *be compelled to* make restitution. If it is hired, it came by its hire.

Various Laws

16 "If a man seduces a virgin who is not ¹betrothed and sleeps with her, he must pay a dowry for her *to be* his wife. 17 If her father absolutely refuses to give her to him, he shall pay money equal to the dowry for virgins. 18 "You shall not allow a sorceress to live.

19 "Whoever has sexual intercourse with an animal must be put to death.

20 "He who sacrifices to any god, other than to the LORD alone, shall be utterly destroyed.

21 "You shall not oppress a stranger nor torment him, for you were strangers in the land of Egypt. 22 You shall not oppress any widow or orphan. 23 If you oppress him at all, *and* if he does cry out to Me, I will assuredly hear his cry; 24 and My anger will be kindled, and I will kill you with the sword, and your wives shall become widows and your children fatherless.

25 "If you lend money to My people, to the poor among you, you are not to act as a creditor to him; you shall not charge him interest. 26 If you ever seize your neighbor's cloak as a pledge, you are to return it to him before the sun sets, 27 for that is his only covering; it is his cloak for his body. What else is he to sleep in? And it will come about that when he cries out to Me, I will listen *to him,* for I am gracious.

28 "You shall not curse God, nor curse a ruler of your people.

29 "You shall not hold back *the offering from* your entire harvest and your wine. The firstborn of your sons you shall give to Me. 30 You shall do the same with your oxen *and* with your sheep. It shall be with its mother for seven days; on the eighth day you shall give it to Me.

31 "You shall be holy people to Me, therefore you shall not eat *any* flesh torn to pieces in the field; you shall throw it to the dogs.

Various Laws

23 "You shall not give a false report; do not join your hand with a wicked person to be a malicious witness. 2 You shall not follow the crowd in doing evil, nor shall you testify in a dispute so as to join together with a crowd in order to pervert *justice;* 3 nor shall you show favor to a poor person in his dispute.

4 "If you encounter your enemy's ox or his donkey wandering away, you must return it to him. 5 If you see the donkey of one who hates you lying *helpless* under its load, you shall not leave it *helpless* for its owner; you must arrange *the load* with him.

6 "You shall not pervert the justice *due* to your needy *brother* in his dispute. 7 Keep far from a false charge, and do not kill the

innocent or the righteous, for I will not acquit the guilty.

8 "You shall not take a bribe, for a bribe blinds the clear-sighted and subverts the cause of the just.

9 "You shall not oppress a stranger, since you yourselves know the feelings of a stranger, for you *also* were strangers in the land of Egypt.

The Sabbath and the Land

10 "Now you shall sow your land for six years and gather in its yield, 11 but *in* the seventh year you shall let it rest and lie uncultivated, so that the needy of your people may eat; and whatever they leave the animal of the field may eat. You are to do the same with your vineyard *and* your olive grove.

12 "For six days you are to do your work, but on the seventh day you shall cease *from labor* so that your ox and your donkey may rest, and the son of your female slave, as well as the stranger *residing with you, may* refresh themselves. 13 Now concerning everything which I have said to you, be careful; and do not mention the name of other gods, nor let *them* be heard from your mouth.

Three National Feasts

14 "Three times a year you shall celebrate a feast to Me. 15 You shall keep the Feast of Unleavened Bread; for seven days you are to eat unleavened bread, as I commanded you, at the appointed time in the month of Abib, for in that month you came out of Egypt. And no one is to appear before Me empty-handed. 16 Also *you shall keep* the Feast of the Harvest *of* the first fruits of your labors *from* what you sow in the field; also the Feast of the Ingathering at the end of the year when you gather in *the fruit of* your labors from the field. 17 Three times a year all your males shall appear before the Lord GOD.

18 "You shall not offer the blood of My sacrifice with leavened bread; nor is the fat of My feast to remain overnight until morning.

19 "You shall bring the choice first fruits of your soil into the house of the LORD your God.

"You are not to boil a young goat in the milk of its mother.

Conquest of the Land

20 "Behold, I am going to send an angel before you to guard you along the way and to bring you into the place which I have prepared. 21 Be attentive to him and obey his voice; do not be rebellious toward him, for he will not pardon your rebellion, since My name is in him. 22 But if you truly obey his voice and do all that I say, then I will be an enemy to your enemies and an adversary to your adversaries. 23 For My angel will go before you and bring you into *the land of* the Amorites, the Hittites, the Perizzites, the Canaanites, the Hivites, and the Jebusites; and I will completely destroy them. 24 You shall not worship their gods, nor serve them, nor do according to their deeds; but you shall utterly overthrow them and break their memorial stones in pieces. 25 And you shall serve the LORD your

---

22:16 ¹ A betrothed couple was considered legally married, but did not yet live together

God, and He will bless your bread and your water; and I will remove sickness from your midst. **26** There will be no one miscarrying or unable to have children in your land; I will fulfill the number of your days. **27** I will send My terror ahead of you, and throw into confusion all the people among whom you come, and I will make all your enemies turn *their* backs to you. **28** And I will send hornets ahead of you so that they will drive out the Hivites, the Canaanites, and the Hittites from you. **29** I will not drive them out from you in a single year, so that the land will not become desolate and the animals of the field become too numerous for you. **30** I will drive them out from you little by little, until you become fruitful and take possession of the land. **31** I will set your boundary from the Red Sea to the sea of the Philistines, and from the wilderness to the *Euphrates* River; for I will hand over the inhabitants of the land to you, and you will drive them out from you. **32** You shall make no covenant with them or with their gods. **33** They shall not live in your land, otherwise they will make you sin against Me; for *if* you serve their gods, it is certain to be a snare to you."

People Affirm Their Covenant with God

24 Then He said to Moses, "Come up to the LORD, you and Aaron, Nadab and Abihu, and seventy of the elders of Israel, and you shall worship at a distance. **2** Moses alone, however, shall approach the LORD, but they shall not approach, nor shall the people come up with him."

3 Then Moses came and reported to the people all the words of the LORD and all the ordinances; and all the people answered with one voice and said, "All the words which the LORD has spoken we will do!" **4** And Moses wrote down all the words of the LORD. Then he got up early in the morning, and built an altar at the foot of the mountain with twelve memorial stones for the twelve tribes of Israel. **5** And he sent young men of the sons of Israel, and they offered burnt offerings and sacrificed bulls as peace offerings to the LORD. **6** Moses took half of the blood and put *it* in basins, and the *other* half of the blood he sprinkled on the altar. **7** Then he took the Book of the Covenant and read *it* as the people listened; and they said, "All that the LORD has spoken we will do, and we will be obedient!" **8** So Moses took the blood and sprinkled *it* on the people, and said, "Behold the blood of the covenant, which the LORD has made with you in accordance with all these words."

9 Then Moses went up with Aaron, Nadab and Abihu, and seventy of the elders of Israel, **10** and they saw the God of Israel; and under His feet there appeared to be a pavement of sapphire, as clear as the sky itself. **11** Yet He did not reach out with His hand against the nobles of the sons of Israel; and they saw God, and they ate and drank.

12 Now the LORD said to Moses, "Come up to Me on the mountain and stay there, and I will give you the stone tablets with the Law and the commandments which I have written for their instruction." **13** So Moses got up along with Joshua his servant, and Moses went up to the mountain of God. **14** But to the elders he said, "Wait here for us until we return to you. And behold, Aaron and Hur are with you; whoever has a legal matter, have him approach them." **15** Then Moses went up to the mountain, and the cloud covered the mountain. **16** The glory of the LORD settled on Mount Sinai, and the cloud covered it for six days; and on the seventh day He called to Moses from the midst of the cloud. **17** And to the eyes of the sons of Israel, the appearance of the glory of the LORD was like a consuming fire on the mountain top. **18** Then Moses entered the midst of the cloud as he went up to the mountain; and Moses was on the mountain for forty days and forty nights.

Offerings for the Sanctuary

25 Then the LORD spoke to Moses, saying, **2** "Tell the sons of Israel to take a contribution for Me; from everyone whose heart moves him you shall take My contribution. **3** This is the contribution which you are to take from them: gold, silver, and bronze, **4** †violet, purple, and scarlet *material,* fine linen, goat *hair,* **5** rams' skins dyed red, †fine leather, acacia wood, **6** oil for lighting, balsam oil for the anointing oil and for the fragrant incense, **7** onyx stones and setting stones for the ephod and for the breastpiece. **8** Have them construct a sanctuary for Me, so that I may dwell among them. **9** According to all that I am going to show you *as* the pattern of the tabernacle and the pattern of all its furniture, so you shall construct *it.*

Ark of the Covenant

10 "Now they shall construct an †ark of acacia wood **2** two and a half cubits long, one and a half cubits wide, and one and a half cubits high. **11** You shall overlay it with pure gold, inside and out you shall overlay it, and you shall make a gold molding around it. **12** You shall also cast four gold rings for it and fasten them on its four feet; two rings shall be on one side of it, and two rings on the other side of it. **13** And you shall make poles of acacia wood and overlay them with gold. **14** You shall put the poles into the rings on the sides of the ark, to carry the ark with them. **15** The poles shall remain in the rings of the ark; they shall not be removed from it. **16** You shall put into the ark the testimony which I shall give you.

17 "And you shall make †an atoning cover of pure gold, **2** two and a half cubits long and one and a half cubits wide. **18** You shall make two cherubim of gold; make them of hammered work at the two ends of the atoning cover. **19** Make one cherub at one end and one cherub at the other end; you shall make the cherubim *of one piece* with the atoning cover at its two

---

25:4 1 Or *bluish;* LXX *hyacinth* in color **25:5** 1 Meaning of the Heb uncertain **25:10** 1 I.e., chest 2 About 3.7 ft. long and 2.2 ft. wide and high or 1.1 m and 68 cm **25:17** 1 Also called *a mercy seat,* and so throughout the ch; i.e., where blood was sprinkled on the Day of Atonement 2 About 3.7 ft. long and 2.2 ft. wide or 1.1 m and 68 cm

ends. 20 And the cherubim shall have *their* wings spread upward, covering the atoning cover with their wings and facing one another; the faces of the cherubim are to be *turned* toward the atoning cover. 21 Then you shall put the atoning cover on top of the ark, and in the ark you shall put the testimony which I will give to you. 22 There I will meet with you; and from above the atoning cover, from between the two cherubim which are upon the ark of the testimony, I will speak to you about every commandment that I will give you for the sons of Israel.

Bread of the Presence

23 "You shall also make a table of acacia wood, [1]two cubits long and one cubit wide, and one and a half cubits high. 24 You shall overlay it with pure gold and make a gold border around it. 25 And you shall make for it a rim of a [1]hand width around *it;* and you shall make a gold border for the rim around it. 26 You shall also make four gold rings for it and put rings on the four corners which are on its four legs. 27 The rings shall be close to the rim, as holders for the poles to carry the table. 28 And you shall make the poles of acacia wood and overlay them with gold, so that with them the table may be carried. 29 You shall also make its dishes, its pans, its jars, and its libation bowls with which to pour drink offerings; you shall make them of pure gold. 30 And you shall set the bread of the Presence on the table before Me continually.

The Golden Lampstand

31 "Then you shall make a lampstand of pure gold. The lampstand, its base and its shaft, are to be made of hammered work; its cups, its bulbs, and its flowers shall be *of one piece* with it. 32 Six branches shall go out from its sides; three branches of the lampstand from its one side and three branches of the lampstand from its other side. 33 Three cups *shall be* shaped like almond blossoms on the one branch, a bulb and a flower, and three cups shaped like almond blossoms on the other branch, a bulb and a flower—the same for six branches going out from the lampstand; 34 and on the lampstand four cups shaped like almond blossoms, its bulbs and its flowers. 35 A bulb shall be under the *first* pair of branches *coming* out of it, and a bulb under the *second* pair of branches *coming* out of it, and a bulb under the *third* pair of branches *coming* out of it, for the six branches coming out of the lampstand. 36 Their bulbs and their branches shall be *of one piece* with it; all of it *shall be* one piece of hammered work of pure gold. 37 Then you shall make its lamps seven *in number;* and they shall mount its lamps so as to shed light on the space in front of it. 38 Its tongs and its trays *shall be* of pure gold. 39 It shall be made from a [1]talent of pure gold, with all these utensils. 40 See that you make *them* by the pattern for them, which was shown to you on the mountain.

Curtains of Linen

26 "Moreover, you shall make the tabernacle with ten curtains of fine twisted linen and [1]violet, purple, and scarlet *material;* you shall make them with cherubim, the work of a skilled embroiderer. 2 The length of each curtain shall be [1]twenty-eight cubits, and the width of each curtain four cubits; all the curtains shall have the same measurements. 3 Five curtains shall be joined to one another, and *the other* five curtains *shall be* joined to one another. 4 You shall make loops of violet on the edge of the outermost curtain in the *first* set, and likewise you shall make *them* on the edge of the curtain that is outermost in the second set. 5 You shall make fifty loops in the one curtain, and you shall make fifty loops on the edge of the curtain that is in the second set; the loops shall be opposite each other. 6 You shall also make fifty clasps of gold, and join the curtains to one another with the clasps so that the [1]tabernacle will be a unit.

Curtains of Goats' Hair

7 "Then you shall make curtains of goats' *hair* as a tent over the tabernacle; you shall make eleven curtains in all. 8 The length of each curtain *shall be* [1]thirty cubits, and the width of each curtain four cubits; the eleven curtains shall have the same measurements. 9 You shall join five curtains by themselves and the *other* six curtains by themselves, and you shall double over the sixth curtain at the front of the tent. 10 You shall make fifty loops on the edge of the curtain that is outermost in the *first* set, and fifty loops on the edge of the curtain *that is outermost in* the second set.

11 "You shall also make fifty clasps of bronze, and you shall put the clasps into the loops and join the tent together so that it will be a unit. 12 The overhanging part that is left over in the curtains of the tent, the half curtain that is left over, shall hang over the back of the tabernacle. 13 The [1]cubit on one side and the cubit on the other, of what is left over in the length of the curtains of the tent, shall hang over the sides of the tabernacle on one side and on the other, to cover it. 14 And you shall make a covering for the tent of rams' skins dyed red and a covering of [1]fine leather above.

Boards and Bases

15 "Then you shall make the boards for the tabernacle of acacia wood, standing upright. 16 [1]Ten cubits *shall be* the length of each board and one and a half cubits the width of each board. 17 *There shall be* two tenons for each board, fitted to one another; that is what you shall do for all the boards of the tabernacle. 18 You shall make the boards for the tabernacle: twenty boards for the south side. 19 You shall make forty bases of silver under the twenty

---

25:23 [1]About 3 ft. long, 1.5 ft. wide, 2.25 ft. high or 90 cm, 45 cm, and 68 cm   25:25 [1]About 3 in. or 7.5 cm   25:39 [1]About 75 lb. or 34 kg   26:1 [1]Or *bluish;* LXX *hyacinth* in color, and so throughout the ch   26:2 [1]About 42 ft. long and 6 ft. wide or 13 m and 1.8 m   26:6 [1]Or *dwelling place,* and so throughout the ch   26:8 [1]About 45 ft. long and 6 ft. wide or 13.5 m and 1.8 m   26:13 [1]About 18 in. or about 45 cm   26:14 [1]Meaning of the Heb uncertain   26:16 [1]About 15 ft. long and 2.2 ft. wide or 4.6 m and 68 cm

boards, two bases under one board for its two tenons and two bases under another board for its two tenons; 20 and for the second side of the tabernacle, on the north side, twenty boards, 21 and their forty bases of silver; two bases under one board and two bases under another board. 22 For the back of the tabernacle, to the west, you shall make six boards. 23 You shall make two boards for the corners of the tabernacle at the back. 24 They shall be double beneath, and together they shall be complete to its top to the first ring; this is how it shall be with both of them: they shall form the two corners. 25 And there shall be eight boards with their bases of silver, sixteen bases; two bases under one board and two bases under another board.

26 "Then you shall make bars of acacia wood, five for the boards of one side of the tabernacle, 27 and five bars for the boards of the other side of the tabernacle, and five bars for the boards of the side of the tabernacle for the back side to the west. 28 The middle bar in the center of the boards shall pass through from end to end. 29 And you shall overlay the boards with gold, and make their rings of gold as holders for the bars; and you shall overlay the bars with gold. 30 Then you shall erect the tabernacle according to its plan which you have been shown on the mountain.

The Veil and Curtain

31 "You shall also make a veil of violet, purple, and scarlet material, and fine twisted linen; it shall be made with cherubim, the work of a skilled embroiderer. 32 Then you shall hang it on four pillars of acacia overlaid with gold, their hooks also of gold, on four bases of silver. 33 You shall hang up the veil under the clasps, and bring in the ark of the testimony there within the veil; and the veil shall serve as a partition for you between the Holy Place and the Most Holy Place. 34 You shall put the ¹atoning cover on the ark of the testimony in the Most Holy Place. 35 And you shall set the table outside the veil, and the lampstand opposite the table on the side of the tabernacle toward the south; and you shall put the table on the north side.

36 "You shall also make a curtain for the doorway of the tent of violet, purple, and scarlet material and fine twisted linen, the work of a weaver. 37 And you shall make five pillars of acacia for the curtain and overlay them with gold, their hooks also of gold; and you shall cast five bases of bronze for them.

The Bronze Altar

27 "Now you shall make the altar of acacia wood, ¹five cubits long and five cubits wide; the altar shall be square, and its height shall be ²three cubits. 2 You shall make its horns on its four corners; its horns shall be of one piece with it, and you shall overlay it with bronze. 3 And you shall make its pails for removing its ashes, and its shovels, its basins,

its forks, and its firepans; you shall make all its utensils of bronze. 4 You shall also make for it a grating, a netting of bronze, and on the netting you shall make four bronze rings at its four corners. 5 And you shall put it under the ledge of the altar, so that the netting will reach halfway up the altar. 6 You shall also make carrying poles for the altar, poles of acacia wood and overlay them with bronze. 7 Its poles shall be inserted into the rings, so that the poles will be on the two sides of the altar when it is carried. 8 You shall make it hollow with planks; as it was shown to you on the mountain, so they shall make it.

Courtyard of the Tabernacle

9 "Now you shall make the courtyard of the tabernacle. On the south side there shall be hangings for the courtyard of fine twisted linen, a ¹hundred cubits long for one side; 10 and its pillars shall be twenty, with their twenty bases of bronze; the hooks of the pillars and their bands shall be of silver. 11 Likewise for the north side in length there shall be hangings a ¹hundred cubits long, and its twenty pillars with their twenty bases of bronze; the hooks of the pillars and their bands shall be of silver. 12 For the width of the courtyard on the west side shall be hangings of ¹fifty cubits, with their ten pillars and their ten bases. 13 The width of the courtyard on the east side shall be fifty cubits. 14 The hangings for the one side of the gate shall be ¹fifteen cubits, with their three pillars and their three bases. 15 And for the other side there shall be hangings of fifteen cubits, with their three pillars and their three bases. 16 And for the gate of the courtyard there shall be a curtain of ¹twenty cubits, of ²violet, purple, and scarlet material and fine twisted linen, the work of a weaver, with their four pillars and their four bases. 17 All the pillars around the courtyard shall be joined together with silver, with their hooks of silver and their bases of bronze. 18 The length of the courtyard shall be a ¹hundred cubits, and the width fifty throughout, and the height five cubits of fine twisted linen, and their bases of bronze. 19 All the utensils of the tabernacle used in all its service, and all its pegs, and all the pegs of the courtyard, shall be of bronze.

20 "And you shall command the sons of Israel that they bring you clear oil of beaten olives for the light, to make a lamp burn continually. 21 In the tent of meeting, outside the veil which is before the testimony, Aaron and his sons shall keep it in order from evening to morning before the LORD; it shall be a permanent statute throughout their generations for the sons of Israel.

Garments of the Priests

28 "Then bring forward to yourself your brother Aaron, and his sons with him, from among the sons of Israel, to serve as priest to Me—Aaron, Nadab and Abihu, Eleazar and Ithamar, Aaron's sons. 2 And you

---

26:34 ¹Also called mercy seat; i.e., where blood was sprinkled on the Day of Atonement   27:1 ¹About 7.5 ft. or 2.3 m   ²About 4.5 ft. or 1.4 m   27:9 ¹About 150 ft. or 46 m   27:11 ¹About 150 ft. or 46 m   27:12 ¹About 75 ft. or 23 m   27:14 ¹About 23 ft. or 6.8 m   27:16 ¹About 30 ft. or 9 m   ²Or bluish; LXX hyacinth in color   27:18 ¹About 150 ft. long, 75 ft. wide, and 7.5 ft. high or about 46 m, 23 m, and 2.3 m

shall make holy garments for Aaron your brother, for glory and for beauty. 3 You shall speak to all the skillful people whom I have endowed with the spirit of wisdom, that they make Aaron's garments to consecrate him, that he may serve as priest to Me. 4 And these are the garments which they shall make: a breastpiece, an ephod, a robe, a tunic of checkered work, a turban, and a sash. They shall make holy garments for your brother Aaron and his sons, so that he may serve as priest to Me. 5 They shall take the gold, the *violet, the purple, the scarlet *material*, and the fine linen.

6 "They shall also make the ephod of gold, of violet, purple, *and* scarlet *material*, and fine twisted linen, the work of the skilled embroiderer. 7 It shall have two shoulder pieces joined to its two ends, so that it may be joined. 8 The skillfully woven band of its overlay, which is on it, shall be like its workmanship, of the same material: of gold, of violet and purple and scarlet *material* and fine twisted linen. 9 And you shall take two onyx stones and engrave on them the names of the sons of Israel, 10 six of their names on the one stone and the names of the remaining six on the other stone, according to their birth. 11 As a jeweler engraves a signet, you shall engrave the two stones according to the names of the sons of Israel; you shall set them in filigree settings of gold. 12 And you shall put the two stones on the shoulder pieces of the ephod, *as* stones of memorial for the sons of Israel, and Aaron shall carry their names before the LORD on his two shoulders as a memorial. 13 And you shall make filigree settings of gold, 14 and two chains of pure gold; you shall make them of twisted cord work, and you shall put the corded chains on the filigree settings.

15 "You shall make a breastpiece of judgment, the work of a skilled embroiderer; like the work of the ephod you shall make it: of gold, of violet, purple, and scarlet *material*, and fine twisted linen you shall make it. 16 It shall be square *and* folded double, a *span in length and a span in width. 17 And you shall mount on it four rows of stones; the first row *shall be* a row of ruby, topaz, and emerald; 18 and the second row a turquoise, a sapphire, and a diamond; 19 and the third row a jacinth, an agate, and an amethyst; 20 and the fourth row a beryl, and an onyx, and a jasper; they shall be set in gold filigree. 21 The stones shall be *engraved* according to the names of the sons of Israel: twelve, according to their names; they shall be *like* the engravings of a signet, each according to his name for the twelve tribes. 22 You shall also make on the breastpiece twisted chains of cord work in pure gold. 23 And you shall make on the breastpiece two rings of gold, and shall put the two rings on the two ends of the breastpiece. 24 And you shall put the two cords of gold on the two rings at the ends of the breastpiece. 25 You shall put the *other* two ends of the two cords on the two filigree *settings*, and put them on the shoulder pieces of the ephod, at the front of it. 26 And you shall

make two rings of gold and place them on the two ends of the breastpiece, on the edge of it, which is toward the inner side of the ephod. 27 And you shall make two rings of gold and put them on the bottom of the two shoulder pieces of the ephod, on the front of it close to the place where it is joined, above the skillfully woven band of the ephod. 28 And they shall bind the breastpiece by its rings to the rings of the ephod with a violet cord, so that it will be on the skillfully woven band of the ephod, and that the breastpiece will not come loose from the ephod. 29 So Aaron shall carry the names of the sons of Israel in the breastpiece of judgment over his heart when he enters the Holy Place, as a memorial before the LORD continually. 30 And you shall put in the breastpiece of judgment the *Urim and the Thummim, and they shall be over Aaron's heart when he goes in before the LORD; and Aaron shall carry the judgment of the sons of Israel over his heart before the LORD continually.

31 "You shall make the robe of the ephod all of violet. 32 There shall be an opening at its top in the middle of it; around its opening there shall be a binding of woven work, like the opening of a coat of mail, so that it will not be torn. 33 You shall make on its hem pomegranates of violet, purple, and scarlet *material* all around on its hem, and bells of gold between them all around: 34 a golden bell and a pomegranate, a golden bell and a pomegranate, all around on the hem of the robe. 35 It shall be on Aaron when he ministers; and its sound shall be heard when he enters and leaves the Holy Place before the LORD, so that he will not die.

36 "You shall also make a plate of pure gold and engrave on it, like the engravings of a signet, 'Holy to the LORD.' 37 You shall fasten it on a violet cord, and it shall be on the turban; it shall be at the front of the turban. 38 It shall be on Aaron's forehead, and Aaron shall take away the guilt of the holy things which the sons of Israel consecrate, regarding all their holy gifts; and it shall always be on his forehead, so that they may be accepted before the LORD.

39 "And you shall weave the tunic of checkered work of fine linen, and shall make a turban of fine linen, and you shall make a sash, the work of a weaver.

40 "For Aaron's sons you shall also make tunics; you shall also make sashes for them, and you shall make caps for them, for glory and for beauty. 41 Then you shall put them on Aaron your brother and on his sons with him; and you shall anoint them and ordain them and consecrate them, so that they may serve Me as priests. 42 You shall make for them linen undergarments to cover *their* bare flesh; they shall reach from the waist even to the thighs. 43 And they shall be on Aaron and on his sons when they enter the tent of meeting, or when they approach the altar to minister in the Holy Place, so that they do not incur guilt and die. It *shall be* a statute forever to him and to his descendants after him.

28:5 1 Or *bluish;* LXX *hyacinth* in color, and so throughout the ch   28:16 1 About 9 in. or 23 cm
28:30 1 I.e., lights and perfections

Consecration of the Priests

29 "Now this is what you shall do to them to consecrate them to serve as priests to Me: take one bull and two rams without blemish, 2 and unleavened bread and unleavened cakes mixed with oil, and unleavened wafers spread with oil; you shall make them of fine wheat flour. 3 And you shall put them in one basket, and present them in the basket along with the bull and the two rams. 4 Then you shall bring Aaron and his sons to the doorway of the tent of meeting and wash them with water. 5 And you shall take the garments, and put on Aaron the tunic and the robe of the ephod, and the ephod and the breastpiece, and wrap his waist with the skillfully woven band of the ephod; 6 and you shall set the turban on his head and put the holy crown on the turban. 7 Then you shall take the anointing oil and pour it on his head, and anoint him. 8 You shall also bring his sons and put tunics on them. 9 And you shall wrap their waists with sashes, Aaron and his sons, and fit caps on them, and they shall have the priesthood by a permanent statute. So you shall ordain Aaron and his sons.

The Sacrifices

10 "Then you shall bring the bull in front of the tent of meeting, and Aaron and his sons shall lay their hands on the head of the bull. 11 And you shall slaughter the bull before the LORD at the doorway of the tent of meeting. 12 Then you shall take some of the blood of the bull and put *it* on the horns of the altar with your finger; and you shall pour out all *the rest of* the blood at the base of the altar. 13 And you shall take all the fat that covers the entrails, and the lobe of the liver, and the two kidneys and the fat that is on them, and offer them up in smoke on the altar. 14 But the flesh of the bull and its hide and its refuse, you shall burn with fire outside the camp; it is a sin offering. 15 "You shall also take the one ram, and Aaron and his sons shall lay their hands on the head of the ram; 16 and you shall slaughter the ram and take its blood and sprinkle it around on the altar. 17 Then you shall cut the ram into its pieces, and wash its entrails and its legs, and put *them* with its pieces and its head. 18 And you shall offer up in smoke the whole ram on the altar; it is a burnt offering to the LORD: it is a soothing aroma, an offering by fire to the LORD. 19 "Then you shall take the other ram, and Aaron and his sons shall lay their hands on the head of the ram. 20 And you shall slaughter the ram, and take some of its blood and put *it* on the lobe of Aaron's right ear and on the lobes of his sons' right ears, and on the thumbs of their right hands, and on the big toes of their right feet, and sprinkle the *rest of the* blood around on the altar. 21 Then you shall take some of the blood that is on the altar and some of the anointing oil, and sprinkle *it* on Aaron and on his garments, and on his sons and on his sons' garments with him; so he and his garments shall be consecrated, as well as his sons and his sons' garments with him.

22 "You shall also take the fat from the ram and the fat tail, and the fat that covers the entrails and the lobe of the liver, and the two kidneys and the fat that is on them, and the right thigh (for it is a ram of ordination), 23 and one loaf of bread, and one cake of bread *mixed with* oil, and one wafer from the basket of unleavened bread which is *set* before the LORD; 24 and you shall put all these in the hands of Aaron and in the hands of his sons, and shall wave them as a wave offering before the LORD. 25 Then you shall take them from their hands, and offer them up in smoke on the altar on the burnt offering for a soothing aroma before the LORD; it is an offering by fire to the LORD. 26 "Then you shall take the breast of Aaron's ram of ordination, and wave it as a wave offering before the LORD; and it shall be your portion. 27 You shall consecrate the breast of the wave offering and the thigh of the contribution which was waved and which was offered from the ram of ordination, from the one which was for Aaron and from the one which was for his sons. 28 It shall be for Aaron and his sons as *their* portion forever from the sons of Israel, for it is a contribution; and it shall be a contribution from the sons of Israel from the sacrifices of their peace offerings, their contribution to the LORD.

29 "The holy garments of Aaron shall be for his sons after him, so that they may be anointed and ordained in them. 30 For seven days the one of his sons who is priest in his place shall put them on when he enters the tent of meeting to minister in the Holy Place.

Food of the Priests

31 "Now you shall take the ram of ordination and boil its flesh in a holy place. 32 Then Aaron and his sons shall eat the flesh of the ram and the bread that is in the basket, at the doorway of the tent of meeting. 33 So they shall eat those things by which atonement was made at their ordination *and* consecration; but a layman shall not eat *them,* because they are holy. 34 And if any of the flesh of ordination or any of the bread remains until morning, then you shall burn the remainder with fire; it shall not be eaten, because it is holy. 35 "So you shall do for Aaron and for his sons, according to all that I have commanded you; you shall ordain them for seven days. 36 Each day you shall offer a bull as a sin offering for atonement, and you shall purify the altar when you make atonement for it, and you shall anoint it to consecrate it. 37 For seven days you shall make atonement for the altar and consecrate it; then the altar shall be most holy, *and* whatever touches the altar shall be holy. 38 "Now this is what you shall offer on the altar: two one-year-old lambs each day, continuously. 39 The one lamb you shall offer in the morning, and the other lamb you shall offer at twilight; 40 and there *shall be a* †tenth *of an* ephah of fine flour mixed with a ²fourth of a hin of beaten oil, and a fourth of a hin of wine for a drink offering with one lamb. 41 The other lamb you shall offer at twilight, and shall offer with it the same grain offering and the same

drink offering as in the morning, for a soothing aroma, an offering by fire to the LORD. 42 It shall be a continual burnt offering throughout your generations at the doorway of the tent of meeting before the LORD, where I will meet with you, to speak to you there. 43 I will meet there with the sons of Israel, and it shall be consecrated by My glory. 44 I will consecrate the tent of meeting and the altar; I will also consecrate Aaron and his sons to serve as priests to Me. 45 And I will dwell among the sons of Israel and will be their God. 46 And they shall know that I am the LORD their God who brought them out of the land of Egypt, so that I might dwell among them; I am the LORD their God.

The Altar of Incense

30 "Now you shall make an altar as a place for burning incense; you shall make it of acacia wood. 2 Its length *shall be* [1]a cubit, and its width a cubit; it shall be square, and its height *shall be* two cubits; its horns *shall be* of one piece with it. 3 You shall overlay it with pure gold, its top and its sides all around, and its horns; and you shall make a gold molding all around for it. 4 You shall also make two gold rings for it under its molding; you shall make *them* on its two sides—on opposite sides—and they shall be holders for poles with which to carry it. 5 And you shall make the poles of acacia wood and overlay them with gold. 6 You shall put this altar in front of the veil that is near the ark of the testimony, in front of the [1]atoning cover that is over *the ark of* the testimony, where I will meet with you. 7 Aaron shall burn fragrant incense on it; he shall burn it every morning when he trims the lamps. 8 And when Aaron sets up the lamps at twilight, he shall burn incense. *There shall be* perpetual incense before the LORD throughout your generations. 9 You shall not offer any strange incense on this altar, or burnt offering, or meal offering; and you shall not pour out a drink offering on it. 10 However, Aaron shall make atonement on its horns once a year; he shall make atonement on it with the blood of the sin offering of atonement once a year throughout your generations. It is most holy to the LORD."

11 The LORD also spoke to Moses, saying, 12 "When you take a census of the sons of Israel to count them, then each one *of them* shall give a ransom for himself to the LORD, when you count them, so that there will be no plague among them when you count them. 13 This *is what* everyone who is counted shall give: half a [1]shekel according to the shekel of the sanctuary (the shekel is twenty gerahs), half a shekel as a contribution to the LORD. 14 Everyone who is counted, from twenty years old and over, shall give the contribution to the LORD. 15 The rich shall not pay more, and the poor shall not pay less, than the half shekel, when you give the contribution to the LORD to make atonement for yourselves. 16 And you shall take the atonement money from the sons of Israel and give it for the service of the tent of meeting, so that it may be a memorial for the sons of Israel before the LORD, to make atonement for yourselves."

17 Then the LORD spoke to Moses, saying, 18 "You shall also make a basin of bronze, with its base of bronze, for washing; and you shall put it between the tent of meeting and the altar, and you shall put water in it. 19 Aaron and his sons shall wash their hands and their feet from it; 20 when they enter the tent of meeting, they shall wash with water, so that they do not die; or when they approach the altar to minister, by offering up in smoke a fire *sacrifice* to the LORD. 21 So they shall wash their hands and their feet, so that they do not die; and it shall be a permanent statute for them, for Aaron and his descendants throughout their generations."

The Anointing Oil

22 Moreover, the LORD spoke to Moses, saying, 23 "Take also for yourself the finest of spices: of liquid myrrh [1]five hundred *shekels,* and of fragrant cinnamon half as much, 250, and of fragrant cane 250, 24 and of cassia 500, according to the shekel of the sanctuary, and of olive oil a [1]hin. 25 You shall make from these a holy anointing oil, a fragrant mixture of ointments, the work of a perfumer; it shall be a holy anointing oil. 26 And you shall anoint the tent of meeting with it, and the ark of the testimony, 27 and the table and all its utensils, and the lampstand and its utensils, and the altar of incense, 28 and the altar of burnt offering and all its utensils, and the basin and its stand. 29 You shall also consecrate them, so that they may be most holy; whatever touches them shall be holy. 30 And you shall anoint Aaron and his sons, and consecrate them, so that they may serve as priests to Me. 31 Furthermore, you shall speak to the sons of Israel, saying, 'This shall be a holy anointing oil to Me throughout your generations. 32 It shall not be poured on anyone's body, nor shall you make *any* like it in the same proportions; it is holy, *and* it shall be holy to you. 33 Whoever mixes *any* like it or whoever puts any of it on a layman shall be cut off from his people.' "

The Incense

34 Then the LORD said to Moses, "Take for yourself spices—stacte, onycha, and galbanum, spices and pure frankincense; there shall be an equal part of each. 35 You shall make incense from it *all,* a skillful mixture, the work of a perfumer, salted, pure, *and* holy. 36 And you shall crush some of it very fine, and put part of it in front of the testimony in the tent of meeting where I will meet with you; it shall be most holy to you. 37 And the incense which you shall make, you shall not make in the same proportions for yourselves; it shall be holy to you for the LORD. 38 Whoever makes *any* like it, to use as perfume, shall be cut off from his people."

30:2 [1] About 1.5 ft. long and wide and 3 ft. high or 45 cm and 90 cm   30:6 [1] Also called *mercy seat;* i.e., where blood was sprinkled on the Day of Atonement   30:13 [1] A shekel was about 0.5 oz. or 14 gm
30:23 [1] About 15.5 and 7.75 lb. or 7 and 3.5 kg   30:24 [1] About 1 gallon or 3.8 liters

The Skilled Craftsmen

31 Now the LORD spoke to Moses, saying, [2] "See, I have called by name Bezalel, the son of Uri, the son of Hur, of the tribe of Judah. [3] And I have filled him with the Spirit of God in wisdom, in understanding, in knowledge, and in all *kinds of* craftsmanship, [4] to create artistic designs for work in gold, in silver, and in bronze, [5] and in the cutting of stones for settings, and in the carving of wood, so that he may work in all *kinds of* craftsmanship. [6] And behold, I Myself have appointed with him Oholiab, the son of Ahisamach, of the tribe of Dan; and in the hearts of all who are skillful I have put skill, so that they may make everything that I have commanded you: [7] the tent of meeting, the ark of testimony, the [1]atoning cover that is on it, and all the furniture of the tent, [8] the table and its utensils, the pure *gold* lampstand with all its utensils, and the altar of incense, [9] the altar of burnt offering with all its utensils, and the basin and its stand, [10] the woven garments as well: the holy garments for Aaron the priest and the garments of his sons, *with which* to carry out their priesthood; [11] the anointing oil also, and the fragrant incense for the Holy Place, they are to make *them* according to everything that I have commanded you."

The Sign of the Sabbath

[12] Now the LORD spoke to Moses, saying, [13] "Now as for you, speak to the sons of Israel, saying, 'You must keep My Sabbaths; for *this* is a sign between Me and you throughout your generations, so that you may know that I am the LORD who sanctifies you. [14] Therefore you are to keep the Sabbath, for it is holy to you. Everyone who profanes it must be put to death; for whoever does *any* work on it, that person shall be cut off from among his people. [15] For six days work may be done, but on the seventh day there is a Sabbath of complete rest, holy to the LORD; whoever does *any* work on the Sabbath day must be put to death. [16] So the sons of Israel shall keep the Sabbath, to celebrate the Sabbath throughout their generations as a permanent covenant.' [17] It is a sign between Me and the sons of Israel forever; for in six days the LORD made heaven and earth, but on the seventh day He ceased *from labor,* and was refreshed."

[18] When He had finished speaking with him on Mount Sinai, He gave Moses the two tablets of the testimony, tablets of stone, written by the finger of God.

The Golden Calf

32 Now when the people saw that Moses delayed to come down from the mountain, the people assembled around Aaron and said to him, "Come, make us a god who will go before us; for this Moses, the man who brought us up from the land of Egypt—we do not know what happened to him." [2] Aaron said to them, "Tear off the gold rings which are in the ears of your wives, your sons, and your daughters, and bring *them* to me." [3] So all the people tore off the gold rings which were in

their ears and brought *them* to Aaron. [4] Then he took *the gold* from their hands, and fashioned it with an engraving tool and made it into a cast metal calf; and they said, "This is your god, Israel, who brought you up from the land of Egypt." [5] Now when Aaron saw *this,* he built an altar in front of it; and Aaron made a proclamation and said, "Tomorrow *shall be* a feast to the LORD." [6] So the next day they got up early and offered burnt offerings, and brought peace offerings; and the people sat down to eat and to drink, and got up to engage in lewd behavior.

[7] Then the LORD spoke to Moses, "Go down at once, for your people, whom you brought up from the land of Egypt, have behaved corruptly. [8] They have quickly turned aside from the way which I commanded them. They have made for themselves a cast metal calf, and have worshiped it and have sacrificed to it and said, 'This is your god, Israel, who brought you up from the land of Egypt!' " [9] Then the LORD said to Moses, "I have seen this people, and behold, they are an obstinate people. [10] So now leave Me alone, that My anger may burn against them and that I may destroy them; and I will make of you a great nation."

Moses' Plea

[11] Then Moses pleaded with the LORD his God, and said, "LORD, why does Your anger burn against Your people whom You have brought out from the land of Egypt with great power and with a mighty hand? [12] Why should the Egyptians talk, saying, 'With evil *motives* He brought them out, to kill them on the mountains and to destroy them from the face of the earth'? Turn from Your burning anger and relent of *doing* harm to Your people. [13] Remember Abraham, Isaac, and Israel, Your servants to whom You swore by Yourself, and said to them, 'I will multiply your descendants as the stars of the heavens, and all this land of which I have spoken I will give to your descendants, and they shall inherit *it* forever.' " [14] So the LORD relented of the harm which He said He would do to His people.

[15] Then Moses turned and went down from the mountain with the two tablets of the testimony in his hand, tablets which were written on both sides; they were written on one *side* and the other. [16] The tablets were God's work, and the writing was God's writing engraved on the tablets. [17] Now when Joshua heard the sound of the people as they shouted, he said to Moses, "*There is* a sound of war in the camp." [18] But he said,

"It is not the sound of the cry of victory,
Nor is it the sound of the cry of defeat;
But I hear the sound of singing."

Moses' Anger

[19] And it came about, as soon as Moses approached the camp, that he saw the calf and *the people* dancing; and Moses' anger burned, and he threw the tablets from his hands and shattered them to pieces at the foot of the mountain. [20] Then he took the calf which they had made and completely burned *it* with fire,

---

31:7 [1] Also called *mercy seat;* i.e., where blood was sprinkled on the Day of Atonement

and ground it to powder, and scattered it over the surface of the water and made the sons of Israel drink *it.*

21 Then Moses said to Aaron, "What did this people do to you, that you have brought *such* a great sin upon them?" 22 And Aaron said, "Do not let the anger of my lord burn; you know the people yourself, that they are prone to evil. 23 For they said to me, 'Make a god for us who will go before us; for this Moses, the man who brought us up from the land of Egypt—we do not know what happened to him.' 24 So I said to them, 'Whoever has any gold, let them tear it off.' Then they gave *it* to me, and I threw it into the fire, and out came this calf."

25 Now when Moses saw that the people were out of control—for Aaron had let them get out of control to *the point of being* an object of ridicule among their enemies— 26 Moses then stood at the gate of the camp, and said, "Whoever is for the LORD, *come* to me!" And all the sons of Levi gathered together to him. 27 And he said to them, "This is what the LORD, the God of Israel says: 'Every man *of you* put his sword on his thigh, and go back and forth from gate to gate in the camp, and kill every man his brother, and every man his friend, and every man his neighbor.' " 28 So the sons of Levi did as Moses instructed, and about three thousand men of the people fell that day. 29 Then Moses said, "Dedicate yourselves today to the LORD—for every man has been against his son and against his brother—in order that He may bestow a blessing upon you today."

30 And on the next day Moses said to the people, "You yourselves have committed a great sin; and now I am going up to the LORD; perhaps I can make atonement for your sin." 31 Then Moses returned to the LORD and said, "Oh, this people has committed a great sin, and they have made a god of gold for themselves! 32 But now, if You will forgive their sin, *very well;* but if not, please wipe me out from Your book which You have written!" 33 However, the LORD said to Moses, "Whoever has sinned against Me, I will wipe him out of My book. 34 But go now, lead the people where I told you. Behold, My angel shall go before you; nevertheless on the day when I punish, I will punish them for their sin." 35 Then the LORD struck the people *with a plague,* because of what they did with the calf which Aaron had made.

The Journey Resumed

33 Then the LORD spoke to Moses, "Depart, go up from here, you and the people whom you have brought up from the land of Egypt, to the land of which I swore to Abraham, Isaac, and Jacob, saying, 'To your descendants I will give it.' 2 And I will send an angel before you and I will drive out the Canaanite, the Amorite, the Hittite, the Perizzite, the Hivite, and the Jebusite. 3 *Go up* to a land flowing with milk and honey; for I will not go up in your midst, because you are an obstinate people, and I might destroy you on the way."

4 When the people heard this sad word, they went into mourning, and none of them put on his jewelry. 5 For the LORD had said to Moses, "Say to the sons of Israel, 'You are an obstinate people; *if* I were to go up in your midst for *just* one moment, I would destroy you. So now, take off your jewelry that I may know what I shall do to you.' " 6 So the sons of Israel stripped themselves of their jewelry, from Mount Horeb *onward.*

7 Now Moses used to take the tent and pitch it outside the camp, a good distance from the camp, and he called it the tent of meeting. And everyone who sought the LORD would go out to the tent of meeting which was outside the camp. 8 And it came about, whenever Moses went out to the tent, that all the people would arise and stand, each at the entrance of his tent, and gaze after Moses until he entered the tent. 9 Whenever Moses entered the tent, the pillar of cloud would descend and stand at the entrance of the tent; and the LORD would speak with Moses. 10 When all the people saw the pillar of cloud standing at the entrance of the tent, all the people would stand and worship, each at the entrance of his tent. 11 So the LORD used to speak to Moses face to face, just as a man speaks to his friend. When Moses returned to the camp, his servant Joshua, the son of Nun, a young man, would not depart from the tent.

Moses Intercedes

12 Then Moses said to the LORD, "See, You say to me, 'Bring up this people!' But You Yourself have not let me know whom You will send with me. Moreover, You have said, 'I have known you by name, and you have also found favor in My sight.' 13 Now then, if I have found favor in Your sight in any way, please let me know Your ways so that I may know You, in order that I may find favor in Your sight. Consider too, that this nation is Your people." 14 And He said, "My presence shall go *with you,* and I will give you rest." 15 Then he said to Him, "If Your presence does not go *with us,* do not lead us up from here. 16 For how then can it be known that I have found favor in Your sight, I and Your people? Is it not by Your going with us, so that we, I and Your people, may be distinguished from all the *other* people who are on the face of the earth?"

17 The LORD said to Moses, "I will also do this thing of which you have spoken; for you have found favor in My sight and I have known you by name." 18 Then *Moses* said, "Please, show me Your glory!" 19 And He said, "I Myself will make all My goodness pass before you, and will proclaim the name of the LORD before you; and I will be gracious to whom I will be gracious, and will show compassion to whom I will show compassion." 20 He further said, "You cannot see My face, for mankind shall not see Me and live!" 21 Then the LORD said, "Behold, there is a place by Me, and you shall stand *there* on the rock; 22 and it will come about, while My glory is passing by, that I will put you in the cleft of the rock and cover you with My hand until I have passed by. 23 Then I will take My hand away and you shall see My back, but My face shall not be seen."

The Two Tablets Replaced

34 Now the LORD said to Moses, "Cut out for yourself two stone tablets like the former ones, and I will write on the tablets the words that were on the former tablets which you smashed. 2 So be ready by morning, and come up in the morning to Mount Sinai, and present yourself there to Me on the top of the mountain. 3 And no one is to come up with you, nor let anyone be seen anywhere on the mountain; even the flocks and the herds are not to graze in front of that mountain." 4 So he cut out two stone tablets like the former ones, and Moses got up early in the morning and went up to Mount Sinai, as the LORD had commanded him, and he took *the* two stone tablets in his hand. 5 And the LORD descended in the cloud and stood there with him as he called upon the name of the LORD. 6 Then the LORD passed by in front of him and proclaimed, "The LORD, the LORD God, compassionate and merciful, slow to anger, and abounding in faithfulness and truth; 7 who keeps faithfulness for thousands, who forgives wrongdoing, violation *of His Law,* and sin; yet He will by no means leave *the guilty* unpunished, inflicting the ʾpunishment of fathers on the children and on the grandchildren to the third and fourth generations." 8 And Moses hurried to bow low toward the ground and worship. 9 Then he said, "If in any way I have found favor in Your sight, Lord, please may the Lord go along in our midst, even though the people are so obstinate, and pardon our wrongdoing and our sin, and take us as Your own possession."

The Covenant Renewed

10 Then God said, "Behold, I am going to make a covenant. Before all your people I will perform miracles which have not been produced in all the earth nor among any of the nations; and all the people among whom you live will see the working of the LORD, for it is a fearful thing that I am going to perform with you. 11 "Be sure to comply with what I am commanding you this day: behold, I am going to drive out the Amorite from you, and the Canaanite, the Hittite, the Perizzite, the Hivite, and the Jebusite. 12 Be careful that you do not make a covenant with the inhabitants of the land into which you are going, or it will become a snare in your midst. 13 But *rather,* you are to tear down their altars and smash their memorial stones, and cut down their ʾAsherim 14—for you shall not worship any other god, because the LORD, whose name is Jealous, is a jealous God— 15 otherwise you might make a covenant with the inhabitants of the land, and they would prostitute themselves with their gods and sacrifice to their gods, and someone might invite you to eat of his sacrifice, 16 and you might take some of his daughters for your sons, and his daughters might prostitute themselves with their gods and cause your sons *also* to prostitute themselves with their gods. 17 You shall not make for yourself *any* gods cast in metal.

18 "You shall keep the Feast of Unleavened Bread. For seven days you are to eat unleavened bread, as I commanded you, at the appointed time in the month of Abib; for in the month of Abib you came out of Egypt. 19 "The firstborn from every womb belongs to Me, and all your male livestock, the firstborn from cattle and sheep. 20 You shall redeem with a lamb the firstborn from a donkey; and if you do not redeem *it,* then you shall break its neck. You shall redeem all the firstborn of your sons. None are to appear before Me empty-handed. 21 "You shall work six days, but on the seventh day you shall rest; *even* during plowing time and harvest you shall rest. 22 And you shall celebrate the Feast of Weeks, *that is,* the first fruits of the wheat harvest, and the Feast of Ingathering at the turn of the year. 23 Three times a year all your males are to appear before the Lord GOD, the God of Israel. 24 For I will drive out nations from you and enlarge your borders, and no one will covet your land when you go up three times a year to appear before the LORD your God. 25 "You shall not offer the blood of My sacrifice with leavened bread, nor is the sacrifice of the Feast of the Passover to be left over until morning. 26 "You shall bring the very first of the first fruits of your soil into the house of the LORD your God.

"You shall not boil a young goat in its mother's milk."

27 Then the LORD said to Moses, "Write down these words, for in accordance with these words I have made a covenant with you and with Israel." 28 So he was there with the LORD for forty days and forty nights; he did not eat bread or drink water. And ʾHe wrote on the tablets the words of the covenant, the Ten Commandments.

Moses' Face Shines

29 And it came about, when Moses was coming down from Mount Sinai (and the two tablets of the testimony *were* in Moses' hand as he was coming down from the mountain), that Moses did not know that the skin of his face shone because of his speaking with Him. 30 So when Aaron and all the sons of Israel saw Moses, behold, the skin of his face shone, and they were afraid to approach him. 31 Then Moses called to them, and Aaron and all the rulers in the congregation returned to him; and Moses spoke to them. 32 Afterward all the sons of Israel came near, and he commanded them *to do* everything that the LORD had spoken to him on Mount Sinai. 33 When Moses had finished speaking with them, he put a veil over his face. 34 But whenever Moses went in before the LORD to speak with Him, he would take off the veil until he came out; and whenever he came out and spoke to the sons of Israel what he had been commanded, 35 the sons of Israel would see the face of Moses, that the skin of Moses' face shone. So Moses would put the veil back over his face until he went in to speak with Him.

34:7 ʾI.e., punishment for the wrongdoing   34:13 ʾI.e., wooden symbols of a female deity (Asherah)
34:28 ʾI.e., the LORD

The Sabbath Emphasized

35 Then Moses assembled all the congregation of the sons of Israel, and said to them, "These are the things that the LORD has commanded *you* to do: 2 "For six days work may be done, but on the seventh day you shall have a holy *day,* a Sabbath of complete rest to the LORD; whoever does any work on it shall be put to death. 3 You shall not kindle a fire in any of your dwellings on the Sabbath day."

4 Moses spoke to all the congregation of the sons of Israel, saying, "This is the thing which the LORD has commanded, saying, 5 'Take from among you a contribution to the LORD; whoever is of a willing heart is to bring it as the LORD's contribution: gold, silver, and bronze, 6 and ¹violet, purple, and scarlet *material,* fine linen, goats' *hair,* 7 and rams' skins dyed red, and ¹fine leather, and acacia wood, 8 and oil for lighting, and spices for the anointing oil, and for the fragrant incense, 9 and onyx stones and setting stones for the ephod and for the breastpiece.

Tabernacle Artisans

10 'Have every skillful person among you come and make all that the LORD has commanded: 11 the tabernacle, its tent and its covering, its hooks and its boards, its bars, its pillars, and its bases; 12 the ark and its poles, the ¹atoning cover, and the covering curtain; 13 the table and its poles, and all its utensils, and the bread of the Presence; 14 the lampstand also for the light and its utensils and its lamps, and the oil for the light; 15 and the altar of incense and its poles, and the anointing oil and the fragrant incense, and the curtain for the doorway at the entrance of the tabernacle; 16 the altar of burnt offering with its bronze grating, its poles, and all its utensils, the basin and its stand; 17 the hangings of the courtyard, its pillars and its bases, and the curtain for the gate of the courtyard; 18 the pegs of the tabernacle and the pegs of the courtyard and their ropes; 19 the woven garments for ministering in the Holy Place, the holy garments for Aaron the priest and the garments of his sons, to serve as priests.'"

Gifts Received

20 Then all the congregation of the sons of Israel departed from Moses' presence. 21 And everyone whose heart stirred him and everyone whose spirit moved him came *and* brought the LORD's contribution for the work of the tent of meeting and for all its service, and for the holy garments. 22 Then all whose hearts moved them, both men and women, came *and* brought brooches and earrings and signet rings and bracelets, all articles of gold; so *did* everyone who presented an offering of gold to the LORD. 23 Everyone who was in possession of violet, purple, or scarlet *material* or fine linen or goats' *hair,* or rams' skins dyed red or fine leather, brought them. 24 Everyone who could make a contribution of silver and bronze

brought the LORD's contribution; and everyone who was in possession of acacia wood for any work of the service brought it. 25 And all the skilled women spun with their hands, and brought what they had spun, *in* violet, purple, *and* scarlet *material,* and *in* fine linen. 26 And all the women whose heart stirred with a skill spun the goats' *hair.* 27 The rulers, moreover, brought the onyx stones and the stones for setting for the ephod and for the breastpiece; 28 and the spice and the oil for the light and for the anointing oil, and for the fragrant incense. 29 The Israelites, all the men and women, whose heart moved them to bring *material* for all the work, which the LORD had commanded through Moses to be done, brought a voluntary offering to the LORD.

30 Then Moses said to the sons of Israel, "See, the LORD has called by name Bezalel the son of Uri, the son of Hur, of the tribe of Judah. 31 And He has filled him with the Spirit of God, in wisdom, in understanding, in knowledge, and in all craftsmanship; 32 to create designs for working in gold, in silver, and in bronze, 33 and in the cutting of stones for settings and in the carving of wood, so as to perform in every inventive work. 34 He also has put in his heart to teach, both he and Oholiab, the son of Ahisamach, of the tribe of Dan. 35 He has filled them with skill to perform every work of an engraver, of a designer, and of an embroiderer, in violet, purple, *and* in scarlet *material,* and in fine linen, and of a weaver, as performers of every work and makers of designs.

The Tabernacle Underwritten

36 "Now Bezalel, Oholiab, and every skillful person in whom the LORD has put skill and understanding to know how to perform all the work in the construction of the sanctuary, shall perform in accordance with everything that the LORD has commanded."

2 Then Moses called Bezalel, Oholiab, and every skillful person in whom the LORD had put skill, everyone whose heart stirred him, to come to the work to perform it. 3 They received from Moses every contribution which the sons of Israel had brought to perform the work in the construction of the sanctuary. And they still *continued* bringing to him voluntary offerings every morning. 4 And all the skillful people who were performing all the work of the sanctuary came, each from the work which they were performing, 5 and they said to Moses, "The people are bringing much more than enough for the construction work which the LORD commanded *us* to perform." 6 So Moses issued a command, and circulated a proclamation throughout the camp, saying, "No man or woman is to perform work any longer for the contributions of the sanctuary." So the people were restrained from bringing *any more.* 7 For the material they had was sufficient and more than enough for all the work, to perform it.

Construction Begins

8 All the skillful people among those who

35:6 ¹Or *bluish;* LXX *hyacinth* in color, and so throughout the ch　35:7 ¹Meaning of the Heb uncertain, and so throughout the ch　35:12 ¹Also called *mercy seat;* i.e., where blood was sprinkled on the Day of Atonement

were performing the work made the tabernacle with ten curtains; of fine twisted linen and ¹violet, purple, and scarlet *material*, with cherubim, the work of a skilled embroiderer, Bezalel made them. 9 The length of each curtain was ¹twenty-eight cubits, and the width of each curtain four cubits; all the curtains had the same measurements. 10 He joined five curtains to one another, and *the other* five curtains he joined to one another. 11 And he made loops of violet on the edge of the outermost curtain in the first set; he did likewise on the edge of the curtain that was outermost in the second set. 12 He made fifty loops in the one curtain, and he made fifty loops on the edge of the curtain that was in the second set; the loops were opposite each other. 13 He also made fifty clasps of gold, and joined the curtains to one another with the clasps, so that the tabernacle was a unit.

14 Then he made curtains of goats' *hair* for a tent over the tabernacle; he made eleven curtains *in all*. 15 The length of each curtain *was* thirty cubits, and four cubits *was* the width of each curtain; the eleven curtains had the same measurements. 16 He joined five curtains by themselves, and *the other* six curtains by themselves. 17 Moreover, he made fifty loops on the edge of the curtain that was outermost in the *first* set, and he made fifty loops on the edge of the curtain *that was out ermost in* the second set. 18 He also made fifty clasps of bronze to join the tent together so that it would be a unit. 19 And he made a covering for the tent of rams' skins dyed red, and a covering of ¹fine leather above.

20 Then he made the boards for the tabernacle of acacia wood, standing upright. 21 Ten cubits *was* the length of each board, and one and a half cubits the width of each board. 22 *There were* two tenons for each board, fitted to one another; he did this to all the boards of the tabernacle. 23 So he made the boards for the tabernacle: twenty boards for the south side; 24 and he made forty bases of silver under the twenty boards; two bases under one board for its two tenons, and two bases under another board for its two tenons. 25 Then for the second side of the tabernacle, on the north side, he made twenty boards, 26 and their forty bases of silver; two bases under one board, and two bases under another board. 27 And for the back of the tabernacle, to the west, he made six boards. 28 He made two boards for the corners of the tabernacle at the back. 29 They were double beneath, and together they were complete to its top, to the first ring; he did this with both of them for the two corners. 30 There were eight boards with their bases of silver, sixteen bases, two bases under every board.

31 Then he made bars of acacia wood, five for the boards for one side of the tabernacle, 32 and five bars for the boards of the other side of the tabernacle, and five bars for the boards of the tabernacle for the back *side* to the west. 33 And he made the middle bar to pass through in the center of the boards from end to end. 34 Then he overlaid the boards with gold, and made their rings of gold *as* holders for the bars, and overlaid the bars with gold.

35 Moreover, he made the veil of violet, purple, and scarlet *material,* and fine twisted linen; he made it with cherubim, the work of a skilled embroiderer. 36 And he made four pillars of acacia for it, and overlaid them with gold, with their hooks of gold; and he cast four bases of silver for them. 37 He also made a curtain for the doorway of the tent, of violet, purple, and scarlet *material,* and fine twisted linen, the work of a weaver; 38 and *he made* its five pillars with their hooks, and he overlaid their tops and their bands with gold; but their five bases were of bronze.

Construction Continues

37 Now Bezalel made the ark of acacia wood; its length was two and a half cubits, its width one and a half cubits, and its height one and a half cubits; 2 and he overlaid it with pure gold inside and out, and made a gold molding for it all around. 3 He cast four rings of gold for it on its four feet; two rings on one side of it, and two rings on the other side of it. 4 And he made poles of acacia wood and overlaid them with gold. 5 He put the poles into the rings on the sides of the ark, to carry it. 6 He also made ¹an atoning cover of pure gold, two and a half cubits long and one and a half cubits wide. 7 And he made two cherubim of gold; he made them of hammered work at the two ends of the atoning cover: 8 one cherub at the one end and one cherub at the other end; he made the cherubim *of one piece* with the atoning cover at the two ends. 9 And the cherubim had *their* wings spread upward, covering the atoning cover with their wings, with their faces toward each other; the faces of the cherubim were toward the atoning cover.

10 Then he made the table of acacia wood, two cubits long, a cubit wide, and one and a half cubits high. 11 He overlaid it with pure gold, and made a gold molding for it all around. 12 And he made a rim for it of a ¹hand width all around, and made a gold molding for its rim all around. 13 He also cast four gold rings for it and put the rings on the four corners that were on its four legs. 14 Close by the rim were the rings, the holders for the poles to carry the table. 15 And he made the poles of acacia wood and overlaid them with gold, to carry the table. 16 He also made the utensils which were on the table, its dishes, its pans, its libation bowls, and its jars, with which to pour out drink offerings, of pure gold.

17 Then he made the lampstand of pure gold. He made the lampstand of hammered work, its base and its shaft; its cups, its bulbs, and its flowers were *of one piece* with it. 18 There were six branches going out of its sides; three branches of the lampstand from the one side of it and three branches of the lampstand from the other side of it; 19 three cups shaped like

---

36:8 ¹Or *bluish;* LXX *hyacinth* in color, and so throughout the ch   **36:9** ¹About 42 ft. long and 6 ft. wide or 13 m and 1.8 m   **36:19** ¹Meaning of the Heb uncertain   **37:6** ¹Also called *a mercy seat,* and so throughout the ch; i.e., where blood was sprinkled on the Day of Atonement
37:12 ¹About 3 in. or 7.5 cm

almond *blossoms,* a bulb and a flower on one branch, and three cups shaped like almond *blossoms,* a bulb and a flower on the other branch—so for the six branches going out of the lampstand. 20 And on the lampstand *there were* four cups shaped like almond *blossoms,* its bulbs and its flowers; 21 and a bulb was under the *first* pair of branches *coming* out of it, and a bulb under the *second* pair of branches *coming* out of it, and a bulb under the *third* pair of branches *coming* out of it, for the six branches coming out of the lampstand. 22 Their bulbs and their branches were *of one piece* with it; the whole of it *was* a single hammered work of pure gold. 23 And he made its seven lamps with its tongs and its trays of pure gold. 24 He made it and all its utensils from a ¹talent of pure gold.

25 Then he made the altar of incense of acacia wood: a cubit long and a cubit wide, square, and two cubits high; its horns were *of one piece* with it. 26 And he overlaid it with pure gold, its top and its sides all around, and its horns; and he made a gold molding for it all around. 27 He also made two golden rings for it under its molding, on its two sides—on opposite sides—as holders for poles with which to carry it. 28 And he made the poles of acacia wood and overlaid them with gold. 29 Then he made the holy anointing oil and the pure, fragrant incense of spices, the work of a perfumer.

The Tabernacle Completed

38 Then he made the altar of burnt offering of acacia wood, five cubits long, and five cubits wide, square, and three cubits high. 2 And he made its horns on its four corners, its horns being *of one piece* with it, and he overlaid it with bronze. 3 He also made all the utensils of the altar, the pails, the shovels, the basins, the meat-forks, and the firepans; he made all its utensils of bronze. 4 And he made for the altar a grating of bronze netting beneath, under its ledge, reaching halfway up. 5 He also cast four rings on the four ends of the bronze grating *as* holders for the poles. 6 He made the poles of acacia wood and overlaid them with bronze. 7 Then he inserted the poles into the rings on the sides of the altar, with which to carry it. He made it hollow with planks.

8 Moreover, he made the basin of bronze with its base of bronze, from the mirrors of the serving women who served at the doorway of the tent of meeting.

9 Then he made the courtyard: for the south side the hangings of the courtyard were of fine twisted linen, a hundred cubits; 10 their twenty pillars, and their twenty bases, *were made* of bronze; the hooks of the pillars and their bands *were* of silver. 11 For the north side *there were* a hundred cubits; their twenty pillars and their twenty bases *were* of bronze, the hooks of the pillars and their bands *were* of silver. 12 For the west side *there were* hangings of fifty cubits *with* their ten pillars and their ten bases; the

hooks of the pillars and their bands *were* of silver. 13 For the east side, fifty cubits. 14 The hangings for the *one* side *of the gate were* fifteen cubits, *with* their three pillars and their three bases, 15 and so for the other side. On both sides of the gate of the courtyard *were* hangings of fifteen cubits, *with* their three pillars and their three bases. 16 All the hangings of the courtyard all around *were* of fine twisted linen. 17 And the bases for the pillars *were* of bronze, the hooks of the pillars and their bands, of silver; and the overlaying of their tops, of silver, and all the pillars of the courtyard were furnished with silver bands. 18 Now the curtain of the gate of the courtyard was the work of the weaver, of ¹violet, purple, and scarlet *material* and fine twisted linen. And the length *was* twenty cubits and the height *was* five cubits, corresponding to the hangings of the courtyard. 19 Their four pillars and their four bases *were* of bronze; their hooks *were* of silver, and the overlaying of their tops and their bands *were* of silver. 20 All the pegs of the tabernacle and of the courtyard all around *were* of bronze.

The Cost of the Tabernacle

21 This is the number of the things for the tabernacle, the tabernacle of the testimony, as they were counted according to the command of Moses, for the service of the Levites, by the hand of Ithamar the son of Aaron the priest. 22 Now Bezalel the son of Uri, the son of Hur, of the tribe of Judah, made everything that the LORD had commanded Moses. 23 With him *was* Oholiab the son of Ahisamach, of the tribe of Dan, an engraver and a skilled embroiderer, and a weaver in¹ violet, in purple, and in scarlet *material,* and fine linen.

24 All the gold that was used for the work, in all the work of the sanctuary, which was the gold of the wave offering, was twenty-nine ¹talents and 730 ²shekels, according to the shekel of the sanctuary. 25 And the silver of those of the congregation who were counted was a hundred talents and 1,775 shekels, according to the shekel of the sanctuary; 26 a beka a head (*that is,* half a shekel according to the shekel of the sanctuary), *assessed* to each one who passed over to those who were counted, from twenty years old and upward, for 603,550 men. 27 The hundred talents of silver were *used* for casting the bases of the sanctuary and the bases of the veil; a hundred bases for the hundred talents, a talent for a base. 28 And of the 1,775 *shekels,* he made hooks for the pillars, and overlaid their tops and made bands for them. 29 And the bronze of the wave offering was seventy talents and 2,400 shekels. 30 With it he made the bases to the doorway of the tent of meeting, and the bronze altar and its bronze grating, and all the utensils of the altar, 31 and the bases of the courtyard all around and the bases of the gate of the courtyard, and all the pegs of the tabernacle and all the pegs of the courtyard all around.

37:24 ¹About 75 lb. or 34 kg   38:18 ¹Or *bluish;* LXX *hyacinth* in color, and so throughout the ch   38:24 ¹A talent was about 75 lb. or 34 kg   ²A shekel was about 0.5 oz. or 14 gm

The Priestly Garments

39 Now from the ᶠviolet, purple, and scarlet *material* they made finely woven garments for ministering in the Holy Place, as well as the holy garments which were for Aaron, just as the LORD had commanded Moses.

2 He made the ephod of gold *and* of violet, purple, and scarlet *material,* and fine twisted linen. 3 Then they hammered out gold sheets and cut *them* into threads to be woven in *with* the violet, the purple, and the scarlet *material,* and the fine linen, the work of a skilled embroiderer. 4 They made attaching shoulder pieces for the ephod; it was attached at its two *upper* ends. 5 And the skillfully woven band of its overlay which was on it was like its workmanship, of the same material: of gold *and* of violet, purple, and scarlet *material,* and fine twisted linen, just as the LORD had commanded Moses.

6 They also made the onyx stones, set in gold filigree *settings;* they were engraved *like* the engravings of a signet, according to the names of the sons of Israel. 7 And he placed them on the shoulder pieces of the ephod *as* memorial stones for the sons of Israel, just as the LORD had commanded Moses.

8 And he made the breastpiece, the work of a skilled embroiderer, like the workmanship of the ephod. of gold *and* of violet, purple, and scarlet *material* and fine twisted linen. 9 It was square; they made the breastpiece folded double, a ᶠspan long and a span wide when folded double. 10 And they mounted four rows of stones on it. The first row *was* a row of ruby, topaz, and emerald; 11 and the second row, a turquoise, a sapphire, and a diamond; 12 and the third row, a jacinth, an agate, and an amethyst; 13 and the fourth row, a beryl, an onyx, and a jasper. They were set in gold filigree *settings* when they were mounted. 14 The stones corresponded to the names of the sons of Israel; they were twelve, corresponding to their names, *engraved with* the engravings of a signet, each with its name for the twelve tribes. 15 And they made for the breastpiece chains like cords, work of twisted cords of pure gold. 16 They made two gold filigree *settings* and two gold rings, and put the two rings on the two ends of the breastpiece. 17 Then they put the two gold cords in the two rings at the ends of the breastpiece. 18 And they put the *other* two ends of the two cords on the two filigree *settings,* and put them on the shoulder pieces of the ephod at the front of it. 19 They made two gold rings and placed *them* on the two ends of the breastpiece, on its inner edge which was next to the ephod. 20 Furthermore, they made two gold rings and placed them on the bottom of the two shoulder pieces of the ephod, on the front of it, close to the place where it joined, above the woven band of the ephod. 21 And they bound the breastpiece by its rings to the rings of the ephod with a violet cord, so that it would be on the woven band of the ephod, and that the breastpiece would not come loose from the ephod, just as the LORD had commanded Moses.

22 Then he made the robe of the ephod of woven work, all of violet; 23 and the opening of the robe was *at the top* in the center, as the opening of a coat of mail, with a binding all around its opening, so that it would not be torn. 24 And they made pomegranates of violet, purple, and scarlet *material and* twisted *linen* on the hem of the robe. 25 They also made bells of pure gold, and put the bells between the pomegranates all around on the hem of the robe, 26 alternating a bell and a pomegranate all around on the hem of the robe for the service, just as the LORD had commanded Moses.

27 They also made the tunics of finely woven linen for Aaron and his sons, 28 and the turban of fine linen, and the decorated caps of fine linen, and the linen undergarments of fine twisted linen, 29 and the sash of fine twisted linen, and violet, purple, and scarlet *material,* the work of the weaver, just as the LORD had commanded Moses.

30 They also made the plate of the holy crown of pure gold, and inscribed it like the engravings of a signet, "Holy to the LORD." 31 Then they fastened a violet cord to it, to fasten it on the turban above, just as the LORD had commanded Moses.

32 So all the work of the tabernacle of the tent of meeting was completed, and the sons of Israel did according to all that the LORD had commanded Moses; so they did. 33 Then they brought the tabernacle to Moses, the tent and all its furnishings: its clasps, its boards, its bars, its pillars, and its bases; 34 and the covering of rams' skins dyed red, and the covering of ᶠfine leather, and the covering curtain; 35 the ark of the testimony, its poles, and the ᶠatoning cover; 36 the table, all its utensils, and the bread of the Presence; 37 the pure *gold* lampstand, with its arrangement of lamps and all its utensils, and the oil for the light; 38 and the gold altar, and the anointing oil and the fragrant incense, and the curtain for the doorway of the tent; 39 the bronze altar and its bronze grating, its poles and all its utensils, the basin and its stand; 40 the hangings for the courtyard, its pillars and its bases, and the curtain for the gate of the courtyard, its ropes and its pegs, and all the equipment for the service of the tabernacle, for the tent of meeting; 41 the woven garments for ministering in the Holy Place, and the holy garments for Aaron the priest and the garments of his sons, to serve as priests. 42 So the sons of Israel did all the work according to everything that the LORD had commanded Moses. 43 And Moses examined all the work, and behold, they had done it; just as the LORD had commanded, this they had done. So Moses blessed them.

The Tabernacle Erected

40 Then the LORD spoke to Moses, saying, 2 "On the first day of the first month you shall set up the tabernacle of the tent of meeting. 3 You shall place the ark of the testimony there, and you shall screen off the ark

---

39:1 ¹ Or *bluish;* LXX *hyacinth* in color, and so throughout the ch   39:9 ¹ About 9 in. or 23 cm
39:34 ¹ Meaning of the Heb uncertain   39:35 ¹ Also called *mercy seat;* i.e., where blood was sprinkled on the Day of Atonement

with the veil. ⁴ Then you shall bring in the table and arrange what belongs on it; and you shall bring in the lampstand and mount its lamps. ⁵ You shall also set the gold altar of incense in front of the ark of the testimony, and set up the curtain for the doorway to the tabernacle. ⁶ And you shall set the altar of burnt offering in front of the doorway of the tabernacle of the tent of meeting. ⁷ Then you shall set the basin between the tent of meeting and the altar, and put water in it. ⁸ You shall also set up the courtyard all around and hang up the curtain for the gate of the courtyard. ⁹ Then you shall take the anointing oil and anoint the tabernacle and everything that is in it, and consecrate it and all its furnishings; and it shall be holy. ¹⁰ You shall also anoint the altar of burnt offering and all its utensils, and consecrate the altar, and the altar shall be most holy. ¹¹ And you shall anoint the basin and its stand, and consecrate it. ¹² Then you shall bring Aaron and his sons to the doorway of the tent of meeting and wash them with water. ¹³ And you shall put the holy garments on Aaron and anoint him and consecrate him, so that he may serve as a priest to Me. ¹⁴ You shall also bring his sons and put tunics on them; ¹⁵ and you shall anoint them just as you have anointed their father, so that they may serve as priests to Me; and their anointing will qualify them for a permanent priesthood throughout their generations." ¹⁶ So Moses did *these things;* according to all that the Lord had commanded him, so he did.

¹⁷ Now in the first month of the second year, on the first *day* of the month, the tabernacle was erected. ¹⁸ Moses erected the tabernacle and laid its bases, and set up its boards, and inserted its bars, and erected its pillars. ¹⁹ And he spread the tent over the tabernacle and put the covering of the tent on top of it, just as the Lord had commanded Moses. ²⁰ Then he took the testimony and put *it* into the ark, and attached the poles to the ark, and put the ¹atoning cover on top of the ark. ²¹ He then brought the ark into the tabernacle, and set up a veil for the covering, and screened off the ark

of the testimony, just as the Lord had commanded Moses. ²² He also put the table in the tent of meeting on the north side of the tabernacle, outside the veil. ²³ And he set the arrangement of bread in order on it before the Lord, just as the Lord had commanded Moses. ²⁴ Then he placed the lampstand in the tent of meeting, opposite the table, on the south side of the tabernacle. ²⁵ And he lighted the lamps before the Lord, just as the Lord had commanded Moses. ²⁶ Then he placed the gold altar in the tent of meeting in front of the veil; ²⁷ and he burned fragrant incense on it, just as the Lord had commanded Moses. ²⁸ Then he set up the curtain for the doorway of the tabernacle. ²⁹ And he set the altar of burnt offering *in front of* the doorway of the tabernacle of the tent of meeting, and offered on it the burnt offering and the meal offering, just as the Lord had commanded Moses. ³⁰ He placed the basin between the tent of meeting and the altar, and put water in it for washing. ³¹ From it Moses and Aaron and his sons washed their hands and their feet. ³² When they entered the tent of meeting, and when they approached the altar, they washed, just as the Lord had commanded Moses. ³³ And he erected the courtyard all around the tabernacle and the altar, and hung up the curtain for the gate of the courtyard. So Moses finished the work.

The Glory of the Lord

³⁴ Then the cloud covered the tent of meeting, and the glory of the Lord filled the tabernacle. ³⁵ And Moses was not able to enter the tent of meeting because the cloud had settled on it, and the glory of the Lord filled the tabernacle. ³⁶ Throughout their journeys, whenever the cloud was taken up from over the tabernacle, the sons of Israel would set out; ³⁷ but if the cloud was not taken up, then they did not set out until the day when it was taken up. ³⁸ For throughout their journeys, the cloud of the Lord was on the tabernacle by day, and there was fire in it by night, in the sight of all the house of Israel.

40:20 ¹ Also called *mercy seat;* i.e., where blood was sprinkled on the Day of Atonement

LEVITICUS

The Law of Burnt Offerings

1 Now the LORD called to Moses and spoke to him from the tent of meeting, saying, 2 "Speak to the sons of Israel and say to them, 'When anyone of you brings an offering to the LORD, you shall bring your offering of livestock from the herd or the flock. 3 If his offering is a burnt offering from the herd, he shall offer a male without defect; he shall offer it at the doorway of the tent of meeting, so that he may be accepted before the LORD. 4 And he shall lay his hand on the head of the burnt offering, so that it may be accepted for him to make atonement on his behalf. 5 Then he shall slaughter the bull before the LORD; and Aaron's sons the priests shall offer up the blood and sprinkle the blood around on the altar that is at the doorway of the tent of meeting. 6 He shall then skin the burnt offering and cut it into its pieces. 7 And the sons of Aaron the priest shall put fire on the altar and arrange wood on the fire. 8 Then Aaron's sons the priests shall arrange the pieces, with the head and the suet, on the wood which is on the fire that is on the altar. 9 Its entrails, however, and its legs he shall wash with water. And the priest shall offer all of it up in smoke on the altar as a burnt offering, an offering by fire as a soothing aroma to the LORD.

10 'But if his offering is from the flock, either from the sheep or from the goats, as a burnt offering, he shall offer a male without defect. 11 And he shall slaughter it on the side of the altar northward before the LORD, and Aaron's sons the priests shall sprinkle its blood around on the altar. 12 He shall then cut it into its pieces with its head and its suet, and the priest shall arrange them on the wood which is on the fire that is on the altar. 13 The entrails, however, and the legs he shall wash with water. And the priest shall offer all of it, and offer it up in smoke on the altar; it is a burnt offering, an offering by fire of a soothing aroma to the LORD.

14 'But if his offering to the LORD is a burnt offering of birds, then he shall bring his offering from the turtledoves or from young doves. 15 The priest shall bring it to the altar, and pinch off its head, and offer it up in smoke on the altar; and its blood is to be drained out on the side of the altar. 16 He shall also remove its craw with its feathers and throw it beside the altar eastward, to the place of the fatty ashes. 17 Then he shall tear it by its wings, but shall not sever it. And the priest shall offer it up in smoke on the altar, on the wood which is on the fire; it is a burnt offering, an offering by fire of a soothing aroma to the LORD.

The Law of Grain Offerings

2 'Now when anyone presents a grain offering as an offering to the LORD, his offering shall be of fine flour, and he shall pour oil on it and put frankincense on it. 2 He shall then bring it to Aaron's sons the priests; and he shall take

from it his handful of its fine flour and of its oil, with all of its frankincense. And the priest shall offer it up in smoke as its memorial portion on the altar, an offering by fire of a soothing aroma to the LORD. 3 The remainder of the grain offering belongs to Aaron and his sons: a most holy part of the offerings to the LORD by fire.

4 'Now when you bring an offering of a grain offering baked in an oven, it shall be unleavened cakes of fine flour mixed with oil, or unleavened wafers spread with oil. 5 And if your offering is a grain offering made on the griddle, it shall be of fine flour, unleavened, mixed with oil; 6 you shall break it into bits and pour oil on it; it is a grain offering. 7 Now if your offering is a grain offering made in a pan, it shall be made of fine flour with oil. 8 When you bring in the grain offering which is made of these things to the LORD, it shall be presented to the priest, and he shall bring it to the altar. 9 The priest then shall take up from the grain offering its memorial portion, and shall offer it up in smoke on the altar as an offering by fire of a soothing aroma to the LORD. 10 The remainder of the grain offering belongs to Aaron and his sons: a most holy part of the offerings to the LORD by fire.

11 'No grain offering, which you bring to the LORD, shall be made with leaven, for you shall not offer up in smoke any leaven or any honey as an offering by fire to the LORD. 12 As an offering of first fruits you shall bring them to the LORD, but they shall not ascend as a soothing aroma on the altar. 13 Every grain offering of yours, moreover, you shall season with salt, so that the salt of the covenant of your God will not be lacking from your grain offering; with all your offerings you shall offer salt.

14 'Also if you bring a grain offering of early ripened things to the LORD, you shall bring fresh heads of grain roasted in the fire, crushed grain of new growth, for the grain offering of your early ripened produce. 15 You shall then put oil on it and place incense on it; it is a grain offering. 16 Then the priest shall offer up in smoke its memorial portion, part of its crushed grain and its oil with all its incense as an offering by fire to the LORD.

The Law of Peace Offerings

3 'Now if his offering is a sacrifice of peace offerings, if he is going to offer from the herd, whether male or female, he shall offer it without defect before the LORD. 2 And he shall lay his hand on the head of his offering and slaughter it at the doorway of the tent of meeting, and Aaron's sons the priests shall sprinkle the blood around on the altar. 3 From the sacrifice of the peace offerings he shall then present an offering by fire to the LORD, the fat that covers the entrails and all the fat that is on the entrails, 4 and the two kidneys with the fat that is on them, which is on the loins, and the lobe of the liver, which he shall

remove with the kidneys. 5 Then Aaron's sons shall offer *it* up in smoke on the altar on the burnt offering, which is on the wood that is on the fire; it is an offering by fire of a soothing aroma to the LORD. 6 But if his offering for a sacrifice of peace offerings to the LORD is from the flock, he shall offer it, male or female, without defect. 7 If he is going to offer a lamb for his offering, then he shall offer it before the LORD, 8 and he shall lay his hand on the head of his offering and slaughter it in front of the tent of meeting, and Aaron's sons shall sprinkle its blood around on the altar. 9 From the sacrifice of peace offerings he shall then bring as an offering by fire to the LORD, its fat, the entire fat tail which he shall remove close to the backbone, the fat that covers the entrails, and all the fat that is on the entrails, 10 and the two kidneys with the fat that is on them, which is on the loins, and the lobe of the liver, which he shall remove with the kidneys. 11 Then the priest shall offer *it* up in smoke on the altar *as* food, an offering by fire to the LORD.

12 'Now if his offering is a goat, then he shall offer it before the LORD, 13 and he shall lay his hand on its head and slaughter it in front of the tent of meeting, and the sons of Aaron shall sprinkle its blood around on the altar. 14 From it he shall present his offering as an offering by fire to the LORD, the fat that covers the entrails and all the fat that is on the entrails, 15 and the two kidneys with the fat that is on them, which is on the loins, and the lobe of the liver, which he shall remove with the kidneys. 16 The priest shall offer them up in smoke on the altar *as* food, an offering by fire as a soothing aroma; all fat is the LORD's. 17 It is a permanent statute throughout your generations in all your dwelling places: you shall not eat any fat or any blood.' "

The Law of Sin Offerings

4 Then the LORD spoke to Moses, saying, 2 "Speak to the sons of Israel, saying, 'If a person sins unintentionally in any of the things which the LORD has commanded not to be done, and commits any of them, 3 if the anointed priest sins so as to bring guilt on the people, then he is to offer to the LORD a bull without defect as a sin offering for his sin which he has committed. 4 He shall bring the bull to the doorway of the tent of meeting before the LORD, and he shall lay his hand on the head of the bull and slaughter the bull before the LORD. 5 Then the anointed priest is to take some of the blood of the bull and bring it to the tent of meeting, 6 and the priest shall dip his finger in the blood and sprinkle some of the blood seven times before the LORD, in front of the veil of the sanctuary. 7 The priest shall also put some of the blood on the horns of the altar of fragrant incense which is before the LORD in the tent of meeting; and all *the rest of* the blood of the bull he shall pour out at the base of the altar of burnt offering, which is at the doorway of the tent of meeting. 8 And he shall remove from it all the fat of the bull of the sin offering: the fat that covers the entrails, and all the fat which is on the entrails, 9 and the two kidneys with the fat that is on them,

which is on the loins, and the lobe of the liver, which he shall remove with the kidneys 10 (just as it is removed from the ox of the sacrifice of peace offerings); and the priest is to offer them up in smoke on the altar of burnt offering. 11 But the hide of the bull and all its flesh, along with its head, its legs, its entrails, and its refuse, 12 that is, all *the rest of* the bull, he is to bring out to a clean place outside the camp where the fatty ashes are poured out, and burn it on wood with fire; where the fatty ashes are poured out it shall be burned.

13 'Now if the entire congregation of Israel does wrong unintentionally and the matter escapes the notice of the assembly, and they commit any of the things which the LORD has commanded not to be done, and they become guilty; 14 when the sin which they have committed becomes known, then the assembly shall offer a bull of the herd as a sin offering and bring it in front of the tent of meeting. 15 Then the elders of the congregation shall lay their hands on the head of the bull before the LORD, and the bull shall be slaughtered before the LORD. 16 Then the anointed priest is to bring some of the blood of the bull to the tent of meeting; 17 and the priest shall dip his finger in the blood and sprinkle *it* seven times before the LORD, in front of the veil. 18 He shall then put some of the blood on the horns of the altar which is before the LORD in the tent of meeting; and all *the rest of* the blood he shall pour out at the base of the altar of burnt offering which is at the doorway of the tent of meeting. 19 And he shall remove all its fat from it and offer it up in smoke on the altar. 20 He shall also do with the bull just as he did with the bull of the sin offering; he shall do the same with it. So the priest shall make atonement for them, and they will be forgiven. 21 Then he is to bring the bull out to *a place* outside the camp and burn it just as he burned the first bull; it is the sin offering for the assembly.

22 'When a leader sins and unintentionally does any of the things which the LORD his God has commanded not to be done, and he becomes guilty, 23 if his sin which he has committed is made known to him, he shall bring as his offering a goat, a male without defect. 24 And he shall lay his hand on the head of the male goat and slaughter it in the place where they slaughter the burnt offering before the LORD; it is a sin offering. 25 Then the priest is to take some of the blood of the sin offering with his finger and put it on the horns of the altar of burnt offering; and *the rest of* its blood he shall pour out at the base of the altar of burnt offering. 26 And he shall offer all its fat up in smoke on the altar as *in the case of* the fat of the sacrifice of peace offerings. So the priest shall make atonement for him regarding his sin, and he will be forgiven.

27 'Now if anyone of the common people sins unintentionally by doing any of the things which the LORD has commanded not to be done, and becomes guilty, 28 if his sin which he has committed is made known to him, then he shall bring as his offering a goat, a female without defect, for his sin which he has committed.

29 And he shall lay his hand on the head of the sin offering and slaughter the sin offering at the place of the burnt offering. 30 The priest shall then take some of its blood with his finger and put it on the horns of the altar of burnt offering; and all *the rest of* its blood he shall pour out at the base of the altar. 31 Then he shall remove all its fat, just as the fat was removed from the sacrifice of peace offerings; and the priest shall offer it up in smoke on the altar as a soothing aroma to the LORD. So the priest shall make atonement for him, and he will be forgiven.

32 'But if he brings a lamb as his offering for a sin offering, he shall bring a female without defect. 33 And he shall lay his hand on the head of the sin offering and slaughter it as a sin offering in the place where they slaughter the burnt offering. 34 And the priest is to take some of the blood of the sin offering with his finger and put it on the horns of the altar of burnt offering, and all *the rest of* its blood he shall pour out at the base of the altar. 35 Then he shall remove all its fat, just as the fat of the lamb is removed from the sacrifice of the peace offerings, and the priest shall offer it up in smoke on the altar, on the offerings by fire to the LORD. So the priest shall make atonement for him regarding his sin which he has committed, and he will be forgiven.

The Law of Guilt Offerings

5 'Now if a person sins after he hears a public order *to testify* when he is a witness, whether he has seen or *otherwise* known, if he does not tell *it*, then he will bear his punishment. 2 Or if a person touches any unclean thing, whether a carcass of an unclean animal, or the carcass of unclean cattle, or a carcass of unclean swarming things, though it is hidden from him and he is unclean, then he will be guilty. 3 Or if he touches human uncleanness, of whatever *sort* his uncleanness *may* be with which he becomes unclean, and it is hidden from him, and then he comes to know *it*, he will be guilty. 4 Or if a person swears thoughtlessly with his lips to do evil or to do good, in whatever *matter* people speak thoughtlessly with an oath, and it is hidden from him, and then he comes to know *it*, he will be guilty of one of these things. 5 So it shall be when he becomes guilty of one of these things, that he shall confess that in which he has sinned. 6 He shall also bring his guilt offering to the LORD for his sin which he has committed, a female from the flock, a lamb or a goat as a sin offering. So the priest shall make atonement on his behalf for his sin.

7 'But if he cannot afford a lamb, then he shall bring to the LORD his guilt offering for that in which he has sinned, two turtledoves or two young doves, one as a sin offering and the other as a burnt offering. 8 He shall bring them to the priest, who shall first offer that which is for the sin offering, and shall pinch off its head at the front of its neck, but he shall not sever *it*. 9 He shall also sprinkle some of the blood of the sin offering on the side of the altar, while the rest of the blood shall be drained out at the base of the altar: it is a sin offering. 10 The second he shall then prepare as a burnt offering according to the ordinance. So the priest shall make atonement on his behalf for his sin which he has committed, and it will be forgiven him.

11 'But if his means are insufficient for two turtledoves or two young doves, then for his offering for that which he has sinned, he shall bring the tenth of an *'ephah* of fine flour as a sin offering; he shall not put oil on it or place incense on it, for it is a sin offering. 12 He shall bring it to the priest, and the priest shall take his handful of it as its memorial portion and offer *it* up in smoke on the altar, with the offerings of the LORD by fire: it is a sin offering. 13 So the priest shall make atonement for him concerning his sin which he has committed from one of these, and it will be forgiven him; then *the rest* shall become the priest's, like the grain offering.' "

14 Then the LORD spoke to Moses, saying, 15 "If a person acts unfaithfully and sins unintentionally against the LORD's holy things, then he shall bring his guilt offering to the LORD: a ram without defect from the flock, according to your assessment in silver by shekels, in *terms of* the shekel of the sanctuary, as a guilt offering. 16 And he shall make restitution for that which he has sinned against the holy thing, and shall add to it a fifth part of it and give it to the priest. The priest shall then make atonement for him with the ram of the guilt offering, and it will be forgiven him.

17 "Now if a person sins and does any of the things which the LORD has commanded not to be done, though he was unaware, he is still guilty and shall bear his punishment. 18 He is then to bring to the priest a ram without defect from the flock, according to your assessment, as a guilt offering. So the priest shall make atonement for him concerning his sin which he committed unintentionally and did not know *it*, and it will be forgiven him. 19 It is a guilt offering; he was certainly guilty before the LORD."

Guilt Offering

6 Then the LORD spoke to Moses, saying, 2 "When a person sins and acts unfaithfully against the LORD, and disavows *the rightful claim of* his neighbor regarding a deposit or a security entrusted *to him*, or regarding robbery, or he has extorted from his neighbor, 3 or has found what was lost and lied about it and sworn falsely, so that he sins regarding any of the things that people do; 4 then it shall be, when he sins and becomes guilty, that he shall restore what he took by robbery or acquired by extortion, or the deposit which was entrusted to him, or the lost property which he found, 5 or anything about which he swore falsely; he shall make restitution for it in full and add to it a fifth more. He shall give it to the one to whom it belongs on the day *he presents* his guilt offering. 6 Then he shall bring to the priest his guilt offering to the LORD, a ram without defect from the flock, according to your assessment, as a guilt offering, 7 and the priest shall

---

5:11 1 About 1 cubic foot or 0.03 cubic meters

make atonement for him before the Lord, and he will be forgiven for any one of the things which he may have done to incur guilt."

The Priest's Part in the Offerings

8 Then the Lord spoke to Moses, saying, 9 "Command Aaron and his sons, saying, 'This is the law for the burnt offering: the burnt offering itself *shall remain* on the hearth on the altar all night until the morning, and the fire on the altar is to be kept burning on it. 10 The priest is to put on his linen robe, and he shall put on linen undergarments next to his body; and he shall take up the fatty ashes *to* which the fire reduces the burnt offering on the altar and place them beside the altar. 11 Then he shall take off his garments and put on other garments, and carry the fatty ashes outside the camp to a clean place. 12 The fire on the altar shall be kept burning on it. It shall not go out, but the priest shall burn wood on it every morning; and he shall lay out the burnt offering on it, and offer up in smoke the fat portions of the peace offerings on it. 13 Fire shall be kept burning continually on the altar; it is not to go out.

14 'Now this is the law of the grain offering: the sons of Aaron shall present it before the Lord in front of the altar. 15 Then one *of them* shall lift up from it a handful of the fine flour of the grain offering, with its oil and all the incense that is on the grain offering, and he shall offer *it* up in smoke on the altar, a soothing aroma, as its memorial offering to the Lord. 16 And Aaron and his sons are to eat what is left of it. It shall be eaten as unleavened cakes in a holy place; they are to eat it in the courtyard of the tent of meeting. 17 It shall not be baked with leaven. I have given it as their share from My offerings by fire; it is most holy, like the sin offering and the guilt offering. 18 Every male among the sons of Aaron may eat it; it is a permanent ordinance throughout your generations, from the offerings by fire to the Lord. Whoever touches them will become consecrated.' "

19 Then the Lord spoke to Moses, saying, 20 "This is the offering which Aaron and his sons are to present to the Lord on the day when he is anointed; the tenth of an ¹ephah of fine flour as a regular grain offering, half of it in the morning and half of it in the evening. 21 It shall be prepared with oil on a griddle. When it is *well* stirred, you shall bring it. You shall present the grain offering in baked pieces as a soothing aroma to the Lord. 22 The anointed priest who will be in his place among his sons shall offer it. By a permanent ordinance it shall be entirely offered up in smoke to the Lord. 23 So every grain offering of the priest shall be burned entirely. It shall not be eaten."

24 Then the Lord spoke to Moses, saying, 25 "Speak to Aaron and to his sons, saying, 'This is the law of the sin offering: in the place where the burnt offering is slaughtered, the sin offering shall be slaughtered before the Lord; it is most holy. 26 The priest who offers it for sin shall eat it. It shall be eaten in a holy place, in the courtyard of the tent of meeting.

27 Whoever touches its flesh will become consecrated; and when any of its blood spatters on a garment, you shall wash what spattered on it in a holy place. 28 Also the earthenware vessel in which it was boiled shall be broken; and if it was boiled in a bronze vessel, then it shall be scoured and rinsed in water. 29 Every male among the priests may eat it; it is most holy. 30 But no sin offering of which any of the blood is brought into the tent of meeting to make atonement in the Holy Place shall be eaten; it shall be burned with fire.

The Priest's Part in the Offerings

7 'Now this is the law of the guilt offering; it is most holy. 2 In the place where they slaughter the burnt offering they are to slaughter the guilt offering, and *the priest* shall sprinkle its blood around on the altar. 3 Then he shall offer from it all its fat: the fat tail and the fat that covers the entrails, 4 and the two kidneys with the fat that is on them, which is on the loins; and he shall remove the lobe on the liver with the kidneys. 5 The priest shall offer them up in smoke on the altar as an offering by fire to the Lord; it is a guilt offering. 6 Every male among the priests may eat it. It shall be eaten in a holy place; it is most holy. 7 The guilt offering is like the sin offering: there is one law for them. The priest who makes atonement with it shall have it. 8 Also the priest who presents anyone's burnt offering, that priest shall have for himself the hide of the burnt offering which he has presented. 9 Likewise, every grain offering that is baked in the oven and everything prepared in a pan or on a griddle shall belong to the priest who presents it. 10 Every grain offering, mixed with oil or dry, shall belong to all the sons of Aaron, to all alike.

11 'Now this is the law of the sacrifice of peace offerings which shall be presented to the Lord. 12 If he offers it by way of thanksgiving, then along with the sacrifice of thanksgiving he shall offer unleavened cakes mixed with oil, and unleavened wafers spread with oil, and cakes *of well* stirred fine flour mixed with oil. 13 With the sacrifice of his peace offerings for thanksgiving, he shall present his offering with cakes of leavened bread. 14 Of this he shall present one of every offering as a contribution to the Lord; it shall belong to the priest who sprinkles the blood of the peace offerings.

15 'Now *as for* the flesh of the sacrifice of his thanksgiving peace offerings, it shall be eaten on the day of his offering; he shall not leave any of it over until morning. 16 But if the sacrifice of his offering is a vow or a voluntary offering, it shall be eaten on the day that he offers his sacrifice, and on the next day what is left of it may be eaten; 17 but what is left over from the flesh of the sacrifice on the third day shall be burned with fire. 18 So if any of the flesh of the sacrifice of his peace offerings is *ever* eaten on the third day, he who offers it will not be accepted, *and* it will not be credited to him. It will be an unclean thing, and the person who eats it shall bear his punishment. 19 'Also the flesh that touches anything

---

6:20 ¹ About 1 cubic foot or 0.03 cubic meters

unclean shall not be eaten; it shall be burned with fire. As for *other* flesh, anyone who is clean may eat *such* flesh. 20 But the person who eats the flesh of the sacrifice of peace offerings which belong to the LORD, when he is unclean, that person shall be cut off from his people. 21 When anyone touches anything unclean, whether human uncleanness, or an unclean animal, or any unclean *'detestable* thing, and eats of the flesh of the sacrifice of peace offerings which belong to the LORD, that person shall be cut off from his people.' "

22 Then the LORD spoke to Moses, saying, 23 "Speak to the sons of Israel, saying, 'You shall not eat any fat *from* an ox, a sheep, or a goat. 24 Also the fat of *an animal* which dies and the fat of an animal torn *by animals* may be put to any *other* use, but you certainly are not to eat it. 25 For whoever eats the fat of the animal from which an offering by fire is offered to the LORD, the person who eats *it* shall also be cut off from his people. 26 And you are not to eat any blood, either of bird or animal, in any of your dwellings. 27 Any person who eats any blood, that person shall also be cut off from his people.' "

28 Then the LORD spoke to Moses, saying, 29 "Speak to the sons of Israel, saying, 'He who offers the sacrifice of his peace offerings to the LORD shall bring his offering to the LORD from the sacrifice of his peace offerings. 30 His own hands are to bring offerings by fire to the LORD. He shall bring the fat with the breast, so that the breast may be presented as a wave offering before the LORD. 31 And the priest shall offer up the fat in smoke on the altar, but the breast shall belong to Aaron and to his sons. 32 And you shall give the right thigh to the priest as a contribution from the sacrifices of your peace offerings. 33 The one among the sons of Aaron who offers the blood of the peace offerings and the fat, the right thigh shall be his as *his* portion. 34 For I have taken from the sons of Israel the breast of the wave offering and the thigh of the contribution from the sacrifices of their peace offerings, and have given them to Aaron the priest and to his sons as *their* allotted portion forever from the sons of Israel. 35 'This is the allotment to Aaron and the allotment to his sons from the offerings by fire to the LORD, on that day when he presented them to serve as priests to the LORD. 36 These the LORD had commanded to be given them from the sons of Israel on the day that He anointed them. It is *their* allotted portion forever throughout their generations.' "

37 This is the law of the burnt offering, the grain offering, the sin offering and the guilt offering, and the ordination offering and the sacrifice of peace offerings, 38 which the LORD commanded Moses on Mount Sinai on the day that He commanded the sons of Israel to present their offerings to the LORD in the wilderness of Sinai.

The Consecration of Aaron and His Sons

8 Then the LORD spoke to Moses, saying, 2 "Take Aaron and his sons with him, and the garments and the anointing oil, and the bull of the sin offering, and the two rams and the basket of unleavened bread, 3 and assemble all the congregation at the doorway of the tent of meeting." 4 So Moses did just as the LORD commanded him. When the congregation was assembled at the doorway of the tent of meeting, 5 Moses said to the congregation, "This is the thing which the LORD has commanded *us* to do."

6 Then Moses had Aaron and his sons come near, and he washed them with water. 7 Then he put the tunic on Aaron and wrapped his waist with the sash, and clothed him with the robe and put the ephod on him; and he wrapped his waist with the artistic band of the ephod, with which he fitted *it* to him. 8 He then placed the breastpiece on him, and in the breastpiece he put the *'Urim* and the Thummim. 9 He also placed the turban on his head, and on the turban, at its front, he placed the golden plate, the holy crown, just as the LORD had commanded Moses.

10 Moses then took the anointing oil and anointed the tabernacle and everything that was in it, and consecrated them. 11 He also sprinkled some of it on the altar seven times and anointed the altar and all its utensils, and the basin and its stand, to consecrate them. 12 Then he poured some of the anointing oil on Aaron's head and anointed him, to consecrate him. 13 Next Moses had Aaron's sons come near, and he clothed them with tunics and wrapped their waists with sashes, and bound caps on them, just as the LORD had commanded Moses.

14 Then he brought the bull of the sin offering, and Aaron and his sons laid their hands on the head of the bull of the sin offering. 15 Next Moses slaughtered *it* and took the blood and with his finger put *some of it* around on the horns of the altar, and purified the altar. Then he poured out *the rest of* the blood at the base of the altar and consecrated it, to make atonement for it. 16 He also took all the fat that was on the entrails and the lobe of the liver, and the two kidneys and their fat; and Moses offered it up in smoke on the altar. 17 But the bull and its hide, its flesh, and its refuse he burned in the fire outside the camp, just as the LORD had commanded Moses.

18 Then he presented the ram of the burnt offering, and Aaron and his sons laid their hands on the head of the ram. 19 And Moses slaughtered *it* and sprinkled the blood around on the altar. 20 When he had cut the ram into its pieces, Moses offered up the head and the pieces and the suet in smoke. 21 After he had washed the entrails and the legs with water, Moses offered up the whole ram in smoke on the altar. It was a burnt offering for a soothing aroma; it was an offering by fire to the LORD, just as the LORD had commanded Moses.

22 Then he presented the second ram, the ram of ordination, and Aaron and his sons laid their hands on the head of the ram. 23 And Moses slaughtered *it* and took some of its blood and put it on the lobe of Aaron's right ear, and on the thumb of his right hand and on the big toe of his right foot. 24 He also had Aaron's sons

come near; and Moses put some of the blood on the lobe of their right ear, and on the thumb of their right hand and on the big toe of their right foot. Moses then sprinkled *the rest of* the blood around on the altar. 25 He then took the fat, and the fat tail, and all the fat that was on the entrails, and the lobe of the liver, the two kidneys and their fat, and the right thigh. 26 And from the basket of unleavened bread that was before the LORD, he took one unleavened cake and one cake of bread *mixed with* oil and one wafer, and placed *them* on the portions of fat and on the right thigh. 27 He then put all *these* on the hands of Aaron and on the hands of his sons, and presented them as a wave offering before the LORD. 28 Then Moses took them from their hands and offered them up in smoke on the altar with the burnt offering. They were an ordination offering for a soothing aroma; it was an offering by fire to the LORD. 29 Moses also took the breast and presented it as a wave offering before the LORD; it was Moses' portion of the ram of ordination, just as the LORD had commanded Moses.

30 So Moses took some of the anointing oil and some of the blood which was on the altar, and sprinkled it on Aaron, on his garments, on his sons, and on the garments of his sons with him; and he consecrated Aaron, his garments, and his sons, and the garments of his sons with him.

31 Then Moses said to Aaron and to his sons, "Boil the flesh at the doorway of the tent of meeting, and eat it there together with the bread which is in the basket of the ordination offering, just as I commanded, saying, 'Aaron and his sons shall eat it.' 32 And the remainder of the flesh and of the bread you shall burn in the fire. 33 And you shall not go outside the doorway of the tent of meeting for seven days, until the day that the period of your ordination is fulfilled; for he will ordain you through seven days. 34 The LORD has commanded *us* to do as has been done this day, to make atonement on your behalf. 35 At the doorway of the tent of meeting, moreover, you shall remain day and night for seven days and fulfill *your* duty to the LORD, so that you will not die; for so I have been commanded." 36 Aaron and his sons did all the things which the LORD had commanded through Moses.

Aaron Offers Sacrifices

9 Now it came about on the eighth day that Moses called Aaron and his sons and the elders of Israel; 2 and he said to Aaron, "Take for yourself a calf, a bull, as a sin offering and a ram as a burnt offering, *both* without defect, and offer *them* before the LORD. 3 Then you shall speak to the sons of Israel, saying, 'Take a male goat as a sin offering, and a calf and a lamb, both one year old, without defect, as a burnt offering, 4 and an ox and a ram for peace offerings, to sacrifice before the LORD, and a grain offering mixed with oil; for today the LORD will appear to you.'" 5 So they took what Moses had commanded to the front of the tent of meeting, and the whole congregation came near and stood before the LORD. 6 And Moses said, "This is the thing which the LORD has

commanded you to do, so that the glory of the LORD may appear to you." 7 Moses then said to Aaron, "Come near to the altar and offer your sin offering and your burnt offering, so that you may make atonement for yourself and for the people; then make the offering for the people, so that you may make atonement for them, just as the LORD has commanded."

8 So Aaron came near to the altar and slaughtered the calf of the sin offering which was for himself. 9 Aaron's sons then presented the blood to him; and he dipped his finger in the blood and put *some* on the horns of the altar, and poured out *the rest of* the blood at the base of the altar. 10 The fat and the kidneys and the lobe of the liver of the sin offering he then offered up in smoke on the altar, just as the LORD had commanded Moses. 11 The flesh and the hide, however, he burned with fire outside the camp.

12 Then he slaughtered the burnt offering; and Aaron's sons brought the blood to him, and he sprinkled it around on the altar. 13 They brought the burnt offering to him in pieces, with the head, and he offered *them* up in smoke on the altar. 14 He also washed the entrails and the legs, and offered *them* up in smoke with the burnt offering on the altar.

15 Then he presented the people's offering, and took the goat of the sin offering which was for the people, and slaughtered it and offered it for sin, like the first. 16 He also presented the burnt offering, and offered it according to the ordinance. 17 Next he presented the grain offering, and filled his hand with some of it and offered *it* up in smoke on the altar, besides the burnt offering of the morning.

18 Then he slaughtered the ox and the ram, the sacrifice of peace offerings which was for the people; and Aaron's sons brought the blood to him, and he sprinkled it around on the altar. 19 As for the portions of fat from the ox and from the ram, the fat tail, the *fat* covering, the kidneys, and the lobe of the liver, 20 they now placed the portions of fat on the breasts; and he offered them up in smoke on the altar. 21 But the breasts and the right thigh Aaron presented as a wave offering before the LORD, just as Moses had commanded.

22 Then Aaron lifted up his hands toward the people and blessed them, and he stepped down after making the sin offering, the burnt offering, and the peace offerings. 23 And Moses and Aaron went into the tent of meeting. When they came out and blessed the people, the glory of the LORD appeared to all the people. 24 Then fire went out from the LORD and consumed the burnt offering and the portions of fat on the altar; and when all the people saw *it,* they shouted and fell face downward.

The Sin of Nadab and Abihu

10 Now Nadab and Abihu, the sons of Aaron, took their respective firepans, and after putting fire in them, placed incense on the fire and offered strange fire before the LORD, which He had not commanded them. 2 And fire came out from the presence of the LORD and consumed them, and they died

before the LORD. 3 Then Moses said to Aaron, "It is what the LORD spoke, saying,

'By those who come near Me I will be treated as holy,
And before all the people I will be honored.'"

So Aaron, therefore, kept silent.

4 Moses called also to Mishael and Elzaphan, the sons of Aaron's uncle Uzziel, and said to them, "Come forward, carry your relatives away from the front of the sanctuary to *an area* outside of the camp." 5 So they came forward and carried them, *still* in their tunics, to *an area* outside the camp, just as Moses had said. 6 Then Moses said to Aaron and to his sons Eleazar and Ithamar, "Do not uncover your heads nor tear your clothes, so that you do not die and He does not become wrathful against all the congregation. But your kinsmen, the entire house of Israel, shall weep for the burning which the LORD has brought about. 7 You shall not even go out from the doorway of the tent of meeting, or you will die; for the LORD's anointing oil is upon you." So they did according to the word of Moses.

8 The LORD then spoke to Aaron, saying, 9 "Do not drink wine or strong drink, neither you nor your sons with you, when you come into the tent of meeting, so that you do not die—it is a permanent statute throughout your generations— 10 and to make a distinction between the holy and the profane, and between the unclean and the clean, 11 and so as to teach the sons of Israel all the statutes which the LORD has spoken to them through Moses."

12 Then Moses spoke to Aaron, and to his surviving sons, Eleazar and Ithamar, "Take the grain offering that is left over from the LORD's offerings by fire and eat it as unleavened bread beside the altar, for it is most holy. 13 You shall eat it in a holy place, because it is your allotted portion and your sons' allotted portion from the LORD's offerings by fire; for so I have been commanded. 14 The breast of the wave offering, however, and the thigh of the offering you may eat in a clean place, you and your sons and your daughters with you; for they have been given as your allotted portion and your sons' allotted portion from the sacrifices of the peace offerings of the sons of Israel. 15 They shall bring the thigh offered by lifting up and the breast offered by waving, along with the offerings by fire of the portions of fat, to present as a wave offering before the LORD; so it shall be a thing perpetually due you and your sons with you, just as the LORD has commanded."

16 But Moses searched carefully for the goat of the sin offering, and behold, it had been burned! So he was angry with Aaron's surviving sons Eleazar and Ithamar, saying, 17 "Why did you not eat the sin offering at the holy place? For it is most holy, and He gave it to you to take away the guilt of the congregation, to make atonement for them before the LORD. 18 Behold, since its blood had not been brought inside, into the sanctuary, you certainly should have eaten it in the sanctuary, just as I commanded!" 19 But Aaron said to Moses, "Behold, this *very* day they presented their sin offering and their burnt offering before the LORD. When things like these happened to me, if I had eaten a sin offering today, would it have been good in the sight of the LORD?" 20 When Moses heard *that,* it was good in his sight.

Laws about Animals for Food

11 The LORD spoke again to Moses and to Aaron, saying to them, 2 "Speak to the sons of Israel, saying, 'These are the creatures which you may eat from all the animals that are on the earth. 3 Whatever has a divided hoof, showing split hoofs, *and* chews the cud, among the animals, that you may eat. 4 Nevertheless, you are not to eat of these, among those which chew the cud, or among those which have a divided hoof: the camel, for though it chews cud, it does not have a divided hoof; it is unclean to you. 5 Likewise, the rock hyrax, for though it chews cud, it does not have a divided hoof; it is unclean to you. 6 The rabbit also, for though it chews cud, it does not have a divided hoof; it is unclean to you. 7 And the pig, for though it has a divided hoof, and *so* it shows a split hoof, it does not chew cud; it is unclean to you. 8 You shall not eat *any* of their flesh nor touch their carcasses; they are unclean to you.

9 'These you may eat, of whatever is in the water: everything that has fins and scales, in the water, in the seas, or in the rivers, you may eat. 10 But whatever is in the seas and in the rivers that does not have fins and scales among all the teeming life of the water, and among all the living creatures that are in the water, they are detestable things to you, 11 and they shall be detestable to you; you may not eat *any* of their flesh, and you shall detest their carcasses. 12 Whatever in the water does not have fins and scales is detestable to you.

Avoid the Unclean

13 'Moreover, these you shall detest among the birds; they are detestable, not to be eaten: the eagle, the vulture, and the buzzard, 14 the red kite, the falcon in its kind, 15 every raven in its kind, 16 the ostrich, the owl, the seagull, and the hawk in its kind, 17 the little owl, the cormorant, and the great owl, 18 the white owl, the pelican, and the carrion vulture, 19 the stork, the heron in its kinds, the hoopoe, and the bat.

20 'All the winged insects that walk on *all* fours are detestable to you. 21 Yet these you may eat among all the winged insects that walk on *all* fours: those which have jointed legs above their feet with which to jump on the earth. 22 These of them you may eat: the locust in its kinds, the devastating locust in its kinds, the cricket in its kinds, and the grasshopper in its kinds. 23 But all *other* winged insects which are four-footed are detestable to you.

24 'By these, moreover, you will be made unclean; whoever touches their carcasses becomes unclean until evening, 25 and whoever picks up any of their carcasses shall wash his clothes and be unclean until evening. 26 As for all the animals which have a divided hoof but do not show a split *hoof,* or do not chew the cud, they are unclean to you; whoever touches

them becomes unclean. 27 Also whatever walks on its paws, among all the creatures that walk on *all* fours, are unclean to you; whoever touches their carcasses becomes unclean until evening, 28 and the one who picks up their carcasses shall wash his clothes and be unclean until evening; they are unclean to you.

29 'Now these are to you the unclean among the swarming things which swarm on the earth: the mole, the mouse, and the great lizard in its kinds, 30 the gecko, the crocodile, the lizard, the sand reptile, and the chameleon. 31 These are to you the unclean among all the swarming things; whoever touches them when they are dead becomes unclean until evening. 32 Also anything on which one of them may fall when they are dead becomes unclean, including any wooden article, or clothing, or a hide, or a sack—any article of which use is made—it shall be put in the water and be unclean until evening, then it becomes clean. 33 As for any earthenware vessel into which one of them may fall, whatever is in it becomes unclean and you shall break the vessel. 34 Any of the food which may be eaten, on which water comes, shall become unclean, and any liquid which may be drunk in every vessel shall become unclean. 35 Moreover, everything on which part of their carcass may fall becomes unclean; an oven or a stove shall be smashed; they are unclean and shall continue as unclean to you. 36 Nevertheless, a spring or a cistern collecting water shall be clean, though the one who touches their carcass shall be unclean. 37 Now if a part of their carcass falls on any seed for sowing which is to be sown, it is clean. 38 But if water is put on the seed and a part of their carcass falls on it, it is unclean to you.

39 'Also if one of the animals dies which you have for food, the one who touches its carcass becomes unclean until evening. 40 He, too, who eats some of its carcass shall wash his clothes and be unclean until evening, and the one who picks up its carcass shall wash his clothes and be unclean until evening.

41 'Now every swarming thing that swarms on the earth is detestable, not to be eaten. 42 Whatever crawls on its belly, and whatever walks on *all* fours, whatever has many feet, in regard to every swarming thing that swarms on the earth, you shall not eat them, because they are detestable. 43 Do not make yourselves detestable through any of the swarming things that swarm; and you shall not make yourselves unclean with them so that you become unclean. 44 For I am the LORD your God. Consecrate yourselves therefore, and be holy, because I am holy. And you shall not make yourselves unclean with any of the swarming things that swarm on the earth. 45 For I am the LORD who brought you up from the land of Egypt, to be your God; so you shall be holy, because I am holy.' "

46 This is the law regarding the animal and the bird, and every living thing that moves in the waters and everything that swarms on the earth, 47 to make a distinction between the unclean and the clean, and between the edible creature and the creature which is not to be eaten.

Laws of Motherhood

12 Then the LORD spoke to Moses, saying, 2 "Speak to the sons of Israel, saying: 'When a woman gives birth and delivers a male *child,* then she shall be unclean for seven days; as *she is* in the days of her menstruation, she shall be unclean. 3 Then on the eighth day the flesh of his foreskin shall be circumcised. 4 And she shall stay *at home* in *her condition of* blood purification for thirty-three days; she shall not touch any consecrated thing, nor enter the sanctuary until the days of her purification are completed. 5 But if she gives birth to a female *child,* then she shall be unclean for two weeks, as in her menstruation; and she shall stay *at home* in *her condition of* blood purification for sixty-six days.

6 'When the days of her purification are completed, for a son or for a daughter, she shall bring to the priest at the doorway of the tent of meeting a one-year-old lamb as a burnt offering and a young pigeon or a turtledove as a sin offering. 7 Then he shall offer it before the LORD and make atonement for her, and she shall be cleansed from the flow of her blood. This is the law for her who gives birth to *a child, whether* a male or a female. 8 But if she cannot afford a lamb, then she shall take two turtledoves or two young doves, the one as a burnt offering and the other as a sin offering; and the priest shall make atonement for her, and she will be clean.' "

The Test for Leprosy

13 Then the LORD spoke to Moses and to Aaron, saying, 2 "When someone has on the skin of his body a swelling, or a scab, or a bright spot, and it becomes an infection of 'leprosy on the skin of his body, then he shall be brought to Aaron the priest or to one of his sons the priests. 3 The priest shall look at the infected area on the skin of the body, and if the hair in the infection has turned white and the infection appears to be deeper than the skin of his body, it is an infection of leprosy; when the priest has looked at him, he shall pronounce him unclean. 4 But if the bright spot is white on the skin of his body, and it does not appear to be deeper than the skin, and the hair on it has not turned white, then the priest shall isolate *the person who has* the infection for seven days. 5 Then the priest shall look at him on the seventh day, and if in his eyes the infection has not changed *and* the infection has not spread on the skin, then the priest shall isolate him for seven more days. 6 The priest shall then look at him again on the seventh day, and if the infected area has faded and the infection has not spread on the skin, then the priest shall pronounce him clean; it is *only* a rash. And he shall wash his clothes and be clean.

7 "But if the rash spreads farther on the skin after he has shown himself to the priest for his cleansing, he shall appear again to the priest. 8 And the priest shall look, and if the rash has

---

13:2 1 I.e., or a serious, unspecified disease, and so throughout the ch

spread on the skin, then the priest shall pronounce him unclean; it is leprosy.

9 "When the infection of leprosy is on someone, then he shall be brought to the priest. 10 The priest shall then look, and if there is a white swelling on the skin, and it has turned the hair white, and there is new raw flesh in the swelling, 11 it is a chronic leprosy on the skin of his body, and the priest shall pronounce him unclean; he shall not isolate him, for he is unclean. 12 If the leprosy breaks out farther on the skin, and the leprosy covers all the skin of *the person who has* the infection from his head even to his feet, as far as the priest can see, 13 then the priest shall look, and behold, *if* the leprosy has covered his entire body, he shall pronounce *the one who has* the infection clean; it has all turned white *and* he is clean. 14 But whenever raw flesh appears on him, he shall be unclean. 15 The priest shall look at the raw flesh, and he shall pronounce him unclean; the raw flesh is unclean, it is leprosy. 16 Or if the raw flesh turns back and is changed to white, then he shall come to the priest, 17 and the priest shall look at him, and behold, *if* the infected area has turned white, then the priest shall pronounce *the one who has* the infection clean; he is clean.

18 "Now when the body has a boil on its skin and it is healed, 19 and in the place of the boil there is a white swelling or a reddish-white, bright spot, then it shall be shown to the priest; 20 and the priest shall look, and behold, *if* it appears to be deeper than the skin, and the hair on it has turned white, then the priest shall pronounce him unclean; it is the infection of leprosy, it has broken out in the boil. 21 But if the priest looks at it, and behold, there are no white hairs in it and it is not deeper than the skin and is faded, then the priest shall isolate him for seven days; 22 and if it spreads farther on the skin, then the priest shall pronounce him unclean; it is an infection. 23 But if the bright spot remains in its place and does not spread, it is *only* the scar of the boil; and the priest shall pronounce him clean.

24 "Or if the body sustains in its skin a burn by fire, and the raw *flesh* of the burn becomes a bright spot, reddish-white, or white, 25 then the priest shall look at it. And if the hair in the bright spot has turned white and it appears to be deeper than the skin, it is leprosy; it has broken out in the burn. Therefore, the priest shall pronounce him unclean; it is an infection of leprosy. 26 But if the priest looks at it, and indeed, there is no white hair in the bright spot and it is no deeper than the skin, but is dim, then the priest shall isolate him for seven days; 27 and the priest shall look at him on the seventh day. If it spreads farther in the skin, then the priest shall pronounce him unclean; it is an infection of leprosy. 28 But if the bright spot remains in its place and has not spread in the skin, but is dim, it is the swelling from the burn; and the priest shall pronounce him clean, for it is *only* the scar of the burn.

29 "Now if a man or woman has an infection on the head or on the beard, 30 then the priest shall look at the infection, and if it appears to be deeper than the skin and there is thin yellowish hair in it, then the priest shall pronounce him unclean; it is a scale, it is leprosy of the head or of the beard. 31 But if the priest looks at the infection of the scale, and indeed, it appears to be no deeper than the skin and there is no black hair in it, then the priest shall isolate *the person* with the scaly infection for seven days. 32 And on the seventh day the priest shall look at the infection, and if the scale has not spread and no yellowish hair has grown in it, and the appearance of the scale is no deeper than the skin, 33 then he shall shave himself, but he shall not shave the scale; and the priest shall isolate *the person* with the scale for seven more days. 34 Then on the seventh day the priest shall look at the scale, and if the scale has not spread in the skin and it appears to be no deeper than the skin, the priest shall pronounce him clean; and he shall wash his clothes and be clean. 35 But if the scale spreads farther in the skin after his cleansing, 36 then the priest shall look at him, and if the scale has spread on the skin, the priest need not look for the yellowish hair; he is unclean. 37 If in his sight the scale has remained, however, and black hair has grown in it, the scale has healed, *and* he is clean; and the priest shall pronounce him clean.

38 "When a man or a woman has bright spots on the skin of the body, white bright spots, 39 then the priest shall look, and if the bright spots on the skin of their bodies are a faint white, it is eczema that has broken out on the skin; he is clean.

40 "Now if a man loses the hair of his head, he is *only* bald; he is clean. 41 And if his head becomes bald at the front and sides, he is bald on the forehead; he is clean. 42 But if on the bald head or the bald forehead there occurs a reddish-white infection, it is leprosy breaking out on his bald head or on his bald forehead. 43 Then the priest shall look at him; and if the swelling of the infection is reddish-white on his bald head or on his bald forehead, like the appearance of leprosy in the skin of the body, 44 he is a leprous man, he is unclean. The priest must pronounce him unclean; his infection is on his head.

45 "As for the person who has the leprous infection, his clothes shall be torn and *the hair of* his head shall be uncovered, and he shall cover his mustache and call out, 'Unclean! Unclean!' 46 He shall remain unclean all the days during which he has the infection; he is unclean. He shall live alone; he shall live outside the camp.

47 "When a garment has a mark of leprosy in it, whether it is a wool garment or a linen garment, 48 whether in ¹warp or ²woof, of linen or of wool, whether in leather or in any article made of leather, 49 if the ¹mark is greenish or reddish in the garment or in the leather, whether in the warp or in the woof, or in any article of leather, it is a leprous mark and it shall be shown to the priest. 50 Then the priest shall look at the mark and shall quarantine the

---

13:48 ¹ I.e., lengthwise material in weaving   ² I.e., material woven crosswise   13:49 ¹ Lit *infestation; possibly material already contaminated prior to weaving*

article with the mark for seven days. 51 He shall then look at the mark on the seventh day; if the mark has spread in the garment, whether in the ¹warp or in the woof, or in the leather, whatever the purpose for which the leather is used, the mark is a leprous malignancy, it is unclean. 52 So he shall burn the garment, whether *it is* the ¹warp or the woof, in wool or in linen, or any article of leather, in which the mark occurs; for it is a leprous malignancy. It shall be burned in the fire.

53 "But if the priest looks, and indeed the mark has not spread in the garment, either in the ¹warp or in the woof, or in any article of leather, 54 then the priest shall order them to wash the thing in which the mark occurs, and he shall quarantine it for seven more days. 55 After the article with the mark has been washed, the priest shall again look, and if the mark has not changed its appearance, even *if* the mark has not spread, it is unclean; you shall burn it in the fire, whether an eating away has produced bareness on the back or on the front of it.

56 "But if the priest looks, and indeed the mark has faded after it has been washed, then he shall tear it out of the garment or out of the leather, whether from the ¹warp or from the woof; 57 yet if it appears again in the garment, whether in the warp or in the woof, or in any article of leather, it is an outbreak; the article with the mark shall be burned in the fire. 58 But the garment, whether the warp or the woof, or any article of leather from which the mark has disappeared when you washed it, shall then be washed a second time and will be clean."

59 This is the law for the mark of leprosy in a garment of wool or linen, whether in the warp or in the woof, or in any article of leather, for pronouncing it clean or unclean.

Law of Cleansing a Person with Leprosy

14 Then the LORD spoke to Moses, saying, 2 "This shall be the law of the person with leprosy on the day of his cleansing. Now he shall be brought to the priest; 3 and the priest shall go out to *a place* outside of the camp. Then the priest shall look, and if the leprous infection has been healed in the person with leprosy, 4 then the priest shall give orders to take two live clean birds, cedar wood, a scarlet string, and hyssop for the one who is to be cleansed. 5 The priest shall also give orders to slaughter the one bird in an earthenware vessel over running water. 6 *As for* the live bird, he shall take it together with the cedar wood, the scarlet string, and the hyssop, and shall dip them and the live bird in the blood of the bird that was slaughtered over the running water. 7 He shall then sprinkle seven times the one who is to be cleansed from the leprosy and shall pronounce him clean, and shall let the live bird go free over the open field. 8 The one to be cleansed shall then wash his clothes and shave off all his hair, and bathe in water and be clean. And afterward he may enter the camp,

but he shall stay outside his tent for seven days. 9 Then it shall be on the seventh day that he shall shave off all his hair: he shall shave his head and his beard and his eyebrows, even all his hair. He shall then wash his clothes and bathe his body in water and be clean.

10 "Now on the eighth day he is to take two male lambs without defect, and a yearling ewe lamb without defect, and three-tenths *of an* ¹ephah of fine flour mixed with oil as a grain offering, and one ²log of oil; 11 and the priest who is going to pronounce *him* clean shall present the person to be cleansed and the offerings before the LORD at the doorway of the tent of meeting. 12 Then the priest shall take the one male lamb and bring it as a guilt offering, with the ¹log of oil, and present them as a wave offering before the LORD. 13 Next he shall slaughter the male lamb in the place where they slaughter the sin offering and the burnt offering, at the place of the sanctuary— for the guilt offering, like the sin offering, belongs to the priest; it is most holy. 14 The priest shall then take some of the blood of the guilt offering, and the priest shall put *it* on the lobe of the right ear of the one to be cleansed, and on the thumb of his right hand, and on the big toe of his right foot. 15 The priest shall also take some of the ¹log of oil, and pour *it* into his left palm; 16 the priest shall then dip his right-hand finger into the oil that is in his left palm, and with his finger sprinkle some of the oil seven times before the LORD. 17 Of the remaining oil which is in his palm, the priest shall put some on the right ear lobe of the one to be cleansed, and on the thumb of his right hand, and on the big toe of his right foot, on the blood of the guilt offering; 18 as for the rest of the oil that is in the priest's palm, he shall put *it* on the head of the one to be cleansed. So the priest shall make atonement on his behalf before the LORD. 19 The priest shall next offer the sin offering and make atonement for the one to be cleansed from his uncleanness. Then afterward, he shall slaughter the burnt offering. 20 The priest shall offer up the burnt offering and the grain offering on the altar. So the priest shall make atonement for him, and he will be clean.

21 "But if he is poor and his means are insufficient, then he is to take one male lamb for a guilt offering as a wave offering to make atonement for him, and a tenth *of an* ¹ephah of fine flour mixed with oil as a grain offering, and a ²log of oil, 22 and two turtledoves or two young doves, which are within his means. The one shall be a sin offering, and the other a burnt offering. 23 Then on the eighth day he shall bring them for his cleansing to the priest, at the doorway of the tent of meeting, before the LORD. 24 The priest shall take the lamb of the guilt offering and the ¹log of oil, and the priest shall offer them as a wave offering before the LORD. 25 Next he shall slaughter the lamb of the guilt offering; and the priest is to take some of the blood of the guilt offering and put *it* on

---

13:51 1 See notes v 48   13:52 1 See notes v 48   13:53 1 See notes v 48   13:56 1 See notes v 48
14:10 1 About 1 cubic foot or 0.03 cubic meters   2 About 0.6 pt. or 0.3 liter   14:12 1 About 0.6 pt. or 0.3 liter   14:15 1 About 0.6 pt. or 0.3 liter   14:21 1 About 1 cubic foot or 0.03 cubic meters   2 About 0.6 pt. or 0.3 liter   14:24 1 About 0.6 pt. or 0.3 liter

the lobe of the right ear of the one to be cleansed, and on the thumb of his right hand, and on the big toe of his right foot. 26 The priest shall also pour some of the oil into his left palm; 27 and with his right-hand finger the priest shall sprinkle some of the oil that is in his left palm seven times before the LORD. 28 The priest shall then put some of the oil that is in his palm on the lobe of the right ear of the one to be cleansed, and on the thumb of his right hand, and on the big toe of his right foot, on the place of the blood of the guilt offering. 29 Moreover, the rest of the oil that is in the priest's palm, he shall put on the head of the one to be cleansed, to make atonement on his behalf before the LORD. 30 He shall then offer one of the turtledoves or young doves, which are within his means. 31 *He shall offer* what he can afford, the one as a sin offering and the other as a burnt offering, together with the grain offering. So the priest shall make atonement before the LORD on behalf of the one to be cleansed. 32 This is the law *for him* in whom there is an infection of leprosy, whose means are limited for his cleansing."

Cleansing a Leprous House

33 The LORD further spoke to Moses and to Aaron, saying:

34 "When you enter the land of Canáan, which I am giving you as a possession, and I put a spot of leprosy on a house in the land of your possession, 35 then the one who owns the house shall come and tell the priest, saying, '*Something* like a spot *of leprosy* has become visible to me in the house.' 36 The priest shall then command that they empty the house before the priest goes in to look at the spot, so that everything in the house need not become unclean; and afterward the priest shall go in to look at the house. 37 So he shall look at the spot, and if the spot on the walls of the house has greenish or reddish depressions and appears deeper than the surface, 38 the priest shall come out of the house, to the doorway, and quarantine the house for seven days. 39 Then the priest shall return on the seventh day and make an inspection. If the spot has indeed spread on the walls of the house, 40 the priest shall order them to pull out the stones with the spot on them and throw them away at an unclean place outside the city. 41 And he shall have the house scraped all around inside, and they shall dump the plaster that they scrape off at an unclean place outside the city. 42 Then they shall take other stones and replace the *discarded* stones, and he shall take other plaster and replaster the house.

43 "If, however, the spot breaks out again in the house after he has pulled out the stones and scraped the house, and after it has been replastered, 44 then the priest shall come in and make an inspection. If he sees that the spot has indeed spread in the house, it is a malignant spot in the house; it is unclean. 45 *The owner* shall therefore tear down the house, its stones, its timbers, and all the plaster of the house, and he shall take *them* outside the city to an unclean place. 46 Moreover, whoever goes into the house during the time that he has quarantined it, becomes unclean until evening. 47 Likewise, whoever lies down in the house shall wash his clothes, and whoever eats in the house shall wash his clothes.

48 "If, on the other hand, the priest comes in and makes an inspection and the spot has not indeed spread in the house after the house has been replastered, then the priest shall pronounce the house clean because the spot has not reappeared. 49 To cleanse the house then, he shall take two birds, cedar wood, a scarlet string, and hyssop, 50 and he shall slaughter the one bird in an earthenware vessel over running water. 51 Then he shall take the cedar wood, the hyssop, and the scarlet string, with the live bird, and dip them in the blood of the slaughtered bird as well as in the running water, and sprinkle the house seven times. 52 So he shall cleanse the house with the blood of the bird and with the running water, along with the live bird, the cedar wood, the hyssop, and the scarlet string. 53 However, he shall let the live bird go free outside the city into the open field. So he shall make atonement for the house, and it will be clean."

54 This is the law for any spot of leprosy— even for a scale, 55 and for the leprous garment or house, 56 and for a swelling, for a scab, and for a bright spot— 57 to teach when they are unclean and when they are clean. This is the law of leprosy.

Cleansing Unhealthiness

15 The LORD also spoke to Moses and to Aaron, saying, 2 "Speak to the sons of Israel, and say to them, 'When any man has a discharge from his body, his discharge is unclean. 3 This, moreover, shall be his uncleanness in his discharge: it is his uncleanness whether his body allows its discharge to flow or whether his body obstructs its discharge. 4 Every bed on which the man with the discharge lies becomes unclean, and everything on which he sits becomes unclean. 5 Anyone, moreover, who touches his bed shall wash his clothes and bathe in water and be unclean until evening; 6 and whoever sits on the thing on which the man with the discharge has been sitting, shall wash his clothes and bathe in water and be unclean until evening. 7 Also whoever touches the man with the discharge shall wash his clothes and bathe in water and be unclean until evening. 8 Or if the man with the discharge spits on one who is clean, he too shall wash his clothes and bathe in water and be unclean until evening. 9 Every saddle on which the man with the discharge rides becomes unclean. 10 Whoever then touches any of the things which were under him shall be unclean until evening, and the one who carries them shall wash his clothes and bathe in water and be unclean until evening. 11 Likewise, whomever the man with the discharge touches without having rinsed his hands in water shall wash his clothes and bathe in water and be unclean until evening. 12 However, an earthenware vessel which the man with the discharge touches shall be broken, and every wooden vessel shall be rinsed in water.

13 'Now when the man with the discharge

becomes cleansed from his discharge, then he shall count off for himself seven days for his cleansing; he shall then wash his clothes and bathe his body in running water and will become clean. 14 Then on the eighth day he shall take for himself two turtledoves or two young doves, and come before the LORD to the doorway of the tent of meeting and give them to the priest; 15 and the priest shall offer them, one as a sin offering and the other as a burnt offering. So the priest shall make atonement on his behalf before the LORD because of his discharge.

16 'Now if a man has a seminal emission, he shall bathe all his body in water and be unclean until evening. 17 As for any garment or any leather on which there is a seminal emission, it shall be washed with water and be unclean until evening. 18 If a man sleeps with a woman *so that* there is a seminal emission, they shall both bathe in water and be unclean until evening.

19 'When a woman has a discharge, *if* her discharge in her body is blood, she shall continue in her menstrual impurity for seven days; and whoever touches her shall be unclean until evening. 20 Everything also on which she lies during her menstrual impurity shall be unclean, and everything on which she sits shall be unclean. 21 Anyone who touches her bed shall wash his clothes and bathe in water and be unclean until evening. 22 Whoever touches any object on which she sits shall wash his clothes and bathe in water and be unclean until evening. 23 Whether it be on the bed or on the thing on which she is sitting, when he touches it, he shall be unclean until evening. 24 If a man actually sleeps with her so that her menstrual impurity is on him, he shall be unclean seven days, and every bed on which he lies shall be unclean.

25 'Now if a woman has a discharge of her blood for many days, not at the period of her menstrual impurity, or if she has a discharge beyond that period, for all the days of her impure discharge she shall continue as though in her menstrual impurity; she is unclean. 26 Any bed on which she lies all the days of her discharge shall be to her like her bed at menstruation; and every object on which she sits shall be unclean, like her uncleanness at that time. 27 Likewise, whoever touches them shall be unclean, and shall wash his clothes and bathe in water and be unclean until evening. 28 When she becomes clean from her discharge, she shall count off for herself seven days; and afterward she will be clean. 29 Then on the eighth day she shall take for herself two turtledoves or two young doves, and bring them to the priest, to the doorway of the tent of meeting. 30 And the priest shall offer the one as a sin offering, and the other as a burnt offering. So the priest shall make atonement on her behalf before the LORD because of her impure discharge.'

31 "And *so* you shall keep the sons of Israel separated from their uncleanness, so that they will not die in their uncleanness by their defiling My tabernacle that is among them." 32 This is the law for the one with a discharge, and for the man who has a seminal emission so that he is unclean by it, 33 and for the woman who is ill because of menstrual impurity, and for the one who has a discharge, whether a male or a female, or a man who sleeps with an unclean woman.

Law of Atonement

16 Now the LORD spoke to Moses after the death of the two sons of Aaron, when they had approached the presence of the LORD and died. 2 The LORD said to Moses:

"Tell your brother Aaron that he shall not enter at any time into the Holy Place inside the veil, before the 1 atoning cover which is on the ark, or he will die; for I will appear in the cloud over the atoning cover. 3 Aaron shall enter the Holy Place with this: with a bull as a sin offering and a ram as a burnt offering. 4 He shall put on the holy linen tunic, and the linen undergarments shall be next to his body, and he shall be wrapped about the waist with the linen sash and the linen turban wound around *his forehead* (these are holy garments). He shall bathe his body in water and put them on. 5 And he shall take from the congregation of the sons of Israel two male goats as a sin offering, and one ram as a burnt offering. 6 Then Aaron shall offer the bull as the sin offering, which is for himself, so that he may make atonement for himself and for his household. 7 He shall then take the two goats and present them before the LORD at the doorway of the tent of meeting. 8 Aaron shall cast lots for the two goats, one lot for the LORD and the other lot for the 1 scapegoat. 9 Then Aaron shall offer the goat on which the lot for the LORD fell, and make it a sin offering. 10 But the goat on which the lot for the scapegoat fell shall be presented alive before the LORD, to make atonement upon it, to send it into the wilderness as the scapegoat.

11 "Then Aaron shall offer the bull of the sin offering which is for himself and make atonement for himself and for his household, and he shall slaughter the bull of the sin offering which is for himself. 12 He shall take a firepan full of coals of fire from upon the altar before the LORD and two handfuls of finely ground sweet incense, and bring *it* inside the veil. 13 He shall put the incense on the fire before the LORD, so that the cloud of incense may cover the atoning cover that is on *the ark of* the testimony, otherwise he will die. 14 Moreover, he shall take some of the blood of the bull and sprinkle *it* with his finger on the atoning cover on the east *side;* also in front of the atoning cover he shall sprinkle some of the blood with his finger seven times.

15 "Then he shall slaughter the goat of the sin offering, which is for the people, and bring its blood inside the veil and do with its blood as he did with the blood of the bull, and sprinkle it on the atoning cover and in front of the atoning cover. 16 He shall make atonement for the Holy Place, because of the impurities of the

sons of Israel and because of their unlawful acts regarding all their sins; and he shall do so for the tent of meeting which remains with them in the midst of their impurities. **17** When he goes in to make atonement in the Holy Place, no one shall be in the tent of meeting until he comes out, so that he may make atonement for himself and for his household, and for all the assembly of Israel. **18** Then he shall go out to the altar that is before the LORD and make atonement for it; he shall take some of the blood from the bull and *some* of the blood from the goat, and put it on the horns of the altar on all sides. **19** With his finger he shall sprinkle some of the blood on it seven times and cleanse it, and consecrate it from the impurities of the sons of Israel.

20 "When he finishes atoning for the Holy Place and the tent of meeting and the altar, he shall offer the live goat. **21** Then Aaron shall lay both of his hands on the head of the live goat, and confess over it all the wrongdoings of the sons of Israel and all their unlawful acts regarding all their sins; and he shall place them on the head of the goat and send *it* away into the wilderness by the hand of a man who *stands* ready. **22** Then the goat shall carry on itself all their wrongdoings to an isolated territory; he shall release the goat in the wilderness.

23 "Then Aaron shall come into the tent of meeting and take off the linen garments which he put on when he went into the Holy Place, and shall leave them there. **24** And he shall bathe his body with water in a holy place and put on his clothes, and come out and offer the burnt offering and the burnt offering of the people, and make atonement for himself and for the people. **25** Then he shall offer up in smoke the fat of the sin offering on the altar. **26** The one who released the goat as the scapegoat shall wash his clothes and bathe his body with water; then afterward he shall come into the camp. **27** But the bull of the sin offering and the goat of the sin offering, whose blood was brought in to make atonement in the Holy Place, shall be taken outside the camp, and they shall burn their hides, their flesh, and their refuse in the fire. **28** Then the one who burns them shall wash his clothes and bathe his body with water; and afterward he shall come into the camp.

An Annual Atonement

29 "*This* shall be a permanent statute for you: in the seventh month, on the tenth day of the month, you shall humble yourselves and not do any work, whether the native, or the stranger who resides among you; **30** for it is on this day that atonement shall be made for you to cleanse you; you will be clean from all your sins before the LORD. **31** It is to be a Sabbath of solemn rest for you, so that you may humble yourselves; it is a permanent statute. **32** So the priest who is anointed and ordained to serve as priest in his father's place shall make atonement: he shall put on the linen garments, the holy garments, **33** and make atonement for the holy sanctuary, and he shall make atonement for the tent of meeting and for the altar. He

shall also make atonement for the priests and for all the people of the assembly. **34** Now you shall have this as a permanent statute, to make atonement for the sons of Israel for all their sins once every year." And just as the LORD had commanded Moses, *so* he did.

Blood for Atonement

17 Then the LORD spoke to Moses, saying, **2** "Speak to Aaron and to his sons and to all the sons of Israel, and say to them, 'This is what the LORD has commanded, saying, **3** "Anyone from the house of Israel who slaughters an ox, a lamb, or a goat in the camp, or slaughters it outside the camp, **4** and has not brought it to the doorway of the tent of meeting to present *it* as an offering to the LORD in front of the tabernacle of the LORD, bloodshed is to be counted against that person. He has shed blood, and that person shall be cut off from among his people. **5** *This shall be done* so that the sons of Israel will bring their sacrifices which they were sacrificing in the open field—so that they will bring them to the LORD at the doorway of the tent of meeting to the priest, and sacrifice them as sacrifices of peace offerings to the LORD. **6** The priest shall sprinkle the blood on the altar of the LORD at the doorway of the tent of meeting, and offer up the fat in smoke as a soothing aroma to the LORD. **7** And they shall no longer offer their sacrifices to the goat demons with which they play the prostitute. This shall be a permanent statute to them throughout their generations."'

8 "Then you shall say to them, 'Anyone from the house of Israel, or from the strangers who reside among them, who offers a burnt offering or sacrifice, **9** and does not bring it to the doorway of the tent of meeting to offer it to the LORD, that person also shall be cut off from his people.

10 'And anyone from the house of Israel, or from the strangers who reside among them, who eats any blood, I will set My face against that person who eats the blood, and will cut him off from among his people. **11** For the life of the flesh is in the blood, and I have given it to you on the altar to make atonement for your souls; for it is the blood by reason of the life that makes atonement.' **12** Therefore I said to the sons of Israel, 'No person among you may eat blood, nor may any stranger who resides among you eat blood.' **13** So when anyone from the sons of Israel, or from the strangers who reside among them, while hunting catches an animal or a bird which may be eaten, he shall pour out its blood and cover it with dirt.

14 "For *as for the* life of all flesh, its blood is *identified* with its life. Therefore I said to the sons of Israel, 'You are not to eat the blood of any flesh, for the life of all flesh is its blood; whoever eats it shall be cut off.' **15** And any person who eats an animal which dies or is torn *by animals,* whether he is a native or a stranger, shall wash his clothes and bathe in water, and remain unclean until evening; then he will become clean. **16** But if he does not wash *his clothes* and bathe his body, then he shall bear *the responsibility for* his guilt."

Laws on Immoral Relations

18 Then the LORD spoke to Moses, saying, 2 "Speak to the sons of Israel and say to them, 'I am the LORD your God. 3 You shall not do what is done in the land of Egypt where you lived, nor are you to do what is done in the land of Canaan where I am bringing you; you shall not walk in their statutes. 4 You are to perform My judgments and keep My statutes, to live in accord with them; I am the LORD your God. 5 So you shall keep My statutes and My judgments, which, *if* a person follows them, then he will live by them; I am the LORD.

6 'None *of you* shall approach any blood relative of his to uncover nakedness; I am the LORD. 7 You shall not uncover the nakedness of your father, that is, the nakedness of your mother. She is your mother; you are not to uncover her nakedness. 8 You shall not uncover the nakedness of your father's wife; it is your father's nakedness. 9 *As for* the nakedness of your sister, *either* your father's daughter or your mother's daughter, *whether* born in the household or born outside *the household,* you shall not uncover their nakedness. 10 The nakedness of your son's daughter or your daughter's daughter, their nakedness you shall not uncover; for their nakedness is yours. 11 The nakedness of your father's wife's daughter, born to your father, she is your sister; you shall not uncover her nakedness. 12 You shall not uncover the nakedness of your father's sister; she is your father's blood relative. 13 You shall not uncover the nakedness of your mother's sister, for she is your mother's blood relative. 14 You shall not uncover the nakedness of your father's brother. You shall not approach his wife; she is your aunt. 15 You shall not uncover the nakedness of your daughter-in-law. She is your son's wife; you shall not uncover her nakedness. 16 You shall not uncover the nakedness of your brother's wife; it is your brother's nakedness. 17 You shall not uncover the nakedness of a woman and of her daughter, nor shall you take her son's daughter or her daughter's daughter, to uncover her nakedness; they are blood relatives. It is an outrageous sin. 18 And you shall not marry a woman in addition to her sister as a second wife while she is alive, to uncover her nakedness.

19 'Also you shall not approach a woman to uncover her nakedness during her menstrual impurity. 20 And you shall not have sexual intercourse with your neighbor's wife, to be defiled with her. 21 You shall not give any of your children to offer them to Molech, nor shall you profane the name of your God; I am the LORD. 22 You shall not sleep with a male as one sleeps with a female; it is an abomination. 23 Also you shall not have sexual intercourse with any animal to be defiled with it, nor shall any woman stand before an animal to mate with it; it is a perversion.

24 'Do not defile yourselves by any of these things; for by all these things the nations which I am driving out from you have become defiled. 25 For the land has become defiled, therefore I have brought its punishment upon it, so the land has vomited out its inhabitants.

26 But as for you, you are to keep My statutes and My judgments, and you shall not do any of these abominations, *neither* the native, nor the stranger who resides among you 27 (for the people of the land who were *there* before you did all these abominations, and the land has become defiled), 28 so that the land will not vomit you out should you defile it, as it has vomited out the nation which was *there* before you. 29 For whoever does any of these abominations, those persons who do *so* shall be cut off from among their people. 30 So you are to keep your commitment to Me not to practice any of the abominable customs which have been practiced before you, so that you do not defile yourselves with them; I am the LORD your God.'"

Idolatry Forbidden

19 Then the LORD spoke to Moses, saying: 2 "Speak to all the congregation of the sons of Israel and say to them, 'You shall be holy, for I the LORD your God am holy. 3 Every one of you shall revere his mother and his father, and you shall keep My Sabbaths; I am the LORD your God. 4 Do not turn to idols or make for yourselves cast metal gods; I am the LORD your God.

5 'Now when you offer a sacrifice of peace offerings to the LORD, you shall offer it so that you may be accepted. 6 It shall be eaten on the same day you offer *it,* and on the next day; but what remains until the third day shall be burned with fire. 7 So if it is eaten at all on the third day, it is unclean; it will not be accepted. 8 And everyone who eats it will bear *the consequences for* his guilt, because he has profaned the holy thing of the LORD; and that person shall be cut off from his people.

Various Laws

9 'Now when you reap the harvest of your land, you shall not reap to the very edges of your field, nor shall you gather the gleanings of your harvest. 10 And you shall not glean your vineyard, nor shall you gather the fallen grapes of your vineyard; you shall leave them for the needy and for the stranger. I am the LORD your God.

11 'You shall not steal, nor deal falsely, nor lie to one another. 12 And you shall not swear falsely by My name, so as to profane the name of your God; I am the LORD.

13 'You shall not oppress your neighbor, nor rob *him.* The wages of a hired worker are not to remain with you all night until morning. 14 You shall not curse a person who is deaf, nor put a stumbling block before a person who is blind, but you shall revere your God; I am the LORD.

15 'You shall not do injustice in judgment; you shall not show partiality to the poor nor give preference to the great, but you are to judge your neighbor fairly. 16 You shall not go about as a slanderer among your people; *and* you are not to jeopardize the life of your neighbor. I am the LORD.

17 'You shall not hate your fellow countryman in your heart; you may certainly rebuke your neighbor, but you are not to incur

sin because of him. 18 You shall not take vengeance, nor hold any grudge against the sons of your people, but you shall love your neighbor as yourself; I am the LORD.

19 'You are to keep My statutes. You shall not cross-breed two kinds of your cattle; you shall not sow your field with two kinds of seed, nor wear a garment of two kinds of material mixed together.

20 'Now if a man has sexual relations with a woman who is a slave acquired for *another* man, but who has in no way been redeemed nor given her freedom, there shall be punishment; they shall not, *however,* be put to death, because she was not free. 21 He shall bring his guilt offering to the LORD to the doorway of the tent of meeting, a ram as a guilt offering. 22 The priest shall also make atonement for him with the ram of the guilt offering before the LORD for his sin which he has committed, and the sin which he has committed will be forgiven him.

23 'Now when you enter the land and plant all kinds of trees for food, then you shall count their fruit as forbidden. For three years it shall be forbidden to you; *it* shall not be eaten. 24 And in the fourth year all its fruit shall be holy, an offering of praise to the LORD. 25 But in the fifth year you shall eat its fruit, so that its yield may increase for you; I am the LORD your God.

26 'You shall not eat *any meat* with the blood. You shall not practice divination nor soothsaying. 27 You shall not round off the hairline of your heads, nor trim the edges of your beard. 28 You shall not make any cuts in your body for the dead, nor make any tattoo marks on yourselves: I am the LORD.

29 'Do not profane your daughter by making her a prostitute, so that the land does not fall into prostitution, and the land *does not* become full of outrageous sin. 30 You shall keep My Sabbaths and revere My sanctuary; I am the LORD.

31 'Do not turn to mediums or spiritists; do not seek them out to be defiled by them. I am the LORD your God.

32 'You shall stand up in the presence of the grayheaded and honor elders, and you shall fear your God; I am the LORD.

33 'When a stranger resides with you in your land, you shall not do him wrong. 34 The stranger who resides with you shall be to you as the native among you, and you shall love him as yourself, for you were strangers in the land of Egypt; I am the LORD your God.

35 'You shall do no wrong in judgment, in measurement of weight, or volume. 36 You shall have accurate balances, accurate weights, an accurate ¹ephah, and an accurate ²hin; I am the LORD your God, who brought you out from the land of Egypt. 37 So you shall keep all My statutes and all My ordinances, and do them; I am the LORD.' "

On Human Sacrifice and Immoralities

20 Then the LORD spoke to Moses, saying, 2 "You shall also say to the sons of Israel:

'Anyone from the sons of Israel or from the strangers residing in Israel who gives any of his children to Molech, shall certainly be put to death; the people of the land shall stone him with stones. 3 I will also set My face against that man and will cut him off from among his people, because he has given some of his children to Molech, so as to defile My sanctuary and to profane My holy name. 4 If the people of the land, however, should ever disregard that man when he gives any of his children to Molech, so as not to put him to death, 5 then I Myself will set My face against that man and against his family, and I will cut off from among their people both him and all those who play the prostitute with him, by playing the prostitute with Molech.

6 'As for the person who turns to mediums and to spiritists, to play the prostitute with them, I will also set My face against that person and will cut him off from among his people. 7 You shall consecrate yourselves therefore and be holy, for I am the LORD your God. 8 So you shall keep My statutes and practice them; I am the LORD who sanctifies you.

9 'If *there is* anyone who curses his father or his mother, he shall certainly be put to death. He has cursed his father or his mother, *and has brought* his own death upon himself.

10 'If *there is* a man who commits adultery with another man's wife, one who commits adultery with his friend's wife, the adulterer and the adulteress must be put to death. 11 If *there is* a man who sleeps with his father's wife, he has uncovered his father's nakedness. Both of them must be put to death, *they have brought* their own deaths upon themselves. 12 If *there is* a man who sleeps with his daughter-in-law, both of them must be put to death. They have committed incest, *and have brought* their own deaths upon themselves. 13 If *there is* a man who sleeps with a male as those who sleep with a woman, both of them have committed a detestable act; they must be put to death. *They have brought* their own deaths upon themselves. 14 If *there is* a man who marries a woman and her mother, it is an outrageous sin; both he and they shall be burned with fire, so that there will be no *such* outrageous sin in your midst. 15 If *there is* a man who has sexual intercourse with an animal, he must be put to death; you shall also kill the animal. 16 If *there is* a woman who approaches any animal to mate with it, you shall kill the woman and the animal; they must be put to death. *They have brought* their own deaths upon themselves.

17 'If *there is* a man who takes his sister, his father's daughter or his mother's daughter, so that he sees her nakedness and she sees his nakedness, it is a disgrace; and they shall be cut off in the sight of the sons of their people. He has uncovered his sister's nakedness; he bears his guilt. 18 If *there is* a man who sleeps with a menstruous woman and uncovers her nakedness, he has exposed her flow, and she has uncovered the flow of her blood; so both of them shall be cut off from among their people.

19:36 ¹I.e., a dry measure, about 1 cubic foot or 0.03 cubic meters   ²I.e., a liquid measure, about 1 gallon or 3.8 liters

19 You shall also not uncover the nakedness of your mother's sister or of your father's sister, for *such a one* has uncovered his blood relative; they will bear their guilt. **20** If *there is* a man who sleeps with his uncle's wife, he has uncovered his uncle's nakedness; they will bear their sin. They will die childless. **21** If *there is* a man who takes his brother's wife, it is detestable; he has uncovered his brother's nakedness. They will be childless.

22 'You are therefore to keep all My statutes and all My ordinances, and do them, so that the land to which I am bringing you to live will not vomit you out. **23** Furthermore, you shall not follow the customs of the nation which I am going to drive out before you, because they did all these things; therefore I have felt disgust for them. **24** So I have said to you, "You are to take possession of their land, and I Myself will give it to you to possess, a land flowing with milk and honey." I am the LORD your God, who has singled you out from the peoples. **25** You are therefore to make a distinction between the clean animal and the unclean, and between the unclean bird and the clean; and you shall not make yourselves detestable by animal or by bird, or by anything that crawls on the ground, which I have distinguished for you as unclean. **26** So you are to be holy to Me, for I the LORD am holy; and I have singled you out from the peoples to be Mine.

27 'Now a man or a woman who is a medium or a spiritist must be put to death. They shall be stoned with stones; *they have brought* their own deaths upon themselves.' "

Regulations concerning Priests

21 Then the LORD said to Moses, "Speak to the priests, the sons of Aaron, and say to them:

'No one shall defile himself for a *dead* person among his people, **2** except for his relatives who are nearest to him, his mother, his father, his son, his daughter, and his brother, **3** also for his virgin sister who is near to him because she has not had a husband; for her, he may defile himself. **4** He shall not defile himself as a relative by marriage among his people, so as to profane himself. **5** They shall not shave any area on their heads bald, nor shave off the edges of their beards, nor make any cuts in their flesh. **6** They shall be holy to their God and not profane the name of their God, because they present the offerings by fire to the LORD, the food of their God; so they shall be holy. **7** They shall not take a woman who is a prostitute and profaned, nor shall they take a woman divorced from her husband; for he is holy to his God. **8** You shall consecrate him, therefore, because he offers the food of your God. He shall be holy to you; for I the LORD, who sanctifies you, am holy. **9** Also the daughter of any priest, if she profanes herself by prostitution, she profanes her father; she shall be burned with fire.

10 'The priest who is ᵗhighest among his brothers, on whose head the anointing oil has been poured and who has been consecrated to wear the garments, shall not uncover his head

nor tear his clothes; **11** nor shall he approach any dead person, nor defile himself *even* for his father or his mother; **12** nor shall he leave the sanctuary nor profane the sanctuary of his God, for the consecration of the anointing oil of his God is on him; I am the LORD. **13** He shall take a wife in her virginity. **14** A widow, or a divorced woman, or one who is profaned by prostitution, these he shall not take; but rather he is to marry a virgin of his own people, **15** so that he will not profane his children among his people; for I am the LORD who sanctifies him.' "

16 Then the LORD spoke to Moses, saying, **17** "Speak to Aaron, saying, 'None of your descendants throughout their generations who has an impairment shall approach to offer the food of his God. **18** For no one who has an impairment shall approach: a man who is blind, or one who limps, or one who has a slit nose, or one with *any* conspicuous feature, **19** or someone who has a broken foot or broken hand, **20** or a contorted back, or *one who is* a dwarf, or *has* a spot in his eye, or a festering rash or scabs, or crushed testicles. **21** No man among the descendants of Aaron the priest who has an impairment is to come forward to offer the LORD's offerings by fire; *since* he has an impairment, he shall not come forward to offer the food of his God. **22** He may eat the food of his God, *both* of the most holy and of the holy, **23** only he shall not come up to the veil or approach the altar, since he has an impairment, so that he does not profane My sanctuaries. For I am the LORD who sanctifies them.' " **24** So Moses spoke to Aaron and to his sons and to all the sons of Israel.

Various Rules for Priests

22 Then the LORD spoke to Moses, saying, **2** "Tell Aaron and his sons to be careful with the holy *gifts* of the sons of Israel, which they dedicate to Me, so as not to profane My holy name; I am the LORD. **3** Say to them, 'Any man among all your descendants throughout your generations who approaches the holy *gifts* which the sons of Israel consecrate to the LORD, while he has an uncleanness, that person shall be cut off from My presence; I am the LORD. **4** No man of the descendants of Aaron, who has leprosy or has a discharge, may eat of the holy *gifts* until he is clean. And one who touches anything made unclean by a corpse, or a man who has a seminal emission, **5** or a man who touches any swarming things by which he is made unclean, or *touches* any person by whom he is made unclean, whatever his uncleanness; **6** a person who touches any such thing shall be unclean until evening, and shall not eat of the holy *gifts* unless he has bathed his body in water. **7** But when the sun sets, he will be clean, and afterward he may eat of the holy *gifts*, for it is his food. **8** He shall not eat *an animal* which dies or is torn *by animals*, becoming unclean by it; I am the LORD. **9** They shall therefore perform *their* duty to Me, so that they do not bear sin because of it and die by it because they profane it; I am the LORD who sanctifies them.

10 'No ¹layman, however, is to eat the holy *gift;* a foreign resident with the priest or a hired worker shall not eat the holy *gift.* 11 But if a priest buys a slave as *his* property with his money, that person may eat of it, and those who are born in his house may eat of his food. 12 If a priest's daughter is married to a layman, she shall not eat of the offering of the holy *gifts.* 13 But if a priest's daughter becomes a widow or divorced, and has no child and returns to her father's house as in her youth, she may eat of her father's food; but no layman shall eat of it. 14 If, however, someone eats a holy *food* unintentionally, then he shall add to it a fifth of it and shall give the holy *food* to the priest. 15 And they shall not profane the holy *gifts* of the sons of Israel, which they offer to the Lord, 16 and *thereby* bring upon them punishment for guilt by eating their holy *gifts;* for I am the Lord who sanctifies them.' "

Flawless Animals for Sacrifice

17 Then the Lord spoke to Moses, saying, 18 "Speak to Aaron and to his sons, and to all the sons of Israel, and say to them, 'Anyone of the house of Israel or of the strangers in Israel who presents his offering, whether it is any of their vows or any of their voluntary offerings, which they present to the Lord as a burnt offering— 19 for you to be accepted—*it must be* a male without defect from the cattle, the sheep, or the goats. 20 Whatever has a defect, you shall not offer, for it will not be accepted for you. 21 When someone offers a sacrifice of peace offerings to the Lord to fulfill a special vow or for a voluntary offering, of the herd or of the flock, it must be without defect to be accepted; there shall be no defect in it. 22 *Those that are* blind, fractured, maimed, or *have* a wart, a festering rash, or scabs, you shall not offer to the Lord, nor make of them an offering by fire on the altar to the Lord. 23 Now *as for* an ox or a lamb which has an overgrown or stunted *member,* you may present it as a voluntary offering, but for a vow it will not be accepted. 24 Also anything *with its testicles* squashed, crushed, torn off, or cut off, you shall not offer to the Lord, nor sacrifice in your land, 25 nor shall you offer any of these *animals taken* from the hand of a foreigner as the food of your God; for their deformity is in them, they have an impairment. They will not be accepted for you.' "

26 Then the Lord spoke to Moses, saying, 27 "When an ox or a sheep or a goat is born, it shall remain seven days with its mother, and from the eighth day on it will be considered acceptable as a sacrifice of an offering by fire to the Lord. 28 But, *whether* it is an ox or a sheep, you shall not slaughter *both* it and its young in one day. 29 When you sacrifice a sacrifice of thanksgiving to the Lord, you shall sacrifice it so that you may be accepted. 30 It shall be eaten on the same day; you shall leave none of it until morning. I am the Lord. 31 So you shall keep My commandments, and do them; I am the Lord. 32 "And you shall not profane My holy name,

but I will be sanctified among the sons of Israel; I am the Lord who sanctifies you, 33 who brought you out from the land of Egypt, to be your God; I am the Lord."

Laws of Holy Days

23 The Lord spoke again to Moses, saying, 2 "Speak to the sons of Israel and say to them, 'The Lord's appointed times which you shall proclaim as holy convocations—My appointed times are these: 3 'For six days work may be done, but on the seventh day there is a Sabbath of complete rest, a holy convocation. You shall not do any work; it is a Sabbath to the Lord in all your dwellings.

4 'These are the appointed times of the Lord, holy convocations which you shall proclaim at the times appointed for them. 5 In the first month, on the fourteenth day of the month at twilight is the Lord's Passover. 6 Then on the fifteenth day of the same month there is the Feast of Unleavened Bread to the Lord; for seven days you shall eat unleavened bread. 7 On the first day you shall have a holy convocation; you shall not do any laborious work. 8 But for seven days you shall present an offering by fire to the Lord. On the seventh day is a holy convocation; you shall not do any laborious work.' "

9 Then the Lord spoke to Moses, saying, 10 "Speak to the sons of Israel and say to them, 'When you enter the land which I am going to give to you and you gather its harvest, then you shall bring in the sheaf of the first fruits of your harvest to the priest. 11 He shall wave the sheaf before the Lord for you to be accepted; on the day after the Sabbath the priest shall wave it. 12 Now on the day when you wave the sheaf, you shall offer a male lamb one year old without defect as a burnt offering to the Lord. 13 Its grain offering shall then be ¹two-tenths *of an ephah* of fine flour mixed with oil, an offering by fire to the Lord *for* a soothing aroma, with its drink offering, a ²fourth of a hin of wine. 14 Until this very day, until you have brought in the offering of your God, you shall eat neither bread nor roasted grain nor new produce. It is to be a permanent statute throughout your generations in all your dwelling places.

15 'You shall also count for yourselves from the day after the Sabbath, from the day when you brought in the sheaf of the wave offering; there shall be seven complete Sabbaths. 16 You shall count fifty days to the day after the seventh Sabbath; then you shall present a new grain offering to the Lord. 17 You shall bring in from your dwelling places two *loaves* of bread as a wave offering, made of ¹two-tenths *of an ephah;* they shall be of a fine flour, baked with leaven as first fruits to the Lord. 18 Along with the bread you shall present seven one-year-old male lambs without defect, and a bull of the herd and two rams; they are to be a burnt offering to the Lord, with their grain offering and their drink offerings, an offering by fire of a soothing aroma to the Lord. 19 You shall also offer one male goat as a sin offering, and two

---

22:10 ¹Or *unauthorized person*   **23:13** ¹About 0.13 cubic feet or 0.004 cubic meters   ²About 0.25 gallon or 1 liter   **23:17** ¹About 0.13 cubic feet or 0.004 cubic meters

male lambs one year old as a sacrifice of peace offerings. 20 The priest shall then wave them with the bread of the first fruits as a wave offering with two lambs before the LORD; they are to be holy to the LORD for the priest. 21 On this very day you shall make a proclamation as well; you are to have a holy convocation. You shall do no laborious work. It is to be a permanent statute in all your dwelling places throughout your generations.

22 'When you reap the harvest of your land, moreover, you shall not reap to the very edges of your field nor gather the gleaning of your harvest; you are to leave them for the needy and the stranger. I am the LORD your God.' "

23 Again the LORD spoke to Moses, saying, 24 "Speak to the sons of Israel, saying, 'In the seventh month on the first of the month you shall have a rest, a reminder by blowing of trumpets, a holy convocation. 25 You shall not do any laborious work, but you shall present an offering by fire to the LORD.' "

The Day of Atonement

26 Then the LORD spoke to Moses, saying, 27 "On exactly the tenth day of this seventh month is the Day of Atonement; it shall be a holy convocation for you, and you shall humble yourselves and present an offering by fire to the LORD. 28 You shall not do any work on this very day, for it is a Day of Atonement, to make atonement on your behalf before the LORD your God. 29 If there is any person who does not humble himself on this very day, he shall be cut off from his people. 30 As for any person who does any work on this very day, that person I will eliminate from among his people. 31 You shall not do any work. It is to be a permanent statute throughout your generations in all your dwelling places. 32 It is to be a Sabbath of complete rest for you, and you shall humble yourselves; on the ninth of the month at evening, from evening until evening, you shall keep your Sabbath."

33 Again the LORD spoke to Moses, saying, 34 "Speak to the sons of Israel, saying, 'On the fifteenth of this seventh month is the Feast of Booths for seven days to the LORD. 35 On the first day is a holy convocation; you shall not do any laborious work. 36 For seven days you shall present an offering by fire to the LORD. On the eighth day you shall have a holy convocation and present an offering by fire to the LORD; it is an assembly. You shall not do any laborious work.

37 'These are the appointed times of the LORD which you shall proclaim as holy convocations, to present offerings by fire to the LORD—burnt offerings and grain offerings, sacrifices and drink offerings, each day's matter on its own day— 38 besides those of the Sabbaths of the LORD, and besides your gifts and besides all your vowed and voluntary offerings, which you give to the LORD.

39 'On exactly the fifteenth day of the seventh month, when you have gathered in the crops of the land, you shall celebrate the feast of the LORD for seven days, with a rest on the first day and a rest on the eighth day. 40 Now on the first day you shall take for yourselves the foliage of beautiful trees, palm branches and branches of trees with thick branches and willows of the brook, and you shall rejoice before the LORD your God for seven days. 41 So you shall celebrate it as a feast to the LORD for seven days in the year. It shall be a permanent statute throughout your generations; you shall celebrate it in the seventh month. 42 You shall live in booths for seven days; all the native-born in Israel shall live in booths, 43 so that your generations may know that I had the sons of Israel live in booths when I brought them out from the land of Egypt. I am the LORD your God.' " 44 So Moses declared to the sons of Israel the appointed times of the LORD.

The Lamp and the Bread of the Sanctuary

24 Then the LORD spoke to Moses, saying, 2 "Command the sons of Israel that they bring to you clear oil from beaten olives for the light, to make a lamp burn continually. 3 Outside the veil of the testimony in the tent of meeting, Aaron shall keep it in order from evening to morning before the LORD continually; it shall be a permanent statute throughout your generations. 4 He shall keep the lamps in order on the pure gold lampstand before the LORD continually.

5 "Then you shall take fine flour and bake twelve cakes with it; 1two-tenths of an ephah shall be in each cake. 6 And you shall set them in two rows, six to a row, on the pure gold table before the LORD. 7 You shall put pure frankincense on each row so that it may be a memorial portion for the bread, an offering by fire to the LORD. 8 Every Sabbath day he shall set it in order before the LORD continually; it is an everlasting covenant for the sons of Israel. 9 And it shall be for Aaron and his sons, and they shall eat it in a holy place; for it is most holy to him from the LORD's offerings by fire, his portion forever."

10 Now the son of an Israelite woman—his father was an Egyptian—went out among the sons of Israel; and the Israelite woman's son and an Israelite man had a fight within the camp. 11 And the son of the Israelite woman blasphemed the Name and cursed. So they brought him to Moses. (Now his mother's name was Shelomith, the daughter of Dibri, of the tribe of Dan.) 12 Then they put him in custody, waiting for Moses to give them a clear decision in accordance with the command of the LORD.

13 Then the LORD spoke to Moses, saying, 14 "Bring the one who has cursed outside the camp, and have all who heard him lay their hands on his head; then have all the congregation stone him. 15 You shall also speak to the sons of Israel, saying, 'If anyone curses his God, then he will bear the responsibility for his sin. 16 Moreover, the one who blasphemes the name of the LORD must be put to death; all the congregation shall certainly stone him. The stranger as well as the native, when he blasphemes the Name, shall be put to death.

An Eye for an Eye

17 'Now if someone takes any human life, he must be put to death. 18 But the one who takes the life of an animal shall make restitution, life for life. 19 If someone injures his neighbor, just as he has done, so shall it be done to him: 20 fracture for fracture, eye for eye, tooth for tooth; just as he has injured a person, so shall it be inflicted on him. 21 So the one who kills an animal shall make restitution, but the one who kills a person shall be put to death. 22 There shall be *only* one standard for you; it shall be for the stranger as well as the native, for I am the LORD your God.' " 23 Then Moses spoke to the sons of Israel, and they brought the one who had cursed outside the camp, and stoned him with stones. So the sons of Israel did just as the LORD had commanded Moses.

The Sabbatical Year and Year of Jubilee

25 The LORD then spoke to Moses on Mount Sinai, saying, 2 "Speak to the sons of Israel and say to them, 'When you come into the land which I am going to give you, then the land shall have a Sabbath to the LORD. 3 For six years you shall sow your field, and for six years you shall prune your vineyard and gather in its produce, 4 but during the seventh year the land shall have a Sabbath rest, a Sabbath to the LORD; you shall not sow your field nor prune your vineyard. 5 You shall not reap your harvest's 1aftergrowth, and you shall not gather your grapes of untrimmed vines; the land shall have a sabbatical year. 6 All of you shall have the Sabbath *produce* of the land as food; for yourself, your male and female slaves, and your hired worker and your foreign resident, those who live as strangers among you. 7 Even your cattle and the animals that are in your land shall have all its produce to eat.

8 'You are also to count off seven Sabbaths of years for yourself, seven times seven years, so that you have the time of the seven Sabbaths of years, *that is,* forty-nine years. 9 You shall then sound a ram's horn abroad on the tenth day of the seventh month; on the Day of Atonement you shall sound a horn all through your land. 10 So you shall consecrate the fiftieth year and proclaim 1a release throughout the land to all its inhabitants. It shall be a jubilee for you, and each of you shall return to his own property, and each of you shall return to his family. 11 You shall have the fiftieth year as a jubilee; you shall not sow, nor harvest its aftergrowth, nor gather grapes *from* its untrimmed vines. 12 For it is a jubilee; it shall be holy to you. You shall eat its produce from the field.

13 'On this year of jubilee each of you shall return to his own property. 14 Furthermore, if you make a sale to your friend, or buy from your friend's hand, you shall not wrong one another. 15 Corresponding to the number of years after the jubilee, you shall buy from your friend; he is to sell to you according to the number of years of crops. 16 In proportion to a greater number of years you shall increase its price, and in proportion to fewer years you shall decrease its price, because *it is* the number of crops *that* he is selling to you. 17 So

you shall not wrong one another, but you shall fear your God; for I am the LORD your God.

18 'You shall therefore follow My statutes and keep My judgments so as to carry them out, so that you may live securely on the land. 19 Then the land will yield its produce, so that you can eat your fill and live securely on it. 20 But if you say, "What are we going to eat in the seventh year if we do not sow nor gather in our produce?" 21 then I will so order My blessing for you in the sixth year that it will bring forth the produce for three years. 22 When you are sowing the eighth year, you can still eat old things from the produce, eating *the old* until the ninth year when its produce comes in.

The Law of Redemption

23 'The land, moreover, shall not be sold permanently, because the land is Mine; for you are *only* strangers and residents with Me. 24 So for every piece of your property, you are to provide for the redemption of the land. 25 'If a fellow countryman of yours becomes so poor that he sells part of his property, then his closest 1redeemer is to come and buy back what his relative has sold. 26 Or in case someone has no redeemer, but recovers to find sufficient means for its redemption, 27 then he shall calculate the years since its sale and refund the balance to the man to whom he sold it, and so return to his property. 28 But if he has not found sufficient means to get it back for himself, then what he has sold shall remain in the hands of its purchaser until the year of jubilee; but at the jubilee it shall revert, so that he may return to his property.

29 'Likewise, if a man sells a dwelling house in a walled city, then his redemption right remains *valid* until a full year after its sale; his right of redemption lasts a full year. 30 But if it is not bought back for him within the space of a full year, then the house that is in the walled city passes permanently to its purchaser throughout his generations; it does not revert in the jubilee. 31 The houses of the villages, however, which have no surrounding wall, shall be regarded as open fields; they have redemption rights and revert in the jubilee. 32 As for the cities of the Levites, the Levites have a permanent right of redemption for the houses of the cities which are their possession. 33 What, therefore, belongs to the Levites may be redeemed, and a house sale in the city of this possession reverts in the jubilee, because the houses of the cities of the Levites are their possession among the sons of Israel. 34 But pasture fields of their cities shall not be sold, for that is their permanent possession.

Of Poor Countrymen

35 'Now in case a countryman of yours becomes poor and his means among you falter, then you are to sustain him, *like* a stranger or a resident, so that he may live with you. 36 Do not take *any kind of* interest from him, but fear your God, so that your countryman may live with you. 37 You shall not give him your silver at interest, nor your food for profit. 38 I am the LORD your God, who brought you out of the

land of Egypt to give you the land of Canaan, *and* to be your God.

39 'Now if a countryman of yours becomes so poor with regard to you that he sells himself to you, you shall not subject him to a slave's service. **40** He shall be with you as a hired worker, as *if he were* a foreign resident; he shall serve with you up to the year of jubilee. **41** He shall then leave you, he and his sons with him, and shall go back to his family, so that he may return to the property of his forefathers. **42** For they are My servants whom I brought out from the land of Egypt; they are not to be sold *in* a slave sale. **43** You shall not rule over him with severity, but are to revere your God. **44** As for your male and female slaves whom you may have—you may acquire male and female slaves from the *pagan* nations that are around you. **45** You may also acquire *them* from the sons of the foreign residents who reside among you, and from their families who are with you, whom they will have produced in your land; they also may become your possession. **46** You may also pass them on as an inheritance to your sons after you, to receive as a possession; you can use them as permanent slaves. But in respect to your countrymen, the sons of Israel, you shall not rule with severity over one another.

Of Redeeming a Person Who Is Poor

47 'Now if the means of a stranger or of a foreign resident with you becomes sufficient, and a countryman of yours becomes poor in relation to him and sells himself to a stranger who is residing with you, or to the descendants of a stranger's family, **48** then he shall have redemption right after he has been sold. One of his brothers may redeem him, **49** or his uncle, or his uncle's son may redeem him, or one of his blood relatives from his family may redeem him; or if he prospers, he may redeem himself. **50** He then, with his purchaser, shall calculate from the year when he sold himself to him up to the year of jubilee; and the price of his sale shall correspond to the number of years *calculated. It is* like the days of a hired worker *that* he will be with him. **51** If there are still many years *remaining,* he shall refund part of his purchase price in proportion to them for his own redemption; **52** but if few years remain until the year of jubilee, he shall so calculate with him. In proportion to his years he is to refund *the amount for* his redemption. **53** He shall be with him like a worker hired year by year; he shall not rule over him with severity in your sight. **54** Even if he is not redeemed by these means, he shall still leave in the year of jubilee, he and his sons with him. **55** For the sons of Israel are My servants; they are My servants whom I brought out from the land of Egypt. I am the LORD your God.

Blessings of Obedience

26 'You shall not make for yourselves idols, nor shall you set up for yourselves a carved image or a memorial stone, nor shall you place a figured stone in your land to bow down to it; for I am the LORD your God. **2** You shall keep My Sabbaths and revere My

sanctuary; I am the LORD. **3** If you walk in My statutes and keep My commandments so as to carry them out, **4** then I shall give you rains in their season, so that the land will yield its produce and the trees of the field will bear their fruit. **5** Indeed, *your* threshing season will last for you until grape gathering, and grape gathering will last until sowing time. So you will eat your food to the full and live securely in your land. **6** I shall also grant peace in the land, so that you may lie down, with no one to make *you* afraid. I shall also eliminate harmful animals from the land, and no sword will pass through your land. **7** Instead, you will chase your enemies, and they will fall before you by the sword; **8** five of you will chase a hundred, and a hundred of you will chase ten thousand; and your enemies will fall before you by the sword. **9** So I will turn toward you and make you fruitful and multiply you, and I will confirm My covenant with you. **10** And you will eat the old supply, and clear out the old because of the new. **11** Moreover, I will make My dwelling among you, and My soul will not reject you. **12** I will also walk among you and be your God, and you shall be My people. **13** I am the LORD your God, who brought you out of the land of Egypt so that *you* would not be their slaves, and I broke your yoke and made you walk erect.

Penalties of Disobedience

14 'But if you do not obey Me and do not carry out all these commandments, **15** if, instead, you reject My statutes, and if your soul loathes My ordinances so as not to carry out all My commandments, *but rather* to break My covenant, **16** I, in turn, will do this to you: I will summon a sudden terror against you, consumption and fever that will make the eyes fail and the soul languish; also, you will sow your seed uselessly, for your enemies will eat it. **17** And I will set My face against you so that you will be defeated before your enemies; and those who hate you will rule over you, and you will flee when no one is pursuing you. **18** If also after these things you do not obey Me, then I will punish you seven times more for your sins. **19** I will also break down your pride of power; and I will make your sky like iron and your earth like bronze. **20** Your strength will be consumed uselessly, for your land will not yield its produce and the trees of the land will not yield their fruit.

21 'Yet if you show hostility toward Me and are unwilling to obey Me, I will increase the plague on you seven times according to your sins. **22** I will also let loose among you the animals of the field, which will deprive you of your children and eliminate your cattle, and reduce your number so that your roads become deserted.

23 'And if by these things you do not learn your lesson regarding Me, but you show hostility toward Me, **24** then I in turn will show hostility toward you; and I, even I, will strike you seven times for your sins. **25** I will also bring upon you a sword which will execute vengeance for the covenant; and when you gather together into your cities, I will send a plague among you, so that you will be handed

over to the enemy. 26 When I break your staff of bread, ten women will bake your bread in one oven, and they will bring back your bread in rationed amounts, so that you will eat and not be satisfied.

27 'Yet if in spite of this you do not obey Me, but act with hostility against Me, 28 then I will act with wrathful hostility against you, and I for My part will punish you seven times for your sins. 29 Further, you will eat the flesh of your sons, and you will eat the flesh of your daughters. 30 I then will destroy your high places, and cut down your incense altars, and pile your remains on the remains of your idols, for My soul will loathe you. 31 I will turn your cities into ruins as well and make your sanctuaries desolate, and I will not smell your soothing aromas. 32 And I will make the land desolate so that your enemies who settle in it will be appalled at it. 33 You, however, I will scatter among the nations, and I will draw out a sword after you, as your land becomes desolate and your cities become ruins.

34 'Then the land will restore its Sabbaths all the days of the desolation, while you are in your enemies' land; then the land will rest and restore its Sabbaths. 35 All the days of its desolation it will have the rest which it did not have on your Sabbaths, while you were living on it. 36 As for those among you who are left, I will also bring despair into their hearts in the lands of their enemies. And the sound of a scattered leaf will chase them, and even when no one is pursuing they will flee as though from the sword, and they will fall. 37 They will then stumble over each other as if running from the sword, although no one is pursuing; and you will have no strength to stand before your enemies. 38 Instead, you will perish among the nations, and your enemies' land will consume you. 39 So those of you who may be left will rot away because of their wrongdoing in the lands of your enemies; and also because of the wrongdoing of their forefathers they will rot away with them.

40 'But if they confess their wrongdoing and the wrongdoing of their forefathers, in their unfaithfulness which they committed against Me, and also in their acting with hostility against Me— 41 I also was acting with hostility against them, to bring them into the land of their enemies—or if their uncircumcised heart is humbled so that they then make amends for their wrongdoing, 42 then I will remember My covenant with Jacob, and I will remember also My covenant with Isaac, and My covenant with Abraham as well, and I will remember the land. 43 For the land will be abandoned by them, and will restore its Sabbaths while it is made desolate without them. They, meanwhile, will be making amends for their wrongdoing, because they rejected My ordinances and their soul loathed My statutes. 44 Yet in spite of this, when they are in the land of their enemies, I will not reject them, nor will I so loathe them as to destroy them, breaking My covenant with them; for I am the LORD their God. 45 But I will remember for them the covenant with their ancestors, whom I brought

out of the land of Egypt in the sight of the nations, so that I might be their God. I am the LORD.'"

46 These are the statutes and ordinances and laws which the LORD established between Himself and the sons of Israel through Moses on Mount Sinai.

Rules concerning Assessments

27 Again, the LORD spoke to Moses, saying, 2 "Speak to the sons of Israel and say to them, 'When someone makes an explicit vow, he shall be valued according to your assessment of persons belonging to the LORD. 3 If your assessment is of a male from twenty years even to sixty years old, then your assessment shall be fifty shekels of silver, by the shekel of the sanctuary. 4 Or if the person is a female, then your assessment shall be thirty shekels. 5 And if the person is from five years even to twenty years old, then your assessment for a male shall be twenty shekels, and for a female, ten shekels. 6 But if the person is from a month even up to five years old, then your assessment shall be five shekels of silver for a male, and for a female your assessment shall be three shekels of silver. 7 If the person is from sixty years old and upward, if a male, then your assessment shall be fifteen shekels, and for a female, ten shekels. 8 But if he is poorer than your assessment, then he shall be presented before the priest, and the priest shall assess him; according to the means of the one who vowed, the priest shall assess him.

9 'Now if it is an animal of the kind that one can present as an offering to the LORD, any such animal that one gives to the LORD shall be holy. 10 He shall not replace it nor exchange it, a good for a bad, or a bad for a good; yet if he does exchange animal for animal, then both it and its substitute shall become holy. 11 If, however, it is any unclean animal of the kind which one does not present as an offering to the LORD, then he shall place the animal before the priest. 12 And the priest shall assess it as either good or bad; as you, the priest, assess it, so shall it be. 13 But if he should ever want to redeem it, then he shall add a fifth of it to your assessment.

14 'Now if someone consecrates his house as holy to the LORD, then the priest shall assess it as either good or bad; as the priest assesses it, so shall it stand. 15 Yet if the one who consecrates it should want to redeem his house, then he shall add a fifth of your assessment price to it, so that it may be his.

16 'Again, if someone consecrates to the LORD part of the field of his own property, then your assessment shall be proportionate to the seed needed for it: a ¹homer of barley seed at fifty shekels of silver. 17 If he consecrates his field as of the year of jubilee, according to your assessment it shall stand. 18 If he consecrates his field after the jubilee, however, then the priest shall calculate the price for him proportionate to the years that are left until the year of jubilee; and it shall be deducted from your assessment. 19 If the one who consecrates it should ever want to redeem the field, then he

---

27:16 ¹ About 7.7 cubic feet or 0.22 cubic meters

shall add a fifth of your assessment price to it, so that it may belong to him. 20 Yet if he does not redeem the field, but has sold the field to another person, it may no longer be redeemed; 21 and when it reverts in the jubilee, the field shall be holy to the LORD, like a field banned from secular use; it shall be for the priest as his property. 22 Or if he consecrates to the LORD a field which he has bought, which is not a part of the field of his own property, 23 then the priest shall calculate for him the amount of your assessment up to the year of jubilee; and he shall on that day give your assessment as holy to the LORD. 24 In the year of jubilee the field shall return to the one from whom he bought it, to whom the possession of the land belongs. 25 Every assessment of yours, moreover, shall be by the shekel of the sanctuary. The shekel shall be twenty gerahs.

26 'However, a firstborn among animals, which as a firstborn belongs to the LORD, no one may consecrate; whether ox or sheep, it is the LORD's. 27 But if it is among the unclean animals, then he shall redeem it according to your assessment and add to it a fifth of it; and if it is not redeemed, then it shall be sold according to your assessment.

28 'Nevertheless, anything which someone sets apart to the LORD for 1destruction out of all that he has, of man or animal or of the field of his own property, shall not be sold nor redeemed. Anything set apart for destruction is most holy to the LORD. 29 No one who may have been set apart among mankind shall be ransomed; he must be put to death.

30 'Now all the tithe of the land, of the seed of the land or of the fruit of the tree, is the LORD's; it is holy to the LORD. 31 If, therefore, someone should ever want to redeem part of his tithe, he shall add to it a fifth of it. 32 For every tenth part of herd or flock, whatever passes under the rod, the tenth one shall be holy to the LORD. 33 He is not to be concerned whether it is good or bad, nor shall he exchange it; yet if he does exchange it, then both it and its substitute shall become holy. It shall not be redeemed.' "

34 These are the commandments which the LORD commanded Moses for the sons of Israel on Mount Sinai.

27:28 1 I.e., as an offering

NUMBERS

The Census of Israel's Warriors

1 Now the LORD spoke to Moses in the wilderness of Sinai, in the tent of meeting, on the first *day* of the second month, in the second year after they had come out of the land of Egypt, saying, 2 "Take a census of all the congregation of the sons of Israel, by their families, by their fathers' households, according to the number of names, every male, head by head 3 from twenty years old and upward, whoever *is able to* go to war in Israel. You and Aaron shall count them by their armies. 4 With you, moreover, there shall be a man of each tribe, each one head of his father's household. 5 These then are the names of the men who shall stand with you: of *the tribe of* Reuben, Elizur the son of Shedeur; 6 of *the tribe of* Simeon, Shelumiel the son of Zurishaddai; 7 of *the tribe of* Judah, Nahshon the son of Amminadab; 8 of Issachar, Nethanel the son of Zuar; 9 of Zebulun, Eliab the son of Helon; 10 of the sons of Joseph: of Ephraim, Elishama the son of Ammihud; of Manasseh, Gamaliel the son of Pedahzur; 11 of Benjamin, Abidan the son of Gideoni; 12 of Dan, Ahiezer the son of Ammishaddai; 13 of Asher, Pagiel the son of Ochran; 14 of Gad, Eliasaph the son of Deuel; 15 of Naphtali, Ahira the son of Enan. 16 These are *the men* who were called *from* the congregation, the leaders of their fathers' tribes; they were the heads of divisions of Israel."

17 So Moses and Aaron took these men who had been designated by name, 18 and they assembled all the congregation on the first *day* of the second month. Then they registered by ancestry in their families, by their fathers' households, according to the number of names, from twenty years old and upward, head by head, 19 just as the LORD had commanded Moses. So he counted them in the wilderness of Sinai.

20 Now the sons of Reuben, Israel's firstborn, their descendants by their families, by their fathers' households, according to the number of names, head by head, every male from twenty years old and upward, whoever *was able to* go to war, 21 their numbered men of the tribe of Reuben *were* 46,500.

22 Of the sons of Simeon, their descendants by their families, by their fathers' households, their numbered men, according to the number of names, head by head, every male from twenty years old and upward, whoever *was able to* go to war, 23 their numbered men of the tribe of Simeon *were* 59,300.

24 Of the sons of Gad, their descendants by their families, by their fathers' households, according to the number of names, from twenty years old and upward, whoever *was able to* go to war, 25 their numbered men of the tribe of Gad *were* 45,650.

26 Of the sons of Judah, their descendants by their families, by their fathers' households, according to the number of names, from twenty years old and upward, whoever *was* able to go to war, 27 their numbered men of the tribe of Judah *were* 74,600.

28 Of the sons of Issachar, their descendants by their families, by their fathers' households, according to the number of names, from twenty years old and upward, whoever *was able to* go to war, 29 their numbered men of the tribe of Issachar *were* 54,400.

30 Of the sons of Zebulun, their descendants by their families, by their fathers' households, according to the number of names, from twenty years old and upward, whoever *was able to* go to war, 31 their numbered men of the tribe of Zebulun *were* 57,400.

32 Of the sons of Joseph, *namely,* of the sons of Ephraim, their descendants by their families, by their fathers' households, according to the number of names, from twenty years old and upward, whoever *was able to* go to war, 33 their numbered men of the tribe of Ephraim *were* 40,500.

34 Of the sons of Manasseh, their descendants by their families, by their fathers' households, according to the number of names, from twenty years old and upward, whoever *was able to* go to war, 35 their numbered men of the tribe of Manasseh *were* 32,200.

36 Of the sons of Benjamin, their descendants by their families, by their fathers' households, according to the number of names, from twenty years old and upward, whoever *was* able to go to war, 37 their numbered men of the tribe of Benjamin *were* 35,400.

38 Of the sons of Dan, their descendants by their families, by their fathers' households, according to the number of names, from twenty years old and upward, whoever *was able to* go to war, 39 their numbered men of the tribe of Dan *were* 62,700.

40 Of the sons of Asher, their descendants by their families, by their fathers' households, according to the number of names, from twenty years old and upward, whoever *was able to* go to war, 41 their numbered men of the tribe of Asher *were* 41,500.

42 Of the sons of Naphtali, their descendants by their families, by their fathers' households, according to the number of names, from twenty years old and upward, whoever *was able to* go to war, 43 their numbered men of the tribe of Naphtali *were* 53,400.

44 These are the ones who were numbered, whom Moses and Aaron counted, with the leaders of Israel, twelve men, each of whom was of his father's household. 45 So all the numbered men of the sons of Israel by their fathers' households, from twenty years old and upward, whoever *was able to* go to war in Israel, 46 all the numbered men were 603,550.

Levites Exempted

47 The Levites, however, were not counted among them by their fathers' tribe. 48 For the LORD had spoken to Moses, saying, 49 "Only the tribe of Levi you shall not count, nor shall you

take their census among the sons of Israel. 50 And you shall appoint the Levites over the ¹tabernacle of the testimony, and over all its furnishings and over everything that belongs to it. They shall carry the tabernacle and all its furnishings, and they shall take care of it; they shall also camp around the tabernacle. 51 So when the tabernacle is to move on, the Levites shall take it down; and when the tabernacle encamps, the Levites shall set it up. But the ¹layman who comes near it shall be put to death. 52 So the sons of Israel shall camp, each man by his own camp, and each man by his own flag, according to their armies. 53 But the Levites shall camp around the tabernacle of the testimony, so that there will be no *divine* wrath against the congregation of the sons of Israel. So the Levites shall be responsible for service to the tabernacle of the testimony." 54 And the sons of Israel did *so;* in accordance with all that the LORD had commanded Moses, so they did.

Arrangement of the Camps

2 Now the LORD spoke to Moses and to Aaron, saying, 2 "The sons of Israel shall camp, each by his own flag, with the banners of their fathers' households; they shall camp around the tent of meeting at a distance. 3 Now those who camp on the east side toward the sunrise *shall be* of the flag of the camp of Judah, by their armies; and the leader of the sons of Judah: Nahshon the son of Amminadab, 4 and his army, their numbered men: 74,600. 5 Those who camp next to him *shall be* the tribe of Issachar; and the leader of the sons of Issachar: Nethanel the son of Zuar, 6 and his army, their numbered men: 54,400. 7 *Then follows* the tribe of Zebulun; and the leader of the sons of Zebulun: Eliab the son of Helon, 8 and his army, his numbered men: 57,400. 9 The total of the numbered men of the camp of Judah: 186,400, by their armies. They shall set out first.

10 "On the south side *shall be* the flag of the camp of Reuben by their armies; and the leader of the sons of Reuben: Elizur the son of Shedeur, 11 and his army, their numbered men: 46,500. 12 And those who camp next to him *shall be* the tribe of Simeon; and the leader of the sons of Simeon: Shelumiel the son of Zurishaddai, 13 and his army, their numbered men: 59,300. 14 Then *follows* the tribe of Gad; and the leader of the sons of Gad: Eliasaph the son of Deuel, 15 and his army, their numbered men: 45,650. 16 The total of the numbered men of the camp of Reuben: 151,450 by their armies. And they shall set out second.

17 "Then the tent of meeting shall set out *with* the camp of the Levites in the midst of the camps; just as they camp, so they shall set out, every man in his place by their flags.

18 "On the west side *shall be* the flag of the camp of Ephraim by their armies; and the leader of the sons of Ephraim: Elishama the son of Ammihud, 19 and his army, their numbered men: 40,500. 20 Next to him *shall be* the tribe of Manasseh; and the leader of the sons of

Manasseh: Gamaliel the son of Pedahzur, 21 and his army, their numbered men, 32,200. 22 Then *follows* the tribe of Benjamin; and the leader of the sons of Benjamin: Abidan the son of Gideoni, 23 and his army, their numbered men, 35,400. 24 The total of the numbered men of the camp of Ephraim: 108,100, by their armies. And they shall set out third.

25 "On the north side *shall be* the flag of the camp of Dan by their armies; and the leader of the sons of Dan: Ahiezer the son of Ammishaddai, 26 and his army, their numbered men: 62,700. 27 Those who camp next to him *shall be* the tribe of Asher; and the leader of the sons of Asher: Pagiel the son of Ochran, 28 and his army, their numbered men: 41,500. 29 Then *follows* the tribe of Naphtali; and the leader of the sons of Naphtali: Ahira the son of Enan, 30 and his army, their numbered men: 53,400. 31 The total of the numbered men of the camp of Dan *was* 157,600. They shall set out last by their flags."

32 These are the numbered men of the sons of Israel by their fathers' households; the total of the numbered men of the camps by their armies, 603,550. 33 The Levites, however, were not counted among the sons of Israel, just as the LORD had commanded Moses. 34 So the sons of Israel did *all this;* according to all that the LORD commanded Moses, so they camped by their flags, and so they set out, everyone by his family according to his father's household.

Levite Priesthood Established

3 Now these are *the records of* the generations of Aaron and Moses at the time when the LORD spoke with Moses on Mount Sinai. 2 These then are the names of the sons of Aaron: Nadab the firstborn, and Abihu, Eleazar and Ithamar. 3 These are the names of the sons of Aaron, the anointed priests, whom he ordained to serve as priests. 4 But Nadab and Abihu died in the presence of the LORD when they offered strange fire before the LORD in the wilderness of Sinai; and they had no children. So Eleazar and Ithamar served as priests in the lifetime of their father Aaron.

5 Then the LORD spoke to Moses, saying, 6 "Bring the tribe of Levi forward and present them before Aaron the priest, that they may serve him. 7 They shall perform the duties for him and for the whole congregation in front of the tent of meeting, to do the service of the tabernacle. 8 They shall also take care of all the furnishings of the tent of meeting, along with the duties of the sons of Israel, to do the service of the tabernacle. 9 So you shall assign the Levites to Aaron and to his sons; they are exclusively assigned to him from the sons of Israel. 10 So you shall appoint Aaron and his sons that they may keep their priesthood, but the layman who comes near shall be put to death."

11 Again the LORD spoke to Moses, saying, 12 "Now, behold, I have taken the Levites from among the sons of Israel instead of every firstborn, the firstborn of the womb among the sons of Israel. So the Levites shall be Mine.

1:50 1 Lit *dwelling place,* and so throughout the ch   **1:51** 1 Lit *stranger*

13 For all the firstborn are Mine; on the day that I fatally struck all the firstborn in the land of Egypt, I sanctified to Myself all the firstborn in Israel, from the human *firstborn* to animals. They shall be Mine; I am the LORD." 14 Then the LORD spoke to Moses in the wilderness of Sinai, saying, 15 "Count the sons of Levi by their fathers' households, by their families; every male from a month old and upward you shall count." 16 So Moses counted them according to the word of the LORD, just as he had been commanded. 17 These, then, are the sons of Levi by their names: Gershon, Kohath, and Merari. 18 And these are the names of the sons of Gershon by their families: Libni and Shimei; 19 and the sons of Kohath by their families: Amram and Izhar, Hebron and Uzziel; 20 and the sons of Merari by their families: Mahli and Mushi. These are the families of the Levites according to their fathers' households.

21 Of Gershon *was* the family of the Libnites and the family of the Shimeites; these *were* the families of the Gershonites. 22 Their numbered men, in the counting of every male from a month old and upward, their numbered men *were* 7,500. 23 The families of the Gershonites were to camp behind the tabernacle westward, 24 and the leader of the fathers' households of the Gershonites: Eliasaph the son of Lael.

Duties of the Levites

25 Now the duties of the sons of Gershon in the tent of meeting *included* the tabernacle and the tent, its covering, and the curtain for the entrance of the tent of meeting, 26 and the curtains of the courtyard, the curtain for the entrance of the courtyard which is around the tabernacle and the altar, and its ropes, according to all the service concerning them. 27 Of Kohath *was* the family of the Amramites, the family of the Izharites, the family of the Hebronites, and the family of the Uzzielites; these were the families of the Kohathites. 28 In the counting of every male from a month old and upward, *there were* 8,600, performing the duties of the sanctuary. 29 The families of the sons of Kohath were to camp on the south side of the tabernacle, 30 and the leader of the fathers' households of the Kohathite families: Elizaphan the son of Uzziel. 31 Now their duties *included* the ark, the table, the lampstand, the altars, the utensils of the sanctuary with which they minister, the curtain, and all the service concerning them; 32 and Eleazar the son of Aaron the priest *was* the head of the leaders of Levi, *and he had* the supervision of those who performed the duties of the sanctuary.

33 Of Merari *was* the family of the Mahlites and the family of the Mushites; these *were* the families of Merari. 34 Their numbered men in the counting of every male from a month old and upward: 6,200. 35 And the leader of the fathers' households of the families of Merari *was* Zuriel the son of Abihail. They were to camp on the northward side of the tabernacle. 36 Now the appointment of duties of the

sons of Merari *included* the framework of the tabernacle, its bars, its pillars, its bases, all its equipment, and all the service concerning them, 37 and the pillars around the courtyard with their bases, their pegs, and their ropes.

38 Now those who were to camp in front of the tabernacle eastward, in front of the tent of meeting toward the sunrise, *were* Moses and Aaron and his sons, performing the duties of the sanctuary for the obligation of the sons of Israel; but the layman coming near was to be put to death. 39 All the numbered men of the Levites, whom Moses and Aaron counted at the command of the LORD by their families, every male from a month old and upward, *were* twenty-two thousand.

Firstborn Redeemed

40 Then the LORD said to Moses, "Count every firstborn male of the sons of Israel from a month old and upward, and make a list of their names. 41 And you shall take the Levites for Me—I am the LORD—instead of all the firstborn among the sons of Israel; and the cattle of the Levites in place of all the firstborn among the cattle of the sons of Israel." 42 So Moses counted all the firstborn among the sons of Israel, just as the LORD had commanded him; 43 and all the firstborn males, by the number of names from a month old and upward for their numbered men, were 22,273. 44 Then the LORD spoke to Moses, saying, 45 "Take the Levites in place of all the firstborn among the sons of Israel, and the cattle of the Levites in place of their cattle. And the Levites shall be Mine; I am the LORD. 46 And as a redemption price for the 273 of the firstborn of the sons of Israel who are in excess of *the number of* the Levites, 47 you shall take five shekels apiece, per head; you shall take *them* in terms of the shekel of the sanctuary (the shekel is twenty *¹gerahs*), 48 and you shall give the money, the redemption price of those who are in excess among them, to Aaron and to his sons." 49 So Moses took the redemption money from those who were in excess of *the number of* those redeemed by the Levites; 50 from the firstborn of the sons of Israel he took the money in terms of the shekel of the sanctuary, 1,365. 51 Then Moses gave the redemption money to Aaron and to his sons, at the command of the LORD, just as the LORD had commanded Moses.

Duties of the Kohathites

4 Then the LORD spoke to Moses and to Aaron, saying, 2 "Take a census of the descendants of Kohath from among the sons of Levi, by their families, by their fathers' households, 3 from thirty years old and upward, even to fifty years old, everyone who can enter the service *of ministry* to do work in the tent of meeting. 4 This is the work of the descendants of Kohath in the tent of meeting, *concerning* the most holy things.

5 "When the camp sets out, Aaron and his sons shall go in and take down the veil of the curtain, and cover the ark of the testimony

---

3:47 ¹A gerah is about 0.025 oz. or 0.7 gm

with it; 6 and they shall place a covering of ¹fine leather on it, and spread over it a cloth of pure ²violet, and insert its carrying poles. 7 Over the table of *the bread of* the Presence they shall also spread a cloth of violet and put on it the dishes, the pans, the sacrificial bowls, and the jugs for the drink offering; and the continual bread shall be on it. 8 And they shall spread over them a cloth of scarlet *material,* and cover the same with a covering of fine leather, and they shall insert its carrying poles. 9 Then they shall take a violet cloth and cover the lampstand for the light, along with its lamps, its tongs, its trays, and all its oil containers, by which they attend to it; 10 and they shall put it and all its utensils in a covering of fine leather, and put it on the carrying bars. 11 Over the golden altar they shall spread a violet cloth, and cover it with a covering of fine leather, and they shall insert its carrying poles; 12 and they shall take all the utensils of service, with which they serve in the sanctuary, and put *them* in a violet cloth and cover them with a covering of fine leather, and put them on the carrying bars. 13 Then they shall clean away the ashes from the altar, and spread a purple cloth over it. 14 They shall also put on it all its utensils by which they serve in connection with it: the firepans, the forks, shovels, and the basins, all the utensils of the altar; and they shall spread a cover of fine leather over it and insert its carrying poles. 15 When Aaron and his sons have finished covering the holy *objects* and all the furnishings of the sanctuary, when the camp is to set out, after that the sons of Kohath shall come to carry *them by the poles,* so that they will not touch the holy *objects* and die. These are the things in the tent of meeting that the sons of Kohath are to carry.

16 "Now the responsibility of Eleazar the son of Aaron the priest is the oil for the light, the fragrant incense, the continual grain offering, and the anointing oil—the responsibility of all the tabernacle and everything that is in it, with the sanctuary and its furnishings."

17 Then the LORD spoke to Moses and to Aaron, saying, 18 "Do not let the tribe of the families of the Kohathites be eliminated from among the Levites. 19 Rather, do this for them so that they will live and not die when they approach the most holy *objects:* Aaron and his sons shall go in and assign each of them to his work and to his load; 20 but they shall not come in to see the holy *objects* even for a moment, or they will die."

Duties of the Gershonites

21 Then the LORD spoke to Moses, saying, 22 "Take a census of the sons of Gershon also, by their fathers' households, by their families; 23 from thirty years old and upward to fifty years old you shall count them: all who can enter to perform service, to do the work in the tent of meeting. 24 This is the service of the families of the Gershonites, in serving and in carrying: 25 they shall carry the curtains of the tabernacle and the tent of meeting *with* its covering and the covering of fine leather that is

on top of it, and the curtain for the entrance of the tent of meeting, 26 and the curtains of the courtyard, the curtain for the entrance of the gate of the courtyard that is around the tabernacle and the altar, and their ropes and all the equipment for their service; and everything that is to be done by them, they shall perform. 27 All the service of the sons of the Gershonites, that is, all their loads and all their work, shall be *performed* at the command of Aaron and his sons; and you shall assign to them as a duty all their loads. 28 This is the service of the families of the sons of the Gershonites in the tent of meeting; and their duties *shall be* under the direction of Ithamar the son of Aaron the priest.

Duties of the Merarites

29 "*As for* the sons of Merari, you shall count them by their families, by their fathers' households; 30 from thirty years old and upward, even to fifty years old, you shall count them, everyone who can enter the service to do the work of the tent of meeting. 31 Now this is the duty of their loads, for all their service in the tent of meeting: the boards of the tabernacle, its bars, its pillars, and its bases, 32 and the pillars around the courtyard and their bases, their pegs, and their ropes, with all their equipment and with all their service; and you shall assign by names *of the men* the items that each is to carry. 33 This is the service of the families of the sons of Merari, according to all their service in the tent of meeting, under the direction of Ithamar the son of Aaron the priest."

34 So Moses, Aaron, and the leaders of the congregation counted the sons of the Kohathites by their families and by their fathers' households, 35 from thirty years old and upward even to fifty years old, everyone who could enter the service for work in the tent of meeting. 36 Their numbered men by their families were 2,750. 37 These were the numbered men of the Kohathite families, everyone who was serving in the tent of meeting, whom Moses and Aaron counted according to the commandment of the LORD through Moses.

38 And the numbered men of the sons of Gershon by their families and by their fathers' households, 39 from thirty years old and upward even to fifty years old, everyone who could enter the service for work in the tent of meeting—40 their numbered men by their families, by their fathers' households, were 2,630. 41 These were the numbered men of the families of the sons of Gershon, everyone who was serving in the tent of meeting, whom Moses and Aaron counted according to the commandment of the LORD.

42 And the numbered men of the families of the sons of Merari by their families, by their fathers' households, 43 from thirty years old and upward even to fifty years old, everyone who could enter the service for work in the tent of meeting—44 their numbered men by their families were 3,200. 45 These were the

---

4:6 1 Meaning of the Heb uncertain, and so throughout the ch   2 Or *bluish;* LXX *hyacinth* in color, and so throughout the ch

numbered men of the families of the sons of Merari, whom Moses and Aaron counted according to the commandment of the LORD through Moses.

46 All the numbered men of the Levites, whom Moses and Aaron, and the leaders of Israel counted, by their families and by their fathers' households, 47 from thirty years old and upward even to fifty years old, everyone who could enter to do the work of service and the work of carrying in the tent of meeting— 48 their numbered men were 8,580. 49 According to the commandment of the LORD through Moses, they were counted, everyone by his serving or carrying; so *these were* his numbered men, just as the LORD had commanded Moses.

On Defilement

5 Then the LORD spoke to Moses, saying, 2 "Command the sons of Israel that they send away from the camp everyone with leprosy, everyone having a discharge, and everyone who is unclean because of *contact with* a *dead* person. 3 You shall send away both male and female; you shall send them outside the camp so that they do not defile their camp where I dwell in their midst." 4 And the sons of Israel did so and sent them outside the camp; just as the LORD had spoken to Moses, that is what the sons of Israel did.

5 Then the LORD spoke to Moses, saying, 6 "Speak to the sons of Israel: 'When a man or woman commits any of the sins of mankind, acting unfaithfully against the LORD, and that person is guilty, 7 then he shall confess his sin which he has committed, and he shall make restitution in full for his wrong and add to it a fifth of it, and give *it* to him whom he has wronged. 8 But if the person has no ¹redeemer to whom restitution may be made for the wrong, the restitution which is made for the wrong *must go* to the LORD for the priest, besides the ram of atonement, by which atonement is made for him. 9 Also every contribution pertaining to all the holy *gifts* of the sons of Israel, which they offer to the priest, shall be his. 10 So every person's holy *gifts* shall be his; whatever anyone gives to the priest, it becomes his.'"

The Adultery Test

11 Then the LORD spoke to Moses, saying, 12 "Speak to the sons of Israel and say to them, 'If any man's wife goes astray and is unfaithful to him, 13 and a man has sexual relations with her and it is hidden from the eyes of her husband and she remains undiscovered, although she has defiled herself, and there is no witness against her and she has not been caught in the act, 14 if an attitude of jealousy comes over him and he is jealous of his wife when she has defiled herself, or if an attitude of jealousy comes over him and he is jealous of his wife when she has not defiled herself, 15 the man shall then bring his wife to the priest, and shall bring *as* an offering for her a tenth of an ¹ephah of barley meal; he shall not pour oil·on it nor put frankincense on it, because it is a grain offering of jealousy, a grain offering of reminder, a reminder of wrongdoing.

16 'Then the priest shall bring her forward and have her stand before the LORD, 17 and the priest shall take holy water in an earthenware container; and he shall take some of the dust that is on the floor of the tabernacle and put *it* in the water. 18 The priest shall then have the woman stand before the LORD and let down *the hair of* the woman's head, and place the grain offering of reminder in her hands, that is, the grain offering of jealousy; and in the hand of the priest is to be the water of bitterness that brings a curse. 19 And the priest shall have her take an oath and shall say to the woman, "If no man has had sexual relations with you and if you have not gone astray into uncleanness, *as you are* under *the authority of* your husband, be immune to this water of bitterness that brings a curse; 20 if, however, you have gone astray, *though* under *the authority of* your husband, and if you have defiled yourself and a man other than your husband has had sexual intercourse with you" 21 (then the priest shall have the woman swear with the oath of the curse, and the priest shall say to the woman), "may the LORD make you a curse and an oath among your people by the LORD's making your thigh shrivel and your ¹belly swollen; ²² and this water that brings a curse shall go into your stomach, to make your belly swell up and your thigh shrivel." And the woman shall say, "Amen, Amen."

23 'The priest shall then write these curses on a scroll, and he shall wash them off into the water of bitterness. 24 Then he shall make the woman drink the water of bitterness that brings a curse, so that the water which brings a curse will go into her and cause bitterness. 25 And the priest shall take the grain offering of jealousy from the woman's hand, and he shall wave the grain offering before the LORD and bring it to the altar; 26 and the priest shall take a handful of the grain offering as its reminder offering and offer *it* up in smoke on the altar, and afterward he shall make the woman drink the water. 27 When he has made her drink the water, then it will come about, if she has defiled herself and has been unfaithful to her husband, that the water which brings a curse will go into her and cause bitterness, and her belly will swell up and her thigh will shrivel, and the woman will become a curse among her people. 28 But if the woman has not defiled herself and is clean, she will be immune and conceive children.

29 'This is the law of jealousy: when a wife, *who is* under *the authority of* her husband, goes astray and defiles herself, 30 or when an attitude of jealousy comes over a man and he is jealous of his wife, he shall then have the woman stand before the LORD, and the priest shall apply all of this law to her. 31 The man, moreover, will be free of guilt, but that woman shall bear *the consequences of* her guilt.'"

Law of the Nazirites

6 Again the LORD spoke to Moses, saying, 2 "Speak to the sons of Israel and say to them, 'When a man or woman makes a special vow, *namely,* the vow of a [1]Nazirite, to live as a Nazirite for the LORD, 3 he shall abstain from wine and strong drink; he shall consume no vinegar, *whether made* from wine or strong drink, nor shall he drink any grape juice nor eat fresh or dried grapes. 4 All the days of his consecration he shall not eat anything that is produced from the grape vine, from *the* seeds even to *the* skin.

5 'All the days of his vow of consecration no razor shall pass over his head. He shall be holy until the days are fulfilled which he lives as a Nazirite for the LORD; he shall let the locks of hair on his head grow long.

6 'All the days of his life as a Nazirite for the LORD he shall not come up to a dead person. 7 He shall not make himself unclean for his father or for his mother, for his brother or for his sister, when they die, because his consecration to God is on his head. 8 All the days of his consecration he is holy to the LORD.

9 'But if *someone* dies very suddenly beside him and he defiles his consecrated head *of hair,* then he shall shave his head on the day when he becomes clean; he shall shave it on the seventh day. 10 Then on the eighth day he shall bring two turtledoves or two young doves to the priest, to the entrance of the tent of meeting. 11 And the priest shall offer one as a sin offering and *the* other as a burnt offering, and make atonement for him regarding his sin because of the *dead* person. And on that same day he shall consecrate his head, 12 and shall live his days of consecration as a Nazirite for the LORD, and shall bring a male lamb a year old as a guilt offering; but the preceding days will not count, because his consecration was defiled.

13 'Now this is the law of the Nazirite when the days of his consecration are fulfilled: he shall bring his offering to the entrance of the tent of meeting. 14 And he shall present his offering to the LORD: one male lamb a year old without defect as a burnt offering, one ewe lamb a year old without defect as a sin offering, one ram without defect as a peace offering, 15 and a basket of unleavened loaves of fine flour mixed with oil and unleavened wafers spread with oil, along with their grain offering and their drink offering. 16 Then the priest shall present *them* before the LORD and offer his sin offering and his burnt offering. 17 He shall also offer the ram as a sacrifice of peace offerings to the LORD, together with the basket of unleavened bread; the priest shall also offer its grain offering and its drink offering. 18 The Nazirite shall then shave his consecrated head *of hair* at the entrance of the tent of meeting, and take the consecrated hair of his head and put *it* on the fire which is under the sacrifice of peace offerings. 19 And the priest shall take the ram's shoulder *when it has been* boiled, and one unleavened loaf from the basket and one unleavened wafer, and shall put *them* on the hands of the Nazirite after he has shaved his consecrated *hair.* 20 Then the priest shall wave them as a wave offering before the LORD. It is holy for the priest, together with the breast *offered as* a wave offering, and the thigh *offered as* a contribution; and afterward the Nazirite may drink wine.'

21 "This is the law of the Nazirite who vows his offering to the LORD according to his consecration, in addition to what *else* he can afford; corresponding to his vow which he makes, so he shall do according to the law of his consecration."

Aaron's Benediction

22 Then the LORD spoke to Moses, saying, 23 "Speak to Aaron and to his sons, saying, 'In this way you shall bless the sons of Israel. You are to say to them:

24¶ The LORD bless you, and keep you;
25¶ The LORD cause His face to shine on you,
   And be gracious to you;
26¶ The LORD lift up His face to you,
   And give you peace.'

27 So they shall invoke My name on the sons of Israel, and *then* I will bless them."

Offerings of the Leaders

7 Now on the day that Moses had finished setting up the tabernacle, he anointed it and consecrated it with all its furnishings, and the altar and all its utensils; he anointed them and consecrated them also. 2 Then the leaders of Israel, the heads of their fathers' households, made an offering (they were the leaders of the tribes; they were the supervisors over the numbered men). 3 When they brought their offering before the LORD, six covered carts and twelve oxen, a cart for *every* two of the leaders and an ox for each one, then they presented them in front of the tabernacle. 4 Then the LORD spoke to Moses, saying, 5 "Accept *these things* from them, that they may be used in the service of the tent of meeting, and you shall give them to the Levites, *to* each man according to his service." 6 So Moses took the carts and the oxen and gave them to the Levites. 7 Two carts and four oxen he gave to the sons of Gershon, according to their service, 8 and four carts and eight oxen he gave to the sons of Merari, according to their service, under the direction of Ithamar the son of Aaron the priest. 9 But he did not give *any* to the sons of Kohath, because theirs *was* the service of the holy *objects, which* they carried on the shoulder.

10 And the leaders offered the dedication *offering* for the altar when it was anointed, so the leaders offered their offering before the altar. 11 Then the LORD said to Moses, "They shall present their offering, one leader each day, for the dedication of the altar."

12 Now the one who presented his offering on the first day was Nahshon the son of Amminadab, of the tribe of Judah; 13 and his offering *was* one silver dish whose weight *was* 130 *shekels, and* one silver bowl of seventy shekels in sanctuary shekels, both of them full of fine flour mixed with oil as a grain offering; 14 one gold pan of ten *shekels,* full of incense;

6:2 [1] I.e., one consecrated to God

15 one bull, one ram, *and* one male lamb one year old, as a burnt offering; **16** one male goat as a sin offering; **17** and for the sacrifice of peace offerings, two oxen, five rams, five male goats, *and* five male lambs one year old. This *was* the offering of Nahshon the son of Amminadab.

18 On the second day Nethanel the son of Zuar, leader of Issachar, presented *an offering;* **19** he presented as his offering one silver dish whose weight *was* 130 *shekels, and* one silver bowl of seventy shekels in sanctuary shekels, both of them full of fine flour mixed with oil as a grain offering; **20** one gold pan of ten *shekels,* full of incense; **21** one bull, one ram, *and* one male lamb one year old, as a burnt offering; **22** one male goat as a sin offering; **23** and for the sacrifice of peace offerings, two oxen, five rams, five male goats, *and* five male lambs one year old. This *was* the offering of Nethanel the son of Zuar.

24 On the third day *it was* Eliab the son of Helon, leader of the sons of Zebulun; **25** his offering *was also* one silver dish whose weight *was* 130 *shekels, and* one silver bowl of seventy shekels in sanctuary shekels, both of them full of fine flour mixed with oil as a grain offering; **26** one gold pan of ten *shekels,* full of incense; **27** one bull, one ram, *and* one male lamb one year old, as a burnt offering; **28** one male goat as a sin offering; **29** and for the sacrifice of peace offerings, two oxen, five rams, five male goats, *and* five male lambs one year old. This *was* the offering of Eliab the son of Helon.

30 On the fourth day *it was* Elizur the son of Shedeur, leader of the sons of Reuben; **31** his offering *was also* one silver dish whose weight *was* 130 *shekels, and* one silver bowl of seventy shekels in sanctuary shekels, both of them full of fine flour mixed with oil as a grain offering; **32** one gold pan of ten *shekels,* full of incense; **33** one bull, one ram, *and* one male lamb one year old, as a burnt offering; **34** one male goat as a sin offering; **35** and for the sacrifice of peace offerings, two oxen, five rams, five male goats, *and* five male lambs one year old. This *was* the offering of Elizur the son of Shedeur.

36 On the fifth day *it was* Shelumiel the son of Zurishaddai, leader of the sons of Simeon; **37** his offering *was also* one silver dish whose weight *was* 130 *shekels, and* one silver bowl of seventy shekels in sanctuary shekels, both of them full of fine flour mixed with oil as a grain offering; **38** one gold pan of ten *shekels,* full of incense; **39** one bull, one ram, *and* one male lamb one year old, as a burnt offering; **40** one male goat as a sin offering; **41** and for the sacrifice of peace offerings, two oxen, five rams, five male goats, *and* five male lambs one year old. This *was* the offering of Shelumiel the son of Zurishaddai.

42 On the sixth day *it was* Eliasaph the son of Deuel, leader of the sons of Gad; **43** his offering *was also* one silver dish whose weight *was* 130 *shekels, and* one silver bowl of seventy shekels in sanctuary shekels, both of them full of fine flour mixed with oil as a grain offering; **44** one gold pan of ten *shekels,* full of incense; **45** one bull, one ram, *and* one male

lamb one year old, as a burnt offering; **46** one male goat as a sin offering; **47** and for the sacrifice of peace offerings, two oxen, five rams, five male goats, *and* five male lambs one year old. This *was* the offering of Eliasaph the son of Deuel.

48 On the seventh day *it was* Elishama the son of Ammihud, leader of the sons of Ephraim; **49** his offering *was also* one silver dish whose weight *was* 130 *shekels, and* one silver bowl of seventy shekels in sanctuary shekels, both of them full of fine flour mixed with oil as a grain offering; **50** one gold pan of ten *shekels,* full of incense; **51** one bull, one ram, *and* one male lamb one year old, as a burnt offering; **52** one male goat as a sin offering; **53** and for the sacrifice of peace offerings, two oxen, five rams, five male goats, *and* five male lambs one year old. This *was* the offering of Elishama the son of Ammihud.

54 On the eighth day *it was* Gamaliel the son of Pedahzur, leader of the sons of Manasseh; **55** his offering *was also* one silver dish whose weight *was* 130 *shekels, and* one silver bowl of seventy shekels in sanctuary shekels, both of them full of fine flour mixed with oil as a grain offering; **56** one gold pan of ten *shekels,* full of incense; **57** one bull, one ram, *and* one male lamb one year old, as a burnt offering; **58** one male goat as a sin offering; **59** and for the sacrifice of peace offerings, two oxen, five rams, five male goats, *and* five male lambs one year old. This *was* the offering of Gamaliel the son of Pedahzur.

60 On the ninth day *it was* Abidan the son of Gideoni, leader of the sons of Benjamin; **61** his offering *was also* one silver dish whose weight *was* 130 *shekels, and* one silver bowl of seventy shekels in sanctuary shekels, both of them full of fine flour mixed with oil as a grain offering; **62** one gold pan of ten *shekels,* full of incense; **63** one bull, one ram, *and* one male lamb one year old, as a burnt offering; **64** one male goat as a sin offering; **65** and for the sacrifice of peace offerings, two oxen, five rams, five male goats, *and* five male lambs one year old. This *was* the offering of Abidan the son of Gideoni.

66 On the tenth day *it was* Ahiezer the son of Ammishaddai, leader of the sons of Dan; **67** his offering *was also* one silver dish whose weight *was* 130 *shekels, and* one silver bowl of seventy shekels in sanctuary shekels, both of them full of fine flour mixed with oil as a grain offering; **68** one gold pan of ten *shekels,* full of incense; **69** one bull, one ram, *and* one male lamb one year old, as a burnt offering; **70** one male goat as a sin offering; **71** and for the sacrifice of peace offerings, two oxen, five rams, five male goats, *and* five male lambs one year old. This *was* the offering of Ahiezer the son of Ammishaddai.

72 On the eleventh day *it was* Pagiel the son of Ochran, leader of the sons of Asher; **73** his offering *was also* one silver dish whose weight *was* 130 *shekels, and* one silver bowl of seventy shekels in sanctuary shekels, both of them full of fine flour mixed with oil as a grain offering; **74** one gold pan of ten *shekels,* full of incense; **75** one bull, one ram, *and* one male

lamb one year old, as a burnt offering; 76 one male goat as a sin offering; 77 and for the sacrifice of peace offerings, two oxen, five rams, five male goats, *and* five male lambs one year old. This *was* the offering of Pagiel the son of Ochran.

78 On the twelfth day *it was* Ahira the son of Enan, leader of the sons of Naphtali; 79 his offering *was also* one silver dish whose weight *was* 130 *shekels,* and one silver bowl of seventy shekels in sanctuary shekels, both of them full of fine flour mixed with oil as a grain offering; 80 one gold pan of ten *shekels,* full of incense; 81 one bull, one ram, *and* one male lamb one year old, as a burnt offering; 82 one male goat as a sin offering; 83 and for the sacrifice of peace offerings, two oxen, five rams, five male goats, *and* five male lambs one year old. This *was* the offering of Ahira the son of Enan.

84 This *was* the dedication *offering* for the altar from the leaders of Israel when it was anointed: twelve silver dishes, twelve silver bowls, *and* twelve gold pans, 85 each silver dish *weighing* 130 *shekels* and each bowl seventy; all the silver of the utensils *totaled* 2,400 in sanctuary shekels; 86 the twelve gold pans full of incense, *weighing* ten *shekels* apiece in sanctuary shekels, all the gold of the pans *totaled* 120 *shekels.* 87 All the oxen for the burnt offering *totaled* twelve bulls, *all* the rams, twelve, the male lambs one year old with their grain offering, twelve, and the male goats as a sin offering, twelve; 88 and all the oxen for the sacrifice of peace offerings *totaled* twenty-four bulls, *all* the rams, sixty, the male goats, sixty, *and* the male lambs one year old, sixty. This *was* the dedication *offering* for the altar after it was anointed.

89 Now when Moses entered the tent of meeting to speak with Him, he heard the voice speaking to him from above the ⟨atoning cover that was on the ark of the testimony, from between the two cherubim; so He spoke to him.

The Seven Lamps

8 Then the LORD spoke to Moses, saying, 2 "Speak to Aaron and say to him, 'When you mount the lamps, the seven lamps will provide light in the front of the lampstand.'" 3 Therefore Aaron did so; he mounted its lamps at the front of the lampstand, just as the LORD had commanded Moses. 4 Now this was the workmanship of the lampstand, hammered work of gold; from its base to its flower ornamentation it was hammered work; according to the pattern which the LORD had shown Moses, so he made the lampstand.

Cleansing the Levites

5 Again the LORD spoke to Moses, saying, 6 "Take the Levites from among the sons of Israel and cleanse them. 7 This is what you shall do to them, for their cleansing: sprinkle purifying water on them, and have them use a razor over their whole body, and they shall wash their clothes and cleanse themselves.

8 Then have them take a bull with its grain offering, fine flour mixed with oil; and you shall take a second bull as a sin offering. 9 So you shall present the Levites in front of the tent of meeting. You shall also assemble the whole congregation of the sons of Israel, 10 and present the Levites before the LORD; and the sons of Israel shall lay their hands on the Levites. 11 Aaron then shall present the Levites before the LORD as a wave offering from the sons of Israel, so that they may qualify to perform the service of the LORD. 12 Now the Levites shall lay their hands on the heads of the bulls; then you are to offer the one as a sin offering and the other as a burnt offering to the LORD, to make atonement for the Levites. 13 And you shall have the Levites stand before Aaron and his sons so as to present them as a wave offering to the LORD.

14 "So you shall single out the Levites from among the sons of Israel, and the Levites shall be Mine. 15 Then after that the Levites may go in to serve the tent of meeting. But you shall cleanse them and present them as a wave offering; 16 for they are exclusively given to Me from among the sons of Israel. I have taken them for Myself instead of the firstborn of every womb, the firstborn of all the sons of Israel. 17 For every firstborn among the sons of Israel is Mine, among the people and among the animals; on the day that I fatally struck all the firstborn in the land of Egypt, I sanctified them for Myself. 18 But I have taken the Levites instead of every firstborn among the sons of Israel. 19 And I have given the Levites as a gift to Aaron and to his sons from among the sons of Israel, to perform the service of the sons of Israel at the tent of meeting and to make atonement on behalf of the sons of Israel, so that there will be no affliction among the sons of Israel due to their approaching the sanctuary."

20 So *this is what* Moses, Aaron, and all the congregation of the sons of Israel did to the Levites; according to everything that the LORD had commanded Moses regarding the Levites, so the sons of Israel did to them. 21 The Levites, too, purified themselves from sin and washed their clothes; and Aaron presented them as a wave offering before the LORD. Aaron also made atonement for them to cleanse them. 22 Then after that the Levites went in to perform their service in the tent of meeting before Aaron and his sons; just as the LORD had commanded Moses concerning the Levites, so they did to them.

Retirement for the Levites

23 Now the LORD spoke to Moses, saying, 24 "This is what *applies* to the Levites: from twenty-five years old and upward they shall enter to perform service in the work of the tent of meeting. 25 But at the age of fifty years they shall retire from service in the work and not work anymore. 26 They may, however, assist their brothers in the tent of meeting, to fulfill an obligation, but they *themselves* shall do no work. In this way you shall deal with the Levites in their obligations."

7:89 ⟨ Also called *mercy seat;* i.e., where blood was sprinkled on the Day of Atonement

The Passover

9 Now the LORD spoke to Moses in the wilderness of Sinai, in the first month of the second year after they had come out of the land of Egypt, saying, **2** "Now the sons of Israel are to celebrate the Passover at its appointed time. **3** On the fourteenth day of this month, at twilight, you shall celebrate it at its appointed time; you shall celebrate it in accordance with all its statutes and all its ordinances." **4** So Moses told the sons of Israel to celebrate the Passover. **5** And they celebrated the Passover in the first *month,* on the fourteenth day of the month, at twilight, in the wilderness of Sinai; in accordance with everything that the LORD had commanded Moses, so the sons of Israel did. **6** But there were *some* men who were unclean because of *contact with a* dead person, so that they could not celebrate Passover on that day; and they came before Moses and Aaron on that day. **7** Those men said to him, "*Though* we are unclean because of a dead person, why are we kept from presenting the offering of the LORD at its appointed time among the sons of Israel?" **8** Moses then said to them, "Wait, and I will listen to what the LORD will command concerning you."

9 Then the LORD spoke to Moses, saying, **10** "Speak to the sons of Israel, saying, 'If any one of you or of your generations becomes unclean because of a *dead* person, or is on a distant journey, he may, however, celebrate the Passover to the LORD. **11** In the second month on the fourteenth day at twilight, they shall celebrate it; they shall eat it with unleavened bread and bitter herbs. **12** They shall not leave any of it until morning, nor break a bone of it; they shall celebrate it in accordance with the whole statute of the Passover. **13** But the person who is clean and is not on a journey, yet refrains from celebrating the Passover, that person shall then be cut off from his people, because he did not present the offering of the LORD at its appointed time. That person will bear *the responsibility for* his sin. **14** And if a stranger resides among you and celebrates the Passover to the LORD, according to the statute of the Passover and its ordinance, so he shall celebrate *it;* you shall have the same statute, both for the stranger and for the native of the land.' "

The Cloud on the Tabernacle

15 Now on the day that the tabernacle was erected, the cloud covered the tabernacle, the tent of the testimony, and in the evening it was like the appearance of fire over the tabernacle until morning. **16** That is how it was continuously; the cloud would cover it *by day,* and the appearance of fire by night. **17** Whenever the cloud was lifted from over the tent, afterward the sons of Israel would set out; and in the place where the cloud settled down, there the sons of Israel would camp. **18** At the command of the LORD the sons of Israel would set out, and at the command of the LORD they would camp; as long as the cloud settled over the tabernacle, they remained camped. **19** Even when the cloud lingered over the tabernacle for many days, the sons of Israel would comply with the LORD's ordinance and not set out. **20** If sometimes the cloud remained a few days over the tabernacle, in accordance with the command of the LORD they remained camped. Then in accordance with the command of the LORD they set out. **21** If sometimes the cloud remained from evening until morning, when the cloud was lifted in the morning they would set out; or *if it remained* in the daytime and at night, whenever the cloud was lifted, they would set out. **22** Whether it was two days, a month, or a year that the cloud lingered over the tabernacle, staying above it, the sons of Israel remained camped and did not set out; but when it was lifted, they did set out. **23** At the command of the LORD they camped, and at the command of the LORD they set out; they did what the LORD required, in accordance with the command of the LORD through Moses.

The Silver Trumpets

10 The LORD spoke further to Moses, saying, **2** "Make yourself two trumpets of silver, you shall make them of hammered work; and you shall use them for summoning the congregation and breaking camp. **3** Now when both are blown, all the congregation shall meet you at the entrance of the tent of meeting. **4** But if *only* one is blown, then the leaders, the heads of the divisions of Israel, shall meet you. **5** And when you blow an alarm, the camps that are pitched on the east side shall set out. **6** Then when you sound an alarm the second time, the camps that are pitched on the south side shall set out; an alarm is to be sounded for them to break camp. **7** When convening the assembly, however, you shall blow *the trumpets* without sounding an alarm. **8** The sons of Aaron, moreover, the priests, shall blow the trumpets; and *this* shall be a permanent statute for you throughout your generations. **9** And when you go to war in your land against the enemy who attacks you, then you shall sound an alarm with the trumpets, so that you will be thought of by the LORD your God, and be saved from your enemies. **10** Also on the day of your joy and at your appointed feasts, and on the first *days* of your months, you shall blow the trumpets over your burnt offerings, and over the sacrifices of your peace offerings; and they shall be as a reminder of you before your God. I am the LORD your God."

The Tribes Leave Sinai

11 Now in the second year, in the second month, on the twentieth of the month, the cloud was lifted from above the tabernacle of the testimony; **12** and the sons of Israel set out on their journeys from the wilderness of Sinai. Then the cloud settled in the wilderness of Paran. **13** So they moved on for the first time in accordance with the command of the LORD through Moses. **14** The flag of the camp of the sons of Judah, by their armies, set out first, with Nahshon the son of Amminadab, over its army, **15** and Nethanel the son of Zuar, over the tribal army of the sons of Issachar; **16** and Eliab the son of Helon over the tribal army of the sons of Zebulun.

17 Then the tabernacle was taken down; and

the sons of Gershon and the sons of Merari, who were carrying the tabernacle, set out. 18 Next the flag of the camp of Reuben, by their armies, set out with Elizur the son of Shedeur, over its army, 19 and Shelumiel the son of Zurishaddai over the tribal army of the sons of Simeon, 20 and Eliasaph the son of Deuel was over the tribal army of the sons of Gad.

21 Then the Kohathites set out, carrying the holy *objects;* and the tabernacle was set up before their arrival. 22 Next the flag of the camp of the sons of Ephraim, by their armies, set out, with Elishama the son of Ammihud over its army, 23 and Gamaliel the son of Pedahzur over the tribal army of the sons of Manasseh; 24 and Abidan the son of Gideoni over the tribal army of the sons of Benjamin.

25 Then the flag of the camp of the sons of Dan, by their armies, *which* formed the rear guard for all the camps, set out, with Ahiezer the son of Ammishaddai over its army, 26 and Pagiel the son of Ochran over the tribal army of the sons of Asher; 27 and Ahira the son of Enan over the tribal army of the sons of Naphtali. 28 This was the order of marching for the sons of Israel by their armies as they set out.

29 Then Moses said to Hobab the son of Reuel the Midianite, Moses' father-in-law, "We are setting out to the place of which the LORD said, 'I will give it to you.' Come with us and we will do you good, for the LORD has promised good concerning Israel." 30 But he said to him, "I will not come, but rather will go to my *own* land and relatives." 31 Then he said, "Please do not leave us, since you know where we should camp in the wilderness, and you will be as eyes for us. 32 So it will be, if you go with us, that whatever good the LORD does for us, we will do for you."

33 So they moved on from the mountain of the LORD three days' journey, with the ark of the covenant of the LORD going on in front of them for the three days, to seek out a resting place for them. 34 And the cloud of the LORD was over them by day when they set out from the camp.

35 Then it came about when the ark set out that Moses said,

"Rise up, LORD!
And may Your enemies be scattered,
And those who hate You flee from Your
    presence."

36 And when it came to rest, he said,

"Return, LORD,
To the myriad thousands of Israel."

The People Complain

11 Now the people became like those who complain of adversity in the ears of the LORD; and the LORD heard *them* and His anger was kindled, and the fire of the LORD burned among them and consumed *some* at the outskirts of the camp. 2 The people then cried out to Moses; and Moses prayed to the LORD, and the fire died out. 3 So that place was named ᵗTaberah, because the fire of the LORD burned among them.

4 Now the rabble who were among them had greedy cravings; and the sons of Israel also wept again and said, "Who will give us meat to eat? 5 We remember the fish which we used to eat for free in Egypt, the cucumbers, the melons, the leeks, the onions, and the garlic; 6 but now our appetite is gone. There is nothing at all to look at except this manna!"

7 Now the manna was like coriander seed, and its appearance like that of ᵗbdellium. 8 The people would roam about and gather *it* and grind *it* between two millstones, or pound *it* in the mortar, and boil *it* in the pot and make loaves with it; and its taste was like the taste of cake *baked with* oil. 9 When the dew came down on the camp at night, the manna would come down with it.

The Complaint of Moses

10 Now Moses heard the people weeping throughout their families, each one at the entrance of his tent; and the anger of the LORD became very hot, and Moses was displeased. 11 So Moses said to the LORD, "Why have You been so hard on Your servant? And why have I not found favor in Your sight, that You have put the burden of all this people on me? 12 Was it I who conceived all this people? Or did I give birth to them, that You should say to me, 'Carry them in your arms, as a nurse carries a nursing infant, to the land which You swore to their fathers'? 13 Where am I to get meat to give to all this people? For they weep before me, saying, 'Give us meat so that we may eat!' 14 I am not able to carry all this people by myself, because it is too burdensome for me. 15 So if You are going to deal with me this way, please kill me now, if I have found favor in Your sight, and do not let me see my misery."

Seventy Elders to Assist Moses

16 The LORD therefore said to Moses, "Gather for Me seventy men from the elders of Israel, whom you know to be the elders of the people and their officers, and bring them to the tent of meeting, and have them take their stand there with you. 17 Then I will come down and speak with you there, and I will take away some of the Spirit who is upon you, and put *Him* upon them; and they shall bear the burden of the people with you, so that you will not bear *it* by yourself. 18 And you shall say to the people, 'Consecrate yourselves for tomorrow, and you shall eat meat; for you have wept in the ears of the LORD, saying, "Oh that someone would give us meat to eat! For we were well-off in Egypt." Therefore the LORD will give you meat and you shall eat. 19 You shall eat, not one day, nor two days, nor five days, nor ten days, nor twenty days, 20 but for a whole month, until it comes out of your nose and makes you nauseated; because you have rejected the LORD who is among you and have wept before Him, saying, "Why did we ever leave Egypt?"'" 21 But Moses said, "The people, among whom I am *included,* are six hundred thousand on foot! Yet You have said, 'I will give them meat, so that they may eat for a whole month.' 22 Are flocks and herds to be slaughtered for them, so that it will be sufficient for them? Or are all the fish of the

---

sea to be caught for them, so that it will be sufficient for them?" 23 Then the LORD said to Moses, "Is the LORD's power too little? Now you shall see whether My word will come true for you or not."

24 So Moses went out and told the people the words of the LORD. He also gathered seventy men of the elders of the people, and positioned them around the tent. 25 Then the LORD came down in the cloud and spoke to him; and He took away some of the Spirit who was upon him and placed *Him* upon the seventy elders. And when the Spirit rested upon them, they prophesied. Yet they did not do *it* again.

26 But two men had remained in the camp; the name of the one was Eldad, and the name of the other, Medad. And the Spirit rested upon them (and they were among those who had been registered, but had not gone out to the tent), and they prophesied in the camp. 27 So a young man ran and informed Moses, and said, "Eldad and Medad are prophesying in the camp." 28 Then Joshua the son of Nun, the personal servant of Moses from his youth, responded and said, "My lord Moses, restrain them!" 29 But Moses said to him, "Are you jealous for my sake? If only all the LORD's people were prophets, that the LORD would put His Spirit upon them!" 30 Then Moses returned to the camp, *both* he and the elders of Israel.

The Quail and the Plague

31 Now a wind burst forth from the LORD and it brought quail from the sea, and dropped *them* beside the camp, about a day's journey on this *side* and a day's journey on the other *side* all around the camp, and about [1]two cubits *deep* on the surface of the ground. 32 And the people spent all that day, all night, and all the next day, and they gathered the quail (the one who gathered least gathered [1]ten homers) and spread *them* out for themselves all around the camp. 33 While the meat was still between their teeth, before it was chewed, the anger of the LORD was kindled against the people, and the LORD struck the people with a very severe plague. 34 So that place was named [1]Kibroth-hattaavah, because there they buried the people who had been greedy. 35 From Kibroth-hattaavah the people set out for Hazeroth, and they remained at Hazeroth.

The Murmuring of Miriam and Aaron

12 Then Miriam and Aaron spoke against Moses because of the Cushite woman whom he had married (for he had married a Cushite woman); 2 and they said, "Is it a fact that the LORD has spoken only through Moses? Has He not spoken through us as well?" And the LORD heard *this.* 3 (Now the man Moses was very humble, more than any person who was on the face of the earth.) 4 And the LORD suddenly said to Moses and to Aaron and Miriam, "You three go out to the tent of meeting." So the three of them went out. 5 Then the LORD came down in a pillar of cloud

and stood at the entrance of the tent; and He called Aaron and Miriam. When they had both come forward, 6 He said,

"Now hear My words:
If there is a prophet among you,
I, the LORD, will make Myself known to
   him in a vision.
I will speak with him in a dream.
7 "*It is* not this way *for* My servant Moses;
He is faithful in all My household;
8 With him I speak mouth to mouth,
That is, openly, and not using mysterious
   language,
And he beholds the form of the LORD.
So why were you not afraid
To speak against My servant, against
   Moses?"

9 And the anger of the LORD burned against them and He departed. 10 But when the cloud had withdrawn from above the tent, behold, Miriam *was* leprous, as *white as* snow. As Aaron turned toward Miriam, behold, she *was* leprous. 11 Then Aaron said to Moses, "Oh, my lord, I beg you, do not hold us responsible for this sin by which we have turned out to be foolish, and by which we have sinned. 12 Oh, do not let her be like a dead person, whose flesh is half eaten away when he comes out of his mother's womb!" 13 So Moses cried out to the LORD, saying, "God, heal her, please!" 14 But the LORD said to Moses, "If her father had only spit in her face, would she not be put to shame for seven days? Have her shut outside the camp for seven days, and afterward she may be received again." 15 So Miriam was shut outside the camp for seven days, and the people did not move on until Miriam was received again.

16 Afterward, however, the people moved on from Hazeroth and camped in the wilderness of Paran.

Spies View the Land

13 Then the LORD spoke to Moses, saying, 2 "Send out men for yourself to spy out the land of Canaan, which I am going to give the sons of Israel; you shall send a man from each of their fathers' tribes, every one a leader among them." 3 So Moses sent them from the wilderness of Paran at the command of the LORD, all of them men who were heads of the sons of Israel. 4 These then *were* their names: from the tribe of Reuben, Shammua the son of Zaccur; 5 from the tribe of Simeon, Shaphat the son of Hori; 6 from the tribe of Judah, Caleb the son of Jephunneh; 7 from the tribe of Issachar, Igal the son of Joseph; 8 from the tribe of Ephraim, Hoshea the son of Nun; 9 from the tribe of Benjamin, Palti the son of Raphu; 10 from the tribe of Zebulun, Gaddiel the son of Sodi; 11 from the tribe of Joseph, from the tribe of Manasseh, Gaddi the son of Susi; 12 from the tribe of Dan, Ammiel the son of Gemalli; 13 from the tribe of Asher, Sethur the son of Michael; 14 from the tribe of Naphtali, Nahbi the son of Vophsi; 15 *and* from the tribe of Gad, Geuel the son of Machi. 16 These are the names of the men whom Moses sent to spy out the

---

11:31 [1] About 3 ft. or 90 cm   11:32 [1] About 77 cubic feet or 2.2 cubic meters   11:34 [1] I.e., the graves of greediness

land; but Moses called Hoshea the son of Nun, Joshua.

17 When Moses sent them to spy out the land of Canaan, he said to them, "Go up there into the 'Negev; then go up into the hill country. 18 See what the land is *like*, and whether the people who live in it are strong or weak, whether they are few or many. 19 And how is the land in which they live, is it good or bad? And how are the cities in which they live, are *the people* in *open* camps or in fortifications? 20 And how is the land, is it productive or unproductive? Are there trees in it or not? And show yourselves courageous and get some of the fruit of the land." Now the time was the season of the first ripe grapes.

21 So they went up and spied out the land from the wilderness of Zin as far as Rehob, at Lebo-hamath. 22 When they had gone up into the Negev, they came to Hebron where Ahiman, Sheshai, and Talmai, the descendants of Anak were. (Hebron was built seven years before Zoan in Egypt.) 23 Then they came to the Valley of 'Eshcol, and from there they cut off a branch with a single cluster of grapes; and they carried it on a pole between two *men,* with some of the pomegranates and the figs. 24 That place was called the Valley of Eshcol, because of the cluster which the sons of Israel cut off from there.

The Spies' Reports

25 When they returned from spying out the land, at the end of forty days, 26 they went on and came to Moses and Aaron and to all the congregation of the sons of Israel, in the wilderness of Paran at Kadesh; and they brought back word to them and to all the congregation, and showed them the fruit of the land. 27 So they reported to him and said, "We came into the land where you sent us, and it certainly does flow with milk and honey, and this is its fruit. 28 Nevertheless, the people who live in the land are strong, and the cities are fortified *and* very large. And indeed, we saw the descendants of Anak there! 29 Amalek is living in the land of the Negev, the Hittites, the Jebusites, and the Amorites are living in the hill country, and the Canaanites are living by the sea and by the side of the Jordan."

30 Then Caleb quieted the people before Moses and said, "We should by all means go up and take possession of it, for we will certainly prevail over it." 31 But the men who had gone up with him said, "We are not able to go up against the people, because they are too strong for us." 32 So they brought a bad report of the land which they had spied out to the sons of Israel, saying, "The land through which we have gone to spy out is a land that devours its inhabitants; and all the people whom we saw in it are people of *great* stature. 33 We also saw the Nephilim there (the sons of Anak are part of the Nephilim); and we were like grasshoppers in our own sight, and so we were in their sight."

The People Rebel

14 Then all the congregation raised their voices and cried out, and the people wept that night. 2 And all the sons of Israel grumbled against Moses and Aaron; and the entire congregation said to them, "If only we had died in the land of Egypt! Or *even* if we had died in this wilderness! 3 So why is the LORD bringing us into this land to fall by the sword? Our wives and our little ones will become plunder! Would it not be better for us to return to Egypt?" 4 So they said to one another, "Let's appoint a leader and return to Egypt!"

5 Then Moses and Aaron fell on their faces in the presence of all the assembly of the congregation of the sons of Israel. 6 And Joshua the son of Nun and Caleb the son of Jephunneh, of those who had spied out the land, tore their clothes; 7 and they spoke to all the congregation of the sons of Israel, saying, "The land which we passed through to spy out is an exceedingly good land. 8 If the LORD is pleased with us, then He will bring us into this land and give it to us—a land which flows with milk and honey. 9 Only do not rebel against the LORD; and do not fear the people of the land, for they will be our prey. Their protection is gone from them, and the LORD is with us; do not fear them." 10 But all the congregation said to stone them with stones. Then the glory of the LORD appeared in the tent of meeting to all the sons of Israel.

Moses Pleads for the People

11 And the LORD said to Moses, "How long will this people be disrespectful to Me? And how long will they not believe in Me, despite all the signs that I have performed in their midst? 12 I will strike them with plague and dispossess them, and I will make you into a nation greater and mightier than they."

13 But Moses said to the LORD, "Then the Egyptians will hear of it, for by Your strength You brought this people up from their midst, 14 and they will tell *it* to the inhabitants of this land. They have heard that You, LORD, are in the midst of this people, because You, LORD, are seen eye to eye, while Your cloud stands over them; and You go before them in a pillar of cloud by day, and in a pillar of fire by night. 15 Now if You put this people to death all at once, then the nations who have heard of Your fame will say, 16 'Since the LORD could not bring this people into the land which He promised them by oath, He slaughtered them in the wilderness.' 17 So now, please, let the power of the Lord be great, just as You have declared, saying, 18 'The LORD is slow to anger and abundant in mercy, forgiving wrongdoing and violation *of His Law;* but He will by no means leave *the guilty* unpunished, inflicting the 'punishment of the fathers on the children to the third and the fourth *generations.'* 19 Please forgive the guilt of this people in accordance with the greatness of Your mercy, just as You also have forgiven this people, from Egypt even until now."

13:17 1 I.e., South country, and so throughout the ch   13:23 1 I.e., cluster (of grapes)
14:18 1 I.e., punishment for the wrongdoing

The Lord Pardons and Rebukes

20 So the Lord said, "I have forgiven *them* in accordance with your word; 21 however, as I live, all the earth will be filled with the glory of the Lord. 22 Certainly all the people who have seen My glory and My signs which I performed in Egypt and in the wilderness, yet have put Me to the test these ten times and have not listened to My voice, 23 shall by no means see the land which I swore to their fathers, nor shall any of those who were disrespectful to Me see it. 24 But as for My servant Caleb, because he has had a different spirit and has followed Me fully, I will bring him into the land which he entered, and his descendants shall take possession of it. 25 Now the Amalekites and the Canaanites live in the valleys; turn tomorrow and set out for the wilderness by the way of the Red Sea."

26 The Lord spoke to Moses and Aaron again, saying, 27 "How long *shall I put up* with this evil congregation who are grumbling against Me? I have heard the complaints of the sons of Israel which they are voicing against Me. 28 Say to them, 'As I live,' declares the Lord, 'just as you have spoken in My hearing, so I will do to you; 29 your dead bodies will fall in this wilderness, all your numbered men according to your complete number from twenty years old and upward, who have grumbled against Mo. 30 By no means will you come into the land where I swore to settle you, except for Caleb the son of Jephunneh and Joshua the son of Nun. 31 Your children, however, whom you said would become plunder—I will bring them in, and they will know the land which you have rejected. 32 But as for you, your dead bodies will fall in this wilderness. 33 Also, your sons will be shepherds in the wilderness for forty years, and they will suffer *for* your unfaithfulness, until your bodies perish in the wilderness. 34 In accordance with the number of days that you spied out the land, forty days, for every day you shall suffer the punishment for your guilt a year, *that is,* forty years, and you will know My opposition. 35 I, the Lord, have spoken, I certainly will do this to all this evil congregation who are gathered together against Me. They shall be worn out in this wilderness, and there they shall die.' "

36 As for the men whom Moses sent to spy out the land, and who returned and led all the congregation to grumble against him by bringing a bad report about the land, 37 those men who brought the bad report of the land also died by a plague in the presence of the Lord. 38 But Joshua the son of Nun and Caleb the son of Jephunneh remained alive out of those men who went to spy out the land.

Israel Repulsed

39 Now when Moses spoke these words to all the sons of Israel, the people mourned greatly. 40 In the morning, however, they got up early and went up to the ridge of the hill country, saying, "Here we are; and we will go up to the place which the Lord has promised, for we have sinned." 41 But Moses said, "Why then are you violating the command of the Lord, when *doing so* will not succeed? 42 Do not go up, for the Lord is not among you, to prevent you from being defeated by your enemies. 43 For the Amalekites and the Canaanites will be there to confront you, and you will fall by the sword, since you have turned back from following the Lord. And the Lord will not be with you." 44 But they *foolishly* dared to go up to the ridge of the hill country; neither the ark of the covenant of the Lord nor Moses left the camp. 45 Then the Amalekites and the Canaanites who lived in that hill country came down, and struck them and scattered them as far as Hormah.

Laws for Canaan

15 Now the Lord spoke to Moses, saying, 2 "Speak to the sons of Israel and say to them, 'When you enter the land where you are going to live, which I am giving you, 3 and you make an offering by fire to the Lord, a burnt offering or a sacrifice to fulfill a special vow, or as a voluntary offering or at your appointed times, to make a soothing aroma to the Lord from the herd or from the flock, 4 then the one who presents his offering shall present to the Lord a grain offering of a tenth *of an 'ephah* of fine flour mixed with a fourth of a ²hin of oil, 5 and you shall prepare wine for the drink offering, a fourth of a hin, with the burnt offering or for the sacrifice, for each lamb. 6 Or for a ram you shall prepare as a grain offering two-tenths *of an ephah* of fine flour mixed with a third of a hin of oil; 7 and for the drink offering you shall offer a third of a hin of wine as a soothing aroma to the Lord. 8 And when you prepare a bull as a burnt offering or a sacrifice, to fulfill a special vow, or for peace offerings to the Lord, 9 then you shall offer with the bull a grain offering of three-tenths *of an ephah* of fine flour mixed with half a hin of oil; 10 and you shall offer as the drink offering half a hin of wine as an offering by fire, as a soothing aroma to the Lord.

11 'This is how it shall be done for each ox, or for each ram, or for each of the male lambs, or of the goats. 12 According to the number that you prepare, so you shall do for each one according to their number. 13 Everyone who is a native shall do these things in this way, in presenting an offering by fire as a soothing aroma to the Lord.

Law for the Stranger

14 Now if a stranger resides among you, or one who *may be* among you throughout your generations, and he *wants to* make an offering by fire, as a soothing aroma to the Lord, just as you do so shall he do. 15 *As for* the assembly, there shall be one statute for you and for the stranger who resides *among you,* a permanent statute throughout your generations; as you are, so shall the stranger be before the Lord. 16 There is to be one law and one ordinance for you and for the stranger who resides with you.' "

17 Then the Lord spoke to Moses, saying, 18 "Speak to the sons of Israel and say to them, 'When you enter the land where I am bringing

---

15:4 1 An ephah was about 7.4 gallons or 28 liters　　2 A hin also was about 1 gallon or 3.8 liters

you, 19 then it shall be, that when you eat from the food of the land, you shall lift up an offering to the LORD. 20 Of the first of your dough you shall lift up a loaf as an offering; as an offering of the threshing floor, so you shall lift it up. 21 From the first of your dough you shall give to the LORD an offering throughout your generations.

22 'But when you unintentionally do wrong and fail to comply with all these commandments which the LORD has spoken to Moses, 23 that is, all that the LORD has commanded you through Moses from the day that the LORD gave commandments and onward, throughout your generations, 24 then it shall be, if it is done unintentionally, without the knowledge of the congregation, that all the congregation shall offer one bull as a burnt offering, as a soothing aroma to the LORD, with its grain offering and its drink offering, according to the ordinance, and one male goat as a sin offering. 25 Then the priest shall make atonement for all the congregation of the sons of Israel, and they will be forgiven; for it was an unintentional wrong, and they have brought their offering, an offering by fire to the LORD, and their sin offering before the LORD, for their unintentional wrong. 26 So all the congregation of the sons of Israel will be forgiven, as well as the stranger who resides among them, for *guilt was attributed* to all the people through an unintentional wrong.

27 'Also, if one person sins unintentionally, then he shall offer a one-year-old female goat as a sin offering. 28 And the priest shall make atonement before the LORD for the person who goes astray by an unintentional sin, making atonement for him so that he may be forgiven. 29 You shall have one law for the native among the sons of Israel and for the stranger who resides among them, for one who does *anything wrong* unintentionally. 30 But the person who does *wrong* defiantly, whether he is a native or a stranger, that one is blaspheming the LORD; and that person shall be cut off from among his people. 31 Since he has despised the word of the LORD and has broken His commandment, that person shall be completely cut off; his guilt *will be* on him.' "

Sabbath-breaking Punished

32 Now while the sons of Israel were in the wilderness, they found a man gathering wood on the Sabbath day. 33 And those who found him gathering wood brought him to Moses and Aaron, and to all the congregation; 34 and they placed him in custody, because it had not been decided what should be done to him. 35 Then the LORD said to Moses, "The man must be put to death; all the congregation shall stone him with stones outside the camp." 36 So all the congregation brought him outside the camp and stoned him to death with stones, just as the LORD had commanded Moses.

37 The LORD also spoke to Moses, saying, 38 "Speak to the sons of Israel and tell them that they shall make for themselves tassels on the corners of their garments throughout their generations, and that they shall put on the tassel of each corner a ¹violet thread. 39 It shall be a tassel for you to look at and remember all the commandments of the LORD, so that you will do them and not follow your own heart and your own eyes, which led you to prostitute yourselves, 40 so that you will remember and do all My commandments and be holy to your God. 41 I am the LORD your God who brought you out from the land of Egypt to be your God; I am the LORD your God."

Korah's Rebellion

16 Now Korah the son of Izhar, the son of Kohath, the son of Levi, with Dathan and Abiram, the sons of Eliab, and On the son of Peleth, sons of Reuben, took *men,* 2 and they stood before Moses, together with some of the sons of Israel, 250 leaders of the congregation chosen in the assembly, men of renown. 3 They assembled together against Moses and Aaron, and said to them, "You have gone far enough! For all the congregation are holy, every one of them, and the LORD is in their midst; so why do you exalt yourselves above the assembly of the LORD?"

4 When Moses heard *this,* he fell on his face; 5 and he spoke to Korah and all his group, saying, "Tomorrow morning the LORD will make known who is His, and who is holy, and will bring *that one* near to Himself; indeed, the one whom He will choose, He will bring near to Himself. 6 Do this: take censers for yourselves, Korah and your whole group, 7 and put fire in them, and place incense upon them in the presence of the LORD tomorrow; and the man whom the LORD chooses *shall be* the one who is holy. You have gone far enough, you sons of Levi!"

8 Then Moses said to Korah, "Hear now, you sons of Levi: 9 Is it too small *an honor* for you that the God of Israel has singled you out from the congregation of Israel, to bring you near to Himself, to perform the service of the tabernacle of the LORD, and to stand before the congregation to minister to them; 10 and that He has brought you near, *Korah,* and all your brothers, sons of Levi, with you? But are you seeking the priesthood as well? 11 Therefore you and your whole group are the ones gathered together against the LORD; but as for Aaron, who is he, that you grumble against him?"

12 Then Moses sent a summons to Dathan and Abiram, the sons of Eliab; but they said, "We will not come up. 13 Is it not enough that you have brought us up out of a land flowing with milk and honey to have us die in the wilderness, but you would also appoint yourself as master over us? 14 Indeed, you have not brought us into a land flowing with milk and honey, nor have you given us an inheritance of fields and vineyards. Would you gouge out the eyes of these men? We will not come up!"

15 Then Moses became very angry and said to the LORD, "Pay no attention to their offering! I have not taken a single donkey from them, nor have I done harm to any of them." 16 Moses said to Korah, "You and all your group be present before the LORD tomorrow, you and they

---

15:38 1 Or *bluish;* LXX *hyacinth* in color, and so throughout the ch

along with Aaron. **17** And each *of you* take his censer and put incense on it, and each *of you* bring his censer before the LORD, 250 censers; also you and Aaron *shall* each *bring* his censer." **18** So they took, each one his *own* censer, and put fire on it, and placed incense on it; and they stood at the entrance of the tent of meeting, with Moses and Aaron. **19** So Korah assembled all the congregation against them at the entrance of the tent of meeting. And the glory of the LORD appeared to all the congregation.

20 Then the LORD spoke to Moses and Aaron, saying, **21** "Separate yourselves from among this congregation, so that I may consume them instantly." **22** But they fell on their faces and said, "God, the God of the spirits of humanity, when one person sins, will You be angry with the entire congregation?"

23 Then the LORD spoke to Moses, saying, **24** "Speak to the congregation, saying, 'Get away from *the areas* around the tents of Korah, Dathan, and Abiram.'"

25 Then Moses arose and went to Dathan and Abiram, with the elders of Israel following him, **26** and he spoke to the congregation, saying, "Get away now from the tents of these wicked men, and do not touch anything that belongs to them, or you will be swept away in all their sin!" **27** So they moved away from *the areas* around the tents of Korah, Dathan, and Abiram; and Dathan and Abiram came out *and* stood at the entrances of their tents, along with their wives, their sons, and their little ones. **28** Then Moses said, "By this you shall know that the LORD has sent me to do all these deeds; for it is not my doing. **29** If these men die the death of all mankind, or if they suffer the fate of all mankind, *then* the LORD has not sent me. **30** But if the LORD brings about an entirely new thing and the ground opens its mouth and swallows them with everything that is theirs, and they descend alive into ¹Sheol, then you will know that these men have been disrespectful to the LORD."

31 And as he finished speaking all these words, the ground that was under them split open; **32** and the earth opened its mouth and swallowed them, their households, and all the people who belonged to Korah with all *their* possessions. **33** So they and all that belonged to them went down alive to Sheol; and the earth closed over them, and they perished from the midst of the assembly. **34** Then all Israel who *were* around them fled at their outcry, for they said, "The earth might swallow us!" **35** Fire also came out from the LORD and consumed the 250 men who were offering the incense.

36 Then the LORD spoke to Moses, saying, **37** "Tell Eleazar, the son of Aaron the priest, that he shall pick up the censers from the midst of the burned area, because they are holy; and you are to scatter the burning coals farther away. **38** As for the censers of these men who have sinned at the cost of their own lives, have them made into hammered sheets as plating for the altar, since they did present them before the LORD and they are holy; and they shall serve as a sign to the sons of Israel."

39 So the priest Eleazar took the bronze censers which the men who were burned had offered, and they hammered them out as plating for the altar, **40** as a reminder to the sons of Israel so that no layman, *anyone* who was not of the descendants of Aaron, would approach to burn incense before the LORD; then he would not become like Korah and his group—just as LORD had spoken to him through Moses.

Murmuring and Plague

41 But on the next day all the congregation of the sons of Israel grumbled against Moses and Aaron, saying, "You are the ones who have caused the death of the LORD's people!" **42** It came about, however, when the congregation had assembled against Moses and Aaron, that they turned toward the tent of meeting, and behold, the cloud covered it and the glory of the LORD appeared. **43** Then Moses and Aaron came to the front of the tent of meeting, **44** and the LORD spoke to Moses, saying, **45** "Get away from among this congregation so that I may consume them instantly." Then they fell on their faces. **46** And Moses said to Aaron, "Take your censer and put fire in it from the altar, and place incense *on it;* then bring it quickly to the congregation and make atonement for them, for wrath has gone out from the LORD, the plague has begun!" **47** Then Aaron took *it* just as Moses had spoken, and he ran into the midst of the assembly; and behold, the plague had begun among the people. So he put *on* the incense and made atonement for the people. **48** And he took his stand between the dead and the living, so that the plague was brought to a halt. **49** But those who died by the plague were 14,700 *in number,* besides those who died on account of Korah. **50** Then Aaron returned to Moses at the entrance of the tent of meeting, for the plague had been brought to a halt.

Aaron's Staff Buds

17 Then the LORD spoke to Moses, saying, **2** "Speak to the sons of Israel, and obtain from them a staff for each father's household: twelve staffs, from all their leaders for their fathers' households. You shall write each man's name on his staff, **3** and write Aaron's name on the staff of Levi; for *there is to be* one staff for the head *of each* of their fathers' households. **4** You shall then leave them in the tent of meeting in front of the testimony, where I meet with you. **5** And it will come about that the staff of the man whom I choose will sprout. So I will relieve Myself of the grumblings of the sons of Israel, who are grumbling against you." **6** So Moses spoke to the sons of Israel, and all their leaders gave him a staff, one for each leader, for their fathers' households, twelve staffs *in all,* with the staff of Aaron among their staffs. **7** Then Moses left the staffs before the LORD in the tent of the testimony.

8 Now on the next day Moses went into the tent of the testimony; and behold, Aaron's staff for the house of Levi had sprouted and produced buds and bloomed with blossoms, and it yielded ripe almonds. **9** Moses then brought out all the staffs from the presence of

---

16:30 ¹ I.e., the netherworld

the LORD to all the sons of Israel; and they looked, and each man took his staff. 10 But the LORD said to Moses, "Put the staff of Aaron back in front of the testimony to be kept as a sign against the rebels, so that you may put an end to their grumblings against Me and they do not die." 11 Moses did *so;* just as the LORD had commanded him, so he did.

12 Then the sons of Israel spoke to Moses, saying, "Behold, we are passing away, we are perishing, we are all perishing! 13 Everyone who comes near, who comes near to the tabernacle of the LORD, must die. Are we to perish completely?"

Duties of Levites

18 So the LORD said to Aaron, "You, your sons, and your father's household with you shall bear the guilt in connection with the sanctuary, and you and your sons with you shall bear the guilt in connection with your priesthood. 2 But also bring your brothers with you, the tribe of Levi, the tribe of your father, so that they may join you and serve you, while you and your sons with you are before the tent of the testimony. 3 And they shall perform duties for you and the duties of the whole tent, but they shall not come near the furnishings of the sanctuary and the altar, or both they and you will die. 4 They shall join you and perform the duties of the tent of meeting, for all the service of the tent; but an unauthorized person shall not come near you. 5 So you shall perform the duties of the sanctuary and the duties of the altar, so that there will no longer be wrath on the sons of Israel. 6 Behold, I Myself have taken your fellow Levites from among the sons of Israel; *they are* a gift to you, dedicated to the LORD, to perform the service for the tent of meeting. 7 But you and your sons with you shall attend to your priesthood for everything that concerns the altar and inside the veil, and you are to perform service. I am giving you the priesthood as a service that is a gift, and the unauthorized person who comes near shall be put to death."

The Priests' Portion

8 Then the LORD spoke to Aaron, "Now behold, I Myself have put you in charge of My offerings, all the holy gifts of the sons of Israel I have given to you as a portion and to your sons as a permanent allotment. 9 This shall be yours from the most holy *gifts reserved* from the fire; every offering of theirs, namely every grain offering, every sin offering, and every guilt offering, with which they shall make restitution to Me, *shall be* most holy for you and for your sons. 10 As the most holy *gifts* you shall eat it; every male shall eat it. It shall be holy to you. 11 This also is yours, the offering of their gift, that is, all the wave offerings of the sons of Israel; I have given them to you and to your sons and daughters with you as a permanent allotment. Everyone of your household who is clean may eat it. 12 All the best of the fresh oil and all the best of the fresh wine and of the grain, the first fruits of what they give to the LORD, I have given them to you. 13 The first

ripe fruits of all that is in their land, which they bring to the LORD, shall be yours; everyone of your household who is clean may eat it. 14 Everything banned from secular use in Israel shall be yours. 15 Every firstborn of the womb of all flesh, whether human or animal, which they offer to the LORD, shall be yours; however you must redeem the human firstborn, and the firstborn of unclean animals you shall redeem. 16 As to their redemption price, from a month old you shall redeem them, by your assessment, five ¹shekels in silver by the shekel of the sanctuary, which is twenty gerahs. 17 But the firstborn of an ox, the firstborn of a sheep, or the firstborn of a goat, you shall not redeem; they are holy. You shall sprinkle their blood on the altar and offer up their fat in smoke *as* an offering by fire, for a soothing aroma to the LORD. 18 However, their meat shall be yours; it shall be yours like the breast of a wave offering and like the right thigh. 19 All the offerings of the holy *gifts,* which the sons of Israel offer to the LORD, I have given to you and your sons and your daughters with you, as a permanent allotment. It is a permanent covenant of salt before the LORD to you and your descendants with you." 20 Then the LORD said to Aaron, "You shall have no inheritance in their land nor own any portion among them; I am your portion and your inheritance among the sons of Israel.

21 "To the sons of Levi, behold, I have given all the tithe in Israel as an inheritance, in return for their service which they perform, the service of the tent of meeting. 22 And the sons of Israel shall not come near the tent of meeting again, or they will bring sin on themselves and die. 23 Only the Levites shall perform the service of the tent of meeting, and they shall bear their *own* guilt; *it shall be* a permanent statute throughout your generations, and among the sons of Israel they shall have no inheritance. 24 For the tithe of the sons of Israel, which they offer as an offering to the LORD, I have given to the Levites as an inheritance; therefore I have said concerning them, 'They shall have no inheritance among the sons of Israel.'"

25 Then the LORD spoke to Moses, saying, 26 "Moreover, you shall speak to the Levites and say to them, 'When you take from the sons of Israel the tithe which I have given you from them for your inheritance, then you shall present an offering from it to the LORD, a tithe of the tithe. 27 Your offering shall be credited to you like the grain from the threshing floor or the full produce from the wine vat. 28 So you shall also present an offering to the LORD from all your tithes, which you receive from the sons of Israel; and from it you shall give the LORD's offering to Aaron the priest. 29 Out of all your gifts you shall present every offering due to the LORD, from all the best of them, the sacred part from them.' 30 And you shall say to them, 'When you have offered from it the best of it, then *the rest* shall be credited to the Levites like the product of the threshing floor, and like the product of the wine vat. 31 You may eat it anywhere, you and your households, for

---

18:16 ¹A shekel is about 0.5 oz. or 14 gm

it is your compensation in return for your service in the tent of meeting. 32 And you will bring on yourselves no sin by reason of it when you have offered the best of it. But you shall not profane the sacred gifts of the sons of Israel, so that you do not die.' "

Ordinance of the Red Heifer

19 Then the LORD spoke to Moses and Aaron, saying, 2 "This is the statute of the law which the LORD has commanded, saying, 'Speak to the sons of Israel that they bring you an unblemished red heifer in which there is no defect *and* on which a yoke has never been mounted. 3 And you shall give it to Eleazar the priest, and it shall be brought outside the camp and be slaughtered in his presence. 4 And Eleazar the priest shall take some of its blood with his finger and sprinkle some of its blood toward the front of the tent of meeting seven times. 5 Then the heifer shall be burned in his sight; its hide, its flesh, and its blood, with its refuse, shall be burned. 6 And the priest shall take cedar wood, hyssop, and scarlet *material,* and throw it into the midst of the burning heifer. 7 The priest shall then wash his clothes and bathe his body in water, and afterward come into the camp; but the priest will be unclean until evening. 8 The one who burns the heifer shall also wash his clothes in water and bathe his body in water, and will be unclean until evening. 9 Now a man who is clean shall gather up the ashes of the heifer and put them outside the camp in a clean place, and the congregation of the sons of Israel shall keep them for water to remove impurity; it is purification from sin. 10 And the one who gathers the ashes of the heifer shall wash his clothes and will be unclean until evening; and it shall be a permanent statute for the sons of Israel and for the stranger who resides among them.

11 'The one who touches the dead body of any person will also be unclean for seven days. 12 That one shall purify himself with the water on the third day and on the seventh day, *and then* he will be clean; but if he does not purify himself on the third day and on the seventh day, he will not be clean. 13 Anyone who touches a dead body, the body of a person who has died, and does not purify himself, defiles the tabernacle of the LORD; and that person shall be cut off from Israel. Since the water for impurity was not sprinkled on him, he will be unclean; his uncleanness is still on him.

14 'This is the law when a person dies in a tent: everyone who comes into the tent and everyone who is in the tent will be unclean for seven days. 15 And every open container, which has no cover tied down on it, will be unclean. 16 Also, anyone who in the open field touches one who has been killed with a sword or one who has died *naturally,* or *touches* a human bone or a grave, will be unclean for seven days. 17 Then for the unclean *person* they shall take some of the ashes of the burnt purification from sin and running water shall be added to them in a container. 18 And a clean person shall take hyssop and dip *it* in the water, and sprinkle *it* on the tent, on all the furnishings, on the

persons who were there, and on the one who touched the bone or the one who was killed or the one who died *naturally,* or the grave. 19 Then the clean *person* shall sprinkle on the unclean on the third day and on the seventh day; and on the seventh day he shall purify him, and he shall wash his clothes and bathe *himself* in water and will be clean by evening.

20 'But the person who is unclean and does not purify himself, that person shall be cut off from the midst of the assembly, because he has defiled the sanctuary of the LORD; the water for impurity has not been sprinkled on him, *so* he is unclean. 21 So it shall be a permanent statute for them. And the one who sprinkles the water for impurity shall wash his clothes, and the one who touches the water for impurity will be unclean until evening. 22 Furthermore, anything that the unclean *person* touches will be unclean; and the person who touches *it* will be unclean until evening.' "

Death of Miriam

20 Then the sons of Israel, the whole congregation, came to the wilderness of Zin in the first month; and the people stayed at Kadesh. Now Miriam died there and was buried there.

2 There was no water for the congregation, and they assembled against Moses and Aaron. 3 Then the people argued with Moses and spoke, saying, "If only we had perished when our brothers perished before the LORD! 4 Why then have you brought the LORD's assembly into this wilderness, for us and our livestock to die here? 5 Why did you make us come up from Egypt, to bring us into this wretched place? It is not a place of grain or figs or vines or pomegranates, nor is there water to drink!" 6 Then Moses and Aaron came in from the presence of the assembly to the entrance of the tent of meeting and fell on their faces. And the glory of the LORD appeared to them; 7 then the LORD spoke to Moses, saying,

The Waters of Meribah

8 "Take the staff; and you and your brother Aaron assemble the congregation and speak to the rock before their eyes, that it shall yield its water. So you shall bring water for them out of the rock, and have the congregation and their livestock drink."

9 So Moses took the staff from before the LORD, just as He had commanded him; 10 and Moses and Aaron summoned the assembly in front of the rock. And he said to them, "Listen now, you rebels; shall we bring water for you out of this rock?" 11 Then Moses raised his hand and struck the rock twice with his staff; and water came out abundantly, and the congregation and their livestock drank. 12 But the LORD said to Moses and Aaron, "Since you did not trust in Me, to treat Me as holy in the sight of the sons of Israel, for that reason you shall not bring this assembly into the land which I have given them." 13 Those *were called* the waters of 'Meribah, because the sons of Israel argued with the LORD, and He proved Himself holy among them.

20:13 1 I.e., contention

14 From Kadesh Moses then sent messengers to the king of Edom *to say,* "This is what your brother Israel has said: 'You know all the hardship that has overtaken us; **15** that our fathers went down to Egypt, and we stayed in Egypt a long time, and the Egyptians treated us and our fathers badly. **16** But when we cried out to the LORD, He heard our voice and sent an angel, and brought us out from Egypt; now behold, we are at Kadesh, a town on the edge of your territory. **17** Please let us pass through your land. We will not pass through field or vineyard; we will not even drink water from a well. We will go along the king's road, not turning to the right or left, until we pass through your territory.' "

18 Edom, however, said to him, "You shall not pass through us, or I will come out with the sword against you." **19** Again, the sons of Israel said to him, "We will go up by the road, and if I and my livestock do drink any of your water, then I will pay its price. Let me only pass through on my feet, nothing *more.*" **20** But he said, "You shall not pass through." And Edom came out against him with a heavy force and a strong hand. **21** So Edom refused to allow Israel to pass through his territory; then Israel turned away from him.

22 Now when they set out from Kadesh, the sons of Israel, the whole congregation, came to Mount Hor.

Death of Aaron

23 Then the LORD spoke to Moses and Aaron at Mount Hor by the border of the land of Edom, saying, **24** "Aaron will be gathered to his people; for he shall not enter the land which I have given to the sons of Israel, because you rebelled against My command at the waters of Meribah. **25** Take Aaron and his son Eleazar, and bring them up to Mount Hor. **26** Then strip Aaron of his garments and put them on his son Eleazar. So Aaron will be gathered *to his people* and will die there." **27** So Moses did just as the LORD had commanded, and they went up to Mount Hor in the sight of all the congregation. **28** And after Moses stripped Aaron of his garments and put them on his son Eleazar, Aaron died there on the mountain top. Then Moses and Eleazar came down from the mountain. **29** When all the congregation saw that Aaron had died, the whole house of Israel wept for Aaron for thirty days.

Arad Conquered

21 When the Canaanite, the king of Arad, who lived in the ¹Negev, heard that Israel was coming by the way of Atharim, he fought against Israel and took some of them captive. **2** So Israel made a vow to the LORD and said, "If You will indeed hand over this people to me, then I will utterly destroy their cities." **3** The LORD heard the voice of Israel and turned over the Canaanites; then they utterly destroyed them and their cities. And the place was named ¹Hormah.

4 Then they set out from Mount Hor by the way of the Red Sea, to go around the land of Edom; and the people became impatient because of the journey. **5** So the people spoke against God and Moses: "Why have you brought us up from Egypt to die in the wilderness? For there is no food and no water, and we are disgusted with this miserable food."

The Bronze Serpent

6 Then the LORD sent fiery serpents among the people and they bit the people, so that many people of Israel died. **7** So the people came to Moses and said, "We have sinned, because we have spoken against the LORD and against you; intercede with the LORD, that He will remove the serpents from us." And Moses interceded for the people. **8** Then the LORD said to Moses, "Make a fiery *serpent,* and put it on a flag *pole;* and it shall come about, that everyone who is bitten, and looks at it, will live." **9** So Moses made a bronze serpent and put it on the flag *pole;* and it came about, that if a serpent bit someone, and he looked at the bronze serpent, he lived.

10 Now the sons of Israel moved out and camped in Oboth. **11** Then they journeyed from Oboth and camped at Iye-abarim, in the wilderness which is opposite Moab, to the east. **12** From there they set out and camped in ¹Wadi Zered. **13** From there they journeyed and camped on the other side of the Arnon, which is in the wilderness that comes out of the border of the Amorites; for the Arnon is the border of Moab, between Moab and the Amorites. **14** For that reason it is said in the Book of the Wars of the LORD,

"Waheb in Suphah,
And the ¹wadis of the Arnon,
15   And the slope of the wadis
That extends to the site of Ar,
And leans to the border of Moab."

16 From there *they continued* to Beer, that is the well where the LORD said to Moses, "Assemble the people, that I may give them water."

17 Then Israel sang this song:
"Spring up, O well! Sing to it!
18 "The well, which the leaders dug,
Which the nobles of the people hollowed out,
With the scepter *and* with their staffs."
And from the wilderness *they continued* to Mattanah, **19** and from Mattanah to Nahaliel, and from Nahaliel to Bamoth, **20** and from Bamoth to the valley that is in the land of Moab, at the top of Pisgah, which overlooks the desert.

Two Victories

21 Then Israel sent messengers to Sihon, king of the Amorites, saying, **22** "Let me pass through your land. We will not turn off into field or vineyard; we will not drink water from wells. We will go by the king's road until we have passed through your border." **23** But Sihon would not permit Israel to pass through his border. Instead, Sihon gathered all his people and went out against Israel in the wilderness, and came to Jahaz and fought against Israel.

21:1 ¹I.e., South country   **21:3** ¹I.e., a devoted thing; or Destruction   **21:12** ¹I.e., a dry stream bed, except in the rainy season   **21:14** ¹I.e., dry stream beds

24 Then Israel struck him with the edge of the sword, and took possession of his land from the Arnon to the Jabbok, as far as the sons of Ammon; for the border of the sons of Ammon *was* Jazer. 25 Israel took all these cities, and Israel lived in all the cities of the Amorites, in Heshbon and in all her villages. 26 For Heshbon was the city of Sihon, king of the Amorites, who had fought against the former king of Moab and had taken all his land out of his hand, as far as the Arnon. 27 For that reason those who use proverbs say,

"Come to Heshbon! Let it be built!
So let the city of Sihon be established.
28 "For a fire spread from Heshbon,
A flame from the town of Sihon;
It devoured Ar of Moab,
The dominant heights of the Arnon.
29 "Woe to you, Moab!
You are destroyed, people of Chemosh!
He has given his sons as fugitives,
And his daughters into captivity,
To an Amorite king, Sihon.
30 "But we have shot them down *with arrows,*
Heshbon is destroyed as far as Dibon,
Then we have laid waste as far as
Nophah,
Which *reaches* to Medeba."

31 So Israel lived in the land of the Amorites. 32 Now Moses sent *men* to spy out Jazer, and they captured its villages and dispossessed the Amorites who *were* there.

33 Then they turned and went up by the way of Bashan, and Og the king of Bashan went out against them with all his people, for battle at Edrei. 34 But the LORD said to Moses, "Do not fear him, for I have handed him over to you, and all his people and his land; and you shall do to him as you did to Sihon, king of the Amorites, who lived in Heshbon." 35 So they killed him and his sons and all his people, until there was no survivor left; and they took possession of his land.

Balak Sends for Balaam

22 Then the sons of Israel journeyed on, and camped in the plains of Moab beyond the Jordan *opposite* Jericho.

2 Now Balak the son of Zippor saw all that Israel had done to the Amorites. 3 So Moab was in great fear because of the people, for they were numerous; and Moab was in dread of the sons of Israel. 4 Moab said to the elders of Midian, "Now this horde will eat up all that is around us, as the ox eats up the grass of the field!" And Balak the son of Zippor was king of Moab at that time. 5 So he sent messengers to Balaam the son of Beor, at Pethor, which is near the *Euphrates* River, *in* the land of the sons of his people, to call for him, saying, "Behold, a people came out of Egypt; behold, they have covered the surface of the land, and they are living opposite me. 6 Now, therefore, please come, curse this people for me since they are too mighty for me; perhaps I will be able to defeat them and drive them out of the land. For I know that he whom you bless is blessed, and he whom you curse is cursed."

7 So the elders of Moab and the elders of Midian left with the *fees for* divination in their hands; and they came to Balaam and repeated Balak's words to him. 8 And he said to them, "Spend the night here, and I will bring word back to you just as the LORD may speak to me." And the leaders of Moab stayed with Balaam. 9 Then God came to Balaam and said, "Who are these men with you?" 10 Balaam said to God, "Balak the son of Zippor, king of Moab, sent *word* to me: 11 'Behold, there is a people who came out of Egypt, and they cover the surface of the land; now come, curse them for me; perhaps I will be able to fight against them and drive them out.' " 12 But God said to Balaam, "Do not go with them; you shall not curse the people, for they are blessed." 13 So Balaam got up in the morning and said to Balak's representatives, "Go *back* to your land, for the LORD has refused to let me go with you." 14 And the representatives from Moab got up and went to Balak, and said, "Balaam refused to come with us."

15 Then Balak sent representatives once again, more numerous and more distinguished than the previous. 16 They came to Balaam and said to him, "This is what Balak the son of Zippor says: 'I beg you, let nothing keep you from coming to me; 17 for I will indeed honor you richly, and I will do whatever you tell me. Please come then, curse this people for me.' " 18 But Balaam replied to the servants of Balak, "*Even* if Balak were to give me his house full of silver and gold, I could not do *anything, either* small or great, contrary to the command of the LORD my God. 19 Now please, you also stay here tonight, and I will find out what else the LORD will say to me." 20 And God came to Balaam at night and said to him, "If the men have come to call you, rise *and* go with them; but you shall do only the thing that I tell you."

21 So Balaam arose in the morning, saddled his donkey, and went with the leaders of Moab.

The Angel and Balaam

22 But God was angry that he was going, and the angel of the LORD took his stand in the road as an adversary against him. Now he was riding on his donkey, and his two servants were with him. 23 When the donkey saw the angel of the LORD standing in the road with his sword drawn in his hand, the donkey turned off from the road and went into the field; and Balaam struck the donkey to guide her back onto the road. 24 Then the angel of the LORD stood in a narrow path of the vineyards, *with* a stone wall on this side and on that side. 25 When the donkey saw the angel of the LORD, she pressed herself against the wall and pressed Balaam's foot against the wall, so he struck her again. 26 Then the angel of the LORD went farther, and stood in a narrow place where there was no way to turn to the right or to the left. 27 When the donkey saw the angel of the LORD, she lay down under Balaam; so Balaam was angry and struck the donkey with his staff. 28 Then the LORD opened the mouth of the donkey, and she said to Balaam, "What have I done to you, that you have struck me these three times?" 29 And Balaam said to the donkey, "*It is* because you have made a mockery of me! If only there had been a sword

in my hand! For I would have killed you by now!" ³⁰ But the donkey said to Balaam, "Am I not your donkey on which you have ridden all your life to this day? Have I ever been in the habit of doing such a thing to you?" And he said, "No."

³¹ Then the LORD opened Balaam's eyes, and he saw the angel of the LORD standing in the way with his sword drawn in his hand; and he bowed all the way to the ground. ³² Then the angel of the LORD said to him, "Why have you struck your donkey these three times? Behold, I have come out as an adversary, because your way was reckless *and* contrary to me. ³³ But the donkey saw me and turned away from me these three times. If she had not turned away from me, I certainly would have killed you just now, and let her live." ³⁴ So Balaam said to the angel of the LORD, "I have sinned, for I did not know that you were standing in the way against me. Now then, if it is displeasing to you, I will turn back." ³⁵ But the angel of the LORD said to Balaam, "Go with the men, but you shall speak only the word that I tell you." So Balaam went along with the representatives of Balak.

³⁶ When Balak heard that Balaam was coming, he went out to meet him at the city of Moab, which is on the Arnon border, at the extreme end of the border. ³⁷ Then Balak said to Balaam, "Did I not urgently send *word* to you to call for you? Why did you not come to me? Am I really unable to honor you?" ³⁸ So Balaam said to Balak, "Behold, I have come to you now! Am I really able to speak anything? The word that God puts in my mouth, that *only* shall I speak." ³⁹ And Balaam went with Balak, and they came to Kiriath-huzoth. ⁴⁰ Balak sacrificed oxen and sheep, and sent *some* to Balaam and the leaders who were with him.

⁴¹ Then it came about in the morning that Balak took Balaam and brought him up to the high places of Baal, and he saw from there a portion of the people.

The Prophecies of Balaam

23 Then Balaam said to Balak, "Build seven altars for me here, and prepare seven bulls and seven rams for me here." ² Balak did just as Balaam had spoken, and Balak and Balaam offered up a bull and a ram on *each* altar. ³ Then Balaam said to Balak, "Stand beside your burnt offering, and I will go; perhaps the LORD will come to meet me, and whatever He shows me I will tell you." So he went to a bare hill.

⁴ Now God met with Balaam, and he said to Him, "I have set up the seven altars, and I have offered up a bull and a ram on *each* altar." ⁵ Then the LORD put a word in Balaam's mouth and said, "Return to Balak, and this is what you shall speak." ⁶ So he returned to him, and behold, he was standing beside his burnt offering, he and all the leaders of Moab. ⁷ And he took up his discourse and said,

"From Aram Balak has brought me,
  Moab's king from the mountains of the East, *saying,*
'Come, declare Jacob cursed for me,
  And come, curse Israel!'

⁸ "How am I to put a curse on him upon
  whom God has not put a curse?
And how am I to curse him whom the
  LORD has not cursed?
⁹ "For I see him from the top of the rocks,
  And I look at him from the hills;
Behold, a people that lives in isolation,
  And does not consider itself *to be* among
  the nations.
¹⁰ "Who has counted the dust of Jacob,
  Or the number of the fourth part of Israel?
May I die the death of the upright,
  And may my end be like his!"

¹¹ Then Balak said to Balaam, "What have you done to me? I took you to put a curse on my enemies, but behold, you have actually blessed *them!*" ¹² He replied, "Must I not be careful to speak what the LORD puts in my mouth?"

¹³ Then Balak said to him, "Please come with me to another place from where you may see them, *although* you will only see the extreme end of them and will not see all of them; and put a curse on them for me from there." ¹⁴ So he took him to the field of Zophim, to the top of Pisgah, and he built seven altars and offered a bull and a ram on *each* altar. ¹⁵ Then he said to Balak, "Stand here beside your burnt offering while I myself meet *the LORD* over there." ¹⁶ Then the LORD met Balaam and put a word in his mouth, and said, "Return to Balak, and this is what you shall speak." ¹⁷ So he came to him, and behold, he was standing beside his burnt offering, and the leaders of Moab with him. And Balak said to him, "What has the LORD spoken?" ¹⁸ Then he took up his discourse and said,

"Arise, Balak, and hear;
  Listen to me, son of Zippor!
¹⁹ "God is not a man, that He would lie,
  Nor a son of man, that He would change
  His mind;
Has He said, and will He not do it?
  Or has He spoken, and will He not make
  it good?
²⁰ "Behold, I have received *a command* to
  bless;
When He has blessed, I cannot revoke it.
²¹ "He has not looked at misfortune in Jacob;
  Nor has He seen trouble in Israel;
The LORD his God is with him,
  And the joyful shout of a king is among
  them.
²² "God brings them out of Egypt,
  He is for them like the horns of the wild
  ox.
²³ "For there is no magic curse against Jacob,
  Nor is there any divination against Israel;
At the *proper* time it shall be said to Jacob
  And to Israel, what God has done!
²⁴ "Behold, a people rises like a lioness,
  And like a lion it raises itself;
It will not lie down until it devours the
  prey,
  And drinks the blood of those slain."

²⁵ Then Balak said to Balaam, "Do not curse them at all nor bless them at all!" ²⁶ But Balaam replied to Balak, "Did I not tell you, 'Whatever the LORD speaks, I must do'?"

²⁷ Then Balak said to Balaam, "Please come,

I will take you to another place; perhaps it will be agreeable with God that you curse them for me from there." 28 So Balak took Balaam to the top of Peor, which overlooks the desert. 29 And Balaam said to Balak, "Build seven altars for me here and prepare seven bulls and seven rams for me here." 30 Balak did just as Balaam had said, and offered up a bull and a ram on *each* altar.

The Prophecy from Peor

24 When Balaam saw that it pleased the LORD to bless Israel, he did not go as at other times to seek omens, rather he turned his attention toward the wilderness. 2 And Balaam raised his eyes and saw Israel camping tribe by tribe; and the Spirit of God came upon him. 3 Then he took up his discourse and said,

"The declaration of Balaam the son of
      Beor,
And the declaration of the man whose eye
      is opened;
4   The declaration of him who hears the
      words of God,
Who sees the vision of the Almighty,
Falling down, yet having his eyes
      uncovered,
5   How pleasant are your tents, Jacob,
Your dwelling places, Israel!
6   "Like valleys that stretch out,
Like gardens beside a river,
Like aloes planted by the LORD,
Like cedars beside the waters.
7   "Water will flow from his buckets,
And his seed *will be* by many waters,
And his king shall be higher than Agag,
And his kingdom shall be exalted.
8   "God brings him out of Egypt,
He is for him like the horns of the wild
      ox.
He will devour the nations *who are* his
      adversaries,
And will crush their bones,
And smash *them* with his arrows.
9   "He crouches, he lies down like a lion,
And like a lioness, who dares to rouse
      him?
Blessed is *everyone* who blesses you,
And cursed is *everyone* who curses you."

10 Then Balak's anger burned against Balaam, and he struck his hands together; and Balak said to Balaam, "I called you to curse my enemies, but behold, you have persisted in blessing them these three times! 11 So flee to your place now. I said I would honor you greatly, but behold, the LORD has held you back from honor." 12 And Balaam said to Balak, "Did I not in fact tell your messengers whom you had sent to me, saying, 13 'If Balak were to give me his house full of silver and gold, I could not do *anything* contrary to the command of the LORD, either good or bad, of my own accord. What the LORD speaks, I will speak'? 14 So now, behold, I am going to my people; come, *and* I will advise you of what this people will do to your people in the days to come."

15 Then he took up his discourse and said,
"The declaration of Balaam the son of Beor,
And the declaration of the man whose eye
      is opened,

16   The declaration of him who hears the
      words of God,
And knows the knowledge of the Most
      High,
Who sees the vision of the Almighty,
Falling down, yet having his eyes
      uncovered:
17   I see him, but not now;
I look at him, but not near;
A star shall appear from Jacob,
A scepter shall rise from Israel,
And shall smash the forehead of Moab,
And overcome all the sons of Sheth.
18   "And Edom shall be a possession,
Seir, its enemies, also will be a possession,
While Israel performs valiantly.
19   "One from Jacob shall rule,
And will eliminate the survivors from the
      city."

20 And he looked at Amalek and took up his discourse and said,
"Amalek was the first of the nations,
But his end *shall be* destruction."
21 And he looked at the Kenite, and took up his discourse and said,
"Your dwelling place is enduring,
And your nest is set in the cliff.
22   "Nevertheless Kain will suffer devastation;
How long will Asshur keep you captive?"
23 Then he took up his discourse and said,
"Oh, who can live unless God has ordained
      it?
24   "But ships *shall come* from the coast of
      Kittim,
And they shall oppress Asshur and
      oppress Eber;
So they also *will come* to destruction."
25 Then Balaam arose, and he departed and returned to his place, and Balak also went on his way.

The Sin of Peor

25 While Israel remained at Shittim, the people began to commit infidelity with the daughters of Moab. 2 For they invited the people to the sacrifices of their gods, and the people ate and bowed down to their gods. 3 So Israel became followers of Baal of Peor, and the LORD was angry with Israel. 4 And the LORD said to Moses, "Take all the leaders of the people and execute them in broad daylight before the LORD, so that the fierce anger of the LORD may turn away from Israel." 5 So Moses said to the judges of Israel, "Each of you kill his men who have become followers of Baal of Peor."

6 Then behold, one of the sons of Israel came and brought to his relatives a Midianite woman, in the sight of Moses and in the sight of the whole congregation of the sons of Israel, while they were weeping at the entrance of the tent of meeting. 7 When Phinehas the son of Eleazar, the son of Aaron the priest, saw it, he rose up from the midst of the congregation and took a spear in his hand, 8 and he went after the man of Israel into the inner room of the tent and pierced both of them, the man of Israel and the woman, through the abdomen. So the plague on the sons of Israel was brought to a halt. 9 But those who died from the plague were twenty-four thousand *in number.*

The Zeal of Phinehas

10 Then the LORD spoke to Moses, saying, 11 "Phinehas the son of Eleazar, the son of Aaron the priest, has averted My wrath from the sons of Israel in that he was jealous with My jealousy among them, so that I did not destroy the sons of Israel in My jealousy. 12 Therefore say, 'Behold, I am giving him My covenant of peace; 13 and it shall be for him and for his descendants after him, a covenant of a permanent priesthood, because he was jealous for his God and made atonement for the sons of Israel.' "

14 Now the name of the dead man of Israel who was killed with the Midianite woman, was Zimri the son of Salu, a leader of a father's household among the Simeonites. 15 And the name of the Midianite woman who was killed was Cozbi the daughter of Zur, who was head of the people of a father's household in Midian.

16 Then the LORD spoke to Moses, saying, 17 "Be hostile to the Midianites and attack them; 18 for they have been hostile to you with their tricks, with which they have deceived you in the matter of Peor and in the matter of Cozbi, the daughter of the leader of Midian, their sister who was killed on the day of the plague because of Peor."

Census of a New Generation

26 Then it came about after the plague, that the LORD spoke to Moses and to Eleazar the son of Aaron the priest, saying, 2 "Take a census of all the congregation of the sons of Israel from twenty years old and upward, by their fathers' households, whoever is able to go to war in Israel." 3 So Moses and Eleazar the priest spoke with them in the plains of Moab by the Jordan at Jericho, saying, 4 "Take a census of the people from twenty years old and upward, as the LORD has commanded Moses."

Now the sons of Israel who came out of the land of Egypt were as follows:

5 Reuben, Israel's firstborn, the sons of Reuben: of Hanoch, the family of the Hanoch-ites; of Pallu, the family of the Palluites; 6 of Hezron, the family of the Hezronites; of Carmi, the family of the Carmites. 7 These are the families of the Reubenites, and those who were counted of them were 43,730. 8 The son of Pallu: Eliab. 9 The sons of Eliab: Nemuel, Dathan, and Abiram. These are the Dathan and Abiram who were called by the congregation, who fought against Moses and against Aaron in the group of Korah, when they fought against the LORD, 10 and the earth opened its mouth and swallowed them up along with Korah, when that group died, when the fire devoured 250 men, so that they became a warning sign. 11 The sons of Korah, however, did not die.

12 The sons of Simeon by their families: of Nemuel, the family of the Nemuelites; of Jamin, the family of the Jaminites; of Jachin, the family of the Jachinites; 13 of Zerah, the family of the Zerahites; of Shaul, the family of the Shaulites. 14 These are the families of the Simeonites, 22,200 in number.

15 The sons of Gad by their families: of Zephon, the family of the Zephonites; of Haggi, the family of the Haggites; of Shuni, the family of the Shunites; 16 of Ozni, the family of the Oznites; of Eri, the family of the Erites; 17 of Arod, the family of the Arodites; of Areli, the family of the Arelites. 18 These are the families of the sons of Gad according to those who were numbered of them, 40,500.

19 The sons of Judah were Er and Onan, but Er and Onan died in the land of Canaan. 20 The sons of Judah by their families were: of Shelah, the family of the Shelanites; of Perez, the family of the Perezites; of Zerah, the family of the Zerahites. 21 The sons of Perez were: of Hezron, the family of the Hezronites; of Hamul, the family of the Hamulites. 22 These are the families of Judah by those who were numbered of them, 76,500.

23 The sons of Issachar by their families: of Tola, the family of the Tolaites; of Puvah, the family of the Punites; 24 of Jashub, the family of the Jashubites; of Shimron, the family of the Shimronites. 25 These are the families of Issachar by those who were numbered of them, 64,300.

26 The sons of Zebulun by their families: of Sered, the family of the Seredites; of Elon, the family of the Elonites; of Jahleel, the family of the Jahleelites. 27 These are the families of the Zebulunites by those who were numbered of them, 60,500.

28 The sons of Joseph by their families: Manasseh and Ephraim. 29 The sons of Manasseh: of Machir, the family of the Machirites; and Machir fathered Gilead: of Gilead, the family of the Gileadites. 30 These are the sons of Gilead: of Iezer, the family of the Iezerites; of Helek, the family of the Helekites; 31 and of Asriel, the family of the Asrielites; and of Shechem, the family of the Shechemites; 32 and of Shemida, the family of the Shemidaites; and of Hepher, the family of the Hepherites. 33 Now Zelophehad the son of Hepher had no sons, only daughters; and the names of the daughters of Zelophehad were Mahlah, Noah, Hoglah, Milcah, and Tirzah. 34 These are the families of Manasseh; and those who were numbered of them were 52,700.

35 These are the sons of Ephraim by their families: of Shuthelah, the family of the Shuthelahites; of Becher, the family of the Becherites; of Tahan, the family of the Tahanites. 36 These are the sons of Shuthelah: of Eran, the family of the Eranites. 37 These are the families of the sons of Ephraim by those who were numbered of them, 32,500. These are the sons of Joseph by their families.

38 The sons of Benjamin by their families: of Bela, the family of the Belaites; of Ashbel, the family of the Ashbelites; of Ahiram, the family of the Ahiramites; 39 of Shephupham, the family of the Shuphamites; of Hupham, the family of the Huphamites. 40 The sons of Bela were Ard and Naaman: of Ard, the family of the Ardites; of Naaman, the family of the Naamites. 41 These are the sons of Benjamin by their families; and those who were numbered of them were 45,600.

42 These are the sons of Dan by their families: of Shuham, the family of the

Shuhamites. These are the families of Dan by their families. 43 All the families of the Shuhamites, by those who were numbered of them, were 64,400.

44 The sons of Asher by their families: of Imnah, the family of the Imnites; of Ishvi, the family of the Ishvites; of Beriah, the family of the Beriites. 45 Of the sons of Beriah: of Heber, the family of the Heberites; of Malchiel, the family of the Malchielites. 46 And the name of the daughter of Asher *was* Serah. 47 These are the families of the sons of Asher by those who were numbered of them, 53,400.

48 The sons of Naphtali by their families: of Jahzeel, the family of the Jahzeelites; of Guni, the family of the Gunites; 49 of Jezer, the family of the Jezerites; of Shillem, the family of the Shillemites. 50 These are the families of Naphtali by their families; and those who were numbered of them were 45,400.

51 These are the ones who were numbered of the sons of Israel, 601,730.

52 Then the LORD spoke to Moses, saying, 53 "Among these the land shall be divided as an inheritance according to the number of names. 54 To a larger *group* you shall increase their inheritance, and to a smaller *group* you shall decrease their inheritance; each shall be given their inheritance corresponding to *the total of* those who were numbered of them. 55 But the land shall be divided by lot. They shall receive their inheritance according to the names of the tribes of their fathers. 56 Corresponding to the selection by lot, their inheritance shall be divided between the larger and the smaller *groups.*"

57 These are those who were numbered of the Levites according to their families: of Gershon, the family of the Gershonites; of Kohath, the family of the Kohathites; of Merari, the family of the Merarites. 58 These are the families of Levi: the family of the Libnites, the family of the Hebronites, the family of the Mahlites, the family of the Mushites, *and* the family of the Korahites. Kohath fathered Amram. 59 And the name of Amram's wife was Jochebed, the daughter of Levi, who was born to Levi in Egypt; and she bore to Amram Aaron and Moses, and their sister Miriam. 60 And to Aaron were born Nadab and Abihu, Eleazar and Ithamar. 61 But Nadab and Abihu died when they offered strange fire before the LORD. 62 Those who were numbered of them were twenty-three thousand, every male from a month old and upward, for they were not numbered among the sons of Israel since no inheritance was given to them among the sons of Israel.

63 These are the ones who were numbered by Moses and Eleazar the priest, who numbered the sons of Israel in the plains of Moab by the Jordan at Jericho. 64 But among these there was not a man of those who were numbered by Moses and Aaron the priest, who numbered the sons of Israel in the wilderness of Sinai. 65 For the LORD had said of them, "They shall certainly die in the wilderness." And not a man was left of them, except Caleb the son of Jephunneh and Joshua the son of Nun.

A Law of Inheritance

27 Then the daughters of Zelophehad, the son of Hepher, the son of Gilead, the son of Machir, the son of Manasseh, of the families of Manasseh the son of Joseph, came forward; and these are the names of his daughters: Mahlah, Noah, Hoglah, Milcah, and Tirzah. 2 They stood before Moses, before Eleazar the priest, before the leaders, and all the congregation at the entrance of the tent of meeting, saying, 3 "Our father died in the wilderness, yet he was not among the group of those who gathered together against the LORD, in the group of Korah; but he died in his own sin, and he had no sons. 4 Why should the name of our father be withdrawn from among his family *simply* because he had no son? Give us property among our father's brothers." 5 So Moses brought their case before the LORD.

6 Then the LORD said to Moses, 7 "The daughters of Zelophehad are right *about their* statements. You shall certainly give them hereditary property among their father's brothers, and you shall transfer the inheritance of their father to them. 8 Further, you shall speak to the sons of Israel, saying, 'If a man dies and has no son, then you shall transfer his inheritance to his daughter. 9 And if he has no daughter, then you shall give his inheritance to his brothers. 10 If he has no brothers, then you shall give his inheritance to his father's brothers. 11 And if his father has no brothers, then you shall give his inheritance to his nearest relative in his own family, and he shall take possession of it; and it shall be a statutory ordinance to the sons of Israel, just as the LORD has commanded Moses.'"

12 Then the LORD said to Moses, "Go up to this mountain of Abarim, and see the land which I have given to the sons of Israel. 13 When you have seen it, you too will be gathered to your people, just as Aaron your brother was; 14 for in the wilderness of Zin, during the strife of the congregation, you rebelled against My command to treat Me as holy before their eyes at the water." (These are the waters of Meribah of Kadesh in the wilderness of Zin.)

Joshua to Succeed Moses

15 Then Moses spoke to the LORD, saying, 16 "May the LORD, the God of the spirits of humanity, appoint a man over the congregation, 17 who will go out and come in before them, and lead them out and bring them in, so that the congregation of the LORD will not be like sheep that have no shepherd." 18 So the LORD said to Moses, "Take Joshua the son of Nun, a man in whom is the Spirit, and lay your hand on him; 19 and have him stand before Eleazar the priest and before all the congregation, and commission him in their sight. 20 And you shall put some of your authority on him, so that all the congregation of the sons of Israel will obey *him.* 21 Moreover, he shall stand before Eleazar the priest, who shall inquire for him by the judgment of the Urim before the LORD. At his command they shall go out, and at his command they shall come in, *both* he and all the sons of Israel with him, all the congregation." 22 Then Moses did just as the LORD

commanded him; he took Joshua and had him stand before Eleazar the priest and before all the congregation. 23 Then he laid his hands on him and commissioned him, just as the LORD had spoken through Moses.

Laws for Offerings

28 Then the LORD spoke to Moses, saying, 2 "Command the sons of Israel and say to them, 'You shall be careful to present to Me My offering, My food for My offerings by fire, of a soothing aroma to Me, at their appointed time.' 3 And you shall say to them, 'This is the offering by fire which you shall offer to the LORD: two male lambs one year old without defect as a continual burnt offering every day. 4 You shall offer the one lamb in the morning, and the other lamb you shall offer at twilight; 5 also a tenth of an ephah of fine flour as a grain offering, mixed with a fourth of a ¹hin of pure oil. 6 It is a continual burnt offering which was ordained on Mount Sinai as a soothing aroma, an offering by fire to the LORD. 7 Then the drink offering with it shall be a fourth of a hin for each lamb; in the Holy Place pour out a drink offering of strong drink to the LORD. 8 The other lamb you shall offer at twilight; as the grain offering of the morning and as its drink offering, you shall offer it, an offering by fire, a soothing aroma to the LORD.

9 'Then on the Sabbath day two male lambs one year old without defect, and two-tenths of an ephah of fine flour mixed with oil as a grain offering, and its drink offering: 10 This is the burnt offering of every Sabbath in addition to the continual burnt offering and its drink offering.

11 'Then at the beginning of each of your months you shall present a burnt offering to the LORD: two bulls and one ram, seven male lambs one year old without defect; 12 and three-tenths of an ephah of fine flour mixed with oil as a grain offering, for each bull; and two-tenths of fine flour mixed with oil as a grain offering, for the one ram; 13 and a tenth of an ephah of fine flour mixed with oil as a grain offering for each lamb, as a burnt offering of a soothing aroma, an offering by fire to the LORD. 14 Their drink offerings shall be half a hin of wine for a bull and a third of a hin for the ram and a fourth of a hin for a lamb; this is the burnt offering of each month throughout the months of the year. 15 And one male goat as a sin offering to the LORD; it shall be offered with its drink offering in addition to the continual burnt offering.

16 'The LORD's Passover shall be on the fourteenth day of the first month. 17 On the fifteenth day of this month there shall be a feast; unleavened bread shall be eaten for seven days. 18 On the first day there shall be a holy assembly; you shall do no laborious work. 19 But you shall present an offering by fire, a burnt offering to the LORD: two bulls and one ram, and seven male lambs one year old, that you have without defect. 20 For their grain offering, you shall offer fine flour mixed with oil: three-tenths of an ephah for a bull, and

two-tenths for the ram. 21 A tenth of an ephah you shall offer for each of the seven lambs; 22 and one male goat as a sin offering to make atonement for you. 23 You shall present these besides the burnt offering of the morning, which is for a continual burnt offering. 24 In this way you shall present daily, for seven days, the food of the offering by fire, of a soothing aroma to the LORD; it shall be presented with its drink offering in addition to the continual burnt offering. 25 On the seventh day you shall have a holy assembly; you shall do no laborious work.

26 'Also on the day of the first fruits, when you present a new grain offering to the LORD in your Feast of Weeks, you shall have a holy assembly; you shall do no laborious work. 27 But you shall offer a burnt offering as a soothing aroma to the LORD: two bulls, one ram, and seven male lambs one year old; 28 and as their grain offering, fine flour mixed with oil: three-tenths of an ephah for each bull, two-tenths for the one ram, 29 and a tenth for each of the seven lambs; 30 also one male goat to make atonement for you. 31 Besides the continual burnt offering and its grain offering, you shall present them with their drink offerings. They shall be without defect.

Offerings of the Seventh Month

29 'Now in the seventh month, on the first day of the month, you shall have a holy assembly; you shall do no laborious work. It will be to you a day for blowing trumpets. 2 And you shall offer a burnt offering as a soothing aroma to the LORD: one bull, one ram, and seven male lambs one year old without defect; 3 also their grain offering, fine flour mixed with oil: three-tenths of an ¹ephah for the bull, two-tenths for the ram, 4 and a tenth for each of the seven lambs, 5 and one male goat as a sin offering, to make atonement for you, 6 besides the burnt offering of the new moon and its grain offering, and the continual burnt offering and its grain offering, and their drink offerings, according to their ordinance, for a soothing aroma, an offering by fire to the LORD.

7 'Then on the tenth day of this seventh month you shall have a holy assembly, and you shall humble yourselves; you shall not do any work. 8 You shall present a burnt offering to the LORD as a soothing aroma: one bull, one ram, and seven male lambs one year old, that you have without defect; 9 and their grain offering, fine flour mixed with oil: three-tenths of an ephah for the bull, two-tenths for the one ram, 10 and a tenth for each of the seven lambs; 11 one male goat as a sin offering, besides the sin offering of atonement and the continual burnt offering, and its grain offering, and their drink offerings.

12 'Then on the fifteenth day of the seventh month you shall have a holy assembly; you shall do no laborious work, and you shall celebrate with a feast to the LORD for seven days. 13 You shall present a burnt offering, an offering by fire as a soothing aroma to the LORD: thirteen bulls, two rams, and fourteen

male lambs one year old, which are without defect; [14] and their grain offering, fine flour mixed with oil: three-tenths *of an ephah* for each of the thirteen bulls, two-tenths for each of the two rams, [15] and a tenth for each of the fourteen lambs; [16] and one male goat as a sin offering, besides the continual burnt offering, its grain offering, and its drink offering.

[17] 'Then on the second day: twelve bulls, two rams, *and* fourteen male lambs one year old without defect; [18] and their grain offering and their drink offerings for the bulls, for the rams, and for the lambs, by their number according to the ordinance; [19] and one male goat as a sin offering, besides the continual burnt offering and its grain offering, and their drink offerings.

[20] 'Then on the third day: eleven bulls, two rams, *and* fourteen male lambs one year old without defect; [21] and their grain offering and their drink offerings for the bulls, for the rams, and for the lambs, by their number according to the ordinance; [22] and one male goat as a sin offering, besides the continual burnt offering and its grain offering, and its drink offering.

[23] 'Then on the fourth day: ten bulls, two rams, *and* fourteen male lambs one year old without defect; [24] their grain offering and their drink offerings for the bulls, for the rams, and for the lambs, by their number according to the ordinance; [25] and one male goat as a sin offering, besides the continual burnt offering, its grain offering, and its drink offering.

[26] 'Then on the fifth day: nine bulls, two rams, *and* fourteen male lambs one year old without defect; [27] and their grain offering and their drink offerings for the bulls, for the rams, and for the lambs, by their number according to the ordinance; [28] and one male goat as a sin offering, besides the continual burnt offering and its grain offering, and its drink offering.

[29] 'Then on the sixth day: eight bulls, two rams, *and* fourteen male lambs one year old without defect; [30] and their grain offering and their drink offerings for the bulls, for the rams, and for the lambs, by their number according to the ordinance; [31] and one male goat as a sin offering, besides the continual burnt offering, its grain offering, and its drink offerings.

[32] 'Then on the seventh day: seven bulls, two rams, *and* fourteen male lambs one year old without defect; [33] and their grain offering and their drink offerings for the bulls, for the rams, and for the lambs, by their number according to the ordinance; [34] and one male goat as a sin offering, besides the continual burnt offering, its grain offering, and its drink offering.

[35] 'On the eighth day you shall have a sacred assembly; you shall do no laborious work. [36] But you shall present a burnt offering, an offering by fire, as a soothing aroma to the LORD: one bull, one ram, *and* seven male lambs one year old without defect; [37] their grain offering and their drink offerings for the bull, for the ram, and for the lambs, by their number according to the ordinance; [38] and one male goat as a sin offering, besides the continual

burnt offering and its grain offering, and its drink offering.

[39] 'You shall present these to the LORD at your appointed times, besides your vowed offerings and your voluntary offerings, for your burnt offerings, your grain offerings, your drink offerings, and for your peace offerings.' " [40] And Moses spoke to the sons of Israel in accordance with everything that the LORD had commanded Moses.

The Law of Vows

30 Then Moses spoke to the heads of the tribes of the sons of Israel, saying, "This is the word which the LORD has commanded: [2] If a man makes a vow to the LORD, or takes an oath to put himself under a binding obligation, he shall not break his word; he shall act in accordance with everything that comes out of his mouth.

[3] "And if a woman makes a vow to the LORD, and puts herself under a binding obligation in her father's house in her youth, [4] and her father hears her vow and her obligation under which she has put herself, and her father says nothing to her, then all her vows shall remain valid and every binding obligation under which she has put herself shall remain valid. [5] But if her father expresses disapproval to her on the day he hears *of it,* none of her vows or her obligations under which she has put herself shall remain valid; and the LORD will forgive her because her father has expressed disapproval to her.

[6] "However, if she happens to marry while under her vows or the impulsive statement of her lips by which she has obligated herself, [7] and her husband hears of it and says nothing to her on the day he hears *it,* then her vows shall remain valid and her binding obligations under which she has put herself shall remain valid. [8] But if on the day her husband hears *of it,* he expresses disapproval to her, then he will annul her vow which she is under and the impulsive statement of her lips by which she has obligated herself; and the LORD will forgive her.

[9] "But *as for* the vow of a widow or of a divorced woman, every binding obligation under which she has put herself, shall remain valid against her. [10] However, if *a married woman* vowed *in* her husband's house, or put herself under a binding obligation with an oath, [11] and her husband heard *it,* but said nothing to her *and* did not express disapproval to her, then all her vows shall remain valid and every binding obligation under which she put herself shall remain valid. [12] But if her husband actually annuls them on the day he hears *them,* then no utterance from her lips concerning her vows or the obligation *she put on* herself shall remain valid; her husband has annulled them, and the LORD will forgive her.

[13] "Every vow and every binding oath to humble herself, her husband may confirm it or her husband may annul it. [14] But if her husband in fact says nothing to her from day to day, then he confirms all her vows or all her binding obligations which are on her; he has confirmed them, because he said nothing to

her on the day he heard them. [15] However, if he actually annuls them 'after he has heard them, then he shall bear *the responsibility for her guilt.*"

[16] These are the statutes which the LORD commanded Moses *concerning matters* between a man and his wife, *and* between a father and his daughter *while she is* in her youth *in* her father's house.

The Slaughter of Midian

31 Then the LORD spoke to Moses, saying, [2] "Take vengeance on the Midianites for the sons of Israel; afterward you will be gathered to your people." [3] So Moses spoke to the people, saying, "Arm men from among you for the war, so that they may go against Midian to execute the LORD's vengeance on Midian. [4] You shall send a thousand from each tribe of all the tribes of Israel to the war." [5] So there were selected from the thousands of Israel, a thousand from each tribe, twelve thousand armed for war. [6] And Moses sent them, a thousand from each tribe, to the war, and Phinehas the son of Eleazar the priest, to the war with them, and the holy implements and the trumpets for the alarm in his hand. [7] So they made war against Midian, just as the LORD had commanded Moses, and they killed every male. [8] They killed the kings of Midian along with the *rest of* those killed: Evi, Rekem, Zur, Hur, and Reba, the five kings of Midian. They also killed Balaam the son of Beor with the sword. [9] And the sons of Israel took captive the women of Midian and their little ones; and they plundered all their cattle, all their flocks, and all their property. [10] Then they burned all their cities where they lived and all their encampments. [11] And they took all the plunder and all the spoils, both of people and of livestock. [12] They brought the captives and the spoils and the plunder to Moses, to Eleazar the priest, and to the congregation of the sons of Israel, to the camp at the plains of Moab which are by the Jordan, *opposite* Jericho.

[13] And Moses, Eleazar the priest, and all the leaders of the congregation went out to meet them outside the camp. [14] But Moses was angry with the officers of the army, the commanders of thousands and the commanders of hundreds, who had come from service in the war. [15] And Moses said to them, "Have you spared all the women? [16] Behold, they caused the sons of Israel, through the counsel of Balaam, to be unfaithful to the LORD in the matter of Peor, so that the plague took place among the congregation of the LORD! [17] Now therefore, kill every male among the little ones, and kill every woman who has known a man intimately. [18] However, all the girls who have not known a man intimately, keep alive for yourselves. [19] And *as for* you, camp outside the camp for seven days; whoever has killed a person and whoever has touched *anyone* killed, purify yourselves, you and your captives, on the third day and on the seventh day. [20] And you shall purify for yourselves every garment, every article of leather, every work of goats' *hair,* and every article of wood."

[21] Then Eleazar the priest said to the men of war who had gone to battle, "This is the statute of the Law which the LORD has commanded Moses: [22] only the gold and the silver, the bronze, the iron, the tin, and the lead, [23] everything that can withstand the fire, you shall pass through the fire, and it will be clean, only it shall be purified with water for impurity. But whatever cannot withstand the fire you shall pass through the water. [24] And you shall wash your clothes on the seventh day and you will be clean; and afterward you may enter the camp."

Division of the Plunder

[25] Then the LORD spoke to Moses, saying, [26] "You and Eleazar the priest and the heads of the fathers' *households* of the congregation take a count of the spoils that were captured, both of people and of livestock; [27] and divide the spoils between the warriors who went to battle and all the congregation. [28] Also, collect a tribute tax for the LORD from the men of war who went to battle, one in five hundred of the persons, of the cattle, of the donkeys, and of the sheep; [29] take it from their half and give it to Eleazar the priest, as an offering to the LORD. [30] And from the sons of Israel's half, you shall take one drawn from every fifty of the persons, of the cattle, of the donkeys, and of the sheep, from all the animals; and give them to the Levites who perform the duty of the tabernacle of the LORD." [31] Moses and Eleazar the priest did just as the LORD had commanded Moses.

[32] Now the spoils that remained from the plunder which the men of war had plundered was 675,000 sheep, [33] seventy-two thousand cattle, [34] sixty-one thousand donkeys, [35] and of *captive* people, of the women who had not known a man intimately, in all were thirty-two thousand people.

[36] The half, the share of those who went to war, was *as follows:* the number of sheep was 337,500, [37] the LORD's tribute tax of the sheep was 675; [38] the cattle were thirty-six thousand, from which the LORD's tribute tax was seventy-two; [39] the donkeys were 30,500, from which the LORD's tribute tax was sixty-one; [40] and the *captive* people were sixteen thousand, from whom the LORD's tribute tax was thirty-two persons. [41] And Moses gave the tribute tax, *which was* the LORD's offering, to Eleazar the priest, just as the LORD had commanded Moses.

[42] As for the sons of Israel's half, which Moses separated from the men who had gone to war— [43] now the congregation's half was 337,500 sheep, [44] thirty-six thousand cattle, [45] 30,500 donkeys, [46] and the *captive* people were sixteen thousand— [47] from the sons of Israel's half Moses took one drawn from every fifty, both of people and of animals, and gave them to the Levites, who performed the duty of the tabernacle of the LORD, just as the LORD had commanded Moses.

[48] Then the officers who were over the thousands of the army, the commanders of thousands and the commanders of hundreds, approached Moses, [49] and they said to Moses, "Your servants have taken a census of the men

---

30:15 [1] I.e., perhaps a long delay before he annuls them

of war who are under our authority, and no man of us is missing. 50 So we have brought as an offering to the LORD what each man found, articles of gold, armlets and bracelets, signet rings, earrings, and necklaces, to make atonement for ourselves before the LORD." 51 Moses and Eleazar the priest took the gold from them, all kinds of crafted articles. 52 All the gold of the offering which they offered up to the LORD, from the commanders of thousands and the commanders of hundreds, was 16,750 shekels. 53 The men of war had taken plunder, every man for himself. 54 So Moses and Eleazar the priest took the gold from the commanders of thousands and of hundreds, and brought it to the tent of meeting as a memorial for the sons of Israel before the LORD.

Reuben and Gad Settle in Gilead

32 Now the sons of Reuben and the sons of Gad had a very large number of livestock. So when they saw the land of Jazer and the land of Gilead, that it was indeed a place suitable for livestock, 2 the sons of Gad and the sons of Reuben came and spoke to Moses, Eleazar the priest, and to the leaders of the congregation, saying, 3 "Ataroth, Dibon, Jazer, Nimrah, Heshbon, Elealeh, Sebam, Nebo, and Beon, 4 the land which the LORD conquered before the congregation of Israel, is a land for livestock, and your servants have livestock." 5 And they said, "If we have found favor in your sight, let this land be given to your servants as our property; do not take us across the Jordan."

6 But Moses said to the sons of Gad and the sons of Reuben, "Should your brothers go to war while you remain here? 7 And why are you discouraging the sons of Israel from crossing over into the land which the LORD has given them? 8 This is what your fathers did when I sent them from Kadesh-barnea to see the land. 9 For when they went up to the Valley of Eshcol and saw the land, they discouraged the sons of Israel so that they did not go into the land which the LORD had given them. 10 So the LORD's anger burned on that day, and He swore, saying, 11 'None of the men who came up from Egypt, from twenty years old and upward, shall see the land which I swore to Abraham, to Isaac, and to Jacob; for they did not follow Me fully, 12 except Caleb the son of Jephunneh the Kenizzite and Joshua the son of Nun; for they have followed the LORD fully.' 13 So the LORD's anger burned against Israel, and He made them wander in the wilderness for forty years, until the entire generation of those who had done evil in the sight of the LORD came to an end. 14 Now behold, you have risen up in your fathers' place, born of sinful men, to add still more to the burning anger of the LORD against Israel. 15 For if you turn away from following Him, He will once more leave them in the wilderness, and you will destroy all these people."

16 Then they approached him and said, "We will build sheepfolds for our livestock here and cities for our little ones; 17 but we ourselves will be armed, hurrying ahead of the sons of Israel, until we have brought them to their place, while our little ones live in the fortified cities because of the inhabitants of the land. 18 We will not return to our homes until every one of the sons of Israel has gained possession of his inheritance. 19 But we will not have an inheritance with them on the other side of the Jordan and beyond, because our inheritance has come to us on this side of the Jordan toward the east."

20 So Moses said to them, "If you will do this, if you will arm yourselves before the LORD for the war, 21 and all of you armed men cross over the Jordan before the LORD until He has driven His enemies out from Him, 22 and the land is subdued before the LORD, then afterward you may return and be free of obligation toward the LORD and toward Israel, and this land shall be yours as property before the LORD. 23 But if you do not do so, behold, you have sinned against the LORD, and be sure that your sin will find you out. 24 Build yourselves cities for your little ones, and sheepfolds for your sheep, and do what you have promised."

25 Then the sons of Gad and the sons of Reuben spoke to Moses, saying, "Your servants will do just as my lord commands. 26 Our little ones, our wives, our livestock, and all our cattle shall remain there in the cities of Gilead, 27 while your servants, that is, everyone who is armed for war, cross over in the presence of the LORD to battle, just as my lord says."

28 So Moses gave the command regarding them to Eleazar the priest, to Joshua the son of Nun, and to the heads of the fathers' households of the tribes of the sons of Israel. 29 And Moses said to them, "If the sons of Gad and the sons of Reuben, everyone who is armed for battle, cross with you over the Jordan in the presence of the LORD, and the land is subdued before you, then you shall give them the land of Gilead as their property; 30 but if they do not cross over with you armed, they shall instead be settled among you in the land of Canaan." 31 And the sons of Gad and the sons of Reuben answered, saying, "As the LORD has said to your servants, so we will do. 32 We ourselves will cross over armed in the presence of the LORD into the land of Canaan, and the property of our inheritance shall remain with us across the Jordan."

33 So Moses gave to them, to the sons of Gad, to the sons of Reuben, and to the half-tribe of Joseph's son Manasseh, the kingdom of Sihon, king of the Amorites and the kingdom of Og, the king of Bashan, the land with its cities with their territories, the cities of the surrounding land. 34 And the sons of Gad built Dibon, Ataroth, Aroer, 35 Atroth-shophan, Jazer, Jogbehah, 36 Beth-nimrah, and Beth-haran as fortified cities, and sheepfolds for sheep. 37 The sons of Reuben built Heshbon, Elealeh, Kiriathaim, 38 Nebo, and Baal-meon—their names being changed—and Sibmah, and they gave other names to the cities which they built. 39 The sons of Machir the son of Manasseh went to Gilead and took it, and dispossessed the Amorites who were in it. 40 So Moses gave Gilead to Machir the son of Manasseh, and he lived in it. 41 Jair the son of

Manasseh went and took its towns, and called them Havvoth-jair. 42 Nobah went and took Kenath and its villages, and named it Nobah, after his own name.

Review of the Journey from Egypt to Jordan

33 These are the journeys of the sons of Israel, by which they came out of the land of Egypt by their armies, under the leadership of Moses and Aaron. 2 Moses recorded their starting places according to their journeys by the command of the LORD, and these are their journeys according to their starting places. 3 Now they journeyed from Rameses in the first month, on the fifteenth day of the first month; on the day after the Passover the sons of Israel started out boldly in the sight of all the Egyptians, 4 while the Egyptians were burying all their firstborn whom the LORD had fatally struck among them. The LORD had also executed judgments against their gods.

5 Then the sons of Israel journeyed from Rameses and camped in Succoth. 6 They journeyed from Succoth and camped in Etham, which is on the edge of the wilderness. 7 Then they journeyed from Etham and turned back to Pi-hahiroth, which faces Baal-zephon; and they camped before Migdol. 8 They journeyed from Pi-hahiroth and passed through the midst of the sea to the wilderness; and they went three days' journey in the wilderness of Etham and camped at Marah. 9 They journeyed from Marah and came to Elim; and in Elim there were twelve springs of water and seventy palm trees, and they camped there. 10 They journeyed from Elim and camped by the Red Sea. 11 And they journeyed from the Red Sea and camped in the wilderness of Sin. 12 They journeyed from the wilderness of Sin and camped at Dophkah. 13 They journeyed from Dophkah and camped at Alush. 14 And they journeyed from Alush and camped at Rephidim; now it was there that the people had no water to drink. 15 And they journeyed from Rephidim and camped in the wilderness of Sinai. 16 They journeyed from the wilderness of Sinai, and camped at Kibroth-hattaavah.

17 They journeyed from Kibroth-hattaavah and camped at Hazeroth. 18 They journeyed from Hazeroth and camped at Rithmah. 19 They journeyed from Rithmah and camped at Rimmon-perez. 20 They journeyed from Rimmon-perez and camped at Libnah. 21 They journeyed from Libnah and camped at Rissah. 22 They journeyed from Rissah and camped in Kehelathah. 23 They journeyed from Kehelathah and camped at Mount Shepher. 24 They journeyed from Mount Shepher and camped at Haradah. 25 They journeyed from Haradah and camped at Makheloth. 26 They journeyed from Makheloth and camped at Tahath. 27 They journeyed from Tahath and camped at Terah. 28 They journeyed from Terah and camped at Mithkah. 29 They journeyed from Mithkah and camped at Hashmonah. 30 They journeyed from Hashmonah and camped at Moseroth. 31 They journeyed from Moseroth and camped at Bene-jaakan. 32 They journeyed from Bene-jaakan and camped at Hor-haggidgad. 33 They journeyed from Hor-haggidgad and camped at Jotbathah.

34 They journeyed from Jotbathah and camped at Abronah. 35 They journeyed from Abronah and camped at Ezion-geber. 36 They journeyed from Ezion-geber and camped in the wilderness of Zin, that is, Kadesh. 37 They journeyed from Kadesh and camped at Mount Hor, at the edge of the land of Edom.

38 Then Aaron the priest went up to Mount Hor at the command of the LORD, and died there in the fortieth year after the sons of Israel had come from the land of Egypt, on the first day in the fifth month. 39 Aaron was 123 years old when he died on Mount Hor.

40 Now the Canaanite, the king of Arad who lived in the Negev in the land of Canaan, heard about the coming of the sons of Israel.

41 Then they journeyed from Mount Hor and camped at Zalmonah. 42 They journeyed from Zalmonah and camped at Punon. 43 They journeyed from Punon and camped at Oboth. 44 They journeyed from Oboth and camped at Iye-abarim, at the border of Moab. 45 They journeyed from Iyim and camped at Dibon-gad. 46 They journeyed from Dibon-gad and camped at Almon-diblathaim. 47 They journeyed from Almon-diblathaim and camped in the mountains of Abarim, before Nebo. 48 They journeyed from the mountains of Abarim and camped in the plains of Moab, by the Jordan opposite Jericho. 49 They camped by the Jordan, from Beth-jeshimoth as far as Abel-shittim, in the plains of Moab.

Law for Possessing the Land

50 Then the LORD spoke to Moses in the plains of Moab by the Jordan opposite Jericho, saying, 51 "Speak to the sons of Israel and say to them, 'When you cross the Jordan into the land of Canaan, 52 you shall drive out all the inhabitants of the land from you, and destroy all their idolatrous sculptures, destroy all their cast metal images, and eliminate all their high places; 53 and you shall take possession of the land and live in it, for I have given the land to you to possess it. 54 You shall maintain the land as an inheritance by lot according to your families; to the larger you shall give more inheritance, and to the smaller you shall give less inheritance. Wherever the lot falls to anyone, that shall be his. You shall pass on land as an inheritance according to the tribes of your fathers. 55 But if you do not drive out the inhabitants of the land from you, then it will come about that those whom you let remain of them will be like thorns in your eyes and like pricks in your sides, and they will trouble you in the land in which you live. 56 And just as I plan to do to them, I will do to you.'"

Instruction for Apportioning Canaan

34 Then the LORD spoke to Moses, saying, 2 "Command the sons of Israel and say to them, 'When you enter the land of Canaan, this is the land that shall fall to you as an inheritance, that is, the land of Canaan according to its borders. 3 Your southern region shall extend from the wilderness of Zin along the side of Edom, and your southern border shall extend from the end of the Salt Sea eastward. 4 Then your border shall change direction from the

south to the ascent of Akrabbim and continue to Zin, and its termination shall be to the south of Kadesh-barnea; and it shall reach Hazaraddar and continue to Azmon. 5 Then the border shall change direction from Azmon to the brook of Egypt, and its termination shall be *at* the sea.

6 'As for the western border, you shall have the Great Sea, that is, *its* coastline; this shall be your western border.

7 'And this shall be your northern border: you shall draw your boundary from the Great Sea to Mount Hor. 8 You shall draw a boundary from Mount Hor to the Lebo-hamath, and the termination of the border shall be at Zedad; 9 and the border shall proceed to Ziphron, and its termination shall be at Hazar-enan. This shall be your northern border.

10 'For your eastern border you shall also draw a boundary from Hazar-enan to Shepham, 11 and the border shall go down from Shepham to Riblah on the east *side* of Ain; and the border shall go down and reach to the slope on the east side of the Sea of Chinnereth. 12 And the border shall go down to the Jordan, and its termination shall be at the Salt Sea. This shall be your land according to its borders on all sides.' "

13 So Moses commanded the sons of Israel, saying, "This is the land that you are to possess by lot, which the LORD has commanded to give to the nine and a half tribes. 14 For the tribe of the sons of Reuben have received *theirs* according to their fathers' households, and the tribe of the sons of Gad according to their fathers' households, and the half-tribe of Manasseh have received their possession. 15 The two and a half tribes have received their possession across the Jordan *opposite* Jericho, eastward toward the sunrise."

16 Then the LORD spoke to Moses, saying, 17 "These are the names of the men who shall assign the land to you as an inheritance: Eleazar the priest, and Joshua the son of Nun. 18 And you shall take one leader of each tribe to assign the land as an inheritance. 19 These are the names of the men: of the tribe of Judah, Caleb the son of Jephunneh. 20 Of the tribe of the sons of Simeon, Samuel the son of Ammihud. 21 Of the tribe of Benjamin, Elidad the son of Chislon. 22 And of the tribe of the sons of Dan, a leader, Bukki the son of Jogli. 23 Of the sons of Joseph: of the tribe of the sons of Manasseh, a leader, Hanniel the son of Ephod. 24 Of the tribe of the sons of Ephraim, a leader, Kemuel the son of Shiphtan. 25 Of the tribe of the sons of Zebulun, a leader, Elizaphan the son of Parnach. 26 Of the tribe of the sons of Issachar, a leader, Paltiel the son of Azzan. 27 Of the tribe of the sons of Asher, a leader, Ahihud the son of Shelomi. 28 Of the tribe of the sons of Naphtali, a leader, Pedahel the son of Ammihud." 29 These are the ones whom the LORD commanded to apportion the inheritance to the sons of Israel in the land of Canaan.

Cities for the Levites

35 Now the LORD spoke to Moses in the plains of Moab, by the Jordan *opposite* Jericho, saying, 2 "Command the sons of Israel that they give to the Levites from the inheritance of their possession cities to live in; and you shall give to the Levites pasture lands around the cities. 3 The cities shall be theirs to live in; and their pasture lands shall be for their cattle and for their equipment and for all their *other* animals.

4 "The pasture lands of the cities which you are to give to the Levites *shall extend* from the wall of the city outward a thousand cubits around. 5 You shall also measure outside the city on the east side two thousand cubits, on the south side two thousand cubits, on the west side two thousand cubits, and on the north side two thousand cubits, with the city in the center. This shall become theirs as pasture lands for the cities.

Cities of Refuge

6 The cities which you shall give to the Levites *shall be* the six cities of refuge, which you shall provide for the one who commits manslaughter to flee to; and in addition to them you shall give forty-two cities. 7 The total *number* of the cities which you are to give to the Levites *shall be* forty-eight cities, together with their pasture lands. 8 As for the cities which you shall give *them* from the possession of the sons of Israel, you shall take more from the larger, and you shall take fewer from the smaller; each shall give some of his cities to the Levites in proportion to his inheritance which he possesses."

9 Then the LORD spoke to Moses, saying, 10 "Speak to the sons of Israel and say to them, 'When you cross the Jordan into the land of Canaan, 11 then you shall select for yourselves cities to be your cities of refuge, so that the one who commits manslaughter *by* killing a person unintentionally may flee there. 12 The cities shall serve you as a refuge from the avenger, so that the one who commits manslaughter does not die until he stands before the congregation for trial. 13 So the cities which you are to provide shall be six cities of refuge for you. 14 You shall provide three cities across the Jordan, and three cities in the land of Canaan; they are to be cities of refuge. 15 These six cities shall be a refuge for the sons of Israel, for the stranger, and for the foreign resident among them; so that anyone who kills a person unintentionally may flee there.

16 'But if he struck him with an iron object, so that he died, he is a murderer; the murderer must be put to death. 17 And if he struck him with a stone in the hand, by which he would die, and *as a result* he did die, he is a murderer; the murderer must be put to death. 18 Or *if* he struck him with a wooden object in the hand, by which he would die, and *as a result* he did die, he is a murderer; the murderer must be put to death. 19 The blood avenger himself shall put the murderer to death; he himself shall put him to death when he meets him. 20 Now if he pushed him in hatred, or he threw *something* at him with malicious intent, and *as a result* he died, 21 or *if* he struck him with his hand with hostility, and *as a result* he died, the one who struck him must be put to death; he is a murderer. The

blood avenger shall put the murderer to death when he meets him.

22 'But if he pushed him suddenly, without hostility, or threw any object at him without malicious intent, 23 or had any deadly stone, and without looking he dropped *it* on him so that he died, while he was not his enemy nor was he seeking to harm him, 24 then the congregation shall judge between the one who fatally struck *the victim* and the blood avenger in accordance with these ordinances. 25 And the congregation shall save the one who committed manslaughter from the hand of the blood avenger, and the congregation shall return him to his city of refuge to which he fled; and he shall live in it until the death of the high priest who was anointed with the holy oil. 26 But if at any time he goes beyond the border of his city of refuge to which he flees, 27 and the blood avenger finds him outside the border of his city of refuge, and the blood avenger kills him, he will not be guilty of bloodshed, 28 because he should have remained in his city of refuge until the death of the high priest. But after the death of the high priest the one who committed manslaughter may return to the land of his property.

29 'These things shall be a statutory ordinance for you throughout your generations in all your dwelling places.

30 'If anyone kills a person, the murderer shall be put to death on the testimony of witnesses, but no person shall be put to death on the testimony of *only* one witness. 31 Moreover, you shall not accept a ransom for the life of a murderer who is condemned to death, but he must be put to death. 32 And you shall not accept a ransom for one who has fled to his city of refuge, so that he may return to live in the land before the death of the priest. 33 So you shall not defile the land in which you *live;* for blood defiles the land, and no atonement can be made for the land for the blood that is shed on it, except by the blood of the one who shed it. 34 So you shall not defile the land in which you live, in the midst of which I dwell; for I the LORD am dwelling in the midst of the sons of Israel.' "

Inheritance by Marriage

36 Now the heads of the fathers' *households* of the family of the sons of Gilead, the son of Machir, the son of Manasseh, of the families of the sons of Joseph, came forward and spoke before Moses and before the leaders, the heads of the fathers' *households* of the sons of Israel, 2 and they said, "The LORD commanded my lord to give the land by lot to the sons of Israel as an inheritance, and my lord was commanded by the LORD to give the inheritance of our brother Zelophehad to his daughters. 3 But *if* they marry one of the sons of the *other* tribes of the sons of Israel, their inheritance will be withdrawn from the inheritance of our fathers and will be added to the inheritance of the tribe to which they belong; so it will be withdrawn from our allotted inheritance. 4 And when the jubilee of the sons of Israel takes place, then their inheritance will be added to the inheritance of the tribe to which they belong; so their inheritance will be withdrawn from the inheritance of the tribe of our fathers."

5 Then Moses commanded the sons of Israel in accordance with the word of the LORD, saying, "The tribe of the sons of Joseph is right in *its* statements. 6 This is what the LORD has commanded regarding the daughters of Zelophehad, saying, 'Let them marry whomever they wish; only they must marry within the family of the tribe of their father.' 7 So no inheritance of the sons of Israel will be transferred from tribe to tribe, for the sons of Israel shall each retain possession of the inheritance of the tribe of his fathers. 8 And every daughter who comes into possession of an inheritance of *any* tribe of the sons of Israel shall marry one of the family of the tribe of her father, so that the sons of Israel may each possess the inheritance of his fathers. 9 So no inheritance will be transferred from one tribe to another tribe, for the tribes of the sons of Israel shall each retain possession of its own inheritance."

10 Just as the LORD had commanded Moses, so the daughters of Zelophehad did: 11 Mahlah, Tirzah, Hoglah, Milcah, and Noah, the daughters of Zelophehad married their uncles' sons. 12 They married *those* from the families of the sons of Manasseh the son of Joseph, and their inheritance remained with the tribe of the family of their father.

13 These are the commandments and the ordinances which the LORD commanded to the sons of Israel through Moses in the plains of Moab, by the Jordan *opposite* Jericho.

DEUTERONOMY

Israel's History after the Exodus

1 These are the words that Moses spoke to all Israel across the Jordan in the wilderness, in the Arabah opposite Suph, between Paran and Tophel, Laban, Hazeroth, and Dizahab. 2 It is eleven days' *journey* from Horeb by way of Mount Seir to Kadesh-barnea. 3 In the fortieth year, on the first *day* of the eleventh month, Moses spoke to the sons of Israel, in accordance with everything that the LORD had commanded him *to declare* to them, 4 after he had defeated Sihon the king of the Amorites, who lived in Heshbon, and Og the king of Bashan, who lived in Ashtaroth and in Edrei. 5 Across the Jordan in the land of Moab, Moses began to explain this Law, saying,

6 "The LORD our God spoke to us at Horeb, saying, 'You have stayed long enough at this mountain. 7 Turn and set out on your journey, and go to the hill country of the Amorites, and to all their neighbors in the Arabah, in the hill country, in the lowland, in the 1Negev, by the seacoast, the land of the Canaanites, and Lebanon, as far as the great river, the river Euphrates. 8 See, I have placed the land before you; go in and take possession of the land which the LORD swore to give to your fathers, to Abraham, to Isaac, and to Jacob, and their descendants after them.'

9 "And I spoke to you at that time, saying, 'I am not able to endure you alone. 10 The LORD your God has multiplied you, and behold, you are this day like the stars of heaven in number. 11 May the LORD, the God of your fathers increase you a thousand times more than you are, and bless you, just as He has promised you! 12 How can I alone endure the burden and weight of you and your strife? 13 Obtain for yourselves men who are wise, discerning, and informed from your tribes, and I will appoint them as your heads.' 14 And you answered me and said, 'The thing which you have said to do is good.' 15 So I took the heads of your tribes, wise and informed men, and appointed them as heads over you, commanders of thousands, hundreds, fifties, and tens, and officers for your tribes.

16 "Then I ordered your judges at that time, saying, 'Hear *the cases* between your fellow countrymen and judge righteously between a person and his fellow countryman, or the stranger who is with him. 17 You are not to show partiality in judgment; you shall hear the small and the great alike. You are not to be afraid of any person, for the judgment is God's. The case that is too difficult for you, you shall bring to me, and I will hear it.' 18 At that time I commanded you all the things that you were to do.

19 "Then we set out from Horeb, and went *through* all that great and terrible wilderness that you saw on the way to the hill country of the Amorites, just as the LORD our God had commanded us; and we came to Kadesh-barnea. 20 And I said to you, 'You have come to the hill country of the Amorites, which the LORD our God is about to give us. 21 See, the LORD your God has placed the land before you; go up, take possession, just as the LORD, the God of your fathers, has spoken to you. Do not fear or be dismayed.'

22 "Then all of you approached me and said, 'Let us send men ahead of us, so that they may spy out the land for us, and bring back to us word of the way by which we should go up, and the cities which we should enter.' 23 The plan pleased me, and I took twelve of your men, one man for each tribe. 24 Then they turned and went up into the hill country, and came to the Valley of Eshcol, and spied it out. 25 And they took *some* of the fruit of the land in their hands and brought it down to us. They also brought us back a report and said, 'The land that the LORD our God is about to give us is good.'

26 "Yet you were unwilling to go up; instead you rebelled against the command of the LORD your God; 27 and you grumbled in your tents and said, 'Because the LORD hates us, He has brought us out of the land of Egypt, to hand us over to the Amorites to destroy us. 28 Where can we go up? Our brothers have made our hearts melt, *by* saying, "The people are bigger and taller than we; the cities are large and fortified *up* to heaven. And besides, we saw the sons of the Anakim there." ' 29 But I said to you, 'Do not be terrified, nor fear them. 30 The LORD your God, who goes before you, will Himself fight for you, just as He did for you in Egypt before your eyes, 31 and in the wilderness where you saw how the LORD your God carried you, just as a man carries his son, on all of the road which you have walked until you came to this place.' 32 Yet in spite of all this, you did not trust the LORD your God, 33 who goes before you on *your* way, to seek out a place for you to make camp, in the fire by night to show you the way by which you should go, and in the cloud by day.

34 "Then the LORD heard the sound of your words, and He was angry and swore an oath, saying, 35 'Not one of these men, this evil generation, shall see the good land which I swore to give your fathers, 36 except Caleb the son of Jephunneh; he shall see it, and to him I will give the land on which he has set foot, and to his sons, because he has followed the LORD fully.' 37 The LORD was angry with me also on your account, saying, 'Not even you shall enter there. 38 Joshua the son of Nun, who stands before you, shall himself enter there; encourage him, for he will give it to Israel as an inheritance. 39 Moreover, your little ones who, you said, would become plunder, and your sons, who this day have no knowledge of good and evil, shall enter there, and I will give it to them and they shall take possession of it.

40 But as for you, turn around and set out for the wilderness by the way of the Red Sea.'

41 "Then you replied to me, 'We have sinned against the LORD; we ourselves will go up and fight, just as the LORD our God commanded us.' And every man of you strapped on his weapons of war, and you viewed it as easy to go up into the hill country. 42 But the LORD said to me, 'Say to them, "Do not go up nor fight, for I am not among you; otherwise you will be defeated by your enemies." ' 43 So I spoke to you, but you would not listen. Instead, you rebelled against the command of the LORD, and acted presumptuously and went up into the hill country. 44 And the Amorites who lived in that hill country came out against you and chased you as bees do, and they scattered you from Seir to Hormah. 45 Then you returned and wept before the LORD; but the LORD did not listen to your voice, nor pay attention to you. 46 So you remained at Kadesh for many days, the days that you spent *there.*

Wanderings in the Wilderness

2 "Then we turned and set out for the wilderness by the way of the Red Sea, as the LORD spoke to me, and we circled Mount Seir for many days. 2 And the LORD spoke to me, saying, 3 'You have circled this mountain long enough. *Now* turn north, 4 and command the people, saying, "You are going to pass through the territory of your brothers the sons of Esau, who live in Seir; and they will be afraid of you. So be very careful; 5 do not provoke them, for I will not give you any of their land, *not even* as much as a footprint, because I have given Mount Seir to Esau as a possession. 6 You are to buy food from them with money so that you may eat, and you shall also purchase water from them with money so that you may drink. 7 For the LORD your God has blessed you in all that you have done; He has known your wandering through this great wilderness. These forty years the LORD your God has been with you; you have not lacked anything." '

8 "So we passed beyond our brothers the sons of Esau, who live in Seir, away from the Arabah road, away from Elath and Ezion-geber. And we turned and passed through by the way of the wilderness of Moab. 9 Then the LORD said to me, 'Do not attack Moab, nor provoke him to war, for I will not give you any of their land as a possession, because I have given Ar to the sons of Lot as a possession.' 10 (The Emim lived there previously, a people as great, numerous, and tall as the Anakim. 11 Like the Anakim, they too are regarded as Rephaim, but the Moabites call them Emim. 12 The Horites previously lived in Seir, but the sons of Esau dispossessed them and destroyed them from before ¹them, and settled in their place; just as Israel did to the land of their possession which the LORD gave them.) 13 'Now arise and cross over the Wadi Zered yourselves.' So we crossed over the Wadi Zered. 14 Now the time that it took for us to come from Kadesh-barnea until we crossed over the Wadi Zered was thirty-eight years, until all the generation of the men of war perished from within the camp, just as

the LORD had sworn to them. 15 Indeed, the hand of the LORD was against them, to destroy them from within the camp until they all perished.

16 "So it came about, when all the men of war had finally perished from among the people, 17 that the LORD spoke to me, saying, 18 'Today you shall cross over Ar, the border of Moab. 19 When you come opposite the sons of Ammon, do not attack them nor provoke them, for I will not give you any of the land of the sons of Ammon as a possession, because I have given it to the sons of Lot as a possession.' 20 (It is also regarded as the land of the Rephaim, *because the* Rephaim previously lived in it, but the Ammonites call them Zamzummin, 21 a people as great, numerous, and tall as the Anakim; but the LORD destroyed them before ¹them. And they dispossessed them and settled in their place, 22 just as He did for the sons of Esau, who live in Seir, when He destroyed the Horites from before them; they dispossessed them and settled in their place, *where they remain* even to this day. 23 And *as for* the Avvim, who lived in villages as far as Gaza, the ¹Caphtorim, who came from ²Caphtor, destroyed them and lived in their place.) 24 'Arise, set out, and pass through the Valley of Arnon. Look! I have handed over to you Sihon the Amorite, king of Heshbon, and his land; start taking possession and plunge into battle with him. 25 This day I will begin to put the dread and fear of you upon the faces of people everywhere, who, when they hear the news of you, will tremble and be in anguish because of you.'

26 "So I sent messengers from the wilderness of Kedemoth to Sihon king of Heshbon with words of peace, saying, 27 'Let me pass through your land; I will travel only on the road. I will not turn aside to the right or to the left. 28 You will sell me food for money so that I may eat, and give me water for money so that I may drink, only let me pass through on foot, 29 just as the sons of Esau who live in Seir and the Moabites who live in Ar did for me, until I cross over the Jordan into the land that the LORD our God is giving us.' 30 But Sihon king of Heshbon was not willing for us to pass through his land; for the LORD your God hardened his spirit and made his heart obstinate, in order to hand him over to you, as *he is* today. 31 And the LORD said to me, 'See, I have begun to turn Sihon and his land over to you. Begin taking possession, so that you may possess his land.'

32 "Then Sihon came out with all his people to meet us in battle at Jahaz. 33 And the LORD our God turned him over to us, and we defeated him with his sons and all his people. 34 So we captured all his cities at that time and utterly destroyed the men, women, and children of every city. We left no survivor. 35 We took only the animals as our plunder, and the spoils of the cities which we had captured. 36 From Aroer which is on the edge of the Valley of Arnon and *from* the city which is in the valley, even to Gilead, there was no city that was too high for us; the LORD our God turned it all over to us. 37 Only you did not go

near the land of the sons of Ammon, all along the river Jabbok and the cities of the hill country, and wherever the Lord our God had commanded us *to avoid.*

Conquests Recounted

3 "Then we turned and went up the road to Bashan, and Og, king of Bashan, came out with all his people to meet us in battle at Edrei. 2 But the Lord said to me, 'Do not fear him, for I have handed him and all his people and his land over to you; and you shall do to him just as you did to Sihon king of the Amorites, who lived in Heshbon.' 3 So the Lord our God also handed over to us Og, king of Bashan, with all his people, and we struck them until no survivor was left. 4 We captured all his cities at that time; there was not a city which we did not take from them: sixty cities, all the region of Argob, the kingdom of Og in Bashan. 5 All these were cities fortified with high walls, gates, and bars, besides a great many unwalled towns. 6 We utterly destroyed them, as we did to Sihon king of Heshbon, utterly destroying the men, women, and children of every city. 7 But all the animals and the spoils of the cities we took as our plunder.

8 "So at that time we took the land from the hand of the two kings of the Amorites who were beyond the Jordan, from the Valley of Arnon to Mount Hermon 9 (Sidonians call Hermon Sirion, and the Amorites call it Senir): 10 all the cities of the plateau, all Gilead, and all Bashan, as far as Salecah and Edrei, cities of the kingdom of Og in Bashan. 11 (For only Og king of Bashan was left of the remnant of the Rephaim. Behold, his bed was a bed of iron; it is in Rabbah of the sons of Ammon. Its length was nine cubits, and its width four cubits by the usual cubit.)

12 "So we took possession of this land at that time. From Aroer, which is by the Valley of Arnon, and half the hill country of Gilead and its cities I gave to the Reubenites and to the Gadites. 13 The rest of Gilead and all Bashan, the kingdom of Og, I gave to the half-tribe of Manasseh, all the region of Argob. (As to all Bashan, it is called the land of Rephaim. 14 Jair the son of Manasseh took all the region of Argob as far as the border of the Geshurites and the Maacathites, *that is,* Bashan, and named it after his own name: Havvoth-jair, *as it is* to this day.) 15 To Machir I gave Gilead. 16 To the Reubenites and the Gadites I gave from Gilead even as far as the Valley of Arnon, the middle of the valley as a border, and as far as the river Jabbok, the border of the sons of Ammon; 17 the Arabah also, with the Jordan as a border, from 'Chinnereth even as far as the sea of the Arabah, the Salt Sea, at the foot of the slopes of Pisgah on the east.

18 "Then I commanded you at that time, saying, 'The Lord your God has given you this land to possess it; all you valiant men shall cross over armed ahead of your brothers, the sons of Israel. 19 However, your wives, your little ones, and your livestock (I know that you have much livestock) shall remain in your cities which I have given you, 20 until the Lord gives rest to your fellow countrymen as to you, and they also take possession of the land which the Lord your God is giving them beyond the Jordan. Then you may return, each man to his possession which I have given you.' 21 And I commanded Joshua at that time, saying, 'Your eyes have seen everything that the Lord your God has done to these two kings; the Lord will do the same to all the kingdoms into which you are about to cross. 22 Do not fear them, for the Lord your God is the One fighting for you.'

23 "I also pleaded with the Lord at that time, saying, 24 'Lord God, You have begun to show Your servant Your greatness and Your strong hand; for what god *is there* in heaven or on earth who can do such works and mighty acts as Yours? 25 Please let me cross over and see the good land that is beyond the Jordan, that good hill country, and Lebanon.' 26 But the Lord was angry with me on your account, and would not listen to me; instead, the Lord said to me, 'Enough! Do not speak to Me any more about this matter. 27 Go up to the top of Pisgah and raise your eyes to the west, the north, the south, and the east, and see *it* with your eyes; for you shall not cross over this Jordan. 28 But commission Joshua and encourage him and strengthen him, for he shall go across leading this people, and he will give to them, as an inheritance, the land which you will see.' 29 So we remained in the valley opposite Beth-peor.

Israel Urged to Obey God's Law

4 "Now, Israel, listen to the statutes and the judgments which I am teaching you to perform, so that you will live and go in and take possession of the land which the Lord, the God of your fathers, is giving you. 2 You shall not add to the word which I am commanding you, nor take away from it, so that you may keep the commandments of the Lord your God which I am commanding you. 3 Your eyes have seen what the Lord has done in the case of Baal-peor, for all the men who followed Baal-peor, the Lord your God has destroyed them from among you. 4 But you who clung to the Lord your God are alive today, every one of you.

5 "See, I have taught you statutes and judgments just as the Lord my God commanded me, that you are to do these things in the land where you are entering to take possession of it. 6 So keep and do *them,* for that is your wisdom and your understanding in the sight of the peoples who will hear all these statutes and say, 'Surely this great nation is a wise and understanding people.' 7 For what great nation *is there* that has a god so near to it as is the Lord our God whenever we call on Him? 8 Or what great nation *is there* that has statutes and judgments as righteous as this whole Law which I am setting before you today?

9 "Only be careful for yourself and watch over your soul diligently, so that you do not forget the things which your eyes have seen and they do not depart from your heart all the days of your life; but make them known to your sons and your grandsons. 10 *Remember* the day you stood before the Lord your God at Horeb,

---

3:17 1 I.e., the Sea of Galilee

when the LORD said to me, 'Assemble the people to Me, that I may have them hear My words so that they may learn to fear Me all the days that they live on the earth, and that they may teach their children.' 11 You came forward and stood at the foot of the mountain, and the mountain was burning with fire to the heart of the heavens: darkness, cloud, and thick gloom. 12 Then the LORD spoke to you from the midst of the fire; you heard the sound of words, but you saw no form—*there was* only a voice. 13 So He declared to you His covenant which He commanded you to perform, *that is,* the Ten Commandments; and He wrote them on two tablets of stone. 14 The LORD commanded me at that time to teach you statutes and judgments, so that you would perform them in the land where you are going over to take possession of it.

15 "So be very careful yourselves, since you did not see any form on the day the LORD spoke to you at Horeb from the midst of the fire, 16 so that you do not act corruptly and make a carved image for yourselves in the form of any figure, a representation of male or female, 17 a representation of any animal that is on the earth, a representation of any winged bird that flies in the sky, 18 a representation of anything that crawls on the ground, *or* a representation of any fish that is in the water below the earth. 19 And *be careful* not to raise your eyes to heaven and look at the sun, the moon, and the stars, all the heavenly lights, and *allow yourself* to be drawn away and worship them and serve them, *things* which the LORD your God has allotted to all the peoples under the whole heaven. 20 But the LORD has taken you and brought you out of the iron furnace, from Egypt, to be a people of His own possession, as today.

21 "Now the LORD was angry with me on your account, and He swore that I would not cross the Jordan, and that I would not enter the good land which the LORD your God is giving you as an inheritance. 22 For I am going to die in this land; I am not crossing the Jordan, but you are going to cross, and you will take possession of this good land. 23 So be careful yourselves, that you do not forget the covenant of the LORD your God which He made with you, and make for yourselves a carved image in the form of anything *against* which the LORD your God has commanded you. 24 For the LORD your God is a consuming fire, a jealous God.

25 "When you father children and *have* grandchildren, and you grow old in the land, and you act corruptly, and make an idol in the form of anything, and do what is evil in the sight of the LORD your God to provoke Him to anger, 26 I call heaven and earth as witnesses against you today, that you will certainly perish quickly from the land where you are going over the Jordan to take possession of it. You will not live long on it, but will be utterly destroyed. 27 The LORD will scatter you among the peoples, and you will be left few in number among the nations where the LORD drives you. 28 There you will serve gods, the work of human hands, wood and stone, which neither see nor hear, nor eat nor smell *anything.* 29 But

from there you will seek the LORD your God, and you will find *Him* if you search for Him with all your heart and all your soul. 30 When you are in distress and all these things happen to you, in the latter days you will return to the LORD your God and listen to His voice. 31 For the LORD your God is a compassionate God; He will not abandon you nor destroy you, nor forget the covenant with your fathers which He swore to them.

32 "Indeed, ask now about the earlier days that were before your time, since the day that God created mankind on the earth, and *inquire* from one end of the heavens to the other. Has *anything* been done like this great thing, or has *anything* been heard like it? 33 Has *any* people heard the voice of God speaking from the midst of the fire, as you have heard *it,* and survived? 34 Or has a god ventured to go to take for himself a nation from within *another* nation by trials, by signs and wonders, by war, by a mighty hand, by an outstretched arm, and by great terrors, just as the LORD your God did for you in Egypt before your eyes? 35 You were shown *these things* so that you might know that the LORD, He is God; there is no other besides Him. 36 Out of the heavens He let you hear His voice to discipline you; and on earth He let you see His great fire, and you heard His words from the midst of the fire. 37 Because He loved your fathers, He chose their descendants after them. And He personally brought you from Egypt by His great power, 38 driving out from before you nations greater and mightier than you, to bring you in *and* to give you their land as an inheritance, as *it is* today. 39 Therefore know today, and take it to your heart, that the LORD, He is God in heaven above and on the earth below; there is no other. 40 So you shall keep His statutes and His commandments which I am giving you today, so that it may go well for you and for your children after you, and that you may live long on the land which the LORD your God is giving you for all time."

41 Then Moses set apart three cities across the Jordan to the east, 42 for one to flee there who unintentionally killed his neighbor, without having hatred for him in time past; and by fleeing to one of these cities he might live: 43 Bezer in the wilderness on the plateau for the Reubenites, Ramoth in Gilead for the Gadites, and Golan in Bashan for the Manassites.

44 Now this is the Law which Moses set before the sons of Israel; 45 these are the testimonies and the statutes, and the ordinances which Moses spoke to the sons of Israel, when they came out of Egypt, 46 across the Jordan, in the valley opposite Beth-peor, in the land of Sihon king of the Amorites who lived in Heshbon, whom Moses and the sons of Israel defeated when they came out of Egypt. 47 And they took possession of his land and the land of Og king of Bashan, the two kings of the Amorites, who *were* across the Jordan to the east, 48 from Aroer, which is on the edge of the Valley of Arnon, even as far as Mount Sion (that is, Hermon), 49 with all the Arabah across the Jordan to the east, even as far as the sea of the Arabah, at the foot of the slopes of Pisgah.

The Ten Commandments Repeated

5 Now Moses summoned all Israel and said to them:

"Listen, Israel, to the statutes and ordinances which I am speaking today for you to hear, so that you may learn them and be careful to do them. 2 The LORD our God made a covenant with us at Horeb. 3 The LORD did not make this covenant with our fathers, but with us, all of us who are alive here today. 4 The LORD spoke with you face to face at the mountain from the midst of the fire, 5 *while* I was standing between the LORD and you at that time, to declare to you the word of the LORD; for you were afraid because of the fire, and you did not go up on the mountain. He said,

6 'I am the LORD your God who brought you out of the land of Egypt, out of the house of slavery.

7 'You shall have no other gods besides Me.

8 'You shall not make for yourself a carved image, *or* any likeness *of* what is in heaven above or on the earth beneath or in the water under the earth. 9 You shall not worship them nor serve them; for I, the LORD your God, am a jealous God, inflicting the *punishment of the fathers on the children, even on the third and fourth *generations* of those who hate Me, 10 but showing favor to thousands, to those who love Me and keep My commandments.

11 'You shall not take the name of the LORD your God in vain, for the LORD will not leave unpunished the one who takes His name in vain.

12 'Keep the Sabbath day to treat it as holy, as the LORD your God commanded you. 13 For six days you shall labor and do all your work, 14 but the seventh day is a Sabbath of the LORD your God; you shall not do any work *that day,* you or your son or your daughter, or your male slave or your female slave, or your ox, your donkey, or any of your cattle, or your resident who stays with you, so that your male slave and your female slave may rest as well as you. 15 And you shall remember that you were a slave in the land of Egypt, and the LORD your God brought you out of there by a mighty hand and an outstretched arm; therefore the LORD your God commanded you to celebrate the Sabbath day.

16 'Honor your father and your mother, just as the LORD your God has commanded you, so that your days may be prolonged and that it may go well for you on the land which the LORD your God is giving you.

17 'You shall not murder.

18 'You shall not commit adultery.

19 'You shall not steal.

20 'You shall not give false testimony against your neighbor.

21 'You shall not covet your neighbor's wife, nor desire your neighbor's house, his field, his male slave or his female slave, his ox, his donkey, or anything that belongs to your neighbor.'

Moses Interceded

22 "These words the LORD spoke to your whole assembly at the mountain from the midst of the fire, *from* the cloud, and *from* the thick darkness, with a great voice, and He added nothing more. He wrote them on two tablets of stone and gave them to me. 23 And when you heard the voice from the midst of the darkness, while the mountain was burning with fire, you approached me, all the heads of your tribes and your elders. 24 You said, 'Behold, the LORD our God has shown us His glory and His greatness, and we have heard His voice from the midst of the fire; we have seen today that God speaks with mankind, yet he lives. 25 Now then, why should we die? For this great fire will consume us; if we hear the voice of the LORD our God any longer, then we will die! 26 For who *is there* of humanity who has heard the voice of the living God speaking from the midst of the fire, as we *have,* and lived? 27 Go near and listen to everything that the LORD our God says; then speak to us everything that the LORD our God speaks to you, and we will listen and do *it.*'

28 "Now the LORD heard the sound of your words when you spoke to me, and the LORD said to me, 'I have heard the sound of the words of this people which they have spoken to you. They have done well in all that they have spoken. 29 If only they had such a heart in them, to fear Me and keep all My commandments always, so that it would go well with them and with their sons forever! 30 Go, say to them, "Return to your tents." 31 But as for you, stand here by Me, that I may speak to you all the commandments, the statutes, and the judgments which you shall teach them, so that they may follow *them* in the land which I am giving them to possess.' 32 So you shall be careful to do just as the LORD your God has commanded you; you shall not turn aside to the right or to the left. 33 You shall walk entirely in the way which the LORD your God has commanded you, so that you may live and that it may be well for you, and that you may prolong *your* days in the land which you will possess.

Obey God and Prosper

6 "Now this is the commandment, the statutes, and the judgments which the LORD your God has commanded *me* to teach you, so that you may do *them* in the land where you are going over to take possession of it, 2 so that you, your son, and your grandson will fear the LORD your God, to keep all His statutes and His commandments which I command you, all the days of your life, and that your days may be prolonged. 3 Now Israel, you shall listen and be careful to do *them,* so that it may go well for you and that you may increase greatly, just as the LORD, the God of your fathers, has promised you, *in* a land flowing with milk and honey.

4 "Hear, Israel! The LORD is our God, the LORD is one! 5 And you shall love the LORD your God with all your heart and with all your soul and with all your strength. 6 These words, which I am commanding you today, shall be on your heart. 7 And you shall repeat them diligently to your sons and speak of them when

---

5:9 1 I.e., punishment for the wrongdoing

you sit in your house, when you walk on the road, when you lie down, and when you get up. [8] You shall also tie them as a sign to your hand, and they shall be as frontlets on your forehead. [9] You shall also write them on the doorposts of your house and on your gates.

[10] "Then it shall come about when the LORD your God brings you into the land that He swore to your fathers, to Abraham, Isaac, and Jacob, to give you, great and splendid cities which you did not build, [11] and houses full of all good things which you did not fill, and carved cisterns which you did not carve out, vineyards and olive trees which you did not plant, and you eat and are satisfied, [12] be careful that you do not forget the LORD who brought you out of the land of Egypt, out of the house of slavery. [13] You shall fear *only* the LORD your God; and you shall worship Him and swear by His name. [14] You shall not follow other gods, any of the gods of the peoples who surround you, [15] for the LORD your God *who is* in the midst of you is a jealous God; *so follow Him,* or else the anger of the LORD your God will be kindled against you, and He will wipe you off the face of the earth.

[16] "You shall not put the LORD your God to the test, as you tested *Him* at Massah. [17] You shall diligently keep the commandments of the LORD your God, and His provisions and His statutes which He has commanded you. [18] You shall do what is right and good in the sight of the LORD, so that it may go well for you and that you may go in and take possession of the good land which the LORD swore to *give* your fathers, [19] by driving out all your enemies from you, as the LORD has spoken.

[20] "When your son asks you in time to come, saying, 'What *do* the provisions and the statutes and the judgments *mean* which the LORD our God commanded you?' [21] then you shall say to your son, 'We were slaves to Pharaoh in Egypt, and the LORD brought us out of Egypt with a mighty hand. [22] Moreover, the LORD provided great and terrible signs and wonders before our eyes against Egypt, Pharaoh, and all his household; [23] He brought us out of there in order to bring us in, to give us the land which He had sworn to our fathers.' [24] So the LORD commanded us to follow all these statutes, to fear the LORD our God for our *own* good always and for our survival, as *it is* today. [25] And it will be righteousness for us if we are careful to follow all this commandment before the LORD our God, just as He commanded us.

Warnings

7 "When the LORD your God brings you into the land where you are entering to take possession of it, and He drives away many nations from before you, the Hittites, the Girgashites, the Amorites, the Canaanites, the Perizzites, the Hivites, and the Jebusites, seven nations greater and mightier than you, [2] and when the LORD your God turns them over to you and you defeat them, you shall utterly destroy them. You shall not make a covenant with them nor be gracious to them. [3] Furthermore, you shall not intermarry with them:

you shall not give your daughters to their sons, nor shall you take their daughters for your sons. [4] For they will turn your sons away from following Me, and they will serve other gods; then the anger of the LORD will be kindled against you and He will quickly destroy you. [5] But this is what you shall do to them: you shall tear down their altars, smash their memorial stones, cut their [1]Asherim to pieces, and burn their carved images in the fire. [6] For you are a holy people to the LORD your God; the LORD your God has chosen you to be a people for His personal possession out of all the peoples who are on the face of the earth.

[7] "The LORD did not make you His beloved nor choose you because you were greater in number than any of the peoples, since you were the fewest of all peoples, [8] but because the LORD loved you and kept the oath which He swore to your forefathers, the LORD brought you out by a mighty hand and redeemed you from the house of slavery, from the hand of Pharaoh king of Egypt. [9] Know therefore that the LORD your God, He is God, the faithful God, who keeps His covenant and His faithfulness to a thousand generations for those who love Him and keep His commandments; [10] but He repays those who hate Him to their faces, to eliminate them; He will not hesitate toward him who hates Him, He will repay him to his face. [11] Therefore, you shall keep the commandment, the statutes, and the judgments which I am commanding you today, to do them.

Promises of God

[12] "Then it shall come about, because you listen to these judgments and keep and do them, that the LORD your God will keep His covenant with you and His faithfulness which He swore to your forefathers. [13] And He will love you, bless you, and make you numerous; He will also bless the fruit of your womb and the fruit of your ground, your grain, your new wine, and your oil, the newborn of your cattle and the offspring of your flock, in the land which He swore to your forefathers to give you. [14] You shall be blessed above all peoples; there will be no sterile male or infertile female among you or among your cattle. [15] And the LORD will remove from you all sickness; and He will not inflict upon you any of the harmful diseases of Egypt which you have known, but He will give them to all who hate you. [16] You shall consume all the peoples whom the LORD your God will turn over to you; your eye shall not pity them, nor shall you serve their gods, for that *would be* a snare to you.

[17] "If you say in your heart, 'These nations are greater than I; how can I dispossess them?' [18] you are not to be afraid of them; you shall remember well what the LORD your God did to Pharaoh and to all Egypt: [19] the great trials which your eyes saw and the signs and the wonders, and the mighty hand and the outstretched arm by which the LORD your God brought you out. The LORD your God will do the same to all the peoples of whom you are afraid. [20] Indeed, the LORD your God will send

---

7:5 [1] I.e., wooden symbols of a female deity (Asherah)

the hornet against them, until those who are left and hide themselves from you perish. [21] You are not to be terrified of them, because the LORD your God is in your midst, a great and awesome God. [22] And the LORD your God will drive away these nations from you little by little; you will not be able to put an end to them quickly, otherwise the wild animals would become too numerous for you. [23] But the LORD your God will turn them over to you, and will throw them into great confusion until they are destroyed. [24] And He will hand over their kings to you, so that you will eliminate their name from under heaven; no one will be able to stand against you until you have destroyed them. [25] The carved images of their gods you are to burn with fire; you shall not covet the silver or the gold that is on them, nor take it for yourselves, or you will be trapped by it; for it is an abomination to the LORD your God. [26] And you shall not bring an abomination into your house and become designated for destruction, like it; you are to utterly detest it, and you are to utterly loathe it, for it is something designated for destruction.

God's Gracious Dealings

8 "All the commandments that I am commanding you today you shall be careful to do, so that you may live and increase, and go in and take possession of the land which the LORD swore to give to your forefathers. [2] And you shall remember all the way which the LORD your God has led you in the wilderness these forty years, in order to humble you, putting you to the test, to know what was in your heart, whether you would keep His commandments or not. [3] And He humbled you and let you go hungry, and fed you with the manna which you did not know, nor did your fathers know, in order to make you understand that man shall not live on bread alone, but man shall live on everything that comes out of the mouth of the LORD. [4] Your clothing did not wear out on you, nor did your foot swell these forty years. [5] So you are to know in your heart that the LORD your God was disciplining you just as a man disciplines his son. [6] Therefore, you shall keep the commandments of the LORD your God, to walk in His ways and to fear Him. [7] For the LORD your God is bringing you into a good land, a land of streams of water, of fountains and springs, flowing out in valleys and hills; [8] a land of wheat and barley, of vines, fig trees, and pomegranates, a land of olive oil and honey; [9] a land where you will eat food without shortage, in which you will not lack anything; a land whose stones are iron, and out of whose hills you can dig copper. [10] When you have eaten and are satisfied, you shall bless the LORD your God for the good land which He has given you.

[11] "Be careful that you do not forget the LORD your God by failing to keep His commandments, His ordinances, and His statutes which I am commanding you today; [12] otherwise, when you eat and are satisfied, and you build good houses and live in them, [13] and when your herds and your flocks increase, and your silver and gold increase, and

everything that you have increases, [14] then your heart will become proud and you will forget the LORD your God who brought you out of the land of Egypt, out of the house of slavery; [15] He who led you through the great and terrible wilderness, with its fiery serpents and scorpions, and its thirsty ground where there was no water; He who brought water for you out of the rock of flint. [16] In the wilderness it was He who fed you manna which your fathers did not know, in order to humble you and in order to put you to the test, to do good for you in the end. [17] Otherwise, you may say in your heart, 'My power and the strength of my hand made me this wealth.' [18] But you are to remember the LORD your God, for it is He who is giving you power to make wealth, in order to confirm His covenant which He swore to your fathers, as it is this day. [19] And it shall come about, if you ever forget the LORD your God and follow other gods and serve and worship them, I testify against you today that you will certainly perish. [20] Like the nations that the LORD eliminates from you, so you shall perish, because you would not listen to the voice of the LORD your God.

Israel Provoked God

9 "Hear, Israel! You are crossing the Jordan today, to go in to dispossess nations greater and mightier than you, cities that are great and fortified to heaven, [2] a people who are great and tall, the sons of the Anakim, whom you know and of whom you have heard it said, 'Who can stand against the sons of Anak?' [3] So be aware today that it is the LORD your God who is crossing over ahead of you as a consuming fire. He will destroy them and He will subdue them before you, so that you may drive them out and eliminate them quickly, just as the LORD has spoken to you.

[4] "Do not say in your heart when the LORD your God has driven them away from you, 'Because of my righteousness the LORD has brought me in to take possession of this land.' Rather, it is because of the wickedness of these nations that the LORD is dispossessing them before you. [5] It is not because of your righteousness or the uprightness of your heart that you are going in to take possession of their land, but it is because of the wickedness of these nations that the LORD your God is driving them out from before you, and in order to confirm the oath which the LORD swore to your fathers, to Abraham, Isaac, and Jacob.

[6] "Know, then, that it is not because of your righteousness that the LORD your God is giving you this good land to possess, for you are a stubborn people. [7] Remember, do not forget how you provoked the LORD your God to anger in the wilderness; from the day that you left the land of Egypt until you arrived at this place, you have been rebellious against the LORD. [8] Even at Horeb you provoked the LORD to anger, and the LORD was so angry with you that He would have destroyed you. [9] When I went up to the mountain to receive the tablets of stone, the tablets of the covenant which the LORD made with you, then I remained on the mountain for forty days and nights; I neither

ate bread nor drank water. 10 The LORD gave me the two tablets of stone written by the finger of God; and on them *were* all the words which the LORD had spoken with you at the mountain from the midst of the fire on the day of the assembly. 11 It came about at the end of forty days and nights that the LORD gave me the two tablets of stone, the tablets of the covenant. 12 Then the LORD said to me, 'Arise, go down from here quickly, because your people, whom you brought out of Egypt, have behaved corruptly. They have quickly turned aside from the way that I commanded them; they have made a cast metal image for themselves.' 13 The LORD also said to me, 'I have seen this people, and indeed, it is a stubborn people. 14 Leave Me alone, that I may destroy them and wipe out their name from under heaven; and I will make of you a nation mightier and greater than they.'

15 "So I turned and came down from the mountain while the mountain was burning with fire, and the two tablets of the covenant were in my two hands. 16 And I saw that you had indeed sinned against the LORD your God. You had made for yourselves a cast metal image of a calf; you had quickly turned aside from the way that the LORD had commanded you. 17 So I took hold of the two tablets and threw them from my two hands, and smashed them to pieces before your eyes! 18 Then I fell down before the LORD like the first *time,* for forty days and nights; I neither ate bread nor drank water, because of all your sin which you had committed by doing what was evil in the sight of the LORD, to provoke Him to anger. 19 For I was afraid of the anger and the rage with which the LORD was angry with you so as to destroy you; but the LORD listened to me that time as well. 20 The LORD was also angry enough with Aaron to destroy him; so I also prayed for Aaron at the same time. 21 And I took your sinful *thing* which you had made, the calf, and burned it in the fire and crushed it, grinding it thoroughly until it was as fine as dust; and I threw its dust into the stream that came down from the mountain.

22 "Then at Taberah, at Massah, and at Kibroth-hattaavah you kept provoking the LORD to anger. 23 And when the LORD sent you from Kadesh-barnea, saying, 'Go up and take possession of the land which I have given you,' you rebelled against the command of the LORD your God; you neither trusted Him nor listened to His voice. 24 You have been rebellious toward the LORD since the day I knew you.

25 "So I fell down before the LORD for the forty days and nights, which I did because the LORD said He would destroy you. 26 And I prayed to the LORD and said, 'Lord GOD, do not destroy Your people, Your inheritance, whom You have redeemed through Your greatness, whom You have brought out of Egypt with a mighty hand! 27 Remember Your servants, Abraham, Isaac, and Jacob; do not turn Your attention to the stubbornness of this people, or to their wickedness, or their sin. 28 Otherwise, the *people of the* land from which You brought us will say, "Since the LORD was not able to bring them into the land which He had promised them, and since He hated them, He has

brought them out to kill them in the wilderness!" 29 Yet they are Your people, and Your inheritance, whom You brought out by Your great power and Your outstretched arm.'

The Tablets Rewritten

10 "At that time the LORD said to me, 'Cut out for yourself two tablets of stone like the first *two,* and come up to Me on the mountain, and make an ark of wood for yourself. 2 Then I will write on the tablets the words that were on the first tablets which you smashed to pieces, and you shall put them in the ark.' 3 So I made an ark of acacia wood and cut out two tablets of stone like the first *two,* and I went up on the mountain with the two tablets in my hand. 4 Then He wrote on the tablets, like the first writing, the Ten Commandments which the LORD had spoken to you on the mountain from the midst of the fire on the day of the assembly; and the LORD gave them to me. 5 Then I turned and came down from the mountain, and I put the tablets in the ark which I had made; and they are there, just as the LORD commanded me."

6 (Now the sons of Israel set out from Beeroth Bene-jaakan to Moserah. There Aaron died and there he was buried, and his son Eleazar served as priest in his place. 7 From there they set out to Gudgodah, and from Gudgodah to Jotbathah, a land of streams of water. 8 At that time the LORD singled out the tribe of Levi to carry the ark of the covenant of the LORD, to stand before the LORD to serve Him and to bless in His name, until this day. 9 Therefore, Levi does not have a portion or inheritance with his brothers; the LORD is his inheritance, just as the LORD your God spoke to him.)

10 "I, moreover, stayed on the mountain for forty days and forty nights like the first time, and the LORD listened to me that time also; the LORD was not willing to destroy you. 11 Then the LORD said to me, 'Arise, proceed on your journey ahead of the people, so that they may go in and take possession of the land which I swore to their fathers to give them.'

12 "And now, Israel, what does the LORD your God require of you, but to fear the LORD your God, to walk in all His ways and love Him, and to serve the LORD your God with all your heart and with all your soul, 13 *and* to keep the LORD's commandments and His statutes which I am commanding you today for your good? 14 Behold, to the LORD your God belong heaven and the highest heavens, the earth and all that is in it. 15 Yet the LORD set His affection on your fathers, to love them, and He chose their descendants after them, you over all the *other* peoples, as *it is* this day. 16 So circumcise your heart, and do not stiffen your neck any longer. 17 For the LORD your God is the God of gods and the Lord of lords, the great, the mighty, and the awesome God, who does not show partiality, nor take a bribe. 18 He executes justice for the orphan and the widow, and shows His love for the stranger by giving him food and clothing. 19 So show your love for the stranger, for you were strangers in the land of Egypt. 20 You shall fear the LORD your God; you shall serve Him, and cling to Him, and you

shall swear by His name. 21 He is your glory and He is your God, who has done these great and awesome things for you which your eyes have seen. 22 Your fathers went down to Egypt seventy persons *in all,* and now the LORD your God has made you as numerous as the stars of heaven.

Rewards of Obedience

11 "You shall therefore love the LORD your God, and always keep His directive, His statutes, His ordinances, and His commandments. 2 Know this day that *I am* not *speaking* with your sons who have not known and who have not seen the discipline of the LORD your God—His greatness, His mighty hand, His outstretched arm, 3 and His signs and His works which He did in the midst of Egypt to Pharaoh the king of Egypt and to all his land; 4 and what He did to Egypt's army, to its horses and its chariots, when He made the water of the Red Sea engulf them while they were pursuing you, and the LORD completely eliminated them; 5 and what He did to you in the wilderness, until you came to this place; 6 and what He did to Dathan and Abiram, the sons of Eliab, the son of Reuben, when the earth opened its mouth and swallowed them, their households, their tents, and every living thing that followed them, among all Israel— 7 but your own eyes have seen all the great work of the LORD which He did.

8 "You shall therefore keep every commandment which I am commanding you today, so that you may be strong and go in and take possession of the land into which you are about to cross to possess it; 9 and so that you may prolong *your* days on the land which the LORD swore to your fathers to give to them and to their descendants, a land flowing with milk and honey. 10 For the land, into which you are entering to possess it, is not like the land of Egypt from which you came, where you used to sow your seed and water it 7 by your foot like a vegetable garden. 11 But the land into which you are about to cross to possess it, a land of hills and valleys, drinks water from the rain of heaven, 12 a land for which the LORD your God cares; the eyes of the LORD your God are continually on it, from the beginning even to the end of the year.

13 "And it shall come about, if you listen obediently to my commandments which I am commanding you today, to love the LORD your God and to serve Him with all your heart and all your soul, 14 that He will provide rain for your land in its season, the 7 early and late rain, so that you may gather your grain, your new wine, and your oil. 15 He will also provide grass in your field for your cattle, and you will eat and be satisfied. 16 Beware that your hearts are not easily deceived, and that you do not turn away and serve other gods, and worship them. 17 Otherwise, the anger of the LORD will be kindled against you, and He will shut up the sky so that there will be no rain, and the ground will not yield its produce; then you will quickly

perish from the good land which the LORD is giving you.

18 "You shall therefore take these words of mine to heart and to soul; and you shall tie them as a sign on your hand, and they shall be as frontlets on your forehead. 19 You shall also teach them to your sons, speaking of them when you sit in your house, when you walk along the road, when you lie down, and when you get up. 20 And you shall write them on the doorposts of your house and on your gates, 21 so that your days and the days of your sons may be increased on the land which the LORD swore to your fathers to give them, as long as the heavens are above the earth. 22 For if you are careful to keep all of this commandment which I am commanding you to do, to love the LORD your God, to walk in all His ways and cling to Him, 23 then the LORD will dispossess all these nations from you, and you will dispossess nations greater and mightier than you. 24 Every place on which the sole of your foot steps shall be yours; your border will be from the wilderness to Lebanon, *and* from the river, the river Euphrates, as far as 7 the western sea. 25 No one will *be able to* stand against you; the LORD your God will instill the dread of you and the fear of you in all the land on which you set foot, just as He has spoken to you.

26 "See, I am placing before you today a blessing and a curse: 27 the blessing, if you listen to the commandments of the LORD your God, which I am commanding you today; 28 and the curse, if you do not listen to the commandments of the LORD your God, but turn aside from the way which I am commanding you today, by following other gods which you have not known.

29 "And it shall come about, when the LORD your God brings you into the land where you are entering to possess it, that you shall place the blessing on Mount Gerizim and the curse on Mount Ebal. 30 Are they not across the Jordan, west of the road toward the sunset, in the land of the Canaanites who live in the Arabah, opposite Gilgal, beside the oaks of Moreh? 31 For you are about to cross the Jordan to go in to take possession of the land which the LORD your God is giving you, and you shall possess it and live in it, 32 and you shall be careful to do all the statutes and the judgments which I am placing before you today.

Laws of the Sanctuary

12 "These are the statutes and the judgments which you shall carefully follow in the land which the LORD, the God of your fathers, has given you to possess as long as you live on the earth. 2 You shall utterly destroy all the places where the nations whom you are going to dispossess serve their gods, on the high mountains, on the hills, and under every leafy tree. 3 And you shall tear down their altars and smash their memorial stones to pieces, and burn their 7 Asherim in the fire, and cut to pieces the carved images of their gods; and you shall eliminate their name from that place. 4 You shall not act this way toward the LORD

11:10 7 I.e., use of foot to facilitate irrigation   **11:14** 7 I.e., autumn   **11:24** 7 I.e., the Mediterranean   **12:3** 7 I.e., wooden symbols of a female deity (Asherah)

your God. 5 But you shall seek *the* LORD at the place which the LORD your God will choose from all your tribes, to establish His name there for His dwelling, and you shall come there. 6 You shall bring there your burnt offerings, your sacrifices, your tithes, the contribution of your hand, your vowed offerings, your voluntary offerings, and the firstborn of your herd and of your flock. 7 There you and your households shall eat before the LORD your God, and rejoice in all your undertakings in which the LORD your God has blessed you.

8 "You shall not do at all what we are doing here today, everyone *doing* whatever is right in his *own* eyes; 9 for you have not as yet come to the resting place and the inheritance which the LORD your God is giving you. 10 When you cross the Jordan and live in the land which the LORD your God is giving you as an inheritance, and He gives you rest from all your enemies around *you* so that you live in security, 11 then it shall come about that the place in which the LORD your God will choose for His name to dwell, there you shall bring everything that I command you: your burnt offerings and your sacrifices, your tithes and the contribution of your hand, and all your choice vowed offerings which you will vow to the LORD. 12 And you shall rejoice before the LORD your God, you and your sons and daughters, your male and female slaves, and the Levite who is within your gates, since he has no portion or inheritance with you.

13 "Be careful that you do not offer your burnt offerings in any *cultic* place that you see, 14 but *only* in the place which the LORD chooses in one of your tribes: there you shall offer your burnt offerings, and there you shall do everything that I command you.

15 "However, you may slaughter and eat meat within any of your gates, whatever you desire, according to the blessing of the LORD your God which He has given you; the unclean and the clean *alike* may eat it, as the gazelle and the deer. 16 Only you shall not eat the blood; you are to pour it out on the ground like water. 17 You are not allowed to eat within your gates the tithe of your grain, new wine, or oil, or the firstborn of your herd or flock, or any of your vowed offerings which you vow, or your voluntary offerings, or the contribution of your hand. 18 But you shall eat them before the LORD your God in the place which the LORD your God will choose, you and your son and daughter, and your male and female slaves, and the Levite who is within your gates; and you shall rejoice before the LORD your God in all your undertakings. 19 Be careful that you do not abandon the Levite as long as you live in your land.

20 "When the LORD your God extends your border as He has promised you, and you say, 'I will eat meat,' because you desire to eat meat, *then* you may eat meat, whatever you desire. 21 If the place where the LORD your God chooses to put His name is too far from you, then you may slaughter *animals* from your herd and flock which the LORD has given you, as I have commanded you; and you may eat within your gates whatever you desire. 22 Just as a

gazelle or a deer is eaten, so you may eat it; the unclean and the clean alike may eat it. 23 Only be sure not to eat the blood, for the blood is the life, and you shall not eat the life with the flesh. 24 You shall not eat it; you shall pour it out on the ground like water. 25 You shall not eat it, so that it may go well for you and your sons after you, since you will be doing what is right in the sight of the LORD. 26 Only your holy things which you may have and your vowed offerings, you shall take and go to the place which the LORD chooses. 27 And you shall offer your burnt offerings, the flesh and the blood, on the altar of the LORD your God; and the blood of your sacrifices shall be poured out on the altar of the LORD your God, and you shall eat the flesh.

28 "Be careful and listen to all these words which I am commanding you, so that it may go well for you and your sons after you forever, for you will be doing what is good and right in the sight of the LORD your God.

29 "When the LORD your God cuts off from you the nations which you are going in to dispossess, and you dispossess them and live in their land, 30 be careful that you are not ensnared to follow them, after they are destroyed from your presence, and that you do not inquire about their gods, saying, 'How do these nations serve their gods, that I also may do likewise?' 31 You shall not behave this way toward the LORD your God, because every abominable act which the LORD hates, they have done for their gods; for they even burn their sons and daughters in the fire for their gods.

32 "Whatever I command you, you shall be careful to do; you shall not add to nor take *anything* away from it.

Reject Idolatry

13 "If a prophet or a dreamer of dreams arises among you and gives you a sign or a wonder, 2 and the sign or the wonder comes *true,* of which he spoke to you, saying, 'Let's follow other gods (whom you have not known) and let's serve them,' 3 you shall not listen to the words of that prophet or dreamer of dreams; for the LORD your God is testing you to find out whether you love the LORD your God with all your heart and with all your soul. 4 You shall follow the LORD your God and fear Him; and you shall keep His commandments, listen to His voice, serve Him, and cling to Him. 5 But that prophet or that dreamer of dreams shall be put to death, because he has spoken falsely against the LORD your God who brought you out of the land of Egypt and redeemed you from the house of slavery, to drive you from the way in which the LORD your God commanded you to walk. So you shall eliminate the evil from among you.

6 "If your brother, your mother's son, or your son or daughter, or the wife you cherish, or your friend who is like your own soul, entices you secretly, saying, 'Let's go and serve other gods' (whom neither you nor your fathers have known, 7 of the gods of the peoples who are around you, near you, or far from you, from one end of the earth to the other end), 8 you

shall not consent to him or listen to him; and your eye shall not pity him, nor shall you spare or conceal him. **9** Instead, you shall most certainly kill him; your hand shall be first against him to put him to death, and afterward the hand of all the people. **10** So you shall stone him to death, because he has attempted to drive you away from the LORD your God who brought you out of the land of Egypt, out of the house of slavery. **11** Then all Israel will hear *about it* and be afraid, and will not do such a wicked thing among you again.

12 "If you hear in one of your cities, which the LORD your God is giving you to live in, *anyone* saying *that* **13** some worthless men have gone out from among you and have seduced the inhabitants of their city, saying, 'Let's go and serve other gods' (whom you have not known), **14** then you shall investigate, search out, and inquire thoroughly. And if it is true *and* the matter is certain that this abomination has been committed among you, **15** you shall most certainly strike the inhabitants of that city with the edge of the sword. Utterly destroy it and all who are in it and its cattle, with the edge of the sword. **16** Then you shall gather all its plunder into the middle of its public square, and burn the city and all its plunder with fire as a whole burnt offering to the LORD your God; and it shall be a ruin forever. It shall never be rebuilt. **17** Nothing at all from what is designated for destruction is to cling to your hand, in order that the LORD may turn from His burning anger and show mercy to you, and have compassion on you and make you increase, just as He has sworn to your fathers, **18** if you will listen to the voice of the LORD your God, keeping all His commandments which I am commanding you today, and doing what is right in the sight of the LORD your God.

Clean and Unclean Animals

14 "You are sons of the LORD your God; you shall not cut yourselves nor shave a bald spot above your forehead for the dead. **2** For you are a holy people to the LORD your God, and the LORD has chosen you to be a people for His personal possession out of all the peoples who are on the face of the earth.

3 "You shall not eat any detestable thing. **4** These are the animals that you may eat: the ox, the sheep, the goat, **5** the deer, the gazelle, the roebuck, the wild goat, the ibex, the antelope, and the mountain sheep. **6** And any animal that has a divided hoof and has *its* hoofs split in two, *and* chews the cud, among the animals, that animal you may eat. **7** However, you are not to eat these among the ones that chew the cud, or among those that have the hoof divided in two: the camel, the rabbit, and the rock hyrax, for though they chew the cud, they do not have a divided hoof; they are unclean to you. **8** And the pig, because it has a divided hoof but *does* not *chew* the cud, it is unclean for you. You shall not eat any of their flesh, nor touch their carcasses.

9 "These you may eat of everything that is in the water: anything that has fins and scales you may eat, **10** but anything that does not have fins and scales, you shall not eat; it is unclean for you.

11 "You may eat any clean bird. **12** But these are the ones that you shall not eat: the eagle and the vulture and the buzzard, **13** and the red kite, the falcon, and the kite in their kinds, **14** and every raven in its kind, **15** and the ostrich, the owl, the seagull, and the hawk in their kinds, **16** the little owl, the great owl, the white owl, **17** the pelican, the carrion vulture, the cormorant, **18** the stork, and the heron in their kinds, and the hoopoe and the bat. **19** And all the swarming insects with wings are unclean to you; they shall not be eaten. **20** You may eat any clean bird.

21 "You shall not eat anything which dies *of itself.* You may give it to the stranger who is in your town, so that he may eat it, or you may sell it to a stranger; for you are a holy people to the LORD your God. You shall not boil a young goat in its mother's milk.

22 "You shall certainly tithe all the produce from what you sow, which comes from the field every year. **23** You shall eat in the presence of the LORD your God, at the place where He chooses to establish His name, the tithe of your grain, your new wine, your oil, and the first-born of your herd and your flock, so that you may learn to fear the LORD your God always. **24** But if the distance is so great for you that you are not able to bring *the tithe,* since the place where the LORD your God chooses to set His name is too far away from you when the LORD your God blesses you, **25** then you shall exchange *it* for money, and bind the money in your hand and go to the place which the LORD your God chooses. **26** And you may spend the money on whatever your heart desires: on oxen, sheep, wine, *other* strong drink, or whatever your heart desires; and there you shall eat in the presence of the LORD your God and rejoice, you and your household. **27** Also you shall not neglect the Levite who is in your town, for he has no portion or inheritance among you.

28 "At the end of every third year you shall bring out all the tithe of your produce in that year, and you shall deposit *it* in your town. **29** And the Levite, because he has no portion or inheritance among you, and the stranger, the orphan, and the widow who are in your town, shall come and eat and be satisfied, in order that the LORD your God may bless you in all the work of your hand which you do.

The Sabbatical Year

15 "At the end of *every* seven years you shall grant a release of debts. **2** And this is the regulation for the release of debts: every creditor is to forgive what he has loaned to his neighbor; he shall not require it of his neighbor and his brother, because the LORD's release has been proclaimed. **3** From a foreigner you may require *it,* but your hand shall forgive whatever of yours is with your brother. **4** However, there will be no poor among you, since the LORD will certainly bless you in the land which the LORD your God is giving you as an inheritance to possess, **5** if only you listen obediently to the voice of the LORD your God, to follow carefully

all this commandment which I am commanding you today. 6 For the LORD your God will have blessed you just as He has promised you, and you will lend to many nations, but you will not borrow; and you will rule over many nations, but they will not rule over you.

7 "If there is a poor person among you, one of your brothers, in any of your towns in your land which the LORD your God is giving you, you shall not harden your heart, nor close your hand from your poor brother; 8 but you shall fully open your hand to him, and generously lend him enough for his need in whatever he lacks. 9 Be careful that there is no mean-spirited thought in your heart, such as, 'The seventh year, the year of release of debts, is near,' and your eye is malicious toward your poor brother, and you give him nothing; then he may cry out to the LORD against you, and it will be a sin in you. 10 You shall generously give to him, and your heart shall not be grudging when you give to him, because for this thing the LORD your God will bless you in all your work, and in all your undertakings. 11 For the poor will not cease to exist in the land; therefore I am commanding you, saying, 'You shall fully open your hand to your brother, to your needy and poor in your land.'

12 "If your fellow countryman, a Hebrew man or woman, is sold to you, then he shall serve you for six years, but in the seventh year you shall set him free. 13 And when you set him free, you shall not send him away empty-handed. 14 You shall give generously to him from your flock, your threshing floor, and from your wine vat; you shall give to him as the LORD your God has blessed you. 15 And you are to remember that you were a slave in the land of Egypt, and the LORD your God redeemed you; therefore I am commanding this of you today. 16 But it shall come about, if he says to you, 'I will not leave you,' because he loves you and your household, since he is doing well with you, 17 then you shall take an 'awl and pierce it through his ear into the door, and he shall be your servant permanently. You shall also do the same to your female slave.

18 "It shall not seem difficult for you when you set him free, because he has given you six years with double the service of a hired worker; so the LORD your God will bless you in whatever you do.

19 "You shall consecrate to the LORD your God all the firstborn males that are born in your herd and in your flock; you shall not work with the firstborn of your herd, nor shear the firstborn of your flock. 20 You and your household shall eat it every year before the LORD your God in the place which the LORD chooses. 21 But if it has any impairment, such as a limp, or blindness, or any serious impairment, you shall not sacrifice it to the LORD your God. 22 You shall eat it within your gates; the unclean and the clean alike may eat it, as a gazelle or a deer. 23 Only you shall not eat its blood; you are to pour it out on the ground like water.

The Feasts of Passover, of Weeks, and of Booths

16 "Observe the month of Abib and celebrate the Passover to the LORD your God, for in the month of Abib the LORD your God brought you out of Egypt by night. 2 You shall sacrifice the Passover to the LORD your God from the flock and the herd, in the place where the LORD chooses to establish His name. 3 You shall not eat leavened bread with it; for seven days you shall eat unleavened bread with it, the bread of affliction (for you came out of the land of Egypt in a hurry), so that you will remember the day when you came out of the land of Egypt all the days of your life. 4 For seven days no leaven shall be seen with you in your entire territory, and none of the meat which you sacrifice on the evening of the first day shall be left overnight until the morning. 5 You are not allowed to sacrifice the Passover in any of your towns which the LORD your God is giving you; 6 but only at the place where the LORD your God chooses to establish His name, you shall sacrifice the Passover in the evening at sunset, at the time that you came out of Egypt. 7 You shall cook and eat it in the place which the LORD your God chooses. In the morning you are to return to your tents. 8 For six days you shall eat unleavened bread, and on the seventh day there shall be a festive assembly to the LORD your God; you shall do no work on it.

9 "You shall count seven weeks for yourself; you shall begin to count seven weeks from the time you begin to put the sickle to the standing grain. 10 Then you shall celebrate the Feast of Weeks to the LORD your God with a voluntary offering of your hand in a proportional amount, which you shall give just as the LORD your God blesses you; 11 and you shall rejoice before the LORD your God, you, your son and your daughter, and your male and female slaves, and the Levite who is in your town, and the stranger, the orphan, and the widow who are in your midst, at the place where the LORD your God chooses to establish His name. 12 You shall also remember that you were a slave in Egypt, and you shall be careful and comply with these statutes.

13 "You shall celebrate the Feast of Booths for seven days when you have gathered in from your threshing floor and your wine vat; 14 and you shall rejoice in your feast, you, your son and your daughter, and your male and female slaves, and the Levite, the stranger, the orphan, and the widow who are in your towns. 15 For seven days you shall celebrate a feast to the LORD your God in the place which the LORD chooses, because the LORD your God will bless you in all your produce and in all the work of your hands, so that you will be altogether joyful.

16 "Three times a year all your males shall appear before the LORD your God at the place which He chooses: at the Feast of Unleavened Bread, at the Feast of Weeks, and at the Feast of Booths; and they are not to appear before the LORD empty-handed. 17 Everyone shall give as he is able, in accordance with the blessing of the LORD your God which He has given you.

15:17 1 I.e., a pointed tool

18 "You shall appoint for yourself judges and officers in all your towns which the LORD your God is giving you, according to your tribes, and they shall judge the people with righteous judgment. 19 You shall not distort justice, you shall not show partiality; and you shall not accept a bribe, because a bribe blinds the eyes of the wise and distorts the words of the righteous. 20 Justice, *and only* justice, you shall pursue, so that you may live and possess the land which the LORD your God is giving you.

21 "You shall not plant for yourself an Asherah of any kind of tree beside the altar of the LORD your God, which you shall make for yourself. 22 And you shall not set up for yourself a memorial stone, which the LORD your God hates.

Administration of Justice

17 "You shall not sacrifice to the LORD your God an ox or a sheep which has a blemish *or* any defect, for that is a detestable thing to the LORD your God.

2 "If there is found in your midst, in any of your towns which the LORD your God is giving you, a man or a woman who does what is evil in the sight of the LORD your God, by violating His covenant, 3 and *that person* has gone and served other gods and worshiped them, or the sun, the moon, or any of the heavenly lights, which I have commanded not to do, 4 and if it is reported to you and you have heard *about it,* then you shall investigate thoroughly. And if it is true and the report is trustworthy that this detestable thing has been done in Israel, 5 then you are to bring out to your gates that man or woman who has done this evil deed, *that is,* the man or the woman, and you shall stone them to death. 6 On the testimony of two witnesses or three witnesses, the condemned shall be put to death; he shall not be put to death on the testimony of *only* one witness. 7 The hands of the witnesses shall be first against him to put him to death, and afterward the hands of all the people. So you shall eliminate the evil from your midst.

8 "If a case is too difficult for you to decide, between one kind of homicide or another, between one kind of lawsuit or another, and between one kind of assault or another, *that are* cases of dispute in your courts, then you shall arise and go up to the place which the LORD your God chooses. 9 So you shall come to the Levitical priests or the judge who is *in office* in those days, and you shall inquire *of them* and they will declare to you the verdict. 10 Then you shall act in accordance with the terms of the verdict which they declare to you from that place which the LORD chooses; and you shall be careful to act in accordance with everything that they instruct you *to do.* 11 In accordance with the terms of the law about which they instruct you, and in accordance with the verdict which they tell you, you shall act; you shall not turn aside from the word which they declare to you, to the right or the left. 12 But the person who acts insolently by not listening to the priest who stands there to serve the LORD your God, nor to the judge, that person shall die; so you shall eliminate the evil

from Israel. 13 Then all the people will hear and be afraid, and will not act insolently again.

14 "When you enter the land which the LORD your God is giving you, and you take possession of it and live in it, and you say, 'I will appoint a king over me like all the nations who are around me,' 15 you shall in fact appoint a king over you whom the LORD your God chooses. *One* from among your countrymen you shall appoint as king over yourselves; you may not put a foreigner over yourselves, *anyone* who is not your countryman. 16 In any case, he is not to acquire many horses for himself, nor shall he make the people return to Egypt in order to acquire many horses, since the LORD has said to you, 'You shall never again return that way.' 17 And he shall not acquire many wives for himself, so that his heart does not turn away; nor shall he greatly increase silver and gold for himself.

18 "Now it shall come about, when he sits on the throne of his kingdom, that he shall write for himself a copy of this Law on a scroll in the presence of the Levitical priests. 19 And it shall be with him, and he shall read it all the days of his life, so that he will learn to fear the LORD his God, by carefully following all the words of this Law and these statutes, 20 so that his heart will not be haughty toward his countrymen, and that he will not turn away from the commandment to the right or the left, so that he and his sons may live long in his kingdom in the midst of Israel.

Portion for the Levites

18 "The Levitical priests, the whole tribe of Levi, shall not have a portion or inheritance with Israel; they shall eat the LORD's offerings by fire and His property. 2 They shall not have an inheritance among their countrymen; the LORD is their inheritance, as He promised them.

3 "Now this shall be the priests' portion from the people, from those who offer a sacrifice, either an ox or a sheep: they shall give the priest the shoulder, the two cheeks, and the stomach. 4 You shall give him the first fruits of your grain, your new wine, and your oil, and the first fleece of your sheep. 5 For the LORD your God has chosen him and his sons from all your tribes, to stand to serve in the name of the LORD always.

6 "Now if a Levite comes from any of your towns throughout Israel where he resides, and he comes whenever he desires to the place which the LORD chooses, 7 then he shall serve in the name of the LORD his God, like all his fellow Levites who stand there before the LORD. 8 They shall eat equal portions, except for *what they receive* from the sale of their fathers' *estates.*

Spiritism Forbidden

9 "When you enter the land which the LORD your God is giving you, you shall not learn to imitate the detestable things of those nations. 10 There shall not be found among you *anyone* who makes his son or his daughter pass through the fire, one who uses divination, a soothsayer, one who interprets omens, or a

sorcerer, **11** or one who casts a spell, or a medium, or a spiritist, or one who consults the dead. **12** For whoever does these things is detestable to the LORD; and because of these detestable things the LORD your God is going to drive them out before you. **13** You are to be blameless before the LORD your God. **14** For these nations, which you are going to dispossess, listen to soothsayers and diviners, but as for you, the LORD your God has not allowed you *to do* so.

15 "The LORD your God will raise up for you a prophet like me from among you, from your countrymen; to him you shall listen. **16** *This is* in accordance with everything that you asked of the LORD your God at Horeb on the day of the assembly, saying, 'Do not let me hear the voice of the LORD my God again, and do not let me see this great fire anymore, or I will die!' **17** And the LORD said to me, 'They have spoken well. **18** I will raise up for them a prophet from among their countrymen like you, and I will put My words in his mouth, and he shall speak to them everything that I command him. **19** And it shall come about that whoever does not listen to My words which he speaks in My name, I Myself will require *it* of him. **20** But the prophet who speaks a word presumptuously in My name, *a word* which I have not commanded him to speak, or which he speaks in the name of other gods, that prophet shall die.' **21** And if you say in your heart, 'How will we recognize the word which the LORD has not spoken?' **22** When the prophet speaks in the name of the LORD, and the thing does not happen or come *true,* that is the thing which the LORD has not spoken. The prophet has spoken it presumptuously; you are not to be afraid of him.

Cities of Refuge

19 "When the LORD your God cuts off the nations whose land the LORD your God is giving you, and you dispossess them and settle in their cities and in their houses, **2** you shall set aside for yourself three cities in the midst of your land which the LORD your God is giving you to possess. **3** You shall prepare the roads for yourself, and divide into three regions the territory of your land which the LORD your God will give you as an inheritance, so that anyone who commits manslaughter may flee there.

4 "Now this is the case of the one who commits manslaughter, who may flee there and live: when he kills his friend unintentionally, not hating him previously— **5** as when *a person* goes into the forest with his friend to cut wood, and his hand swings the axe to cut down the tree, and the iron *head* slips off the handle and strikes his friend so that he dies— he may flee to one of these cities and live. **6** Otherwise, the avenger of blood might pursue him in the heat of his anger, and overtake him because the way is long, and take his life, though he was not sentenced to death since he had not hated him previously. **7** Therefore I command you, saying, 'You shall set aside for yourself three cities.'

8 "And if the LORD your God enlarges your territory, just as He has sworn to your fathers,

and gives you all the land that He promised to give your fathers— **9** if you carefully follow all of this commandment which I am commanding you today, to love the LORD your God, and to walk in His ways always—then you shall add three more cities for yourself, besides these three. **10** So innocent blood will not be shed in the midst of your land which the LORD your God is giving you as an inheritance, and guilt for bloodshed will *not* be on you.

11 "But if there is a person who hates his neighbor, and waits in ambush for him and rises up against him and strikes him so that he dies, and he flees to one of these cities, **12** then the elders of his city shall send *men* and take him from there, and hand him over to the avenger of blood, so that he may die. **13** You shall not pity him, but you shall eliminate the guilt for the bloodshed of the innocent from Israel, so that it may go well for you.

Laws of Landmark and Testimony

14 "You shall not displace your neighbor's boundary marker, which the ancestors have set, in your inheritance which you will inherit in the land that the LORD your God is giving you to possess.

15 "A single witness shall not rise up against a person regarding any wrongdoing or any sin that he commits; on the testimony of two or three witnesses a matter shall be confirmed. **16** If a malicious witness rises up against a person to testify against him of wrongdoing, **17** then both people who have the dispute shall stand before the LORD, before the priests and the judges who will be *in office* in those days. **18** And the judges shall investigate thoroughly, and if the witness is a false witness *and* he has testified against his brother falsely, **19** then you shall do to him just as he had planned to do to his brother. So you shall eliminate the evil from among you. **20** And the rest *of the people* will hear and be afraid, and will never again do such an evil thing among you. **21** So you shall not show pity: life for life, eye for eye, tooth for tooth, hand for hand, *and* foot for foot.

Laws of Warfare

20 "When you go out to battle against your enemies and see horses, chariots, *and* people more numerous than you, do not be afraid of them; for the LORD your God, who brought you up from the land of Egypt, is with you. **2** When you are approaching the battle, the priest shall come forward and speak to the people. **3** He shall say to them, 'Hear, Israel, you are approaching the battle against your enemies today. Do not be fainthearted. Do not be afraid, or panic, or be terrified by them, **4** for the LORD your God is the One who is going with you, to fight for you against your enemies, to save you.' **5** The officers also shall speak to the people, saying, 'Who is the man that has built a new house but has not dedicated it? Let him go and return to his house, otherwise he might die in the battle and another man would dedicate it. **6** And who is the man that has planted a vineyard but has not put it to use? Let him go and return to his house, otherwise he might die in the battle and another man

would put it to use. 7 And who is the man that is 1betrothed to a woman and has not married her? Let him go and return to his house, otherwise he might die in the battle and another man would marry her.' 8 Then the officers shall speak further to the people and say, 'Who is the man that is afraid and faint-hearted? Let him go and return to his house, so that he does not make his brothers' hearts melt like his heart!' 9 And when the officers have finished speaking to the people, they shall appoint commanders of armies at the head of the people.

10 "When you approach a city to fight against it, you shall offer it terms of peace. 11 And if it agrees to make peace with you and opens to you, then all the people who are found in it shall become your forced labor and serve you. 12 However, if it does not make peace with you, but makes war against you, then you shall besiege it. 13 When the LORD your God gives it into your hand, you shall strike all the men in it with the edge of the sword. 14 However, the women, the children, the animals, and everything that is in the city, all of its spoils, you shall take as plunder for yourself; and you shall use the spoils of your enemies which the LORD your God has given you. 15 This is what you shall do to all the cities that are very far from you, which are not of the cities of these nations nearby. 16 Only in the cities of these peoples that the LORD your God is giving you as an inheritance, you shall not leave anything that breathes alive. 17 Instead, you shall utterly destroy them, the Hittite and the Amorite, the Canaanite and the Perizzite, the Hivite and the Jebusite, just as the LORD your God has commanded you, 18 so that they will not teach you to do all the same detestable practices of theirs which they have done for their gods, by which you would sin against the LORD your God.

19 "When you besiege a city for a long time, to make war against it in order to capture it, you shall not destroy its trees by swinging an axe against them; for you may eat from them, so you shall not cut them down. For is the tree of the field a human, that it should be besieged by you? 20 Only the trees that you know are not fruit trees you shall destroy and cut down, so that you may construct siegeworks against the city that is making war against you until it falls.

Expiation of a Crime

21 "If a person who has been killed *by someone* is found lying in the open country in the land which the LORD your God is giving you to possess, *and* it is not known who struck him, 2 then your elders and your judges shall go out and measure *the distance* to the cities which are around the one who was killed. 3 And it shall be that the city which is nearest to the person killed, that is, that the elders of that city shall take a heifer of the herd that has not been worked and has not pulled in a yoke; 4 and the elders of that city shall bring the heifer down to a valley with running water, which has not been plowed or sown, and they

shall break the heifer's neck there in the valley. 5 Then the priests, the sons of Levi, shall come forward, because the LORD your God has chosen them to serve Him and to bless in the name of the LORD; and every dispute and violent crime shall be settled by them. 6 And all the elders of that city which is nearest to the person killed shall wash their hands over the heifer whose neck was broken in the valley; 7 and they shall respond and say, 'Our hands did not shed this blood, nor did our eyes see *who did.* 8 Forgive Your people Israel whom You have redeemed, LORD, and do not place the guilt for innocent blood in the midst of Your people Israel.' And the guilt for bloodshed shall be forgiven them. 9 So you shall remove the guilt for innocent blood from your midst, when you do what is right in the eyes of the LORD.

Domestic Relations

10 "When you go out to battle against your enemies, and the LORD your God hands them over to you and you take them away captive, 11 and you see among the captives a beautiful woman, and are strongly attracted to her and would take her as a wife for yourself, 12 then you shall bring her into your home, and she shall shave her head and trim her nails. 13 She shall also remove the clothes of her captivity and shall remain in your house, and weep for her father and mother a full month; and after that you may have relations with her and become her husband and she shall be your wife. 14 But it shall be, if you are not pleased with her, then you shall let her go wherever she wishes; and you certainly shall not sell her for money, you shall not treat her as merchandise, since you have 1humiliated her.

15 "If a man has two wives, the one loved and the other unloved, and *both* the loved and the unloved have borne him sons, and the first-born son belongs to the unloved, 16 then it shall be on the day that he wills what he owns as an inheritance to his sons, he is not allowed to treat the son of the loved *wife* as the firstborn, at the expense of the son of the unloved, *who actually is* the firstborn *son.* 17 On the contrary, he shall acknowledge the firstborn, the son of the unloved *wife,* by giving him a double portion of everything that he owns, for he *was* the beginning of his strength; to him belongs the right of the firstborn.

18 "If any person has a stubborn and rebellious son who does not obey his father or his mother, and when they discipline him, he does not listen to them, 19 then his father and mother shall seize him, and bring him out to the elders of his city at the gateway of his hometown. 20 And they shall say to the elders of his city, 'This son of ours is stubborn and rebellious; he does not obey us, he is thoughtless and given to drinking.' 21 Then all the men of his city shall stone him to death; so you shall eliminate the evil from your midst, and all Israel will hear *about it* and fear.

22 "Now if a person has committed a sin *carrying* a sentence of death and he is put to death, and you hang him on 1a tree,

20:7 1A betrothed couple was considered legally married, but did not yet live together 21:14 1I.e., by a forced marriage 21:22 1Lit wood

23 his body is not to be left overnight on the ¹tree, but you shall certainly bury him on the same day (for he who is hanged is cursed of God), so that you do not defile your land which the LORD your God is giving you as an inheritance.

Various Laws

22 "You shall not see your countryman's ox or his sheep straying away, and avoid them; you shall certainly bring them back to your countryman. ² And if your countryman is not near you, or if you do not know him, then you shall bring it to your house, and it shall remain with you until your countryman looks for it; then you shall restore it to him. ³ You shall also do this with his donkey, and you shall do the same with his garment, and you shall do likewise with any lost property of your countryman, which has been lost by him and you have found. You are not allowed to avoid *them.* ⁴ You shall not see your countryman's donkey or his ox fallen down on the road, and avoid them; you shall certainly help him raise *them* up.

⁵ "A woman shall not wear a man's clothing, nor shall a man put on a woman's clothing; for whoever does these things is an abomination to the LORD your God.

⁶ "If you happen to come upon a bird's nest along the way, in any tree or on the ground, with young ones or eggs *in it,* and the mother sitting on the young or on the eggs, you shall not take the mother with the young; ⁷ you shall certainly let the mother go, but the young you may take for yourself, in order that it may go well for you and that you may prolong your days.

⁸ "When you build a new house, you shall make a parapet for your roof, so that you will not bring guilt for bloodshed on your house if anyone falls from it.

⁹ "You shall not sow your vineyard with two kinds of seed, otherwise all the produce of the seed which you have sown and the yield of the vineyard will be forfeited to the sanctuary.

10 "You shall not plow with an ox and a donkey together.

11 "You shall not wear a material of wool and linen combined together.

12 "You shall make yourself tassels on the four corners of your garment with which you cover yourself.

Laws on Morality

13 "If any man takes a wife and goes in to her and *then* turns against her, 14 and he charges her with shameful behavior and publicly defames her, and says, 'I took this woman, *but* when I came near her, I did not find her to have evidence of virginity,' 15 then the girl's father and her mother shall take and bring out the evidence of the girl's virginity to the elders of the city at the gate. 16 And the girl's father shall say to the elders, 'I gave my daughter to this man as a wife, but he turned against her; 17 and behold, he has charged her with shameful behavior, saying, "I did not find your daughter to have evidence of virginity." But this is the evidence of my daughter's virginity.' And they shall spread out the garment before the elders of the city. 18 Then the elders of that city shall take the man and rebuke him, 19 and they shall fine him a hundred *shekels* of silver and give it to the girl's father, because he publicly defamed a virgin of Israel. And she shall remain his wife; he is not allowed to divorce her all his days.

20 "But if this charge is true, *and* they did not find the girl to have evidence of virginity, 21 then they shall bring the girl out to the doorway of her father's house, and the men of her city shall stone her to death, because she has committed a disgraceful sin in Israel by playing the prostitute in her father's house; so you shall eliminate the evil from among you.

22 "If a man is found sleeping with a married woman, then both of them shall die, the man who slept with the woman, and the woman; so you shall eliminate the evil from Israel.

23 "If there is a girl who is a virgin ¹betrothed to a man, and *another* man finds her in the city and sleeps with her, 24 then you shall bring them both out to the gate of that city and you shall stone them to death: the girl, because she did not cry out for help *though she was* in the city, and the man, because he has violated his neighbor's wife. So you shall eliminate the evil from among you.

25 "But if the man finds the girl who is betrothed in the field, and the man seizes her and rapes her, then only the man who raped her shall die. 26 And you are not to do anything to the girl; there is no sin in the girl *worthy of* death, for just as a man rises against his neighbor and murders him, so is this case. 27 When he found her in the field, the betrothed girl cried out, but there was no one to save her.

28 "If a man finds a girl who is a virgin, who is not betrothed, and he seizes her and has sexual relations with her, and they are discovered, 29 then the man who had sexual relations with her shall give the girl's father fifty *shekels* of silver, and she shall become his wife, because he has violated her; he is not allowed to divorce her all his days.

30 "A man shall not take his father's wife *in marriage,* so that he does not ¹uncover his father's garment.

Persons Excluded from the Assembly

23 "No one who is emasculated or has his male organ cut off may enter the assembly of the LORD. ² No one of illegitimate birth may enter the assembly of the LORD; none of his *descendants,* even to the tenth generation, may enter the assembly of the LORD. ³ No Ammonite or Moabite may enter the assembly of the LORD; none of their *descendants,* even to the tenth generation, may ever enter the assembly of the LORD, ⁴ because they did not meet you with food and water on the way when you came out of Egypt, and because they hired against you Balaam the son of Beor from Pethor of Mesopotamia, to curse you.

21:23 ¹ Lit *wood*   **22:23** ¹ A betrothed couple was considered legally married, but did not yet live together   **22:30** ¹ Idiom for violating his father's marriage

5 Nevertheless, the LORD your God was unwilling to listen to Balaam, but the LORD your God turned the curse into a blessing for you because the LORD your God loves you. 6 You shall never seek their peace or their prosperity all your days.

7 "You shall not loathe an Edomite, for he is your brother; you shall not loathe an Egyptian, because you were a stranger in his land. 8 The sons of the third generation who are born to them may enter the assembly of the LORD.

9 "When you go out as an army against your enemies, you shall be on guard against every evil thing.

10 "If there is among you any man who is unclean because of a nocturnal emission, then he must go outside the camp; he may not reenter the camp. 11 But when evening approaches, he shall bathe himself with water, and at sundown he may reenter the camp.

12 "You shall also have a place *allocated* outside the camp, so that you may go out there *to relieve yourself,* 13 and you shall have a spade among your tools, and it shall be when you sit down outside, you shall dig with it and shall turn and cover up your excrement. 14 Since the LORD your God walks in the midst of your camp to save you and to defeat your enemies before you, your camp must be holy; so He must not see anything indecent among you or He will turn away from you.

15 "You shall not hand over to his master a slave who has escaped from his master to you. 16 He shall live with you in your midst, in the place that he chooses in one of your towns where it pleases him; you shall not mistreat him.

17 "None of the daughters of Israel shall be a cult prostitute, nor shall any of the sons of Israel be a cult prostitute. 18 You shall not bring the earnings of a prostitute or the money for a ¹dog into the house of the LORD your God *as payment* for any vowed offering, because both of these are an abomination to the LORD your God.

19 "You are not to charge interest to your countrymen: interest on money, food, *or* anything that may be loaned on interest. 20 You may charge interest to a foreigner, but to your countrymen you shall not charge interest, so that the LORD your God may bless you in all that you undertake in the land which you are about to enter to possess.

21 "When you make a vow to the LORD your God, you shall not delay to pay it, for the LORD your God will certainly require it of you, and it will be a sin for you. 22 However, if you refrain from making vows, it will not be a sin for you. 23 You shall be careful and perform what goes out of your lips, since in fact you have vowed a voluntary offering to the LORD your God, whatever you have promised.

24 "When you enter your neighbor's vineyard, you may eat grapes until you are satisfied; but you are not to put *any* in your basket.

25 "When you enter your neighbor's standing grain, you may pluck the heads of grain with your hand, but you are not to use a sickle on your neighbor's standing grain.

Law of Divorce

24 "When a man takes a wife and marries her, and it happens, if she finds no favor in his eyes because he has found some indecency in her, that he writes her a certificate of divorce, puts *it* in her hand, and sends her away from his house, 2 and she leaves his house and goes and becomes another man's *wife,* 3 and the latter husband turns against her, writes her a certificate of divorce and puts *it* in her hand, and sends her away from his house, or if the latter husband who took her to be his wife dies, 4 *then* her former husband who sent her away is not allowed to take her again to be his wife, after she has been defiled; for that is an abomination before the LORD, and you shall not bring sin on the land which the LORD your God is giving you as an inheritance.

5 "When a man takes a new wife, he is not to go out with the army, nor be assigned any duty; he shall be free at home for one year and shall make his wife whom he has taken happy.

Various Laws

6 "No one shall seize a handmill or an upper millstone as a pledge *for a loan,* since he would be seizing *the debtor's* means of life as a pledge.

7 "If someone is caught kidnapping any of his countrymen of the sons of Israel, and he treats him as merchandise and sells him, then that thief shall die; so you shall eliminate the evil from among you.

8 "Be careful about an infestation of leprosy, that you are very attentive and act in accordance with everything that the Levitical priests teach you; just as I have commanded them, you shall be careful to act. 9 Remember what the LORD your God did to Miriam on the way as you came out of Egypt.

10 "When you make your neighbor a loan of any kind, you shall not enter his house to take his pledge. 11 You shall stand outside, and the person to whom you are making the loan shall bring the pledge outside to you. 12 And if he is a poor man, you shall not sleep with his pledge. 13 When the sun goes down you shall certainly return the pledge to him, so that he may sleep in his cloak and bless you; and it will be righteousness for you before the LORD your God.

14 "You shall not exploit a hired worker *who is* poor and needy, whether *he is* one of your countrymen or one of your strangers who are in your land in your towns. 15 You shall give him his wages on his day before the sun sets—for he is poor and sets his heart on it—so that he does not cry out against you to the LORD, and it becomes a sin in you.

16 "Fathers shall not be put to death for *their* sons, nor shall sons be put to death for *their* fathers; everyone shall be put to death for his own sin *alone.*

17 "You shall not pervert the justice due a stranger *or* an orphan, nor seize a widow's garment as a pledge. 18 But you are to remember

---

that you were a slave in Egypt, and that the LORD your God redeemed you from there; therefore I am commanding you to do this thing.

19 "When you reap your harvest in your field and forget a sheaf in the field, you are not to go back to get it; it shall belong to the stranger, the orphan, and to the widow, in order that the LORD your God may bless you in all the work of your hands. 20 When you beat *the olives* off your olive tree, you are not to search through the branches again; *that* shall be *left* for the stranger, the orphan, and for the widow.

21 "When you gather the grapes of your vineyard, you are not to go over it again; *that* shall be *left* for the stranger, the orphan, and the widow. 22 And you shall remember that you were a slave in the land of Egypt; therefore I am commanding you to do this thing.

Various Laws

25 "If there is a dispute between people and they go to court, and the judges decide their case, and they declare the righteous innocent and pronounce the wicked guilty, 2 then it shall be if the wicked person deserves to be beaten, the judge shall then make him lie down and have him beaten in his presence with the number *of lashes* according to his wrongful act. 3 He may have him beaten forty times, *but* not more, so that he does not have him beaten with many more lashes than these, and that your brother does not become contemptible in your eyes.

4 "You shall not muzzle the ox while it is threshing.

5 "When brothers live together, and one of them dies and has no son, the wife of the deceased shall not be *married* outside *the family* to a strange man. Her husband's brother shall have relations with her and take her to himself as *his* wife, and perform the duty of a husband's brother to her. 6 It shall then be that the firstborn to whom she gives birth shall assume the name of his *father's* deceased brother, so that his name will not be wiped out from Israel. 7 But if the man does not desire to take his brother's widow, then his brother's widow shall go up to the gate to the elders, and say, 'My husband's brother refuses to establish a name for his brother in Israel; he is not willing to perform the duty of a husband's brother to me.' 8 Then the elders of his city shall summon him and speak to him. And *if* he persists and says, 'I do not desire to take her,' 9 then his brother's widow shall come up to him in the sight of the elders, and pull his sandal off his foot and spit in his face; and she shall declare, 'This is what is done to the man who does not build up his brother's house!' 10 And in Israel his family shall be called by the name, 'The house of him whose sandal was removed.'

11 "If *two* men, a man and his countryman, have a fight with each other, and the wife of one comes up to save her husband from the hand of the one who is hitting him, and she reaches out with her hand and grasps that man's genitals, 12 then you shall cut off her hand; you shall not show pity.

13 "You shall not have in your bag differing weights, a large and a small. 14 You shall not have in your house differing measures, a large and a small. 15 You shall have a correct and honest weight; you shall have a correct and honest measure, so that your days may be prolonged in the land which the LORD your God is giving you. 16 For everyone who does these things, everyone who acts unjustly is an abomination to the LORD your God.

17 "Remember what Amalek did to you on the way when you came out of Egypt, 18 how he confronted you on the way and attacked among you all the stragglers at your rear when you were tired and weary; and he did not fear God. 19 So it shall come about, when the LORD your God has given you rest from all your surrounding enemies in the land which the LORD your God is giving you as an inheritance to possess, that you shall wipe out the mention of *the name* Amalek from under heaven; you must not forget.

Offering First Fruits

26 "Then it shall be, when you enter the land which the LORD your God is giving you as an inheritance, and you take possession of it and live in it, 2 that you shall take some of the first of all the produce of the ground which you bring in from your land that the LORD your God gives you, and you shall put *it* in a basket and go to the place where the LORD your God chooses to establish His name. 3 And you shall go to the priest who is *in office* at that time and say to him, 'I declare today to the LORD my God that I have entered the land which the LORD swore to our fathers to give us.' 4 Then the priest shall take the basket from your hand and set it before the altar of the LORD your God. 5 And you shall respond and say before the LORD your God, 'My father was a wandering Aramean, and he went down to Egypt and resided there, few in number; but there he became a great, mighty, and populous nation. 6 And the Egyptians treated us badly and oppressed us, and imposed hard labor on us. 7 Then we cried out to the LORD, the God of our fathers, and the LORD heard our voice and saw our wretched condition, our trouble, and our oppression; 8 and the LORD brought us out of Egypt with a mighty hand, an outstretched arm, and with great terror, and with signs and wonders; 9 and He has brought us to this place, and has given us this land, a land flowing with milk and honey. 10 And now behold, I have brought the first of the produce of the ground which You, LORD have given me.' Then you shall set it before the LORD your God, and worship before the LORD your God; 11 and you, the Levite, and the stranger who is among you shall rejoice in all the good which the LORD your God has given you and your household.

12 "When you have finished paying all the tithe of your produce in the third year, the year of the tithe, then you shall give it to the Levite, to the stranger, to the orphan, and to the widow, so that they may eat in your towns and be satisfied. 13 And you shall say before the LORD your God, 'I have removed the sacred *portion* from *my* house, and have also given it

to the Levite, the stranger, the orphan, and the widow, in accordance with all Your commandments which You have commanded me; I have not violated or forgotten any of Your commandments. 14 I have not eaten of it while mourning, nor have I removed any of it while I was unclean, nor offered any of it to the dead. I have listened to the voice of the LORD my God; I have acted in accordance with everything that You have commanded me. 15 Look down from Your holy dwelling place, from heaven, and bless Your people Israel, and the ground which You have given us, a land flowing with milk and honey just as You swore to our fathers.'

16 "This day the LORD your God commands you to perform these statutes and ordinances. Therefore you shall be careful to perform them with all your heart and with all your soul. 17 Today you have declared the LORD to be your God, and that you will walk in His ways and keep His statutes, His commandments, and His ordinances, and listen to His voice. 18 And the LORD has today declared you to be His people, *His* personal possession, just as He promised you, and that you are to keep all His commandments; 19 and that He will put you high above all the nations which He has made, for glory, fame, and honor; and that you shall be a consecrated people to the LORD your God, just as He has spoken."

The Curses at Mount Ebal

27 Then Moses and the elders of Israel commanded the people, saying, "Keep all the commandments which I am commanding you today. 2 So it shall be on the day when you cross the Jordan to the land which the LORD your God is giving you, that you shall set up for yourself large stones and coat them with lime 3 and write on them all the words of this Law, when you cross over, so that you may enter the land which the LORD your God is giving you, a land flowing with milk and honey, just as the LORD, the God of your fathers, promised you. 4 So it shall be when you cross the Jordan, you shall set up these stones on Mount Ebal, as I am commanding you today, and you shall coat them with lime. 5 Moreover, you shall build there an altar to the LORD your God, an altar of stones; you shall not wield an iron *tool* on them. 6 You shall build the altar of the LORD your God of uncut stones, and you shall offer on it burnt offerings to the LORD your God; 7 and you shall sacrifice peace offerings and eat there, and rejoice before the LORD your God. 8 You shall write on the stones all the words of this Law very clearly."

9 Then Moses and the Levitical priests spoke to all Israel, saying, "Be silent and listen, Israel! This day you have become a people for the LORD your God. 10 So you shall obey the LORD your God, and do His commandments and His statutes which I am commanding you today."

11 Moses also commanded the people on that day, saying, 12 "When you cross the Jordan, these *tribes* shall stand on Mount Gerizim to bless the people: Simeon, Levi, Judah, Issachar, Joseph, and Benjamin. 13 For the curse, these *tribes* shall stand on Mount Ebal: Reuben, Gad,

Asher, Zebulun, Dan, and Naphtali. 14 The Levites shall then respond and say to all the people of Israel with a loud voice,

15 'Cursed is the person who makes a carved image or cast metal image, an abomination to the LORD, the work of the hands of a craftsman, and sets *it* up in secret.' And all the people shall reply and say, 'Amen.'

16 'Cursed is one who treats his father or mother contemptuously.' And all the people shall say, 'Amen.'

17 'Cursed is one who displaces his neighbor's boundary marker.' And all the people shall say, 'Amen.'

18 'Cursed is one who misleads a person who is blind on the road.' And all the people shall say, 'Amen.'

19 'Cursed is one who distorts the justice *due* a stranger, an orphan, or a widow.' And all the people shall say, 'Amen.'

20 'Cursed is he who sleeps with his father's wife, because he has 1 uncovered his father's garment.' And all the people shall say, 'Amen.'

21 'Cursed is one who has sexual intercourse with any animal.' And all the people shall say, 'Amen.'

22 'Cursed is he who sleeps with his sister, the daughter of his father or of his mother.' And all the people shall say, 'Amen.'

23 'Cursed is he who sleeps with his mother-in-law.' And all the people shall say, 'Amen.'

24 'Cursed is he who attacks his neighbor in secret.' And all the people shall say, 'Amen.'

25 'Cursed is he who accepts a bribe to attack an innocent person.' And all the people shall say, 'Amen.'

26 'Cursed is *anyone* who does not fulfill the words of this Law by doing them.' And all the people shall say, 'Amen.'

The Blessings at Mount Gerizim

28 "Now it shall be, if you diligently obey the LORD your God, being careful to do all His commandments which I am commanding you today, that the LORD your God will put you high above all the nations of the earth. 2 And all these blessings will come to you and reach you if you obey the LORD your God:

3 "Blessed *will* you *be* in the city, and blessed *will* you *be* in the country.

4 "Blessed *will be* the children of your womb, the produce of your ground, and the offspring of your animals: the newborn of your herd and the young of your flock.

5 "Blessed *will be* your basket and your kneading bowl.

6 "Blessed *will* you *be* when you come in, and blessed *will* you *be* when you go out.

7 "The LORD will cause your enemies who rise up against you to be defeated by you; they will go out against you one way and will flee at your presence seven ways. 8 The LORD will command the blessing for you in your barns and in everything that you put your hand to, and He will bless you in the land that the LORD your God is giving you. 9 The LORD will establish you as a holy people to Himself, as He swore to you, if you keep the commandments

---

27:20 1 Idiom for violated his father's marriage

of the LORD your God and walk in His ways. ¹⁰ So all the peoples of the earth will see that you are called by the name of the LORD, and they will be afraid of you. ¹¹ And the LORD will give you more than enough prosperity, in the children of your womb, in the offspring of your livestock, and in the produce of your ground, in the land which the LORD swore to your fathers to give you. ¹² The LORD will open for you His good storehouse, the heavens, to give rain to your land in its season and to bless every work of your hand; and you will lend to many nations, but you will not borrow. ¹³ And the LORD will make you the head and not the tail, and you will only be above, and not be underneath, if you listen to the commandments of the LORD your God which I am commanding you today, to follow *them* carefully, ¹⁴ and do not turn aside from any of the words which I am commanding you today, to the right or the left, to pursue other gods to serve them.

Consequences of Disobedience

¹⁵ "But it shall come about, if you do not obey the LORD your God, to be careful to follow all His commandments and His statutes which I am commanding you today, that all these curses will come upon you and overtake you:

¹⁶ "Cursed *will* you *be* in the city, and cursed *will* you *be* in the country.

¹⁷ "Cursed *will be* your basket and your kneading bowl.

¹⁸ "Cursed *will be* the children of your womb, the produce of your ground, the newborn of your herd, and the offspring of your flock.

¹⁹ "Cursed *will* you *be* when you come in, and cursed *will* you *be* when you go out.

²⁰ "The LORD will send against you curses, panic, and rebuke, in everything you undertake to do, until you are destroyed and until you perish quickly, on account of the evil of your deeds, because you have abandoned Me. ²¹ The LORD will make the plague cling to you until He has eliminated you from the land where you are entering to take possession of it. ²² The LORD will strike you with consumption, inflammation, fever, feverish heat, and with ¹the sword, with blight, and with mildew, and they will pursue you until you perish. ²³ The heaven which is over your head shall be bronze, and the earth which is under you, iron. ²⁴ The LORD will make the rain of your land powder and dust; from heaven it shall come down on you until you are destroyed.

²⁵ "The LORD will cause you to be defeated by your enemies; you will go out one way against them, but you will flee seven ways from their presence, and you will be *an example of* terror to all the kingdoms of the earth. ²⁶ Your dead bodies will serve as food for all birds of the sky and for the animals of the earth, and there will be no one to frighten *them away.*

²⁷ "The LORD will strike you with the boils of Egypt and with tumors, the festering rash, and with scabies, from which you cannot be healed. ²⁸ The LORD will strike you with

insanity, blindness, and with confusion of mind; ²⁹ and you will be groping about at noon, just as a person who is blind gropes in the darkness, and you will not be successful in your ways; but you will only be oppressed and robbed all the time, with no one to save you. ³⁰ You will ¹betroth a woman, but another man will violate her; you will build a house, but you will not live in it; you will plant a vineyard, but you will not make use of its fruit. ³¹ Your ox *will be* slaughtered before your eyes, but you will not eat of it; your donkey *will be* snatched away from you, and will not be restored to you; your sheep *will be* given to your enemies, and you will have no one to save you. ³² Your sons and your daughters *will be* given to another people, while your eyes look on and long for them constantly; but there will be nothing you can do. ³³ A people whom you do not know will eat the produce of your ground and every product of your labor, and you will never be anything but oppressed and mistreated continually. ³⁴ You will also be driven insane by the sight of what you see. ³⁵ The LORD will strike you on the knees and thighs with severe boils from which you cannot be healed, *and strike you* from the sole of your foot to the top of your head. ³⁶ The LORD will bring you and your king, whom you appoint over you, to a nation that neither you nor your fathers have known, and there you shall serve other gods, *made of* wood and stone. ³⁷ And you will become an *object of* horror, a song of mockery, and an object of taunting among all the peoples where the LORD drives you.

³⁸ "You will bring out a great amount of seed to the field, but you will gather in little, because the locust will devour it. ³⁹ You will plant and cultivate vineyards, but you will neither drink of the wine nor bring in *the harvest,* because the worm will eat it. ⁴⁰ You will have olive trees throughout your territory but you will not anoint yourself with the oil, because your olives will drop off *prematurely.* ⁴¹ You will father sons and daughters but they will not remain yours, because they will go into captivity. ⁴² The cricket will take possession of all your trees and the produce of your ground. ⁴³ The stranger who is among you will rise above you higher and higher, and you will go down lower and lower. ⁴⁴ He will lend to you, but you will not lend to him; he will be the head, and you will be the tail.

⁴⁵ "So all these curses shall come upon you and pursue you and overtake you until you are destroyed, because you would not obey the LORD your God by keeping His commandments and His statutes which He commanded you. ⁴⁶ And they will become a sign and a wonder against you and your descendants forever.

⁴⁷ "Since you did not serve the LORD your God with joy and a cheerful heart, *in gratitude* for the abundance of all *things,* ⁴⁸ you will serve your enemies whom the LORD will send against you, in hunger, thirst, nakedness, and devoid of all *things;* and He will put an iron yoke on your neck until He has destroyed you. ⁴⁹ "The LORD will bring a nation against you

---

28:22 ¹Another reading is *drought*   28:30 ¹A betrothed couple was considered legally married, but did not yet live together

from far away, from the end of the earth, as the eagle swoops down; a nation whose language you will not understand, [50] a nation with a defiant attitude, who will have no respect for the old, nor show favor to the young. [51] Furthermore, it will eat the offspring of your herd and the produce of your ground until you are destroyed; a *nation* that will leave you no grain, new wine, or oil, nor the newborn of your cattle or the young of your flock, until they have eliminated you. [52] And it will besiege you in all your towns until your high and fortified walls in which you trusted come down throughout your land, and it will besiege you in all your towns throughout your land which the LORD your God has given you. [53] Then you will eat the offspring of your own body, the flesh of your sons and of your daughters whom the LORD your God has given you, during the siege and the hardship by which your enemy will oppress you. [54] The man who is refined and very delicate among you will be hostile toward his brother, toward the wife he cherishes, and toward the rest of his children who are left, [55] so that he will not give *even* one of them any of the flesh of his children which he will eat, since he has nothing *else* left, during the siege and the hardship by which your enemy will oppress you in all your towns. [56] The refined and delicate woman among you, who would not venture to set the sole of her foot on the ground because of her delicateness and tenderness, will be hostile toward the husband she cherishes and toward her son and daughter, [57] and toward her afterbirth that comes from between her legs, and toward her children to whom she gives birth, because she will eat them secretly for lack of anything *else,* during the siege and the hardship with which your enemy will oppress you in your towns.

[58] "If you are not careful to follow all the words of this Law that are written in this book, to fear this honored and awesome name, the LORD your God, [59] then the LORD will bring extraordinary plagues on you and your descendants, severe and lasting plagues, and miserable and chronic sicknesses. [60] And He will bring back on you every disease of Egypt of which you were afraid, and they will cling to you. [61] Also every sickness and every plague, which are not written in the book of this Law, the LORD will bring on you until you are destroyed. [62] Then you will be left few in number, whereas you were as numerous as the stars of heaven, because you did not obey the LORD your God. [63] And it will come about that, just as the LORD rejoiced over you to be good to you, and make you numerous, so will the LORD rejoice over you to wipe you out and destroy you; and you will be torn away from the land which you are entering to possess. [64] Furthermore, the LORD will scatter you among all the peoples, from *one* end of the earth to the other; and there you will serve other gods, *made of* wood and stone, which you and your fathers have not known. [65] Among those nations you will find no peace, and there will be no resting place for the sole of your foot; but there the LORD will give you a trembling heart, failing of eyes, and despair of soul. [66] So your

lives will be hanging in doubt before you; and you will be terrified night and day, and have no assurance of your life. [67] In the morning you will say, 'If only it were evening!' And at evening you will say, 'If only it were morning!' because of the terror of your heart which you fear, and the sight of your eyes which you will see. [68] And the LORD will bring you back to Egypt in ships, by the way about which I said to you, 'You will never see it again!' And there you will offer yourselves for sale to your enemies as male and female slaves, but there will be no buyer."

The Covenant in Moab

29 These are the words of the covenant which the LORD commanded Moses to make with the sons of Israel in the land of Moab, besides the covenant which He had made with them at Horeb.

[2] And Moses summoned all Israel and said to them, "You have seen all that the LORD did before your eyes in the land of Egypt to Pharaoh and all his servants, and to all his land; [3] the great trials which your eyes have seen, those great signs and wonders. [4] Yet to this day the LORD has not given you a heart to know, nor eyes to see, nor ears to hear. [5] And I have led you in the wilderness for forty years; your clothes have not worn out on you, and your sandal has not worn out on your foot. [6] You have not eaten bread, nor have you drunk wine or *other* strong drink, in order that you might know that I am the LORD your God. [7] When you reached this place, Sihon the king of Heshbon and Og the king of Bashan came out to meet us for battle, but we defeated them; [8] and we took their land and gave it as an inheritance to the Reubenites, the Gadites, and the half-tribe of the Manassites. [9] So you will keep the words of this covenant and do them, in order that you may be successful in everything that you do.

[10] "You stand today, all of you, before the LORD your God: your heads, your tribes, your elders and your officers, *that is,* all the men of Israel, [11] your little ones, your wives, and the stranger who is within your camps, from the one who gathers your firewood to the one who draws your water, [12] so that you may enter into the covenant with the LORD your God, and into His oath which the LORD your God is making with you today, [13] in order that He may establish you today as His people, and that He may be your God, just as He spoke to you and as He swore to your fathers, to Abraham, Isaac, and Jacob. [14] "Now *it is* not with you alone *that* I am making this covenant and this oath, [15] but *both* with those who stand here with us today in the presence of the LORD our God, and with those who are not with us here today [16] (for you know how we lived in the land of Egypt, and how we passed through the midst of the nations through which you passed; [17] moreover, you have seen their abominations and their idols *made of* wood and stone, silver and gold, which *they had* with them); [18] so that there will not be among you a man or woman, or family or tribe, whose heart turns away today from

the LORD our God, to go to serve the gods of those nations; that there will not be among you a root bearing poisonous fruit and wormwood. 19 And it shall be when he hears the words of this curse, that he will consider himself fortunate in his heart, saying, 'I will do well though I walk in the stubbornness of my heart in order to destroy the watered *land* along with the dry.' 20 The LORD will not be willing to forgive him, but rather the anger of the LORD and His wrath will burn against that person, and every curse that is written in this book will lie upon him, and the LORD will wipe out his name from under heaven. 21 Then the LORD will single him out for disaster from all the tribes of Israel, in accordance with all the curses of the covenant which is written in this Book of the Law.

22 "Now the future generation, your sons who rise up after you and the foreigner who comes from a distant land, when they see the plagues of that land and the diseases with which the LORD has afflicted it, will say, 23 'All its land is brimstone and salt, burned debris, unsown and unproductive, and no grass grows on it, like the overthrow of Sodom and Gomorrah, Admah and Zeboiim, which the LORD overthrew in His anger and in His wrath.' 24 All the nations will say, 'Why has the LORD done *all* this to this land? Why this great outburst of anger?' 25 Then *people* will say, '*It is* because they abandoned the covenant of the LORD, the God of their fathers, which He made with them when He brought them out of the land of Egypt. 26 And they went and served other gods and worshiped them, gods that they have not known and whom He had not assigned to them. 27 Therefore, the anger of the LORD burned against that land, to bring upon it every curse which is written in this book; 28 and the LORD uprooted them from their land in anger, fury, and in great wrath, and hurled them into another land, as *it is* this day.'

29 "The secret things belong to the LORD our God, but the things revealed belong to us and to our sons forever, so that we may follow all the words of this Law.

Restoration Promised

30 "So it will be when all of these things have come upon you, the blessing and the curse which I have placed before you, and you call *them* to mind in all the nations where the LORD your God has scattered you, 2 and you return to the LORD your God and obey Him with all your heart and soul in accordance with everything that I am commanding you today, you and your sons, 3 then the LORD your God will restore you from captivity, and have compassion on you, and will gather you again from all the peoples where the LORD your God has scattered you. 4 If any of your scattered *countrymen* are at the ends of the earth, from there the LORD your God will gather you, and from there He will bring you back. 5 The LORD your God will bring you into the land which your fathers possessed, and you shall possess it; and He will be good to you and make you more numerous than your fathers.

6 "Moreover, the LORD your God will

circumcise your heart and the hearts of your descendants, to love the LORD your God with all your heart and all your soul, so that you may live. 7 And the LORD your God will inflict all these curses on your enemies and on those who hate you, who persecuted you. 8 And you will again obey the LORD, and follow all His commandments which I am commanding you today. 9 Then the LORD your God will prosper you abundantly in every work of your hand, in the children of your womb, the offspring of your cattle, and in the produce of your ground, for the LORD will again rejoice over you for good, just as He rejoiced over your fathers; 10 if you obey the LORD your God, to keep His commandments and His statutes which are written in this Book of the Law, if you turn to the LORD your God with all your heart and soul.

11 "For this commandment which I am commanding you today is not too difficult for you, nor is it far away. 12 It is not in heaven, that you could say, 'Who will go up to heaven for us and get it for us, and proclaim it to us, so that we may follow it?' 13 Nor is it beyond the sea, that you could say, 'Who will cross the sea for us and get it for us and proclaim it to us, so that we may follow it?' 14 On the contrary, the word is very near you, in your mouth and in your heart, that you may follow it.

Choose Life

15 "See, I have placed before you today life and happiness, and death and adversity, 16 in that I am commanding you today to love the LORD your God, to walk in His ways and to keep His commandments, His statutes, and His judgments, so that you may live and become numerous, and that the LORD your God may bless you in the land where you are entering to take possession of it. 17 But if your heart turns away and you will not obey, but allow yourself to be led astray and you worship other gods and serve them, 18 I declare to you today that you will certainly perish. You will not prolong *your* days in the land where you are crossing the Jordan to enter and take possession of it. 19 I call heaven and earth to witness against you today, that I have placed before you life and death, the blessing and the curse. So choose life in order that you may live, you and your descendants, 20 by loving the LORD your God, by obeying His voice, and by holding close to Him; for this is your life and the length of your days, so that you may live in the land which the LORD swore to your fathers, to Abraham, Isaac, and Jacob, to give them."

Moses' Last Counsel

31 So Moses went and spoke these words to all Israel. 2 And he said to them, "I am 120 years old today; I am no longer able to go out and come in, and the LORD has told me, 'You shall not cross this Jordan.' 3 It is the LORD your God who is going to cross ahead of you; He Himself will destroy these nations before you, and you shall dispossess them. Joshua is the one who is going to cross ahead of you, just as the LORD has spoken. 4 And the LORD will do to them just as He did to Sihon and Og, the

kings of the Amorites, and to their land, when He destroyed them. 5 The LORD will turn them over to you, and you will do to them in accordance with all the commandments which I have commanded you. 6 Be strong and courageous, do not be afraid or in dread of them, for the LORD your God is the One who is going with you. He will not desert you or abandon you."

7 Then Moses called to Joshua and said to him in the sight of all Israel, "Be strong and courageous, for you will go with this people into the land which the LORD has sworn to their fathers to give them, and you will give it to them as an inheritance. 8 And the LORD is the one who is going ahead of you; He will be with you. He will not desert you or abandon you. Do not fear and do not be dismayed."

9 So Moses wrote this Law and gave it to the priests, the sons of Levi who carried the ark of the covenant of the LORD, and to all the elders of Israel. 10 Then Moses commanded them, saying, "At the end of *every* seven years, at the time of the year of the release of debts, at the Feast of Booths, 11 when all Israel comes to appear before the LORD your God at the place which He will choose, you shall read this Law before all Israel so that they hear *it*. 12 Assemble the people, the men, the women, the children, and the stranger who is in your town, so that they may hear and learn and fear the LORD your God, and be careful to follow all the words of this Law. 13 And their children, who have not known, will hear and learn to fear the LORD your God, as long as you live on the land which you are about to cross the Jordan to possess."

Israel Will Fall Away

14 Then the LORD said to Moses, "Behold, the time for you to die is near; call Joshua and present yourselves at the tent of meeting, and I will commission him." So Moses and Joshua went and presented themselves at the tent of meeting. 15 And the LORD appeared in the tent in a pillar of cloud, and the pillar of cloud stood at the entrance of the tent. 16 The LORD said to Moses, "Behold, you are about to 1lie down with your fathers; and this people will arise and play the prostitute with the foreign gods of the land into the midst of which they are going, and they will abandon Me and break My covenant which I have made with them. 17 Then My anger will be kindled against them on that day, and I will abandon them and hide My face from them, and they will be consumed, and many evils and troubles will find them; so they will say on that day, 'Is it not because our God is not among us that these evils have found us?' 18 But I will assuredly hide My face on that day because of all the evil that they will have done, for they will have turned away to other gods. 19 "Now then, write this song for yourselves, and teach it to the sons of Israel; put it on their lips, so that this song may be a witness for Me against the sons of Israel. 20 For when I bring them into the land flowing with milk and

honey, which I swore to their fathers, and they eat and are satisfied and become prosperous, then they will turn to other gods and serve them, and spurn Me and break My covenant. 21 Then it will come about, when many evils and troubles find them, that this song will testify before them as a witness (for it shall not be forgotten from the mouth of their descendants); for I know their inclination which they are developing today, before I bring them into the land which I swore." 22 So Moses wrote down this song on the same day, and taught it to the sons of Israel.

Joshua Is Commissioned

23 Then He commissioned Joshua the son of Nun, and said, "Be strong and courageous, for you will bring the sons of Israel into the land which I swore to them, and I will be with you."

24 It came about, when Moses finished writing the words of this Law in a book until they were complete, 25 that Moses commanded the Levites who carried the ark of the covenant of the LORD, saying, 26 "Take this Book of the Law and place it beside the ark of the covenant of the LORD your God, so that it may remain there as a witness against you. 27 For I know your rebellion and your stubbornness; behold, as long as I have been alive with you *until* today, you have been rebellious against the LORD; how much more, then, after my death? 28 Assemble to me all the elders of your tribes and your officers, that I may speak these words in their hearing and call the heavens and the earth as witnesses against them. 29 For I know that after my death you will behave very corruptly and turn from the way which I have commanded you; and evil will confront you in the latter days, because you will do that which is evil in the sight of the LORD, provoking Him to anger with the work of your hands."

30 Then Moses spoke in the hearing of all the assembly of Israel the words of this song, until they were complete:

The Song of Moses

32 "Listen, you heavens, and I will speak;
And let the earth hear the words of my mouth!

2 "May my teaching drip as the rain,
My speech trickle as the dew,
As droplets on the fresh grass,
And as the showers on the vegetation.

3 "For I proclaim the name of the LORD;
Ascribe greatness to our God!

4 "The Rock! His work is perfect,
For all His ways are just;
A God of faithfulness and without injustice,
Righteous and just is He.

5 "They have acted corruptly against Him,
They are not His children, *because of* their defect;
But are a perverse and crooked generation.

6 "*Is* this *what* you do to the LORD,
You foolish and unwise people?

Is He not your Father *who has* purchased
you?
He has made you and established you.
7 "Remember the days of old,
Consider the years of all generations.
Ask your father and he will inform you,
Your elders, and they will tell you.
8 "When the Most High gave the nations
their inheritance,
When He separated the sons of mankind,
He set the boundaries of the peoples
According to the number of the ¹sons of
Israel.
9 "For the LORD's portion is His people;
Jacob is the allotment of His inheritance.
10 "He found him in a desert land,
And in the howling wasteland of a
wilderness;
He encircled him, He cared for him,
He guarded him as the apple of His eye.
11 "As an eagle stirs up its nest,
And hovers over its young,
He spread His wings, He caught them,
He carried them on His pinions.
12 "The LORD alone guided him,
And there was no foreign god with him.
13 "He had him ride on the high places of the
earth,
And he ate the produce of the field;
And He had him suck honey from the
rock,
And oil from the flinty rock,
14 Curds of the herd, and milk of the flock,
With fat of lambs
And rams, the breed of Bashan, and *of*
goats,
With the best of the wheat;
And you drank wine of the blood of
grapes.
15¶ "But ¹Jeshurun became fat and kicked—
You have become fat, thick, *and*
obstinate—
Then he abandoned God who made him,
And rejected the Rock of his salvation.
16 "They made Him jealous with strange
gods;
With abominations they provoked Him to
anger.
17 "They sacrificed to demons, *who were* not
God,
To gods *whom* they have not known,
New *gods* who came lately,
Whom your fathers did not know.
18 "You forgot the Rock who fathered you,
And forgot the God who gave you birth.
19¶ "The LORD saw *this,* and spurned *them*
Because of the provocation *by* His sons
and daughters.
20 "Then He said, 'I will hide My face from
them,
I will see what their end *will be;*
For they are a perverse generation,
Sons in whom there is no faithfulness.
21 'They have made Me jealous with *what* is
not God;
They have provoked Me to anger with
their idols.
So I will make them jealous with *those*
who are not a people;

I will provoke them to anger with a
foolish nation,
22 For a fire has flared in My anger,
And it burns to the lowest part of ¹Sheol,
And devours the earth with its yield,
And sets on fire the foundations of the
mountains.
23¶ 'I will add misfortunes to them;
I will use up My arrows on them.
24 *They will be* wasted by famine, and
emaciated by plague
And a bitter epidemic;
And the teeth of beasts I will send against
them,
With the venom of crawling things of the
dust.
25 'Outside the sword will make *them*
childless,
And inside, terror—
Both young man and virgin,
The nursing child with the man of gray
hair.
26 'I would have said, "I will wipe them out,
I will remove the mention of their name
from humanity,"
27 Had I not feared the provocation by the
enemy,
That their adversaries would misjudge,
That they would say, "Our hand is
triumphant,
And the LORD has not performed all
this." '
28¶ "For they are a nation destitute of counsel,
And there is no understanding in them.
29 "If only they were wise *and* they
understood this;
If only they would discern their future!
30 "How could one chase a thousand,
And two put ten thousand to flight,
Unless their Rock had sold them,
And the LORD had given them up?
31 "Indeed, their rock is not like our Rock;
Even our enemies themselves judge this.
32 "For their vine is from the vine of Sodom,
And from the fields of Gomorrah;
Their grapes are grapes of poison,
Their clusters, bitter.
33 "Their wine is the venom of serpents,
And the deadly poison of vipers.
34¶ 'Is it not stored up with Me,
Sealed up in My treasuries?
35 'Vengeance is Mine, and retribution;
In *due* time their foot will slip.
For the day of their disaster is near,
And the impending things are hurrying to
them.'
36 "For the LORD will vindicate His people,
And will have compassion on His
servants,
When He sees that *their* strength is gone,
And there is none *remaining,* bond or
free.
37 "And He will say, 'Where are their gods,
The rock in which they took refuge?
38 'Those who ate the fat of their sacrifices,
And drank the wine of their drink
offering?
Let them rise up and help you,
Let them be your protection!

39 'See now that I, I am He,
And there is no god besides Me;
It is I who put to death and give life.
I have wounded and it is I who heal,
And there is no one who can save anyone
from My hand.
40 'Indeed, I raise My hand to heaven,
And say, as I live forever,
41 If I have sharpened My flashing sword,
And My hand has taken hold of justice,
I will return vengeance on My
adversaries,
And I will repay those who hate Me.
42 'I will make My arrows drunk with blood,
And My sword will devour flesh,
With the blood of the slain and the
captives,
From the long-haired leaders of the
enemy.'
43 "Rejoice, you nations, with His people;
For He will avenge the blood of His
servants,
And will return vengeance on His
adversaries,
And will atone for His land and His
people."

44 Then Moses came and spoke all the words
of this song in the hearing of the people, he,
with Joshua the son of Nun. 45 When Moses
had finished speaking all these words to all
Israel, 46 he said to them, "Take to your heart
all the words with which I am warning you
today, which you will command your sons to
follow carefully, all the words of this Law. 47 For
it is not a trivial matter for you; indeed it is
your life. And by this word you will prolong
your days in the land, which you are about to
cross the Jordan to possess."

48 Now the LORD spoke to Moses that very
same day, saying, 49 "Go up to this mountain of
the Abarim, Mount Nebo, which is in the land
of Moab opposite Jericho, and look at the land
of Canaan, which I am giving to the sons of
Israel as a possession. 50 Then you are to die
on the mountain where you ascend, and be
gathered to your people, as Aaron your brother
died on Mount Hor and was gathered to his
people, 51 because you broke faith with Me in
the midst of the sons of Israel at the waters of
Meribah-kadesh, in the wilderness of Zin,
because you did not treat Me as holy in the
midst of the sons of Israel. 52 For you will see
the land at a distance but you will not go there,
into the land which I am giving the sons of
Israel."

The Blessing by Moses

33 Now this is the blessing with which
Moses the man of God blessed the sons
of Israel before his death. 2 He said,
"The LORD came from Sinai,
And dawned on them from Seir;
He shone from Mount Paran,
And He came from the midst of myriads of
holy ones;
At His right hand there was flashing
lightning for them.
3 "Indeed, He loves the people;
All Your holy ones are in Your hand,
And they followed in Your steps;

Everyone takes of Your words.
4 "Moses issued to us the Law,
A possession for the assembly of Jacob.
5 "And He was king in Jeshurun,
When the heads of the people gathered,
The tribes of Israel together.
6¶ "May Reuben live and not die,
Nor may his people be few."
7 And this was regarding Judah; so he said:
"Hear, LORD, the voice of Judah,
And bring him to his people.
With his hands he contended for them,
And may You be a help against his
adversaries."
8 Of Levi he said,
"Let Your Thummim and Your Urim belong
to Your godly man,
Whom You tested at Massah,
With whom You contended at the waters
of Meribah;
9 Who said of his father and his mother,
'I did not consider them';
And he did not acknowledge his brothers,
Nor did he regard his own sons,
For they kept Your word,
And complied with Your covenant.
10 "They will teach Your ordinances to Jacob,
And Your Law to Israel.
They shall put incense before You,
And whole burnt offerings on Your altar.
11 "LORD, bless his strength,
And accept the work of his hands;
Smash the hips of those who rise up
against him,
And those who hate him, so that they do
not rise again."
12 Of Benjamin he said,
"May the beloved of the LORD live in
security beside Him
Who shields him all the day long,
And he lives between His shoulders."
13 Of Joseph he said,
"Blessed of the LORD be his land,
With the choice things of heaven, with
the dew,
And from the deep waters lying beneath,
14 And with the choice yield of the sun,
And the choice produce of the months;
15 And with the best things of the ancient
mountains,
With the choice things of the everlasting
hills,
16 And with the choice things of the earth
and its fullness,
And the favor of Him who dwelt in the
bush.
Let it come to the head of Joseph,
And to the top of the head of the one who
was prince among his brothers.
17 "As the firstborn of his ox, majesty is his,
And his horns are the horns of the wild
ox;
With them he will gore the peoples
All at once, to the ends of the earth.
And those are the ten thousands of
Ephraim,
And those are the thousands of
Manasseh."
18 Of Zebulun he said,
"Rejoice, Zebulun, in your going out,

And, Issachar, in your tents.

19 "They will call peoples *to* the mountain;
There they will offer righteous sacrifices;
For they will draw out the abundance of
the seas,
And the hidden treasures of the sand."

20 Of Gad he said,
"Blessed is the one who enlarges Gad;
He lies down as a lion,
And tears the arm, also the crown of the
head.

21 "Then he selected the choicest *part* for
himself,
For there the ruler's portion was reserved;
And he came *with* the leaders of the
people;
He executed the justice of the LORD,
And His ordinances with Israel."

22 Of Dan he said,
"Dan is a lion's cub;
He leaps out from Bashan."

23 Of Naphtali he said,
"Naphtali, satisfied with favor,
And full of the blessing of the LORD,
Take possession of the sea and the south."

24 Of Asher he said,
"More blessed than sons is Asher;
May he be favored by his brothers,
And may he dip his foot in olive oil.

25 "Your bars will be iron and bronze,
And as your days, *so will* your strength *be.*

26 ¶ "There is no one like the God of 'Jeshurun,
Who rides the heavens to your help,
And the clouds in His majesty.

27 "The eternal God is a hiding place,
And underneath are the everlasting arms;
And He drove out the enemy from you,
And said, 'Destroy!'

28 "So Israel lives in security,
The fountain of Jacob secluded,
In a land of grain and new wine;
His heavens also drip down dew.

29 "Blessed are you, Israel;
Who is like you, a people saved by the
LORD,

The shield of your help,
And He who is the sword of your
majesty!
So your enemies will cringe before you,
And you will trample on their high
places."

The Death of Moses

34 Now Moses went up from the plains of
Moab to Mount Nebo, to the top of
Pisgah, which is opposite Jericho. And the
LORD showed him all the land, Gilead as far as
Dan, 2 and all Naphtali and the land of Ephraim
and Manasseh, and all the land of Judah as far
as the 'western sea, 3 and the Negev and the
territory in the Valley of Jericho, the city of
palm trees, as far as Zoar. 4 Then the LORD said
to him, "This is the land which I swore to
Abraham, Isaac, and Jacob, saying, 'I will give
it to your descendants'; I have let you see *it*
with your eyes, but you will not go over
there." 5 So Moses the servant of the LORD died
there in the land of Moab, in accordance with
the word of the LORD. 6 And He buried him in
the valley in the land of Moab, opposite Beth-
peor; but no one knows his burial place to this
day. 7 Although Moses was 120 years old when
he died, his eyesight was not dim, nor *had* his
vigor left *him.* 8 So the sons of Israel wept for
Moses in the plains of Moab for thirty days;
then the days of weeping *and* mourning for
Moses came to an end.

9 Now Joshua the son of Nun was filled with
the spirit of wisdom, because Moses had laid
his hands on him; and the sons of Israel
listened to him and did as the LORD had
commanded Moses. 10 Since that time no
prophet has risen in Israel like Moses, whom
the LORD knew face to face, 11 for all the signs
and wonders which the LORD sent him to
perform in the land of Egypt against Pharaoh,
all his servants, and all his land— 12 and for all
the mighty power and all the great terror
which Moses performed in the sight of all
Israel.

33:26 1 I.e., Israel   34:2 1 I.e., Mediterranean Sea

The Book of
JOSHUA

God's Orders to Joshua

1 Now it came about after the death of Moses the servant of the LORD, that the LORD spoke to Joshua the son of Nun, Moses' servant, saying, **2** "Moses My servant is dead; so now arise, cross this Jordan, you and all this people, to the land which I am giving to them, to the sons of Israel. **3** Every place on which the sole of your foot steps, I have given it to you, just as I spoke to Moses. **4** From the wilderness and this Lebanon, even as far as the great river, the river Euphrates, all the land of the Hittites, and as far as the Great Sea toward the setting of the sun will be your territory. **5** No one will *be able to* oppose you all the days of your life. Just as I have been with Moses, I will be with you; I will not desert you nor abandon you. **6** Be strong and courageous, for you shall give this people possession of the land which I swore to their fathers to give them. **7** Only be strong and very courageous; be careful to do according to all the Law which Moses My servant commanded you; do not turn from it to the right or to the left, so that you may achieve success wherever you go. **8** This Book of the Law shall not depart from your mouth, but you shall meditate on it day and night, so that you may be careful to do according to all that is written in it; for then you will make your way prosperous, and then you will achieve success. **9** Have I not commanded you? Be strong and courageous! Do not be terrified nor dismayed, for the LORD your God is with you wherever you go."

Joshua Assumes Command

10 Then Joshua commanded the officers of the people, saying, **11** "Pass through the midst of the camp and command the people, saying, 'Prepare provisions for yourselves, for within three days you are going to cross this Jordan, to go in to take possession of the land which the LORD your God is giving you, to possess it.'" **12** But to the Reubenites, to the Gadites, and to the half-tribe of Manasseh, Joshua said, **13** "Remember the word which Moses the servant of the LORD commanded you, saying, 'The LORD your God is giving you rest, and will give you this land.' **14** Your wives, your little ones, and your livestock shall remain in the land which Moses gave you beyond the Jordan, but you shall cross ahead of your brothers in battle formation, all your valiant warriors, and shall help them, **15** until the LORD gives your brothers rest, as *He is giving* you, and they also possess the land which the LORD your God is giving them. Then you may return to your own land, and take possession of that which Moses the servant of the LORD gave you beyond the Jordan toward the sunrise." **16** They answered Joshua, saying, "All that you have commanded us we will do, and wherever you send us we will go. **17** Just as we obeyed Moses in all things, so we will obey you; only may the LORD your God be with you as He was with Moses. **18** Anyone who rebels against your command and does not obey your words in all that you command him, shall be put to death; only be strong and courageous."

Rahab Shelters Spies

2 Then Joshua the son of Nun sent two men as spies secretly from Shittim, saying, "Go, view the land, especially Jericho." So they went and entered the house of a prostitute whose name was Rahab, and rested there. **2** But it was told to the king of Jericho, saying, "Behold, men from the sons of Israel have come here tonight to spy out the land." **3** And the king of Jericho sent *word* to Rahab, saying, "Bring out the men who have come to you, who have entered your house, for they have come to spy out all the land." **4** But the woman had taken the two men and hidden them, and she said, "Yes, the men came to me, but I did not know where they were from. **5** It came about, when *it was time* to shut the gate at dark, that the men went out; I do not know where the men went. Pursue them quickly, for you will overtake them." **6** But she had brought them up to the roof and hidden them in the stalks of flax which she had laid in order on the roof. **7** So the men pursued them on the road to the Jordan, to the crossing places; and as soon as those who were pursuing them had gone out, they shut the gate.

8 Now before the spies lay down, she came up to them on the roof, **9** and said to the men, "I know that the LORD has given you the land, and that the terror of you has fallen on us, and that all the inhabitants of the land have despaired because of you. **10** For we have heard how the LORD dried up the water of the Red Sea before you when you came out of Egypt, and what you did to the two kings of the Amorites who were beyond the Jordan, to Sihon and Og, whom you utterly destroyed. **11** When we heard *these reports,* our hearts melted and no courage remained in anyone any longer because of you; for the LORD your God, He is God in heaven above and on earth below. **12** Now then, please swear to me by the LORD, since I have dealt kindly with you, that you also will deal kindly with my father's household, and give me a pledge of truth, **13** and spare my father and my mother, and my brothers and my sisters, and all who belong to them, and save our lives from death." **14** So the men said to her, "Our life for yours if you do not tell this business of ours; and it shall come about when the LORD gives us the land that we will deal kindly and faithfully with you."

The Promise to Rahab

15 Then she let them down by a rope through the window, for her house was on the

city wall, so that she was living on the wall. ¹⁶ And she said to them, "Go to the hill country, so that the pursuers will not encounter you, and hide yourselves there for three days until the pursuers return. Then afterward you may go on your way." ¹⁷ And the men said to her, "We *shall be* exempt from this oath to you which you have made us swear, ¹⁸ unless, when we come into the land, you tie this cord of scarlet thread in the window through which you let us down, and gather into your house your father, your mother, your brothers, and all your father's household. ¹⁹ And it shall come about that anyone who goes out of the doors of your house outside *will have* his blood on his own head, and we *will be* innocent; but anyone who is with you in the house, his blood *will be* on our head if a hand is *laid* on him. ²⁰ But if you tell this business of ours, then we shall be exempt from the oath which you have made us swear." ²¹ She then said, "According to your words, so be it." So she sent them away, and they departed; and she tied the scarlet cord in the window.

²² So they departed and came to the hill country, and remained there for three days, until the pursuers returned. Now the pursuers had searched for *them* all along the road, but had not found *them*. ²³ Then the two men returned and came down from the hill country, and they crossed over and came to Joshua the son of Nun. Then they reported to him all that had happened to them. ²⁴ And they said to Joshua, "The LORD has indeed handed over to us all the land; furthermore, all the inhabitants of the land have despaired because of us."

Israel Crosses the Jordan

3 Then Joshua got up early in the morning; and he and all the sons of Israel set out from Shittim and came to the Jordan, and they spent the night there before they crossed. ² Then at the end of three days the officers went through the midst of the camp; ³ and they commanded the people, saying, "When you see the ark of the covenant of the LORD your God with the Levitical priests carrying it, then you shall set out from your place and go after it. ⁴ However, there shall be a distance between you and it of about two thousand cubits by measurement. Do not come near it, so that you may know the way by which you shall go, for you have not passed this way before."

⁵ Then Joshua said to the people, "Consecrate yourselves, for tomorrow the LORD will do miracles among you." ⁶ And Joshua spoke to the priests, saying, "Take up the ark of the covenant and cross over ahead of the people." So they took up the ark of the covenant and went ahead of the people.

⁷ Now the LORD said to Joshua, "This day I will begin to exalt you in the sight of all Israel, so that they will know that just as I have been with Moses, I will be with you. ⁸ So you shall command the priests who are carrying the ark of the covenant, saying, 'When you come to the edge of the waters of the Jordan, you shall stand *still* in the Jordan.'" ⁹ Then Joshua said to the sons of Israel, "Come here, and hear the words of the LORD your God." ¹⁰ And Joshua

said, "By this you will know that the living God is among you, and that He will assuredly drive out from you the Canaanite, the Hittite, the Hivite, the Perizzite, the Girgashite, the Amorite, and the Jebusite. ¹¹ Behold, the ark of the covenant of the Lord of all the earth is crossing over ahead of you into the Jordan. ¹² Now then, take for yourselves twelve men from the tribes of Israel, one man for each tribe. ¹³ And it will come about when the soles of the feet of the priests who carry the ark of the LORD, the Lord of all the earth, rest in the waters of the Jordan, the waters of the Jordan will be cut off, *that is,* the waters which are flowing down from above; and they will stand in one heap."

¹⁴ So when the people set out from their tents to cross the Jordan, with the priests carrying the ark of the covenant before the people, ¹⁵ and when those who were carrying the ark came up to the Jordan and the feet of the priests carrying the ark stepped down into the edge of the water (for the Jordan overflows all its banks all the days of harvest), ¹⁶ then the waters which were flowing down from above stood *and* rose up in one heap, a great distance away at Adam, the city that is beside Zarethan; and those which were flowing down toward the sea of the Arabah, the Salt Sea, were completely cut off. So the people crossed opposite Jericho. ¹⁷ And the priests who carried the ark of the covenant of the LORD stood firm on dry ground in the middle of the Jordan while all Israel crossed on dry ground, until all the nation had finished crossing the Jordan.

Memorial Stones from the Jordan

4 Now when the entire nation had finished crossing the Jordan, the LORD spoke to Joshua, saying, ² "Take for yourselves twelve men from the people, one man from each tribe, ³ and command them, saying, 'Take up for yourselves twelve stones from here out of the middle of the Jordan, from the place where the priests' feet are standing firmly, and carry them over with you and lay them down in the encampment where you will spend the night.'" ⁴ So Joshua called the twelve men whom he had appointed from the sons of Israel, one man from each tribe; ⁵ and Joshua said to them, "Cross again to the ark of the LORD your God into the middle of the Jordan, and each of you take up a stone on his shoulder, according to the number of the tribes of the sons of Israel. ⁶ This shall be a sign among you; when your children ask later, saying, 'What do these stones mean to you?' ⁷ then you shall say to them, 'That the waters of the Jordan were cut off before the ark of the covenant of the LORD; when it crossed the Jordan, the waters of the Jordan were cut off.' So these stones shall become a memorial to the sons of Israel forever."

⁸ So the sons of Israel did exactly as Joshua commanded, and took up twelve stones from the middle of the Jordan, just as the LORD spoke to Joshua, according to the number of the tribes of the sons of Israel; and they carried them over with them to the encampment and put them down there. ⁹ Then Joshua set up

twelve stones in the middle of the Jordan at the place where the feet of the priests who carried the ark of the covenant were standing, and they are there to this day. 10 For the priests who carried the ark were standing in the middle of the Jordan until everything was completed that the LORD had commanded Joshua to speak to the people, according to all that Moses had commanded Joshua. And the people hurried and crossed; 11 and when all the people had finished crossing, *then* the ark of the LORD and the priests crossed in front of the people. 12 The sons of Reuben, the sons of Gad, and the half-tribe of Manasseh crossed over in battle formation before the sons of Israel, just as Moses had spoken to them; 13 about forty thousand equipped for war, crossed for battle before the LORD to the desert plains of Jericho.

14 On that day the LORD exalted Joshua in the sight of all Israel, so that they revered him, just as they had revered Moses all the days of his life.

15 Now the LORD said to Joshua, 16 "Command the priests who carry the ark of the testimony that they come up from the Jordan." 17 So Joshua commanded the priests, saying, "Come up from the Jordan." 18 It came about when the priests who carried the ark of the covenant of the LORD had come up from the middle of the Jordan, and the soles of the priests' feet were lifted up to the dry ground, that the waters of the Jordan returned to their place, and went over all its banks as before.

19 Now the people came up from the Jordan on the tenth of the first month and camped at Gilgal, on the eastern edge of Jericho. 20 As for those twelve stones which they had taken from the Jordan, Joshua set *them* up at Gilgal. 21 And he said to the sons of Israel, "When your children ask their fathers in time to come, saying, 'What are these stones?' 22 then you shall inform your children, saying, 'Israel crossed this Jordan on dry ground.' 23 For the LORD your God dried up the waters of the Jordan before you until you had crossed, just as the LORD your God had done to the Red Sea, which He dried up before us until we had crossed; 24 so that all the peoples of the earth may know that the hand of the LORD is mighty, so that you may fear the LORD your God forever."

Israel Is Circumcised

5 Now it came about when all the kings of the Amorites who *were* beyond the Jordan to the west, and all the kings of the Canaanites who *were* by the sea, heard how the LORD had dried up the waters of the Jordan before the sons of Israel until they had crossed, that their hearts melted, and there was no spirit in them any longer because of the sons of Israel.

2 At that time the LORD said to Joshua, "Make for yourself flint knives and circumcise again the sons of Israel the second time." 3 So Joshua made himself flint knives and circumcised the sons of Israel at 1Gibeath-haaraloth. 4 This is the reason why Joshua circumcised them: all the people who came out of Egypt who were males, all the men of war, died in the wilderness along the way after they

came out of Egypt. 5 For all the people who came out were circumcised, but all the people who were born in the wilderness along the way as they came out of Egypt had not been circumcised. 6 For the sons of Israel walked forty years in the wilderness, until all the nation, *that is,* the men of war who came out of Egypt, perished because they did not listen to the voice of the LORD, to whom the LORD had sworn that He would not let them see the land which the LORD had sworn to their fathers to give us, a land flowing with milk and honey. 7 So their children whom He raised up in their place, Joshua circumcised; for they were uncircumcised, because they had not circumcised them along the way.

8 Now when they had finished circumcising all the nation, they remained in their places in the camp until they recovered. 9 Then the LORD said to Joshua, "Today I have rolled away the shame of Egypt from you." So the name of that place is called 1Gilgal to this day.

10 While the sons of Israel camped at Gilgal they celebrated the Passover on the evening of the fourteenth day of the month on the desert plains of Jericho. 11 Then on the day after the Passover, on that very day, they ate some of the produce of the land, unleavened cakes and roasted *grain.* 12 And the manna ceased on the day after they had eaten some of the produce of the land, so that the sons of Israel no longer had manna, but they ate some of the yield of the land of Canaan during that year.

13 Now it came about when Joshua was by Jericho, he raised his eyes and looked, and behold, a man was standing opposite him with his sword drawn in his hand, and Joshua went to him and said to him, "Are you for us or for our enemies?" 14 He said, "No; rather I have come now *as* captain of the army of the LORD." And Joshua fell on his face to the ground, and bowed down, and said to him, "What has my lord to say to his servant?" 15 And the captain of the LORD's army said to Joshua, "Remove your sandals from your feet, for the place where you are standing is holy." And Joshua did so.

The Conquest of Jericho

6 Now Jericho was tightly shut because of the sons of Israel; no one went out and no one came in. 2 But the LORD said to Joshua, "See, I have handed Jericho over to you, with its king *and* the valiant warriors. 3 And you shall march around the city, all the men of war circling the city once. You shall do so for six days. 4 Also seven priests shall carry seven trumpets of rams' horns in front of the ark; then on the seventh day you shall march around the city seven times, and the priests shall blow the trumpets. 5 It shall be that when they make a long blast with the ram's horn, and when you hear the sound of the trumpet, all the people shall shout with a great shout; and the wall of the city will fall down flat, and the people shall go up, everyone straight ahead."

6 So Joshua the son of Nun called the priests and said to them, "Take up the ark of the covenant, and have seven priests carry seven trumpets of rams' horns in front of the ark of

---

5:3 1 I.e., the hill of the foreskins   5:9 1 I.e., wheel, or stone circle

the LORD." 7 Then he said to the people, "Go forward and march around the city, and the armed men shall go on ahead of the ark of the LORD." 8 And it was *so,* that when Joshua had spoken to the people, the seven priests carrying the seven trumpets of rams' horns before the LORD went forward and blew the trumpets; and the ark of the covenant of the LORD followed them. 9 And the armed men went ahead of the priests who blew the trumpets, and the rear guard came after the ark, while they continued to blow the trumpets. 10 But Joshua commanded the people, saying, "You shall not shout nor let your voice be heard, nor let a word proceed from your mouth, until the day I tell you, 'Shout!' Then you shall shout!" 11 So he had the ark of the LORD taken around the city, circling *it* once; then they came into the camp and spent the night in the camp.

12 Now Joshua got up early in the morning, and the priests took up the ark of the LORD. 13 Then the seven priests carrying the seven trumpets of rams' horns in front of the ark of the LORD went on continually, and blew the trumpets; and the armed men went ahead of them, and the rear guard came after the ark of the LORD, while they continued to blow the trumpets. 14 So the second day they marched around the city once and returned to the camp; they did the same for six days.

15 Then on the seventh day they got up early at the dawning of the day and marched around the city in the same way seven times; only on that day did they march around the city seven times. 16 And at the seventh time, when the priests blew the trumpets, Joshua said to the people, "Shout! For the LORD has given you the city. 17 But the city shall be designated for ⁱdestruction, it and everything that is in it belongs to the LORD; only Rahab the prostitute and all who are with her in the house shall live, because she hid the messengers whom we sent. 18 But as for you, only keep yourselves from the things designated for destruction, so that you do not covet *them* and take some of the designated things, and turn the camp of Israel into something designated for destruction and bring disaster on it. 19 But all the silver and gold, and articles of bronze and iron are holy to the LORD; they shall go into the treasury of the LORD." 20 So the people shouted, and the priests blew the trumpets; and when the people heard the sound of the trumpet, the people shouted with a great shout, and the wall fell down flat, so that the people went up into the city, everyone straight ahead, and they took the city. 21 They utterly destroyed everything in the city, both man and woman, young and old, and ox, sheep, and donkey, with the edge of the sword.

22 And Joshua said to the two men who had spied out the land, "Go into the prostitute's house and bring the woman and all she has out of there, just as you have sworn to her." 23 So the young men who were spies went in and brought out Rahab, her father, her mother, her brothers, and all she had; they also brought out all her relatives, and placed them outside the camp of Israel. 24 Then they burned the city with fire, and all that was in it. Only the silver and gold, and the articles of bronze and iron, they put into the treasury of the ⁱhouse of the LORD. 25 However, Rahab the prostitute and her father's household and all she had, Joshua spared; and she has lived in the midst of Israel to this day, because she hid the messengers whom Joshua sent to spy out Jericho.

26 Then Joshua made them take an oath at that time, saying, "Cursed before the LORD is the man who rises up and builds this city Jericho; with *the loss of* his firstborn he will lay its foundation, and with *the loss of* his youngest son he will set up its gates." 27 So the LORD was with Joshua, and his fame was in all the land.

Israel Is Defeated at Ai

7 But the sons of Israel acted unfaithfully regarding the things designated for destruction, for Achan, the son of Carmi, the son of Zabdi, the son of Zerah, from the tribe of Judah, took some of the designated things; therefore the anger of the LORD burned against the sons of Israel.

2 Now Joshua sent men from Jericho to Ai, which is near Beth-aven, east of Bethel, and said to them, "Go up and spy out the land." So the men went up and spied out Ai. 3 Then they returned to Joshua and said to him, "Do not have all the people go up; have *only* about two or three thousand men go up and attack Ai; do not trouble all the people there, for they are few." 4 So about three thousand men from the people went up there, but they fled from the men of Ai. 5 And the men of Ai struck and killed about thirty-six of their men, and pursued them from the gate as far as Shebarim and struck them on the mountainside; and the hearts of the people melted and became like water.

6 Then Joshua tore his clothes and fell to the ground on his face before the ark of the LORD until the evening, *both* he and the elders of Israel; and they put dust on their heads. 7 And Joshua said, "Oh, Lord GOD! Why did You ever bring this people across the Jordan, *only* to hand us over to the Amorites, to eliminate us? If only we had been willing to live beyond the Jordan! 8 O Lord, what can I say since Israel has turned *their* back before their enemies? 9 For the Canaanites and all the inhabitants of the land will hear about it, and they will surround us and eliminate our name from the earth. And what will You do for Your great name?"

10 So the LORD said to Joshua, "Stand up! Why is it that you have fallen on your face? 11 Israel has sinned, and they have also violated My covenant which I commanded them. And they have even taken some of the things designated for destruction, and have both stolen and kept *it* a secret. Furthermore, they have also put *them* among their own things. 12 Therefore the sons of Israel cannot stand against their enemies; they turn *their* backs before their enemies, because they have become designated for destruction. I will not

be with you anymore unless you eliminate from your midst the things designated for destruction. 13 Stand up! Consecrate the people and say, 'Consecrate yourselves for tomorrow, because the LORD, the God of Israel, has said this: "There are things designated for destruction in your midst, Israel. You cannot stand against your enemies until you have removed the designated things from your midst." 14 So in the morning you shall come forward by your tribes. And it shall be that the tribe which the LORD selects by lot shall come forward by families, and the family which the LORD selects shall come forward by households, and the household which the LORD selects shall come forward man by man. 15 And it shall be that the one who is selected with the things designated for destruction shall be burned with fire, he and all that belongs to him, because he has violated the covenant of the LORD, and because he has committed a disgraceful thing in Israel.' "

The Sin of Achan

16 So Joshua got up early in the morning and brought Israel forward by tribes, and the tribe of Judah was selected. 17 So he brought the family of Judah forward, and he selected the family of the Zerahites; then he brought the family of the Zerahites forward man by man, and Zabdi was selected. 18 And he brought his household forward man by man; and Achan, son of Carmi, son of Zabdi, son of Zerah, from the tribe of Judah, was selected. 19 Then Joshua said to Achan, "My son, I implore you, give glory to the LORD, the God of Israel, and give praise to Him; and tell me now what you have done. Do not hide it from me." 20 So Achan answered Joshua and said, "Truly, I have sinned against the LORD, the God of Israel, and this is what I did: 21 when I saw among the spoils a beautiful robe from Shinar, two hundred shekels of silver, and a bar of gold fifty shekels in weight, then I wanted them and took them; and behold, they are hidden in the ground inside my tent, with the silver underneath."

22 So Joshua sent messengers, and they ran to the tent; and behold, it was hidden in his tent with the silver underneath it. 23 So they took them from inside the tent and brought them to Joshua and to all the sons of Israel; and they laid them out before the LORD. 24 Then Joshua, and all Israel with him, took Achan the son of Zerah, the silver, the robe, the bar of gold, his sons, his daughters, his oxen, his donkeys, his sheep, his tent, and all that belonged to him; and they brought them up to the Valley of 1Achor. 25 And Joshua said, "Why have you brought disaster on us? The LORD will bring disaster on you this day." And all Israel stoned them with stones; and they burned them with fire after they had stoned them with stones. 26 Then they erected over him a large heap of stones that stands to this day, and the LORD turned from the fierceness of His anger. Therefore the name of that place has been called the Valley of 1Achor to this day.

The Conquest of Ai

8 Now the LORD said to Joshua, "Do not fear or be dismayed. Take all the people of war with you. Arise, go up to Ai; see, I have handed over to you the king of Ai, his people, his city, and his land. 2 You shall do to Ai and its king just as you did to Jericho and its king; you shall take only its spoils and its cattle as plunder for yourselves. Set an ambush for the city behind it."

3 So Joshua rose up with all the people of war to go up to Ai; and Joshua chose thirty thousand men, valiant warriors, and sent them out at night. 4 He commanded them, saying, "See, you are going to ambush the city from behind it. Do not go very far from the city, but all of you be ready. 5 Then I and all the people who are with me will approach the city. And when they come out to meet us as they did the first time, we will flee before them. 6 They will come out after us until we have lured them away from the city, for they will say, 'They are fleeing before us just as they did the first time.' So we will flee before them. 7 Then you shall rise from your ambush and take possession of the city, for the LORD your God will hand it over to you. 8 Then it will be when you have seized the city, that you shall set the city on fire. You shall do it in accordance with the word of the LORD. See, I have commanded you." 9 So Joshua sent them away, and they went to the place of ambush and remained between Bethel and Ai, on the west side of Ai; but Joshua spent that night among the people.

10 Now Joshua got up early in the morning and mustered the people, and he went up with the elders of Israel before the people to Ai. 11 Then all the people of war who were with him went up and approached, and arrived in front of the city; and they camped on the north side of Ai. And there was a valley between him and Ai. 12 Then he took about five thousand men and set them in ambush between Bethel and Ai, on the west side of the city. 13 So they stationed the people, all the army that was on the north side of the city, and its rear guard on the west side of the city, and Joshua spent that night in the midst of the valley. 14 And it came about, when the king of Ai saw them, that the men of the city hurried and got up early, and went out to meet Israel in battle, he and all his people at the appointed place before the desert plain. But he did not know that there was an ambush against him behind the city. 15 Then Joshua and all Israel pretended to be defeated before them, and fled by the way of the wilderness. 16 And all the people who were in the city were called together to pursue them, and they pursued Joshua and were lured away from the city. 17 So not a man was left in Ai or Bethel, but they had all gone out after Israel, and they left the city unguarded and pursued Israel.

18 Then the LORD said to Joshua, "Reach out with the sword that is in your hand toward Ai, for I will hand it over to you." So Joshua reached out with the sword that was in his hand toward the city. 19 Then the men in

ambush rose quickly from their place, and when he had reached out with his hand, they ran and entered the city and captured it, and they quickly set the city on fire. 20 When the men of Ai turned back and looked, behold, the smoke of the city ascended to the sky, and they had no place to flee this way or that, for the people who had been fleeing to the wilderness turned against the pursuers. 21 When Joshua and all Israel saw that the *men in* ambush had captured the city and that the smoke of the city ascended, they turned back and killed the men of Ai. 22 The others came out from the city to confront them, so that they were *trapped* in the midst of Israel, some on this side and some on that side; and they killed them until there was not one left who escaped or survived. 23 But they captured the king of Ai alive and brought him to Joshua.

24 Now when Israel had finished killing all the inhabitants of Ai in the field in the wilderness where they pursued them, and all of them had fallen by the edge of the sword until they were destroyed, then all Israel returned to Ai and struck it with the edge of the sword. 25 So all who fell that day, both men and women, were twelve thousand—all the people of Ai. 26 For Joshua did not withdraw his hand with which he reached out with the sword until he had utterly destroyed all the inhabitants of Ai. 27 Israel took only the cattle and the spoils of that city as plunder for themselves, in accordance with the word of the LORD which He had commanded Joshua. 28 So Joshua burned Ai and made it a refuse heap forever, a desolation until this day. 29 And he hanged the king of Ai on ¹a tree until evening; but at sunset Joshua gave the command and they took his body down from ²the tree and threw it at the entrance of the city gate, and erected over it a large heap of stones *that stands* to this day.

30 Then Joshua built an altar to the LORD, the God of Israel, on Mount Ebal, 31 just as Moses the servant of the LORD had commanded the sons of Israel, as it is written in the Book of the Law of Moses, an altar of uncut stones on which no one had wielded an iron *tool;* and they offered burnt offerings on it to the LORD, and sacrificed peace offerings. 32 And he wrote there on the stones a copy of the Law of Moses, which ¹he had written, in the presence of the sons of Israel. 33 And all Israel with their elders, officers, and their judges were standing on both sides of the ark before the Levitical priests who carried the ark of the covenant of the LORD, the stranger as well as the native. Half of them *stood* in front of Mount Gerizim, and half of them in front of Mount Ebal, just as Moses the servant of the LORD had commanded at first to bless the people of Israel. 34 Then afterward he read all the words of the Law, the blessing and the curse, according to everything that is written in the Book of the Law. 35 There was not a word of all that Moses had commanded which Joshua did not read before all the assembly of Israel with the women, the little ones, and the strangers who were living among them.

Deception by the Gibeonites

9 Now it came about when all the kings who were beyond the Jordan, in the hill country, the lowland, and on all the coast of the Great Sea toward Lebanon, the Hittite and the Amorite, the Canaanite, the Perizzite, the Hivite, and the Jebusite, heard about it, 2 that they met together with one purpose, to fight with Joshua and with Israel.

3 The inhabitants of Gibeon also heard what Joshua had done to Jericho and to Ai, 4 but they on their part acted craftily and went and took provisions for a journey, and took worn-out sacks on their donkeys, and wineskins *that were* worn out, split open, and patched, 5 and worn-out and patched sandals on their feet, and worn-out clothes on themselves; and all the bread of their provision was dry *and* had become crumbled. 6 And they went to Joshua at the camp at Gilgal and said to him and to the men of Israel, "We have come from a far country; now then, make a covenant with us." 7 But the men of Israel said to the Hivites, "Perhaps you are living within our land; how then are we to make a covenant with you?" 8 So they said to Joshua, "We are your servants." Then Joshua said to them, "Who are you and where do you come from?" 9 They said to him, "Your servants have come from a very distant country because of the fame of the LORD your God; for we have heard the report about Him and all that He did in Egypt, 10 and all that He did to the two kings of the Amorites who were beyond the Jordan, to Sihon king of Heshbon and to Og king of Bashan who was in Ashtaroth. 11 So our elders and all the inhabitants of our country spoke to us, saying, 'Take provisions in your hand for the journey, and go to meet them, and say to them, "We are your servants; now then, make a covenant with us." ' 12 This bread of ours *was* hot *when* we took it for our provisions from our houses on the day that we left to come to you; but now behold, it is dry and has become crumbled. 13 And these wineskins which we filled were new, and behold, they are split open; and these clothes of ours and our sandals are worn out from the very long journey." 14 So the men *of Israel* took some of their provisions, and did not ask for the counsel of the LORD. 15 And Joshua made peace with them and made a covenant with them, to let them live; and the leaders of the congregation swore *an oath* to them.

16 However, it came about at the end of three days after they had made a covenant with them, that they heard that they were neighbors and that they were living within their land. 17 Then the sons of Israel set out and came to their cities on the third day. Now their cities *were* Gibeon, Chephirah, Beeroth, and Kiriath-jearim. 18 But the sons of Israel did not attack them because the leaders of the congregation had sworn to them by the LORD, the God of Israel. And the whole congregation grumbled against the leaders. 19 But all the leaders said to the whole congregation, "We have sworn to them by the LORD, the God of Israel, and now we cannot touch them. 20 This we will do to them, even let them live, so that wrath will not

---

8:29 ¹Lit *the wood*   ²Lit *the wood*   8:32 ¹I.e., Moses

be on us because of the oath which we swore to them." 21 So the leaders said to them, "Let them live." And they became gatherers of firewood and labor to draw water for the whole congregation, just as the leaders had spoken to them.

22 Then Joshua called for them and spoke to them, saying, "Why have you deceived us, saying, 'We are very far from you,' when you are living within our land? 23 Now therefore, you are cursed, and you will never cease to be slaves, both gatherers of firewood and labor to draw water for the house of my God." 24 So they answered Joshua and said, "Since your servants were fully informed that the LORD your God had commanded His servant Moses to give you all the land, and to destroy all the inhabitants of the land before you, we feared greatly for our lives because of you, and did this thing. 25 And now behold, we are in your hands; do to us as it seems good and right in your sight to do." 26 This he did to them, and saved them from the hands of the sons of Israel, and they did not kill them. 27 But on that day Joshua made them gatherers of firewood and labor to draw water for the congregation and for the altar of the LORD, to this day, in the place which He would choose.

Five Kings Attack Gibeon

10 Now it came about when Adoni-zedek king of Jerusalem heard that Joshua had captured Ai, and had utterly destroyed it (just as he had done to Jericho and its king, so he had done to Ai and its king), and that the inhabitants of Gibeon had made peace with Israel and were within their land, 2 that he feared greatly because Gibeon *was* a great city, like one of the royal cities, and because it was greater than Ai, and all its men *were* mighty. 3 Therefore Adoni-zedek king of Jerusalem sent *word* to Hoham king of Hebron, to Piram king of Jarmuth, to Japhia king of Lachish, and to Debir king of Eglon, saying, 4 "Come up to me and help me, and let's attack Gibeon, for it has made peace with Joshua and with the sons of Israel." 5 So the five kings of the Amorites, the king of Jerusalem, the king of Hebron, the king of Jarmuth, the king of Lachish, *and* the king of Eglon, gathered together and went up, they with all their armies, and camped by Gibeon and fought against it.

6 Then the men of Gibeon sent *word* to Joshua at the camp at Gilgal, saying, "Do not abandon your servants; come up to us quickly and save us and help us, for all the kings of the Amorites that live in the hill country have assembled against us." 7 So Joshua went up from Gilgal, he and all the people of war with him, and all the valiant warriors. 8 And the LORD said to Joshua, "Do not fear them, for I have handed them over to you; not one of them will stand against you." 9 So Joshua came upon them suddenly by marching all night from Gilgal. 10 And the LORD brought them into confusion before Israel, and He struck them down in a great defeat at Gibeon, and pursued them by the way of the ascent to Beth-horon and struck them as far as Azekah and

Makkedah. 11 And as they fled from Israel, *while* they were at the descent of Beth-horon, the LORD hurled large stones from heaven on them as far as Azekah, and they died; *there were* more who died from the hailstones than those whom the sons of Israel killed with the sword.

12 Then Joshua spoke to the LORD on the day when the LORD turned the Amorites over to the sons of Israel, and he said in the sight of Israel,

"Sun, stand still at Gibeon,
   And moon, at the Valley of Aijalon!"
13   So the sun stood still, and the moon
      stopped,
   Until the nation avenged themselves of
      their enemies.

Is it not written in the Book of Jashar? And the sun stopped in the middle of the sky and did not hurry to go *down* for about a whole day. 14 There was no day like that before it or after it, when the LORD listened to the voice of a man; for the LORD fought for Israel.

15 Then Joshua and all Israel with him returned to the camp at Gilgal.

Victory at Makkedah

16 Now these five kings had fled and hidden themselves in the cave at Makkedah. 17 And it was told to Joshua, saying, "The five kings have been found hidden in the cave at Makkedah." 18 So Joshua said, "Roll large stones against the mouth of the cave, and post men by it to guard them, 19 but do not stay *there* yourselves; pursue your enemies and attack them from behind. Do not allow them to enter their cities, for the LORD your God has handed them over to you." 20 It came about when Joshua and the sons of Israel had finished striking them down in a very great defeat, until they were destroyed, and the survivors of them *who* escaped had entered the fortified cities, 21 that all the people returned to the camp, to Joshua at Makkedah in peace. No one uttered a word against any of the sons of Israel.

22 Then Joshua said, "Open the mouth of the cave and bring these five kings out to me from the cave." 23 They did so, and brought these five kings out to him from the cave: the king of Jerusalem, the king of Hebron, the king of Jarmuth, the king of Lachish, *and* the king of Eglon. 24 When they brought these kings out to Joshua, Joshua called for all the men of Israel, and said to the leaders of the men of war who had gone with him, "Come forward, put your feet on the necks of these kings." So they came forward and put their feet on their necks. 25 Joshua then said to them, "Do not fear or be dismayed! Be strong and courageous, for the LORD will do this to all your enemies with whom you fight." 26 So afterward Joshua struck them and put them to death, and he hanged them on five ¹trees; and they were hung on the ²trees until evening. 27 Then it came about at sunset that Joshua gave the command, and they took them down from the ¹trees and threw them into the cave where they had hidden themselves, and put large stones over the mouth of the cave, to this very day.

10:26 ¹Or *wooden* posts   2 Or *wooden* posts   10:27 ¹Or *wooden* posts

28 Now Joshua captured Makkedah on that day, and struck it and its king with the edge of the sword; he utterly destroyed it and every 'person who was in it. He left no survivor. So he did to the king of Makkedah just as he had done to the king of Jericho.

Joshua's Conquest of Southern Canaan

29 Then Joshua and all Israel with him passed on from Makkedah to Libnah, and fought against Libnah. 30 And the LORD also handed it over to Israel, with its king, and he struck it and every person who was in it with the edge of the sword. He left no survivor in it. So he did to its king just as he had done to the king of Jericho.

31 And Joshua and all Israel with him passed on from Libnah to Lachish, and they camped by it and fought against it. 32 And the LORD handed Lachish over to Israel; and he captured it on the second day, and struck it and every person who was in it with the edge of the sword, according to all that he had done to Libnah.

33 Then Horam king of Gezer came up to help Lachish, and Joshua defeated him and his people until he had left him no survivor.

34 And Joshua and all Israel with him passed on from Lachish to Eglon, and they camped by it and fought against it. 35 They captured it on that day and struck it with the edge of the sword; and he utterly destroyed on that day every person who was in it, according to all that he had done to Lachish.

36 Then Joshua and all Israel with him went up from Eglon to Hebron, and they fought against it. 37 And they captured it and struck it and its king and all its cities and all the persons who were in it with the edge of the sword. He left no survivor, according to all that he had done to Eglon. And he utterly destroyed it and every person who was in it.

38 Then Joshua and all Israel with him returned to Debir, and they fought against it. 39 He captured it and its king and all its cities, and they struck them with the edge of the sword, and utterly destroyed every person who was in it. He left no survivor. Just as he had done to Hebron, so he did to Debir and its king, as he had also done to Libnah and its king.

40 So Joshua struck all the land, the hill country and the 'Negev and the lowland and the slopes, and all their kings. He left no survivor, but he utterly destroyed all who breathed, just as the LORD, the God of Israel, had commanded. 41 Joshua struck them from Kadesh-barnea even as far as Gaza, and all the country of Goshen even as far as Gibeon. 42 Joshua captured all these kings and their lands at one time, because the LORD, the God of Israel, fought for Israel. 43 So Joshua and all Israel with him returned to the camp at Gilgal.

Northern Canaan Taken

11 Then it came about, when Jabin king of Hazor heard about it, that he sent word to Jobab king of Madon, to the king of Shimron, to the king of Achshaph, 2 and to the kings who were of the north in the hill country, and in the Arabah—south of 'Chinneroth and in the lowland, and on the heights of Dor on the west— 3 to the Canaanite on the east and on the west, and the Amorite, the Hittite, the Perizzite, and the Jebusite in the hill country, and the Hivite at the foot of Hermon in the land of Mizpeh. 4 Then they came out, they and all their armies with them, as many people as the sand that is on the seashore, with very many horses and chariots. 5 So all of these kings gathered together, and came and encamped together at the waters of Merom, to fight against Israel.

6 Yet the LORD said to Joshua, "Do not be afraid because of them, for tomorrow at this time I am going to turn all of them over to Israel as good as dead; you shall hamstring their horses and burn their chariots with fire." 7 So Joshua and all the people of war with him came upon them suddenly at the waters of Merom, and attacked them. 8 And the LORD handed them over to Israel, so that they defeated them, and pursued them as far as Great Sidon, and Misrephoth-maim, and the Valley of Mizpeh to the east; and they struck them until no survivor was left to them. 9 And Joshua did to them just as the LORD had told him; he hamstrung their horses and burned their chariots with fire.

10 Then Joshua turned back at that time and captured Hazor, and struck its king with the sword; for Hazor previously was the head of all these kingdoms. 11 They struck every person who was in it with the edge of the sword, utterly destroying them; there was no one left who breathed. And he burned Hazor with fire. 12 Joshua captured all the cities of these kings, and all their kings; and he struck them with the edge of the sword and utterly destroyed them, just as Moses the servant of the LORD had commanded. 13 However, Israel did not burn any cities that stood on their mounds, except Hazor alone, which Joshua burned. 14 And all the spoils of these cities and the cattle, the sons of Israel took as their plunder; but they struck every person with the edge of the sword, until they had destroyed them. They left no one breathing. 15 Just as the LORD had commanded His servant Moses, so Moses commanded Joshua, and so Joshua did; he left nothing undone of all that the LORD had commanded Moses.

16 So Joshua took all that land: the hill country and all the Negev, all the land of Goshen, the lowland, the Arabah, the hill country of Israel and its lowland 17 from Mount Halak, that rises toward Seir, even as far as Baal-gad in the Valley of Lebanon at the foot of Mount Hermon. And he captured all their kings, and struck them and put them to death. 18 Joshua waged war a long time with all these kings. 19 There was not a city which made peace with the sons of Israel except the Hivites living in Gibeon; they took them all in battle. 20 For it was of the LORD to harden their hearts, to meet Israel in battle in order that he might utterly destroy them, that they might receive no

---

mercy, but that he might destroy them, just as the LORD had commanded Moses.

21 Then Joshua came at that time and eliminated the Anakim from the hill country, from Hebron, Debir, Anab, and from all the hill country of Judah and all the hill country of Israel. Joshua utterly destroyed them with their cities. 22 There were no Anakim left in the land of the sons of Israel; only in Gaza, Gath, and Ashdod *some* remained. 23 So Joshua took the whole land, in accordance with everything that the LORD had spoken to Moses; and Joshua gave it as an inheritance to Israel according to their divisions by their tribes. So the land was at rest from war.

Kings Defeated by Israel

12 Now these are the kings of the land whom the sons of Israel defeated, and they took possession of their land beyond the Jordan toward the sunrise, from the Valley of the Arnon as far as Mount Hermon, and all the Arabah to the east: 2 Sihon king of the Amorites, who lived in Heshbon *and* ruled from Aroer, which is on the edge of the Valley of the Arnon, both the middle of the valley and half of Gilead, even as far as the brook Jabbok, the border of the sons of Ammon; 3 and the Arabah as far as the Sea of 1Chinneroth toward the east, and as far as the Sea of the Arabah, *that is,* the Salt Sea, eastward toward Beth jeshimoth, and on the south, at the foot of the slopes of Pisgah; 4 and the territory of Og king of Bashan, one of the remnant of Rephaim, who lived at Ashtaroth and at Edrei, 5 and ruled over Mount Hermon, Salecah, and all Bashan, as far as the border of the Geshurites and the Maacathites, and half of Gilead, *as far as* the border of Sihon king of Heshbon. 6 Moses the servant of the LORD and the sons of Israel defeated them; and Moses the servant of the LORD gave it to the Reubenites, the Gadites, and the half-tribe of Manasseh as a possession.

7 Now these are the kings of the land whom Joshua and the sons of Israel defeated beyond the Jordan toward the west, from Baal-gad in the Valley of Lebanon even as far as Mount Halak, which rises toward Seir; and Joshua gave it to the tribes of Israel as a possession according to their divisions, 8 in the hill country, in the lowland, in the Arabah, on the slopes, in the wilderness, and in the Negev; the Hittite, the Amorite and the Canaanite, the Perizzite, the Hivite, and the Jebusite: 9 the king of Jericho, one; the king of Ai, which is beside Bethel, one; 10 the king of Jerusalem, one; the king of Hebron, one; 11 the king of Jarmuth, one; the king of Lachish, one; 12 the king of Eglon, one; the king of Gezer, one; 13 the king of Debir, one; the king of Geder, one; 14 the king of Hormah, one; the king of Arad, one; 15 the king of Libnah, one; the king of Adullam, one; 16 the king of Makkedah, one; the king of Bethel, one; 17 the king of Tappuah, one; the king of Hepher, one; 18 the king of Aphek, one; the king of Lasharon, one; 19 the king of Madon, one; the king of Hazor, one; 20 the king of Shimron-meron, one; the king of Achshaph, one; 21 the king of Taanach, one; the king of Megiddo, one; 22 the king of Kedesh, one; the king of Jokneam in Carmel, one; 23 the king of Dor in the heights of Dor, one; the king of Goiim in Gilgal, one; 24 the king of Tirzah, one: in all, thirty-one kings.

Canaan Divided among the Tribes

13 Now Joshua was old *and* advanced in years when the LORD said to him, "You are old *and* advanced in years, and a very large *amount* of the land remains to be possessed. 2 This is the land that remains: all the regions *of* the Philistines and all *those of* the Geshurites; 3 from the Shihor which is east of Egypt, even as far as the border of Ekron to the north (it is counted as Canaanite); the five lords of the Philistines: the Gazite, the Ashdodite, the Ashkelonite, the Gittite, the Ekronite; and the Avvite 4 to the south, all the land of the Canaanite, and Mearah that belongs to the Sidonians, as far as Aphek, to the border of the Amorite; 5 and the land of the Gebalite, and all of Lebanon, toward the east, from Baal-gad below Mount Hermon as far as Lebo-hamath. 6 All the inhabitants of the hill country from Lebanon as far as Misrephoth-maim, all the Sidonians, I will drive out from the sons of Israel; only allot it to Israel as an inheritance as I have commanded you. 7 Now therefore, apportion this land as an inheritance to the nine tribes and the half-tribe of Manasseh."

8 With the other half-tribe, the Reubenites and the Gadites received their inheritance which Moses gave them beyond the Jordan to the east, just as Moses the servant of the LORD gave to them; 9 from Aroer, which is on the edge of the Valley of the Arnon, with the city which is in the middle of the valley, and all the plain of Medeba, as far as Dibon; 10 and all the cities of Sihon king of the Amorites, who reigned in Heshbon, as far as the border of the sons of Ammon; 11 and Gilead, and the territory of the Geshurites and Maacathites, and all Mount Hermon, and all Bashan as far as Salecah; 12 all the kingdom of Og in Bashan, who reigned in Ashtaroth and in Edrei (he *alone* was left of the remnant of the Rephaim); for Moses struck them and drove them out. 13 But the sons of Israel did not drive out the Geshurites or the Maacathites; instead, Geshur and Maacath live among Israel to this day. 14 Only to the tribe of Levi he did not give an inheritance; the offerings by fire to the LORD, the God of Israel, are their inheritance, as He spoke to him.

15 So Moses gave *an inheritance* to the tribe of the sons of Reuben according to their families. 16 Their territory was from Aroer, which is on the edge of the Valley of the Arnon, with the city which is in the middle of the valley and all the plain by Medeba; 17 Heshbon and all its cities which are on the plain: Dibon, Bamoth-baal, Beth-baal-meon, 18 Jahaz, Kedemoth, Mephaath, 19 Kiriathaim, Sibmah, Zereth-shahar on the hill of the valley, 20 Beth-peor, the slopes of Pisgah, Beth-jeshimoth, 21 even all the cities of the plain, and all the kingdom of Sihon king of the Amorites, who reigned in Heshbon, whom

Moses struck with the leaders of Midian, Evi, Rekem, Zur, Hur, and Reba, the leaders of Sihon, who lived in the land. 22 The sons of Israel also killed Balaam the son of Beor, the diviner, with the sword among *the rest of* their dead. 23 The border of the sons of Reuben was the Jordan. This was the inheritance of the sons of Reuben according to their families, the cities and their villages.

24 Moses also gave *an inheritance* to the tribe of Gad, to the sons of Gad according to their families. 25 Their territory was Jazer and all the cities of Gilead, and half the land of the sons of Ammon, as far as Aroer which is opposite Rabbah; 26 and from Heshbon as far as Ramath-mizpeh and Betonim, and from Mahanaim as far as the border of Debir; 27 and in the valley, Beth-haram, Beth-nimrah, Succoth, and Zaphon, the rest of the kingdom of Sihon king of Heshbon, with the Jordan as a border, as far as the *lower* end of the Sea of 1Chinnereth beyond the Jordan to the east. 28 This is the inheritance of the sons of Gad according to their families, the cities and their villages.

29 Moses also gave *an inheritance* to the half-tribe of Manasseh; and it was for the half-tribe of the sons of Manasseh according to their families. 30 Their territory was from Mahanaim, all Bashan, all the kingdom of Og king of Bashan, and all the towns of Jair, which are in Bashan, sixty cities; 31 also half of Gilead, with Ashtaroth and Edrei, the cities of the kingdom of Og in Bashan, *were* for the sons of Machir the son of Manasseh, for half of the sons of Machir according to their families.

32 These are *the territories* which Moses apportioned as an inheritance in the plains of Moab, beyond the Jordan at Jericho to the east. 33 But to the tribe of Levi, Moses did not give an inheritance; the LORD, the God of Israel, is their inheritance, as He had promised to them.

Caleb's Request

14 Now these are *the territories* which the sons of Israel inherited in the land of Canaan, which Eleazar the priest, Joshua the son of Nun, and the heads of the fathers' *households* of the tribes of the sons of Israel apportioned to them as inheritances, 2 by the lot of their inheritance, just as the LORD commanded through Moses, for the nine tribes and the half-tribe. 3 For Moses had given the inheritance of the two tribes and the half-tribe beyond the Jordan; but he did not give an inheritance to the Levites among them. 4 For the sons of Joseph were two tribes, Manasseh and Ephraim, and they did not give a portion to the Levites in the land, except cities to live in, with their pasture lands for their livestock and for their property. 5 The sons of Israel did exactly as the LORD had commanded Moses, and they divided the land.

6 Then the sons of Judah approached Joshua in Gilgal, and Caleb the son of Jephunneh the Kenizzite said to him, "You know the word which the LORD spoke to Moses the man of God on account of you and me in Kadesh-barnea. 7 I was forty years old when Moses the

servant of the LORD sent me from Kadesh-barnea to spy out the land, and I brought word back to him as *it was* in my heart. 8 Nevertheless my brothers who went up with me made the heart of the people melt *with fear;* but I followed the LORD my God fully. 9 So Moses swore on that day, saying, 'The land on which your foot has walked shall certainly be an inheritance to you and to your children forever, because you have followed the LORD my God fully.' 10 And now behold, the LORD has let me live, just as He spoke, these forty-five years, from the time that the LORD spoke this word to Moses, when Israel walked in the wilderness; and now behold, I am eighty-five years old today. 11 I am still as strong today as I was on the day Moses sent me; as my strength was then, so my strength is now, for war and for going out and coming in. 12 Now then, give me this hill country about which the LORD spoke on that day, for you heard on that day that Anakim *were* there, with great fortified cities; perhaps the LORD will be with me, and I will drive them out just as the LORD has spoken."

13 So Joshua blessed him and gave Hebron to Caleb the son of Jephunneh as an inheritance. 14 Therefore, Hebron became the inheritance of Caleb the son of Jephunneh the Kenizzite to this day, because he followed the LORD God of Israel fully. 15 Now the name of Hebron was previously Kiriath-arba; *for Arba* was the greatest man among the Anakim. Then the land was at rest from war.

Territory of Judah

15 Now the lot for the tribe of the sons of Judah according to their families reached the border of Edom, southward to the wilderness of Zin at the extreme south. 2 Their southern border was from the *lower* end of the Salt Sea, from the bay that turns to the south. 3 Then it proceeded southward to the ascent of Akrabbim and continued to Zin, then went up by the south of Kadesh-barnea and continued to Hezron, and went up to Addar and turned to Karka. 4 It continued to Azmon and proceeded to the brook of Egypt, and the border ended at the sea. This shall be your southern border. 5 The eastern border *was* the Salt Sea, as far as the mouth of the Jordan. And the border of the north side was from the bay of the sea at the mouth of the Jordan. 6 Then the border went up to Beth-hoglah, and continued on the north of Beth-arabah, and the border went up to the stone of Bohan the son of Reuben. 7 And the border went up to Debir from the Valley of Achor, and turned northward toward Gilgal which is opposite the ascent of Adummim, which is on the south of the valley; and the border continued to the waters of En-shemesh and it ended at En-rogel. 8 Then the border went up the Valley of Ben-hinnom to the slope of the Jebusite on the south (that is, Jerusalem); and the border went up to the top of the mountain which is opposite the Valley of Hinnom to the west, which is at the end of the Valley of Rephaim toward the north. 9 And from the top of the mountain the border turned to

the spring of the waters of Nephtoah and proceeded to the cities of Mount Ephron, then the border turned to Baalah (that is, Kiriath-jearim). 10 The border turned from Baalah westward to Mount Seir, and continued to the slope of Mount Jearim on the north (that is, Chesalon), and went down to Beth-shemesh and continued through Timnah. 11 Then the border proceeded to the side of Ekron north-ward. And the border turned to Shikkeron and continued to Mount Baalah and proceeded to Jabneel, and the border ended at the sea. 12 The western border *was* at the Great Sea, even *its* coastline. This is the border around the sons of Judah according to their families.

13 Now he gave to Caleb the son of Jephun-neh a portion among the sons of Judah, in accordance with the command of the LORD to Joshua, *namely,* Kiriath-arba, *Arba being* the father of Anak (that is, Hebron). 14 And Caleb drove out from there the three sons of Anak: Sheshai, Ahiman, and Talmai, the children of Anak. 15 Then he went up from there against the inhabitants of Debir; now the name of Debir previously was Kiriath-sepher. 16 And Caleb said, "The one who attacks Kiriath-sepher and captures it, I will give him Achsah my daughter as a wife." 17 Othniel the son of Kenaz, the brother of Caleb, captured it; so he gave him Achsah his daughter as a wife. 18 And it happened that when she came *to him,* she incited him to ask her father for a field. So she dismounted from the donkey, and Caleb said to her, "What do you want?" 19 Then she said, "Give me a blessing; since you have given me the land of the Negev, give me springs of water also." So he gave her the upper springs and the lower springs.

20 This is the inheritance of the tribe of the sons of Judah according to their families.

21 Now the cities at the extremity of the tribe of the sons of Judah toward the border of Edom in the south were Kabzeel, Eder, and Jagur, 22 Kinah, Dimonah, and Adadah, 23 Kedesh, Hazor, and Ithnan, 24 Ziph, Telem, and Bealoth, 25 Hazor-hadattah, Kerioth-hezron (that is, Hazor), 26 Amam, Shema, and Moladah, 27 Hazar-gaddah, Heshmon, and Beth-pelet, 28 Hazar-shual, Beersheba, and Biziothiah, 29 Baalah, Iim, and Ezem, 30 Eltolad, Chesil, and Hormah, 31 Ziklag, Madmannah, and Sansan-nah, 32 Lebaoth, Shilhim, Ain, and Rimmon; in all, twenty-nine cities with their villages.

33 In the lowland: Eshtaol, Zorah, and Ashnah, 34 Zanoah, En-gannim, Tappuah, and Enam, 35 Jarmuth, Adullam, Socoh, and Azekah, 36 Shaaraim, Adithaim, Gederah, and Gederothaim; fourteen cities with their villages.

37 Zenan, Hadashah, and Migdal-gad, 38 Dilean, Mizpeh, and Joktheel, 39 Lachish, Bozkath, and Eglon, 40 Cabbon, Lahmas, and Chitlish, 41 Gederoth, Beth-dagon, Naamah, and Makkedah; sixteen cities with their villages.

42 Libnah, Ether, and Ashan, 43 Iphtah, Ashnah, and Nezib, 44 Keilah, Achzib, and Mareshah; nine cities with their villages.

45 Ekron, with its towns and its villages; 46 from Ekron even to the sea, all that were by the side of Ashdod, with their villages.

47 Ashdod, its towns and its villages; Gaza, its towns and its villages, as far as the brook of Egypt and the Great Sea, even *its* coastline.

48 In the hill country: Shamir, Jattir, and Socoh, 49 Dannah, Kiriath-sannah (that is, Debir), 50 Anab, Eshtemoh, Anim, 51 Goshen, Holon, and Giloh; eleven cities with their villages.

52 Arab, Dumah, and Eshan, 53 Janum, Beth-tappuah, and Aphekah, 54 Humtah, Kiriath-arba (that is, Hebron), and Zior; nine cities with their villages.

55 Maon, Carmel, Ziph, and Juttah, 56 Jezreel, Jokdeam, and Zanoah, 57 Kain, Gibeah, and Timnah; ten cities with their villages.

58 Halhul, Beth-zur, and Gedor, 59 Maarath, Beth-anoth, and Eltekon; six cities with their villages.

60 Kiriath-baal (that is, Kiriath-jearim), and Rabbah; two cities with their villages.

61 In the wilderness: Beth-arabah, Middin, and Secacah, 62 Nibshan, the City of Salt, and Engedi; six cities with their villages.

63 Now as for the Jebusites, the inhabitants of Jerusalem, the sons of Judah could not drive them out; so the Jebusites live with the sons of Judah in Jerusalem to this day.

Territory of Ephraim

16 Then the lot for the sons of Joseph went from the Jordan at Jericho to the waters of Jericho on the east *into* the wilderness, going up from Jericho through the hill country to Bethel. 2 It went from Bethel to Luz, and continued to the border of the Archites at Ataroth. 3 Then it went down westward to the territory of the Japhletites, as far as the terri-tory of lower Beth-horon even to Gezer, and it ended at the sea.

4 The sons of Joseph, Manasseh and Ephraim, received their inheritance. 5 Now *this* was the territory of the sons of Ephraim accord-ing to their families: the border of their inheri-tance eastward was Ataroth-addar, as far as upper Beth-horon. 6 Then the border went westward at Michmethath on the north, and the border turned eastward to Taanath-shiloh and continued *beyond* it to the east of Janoah. 7 Then it went down from Janoah to Ataroth and to Naarah, then reached Jericho and came out at the Jordan. 8 From Tappuah the border continued westward to the brook of Kanah, and it ended at the sea. This is the inheritance of the tribe of the sons of Ephraim according to their families, 9 *together* with the cities which were set apart for the sons of Ephraim in the midst of the inheritance of the sons of Manasseh, all the cities with their villages. 10 But they did not drive out the Canaanites who lived in Gezer, so the Canaanites live in the midst of Ephraim to this day, and they became forced laborers.

Territory of Manasseh

17 Now *this* was the lot for the tribe of Manasseh, for he was the firstborn of Joseph. To Machir the firstborn of Manasseh, the father of Gilead, were allotted Gilead and Bashan, because he was a man of war. 2 So *the lot* was *made* for the rest of the sons of

Manasseh according to their families: for the sons of Abiezer, the sons of Helek, the sons of Asriel, the sons of Shechem, the sons of Hepher, and the sons of Shemida; these *were* the male descendants of Manasseh the son of Joseph according to their families.

3 However, Zelophehad, the son of Hepher, the son of Gilead, the son of Machir, the son of Manasseh, had no sons, only daughters; and these are the names of his daughters: Mahlah, Noah, Hoglah, Milcah, and Tirzah. 4 They approached Eleazar the priest, Joshua the son of Nun, and the leaders, saying, "The LORD commanded Moses to give us an inheritance among our brothers." So in accordance with the command of the LORD he gave them an inheritance among their father's brothers. 5 So ten portions fell to Manasseh, besides the land of Gilead and Bashan, which is beyond the Jordan, 6 because the daughters of Manasseh received an inheritance among his sons. And the land of Gilead belonged to the rest of the sons of Manasseh.

7 The border of Manasseh ran from Asher to Michmethath which was east of Shechem; then the border went southward to the inhabitants of En-tappuah. 8 The land of Tappuah belonged to Manasseh, but Tappuah on the border of Manasseh *belonged* to the sons of Ephraim. 9 And the border went down to the brook of Kanah, southward of the brook (these cities *belonged* to Ephraim among the cities of Manasseh), and the border of Manasseh *was* on the north side of the brook, and it ended at the sea. 10 The south side *belonged* to Ephraim and the north side to Manasseh, and the sea was their border; and they reached to Asher on the north and to Issachar on the east. 11 In Issachar and in Asher, Manasseh had Beth-shean and its towns and Ibleam and its towns, and the inhabitants of Dor and its towns, and the inhabitants of En-dor and its towns, and the inhabitants of Taanach and its towns, and the inhabitants of Megiddo and its towns; the third is Napheth. 12 But the sons of Manasseh could not take possession of these cities, because the Canaanites persisted in living in this land. 13 And it came about when the sons of Israel became strong, they put the Canaanites to forced labor, but they did not drive them out completely.

14 Then the sons of Joseph spoke to Joshua, saying, "Why have you given me *only* one lot and one portion as an inheritance, though I am a numerous people whom the LORD has blessed up to this point?" 15 And Joshua said to them, "If you are a numerous people, go up to the forest and clear *a place* for yourself there in the land of the Perizzites and of the Rephaim, since the hill country of Ephraim is too narrow for you." 16 The sons of Joseph then said, "The hill country is not enough for us, but all the Canaanites who live in the valley land have iron chariots, both those who are in Beth-shean and its towns and those who are in the Valley of Jezreel." 17 But Joshua spoke to the house of Joseph, to Ephraim and Manasseh, saying, "You are a numerous people and have great power; you shall not have one lot *only,* 18 but the hill country shall be yours. For

though it is a forest, you shall clear it, and to its farthest borders it shall be yours; for you shall drive out the Canaanites, even though they have iron chariots *and* though they are strong."

Rest of the Land Divided

18 Then the whole congregation of the sons of Israel assembled at Shiloh, and set up the tent of meeting there; and the land was subdued before them.

2 But there remained among the sons of Israel seven tribes who had not divided their inheritance. 3 So Joshua said to the sons of Israel, "How long will you put off entering to take possession of the land which the LORD, the God of your fathers, has given you? 4 Provide for yourselves three men from each tribe so that I may send them, and that they may arise and walk through the land and write *a description of* it according to their inheritance; then they shall return to me. 5 And they shall divide it into seven portions; Judah shall stay in its territory on the south, and the house of Joseph shall stay in their territory on the north. 6 And you shall write *a description of* the land in seven divisions, and bring *the description* here to me. Then I will cast lots for you here before the LORD our God. 7 For the Levites have no portion among you, because the priesthood of the LORD is their inheritance. Gad, Reuben, and the half-tribe of Manasseh also have received their inheritance eastward beyond the Jordan, which Moses the servant of the LORD gave them."

8 Then the men arose and went, and Joshua commanded those who went to write *a description of* the land, saying, "Go and walk through the land and write *a description of* it, and return to me; then I will cast lots for you here before the LORD in Shiloh." 9 So the men went and passed through the land, and wrote *a description of* it by cities in seven divisions in a book; and they came to Joshua at the camp at Shiloh. 10 Joshua then cast lots for them in Shiloh before the LORD, and there Joshua divided the land for the sons of Israel according to their divisions.

The Territory of Benjamin

11 Now the lot of the tribe of the sons of Benjamin came up according to their families, and the territory of their lot lay between the sons of Judah and the sons of Joseph. 12 Their border on the north side was from the Jordan, then the border went up to the side of Jericho on the north, and went up through the hill country westward, and it ended at the wilderness of Beth-aven. 13 Then from there the border continued to Luz, to the side of Luz (that is, Bethel) southward; and the border went down to Ataroth-addar, near the hill which *lies* on the south of lower Beth-horon. 14 And the border changed direction *from there* and turned around on the west side southward, from the hill which *lies* opposite Beth-horon southward; and it ended at Kiriath-baal (that is, Kiriath-jearim), a city of the sons of Judah. This *was* the west side. 15 Then the south side *was* from the edge of Kiriath-jearim, and the border went westward and went to the fountain of the

waters of Nephtoah. **16** Then the border went down to the edge of the hill which is in the Valley of Ben-hinnom, which is in the Valley of Rephaim northward; and it went down to the Valley of Hinnom, to the slope of the Jebusite southward, and went down to En-rogel. **17** Then it turned northward and went to En-shemesh, and went to Geliloth, which is opposite the ascent of Adummim, and it went down to the stone of Bohan the son of Reuben. **18** And it continued to the side in front of the Arabah northward, and went down to the Arabah. **19** Then the border continued to the side of Beth-hoglah northward; and the border ended at the north bay of the Salt Sea, at the south end of the Jordan. This *was* the southern border. **20** Moreover, the Jordan was its border on the east side. This *was* the inheritance of the sons of Benjamin according to their families, *and* according to its borders all around.

21 Now the cities of the tribe of the sons of Benjamin according to their families were Jericho, Beth-hoglah, and Emek-keziz, **22** Beth-arabah, Zemaraim, and Bethel, **23** Avvim, Parah, and Ophrah, **24** Chephar-ammoni, Ophni, and Geba; twelve cities with their villages. **25** Gibeon, Ramah, and Beeroth, **26** Mizpeh, Chephirah, and Mozah, **27** Rekem, Irpeel, and Taralah, **28** Zelah, Haeleph, the Jebusite *city* (that is, Jerusalem), Gibeah, Kiriath; fourteen cities with their villages. This is the inheritance of the sons of Benjamin according to their families.

Territory of Simeon

19 Then the second lot went to Simeon, to the tribe of the sons of Simeon according to their families; and their inheritance was in the midst of the inheritance of the sons of Judah. **2** So they had in their inheritance Beersheba or Sheba and Moladah, **3** Hazar-shual, Balah, and Ezem, **4** Eltolad, Bethul, and Hormah, **5** Ziklag, Beth-marcaboth, and Hazar-susah, **6** Beth-lebaoth, and Sharuhen; thirteen cities with their villages; **7** Ain, Rimmon, Ether, and Ashan; four cities with their villages; **8** and all the villages which *were* around these cities as far as Baalath-beer, Ramah of the Negev. This *was* the inheritance of the tribe of the sons of Simeon according to their families. **9** The inheritance of the sons of Simeon *was taken* from the portion of the sons of Judah, because the share of the sons of Judah was too large for them; so the sons of Simeon received an inheritance in the midst of Judah's inheritance.

Territory of Zebulun

10 Now the third lot came up for the sons of Zebulun according to their families. And the territory of their inheritance was as far as Sarid. **11** Then their border went up to the west and to Maralah, and it reached Dabbesheth and reached to the brook that is opposite Jokneam. **12** Then it turned from Sarid to the east toward the sunrise as far as the border of Chisloth-tabor, and it proceeded to Daberath and up to Japhia. **13** From there it continued eastward toward the sunrise to Gath-hepher, to Eth-kazin, and it proceeded to Rimmon which

stretches to Neah. **14** Then the border circled around it on the north to Hannathon, and it ended at the Valley of Iphtahel. **15** *Included* also *were* Kattah, Nahalal, Shimron, Idalah, and Bethlehem; twelve cities with their villages. **16** This *was* the inheritance of the sons of Zebulun according to their families, these cities with their villages.

Territory of Issachar

17 The fourth lot went to Issachar, to the sons of Issachar according to their families. **18** Their territory was to Jezreel and *included* Chesulloth, Shunem, **19** Hapharaim, Shion, and Anaharath, **20** Rabbith, Kishion, and Ebez, **21** Remeth, En-gannim, En-haddah, and Beth-pazzez. **22** The border reached to Tabor, Shahazumah, and Beth-shemesh, and their border ended at the Jordan; sixteen cities with their villages. **23** This *was* the inheritance of the tribe of the sons of Issachar according to their families, the cities with their villages.

Territory of Asher

24 Now the fifth lot went to the tribe of the sons of Asher according to their families. **25** Their territory was Helkath, Hali, Beten, and Achshaph, **26** Allammelech, Amad, and Mishal; and it reached to Carmel on the west and Shihor-libnath. **27** It turned toward the east to Beth-dagon and reached Zebulun, and to the Valley of Iphtahel northward to Beth-emek and Neiel; then it proceeded on north to Cabul, **28** Ebron, Rehob, Hammon, and Kanah, as far as Great Sidon. **29** The border turned to Ramah and to the fortified city of Tyre; then the border turned to Hosah, and it ended at the sea by the region of Achzib. **30** *Included* also *were* Ummah, Aphek, and Rehob; twenty-two cities with their villages. **31** This *was* the inheritance of the tribe of the sons of Asher according to their families, these cities with their villages.

Territory of Naphtali

32 The sixth lot went to the sons of Naphtali; to the sons of Naphtali according to their families. **33** Their border was from Heleph, from the oak in Zaanannim, and Adami-nekeb and Jabneel, as far as Lakkum, and it ended at the Jordan. **34** Then the border turned westward to Aznoth-tabor and proceeded from there to Hukkok; and it reached Zebulun on the south and reached Asher on the west, and Judah at the Jordan toward the east. **35** The fortified cities *were* Ziddim, Zer, Hammath, Rakkath, and Chinnereth, **36** Adamah, Ramah, and Hazor, **37** Kedesh, Edrei, and En-hazor, **38** Yiron, Migdal-el, Horem, Beth-anath, and Beth-shemesh; nineteen cities with their villages. **39** This *was* the inheritance of the tribe of the sons of Naphtali according to their families, the cities with their villages.

Territory of Dan

40 The seventh lot went to the tribe of the sons of Dan according to their families. **41** The territory of their inheritance was Zorah, Eshtaol, and Ir-shemesh, **42** Shaalabbin, Aijalon, and Ithlah, **43** Elon, Timnah, and Ekron, **44** Eltekeh, Gibbethon, and Baalath, **45** Jehud,

Bene-berak, and Gath-rimmon, 46 Me-jarkon, and Rakkon, with the territory opposite Joppa. 47 The territory of the sons of Dan proceeded beyond them; for the sons of Dan went up and fought with Leshem and captured it. Then they struck it with the edge of the sword and took possession of it and settled in it; and they named Leshem Dan after the name of their father Dan. 48 This *was* the inheritance of the tribe of the sons of Dan according to their families, these cities with their villages.

49 When they finished apportioning the land for inheritance by its borders, the sons of Israel gave an inheritance among them to Joshua the son of Nun. 50 In accordance with the command of the LORD, they gave him the city for which he asked, Timnath-serah in the hill country of Ephraim. So he built the city and settled in it.

51 These are the inheritances which Eleazar the priest, Joshua the son of Nun, and the heads of the fathers' *households* of the tribes of the sons of Israel apportioned by lot in Shiloh before the LORD at the doorway of the tent of meeting. So they finished dividing the land.

Six Cities of Refuge

20 Then the LORD spoke to Joshua, saying, 2 "Speak to the sons of Israel, saying, 'Designate the cities of refuge, of which I spoke to you through Moses, 3 so that one who commits manslaughter *by* killing a person unintentionally, without premeditation, may flee there, and they shall become your refuge from the avenger of blood. 4 Then he shall flee to one of these cities, and shall stand at the entrance of the gate of the city, and state his case in the presence of the elders of that city; and they shall receive him into the city to them and give him a place, so that he may remain among them. 5 Now if the avenger of blood pursues him, then they are not to hand the one who committed manslaughter over to him, since he struck his neighbor without premeditation and did not hate him previously. 6 And he shall remain in that city until he stands before the congregation for judgment, until the death of the one who is high priest in those days. Then he shall return to his own city and to his own house, to the city from which he fled.' "

7 So they set apart Kedesh in Galilee in the hill country of Naphtali, and Shechem in the hill country of Ephraim, and Kiriath-arba (that is, Hebron) in the hill country of Judah. 8 And beyond the Jordan east of Jericho, they designated Bezer in the wilderness on the plain from the tribe of Reuben, and Ramoth in Gilead from the tribe of Gad, and Golan in Bashan from the tribe of Manasseh. 9 These were the designated cities for all the sons of Israel and for the stranger who resides among them, so that whoever kills a person unintentionally may flee there, and not die by the hand of the avenger of blood until he stands before the congregation.

Forty-eight Cities of the Levites

21 Then the heads of fathers' *households* of the Levites approached Eleazar the priest, Joshua the son of Nun, and the heads of fathers' *households* of the tribes of the sons of Israel. 2 And they spoke to them at Shiloh in the land of Canaan, saying, "The LORD commanded through Moses to give us cities to live in, with their pasture lands for our cattle." 3 So the sons of Israel gave the Levites from their inheritance these cities with their pasture lands, in accordance with the command of the LORD. 4 Then the lot came out for the families of the Kohathites. And to the sons of Aaron the priest, who were of the Levites, thirteen cities were *given* by lot from the tribe of Judah, from the tribe of the Simeonites, and from the tribe of Benjamin.

5 And to the rest of the sons of Kohath ten cities *were given* by lot from the families of the tribe of Ephraim, from the tribe of Dan, and from the half-tribe of Manasseh.

6 And to the sons of Gershon thirteen cities *were given* by lot from the families of the tribe of Issachar, from the tribe of Asher, from the tribe of Naphtali, and from the half-tribe of Manasseh in Bashan.

7 To the sons of Merari according to their families twelve cities *were given* from the tribe of Reuben, from the tribe of Gad, and from the tribe of Zebulun.

8 Now the sons of Israel gave by lot to the Levites these cities with their pasture lands, as the LORD had commanded through Moses.

9 They gave these cities which are mentioned *here* by name from the tribe of the sons of Judah and from the tribe of the sons of Simeon; 10 and they were for the sons of Aaron, one of the families of the Kohathites, of the sons of Levi, because the lot was theirs first. 11 So they gave them Kiriath-arba (*Arba* being the father of Anak), that is, Hebron, in the hill country of Judah, with its surrounding pasture lands. 12 But the fields of the city and its villages they gave to Caleb the son of Jephunneh as his possession.

13 So to the sons of Aaron the priest they gave Hebron, the city of refuge for the one who commits manslaughter, with its pasture lands, Libnah with its pasture lands, 14 Jattir with its pasture lands, Eshtemoa with its pasture lands, 15 Holon with its pasture lands, Debir with its pasture lands, 16 Ain with its pasture lands, Juttah with its pasture lands, *and* Beth-shemesh with its pasture lands; nine cities from these two tribes. 17 From the tribe of Benjamin, Gibeon with its pasture lands, Geba with its pasture lands, 18 Anathoth with its pasture lands, and Almon with its pasture lands; four cities. 19 All the cities of the sons of Aaron, the priests, were thirteen cities with their pasture lands.

20 Then the cities from the tribe of Ephraim were allotted to the families of the sons of Kohath, the Levites, *that is, to* the rest of the sons of Kohath. 21 They gave them Shechem, the city of refuge for the one who commits manslaughter, with its pasture lands, in the hill country of Ephraim, and Gezer with its pasture lands, 22 and Kibzaim with its pasture lands, and Beth-horon with its pasture lands; four cities. 23 And from the tribe of Dan, Elteke with its pasture lands, Gibbethon with its

pasture lands, 24 Aijalon with its pasture lands, Gath-rimmon with its pasture lands; four cities. 25 From the half-tribe of Manasseh, *they allotted* Taanach with its pasture lands and Gath-rimmon with its pasture lands; two cities. 26 All the cities with their pasture lands for the families of the rest of the sons of Kohath were ten.

27 And to the sons of Gershon, one of the families of the Levites, from the half-tribe of Manasseh, *they gave* Golan in Bashan, the city of refuge for the one who commits manslaughter, with its pasture lands, and Be-eshterah with its pasture lands; two cities. 28 And from the tribe of Issachar *they gave* Kishion with its pasture lands, Daberath with its pasture lands, 29 Jarmuth with its pasture lands, *and* En-gannim with its pasture lands; four cities. 30 From the tribe of Asher, *they gave* Mishal with its pasture lands, Abdon with its pasture lands, 31 Helkath with its pasture lands, and Rehob with its pasture lands; four cities. 32 And from the tribe of Naphtali, *they gave* Kedesh in Galilee, the city of refuge for the one who commits manslaughter, with its pasture lands, Hammoth-dor with its pasture lands, and Kartan with its pasture lands; three cities. 33 All the cities of the Gershonites according to their families were thirteen cities with their pasture lands.

34 And to the families of the sons of Merari, the rest of the Levites, *they gave* from the tribe of Zebulun, Jokneam with its pasture lands, Kartah with its pasture lands, 35 Dimnah with its pasture lands, *and* Nahalal with its pasture lands; four cities. 36 From the tribe of Reuben *they gave* Bezer with its pasture lands, Jahaz with its pasture lands, 37 Kedemoth with its pasture lands, and Mephaath with its pasture lands; four cities. 38 And from the tribe of Gad, *they gave* Ramoth in Gilead, the city of refuge for the one who commits manslaughter, with its pasture lands, Mahanaim with its pasture lands, 39 Heshbon with its pasture lands, *and* Jazer with its pasture lands; four cities in all. 40 All *these were* the cities of the sons of Merari according to their families, the rest of the families of the Levites; and their lot was twelve cities.

41 All the cities of the Levites in the midst of the possession of the sons of Israel were forty-eight cities with their pasture lands. 42 These cities individually had their surrounding pasture lands; this is how *it was* with all these cities.

43 So the Lord gave Israel all the land which He had sworn to give to their fathers, and they took possession of it and lived in it. 44 And the Lord gave them rest on every side, in accordance with everything that He had sworn to their fathers, and no one of all their enemies stood before them; the Lord handed all their enemies over to them. 45 Not one of the good promises which the Lord had made to the house of Israel failed; everything came to pass.

Tribes beyond Jordan Return

22 Then Joshua summoned the Reubenites and the Gadites, and the half-tribe of Manasseh, 2 and said to them, "You have kept all that Moses the servant of the Lord commanded you, and have listened to my voice in all that I commanded you. 3 You have not abandoned your brothers these many days to this day, but have fulfilled the obligation of the commandment of the Lord your God. 4 And now the Lord your God has given rest to your brothers, as He spoke to them; therefore turn now and go to your tents, to the land of your possession, which Moses the servant of the Lord gave you beyond the Jordan. 5 Only be very careful to follow the commandment and the Law which Moses the servant of the Lord commanded you, to love the Lord your God and walk in all His ways, and keep His commandments and cling to Him, and serve Him with all your heart and with all your soul." 6 So Joshua blessed them and sent them away, and they went to their tents.

7 Now to the one half-tribe of Manasseh Moses had given *a possession* in Bashan, but to the other half Joshua gave *a possession* among their brothers westward beyond the Jordan. So when Joshua sent them away to their tents, he also blessed them, 8 and said to them, "Return to your tents with great riches and with very many livestock, with silver, gold, bronze, iron, and with very many clothes; divide the spoils of your enemies with your brothers." 9 So the sons of Reuben, the sons of Gad, and the half-tribe of Manasseh returned *home,* leaving the sons of Israel at Shiloh, which is in the land of Canaan, to go to the land of Gilead, to the land of their possession in which they had settled, in accordance with the command of the Lord through Moses.

The Offensive Altar

10 When they came to the region of the Jordan which is in the land of Canaan, the sons of Reuben, the sons of Gad, and the half-tribe of Manasseh built an altar there by the Jordan, a large altar in appearance. 11 But the sons of Israel heard a report: "Behold, the sons of Reuben, the sons of Gad, and the half-tribe of Manasseh have built an altar at the frontier of the land of Canaan, in the region of the Jordan, on the side *belonging to* the sons of Israel." 12 And when the sons of Israel heard *about it,* the entire congregation of the sons of Israel assembled at Shiloh to go up against them in battle.

13 Then the sons of Israel sent to the sons of Reuben, to the sons of Gad, and to the half-tribe of Manasseh, in the land of Gilead, Phinehas the son of Eleazar the priest, 14 and with him ten leaders, one leader for each father's household from each of the tribes of Israel; and each one of them *was* the head of his father's household among the thousands of Israel. 15 They came to the sons of Reuben, the sons of Gad, and to the half-tribe of Manasseh, in the land of Gilead, and they spoke with them, saying, 16 "This is what the whole congregation of the Lord says: 'What is this unfaithful act which you have committed against the God of Israel, turning away from following the Lord this day, by building yourselves an altar, to rebel against the Lord this day? 17 Is the wrongdoing of Peor not

enough for us, from which we have not cleansed ourselves to this day, although a plague came on the congregation of the LORD, [18] that you must turn away this day from following the LORD? If you rebel against the LORD today, He will be angry with the entire congregation of Israel tomorrow. [19] If, however, the land of your possession is unclean, then cross into the land of the possession of the LORD, where the LORD's tabernacle stands, and settle among us. Only do not rebel against the LORD, or rebel against us, by building an altar for yourselves besides the altar of the LORD our God. [20] Did Achan the son of Zerah not act unfaithfully in the things designated for destruction, and wrath fall on the entire congregation of Israel? So that man did not perish alone in his guilt.' "

[21] Then the sons of Reuben, the sons of Gad, and the half-tribe of Manasseh answered and spoke to the heads of the families of Israel. [22] "The Mighty One, God, the LORD, the Mighty One, God, the LORD! He knows, and may Israel itself know. If *it was* in rebellion, or if in an unfaithful act against the LORD, do not save us this day! [23] If we have built us an altar to turn away from following the LORD, or if to offer a burnt offering or grain offering on it, or if to offer sacrifices of peace offerings on it, may the LORD Himself demand it. [24] But truly we have done this out of concern, for a reason, saying, 'In time to come your sons may say to our sons, "What have you to do with the LORD, the God of Israel? [25] For the LORD has made the Jordan a border between us and you, *you* sons of Reuben and sons of Gad; you have no portion in the LORD." So your sons may make our sons stop fearing the LORD.'

[26] "Therefore we said, 'Let's build an altar, not for burnt offering or for sacrifice; [27] rather, it *shall be* a witness between us and you and between our generations after us, that we are to perform the service of the LORD before Him with our burnt offerings, our sacrifices, and with our peace offerings, so that your sons will not say to our sons in time to come, "You have no portion in the LORD." ' [28] Therefore we said, 'It shall also come about if they say *this* to us or to our generations in time to come, then we shall say, "See the copy of the altar of the LORD which our fathers made, not for burnt offering or for sacrifice; rather, it is a witness between us and you." ' [29] Far be it from us that we should rebel against the LORD and turn away from following the LORD this day, by building an altar for burnt offering, for grain offering, or for sacrifice, besides the altar of the LORD our God which is before His tabernacle."

[30] So when Phinehas the priest and the leaders of the congregation, that is, the heads of the families of Israel who *were* with him, heard the words which the sons of Reuben, the sons of Gad, and the sons of Manasseh spoke, it pleased them. [31] And Phinehas the son of Eleazar the priest said to the sons of Reuben, the sons of Gad, and to the sons of Manasseh, "Today we know that the LORD is in our midst, because you have not committed this unfaithful act against the LORD; now you have saved the sons of Israel from the hand of the LORD."

[32] Then Phinehas the son of Eleazar the priest and the leaders returned from the sons of Reuben and from the sons of Gad, from the land of Gilead to the land of Canaan, to the sons of Israel, and brought back word to them. [33] The word pleased the sons of Israel, and the sons of Israel blessed God; and they did not speak of going up against them in battle to destroy the land in which the sons of Reuben and the sons of Gad were living. [34] And the sons of Reuben and the sons of Gad called the altar *Witness;* "For," *they said,* "it is a witness between us that the LORD is God."

Joshua's Farewell Address

23 Now it came about after many days, when the LORD had given rest to Israel from all their enemies on every side, and Joshua was old, advanced in years, [2] that Joshua called for all Israel, for their elders, their heads, their judges, and their officers, and said to them, "I am old, advanced in years. [3] And you have seen all that the LORD your God has done to all these nations because of you, for the LORD your God is He who has been fighting for you. [4] See, I have apportioned to you these nations which remain as an inheritance for your tribes, with all the nations which I have eliminated, from the Jordan even to the Great Sea toward the west. [5] And the LORD your God, He will thrust them away from you and drive them from you; and you will take possession of their land, just as the LORD your God promised you. [6] Be very determined, then, to keep and do everything that is written in the Book of the Law of Moses, so that you will not turn aside from it to the right or to the left, [7] so that you will not associate with these nations, these which remain with you, or mention the name of their gods, or make *anyone* swear *by them,* or serve them, or bow down to them. [8] But you are to cling to the LORD your God, as you have done to this day. [9] For the LORD has driven out great and mighty nations from before you; and as for you, no one has stood against you to this day. [10] One of your men puts to flight a thousand, for the LORD your God is He who fights for you, just as He promised you. [11] So take great care for yourselves that you love the LORD your God. [12] For if you ever go back and cling to the rest of these nations, these which remain with you, and intermarry with them, so that you associate with them and they with you, [13] know with certainty that the LORD your God will not continue to drive these nations out from before you; but they will be a snare and a trap to you, and a whip on your sides and thorns in your eyes, until you perish from this good land which the LORD your God has given you.

[14] "Now behold, today I am going the way of all the earth, and you know in all your hearts and in all your souls that not one word of all the good words which the LORD your God spoke concerning you has failed; they all have been fulfilled for you, not one of them has failed. [15] But it will come about that just as all the good words which the LORD your God spoke to you have come upon you, so the LORD will bring upon you all the warnings, until He

has eliminated you from this good land which the LORD your God has given you. 16 When you violate the covenant of the LORD your God, which He commanded you, and you go and serve other gods and bow down to them, then the anger of the LORD will burn against you, and you will perish quickly from the good land which He has given you."

Joshua Reviews Israel's History

24 Then Joshua gathered all the tribes of Israel at Shechem, and called for the elders of Israel, their heads, their judges, and their officers; and they presented themselves before God. 2 Joshua said to all the people, "This is what the LORD, the God of Israel says: 'From ancient times your fathers lived beyond the *Euphrates* River, *namely,* Terah, the father of Abraham and the father of Nahor, and they served other gods. 3 Then I took your father Abraham from beyond the *Euphrates* River and led him through all the land of Canaan, and multiplied his descendants and gave him Isaac. 4 To Isaac I gave Jacob and Esau, and to Esau I gave Mount Seir, to possess it; but Jacob and his sons went down to Egypt. 5 Then I sent Moses and Aaron, and I plagued Egypt by what I did in its midst; and afterward I brought you out. 6 So I brought your fathers out of Egypt, and you came to the sea; and Egypt pursued your fathers with chariots and horsemen to the Red Sea. 7 But when they cried out to the LORD, He put darkness between you and the Egyptians, and brought the sea upon them and covered them; and your own eyes saw what I did in Egypt. And you lived in the wilderness for a long time. 8 Then I brought you into the land of the Amorites, who lived beyond the Jordan, and they fought with you; but I handed them over to you, and you took possession of their land when I eliminated them before you. 9 Then Balak the son of Zippor, king of Moab, rose up and fought against Israel, and he sent *messengers* and summoned Balaam the son of Beor to curse you. 10 But I was not willing to listen to Balaam. So he had to bless you, and I saved you from his hand. 11 You crossed the Jordan and came to Jericho; and the citizens of Jericho fought against you, *and* the Amorite, the Perizzite, the Canaanite, the Hittite, the Girgashite, the Hivite, and the Jebusite. Therefore I handed them over to you. 12 Then I sent the hornet before you and it drove out the two kings of the Amorites from you—not by your sword nor your bow. 13 And I gave you a land on which you had not labored, and cities which you had not built, and you have lived in them; you are eating of vineyards and olive groves which you did not plant.'

"We Will Serve the LORD"

14 "Now, therefore, fear the LORD and serve Him in sincerity and truth; and do away with the gods which your fathers served beyond the *Euphrates* River and in Egypt, and serve the LORD. 15 But if it is disagreeable in your sight to serve the LORD, choose for yourselves today whom you will serve: whether the gods which your fathers served, which were beyond the *Euphrates* River, or the gods of the Amorites in whose land you are living; but as for me and my house, we will serve the LORD."

16 The people answered and said, "Far be it from us that we would abandon the LORD to serve other gods; 17 for the LORD our God is He who brought us and our fathers up out of the land of Egypt, from the house of slaves, and did these great signs in our sight and watched over us through all the way in which we went and among all the peoples through whose midst we passed. 18 The LORD drove out from before us all the peoples, even the Amorites who lived in the land. We also will serve the LORD, for He is our God."

19 Then Joshua said to the people, "You will not be able to serve the LORD, for He is a holy God. He is a jealous God; He will not forgive your wrongdoing or your sins. 20 If you abandon the LORD and serve foreign gods, then He will turn and do you harm and destroy you after He has done good to you." 21 And the people said to Joshua, "No, but we will serve the LORD." 22 So Joshua said to the people, "You are witnesses against yourselves that you have chosen for yourselves the LORD, to serve Him." And they said, "*We are* witnesses." 23 "Now then, do away with the foreign gods which are in your midst, and incline your hearts to the LORD, the God of Israel." 24 And the people said to Joshua, "We will serve the LORD our God and obey His voice." 25 So Joshua made a covenant with the people that day, and made for them a statute and an ordinance in Shechem. 26 And Joshua wrote these words in the Book of the Law of God; and he took a large stone and set it up there under the oak that was by the sanctuary of the LORD. 27 Then Joshua said to all the people, "Behold, this stone shall be a witness against us, because it has heard all the words of the LORD which He spoke to us; so it shall be a witness against you, so that you do not deny your God." 28 Then Joshua dismissed the people, each to his inheritance.

Joshua's Death and Burial

29 Now it came about after these things that Joshua the son of Nun, the servant of the LORD, died, being 110 years old. 30 And they buried him in the territory of his inheritance, in Timnath-serah, which is in the hill country of Ephraim, on the north of Mount Gaash.

31 Israel served the LORD all the days of Joshua and all the days of the elders who survived Joshua, and had known every deed of the LORD which He had done for Israel.

32 Now they buried the bones of Joseph, which the sons of Israel brought up from Egypt, at Shechem, in the plot of land which Jacob had bought from the sons of Hamor the father of Shechem for a hundred pieces of money; and they became the inheritance of Joseph's sons. 33 And Eleazar the son of Aaron died; and they buried him at Gibeah, *the town* of his son Phinehas, which was given to him in the hill country of Ephraim.

The Book of
JUDGES

Jerusalem Is Captured

1 Now it came about after the death of Joshua that the sons of Israel inquired of the LORD, saying, "Who shall go up first for us against the Canaanites, to fight against them?" 2 The LORD said, "Judah shall go up; behold, I have handed the land over to him." 3 Then Judah said to his brother Simeon, "Go up with me into the territory allotted me, and let's fight the Canaanites; and I in turn will go with you into the territory allotted you." So Simeon went with him. 4 Judah went up, and the LORD handed over to them the Canaanites and the Perizzites, and they defeated ten thousand men at Bezek. 5 They found Adoni-bezek in Bezek and fought against him, and they defeated the Canaanites and the Perizzites. 6 But Adoni-bezek fled; and they pursued him and caught him, and cut off his thumbs and big toes. 7 And Adoni-bezek said, "Seventy kings with their thumbs and their big toes cut off used to gather up *scraps* under my table; as I have done, so God has repaid me." So they brought him to Jerusalem, and he died there.

8 Then the sons of Judah fought against Jerusalem and captured it, and struck it with the edge of the sword, and set the city on fire. 9 Afterward, the sons of Judah went down to fight against the Canaanites living in the hill country, and in the ¹Negev, and in the lowland. 10 So Judah went against the Canaanites who lived in Hebron (the name of Hebron *was* previously Kiriath-arba); and they struck Sheshai, Ahiman, and Talmai.

Capture of Other Cities

11 Then from there he went against the inhabitants of Debir (the name of Debir *was* previously Kiriath-sepher). 12 And Caleb said, "Whoever attacks Kiriath-sepher and captures it, I will give him my daughter Achsah as a wife." 13 Now Othniel the son of Kenaz, Caleb's younger brother, captured it; so he gave him his daughter Achsah as a wife. 14 Then it happened that when she came *to him,* she incited him to ask her father for a field. Then *later,* she dismounted from her donkey, and Caleb said to her, "What do you want?" 15 She said to him, "Give me a blessing: since you have given me the land of the ¹Negev, give me springs of water also." So Caleb gave her the upper springs and the lower springs.

16 Now the descendants of the Kenite, Moses' father-in-law, went up from the city of palms with the sons of Judah, to the wilderness of Judah which is in the south of Arad; and they went and lived with the people. 17 Then Judah went with his brother Simeon, and they struck the Canaanites living in Zephath, and utterly destroyed it. So the name of the city was called Hormah. 18 And Judah took Gaza with its territory, Ashkelon with its territory,

and Ekron with its territory. 19 Now the LORD was with Judah, and they took possession of the hill country; but *they could* not drive out the inhabitants of the valley, because they had iron chariots. 20 Then they gave Hebron to Caleb, as Moses had promised; and he drove out from there the three sons of Anak. 21 But the sons of Benjamin did not drive out the Jebusites who lived in Jerusalem; so the Jebusites have lived with the sons of Benjamin in Jerusalem to this day.

22 Likewise the house of Joseph went up against Bethel, and the LORD was with them. 23 The house of Joseph had *men* spy out Bethel (the name of the city previously was Luz). 24 And the spies saw a man coming out of the city, and they said to him, "Please show us the entrance to the city, and we will treat you kindly." 25 So he showed them the entrance to the city, and they struck the city with the edge of the sword, but they let the man and all his family go free. 26 Then the man went to the land of the Hittites and built a city, and named it Luz, which is its name to this day.

Places Not Conquered

27 But Manasseh did not take possession of Beth-shean and its villages, or Taanach and its villages, or the inhabitants of Dor and its villages, or the inhabitants of Ibleam and its villages, or the inhabitants of Megiddo and its villages; so the Canaanites persisted in living in this land. 28 And it came about, when Israel became strong, that they put the Canaanites to forced labor; but they did not drive them out completely.

29 And Ephraim did not drive out the Canaanites who were living in Gezer; so the Canaanites lived in Gezer among them.

30 Zebulun did not drive out the inhabitants of Kitron, or the inhabitants of ¹Nahalol; so the Canaanites lived among them and became subject to forced labor.

31 Asher did not drive out the inhabitants of Acco, or the inhabitants of Sidon, or of Ahlab, or of Achzib, Helbah, Aphik, or of Rehob. 32 So the Asherites lived among the Canaanites, the inhabitants of the land; for they did not drive them out.

33 Naphtali did not drive out the inhabitants of Beth-shemesh, or the inhabitants of Beth-anath, but lived among the Canaanites, the inhabitants of the land; and the inhabitants of Beth-shemesh and Beth-anath became forced labor for them.

34 Then the Amorites forced the sons of Dan into the hill country, for they did not allow them to come down to the valley; 35 yet the Amorites persisted in living on Mount Heres, in Aijalon and Shaalbim; but when the power of the house of Joseph grew strong, they became forced labor. 36 The border of the

Amorites *ran* from the ascent of Akrabbim, from Sela and upward.

Israel Rebuked

2 Now the angel of the LORD came up from Gilgal to Bochim. And he said, "I brought you up out of Egypt and led you into the land which I have sworn to your fathers; and I said, 'I will never break My covenant with you, 2 and as for you, you shall not make a covenant with the inhabitants of this land; you shall tear down their altars.' But you have not obeyed Me; what is this *thing that* you have done? 3 Therefore I also said, 'I will not drive them out from you; but they will ¹become *like thorns* in your sides, and their gods will be a snare to you.' " 4 Now when the angel of the LORD spoke these words to all the sons of Israel, the people raised their voices and wept. 5 So they named that place ¹Bochim; and there they sacrificed to the LORD.

Joshua Dies

6 When Joshua had dismissed the people, the sons of Israel went, each one to his inheritance, to take possession of the land. 7 The people served the LORD all the days of Joshua, and all the days of the elders who survived Joshua, who had seen all the great work of the LORD which He had done for Israel. 8 Then Joshua the son of Nun, the servant of the LORD, died at the age of 110. 9 And they buried him in the territory of his inheritance in Timnath-heres, in the hill country of Ephraim, north of Mount Gaash. 10 All that generation also were gathered to their fathers; and another generation rose up after them who did not know the LORD, nor even the work which He had done for Israel.

Israel Serves the Baals

11 Then the sons of Israel did evil in the sight of the LORD and served the Baals, 12 and they abandoned the LORD, the God of their fathers, who had brought them out of the land of Egypt, and they followed other gods from the gods of the peoples who were around them, and bowed down to them; so they provoked the LORD to anger. 13 They abandoned the LORD and served Baal and the Ashtaroth. 14 Then the anger of the LORD burned against Israel, and He handed them over to plunderers, and they plundered them; and He sold them into the hands of their enemies around *them,* so that they could no longer stand against their enemies. 15 Wherever they went, the hand of the LORD was against them for evil, as the LORD had spoken and just as the LORD had sworn to them, so that they were severely distressed. 16 Then the LORD raised up judges who saved them from the hands of those who plundered them. 17 Yet they did not listen to their judges, for they ¹committed infidelity with other gods and bowed down to them. They turned aside quickly from the way in which their fathers had walked in obeying the commandments of the LORD; they did not do the same *as their fathers.* 18 And when the

LORD raised up judges for them, the LORD was with the judge and saved them from the hand of their enemies all the days of the judge; for the LORD was moved to pity by their groaning because of those who tormented and oppressed them. 19 But it came about, when the judge died, that they would turn back and act more corruptly than their fathers, in following other gods to serve them and bow down to them; they did not abandon their practices or their obstinate ways. 20 So the anger of the LORD burned against Israel, and He said, "Because this nation has violated My covenant which I commanded their fathers, and has not listened to My voice, 21 I in turn will no longer drive out from them any of the nations which Joshua left when he died, 22 in order to test Israel by them, whether they will keep the way of the LORD to walk in it as their fathers did, or not." 23 So the LORD allowed those nations to remain, not driving them out quickly; and He did not hand them over to Joshua.

Idolatry Leads to Servitude

3 Now these are the nations that the LORD left, to test Israel by them *(that is,* all *the Israelites* who had not experienced any of the wars of Canaan; 2 only in order that the generations of the sons of Israel might be taught war, those who had not experienced it previously). ³ *These nations are.* the five governors of the Philistines and all the Canaanites and the Sidonians, and the Hivites who lived on Mount Lebanon, from Mount Baal-hermon as far as Lebo-hamath. 4 They were *left* to test Israel by them, to find out if they would obey the commandments of the LORD, which He had commanded their fathers through Moses. 5 The sons of Israel lived among the Canaanites, the Hittites, the Amorites, the Perizzites, the Hivites, and the Jebusites; 6 and they took their daughters for themselves as wives, and gave their own daughters to their sons, and served their gods.

7 So the sons of Israel did what was evil in the sight of the LORD, and they forgot the LORD their God and served the Baals and the ¹Asheroth. 8 Then the anger of the LORD was kindled against Israel, so that He sold them into the hand of Cushan-rishathaim, king of Mesopotamia; and the sons of Israel served Cushan-rishathaim for eight years.

The First Judge Frees Israel

9 But the sons of Israel cried out to the LORD, and the LORD raised up a deliverer for the sons of Israel to set them free, Othniel the son of Kenaz, Caleb's younger brother. 10 And the Spirit of the LORD came upon him, and he judged Israel. When he went to war, the LORD handed over to him Cushan-rishathaim king of Mesopotamia, so that he prevailed over Cushan-rishathaim. 11 Then the land was at rest for forty years. And Othniel the son of Kenaz died.

12 Now the sons of Israel again did evil in the sight of the LORD. So the LORD strengthened Eglon the king of Moab against Israel,

---

2:3 ¹Some ancient mss *become adversaries to you and*   2:5 ¹I.e., weepers   2:17 ¹I.e., against God
3:7 ¹I.e., wooden symbols of a female deity (Asherah)

because they had done evil in the sight of the LORD. 13 And he gathered to himself the sons of Ammon and Amalek; and he went and defeated Israel, and they took possession of the city of the palm trees. 14 And the sons of Israel served Eglon the king of Moab for eighteen years.

Ehud Kills Eglon

15 But when the sons of Israel cried out to the LORD, the LORD raised up a deliverer for them, Ehud the son of Gera, the Benjaminite, a left-handed man. And the sons of Israel sent tribute by him to Eglon the king of Moab. 16 Now Ehud made himself a sword which had two edges, a cubit in length, and he strapped it on his right thigh under his cloak. 17 Then he presented the tribute to Eglon king of Moab. Now Eglon was a very fat man. 18 And it came about, when he had finished presenting the tribute, that *Ehud* sent away the people who had carried the tribute. 19 But he himself turned back from the idols which were at Gilgal, and said, "I have a secret message for you, O king." And *the king* said, "Silence!" And all who were attending him left him. 20 Then Ehud came to him while he was sitting in his cool roof chamber alone. And Ehud said, "I have a message from God for you." And he got up from his seat. 21 Then Ehud reached out with his left hand and took the sword from his right thigh, and thrust it into his belly. 22 The hilt *of the sword* also went in after the blade, and the fat closed over the blade because he did not pull the sword out of his belly; and the refuse came out. 23 Then Ehud went out into the vestibule, and shut the doors of the roof chamber behind him, and locked *them*.

24 When he had left, the king's servants came and looked, and behold, the doors of the roof chamber were locked; and they said, "Undoubtedly he is relieving himself in the cool room." 25 So they waited until it would have been shameful *to wait longer;* but behold, he did not open the doors of the roof chamber. So they took the key and opened *them*, and behold, their master had fallen to the floor dead.

26 Now Ehud escaped while they were hesitating, and he passed by the idols and escaped to Seirah. 27 And when he arrived, he blew the trumpet in the hill country of Ephraim; and the sons of Israel went down with him from the hill country, and he *was* leading them. 28 Then he said to them, "Pursue *them,* for the LORD has handed your enemies the Moabites over to you." So they went down after him and took control of the crossing places of the Jordan opposite Moab, and did not allow anyone to cross. 29 They struck and killed about ten thousand Moabites at that time, all robust and valiant men; and no one escaped. 30 So Moab was subdued that day under the hand of Israel. And the land was at rest for eighty years.

Shamgar Saves Israel

31 Now after him came Shamgar the son of Anath, who struck and killed six hundred Philistines with an †oxgoad; and he also saved Israel.

Deborah and Barak

4 Then the sons of Israel again did evil in the sight of the LORD, after Ehud died. 2 So the LORD sold them into the hand of Jabin king of Canaan, who reigned in Hazor; and the commander of his army was Sisera, who lived in Harosheth-hagoyim. 3 The sons of Israel cried out to the LORD; for he had nine hundred iron chariots, and he oppressed the sons of Israel severely for twenty years.

4 Now Deborah, a prophetess, the wife of Lappidoth, was judging Israel at that time. 5 She used to sit under the palm tree of Deborah between Ramah and Bethel in the hill country of Ephraim; and the sons of Israel went up to her for judgment. 6 Now she sent *word* and summoned Barak the son of Abinoam from Kedesh-naphtali, and said to him, "The LORD, the God of Israel, has indeed commanded, 'Go and march to Mount Tabor, and take with you ten thousand men from the sons of Naphtali and from the sons of Zebulun. 7 I will draw out to you Sisera, the commander of Jabin's army, with his chariots and his many *troops* to the river Kishon, and I will hand him over to you.'" 8 Then Barak said to her, "If you will go with me, then I will go; but if you will not go with me, I will not go." 9 She said, "I will certainly go with you; however, the fame shall not be yours on the journey that you are about to take, for the LORD will sell Sisera into the hand of a woman." Then Deborah got up and went with Barak to Kedesh. 10 Barak summoned Zebulun and Naphtali to Kedesh, and ten thousand men went up with him; Deborah also went up with him.

11 Now Heber the Kenite had separated himself from the Kenites, from the sons of Hobab the father-in-law of Moses, and had pitched his tent as far away as the oak in Zaanannim, which is near Kedesh.

12 Then they told Sisera that Barak the son of Abinoam had gone up to Mount Tabor. 13 Sisera summoned all his chariots, nine hundred iron chariots, and all the people who *were* with him, from Harosheth-hagoyim to the river Kishon. 14 Then Deborah said to Barak, "Arise! For this is the day on which the LORD has handed Sisera over to you; behold, the LORD has gone out before you." So Barak went down from Mount Tabor with ten thousand men following him. 15 And the LORD routed Sisera and all *his* chariots and all *his* army with the edge of the sword before Barak; and Sisera got down from *his* chariot and fled on foot. 16 But Barak pursued the chariots and the army as far as Harosheth-hagoyim, and all the army of Sisera fell by the edge of the sword; not even one was left.

17 Now Sisera fled on foot to the tent of Jael the wife of Heber the Kenite, because *there was* peace between Jabin the king of Hazor and the house of Heber the Kenite. 18 And Jael went out to meet Sisera, and said to him, "Turn aside, my master, turn aside to me! Do not be afraid." So he turned aside to her into the tent,

---

3:31 †I.e., a spiked stick for driving livestock

and she covered him with a rug. 19 And he said to her, "Please give me a little water to drink, for I am thirsty." So she opened a leather bottle of milk and gave him a drink; then she covered him. 20 And he said to her, "Stand in the doorway of the tent, and it shall be if anyone comes and inquires of you, and says, 'Is there anyone here?' that you shall say, 'No.'" 21 But Jael, Heber's wife, took a tent peg and a hammer in her hand, and went secretly to him and drove the peg into his temple, and it went through into the ground; for he was sound asleep and exhausted. So he died. 22 And behold, while Barak was pursuing Sisera, Jael came out to meet him and said to him, "Come, and I will show you the man whom you are seeking." So he entered with her, and behold, Sisera was lying dead with the tent peg in his temple.

23 So God subdued Jabin the king of Canaan on that day before the sons of Israel. 24 And the hand of the sons of Israel pressed harder and harder upon Jabin the king of Canaan, until they had eliminated Jabin the king of Canaan.

The Song of Deborah and Barak

5 Then Deborah and Barak the son of Abinoam sang on that day, saying,

2 "For the leaders leading in Israel,
For the people volunteering,
Bless the LORD!

3 "Hear, you kings; listen, you dignitaries!
I myself—to the LORD, I myself will sing,
I will sing praise to the LORD, the God of
Israel!

4 "LORD, when You went out from Seir,
When You marched from the field of
Edom,
The earth quaked, the heavens also
dripped,
The clouds also dripped water.

5 "The mountains flowed *with water* at the
presence of the LORD,
This Sinai, at the presence of the LORD,
the God of Israel.

6¶ "In the days of Shamgar the son of Anath,
In the days of Jael, the roads were
deserted,
And travelers went by roundabout ways.

7 "The peasantry came to an end, they came
to an end in Israel,
Until I, Deborah, arose,
Until I arose, a mother in Israel.

8 "New gods were chosen;
Then war *was in* the gates.
Not a shield or a spear was seen
Among forty thousand in Israel.

9 "My heart *goes out* to the commanders of
Israel,
The volunteers among the people;
Bless the LORD!

10 "You who ride on white donkeys,
You who sit on *rich* carpets,
And you who travel on the road—shout in
praise!

11 "At the sound of those who distribute
water among the watering places,
There they will recount the righteous
deeds of the LORD,

The righteous deeds for His peasantry in
Israel.
Then the people of the LORD went down
to the gates.

12¶ "Awake, awake, Deborah;
Awake, awake, sing a song!
Arise, Barak, and lead away your captives,
son of Abinoam.

13 "Then survivors came down to the nobles;
The people of the LORD came down to me
as warriors.

14 "From Ephraim those whose root is in
Amalek *came down,*
Following you, Benjamin, with your
peoples;
From Machir commanders came down,
And from Zebulun those who wield the
staff of office.

15 "And the princes of Issachar *were* with
Deborah;
As *was* Issachar, so *was* Barak;
Into the valley they rushed at his heels;
Among the divisions of Reuben
There were great determinations of heart.

16 "Why did you sit among the †sheepfolds,
To hear the piping for the flocks?
Among the divisions of Reuben
There were great searchings of heart.

17 "Gilead remained across the Jordan;
And why did Dan stay on ships?
Asher sat at the seashore,
And remained by its landings.

18 "Zebulun *was* a people who risked their
lives,
And Naphtali *too,* on the high places of
the field.

19¶ "The kings came *and* fought;
Then the kings of Canaan fought
At Taanach near the waters of Megiddo;
They took no plunder in silver.

20 "The stars fought from heaven,
From their paths they fought against
Sisera.

21 "The torrent of Kishon swept them away,
The ancient torrent, the torrent Kishon.
My soul, march on with strength!

22 "Then the horses' hoofs beat
From the galloping, the galloping of his
mighty stallions.

23 'Curse Meroz,' said the angel of the LORD,
'Utterly curse its inhabitants,
Because they did not come to the help of
the LORD,
To the help of the LORD against the
warriors.'

24¶ "Most blessed of women is Jael,
The wife of Heber the Kenite;
Most blessed is she of women in the tent.

25 "He asked for water, she gave him milk;
In a magnificent bowl she brought him
curds.

26 "She reached out her hand for the tent peg,
And her right hand for the workmen's
hammer.
Then she struck Sisera, she smashed his
head;
And she shattered and pierced his temple.

27 "Between her feet he bowed, he fell, he
lay;

5:16 ¹ Or *saddlebags*

Between her feet he bowed, he fell;
Where he bowed, there he fell dead.
28¶ "Out of the window she looked and wailed,
The mother of Sisera through the lattice,
'Why does his chariot delay in coming?
Why do the hoofbeats of his chariots
delay?'
29 "Her wise princesses would answer her,
Indeed she repeats her words to herself,
30 'Are they not finding, are they not dividing
the spoils?
A concubine, two concubines for every
warrior;
To Sisera a spoil of dyed cloth,
A spoil of dyed cloth embroidered,
Dyed cloth of double embroidery on the
neck of the plunderer?'
31 "May all Your enemies perish in this way,
LORD;
But may those who love Him be like the
rising of the sun in its might."
And the land was at rest for forty years.

Israel Oppressed by Midian

6 Then the sons of Israel did what was evil in the sight of the LORD; and the LORD handed them over to Midian for seven years. 2 The power of Midian prevailed against Israel. Because of Midian the sons of Israel made for themselves the dens which were in the mountains and the caves and the strongholds. 3 For whenever Israel had sown, the Midianites would come up with the Amalekites and the people of the east and march against them. 4 So they would camp against them and destroy the produce of the earth as far as Gaza, and leave no sustenance in Israel, nor a sheep, ox, or donkey. 5 For they would come up with their livestock and their tents, they would come in like locusts in number, and both they and their camels were innumerable; and they came into the land to ruin it. 6 So Israel was brought very low because of Midian, and the sons of Israel cried out to the LORD.

7 Now it came about, when the sons of Israel cried out to the LORD on account of Midian, 8 that the LORD sent a prophet to the sons of Israel, and he said to them, "This is what the LORD, the God of Israel says: 'It was I who brought you up from Egypt, and brought you out of the house of slavery. 9 And I rescued you from the hands of the Egyptians, and from the hands of all your oppressors, and I drove them out from you and gave you their land, 10 and I said to you, "I am the LORD your God; you shall not fear the gods of the Amorites in whose land you live." But you have not obeyed Me.' "

Gideon Is Visited

11 Then the angel of the LORD came and sat under the oak that was in Ophrah, which belonged to Joash the Abiezrite, as his son Gideon was beating out wheat in the wine press in order to save it from the Midianites. 12 And the angel of the LORD appeared to him and said to him, "The LORD is with you, valiant warrior." 13 Then Gideon said to him, "O my lord, if the LORD is with us, why then has all

this happened to us? And where are all His miracles which our fathers told us about, saying, 'Did the LORD not bring us up from Egypt?' But now the LORD has abandoned us and handed us over to Midian." 14 And the LORD looked at him and said, "Go in this strength of yours and save Israel from the hand of Midian. Have I not sent you?" 15 But he said to Him, "O Lord, how am I to save Israel? Behold, my family is the least in Manasseh, and I am the youngest in my father's house." 16 Yet the LORD said to him, "I will certainly be with you, and you will defeat Midian as one man." 17 So Gideon said to Him, "If now I have found favor in Your sight, then perform for me a sign that it is You speaking with me. 18 Please do not depart from here until I come back to You, and bring out my offering and lay it before You." And He said, "I will remain until you return."

19 Then Gideon went in and prepared a young goat and unleavened bread from an 1ephah of flour; he put the meat in a basket and the broth in a pot, and brought them out to him under the oak and presented them. 20 And the angel of God said to him, "Take the meat and the unleavened bread and lay them on this rock, and pour out the broth." And he did so. 21 Then the angel of the LORD put out the end of the staff that was in his hand and touched the meat and the unleavened bread; and fire came up from the rock and consumed the meat and the unleavened bread. Then the angel of the LORD vanished from his sight. 22 When Gideon perceived that he was the angel of the LORD, he said, "Oh, Lord GOD! For I have seen the angel of the LORD face to face!" 23 But the LORD said to him, "Peace to you, do not be afraid; you shall not die." 24 Then Gideon built an altar there to the LORD and named it The LORD is Peace. To this day it is still in Ophrah of the Abiezrites.

25 Now on the same night the LORD said to him, "Take your father's bull and a second bull seven years old, and tear down the altar of Baal which belongs to your father, and cut down the 1Asherah that is beside it; 26 and build an altar to the LORD your God on the top of this stronghold in an orderly way, and take a second bull and offer a burnt offering with the wood of the Asherah which you shall cut down." 27 Then Gideon took ten men from his servants and did as the LORD had spoken to him; and because he was too afraid of his father's household and the men of the city to do it by day, he did it by night.

The Altar of Baal Destroyed

28 When the people of the city got up early in the morning, behold, the altar of Baal had been torn down, and the Asherah which had been beside it had been cut down, and the second bull had been offered on the altar which had been built. 29 So they said to one another, "Who did this thing?" And when they searched and inquired, they said, "Gideon the son of Joash did this thing." 30 Then the men of the city said to Joash, "Bring out your son, that he may die, for he has torn down the altar of Baal,

---

6:19 1About 1 cubic foot or 0.03 cubic meters 6:25 1I.e., wooden symbol of a female deity; also vv 26, 28, 30

and indeed, he has cut down the Asherah which was beside it." 31 But Joash said to all who stood against him, "Will you contend for Baal, or will you save him? Whoever will contend for him shall be put to death by morning. If he is a god, let him contend for himself, since *someone* has torn down his altar!" 32 Therefore on that day he named Gideon Jerubbaal, that is to say, "Let Baal contend against him," because he had torn down his altar.

33 Then all the Midianites, the Amalekites, and the people of the east assembled together; and they crossed over and camped in the Valley of Jezreel. 34 So the Spirit of the LORD covered Gideon like clothing; and he blew a trumpet, and the Abiezrites were called together to follow him. 35 And he sent messengers throughout Manasseh, and they also were called together to follow him; and he sent messengers to Asher, Zebulun, and Naphtali, and they came up to meet them.

Sign of the Fleece

36 Then Gideon said to God, "If You are going to save Israel through me, as You have spoken, 37 behold, I am putting a fleece of wool on the threshing floor. If there is dew on the fleece only, and it is dry on all the ground, then I will know that You will save Israel through me, as You have spoken." 38 And it was so. When he got up early the next morning and wrung out the fleece, he wrung the dew from the fleece, a bowl full of water. 39 Then Gideon said to God, "Do not let Your anger burn against me, so that I may speak only one *more* time; please let me put *You* to the test only one *more* time with the fleece: let it now be dry only on the fleece, and let there be dew on all the ground." 40 And God did so that night; for it was dry only on the fleece, and dew was on all the ground.

Gideon's Three Hundred Chosen Men

7 Then Jerubbaal (that is, Gideon) and all the people who were with him got up early, and camped beside the spring of Harod; and the camp of Midian was on the north side of them by the hill of Moreh in the valley. 2 And the LORD said to Gideon, "The people who are with you are too many for Me to hand Midian over to them, otherwise Israel would become boastful, saying, 'My own power has saved me.' 3 Now therefore come, proclaim in the hearing of the people, saying, 'Whoever is afraid and worried, is to return and leave Mount Gilead.'" So twenty-two thousand from the people returned, but ten thousand remained. 4 Then the LORD said to Gideon, "The people are still too many; bring them down to the water and I will test them for you there. So it shall be that he of whom I say to you, 'This one shall go with you,' he shall go with you; but everyone of whom I say to you, 'This one shall not go with you,' he shall not go." 5 So he brought the people down to the water. Then the LORD said to Gideon, "You shall put everyone who laps the water with his tongue as a dog laps in one group, and everyone who

kneels down to drink *in another*." 6 Now the number of those who lapped, putting their hand to their mouth, was three hundred men; but all the rest of the people kneeled down to drink water. 7 And the LORD said to Gideon, "I will save you with the three hundred men who lapped, and will hand the Midianites over to you; so have all the *other* people go, each man to his home." 8 So the three hundred men took the people's provisions and their trumpets in their hands. And Gideon dismissed all the *other* men of Israel, each to his tent, but retained the three hundred men; and the camp of Midian was below him in the valley.

9 Now on the same night it came about that the LORD said to him, "Arise, go down against the camp, for I have handed it over to you. 10 But if you are afraid to go down, go with Purah your servant down to the camp, 11 so that you will hear what they say; and afterward you will have the courage to go down against the camp." So he went down with Purah his servant to the outposts of the army that was in the camp. 12 Now the Midianites, the Amalekites, and all the people of the east were lying in the valley as numerous as locusts; and their camels were without number, as numerous as the sand on the seashore. 13 When Gideon came, behold, a man was relating a dream to his friend. And he said, "Behold, I had a dream; a loaf of barley bread was tumbling into the camp of Midian, and it came to the tent and struck it so that it fell, and turned it upside down so that the tent collapsed." 14 And his friend replied, "This is nothing other than the sword of Gideon the son of Joash, a man of Israel; God has handed over to him Midian and all the camp."

15 When Gideon heard the account of the dream and its interpretation, he bowed in worship. Then he returned to the camp of Israel and said, "Arise, for the LORD has handed over to you the camp of Midian!" 16 And he divided the three hundred men into three units, and he put trumpets and empty pitchers into the hands of all of them, with torches inside the pitchers. 17 Then he said to them, "Look at me and do likewise. And behold, when I come to the outskirts of the camp, do as I do. 18 When I and all who are with me blow the trumpet, then you also blow the trumpets around the entire camp and say, 'For the LORD and for Gideon!'"

Confusion of the Enemy

19 So Gideon and the hundred men who were with him came to the outskirts of the camp at the beginning of the middle night watch, when they had just posted the watch; and they blew the trumpets and smashed the pitchers that were in their hands. 20 When the three units blew the trumpets and broke the pitchers, they held the torches in their left hands and the trumpets in their right hands for blowing, and shouted, "A sword for the LORD and for Gideon!" 21 And each stood in his place around the camp; and all the army ran, crying out as they fled. 22 And when they blew the three hundred trumpets, the LORD set the sword of one against another even throughout the entire army; and the army fled as far as

Beth-shittah toward Zererah, as far as the edge of Abel-meholah, by Tabbath. 23 And the men of Israel were summoned from Naphtali, Asher, and all Manasseh, and they pursued Midian.

24 Then Gideon sent messengers throughout the hill country of Ephraim, saying, "Come down against Midian and take control of the waters ahead of them, as far as Beth-barah and the Jordan." So all the men of Ephraim were summoned, and they took control of the waters as far as Beth-barah and the Jordan. 25 And they captured the two leaders of Midian, Oreb and Zeeb, and they killed Oreb at the rock of Oreb, and they killed Zeeb at the wine press of Zeeb, while they pursued Midian; and they brought the heads of Oreb and Zeeb to Gideon from across the Jordan.

Zebah and Zalmunna Routed

8 Then the men of Ephraim said to Gideon, "What is this thing *that* you have done to us, not calling upon us when you went to fight against Midian?" And they quarreled with him vehemently. 2 But he said to them, "What have I done now in comparison with you? Is the gleaning *of the grapes* of Ephraim not better than the vintage of Abiezer? 3 God has handed over to you the leaders of Midian, Oreb and Zeeb; and what was I able to do in comparison with you?" Then their anger toward him subsided when he said that.

4 Then Gideon and the three hundred men who were with him came to the Jordan *and* crossed over, exhausted yet *still* pursuing. 5 And he said to the men of Succoth, "Please give loaves of bread to the people who are following me, for they are exhausted, and I am pursuing Zebah and Zalmunna, the kings of Midian." 6 But the leaders of Succoth said, "Are the hands of Zebah and Zalmunna already in your hand, that we should give bread to your army?" 7 So Gideon said, "For this *answer,* when the LORD has handed over to me Zebah and Zalmunna, I will thrash your bodies with the thorns of the wilderness and with briers." 8 Then he went up from there to Penuel and spoke similarly to them; and the men of Penuel answered him just as the men of Succoth had answered. 9 So he said also to the men of Penuel, "When I return safely, I will tear down this tower."

10 Now Zebah and Zalmunna were in Karkor, and their armies with them, about fifteen thousand men, all who were left of the entire army of the people of the east; for the fallen were 120,000 swordsmen. 11 Gideon went up by the way of those who lived in tents to the east of Nobah and Jogbehah, and he attacked the camp when the camp was unsuspecting. 12 When Zebah and Zalmunna fled, he pursued them and captured the two kings of Midian, Zebah and Zalmunna, and routed the entire army.

13 Then Gideon the son of Joash returned from the battle by the ascent of Heres. 14 And he captured a youth from Succoth and questioned him. Then *the youth* wrote down for him the leaders of Succoth and its elders, seventy-seven men. 15 And he came to the men of Succoth and said, "Behold Zebah and Zalmunna, about whom you taunted me, saying, 'Are the hands of Zebah and Zalmunna already in your hand, that we should give bread to your men who are weary?' " 16 Then he took the elders of the city, and thorns of the wilderness and briers, and he disciplined the men of Succoth with them. 17 And he tore down the tower of Penuel and killed the men of the city.

18 Then he said to Zebah and Zalmunna, "Where *were* the men whom you killed at Tabor?" But they said, "You and they were alike, each one resembling the son of a king." 19 And he said, "They *were* my brothers, the sons of my mother. *As* the LORD lives, if only you had let them live, I would not kill you." 20 So he said to Jether his firstborn, "Rise, kill them." But the youth did not draw his sword, for he was afraid, because he was still a youth. 21 Then Zebah and Zalmunna said, "Rise up yourself, and attack us; for as the man, so is his strength." So Gideon arose and killed Zebah and Zalmunna, and took the crescent amulets which were on their camels' necks.

22 Then the men of Israel said to Gideon, "Rule over us, both you and your son, your son's son as well, for you have saved us from the hand of Midian!" 23 But Gideon said to them, "I will not rule over you, nor shall my son rule over you; the LORD shall rule over you." 24 Yet Gideon said to them, "I would request of you, that each of you give me an earring from his plunder." (For they had gold earrings, because they were Ishmaelites.) 25 And they said, "We will certainly give *them to you.*" So they spread out a garment, and every one of them tossed an earring there from his plunder. 26 The weight of the gold earrings that he requested was 1,700 *shekels* of gold, apart from the crescent amulets, the ear pendants, and the purple robes which *were* on the kings of Midian, and apart from the neck chains that *were* on their camels' necks. 27 Gideon made it into an ephod, and placed it in his city, Ophrah; but all Israel 1 committed infidelity with it there, and it became a snare to Gideon and his household.

Forty Years of Peace

28 So Midian was subdued before the sons of Israel, and they did not lift up their heads anymore. And the land was undisturbed for forty years in the days of Gideon.

29 Then Jerubbaal the son of Joash went and lived in his own house. 30 Now Gideon had seventy sons who were his direct descendants, for he had many wives. 31 And his concubine who was in Shechem also bore him a son, and he named him Abimelech. 32 And Gideon the son of Joash died at a good old age and was buried in the tomb of his father Joash, in Ophrah of the Abiezrites.

33 Then it came about, as soon as Gideon was dead, that the sons of Israel again 1 committed infidelity with the Baals, and made Baal-berith their god. 34 So the sons of Israel did not remember the LORD their God, who had

saved them from the hands of all their enemies on every side; 35 nor did they show kindness to the household of Jerubbaal (*that is,* Gideon) in accordance with all the good that he had done for Israel.

Abimelech's Conspiracy

9 Now Abimelech the son of Jerubbaal went to Shechem, to his mother's relatives, and spoke to them and to the entire family of the household of his mother's father, saying, 2 "Speak, now, in the hearing of all the leaders of Shechem, 'Which is better for you: for seventy men, all the sons of Jerubbaal, to rule over you, or for one man to rule over you?' Also, remember that I am your bone and your flesh." 3 So his mother's relatives spoke all these words on his behalf in the hearing of all the leaders of Shechem; and they were inclined to follow Abimelech, for they said, "He is our relative." 4 And they gave him seventy *pieces* of silver from the house of Baal-berith, with which Abimelech hired worthless and reckless men, and they followed him. 5 Then he went to his father's house in Ophrah and killed his brothers the sons of Jerubbaal, seventy men, on one stone. But Jotham the youngest son of Jerubbaal was left, because he hid himself. 6 All the leaders of Shechem and all Beth-millo assembled together, and they went and made Abimelech king, by the oak of the memorial stone which was in Shechem.

7 Now when they told Jotham, he went and stood on the top of Mount Gerizim, and raised his voice and called out. And he said to them, "Listen to me, you leaders of Shechem, that God may listen to you. 8 Once the trees went to anoint a king over them, and they said to the olive tree, 'Reign over us!' 9 But the olive tree said to them, 'Shall I give up my fatness with which God and mankind are honored, and go to wave over the trees?' 10 Then the trees said to the fig tree, 'You, come, reign over us!' 11 But the fig tree said to them, 'Shall I give up my sweetness and my good fruit, and go to wave over the trees?' 12 Then the trees said to the vine, 'You, come, reign over us!' 13 But the vine said to them, 'Shall I give up my new wine, which cheers God and mankind, and go to wave over the trees?' 14 Then all the trees said to the bramble, 'You, come, reign over us!' 15 And the bramble said to the trees, 'If you really are anointing me as king over you, come and take refuge in my shade; but if not, may fire come out of the bramble and consume the cedars of Lebanon.'

16 "Now then, if you have acted with honesty and integrity in making Abimelech king, and if you have dealt well with Jerubbaal and his house, and have dealt with him as he deserved— 17 for my father fought for you, and risked his life and saved you from the hand of Midian; 18 but *in fact* you have risen against my father's house today and have killed his sons, seventy men, on one stone, and have made Abimelech, the son of his female slave, king over the leaders of Shechem, because he is your relative— 19 so if you have acted with honesty and integrity toward Jerubbaal and his

house this day, be joyful about Abimelech, and may he also be joyful about you. 20 But if not, may fire come out of Abimelech and consume the leaders of Shechem and Beth-millo; and may fire come out of the leaders of Shechem and from Beth-millo, and consume Abimelech." 21 Then Jotham escaped and fled, and went to Beer; and he stayed there because of his brother Abimelech.

Shechem and Abimelech Fall

22 Now Abimelech ruled over Israel for three years. 23 Then God sent an evil spirit between Abimelech and the leaders of Shechem; and the leaders of Shechem dealt treacherously with Abimelech, 24 so that the violence done to the seventy sons of Jerubbaal would come, and *the responsibility for* their blood would be placed on their brother Abimelech, who killed them, and on the leaders of Shechem, who encouraged him to kill his brothers. 25 The leaders of Shechem set up men in ambush against him on the tops of the mountains, and they robbed everyone who would pass by them on the road; and it was reported to Abimelech.

26 Now Gaal the son of Ebed came with his relatives, and crossed over into Shechem; and the leaders of Shechem trusted him. 27 So they went out to the field and gathered the grapes of their vineyards and trampled *them,* and held a festival; and they went into the house of their god, and ate and drank and cursed Abimelech. 28 Then Gaal the son of Ebed said, "Who is Abimelech, and who is Shechem, that we should serve him? Is he not the son of Jerubbaal, and *is* Zebul *not* his governor? Serve the men of Hamor the father of Shechem; but why should we serve him? 29 If only this people were under my authority! Then I would do away with Abimelech." And he said to Abimelech, "Enlarge your army and come out!"

30 When Zebul the leader of the city heard the words of Gaal the son of Ebed, his anger burned. 31 So using deception, he *successfully* sent messengers to Abimelech, saying, "Behold, Gaal the son of Ebed and his relatives have come to Shechem; and behold, they are stirring up the city against you. 32 So now, arise by night, you and the people who are with you, and lie in wait in the field. 33 Then in the morning, as soon as the sun is up, you shall rise early and attack the city; and behold, when he and the people who are with him come out against you, you shall do to them whatever you can."

34 So Abimelech and all the people who *were* with him got up at night, and lay in wait against Shechem, in four units. 35 Now Gaal the son of Ebed went out and stood at the entrance of the city gate; and Abimelech and the people who *were* with him arose from the ambush. 36 When Gaal saw the people, he said to Zebul, "Look, people are coming down from the tops of the mountains." But Zebul said to him, "You are seeing the shadow of the mountains as *if they were* people." 37 And Gaal spoke yet again and said, "Look, people are coming down from the highest part of the land, and one unit is

coming by way of the diviners' oak." **38** Then Zebul said to him, "Where then is your boasting with which you said, 'Who is Abimelech that we should serve him?' Is this not the people whom you rejected? Go out now and fight them!" **39** So Gaal went out in the sight of the leaders of Shechem and fought Abimelech. **40** But Abimelech chased him, and he fled from him; and many fell wounded up to the entrance of the gate. **41** Then Abimelech stayed in Arumah, but Zebul drove out Gaal and his relatives so that they could not stay in Shechem.

42 Now it came about the next day, that the people went out to the field, and it was reported to Abimelech. **43** So he took his people and divided them into three units, and lay in wait in the field; when he looked and saw the people coming out from the city, he attacked them and killed them. **44** Then Abimelech and the company who was with him rushed forward and stood at the entrance of the city gate; the *other* two companies then attacked all who *were* in the field and killed them. **45** Abimelech fought against the city that whole day, and he captured the city and killed the people who *were* in it; then he tore down the city and sowed it with salt.

46 When all the leaders of the tower of Shechem heard *about it,* they entered the inner chamber of the temple of El-berith. **47** And it was reported to Abimelech that all the leaders of the tower of Shechem were gathered together. **48** So Abimelech went up to Mount Zalmon, he and all the people who *were* with him; and Abimelech took an axe in his hand and cut down a branch *from the* trees, and lifted it and put *it* on his shoulder. Then he said to the people who *were* with him, "What you saw me do, hurry *and* do likewise." **49** So all the people also cut down, each one, his branch and followed Abimelech, and put *them* on top of the inner chamber and set the inner chamber on fire over those *inside,* so that all the people of the tower of Shechem also died, about a thousand men and women.

50 Then Abimelech went to Thebez, and he camped against Thebez and captured it. **51** But there was a strong tower in the center of the city, and all the men and women with all the leaders of the city fled there and shut themselves in; and they went up on the roof of the tower. **52** So Abimelech came to the tower and fought against it, and approached the entrance of the tower to burn it down with fire. **53** But a woman threw an upper millstone on Abimelech's head, crushing his skull. **54** Then he called quickly to the young man, his armor bearer, and said to him, "Draw your sword and kill me, so that it will not be said of me, 'A woman killed him.'" So the young man pierced him through, and he died. **55** Now when the men of Israel saw that Abimelech was dead, each left for his home. **56** So God repaid the wickedness of Abimelech, which he had done to his father in killing his seventy brothers. **57** God also returned all the wickedness of the men of Shechem on their heads, and the curse of Jotham the son of Jerubbaal came upon them.

Oppression by Philistines and Ammonites

10 Now after Abimelech *died,* Tola the son of Puah, the son of Dodo, a man of Issachar, rose up to save Israel; and he lived in Shamir in the hill country of Ephraim. **2** He judged Israel for twenty-three years. Then he died and was buried in Shamir.

3 After him, Jair the Gileadite rose up and judged Israel for twenty-two years. **4** And he had thirty sons who rode on thirty donkeys, and they had thirty cities in the land of Gilead that are called Havvoth-jair to this day. **5** And Jair died and was buried in Kamon.

6 Then the sons of Israel again did evil in the sight of the LORD, and they served the Baals and the Ashtaroth, the gods of Aram, the gods of Sidon, the gods of Moab, the gods of the sons of Ammon, and the gods of the Philistines; so they abandoned the LORD and did not serve Him. **7** And the anger of the LORD burned against Israel, and He sold them into the hands of the Philistines, and into the hands of the sons of Ammon. **8** And they afflicted and oppressed the sons of Israel that year; for eighteen years they *oppressed* all the sons of Israel who were beyond the Jordan, in Gilead in the land of the Amorites. **9** And the sons of Ammon crossed the Jordan to fight also against Judah, Benjamin, and the house of Ephraim, so that Israel was in great difficulty.

10 Then the sons of Israel cried out to the LORD, saying, "We have sinned against You, for indeed, we have abandoned our God and served the Baals." **11** And the LORD said to the sons of Israel, "*Did I* not *save you* from the Egyptians, the Amorites, the sons of Ammon, and the Philistines? **12** And when the Sidonians, the Amalekites, and the Maonites oppressed you, you cried out to Me, and I saved you from their hands. **13** Yet you abandoned Me and served other gods; therefore I will no longer save you. **14** Go and cry out to the gods which you have chosen; let them save you in the time of your distress." **15** Then the sons of Israel said to the LORD, "We have sinned, do to us whatever seems good to You; only please save us this day." **16** So they removed the foreign gods from among them and served the LORD; and He could no longer endure the misery of Israel.

17 Then the sons of Ammon were summoned, and they camped in Gilead. And the sons of Israel gathered together and camped in Mizpah. **18** And the people, the leaders of Gilead, said to one another, "Who is the man who will begin to fight against the sons of Ammon? He shall become head over all the inhabitants of Gilead."

Jephthah, the Ninth Judge

11 Now Jephthah the Gileadite was a valiant warrior, but he was the son of a prostitute. And Gilead had fathered Jephthah. **2** Gilead's wife bore him sons; and when his wife's sons grew up, they drove Jephthah out and said to him, "You shall not have an inheritance in our father's house, for you are the son of another woman." **3** So Jephthah fled from his brothers and lived in the land of Tob; and

worthless men gathered around Jephthah, and they went wherever he did. **4** Now it came about, after a while, that the sons of Ammon fought against Israel. **5** When the sons of Ammon fought against Israel, the elders of Gilead went to get Jephthah from the land of Tob; **6** and they said to Jephthah, "Come and be our leader, that we may fight against the sons of Ammon." **7** But Jephthah said to the elders of Gilead, "Did you not hate me and drive me from my father's house? So why have you come to me now when you are in trouble?" **8** The elders of Gilead said to Jephthah, "For this reason we have now returned to you, that you may go with us and fight the sons of Ammon, and become our head over all the inhabitants of Gilead." **9** So Jephthah said to the elders of Gilead, "If you bring me back to fight against the sons of Ammon and the LORD gives them up to me, will I become your head?" **10** And the elders of Gilead said to Jephthah, "The LORD is witness between us; be assured we will do as you have said." **11** Then Jephthah went with the elders of Gilead, and the people made him head and leader over them; and Jephthah spoke all his words before the LORD at Mizpah.

12 So Jephthah sent messengers to the king of the sons of Ammon, saying, "What *conflict* do you and I have, that you have come to me to fight against my land?" **13** And the king of the sons of Ammon said to the messengers of Jephthah, "*It is* because Israel took my land when they came up from Egypt, from the Arnon as far as the Jabbok and the Jordan; so return them peaceably now." **14** But Jephthah sent messengers once again to the king of the sons of Ammon, **15** and they said to him, "This is what Jephthah says: 'Israel did not take the land of Moab nor the land of the sons of Ammon. **16** For when they came up from Egypt, and Israel went through the wilderness to the Red Sea, and came to Kadesh, **17** then Israel sent messengers to the king of Edom, saying, "Please let us pass through your land"; but the king of Edom would not listen. And they also sent *messengers* to the king of Moab, but he would not consent. So Israel remained at Kadesh. **18** Then they went through the wilderness and around the land of Edom and the land of Moab, and came to the east side of the land of Moab, and they camped beyond the Arnon; but they did not enter the territory of Moab, for the Arnon *was* the border of Moab. **19** And Israel sent messengers to Sihon king of the Amorites, the king of Heshbon; and Israel said to him, "Please let us pass through your land to our place." **20** But Sihon did not trust Israel to pass through his territory; so Sihon gathered all his people and camped in Jahaz, and fought with Israel. **21** And the LORD, the God of Israel, handed Sihon and all his people over to Israel, and they defeated them; so Israel took possession of all the land of the Amorites, the inhabitants of that country. **22** So they possessed all the territory of the Amorites, from the Arnon as far as the Jabbok, and from the wilderness as far as the Jordan. **23** And now the LORD, the God of Israel, has driven out the Amorites from His people Israel; so should you possess it? **24** Do

you not possess what Chemosh your god gives you to possess? So whatever the LORD our God has dispossessed before us, we will possess it. **25** Now then, are you any better than Balak the son of Zippor, king of Moab? Did he ever contend with Israel, or did he ever fight against them? **26** While Israel was living in Heshbon and its villages, and in Aroer and its villages, and in all the cities that are on the banks of the Arnon, three hundred years, why did you not recover them within that time? **27** So I have not sinned against you, but you are doing me wrong by making war against me. May the LORD, the Judge, judge today between the sons of Israel and the sons of Ammon.'" **28** But the king of the sons of Ammon disregarded the message which Jephthah sent him.

Jephthah's Tragic Vow

29 Now the Spirit of the LORD came upon Jephthah, and he passed through Gilead and Manasseh; then he passed through Mizpah of Gilead, and from Mizpah of Gilead he went on to the sons of Ammon. **30** And Jephthah made a vow to the LORD and said, "If You will indeed hand over to me the sons of Ammon, **31** then whatever comes out the doors of my house to meet me when I return safely from the sons of Ammon, it shall be the LORD's, and I will offer it up as a burnt offering." **32** So Jephthah crossed over to the sons of Ammon to fight against them; and the LORD handed them over to him. **33** He inflicted a very great defeat on them from Aroer to the entrance of Minnith, twenty cities, and as far as Abel-keramim. So the sons of Ammon were subdued before the sons of Israel.

34 But Jephthah came to his house at Mizpah, and behold, his daughter was coming out to meet him with tambourines and with dancing. And she was his one *and* only child; besides her he had no son or daughter. **35** So when he saw her, he tore his clothes and said, "Oh, my daughter! You have brought me disaster, and you are among those who trouble me; for I have given my word to the LORD, and I cannot take *it* back." **36** So she said to him, "My father, you have given your word to the LORD; do to me just as you have said, since the LORD has brought you vengeance on your enemies, the sons of Ammon." **37** And she said to her father, "Let this thing be done for me; allow me two months, so that I may go to the mountains and weep because of my virginity, I and my friends." **38** Then he said, "Go." So he let her go for two months; and she left with her friends, and wept on the mountains because of her virginity. **39** And at the end of two months she returned to her father, who did to her what he had vowed; and she had no relations with a man. And it became a custom in Israel, **40** that the daughters of Israel went annually to commemorate the daughter of Jephthah the Gileadite for four days in the year.

Jephthah and His Successors

12 Now the men of Ephraim were summoned, and they crossed to Zaphon; and they said to Jephthah, "Why did you cross over to fight against the sons of Ammon

without calling us to go with you? We will burn your house down on you!" 2 So Jephthah said to them, "I and my people were in a major dispute with the sons of Ammon; and I did call you, but you did not save me from their hand. 3 When I saw that you were no deliverer, I took my life in my hands and crossed over against the sons of Ammon, and the LORD handed them over to me. Why then have you come up to me this day to fight against me?" 4 Then Jephthah gathered all the men of Gilead and fought Ephraim; and the men of Gilead defeated Ephraim, because they said, "You are survivors of Ephraim, you Gileadites, in the midst of Ephraim *and* in the midst of Manasseh." 5 And the Gileadites took control of the crossing places of the Jordan opposite Ephraim. And it happened whenever *any of* the survivors of Ephraim said, "Let me cross over," that the men of Gilead would say to him, "Are you an Ephraimite?" If he said, "No," 6 then they would say to him, "Just say, 'Shibboleth.'" But he said, "Sibboleth," for he was not prepared to pronounce it correctly. Then they seized him and slaughtered him at the crossing places of the Jordan. So at that time forty-two thousand from Ephraim fell.

7 Jephthah judged Israel for six years. Then Jephthah the Gileadite died and was buried in *one of* the cities of Gilead.

8 Now Ibzan of Bethlehem judged Israel after him. 9 He had thirty sons, and thirty daughters *whom* he gave in marriage outside *the family,* and he brought in thirty daughters from outside for his sons. And he judged Israel for seven years. 10 Then Ibzan died and was buried in Bethlehem.

11 Now Elon the Zebulunite judged Israel after him; he judged Israel for ten years. 12 Then Elon the Zebulunite died and was buried at Aijalon in the land of Zebulun.

13 Now Abdon the son of Hillel the Pirathonite judged Israel after him. 14 He had forty sons and thirty grandsons who rode on seventy donkeys; and he judged Israel for eight years. 15 Then Abdon the son of Hillel the Pirathonite died and was buried at Pirathon in the land of Ephraim, in the hill country of the Amalekites.

Philistines Oppress Again

13 Now the sons of Israel again did evil in the sight of the LORD, and the LORD handed them over to the Philistines for forty years.

2 And there was a man of Zorah, of the family of the Danites, whose name was Manoah; and his wife was infertile and had not given birth *to any children.* 3 Then the angel of the LORD appeared to the woman and said to her, "Behold now, you are infertile and have not given birth; but you will conceive and give birth to a son. 4 And now, be careful not to drink wine or strong drink, nor eat any unclean thing. 5 For behold, you will conceive and give birth to a son, and no razor shall come upon his head, for the boy shall be a Nazirite to God from the womb; and he will begin to save Israel from the hands of the Philistines." 6 Then

the woman came and told her husband, saying, "A man of God came to me, and his appearance was like the appearance of the angel of God, very awesome. So I did not ask him where he *came* from, nor did he tell me his name. 7 But he said to me, 'Behold, you shall conceive and give birth to a son, and now you shall not drink wine or strong drink, nor eat any unclean thing, for the boy shall be a Nazirite to God from the womb to the day of his death.'"

8 Then Manoah pleaded with the LORD and said, "Lord, please let the man of God whom You have sent come to us again so that he may teach us what we are to do for the boy who is to be born." 9 And God listened to the voice of Manoah; and the angel of God came again to the woman as she was sitting in the field, but Manoah her husband was not with her. 10 So the woman hurried and ran, and told her husband, "Behold, the man who came the *other* day has appeared to me!" 11 So Manoah got up and followed his wife, and when he came to the man he said to him, "Are you the man who spoke to the woman?" And he said, "I am." 12 Then Manoah said, "Now *when* your words are fulfilled, what shall be the boy's way of life and his vocation?" 13 And the angel of the LORD said to Manoah, "The woman shall pay attention to all that I said. 14 She shall not eat anything that comes from the vine nor drink wine or strong drink, nor eat any unclean thing; she shall keep all that I commanded."

15 Then Manoah said to the angel of the LORD, "Please let us detain you so that we may prepare a young goat for you." 16 But the angel of the LORD said to Manoah, "Though you detain me, I will not eat your food, but if you prepare a burnt offering, offer it to the LORD." For Manoah did not know that he was the angel of the LORD. 17 And Manoah said to the angel of the LORD, "What is your name, so that when your words are fulfilled, we may honor you?" 18 But the angel of the LORD said to him, "Why do you ask my name, for it is 'wonderful?" 19 So Manoah took the young goat along with the grain offering and offered it on the rock to the LORD; and He performed wonders while Manoah and his wife looked on. 20 For it came about when the flame went up from the altar toward heaven, that the angel of the LORD ascended in the flame of the altar. When Manoah and his wife saw *this,* they fell on their faces to the ground.

21 Now the angel of the LORD did not appear to Manoah or his wife again. Then Manoah knew that he was the angel of the LORD. 22 So Manoah said to his wife, "We will certainly die, for we have seen God." 23 But his wife said to him, "If the LORD had desired to kill us, He would not have accepted a burnt offering and a grain offering from our hands, nor would He have shown us all these things, nor would He have let us hear *things* like this at this time."

24 So the woman gave birth to a son, and named him Samson; and the child grew up and the LORD blessed him. 25 And the Spirit of the

---

13:18 1 I.e., incomprehensible

LORD began to stir him *when he was* in ¹Mahaneh-dan, between Zorah and Eshtaol.

Samson's Marriage

14 Then Samson went down to Timnah, and he saw a woman in Timnah, *one* of the daughters of the Philistines. ²So he came back and told his father and mother, "I saw a woman in Timnah, *one* of the daughters of the Philistines; so now, get her for me as a wife." ³But his father and his mother said to him, "Is there no woman among the daughters of your relatives, or among all our people, that you go to take a wife from the uncircumcised Philistines?" Yet Samson said to his father, "Get her for me, because she is right for me." ⁴However, his father and mother did not know that this was of the LORD, for He was seeking an occasion against the Philistines. And at that time the Philistines were ruling over Israel.

⁵Then Samson went down to Timnah with his father and mother, and came as far as the vineyards of Timnah; and behold, a young lion *came* roaring toward him. ⁶And the Spirit of the LORD rushed upon him, so that he tore it apart as one tears apart a young goat, though he had nothing in his hand; but he did not tell his father or mother what he had done. ⁷So he went down and talked to the woman; and she looked pleasing to Samson. ⁸When he returned later to take her, he turned aside to look at the carcass of the lion; and behold, a swarm of bees and honey were in the body of the lion. ⁹So he took out the honey on his hands and went on, eating as he went. When he came to his father and mother, he gave *some* to them and they ate *it;* but he did not tell them that he had taken the honey out of the body of the lion.

¹⁰Then his father went down to the woman; and Samson held a feast there, for the young men customarily did this. ¹¹When they saw him, they brought thirty companions to be with him.

Samson's Riddle

¹²Then Samson said to them, "Let me now propose a riddle for you; if you actually tell me the answer within the seven days of the feast, and solve it, then I will give you thirty linen wraps and thirty outfits of clothes. ¹³But if you are unable to tell me, then you shall give me thirty linen wraps and thirty outfits of clothes." And they said to him, "Propose your riddle, so that we may hear it." ¹⁴So he said to them,

"Out of the eater came something to eat,
And out of the strong came something sweet."

But they could not tell *the answer to* the riddle in three days.

¹⁵Then it came about on the fourth day that they said to Samson's wife, "Entice your husband, so that he will tell us the riddle, or we will burn you and your father's house with fire. Have you invited us to impoverish us? *Is this* not *so?*" ¹⁶So Samson's wife wept in front of him and said, "You only hate me, and you do not love me; you have proposed a riddle to the sons of my people, and have not told *it* to me." And he said to her, "Behold, I have not told *it*

to my father or mother; so should I tell you?" ¹⁷However she wept before him for seven days while their feast lasted. And on the seventh day he told her because she pressed him so hard. She then told the riddle to the sons of her people. ¹⁸So the men of the city said to him on the seventh day before the sun went down,

"What is sweeter than honey?
And what is stronger than a lion?"

And he said to them,

"If you had not plowed with my heifer,
You would not have found out my riddle."

¹⁹Then the Spirit of the LORD rushed upon him, and he went down to Ashkelon and killed thirty men of them and took what they were wearing and gave the outfits of clothes to those who told the riddle. And his anger burned, and he went up 3to his father's house. ²⁰But Samson's wife was *given* to his companion who had been his friend.

Samson Burns Philistine Crops

15 But after a while, in the time of wheat harvest, Samson visited his wife with a young goat, and said, "I will go in to my wife in *her* room." But her father did not let him enter. ²Her father said, "I really thought that you hated her intensely; so I gave her to your companion. Is her younger sister not more beautiful than she? Please let her be yours instead." ³Samson then said to them, "This time I will have been blameless regarding the Philistines when I do them harm." ⁴And Samson went and caught three hundred jackals, and took torches, and turned *the jackals* tail to tail and put one torch in the middle between two tails. ⁵When he had set fire to the torches, he released *the jackals* into the standing grain of the Philistines and set fire to both the bundled heaps and the standing grain, along with the vineyards *and* olive groves. ⁶Then the Philistines said, "Who did this?" And *some* said, "Samson, the son-in-law of the Timnite, because he took his wife and gave her to his companion." So the Philistines came up and burned her and her father *to death* with fire. ⁷Then Samson said to them, "If this is how you act, I will certainly take revenge on you, and *only* after *that* will I stop." ⁸So he struck them ruthlessly with a great slaughter; and *afterward* he went down and lived in the cleft of the rock of Etam.

⁹Then the Philistines went up and camped in Judah, and spread out in Lehi. ¹⁰So the men of Judah said, "Why have you come up against us?" And they said, "We have come up to bind Samson in order to do to him as he did to us." ¹¹Then three thousand men of Judah went down to the cleft of the rock of Etam and said to Samson, "Do you not know that the Philistines are rulers over us? What then is this that you have done to us?" And he said to them, "Just as they did to me, so I have done to them." ¹²Then they said to him, "We have come down to bind you so that we may hand you over to the Philistines." And Samson said to them, "Swear to me that you will not kill me." ¹³So they said to him, "No, but we will

bind you tightly and give you into their hands; but we certainly will not kill you." Then they bound him with two new ropes, and brought him up from the rock.

14 When he came to Lehi, the Philistines shouted as they met him. And the Spirit of the LORD rushed upon him so that the ropes that were on his arms were like flax that has burned with fire, and his restraints dropped from his hands. 15 Then he found a fresh jawbone of a donkey, so he reached out with his hand and took it, and killed a thousand men with it. 16 And Samson said,

"With the jawbone of a donkey,
Heaps upon heaps,
With the jawbone of a donkey
I have killed a thousand men."

17 When he had finished speaking, he threw the jawbone from his hand; and he named that place 1Ramath-lehi. 18 Then he became very thirsty, and he called to the LORD and said, "You have handed this great victory over to Your servant, and now am I to die of thirst and fall into the hands of the uncircumcised?" 19 But God split the hollow place that is in Lehi so that water came out of it. When he drank, his strength returned and he revived. Therefore he named it En-hakkore, which is in Lehi to this day. 20 So he judged Israel for twenty years in the days of the Philistines.

Samson's Weakness

16 Now Samson went to Gaza and saw a prostitute there, and had relations with her. 2 When it was reported to the Gazites, saying, "Samson has come here," they surrounded the place and lay in wait for him all night at the gate of the city. And they kept silent all night, saying, "Let's wait until the morning light, then we will kill him." 3 Now Samson lay asleep until midnight, and at midnight he got up and took hold of the doors of the city gate and the two doorposts, and pulled them up along with the bars; then he put them on his shoulders, and carried them up to the top of the mountain which is opposite Hebron.

4 After this it came about that he was in love with a woman in the Valley of Sorek, whose name was Delilah. 5 So the governors of the Philistines came up to her and said to her, "Entice him, and see where his great strength lies and how we can overpower him so that we may bind him to humble him. Then we will each give you 1,100 pieces of silver." 6 So Delilah said to Samson, "Please tell me where your great strength lies, and how you can be bound to humble you." 7 And Samson said to her, "If they bind me with seven fresh 1animal tendons that have not been dried, then I will become weak and be like any other man." 8 Then the governors of the Philistines brought up to her seven fresh 1animal tendons that had not been dried, and she bound him with them. 9 Now she had men prepared for an ambush in an inner room. And she said to him, "The Philistines are upon you, Samson!" But he tore the tendons to pieces just like a thread of flax

is torn apart when it comes too close to fire. So his strength was not discovered.

10 Then Delilah said to Samson, "Behold, you have toyed with me and told me lies; now please tell me how you may be bound." 11 Then He said to her, "If they bind me tightly with new ropes which have not been used, then I will become weak and be like any other man." 12 So Delilah took new ropes and bound him with them and said to him, "The Philistines are upon you, Samson!" For the men in the ambush were waiting in the inner room. But he tore the ropes from his arms like thread.

13 Then Delilah said to Samson, "Up to now you have toyed with me and told me lies; tell me how you may be bound." And he said to her, "If you weave the seven locks of my hair with the 1web 2[and fasten it with the pin, then I will be weak like any other man." 14 So while he slept, Delilah wove the seven locks of his hair with the web]. And she fastened it with the pin and said to him, "The Philistines are upon you, Samson!" But he awoke from his sleep and pulled out the pin of the loom and the web.

Delilah Extracts His Secret

15 Then she said to him, "How can you say, 'I love you,' when your heart is not with me? You have toyed with me these three times and have not told me where your great strength is." 16 And it came about, when she pressed him daily with her words and urged him, that his soul was annoyed to death. 17 So he told her all that was in his heart and said to her, "A razor has never come on my head, for I have been a Nazirite to God from my mother's womb. If I am shaved, then my strength will leave me and I will become weak and be like any other man."

18 When Delilah saw that he had told her all that was in his heart, she sent word and called the governors of the Philistines, saying, "Come up once more, for he has told me all that is in his heart." Then the governors of the Philistines came up to her and brought up the money in their hands. 19 And she made him sleep on her knees, and called for a man and had him shave off the seven locks of his head. Then she began to humble him, and his strength left him. 20 She said, "The Philistines are upon you, Samson!" And he awoke from his sleep and said, "I will go out as at other times and shake myself free." But he did not know that the LORD had departed from him. 21 Then the Philistines seized him and gouged out his eyes; and they brought him down to Gaza and restrained him with bronze chains, and he became a grinder in the prison. 22 However, the hair of his head began to grow again after it was shaved off.

23 Now the governors of the Philistines assembled to offer a great sacrifice to Dagon their god, and to celebrate, for they said,

"Our god has handed Samson our enemy
over to us."

15:17 1 I.e., the high place of the jawbone   16:7 1 I.e., of a butchered animal, that shrink and hold when drying   16:8 1 See note v 7   16:13 1 I.e., in weaving, the warp of a loom   2 The passage in brackets is found in LXX but not in any Heb mss

24 When the people saw him, they praised their god, for they said,

"Our god has handed our enemy over to us,
Even the destroyer of our country,
Who has killed many of us."

25 It so happened when they were in high spirits, that they said, "Call for Samson, that he may amuse us." So they called for Samson from the prison, and he entertained them. And they made him stand between the pillars. **26** Then Samson said to the boy who was holding his hand, "Let me feel the pillars on which the house rests, so that I may lean against them." **27** Now the house was full of men and women, and all the governors of the Philistines were there. And about three thousand men and women were on the roof looking on while Samson was entertaining *them.*

Samson Is Avenged

28 Then Samson called to the LORD and said, "Lord GOD, please remember me and please strengthen me just this time, O God, that I may at once take vengeance on the Philistines for my two eyes." **29** Then Samson grasped the two middle pillars on which the house rested, and braced himself against them, the one with his right hand and the other with his left. **30** And Samson said, "Let me die with the Philistines!" And he pushed outwards powerfully, so that the house fell on the governors and all the people who were in it. And the dead whom he killed at his death were more than those whom he killed during his lifetime. **31** Then his brothers and all his father's household came down and took him, and brought him up and buried him between Zorah and Eshtaol in the tomb of his father Manoah. So he had judged Israel for twenty years.

Micah's Idolatry

17 Now there was a man of the hill country of Ephraim whose name was Micah. **2** And he said to his mother, "The 1,100 *pieces* of silver that were taken from you, about which you uttered a curse and also spoke *it* in my hearing, behold, the silver is with me; I took it." And his mother said, "Blessed be my son by the LORD." **3** He then returned the 1,100 *pieces* of silver to his mother, and his mother said, "I wholly consecrate the silver from my hand to the LORD for my son to make a carved image and a cast metal image; so now I will return them to you." **4** So when he returned the silver to his mother, his mother took two hundred *pieces* of silver and gave them to the silversmith, who made them into a carved image and a cast metal image, and they were in the house of Micah. **5** And the man Micah had a ¹shrine and he made an ephod and household idols, and consecrated one of his sons, so that he might become his priest. **6** In those days there was no king in Israel; everyone did what was right in his own eyes.

7 Now there was a young man from Bethlehem in Judah, of the family of Judah,

who was a Levite; and he was staying there. **8** Then the man left the city, Bethlehem in Judah, to stay wherever he would find *a place;* and as he made his journey, he came to the hill country of Ephraim, to the house of Micah. **9** Micah said to him, "Where do you come from?" And he said to him, "I am a Levite from Bethlehem in Judah, and I am going to stay wherever I may find *a place.*" **10** Micah then said to him, "Stay with me and be a father and a priest to me, and I will give you ten *pieces* of silver a year, a supply of clothing, and your sustenance." So the Levite went *in.* **11** The Levite agreed to live with the man, and the young man became to him like one of his sons. **12** So Micah consecrated the Levite, and the young man became his priest and lived in the house of Micah. **13** Then Micah said, "Now I know that the LORD will prosper me, because I have a Levite as a priest."

Danites Seek Territory

18 In those days there was no king of Israel; and in those days the tribe of the Danites was seeking an inheritance for themselves to live in, for until that day an inheritance had not been allotted to them as a possession among the tribes of Israel. **2** So the sons of Dan sent from their family five men out of their whole number, valiant men from Zorah and Eshtaol, to spy out the land and to explore it; and they said to them, "Go, explore the land." And they came to the hill country of Ephraim, to the house of Micah, and stayed overnight there. **3** When they were near the house of Micah, they recognized the voice of the young man, the Levite; and they turned aside there and said to him, "Who brought you here? And what are you doing in this *place?* And what do you have here?" **4** He said to them, "Micah has done this and that for me, and he has hired me and I have become his priest." **5** Then they said to him, "Inquire of God, please, that we may know whether our way on which we are going will be successful." **6** And the priest said to them, "Go in peace; your way in which you are going has the LORD's approval."

7 So the five men departed and came to Laish, and saw the people who were in it living in security, in the way of the Sidonians, quiet and unsuspecting; for there was no oppressive ruler humiliating *them* for anything in the land, and they were far from the Sidonians and had no dealings with anyone. **8** When they came back to their brothers at Zorah and Eshtaol, their brothers said to them, "What *do* you say?" **9** And they said, "Arise, and let's go up against them; for we have seen the land, and behold, it is very good. And will you sit still? Do not hesitate to go, to enter, to take possession of the land. **10** When you enter, you will come to an unsuspecting people with a spacious land; for God has handed it over to you, a place where there is no lack of anything that is on the earth."

11 Then from the family of the Danites, from Zorah and from Eshtaol, six hundred men armed with weapons of war set out. **12** They

---

17:5 ¹Lit *house of gods*

went up and camped at Kiriath-jearim in Judah. Therefore they called that place ¹Mahaneh-dan to this day; behold, it is west of Kiriath-jearim. 13 And they passed from there to the hill country of Ephraim and came to the house of Micah.

Danites Take Micah's Idols

14 Then the five men who went to spy out the country of Laish said to their kinsmen, "Do you know that there are in these houses an ephod and ¹household idols, and a carved image and a cast metal image? Now then, consider what you should do." 15 So they turned aside there and came to the house of the young man, the Levite, to the house of Micah, and asked him how he was doing. 16 Meanwhile, the six hundred men armed with their weapons of war, who were of the sons of Dan, were positioned at the entrance of the gate. 17 Now the five men who went to spy out the land went up and entered there; they took the carved image, the ephod, the household idols, and the cast metal image, while the priest was standing at the entrance of the gate with the six hundred men armed with weapons of war. 18 When these men entered Micah's house and took the carved image, the ephod, household idols, and the cast metal image, the priest said to them, "What are you doing?" 19 And they said to him, "Be silent, put your hand over your mouth, and go with us, and be to us a father and a priest. Is it better for you to be a priest to the house of one man, or to be priest to a tribe and a family in Israel?" 20 The priest's heart was glad, and he took the ephod, the household idols, and the carved image, and went among the people. 21 Then they turned and left, and put the children, the livestock, and the valuables in front of them. 22 When they had distanced themselves from Micah's house, the men who were in the houses near Micah's house assembled by command and overtook the sons of Dan. 23 Then they called out to the sons of Dan, who turned around and said to Micah, "What is the matter with you, that you have assembled together?" 24 And he said, "You have taken my gods which I made, and the priest, and have gone away; what more do I have? So how can you say to me, 'What is the matter with you?'" 25 Then the sons of Dan said to him, "Do not let your voice be heard among us, or else fierce men will attack you, and you will lose your life and the lives of your household." 26 So the sons of Dan went on their way; and when Micah saw that they were too strong for him, he turned and went back to his house. 27 Then they took what Micah had made and the priest who had belonged to him, and came to Laish, to a people quiet and unsuspecting, and struck them with the edge of the sword; and they burned the city with fire. 28 And there was no one to save them, because it was far from Sidon and they had no dealings with anyone, and it was in the valley which is near Beth-rehob. So they rebuilt the city and lived in it. 29 And they named the city Dan, after

the name of Dan their father who was born to Israel; however, the name of the city was previously Laish. 30 The sons of Dan set up for themselves the carved image; and Jonathan, the son of Gershom, the son of ¹Manasseh, he and his sons were priests to the tribe of the Danites until the day of the captivity of the land. 31 So they set up for themselves Micah's carved image which he had made, all the time that the house of God was in Shiloh.

A Levite's Concubine Raped and Killed

19 Now it came about in those days, when there was no king in Israel, that there was a certain Levite staying in the remote part of the hill country of Ephraim, who took a concubine for himself from Bethlehem in Judah. 2 But his concubine ¹found him repugnant, and she left him and went to her father's house in Bethlehem in Judah, and remained there for a period of four months. 3 Then her husband set out and went after her to speak gently to her in order to bring her back, taking with him his servant and a pair of donkeys. And she brought him into her father's house, and when the girl's father saw him, he was glad to meet him. 4 His father-in-law, the girl's father, prevailed upon him, and he remained with him for three days. So they ate and drank and stayed there. 5 Now on the fourth day they got up early in the morning, and he prepared to go; but the girl's father said to his son-in-law, "Strengthen yourself with a piece of bread, and afterward you may go." 6 So both of them sat down and ate and drank together; and the girl's father said to the man, "Please be so kind as to spend the night, and let your heart be cheerful." 7 However, the man got up to go; but his father-in-law urged him, and he spent the night there again. 8 Now on the fifth day he got up to go early in the morning, but the girl's father said, "Please strengthen yourself, and wait until late afternoon"; so both of them ate. 9 When the man got up to go, along with his concubine and servant, his father-in-law, the girl's father, said to him, "Behold now, the day has drawn to a close; please spend the night. Behold, the day is coming to an end; spend the night here so that your heart may be cheerful. Then tomorrow you may arise early for your journey and go home." 10 But the man was unwilling to spend the night, so he got up and left, and came to a place opposite Jebus (that is, Jerusalem). And with him was a pair of saddled donkeys; his concubine also was with him. 11 When they were near Jebus, the day was almost gone; and the servant said to his master, "Please come, and let's turn aside into this city of the Jebusites and spend the night in it." 12 However, his master said to him, "We will not turn aside into a city of foreigners who are not of the sons of Israel; instead, we will go on as far as Gibeah." 13 And he said to his servant, "Come, and let's approach one of these places; and we will spend the night in Gibeah or Ramah." 14 So they passed along and went their way, and the sun set on them near Gibeah

---

18:12 ¹ I.e., the camp of Dan   18:14 ¹ Heb teraphim   18:30 ¹ Some ancient versions Moses
19:2 ¹ Or was unfaithful to him (a Hebrew homonym); LXX became angry at him

which belongs to Benjamin. **15** They turned aside there to enter *and* spend the night in Gibeah. When they entered, they sat down in the public square of the city, for no one took them into *his* house to spend the night.

16 Then behold, an old man was coming out of the field from his work at evening. Now the man was from the hill country of Ephraim, and he was staying in Gibeah, but the men of the place were Benjaminites. **17** And he raised his eyes and saw the traveler in the public square of the city; and the old man said, "Where are you going, and where do you come from?" **18** And he said to him, "We are passing from Bethlehem in Judah to the remote part of the hill country of Ephraim, *for* I am from there, and I went to Bethlehem in Judah. But I am *now* going to my house, and no one will take me into his house. **19** Yet there is both straw and feed for our donkeys, and also bread and wine for me, and your female slave, and the young man who is with your servants; there is no lack of anything." **20** Then the old man said, "Peace to you. Only let me *take care of* all your needs; however, do not spend the night in the public square." **21** So he took him into his house and fed the donkeys, and they washed their feet and ate and drank.

22 While they were celebrating, behold, the men of the city, certain worthless men, surrounded the house, pushing one another at the door; and they spoke to the owner of the house, the old man, saying, "Bring out the man who entered your house that we may have relations with him." **23** Then the man, the owner of the house, went out to them and said to them, "No, my brothers, please do not act *so* wickedly. Since this man has come into my house, do not commit this vile sin. **24** Here is my virgin daughter and the man's concubine. Please let me bring them out, then rape them and do to them whatever you wish. But do not commit this act of vile sin against this man." **25** But the men would not listen to him. So the man seized his concubine and brought *her* outside to them; and they raped her and abused her all night until morning, then let her go at the approach of dawn. **26** As the day began to dawn, the woman came and fell down at the doorway of the man's house where her master was, until *full* daylight.

27 When her master got up in the morning and opened the doors of the house and went out to go on his way, then behold, his concubine was lying at the doorway of the house with her hands on the threshold. **28** And he said to her, "Get up and let's go," but there was no answer. Then he put her on the donkey; and the man set out and went to his home. **29** When he entered his house, he took a knife and seized his concubine, and cut her in twelve pieces, limb by limb. Then he sent her throughout the territory of Israel. **30** All who saw *it* said, "Nothing like this has *ever* happened or been seen from the day when the sons of Israel came up from the land of Egypt to this day. Consider it, make a plan, and speak up!"

Resolve to Punish the Guilty

20 Then all the sons of Israel from Dan to Beersheba, including the land of Gilead, came out, and the congregation assembled as one person to the LORD at Mizpah. **2** And the leaders of all the people, all the tribes of Israel, took their stand in the assembly of the people of God, four hundred thousand foot soldiers who drew the sword. **3** (Now the sons of Benjamin heard that the sons of Israel had gone up to Mizpah.) And the sons of Israel said, "Tell *us,* how did this wickedness take place?" **4** So the Levite, the husband of the woman who was murdered, answered and said, "I came with my concubine to spend the night at Gibeah which belongs to Benjamin. **5** But the citizens of Gibeah rose up against me and surrounded the house at night, threatening me. They intended to kill me; instead, they raped my concubine so that she died. **6** And I took hold of my concubine and cut her in pieces, and sent her throughout the land of Israel's inheritance; for they have committed an outrageous sin and vile act in Israel. **7** Behold, all you sons of Israel, give your response and advice here."

8 Then all the people rose up as one person, saying, "Not one of us will go to his tent, nor will any of us go home. **9** But now this is the thing which we will do to Gibeah; *we will go up* against it by lot. **10** And we will take ten men out of a hundred throughout the tribes of Israel, and a hundred out of a thousand, and a thousand out of ten thousand to supply provisions for the people, so that when they come to Gibeah of Benjamin, they may punish *them* for all the vile sin that they have committed in Israel." **11** So all the men of Israel were gathered against the city, united as one man.

12 Then the tribes of Israel sent men through the entire tribe of Benjamin, saying, "What is this wickedness that has taken place among you? **13** Now then, turn over the men, the worthless men who are in Gibeah, so that we may put them to death and remove *this* wickedness from Israel." But the sons of Benjamin would not listen to the voice of their brothers, the sons of Israel. **14** Instead, the sons of Benjamin gathered from the cities to Gibeah, to go out to battle against the sons of Israel. **15** From the cities on that day the sons of Benjamin were counted, twenty-six thousand men who drew the sword, besides the inhabitants of Gibeah who were counted, seven hundred choice men. **16** Out of all these people seven hundred choice men were left-handed; each one could sling a stone at a hair and not miss.

17 Then the men of Israel besides Benjamin were counted, four hundred thousand men who drew the sword; all of these were men of war.

Civil War, Benjamin Defeated

18 Now the sons of Israel set out, went up to Bethel, and inquired of God and said, "Who shall go up first for us to battle against the sons of Benjamin?" Then the LORD said, "Judah *shall go up* first."

19 So the sons of Israel got up in the morning and camped against Gibeah. 20 The men of Israel went to battle against Benjamin, and the men of Israel lined up for battle against them at Gibeah. 21 Then the sons of Benjamin came out of Gibeah and struck to the ground on that day twenty-two thousand men of Israel. 22 But the people, the men of Israel, showed themselves courageous and lined up for battle again in the place where they had lined themselves up on the first day. 23 And the sons of Israel went up and wept before the LORD until evening, and inquired of the LORD, saying, "Shall we again advance for battle against the sons of my brother Benjamin?" And the LORD said, "Go up against him."

24 So the sons of Israel came against the sons of Benjamin on the second day. 25 And Benjamin went out against them from Gibeah the second day and struck to the ground again eighteen thousand men of the sons of Israel; all of these drew the sword. 26 Then all the sons of Israel and all the people went up and came to Bethel, and they wept and remained there before the LORD, and fasted that day until evening. And they offered burnt offerings and peace offerings before the LORD. 27 And the sons of Israel inquired of the LORD (for the ark of the covenant of God was there in those days, 28 and Phinehas the son of Eleazar, Aaron's son, stood before it to minister in those days), saying, "Shall I yet again go out to battle against the sons of my brother Benjamin, or shall I stop?" And the LORD said, "Go up, for tomorrow I will hand them over to you."

29 So Israel set men in ambush around Gibeah. 30 And the sons of Israel went up against the sons of Benjamin on the third day and lined up against Gibeah as at other times. 31 When the sons of Benjamin went out against the people, they were lured away from the city, and they began to strike and kill some of the people as at other times, on the roads (one of which goes up to Bethel, and the other to Gibeah), and in the field, about thirty men of Israel. 32 And the sons of Benjamin said, "They are defeated before us, like the first time." But the sons of Israel said, "Let's flee, so that we may draw them away from the city to the roads." 33 Then all the men of Israel rose from their place and lined up at Baal-tamar; and the men of Israel in ambush charged from their place, from Maareh-geba. 34 When ten thousand choice men from all Israel came against Gibeah, the battle became fierce; but Benjamin did not know that disaster was close to them. 35 And the LORD struck Benjamin before Israel, so that the sons of Israel destroyed 25,100 men of Benjamin that day, all who drew the sword.

36 So the sons of Benjamin saw that they were defeated. When the men of Israel gave ground to Benjamin because they relied on the men in ambush whom they had set against Gibeah, 37 the men in ambush hurried and rushed against Gibeah; the men in ambush also deployed and struck all the city with the edge of the sword. 38 Now the agreed sign between the men of Israel and the men in ambush was that they would make a great cloud of smoke rise from the city. 39 Then the men of Israel turned in the battle, and Benjamin began to strike and kill about thirty men of Israel, for they said, "Undoubtedly they are defeated before us, as in the first battle." 40 But when the cloud began to rise from the city *in* a column of smoke, Benjamin looked behind them; and behold, the entire city was going up *in smoke* to heaven. 41 Then the men of Israel turned, and the men of Benjamin were terrified; for they saw that disaster was close to them. 42 Therefore, they turned their backs before the men of Israel *to flee* in the direction of the wilderness, but the battle overtook them while those who *attacked* from the cities were annihilating them in the midst of them. 43 They surrounded Benjamin, pursued them without rest, *and* trampled them down opposite Gibeah toward the east. 44 So eighteen thousand men of Benjamin fell; all of these *were* valiant men. 45 The rest turned and fled toward the wilderness to the rock of Rimmon, but they caught five thousand of them on the roads and overtook them at Gidom, and killed two thousand of them. 46 So all those of Benjamin who fell that day were twenty-five thousand men who drew the sword; all of these were valiant men. 47 But six hundred men turned and fled toward the wilderness to the rock of Rimmon; and they remained at the rock of Rimmon for four months. 48 The men of Israel then turned back against the sons of Benjamin and struck them with the edge of the sword, both the entire city with the cattle and all that they found; they also set on fire all the cities which they found.

Mourning a Lost Tribe

21 Now the men of Israel had sworn in Mizpah, saying, "None of us shall give his daughter to Benjamin in marriage." 2 So the people came to Bethel and sat there before God until evening, and raised their voices and wept profusely. 3 And they said, "Why, LORD, God of Israel, has this happened in Israel, that one tribe is missing today from Israel?" 4 And it came about the next day that the people got up early and built an altar there, and offered burnt offerings and peace offerings.

5 Then the sons of Israel said, "Who is there among all the tribes of Israel who did not go up to the LORD in the assembly?" For they had taken a solemn oath concerning *anyone* who did not go up to the LORD at Mizpah, saying, "He shall certainly be put to death." 6 And the sons of Israel were sorry for their brother Benjamin, and said, "Today one tribe is cut off from Israel! 7 What are we to do for wives for those who are left, since we have sworn by the LORD not to give them any of our daughters as wives?"

Provision for Their Survival

8 And they said, "What one is there of the tribes of Israel that did not go up to the LORD at Mizpah?" And behold, no one had come to the camp from Jabesh-gilead to the assembly. 9 For when the people were counted, behold, not one of the inhabitants of Jabesh-gilead was there. 10 And the congregation sent twelve

thousand of the valiant warriors there, and commanded them, saying, "Go and strike the inhabitants of Jabesh-gilead with the edge of the sword, along with the women and the children. **11** And this is the thing that you shall do: you shall utterly destroy every male, and every woman who has slept with a male." **12** And they found among the inhabitants of Jabesh-gilead four hundred young virgins who had not known a man by sleeping with him; and they brought them to the camp at Shiloh, which is in the land of Canaan.

13 Then the whole congregation sent *word* and spoke to the sons of Benjamin who were at the rock of Rimmon, and proclaimed peace to them. **14** And *the tribe of* Benjamin returned at that time, and they gave them the women whom they had allowed to live from the women of Jabesh-gilead; but they were not enough for them. **15** And the people were sorry for Benjamin, because the LORD had created a gap in the tribes of Israel.

16 Then the elders of the congregation said, "What are we to do for wives for those who are left, since the women have been eliminated from Benjamin?" **17** And they said, "*There must be* an inheritance for the survivors of Benjamin, so that a tribe will not be wiped out from Israel. **18** But we cannot give them wives from our daughters." For the sons of Israel had

sworn, saying, "Cursed is he who gives a wife to Benjamin!"

19 So they said, "Behold, there is a feast of the LORD from year to year in Shiloh, which is on the north side of Bethel, on the east side of the road that goes up from Bethel to Shechem, and on the south side of Lebonah." **20** And they commanded the sons of Benjamin, saying, "Go and lie in wait in the vineyards, **21** and watch; and behold, if the daughters of Shiloh come out to take part in the dances, then you shall come out of the vineyards, and each of you shall seize his wife from the daughters of Shiloh, and go to the land of Benjamin. **22** And when their fathers or their brothers come to complain to us, we shall say to them, 'Give them to us voluntarily, because we did not take for each man *of Benjamin* a wife in battle, nor did you give *them* to them, otherwise you would now be guilty.'" **23** The sons of Benjamin did so, and took wives according to their number from those who danced, whom they seized. And they went and returned to their inheritance, and rebuilt the cities and lived in them. **24** And the sons of Israel departed from there at that time, every man to his tribe and family, and each one departed from there to his inheritance.

25 In those days there was no king in Israel; everyone did what was right in his own eyes.

The Book of
RUTH

Naomi Widowed

1 Now it came about in the days when the judges governed, that there was a famine in the land. And a man of Bethlehem in Judah went to reside in the land of Moab with his wife and his two sons. 2 The name of the man *was* Elimelech, and the name of his wife, Naomi; and the names of his two sons *were* Mahlon and Chilion, Ephrathites of Bethlehem in Judah. So they entered the land of Moab and remained there. 3 Then Elimelech, Naomi's husband, died; and she was left with her two sons. 4 And they took for themselves Moabite women *as* wives; the name of the one was Orpah, and the name of the other, Ruth. And they lived there about ten years. 5 Then both Mahlon and Chilion also died, and the woman was left without her two sons and her husband.

6 Then she arose with her daughters-in-law to return from the land of Moab, because she had heard in the land of Moab that the LORD had visited His people by giving them food. 7 So she departed from the place where she was, and her two daughters-in-law with her; and they went on the way to return to the land of Judah. 8 But Naomi said to her two daughters-in-law, "Go, return each of you to your mother's house. May the LORD deal kindly with you as you have dealt with the dead and with me. 9 May the LORD grant that you may find a place of rest, each one in the house of her husband." Then she kissed them, and they raised their voices and wept. 10 However, they said to her, "*No*, but we will return with you to your people." 11 But Naomi said, "Return, my daughters. Why should you go with me? Do I still have sons in my womb, that they may be your husbands? 12 Return, my daughters! Go, for I am too old to have a husband. If I said I have hope, if I were even to have a husband tonight and also give birth to sons, 13 would you therefore wait until they were grown? Would you therefore refrain from marrying? No, my daughters; for it is much more bitter for me than for you, because the hand of the LORD has come out against me."

Ruth's Loyalty

14 And they raised their voices and wept again; and Orpah kissed her mother-in-law, but Ruth clung to her. 15 Then she said, "Behold, your sister-in-law has gone back to her people and her gods; return after your sister-in-law." 16 But Ruth said, "Do not plead with me to leave you *or* to turn back from following you; for where you go, I will go, and where you sleep, I will sleep. Your people *shall be* my people, and your God, my God. 17 Where you die, I will die, and there I will be buried. May the LORD do so to me, and worse, if *anything but* death separates me from

you." 18 When she saw that she was determined to go with her, she stopped speaking to her *about it.*

19 So they both went on until they came to Bethlehem. And when they had come to Bethlehem, all the city was stirred because of them, and the women said, "Is this Naomi?" 20 But she said to them, "Do not call me ¹Naomi; call me ²Mara, for the Almighty has dealt very bitterly with me. 21 I went *away* full, but the LORD has brought me back empty. Why do you call me Naomi, since the LORD has testified against me and the Almighty has afflicted me?"

22 So Naomi returned, and with her Ruth the Moabitess, her daughter-in-law, who returned from the land of Moab. And they came to Bethlehem at the beginning of barley harvest.

Ruth Gleans in Boaz's Field

2 Now Naomi had a relative of her husband, a man of great wealth, of the family of Elimelech, whose name was Boaz. 2 And Ruth the Moabitess said to Naomi, "Please let me go to the field and glean among the ears of grain following one in whose eyes I may find favor." And she said to her, "Go, my daughter." 3 So she left and went and gleaned in the field after the reapers; and she happened to come to the portion of the field belonging to Boaz, who was of the family of Elimelech. 4 Now behold, Boaz came from Bethlehem and said to the reapers, "May the LORD be with you." And they said to him, "May the LORD bless you." 5 Then Boaz said to his servant who was in charge of the reapers, "Whose young woman is this?" 6 And the servant in charge of the reapers replied, "She is the young Moabite woman who returned with Naomi from the land of Moab. 7 And she said, 'Please let me glean and gather after the reapers among the sheaves.' So she came and has remained from the morning until now; she has been sitting in the house for a little while."

8 Then Boaz said to Ruth, "Listen carefully, my daughter. Do not go to glean in another field; furthermore, do not go on from this one, but join my young women here. 9 *Keep* your eyes on the field which they reap, and go after them. Indeed, I have ordered the servants not to touch you. When you are thirsty, go to the water jars and drink from what the servants draw." 10 Then she fell on her face, bowing to the ground, and said to him, "Why have I found favor in your sight that you should take notice of me, since I am a foreigner?" 11 Boaz replied to her, "All that you have done for your mother-in-law after the death of your husband has been fully reported to me, and how you left your father and your mother and the land of your birth, and came to a people that you did not previously know. 12 May the LORD reward

---

your work, and may your wages be full from the LORD, the God of Israel, under whose wings you have come to take refuge." ¹³ Then she said, "I have found favor in your sight, my lord, for you have comforted me and indeed have spoken kindly to your servant, though I am not like one of your female servants."

¹⁴ And at mealtime Boaz said to her, "Come here, that you may eat of the bread and dip your piece of bread in the vinegar." So she sat beside the reapers; and he served her roasted grain, and she ate and was satisfied and had some left. ¹⁵ When she got up to glean, Boaz commanded his servants, saying, "Let her glean even among the sheaves, and do not insult her. ¹⁶ Also you are to purposely slip out for her *some grain* from the bundles and leave *it* so that she may glean, and do not rebuke her."

¹⁷ So she gleaned in the field until evening. Then she beat out what she had gleaned, and it was about an ¹ephah of barley. ¹⁸ And she picked *it* up and went into the city, and her mother-in-law saw what she had gleaned. She also took *some* out and gave Naomi what she had left after she was satisfied. ¹⁹ Her mother-in-law then said to her, "Where did you glean today and where did you work? May he who took notice of you be blessed." So she told her mother-in-law with whom she had worked, and said, "The name of the man with whom I worked today is Boaz." ²⁰ Naomi said to her daughter-in-law, "May he be blessed of the LORD who has not withdrawn His kindness from the living and from the dead." Again Naomi said to her, "The man is our relative; he is one of our redeemers." ²¹ Then Ruth the Moabitess said, "Furthermore, he said to me, 'You are to stay close to my servants until they have finished all my harvest.' " ²² And Naomi said to her daughter-in-law Ruth, "It is good, my daughter, that you go out with his young women, so that *others* do not assault you in another field." ²³ So she stayed close by the young women of Boaz in order to glean until the end of the barley harvest and the wheat harvest. And she lived with her mother-in-law.

Boaz Will Redeem Ruth

3 Then her mother-in-law Naomi said to her, "My daughter, shall I not seek security for you, that it may go well for you? ² Now then, is Boaz not our relative, with whose young women you were? Behold, he is winnowing barley at the threshing floor tonight. ³ Wash yourself therefore, and anoint yourself, and put on your *best* clothes, and go down to the threshing floor; *but* do not reveal yourself to the man until he has finished eating and drinking. ⁴ And it shall be when he lies down, that you shall take notice of the place where he lies, and you shall go and uncover his feet and lie down; then he will tell you what you should do." ⁵ And she said to her, "All that you say I will do."

⁶ So she went down to the threshing floor and did according to all that her mother-in-law had commanded her. ⁷ When Boaz had eaten and drunk and his heart was cheerful, he went to lie down at the end of the heap of grain; and

she came secretly, and uncovered his feet and lay down. ⁸ And it happened in the middle of the night that the man was startled and bent forward; and behold, a woman was lying at his feet. ⁹ So he said, "Who are you?" And she answered, "I am Ruth your slave. Now spread your garment over your slave, for you are a redeemer." ¹⁰ Then he said, "May you be blessed of the LORD, my daughter. You have shown your last kindness to be better than the first, by not going after young men, whether poor or rich. ¹¹ So now, my daughter, do not fear. I will do for you whatever you say, for all my people in the city know that you are a woman of excellence. ¹² But now, although it is true that I am a redeemer, yet there is also a redeemer more closely related than I. ¹³ Remain this night, and when morning comes, if he will redeem you, good; let him redeem you. But if he does not wish to redeem you, then I will redeem you, as the LORD lives. Lie down until morning."

¹⁴ So she lay at his feet until morning, and got up before one person could recognize another; and he said, "Do not let it be known that the woman came to the threshing floor." ¹⁵ Again he said, "Give me the shawl that is on you and hold it." So she held it, and he measured six *measures* of barley and laid *it* on her. Then she went into the city. ¹⁶ When she came to her mother-in-law, she said, "How did it go, my daughter?" And she told her all that the man had done for her. ¹⁷ She also said, "These six *measures* of barley he gave to me, for he said, 'Do not go to your mother-in-law empty-handed.' " ¹⁸ Then she said, "Wait, my daughter, until you know how the matter turns out; for the man will not rest until he has settled it today."

The Marriage of Ruth

4 Now Boaz went up to the gate and sat down there, and behold, the redeemer of whom Boaz spoke was passing by, so he said, "Come over here, friend, sit down here." And he came over and sat down. ² Then he took ten men of the elders of the city and said, "Sit down here." So they sat down. ³ And he said to the redeemer, "Naomi, who has returned from the land of Moab, has to sell the plot of land which belonged to our brother Elimelech. ⁴ So I thought that I would inform you, saying, 'Buy *it* before those who are sitting *here,* and before the elders of my people. If you will redeem *it,* redeem *it;* but if not, tell me so that I may know; for there is no one except you to redeem *it,* and I am after you.' " And he said, "I will redeem *it.*" ⁵ Then Boaz said, "On the day you buy the field from the hand of Naomi, you must also acquire Ruth the Moabitess, the widow of the deceased, in order to raise up the name of the deceased on his inheritance." ⁶ Then the redeemer said, "I cannot redeem *it* for myself, otherwise I would jeopardize my own inheritance. Redeem *it* for yourself; you *may have* my right of redemption, since I cannot redeem *it.*"

⁷ Now this was *the custom* in former times in Israel concerning the redemption and the

---

2:17 ¹ About 1 cubic foot or 0.03 cubic meters

exchange *of land* to confirm any matter: a man removed his sandal and gave *it* to another; and this was the *way of* confirmation in Israel. **8** So the redeemer said to Boaz, "Buy *it* for yourself." And he removed his sandal. **9** Then Boaz said to the elders and all the people, "You are witnesses today that I have bought from the hand of Naomi all that belonged to Elimelech and all that belonged to Chilion and Mahlon. **10** Furthermore, I have acquired Ruth the Moabitess, the widow of Mahlon, to be my wife in order to raise up the name of the deceased on his inheritance, so that the name of the deceased will not be eliminated from his brothers or from the court of his *birth* place; you are witnesses today." **11** And all the people who were in the court, and the elders, said, "*We are* witnesses. May the LORD make the woman who is coming into your home like Rachel and Leah, both of whom built the house of Israel; and may you achieve wealth in Ephrathah and become famous in Bethlehem. **12** Moreover, may your house be like the house of Perez whom Tamar bore to Judah, through the descendants whom the LORD will give you by this young woman."

13 So Boaz took Ruth, and she became his wife, and he had relations with her. And the LORD enabled her to conceive, and she gave birth to a son. **14** Then the women said to Naomi, "Blessed is the LORD who has not left you without a redeemer today, and may his name become famous in Israel. **15** May he also be to you one who restores life and sustains your old age; for your daughter-in-law, who loves you and is better to you than seven sons, has given birth to him."

The Line of David

16 Then Naomi took the child and laid him in her lap, and became his nurse. **17** And the neighbor women gave him a name, saying, "A son has been born to Naomi!" So they named him Obed. He is the father of Jesse, the father of David.

18 Now these are the generations of Perez: Perez fathered Hezron, **19** Hezron fathered Ram, and Ram fathered Amminadab, **20** and Amminadab fathered Nahshon, and Nahshon fathered Salmon, **21** and Salmon fathered Boaz, and Boaz fathered Obed, **22** and Obed fathered Jesse, and Jesse fathered David.

The First Book of
SAMUEL

Elkanah and His Wives

1 Now there was a man from Ramathaim-zophim from the hill country of Ephraim, and his name was Elkanah the son of Jeroham, the son of Elihu, the son of Tohu, the son of Zuph, an Ephraimite. 2 And he had two wives: the name of one was Hannah and the name of the other Peninnah; and Peninnah had children, but Hannah had no children.

3 Now this man would go up from his city yearly to worship and to sacrifice to the LORD of armies in Shiloh. And the two sons of Eli, Hophni and Phinehas, were priests to the LORD there. 4 When the day came that Elkanah sacrificed, he would give portions to his wife Peninnah and to all her sons and daughters; 5 but to Hannah he would give a double portion, because he loved Hannah, but the LORD had closed her womb. 6 Her rival, moreover, would provoke her bitterly to irritate her, because the LORD had closed her womb. 7 And it happened year after year, as often as she went up to the house of the LORD, that she would provoke her; so she wept and would not eat. 8 Then Elkanah her husband would say to her, "Hannah, why do you weep, and why do you not eat, and why is your heart sad? Am I not better to you than ten sons?"

9 Then Hannah got up after eating and drinking in Shiloh. Now Eli the priest was sitting on the seat by the doorpost of the temple of the LORD. 10 She, greatly distressed, prayed to the LORD and wept bitterly. 11 And she made a vow and said, "LORD of armies, if You will indeed look on the affliction of Your bondservant and remember me, and not forget Your bond-servant, but will give Your bond-servant a son, then I will give him to the LORD all the days of his life, and a razor shall never come on his head."

12 Now it came about, as she continued praying before the LORD, that Eli was watching her mouth. 13 As for Hannah, she was speaking in her heart, only her lips were quivering, but her voice was not heard. So Eli thought that she was drunk. 14 Then Eli said to her, "How long will you behave like a drunk? Get rid of your wine!" 15 But Hannah answered and said, "No, my lord, I am a woman despairing in spirit; I have drunk neither wine nor strong drink, but I have poured out my soul before the LORD. 16 Do not consider your bond-servant a useless woman, for I have spoken until now out of my great concern and provocation." 17 Then Eli answered and said, "Go in peace; and may the God of Israel grant your request that you have asked of Him." 18 She said, "Let your bond-servant find favor in your sight." So the woman went on her way and ate, and her face was no longer sad.

Samuel Is Born to Hannah

19 Then they got up early in the morning and worshiped before the LORD, and returned again to their house in Ramah. And Elkanah had relations with Hannah his wife, and the LORD remembered her. 20 It came about in due time, after Hannah had conceived, that she gave birth to a son; and she named him Samuel, saying, "Because I have asked for him of the LORD."

21 Then the man Elkanah went up with all his household to offer to the LORD the yearly sacrifice and to pay his vow. 22 But Hannah did not go up, for she said to her husband, "I will not go until the child is weaned; then I will bring him, so that he may appear before the LORD and stay there for life." 23 Elkanah her husband said to her, "Do what seems best to you. Stay until you have weaned him; only may the LORD confirm His word." So the woman stayed and nursed her son until she weaned him. 24 Now when she had weaned him, she took him up with her, with a three-year-old bull, one ephah of flour, and a jug of wine, and brought him to the house of the LORD in Shiloh, although the child was young. 25 Then they slaughtered the bull, and brought the boy to Eli. 26 And she said, "Pardon me, my lord! As your soul lives, my lord, I am the woman who stood here beside you, praying to the LORD. 27 For this boy I prayed, and the LORD has granted me my request which I asked of Him. 28 So I have also dedicated him to the LORD; as long as he lives he is dedicated to the LORD." And he worshiped the LORD there.

Hannah's Song of Thanksgiving

2 Then Hannah prayed and said,
"My heart rejoices in the LORD;
My horn is exalted in the LORD,
My mouth speaks boldly against my
    enemies,
Because I rejoice in Your salvation.
2 "There is no one holy like the LORD,
Indeed, there is no one besides You,
Nor is there any rock like our God.
3 "Do not go on boasting so very proudly,
Do not let arrogance come out of your
    mouth;
For the LORD is a God of knowledge,
And with Him actions are weighed.
4 "The bows of the mighty are broken to
    pieces,
But those who have stumbled strap on
    strength.
5 "Those who were full hire themselves out
    for bread,
But those who were hungry cease to be
    hungry.
Even the infertile woman gives birth to
    seven,

But she who has many children
languishes.

6 "The LORD puts to death and makes alive;
He brings down to 'Sheol and brings up.

7 "The LORD makes poor and rich;
He humbles, He also exalts.

8 "He raises the poor from the dust,
He lifts the needy from the garbage heap
To seat *them* with nobles,
And He gives them a seat of honor as an
inheritance;
For the pillars of the earth are the LORD's,
And He set the world on them.

9 "He watches over the feet of His godly
ones,
But the wicked ones are silenced in darkness;
For not by might shall a person prevail.

10 "Those who contend with the LORD will be
terrified;
Against them He will thunder in the
heavens,
The LORD will judge the ends of the
earth;
And He will give strength to His king,
And will exalt the 'horn of His anointed."

11 Then Elkanah went to his home at Ramah.
But the boy continued to attend to the service
of the LORD before Eli the priest.

The Sin of Eli's Sons

12 Now the sons of Eli were useless men;
they did not know the LORD. 13 And *this was*
the custom of the priests with the people:
when anyone was offering a sacrifice, the
priest's servant would come while the meat
was cooking, with a three-pronged fork in his
hand. 14 And he would thrust it into the pan, or
kettle, or caldron, or pot; everything that the
fork brought up, the priest would take for
himself. They did so in Shiloh to all the
Israelites who came there. 15 Also, before they
burned the fat, the priest's servant would come
and say to the man who was sacrificing, "Give
the priest meat for roasting, as he will not take
cooked meat from you, only raw." 16 And *if* the
man said to him, "They must burn the fat first,
then take as much as you desire," then he
would say, "No, but you must give *it to me*
now; and if not, I am taking it by force!" 17 And
so the sin of the young men was very great
before the LORD, for the men treated the
offering of the LORD disrespectfully.

Samuel before the LORD as a Boy

18 Now Samuel was ministering before the
LORD, *as* a boy wearing a linen ephod. 19 And
his mother would make for him a little robe
and bring it up to him from year to year when
she would come up with her husband to offer
the yearly sacrifice. 20 Then Eli would bless
Elkanah and his wife, and say, "May the LORD
give you children from this woman in place of
the one she requested of the LORD." And they
went to their own home.

21 The LORD indeed visited Hannah, and she
conceived and gave birth to three sons and two
daughters. And the boy Samuel grew up before
the LORD.

Eli Rebukes His Sons

22 Now Eli was very old; and he heard *about*
everything that his sons were doing to all
Israel, and that they slept with the women who
served at the doorway of the tent of meeting.
23 So he said to them, "Why are you doing such
things as these, the evil things that I hear from
all these people? 24 No, my sons; for the report
is not good which I hear the LORD's people cir-
culating. 25 If one person sins against another,
God will mediate for him; but if a person sins
against the LORD, who can intercede for him?"
But they would not listen to the voice of their
father, for the LORD desired to put them to
death.

26 Now the boy Samuel was continuing to
grow and to be in favor both with the LORD and
with people.

27 Then a man of God came to Eli and said to
him, "This is what the LORD says: 'Did I *not*
indeed reveal Myself to the house of your
father when they were in Egypt *in bondage* to
Pharaoh's house? 28 Did I *not* choose them from
all the tribes of Israel to be My priests, to go up
to My altar, to burn incense, to carry an ephod
before Me? And did I *not* give to the house of
your father all the fire *offerings* of the sons of
Israel? 29 Why are you showing contempt for
My sacrifice and My offering which I have
commanded *for My* dwelling, and *why* are you
honoring your sons above Me, by making
yourselves fat with the choicest of every
offering of My people Israel?' 30 Therefore the
LORD God of Israel declares, 'I did indeed say
that your house and the house of your father
was to walk before Me forever'; but now the
LORD declares, 'Far be it from Me—for those
who honor Me I will honor, and those who
despise Me will be insignificant. 31 Behold, the
days are coming when I will eliminate your
strength and the strength of your father's
house, so that there will not be an old man in
your house. 32 And you will look at the distress
of *My* dwelling, in *spite of* all the good that I do
for Israel; and there will never be an old man
in your house. 33 Yet I will not cut off every
man of yours from My altar, so that your eyes
will fail *from weeping* and your soul grieve,
and all the increase of your house will die in
the prime of life. 34 And this will be the sign to
you which will come in regard to your two
sons, Hophni and Phinehas: on the same day
both of them will die. 35 But I will raise up for
Myself a faithful priest who will do according
to what is in My heart and My soul; and I will
build him an enduring house, and he will walk
before My anointed always. 36 And everyone
who is left in your house will come to bow
down to him for a silver coin or a loaf of bread
and say, "Please assign me to one of the priest's
offices so that I may eat a piece of bread." ' "

The Prophetic Call to Samuel

3 Now the boy Samuel was attending to the
service of the LORD before Eli. And word
from the LORD was rare in those days; visions
were infrequent.

2 But it happened at that time as Eli was
lying down in his place (now his eyesight had

2:6 ¹I.e., the netherworld   2:10 ¹I.e., strength

begun to be poor *and* he could not see *well)*, **3** and the lamp of God had not yet gone out, and Samuel was lying down in the temple of the LORD where the ark of God *was*, **4** that the LORD called Samuel; and he said, "Here I am." **5** Then he ran to Eli and said, "Here I am, for you called me." But he said, "I did not call, go back *and* lie down." So he went and lay down. **6** And the LORD called yet again, "Samuel!" So Samuel got up and went to Eli and said, "Here I am, for you called me." But he said, "I did not call, my son, go back *and* lie down." **7** Now Samuel did not yet know the LORD, nor had the word of the LORD yet been revealed to him. **8** So the LORD called Samuel again for the third time. And he got up and went to Eli and said, "Here I am, for you called me." Then Eli realized that the LORD was calling the boy. **9** And Eli said to Samuel, "Go lie down, and it shall be if He calls you, that you shall say, 'Speak, LORD, for Your servant is listening.'" So Samuel went and lay down in his place.

10 Then the LORD came and stood, and called as at *the* other times: "Samuel! Samuel!" And Samuel said, "Speak, for Your servant is listening." **11** Then the LORD said to Samuel, "Behold, I am going to do a thing in Israel, *and* both ears of everyone who hears *about* it will ring. **12** On that day I will carry out against Eli everything that I have spoken in regard to his house, from beginning to end. **13** For I have told him that I am going to judge his house forever for the wrongdoing that he knew, because his sons were bringing a curse on themselves and he did not rebuke them. **14** Therefore I have sworn to the house of Eli that the wrongdoing of Eli's house shall never be atoned for by sacrifice or offering."

15 So Samuel lay down until morning. Then he opened the doors of the house of the LORD. But Samuel was afraid to tell the vision to Eli. **16** Then Eli called Samuel and said, "Samuel, my son." And he said, "Here I am." **17** He said, "What is the word that He spoke to you? Please do not hide it from me. May God do the same to you, and more so, if you hide a *single* word from me of all the words that He spoke to you!" **18** So Samuel told him everything and hid nothing from him. And he said, "He is the LORD; let Him do what seems good to Him."

19 Now Samuel grew, and the LORD was with him, and He let none of his words fail. **20** And all Israel from Dan even to Beersheba knew that Samuel was confirmed as a prophet of the LORD. **21** And the LORD appeared again at Shiloh, because the LORD revealed Himself to Samuel at Shiloh by the word of the LORD.

Philistines Take the Ark in Victory

4 So the word of Samuel came to all Israel. Now Israel went out to meet the Philistines in battle, and they camped beside Ebenezer, while the Philistines camped in Aphek. **2** Then the Philistines drew up in battle formation to meet Israel. When the battle spread, Israel was defeated by the Philistines, who killed about four thousand men on the battlefield. **3** When the people came into the camp, the elders of Israel said, "Why has the LORD defeated us today before the Philistines? Let's take the ark of the covenant of the LORD from Shiloh, so that He may come among us and save us from the power of our enemies." **4** So the people sent *men* to Shiloh, and from there they carried the ark of the covenant of the LORD of armies who is enthroned *above* the cherubim; and the two sons of Eli, Hophni and Phinehas, *were* there with the ark of the covenant of God.

5 And as the ark of the covenant of the LORD was coming into the camp, all Israel shouted with a great shout, so that the earth resounded. **6** And when the Philistines heard the noise of the shout, they said, "What *does* the noise of this great shout in the camp of the Hebrews *mean?*" Then they understood that the ark of the LORD had come into the camp. **7** So the Philistines were afraid, for they said, "God has come into the camp!" And they said, "Woe to us! For nothing like this has happened before. **8** Woe to us! Who will save us from the hand of these mighty gods? These are the gods who struck the Egyptians with all *kinds of* plagues in the wilderness. **9** Take courage and be men, Philistines, or you will become slaves to the Hebrews, as they have been slaves to you; so be men and fight!"

10 So the Philistines fought and Israel was defeated, and every man fled to his tent; and the defeat was very great, for thirty thousand foot soldiers of Israel fell. **11** Moreover, the ark of God was taken; and the two sons of Eli, Hophni and Phinehas, died.

12 Now a man of Benjamin ran from the battle line and came to Shiloh the same day with his clothes torn, and dust on his head. **13** When he came, behold, Eli was sitting on *his* seat by the road keeping watch, because his heart was anxious about the ark of God. And the man came to give a report in the city, and all the city cried out. **14** When Eli heard the noise of the outcry, he said, "What *does* the noise of this commotion *mean?*" Then the man came hurriedly and told Eli. **15** Now Eli was ninety-eight years old, and his eyes were fixed and he could not see. **16** The man said to Eli, "I am the one who came from the battle line. Indeed, I escaped from the battle line today." And he said, "How are things, my son?" **17** Then the one who brought the news replied, "Israel has fled before the Philistines and there has also been a great defeat among the people, and your two sons, Hophni and Phinehas are also dead; and the ark of God has been taken." **18** When he mentioned the ark of God, Eli fell off the seat backward beside the gate, and his neck was broken and he died, for he was old and heavy. And *so* he judged Israel for forty years.

19 Now his daughter-in-law, Phinehas' wife, was pregnant *and about* to give birth; and when she heard the news that the ark of God had been taken and that her father-in-law and her husband had died, she kneeled down and gave birth, because her pains came upon her. **20** And about the time of her death the women who were standing by her said to her, "Do not be afraid, for you have given birth to a son."

But she did not answer or pay attention. 21 And she named the boy 'Ichabod, saying, "The glory has departed from Israel," because the ark of God had been taken and because of her father-in-law and her husband. 22 So she said, "The glory has departed from Israel, because the ark of God has been taken."

Capture of the Ark Provokes God

5 Now the Philistines took the ark of God and brought it from Ebenezer to Ashdod. 2 Then the Philistines took the ark of God and brought it into the house of Dagon, and placed it beside Dagon. 3 When the Ashdodites got up early the next day, behold, Dagon had fallen on his face to the ground before the ark of the LORD. So they took Dagon and set him back in his place. 4 But when they got up early the next morning, behold, Dagon had fallen on his face to the ground before the ark of the LORD. And the head of Dagon and both palms of his hands *were* cut off on the threshold; only the torso of Dagon was left. 5 For that reason neither the priests of Dagon nor any who enter Dagon's house step on the threshold of Dagon in Ashdod to this day.

6 Now the hand of the LORD was heavy on the Ashdodites, and He made them feel devastated and struck them with tumors, *both* Ashdod and its territories. 7 When the men of Ashdod saw that it was so, they said, "The ark of the God of Israel must not remain with us, because His hand is severe on us and on Dagon our god." 8 So they sent *word* and gathered all the governors of the Philistines to them, and said, "What shall we do with the ark of the God of Israel?" And they said, "Have the ark of the God of Israel brought to Gath." So they took the ark of the God of Israel away. 9 After they had taken it away, the hand of the LORD was against the city, *creating* a very great panic; and He struck the people of the city, from the young to the old, so that tumors broke out on them. 10 So they sent the ark of God to Ekron. And as the ark of God came to Ekron, the Ekronites cried out, saying, "They have brought the ark of the God of Israel to us, to kill us and our people!" 11 Therefore they sent *word* and gathered all the governors of the Philistines, and said, "Send away the ark of the God of Israel and let it return to its own place, so that it will not kill us and our people!" For there was a deadly panic throughout the city; the hand of God was very heavy there. 12 And the people who did not die were struck with tumors, and the outcry of the city went up to heaven.

The Ark Returned to Israel

6 Now the ark of the LORD had been in the territory of the Philistines for seven months. 2 And the Philistines called for the priests and the diviners, saying, "What are we to do with the ark of the LORD? Tell us how we may send it to its place." 3 And they said, "If you are going to send the ark of the God of Israel away, do not send it empty; but you shall certainly return to Him a guilt offering. Then you will be healed, and it will be revealed to you why His

hand does not leave you." 4 Then they said, "What is to be the guilt offering that we shall return to Him?" And they said, "Five gold tumors and five gold mice *corresponding to* the number of the governors of the Philistines, since one plague was on all of you and on your governors. 5 So you shall make likenesses of your tumors and likenesses of your mice that are ruining the land, and you shall give glory to the God of Israel; perhaps He will lighten His hand from you, your gods, and your land. 6 Why then do you harden your hearts as the Egyptians and Pharaoh hardened their hearts? When He had severely dealt with them, did they not let the people go, and they left? 7 Now then, take and prepare a new cart and two milk cows on which there has never been a yoke; and hitch the cows to the cart and take their calves back home, away from them. 8 Then take the ark of the LORD and place it on the cart; and put the articles of gold which you return to Him as a guilt offering in a saddlebag by its side. Then send it away that it may go. 9 But watch: if it goes up by the way of its own territory to Beth-shemesh, then He has done this great evil to us. But if not, then we will know that it was not His hand that struck us; it happened to us by chance."

10 Then the men did so: they took two milk cows and hitched them to the cart, and shut in their calves at home. 11 And they put the ark of the LORD on the cart, and the saddlebag with the gold mice and the likenesses of their tumors. 12 Now the cows went straight in the direction of Beth-shemesh; they went on the same road, bellowing as they went, and did not turn off to the right or to the left. And the governors of the Philistines followed them to the border of Beth-shemesh.

13 Now *the people of* Beth-shemesh were gathering in their wheat harvest in the valley, and they raised their eyes and saw the ark, and rejoiced at seeing *it*. 14 And the cart came into the field of Joshua the Beth-shemite and stopped there where *was* a large stone; and they split the wood of the cart and offered the cows as a burnt offering to the LORD. 15 And the Levites took down the ark of the LORD and the saddlebag that was with it, in which were the articles of gold, and put them on the large stone; and the men of Beth-shemesh offered burnt offerings and sacrificed sacrifices that day to the LORD. 16 When the five governors of the Philistines saw *it,* they returned to Ekron that day.

17 Now these are the gold tumors which the Philistines returned as a guilt offering to the LORD: one for Ashdod, one for Gaza, one for Ashkelon, one for Gath, *and* one for Ekron; 18 and the gold mice, *corresponding* to the number of all the cities of the Philistines belonging to the five governors, both of fortified cities and of country villages. The large stone on which they placed the ark of the LORD *is a witness* to this day in the field of Joshua the Beth-shemite.

19 Now He fatally struck some of the men of Beth-shemesh because they had looked into the ark of the LORD. He struck 50,070 men

---

4:21 1 I.e., no glory, or where is the glory?

among the people, and the people mourned because the LORD had struck the people with a great slaughter. 20 And the men of Beth-shemesh said, "Who is able to stand before the LORD, this holy God? And to whom will He go up from us?" 21 So they sent messengers to the inhabitants of Kiriath-jearim, saying, "The Philistines have brought back the ark of the LORD; come down and take it up to yourselves."

Israel Saved from the Philistines

7 And the men of Kiriath-jearim came and took the ark of the LORD and brought it into the house of Abinadab on the hill, and they consecrated his son Eleazar to watch over the ark of the LORD. 2 From the day that the ark remained at Kiriath-jearim, the time was long, for it was twenty years; and all the house of Israel mourned after the LORD.

3 Then Samuel spoke to all the house of Israel, saying, "If you are returning to the LORD with all your heart, then remove the foreign gods and the Ashtaroth from among you, and direct your hearts to the LORD and serve Him alone; and He will save you from the hand of the Philistines." 4 So the sons of Israel removed the Baals and the Ashtaroth, and served the LORD alone.

5 Then Samuel said, "Gather all Israel to Mizpah and I will pray to the LORD for you." 6 So they gathered to Mizpah, and drew water and poured it out before the LORD, and fasted on that day and said there, "We have sinned against the LORD." And Samuel judged the sons of Israel at Mizpah.

7 Now when the Philistines heard that the sons of Israel had gathered at Mizpah, the governors of the Philistines went up against Israel. And when the sons of Israel heard about it, they were afraid of the Philistines. 8 So the sons of Israel said to Samuel, "Do not stop crying out to the LORD our God for us, that He will save us from the hand of the Philistines!" 9 Samuel took a nursing lamb and offered it as a whole burnt offering to the LORD; and Samuel cried out to the LORD for Israel, and the LORD answered him. 10 Now Samuel was offering up the burnt offering, and the Philistines advanced to battle Israel. But the LORD thundered with a great thunder on that day against the Philistines and confused them, so that they were struck down before Israel. 11 And the men of Israel came out of Mizpah and pursued the Philistines, and killed them as far as below Beth-car.

12 Then Samuel took a stone and placed it between Mizpah and Shen, and named it 'Ebenezer, saying, "So far the LORD has helped us." 13 So the Philistines were subdued, and they did not come anymore within the border of Israel. And the hand of the LORD was against the Philistines all the days of Samuel. 14 The cities which the Philistines had taken from Israel were restored to Israel, from Ekron even to Gath; and Israel recovered their territory from the hand of the Philistines. So there was peace between Israel and the Amorites.

Samuel's Ministry

15 Now Samuel judged Israel all the days of his life. 16 And he used to go annually on a circuit to Bethel, Gilgal, and Mizpah, and he judged Israel in all these places. 17 Then *he would make* his return to Ramah, because his house *was* there, and there he *also* judged Israel; and there he built an altar to the LORD.

Israel Demands a King

8 Now it came about, when Samuel was old, that he appointed his sons as judges over Israel. 2 The name of his firstborn was Joel, and the name of his second, Abijah; *they were* judging in Beersheba. 3 His sons, however, did not walk in his ways but turned aside after dishonest gain, and they took bribes and perverted justice.

4 Then all the elders of Israel gathered together and came to Samuel at Ramah; 5 and they said to him, "Behold, you have grown old, and your sons do not walk in your ways. Now appoint us a king to judge us like all the nations." 6 But the matter was displeasing in the sight of Samuel when they said, "Give us a king to judge us." And Samuel prayed to the LORD. 7 And the LORD said to Samuel, "Listen to the voice of the people regarding all that they say to you, because they have not rejected you, but they have rejected Me from being King over them. 8 Like all the deeds which they have done since the day that I brought them up from Egypt even to this day—in that they have abandoned Me and served other gods—so they are doing to you as well. 9 Now then, listen to their voice; however, you shall warn them strongly and tell them of the practice of the king who will reign over them."

Warning concerning a King

10 So Samuel spoke all the words of the LORD to the people who had asked him for a king. 11 And he said, "This will be the practice of the king who will reign over you: he will take your sons and put *them* in his chariots for himself and among his horsemen, and they will run before his chariots. 12 He will appoint for himself commanders of thousands and commanders of fifties, and *some* to do his plowing and to gather in his harvest, and to make his weapons of war and equipment for his chariots. 13 He will also take your daughters *and use them* as perfumers, cooks, and bakers. 14 He will take the best of your fields, your vineyards, and your olive groves, and give *them* to his servants. 15 And he will take a tenth of your seed and your vineyards and give *it* to his high officials and his servants. 16 He will also take your male servants and your female servants, and your best young men, and your donkeys, and use *them* for his work. 17 He will take a tenth of your flocks, and you yourselves will become his servants. 18 Then you will cry out on that day because of your king whom you have chosen for yourselves, but the LORD will not answer you on that day."

19 Yet the people refused to listen to the voice of Samuel, and they said, "No, but there shall be a king over us, 20 so that we also may

---

7:12 1 I.e., the stone of help

be like all the nations, and our king may judge us and go out before us and fight our battles." 21 Now after Samuel had heard all the words of the people, he repeated them in the LORD's hearing. 22 And the LORD said to Samuel, "Listen to their voice and appoint a king for them." So Samuel said to the men of Israel, "Go, every man to his city."

Saul's Search

9 Now there was a man of Benjamin whose name was Kish the son of Abiel, son of Zeror, son of Becorath, son of Aphiah, son of a Benjaminite, a 'valiant mighty man. 2 He had a son whose name was Saul, a young and handsome *man,* and there was not a more handsome man than he among the sons of Israel; from his shoulders and up he was taller than any of the people.

3 Now the donkeys of Kish, Saul's father, had wandered off. So Kish said to his son Saul, "Now take with you one of the servants and arise, go search for the donkeys." 4 So he passed through the hill country of Ephraim and passed through the land of Shalishah, but they did not find *them.* Then they passed through the land of Shaalim, but they were not *there.* Then he passed through the land of the Benjaminites, but they did not find *them.*

5 When they came to the land of Zuph, Saul said to his servant who was with him, "Come, and let's return, or else my father will stop *being concerned* about the donkeys and will become anxious about us." 6 But he said to him, "Behold now, *there is* a man of God in this city, and the man is held in honor; everything that he says definitely comes *true.* Now let's go there, perhaps he can tell us about our journey on which we have set out." 7 Then Saul said to his servant, "But look, if we go, what shall we bring the man? For the bread is gone from our sacks and there is no gift to bring to the man of God. What do we have?" 8 The servant answered Saul again and said, "Look, I have in my hand a fourth of a shekel of silver; I will give *it* to the man of God and he will tell us our way." 9 (Previously in Israel, when a man went to inquire of God, he used to say, "Come, and let's go to the seer"; for *he who is called* a prophet now was previously called a seer.) 10 Then Saul said to his servant, "Good idea; come, let's go." So they went to the city where the man of God was.

11 As they went up the slope to the city, they found young women going out to draw water, and they said to them, "Is the seer here?" 12 They answered them and said, "He is; see, *he is* ahead of you. Hurry now, for he has come into the city today, because the people have a sacrifice on the high place today. 13 As soon as you enter the city you will find him before he goes up to the high place to eat, for the people will not eat until he comes, because he must bless the sacrifice; afterward those who are invited will eat. Now then, go up, for you will find him about this time." 14 So they went up to the city. As they came into the city, behold, Samuel was coming out toward them to go up to the high place.

God's Choice for King

15 Now a day before Saul's coming, the LORD had revealed *this* to Samuel, saying, 16 "About this time tomorrow I will send you a man from the land of Benjamin, and you shall anoint him as ruler over My people Israel; and he will save My people from the hand of the Philistines. For I have considered My people, because their outcry has come to Me." 17 When Samuel saw Saul, the LORD said to him, "Behold, the man of whom I spoke to you! This one shall rule over My people." 18 Then Saul approached Samuel at the gateway and said, "Please tell me where the seer's house is." 19 And Samuel answered Saul and said, "I am the seer. Go up ahead of me to the high place, for you shall eat with me today; and in the morning I will let you go, and will tell you everything that is on your mind. 20 And as for your donkeys that wandered off three days ago, do not be concerned about them, for they have been found. And for whom is everything that is desirable in Israel? Is it not for you and for all your father's household?" 21 Saul replied, "Am I not a Benjaminite, of the smallest of the tribes of Israel, and my family the least of all the families of the tribe of Benjamin? Why then have you spoken to me in this way?"

22 Then Samuel took Saul and his servant and brought them into the hall, and gave them a place at the head of those who were invited, who were about thirty men. 23 And Samuel said to the cook, "Serve the portion that I gave you about which I said to you, 'Set it aside.'" 24 Then the cook took up the leg with what was on it and placed *it* before Saul. And Samuel said, "Here is what has been reserved! Place *it* before you *and* eat, because it has been kept for you until the appointed time, since I said I have invited the people." So Saul ate with Samuel that day.

25 When they came down from the high place *into* the city, *Samuel* spoke with Saul on the roof. 26 And they got up early; and at daybreak Samuel called to Saul on the roof, saying, "Get up, so that I may send you on your way." So Saul got up, and both he and Samuel went out into the street. 27 As they were going down to the edge of the city, Samuel said to Saul, "Speak to the servant and have him go on ahead of us and pass by; but you stand *here* now, so that I may proclaim the word of God to you."

Saul among the Prophets

10 Then Samuel took the flask of oil, poured it on Saul's head, kissed him, and said, "Has the LORD not anointed you as ruler over His inheritance? 2 When you leave me today, then you will find two men close to Rachel's tomb in the territory of Benjamin at Zelzah; and they will say to you, 'The donkeys which you went to look for have been found. Now behold, your father has stopped talking about the donkeys and is anxious about you, saying, "What am I to do about my son?"' 3 Then you will go on farther from there, and you will come as far as the oak of Tabor, and there three men going up to God at Bethel will meet you:

9:1 1 Or *man of wealth and influence*   9:25 1 LXX *they spread a bed for Saul on the roof*

one carrying three young goats, another carrying three loaves of bread, and another carrying a jug of wine. 4 And they will greet you and give you two *loaves* of bread, *which* you will accept from their hand. 5 Afterward you will come to the hill of God where the Philistine garrison is; and it shall be as soon as you have come there to the city, that you will meet a group of prophets coming down from the high place with harp, tambourine, flute, and a lyre in front of them, and they will be prophesying. 6 Then the Spirit of the LORD will rush upon you, and you will prophesy with them and be changed into a different man. 7 And it shall be when these signs come to you, do for yourself what the occasion requires, because God is with you. 8 And you shall go down ahead of me to Gilgal; and behold, I will be coming down to you to offer burnt offerings and sacrifice peace offerings. You shall wait seven days until I come to you and inform you of what you should do."

9 Then it happened, when he turned his back to leave Samuel, that God changed his heart; and all those signs came about on that day. 10 When they came there to the hill, behold, a group of prophets met him; and the Spirit of God rushed upon him, so that he prophesied among them. 11 And it came about, when all who previously knew him saw that he was indeed prophesying with the prophets, that the people said to one another, "What is this that has happened to the son of Kish? Is Saul also among the prophets?" 12 And a man from there responded and said, "And who is their father?" Therefore it became a saying: "Is Saul also among the prophets?" 13 When he had finished prophesying, he came to the high place.

14 Now Saul's uncle said to him and his servant, "Where did you go?" And he said, "To look for the donkeys. When we saw that they were nowhere *to be found,* we went to Samuel." 15 Saul's uncle said, "Please tell me what Samuel said to you." 16 So Saul said to his uncle, "He told us plainly that the donkeys had been found." But he did not tell him about the matter of the kingdom which Samuel had mentioned.

Saul Publicly Chosen King

17 Now Samuel called the people together to the LORD at Mizpah; 18 and he said to the sons of Israel, "This is what the LORD, the God of Israel says: 'I brought Israel up from Egypt, and I rescued you from the hand of the Egyptians and from the power of all the kingdoms that were oppressing you.' 19 But today you have rejected your God, who saves you from all your catastrophes and your distresses; yet you have said, 'No, but put a king over us!' Now then, present yourselves before the LORD by your tribes and by your groups of thousands."

20 So Samuel brought all the tribes of Israel forward; and the tribe of Benjamin was selected by lot. 21 Then he brought the tribe of Benjamin forward by its families, and the Matrite family was selected by lot. And Saul the son of Kish was selected by lot; but when they looked for him, he could not be found.

22 Therefore they inquired further of the LORD: "Has the man come here yet?" And the LORD said, "Behold, he is hiding himself among the baggage." 23 So they ran and took him from there, and when he stood among the people, he was taller than any of the people from his shoulders upward. 24 Samuel said to all the people, "Do you see him whom the LORD has chosen? Surely there is no one like him among all the people." So all the people shouted and said, "*Long* live the king!"

25 Then Samuel told the people the ordinances of the kingdom, and wrote *them* in the book, and placed *it* before the LORD. And Samuel sent all the people away, each one to his house. 26 Saul also went to his house in Gibeah; and the valiant *men* whose hearts God had touched went with him. 27 But certain useless men said, "How can this one save us?" And they despised him and did not bring him a gift. But he kept silent *about it.*

Saul Defeats the Ammonites

11 Now Nahash the Ammonite went up and besieged Jabesh-gilead; and all the men of Jabesh said to Nahash, "Make a covenant with us and we will serve you." 2 But Nahash the Ammonite said to them, "I will make *it* with you on this condition, that I will gouge out the right eye of every one of you, and *thereby* I will inflict a disgrace on all Israel." 3 So the elders of Jabesh said to him, "Allow us seven days to send messengers throughout the territory of Israel. Then, if there is no one to save us, we will come out to you." 4 Then the messengers came to Gibeah of Saul and spoke *these* words in the hearing of the people, and all the people raised their voices and wept.

5 Now behold, Saul was coming from the field behind the oxen, and Saul said, "What is *the matter* with the people that they weep?" So they reported to him the words of the men of Jabesh. 6 Then the Spirit of God rushed upon Saul when he heard these words, and he became very angry. 7 He then took a yoke of oxen and cut them in pieces, and sent *them* throughout the territory of Israel by the hand of messengers, saying, "Whoever does not come out after Saul and after Samuel, the same shall be done to his oxen." Then the dread of the LORD fell on the people, and they came out as one person. 8 He counted them in Bezek; and the sons of Israel were three hundred thousand, and the men of Judah, thirty thousand. 9 They said to the messengers who had come, "This is what you shall say to the men of Jabesh-gilead: 'Tomorrow, by the time the sun is hot, you will be saved.' " So the messengers went and told the men of Jabesh; and they rejoiced. 10 Then the men of Jabesh said, "Tomorrow we will come out to you, and you may do to us whatever seems good to you." 11 The next morning Saul put the people in three companies; and they came into the midst of the camp at the morning watch, and struck and killed the Ammonites until the heat of the day. And those who survived scattered, so that no two of them were left together.

12 Then the people said to Samuel, "Who is he that said, 'Shall Saul reign over us?' Bring

the men, so that we may put them to death!" [13] But Saul said, "Not a single person shall be put to death this day, for today the LORD has brought about victory in Israel."

[14] Then Samuel said to the people, "Come, and let us go to Gilgal and renew the kingdom there." [15] So all the people went to Gilgal, and there they made Saul king before the LORD in Gilgal. There they also offered sacrifices of peace offerings before the LORD; and there Saul and all the men of Israel rejoiced greatly.

Samuel Addresses Israel

12 Then Samuel said to all Israel, "Behold, I have listened to your voice for all that you said to me, and I have appointed a king over you. [2] Now, here is the king walking before you, but as for me, I am old and gray, and my sons are here with you. And I have walked before you since my youth to this day. [3] Here I am; testify against me before the LORD and His anointed. Whose ox have I taken, or whose donkey have I taken, or whom have I exploited? Whom have I oppressed, or from whose hand have I taken a bribe to close my eyes with it? I will return it to you." [4] And they said, "You have not exploited us or oppressed us, or taken anything from anyone's hand." [5] So he said to them, "The LORD is witness against you, and His anointed is witness this day that you have found nothing in my hand." And they said, "He is witness."

[6] Then Samuel said to the people, "It is the LORD who appointed Moses and Aaron and who brought your fathers up from the land of Egypt. [7] Now then, take your stand, so that I may enter into judgment with you before the LORD concerning all the righteous acts of the LORD that He did for you and your fathers. [8] When Jacob went into Egypt and your fathers cried out to the LORD, then the LORD sent Moses and Aaron who brought your fathers out of Egypt and settled them in this place. [9] But they forgot the LORD their God, so He sold them into the hand of Sisera, commander of the army of Hazor, and into the hand of the Philistines, and into the hand of the king of Moab, and they fought against them. [10] They cried out to the LORD and said, 'We have sinned, because we have abandoned the LORD and have served the Baals and the Ashtaroth; but now save us from the hands of our enemies, and we will serve You.' [11] Then the LORD sent Jerubbaal, [1]Bedan, Jephthah, and Samuel, and saved you from the hands of your enemies all around, so that you lived in security.

The King Confirmed

[12] But when you saw that Nahash the king of the sons of Ammon was coming against you, you said to me, 'No, but a king shall reign over us!' Yet the LORD your God was your king. [13] And now, behold, the king whom you have chosen, whom you have asked for, and behold, the LORD has put a king over you. [14] If you will fear the LORD and serve Him, and listen to His voice and not rebel against the command of the

LORD, then both you and the king who reigns over you will follow the LORD your God. [15] But if you do not listen to the voice of the LORD, but rebel against the command of the LORD, then the hand of the LORD will be against you, even as it was against your fathers. [16] Even now, take your stand and see this great thing which the LORD is going to do before your eyes. [17] Is it not the wheat harvest today? I will call to the LORD, that He will send thunder and rain. Then you will know and see that your wickedness is great which you have done in the sight of the LORD, by asking for yourselves a king." [18] So Samuel called to the LORD, and the LORD sent thunder and rain that day; and all the people greatly feared the LORD and Samuel.

[19] Then all the people said to Samuel, "Pray to the LORD your God for your servants, so that we do not die; for we have added to all our sins this evil, by asking for ourselves a king." [20] Samuel said to the people, "Do not fear. You have committed all this evil, yet do not turn aside from following the LORD, but serve the LORD with all your heart. [21] But you must not turn aside, for then you would go after useless things which cannot benefit or save, because they are useless. [22] For the LORD will not abandon His people on account of His great name, because the LORD has been pleased to make you a people for Himself. [23] Furthermore, as for me, far be it from me that I would sin against the LORD by ceasing to pray for you; but I will instruct you in the good and right way. [24] Only fear the LORD and serve Him in truth with all your heart; for consider what great things He has done for you. [25] But if you still do evil, both you and your king will be swept away."

War with the Philistines

13 Saul was [1]thirty years old when he began to reign, and he reigned for [2]forty-two years over Israel.

[2] Now Saul chose for himself three thousand men of Israel, of whom two thousand were with Saul in Michmash and in the hill country of Bethel, while a thousand were with Jonathan at Gibeah of Benjamin. But he sent the rest of the people away, each to his tent. [3] And Jonathan attacked the garrison of the Philistines that was in Geba, and the Philistines heard about it. Then Saul blew the trumpet throughout the land, saying, "Let the Hebrews hear!" [4] And all Israel heard the news that Saul had attacked the garrison of the Philistines, and also that Israel had become repulsive to the Philistines. Then the people were summoned to Saul at Gilgal.

[5] Now the Philistines assembled to fight with Israel, thirty thousand chariots and six thousand horsemen, and people like the sand which is on the seashore in abundance; and they came up and camped in Michmash, east of Beth-aven. [6] When the men of Israel saw that they were in trouble (for the people were hard-pressed), then the people kept themselves hidden in caves, in crevices, in cliffs, in crypts,

---

12:11 [1]LXX and Syriac Barak   13:1 [1]As in some LXX mss, but very uncertain; MT one year old   [2]See Acts 13:21; Heb two years

and in pits. 7 And *some of* the Hebrews crossed the Jordan *into* the land of Gad and Gilead. But as for Saul, he was still in Gilgal, and all the people followed him, trembling.

8 Now he waited for seven days, until the appointed time that Samuel *had set*, but Samuel did not come to Gilgal; and the people were scattering from him. 9 So Saul said, "Bring me the burnt offering and the peace offerings." And he offered the burnt offering. 10 But as soon as he finished offering the burnt offering, behold, Samuel came; and Saul went out to meet him *and* to greet him. 11 But Samuel said, "What have you done?" And Saul said, "Since I saw that the people were scattering from me, and that you did not come at the appointed time, and that the Philistines were assembling at Michmash, 12 I thought, 'Now the Philistines will come down against me at Gilgal, and I have not asked the favor of the LORD.' So I worked up the courage and offered the burnt offering." 13 But Samuel said to Saul, "You have acted foolishly! You have not kept the commandment of the LORD your God, which He commanded you, for the LORD would now have established your kingdom over Israel forever. 14 But now your kingdom shall not endure. The LORD has sought for Himself a man after His own heart, and the LORD has appointed him ruler over His people, because you have not kept what the LORD commanded you."

15 Then Samuel set out and went up from Gilgal to Gibeah of Benjamin. And Saul counted the people who were present with him, about six hundred men. 16 Now Saul, his son Jonathan, and the people who were present with them were staying in Geba of Benjamin while the Philistines camped at Michmash. 17 Then raiders came from the camp of the Philistines in three companies: one company turned toward Ophrah, to the land of Shual, 18 and another company turned toward Beth-horon, and another company turned toward the border that overlooks the Valley of Zeboim toward the wilderness.

19 Now no blacksmith could be found in all the land of Israel, because the Philistines said, "Otherwise the Hebrews will make swords or spears." 20 So all Israel went down to the Philistines, each to sharpen his plowshare, his mattock, his axe, and his hoe. 21 The charge was two-thirds of a shekel for the plowshares, the mattocks, the forks, and the axes, and to fix the 1cattle goads. 22 So it came about on the day of battle that neither sword nor spear was found in the hands of any of the people who *were* with Saul and Jonathan, but they were found with Saul and his son Jonathan. 23 And the garrison of the Philistines went out to the gorge of Michmash.

Jonathan's Victory

14 Now the day came that Jonathan, the son of Saul, said to the young man who was carrying his armor, "Come, and let's cross over to the Philistines' garrison that is on the other side." But he did not tell his father. 2 Saul was staying on the outskirts of Gibeah under

the pomegranate tree that is in Migron. And the people who *were* with him *numbered* about six hundred men; 3 and Ahijah, the son of Ahitub, Ichabod's brother, the son of Phinehas, the son of Eli, the priest of the LORD at Shiloh, was wearing an ephod. And the people did not know that Jonathan had gone. 4 Now between the gorges by which Jonathan sought to cross over to the Philistines' garrison there was a rocky crag on the one side, and a rocky crag on the other side; and the name of the one was Bozez, and the name of the other, Seneh. 5 The one crag *rose* on the north opposite Michmash, and the other on the south opposite Geba.

6 Then Jonathan said to the young man who was carrying his armor, "Come, and let's cross over to the garrison of these uncircumcised *men;* perhaps the LORD will work for us, because the LORD is not limited to saving by many or by few!" 7 His armor bearer said to him, "Do everything that is in your heart; turn yourself *to it, and* here I am with you, as your heart *desires.*" 8 Then Jonathan said, "Behold, we are going to cross over to the men and reveal ourselves to them. 9 If they say to us, 'Wait until we come to you'; then we will stand in our place and not go up to them. 10 But if they say, 'Come up to us,' then we will go up, for the LORD has handed them over to us; and this *shall be* the sign to us." 11 When the two of them revealed themselves to the garrison of the Philistines, the Philistines said, "Behold, Hebrews are coming out of the holes where they have kept themselves hidden." 12 So the men of the garrison responded to Jonathan and his armor bearer and said, "Come up to us and we will inform you of something." And Jonathan said to his armor bearer, "Come up after me, for the LORD has handed them over to Israel." 13 Then Jonathan climbed up on his hands and feet, with his armor bearer behind him; and *the men* fell before Jonathan, and his armor bearer put some to death after him. 14 Now that first slaughter which Jonathan and his armor bearer inflicted was about twenty men within about half a furrow in an acre of land. 15 And there was a trembling in the camp, in the field, and among all the people. Even the garrison and the raiders trembled, and the earth quaked so that it became a great trembling.

16 Now Saul's watchmen in Gibeah of Benjamin looked, and behold, the multitude dissolved; they went here *and there.* 17 So Saul said to the people who *were* with him, "Look carefully now and see who has left us." And when they had looked, behold, Jonathan and his armor bearer were not *there.* 18 Then Saul said to Ahijah, "Bring the ark of God here." For at that time the ark of God was with the sons of Israel. 19 While Saul talked to the priest, the commotion in the camp of the Philistines continued and increased; so Saul said to the priest, "Withdraw your hand." 20 Then Saul and all the people who *were* with him rallied and came to the battle; and behold, every man's sword was against his fellow *Philistine, and there was* very great confusion. 21 Now the Hebrews *who* were with the Philistines previously, who went

---

13:21 1 I.e., spiked sticks for driving cattle

up with them all around in the camp, even they also *returned* to be with the Israelites who *were* with Saul and Jonathan. 22 When all the men of Israel who had kept themselves hidden in the hill country of Ephraim heard that the Philistines had fled, they also closely pursued them in the battle. 23 So the LORD saved Israel that day, and the battle spread beyond Beth-aven.

Saul's Foolish Order

24 Now the men of Israel were hard-pressed on that day, for Saul had put the people under oath, saying, "Cursed be the man who eats food before evening, and *before* I have avenged myself on my enemies." So none of the people tasted food. 25 All *the people of* the land entered the forest, and there was honey on the ground. 26 When the people entered the forest, behold, *there was* honey dripping; but no man put his hand to his mouth, because the people feared the oath. 27 However, Jonathan had not heard *it* when his father put the people under oath; so he put out the end of the staff that *was* in his hand and dipped it in the honeycomb, and put his hand to his mouth, and his eyes brightened. 28 Then one of the people responded and said, "Your father strictly put the people under oath, saying, 'Cursed be the man who eats food today.'" And the people were weary. 29 Then Jonathan said, "My father has troubled the land. See now that my eyes have brightened because I tasted a little of this honey. 30 How much more, if only the people had freely eaten today of the spoils of their enemies which they found! For now the defeat among the Philistines has not been great."

31 They attacked the Philistines that day from Michmash to Aijalon. But the people were very tired. 32 So the people loudly rushed upon the spoils, and took sheep, oxen, and calves, and slaughtered *them* on the ground; and the people ate *them* with the blood. 33 Then *observers* informed Saul, saying, "Look, the people are sinning against the LORD by eating *meat* with the blood." And he said, "You have acted treacherously; roll a large rock to me today." 34 Then Saul said, "Disperse yourselves among the people and say to them, 'Each one of you bring me his ox or his sheep, and slaughter *it* here and eat; and do not sin against the LORD by eating *it* with the blood.'" So all the people brought *them* that night, each one his ox with him, and they slaughtered *them* there. 35 And Saul built an altar to the LORD; it was the first altar that he built to the LORD.

36 Then Saul said, "Let's go down after the Philistines by night and take plunder among them until the morning light, and let's not leave a man among them alive." And they said, "Do whatever seems good to you." So the priest said, "Let's approach God here." 37 So Saul inquired of God: "Shall I go down after the Philistines? Will You hand them over to Israel?" But He did not answer him on that day. 38 Then Saul said, "Come here, all you leaders of the people, and investigate and see how this sin has happened today. 39 For as the LORD lives, who saves Israel, even if it is in my son

Jonathan, he shall assuredly die!" But not one of all the people answered him. 40 Then he said to all Israel, "You shall be on one side, and I and my son Jonathan will be on the other side." And the people said to Saul, "Do what seems good to you." 41 Therefore, Saul said to the LORD, the God of Israel, "Give a perfect *lot*." And Jonathan and Saul were selected by lot, but the people were exonerated. 42 Then Saul said, "Cast *lots* between me and my son Jonathan." And Jonathan was selected by lot.

43 So Saul said to Jonathan, "Tell me what you have done." And Jonathan told him, and said, "I did indeed taste a little honey with the end of the staff that was in my hand. Here I am, I must die!" 44 And Saul said, "May God do the same *to me* and more also, for you shall certainly die, Jonathan!" 45 But the people said to Saul, "Must Jonathan die, he who has brought about this great victory in Israel? Far from it! As the LORD lives, not *even* a hair of his head shall fall to the ground, because he has worked with God this day." So the people rescued Jonathan and he did not die. 46 Then Saul went up from pursuing the Philistines, and the Philistines went to their own place.

Constant Warfare

47 Now when Saul had taken control of the kingdom over Israel, he fought against all his enemies on every side, against Moab, the sons of Ammon, Edom, the kings of Zobah, and the Philistines; and wherever he turned, he inflicted punishment. 48 And he acted valiantly and defeated the Amalekites, and saved Israel from the hands of those who plundered them.

49 Now the sons of Saul were Jonathan, Ishvi, and Malchi-shua; and the names of his two daughters *were these:* the name of the firstborn *was* Merab, and the name of the younger, Michal. 50 And the name of Saul's wife was Ahinoam the daughter of Ahimaaz. And the name of the commander of his army was Abner the son of Ner, Saul's uncle. 51 Kish *was* the father of Saul, and Ner the father of Abner *was* the son of Abiel.

52 Now the war against the Philistines was severe all the days of Saul; and when Saul saw any warrior or any valiant man, he attached him to his staff.

Saul's Disobedience

15 Then Samuel said to Saul, "The LORD sent me to anoint you as king over His people, over Israel; now therefore, listen to the words of the LORD. 2 This is what the LORD of armies says: 'I will punish Amalek *for* what he did to Israel, in that he obstructed him on the way while he was coming up from Egypt. 3 Now go and strike Amalek and completely destroy everything that he has, and do not spare him; but put to death both man and woman, child and infant, ox and sheep, camel and donkey.'"

4 Then Saul summoned the people and counted them in Telaim: two hundred thousand foot soldiers and ten thousand men of Judah. 5 And Saul came to the city of Amalek and set an ambush in the ʰwadi. 6 But Saul said to the Kenites, "Go, get away, go down from

---

15:5 ¹ Or *valley*

among the Amalekites, so that I do not destroy you along with them; for you showed kindness to all the sons of Israel when they went up from Egypt." So the Kenites got away from among the Amalekites. 7 Then Saul defeated the Amalekites, from Havilah going toward Shur, which is east of Egypt. 8 He captured Agag the king of the Amalekites alive, and completely destroyed all the people with the edge of the sword. 9 But Saul and the people spared Agag and the best of the sheep, the oxen, the more valuable *animals*, the lambs, and everything that was good, and were unwilling to destroy them completely; but everything despicable and weak, that they completely destroyed.

Samuel Rebukes Saul

10 Then the word of the LORD came to Samuel, saying, 11 "I regret that I have made Saul king, because he has turned back from following Me and has not carried out My commands." And Samuel was furious and cried out to the LORD all night. 12 Samuel got up early in the morning to meet Saul; and it was reported to Samuel, saying, "Saul came to Carmel, and behold, he set up a monument for himself, then turned and proceeded on down to Gilgal." 13 So Samuel came to Saul, and Saul said to him, "Blessed are you of the LORD! I have carried out the command of the LORD." 14 But Samuel said, "What then is this bleating of the sheep in my ears, and the bellowing of the oxen which I hear?" 15 Saul said, "They have brought them from the Amalekites, for the people spared the best of the sheep and oxen to sacrifice to the LORD your God; but the rest we have completely destroyed." 16 Then Samuel said to Saul, "Stop, and let me inform you of what the LORD said to me last night." And he said to him, "Speak!"

17 So Samuel said, "Is it not *true,* though you were insignificant in your own eyes, *that* you *became* the head of the tribes of Israel? For the LORD anointed you as king over Israel. 18 And the LORD sent you on a mission, and said, 'Go and completely destroy the sinners, the Amalekites, and fight against them until they are eliminated.' 19 Why then did you not obey the voice of the LORD? Instead, you loudly rushed upon the spoils and did what was evil in the sight of the LORD!"

20 Then Saul said to Samuel, "I did obey the voice of the LORD, for I went on the mission on which the LORD sent me; and I have brought Agag the king of Amalek, and have completely destroyed the Amalekites. 21 But the people took *some* of the spoils, sheep and oxen, the choicest of the things designated for destruction, to sacrifice to the LORD your God at Gilgal." 22 Samuel said,

"Does the LORD have as much delight in
   burnt offerings and sacrifices
As in obeying the voice of the LORD?
Behold, to obey is better than a sacrifice,
And to pay attention is *better* than the fat
   of rams.
23 "For rebellion is *as reprehensible as* the sin
   of divination,
And insubordination is *as reprehensible
   as* false religion and idolatry.

Since you have rejected the word of the LORD,
He has also rejected you from *being* king."
24 Then Saul said to Samuel, "I have sinned, for I have violated the command of the LORD and your words, because I feared the people and listened to their voice. 25 Now then, please pardon my sin and return with me, so that I may worship the LORD." 26 But Samuel said to Saul, "I will not return with you; for you have rejected the word of the LORD, and the LORD has rejected you from being king over Israel." 27 Then Samuel turned to go, but *Saul* grasped the edge of his robe, and it tore off. 28 So Samuel said to him, "The LORD has torn the kingdom of Israel from you today and has given it to your neighbor, who is better than you. 29 Also the Glory of Israel will not lie nor change His mind; for He is not a man, that He would change His mind." 30 Then *Saul* said, "I have sinned; *but* please honor me now before the elders of my people and before *all* Israel, and go back with me, so that I may worship the LORD your God." 31 So Samuel went back following Saul, and Saul worshiped the LORD.

32 Then Samuel said, "Bring me Agag, the king of the Amalekites." And Agag came to him cheerfully. And Agag said, "Surely the bitterness of death is gone!" 33 But Samuel said, "As your sword has made women childless, so shall your mother be childless among women." And Samuel cut Agag to pieces before the LORD at Gilgal.

34 Then Samuel went to Ramah, but Saul went up to his house at Gibeah of Saul. 35 And Samuel did not see Saul again until the day of his death, though Samuel mourned for Saul. And the LORD regretted that He had made Saul king over Israel.

Samuel Goes to Bethlehem

16 Now the LORD said to Samuel, "How long are you going to mourn for Saul, since I have rejected him from being king over Israel? Fill your horn with oil and go; I will send you to Jesse the Bethlehemite, because I have chosen a king for Myself among his sons." 2 But Samuel said, "How can I go? When Saul hears *about it,* he will kill me." But the LORD said, "Take a heifer with you and say, 'I have come to sacrifice to the LORD.' 3 And you shall invite Jesse to the sacrifice, and I will let you know what you shall do; and you shall anoint for Me the one whom I designate to you." 4 So Samuel did what the LORD told *him,* and he came to Bethlehem. Then the elders of the city came trembling to meet him and said, "Do you come in peace?" 5 And he said, "In peace; I have come to sacrifice to the LORD. Consecrate yourselves and come with me to the sacrifice." He also consecrated Jesse and his sons and invited them to the sacrifice.

6 When they entered, he looked at Eliab and thought, "Surely the LORD's anointed is *standing* before Him." 7 But the LORD said to Samuel, "Do not look at his appearance or at the height of his stature, because I have rejected him; for God does not *see* as man sees, since man looks at the outward appearance, but the LORD looks at the heart." 8 Then Jesse called Abinadab and

had him pass before Samuel. But he said, "The LORD has not chosen this one, either." 9 Next Jesse had Shammah pass by. And he said, "The LORD has not chosen this one, either." 10 So Jesse had seven of his sons pass before Samuel. But Samuel said to Jesse, "The LORD has not chosen these." 11 Then Samuel said to Jesse, "Are these all the boys?" And he said, "The youngest is still left, but behold, he is tending the sheep." So Samuel said to Jesse, "Send word and bring him; for we will not take our places at the table until he comes here."

David Anointed

12 So he sent word and brought him in. Now he was reddish, with beautiful eyes and a handsome appearance. And the LORD said, "Arise, anoint him; for this is he." 13 So Samuel took the horn of oil and anointed him in the midst of his brothers; and the Spirit of the LORD rushed upon David from that day forward. And Samuel set out and went to Ramah.

14 Now the Spirit of the LORD left Saul, and an evil spirit from the LORD terrified him. 15 Saul's servants then said to him, "Behold now, an evil spirit from God is terrifying you. 16 May our lord now command your servants who are before you. Have them search for a man who is a skillful musician on the harp; and it shall come about whenever the evil spirit from God is upon you, that he shall play the harp with his hand, and you will become well." 17 So Saul said to his servants, "Now select for me a man who can play well, and bring him to me." 18 Then one of the young men responded and said, "Behold, I have seen a son of Jesse the Bethlehemite who is a skillful musician, a valiant mighty man, a warrior, skillful in speech, and a handsome man; and the LORD is with him." 19 So Saul sent messengers to Jesse to say, "Send me your son David, who is with the flock." 20 And Jesse took a donkey loaded with bread and a jug of wine, and he took a young goat, and sent them to Saul by his son David. 21 Then David came to Saul and attended him; and Saul greatly loved him, and he became his armor bearer. 22 So Saul sent word to Jesse, saying, "Let David now be my attendant for he has found favor in my sight." 23 So it came about whenever the evil spirit from God came to Saul, David would take the harp and play it with his hand; and Saul would feel relieved and become well, and the evil spirit would leave him.

Goliath's Challenge

17 Now the Philistines gathered their armies for battle; and they were gathered at Socoh which belongs to Judah, and they camped between Socoh and Azekah, in Ephesdammim. 2 Saul and the men of Israel were assembled and camped in the Valley of Elah, and they drew up in battle formation to confront the Philistines. 3 The Philistines were standing on the mountain on one side, while Israel was standing on the mountain on the other side, with the valley between them. 4 Then a champion came forward from the army encampment of the Philistines, named Goliath, from Gath. His height was ¹six cubits and a ²span. 5 And he had a bronze helmet on his head, and he wore scale-armor which weighed five thousand shekels of bronze. 6 He also had bronze ¹greaves on his legs and a bronze saber slung between his shoulders. 7 The shaft of his spear was like a weaver's beam, and the head of his spear weighed six hundred shekels of iron; and his shield-carrier walked in front of him. 8 He stood and shouted to the ranks of Israel and said to them, "Why do you come out to draw up in battle formation? Am I not the Philistine, and you the servants of Saul? Choose a man as your representative and have him come down to me. 9 If he is able to fight me and kill me, then we will become your servants; but if I prevail against him and kill him, then you shall become our servants and serve us." 10 Then the Philistine said, "I have defied the ranks of Israel this day! Give me a man, so that we may fight together." 11 When Saul and all Israel heard these words of the Philistine, they were dismayed and very fearful.

12 Now David was the son of the Ephrathite of Bethlehem in Judah, the man whose name was Jesse, and he had eight sons. And Jesse was old in the days of Saul, advanced in years among men. 13 The three older sons of Jesse had followed Saul to the battle. And the names of his three sons who had gone into the battle were Eliab the firstborn, and second to him, Abinadab, and the third, Shammah. 14 So David was the youngest. Now the three oldest followed Saul, 15 but David went back and forth from Saul to tend his father's flock at Bethlehem. 16 And the Philistine came forward morning and evening, and took his stand for forty days.

17 Then Jesse said to his son David, "Take now for your brothers an ephah of this roasted grain and these ten loaves, and run to the camp to your brothers. 18 Bring also these ten slices of cheese to the commander of their thousand, and look into the well-being of your brothers and bring back confirmation from them. 19 For Saul and they and all the men of Israel are in the Valley of Elah, fighting the Philistines."

David Accepts the Challenge

20 So David got up early in the morning and left the flock with a keeper, and took the supplies and went as Jesse had commanded him. And he came to the entrenchment encircling the camp while the army was going out in battle formation, shouting the war cry. 21 Israel and the Philistines drew up in battle formation, army against army. 22 Then David left the baggage in the care of the baggage keeper and ran to the battle line. And he entered and greeted his brothers. 23 As he was speaking with them, behold, the champion, the Philistine from Gath named Goliath, was coming up from the army of the Philistines, and he spoke these same words; and David heard him. 24 When all the men of Israel saw the man, they fled from him and were very fearful.

17:4 ¹ About 9 ft. or 2.7 m   ² About 9 in. or 23 cm   **17:6** ¹ I.e., shin guards

25 And the men of Israel said, "Have you seen this man who is coming up? Surely he is coming up to defy Israel. And it will be that the king will make the man who kills him wealthy with great riches, and will give him his daughter and make his father's house [f]free in Israel."

26 Then David said to the men who were standing by him, "What will be done for the man who kills this Philistine and rids Israel of the disgrace? For who is this uncircumcised Philistine, that he has *dared to* defy the armies of the living God?" 27 The people answered him in agreement with this statement, saying, "This is what will be done for the man who kills him."

28 Now Eliab his oldest brother heard *him* when he spoke to the men; and Eliab's anger burned against David and he said, "Why is it that you have come down? And with whom have you left those few sheep in the wilderness? I myself know your insolence and the wickedness of your heart; for you have come down in order to see the battle." 29 But David said, "What have I done now? Was it not *just* a question?" 30 Then he turned away from him to another and said the same thing; and the people replied with the same words as before.

David Kills Goliath

31 When the words that David spoke were heard, they informed Saul, and he sent for him. 32 And David said to Saul, "May no one's heart fail on account of him; your servant will go and fight this Philistine!" 33 But Saul said to David, "You are not able to go against this Philistine to fight him; for you are *only* a youth, while he has been a warrior since his youth." 34 But David said to Saul, "Your servant was tending his father's sheep. When a lion or a bear came and took a sheep from the flock, 35 I went out after it and attacked it, and rescued *the sheep* from its mouth; and when it rose up against me, I grabbed *it* by its mane and struck it and killed it. 36 Your servant has killed both the lion and the bear; and this uncircumcised Philistine will be like one of them, since he has defied the armies of the living God." 37 And David said, "The LORD who saved me from the paw of the lion and the paw of the bear, He will save me from the hand of this Philistine." So Saul said to David, "Go, and may the LORD be with you." 38 Then Saul clothed David with his military attire and put a bronze helmet on his head, and outfitted him with armor. 39 And David strapped on his sword over his military attire and struggled at walking, for he had not trained *with the armor.* So David said to Saul, "I cannot go with these, because I have not trained *with them.*" And David took them off. 40 Then he took his staff in his hand and chose for himself five smooth stones from the brook, and put them in the shepherd's bag which he had, that is, in *his* shepherd's pouch, and his sling was in his hand; and he approached the Philistine.

41 Then the Philistine came and approached David, with the shield-bearer in front of him. 42 When the Philistine looked and saw David, he was contemptuous of him; for he was *only* a youth, and reddish, with a handsome appearance. 43 So the Philistine said to David, "Am I a dog, that you come to me with sticks?" And the Philistine cursed David by his gods. 44 The Philistine also said to David, "Come to me, and I will give your flesh to the birds of the sky and the wild animals." 45 But David said to the Philistine, "You come to me with a sword, a spear, and a saber, but I come to you in the name of the LORD of armies, the God of the armies of Israel, whom you have defied. 46 This day the LORD will hand you over to me, and I will strike you and remove your head from you. Then I will give the dead bodies of the army of the Philistines this day to the birds of the sky and the wild animals of the earth, so that all the earth may know that there is a God in Israel, 47 and that this entire assembly may know that the LORD does not save by sword or by spear; for the battle is the LORD's, and He will hand you over to us!"

48 Then it happened, when the Philistine came closer to meet David, that David ran quickly toward the battle line to meet the Philistine. 49 And David put his hand into his bag and took from it a stone and slung *it,* and struck the Philistine on his forehead. And the stone penetrated his forehead, and he fell on his face to the ground.

50 So David prevailed over the Philistine with the sling and the stone: he struck the Philistine and killed him, and there was no sword in David's hand. 51 Then David ran and stood over the Philistine, and took his sword and drew it out of its sheath and finished him, and cut off his head with it. When the Philistines saw that their champion was dead, they fled. 52 Then the men of Israel and Judah rose up and shouted, and they pursued the Philistines as far as the valley, and to the gates of Ekron. And the Philistine dead lay along the way to Shaaraim, even to Gath and Ekron. 53 Then the sons of Israel returned from their close pursuit of the Philistines, and plundered their camps. 54 And David took the Philistine's head and brought it to Jerusalem, but he put his weapons in his tent.

55 Now when Saul had seen David going out against the Philistine, he said to Abner the commander of the army, "Abner, whose son is this young man?" And Abner said, "By your life, O king, I do not know." 56 And the king said, "You *then,* ask whose son the youth is." 57 So when David returned from killing Philistine, Abner took him and brought him before Saul with the Philistine's head in his hand. 58 Then Saul said to him, "Whose son are you, young man?" And David answered, "*I am* the son of your servant Jesse the Bethlehemite."

Jonathan and David

18 Now it came about, when he had finished speaking to Saul, that Jonathan committed himself to David, and Jonathan loved him as himself. 2 And Saul took him that day and did not let him return to his father's house. 3 Then Jonathan made a covenant with

---

17:25 [1] I.e., exempt from taxes and public service

David because he loved him as himself. 4 Jonathan stripped himself of the robe that was on him and gave it to David, with his military gear, including his sword, his bow, and his belt. 5 And David went *into battle* wherever Saul sent him, *and always* achieved success; so Saul put him in charge of the men of war. And it was pleasing in the sight of all the people, and also in the sight of Saul's servants.

6 Now it happened as they were coming, when David returned from killing the Philistine, that the women came out of all the cities of Israel, singing and dancing, to meet King Saul, with tambourines, with joy and with *other* ¹musical instruments. 7 The women sang as they played, and said,

"Saul has slain his thousands,
    And David his ten thousands."

8 Then Saul became very angry, for this lyric displeased him; and he said, "They have given David *credit for* ten thousands, but to me they have given *credit for only* thousands! Now *what* more can he have but the kingdom?" 9 And Saul eyed David with suspicion from that day on.

Saul Turns against David

10 Now it came about on the next day that an evil spirit from God rushed upon Saul, and he raved in the midst of the house while David was playing *the harp* with his hand, as usual; and a spear *was* in Saul's hand. 11 Then Saul hurled the spear, for he thought, "I will pin David to the wall." But David escaped from his presence, twice.

12 Now Saul was afraid of David, because the LORD was with him but had left Saul. 13 So Saul removed him from his presence and appointed him as his commander of a thousand; and he went out and came in before the people. 14 David was successful in all his ways, for the LORD *was* with him. 15 When Saul saw that he was very successful, he was afraid of him. 16 But all Israel and Judah loved David, for he would go out *to battle* and return before them.

17 Then Saul said to David, "Here is my older daughter Merab; I will give her to you as a wife, only be a valiant man for me and fight the LORD's battles." For Saul thought, "My hand shall not be against him, but let the hand of the Philistines be against him." 18 But David said to Saul, "Who am I, and who is my family, *or* my father's family in Israel, that I should be the king's son-in-law?" 19 So it came about at the time that Merab, Saul's daughter, was to be given to David, that she was given *instead* to Adriel the Meholathite as a wife.

David Marries Saul's Daughter

20 Now Michal, Saul's daughter, loved David. When they informed Saul, the thing was pleasing to him. 21 For Saul thought, "I will give her to him so that she may become a trap for him, and that the hand of the Philistines may be against him." Therefore Saul said to David, "For a second time you may become my son-in-law, today." 22 Then Saul commanded his servants, "Speak to David in secret, saying, 'Behold, the king delights in you, and all his servants love you; now then, become the king's son-in-law.'" 23 So Saul's servants spoke these words to David. But David said, "Is it trivial in your sight to become the king's son-in-law, since I am *only* a poor man and insignificant?" 24 Then Saul's servants reported to him, saying, "These are the words David spoke." 25 Saul then said, "This is what you shall say to David: 'The king does not desire any dowry except a hundred foreskins of the Philistines, to take vengeance on the king's enemies.'" But Saul plotted to have David fall by the hand of the Philistines. 26 When his servants told David these words, it pleased David to become the king's son-in-law. So before the time had expired, 27 David set out and went, he and his men, and fatally struck two hundred men among the Philistines. Then David brought their foreskins, and they presented all *two hundred* of them to the king, so that he might become the king's son-in-law. And Saul gave him his daughter Michal as a wife. 28 When Saul saw and realized that the LORD was with David, and *that* Michal, Saul's daughter, loved him, 29 then Saul was even more afraid of David. So Saul was David's enemy continually. 30 Then the commanders of the Philistines went *to battle,* and it happened as often as they went out, that David was more successful than all the servants of Saul. So his name was held in high esteem.

David Protected from Saul

19 Now Saul told his son Jonathan and all his servants to put David to death. But Jonathan, Saul's son, greatly delighted in David. 2 So Jonathan informed David, saying, "My father Saul is seeking to put you to death. Now then, please be on your guard in the morning, and stay in a hiding place and conceal yourself. 3 And as for me, I will go out and stand beside my father in the field where you are *hiding,* and I will speak with my father about you; and whatever I find out, I will tell you." 4 Then Jonathan spoke well of David to his father Saul and said to him, "May the king not sin against his servant David, since he has not sinned against you, and since his deeds *have been* very beneficial to you. 5 For he took his life in his hand and struck the Philistine, and the LORD brought about a great victory for all Israel; you saw *it* and rejoiced. Why then would you sin against innocent blood by putting David to death for no reason?" 6 Saul listened to the voice of Jonathan, and Saul vowed, "As the LORD lives, *David* shall not be put to death." 7 Then Jonathan called David, and Jonathan told him all these words. And Jonathan brought David to Saul, and he was in his presence as before.

8 When there was war again, David went out and fought the Philistines and defeated them with great slaughter, so that they fled from him. 9 Now there was an evil spirit from the LORD on Saul as he was sitting in his house with his spear in his hand, and David was playing *the harp* with his hand. 10 And Saul tried to pin David to the wall with the spear, but he escaped from Saul's presence, so that he stuck

---

the spear into the wall. And David fled and escaped that night.

11 Then Saul sent messengers to David's house to watch him, in order to put him to death in the morning. But Michal, David's wife, informed him, saying, "If you do not save your life tonight, tomorrow you will be put to death!" **12** So Michal let David down through a window, and he went and fled, and escaped. **13** And Michal took the household idol and laid *it* on the bed, and put a quilt of goats' hair at its head, and covered *it* with clothing. **14** When Saul sent messengers to take David, she said, "He is sick." **15** Then Saul sent messengers to see David, saying, "Bring him up to me on his bed, so that I may put him to death." **16** When the messengers entered, behold, the household idol *was* on the bed with the quilt of goats' hair at its head. **17** So Saul said to Michal, "Why have you betrayed me like this and let my enemy go, so that he has escaped?" And Michal said to Saul, "He said to me, 'Let me go! Why should I put you to death?'"

18 So David fled and escaped, and came to Samuel at Ramah; and he informed him of everything that Saul had done to him. And he and Samuel went and stayed in Naioth. **19** But it was reported to Saul, saying, "Behold, David is at Naioth in Ramah." **20** Then Saul sent messengers to take David, but when they saw the company of prophets prophesying, with Samuel standing *and* presiding over them, the Spirit of God came upon the messengers of Saul; and they also prophesied. **21** When Saul was informed *of this,* he sent other messengers, but they also prophesied. So Saul sent messengers again the third time, yet they prophesied. **22** Then he went to Ramah himself and came as far as the large well that is in Secu; and he asked, "Where are Samuel and David?" And *someone* said, "Behold, they are at Naioth in Ramah." **23** So he proceeded there to Naioth in Ramah; but the Spirit of God came upon him also, so that he went along prophesying continually until he came to Naioth in Ramah. **24** He also stripped off his clothes, and he too prophesied before Samuel and lay down naked all that day and all night. Therefore they say, "Is Saul also among the prophets?"

David and Jonathan's Covenant

20 Then David fled from Naioth in Ramah, and he came and said to Jonathan, "What have I done? What is my guilt? And what is my sin before your father, that he is seeking my life?" **2** He said to him, "Far from it, you shall not die! Behold, my father does nothing either great or small without informing me. So why would my father hide this thing from me? It is not so!" **3** Yet David vowed again, saying, "Your father is well aware that I have found favor in your sight, and he has said, 'Jonathan is not to know this, otherwise he will be worried.' But indeed as the LORD lives and as your soul lives, there is just a step between me and death." **4** Then Jonathan said to David, "Whatever you say, I will do for you." **5** So David said to Jonathan, "Behold, tomorrow is the new moon, and I am obligated to sit down to eat with the king. But let me go so that I may hide myself in the field until the third evening. **6** If your father misses me at all, then say, 'David earnestly requested *leave* of me to run to Bethlehem, his city, because it is the yearly sacrifice there for the whole family.' **7** If he says, '*That is* good,' your servant *will be* safe; but if he is very angry, be aware that he has decided on evil. **8** So deal kindly with your servant, for you have brought your servant into a covenant of the LORD with you. But if I am guilty of wrongdoing, kill me yourself; for why then should you bring me to your father?" **9** Jonathan said, "Far be it from you! For if I in fact learn that my father has decided to inflict harm on you, would I not inform you?" **10** Then David said to Jonathan, "Who will inform me if your father answers you harshly?" **11** Jonathan said to David, "Come, and let's go out to the field." So both of them went out to the field.

12 Then Jonathan said to David, "The LORD, the God of Israel, *is my witness!* When I have sounded out my father about this time tomorrow *or* the third day, behold, *if he has a good feeling* toward you, shall I not then send *word* to you and inform you? **13** If it pleases my father *to do* you harm, may the LORD do so to me and more so, if I *fail to* inform you and send you away, so that you may go in safety. And may the LORD be with you as He has been with my father. **14** And if I am still alive, will you not show me the faithfulness of the LORD, so that I do not die? **15** And you shall never cut off your loyalty to my house, not even when the LORD cuts off every one of the enemies of David from the face of the earth." **16** So Jonathan made a *covenant* with the house of David, *saying,* "May the LORD demand *it* from the hands of David's enemies." **17** And Jonathan made David vow again because of his love for him, because he loved him as he loved his own life.

18 Then Jonathan said to him, "Tomorrow is the new moon, and you will be missed since your seat will be empty. **19** When you have stayed for three days, you shall go down quickly and come to the place where you hid yourself on that eventful day, and you shall remain beside the stone Ezel. **20** And I will shoot three arrows to the side, as though I shot at a target. **21** Then behold, I will send the boy, *telling him,* 'Go, find the arrows.' If I specifically say to the boy, 'Behold, the arrows are on this side of you, get them,' then come, because it is safe for you and there is nothing *to harm you,* as the LORD lives. **22** But if I say to the youth, 'Behold, the arrows are beyond you,' go, because the LORD has sent you away. **23** As for the agreement of which you and I have spoken, behold, the LORD is between you and me forever."

24 So David hid himself in the field; and when the new moon came, the king sat down to eat food. **25** Now the king sat on his seat as usual, the seat by the wall; then Jonathan stood up and Abner sat down by Saul's side; but David's place was empty. **26** Nevertheless Saul did not say anything that day, because he thought, "It *must have been* an accident; he is not clean, undoubtedly *he is* not clean." **27** But

it came about the next day, the second *day* of the new moon, that David's place was empty *again;* so Saul said to his son Jonathan, "Why has the son of Jesse not come to the meal, either yesterday or today?" 28 And Jonathan answered Saul, "David earnestly requested leave of me *to go* to Bethlehem. 29 He said, 'Please let me go, because our family has a sacrifice in the city, and my brother has ordered me *to attend.* So now, if I have found favor in your sight, please let me slip away so that I may see my brothers.' For this reason he has not come to the king's table."

Saul Is Angry with Jonathan

30 Then Saul's anger burned against Jonathan, and he said to him, "You son of a perverse, rebellious woman! Do I not know that you are choosing the son of Jesse to your own shame, and to the shame of your mother's nakedness? 31 For, as long as the son of Jesse lives on the earth, neither you nor your kingdom will be established. Now then, send *men* and bring him to me, for he is doomed to die!" 32 But Jonathan replied to his father Saul and said to him, "Why must he be put to death? What has he done?" 33 Then Saul hurled his spear at him to strike and kill him; so Jonathan knew that his father had decided to put David to death. 34 Then Jonathan got up from the table in the heat of anger, and did not eat food on the second day of the new moon, because he was worried about David since his father had insulted him.

35 Now it came about in the morning that Jonathan went out to the field at the time agreed upon with David, and a little boy *was* with him. 36 He said to his boy, "Run, find now the arrows which I am about to shoot." The boy ran, and he shot an arrow past him. 37 When the boy reached the location of the arrow which Jonathan had shot, Jonathan called after the boy and said, "Is the arrow not beyond you?" 38 Then Jonathan called after the boy, "Hurry, be quick, do not stay!" And Jonathan's boy picked up the arrow and came to his master. 39 But the boy was not aware of anything; only Jonathan and David knew about the matter. 40 Then Jonathan gave his weapons to his boy and said to him, "Go, bring *them* to the city." 41 When the boy was gone, David got up from the south side, then he fell on his face to the ground and bowed three times. And they kissed each other and wept together, until David *wept* immeasurably. 42 Then Jonathan said to David, "Go in safety, since we have sworn to each other in the name of the LORD, saying, 'The LORD will be between me and you, and between my descendants and your descendants forever.'" So *David* set out and went *on his way,* while Jonathan went into the city.

David Takes Consecrated Bread

21 Then David came to Nob, to Ahimelech the priest; and Ahimelech came trembling to meet David and said to him, "Why are you alone, and no one with you?" 2 David said to Ahimelech the priest, "The king has commissioned me with a matter and has said to me, 'No one is to know anything about the matter on which I am sending you and with which I have commissioned you; and I have directed the young men to a certain place.' 3 Now then, what do you have on hand? Give me five loaves of bread, or whatever can be found." 4 The priest answered David and said, "There is no ordinary bread on hand, but there is consecrated bread, if only the young men have kept themselves from women." 5 David answered the priest and said to him, "Be assured, women have been denied to us as previously when I left and the bodies of the young men were consecrated, though it was an ordinary journey; how much more then will their bodies be consecrated today?" 6 So the priest gave him consecrated *bread;* for there was no bread there except the bread of the Presence which was removed from *its place* before the LORD, in order to put hot bread *in its place* on the day it was taken away.

7 Now one of the servants of Saul was there that day, detained before the LORD; and his name was Doeg the Edomite, the chief of Saul's shepherds.

8 David said to Ahimelech, "Now is there no spear or sword on hand? For I brought neither my sword nor my weapons with me, because the king's matter was urgent." 9 Then the priest said, "The sword of Goliath the Philistine, whom you killed in the Valley of Elah, behold, it is wrapped in a cloth behind the ephod; if you would take it for yourself, take *it.* For there is no other except it here." And David said, "There is none like it; give it to me."

10 Then David set out and fled that day from Saul, and went to Achish king of Gath. 11 But the servants of Achish said to him, "Is this not David, the king of the land? Did they not sing of this one as they danced, saying,

'Saul has slain his thousands,
And David his ten thousands'?"

12 David took these words to heart and greatly feared Achish king of Gath. 13 So he disguised his sanity *while* in their sight and acted insanely in their custody, and he scribbled on the doors of the gate, and drooled on his beard. 14 Then Achish said to his servants, "Look, you see the man is behaving like an insane person. Why do you bring him to me? 15 Do I lack insane people, that you have brought this one to behave like an insane person in my presence? Shall this one come into my house?"

Priests Killed at Nob

22 So David departed from there and escaped to the cave of Adullam; and when his brothers and all his father's household heard *about it,* they went down there to him. 2 Then everyone who was in distress, and everyone who was in debt, and everyone who was discontented gathered to him; and he became captain over them. Now there were about four hundred men with him.

3 And David went from there to Mizpah of Moab; and he said to the king of Moab, "Please let my father and my mother come *and stay* with you until I know what God will do for me." 4 Then he left them with the king of Moab; and they stayed with him all the time that David was in the stronghold. 5 But Gad the

prophet said to David, "Do not stay in the stronghold; leave, and go into the land of Judah." So David left and went into the forest of Hereth.

6 Then Saul heard that David and the men who were with him had been discovered. Now Saul was in Gibeah, sitting under the tamarisk tree on the height with his spear in his hand, and all his servants were standing in front of him. 7 Saul said to his servants who were standing in front of him, "Hear now, you Benjaminites! Will the son of Jesse really give all of you fields and vineyards? Will he make you all commanders of thousands and commanders of hundreds? 8 For all of you have conspired against me so that there is no one who informs me when my son makes a *covenant* with the son of Jesse, and there is none of you who cares about me or informs me that my son has stirred up my servant against me to lie in ambush, as *it is* this day." 9 Then Doeg the Edomite, who was standing in front of the servants of Saul, responded and said, "I saw the son of Jesse coming to Nob, to Ahimelech the son of Ahitub. 10 And he inquired of the Lord for him, gave him provisions, and gave him the sword of Goliath the Philistine."

11 Then the king sent a *messenger* to summon Ahimelech the priest, the son of Ahitub, and all his father's household, the priests who were in Nob; and all of them came to the king. 12 Saul said, "Listen now, son of Ahitub." And he replied, "Here I am, my lord." 13 Saul then said to him, "Why have you and the son of Jesse conspired against me, in that you have given him bread and a sword, and have inquired of God for him, so that he would rise up against me by lying in ambush as *it is* this day?"

14 Then Ahimelech answered the king and said, "And who among all your servants is as faithful as David, the king's *own* son-in-law, who is commander over your bodyguard, and is honored in your house? 15 Did I *just* begin to inquire of God for him today? Far be it from me! Do not let the king impute anything against his servant or against any of the household of my father, because your servant knows nothing at all of this whole affair." 16 But the king said, "You shall certainly die, Ahimelech, you and all your father's household!" 17 And the king said to the guards who were attending him, "Turn around and put the priests of the Lord to death, because their hand also is with David and because they knew that he was fleeing and did not inform me." But the servants of the king were unwilling to reach out with their hands to attack the priests of the Lord. 18 Then the king said to Doeg, "You, turn around and attack the priests!" And Doeg the Edomite turned around and attacked the priests, and he killed on that day eighty-five men who wore the linen ephod. 19 He also struck Nob the city of the priests with the edge of the sword, both men and women, children and infants; *he* also *struck* oxen, donkeys, and sheep with the edge of the sword.

20 But one son of Ahimelech the son of Ahitub, named Abiathar, escaped and fled to David. 21 Abiathar informed David that Saul had killed the priests of the Lord. 22 Then David said to Abiathar, "I knew on that day, when Doeg the Edomite was there, that he would certainly tell Saul. I myself have turned against every person in your father's household. 23 Stay with me; do not be afraid, even though he who is seeking my life is seeking your life. For you are safe with me."

David Saves Keilah

23 Then they informed David, saying, "Behold, the Philistines are fighting against Keilah and are plundering the threshing floors." 2 So David inquired of the Lord, saying, "Shall I go and attack these Philistines?" And the Lord said to David, "Go and attack the Philistines and save Keilah." 3 But David's men said to him, "Behold, we are fearful here in Judah. How much more then if we go to Keilah against the ranks of the Philistines?" 4 So David inquired of the Lord once more. And the Lord answered him and said, "Arise, go down to Keilah, for I am going to hand the Philistines over to you." 5 Then David and his men went to Keilah and fought the Philistines; and he drove away their livestock and struck them with a great slaughter. So David saved the inhabitants of Keilah.

6 Now it came about, when Abiathar the son of Ahimelech fled to David at Keilah, *that* he came down *with* an ephod in his hand. 7 When it was reported to Saul that David had come to Keilah, Saul said, "God has handed him over to me, for he shut himself in by entering a city with double gates and bars." 8 So Saul summoned all the people for war, to go down to Keilah to besiege David and his men. 9 But David knew that Saul was plotting evil against him; so he said to Abiathar the priest, "Bring the ephod here." 10 Then David said, "Lord God of Israel, Your servant has heard for certain that Saul is seeking to come to Keilah to destroy the city on my account. 11 Will the citizens of Keilah hand me over to him? Will Saul come down just as Your servant has heard? Lord God of Israel, please, tell Your servant." And the Lord said, "He will come down." 12 Then David said, "Will the citizens of Keilah hand me and my men over to Saul?" And the Lord said, "They will hand you over." 13 Then David and his men, about six hundred, rose up and departed from Keilah, and they went wherever they could go. When it was reported to Saul that David had escaped from Keilah, he gave up the pursuit. 14 David stayed in the wilderness in the strongholds, and remained in the hill country in the wilderness of Ziph. And Saul searched for him every day, but God did not hand him over to him.

Saul Pursues David

15 Now David saw that Saul had come out to seek his life while David was in the wilderness of Ziph, at Horesh. 16 And Jonathan, Saul's son, set out and went to David at Horesh, and encouraged him in God. 17 He said to him, "Do not be afraid, because the hand of Saul my father will not find you, and you will be king over Israel, and I will be second in command to you; and Saul my father knows that as well."

18 So the two of them made a covenant before the LORD; and David stayed at Horesh, while Jonathan went to his house.

19 Then Ziphites came up to Saul at Gibeah, saying, "Is David not keeping himself hidden with us in the strongholds at Horesh, on the hill of Hachilah, which is south of Jeshimon? 20 Now then, O king, come down, since you fully desire to do so; and our part *shall be* to hand him over to the king." 21 Saul said, "May you be blessed of the LORD, since you have had compassion on me. 22 Go now, be more persistent, and investigate and see his place where he is hiding, *and* who has seen him there; for I am told that he is very cunning. 23 So look, and learn about all the hiding places where he keeps himself hidden, and return to me with certainty, and I will go with you; and if he is in the land, I will search him out among all the thousands of Judah."

24 So they set out and went to Ziph ahead of Saul. Now David and his men were in the wilderness of Maon, in the Arabah to the south of Jeshimon. 25 When Saul and his men went to seek *him,* they informed David, and he came down to the rock and stayed in the wilderness of Maon. And when Saul heard *about it,* he pursued David in the wilderness of Maon. 26 Saul went on one side of the mountain, and David and his men on the other side of the mountain; and David was hurrying to get away from Saul, while Saul and his men were surrounding David and his men to apprehend them. 27 But a messenger came to Saul, saying, "Hurry and come, for the Philistines have launched an attack against the land!" 28 So Saul returned from pursuing David and went to confront the Philistines; therefore they called that place the Rock of Division. 29 And David went up from there and stayed in the strongholds of Engedi.

David Spares Saul's Life

24 Now when Saul returned from pursuing the Philistines, it was reported to him, saying, "Behold, David is in the wilderness of Engedi." 2 Then Saul took three thousand chosen men from all Israel and went to search for David and his men in front of the Rocks of the Mountain Goats. 3 And he came to the sheepfolds on the way, where there *was* a cave; and Saul went in to relieve himself. Now David and his men were sitting in the inner recesses of the cave. 4 Then David's men said to him, "Behold, *this is* the day of which the LORD said to you, 'Behold; I am about to hand your enemy over to you, and you shall do to him as it seems good to you.'" Then David got up and cut off the edge of Saul's robe secretly. 5 But it came about afterward that David's conscience bothered him because he had cut off the edge of Saul's *robe.* 6 So he said to his men, "Far be it from me because of the LORD that I would do this thing to my lord, the LORD's anointed, to reach out with my hand against him, since he is the LORD's anointed." 7 And David rebuked his men with *these* words and did not allow them to rise up against Saul. And Saul got up, left the cave, and went on *his* way.

8 Afterward, however, David got up and went out of the cave, and called after Saul, saying, "My lord the king!" And when Saul looked behind him, David bowed with his face to the ground and prostrated himself. 9 And David said to Saul, "Why do you listen to the words of men who say, 'Behold, David is seeking to harm you'? 10 Behold, this day your eyes have seen that the LORD had handed you over to me today in the cave, and *someone* said to kill you, but I spared you; and I said, 'I will not reach out with my hand against my lord, because he is the LORD's anointed.' 11 So, my father, look! Indeed, look at the edge of your robe in my hand! For by *the fact* that I cut off the edge of your robe but did not kill you, know and understand that there is no evil or rebellion in my hands, and I have not sinned against you, though you are lying in wait for my life, to take it. 12 May the LORD judge between you and me, and may the LORD take vengeance on you for me; but my hand shall not be against you. 13 As the proverb of the ancients says, 'Out of the wicked comes wickedness'; but my hand shall not be against you. 14 After whom has the king of Israel gone out? Whom are you pursuing? A dead dog, a single flea? 15 May the LORD therefore be judge and decide between you and me; and may He see and plead my cause and save me from your hand."

16 When David had finished speaking these words to Saul, Saul said, "Is this your voice, my son David?" Then Saul raised his voice and wept. 17 And he said to David, "You are more righteous than I; for you have dealt well with me, while I have dealt maliciously with you. 18 You have declared today that you have done good to me, that the LORD handed me over to you and *yet* you did not kill me. 19 Though if a man finds his enemy, will he let him go away unharmed? May the LORD therefore reward you with good in return for what you have done to me this day. 20 Now, behold, I know that you will certainly be king, and that the kingdom of Israel will be established in your hand. 21 So now swear to me by the LORD that you will not cut off my descendants after me, and that you will not eliminate my name from my father's household." 22 And David swore *an oath* to Saul. Then Saul went to his home, but David and his men went up to the stronghold.

Samuel's Death

25 Then Samuel died; and all Israel assembled and mourned for him, and they buried him at his house in Ramah. And David set out and went down to the wilderness of Paran.

Nabal and Abigail

2 Now *there was* a man in Maon whose business was in Carmel; and the man was very rich, and he had three thousand sheep and a thousand goats. And it came about while he was shearing his sheep in Carmel 3 (now the man's name was Nabal, and his wife's name was Abigail. And the woman was intelligent and beautiful in appearance, but the man was harsh and evil in *his* dealings, and he was a Calebite), 4 that David heard in the wilderness

that Nabal was shearing his sheep. 5 So David sent ten young men; and David said to the young men, "Go up to Carmel and visit Nabal, and greet him in my name; 6 and this is what you shall say: 'Have a long life, peace to you, and peace to your house, and peace to all that you have! 7 Now then, I have heard that you have shearers. Now, your shepherds have been with us; we have not harmed them, nor has anything of theirs gone missing all the days they were in Carmel. 8 Ask your young men and they will tell you. Therefore let *my* young men find favor in your eyes, for we have come on a festive day. Please give whatever you find at hand to your servants and to your son David.' "

9 When David's young men came, they spoke to Nabal in accordance with all these words in David's name; then they waited. 10 But Nabal answered David's servants and said, "Who is David? And who is the son of Jesse? There are many servants today who are each breaking away from his master. 11 Shall I then take my bread and my water and my meat that I have slaughtered for my shearers, and give it to men whose origin I do not know?" 12 So David's young men made their way back and returned; and they came and informed him in accordance with all these words. 13 Then David said to his men, "Each *of you* strap on his sword." So each man strapped on his sword. And David also strapped on his sword, and about four hundred men went up behind David, while two hundred stayed with the baggage.

14 Now one of the young men told Abigail, Nabal's wife, saying, "Behold, David sent messengers from the wilderness to greet our master, and he spoke to them in anger. 15 Yet the men were very good to us, and we were not harmed, nor did anything go missing as long as we went with them, while we were in the fields. 16 They were a wall to us both by night and by day, all the time we were with them tending the sheep. 17 Now then, be aware and consider what you should do, because harm is plotted against our master and against all his household; and he is such a worthless man that no one can speak to him."

Abigail Intercedes

18 Then Abigail hurried and took two hundred *loaves* of bread and two jugs of wine, and five sheep *already* prepared and five measures of roasted grain, and a hundred cakes of raisins and two hundred cakes of figs, and she loaded *them* on donkeys. 19 Then she said to her young men, "Go on ahead of me; behold, I am coming after you." But she did not tell her husband Nabal. 20 And it happened as she was riding on her donkey and coming down by the hidden part of the mountain, that behold, David and his men were coming down toward her; so she met them. 21 Now David had said, "It is certainly for nothing that I have guarded everything that this *man* has in the wilderness, so that nothing has gone missing of all that belonged to him! For he has returned me evil for good. 22 May God do so to the enemies of David, and more so, if by morning I leave alive

as much as one male of any who belong to him."

23 When Abigail saw David, she hurried and dismounted from her donkey, and fell on her face in front of David and bowed herself to the ground. 24 She fell at his feet and said, "On me alone, my lord, be the blame. And please let your slave speak to you, and listen to the words of your slave. 25 Please do not let my lord pay attention to this worthless man, Nabal, for as his name is, so is he. Nabal is his name, and stupidity is with him; but I your slave did not see the young men of my lord whom you sent.

26 "Now then, my lord, as the LORD lives, and as your soul lives, since the LORD has restrained you from shedding blood, and from avenging yourself by your own hand, now then, may your enemies and those who seek evil against my lord, be like Nabal. 27 And now let this gift which your servant has brought to my lord be given to the young men who accompany my lord. 28 Please forgive the offense of your slave; for the LORD will certainly make for my lord an enduring house, because my lord is fighting the battles of the LORD, and evil will not be found in you all your days. 29 Should anyone rise up to pursue you and to seek your life, then the life of my lord shall be bound in the bundle of the living with the LORD your God; but the lives of your enemies He will sling out as from the hollow of a sling. 30 And when the LORD does for my lord in accordance with all the good that He has spoken concerning you, and appoints you ruler over Israel, 31 this will not become an obstacle to you, or a troubled heart to my lord, both by having shed blood without cause and by my lord's having avenged himself. When the LORD deals well with my lord, then remember your slave."

32 Then David said to Abigail, "Blessed be the LORD God of Israel, who sent you this day to meet me, 33 and blessed be your discernment, and blessed be you, who have kept me this day from bloodshed and from avenging myself by my own hand. 34 Nevertheless, as the LORD God of Israel lives, who has restrained me from harming you, if you had not come quickly to meet me, there certainly would not have been left to Nabal until the morning light as much as one male." 35 So David accepted from her hand what she had brought him, and said to her, "Go up to your house in peace. See, I have listened to you and granted your request."

36 Then Abigail came to Nabal, and behold, he was having a feast in his house, like the feast of a king. And Nabal's heart was cheerful within him, for he was very drunk; so she did not tell him anything at all until the morning light. 37 But in the morning, when the wine had gone out of Nabal, his wife told him these things, and his heart died within him so that he became *like* a stone. 38 About ten days later, the LORD struck Nabal and he died.

David Marries Abigail

39 When David heard that Nabal was dead, he said, "Blessed be the LORD, who has pleaded the cause of the shame inflicted on me by the

hand of Nabal, and has kept back His servant from evil. The LORD has also returned the evildoing of Nabal on his own head." Then David sent a proposal to Abigail, to take her as his wife. **40** When the servants of David came to Abigail at Carmel, they spoke to her, saying, "David has sent us to you to take you to him as *his* wife." **41** And she got up and bowed with her face to the ground, and said, "Behold, your slave is a servant to wash the feet of my lord's servants." **42** Then Abigail got up quickly, and rode on a donkey, with her five female attendants who accompanied her; and she followed the messengers of David and became his wife.

43 David had also taken Ahinoam of Jezreel, and they both became his wives.

44 But Saul had given his daughter Michal, David's wife, to Palti the son of Laish, who was from Gallim.

David Again Spares Saul

26 Then the Ziphites came to Saul at Gibeah, saying, "Is David not keeping himself hidden on the hill of Hachilah, *which is* opposite Jeshimon?" **2** So Saul set out and went down to the wilderness of Ziph, taking with him three thousand chosen men of Israel, to search for David in the wilderness of Ziph. **3** And Saul camped on the hill of Hachilah, which is opposite Jeshimon, beside the road, and David was staying in the wilderness. When he saw that Saul had come after him into the wilderness, **4** David sent out spies, and he learned that Saul was definitely coming. **5** David then set out and came to the place where Saul had camped. And David saw the place where Saul lay, and Abner the son of Ner, the commander of his army; and Saul was lying in the circle of the camp, and the people were camped around him.

6 Then David said to Ahimelech the Hittite and to Abishai the son of Zeruiah, Joab's brother, saying, "Who will go down with me to Saul in the camp?" And Abishai said, "I will go down with you." **7** So David and Abishai came to the people by night, and behold, Saul lay sleeping inside the circle of the camp with his spear stuck in the ground at his head; and Abner and the people were lying around him. **8** Then Abishai said to David, "Today God has handed your enemy over to you; now then, please let me pin him with the spear to the ground with one thrust, and I will not do it to him a second time." **9** But David said to Abishai, "Do not kill him, for who can reach out with his hand against the LORD's anointed and remain innocent?" **10** David also said, "As the LORD lives, the LORD certainly will strike him, or his day will come that he dies, or he will go down in battle and perish. **11** The LORD forbid that I would reach out with my hand against the LORD's anointed! But now please take the spear that is at his head and the jug of water, and let's go." **12** So David took the spear and the jug of water *that were* at Saul's head, and they left; and no one saw or knew *about it,* nor did anyone awaken, for they were all asleep, because a deep sleep from the LORD had fallen on them.

13 Then David crossed over to the other side and stood on top of the mountain at a distance *with* a large area between them. **14** And David called to the people and to Abner the son of Ner, saying, "Will you not answer, Abner?" Then Abner replied, "Who are you who calls to the king?" **15** So David said to Abner, "Are you not a man? And who is like you in Israel? Why then have you not guarded your lord the king? For one of the people came to kill the king your lord! **16** This thing that you have done is not good. As the LORD lives, *all of* you undoubtedly must die, because you did not guard your lord, the LORD's anointed. And now, see where the king's spear is and the jug of water that was at his head!"

17 Then Saul recognized David's voice and said, "Is this your voice, my son David?" And David said, "It is my voice, my lord the king." **18** He also said, "Why then is my lord pursuing his servant? For what have I done? Or what evil is in my hand? **19** Now then, please let my lord the king listen to the words of his servant. If the LORD has incited you against me, may He accept an offering; but if it is people, cursed are they before the LORD, because they have driven me out today so that I would have no share in the inheritance of the LORD, saying, 'Go, serve other gods.' **20** Now then, do not let my blood fall to the ground far from the presence of the LORD; for the king of Israel has come out to search for a single flea, just as one hunts a partridge in the mountains."

21 Then Saul said, "I have sinned. Return, my son David, for I will not harm you again since my life was precious in your sight this day. Behold, I have played the fool and have made a very great mistake." **22** David replied, "Behold, the spear of the king! Now have one of the young men come over and take it. **23** And the LORD will repay each man *for* his righteousness and his faithfulness; for the LORD handed you over to me today, but I refused to reach out with my hand against the LORD's anointed. **24** Therefore behold, just as your life was highly valued in my sight this day, so may my life be highly valued in the sight of the LORD, and may He rescue me from all distress." **25** Then Saul said to David, "Blessed are you, my son David; you will both accomplish much and assuredly prevail." So David went on his way, and Saul returned to his place.

David Flees to the Philistines

27 Then David said to himself, "Now I will perish one day by the hand of Saul. There is nothing better for me than to safely escape into the land of the Philistines. Then Saul will despair of searching for me anymore in all the territory of Israel, and I will escape from his hand." **2** So David set out and went over, he and the six hundred men who were with him, to Achish the son of Maoch, king of Gath. **3** And David lived with Achish in Gath, he and his men, each with his *own* household—David with his two wives, Ahinoam the Jezreelitess, and Abigail the Carmelitess, Nabal's widow. **4** Now it was reported to Saul that David had fled to Gath, so he no longer searched for him.

5 Then David said to Achish, "If now I have

found favor in your sight, have them give me a place in one of the cities in the country, so that I may live there; for why should your servant live in the royal city with you?" **6** So Achish gave him Ziklag that day; therefore Ziklag has belonged to the kings of Judah to this day. **7** The number of days that David lived in the country of the Philistines was a year and four months.

8 Now David and his men went up and attacked the Geshurites, the Girzites, and the Amalekites; for they were the inhabitants of the land from ancient times, as you come to Shur even as far as the land of Egypt. **9** David attacked the land and did not leave a man or a woman alive, and he took the sheep, the cattle, the donkeys, the camels, and the clothing. Then he returned and came to Achish. **10** Now Achish said, "Where did you carry out an attack today?" And David said, "Against the ᶦNegev of Judah, against the Negev of the Jerahmeelites, and against the Negev of the Kenites." **11** And David did not leave a man or a woman alive to bring to Gath, saying, "Otherwise they will tell about us, saying, 'This is what David has done, and this *has been* his practice all the time that he has lived in the country of the Philistines.'" **12** So Achish believed David, saying, "He has undoubtedly made himself repulsive among his people Israel; therefore he will become my servant forever."

Saul and the Spirit Medium

28 Now it came about in those days that the Philistines gathered their armed camps for war, to fight against Israel. And Achish said to David, "Know for certain that you will go out with me in the camp, you and your men." **2** David said to Achish, "Very well, you will learn what your servant can do." So Achish said to David, "*Then* I will assuredly make you my bodyguard for life!"

3 Now Samuel was dead, and all Israel had mourned him and buried him in Ramah, his own city. And Saul had removed the mediums and spiritists from the land. **4** So the Philistines assembled and came and camped in Shunem; and Saul gathered all Israel together, and they camped in Gilboa. **5** When Saul saw the camp of the Philistines, he was afraid and his heart trembled greatly. **6** So Saul inquired of the LORD, but the LORD did not answer him, either in dreams, or by the Urim, or by the prophets. **7** Then Saul said to his servants, "Find for me a woman who is a medium, so that I may go to her and inquire of her." And his servants said to him, "Behold, there is a woman who is a medium at En-dor."

8 Then Saul disguised himself by putting on different clothes, and went, he and two men with him, and they came to the woman by night; and he said, "Consult the spirit for me, please, and bring up for me *the one* whom I shall name for you." **9** But the woman said to him, "Behold, you know what Saul has done, that he has eliminated the mediums and spiritists from the land. Why are you then setting a trap for my life, to bring about my death?" **10** So Saul swore an oath to her by the

LORD, saying, "As the LORD lives, no punishment shall come upon you for this thing." **11** Then the woman said, "Whom shall I bring up for you?" And he said, "Bring up Samuel for me." **12** When the woman saw Samuel, she cried out with a loud voice; and the woman spoke to Saul, saying, "Why have you deceived me? For you are Saul!" **13** But the king said to her, "Do not be afraid; but what do you see?" And the woman said to Saul, "I see a divine being coming up from the earth." **14** He said to her, "How does he appear?" And she said, "An old man is coming up, and he is wrapped in a robe." Then Saul knew that it was Samuel, and he bowed with his face to the ground and paid ᶦhomage.

15 And Samuel said to Saul, "Why have you disturbed me by bringing me up?" Saul replied, "I am very distressed, for the Philistines are waging war against me, and God has abandoned me and no longer answers me, either through prophets or in dreams; therefore I have called you, so that you may let me know what I should do." **16** Samuel said, "But why ask me, since the LORD has abandoned you and has become your enemy? **17** And the LORD has done just as He spoke through me; for the LORD has torn the kingdom from your hand and given it to your neighbor, to David. **18** Just as you did not obey the LORD and did not execute His fierce wrath on Amalek, so the LORD has done this thing to you this day. **19** Furthermore, the LORD will also hand Israel along with you over to the Philistines; so tomorrow you and your sons *will be* with me. Indeed, the LORD will hand the army of Israel over to the Philistines!"

20 Then Saul immediately fell full length to the ground and was very afraid because of Samuel's words; there was no strength in him either, because he had eaten no food all day and all night. **21** The woman came to Saul and saw that he was utterly horrified, and she said to him, "Behold, your servant has obeyed you, and I have taken my life in my hand and have listened to your words which you spoke to me. **22** So now you too, please listen to the voice of your servant, and let me serve you a piece of bread, and eat *it,* so that you will have strength when you go on *your* way." **23** But he refused and said, "I will not eat." However, his servants together with the woman urged him, and he listened to them. So he got up from the ground and sat on the bed. **24** Now the woman had a fattened calf in the house, and she quickly slaughtered it; then she took flour, kneaded it and baked unleavened bread *from it.* **25** She then served *it* to Saul and his servants, and they ate. Then they got up and left that night.

The Philistines Mistrust David

29 Now the Philistines gathered together all their armies to Aphek, while the Israelites were camping by the spring which is in Jezreel. **2** And the governors of the Philistines were proceeding on, *leading* hundreds and thousands, and David and his men were proceeding in the back with Achish. **3** Then the

---

27:10 ᶦI.e., South country **28:14** ᶦI.e., great respect and honor to a superior

commanders of the Philistines said, "What *are* these Hebrews *doing here?*" And Achish said to the commanders of the Philistines, "Is this not David, the servant of Saul the king of Israel, who has been with me these days, or *rather* these years, and I have found nothing at all *suspicious* in him since the day he deserted *to me* to this day?" 4 But the commanders of the Philistines were angry with him, and the commanders of the Philistines said to him, "Make the man go back, so that he will return to his place where you have assigned him, and do not let him go down to battle with us, or in the battle he may become an adversary to us. For how could this *man* find favor with his lord? *Would it* not *be* with the heads of these men? 5 Is this not David, of whom they sing in the dances, saying,

'Saul has slain his thousands,
   And David his ten thousands'?"

6 Then Achish called David and said to him, "*As* the LORD lives, you *have* indeed *been* honest, and your 1going out and your coming in with me in the army are pleasing in my sight; for I have not found evil in you since the day of your coming to me to this day. Nevertheless, you are not pleasing in the sight of the governors. 7 Now then, return and go in peace, so that you will not do *anything* wrong in the sight of the governors of the Philistines." 8 However, David said to Achish, "But what have I done? And what have you found in your servant since the day that I came before you, to this day, that I cannot go and fight against the enemies of my lord the king?" 9 But Achish replied to David, "I know that you are pleasing in my sight, like an angel of God; nevertheless the commanders of the Philistines have said, 'He must not go up with us into the battle.' 10 Now then, rise early in the morning with the servants of your lord who have come with you, and *as soon as* you have risen early in the morning and have light, leave." 11 So David got up early, he and his men, to leave in the morning to return to the land of the Philistines. And the Philistines went up to Jezreel.

David's Victory over the Amalekites

30 Then it happened, when David and his men came to Ziklag on the third day, that the Amalekites had carried out an attack on the Negev and on Ziklag, and had overthrown Ziklag and burned it with fire; 2 and they took captive the women *and all* who were in it, from the small to the great, without killing anyone, and drove *them* off and went their way. 3 When David and his men came to the city, behold, it was burned with fire, and their wives, their sons, and their daughters had been taken captive. 4 Then David and the people who were with him raised their voices and wept until there was no strength in them to weep. 5 Now David's two wives had been taken captive, Ahinoam the Jezreelitess and Abigail the widow of Nabal the Carmelite. 6 Also, David was in great distress because the people spoke of stoning him, for all the people were embittered, each one because of his sons and his daughters. But David felt strengthened in the LORD his God.

7 Then David said to Abiathar the priest, the son of Ahimelech, "Please bring me the ephod." So Abiathar brought the ephod to David. 8 And David inquired of the LORD, saying, "Shall I pursue this band of raiders? Will I overtake them?" And He said to him, "Pursue, for you will certainly overtake them, and you will certainly rescue *everyone.*" 9 So David left, he and the six hundred men who were with him, and they came to the brook Besor, *where some* who were left behind stayed. 10 But David pursued, he and four hundred men, for two hundred who were too exhausted to cross the brook Besor stayed *behind.*

11 Now they found an Egyptian in the field and brought him to David, and gave him bread and he ate, and they provided him water to drink. 12 They also gave him a slice of fig cake and two cakes of raisins, and he ate; then his spirit revived. For he had not eaten bread or drunk water for three days and three nights. 13 Then David said to him, "To whom do you belong? And where are you from?" And he said, "I am a young man of Egypt, a servant of an Amalekite; and my master abandoned me when I became sick three days ago. 14 We carried out an attack on the Negev of the Cherethites, and on that which belongs to Judah, and on the Negev of Caleb, and we burned Ziklag with fire." 15 Then David said to him, "Will you bring me down to this band of raiders?" And he said, "Swear to me by God that you will not kill me or hand me over to my master, and I will bring you down to this band."

16 Now when he had brought him down, behold, they were dispersed over all the land, eating and drinking and celebrating because of all the great plunder that they had taken from the land of the Philistines and from the land of Judah. 17 And David slaughtered them from the twilight until the evening of the next day; and not a man of them escaped, except four hundred young men who rode on camels and fled. 18 So David recovered all that the Amalekites had taken, and rescued his two wives. 19 And nothing of theirs was missing, whether small or great, sons or daughters, plunder, or anything that they had taken for themselves; David brought *it* all back. 20 So David had captured all the sheep and the cattle *which the people* drove ahead of the *other* livestock, and they said, "This is David's plunder."

The Plunder Is Divided

21 When David came to the two hundred men who were too exhausted to follow David and had been left behind at the brook Besor, and they went out to meet David and to meet the people who were with him, then David approached the people and greeted them. 22 Then all the wicked and worthless men among those who went with David said, "Since they did not go with us, we will not give them any of the spoils that we have recovered, except to every man his wife and his children, so that they may lead *them* away and leave."

29:6 1 I.e., performance of duties

23 But David said, "You must not do so, my brothers, with what the LORD has given us, for He has protected us and handed over to us the band of raiders that came against us. 24 And who will listen to you in this matter? For as *is* the share of the one who goes down into the battle, so *shall be* the share of the one who stays by the baggage; they shall share alike." 25 So it has been from that day forward, that he made it a statute and an ordinance for Israel to this day.

26 Now when David came to Ziklag, he sent *some* of the spoils to the elders of Judah, to his friends, saying, "Behold, a gift for you from the spoils of the enemies of the LORD: 27 to those who were in Bethel, to those who were in Ramoth of the Negev, to those who were in Jattir, 28 to those who were in Aroer, to those who were in Siphmoth, to those who were in Eshtemoa, 29 to those who were in Racal, to those who were in the cities of the Jerahmeelites, to those who were in the cities of the Kenites, 30 to those who were in Hormah, to those who were in Bor-ashan, to those who were in Athach, 31 to those who were in Hebron, and to all the places where David himself and his men walked."

Saul and His Sons Killed in Battle

31 Now the Philistines were fighting against Israel, and the men of Israel fled from the Philistines but fell fatally wounded on Mount Gilboa. 2 And the Philistines also overtook Saul and his sons, and the Philistines killed Jonathan, Abinadab, and Malchi-shua, the sons of Saul. 3 The battle went heavily against Saul, and the archers found him; and

he was gravely wounded by the archers. 4 Then Saul said to his armor bearer, "Draw your sword and pierce me through with it, otherwise these uncircumcised *Philistines* will come and pierce me through, and abuse me." But his armor bearer was unwilling, because he was very fearful. So Saul took his sword and fell on it. 5 When his armor bearer saw that Saul was dead, he also fell on his sword and died with him. 6 So Saul died with his three sons, his armor bearer, and all his men on that day together.

7 Now when the people of Israel who were on the other side of the valley, with those who were beyond the Jordan, saw that the men of Israel had fled and that Saul and his sons were dead, they abandoned the cities and fled; then the Philistines came and settled in them.

8 It came about on the next day, when the Philistines came to strip those killed, that they found Saul and his three sons fallen on Mount Gilboa. 9 They cut off his head and stripped off his weapons, and sent *them* throughout the land of the Philistines, to bring the good news to the house of their idols and to the people. 10 They put his weapons in the temple of Ashtaroth, and they nailed his body to the wall of Beth-shan. 11 Now when the inhabitants of Jabesh-gilead heard what the Philistines had done to Saul, 12 all the valiant men got up and walked all night, and they took the body of Saul and the bodies of his sons from the wall of Beth-shan, and they came to Jabesh and burned them there. 13 And they took their bones and buried them under the tamarisk tree in Jabesh, and fasted for seven days.

The Second Book of
SAMUEL

David Learns of Saul's Death

1 Now it came about after the death of Saul, when David had returned from the slaughter of the Amalekites, that David stayed two days in Ziklag. 2 And on the third day, behold, a man came from Saul's camp with his clothes torn and dust on his head. And it happened when he came to David, he fell to the ground and prostrated himself. 3 Then David said to him, "From where do you come?" And he said to him, "I have escaped from the camp of Israel." 4 David said to him, "How did things go? Please tell me." And he said, "The people have fled from the battle, and many of the people also have fallen and are dead; and Saul and his son Jonathan are also dead." 5 Then David said to the young man who told him, "How do you know that Saul and his son Jonathan are dead?" 6 The young man who told him said, "By chance I happened to be on Mount Gilboa, and behold, Saul was leaning on his spear. And behold, the chariots and the horsemen had overtaken him. 7 When he looked behind himself, he saw me, and called to me. And I said, 'Here I am.' 8 Then he said to me, 'Who are you?' And I answered him, 'I am an Amalekite.' 9 And he said to me, 'Please stand next to me and finish me off, for agony has seized me because my life still lingers in me.' 10 So I stood next to him and finished him off, because I knew that he could not live after he had fallen. And I took the crown which was on his head and the band which was on his arm, and I have brought them here to my lord."

11 Then David took hold of his clothes and tore them, and so also did all the men who were with him. 12 And they mourned and wept and fasted until evening for Saul and his son Jonathan, and for the people of the LORD and the house of Israel, because they had fallen by the sword. 13 Then David said to the young man who informed him, "Where are you from?" And he answered, "I am the son of a stranger, an Amalekite." 14 And David said to him, "How is it you were not afraid to reach out with your hand to destroy the LORD's anointed?" 15 Then David called one of the young men and said, "Come forward, put him to death." So he struck him and he died. 16 And David said to him, "*Your blood is on your head, because your own mouth has testified against you, saying, 'I have finished off the LORD's anointed.'"

David's Song of Mourning for Saul and Jonathan

17 Then David sang this song of mourning over Saul and his son Jonathan, 18 and he told them to teach the sons of Judah the mourning song of the bow; behold, it is written in the Book of Jashar.

19 "Your beauty, Israel, is slaughtered on your high places!
How the mighty have fallen!
20 "Tell it not in Gath,
Proclaim it not in the streets of Ashkelon,
Or the daughters of the Philistines will rejoice,
The daughters of the uncircumcised will celebrate.
21 "Mountains of Gilboa,
May there be no dew nor rain on you, or fields of offerings!
For there the shield of the mighty was defiled,
The shield of Saul, not anointed with oil.
22 "From the blood of those slaughtered, from the fat of the mighty,
The bow of Jonathan did not turn back,
And the sword of Saul did not return unstained.
23 "Saul and Jonathan, beloved and delightful in life,
And in their deaths they were not separated;
They were swifter than eagles,
They were mightier than lions.
24 "Daughters of Israel, weep over Saul,
Who clothed you in scarlet, with jewelry,
Who put gold jewelry on your apparel.
25 "How the mighty have fallen in the midst of the battle!
Jonathan is slaughtered on your high places.
26 "I am distressed for you, my brother Jonathan;
You have been a close friend to me.
Your love for me was more wonderful Than the love of women.
27 "How the mighty have fallen,
And the weapons of war have perished!"

David Made King over Judah

2 Then it came about afterward that David inquired of the LORD, saying, "Shall I go up to one of the cities of Judah?" And the LORD said to him, "Go up." So David said, "Where shall I go up?" And He said, "To Hebron." 2 So David went up there, and his two wives also, Ahinoam the Jezreelitess and Abigail the widow of Nabal the Carmelite. 3 And David brought up his men who were with him, each with his household; and they settled in the cities of Hebron. 4 Then the men of Judah came, and there they anointed David king over the house of Judah.

And they told David, saying, "It was the men of Jabesh-gilead who buried Saul." 5 So David sent messengers to the men of Jabesh-gilead, and said to them, "May you be blessed of the LORD because you have shown this kindness to Saul your lord, and have buried him. 6 And now may the LORD show kindness

---

1:16 1 I.e., his death was his own responsibility

and truth to you; and I also will show this goodness to you, because you have done this thing. 7 Now then, let your hands be strong and be valiant, since Saul your lord is dead, and also the house of Judah has anointed me king over them."

Ish-bosheth Made King over Israel

8 But Abner the son of Ner, commander of Saul's army, had taken 'Ish-bosheth the son of Saul and brought him over to Mahanaim. 9 And he made him king over Gilead, over the Ashurites, over Jezreel, over Ephraim, and over Benjamin, even over all Israel. 10 Ish-bosheth, Saul's son, was forty years old when he became king over Israel, and he was king for two years. The house of Judah, however, followed David. 11 And the time that David was king in Hebron over the house of Judah was seven years and six months.

Civil War

12 Now Abner the son of Ner, went from Mahanaim to Gibeon with the servants of Ish-bosheth the son of Saul. 13 And Joab the son of Zeruiah and the servants of David went out and met them by the pool of Gibeon; and they sat down, *Abner's men* on the one side of the pool and Joab's men on the other side of the pool. 14 Then Abner said to Joab, "Now have the young men arise and hold a martial skills match in our presence." And Joab said, "Have them arise!" 15 So they got up and went over by count, twelve for Benjamin and Ish-bosheth the son of Saul, and twelve from the servants of David. 16 And each one of them seized his opponent by the head and *thrust* his sword in his opponent's side; so they fell down together. Therefore that place was called 'Helkath-hazzurim, which is in Gibeon. 17 That day the battle was very severe, and Abner and the men of Israel were defeated by the servants of. David.

18 Now the three sons of Zeruiah were there, Joab, Abishai, and Asahel; and Asahel *was as* swift-footed as one of the gazelles that is in the field. 19 Asahel pursued Abner and did not turn to the right or to the left from following Abner. 20 Then Abner looked behind himself and said, "Is that you, Asahel?" And he said, "It is I!" 21 So Abner said to him, "Turn aside for your *own good* to your right or to your left, and take hold of one of the young men for yourself, and take for yourself his equipment." But Asahel was unwilling to turn aside from following him. 22 Then Abner repeated again to Asahel, "Turn aside for your *own good* from following me. Why should I strike you to the ground? How then could I show my face to your brother Joab?"

23 However, he refused to turn aside; so Abner struck him in the belly with the butt end of the spear, so that the spear came out at his back. And he fell there and died on the spot. And it happened that all who came *thereafter* to the place where Asahel had fallen and died, stood still.

24 But Joab and Abishai pursued Abner, and when the sun was going down, they came to the hill of Ammah, which is opposite Giah by way of the wilderness of Gibeon. 25 And the sons of Benjamin gathered together behind Abner and became one troop, and they stood on the top of a hill. 26 Then Abner called to Joab and said, "Should the sword devour forever? Do you not realize that it will be bitter in the end? So how long will you refrain from telling the people to turn back from pursuing their kinsmen?" 27 Joab said, "As God lives, if you had not spoken, then the people *of Judah* certainly would have withdrawn in the morning, each from pursuing his brother." 28 So Joab blew the trumpet, and all the people halted and no longer pursued Israel, nor did they continue to fight anymore. 29 Abner and his men then went through the Arabah all that night; so they crossed the Jordan, walked all morning, and came to Mahanaim.

30 Then Joab returned from pursuing Abner; but he gathered all the people together, and nineteen of David's servants were missing, besides Asahel. 31 However, the servants of David had struck and killed *many* of Benjamin and Abner's men; 360 men were dead. 32 And they carried Asahel *away* and buried him in his father's tomb, which was in Bethlehem. Then Joab and his men traveled all night until *the day* dawned at Hebron.

The House of David Strengthened

3 Now there was a long war between the house of Saul and the house of David; and David became steadily stronger, while the house of Saul became steadily weaker.

2 Sons were born to David in Hebron: his firstborn was Amnon, by Ahinoam the Jezreelitess; 3 and his second, Chileab, by Abigail the widow of Nabal the Carmelite; and the third, Absalom the son of Maacah, the daughter of Talmai, king of Geshur; 4 and the fourth, Adonijah the son of Haggith; and the fifth, Shephatiah the son of Abital; 5 and the sixth, Ithream, by David's wife Eglah. These *sons* were born to David in Hebron.

Abner Joins David

6 Now it happened that while there was war between the house of Saul and the house of David, Abner was strengthening himself in the house of Saul. 7 And Saul had a concubine whose name was Rizpah, the daughter of Aiah; and Ish-bosheth said to Abner, "Why have you gone in to my father's concubine?" 8 Then Abner became very angry over Ish-bosheth's question and said, "Am I a dog's head that belongs to Judah? Today I show kindness to the house of Saul your father, to his brothers and to his friends, and have not let you fall into the hands of David; yet today you call me to account for wrongdoing with that woman? 9 May God do so to me, and more so, if as the LORD has sworn to David, I do not accomplish this for him: 10 to transfer the kingdom from the house of Saul, and to establish the throne of David over Israel and over Judah, from Dan even to Beersheba." 11 And Ish-bosheth could no longer say a word in response to Abner, because he was afraid of him.

2:8 1 I.e., man of shame; cf. 1 Chr 8:33, *Eshbaal*　　2:16 1 I.e., the field of sword-edges

12 Then Abner sent messengers to David at his place, saying, "Whose is the land? Make your covenant with me, and behold, my hand shall be with you to bring all Israel over to you." **13** And he said, "Good! I will make a covenant with you, only I require one thing of you, namely, that you shall not see my face unless you first bring Michal, Saul's daughter, when you come to see me." **14** So David sent messengers to Ish-bosheth, Saul's son, saying, "Give me my wife Michal, to whom I was betrothed for a hundred foreskins of the Philistines." **15** Ish-bosheth sent *men* and had her taken from *her* husband, from Paltiel the son of Laish. **16** And her husband went with her, weeping as he went, following her as far as Bahurim. Then Abner said to him, "Go, return." So he returned.

17 Now Abner had a consultation with the elders of Israel, saying, "In times past you were seeking for David to be king over you. **18** Now then, do *it!* For the LORD has spoken regarding David, saying, 'By the hand of My servant David I will save My people Israel from the hand of the Philistines, and from the hands of all their enemies.'" **19** Abner also spoke to Benjamin; and in addition Abner went to speak to David in Hebron everything that seemed good to Israel and to the entire house of Benjamin.

20 Then Abner and twenty men with him came to David at Hebron. And David held a feast for Abner and the men who were with him. **21** Abner said to David, "Let me set out and go and gather all Israel to my lord the king, so that they may make a covenant with you, and that you may be king over all that your soul desires." So David let Abner go, and he went in peace.

22 And behold, the servants of David and Joab came from a raid and brought a large amount of plunder with them; but Abner was not with David in Hebron, since he had let him go, and he had gone in peace. **23** When Joab and all the army that was with him arrived, they informed Joab, saying, "Abner the son of Ner came to the king, and he has let him go *on his way,* and he has gone in peace." **24** Then Joab came to the king and said, "What have you done? Behold, Abner came to you; why then have you let him go, so that he is already gone? **25** You know Abner the son of Ner, that he came to gain your confidence, and to learn of your going out and coming in and to find out everything that you are doing."

Joab Murders Abner

26 When Joab left David's presence, he sent messengers after Abner, and they brought him back from the well of Sirah; but David did not know *about it.* **27** So when Abner returned to Hebron, Joab took him aside into the middle of the gate to speak with him privately, and there he struck him in the belly, so that he died on account of the blood of his brother Asahel. **28** Afterward, when David heard *about* this, he said, "I and my kingdom are innocent before the LORD forever of the blood of Abner the son of Ner. **29** May it turn upon the head of Joab and on all his father's house; and may there not be

eliminated from the house of Joab someone who suffers a discharge, or has leprosy, or holds the spindle, or falls by the sword, or lacks bread." **30** So Joab and his brother Abishai killed Abner because he had put their brother Asahel to death in the battle at Gibeon.

David Mourns Abner

31 Then David said to Joab and to all the people who were with him, "Tear your clothes and put on sackcloth, and mourn before Abner." And King David walked behind the bier. **32** And they buried Abner in Hebron; and the king raised his voice and wept at the grave of Abner, and all the people wept. **33** And the king sang a song of mourning for Abner and said,

"Should Abner die as a fool dies?
34　"Your hands were not bound, nor your feet
　　　put in bronze shackles;
　　As one falls before the wicked, you have
　　　fallen."

And all the people wept over him again. **35** Then all the people came to provide food for David *in his distress* while it was still day; but David vowed, saying, "May God do so to me, and more so, if I taste bread or anything else before the sun goes down." **36** Now all the people took note *of David's vow,* and it pleased them, just as everything that the king did pleased all the people. **37** So all the people and all Israel understood on that day that it had not been *the desire* of the king to put Abner the son of Ner to death. **38** Then the king said to his servants, "Do you not know that a leader and a great man has fallen in Israel this day? **39** And I am weak today, though anointed king; and these men, the sons of Zeruiah, are too difficult for me. May the LORD repay the evildoer in proportion to his evil."

Ish-bosheth Murdered

4 Now when Ish-bosheth, Saul's son, heard that Abner had died in Hebron, his courage failed, and all Israel was horrified. **2** And Saul's son had two men *who were* commanders of troops: the name of the one was Baanah, and the name of the other Rechab, sons of Rimmon the Beerothite, of the sons of Benjamin (for Beeroth is also considered *part* of Benjamin, **3** and the Beerothites fled to Gittaim and have lived there *as* strangers until this day).

4 Now Jonathan, Saul's son, had a son who was disabled in both feet. He was five years old when the news of Saul and Jonathan came from Jezreel, and his nurse picked him up and fled. But it happened that in her hurry to flee, he fell and could no longer walk. And his name was Mephibosheth.

5 So the sons of Rimmon the Beerothite, Rechab and Baanah, departed and came to the house of Ish-bosheth in the heat of the day, while he was taking his midday rest. **6** And they came to the interior of the house *as if* to get wheat, and they struck him in the belly; and Rechab and his brother Baanah escaped. **7** Now when they had come into the house, as he was lying on his bed in his bedroom, they struck him and killed him, and they beheaded him.

And they took his head and traveled by way of the Arabah all night. **8** Then they brought the head of Ish-bosheth to David at Hebron, and said to the king, "Behold, the head of Ish-bosheth the son of Saul, your enemy, who sought your life; so the LORD has given my lord the king vengeance this day on Saul and his descendants."

9 But David replied to Rechab and his brother Baanah, sons of Rimmon the Beerothite, and said to them, "As the LORD lives, who has redeemed my life from all distress, **10** when the one who informed me, saying, 'Behold, Saul is dead,' also viewed himself as the bearer of good news, I seized him and killed him in Ziklag, which was the reward I gave him for *his* news. **11** How much more, when wicked men have killed a righteous man in his *own* house on his bed, shall I not now require his blood from your hands and eliminate you *both* from the earth?" **12** Then David commanded the young men, and they killed them and cut off their hands and feet, and hung them up beside the pool in Hebron. But they took the head of Ish-bosheth and buried it in the grave of Abner in Hebron.

David King over All Israel

5 Then all the tribes of Israel came to David at Hebron and said, "Behold, we are your bone and your flesh. **2** Previously, when Saul was king over us, you were the one who led Israel out and in. And the LORD said to you, 'You will shepherd My people Israel, and you will be a leader over Israel.' " **3** So all the elders of Israel came to the king at Hebron, and King David made a covenant with them before the LORD in Hebron; then they anointed David king over Israel. **4** David was thirty years old when he became king, *and* he reigned for forty years. **5** At Hebron he reigned over Judah for seven years and six months, and in Jerusalem he reigned for thirty-three years over all Israel and Judah.

6 Now the king and his men went to Jerusalem against the Jebusites, the inhabitants of the land; and they said to David, "You shall not come in here, but *even* those who are blind and those who limp will turn you away," thinking, "David cannot enter here." **7** Nevertheless, David captured the stronghold of Zion, that is, the city of David. **8** And David said on that day, "Whoever strikes the Jebusites is to reach those who limp and those who are blind, who are hated by David's soul, through the water tunnel." For that reason they say, "People who are blind and people who limp shall not come into the house." **9** So David lived in the stronghold, and called it the city of David. And David built all around from the *Millo and inward. **10** David became greater and greater, for the LORD God of armies was with him.

11 Then Hiram king of Tyre sent messengers to David with cedar trees, carpenters, and stonemasons; and they built a house for David. **12** And David realized that the LORD had appointed him as king over Israel, and that He had exalted his kingdom for the sake of His people Israel.

13 Meanwhile David took more concubines and wives from Jerusalem, after he came from Hebron; and more sons and daughters were born to David. **14** Now these are the names of those who were born to him in Jerusalem: Shammua, Shobab, Nathan, Solomon, **15** Ibhar, Elishua, Nepheg, Japhia, **16** Elishama, Eliada, and Eliphelet.

War with the Philistines

17 Now when the Philistines heard that they had anointed David king over Israel, all the Philistines went up to seek out David; and when David heard *about it,* he went down to the stronghold. **18** Now the Philistines came and overran the Valley of Rephaim. **19** So David inquired of the LORD, saying, "Shall I go up against the Philistines? Will You hand them over to me?" And the LORD said to David, "Go up, for I will certainly hand the Philistines over to you." **20** Then David came to Baal-perazim and defeated them there; and he said, "The LORD has broken through my enemies before me like the breakthrough of waters." Therefore he named that place *Baal-perazim. **21** And *the Philistines* abandoned their idols there, so David and his men carried them away.

22 Now the Philistines came up once again and overran the Valley of Rephaim. **23** So David inquired of the LORD, but He said, "You shall not go *directly* up; circle around behind them and come at them in front of the baka-shrubs. **24** And it shall be, when you hear the sound of marching in the tops of the baka-shrubs, then you shall act promptly, for then the LORD will have gone out before you to strike the army of the Philistines." **25** Then David did so, just as the LORD had commanded him; he struck and killed the Philistines from Geba as far as Gezer.

Peril in Moving the Ark

6 Now David again gathered all the chosen men of Israel, thirty thousand. **2** And David departed from Baale-judah, with all the people who were with him, to bring up from there the ark of God which is called by the Name, the *very* name of the LORD of armies who is enthroned *above* the cherubim. **3** They had mounted the ark of God on a new cart and moved it from the house of Abinadab, which was on the hill; and Uzzah and Ahio, the sons of Abinadab, were leading the new cart. **4** So they brought it with the ark of God from the house of Abinadab, which was on the hill; and Ahio was walking ahead of the ark. **5** Meanwhile, David and all the house of Israel were celebrating before the LORD with all kinds of *instruments made of* juniper wood, and with lyres, harps, tambourines, castanets, and cymbals.

6 But when they came to the threshing floor of Nacon, Uzzah reached out toward the ark of God and took hold of it, because the oxen nearly overturned *it.* **7** And the anger of the LORD burned against Uzzah, and God struck

---

5:9 1 I.e., terraced structure　**5:20** 1 I.e., the master of breakthroughs

him down there for his irreverence; and he died there by the ark of God. [8] Then David became angry because of the LORD's outburst against Uzzah; and that place has been called [7]Perez-uzzah to this day. [9] So David was afraid of the LORD that day; and he said, "How can the ark of the LORD come to me?" [10] And David was unwilling to move the ark of the LORD into the city of David with him; but David took it aside to the house of Obed-edom, the Gittite. [11] The ark of the LORD remained in the house of Obed-edom the Gittite for three months, and the LORD blessed Obed-edom and all his household.

The Ark Is Brought to Jerusalem
[12] Now it was reported to King David, saying, "The LORD has blessed the house of Obed-edom and all that belongs to him, on account of the ark of God." So David went and brought the ark of God up from the house of Obed-edom to the city of David with joy. [13] And *so* it was, that when those carrying the ark of the LORD marched six paces, he sacrificed an ox and a fattened steer. [14] And David was dancing before the LORD with all *his* strength, and David was wearing a linen ephod. [15] So David and all the house of Israel were bringing up the ark of the LORD with joyful shouting and the sound of the trumpet.

[16] Then it happened, *as* the ark of the LORD was coming into the city of David, that Michal the daughter of Saul looked down through the window and saw King David leaping and dancing before the LORD; and she was contemptuous of him in her heart.

[17] Now they brought in the ark of the LORD and set it in its place inside the tent which David had pitched for it; and David offered burnt offerings and peace offerings before the LORD. [18] When David had finished offering the burnt offering and the peace offerings, he blessed the people in the name of the LORD of armies. [19] Further, he distributed to all the people, to all the multitude of Israel, both to men and women, a cake of bread, one of dates, and one of raisins to each one. Then all the people left, each to his house.

[20] But when David returned to bless his *own* household, Michal the daughter of Saul came out to meet David and said, "How the king of Israel dignified himself today! For he exposed himself today in the sight of his servants' female slaves, as one of the rabble shamelessly exposes himself!" [21] But David said to Michal, "*I was* before the LORD, who preferred me to your father and to all his house, to appoint me as ruler over the people of the LORD, over Israel. So I will celebrate before the LORD! [22] And I might demean myself *even* more than this and be lowly in my own sight, but with the female slaves of whom you have spoken, with them I am to be held in honor!" [23] And Michal the daughter of Saul had no child to the day of her death.

David Plans to Build a Temple
7 Now it came about, when the king lived in his house, and the LORD had given him rest on every side from all his enemies, [2] that the king said to Nathan the prophet, "See now, I live in a house of cedar, but the ark of God remains within the tent." [3] Nathan said to the king, "Go, do all that is in your mind, for the LORD is with you."

[4] But in the same night, the word of the LORD came to Nathan, saying, [5] "Go and say to My servant David, 'This is what the LORD says: "Should you build Me a house for My dwelling? [6] For I have not dwelt in a house since the day I brought up the sons of Israel from Egypt, even to this day; rather, I have been moving about in a tent, that is, in a dwelling place. [7] Wherever I have gone with all the sons of Israel, did I speak a word with one of the tribes of Israel, whom I commanded to shepherd My people Israel, saying, 'Why have you not built Me a house of cedar?'"'

God's Covenant with David
[8] Now then, this is what you shall say to My servant David: 'This is what the LORD of armies says: "I Myself took you from the pasture, from following the sheep, to be leader over My people Israel. [9] And I have been with you wherever you have gone, and have eliminated all your enemies from you; I will also make a great name for you, like the names of the great men who are on the earth. [10] And I will establish a place for My people Israel, and will plant them, so that they may live in their own place and not be disturbed again, nor will malicious people oppress them anymore as previously, [11] even from the day that I appointed judges over My people Israel; and I will give you rest from all your enemies. The LORD also declares to you that the LORD will make a house for you. [12] When your days are finished and you [7]lie down with your fathers, I will raise up your descendant after you, who will come from you, and I will establish his kingdom. [13] He shall build a house for My name, and I will establish the throne of his kingdom forever. [14] I will be a father to him and he will be a son to Me; when he does wrong, I will discipline him with a rod of men and with strokes of sons of mankind, [15] but My favor shall not depart from him, as I took *it* away from Saul, whom I removed from you. [16] Your house and your kingdom shall endure before Me forever; your throne shall be established forever."'" [17] In accordance with all these words and all of this vision, so Nathan spoke to David.

David's Prayer
[18] Then David the king came in and sat before the LORD, and he said, "Who *am* I, Lord GOD, and who *are the members of* my household, that You have brought me this far? [19] And yet this was insignificant in Your eyes, Lord GOD, for You have spoken also of the house of Your servant regarding the distant future. And this is the custom of mankind, Lord GOD. [20] Again what more can David say to You? For You know Your servant, Lord GOD! [21] For the sake of Your word, and according to Your heart, You have done all this greatness, to let Your

---

6:8 [1] I.e., outburst *against* Uzzah 7:12 [1] I.e., die

servant know. 22 For this reason You are great, Lord GOD; for there is no one like You, and there is no God except You, according to all that we have heard with our ears. 23 And what one nation on the earth is like Your people Israel, whom God went to redeem for Himself as a people, and to make a name for Himself, and to do a great thing for You and awesome things for Your land, because of Your people whom You have redeemed for Yourself from Egypt, *from other* nations and their gods? 24 For You have established for Yourself Your people Israel as Your *own* people forever, and You, LORD, have become their God. 25 Now then, LORD God, the word that You have spoken about Your servant and his house, confirm *it* forever, and do just as You have spoken, 26 so that Your name may be great forever, by saying, 'The LORD of armies *is* God over Israel'; and may the house of Your servant David be established before You. 27 For You, LORD of armies, God of Israel, have given a revelation to Your servant, saying, 'I will build you a house'; therefore Your servant has found courage to pray this prayer to You. 28 Now then, Lord GOD, You are God, and Your words are truth; and You have promised this good thing to Your servant. 29 And now, may it please You to bless the house of Your servant, so that it may continue forever before You. For You, Lord GOD, have spoken; and with Your blessing may the house of Your servant be blessed forever."

David's Triumphs

8 Now it happened afterward that David defeated the Philistines and subdued them; and David took control of the chief city from the hand of the Philistines.

2 And He defeated Moab, and measured them with the line, making them lie down on the ground; and he measured two lines to put to death, and a full line to keep alive. And the Moabites became servants to David, bringing tribute.

3 Then David defeated Hadadezer, the son of Rehob king of Zobah, as he went to restore his power at the *Euphrates* River. 4 And David captured from him 1,700 horsemen and twenty thousand foot soldiers; and David hamstrung *almost* all the chariot horses, but left *enough* of them *for* a hundred chariots. 5 When the Arameans of Damascus came to help Hadadezer, king of Zobah, David killed twenty-two thousand men among the Arameans. 6 Then David put garrisons among the Arameans of Damascus, and the Arameans became servants to David, bringing tribute. And the LORD helped David wherever he went. 7 David took the shields of gold which were carried by the servants of Hadadezer, and brought them to Jerusalem. 8 And from Betah and Berothai, cities of Hadadezer, King David took a very large amount of bronze.

9 Now when Toi king of Hamath heard that David had defeated the whole army of Hadadezer, 10 Toi sent his son Joram to King David to greet him and bless him, because he had fought Hadadezer and defeated him; for Hadadezer had been at war with Toi. And

Joram brought with him articles of silver, gold, and bronze. 11 King David also consecrated these *gifts* to the LORD, with the silver and gold that he had consecrated from all the nations which he had subdued: 12 from 1Aram, Moab, the sons of Ammon, the Philistines, Amalek, and from the spoils of Hadadezer, son of Rehob, king of Zobah.

13 So David made a name *for himself* when he returned from killing eighteen thousand 1Arameans in the Valley of Salt. 14 He also put garrisons in Edom. In all Edom he put garrisons, and all the Edomites became servants to David. And the LORD helped David wherever he went.

15 So David reigned over all Israel; and David administered justice and righteousness for all his people. 16 Joab the son of Zeruiah *was* commander over the army, and Jehoshaphat the son of Ahilud *was* secretary. 17 Zadok the son of Ahitub and Ahimelech the son of Abiathar *were* priests, and Seraiah *was* scribe. 18 Benaiah the son of Jehoiada was over the Cherethites and the Pelethites; and David's sons were chief ministers.

David's Kindness to Mephibosheth

9 Then David said, "Is there anyone still left of the house of Saul, so that I could show him kindness for Jonathan's sake?" 2 Now *there was a servant of the house of Saul whose name* was Ziba, and they summoned him to David; and the king said to him, "Are you Ziba?" And he said, "*I am* your servant." 3 Then the king said, "Is there no one remaining of the house of Saul to whom I could show the kindness of God?" And Ziba said to the king, "There is still a son of Jonathan, one who is disabled in both feet." 4 So the king said to him, "Where is he?" And Ziba said to the king, "Behold, he is in the house of Machir the son of Ammiel, in Lo-debar." 5 Then King David sent messengers who brought him from the house of Machir the son of Ammiel, from Lo-debar. 6 Mephibosheth, the son of Jonathan the son of Saul, came to David and fell on his face and prostrated himself. And David said, "Mephibosheth." And he said, "Here is your servant!" 7 Then David said to him, "Do not be afraid, for I will assuredly show kindness to you for the sake of your father Jonathan, and I will restore to you all the land of your grandfather Saul; and you yourself shall eat at my table regularly." 8 Again he prostrated himself, and said, "What is your servant, that you should be concerned about a dead dog like me?"

9 Then the king summoned Saul's servant Ziba and said to him, "Everything that belonged to Saul and to all his house I have given to your master's grandson. 10 You and your sons and your servants shall cultivate the land for him, and you shall bring in *the produce* so that your master's grandson will have food to eat; nevertheless Mephibosheth, your master's grandson, shall eat at my table regularly." Now Ziba had fifteen sons and twenty servants. 11 Then Ziba said to the king, "In accordance with everything that my lord the king commands his servant, so your

servant will do." So Mephibosheth ate at David's table as one of the king's sons. 12 Mephibosheth had a young son whose name was Mica. And all who lived in the house of Ziba were servants to Mephibosheth. 13 So Mephibosheth lived in Jerusalem, because he ate at the king's table regularly. And he was disabled in his two feet.

Ammon and Aram Defeated

10 Now it happened afterward that the king of the Ammonites died, and his son Hanun became king in his place. 2 Then David said, "I will show kindness to Hanun the son of Nahash, just as his father showed kindness to me." So David sent some of his servants to console him about his father. But when David's servants came to the land of the Ammonites, 3 the commanders of the Ammonites said to their lord Hanun, "Do you think that David is *simply* honoring your father since he has sent you *servants* to console you? Has David not sent his servants to you in order to explore the city, to spy it out and overthrow it?" 4 So Hanun took David's servants and shaved off half of their beards, and cut off their robes in the middle as far as their buttocks, and sent them away. 5 When *messengers* informed David, he sent *servants* to meet them, because the men were extremely humiliated. And the king said, "Stay in Jericho until your beards grow *back,* and *then* you shall return."

6 Now when the sons of Ammon saw that they had become repulsive to David, the sons of Ammon sent *messengers* and hired the Arameans of Beth-rehob and the Arameans of Zobah, twenty thousand foot soldiers, and the king of Maacah *with* a thousand men, and the men of Tob *with* twelve thousand men. 7 When David heard *about this,* he sent Joab and all the army, the warriors. 8 And the sons of Ammon came out and lined up for battle at the entrance of the city, while the Arameans of Zobah and of Rehob and the men of Tob and Maacah *were stationed* by themselves in the field.

9 Now when Joab saw that the battle was set against him at the front and at the rear, he selected *warriors* from all the choice men in Israel, and lined *them* up against the Arameans. 10 But the remainder of the people he placed under the command of his brother Abishai, and he lined *them* up against the sons of Ammon. 11 And he said, "If the Arameans are too strong for me, then you shall help me; but if the sons of Ammon are too strong for you, then I will come to help you. 12 Be strong, and let's show ourselves courageous for the sake of our people and the cities of our God; and may the LORD do what is good in His sight." 13 So Joab and the people who were with him advanced to the battle against the Arameans, and they fled from him. 14 When the sons of Ammon saw that the Arameans had fled, they *also* fled from Abishai and entered the city. Then Joab returned from *fighting* against the sons of Ammon and came to Jerusalem.

15 When the Arameans saw that they had been defeated by Israel, they assembled together. 16 And Hadadezer sent *word* and brought out the Arameans who were beyond the *Euphrates* River, and they came to Helam; and Shobach the commander of the army of Hadadezer led them. 17 Now when it was reported to David, he gathered all Israel together and crossed the Jordan, and came to Helam. And the Arameans lined up against David and fought him. 18 But the Arameans fled from Israel, and David killed seven hundred charioteers of the Arameans and forty thousand horsemen, and struck Shobach the commander of their army, and he died there. 19 When all the kings, servants of Hadadezer, saw that they had been defeated by Israel, they made peace with Israel and served them. So the Arameans were afraid to help the sons of Ammon anymore.

Bathsheba, David's Great Sin

11 Then it happened in the spring, at the time when kings go out *to battle,* that David sent Joab and his servants with him and all Israel, and they brought destruction on the sons of Ammon and besieged Rabbah. But David stayed in Jerusalem.

2 Now at evening time David got up from his bed and walked around on the roof of the king's house, and from the roof he saw a woman bathing; and the woman was very beautiful in appearance. 3 So David sent *servants* and inquired about the woman. And *someone* said, "Is this not Bathsheba, the daughter of Eliam, the wife of Uriah the Hittite?" 4 Then David sent messengers and had her brought, and when she came to him, he slept with her; and when she had purified herself from her uncleanness, she returned to her house. 5 But the woman conceived; so she sent *word* and informed David, and said, "I am pregnant."

6 Then David sent *word* to Joab: "Send me Uriah the Hittite." So Joab sent Uriah to David. 7 When Uriah came to him, David asked about Joab's well-being and that of the people, and the condition of the war. 8 Then David said to Uriah, "Go down to your house, and wash your feet." So Uriah left the king's house, and a gift from the king was sent after him. 9 But Uriah slept at the door of the king's house with all the servants of his lord, and did not go down to his house. 10 Now when they informed David, saying, "Uriah did not go down to his house," David said to Uriah, "Did you not come from a journey? Why did you not go down to your house?" 11 And Uriah said to David, "The ark and Israel and Judah are staying in temporary shelters, and my lord Joab and the servants of my lord are camping in the open field. Should I then go to my house to eat and drink and to sleep with my wife? By your life and the life of your soul, I will not do this thing." 12 Then David said to Uriah, "Stay here today also, and tomorrow I will let you go *back.*" So Uriah remained in Jerusalem that day and the day after. 13 Now David summoned Uriah, and he ate and drank in his presence, and he made Uriah drunk; and in the evening *Uriah* went out to lie on his bed with his lord's servants, and he *still* did not go down to his house.

14 So in the morning David wrote a letter to Joab and sent *it* by the hand of Uriah. **15** He had written in the letter the following: "Station Uriah on the front line of the fiercest battle and pull back from him, so that he may be struck and killed." **16** So it was as Joab kept watch on the city, that he stationed Uriah at the place where he knew there *were* valiant men. **17** And the men of the city went out and fought against Joab, and some of the people among David's servants fell; and Uriah the Hittite also died. **18** Then Joab sent *a messenger* and reported to David all the events of the war. **19** He ordered the messenger, saying, "When you have finished telling all the events of the war to the king, **20** then it shall be that if the king's wrath rises and he says to you, 'Why did you move against the city to fight? Did you not know that they would shoot from the wall? **21** Who struck Abimelech the son of Jerubbesheth? Did a woman not throw an upper millstone on him from the wall so that he died at Thebez? Why did you move against the wall?'—then you shall say, 'Your servant Uriah the Hittite also died.'"

22 So the messenger departed and came and reported to David everything that Joab had sent him *to tell.* **23** The messenger said to David, "The men prevailed against us and came out against us in the field, but we pressed them as far as the entrance of the gate. **24** Also, the archers shot at your servants from the wall; so some of the king's servants died, and your servant Uriah the Hittite also died." **25** Then David said to the messenger, "This is what you shall say to Joab: 'Do not let this thing displease you, for the sword devours one as well as another; fight with determination against the city and overthrow it'; and *thereby* encourage him."

26 Now when Uriah's wife heard that her husband Uriah was dead, she mourned for her husband. **27** When the *time of* mourning was over, David sent *servants* and had her brought to his house and she became his wife; then she bore him a son. But the thing that David had done was evil in the sight of the LORD.

Nathan Rebukes David

12 Then the LORD sent Nathan to David. And he came to him and said,
"There were two men in a city, the one
  wealthy and the other poor.
2 "The wealthy man had a great many flocks
  and herds.
3 "But the poor man had nothing at all
  except one little ewe lamb
Which he bought and nurtured;
And it grew up together with him and his
  children.
It would eat scraps from him and drink
  from his cup and lie in his lap,
And was like a daughter to him.
4 "Now a visitor came to the wealthy man,
And he could not bring himself to take
  any animal from his own flock or his
  own herd,
To prepare for the traveler who had come
  to him;
So he took the poor man's ewe lamb and

prepared it for the man who had come to him."

5 Then David's anger burned greatly against the man, and he said to Nathan, "As the LORD lives, the man who has done this certainly deserves to die! **6** So he must make restitution for the lamb four times over, since he did this thing and had no compassion."

7 Nathan then said to David, "You yourself are the man! This is what the LORD, the God of Israel says: 'It is I who anointed you as king over Israel, and it is I who rescued you from the hand of Saul. **8** I also gave you your master's house and *put* your master's wives into your care, and I gave you the house of Israel and Judah; and if *that had been* too little, I would have added to you many more things like these! **9** Why have you despised the word of the LORD, by doing evil in His sight? You have struck and killed Uriah the Hittite with the sword, you have taken his wife as your wife, and you have slaughtered him with the sword of the sons of Ammon. **10** Now then, the sword shall never leave your house, because you have despised Me and have taken the wife of Uriah the Hittite to be your wife.' **11** This is what the LORD says: 'Behold, I am going to raise up evil against you from your own household; I will even take your wives before your eyes and give *them* to your companion, and he will sleep with your wives in broad daylight. **12** Indeed, you did it secretly, but I will do this thing before all Israel, and in open daylight.'" **13** Then David said to Nathan, "I have sinned against the LORD." And Nathan said to David, "The LORD also has allowed your sin to pass; you shall not die. **14** However, since by this deed you have shown utter disrespect for the LORD, the child himself who is born to you shall certainly die." **15** Then Nathan went to his house.

Loss of a Child

Later the LORD struck the child that Uriah's widow bore to David, so that he was *very* sick. **16** David therefore pleaded with God for the child; and David fasted and went and lay all night on the ground. **17** The elders of his household stood beside him in order to help him up from the ground, but he was unwilling and would not eat food with them. **18** Then it happened on the seventh day that the child died. And David's servants were afraid to tell him that the child was dead, for they said, "Behold, while the child was *still* alive, we spoke to him and he did not listen to us. How then can we tell him that the child is dead, since he might do *himself* harm?" **19** But when David saw that his servants were whispering together, David perceived that the child was dead; so David said to his servants, "Is the child dead?" And they said, "He is dead." **20** So David got up from the ground, washed, anointed *himself,* and changed his clothes; and he went into the house of the LORD and worshiped. Then he went to his own house, and when he asked, they served him food, and he ate.

21 Then his servants said to him, "What is this thing that you have done? You fasted and

wept for the child *while he was* alive; but when the child died, you got up and ate food." 22 And he said, "While the child was still alive, I fasted and wept; for I said, 'Who knows, the LORD may be gracious to me, and the child may live.' 23 But now he has died; why should I fast? Can I bring him back again? I am going to him, but he will not return to me."

Solomon Born

24 Then David comforted his wife Bathsheba, and went in to her and slept with her; and she gave birth to a son, and he named him Solomon. Now the LORD loved him, 25 and sent *word* through Nathan the prophet, and he named him 1Jedidiah for the LORD's sake.

War Again

26 Now Joab fought against Rabbah of the sons of Ammon, and captured the royal city. 27 Then Joab sent messengers to David and said, "I have fought against Rabbah, I have even captured the city of waters. 28 Now then, gather the rest of the people and camp opposite the city and capture it, or I will capture the city myself and it will be named after me." 29 So David gathered all the people and went to Rabbah, and he fought against it and captured it. 30 Then he took the crown of their king from his head; and its weight *was* a 1talent of gold, and *it had* a precious stone; and it was *placed* on David's head. And he brought out the plunder of the city in great amounts. 31 He also brought out the people who were in it, and put *some to work* at saws, iron picks, and iron axes, and made others serve at the brick works. And he did the same to all the cities of the sons of Ammon. Then David and all the people returned *to* Jerusalem.

Amnon and Tamar

13 Now it was after this that Absalom the son of David had a beautiful sister whose name was Tamar, and Amnon the son of David was in love with her. 2 But Amnon was so frustrated on account of his sister Tamar that he made himself ill, for she was a virgin, and it seemed too difficult to Amnon to do anything to her. 3 But Amnon had a friend whose name was Jonadab, the son of Shimeah, David's brother; and Jonadab was a very clever man. 4 And he said to him, "Why are you, the king's son, so depressed morning after morning? Will you not tell me?" So Amnon said to him, "I am in love with Tamar, the sister of my brother Absalom." 5 Jonadab then said to him, "Lie down on your bed and pretend to be ill; when your father comes to see you, say to him, 'Please have my sister Tamar come and give me food to eat, and have her prepare the food in my sight, so that I may see *it* and eat from her hand.'" 6 So Amnon lay down and pretended to be ill; when the king came to see him, Amnon said to the king, "Please have my sister Tamar come and make me a couple of pastries in my sight, so that I may eat from her hand." 7 Then David sent *a messenger* to the house for Tamar, saying, "Go now to your brother Amnon's house, and prepare food for him." 8 So

Tamar went to her brother Amnon's house, and he was lying *in bed.* And she took dough, kneaded *it,* made pastries in his sight, and baked the pastries. 9 Then she took the tray and served *them* to him, but he refused to eat. And Amnon said, "Have everyone leave me." So everyone left him. 10 Then Amnon said to Tamar, "Bring the food into the bedroom, so that I may eat from your hand." So Tamar took the pastries which she had made and brought them into the bedroom to her brother Amnon. 11 When she brought *them* to him to eat, he took hold of her and said to her, "Come, sleep with me, my sister." 12 But she said to him, "No, my brother, do not violate me, for such a thing is not done in Israel; do not do this disgraceful sin! 13 As for me, where could I get rid of my shame? And as for you, you will be like one of the fools in Israel. Now then, please speak to the king, for he will not withhold me from you." 14 However, he would not listen to her; since he was stronger than she, he violated her and slept with her.

15 Then Amnon hated her with a very great hatred; indeed, the hatred with which he hated her was greater than the love with which he had loved her. And Amnon said to her, "Get up, go *away!*" 16 But she said to him, "No, because this wrong in sending me away is greater than the other that you have done to me!" Yet he would not listen to her. 17 Then he called his young man who attended him and said, "Now throw this woman out of my *presence,* and lock the door behind her!" 18 Now she had on a long-sleeved garment; for this is how the virgin daughters of the king dressed themselves in robes. Then his attendant took her out and locked the door behind her. 19 Tamar took ashes *and put them* on her head, and tore her long-sleeved garment which *was* on her; and she put her hand on her head and went *on her way,* crying out as she went.

20 Then Absalom her brother said to her, "Has Amnon your brother been with you? But now keep silent, my sister, he is your brother; do not take this matter to heart." So Tamar remained and was isolated in her brother Absalom's house. 21 Now when King David heard about all these matters, he became very angry. 22 But Absalom did not speak with Amnon either good or bad; for Absalom hated Amnon because he had violated his sister Tamar.

23 Now it came about after two full years that Absalom had sheepshearers in Baal-hazor, which is near Ephraim, and Absalom invited all the king's sons *to celebrate.*

Absalom Avenges Tamar

24 And Absalom came to the king and said, "Behold now, your servant has sheepshearers; may the king and his servants please go with your servant." 25 But the king said to Absalom, "No, my son, we should not all go, so that we will not be a burden to you." Though he urged him, he would not go; but he blessed him. 26 Then Absalom said, "If not, please have my brother Amnon go with us." But the king said to him, "Why should he go with you?"

12:25 1 I.e., beloved of the LORD   12:30 1 About 75 lb. or 34 kg

27 Nevertheless Absalom urged him, so he let Amnon and all the king's sons go with him. 28 Then Absalom commanded his servants, saying, "See now, when Amnon's heart is cheerful with wine, and I say to you, 'Strike Amnon,' then put him to death. Do not fear; have I not commanded you myself? Be courageous and be valiant." 29 And the servants of Absalom did to Amnon just as Absalom had commanded. Then all the king's sons got up and each mounted his mule and fled.

30 Now it was while they were on the way that the report came to David, saying, "Absalom has struck and killed all the king's sons, and not one of them is left." 31 Then the king stood up, tore his clothes, and lay on the ground; and all his servants were standing by with clothes torn. 32 And Jonadab, the son of Shimeah, David's brother, responded, "Let my lord not assume that they have put to death all the young men, the king's sons, for only Amnon is dead; because this has been set up by the intent of Absalom since the day that he violated his sister Tamar. 33 So now, may my lord the king not take the report to heart, claiming, 'all the king's sons are dead'; but only Amnon is dead."

34 Now Absalom had fled. And the young man who was the watchman raised his eyes and looked, and behold, many people were coming from the road behind him by the side of the mountain. 35 And Jonadab said to the king, "Behold, the king's sons have come; so it has happened according to your servant's word." 36 As soon as he had finished speaking, behold, the king's sons came and raised their voices and wept; and the king and all his servants also wept very profusely.

37 Now Absalom had fled and gone to Talmai the son of Ammihud, the king of Geshur. And David mourned for his son every day. 38 So Absalom had fled and gone to Geshur, and was there for three years. 39 And *the heart of* King David longed to go out to Absalom; for he was comforted regarding Amnon, since he was dead.

The Woman of Tekoa

14 Now Joab the son of Zeruiah perceived that the king's heart *was drawn* toward Absalom. 2 So Joab sent *a messenger* to Tekoa and brought a wise woman from there, and said to her, "Please follow mourning rites, and put on mourning garments now, and do not anoint yourself with oil but be like a woman who has been mourning for the dead for many days. 3 Then go to the king and speak to him in this way." So Joab put the words in her mouth.

4 Now when the woman of Tekoa ¹spoke to the king, she fell on her face to the ground and prostrated herself, and said, "Help, O king!" 5 And the king said to her, "What is *troubling* you?" And she answered, "Truly I am a widow, for my husband is dead. 6 And your servant had two sons, but the two of them fought in the field, and there was no one to save them from each other, so one struck the other and killed him. 7 Now behold, the entire family has risen against your servant, and they have said, 'Hand

over the one who struck his brother, so that we may put him to death for the life of his brother whom he killed, and eliminate the heir as well.' So they will extinguish my coal which is left, so as to leave my husband neither name nor remnant on the face of the earth."

8 Then the king said to the woman, "Go to your home, and I will issue orders concerning you." 9 The woman of Tekoa said to the king, "My lord, the king, the guilt is on me and my father's house, but the king and his throne are guiltless." 10 So the king said, "Whoever speaks to you, bring him to me, and he will not touch you anymore." 11 Then she said, "May the king please remember the LORD your God, *so that* the avenger of blood will not continue to destroy, otherwise they will destroy my son." And he said, "As the LORD lives, not one hair of your son shall fall to the ground."

12 Then the woman said, "Please let your servant speak a word to my lord the king." And he said, "Speak." 13 The woman said, "Why then have you planned such a thing against the people of God? For in speaking this word the king is like one who is guilty, *in that* the king does not bring back his banished one. 14 For we will surely die and are like water spilled on the ground, which cannot be gathered up. Yet God does not take away life, but makes plans so that the banished one will not be cast out from Him. 15 Now then, the reason I have come to speak this word to my lord the king is that the people have made me afraid; so your servant said, 'Let me now speak to the king, perhaps the king will perform the request of his slave. 16 For the king will listen, to save his slave from the hand of the man who would eliminate both me and my son from the inheritance of God.' 17 Then your servant said, 'Please let the word of my lord the king be comforting, for as the angel of God, so is my lord the king to discern good and evil. And may the LORD your God be with you.'"

18 Then the king answered and said to the woman, "Please do not hide anything from me that I am about to ask you." And the woman said, "Let my lord the king please speak." 19 So the king said, "Is the hand of Joab with you in all this?" And the woman replied, "As your soul lives, my lord the king, no one can turn to the right or to the left from anything that my lord the king has spoken. Indeed, it was your servant Joab who commanded me, and it was he who put all these words in the mouth of your servant. 20 In order to change the appearance of things your servant Joab has done this thing. But my lord is wise, like the wisdom of the angel of God, to know all that is on the earth."

Absalom Returns

21 Then the king said to Joab, "Behold now, I will certainly do this thing; go then, bring back the young man Absalom." 22 And Joab fell on his face to the ground, prostrated himself, and blessed the king; then Joab said, "Today your servant knows that I have found favor in your sight, my lord the king, in that the king has performed the request of his

---

14:4 ¹Many mss and ancient versions *came*

servant." 23 So Joab arose and went to Geshur, and brought Absalom to Jerusalem. 24 However, the king said, "He shall return to his own house, but he shall not see my face." So Absalom returned to his own house and did not see the king's face.

25 Now in all Israel there was no one as handsome as Absalom, so highly praised; from the sole of his foot to the top of his head there was no impairment in him. 26 And when he cut the hair of his head (and it was at the end of every year that he cut *it,* because it was heavy on him, so he cut it), he weighed the hair of his head at ʰtwo hundred shekels by the king's weight. 27 And to Absalom there were born three sons, and one daughter whose name was Tamar; she was a woman of beautiful appearance.

28 Now Absalom lived two full years in Jerusalem, yet he did not see the king's face. 29 Then Absalom sent for Joab, to send him to the king, but he would not come to him. So he sent *word* again a second time, but he would not come. 30 Therefore he said to his servants, "See, Joab's plot is next to mine, and he has barley there; go and set it on fire." So Absalom's servants set the plot on fire. 31 Then Joab got up, came to Absalom at his house, and said to him, "Why have your servants set my plot on fire?" 32 Absalom answered Joab, "Behold, I sent for you, saying, 'Come here, so that I may send you to the king, to say, "Why have I come from Geshur? It would be better for me still to be there." ' Now then, let me see the king's face, and if there is guilt in me, he can have me executed." 33 So when Joab came to the king and told him, he summoned Absalom. Then *Absalom* came to the king and prostrated himself with his face to the ground before the king; and the king kissed Absalom.

Absalom's Conspiracy

15 Now it came about after this that Absalom provided for himself a chariot and horses, and fifty men to run ahead of him. 2 And Absalom used to rise early and stand beside the road to the gate; and when any man who had a lawsuit was to come before the king for judgment, Absalom would call out to him and say, "From what city are you?" And he would say, "Your servant is from one of the tribes of Israel." 3 Then Absalom would say to him, "See, your claims are good and right, but you have no one to listen to you on the part of the king." 4 Moreover, Absalom would say, "Oh that someone would appoint me judge in the land, then every man who has a lawsuit or claim could come to me, and I would give him justice!" 5 And whenever a man approached to prostrate himself before him, he would put out his hand and take hold of him and kiss him. 6 Absalom dealt this way with all Israel who came to the king for judgment; so Absalom stole the hearts of the people of Israel.

7 Now it came about at the end of ʰfour years that Absalom said to the king, "Please let me go and pay my vow which I have made to the LORD, in Hebron. 8 For your servant made a vow while I was living in Geshur in Aram, saying, 'If the LORD will indeed bring me back to Jerusalem, then I will serve the LORD.' " 9 The king said to him, "Go in peace." So he got up and went to Hebron. 10 But Absalom sent spies throughout the tribes of Israel, saying, "As soon as you hear the sound of the trumpet, then you shall say, 'Absalom is king in Hebron!' " 11 Then two hundred men went with Absalom from Jerusalem, who were invited and went innocently, for they did not know anything. 12 And Absalom sent for Ahithophel the Gilonite, David's counselor, from his city Giloh, while he was offering the sacrifices. And the conspiracy was strong, for the people continually increased with Absalom.

David Flees Jerusalem

13 Then a messenger came to David, saying, "The hearts of the people of Israel are with Absalom." 14 So David said to all his servants who were with him in Jerusalem, "Arise and let's flee, for *otherwise* none of us will escape from Absalom. Go quickly, or he will hurry and overtake us, and bring disaster on us and strike the city with the edge of the sword." 15 Then the king's servants said to the king, "Behold, your servants *will do* whatever my lord the king chooses." 16 So the king left, and all his household with him; but the king left ten concubines behind to take care of the house. 17 The king left, and all the people with him, and they stopped at the last house. 18 Now all of his servants passed by beside him, and all the Cherethites, all the Pelethites, and all the Gittites, six hundred men who had come with him from Gath, passed by before the king.

19 Then the king said to Ittai the Gittite, "Why should you go with us too? Return and stay with your king, since you are a foreigner and an exile as well; *return* to your own place. 20 You came *only* yesterday, so should I make you wander with us today, while I go wherever I go? Return and take your brothers back; mercy and truth be with you." 21 But Ittai answered the king and said, "As the LORD lives, and as my lord the king lives, wherever my lord the king may be, whether for death or for life, there assuredly shall your servant be!" 22 Then David said to Ittai, "Go and cross over the brook Kidron." So Ittai the Gittite crossed over with all his men and all the ʰlittle ones who *were* with him. 23 While all the country was weeping with a loud voice, all the people were crossing over. The king was also crossing over the brook Kidron, and all the people were crossing over toward the way of the wilderness.

24 Now behold, Zadok also *came,* and all the Levites with him, carrying the ark of the covenant of God. And they set down the ark of God, and Abiathar came up until all the people had finished crossing over from the city. 25 And the king said to Zadok, "Return the ark of God to the city. If I find favor in the sight of the LORD, then He will bring me back and show me *both* it and His habitation. 26 But if He says this: 'I have no delight in you,' *then* here I am,

let Him do to me as seems good to Him." 27 The king also said to Zadok the priest, "Are you *not* a seer? Return to the city in peace, and your two sons with you, your son Ahimaaz and Jonathan the son of Abiathar. 28 See, I am going to wait at the river crossing places of the wilderness until word comes from you to inform me." 29 So Zadok and Abiathar returned the ark of God to Jerusalem and remained there.

30 And David was going up the ascent of the *Mount of* Olives, weeping as he went, and his head was covered, and he was walking barefoot. Then all the people who were with him each covered his own head, and they were going up, weeping as they went. 31 Now *someone* informed David, saying, "Ahithophel is among the conspirators with Absalom." And David said, "LORD, please make the advice of Ahithophel foolish."

32 It happened as David was coming to the summit, where God was worshiped, that behold, Hushai the Archite met him with his coat torn, and dust on his head. 33 And David said to him, "If you go over with me, then you will become a burden to me. 34 But if you return to the city and say to Absalom, 'I will be your servant, O king; even *as* I was your father's servant in time past, so now I will also be your servant,' then you can foil the advice of Ahithophel for me. 35 Are Zadok and Abiathar the priests not with you there? So it shall be that whatever you hear from the king's house, you shall report to Zadok and Abiathar the priests. 36 Behold their two sons are there with them, Ahimaaz, Zadok's *son* and Jonathan, Abiathar's *son;* and by them you shall send me everything that you hear." 37 So Hushai, David's friend, came into the city, and Absalom came into Jerusalem.

Ziba, a False Servant

16 Now when David had gone on a little beyond the summit, behold, Ziba the servant of Mephibosheth met him with a team of saddled donkeys, and on them *were* two hundred loaves of bread, a hundred cakes of raisins, a hundred summer fruits, and a jug of wine. 2 And the king said to Ziba, "Why do you have these?" And Ziba said, "The donkeys are for the king's household to ride, the bread and summer fruit are for the young men to eat, and the wine, for whoever is weary in the wilderness to drink." 3 Then the king said, "And where is your master's son?" And Ziba said to the king, "Behold, he is staying in Jerusalem, for he said, 'Today the house of Israel will restore the kingdom of my father to me.'" 4 So the king said to Ziba, "Behold, all that belongs to Mephibosheth is yours." And Ziba said, "I prostrate myself; may I find favor in your sight, my lord, the king!"

David Is Cursed

5 When King David came to Bahurim, behold, a man was coming out from there from the family of the house of Saul, and his name was Shimei, the son of Gera; he was coming out, cursing as he came. 6 He also threw stones at David and all the servants of King David; and

all the people and all the warriors were on his right and on his left. 7 This is what Shimei said when he cursed: "Go away, go away, you man of bloodshed and worthless man! 8 The LORD has brought back upon you all the bloodshed of the house of Saul, in whose place you have become king; and the LORD has handed the kingdom over to your son Absalom. And behold, you are *caught* in your own evil, for you are a man of bloodshed!"

9 Then Abishai the son of Zeruiah said to the king, "Why should this dead dog curse my lord the king? Now let me go over and cut off his head." 10 But the king said, "What *business* of mine is yours, you sons of Zeruiah? If he curses, and if the LORD has told him, 'Curse David,' then who should say, 'Why have you done so?' " 11 Then David said to Abishai and to all his servants, "Behold, my son who came out of my own body seeks my life; how much more now *this* Benjaminite? Leave him alone and let him curse, for the LORD has told him. 12 Perhaps the LORD will look on my misery and return good to me instead of his cursing this day." 13 So David and his men went on the road; and Shimei kept going on the hillside close beside him, and as he went he cursed and threw stones and dirt at him. 14 And the king and all the people who were with him arrived exhausted, and he refreshed himself there.

Absalom Enters Jerusalem

15 Then Absalom and all the people, the men of Israel, entered Jerusalem, and Ahithophel with him. 16 Now it came about, when Hushai the Archite, David's friend, came to Absalom, that Hushai said to Absalom, "*Long* live the king! *Long* live the king!" 17 But Absalom said to Hushai, "Is this your loyalty to your friend? Why did you not go with your friend?" 18 So Hushai said to Absalom, "No! For whomever the LORD, this people, and all the men of Israel have chosen, his I shall be, and with him I shall remain. 19 Besides, whom should I serve? *Should I* not *serve* in the presence of his son? Just as I have served in your father's presence, so I shall be in your presence."

20 Then Absalom said to Ahithophel, "Give your advice. What should we do?" 21 Ahithophel said to Absalom, "Have relations with your father's concubines, whom he has left behind to take care of the house; then all Israel will hear that you have made yourself repulsive to your father. The hands of all who are with you will also be strengthened." 22 So they pitched a tent for Absalom on the roof, and Absalom had relations with his father's concubines in the sight of all Israel. 23 Now the advice of Ahithophel, which he gave in those days, *was taken* as though one inquired of the word of God; so *was* all the advice of Ahithophel *regarded* by both David and Absalom.

Hushai's Counsel

17 Furthermore, Ahithophel said to Absalom, "Please let me choose twelve thousand men and let me set out and pursue David tonight. 2 And I will attack him while he is weary and exhausted and startle him, so that

all the people who are with him will flee. Then I will strike and kill the king *when he is* alone, **3** and I will bring all the people back to you. The return of everyone depends on the man whom you are seeking; *then* all the people will be at peace." **4** And the plan pleased Absalom and all the elders of Israel.

5 Nevertheless, Absalom said, "Now call Hushai the Archite also, and let's hear what he has to say." **6** When Hushai had come to Absalom, Absalom said to him, "Ahithophel has proposed this plan. Should we carry out his plan? If not, say *so* yourself." **7** So Hushai said to Absalom, "This time the advice that Ahithophel has given is not good." **8** Then Hushai said, "You yourself know your father and his men, that they are warriors and they are fierce, like a bear deprived of her cubs in the field. And your father is an expert in warfare, and he will not spend the night with the people. **9** Behold, he has now hidden himself in one of the ravines, or in another place; and it will be that when he falls on them at the first *attack,* whoever hears *it* will say, 'There has been a slaughter among the people who follow Absalom!' **10** And even the one who is valiant, whose heart is like the heart of a lion, will completely despair; for all Israel knows that your father is a mighty man, and those who are with him are valiant men. **11** But I advise that all Israel be fully gathered to you, from Dan even to Beersheba, like the sand that is by the sea in abundance; and that you personally go into battle. **12** Then we will come to him in one of the places where he can be found, and we will fall on him just as the dew falls on the ground; and of him and of all the men who are with him, not even one will be left. **13** And if he withdraws into a city, then all Israel shall bring ropes to that city, and we will drag it into the ʾvalley until not even a pebble is found there." **14** Then Absalom and all the men of Israel said, "The advice of Hushai the Archite is better than the advice of Ahithophel." For the LORD had ordained to foil the good advice of Ahithophel, in order for the LORD to bring disaster on Absalom.

Hushai's Warning Saves David

15 Then Hushai said to Zadok and to Abiathar the priests, "This is what Ahithophel advised Absalom and the elders of Israel *to do,* and this is what I have advised. **16** Now then, send *a messenger* quickly and tell David, saying, 'Do not spend the night at the river crossing places of the wilderness, but by all means cross over, or else the king and all the people who are with him will be destroyed.'" **17** Now Jonathan and Ahimaaz were staying at En-rogel, and a female servant would go and inform them, and they would go and inform King David, for they could not allow themselves to be seen entering the city. **18** But a boy did see them, and he told Absalom; so the two of them left quickly and came to the house of a man in Bahurim, who had a well in his court-yard, and they went down into it. **19** And the woman took a cover and spread it over the well's mouth and scattered barley meal on it,

so that nothing was known. **20** Then Absalom's servants came to the woman at the house and said, "Where are Ahimaaz and Jonathan?" And the woman said to them, "They have crossed the brook of water." And when they searched and did not find *them,* they returned to Jerusalem.

21 It came about after they had departed, that they came up out of the well and went and reported to King David; and they said to David, "Set out and cross over the water quickly, because this is what Ahithophel has advised against you." **22** Then David and all the people who *were* with him set out and crossed the Jordan; by dawn not even one remained who had not crossed the Jordan.

23 Now when Ahithophel saw that his advice had not been followed, he saddled *his* donkey and set out and went to his home, to his city, and set his house in order, and hanged himself; so he died and was buried in his father's grave.

24 Then David came to Mahanaim. And Absalom crossed the Jordan, he and all the men of Israel with him. **25** Absalom put Amasa in command of the army in place of Joab. Now Amasa was the son of a man whose name was Ithra the Israelite, who had relations with Abigail the daughter of Nahash, sister of Zeruiah, Joab's mother. **26** And Israel and Absalom camped in the land of Gilead.

27 Now when David had come to Mahanaim, Shobi the son of Nahash from Rabbah of the sons of Ammon, Machir the son of Ammiel from Lo-debar, and Barzillai the Gileadite from Rogelim, **28** brought beds, basins, pottery, wheat, barley, flour, roasted *grain,* beans, lentils, roasted *seeds,* **29** honey, curds, sheep, and cheese of the herd, for David and the people who *were* with him, to eat. For they said, "The people are hungry and exhausted and thirsty in the wilderness."

Absalom Killed

18 Then David took a count of the people who were with him and appointed over them commanders of thousands and command-ers of hundreds. **2** And David sent the people out, a third under the command of Joab, a third under the command of Abishai the son of Zeruiah, Joab's brother, and a third under the command of Ittai the Gittite. And the king said to the people, "I myself will certainly go out with you also." **3** But the people said, "You should not go out; for if in fact we flee, they will not care about us; and if half of us die, they will not care about us. But you are worth ten thousand of us; so now it is better that you will be *ready* to help us from the city." **4** Then the king said to them, "Whatever seems best to you I will do." So the king stood beside the gate, and all the people went out by hundreds and thousands. **5** But the king commanded Joab, Abishai, and Ittai, saying, "*Deal* gently with the young man Absalom for my sake." And all the people heard when the king commanded all the commanders regarding Absalom.

6 Then the people went out to the field against Israel, and the battle took place in the forest of Ephraim. **7** The people of Israel were

---

17:13 ¹ Or *wadi;* i.e., a dry stream bed

defeated there by the servants of David, and the slaughter there that day was great, twenty thousand *men.* [8] For the battle there was spread over the whole countryside, and the forest devoured more people that day than the sword devoured.

[9] Now Absalom encountered the servants of David. Absalom was riding on *his* mule, and the mule went under the branches of a massive oak. Then his head caught firmly in the oak, and he was left hanging between the sky and earth, while the mule that was under him kept going. [10] When a certain man saw *him,* he informed Joab and said, "Behold, I saw Absalom hanging in an oak." [11] Then Joab said to the man who had informed him, "So behold, you saw *him!* Why then did you not strike him there to the ground? And *it would have been* my duty to give you ten *pieces* of silver and a belt." [12] But the man said to Joab, "Even if I were to receive a thousand *pieces of* silver in my hand, I would not put out my hand against the king's son; for in our hearing the king commanded you, Abishai, and Ittai, saying, 'Protect the young man Absalom for me!' [13] Otherwise, if I had dealt treacherously against his life (and there is nothing hidden from the king), then you yourself would have avoided *me."* [14] Then Joab said, "I will not waste time here with you." So he took three spears in his hand and thrust them through the heart of Absalom while he was still alive in the midst of the oak. [15] And ten young men who carried Joab's armor gathered around and struck Absalom and killed him.

[16] Then Joab blew the trumpet, and the people returned from pursuing Israel, for Joab restrained the people. [17] And they took Absalom and threw him into a deep pit in the forest, and erected over him a very large pile of stones. And all Israel fled, each to his *own* tent. [18] Now Absalom in his lifetime had taken and set up for himself a memorial stone, which is in the King's Valley, for he said, "I have no son to continue my name." So he named the memorial stone after his own name, and it is called Absalom's Monument to this day.

David Is Grief-stricken

[19] Then Ahimaaz the son of Zadok said, "Please let me run and bring the king news that the LORD has freed him from the hand of his enemies!" [20] But Joab said to him, "You are not the man *to bring* news this day, but you shall bring news another day; however, you shall bring no news this day, because the king's son is dead." [21] Then Joab said to the Cushite, "Go, tell the king what you have seen." So the Cushite bowed to Joab and ran. [22] However, Ahimaaz the son of Zadok said once more to Joab, "But whatever happens, please let me also run after the Cushite." And Joab said, "Why would you run, my son, since you will have no messenger's reward for going?" [23] "But whatever happens," *he said,* "I will run." So he said to him, "Run." Then Ahimaaz ran by way of the plain and passed by the Cushite.

[24] Now David was sitting between the two gates; and the watchman went to the roof of the gate by the wall, and raised his eyes and looked; and behold, a man was running by himself. [25] So the watchman called out and told the king. And the king said, "If he is by himself there is good news in his mouth." And he came nearer and nearer. [26] Then the watchman saw another man running; and the watchman called to the gatekeeper and said, "Behold, *another* man is running by himself." And the king said, "This one also is bringing good news." [27] The watchman said, "I think the running form of the first one is like the running form of Ahimaaz the son of Zadok." And the king said, "This is a good man, and he is coming with good news."

[28] Then Ahimaaz called out and said to the king, "Ali is well." And he prostrated himself before the king with his face to the ground. And he said, "Blessed is the LORD your God, who has turned over the men who raised their hands against my lord the king." [29] But the king said, "Is it well with the young man Absalom?" And Ahimaaz answered, "When Joab sent the king's servant, and your servant, I saw a great commotion, but I did not know what *it was."* [30] Then the king said, "Turn aside and stand here." So he turned aside and stood still.

[31] Then behold, the Cushite arrived, and the Cushite said, "Let my lord the king receive good news, for the LORD has freed you this day from the hand of all those who rose up against you." [32] Then the king said to the Cushite, "Is it well with the young man Absalom?" And the Cushite answered, "May the enemies of my lord the king, and all who rise up against you for evil, be like *that* young man!"

[33] Then the king trembled and went up to the chamber over the gate and wept. And this is what he said as he walked: "My son Absalom, my son, my son Absalom! If only I had died instead of you, Absalom, my son, my son!"

Joab Disapproves of David's Mourning

19 Then it was reported to Joab, "Behold, the king is weeping and he mourns for Absalom." [2] So the victory that day was turned into mourning for all the people, because the people heard *it* said that day, "The king is in mourning over his son." [3] And the people entered the city surreptitiously that day, just as people who are humiliated surreptitiously flee in battle. [4] And the king covered his face and cried out with a loud voice, "My son Absalom, Absalom, my son, my son!" [5] Then Joab came into the house to the king and said, "Today you have shamed all your servants, who have saved your life today and the lives of your sons and daughters, the lives of your wives, and the lives of your concubines, [6] by loving those who hate you, and by hating those who love you. For you have revealed today that commanders and servants are nothing to you; for I know today that if Absalom were alive and all of us were dead today, then it would be right as far as you are concerned. [7] Now therefore arise, go out and speak kindly to your servants, for I swear by the LORD, if you do not go out, no man will stay the night with you, and this will be worse for you than all the misfortune that has happened to you from your youth until now!"

David Restored as King

8 So the king got up and sat at the gate. When they told all the people, saying, "Behold, the king is sitting at the gate," then all the people came before the king.

Now Israel had fled, each to his tent. **9** And all the people were quarreling throughout the tribes of Israel, saying, "The king rescued us from the hands of our enemies and saved us from the hands of the Philistines, but now he has fled out of the land from Absalom. **10** However, Absalom, whom we anointed over us, has died in battle. Now then, why are you silent about bringing the king back?"

11 Then King David sent *word* to Zadok and Abiathar the priests, saying, "Speak to the elders of Judah, saying, 'Why are you the last to bring the king back to his house, since the word of all Israel has come to the king, *even* to his house? **12** You are my brothers; you are my bone and my flesh. Why then should you be the last to bring back the king?' **13** And say to Amasa, 'Are you not my bone and my flesh? May God do so to me, and more so, if you will not be commander of the army for me continually, in place of Joab.'" **14** So he turned the hearts of all the men of Judah as one man, so that they sent *word* to the king, *saying,* "Return, you and all your servants." **15** The king then returned and came as far as the Jordan. And *the men of* Judah came to Gilgal in order to go to meet the king, to escort the king across the Jordan.

16 Then Shimei the son of Gera, the Benjaminite who was from Bahurim, hurried and came down with the men of Judah to meet King David. **17** And there were a thousand men of Benjamin with him, and Ziba the servant of the house of Saul, and his fifteen sons and his twenty servants with him; and they rushed to the Jordan before the king. **18** Then they crossed the shallow places *repeatedly* to bring over the king's household, and to do what was good in his sight. And Shimei the son of Gera fell down before the king as he was about to cross the Jordan. **19** And he said to the king, "May my lord not consider me guilty, nor call to mind what your servant did wrong on the day when my lord the king went out from Jerusalem, so that the king would take *it* to heart. **20** For your servant knows that I have sinned; so behold, I have come today, the first of all the house of Joseph to go down to meet my lord the king." **21** But Abishai the son of Zeruiah responded, "Should Shimei not be put to death for this, the fact that he cursed the LORD's anointed?" **22** David then said, "What is there between you and me, you sons of Zeruiah, that you should be an adversary to me today? Should anyone be put to death in Israel today? For do I not know that I am king over Israel today?" **23** So the king said to Shimei, "You shall not die." The king also swore to him.

24 Then Mephibosheth the grandson of Saul came down to meet the king; but he had neither tended to his feet, nor trimmed his mustache, nor washed his clothes since the day the king departed until the day he came *home* in peace. **25** And it was when he came *from* Jerusalem to meet the king, that the king said to him, "Why did you not go with me, Mephibosheth?" **26** So he said, "My lord the king, my servant betrayed me; for your servant said, 'I will saddle the donkey for myself so that I may ride on it and go with the king,' since your servant cannot walk. **27** Furthermore, he has slandered your servant to my lord the king; but my lord the king is like the angel of God, therefore do what is good in your sight. **28** For all my father's household was only people *worthy* of death to my lord the king; yet you placed your servant among those who ate at your own table. So what right do I still have, that I should complain anymore to the king?" **29** So the king said to him, "Why do you still speak of your affairs? I have decided, 'You and Ziba shall divide the land.'" **30** And Mephibosheth said to the king, "Let him even take it all, since my lord the king has come safely to his own house."

31 Now Barzillai the Gileadite had come down from Rogelim; and he went on to the Jordan with the king to escort him over the Jordan. **32** Barzillai was very old: eighty years old; and he had provided the king food while he stayed in Mahanaim, for he was a very great man. **33** So the king said to Barzillai, "You cross over with me, and I will provide you food in Jerusalem with me." **34** But Barzillai said to the king, "How long do I still have to live, that I should go up with the king to Jerusalem? **35** I am now eighty years old. Can I distinguish between good and bad? Or can your servant taste what I eat or what I drink? Or can I still hear the voice of men and women singing? Why then should your servant be an added burden to my lord the king? **36** Your servant would merely cross over the Jordan with the king. So why should the king compensate me *with* this reward? **37** Please let your servant return, so that I may die in my *own* city near the grave of my father and my mother. However, here is your servant Chimham; let him cross over with my lord the king, and do for him what is good in your sight." **38** And the king answered, "Chimham shall cross over with me, and I will do for him what is good in your sight; and whatever you require of me, I will do for you." **39** All the people crossed over the Jordan and the king crossed *too.* The king then kissed Barzillai and blessed him, and he returned to his place.

40 Now the king went on to Gilgal, and Chimham went on with him; and all the people of Judah and also half the people of Israel accompanied the king. **41** And behold, all the men of Israel came to the king and said to the king, "Why have our brothers, the men of Judah, abducted you and brought the king and his household and all David's men with him, over the Jordan?" **42** Then all the men of Judah answered the men of Israel, "Because the king is a close relative to us. Why then are you angry about this matter? Have we eaten at all at the king's expense, or has anything been taken for us?" **43** But the men of Israel answered the men of Judah and said, "We have ten parts in the king, therefore we also *have* more *claim* on David than you. Why then did you treat us with contempt? Was it not our

advice first to bring back our king?" Yet the words of the men of Judah were harsher than the words of the men of Israel.

Sheba's Revolt

20 Now a worthless man happened to be there whose name was Sheba, the son of Bichri, a Benjaminite; and he blew the trumpet and said,

"We have no share in David,
Nor do we have an inheritance in the son of Jesse;
Every man to his tents, Israel!"

2 So all the men of Israel withdrew from following David and followed Sheba the son of Bichri; but the men of Judah remained loyal to their king, from the Jordan even to Jerusalem.

3 Then David came to his house in Jerusalem, and the king took the ten women, the concubines whom he had left behind to take care of the house, and put them in custody and provided them with food, but did not have relations with them. So they were locked up until the day of their death, living as widows.

4 Now the king said to Amasa, "Summon the men of Judah for me within three days, and be present here yourself." 5 So Amasa went to summon the men of Judah, but he was delayed longer than the set time which he had designated for him. 6 And David said to Abishai, "Now Sheba the son of Bichri will do us more harm than Absalom; take your lord's servants and pursue him, so that he does not find for himself fortified cities and escape from our sight." 7 So Joab's men went out after him, along with the Cherethites, the Pelethites, and all the warriors; and they left Jerusalem to pursue Sheba the son of Bichri. 8 When they were at the large stone which is in Gibeon, Amasa came to meet them. Now Joab was dressed in his military attire, and over it he had a belt with a sword in its sheath strapped on at his waist; and as he went forward, it fell out. 9 And Joab said to Amasa, "Is it going well for you, my brother?" And Joab took hold of Amasa by the beard with his right hand to kiss him.

Amasa Murdered

10 But Amasa was not on guard against the sword which was in Joab's hand, so he struck him in the belly with it and spilled out his intestines on the ground, and did not strike him again, and he died. Then Joab and his brother Abishai pursued Sheba the son of Bichri. 11 Now one of Joab's young men stood by him and said, "Whoever favors Joab and whoever is for David, follow Joab!" 12 But Amasa was wallowing in his own blood in the middle of the road. And when the man saw that all the people stood still, he removed Amasa from the road to the field and threw a garment over him when he saw that everyone who came by him stood still.

Revolt Put Down

13 As soon as he was removed from the road, all the men went on after Joab to pursue Sheba the son of Bichri.

14 Now he went on through all the tribes of Israel to Abel, that is, Beth-maacah, and all the Berites; and they assembled and went after him as well. 15 And they came and besieged him in Abel Beth-maacah, and they built up an assault ramp against the city, and it stood against the outer rampart; and all the people who were with Joab were wreaking destruction in order to topple the wall. 16 Then a wise woman called out from the city, "Listen, listen! Please tell Joab, 'Come here that I may speak with you.'" 17 So he approached her, and the woman said, "Are you Joab?" And he answered, "I am." Then she said to him, "Listen to the words of your slave." And he said, "I am listening." 18 Then she spoke, saying, "In the past they used to say, 'They will undoubtedly ask advice at Abel,' and that is how they ended a dispute. 19 I am one of those who are ready for peace and faithful in Israel. You are trying to destroy a city, even a mother in Israel. Why would you swallow up the inheritance of the LORD?" 20 Joab replied, "Far be it, far be it from me that I would consume or destroy! 21 Such is not the case. But a man from the hill country of Ephraim, Sheba the son of Bichri by name, has raised his hand against King David. Only turn him over, and I will depart from the city." And the woman said to Joab, "Behold, his head will be thrown to you over the wall." 22 Then the woman wisely came to all the people. And they cut off the head of Sheba the son of Bichri and threw it to Joab. So he blew the trumpet, and they were dispersed from the city, each to his tent. Joab also returned to the king at Jerusalem.

23 Now Joab was in command of the entire army of Israel, and Benaiah the son of Jehoiada was over the Cherethites and the Pelethites; 24 and Adoram was over the forced labor, and Jehoshaphat the son of Ahilud was the secretary; 25 and Sheva was scribe, and Zadok and Abiathar were priests; 26 Ira the Jairite also was a priest to David.

Gibeonite's Revenge

21 Now there was a famine in the days of David for three years, year after year; and David sought the presence of the LORD. And the LORD said, "It is because of Saul and his bloody house, because he put the Gibeonites to death." 2 So the king called the Gibeonites and spoke to them (now the Gibeonites were not of the sons of Israel, but of the remnant of the Amorites, and the sons of Israel had made a covenant with them, but Saul had sought to kill them in his zeal for the sons of Israel and Judah). 3 David said to the Gibeonites, "What should I do for you? And how can I make amends, so that you will bless the inheritance of the LORD?" 4 Then the Gibeonites said to him, "For us it is not a matter of silver or gold with Saul or his house, nor is it for us to put anyone to death in Israel." Nevertheless David said, "I will do for you whatever you say." 5 So they said to the king, "The man who destroyed us and who planned to eliminate us so that we would not exist within any border of Israel— 6 let seven men from his sons be given to us, and we will hang them

before the LORD in Gibeah of Saul, the chosen of the LORD." And the king said, "I will give *them."*

7 But the king spared Mephibosheth, the son of Jonathan, the son of Saul, because of the oath of the LORD which was between them, between David and Saul's son Jonathan. **8** So the king took the two sons of Rizpah the daughter of Aiah, Armoni and Mephibosheth whom she had borne to Saul, and the five sons of Merab the daughter of Saul, whom she had borne to Adriel the son of Barzillai the Meholathite. **9** Then he handed them over to the Gibeonites, and they hanged them on the mountain before the LORD, so that the seven of them fell together; and they were put to death in the first days of harvest at the beginning of barley harvest.

10 And Rizpah the daughter of Aiah took sackcloth and spread it out for herself on the rock, from the beginning of harvest until it rained on them from the sky; and she allowed neither the birds of the sky to rest on them by day nor the wild animals by night. **11** When it was reported to David what Rizpah the daughter of Aiah, the concubine of Saul, had done, **12** then David went and took the bones of Saul and the bones of his son Jonathan from the citizens of Jabesh-gilead, who had stolen them from the public square of Beth-shan, where the Philistines had hanged them on the day the Philistines struck and killed Saul in Gilboa. **13** He brought up from there the bones of Saul and the bones of his son Jonathan, and they gathered the bones of those who had been hanged. **14** Then they buried the bones of Saul and his son Jonathan in the country of Benjamin in Zela, in the grave of his father Kish; So they did everything that the king commanded, and after that God responded to prayer for the land.

15 Now when the Philistines were at war with Israel again, David went down, and his servants with him; and when they fought against the Philistines, David became weary. **16** Then Ishbi-benob, who was among the descendants of the giant, the weight of whose spear was ¹three hundred *shekels* of bronze in weight, had strapped on a new *sword,* and he intended to kill David. **17** But Abishai the son of Zeruiah helped him, and struck the Philistine and killed him. Then David's men swore to him, saying, "You shall not go out again with us to battle, so that you do not extinguish the lamp of Israel."

18 Now it came about after this that there was war again with the Philistines at Gob; then Sibbecai the Hushathite struck and killed Saph, who was among the descendants of the giant. **19** And there was war with the Philistines again at Gob, and Elhanan the son of Jaare-oregim the Bethlehemite killed ¹Goliath the Gittite, the shaft of whose spear was like a weaver's beam. **20** And there was war at Gath again, where there was a man of *great* stature who had six fingers on each hand and six toes on each foot, twenty-four in number; and he also had been born to the giant. **21** When he defied Israel, Jonathan the son of Shimei, David's

brother, struck and killed him. **22** These four were born to the giant at Gath, and they fell by the hand of David and by the hand of his servants.

David's Psalm of Deliverance

22 Now David spoke the words of this song to the LORD on the day that the LORD had saved him from the hand of all his enemies and from the hand of Saul. **2** He said,

"The LORD is my rock and my fortress and my deliverer;

3 My God, my rock, in whom I take refuge, My shield and the horn of my salvation, my stronghold and my refuge; My savior, You save me from violence.

4 "I call upon the LORD, who is worthy to be praised, And I am saved from my enemies.

5 "For the waves of death encompassed me; The floods of destruction terrified me;

6 The ropes of ¹Sheol surrounded me; The snares of death confronted me.

7 "In my distress I called upon the LORD, Yes, I called out to my God; And from His temple He heard my voice, And my cry for help *came* into His ears.

8 "Then the earth shook and quaked, The foundations of heaven were trembling And were shaken, because He was angry.

9 "Smoke went up out of His nostrils, And fire from His mouth was devouring; Coals were kindled by it.

10 "He also bowed the heavens down low, and came down With thick darkness under His feet.

11 "He rode on a cherub and flew; He appeared on the wings of the wind.

12 "He made darkness canopies around Him, A mass of waters, thick clouds of the sky.

13 "From the brightness before Him Coals of fire were kindled.

14 "The LORD thundered from heaven, And the Most High uttered His voice.

15 "And He shot arrows and scattered them, Lightning, and routed them.

16 "Then the channels of the sea appeared, The foundations of the world were exposed By the rebuke of the LORD, From the blast of the breath of His nostrils.

17 "He sent from on high, He took me; He drew me out of many waters.

18 "He rescued me from my strong enemy, From those who hated me, for they were too strong for me.

19 "They confronted me on the day of my disaster, But the LORD was my support.

20 "He also brought me out into an open place; He rescued me, because He delighted in me.

21 "The LORD has treated me in accordance with my righteousness; In accordance with the cleanliness of my hands He has repaid me.

21:16 ¹About 9 lb. or 4 kg   **21:19** ¹In 1 Chr 20:5, *Lahmi, the brother of Goliath*   **22:6** ¹I.e., the netherworld

22 "For I have kept the ways of the LORD,
And have not acted wickedly against my
God.
23 "For all His ordinances *were* before me,
And *as for* His statutes, I did not deviate
from them.
24 "I was also blameless toward Him,
And I have kept myself from my
wrongdoing.
25 "So the LORD has repaid me in accordance
with my righteousness,
In accordance with my cleanliness before
His eyes.
26 "With *the one who is* faithful You show
Yourself faithful,
With the blameless one You prove
Yourself blameless;
27 With the *one who is* pure You show
Yourself pure,
But with the perverted You show Yourself
astute.
28 "And You save an afflicted people;
But Your eyes are on the haughty *whom*
You humiliate.
29 "For You are my lamp, LORD;
And the LORD illuminates my darkness.
30 "For by You I can run at a troop of warriors;
By my God I can leap over a wall.
31 "As for God, His way is blameless;
The word of the LORD is refined;
He is a shield to all who take refuge in
Him.
32 "For who is God, except the LORD?
And who is a rock, except our God?
33 "God is my strong fortress;
And He sets the blameless on His way.
34 "He makes my feet like deer's *feet,*
And sets me on my high places.
35 "He trains my hands for battle,
So that my arms can bend a bow of
bronze.
36 "You have also given me the shield of Your
salvation,
And Your help makes me great.
37 "You enlarge my steps under me,
And my feet have not slipped.
38 "I pursued my enemies and eliminated
them,
And I did not turn back until they were
finished off.
39 "And I have devoured them and smashed
them, so that they would not rise;
And they fell under my feet.
40 "For You have encircled me with strength
for battle;
You have forced those who rose up against
me to bow down under me.
41 "You have also made my enemies turn *their*
backs to me,
And I destroyed those who hated me.
42 "They looked, but there was no one to save
them;
Even to the LORD, but He did not answer
them.
43 "Then I pulverized them as the dust of the
earth;
I crushed *and* trampled them like the mud
of the streets.
44 "You have also saved me from the contentions of my people;

You have kept me as head of the nations;
A people I have not known serve me.
45 "Foreigners pretend to obey me;
As soon as they hear, they obey me.
46 "Foreigners lose heart,
And come trembling out of their fortresses.
47 "The LORD lives, and blessed be my Rock;
And exalted be my God, the rock of my
salvation,
48 The God who executes vengeance for me,
And brings down peoples under me,
49 Who also brings me out from my enemies;
You also raise me above those who rise up
against me;
You rescue me from the violent person.
50 "Therefore I will give thanks to You, LORD,
among the nations,
And I will sing praises to Your name.
51 "*He is* a tower of salvation *to* His king,
And shows favor to His anointed,
To David and his descendants forever."

David's Last Song

23 Now these are the last words of David.
David the son of Jesse declares,
The man who was raised on high,
The anointed of the God of Jacob
And the sweet psalmist of Israel,
declares,
2 "The Spirit of the LORD spoke through me,
And His word was on my tongue.
3 "The God of Israel said *it;*
The Rock of Israel spoke to me:
'He who rules over mankind righteously,
Who rules *in* the fear of God,
4 Is like the light of the morning *when* the
sun rises,
A morning without clouds,
When the fresh grass *springs* out of the
earth
From sunshine after rain.'
5 "Is my house not indeed so with God?
For He has made an everlasting covenant
with me,
Properly ordered in all things, and
secured;
For will He not indeed make
All my salvation and all *my* delight grow?
6 "But the worthless, every one of them, are
like scattered thorns,
Because they cannot be taken in hand;
7 Instead, the man *who* touches them
Must be armed with iron and the shaft of
a spear,
And they will be completely burned with
fire in *their* place."

David's Mighty Men

8 These are the names of the mighty men
whom David had: Josheb-basshebeth, a
Tahchemonite, chief of the captains; he was
called Adino the Eznite because of eight hundred who were killed *by him* at one time. 9 And
after him was Eleazar the son of Dodo the
Ahohite, one of the three mighty men with
David when they defied the Philistines who
were gathered there to battle and the men of
Israel had withdrawn. 10 He rose up and struck
the Philistines until his hand was weary and it

clung to the sword, and the LORD brought about a great victory that day; and the people returned after him only to plunder *the dead.*

11 Now after him was Shammah the son of Agee, a Hararite. And the Philistines were gathered into an army where there was a plot of land full of lentils, and the people fled from the Philistines. 12 But he took his stand in the midst of the plot, defended it, and struck the Philistines; and the LORD brought about a great victory.

13 Then three of the thirty chief men went down and came to David at harvest time to the cave of Adullam, while the army of the Philistines was camping in the Valley of Rephaim. 14 David was then in the stronghold, while the garrison of the Philistines was then in Bethlehem. 15 And David had a craving and said, "Oh that someone would give me water to drink from the well of Bethlehem which is by the gate!" 16 So the three mighty men forced their way into the camp of the Philistines, and drew water from the well of Bethlehem which was by the gate, and carried *it* and brought *it* to David. Yet he would not drink it, but poured it out as an offering to the LORD; 17 and he said, "Far be it from me, LORD, that I would do this! *Should I drink* the blood of the men who went at *the risk of* their lives?" So he would not drink it. These things the three mighty men did.

18 Now Abishai, the brother of Joab, the son of Zeruiah, was chief of the thirty. And he swung his spear against three hundred and killed *them,* and had a name as well as the three. 19 He was the most honored among the thirty, so he became their commander; however, he did not attain to *the reputation* of the three.

20 Then Benaiah the son of Jehoiada, the son of a valiant man of Kabzeel, who had done great deeds, killed the two *sons of* Ariel of Moab. He also went down and killed a lion in the middle of a pit on a snowy day. 21 And he killed an Egyptian, an impressive man. Now the Egyptian *had* a spear in his hand, but he went down to him with a club and snatched the spear from the Egyptian's hand, and killed him with his own spear. 22 These *things* Benaiah the son of Jehoiada did, and had a name as well as the three mighty men. 23 He was honored among the thirty, but he did not attain *the reputation* of the three. And David appointed him over his bodyguard.

24 Asahel the brother of Joab was among the thirty; *and there was* Elhanan the son of Dodo of Bethlehem, 25 Shammah the Harodite, Elika the Harodite, 26 Helez the Paltite, Ira the son of Ikkesh the Tekoite, 27 Abiezer the Anathothite, Mebunnai the Hushathite, 28 Zalmon the Ahohite, Maharai the Netophathite, 29 Heleb the son of Baanah the Netophathite, Ittai the son of Ribai of Gibeah of the sons of Benjamin, 30 Benaiah a Pirathonite, Hiddai of the brooks of Gaash, 31 Abi-albon the Arbathite, Azmaveth the Barhumite, 32 Eliahba the Shaalbonite, the sons of Jashen, Jonathan, 33 Shammah the Hararite, Ahiam the son of Sharar the Ararite, 34 Eliphelet the son of Ahasbai, the son of the Maacathite, Eliam the son of Ahithophel the Gilonite, 35 Hezro the Carmelite, Paarai the Arbite, 36 Igal the son of Nathan of Zobah, Bani the Gadite, 37 Zelek the Ammonite, Naharai the Beerothite, armor bearers of Joab the son of Zeruiah, 38 Ira the Ithrite, Gareb the Ithrite, 39 *and* Uriah the Hittite; thirty-seven in all.

The Census Taken

24 Now the anger of the LORD burned against Israel again, and He incited David against them to say, "Go, count Israel and Judah." 2 So the king said to Joab the commander of the army, who was with him, "Roam about now through all the tribes of Israel, from Dan to Beersheba, and conduct a census of the people, so that I may know the number of the people." 3 But Joab said to the king, "May the LORD your God add to the people a hundred times as many as they are, while the eyes of my lord the king *can still* see; but why does my lord the king delight in this thing?" 4 Nevertheless, the king's order prevailed against Joab and against the commanders of the army. So Joab and the commanders of the army left the presence of the king to conduct a census of the people of Israel. 5 They crossed the Jordan and camped in Aroer, on the right side of the city that is in the middle of the Valley of Gad and toward Jazer. 6 Then they came to Gilead and to 'the land of Tahtim-hodshi, and they came to Dan-jaan and around to Sidon, 7 then they came to the fortress of Tyre and to all the cities of the Hivites and of the Canaanites, and they went out to the south of Judah, *to* Beersheba. 8 So when they had roamed about through the whole land, they came to Jerusalem at the end of nine months and twenty days. 9 And Joab gave the number of the census of the people to the king: in Israel there were eight hundred thousand valiant men who drew the sword, and the men of Judah were five hundred thousand men.

10 Now David's heart troubled him after he had counted the people. So David said to the LORD, "I have sinned greatly in what I have done. But now, LORD, please overlook the guilt of Your servant, for I have acted very foolishly." 11 When David got up in the morning, the word of the LORD came to Gad the prophet, David's seer, saying, 12 "Go and speak to David, 'This is what the LORD says: "I am imposing upon you three *choices;* choose for yourself one of them, and I will do *it* to you."'" 13 So Gad came to David and told him, and said to him, "Shall seven years of famine come to you in your land? Or will you flee for three months before your enemies while they pursue you? Or shall there be three days' of plague in your land? Now consider and see what answer I shall return to Him who sent me." 14 Then David said to Gad, "I am in great distress. Let us now fall into the hand of the LORD, for His mercies are great; but do not let me fall into human hands."

Plague Sent

15 So the LORD sent a plague upon Israel from the morning until the appointed time,

---

24:6 1 Another reading is *Kadesh in the land of the Hittite*

and seventy thousand men of the people from Dan to Beersheba died. 16 When the angel extended his hand *toward* Jerusalem to destroy it, the LORD relented of the disaster and said to the angel who destroyed the people, "It is enough! Now drop your hand!" And the angel of the LORD was by the threshing floor of Araunah the Jebusite. 17 Then David spoke to the LORD when he saw the angel who was striking down the people, and said, "Behold, it is I who have sinned, and it is I who have done wrong; but these sheep, what have they done? Please let Your hand be against me and against my father's house!"

David Builds an Altar

18 So Gad came to David that day and said to him, "Go up, erect an altar to the LORD on the threshing floor of Araunah the Jebusite." 19 Then David went up in accordance with the word of Gad, just as the LORD had commanded. 20 And Araunah looked down and saw the king and his servants crossing over toward him; so Araunah went out and bowed his face to the ground before the king. 21 Then Araunah said, "Why has my lord the king come to his servant?" And David said, "To buy the threshing floor from you, in order to build an altar to the LORD, so that the plague may be withdrawn from the people." 22 Araunah then said to David, "Let my lord the king take and offer up what is good in his sight. Look, *here are* the oxen for the burnt offering, the threshing sledges and the yokes of the oxen for the wood. 23 Everything, O king, Araunah gives to the king." And Araunah said to the king, "May the LORD your God be favorable to you." 24 However, the king said to Araunah, "No, but I will certainly buy *it* from you for a price; for I will not offer burnt offerings to the LORD my God that cost me nothing." So David bought the threshing floor and the oxen for fifty shekels of silver. 25 Then David built there an altar to the LORD, and he offered burnt offerings and peace offerings. And the LORD responded to prayer for the land, and the plague was withdrawn from Israel.

The First Book of the
KINGS

David in Old Age

1 Now King David was old, advanced in age; and they covered him with garments, but he could not keep warm. 2 So his servants said to him, "Have them search for a young virgin for my lord the king, and have her attend the king and become his nurse; and have her lie on your chest, so that my lord the king may keep warm." 3 So they searched for a beautiful girl throughout the territory of Israel, and found Abishag the Shunammite, and brought her to the king. 4 The girl was very beautiful; and she became the king's nurse and served him, but the king did not become intimate with her.

5 Now Adonijah the son of Haggith exalted himself, saying, "I will be king." So he prepared for himself chariots and horsemen, with fifty men to run before him. 6 And his father had never rebuked him at any time by asking, "Why have you done so?" And he was also a very handsome man, and he was born after Absalom. 7 Now he had conferred with Joab the son of Zeruiah and with Abiathar the priest; and they allied themselves with Adonijah. 8 But Zadok the priest, Benaiah the son of Jehoiada, Nathan the prophet, Shimei, Rei, and the mighty men who belonged to David, were not with Adonijah.

9 Adonijah sacrificed sheep, oxen, and fattened steers by the stone of Zoheleth, which is beside En-rogel; and he invited all his brothers, the king's sons, and all the men of Judah, the king's servants. 10 But he did not invite Nathan the prophet, Benaiah, the mighty men, or his brother Solomon.

Nathan and Bathsheba

11 Then Nathan spoke to Bathsheba the mother of Solomon, saying, "Have you not heard that Adonijah the son of Haggith has become king, and David our lord does not know it? 12 So now come, please let me give you advice, and save your life and the life of your son Solomon. 13 Go at once to King David and say to him, 'Have you not, my lord the king, sworn to your servant, saying, "Solomon your son certainly shall be king after me, and he shall sit on my throne"? Why then has Adonijah become king?' 14 Behold, while you are still there speaking with the king, I will come in after you and confirm your words."

15 So Bathsheba entered to the king in the bedroom. Now the king was very old, and Abishag the Shunammite was serving the king. 16 Then Bathsheba bowed and prostrated herself before the king. And the king said, "What is on your mind?" 17 So she said to him, "My lord, you yourself swore to your servant by the LORD your God, saying, 'Your son Solomon certainly shall be king after me, and he shall sit on my throne.' 18 But now, behold, Adonijah is king; and now, my lord the king,

you do not know it. 19 He has sacrificed oxen and fattened steers and sheep in abundance, and has invited all the sons of the king, Abiathar the priest, and Joab the commander of the army, but he has not invited Solomon your servant. 20 And as for you, my lord the king, the eyes of all Israel are upon you, to announce to them who shall sit on the throne of my lord the king after him. 21 Otherwise it will come about, as soon as my lord the king 1lies down with his fathers, that I and my son Solomon will be considered offenders."

22 And behold, while she was still speaking with the king, Nathan the prophet came in. 23 They informed the king, saying, "Nathan the prophet is here." And when he came into the king's presence, he prostrated himself before the king with his face to the ground. 24 Then Nathan said, "My lord the king, have you yourself said, 'Adonijah shall be king after me, and he shall sit on my throne'? 25 For he has gone down today and has sacrificed oxen and fattened steers and sheep in abundance, and has invited all the king's sons, the commanders of the army, and Abiathar the priest, and behold, they are eating and drinking in his presence; and they say, 'Long live King Adonijah!' 26 But me, even me your servant, Zadok the priest, Benaiah the son of Jehoiada, and your servant Solomon, he has not invited. 27 Has this thing been done by my lord the king, and you have not let your servants know who shall sit on the throne of my lord the king after him?"

28 Then King David responded and said, "Summon Bathsheba to me." And she came into the king's presence and stood before the king. 29 Then the king vowed and said, "As the LORD lives, who has redeemed my life from all distress, 30 certainly as I vowed to you by the LORD, the God of Israel, saying, 'Your son Solomon certainly shall be king after me, and he shall sit on my throne in my place'; I will indeed do so this day." 31 Then Bathsheba bowed with her face to the ground, and prostrated herself before the king and said, "May my lord King David live forever."

32 Then King David said, "Summon to me Zadok the priest, Nathan the prophet, and Benaiah the son of Jehoiada." And they came into the king's presence. 33 And the king said to them, "Take with you the servants of your lord, and have my son Solomon ride on my own mule, and bring him down to Gihon. 34 And have Zadok the priest and Nathan the prophet anoint him there as king over Israel, and blow the trumpet and say, 'Long live King Solomon!' 35 Then you shall come up after him, and he shall come and sit on my throne; and he shall be king in my place; for I have appointed him to be ruler over Israel and Judah." 36 Benaiah the son of Jehoiada answered the king and said,

"Amen! May the LORD, the God of my lord the king, say the same. 37 Just as the LORD has been with my lord the king, so may He be with Solomon, and make his throne greater than the throne of my lord King David!"

Solomon Anointed King

38 So Zadok the priest, Nathan the prophet, Benaiah the son of Jehoiada, the Cherethites, and the Pelethites went down and had Solomon ride on King David's mule, and brought him to Gihon. 39 And Zadok the priest then took the horn of oil from the tent and anointed Solomon. Then they blew the trumpet, and all the people said, "*Long* live King Solomon!" 40 And all the people went up after him, and the people were playing on flutes and rejoicing with great joy, so that the earth shook at their noise.

41 Now Adonijah and all the guests who *were* with him heard *this* as they finished eating. When Joab heard the sound of the trumpet, he said, "Why is the city making such an uproar?" 42 While he was still speaking, behold, Jonathan the son of Abiathar the priest came. Then Adonijah said, "Come in, for you are a valiant man and you bring good news." 43 But Jonathan replied to Adonijah, "On the contrary! Our lord King David has made Solomon king! 44 The king has also sent with him Zadok the priest, Nathan the prophet, Benaiah the son of Jehoiada, the Cherethites, and the Pelethites; and they have mounted him on the king's mule. 45 Furthermore, Zadok the priest and Nathan the prophet have anointed him king in Gihon, and they have come up from there rejoicing, so that the city is going wild. This is the noise which you have heard. 46 Besides, Solomon has even taken his seat on the throne of the kingdom. 47 Moreover, the king's servants came to bless our lord King David, saying, 'May your God make the name of Solomon better than your name, and his throne greater than your throne!' And the king bowed himself on the bed. 48 The king has also said this: 'Blessed be the LORD, the God of Israel, who has granted one to sit on my throne today while my own eyes see *it.*' "

49 Then all the guests of Adonijah trembled and got up, and each went on his way. 50 Adonijah also was afraid of Solomon, and he got up, and went, and took hold of the horns of the altar. 51 Now it was reported to Solomon, saying, "Behold, Adonijah is afraid of King Solomon, for behold, he has taken hold of the horns of the altar, saying, 'May King Solomon swear to me today that he will not put his servant to death with the sword.'" 52 And Solomon said, "If he is a worthy man, not one of his hairs will fall to the ground; but if wickedness is found in him, he will die." 53 So King Solomon sent *men,* and they brought him down from the altar. And he came and prostrated himself before King Solomon, and Solomon said to him, "Go to your house."

David's Command to Solomon

2 As David's time to die drew near, he commanded his son Solomon, saying, 2 "I am going the way of all the earth. So be strong, and prove yourself a man. 3 Do your duty to the LORD your God, to walk in His ways, to keep His statutes, His commandments, His ordinances, and His testimonies, according to what is written in the Law of Moses, so that you may succeed in all that you do and wherever you turn, 4 so that the LORD may fulfill His promise which He spoke regarding me, saying, 'If your sons are careful about their way, to walk before Me in truth with all their heart and all their soul, you shall not be deprived of a man to occupy the throne of Israel.'

5 "Now you yourself also know what Joab the son of Zeruiah did to me, what he did to the two commanders of the armies of Israel, to Abner the son of Ner and to Amasa the son of Jether, whom he killed; he also shed the blood of war in peace. And he put the blood of war on his belt that was on his waist, and on his sandals that were on his feet. 6 So act as your wisdom *dictates,* and do not let his gray hair go down to 1 Sheol in peace. 7 However, show kindness to the sons of Barzillai the Gileadite, and let them be among those who eat at your table; for they assisted me when I fled from Absalom your brother. 8 And behold, *you have* with you Shimei the son of Gera the Benjaminite, of Bahurim; now it was he who cursed me with a painful curse on the day I went to Mahanaim. But when he came down to meet me at the Jordan, I swore to him by the LORD, saying, 'I will not put you to death with the sword.' 9 But now do not leave him unpunished, for you are a wise man; and you will know what to do to him, and you will bring his gray hair down to Sheol with blood."

Death of David

10 Then David 1 lay down with his fathers, and he was buried in the city of David. 11 Now the days that David reigned over Israel *were* forty years: in Hebron he reigned for seven years, and in Jerusalem he reigned for thirty-three years. 12 Then Solomon sat on the throne of his father David, and his kingdom was firmly established.

13 Now Adonijah the son of Haggith came to Bathsheba the mother of Solomon. So she said, "Do you come peacefully?" And he said, "Peacefully." 14 Then he said, "I have something *to say* to you." And she said, "Speak." 15 So he said, "You yourself know that the kingdom was mine and that all Israel intended for me to be king; however, the kingdom has turned around and become my brother's, for it was his from the LORD. 16 So now I am making one request of you; do not refuse me." And she said to him, "Speak." 17 Then he said, "Please speak to Solomon the king—for he will not refuse you—that he may give me Abishag the Shunammite as a wife." 18 And Bathsheba said, "Very well; I will speak to the king for you."

Adonijah Executed

19 So Bathsheba went to King Solomon, to speak to him for Adonijah. And the king stood

to meet her, bowed to her, and sat on his throne; then he had a throne set up for the king's mother, and she sat on his right. 20 Then she said, "I am making one small request of you; do not refuse me." And the king said to her, "Ask, my mother, for I will not refuse you." 21 So she said, "Let Abishag the Shunammite be given to Adonijah your brother as a wife." 22 But King Solomon answered and said to his mother, "And why are you requesting Abishag the Shunammite for Adonijah? Request for him the kingdom as well—since he is my older brother—for him, for Abiathar the priest, and for Joab the son of Zeruiah!" 23 Then King Solomon swore by the LORD, saying, "May God do so to me and more so, if Adonijah has not spoken this word against his own life! 24 Now then, as the LORD lives, who has established me and set me on the throne of David my father, and has made me a house just as He promised, Adonijah certainly shall be put to death today!" 25 Then King Solomon sent *the order* by Benaiah the son of Jehoiada; and he struck him so that he died.

26 Then to Abiathar the priest the king said, "Go to Anathoth to your own field, for you deserve to die; but I will not put you to death at this time, because you carried the ark of the Lord GOD before my father David, and because you were afflicted in everything with which my father was afflicted." 27 So Solomon dismissed Abiathar from being priest to the LORD, to fulfill the word of the LORD, which He had spoken regarding the house of Eli in Shiloh.

Joab Executed

28 Now the news came to Joab because Joab had followed Adonijah, though he had not followed Absalom. So Joab fled to the tent of the LORD and took hold of the horns of the altar. 29 And it was reported to King Solomon that Joab had fled to the tent of the LORD, and was beside the altar. Then Solomon sent Benaiah the son of Jehoiada, saying, "Go, execute him." 30 So Benaiah came to the tent of the LORD and said to him, "This is what the king has said: 'Come out.'" But he said, "No, for I will die here." So Benaiah brought back word to the king, saying, "This is what Joab spoke, and so he answered me." 31 And the king said to him, "Do just as he has spoken, and execute him and bury him, so that you may remove from me and from my father's house the blood which Joab shed without justification. 32 The LORD will return his blood on his own head, because he struck two men more righteous and better than he, and killed them with the sword, while my father David did not know *about it:* Abner the son of Ner, commander of the army of Israel, and Amasa the son of Jether, commander of the army of Judah. 33 So their blood shall return on the head of Joab and on the head of his descendants forever; but for David and his descendants, and his house and his throne, may there be peace from the LORD forever." 34 Then Benaiah the son of Jehoiada went up and struck him and

put him to death, and he was buried at his own house in the wilderness. 35 And the king appointed Benaiah the son of Jehoiada over the army in his place, and the king appointed Zadok the priest in place of Abiathar.

Shimei Executed

36 Now the king sent *men* and summoned Shimei, and said to him, "Build yourself a house in Jerusalem and live there, and do not leave there for any *other* place. 37 For on the day you leave and cross the brook Kidron, you will know for certain that you will assuredly die; your blood will be 1 on your own head." 38 Shimei then said to the king, "The word is good. Just as my lord the king has spoken, so your servant shall do." So Shimei lived in Jerusalem for many days.

39 But it came about at the end of three years, that two of Shimei's servants ran away to Achish son of Maacah, king of Gath. And *others* told Shimei, saying, "Behold, your servants are in Gath." 40 Then Shimei got up and saddled his donkey, and went to Gath to Achish, to search for his servants. And Shimei went and brought his servants from Gath. 41 And it was reported to Solomon that Shimei had gone from Jerusalem to Gath, and had returned. 42 So the king sent *men* and summoned Shimei, and said to him, "Did I not make you swear by the LORD, and solemnly warn you, saying, 'Know for certain that on the day you depart and go anywhere, you shall assuredly die'? And you said to me, 'The word I have heard is good.' 43 Why then have you not kept the oath of the LORD, and the command which I imposed on you?" 44 The king also said to Shimei, "You yourself know all the evil that you acknowledge in your heart, which you did to my father David; therefore the LORD will return your evil on your own head. 45 But King Solomon will be blessed, and the throne of David will be established before the LORD forever." 46 So the king commanded Benaiah the son of Jehoiada, and he went out and struck him so that he died.

And the kingdom was established in the hands of Solomon.

Solomon's Rule Consolidated

3 Now Solomon formed a marriage alliance with Pharaoh king of Egypt, and took Pharaoh's daughter and brought her to the city of David until he had finished building his own house and the house of the LORD, and the wall around Jerusalem. 2 The people were still sacrificing on the high places, because there was no house built for the name of the LORD until those days.

3 Now Solomon loved the LORD, walking in the statutes of his father David, except that he was sacrificing and burning incense on the high places. 4 And the king went to Gibeon to sacrifice there, because that was the great high place; Solomon offered a thousand burnt offerings on that altar. 5 In Gibeon the LORD appeared to Solomon in a dream at night; and God said, "Ask what *you wish* Me to give you."

Solomon's Prayer

6 Then Solomon said, "You have shown great faithfulness to Your servant David my father, according as he walked before You in truth, righteousness, and uprightness of heart toward You; and You have reserved for him this great faithfulness, that You have given him a son to sit on his throne, as *it is* this day. 7 And now, LORD my God, You have made Your servant king in place of my father David, yet I am *like* a little boy; I do not know how to ¹go out or come in. 8 And Your servant is in the midst of Your people whom You have chosen, a great people who are too many to be numbered or counted. 9 So give Your servant an understanding heart to judge Your people, to discern between good and evil. For who is capable of judging this great people of Yours?"

God's Answer

10 Now it was pleasing in the sight of the Lord that Solomon had asked this thing. 11 And God said to him, "Because you have asked this thing, and have not asked for yourself a long life, nor have asked riches for yourself, nor have you asked for the lives of your enemies, but have asked for yourself discernment to understand justice, 12 behold, I have done according to your words. Behold, I have given you a wise and discerning heart, so that there has been no one like you before you, nor shall one like you arise after you. 13 I have also given you what you have not asked, both riches and honor, so that there will not be any among the kings like you all your days. 14 And if you walk in My ways, keeping My statutes and commandments, as your father David walked, then I will prolong your days."

15 Then Solomon awoke, and behold, it was a dream. And he came to Jerusalem and stood before the ark of the covenant of the Lord, and offered burnt offerings and made peace offerings, and held a feast for all his servants.

Solomon Wisely Judges

16 Then two women who were prostitutes came to the king and stood before him. 17 The one woman said, "Pardon me, my lord: this woman and I live in the same house; and I gave birth to a child while she was in the house. 18 And it happened on the third day after I gave birth, that this woman also gave birth to a child, and we were together. There was no stranger with us in the house, only the two of us in the house. 19 Then this woman's son died in the night, because she lay on him. 20 So she got up in the middle of the night and took my son from beside me while your servant was asleep, and she laid him at her breast, and laid her dead son at my breast. 21 When I got up in the morning to nurse my son, behold, he was dead! But when I examined him closely in the morning, behold, he was not my son, whom I had borne!" 22 Then the other woman said, "No! For the living one is my son, and the dead one is your son." But the first woman said, "No! For the dead one is your son, and the living one is my son." So they spoke before the king.

23 Then the king said, "The one says, 'This is my son who is living, and your son is the dead one'; and the other says, 'No! For your son is the dead one, and my son is the living one.'" 24 And the king said, "Get me a sword." So they brought a sword before the king. 25 And the king said, "Cut the living child in two, and give half to the one and half to the other." 26 But the woman whose child *was* the living one spoke to the king, for she was deeply stirred over her son, and she said, "Pardon me, my lord! Give her the living child, and by no means kill him!" But the other *woman* was saying, "He shall be neither mine nor yours; cut *him!*" 27 Then the king replied, "Give the first woman the living child, and by no means kill him. She is his mother." 28 When all Israel heard about the judgment which the king had handed down, they feared the king, because they saw that the wisdom of God was in him to administer justice.

Solomon's Officials

4 Now King Solomon was king over all Israel. 2 These were his officials: Azariah the son of Zadok *was* the priest; 3 Elihoreph and Ahijah, the sons of Shisha *were* scribes; Jehoshaphat the son of Ahilud *was* the secretary; 4 and Benaiah the son of Jehoiada *was* over the army; and Zadok and Abiathar *were* priests; 5 and Azariah the son of Nathan *was* over the deputies; and Zabud the son of Nathan, a priest, *was* the king's confidant; 6 and Ahishar was over the household; and Adoniram the son of Abda *was* over the forced labor.

7 Solomon had twelve deputies over all Israel, who provided food for the king and his household; each *deputy* had to provide food for a month in the year. 8 And these *were* their names: Ben-hur, in the hill country of Ephraim; 9 Ben-deker in Makaz and Shaalbim, and Beth-shemesh, and Elonbeth-hanan; 10 Ben-hesed in Arubboth (Socoh *was* his and all the land of Hepher); 11 Ben-abinadab *in* all the hills of Dor (Taphath the daughter of Solomon was his wife); 12 Baana the son of Ahilud *in* Taanach and Megiddo, and all Beth-shean which is beside Zarethan below Jezreel, from Beth-shean to Abel-meholah as far as the other side of Jokmeam; 13 Ben-geber in Ramoth-gilead (the villages of Jair, the son of Manasseh, which are in Gilead were his: the region of Argob, which is in Bashan, sixty great cities with walls and bronze bars *were* his); 14 Ahinadab the son of Iddo *in* Mahanaim; 15 Ahimaaz in Naphtali (he also married Basemath the daughter of Solomon); 16 Baana the son of Hushai in Asher and Bealoth; 17 Jehoshaphat the son of Paruah in Issachar; 18 Shimei the son of Ela in Benjamin; 19 Geber the son of Uri in the land of Gilead, the country of Sihon king of the Amorites and of Og king of Bashan; and *he was* the only deputy who *was* in the land.

Solomon's Power, Wealth, and Wisdom

20 Judah and Israel *were* as numerous as the sand that is on the seashore in abundance; *they* were eating, drinking, and rejoicing.

3:7 ¹ I.e., conduct daily business

21 Now Solomon was ruling over all the kingdoms from the *Euphrates* River *to* the land of the Philistines and to the border of Egypt; *they* brought tribute and served Solomon all the days of his life.

22 Solomon's provision for one day was [1]thirty kors of fine flour and [2]sixty kors of meal, 23 ten fat oxen, twenty pasture-fed oxen, and a hundred sheep, besides deer, gazelles, roebucks, and fattened geese. 24 For he was ruling over everything west of the *Euphrates* River, from Tiphsah even to Gaza, over all the kings west of the River; and he had peace on all sides surrounding him. 25 So Judah and Israel lived securely, everyone under his vine and his fig tree, from Dan even to Beersheba, all the days of Solomon. 26 Solomon had forty thousand stalls of horses for his chariots, and twelve thousand horsemen. 27 And those deputies provided food for King Solomon and all who came to King Solomon's table, each in his month; they allowed nothing to be lacking. 28 They also brought barley and straw for the *war* horses and baggage horses to the place where it was *required,* each *deputy* according to his duty.

29 Now God gave Solomon wisdom and very great discernment and breadth of mind, like the sand that is on the seashore. 30 Solomon's wisdom surpassed the wisdom of all the people of the east and all the wisdom of Egypt. 31 For he was wiser than all *other* people, *more* than Ethan the Ezrahite, Heman, Calcol, and Darda, the sons of Mahol; and his fame was *known* in all the surrounding nations. 32 He also told three thousand proverbs, and his songs *numbered* 1,005. 33 He told of trees, from the cedar that is in Lebanon even to the hyssop that grows on the wall; he told also of animals, birds, crawling things, and fish. 34 *People* came from all the nations to hear the wisdom of Solomon, from all the kings of the earth who had heard of his wisdom.

Alliance with King Hiram

5 Now Hiram king of Tyre sent his servants to Solomon when he heard that they had anointed him king in place of his father, for Hiram had always been a friend of David. 2 Then Solomon sent *word* to Hiram, saying, 3 "You know that David my father was unable to build a house for the name of the LORD his God because of the wars which surrounded him, until the LORD put them under the soles of his feet. 4 But now the LORD my God has secured me rest on every side; there is neither adversary nor misfortune. 5 So behold, I intend to build a house for the name of the LORD my God, just as the LORD spoke to David my father, saying, 'Your son, whom I will put on your throne in your place, he will build the house for My name.' 6 Now then, issue orders that they cut cedars from Lebanon for me, and my servants will be with your servants; and I will give you wages for your servants in accordance with all that you say, for you yourself know that

there is no one among us who knows how to cut timber like the Sidonians."

7 When Hiram heard the words of Solomon, he greatly rejoiced; and he said, "Blessed be the LORD today, who has given to David a wise son over this great people." 8 So Hiram sent *word* to Solomon, saying, "I have heard *the message* which you sent me; I will do everything you wish concerning the cedar and juniper timber. 9 My servants will bring *the* timbers down from Lebanon to the sea; and I will have them made into rafts *to go* by sea to the place where you direct me, and I will have them broken up there, and you will carry *them* away. Then you shall do what I wish, by giving food to my household." 10 So Hiram gave Solomon all that he wished of the cedar and juniper timber. 11 Solomon then gave Hiram [1]twenty thousand kors of wheat as food for his household, and [2]twenty kors of pure oil; this is what Solomon would give Hiram year by year. 12 And the LORD gave wisdom to Solomon, just as He promised him; and there was peace between Hiram and Solomon, and the two of them made a covenant.

Conscription of Laborers

13 Now King Solomon conscripted forced laborers from all Israel; and the forced laborers *numbered* thirty thousand men. 14 Then he sent them to Lebanon, ten thousand a month in shifts; they were in Lebanon for a month, *and* two months at home. And Adoniram *was* in charge of the forced laborers. 15 Now Solomon had seventy thousand porters, and eighty thousand stonemasons in the mountains, 16 besides Solomon's 3,300 chief deputies who *were* in charge of the project *and* ruled over the people who were doing the work. 17 Then the king issued orders, and they quarried large stones, valuable stones, to lay the foundation of the house with cut stones. 18 So Solomon's builders and Hiram's builders and the Gebalites cut *the stones,* and they prepared the timbers and the stones to build the house.

The Building of the Temple

6 Now it came about in the four hundred and eightieth year after the sons of Israel came out of the land of Egypt, in the fourth year of Solomon's reign over Israel, in the month of Ziv, that is, the second month, that he began to build the house of the LORD. 2 And the house which King Solomon built for the LORD *was* [1]sixty cubits *in* its length, and twenty *cubits in* its width, and its height *was* thirty cubits. 3 The porch in front of the main room of the house *was* [1]twenty cubits in length, corresponding to the width of the house, *and* its width along the front of the house *was* ten cubits. 4 Also for the house he made windows with *artistic* frames. 5 Against the wall of the house he built stories encompassing the walls of the house around both the main room and the inner sanctuary; so he made side chambers all around. 6 The

---

4:22 [1]About 231 cubic feet or 6.5 cubic meters   [2]About 462 cubic feet or 13 cubic meters   5:11 [1]About 154,000 cubic feet or 4,360 cubic meters   [2]About 154 cubic feet or 4.4 cubic meters   6:2 [1]About 90 ft. long, 30 ft. wide, and 45 ft. high or 27 m, 9 m, and 14 m   6:3 [1]About 30 ft. long and 15 ft. deep or 9 m and 4.6 m

lowest story *was* [1]five cubits wide, the middle *was* six cubits wide, and the third *was* seven cubits wide; for on the outside he made offsets *in the wall* of the house all around so that *the beams* would not be inserted into the walls of the house.

7 The house, while it was being built, was built of stone finished at the quarry, and neither hammer, nor axe, nor any iron tool was heard in the house while it was being built.

8 The doorway for the [1]lowest side chamber *was* on the right side of the house; and they would go up by a winding staircase to the middle *story*, and from the middle to the third. 9 So he built the house and finished it; and he covered the house with beams and planks of cedar. 10 He also built the stories against the whole house, *each* [1]five cubits high; and they were attached to the house with timbers of cedar.

11 Now the word of the LORD came to Solomon, saying, 12 "*As for* this house which you are building, if you will walk in My statutes and execute My ordinances and keep all My commandments by walking in them, then I will fulfill My word with you which I spoke to David your father. 13 And I will dwell among the sons of Israel, and will not abandon My people Israel."

14 So Solomon built the house and finished it. 15 He built the walls of the house on the inside with boards of cedar; from the floor of the house to the ceiling he paneled *the walls* on the inside with wood, and he paneled the floor of the house with boards of juniper. 16 He also built [1]twenty cubits on the rear part of the house with boards of cedar from the floor to the ceiling; he built *them* for it on the inside as an inner sanctuary, as the Most Holy Place. 17 The house, that is, the main room in front of *the inner sanctuary*, was [1]forty cubits *long*. 18 There was cedar inside the house, carved *in the shape* of gourds and open flowers; everything was cedar, there was no stone visible. 19 Then he prepared an inner sanctuary inside the house in order to place there the ark of the covenant of the LORD. 20 The inner sanctuary *was* twenty cubits in length, twenty cubits in width, and twenty cubits in height; and he overlaid it with pure gold. He also paneled the altar with cedar. 21 So Solomon overlaid the inside of the house with pure gold. And he extended chains of gold across the front of the inner sanctuary, and he overlaid it with gold. 22 He overlaid the entire house with gold, until all the house was finished. Also the entire altar which was by the inner sanctuary he overlaid with gold.

23 And in the inner sanctuary he made two [1]cherubim of olive wood, each ten cubits high. 24 The one wing of the *first* cherub *was* five cubits, and the other wing of the *first* cherub *was* five cubits; from the end of one wing to the end of the other wing *were* ten cubits. 25 The second cherub *was* ten cubits; both of the cherubim were of the same measurement and the same form. 26 The height of the one cherub *was* ten cubits, and so *was that of* the other cherub. 27 He placed the cherubim in the midst of the inner house, and the wings of the one was touching the *one* wall, and the wing of the other cherub was touching the other wall. And their wings were touching end to end in the center of the house. 28 He also overlaid cherubim with gold.

29 Then he carved all the surrounding walls of the house with engravings of cherubim, palm trees, and open flowers, for the inner and outer *sanctuaries*. 30 And he overlaid the floor of the house with gold, for the inner and outer *sanctuaries*.

31 And for the entrance of the inner sanctuary he made doors of olive wood, the lintel, *and* five-sided doorposts. 32 So *he made* two doors of olive wood, and he carved on them carvings of cherubim, palm trees, and open flowers, and overlaid them with gold; and he overlaid the cherubim and the palm trees with gold.

33 So too he made for the entrance of the main room four-sided doorposts of olive wood, 34 and two doors of juniper wood; the two leaves of the one door turned on pivots, and the two leaves of the other door turned on pivots. 35 He carved *on it* cherubim, palm trees, and open flowers; and he overlaid *them* with gold plated on the carved work. 36 And he built the inner courtyard with three rows of cut stone and a row of cedar beams.

37 In the fourth year the foundation of the house of the LORD was laid, in the month of Ziv. 38 And in the eleventh year, in the month of Bul, that is, the eighth month, the house was finished in all its parts and in accordance with all its plans. So he was seven years in building it.

Solomon's Palace

7 Now Solomon built his own house *over the course of* thirteen years, and he finished all of his house. 2 He built the house of the timber from Lebanon; its length was [1]a hundred cubits, its width fifty cubits, and its height thirty cubits, on four rows of cedar pillars with cedar beams on the pillars. 3 And it was paneled with cedar above the side chambers which were on the forty-five pillars, fifteen *in each* row. 4 *There were artistic window* frames *in* three rows, and window was opposite window at three intervals. 5 And all the doorways and doorposts *had* squared *artistic* frames, and window was opposite window at three intervals.

6 Then he made the hall of pillars; its length was [1]fifty cubits and its width thirty cubits, and a porch *was* in front of them and pillars and a threshold in front of them.

7 And he made the hall of the throne where he was to judge, the hall of judgment, and it was paneled with cedar from floor to floor. 8 And his house where he was to live, the

other courtyard inward from the hall, was of this *same* workmanship. He also made a house like this hall for Pharaoh's daughter, whom Solomon had married.

9 All of these were *made* of valuable stones, of stone cut according to measure, sawed with saws, inside and outside; even from the foundation to the *[1]*coping, and from the outside to the large courtyard.

10 And the foundation was of valuable stones, large stones, stones of *[1]*ten cubits and stones of eight cubits. 11 And above were valuable stones, cut according to measure, and cedar. 12 So the large courtyard all around *had* three rows of cut stone and a row of cedar beams as well as the inner courtyard of the house of the LORD, and the porch of the house.

Hiram's Work in the Temple

13 Now King Solomon sent *word* and had Hiram brought from Tyre. 14 He was a widow's son from the tribe of Naphtali, and his father was a man of Tyre, an artisan in bronze; and he was filled with wisdom, skill, and knowledge for doing any work in bronze. So he came to King Solomon and performed all his work.

15 He fashioned the two pillars of bronze; *[1]*eighteen cubits was the height of each pillar, and a line of *[2]*twelve cubits measured the circumference of both. 16 He also made two capitals of cast bronze to put on the tops of the pillars; the height of the one capital was *[1]*five cubits and the height of the other capital was five cubits. 17 *There were* lattices of latticework and wreaths of chainwork for the capitals which were on the top of the pillars; seven for the one capital and seven for the other capital. 18 So he made the pillars, and two rows around on the one lattice to cover the capitals which were on the top of the pomegranates; and so he did for the other capital. 19 The capitals which *were* on the tops of the pillars in the porch were of lily design, four cubits. 20 So *there were* capitals on the two pillars, also above *and* close to the rounded projection which was beside the lattice; and the pomegranates *totaled* two hundred in rows around both capitals. 21 And he set up the pillars at the porch of the main room: he set up the right pillar and named it *[1]*Jachin, and he set up the left pillar and named it *[2]*Boaz. 22 On the top of the pillars was *the* lily design. So the work of the pillars was finished.

23 He also he made the *[1]*Sea of cast *metal* *[2]*ten cubits from brim to brim, circular *in* shape, and its height was five cubits, and it was *[3]*thirty cubits in circumference. 24 Under its brim gourds *went* around encircling it ten to a cubit, completely surrounding the Sea; the gourds were in two rows, cast with the rest. 25 It was standing on twelve oxen, three facing north, three facing west, three facing south, and three facing east; and the Sea *was set* on top of them, and all their rear parts *turned*

inward. 26 And it was a *[1]*hand width thick, and its brim was made like the brim of a cup, *like* a lily blossom; it could hold *[2]*two thousand baths.

27 Then he made the ten stands of bronze; the length of each stand was *[1]*four cubits, its width four cubits, and its height was three cubits. 28 This was the design of the stands: they had borders, that is, borders between the crossbars, 29 and on the borders which were between the crossbars *were* lions, oxen, and cherubim; and on the crossbars there *was* a pedestal above, and beneath the lions and oxen *were* wreaths of hanging work. 30 Now each stand had four bronze wheels with bronze axles, and its four feet had supports; beneath the basin *were* cast supports with wreaths at each side. 31 And its opening inside the crown at the top *was* a *[1]*cubit, and its opening *was* round *like* the design of a pedestal, a cubit and a half; and on its opening also *there were* engravings, and their borders were square, not round. 32 The four wheels *were* underneath the borders, and the axles of the wheels *were* on the stand. And the height of a wheel *was* a cubit and a half. 33 The workmanship of the wheels *was* like the workmanship of a chariot wheel. Their axles, their rims, their spokes, and their hubs *were* all cast. 34 Now *there were* four supports at the four corners of each stand; its supports *were* part of the stand itself. 35 And on the top of the stand *there was* a circular *form* half a cubit high, and on the top of the stand its stays and its borders *were* part of it. 36 And he engraved on the plates of its stays and on its borders cherubim, lions, and palm trees, as *there was* clear space on each, with wreaths *all* around. 37 He made the ten stands like this: all of them had the same casting, same measure, *and* same form.

38 And he made ten basins of bronze, each holding *[1]*forty baths; each basin *was* *[2]*four cubits, *and* on each of the ten stands *was* one basin. 39 Then he placed the stands, five on the right side of the house and five on the left side of the house; and he set the *[1]*Sea *of cast metal* on the right side of the house eastward toward the south.

40 Now Hiram made the basins and the shovels and the bowls. So Hiram finished doing all the work which he performed for King Solomon *in* the house of the LORD: 41 the two pillars and the *two* bowls of the capitals which *were* on the top of the two pillars, and the two lattices to cover the two bowls of the capitals which *were* on the top of the pillars; 42 and the four hundred pomegranates for the two lattices, two rows of pomegranates for each lattice to cover the two bowls of the capitals which *were* on the tops of the pillars; 43 and the ten stands with the ten basins on the stands; 44 and the one *[1]*Sea and the twelve oxen under the Sea; 45 and the buckets, the shovels, and the bowls; indeed, all these utensils which Hiram made for King Solomon *in* the house of

---

7:9 1 I.e., top sloping course of stone   7:10 1 About 15 and 12 ft. or 4.5 and 3.7 m   7:15 1 About 27 ft. or 8 m   2 About 18 ft. or 5.5 m   7:16 1 About 7.5 ft. or 2.3 m   7:21 1 I.e., he shall establish   2 I.e., in it is strength   7:23 1 I.e., large basin   2 About 15 ft. in diameter and 7.5 ft. high or 4.6 m and 2.3 m high   3 About 45 ft. or 14 m   7:26 1 About 3 in. or 7.6 cm   2 About 12,000 gallons or 45,424 liters   7:27 1 About 6 ft. long and wide and 4.5 ft. high or 1.8 m and 1.4 m   7:31 1 About 18 in. or 45 cm   7:38 1 About 240 gallons or 908 liters   2 About 6 ft. or 1.8 m   7:39 1 I.e., large basin   7:44 1 I.e., large basin

the LORD were of polished bronze. 46 The king had them cast in the plain of the Jordan, in the clay ground between Succoth and Zarethan. 47 However, Solomon left all the utensils unweighed, because they were too many; the weight of the bronze could not be determined. 48 Solomon also made all the furniture that was in the house of the LORD: the golden altar and the golden table on which was set the bread of the Presence; 49 and the lampstands of pure gold, five on the right side and five on the left, in front of the inner sanctuary; and the flowers, the lamps, and the tongs, of gold; 50 also the cups, the shears, the bowls, the ladles, and the firepans, of pure gold; and the hinges both for the doors of the inner house, the Most Holy Place, and for the doors of the house, that is, for the main room, of gold.

51 So all the work that King Solomon performed in the house of the LORD was finished. And Solomon brought in the offerings vowed by his father David, the silver and the gold and the utensils, and he put them in the treasuries of the house of the LORD.

The Ark Brought into the Temple

8 Then Solomon assembled the elders of Israel and all the heads of the tribes, the leaders of the fathers' households of the sons of Israel, to King Solomon in Jerusalem, to bring up the ark of the covenant of the LORD from the city of David, that is, Zion. 2 So all the men of Israel assembled themselves before King Solomon at the feast, in the month Ethanim, that is, the seventh month. 3 Then all the elders of Israel came, and the priests took up the ark. 4 And they brought up the ark of the LORD, the tent of meeting, and all the holy utensils which were in the tent; the priests and the Levites brought them up. 5 And King Solomon and all the congregation of Israel, who were gathered together to him, were with him before the ark, sacrificing so many sheep and oxen that they could not be counted or numbered. 6 Then the priests brought the ark of the covenant of the LORD to its place, into the inner sanctuary of the house, to the Most Holy Place, under the wings of the cherubim. 7 For the cherubim spread their wings over the place of the ark, and the cherubim made a covering over the ark and its carrying poles from above. 8 But the poles were so long that the ends of the poles could be seen from the holy place in front of the inner sanctuary, but they could not be seen outside; they are there to this day. 9 There was nothing in the ark except the two tablets of stone which Moses put there at Horeb, where the LORD made a covenant with the sons of Israel, when they came out of the land of Egypt. 10 And it happened that when the priests came from the holy place, the cloud filled the house of the LORD, 11 so that the priests could not stand to minister because of the cloud, for the glory of the LORD filled the house of the LORD.

Solomon Addresses the People

12 Then Solomon said,
"The LORD has said that He would dwell in the thick darkness.

13 "I have truly built You a lofty house,
A place for Your dwelling forever."

14 Then the king turned around and blessed all the assembly of Israel, while all the assembly of Israel was standing. 15 He said, "Blessed be the LORD, the God of Israel, who spoke with His mouth to my father David, and fulfilled it with His hands, saying, 16 'Since the day that I brought My people Israel from Egypt, I did not choose a city out of all the tribes of Israel in which to build a house so that My name would be there, but I chose David to be over My people Israel.' 17 Now it was in the heart of my father David to build a house for the name of the LORD, the God of Israel. 18 But the LORD said to my father David, 'Because it was in your heart to build a house for My name, you did well that it was in your heart. 19 Nevertheless you shall not build the house, but your son who will be born to you, he will build the house for My name.' 20 Now the LORD has fulfilled His word which He spoke; for I have risen in place of my father David and I sit on the throne of Israel, just as the LORD promised, and I have built the house for the name of the LORD, the God of Israel. 21 And there I have set a place for the ark, in which is the covenant of the LORD, which He made with our fathers when He brought them out of the land of Egypt."

The Prayer of Dedication

22 Then Solomon stood before the altar of the LORD in the presence of all the assembly of Israel, and he spread out his hands toward heaven. 23 And he said, "LORD, God of Israel, there is no God like You in heaven above or on earth beneath, keeping the covenant and showing faithfulness to Your servants who walk before You with all their heart, 24 You who have kept with Your servant, my father David, that which You promised him; You have spoken with Your mouth and have fulfilled it with Your hand, as it is this day. 25 Now then, LORD, God of Israel, keep with Your servant David my father that which You have promised him, saying, 'You shall not be deprived of a man to sit on the throne of Israel, if only your sons are careful about their way, to walk before Me as you have walked.' 26 Now then, God of Israel, let Your words, please, be confirmed, which You have spoken to Your servant, my father David.

27 "But will God indeed dwell on the earth? Behold, heaven and the highest heaven cannot contain You, how much less this house which I have built! 28 Nevertheless, turn Your attention to the prayer of Your servant and to his plea, LORD, my God, to listen to the cry and to the prayer which Your servant prays before You today, 29 so that Your eyes may be open toward this house night and day, toward the place of which You have said, 'My name shall be there,' to listen to the prayer which Your servant will pray toward this place. 30 And listen to the plea of Your servant and of Your people Israel, when they pray toward this place; hear in heaven Your dwelling place; hear and forgive! 31 "If a person sins against his neighbor and is compelled to take an oath of innocence, and

he comes *and* takes an oath before Your altar in this house, 32 then hear in heaven and act and judge Your servants, condemning the wicked by bringing his way on his own head, and acquitting the righteous by giving him according to his righteousness.

33 "When Your people Israel are defeated before an enemy because they have sinned against You, if they turn to You again and confess Your name and pray and implore Your favor in this house, 34 then hear in heaven, and forgive the sin of Your people Israel, and bring them back to the land which You gave their fathers.

35 "When the heavens are shut up and there is no rain because they have sinned against You, and they pray toward this place and praise Your name, and turn from their sin when You afflict them, 36 then hear in heaven and forgive the sin of Your servants and Your people Israel; indeed, teach them the good way in which they are to walk. And provide rain on Your land, which You have given to Your people as an inheritance.

37 "If there is a famine in the land, if there is a plague, if there is blight *or* mildew, locust *or* grasshopper, if their enemy harasses them in the land of their cities, whatever plague, whatever sickness *there is,* 38 whatever prayer or plea is offered by any person *or* by all Your people Israel, each knowing the affliction of his own heart, and spreading his hands toward this house; 39 then hear in heaven, Your dwelling place, and forgive and act, and give to each in accordance with all his ways, whose heart You know—for You alone know the hearts of all mankind— 40 so that they will fear You all the days that they live on the land which You have given to our fathers.

41 "Also regarding the foreigner who is not of Your people Israel, when he comes from a far country on account of Your name 42 (for they will hear of Your great name and Your mighty hand, and of Your outstretched arm); when he comes and prays toward this house, 43 hear in heaven Your dwelling place, and act in accordance with all for which the foreigner calls to You, in order that all the peoples of the earth may know Your name, to fear You, as *do* Your people Israel, and that they may know that this house which I have built is called by Your name.

44 "When Your people go out to battle against their enemy, by whatever way You send them, and they pray to the LORD toward the city which You have chosen and the house which I have built for Your name, 45 then hear in heaven their prayer and their pleading, and maintain their cause.

46 "When they sin against You (for there is no person who does not sin) and You are angry with them and turn them over to an enemy, so that they take them away captive to the land of the enemy, distant or near; 47 if they take it to heart in the land where they have been taken captive, and repent and implore Your favor in the land of those who have taken them captive, saying, 'We have sinned and done wrong, we have acted wickedly'; 48 if they return to You with all their heart and with all their soul in the land of their enemies who have taken them captive, and pray to You toward their land which You have given to their fathers, the city which You have chosen, and the house which I have built for Your name; 49 then hear their prayer and their pleading in heaven, Your dwelling place, and maintain their cause, 50 and forgive Your people who have sinned against You and all their wrongdoings which they have committed against You, and make them *objects of* compassion before those who have taken them captive, so that they will have compassion on them 51 (for they are Your people and Your inheritance which You have brought out of Egypt, from the midst of the iron furnace), 52 so that Your eyes may be open to the pleading of Your servant and to the pleading of Your people Israel, to listen to them whenever they call to You. 53 For You have singled them out from all the peoples of the earth as Your inheritance, just as You spoke through Moses Your servant, when You brought our fathers out of Egypt, Lord GOD."

Solomon's Benediction

54 When Solomon had finished praying this entire prayer and plea to the LORD, he stood up from the altar of the LORD, from kneeling on his knees with his hands spread toward heaven. 55 And he stood and blessed all the assembly of Israel with a loud voice, saying:

56 "Blessed be the LORD, who has given rest to His people Israel in accordance with everything that He promised; not one word has failed of all His good promise, which He promised through Moses His servant. 57 May the LORD our God be with us, as He was with our fathers; may He not leave us nor forsake us, 58 so that He may guide our hearts toward Himself, to walk in all His ways and to keep His commandments, His statutes, and His ordinances, which He commanded our fathers. 59 And may these words of mine, with which I have implored the favor of the LORD, be near to the LORD our God day and night, so that He will maintain the cause of His servant and the cause of His people Israel, as each day requires, 60 so that all the peoples of the earth may know that the LORD is God; there is no one else. 61 Your hearts therefore shall be wholly devoted to the LORD our God, to walk in His statutes and to keep His commandments, as at this day."

Dedicatory Sacrifices

62 Then the king and all Israel with him offered sacrifice before the LORD. 63 And Solomon offered for the sacrifice of peace offerings, which he offered to the LORD, twenty-two thousand oxen and 120,000 sheep. So the king and all the sons of Israel dedicated the house of the LORD. 64 On the same day the king consecrated the middle of the courtyard that *was* in front of the house of the LORD, because there he offered the burnt offering, the grain offering, and the fat of the peace offerings; for the bronze altar that *was* before the LORD *was* too small to hold the burnt offering, the grain offering, and the fat of the peace offerings.

65 So Solomon held the *feast at that time, and all Israel with him, a great assembly from the entrance of Hamath to the brook of Egypt, before the Lord our God, for seven days and seven *more* days, *that is,* fourteen days. 66 On the eighth day he dismissed the people, and they blessed the king. Then they went to their tents joyful and with happy hearts for all the goodness that the Lord had shown to David His servant, and to Israel His people.

God's Promise and Warning

9 Now it came about when Solomon had finished building the house of the Lord and the king's house, and all that Solomon desired to do, 2 that the Lord appeared to Solomon a second time, as He had appeared to him at Gibeon. 3 And the Lord said to him, "I have heard your prayer and your plea which you have offered before Me; I have consecrated this house which you have built, by putting My name there forever, and My eyes and My heart will be there always. 4 As for you, if you walk before Me as your father David walked, in integrity of heart and honesty, acting in accordance with everything that I have commanded you, *and if* you keep My statutes and My ordinances, 5 then I will establish the throne of your kingdom over Israel forever, just as I promised to your father David, saying, 'You shall not be deprived of a man on the throne of Israel.'

6 "But if you or your sons indeed turn away from following Me, and do not keep My commandments and My statutes which I have placed before you, but you go and serve other gods and worship them, 7 then I will cut Israel off from the land which I have given them, and the house which I have consecrated for My name, I will expel from My sight. So Israel will become a saying and an object of derision among all peoples. 8 And this house will become a heap of ruins; everyone who passes by it will be appalled and hiss and say, 'Why has the Lord done such a thing to this land and this house?' 9 And they will say, 'Because they abandoned the Lord their God, who brought their fathers out of the land of Egypt, and they adopted other gods and worshiped and served them, for that reason the Lord has brought all this adversity on them.'"

Cities Given to Hiram

10 Now it came about at the end of twenty years in which Solomon had built the two houses, the house of the Lord and the king's house 11 (Hiram king of Tyre had supplied Solomon with cedar and juniper timber and gold, satisfying all his desire), that King Solomon then gave Hiram twenty cities in the land of Galilee. 12 So Hiram left Tyre to see the cities which Solomon had given him, and they did not please him. 13 And he said, "What are these cities which you have given me, my brother?" So they have been called the land of *Cabul to this day. 14 And Hiram sent to the king *120 talents of gold.

15 Now this is the account of the forced labor which King Solomon conscripted to build the house of the Lord, his own house, the *Millo, the wall of Jerusalem, Hazor, Megiddo, and Gezer. 16 For Pharaoh king of Egypt had gone up and overthrown Gezer and burned it with fire, and killed the Canaanites who lived in the city; and he had given it *as* a dowry to his daughter, Solomon's wife. 17 So Solomon rebuilt Gezer and the lower Beth-horon, 18 and Baalath and Tamar in the wilderness, in the land *of Judah,* 19 and all the storage cities which Solomon had, that is, the cities for his chariots and the cities for his horsemen, and everything that it pleased Solomon to build in Jerusalem, in Lebanon, and in all the land under his rule. 20 *As for* all the people who were left of the Amorites, the Hittites, the Perizzites, the Hivites, and the Jebusites, who were not of the sons of Israel, 21 their descendants who were left after them in the land, whom the sons of Israel were unable to completely eliminate, from them Solomon conscripted forced laborers, *as they are* to this day. 22 But Solomon did not make slaves of the sons of Israel; for they were men of war, his servants, his commanders, his charioteers, his chariot commanders, and his horsemen.

23 These *were* the chief officers who *were* in charge of Solomon's work, 550, who ruled over the people doing the work. 24 As soon as Pharaoh's daughter came up from the city of David to her house which *Solomon* had built for her, he then built the Millo.

25 Now three times a year Solomon offered burnt offerings and peace offerings on the altar which he had built for the Lord, burning incense with them *on the altar* which *was* before the Lord. So he finished the house.

26 King Solomon also built a fleet of ships in Ezion-geber, which is near Eloth on the shore of the Red Sea, in the land of Edom. 27 And Hiram sent his servants with the fleet, sailors who knew the sea, along with the servants of Solomon. 28 And they went to Ophir and received *420 talents of gold from there, and brought *it* to King Solomon.

The Queen of Sheba

10 Now when the queen of Sheba heard about the fame of Solomon *in relation* to the name of the Lord, she came to test him with riddles. 2 So she came to Jerusalem with a very large entourage, with camels carrying balsam oil and a very large *quantity of* gold and precious stones. When she came to Solomon, she spoke to him about everything that was in her heart. 3 And Solomon answered all her questions; nothing was concealed from the king which he did not explain to her. 4 When the queen of Sheba saw all the wisdom of Solomon, and the house that he had built, 5 and the food of his table, the seating of his servants, the service of his waiters and their attire, his cupbearers, and his burnt offerings which he offered at the house of the Lord, she was breathless. 6 Then she said to the king, "It was a true story that I heard in my own land

---

8:65 1 I.e., of Booths 9:13 1 I.e., like nothing 9:14 1 About 4.5 tons or 4 metric tons 9:15 1 I.e., terraced structure 9:28 1 About 16 tons or 14 metric tons

about your words and your wisdom. 7 But I did not believe the stories until I came and my *own* eyes saw *it all*. And behold, the half *of it* was not reported to me. You have exceeded *in* wisdom and prosperity the report which I heard. 8 Blessed are your men, *and* blessed are these servants of yours who stand before you continually *and* hear your wisdom! 9 Blessed be the LORD your God who delighted in you to put you on the throne of Israel; because the LORD loves Israel forever, He made you king, to do justice and righteousness." 10 Then she gave the king *1*120 talents of gold, and a very large *amount* of balsam oil and precious stones. Never again did such a large quantity of balsam oil come in as that which the queen of Sheba gave King Solomon.

11 And the ships of Hiram as well, which brought gold from Ophir, brought in from Ophir a very great *number of* almug trees and precious stones. 12 The king made from the almug trees supports for the house of the LORD and for the king's house, and lyres and harps for the singers; such almug trees have not come in *again,* nor have they been seen to this day.

13 And King Solomon granted the queen of Sheba everything she desired, whatever she requested, besides what he gave her in proportion to his royal bounty. Then she departed and went to her own land together with her servants.

Wealth, Splendor, and Wisdom

14 Now the weight of gold that came to Solomon in one year was *1*666 talents of gold, 15 besides *that* from the traders, and the wares of the merchants and all the kings of the Arabs and the governors of the country. 16 King Solomon made two hundred large shields of beaten gold, using six hundred *shekels of* gold on each large shield. 17 And *he made* three hundred *small* shields of beaten gold, using *1*three minas of gold on each shield; and the king put them in the house of the timber of Lebanon. 18 Moreover, the king made a large throne of ivory and overlaid it with fine gold. 19 *There were* six steps to the throne and a round top to the throne at its back, and armrests on each side of the seat, and two lions standing beside the armrests. 20 Twelve lions were standing there on the six steps on the one side and on the other; nothing like *it* was made for any other kingdom. 21 Now all King Solomon's drinking utensils *were* of gold, and all the utensils of the house of the timber of Lebanon *were* of pure gold. None was of silver; it was not considered *as* amounting to anything in the days of Solomon. 22 For the king had the ships of Tarshish at sea with Hiram's ships; once every three years the ships of Tarshish would come carrying gold and silver, ivory, monkeys, and peacocks.

23 So King Solomon became greater than all the kings of the earth in wealth and wisdom. 24 And all the earth was seeking the attention of Solomon, to hear his wisdom, which God had put in his heart. 25 And they were bringing, everyone, a gift: articles of silver and gold, garments, weapons, balsam oil, horses, and mules, so much year by year.

26 Now Solomon gathered chariots and horsemen; and he had 1,400 chariots and twelve thousand horsemen, and he stationed them in the chariot cities and with the king in Jerusalem. 27 And the king made silver *as common* as stones in Jerusalem, and he made cedars as plentiful as sycamore trees that are in the lowland. 28 Also Solomon's import of horses was from Egypt and Kue, *and* the king's merchants acquired *them* from Kue for a price. 29 A chariot was imported from Egypt for six hundred *shekels* of silver, and a horse for 150; and by the same means they exported them to all the kings of the Hittites and to the kings of the Arameans.

Solomon Turns from God

11 Now King Solomon loved many foreign women along with the daughter of Pharaoh: Moabite, Ammonite, Edomite, Sidonian, *and* Hittite women, 2 from the nations of which the LORD had said to the sons of Israel, "You shall not associate with them, nor shall they associate with you; they will certainly turn your heart away to follow their gods." Solomon clung to these in love. 3 He had seven hundred wives, *who were* princesses, and three hundred concubines; and his wives turned his heart away. 4 For when Solomon was old, his wives turned his heart away to follow other gods; and his heart was not wholly devoted to the LORD his God, as the heart of his father David *had been.* 5 For Solomon became a follower of Ashtoreth the goddess of the Sidonians, and of Milcom the abhorrent idol of the Ammonites. 6 So Solomon did what was evil in the sight of the LORD, and did not follow the LORD fully, as his father David *had done.* 7 Then Solomon built a high place for Chemosh, the abhorrent idol of Moab, on the mountain that is east of Jerusalem, and for Molech, the abhorrent idol of the sons of Ammon. 8 He also did the same for all his foreign wives, who burned incense and sacrificed to their gods.

9 Now the LORD was angry with Solomon because his heart had turned away from the LORD, the God of Israel, who had appeared to him twice, 10 and had commanded him regarding this thing, that he was not to follow other gods; but he did not comply with what the LORD had commanded. 11 So the LORD said to Solomon, "Since you have done this, and you have not kept My covenant and My statutes, which I have commanded you, I will certainly tear the kingdom away from you, and will give it to your servant. 12 However, I will not do it in your days, *only* for the sake of your father David; *but* I will tear it away from the hand of your son. 13 Yet I will not tear away all the kingdom, *but* I will give one tribe to your son for the sake of My servant David, and for the sake of Jerusalem, which I have chosen."

10:10 1 About 4.5 tons or 4 metric tons   10:14 1 About 25 tons or 23 metric tons
10:17 1 About 3.8 lb. or 1.7 kg

God Raises Adversaries

14 Then the LORD raised up an adversary against Solomon, Hadad the Edomite; he was of the royal line in Edom. 15 For it came about, when David was in Edom and Joab the commander of the army had gone up to bury those killed *in battle,* and had struck and killed every male in Edom 16 (for Joab and all Israel stayed there for six months, until he had eliminated every male in Edom), 17 that Hadad fled to Egypt, he and certain Edomites of his father's servants with him, while Hadad *was* a young boy. 18 They set out from Midian and came to Paran; and they took men with them from Paran and came to Egypt, to Pharaoh king of Egypt, who gave him a house and assigned him food and gave him land. 19 Now Hadad found great favor in the sight of Pharaoh, so that he gave him in marriage the sister of his own wife, the sister of Tahpenes the queen. 20 And the sister of Tahpenes gave birth to his son Genubath, whom Tahpenes weaned in Pharaoh's house; and Genubath was in Pharaoh's house among the sons of Pharaoh. 21 But when Hadad heard in Egypt that David ¹lay down with his fathers and that Joab the commander of the army was dead, Hadad said to Pharaoh, "Let me go, so that I may go to my own country." 22 However, Pharaoh said to him, "But what have you lacked with me that you are here, requesting to go to your own country?" And he answered, "Nothing; nevertheless you must let me go."

23 God also raised up *another* adversary against him, Rezon the son of Eliada, who had fled from his master Hadadezer, king of Zobah. 24 And he gathered men to himself and became leader of a marauding band, after David killed those *of Zobah;* and they went to Damascus and stayed there, and reigned in Damascus. 25 So he was an adversary to Israel all the days of Solomon, along with the harm that Hadad *inflicted;* and he felt disgust for Israel and reigned over Aram.

26 Then Jeroboam the son of Nebat, an Ephraimite of Zeredah, Solomon's servant, whose mother's name was Zeruah, a widow, also rebelled against the king. 27 Now this was the reason why he rebelled against the king: Solomon built the ¹Millo, and closed up the breach of the city of his father David. 28 Now the man Jeroboam was a valiant warrior, and when Solomon saw that the young man was industrious, he appointed him over all the forced labor of the house of Joseph. 29 And it came about at that time, when Jeroboam went out of Jerusalem, that the prophet Ahijah the Shilonite found him on the road. Now Ahijah had clothed himself with a new cloak; and both of them were alone in the field. 30 Then Ahijah took hold of the new cloak which was on him and tore it into twelve pieces. 31 And he said to Jeroboam, "Take for yourself ten pieces; for this is what the LORD, the God of Israel says: 'Behold, I am going to tear the kingdom away from the hand of Solomon and give you ten tribes 32 (but he shall have one tribe, for the sake of My servant David and for the sake of Jerusalem, the city which I have chosen from all the tribes of Israel), 33 because they have abandoned Me, and have worshiped Ashtoreth the goddess of the Sidonians, Chemosh the god of Moab, and Milcom the god of the sons of Ammon; and they have not walked in My ways, doing what is right in My sight and *keeping* My statutes and My ordinances, as his father David *did.* 34 Nevertheless I will not take the whole kingdom out of his hand, but I will make him ruler all the days of his life, for the sake of My servant David whom I chose, who kept My commandments and My statutes; 35 but I will take the kingdom from his son's hand and give it to you; *that is,* ten tribes. 36 But to his son I will give one tribe, so that My servant David may always have a lamp before Me in Jerusalem, the city where I have chosen for Myself to put My name. 37 However I will take you, and you shall reign over all that you desire, and you shall be king over Israel. 38 Then it shall be, that if you listen to all that I command you and walk in My ways, and do what is right in My sight by keeping My statutes and My commandments, as My servant David did, then I will be with you and build you an enduring house as I built for David, and I will give Israel to you. 39 So I will oppress the descendants of David for this, but not always.' " 40 Solomon sought therefore to put Jeroboam to death; but Jeroboam set out and fled to Egypt to Shishak king of Egypt, and he was in Egypt until the death of Solomon.

The Death of Solomon

41 Now the rest of the acts of Solomon and whatever he did, and his wisdom, are they not written in the Book of the Acts of Solomon? 42 So the time that Solomon reigned in Jerusalem over all Israel was forty years. 43 Then Solomon ¹lay down with his fathers and was buried in the city of his father David, and his son Rehoboam reigned in his place.

King Rehoboam Acts Foolishly

12 Then Rehoboam went to Shechem, because all Israel had come to Shechem to make him king. 2 Now when Jeroboam the son of Nebat heard *about this,* he was living in Egypt (for he was still in Egypt, where he had fled from the presence of King Solomon). 3 Then they sent *word* and summoned him, and Jeroboam and all the assembly of Israel came and spoke to Rehoboam, saying, 4 "Your father made our yoke hard; but now, lighten the hard labor *imposed by* your father and his heavy yoke which he put on us, and we will serve you." 5 Then he said to them, "Depart for three days, then return to me." So the people departed.

6 And King Rehoboam consulted with the elders who had served his father Solomon while he was still alive, saying, "How do you advise *me* to answer this people?" 7 Then they spoke to him, saying, "If you will be a servant to this people today, and will serve them and grant them their request, and speak pleasant words to them, then they will be your servants always." 8 But he ignored the advice of the elders which they had given him, and consulted

with the young men who had grown up with him and served him. 9 He said to them, "What advice do you give, so that we may answer this people who have spoken to me, saying, 'Lighten the yoke which your father put on us'?" 10 And the young men who had grown up with him spoke to him, saying, "This is what you should say to this people who spoke to you, saying: 'Your father made our yoke heavy, now you make it lighter for us!' You should speak this way to them: 'My little finger is thicker than my father's waist! 11 Now then, my father loaded you with a heavy yoke; yet I will add to your yoke. My father disciplined you with whips, but I will discipline you with scorpions!' "

12 Then Jeroboam and all the people came to Rehoboam on the third day, just as the king had directed, saying, "Return to me on the third day." 13 And the king answered the people harshly, for he ignored the advice of the elders which they had given him, 14 and he spoke to them according to the advice of the young men, saying, "My father made your yoke heavy, but I will add to your yoke; my father disciplined you with whips, but I will discipline you with scorpions!" 15 So the king did not listen to the people; because it was a turn of events from the Lord, in order to establish His word which the Lord spoke through Ahijah the Shilonite to Jeroboam the son of Nebat.

The Kingdom Divided; Jeroboam Rules Israel

16 When all Israel saw that the king had not listened to them, the people replied to the king, saying,

"What share do we have in David?
We have no inheritance in the son of Jesse;
To your tents, Israel!
Now look after your own house, David!"

So Israel went away to their tents. 17 But as for the sons of Israel who lived in the cities of Judah, Rehoboam reigned over them. 18 Then King Rehoboam sent Adoram, who was in charge of the forced labor, and all Israel stoned him to death. And King Rehoboam hurried to mount his chariot to flee to Jerusalem. 19 So Israel has broken with the house of David to this day.

20 And it came about, when all Israel heard that Jeroboam had returned, that they sent word and called him to the assembly, and made him king over all Israel. None except the tribe of Judah alone followed the house of David.

21 Now when Rehoboam had come to Jerusalem, he assembled all the house of Judah and the tribe of Benjamin, 180,000 chosen warriors, to fight against the house of Israel to restore the kingdom to Rehoboam the son of Solomon. 22 But the word of God came to Shemaiah the man of God, saying, 23 "Tell Rehoboam the son of Solomon, king of Judah, and all the house of Judah and Benjamin, and the rest of the people, saying, 24 'This is what the Lord says: "You shall not go up nor fight against your relatives the sons of Israel; return, every man to his house, for this thing has come from Me." ' " So they listened to the word of

the Lord, and returned to go their way in accordance with the word of the Lord.

Jeroboam's Idolatry

25 Then Jeroboam built Shechem in the hill country of Ephraim, and lived there. And he went out from there and built Penuel. 26 And Jeroboam said in his heart, "Now the kingdom will return to the house of David. 27 If this people go up to offer sacrifices in the house of the Lord in Jerusalem, then the heart of this people will return to their lord, to Rehoboam king of Judah; and they will kill me and return to Rehoboam king of Judah." 28 So the king consulted, and he made two golden calves; and he said to the people, "It is too much for you to go up to Jerusalem; behold your gods, Israel, that brought you up from the land of Egypt." 29 And he set up one in Bethel, and the other he put in Dan. 30 Now this thing became a sin, for the people went to worship before the one as far as Dan. 31 And he made houses on high places, and appointed priests from all the people who were not of the sons of Levi. 32 Jeroboam also instituted a feast in the eighth month on the fifteenth day of the month, like the feast that is in Judah, and he went up to the altar. So he did in Bethel, sacrificing to the calves which he had made. And he stationed in Bethel the priests of the high places which he had made. 33 Then he went up to the altar which he had made in Bethel on the fifteenth day in the eighth month, the month that he had devised in his own heart; and he instituted a feast for the sons of Israel and went up to the altar to burn incense.

Jeroboam Warned, Stricken

13 Now behold, a man of God came from Judah to Bethel by the word of the Lord, while Jeroboam was standing at the altar to burn incense. 2 And he cried out against the altar by the word of the Lord and said, "Altar, altar, this is what the Lord says: 'Behold, a son shall be born to the house of David, Josiah by name; and on you he shall sacrifice the priests of the high places who burn incense on you, and human bones shall burn on you.' " 3 Then he gave a sign on the same day, saying, "This is the sign which the Lord has spoken: 'Behold, the altar shall be torn to pieces and the ashes which are on it shall be poured out.' " 4 Now when the king heard the statement of the man of God which he cried out against the altar in Bethel, Jeroboam stretched out his hand from the altar, saying, "Seize him!" But his hand which he had stretched out toward him dried up, and he could not draw it back to himself. 5 The altar also was torn to pieces and the ashes were poured out from the altar, in accordance with the sign which the man of God had given by the word of the Lord. 6 And the king responded and said to the man of God, "Please appease the Lord your God and pray for me, so that my hand may be restored to me." So the man of God appeased the Lord, and the king's hand was restored to him, and it became as it was before. 7 Then the king said to the man of God, "Come home with me and refresh yourself, and I will give you a gift." 8 But the

man of God said to the king, "If you were to give me half your house, I would not go with you, nor would I eat bread or drink water in this place. 9 For so it was commanded me by the word of the LORD, saying, 'You shall not eat bread nor drink water, nor return by the way that you came.' " 10 So he went another way and did not return by the way that he had come to Bethel.

The Disobedient Prophet

11 Now an old prophet was living in Bethel; and his sons came and told him all the deeds which the man of God had done that day in Bethel; the words which he had spoken to the king, these also they reported to their father. 12 And their father said to them, "Which way did he go?" Now his sons had seen the way that the man of God who came from Judah had gone. 13 Then he said to his sons, "Saddle the donkey for me." So they saddled the donkey for him and he rode *away* on it. 14 So he went after the man of God and found him sitting under an oak; and he said to him, "Are you the man of God who came from Judah?" And he said, "I am." 15 Then he said to him, "Come home with me and eat bread." 16 But he said, "I cannot return with you, nor come in with you, nor will I eat bread or drink water with you in this place. 17 For a command *came* to me by the word of the LORD: 'You shall not eat bread, nor drink water there; do not return by going the way that you came.' " 18 Then he said to him, "I too am a prophet like you, and an angel spoke to me by the word of the LORD, saying, 'Bring him back with you to your house, so that he may eat bread and drink water.' " *But* he lied to him. 19 So he went back with him, and ate bread in his house and drank water.

20 Now it came about, as they were sitting down at the table, that the word of the LORD came to the prophet who had brought him back; 21 and he cried out to the man of God who came from Judah, saying, "This is what the LORD says: 'Because you have disobeyed the command of the LORD, and have not kept the commandment which the LORD your God commanded you, 22 but have returned and eaten bread and drunk water in the place of which He said to you, "You are not to eat bread nor drink water"; your dead body will not come to the grave of your fathers.' " 23 It came about after he had eaten bread and after he had drunk, that he saddled the donkey for him, for the prophet whom he had brought back. 24 Now when he had gone, a lion met him on the way and killed him, and his body was thrown on the road, with the donkey standing beside it; the lion also was standing beside the body. 25 And behold, men passed by and saw the body thrown on the road, and the lion standing beside the body; so they came and told *about it* in the city where the old prophet had lived. 26 Now when the prophet who had brought him back from the way heard *about it,* he said, "It is the man of God, who disobeyed the command of the LORD; therefore the LORD has given him to the lion, which has torn him and killed him, in accordance with the word of the

LORD which He spoke to him." 27 Then he spoke to his sons, saying, "Saddle the donkey for me." And they saddled *it.* 28 Then he went and found his body thrown on the road, with the donkey and the lion standing beside the body; the lion had not eaten the body nor harmed the donkey. 29 So the prophet picked up the body of the man of God and laid it on the donkey and brought it back; and he came to the city of the old prophet to mourn and to bury him. 30 He laid his body in his own grave, and they mourned over him, *saying,* "Oh, my brother!" 31 And after he had buried him, he talked to his sons, saying, "When I die, bury me in the grave in which the man of God is buried; lay my bones beside his bones. 32 For the thing will certainly come to pass which he cried out by the word of the LORD against the altar that is in Bethel, and against all the houses of the high places which are in the cities of Samaria."

33 After this event, Jeroboam did not abandon his evil way, but he again appointed priests of the high places from all the people; anyone who wanted, he ordained, and he became *one of the* priests of the high places. 34 This event also became a sin of the house of Jeroboam, even to wipe *it* out and eliminate *it* from the face of the earth.

Ahijah Prophesies against the King

14 At that time Abijah the son of Jeroboam became sick. 2 And Jeroboam said to his wife, "Now arise and disguise yourself so that they will not know that you are the wife of Jeroboam, and go to Shiloh. Behold, Ahijah the prophet is there, who said regarding me *that I would be* king over this people. 3 Take ten loaves with you, *some* pastries, and a jar of honey, and go to him. He will tell you what will happen to the boy."

4 And Jeroboam's wife did so, and set out and went to Shiloh, and came to the house of Ahijah. Now Ahijah could not see because his eyes were glossy from his old age. 5 Now the LORD had said to Ahijah, "Behold, the wife of Jeroboam is coming to inquire of you about her son, because he is sick. You shall say such and such to her, for it will be when she arrives, that she is going to make herself unrecognizable."

6 So when Ahijah heard the sound of her feet coming in the doorway, he said, "Come in, wife of Jeroboam; why do you make yourself unrecognizable? Nevertheless, I am sent to you *with* a harsh *message.* 7 Go, say to Jeroboam, 'This is what the LORD, the God of Israel says: "Because I exalted you from among the people and made you leader over My people Israel, 8 and tore the kingdom away from the house of David and gave it to you—yet you have not been like My servant David, who kept My commandments and followed Me with all his heart, to do only that which was right in My sight; 9 you also have done more evil than all who were before you, and you have gone and made for yourself other gods and cast metal images to provoke Me to anger, and have thrown Me behind your back— 10 therefore behold, I am bringing disaster on the house of

Jeroboam, and I will eliminate from Jeroboam every male person, both bond and free in Israel, and I will make a clean sweep of the house of Jeroboam, just as one sweeps away dung until it is all gone. [11] Anyone belonging to Jeroboam who dies in the city, the dogs will eat. And anyone who dies in the field, the birds of the sky will eat; for the LORD has spoken *it.*" ' [12] Now you, arise, go to your house. When your feet enter the city the child will die. [13] Then all Israel will mourn for him and bury him, for he alone of Jeroboam's *family* will come to the grave, because in him something good was found toward the LORD God of Israel in the house of Jeroboam. [14] Moreover, the LORD will raise up for Himself a king over Israel who will eliminate the house of Jeroboam this day and from now on.

[15] "For the LORD will strike Israel, just as a reed sways in the water; and He will uproot Israel from this good land which He gave to their fathers, and will scatter them beyond the *Euphrates* River, because they have made their [1]Asherim, provoking the LORD to anger. [16] He will give up Israel because of the sins of Jeroboam, which he committed and with which he misled Israel into sin."

[17] Then Jeroboam's wife arose and departed, and came to Tirzah. As she was entering the threshold of the house, the child died. [18] Then all Israel buried him and mourned for him, in accordance with the word of the LORD which He had spoken through His servant Ahijah the prophet.

[19] Now *as for* the rest of the acts of Jeroboam, how he made war and how he reigned, behold, they are written in the Book of the Chronicles of the Kings of Israel. [20] And the time that Jeroboam reigned *was* twenty-two years; and he [1]lay down with his fathers, and his son Nadab reigned in his place.

Rehoboam Misleads Judah

[21] Now Rehoboam the son of Solomon reigned in Judah. Rehoboam was forty-one years old when he became king, and he reigned for seventeen years in Jerusalem, the city which the LORD had chosen from all the tribes of Israel to put His name there. And his mother's name was Naamah the Ammonitess. [22] And *the people of* Judah did evil in the sight of the LORD, and they provoked Him to jealousy with their sins which they committed, more than all that their fathers had done. [23] For they, too, built for themselves high places, memorial stones, and [1]Asherim on every high hill and under every luxuriant tree. [24] There were also male cult prostitutes in the land. They committed all the same abominations of the nations which the LORD dispossessed before the sons of Israel.

[25] Now it happened in the fifth year of King Rehoboam, that Shishak the king of Egypt marched against Jerusalem. [26] And he took away the treasures of the house of the LORD and the treasures of the king's house, and he took everything; he even took all the shields of gold which Solomon had made. [27] So King Rehoboam made shields of bronze in their place, and entrusted them to the care of the commanders of the guard who guarded the doorway of the king's house. [28] And it happened as often as the king entered the house of the LORD, that the guards would carry them and would bring them back into the guards' room.

[29] Now *as for* the rest of the acts of Rehoboam and all that he did, are they not written in the Book of the Chronicles of the Kings of Judah? [30] And there was war between Rehoboam and Jeroboam continually. [31] And Rehoboam [1]lay down with his fathers and was buried with his fathers in the city of David; and his mother's name was Naamah the Ammonitess. And his son Abijam became king in his place.

Abijam Reigns over Judah

15 Now in the eighteenth year of King Jeroboam, the son of Nebat, Abijam became king over Judah. [2] He reigned for three years in Jerusalem; and his mother's name was Maacah the daughter of Abishalom. [3] He walked in all the sins of his father which he had committed before him; and his heart was not wholly devoted to the LORD his God, like the heart of his father David. [4] But for David's sake the LORD his God gave him a lamp in Jerusalem, to raise up his son after him and to establish Jerusalem, [5] because David did what was right in the sight of the LORD, and did not deviate from anything that He commanded him all the days of his life, except in the case of Uriah the Hittite. [6] And there was war between Rehoboam and Jeroboam all the days of his life.

[7] Now *as for* the rest of the acts of Abijam and all that he did, are they not written in the Book of the Chronicles of the Kings of Judah? And there was war between Abijam and Jeroboam.

Asa Succeeds Abijam

[8] And Abijam [1]lay down with his fathers, and they buried him in the city of David; and his son Asa became king in his place.

[9] So in the twentieth year of Jeroboam the king of Israel, Asa began to reign as king of Judah. [10] He reigned for forty-one years in Jerusalem; and his mother's name was Maacah the daughter of Abishalom. [11] Now Asa did what was right in the sight of the LORD, like his father David. [12] He also removed the male cult prostitutes from the land and removed all the idols which his fathers had made. [13] And even his mother Maacah, he also removed her from *the position of* queen mother, because she had made an abominable image [1]as an Asherah; and Asa cut down her abominable image and burned *it* at the brook Kidron. [14] But the high places were not eliminated; nevertheless Asa's heart was wholly devoted to the LORD all his days. [15] And he brought into the house of the LORD the holy gifts of his father and his own holy gifts: silver, gold, and *valuable* utensils.

14:15 [1]I.e., wooden symbols of a female deity (Asherah) **14:20** [1]I.e., died **14:23** [1]I.e., wooden symbols of a female deity (Asherah) **14:31** [1]I.e., died **15:8** [1]I.e., died **15:13** [1]Or *for Asherah;* i.e., wooden symbol of a female deity

16 Now there was war between Asa and Baasha king of Israel all their days. **17** Baasha king of Israel marched against Judah and fortified Ramah in order to prevent *anyone* from going out or coming in to Asa king of Judah. **18** Then Asa took all the silver and the gold that was left in the treasuries of the house of the LORD and the treasuries of the king's house, and handed it over to his servants. And King Asa sent them to Ben-hadad the son of Tabrimmon, the son of Hezion, king of Aram, who lived in Damascus, saying, **19** *"Let's make* a treaty between you and me, *as there was* between my father and your father. Behold, I have sent you a gift of silver and gold; go, break your treaty with Baasha king of Israel so that he will withdraw from me." **20** So Ben-hadad listened to King Asa and sent the commanders of his armies against the cities of Israel, and conquered Ijon, Dan, Abel-beth-maacah, and all Chinneroth, besides all the land of Naphtali. **21** When Baasha heard *about it,* he stopped fortifying Ramah and remained in Tirzah. **22** Then King Asa made a proclamation to all Judah—no one was exempt—and they carried away the stones of Ramah and its timber with which Baasha had built *fortifications.* And King Asa built with them Geba of Benjamin and Mizpah.

Jehoshaphat Succeeds Asa

23 Now *as for* the rest of all the acts of Asa and all his might, and all that he did and the cities which he built, are they not written in the Book of the Chronicles of the Kings of Judah? But in the time of his old age he was diseased in his feet. **24** And Asa *¹lay down with his fathers and was buried with his fathers in the city of his father David; and his son Jehoshaphat reigned in his place.

Nadab and Then Baasha Rule over Israel

25 Now Nadab the son of Jeroboam became king over Israel in the second year of Asa king of Judah, and he reigned over Israel for two years. **26** He did evil in the sight of the LORD, and walked in the way of his father and in his sin into which he misled Israel. **27** Then Baasha the son of Ahijah of the house of Issachar conspired against him, and Baasha struck and killed him at Gibbethon, which belonged to the Philistines, while Nadab and all Israel were laying siege to Gibbethon. **28** So Baasha killed him in the third year of Asa king of Judah, and reigned in his place. **29** And as soon as he was king, he struck and killed all the household of Jeroboam. He did not leave Jeroboam any persons alive, *but kept killing* until he had eliminated them, in accordance with the word of the LORD which He spoke by His servant Ahijah the Shilonite, **30** *and* because of the sins of Jeroboam which he committed, and into which he misled Israel, because of his provocation with which he provoked the LORD God of Israel to anger.

31 Now *as for* the rest of the acts of Nadab and all that he did, are they not written in the Book of the Chronicles of the Kings of Israel?

War with Judah

32 And there was war between Asa and Baasha king of Israel all their days.

33 In the third year of Asa king of Judah, Baasha the son of Ahijah became king over all Israel at Tirzah, *and he reigned* for twenty-four years. **34** And he did evil in the sight of the LORD, and walked in the way of Jeroboam and in his sin into which he misled Israel.

Prophecy against Baasha

16 Now the word of the LORD came to Jehu the son of Hanani against Baasha, saying, **2** "Since I exalted you from the dust and made you leader over My people Israel, and you have walked in the way of Jeroboam and have misled My people Israel into sin, provoking Me to anger with their sins, **3** behold, I am going to burn Baasha and his house, and I will make your house like the house of Jeroboam the son of Nebat. **4** Anyone belonging to Baasha who dies in the city, the dogs will eat; and anyone belonging to him who dies in the field, the birds of the sky will eat."

5 Now *as for* the rest of the acts of Baasha and what he did and his might, are they not written in the Book of the Chronicles of the Kings of Israel?

The Israelite Kings

6 And Baasha ²lay down with his fathers and was buried in Tirzah, and his son Elah became king in his place. **7** Moreover, the word of the LORD through the prophet Jehu the son of Hanani came against Baasha and his household, both because of all the evil that he did in the sight of the LORD, provoking Him to anger with the work of his hands, by being like the house of Jeroboam, and because he struck it.

8 In the twenty-sixth year of Asa king of Judah, Elah the son of Baasha became king over Israel at Tirzah, *and reigned* for two years. **9** And his servant Zimri, commander of half his chariots, conspired against him. Now Elah *was* in Tirzah drinking himself drunk in the house of Arza, who *was* in charge of the household in Tirzah. **10** Then Zimri came in and struck him and put him to death in the twenty-seventh year of Asa king of Judah, and he became king in his place. **11** And when he became king, as soon as he sat on his throne, he killed all the household of Baasha; he did not leave a single male alive, either of his relatives or of his friends.

12 So Zimri eliminated all the household of Baasha, in accordance with the word of the LORD which He spoke against Baasha through Jehu the prophet, **13** for all the sins of Baasha and the sins of his son Elah, which they committed and into which they misled Israel, provoking the LORD God of Israel to anger with their idols. **14** Now *as for* the rest of the acts of Elah and all that he did, are they not written in the Book of the Chronicles of the Kings of Israel?

15 In the twenty-seventh year of Asa king of Judah, Zimri reigned for seven days in Tirzah. Now the people were camped against Gibbethon, which belonged to the Philistines.

15:24 ¹I.e., died   **16:6** ¹I.e., died

16 And the people who were camped heard it being said, "Zimri has conspired and has also struck and killed the king!" Therefore all Israel made Omri, the commander of the army, king over Israel that day in the camp. 17 Then Omri and all Israel with him went up from Gibbethon and besieged Tirzah. 18 When Zimri saw that the city was taken, he went into the citadel of the king's house and burned the king's house over himself with fire, and died, 19 because of his sins which he committed, doing evil in the sight of the LORD, walking in the way of Jeroboam, and in his sin which he committed, misleading Israel into sin. 20 Now as for the rest of the acts of Zimri and his conspiracy which he carried out, are they not written in the Book of the Chronicles of the Kings of Israel?

21 Then the people of Israel were divided into two parts: half of the people followed Tibni the son of Ginath, to make him king; the other half followed Omri. 22 But the people who followed Omri prevailed over the people who followed Tibni the son of Ginath. And Tibni died and Omri became king. 23 In the thirty-first year of Asa king of Judah, Omri became king over Israel and reigned for twelve years; he reigned for six years at Tirzah. 24 And he purchased the hill Samaria from Shemer for 1two talents of silver; and he built on the hill, and named the city which he built Samaria, after the name of Shemer, the owner of the hill.

25 Now Omri did evil in the sight of the LORD, and acted more wickedly than all who were before him. 26 For he walked entirely in the way of Jeroboam the son of Nebat and in his sins into which he misled Israel, provoking the LORD God of Israel to anger with their idols. 27 Now as for the rest of the acts of Omri which he did and his might which he displayed, are they not written in the Book of Chronicles of the Kings of Israel? 28 And Omri 1lay down with his fathers and was buried in Samaria; and his son Ahab became king in his place.

29 Now Ahab the son of Omri became king over Israel in the thirty-eighth year of Asa king of Judah, and Ahab the son of Omri reigned over Israel in Samaria for twenty-two years. 30 Ahab the son of Omri did evil in the sight of the LORD more than all who were before him.

31 And as though it had been a trivial thing for him to walk in the sins of Jeroboam the son of Nebat, he married Jezebel the daughter of Ethbaal king of the Sidonians, and went and served Baal, and worshiped him. 32 So he erected an altar for Baal at the house of Baal, which he built in Samaria. 33 Ahab also made the 1Asherah. So Ahab did more to provoke the LORD God of Israel to anger than all the kings of Israel who were before him. 34 In his days Hiel the Bethelite rebuilt Jericho; he laid its foundations with the loss of Abiram his first-born, and set up its gates with the loss of his youngest son Segub, in accordance with the word of the LORD, which He spoke by Joshua the son of Nun.

Elijah Predicts Drought

17 Now Elijah the Tishbite, who was of the settlers of Gilead, said to Ahab, "As the LORD, the God of Israel lives, before whom I stand, there shall certainly be neither dew nor rain during these years, except by my word." 2 Then the word of the LORD came to him, saying, 3 "Go away from here and turn eastward, and hide yourself by the brook Cherith, which is east of the Jordan. 4 And it shall be that you will drink from the brook, and I have commanded the ravens to provide food for you there." 5 So he went and did everything according to the word of the LORD, for he went and lived by the brook Cherith, which is east of the Jordan. 6 And the ravens brought him bread and meat in the morning and bread and meat in the evening, and he would drink from the brook. 7 But it happened after a while that the brook dried up, because there was no rain in the land.

8 Then the word of the LORD came to him, saying, 9 "Arise, go to Zarephath, which belongs to Sidon, and stay there; behold, I have commanded a widow there to provide food for you." 10 So he arose and went to Zarephath, and when he came to the entrance of the city, behold, a widow was there gathering sticks; and he called to her and said, "Please get me a little water in a cup, so that I may drink." 11 As she was going to get it, he called to her and said, "Please bring me a piece of bread in your hand." 12 But she said, "As the LORD your God lives, I have no food, only a handful of flour in the bowl and a little oil in the jar; and behold, I am gathering a few sticks so that I may go in and prepare it for me and my son, so that we may eat it and die." 13 However, Elijah said to her, "Do not fear; go, do as you have said. Just make me a little bread loaf from it first and bring it out to me, and afterward you may make one for yourself and for your son. 14 For this is what the LORD, the God of Israel says: 'The bowl of flour shall not be used up, nor shall the jar of oil become empty, until the day that the LORD provides rain on the face of the earth.' " 15 So she went and did everything in accordance with the word of Elijah, and she and he and her household ate for many days. 16 The bowl of flour was not used up, nor did the jar of oil become empty, in accordance with the word of the LORD which He spoke through Elijah.

Elijah Raises the Widow's Son

17 Now it happened after these things that the son of the woman, the mistress of the house, became sick; and his condition became very grave, until at the end he was no longer breathing. 18 So she said to Elijah, "Why is my business any of yours, you man of God? Yet you have come to me to bring my wrongdoing to remembrance, and to put my son to death!" 19 But he said to her, "Give me your son." Then he took him from her arms and carried him up to the upstairs room where he was living, and laid him on his own bed. 20 And he called to the LORD and said, "LORD, my God, have You also brought catastrophe upon the

---

16:24 1About 150 lb. or 68 kg   16:28 1I.e., died   16:33 1I.e., wooden symbol of a female deity

widow with whom I am staying, by causing her son to die?" 21 Then he stretched himself out over the boy three times, and called to the LORD and said, "LORD, my God, please, let this boy's life return to him." 22 And the LORD listened to the voice of Elijah, and the life of the boy returned to him and he revived. 23 Elijah then took the boy and brought him down from the upstairs room into the house and gave him to his mother; and Elijah said, "See, your son is alive." 24 Then the woman said to Elijah, "Now I know that you are a man of God, and that the word of the LORD in your mouth is truth."

Obadiah Meets Elijah

18 Now it happened *after* many days that the word of the LORD came to Elijah in the third year, saying, "Go, present yourself to Ahab, and I will provide rain on the face of the earth." 2 So Elijah went to present himself to Ahab. Now the famine *was* severe in Samaria. 3 Ahab summoned Obadiah, who *was* in charge of the household. (Now Obadiah feared the LORD greatly; 4 for when Jezebel killed the prophets of the LORD, Obadiah took a hundred prophets and hid them by fifties in a cave, and provided them with bread and water.) 5 Then Ahab said to Obadiah, "Go through the land to all the springs of water and to all the river valleys; perhaps wo will find grass and keep the horses and mules alive, and not *have to* kill some of the cattle." 6 So they divided the land between them to survey it; Ahab went one way by himself, and Obadiah went another way by himself.

7 Now as Obadiah was on the way, behold, Elijah met him, and he recognized him and fell on his face and said, "Is it you, Elijah my master?" 8 And he said to him, "It is I. Go, say to your master, 'Behold, Elijah *is here.*'" 9 But he said, "What sin have I committed, that you are handing your servant over to Ahab, to put me to death? 10 As *surely as* the LORD your God lives, there is no nation or kingdom to which my master has not sent *word* to search for you; and whenever they say, 'He is not *here,*' he makes the kingdom or nation swear that they could not find you. 11 Yet now you are saying, 'Go, say to your master, "Behold, Elijah *is here!*"' 12 And it will come about when I leave you that the Spirit of the LORD will carry you to where I do not know; so when I come and inform Ahab and he cannot find you, he will kill me, though *I,* your servant, have feared the LORD from my youth. 13 Has it not been reported to my master what I did when Jezebel killed the prophets of the LORD, that I hid a hundred prophets of the LORD by fifties in a cave, and provided them with bread and water? 14 Yet now you are saying, 'Go, say to your master, "Behold, Elijah *is here*"'; he will then kill me!" 15 Then Elijah said, "As *surely as* the LORD of armies lives, before whom I stand, I will certainly present myself to him today." 16 So Obadiah went to meet Ahab and informed him; then Ahab went to meet Elijah.

17 When Ahab saw Elijah, Ahab said to him, "Is this you, the cause of disaster to Israel?"

18 He said, "I have not brought disaster to Israel, but you and your father's house *have,* because you have abandoned the commandments of the LORD and you have followed the Baals. 19 Now then, send *orders and* gather to me all Israel at Mount Carmel, *together* with 450 prophets of Baal and four hundred prophets of 'the Asherah, who eat at Jezebel's table."

God or Baal on Mount Carmel

20 So Ahab sent *orders* among all the sons of Israel and brought the prophets together at Mount Carmel. 21 Then Elijah approached all the people and said, "How long are you going to struggle with the two choices? If the LORD is God, follow Him; but if Baal, follow him." But the people did not answer him *so much as* a word. 22 Then Elijah said to the people, "I alone am left as a prophet of the LORD, while Baal's prophets are 450 men. 23 Now have them give us two oxen; and have them choose the one ox for themselves and cut it up, and place it on the wood, but put no fire *under it;* and I will prepare the other ox and lay it on the wood, and I will not put a fire *under it.* 24 Then you call on the name of your god, and I will call on the name of the LORD; and the God who answers by fire, He is God." And all the people replied, "That is a good idea."

23 So Elijah said to the prophets of Baal, "Choose the one ox for yourselves and prepare it first, since *there are* many *of* you, and call on the name of your god, but put no fire *under the ox.*" 26 Then they took the ox which was given them and they prepared it, and they called on the name of Baal from morning until noon, saying, "O Baal, answer us!" But there was no voice and no one answered. And they 'limped about the altar which they had made. 27 And at noon Elijah ridiculed them and said, "Call out with a loud voice, since he is a god; undoubtedly he is attending to business, or is on the way, or is on a journey. Perhaps he is asleep, and will awaken." 28 So they cried out with a loud voice, and cut themselves according to their custom with swords and lances until blood gushed out on them. 29 When midday was past, they raved until the time of the offering of the *evening* sacrifice; but there was no voice, no one answered, and no one paid attention.

30 Then Elijah said to all the people, "Come forward to me." So all the people came forward to him. And he repaired the altar of the LORD which had been torn down. 31 Then Elijah took twelve stones, corresponding to the number of the tribes of the sons of Jacob, to whom the word of the LORD had come, saying, "Israel shall be your name." 32 And with the stones he built an altar in the name of the LORD; and he made a trench around the altar, large enough to hold two measures of seed. 33 Then he laid out the wood, and he cut the ox in pieces and placed *it* on the wood. 34 And he said, "Fill four large jars with water and pour *it* on the burnt offering and on the wood." And he said, "Do it a second time," so they did it a second time. Then he said, "Do it a third time," so they did

---

18:19 1 I.e., wooden symbol of a female deity   18:26 1 I.e., in a type of ceremonial dance

it a third time. 35 The water flowed around the altar, and he also filled the trench with water.

Elijah's Prayer

36 Then at the time of the offering of the *evening* sacrifice, Elijah the prophet approached and said, "LORD, God of Abraham, Isaac, and Israel, today let it be known that You are God in Israel and that I am Your servant, and *that* I have done all these things at Your word. 37 Answer me, LORD, answer me, so that this people may know that You, LORD, are God, and *that* You have turned their heart back." 38 Then the fire of the LORD fell and consumed the burnt offering and the wood, and the stones and the dust; and it licked up the water that was in the trench. 39 When all the people saw *this,* they fell on their faces; and they said, "The LORD, He is God; the LORD, He is God!" 40 Then Elijah said to them, "Seize the prophets of Baal; do not let one of them escape." So they seized them; and Elijah brought them down to the brook Kishon, and slaughtered them there.

41 Now Elijah said to Ahab, "Go up, eat and drink; for there is the sound of the roar of a *heavy* shower." 42 So Ahab went up to eat and drink. But Elijah went up to the top of Carmel; and he bent down to the earth and put his face between his knees. 43 And he said to his servant, "Go up now, look toward the sea." So he went up and looked, but he said, "There is nothing." Yet *Elijah* said, "Go back" seven times. 44 And *when he returned* the seventh *time,* he said, "Behold, a cloud as small as a person's hand is coming up from the sea." And *Elijah* said, "Go up, say to Ahab, 'Harness *your chariot horses* and go down, so that the *heavy* shower does not stop you.'" 45 Meanwhile the sky became dark with clouds and wind *came up,* and there was a heavy shower. And Ahab rode and went to Jezreel. 46 Then the hand of the LORD was on Elijah, and he belted *his cloak* around his waist and outran Ahab to Jezreel.

Elijah Flees from Jezebel

19 Now Ahab told Jezebel everything that Elijah had done, and how he had killed all the prophets with the sword. 2 Then Jezebel sent a messenger to Elijah, saying, "So may the gods do to me and more so, if *by* about this time tomorrow I do not make your life like the life of one of them." 3 And he was afraid, and got up and ran for his life and came to Beersheba, which belongs to Judah; and he left his servant there. 4 But he himself went a day's journey into the wilderness, and came and sat down under a broom tree; and he asked for himself to die, and said, "Enough! Now, LORD, take my life, for I am no better than my fathers." 5 Then he lay down and fell asleep under a broom tree; but behold, there was an angel touching him, and he said to him, "Arise, eat!" 6 And he looked, and behold, there was at his head a round loaf of bread *baked on* hot coals, and a pitcher of water. So he ate and drank, and lay down again. 7 But the angel of the LORD came back a second time and touched him, and said, "Arise, eat; because the journey is too long for you." 8 So he arose and ate and drank, and he journeyed in the strength of that food for forty days and forty nights to Horeb, the mountain of God.

Elijah at Horeb

9 Then he came there to a cave and spent the night there; and behold, the word of the LORD *came* to him, and He said to him, "What are you doing here, Elijah?" 10 And he said, "I have been very zealous for the LORD, the God of armies; for the sons of Israel have abandoned Your covenant, torn down Your altars, and killed Your prophets with the sword. And I alone am left; and they have sought to take my life."

11 So He said, "Go out and stand on the mountain before the LORD." And behold, the LORD was passing by! And a great and powerful wind was tearing out the mountains and breaking the rocks in pieces before the LORD; *but* the LORD *was* not in the wind. And after the wind *there was* an earthquake, *but* the LORD *was* not in the earthquake. 12 And after the earthquake, a fire, *but* the LORD *was* not in the fire; and after the fire, a sound of a gentle blowing. 13 When Elijah heard *it,* he wrapped his face in his cloak and went out and stood in the entrance of the cave. And behold, a voice *came* to him and said, "What are you doing here, Elijah?" 14 Then he said, "I have been very zealous for the LORD, the God of armies; for the sons of Israel have abandoned Your covenant, torn down Your altars, and killed Your prophets with the sword. And I alone am left; and they have sought to take my life."

15 The LORD said to him, "Go, return on your way to the wilderness of Damascus; and when you have arrived, you shall anoint Hazael king over Aram. 16 You shall also anoint Jehu the son of Nimshi king over Israel; and you shall anoint Elisha the son of Shaphat of Abel-meholah as prophet in your place. 17 And it shall come about that the one who escapes from the sword of Hazael, Jehu shall put to death, and the one who escapes from the sword of Jehu, Elisha shall put to death. 18 Yet I will leave seven thousand in Israel, all the knees that have not bowed to Baal and every mouth that has not kissed him."

19 So he departed from there and found Elisha the son of Shaphat while he was plowing, with twelve yoke *of oxen* in front of him, and he with the twelfth. And Elijah came over to him and threw his cloak on him. 20 Then he left the oxen behind and ran after Elijah, and said, "Please let me kiss my father and my mother, then I will follow you." And he said to him, "Go back, for 'what have I done to you?" 21 So he returned from following him, and took the pair of oxen and sacrificed them, and cooked their meat with the implements of the oxen, and gave *it* to the people and they ate. Then he got up and followed Elijah and served him.

War with Aram

20 Now Ben-hadad, king of Aram, gathered all his army, and *there were* thirty-two

---

19:20 1 I.e., so as to influence Elisha's decision

kings with him, and horses and chariots. And he went up and besieged Samaria, and fought against it. [2] Then he sent messengers to the city to Ahab, king of Israel, and said to him, "This is what Ben-hadad says: [3] 'Your silver and your gold are mine; your most beautiful wives and children are also mine.' " [4] And the king of Israel replied, "As you say, my lord, O king; I am yours, as well as all that I have." [5] Then the messengers returned and said, "Ben-hadad says this: 'I did indeed send *word* to you, saying, "You shall give me your silver, your gold, your wives, and your children"; [6] but about this time tomorrow I will send my servants to you, and they will search your house and the houses of your servants; and they will take in their hands everything that is pleasing to your eyes, and take *it all* away.' "

[7] Then the king of Israel summoned all the elders of the land and said, "Please be aware and see that this man is looking for trouble; for he sent me *his demand* for my wives, my children, my silver, and my gold, and I did not refuse him." [8] Then all the elders and all the people said to him, "Do not listen nor consent." [9] So he said to the messengers of Ben-hadad, "Tell my lord the king, 'Everything that you sent *as a demand* to your servant at the first, I will do; but this thing I cannot do.' " Then the messengers departed, and brought him word again. [10] Ben-hadad sent *word* to him and said, "May the gods do so to me and more so, [1]if the dust of Samaria will be enough for handfuls for all the people who follow me." [11] Then the king of Israel replied, "Tell *him*, 'He who straps on *his weapons* had better not boast like one who takes *them* off.' " [12] And when *Ben-hadad* heard this message, while he was drinking with the kings in the temporary shelters, he said to his servants, "Take *your* positions." So they took *their* positions against the city.

Ahab Victorious

[13] Now behold, a prophet approached Ahab king of Israel, and said, "This is what the Lord says: 'Have you seen all this great multitude? Behold, I am going to hand them over to you today, and you shall know that I am the Lord.' " [14] But Ahab said, "By whom?" So he said, "The Lord says this: 'By the young men of the leaders of the provinces.' " Then he said, "Who will begin the battle?" And he said, "You *will.*" [15] So he mustered the young men of the leaders of the provinces, and there were 232; and after them he mustered all the people, all the sons of Israel: seven thousand.

[16] They went out at noon, while Ben-hadad was drinking himself drunk in the temporary shelters with the thirty-two kings who were helping him. [17] The young men of the leaders of the provinces went out first; and Ben-hadad sent out *scouts,* and they reported to him, saying, "Men have come out from Samaria." [18] Then he said, "If they have come out for peace, take them alive; or if they have come out for war, take them alive *as well.*"

[19] So these *men* went out from the city, the young men of the leaders of the provinces, and the army which followed them. [20] And they killed, each one, his man; and the Arameans fled and Israel pursued them, and Ben-hadad the king of Aram escaped on a horse with horsemen. [21] The king of Israel also went out and struck the horses and chariots, and killed the Arameans in a great slaughter.

[22] Then the prophet approached the king of Israel and said to him, "Go, show yourself courageous and be aware and see what you have to do; for at [1]the turn of the year the king of Aram will march against you."

[23] Now the servants of the king of Aram said to him, "Their gods are gods of the mountains; for that reason they were stronger than we. But let us fight them in the plain, *and* we will certainly be stronger than they. [24] Carry out this plan: remove the kings, each from his place, and put governors in their place, [25] and muster an army like the army that you have lost, horse for horse and chariot for chariot. Then we will fight against them in the plain, *and* we will certainly be stronger than they." And he listened to their voice and did so.

Another Aramean War

[26] So at the turn of the year Ben-hadad mustered the Arameans and went up to Aphek to fight against Israel. [27] And the sons of Israel were mustered and given provisions, and they went to meet them; and the sons of Israel camped opposite them like two little flocks of goats, while the Arameans filled the country. [28] Then a man of God approached and spoke to the king of Israel, and said, "This is what the Lord says: 'Since the Arameans have said, "The Lord is a god of mountains, but He is not a god of valleys," therefore I will hand over to you all this great multitude, and you shall know that I am the Lord.' " [29] So they camped, one opposite the other, for seven days. And on the seventh day the battle was joined, and the sons of Israel killed *of* the Arameans a hundred thousand foot soldiers in a single day. [30] But the rest fled to Aphek into the city, and the wall fell on twenty-seven thousand men who were left. And Ben-hadad fled and came into the city, *going from one* inner room to another.

[31] But his servants said to him, "Behold now, we have heard that the kings of the house of Israel are merciful kings. Please let's put sackcloth around our waists and ropes on our heads, and go out to the king of Israel; perhaps he will let you live." [32] So they put sackcloth around their waists and ropes on their heads, and came to the king of Israel and said, "Your servant Ben-hadad says, 'Please let me live.' " And *Ahab* said, "Is he still alive? He is my brother." [33] Now the men took this as a *good* omen, and quickly accepting it from him, they said, "Your brother Ben-hadad." Then he said, "Go, bring him." Then Ben-hadad came out to him, and he had him mount the chariot. [34] And *Ben-hadad* said to him, "The cities which my father took from your father I will restore, and you can make streets for yourself in Damascus, as my father made in Samaria." *Ahab said,* "And I will let you go with this covenant." So he made a covenant with him and let him go.

20:10 [1] I.e., what is left of Samaria after it is destroyed   20:22 [1] I.e., spring

35 Now a man from the sons of the prophets said to another by the word of the LORD, "Please strike me." But the man refused to strike him. 36 Then he said to him, "Because you have not listened to the voice of the LORD, behold, as soon as you leave me, a lion will kill you." And as soon as he left him a lion found him and killed him. 37 Then he found another man and said, "Please strike me." And the man struck him, injuring him. 38 So the prophet departed and waited for the king by the road, and disguised himself with a bandage over his eyes. 39 And as the king passed by, he cried out to the king and said, "Your servant went out into the midst of the battle; and behold, a man turned aside and brought a man to me and said, 'Guard this man; if for any reason he goes missing, then your life shall be forfeited in place of his life, or else you shall pay a ⸆talent of silver.' 40 Now while your servant was busy here and there, he disappeared." And the king of Israel said to him, "So shall your judgment be; you yourself determined it." 41 Then he quickly took the bandage away from his eyes, and the king of Israel recognized him, that he was one of the prophets. 42 And the prophet said to him, "This is what the LORD says: 'Since you have let go from your hand the man I had designated for destruction, your life shall be forfeited in place of his life, and your people in place of his people.'" 43 So the king of Israel went to his house sullen and furious, and came to Samaria.

Ahab Covets Naboth's Vineyard

21 Now it came about after these things that Naboth the Jezreelite had a vineyard which was in Jezreel beside the palace of Ahab, the king of Samaria. 2 And Ahab spoke to Naboth, saying, "Give me your vineyard so that I may have it for a vegetable garden, because it is close beside my house, and I will give you a better vineyard in place of it; if you prefer, I will give you what it is worth in money." 3 But Naboth said to Ahab, "The LORD forbid me that I would give you the inheritance of my fathers!" 4 So Ahab entered his house sullen and furious because of the answer that Naboth the Jezreelite had given to him, since he said, "I will not give you the inheritance of my fathers." And he lay down on his bed and turned his face away, and ate no food. 5 But Jezebel his wife came to him and said to him, "How is it that your spirit is so sullen that you are not eating food?" 6 So he said to her, "It is because I was speaking to Naboth the Jezreelite and saying to him, 'Give me your vineyard for money; or else, if it pleases you, I will give you a vineyard in place of it.' But he said, 'I will not give you my vineyard.'" 7 Jezebel his wife said to him, "Do you now reign over Israel? Arise, eat bread, and let your heart be joyful; I will give you the vineyard of Naboth the Jezreelite." 8 So she wrote letters in Ahab's name and sealed them with his seal, and sent the letters to the elders and to the nobles who were living with Naboth in his city. 9 Now she had written in the letters, saying, "Proclaim a fast and seat Naboth at the head of the people; 10 and seat two worthless men opposite him, and have them testify against him, saying, 'You cursed God and the king.' Then take him out and stone him to death."

Jezebel's Plot

11 So the men of his city, the elders and the nobles who lived in his city, did just as Jezebel had sent word to them, just as it was written in the letters which she had sent them. 12 They proclaimed a fast, and seated Naboth at the head of the people. 13 Then the two worthless men came in and sat opposite him; and the worthless men testified against him, against Naboth, before the people, saying, "Naboth cursed God and the king." So they took him outside the city and stoned him to death with stones. 14 Then they sent word to Jezebel, saying, "Naboth has been stoned and is dead." 15 And when Jezebel heard that Naboth had been stoned and was dead, Jezebel said to Ahab, "Arise, take possession of the vineyard of Naboth, the Jezreelite, which he refused to give you for money; for Naboth is not alive, but dead." 16 When Ahab heard that Naboth was dead, Ahab got up to go down to the vineyard of Naboth the Jezreelite, to take possession of it.

17 Then the word of the LORD came to Elijah the Tishbite, saying, 18 "Arise, go down to meet Ahab king of Israel, who is in Samaria; behold, he is in the vineyard of Naboth, where he has gone down to take possession of it. 19 And you shall speak to him, saying, 'This is what the LORD says: "Have you murdered and also taken possession?"' And you shall speak to him, saying, 'The LORD says this: "In the place where the dogs licked up the blood of Naboth, the dogs will lick up your blood, yours as well."'" 20 Then Ahab said to Elijah, "Have you found me, enemy of mine?" And he answered, "I have found you, because you have given yourself over to do evil in the sight of the LORD. 21 Behold, I am bringing disaster upon you, and I will utterly sweep you away, and will eliminate from Ahab every male, both bond and free in Israel; 22 and I will make your house like the house of Jeroboam the son of Nebat, and like the house of Baasha the son of Ahijah, because of the provocation with which you have provoked Me to anger, and because you have misled Israel into sin. 23 The LORD has also spoken of Jezebel, saying, 'The dogs will eat Jezebel in the territory of Jezreel.' 24 The one belonging to Ahab, who dies in the city, the dogs will eat; and the one who dies in the field, the birds of the sky will eat."

25 There certainly was no one like Ahab who gave himself over to do evil in the sight of the LORD, because Jezebel his wife incited him. 26 He also acted very despicably in following idols, conforming to everything that the Amorites had done, whom the LORD drove out from the sons of Israel.

27 Yet it came about, when Ahab heard these words, that he tore his clothes and put on sackcloth and fasted, and he lay in sackcloth and went about despondently. 28 Then the word of

---

20:39 1 About 75 lb. or 34 kg

the Lord came to Elijah the Tishbite, saying, **29** "Do you see how Ahab has humbled himself before Me? Because he has humbled himself before Me, I will not bring the disaster in his days; I will bring the disaster upon his house in his son's days."

Ahab's Third Campaign against Aram

22 Now three years passed without war between Aram and Israel. **2** In the third year, Jehoshaphat the king of Judah came down to the king of Israel. **3** Now the king of Israel said to his servants, "Are you aware that Ramoth-gilead belongs to us, yet we are hesitant to take it out of the hand of the king of Aram?" **4** So he said to Jehoshaphat, "Will you go to battle with me at Ramoth-gilead?" And Jehoshaphat said to the king of Israel, "Consider me yours, my people yours, and my horses yours!"

5 However, Jehoshaphat said to the king of Israel, "Please request the word of the Lord first." **6** So the king of Israel assembled the †prophets, about four hundred men, and said to them, "Should I go to battle against Ramoth-gilead or should I refrain?" And they said, "Go up, for the Lord will hand *it* over to the king." **7** But Jehoshaphat said, "Is there no longer a prophet of the Lord here, that we may inquire of him?" **8** And the king of Israel said to Jehoshaphat, "There is still one man by whom we may inquire of the Lord, but I hate him, because he does not prophesy *anything* good regarding me, but *only* bad. *He is* Micaiah the son of Imlah." But Jehoshaphat said, "May the king not say so." **9** Then the king of Israel summoned an officer and said, "Bring Micaiah son of Imlah quickly." **10** Now the king of Israel and Jehoshaphat the king of Judah were sitting, each on his throne, dressed in *their* robes, at the threshing floor at the entrance of the gate of Samaria; and all the prophets were prophesying before them. **11** Then Zedekiah the son of Chenaanah made horns of iron for himself and said, "This is what the Lord says: 'With these you will gore the Arameans until they are destroyed!' " **12** All the prophets were prophesying this as well, saying, "Go up to Ramoth-gilead and succeed, for the Lord will hand *it* over to the king."

Micaiah Predicts Defeat

13 Then the messenger who went to summon Micaiah spoke to him saying, "Behold now, the words of the prophets are unanimously favorable to the king. Please let your word be like the word of one of them, and speak favorably." **14** But Micaiah said, "As the Lord lives, whatever the Lord says to me, I shall speak it."

15 When he came to the king, the king said to him, "Micaiah, should we go to battle against Ramoth-gilead, or should we refrain?" And he said, "Go up and succeed, for the Lord will hand *it* over to the king!" **16** Then the king said to him, "How many times must I make you swear that you will tell me nothing but the truth in the name of the Lord?" **17** So he said, "I saw all Israel

Scattered on the mountains,
Like sheep that have no shepherd.
And the Lord said,
'These *people* have no master.
Each of them is to return to his house in
    peace.' "
18 Then the king of Israel said to Jehoshaphat, "Did I not tell you that he would not prophesy *anything* good regarding me, but *only* bad?" **19** And *Micaiah* said, "Therefore, hear the word of the Lord. I saw the Lord sitting on His throne, and all the angels of heaven standing by Him on His right and on His left. **20** And the Lord said, 'Who will entice Ahab to go up and fall at Ramoth-gilead?' And one *spirit* said this, while another said that. **21** Then a spirit came forward and stood before the Lord, and said, 'I will entice him.' **22** And the Lord said to him, 'How?' And he said, 'I will go out and be a deceiving spirit in the mouths of all his prophets.' Then He said, 'You shall entice *him,* and you will also prevail. Go and do so.' **23** Now then, behold, the Lord has put a deceiving spirit in the mouth of all these prophets of yours; and the Lord has declared disaster against you."

24 Then Zedekiah the son of Chenaanah approached and struck Micaiah on the cheek; and he said, "How did the Spirit of the Lord pass from me to speak to you?" **25** And Micaiah said, "Behold, you are going to see *how* on that day when you go *from one* inner room to another *trying* to hide yourself." **26** Then the king of Israel said, "Take Micaiah and return him to Amon the governor of the city, and to Joash the king's son; **27** and say, 'This is what the king says: "Put this *man* in prison, and feed him enough bread and water to survive until I return safely." ' " **28** But Micaiah said, "If you actually return safely, the Lord has not spoken by me." And he said, "Listen, all you people!"

Defeat and Death of Ahab

29 So the king of Israel and Jehoshaphat king of Judah went up *against* Ramoth-gilead. **30** And the king of Israel said to Jehoshaphat, "I will disguise myself and go into the battle, but you put on your robes." So the king of Israel disguised himself and went into the battle. **31** Now the king of Aram had commanded the thirty-two commanders of his chariots, saying, "Do not fight with the small *or* great, but only with the king of Israel." **32** So when the commanders of the chariots saw Jehoshaphat, they said, "Surely he is the king of Israel!" And they turned aside to fight against him, and Jehoshaphat cried out. **33** Then, when the commanders of the chariots saw that it was not the king of Israel, they turned back from pursuing him.

34 Now one man drew his bow at random and struck the king of Israel in a joint of the armor. So he said to the driver of his chariot, "Turn around and take me out of the battle, for I am severely wounded." **35** The battle raged on that day, and the king was propped up in his chariot in front of the Arameans, and he died at evening, and the blood from the wound ran

---

22:6 †I.e., official prophets who at that time were false

into the bottom of the chariot. **36** Then the word passed throughout the army close to sunset, saying, "Every man to his city, and every man to his country!"

37 So the king died and was brought to Samaria, and they buried the king in Samaria. **38** They washed out the chariot by the pool of Samaria, and the dogs licked up his blood (*it was there that* the prostitutes bathed themselves) in accordance with the word of the LORD which He had spoken. **39** Now *as for* the rest of the acts of Ahab and everything that he did, and the ivory house which he built and all the cities which he built, are they not written in the Book of the Chronicles of the Kings of Israel? **40** So Ahab 1lay down with his fathers, and his son Ahaziah became king in his place.

The New Rulers

41 Now Jehoshaphat the son of Asa became king over Judah in the fourth year of Ahab king of Israel. **42** Jehoshaphat was thirty-five years old when he became king, and he reigned for twenty-five years in Jerusalem. And his mother's name was Azubah the daughter of Shilhi. **43** He walked entirely in the way of his father Asa; he did not turn aside from it, doing what was right in the sight of the LORD. However, the high places were not taken away; the people still sacrificed and burned incense

on the high places. **44** Jehoshaphat also made peace with the king of Israel.

45 Now *as for* the rest of the acts of Jehoshaphat, and his might which he showed and how he made war, are they not written in the Book of the Chronicles of the Kings of Judah? **46** And the remnant of the cult prostitutes who remained in the days of his father Asa, he eliminated from the land.

47 Now there was no king in Edom; a governor *served as* king. **48** Jehoshaphat built ships of Tarshish to go to Ophir for gold, but they did not go, because the ships were destroyed at Ezion-geber. **49** Then Ahaziah the son of Ahab said to Jehoshaphat, "Let my servants go with your servants in the ships." But Jehoshaphat was not willing. **50** And Jehoshaphat 1lay down with his fathers and was buried with his fathers in the city of his father David, and his son Jehoram became king in his place.

51 Ahaziah the son of Ahab became king over Israel in Samaria in the seventeenth year of Jehoshaphat king of Judah, and he reigned over Israel for two years. **52** He did evil in the sight of the LORD and walked in the way of his father and in the way of his mother, and in the way of Jeroboam the son of Nebat, who misled Israel into sin. **53** So he served Baal and worshiped him, and provoked the LORD God of Israel to anger, according to all that his father had done.

22:40 1 I.e., died   22:50 1 I.e., died

The Second Book of the
KINGS

Ahaziah's Messengers Meet Elijah

1 Now Moab broke with Israel after the death of Ahab. 2 And Ahaziah fell through the *window* lattice in his upper chamber which *was* in Samaria, and became ill. So he sent messengers and said to them, "Go, inquire of Baal-zebub, the god of Ekron, whether I will recover from this sickness." 3 But the angel of the LORD said to Elijah the Tishbite, "Arise, go up to meet the messengers of the king of Samaria and say to them, 'Is it because there is no God in Israel *that* you are going to inquire of Baal-zebub, the god of Ekron?' 4 Now therefore, this is what the LORD says: 'You will not get down from the bed upon which you have lain, but you shall certainly die.'" Then Elijah departed.

5 When the messengers returned to Ahaziah, he said to them, "Why have you returned?" 6 They said to him, "A man came up to meet us and said to us, 'Go, return to the king who sent you and say to him, "This is what the LORD says: 'Is it because there is no God in Israel *that* you are sending *messengers* to inquire of Baal-zebub, the god of Ekron? Therefore you will not get down from the bed upon which you have lain, but you shall certainly die.'"'" 7 Then he said to them, "What did the man look like, who came up to meet you and spoke these words to you?" 8 And they said to him, "*He was* a hairy man with a leather belt worn around his waist." And he said, "It is Elijah the Tishbite."

9 Then *the king* sent to him a captain of fifty with his fifty *men.* And he went up to him, and behold, he was sitting on the top of the hill. And he said to him, "You man of God, the king says, 'Come down.'" 10 But Elijah replied to the captain of fifty, "If I am a man of God, may fire come down from heaven and consume you and your fifty." Then fire came down from heaven and consumed him and his fifty *men.*

11 So *the king* again sent to him another captain of fifty with his fifty *men.* And he said to him, "You man of God, this is what the king says: 'Come down quickly!'" 12 But Elijah replied to them, "If I am a man of God, may fire come down from heaven and consume you and your fifty." Then the fire of God came down from heaven and consumed him and his fifty *men.*

13 So *the king* again sent the captain of a third fifty with his fifty *men.* When the third captain of fifty went up, he came and bowed down on his knees before Elijah, and begged him and said to him, "You man of God, please let my life and the lives of these fifty servants of yours be precious in your sight. 14 Behold, fire came down from heaven and consumed the first two captains of fifty with their fifties; but now let my life be precious in your sight." 15 And the angel of the LORD said to Elijah, "Go down with him; do not be afraid of him." So he got up and went down with him to the king. 16 Then he said to him, "This is what the LORD says: 'Since you have sent messengers to inquire of Baal-zebub, the god of Ekron—is it because there is no God in Israel to inquire of His word? Therefore you will not get down from the bed upon which you have lain, but you shall certainly die.'"

Jehoram Reigns over Israel

17 So Ahaziah died in accordance with the word of the LORD which Elijah had spoken. And since he had no son, Jehoram became king in his place in the second year of Jehoram the son of Jehoshaphat, king of Judah. 18 Now *as for* the rest of the acts of Ahaziah which he did, are they not written in the Book of the Chronicles of the Kings of Israel?

Elijah Taken to Heaven

2 Now it came about, when the LORD was about to bring Elijah up by a whirlwind to heaven, that Elijah left Gilgal with Elisha. 2 And Elijah said to Elisha, "Stay here please, for the LORD has sent me as far as Bethel." But Elisha said, "As *surely as* the LORD lives and as you yourself live, I will not leave you." So they went down to Bethel. 3 Then the sons of the prophets who *were at* Bethel went out to Elisha and said to him, "Are you aware that the LORD will take away your master from over you today?" And he said, "Yes, I am aware; say nothing *about it.*"

4 And Elijah said to him, "Elisha, please stay here, for the LORD has sent me to Jericho." But he said, "As *surely as* the LORD lives, and as you yourself live, I will not leave you." So they came to Jericho. 5 Then the sons of the prophets who *were* at Jericho approached Elisha and said to him, "Do you know that the LORD will take away your master from over you today?" And he answered, "Yes, I know; say nothing *about it.*" 6 And Elijah said to him, "Please stay here, for the LORD has sent me to the Jordan." But he said, "As *surely as* the LORD lives, and as you yourself live, I will not leave you." So the two of them went on.

7 Now fifty men of the sons of the prophets went and stood opposite *them* at a distance, while the two of them stood by the Jordan. 8 And Elijah took his coat, folded it, and struck the waters, and they were divided here and there, so that the two of them crossed over on dry ground.

9 When they had crossed over, Elijah said to Elisha, "Ask *me* what I should do for you before I am taken from you." And Elisha said, "Please let a double portion of your spirit be upon me." 10 He said, "You have asked a hard thing. *Nevertheless,* if you see me when I am taken from you, it shall be so for you; but if not, it shall not be *so.*" 11 And as they were walking along and talking, behold, a chariot of

fire *appeared* with horses of fire, and they separated the two of them. Then Elijah went up by a whirlwind to heaven. 12 And Elisha was watching *it* and he was crying out, "My father, my father, the chariot of Israel and its horsemen!" And he did not see Elijah again. Then he took hold of his own clothes and tore them in two pieces. 13 He also took up the coat of Elijah that had fallen from him, and he went back and stood by the bank of the Jordan. 14 Then he took the coat of Elijah that had fallen from him and struck the waters, and said, "Where is the LORD, the God of Elijah?" And when he also had struck the waters, they were divided here and there; and Elisha crossed over.

Elisha Succeeds Elijah

15 Now when the sons of the prophets who *were* at Jericho opposite *him* saw him, they said, "The spirit of Elijah has settled on Elisha." And they came to meet him and bowed down to the ground before him. 16 Then they said to him, "Behold now, there are with your servants fifty strong men; please let them go and search for your master, in case the Spirit of the LORD has taken him up and cast him on some mountain or into some valley." But he said, "You shall not send *anyone.*" 17 Yet when they urged him until he was ashamed *to refuse,* he said, "Send *them.*" So they sent fifty men; and they searched for three days, but did not find him. 18 They returned to him while he was staying in Jericho; and he said to them, "Did I not say to you, 'Do not go'?"

19 Then the men of the city said to Elisha, "Behold now, the site of the city is pleasant, as my lord sees; but the water is bad and the land is unfruitful." 20 And he said, "Bring me a new jar, and put salt in it." So they brought *it* to him. 21 Then he went out to the spring of water and threw salt in it and said, "This is what the LORD says: 'I have purified these waters; there shall not come from there death or unfruitfulness any longer.' " 22 So the waters have been purified to this day, in accordance with the word of Elisha which he spoke.

23 Now he went up from there to Bethel; and as he was going up by the road, *some* young boys came out from the city and ridiculed him and said to him, "Go up, you baldhead; go up, you baldhead!" 24 When he looked behind him and saw them, he cursed them in the name of the LORD. Then two female bears came out of the woods and tore up forty-two of the boys. 25 He then went on from there to Mount Carmel, and from there he returned to Samaria.

Jehoram Meets Moabite Rebellion

3 Now Jehoram the son of Ahab became king over Israel at Samaria in the eighteenth year of Jehoshaphat king of Judah, and he reigned for twelve years. 2 He did evil in the sight of the LORD, though not like his father and his mother; for he removed the memorial stone of Baal which his father had made. 3 Nevertheless, he clung to the sins of Jeroboam the son of

Nebat, into which he misled Israel; he did not abandon them.

4 Now Mesha the king of Moab was a sheep breeder, and he used to make *tribute* payments to the king of Israel of a hundred thousand lambs, and the wool of a hundred thousand rams. 5 However, when *King* Ahab died, the king of Moab broke with the 1king of Israel. 6 So King Jehoram left Samaria *for battle* at that time and mustered all Israel. 7 Then he went and sent *word* to Jehoshaphat the king of Judah, saying, "The king of Moab has broken away from me. Will you go with me to fight against Moab?" And he said, "I will go up. Consider me yours, my people as your people, my horses as your horses." 8 Then he said, "Which way shall we go up?" And he answered, "The way of the wilderness of Edom."

9 So the king of Israel went with the king of Judah and the king of Edom, and they made a circuit of seven days' journey. But there was no water for the army or for the cattle that followed them. 10 Then the king of Israel said, "It is hopeless! For the LORD has called these three kings to hand them over to Moab!" 11 But Jehoshaphat said, "Is there no prophet of the LORD here, that we may inquire of the LORD by him?" And one of the king of Israel's servants answered and said, "Elisha the son of Shaphat is here, who used to pour water on the hands of Elijah." 12 And Jehoshaphat said, "The word of the LORD is with him." So the king of Israel and Jehoshaphat and the king of Edom went down to him.

13 Now Elisha said to the king of Israel, "What business do you have with me? Go to your father's prophets and your mother's prophets." But the king of Israel said to him, "No, for the LORD has called these three kings *together* to hand them over to Moab." 14 Elisha said, "As *surely as* the LORD of armies lives, before whom I stand, if I did not respect Jehoshaphat the king of Judah, I would not look at you nor see you. 15 But now bring me a musician." And it came about, when the musician played, that the hand of the LORD came upon him. 16 And he said, "This is what the LORD says: 'Make this valley full of trenches.' 17 For the LORD says this: 'You will not see wind, nor will you see rain; yet that valley shall be filled with water, so that you will drink, you, your livestock, and your *other* animals. 18 And this is an insignificant thing in the sight of the LORD; He will also give the Moabites into your hand. 19 Then you shall strike every fortified city and every choice city, and cut down every good tree and stop up all the springs of water, and spoil every good plot of land with stones.' " 20 And it happened in the morning about *the time of* offering the sacrifice, that, behold, water came from the direction of Edom, and the country was filled with water.

21 Now all the Moabites heard that the kings had come up to fight against them. And all who were able to put on armor and older were summoned and they took their positions on the border. 22 Then they got up early in the

morning, and the sun shone on the water, and the Moabites saw the water opposite *them* as red as blood. 23 So they said, "This is blood; the kings must have fought each other, and they have killed one another. Now then, Moab, to the spoils!" 24 But when they came to the camp of Israel, the Israelites rose up and struck the Moabites, so that they fled from them; and *the Israelites* invaded the land, killing the Moabites. 25 So they destroyed the cities; and each one threw a stone on every plot of good land and filled it. So they stopped up every spring of water and cut down every good tree, until in Kir-hareseth *only* they left its stones; however, the rock slingers surrounded *it* and struck it. 26 When the king of Moab saw that the battle was too fierce for him, he took with him seven hundred men who drew swords, to break through to the king of Edom; but they could not. 27 Then *the king of Moab* took his oldest son who was to reign in his place, and offered him as a burnt offering on the wall. And great anger came upon Israel, and they departed from him and returned to their own land.

The Widow's Oil

4 Now a woman of the wives of the sons of the prophets cried out to Elisha, saying, "Your servant my husband is dead, and you know that your servant feared the LORD; and the creditor has come to take my two children to be his slaves." 2 So Elisha said to her, "What shall I do for you? Tell me, what do you have in the house?" And she said, "Your servant has nothing in the house except a jar of oil." 3 Then he said, "Go, borrow containers elsewhere for yourself, *empty* containers from all your neighbors—do not get *too* few. 4 Then you shall come in and shut the door behind you and your sons, and pour into all these containers; and you shall set aside what is full." 5 So she left him and shut the door behind her and her sons; they *began* bringing *the containers* to her, and she poured *the oil.* 6 When the containers were full, she said to her son, "Bring me another container." But he said to her, "There are no more containers." Then the oil stopped. 7 So she came and told the man of God. And he said, "Go, sell the oil and pay your debt, and you *and* your sons can live on the rest."

The Shunammite Woman

8 Now a day came when Elisha went over to Shunem, where there was a prominent woman, and she urged him to eat food. And so it was, as often as he passed by, *that* he turned in there to eat food. 9 And she said to her husband, "Behold now, I am aware that this is a holy man of God passing by us repeatedly. 10 Please, let's make a little walled upper room, and let's set up a bed for him there, and a table, a chair, and a lampstand; then it shall be, when he comes to us, *that* he can turn in there."

11 Now one day he came there, and turned in to the upper room and rested. 12 Then he said to his servant Gehazi, "Call this Shunammite." And when he had called her,

she stood before him. 13 And he said to him, "Say now to her, 'Behold, you have taken trouble for us with all this care; what can I do for you? Would you like me to speak for you to the king or to the commander of the army?'" But she answered, "I live among my own people." 14 So he said, "What then is to be done for her?" And Gehazi answered, "It is a fact that she has no son, and her husband is old." 15 He then said, "Call her." When he had called her, she stood in the doorway. 16 Then he said, "At this season next year, you are going to embrace a son." And she said, "No, my lord, you man of God, do not lie to your servant."

17 Now the woman conceived and gave birth to a son at that season the next year, as Elisha had told her.

The Shunammite's Son

18 When the child was grown, the day came that he went out to his father, to the reapers. 19 And he said to his father, "My head, my head!" And *his father* said to his servant, "Carry him to his mother." 20 When he had carried him and brought him to his mother, he sat on her lap until noon, and *then* he died. 21 And she went up and laid him on the bed of the man of God, and shut *the door* behind him and left. 22 Then she called to her husband and said, "Please send me one of the servants and one of the donkeys, so that I may run to the man of God and return." 23 But he said, "Why are you going to him today? It is neither new moon nor Sabbath." So she *just* said, "*It will be* fine." 24 Then she saddled the donkey and said to her servant, "Drive *the donkey* and go on; do not slow down the pace for me unless I tell you." 25 So she went on and came to the man of God at Mount Carmel.

When the man of God saw her at a distance, he said to Gehazi his servant, "Behold, that person there is the Shunammite. 26 Please run now to meet her and say to her, 'Is it *going* well for you? Is it *going* well for your husband? Is it *going* well for the child?'" Then she answered, "It is *going* well." 27 But she came to the man of God at the hill and took hold of his feet. And Gehazi came up to push her away, but the man of God said, "Leave her alone, for her soul is troubled within her; and the LORD has concealed *it* from me and has not informed me." 28 Then she said, "Did I ask for a son from my lord? Did I not say, 'Do not give me false hope'?"

29 Then he said to Gehazi, "Get ready and take my staff in your hand, and go; if you meet anyone, do not greet him, and if anyone greets you, do not reply to him. And lay my staff on the boy's face." 30 The mother of the boy said, "As *surely as* the LORD lives and you yourself live, I will not leave you." So he got up and followed her. 31 Then Gehazi went on ahead of them and laid the staff on the boy's face, but there was no sound or response. So he returned to meet him and informed him, saying, "The boy has not awakened."

32 When Elisha entered the house, behold the boy was dead, laid on his bed. 33 So he entered and shut the door behind them both, and he prayed to the LORD. 34 Then he got up

on the bed and lay on the child, and put his mouth on his mouth, his eyes on his eyes, his hands on his hands, and he bent down on him; and the flesh of the child became warm. 35 Then he returned and walked in the house back and forth once, and went up and bent down on him; and the boy sneezed seven times, then the boy opened his eyes. 36 And he called Gehazi and said, "Call this Shunammite." So he called her. And when she came to him, he said, "Pick up your son." 37 Then she came in and fell at his feet and bowed down to the ground, and she picked up her son and left.

The Poisonous Stew

38 When Elisha returned to Gilgal, *there was* a famine in the land. As the sons of the prophets were sitting in front of him, he said to his servant, "Put on the large pot and boil stew for the sons of the prophets." 39 Then one went out into the field to gather mallow, and found a wild vine and gathered from it his lap full of wild gourds; and he came and sliced them into the pot of stew, because they did not know *what they were.* 40 So they poured *it* out for the men to eat. But as they were eating the stew, they cried out and said, "You man of God, there is death in the pot!" And they were unable to eat. 41 Then he said, "Bring flour." And he threw it into the pot, and said, "Pour *it* out for the people that they may eat." Then there was nothing harmful in the pot.

42 Now a man came from Baal-shalishah, and brought the man of God bread of the first fruits, twenty loaves of barley and fresh grain in his sack. And *Elisha* said, "Give *them* to the people that they may eat." 43 But his attendant said, "How am I to serve this to a hundred men?" Nevertheless he said, "Give *them* to the people that they may eat, for this is what the LORD says: 'They shall eat and have *some* left over.'" 44 So he served *it* to them, and they ate and had *some* left over, in accordance with the word of the LORD.

Naaman Is Healed

5 Now Naaman, commander of the army of the king of Aram, was a great man in the view of his master, and eminent, because by him the LORD had given victory to Aram. The man was also a valiant warrior, *but* afflicted with leprosy. 2 Now the Arameans had gone out in bands and had taken captive a little girl from the land of Israel; and she waited on Naaman's wife. 3 And she said to her mistress, "If only my master were with the prophet who is in Samaria! Then he would cure him of his leprosy." 4 And Naaman went in and told his master, saying, "The girl who is from the land of Israel spoke such and such." 5 Then the king of Aram said, "Go now, and I will send a letter to the king of Israel." So he departed and took with him ten ¹talents of silver, six thousand ²shekels of gold, and ten changes of clothes. 6 And he brought the letter to the king of Israel, which said, "And now as this letter comes to you, behold, I have sent Naaman my servant to you, so that you may cure him of his

leprosy." 7 But when the king of Israel read the letter, he tore his clothes and said, "Am I God, to kill and to keep alive, that this man is sending *word* to me to cure a man of his leprosy? But consider now, and see how he is seeking a quarrel against me."

8 Now it happened, when Elisha the man of God heard that the king of Israel had torn his clothes, that he sent *word* to the king, saying, "Why did you tear your clothes? Just have him come to me, and he shall learn that there is a prophet in Israel." 9 So Naaman came with his horses and his chariots, and stood at the doorway of Elisha's house. 10 And Elisha sent a messenger to him, saying, "Go and wash in the Jordan seven times, and your flesh will be restored to you and *you will* be clean." 11 But Naaman was furious and went away, and he said, "Behold, I thought, 'He will certainly come out to me, and stand and call on the name of the LORD his God, and wave his hand over the site and cure the leprosy.' 12 Are Abanah and Pharpar, the rivers of Damascus, not better than all the waters of Israel? Could I not wash in them and be clean?" So he turned and went away in a rage. 13 Then his servants approached and spoke to him, saying, "My father, had the prophet told you *to do some* great thing, would you not have done *it?* How much more *then,* when he says to you, 'Wash, and be clean'?" 14 So he went down and dipped *himself* in the Jordan seven times, in accordance with the word of the man of God; and his flesh was restored like the flesh of a little child, and he was clean.

Gehazi's Greed

15 Then he returned to the man of God with all his company, and came and stood before him. And he said, "Behold now, I know that there is no God in all the earth, except in Israel; so please accept a gift from your servant now." 16 But he said, "As *surely as* the LORD lives, before whom I stand, I will accept nothing." And he urged him to accept *it,* but he refused. 17 Then Naaman said, "If not, please let your servant be given two mules' load of earth; for your servant will no longer offer a burnt offering nor a sacrifice to other gods, but to the LORD. 18 Regarding this matter may the LORD forgive your servant: when my master goes into the house of Rimmon to worship there, and he leans on my hand and I bow down in the house of Rimmon, when I bow down in the house of Rimmon, may the LORD please forgive your servant in this matter." 19 He said to him, "Go in peace." So he went some distance from him.

20 But Gehazi, the servant of Elisha the man of God, thought, "Behold, my master has spared this Naaman the Aramean, by not accepting from his hand what he brought. As the LORD lives, I will run after him and take something from him." 21 So Gehazi pursued Naaman. When Naaman saw *someone* running after him, he came down from the chariot to meet him and said, "*Is everything* well?" 22 And he said, "*Everything is* well. My master has sent me, saying, 'Behold, just now two young

---

5:5 ¹A talent was about 75 lb. or 34 kg   ²A shekel was about 0.5 oz. or 14 gm

men of the sons of the prophets have come to me from the hill country of Ephraim. Please give them a talent of silver and two changes of clothes.'" 23 Naaman said, "Be sure to take two talents." And he urged him, and tied up two talents of silver in two bags with two changes of clothes, and gave *them* to two of his servants; and they carried *them* before him. 24 When he came to the hill, he took them from their hand and deposited them in the house, and he sent the men away, and they departed. 25 But he went in and stood before his master. And Elisha said to him, "Where have you been, Gehazi?" And he said, "Your servant went nowhere." 26 Then he said to him, "Did my heart not go *with you,* when the man turned from his chariot to meet you? Is it a time to accept money and to accept clothes, olive groves, vineyards, sheep, oxen, and male and female slaves? 27 Therefore, the leprosy of Naaman shall cling to you and to your descendants forever." So he went out from his presence afflicted with leprosy, *as white* as snow.

The Axe Head Recovered

6 Now the sons of the prophets said to Elisha, "Behold now, the place before you where we are living is too cramped for us. 2 Please let us go to the Jordan, and let us each take from there a beam, and let us construct a place there for ourselves, to live there." So he said, "Go." 3 Then one *of them* said, "Please agree and go with your servants." And he said, "I will go." 4 So he went with them; and when they came to the Jordan, they cut down trees. 5 But it happened that as one *of them* was cutting down a beam, the axe head fell into the water; and he cried out and said, "Oh, my master! It was borrowed!" 6 Then the man of God said, "Where did it fall?" And when he showed him the place, he cut off a stick and threw *it* in there, and made the iron float. 7 Then he said, "Pick it up for yourself." So he reached out his hand and took it.

The Arameans Plot to Capture Elisha

8 Now the king of Aram was making war against Israel; and he consulted with his servants, saying, "In such and such a place shall be my camp." 9 But the man of God sent *word* to the king of Israel, saying, "Be careful that you do not pass this place, because the Arameans are coming down there." 10 And the king of Israel sent *scouts* to the place about which the man of God had told him; so he warned him, so that he was on his guard there, more than once or twice.

11 Now the heart of the king of Aram was enraged over this matter; and he called his servants and said to them, "Will you not tell me which of us is for the king of Israel?" 12 One of his servants said, "No, my lord, the king; but Elisha, the prophet who is in Israel, tells the king of Israel the words that you speak in your bedroom." 13 So he said, "Go and see where he is, so that I may send *men* and take him." And it was told to him, saying, "Behold, *he is* in Dothan." 14 So he sent horses and chariots and a substantial army there, and they came by night and surrounded the city.

15 Now when the attendant of the man of God had risen early and gone out, behold, an army with horses and chariots was circling the city. And his servant said to him, "This is hopeless, my master! What are we to do?" 16 And he said, "Do not be afraid, for those who are with us are greater than those who are with them." 17 Then Elisha prayed and said, "LORD, please, open his eyes so that he may see." And the LORD opened the servant's eyes, and he saw; and behold, the mountain was full of horses and chariots of fire all around Elisha. 18 And when they came down to him, Elisha prayed to the LORD and said, "Please strike this people with blindness." So He struck them with blindness in accordance with the word of Elisha. 19 Then Elisha said to them, "This is not the way, nor is this the city; follow me and I will bring you to the man whom you seek." And he brought them to Samaria.

20 When they had come into Samaria, Elisha said, "LORD, open the eyes of these *men,* so that they may see." So the LORD opened their eyes, and they saw; and behold, *they were* in the midst of Samaria. 21 Then the king of Israel when he saw them, said to Elisha, "My father, shall I kill them? Shall I kill them?" 22 But he answered, "You shall not kill *them.* Would you kill those whom you have taken captive with your sword and your bow? Set bread and water before them, so that they may eat and drink, and go to their master." 23 So he provided a large feast for them; and when they had eaten and drunk, he sent them away, and they went to their master. And the marauding bands of Arameans did not come again into the land of Israel.

The Siege of Samaria—Cannibalism

24 Now it came about after this, that Ben-hadad the king of Aram gathered all his army, and went up and besieged Samaria. 25 So there was a severe famine in Samaria; and behold, they kept besieging it until a donkey's head was *sold* for eighty *shekels* of silver, and a fourth of a ʳkab of dove's dung for five *shekels* of silver. 26 And as the king of Israel was passing by on the wall, a woman cried out to him, saying, "Help, my lord the king!" 27 But he said, "If the LORD does not help you, from where am I to help you? From the threshing floor, or from the wine press?" 28 Then the king said to her, "What is on your mind?" And she said, "This woman said to me, 'Give your son so that we may eat him today, and we will eat my son tomorrow.' 29 So we cooked my son and ate him; and I said to her on the next day, 'Give your son, so that we may eat him'; but she has hidden her son." 30 When the king heard the woman's words, he tore his clothes—and he was passing by on the wall—and the people looked, and behold, *he had* sackcloth underneath on his body. 31 Then he said, "May God do so to me and more so, if the head of Elisha the son of Shaphat remains on him today."

32 Now Elisha was sitting in his house, and

the elders were sitting with him. And *the king* sent a man from his presence; but before the messenger came to him, he said to the elders, "Do you see how this son of a murderer has sent *a man* to cut off my head? Look, when the messenger comes, shut the door and hold the door shut against him. Is the sound of his master's feet not behind him?" **33** While he was still talking with them, behold, the messenger came down to him and he said, "Behold, this evil is from the LORD; why should I wait for the LORD any longer?"

Elisha Promises Food

7 Then Elisha said, "Listen to the word of the LORD; this is what the LORD says: 'About this time tomorrow a measure of fine flour *will be sold* for a shekel, and two measures of barley for a shekel, at the gate of Samaria.'" **2** The royal officer on whose hand the king was leaning responded to the man of God and said, "Even if the LORD were to make windows in heaven, could this thing happen?" Then he said, "Behold, you are going to see it with your own eyes, but you will not eat any of it."

Four Men with Leprosy Report Arameans' Flight

3 Now there were four leprous men at the entrance of the gate; and they said to one another, "Why are we sitting here until we die? **4** If we say, 'We will enter the city,' then the famine is in the city and we will die there; but if we sit here, we will also die. Now then come, and let's go over to the camp of the Arameans. If they spare us, we will live; and if they kill us, then we will die." **5** So they got up at twilight to go to the camp of the Arameans; when they came to the outskirts of the camp of the Arameans, behold, there was no one there. **6** For the Lord had made the army of the Arameans hear a sound of chariots, a sound of horses, *that is,* the sound of a great army; and they said to one another, "Behold, the king of Israel has hired the kings of the Hittites and the kings of the Egyptians against us, to attack us!" **7** So they got up and fled at twilight, and abandoned their tents, their horses, and their donkeys—*indeed* the camp *itself,* just as it was; and they fled for their lives. **8** When these men with leprosy came to the outskirts of the camp, they entered one tent and ate and drank, and carried from there silver, gold, and clothes, and they went and hid *them;* then they returned and entered another tent, and carried *valuables* from there *also,* and went and hid *them.*

9 Then they said to one another, "We are not doing the right thing. This day is a day of good news, but we are keeping silent *about it;* if we wait until the morning light, punishment will overtake us. Now then come, let's go and inform the king's household." **10** So they came and called to the gatekeepers of the city, and told them, saying, "We came to the camp of the Arameans, and behold, there was no one there, nor a human voice; only the horses tied and the donkeys tied, and the tents just as they were." **11** And the gatekeepers called and announced *it* inside the king's house. **12** Then the king got up in the night and said to his servants, "I will now tell you what the

Arameans have done to us. They know that we are hungry; so they have left the camp to hide themselves in the field, saying, 'When they come out of the city, we will capture them alive and get into the city.'" **13** One of his servants responded and said, "Please, have some *men* take five of the horses that remain, which are left in the city. Behold, they *will be in any case* like all the multitude of Israel who are left in it; behold, they *will be* like all the multitude of Israel who have *already* perished, so let us send *them* and see." **14** Therefore they took two chariots with horses, and the king sent *them* after the army of the Arameans, saying, "Go and see."

The Promise Fulfilled

15 They went after them to the Jordan, and behold, all the way was full of clothes and equipment which the Arameans had thrown away when they fled in a hurry. Then the messengers returned and informed the king. **16** So the people went out and plundered the camp of the Arameans. Then a measure of fine flour *was sold* for a shekel, and two measures of barley for a shekel, in accordance with the word of the LORD. **17** Now the king appointed the royal officer on whose hand he leaned to be in charge of the gate; but the people trampled on him at the gate, and he died, just as the man of God had said, who spoke when the king came down to him. **18** So it happened just as the man of God had spoken to the king, saying, "Two measures of barley for a shekel and a measure of fine flour for a shekel, will be *sold* about this time tomorrow at the gate of Samaria." **19** *At that time* the royal officer had responded to the man of God and said, "Now even if the LORD were to make windows in heaven, could such a thing as this happen?" And he had said, "Behold, you are going to see it with your own eyes, but you will not eat any of it." **20** And this is what happened to him, for the people trampled on him at the gate and he died.

Jehoram Restores the Shunammite's Land

8 Now Elisha spoke to the woman whose son he had restored to life, saying, "Arise and go with your household, and live wherever you can live; for the LORD has called for a famine, and it will indeed come on the land for seven years." **2** So the woman arose and acted in accordance with the word of the man of God: she went with her household and resided in the land of the Philistines for seven years. **3** Then at the end of seven years, the woman returned from the land of the Philistines; and she went to appeal to the king for her house and for her field. **4** Now the king was speaking with Gehazi, the servant of the man of God, saying, "Please report to me all the great things that Elisha has done." **5** And as he was reporting to the king how he had restored to life the one who was dead, behold, the woman whose son he had restored to life appealed to the king for her house and for her field. And Gehazi said, "My lord the king, this is the woman and this is her son, whom Elisha restored to life." **6** When the king asked the

woman, she told *everything* to him. So the king appointed an officer for her, saying, "Restore all that was hers and all the produce of the field from the day that she left the land even until now."

Elisha Predicts Evil from Hazael

7 Then Elisha came to Damascus. Now Ben-hadad, the king of Aram, was sick, and it was told to him, saying, "The man of God has come here." 8 And the king said to Hazael, "Take a gift in your hand and go to meet the man of God, and inquire of the LORD by him, saying, 'Will I recover from this sickness?' " 9 So Hazael went to meet him and took a gift in his hand, even every kind of good thing of Damascus, forty camels' loads; and he came and stood before him and said, "Your son Ben-hadad king of Aram has sent me to you, saying, 'Will I recover from this sickness?' " 10 Then Elisha said to him, "Go, say to him, 'You will certainly recover'; but the LORD has shown me that he will certainly die." 11 And he stared steadily *at him* until Hazael was embarrassed, and *then* the man of God wept. 12 And Hazael said, "Why is my lord weeping?" And he answered, "Because I know the evil that you will do to the sons of Israel: you will set their fortified cities on fire, you will kill their young men with the sword, their little ones you will smash to pieces, and you will rip up their pregnant women." 13 Then Hazael said, "But what is your servant—a *lowly* dog—that he could do this great thing?" And Elisha answered, "The LORD has shown me that you *will be* king over Aram." 14 So he left Elisha and came to his master, who said to him, "What did Elisha say to you?" And he answered, "He told me that you would certainly recover." 15 But on the following day, he took the †cover and dipped it in water, and spread it over his face, so that he died. And Hazael became king in his place.

Another Jehoram Reigns in Judah

16 Now in the fifth year of Joram the son of Ahab king of Israel, when Jehoshaphat was the king of Judah, Jehoram the son of Jehoshaphat king of Judah became king. 17 He was thirty-two years old when he became king, and he reigned for eight years in Jerusalem. 18 He walked in the way of the kings of Israel, just as the house of Ahab had done, for Ahab's daughter was his wife; and he did evil in the sight of the LORD. 19 However, the LORD did not want to destroy Judah, for the sake of David His servant, since He had promised him to give him a †lamp through his sons always. 20 In his days Edom broke away from the rule of Judah, and appointed a king over themselves. 21 Then Joram crossed over to Zair, and all his chariots with him. And he got up at night and struck the Edomites who had surrounded him and the captains of the chariots; but his army fled to their tents. 22 So Edom has broken away from Judah to this day. Then Libnah broke away at the same time. 23 Now the rest of the acts of Joram and everything that he did, are they not written in the Book of the Chronicles of the Kings of Judah?

Ahaziah Succeeds Jehoram in Judah

24 So Joram †lay down with his fathers and was buried with his fathers in the city of David; and his son Ahaziah became king in his place.

25 In the twelfth year of Joram the son of Ahab king of Israel, Ahaziah the son of Jehoram king of Judah began to reign. 26 Ahaziah *was* twenty-two years old when he became king, and he reigned for one year in Jerusalem. And his mother's name *was* Athaliah the granddaughter of Omri king of Israel. 27 He walked in the way of the house of Ahab and did evil in the sight of the LORD, like the house of Ahab, because he was a son-in-law of the house of Ahab.

28 Then he went with Joram the son of Ahab to war against Hazael king of Aram at Ramoth-gilead, and the Arameans wounded Joram. 29 So King Joram returned to have himself healed in Jezreel of the wounds which the Arameans had inflicted on him at Ramah when he fought against Hazael king of Aram. Then Ahaziah the son of Jehoram king of Judah went down to see Joram the son of Ahab in Jezreel because he was sick.

Jehu Reigns over Israel

9 Now Elisha the prophet summoned one of the sons of the prophets and said to him, "Get ready and take this flask of oil in your hand, and go to Ramoth-gilead. 2 When you arrive there, then look there for Jehu the son of Jehoshaphat the son of Nimshi, and go in and have him get up from among his brothers, and bring him to an inner room. 3 Then take the flask of oil and pour it on his head, and say, 'This is what the LORD says: "I have anointed you king over Israel." ' Then open the door and flee, and do not wait."

4 So the young man, the servant of the prophet, went to Ramoth-gilead. 5 When he arrived, behold, the commanders of the army were sitting, and he said, "I have a word for you, commander." And Jehu said, "For which *one* of us?" And he said, "For you, commander." 6 He then got up and went into the house, and *the prophet's servant* poured the oil on his head and said to him, "This is what the LORD, the God of Israel says: 'I have anointed you king over the people of the LORD, over Israel. 7 And you shall strike the house of Ahab your master, so that I may avenge the blood of My servants the prophets, and the blood of all the servants of the LORD, at the hand of Jezebel. 8 For the entire house of Ahab shall perish, and I will eliminate from Ahab every male person both slave and free in Israel. 9 I will make the house of Ahab like the house of Jeroboam the son of Nebat, and like the house of Baasha the son of Ahijah. 10 The dogs will eat Jezebel in the territory of Jezreel, and no one will bury *her*.' " Then he opened the door and fled.

11 Now Jehu went out to the servants of his master, and one said to him, "Is everything well? Why did this crazy fellow come to you?" And he said to them, "You know *very well* the man and his talk." 12 And they said, "It is a lie; tell us now." And he said, "Such and such he

---

said to me, saying, 'This is what the LORD says: "I have anointed you king over Israel." ' "

13 Then they hurried, and each man took his garment and put it under him on the bare steps, and blew the trumpet, saying, "Jehu is king!"

Jehu Assassinates Jehoram (Joram)

14 So Jehu the son of Jehoshaphat the son of Nimshi conspired against Joram. Now Joram with all Israel was defending Ramoth-gilead against Hazael king of Aram, 15 but King 1Joram had returned to Jezreel to have himself healed of the wounds which the Arameans had inflicted on him when he fought Hazael king of Aram. So Jehu said to the other men, "If this is your intent, then let no one escape from the city to go tell about it in Jezreel." 16 Then Jehu rode in a chariot and went to Jezreel, since Joram was lying there recovering. And Ahaziah the king of Judah had come down to see Joram.

17 Now the watchman was standing on the tower in Jezreel and he saw the company of Jehu as he came, and he said, "I see a company." And 1Joram said, "Take a horseman and send him to meet them and have him ask, 'Is your intention peace?' " 18 So a horseman went to meet him and said, "This is what the king says: 'Is your intention peace?' " But Jehu said, "How is peace any business of yours? Turn and follow me." And the watchman reported, "The messenger came to them, but he did not return." 19 Then he sent a second horseman, and he came to them and said, "This is what the king says: 'Is your intention peace?' " And Jehu answered, "How is peace any business of yours? Turn and follow me." 20 And the watchman reported, "He came up to them, but he did not return; and the 1driving is like the driving of Jehu the son of Nimshi, for he drives furiously."

21 Then Joram said, "Get ready." And they made his chariot ready. Then Joram king of Israel and Ahaziah king of Judah went out, each in his chariot, and they went out to meet Jehu and found him on the property of Naboth the Jezreelite. 22 When Joram saw Jehu, he said, "Is your intention peace, Jehu?" And he answered, "What 'peace,' so long as your mother Jezebel's acts of prostitution and witchcraft are so many?" 23 So Joram turned back and fled, and he said to Ahaziah, "There is treachery, Ahaziah!" 24 Then Jehu drew his bow with his full strength and shot Joram between his arms; and the arrow went through his heart, and he sank in his chariot. 25 And Jehu said to Bidkar his officer, "Pick him up and throw him on the property of the field of Naboth the Jezreelite; for remember, when you and I were riding together after his father Ahab, that the LORD brought this pronouncement against him: 26 'I have certainly seen yesterday the blood of Naboth and the blood of his sons,' declares the LORD, 'and I will repay you on this property,' declares the LORD. Now then, pick him up and throw him on the property, in accordance with the word of the LORD."

Jehu Assassinates Ahaziah

27 When Ahaziah the king of Judah saw this, he fled by way of the garden house. But Jehu pursued him and said, "Shoot him too, in the chariot." So they shot him at the ascent of Gur, which is at Ibleam. But he fled to Megiddo and died there. 28 Then his servants carried him in a chariot to Jerusalem, and buried him in his grave with his fathers in the city of David. 29 Now in the eleventh year of Joram, the son of Ahab, Ahaziah became king over Judah.

30 When Jehu came to Jezreel, Jezebel heard about it, and she put makeup on her eyes and adorned her head, and looked down through the window. 31 As Jehu entered the gate, she said, "Is your intention peace, Zimri, his master's murderer?" 32 Then he raised his face toward the window and said, "Who is with me, who?" And two or three officials looked down at him.

Jezebel Is Killed

33 Then he said, "Throw her down." So they threw her down, and some of her blood spattered on the wall and on the horses, and he trampled her underfoot. 34 When he came in, he ate and drank; and he said, "See now to this cursed woman and bury her, for she is a king's daughter." 35 So they went to bury her, but they found nothing of her except the skull, the feet, and the palms of her hands. 36 Therefore they returned and informed him. And he said, "This is the word of the LORD, which He spoke by His servant Elijah the Tishbite, saying, 'On the property of Jezreel the dogs shall eat the flesh of Jezebel; 37 and the corpse of Jezebel will be like dung on the face of the field in the property of Jezreel, so they cannot say, "This is Jezebel." ' "

Judgment upon Ahab's House

10 Now Ahab had seventy sons in Samaria. And Jehu wrote letters and sent them to Samaria, to the officials of Jezreel, the elders, and to the guardians of the children of Ahab, saying, 2 "And now, when this letter comes to you, since your master's sons are with you, as well as the chariots and horses, and a fortified city and the weapons, 3 select the best and most capable of your master's sons and seat him on his father's throne, and fight for your master's house." 4 But they feared greatly and said, "Behold, the two kings did not stand firm before him; how then can we stand?" 5 And the one who was in charge of the household, and the one who was in charge of the city, and the elders, and the guardians of the children, sent word to Jehu, saying, "We are your servants, and everything that you tell us we will do. We will not appoint any man king; do what is good in your sight." 6 Then he wrote them a letter a second time, saying, "If you are on my side, and will listen to my voice, take the heads of the men, your master's sons, and come to me at Jezreel about this time tomorrow." Now the king's sons, seventy men, were with the great people of the city, who were raising them. 7 When the letter came to them, they took the king's sons and slaughtered them, seventy

---

9:15 1 Heb Jehoram   **9:17** 1 Heb Jehoram   **9:20** 1 I.e., of the chariot

men, and put their heads in baskets, and sent *them* to him at Jezreel. [8] When the messenger came and informed him, saying, "They have brought the heads of the king's sons," he said, "Put them in two heaps at the entrance of the gate until morning." [9] Now in the morning he went out and stood and said to all the people, "You are innocent; behold, I conspired against my master and killed him, but who killed all these? [10] Know then that nothing of the word of the LORD, which the LORD spoke concerning the house of Ahab, shall 'fall to the earth, for the LORD has done what He spoke through His servant Elijah." [11] So Jehu killed all who remained of the house of Ahab in Jezreel, and all his great men, his acquaintances, and his priests, until he left him without a survivor.

[12] Then he set out and went to Samaria. On the way while he was at 'Beth-eked of the shepherds, [13] Jehu encountered the relatives of Ahaziah king of Judah, and he said, "Who are you?" And they answered, "We are the relatives of Ahaziah; and we have come down to greet the sons of the king and the sons of the queen mother." [14] Then he said, "Take them alive." So they took them alive, and slaughtered them at the pit of Beth-eked, forty-two men; and he left none of them.

[15] Now when he had gone from there, he encountered Jehonadab the son of Rechab coming to meet him; and he greeted him and said to him, "Is your heart right, just as my heart *is* with your heart?" And Jehonadab answered, "It is." *Jehu said,* "If it is, give *me* your hand." And he gave *him* his hand, and he pulled him up to him into the chariot. [16] Then he said, "Come with me and see my zeal for the LORD." So he had him ride in his chariot. [17] When he came to Samaria, he killed all who remained to Ahab in Samaria, until he had eliminated them, in accordance with the word of the LORD which He spoke to Elijah.

Jehu Destroys Baal Worshipers

[18] Then Jehu gathered all the people and said to them, "Ahab served Baal a little; Jehu will serve him much. [19] Now, summon to me all the prophets of Baal, all his worshipers and all his priests; let no one go missing, because I have a great sacrifice for Baal; whoever is missing shall not live." But Jehu did it in deception, in order to eliminate the worshipers of Baal. [20] And Jehu said, "Proclaim a holy assembly for Baal." And they proclaimed *it*. [21] Then Jehu sent *word* throughout Israel, and all the worshipers of Baal came, so that there was not a person left who did not come. And when they entered the house of Baal, the house of Baal was filled from one end to the other. [22] And he said to the one who *was* in charge of the wardrobe, "Bring out garments for all the worshipers of Baal." So he brought out the garments for them. [23] Then Jehu entered the house of Baal with Jehonadab the son of Rechab; and he said to the worshipers of Baal, "Search carefully and see to it that there is here with you none of the servants of the LORD, but only the worshipers of Baal." [24] Then

they entered to offer sacrifices and burnt offerings.

Now Jehu had stationed for himself eighty men outside, and he had said, "The one who allows any of the men whom I bring into your hands to escape shall give up his life in exchange."

[25] Then it came about, as soon as he had finished offering the burnt offering, that Jehu said to the guard and to the royal officers, "Go in, kill them; let none come out." So they killed them with the edge of the sword; and the guard and the royal officers threw *them* out, and went to the sanctuary of the house of Baal. [26] They brought out the memorial stones of the house of Baal and burned them. [27] They also tore down the memorial stone of Baal and tore down the house of Baal, and made it a latrine *as it is* to this day.

[28] So Jehu eradicated Baal from Israel. [29] However, *as for* the sins of Jeroboam the son of Nebat, into which he misled Israel, from these Jehu did not desist, *including* the golden calves that *were* at Bethel and at Dan. [30] Yet the LORD said to Jehu, "Because you have done well in performing what is right in My eyes, *and* have done to the house of Ahab in accordance with everything that *was* in My heart, your sons to the fourth *generation* shall sit on the throne of Israel." [31] But Jehu was not careful to walk in the Law of the LORD, the God of Israel, with all his heart; he did not desist from the sins of Jeroboam, into which he misled Israel.

[32] In those days the LORD began to cut off *pieces* from Israel; and Hazael defeated *them* throughout the territory of Israel: [33] from the Jordan eastward, all the land of Gilead, the Gadites, the Reubenites, and the Manassites; from Aroer, which is by the Valley of the Arnon, that is, Gilead and Bashan.

Jehoahaz Succeeds Jehu

[34] Now *as for* the rest of the acts of Jehu and everything that he did and all his might, are they not written in the Book of the Chronicles of the Kings of Israel? [35] And Jehu 'lay down with his fathers, and they buried him in Samaria. And his son Jehoahaz became king in his place. [36] So the time which Jehu reigned over Israel in Samaria *was* twenty-eight years.

Athaliah Queen of Judah

11 When Athaliah the mother of Ahaziah saw that her son was dead, she arose and eliminated all the royal children. [2] But Jehosheba, the daughter of King Joram, sister of Ahaziah, took Joash the son of Ahaziah and abducted him from among the king's sons who were being put to death, *and put* him and his nurse in the bedroom. So they hid him from Athaliah, and he was not put to death. [3] So he was kept hidden with her in the house of the LORD for six years, while Athaliah was reigning over the land.

[4] Now in the seventh year Jehoiada sent *orders* and brought the captains of hundreds of the Carites and of the guards, and brought them to himself at the house of the LORD. Then

he made a covenant with them and put them under oath at the house of the LORD, and showed them the king's son. [5] And he commanded them, saying, "This is the thing that you shall do: a third of you, who come in on the Sabbath and keep watch over the king's house [6] (a third also *shall be* at the gate Sur, and a third at the gate behind the guards), shall keep watch over the house for defense. [7] And two parts of you, all who go out on the Sabbath, shall also keep watch over the house of the LORD for the king. [8] Then you shall surround the king, each with his weapons in his hand; and whoever comes within the ranks shall be put to death. And you are to be with the king when he goes out and when he comes in."

[9] So the captains of hundreds acted in accordance with everything that Jehoiada the priest commanded. And each one of them took his men who were to come in on the Sabbath, along with those who were to go out on the Sabbath, and they came to Jehoiada the priest. [10] Then the priest gave the captains of hundreds the spears and shields that *had been* King David's, which *were* in the house of the LORD. [11] The guards stood, each with his weapons in his hand, from the right side of the house to the left side of the house, by the altar and by the house, around the king. [12] Then he brought the king's son out, and put the crown on him and *gave him* the testimony; and they made him king and anointed him, and they clapped their hands and said, "*Long* live the king!"

[13] When Athaliah heard the noise of the guards *and of* the people, she came to the people at the house of the LORD. [14] And she looked, and behold, the king was standing by the pillar according to the custom, with the captains and the trumpeters beside the king; and all the people of the land were joyful and were blowing trumpets. Then Athaliah tore her clothes and cried out, "Conspiracy! Conspiracy!" [15] And Jehoiada the priest commanded the captains of hundreds who were appointed over the army and said to them, "Bring her out between the ranks, and whoever follows her, put to death with the sword!" For the priest said, "She is not to be put to death at the house of the LORD." [16] So they seized her, and when they brought her to the horses' entrance of the king's house, she was put to death there.

[17] Then Jehoiada made a covenant between the LORD, the king, and the people, that they would be the LORD's people, and between the king and the people. [18] And all the people of the land came to the house of Baal and tore it down; they thoroughly smashed his altars and his images in pieces, and they killed Mattan the priest of Baal before the altars. Then the priest appointed sentries over the house of the LORD. [19] And he took the captains of hundreds and the Carites, and the guards and all the people of the land; and they brought the king down from the house of the LORD, and came by way of the gate of the guards to the king's

house. And he sat on the throne of the kings. [20] So all the people of the land rejoiced and the city was peaceful. For they had put Athaliah to death with the sword at the king's house. [21] [1]Jehoash was seven years old when he became king.

Jehoash (Joash) Reigns over Judah

12 In the seventh year of Jehu, [1]Jehoash became king, and he reigned for forty years in Jerusalem; and his mother's name was Zibiah of Beersheba. [2] Jehoash did what was right in the sight of the LORD all his days that Jehoiada the priest instructed him. [3] Only the high places did not end; the people still sacrificed and burned incense on the high places.

The Temple to Be Repaired

[4] Then Jehoash said to the priests, "All the money of the sacred offerings which is brought into the house of the LORD, in current money, *both* the money of each man's assessment *and* all the money which anyone's heart prompts him to bring into the house of the LORD, [5] The priests are to take it for themselves, each from his acquaintance; and they shall repair damage to the house wherever any damage is found."

[6] But it came about that in the twenty-third year of King Jehoash, the priests had not repaired *any* damage to the house. [7] So King Jehoash summoned Jehoiada the priest, and the *other* priests, and said to them, "Why do you not repair damage to the house? Now then, you are not to take *any more* money from your acquaintances, but give it up for the damage to the house." [8] The priests then agreed that they would not take *any more* money from the people, nor would they repair damage to the house.

[9] Instead, Jehoiada the priest took a chest and drilled a hole in its lid and put it beside the altar, on the right side as one comes into the house of the LORD; and the priests who guarded the threshold put in it all the money that was brought into the house of the LORD. [10] When they saw that there was a great *amount of* money in the chest, the king's scribe and the high priest went up and tied *it* up in bags, and counted the money that was found in the house of the LORD. [11] And they handed the money which was assessed over to those who did the work, who had the oversight of the house of the LORD; and they paid it out to the carpenters and the builders who worked on the house of the LORD; [12] and to the masons and the stonecutters, and for buying timber and cut stone to repair the damage to the house of the LORD, and for everything that was laid out for the house to repair it. [13] However there were not made for the house of the LORD silver cups, shears, bowls, trumpets, any receptacles of gold, or receptacles of silver from the money which was brought into the house of the LORD; [14] for they gave that to those who did the work, and with it they repaired the house of the LORD. [15] Moreover, they did not require an accounting from the men into whose hands they gave the money to pay to

11:21 1 Ch 12:1 in Heb; Jehoash is another spelling of Joash in Heb   **12:1** 1 Jehoash is another spelling of Joash in Heb

those who did the work, because they acted faithfully. [16] The money from the guilt offerings and the money from the sin offerings was not brought into the house of the LORD; it belonged to the priests.

[17] Then Hazael the king of Aram went up and fought against Gath and captured it, and Hazael was intent on going up against Jerusalem. [18] So Jehoash king of Judah took all the sacred offerings that Jehoshaphat, Jehoram, and Ahaziah, his fathers, kings of Judah, had consecrated, and his own sacred offerings, and all the gold that was found among the treasuries of the house of the LORD and of the king's house, and sent *them* to Hazael king of Aram. Then he withdrew from Jerusalem.

Joash (Jehoash) Succeeded by Amaziah in Judah

[19] Now *as for* the rest of the acts of Joash and everything that he did, are they not written in the Book of the Chronicles of the Kings of Judah? [20] And his servants rose up and formed a conspiracy; and they struck and killed Joash at the house of Millo *as he was* going down to Silla. [21] For Jozacar the son of Shimeath and Jehozabad the son of Shomer, his servants, struck *him* and he died; and they buried him with his fathers in the city of David, and his son Amaziah became king in his place.

Kings of Israel: Jehoahaz and Jehoash

13 In the twenty-third year of Joash the son of Ahaziah, king of Judah, Jehoahaz the son of Jehu became king over Israel at Samaria, *and he reigned* for seventeen years. [2] He did evil in the sight of the LORD, and followed the sins of Jeroboam the son of Nebat, into which he misled Israel; he did not turn from them. [3] So the anger of the LORD was kindled against Israel, and He continually handed them over to Hazael king of Aram, and to Ben-hadad, the son of Hazael. [4] Then Jehoahaz appeased the LORD, and the LORD listened to him; for He saw the oppression of Israel, how the king of Aram oppressed them. [5] And the LORD gave Israel a savior, so that they escaped from under the hand of the Arameans; and the sons of Israel lived in their tents as previously. [6] Nevertheless they did not abandon the sins of the house of Jeroboam, into which he misled Israel; *rather,* they walked in them; and the [1]Asherah also remained standing in Samaria. [7] For he left to Jehoahaz no more of the army than fifty horsemen, ten chariots, and ten thousand infantry, because the king of Aram had eliminated them and made them like the dust at threshing. [8] Now *as for* the rest of the acts of Jehoahaz, and all that he did and his might, are they not written in the Book of the Chronicles of the Kings of Israel? [9] And Jehoahaz [1]lay down with his fathers, and they buried him in Samaria; and his son Joash became king in his place.

[10] In the thirty-seventh year of Joash king of Judah, [1]Jehoash the son of Jehoahaz became king over Israel in Samaria, *and he reigned* for sixteen years. [11] He did evil in the sight of the

LORD; he did not turn away from all the sins of Jeroboam the son of Nebat, into which he misled Israel; *rather,* he walked in them. [12] Now *as for* the rest of the acts of Joash and all that he did, and his might with which he fought against Amaziah king of Judah, are they not written in the Book of the Chronicles of the Kings of Israel? [13] So Joash [1]lay down with his fathers, and Jeroboam sat on his throne; and Joash was buried in Samaria with the kings of Israel.

Death of Elisha

[14] When Elisha became sick with the illness of which he was to die, Joash the king of Israel came down to him, and wept over him and said, "My father, my father, the chariots of Israel and its horsemen!" [15] And Elisha said to him, "Take a bow and arrows." So he took a bow and arrows. [16] Then *Elisha* said to the king of Israel, "Lay your hand on the bow." And he laid his hand *on it,* then Elisha put his hands on the king's hands. [17] And he said, "Open the window toward the east," and he opened *it.* Then Elisha said, "Shoot!" So he shot. And he said, "The LORD's arrow of victory, and the arrow of victory over Aram; for you will defeat the Arameans at Aphek until you have put an end *to them.*" [18] Then he said, "Take the arrows," and he took *them.* And he said to the king of Israel, "Strike the ground," and he struck *it* three times and stopped. [19] Then the man of God became angry at him and said, "You should have struck five or six times, then you would have struck Aram until you put an end *to it.* But now you shall strike Aram *only* three times."

[20] And Elisha died, and they buried him. Now the marauding bands of the Moabites would invade the land in the spring of the year. [21] And as they were burying a man, behold, they saw a marauding band; and they threw the man into the grave of Elisha. And when the man touched the bones of Elisha he revived and stood up on his feet.

[22] Now Hazael king of Aram had oppressed Israel all the days of Jehoahaz. [23] But the LORD was gracious to them and had compassion on them and turned to them because of His covenant with Abraham, Isaac, and Jacob; and He was unwilling to eliminate them or cast them away from His presence until now. [24] When Hazael king of Aram died, his son Ben-hadad became king in his place. [25] Then Jehoash the son of Jehoahaz again took from the hand of Ben-hadad the son of Hazael the cities which he had taken in war from the hand of his father Jehoahaz. Three times Joash defeated him and recovered the cities of Israel.

Amaziah Reigns over Judah

14 In the second year of Joash son of Joahaz king of Israel, Amaziah the son of Joash king of Judah became king. [2] He was twenty-five years old when he became king, and he reigned for twenty-nine years in Jerusalem. And his mother's name was Jehoaddin of Jerusalem. [3] He did what was right in the sight

---

13:6 [1]I.e., wooden symbol of a female deity   **13:9** [1]I.e., died   **13:10** [1]In Heb Jehoash is another spelling of Joash   **13:13** [1]I.e., died

of the LORD, yet not like his father David; he acted in accordance with everything that his father Joash had done. 4 Only the high places were not eliminated; the people still sacrificed and burned incense on the high places. 5 Now it came about, as soon as the kingdom was firmly in his hand, that he killed his servants who had killed the king, his father. 6 But he did not put the sons of the murderers to death, in obedience to what is written in the Book of the Law of Moses, as the LORD commanded, saying, "The fathers shall not be put to death for the sons, nor the sons be put to death for the fathers; but each shall be put to death for his own sin."

7 He killed ten thousand *of* the Edomites in the Valley of Salt, and took Sela by war, and named it Joktheel, *as it is* to this day.

8 Then Amaziah sent messengers to 1Jehoash, the son of Jehoahaz son of Jehu, king of Israel, saying, "Come, let's face each other *in combat.*" 9 But Jehoash king of Israel sent *messengers* to Amaziah king of Judah, saying, "The thorn bush that was in Lebanon sent *word* to the cedar that was in Lebanon, saying, 'Give your daughter to my son in marriage.' But a wild animal that was in Lebanon passed by and trampled the thorn bush. 10 You have indeed defeated Edom, and your heart is elated. Enjoy the glory and stay home; for why should you get involved in trouble so that you would fall, you and Judah with you?"

11 But Amaziah would not listen. So Jehoash king of Israel went up; and they faced each other, he and Amaziah king of Judah, at Beth-shemesh, which belongs to Judah. 12 And Judah was defeated by Israel, and they fled, every man to his tent. 13 Then Jehoash king of Israel captured Amaziah king of Judah, the son of Jehoash the son of Ahaziah, at Beth-shemesh, and came to Jerusalem and tore down the wall of Jerusalem from the Gate of Ephraim to the Corner Gate, 1four hundred cubits. 14 And he took all the gold and silver and all the utensils which were found in the house of the LORD, and in the treasuries of the king's house, the hostages as well, and returned to Samaria.

Jeroboam II Succeeds Jehoash (Joash) in Israel

15 Now *as for* the rest of the acts of Jehoash that he did, and his might and how he fought with Amaziah king of Judah, are they not written in the Book of the Chronicles of the Kings of Israel? 16 So Jehoash 1lay down with his fathers and was buried in Samaria with the kings of Israel; and his son Jeroboam became king in his place.

Azariah (Uzziah) Succeeds Amaziah in Judah

17 Amaziah the son of Joash king of Judah lived for fifteen years after the death of Jehoash son of Jehoahaz king of Israel. 18 Now *as for* the rest of the acts of Amaziah, are they not written in the Book of the Chronicles of the Kings of Judah? 19 They formed a conspiracy against him in Jerusalem, and he fled to Lachish; but they sent *men* to Lachish after

him and they killed him there. 20 Then they carried him on horses, and he was buried in Jerusalem with his fathers in the city of David. 21 And all the people of Judah took Azariah, who *was* sixteen years old, and made him king in place of his father Amaziah. 22 He built Elath and restored it to Judah after the king 1lay down with his fathers.

23 In the fifteenth year of Amaziah the son of Joash king of Judah, Jeroboam the son of Joash king of Israel became king in Samaria, *and* reigned for forty-one years. 24 He did evil in the sight of the LORD; he did not abandon all the sins of Jeroboam the son of Nebat, into which he misled Israel. 25 He restored the border of Israel from the entrance of Hamath as far as the Sea of the Arabah, in accordance with the word of the LORD, the God of Israel, which He spoke through His servant Jonah the son of Amittai, the prophet, who was from Gath-hepher. 26 For the LORD saw the misery of Israel, *which was* very bitter; for there was neither bond nor free *spared,* nor was there any helper for Israel. 27 Yet the LORD did not say that He would wipe out the name of Israel from under heaven, but He saved them by the hand of Jeroboam the son of Joash.

Zechariah Reigns over Israel

28 Now *as for* the rest of the acts of Jeroboam and all that he did and his might, how he fought and how he recovered for Israel Damascus and Hamath, *which had belonged* to Judah, are they not written in the Book of the Chronicles of the Kings of Israel? 29 And Jeroboam 1lay down with his fathers, with the kings of Israel, and his son Zechariah became king in his place.

Series of Kings: Azariah (Uzziah) over Judah

15 In the twenty-seventh year of Jeroboam king of Israel, Azariah son of Amaziah king of Judah became king. 2 He was sixteen years old when he became king, and he reigned for fifty-two years in Jerusalem; and his mother's name was Jecoliah of Jerusalem. 3 He did what was right in the sight of the LORD, in accordance with everything that his father Amaziah had done. 4 Only the high places were not eliminated; the people still sacrificed and burned incense on the high places. 5 And the LORD afflicted the king, so that he had leprosy to the day of his death. And he lived in a separate house, while Jotham the king's son was in charge of the household, judging the people of the land. 6 Now *as for* the rest of the acts of Azariah and all that he did, are they not written in the Book of the Chronicles of the Kings of Judah? 7 And Azariah 1lay down with his fathers, and they buried him with his fathers in the city of David, and his son Jotham became king in his place.

Zechariah over Israel

8 In the thirty-eighth year of Azariah king of Judah, Zechariah the son of Jeroboam became king over Israel in Samaria for six months. 9 He did evil in the sight of the LORD, just as his

fathers had done; he did not desist from the sins of Jeroboam the son of Nebat, into which he misled Israel. [10] Then Shallum the son of Jabesh conspired against him, and struck him in the presence of the people and killed him, and reigned in his place. [11] Now *as for* the rest of the acts of Zechariah, behold they are written in the Book of the Chronicles of the Kings of Israel. [12] This is the word of the LORD which He spoke to Jehu, saying, "Your sons *to* the fourth *generation* shall sit on the throne of Israel." And so it was.

[13] Shallum the son of Jabesh became king in the thirty-ninth year of Uzziah king of Judah, and he reigned for one month in Samaria. [14] Then Menahem the son of Gadi went up from Tirzah and came to Samaria, and struck Shallum son of Jabesh in Samaria, and killed him and became king in his place. [15] Now *as for* the rest of the acts of Shallum and his conspiracy which he formed, behold, they are written in the Book of the Chronicles of the Kings of Israel. [16] Then Menahem attacked Tiphsah and all who were in it and its borders from Tirzah, because they did not open up *to him;* so he attacked *it* and ripped up all its women who were pregnant.

Menahem over Israel

[17] In the thirty-ninth year of Azariah king of Judah, Menahem the son of Gadi became king over Israel *and reigned* for ten years in Samaria. [18] He did evil in the sight of the LORD; for all his days he did not desist from the sins of Jeroboam the son of Nebat, into which he misled Israel.

[19] Pul, the king of Assyria, came against the land, and Menahem gave Pul a ¹thousand talents of silver so that his hand might be with him to strengthen the kingdom under his rule. [20] Then Menahem collected the money from Israel, from all the ¹mighty men of wealth, from each man fifty shekels of silver to pay the king of Assyria. So the king of Assyria returned and did not stay there in the land. [21] Now *as for* the rest of the acts of Menahem and all that he did, are they not written in the Book of the Chronicles of the Kings of Israel? [22] And Menahem ¹lay down with his fathers, and his son Pekahiah became king in his place.

Pekahiah over Israel

[23] In the fiftieth year of Azariah king of Judah, Pekahiah the son of Menahem became king over Israel in Samaria, *and reigned* for two years. [24] He did evil in the sight of the LORD; he did not desist from the sins of Jeroboam the son of Nebat, into which he misled Israel. [25] Then Pekah the son of Remaliah, his officer, conspired against him and struck him in Samaria, in the castle of the king's house with Argob and Arieh; and with him were fifty men of the Gileadites, and he killed him and became king in his place. [26] Now *as for* the rest of the acts of Pekahiah and everything that he did, behold, they are written in the Book of the Chronicles of the Kings of Israel.

Pekah over Israel

[27] In the fifty-second year of Azariah king of Judah, Pekah the son of Remaliah became king over Israel in Samaria, *and he reigned* for twenty years. [28] He did evil in the sight of the LORD; he did not desist from the sins of Jeroboam son of Nebat, into which he misled Israel.

[29] In the days of Pekah king of Israel, Tiglath-pileser the king of Assyria came and took Ijon, Abel-beth-maacah, Janoah, Kedesh, Hazor, Gilead, and Galilee, all the land of Naphtali; and he led their populations into exile to Assyria. [30] And Hoshea the son of Elah formed a conspiracy against Pekah the son of Remaliah, and struck him and put him to death, and he became king in his place, in the twentieth year of Jotham the son of Uzziah. [31] Now *as for* the rest of the acts of Pekah and all that he did, behold, they are written in the Book of the Chronicles of the Kings of Israel.

Jotham over Judah

[32] In the second year of Pekah the son of Remaliah king of Israel, Jotham the son of Uzziah king of Judah became king. [33] He was twenty-five years old when he became king, and he reigned for sixteen years in Jerusalem; and his mother's name *was* Jerusha the daughter of Zadok. [34] He did what was right in the sight of the LORD; he acted in accordance with everything that his father Uzziah had done. [35] Only the high places were not eliminated; the people still sacrificed and burned incense on the high places. He built the upper gate of the house of the LORD. [36] Now *as for* the rest of the acts of Jotham which he did, are they not written in the Book of the Chronicles of the Kings of Judah? [37] In those days the LORD began to send Rezin the king of Aram and Pekah the son of Remaliah against Judah. [38] And Jotham ¹lay down with his fathers, and he was buried with his fathers in the city of his father David; and his son Ahaz became king in his place.

Ahaz Reigns over Judah

16 In the seventeenth year of Pekah the son of Remaliah, Ahaz the son of Jotham, king of Judah, became king. [2] Ahaz *was* twenty years old when he became king, and he reigned for sixteen years in Jerusalem; and he did not do what was right in the sight of the LORD his God, as his father David *had done.* [3] But he walked in the way of the kings of Israel, and he even made his son pass through the fire, in accordance with the abominations of the nations whom the LORD had driven out before the sons of Israel. [4] And he sacrificed and burned incense on the high places, on the hills, and under every green tree.

[5] Then Rezin the king of Aram and Pekah the son of Remaliah, king of Israel, went up to Jerusalem for war; and they besieged Ahaz, but were not capable of fighting him. [6] At that time Rezin king of Aram restored Elath to Aram, and drove the Judeans away from Elath; and

the Arameans came to Elath and have lived there to this day.

Ahaz Seeks Help of Assyria

7 So Ahaz sent messengers to Tiglath-pileser king of Assyria, saying, "I am your servant and your son; come up and save me from the hand of the king of Aram, and from the hand of the king of Israel, who are rising up against me." 8 And Ahaz took the silver and gold that was found in the house of the LORD and in the treasuries of the king's house, and sent a gift to the king of Assyria. 9 So the king of Assyria listened to him; and the king of Assyria went up against Damascus and captured it, and led *the people of* it into exile to Kir, and put Rezin to death.

Damascus Falls

10 Now King Ahaz went to Damascus to meet Tiglath-pileser king of Assyria, and he saw the altar which *was* at Damascus; and King Ahaz sent to Urijah the priest the pattern of the altar and its model, according to all its workmanship. 11 So Urijah the priest built an altar; according to everything that King Ahaz had sent from Damascus, in that way Urijah the priest made *it,* before the coming of King Ahaz from Damascus. 12 And when the king came from Damascus, the king saw the altar; then the king approached the altar and went up to it, 13 and burned his burnt offering and his meal offering, and poured out his drink offering and sprinkled the blood of his peace offerings on the altar. 14 And the bronze altar, which *was* before the LORD, he brought from the front of the house, from between *his* altar and the house of the LORD, and he put it on the north side of *his* altar. 15 Then King Ahaz commanded Urijah the priest, saying, "Upon the great altar burn the morning burnt offering, the evening meal offering, the king's burnt offering and his meal offering, with the burnt offering of all the people of the land, their meal offering, and their drink offerings; and sprinkle on it all the blood of the burnt offering and all the blood of the sacrifice. But the bronze altar shall be for me, for making inquiries." 16 So Urijah the priest acted in accordance with everything that King Ahaz commanded.

17 Then King Ahaz cut off the borders of the stands, and removed the wash basin from them; he also took down the [1]Sea from the bronze oxen which were under it and put it on a pavement of stone. 18 And the covered way for the Sabbath which they had built in the house, and the outer entry of the king, he removed *from* the house of the LORD because of the king of Assyria.

Hezekiah Reigns over Judah

19 Now *as for* the rest of the acts of Ahaz which he did, are they not written in the Book of the Chronicles of the Kings of Judah? 20 So Ahaz [1]lay down with his fathers, and was buried with his fathers in the city of David; and his son Hezekiah reigned in his place.

Hoshea Reigns over Israel

17 In the twelfth year of Ahaz king of Judah, Hoshea the son of Elah became king over Israel in Samaria, *and reigned* for nine years. 2 He did evil in the sight of the LORD, only not as the kings of Israel who preceded him. 3 Shalmaneser the king of Assyria marched against him, and Hoshea became his servant and paid him tribute. 4 But the king of Assyria uncovered a conspiracy by Hoshea, who had sent messengers to So, king of Egypt, and had *then* brought no tribute to the king of Assyria, as *he had done* year by year; so the king of Assyria arrested him and confined him in prison.

5 Then the king of Assyria invaded the entire land, and went up to Samaria and besieged it for three years.

Israel Captive

6 In the ninth year of Hoshea, the king of Assyria captured Samaria and led *the people of* Israel into exile to Assyria, and settled them in Halah and Habor, *on* the river of Gozan, and in the cities of the Medes.

Why Israel Fell

7 Now *this* came about because the sons of Israel had sinned against the LORD their God, who had brought them up from the land of Egypt, from under the hand of Pharaoh, king of Egypt; and they had feared other gods. 8 They also followed the customs of the nations whom the LORD had driven out from the sons of Israel, and *in the customs* of the kings of Israel which they had introduced. 9 And the sons of Israel did things secretly against the LORD their God which were not right. Moreover, they built for themselves high places in all their towns, from watchtower to fortified city. 10 And they set up for themselves memorial stones and [1]Asherim on every high hill and under every green tree, 11 and there they burned incense on all the high places as the nations *did* that the LORD had taken into exile before them; and they did evil things, provoking the LORD. 12 They served idols, concerning which the LORD had said to them, "You shall not do this thing." 13 Yet the LORD warned Israel and Judah through all His prophets *and* every seer, saying, "Turn back from your evil ways and keep My commandments *and* My statutes in accordance with all the Law which I commanded your fathers, and which I sent to you through My servants the prophets." 14 However, they did not listen, but stiffened their neck like their fathers, who did not believe in the LORD their God. 15 They rejected His statutes and His covenant which He made with their fathers, and His warnings which He gave them. And they followed idols and became empty, and followed the nations that surrounded them, *about* which the LORD had commanded them not to do as they *did.* 16 And they abandoned all the commandments of the LORD their God and made for themselves cast metal images: two calves. And they made a [1]Asherah, and worshiped all the heavenly

---

16:17 [1]I.e., a very large basin   **16:20** [1]I.e., died   **17:10** [1]I.e., wooden symbols of a female deity (Asherah)   **17:16** [1]I.e., a wooden symbol of a female deity

lights, and served Baal. 17 Then they made their sons and their daughters pass through the fire, and they practiced divination and interpreting omens, and gave themselves over to do evil in the sight of the LORD, provoking Him. 18 So the LORD was very angry with Israel, and He removed them from His sight; no one was left except the tribe of Judah.

19 Judah did not keep the commandments of the LORD their God either, but they followed the customs which Israel had introduced. 20 So the LORD rejected all the descendants of Israel and afflicted them and handed them over to plunderers, until He had cast them out of His sight.

21 When He had torn Israel from the house of David, they made Jeroboam the son of Nebat king. Then Jeroboam drove Israel away from following the LORD and misled them into a great sin. 22 And the sons of Israel walked in all the sins of Jeroboam which he committed; they did not desist from them 23 until the LORD removed Israel from His sight, just as He had spoken through all His servants the prophets. So Israel went into exile from their own land to Assyria until this day.

Cities of Israel Filled with Strangers

24 Then the king of Assyria brought *people* from Babylon, Cuthah, Avva, Hamath, and Sepharvaim, and settled *them* in the cities of Samaria in place of the sons of Israel. So they took possession of Samaria and lived in its cities. 25 And at the beginning of their living there, they did not fear the LORD; therefore the LORD sent lions among them that were killing some of them. 26 So they spoke to the king of Assyria, saying, "The nations whom you have taken into exile and settled in the cities of Samaria do not know the custom of the God of the land; so He has sent lions among them, and behold, they are killing them because they do not know the custom of the God of the land."

27 Then the king of Assyria issued commands, saying, "Take one of the priests there whom you led into exile, and have him go and live there; and have him teach them the custom of the God of the land." 28 So one of the priests whom they had led into exile from Samaria came and lived in Bethel, and taught them how they were to fear the LORD.

29 But every nation was *still* making gods of its own, and they put them in the houses of the high places which the people of Samaria had made, every nation in their cities in which they lived. 30 The men of Babylon made Succoth-benoth, the men of Cuth made Nergal, the men of Hamath made Ashima, 31 and the Avvites made Nibhaz and Tartak; and the Sepharvites were burning their children in the fire to Adrammelech and Anammelech, the gods of Sepharvaim. 32 They also feared the LORD and appointed from their entire population priests of the high places, who acted for them in the houses of the high places. 33 They feared the LORD, yet they were serving their own gods in accordance with the custom of the nations from among whom they had been taken into exile.

34 To this day they act in accordance with the earlier customs: they do not fear the LORD, nor do they follow their statutes, their ordinances, the Law, or the commandments which the LORD commanded the sons of Jacob, whom He named Israel. 35 The LORD made a covenant with them and commanded them, saying, "You shall not fear other gods, nor bow down to them, nor serve them, nor sacrifice to them. 36 But the LORD, who brought you up from the land of Egypt with great power and with an outstretched arm, Him you shall fear, and to Him you shall bow down, and to Him you shall sacrifice. 37 And the statutes, the ordinances, the Law, and the commandment which He wrote for you, you shall take care to do always; and you shall not fear other gods. 38 The covenant that I have made with you, you shall not forget, nor shall you fear other gods. 39 But you shall fear the LORD your God; and He will save you from the hand of all your enemies." 40 However, they did not listen, but they kept acting in accordance with their earlier custom. 41 So while these nations feared the LORD, they also served their idols; their children likewise and their grandchildren, just as their fathers did, they do to this day.

Hezekiah Reigns over Judah

18 Now it came about in the third year of Hoshea, the son of Elah king of Israel, that Hezekiah the son of Ahaz king of Judah became king. 2 He was twenty-five years old when he became king, and he reigned for twenty-nine years in Jerusalem; and his mother's name was Abi the daughter of Zechariah. 3 He did what was right in the sight of the LORD, in accordance with everything that his father David had done. 4 He removed the high places and smashed the memorial stones to pieces, and cut down the 1Asherah. He also crushed to pieces the bronze serpent that Moses had made, for until those days the sons of Israel had been burning incense to it; and it was called 2Nehushtan. 5 He trusted in the LORD, the God of Israel; and after him there was no one like him among all the kings of Judah, nor *among those* who came before him. 6 For he clung to the LORD; he did not desist from following Him, but kept His commandments, which the LORD had commanded Moses.

Hezekiah Victorious

7 And the LORD was with him; wherever he went he was successful. And he revolted against the king of Assyria and did not serve him. 8 He defeated the Philistines as far as Gaza and its territory, from watchtower to fortified city.

9 Now in the fourth year of King Hezekiah, which was the seventh year of Hoshea son of Elah king of Israel, Shalmaneser king of Assyria marched against Samaria and besieged it. 10 And at the end of three years they captured it; in the sixth year of Hezekiah, which was the ninth year of Hoshea king of Israel, Samaria was captured. 11 Then the king of Assyria led Israel into exile to Assyria, and put them in

---

18:4 1 I.e., a wooden symbol of a female deity   2 I.e., a bronze sculpture

Halah and on the Habor, the river of Gozan, and in the cities of the Medes. 12 This happened because they did not obey the voice of the LORD their God, but violated His covenant, all that Moses the servant of the LORD had commanded; they would neither listen nor do it.

Invasion of Judah

13 Now in the fourteenth year of King Hezekiah, Sennacherib king of Assyria marched against all the fortified cities of Judah and seized them. 14 Then Hezekiah king of Judah sent messengers to the king of Assyria at Lachish, saying, "I have done wrong. Withdraw from me; whatever you impose on me I will endure." So the king of Assyria imposed on Hezekiah king of Judah the payment of three hundred 1 talents of silver and thirty talents of gold. 15 Hezekiah then gave him all the silver that was found in the house of the LORD, and in the treasuries of the king's house. 16 At that time Hezekiah cut off the gold from the doors of the temple of the LORD, and from the doorposts, which Hezekiah king of Judah had overlaid, and he gave it to the king of Assyria.

17 Then the king of Assyria sent Tartan, Rab-saris, and Rabshakeh from Lachish to King Hezekiah with a large army to Jerusalem. So they went up and came to Jerusalem. And when they went up, they came and stood by the conduit of the upper pool, which is on the road of the 1 fuller's field. 18 Then they called to the king, and Eliakim the son of Hilkiah, who was in charge of the household, Shebnah the scribe, and Joah the son of Asaph the secretary, went out to them.

19 And Rabshakeh said to them, "Say now to Hezekiah, 'This is what the great king, the king of Assyria says: "What is this confidence that you have? 20 You say—but they are only empty words—'I have a plan and strength for the war.' Now on whom have you relied, that you have revolted against me? 21 Now behold, you have relied on the support of this broken reed, on Egypt; on which if a man leans, it will go into his hand and pierce it. That is how Pharaoh king of Egypt is to all who rely on him. 22 However, if you say to me, 'We have trusted in the LORD our God,' is it not He whose high places and whose altars Hezekiah has removed, and has said to Judah and to Jerusalem, 'You shall worship before this altar in Jerusalem'? 23 Now then, come make a wager with my master the king of Assyria: I will give you two thousand horses, if you are able on your part to put riders on them! 24 How then can you drive back even one official of the least of my master's servants, and rely on Egypt for chariots and horsemen? 25 Have I now come up without the LORD's approval against this place to destroy it? The LORD said to me, 'Go up against this land and destroy it.' " ' "

26 Then Eliakim the son of Hilkiah, Shebnah, and Joah, said to Rabshakeh, "Speak now to your servants in Aramaic, because we understand it; and do not speak with us in 1 Judean so that the people who are on the wall hear you." 27 But Rabshakeh said to them, "Has my master

sent me only to your master and to you to speak these words? Has he not also sent me to the men who sit on the wall, doomed to eat their own dung and drink their own urine with you?"

28 Then Rabshakeh stood up and shouted with a loud voice in Judean, saying, "Hear the word of the great king, the king of Assyria! 29 This is what the king says: 'Do not let Hezekiah deceive you, for he will not be able to save you from my hand. 30 And do not let Hezekiah lead you to trust in the LORD by saying, "The LORD will certainly save us, and this city will not be handed over to the king of Assyria." 31 Do not listen to Hezekiah, for this is what the king of Assyria says: "Make your peace with me and come out to me, and eat, each one, from his vine and each from his fig tree, and drink, each one, the waters of his own cistern, 32 until I come and take you to a land like your own land, a land of grain and new wine, a land of bread and vineyards, a land of olive trees producing oil, and of honey, so that you will live and not die." But do not listen to Hezekiah, because he misleads you by saying, "The LORD will save us." 33 Has any of the gods of the nations actually saved his land from the hand of the king of Assyria? 34 Where are the gods of Hamath and Arpad? Where are the gods of Sepharvaim, Hena, and Ivvah? Have they saved Samaria from my hand? 35 Who among all the gods of the lands are there who have saved their land from my hand, that the LORD would save Jerusalem from my hand?' "

36 But the people were silent and did not answer him with even a word, because it was the king's command: "Do not answer him." 37 Then Eliakim the son of Hilkiah, who was in charge of the household, and Shebna the scribe and Joah the son of Asaph, the secretary, came to Hezekiah with their clothes torn, and they reported to him the words of Rabshakeh.

Isaiah Encourages Hezekiah

19 Now when King Hezekiah heard the report, he tore his clothes, covered himself with sackcloth, and entered the house of the LORD. 2 Then he sent Eliakim, who was in charge of the household, with Shebna the scribe and the elders of the priests, covered with sackcloth, to Isaiah the prophet, the son of Amoz. 3 And they said to him, "This is what Hezekiah says: 'This day is a day of distress, rebuke, and humiliation; for children have come to the point of birth, and there is no strength to deliver them. 4 Perhaps the LORD your God will hear all the words of Rabshakeh, whom his master the king of Assyria has sent to taunt the living God, and will avenge the words which the LORD your God has heard. Therefore, offer a prayer for the remnant that is left.' " 5 So the servants of King Hezekiah came to Isaiah. 6 And Isaiah said to them, "This is what you shall say to your master: 'The LORD says this: "Do not be fearful because of the words that you have heard, with which the servants of the king of Assyria have blasphemed Me. 7 Behold, I am going to put a spirit in him so that he will hear news and return to

---

18:14 1 A talent was about 75 lb. or 34 kg   18:17 1 I.e., launderer's   18:26 1 I.e., Hebrew

his own land. And I will make him fall by the sword in his own land."'"

Sennacherib Defies God

8 Then Rabshakeh returned and found the king of Assyria fighting against Libnah, for he had heard that *the king* had left Lachish. **9** When he heard *them* say about Tirhakah king of Cush, "Behold, he has come out to fight you," he sent messengers again to Hezekiah, saying, **10** "This is what you shall say to Hezekiah king of Judah: 'Do not let your God in whom you trust deceive you by saying, "Jerusalem will not be handed over to the king of Assyria." **11** Behold, you yourself have heard what the kings of Assyria have done to all the lands, destroying them completely. So will you be saved? **12** Did the gods of the nations which my fathers destroyed save them: Gozan, Haran, Rezeph, and the sons of Eden who *were* in Telassar? **13** Where is the king of Hamath, the king of Arpad, the king of the city of Sepharvaim, and *of* Hena and Ivvah?'"

Hezekiah's Prayer

14 Then Hezekiah took the letter from the hand of the messengers and read it, and he went up to the house of the LORD and spread it out before the LORD. **15** Hezekiah prayed before the LORD and said, "LORD, God of Israel, enthroned *above* the cherubim, You are the God, You alone, of all the kingdoms of the earth. You have made heaven and earth. **16** Incline Your ear, LORD, and hear; open Your eyes, LORD, and see; and listen to the words of Sennacherib, which he has sent to taunt the living God. **17** It is true, LORD; the kings of Assyria have laid waste the nations and their lands, **18** and have hurled their gods into the fire; for they were not gods, but *only* the work of human hands, wood and stone. So they have destroyed them. **19** But now, LORD our God, please, save us from his hand, so that all the kingdoms of the earth may know that You alone, LORD, are God."

God's Answer through Isaiah

20 Then Isaiah the son of Amoz sent *word* to Hezekiah, saying, "This is what the LORD, the God of Israel says: 'Because you have prayed to Me about Sennacherib king of Assyria, I have heard *you.*' **21** This is the word that the LORD has spoken against him:

'She, the virgin daughter of Zion, has
　shown contempt for you *and* mocked
　you;
She, the daughter of Jerusalem, has
　shaken *her* head behind you!

22 'Whom have you taunted and blasphemed?
And against whom have you raised *your*
　voice,
And haughtily raised your eyes?
Against the Holy One of Israel!

23 'Through your messengers you have
　taunted the Lord,
And you have said, "With my many
　chariots
I went up to the heights of the mountains,
To the remotest parts of Lebanon;

And I cut down its tall cedars *and* its
　choicest junipers.
And I entered its farthest resting place, its
　thickest forest.

24 "I dug *wells* and drank foreign waters,
And with the soles of my feet I dried up
All the streams of Egypt."

25¶ 'Have you not heard?
Long ago I did it;
From ancient times I planned it.
Now I have brought it about,
That you would turn fortified cities into
　ruined heaps.

26 'Therefore their inhabitants were
　powerless,
They were shattered and put to shame.
They were *like* the vegetation of the field
　and the green grass,
Like grass on the housetops that is
　scorched before it has grown.

27 'But I know your sitting down,
Your going out, your coming in,
And your raging against Me.

28 'Because of your raging against Me,
And because your complacency has come
　up to My ears,
I will put My hook in your nose,
And My bridle in your lips,
And I will turn you back by the way by
　which you came.

20 'Then this shall be the sign for you: you will eat this year what grows of itself, in the second year what grows by itself, and in the third year sow, harvest, plant vineyards, and eat their fruit. **30** The survivors that are left of the house of Judah will again *take* root downward and bear fruit upward. **31** For out of Jerusalem will go a remnant, and survivors out of Mount Zion. The zeal of 'the LORD will perform this.

32 'Therefore this is what the LORD says about the king of Assyria: "He will not come to this city nor shoot an arrow there; and he will not come before it with a shield nor heap up an assault ramp against it. **33** By the way that he came, by the same he will return, and he shall not come to this city,"' declares the LORD. **34** 'For I will protect this city to save it for My own sake, and for My servant David's sake.'"

35 Then it happened that night that the angel of the LORD went out and struck 185,000 in the camp of the Assyrians; and when *the rest* got up early in the morning, behold, all of the 185,000 were dead. **36** So Sennacherib the king of Assyria departed and returned *home,* and lived at Nineveh. **37** Then it came about, as he was worshiping in the house of Nisroch his god, that Adrammelech and Sharezer killed him with the sword; and they escaped to the land of Ararat. And his son Esarhaddon became king in his place.

Hezekiah's Illness and Recovery

20 In those days Hezekiah became mortally ill. And Isaiah the prophet, the son of Amoz, came to him and said to him, "This is what the LORD says: 'Set your house in order, for you are going to die and not live.'" **2** Then he turned his face to the wall and prayed to the

LORD, saying, 3 "Please, LORD, just remember how I have walked before You wholeheartedly and in truth, and have done what is good in Your sight!" And Hezekiah wept profusely. 4 And even before Isaiah had left the middle courtyard, the word of the LORD came to him, saying, 5 "Return and say to Hezekiah the leader of My people, 'This is what the LORD, the God of your father David says: "I have heard your prayer, I have seen your tears; behold, I am going to heal you. On the third day you shall go up to the house of the LORD. 6 And I will add fifteen years to your life, and I will save you and this city from the hand of the king of Assyria; and I will protect this city for My own sake and for My servant David's sake." ' " 7 Then Isaiah said, "Take a cake of figs." And they took it and placed it on the inflamed spot, and he recovered.

8 Now Hezekiah said to Isaiah, "What will be the sign that the LORD will heal me, and that I will go up to the house of the LORD on the third day?" 9 Isaiah said, "This shall be the sign to you from the LORD, that the LORD will perform the word that He has spoken: shall the shadow go forward ten steps or go back ten steps?" 10 So Hezekiah said, "It is easy for the shadow to decline ten steps; no, but have the shadow turn backward ten steps." 11 Then Isaiah the prophet called out to the LORD, and He brought the shadow on the stairway back ten steps by which it had gone down on the stairway of Ahaz.

Hezekiah Shows Babylon His Treasures

12 At that time Berodach-baladan, a son of Baladan, king of Babylon, sent letters and a gift to Hezekiah, because he heard that Hezekiah had been sick. 13 And Hezekiah listened to 1them, and showed them all his treasure house, the silver, the gold, the balsam oil, the scented oil, the house of his armor, and everything that was found in his treasuries. There was nothing in his house nor in all his realm that Hezekiah did not show them. 14 Then Isaiah the prophet came to King Hezekiah and said to him, "What did these men say, and from where have they come to you?" And Hezekiah said, "They have come from a far country, from Babylon." 15 Isaiah said, "What have they seen in your house?" So Hezekiah answered, "They have seen everything that is in my house; there is nothing among my treasuries that I have not shown them."

16 Then Isaiah said to Hezekiah, "Hear the word of the LORD: 17 'Behold, the days are coming when everything that is in your house, and what your fathers have stored up to this day, will be carried to Babylon; nothing will be left,' says the LORD. 18 'And some of your sons who will come from you, whom you will father, will be taken away; and they will become officials in the palace of the king of Babylon.' " 19 Then Hezekiah said to Isaiah, "The word of the LORD which you have spoken is good." For he thought, "Is it not good, if there will be peace and security in my days?"

20 Now the rest of the acts of Hezekiah and all his might, and how he constructed the pool and the conduit and brought water into the city, are they not written in the Book of the Chronicles of the Kings of Judah? 21 So Hezekiah 1lay down with his fathers, and his son Manasseh became king in his place.

Manasseh Succeeds Hezekiah

21 Manasseh was twelve years old when he became king, and he reigned for fifty-five years in Jerusalem; and his mother's name was Hephzibah. 2 He did evil in the sight of the LORD, in accordance with the abominations of the nations whom the LORD dispossessed before the sons of Israel. 3 For he rebuilt the high places which his father Hezekiah had destroyed; and he erected altars for Baal and made an 1Asherah, just as Ahab king of Israel had done, and he worshiped all the heavenly lights and served them. 4 And he built altars in the house of the LORD, of which the LORD had said, "In Jerusalem I will put My name." 5 He built altars for all the heavenly lights in the two courtyards of the house of the LORD. 6 And he made his son pass through the fire, interpreted signs, practiced divination, and used mediums and spiritists. He did great evil in the sight of the LORD, provoking Him to anger. 7 Then he put the carved image of Asherah that he had made in the house of which the LORD had said to David and to his son Solomon, "In this house and in Jerusalem, which I have chosen from all the tribes of Israel, I will put My name forever. 8 And I will not make the feet of Israel wander anymore from the land which I gave their fathers, if only they will take care to act in accordance with everything that I have commanded them, and with all the Law that My servant Moses commanded them." 9 But they did not listen, and Manasseh encouraged them to do evil, more than the nations whom the LORD eliminated from the presence of the sons of Israel.

The King's Idolatries Rebuked

10 Now the LORD spoke through His servants the prophets, saying, 11 "Since Manasseh king of Judah has committed these abominations, having done more evil than all that the Amorites did who were before him, and has also misled Judah into sin with his idols, 12 therefore this is what the LORD, the God of Israel says: 'Behold, I am bringing such a disaster on Jerusalem and Judah that whoever hears about it, both of his ears will ring. 13 I will stretch over Jerusalem the line of Samaria and the plummet of the house of Ahab, and I will wipe Jerusalem clean just as one wipes a bowl, wiping it and turning it upside down. 14 And I will abandon the remnant of My inheritance and hand them over to their enemies, and they will become as plunder and spoils to all their enemies, 15 because they have done evil in My sight, and have been provoking Me to anger since the day their fathers came from Egypt, even to this day.' "

16 Furthermore, Manasseh shed very much innocent blood until he had filled Jerusalem from one end to another, besides his sin into

---

20:13 1 I.e., messengers   20:21 1 I.e., died   21:3 1 I.e., a wooden symbol of a female deity

which he misled Judah, in doing evil in the sight of the LORD. 17 Now the rest of the acts of Manasseh and all that he did, and his sin which he committed, are they not written in the Book of the Chronicles of the Kings of Judah? 18 And Manasseh [1]lay down with his fathers and was buried in the garden of his own house, in the garden of Uzza, and his son Amon became king in his place.

Amon Succeeds Manasseh

19 Amon was twenty-two years old when he became king, and he reigned for two years in Jerusalem; and his mother's name *was* Meshullemeth the daughter of Haruz of Jotbah. 20 He did evil in the sight of the LORD, just as his father Manasseh had done. 21 For he walked entirely in the way that his father had walked, and served the idols that his father had served, and worshiped them. 22 So he abandoned the LORD, the God of his fathers, and did not walk in the way of the LORD. 23 And the servants of Amon conspired against him and killed the king in his own house. 24 Then the people of the land killed all those who had conspired against King Amon, and the people of the land made his son Josiah king in his place. 25 Now the rest of the acts of Amon which he did, are they not written in the Book of the Chronicles of the Kings of Judah? 26 He was buried in his grave in the garden of Uzza, and his son Josiah became king in his place.

Josiah Succeeds Amon

22 Josiah was eight years old when he became king, and he reigned for thirty-one years in Jerusalem; and his mother's name *was* Jedidah the daughter of Adaiah of Bozkath. 2 He did what was right in the sight of the LORD and walked entirely in the way of his father David, and did not turn aside to the right or to the left. 3 Now in the eighteenth year of King Josiah, the king sent Shaphan, the son of Azaliah the son of Meshullam the scribe, to the house of the LORD, saying, 4 "Go up to Hilkiah the high priest, and have him count all the money brought into the house of the LORD, which the doorkeepers have collected from the people. 5 And have them hand it over to the workmen who have the oversight of the house of the LORD, and have them give it to the workmen who are in the house of the LORD to repair the damage to the house: 6 to the carpenters, the builders, the masons, and for buying timber and cut stone to repair the house. 7 However, no accounting shall be made with them for the money handed over to them, because they deal honestly."

The Lost Book

8 Then Hilkiah the high priest said to Shaphan the scribe, "I have found the Book of the Law in the house of the LORD." And Hilkiah gave the book to Shaphan, who read it. 9 Then Shaphan the scribe came to the king and brought back word to the king and said, "Your servants have emptied out the money that was found in the house, and have handed it over to

the workmen who have the oversight of the house of the LORD." 10 Moreover, Shaphan the scribe informed the king, saying, "Hilkiah the priest has given me a book." And Shaphan read it in the presence of the king.

11 When the king heard the words of the Book of the Law, he tore his clothes. 12 Then the king commanded Hilkiah the priest, Ahikam the son of Shaphan, Achbor the son of Micaiah, Shaphan the scribe, and Asaiah the king's servant, saying, 13 "Go, inquire of the LORD for me and for the people and all Judah concerning the words of this book that has been found, for the wrath of the LORD that burns against us is great, because our fathers did not listen to the words of this book, to act in accordance with everything that is written regarding us."

Huldah Predicts

14 So Hilkiah the priest, Ahikam, Achbor, Shaphan, and Asaiah went to Huldah the prophetess, the wife of Shallum the son of Tikvah, the son of Harhas, keeper of the wardrobe (and she lived in Jerusalem in the Second Quarter); and they spoke to her. 15 Then she said to them, "This is what the LORD, the God of Israel says: 'Tell the man who sent you to Me, 16 "This is what the LORD says: 'Behold, I am going to bring disaster on this place and on its inhabitants, all the words of the book which the king of Judah has read. 17 Since they have abandoned Me and have burned incense to other gods so that they may provoke Me to anger with all the work of their hands, My wrath burns against this place, and it shall not be quenched.'" 18 But to the king of Judah who sent you to inquire of the LORD, this is what you shall say to him: "This is what the LORD, the God of Israel says: '*Regarding* the words which you have heard, 19 since your heart was tender and you humbled yourself before the LORD when you heard what I spoke against this place and against its inhabitants, that they would become an object of horror and a curse, and you have torn your clothes and wept before Me, I have indeed heard you,' declares the LORD." 20 Therefore, behold, I am going to gather you to your fathers, and you will be gathered to your grave in peace, and your eyes will not look at all the devastation that I am going to bring on this place.'" So they brought back word to the king.

Josiah's Covenant

23 Then the king sent *messengers,* and they gathered to him all the elders of Judah and Jerusalem. 2 And the king went up to the house of the LORD and every man of Judah and all the inhabitants of Jerusalem with him, and the priests, the prophets, and all the people, from the small to the great; and he read in their presence all the words of the Book of the Covenant which was found in the house of the LORD. 3 And the king stood by the pillar and made a covenant before the LORD, to walk after the LORD, and to keep His commandments, His provisions, and His statutes with all *his* heart and all *his* soul, to carry out the words of this

---

21:18 [1]i.e., died

covenant that were written in this book. And all the people entered into the covenant.

Reforms under Josiah

4 Then the king commanded Hilkiah the high priest, the priests of the second order, and the doorkeepers to bring out of the temple of the Lord all the utensils that had been made for Baal, for [1]Asherah, and for all the heavenly lights; and he burned them outside Jerusalem in the fields of the Kidron *Valley,* and carried their ashes to Bethel. **5** Then he did away with the idolatrous priests whom the kings of Judah had appointed to burn incense on the high places in the cities of Judah and in the surrounding area of Jerusalem, as well as those who burned incense to Baal, to the sun, to the moon, to the constellations, and to all the *remaining* heavenly lights. **6** He also brought out the Asherah from the house of the Lord outside Jerusalem to the brook Kidron, and burned it at the brook Kidron, and ground *it* to dust, and threw its dust on the graves of the common people. **7** And he tore down the cubicles of the *male* cult prostitutes which *were* in the house of the Lord, where the women were weaving hangings for the Asherah. **8** Then he brought all the priests from the cities of Judah, and defiled the high places where the priests had burned incense, from Geba to Beersheba; and he tore down the high places of the gates that *were* at the entrance of the gate of Joshua the governor of the city, which *were* on one's left at the city gate. **9** Nevertheless the priests of the high places did not go up to the altar of the Lord in Jerusalem, but they ate unleavened bread among their brothers. **10** He also defiled [1]Topheth, which is in the Valley of the Son of Hinnom, so that no one would make his son or his daughter pass through the fire for Molech. **11** And he did away with the horses that the kings of Judah had given to the sun, at the entrance of the house of the Lord, by the chamber of Nathan-melech the official, which *was* at the covered courtyard; and he burned the chariots of the sun with fire. **12** The king also tore down the altars that *were* on the roof, the upper chamber of Ahaz, which the kings of Judah had made, and the altars which Manasseh had made in the two courtyards of the house of the Lord; and he smashed them there and threw their dust into the brook Kidron. **13** And the king defiled the high places that *were* opposite Jerusalem, which *were* on the right of the mount of destruction which Solomon the king of Israel had built for Ashtoreth the abomination of the Sidonians, for Chemosh the abomination of Moab, and for Milcom the abomination of the sons of Ammon. **14** He also smashed to pieces the memorial stones and cut down the [1]Asherim, and filled their places with human bones.

15 Furthermore, the altar that *was* at Bethel *and* the high place which Jeroboam the son of Nebat, who misled Israel into sin, had made, even that altar and the high place he tore down. Then he burned the high place, ground

the remains to dust, and burned the Asherah. **16** Now when Josiah turned, he saw the graves that *were* there on the mountain, and he sent *men* and took the bones from the graves, and burned *them* on the altar and defiled it in accordance with the word of the Lord which the man of God proclaimed, *the one* who proclaimed these things. **17** Then he said, "What is this gravestone there that I see?" And the men of the city told him, "*It is* the grave of the man of God who came from Judah and proclaimed these things which you have done against the altar of Bethel." **18** And he said, "Leave him alone; no one is to disturb his bones." So they left his bones undisturbed with the bones of the prophet who came from Samaria. **19** Then Josiah also removed all the houses of the high places which *were* in the cities of Samaria, which the kings of Israel had constructed, provoking the Lord to anger; and he did to them just as he had done in Bethel. **20** And he slaughtered all the priests of the high places who *were* there on the altars, and burned human bones on them; then he returned to Jerusalem.

Passover Reinstituted

21 Then the king commanded all the people, saying, "Celebrate the Passover to the Lord your God as it is written in this Book of the Covenant." **22** Truly such a Passover had not been celebrated since the days of the judges who judged Israel, nor in all the days of the kings of Israel and the kings of Judah. **23** But in the eighteenth year of King Josiah, this Passover was celebrated to the Lord in Jerusalem.

24 Moreover, Josiah removed the mediums, the spiritists, the [1]household idols, the idols, and all the abominations that were seen in the land of Judah and in Jerusalem, so that he might fulfill the words of the Law which were written in the book that Hilkiah the priest found in the house of the Lord. **25** Before him there was no king like him who turned to the Lord with all his heart, all his soul, and all his might, in conformity to all the Law of Moses; nor did any like him arise after him.

26 Nevertheless, the Lord did not turn from the fierceness of His great wrath with which His anger burned against Judah, because of all the provocations with which Manasseh had provoked Him. **27** And the Lord said, "I will also remove Judah from My sight, just as I have removed Israel. And I will reject this city which I have chosen, Jerusalem, and the temple of which I said, 'My name shall be there!' "

Jehoahaz Succeeds Josiah

28 Now the rest of the acts of Josiah and all that he did, are they not written in the Book of the Chronicles of the Kings of Judah? **29** In his days Pharaoh Neco king of Egypt went up to the king of Assyria at the river Euphrates. And King Josiah went to meet him, and when *Pharaoh Neco* saw him he killed him at Megiddo. **30** His servants carried his body in a chariot from Megiddo, and brought him to Jerusalem and buried him in his own tomb.

23:4 [1] I.e., a wooden symbol of a female deity, and so throughout the ch   23:10 [1] I.e., place of burning   23:14 [1] I.e., wooden symbols of a female deity (Asherah)   23:24 [1] Heb *teraphim*

Then the people of the land took Jehoahaz the son of Josiah and anointed him and made him king in place of his father.

31 Jehoahaz was twenty-three years old when he became king, and he reigned for three months in Jerusalem; and his mother's name was Hamutal the daughter of Jeremiah of Libnah. 32 He did evil in the sight of the LORD, in accordance with all that his forefathers had done. 33 And Pharaoh Neco imprisoned him at Riblah in the land of Hamath, so that he would not reign in Jerusalem; and he imposed on the land a fine of ¹a hundred talents of silver and ²a talent of gold.

Jehoiakim Made King by Pharaoh

34 Then Pharaoh Neco made Eliakim the son of Josiah king in the place of his father Josiah, and he changed his name to Jehoiakim. But he took Jehoahaz and brought *him* to Egypt, and he died there. 35 So Jehoiakim gave the silver and gold to Pharaoh, but he assessed the land in order to give the money at the command of Pharaoh. He collected the silver and gold from the people of the land, each according to his assessment, to give to Pharaoh Neco.

36 Jehoiakim was twenty-five years old when he became king, and he reigned for eleven years in Jerusalem; and his mother's name *was* Zebidah the daughter of Pedaiah of Rumah. 37 He did evil in the sight of the LORD, in accordance with all that his forefathers had done.

Babylon Controls Jehoiakim

24 In his days Nebuchadnezzar king of Babylon came up, and Jehoiakim became his servant for three years; then he turned and revolted against him. 2 And the LORD sent against him bands of Chaldeans, bands of Arameans, bands of Moabites, and bands of Ammonites. He sent them against Judah to destroy it, in accordance with the word of the LORD which He had spoken through His servants the prophets. 3 It indeed came upon Judah at the command of the LORD, to remove *them* from His sight due to the sins of Manasseh, in accordance with everything that he had done, 4 and also for the innocent blood which he shed, for he filled Jerusalem with innocent blood; and the LORD was unwilling to forgive. 5 Now the rest of the acts of Jehoiakim and all that he did, are they not written in the Book of the Chronicles of the Kings of Judah?

Jehoiachin Reigns

6 So Jehoiakim ¹lay down with his fathers, and his son Jehoiachin became king in his place. 7 Now the king of Egypt did not come out of his land again, because the king of Babylon had taken everything that belonged to the king of Egypt from the brook of Egypt to the river Euphrates.

8 Jehoiachin was eighteen years old when he became king, and he reigned for three months in Jerusalem; and his mother's name *was* Nehushta the daughter of Elnathan of Jerusalem. 9 He did evil in the sight of the LORD, in accordance with all that his father had done.

Deportation to Babylon

10 At that time the servants of Nebuchadnezzar the king of Babylon went up to Jerusalem, and the city came under siege. 11 And Nebuchadnezzar the king of Babylon came to the city, while his servants were besieging it. 12 Then Jehoiachin the king of Judah went out to the king of Babylon, he, his mother, his servants, his commanders, and his officials. And the king of Babylon took him *prisoner* in the eighth year of his reign. 13 He also brought out from there all the treasures of the house of the LORD, and the treasures of the king's house, and he smashed all the articles of gold that Solomon king of Israel had made in the temple of the LORD, just as the LORD had said. 14 Then he led into exile all *the people of* Jerusalem and all the commanders and all the valiant warriors, ten thousand exiles, and all the craftsmen and the smiths. None were left except the poorest people of the land.

15 So he led Jehoiachin into exile to Babylon; also the king's mother, the king's wives, and his officials, and the leading men of the land, he led into exile from Jerusalem to Babylon. 16 And all the valiant men, seven thousand, and the craftsmen and the smiths, a thousand, all strong *and* fit for war, these too the king of Babylon brought into exile to Babylon.

Zedekiah Made King

17 Then the king of Babylon made his uncle Mattaniah king in his place, and changed his name to Zedekiah.

18 Zedekiah was twenty-one years old when he became king, and he reigned for eleven years in Jerusalem; and his mother's name was Hamutal the daughter of Jeremiah of Libnah. 19 He did evil in the sight of the LORD, in accordance with everything that Jehoiakim had done. 20 For *it was* due to the anger of the LORD *that this* happened in Jerusalem and Judah, until He cast them out of His presence. And Zedekiah revolted against the king of Babylon.

Nebuchadnezzar Besieges Jerusalem

25 Now in the ninth year of his reign, on the tenth day of the tenth month, Nebuchadnezzar the king of Babylon came, he and all his army, against Jerusalem, camped against it, and built a siege wall all around it. 2 So the city was under siege until the eleventh year of King Zedekiah. 3 On the ninth day of the *fourth* month the famine was so severe in the city that there was no food for the people of the land. 4 Then the city was broken into, and all the men of war *fled* by night by way of the gate between the two walls that were beside the king's garden, though the Chaldeans were all around the city. And they went by way of the Arabah. 5 But the army of the Chaldeans pursued the king and overtook him in the plains of Jericho, and all his army was scattered from him. 6 Then they captured the king and brought him up to the king of Babylon at Riblah, and he passed sentence on him. 7 And they slaughtered the sons of Zedekiah before his eyes, then put out Zedekiah's eyes

and bound him with bronze shackles, and brought him to Babylon.

Jerusalem Burned and Plundered

8 Now on the seventh *day* of the fifth month, which was the nineteenth year of King Nebuchadnezzar, king of Babylon, Nebuzaradan the captain of the bodyguards, a servant of the king of Babylon, came to Jerusalem. 9 And he burned the house of the LORD, the king's house, and all the houses of Jerusalem; even every great house he burned with fire. 10 So all the army of the Chaldeans who *were with* the captain of the bodyguards tore down the walls around Jerusalem. 11 Then Nebuzaradan, the captain of the bodyguards, led into exile the rest of the people who were left in the city and the deserters who had deserted to the king of Babylon, and the rest of the people. 12 But the captain of the bodyguards left some of the poorest of the land to be vinedressers and farmers.

13 Now the Chaldeans smashed to pieces the bronze pillars which were in the house of the LORD, and the stands and the bronze ⁷Sea which were in the house of the LORD, and carried the bronze to Babylon. 14 And they took away the pots, the shovels, the shears, the spoons, and all the bronze utensils which were used in temple service. 15 The captain of the bodyguards also took away the firepans and the basins, what was fine gold and what was fine silver. 16 The two pillars, the one Sea, and the stands which Solomon had made for the house of the LORD—the bronze of all these articles was too heavy to weigh. 17 The height of the one pillar was ¹eighteen cubits, and a bronze capital was on it; the height of the capital was ²three cubits, with latticework and pomegranates on the capital all around, all of bronze. And the second pillar was like these, same *features* with latticework. 18 Then the captain of the bodyguards took Seraiah the chief priest and Zephaniah the second priest, with the three doorkeepers. 19 And from the city he took one official who was overseer of the men of war, and five of the king's advisers who were found in the city; and the scribe of the captain of the army who mustered the people of the land; and sixty men of the people of the land who were found in the city. 20 Nebuzaradan the captain of the bodyguards took them and brought them to the king of Babylon at Riblah. 21 Then the king of Babylon struck them down and put them to death at Riblah in the land of Hamath. So Judah went into exile from its land.

Gedaliah Made Governor

22 Now *as for* the people who were left in the land of Judah, whom Nebuchadnezzar king of Babylon had left, he appointed Gedaliah the son of Ahikam, the son of Shaphan over them. 23 When all the captains of the forces, they and *their* men, heard that the king of Babylon had appointed Gedaliah *governor,* they came to Gedaliah at Mizpah, namely, Ishmael the son of Nethaniah, Johanan the son of Kareah, Seraiah the son of Tanhumeth the Netophathite, and Jaazaniah the son of the Maacathite, they and their men. 24 And Gedaliah swore to them and their men and said to them, "Do not be afraid of the servants of the Chaldeans; live in the land and serve the king of Babylon, and it will go well for you."

25 But it happened in the seventh month, that Ishmael the son of Nethaniah, the son of Elishama, of the royal family, came with ten men and struck Gedaliah down so that he died along with the Jews and the Chaldeans who were with him at Mizpah. 26 Then all the people, from the small to the great, and the captains of the forces set out and came to Egypt; for they were afraid of the Chaldeans.

27 Now it came about in the thirty-seventh year of the exile of Jehoiachin king of Judah, in the twelfth month, on the twenty-seventh *day* of the month, that Evil-merodach king of Babylon, in the year that he became king, released Jehoiachin king of Judah from prison; 28 and he spoke kindly to him and set his throne above the throne of the kings who *were* with him in Babylon. 29 So Jehoiachin changed his prison clothes, and had his meals in the king's presence regularly all the days of his life; 30 and as his allowance, a regular allowance was given to him by the king, a portion for each day, all the days of his life.

25:13 ¹ I.e., a very large basin   25:17 ¹ About 27 ft. or 8 m   ² About 4.5 ft. or 1.3 m

Genealogy from Adam

1 Adam, Seth, Enosh, 2 Kenan, Mahalalel, Jared, 3 Enoch, Methuselah, Lamech, 4 Noah, Shem, Ham, and Japheth.

5 The sons of Japheth were Gomer, Magog, Madai, Javan, Tubal, Meshech, and Tiras. 6 The sons of Gomer were Ashkenaz, Diphath, and Togarmah. 7 The sons of Javan were Elishah, Tarshish, Kittim, and Rodanim.

8 The sons of Ham were Cush, Mizraim, Put, and Canaan. 9 The sons of Cush were Seba, Havilah, Sabta, Raama, and Sabteca; and the sons of Raamah were Sheba and Dedan. 10 Cush fathered Nimrod; he began to be a mighty one on the earth.

11 Mizraim fathered the people of Lud, Anam, Lehab, Naphtuh, 12 Pathrus, and Casluh, from whom the Philistines came, and the Caphtorim.

13 Canaan fathered Sidon his firstborn, and Heth, 14 and the Jebusites, the Amorites, the Girgashites, 15 the Hivites, the Arkites, the Sinites, 16 the Arvadites, the Zemarites, and the Hamathites.

17 The sons of Shem were Elam, Asshur, Arpachshad, Lud, Aram, Uz, Hul, Gether, and Meshech. 18 Arpachshad fathered Shelah, and Shelah fathered Eber. 19 Two sons were born to Eber: the name of the one was Peleg, for in his days the earth was divided; and his brother's name was Joktan. 20 Joktan fathered Almodad, Sheleph, Hazarmaveth, Jerah, 21 Hadoram, Uzal, Diklah, 22 Ebal, Abimael, Sheba, 23 Ophir, Havilah, and Jobab; all these were the sons of Joktan.

24 Shem, Arpachshad, Shelah, 25 Eber, Peleg, Reu, 26 Serug, Nahor, Terah, 27 and Abram, that is Abraham.

Descendants of Abraham

28 The sons of Abraham were Isaac and Ishmael. 29 These are their genealogies: the firstborn of Ishmael was Nebaioth, then Kedar, Adbeel, Mibsam, 30 Mishma, Dumah, Massa, Hadad, Tema, 31 Jetur, Naphish, and Kedemah; these were the sons of Ishmael. 32 The sons of Keturah, Abraham's concubine, to whom she gave birth, were Zimran, Jokshan, Medan, Midian, Ishbak, and Shuah. And the sons of Jokshan were Sheba and Dedan. 33 The sons of Midian were Ephah, Epher, Hanoch, Abida, and Eldaah. All these were the sons of Keturah.

34 Abraham fathered Isaac. The sons of Isaac were Esau and ¹Israel. 35 The sons of Esau were Eliphaz, Reuel, Jeush, Jalam, and Korah. 36 The sons of Eliphaz were Teman, Omar, Zephi, Gatam, Kenaz, Timna, and Amalek. 37 The sons of Reuel were Nahath, Zerah, Shammah, and Mizzah. 38 The sons of Seir were Lotan, Shobal, Zibeon, Anah, Dishon, Ezer, and Dishan. 39 The sons of Lotan were Hori and Homam; and Lotan's sister was Timna. 40 The sons of Shobal were Alian, Manahath, Ebal, Shephi, and Onam. And the sons of Zibeon were Aiah and Anah. 41 The son of Anah was Dishon. And the sons of Dishon were Hamran, Eshban, Ithran, and Cheran. 42 The sons of Ezer were Bilhan, Zaavan, and Jaakan. The sons of Dishan were Uz and Aran.

43 Now these are the kings who reigned in the land of Edom before any king from the sons of Israel reigned. Bela was the son of Beor, and the name of his city was Dinhabah. 44 When Bela died, Jobab the son of Zerah of Bozrah became king in his place. 45 When Jobab died, Husham of the land of the Temanites became king in his place. 46 When Husham died, Hadad the son of Bedad, who defeated Midian in the field of Moab, became king in his place; and the name of his city was Avith. 47 When Hadad died, Samlah of Masrekah became king in his place. 48 When Samlah died, Shaul of Rehoboth by the Euphrates River became king in his place. 49 When Shaul died, Baal-hanan the son of Achbor became king in his place, 50 When Baal-hanan died, Hadad became king in his place; and the name of his city was Pai, and his wife's name was Mehetabel, the daughter of Matred, the daughter of Mezahab. 51 Then Hadad died.

Now the tribal chiefs of Edom were chief Timna, chief Aliah, chief Jetheth, 52 chief Oholibamah, chief Elah, chief Pinon, 53 chief Kenaz, chief Teman, chief Mibzar, 54 chief Magdiel, and chief Iram. These were the chiefs of Edom.

Genealogy: Twelve Sons of Israel (Jacob)

2 These were the sons of Israel: Reuben, Simeon, Levi, Judah, Issachar, Zebulun, 2 Dan, Joseph, Benjamin, Naphtali, Gad, and Asher.

3 The sons of Judah were Er, Onan, and Shelah; these three were born to him by Bathshua the Canaanitess. But Er, Judah's firstborn, was evil in the sight of the LORD, so He put him to death. 4 His daughter-in-law Tamar bore him Perez and Zerah. Judah had five sons in all.

5 The sons of Perez were Hezron and Hamul. 6 The sons of Zerah were Zimri, Ethan, Heman, Calcol, and Dara; five of them in all. 7 The son of Carmi was Achar, the one who brought disaster on Israel by violating the ⁷ban. 8 The son of Ethan was Azariah.

Genealogy of David

9 Now the sons of Hezron who were born to him were Jerahmeel, Ram, and Chelubai. 10 Ram fathered Amminadab, and Amminadab fathered Nahshon, leader of the sons of Judah; 11 Nahshon fathered Salma, Salma fathered Boaz, 12 Boaz fathered Obed, and Obed fathered Jesse; 13 and Jesse fathered Eliab his firstborn,

---

1:34 ¹I.e., Jacob 2:7 ¹I.e., the ban against forbidden spoils

then Abinadab, the second, Shimea, the third, 14 Nethanel, the fourth, Raddai, the fifth, 15 Ozem, the sixth, *and* David, the seventh. 16 Their sisters *were* Zeruiah and Abigail. And the three sons of Zeruiah *were* Abshai, Joab, and Asahel. 17 Abigail gave birth to Amasa, and the father of Amasa was Jether the Ishmaelite.

18 Now Caleb the son of Hezron had sons by Azubah *his* wife, and by Jerioth; and these were her sons: Jesher, Shobab, and Ardon. 19 When Azubah died, Caleb married Ephrath, who bore to him Hur. 20 Hur fathered Uri, and Uri fathered Bezalel.

21 Later, Hezron had relations with the daughter of Machir the father of Gilead, whom he married when he was sixty years old; and she bore to him Segub. 22 Segub fathered Jair, who had twenty-three cities in the land of Gilead. 23 But Geshur and Aram took the villages of Jair from them, with Kenath and its villages, sixty settlements. All of these were the sons of Machir, the father of Gilead. 24 After the death of Hezron in Caleb-ephrathah, Abijah, Hezron's wife, bore to him Ashhur the father of Tekoa.

25 Now the sons of Jerahmeel, the firstborn of Hezron, *were* Ram the firstborn, then Bunah, Oren, Ozem, *and* Ahijah. 26 Jerahmeel had another wife, whose name was Atarah; she was the mother of Onam. 27 The sons of Ram, the firstborn of Jerahmeel, were Maaz, Jamin, and Eker. 28 The sons of Onam were Shammai and Jada. And the sons of Shammai *were* Nadab and Abishur. 29 The name of Abishur's wife *was* Abihail, and she bore to him Ahban and Molid. 30 The sons of Nadab *were* Seled and Appaim, and Seled died without sons. 31 The son of Appaim *was* Ishi. And the son of Ishi *was* Sheshan, and the son of Sheshan, Ahlai. 32 The sons of Jada the brother of Shammai *were* Jether and Jonathan, and Jether died without sons. 33 The sons of Jonathan *were* Peleth and Zaza. These were the descendants of Jerahmeel. 34 Now Sheshan had no sons, only daughters. Sheshan also had an Egyptian servant, whose name was Jarha. 35 Sheshan gave his daughter to his servant Jarha in marriage, and she bore to him Attai. 36 Attai fathered Nathan, Nathan fathered Zabad, 37 Zabad fathered Ephlal, Ephlal fathered Obed, 38 Obed fathered Jehu, Jehu fathered Azariah, 39 Azariah fathered Helez, Helez fathered Eleasah, 40 Eleasah fathered Sismai, Sismai fathered Shallum, 41 Shallum fathered Jekamiah, and Jekamiah fathered Elishama.

42 Now the sons of Caleb, the brother of Jerahmeel, *were* Mesha his firstborn, who was the father of Ziph; and his son was Mareshah, the father of Hebron. 43 The sons of Hebron *were* Korah, Tappuah, Rekem, and Shema. 44 Shema fathered Raham, the father of Jorkeam; and Rekem fathered Shammai. 45 The son of Shammai was Maon, and Maon *was* the father of Bethzur. 46 Ephah, Caleb's concubine, gave birth to Haran, Moza, and Gazez; and Haran fathered Gazez. 47 The sons of Jahdai *were* Regem, Jotham, Geshan, Pelet, Ephah, and Shaaph. 48 Maacah, Caleb's concubine, gave birth to Sheber and Tirhanah. 49 She also

gave birth to Shaaph the father of Madmannah, Sheva the father of Machbena and the father of Gibea; and the daughter of Caleb *was* Achsah. 50 These were the sons of Caleb.

The sons of Hur, the firstborn of Ephrathah, *were* Shobal the father of Kiriath-jearim, 51 Salma the father of Bethlehem, *and* Hareph the father of Beth-gader. 52 Shobal the father of Kiriath-jearim had sons: Haroeh, half of the Manahathites, 53 and the families of Kiriath-jearim: the Ithrites, the Puthites, the Shumathites, and the Mishraites; from these came the Zorathites and the Eshtaolites. 54 The sons of Salma *were* Bethlehem and the Netophathites, Atroth-beth-joab, and half of the Manahathites, the Zorites. 55 The families of scribes who lived at Jabez *were* the Tirathites, the Shimeathites, *and* the Sucathites. Those are the Kenites who came from Hammath, the father of the house of Rechab.

Family of David

3 Now these were the sons of David who were born to him in Hebron: the firstborn *was* Amnon, by Ahinoam the Jezreelitess; the second *was* Daniel, by Abigail the Carmelitess; 2 the third *was* Absalom the son of Maacah, the daughter of Talmai king of Geshur; the fourth *was* Adonijah the son of Haggith; 3 the fifth *was* Shephatiah, by Abital; the sixth *was* Ithream, by his wife Eglah. 4 Six were born to him in Hebron, and he reigned there for seven years and six months. And in Jerusalem he reigned for thirty-three years. 5 These were *the children* born to him in Jerusalem: Shimea, Shobab, Nathan, and Solomon, four by Bath-shua the daughter of Ammiel; 6 and Ibhar, Elishama, Eliphelet, 7 Nogah, Nepheg, Japhia, 8 Elishama, Eliada, and Eliphelet, nine. 9 All *of these were* the sons of David, besides the sons of the concubines; and Tamar was their sister.

10 Now Solomon's son *was* Rehoboam, *then* Abijah *was* his son, Asa, his son, Jehoshaphat, his son, 11 Joram, his son, Ahaziah, his son, Joash, his son, 12 Amaziah, his son, Azariah, his son, Jotham, his son, 13 Ahaz, his son, Hezekiah, his son, Manasseh, his son, 14 Amon, his son, *and* Josiah, his son. 15 The sons of Josiah *were* Johanan, the firstborn, the second *was* Jehoiakim, the third, Zedekiah, *and* the fourth, Shallum. 16 The sons of Jehoiakim *were* his son Jeconiah *and* his son Zedekiah. 17 The sons of Jeconiah, the prisoner, *were* his son Shealtiel 18 and Malchiram, Pedaiah, Shenazzar, Jekamiah, Hoshama, and Nedabiah. 19 The sons of Pedaiah *were* Zerubbabel and Shimei. And the sons of Zerubbabel *were* Meshullam and Hananiah, and Shelomith *was* their sister; 20 and Hashubah, Ohel, Berechiah, Hasadiah, and Jushab-hesed, five. 21 The sons of Hananiah *were* Pelatiah and Jeshaiah, the sons of Rephaiah, the sons of Arnan, the sons of Obadiah, the sons of Shecaniah. 22 The descendants of Shecaniah *were* Shemaiah, and the sons of Shemaiah: Hattush, Igal, Bariah, Neariah, and Shaphat, six. 23 The sons of Neariah *were* Elioenai, Hizkiah, and Azrikam, three. 24 The sons of Elioenai *were* Hodaviah, Eliashib, Pelaiah, Akkub, Johanan, Delaiah, and Anani, seven.

Descendants of Judah

4 The sons of Judah *were* Perez, Hezron, Carmi, Hur, and Shobal. 2 Reaiah the son of Shobal fathered Jahath, and Jahath fathered Ahumai and Lahad. These *were* the families of the Zorathites. 3 These *were* the sons of Etam: Jezreel, Ishma, and Idbash; and the name of their sister *was* Hazzelelponi. 4 Penuel *was* the father of Gedor, and Ezer the father of Hushah. These *were* the sons of Hur, the firstborn of Ephrathah, the father of Bethlehem. 5 Ashhur, the father of Tekoa, had two wives, Helah and Naarah. 6 Naarah bore to him Ahuzzam, Hepher, Temeni, and Haahashtari. These were the sons of Naarah. 7 The sons of Helah *were* Zereth, Izhar, and Ethnan. 8 Koz fathered Anub and Zobebah, and the families of Aharhel, the son of Harum. 9 Jabez was more honorable than his brothers, and his mother named him Jabez, saying, "Because I gave birth *to him* in pain." 10 Now Jabez called on the God of Israel, saying, "Oh that You would greatly bless me and extend my border, and that Your hand might be with me, and that You would keep *me* from harm so that *it* would not hurt me!" And God brought about what he requested.

11 Chelub the brother of Shuhah fathered Mehir, who was the father of Eshton. 12 Eshton fathered Beth-rapha and Paseah, and Tehinnah the father of Ir-nahash. These are the men of Recah.

13 Now the sons of Kenaz *were* Othniel and Seraiah. And the sons of Othniel *were* Hathath and Meonothai. 14 Meonothai fathered Ophrah, and Seraiah fathered Joab the father of Geharashim, for they were craftsmen. 15 The sons of Caleb the son of Jephunneh *were* Iru, Elah, and Naam; and the son of Elah *was* Kenaz. 16 The sons of Jehallelel *were* Ziph and Ziphah, Tiria and Asarel. 17 The sons of Ezrah *were* Jether, Mered, Epher, and Jalon. And *Mered's wife* conceived *and gave birth to* Miriam, Shammai, and Ishbah the father of Eshtemoa. 18 (His Jewish wife gave birth to Jered, the father of Gedor, Heber the father of Soco, and Jekuthiel the father of Zanoah.) These were the sons of Bithia the daughter of Pharaoh, whom Mered married. 19 The sons of the wife of Hodiah, the sister of Naham, *were* the fathers of Keilah the Garmite and Eshtemoa the Maacathite. 20 The sons of Shimon *were* Amnon and Rinnah, *and* Benhanan and Tilon. And the sons of Ishi *were* Zoheth and Ben-zoheth. 21 The sons of Shelah the son of Judah *were* Er the father of Lecah and Laadah the father of Mareshah, and the families of the house of the linen workers at Beth-ashbea; 22 and Jokim, the men of Cozeba, Joash, Saraph, who ruled in Moab, and Jashubi-lehem. And the records are ancient. 23 These were the potters and the inhabitants of Netaim and Gederah; they lived there with the king for his work.

Descendants of Simeon

24 The sons of Simeon *were* Nemuel and Jamin, Jarib, Zerah, *and* Shaul; 25 Shallum *was* his son, Mibsam his son, *and* Mishma his son. 26 The sons of Mishma *were* Hammuel his son, Zaccur his son, *and* Shimei his son. 27 Now Shimei had sixteen sons and six daughters; but

his brothers did not have many sons, nor did all their family increase like the sons of Judah. 28 They lived in Beersheba, Moladah, and Hazar-shual, 29 in Bilhah, Ezem, Tolad, 30 Bethuel, Hormah, Ziklag, 31 Beth-marcaboth, Hazar-susim, Beth-biri, and Shaaraim. These *were* their cities until the reign of David. 32 Their villages *were* Etam, Ain, Rimmon, Tochen, and Ashan, five cities, 33 and all their settlements that *were* around the same cities as far as Baal. These *were* their dwellings, and they have their genealogy.

34 Meshobab, Jamlech, Joshah the son of Amaziah, 35 Joel, Jehu the son of Joshibiah, the son of Seraiah, the son of Asiel, 36 and Elioenai, Jaakobah, Jeshohaiah, Asaiah, Adiel, Jesimiel, Benaiah, 37 and Ziza the son of Shiphi, the son of Allon, the son of Jedaiah, the son of Shimri, the son of Shemaiah— 38 these mentioned by name *were* leaders in their families; and their fathers' houses spread out greatly. 39 They went to the entrance of Gedor, as far as the east side of the valley, to seek pasture for their flocks. 40 They found pasture that was rich and good, and the land was spread out on both sides, and peaceful and undisturbed; for those who lived there previously *were* Hamites. 41 These *people,* recorded by name, came in the days of Hezekiah king of Judah, and they attacked their tents and the Meunites who were found there, and utterly destroyed them to this day; and they lived in their place, because there was pasture there for their flocks. 42 From them, from the sons of Simeon, five hundred men went to Mount Seir, with Pelatiah, Neariah, Rephaiah, and Uzziel, the sons of Ishi, as their leaders. 43 They destroyed the remnant of the Amalekites who escaped, and they have lived there to this day.

Genealogy from Reuben

5 Now the sons of Reuben, the firstborn of Israel (for he was the firstborn, but because he defiled his father's bed, his birthright was given to the sons of Joseph, the son of Israel; so he is not enrolled in the genealogy according to the birthright. 2 Though Judah prevailed over his brothers, and from him *came* the leader, yet the birthright belonged to Joseph), 3 the sons of Reuben the firstborn of Israel *were* Hanoch and Pallu, *and* Hezron and Carmi. 4 The sons of Joel *were* Shemaiah his son, Gog his son, Shimei his son, 5 Micah his son, Reaiah his son, Baal his son, 6 and Beerah his son, whom Tilgath-pilneser king of Assyria took into exile; he was leader of the Reubenites. 7 His relatives by their families, in the genealogy of their generations, *were* Jeiel the chief, then Zechariah 8 and Bela, the son of Azaz, the son of Shema, the son of Joel, who lived in Aroer, as far as Nebo and Baal-meon. 9 Toward the east he settled as far as the entrance of the wilderness from the river Euphrates, because their livestock had increased in the land of Gilead. 10 In the days of Saul they made war with the Hagrites, who fell by their hand, so that they occupied their tents throughout the land east of Gilead.

11 Now the sons of Gad lived opposite them in the land of Bashan, as far as Salecah. 12 Joel

was the head and Shapham the second, then Janai and Shaphat in Bashan. [13] Their relatives of their fathers' households *were* Michael, Meshullam, Sheba, Jorai, Jacan, Zia, and Eber, seven. [14] These *were* the sons of Abihail, the son of Huri, the son of Jaroah, the son of Gilead, the son of Michael, the son of Jeshishai, the son of Jahdo, the son of Buz; [15] Ahi the son of Abdiel, the son of Guni, *was* head of their fathers' households. [16] They lived in Gilead, in Bashan and in its towns, and in all the pasture lands of Sharon, as far as their borders. [17] All of these were enrolled in the genealogies in the days of Jotham king of Judah, and in the days of Jeroboam king of Israel.

[18] The sons of Reuben, the Gadites, and the half-tribe of Manasseh, *consisting* of valiant men, men who carried shield and sword and shot with a bow and *were* skillful in battle, *totaled* 44,760 who went to war. [19] They made war against the Hagrites, Jetur, Naphish, and Nodab. [20] They were helped against them, and the Hagrites and all who *were* with them were handed over to them; for they cried out to God in the battle, and He answered their prayers because they trusted in Him. [21] They took away their livestock: their fifty thousand camels, 250,000 sheep, *and* two thousand donkeys; and a hundred thousand people. [22] For many fell mortally wounded, because the war *was* of God. And they settled in their place until the exile.

[23] Now the sons of the half-tribe of Manasseh lived in the land; from Bashan to Baal-hermon, Senir, and Mount Hermon they were numerous. [24] These were the heads of their fathers' households: Epher, Ishi, Eliel, Azriel, Jeremiah, Hodaviah, and Jahdiel, valiant mighty men, famous men, heads of their fathers' households.

[25] But they were untrue to the God of their fathers and prostituted themselves with the gods of the peoples of the land, whom God had destroyed before them. [26] So the God of Israel stirred up the spirit of Pul, king of Assyria, that is, the spirit of Tilgath-pilneser king of Assyria, and he took them into exile, namely the Reubenites, the Gadites, and the half-tribe of Manasseh, and brought them to Halah, Habor, Hara, and to the river of Gozan, *where they are* to this day.

Genealogy: The Priestly Line

6 The sons of Levi *were* Gershon, Kohath, and Merari. [2] The sons of Kohath *were* Amram, Izhar, Hebron, and Uzziel. [3] The children of Amram *were* Aaron, Moses, and Miriam. And the sons of Aaron *were* Nadab, Abihu, Eleazar, and Ithamar. [4] Eleazar fathered Phinehas, Phinehas fathered Abishua, [5] Abishua fathered Bukki, Bukki fathered Uzzi, [6] Uzzi fathered Zerahiah, Zerahiah fathered Meraioth, [7] Meraioth fathered Amariah, Amariah fathered Ahitub, [8] Ahitub fathered Zadok, Zadok fathered Ahimaaz, [9] Ahimaaz fathered Azariah, Azariah fathered Johanan, [10] Johanan fathered Azariah (it was he who served as the priest in the house which Solomon built in Jerusalem), [11] Azariah fathered Amariah,

Amariah fathered Ahitub, [12] Ahitub fathered Zadok, Zadok fathered Shallum, [13] Shallum fathered Hilkiah, Hilkiah fathered Azariah, [14] Azariah fathered Seraiah, and Seraiah fathered Jehozadak; [15] Jehozadak went *along* when the LORD led Judah and Jerusalem into exile by Nebuchadnezzar.

[16] The sons of Levi *were* Gershom, Kohath, and Merari. [17] These are the names of the sons of Gershom: Libni and Shimei. [18] The sons of Kohath *were* Amram, Izhar, Hebron, and Uzziel. [19] The sons of Merari *were* Mahli and Mushi. And these are the families of the Levites according to their fathers' *households.* [20] Of Gershom: Libni his son, Jahath his son, Zimmah his son, [21] Joah his son, Iddo his son, Zerah his son, *and* Jeatherai his son. [22] The sons of Kohath *were* Amminadab his son, Korah his son, Assir his son, [23] Elkanah his son, Ebiasaph his son, Assir his son, [24] Tahath his son, Uriel his son, Uzziah his son, and Shaul his son. [25] The sons of Elkanah *were* Amasai and Ahimoth. [26] *As for* Elkanah, the sons of Elkanah *were* Zophai his son, Nahath his son, [27] Eliab his son, Jeroham his son, *and* Elkanah his son. [28] The sons of Samuel *were* Joel, the firstborn, and Abijah, the second. [29] The sons of Merari *were* Mahli, Libni his son, Shimei his son, Uzzah his son, [30] Shimea his son, Haggiah his son, *and* Asaiah his son.

[31] Now these are the ones whom David appointed over the service of song in the house of the LORD, after the ark rested *there.* [32] They were ministering in song in front of the tabernacle of the tent of meeting until Solomon's building of the house of the LORD in Jerusalem; and they served in their office according to their order. [33] These are the ones who served with their sons: From the sons of the Kohathites *were* Heman the singer, the son of Joel, the son of Samuel, [34] the son of Elkanah, the son of Jeroham, the son of Eliel, the son of Toah, [35] the son of Zuph, the son of Elkanah, the son of Mahath, the son of Amasai, [36] the son of Elkanah, the son of Joel, the son of Azariah, the son of Zephaniah, [37] the son of Tahath, the son of Assir, the son of Ebiasaph, the son of Korah, [38] the son of Izhar, the son of Kohath, the son of Levi, the son of Israel. [39] *Heman's* brother Asaph stood at his right hand, Asaph the son of Berechiah, the son of Shimea, [40] the son of Michael, the son of Baaseiah, the son of Malchijah, [41] the son of Ethni, the son of Zerah, the son of Adaiah, [42] the son of Ethan, the son of Zimmah, the son of Shimei, [43] the son of Jahath, the son of Gershom, the son of Levi. [44] On the left hand *were* their kinsmen the sons of Merari: Ethan the son of Kishi, the son of Abdi, the son of Malluch, [45] the son of Hashabiah, the son of Amaziah, the son of Hilkiah, [46] the son of Amzi, the son of Bani, the son of Shemer, [47] the son of Mahli, the son of Mushi, the son of Merari, the son of Levi. [48] Their kinsmen the Levites were appointed for all the service of the tabernacle of the house of God.

[49] But Aaron and his sons offered on the altar of burnt offering and on the altar of incense, for all the work of the Most Holy Place, and to make atonement for Israel, in

accordance with everything that Moses the servant of God had commanded. 50 These are the sons of Aaron: Eleazar his son, Phinehas his son, Abishua his son, 51 Bukki his son, Uzzi his son, Zerahiah his son, 52 Meraioth his son, Amariah his son, Ahitub his son, 53 Zadok his son, *and* Ahimaaz his son.

54 Now these are their settlements according to their camps within their borders. To the sons of Aaron of the families of the Kohathites (for theirs was the *first* lot), 55 to them they gave Hebron in the land of Judah and its pasture lands around it; 56 but they gave the fields of the city and its settlements to Caleb the son of Jephunneh. 57 To the sons of Aaron they gave the *following* cities of refuge: Hebron, Libnah *together* with its pasture lands, Jattir, Eshtemoa with its pasture lands, 58 Hilen with its pasture lands, Debir with its pasture lands, 59 Ashan with its pasture lands, and Beth-shemesh with its pasture lands; 60 and from the tribe of Benjamin: Geba with its pasture lands, Allemeth with its pasture lands, and Anathoth with its pasture lands. Their cities throughout their families were thirteen cities in all.

61 Then to the rest of the sons of Kohath *were given* by lot, from the family of the tribe, from the half-tribe, the half of Manasseh, ten cities. 62 To the sons of Gershom, according to their families, *were given* from the tribe of Issachar, the tribe of Asher, the tribe of Naphtali, and the tribe of Manasseh, thirteen cities in Bashan. 63 To the sons of Merari *were given* by lot, according to their families, from the tribe of Reuben, the tribe of Gad, and the tribe of Zebulun, twelve cities. 64 So the sons of Israel gave the Levites the cities with their pasture lands. 65 They gave by lot from the tribe of the sons of Judah, the tribe of the sons of Simeon, and the tribe of the sons of Benjamin, these cities which are mentioned by name.

66 Now some of the families of the sons of Kohath had cities of their territory from the tribe of Ephraim. 67 They gave to them the *following* cities of refuge: Shechem in the hill country of Ephraim with its pasture lands, Gezer with its pasture lands, 68 Jokmeam with its pasture lands, Beth-horon with its pasture lands, 69 Aijalon with its pasture lands, and Gath-rimmon with its pasture lands; 70 and from the half-tribe of Manasseh: Aner with its pasture lands and Bileam with its pasture lands, for the rest of the family of the sons of Kohath.

71 To the sons of Gershom *were given,* from the family of the half-tribe of Manasseh: Golan in Bashan with its pasture lands and Ashtaroth with its pasture lands; 72 and from the tribe of Issachar: Kedesh with its pasture lands, Daberath with its pasture lands, 73 Ramoth with its pasture lands, and Anem with its pasture lands; 74 and from the tribe of Asher: Mashal with its pasture lands, Abdon with its pasture lands, 75 Hukok with its pasture lands, and Rehob with its pasture lands; 76 and from the tribe of Naphtali: Kedesh in Galilee with its pasture lands, Hammon with its pasture lands, and Kiriathaim with its pasture lands.

77 To the rest of *the Levites,* the sons of Merari, *were given,* from the tribe of Zebulun: Rimmono with its pasture lands, Tabor with its pasture lands, 78 and beyond the Jordan at Jericho, on the east side of the Jordan, *were given them,* from the tribe of Reuben: Bezer in the wilderness with its pasture lands, Jahzah with its pasture lands, 79 Kedemoth with its pasture lands, and Mephaath with its pasture lands; 80 and from the tribe of Gad: Ramoth in Gilead with its pasture lands, Mahanaim with its pasture lands, 81 Heshbon with its pasture lands, and Jazer with its pasture lands.

Genealogy from Issachar

7 Now the sons of Issachar *were* four: Tola, Puah, Jashub, and Shimron. 2 The sons of Tola *were* Uzzi, Rephaiah, Jeriel, Jahmai, Ibsam, and Samuel, heads of their fathers' households. *The sons* of Tola *were* valiant warriors in their generations. Their number in the days of David was 22,600. 3 The son of Uzzi *was* Izrahiah. And the sons of Izrahiah *were* Michael, Obadiah, Joel, *and* Isshiah; all five of them *were* chief men. 4 And with them by their generations according to their fathers' households were thirty-six thousand troops of the army for war; for they had many wives and sons. 5 Their relatives among all the families of Issachar *were* valiant warriors, registered by genealogy, eighty-seven thousand in all.

Descendants of Benjamin

6 Benjamin *had* three *sons:* Bela, Becher, and Jediael. 7 The sons of Bela were five: Ezbon, Uzzi, Uzziel, Jerimoth, and Iri. They *were* heads of fathers' households, valiant warriors, 22,034 registered by genealogy. 8 The sons of Becher *were* Zemirah, Joash, Eliezer, Elioenai, Omri, Jeremoth, Abijah, Anathoth, and Alemeth. All these *were* the sons of Becher. 9 They were registered by genealogy according to their generations, heads of their fathers' households, 20,200 valiant warriors. 10 The son of Jediael *was* Bilhan. And the sons of Bilhan *were* Jeush, Benjamin, Ehud, Chenaanah, Zethan, Tarshish, and Ahishahar. 11 All these *were* sons of Jediael, according to the heads of their fathers' households, 17,200 valiant warriors who were ready to go out with the army to war. 12 Shuppim and Huppim *were* the sons of Ir; Hushim *was* the son of Aher.

Sons of Naphtali

13 The sons of Naphtali *were* Jahziel, Guni, Jezer, and Shallum, the sons of Bilhah.

Descendants of Manasseh

14 The sons of Manasseh *were* Asriel, to whom his Aramean concubine gave birth; she *also* gave birth to Machir, the father of Gilead. 15 Machir took a wife from Huppim and Shuppim, whose name was Maacah. And the name of the second was Zelophehad, and Zelophehad had daughters. 16 Maacah the wife of Machir gave birth to a son, and she named him Peresh; the name of his brother *was* Sheresh, and his sons *were* Ulam and Rakem. 17 The son of Ulam *was* Bedan. These *were* the sons of Gilead the son of Machir, the son of Manasseh. 18 His sister Hammolecheth gave birth to Ishhod, Abiezer, and Mahlah. 19 The

sons of Shemida were Ahian, Shechem, Likhi, and Aniam.

Descendants of Ephraim

20 The sons of Ephraim were Shuthelah and Bered his son, Tahath his son, Eleadah his son, Tahath his son, 21 Zabad his son, Shuthelah his son, and Ezer and Elead, whom the men of Gath who were born in the land killed, because they came down to take their live-stock. 22 Their father Ephraim mourned for many days, and his relatives came to comfort him. 23 Then he went in to his wife, and she conceived and gave birth to a son, and he named him Beriah, because misfortune had come upon his house. 24 His daughter was Sheerah, who built lower and upper Beth-horon, as well as Uzzen-sheerah. 25 Rephah was his son along with Resheph, Telah his son, Tahan his son, 26 Ladan his son, Ammihud his son, Elishama his son, 27 Non his son, and Joshua his son.

28 Their possessions and dwelling places were Bethel with its towns, and to the east, Naaran, and to the west, Gezer with its towns, and Shechem with its towns, as far as Ayyah with its towns, 29 and along the borders of the sons of Manasseh, Beth-shean with its towns, Taanach with its towns, Megiddo with its towns, and Dor with its towns. In these regions lived the sons of Joseph the son of Israel.

Descendants of Asher

30 The sons of Asher were Imnah, Ishvah, Ishvi, and Beriah; and Serah was their sister. 31 The sons of Beriah were Heber and Malchiel, who was the father of Birzaith. 32 Heber fathered Japhlet, Shomer, and Hotham, and their sister Shua. 33 The sons of Japhlet were Pasach, Bimhal, and Ashvath. These were the sons of Japhlet. 34 The sons of Shemer were Ahi and Rohgah, and Jehubbah and Aram. 35 The sons of his brother Helem were Zophah, Imna, Shelesh, and Amal. 36 The sons of Zophah were Suah, Harnepher, Shual, Beri, Imrah, 37 Bezer, Hod, Shamma, Shilshah, Ithran, and Beera. 38 The sons of Jether were Jephunneh, Pispa, and Ara. 39 The sons of Ulla were Arah, Han-niel, and Rizia. 40 All these were the sons of Asher, heads of the fathers' houses, choice, valiant mighty men, and heads of the leaders. And the number of them registered by genealogy for service in war was twenty-six thousand men.

Genealogy from Benjamin

8 And Benjamin fathered Bela his firstborn, Ashbel the second, Aharah the third, 2 Nohah the fourth, and Rapha the fifth. 3 Bela had sons: Addar, Gera, Abihud, 4 Abishua, Naaman, Ahoah, 5 Gera, Shephuphan, and Huram. 6 These are the sons of Ehud: these are the heads of fathers' households of the inhabi-tants of Geba, and they took them into exile to Manahath, 7 namely, Naaman, Ahijah, and Gera—he exiled them; and he fathered Uzza and Ahihud. 8 Shaharaim fathered children in the country of Moab after he had sent his wives Hushim and Baara away. 9 By Hodesh his wife he fathered Jobab, Zibia, Mesha, Malcam, 10 Jeuz, Sachia, and Mirmah. These were his sons, heads of fathers' households. 11 By Hushim he fathered Abitub and Elpaal. 12 The sons of Elpaal were Eber, Misham, and Shemed, who built Ono and Lod, with its towns; 13 and Beriah and Shema, who were heads of fathers' households of the inhabitants of Aijalon, who put the inhabitants of Gath to flight; 14 and Ahio, Shashak, and Jeremoth. 15 Zebadiah, Arad, Eder, 16 Michael, Ishpah, and Joha were the sons of Beriah. 17 Zebadiah, Meshullam, Hizki, Heber, 18 Ishmerai, Izliah, and Jobab were the sons of Elpaal. 19 Jakim, Zichri, Zabdi, 20 Elienai, Zillethai, Eliel, 21 Adaiah, Beraiah, and Shimrath were the sons of Shimei. 22 Ishpan, Eber, Eliel, 23 Abdon, Zichri, Hanan, 24 Hananiah, Elam, Anthothijah, 25 Iphdeiah, and Penuel were the sons of Shashak. 26 Shamsherai, Shehariah, Athaliah, 27 Jaareshiah, Elijah, and Zichri were the sons of Jeroham. 28 These were heads of the fathers' households according to their generations, chief men who lived in Jerusalem.

29 Now, Jeiel, the father of Gibeon lived in Gibeon, and his wife's name was Maacah; 30 and his firstborn son was Abdon, then Zur, Kish, Baal, Nadab, 31 Gedor, Ahio, and Zecher. 32 Mikloth fathered Shimeah. They also lived with their relatives in Jerusalem opposite their other relatives.

Genealogy from King Saul

33 Ner fathered Kish, Kish fathered Saul, and Saul fathered Jonathan, Malchi-shua, Abinadab, and Eshbaal. 34 The son of Jonathan was Merib-baal, and Merib-baal fathered Micah. 35 The sons of Micah were Pithon, Melech, Tarea, and Ahaz. 36 Ahaz fathered Jehoaddah, Jehoaddah fathered Alemeth, Azmaveth, and Zimri; and Zimri fathered Moza. 37 Moza fathered Binea; Raphah was his son, Eleasah, his son, and Azel, his son. 38 Azel had six sons, and these were their names: Azrikam, Bocheru, Ishmael, Sheariah, Obadiah, and Hanan. All these were the sons of Azel. 39 The sons of his brother Eshek were Ulam his firstborn, Jeush the second, and Eliphelet the third. 40 The sons of Ulam were valiant mighty men, archers, and they had many sons and grandsons, 150 of them. All these were among the sons of Benjamin.

People of Jerusalem

9 So all Israel was enrolled in genealogies; and behold, they are written in the Book of the Kings of Israel. And Judah was taken into exile to Babylon for their infidelity.

2 Now the first inhabitants who lived on their own property in their cities were people of Israel, including the priests, the Levites, and the temple servants. 3 Some of the sons of Judah, some of the sons of Benjamin, and some of the sons of Ephraim and Manasseh lived in Jerusalem: 4 Uthai the son of Ammihud, the son of Omri, the son of Imri, the son of Bani, from the sons of Perez the son of Judah. 5 From the Shilonites were Asaiah the firstborn and his sons. 6 From the sons of Zerah were Jeuel and their relatives, 690 of them. 7 From the sons of

Benjamin *were* Sallu the son of Meshullam, the son of Hodaviah, the son of Hassenuah, 8 and Ibneiah the son of Jeroham, and Elah the son of Uzzi, the son of Michri, and Meshullam the son of Shephatiah, the son of Reuel, the son of Ibnijah; 9 and their relatives according to their generations, 956. All these men *were* heads of fathers' *households* according to their fathers' houses.

10 From the priests *were* Jedaiah, Jehoiarib, Jachin, 11 and Azariah the son of Hilkiah, the son of Meshullam, the son of Zadok, the son of Meraioth, the son of Ahitub, the chief officer of the house of God; 12 and Adaiah the son of Jeroham, the son of Pashhur, the son of Malchijah, and Maasai the son of Adiel, the son of Jahzerah, the son of Meshullam, the son of Meshillemith, the son of Immer; 13 and their relatives, heads of their fathers' households, 1,760 competent men for the work of the service of the house of God.

14 Of the Levites, *there were* Shemaiah the son of Hasshub, the son of Azrikam, the son of Hashabiah, of the sons of Merari; 15 and Bakbakkar, Heresh, and Galal; and Mattaniah the son of Mica, the son of Zichri, the son of Asaph, 16 and Obadiah the son of Shemaiah, the son of Galal, the son of Jeduthun; and Berechiah the son of Asa, the son of Elkanah, who lived in the settlements of the Netophathites.

17 Now the gatekeepers *were* Shallum, Akkub, Talmon, Ahiman, and their relatives (Shallum the chief 18 *being stationed* until now at the king's gate to the east). These *were* the gatekeepers for the camp of the sons of Levi. 19 Shallum the son of Kore, the son of Ebiasaph, the son of Korah, and his relatives of his father's house, the Korahites, *were* in charge of the work of the service, doorkeepers of the tent; and their fathers had been in charge of the camp of the LORD, keepers of the entrance. 20 Phinehas the son of Eleazar was supervisor over them previously, *and* the LORD was with him. 21 Zechariah the son of Meshelemiah was gatekeeper of the entrance of the tent of meeting. 22 Those who were chosen to be gatekeepers at the thresholds were 212 in all. They were registered by genealogy in their settlements, those whom David and Samuel the seer appointed in their official capacity. 23 So they and their sons were in charge of the gates of the house of the LORD, the house of the tent, in their divisions of service. 24 The gatekeepers were on the four sides, to the east, west, north, and south. 25 Their relatives in their settlements *were* to come in every seven days from time to time *to be* with them; 26 for the four chief gatekeepers, who *were* Levites, *served* in an official capacity, and were in charge of the chambers and in charge of the treasuries in the house of God. 27 They spent the night around the house of God, because the watch was committed to them; and they were in charge of opening *it* morning by morning.

28 Now some of them were in charge of the utensils of the service, for they counted them when they brought them in and when they took them out. 29 Some of them also were appointed over the furniture and over all the utensils of the sanctuary, and over the finely milled flour, the wine, the olive oil, the frankincense, and the balsam oil. 30 Some of the sons of the priests prepared the mixing of the balsam oil. 31 Mattithiah, one of the Levites, who was the firstborn of Shallum the Korahite, had the responsibility for the baking of cakes in pans. 32 Some of their relatives of the sons of the Kohathites were in charge of the showbread to prepare it every Sabbath.

33 Now these are the singers, heads of fathers' *households* of the Levites, *who lived* in the chambers *of the temple* free *of other duties;* for they were engaged in their work day and night. 34 These were heads of fathers' *households* of the Levites according to their generations, chief men who lived in Jerusalem.

Ancestry and Descendants of Saul

35 Jeiel the father of Gibeon lived in Gibeon, and his wife's name was Maacah, 36 and his firstborn son *was* Abdon, then Zur, Kish, Baal, Ner, Nadab, 37 Gedor, Ahio, Zechariah, and Mikloth. 38 Mikloth fathered Shimeam. And they also lived with their relatives in Jerusalem opposite their *other* relatives. 39 Ner fathered Kish, Kish fathered Saul, and Saul fathered Jonathan, Malchi-shua, Abinadab, and Eshbaal. 40 The son of Jonathan *was* Merib-baal; and Merib-baal fathered Micah. 41 The sons of Micah *were* Pithon, Melech, Tahrea, *and Ahaz.* 42 Ahaz fathered Jarah, Jarah fathered Alemeth, Azmaveth, and Zimri; and Zimri fathered Moza. 43 Moza fathered Binea, and Rephaiah *was* his son, Eleasah his son, Azel his son. 44 Azel had six sons whose names were these: Azrikam, Bocheru, Ishmael, Sheariah, Obadiah, and Hanan. These were the sons of Azel.

Defeat and Death of Saul and His Sons

10 Now the Philistines fought against Israel, and the men of Israel fled from the Philistines but fell fatally wounded on Mount Gilboa. 2 And the Philistines also overtook Saul and his sons, and the Philistines killed Jonathan, Abinadab, and Malchi-shua, the sons of Saul. 3 The battle became severe against Saul, and the archers found him; and he was wounded by the archers. 4 Then Saul said to his armor bearer, "Draw your sword and thrust me through with it, otherwise these uncircumcised *Philistines* will come and abuse me." But his armor bearer would not, for he was very afraid. So Saul took his *own* sword and fell on it. 5 When his armor bearer saw that Saul was dead, he likewise fell on his sword and died. 6 So Saul died with his three sons, and all *those* of his house died together.

7 When all the people of Israel who were in the valley saw that they had fled, and that Saul and his sons were dead, they abandoned their cities and fled; and the Philistines came and lived in them.

8 It came about the next day, when the Philistines came to strip those killed, that they found Saul and his sons fallen on Mount Gilboa. 9 So they stripped him and took his head and his armor and sent *messengers* around the land of the Philistines to carry the

good news to their idols and to the people. 10 They put his armor in the house of their gods and impaled his head in the house of Dagon.

Jabesh-gilead's Tribute to Saul

11 When all Jabesh-gilead heard everything that the Philistines had done to Saul, 12 all the valiant men got up and took away the body of Saul and the bodies of his sons, and brought them to Jabesh; and they buried their bones under the oak in Jabesh, and fasted for seven days.

13 So Saul died for his unfaithfulness which he committed against the LORD, because of the word of the LORD which he did not keep; and also because he asked *counsel* of a medium, making inquiry *of her,* 14 and did not inquire of the LORD. Therefore He killed him and turned the kingdom over to David, the son of Jesse.

David Made King over All Israel

11 Then all Israel gathered to David at Hebron and said, "Behold, we are your bone and your flesh. 2 In times past, even when Saul was king, you *were* the one who led out and brought in Israel; and the LORD your God said to you, 'You shall shepherd My people Israel, and you shall be leader over My people Israel.' " 3 So all the elders of Israel came to the king at Hebron, and David made a covenant with them in Hebron before the LORD; and they anointed David king over Israel, in accordance with the word of the LORD through Samuel.

Jerusalem Is the Capital City

4 Then David and all Israel went to Jerusalem (that is, Jebus); and the Jebusites, the inhabitants of the land, *were* there. 5 The inhabitants of Jebus said to David, "You shall not enter here." Nevertheless David took the mountain stronghold of Zion (that is, the city of David). 6 Now David had said, "Whoever is first to kill a Jebusite shall be chief and commander." Joab the son of Zeruiah went up first, so he became chief. 7 Then David lived in the stronghold; therefore it was called the city of David. 8 He built the city all around, from the ¹Millo to the surrounding area; and Joab repaired the rest of the city. 9 And David became greater and greater, for the LORD of armies *was* with him.

David's Mighty Men

10 Now these are the heads of the mighty men whom David had, who remained faithful to him in his kingdom, together with all Israel, to make him king, in accordance with the word of the LORD concerning Israel. 11 These *constitute* the list of David's mighty men: Jashobeam, the son of a Hachmonite, the chief of the thirty; he wielded his spear against three hundred whom he killed at one time.

12 After him was Eleazar the son of Dodo, the Ahohite, who *was* one of the three mighty men. 13 He was with David at Pas-dammim when the Philistines were gathered together there to battle, and there was a plot of land full of barley; and the people fled from the Philistines. 14 But they took their stand in the midst of the plot and defended it, and defeated the Philistines; and the LORD saved them with a great victory.

15 Now three of the thirty chief men went down to the rock to David, into the cave of Adullam, while the army of the Philistines was camping in the Valley of Rephaim. 16 David was then in the stronghold, while the garrison of the Philistines *was* then in Bethlehem. 17 And David had a craving and said, "Oh that someone would give me water to drink from the well of Bethlehem, which is by the gate!" 18 So the three broke through the camp of the Philistines and drew water from the well of Bethlehem which *was* by the gate, and took *it* and brought *it* to David; however, David would not drink it, but poured it out to the LORD; 19 and he said, "Far be it from me before my God that I would do this. Shall I drink the blood of these men *who went* at the risk of their lives? For they brought it at the risk of their lives." Therefore he would not drink it. The three mighty men did these things.

20 As for Abshai the brother of Joab, he was chief of the thirty, and he wielded his spear against three hundred and killed them; and he had a name as well as the thirty. 21 Of the three in the second *rank* he was the most honored, and he became their commander; however, he did not attain *the reputation* of the *first* three.

22 Benaiah the son of Jehoiada, the son of a warrior of Kabzeel, mighty in deeds, struck and killed the two *sons of* Ariel of Moab. He also went down and struck and killed a lion inside a pit on a snowy day. 23 And he killed an Egyptian, a man of *great* stature ¹five cubits tall. Now in the Egyptian's hand *was* a spear like a weaver's beam, but he went down to him with a club and snatched the spear from the Egyptian's hand and killed him with his own spear. 24 Benaiah the son of Jehoiada did these things, and had a name as well as the three mighty men. 25 Behold, he was honored among the thirty, but he did not attain *the reputation* of the *first* three; and David appointed him over his bodyguard.

26 Now the mighty men of the armies *were* Asahel the brother of Joab, Elhanan the son of Dodo of Bethlehem, 27 Shammoth the Harorite, Helez the Pelonite, 28 Ira the son of Ikkesh the Tekoite, Abiezer the Anathothite, 29 Sibbecai the Hushathite, Ilai the Ahohite, 30 Maharai the Netophathite, Heled the son of Baanah the Netophathite, 31 Ithai the son of Ribai of Gibeah of the sons of Benjamin, Benaiah the Pirathonite, 32 Hurai of the brooks of Gaash, Abiel the Arbathite, 33 Azmaveth the Baharumite, Eliahba the Shaalbonite, 34 the sons of Hashem the Gizonite, Jonathan the son of Shagee the Hararite, 35 Ahiam the son of Sacar the Hararite, Eliphal the son of Ur, 36 Hepher the Mecherathite, Ahijah the Pelonite, 37 Hezro the Carmelite, Naarai the son of Ezbai, 38 Joel the brother of Nathan, Mibhar the son of Hagri, 39 Zelek the Ammonite, Naharai the Berothite, the armor bearer of Joab the son of Zeruiah, 40 Ira the Ithrite, Gareb the Ithrite, 41 Uriah the Hittite, Zabad the son of

---

11:8 ¹ I.e., terraced structure   11:23 ¹ About 7.5 ft. or 2.3 m

Ahlai, **42** Adina the son of Shiza the Reubenite, a chief of the Reubenites, and thirty with him, **43** Hanan the son of Maacah and Joshaphat the Mithnite, **44** Uzzia the Ashterathite, Shama and Jeiel the sons of Hotham the Aroerite, **45** Jediael the son of Shimri and his brother Joha the Tizite, **46** Eliel the Mahavite, and Jeribai and Joshaviah, the sons of Elnaam, Ithmah the Moabite, **47** Eliel, Obed, and Jaasiel the Mezobaite.

David's Supporters in Ziklag

12 Now these are the *men* who came to David at Ziklag, while he was still restricted because of Saul the son of Kish; and they were among the mighty men who helped *him* in war. **2** They were equipped with bows, using both the right hand and the left *to sling* stones and *shoot* arrows with the bow; *they were* Saul's kinsmen from Benjamin. **3** The chief was Ahiezer, then Joash, the sons of Shemaah the Gibeathite; and Jeziel and Pelet, the sons of Azmaveth, and Beracah, and Jehu the Anathothite, **4** and Ishmaiah the Gibeonite, a mighty man among the thirty, and in charge of the thirty. Then Jeremiah, Jahaziel, Johanan, Jozabad the Gederathite, **5** Eluzai, Jerimoth, Bealiah, Shemariah, Shephatiah the Haruphite, **6** Elkanah, Isshiah, Azarel, Joezer, Jashobeam, the Korahites, **7** and Joelah and Zebadiah, the sons of Jeroham of Gedor.

8 From the Gadites valiant mighty men went over to David at the stronghold in the wilderness, men trained for war who could handle a large shield and spear, whose faces were *like* the faces of lions, and *they were* as swift as the gazelles on the mountains. **9** Ezer *was* the first, Obadiah the second, Eliab the third, **10** Mishmannah the fourth, Jeremiah the fifth, **11** Attai the sixth, Eliel the seventh, **12** Johanan the eighth, Elzabad the ninth, **13** Jeremiah the tenth, *and* Machbannai, the eleventh. **14** These men from the sons of Gad were captains of the army; the one who was least was *equal* to a hundred, and the greatest, to a thousand. **15** These are the ones who crossed the Jordan in the first month, when it was overflowing all its banks, and they put to flight all those in the valleys, to the east and to the west.

16 Then some of the sons of Benjamin and Judah came to the stronghold to David. **17** David went out to meet them, and said to them, "If you come peacefully to help me, my heart shall be united with you; but if to betray me to my enemies, since there is no wrong in my hands, may the God of our fathers look on *it* and decide." **18** Then the Spirit covered Amasai like clothing, the chief of the thirty; *and he said,*

"*We are* yours, David,
And *are* with you, son of Jesse!
Peace, peace to you,
And peace to him who helps you;
Indeed, your God helps you!"

Then David received them and made them captains of the troops.

19 From Manasseh some also defected to David when he was about to go to battle with the Philistines against Saul. But they did not help them, because the governors of the Philistines sent him away after consultation, saying, "At *the cost of* our heads he might defect to his master Saul." **20** As he was going to Ziklag, *men* from Manasseh defected to him: Adnah, Jozabad, Jediael, Michael, Jozabad, Elihu, and Zillethai, captains of thousands who belonged to Manasseh. **21** They helped David against the band of raiders, for they were all valiant mighty men, and were captains in the army. **22** For day by day *men* came to David to help him, until there was a great army like the army of God.

Supporters Gathered at Hebron

23 Now these are the numbers of the divisions equipped for war, who came to David at Hebron, to turn the kingdom of Saul to him, according to the word of the LORD. **24** The sons of Judah who carried shield and spear *numbered* 6,800, equipped for war. **25** From the sons of Simeon, valiant mighty men of war, 7,100. **26** From the sons of Levi, 4,600. **27** Now Jehoiada was the leader of *the house of* Aaron, and with him were 3,700, **28** also Zadok, a young valiant mighty man, and *from* his father's house, twenty-two captains. **29** From the sons of Benjamin, Saul's kinsmen, three thousand; for until now the majority of them had kept their allegiance to the house of Saul. **30** From the sons of Ephraim 20,800, valiant mighty men, famous men in their fathers' households. **31** From the half-tribe of Manasseh eighteen thousand, who were designated by name to come and make David king. **32** From the sons of Issachar, men who understood the times, with knowledge of what Israel should do, their chiefs *were* two hundred; and all their kinsmen *were* at their command. **33** From Zebulun, there were fifty thousand who went out in the army, who could draw up in battle formation with all kinds of weapons of war and helped *David* with an undivided heart. **34** From Naphtali *there were* a thousand captains, and with them thirty-seven thousand with shield and spear. **35** From the Danites who could draw up in battle formation, *there were* 28,600. **36** From Asher *there were* forty thousand who went out in the army to draw up in battle formation. **37** From the other side of the Jordan, from the Reubenites, the Gadites, and the half-tribe of Manasseh, *there were* 120,000 with all *kinds* of weapons of war for the battle.

38 All of these, being men of war who helped in battle formation, came to Hebron with a perfect heart to make David king over all Israel; and all the rest of Israel also were of one mind to make David king. **39** They were there with David for three days, eating and drinking, for their kinsmen had prepared for them. **40** Moreover, those who were near to them, as far as Issachar, Zebulun, and Naphtali, brought food on donkeys, camels, mules, and on oxen, great quantities of flour cakes, fig cakes and bunches of raisins, wine, oil, oxen, and sheep. There was joy indeed in Israel.

Peril in Transporting the Ark

13 Then David consulted with the captains of the thousands and the hundreds, with

every leader. 2 David said to all the assembly of Israel, "If it *seems* good to you, and if it is from the LORD our God, 7let us send *word* everywhere to our kinsmen who remain in all the land of Israel, and to the priests and Levites who are with them in their cities with pasture lands, that they meet with us; 3 and 7let us bring back the ark of our God to us, since we did not seek it in the days of Saul." 4 Then all the assembly said that they would do so, for this was right in the eyes of all the people.

5 So David assembled all Israel together, from the Shihor of Egypt to the entrance of Hamath, to bring the ark of God from Kiriath-jearim. 6 David and all Israel went up to Baalah, *that is,* to Kiriath-jearim, which belongs to Judah, to bring up from there the ark of God, the LORD who is enthroned *above* the cherubim, where His name is called. 7 And they carried the ark of God on a new cart from the house of Abinadab, and Uzza and Ahio drove the cart. 8 David and all Israel were celebrating before God with all *their* might, with songs and with lyres, harps, tambourines, cymbals, and trumpets.

9 When they came to the threshing floor of Chidon, Uzza put out his hand to hold the ark, because the oxen nearly overturned *it.* 10 But the anger of the LORD burned against Uzza, so He struck him because he had put out his hand toward the ark; and he died there before God. 11 Then David became angry because of the LORD's outburst against Uzza; and he called that place 7Perez-uzza *as it is* to this day. 12 David was afraid of God that day, saying, "How can I bring the ark of God *home* to me?" 13 So David did not take the ark with him to the city of David, but took it aside to the house of Obed-edom the Gittite. 14 And the ark of God remained with the family of Obed-edom in his house for three months; and the LORD blessed the family of Obed-edom and all that he had.

David's Family Enlarged

14 Now Hiram king of Tyre sent messengers to David with cedar trees, masons, and carpenters, to build a house for him. 2 And David realized that the LORD had established him as king over Israel, *and* that his kingdom was highly exalted, for the sake of His people Israel. 3 Then David took more wives in Jerusalem, and David fathered more sons and daughters. 4 These are the names of the children born to him in Jerusalem: Shammua, Shobab, Nathan, Solomon, 5 Ibhar, Elishua, Elpelet, 6 Nogah, Nepheg, Japhia, 7 Elishama, Beeliada, and Eliphelet.

Philistines Defeated

8 When the Philistines heard that David had been anointed king over all Israel, all the Philistines went up in search of David; and David heard about it and went out against them. 9 Now the Philistines had come and carried out a raid in the Valley of Rephaim. 10 David inquired of God, saying, "Shall I go up against the Philistines? And will You hand them over to me?" Then the LORD said to him,

"Go up, for I will hand them over to you." 11 So they came up to Baal-perazim, and David defeated them there; and David said, "God has broken through my enemies by my hand, like the breakthrough of waters." Therefore they named that place 1Baal-perazim. 12 They abandoned their gods there; so David gave the order and they were burned with fire.

13 The Philistines carried out yet another raid in the valley. 14 David inquired again of God, and God said to him, "You shall not go up after them; circle around behind them and come at them in front of the baka-shrubs. 15 When you hear the sound of marching in the tops of the baka-shrubs, then you shall go out to battle, for God will have gone out before you to strike the army of the Philistines." 16 David did just as God had commanded him, and they defeated the army of the Philistines from Gibeon even as far as Gezer. 17 Then the fame of David spread in all the lands; and the LORD brought the fear of him on all the nations.

Plans to Move the Ark to Jerusalem

15 Now *David* built houses for himself in the city of David; and he prepared a place for the ark of God and pitched a tent for it. 2 Then David said, "No one is to carry the ark of God except the Levites; for the LORD chose them to carry the ark of the LORD and to serve Him forever." 3 And David assembled all Israel at Jerusalem to bring up the ark of the LORD to its place which he had prepared for it. 4 David gathered together the sons of Aaron and the Levites: 5 of the sons of Kohath, Uriel the chief, and 120 of his relatives; 6 of the sons of Merari, Asaiah the chief, and 220 of his relatives; 7 of the sons of Gershom, Joel the chief, and 130 of his relatives; 8 of the sons of Elizaphan, Shemaiah the chief, and two hundred of his relatives; 9 of the sons of Hebron, Eliel the chief, and eighty of his relatives; 10 of the sons of Uzziel, Amminadab the chief, and 112 of his relatives.

11 Then David called for the priests Zadok and Abiathar, and for the Levites, for Uriel, Asaiah, Joel, Shemaiah, Eliel, and Amminadab; 12 and he said to them, "You are the heads of the fathers' *households* of the Levites; consecrate yourselves, you and your relatives, so that you may bring up the ark of the LORD God of Israel to *the place* that I have prepared for it. 13 Because you did not *carry it* at the first, the LORD our God made an outburst against us, since we did not seek Him according to the ordinance." 14 So the priests and the Levites consecrated themselves to bring up the ark of the LORD God of Israel. 15 The sons of the Levites carried the ark of God on their shoulders with the poles on them, just as Moses had commanded in accordance with the word of the LORD.

16 Then David spoke to the chiefs of the Levites to appoint their relatives *as* the singers, with musical instruments, harps, lyres, and cymbals, playing to raise sounds of joy. 17 So the Levites appointed Heman the son of Joel, and from his relatives, Asaph the son of Berechiah;

13:2 1 Indicating a proposal, not a request　**13:3** 1 See note v 2　**13:11** 1 I.e., the outburst *against* Uzza
14:11 1 I.e., the master of breakthroughs

and from the sons of Merari their relatives, Ethan the son of Kushaiah, 18 and with them their relatives of the second rank, Zechariah, Ben, Jaaziel, Shemiramoth, Jehiel, Unni, Eliab, Benaiah, Maaseiah, Mattithiah, Eliphelehu, Mikneiah, Obed-edom, and Jeiel, the gatekeepers. 19 So the singers, Heman, Asaph, and Ethan, *were appointed* to sound aloud cymbals of bronze; 20 and Zechariah, Aziel, Shemiramoth, Jehiel, Unni, Eliab, Maaseiah, and Benaiah, with harps *tuned* to alamoth; 21 and Mattithiah, Eliphelehu, Mikneiah, Obed-edom, Jeiel, and Azaziah, to lead with lyres *tuned* to the sheminith. 22 Chenaniah, chief of the Levites, was *in charge of* the singing; he gave instruction in singing because he was skillful. 23 Berechiah and Elkanah were gatekeepers for the ark. 24 Shebaniah, Joshaphat, Nethanel, Amasai, Zechariah, Benaiah, and Eliezer, the priests, blew the trumpets before the ark of God. Obed-edom and Jehiah also *were* gatekeepers for the ark.

25 So *it was* David, with the elders of Israel and the captains of thousands, who went to bring up the ark of the covenant of the Lord from the house of Obed-edom with joy. 26 Because God was helping the Levites who were carrying the ark of the covenant of the Lord, they sacrificed seven bulls and seven rams. 27 Now David was clothed with a robe of fine linen with all the Levites who were carrying the ark, and the singers, and Chenaniah the leader of the singing *with* the singers. David also wore an ephod of linen. 28 So all Israel brought up the ark of the covenant of the Lord with shouting, and with *the* sound of the horn, with trumpets, with loud-sounding cymbals, with harps, and lyres.

29 When the ark of the covenant of the Lord came to the city of David, Michal the daughter of Saul looked out of the window and saw King David dancing and celebrating; and she despised him in her heart.

A Tent for the Ark

16 And they brought in the ark of God and placed it inside the tent which David had pitched for it, and they offered burnt offerings and peace offerings before God. 2 When David had finished offering the burnt offering and the peace offerings, he blessed the people in the name of the Lord. 3 Then he distributed to everyone of Israel, both men and women, to everyone a loaf of bread, a portion *of meat,* and a raisin cake.

4 He appointed some of the Levites *as* ministers before the ark of the Lord, to celebrate and to thank and praise the Lord God of Israel: 5 Asaph the chief, and second to him Zechariah, *then* Jeiel, Shemiramoth, Jehiel, Mattithiah, Eliab, Benaiah, Obed-edom, and Jeiel, with *musical* instruments, harps, *and* lyres; also Asaph *played* loud-sounding cymbals, 6 and the priests Benaiah and Jahaziel *blew* trumpets continually before the ark of the covenant of God.

7 Then on that day David first assigned Asaph and his relatives to give thanks to the Lord.

Psalm of Thanksgiving

8 Give thanks to the Lord, call upon His name;
Make His deeds known among the peoples.
9 Sing to Him, sing praises to Him;
Speak of all His wonders.
10 Boast in His holy name;
Let the heart of those who seek the Lord be joyful.
11 Seek the Lord and His strength;
Seek His face continually.
12 Remember His wonderful deeds which He has done,
His marvels and the judgments from His mouth,
13 *You* descendants of Israel His servant,
Sons of Jacob, His chosen ones!
14 He is the Lord our God;
His judgments are in all the earth.
15 Remember His covenant forever,
The word which He commanded to a thousand generations,
16 *The covenant* which He made with Abraham,
And His oath to Isaac.
17 He also confirmed it to Jacob as a statute,
To Israel as an everlasting covenant,
18 Saying, "To you I will give the land of Canaan,
As the portion of your inheritance."
19 When they were only a few in number,
Very few, and strangers in it,
20 And they wandered from nation to nation,
And from *one* kingdom to another people,
21 He allowed no one to oppress them,
And He rebuked kings for their sakes,
saying,
22 "Do not touch My anointed ones,
And do not harm My prophets."
23 Sing to the Lord, all the earth;
Proclaim good news of His salvation from day to day.
24 Tell of His glory among the nations,
His wonderful deeds among all the peoples.
25 For great is the Lord, and greatly to be praised;
He also is to be feared above all gods.
26 For all the gods of the peoples are idols,
But the Lord made the heavens.
27 Splendor and majesty are before Him,
Strength and joy are in His place.
28 Ascribe to the Lord, you families of the peoples,
Ascribe to the Lord glory and strength.
29 Ascribe to the Lord the glory due His name;
Bring an offering, and come before Him;
Worship the Lord in holy attire.
30 Tremble before Him, all the earth;
Indeed, the world is firmly established, it will not be moved.
31 ¹Let the heavens be joyful, and the earth rejoice;
And let them say among the nations, "The Lord reigns."
32 Let the sea roar, and everything it contains;

16:31 ¹ Hopeful command or wish, not a request; and so through v 32

Let the field rejoice, and everything that is
in it.
33 Then the trees of the forest will sing for
joy in the presence of the LORD;
For He is coming to judge the earth.
34 Give thanks to the LORD, for *He is* good;
For His faithfulness is everlasting.
35 Then say, "Save us, God of our salvation,
And gather us and save us from the
nations,
To give thanks to Your holy name,
And glory in Your praise."
36 Blessed be the LORD, the God of Israel,
From everlasting to everlasting!
Then all the people said, "Amen," and praised
the LORD.

Worship before the Ark

37 So he left Asaph and his relatives there
before the ark of the covenant of the LORD, to
minister before the ark continually, as every
day's work required, **38** and Obed-edom with
his sixty-eight relatives; Obed-edom, the son of
Jeduthun, and Hosah as gatekeepers. **39** *He left*
Zadok the priest and his relatives the priests
before the tabernacle of the LORD in the high
place which *was* at Gibeon, **40** to offer burnt
offerings to the LORD on the altar of burnt
offering continually morning and evening, even
according to everything that is written in the
Law of the LORD, which He commanded
Israel. **41** With them *were* Heman and Jeduthun,
and the rest who were chosen, who were designated by name, to give thanks to the LORD,
because His kindness is everlasting. **42** And
with them *were* Heman and Jeduthun *with*
trumpets and cymbals for those who *were to*
play *them,* and *with* instruments *for* the songs
of God, and the sons of Jeduthun for the gate.
43 Then all the people departed, each to his
house; and David returned to bless his household.

God's Covenant with David

17 And it came about, when David lived in
his house, that David said to Nathan the
prophet, "Look, I am living in a house of cedar,
but the ark of the covenant of the LORD is
under tent curtains." **2** Then Nathan said to
David, "Do whatever is in your heart, for God
is with you."

3 But it happened that same night, that the
word of God came to Nathan, saying, **4** "Go and
tell David My servant, 'This is what the LORD
says: "You shall not build a house for Me to
dwell in; **5** for I have not dwelt in a house since
the day that I brought up Israel to this day, but
I have gone from tent to tent and from *one*
dwelling place *to another.* **6** In all places where
I have walked with all Israel, have I spoken a
word with any of the judges of Israel, whom I
commanded to shepherd My people, saying,
'Why have you not built Me a house of
cedar?' " ' **7** Now, therefore, this is what you
shall say to My servant David: 'This is what the
LORD of armies says: "I took you from the
pasture, from following the sheep, to be leader
over My people Israel. **8** I have been with you
wherever you have gone, and have eliminated

all your enemies from you; and I will make for
you a name like the name of the great ones
who are on the earth. **9** And I will appoint a
place for My people Israel, and will plant them
there, so that they may live in their own place
and not tremble *with anxiety* again; and the
wicked will not make them waste away
anymore as *they did* previously, **10** even from
the day that I commanded judges *to be* over
My people Israel. And I will subdue all your
enemies.

Moreover, I tell you that the LORD will build
a house for you. **11** When your days are fulfilled
that you must ¹go *to be* with your fathers, then
I will set up *one of* your descendants after you,
who will be from your sons; and I will establish
his kingdom. **12** He shall build for Me a house,
and I will establish his throne forever. **13** I will
be his father and he shall be My son; and I will
not take My favor away from him, as I took it
from him who was before you. **14** But I will settle him in My house and in My kingdom
forever, and his throne will be established
forever." ' " **15** According to all these words and
according to all of this vision, so Nathan spoke
to David.

David's Prayer in Response

16 Then King David came in and sat before
the LORD, and said, "Who am I, LORD God, and
what is my house that You have brought me
this far? **17** This was a small thing in Your eyes,
God; but You have spoken of Your servant's
house for a great while to come, and have
viewed me according to the standard of a
person of high degree, LORD God. **18** What more
can David still *say* to You concerning the honor
bestowed on Your servant? For You know Your
servant. **19** LORD, for Your servant's sake, and
according to Your own heart, You have accomplished all this greatness, to make known all
these great things. **20** LORD, there is none like
You, nor is there any God besides You, according to everything that we have heard with our
ears. **21** And what one nation on the earth is
like Your people Israel, whom God went to
redeem for Himself *as* a people, to make for
You a name by great and awesome things, by
driving out nations from before Your people,
whom You redeemed from Egypt? **22** For You
have made Your people Israel Your own people
forever, and You, LORD, became their God.

23 "Now, LORD, let the word that You have
spoken concerning Your servant and concerning his house be established forever, and
do just as You have spoken. **24** Let Your name be
established and be great forever, saying, 'The
LORD of armies is the God of Israel, a God to
Israel; and the house of Your servant David is
established before You.' **25** For You, my God,
have revealed to Your servant that You will
build him a house; therefore Your servant has
found *courage* to pray before You. **26** Now,
LORD, You are God, and have promised this
good thing to Your servant. **27** And now You
have decided to bless the house of Your
servant, that it may continue forever before
You; for You, LORD, have blessed, and it is
blessed forever."

17:11 ¹I.e., die

David's Kingdom Strengthened

18 Now after this it came about that David defeated the Philistines and subdued them and took Gath and its towns from the hand of the Philistines. [2] And he defeated Moab, and the Moabites became servants to David, bringing tribute.

[3] David also defeated Hadadezer king of Zobah *as far as* Hamath, as he went to establish his rule to the river Euphrates. [4] David took from him a thousand chariots and seven thousand horsemen and twenty thousand foot soldiers, and David hamstrung *almost* all the chariot horses, but left *enough* of them for a hundred chariots.

[5] When the Arameans of Damascus came to help Hadadezer king of Zobah, David killed twenty-two thousand men of the Arameans. [6] Then David put *garrisons* among the Arameans of Damascus; and the Arameans became servants to David, bringing tribute. And the LORD helped David wherever he went. [7] And David took the shields of gold which were carried by the servants of Hadadezer, and brought them to Jerusalem. [8] Also from Tibhath and Cun, cities of Hadadezer, David took a very large amount of bronze, with which Solomon made the bronze *Sea and the pillars and the bronze utensils.

[9] Now when Tou king of Hamath heard that David had defeated all the army of Hadadezer king of Zobah, [10] he sent Hadoram his son to King David to greet him and to bless him, because he had fought against Hadadezer and had defeated him; for Hadadezer had been at war with Tou. And *Hadoram brought* all kinds of articles of gold and silver and bronze. [11] King David also dedicated these to the LORD, with the silver and the gold which he had carried away from all the nations: from Edom, Moab, the sons of Ammon, the Philistines, and from Amalek.

[12] Moreover, Abishai the son of Zeruiah defeated eighteen thousand Edomites in the Valley of Salt. [13] Then he put garrisons in Edom, and all the Edomites became servants to David. And the LORD helped David wherever he went.

[14] So David reigned over all Israel; and he administered justice and righteousness for all his people. [15] Joab the son of Zeruiah *was* over the army, and Jehoshaphat the son of Ahilud *was* secretary; [16] and Zadok the son of Ahitub and Abimelech the son of Abiathar *were* priests, and Shavsha *was* secretary; [17] and Benaiah the son of Jehoiada *was* over the Cherethites and the Pelethites, and the sons of David *were* chiefs at the king's side.

David's Messengers Abused

19 Now it came about after this, that Nahash the king of the sons of Ammon died, and his son became king in his place. [2] Then David said, "I will show kindness to Hanun the son of Nahash, because his father showed kindness to me." So David sent messengers to console him concerning his father. And David's servants came into the land of the sons of Ammon to Hanun to console him. [3] But the commanders among the sons of Ammon said to Hanun, "Do you think that David is honoring your father, in that he has sent comforters to you? Have his servants not come to you to search, to demolish, and to spy out the land?" [4] So Hanun took David's servants and shaved them, and cut off their robes in the middle as far as their buttocks, and sent them away. [5] Then *certain people* went and told David about the men. And he sent *messengers* to meet them, because the men were very humiliated. And the king said, "Stay at Jericho until your beards grow *back,* then return."

[6] When the sons of Ammon saw that they had made themselves repulsive to David, Hanun and the sons of Ammon sent [1]a thousand talents of silver to hire for themselves chariots and horsemen from Mesopotamia, Aram-maacah, and Zobah. [7] So they hired for themselves thirty-two thousand chariots, and the king of Maacah and his people, who came and camped opposite Medeba. And the sons of Ammon gathered together from their cities and came to the battle. [8] When David heard *about it,* he sent Joab and all the army, the mighty men. [9] The sons of Ammon came out and drew up in battle formation at the entrance of the city; and the kings who had come were by themselves in the field.

Ammon and Aram Defeated

[10] Now when Joab saw that the battle was set against him at the front and at the rear, he selected *warriors* from all the choice men in Israel and lined *them* up against the Arameans. [11] But the remainder of the people he placed under the command of Abshai his brother; and they lined up against the sons of Ammon. [12] He said, "If the Arameans are too strong for me, then you shall help me; but if the sons of Ammon are too strong for you, then I will help you. [13] Be strong, and let's show ourselves courageous for the benefit of our people and the cities of our God; and may the LORD do what is good in His sight." [14] So Joab and the people who were with him advanced to battle against the Arameans, and they fled from him. [15] When the sons of Ammon saw that the Arameans had fled, they also fled from his brother Abshai and entered the city. Then Joab came to Jerusalem.

[16] When the Arameans saw that they had been defeated by Israel, they sent messengers and brought out the Arameans who were beyond the *Euphrates* River, with Shophach the commander of the army of Hadadezer leading them. [17] When it was reported to David, he gathered all Israel together and crossed the Jordan, and came upon them and drew up in formation against them. And when David drew up in battle formation against the Arameans, they fought against him. [18] And the Arameans fled from Israel, and David killed of the Arameans seven thousand charioteers and forty thousand foot soldiers; and he put Shophach the commander of the army to death. [19] So when the servants of Hadadezer saw that they had been defeated by Israel, they made peace with David and served him. So the

---

18:8 [1]I.e., large basin   **19:6** [1]About 38 tons or 34 metric tons

Arameans were not willing to help the sons of Ammon anymore.

War with Philistine Giants

20 Then it happened in the spring, at the time when kings go out *to battle,* that Joab led out the army and ravaged the land of the sons of Ammon, and came and besieged Rabbah. But David stayed in Jerusalem. And Joab struck Rabbah and overthrew it. 2 David took the crown of their king from his head, and he found it to weigh a ¹talent of gold, and there was a precious stone in it; and it was placed on David's head. And he brought out the spoils of the city, a very great amount. 3 He brought out the people who *were* in it, and ¹put *them to work* at saws, iron picks, and axes. And David did the same to all the cities of the sons of Ammon. Then David and all the people returned *to* Jerusalem.

4 Now it came about after this, that war broke out at Gezer with the Philistines; then Sibbecai the Hushathite killed Sippai, one of the descendants of the giants, and they were subdued. 5 And there was war with the Philistines again, and Elhanan the son of Jair killed Lahmi the brother of Goliath the Gittite, the shaft of whose spear *was* like a weaver's beam. 6 Again there was war at Gath, where there was a man of *great* stature who had twenty-four fingers and toes, six *fingers on each hand* and six *toes on each foot;* and he also was descended from the giants. 7 When he taunted Israel, Jonathan the son of Shimea, David's brother, killed him. 8 These were descended from the giants in Gath, and they fell by the hand of David and by the hand of his servants.

Census Brings Plague

21 Then Satan stood up against Israel and incited David to count Israel. 2 So David said to Joab and to the leaders of the people, "Go, count Israel from Beersheba to Dan, and bring me *word* so that I may know their number." 3 But Joab said, "May the LORD add to His people a hundred times as many as they are! My lord the king, are they not all my lord's servants? Why does my lord seek this thing? Why should he be a cause of guilt to Israel?" 4 Nevertheless, the king's word prevailed against Joab. Therefore, Joab departed and went throughout Israel, and came to Jerusalem. 5 Then Joab gave the number of the census of the people to David. Israel was 1,100,000 men in all who drew the sword; and Judah *was* 470,000 men who drew the sword. 6 But he did not count Levi and Benjamin among them, because the king's command was abhorrent to Joab.

7 Now God was displeased with this thing, so He struck Israel. 8 David said to God, "I have sinned greatly, by doing this thing. But now, please overlook Your servant's guilt, for I have behaved very foolishly."

9 The LORD spoke to Gad, David's seer, saying, 10 "Go and speak to David, saying, 'This is what the LORD says: "I extend to you three *choices;* choose for yourself one of them, which I will do to you." ' " 11 So Gad came to

David and said to him, "This is what the LORD says: 'Take for yourself 12 three years of famine, or three months to be swept away before your foes while the sword of your enemies overtakes *you,* or else three days of the sword of the LORD: a plague in the land, and the angel of the LORD destroying throughout the territory of Israel.' Now, therefore, consider what answer I shall bring back to Him who sent me." 13 David said to Gad, "I am in great distress; please let me fall into the hand of the LORD, for His mercies are very great. But do not let me fall into human hands."

14 So the LORD sent a plague on Israel; seventy thousand men of Israel fell. 15 And God sent an angel to Jerusalem to destroy it; but as he was about to destroy *it,* the LORD saw and was sorry about the catastrophe, and said to the destroying angel, "It is enough; now relax your hand." And the angel of the LORD was standing by the threshing floor of Ornan the Jebusite. 16 Then David raised his eyes and saw the angel of the LORD standing between earth and heaven, with his drawn sword in his hand stretched out over Jerusalem. Then David and the elders, covered with sackcloth, fell on their faces. 17 And David said to God, "Is it not I who commanded to count the people? Indeed, I am the one who has sinned and acted very wickedly, but these sheep, what have they done? LORD, my God, just let Your hand be against me and my father's household, and not against Your people as a plague."

David's Altar

18 Then the angel of the LORD commanded Gad to say to David, that David was to go up and build an altar to the LORD on the threshing floor of Ornan the Jebusite. 19 So David went up at the word of Gad, which he spoke in the name of the LORD. 20 Now Ornan turned back and saw the angel, and his four sons *who were* with him hid themselves. And Ornan was threshing wheat. 21 As David came to Ornan, Ornan looked and saw David, and went out from the threshing floor and prostrated himself to David with his face to the ground. 22 Then David said to Ornan, "Give me the site of *this* threshing floor, so that I may build on it an altar to the LORD; you shall give it to me for the full price, so that the plague may be brought to a halt from the people." 23 But Ornan said to David, "Take *it* for yourself, and may my lord the king do what is good in his sight. See, I am giving the oxen for burnt offerings, and the threshing sledges for wood and the wheat for the grain offering; I am giving *it* all." 24 Nevertheless, King David said to Ornan, "No, but I will certainly buy *it* for the full price; for I will not take what is yours for the LORD, nor offer a burnt offering which costs me nothing." 25 So David gave Ornan six hundred shekels of gold by weight for the site. 26 Then David built an altar there to the LORD, and offered burnt offerings and peace offerings. And he called to the LORD, and He answered him with fire from heaven on the altar of burnt offering. 27 The LORD commanded the angel, and he returned his sword to its sheath.

20:2 ¹About 75 lb. or 34 kg   20:3 ¹So 2 Sam 12:31; MT *sawed* them *apart with*

28 At that time, when David saw that the LORD had answered him on the threshing floor of Ornan the Jebusite, he offered sacrifice there. 29 For the tabernacle of the LORD, which Moses had made in the wilderness, and the altar of burnt offering *were* on the high place at Gibeon at that time. 30 But David could not go before it to inquire of God, for he was terrified by the sword of the angel of the LORD.

David Prepares for Temple Building

22 Then David said, "This is the house of the LORD God, and this is the altar of burnt offering for Israel."

2 So David gave orders to gather the strangers who were in the land of Israel, and he set stonecutters to cut out stones to build the house of God. 3 And David prepared large quantities of iron to make the nails for the doors of the gates and for the clamps, and more bronze than could be weighed; 4 and timbers of cedar beyond number, for the Sidonians and Tyrians brought large quantities of cedar timber to David. 5 David said, "My son Solomon is young and inexperienced, and the house that is to be built for the LORD shall be exceedingly magnificent, famous, and glorious throughout the lands. *Therefore* I now will make preparations for it." So David made ample preparations before his death.

Solomon Commanded to Build the Temple

6 Then he called for his son Solomon, and commanded him to build a house for the LORD God of Israel. 7 David said to Solomon, "My son, I had intended to build a house for the name of the LORD my God. 8 But the word of the LORD came to me, saying, 'You have shed much blood and have waged great wars; you shall not build a house to My name, because you have shed so much blood on the earth before Me. 9 Behold, a son will be born to you, who shall be a man of rest, and I will give him rest from all his enemies on every side; for his name will be 'Solomon, and I will give peace and quiet to Israel in his days. 10 He shall build a house for My name, and he shall be My son and I will be his Father; and I will establish the throne of his kingdom over Israel forever.' 11 Now, my son, the LORD be with you that you may be successful, and build the house of the LORD your God just as He has spoken concerning you. 12 Only the LORD give you discretion and understanding, and put you in charge of Israel, so that you may keep the Law of the LORD your God. 13 Then you will prosper, if you are careful to follow the statutes and the ordinances which the LORD commanded Moses concerning Israel. Be strong and courageous, do not fear nor be dismayed. 14 Now behold, with great pains I have prepared for the house of the LORD a hundred thousand ¹talents of gold and a million talents of silver, and bronze and iron beyond measure, for they are in great quantity; I have also prepared timber and stone, and you may add to that. 15 Moreover there are many workmen with you, stonecutters, masons of stone, and carpenters; and all *of them* are skillful in every kind of work.

16 Of the gold, silver, bronze, and iron there is no limit. Arise and work, and may the LORD be with you."

17 David also commanded all the leaders of Israel to help his son Solomon, *saying,* 18 "Is the LORD your God not with you? And has He not given you rest on every side? For He has handed over to me the inhabitants of the land, and the land is subdued before the LORD and before His people. 19 Now set your heart and your soul to seek the LORD your God; then arise, and build the sanctuary of the LORD God, so that you may bring the ark of the covenant of the LORD and the holy vessels of God into the house that is to be built for the name of the LORD."

Solomon Reigns

23 Now when David reached old age, he made his son Solomon king over Israel. 2 And he gathered together all the leaders of Israel with the priests and the Levites.

Offices of the Levites

3 Now the Levites were counted from thirty years old and upward, and their number by head count of men was thirty-eight thousand. 4 Of these, twenty-four thousand were to oversee the work of the house of the LORD; and six thousand *were* officers and judges, 5 and four thousand *were* gatekeepers, and four thousand *were* praising the LORD with the instruments which David made for giving praise. 6 David divided them into divisions according to the sons of Levi: Gershon, Kohath, and Merari.

Gershonites

7 Of the Gershonites *there were* Ladan and Shimei. 8 The sons of Ladan *were* Jehiel the first, and Zetham and Joel, three. 9 The sons of Shimei *were* Shelomoth, Haziel, and Haran, three. These were the heads of the fathers' *households* of Ladan. 10 The sons of Shimei *were* Jahath, Zina, Jeush, and Beriah. These four *were* the sons of Shimei. 11 Jahath was the first and Zizah the second; but Jeush and Beriah did not have many sons, so they became a father's household, one group for duty.

Kohathites

12 The sons of Kohath were four *in number:* Amram, Izhar, Hebron, and Uzziel. 13 The sons of Amram were Aaron and Moses. And Aaron was set apart to sanctify him as most holy, he and his sons forever, to burn incense before the LORD, to serve Him and bless in His name forever. 14 But *as for* Moses, the man of God, his sons were named among the tribe of Levi. 15 The sons of Moses *were* Gershom and Eliezer. 16 The son of Gershom *was* Shebuel the chief. 17 The son of Eliezer was Rehabiah the chief; and Eliezer had no other sons, but the sons of Rehabiah were very many. 18 The son of Izhar was Shelomith the chief. 19 The sons of Hebron *were* Jeriah the first, Amariah the second, Jahaziel the third, and Jekameam the fourth. 20 The sons of Uzziel *were* Micah the first and Isshiah the second.

Merarites

21 The sons of Merari were Mahli and Mushi. The sons of Mahli *were* Eleazar and Kish. 22 Eleazar died and had no sons, but only daughters; so their relatives, the sons of Kish, took them *as wives.* 23 The sons of Mushi *were* three: Mahli, Eder, and Jeremoth.

Duties Revised

24 These were the sons of Levi according to their fathers' households, the heads of the fathers' *households* of those among them who were counted, in the number of names by their head count, doing the work for the service of the house of the LORD, from twenty years old and upward. 25 For David said, "The LORD God of Israel has given rest to His people, and He dwells in Jerusalem forever. 26 Also, the Levites will no longer need to carry the tabernacle and all its utensils for its service." 27 For by the last words of David, the sons of Levi *were* counted from twenty years old and upward. 28 For their office is to assist the sons of Aaron with the service of the house of the LORD, in the courtyards and in the chambers, and in the purification of all holy things, and the work of the service of the house of God, 29 and with the showbread, and the fine flour for a grain offering, and unleavened wafers, or *what is baked in* the pan or what is well-mixed, and all measures of volume and size. 30 They are to stand every morning to thank and to praise the LORD, and likewise at evening, 31 and to offer all burnt offerings to the LORD, on the Sabbaths, the new moons and the appointed festivals, in the number *determined* by the ordinance concerning them, continually before the LORD. 32 So they are to perform the duties of the tent of meeting, the holy place, and *of assisting* the sons of Aaron their relatives, for the service of the house of the LORD.

Divisions of the Levites

24 Now the divisions of the descendants of Aaron *were these:* the sons of Aaron *were* Nadab, Abihu, Eleazar, and Ithamar. 2 But Nadab and Abihu died before their father and had no sons. So Eleazar and Ithamar served as priests. 3 David, with Zadok of the sons of Eleazar and Ahimelech of the sons of Ithamar, divided them according to their offices for their ministry. 4 Since more chief men were found from the descendants of Eleazar than the descendants of Ithamar, they divided them this way: *there were* sixteen heads of fathers' households of the descendants of Eleazar, and eight of the descendants of Ithamar according to their fathers' households. 5 So they were divided by lot, the one as the other; for they were officers of the sanctuary and officers of God, both from the descendants of Eleazar and the descendants of Ithamar. 6 Shemaiah, the son of Nethanel the scribe, from the Levites, recorded them in the presence of the king, the leaders, Zadok the priest, Ahimelech the son of Abiathar, and the heads of the fathers' *households* of the priests and the Levites; one father's household taken for Eleazar and one taken for Ithamar.

7 Now the first lot came out for Jehoiarib, the second for Jedaiah, 8 the third for Harim, the fourth for Seorim, 9 the fifth for Malchijah, the sixth for Mijamin, 10 the seventh for Hakkoz, the eighth for Abijah, 11 the ninth for Jeshua, the tenth for Shecaniah, 12 the eleventh for Eliashib, the twelfth for Jakim, 13 the thirteenth for Huppah, the fourteenth for Jeshebeab, 14 the fifteenth for Bilgah, the sixteenth for Immer, 15 the seventeenth for Hezir, the eighteenth for Happizzez, 16 the nineteenth for Pethahiah, the twentieth for Jehezkel, 17 the twenty-first for Jachin, the twenty-second for Gamul, 18 the twenty-third for Delaiah, *and* the twenty-fourth for Maaziah. 19 These were their offices for their ministry when *they* entered the house of the LORD according to the ordinance *given* to them through their father Aaron, just as the LORD God of Israel had commanded him.

20 Now for the rest of the sons of Levi: of the sons of Amram, Shubael; of the sons of Shubael, Jehdeiah. 21 Of Rehabiah: of the sons of Rehabiah, Isshiah, the first. 22 Of the Izharites, Shelomoth; of the sons of Shelomoth, Jahath. 23 The sons *of Hebron:* Jeriah *the first,* Amariah the second, Jahaziel the third, Jekameam the fourth. 24 *Of* the sons of Uzziel, Micah; of the sons of Micah, Shamir. 25 The brother of Micah, Isshiah; of the sons of Isshiah, Zechariah. 26 The sons of Merari, Mahli and Mushi; the sons of Jaaziah, Beno. 27 The sons of Merari: by Jaaziah *were* Beno, Shoham, Zaccur, and Ibri. 28 By Mahli: Eleazar, who had no sons. 29 By Kish: the sons of Kish, Jerahmeel. 30 The sons of Mushi: Mahli, Eder, and Jerimoth. These *were* the sons of the Levites according to their fathers' households. 31 These also cast lots just as their relatives, the sons of Aaron *did* in the presence of David the king, Zadok, Ahimelech, and the heads of the fathers' *households* of the priests and of the Levites— the head of fathers' *households* as well as those of his younger brother.

Number and Services of Musicians

25 Moreover, David and the commanders of the army set apart for the service *some* of the sons of Asaph, Heman, and Jeduthun, who *were* to prophesy with lyres, harps, and cymbals; and the number of those who performed this service was: 2 Of the sons of Asaph: Zaccur, Joseph, Nethaniah, and Asharelah; the sons of Asaph *were* under the direction of Asaph, who prophesied under the direction of the king. 3 Of Jeduthun, the sons of Jeduthun: Gedaliah, Zeri, Jeshaiah, Shimei, Hashabiah, and Mattithiah, six *in all,* under the direction of their father Jeduthun with the harp, who prophesied in giving thanks and praising the LORD. 4 Of Heman, the sons of Heman: Bukkiah, Mattaniah, Uzziel, Shebuel and Jerimoth, Hananiah, Hanani, Eliathah, Giddalti and Romamti-ezer, Joshbekashah, Mallothi, Hothir, *and* Mahazioth. 5 All these *were* the sons of Heman the king's seer to exalt him according to the words of God, for God gave fourteen sons and three daughters to Heman. 6 All of these were under the direction of their father to sing in the house of the LORD, with cymbals, harps, and lyres, for the service of the

house of God. Asaph, Jeduthun, and Heman *were* under the direction of the king. [7] Their number who were trained in singing to the LORD, with their relatives, all who were skillful, *was* 288.

Divisions of the Musicians

[8] They cast lots for their duties, all alike, the small as well as the great, the teacher *as well as* the pupil.

[9] Now the first lot came out for Asaph to Joseph, the second for Gedaliah, he with his relatives and sons *were* twelve; [10] the third to Zaccur, his sons and his relatives, twelve; [11] the fourth to Izri, his sons and his relatives, twelve; [12] the fifth to Nethaniah, his sons and his relatives, twelve; [13] the sixth to Bukkiah, his sons and his relatives, twelve; [14] the seventh to Jesharelah, his sons and his relatives, twelve; [15] the eighth to Jeshaiah, his sons and his relatives, twelve; [16] the ninth to Mattaniah, his sons and his relatives, twelve; [17] the tenth to Shimei, his sons and his relatives, twelve; [18] the eleventh to Azarel, his sons and his relatives, twelve; [19] the twelfth to Hashabiah, his sons and his relatives, twelve; [20] for the thirteenth, Shubael, his sons and his relatives, twelve; [21] for the fourteenth, Mattithiah, his sons and his relatives, twelve; [22] for the fifteenth to Jeremoth, his sons and his relatives, twelve; [23] for the sixteenth to Hananiah, his sons and his relatives, twelve; [24] for the seventeenth to Joshbekashah, his sons and his relatives, twelve; [25] for the eighteenth to Hanani, his sons and his relatives, twelve; [26] for the nineteenth to Mallothi, his sons and his relatives, twelve; [27] for the twentieth to Eliathah, his sons and his relatives, twelve; [28] for the twenty-first to Hothir, his sons and his relatives, twelve; [29] for the twenty-second to Giddalti, his sons and his relatives, twelve; [30] for the twenty-third to Mahazioth, his sons and his relatives, twelve; [31] for the twenty-fourth to Romamti-ezer, his sons and his relatives, twelve.

Divisions of the Gatekeepers

26 For the divisions of the gatekeepers *there were* of the Korahites, Meshelemiah the son of Kore, of the sons of Asaph. [2] Meshelemiah had sons: Zechariah the firstborn, Jediael the second, Zebadiah the third, Jathniel the fourth, [3] Elam the fifth, Johanan the sixth, *and* Eliehoenai the seventh. [4] Obed-edom had sons: Shemaiah the firstborn, Jehozabad the second, Joah the third, Sacar the fourth, Nethanel the fifth, [5] Ammiel the sixth, Issachar the seventh, *and* Peullethai the eighth; God had indeed blessed him. [6] Also to his son Shemaiah sons were born who ruled over the house of their father, for they were valiant mighty men. [7] The sons of Shemaiah *were* Othni, Rephael, Obed, and Elzabad, whose brothers, Elihu and Semachiah, were valiant men. [8] All these *were* of the sons of Obed-edom; they and their sons and relatives *were* able men with strength for the service, sixty-two from Obed-edom. [9] Meshelemiah had sons and relatives, eighteen valiant men. [10] Also

Hosah, *one* of the sons of Merari had sons: Shimri the first (although he was not the firstborn, his father made him first), [11] Hilkiah the second, Tebaliah the third, *and* Zechariah the fourth; the sons and relatives of Hosah *were* thirteen in all.

[12] To these divisions of the gatekeepers, to the chief men, *were given* duties like their relatives, to serve in the house of the LORD. [13] They cast lots, the small and the great alike, according to their fathers' households, for every gate. [14] The lot to the east fell to Shelemiah. Then they cast lots *for* his son Zechariah, a counselor with insight, and his lot came out to the north. [15] For Obed-edom *it fell* to the south, and to his sons went the storehouse. [16] For Shuppim and Hosah *it was* to the west, by the gate of Shallecheth, on the ascending highway. Guard corresponded to guard. [17] On the east there were six Levites, on the north four daily, on the south four daily, and at the storehouse two by two. [18] At the *annex on the west *there were* four at the highway and two at the annex. [19] These were the divisions of the gatekeepers of the sons of Korah and of the sons of Merari.

Keepers of the Treasure

[20] *The Levites, their relatives, were in charge of the treasures of the house of God and of the treasures of the dedicated gifts. [21] The sons of Ladan, the sons of the Gershonites belonging to Ladan, *namely,* the Jehielites, *were* the heads of the fathers' *households,* belonging to Ladan the Gershonite.

[22] The sons of Jehieli, Zetham, and his brother Joel, were in charge of the treasures of the house of the LORD. [23] As for the Amramites, the Izharites, the Hebronites, and the Uzzielites, [24] Shebuel the son of Gershom, the son of Moses, was officer over the treasures. [25] His relatives by Eliezer *were* Rehabiah his son, Jeshaiah his son, Joram his son, Zichri his son, and Shelomoth his son. [26] This Shelomoth and his relatives were in charge of all the treasures of the dedicated gifts which King David and the heads of the fathers' *households,* the commanders of thousands and hundreds, and the commanders of the army, had dedicated. [27] They dedicated part of the spoils won in battles to repair the house of the LORD. [28] And all that Samuel the seer had dedicated, and Saul the son of Kish, Abner the son of Ner, and Joab the son of Zeruiah, everyone who had dedicated *anything, all of this* was under the care of Shelomoth and his relatives.

Outside Duties

[29] As for the Izharites, Chenaniah and his sons were *assigned* to outside duties for Israel, as officers and judges. [30] As for the Hebronites, Hashabiah and his relatives, 1,700 capable men, were responsible for the affairs of Israel west of the Jordan, for all the work of the LORD and the service of the king. [31] As for the Hebronites, Jerijah the chief (these Hebronites were sought out according to their genealogies and fathers' *households,* in the fortieth year of David's reign, and men of outstanding

capability were found among them at Jazer of Gilead) 32 and his relatives, capable men, *numbered* 2,700, heads of fathers' *households.* And King David appointed them as overseers of the Reubenites, the Gadites, and the half-tribe of the Manassites concerning all the affairs of God and of the king.

Commanders of the Army

27 Now *this is* the number of the sons of Israel, the heads of fathers' *households,* the commanders of thousands and of hundreds, and their officers who served the king in all the affairs of the divisions which came in and went out month by month throughout the months of the year, each division *numbering* twenty-four thousand: 2 Jashobeam the son of Zabdiel was in charge of the first division for the first month; and in his division *were* twenty-four thousand. 3 *He was* from the sons of Perez, *and was* chief of all the commanders of the army for the first month. 4 Dodai the Ahohite and his division was in charge of the division for the second month, Mikloth *being* the chief officer; and in his division *were* twenty-four thousand. 5 The third commander of the army for the third month *was* Benaiah, the son of Jehoiada the priest, *as* chief; and in his division *were* twenty-four thousand. 6 This Benaiah *was* the mighty man of the thirty, and was in charge of thirty; and over his division was his son Ammizabad. 7 The fourth, for the fourth month *was* Asahel the brother of Joab, and Zebadiah his son after him; and in his division *were* twenty-four thousand. 8 The fifth, for the fifth month *was* the commander Shamhuth the Izrahite; and in his division *were* twenty-four thousand. 9 The sixth, for the sixth month *was* Ira the son of Ikkesh the Tekoite; and in his division *were* twenty-four thousand. 10 The seventh, for the seventh month *was* Helez the Pelonite for the sons of Ephraim; and in his division *were* twenty-four thousand. 11 The eighth, for the eighth month *was* Sibbecai the Hushathite of the Zerahites; and in his division *were* twenty-four thousand. 12 The ninth, for the ninth month *was* Abiezer the Anathothite of the Benjaminites; and in his division *were* twenty-four thousand. 13 The tenth, for the tenth month *was* Maharai the Netophathite of the Zerahites; and in his division *were* twenty-four thousand. 14 The eleventh, for the eleventh month *was* Benaiah the Pirathonite of the sons of Ephraim; and in his division *were* twenty-four thousand. 15 The twelfth, for the twelfth month *was* Heldai the Netophathite of Othniel; and in his division *were* twenty-four thousand.

Chief Officers of the Tribes

16 Now in charge of the tribes of Israel: chief officer for the Reubenites was Eliezer the son of Zichri; for the Simeonites, Shephatiah the son of Maacah; 17 for Levi, Hashabiah the son of Kemuel; for Aaron, Zadok; 18 for Judah, Elihu, *one* of David's brothers; for Issachar, Omri the son of Michael; 19 for Zebulun, Ishmaiah the son of Obadiah; for Naphtali, Jeremoth the son of Azriel; 20 for the sons of Ephraim, Hoshea

the son of Azaziah; for the half-tribe of Manasseh, Joel the son of Pedaiah; 21 for the half-tribe of Manasseh in Gilead, Iddo the son of Zechariah; for Benjamin, Jaasiel the son of Abner; 22 for Dan, Azarel the son of Jeroham. These *were* the leaders of the tribes of Israel. 23 But David did not count those twenty years of age and under, because the Lord had said He would multiply Israel as the stars of heaven. 24 Joab the son of Zeruiah had begun to count *them,* but did not finish; and because of this, wrath came upon Israel, and the number was not included in the account of the chronicles of King David.

Various Overseers

25 Now Azmaveth the son of Adiel was responsible for the king's storehouses. And Jonathan the son of Uzziah was responsible for the storehouses in the country, the cities, the villages, and the towers. 26 Ezri the son of Chelub was responsible for the agricultural workers who tilled the soil. 27 Shimei the Ramathite was responsible for the vineyards; and Zabdi the Shiphmite was responsible for the produce of the vineyards *stored* in the wine cellars. 28 Baal-hanan the Gederite was responsible for the olive and sycamore trees in the *[†]*Shephelah; and Joash was responsible for the stores of oil. 29 Shitrai the Sharonite was responsible for the cattle which were grazing in Sharon; and Shaphat the son of Adlai was responsible for the cattle in the valleys. 30 Obil the Ishmaelite was responsible for the camels; and Jehdeiah the Meronothite was responsible for the donkeys. 31 Jaziz the Hagrite was responsible for the flocks. All these were overseers of the property which belonged to King David.

Counselors

32 Also Jonathan, David's uncle, *was* a counselor, a man of understanding, and a scribe; and Jehiel the son of Hachmoni tutored the king's sons. 33 Ahithophel *was* counselor to the king; and Hushai the Archite *was* the king's friend. 34 Jehoiada the son of Benaiah, and Abiathar succeeded Ahithophel; and Joab was the commander of the king's army.

David's Address about the Temple

28 Now David assembled at Jerusalem all the officials of Israel, the leaders of the tribes, and the commanders of the divisions that served the king, the commanders of thousands, and the commanders of hundreds, and the overseers of all the property and live-stock belonging to the king and his sons, with the officials and the mighty men, all the valiant warriors. 2 Then King David rose to his feet and said, "Listen to me, my brothers and my people; I *had* intended to build a permanent home for the ark of the covenant of the Lord and for the footstool of our God. So I had made preparations to build *it.* 3 But God said to me, 'You shall not build a house for My name, because you are a man of war and have shed blood.' 4 Yet, the Lord, the God of Israel, chose me from all the household of my father to be

king over Israel forever. For He has chosen Judah to be a leader; and in the house of Judah, my father's house, and among the sons of my father He took pleasure in me to make *me* king over all Israel. **5** Of all my sons (for the LORD has given me many sons), He has chosen my son Solomon to sit on the throne of the kingdom of the LORD over Israel. **6** He said to me, 'Your son Solomon is the one who shall build My house and My courtyards; for I have chosen him to be a son to Me, and I will be a Father to him. **7** I will establish his kingdom forever if he resolutely performs My commandments and My ordinances, as is done now.' **8** So now, in the sight of all Israel, the assembly of the LORD, and in the presence of our God, keep and seek after all the commandments of the LORD your God so that you may possess the good land and leave it as an inheritance to your sons after you forever.

9 "As for you, my son Solomon, know the God of your father, and serve Him wholeheartedly and with a willing mind; for the LORD searches all hearts, and understands every intent of the thoughts. If you seek Him, He will let you find Him; but if you forsake Him, He will reject you forever. **10** Consider now, for the LORD has chosen you to build a house for the sanctuary; be courageous and act."

11 Then David gave to his son Solomon the plan of the porch *of the temple,* its buildings, its storehouses, its upper rooms, its inner rooms, and the room for the *'atoning cover;* **12** and the plan of all that he had in mind, for the courtyards of the house of the LORD, and for all the surrounding rooms, for the storehouses of the house of God and for the storehouses of the dedicated things; **13** also for the divisions of the priests and the Levites and for all the work of the service of the house of the LORD and for all the utensils of service in the house of the LORD; **14** for the golden *utensils,* by weight of gold for all utensils for every service; for all the silver utensils, by weight *of silver* for all utensils for every service; **15** and the weight *of gold* for the golden lampstands and their golden lamps, with the weight of each lampstand and its lamps; and *the weight of silver* for the silver lampstands, with the weight of each lampstand and its lamps according to the use of each lampstand; **16** and the gold by weight for the tables of the showbread, for each table; and silver for the silver tables; **17** and the forks, the basins, and the pitchers of pure gold; and for the golden bowls with the weight for each bowl; and for the silver bowls with the weight for each bowl; **18** and for the altar of incense, refined gold by weight; and gold for the model of the chariot, and the cherubim that spread out *their wings* and covered the ark of the covenant of the LORD.

19 "All *this," said David,* "the LORD made me understand in writing by *His* hand upon me, all the details of this pattern."

20 Then David said to his son Solomon, "Be strong and courageous, and act; do not fear nor be dismayed, for the LORD God, my God, is with you. He will not fail you nor forsake you until all the work for the service of the house of the LORD is finished. **21** Now behold, *there are* the divisions of the priests and the Levites for all the service of the house of God, and every willing man of any skill will be with you in all the work for all kinds of service. The officials also and all the people will be entirely at your command."

Offerings for the Temple

29 Then King David said to the entire assembly, "My son Solomon, whom alone God has chosen, is still young and inexperienced, and the work is great; for the temple is not for mankind, but for the LORD God. **2** Now with all my ability I have provided for the house of my God the gold for the *things of* gold, the silver for the *things of* silver, the bronze for the *things of* bronze, the iron for the *things of* iron, wood for the *things of* wood, onyx stones and inlaid *stones,* stones of antimony and stones of various colors, and all kinds of precious stones and alabaster in abundance. **3** In addition, in my delight in the house of my God, the treasure I have of gold and silver, I give to the house of my God, over and above all that I have *already* provided for the holy temple, **4** *namely,* three thousand *'*talents of gold, from the gold of Ophir, and seven thousand talents of refined silver, to overlay the walls of the buildings; **5** gold for the *things of* gold and silver for the *things of* silver, that is, for all the work done by the craftsmen. Who then is willing to consecrate himself this day to the LORD?"

6 Then the rulers of the fathers' *households,* the leaders of the tribes of Israel, and the commanders of thousands and hundreds, with the supervisors of the king's work, offered willingly; **7** and for the service of the house of God they gave five thousand talents and ten thousand *'*darics of gold, ten thousand talents of silver, eighteen thousand talents of brass, and a hundred thousand talents of iron. **8** Whoever possessed *precious* stones gave *them* to the treasury of the house of the LORD, in care of Jehiel the Gershonite. **9** Then the people rejoiced because they had offered so willingly, for they made their offering to the LORD wholeheartedly, and King David also rejoiced greatly.

David's Prayer

10 So David blessed the LORD in the sight of all the assembly; and David said, "Blessed are You, LORD God of Israel our father, forever and ever. **11** Yours, LORD, is the greatness, the power, the glory, the victory, and the majesty, indeed everything that is in the heavens and on the earth; Yours is the dominion, LORD, and You exalt Yourself as head over all. **12** Both riches and honor *come* from You, and You rule over all, and in Your hand is power and might; and it lies in Your hand to make great and to strengthen everyone. **13** Now therefore, our God, we thank You, and praise Your glorious name.

14 "But who am I and who are my people

28:11 [1] Also called *mercy seat;* i.e., where blood was sprinkled on the Day of Atonement　**29:4** [1] A talent was about 75 lb. or 34 kg　**29:7** [1] A coin weighing about 0.25 oz. or 7 gm

that we should be able to offer as generously as this? For all things come from You, and from Your hand we have given to You. 15 For we are strangers before You, and temporary residents, as all our fathers were; our days on the earth are like a shadow, and there is no hope. 16 LORD our God, all this abundance that we have provided to build You a house for Your holy name, it is from Your hand, and everything is Yours. 17 Since I know, my God, that You put the heart to the test and delight in uprightness, I, in the integrity of my heart, have willingly offered all these *things;* so now with joy I have seen Your people, who are present here, make *their* offerings willingly to You. 18 LORD, God of Abraham, Isaac, and Israel, our fathers, keep this forever in the intentions of the hearts of Your people, and direct their hearts to You; 19 and give my son Solomon a perfect heart to keep Your commandments, Your testimonies, and Your statutes, and to do *them* all, and to build the temple for which I have made provision."

20 Then David said to all the assembly, "Now bless the LORD your God." And all the assembly blessed the LORD, the God of their fathers, and bowed down and paid 1homage to the LORD and the king.

Sacrifices

21 On the next day they made sacrifices to the LORD and offered burnt offerings to the LORD, a thousand bulls, a thousand rams, *and* a thousand lambs, with their drink offerings and sacrifices in abundance for all Israel. 22 So they ate and drank that day before the LORD with great gladness.

Solomon Again Made King

And they made Solomon the son of David king a second time, and they anointed *him* as ruler for the LORD and Zadok as priest. 23 Then Solomon sat on the throne of the LORD as king instead of his father David; and he prospered, and all Israel obeyed him. 24 And all the officials, the mighty men, and also all the sons of King David pledged allegiance to King Solomon. 25 The LORD highly honored Solomon in the sight of all Israel, and bestowed on him royal majesty which had not been *bestowed* on any king before him in Israel.

26 Now David the son of Jesse reigned over all Israel. 27 The period which he reigned over Israel *was* forty years; he reigned in Hebron seven years and in Jerusalem thirty-three *years.*

Death of David

28 Then he died at a good old age, full of days, riches, and honor; and his son Solomon reigned in his place. 29 Now the acts of King David, from the first to the last, are written in the chronicles of Samuel the seer, in the chronicles of Nathan the prophet, and in the chronicles of Gad the seer, 30 with all of his reign, his power, and the circumstances which came upon him, Israel, and all the kingdoms of the lands.

29:20 1 I.e., great respect and honor to a superior

The Second Book of the
CHRONICLES

Solomon Worships at Gibeon

1 Now Solomon the son of David established himself securely over his kingdom, and the LORD his God *was* with him and exalted him greatly.

2 And Solomon spoke to all Israel, to the commanders of thousands, of hundreds, and to the judges and to every leader in all Israel, the heads of the fathers' *households.* 3 Then Solomon and all the assembly with him went to the high place which was at Gibeon, because God's tent of meeting was there which Moses, the servant of the LORD had made in the wilderness. 4 However, David had brought up the ark of God from Kiriath-jearim to the place he had prepared for it, for he had pitched a tent for it in Jerusalem. 5 Now the bronze altar which Bezalel, the son of Uri, the son of Hur, had made was there before the tabernacle of the LORD, and Solomon and the assembly sought it *out.* 6 And Solomon went up there before the LORD to the bronze altar which *was* at the tent of meeting, and offered a thousand burnt offerings on it.

7 In that night God appeared to Solomon and said to him, "Ask what I shall give you."

Solomon's Prayer for Wisdom

8 And Solomon said to God, "You have dealt with my father David with great faithfulness, and have made me king in his place. 9 Now, LORD God, Your promise to my father David is fulfilled, for You have made me king over a people as numerous as the dust of the earth. 10 Now give me wisdom and knowledge, so that I may go out and come in before this people, for who can rule this great people of Yours?" 11 Then God said to Solomon, "Because this was in your heart, and you did not ask for riches, wealth, or honor, or the life of those who hate you, nor did you even ask for long life, but you asked for yourself wisdom and knowledge so that you may rule My people over whom I have made you king, 12 wisdom and knowledge have been granted to you. I will also give you riches, wealth, and honor, such as none of the kings who were before you has possessed, nor *will* those who will come after you." 13 So Solomon went from the high place which was at Gibeon, from the tent of meeting, to Jerusalem, and he reigned over Israel.

Solomon's Wealth

14 Solomon amassed chariots and horsemen. He had 1,400 chariots and twelve thousand horsemen, and he stationed them in the chariot cities and with the king in Jerusalem. 15 The king made silver and gold as plentiful in Jerusalem as stones, and he made cedars as plentiful as sycamores in the lowland. 16 Solomon's horses were imported from Egypt and from Kue; the king's traders acquired them from Kue for a price. 17 They imported chariots from Egypt for six hundred *shekels* of silver apiece, horses for 150 apiece, and by the same means they exported them to all the kings of the Hittites and the kings of Aram.

Solomon Will Build a Temple and a Palace

2 Now Solomon decided to build a house for the name of the LORD, and a royal palace for himself. 2 So Solomon assigned seventy thousand men to carry loads, eighty thousand men to quarry *stone* in the mountains, and 3,600 to supervise them.

3 Then Solomon sent *word* to Huram the king of Tyre, saying, "As you dealt with my father David and sent him cedars to build him a house to live in, do *it for me.* 4 Behold, I am about to build a house for the name of the LORD my God, dedicating it to Him, to burn fragrant incense before Him and *to set out* the showbread continually, and to offer burnt offerings morning and evening, on Sabbaths, on new moons, and on the appointed feasts of the LORD our God. This *is to be done* in Israel forever. 5 The house which I am about to build *will be* great, for our God is greater than all the gods. 6 But who is able to build a house for Him, since the heavens and the highest heavens cannot contain Him? And who am I, that I should build a house for Him, except to burn *incense* before Him? 7 Now send me a skilled man to work in gold, silver, brass, iron, and in purple, crimson, and violet *fabrics,* one who knows how to make engravings, to *work* with the skilled workers whom I have in Judah and Jerusalem, whom my father David provided. 8 Send me also cedar, juniper, and algum timber from Lebanon, for I know that your servants know how to cut timber of Lebanon; and indeed my servants *will work* with your servants, 9 to prepare timber in abundance for me, for the house which I am about to build *will be* great and wonderful. 10 Now behold, I will give your servants, the woodsmen who cut the timber, [1]twenty thousand kors of crushed wheat, twenty thousand kors of barley, [2]twenty thousand baths of wine, and twenty thousand baths of oil."

Huram to Assist

11 Then Huram, king of Tyre, answered in a letter sent to Solomon: "Because the LORD loves His people, He has made you king over them." 12 Then Huram continued, "Blessed be the LORD, the God of Israel, who made heaven and earth, who has given King David a wise son, endowed with discretion and understanding, who will build a house for the LORD and a royal palace for himself.

13 "Now then, I am sending Huram-abi, a skilled man, endowed with understanding,

---

2:10 [1]About 154,000 cubic feet or 4,360 cubic meters   [2]About 120,000 gallons or 454,249 liters

14 the son of a Danite woman and a Tyrian father, who knows how to work in gold, silver, bronze, iron, stone, and wood, *and* in purple, violet, linen, and crimson fabrics, and *who knows how* to make all kinds of engravings and to execute any design which is assigned to him, *to work* with your skilled workers and with those of my lord, your father David. 15 Now then, let my lord send his servants wheat and barley, oil and wine, of which he has spoken. 16 We will cut whatever timber you need from Lebanon and bring it to you as rafts by sea to Joppa, so that you may carry it up to Jerusalem."

17 Solomon counted all the foreigners who *were* in the land of Israel, following the census which his father David had taken; and 153,600 were found. 18 He appointed seventy thousand of them to carry loads and eighty thousand to quarry *stones* in the mountains, and 3,600 supervisors to make the people work.

The Temple Construction in Jerusalem

3 Then Solomon began to build the house of the LORD in Jerusalem on Mount Moriah, where the L ORD had appeared to his father David, at the place that David had prepared on the threshing floor of Ornan the Jebusite. 2 He began to build on the second *day* in the second month of the fourth year of his reign.

Dimensions and Materials of the Temple

3 Now these are the foundations which Solomon laid for building the house of God. The length in cubits, according to the old standard, *was* ¹sixty cubits, and the width, twenty cubits. 4 The porch which was in front *of the house* was as long as the width of the house, ¹twenty cubits, and the height ²twenty; and inside he overlaid it with pure gold. 5 He overlaid the main room with juniper wood and overlaid it with fine gold; and he ornamented it with palm trees and chains. 6 Further, he overlaid the house with precious stones; and the gold was gold from Parvaim. 7 He also overlaid the house with gold—the beams, the thresholds, and its walls and doors; and he carved cherubim on the walls.

8 Then he made the room of the Most Holy Place: its length across the width of the house *was* ¹twenty cubits, and its width *was* twenty cubits; and he overlaid it with fine gold, *amounting* to ²six hundred talents. 9 The weight of the nails was fifty shekels of gold. He also overlaid the upper rooms with gold.

10 Then he made two sculptured cherubim in the room of the Most Holy Place and overlaid them with gold. 11 The wingspan of the ¹cherubim *was* twenty ²cubits; the wing of one, of five cubits, touched the wall of the house, and *its* other wing, of five cubits, touched the wing of the other cherub. 12 The wing of the other cherub, of five cubits, touched the wall of the house; and *its* other wing, of five cubits, was attached to the wing of the first cherub.

13 The wings of these cherubim extended twenty cubits, and they stood on their feet facing the *main* room. 14 He made the veil of violet, purple, crimson, and fine linen, and he worked cherubim into it.

15 He also made two pillars for the front of the house, thirty-five cubits high, and the capital on the top of each *was* five cubits. 16 He made chains in the inner sanctuary and placed *them* on the tops of the pillars; and he made a hundred pomegranates and placed *them* on the chains. 17 He erected the pillars in front of the temple, one on the right and the other on the left, and named the one on the right Jachin and the one on the left Boaz.

Furnishings of the Temple

4 Then he made a bronze altar, ¹twenty cubits in length, twenty cubits in width, and ²ten cubits in height. 2 He also made the ¹Sea of cast metal, ²ten cubits from brim to brim, circular in form, and its height *was* ³five cubits and its circumference ⁴thirty cubits. 3 Now figures like oxen *were* under it *and* all around it, ¹ten cubits, entirely encircling the Sea. ¹The oxen *were* in two rows, cast in one piece. 4 It was standing on twelve oxen, three facing north, three facing west, three facing south, and three facing east; and the Sea *was set* on top of them and all their hindquarters turned inward. 5 It was a ¹hand width thick, and its brim was made like the brim of a cup, *like* a lily blossom; it could hold three thousand ²baths. 6 He also made ten basins in which to wash, and he set five on the right side and five on the left to rinse things for the burnt offering; but the Sea *was* for the priests to wash in.

7 Then he made the ten golden lampstands in the way prescribed for them, and he set them in the temple, five on the right side and five on the left. 8 He also made ten tables and placed them in the temple, five on the right side and five on the left. And he made a hundred golden bowls. 9 Then he made the courtyard of the priests and the great courtyard, and doors for the courtyard, and overlaid their doors with bronze. 10 He put the Sea on the right side *of the house* toward the southeast.

11 Huram also made the pails, the shovels, and the bowls. So Huram finished the work that he did for King Solomon in the house of God: 12 the two pillars, the bowls and the two capitals on top of the pillars, and the two latticeworks to cover the two bowls of the capitals which were on top of the pillars, 13 and the four hundred pomegranates for the two latticeworks, two rows of pomegranates for each latticework to cover the two bowls of the capitals which were on the pillars. 14 He also made the stands and he made the basins on the stands, 15 *and* the one Sea with the twelve oxen under it. 16 The pails, the shovels, the forks, and all its utensils, Huram-abi made of polished bronze for King Solomon, for the house of the LORD. 17 On the plain of the Jordan the king

---

3:3 1 About 90 ft. long and 30 ft. wide or 27 m long and 9 m wide   3:4 1 About 30 ft. or 9 m   2 As in ancient versions; MT *120 cubits* or about 180 ft. or 55 m   3:8 1 About 30 ft. or 9 m   2 About 23 tons or 21 metric tons   3:11 1 Heb plural of *cherub*   2 About 18 in. or 45 cm   4:1 1 About 30 ft. or 9 m   2 About 15 ft. or 4.6 m   4:2 1 I.e., large basin m   2 About 15 ft. or 4.6 m   3 About 7.5 ft. or 2.3 m   4 About 45 ft. or 14 m   4:3 1 About 15 ft. or 4.6 m   4:5 1 About 3 in. or 7.6 cm   2 About 18,000 gallons or 68,137 liters

cast them in the clay ground between Succoth and Zeredah. 18 So Solomon made all these utensils in great quantities, for the weight of the bronze could not be determined.

19 Solomon also made all the things that *were* in the house of God: the golden altar, the tables with the bread of the Presence on them, 20 the lampstands with their lamps of pure gold, to burn in front of the inner sanctuary in the way prescribed; 21 the flowers, the lamps, and the tongs of gold, that is, of purest gold; 22 and the snuffers, the bowls, the spoons, and the firepans of pure gold; and the entrance of the house, its inner doors for the Most Holy Place and the doors of the house, *that is,* of the main room, of gold.

The Ark Is Brought into the Temple

5 So all the work that Solomon performed for the house of the LORD was finished. And Solomon brought in the things that his father David had dedicated, the silver, the gold, and all the utensils, *and he* put *them* in the treasuries of the house of God.

2 Then Solomon assembled at Jerusalem the elders of Israel, all the heads of the tribes, *and* the leaders of the fathers' *households* of the sons of Israel, to bring the ark of the covenant of the LORD up from the city of David, which is Zion. 3 All the men of Israel assembled themselves before the king at the feast, that is in the seventh month. 4 Then all the elders of Israel came, and the Levites picked up the ark. 5 They brought up the ark, the tent of meeting, and all the holy utensils that *were* in the tent. The Levitical priests brought them up. 6 And King Solomon and all the congregation of Israel who had assembled with him before the ark were sacrificing so many sheep and oxen that they could not be counted or numbered. 7 Then the priests brought the ark of the covenant of the LORD to its place, into the inner sanctuary of the house, to the Most Holy Place, under the wings of the cherubim. 8 For the cherubim spread their wings over the place of the ark, so that the cherubim made a covering over the ark and its poles. 9 The poles were so long that the ends of the poles of the ark could be seen in front of the inner sanctuary, but they could not be seen outside; and they are there to this day. 10 There was nothing in the ark except the two tablets which Moses put *there* at Horeb, where the LORD made *a covenant* with the sons of Israel, when they came out of Egypt.

The Glory of God Fills the Temple

11 When the priests came out from the holy place (for all the priests who were present had sanctified themselves, without regard to divisions), 12 and all the Levitical singers, Asaph, Heman, Jeduthun, and their sons and kinsmen, clothed in fine linen, with cymbals, harps, and lyres, standing east of the altar, and with them 120 priests blowing trumpets 13 in unison when the trumpeters and the singers were to make themselves heard with one voice to praise and to glorify the LORD, and when they raised their voices accompanied by trumpets, cymbals, and *other* musical

instruments, and when they praised the LORD saying, "He indeed is good for His kindness is everlasting," then the house, the house of the LORD, was filled with a cloud, 14 so that the priests could not rise to minister because of the cloud, for the glory of the LORD filled the house of God.

Solomon's Dedication of the Temple

6 Then Solomon said,
"The LORD has said that He would dwell in the thick darkness.
2 "I have built You a lofty house,
And a place for Your dwelling forever."
3 Then the king turned around and blessed all the assembly of Israel, while all the assembly of Israel was standing. 4 He said, "Blessed be the LORD, the God of Israel, who spoke with His mouth to my father David, and fulfilled *it* with His hands, saying, 5 'Since the day that I brought My people from the land of Egypt, I did not choose a city out of all the tribes of Israel *in which* to build a house, so that My name might be there, nor did I choose a man to be *the* leader over My people Israel; 6 but I have chosen Jerusalem so that My name might be there, and I have chosen David to be over My people Israel.' 7 Now it was in the heart of my father David to build a house for the name of the LORD, the God of Israel. 8 But the LORD said to my father David, 'Because it was in your heart to build a house for My name, you did well that it was in your heart. 9 Nevertheless you shall not build the house, but your son who will be born to you, he shall build the house for My name.' 10 Now the LORD has fulfilled His word which He spoke; for I have risen in place of my father David and sit on the throne of Israel, as the LORD promised, and have built the house for the name of the LORD, the God of Israel. 11 There I have placed the ark in which is the covenant of the LORD, which He made with the sons of Israel."

Solomon's Prayer of Dedication

12 Then he stood before the altar of the LORD in the presence of all the assembly of Israel and spread out his hands. 13 For Solomon had made a bronze platform, ¹five cubits long, five cubits wide, and three cubits high, and had set it in the midst of the courtyard; and he stood on it, knelt on his knees in the presence of all the assembly of Israel and spread out his hands toward heaven. 14 He said, "LORD, God of Israel, there is no god like You in heaven or on earth, keeping Your covenant and Your faithfulness to Your servants who walk before You with all their heart; 15 You who have kept with Your servant, my father David, that which You promised him; You have spoken with Your mouth and have fulfilled it with Your hand, as *it is* this day. 16 Now then, LORD, God of Israel, keep to Your servant David, my father, that which You promised him, saying, 'You shall not lack a man to sit on the throne of Israel, if only your sons pay attention to their way, to walk in My Law as you have walked before Me.' 17 Now then, LORD, God of Israel, let Your word be

---

6:13 ¹About 7.5 ft. long and wide and 4.5 ft. high or 2.3 m and 1.4 m

confirmed which You have spoken to Your servant David. **18** "But will God really dwell with mankind on the earth? Behold, heaven and the highest heaven cannot contain You; how much less this house which I have built! **19** Nevertheless, turn Your attention to the prayer of Your servant and to his plea, LORD, my God, to listen to the cry and to the prayer which Your servant prays before You; **20** that Your eye will be open toward this house day and night, toward the place of which You have said that *You would* put Your name there, to listen to the prayer which Your servant shall pray toward this place. **21** Listen to the pleadings of Your servant and of Your people Israel when they pray toward this place; hear from Your dwelling place, from heaven; hear and forgive.

22 "If someone sins against his neighbor and is made to take an oath, and he comes *and* takes an oath before Your altar in this house, **23** then hear from heaven and take action and judge Your servants, punishing the wicked by bringing his way on his own head, and justifying the righteous by repaying him according to his righteousness.

24 "If Your people Israel are defeated before an enemy because they have sinned against You, and they return *to You* and praise Your name, and pray and plead before You in this house, **25** then hear from heaven and forgive the sin of Your people Israel, and bring them back to the land which You have given to them and to their fathers.

26 "When the heavens are shut up and there is no rain because they have sinned against You, and they pray toward this place and praise Your name, and turn from their sin when You afflict them, **27** then hear in heaven and forgive the sin of Your servants and Your people Israel; indeed, teach them the good way in which they are to walk. And provide rain on Your land, which You have given to Your people as an inheritance.

28 "If there is a famine in the land, if there is a plague, if there is blight or mildew, if there is locust or grasshopper, if their enemies besiege them in the land of their cities, whatever plague or whatever sickness *there is,* **29** whatever prayer or plea is made by anyone or by all Your people Israel, each knowing his own affliction and his own pain, and spreading his hands toward this house, **30** then hear from heaven, Your dwelling place, and forgive, and render to each according to all his ways, whose heart You know—for You alone know the hearts of the sons of mankind—**31** so that they may fear You, to walk in Your ways as long as they live in the land which You have given to our fathers.

32 "Also concerning the foreigner who is not from Your people Israel, when he comes from a far country on account of Your great name and Your mighty hand and Your outstretched arm, when they come and pray toward this house, **33** then hear from heaven, from Your dwelling place, and do according to all for which the foreigner calls to You, so that all the peoples of the earth may know Your name, and fear You as *do* Your people Israel, and that they may

know that this house which I have built is called by Your name. **34** "When Your people go out to battle against their enemies, by whatever way You send them, and they pray to You toward this city which You have chosen and the house which I have built for Your name, **35** then hear from heaven their prayer and their pleading, and maintain their cause.

36 "When they sin against You (for there is no one who does not sin), and You are angry with them and turn them over to an enemy, so that they take them away captive to a land far off or near, **37** if they take it to heart in the land where they are taken captive, and repent and plead to You in the land of their captivity, saying, 'We have sinned, we have done wrong and have acted wickedly'; **38** *if* they return to You with all their heart and with all their soul in the land of their captivity, where they have been taken captive, and pray toward their land which You have given to their fathers and the city which You have chosen, and toward the house which I have built for Your name, **39** then hear from heaven, from Your dwelling place, their prayer and pleadings, and maintain their cause, and forgive Your people who have sinned against You.

40 "Now, my God, please, let Your eyes be open and Your ears attentive to the prayer *offered* in this place.

41 "Now then arise, LORD God, to Your resting place, You and the ark of Your might; let Your priests, LORD God, be clothed with salvation, and let Your godly ones rejoice in what is good.

42 "LORD God, do not turn away the face of Your anointed; remember *Your* faithfulness to Your servant David."

The Shekinah Glory

7 Now when Solomon had finished praying, fire came down from heaven and consumed the burnt offering and the sacrifices, and the glory of the LORD filled the house. **2** And the priests could not enter the house of the LORD because the glory of the LORD filled the LORD's house. **3** All the sons of Israel, seeing the fire come down and the glory of the LORD upon the house, bowed down on the pavement with their faces to the ground, and they worshiped and gave praise to the LORD, *saying,* "Certainly He is good, certainly His faithfulness is everlasting."

Sacrifices Offered

4 Then the king and all the people offered sacrifice before the LORD. **5** King Solomon offered a sacrifice of twenty-two thousand oxen and 120,000 sheep. So the king and all the people dedicated the house of God. **6** The priests stood at their posts, and the Levites also, with the musical instruments for the LORD, which King David had made for giving praise to the LORD—"for His faithfulness is everlasting"—whenever David gave praise through their ministry; the priests on the other side blew trumpets and all Israel was standing.

7 Then Solomon consecrated the middle of

the courtyard that *was* before the house of the LORD, for he offered the burnt offerings and the fat of the peace offerings there, because the bronze altar which Solomon had made was not able to contain the burnt offering, the grain offering, and the fat.

The Feast of Dedication

8 So Solomon held the feast at that time for seven days, and all Israel with him, a very great assembly *that came* from the entrance of Hamath to the brook of Egypt. 9 And on the eighth day they held a solemn assembly, because they held the dedication of the altar for seven days, and the feast for seven days. 10 Then on the twenty-third day of the seventh month he sent the people to their tents, rejoicing and happy in heart because of the goodness that the LORD had shown to David, to Solomon, and to His people Israel.

God's Promise and Warning

11 So Solomon finished the house of the LORD and the king's palace, and successfully completed everything that he had planned on doing in the house of the LORD and in his palace. 12 Then the LORD appeared to Solomon at night and said to him, "I have heard your prayer and have chosen this place for Myself as a house of sacrifice. 13 If I shut up the heavens so that there is no rain, or if I command the locust to devour the land, or if I send a plague among My people, 14 and My people who are called by My name humble themselves, and pray and seek My face, and turn from their wicked ways, then I will hear from heaven, and I will forgive their sin and will heal their land. 15 Now My eyes will be open and My ears attentive to the prayer *offered in* this place. 16 For now I have chosen and consecrated this house so that My name may be there forever, and My eyes and My heart will be there always. 17 As for you, if you walk before Me as your father David walked, to do according to everything that I have commanded you, and keep My statutes and My ordinances, 18 then I will establish your royal throne as I covenanted with your father David, saying, 'You shall not lack a man *to be* ruler in Israel.'

19 "But if you turn away and abandon My statutes and My commandments which I have set before you, and go and serve other gods and worship them, 20 then I will uproot you from My land which I have given you, and this house which I have consecrated for My name I will cast out of My sight; and I will make it a proverb and an object of scorn among all peoples. 21 As for this house, which was exalted, everyone who passes by it will be astonished and say, 'Why has the LORD done these things to this land and to this house?' 22 And they will say, 'Because they abandoned the LORD, the God of their fathers, who brought them from the land of Egypt, and they adopted other gods, and worshiped and served them; therefore He has brought all this adversity on them.' "

Solomon's Activities and Accomplishments

8 Now it came about at the end of the twenty years in which Solomon had built the house of the LORD and his own house, 2 that he built the cities which Huram had given him, and settled the sons of Israel there.

3 Then Solomon went to Hamath-zobah and captured it. 4 He built Tadmor in the wilderness and all the storage cities which he had built in Hamath. 5 He also built upper Beth-horon and lower Beth-horon, *which were* fortified cities *with* walls, gates, and bars; 6 and Baalath and all the storage cities that Solomon had, and all the cities for his chariots and cities for his horsemen, and everything that it pleased Solomon to build in Jerusalem, Lebanon, and all the land under his rule.

7 All of the people who were left of the Hittites, the Amorites, the Perizzites, the Hivites, and the Jebusites, who were not of Israel, 8 *that is,* from their descendants who were left after them in the land, whom the sons of Israel had not destroyed, Solomon raised them as forced laborers to this day. 9 But Solomon did not make slaves from the sons of Israel for his work; for they were men of war, his chief captains and commanders of his chariots and his horsemen. 10 These were the chief officers of King Solomon, 250 who ruled over the people.

11 Then Solomon brought Pharaoh's daughter up from the city of David to the house which he had built for her, for he said, "My wife shall not live in the house of David king of Israel, because the places where the ark of the LORD has entered are holy."

12 Then Solomon offered burnt offerings to the LORD on the altar of the LORD which he had built in front of the porch; 13 and *he did so* according to the daily rule, offering *them* up according to the commandment of Moses, for the Sabbaths, the new moons, and the three annual feasts—the Feast of Unleavened Bread, the Feast of Weeks, and the Feast of Booths.

14 Now according to the ordinance of his father David, he appointed the divisions of the priests for their service, and the Levites for their duties of praise and ministering before the priests according to the daily rule, and the gatekeepers by their divisions at every gate; for this is what David, the man of God, had commanded. 15 And they did not deviate from the commandment of the king to the priests and Levites in any matter or regarding the storehouses.

16 So all the work of Solomon was carried out from the day of the foundation of the house of the LORD, until it was finished. *So* the house of the LORD was completed.

17 Then Solomon went to Ezion-geber and to Eloth on the seashore in the land of Edom. 18 And by his servants Huram sent him ships and servants who knew the sea; and they went with Solomon's servants to Ophir and took from there 1450 talents of gold, and brought it to King Solomon.

8:18 1 About 17 tons or 15 metric tons

Visit of the Queen of Sheba

9 Now when the queen of Sheba heard about the fame of Solomon, she came to Jerusalem to test Solomon with riddles. She had a very large entourage, with camels carrying balsam oil and a large amount of gold and precious stones; and when she came to Solomon, she spoke with him about everything that was on her heart. 2 Solomon answered all her questions; nothing was hidden from Solomon which he did not explain to her. 3 When the queen of Sheba had seen the wisdom of Solomon, the house which he had built, 4 the food at his table, the seating of his servants, the attendance of his ministers and their attire, his cupbearers and their attire, and his stairway by which he went up to the house of the LORD, she was breathless. 5 Then she said to the king, "It was a true story that I heard in my own land about your words and your wisdom. 6 But I did not believe their stories until I came and my own eyes saw it all. And behold, not even half of the greatness of your wisdom was reported to me. You have surpassed the report that I heard. 7 How blessed are your men, how blessed are these servants of yours, who stand before you continually and hear your wisdom! 8 Blessed be the LORD your God who delighted in you, setting you on His throne as king for the LORD your God; because your God loved Israel, establishing them forever, He made you king over them, to carry out justice and righteousness." 9 Then she gave the king *1120 talents of gold and a very great *amount of* balsam oil and precious stones; there had never been balsam oil like that which the queen of Sheba gave King Solomon.

10 The servants of Huram and the servants of Solomon who brought gold from Ophir, also brought algum trees and precious stones. 11 From the algum trees the king made steps to the house of the LORD and for the king's palace, and lyres and harps for the singers; and nothing like them was seen before in the land of Judah.

12 King Solomon gave the queen of Sheba her every desire, whatever she requested, besides *gifts equal to* what she had brought to the king. Then she turned and went to her own land with her servants.

Solomon's Wealth and Power

13 Now the weight of gold that came to Solomon in one year was *1666 talents of gold, 14 besides *what* the traders and merchants brought; and all the kings of Arabia and the governors of the country brought gold and silver to Solomon. 15 King Solomon made two hundred large shields of beaten gold, using six hundred *shekels of* beaten gold on each large shield. 16 *He made* three hundred shields of beaten gold, using three hundred *shekels of* gold on each shield; and the king put them in the house of the forest of Lebanon. 17 Moreover, the king made a great throne of ivory, and overlaid it with pure gold. 18 *There were* six steps to the throne and a footstool in gold attached to the throne, and arms on each side of the seat, and two lions standing beside

the arms. 19 Twelve lions were standing there on the six steps on the one side and on the other; nothing like *it* was made for any *other* kingdom. 20 All King Solomon's drinking vessels *were* of gold, and all the vessels of the house of the forest of Lebanon *were* of pure gold; silver was not considered valuable in the days of Solomon. 21 For the king had ships which went to Tarshish with the servants of Huram; once *every* three years the ships of Tarshish came bringing gold and silver, ivory, apes, and peacocks.

22 So King Solomon became greater than all the kings of the earth in wealth and wisdom. 23 And all the kings of the earth were seeking the presence of Solomon, to hear his wisdom which God had put in his heart. 24 They were bringing, each *of them* his gift: articles of silver and gold, garments, weapons, balsam oil, horses, and mules, so much year by year. 25 Now Solomon had four thousand stalls for horses and chariots and twelve thousand horsemen, and he stationed them in the chariot cities and with the king in Jerusalem. 26 He was ruler over all the kings from the *Euphrates* River to the land of the Philistines, and as far as the border of Egypt. 27 And the king made silver *as common* as stones in Jerusalem, and he made cedars as plentiful as sycamore trees that are in the lowland. 28 And they were bringing horses for Solomon from Egypt and from all countries.

29 Now the rest of the acts of Solomon, *from* the first to the last, are they not written in the records of Nathan the prophet, in the prophecy of Ahijah the Shilonite, and in the visions of Iddo the seer concerning Jeroboam the son of Nebat? 30 Solomon reigned in Jerusalem over all Israel for forty years.

Death of Solomon

31 And Solomon *1lay down with his fathers and was buried in the city of his father David; and his son Rehoboam reigned in his place.

Rehoboam's Reign of Foolishness

10 Then Rehoboam went to Shechem, because all Israel had come to Shechem to make him king. 2 When Jeroboam the son of Nebat heard *about it* (he was in Egypt where he had fled from the presence of King Solomon), Jeroboam returned from Egypt. 3 So they sent *word* and summoned him. When Jeroboam and all Israel came, they spoke to Rehoboam, saying, 4 "Your father made our yoke hard; but now, lighten the hard labor *imposed by* your father and his heavy yoke which he put on us, and we will serve you." 5 He said to them, "Return to me again in three days." So the people departed.

6 And then King Rehoboam consulted with the elders who had served his father Solomon while he was still alive, saying, "How do you advise *me* to answer this people?" 7 They spoke to him, saying, "If you are kind to this people and please them and speak pleasant words to them, then they will be your servants always." 8 But he ignored the advice of the elders which they had given him, and consulted with the

young men who had grown up with him and served him. 9 He said to them, "What advice do you give, so that we may answer this people, who have spoken to me, saying, 'Lighten the yoke which your father put on us'?" 10 The young men who had grown up with him spoke to him, saying, "This is what you should say to the people who spoke to you, saying: 'Your father made our yoke heavy, but you make it lighter for us!' You should speak this way to them: 'My little finger is thicker than my father's waist! 11 Now then, my father loaded you with a heavy yoke; yet I will add to your yoke. My father disciplined you with whips, but I *will discipline you* with 'scorpions!' "

12 So Jeroboam and all the people came to Rehoboam on the third day, just as the king had directed, saying, "Return to me on the third day." 13 The king answered them harshly, and King Rehoboam ignored the advice of the elders. 14 He spoke to them according to the advice of the young men, saying, "My father made your yoke heavy, but I will add to it; my father disciplined you with whips, but I *will discipline you* with 'scorpions." 15 So the king did not listen to the people, because it was a turn of events from God so that the LORD might establish His word, which He spoke through Ahijah the Shilonite to Jeroboam the son of Nebat.

16 When all Israel *saw* that the king had not listened to them, the people replied to the king, saying,

"What share do we have in David?
 We have no inheritance in the son of Jesse.
Everyone to your tents, Israel!
Now look after your own house, David!"

So all Israel went *away* to their tents. 17 But as for the sons of Israel who lived in the cities of Judah, Rehoboam reigned over them. 18 Then King Rehoboam sent Hadoram, who was in charge of the forced labor, and the sons of Israel stoned him to death. And King Rehoboam hurried to mount his chariot to flee to Jerusalem. 19 So Israel has been in rebellion against the house of David to this day.

Rehoboam Reigns over Judah and Builds Cities

11 Now when Rehoboam had come to Jerusalem, he assembled the house of Judah and Benjamin, 180,000 chosen warriors, to fight against Israel to restore the kingdom to Rehoboam. 2 But the word of the LORD came to Shemaiah the man of God, saying, 3 "Tell Rehoboam the son of Solomon, king of Judah, and all Israel in Judah and Benjamin, saying, 4 'This is what the LORD says: "You shall not go up nor fight against your relatives; return, every man, to his house, for this event is from Me." ' " So they listened to the words of the LORD and returned from going against Jeroboam.

5 Rehoboam lived in Jerusalem and built cities for defense in Judah. 6 He built Bethlehem, Etam, Tekoa, 7 Beth-zur, Soco, Adullam, 8 Gath, Mareshah, Ziph, 9 Adoraim, Lachish, Azekah, 10 Zorah, Aijalon, and Hebron, which are fortified cities in Judah

and Benjamin. 11 He also strengthened the fortresses and put officers in them and supplies of food, oil, and wine. 12 *He put* shields and spears in every city and strengthened them greatly. So he held Judah and Benjamin.

13 Moreover, the priests and the Levites who were in all Israel also stood with him from all their districts.

Jeroboam Appoints False Priests

14 For the Levites left their pasture lands and their property and went to Judah and Jerusalem, because Jeroboam and his sons had excluded them from serving as priests to the LORD. 15 He set up priests of his own for the high places, for the satyrs and the calves which he had made. 16 Those from all the tribes of Israel who set their hearts on seeking the LORD God of Israel followed them to Jerusalem, to sacrifice to the LORD God of their fathers. 17 They strengthened the kingdom of Judah and supported Rehoboam the son of Solomon for three years, for they walked in the way of David and Solomon for three years.

Rehoboam's Family

18 Then Rehoboam married Mahalath the daughter of Jerimoth the son of David *and of* Abihail the daughter of Eliab the son of Jesse, 19 and she bore to him sons: Jeush, Shemariah, and Zaham. 20 After her he married Maacah the daughter of Absalom, and she bore to him Abijah, Attai, Ziza, and Shelomith. 21 Rehoboam loved Maacah the daughter of Absalom more than all his *other* wives and concubines. For he had taken eighteen wives and sixty concubines, and fathered twenty-eight sons and sixty daughters. 22 Rehoboam appointed Abijah the son of Maacah as head and leader among his brothers, for he *intended* to make him king. 23 He acted wisely and distributed some of his sons through all the territories of Judah and Benjamin to all the fortified cities, and he gave them plenty of provisions. And he sought many wives *for them.*

Shishak of Egypt Invades Judah

12 When the kingdom of Rehoboam was established and strong, he and all Israel with him abandoned the Law of the LORD. 2 And it came about in King Rehoboam's fifth year, because they had been unfaithful to the LORD, that Shishak king of Egypt came up against Jerusalem 3 with 1,200 chariots and sixty thousand horsemen. And the people who came with him from Egypt were innumerable: the Lubim, the Sukkiim, and the Ethiopians. 4 And he captured the fortified cities of Judah and came as far as Jerusalem. 5 Then Shemaiah the prophet came to Rehoboam and the princes of Judah who had gathered at Jerusalem because of Shishak, and he said to them, "This is what the LORD says: 'You have abandoned Me, so I also have abandoned you to Shishak.' " 6 So the princes of Israel and the king humbled themselves and said, "The LORD is righteous." 7 When the LORD saw that they had humbled themselves, the word of the LORD came to Shemaiah, saying, "They have humbled

---

10:11 1 Prob. a brutal type of whip   10:14 1 Prob. a brutal type of whip

themselves, *so* I will not destroy them; and I will grant them a little deliverance, and My wrath will not be poured out on Jerusalem by means of Shishak. ⁸ But they will become his slaves, so that they may learn *the difference between* My service and the service of the kingdoms of the countries."

Plunder Impoverishes Judah

⁹ So Shishak king of Egypt went up against Jerusalem, and he took the treasures of the house of the Lord and the treasures of the king's palace. He took everything; he even took the gold shields which Solomon had made. ¹⁰ Then King Rehoboam made shields of bronze in their place and committed them to the care of the commanders of the guards who guarded the entrance of the king's house. ¹¹ As often as the king entered the house of the Lord, the guards came and carried them and *then* brought them back into the guards' room. ¹² And when he humbled himself, the anger of the Lord turned away from him, so as not to destroy *him* completely; and conditions were also good in Judah.

¹³ So King Rehoboam became powerful in Jerusalem and reigned *there*. For Rehoboam was forty-one years old when he began to reign, and he reigned for seventeen years in Jerusalem, the city which the Lord had chosen from all the tribes of Israel, to put His name there. And his mother's name was Naamah the Ammonitess. ¹⁴ But he did evil because he did not set his heart to seek the Lord.

¹⁵ Now the acts of Rehoboam, from the first to the last, are they not written in the records of Shemaiah the prophet and of Iddo the seer, according to genealogical enrollment? And *there were* wars between Rehoboam and Jeroboam continually. ¹⁶ And Rehoboam ¹lay down with his fathers and was buried in the city of David; and his son Abijah became king in his place.

Abijah Succeeds Rehoboam

13 In the eighteenth year of King Jeroboam, Abijah became king over Judah. ² He reigned in Jerusalem for three years; and his mother's name was Micaiah the daughter of Uriel of Gibeah.

Now there was war between Abijah and Jeroboam. ³ Abijah began the battle with an army of warriors, four hundred thousand chosen men, while Jeroboam drew up in battle formation against him with eight hundred thousand chosen men *who were* valiant warriors.

Civil War

⁴ Then Abijah stood on Mount Zemaraim, which is in the hill country of Ephraim, and said, "Listen to me, Jeroboam and all Israel: ⁵ Do you not know that the Lord God of Israel gave the rule over Israel forever to David and his sons by a covenant of salt? ⁶ Yet Jeroboam the son of Nebat, the servant of Solomon the son of David, rose up and rebelled against his master, ⁷ and worthless men gathered to him, wicked men, who proved too strong for

Rehoboam, the son of Solomon, when he was young and timid and could not hold his own against them.

⁸ "So now you intend to assert yourselves against the kingdom of the Lord through the sons of David, being a great multitude and *having* with you the golden calves which Jeroboam made for you as gods. ⁹ Have you not driven out the priests of the Lord, the sons of Aaron and the Levites, and made for yourselves priests like the peoples of *other* lands? Whoever comes to consecrate himself with a bull and seven rams, even he may become a priest of *things that are* not gods. ¹⁰ But as for us, the Lord is our God, and we have not abandoned Him; and the sons of Aaron are ministering to the Lord as priests, and the Levites attend to their work. ¹¹ Every morning and evening they burn to the Lord burnt offerings and fragrant incense, and the show-bread is *set* on the clean table, and the golden lampstand with its lamps is *ready* to light every evening; for we perform *our* duty to the Lord our God, but you have abandoned Him. ¹² Now behold, God is with us at *our* head, and His priests with the signal trumpets to sound the war cry against you. Sons of Israel, do not fight against the Lord God of your fathers, for you will not succeed."

¹³ But Jeroboam had set an ambush to come from behind, so that *Israel* was in front of Judah and the ambush was behind them. ¹⁴ When Judah turned around, behold, they were attacked both from front and rear; so they cried out to the Lord, and the priests blew the trumpets. ¹⁵ Then the men of Judah raised a war cry, and when the men of Judah raised the war cry, God defeated Jeroboam and all Israel before Abijah and Judah. ¹⁶ When the sons of Israel fled from Judah, God handed them over to them. ¹⁷ Abijah and his people defeated them with a great slaughter, so that five hundred thousand chosen men of Israel fell slain. ¹⁸ The sons of Israel were subdued at that time, and the sons of Judah conquered because they trusted in the Lord, the God of their fathers. ¹⁹ Abijah pursued Jeroboam and captured from him *several* cities, Bethel with its villages, Jeshanah with its villages, and Ephron with its villages.

Death of Jeroboam

²⁰ Jeroboam did not again recover strength in the days of Abijah; and the Lord struck him and he died.

²¹ But Abijah became powerful, and he took fourteen wives for himself, and fathered twenty-two sons and sixteen daughters. ²² Now the rest of the acts of Abijah, and his ways and his words are written in the treatise of Iddo the prophet.

Asa Succeeds Abijah in Judah

14 So Abijah ¹lay down with his fathers, and they buried him in the city of David, and his son Asa became king in his place. The land was undisturbed for ten years during his days.

² And Asa did *what was* good and right in the sight of the Lord his God, ³ for he removed

---

12:16 ¹ l.e., died   **14:1** ¹ l.e., died

the foreign altars and high places, tore down the memorial stones, cut down the [1]Asherim, [4]and commanded Judah to seek the LORD God of their fathers and to comply with the Law and the commandment. [5]He also removed the high places and the incense altars from all the cities of Judah. And the kingdom was undisturbed under him. [6]He built fortified cities in Judah, since the land was undisturbed, and there was no one at war with him during those years, because the LORD had given him rest. [7]For he said to Judah, "Let's build these cities and surround *them* with walls and towers, gates and bars. The land is still ours because we have sought the LORD our God; we have sought Him, and He has given us rest on every side." So they built and prospered. [8]Now Asa had an army of three hundred thousand from Judah, carrying large shields and spears, and 280,000 from Benjamin, carrying shields and wielding bows; all of them were valiant warriors.

[9]Now Zerah the Ethiopian went out against them with an army of a million men and three hundred chariots, and he came to Mareshah. [10]So Asa went out to meet him, and they drew up in battle formation in the Valley of Zephathah at Mareshah. [11]Then Asa called to the LORD his God and said, "LORD, there is no one besides You to help *in the battle* between the powerful and those who have no strength; help us, LORD our God, for we trust in You, and in Your name have come against this multitude. LORD, You are our God; do not let man prevail against You." [12]So the LORD routed the Ethiopians before Asa and before Judah, and the Ethiopians fled. [13]Asa and the people who *were* with him pursued them as far as Gerar; and so many Ethiopians fell that they could not recover, for they were shattered before the LORD and before His army. And they carried away a very large *amount of* plunder. [14]They destroyed all the cities around Gerar, for the dread of the LORD had fallen on them; and they pillaged all the cities, for there was much plunder in them. [15]They also fatally struck those who owned livestock, and they led away large numbers of sheep and camels. Then they returned to Jerusalem.

Azariah the Prophet Warns Asa

15 Now the Spirit of God came on Azariah the son of Oded, [2]and he went out to meet Asa and said to him, "Listen to me, Asa, and all Judah and Benjamin: the LORD is with you when you are with Him. And if you seek Him, He will let you find Him; but if you abandon Him, He will abandon you. [3]For many days Israel was without the true God and without a teaching priest and without *the* Law. [4]But in their distress they turned to the LORD God of Israel, and they sought Him, and He let them find Him. [5]In those times there was no peace for him who went out or him who came in, because many disturbances afflicted all the inhabitants of the lands. [6]Nation was crushed by nation, and city by city, for God troubled them with every kind of distress. [7]But you, be

strong and do not lose courage, for there is a reward for your work."

Asa's Reforms

[8]Now when Asa heard these words and the prophecy which Azariah the son of Oded the prophet spoke, he took courage and removed the abominable idols from all the land of Judah and Benjamin, and from the cities which he had captured in the hill country of Ephraim. He then restored the altar of the LORD which was in front of the porch of the LORD. [9]And he gathered all Judah and Benjamin, and those from Ephraim, Manasseh, and Simeon who resided with them, for many defected to him from Israel when they saw that the LORD his God was with him. [10]So they assembled at Jerusalem in the third month of the fifteenth year of Asa's reign. [11]They sacrificed to the LORD on that day seven hundred oxen and seven thousand sheep from the spoils they had brought. [12]They entered into the covenant to seek the LORD God of their fathers with all their heart and soul; [13]and whoever would not seek the LORD God of Israel was to be put to death, whether small or great, man or woman. [14]Moreover, they made an oath to the LORD with a loud voice, with shouting, trumpets, and with horns. [15]All Judah rejoiced concerning the oath, for they had sworn with all their heart and had sought Him earnestly, and He let them find Him. So the LORD gave them rest on every side.

[16]He also removed Maacah, the mother of King Asa, from the *position of* queen mother, because she had made an abominable image [1]as an Asherah, and Asa cut down her abominable image, crushed *it*, and burned *it* at the brook Kidron. [17]But the high places were not removed from Israel; nevertheless Asa's heart was blameless all his days. [18]He brought into the house of God the dedicated things of his father and his own dedicated things: silver, gold, and utensils. [19]And there was no *more* war until the thirty-fifth year of Asa's reign.

Asa Wars against Baasha

16 In the thirty-sixth year of Asa's reign, Baasha king of Israel came up against Judah and fortified Ramah in order to prevent *anyone* from going out or coming in to Asa king of Judah. [2]Then Asa brought out silver and gold from the treasuries of the house of the LORD and the king's house, and sent it to Ben-hadad king of Aram, who lived in Damascus, saying, [3]"A treaty *must be made* between you and me, *as there was* between my father and your father. Behold, I have sent you silver and gold; go, break your treaty with Baasha king of Israel so that he will withdraw from me." [4]And Ben-hadad listened to King Asa, and he sent the commanders of his armies against the cities of Israel, and they conquered Ijon, Dan, Abel-maim, and all the storage cities of Naphtali. [5]When Baasha heard *about it,* he stopped fortifying Ramah and put an end to his work. [6]Then King Asa brought all Judah, and they carried away the stones of Ramah and its

---

14:3 [1]I.e., wooden symbols of a female deity (Asherah)   **15:16** [1]Or for *Asherah;* i.e., a wooden symbol of a female deity

timber with which Baasha had been building, and with it he fortified Geba and Mizpah.

Asa Imprisons the Prophet

7 At that time Hanani the seer came to Asa king of Judah and said to him, "Because you have relied on the king of Aram and have not relied on the LORD your God, for that reason the army of the king of Aram has escaped from your hand. 8 Were not the Ethiopians and the Lubim an immense army with very many chariots and horsemen? Yet because you relied on the LORD, He handed them over to you. 9 For the eyes of the LORD roam throughout the earth, so that He may strongly support those whose heart is completely His. You have acted foolishly in this. Indeed, from now on you will have wars." 10 Then Asa was angry with the seer and put him in prison, for he was enraged at him for this. And Asa mistreated some of the people at the same time.

11 Now, the acts of Asa *from* the first to the last, behold, they are written in the Book of the Kings of Judah and Israel. 12 In the thirty-ninth year of his reign Asa became diseased in his feet. His disease was severe, yet even in his disease he did not seek the LORD, but the physicians. 13 So Asa 1lay down with his fathers, and died in the forty-first year of his reign. 14 They buried him in his own tomb which he had cut out for himself in the city of David, and they laid him in the resting place which he had filled with spices of various kinds blended by the perfumers' art; and they made a very great fire for him.

Jehoshaphat Succeeds Asa

17 His son Jehoshaphat then became king in his place, and he proved himself strong over Israel. 2 He placed troops in all the fortified cities of Judah, and placed garrisons in the land of Judah and in the cities of Ephraim which his father Asa had captured.

His Good Reign

3 And the LORD was with Jehoshaphat because he followed the example of his father David's earlier days and did not seek the Baals, 4 but sought the God of his father, followed His commandments, and did not *act* as Israel did. 5 So the LORD established the kingdom in his control, and all Judah gave tribute to Jehoshaphat, and he had great riches and honor. 6 He took great pride in the ways of the LORD, and again removed the high places and the 1Asherim from Judah.

7 Then in the third year of his reign he sent his officials, Ben-hail, Obadiah, Zechariah, Nethanel, and Micaiah, to teach in the cities of Judah; 8 and with them the Levites, Shemaiah, Nethaniah, Zebadiah, Asahel, Shemiramoth, Jehonathan, Adonijah, Tobijah, and Tobadonijah, the Levites; and with them the priests Elishama and Jehoram. 9 They taught in Judah, *having* the Book of the Law of the LORD with them; and they went throughout the cities of Judah and taught among the people.

10 Now the dread of the LORD was on all the kingdoms of the lands which *were* around Judah, so that they did not make war against Jehoshaphat. 11 Some of the Philistines brought gifts and silver as tribute to Jehoshaphat; the Arabians also brought him flocks, 7,700 rams and 7,700 male goats. 12 So Jehoshaphat grew greater and greater, and he built fortresses and storage cities in Judah. 13 He had large supplies in the cities of Judah, and warriors, valiant mighty men, in Jerusalem. 14 This was their muster according to their fathers' households: of Judah, commanders of thousands, Adnah *was* the commander, and with him three hundred thousand valiant warriors; 15 and next to him *was* Johanan the commander, and with him 280,000; 16 and next to him Amasiah the son of Zichri, who volunteered for the LORD, and with him two hundred thousand valiant warriors; 17 and of Benjamin, Eliada, a valiant warrior, and with him two hundred thousand armed with bow and shield; 18 and next to him Jehozabad, and with him 180,000 equipped for war. 19 These are the ones who served the king, apart from those whom the king put in the fortified cities throughout Judah.

Jehoshaphat Allies with Ahab

18 Now Jehoshaphat had great riches and honor; and he allied himself by marriage to Ahab. 2 Some years later he went down to *visit* Ahab at Samaria, and Ahab slaughtered many sheep and oxen for him and the people who were with him. And he incited him to go up against Ramoth-gilead. 3 Ahab king of Israel said to Jehoshaphat king of Judah, "Will you go with me *against* Ramoth-gilead?" And he said to him, "I am as you are, and my people as your people, and *we will be* with you in the battle."

4 However, Jehoshaphat said to the king of Israel, "Please request the word of the LORD first." 5 So the king of Israel assembled the 1prophets, four hundred men, and said to them, "Should we go to battle against Ramoth-gilead, or should I refrain?" And they said, "Go up, for God will hand *it* over to the king." 6 But Jehoshaphat said, "Is there no longer a prophet of the LORD here, that we may inquire of him?" 7 And the king of Israel said to Jehoshaphat, "There is still one man by whom we may inquire of the LORD, but I hate him, for he never prophesies *anything* good regarding me, but always bad. He is Micaiah the son of Imlah." But Jehoshaphat said, "May the king not say so."

Ahab's False Prophets Assure Victory

8 Then the king of Israel summoned an officer and said, "Bring Micaiah son of Imlah quickly." 9 Now the king of Israel and Jehoshaphat the king of Judah were sitting, each on his throne, dressed in *their* robes, and *they* were sitting at the threshing floor at the entrance of the gate of Samaria; and all the prophets were prophesying before them. 10 Then Zedekiah the son of Chenaanah made horns of iron for himself and said, "This is what the LORD says: 'With these you will gore the Arameans until

---

16:13 1 I.e., died   17:6 1 I.e., wooden symbols of a female deity (Asherah)   18:5 1 I.e., official prophets who at that time were false

they are destroyed!'" **11** All the prophets were prophesying this as well, saying, "Go up to Ramoth-gilead and be successful, for the LORD will hand *it* over to the king."

Micaiah Brings Word from God

12 Then the messenger who went to summon Micaiah spoke to him saying, "Behold, the words of the prophets are unanimously favorable to the king. So please let your word be like one of them, and speak favorably." **13** But Micaiah said, "As the LORD lives, whatever my God says, I will speak it."

14 When he came to the king, the king said to him, "Micaiah, should we go to battle against Ramoth-gilead, or should I refrain?" He said, "Go up and succeed, for they will be handed over to you!" **15** Then the king said to him, "How many times must I make you swear that you will tell me nothing but the truth in the name of the LORD?" **16** So he said,

"I saw all Israel
    Scattered on the mountains,
    Like sheep that have no shepherd.
And the LORD said,
    'These *people* have no master.
    Each of them is to return to his house in peace.' "

17 Then the king of Israel said to Jehoshaphat, "Did I not tell you that he would not prophesy anything good regarding me, but only bad?" **18** And *Micaiah* said, "Therefore, hear the word of the LORD. I saw the LORD sitting on His throne, and all the angels of heaven standing on His right and on His left. **19** And the LORD said, 'Who will entice Ahab king of Israel to go up and fall at Ramoth-gilead?' And one *spirit* said this, while another said that. **20** Then a spirit came forward and stood before the LORD and said, 'I will entice him.' And the LORD said to him, 'How?' **21** He said, 'I will go out and be a deceiving spirit in the mouths of all his prophets.' Then He said, 'You shall entice *him*, and you will also prevail. Go out and do so.' **22** Now therefore, behold, the LORD has put a deceiving spirit in the mouths of these prophets of yours, for the LORD has declared disaster against you."

23 Then Zedekiah the son of Chenaanah approached and struck Micaiah on the cheek; and he said, "How did the Spirit of the LORD pass from me to speak to you?" **24** And Micaiah said, "Behold, you are going to see *how* on that day when you go *from one* inner room to another *trying* to hide yourself." **25** Then the king of Israel said, "Take Micaiah and return him to Amon the governor of the city, and to Joash the king's son; **26** and say, 'This is what the king says: "Put this *man* in prison, and feed him enough bread and water to survive until I return safely." ' " **27** But Micaiah said, "If you actually return safely, the LORD has not spoken by me." And he said, "Listen, all you people!"

Ahab's Defeat and Death

28 So the king of Israel and Jehoshaphat king of Judah went up against Ramoth-gilead. **29** And the king of Israel said to Jehoshaphat, "I will disguise myself and go into battle, but you put on your robes." So the king of Israel disguised himself, and they went into battle. **30** Now the king of Aram had commanded the commanders of his chariots, saying, "Do not fight with the small *or* great, but only with the king of Israel." **31** So when the commanders of the chariots saw Jehoshaphat, they said, "He is the king of Israel!" And they turned aside to fight against him. But Jehoshaphat cried out, and the LORD helped him, and God diverted them from him. **32** When the commanders of the chariots saw that it was not the king of Israel, they turned back from pursuing him. **33** Now one man drew his bow at random and struck the king of Israel in a joint of the armor. So he said to the driver of his chariot, "Turn around and take me out of the battle, for I am severely wounded." **34** The battle raged on that day, and the king of Israel propped himself up in his chariot in front of the Arameans until the evening; and at sunset he died.

Jehu Rebukes Jehoshaphat

19 Then Jehoshaphat the king of Judah returned in safety to his house in Jerusalem. **2** And Jehu the son of Hanani the seer went out to meet him and said to King Jehoshaphat, "Should you help the wicked and love those who hate the LORD, and by doing so *bring* wrath on yourself from the LORD? **3** But there is *some* good in you, for you have removed the *Asheroth from the land and you have set your heart to seek God."

4 So Jehoshaphat lived in Jerusalem and went out again among the people from Beersheba to the hill country of Ephraim, and brought them back to the LORD, the God of their fathers.

Reforms Instituted

5 He appointed judges in the land in all the fortified cities of Judah, city by city. **6** He said to the judges, "Consider what you are doing, for you do not judge for mankind but for the LORD who is with you when you render judgment. **7** Now then, let the fear of the LORD be upon you; be careful about what you do, for the LORD our God will have no part in injustice or partiality, or in the taking of a bribe."

8 In Jerusalem Jehoshaphat also appointed some of the Levites and priests, and some of the heads of the fathers' *households* of Israel, for the judgment of the LORD, and to judge disputes among the inhabitants of Jerusalem. **9** Then he commanded them, saying, "This is what you shall do in the fear of the LORD, faithfully and wholeheartedly. **10** Whenever any dispute comes to you from your countrymen who live in their cities, between blood and blood, between law and commandment, statutes and ordinances, you shall warn them so that they will not be guilty before the LORD, and wrath will *not* come on you and your countrymen. This you shall do and you will not be guilty. **11** Behold, Amariah the chief priest will be over you in every matter that pertains to the LORD, and Zebadiah the son of Ishmael, the ruler of the house of Judah, in all that pertains to the king. Also the Levites shall be officers

---

19:3 1 I.e., wooden symbols of a female deity

before you. Act resolutely, and may the LORD be with the upright."

Judah Invaded

20 Now it came about after this, that the sons of Moab and the sons of Ammon, together with some of the Meunites, came to make war against Jehoshaphat. 2 Then some came and reported to Jehoshaphat, saying, "A great multitude is coming against you from beyond the sea, from Aram; and behold, they are in Hazazon-tamar (that is Engedi)." 3 Jehoshaphat was afraid and turned his attention to seek the LORD; and he proclaimed a period of fasting throughout Judah. 4 So Judah gathered together to seek help from the LORD; they even came from all the cities of Judah to seek the LORD.

Jehoshaphat's Prayer

5 Then Jehoshaphat stood in the assembly of Judah and Jerusalem, in the house of the LORD in front of the new courtyard; 6 and he said, "LORD, God of our fathers, are You not God in the heavens? And are You not ruler over all the kingdoms of the nations? Power and might are in Your hand so that no one can stand against You. 7 Did You not, our God, drive out the inhabitants of this land from Your people Israel, and give it to the descendants of Your friend Abraham forever? 8 They have lived in it, and have built You a sanctuary in it for Your name, saying, 9 'If disaster comes upon us, the sword, or judgment, or plague, or famine, we will stand before this house and before You (for Your name is in this house), and cry out to You in our distress, and You will hear and save us.' 10 Now behold, the sons of Ammon, Moab, and Mount Seir, whom You did not allow Israel to invade when they came out of the land of Egypt (for they turned aside from them and did not destroy them), 11 see how they are rewarding us by coming to drive us out from Your possession which You have given us as an inheritance. 12 Our God, will You not judge them? For we are powerless before this great multitude that is coming against us; nor do we know what to do, but our eyes are on You."

13 All Judah was standing before the LORD, with their infants, their wives, and their children.

Jahaziel Answers the Prayer

14 Then in the midst of the assembly the Spirit of the LORD came upon Jahaziel the son of Zechariah, the son of Benaiah, the son of Jeiel, the son of Mattaniah, the Levite of the sons of Asaph; 15 and he said, "Listen, all you of Judah and the inhabitants of Jerusalem, and King Jehoshaphat: This is what the LORD says to you: 'Do not fear or be dismayed because of this great multitude, for the battle is not yours but God's. 16 Tomorrow, go down against them. Behold, they will come up by the ascent of Ziz, and you will find them at the end of the valley in front of the wilderness of Jeruel. 17 You need not fight in this battle; take your position, stand and watch the salvation of the LORD in your behalf, Judah and Jerusalem.' Do not fear

or be dismayed; tomorrow, go out to face them, for the LORD is with you."

18 Jehoshaphat bowed his head with his face to the ground, and all Judah and the inhabitants of Jerusalem fell down before the LORD, worshiping the LORD. 19 The Levites, from the sons of the Kohathites and from the sons of the Korahites, stood up to praise the LORD God of Israel, with a very loud voice.

Enemies Destroy Themselves

20 They rose early in the morning and went out to the wilderness of Tekoa; and when they went out, Jehoshaphat stood and said, "Listen to me, Judah and inhabitants of Jerusalem: Put your trust in the LORD your God and you will endure. Put your trust in His prophets, and succeed." 21 When he had consulted with the people, he appointed those who sang to the LORD and those who praised Him in holy attire, as they went out before the army and said, "Give thanks to the LORD, for His faithfulness is everlasting." 22 When they began singing and praising, the LORD set ambushes against the sons of Ammon, Moab, and Mount Seir, who had come against Judah; so they were struck down. 23 For the sons of Ammon and Moab rose up against the inhabitants of Mount Seir, completely destroying them; and when they had finished with the inhabitants of Seir, they helped to destroy one another.

24 When Judah came to the watchtower of the wilderness, they turned toward the multitude, and behold, they were corpses lying on the ground, and there was no survivor. 25 When Jehoshaphat and his people came to take their spoils, they found much among them, including goods, garments, and valuable things which they took for themselves, more than they could carry. And they were taking the spoils for three days because there was so much.

Triumphant Return to Jerusalem

26 Then on the fourth day they assembled in the Valley of Beracah, for they blessed the LORD there. Therefore they have named that place "The Valley of 1Beracah" until today. 27 Every man of Judah and Jerusalem returned, with Jehoshaphat at their head, returning to Jerusalem with joy, for the LORD had helped them to rejoice over their enemies. 28 They came to Jerusalem with harps, lyres, and trumpets, to the house of the LORD. 29 And the dread of God was on all the kingdoms of the lands when they heard that the LORD had fought against the enemies of Israel. 30 So the kingdom of Jehoshaphat was at peace, for his God gave him rest on all sides.

31 Now Jehoshaphat reigned over Judah. He was thirty-five years old when he became king, and he reigned in Jerusalem for twenty-five years. And his mother's name was Azubah the daughter of Shilhi. 32 He walked in the way of his father Asa and did not deviate from it, doing right in the sight of the LORD. 33 The high places, however, were not removed; the people had not yet directed their hearts to the God of their fathers.

34 Now the rest of the acts of Jehoshaphat, first to last, behold, they are written in the annals of Jehu the son of Hanani, which is recorded in the Book of the Kings of Israel.

Alliance Displeases God

35 After this Jehoshaphat king of Judah allied himself with Ahaziah king of Israel. He acted wickedly in so doing. 36 So he allied himself with him to make ships to go to Tarshish, and they made the ships in Ezion-geber. 37 Then Eliezer the son of Dodavahu of Mareshah prophesied against Jehoshaphat, saying, "Because you have allied yourself with Ahaziah, the LORD has destroyed your works." So the ships were wrecked and could not go to Tarshish.

Jehoram Succeeds Jehoshaphat in Judah

21 Then Jehoshaphat ¹lay down with his fathers and was buried with his fathers in the city of David, and his son Jehoram became king in his place. 2 He had brothers, the sons of Jehoshaphat: Azariah, Jehiel, Zechariah, Azaryahu, Michael, and Shephatiah. All these *were* the sons of Jehoshaphat king of Israel. 3 Their father gave them many gifts of silver, gold, and precious things, with fortified cities in Judah; but he gave the kingdom to Jehoram because he was the firstborn.

4 Now when Jehoram had taken over the kingdom of his father and gathered courage, he killed all his brothers with the sword, and some of the leaders of Israel as well. 5 Jehoram *was* thirty-two years old when he became king, and he reigned for eight years in Jerusalem. 6 He walked in the way of the kings of Israel, just as the house of Ahab had done, for Ahab's daughter was his wife; and he did evil in the sight of the LORD. 7 Yet the LORD was not willing to destroy the house of David because of the covenant which He had made with David, and because He had promised to give a lamp to him and his sons forever.

Revolt against Judah

8 In his days Edom broke away from the rule of Judah, and appointed a king over themselves. 9 Then Jehoram crossed over with his commanders and all his chariots with him. And he got up at night and struck and killed the Edomites who were surrounding him, and the commanders of the chariots. 10 So Edom revolted against Judah to this day. Then Libnah revolted at the same time against his rule because he had abandoned the LORD God of his fathers. 11 Furthermore, he made high places in the mountains of Judah, and caused the inhabitants of Jerusalem to be unfaithful, and led Judah astray.

12 Then a letter came to him from Elijah the prophet, saying, "This is what the LORD, the God of your father David says: 'Because you have not walked in the ways of your father Jehoshaphat and the ways of Asa king of Judah, 13 but have walked in the way of the kings of Israel, and have caused Judah and the inhabitants of Jerusalem to be unfaithful as the house of Ahab was unfaithful, and you have also

killed your brothers, your own family, who were better than you, 14 behold, the LORD is going to strike your people, your sons, your wives, and all your possessions with a great plague; 15 and you will suffer severe sickness, a disease of your bowels, until your bowels come out because of the sickness, day by day.' "

16 Then the LORD stirred up against Jehoram the spirit of the Philistines and the Arabs who bordered the Ethiopians; 17 and they came against Judah and invaded it, and carried away all the possessions found in the king's house together with his sons and his wives, so that no son was left to him except Jehoahaz, the youngest of his sons.

18 So after all this the LORD struck him in his intestines with an incurable sickness. 19 Now it came about in the course of time, at the end of two years, that his bowels came out because of his sickness, and he died in great pain. And his people did not make a *funeral* fire for him like the fire for his fathers. 20 He was thirty-two years old when he became king, and he reigned in Jerusalem for eight years; and he departed with no one's regret, and they buried him in the city of David, but not in the tombs of the kings.

Ahaziah Succeeds Jehoram in Judah

22 Then the inhabitants of Jerusalem made Ahaziah, his youngest son, king in his place, for the band of men who came with the Arabs to the camp had killed all the older *sons.* So Ahaziah the son of Jehoram king of Judah began to reign. 2 Ahaziah *was* twenty-two years old when he became king, and he reigned for one year in Jerusalem. And his mother's name was Athaliah, the granddaughter of Omri. 3 He also walked in the ways of the house of Ahab, for his mother was his counselor to act wickedly. 4 So he did evil in the sight of the LORD like the house of Ahab, for they were his counselors after the death of his father, to his own destruction.

Ahaziah Allies with Jehoram of Israel

5 He also walked by their counsel, and went with Jehoram the son of Ahab king of Israel to wage war against Hazael king of Aram at Ramoth-gilead. But the Arameans wounded Joram. 6 So he returned to be healed in Jezreel of the wounds which they had inflicted on him at Ramah, when he fought against Hazael king of Aram. And Ahaziah, the son of Jehoram king of Judah, went down to see Jehoram the son of Ahab in Jezreel, because he was sick.

7 Now the destruction of Ahaziah was from God, in that he went to Joram. For when he arrived, he went out with Jehoram against Jehu the son of Nimshi, whom the LORD had anointed to eliminate the house of Ahab.

Jehu Murders Princes of Judah

8 And it came about, when Jehu was executing judgment on the house of Ahab, that he found the princes of Judah and the sons of Ahaziah's brothers attending to Ahaziah, and killed them. 9 He also searched for Ahaziah, and they caught

him while he was hiding in Samaria; they brought him to Jehu, put him to death, and buried him. For they said, "He is the son of Jehoshaphat, who sought the LORD with all his heart." So there was no one of the house of Ahaziah to retain the power of the kingdom.

10 Now when Athaliah the mother of Ahaziah saw that her son was dead, she rose and eliminated all the royal children of the house of Judah. 11 But Jehoshabeath the king's daughter took Joash the son of Ahaziah, and stole him from among the king's sons who were being put to death, and placed him and his nurse in the bedroom. So Jehoshabeath, the daughter of King Jehoram, the wife of Jehoiada the priest (for she was the sister of Ahaziah), hid him from Athaliah so that she would not put him to death. 12 He kept himself hidden with them in the house of God for six years while Athaliah reigned over the land.

Jehoiada Sets Joash on the Throne of Judah

23 Now in the seventh year, Jehoiada gathered his courage, and took captains of hundreds: Azariah the son of Jeroham, Ishmael the son of Johanan, Azariah the son of Obed, Maaseiah the son of Adaiah, and Elishaphat the son of Zichri, *and they entered* into a covenant with him. 2 And they went throughout Judah and gathered the Levites from all the cities of Judah, and the heads of the fathers' *households* of Israel, and they came to Jerusalem. 3 Then all the assembly made a covenant with the king in the house of God. And Jehoiada said to them, "Behold, the king's son shall reign, as the LORD has spoken concerning the sons of David. 4 This is the thing which you shall do: a third of you, of the priests and Levites who come in on the Sabbath, *shall be* gatekeepers, 5 and a third *shall be* at the king's house, and a third at the Gate of the Foundation; and all the people *shall be* in the courtyards of the house of the LORD. 6 But no one is to enter the house of the LORD except the priests and the ministering Levites; they may enter, for they are holy. And all the people are to keep the command of the LORD. 7 The Levites will surround the king, each man with his weapons in his hand; and whoever enters the house is to be put to death. Therefore be with the king when he comes in and when he goes out."

8 The Levites and all Judah did according to all that Jehoiada the priest commanded. And each one of them took his men who were to come in on the Sabbath, with those who were to go out on the Sabbath, for Jehoiada the priest did not dismiss *any of* the divisions. 9 Then Jehoiada the priest gave the captains of hundreds the spears and the shields and quivers which had been King David's, which were in the house of God. 10 He stationed all the people, each man with his weapon in his hand, from the right side of the house to the left side of the house, by the altar and by the house, around the king. 11 Then they brought out the king's son and put the crown on him, and *gave him* the testimony and made him king. And Jehoiada and his sons anointed him and said, "*Long* live the king!"

Athaliah Murdered

12 When Athaliah heard the noise of the people running and praising the king, she went into the house of the LORD to the people. 13 She looked, and behold, the king was standing by his pillar at the entrance, and the captains and the trumpeters *were* beside the king. And all the people of the land rejoiced and blew trumpets, the singers with *their* musical instruments leading the praise. Then Athaliah tore her clothes and said, "Conspiracy! Conspiracy!" 14 And Jehoiada the priest brought out the captains of hundreds who were appointed over the army, and said to them, "Bring her out between the ranks, and whoever follows her is to be put to death with the sword." For the priest said, "You shall not put her to death in the house of the LORD." 15 So they seized her, and when she arrived at the entrance of the Horse Gate of the king's house, they put her to death there.

Reforms Carried Out

16 Then Jehoiada made a covenant between himself and all the people and the king, that they would be the LORD's people. 17 And all the people went to the house of Baal and tore it down, and they broke in pieces his altars and his images, and killed Mattan the priest of Baal before the altars. 18 Moreover, Jehoiada placed the offices of the house of the LORD under the authority of the Levitical priests, whom David had assigned over the house of the LORD, to offer the burnt offerings of the LORD, as it is written in the Law of Moses—with rejoicing and singing according to the order of David. 19 He stationed the gatekeepers of the house of the LORD, so that no one would enter *who was* in any way unclean. 20 He took the captains of hundreds, the nobles, the rulers of the people, and all the people of the land, and brought the king down from the house of the LORD, and went through the upper gate to the king's house. And they seated the king upon the royal throne. 21 So all of the people of the land rejoiced and the city was at rest. For they had put Athaliah to death with the sword.

Young Joash Influenced by Jehoiada

24 Joash *was* seven years old when he became king, and he reigned for forty years in Jerusalem; and his mother's name *was* Zibiah from Beersheba. 2 Joash did what was right in the sight of the LORD all the days of Jehoiada the priest. 3 Jehoiada took two wives for him, and he fathered sons and daughters.

Faithless Priests

4 Now it came about after this that Joash decided to restore the house of the LORD. 5 He gathered the priests and Levites and said to them, "Go out to the cities of Judah and collect money from all Israel to repair the house of your God annually, and you shall do the work quickly." But the Levites did not act quickly. 6 So the king summoned Jehoiada, the chief *priest*, and said to him, "Why have you not required the Levites to bring in from Judah and from Jerusalem the contribution of Moses, the servant of the LORD, and the congregation of

Israel, for the tent of the testimony?" 7 For the sons of the wicked Athaliah had broken into the house of God, and even used the holy things of the house of the LORD for the Baals.

Temple Repaired

8 So the king commanded, and they made a chest and set it outside by the gate of the house of the LORD. 9 And they made a proclamation in Judah and Jerusalem to bring to the LORD the contribution commanded by Moses the servant of God on Israel in the wilderness. 10 All the officers and all the people rejoiced, and they brought in their contribution and dropped it into the chest until they had finished. 11 It happened that whenever the chest was brought to the king's officer by the Levites, and they saw that the money was substantial, the king's scribe and the chief priest's officer would come and empty the chest, and pick it up and return it to its place. They did this daily and collected a large amount of money. 12 The king and Jehoiada gave it to those who did the work of the service of the house of the LORD; and they hired masons and carpenters to restore the house of the LORD, and also workers in iron and bronze to repair the house of the LORD. 13 So the workmen labored, and the repair work progressed in their hands, and they restored the house of God according to its specifications and strengthened it. 14 When they had finished, they brought the rest of the money before the king and Jehoiada; and it was made into utensils for the house of the LORD, utensils for the service and the burnt offerings, and pans and utensils of gold and silver. And they offered burnt offerings in the house of the LORD continually, all the days of Jehoiada.

15 Now Jehoiada reached a good old age and he died; he was 130 years old at his death. 16 And they buried him in the city of David with the kings, because he had done well in Israel and for God and His house.

17 But after the death of Jehoiada the officials of Judah came and bowed down to the king, and the king listened to them. 18 And they abandoned the house of the LORD, the God of their fathers, and served the 1Asherim and the idols; so wrath came upon Judah and Jerusalem for this guilt of theirs. 19 Yet He sent prophets to them to bring them back to the LORD; and they testified against them, but they would not listen.

Joash Murders Son of Jehoiada

20 Then the Spirit of God covered Zechariah, the son of Jehoiada the priest like clothing; and he stood above the people and said to them, "This is what God has said, 'Why do you break the commandments of the LORD and do not prosper? Because you have abandoned the LORD, He has also abandoned you.'" 21 So they conspired against him, and at the command of the king they stoned him to death in the courtyard of the house of the LORD. 22 So Joash the king did not remember the kindness which Zechariah's father Jehoiada had shown him,

but he murdered his son. And as Zechariah died he said, "May the LORD see and avenge!"

Aram Invades and Defeats Judah

23 Now it happened at the turn of the year that the army of the Arameans came up against Joash; and they came to Judah and Jerusalem, destroyed all the officials of the people from among the people, and sent all their spoils to the king of Damascus. 24 Indeed, the army of the Arameans came with a small number of men; yet the LORD handed a very great army over to them, because Judah and Joash had abandoned the LORD, the God of their fathers. So they executed judgment on Joash.

25 When they left him (for they left him very sick), his own servants conspired against him because of the blood of the son of Jehoiada the priest, and they murdered him on his bed. So he died, and they buried him in the city of David, but they did not bury him in the tombs of the kings. 26 Now these are the men who conspired against him: Zabad the son of Shimeath the Ammonitess, and Jehozabad the son of Shimrith the Moabitess. 27 As to his sons and the many pronouncements against him and the rebuilding of the house of God, behold, they are written in the treatise of the Book of the Kings. Then his son Amaziah became king in his place.

Amaziah Succeeds Joash in Judah

25 Amaziah was twenty-five years old when he became king, and he reigned for twenty-nine years in Jerusalem. And his mother's name was Jehoaddan of Jerusalem. 2 He did what was right in the sight of the LORD, only not wholeheartedly. 3 Now it came about, as soon as the kingdom was firmly in his grasp, that he killed his servants who had killed his father the king. 4 However, he did not put their children to death, but did as it is written in the Law in the Book of Moses, which the LORD commanded, saying, "Fathers shall not be put to death for sons, nor sons be put to death for fathers; but each shall be put to death for his own sin."

Amaziah Defeats Edomites

5 Moreover, Amaziah assembled Judah and appointed them according to their fathers' households under commanders of thousands and commanders of hundreds throughout Judah and Benjamin; and he took a census of those from twenty years old and upward and found them to be three hundred thousand choice men, able to go to war and handle spear and shield. 6 He also hired a hundred thousand valiant warriors from Israel for 1a hundred talents of silver. 7 But a man of God came to him saying, "O king, do not let the army of Israel come with you, for the LORD is not with Israel nor with any of the sons of Ephraim. 8 But if you do go, do it, be strong for the battle; yet God will bring you down before the enemy, for God has the power to help and to bring down." 9 Amaziah said to the man of God, "But what are we to do about the 1hundred talents which

---

24:18 1I.e., wooden symbols of a female deity (Asherah) 25:6 1About 3.75 tons or 3.4 metric tons
25:9 1About 3.75 tons or 3.4 metric tons

I have given to the troops of Israel?" And the man of God answered, "The LORD has much more to give you than this." 10 Then Amaziah dismissed the troops which came to him from Ephraim, to go home; so their anger burned against Judah, and they returned home in fierce anger.

11 Now Amaziah gathered his courage and led his people out, and went to the Valley of Salt, and struck and killed ten thousand of the sons of Seir. 12 The sons of Judah also captured ten thousand alive and brought them to the top of the cliff, and threw them down from the top of the cliff so that they were all dashed to pieces. 13 But the troops whom Amaziah sent back, *those* not going with him to battle, raided the cities of Judah from Samaria to Beth-horon, and struck and killed three thousand of them, and plundered a large amount of spoils.

Amaziah Rebuked for Idolatry

14 Now after Amaziah came from slaughtering the Edomites, he brought the gods of the sons of Seir and set them up as his gods. Then he bowed down before them and burned incense to them. 15 So the anger of the LORD burned against Amaziah, and He sent him a prophet who said to him, "Why have you sought the gods of the people who have not saved their own people from your hand?" 16 As he was talking with him, the king said to him, "Have we appointed you to be a royal counselor? Stop! Why should you be put to death?" Then the prophet stopped and said, "I know that God has planned to destroy you, because you have done this and have not listened to my counsel."

Amaziah Defeated by Joash of Israel

17 Then Amaziah king of Judah took counsel and sent *word* to Joash the son of Jehoahaz the son of Jehu, king of Israel, saying, "Come, let's face each other." 18 But Joash the king of Israel sent *a reply* to Amaziah king of Judah, saying, "The thorn bush that was in Lebanon sent *word* to the cedar that was in Lebanon, saying, 'Give your daughter to my son in marriage.' But a wild beast that was in Lebanon passed by and trampled the thorn bush. 19 You said, 'Behold, you have defeated Edom.' And your heart has lifted you up in boasting. Now stay home; why should you provoke trouble so that you, would fall, you and Judah with you?"

20 But Amaziah would not listen, for it was from God, so that He might hand them over *to Joash,* because they had sought the gods of Edom. 21 So Joash king of Israel went up, and he and Amaziah king of Judah faced each other at Beth-shemesh, which belonged to Judah. 22 And Judah was defeated by Israel, and they fled, every man to his tent. 23 Then Joash king of Israel captured Amaziah king of Judah, the son of Joash the son of Jehoahaz, at Beth-shemesh, and brought him to Jerusalem and tore down the wall of Jerusalem from the Gate of Ephraim to the Corner Gate, ¹four hundred cubits. 24 *He took* all the gold and silver and all the utensils which were found in the house of

God with Obed-edom, and the treasures of the king's house, the hostages too, and returned to Samaria.

25 And Amaziah, the son of Joash king of Judah, lived fifteen years after the death of Joash, son of Jehoahaz, king of Israel. 26 Now the rest of the acts of Amaziah, from the first to the last, behold, are they not written in the Book of the Kings of Judah and Israel? 27 From the time that Amaziah turned away from following the LORD they conspired against him in Jerusalem, and he fled to Lachish; but they sent *men* after him to Lachish, and they killed him there. 28 Then they brought him on horses and buried him with his fathers in the city of Judah.

Uzziah Succeeds Amaziah in Judah

26 Now all the people of Judah took Uzziah, who *was* sixteen years old, and made him king in place of his father Amaziah. 2 He built Eloth and restored it to Judah after the king ¹lay down with his fathers. 3 Uzziah was sixteen years old when he became king, and he reigned for fifty-two years in Jerusalem; and his mother's name was Jechiliah of Jerusalem. 4 He did what was right in the sight of the LORD, in accordance with everything that his father Amaziah had done. 5 He continued to seek God in the days of Zechariah, who had understanding through the vision of God; and as long as he sought the LORD, God made him successful.

Uzziah Succeeds in War

6 Now he went out and fought against the Philistines, and broke down the wall of Gath, the wall of Jabneh, and the wall of Ashdod; and he built cities in *the area of* Ashdod and among the Philistines. 7 God helped him against the Philistines, and against the Arabians who lived in Gur-baal, and the Meunites. 8 The Ammonites gave tribute to Uzziah, and his fame extended to the border of Egypt, for he became very strong. 9 Moreover, Uzziah built towers in Jerusalem at the Corner Gate, the Valley Gate, and at the corner buttress, and he fortified them. 10 He also built towers in the wilderness and carved out many cisterns, for he had much livestock, both in the lowland and in the plain. *He also had* plowmen and vinedressers in the hill country and the fertile fields, for he loved the soil. 11 Moreover, Uzziah had an army ready for battle, which entered combat by divisions according to the number of their muster, recorded by Jeiel the scribe and Maaseiah the official, under the direction of Hananiah, one of the king's officers. 12 The total number of the heads of the households, of valiant warriors, was 2,600. 13 Under their direction was an army of 307,500, who could wage war with great power, to help the king against the enemy. 14 Moreover, Uzziah prepared for all the army shields, spears, helmets, body armor, bows, and slingstones. 15 In Jerusalem he made machines *of war* invented by skillful workmen to be on the towers and the corners, for the purpose of shooting arrows and great stones. So his fame

---

25:23 ¹About 600 ft. or 183 m   26:2 ¹I.e., died

spread far, for he was marvelously helped until he *was* strong.

Pride Is Uzziah's Undoing

16 But when he became strong, his heart was so proud that he acted corruptly, and he was untrue to the LORD his God, for he entered the temple of the LORD to burn incense on the altar of incense. **17** Then Azariah the priest entered after him, and with him eighty priests of the LORD, valiant men. **18** They opposed Uzziah the king and said to him, "It is not for you, Uzziah, to burn incense to the LORD, but for the priests, the sons of Aaron who have been consecrated to burn incense. Leave the sanctuary, for you have been untrue and will have no honor from the LORD God." **19** But Uzziah, with a censer in his hand for burning incense, was enraged; and while he was enraged with the priests, leprosy broke out on his forehead in the presence of the priests in the house of the LORD, beside the altar of incense. **20** Azariah the chief priest and all the priests looked at him, and behold, he *was* leprous on his forehead; and they quickly removed him from there, and he himself also hurried to get out because the LORD had stricken him. **21** King Uzziah had leprosy to the day of his death; and he lived in a separate house, afflicted *as he was* with leprosy, for he was cut off from the house of the LORD. And his son Jotham *was* over the king's house, judging the people of the land.

22 Now the rest of the acts of Uzziah, the first to the last, the prophet Isaiah, the son of Amoz, has written. **23** So Uzziah [1] lay down with his fathers, and they buried him with his fathers in the field of the grave which belonged to the kings, for they said, "He had leprosy." And his son Jotham became king in his place.

Jotham Succeeds Uzziah in Judah

27 Jotham was twenty-five years old when he became king, and he reigned for sixteen years in Jerusalem. And his mother's name was Jerushah the daughter of Zadok. **2** He did what was right in the sight of the LORD, according to all that his father Uzziah had done; however he did not enter the temple of the LORD. But the people continued acting corruptly. **3** He built the upper gate of the house of the LORD, and he built the wall of Ophel extensively. **4** Moreover, he built cities in the hill country of Judah, and he built fortresses and towers on the wooded *hills.* **5** He fought with the king of the Ammonites and prevailed over them so that during that year the Ammonites gave him [1] a hundred talents of silver, [2] ten thousand kors of wheat, and ten thousand of barley. The Ammonites also paid him this *amount* in the second year and in the third. **6** So Jotham became powerful because he directed his ways before the LORD his God. **7** Now the rest of the acts of Jotham, all his wars and his ways, behold, they are written in the Book of the Kings of Israel and Judah. **8** He was twenty-five years old when he became king, and he reigned in Jerusalem for sixteen years. **9** And Jotham [1] lay down with his fathers, and they buried him in the city of David; and his son Ahaz became king in his place.

Ahaz Succeeds Jotham in Judah

28 Ahaz *was* twenty years old when he became king, and he reigned in Jerusalem for sixteen years. He did not do what was right in the sight of the LORD as his father David *had done.* **2** But he walked in the ways of the kings of Israel; he also made cast metal images for the Baals. **3** Furthermore, he burned incense in the Valley of Ben-hinnom, and burned his sons in fire, according to the abominations of the nations whom the LORD had driven out from the sons of Israel. **4** He sacrificed and burned incense on the high places, on the hills, and under every green tree.

Judah Is Invaded

5 Therefore the LORD his God handed him over to the king of Aram; and they defeated him and carried from him a great number of captives, and brought *them* to Damascus. And he was also handed over to the king of Israel, who struck him with heavy casualties. **6** For Pekah the son of Remaliah killed 120,000 in Judah in one day, all valiant men, because they had abandoned the LORD God of their fathers. **7** And Zichri, a mighty man of Ephraim, killed Maaseiah the king's son, Azrikam the ruler of the house, and Elkanah the second to the king. **8** The sons of Israel led away captive two hundred thousand of their relatives, women, sons, and daughters; and they also took a great deal of spoils from them, and brought the spoils to Samaria. **9** But a prophet of the LORD was there, whose name *was* Oded; and he went out to meet the army which came to Samaria and said to them, "Behold, because the LORD, the God of your fathers, was angry with Judah, He has handed them over to you, and you have killed them in a rage *which* has even reached heaven. **10** Now you are proposing to subjugate the people of Judah and Jerusalem as male and female slaves for yourselves. *Are* you not, however guilty yourselves of offenses against the LORD your God? **11** Now then, listen to me and return the captives whom you captured from your brothers, for the burning anger of the LORD is against you." **12** Then some of the leading men of the sons of Ephraim—Azariah the son of Johanan, Berechiah the son of Meshillemoth, Jehizkiah the son of Shallum, and Amasa the son of Hadlai—rose up against those who were coming from the battle, **13** and said to them, "You must not bring the captives in here, for you are proposing *to bring* guilt upon us before the LORD, adding to our sins and our guilt; for our guilt is great, and *His* burning anger is against Israel." **14** So the armed men left the captives and the spoils before the officers and all the assembly. **15** Then the men who were designated by name got up, took the captives, and they clothed all their naked people from the spoils; they gave them clothes and sandals, fed them and gave them drink, anointed them

---

26:23 [1] I.e., died   **27:5** [1] About 3.75 tons or 3.4 metric tons   [2] About 77,000 cubic feet or 2,180 cubic meters   **27:9** [1] I.e., died

with oil, led all their feeble ones on donkeys, and brought them to Jericho, the city of palm trees, to their brothers; then they returned to Samaria.

Compromise with Assyria

16 At that time King Ahaz sent *word* to the 'kings of Assyria for help. 17 For the Edomites had come again and attacked Judah, and led away captives. 18 The Philistines had also invaded the cities of the lowland and of the Negev of Judah, and had taken Beth-shemesh, Aijalon, Gederoth, and Soco with its villages, Timnah with its villages, and Gimzo with its villages; and they had settled there. 19 For the LORD had humbled Judah because of Ahaz king of Israel, for he had brought about a lack of restraint in Judah and was very unfaithful to the LORD. 20 So Tilgath-pilneser king of Assyria came against him and afflicted him instead of strengthening him. 21 Although Ahaz took a portion out of the house of the LORD and out of the palace of the king and of the princes, and gave *it* to the king of Assyria, it did not help him.

22 Now during the time of his distress, this same King Ahaz became even more unfaithful to the LORD. 23 For he sacrificed to the gods of Damascus who had defeated him, and said, "Because the gods of the kings of Aram helped them, I will sacrifice to them so that they may help me." But they became the downfall of him and all Israel. 24 Moreover, when Ahaz gathered together the utensils of the house of God, he cut the utensils of the house of God in pieces; and he closed the doors of the house of the LORD, and made altars for himself in every corner of Jerusalem. 25 In every city of Judah he made high places to burn incense to other gods, and provoked the LORD, the God of his fathers, to anger. 26 Now the rest of his acts and all his ways, from the first to the last, behold, they are written in the Book of the Kings of Judah and Israel. 27 So Ahaz 'lay down with his fathers, and they buried him in the city, in Jerusalem, for they did not bring him to the tombs of the kings of Israel; and his son Hezekiah reigned in his place.

Hezekiah Succeeds Ahaz in Judah

29 Hezekiah became king *when he was* twenty-five years old; and he reigned for twenty-nine years in Jerusalem. And his mother's name *was* Abijah, the daughter of Zechariah. 2 He did what was right in the sight of the LORD, in accordance with everything that his father David had done.

3 In the first year of his reign, in the first month, he opened the doors of the house of the LORD and repaired them. 4 He brought in the priests and the Levites and gathered them into the public square on the east.

Reforms Begun

5 Then he said to them, "Listen to me, you Levites. Consecrate yourselves now, and consecrate the house of the LORD, the God of your fathers, and carry the uncleanness out of the holy place. 6 For our fathers have been

unfaithful and have done evil in the sight of the LORD our God, and they have abandoned Him and turned their faces away from the dwelling place of the LORD, and have turned *their* backs. 7 They have also shut the doors of the porch and extinguished the lamps, and have not burned incense nor offered burnt offerings in the holy place to the God of Israel. 8 Therefore the wrath of the LORD was against Judah and Jerusalem, and He has made them an object of terror, of horror, and of hissing, as you see with your own eyes. 9 For behold, our fathers have fallen by the sword, and our sons, our daughters, and our wives are in captivity because of this. 10 Now it is in my heart to make a covenant with the LORD God of Israel, so that His burning anger may turn away from us. 11 My sons, do not be negligent now, for the LORD has chosen you to stand before Him, to serve Him, and to be His ministers and burn incense."

12 Then the Levites arose: Mahath the son of Amasai and Joel the son of Azariah, from the sons of the Kohathites; and from the sons of Merari, Kish the son of Abdi and Azariah the son of Jehallelel; and from the Gershonites, Joah the son of Zimmah and Eden the son of Joah; 13 and from the sons of Elizaphan, Shimri and Jeiel; and from the sons of Asaph, Zechariah and Mattaniah; 14 and from the sons of Heman, Jehiel and Shimei; and from the sons of Jeduthun, Shemaiah and Uzziel. 15 They assembled their brothers, consecrated themselves, and went in to cleanse the house of the LORD, according to the commandment of the king by the words of the LORD. 16 So the priests went into the inner part of the house of the LORD to cleanse *it,* and they brought every unclean thing which they found in the temple of the LORD out to the courtyard of the house of the LORD. Then the Levites received *it* to carry out to the Kidron Valley. 17 Now they began the consecration on the first *day* of the first month, and on the eighth day of the month they entered the porch of the LORD. Then they consecrated the house of the LORD in eight days, and finished on the sixteenth day of the first month. 18 Then they went in to King Hezekiah and said, "We have cleansed the whole house of the LORD, the altar of burnt offering with all its utensils, and the table of the showbread with all of its utensils. 19 Moreover, all the utensils which King Ahaz had discarded during his reign in his unfaithfulness, we have prepared and consecrated; and behold, they are before the altar of the LORD."

Hezekiah Restores Temple Worship

20 Then King Hezekiah got up early and assembled the princes of the city, and went up to the house of the LORD. 21 They brought seven bulls, seven rams, seven lambs, and seven male goats as a sin offering for the kingdom, the sanctuary, and Judah. And he ordered the priests, the sons of Aaron, to offer *them* on the altar of the LORD. 22 So they slaughtered the bulls, and the priests took the blood and sprinkled it on the altar. They also slaughtered the rams and sprinkled the blood on the altar; they

slaughtered the lambs as well, and sprinkled the blood on the altar. 23 Then they brought the male goats of the sin offering before the king and the assembly, and they laid their hands on them. 24 The priests slaughtered them and purified the altar with their blood to atone for all Israel, because the king ordered the burnt offering and the sin offering for all Israel.

25 He then stationed the Levites in the house of the LORD with cymbals, harps, and lyres, according to the command of David and of Gad, the king's seer, and of Nathan the prophet; for the command was from the LORD through His prophets. 26 The Levites stood with the *musical* instruments of David, and the priests with the trumpets. 27 Then Hezekiah gave the order to offer the burnt offering on the altar. When the burnt offering began, the song to the LORD *also* began with the trumpets, *accompanied* by the instruments of David, king of Israel. 28 While the whole assembly worshiped, the singers also sang and the trumpets sounded; all this *continued* until the burnt offering was finished.

29 Now at the completion of the burnt offerings, the king and all who were present with him bowed down and worshiped. 30 Moreover, King Hezekiah and the officials ordered the Levites to sing praises to the LORD with the words of David and Asaph the seer. So they sang praises with joy, and bowed down and worshiped.

31 Then Hezekiah said, "Now *that* you have consecrated yourselves to the LORD, come forward and bring sacrifices and thanksgiving offerings to the house of the LORD." So the assembly brought sacrifices and thanksgiving offerings, and everyone who was willing *brought* burnt offerings. 32 The number of the burnt offerings which the assembly brought was seventy bulls, a hundred rams, and two hundred lambs; all of these were for a burnt offering to the LORD. 33 The consecrated *offerings* were six hundred bulls and three thousand sheep. 34 But the priests were too few, so that they were unable to skin all the burnt offerings; therefore their brothers the Levites helped them until the work was finished and the *other* priests had consecrated themselves. For the Levites were more conscientious to consecrate themselves than the priests. 35 There *were* also many burnt offerings with the fat of the peace offerings and the drink offerings for the burnt offerings. So the service of the house of the LORD was established *again*. 36 Then Hezekiah and all the people rejoiced over what God had prepared for the people, because the thing came about suddenly.

All Israel Invited to the Passover

30 Now Hezekiah sent *word* to all Israel and Judah and also wrote letters to Ephraim and Manasseh, that they should come to the house of the LORD in Jerusalem to celebrate the Passover to the LORD God of Israel. 2 For the king and his princes and all the assembly in Jerusalem had decided to celebrate the Passover in the second month, 3 since they could not celebrate it at that time, because

the priests had not consecrated themselves in sufficient numbers, nor had the people been gathered to Jerusalem. 4 So the decision was right in the sight of the king and all the assembly. 5 So they established a decree to circulate a proclamation throughout Israel from Beersheba to Dan, that they are to come to celebrate the Passover to the LORD God of Israel in Jerusalem. For they had not celebrated *it* in great numbers as was written. 6 The couriers went throughout Israel and Judah with the letters from the hand of the king and his princes, even according to the command of the king, saying, "Sons of Israel, return to the LORD God of Abraham, Isaac, and Israel, that He may return to those of you who escaped *and* are left from the hand of the kings of Assyria. 7 Do not be like your fathers and your brothers, who were untrue to the LORD God of their fathers, so that He made them an object of horror, just as you see. 8 Now do not stiffen your neck like your fathers, *but* yield to the LORD and enter His sanctuary which He has consecrated forever, and serve the LORD your God, that His burning anger may turn away from you. 9 For if you return to the LORD, your brothers and your sons *will find* compassion in the presence of those who led them captive, and will return to this land. For the LORD your God is gracious and compassionate, and will not turn *His* face away from you if you return to Him."

10 So the couriers passed from city to city through the country of Ephraim and Manasseh, and as far as Zebulun, but they laughed at them with scorn and mocked them. 11 Nevertheless, some men of Asher, Manasseh, and Zebulun humbled themselves and came to Jerusalem. 12 The hand of God was also on Judah to give them one heart to do what the king and the princes commanded by the word of the LORD.

Passover Reinstituted

13 Now many people were gathered at Jerusalem to celebrate the Feast of Unleavened Bread in the second month, a very large assembly. 14 They got up and removed the altars which *were* in Jerusalem; they also removed all the incense altars and threw *them* into the brook Kidron. 15 Then they slaughtered the Passover *lambs* on the fourteenth of the second month. And the priests and Levites were ashamed of themselves, and consecrated themselves and brought burnt offerings to the house of the LORD. 16 They stood at their stations following their custom, according to the Law of Moses the man of God; the priests sprinkled the blood *which they received* from the hand of the Levites. 17 For *there were* many in the assembly who had not consecrated themselves; therefore, the Levites *were* in charge of the slaughter of the Passover *lambs* for everyone who *was* unclean, in order to consecrate *them* to the LORD. 18 For a multitude of the people, many from Ephraim and Manasseh, *and* Issachar and Zebulun, had not purified themselves, yet they ate the Passover contrary to *what was* written. For Hezekiah prayed for them, saying, "May the good LORD pardon 19 everyone who prepares his heart to seek God, the LORD God of his fathers, though

not according to the purification *rules* of the sanctuary." 20 So the LORD heard Hezekiah and healed the people. 21 The sons of Israel present in Jerusalem celebrated the Feast of Unleavened Bread for seven days with great joy, and the Levites and the priests were praising the LORD day after day with loud instruments to the LORD. 22 Then Hezekiah spoke encouragingly to all the Levites who showed good insight *in the things* of the LORD. So they ate for the appointed seven days, sacrificing peace offerings and giving thanks to the LORD God of their fathers.

23 Then the whole assembly decided to celebrate *the feast* another seven days, so they celebrated the seven days with joy. 24 For Hezekiah king of Judah had contributed to the assembly a thousand bulls and seven thousand sheep, and the princes had contributed to the assembly a thousand bulls and ten thousand sheep; and a large number of priests consecrated themselves. 25 All the assembly of Judah rejoiced, with the priests and the Levites and all the assembly that came from Israel, both the strangers who came from the land of Israel and those living in Judah. 26 So there was great joy in Jerusalem, because there was nothing like this in Jerusalem since the days of Solomon the son of David, king of Israel. 27 Then the Levitical priests stood and blessed the people; and their voice was heard and their prayer came to His holy dwelling place, to heaven.

Idols Are Destroyed

31 Now when all this was finished, all Israel who were present went out to the cities of Judah, broke the memorial stones in pieces, cut down the *Asherim and pulled down the high places and the altars throughout Judah and Benjamin, as well as in Ephraim and Manasseh, until they had destroyed them all. Then all the sons of Israel returned to their cities, each to his possession.

2 And Hezekiah appointed the divisions of the priests and the Levites by their divisions, each according to his service, *both* the priests and the Levites, for burnt offerings and for peace offerings, to serve and to give thanks and to praise in the gates of the camp of the LORD.

Reforms Continued

3 *He* also *appointed* the king's portion of his property for the burnt offerings, *namely,* for the morning and evening burnt offerings, and the burnt offerings for the Sabbaths and for the new moons and for the appointed festivals, as it is written in the Law of the LORD. 4 Also he told the people who lived in Jerusalem to give the portion due to the priests and the Levites, so that they might devote themselves to the Law of the LORD. 5 As soon as the order spread, the sons of Israel abundantly provided the first fruits of grain, new wine, oil, honey, and of all the produce of the field; and they brought in abundantly the tithe of everything. 6 The sons of Israel and Judah who lived in the cities of Judah also brought in the tithe of oxen and sheep, and the tithe of sacred gifts which were

consecrated to the LORD their God, and placed *them* in heaps. 7 In the third month they began to make the heaps, and they finished *them* by the seventh month. 8 When Hezekiah and the rulers came and saw the heaps, they blessed the LORD and His people Israel. 9 Then Hezekiah questioned the priests and the Levites concerning the heaps. 10 Azariah, the chief priest of the house of Zadok, said to him, "Since the contributions started coming into the house of the LORD, we have had enough to eat with plenty left over, for the LORD has blessed His people, and this great quantity is left over."

11 Then Hezekiah commanded *them* to prepare rooms in the house of the LORD, and they prepared *them*. 12 They faithfully brought in the contributions, the tithes, and the consecrated things; and Conaniah the Levite *was* the officer in charge of them, and his brother Shimei *was* second. 13 Jehiel, Azaziah, Nahath, Asahel, Jerimoth, Jozabad, Eliel, Ismachiah, Mahath, and Benaiah *were* overseers under the authority of Conaniah and his brother Shimei by the appointment of King Hezekiah, and Azariah *was* the *chief* officer of the house of God. 14 Kore the son of Imnah the Levite, the keeper of the eastern *gate, was* in charge of the voluntary offerings for God, to distribute the contributions for the LORD and the most holy things. 15 Under his authority *were* Eden, Miniamin, Jeshua, Shemaiah, Amariah, and Shecaniah, in the cities of the priests, to distribute *their portions* faithfully to their brothers by divisions, whether great or small, 16 without regard to their genealogical enrollment, to the males from thirty years old and upward—everyone who entered the house of the LORD for his daily obligations—for their work in their duties according to their divisions; 17 as well as the priests who were enrolled genealogically according to their fathers' households, and the Levites from twenty years old and upward, by their duties *and* their divisions. 18 The genealogical enrollment *included* all their little children, their wives, their sons, and their daughters, for the whole assembly, for they consecrated themselves faithfully in holiness. 19 Also for the sons of Aaron, the priests, *who were* in the pasture lands of their cities, *or* in each and every city, *there were* men who were designated by name to distribute portions to every male among the priests and to everyone genealogically enrolled among the Levites.

20 Hezekiah did this throughout Judah; and he did what *was* good, right, and true before the LORD his God. 21 Every work which he began in the service of the house of God in the Law and in the commandment, seeking his God, he did with all his heart and prospered.

Sennacherib Invades Judah

32 After these acts of faithfulness Sennacherib king of Assyria came and invaded Judah and besieged the fortified cities, and intended to break into them for himself. 2 Now when Hezekiah saw that Sennacherib

---

31:1 1 I.e., wooden symbols of a female deity (Asherah)

had come and that he intended to *wage* war against Jerusalem, 3 he decided with his officers and his warriors to cut off the *supply of* water from the springs which *were* outside the city, and they helped him. 4 So many people assembled and stopped up all the springs and the stream which flowed through the region, saying, "Why should the kings of Assyria come and find abundant water?" 5 And he resolutely set to work and rebuilt all of the wall that had been broken down and erected towers on it, and *built* another outside wall and strengthened the *¹*Millo *in* the city of David, and made weapons and shields in great numbers. 6 He appointed military officers over the people and gathered them to him in the public square at the city gate, and spoke encouragingly to them, saying, 7 "Be strong and courageous, do not fear or be dismayed because of the king of Assyria nor because of all the horde that is with him; for *the One* with us is greater than *the one* with him. 8 With him is *only* an arm of flesh, but with us is the Lord our God to help us and to fight our battles." And the people relied on the words of Hezekiah king of Judah.

Sennacherib Undermines Hezekiah

9 After this Sennacherib king of Assyria sent his servants to Jerusalem while he *was* besieging Lachish with all his forces with him, against Hezekiah king of Judah and against all of Judah who *were* in Jerusalem, saying, 10 "This is what Sennacherib king of Assyria says: 'On what are you trusting that you are staying in Jerusalem under siege? 11 Is Hezekiah not misleading you to give yourselves over to die by hunger and by thirst, saying, "The Lord our God will save us from the hand of the king of Assyria"? 12 Is it not the same Hezekiah who removed His high places and His altars, and said to Judah and Jerusalem, "You shall worship before one altar, and on it you shall burn incense"? 13 Do you not know what I and my fathers have done to all the peoples of the lands? Were the gods of the nations of those lands at all able to save their land from my hand? 14 Who *was there* among all the gods of those nations which my fathers utterly destroyed who could save his people from my hand, that your God would be able to save you from my hand? 15 Now then, do not let Hezekiah deceive you or mislead you like this, and do not believe him, for no god of any nation or kingdom was able to save his people from my hand or from the hand of my fathers. How much less will your God save you from my hand?'" 16 His servants spoke further against the Lord God and against His servant Hezekiah. 17 He also wrote letters to insult the Lord God of Israel, and to speak against Him, saying, "As the gods of the nations of the lands have not saved their people from my hand, so the God of Hezekiah will not save His people from my hand." 18 They called *this* out with a loud voice in the language of Judah to the people of Jerusalem who were on the wall, to frighten and terrify them, so that they might take the city. 19 They spoke of the God of Jerusalem as *they did* against the gods of the peoples of the earth, the work of human hands.

Hezekiah's Prayer Is Answered

20 But King Hezekiah and Isaiah the prophet, the son of Amoz, prayed about this and called out to heaven for help. 21 And the Lord sent an angel who destroyed every warrior, commander, and officer in the camp of the king of Assyria. So he returned in shame to his own land. And when he had entered the temple of his god, some of his own sons killed him there with the sword. 22 So the Lord saved Hezekiah and the inhabitants of Jerusalem from the hand of Sennacherib the king of Assyria and from the hand of all *others,* and guided them on every side. 23 And many were bringing gifts to the Lord at Jerusalem and valuable presents to Hezekiah king of Judah; so thereafter he rose in the sight of all nations.

24 In those days Hezekiah became mortally ill; and he prayed to the Lord, and the Lord spoke to him and gave him a sign. 25 But Hezekiah did nothing in return for the benefit he received, because his heart was proud; therefore wrath came upon him and upon Judah and Jerusalem. 26 However, Hezekiah humbled the pride of his heart, both he and the inhabitants of Jerusalem, so that the wrath of the Lord did not come on them in the days of Hezekiah.

27 Now Hezekiah had immense riches and honor; and he made for himself treasuries for silver, gold, precious stones, spices, shields, and all kinds of valuable articles, 28 also storehouses for the produce of grain, wine, and oil; stalls for all kinds of cattle, and sheepfolds for the flocks. 29 He made cities for himself and acquired flocks and herds in abundance, because God had given him very great wealth. 30 It was Hezekiah who stopped the upper outlet of the waters of Gihon and directed them to the west side of the city of David. And Hezekiah was successful in everything that he did. 31 Even *in the matter of* the messengers of the rulers of Babylon, who were sent to him to inquire about the wonder that had happened in the land; God left him alone *only* to test him, so that He might know everything that was in his heart.

32 Now the rest of the acts of Hezekiah and his deeds of devotion, behold, they are written in the vision of Isaiah the prophet, the son of Amoz, in the Book of the Kings of Judah and Israel. 33 So Hezekiah *¹*lay down with his fathers, and they buried him in the upper section of the tombs of the sons of David; and all Judah and the inhabitants of Jerusalem honored him at his death. And his son Manasseh became king in his place.

Manasseh Succeeds Hezekiah in Judah

33 Manasseh was twelve years old when he became king, and he reigned for fifty-five years in Jerusalem. 2 He did evil in the sight of the Lord according to the abominations of the nations whom the Lord dispossessed before the sons of Israel. 3 For he rebuilt the high

---

32:5 ¹I.e., terraced structure   32:33 ¹I.e., died

places which his father Hezekiah had torn down; he also set up altars for the Baals and made ⁷Asherim, and he worshiped all the heavenly lights and served them. 4 He built altars in the house of the LORD of which the LORD had said, "My name shall be in Jerusalem forever." 5 He built altars for all the heavenly lights in the two courtyards of the house of the LORD. 6 He also made his sons pass through the fire in the Valley of Ben-hinnom; and he practiced witchcraft, used divination, practiced sorcery, and dealt with mediums and spiritists. He did much evil in the sight of the LORD, provoking Him to anger. 7 Then he put the carved image of the idol which he had made in the house of God, of which God had said to David and his son Solomon, "In this house and in Jerusalem, which I have chosen from all the tribes of Israel, I will put My name forever; 8 and I will not remove the foot of Israel again from the land which I have appointed for your fathers, if only they will take care to do everything that I have commanded them according to all the Law, the statutes, and the ordinances *given* through Moses." 9 So Manasseh encouraged Judah and the inhabitants of Jerusalem to do more evil than the nations whom the LORD destroyed before the sons of Israel.

Manasseh's Idolatry Rebuked

10 So the LORD spoke to Manasseh and his people, but they paid no attention. 11 Therefore the LORD brought the commanders of the army of the king of Assyria against them, and they captured Manasseh with hooks, bound him with bronze *chains,* and led him to Babylon. 12 When he was in distress, he appeased the LORD his God and humbled himself greatly before the God of his fathers. 13 When he prayed to Him, He was moved by him and heard his pleading, and brought him back to Jerusalem to his kingdom. Then Manasseh knew that the LORD *alone is* God.

14 Now after this he built the outer wall of the city of David on the west side of Gihon, in the valley, up to the entrance of the Fish Gate; and he encircled the Ophel *with it* and made it very high. Then he put army commanders in all the fortified cities in Judah. 15 He also removed the foreign gods and the idol from the house of the LORD, as well as all the altars which he had built on the mountain of the house of the LORD and in Jerusalem, and he threw *them* outside the city. 16 He set up the altar of the LORD and sacrificed peace offerings and thanksgiving offerings on it; and he ordered Judah to serve the LORD God of Israel. 17 However, the people still sacrificed on the high places, *although* only to the LORD their God.

18 Now the rest of the acts of Manasseh and his prayer to his God, and the words of the seers who spoke to him in the name of the LORD God of Israel, behold, they are among the records of the kings of Israel. 19 His prayer also and *how God* was moved by him, and all his sin, his unfaithfulness, and the sites on which he built high places and erected the ⁷Asherim and the carved images, before he humbled himself, behold, they are written in the records of ²Hozai. 20 So Manasseh ⁷lay down with his fathers, and they buried him in his own house. And his son Amon became king in his place.

Amon Becomes King in Judah

21 Amon *was* twenty-two years old when he became king, and he reigned for two years in Jerusalem. 22 He did evil in the sight of the LORD, just as his father Manasseh had done, and Amon sacrificed to all the carved images which his father Manasseh had made, and he served them. 23 Furthermore, he did not humble himself before the LORD as his father Manasseh had done, but Amon multiplied *his* guilt. 24 Finally, his servants conspired against him and put him to death in his own house. 25 But the people of the land killed all the conspirators against King Amon, and the people of the land made his son Josiah king in his place.

Josiah Succeeds Amon in Judah

34 Josiah *was* eight years old when he became king, and he reigned for thirty-one years in Jerusalem. 2 He did what was right in the sight of the LORD, and walked in the ways of his father David and did not turn aside to the right or the left. 3 For in the eighth year of his reign while he was still a youth, he began to seek the God of his father David; and in the twelfth year he began to purge Judah and Jerusalem of the high places, the ⁷Asherim, the carved images, and the cast metal images. 4 They tore down the altars of the Baals in his presence, and he chopped down the incense altars that were high above them; also he broke in pieces the Asherim, the carved images, and the cast metal images, and ground *them* to powder, and scattered *it* on the graves of those who had sacrificed to them. 5 Then he burned the bones of the priests on their altars and purged Judah and Jerusalem. 6 In the cities of Manasseh, Ephraim, Simeon, and as far as Naphtali, in their surrounding spaces, 7 he also tore down the altars and crushed the Asherim and the carved images into powder, and chopped down all the incense altars throughout the land of Israel. Then he returned to Jerusalem.

Josiah Repairs the Temple

8 Now in the eighteenth year of his reign, when he had purged the land and the house, he sent Shaphan the son of Azaliah, Maaseiah an official of the city, and Joah the son of Joahaz the secretary, to repair the house of the LORD his God. 9 They came to Hilkiah the high priest and gave him the money that was brought into the house of God, which the Levites, the doorkeepers, had collected from Manasseh and Ephraim, and from all the remnant of Israel, from all Judah and Benjamin and the inhabitants of Jerusalem. 10 Then they handed it over to the workmen who had the oversight of the house of the LORD, and the workmen who were working in the house of

---

33:3 ¹I.e., wooden symbols of a female deity (Asherah)   33:19 ¹I.e., wooden symbols of a female deity (Asherah)   ²LXX *seers*   33:20 ¹I.e., died   34:3 ¹I.e., wooden symbols of a female deity (Asherah)

the LORD used it to restore and repair the house. 11 They in turn gave *it* to the carpenters and the builders to buy quarried stone and timber for couplings, and to make beams for the houses which the kings of Judah had let go to ruin. 12 The men did the work faithfully with foremen over them to supervise: Jahath and Obadiah, the Levites of the sons of Merari, Zechariah and Meshullam of the sons of the Kohathites, and the Levites, all who were skillful with musical instruments. 13 *They were* also in charge of the burden bearers, and supervised all the workmen from job to job; and some of the Levites *were* scribes, and officials, and gatekeepers.

Hilkiah Discovers the Lost Book of the Law

14 When they were bringing out the money which had been brought into the house of the LORD, Hilkiah the priest found the Book of the Law of the LORD *given* by Moses. 15 Hilkiah responded and said to Shaphan the scribe, "I have found the Book of the Law in the house of the LORD." And Hilkiah gave the book to Shaphan. 16 Then Shaphan brought the book to the king and reported further word to the king, saying, "Everything that was entrusted to your servants, they are doing. 17 They have also emptied out the money which was found in the house of the LORD, and have handed it over to the supervisors and the workmen." 18 Moreover, Shaphan the scribe informed the king, saying, "Hilkiah the priest gave me a book." And Shaphan read from it in the presence of the king.

19 When the king heard the words of the Law, he tore his clothes. 20 Then the king commanded Hilkiah, Ahikam the son of Shaphan, Abdon the son of Micah, Shaphan the scribe, and Asaiah the king's servant, saying, 21 "Go, inquire of the LORD for me and for those who are left in Israel and Judah, concerning the words of the book which has been found; for the wrath of the LORD which has poured out on us is great, because our fathers have not kept the word of the LORD, to act in accordance with everything that is written in this book."

Huldah, the Prophetess, Speaks

22 So Hilkiah and *those* whom the king had told went to Huldah the prophetess, the wife of Shallum the son of Tokhath, the son of Hasrah, the keeper of the wardrobe (she lived in Jerusalem in the Second Quarter); and they spoke to her regarding this. 23 Then she said to them, "This is what the LORD, the God of Israel says: 'Tell the man who sent you to Me, 24 this is what the LORD says: "Behold, I am bringing evil on this place and on its inhabitants, all the curses written in the book which they have read in the presence of the king of Judah. 25 Since they have abandoned Me and have burned incense to other gods, so that they may provoke Me to anger with all the works of their hands, My wrath will be poured out on this place and it will not be quenched." ' 26 But to the king of Judah who sent you to inquire of the LORD, this is what you shall say to him: 'This is what the LORD, the God of Israel says:

In regard to the words which you have heard, 27 "Because your heart was tender and you humbled yourself before God when you heard His words against this place and its inhabitants, and *because* you humbled yourself before Me, tore your clothes, and wept before Me, I have indeed heard you," declares the LORD. 28 "Behold, I will gather you to your fathers, and you will be gathered to your grave in peace, so your eyes will not see all the evil which I am bringing on this place and its inhabitants." ' " And they brought back word to the king.

29 Then the king sent *word* and gathered all the elders of Judah and Jerusalem. 30 The king went up to the house of the LORD with all the men of Judah, the inhabitants of Jerusalem, the priests, the Levites, and all the people, from the greatest to the least; and he read in their presence all the words of the Book of the Covenant which was found in the house of the LORD.

Josiah's Good Reign

31 Then the king stood in his place and made a covenant before the LORD to walk after the LORD, and to keep His commandments, His testimonies, and His statutes with all his heart and with all his soul, to perform the words of the covenant that are written in this book. 32 Furthermore, he made all who were present in Jerusalem and Benjamin stand *with him.* So the inhabitants of Jerusalem acted in accordance with the covenant of God, the God of their fathers. 33 Josiah removed all the abominations from all the lands belonging to the sons of Israel, and made all who were present in Israel serve the LORD their God. Throughout his lifetime they did not turn from following the LORD God of their fathers.

The Passover Held Again

35 Then Josiah celebrated the Passover to the LORD in Jerusalem, and they slaughtered the Passover *animals* on the fourteenth *day* of the first month. 2 He appointed the priests to their offices and encouraged them in the service of the house of the LORD. 3 He also said to the Levites who taught all Israel *and* who were holy to the LORD, "Put the holy ark in the house which Solomon the son of David king of Israel built; it will not be a burden on *your* shoulders. Now serve the LORD your God and His people Israel. 4 Prepare *yourselves* by your fathers' households in your divisions, according to the writing of David king of Israel and according to the writing of his son Solomon. 5 Furthermore, stand in the holy place according to the sections of the fathers' households of your countrymen, the lay people, and according to the Levites, by division of a father's household. 6 Now slaughter the Passover *animals,* keep one another consecrated, and prepare for your countrymen to act in accordance with the word of the LORD by Moses."

7 Josiah contributed to the lay people, to all who were present, flocks of lambs and young goats, all for the Passover offerings, numbering thirty thousand, plus three thousand bulls;

these were from the king's property. 8 His officers also contributed a voluntary offering to the people, the priests, and the Levites. Hilkiah, Zechariah, and Jehiel, the officials of the house of God, gave the priests 2,600 *from the flocks* and three hundred bulls, for the Passover offerings. 9 Conaniah also, and his brothers Shemaiah and Nethanel, and Hashabiah and Jeiel and Jozabad, the officers of the Levites, contributed five thousand *from the flocks* and five hundred bulls to the Levites for the Passover offerings.

10 So the service was prepared, and the priests stood at their positions and the Levites by their divisions according to the king's command. 11 They slaughtered the Passover *animals,* and while the priests sprinkled the blood *received* from their hand, the Levites skinned *the animals.* 12 Then they removed the burnt offerings so that *they* might give them to the sections of the fathers' households of the lay people to present to the LORD, as it is written in the Book of Moses. *They did* this with the bulls as well. 13 So they roasted the Passover *animals* on the fire according to the ordinance, and they boiled the holy things in pots, in kettles, and in pans and carried *them* quickly to all the lay people. 14 Afterward they prepared for themselves and for the priests, because the priests, the sons of Aaron, *were* offering the burnt offerings and the fat until night; so the Levites prepared for themselves and for the priests, the sons of Aaron. 15 The singers, the sons of Asaph, *were* also at their positions according to the command of David, Asaph, Heman, and Jeduthun the king's seer; and the gatekeepers at each gate did not have to leave their service, because their kinsmen the Levites prepared for them.

16 So all the service of the LORD was prepared on that day to celebrate the Passover, and to offer burnt offerings on the altar of the LORD according to the command of King Josiah. 17 And the sons of Israel who were present celebrated the Passover at that time, and the Feast of Unleavened Bread for seven days. 18 There had not been a Passover celebrated like it in Israel since the days of Samuel the prophet; nor had any of the kings of Israel celebrated such a Passover as Josiah did with the priests, the Levites, all Judah and Israel who were present, and the inhabitants of Jerusalem. 19 In the eighteenth year of Josiah's reign this Passover was celebrated.

Josiah Dies in Battle

20 After all this, when Josiah had set the temple in order, Neco king of Egypt came up to wage war at Carchemish on the Euphrates, and Josiah went out to engage him. 21 But Neco sent messengers to him, saying, "What business do you have with me, King of Judah? *I am* not *coming* against you today, but against the house with which I am at war, and God has told me to hurry. For your own sake, stop *interfering with* God who is with me, so that He does not destroy you." 22 However, Josiah would not turn away from him, but disguised

himself in order to fight against him; nor did he listen to the words of Neco from the mouth of God, but he came to wage war on the plain of Megiddo. 23 The archers shot King Josiah, and the king said to his servants, "Take me away, for I am badly wounded." 24 So his servants took him out of the chariot and carried him on the second chariot which he had, and brought him to Jerusalem where he died and was buried in the tombs of his fathers. All Judah and Jerusalem mourned for Josiah. 25 Then Jeremiah chanted a song of mourning for Josiah. And all the male and female singers speak about Josiah in their songs of mourning to this day. And they made them an ordinance in Israel; behold, they are also written in the Lamentations. 26 Now the rest of the acts of Josiah and his deeds of devotion as written in the Law of the LORD, 27 and his acts, the first to the last, behold, they are written in the Book of the Kings of Israel and Judah.

Joahaz, Jehoiakim, Then Jehoiachin Rule

36 Then the people of the land took [1]Joahaz the son of Josiah and made him king in place of his father in Jerusalem. 2 Joahaz was twenty-three years old when he became king, and he reigned for three months in Jerusalem. 3 Then the king of Egypt deposed him in Jerusalem, and imposed a fine on the land of [1]a hundred talents of silver and [2]one talent of gold. 4 The king of Egypt made Joahaz's brother Eliakim king over Judah and Jerusalem, and changed his name to Jehoiakim. But Neco took his brother Joahaz and brought him to Egypt.

5 Jehoiakim was twenty-five years old when he became king, and he reigned for eleven years in Jerusalem; and he did evil in the sight of the LORD his God. 6 Nebuchadnezzar king of Babylon came up against him and bound him with bronze *chains* to take him to Babylon. 7 Nebuchadnezzar also brought *some* of the articles of the house of the LORD to Babylon, and he put them in his temple in Babylon. 8 Now the rest of the acts of Jehoiakim and the abominations which he committed, and what was found against him, behold, they are written in the Book of the Kings of Israel and Judah. And his son Jehoiachin became king in his place.

9 Jehoiachin was [1]eighteen years old when he became king, and he reigned for three months and ten days in Jerusalem. He did evil in the sight of the LORD.

Captivity in Babylon Begun

10 At the turn of the year King Nebuchadnezzar sent *men* and had him brought to Babylon with the valuable articles of the house of the LORD; and he made his relative Zedekiah king over Judah and Jerusalem.

Zedekiah Rules in Judah

11 Zedekiah was twenty-one years old when he became king, and he reigned for eleven years in Jerusalem. 12 He did evil in the sight of the LORD his God; he did not humble himself

---

36:1 1 I.e., short form of Jehoahaz   **36:3** 1 About 3.75 tons or 3.4 metric tons   2 About 75 lb. or 34 kg
36:9 1 As in LXX and some Heb mss; MT *eight years*

before Jeremiah the prophet who spoke for the Lord. 13 He also rebelled against King Nebuchadnezzar, who had made him swear *allegiance* by God. But he stiffened his neck and hardened his heart against turning to the Lord God of Israel. 14 Furthermore, all the officials of the priests and the people were very unfaithful, *following* all the abominations of the nations; and they defiled the house of the Lord which He had sanctified in Jerusalem.

15 Yet the Lord, the God of their fathers, sent *word* to them again and again by His messengers, because He had compassion on His people and on His dwelling place; 16 but they *continually* mocked the messengers of God, despised His words, and scoffed at His prophets, until the wrath of the Lord rose against His people, until there was no remedy. 17 So He brought up against them the king of the Chaldeans, who killed their young men with the sword in the house of their sanctuary, and had no compassion on young man or virgin, old man or frail; He handed *them* all over to him. 18 He brought all the articles of the house of God, great and small, and the treasures of the house of the Lord, and the treasures of the king and his officers, to Babylon.

19 Then they burned the house of God and broke down the wall of Jerusalem, and burned all its fortified buildings with fire and destroyed all its valuable articles. 20 He took into exile those who had escaped from the sword to Babylon; and they were servants to him and to his sons until the rule of the kingdom of Persia, 21 to fulfill the word of the Lord by the mouth of Jeremiah, until the land had enjoyed its Sabbaths. All the days of its desolation it kept the Sabbath until seventy years were complete.

Cyrus Permits Return

22 Now in the first year of Cyrus king of Persia—in order to fulfill the word of the Lord by the mouth of Jeremiah—the Lord stirred up the spirit of Cyrus king of Persia so that he sent a proclamation throughout his kingdom, and also *put it* in writing, saying, 23 "This is what Cyrus king of Persia says: 'The Lord, the God of heaven, has given me all the kingdoms of the earth, and He has appointed me to build Him a house in Jerusalem, which is in Judah. Whoever there is among you of all His people, may the Lord his God be with him; ¹go up then!' "

36:23 1 Lit *and he is to go up;* i.e., go to Jerusalem

The Book of
EZRA

Cyrus' Proclamation

1 Now in the first year of Cyrus king of Persia, in order to fulfill the word of the LORD by the mouth of Jeremiah, the LORD stirred up the spirit of Cyrus king of Persia, so that he sent a proclamation throughout his kingdom, and also *put it* in writing, saying: 2 "This is what Cyrus king of Persia says: 'The LORD, the God of heaven, has given me all the kingdoms of the earth, and He has appointed me to rebuild for Him a house in Jerusalem, which is in Judah. 3 Whoever there is among you of all His people, may his God be with him! Go up to Jerusalem which is in Judah and rebuild the house of the LORD, the God of Israel; He is the God who is in Jerusalem. 4 And every survivor, at whatever place he may live, the people of that place are to support him with silver and gold, with equipment and cattle, together with a voluntary offering for the house of God which is in Jerusalem.' "

Holy Vessels Restored

5 Then the heads of fathers' *households* of Judah and Benjamin and the priests and the Levites rose up, everyone whose spirit God had stirred to go up to rebuild the house of the LORD which is in Jerusalem. 6 And all of those around them encouraged them with articles of silver, with gold, with equipment, cattle, and with valuables, aside from everything that was given as a voluntary offering. 7 Also King Cyrus brought out the articles of the house of the LORD, which Nebuchadnezzar had carried away from Jerusalem and put in the house of his gods; 8 and Cyrus, king of Persia, had them brought out by the hand of Mithredath the treasurer, and he counted them out to Sheshbazzar, the leader of Judah. 9 Now this *was* their number: thirty gold dishes, a thousand silver dishes, twenty nine duplicates; 10 thirty gold bowls, 410 silver bowls of a second *kind, and* a thousand other articles. 11 All the articles of gold and silver *totaled* 5,400. Sheshbazzar brought them all up with the exiles who went up from Babylon to Jerusalem.

Number of Those Returning

2 Now these are the people of the province who came up out of the captivity of the exiles whom Nebuchadnezzar the king of Babylon had taken into exile to Babylon, and they returned to Jerusalem and Judah, each to his city. 2 These came with Zerubbabel, Jeshua, Nehemiah, Seraiah, Reelaiah, Mordecai, Bilshan, Mispar, Bigvai, Rehum, *and* Baanah.

This is the number of the men of the people of Israel: 3 the sons of Parosh, 2,172; 4 the sons of Shephatiah, 372; 5 the sons of Arah, 775; 6 the sons of Pahath-moab of the sons of Jeshua *and* Joab, 2,812; 7 the sons of Elam, 1,254; 8 the sons of Zattu, 945; 9 the sons of Zaccai, 760;

10 the sons of Bani, 642; 11 the sons of Bebai, 623; 12 the sons of Azgad, 1,222; 13 the sons of Adonikam, 666; 14 the sons of Bigvai, 2,056; 15 the sons of Adin, 454; 16 the sons of Ater, of Hezekiah, 98; 17 the sons of Bezai, 323; 18 the sons of Jorah, 112; 19 the sons of Hashum, 223; 20 the sons of Gibbar, 95; 21 the men of Bethlehem, 123; 22 the men of Netophah, 56; 23 the men of Anathoth, 128; 24 the sons of Azmaveth, 42; 25 the sons of Kiriath-arim, Chephirah, and Beeroth, 743; 26 the sons of Ramah and Geba, 621; 27 the men of Michmas, 122; 28 the men of Bethel and Ai, 223; 29 the sons of Nebo, 52; 30 the sons of Magbish, 156; 31 the sons of the other Elam, 1,254; 32 the sons of Harim, 320; 33 the sons of Lod, Hadid, and Ono, 725; 34 the men of Jericho, 345; 35 the sons of Senaah, 3,630.

Priests Returning

36 The priests: the sons of Jedaiah of the house of Jeshua, 973; 37 the sons of Immer, 1,052; 38 the sons of Pashhur, 1,247; 39 the sons of Harim, 1,017.

Levites Returning

40 The Levites: the sons of Jeshua and Kadmiel, of the sons of Hodaviah, 74. 41 The singers: the sons of Asaph, 128. 42 The sons of the gatekeepers: the sons of Shallum, the sons of Ater, the sons of Talmon, the sons of Akkub, the sons of Hatita, *and* the sons of Shobai, 139 in all.

43 The temple servants: the sons of Ziha, the sons of Hasupha, the sons of Tabbaoth, 44 the sons of Keros, the sons of Siaha, the sons of Padon, 45 the sons of Lebanah, the sons of Hagabah, the sons of Akkub, 46 the sons of Hagab, the sons of Shalmai, the sons of Hanan, 47 the sons of Giddel, the sons of Gahar, the sons of Reaiah, 48 the sons of Rezin, the sons of Nekoda, the sons of Gazzam, 49 the sons of Uzza, the sons of Paseah, the sons of Besai, 50 the sons of Asnah, the sons of Meunim, the sons of Nephisim, 51 the sons of Bakbuk, the sons of Hakupha, the sons of Harhur, 52 the sons of Bazluth, the sons of Mehida, the sons of Harsha, 53 the sons of Barkos, the sons of Sisera, the sons of Temah, 54 the sons of Neziah, *and* the sons of Hatipha.

55 The sons of Solomon's servants: the sons of Sotai, the sons of Hassophereth, the sons of Peruda, 56 the sons of Jaalah, the sons of Darkon, the sons of Giddel, 57 the sons of Shephatiah, the sons of Hattil, the sons of Pochereth-hazzebaim, *and* the sons of Ami.

58 All the temple servants and the sons of Solomon's servants *totaled* 392.

59 Now these *were* the ones who came up from Tel-melah, Tel-harsha, Cherub, Addan, *and* Immer, but they were not able to provide evidence of their fathers' households and their

descendants, whether they *were* of Israel: 60 the sons of Delaiah, the sons of Tobiah, *and* the sons of Nekoda, 652.

Priests Removed

61 Of the sons of the priests: the sons of Hobaiah, the sons of Hakkoz, the sons of Barzillai, who took a wife from the daughters of Barzillai the Gileadite, and he was called by their name. 62 These searched *among* their genealogical registration but they could not be located; so they were considered defiled *and excluded* from the priesthood. 63 The governor said to them that they were not to eat from the most holy things until a priest stood up with Urim and Thummim.

64 The whole assembly together *totaled* 42,360, 65 besides their male and female slaves who *totaled* 7,337; and they had two hundred singing men and women. 66 Their horses *numbered* 736; their mules, 245; 67 their camels, 435; *their* donkeys, 6,720.

68 Some of the heads of fathers' *households,* when they arrived at the house of the LORD which is in Jerusalem, offered willingly for the house of God to erect it on its site. 69 According to their ability they gave to the treasury *for* the work sixty-one thousand gold drachmas, five thousand silver minas, and a hundred priestly garments.

70 Now the priests and the Levites, some of the people, the singers, the gatekeepers, and the temple servants lived in their cities, and all Israel in their cities.

Altar and Sacrifices Restored

3 Now when the seventh month came, and the sons of Israel *were* in the cities, the people gathered together as one person to Jerusalem. 2 Then Jeshua the son of Jozadak and his brothers the priests, and Zerubbabel the son of Shealtiel and his brothers, rose up and built the altar of the God of Israel to offer burnt offerings on it, as it is written in the Law of Moses, the man of God. 3 So they set up the altar on its foundation, because they were terrified of the peoples of the lands; and they offered burnt offerings on it to the LORD, burnt offerings morning and evening. 4 They also celebrated the Feast of Booths, as it is written, and *offered* the prescribed number of burnt offerings daily, according to the ordinance, as each day required; 5 and afterward *there was* a continual burnt offering, also for the new moons and for all the appointed festivals of the LORD that were consecrated, and from everyone who offered a voluntary offering to the LORD. 6 From the first day of the seventh month they began to offer burnt offerings to the LORD, but the foundation of the temple of the LORD had not been laid. 7 Then they gave money to the masons and carpenters, and food, drink, and oil to the Sidonians and the Tyrians to bring cedar wood from Lebanon to the sea at Joppa, according to the permission they had from Cyrus king of Persia.

Temple Restoration Begun

8 Now in the second year of their coming to the house of God at Jerusalem, in the second month, Zerubbabel the son of Shealtiel, Jeshua the son of Jozadak, and the rest of their brothers the priests and the Levites, and all who came from the captivity to Jerusalem, began *the work* and appointed the Levites who were twenty years old and upward to oversee the work of the house of the LORD. 9 Then Jeshua *with* his sons and brothers stood united *with* Kadmiel and his sons, the sons of Judah and the sons of Henadad *with* their sons and brothers the Levites, to oversee the workmen in the temple of God.

10 Now when the builders had laid the foundation of the temple of the LORD, the priests stood in their apparel with trumpets, and the Levites, the sons of Asaph, with cymbals, to praise the LORD according to the directions of King David of Israel. 11 And they sang, praising and giving thanks to the LORD, *saying,* "For *He is* good, for His favor *is* upon Israel forever." And all the people shouted with a great shout of joy when they praised the LORD, because the foundation of the house of the LORD was laid. 12 Yet many of the priests and Levites and heads of fathers' *households,* the old men who had seen the first temple, wept with a loud voice when the foundation of this house was laid before their eyes, while many shouted aloud for joy, 13 so that the people could not distinguish the sound of the shout of joy from the sound of the weeping of the people, because the people were shouting with a loud shout, and the sound was heard far away.

Enemies Hinder the Work

4 Now when the enemies of Judah and Benjamin heard that the people of the exile were building a temple to the LORD God of Israel, 2 they approached Zerubbabel and the heads of fathers' *households,* and said to them, "Let us build with you, for like you, we seek your God; and we have been sacrificing to Him since the days of Esarhaddon king of Assyria, who brought us up here." 3 But Zerubbabel and Jeshua and the rest of the heads of fathers' *households* of Israel said to them, "You have nothing *in common* with us in building a house to our God; but we ourselves will together build for the LORD God of Israel, just as King Cyrus, the king of Persia, has commanded us."

4 Then the people of the land discouraged the people of Judah, and frightened them from building, 5 and bribed advisers against them to frustrate their advice all the days of Cyrus king of Persia, even until the reign of Darius king of Persia.

6 Now in the reign of ¹Ahasuerus, in the beginning of his reign, they wrote an accusation against the inhabitants of Judah and Jerusalem.

7 And in the days of Artaxerxes, Bishlam, Mithredath, Tabeel, and the rest of his colleagues wrote to Artaxerxes king of Persia; and the text of the letter was written in Aramaic and translated *from* Aramaic.

4:6 ¹ Or *Xerxes;* Heb *Ahash-verosh*

The Letter to King Artaxerxes

8 Rehum the commander and Shimshai the scribe wrote a letter against Jerusalem to King Artaxerxes, as follows— 9 Rehum the commander, Shimshai the scribe, and the rest of their colleagues, the judges and the lesser governors, the officials, the secretaries, the men of Erech, the Babylonians, the men of Susa, that is, the Elamites, 10 and the rest of the nations which the great and honorable Osnappar deported and settled in the city of Samaria, and in the rest of the region beyond the *Euphrates* River. And now 11 this is a copy of the letter which they sent to him:

"To King Artaxerxes: Your servants, the men of the region beyond the *Euphrates* River; and now 12 let it be known to the king that the Jews who came up from you have come to us at Jerusalem; they are rebuilding the rebellious and evil city and are finishing the walls and repairing the foundations. 13 Now let it be known to the king, that if that city is rebuilt and the walls are finished, they will not pay tribute, custom tax, or toll, and it will be detrimental to the revenue of the kings. 14 Now because we are in the service of the palace, and it is not fitting for us to see the king's shame, for this reason we have sent *word* and informed the king, 15 so that a search may be conducted in the record books of your fathers. And you will discover in the record books and learn that that city is a rebellious city and detrimental to kings and provinces, and that they have revolted within it in past days; for this reason that city was laid waste. 16 We are informing the king that if that city is rebuilt and the walls finished, then as a result of this you will have no possession in *the province* beyond the *Euphrates* River."

The King Replies and Work Stops

17 *Then* the king sent a response to Rehum the commander, Shimshai the scribe, and to the rest of their colleagues who live in Samaria and in the rest of *the provinces* beyond the *Euphrates* River: "Peace. And now, 18 the document which you sent to us has been translated *and* read before me. 19 And a decree has been issued by me, and a search has been conducted and it has been discovered that that city has risen up against the kings in past days, and that rebellion and revolt have been perpetrated in it, 20 that mighty kings have ruled over Jerusalem, governing all *the provinces* beyond the *Euphrates* River, and that tribute, custom tax, and toll were paid to them. 21 Now issue a decree to make those men stop *work,* so that this city will not be rebuilt until a decree is issued by me. 22 And beware of being negligent in carrying out this *matter;* why should there be great damage, to the detriment of the kings?"

23 Then as soon as the copy of King Artaxerxes' decree was read before Rehum and Shimshai the scribe and their colleagues, they went in a hurry to Jerusalem to the Jews and stopped them by military force. 24 Then work on the house of God in Jerusalem was discontinued, and it was stopped until the second year of the reign of Darius king of Persia.

Temple Work Resumed

5 When the prophets, Haggai the prophet and Zechariah the son of Iddo, prophesied to the Jews who were in Judah and Jerusalem in the name of the God of Israel, who was over them, 2 then Zerubbabel the son of Shealtiel and Jeshua the son of Jozadak rose up and began to rebuild the house of God which is in Jerusalem; and the prophets of God were with them, supporting them.

3 At that time Tattenai, the governor of *the province* beyond the *Euphrates* River, and Shethar-bozenai and their colleagues came to them and spoke to them as follows: "Who issued you a decree to rebuild this temple and to finish this structure?" 4 Then we told them accordingly what the names of the men were who were reconstructing this building. 5 But the eye of their God was on the elders of the Jews, and they did not stop them until the report could reach Darius, and then the decree concerning it could be sent back.

Enemies Write to Darius

6 *This is* the copy of the letter that Tattenai, the governor of *the province* beyond the *Euphrates* River, and Shethar-bozenai and his colleagues the officials, who were beyond the River, sent to him in which it was written as follows: "To Darius the king, all peace. 8 May it be known to the king that we have gone to the province of Judah, to the house of the great God which is being built with large stones, and beams are being laid in the walls; and this work is being performed with great care and is succeeding in their hands. 9 Then we asked those elders and said to them as follows: 'Who issued you a decree to rebuild this temple and to finish this structure?' 10 We also asked them their names so as to inform you, in order that we might write down the names of the men who were in charge. 11 So they answered us as follows, saying, 'We are the servants of the God of heaven and earth, and are rebuilding the temple that was built many years ago, which a great king of Israel built and finished. 12 But because our fathers provoked the God of heaven to wrath, He handed them over to Nebuchadnezzar king of Babylon, the Chaldean, *who* destroyed this temple and deported the people to Babylon. 13 However, in the first year of Cyrus king of Babylon, King Cyrus issued a decree to rebuild this house of God. 14 Also the gold and silver utensils of the house of God which Nebuchadnezzar had taken from the temple in Jerusalem and brought them to the temple of Babylon, King Cyrus took them from the temple of Babylon and they were given to one whose name was Sheshbazzar, whom he had appointed governor. 15 And he said to him, "Take these utensils, go *and* deposit them in the temple in Jerusalem, and have the house of God rebuilt in its place." 16 Then that Sheshbazzar came *and* laid the foundations of the house of God in Jerusalem; and from then until now it has been

under construction and it is not *yet* completed.'
17 And now, if it pleases the king, let a search
be conducted in the king's treasure house,
which is there in Babylon, as to whether a
decree was issued by King Cyrus to rebuild
this house of God in Jerusalem; and let the
king send to us his decision concerning this
matter."

Darius Finds Cyrus' Decree

6 Then King Darius issued a decree, and a
search was conducted in the archives,
where the treasures were stored in Babylon.
2 And in 'Ecbatana, in the fortress which is in
the province of Media, a scroll was found;
and the following was written in it: "Mem-
orandum— 3 In the first year of King Cyrus,
Cyrus the king issued a decree: '*Concerning*
the house of God in Jerusalem, let the temple,
the place where sacrifices are offered, be
rebuilt, and let its foundations be repaired, its
height *being* 'sixty cubits *and* its width sixty
cubits, 4 *with* three layers of large stones and
one layer of timber. And the cost is to be paid
from the royal treasury. 5 Also the gold and
silver utensils of the house of God, which
Nebuchadnezzar took from the temple in
Jerusalem and brought to Babylon, are to be
returned and brought to their places in the
temple in Jerusalem; and you shall put *them* in
the house of God.'

6 "Now *as for you,* Tattenai, governor of *the
province* beyond the *Euphrates* River, Shethar-
bozenai, and your colleagues, the officials of
the provinces beyond the River, stay away from
there. 7 Leave that work on the house of God
alone; let the governor of the Jews and the
elders of the Jews rebuild that house of God
on its site. 8 Furthermore, I issue a decree
concerning what you are to do for these elders
of Judah in the rebuilding of that house of God:
the full cost is to be paid to those people from
the royal treasury out of the taxes of *the
provinces* beyond the *Euphrates* River, *and*
that without interruption. 9 And whatever is
needed, bulls, rams, and lambs for burnt
offerings to the God of heaven, and wheat,
salt, wine, and anointing oil, as the priests in
Jerusalem order, *it* is to be given to them daily
without fail, 10 so that they may offer acceptable
sacrifices to the God of heaven and pray for the
lives of the king and his sons. 11 And I issued
a decree that any person who violates this
decree, a timber shall be pulled out of his
house and he shall be impaled on it; and his
house shall be turned into a refuse heap on
account of this. 12 May the God who has caused
His name to dwell there overthrow any king or
people who attempts to change *it,* so as to
destroy that house of God in Jerusalem. I,
Darius, have issued *this* decree; *it* is to be
carried out with all diligence!"

The Temple Completed and Dedicated

13 Then Tattenai, the governor of *the
province* beyond the *Euphrates* River, Shethar-
bozenai, and their colleagues carried out *the
decree* with all diligence, just as King Darius
had ordered. 14 And the elders of the Jews were

successful in building through the prophecy of
Haggai the prophet and Zechariah the son of
Iddo. And they finished building following the
command of the God of Israel and the decree
of Cyrus, Darius, and Artaxerxes king of Persia.
15 Now this temple was completed on the third
day of the month Adar; it was the sixth year of
the reign of King Darius.

16 And the sons of Israel, the priests, the
Levites, and the rest of the exiles, celebrated
the dedication of this house of God with joy.
17 They offered for the dedication of this temple of God a hundred bulls, two hundred rams,
four hundred lambs, and as a sin offering for all
Israel twelve male goats, corresponding to the
number of the tribes of Israel. 18 Then they
appointed the priests to their divisions and the
Levites in their sections for the service of God
in Jerusalem, as it is written in the Book of
Moses.

The Passover Held

19 The exiles held the Passover on the
fourteenth of the first month. 20 For the priests
and the Levites had purified themselves
together; all of them were pure. Then they
slaughtered the Passover *lambs* for all the
exiles, both for their brothers the priests and
for themselves. 21 And the sons of Israel who
returned from exile and all those who had
separated themselves from the impurity of the
nations of the land to *join* them, to seek the
LORD God of Israel, ate *the Passover.* 22 And
they held the Feast of Unleavened Bread for
seven days with joy, because the LORD had
made them happy, and had turned the heart of
the king of Assyria toward them to encourage
them in the work of the house of God, the God
of Israel.

Ezra Journeys from Babylon to Jerusalem

7 Now after these things, in the reign of
Artaxerxes king of Persia, Ezra *went up to
Jerusalem; Ezra was* the son of Seraiah, son of
Azariah, son of Hilkiah, 2 son of Shallum, son of
Zadok, son of Ahitub, 3 son of Amariah, son of
Azariah, son of Meraioth, 4 son of Zerahiah, son
of Uzzi, son of Bukki, 5 son of Abishua, son of
Phinehas, son of Eleazar, son of Aaron the chief
priest. 6 *So* this Ezra went up from Babylon, and
he was a scribe skilled in the Law of Moses,
which the LORD God of Israel had given; and
the king granted him all he requested because
the hand of the LORD his God *was* upon him.
7 Some of the sons of Israel and some of the
priests, the Levites, the singers, the gatekeepers, and the temple servants went up
to Jerusalem in the seventh year of King
Artaxerxes.

8 And he came to Jerusalem in the fifth
month, which was in the seventh year of the
king. 9 For on the first *day* of the first month
he began to go up from Babylon; and on the
first of the fifth month he came to Jerusalem,
because the good hand of his God *was* upon
him. 10 For Ezra had firmly resolved to study
the Law of the LORD and to practice *it,* and
to teach *His* statutes and ordinances in
Israel.

6:2 1 Aram *Achmetha*   6:3 1 About 90 ft. or 27 m

King's Decree on Behalf of Ezra

11 Now this is the copy of the letter which King Artaxerxes gave to Ezra the priest, the scribe, learned in the words of the commandments of the LORD and His statutes to Israel: **12** "Artaxerxes, king of kings, to Ezra the priest, the scribe of the Law of the God of heaven, perfect *peace.* And now **13** I have issued a decree that any of the people of Israel and their priests and the Levites in my kingdom who are willing to go to Jerusalem, may go with you. **14** Since you are sent on the part of the king and his seven advisers to inquire about Judah and Jerusalem according to the Law of your God which is in your hand, **15** and to bring the silver and gold, which the king and his advisers have voluntarily given to the God of Israel, whose dwelling is in Jerusalem, **16** with all the silver and gold which you find in the entire province of Babylon, along with the voluntary offering of the people and of the priests, who offered willingly for the house of their God which is in Jerusalem; **17** with this money, therefore, you shall diligently buy bulls, rams, *and* lambs, with their grain offerings and their drink offerings, and offer them on the altar of the house of your God which is in Jerusalem. **18** And whatever seems good to you and your brothers to do with the rest of the silver and gold, you may do according to the will of your God. **19** Also the utensils which are given to you for the service of the house of your God, deliver in full before the God of Jerusalem. **20** And the rest of the needs of the house of your God, for which it may be incumbent upon you to provide, provide *for them* from the royal treasury.

21 "I myself, King Artaxerxes, issue a decree to all the treasurers who are *in the provinces* beyond the *Euphrates* River, that whatever Ezra the priest, the scribe of the Law of the God of heaven, may require of you, it shall be done diligently, **22** up to ¹a hundred talents of silver, ²a hundred kors of wheat, ³a hundred baths of wine, a hundred baths of anointing oil, and salt as needed. **23** Whatever is commanded by the God of heaven, it shall be done with zeal for the house of the God of heaven, so that there will not be wrath against the kingdom of the king and his sons. **24** We also inform you that it is not allowed to impose tax, tribute, or toll *on* any of the priests, Levites, singers, doorkeepers, temple servants, or *other* servants of this house of God.

25 "And you, Ezra, according to the wisdom of your God which is in your hand, appoint magistrates and judges so that they may judge all the people who are in *the province* beyond the *Euphrates* River, that is, all those who know the laws of your God; and you may teach anyone who is ignorant *of them.* **26** And whoever does not comply with the Law of your God and the law of the king, judgment is to be executed upon him strictly, whether for death or for banishment, or for confiscation of property or for imprisonment."

The King's Kindness

27 Blessed be the LORD, the God of our fathers, who has put *such a thing* as this in the king's heart, to glorify the house of the LORD which is in Jerusalem, **28** and has extended favor to me before the king and his counselors and before all the king's mighty officials. So I was strengthened according to the hand of the LORD my God *that was* upon me, and I gathered leading men from Israel to go up with me.

People Who Went with Ezra

8 Now these are the heads of their fathers' *households* and the genealogical enrollment of those who went up with me from Babylon in the reign of King Artaxerxes: **2** of the sons of Phinehas, Gershom; of the sons of Ithamar, Daniel; of the sons of David, Hattush; **3** of the sons of Shecaniah *who was* of the sons of Parosh, Zechariah, and with him 150 males *who were in* the genealogical list; **4** of the sons of Pahath-moab, Eliehoenai the son of Zerahiah and two hundred males with him; **5** of the sons of Zattu, Shecaniah, the son of Jahaziel and three hundred males with him; **6** and of the sons of Adin, Ebed the son of Jonathan and fifty males with him; **7** and of the sons of Elam, Jeshaiah the son of Athaliah and seventy males with him; **8** and of the sons of Shephatiah, Zebadiah the son of Michael and eighty males with him; **9** of the sons of Joab, Obadiah the son of Jehiel and 218 males with him; **10** and of the sons of Bani, Shelomith, the son of Josiphiah and 160 males with him; **11** and of the sons of Bebai, Zechariah the son of Bebai and twenty-eight males with him; **12** and of the sons of Azgad, Johanan the son of Hakkatan and 110 males with him; **13** and of the sons of Adonikam, the last ones, these being their names: Eliphelet, Jeiel, and Shemaiah, and sixty males with them; **14** and of the sons of Bigvai, Uthai and Zabbud, and seventy males with them.

Ezra Sends for Levites

15 Now I assembled them at the river that runs to Ahava, where we camped for three days; and when I paid close attention to the people and the priests, I did not find any Levites there. **16** So I sent for Eliezer, Ariel, Shemaiah, Elnathan, Jarib, Elnathan, Nathan, Zechariah, and Meshullam, leading men, and for Joiarib and Elnathan, teachers. **17** And I sent them to Iddo the leading man at the place *called* Casiphia; and I told them what to say to Iddo and his brothers, the temple servants at the place Casiphia, *that is,* to bring ministers to us for the house of our God. **18** And as the good hand of our God *was* upon us, they brought us a man of insight from the sons of Mahli, the son of Levi, the son of Israel, namely Sherebiah, and his sons and brothers, eighteen men; **19** and Hashabiah and Jeshaiah of the sons of Merari, *with* his brothers and their sons, twenty men; **20** and 220 of the temple servants, whom David and the officials had provided for the service of the Levites, all of them designated by name.

7:22 ¹About 3.75 tons or 3.4 metric tons   ²About 770 cubic feet or 22 cubic meters   ³About 600 gallons or 2,271 liters

Protection of God Invoked

21 Then I proclaimed a fast there at the river of Ahava, to humble ourselves before our God, to seek from Him a safe journey for us, our little ones, and all our possessions. 22 For I was ashamed to request from the king troops and horsemen to protect us from the enemy on the way, because we had said to the king, "The hand of our God is favorably disposed to all who seek Him, but His power and His anger are against all those who abandon Him." 23 So we fasted and sought our God concerning this *matter,* and He listened to our pleading.

24 Then I selected twelve of the leading priests: Sherebiah, Hashabiah, and with them ten of their brothers; 25 and I weighed out to them the silver, the gold, and the utensils, the offering for the house of our God which the king, his counselors, his officials, and all Israel who were present *there* had contributed. 26 So I weighed into their hands ¹650 talents of silver, and silver utensils *worth* ²a hundred talents, *and* a hundred gold talents, 27 and twenty gold bowls *worth* a thousand ¹darics, and two utensils of fine shiny bronze, precious as gold. 28 Then I said to them, "You are holy to the LORD, and the utensils are holy; and the silver and the gold are a voluntary offering to the LORD God of your fathers. 29 Watch and keep *them* until you weigh *them* before the leading priests, the Levites, and the leaders of the fathers' *households* of Israel in Jerusalem, *in* the chambers of the house of the LORD." 30 So the priests and the Levites accepted the weight of silver and gold and the utensils, to bring *them* to Jerusalem to the house of our God.

31 Then we journeyed from the river Ahava on the twelfth of the first month to go to Jerusalem; and the hand of our God was upon us, and He rescued us from the hand of the enemy and the ambushes by the road. 32 So we came to Jerusalem and remained there for three days.

Treasure Placed in the Temple

33 And on the fourth day the silver, the gold, and the utensils were weighed out in the house of our God into the hand of Meremoth the son of Uriah the priest, and with him *was* Eleazar the son of Phinehas; and with them *were* the Levites, Jozabad the son of Jeshua and Noadiah the son of Binnui. 34 *A notation was made* for everything by number and weight, and all the weight was recorded at that time.

35 The exiles who had come from the captivity offered burnt offerings to the God of Israel: twelve bulls for all Israel, ninety-six rams, seventy-seven lambs, twelve male goats for a sin offering, all as a burnt offering to the LORD. 36 Then they delivered the king's edicts to the king's satraps and the governors *in the provinces* beyond the *Euphrates* River, and they supported the people and the house of God.

Mixed Marriages

9 Now when these things had been completed, the officials approached me, saying,

"The people of Israel and the priests and the Levites have not separated themselves from the peoples of the lands, as to their abominations, *those* of the Canaanites, the Hittites, the Perizzites, the Jebusites, the Ammonites, the Moabites, the Egyptians, and the Amorites. 2 For they have taken some of their daughters *as wives* for themselves and for their sons, so that the holy race has intermingled with the peoples of the lands; indeed, the hands of the officials and the leaders have taken the lead in this unfaithfulness." 3 When I heard about this matter, I tore my garment and my robe, and pulled out some of the hair from my head and my beard, and sat down appalled. 4 Then everyone who was frightened by the words of the God of Israel on account of the unfaithfulness of the exiles gathered to me, and I sat appalled until the evening offering.

Prayer of Confession

5 But at the evening offering I stood up from my humiliation, even with my garment and my robe torn, and I bowed down on my knees and spread out my hands to the LORD my God; 6 and I said, "My God, I am ashamed and humiliated to lift up my face to You, my God, for our wrongful deeds have risen above our heads, and our guilt has grown even to the heavens. 7 Since the days of our fathers to this day we *have been* in great guilt, and because of our wrongful deeds we, our kings, *and* our priests have been handed over to the kings of the lands, to the sword, to captivity, to plunder, and to open shame, as *it is* this day. 8 But now for a brief moment grace has been *shown* from the LORD our God, to leave us an escaped remnant and to give us a ¹peg in His holy place, so that our God may enlighten our eyes and grant us a little reviving in our bondage. 9 For we are slaves; yet in our bondage our God has not abandoned us, but has extended favor to us in the sight of the kings of Persia, to give us reviving to erect the house of our God, to restore its ruins, and to give us a wall in Judah and Jerusalem.

10 "And now, our God, what shall we say after this? For we have abandoned Your commandments, 11 which You have commanded by Your servants the prophets, saying, 'The land which you are entering to possess is an unclean land with the uncleanness of the peoples of the lands, with their abominations which have filled it from end to end, *and* with their impurity. 12 So now do not give your daughters to their sons nor take their daughters for your sons, and never seek their peace or their prosperity, so that you may be strong and may eat the good *things* of the land, and leave *it* as an inheritance to your sons forever.' 13 And after everything that has come upon us for our evil deeds and our great guilt, since You our God have spared *us by inflicting* less than our wrongdoing *deserves,* and have given us *such* an escaped remnant as this, 14 shall we again break Your commandments and intermarry with the peoples who commit these abominations? Would You not be angry

---

8:26 ¹About 24 tons or 22 metric tons   ²About 3.75 tons or 3.4 metric tons   8:27 ¹A coin weighing about 0.25 oz. or 7 gm   9:8 ¹I.e., a foothold

with us to the point of destruction, until there would be no remnant nor any who would escape? [15] LORD God of Israel, You are righteous, for we have been left an escaped remnant, as *it is* this day; behold, we are before You in our guilt, for no one can stand before You because of this."

Reconciliation with God

10 Now while Ezra was praying and making confession, weeping and prostrating himself before the house of God, a very large assembly, men, women, and children, gathered to him from Israel; for the people wept greatly. [2] Shecaniah the son of Jehiel, one of the sons of Elam, said to Ezra, "We have been unfaithful to our God and have married foreign women from the peoples of the land; yet now there is hope for Israel in spite of this. [3] So now let's make a covenant with our God to send away all the wives and their children, following the counsel of [1]my lord and of those who fear the commandment of our God; and let it be done according to the Law. [4] Arise! For *this* matter is your responsibility, but we will be with you; be courageous and act."

[5] Then Ezra stood and made the leading priests, the Levites, and all Israel take an oath that they would do according to this proposal; so they took the oath. [6] Then Ezra rose from before the house of God and went into the chamber of Jehohanan the son of Eliashib. Although he went there, he did not eat bread nor drink water, because he was mourning over the unfaithfulness of the exiles. [7] So they made a proclamation throughout Judah and Jerusalem to all the exiles, that they were to assemble at Jerusalem, [8] and that whoever did not come within three days, in accordance with the counsel of the leaders and the elders, all his property would be forfeited, and he himself would be excluded from the assembly of the exiles.

[9] So all the men of Judah and Benjamin assembled at Jerusalem within the three days. It was the ninth month on the twentieth of the month, and all the people sat in the public square *before* the house of God, trembling because of this matter and the *heavy* rain. [10] Then Ezra the priest stood up and said to them, "You have been unfaithful and have married foreign wives, adding to the guilt of Israel. [11] Now therefore, make confession to the LORD God of your fathers and do His will; and separate yourselves from the peoples of the land and from the foreign wives." [12] Then all the assembly replied with a loud voice, "It is our duty to do exactly as you have said! [13] However, there are many people, it is the rainy season, and we are not able to stand in the open. Nor *can* the task *be done* in one or two days, because we have done a great wrong in this matter. [14] Please let our leaders represent all the assembly and have all those in our cities who have married foreign wives come at

appointed times, together with the elders and judges of each city, until the fierce anger of our God on account of this matter is turned away from us." [15] Only Jonathan the son of Asahel and Jahzeiah the son of Tikvah opposed this, with Meshullam and Shabbethai the Levite supporting them.

[16] But the exiles did so. And Ezra the priest selected men *who were* the heads of fathers' *households* for *each of* their father's households, all of them by name. So they convened on the first day of the tenth month to investigate the matter. [17] And they finished *investigating* all the men who had married foreign wives by the first day of the first month.

List of Offenders

[18] Now among the sons of the priests who had married foreign wives were found of the sons of Jeshua the son of Jozadak, and his brothers: Maaseiah, Eliezer, Jarib, and Gedaliah. [19] They pledged to send away their wives, and being guilty, *they offered* a ram of the flock for their guilt. [20] Of the sons of Immer, *there were* Hanani and Zebadiah; [21] and of the sons of Harim: Maaseiah, Elijah, Shemaiah, Jehiel, and Uzziah; [22] and of the sons of Pashhur: Elioenai, Maaseiah, Ishmael, Nethanel, Jozabad, and Elasah.

[23] Of the Levites *there were* Jozabad, Shimei, Kelaiah (that is, Kelita), Pethahiah, Judah, and Eliezer.

[24] Of the singers *there was* Eliashib; and of the gatekeepers: Shallum, Telem, and Uri.

[25] Of Israel, of the sons of Parosh *there were* Ramiah, Izziah, Malchijah, Mijamin, Eleazar, Malchijah, and Benaiah; [26] and of the sons of Elam: Mattaniah, Zechariah, Jehiel, Abdi, Jeremoth, and Elijah; [27] and of the sons of Zattu: Elioenai, Eliashib, Mattaniah, Jeremoth, Zabad, and Aziza; [28] and of the sons of Bebai: Jehohanan, Hananiah, Zabbai, *and* Athlai; [29] and of the sons of Bani: Meshullam, Malluch and Adaiah, Jashub, Sheal, *and* Jeremoth; [30] and of the sons of Pahath-moab: Adna and Chelal, Benaiah, Maaseiah, Mattaniah, Bezalel, Binnui, and Manasseh; [31] and *of* the sons of Harim: Eliezer, Isshijah, Malchijah, Shemaiah, Shimeon, [32] Benjamin, Malluch, *and* Shemariah; [33] of the sons of Hashum: Mattenai, Mattattah, Zabad, Eliphelet, Jeremai, Manasseh, *and* Shimei; [34] of the sons of Bani: Maadai, Amram, Uel, [35] Benaiah, Bedeiah, Cheluhi, [36] Vaniah, Meremoth, Eliashib, [37] Mattaniah, Mattenai, Jaasu, [38] Bani, Binnui, Shimei, [39] Shelemiah, Nathan, Adaiah, [40] Machnadebai, Shashai, Sharai, [41] Azarel, Shelemiah, Shemariah, [42] Shallum, Amariah, *and* Joseph. [43] Of the sons of Nebo *there were* Jeiel, Mattithiah, Zabad, Zebina, Jaddai, Joel, *and* Benaiah. [44] All of these men had married foreign wives, and some of them had wives *by whom* they had children.

The Book of
NEHEMIAH

Nehemiah's Grief for the Exiles

1 The words of Nehemiah the son of Hacaliah.

Now it happened in the month Chislev, *in* the twentieth year, while I was in Susa the capitol, 2 that Hanani, one of my brothers, and some men from Judah came; and I asked them about the Jews who had escaped and had survived the captivity, and about Jerusalem. 3 And they said to me, "The remnant there in the province who survived the captivity are in great distress and disgrace, and the wall of Jerusalem is broken down and its gates have been burned with fire."

4 Now when I heard these words, I sat down and wept and mourned for days; and I was fasting and praying before the God of heaven. 5 I said, "Please, LORD God of heaven, the great and awesome God, who keeps the covenant and faithfulness for those who love Him and keep His commandments: 6 let Your ear now be attentive and Your eyes open, to hear the prayer of Your servant which I am praying before You now, day and night, on behalf of the sons of Israel Your servants, confessing the sins of the sons of Israel which we have committed against You; I and my father's house have sinned. 7 We have acted very corruptly against You and have not kept the commandments, nor the statutes, nor the ordinances which You commanded Your servant Moses. 8 Remember, please, the word which You commanded Your servant Moses, saying, '*If* you are unfaithful, I will scatter you among the peoples; 9 but *if* you return to Me and keep My commandments and do them, though those of you who have been scattered were in the most remote part of the heavens, I will gather them from there and bring them to the place where I have chosen to have My name dwell.' 10 They are Your servants and Your people whom You redeemed by Your great power and by Your strong hand. 11 Please, Lord, may Your ear be attentive to the prayer of Your servant and the prayer of Your servants who delight to revere Your name, and please make Your servant successful today and grant him mercy before this man."

Now I was the cupbearer to the king.

Nehemiah's Prayer Answered

2 And it came about in the month Nisan, in the twentieth year of King Artaxerxes, that wine *was* before him, and I picked up the wine and gave it to the king. Now I had not been sad in his presence. 2 So the king said to me, "Why is your face sad, though you are not ill? This is nothing but sadness of heart." Then I was very much afraid. 3 And I said to the king, "May the king live forever. Why should my face not be sad when the city, the site of my fathers' tombs, is desolate and its gates have been consumed by fire?" 4 Then the king said to me, "What would you request?" So I prayed to the God of heaven. 5 Then I said to the king, "If it pleases the king, and if your servant has found favor before you, *I request* that you send me to Judah, to the city of my fathers' tombs, that I may rebuild it." 6 Then the king said to me, with the queen sitting beside him, "How long will your journey be, and when will you return?" So it pleased the king to send me, and I gave him a definite time. 7 And I said to the king, "If it pleases the king, let letters be given me for the governors *of the provinces* beyond the River, so that they will allow me to pass through until I come to Judah, 8 and a letter to Asaph the keeper of the king's forest, so that he will give me timber to make beams for the gates of the citadel which is by the temple, for the wall of the city, and for the house to which I will go." And the king granted *them* to me because the good hand of my God *was* on me.

9 Then I came to the governors *of the provinces* beyond the *Euphrates* River and gave them the king's letters. Now the king had sent with me officers of the army and horsemen. 10 And when Sanballat the Horonite and Tobiah the Ammonite official heard *about it,* it was very displeasing to them that someone had come to seek the welfare of the sons of Israel.

Nehemiah Inspects Jerusalem's Walls

11 So I came to Jerusalem and was there for three days. 12 And I got up in the night, I and a few men with me. I did not tell anyone what my God was putting into my mind to do for Jerusalem, and there was no animal with me except the animal on which I was riding. 13 So I went out at night by the Valley Gate in the direction of the Dragon's Spring and *on* to the Dung Gate, and I was inspecting the walls of Jerusalem which were broken down and its gates which had been consumed by fire. 14 Then I passed on to the Fountain Gate and the King's Pool, but there was no place for my mount to pass. 15 So I was going up at night by the ravine and inspecting the wall. Then I entered the Valley Gate again and returned. 16 However, the officials did not know where I had gone or what I was doing; nor had I as yet told the Jews, the priests, the nobles, the officials, or the rest who were doing the work.

17 Then I said to them, "You see the bad situation we are in, that Jerusalem is desolate and its gates have been burned by fire. Come, let's rebuild the wall of Jerusalem so that we will no longer be a disgrace." 18 And I told them how the hand of my God had been favorable to me and also about the king's words which he had spoken to me. Then they said, "Let's arise and build." So they put their hands to the good *work.* 19 But when Sanballat the Horonite and Tobiah the Ammonite official, and Geshem the Arab heard *about it,* they mocked us and despised us, and said, "What is this thing that you are doing? Are you rebelling

against the king?" 20 So I answered them and said to them, "The God of heaven will make us successful; therefore we His servants will arise and build, but you have no part, right, or memorial in Jerusalem."

Builders of the Walls

3 Then Eliashib the high priest arose with his brothers the priests and built the Sheep Gate; they consecrated it and installed its doors. They consecrated the wall to the Tower of the Hundred *and* the Tower of Hananel. 2 And next to him the men of Jericho built, and next to them Zaccur the son of Imri built.

3 Now the sons of Hassenaah built the Fish Gate; they laid its beams and installed its doors with its bolts and bars. 4 Next to them Meremoth the son of Uriah the son of Hakkoz made repairs. And next to him Meshullam the son of Berechiah the son of Meshezabel made repairs. And next to him Zadok the son of Baana *also* made repairs. 5 Moreover, next to him the Tekoites made repairs, but their nobles did not support the work of their masters.

6 Now Joiada the son of Paseah and Meshullam the son of Besodeiah repaired the Ancient Gate; they laid its beams and installed its doors with its bolts and its bars. 7 Next to them Melatiah the Gibeonite and Jadon the Meronothite, the men of Gibeon and of Mizpah, also made repairs for the official seat of the governor *of the province* beyond the *Euphrates* River. 8 Next to him Uzziel the son of Harhaiah of the goldsmiths made repairs. And next to him Hananiah, one of the perfumers, made repairs, and they restored Jerusalem as far as the Broad Wall. 9 And next to them Rephaiah the son of Hur, the official of half the district of Jerusalem, made repairs. 10 Next to them Jedaiah the son of Harumaph made repairs opposite his house. And next to him Hattush the son of Hashabneiah made repairs. 11 Malchijah the son of Harim and Hasshub the son of Pahath-moab repaired another section and the Tower of Furnaces. 12 Next to him Shallum the son of Hallohesh, the official of half the district of Jerusalem, made repairs, he and his daughters.

13 Hanun and the inhabitants of Zanoah repaired the Valley Gate. They built it and installed its doors with its bolts and its bars, and a ¹thousand cubits of the wall to the Dung Gate.

14 And Malchijah the son of Rechab, official of the district of Beth-haccherem repaired the Dung Gate. He built it and installed its doors with its bolts and its bars.

15 Shallum the son of Col-hozeh, the official of the district of Mizpah, repaired the Fountain Gate. He built it, made a roof for it, and installed its doors with its bolts and its bars, and the wall of the Pool of Shelah at the king's garden as far as the steps that descend from the city of David. 16 After him Nehemiah the son of Azbuk, official of half the district of Beth-zur, made repairs as far as *a point* opposite the tombs of David, and as far as the artificial pool and the house of the mighty men. 17 After him the Levites carried out repairs *under* Rehum

the son of Bani. Next to him Hashabiah, the official of half the district of Keilah, carried out repairs for his district. 18 After him their brothers carried out repairs *under* Bavvai the son of Henadad, official of *the other* half of the district of Keilah. 19 And next to him Ezer the son of Jeshua, the official of Mizpah, repaired another section in front of the ascent of the armory at the Angle. 20 After him Baruch the son of Zabbai zealously repaired another section, from the Angle to the doorway of the house of Eliashib the high priest. 21 After him Meremoth the son of Uriah the son of Hakkoz repaired another section, from the doorway of Eliashib's house even as far as the end of his house. 22 And after him the priests, the men of the ¹vicinity, carried out repairs. 23 After them Benjamin and Hasshub carried out repairs in front of their house. After them Azariah the son of Maaseiah, son of Ananiah, carried out repairs beside his house. 24 After him Binnui the son of Henadad repaired another section, from the house of Azariah as far as the Angle and as far as the corner. 25 Palal the son of Uzai *made repairs* in front of the Angle and the tower projecting from the upper house of the king, which is by the courtyard of the guard. After him Pedaiah the son of Parosh *made repairs.* 26 Now the temple servants living in Ophel *made repairs* as far as the front of the Water Gate toward the east and the projecting tower. 27 After them the Tekoites repaired another section in front of the great projecting tower and as far as the wall of Ophel.

28 Above the Horse Gate the priests carried out repairs, each in front of his house. 29 After them Zadok the son of Immer carried out repairs in front of his house. And after him Shemaiah the son of Shecaniah, the keeper of the East Gate, carried out repairs. 30 After him Hananiah the son of Shelemiah, and Hanun the sixth son of Zalaph, repaired another section. After him Meshullam the son of Berechiah carried out repairs in front of his own quarters. 31 After him Malchijah, one of the goldsmiths, carried out repairs as far as the house of the temple servants and of the merchants, in front of the Inspection Gate and as far as the upper room of the corner. 32 And between the upper room of the corner and the Sheep Gate the goldsmiths and the merchants carried out repairs.

Work Is Ridiculed

4 Now it came about that when Sanballat heard that we were rebuilding the wall, he became furious and very angry, and he mocked the Jews. 2 And he spoke in the presence of his brothers and the wealthy people of Samaria and said, "What are these feeble Jews doing? Are they going to restore *the temple* for themselves? Can they offer sacrifices? Can they finish *it* in a day? Can they revive the stones from the heaps of rubble, even the burned ones?" 3 Now Tobiah the Ammonite *was* near him, and he said, "Even what they are building—if a fox were to jump *on it,* it would break their stone wall down!"

4 Hear, O our God, how we are *an object of*

3:13 ¹About 1,500 ft. or 457 m   3:22 ¹I.e., the lower Jordan Valley

contempt! Return their taunting on their own heads, and turn them into plunder in a land of captivity. 5 Do not forgive their guilt and do not let their sin be wiped out before You, for they have demoralized the builders.

6 So we built the wall, and the entire wall was joined together to half its *height,* for the people had a mind to work.

7 Now when Sanballat, Tobiah, the Arabs, the Ammonites, and the Ashdodites heard that the repair of the walls of Jerusalem went on, *and* that the breaches began to be closed, they were very angry. 8 So all of them conspired together to come to fight against Jerusalem and to cause confusion in it.

Discouragement Overcome

9 But we prayed to our God, and because of them we set up a guard against them day and night.

10 And so in Judah it was said:

"The strength of the burden bearers is failing,
Yet there is much rubble;
And we ourselves are unable
To rebuild the wall."

11 And our enemies said, "They will not know or see until we come among them, kill them, and put a stop to the work." 12 When the Jews who lived near them came and told us ten times, "They will come up against us from every place where you may turn," 13 then I stationed *men* in the lowest parts of the space behind the wall, the exposed places, and I stationed the people in families with their swords, spears, and bows. 14 When I saw *their fear,* I stood and said to the nobles, the officials, and the rest of the people: "Do not be afraid of them; remember the Lord who is great and awesome, and fight for your brothers, your sons, your daughters, your wives, and your houses."

15 Now when our enemies heard that it was known to us, and that God had frustrated their plan, then all of us returned to the wall, each one to his work. 16 And from that day *on,* half of my servants carried on the work while half of them kept hold of the spears, the shields, the bows, and the coats of mail; and the captains *were* behind all the house of Judah. 17 Those who were rebuilding the wall and those who carried burdens carried with one hand doing the work, and the other keeping hold of a weapon. 18 As for the builders, each *wore* his sword strapped to his waist as he built, while the trumpeter *stood* near me.
19 And I said to the nobles, the officials, and the rest of the people, "The work is great and extensive, and we are separated on the wall far from one another. 20 At whatever place you hear the sound of the trumpet, assemble to us there. Our God will fight for us."

21 So we carried on the work with half of them holding spears from dawn until the stars appeared. 22 At that time I also said to the people, "Each man with his servant shall spend the night within Jerusalem, so that they may be a guard for us by night and a laborer by day." 23 So neither I, my brothers, my servants, nor the men of the guard who followed me—none

of us removed our clothes; each *took* his weapon *even to* the water.

Charging Interest Abolished

5 Now there was a great outcry of the people and of their wives against their Jewish brothers. 2 For there were those who said, "We, our sons, and our daughters are many; therefore let's get grain so that we may eat and live." 3 And there were *others* who said, "We are mortgaging our fields, our vineyards, and our houses so that we might get grain because of the famine." 4 There also were those who said, "We have borrowed money for the king's tax *on* our fields and our vineyards. 5 And now our flesh is like the flesh of our brothers, our children like their children. Yet behold, we are forcing our sons and our daughters to be slaves, and some of our daughters are forced into bondage *already,* and we are helpless because our fields and vineyards belong to others."

6 Then I was very angry when I heard their outcry and these words. 7 So I thought it over and contended with the nobles and the leading people, and said to them, "You are lending at interest, each to his brother!" Therefore, I held a great assembly against them. 8 And I said to them, "We, according to our ability, have redeemed our Jewish brothers who were sold to the nations; now would you even sell your brothers that they may be sold to us?" Then they were silent and could not find a word *to say.* 9 So I said, "The thing which you are doing is not good; should you not walk in the fear of our God because of the taunting of the nations, our enemies? 10 And likewise I, my brothers, and my servants are lending them money and grain. Please, let's do without this interest. 11 Please, give back to them this very day their fields, their vineyards, their olive groves, and their houses, as well as the hundredth *part* of the money and of the grain, the new wine, and the oil that you are charging as interest from them." 12 Then they said, "We will give *it* back and will require nothing from them; we will do exactly as you say." So I called the priests and made them take an oath to act in accordance with this promise. 13 I also shook out the front of my garment and said, "So may God shake out every person from his house and from his possessions who does not keep this promise; just so may he be shaken out and emptied." And all the assembly said, "Amen!" And they praised the Lord. Then the people acted in accordance with this promise.

Nehemiah's Example

14 Furthermore, since the day that I was appointed to be their governor in the land of Judah, from the twentieth year to the thirty-second year of King Artaxerxes, for twelve years, neither I nor my kinsmen have eaten the governor's food *allowance.* 15 But the previous governors who were before me laid burdens on the people and took from them bread and wine besides forty shekels of silver; even their servants domineered the people. But I did not do so because of *my* fear of God. 16 I also applied myself to the work on this wall; we did not buy any land, and all my servants were

gathered there for the work. 17 Moreover, *there were* at my table 150 Jews and officials, besides those who came to us from the nations that were around us. 18 Now that which was prepared for each day was one ox *and* six choice sheep; also birds were prepared for me, and every ten days all *sorts of* wine *were provided* in abundance. Yet for *all* this I did not request the governor's food *allowance,* because the forced labor was heavy on this people. 19 Remember me, my God, for good, *in return for* all that I have done for this people.

The Enemy's Plot

6 Now when it was reported to Sanballat, Tobiah, Geshem the Arab, and to the rest of our enemies that I had rebuilt the wall, and *that* no breach was left in it, although at that time I had not installed the doors in the gates, 2 Sanballat and Geshem sent *a message* to me, saying, "Come, let's meet together ¹at Chephirim in the plain of Ono." But they were plotting to harm me. 3 So I sent messengers to them, saying, "I am doing a great work and am unable to come down. Why should the work stop while I leave it and come down to you?" 4 Then they sent *messages* to me four times worded in this way, and I answered them with the same wording. 5 Then Sanballat sent his servant to me in the same way a fifth time with an open letter in his hand. 6 In it was written: "It is reported among the nations, and Gashmu says, that you and the Jews intend to rebel; for that reason you are rebuilding the wall. And you are to be their king, according to these reports. 7 You have also appointed prophets to proclaim in Jerusalem concerning you, 'A king is in Judah!' And now it will be reported to the king according to these reports. So come now, let's consult together." 8 Then I sent *a message* to him saying, "*Nothing* like these things that you are saying has been done, but you are inventing them in your own mind." 9 For all of them were *trying* to frighten us, thinking, "They will become discouraged with the work and it will not be done." But now, *God,* strengthen my hands.

10 When I entered the house of Shemaiah the son of Delaiah, son of Mehetabel, who was confined *at home,* he said, "Let's meet together in the house of God, within the temple, and let's close the doors of the temple, for they are coming to kill you, and they are coming to kill you at night." 11 But I said, "Should a man like me flee? And who is there like me who would go into the temple to save his own life? I will not go in." 12 Then I realized that God certainly had not sent him, but he uttered *his* prophecy against me because Tobiah and Sanballat had hired him. 13 He was hired for this reason, that I would become frightened and act accordingly and sin, so that they might have an evil report in order that they could taunt me. 14 Remember, my God, Tobiah and Sanballat in accordance with these works of theirs, and also Noadiah the prophetess and the rest of the prophets, who were *trying* to frighten me.

The Wall Is Finished

15 So the wall was completed on the twenty-fifth of *the month* Elul, in fifty-two days. 16 When all our enemies heard *about it,* and all the nations surrounding us saw *it,* they lost their confidence; for they realized that this work had been accomplished with the help of our God. 17 Also in those days many letters went from the nobles of Judah to Tobiah, and Tobiah's letters came to them. 18 For many in Judah were bound by oath to him because he was the son-in-law of Shecaniah the son of Arah, and his son Jehohanan had married the daughter of Meshullam the son of Berechiah. 19 Moreover, they were speaking about his good deeds in my presence, and were reporting my words to him. Then Tobiah sent letters to frighten me.

Census of First Returned Exiles

7 Now when the wall was rebuilt and I had installed the doors, and the gatekeepers, the singers, and the Levites were appointed, 2 then I put Hanani my brother, and Hananiah the commander of the citadel, in charge of Jerusalem, for he was a faithful man and feared God more than many. 3 Then I said to them, "The gates of Jerusalem are not to be opened until the sun is hot, and while they are standing *guard, the gatekeepers* are to keep the doors shut and bolted. Also appoint guards from the inhabitants of Jerusalem, each at his post, and each in front of his own house." 4 Now the city was large and spacious, but the people in it were few and the houses were not built.

5 Then my God put it into my heart to assemble the nobles, the officials, and the *other* people to be enrolled by genealogies. Then I found the book of the genealogy of those who came up first, in which I found the following record:

6 These are the people of the province who came up from the captivity of the exiles whom Nebuchadnezzar the king of Babylon had taken into exile, and who returned to Jerusalem and Judah, each to his city, 7 who came with Zerubbabel, Jeshua, Nehemiah, Azariah, Raamiah, Nahamani, Mordecai, Bilshan, Mispereth, Bigvai, Nehum, *and* Baanah.

The number of men of the people of Israel: 8 the sons of Parosh, 2,172; 9 the sons of Shephatiah, 372; 10 the sons of Arah, 652; 11 the sons of Pahath-moab of the sons of Jeshua and Joab, 2,818; 12 the sons of Elam, 1,254; 13 the sons of Zattu, 845; 14 the sons of Zaccai, 760; 15 the sons of Binnui, 648; 16 the sons of Bebai, 628; 17 the sons of Azgad, 2,322; 18 the sons of Adonikam, 667; 19 the sons of Bigvai, 2,067; 20 the sons of Adin, 655; 21 the sons of Ater, of Hezekiah, 98; 22 the sons of Hashum, 328; 23 the sons of Bezai, 324; 24 the sons of Hariph, 112; 25 the sons of Gibeon, 95; 26 the men of Bethlehem and Netophah, 188; 27 the men of Anathoth, 128; 28 the men of Beth-azmaveth, 42; 29 the men of Kiriath-jearim, Chephirah, and Beeroth, 743; 30 the men of Ramah and Geba, 621; 31 the men of Michmas, 122; 32 the men of Bethel and Ai, 123; 33 the men of the

---

6:2 ¹LXX *in the villages in*

other Nebo, 52; [34] the sons of the other Elam, 1,254; [35] the sons of Harim, 320; [36] the men of Jericho, 345; [37] the sons of Lod, Hadid, and Ono, 721; [38] the sons of Senaah, 3,930.

[39] The priests: the sons of Jedaiah of the house of Jeshua, 973; [40] the sons of Immer, 1,052; [41] the sons of Pashhur, 1,247; [42] the sons of Harim, 1,017.

[43] The Levites: the sons of Jeshua, of Kadmiel, of the sons of Hodevah, 74. [44] The singers: the sons of Asaph, 148. [45] The gatekeepers: the sons of Shallum, the sons of Ater, the sons of Talmon, the sons of Akkub, the sons of Hatita, the sons of Shobai, 138.

[46] The temple servants: the sons of Ziha, the sons of Hasupha, the sons of Tabbaoth, [47] the sons of Keros, the sons of Sia, the sons of Padon, [48] the sons of Lebana, the sons of Hagaba, the sons of Shalmai, [49] the sons of Hanan, the sons of Giddel, the sons of Gahar, [50] the sons of Reaiah, the sons of Rezin, the sons of Nekoda, [51] the sons of Gazzam, the sons of Uzza, the sons of Paseah, [52] the sons of Besai, the sons of Meunim, the sons of Nephushesim, [53] the sons of Bakbuk, the sons of Hakupha, the sons of Harhur, [54] the sons of Bazlith, the sons of Mehida, the sons of Harsha, [55] the sons of Barkos, the sons of Sisera, the sons of Temah, [56] the sons of Neziah, the sons of Hatipha.

[57] The sons of Solomon's servants: the sons of Sotai, the sons of Sophereth, the sons of Perida, [58] the sons of Jaala, the sons of Darkon, the sons of Giddel, [59] the sons of Shephatiah, the sons of Hattil, the sons of Pochereth-hazzebaim, *and* the sons of Amon.

[60] All the temple servants and the sons of Solomon's servants *totaled* 392.

[61] These *were* the ones who came up from Tel-melah, Tel-harsha, Cherub, Addon, and Immer; but they could not provide evidence for their fathers' households or their descendants, whether they *were* of Israel: [62] the sons of Delaiah, the sons of Tobiah, the sons of Nekoda, 642. [63] And of the priests: the sons of Hobaiah, the sons of Hakkoz, the sons of Barzillai, who took a wife of the daughters of Barzillai, the Gileadite, and was named after them. [64] These searched *among* their ancestral registration, but it could not be located; therefore they were considered unclean and *disqualified* from the priesthood. [65] And the governor said to them that they were not to eat from the most holy things until a priest arose with Urim and Thummim.

Total of People and Gifts

[66] The whole assembly together *totaled* 42,360, [67] besides their male slaves and their female slaves, of whom *there were* 7,337; and they had 245 male and female singers. [68] *Their* horses were 736; *their* mules, 245; [69] *their* camels, 435; *their* donkeys, 6,720.

[70] Some of the heads of fathers' *households* gave to the work. The governor gave to the treasury a thousand gold drachmas, fifty basins, *and* 530 priests' garments. [71] And some of the heads of fathers' *households* gave to the treasury *for* the work twenty thousand gold drachmas and 2,200 silver minas. [72] What the rest of the people gave was twenty thousand gold drachmas, two thousand silver minas, and sixty-seven priests' garments.

[73] Now the priests, the Levites, the gatekeepers, the singers, some of the people, the temple servants, and all Israel lived in their cities.

And when the seventh month came, the sons of Israel *were* in their cities.

Ezra Reads the Law

8 And all the people gathered as one person at the public square which was in front of the Water Gate, and they asked Ezra the scribe to bring the Book of the Law of Moses which the LORD had given to Israel. [2] Then Ezra the priest brought the Law before the assembly of men, women, and all who *could* listen with understanding, on the first day of the seventh month. [3] And he read from it before the public square which was in front of the Water Gate, from early morning until midday, in the presence of men and women, those who could understand; and all the people were attentive to the Book of the Law. [4] Ezra the scribe stood at a wooden podium which they had made for the purpose. And beside him stood Mattithiah, Shema, Anaiah, Uriah, Hilkiah, and Maaseiah on his right; and Pedaiah, Mishael, Malchijah, Hashum, Hashbaddanah, Zechariah, *and* Meshullam on his left. [5] Then Ezra opened the book in the sight of all the people, for he was *standing* above all the people; and when he opened it, all the people stood up. [6] Then Ezra blessed the LORD, the great God. And all the people answered, "Amen, Amen!" with the raising of their hands; then they kneeled down and worshiped the LORD with *their* faces to the ground. [7] Also Jeshua, Bani, Sherebiah, Jamin, Akkub, Shabbethai, Hodiah, Maaseiah, Kelita, Azariah, Jozabad, Hanan, Pelaiah, and the Levites explained the Law to the people while the people *remained* in their place. [8] They read from the book, from the Law of God, translating to give the sense so that they understood the reading.

This Day Is Holy

[9] Then Nehemiah, who was the governor, and Ezra the priest *and* scribe, and the Levites who taught the people said to all the people, "This day is holy to the LORD your God; do not mourn or weep." For all the people were weeping when they heard the words of the Law. [10] Then he said to them, "Go, eat the festival foods, drink the sweet drinks, and send portions to him who has nothing prepared; for this day is holy to our Lord. Do not be grieved, for the joy of the LORD is your refuge." [11] So the Levites silenced all the people, saying, "Be still, for the day is holy; do not be grieved." [12] Then all the people went away to eat, drink, to send portions, and to celebrate a great feast, because they understood the words which had been made known to them.

Feast of Booths Restored

[13] Then on the second day the heads of fathers' *households* of all the people, the priests, and the Levites were gathered to Ezra the scribe so that they might gain insight into

the words of the Law. 14 And they found written in the Law how the LORD had commanded through Moses that the sons of Israel were to live in booths during the feast of the seventh month. 15 And that they were to proclaim and circulate a proclamation in all their cities and in Jerusalem, saying, "Go out to the hills, and bring olive branches and wild olive branches, myrtle branches, palm branches, and branches of *other* trees with thick branches, to make booths, as it is written." 16 So the people went out and brought *them* and made booths for themselves, each on his roof, and in their courtyards and in the courtyards of the house of God, and in the public square at the Water Gate, and in the square at the Gate of Ephraim. 17 The entire assembly of those who had returned from the captivity made booths and lived in the booths. Indeed, the sons of Israel had not done so since the days of Joshua the son of Nun to that day. And there was very great rejoicing. 18 He read from the Book of the Law of God daily, from the first day to the last day. And they celebrated the feast seven days, and on the eighth day *there was* a festive assembly in accordance with the ordinance.

The People Confess Their Sin

9 Now on the twenty-fourth day of this month the sons of Israel assembled with fasting, in sackcloth and with dirt upon them. 2 The descendants of Israel separated themselves from all foreigners, and they stood and confessed their sins and the wrongdoings of their fathers. 3 While they stood in their place, they read from the Book of the Law of the LORD their God for a fourth of the day; and for *another* fourth they confessed and worshiped the LORD their God. 4 Now on the Levites' platform stood Jeshua, Bani, Kadmiel, Shebaniah, Bunni, Sherebiah, Bani, *and* Chenani, and they cried out with a loud voice to the LORD their God.

5 Then the Levites, Jeshua, Kadmiel, Bani, Hashabneiah, Sherebiah, Hodiah, Shebaniah, *and* Pethahiah said, "Arise, bless the LORD your God forever and ever!
May Your glorious name be blessed
And exalted above all blessing and praise!
6 "You alone are the LORD.
You have made the heavens,
The heaven of heavens with all
their ¹lights,
The earth and everything that is on it,
The seas and everything that are in them.
You give life to all of them,
And the heavenly lights bow down before
You.
7 "You are the LORD God,
Who chose Abram
And brought him out from Ur of the
Chaldees,
And gave him the name Abraham.
8 "You found his heart faithful before You,
And made a covenant with him
To give *him* the land of the Canaanite,
Of the Hittite and the Amorite,
Of the Perizzite, the Jebusite, and the
Girgashite—

To give *it* to his descendants.
And You have fulfilled Your promise,
Because You are righteous.
9 ¶ "You saw the affliction of our fathers in
Egypt,
And heard their cry by the Red Sea.
10 "Then You performed signs and wonders
against Pharaoh,
Against all his servants and all the people
of his land;
For You knew that they acted arrogantly
toward them,
And You made a name for Yourself as *it is*
this day.
11 "You divided the sea before them,
So they passed through the midst of the
sea on dry ground;
And You hurled their pursuers into the
depths,
Like a stone into raging waters.
12 "And with a pillar of cloud You led them by
day,
And with a pillar of fire by night
To light for them the way
In which they were to go.
13 "Then You came down on Mount Sinai,
And spoke with them from heaven;
You gave them just ordinances and true
laws,
Good statutes and commandments.
14 "So You made known to them Your holy
Sabbath,
And gave them commandments, statutes,
and law,
Through Your servant Moses.
15 "You provided bread from heaven for them
for their hunger,
You brought out water from a rock for
them for their thirst,
And You told them to enter in order to
take possession of
The land which You swore to give them.
16 ¶ "But they, our fathers, acted arrogantly;
They became stubborn and would not
listen to Your commandments.
17 "They refused to listen,
And did not remember Your wondrous
deeds which You performed among
them;
So they became stubborn and appointed a
leader to return to their slavery in
Egypt.
But You are a God of forgiveness,
Gracious and compassionate,
Slow to anger and abounding in mercy;
And You did not abandon them.
18 "Even when they made for themselves
A calf of cast metal
And said, 'This is your ¹god
Who brought you up from Egypt,'
And committed great blasphemies,
19 You, in Your great compassion,
Did not abandon them in the wilderness;
The pillar of cloud did not leave them by
day,
To guide them on their way,
Nor the pillar of fire by night, to light
for them the way in which they were
to go.

9:6 ¹Lit *host;* i.e., sun, stars, etc.   9:18 ¹Or *God;* i.e., an idol intended to represent God

20 "Instead, You gave Your good Spirit to instruct them,
You did not withhold Your manna from their mouth,
And You gave them water for their thirst.

21 "Indeed, for forty years You provided for them in the wilderness *and* they were not lacking;
Their clothes did not wear out, nor did their feet swell up.

22 "You also gave them kingdoms and peoples,
And allotted *them* to them as a boundary.
They took possession of the land of Sihon the king of Heshbon
And the land of Og the king of Bashan.

23 "You made their sons *as* numerous as the stars of heaven,
And You brought them into the land
Which You had told their fathers to enter and possess.

24 "So their sons entered and took possession of the land.
And You subdued before them the inhabitants of the land, the Canaanites,
And You handed them over to them, with their kings and the peoples of the land,
To do with them as they desired.

25 "They captured fortified cities and a fertile land.
They took possession of houses full of every good thing,
Carved out cisterns, vineyards, olive groves,
Fruit trees in abundance.
So they ate, were filled and put on fat,
And lived luxuriously in Your great goodness.

26¶ "But they became rebellious and revolted against You,
And threw Your Law behind their backs
And killed Your prophets who had admonished them
In order to bring them back to You,
And they committed great blasphemies.

27 "Therefore You handed them over to their enemies who oppressed them,
But when they cried out to You in the time of their distress,
You heard from heaven, and according to Your great compassion
You gave them people who saved them from the hand of their enemies.

28 "But as soon as they had rest, they did evil again before You;
Therefore You abandoned them to the hand of their enemies, so that they ruled over them.
When they cried out again to You, You heard from heaven,
And many times You rescued them according to Your compassion.

29 And admonished them in order to turn them back to Your Law.
Yet they acted arrogantly and did not listen to Your commandments but sinned against Your ordinances,
Which, *if* a person follows them, then he will live by them.
And they turned a stubborn shoulder and

stiffened their neck, and would not listen.

30 "However, You remained patient with them for many years,
And admonished them by Your Spirit through Your prophets,
Yet they would not listen.
Therefore You handed them over to the peoples of the lands.

31 "Nevertheless, in Your great compassion You did not make an end of them or abandon them,
For You are a gracious and compassionate God.

32¶ "Now then, our God, the great, the mighty, and the awesome God, who keeps *His* covenant and faithfulness,
Do not let all the hardship seem insignificant before You,
Which has happened to us, our kings, our leaders, our priests, our prophets, our fathers, and to all Your people,
From the days of the kings of Assyria to this day.

33 "However, You are righteous in everything that has happened to us;
For You have dealt faithfully, but we have acted wickedly.

34 "For our kings, our leaders, our priests, and our fathers have not kept Your Law
Or paid attention to Your commandments and Your admonitions with which You have admonished them.

35 "But they, in their own kingdom,
With Your great goodness which You gave them,
With the broad and rich land which You placed before them,
Did not serve You or turn from their evil deeds.

36 "Behold, we are slaves today,
And as for the land which You gave to our fathers to eat its fruit and its bounty,
Behold, we are slaves on it.

37 "And its abundant produce is for the kings Whom You have set over us because of our sins;
They also rule over our bodies
And over our cattle as they please,
So we are in great distress.

A Covenant Results

38¶ "Now because of all this
We are making an agreement in writing;
And on the sealed *document are the names of* our leaders, our Levites, *and* our priests."

Signers of the Document

10 Now on the sealed *document were the names of:* Nehemiah the governor, the son of Hacaliah, and Zedekiah, 2 Seraiah, Azariah, Jeremiah, 3 Pashhur, Amariah, Malchijah, 4 Hattush, Shebaniah, Malluch, 5 Harim, Meremoth, Obadiah, 6 Daniel, Ginnethon, Baruch, 7 Meshullam, Abijah, Mijamin, 8 Maaziah, Bilgai, *and* Shemaiah. These *were* the priests. 9 And the Levites: Jeshua the son of Azaniah, Binnui of the sons of Henadad, *and* Kadmiel; 10 also their brothers Shebaniah,

Hodiah, Kelita, Pelaiah, Hanan, 11 Mica, Rehob, Hashabiah, 12 Zaccur, Sherebiah, Shebaniah, 13 Hodiah, Bani, *and* Beninu. 14 The leaders of the people: Parosh, Pahath-moab, Elam, Zattu, Bani, 15 Bunni, Azgad, Bebai, 16 Adonijah, Bigvai, Adin, 17 Ater, Hezekiah, Azzur, 18 Hodiah, Hashum, Bezai, 19 Hariph, Anathoth, Nebai, 20 Magpiash, Meshullam, Hezir, 21 Meshezabel, Zadók, Jaddua, 22 Pelatiah, Hanan, Anaiah, 23 Hoshea, Hananiah, Hasshub, 24 Hallohesh, Pilha, Shobek, 25 Rehum, Hashabnah, Maaseiah, 26 Ahiah, Hanan, Anan, 27 Malluch, Harim, *and* Baanah.

Obligations of the Document

28 Now the rest of the people, the priests, the Levites, the gatekeepers, the singers, the temple servants, and all those who had separated themselves from the peoples of the lands to the Law of God, their wives, their sons, and their daughters, all those who had knowledge and understanding, 29 are joining with their kinsmen, their nobles, and are taking on themselves a curse and an oath to walk in God's Law, which was given through Moses, God's servant, and to keep and to comply with all the commandments of GOD our Lord, and His ordinances and statutes; 30 and that we will not give our daughters to the peoples of the land or take their daughters for our sons. 31 As for the peoples of the land who bring wares or any grain on the Sabbath day to sell, we will not buy from them on the Sabbath or on *any* holy day; and we will forgo *the crops of* the seventh year and every debt.

32 We also imposed on ourselves the obligation to contribute yearly a third of a shekel for the service of the house of our God: 33 for the showbread, for the continual grain offering, for the continual burnt offering, the Sabbaths, the new moons, for the appointed times, for the holy things, and for the sin offerings to make atonement for Israel, and all the work of the house of our God.

34 Likewise we cast lots for the supply of wood *among* the priests, the Levites, and the people so that they could bring it to the house of our God, according to our fathers' households, at set times annually, to burn on the altar of the LORD our God, as it is written in the Law; 35 and so that they could bring the first fruits of our ground and the first fruits of all the fruit of every tree to the house of the LORD annually, 36 and bring to the house of our God the firstborn of our sons and of our cattle, and the firstborn of our herds and our flocks as it is written in the Law, for the priests who are ministering in the house of our God. 37 We will also bring the first of our dough, our contributions, the fruit of every tree, the new wine, and the oil to the priests at the chambers of the house of our God, and the tithe of our ground to the Levites, for the Levites are they who receive the tithes in all the rural towns. 38 And the priest, the son of Aaron, shall be with the Levites when the Levites receive tithes, and the Levites shall bring up the tenth of the tithes to the house of our God, to the chambers of the storehouse. 39 For the sons of Israel and the sons of Levi shall bring the contribution of the grain, the new wine, and the oil to the chambers; the utensils of the sanctuary, the priests who are ministering, the gatekeepers, and the singers are there. So we will not neglect the house of our God.

Time Passes; Heads of Provinces

11 Now the leaders of the people lived in Jerusalem, but the rest of the people cast lots to bring one out of ten to live in Jerusalem, the holy city, while nine-tenths *remained* in the *other* cities. 2 And the people blessed all the men who volunteered to live in Jerusalem.

3 Now these are the heads of the provinces who lived in Jerusalem, but in the cities of Judah each lived on his own property in their cities—the Israelites, the priests, the Levites, the temple servants, and the descendants of Solomon's servants. 4 Some of the sons of Judah and some of the sons of Benjamin lived in Jerusalem. From the sons of Judah: Athaiah the son of Uzziah, the son of Zechariah, the son of Amariah, the son of Shephatiah, the son of Mahalalel, of the sons of Perez; 5 and Maaseiah the son of Baruch, the son of Col-hozeh, the son of Hazaiah, the son of Adaiah, the son of Joiarib, the son of Zechariah, the son of the Shilonite. 6 All the sons of Perez who lived in Jerusalem were 468 able men.

7 Now these are the sons of Benjamin: Sallu the son of Meshullam, the son of Joed, the son of Pedaiah, the son of Kolaiah, the son of Maaseiah, the son of Ithiel, the son of Jeshaiah; 8 and after him Gabbai *and* Sallai, 928. 9 Joel the son of Zichri was their overseer, and Judah the son of Hassenuah was second in command of the city.

10 From the priests: Jedaiah the son of Joiarib, Jachin, 11 Seraiah the son of Hilkiah, the son of Meshullam, the son of Zadok, the son of Meraioth, the son of Ahitub, the overseer of the house of God, 12 and their kinsmen who did the work of the temple, 822; and Adaiah the son of Jeroham, the son of Pelaliah, the son of Amzi, the son of Zechariah, the son of Pashhur, the son of Malchijah, 13 and his kinsmen, heads of fathers' *households,* 242; and Amashsai the son of Azarel, the son of Ahzai, the son of Meshillemoth, the son of Immer, 14 and their brothers, valiant warriors, 128. And their overseer was Zabdiel, the son of Haggedolim.

15 Now from the Levites: Shemaiah the son of Hasshub, the son of Azrikam, the son of Hashabiah, the son of Bunni; 16 and Shabbethai and Jozabad, from the leaders of the Levites, who were in charge of the outside work of the house of God; 17 and Mattaniah the son of Mica, the son of Zabdi, the son of Asaph, who was the leader in beginning the thanksgiving at prayer, and Bakbukiah, the second among his kinsmen; and Abda the son of Shammua, the son of Galal, the son of Jeduthun. 18 All the Levites in the holy city *were* 284.

19 Also the gatekeepers: Akkub, Talmon, and their kinsmen who kept watch at the gates, *were* 172.

Outside Jerusalem

20 The rest of Israel, of the priests *and* of the

Levites, *were* in all the cities of Judah, each on his own inheritance. 21 But the temple servants were living in Ophel, and Ziha and Gishpa were in charge of the temple servants.

22 Now the overseer of the Levites in Jerusalem was Uzzi the son of Bani, the son of Hashabiah, the son of Mattaniah, the son of Mica, from the sons of Asaph, *who were* the singers for the service of the house of God. 23 For *there was* a commandment from the king concerning them and a royal command for the singers day by day. 24 And Pethahiah the son of Meshezabel, of the sons of Zerah the son of Judah, was the king's representative for every matter concerning the people.

25 Now as for the villages with their fields, some of the sons of Judah lived in Kiriath-arba and its towns, in Dibon and its towns, and in Jekabzeel and its villages, 26 and in Jeshua, in Moladah, and Beth-pelet, 27 and in Hazar-shual, in Beersheba and its towns, 28 and in Ziklag, in Meconah and in its towns, 29 and in En-rimmon, in Zorah, and in Jarmuth, 30 Zanoah, Adullam, and their villages, Lachish and its fields, Azekah and its towns. So they camped from Beersheba as far as the Valley of Hinnom. 31 The sons of Benjamin also *lived* from Geba onward, at Michmash and Aija, at Bethel and its towns, 32 at Anathoth, Nob, Ananiah, 33 Hazor, Ramah, Gittaim, 34 Hadid, Zeboim, Neballat, 35 Lod, and Ono, the Valley of Craftsmen. 36 And from the Levites, *some* divisions in Judah *belonged* to Benjamin.

Priests and Levites Who Returned to Jerusalem with Zerubbabel

12 Now these are the priests and the Levites who came up with Zerubbabel the son of Shealtiel, and Jeshua: Seraiah, Jeremiah, Ezra, 2 Amariah, Malluch, Hattush, 3 Shecaniah, Rehum, Meremoth, 4 Iddo, Ginnethoi, Abijah, 5 Mijamin, Maadiah, Bilgah, 6 Shemaiah and Joiarib, Jedaiah, 7 Sallu, Amok, Hilkiah, *and* Jedaiah. These were the heads of the priests and their kinsmen in the days of Jeshua.

8 And the Levites *were* Jeshua, Binnui, Kadmiel, Sherebiah, Judah, *and* Mattaniah *who was* in charge of the songs of thanksgiving, he and his brothers. 9 Also Bakbukiah and Unni, their brothers, *stood* opposite them in *their* service divisions. 10 Jeshua fathered Joiakim, Joiakim fathered Eliashib, Eliashib *fathered* Joiada, 11 Joiada fathered Jonathan, and Jonathan fathered Jaddua.

12 Now in the days of Joiakim, the priests, the heads of fathers' *households* were: of Seraiah, Meraiah; of Jeremiah, Hananiah; 13 of Ezra, Meshullam; of Amariah, Jehohanan; 14 of Malluchi, Jonathan; of Shebaniah, Joseph; 15 of Harim, Adna; of Meraioth, Helkai; 16 of Iddo, Zechariah; of Ginnethon, Meshullam; 17 of Abijah, Zichri; of Miniamin, of Moadiah, Piltai; 18 of Bilgah, Shammua; of Shemaiah, Jehonathan; 19 of Joiarib, Mattenai; of Jedaiah, Uzzi; 20 of Sallai, Kallai; of Amok, Eber; 21 of Hilkiah, Hashabiah; *and* of Jedaiah, Nethanel.

The Chief Levites

22 As for the Levites, the heads of fathers'

households were registered in the days of Eliashib, Joiada, and Johanan, and Jaddua; so *were* the priests in the reign of Darius the Persian. 23 The sons of Levi, the heads of fathers' *households,* were registered in the Book of the Chronicles up to the days of Johanan the son of Eliashib. 24 And the heads of the Levites *were* Hashabiah, Sherebiah, and Jeshua the son of Kadmiel, with their brothers opposite them, to praise *and* give thanks, as prescribed by David the man of God, division corresponding to division. 25 Mattaniah, Bakbukiah, Obadiah, Meshullam, Talmon, *and* Akkub *were* gatekeepers keeping watch at the storerooms of the gates. 26 These men *served* in the days of Joiakim the son of Jeshua, the son of Jozadak, and in the days of Nehemiah the governor and Ezra the priest *and* scribe.

Dedication of the Wall

27 Now at the dedication of the wall of Jerusalem they sought out the Levites from all their places, to bring them to Jerusalem so that they could celebrate the dedication with joy, with songs of thanksgiving and with songs *to the accompaniment* of cymbals, harps, and lyres. 28 So the sons of the singers were assembled from the territory around Jerusalem, and from the villages of the Netophathites, 29 from Beth-gilgal and from *their* fields in Geba and Azmaveth, because the singers had built themselves villages around Jerusalem. 30 The priests and the Levites purified themselves; they also purified the people, the gates, and the wall.

Procedures for the Temple

31 Then I had the leaders of Judah come up on top of the wall, and I appointed two large choirs, the first proceeding to the right on top of the wall toward the Dung Gate. 32 Hoshaiah and half of the leaders of Judah followed them, 33 with Azariah, Ezra, Meshullam, 34 Judah, Benjamin, Shemaiah, Jeremiah, 35 and some of the sons of the priests with trumpets; *and* Zechariah the son of Jonathan, the son of Shemaiah, the son of Mattaniah, the son of Micaiah, the son of Zaccur, the son of Asaph, 36 and his kinsmen, Shemaiah, Azarel, Milalai, Gilalai, Maai, Nethanel, Judah, *and* Hanani, with the musical instruments of David the man of God. And Ezra the scribe *went* before them. 37 At the Fountain Gate they went directly up the steps of the city of David by the stairway of the wall, above the house of David to the Water Gate on the east.

38 The second choir proceeded to the left, while I followed them with half of the people on the wall, above the Tower of Furnaces, to the Broad Wall, 39 and above the Gate of Ephraim, by the Ancient Gate, by the Fish Gate, the Tower of Hananel, and the Tower of the Hundred, as far as the Sheep Gate; and they stopped at the Gate of the Guard. 40 Then the two choirs took their positions in the house of God. So did I and half of the officials with me; 41 and the priests, Eliakim, Maaseiah, Miniamin, Micaiah, Elioenai, Zechariah, and Hananiah, with the trumpets; 42 and Maaseiah, Shemaiah, Eleazar, Uzzi, Jehohanan, Malchijah,

Elam, and Ezer. And the singers sang, with Jezrahiah *their* leader, 43 and on that day they offered great sacrifices and rejoiced because God had given them great joy, and the women and children rejoiced as well, so that the joy of Jerusalem was heard from far away.

44 On that day men were also appointed over the chambers for the supplies, the contributions, the first fruits, and the tithes, to gather into them from the fields of the cities the portions *required by* the Law for the priests and Levites; for Judah rejoiced over the priests and the Levites who served. 45 For they performed the worship of their God and the service of purification, together with the singers and the gatekeepers in accordance with the command of David *and* of his son Solomon. 46 For in the days of David and Asaph, in ancient times, *there were* leaders of the singers, songs of praise and songs of thanksgiving to God. 47 So all Israel in the days of Zerubbabel and Nehemiah gave the portions *due* the singers and the gatekeepers as each day required, and they set apart the consecrated *portion* for the Levites, and the Levites set apart the consecrated *portion* for the sons of Aaron.

Foreigners Excluded

13 On that day the Book of Moses was read aloud as the people listened; and there was found written in it that no Ammonite or Moabite was ever to enter the assembly of God, 2 because they did not meet the sons of Israel with bread and water, but hired Balaam against them to curse them. However, our God turned the curse into a blessing. 3 So when they heard the Law, they excluded all foreigners from Israel.

Tobiah Expelled and the Temple Cleansed

4 Now prior to this, Eliashib the priest, who was appointed over the chambers of the house of our God, being related to Tobiah, 5 had prepared a large room for him, where previously they used to put the grain offerings, the frankincense, the utensils and the tithes of grain, wine, and oil prescribed for the Levites, the singers, and the gatekeepers, and the contributions for the priests. 6 But during all this *time* I was not in Jerusalem, for in the thirty-second year of Artaxerxes king of Babylon I had come to the king. After some time, however, I requested a leave of absence from the king, 7 and I came to Jerusalem and learned about the evil that Eliashib had committed for Tobiah, by preparing a room for him in the courtyards of the house of God. 8 It was very displeasing to me, so I threw all of Tobiah's household articles out of the room. 9 Then I gave an order, and they cleansed the rooms; and I returned the utensils of the house of God there with the grain offering and the frankincense.

Tithes Restored

10 I also discovered that the portions of the Levites had not been given *to them,* so the Levites and the singers who performed the service had gone away, each to his own field.

11 So I reprimanded the officials and said, "Why has the house of God been neglected?" Then I gathered them together and stationed them at their posts. 12 All Judah then brought the tithe of the grain, wine, and oil into the storehouses. 13 *To be* in charge of the storehouses, I appointed Shelemiah the priest, Zadok the scribe, and Pedaiah from the Levites, and in addition to them was Hanan the son of Zaccur, the son of Mattaniah; for they were considered reliable, and it was their task to distribute to their kinsmen. 14 Remember me for this, my God, and do not wipe out my loyal deeds which I have performed for the house of my God and its services.

Sabbath Restored

15 In those days I saw in Judah *people* who were treading wine presses on the Sabbath, and bringing in sacks of grain and loading *them* on donkeys, as well as wine, grapes, figs, and every *kind of* load, and they were bringing *them* into Jerusalem on the Sabbath day. So I admonished *them* on the day they sold food. 16 Also people of Tyre were living there *who* imported fish and all *kinds of* merchandise, and sold *them* to the sons of Judah on the Sabbath, even in Jerusalem. 17 Then I reprimanded the nobles of Judah and said to them, "What is this evil thing that you are doing, by profaning the Sabbath day? 18 Did your fathers not do the same, so that our God brought on us and on this city all this trouble? Yet you are adding to the wrath against Israel by profaning the Sabbath."

19 And it came about that just as it became dark at the gates of Jerusalem before the Sabbath, I ordered that the doors be shut, and that they were not to open them until after the Sabbath. Then I stationed some of my servants at the gates *so that* no load would enter on the Sabbath day. 20 Once or twice the traders and merchants of every *kind of* merchandise spent the night outside Jerusalem. 21 Then I warned them and said to them, "Why do you spend the night in front of the wall? If you do so again, I will use force against you." From that time *on* they did not come on the Sabbath. 22 And I ordered the Levites that they were to purify themselves and come as gatekeepers to sanctify the Sabbath day. *For* this also remember me, my God, and have compassion on me according to the greatness of Your mercy.

Mixed Marriages Forbidden

23 In those days I also saw that the Jews had married women from Ashdod, Ammon, *and* Moab. 24 As for their children, half spoke in the language of Ashdod, and none of them knew how to speak the language of Judah, but only the language of his own people. 25 So I quarreled with them and cursed them, and struck some of them and pulled out their hair, and made them swear by God, "You shall not give your daughters to their sons, nor take *any* of their daughters for your sons or for yourselves. 26 Did Solomon the king of Israel not sin regarding these things? Yet among the many nations there was no king like him, and

he was loved by his God, and God made him king over all Israel; *yet* the foreign women caused even him to sin. [27] Has it not then been reported about you that you have committed all this great evil by acting unfaithfully against our God, by marrying foreign women?" [28] Even one of the sons of Joiada, the son of Eliashib the high priest, *became* a son-in-law of Sanballat the Horonite, so I chased him away from me.

[29] Remember them, my God, because they have defiled the priesthood and the covenant of the priesthood and the Levites.

[30] So I purified them from everything foreign, and assigned duties to the priests and the Levites, each in his work, [31] and *I arranged* for the delivery of wood at appointed times and for the first fruits. Remember me, my God, for good.

The Book of
ESTHER

The Banquets of the King

1 Now it happened in the days of Ahasuerus, the Ahasuerus who reigned from India to Cush over 127 provinces, 2 in those days as King Ahasuerus sat on his royal throne which *was* at the citadel in Susa, 3 in the third year of his reign he held a banquet for all his officials and attendants, the army *officers* of Persia and Media, the nobles and the officials of his provinces, in his presence. 4 At that time he displayed the riches of his royal glory and the splendor of his great majesty for many days, 180 days.

5 When these days were finished, the king held a banquet lasting seven days for all the people who were present at the citadel in Susa, from the greatest to the least, in the courtyard of the garden of the king's palace. 6 *There were curtains of* fine white and violet linen held by cords of fine purple linen on silver rings and marble columns, *and* couches of gold and silver on a mosaic floor of porphyry, marble, mother-of-pearl, and mineral stones. 7 Drinks were served in golden vessels of various kinds, and the royal wine was plentiful in proportion to the king's bounty. 8 But the drinking was *done* according to the *royal* law; there was no compulsion, for so the king had given orders to each official of his household, that he was to do as each person pleased. 9 Queen Vashti also held a banquet for the women in the palace which belonged to King Ahasuerus.

Queen Vashti's Refusal

10 On the seventh day, when the heart of the king was cheerful with wine, he ordered Mehuman, Biztha, Harbona, Bigtha, Abagtha, Zethar, and Carkas, the seven eunuchs who served in the presence of King Ahasuerus, 11 to bring Queen Vashti before the king with *her* royal turban in order to display her beauty to the people and the officials, for she was beautiful. 12 But Queen Vashti refused to come at the king's order delivered by the eunuchs. So the king became very angry, and his wrath burned within him.

13 Then the king said to the wise men who understood the times—for it was the custom of the king *to speak* this way before all who knew *Persian* law and justice 14 and were close to him, *namely,* Carshena, Shethar, Admatha, Tarshish, Meres, Marsena, and Memucan, the seven officials of Persia and Media who had access to the king's presence and sat in the first place in the kingdom— 15 "According to law, what is to be done with Queen Vashti, since she did not obey the command of King Ahasuerus delivered by the eunuchs?" 16 And in the presence of the king and the *other* officials, Memucan said, "Queen Vashti has wronged not only the king but *also* all the officials and all the peoples who are in all the provinces of King Ahasuerus. 17 For the queen's conduct will become known to all the women so as to make their own husbands despicable in their sight, when they say, 'King Ahasuerus commanded that Queen Vashti be brought in to his presence, but she did not come.' 18 And this day the wives of the officials of Persia and Media who have heard about the queen's conduct will talk *about it* to all the king's officials, and there will be plenty of contempt and anger. 19 If it pleases the king, let a royal edict be issued by him and let it be written in the laws of Persia and Media so that it cannot be repealed, that Vashti may not come into the presence of King Ahasuerus, and let the king give her royal position to another who is more worthy than she. 20 When the king's edict which he will make is heard throughout his kingdom, great as it is, then all women will give honor to their husbands, great and small."

21 Now *this* word pleased the king and the officials, and the king did as Memucan proposed. 22 So he sent letters to all the king's provinces, to each province according to its script and to every people according to their language, that every man was to be the ruler in his own house and the one who speaks in the language of his own people.

Vashti's Successor Sought

2 After these things, when the anger of King Ahasuerus had subsided, he remembered Vashti and what she had done, and what had been decided regarding her. 2 Then the king's attendants, who served him, said, "Let beautiful young virgins be sought for the king. 3 And may the king appoint overseers in all the provinces of his kingdom, and have them bring every beautiful young virgin to the citadel of Susa, to the harem, into the custody of Hegai, the king's eunuch, who is in charge of the women; and let their cosmetics be given *to them.* 4 Then let the young woman who pleases the king be queen in place of Vashti." And the suggestion pleased the king, and he did accordingly.

5 There was a Jew at the citadel in Susa whose name was Mordecai, the son of Jair, the son of Shimei, the son of Kish, a Benjaminite, 6 who had been taken from Jerusalem with the exiles who had been deported with Jeconiah king of Judah, whom Nebuchadnezzar the king of Babylon had deported. 7 He was the guardian to Hadassah, that is Esther, his uncle's daughter, for she had no father or mother. Now the young woman was beautiful of form and face, and when her father and her mother died, Mordecai took her as his own daughter.

Esther Finds Favor

8 So it came about, when the command and decree of the king were heard and many young ladies were gathered to the citadel of Susa into the custody of Hegai, that Esther was taken to

the king's palace into the custody of Hegai, who was in charge of the women. ⁹Now the young lady pleased him and found favor with him. So he quickly provided her with her cosmetics and food, gave her seven choice female attendants from the king's palace, and transferred her and her attendants to the best place in the harem. ¹⁰Esther did not reveal her people or her kindred, because Mordecai had instructed her that she was not to reveal *them.* ¹¹And every day Mordecai walked back and forth in front of the courtyard of the harem to learn how Esther was and what was happening to her.

¹²Now when the turn came for each young woman to go in to King Ahasuerus, after the end of her twelve months under the regulations for the women—for the days of their beauty treatment were completed as follows: six months with oil of myrrh and six months with balsam oil and the cosmetics for women—¹³the young woman would go in to the king in this way: anything that she desired was given her to take with her from the harem to the king's palace. ¹⁴In the evening she would enter and in the morning she would return to the second harem, to the custody of Shaashgaz, the king's eunuch who was in charge of the concubines. She would not go in to the king again, unless the king delighted in her and she was summoned by name.

¹⁵Now when the turn of Esther, the daughter of Abihail the uncle of Mordecai who had taken her as his daughter, came to go in to the king, she did not request anything except what Hegai, the king's eunuch who was in charge of the women, advised. And Esther was finding favor in the eyes of all who saw her. ¹⁶So Esther was taken to King Ahasuerus in his royal palace in the tenth month, which is the month Tebeth, in the seventh year of his reign.

Esther Becomes Queen

¹⁷The king loved Esther more than all the women, and she found favor and kindness with him more than all the virgins, so that he set the royal turban on her head and made her queen in place of Vashti. ¹⁸Then the king held a great banquet, Esther's banquet, for all his officials and his servants; he also made a holiday for the provinces and gave gifts in proportion to the king's bounty.

¹⁹Now when the virgins were gathered together for the second time, then Mordecai was sitting at the king's gate. ²⁰Esther *still* had not revealed her relatives or her people, just as Mordecai had instructed her; for Esther did what Mordecai told her just as she had when under his care.

Mordecai Saves the King

²¹In those days, while Mordecai was sitting at the king's gate, Bigthan and Teresh, two of the king's officials from those who guarded the door, became angry and sought to attack King Ahasuerus. ²²But the plot became known to Mordecai and he informed Queen Esther, and Esther told the king in Mordecai's name.

²³Then when the plot was investigated and found *to be so,* they were both hanged on a wooden *gallows;* and it was written in the Book of the Chronicles in the king's presence.

Haman's Plot against the Jews

3 After these events King Ahasuerus honored Haman, the son of Hammedatha the Agagite, and promoted him and established his authority over all the officials who *were* with him. ²All the king's servants who were at the king's gate bowed down and paid ᵗhomage to Haman; for so the king had commanded regarding him. But Mordecai neither bowed down nor paid ²homage. ³Then the king's servants who were at the king's gate said to Mordecai, "Why are you violating the king's command?" ⁴Now it was when they had spoken daily to him and he would not listen to them, that they told Haman to see whether Mordecai's reason would stand; for he had told them that he was a Jew. ⁵When Haman saw that Mordecai neither bowed down nor paid ᵗhomage to him, Haman was filled with rage. ⁶But he considered it beneath his dignity to kill Mordecai alone, for they had told him *who* the people of Mordecai *were;* so Haman sought to annihilate all the Jews, the people of Mordecai, who *were found* throughout the kingdom of Ahasuerus.

⁷In the first month, which is the month Nisan, in the twelfth year of King Ahasuerus, Pur, that is the lot, was cast before Haman from day to day and from month *to month,* until the twelfth month, that is the month Adar. ⁸Then Haman said to King Ahasuerus, "There is a certain people scattered and dispersed among the peoples in all the provinces of your kingdom; their laws are different from *those* of all *other* people and they do not comply with the king's laws, so it is not in the king's interest to let them remain. ⁹If it is pleasing to the king, let it be decreed that they be eliminated, and I will pay ᵗten thousand talents of silver into the hands of those who carry out the *king's* business, to put into the king's treasuries." ¹⁰Then the king took his signet ring from his hand and gave it to Haman, the son of Hammedatha the Agagite, the enemy of the Jews. ¹¹And the king said to Haman, "The silver is yours, and the people *also,* to do with them as you please."

¹²Then the king's scribes were summoned on the thirteenth day of the first month, and it was written just as Haman commanded to the king's satraps, to the governors who were over each province and to the officials of each people, each province according to its script, each people according to its language, being written in the name of King Ahasuerus and sealed with the king's signet ring. ¹³Letters were sent by couriers to all the king's provinces to annihilate, kill, and destroy all the Jews, both young and old, women and children, in one day, the thirteenth *day* of the twelfth month, which is the month Adar, and to seize their possessions as plunder. ¹⁴A copy of the edict to be issued as law in

---

3:2 ¹ I.e., great respect and honor to a superior   2 I.e., great respect and honor to a superior
3:5 ¹ I.e., great respect and honor to a superior   3:9 ¹ About 375 tons or 340 metric tons

every province was published to all the peoples so that they would be ready for this day. 15 The couriers went out, speeded by the king's order while the decree was issued at the citadel in Susa; and while the king and Haman sat down to drink, the city of Susa was agitated.

Esther Learns of Haman's Plot

4 When Mordecai learned of everything that had been done, he tore his clothes, put on sackcloth and ashes, and went out into the midst of the city and wailed loudly and bitterly. 2 And he came as far as the king's gate, for no one was to enter the king's gate clothed in sackcloth. 3 In each and every province where the command and decree of the king came, there was great mourning among the Jews, with fasting, weeping, and mourning rites; and many had sackcloth and ashes spread out as a bed.

4 Then Esther's attendants and her eunuchs came and informed her, and the queen was seized by great fear. And she sent garments to clothe Mordecai so that he would remove his sackcloth from him, but he did not accept them. 5 Then Esther summoned Hathach from the king's eunuchs, whom the king had appointed to attend her, and ordered him to go to Mordecai to learn what this mourning was and why it was happening. 6 So Hathach went out to Mordecai in the city square, in front of the king's gate. 7 Mordecai told him everything that had happened to him, and the exact amount of money that Haman had promised to pay to the king's treasuries for the elimination of the Jews. 8 He also gave him a copy of the text of the edict which had been issued in Susa for their annihilation, so that he might show Esther and inform her, and to order her to go in to the king to implore his favor and plead with him for her people.

9 So Hathach came back and reported Mordecai's words to Esther. 10 Then Esther spoke to Hathach and ordered him to reply to Mordecai: 11 "All the king's servants and the people of the king's provinces know that for any man or woman who comes to the king in the inner courtyard, who is not summoned, he has only one law, that he be put to death, unless the king holds out to him the golden scepter so that he may live. And I have not been summoned to come to the king for these thirty days." 12 And they reported Esther's words to Mordecai.

13 Then Mordecai told them to reply to Esther, "Do not imagine that you in the king's palace can escape any more than all the other Jews. 14 For if you keep silent at this time, liberation and rescue will arise for the Jews from another place, and you and your father's house will perish. And who knows whether you have not attained royalty for such a time as this?"

Esther Plans to Intercede

15 Then Esther told them to reply to Mordecai, 16 "Go, gather all the Jews who are found in Susa, and fast for me; do not eat or drink for three days, night or day. I and my attendants also will fast in the same way. And then I will go in to the king, which is not in accordance with the law; and if I perish, I perish." 17 So Mordecai went away and did just as Esther had commanded him.

Esther Plans a Banquet

5 Now it came about on the third day that Esther put on her royal robes and stood in the inner courtyard of the king's palace in front of the king's rooms, and the king was sitting on his royal throne in the throne room, opposite the entrance to the palace. 2 When the king saw Esther the queen standing in the courtyard, she obtained favor in his sight; and the king extended to Esther the golden scepter which was in his hand. So Esther approached and touched the top of the scepter. 3 Then the king said to her, "What is troubling you, Queen Esther? And what is your request? Up to half of the kingdom it shall be given to you." 4 Esther said, "If it pleases the king, may the king and Haman come this day to the banquet that I have prepared for him."

5 Then the king said, "Bring Haman quickly so that we may do as Esther desires." So the king and Haman came to the banquet which Esther had prepared. 6 As they drank their wine at the banquet, the king said to Esther, "What is your request, for it shall be granted to you. And what is your wish? Up to half of the kingdom it shall be done." 7 So Esther replied, "My request and my wish is: 8 if I have found favor in the sight of the king, and if it pleases the king to grant my request and do what I wish, may the king and Haman come to the banquet which I will prepare for them, and tomorrow I will do as the king says."

Haman's Pride

9 Then Haman went out that day joyful and pleased of heart; but when Haman saw Mordecai at the king's gate and that he did not stand up or tremble before him, Haman was filled with anger against Mordecai. 10 Haman controlled himself, however, and went to his house. But he sent for his friends and his wife Zeresh. 11 Then Haman told them of the glory of his riches, and his many sons, and every occasion on which the king had honored him and how he had promoted him above the officials and servants of the king. 12 Haman also said, "Even Esther the queen let no one except me come with the king to the banquet which she had prepared; and tomorrow also I am invited by her with the king. 13 Yet all of this does not satisfy me every time I see Mordecai the Jew sitting at the king's gate." 14 Then Zeresh his wife and all his friends said to him, "Have a wooden gallows 1 fifty cubits high made, and in the morning ask the king to have Mordecai hanged on it; then go joyfully with the king to the banquet." And the advice pleased Haman, so he had the wooden gallows made.

The King Plans to Honor Mordecai

6 During that night the king could not sleep, so he gave an order to bring the book of records, the chronicles, and they were read

5:14 1 About 75 ft. or 23 m

before the king. [2] And it was found written what Mordecai had reported about Bigthana and Teresh, two of the king's eunuchs who were doorkeepers, that they had sought to attack King Ahasuerus. [3] Then the king said, "What honor or dignity has been bestowed on Mordecai for this?" And the king's servants who attended him said, "Nothing has been done for him." [4] So the king said, "Who is in the courtyard?" Now Haman had *just* entered the outer courtyard of the king's palace in order to speak to the king about hanging Mordecai on the wooden *gallows* which he had prepared for him. [5] So the king's servants said to him, "Behold, Haman is standing in the courtyard." And the king said, "Have him come in." [6] Haman then came in and the king said to him, "What is to be done for the man whom the king desires to honor?" And Haman said to himself, "Whom would the king desire to honor more than me?" [7] Therefore Haman said to the king, "For the man whom the king desires to honor, [8] have them bring a royal robe which the king has worn, and the horse on which the king has ridden, and on whose head a royal turban has been placed; [9] then *order them* to hand the robe and the horse over to one of the king's noble officials, and have them dress the man whom the king desires to honor, and lead him on horseback through the city square, and proclaim before him, 'So it shall be done for the man whom the king desires to honor.' "

Haman Must Honor Mordecai

[10] Then the king said to Haman, "Quickly, take the robe and the horse just as you have said, and do so for Mordecai the Jew, who is sitting at the king's gate; do not fail to do anything of all that you have said." [11] So Haman took the robe and the horse, and dressed Mordecai, and led him *on horseback* through the city square, and proclaimed before him, "So it shall be done for the man whom the king desires to honor." [12] Then Mordecai returned to the king's gate, while Haman hurried home, mourning, with *his* head covered. [13] And Haman informed Zeresh his wife and all his friends of everything that had happened to him. Then his wise men and Zeresh his wife said to him, "If Mordecai, before whom you have begun to fall, is of Jewish origin, you will not prevail over him, but will certainly fall before him."

[14] While they were still talking with him, the king's eunuchs arrived and quickly brought Haman to the banquet which Esther had prepared.

Esther's Plea

7 Now the king and Haman came to drink *wine* with Esther the queen. [2] And the king said to Esther on the second day also as they drank their wine at the banquet, "What is your request, Queen Esther? It shall be granted you. And what is your wish? Up to half of the kingdom it shall be done." [3] Then Queen Esther replied, "If I have found favor in your sight, O king, and if it pleases the king, let my

life be given me as my request, and my people as my wish; [4] for we have been sold, I and my people, to be destroyed, killed, and eliminated. Now if we had only been sold as slaves, men and women, I would have kept silent, because the distress would not be sufficient *reason* to burden the king." [5] Then King Ahasuerus asked Queen Esther, "Who is he, and where is he, who would presume to do such *a thing?*" [6] And Esther said, "A foe and an enemy is this wicked Haman!" Then Haman became terrified before the king and queen.

Haman Is Hanged

[7] The king then got up in his anger from drinking wine *and went* into the palace garden; but Haman stayed to beg for his life from Queen Esther, for he saw that harm had been determined against him by the king. [8] Now when the king returned from the palace garden into the place where they had been drinking wine, Haman was falling on the couch where Esther was. Then the king said, "Will he even assault the queen with me in the house?" As the word went out of the king's mouth, they covered Haman's face. [9] Then Harbonah, one of the eunuchs who *stood* before the king, said, "Indeed, behold, the wooden *gallows* standing at Haman's house [1]fifty cubits high, which Haman made for Mordecai who spoke good in behalf of the king!" And the king said, "Hang him on it." [10] So they hanged Haman on the wooden *gallows* which he had prepared for Mordecai, and the king's anger subsided.

Mordecai Promoted

8 On that day King Ahasuerus gave the house of Haman, the enemy of the Jews, to Queen Esther; and Mordecai came before the king, because Esther had disclosed what he was to her. [2] Then the king took off his signet ring, which he had taken away from Haman, and gave it to Mordecai. And Esther set Mordecai over the house of Haman.

[3] Then Esther spoke again to the king, fell at his feet, wept, and pleaded for his compassion to avert the evil *scheme* of Haman the Agagite and his plot which he had devised against the Jews. [4] And the king extended the golden scepter to Esther. So Esther got up and stood before the king. [5] Then she said, "If it pleases the king and if I have found favor before him, and the matter *seems* proper to the king and I am pleasing in his sight, let it be written to revoke the letters devised by Haman, the son of Hammedatha the Agagite, which he wrote to eliminate the Jews who are in all the king's provinces. [6] For how can I endure to see the disaster which will happen to my people, and how can I endure to see the destruction of my kindred?" [7] So King Ahasuerus said to Queen Esther and to Mordecai the Jew, "Behold, I have given the house of Haman to Esther, and they have hanged him on the wooden *gallows* because he had reached out with his hand against the Jews.

The King's Decree Avenges the Jews

[8] Now you write to the Jews as you see fit, in

7:9 [1] About 75 ft. or 23 m

the king's name, and seal *it* with the king's signet ring; for a decree which is written in the name of the king and sealed with the king's signet ring may not be revoked."

9 So the king's scribes were summoned at that time in the third month (that is, the month Sivan), on the twenty-third day; and it was written in accordance with everything that Mordecai commanded the Jews, the satraps, the governors, and the officials of the provinces which *extended* from India to Cush, 127 provinces, to every province according to its script, and to every people according to their language, as well as to the Jews according to their script and their language. 10 He wrote in the name of King Ahasuerus, and sealed it with the king's signet ring, and sent letters by couriers on horses, riding on royal relay horses, offspring of racing mares. 11 In the letters the king granted the Jews who were in each and every city *the right* to assemble and to defend their lives, to destroy, kill, and eliminate the entire army of *any* people or province which was going to attack them, *including* children and women, and to plunder their spoils, 12 on one day in all the provinces of King Ahasuerus, on the thirteenth *day* of the twelfth month (that is, the month Adar). 13 A copy of the edict to be issued as law in each and every province was published to all the peoples, so that the Jews would be ready for this day to avenge themselves on their enemies. 14 The couriers, hurrying and speeded by the king's command, left, riding on the royal relay horses; and the decree was issued at the citadel in Susa.

15 Then Mordecai went out from the presence of the king in a royal robe of violet and white, with a large crown of gold and a garment of fine linen and purple; and the city of Susa shouted and rejoiced. 16 For the Jews there was light, joy, jubilation, and honor. 17 In each and every province and in each and every city, wherever the king's commandment and his decree arrived, there was joy and jubilation for the Jews, a feast and a holiday. And many among the peoples of the land became Jews, because the dread of the Jews had fallen on them.

The Jews Destroy Their Enemies

9 Now in the twelfth month (that is, the month Adar), on the thirteenth day, when the king's command and edict were to be put into effect, on the day when the enemies of the Jews hoped to gain the mastery over them, it turned out to the contrary so that the Jews themselves gained mastery over those who hated them. 2 The Jews assembled in their cities throughout the provinces of King Ahasuerus to attack those who sought to harm them; and no one could stand against them, because the dread of them had fallen on all the peoples. 3 Even all the officials of the provinces, the satraps, the governors, and those who were doing the king's business were supporting the Jews, because the dread of Mordecai had fallen on them. 4 For Mordecai was great in the king's house, and the news about him spread throughout the provinces; for the man Mordecai became greater and greater. 5 So the

Jews struck all their enemies with the sword, killing and destroying; and they did as they pleased to those who hated them. 6 At the citadel in Susa the Jews killed and eliminated five hundred men, 7 and they killed Parshandatha, Dalphon, Aspatha, 8 Poratha, Adalia, Aridatha, 9 Parmashta, Arisai, Aridai, and Vaizatha, 10 the ten sons of Haman the son of Hammedatha, the Jews' enemy; but they did not lay their hands on the plunder.

11 On that day the number of those who were killed at the citadel in Susa was reported to the king. 12 And the king said to Queen Esther, "The Jews have killed and eliminated five hundred men and the ten sons of Haman at the citadel in Susa. What have they done in the rest of the king's provinces! Now what is your request? It shall also be granted you. And what is your further wish? It shall also be done." 13 Then Esther said, "If it pleases the king, let tomorrow also be granted to the Jews who are in Susa to do according to the edict of today; and let Haman's ten sons be hanged on the wooden *gallows.*" 14 So the king commanded that it was to be done so; and an edict was issued in Susa, and Haman's ten sons were hanged. 15 The Jews who were in Susa assembled also on the fourteenth day of the month Adar and killed three hundred men in Susa, but they did not lay their hands on the plunder.

16 Now the rest of the Jews who *were* in the king's provinces assembled, to defend their lives and rid themselves of their enemies, and to kill seventy-five thousand of those who hated them; but they did not lay their hands on the plunder. 17 *This was done* on the thirteenth day of the month Adar, and on the fourteenth day they rested and made it a day of feasting and rejoicing.

18 But the Jews who were in Susa assembled on the thirteenth and the fourteenth of the same month, and they rested on the fifteenth day and made it a day of feasting and rejoicing. 19 Therefore the Jews of the rural areas, who live in the rural towns, make the fourteenth day of the month Adar *a* holiday for rejoicing and feasting and sending portions *of food* to one another.

The Feast of Purim Instituted

20 Then Mordecai recorded these events, and he sent letters to all the Jews who were in all the provinces of King Ahasuerus, *both* near and far, 21 obliging them to celebrate the fourteenth day of the month Adar, and the fifteenth day of the same month, annually, 22 because on those days the Jews rid themselves of their enemies, and *it was a* month which was turned for them from grief into joy, and from mourning into a holiday; that they were to make them days of feasting and rejoicing, and sending portions *of food* to one another, and gifts to the poor.

23 So the Jews undertook what they had started to do, and what Mordecai had written to them. 24 For Haman the son of Hammedatha, the Agagite, the adversary of all the Jews, had schemed against the Jews to eliminate them, and had cast Pur, that is the lot, to disturb

them and eliminate them. 25 But when it came to the king's attention, he commanded by letter that his wicked scheme which he had devised against the Jews was to return on his own head, and that he and his sons were to be hanged on the wooden *gallows*. 26 Therefore they called these days Purim after the name of Pur. And because of the instructions in this letter, both what they had seen in this regard and what had happened to them, 27 the Jews established and made a custom for themselves, their descendants, and for all those who allied themselves with them, so that they would not fail to celebrate these two days according to their regulation and according to their appointed time annually. 28 So these days were to be remembered and celebrated throughout every generation, every family, every province, and every city; and these days of Purim were not to be neglected by the Jews, or their memory fade from their descendants.

29 Then Queen Esther, daughter of Abihail, with Mordecai the Jew, wrote with full authority to confirm this second letter about Purim. 30 He sent letters to all the Jews, to the 127 provinces of the kingdom of Ahasuerus, *namely,* words of peace and truth, 31 to establish these days of Purim at their appointed times, just as Mordecai the Jew and Queen Esther had established for them, and just as they had established for themselves and for their descendants, *with* instructions for their times of fasting and their mourning. 32 The command of Esther established these customs for Purim, and it was written in the book.

Mordecai's Greatness

10 Now King Ahasuerus imposed a tax on the land and the coastlands of the sea. 2 And every accomplishment of his authority and power, and the full account of the greatness of Mordecai with which the king honored him, are they not written in the Book of the Chronicles of the Kings of Media and Persia? 3 For Mordecai the Jew was second *only* to King Ahasuerus, and great among the Jews and in favor with his many kinsmen, one who sought the good of his people and one who spoke for the welfare of his entire nation.

The Book of
JOB

Job's Character and Wealth

1 There was a man in the land of Uz whose name was Job; and that man was blameless, upright, fearing God and turning away from evil. 2 Seven sons and three daughters were born to him. 3 His possessions were seven thousand sheep, three thousand camels, five hundred yoke of oxen, five hundred female donkeys, and very many servants; and that man was the greatest of all the men of the east. 4 His sons used to go and hold a feast in the house of each one on his day, and they would send *word* and invite their three sisters to eat and drink with them. 5 When the days of feasting had completed their cycle, Job would send *word to them* and consecrate them, getting up early in the morning and offering burnt offerings *according to* the number of them all; for Job said, "Perhaps my sons have sinned and cursed God in their hearts." Job did so continually.

6 Now there was a day when the ¹sons of God came to present themselves before the Lord, and ²Satan also came among them. 7 The Lord said to Satan, "From where do you come?" Satan answered the Lord and said, "From roaming about on the earth and walking around on it." 8 The Lord said to Satan, "Have you considered My servant Job? For there is no one like him on the earth, a blameless and upright man, fearing God and turning away from evil." 9 Then Satan answered the Lord, "Does Job fear God for nothing? 10 Have You not made a fence around him and his house and all that he has, on every side? You have blessed the work of his hands, and his possessions have increased in the land. 11 But reach out with Your hand now and touch all that he has; he will certainly curse You to Your face." 12 Then the Lord said to Satan, "Behold, all that he has is in your power; only do not reach out *and put* your hand on him." So Satan departed from the presence of the Lord.

Satan Allowed to Test Job

13 Now on the day when his sons and his daughters were eating and drinking wine in their oldest brother's house, 14 a messenger came to Job and said, "The oxen were plowing and the female donkeys feeding beside them, 15 and the Sabeans attacked and took them. They also killed the servants with the edge of the sword, and I alone have escaped to tell you." 16 While he was still speaking, another came and said, "The fire of God fell from heaven and burned up the sheep and the servants and consumed them, and I alone have escaped to tell you." 17 While he was still speaking, another came and said, "The Chaldeans formed three units and made a raid on the camels and took them, and killed the servants with the edge of the sword, and I alone have escaped to tell you." 18 While he was still speaking, another also came and said, "Your sons and your daughters were eating and drinking wine in their oldest brother's house, 19 and behold, a great wind came from across the wilderness and struck the four corners of the house, and it fell on the young people and they died, and I alone have escaped to tell you."

20 Then Job got up, tore his robe, and shaved his head; then he fell to the ground and worshiped. 21 He said,

"Naked I came from my mother's womb,
And naked I shall return there.
The Lord gave and the Lord has taken away.
Blessed be the name of the Lord."

22 Despite all this, Job did not sin, nor did he blame God.

Job Loses His Health

2 Again, there was a day when the sons of God came to present themselves before the Lord, and ¹Satan also came among them to present himself before the Lord. 2 The Lord said to Satan, "Where have you come from?" Then Satan answered the Lord and said, "From roaming about on the earth and walking around on it." 3 The Lord said to Satan, "Have you considered My servant Job? For there is no one like him on the earth, a blameless and upright man fearing God and turning away from evil. And he still holds firm to his integrity, although you incited Me against him to ruin him without cause." 4 Satan answered the Lord and said, "Skin for skin! Yes, all that a man has, he will give for his life. 5 However, reach out with Your hand now, and touch his bone and his flesh; he will curse You to Your face!" 6 So the Lord said to Satan, "Behold, he is in your power, only spare his life."

7 Then Satan went out from the presence of the Lord and struck Job with severe boils from the sole of his foot to the top of his head. 8 And *Job* took a piece of pottery to scrape himself while he was sitting in the ashes.

9 Then his wife said to him, "Do you still hold firm your integrity? Curse God and die!" 10 But he said to her, "You are speaking as one of the foolish women speaks. Shall we actually accept good from God but not accept adversity?" Despite all this, Job did not sin with his lips.

11 Now when Job's three friends heard about all this adversity that had come upon him, they came, each one from his own place—Eliphaz the Temanite, Bildad the Shuhite, and Zophar the Naamathite; and they made an appointment together to come to sympathize with him and comfort him. 12 When they looked from a

---

1:6 ¹ I.e., prob. angels   2 Heb *ha-satan;* i.e., the adversary, and so throughout the ch   2:1 ¹ Heb *ha-satan;* i.e., the adversary, and so throughout the ch

distance and did not recognize him, they raised their voices and wept. And each of them tore his robe, and they threw dust over their heads toward the sky. 13 Then they sat down on the ground with him for seven days and seven nights, with no one speaking a word to him, for they saw that *his* pain was very great.

Job's Lament

3 Afterward Job opened his mouth and cursed the day of his *birth.* 2 And Job said,
3 "May the day on which I was to be born perish,
As well as the night *which* said, 'A boy is conceived.'
4 "May that day be darkness;
May God above not care for it,
Nor light shine on it.
5 "May darkness and black gloom claim it;
May a cloud settle on it;
May the blackness of the day terrify it.
6 "*As for* that night, may darkness seize it;
May it not rejoice among the days of the year;
May it not come into the number of the months.
7 "Behold, may that night be barren;
May no joyful shout enter it.
8 "May those curse it who curse the day,
Who are prepared to disturb Leviathan.
9 "May the stars of its twilight be darkened;
May it wait for light but have none,
And may it not see the breaking dawn;
10 Because it did not shut the opening of my *mother's* womb,
Or hide trouble from my eyes.
11¶ "Why did I not die at birth,
Come out of the womb and pass away?
12 "Why were the knees *there* in front of me,
And why the breasts, that I would nurse?
13 "For now I would have lain down and been quiet;
I would have slept then, I would have been at rest,
14 With kings and counselors of the earth,
Who rebuilt ruins for themselves;
15 Or with rulers who had gold,
Who were filling their houses *with* silver.
16 "Or like a miscarriage which is hidden, I would not exist,
As infants that never saw light.
17 "There the wicked cease from raging,
And there the weary are at rest.
18 "The prisoners are at ease together;
They do not hear the voice of the taskmaster.
19 "The small and the great are there,
And the slave is free from his master.
20¶ "Why is light given to one burdened with grief,
And life to the bitter of soul,
21 Who long for death, but there is none,
And dig for it more than for hidden treasures;
22 Who are filled with jubilation,
And rejoice when they find the grave?
23 "*Why is light given* to a man whose way is hidden,
And whom God has shut off?

24 "For my groaning comes at the sight of my food,
And my cries pour out like water.
25 "For what I fear comes upon me,
And what I dread encounters me.
26 "I am not at ease, nor am I quiet,
And I am not at rest, but turmoil comes."

Eliphaz Says the Innocent Do Not Suffer

4 Then Eliphaz the Temanite responded,
2 "If one ventures a word with you, will you become impatient?
But who can refrain from speaking?
3 "Behold, you have taught many,
And you have strengthened weak hands.
4 "Your words have helped the stumbling to stand,
And you have strengthened feeble knees.
5 "But now it comes to you, and you are impatient;
It touches you, and you are horrified.
6 "Is your fear *of God* not your confidence,
And the integrity of your ways your hope?
7¶ "Remember now, who *ever* perished being innocent?
Or where were the upright destroyed?
8 "According to what I have seen, those who 'plow wrongdoing
And those who sow trouble harvest it.
9 "By the breath of God they perish,
And by the blast of His anger they come to an end.
10 "The roaring of the lion and the voice of the *fierce* lion,
And the teeth of the young lions are broken out.
11 "The lion perishes for lack of prey,
And the cubs of the lioness are scattered.
12¶ "Now a word was brought to me secretly,
And my ear received a whisper of it.
13 "Amid disquieting thoughts from visions of the night,
When deep sleep falls on people,
14 Dread came upon me, and trembling,
And made all my bones shake.
15 "Then a spirit passed by my face;
The hair of my flesh stood up.
16 "*Something* was standing still, but I could not recognize its appearance;
A form *was* before my eyes;
There was silence, then I heard a voice:
17 'Can mankind be righteous before God?
Can a man be pure before his Maker?
18 'He puts no trust even in His servants;
And He accuses His angels of error.
19 'How much more those who live in houses of clay,
Whose foundation is in the dust,
Who are crushed before the moth!
20 'Between morning and evening they are broken in pieces;
Unregarded, they perish forever.
21 'Is their tent-cord not pulled out within them?
They die, yet without wisdom.'

4:8 ¹I.e., devise

God Is Just

5 "Call now, is there anyone who will answer you?
  And to which of the holy ones will you turn?

2 "For irritation kills the fool,
   And jealousy brings death to the simple.
3 "I have seen the fool taking root,
   And I cursed his home immediately.
4 "His sons are far from safety,
   They are also oppressed at the gate,
   And there is no one to save *them.*
5 "The hungry devour his harvest
   And take it to a *place of* thorns,
   And the schemer is eager for their wealth.
6 "For disaster does not come from the dust,
   Nor does trouble sprout from the ground,
7 For man is born for trouble,
   As sparks fly upward.
8¶ "But as for me, I would seek God,
   And I would make my plea before God,
9 Who does great and unsearchable things,
   Wonders without number.
10 "He gives rain on the earth,
   And sends water on the fields,
11 So that He sets on high those who are lowly,
   And those who mourn are lifted to safety.
12 "He frustrates the schemes of the shrewd,
   So that their hands cannot attain success.
13 "He captures the wise by their own cleverness,
   And the advice of the cunning is quickly thwarted.
14 "By day they meet with darkness,
   And grope at noon as in the night.
15 "But He saves from the sword of their mouth,
   And the poor from the hand of the strong.
16 "So the helpless has hope,
   And injustice has shut its mouth.
17¶ "Behold, happy is the person whom God disciplines,
   So do not reject the discipline of the Almighty.
18 "For He inflicts pain, and gives relief;
   He wounds, but His hands *also* heal.
19 "In six troubles He will save you;
   Even in seven, evil will not touch you.
20 "In famine He will redeem you from death,
   And in war, from the power of the sword.
21 "You will be hidden from the scourge of the tongue,
   And you will not be afraid of violence when it comes.
22 "You will laugh at violence and hunger,
   And you will not be afraid of wild animals.
23 "For you will be in league with the stones of the field,
   And the animals of the field will be at peace with you.
24 "You will know that your tent is secure,
   For you will visit your home and have nothing missing.
25 "You will also know that your descendants will be many,
   And your offspring as the grass of the earth.
26 "You will come to the grave at a ripe age,

Like the stacking of grain in its season.
27 "Behold this; we have investigated it, *and* so it is.
   Hear it, and know for yourself."

Job's Friends Are No Help

6 Then Job responded,
2 "Oh if only my grief were actually weighed
  And laid in the balances together with my disaster!
3 "For then it would be heavier than the sand of the seas;
   For that reason my words have been rash.
4 "For the arrows of the Almighty are within me,
   My spirit drinks their poison;
   The terrors of God line up against me.
5 "Does the wild donkey bray over *his* grass,
   Or does the ox low over his feed?
6 "Can something tasteless be eaten without salt,
   Or is there any taste in the juice of an alkanet *plant?*
7 "My soul refuses to touch *them;*
   They are like loathsome food to me.
8¶ "Oh, that my request might come to pass,
   And that God would grant my hope!
9 "*Oh,* that God would decide to crush me,
   That He would let loose His hand and cut me off!
10 "But it is still my comfort,
   And I rejoice in unsparing pain,
   That I have not denied the words of the Holy One.
11 "What is my strength, that I should wait?
   And what is my end, that I should endure?
12 "Is my strength the strength of stones,
   Or is my flesh bronze?
13 "Is it that my help is not within me,
   And that a good outcome is driven away from me?
14¶ "For the despairing man *there should be* kindness from his friend;
   So that he does not abandon the fear of the Almighty.
15 "My brothers have acted deceitfully like a ʾwadi,
   Like the torrents of wadis which drain away,
16 Which are darkened because of ice,
   And into which the snow melts.
17 "When they dry up, they vanish;
   When it is hot, they disappear from their place.
18 "The paths of their course wind along,
   They go up into wasteland and perish.
19 "The caravans of Tema looked,
   The travelers of Sheba hoped for them.
20 "They were put to shame, for they had trusted,
   They came there and were humiliated.
21 "Indeed, you have now become such,
   You see terrors and are afraid.
22 "Have I said, 'Give me *something,*'
   Or, 'Offer a bribe for me from your wealth,'
23 Or, 'Save me from the hand of the enemy,'

6:15 ¹I.e., dry stream bed(s), except in the rainy season

Or, 'Redeem me from the hand of the tyrants'?

24 ¶ "Teach me, and I will be silent;
And show me how I have done wrong.

25 "How painful are honest words!
But what does your argument prove?

26 "Do you intend to rebuke *my* words,
When the words of one in despair belong to the wind?

27 "You would even cast *lots* for the orphans,
And barter over your friend.

28 "Now please look at me,
And *see* if I am lying to your face.

29 "Please turn away, let there be no injustice;
Turn away, my righteousness is still in it.

30 "Is there injustice on my tongue?
Does my palate not discern disasters?

Job's Life Seems Futile

7 "Is a person not forced to labor on earth,
And *are* his days not like the days of a hired worker?

2 "As a slave pants for the shade,
And as a hired worker who eagerly waits for his wages,

3 So I am allotted worthless months,
And nights of trouble are apportioned to me.

4 "When I lie down, I say,
'When shall I arise?'
But the night continues,
And I am continually tossing until dawn.

5 "My flesh is clothed with maggots and a crust of dirt,
My skin hardens and oozes.

6 "My days are swifter than a weaver's shuttle,
And they come to an end without hope.

7 ¶ "Remember that my life is a *mere* breath;
My eye will not see goodness again.

8 "The eye of him who sees me will no *longer* look at me;
Your eyes *will be* on me, but I will not exist.

9 "When a cloud vanishes, it is gone;
In the same way one who goes down to ¹Sheol does not come up.

10 "He will not return to his house again,
Nor will his place know about him anymore.

11 ¶ "Therefore I will not restrain my mouth;
I will speak in the anguish of my spirit,
I will complain in the bitterness of my soul.

12 "Am I the sea, or the sea monster,
That You set a guard over me?

13 "If I say, 'My couch will comfort me,
My bed will ease my complaint,'

14 Then You frighten me with dreams,
And terrify me by visions,

15 So that my soul would choose suffocation,
Death rather than my pains.

16 "I waste away; I will not live forever.
Leave me alone, for my days are *only* a breath.

17 "What is man that You exalt him,
And that You are concerned about him,

18 That You examine him every morning

And put him to the test every moment?

19 "Will You never turn Your gaze away from me,
Nor leave me alone until I swallow my spittle?

20 "Have I sinned? What have I done to You,
Watcher of mankind?
Why have You made me Your target,
So that I am a burden to myself?

21 "Why then do You not forgive my wrongdoing
And take away my guilt?
For now I will lie down in the dust;
And You will search for me, but I will no *longer* exist."

Bildad Says God Rewards the Good

8 Then Bildad the Shuhite responded,

2 "How long will you say these things,
And the words of your mouth be a mighty wind?

3 "Does God pervert justice?
Or does the Almighty pervert what is right?

4 "If your sons sinned against Him,
Then He turned them over to the power of their wrongdoing.

5 "If you will search for God
And implore the compassion of the Almighty,

6 If you are pure and upright,
Surely now He will stir Himself for you
And restore your righteous estate.

7 "Though your beginning was insignificant,
Yet your end will increase greatly.

8 ¶ "Please inquire of past generations,
And consider the things searched out by their fathers.

9 "For we are *only* of yesterday and know nothing,
Because our days on earth are as a shadow.

10 "Will they not teach you *and* tell you,
And bring forth words from their minds?

11 ¶ "Can papyrus grow tall without a marsh?
Can the rushes grow without water?

12 "While it is still green *and* not cut down,
Yet it withers before any *other* plant.

13 "So are the paths of all who forget God;
And the hope of the godless will perish,

14 His confidence is fragile,
And his trust is a spider's web.

15 "He depends on his house, but it does not stand;
He holds on to it, but it does not endure.

16 "He flourishes before the sun,
And his shoots spread out over his garden.

17 "His roots wrap around a rock pile,
He grasps a house of stones.

18 "If he is removed from his place,
Then it will deny him, *saying,* 'I never saw you.'

19 "Behold, this is the joy of His way;
And out of the dust others will spring.

20 "Behold, God will not reject *a person of* integrity,
Nor will He help evildoers.

21 "He will yet fill your mouth with laughter,

7:9 ¹I.e., the netherworld

And your lips with joyful shouting.
22 "Those who hate you will be clothed with
shame,
And the tent of the wicked will no *longer*
exist."

Job Says There Is No Arbitrator between God and Mankind

9 Then Job responded,
2 "In truth I know that this is so;
But how can a person be in the right with
God?
3 "If one wished to dispute with Him,
He could not answer Him once in a
thousand *times.*
4 "Wise in heart and mighty in strength,
Who has defied Him without harm?
5 "*It is God* who removes the mountains,
and they do not know *how,*
When He overturns them in His anger.
6 "*It is He* who shakes the earth from its
place,
And its pillars tremble;
7 Who commands the sun not to shine,
And puts a seal on the stars;
8 Who alone stretches out the heavens,
And tramples down the waves of the sea;
9 Who makes the Bear, Orion, and the
Pleiades,
And the constellations of the south.
10 "*It is He* who does great things, the
unfathomable,
And wondrous works without number.
11 "If He were to pass by me, I would not see
Him;
Were He to move past *me,* I would not
perceive Him.
12 "If He were to snatch away, who could
restrain Him?
Who could say to Him, 'What are You
doing?'
13¶ "God will not turn back His anger;
Beneath Him the helpers of 'Rahab cower.
14 "How then can I answer Him,
And choose my words before Him?
15 "For though I were right, I could not
answer;
I would have to implore the mercy of my
Judge.
16 "If I called and He answered me,
I could not believe that He was listening
to my voice.
17 "For He bruises me with a storm
And multiplies my wounds without cause.
18 "He will not allow me to get my breath,
But He saturates me with bitterness.
19 "If *it is a matter* of power, behold, *He is* the
strong one!
And if *it is a matter* of justice, who can
summon Him?
20 "Though I am righteous, my mouth will
condemn me;
Though I am guiltless, He will declare me
guilty.
21 "I am guiltless;
I do not take notice of myself;
I reject my life.
22 "It is *all* one; therefore I say,
'He destroys the guiltless and the wicked.'

23 "If the whip kills suddenly,
He mocks the despair of the innocent.
24 "The earth is handed over to the wicked;
He covers the faces of its judges.
If *it is* not *He,* then who is it?
25¶ "Now my days are swifter than a runner;
They flee away, they see no good.
26 "They slip by like reed boats,
Like an eagle that swoops on its prey.
27 "Though I say, 'I will forget my complaint,
I will put my face in order and be
cheerful,'
28 I am afraid of all my pains,
I know that You will not acquit me.
29 "I am guilty,
Why then should I struggle in vain?
30 "If I washed myself with snow,
And cleansed my hands with lye,
31 Then You would plunge me into the pit,
And my own clothes would loathe me.
32 "For *He is* not a man, as I am, that I may
answer Him—
That we may go to court together!
33 "There is no arbitrator between us,
Who can place his hand upon us both.
34 "Let Him remove His rod from me,
And let not the dread of Him terrify me.
35 "*Then* I would speak and not fear Him;
But I am not like that in myself.

Job Despairs of God's Dealings

10 "I am disgusted with my own
life;
I will express my complaint freely;
I will speak in the bitterness of my soul.
2 "I will say to God, 'Do not condemn me;
Let me know why You contend with me.
3 'Is it right for You indeed to oppress,
To reject the work of Your hands,
And to look favorably on the plan of the
wicked?
4 'Do You have eyes of flesh?
Or do You see as mankind sees?
5 'Are Your days like the days of a mortal,
Or Your years like a man's year,
6 That You should search for my guilt
And carefully seek my sin?
7 'According to Your knowledge I am indeed
not guilty,
Yet there is no one to save *me* from Your
hand.
8¶ 'Your hands fashioned and made me
altogether,
Yet would You destroy me?
9 'Remember that You have made me as
clay;
Yet would You turn me into dust again?
10 'Did You not pour me out like milk,
And curdle me like cheese,
11 Clothe me with skin and flesh,
And intertwine me with bones and
tendons?
12 'You have granted me life and goodness;
And Your care has guarded my spirit.
13 'Yet You have concealed these things in
Your heart;
I know that this is within You:
14 If I have sinned, You will take note of me,
And will not acquit me of my guilt.

9:13 ¹ I.e., a sea monster, not to be confused with Rahab in Joshua 2

15 'If I am wicked, woe to me!
But *if* I am righteous, I *dare* not lift up my head.
I am full of shame, and conscious of my misery.

16 'And should *my head* be high, You would hunt me like a lion;
And You would show Your power against me again.

17 'You renew Your witnesses against me
And increase Your anger toward me;
Hardship after hardship is with me.

18¶ 'Why then did You bring me out of the womb?
If only I had died and no eye had seen me!

19 'I should have been as though I had not been,
Brought from womb to tomb.'

20 "Would He not leave my few days alone?
Withdraw from me so that I may have a little cheerfulness

21 Before I go—and I shall not return—
To the land of darkness and deep shadow,

22 The land of utter gloom like darkness *itself,*
Of deep shadow without order,
And it shines like darkness."

Zophar Rebukes Job

11 Then Zophar the Naamathite responded,

2 "Shall a multitude of words go unanswered,
And a talkative man be acquitted?

3 "Shall your boasts silence people?
And will you scoff, and no one rebuke?

4 "For you have said, 'My teaching is pure,
And I am innocent in your eyes.'

5 "But if only God would speak,
And open His lips against you,

6 And show you the secrets of wisdom!
For sound wisdom has two sides.
Know then that God forgets part of your guilt.

7¶ "Can you discover the depths of God?
Can you discover the limits of the Almighty?

8 "*They are as* high *as* the heavens; what can you do?
Deeper than ¹Sheol; what can you know?

9 "Its measurement is longer than the earth
And broader than the sea.

10 "If He passes by or apprehends *people,*
Or calls an assembly, who can restrain Him?

11 "For He knows false people,
And He sees injustice without investigating.

12 "An idiot will become intelligent
When a wild donkey is born a human.

13¶ "If you would direct your heart *rightly*
And spread out your hands to Him,

14 If wrongdoing is in your hand, put it far away,
And do not let malice dwell in your tents;

15 Then, indeed, you could lift up your face without *moral* blemish,
And you would be firmly established and not fear.

16 "For you would forget *your* trouble;
Like waters that have passed by, you would remember *it.*

17 "Your life would be brighter than noonday;
Darkness would be like the morning.

18 "Then you would trust, because there is hope;
And you would look around and rest securely.

19 "You would lie down and none would disturb *you,*
And many would flatter you.

20 "But the eyes of the wicked will fail,
And there will be no escape for them;
And their hope is to breathe their last."

Job Chides His Accusers

12 Then Job responded,

2 "Truly then you are the people,
And with you wisdom will die!

3 "But I have intelligence as well as you;
I am not inferior to you.
And who does not know such things as these?

4 "I am a joke to my friends,
The one who called on God and He answered him;
The just *and* blameless *man* is a joke.

5 "He who is at ease holds disaster in contempt,
As prepared for those whose feet slip.

6 "The tents of the destroyers prosper,
And those who provoke God are secure,
Whom God brings into their power.

7¶ "But just ask the animals, and have them teach you;
And the birds of the sky, and have them tell you.

8 "Or speak to the earth, and have it teach you;
And have the fish of the sea tell you.

9 "Who among all these does not know
That the hand of the LORD has done this,

10 In whose hand is the life of every living thing,
And the breath of all mankind?

11 "Does the ear not put words to the test,
As the palate tastes its food?

12 "Wisdom is with the aged,
And with long life *comes* understanding.

Job Speaks of the Power of God

13¶ "Wisdom and might are with Him;
Advice and understanding *belong* to Him.

14 "Behold, He tears down, and it cannot be rebuilt;
He imprisons a person, and there is no release.

15 "Behold, He restrains the waters, and they dry up;
And He sends them out, and they inundate the earth.

16 "Strength and sound wisdom are with Him.
One who goes astray and one who leads astray belong to Him.

17 "He makes advisers walk barefoot
And makes fools of judges.

18 "He undoes the binding of kings,
And ties a loincloth around their waist.

19 "He makes priests walk barefoot,
And overthrows the secure ones.
20 "He deprives the trusted ones of speech,
And takes away the discernment of the
elders.
21 "He pours contempt on nobles,
And loosens the belt of the strong.
22 "He reveals mysteries from the darkness,
And brings the deep darkness into light.
23 "He makes the nations great, then destroys
them;
He enlarges the nations, then leads them
away.
24 "He deprives the leaders of the earth's
people of intelligence
And makes them wander in a pathless
wasteland.
25 "They grope in darkness with no light,
And He makes them stagger like a
drunken person.

Job Says His Friends' Proverbs Are Ashes

13 "Behold, my eye has seen all *this*,
My ear has heard and understood it.
2 "What you know I also know;
I am not inferior to you.
3¶ "But I would speak to the Almighty,
And I desire to argue with God.
4 "But you smear *me* with lies;
You are all worthless physicians.
5 "Oh that you would be completely silent,
And that it would become your wisdom!
6 "Please hear my argument,
And give your attention to the contentions
of my lips.
7 "Will you speak what is unjust for God,
And speak what is deceitful for Him?
8 "Will you show partiality for Him?
Will you contend for God?
9 "*Will it go* well when He examines you?
Or will you deceive Him as one deceives a
man?
10 "He will certainly punish you
If you secretly show partiality.
11 "Will His majesty not terrify you,
And the dread of Him fall upon you?
12 "Your memorable sayings are proverbs of
ashes,
Your defenses are defenses of clay.

Job Is Sure He Will Be Vindicated

13¶ "Be silent before me so that I may speak;
Then let come upon me what *may*.
14 "Why should I take my flesh in my teeth,
And put my life in my hands?
15 "Though He slay me,
I will hope in Him.
Nevertheless I will argue my ways before
Him.
16 "This also *will be* my salvation,
For a godless person cannot come before
His presence.
17 "Listen carefully to my speech,
And let my declaration *fill* your ears.
18 "Behold now, I have prepared my case;
I know that I will be vindicated.
19 "Who could contend with me?
For then I would be silent and die.

20¶ "Only two things *I ask that You* do not do
to me,
Then I will not hide from Your face:
21 Remove Your hand from me,
And may the dread of You not terrify me.
22 "Then call and I will answer;
Or let me speak, then reply to me.
23 "How many are my guilty deeds and sins?
Make known to me my wrongdoing and
my sin.
24 "Why do You hide Your face
And consider me Your enemy?
25 "Will You scare away a scattered leaf?
Or will You pursue the dry chaff?
26 "For You write bitter things against me
And make me inherit the guilty deeds of
my youth.
27 "You put my feet in the stocks
And watch all my paths;
You set a limit for the soles of my feet,
28 While I am decaying like a rotten thing,
Like a garment that is moth-eaten.

Job Speaks of the Finality of Death

14 "Man, who is born of woman,
Is short-lived and full of turmoil.
2 "Like a flower he comes out and withers.
He also flees like a shadow and does not
remain.
3 "You also open Your eyes on him
And bring him into judgment with
Yourself.
4 "Who can make the clean out of the
unclean?
No one!
5 "Since his days are determined,
The number of his months is with You;
And You have set his limits so that he
cannot pass.
6 "Look away from him so that he may rest,
Until he fulfills his day like a hired
worker.
7¶ "For there is hope for a tree,
When it is cut down, that it will sprout
again,
And its shoots will not fail.
8 "Though its roots grow old in the ground,
And its stump dies in the dry soil,
9 At the scent of water it will flourish
And produce sprigs like a plant.
10 "But a man dies and lies prostrate.
A person passes away, and where is he?
11 "*As* water evaporates from the sea,
And a river becomes parched and dried
up,
12 So a man lies down and does not rise.
Until the heavens no longer exist,
He will not awake nor be woken from his
sleep.
13¶ "Oh that You would hide me in ˢSheol,
That You would conceal me until Your
wrath returns *to You*,
That You would set a limit for me and
remember me!
14 "If a man dies, will he live *again*?
All the days of my struggle I will wait
Until my relief comes.
15 "You will call, and I will answer You;
You will long for the work of Your hands.

14:13 ˢI.e., the netherworld

16 "For now You number my steps,
You do not observe my sin.

17 "My wrongdoing is sealed up in a bag,
And You cover over my guilt.

18 ¶ "But the falling mountain crumbles away,
And the rock moves from its place;

19 Water wears away stones,
Its torrents wash away the dust of the
earth;
So You destroy a man's hope.

20 "You forever overpower him and he
departs;
You change his appearance and send him
away.

21 "His sons achieve honor, but he does not
know *it;*
Or they become insignificant, and he does
not perceive it.

22 "However, his body pains him,
And his soul mourns for himself."

Eliphaz Says Job Presumes Much

15 Then Eliphaz the Temanite
responded,

2 "Should a wise man answer with windy
knowledge,
And fill himself with the east wind?

3 "Should he argue with useless talk,
Or with words which do not benefit?

4 "Indeed, you do away with reverence,
And hinder meditation before God.

5 "For your wrongdoing teaches your mouth,
And you choose the language of the
cunning.

6 "Your own mouth condemns you, and
not I;
And your own lips testify against you.

7 ¶ "Were you the first person to be born,
Or were you brought forth before the
hills?

8 "Do you hear the secret discussion of God,
And limit wisdom to yourself?

9 "What do you know that we do not know?
What do you understand that we do not?

10 "Both the gray-haired and the aged are
among us,
Older than your father.

11 "Are the consolations of God too little for
you,
Or the word *spoken* gently to you?

12 "Why does your heart take you away?
And why do your eyes wink,

13 That you can turn your spirit against God
And produce *such* words from your
mouth?

14 "What is man, that he would be pure,
Or he who is born of a woman, that he
would be righteous?

15 "Behold, He has no trust in His holy ones,
And the heavens are not pure in His sight;

16 How much less one who is detestable and
corrupt:
A person who drinks malice like water!

What Eliphaz Has Seen of Life

17 ¶ "I will tell you, listen to me;
And what I have seen I will also declare;

18 What wise people have told,
And have not concealed from their
fathers,

19 To whom alone the land was given,
And no stranger passed among them.

20 "The wicked person writhes in pain all *his*
days,
And the years reserved for the ruthless
are numbered.

21 "Sounds of terror are in his ears;
While he is at peace the destroyer comes
upon him.

22 "He does not believe that he will return
from darkness,
And he is destined for the sword.

23 "He wanders about for food, *saying,*
'Where *is it?'*
He knows that a day of darkness is at
hand.

24 "Distress and anguish terrify him,
They overpower him like a king ready for
the attack,

25 Because he has reached out with his hand
against God,
And is arrogant toward the Almighty.

26 "He rushes headlong at Him
With his massive shield.

27 "For he has covered his face with his fat,
And put fat on his waist.

28 "He has lived in desolate cities,
In houses no one would inhabit,
Which are destined to become ruins.

29 "He will not become rich, nor will his
wealth endure;
And his property will not stretch out on
the earth.

30 "He will not escape from darkness;
The flame will dry up his shoot,
And he will go away by the breath of His
mouth.

31 "Let him not trust in emptiness, deceiving
himself;
For his reward will be emptiness.

32 "It will be accomplished before his time,
And his palm branch will not be green.

33 "He will drop off his unripe grape like the
vine,
And will cast off his flower like the olive
tree.

34 "For the company of the godless is barren,
And fire consumes the tents of the
corrupt.

35 "They conceive harm and give birth to
wrongdoing,
And their mind prepares deception."

Job Says Friends Are Miserable Comforters

16 Then Job responded,

2 "I have heard many things like these;
Miserable comforters are you all!

3 "Is there *no* end to windy words?
Or what provokes you that you answer?

4 "I too could speak like you,
If only I were in your place.
I could compose words against you
And shake my head at you.

5 "*Or* I could strengthen you with my mouth,
And the condolence of my lips could
lessen *your* pain.

Job Says God Shattered Him

6 ¶ "If I speak, my pain is not lessened,
And if I refrain, what *pain* leaves me?

7 "But now He has exhausted me;
   You have laid waste all my group *of loved
   ones.*
8 "And you have shriveled me up,
   It has become a witness;
   And my infirmity rises up against me,
   It testifies to my face.
9 "His anger has torn me and hunted me
   down,
   He has gnashed at me with His teeth;
   My enemy glares at me.
10 "They have gaped at me with their mouths,
   They have slapped me on the cheek with
   contempt;
   They have massed themselves against me.
11 "God hands me over to criminals,
   And tosses me into the hands of the
   wicked.
12 "I was at ease, but He shattered me,
   And He has grasped me by my neck and
   shaken me to pieces;
   He has also set me up as His target.
13 "His arrows surround me.
   He splits my kidneys open without mercy;
   He pours out my bile on the ground.
14 "He breaks through me with breach after
   breach;
   He runs at me like a warrior.
15 "I have sewed sackcloth over my skin,
   And thrust my horn in the dust.
16 "My face is flushed from weeping,
   And deep darkness is on my eyelids,
17 Although there is no violence in my
   hands,
   And my prayer is pure.
18¶ "Earth, do not cover my blood,
   And may there be no *resting* place for my
   cry.
19 "Even now, behold, my witness is in
   heaven,
   And my advocate is on high.
20 "My friends are my scoffers;
   My eye weeps to God,
21 That one might plead for a man with God
   As a son of man with his neighbor!
22 "For when a few years are past,
   I shall go the way of no return.

Job Says He Has Become a Proverb

17 "My spirit is broken, my days are
   extinguished,
   The grave is *ready* for me.
2 "Mockers are certainly with me,
   And my eye gazes on their provocation.
3¶ "Make a pledge for me with Yourself;
   Who is there that will be my guarantor?
4 "For You have kept their hearts away from
   understanding;
   Therefore You will not exalt *them.*
5 "He who informs against friends for a share
   of the spoils,
   The eyes of his children also will perish.
6¶ "But He has made me a proverb *among* the
   people,
   And I am one at whom people spit.
7 "My eye has also become inexpressive
   because of grief,
   And all my body parts are like a shadow.
8 "The upright will be appalled at this,

And the innocent will stir himself up
   against the godless.
9 "Nevertheless the righteous will hold to his
   way,
   And the one who has clean hands will
   grow stronger and stronger.
10 "But come again all of you now,
   For I do not find a wise man among you.
11 "My days are past, my plans are torn apart,
   The wishes of my heart.
12 "They make night into day, *saying,*
   'The light is near,' in the presence of darkness.
13 "If I hope for †Sheol as my home,
   I make my bed in the darkness;
14 *If* I call to the grave, 'You are my father';
   To the maggot, 'my mother and my sister';
15 Where then is my hope?
   And who looks at my hope?
16 "Will it go down with me to Sheol?
   Shall we together go down into the dust?"

Bildad Speaks of the Wicked

18 Then Bildad the Shuhite
   responded,
2 "How long will you hunt for words?
   Show understanding, and then we can
   talk.
3 "Why are we regarded as animals,
   As stupid in your eyes?
4 "You who tear yourself in your anger—
   Should the earth be abandoned for your
   sake,
   Or the rock moved from its place?
5¶ "Indeed, the light of the wicked goes out,
   And the spark from his fire does not
   shine.
6 "The light in his tent is darkened,
   And his lamp goes out above him.
7 "His vigorous stride is shortened,
   And his own plan brings him down.
8 "For he is thrown into the net by his own
   feet,
   And he steps on the webbing.
9 "A snare seizes *him* by the heel,
   And a trap snaps shut on him.
10 "A noose for him is hidden in the ground,
   And a trap for him on the pathway.
11 "All around sudden terrors frighten him,
   And harass him at every step.
12 "His strength is famished,
   And disaster is ready at his side.
13 "It devours parts of his skin,
   The firstborn of death devours his limbs.
14 "He is torn from the security of his tent,
   And they march him before the king of
   terrors.
15 "Nothing of his dwells in his tent;
   Brimstone is scattered on his home.
16 "His roots are dried below,
   And his branch withers above.
17 "The memory of him perishes from the
   earth,
   And he has no name abroad.
18 "He is driven from light into darkness,
   And chased from the inhabited world.
19 "He has no offspring or descendants among
   his people,
   Nor any survivor where he resided.

17:13 †I.e., the netherworld

20 "Those in the west are appalled at his fate,
  And those in the east are seized with
    horror.
21 "Certainly these are the dwellings of the
    wicked,
  And this is the place of him who does not
    know God.'"

Job Feels Insulted
19 Then Job responded,
²"How long will you torment me
  And crush me with words?
3 "These ten times you have insulted me;
  You are not ashamed to wrong me.
4 "Even *if* I have truly done wrong,
  My error stays with me.
5 "If indeed you exalt yourselves against me
  And prove my disgrace to me,
6 Know then that God has wronged me
  And has surrounded me with His net.

Everything Is Against Him
7¶ "Behold, I cry, 'Violence!' but I get no
    answer;
  I shout for help, but there is no justice.
8 "He has blocked my way so that I cannot
    pass,
  And He has put darkness on my paths.
9 "He has stripped my honor from me
  And removed the crown from my head.
10 "He breaks me down on every side, and I
    am gone;
  And He has uprooted my hope like a
    tree.
11 "He has also kindled His anger against me
  And considered me as His enemy.
12 "His troops come together
  And build up their way against me
  And camp around my tent.
13¶ "He has removed my brothers far from me,
  And my acquaintances have completely
    turned away from me.
14 "My relatives have failed,
  And my close friends have forgotten me.
15 "Those who live in my house and my
    servant women consider me a stranger.
  I am a foreigner in their sight.
16 "I call to my servant, but he does not
    answer;
  I have to implore his favor with my
    mouth.
17 "My breath is offensive to my wife,
  And I am loathsome to my own brothers.
18 "Even young children despise me;
  I stand up and they speak against me.
19 "All my associates loathe me,
  And those I love have turned against me.
20 "My bone clings to my skin and my flesh,
  And I have escaped *only* by the skin of my
    teeth.
21 "Pity me, pity me, you friends of mine,
  For the hand of God has struck me.
22 "Why do you persecute me as God *does,*
  And are not satisfied with my flesh?

Job Says My Redeemer Lives
23¶ "Oh that my words were written!
  Oh that they were recorded in a book!
24 "That with an iron stylus and lead
  They were engraved in the rock forever!

25 "Yet as for me, I know that my Redeemer
    lives,
  And at the last, He will take His stand on
    the earth.
26 "Even after my skin is destroyed,
  Yet from my flesh I will see God,
27 Whom I, on my part, shall behold for
    myself,
  And *whom* my eyes will see, and not
    another.
  My heart faints within me!
28 "If you say, 'How shall we persecute him?'
  And 'What pretext for a case against him
    can we find?'
29 "*Then* be afraid of the sword for yourselves,
  For wrath *brings* the punishment of the
    sword,
  So that you may know there is judgment."

Zophar Says the Rejoicing of the Wicked Is Short
20 Then Zophar the Naamathite
  responded,
2 "Therefore my disquieting thoughts make
    me respond,
  Even because of my inward agitation.
3 "I listened to the reprimand which insults
    me,
  And the spirit of my understanding makes
    me answer.
4 "Do you know this from ancient times,
  From the establishment of mankind on
    earth,
5 That the rejoicing of the wicked is short,
  And the joy of the godless momentary?
6 "Though his arrogance reaches the
    heavens,
  And his head touches the clouds,
7 He perishes forever like his refuse;
  Those who have seen him will say,
    'Where is he?'
8 "He flies away like a dream, and they
    cannot find him;
  Like a vision of the night he is chased
    away.
9 "The eye which saw him sees him no
    longer,
  And his place no longer beholds him.
10 "His sons favor the poor,
  And his hands give back his wealth.
11 "His bones are full of his youthful strength,
  But it lies down with him in the dust.
12¶ "Though evil tastes sweet in his mouth
  And he hides it under his tongue,
13 *Though* he desires it and will not let it go,
  But holds it in his mouth,
14 *Yet* his food in his stomach is changed
  To the venom of cobras within him.
15 "He swallows riches,
  But will vomit them up;
  God will expel them from his belly.
16 "He sucks the poison of cobras;
  The viper's tongue kills him.
17 "He does not look at the streams,
  The rivers flowing with honey and curds.
18 "He returns the product of his labor
  And cannot swallow *it;*
  As to the riches of his trading,
  He cannot even enjoy *them.*
19 "For he has oppressed *and* neglected the
    poor;

He has seized a house which he has not built.

20¶ "Because he knew no quiet within him,
He does not retain anything he desires.

21 "Nothing remains for him to devour,
Therefore his prosperity does not endure.

22 "In the fullness of his excess he will be cramped;
The hand of everyone who suffers will come *against* him.

23 "When he fills his belly,
God will send His fierce anger on him
And rain *it* on him while he is eating.

24 "He may flee from the iron weapon,
But the bronze bow will pierce him.

25 "It is drawn and comes out of his back,
Even the flashing *point* from his gall-bladder;
Terrors come upon him,

26 Complete darkness is held in reserve for his treasures,
And unfanned fire will devour him;
It will consume the survivor in his tent.

27 "The heavens will reveal his guilt,
And the earth will rise up against him.

28 "The increase of his house will disappear;
His possessions will flow away on the day of His anger.

29 "This is a wicked person's portion from God,
The inheritance decreed to him by God."

Job Says God Will Deal with the Wicked

21 Then Job responded,

2 "Listen carefully to my speech,
And let this be your *way of* consolation.

3 "Bear with me that I may speak;
Then after I have spoken, you may mock *me.*

4 "As for me, is my complaint to a mortal?
Or why should I not be impatient?

5 "Look at me, and be astonished,
And put *your* hand over *your* mouth.

6 "Even when I remember, I am disturbed,
And horror takes hold of my flesh.

7 "Why do the wicked *still* live,
Grow old, *and* also become very powerful?

8 "Their descendants endure with them in their sight,
And their offspring before their eyes,

9 Their houses are safe from fear,
And the rod of God is not on them.

10 "His ox mates without fail;
His cow calves and does not miscarry.

11 "They send out their boys like the flock,
And their children dance.

12 "They sing with the tambourine and harp,
And rejoice at the sound of the flute.

13 "They spend their days in prosperity,
And suddenly they go down to ʾSheol.

14 "Yet they say to God, 'Go away from us!
We do not even desire the knowledge of Your ways.

15 'Who is the Almighty, that we should serve Him,
And what would we gain if we plead with Him?'

16 "Behold, their prosperity is not in their hand;
The advice of the wicked is far from me.

17¶ "How often is the lamp of the wicked put out,
Or does their disaster fall on them?
Does God apportion destruction in His anger?

18 "Are they as straw before the wind,
And like chaff which the storm carries away?

19 "*You say,* 'God saves up a person's wrongdoing for his sons.'
Let God repay him so that he may know *it.*

20 "Let his own eyes see his destruction,
And let him drink of the wrath of the Almighty.

21 "For what does he care about his household after him,
When the number of his months is at an end?

22 "Can anyone teach God knowledge,
In that He judges those on high?

23 "One dies in his full strength,
Being wholly undisturbed and at ease;

24 His sides are filled with fat,
And the marrow of his bones is wet,

25 While another dies with a bitter soul,
Never even tasting *anything* good.

26 "Together they lie down in the dust,
And maggots cover them.

27¶ "Behold, I know your thoughts,
And the plots you devise against me.

28 "For you say, 'Where is the house of the nobleman,
And where is the tent, the dwelling places of the wicked?'

29 "Have you not asked travelers,
And do you not examine their evidence?

30 "For the wicked person is spared a day of disaster;
They are led *away* from a day of fury.

31 "Who confronts him with his actions,
And who repays him for what he has done?

32 "When he is carried to the grave,
People will keep watch over *his* tomb.

33 "The clods of the valley will gently cover him;
Moreover, all mankind will follow after him,
While countless *others* go before him.

34 "So how dare you give me empty comfort?
For your answers remain *nothing but* falsehood!"

Eliphaz Accuses and Exhorts Job

22 Then Eliphaz the Temanite responded,

2 "Can a strong man be of use to God,
Or a wise one be useful to himself?

3 "Is *it any* pleasure to the Almighty if you are righteous,
Or gain if you make your ways blameless?

4 "Is it because of your reverence that He punishes you,
That He enters into judgment against you?

5 "Is your wickedness not abundant,

And is there no end to your guilty deeds?
6 "For you have seized pledges from your
brothers without cause,
And stripped people naked.
7 "You have given the weary no water to
drink,
And you have withheld bread from the
hungry.
8 "But the earth belongs to the powerful
man,
And the one who is honorable dwells on
it.
9 "You have sent widows away empty,
And the strength of orphans has been
crushed.
10 "Therefore traps surround you,
And sudden dread terrifies you,
11 Or darkness, *so that* you cannot see,
And a flood of water covers you.
12¶ "Is God not *in* the height of heaven?
Look also at the highest stars, how high
they are!
13 "But you say, 'What does God know?
Can He judge through the thick darkness?
14 'Clouds are a hiding place for Him, so that
He cannot see;
And He walks on the vault of heaven.'
15 "Will you keep to the ancient path
Which wicked people have walked,
16 Who were snatched away before their
time,
Whose foundations were washed away *by*
a river?
17 "They said to God, 'Go away from us!'
And 'What can the Almighty do to them?'
18 "Yet He filled their houses with good
things;
But the advice of the wicked is far from
me.
19 "The righteous see and are glad,
And the innocent mock them, *saying,*
20 'Truly our enemies are eliminated,
And fire has consumed their abundance.'
21¶ "Be reconciled with Him, and be at peace;
Thereby good will come to you.
22 "Please receive instruction from His
mouth,
And put His words in your heart.
23 "If you return to the Almighty, you will be
restored;
If you remove injustice far from your tent,
24 And put *your* gold in the dust,
And *the gold of* Ophir among the stones
of the brooks,
25 Then the Almighty will be your gold
And abundant silver to you.
26 "For then you will take pleasure in the
Almighty
And lift up your face to God.
27 "You will pray to Him, and He will hear
you;
And you will pay your vows.
28 "You will also decide something, and it will
be established for you;
And light will shine on your ways.
29 "When they have brought *you* low, you will
speak with confidence,
And He will save the humble person.
30 "He will rescue one who is not innocent,

And he will be rescued due to the
cleanness of your hands."

Job Says He Longs for God

23 Then Job responded,
2 "Even today my complaint is rebellion;
His hand is heavy despite my groaning.
3 "Oh that I knew how to find Him,
That I might come to His home!
4 "I would present *my* case before Him
And fill my mouth with arguments.
5 "I would learn the words *which* He would
answer,
And perceive what He would tell me.
6 "Would He contend with me by the
greatness of *His* power?
No, surely He would pay attention to me.
7 "There the upright would argue with Him;
And I would be free of my Judge forever.
8¶ "Behold, I go forward but He is not *there,*
And backward, but I cannot perceive Him;
9 When He acts on the left, I cannot see
Him;
He turns to the right, but I cannot see
Him.
10 "But He knows the way I take;
When He has put me to the test, I will
come out as gold.
11 "My foot has held on to His path;
I have kept His way and not turned aside.
12 "I have not failed the command of His lips;
I have treasured the words of His mouth
more than my necessary food.
13 "But He is unique, and who can make Him
turn?
Whatever His soul desires, He does *it.*
14 "For He carries out what is destined for
me,
And many such *destinies* are with Him.
15 "Therefore, I would be terrified at His
presence;
When I consider *this,* I am frightened of
Him.
16 "*It is* God *who* has made my heart faint,
And the Almighty *who* has terrified me,
17 But I am not destroyed by darkness,
Nor by deep gloom *which* covers me.

Job Says God Seems to Ignore Wrongs

24 "Why are [1]times not stored up by the
Almighty,
And *why* do those who know Him not see
His [2]days?
2 "*People* remove landmarks;
They seize and devour flocks.
3 "They drive away the donkeys of orphans;
They seize the widow's ox as a pledge.
4 "They push the needy aside from the road;
The poor of the land have to hide
themselves together.
5 "Behold, *like* wild donkeys in the
wilderness
They go out scavenging for food in their
activity,
As bread for *their* children in the desert.
6 "They harvest their feed in the field
And glean the vineyard of the wicked.
7 "They spend the night naked, without
clothing,

24:1 [1]I.e., of judgment for the wicked   [2]I.e., of judgment for the wicked

And have no covering against the cold.
8 "They are wet from the mountain rains,
And they hug the rock for lack of a
shelter.
9 "*Others* snatch an orphan from the breast,
And they seize *it* as a pledge against the
poor.
10 "*The poor* move about naked without
clothing,
And they carry sheaves, *while going*
hungry.
11 "Within the walls they produce oil;
They tread wine presses but go thirsty.
12 "From the city people groan,
And the souls of the wounded cry for
help;
Yet God does not pay attention to the
offensiveness.
13¶ "Others have been with those who rebel
against the light;
They do not want to know its ways
Nor stay in its paths.
14 "The murderer arises at dawn;
He kills the poor and the needy,
And at night he is like a thief.
15 "The eye of the adulterer watches for
twilight,
Saying, 'No eye will see me.'
And he disguises his face.
16 "In the darkness they dig into houses,
They shut themselves up by day;
They do not know the light.
17 "For the morning is the same to him as
thick darkness,
For he is familiar with the terrors of thick
darkness.
18¶ "They are insignificant on the surface of
the water;
Their plot of land on the earth is cursed.
They do not turn toward the vineyards.
19 "Dryness and heat snatch away the snow
waters,
As ¹Sheol *snatches those who* have
sinned.
20 "A mother will forget him;
The maggot feeds sweetly until he is no
longer remembered.
And injustice will be broken like a tree.
21 "He wrongs the infertile woman,
And does no good for the widow.
22 "But He drags off the mighty by His power;
He rises, but no one has assurance of life.
23 "He provides them with security, and they
are supported;
And His eyes are on their ways.
24 "They are exalted a little while, then they
are gone;
Moreover, they are brought low, *and* like
everything they are gathered up;
Like the heads of grain they wither.
25 "Now if it is not so, who can prove me a
liar,
And make my speech worthless?"

Bildad Says Mankind Is Inferior

25 Then Bildad the Shuhite
responded,
2 "Dominion and awe belong to Him

Who makes peace in His heights.
3 "Is there any number to His troops?
And upon whom does His light not rise?
4 "How then can mankind be righteous with
God?
Or how can *anyone* who is born of
woman be pure?
5 "If even the moon has no brightness
And the stars are not pure in His sight,
6 How much less man, *that* maggot,
And a son of man, *that* worm!"

Job Rebukes Bildad

26 Then Job responded,
2 "What a help you are to the weak!
You have saved the arm without strength!
3 "What advice you have given to *one*
without wisdom!
What helpful insight you have abundantly
provided!
4 "To whom have you uttered words?
And whose spirit was expressed through
you?

The Greatness of God

5¶ "The departed spirits are made to tremble
Under the waters and their inhabitants.
6 "¹Sheol is naked before Him,
And ²Abaddon has no covering.
7 "He stretches out the north over empty
space
And hangs the earth on nothing.
8 "He wraps up the waters in His clouds,
And the cloud does not burst under them.
9 "He obscures the face of the full moon
And spreads His cloud over it.
10 "He has inscribed a circle on the surface of
the waters
At the boundary of light and darkness.
11 "The pillars of heaven tremble
And are amazed at His rebuke.
12 "With His power He quieted the sea,
And by His understanding He shattered
¹Rahab.
13 "By His breath the heavens are cleared;
His hand has pierced the fleeing serpent.
14 "Behold, these are the fringes of His ways;
And how faint a word we hear of Him!
But His mighty thunder, who can
understand?"

Job Affirms His Righteousness

27 Job again took up his discourse
and said,
2 "As God lives, who has taken away my
right,
And the Almighty, who has embittered my
soul,
3 For as long as life is in me,
And the breath of God is in my nostrils,
4 My lips certainly will not speak unjustly,
Nor will my tongue mutter deceit.
5 "Far be it from me that I should declare
you right;
Until I die, I will not give up my integrity.
6 "I have kept hold of my righteousness and
will not let it go.
My heart does not rebuke any of my days.

24:19 ¹I.e., the netherworld   26:6 ¹I.e., the netherworld   ²I.e., the place of destruction
26:12 ¹I.e., a sea monster, not to be confused with Rahab in Joshua 2

The State of the Godless

7¶ "May my enemy be as the wicked,
　And my opponent as the criminal.
8 "For what is the hope of the godless when
　　he makes an end *of life,*
　When God requires his life?
9 "Will God hear his cry
　When distress comes upon him?
10 "Or will he take pleasure in the Almighty?
　Will he call on God at all times?
11 "I will instruct you in the power of God;
　What is with the Almighty I will not
　　conceal.
12 "Behold, all of you have seen *it;*
　Why then do you talk of nothing?
13¶ "This is the portion of a wicked person
　　from God,
　And the inheritance *which* tyrants receive
　　from the Almighty:
14 Though his sons are many, they are
　　destined for the sword;
　And his descendants will not be satisfied
　　with bread.
15 "His survivors will be buried because of the
　　plague,
　And their widows will not *be able to*
　　weep.
16 "Though he piles up silver like dust,
　And prepares garments as *plentiful as* the
　　clay,
17 He may prepare *it,* but the righteous will
　　wear *it*
　And the innocent will divide the silver.
18 "He has built his house like the spider's
　　web,
　Or a hut *which* the watchman has made.
19 "He lies down rich, but never again;
　He opens his eyes, and it no *longer* exists.
20 "Terrors overtake him like a flood;
　A storm steals him away in the night.
21 "The east wind carries him away, and he is
　　gone;
　For it sweeps him away from his place.
22 "For it will hurl at him without mercy;
　He will certainly try to flee from its
　　power.
23 "*People* will ¹clap their hands at him,
　And will whistle at him from their places.

Job Tells of Earth's Treasures

28 "Certainly there is a mine
　for silver
　And a place for refining gold.
2 "Iron is taken from the dust,
　And copper is smelted from rock.
3 "*Man* puts an end to darkness,
　And to the farthest limit he searches out
　The rock in gloom and deep shadow.
4 "He sinks a shaft away from inhabited
　　areas,
　Forgotten by the foot;
　They hang *and* swing, away from people.
5 "From the earth comes food,
　And underneath, it is turned over like
　　fire.
6 "Its rocks are the source of sapphires,
　And its dust *contains* gold.
7 "No bird of prey knows the path,
　Nor has the falcon's eye caught sight of it.

8 "The proud animals have not trodden it,
　Nor has the lion passed over it.
9 "He puts his hand on the flint;
　He overturns the mountains at the base.
10 "He carves out channels through the rocks,
　And his eye sees anything precious.
11 "He dams up the streams from flowing,
　And brings to light what is hidden.

The Search for Wisdom Is Harder

12¶ "But where can wisdom be found?
　And where is the place of understanding?
13 "Mankind does not know its value,
　Nor is it found in the land of the living.
14 "The ocean depth says, 'It is not in me';
　And the sea says, 'It is not with me.'
15 "Pure gold cannot be given in exchange for
　　it,
　Nor can silver be weighed as its price.
16 "It cannot be valued in the gold of Ophir,
　In precious onyx, or sapphire.
17 "Gold or glass cannot equal it,
　Nor can it be exchanged for articles of
　　pure gold.
18 "Coral and crystal are not to be mentioned;
　And the acquisition of wisdom is more
　　valuable than pearls.
19 "The topaz of Cush cannot equal it,
　Nor can it be valued in pure gold.
20 "Where then does wisdom come from?
　And where is this place of understanding?
21 "It is hidden from the eyes of every living
　　creature,
　And concealed from the birds of the sky.
22 "¹Abaddon and Death say,
　'With our ears we have heard a report
　　of it.'
23¶ "God understands its way,
　And He knows its place.
24 "For He looks to the ends of the earth;
　He sees everything under the heavens.
25 "When He imparted weight to the wind,
　And assessed the waters by measure,
26 When He made a limit for the rain,
　And a course for the thunderbolt,
27 Then He saw it and declared it;
　He established it and also searched it out.
28 "And to mankind He said, 'Behold, the fear
　　of the Lord, that is wisdom;
　And to turn away from evil is
　　understanding.' "

Job's Past Was Glorious

29 Job again took up his discourse
　and said,
2 "Oh that I were as in months gone by,
　As in the days when God watched over
　　me;
3 When His lamp shone over my head,
　And by His light I walked *through* dark-
　　ness;
4 Just as I was in the days of my youth,
　When the protection of God *was* over my
　　tent;
5 When the Almighty was still with me,
　And my children were around me;
6 When my steps were bathed in cream,
　And the rock poured out streams of oil
　　for me!

27:23 ¹I.e., mock and ridicule him　28:22 ¹I.e., Destruction

7   "When I went out to the gate of the city,
    When I took my seat in the public square,
8   The young men saw me and hid
    themselves,
    And the old men arose *and* stood.
9   "The leaders stopped talking
    And put *their* hands on their mouths;
10   The voices of the prominent people were
    hushed,
    And their tongues stuck to their palates.
11   "For *when* an ear heard, it called me
    blessed,
    And when an eye saw, it testified in
    support of me,
12   Because I saved the poor who cried for
    help,
    And the orphan who had no helper.
13   "The blessing of the one who was about to
    perish came upon me,
    And I made the widow's heart sing for joy.
14   "I put on righteousness, and it clothed me;
    My justice was like a robe and a head-
    band.
15   "I was eyes to those who were blind,
    And feet to those who could not walk.
16   "I was a father to the poor,
    And I investigated the case which I did
    not know.
17   "I broke the jaws of the wicked
    And rescued the prey from his teeth.
18   "Then I thought, 'I will die with my family,
    And I will multiply *my* days as the sand.
19   'My root is spread out to the waters,
    And dew lies on my branch all night.
20   'My glory is *ever* new with me,
    And my bow is renewed in my hand.'
21¶   "To me they listened and waited,
    And they kept silent for my advice.
22   "After my words they did not *speak* again,
    And my speech dropped on them.
23   "They waited for me as for the rain,
    And opened their mouths as for the late
    rain.
24   "I smiled at them *when* they did not
    believe,
    And they did not look at my kindness
    ungraciously.
25   "I chose a way for them and sat as chief,
    And lived as a king among the troops,
    As one who comforted the mourners.

Job's Present State Is Humiliating

30   "But now those who are younger than I
    mock me,
    Whose fathers I refused to put with the
    dogs of my flock.
2   "Indeed, what *good was* the strength of
    their hands to me?
    Vigor had perished from them.
3   "From poverty and famine they are gaunt,
    They who gnaw at the dry ground by
    night in waste and desolation,
4   Who pluck saltweed by the bushes,
    And whose food is the root of the broom
    shrub.
5   "They are driven from the community;
    They shout against them as *against* a
    thief,
6   So that they live on the slopes of ravines,

In holes *in* the ground and *among* the
    rocks.
7   "Among the bushes they cry out;
    Under the weeds they are gathered
    together.
8   "Worthless fellows, even those without a
    name,
    They were cast out from the land.
9¶   "And now I have become their taunt,
    And I have become a ʰbyword to them.
10   "They loathe me *and* stand aloof from me,
    And they do not refrain from spitting in
    my face.
11   "Because He has undone my bowstring and
    afflicted me,
    They have cast off the bridle before me.
12   "On the right hand their mob arises;
    They push aside my feet and pile up their
    ways of destruction against me.
13   "They break up my path,
    They promote my destruction;
    No one restrains them.
14   "As *through* a wide gap they come,
    Amid the storm they roll on.
15   "Sudden terrors are turned upon me;
    They chase *away* my dignity like the
    wind,
    And my prosperity has passed away like a
    cloud.
16¶   "And now my soul is poured out within
    me;
    Days of misery have seized me.
17   "At night it pierces my bones within me,
    And my gnawing *pains* do not rest.
18   "By a great force my garment is distorted;
    It ties me up like the collar of my coat.
19   "He has thrown me into the mire,
    And I have become like dust and ashes.
20   "I cry out to You for help, but You do not
    answer me;
    I stand up, and You turn Your attention
    against me.
21   "You have become cruel to me;
    With the strength of Your hand You
    persecute me.
22   "You lift me up to the wind *and* make me
    ride *it;*
    And You dissolve me in a storm.
23   "For I know that You will bring me to
    death,
    And to the house of meeting for all living.
24¶   "Yet does one in a heap of ruins not reach
    out *with his* hand,
    Or in his disaster does he not cry out for
    help?
25   "Have I not wept for the one whose life is
    hard?
    Was my soul not grieved for the needy?
26   "When I expected good, evil came;
    When I waited for light, darkness came.
27   "I am seething within and cannot rest;
    Days of misery confront me.
28   "I go about mourning without comfort;
    I stand up in the assembly *and* cry out for
    help.
29   "I have become a brother to jackals,
    And a companion of ostriches.
30   "My skin turns black on me,
    And my bones burn with fever.

30:9 ¹I.e., prob. a word of insult

31 "Therefore my harp is turned to mourning,
And my flute to the sound of those who weep.

Job Asserts His Integrity

31 "I have made a covenant with my eyes;
How then could I look at a virgin?

2 "And what is the portion of God from above,
Or the inheritance of the Almighty from on high?

3 "Is it not disaster to the criminal,
And misfortune to those who practice injustice?

4 "Does He not see my ways,
And count all my steps?

5 ¶ "If I have walked with deception,
And my foot has hurried after deceit,

6 Let Him weigh me with accurate scales,
And let God know my integrity.

7 "If my step has turned from the way,
Or my heart followed my eyes,
Or if any spot has stuck to my hands,

8 Let me sow and another eat,
And let my crops be uprooted.

9 ¶ "If my heart has been enticed by a woman,
Or I have lurked at my neighbor's doorway,

10 May my wife grind grain for another,
And let others ¹kneel down over her.

11 "For that would be a lustful crime;
Moreover, it would be wrongdoing punishable by judges.

12 "For it would be fire that consumes to ¹Abaddon,
And would uproot all my increase.

13 ¶ "If I have rejected the claim of my male or female slaves
When they filed a complaint against me,

14 What then could I do when God arises?
And when He calls me to account, how am I to answer Him?

15 "Did He who made me in the womb not make him,
And the same one create us in the womb?

16 ¶ "If I have kept the poor from their desire,
Or have caused the eyes of the widow to fail,

17 Or have eaten my morsel alone,
And the orphan has not shared it

18 (But from my youth he grew up with me as with a father,
And from my infancy I guided her),

19 If I have seen anyone perish for lack of clothing,
Or that the needy had no covering,

20 If his waist has not ¹thanked me,
And if he has not been warmed with the fleece of my sheep,

21 If I have lifted up my hand against the orphan,
Because I saw I had support in the gate,

22 May my shoulder fall from its socket,
And my arm be broken off at the elbow.

23 "For disaster from God is a terror to me,
And because of His majesty I can do nothing.

24 ¶ "If I have put my confidence in gold,
And called fine gold my trust,

25 If I have gloated because my wealth was great,
And because my hand had obtained so much;

26 If I have looked at the sun when it shone,
Or the moon going in splendor,

27 And my heart was secretly enticed,
And my hand threw a kiss from my mouth,

28 That too would have been a guilty deed calling for judgment,
For I would have denied God above.

29 ¶ "Have I rejoiced at the misfortune of my enemy,
Or become excited when evil found him?

30 "No, I have not allowed my mouth to sin
By asking for his life in a curse.

31 "Have the people of my tent not said,
'Who can find one who has not been satisfied with his meat'?

32 "The stranger has not spent the night outside,
For I have opened my doors to the traveler.

33 "Have I covered my wrongdoings like a man,
By hiding my guilt in my shirt pocket,

34 Because I feared the great multitude
And the contempt of families terrified me,
And I kept silent and did not go out of doors?

35 "Oh that I had one to hear me!
Here is my signature;
Let the Almighty answer me!
And the indictment which my adversary has written,

36 I would certainly carry it on my shoulder,
I would tie it to myself like a garland.

37 "I would declare to Him the number of my steps;
Like a prince, I would approach Him.

38 ¶ "If my land cries out against me,
And its furrows weep together;

39 If I have eaten its fruit without money,
Or have caused its owners to lose their lives,

40 May the thorn-bush grow instead of wheat,
And stinkweed instead of barley."
The words of Job are ended.

Elihu Rebukes Job in Anger

32 Then these three men stopped answering Job, because he was righteous in his own eyes. 2 But the anger of Elihu the son of Barachel the Buzite, of the family of Ram, burned against Job; his anger burned because he justified himself before God. 3 And his anger burned against his three friends because they had found no answer, yet they had condemned Job. 4 Now Elihu had waited to speak to Job because they were years older than he. 5 But when Elihu saw that there was no answer in the mouth of the three men, his anger burned.

31:10 ¹ I.e., have sexual relations with her   **31:12** ¹ I.e., the place of destruction
31:20 ¹ Lit *blessed;* i.e., for clothing

6 So Elihu the son of Barachel the Buzite spoke out and said,
"I am young in years and you are old;
Therefore I was shy and afraid to tell you what I think.

7 "I thought age should speak,
And increased years should teach wisdom.

8 "But it is a spirit *that is* in mankind,
And the breath of the Almighty gives them understanding.

9 "The abundant *in years* may not be wise,
Nor may elders understand justice.

10 "So I say, 'Listen to me,
I too will tell what I think.'

11¶ "Behold, I waited for your words,
I listened to your skillful speech,
While you pondered what to say.

12 "I also paid close attention to you;
But indeed, there was no one who refuted Job,
Not one of you who answered his words.

13 "So do not say,
'We have found wisdom:
God will defeat him, not man.'

14 "But he has not presented *his* words against me,
Nor will I reply to him with your arguments.

15¶ "They are dismayed, they no longer answer;
Words have failed them.

16 "Should I wait, because they are not speaking,
Because they have stopped *and* no longer answer?

17 "I too will give my share of answers;
I also will tell my opinion.

18 "For I am full of words;
The spirit within me compels me.

19 "Behold, my belly is like unvented wine;
Like new wineskins, it is about to burst.

20 "Let me speak so that I may get relief;
Let me open my lips and answer.

21 "Let me be partial to no one,
Nor flatter *any* man.

22 "For I do not know how to flatter,
Otherwise my Maker would quickly take me away.

Elihu Claims to Speak for God

33 "However, please hear my speech, Job,
And listen to all my words.

2 "Behold now, I open my mouth,
My tongue in my mouth speaks.

3 "My words are *from* the integrity of my heart,
And my lips speak knowledge sincerely.

4 "The Spirit of God has made me,
And the breath of the Almighty gives me life.

5 "Refute me if you can;
Line up against me, take your stand.

6 "Behold, I belong to God, like you;
I too have been formed out of the clay.

7 "Behold, no fear of me should terrify you,
Nor should my pressure weigh heavily on you.

8¶ "You have in fact spoken while I listened,
And I heard the sound of *your* words:

9 'I am pure, without wrongdoing;
I am innocent and there is no guilt in me.

10 'Behold, He invents criticisms against me;
He counts me as His enemy.

11 'He puts my feet in the stocks;
He watches all my paths.'

12 "Behold, let me respond to you, you are not right in this,
For God is greater than mankind.

13¶ "Why do you complain to Him
That He does not give an account of all His doings?

14 "Indeed God speaks once,
Or twice, *yet* no one notices it.

15 "In a dream, a vision of the night,
When deep sleep falls on people,
While they slumber in their beds,

16 Then He opens the ears of people,
And horrifies them with warnings,

17 So that He may turn a person away *from bad* conduct,
And keep a man from pride;

18 He keeps his soul back from the pit,
And his life from perishing by the spear.

19¶ "*A person* is also rebuked by pain in his bed,
And with constant complaint in his bones,

20 So that his life loathes bread,
And his soul, food that he should crave.

21 "His flesh wastes away from sight,
And his bones, *which* were not seen, stick out.

22 "Then his soul comes near to the pit,
And his life to those who bring death.

23¶ "If there is an interceding angel for him,
One out of a thousand,
To remind a person of what is right for him,

24 And he is gracious to him, and says,
'Free him from going down to the pit,
I have found a ransom';

25 Let his flesh become fresher than in youth,
Let him return to the days of his youthful vigor;

26 *Then* he will pray to God, and He will accept him,
So that he may see His face with joy,
And He will restore His righteousness to *that* person.

27 "He will sing to people and say,
'I have sinned and perverted what is right,
And it is not proper for me.

28 'He has redeemed my soul from going to the pit,
And my life will see the light.'

29¶ "Behold, God does all these *things* for a man two or three times,

30 To bring back his soul from the pit,
So that he may be enlightened with the light of life.

31 "Pay attention, Job, listen to me;
Keep silent, and let me speak.

32 "*Then* if you have anything to say, answer me;
Speak, for I would take pleasure in justifying you.

33 "If not, listen to me;
Keep silent, and I will teach you wisdom."

Elihu Vindicates God's Justice

34 Then Elihu continued and said,
2 "Hear my words, you wise men,
And listen to me, you who understand.
3 "For the ear tests words
As the palate tastes food.
4 "Let us choose for ourselves what is right;
Let us understand among ourselves what
is good.
5 "For Job has said, 'I am righteous,
But God has taken away my right;
6 Should I lie about my right?
My wound is incurable, *though I am*
without wrongdoing.'
7 "What man is like Job,
Who drinks up derision like water,
8 Who goes in company with the workers of
injustice,
And walks with wicked people?
9 "For he has said, 'It is of no use to a man
When he becomes friends with God.'
10¶ "Therefore, listen to me, you men of
understanding.
Far be it from God to do evil,
And from the Almighty to do wrong.
11 "For He repays a person for his work,
And lets *things* happen in correspondence
to a man's behavior.
12 "God certainly will not act wickedly,
And the Almighty will not pervert justice.
13 "Who gave Him authority over the earth?
And who has placed the whole world *on*
Him?
14 "If He were to determine to do so,
If He were to gather His spirit and His
breath to Himself,
15 Humanity would perish together,
And mankind would return to dust.
16¶ "But if *you have* understanding, hear this;
Listen to the sound of my words.
17 "Shall one who hates justice rule?
And will you condemn the righteous
mighty One,
18 Who says to a king, 'You worthless one,'
To nobles, 'You wicked one';
19 Who shows no partiality to the
prominent,
Nor regards the rich as above the poor,
Since they are all the work of His hands?
20 "In a moment they die, and at midnight
People are shaken and pass away,
And the powerful are taken away without
a hand.
21¶ "For His eyes are upon the ways of a
person,
And He sees all his steps.
22 "There is no darkness or deep shadow
Where the workers of injustice can hide
themselves.
23 "For He does not *need to* consider a person
further,
That he should go before God in
judgment.
24 "He breaks in pieces the mighty without
investigation,
And sets others in their place.
25 "Therefore He knows their deeds,
And He overthrows *them* in the night,
And they are crushed.
26 "He strikes them like the wicked
In a public place,
27 Because they turned aside from following
Him,
And had no regard for any of His ways,
28 So that they caused the cry of the poor to
come to Him,
And that He would hear the cry of the
afflicted—
29 When He keeps quiet, who can condemn?
And when He hides His face, who then
can look at Him,
That is, regarding both nation and a
person?—
30 "So that godless people would not rule,
Nor be snares for the people.
31¶ "For has anyone said to God,
'I have endured *punishment;*
I will not offend *anymore;*
32 Teach me what I do not see;
If I have done wrong,
I will not do it again'?
33 "Shall *God* repay on your terms, because
you have rejected *His?*
For you must choose, and not I;
Therefore declare what you know.
34 "Men of understanding will say to me,
And a wise man who hears me,
35 'Job speaks without knowledge,
And his words are without wisdom.
36 'Oh that Job were tested to the limit,
Because he answers like sinners.
37 'For he adds rebellion to his sin;
He claps his hands among us,
And multiplies his words against God.'"

Elihu Sharply Rebukes Job

35 Then Elihu continued and said,
2 "Do you think this is in accordance
with justice?
Do you say, 'My righteousness is more
than God's'?
3 "For you say, 'What advantage will it be to
You?
What benefit will I have, more than *if* I
had sinned?'
4 "I will answer you,
And your friends with you.
5 "Look at the heavens and see;
And look at the clouds—they are higher
than you.
6 "If you have sinned, what do you accomplish against Him?
And if your wrongdoings are many, what
do you do to Him?
7 "If you are righteous, what do you give to
Him,
Or what does He receive from your hand?
8 "Your wickedness is for a man like yourself,
And your righteousness is for a son of
man.
9¶ "Because of the multitude of oppressions
they cry out;
They cry for help because of the arm of
the mighty.
10 "But no one says, 'Where is God my Maker,
Who gives songs in the night,
11 Who teaches us more than the animals of
the earth
And makes us wiser than the birds of the
sky?'

12 "There they cry out, but He does not answer
Because of the pride of evil people.
13 "God certainly will not listen to an empty *cry,*
Nor will the Almighty regard it.
14 "How much less when you say you do not look at Him,
The case is before Him, and you must wait for Him!
15 "And now, because He has not avenged His anger,
Nor has He acknowledged wrongdoing well,
16 So Job opens his mouth *with* empty *words;*
He multiplies words without knowledge."

Elihu Speaks of God's Dealings with Mankind

36 Then Elihu continued and said,
2 "Wait for me a little, and I will show you
That there is still more to be said on God's behalf.
3 "I will bring my knowledge from afar,
And ascribe righteousness to my Maker.
4 "For truly my words are not false;
One who is perfect in knowledge is with you.
5 "Behold, God is mighty but does not reject *anyone;*
He is mighty in strength of understanding.
6 "He does not keep the wicked alive,
But gives justice to the afflicted.
7 "He does not withdraw His eyes from the righteous,
But with kings on the throne
He has seated them forever, and they are exalted.
8 "And if they are bound in shackles,
And are caught in the snares of misery,
9 Then He declares to them their work
And their wrongdoings, that they have been arrogant.
10 "He opens their ears to instruction,
And commands that they return from injustice.
11 "If they listen and serve *Him,*
They will end their days in prosperity,
And their years in happiness.
12 "But if they do not listen, they will perish by the sword,
And die without knowledge.
13 "But the godless in heart nurture anger;
They do not call for help when He binds them.
14 "They die in youth,
And their life *perishes* among the cult prostitutes.
15 "He rescues the afflicted in their misery,
And opens their ears in *time of* oppression.
16 "Then indeed, He induced you away from the mouth of distress,
And instead of it, a broad place with no constraint;
And your table was full of rich food.
17¶ "But you were full of judgment on the wicked;
Judgment and justice take hold *of you.*

18 "*Beware* that wrath does not entice you to mockery;
And do not let the greatness of the ransom turn you aside.
19 "Will your cry for help keep you from distress,
Or all the exertions of *your* strength?
20 "Do not long for the night,
When people vanish in their places.
21 "Be careful, do not turn to evil,
For you preferred this to misery.
22 "Behold, God is exalted in His power;
Who is a teacher like Him?
23 "Who has appointed Him His way,
And who has said, 'You have done wrong'?
24¶ "Remember that you are to exalt His work,
Of which people have sung.
25 "All people have seen it;
Mankind looks at it from afar.
26 "Behold, God is exalted, and we do not know *Him;*
The number of His years is unsearchable.
27 "For He draws up the drops of water;
They distill rain from its celestial stream,
28 Which clouds pour down;
They drip upon mankind abundantly.
29 "Can anyone understand the spreading of the clouds,
The thundering of His pavilion?
30 "Behold, He spreads His lightning about Him,
And He covers the depths of the sea.
31 "For by them He judges peoples;
He gives food in abundance.
32 "He covers *His* hands with the lightning,
And commands it to strike the target.
33 "Its thundering voice declares His presence;
The livestock also, concerning what is coming up.

Elihu Says God Has Authority Over the Storm

37 "At this also my heart trembles,
And leaps from its place.
2 "Listen closely to the thunder of His voice,
And the rumbling that goes out from His mouth.
3 "Under the whole heaven He lets it loose,
And His lightning *travels* to the ends of the earth.
4 "After it, a voice roars;
He thunders with His majestic voice,
And He does not restrain the lightning when His voice is heard.
5 "God thunders wondrously with His voice,
Doing great things which we do not comprehend.
6 "For to the snow He says, 'Fall on the earth,'
And to the downpour and the rain, 'Be strong.'
7 "He seals the hand of every person,
So that all people may know His work.
8 "Then the animal goes into its lair
And remains in its den.
9 "From the south comes the storm,
And from the north wind the cold.
10 "From the breath of God ice is made,
And the expanse of the waters is frozen.

11 "He also loads the clouds with moisture;
He disperses the cloud of His lightning.
12 "It changes direction, turning around by
His guidance,
That it may do whatever He commands it
On the face of the inhabited earth.
13 "Whether for correction, or for His earth,
Or for goodness, He causes it to happen.
14¶ "Listen to this, Job;
Stand and consider the wonders of God.
15 "Do you know how God establishes them,
And makes the lightning of His clouds to
shine?
16 "Do you know about the hovering of the
clouds,
The wonders of One who is perfect in
knowledge,
17 You whose garments are hot
When the land is still because of the south
wind?
18 "Can you, with Him, spread out the skies,
Strong as a cast metal mirror?
19 "Teach us what we are to say to Him;
We cannot present *our case* because of
darkness.
20 "Shall it be told Him that I would speak?
Or should a man say that he would be
swallowed up?
21¶ "Now *people* do not see the light which is
bright in the skies;
But the wind has passed and cleared
them.
22 "From the north comes golden *splendor;*
Around God is awesome majesty.
23 "The Almighty—we cannot find Him;
He is exalted in power
And He will not violate justice and
abundant righteousness.
24 "Therefore people fear Him;
He does not regard any who are wise of
heart."

God Speaks Now to Job

38 Then the Lord answered Job from the
whirlwind and said,
2 "Who is this who darkens *the divine* plan
By words without knowledge?
3 "Now tighten the belt on your waist like a
man,
And I shall ask you, and you inform Me!
4 "Where were you when I laid the
foundation of the earth?
Tell *Me,* if you have understanding,
5 Who set its measurements? Since you
know.
Or who stretched the measuring line over
it?
6 "On what were its bases sunk?
Or who laid its cornerstone,
7 When the morning stars sang together
And all the sons of God shouted for joy?
8¶ "Or *who* enclosed the sea with doors
When it went out from the womb,
bursting forth;
9 When I made a cloud its garment,
And thick darkness its swaddling bands,
10 And I placed boundaries on it
And set a bolt and doors,
11 And I said, 'As far as this point you shall
come, but no farther;

And here your proud waves shall stop'?

God's Mighty Power

12¶ "Have you ever in your life commanded the
morning,
And made the dawn know its place,
13 So that it would take hold of the ends of
the earth,
And the wicked would be shaken off from
it?
14 "It is changed like clay *under* the seal;
And they stand out like a garment.
15 "Their light is withheld from the wicked,
And the uplifted arm is broken.
16¶ "Have you entered the springs of the sea,
And walked in the depth of the ocean?
17 "Have the gates of death been revealed to
you,
And have you seen the gates of deep
darkness?
18 "Have you understood the expanse of the
earth?
Tell *Me,* if you know all this.
19¶ "Where is the way to the dwelling of light?
And darkness, where is its place,
20 That you would take it to its territory,
And discern the paths to its home?
21 "You know, for you were born then,
And the number of your days is great!
22 "Have you entered the storehouses of the
snow,
And have you seen the storehouses of the
hail,
23 Which I have reserved for a time of
distress,
For a day of war and battle?
24 "Where is the way that the light is divided,
And the east wind scattered on the earth?
25¶ "Who has split *open* a channel for the
flood,
And a way for the thunderbolt,
26 To bring rain on a land without people,
On a desert without a person in it,
27 To satisfy the waste and desolate land,
And to make the seeds of grass to sprout?
28 "Does the rain have a father?
Or who has fathered the drops of dew?
29 "From whose womb has come the ice?
And the frost of heaven, who has given it
birth?
30 "Water becomes hard like stone,
And the surface of the deep is imprisoned.
31¶ "Can you tie up the chains of the Pleiades,
Or untie the cords of Orion?
32 "Can you bring out a constellation in its
season,
And guide the Bear with her satellites?
33 "Do you know the ordinances of the
heavens,
Or do you establish their rule over the
earth?
34¶ "Can you raise your voice to the clouds,
So that an abundance of water will cover
you?
35 "Can you send flashes of lightning, so that
they may go
And say to you, 'Here we are'?
36 "Who has put wisdom in the innermost
being,
Or given understanding to the mind?

37   "Who can count the clouds by wisdom,
     And pour out the water jars of the
       heavens,
38   When the dust hardens into a mass
     And the clods stick together?
39¶ "Can you hunt the prey for the lioness,
     Or satisfy the appetite of young lions,
40   When they crouch in *their* hiding places,
     And lie in wait in *their* lair?
41   "Who prepares feed for the raven
     When its young cry to God,
     And wander about without food?

God Speaks of Nature and Its Beings

39 "Do you know the time the mountain
     goats give birth?
     Do you observe the calving of the deer?
2   "Can you count the months they fulfill,
     Or do you know the time they give birth?
3   "They kneel down, they deliver their
       young,
     They get rid of their labor pains.
4   "Their offspring become strong, they grow
     up in the open field;
     They leave and do not return to them.
5¶ "Who sent the wild donkey out free?
     And who opened the bonds of the swift
       donkey,
6   To whom I gave the wilderness as his
       home,
     And the salt land as his dwelling place?
7   "He laughs at the turmoil of the city,
     He does not hear the shouting of the
       taskmaster.
8   "He explores the mountains of his pasture,
     And searches after every green thing.
9   "Will the wild bull be willing to serve you,
     Or will he spend the night at your feeding
       trough?
10   "Can you tie down the wild bull in a
     furrow with ropes,
     Or will he plow the valleys after you?
11   "Will you trust him because his strength is
     great,
     And leave your labor to him?
12   "Will you have faith in him that he will
     return your grain
     And gather *it from* your threshing floor?
13¶ "The wings of the ostrich flap joyously,
     With the pinion and feathers of love,
14   For she abandons her eggs to the earth
     And warms them in the dust,
15   And she forgets that a foot may crush
     them,
     Or that a wild animal may trample them.
16   "She treats her young cruelly, as if *they*
     were not hers;
     Though her labor is for nothing, *she* is
       unconcerned;
17   Because God has made her forget wisdom,
     And has not given her a share of
       understanding.
18   "When she rushes away on high,
     She laughs at the horse and his rider.
19¶ "Do you give the horse *his* might?
     Do you clothe his neck with a mane?
20   "Do you make him leap like locusts?
     His majestic snorting is frightening.
21   "He paws in the valley, and rejoices in *his*
     strength;

     He goes out to meet the battle.
22   "He laughs at fear and is not dismayed;
     And he does not turn back from the
       sword.
23   "The quiver rattles against him,
     The flashing spear and javelin.
24   "He races over the ground with a roar and
     fury,
     And he does not stand still when *he hears*
     the sound of the trumpet.
25   "As often as the trumpet *sounds* he says,
     'Aha!'
     And he senses the battle from afar,
     And the thunder of the captains and the
       war cry.
26¶ "Is it by your understanding that the hawk
     soars,
     Stretching his wings toward the south?
27   "Is it at your command that the eagle flies
     high,
     And makes his nest on high?
28   "He dwells and spends his nights on the
     cliff,
     On the rocky cliff, an inaccessible
       place.
29   "From there he tracks food;
     His eyes look at *it* from afar.
30   "His young ones also lick up blood
     greedily;
     And where the slain are, there he is."

Job Says What Can I Say?

40 Then the Lord said to Job,
2   "Will the faultfinder contend with the
     Almighty?
     Let him who rebukes God give an
       answer."
     3 Then Job answered the Lord and said,
4   "Behold, I am insignificant; what can I say
     in response to You?
     I put my hand on my mouth.
5   "I have spoken once, and I will not reply;
     Or twice, and I will add nothing *more.*"

God Questions Job

     6 Then the Lord answered Job from the
whirlwind and said,
7   "Now tighten the belt on your waist like a
     man;
     I will ask you, and you instruct Me.
8   "Will you really nullify My judgment?
     Will you condemn Me so that you may be
     justified?
9   "Or do you have an arm like God,
     And can you thunder with a voice like
     His?
10¶ "Adorn yourself with pride and dignity,
     And clothe yourself with honor and
     majesty.
11   "Let out your outbursts of anger,
     And look at everyone who is arrogant, and
     humble him.
12   "Look at everyone who is arrogant, *and*
     humble him,
     And trample down the wicked where they
     stand.
13   "Hide them together in the dust;
     Imprison them in the hidden *place.*
14   "Then I will also confess to you,
     That your own right hand can save you.

God's Power Shown in Creatures

15¶ "Behold, [1]Behemoth, which I made as well
as you;
He eats grass like an ox.

16 "Behold, his strength in his waist,
And his power in the muscles of his belly.

17 "He hangs his tail like a cedar;
The tendons of his thighs are knit
together.

18 "His bones are tubes of bronze;
His limbs are like bars of iron.

19¶ "He is the first of the ways of God;
Let his Maker bring His sword near.

20 "Indeed the [1]mountains bring him food,
And all the animals of the field play there.

21 "He lies down under the lotus plants,
In the hiding place of the reeds and the
marsh.

22 "The lotus plants cover him with shade;
The willows of the brook surround him.

23 "If a river rages, he is not alarmed;
He is confident, though the Jordan rushes
to his mouth.

24 "Can anyone capture him when he is on
watch,
Can anyone pierce *his* nose with barbs?

God's Power Shown in Creatures

41 "Can you drag out [1]Leviathan with a
fishhook,
And press down his tongue with a rope?

2 "Can you put a rope in his nose,
And pierce his jaw with a hook?

3 "Will he make many pleas to you,
Or will he speak to you gentle words?

4 "Will he make a covenant with you?
Will you take him as a servant forever?

5 "Will you play with him as with a bird,
And tie him down for your young girls?

6 "Will the traders bargain for him?
Will they divide him among the
merchants?

7 "Can you fill his skin with harpoons,
Or his head with fishing spears?

8 "Lay your hand on him.
Remember the battle; you will not do it
again!

9 "Behold, your expectation is false;
Will you be hurled down even at the sight
of him?

10 "No one is so reckless that he dares to stir
him;
Who then is he who opposes Me?

11 "Who has been first *to give* to Me, that I
should repay *him?*
Whatever is under the entire heaven is
Mine.

12¶ "I will not be silent about his limbs,
Or his mighty strength, or his graceful
frame.

13 "Who can strip off his outer covering?
Who can pierce his double armor?

14 "Who can open the doors of his face?
Around his teeth there is terror.

15 "*His* strong scales are *his* pride,
Locked *as with* a tight seal.

16 "One is so close to another
That no air can come between them.

17 "They are joined one to another;
They clasp each other and cannot be
separated.

18 "His sneezes flash forth light,
And his eyes are like the eye of dawn.

19 "From his mouth go burning torches;
Sparks of fire leap forth.

20 "From his nostrils smoke goes out
As *from* a boiling pot and *burning* reeds.

21 "His breath sets coals aglow,
And a flame goes forth from his mouth.

22 "In his neck dwells strength,
And dismay leaps before him.

23 "The folds of his flesh are joined together,
Firm and immovable on him.

24 "His heart is as firm as a stone,
And as firm as a lower millstone.

25 "When he rises up, the mighty are afraid;
Because of the crashing they are
bewildered.

26 "The sword that reaches him cannot
prevail,
Nor the spear, the dart, or the javelin.

27 "He regards iron as straw,
Bronze as rotten wood.

28 "The arrow cannot make him flee;
Slingstones are turned into stubble for
him.

29 "Clubs are regarded as stubble;
He laughs at the rattling of the javelin.

30 "His underparts are *like* sharp pieces of
pottery;
He spreads out *like* a threshing sledge on
the mud.

31 "He makes the depths boil like a pot;
He makes the sea like a jar of ointment.

32 "Behind him he illuminates a pathway;
One would think the deep to be
gray-haired.

33 "Nothing on earth is like him,
One made without fear.

34 "He looks on everything that is high;
He is king over all the sons of pride."

Job's Confession

42 Then Job answered the LORD
and said,

2 "I know that You can *do* all things,
And that no plan is impossible for You.

3 'Who is this who conceals advice without
knowledge?'
Therefore I have declared that which I did
not understand,
Things too wonderful for me, which I do
not know.

4 'Please listen, and I will speak;
I will ask You, and You instruct me.'

5 "I have heard of You by the hearing of the
ear;
But now my eye sees You;

6 Therefore I retract,
And I repent, *sitting* on dust and ashes."

God Is Displeased with Job's Friends

7 It came about after the LORD had spoken
these words to Job, that the LORD said to Eliphaz the Temanite, "My wrath is kindled
against you and against your two friends,

40:15 [1] I.e., a powerful animal, possibly a hippopotamus   **40:20** [1] I.e., the mountain streams
41:1 [1] I.e., a sea monster or crocodile

because you have not spoken of Me what is trustworthy, as My servant Job *has.* **8** Now therefore, take for yourselves seven bulls and seven rams, and go to My servant Job, and offer up a burnt offering for yourselves, and My servant Job will pray for you. For I will accept him so as not to do with you *as your* foolishness *deserves,* because you have not spoken of Me what is trustworthy, as My servant Job *has.*" **9** So Eliphaz the Temanite, Bildad the Shuhite, *and* Zophar the Naamathite went and did as the LORD told them; and the LORD accepted Job.

God Restores Job's Fortunes

10 The LORD also restored the fortunes of Job when he prayed for his friends, and the LORD increased double all that Job had. **11** Then all his brothers, all his sisters, and all who had known

him before came to him, and they ate bread with him in his house; and they sympathized with him and comforted him for all the adversities that the LORD had brought on him. And each one gave him a piece of money, and each a ring of gold. **12** The LORD blessed the latter *days* of Job more than his beginning; and he had fourteen thousand sheep, six thousand camels, a thousand yoke of oxen, and a thousand female donkeys. **13** He also had seven sons and three daughters. **14** He named the first Jemimah, the second Keziah, and the third Keren-happuch. **15** In all the land no women were found as beautiful as Job's daughters; and their father gave them inheritances among their brothers. **16** After this, Job lived 140 years, and saw his sons and his grandsons, four generations. **17** And Job died, an old man and full of days.

THE PSALMS

The following expressions occur often in the Psalms:
Selah Might mean *Higher pitch, Pause, Always,* or *From the beginning*
Maskil Possibly *Contemplative,* or *Didactic,* or *Skillful Psalm*
Mikhtam Possibly *Epigrammatic Poem,* or *Atonement Psalm*
Sheol The netherworld

BOOK 1

PSALM 1

The Righteous and the Wicked Contrasted.
1 Blessed is the person who does not walk
in the counsel of the wicked,
Nor stand in the path of sinners,
Nor sit in the seat of scoffers!
2 But his delight is in the Law of the
LORD,
And on His Law he meditates day and
night.
3 He will be like a tree planted by streams
of water,
Which yields its fruit in its season,
And its leaf does not wither;
And in whatever he does, he prospers.
4¶ The wicked are not so,
But they are like chaff which the wind
blows away.
5 Therefore the wicked will not stand in the
judgment,
Nor sinners in the assembly of the
righteous.
6 For the LORD knows the way of the
righteous,
But the way of the wicked will perish.

PSALM 2

The Reign of the LORD's Anointed.
1 Why are the nations restless
And the peoples plotting in vain?
2 The kings of the earth take their stand
And the rulers conspire together
Against the LORD and against
His ¹Anointed, *saying,*
3 "Let's tear their shackles apart
And throw their ropes away from us!"
4¶ He who sits in the heavens laughs,
The Lord scoffs at them.
5 Then He will speak to them in His
anger
And terrify them in His fury, *saying,*
6 "But as for Me, I have installed My King
Upon Zion, My holy mountain."
7¶ "I will announce the decree of the LORD:
He said to Me, 'You are My Son,
Today I have fathered You.
8 'Ask *it* of Me, and I will certainly give the
nations as Your inheritance,
And the ends of the earth as Your
possession.
9 'You shall ¹break them with a rod of iron,
You shall shatter them like
earthenware.'"
10¶ Now then, you kings, use insight;

Let yourselves be instructed, you judges of
the earth.
11 Serve the LORD with reverence
And rejoice with trembling.
12 ¹Kiss the Son, that He not be angry and
you perish *on* the way,
For His wrath may be kindled quickly.
How blessed are all who take refuge in
Him!

PSALM 3

Morning Prayer of Trust in God.
*A Psalm of David, when he fled from his son
Absalom.*
1 LORD, how my enemies have increased!
Many are rising up against me.
2 Many are saying of my soul,
"There is no salvation for him in God."
Selah
3¶ But You, LORD, are a shield around me,
My glory, and the One who lifts my head.
4 I was crying out to the LORD with my
voice,
And He answered me from His holy
mountain. Selah
5 I lay down and slept;
I awoke, for the LORD sustains me.
6 I will not be afraid of ten thousands of
people
Who have set themselves against me all
around.
7¶ Arise, LORD; save me, my God!
For You have struck all my enemies on the
cheek;
You have shattered the teeth of the
wicked.
8 Salvation belongs to the LORD;
May Your blessing *be* upon Your people!
Selah

PSALM 4

Evening Prayer of Trust in God.
*For the music director; on stringed instruments.
A Psalm of David.*
1 Answer me when I call, God of my
righteousness!
You have relieved me in my distress;
Be gracious to me and hear my prayer.
2¶ You sons of man, how long will my honor
be *treated as* an insult?
How long will you love what is worthless
and strive for a lie? Selah
3 But know that the LORD has set apart the
godly person for Himself;
The LORD hears when I call to Him.
4¶ Tremble, and do not sin;

2:2 ¹Or *Messiah*   **2:9** ¹Another reading is *rule*   **2:12** ¹I.e., probably kiss the feet of the Son

Meditate in your heart upon your bed,
and be still.   *Selah*

5 Offer the sacrifices of righteousness,
And trust in the LORD.

6¶ Many are saying, "Who will show us
anything good?"
Lift up the light of Your face upon us,
LORD!

7 You have put joy in my heart,
More than when their grain and new
wine are abundant.

8 In peace I will both lie down and
sleep,
For You alone, LORD, have me dwell in
safety.

PSALM 5

Prayer for Protection from the Wicked.
For the music director; for flute accompaniment.
A Psalm of David.

1 Listen to my words, LORD,
Consider my sighing.

2 Listen to the sound of my cry for help, my
King and my God,
For to You I pray.

3 In the morning, LORD, You will hear my
voice;
In the morning I will present *my prayer* to
You and be on the watch.

4¶ For You are not a God who takes pleasure
in wickedness;
No evil can dwell with You.

5 The boastful will not stand before Your
eyes;
You hate all who do injustice.

6 You destroy those who speak lies;
The LORD loathes the person of bloodshed
and deceit.

7 But as for me, by Your abundant
graciousness I will enter Your house,
At Your holy temple I will bow in
reverence for You.

8¶ LORD, lead me in Your righteousness
because of my enemies;
Make Your way straight before me.

9 For there is nothing trustworthy in their
mouth;
Their inward part is destruction
itself.
Their throat is an open grave;
They flatter with their tongue.

10 Make them pay, God;
Have them fall by their own
schemes!
Scatter them in the multitude of their
wrongdoings,
For they are rebellious against You.

11¶ But rejoice, all who take refuge in
You,
Sing for joy forever!
And may You shelter them,
That those who love Your name may
rejoice in You.

12 For You bless the righteous person,
LORD,
You surround him with favor as with a
shield.

PSALM 6

Prayer for Mercy in Time of Trouble.
For the music director; with stringed instruments,
upon an eight-string lyre. A Psalm of David.

1 LORD, do not rebuke me in Your anger,
Nor discipline me in Your wrath.

2 Be gracious to me, LORD, for I *am* frail;
Heal me, LORD, for my bones are
horrified.

3 And my soul is greatly horrified;
But You, LORD—how long?

4¶ Return, LORD, rescue my soul;
Save me because of Your mercy.

5 For there is no mention of You in death;
In ⁱSheol, who will praise You?

6¶ I am weary with my sighing;
Every night I make my bed swim,
I flood my couch with my tears.

7 My eye has wasted away with grief;
It has grown old because of all my
enemies.

8¶ Leave me, all you who practice injustice,
For the LORD has heard the sound of my
weeping.

9 The LORD has heard my pleading,
The LORD receives my prayer.

10 All my enemies will be put to shame and
greatly horrified;
They shall turn back, they will suddenly
be put to shame.

PSALM 7

The LORD Implored to Defend the Psalmist
against the Wicked.
A ⁺Shiggaion of David, which he sang to the LORD
concerning Cush, a Benjaminite.

1 O LORD my God, in You I have taken
refuge;
Save me from all those who pursue me,
and rescue me,

2 Or he will tear my soul like a lion,
Dragging me away, while there is no one
to rescue *me.*

3¶ O LORD my God, if I have done this,
If there is injustice in my hands,

4 If I have done evil to my friend,
Or have plundered my enemy for no
reason,

5 Let the enemy pursue my soul and
overtake *it;*
And let him trample my life to the ground
And lay my glory in the dust.   *Selah*

6¶ Arise, LORD, in Your anger;
Raise Yourself against the rage of my
enemies,
And stir Yourself for me; You have ordered
judgment.

7 Let the assembly of the peoples
encompass You,
And return on high over it.

8 The LORD judges the peoples;
Vindicate me, LORD, according to my
righteousness and my integrity that is
in me.

9 Please let the evil of the wicked come to
an end, but establish the righteous;

6:5 ¹ I.e., the netherworld   7:1 † I.e., Dithyrambic rhythm; or wild, passionate song

For the righteous God puts hearts and minds to the test.

10 My shield is with God,
Who saves the upright in heart.

11 God is a righteous judge,
And a God who shows indignation every day.

12¶ If one does not repent, He will sharpen His sword;
He has bent His bow and taken aim.

13 He has also prepared deadly weapons for Himself;
He makes His arrows fiery *shafts.*

14 Behold, *an evil person* is pregnant with injustice,
And he conceives harm and gives birth to lies.

15 He has dug a pit and hollowed it out,
And has fallen into the hole which he made.

16 His harm will return on his own head,
And his violence will descend on the top of his own head.

17¶ I will give thanks to the LORD according to His righteousness
And will sing praise to the name of the LORD Most High.

PSALM 8

The LORD's Glory and Mankind's Dignity.
For the music director; on the Gittith. A Psalm of David.

1 LORD, our Lord,
How majestic is Your name in all the earth,
You who have displayed Your splendor above the heavens!

2 From the mouths of infants and nursing babies You have established strength
Because of Your enemies,
To do away with the enemy and the revengeful.

3¶ When I consider Your heavens, the work of Your fingers,
The moon and the stars, which You have set in place;

4 What is man that You think of him,
And a son of man that You are concerned about him?

5 Yet You have made him a little lower than *God,
And You crown him with glory and majesty!

6 You have him rule over the works of Your hands;
You have put everything under his feet,

7 All sheep and oxen,
And also the animals of the field,

8 The birds of the sky, and the fish of the sea,
Whatever passes through the paths of the seas.

9¶ LORD, our Lord,
How majestic is Your name in all the earth!

PSALM 9

Thanksgiving for God's Justice.
For the music director; on †Muth-labben. A Psalm of David.

1 I will give thanks to the LORD with all my heart;
I will tell of all Your wonders.

2 I will rejoice and be jubilant in You;
I will sing praise to Your name, O Most High.

3¶ When my enemies turn back,
They stumble and perish before You.

4 For You have maintained my just cause;
You have sat on the throne judging righteously.

5 You have rebuked the nations, You have eliminated the wicked;
You have wiped out their name forever and ever.

6 The enemy has come to an end *in* everlasting ruins,
And You have uprooted the cities;
The very memory of them has perished.

7¶ But the LORD sits *as King* forever;
He has established His throne for judgment,

8 And He will judge the world in righteousness;
He will execute judgment for the peoples fairly.

9 The LORD will also be a stronghold for the oppressed,
A stronghold in times of trouble;

10 And those who know Your name will put their trust in You,
For You, LORD, have not abandoned those who seek You.

11¶ Sing praises to the LORD, who dwells in Zion;
Declare His deeds among the peoples.

12 For He who ¹requires blood remembers them;
He does not forget the cry of the needy.

13 Be gracious to me, LORD;
See my oppression from those who hate me,
You who lift me up from the gates of death,

14 So that I may tell of all Your praises,
That in the gates of the daughter of Zion
I may rejoice in Your salvation.

15 The nations have sunk down into the pit *which* they have made;
In the net which they hid, their own foot has been caught.

16 The LORD has made Himself known;
He has executed judgment.
A wicked one is ensnared in the work of his own hands. *Higgaion Selah*

17¶ The wicked will return to ¹Sheol,
All the nations who forget God.

18 For the needy will not always be forgotten,
Nor the hope of the afflicted perish forever.

19 Arise, LORD, do not let mankind prevail;

Let the nations be judged before You.
20 Put them in fear, LORD;
Let the nations know that they are *merely*
human.   *Selah*

PSALM 10

A Prayer for the Overthrow of the Wicked.
1 Why do You stand far away, LORD?
Why do You hide *Yourself* in times of
trouble?
2 In arrogance the wicked hotly pursue the
needy;
Let them be caught in the plots which
they have devised.
3¶ For the wicked boasts of his soul's desire,
And the greedy person curses *and* shows
disrespect to the LORD.
4 The wicked, in his haughtiness, does not
seek *Him.*
There is no God *in* all his schemes.
5¶ His ways succeed at all times;
Yet Your judgments are on high, out of his
sight;
As for all his enemies, he snorts at them.
6 He says to himself, "I will not be moved;
Throughout the generations I will not be
in adversity."
7 His mouth is full of cursing, deceit, and
oppression;
Under his tongue is harm and injustice.
8 He sits in the lurking places of the
villages;
He kills the innocent in the secret
places;
His eyes surreptitiously watch for the
unfortunate.
9 He lurks in secret like a lion in his lair;
He lurks to catch the needy;
He catches the needy when he pulls him
into his net.
10 Then he crushes *the needy one, who*
cowers;
And unfortunate people fall by his mighty
power.
11 He says to himself, "God has forgotten;
He has hidden His face; He will never see
it."
12¶ Arise, LORD; God, lift up Your hand.
Do not forget the humble.
13 Why has the wicked treated God
disrespectfully?
He has said to himself, "You will not
require *an account.*"
14 You have seen *it,* for You have looked at
harm and provocation to take it into
Your hand.
The unfortunate commits *himself* to You;
You have been the helper of the orphan.
15 Break the arm of the wicked and the
evildoer,
Seek out his wickedness until You find
none.
16¶ The LORD is King forever and ever;
Nations have perished from His land.
17 LORD, You have heard the desire of the
humble;
You will strengthen their heart, You will
make Your ear attentive

18 To vindicate the orphan and the
oppressed,
So that mankind, which is of the earth,
will no longer cause terror.

PSALM 11

The LORD, a Refuge and Defense.
For the music director. A Psalm of David.
1 In the LORD I take refuge;
How can you say to my soul, "Flee *as* a
bird to your mountain?
2 "For, behold, the wicked bend the bow,
They have set their arrow on the
string
To shoot in darkness at the upright in
heart.
3 "If the foundations are destroyed,
What can the righteous do?"
4¶ The LORD is in His holy temple; the
LORD's throne is in heaven;
His eyes see, His eyelids test the sons of
mankind.
5 The LORD tests the righteous and the
wicked,
And His soul hates one who loves
violence.
6 He will rain ¹coals of fire upon the
wicked,
And brimstone and burning wind will be
the portion of their cup.
7 For the LORD is righteous, He loves
righteousness;
The upright will see His face.

PSALM 12

God, a Helper against the Treacherous.
For the music director; upon an eight-stringed lyre.
A Psalm of David.
1 Help, LORD, for the godly person has come
to an end,
For the faithful have disappeared from the
sons of mankind.
2 They speak lies to one another;
They speak with flattering lips and a
double heart.
3 May the LORD cut off all flattering lips,
The tongue that speaks great things;
4 Who have said, "With our tongue we will
prevail;
Our lips are our own; who is lord over
us?"
5 "Because of the devastation of the poor,
because of the groaning of the
needy,
Now I will arise," says the LORD; "I will
put him in the safety for which he
longs."
6¶ The words of the LORD are pure
words;
Like silver refined in a furnace on the
ground, filtered seven times.
7 You, LORD, will keep them;
You will protect him from this generation
forever.
8 The wicked strut about on every side
When vileness is exalted among the sons
of mankind.

11:6 ¹As in a Gr version; MT *snares; Fire and*

PSALM 13

Prayer for Help in Trouble.
For the music director. A Psalm of David.

1 How long, LORD? Will You forget me
   forever?
   How long will You hide Your face from
   me?

2 How long am I to feel anxious in my soul,
   With grief in my heart all the day?
   How long will my enemy be exalted over
   me?

3 ¶ Consider *and* answer me, O LORD my
   God;
   Enlighten my eyes, or I will sleep the
   sleep of death,

4 And my enemy will say, "I have overcome
   him,"
   And my adversaries will rejoice when I
   am shaken.

5 ¶ But I have trusted in Your faithfulness;
   My heart shall rejoice in Your salvation.

6 I will sing to the LORD,
   Because He has looked after me.

PSALM 14

Foolishness and Wickedness of People.
For the music director. A Psalm of David.

1 The fool has said in his heart, "There is
   no God."
   They are corrupt, they have committed
   detestable acts;
   There is no one who does good.

2 The LORD has looked down from heaven
   upon the sons of mankind
   To see if there are any who understand,
   Who seek God.

3 They have all turned aside, together they
   are corrupt;
   There is no one who does good, not even
   one.

4 ¶ Do all the workers of injustice not know,
   Who devour my people *as* they eat bread,
   And do not call upon the LORD?

5 There they are in great dread,
   For God is with a righteous generation.

6 You would put to shame the plan of the
   poor,
   But the LORD is his refuge.

7 ¶ Oh, that the salvation of Israel *would
   come* out of Zion!
   When the LORD restores the fortunes of
   His people,
   Jacob will rejoice, Israel will be glad.

PSALM 15

Description of a Citizen of Zion.
A Psalm of David.

1 LORD, who may reside in Your tent?
   Who may settle on Your holy hill?

2 One who walks with integrity, practices
   righteousness,
   And speaks truth in his heart.

3 He does not slander with his tongue,
   Nor do evil to his neighbor,
   Nor bring shame on his friend;

4 A despicable person is despised in his
   eyes,
   But he honors those who fear the LORD;
   He takes an oath to his own detriment,
   and does not change;

5 He does not lend his money ¹at interest,
   Nor does he take a bribe against the
   innocent.
   One who does these things will never be
   shaken.

PSALM 16

***The LORD, the Psalmist's Portion in Life and
Salvation in Death.***
A ¹Mikhtam of David.

1 Protect me, God, for I take refuge in You.

2 I said to the LORD, "You are my Lord;
   I have nothing good besides You."

3 As for the ¹saints who are on the earth,
   They are the majestic ones; all my delight
   is in them.

4 The pains of those who have acquired
   another *god* will be multiplied;
   I will not pour out their drink offerings of
   blood,
   Nor will I take their names upon my lips.

5 ¶ The LORD is the portion of my inheritance
   and my cup;
   You support my lot.

6 The measuring lines have fallen for me in
   pleasant places;
   Indeed, my inheritance is beautiful to me.

7 ¶ I will bless the LORD who has advised me;
   Indeed, my mind instructs me in the
   night.

8 I have set the LORD continually before me;
   Because He is at my right hand, I will not
   be shaken.

9 Therefore my heart is glad and my glory
   rejoices;
   My flesh also will dwell securely.

10 For You will not abandon my soul to
    ¹Sheol;
    You will not allow Your Holy One to
    undergo decay.

11 You will make known to me the way of
    life;
    In Your presence is fullness of joy;
    In Your right hand there are pleasures
    forever.

PSALM 17

Prayer for Protection against Oppressors.
A Prayer of David.

1 Hear a just cause, LORD, give *Your*
   attention to my cry;
   Listen to my prayer, which is not from
   deceitful lips.

2 Let my judgment come forth from Your
   presence;
   Let Your eyes look with integrity.

3 You have put my heart to the test;
   You have visited *me* by night;
   You have sifted me and You find nothing;
   My intent is that my mouth will not
   offend.

15:5 ¹I.e., to a fellow Israelite   **16:1** †*Possibly* Epigrammatic Poem *or* Atonement Psalm   **16:3** ¹Lit *holy
ones;* i.e., God's people   **16:10** ¹I.e., the netherworld

4 As for the works of mankind, by the word
of Your lips
I have kept from the ways of the violent.
5 My steps have held to Your paths.
My feet have not slipped.
6¶ I have called upon You, for You will
answer me, God;
Incline Your ear to me, hear my speech.
7 Show Your wonderful faithfulness,
Savior of those who take refuge at Your
right hand
From those who rise up *against them.*
8 Keep me as the apple of the eye;
Hide me in the shadow of Your wings
9 From the wicked who deal violently with
me,
My deadly enemies who surround me.
10 They have closed their unfeeling *hearts,*
With their mouths they speak proudly.
11 They have now surrounded us in our
steps;
They set their eyes to cast *us* down to the
ground.
12 He is like a lion that is eager to tear,
And as a young lion lurking in secret
places.
13¶ Arise, LORD, confront him, make him bow
down;
Save my soul from the wicked with Your
sword,
14 From people by Your hand, LORD,
From people of the world, whose portion
is in *this* life,
And whose belly You fill with Your
treasure;
They are satisfied with children,
And leave their abundance to their babies.
15 As for me, I shall behold Your face in
righteousness;
I shall be satisfied with Your likeness
when I awake.

PSALM 18

The LORD Praised for Rescuing David.
For the music director. A Psalm of David, the servant
of the LORD, who spoke to the LORD the words of this
song on the day that the LORD rescued him from the
hand of all his enemies and from the hand of Saul.
And he said,
1 "I love You, LORD, my strength."
2 The LORD is my rock and my fortress and
my savior,
My God, my rock, in whom I take refuge;
My shield and the horn of my salvation,
my stronghold.
3 I call upon the LORD, who is worthy to be
praised,
And I am saved from my enemies.
4¶ The ropes of death encompassed me,
And the torrents of destruction terrified
me.
5 The ropes of ¹Sheol surrounded me;
The snares of death confronted me.
6 In my distress I called upon the LORD,
And cried to my God for help;
He heard my voice from His temple,
And my cry for help before Him came into
His ears.

7¶ Then the earth shook and quaked;
And the foundations of the mountains
were trembling
And were shaken, because He was angry.
8 Smoke went up out of His nostrils,
And fire from His mouth was devouring;
Coals burned from it.
9 He also bowed the heavens down low,
and came down
With thick darkness under His feet.
10 He rode on a cherub and flew;
And He sped on the wings of the wind.
11 He made darkness His hiding place, His
canopy around Him,
Darkness of waters, thick clouds.
12 From the brightness before Him passed
His thick clouds,
Hailstones and coals of fire.
13 The LORD also thundered in the heavens,
And the Most High uttered His voice,
Hailstones and coals of fire.
14 He sent out His arrows, and scattered
them,
And lightning flashes in abundance, and
routed them.
15 Then the channels of water appeared,
And the foundations of the world were
exposed
By Your rebuke, LORD,
At the blast of the breath of Your nostrils.
16¶ He sent from on high, He took me;
He drew me out of many waters.
17 He saved me from my strong enemy,
And from those who hated me, for they
were too mighty for me.
18 They confronted me in the day of my
disaster,
But the LORD was my support.
19 He also brought me out into an open
place;
He rescued me, because He delighted in
me.
20¶ The LORD has rewarded me according to
my righteousness;
According to the cleanness of my hands
He has repaid me.
21 For I have kept the ways of the LORD,
And have not acted wickedly against my
God.
22 For all His judgments were before me,
And I did not put away His statutes from
me.
23 I was also blameless with Him,
And I kept myself from my wrongdoing.
24 Therefore the LORD has repaid me
according to my righteousness,
According to the cleanness of my hands in
His eyes.
25¶ With the faithful You show Yourself
faithful;
With the blameless You prove Yourself
blameless;
26 With the pure You show Yourself pure,
And with the crooked You show Yourself
astute.
27 For You save an afflicted people,
But You humiliate haughty eyes.
28 For You light my lamp;
The LORD my God illumines my darkness.

18:5 ¹I.e., the netherworld

29 For by You I can run at a troop of
　　warriors;
　　And by my God I can leap over a wall.
30¶ As for God, His way is blameless;
　　The word of the LORD is refined;
　　He is a shield to all who take refuge in
　　Him.
31 For who is God, but the LORD?
　　And who is a rock, except our God,
32 The God who encircles me with strength,
　　And makes my way blameless?
33 He makes my feet like deer's *feet,*
　　And sets me up on my high places.
34 He trains my hands for battle,
　　So that my arms can bend a bow of
　　bronze.
35 You have also given me the shield of Your
　　salvation,
　　And Your right hand upholds me;
　　And Your gentleness makes me great.
36 You enlarge my steps under me,
　　And my feet have not slipped.
37¶ I pursued my enemies and overtook
　　them,
　　And I did not turn back until they were
　　consumed.
38 I shattered them, so that they were not
　　able to rise;
　　They fell under my feet.
39 For You have encircled me with strength
　　for battle;
　　You have forced those who rose up against
　　me to bow down under me.
40 You have also made my enemies turn
　　their backs to me,
　　And I destroyed those who hated me.
41 They cried for help, but there was no one
　　to save,
　　They cried to the LORD, but He did not
　　answer them.
42 Then I beat them fine like the dust before
　　the wind;
　　I emptied them out like the mud of the
　　streets.
43¶ You have rescued me from the
　　contentions of the people;
　　You have placed me as head of the
　　nations;
　　A people whom I have not known serve
　　me.
44 As soon as they hear, they obey me;
　　Foreigners pretend to obey me.
45 Foreigners lose heart,
　　And come trembling out of their
　　fortresses.
46¶ The LORD lives, and blessed be my rock;
　　And exalted be the God of my salvation,
47 The God who executes vengeance for me,
　　And subdues peoples under me.
48 He rescues me from my enemies;
　　You indeed lift me above those who rise
　　up against me;
　　You rescue me from a violent man.
49 Therefore I will give thanks to You among
　　the nations, LORD,
　　And I will sing praises to Your name.
50 He gives great ¹salvation to His king,
　　And shows faithfulness to His anointed,
　　To David and his descendants forever.

PSALM 19

The Works and the Word of God.
For the music director. A Psalm of David.
1 The heavens tell of the glory of God;
　　And their expanse declares the work of
　　His hands.
2 Day to day pours forth speech,
　　And night to night reveals knowledge.
3 There is no speech, nor are there words;
　　Their voice is not heard.
4 Their ¹line has gone out into all the earth,
　　And their words to the end of the world.
　　In them He has placed a tent for the sun,
5 Which is like a groom coming out of his
　　chamber;
　　It rejoices like a strong person to run his
　　course.
6 Its rising is from one end of the heavens,
　　And its circuit to the other end of them;
　　And there is nothing hidden from its
　　heat.
7¶ The Law of the LORD is ¹perfect, restoring
　　the soul;
　　The testimony of the LORD is sure, making
　　wise the simple.
8 The precepts of the LORD are right,
　　rejoicing the heart;
　　The commandment of the LORD is pure,
　　enlightening the eyes.
9 The fear of the LORD is clean, enduring
　　forever;
　　The judgments of the LORD are true; they
　　are righteous altogether.
10 They are more desirable than gold, yes,
　　than much pure gold;
　　Sweeter also than honey and drippings of
　　the honeycomb.
11 Moreover, Your servant is warned by
　　them;
　　In keeping them there is great reward.
12 Who can discern *his* errors? Acquit me of
　　hidden *faults.*
13 Also keep Your servant back from
　　presumptuous *sins;*
　　Let them not rule over me;
　　Then I will be innocent,
　　And I will be blameless of great
　　wrongdoing.
14 May the words of my mouth and the
　　meditation of my heart
　　Be acceptable in Your sight,
　　LORD, my rock and my Redeemer.

PSALM 20

Prayer for Victory over Enemies.
For the music director. A Psalm of David.
1 May the LORD answer you on a day of
　　trouble!
　　May the name of the God of Jacob protect
　　you!
2 May He send you help from the sanctuary,
　　And support you from Zion!
3 May He remember all your meal offerings
　　And accept your burnt offering!　　*Selah*
4¶ May He grant you your heart's desire
　　And fulfill your whole plan!
5 We will sing for joy over your victory,

18:50 ¹I.e., victories; lit *salvations*　　19:4 ¹Another reading is *sound*　　19:7 ¹I.e., blameless

And in the name of our God we will set
up our banners.
May the LORD fulfill all your desires.
6¶ Now I know that the LORD saves His
anointed;
He will answer him from His holy
heaven
With the saving strength of His right
hand.
7 Some *praise their* chariots and some *their*
horses,
But we will praise the name of the LORD,
our God.
8 They have bowed down and fallen,
But we have risen and stood
upright.
9 Save, LORD;
May the King answer us on the day we
call.

PSALM 21

Praise for Salvation.
For the music director. A Psalm of David.
1 LORD, in Your strength the king will be
glad,
And in Your salvation how greatly he will
rejoice!
2 You have given him his heart's desire,
And You have not withheld the request of
his lips.   *Selah*
3 For You meet him with the blessings of
good things;
You set a crown of pure gold on his
head.
4 He asked for life from You,
You gave it to him,
Length of days forever and ever.
5 His glory is great through Your
salvation,
Splendor and majesty You place upon
him.
6 For You make him most blessed
forever;
You make him joyful with the joy of Your
presence.
7¶ For the king trusts in the LORD,
And through the faithfulness of the Most
High he will not be shaken.
8 Your hand will find all your enemies;
Your right hand will find those who hate
you.
9 You will make them as a fiery oven in the
time of your anger;
The LORD will swallow them up in His
wrath,
And fire will devour them.
10 You will eliminate their descendants from
the earth,
And their children from among the sons
of mankind.
11 Though they intended evil against You
And devised a plot,
They will not succeed.
12 For You will make them turn their
back;
You will take aim at their faces with Your
bowstrings.
13 Be exalted, LORD, in Your strength;
We will sing and praise Your power.

PSALM 22

A Cry of Anguish and a Song of Praise.
For the music director; upon Aijeleth Hashshahar.
A Psalm of David.
1 My God, my God, why have You forsaken
me?
Far from my help are the words of my
groaning.
2 My God, I cry out by day, but You do not
answer;
And by night, but I have no rest.
3 Yet You are holy,
You who are enthroned upon the praises
of Israel.
4 In You our fathers trusted;
They trusted and You rescued them.
5 To You they cried out and they fled to
safety;
In You they trusted and were not
disappointed.
6¶ But I am a worm and not a person,
A disgrace of mankind and despised by
the people.
7 All who see me deride me;
They sneer, they shake their heads,
saying,
8 "Turn *him* over to the LORD; let Him save
him;
Let Him rescue him, because He delights
in him."
9¶ Yet You are He who brought me forth
from the womb;
You made me trust *when* upon my
mother's breasts.
10 I was cast upon You from birth;
You have been my God from my mother's
womb.
11¶ Do not be far from me, for trouble is near;
For there is no one to help.
12 Many bulls have surrounded me;
Strong *bulls* of Bashan have encircled me.
13 They open their mouths wide at me,
As a ravening and roaring lion.
14 I am poured out like water,
And all my bones are out of joint;
My heart is like wax;
It is melted within me.
15 My strength is dried up like a piece of
pottery,
And my tongue clings to my jaws;
And You lay me in the dust of death.
16 For dogs have surrounded me;
A band of evildoers has encompassed me;
They pierced my hands and my feet.
17 I can count all my bones.
They look, they stare at me;
18 They divide my garments among them,
And they cast lots for my clothing.
19¶ But You, LORD, do not be far away;
You who are my help, hurry to my
assistance.
20 Save my soul from the sword,
My only *life* from the power of the dog.
21 Save me from the lion's mouth;
From the horns of the wild oxen You
answer me.
22¶ I will proclaim Your name to my brothers;
In the midst of the assembly I will praise
You.

23 You who fear the LORD, praise Him;
All you descendants of Jacob, glorify Him,
And stand in awe of Him, all you descen-
dants of Israel.

24 For He has not despised nor scorned the
suffering of the afflicted;
Nor has He hidden His face from him;
But when he cried to Him for help, He
heard.

25¶ From You *comes* my praise in the great
assembly;
I shall pay my vows before those who fear
Him.

26 The afflicted will eat and be satisfied;
Those who seek Him will praise the
LORD.
May your heart live forever!

27 All the ends of the earth will remember
and turn to the LORD,
And all the families of the nations will
worship before You.

28 For the kingdom is the LORD's
And He rules over the nations.

29 All the prosperous of the earth will eat
and worship,
All those who go down to the dust will
kneel before Him,
Even he who cannot keep his soul alive.

30 A posterity will serve Him;
It will be told of the Lord to the *coming*
generation.

31 They will come and will declare His
righteousness
To a people who will be born, that He has
performed *it*.

PSALM 23

The LORD, the Psalmist's Shepherd.
A Psalm of David.

1 The LORD is my shepherd,
I will not be in need.

2 He lets me lie down in green pastures;
He leads me beside quiet waters.

3 He restores my soul;
He guides me in the paths of
righteousness
For the sake of His name.

4¶ Even though I walk through the valley of
the shadow of death,
I fear no evil, for You are with me;
Your rod and Your staff, they comfort me.

5 You prepare a table before me in the
presence of my enemies;
You have anointed my head with oil;
My cup overflows.

6 Certainly goodness and faithfulness will
follow me all the days of my life,
And my dwelling *will be* in the house of
the LORD forever.

PSALM 24

The King of Glory Entering Zion.
A Psalm of David.

1 The earth is the LORD's, and all it
contains,
The world, and those who live in it.

2 For He has founded it upon the seas
And established it upon the rivers.

3 Who may ascend onto the hill of the
LORD?
And who may stand in His holy place?

4 One who has clean hands and a pure
heart,
Who has not lifted up his soul to deceit
And has not sworn deceitfully.

5 He will receive a blessing from the
LORD
And righteousness from the God of his
salvation.

6 This is the generation of those who seek
Him,
Who seek Your face—*even* Jacob.   *Selah*

7¶ Lift up your heads, you gates,
And be lifted up, you ancient doors,
That the King of glory may come in!

8 Who is the King of glory?
The LORD strong and mighty,
The LORD mighty in battle.

9 Lift up your heads, you gates,
And lift *them* up, you ancient doors,
That the King of glory may come in!

10 Who is this King of glory?
The LORD of armies,
He is the King of glory.   *Selah*

PSALM 25

Prayer for Protection, Guidance, and Pardon.
A Psalm of David.

1 To You, LORD, I lift up my soul.

2 My God, in You I trust,
Do not let me be ashamed;
Do not let my enemies rejoice over me.

3 Indeed, none of those who wait for You
will be ashamed;
Those who deal treacherously without
cause will be ashamed.

4¶ Make me know Your ways, LORD;
Teach me Your paths.

5 Lead me in Your truth and teach me,
For You are the God of my salvation;
For You I wait all the day.

6 Remember, LORD, Your compassion and
Your faithfulness,
For they have been from of old.

7 Do not remember the sins of my youth
or my wrongdoings;
Remember me according to Your
faithfulness,
For Your goodness' sake, LORD.

8¶ The LORD is good and upright;
Therefore He instructs sinners in the
way.

9 He leads the humble in justice,
And He teaches the humble His way.

10 All the paths of the LORD are faithfulness
and truth
To those who comply with His covenant
and His testimonies.

11 For the sake of Your name, LORD,
Forgive my wrongdoing, for it is great.

12¶ Who is the person who fears the LORD?
He will instruct him in the way he should
choose.

13 His soul will dwell in prosperity,
And his descendants will inherit the land.

14 The secret of the LORD is for those who
fear Him,

And He will make them know His
covenant.
15 My eyes are continually toward the LORD,
For He will rescue my feet from the net.
16¶ Turn to me and be gracious to me,
For I am lonely and afflicted.
17 The troubles of my heart are enlarged;
Bring me out of my distresses.
18 Look at my misery and my trouble,
And forgive all my sins.
19 Look at my enemies, for they are many,
And they hate me with violent hatred.
20 Guard my soul and save me;
Do not let me be ashamed, for I take
refuge in You.
21 Let integrity and uprightness protect me,
For I wait for You.
22 Redeem Israel, God,
From all his distress.

PSALM 26

*Protestation of Integrity and Prayer for
Protection.*
A Psalm *of David.*
1 Vindicate me, LORD, for I have walked in
my integrity,
And I have trusted in the LORD without
wavering.
2 Examine me, LORD, and put me to the
test;
Refine my mind and my heart.
3 For Your goodness is before my eyes,
And I have walked in Your truth.
4 I do not sit with deceitful people,
Nor will I go with pretenders.
5 I hate the assembly of evildoers,
And I will not sit with the wicked.
6 I will wash my hands in innocence,
And I will go around Your altar, LORD,
7 That I may proclaim with the voice of
thanksgiving
And declare all Your wonders.
8¶ LORD, I love the dwelling of Your house,
And the place where Your glory remains.
9 Do not take my soul away *along* with
sinners,
Nor my life with men of bloodshed,
10 In whose hands is a wicked scheme,
And whose right hand is full of bribes.
11 But as for me, I will walk in my integrity;
Redeem me, and be gracious to me.
12 My foot stands on level ground;
In the congregations I will bless the LORD.

PSALM 27

A Psalm of Fearless Trust in God.
A Psalm *of David.*
1 The LORD is my light and my salvation;
Whom should I fear?
The LORD is the defense of my life;
Whom should I dread?
2 When evildoers came upon me to devour
my flesh,
My adversaries and my enemies, they
stumbled and fell.
3 If an army encamps against me,
My heart will not fear;
If war arises against me,

In *spite of* this I am confident.
4¶ One thing I have asked from the LORD,
that I shall seek:
That I may dwell in the house of the LORD
all the days of my life,
To behold the beauty of the LORD
And to meditate in His temple.
5 For on the day of trouble He will conceal
me in His tabernacle;
He will hide me in the secret place of His
tent;
He will lift me up on a rock.
6 And now my head will be lifted up above
my enemies around me,
And I will offer sacrifices in His tent with
shouts of joy;
I will sing, yes, I will sing praises to the
LORD.
7¶ Hear, LORD, when I cry with my voice,
And be gracious to me and answer me.
8 *When You said,* "Seek My face," my heart
said to You,
"I shall seek Your face, LORD."
9 Do not hide Your face from me,
Do not turn Your servant away in anger;
You have been my help;
Do not abandon me nor forsake me,
God of my salvation!
10 For my father and my mother have
forsaken me,
But the LORD will take me up.
11¶ Teach me Your way, LORD,
And lead me on a level path
Because of my enemies.
12 Do not turn me over to the desire of my
enemies,
For false witnesses have risen against me,
And *the* violent witness.
13 I certainly believed that I would see the
goodness of the LORD
In the land of the living.
14 Wait for the LORD;
Be strong and let your heart take courage;
Yes, wait for the LORD.

PSALM 28

A Prayer for Help, and Praise for Its Answer.
A Psalm *of David.*
1 To You, LORD, I call;
My rock, do not be deaf to me,
For if You are silent to me,
I will become like those who go down to
the pit.
2 Hear the sound of my pleadings when I
cry to You for help,
When I raise my hands toward Your holy
sanctuary.
3 Do not drag me away with the wicked
And with those who practice injustice,
Who speak peace with their neighbors,
While evil is in their hearts.
4 Give *back* to them according to their work
and according to the evil of their
practices;
Give *back* to them according to the work
of their hands;
Repay them what is due them.
5 Because they do not regard the works of
the LORD

Nor the deeds of His hands,
He will tear them down and not build
   them up.
6¶ Blessed be the LORD,
Because He has heard the sound of my
   pleading.
7 The LORD is my strength and my shield;
My heart trusts in Him, and I am
   helped;
Therefore my heart triumphs,
And with my song I shall thank Him.
8 The LORD is their strength,
And He is a refuge of salvation to His
   anointed.
9 Save Your people and bless Your inheritance;
Be their shepherd also, and carry them
   forever.

PSALM 29

The Voice of the LORD in the Storm.
A Psalm of David.
1 Ascribe to the LORD, sons of the mighty,
Ascribe to the LORD glory and strength.
2 Ascribe to the LORD the glory due His
   name;
Worship the LORD in holy attire.
3¶ The voice of the LORD is on the waters;
The God of glory thunders,
The LORD is over many waters.
4 The voice of the LORD is powerful,
The voice of the LORD is majestic.
5 The voice of the LORD breaks the cedars;
Yes, the LORD breaks the cedars of
   Lebanon in pieces.
6 He makes Lebanon skip like a calf,
And Sirion like a young wild ox.
7 The voice of the LORD divides ⁱflames of
   fire.
8 The voice of the LORD shakes the wilderness;
The LORD shakes the wilderness of
   Kadesh.
9 The voice of the LORD makes the deer give
   birth
And strips the forests bare;
And in His temple everything says,
   "Glory!"
10¶ The LORD sat *as King* at the flood;
Yes, the LORD sits as King forever.
11 The LORD will give strength to His people;
The LORD will bless His people with
   peace.

PSALM 30

Thanksgiving for Rescue from Death.
A Psalm; a Song at the Dedication of the House.
A Psalm of David.
1 I will exalt You, LORD, for You have lifted
   me up,
And have not let my enemies rejoice over
   me.
2 LORD my God,
I cried to You for help, and You healed
   me.
3 LORD, You have brought up my soul from
   ⁱSheol;

You have kept me alive, that I would not
   go down to the pit.
4 Sing praise to the LORD, you His godly
   ones,
And praise the mention of His holiness.
5 For His anger is but for a moment,
His favor is for a lifetime;
Weeping may last for the night,
But a shout of joy *comes* in the morning.
6¶ Now as for me, I said in my prosperity,
   "I will never be moved."
7 LORD, by Your favor You have made my
   mountain to stand strong;
You hid Your face, I was dismayed.
8 To You, LORD, I called,
And to the Lord I pleaded for compassion:
9 "What gain is there in my blood, if I go
   down to the pit?
Will the dust praise You? Will it declare
   Your faithfulness?
10¶ "Hear, LORD, and be gracious to me;
LORD, be my helper."
11 You have turned my mourning into
   dancing for me;
You have untied my sackcloth and
   encircled me with joy,
12 That *my* soul may sing praise to You and
   not be silent.
LORD my God, I will give thanks to You
   forever.

PSALM 31

A Psalm of Complaint and of Praise.
For the music director. A Psalm of David.
1 In You, LORD, I have taken refuge;
Let me never be put to shame;
In Your righteousness rescue me.
2 Incline Your ear to me, rescue me quickly;
Be a rock of strength for me,
A stronghold to save me.
3 For You are my rock and my fortress;
For the sake of Your name You will lead
   me and guide me.
4 You will pull me out of the net which they
   have secretly laid for me,
For You are my strength.
5 Into Your hand I entrust my spirit;
You have redeemed me, LORD, God of
   truth.
6¶ I hate those who devote themselves to
   worthless idols,
But I trust in the LORD.
7 I will rejoice and be glad in Your
   faithfulness,
Because You have seen my misery;
You have known the troubles of my soul,
8 And You have not handed me over to the
   enemy;
You have set my feet in a large place.
9¶ Be gracious to me, LORD, for I am in
   distress;
My eye is wasted away from grief, my soul
   and my body *too.*
10 For my life is spent with sorrow
And my years with sighing;
My strength has failed because of my
   guilt,
And my body has wasted away.

29:7 ¹I.e., lightning   30:3 ¹I.e., the netherworld

11 Because of all my adversaries, I have
become a disgrace,
Especially to my neighbors,
And an object of dread to my
acquaintances;
Those who see me in the street flee
from me.
12 I am forgotten like a dead person, out of
mind;
I am like a broken vessel.
13 For I have heard the slander of many,
Terror is on every side;
While they took counsel together against
me,
They schemed to take away my life.
14¶ But as for me, I trust in You, LORD,
I say, "You are my God."
15 My times are in Your hand;
Rescue me from the hand of my enemies
and from those who persecute me.
16 Make Your face shine upon Your servant;
Save me in Your faithfulness.
17 Let me not be put to shame, LORD, for I
call upon You;
Let the wicked be put to shame, let them
be silent in †Sheol.
18 Let the lying lips be speechless,
Which speak arrogantly against the
righteous
With pride and contempt.
19¶ How great is Your goodness,
Which You have stored up for those who
fear You,
Which You have performed for those who
take refuge in You,
Before the sons of mankind!
20 You hide them in the secret place of Your
presence from the conspiracies of
mankind;
You keep them secretly in a shelter from
the strife of tongues.
21 Blessed be the LORD,
For He has shown His marvelous
faithfulness to me in a besieged city.
22 As for me, I said in my alarm,
"I am cut off from Your eyes";
Nevertheless You heard the sound of my
pleadings
When I called to You for help.
23¶ Love the LORD, all His godly ones!
The LORD watches over the faithful
But fully repays the one who acts
arrogantly.
24 Be strong and let your heart take courage,
All you who wait for the LORD.

PSALM 32

Blessedness of Forgiveness and of Trust in God.
A Psalm *of David. A †Maskil.*
1 How blessed is he whose wrongdoing is
forgiven,
Whose sin is covered!
2 How blessed is a person whose guilt the
LORD does not take into account,
And in whose spirit there is no deceit!
3¶ When I kept silent *about my sin,* my body
wasted away

Through my groaning all day long.
4 For day and night Your hand was heavy
upon me;
My vitality failed *as* with the dry heat of
summer.　　　　　　　　　*Selah*
5 I acknowledged my sin to You,
And I did not hide my guilt;
I said, "I will confess my wrongdoings to
the LORD";
And You forgave the guilt of my sin.　*Selah*
6 Therefore, let everyone who is godly pray
to You in a time when You may be
found;
Certainly in a flood of great waters, they
will not reach him.
7 You are my hiding place; You keep me
from trouble;
You surround me with songs of
deliverance.　　　　　　*Selah*
8¶ I will instruct you and teach you in the
way which you should go;
I will advise you with My eye upon you.
9 Do not be like the horse or like the mule,
which have no understanding,
Whose trappings include bit and bridle to
hold them in check,
Otherwise they will not come near to you.
10 The sorrows of the wicked are many,
But the one who trusts in the LORD,
goodness will surround him.
11 Be glad in the LORD and rejoice, you
righteous ones;
And shout for joy, all you who are upright
in heart.

PSALM 33

Praise to the Creator and Protector.
1 Sing for joy in the LORD, you righteous
ones;
Praise is becoming to the upright.
2 Give thanks to the LORD with the lyre;
Sing praises to Him with a harp of ten
strings.
3 Sing to Him a new song;
Play skillfully with a shout of joy.
4 For the word of the LORD is right,
And all His work is *done* in faithfulness.
5 He loves righteousness and justice;
The earth is full of the goodness of the
LORD.
6¶ By the word of the LORD the heavens
were made,
And by the breath of His mouth all their
†lights.
7 He gathers the waters of the sea together
as a heap;
He puts the depths in storehouses.
8 Let all the earth fear the LORD;
Let all the inhabitants of the world stand
in awe of Him.
9 For He spoke, and it was done;
He commanded, and it stood firm.
10 The LORD nullifies the plan of nations;
He frustrates the plans of peoples.
11 The plan of the LORD stands forever,
The plans of His heart from generation to
generation.

---

12 Blessed is the nation whose God is the
   LORD,
   The people He has chosen for His own
   inheritance.
13¶ The LORD looks from heaven;
   He sees all the sons of mankind;
14 From His dwelling place He looks out
   On all the inhabitants of the earth,
15 He who fashions the hearts of them all,
   He who understands all their works.
16 The king is not saved by a mighty army;
   A warrior is not rescued by great
   strength.
17 A horse is a false hope for victory;
   Nor does it rescue anyone by its great
   strength.
18¶ Behold, the eye of the LORD is on those
   who fear Him,
   On those who wait for His faithfulness,
19 To rescue their soul from death
   And to keep them alive in famine.
20 Our soul waits for the LORD;
   He is our help and our shield.
21 For our heart rejoices in Him,
   Because we trust in His holy name.
22 Let Your favor, LORD, be upon us,
   Just as we have waited for You.

PSALM 34

**The LORD, a Provider and the One Who
Rescues Me.**
A Psalm *of David, when he pretended to be insane
before Abimelech, who drove him away, and he
departed.*
1 I will bless the LORD at all times;
   His praise shall continually be in my
   mouth.
2 My soul will make its boast in the LORD;
   The humble will hear it and rejoice.
3 Exalt the LORD with me,
   And let's exalt His name together.
4¶ I sought the LORD and He answered me,
   And rescued me from all my fears.
5 They looked to Him and were radiant,
   And their faces will never be ashamed.
6 This wretched man cried out, and the
   LORD heard *him,*
   And saved him out of all his troubles.
7 The angel of the LORD encamps around
   those who fear Him,
   And rescues them.
8¶ Taste and see that the LORD is good;
   How blessed is the man who takes refuge
   in Him!
9 Fear the LORD, you His saints;
   For to those who fear Him there is no lack
   of anything.
10 The young lions do without and suffer
   hunger;
   But they who seek the LORD will not lack
   any good thing.
11 Come, you children, listen to me;
   I will teach you the fear of the LORD.
12 Who is the person who desires life
   And loves *length of* days, that he may see
   good?
13 Keep your tongue from evil
   And your lips from speaking deceit.

14 Turn from evil and do good;
   Seek peace and pursue it.
15¶ The eyes of the LORD are toward the
   righteous,
   And His ears are toward their cry for help.
16 The face of the LORD is against evildoers,
   To eliminate the memory of them from
   the earth.
17 *The righteous* cry out, and the LORD hears
   And rescues them from all their troubles.
18 The LORD is near to the brokenhearted
   And saves those who are crushed in spirit.
19¶ The afflictions of the righteous are many,
   But the LORD rescues him from them all.
20 He protects all his bones,
   Not one of them is broken.
21 Evil will bring death to the wicked,
   And those who hate the righteous will
   suffer for their guilt.
22 The LORD redeems the souls of His
   servants,
   And none of those who take refuge in
   Him will suffer for their guilt.

PSALM 35

Prayer for Rescue from Enemies.
A Psalm *of David.*
1 Contend, LORD, with those who contend
   with me;
   Fight against those who fight against me.
2 Take hold of ¹buckler and shield
   And rise up as my help.
3 Draw also the spear and the battle-axe to
   meet those who pursue me;
   Say to my soul, "I am your salvation."
4 Let those be ashamed and dishonored
   who seek my life;
   Let those be turned back and humiliated
   who devise evil against me.
5 Let them be like chaff before the wind,
   With the angel of the LORD driving *them*
   on.
6 Let their way be dark and slippery,
   With the angel of the LORD pursuing
   them.
7 For they hid their net for me without
   cause;
   Without cause they dug a pit for my soul.
8 Let destruction come upon him when he
   is unaware,
   And let the net which he hid catch him;
   Let him fall into that very destruction.
9¶ So my soul shall rejoice in the LORD;
   It shall rejoice in His salvation.
10 All my bones will say, "LORD, who is like
   You,
   Who rescues the afflicted from one who is
   too strong for him,
   And the afflicted and the poor from one
   who robs him?"
11 Malicious witnesses rise up;
   They ask me things that I do not know.
12 They repay me evil for good,
   To the bereavement of my soul.
13 But as for me, when they were sick, my
   clothing was sackcloth;
   I humbled my soul with fasting,
   But my prayer kept returning to me.

35:2 ¹I.e., small shield

14 I went about as though it were my friend
    or brother;
    I bowed down in mourning, like one who
    mourns for a mother.
15 But at my stumbling they rejoiced and
    gathered themselves together;
    The afflicted people whom I did not know
    gathered together against me,
    They slandered me without ceasing.
16 Like godless jesters at a feast,
    They gnashed at me with their teeth.
17¶ Lord, how long will You look on?
    Rescue my soul from their ravages,
    My only *life* from the lions.
18 I will give You thanks in the great
    congregation;
    I will praise You among a mighty people.
19 Do not let those who are wrongfully my
    enemies rejoice over me;
    Nor let those who hate me for no reason
    wink maliciously.
20 For they do not speak peace,
    But they devise deceitful words against
    those who are quiet in the land.
21 They opened their mouth wide against
    me;
    They said, "Aha, aha! Our eyes have seen
    it!"
22¶ You have seen it, Lord, do not keep silent;
    Lord, do not be far from me.
23 Stir Yourself, and awake to my right
    And to my cause, my God and my Lord.
24 Judge me, Lord my God, according to
    Your righteousness,
    And do not let them rejoice over me.
25 Do not let them say in their heart, "Aha,
    our desire!"
    Do not let them say, "We have swallowed
    him up!"
26 May those be ashamed and altogether
    humiliated who rejoice at my distress;
    May those who exalt themselves over me
    be clothed with shame and dishonor.
27¶ May those shout for joy and rejoice, who
    take delight in my vindication;
    And may they say continually, "The Lord
    be exalted,
    Who delights in the prosperity of His
    servant."
28 And my tongue shall proclaim Your
    righteousness
    And Your praise all day long.

PSALM 36

Wickedness of Humanity and Goodness of God.
For the music director. A Psalm *of David the servant
of the* LORD.
1 Wrongdoing speaks to the ungodly within
    his heart;
    There is no fear of God before his eyes.
2 For it flatters him in his *own* eyes
    Concerning the discovery of his wrongful
    deed *and* the hatred *of it.*
3 The words of his mouth are wickedness
    and deceit;
    He has ceased to be wise *and* to do good.
4 He plans wickedness on his bed;
    He sets himself on a path that is not good;
    He does not reject evil.

5¶ Your mercy, Lord, extends to the heavens,
    Your faithfulness *reaches* to the skies.
6 Your righteousness is like the mountains
    of God;
    Your judgments are *like* the great deep.
    Lord, You protect mankind and animals.
7 How precious is Your mercy, God!
    And the sons of mankind take refuge in
    the shadow of Your wings.
8 They drink their fill of the abundance of
    Your house;
    And You allow them to drink *from* the
    river of Your delights.
9 For the fountain of life is with You;
    In Your light we see light.
10¶ Prolong Your mercy to those who know
    You,
    And Your righteousness to the upright of
    heart.
11 May the foot of pride not come upon me,
    And may the hand of the wicked not drive
    me away.
12 Those who do injustice have fallen there;
    They have been thrust down and cannot
    rise.

PSALM 37

**Security of Those Who Trust in the Lord, and
Insecurity of the Wicked.**
A Psalm *of David.*
1 Do not get upset because of evildoers,
    Do not be envious of wrongdoers.
2 For they will wither quickly like the grass,
    And decay like the green plants.
3 Trust in the Lord and do good;
    Live in the land and cultivate faithfulness.
4 Delight yourself in the Lord;
    And He will give you the desires of your
    heart.
5 Commit your way to the Lord,
    Trust also in Him, and He will do it.
6 He will bring out your righteousness as
    the light,
    And your judgment as the noonday.
7¶ Rest in the Lord and wait patiently for
    Him;
    Do not get upset because of one who is
    successful in his way,
    Because of the person who carries out
    wicked schemes.
8 Cease from anger and abandon wrath;
    Do not get upset; *it leads* only to
    evildoing.
9 For evildoers will be eliminated,
    But those who wait for the Lord, they will
    inherit the land.
10 Yet a little while and the wicked person
    will be no more;
    And you will look carefully for his place
    and he will not be *there.*
11 But the humble will inherit the land
    And will delight themselves in abundant
    prosperity.
12¶ The wicked plots against the righteous,
    And gnashes at him with his teeth.
13 The Lord laughs at him,
    For He sees that his day is coming.
14 The wicked have drawn the sword and
    bent their bow

To take down the afflicted and the needy,
To kill off those who are upright in conduct.

15 Their sword will enter their own heart,
And their bows will be broken.

16¶ Better is the little of the righteous
Than the abundance of many wicked.

17 For the arms of the wicked will be broken,
But the Lord sustains the righteous.

18 The Lord knows the days of the blameless,
And their inheritance will be forever.

19 They will not be ashamed in the time of evil,
And in the days of famine they will have plenty.

20 But the wicked will perish;
And the enemies of the Lord will be like the ¹glory of the pastures,
They vanish—like smoke they vanish away.

21 The wicked borrows and does not pay back,
But the righteous is gracious and gives.

22 For those blessed by Him will inherit the land,
But those cursed by Him will be eliminated.

23¶ The steps of a man are established by the Lord,
And He delights in his way.

24 When he falls, he will not be hurled down,
Because the Lord is the One who holds his hand.

25 I have been young and now I am old,
Yet I have not seen the righteous forsaken
Or his descendants begging for bread.

26 All day long he is gracious and lends,
And his descendants are a blessing.

27¶ Turn from evil and do good,
So that you will dwell forever.

28 For the Lord loves justice
And does not abandon His godly ones;
They are protected forever,
But the descendants of the wicked will be eliminated.

29 The righteous will inherit the land
And dwell in it forever.

30 The mouth of the righteous utters wisdom,
And his tongue speaks justice.

31 The Law of his God is in his heart;
His steps do not slip.

32 The wicked spies upon the righteous
And seeks to kill him.

33 The Lord will not leave him in his hand
Or let him be condemned when he is judged.

34 Wait for the Lord and keep His way,
And He will exalt you to inherit the land;
When the wicked are eliminated, you will see it.

35¶ I have seen a wicked, violent person
Spreading himself like a luxuriant tree in its native soil.

36 Then he passed away, and behold, he was no more;

I searched for him, but he could not be found.

37 Observe the blameless person, and look at the upright;
For the person of peace will have a future.

38 But wrongdoers will altogether be destroyed;
The future of the wicked will be eliminated.

39 But the salvation of the righteous is from the Lord;
He is their strength in time of trouble.

40 The Lord helps them and rescues them;
He rescues them from the wicked and saves them,
Because they take refuge in Him.

PSALM 38

Prayer of a Suffering Penitent.
A Psalm of David, for a memorial.

1 Lord, do not rebuke me in Your wrath,
And do not punish me in Your burning anger.

2 For Your arrows have sunk deep into me,
And Your hand has pressed down on me.

3 There is no healthy part in my flesh because of Your indignation;
There is no health in my bones because of my sin.

4 For my guilty deeds have gone over my head;
Like a heavy burden they weigh too much for me.

5 My wounds grow foul *and* fester
Because of my foolishness.

6 I am bent over and greatly bowed down;
I go in mourning all day long.

7 For my sides are filled with burning,
And there is no healthy part in my flesh.

8 I feel faint and badly crushed;
I groan because of the agitation of my heart.

9¶ Lord, all my desire is before You;
And my sighing is not hidden from You.

10 My heart throbs, my strength fails me;
And the light of my eyes, even that has gone from me.

11 My loved ones and my friends stand aloof from my plague;
And my kinsmen stand far away.

12 Those who seek my life lay snares *for me;*
And those who seek to injure me have threatened destruction,
And they plot deception all day long.

13¶ But I, like a person who is deaf, do not hear;
And *I am* like a person who cannot speak,
who does not open his mouth.

14 Yes, I am like a person who does not hear,
And in whose mouth are no arguments.

15 For I wait for You, Lord;
You will answer, Lord my God.

16 For I said, "May they not rejoice over me,
Who, when my foot slips, would exalt themselves over me."

17 For I am ready to fall,
And my sorrow is continually before me.

18 For I admit my guilt;

37:20 ¹I.e., flowers

I am full of anxiety because of my sin.
19 But my enemies are vigorous *and* strong,
And those who wrongfully hate me are
many.
20 And those who repay evil for good,
They become my enemies, because I
follow what is good.
21 Do not abandon me, LORD;
My God, do not be far from me!
22 Hurry to help me,
Lord, my salvation!

PSALM 39

The Futility of Life.
*For the music director, for Jeduthun. A Psalm
of David.*
1 I said, "I will keep watch over my ways
So that I do not sin with my tongue;
I will keep watch over my mouth as with
a muzzle
While the wicked are in my presence."
2 I was mute and silent,
I refused to say *even something* good,
And my pain was stirred up.
3 My heart was hot within me,
While I was musing the fire burned;
Then I spoke with my tongue:
4 "LORD, let me know my end,
And what is the extent of my days;
Let me know how transient I am.
5 "Behold, You have made my days
like 'hand widths,
And my lifetime as nothing in Your
sight;
Certainly all mankind standing is a mere
breath.   *Selah*
6 "Certainly every person walks around as a
fleeting shadow;
They certainly make an uproar for
nothing;
He amasses *riches* and does not know
who will gather them.
7¶ "And now, Lord, for what do I wait?
My hope is in You.
8 "Save me from all my wrongdoings;
Do not make me an *object of* reproach for
the foolish.
9 "I have become mute, I do not open my
mouth,
Because it is You who have done *it.*
10 "Remove Your plague from me;
Because of the opposition of Your hand I
am perishing.
11 "With rebukes You punish a person for
wrongdoing;
You consume like a moth what is precious
to him;
Certainly all mankind is mere breath!
     Selah
12¶ "Hear my prayer, LORD, and listen to my
cry for help;
Do not be silent to my tears;
For I am a stranger with You,
One who lives abroad, like all my
fathers.
13 "Turn Your eyes away from me, that I may
become cheerful *again*.
Before I depart and am no more."

PSALM 40

God Sustains His Servant.
For the music director. A Psalm of David.
1 I waited patiently for the LORD;
And He reached down to me and heard
my cry.
2 He brought me up out of the pit of
destruction, out of the mud;
And He set my feet on a rock, making my
footsteps firm.
3 He put a new song in my mouth, a song of
praise to our God;
Many will see and fear
And will trust in the LORD.
4¶ How blessed is the man who has made
the LORD his trust,
And has not turned to the proud, nor to
those who become involved in
falsehood.
5 Many, LORD my God, are the wonders
which You have done,
And Your thoughts toward us;
There is no one to compare with You.
If I would declare and speak of them,
They would be too numerous to count.
6¶ You have not desired sacrifice and meal
offering;
You have opened my ears;
You have not required burnt offering and
sin offering.
7 Then I said, "Behold, I have come;
It is written of me in the scroll of the
book.
8 "I delight to do Your will, my God;
Your Law is within my heart."
9¶ I have proclaimed good news of righteousness in the great congregation;
Behold, I will not restrain my lips,
LORD, You know.
10 I have not hidden Your righteousness
within my heart;
I have spoken of Your faithfulness and
Your salvation;
I have not concealed Your mercy and Your
truth from the great congregation.
11¶ You, LORD, will not withhold Your
compassion from me;
Your mercy and Your truth will
continually watch over me.
12 For evils beyond number have surrounded
me;
My guilty deeds have overtaken me, so
that I am not able to see;
They are more numerous than the hairs of
my head,
And my heart has failed me.
13¶ Be pleased, LORD, to rescue me;
Hurry, LORD, to help me.
14 May those be ashamed and humiliated
together
Who seek my life to destroy it;
May those be turned back and dishonored
Who delight in my hurt.
15 May those be appalled because of their
shame
Who say to me, "Aha, aha!"
16 May all who seek You rejoice and be glad
in You;

May those who love Your salvation
continually say,
"The LORD be exalted!"
17 But I am afflicted and needy;
May the Lord be mindful of me.
You are my help and my savior;
Do not delay, my God.

PSALM 41

The Psalmist in Sickness Complains of Enemies and False Friends.

For the music director. A Psalm of David.
1 Blessed is one who considers the helpless;
The LORD will save him on a day of
trouble.
2 The LORD will protect him and keep him
alive,
And he will be called blessed upon the
earth;
And do not turn him over to the desire of
his enemies.
3 The LORD will sustain him upon his
sickbed;
In his illness, You restore him to health.
4¶ As for me, I said, "LORD, be gracious to
me;
Heal my soul, for I have sinned against
You."
5 My enemies speak evil against me,
"When will he die, and his name perish?"
6 And when he comes to see me, he speaks
empty words;
His heart gathers wickedness to itself;
When he goes outside, he tells it.
7 All who hate me whisper together against
me;
They plot my harm against me, *saying,*
8 "A wicked thing is poured out upon him,
So that when he lies down, he will not get
up again."
9 Even my close friend in whom I trusted,
Who ate my bread,
Has lifted up his heel against me.
10¶ But You, LORD, be gracious to me and
raise me up,
That I may repay them.
11 By this I know that You are pleased with
me,
Because my enemy does not shout in
triumph over me.
12 As for me, You uphold me in my integrity,
And You place me in Your presence
forever.
13¶ Blessed be the LORD, the God of Israel,
From everlasting to everlasting.
Amen and Amen.

BOOK 2

PSALM 42

Thirsting for God in Trouble and Exile.

For the music director. A Maskil of the sons of Korah.
1 As the deer pants for the water brooks,
So my soul pants for You, God.
2 My soul thirsts for God, for the living
God;

When shall I come and appear before
God?
3 My tears have been my food day and
night,
While *they* say to me all day long, "Where
is your God?"
4 I remember these things and pour out my
soul within me.
For I used to go over with the multitude
and walk them to the house of God,
With a voice of joy and thanksgiving, a
multitude celebrating a festival.
5¶ Why are you in despair, my soul?
And *why* are you restless within me?
Wait for God, for I will again praise Him
For the help of His presence, my God.
6 My soul is in despair within me;
Therefore I remember You from the land
of the Jordan
And the peaks of Hermon, from Mount
Mizar.
7 Deep calls to deep at the sound of Your
waterfalls;
All Your breakers and Your waves have
passed over me.
8 The LORD will send His goodness in the
daytime;
And His song will be with me in the
night,
A prayer to the God of my life.
9¶ I will say to God my rock, "Why have You
forgotten me?
Why do I go about mourning because
of the oppression of the enemy?"
10 As a shattering of my bones, my
adversaries taunt me,
While they say to me all day long,
"Where is your God?"
11 Why are you in despair, my soul?
And why are you restless within me?
Wait for God, for I will again praise
[1]Him
For the [2]help of His presence, my God.

PSALM 43

Prayer for Help.

1 Vindicate me, God, and plead my case
against an ungodly nation;
Save me from the deceitful and unjust
person!
2 For You are the God of my strength; why
have You rejected me?
Why do I go about mourning because of
the oppression of the enemy?
3¶ Send out Your light and Your truth, they
shall lead me;
They shall bring me to Your holy hill
And to Your dwelling places.
4 Then I will go to the altar of God,
To God my exceeding joy;
And I will praise You on the lyre, God, my
God.
5¶ Why are you in despair, my soul?
And why are you restless within me?
Wait for God, for I will again praise
[1]Him
For the [2]help of His presence, my God.

42:11 [1]As in some ancient mss, cf. v 5; MT *Him, the help of my face and my God*   [2]Or *saving acts of*
43:5 [1]As in some ancient mss; MT *Him, the help of my face and my God*   [2]Or *saving acts of*

PSALM 44

Former Times of Help and Present Troubles.
For the music director. A Maskil of the sons of Korah.

1 God, we have heard with our ears,
Our fathers have told us
The work that You did in their days,
In the days of old.
2 You with Your own hand drove out the
nations;
Then You planted them;
You afflicted the peoples,
Then You let them go free.
3 For by their own sword they did not
possess the land,
And their own arm did not save them,
But Your right hand and Your arm and the
light of Your presence,
For You favored them.
4¶ You are my King, God;
Command victories for Jacob.
5 Through You we will push back our
adversaries;
Through Your name we will trample down
those who rise up against us.
6 For I will not trust in my bow,
Nor will my sword save me.
7 But You have saved us from our
adversaries,
And You have put to shame those who
hate us.
8 In God we have boasted all day long,
And we will give thanks to Your name
forever.   *Selah*
9¶ Yet You have rejected *us* and brought us to
dishonor,
And do not go out with our armies.
10 You cause us to turn back from the
enemy;
And those who hate us have taken spoils
for themselves.
11 You turn us over to be eaten like sheep,
And have scattered us among the nations.
12 You sell Your people cheaply,
And have not profited by their sale.
13 You make us an *object of* reproach to our
neighbors,
Of scoffing and ridicule to those around
us.
14 You make us a proverb among the nations,
A laughingstock among the peoples.
15 All day long my dishonor is before me
And I am covered with my humiliation,
16 Because of the voice of one who taunts
and reviles,
Because of the presence of the enemy and
the avenger.
17¶ All this has come upon us, but we have
not forgotten You,
And we have not dealt falsely with Your
covenant.
18 Our heart has not turned back,
And our steps have not deviated from
Your way,
19 Yet You have crushed us in a place of
jackals
And covered us with deep darkness.
20¶ If we had forgotten the name of our God
Or extended our hands to a strange god,
21 Would God not find this out?

22 For He knows the secrets of the heart.
But for Your sake we are killed all day
long;
We are regarded as sheep to be
slaughtered.
23 Wake Yourself up, why do You sleep,
Lord?
Awake, do not reject us forever.
24 Why do You hide Your face
And forget our affliction and oppression?
25 For our souls have sunk down into the
dust;
Our bodies cling to the earth.
26 Rise up, be our help,
And redeem us because of Your mercy.

PSALM 45

A Song Celebrating the King's Marriage.
For the music director; according to the Shoshan-
nim. A Maskil of the sons of Korah. A Song of Love.

1 My heart is moved with a good theme;
I address my verses to the King;
My tongue is the pen of a ready writer.
2 You are the most handsome of the sons of
mankind;
Grace is poured upon Your lips;
Therefore God has blessed You forever.
3¶ Strap Your sword on *Your* thigh, Mighty
One,
In Your splendor and majesty!
4 And in Your majesty ride on victoriously,
For the cause of truth, humility, *and*
righteousness;
Let Your right hand teach You awesome
things.
5 Your arrows are sharp;
The peoples fall under You;
Your arrows are in the heart of the King's
enemies.
6¶ Your throne, God, is forever and ever;
The scepter of Your kingdom is a scepter
of justice.
7 You have loved righteousness and hated
wickedness;
Therefore God, Your God, has anointed
You
With the oil of joy above Your
companions.
8 All Your garments are *fragrant with*
myrrh, aloes, *and* cassia;
From ivory palaces stringed instruments
have made You joyful.
9 Kings' daughters are among Your noble
women;
At Your right hand stands the queen in
gold from Ophir.
10¶ Listen, daughter, look and incline your
ear:
Forget your people and your father's
house;
11 Then the King will crave your beauty.
Because He is your Lord, bow down to
Him.
12 The daughter of Tyre *will come* with a
gift;
The wealthy among the people will seek
your favor.
13¶ The King's daughter is all glorious within;
Her clothing is interwoven with gold.

14 She will be brought to the King in colorful
  garments;
  The virgins, her companions who follow
  her,
  Will be brought to You.
15 They will be brought with joy and
  rejoicing;
  They will enter into the King's palace.
16¶ In place of your fathers will be your sons;
  You shall make them princes in all the
  earth.
17 I will make Your name known among all
  generations;
  Therefore the peoples will praise You
  forever and ever.

PSALM 46

God, the Refuge of His People.
*For the music director. A Psalm of the sons of
Korah, †set to Alamoth. A Song.*
1 God is our refuge and strength,
  A very ready help in trouble.
2 Therefore we will not fear, though the
  earth shakes
  And the mountains slip into the heart of
  the sea;
3 Though its waters roar *and* foam,
  Though the mountains quake at its
  swelling pride.   *Selah*
4¶ There is a river whose streams make the
  city of God happy,
  The holy dwelling places of the Most
  High.
5 God is in the midst of her, she will not be
  moved;
  God will help her when morning dawns.
6 The nations made an uproar, the
  kingdoms tottered;
  He raised His voice, the earth quaked.
7 The LORD of armies is with us;
  The God of Jacob is our stronghold. *Selah*
8¶ Come, behold the works of the LORD,
  Who has inflicted horrific events on the
  earth.
9 He makes wars to cease to the end of the
  earth;
  He breaks the bow and cuts the spear in
  two;
  He burns the chariots with fire.
10 "Stop *striving* and know that I am God;
  I will be exalted among the nations, I will
  be exalted on the earth."
11 The LORD of armies is with us;
  The God of Jacob is our stronghold. *Selah*

PSALM 47

God, the King of the Earth.
For the music director. A Psalm of the sons of Korah.
1 Clap your hands, all you peoples;
  Shout to God with a voice of joy.
2 For the LORD Most High is to be feared,
  A great King over all the earth.
3 He subdues peoples under us
  And nations under our feet.
4 He chooses our inheritance for us,
  The pride of Jacob whom He loves. *Selah*
5¶ God has ascended with a shout,

The LORD, with the sound of a trumpet.
6 Sing praises to God, sing praises;
  Sing praises to our King, sing praises.
7 For God is the King of all the earth;
  Sing praises with a psalm of wisdom.
8 God reigns over the nations,
  God sits on His holy throne.
9 The princes of the people have assembled
  as the people of the God of Abraham,
  For the shields of the earth belong to God;
  He is highly exalted.

PSALM 48

The Beauty and Glory of Zion.
A Song; a Psalm of the sons of Korah.
1 Great is the LORD, and greatly to be
  praised
  In the city of our God, His holy mountain.
2 Beautiful in elevation, the joy of the
  whole earth,
  Is Mount Zion *in* the far north,
  The city of the great King.
3 In its palaces,
  God has made Himself known as a
  stronghold.
4¶ For, behold, the kings arrived,
  They passed by together.
5 They saw *it,* then they were amazed;
  They were terrified, they fled in a hurry,
6 Panic seized them there,
  Anguish, as *that* of a woman in childbirth.
7 With the east wind
  You smash the ships of Tarshish.
8 Just as we have heard, so have we seen
  In the city of the LORD of armies, in the
  city of our God;
  God will establish her forever. *Selah*
9¶ We have thought over Your goodness,
  God,
  In the midst of Your temple.
10 As is Your name, God,
  So is Your praise to the ends of the earth;
  Your right hand is full of righteousness.
11 Mount Zion shall be glad,
  The daughters of Judah shall rejoice
  Because of Your judgments.
12 Walk around Zion and encircle her;
  Count her towers;
13 Consider her ramparts;
  Go through her palaces,
  So that you may tell *of her* to the next
  generation.
14 For such is God,
  Our God forever and ever;
  He will lead us until death.

PSALM 49

The Foolishness of Trusting in Riches.
For the music director. A Psalm of the sons of Korah.
1 Hear this, all peoples;
  Listen, all inhabitants of the world,
2 Both low and high,
  Rich and poor together.
3 My mouth will speak wisdom,
  And the meditation of my heart *will be*
  understanding.
4 I will incline my ear to a proverb;

I will express my riddle on the harp.

5¶ Why should I fear in days of adversity,
When the injustice of those who betray
me surrounds me,

6 Those who trust in their wealth
And boast in the abundance of their
riches?

7 No one can by any means redeem another
Or give God a ransom for him—

8 For the redemption of his soul is priceless,
And he should cease *imagining* forever—

9 That he might live on eternally,
That he might not undergo decay.

10¶ For he sees *that even* wise people die;
The foolish and the stupid alike perish
And leave their wealth to others.

11 Their inner thought is *that* their houses
are forever
And their dwelling places to all
generations;
They have named their lands after their
own names.

12 But man in *his* splendor will not endure;
He is like the animals that perish.

13¶ This is the way of those who are foolish,
And of those after them who approve
their words.   *Selah*

14 Like sheep they sink down to 'Sheol;
Death will be their shepherd;
And the upright will rule over them in the
morning,
And their form shall be for Sheol to
consume
So that they have no lofty home.

15 But God will redeem my soul from the
power of Sheol,
For He will receive me.   *Selah*

16¶ Do not be afraid when a person becomes
rich,
When the splendor of his house is
increased;

17 For when he dies, he will take nothing
with him;
His wealth will not descend after him.

18 Though while he lives he congratulates
himself—
And though *people* praise you when you
do well for yourself—

19 He will go to the generation of his fathers;
They will never see the light.

20 Mankind in *its* splendor, yet without
understanding,
Is like the animals *that* perish.

PSALM 50

**God, the Judge of the Righteous and
the Wicked.**

A Psalm of Asaph.

1 The Mighty One, God, the LORD, has
spoken
And summoned the earth, from the rising
of the sun to its setting.

2 Out of Zion, the perfection of beauty,
God has shone.

3 May our God come and not keep silent;
Fire devours before Him,
And a storm is violently raging around
Him.

4 He summons the heavens above,
And the earth, to judge His people:

5 "Gather My godly ones to Me,
Those who have made a covenant
with Me by sacrifice."

6 And the heavens declare His
righteousness,
For God Himself is judge.   *Selah*

7¶ "Hear, My people, and I will speak;
Israel, I will testify against you;
I am God, your God.

8 "I do not rebuke you for your sacrifices,
And your burnt offerings are continually
before Me.

9 "I will not take a bull from your house,
Nor male goats from your folds.

10 "For every animal of the forest is Mine,
The cattle on a thousand hills.

11 "I know every bird of the mountains,
And everything that moves in the field is
Mine.

12 "If I were hungry I would not tell you,
For the world is Mine, and everything it
contains.

13 "Shall I eat the flesh of bulls
Or drink the blood of male goats?

14 "Offer God a sacrifice of thanksgiving
And pay your vows to the Most High;

15 Call upon Me on the day of trouble;
I will rescue you, and you will honor Me."

16¶ But to the wicked God says,
"What *right* do you have to tell of My
statutes
And to take My covenant in your mouth?

17 "For you yourself hate discipline,
And you throw My words behind you.

18 "When you see a thief, you become friends
with him,
And you associate with adulterers.

19 "You let your mouth loose in evil,
And your tongue harnesses deceit.

20 "You sit and speak against your brother;
You slander your own mother's son.

21 "These things you have done *and* I kept
silent;
You thought that I was *just* like you;
I will rebuke you and present *the case*
before your eyes.

22¶ "Now consider this, you who forget God,
Or I will tear *you* in pieces, and there will
be no one to save *you.*

23 "He who offers a sacrifice of thanksgiving
honors Me;
And to him who sets *his* way *properly*
I will show the salvation of God."

PSALM 51

A Contrite Sinner's Prayer for Pardon.

*For the music director. A Psalm of David, when
Nathan the prophet came to him, after he had gone
in to Bathsheba.*

1 Be gracious to me, God, according to Your
faithfulness;
According to the greatness of Your
compassion, wipe out my wrongdoings.

2 Wash me thoroughly from my guilt
And cleanse me from my sin.

3 For I know my wrongdoings,

And my sin is constantly before me.
4 Against You, You only, I have sinned
And done what is evil in Your sight,
So that You are justified when You speak
And blameless when You judge.
5¶ Behold, I was brought forth in guilt,
And in sin my mother conceived me.
6 Behold, You desire truth in the innermost
being,
And in secret You will make wisdom
known to me.
7 Purify me with hyssop, and I will be clean;
Cleanse me, and I will be whiter than
snow.
8 Let me hear joy and gladness,
Let the bones You have broken rejoice.
9 Hide Your face from my sins
And wipe out all my guilty deeds.
10¶ Create in me a clean heart, God,
And renew a steadfast spirit within me.
11 Do not cast me away from Your presence,
And do not take Your Holy Spirit from me.
12 Restore to me the joy of Your salvation,
And sustain me with a willing spirit.
13 *Then* I will teach wrongdoers Your ways,
And sinners will be converted to You.
14¶ Save me from the guilt of bloodshed, God,
the God of my salvation;
Then my tongue will joyfully sing of Your
righteousness.
15 Lord, open my lips,
So that my mouth may declare Your
praise.
16 For You do not delight in sacrifice,
otherwise I would give it;
You do not take pleasure in burnt offering.
17 The sacrifices of God are a broken spirit;
A broken and a contrite heart, God, You
will not despise.
18¶ By Your favor do good to Zion;
Build the walls of Jerusalem.
19 Then You will delight in righteous
sacrifices,
In burnt offering and whole burnt offering;
Then bulls will be offered on Your altar.

PSALM 52

Futility of Boastful Wickedness.
*For the music director. A Maskil of David, when
Doeg the Edomite came and told Saul and said to
him, "David has come to the house of Ahimelech."*
1 Why do you boast in evil, you mighty
man?
The faithfulness of God *endures* all day
long.
2 Your tongue devises destruction,
Like a sharp razor, you worker of deceit.
3 You love evil more than good,
Lies more than speaking what is right.
Selah
4 You love all words that devour,
You deceitful tongue.
5¶ But God will break you down forever;
He will snatch you up and tear you away
from *your* tent,
And uproot you from the land of the
living. *Selah*
6 The righteous will see and fear,

And they will laugh at him, *saying,*
7 "Behold, the man who would not make
God his refuge,
But trusted in the abundance of his
riches
And was strong in his *evil* desire."
8¶ But as for me, I am like a green olive tree
in the house of God;
I trust in the faithfulness of God forever
and ever.
9 I will praise You forever, because You have
done *it,*
And I will wait on Your name, for *it is*
good, in the presence of Your godly
ones.

PSALM 53

Foolishness and Wickedness of People.
For the music director; according to †*Mahalath.
A Maskil of David.*
1 The fool has said in his heart, "There is
no God."
They are corrupt, and have committed
abominable injustice;
There is no one who does good.
2 God has looked down from heaven
upon the sons of mankind
To see if there is anyone who
understands,
Who seeks after God.
3 Every one of them has turned aside;
together they have become corrupt;
There is no one who does good, not even
one.
4¶ Have the workers of injustice no
knowledge,
Who eat up My people *like* they ate
bread,
And have not called upon God?
5 They were in great fear there, *where* no
fear had been;
For God scattered the bones of him who
encamped against you;
You put *them* to shame, because God had
rejected them.
6 Oh, that the salvation of Israel *would
come* from Zion!
When God restores the fortunes of His
people,
Jacob shall rejoice, Israel shall be glad.

PSALM 54

Prayer for Defense against Enemies.
*For the music director; on stringed instruments.
A Maskil of David, when the Ziphites came and
said to Saul, "Is David not keeping himself hidden
among us?"*
1 Save me, God, by Your name,
And vindicate me by Your power.
2 Hear my prayer, God;
Listen to the words of my mouth.
3 For strangers have risen against me
And violent men have sought my life;
They have not set God before them.
Selah
4¶ Behold, God is my helper;
The Lord is the sustainer of my soul.

53:1 †*I.e., sickness, a sad tone*

5   He will pay back the evil to my enemies;
     Destroy them in Your faithfulness.
6¶   Willingly I will sacrifice to You;
     I will praise Your name, LORD, for it is
        good.
7   For He has saved me from all trouble,
     And my eye has looked *with satisfaction*
        upon my enemies.

PSALM 55

Prayer for the Destruction of the Treacherous.
For the music director; on stringed instruments.
A Maskil of David.
1   Listen to my prayer, God;
     And do not hide Yourself from my
        pleading.
2   Give *Your* attention to me and answer me;
     I am restless in my complaint and severely
        distracted,
3   Because of the voice of the enemy,
     Because of the pressure of the wicked;
     For they bring down trouble upon me
     And in anger they hold a grudge against
        me.
4¶   My heart is in anguish within me,
     And the terrors of death have fallen upon
        me.
5   Fear and trembling come upon me,
     And horror has overwhelmed me.
6   I said, "Oh, that I had wings like a dove!
     I would fly away and be at rest.
7   "Behold, I would flee far away,
     I would spend my nights in the wilder-
        ness.   *Selah*
8   "I would hurry to my place of refuge
     From the stormy wind *and* heavy gale."
9¶   Confuse them, Lord, divide their tongues,
     For I have seen violence and strife in the
        city.
10   Day and night they go around her upon
        her walls,
     And evil and harm are in her midst.
11   Destruction is in her midst;
     Oppression and deceit do not depart from
        her streets.
12¶ For it is not an enemy who taunts me,
     Then I could endure *it;*
     Nor is it one who hates me who has
        exalted himself against me,
     Then I could hide myself from him.
13   But it is you, a man my equal,
     My companion and my confidant;
14   We who had sweet fellowship together,
     Walked in the house of God among the
        commotion.
15   *May* death *come* deceitfully upon them;
     May they go down alive to ¹Sheol,
     For evil is in their dwelling, in their
        midst.
16¶ As for me, I shall call upon God,
     And the LORD will save me.
17   Evening and morning and at noon, I will
        complain and moan,
     And He will hear my voice.
18   He will redeem my soul in peace from the
        battle *which is* against me,
     For they are many *who are aggressive*
        toward me.

19   God will hear and humiliate them—
     Even the one who sits enthroned from
        ancient times—   *Selah*
     With whom there is no change,
     And who do not fear God.
20   He has put forth his hands against those
        who were at peace with him;
     He has violated his covenant.
21   His speech was smoother than butter,
     But his heart was war;
     His words were softer than oil,
     Yet they were drawn swords.
22¶ Cast your burden upon the LORD and He
        will sustain you;
     He will never allow the righteous to be
        shaken.
23   But You, God, will bring them down to
        the pit of destruction;
     Men of bloodshed and deceit will not live
        out half their days.
     But I will trust in You.

PSALM 56

Pleading for Help and Grateful Trust in God.
For the music director; according to Jonath elem
rehokim. A Mikhtam of David, when the Philistines
seized him in Gath.
1   Be gracious to me, God, for a man has
        trampled upon me;
     Fighting all day long he oppresses me.
2   My enemies have trampled upon me all
        day long,
     For they are many who fight proudly
        against me.
3   When I am afraid,
     I will put my trust in You.
4   In God, whose word I praise,
     In God I have put my trust;
     I shall not be afraid.
     What can *mere* mortals do to me?
5   All day long they distort my words;
     All their thoughts are against me for
        evil.
6   They attack, they lurk,
     They watch my steps,
     As they have waited *to take* my life.
7   Because of *their* wickedness, *will there be*
        an escape for them?
     In anger make the peoples fall down,
        God!
8¶   You have taken account of my miseries;
     Put my tears in Your bottle.
     Are they not in Your book?
9   Then my enemies will turn back on the
        day when I call;
     This I know, that God is for me.
10   In God, *whose* word I praise,
     In the LORD, *whose* word I praise,
11   In God I have put my trust, I shall not be
        afraid.
     What can mankind do to me?
12   Your vows are *binding* upon me, God;
     I will render thanksgiving offerings to
        You.
13   For You have saved my soul from death,
     Indeed my feet from stumbling,
     So that I may walk before God
     In the light of the living.

55:15 ¹I.e., the netherworld

PSALM 57

Prayer for Rescue from Persecutors.
For the music director; set to *Al-tashheth.*
A Mikhtam of David, when he fled from Saul in
the cave.

1 Be gracious to me, God, be gracious to
me,
For my soul takes refuge in You;
And in the shadow of Your wings I will
take refuge
Until destruction passes by.
2 I will cry to God Most High,
To God who accomplishes *all things* for
me.
3 He will send from heaven and save me;
He rebukes the one who tramples upon
me.   *Selah*
God will send His favor and His truth.
4¶ My soul is among lions;
I must lie *among* those who devour,
Among sons of mankind whose teeth are
spears and arrows,
And their tongue is a sharp sword.
5 Be exalted above the heavens, God;
May Your glory *be* above all the earth.
6 They have prepared a net for my steps;
My soul is bowed down;
They dug a pit before me;
They *themselves* have fallen into the
midst of it.   *Selah*
7¶ My heart is steadfast, God, my heart is
steadfast;
I will sing, yes, I will sing praises!
8 Awake, my glory!
Awake, harp and lyre!
I will awaken the dawn.
9 I will praise You, Lord, among the
peoples;
I will sing praises to You among the
nations.
10 For Your goodness is great to the heavens
And Your truth to the clouds.
11 Be exalted above the heavens, God;
May Your glory *be* above all the earth.

PSALM 58

Prayer for the Punishment of the Wicked.
For the music director; set to *Al-tashheth.*
A Mikhtam of David.

1 Do you indeed speak righteousness, you
gods?
Do you judge fairly, you sons of mankind?
2 No, in heart you practice injustice;
On earth you clear a way for the violence
of your hands.
3 The wicked have turned away from the
womb;
These who speak lies go astray from birth.
4 They have venom like the venom of a
serpent;
Like a deaf cobra that stops up its ear,
5 So that it does not hear the voice of
charmers,
Or a skillful caster of spells.
6¶ God, shatter their teeth in their mouth;
Break out the fangs of the young lions,
Lord.

7 May they flow away like water that runs
off;
When he aims his arrows, *may they be* as
headless shafts.
8 *May they be* like a snail which goes along
in slime,
Like the miscarriage of a woman that
never sees the sun.
9 Before your pots can feel *the fire of* thorns
He will sweep them away with a whirlwind, the green and the burning alike.
10¶ The righteous will rejoice when he sees
vengeance;
He will wash his feet in the blood of the
wicked.
11 And people will say, "There certainly is a
reward for the righteous;
There certainly is a God who judges on
the earth!"

PSALM 59

Prayer for Rescue from Enemies.
For the music director; set to *Al-tashheth.*
A Mikhtam of David, when Saul sent men *and they*
watched the house in order to kill him.

1 Rescue me from my enemies, my God;
Set me *securely* on high away from those
who rise up against me.
2 Rescue me from those who practice
injustice,
And save me from men of bloodshed.
3 For behold, they have set an ambush for
my life;
Fierce men attack me,
Not for my wrongdoing nor for my sin,
Lord,
4 For no guilt *of mine,* they run and take
their stand against me.
Stir Yourself to help me, and see!
5 You, Lord God of armies, the God of
Israel,
Awake to punish all the nations;
Do not be gracious to any *who* deal
treacherously in wrongdoing.   *Selah*
6 They return at evening, they howl like a
dog,
And prowl around the city.
7 Behold, they gush forth with their
mouths;
Swords are in their lips,
For, *they say,* "Who hears?"
8 But You, Lord, laugh at them;
You scoff at all the nations.
9¶ *Because of* [1]his strength I will watch for
You,
For God is my refuge.
10 My God in His faithfulness will meet me;
God will let me look *triumphantly* upon
my enemies.
11 Do not kill them, or my people will forget;
Scatter them by Your power and bring
them down,
Lord, our shield.
12 *On account of* the sin of their mouths *and*
the words of their lips,
May they even be caught in their pride,
And on account of curses and lies which
they tell.

59:9 [1]LXX, some mss and some ancient versions *my strength* (cf. v 17)

13 Destroy *them* in wrath, destroy *them* so
     that they will no longer exist;
     So that *people* may know that God rules
     in Jacob,
     To the ends of the earth.   *Selah*
14 They return at evening, they howl like a
     dog,
     And prowl around the city.
15 They wander about for food
     And murmur if they are not satisfied.
16¶ But as for me, I will sing of Your
     strength;
     Yes, I will joyfully sing of Your faithfulness
     in the morning,
     For You have been my refuge
     And a place of refuge on the day of my
     distress.
17 My strength, I will sing praises to You;
     For God is my refuge, the God who shows
     me favor.

PSALM 60

***Grieving over Defeat in Battle, and Prayer
for Help.***
*For the music director; according to Shushan Eduth.
A Mikhtam of David, to teach; when he fought with
Aram-naharaim and Aram-zobah, and Joab
returned, and killed twelve thousand of Edom in the
Valley of Salt.*
1   God, You have rejected us. You have
     broken us;
     You have been angry; restore us!
2   You have made the land quake, You have
     split it open;
     Heal its cracks, for it sways.
3   You have made Your people experience
     hardship;
     You have given us wine to drink that
     makes us stagger.
4   You have given a banner to those who fear
     You,
     That it may be displayed because of the
     truth.   *Selah*
5   That Your beloved may be rescued,
     Save *us* with Your right hand, and answer
     us!
6¶ God has spoken in His holiness:
     "I will triumph, I will divide up Shechem,
     and measure out the Valley of
     Succoth.
7   "Gilead is Mine, and Manasseh is Mine;
     Ephraim also is the helmet of My head;
     Judah is My scepter.
8   "Moab is My washbowl;
     I will throw My sandal over Edom;
     Shout loud, Philistia, because of Me!"
9¶ Who will bring me into the besieged
     city?
     Who will lead me to Edom?
10 Have You Yourself not rejected us,
     God?
     And will You not go out with our armies,
     God?
11 Oh give us help against the enemy,
     For rescue by man is worthless.
12 Through God we will do valiantly,
     And it is He who will trample down our
     enemies.

PSALM 61

Confidence in God's Protection.
*For the music director; on a stringed instrument.
A Psalm of David.*
1   Hear my cry, God;
     Give *Your* attention to my prayer.
2   From the end of the earth I call to You
     when my heart is faint;
     Lead me to the rock that is higher than I.
3   For You have been a refuge for me,
     A tower of strength against the enemy.
4   Let me dwell in Your tent forever;
     Let me take refuge in the shelter of Your
     wings.   *Selah*
5¶ For You have heard my vows, God;
     You have given *me* the inheritance of
     those who fear Your name.
6   You will prolong the king's life;
     His years will be like generations.
7   He will sit *enthroned* before God forever;
     Appoint faithfulness and truth that they
     may watch over him.
8   So I will sing praise to Your name forever,
     That I may pay my vows day by day.

PSALM 62

***God Alone a Refuge from Treachery and
Oppression.***
*For the music director; according to Jeduthun.
A Psalm of David.*
1   My soul *waits in* silence for God alone;
     From Him *comes* my salvation.
2   He alone is my rock and my salvation,
     My stronghold; I will not be greatly
     shaken.
3¶ How long will you attack a man,
     That you may murder *him*, all of you,
     Like a leaning wall, like a tottering fence?
4   They have planned only to thrust him
     down from his high position;
     They delight in falsehood;
     They bless with their mouth,
     But inwardly they curse.   *Selah*
5¶ My soul, wait in silence for God alone,
     For my hope is from Him.
6   He alone is my rock and my salvation,
     My refuge; I will not be shaken.
7   My salvation and my glory *rest* on God;
     The rock of my strength, my refuge is in
     God.
8   Trust in Him at all times, you people;
     Pour out your hearts before Him;
     God is a refuge for us.   *Selah*
9¶ People of low standing are only breath,
     and people of rank are a lie;
     In the balances they go up.
     Together they are *lighter* than breath.
10 Do not trust in oppression,
     And do not vainly rely on robbery;
     If wealth increases, do not set *your* heart
     on it.
11¶ God has spoken ¹once;
     ²Twice I have heard this:
     That power belongs to God;
12 And faithfulness is Yours, Lord,
     For You reward a person according to his
     work.

62:11 ¹Or *one thing*   ²Or *These two things I have heard*

PSALM 63

The Thirsting Soul Satisfied in God.
A Psalm of David, when he was in the wilderness of Judah.

1 God, You are my God; I shall be watching
for You;
My soul thirsts for You, my flesh yearns
for You,
In a dry and exhausted land where there
is no water.
2 So have I seen You in the sanctuary,
To see Your power and glory.
3 Because Your favor is better than life,
My lips will praise You.
4 So I will bless You as long as I live;
I will lift up my hands in Your name.
5 My soul is satisfied as with fat and fatness,
And my mouth offers praises with joyful
lips.
6¶ When I remember You on my bed,
I meditate on You in the night watches,
7 For You have been my help,
And in the shadow of Your wings I sing
for joy.
8 My soul clings to You;
Your right hand takes hold of me.
9¶ But those who seek my life to destroy it,
Will go into the depths of the earth.
10 They will be turned over to the power of
the sword;
They will be a prey for foxes.
11 But the king will rejoice in God;
Everyone who swears by Him will boast,
For the mouths of those who speak lies
will be stopped.

PSALM 64

Prayer for Rescue from Secret Enemies.
For the music director. A Psalm of David.

1 Hear my voice, God, in my ¹complaint;
Protect my life from dread of the enemy.
2 Hide me from the secret discussion of
evildoers,
From the restlessness of the workers of
injustice,
3 Who have sharpened their tongues like a
sword.
They aimed bitter speech *as* their arrows,
4 To shoot from concealment at the
innocent;
Suddenly they shoot at him, and do not
fear.
5 They make firm for themselves an evil
purpose;
They talk of setting snares secretly;
They say, "Who can see them?"
6 They devise injustices, *saying,*
"We are ready *with* a well-conceived plot";
For the inward thought and the heart of a
person are deep.
7¶ But God will shoot an arrow at them;
Suddenly they will be wounded.
8 So they will make him stumble;
Their own tongue is against them;
All who see *them* will shake their heads.
9 Then all people will fear,
And they will declare the work of God,

And will consider what He has done.
10 The righteous person will be glad in the
LORD and take refuge in Him;
And all the upright in heart will boast.

PSALM 65

God's Abundant Favor to Earth and Mankind.
For the music director. A Psalm of David. A Song.

1 There will be silence before You, *and*
praise in Zion, God,
And the vow will be fulfilled for You.
2 You who hear prayer,
To You all mankind comes.
3 Wrongdoings prevail against me;
As for our offenses, You forgive them.
4 Blessed *is the one* You choose and allow
to approach *You;*
He will dwell in Your courtyards.
We will be satisfied with the goodness of
Your house,
Your holy temple.
5¶ By awesome *deeds* You answer us in
righteousness, God of our salvation,
You who are the trust of all the ends of
the earth and the farthest sea;
6 Who establishes the mountains by His
strength,
Who is encircled with might;
7 Who stills the roaring of the seas,
The roaring of their waves,
And the turmoil of the nations.
8 They who dwell at the ends *of the earth*
stand in awe of Your signs;
You make the sunrise and the sunset
shout for joy.
9¶ You visit the earth and cause it to
overflow;
You greatly enrich it;
The stream of God is full of water;
You prepare their grain, for so You prepare
the earth.
10 You water its furrows abundantly,
You settle its ridges,
You soften it with showers,
You bless its growth.
11 You have crowned the year with Your
goodness,
And Your paths drip *with* fatness.
12 The pastures of the wilderness drip,
And the hills encircle themselves with
rejoicing.
13 The meadows are clothed with flocks
And the valleys are covered with grain;
They shout for joy, yes, they sing.

PSALM 66

Praise for God's Mighty Deeds and for His
Answer to Prayer.
For the music director. A Song. A Psalm.

1 Shout joyfully to God, all the earth;
2 Sing the glory of His name;
Make His praise glorious.
3 Say to God, "How awesome are Your
works!
Because of the greatness of Your power
Your enemies will pretend to obey You.
4 "All the earth will worship You,

64:1 ¹Or *concern*

And will sing praises to You;
They will sing praises to Your name."
Selah

5¶ Come and see the works of God,
Who is awesome in *His* deeds toward the
sons of mankind.

6 He turned the sea into dry land;
They passed through the river on foot;
Let's rejoice there, in Him!

7 He rules by His might forever;
His eyes keep watch on the nations;
The rebellious shall not exalt themselves!
Selah

8¶ Bless our God, you peoples,
And sound His praise abroad,

9 Who keeps us in life,
And does not allow our feet to slip.

10 For You have put us to the test, God;
You have refined us as silver is refined.

11 You brought us into the net;
You laid an oppressive burden upon us.

12 You made men ride over our heads;
We went through fire and through water.
Yet You brought us out into *a place of*
abundance.

13 I shall come into Your house with burnt
offerings;
I shall pay You my vows,

14 Which my lips uttered
And my mouth spoke when I was in
distress.

15 I shall offer to You burnt offerings of fat
animals,
With the smoke of rams;
I shall make *an offering of* bulls with male
goats.   *Selah*

16¶ Come *and* hear, all who fear God,
And I will tell of what He has done for my
soul.

17 I cried to Him with my mouth,
And He was exalted with my tongue.

18 If I regard wickedness in my heart,
The Lord will not hear;

19 But God has heard;
He has given attention to the sound of my
prayer.

20 Blessed be God;
Who has not turned away my prayer
Nor His favor from me.

PSALM 67

The Nations Exhorted to Praise God.
For the music director; with stringed instruments.
A Psalm. A Song.

1 God be gracious to us and bless us,
And cause His face to shine upon us—
Selah

2 That Your way may be known on the
earth,
Your salvation among all nations.

3 May the peoples praise You, God;
May all the peoples praise You.

4 May the nations be glad and sing for joy;
For You will judge the peoples with
fairness
And guide the nations on the earth.
Selah

5 May the peoples praise You, God;
May all the peoples praise You.

6 The earth has yielded its produce;
God, our God, blesses us.

7 God blesses us,
So that all the ends of the earth may fear
Him.

PSALM 68

The God of Sinai and of the Sanctuary.
For the music director. A Psalm of David. A Song.

1 May God arise, may His enemies be
scattered,
And may those who hate Him flee from
His presence.

2 As smoke is driven away, *so* drive *them*
away;
As wax melts before a fire,
So the wicked will perish before God.

3 But the righteous will be joyful; they will
rejoice before God;
Yes, they will rejoice with gladness.

4 Sing to God, sing praises to His name;
Exalt Him who rides through the
deserts,
Whose name is the LORD, and be jubilant
before Him.

5¶ A father of the fatherless and a judge for
the widows,
Is God in His holy dwelling.

6 God makes a home for the lonely;
He leads out the prisoners into prosperity,
Only the rebellious live in parched lands.

7¶ God, when You went forth before Your
people,
When You marched through the desert,
Selah

8 The earth quaked;
The heavens also dropped *rain* at the
presence of God;
Sinai itself *quaked* at the presence of God,
the God of Israel.

9 You made plentiful rain fall, God;
You confirmed Your inheritance when it
was parched.

10 Your creatures settled in it;
In Your kindness You provided for the
poor, God.

11¶ The Lord gives the command;
The women who proclaim good news are
a great army:

12 "Kings of armies flee, they flee,
And she who remains at home will divide
the spoils!"

13 When you lie down among the
sheepfolds,
You are like the wings of a dove covered
with silver,
And its pinions with glistening gold.

14 When the Almighty scattered the kings
there,
It was snowing in Zalmon.

15¶ The mountain of Bashan is a mountain of
God;
The mountain of Bashan is a mountain of
many peaks.

16 Why do you look with envy, you
mountains of many peaks,
At the mountain God has desired as His
dwelling?
Indeed, the LORD will dwell *there* forever.

17 The chariots of God are myriads,
    thousands upon thousands;
    The Lord is among them *as at* Sinai, in
    holiness.
18 You have ascended on high, You have led
    captive *Your* captives;
    You have received gifts among people,
    Even *among* the rebellious as well, that
    the LORD God may dwell *there.*
19¶ Blessed be the Lord, who daily bears our
    burden,
    The God *who* is our salvation.   *Selah*
20 God is to us a God of salvation;
    And to GOD the Lord belong ways of
    escape from death.
21 God certainly will shatter the heads of His
    enemies,
    The hairy head of one who goes about in
    his guilt.
22 The Lord said, "I will bring *them* back
    from Bashan.
    I will bring *them* back from the depths of
    the sea,
23 So that your foot may shatter *them* in
    blood,
    And the tongue of your dogs *may have* its
    portion from *your* enemies."
24¶ They have seen Your procession, God,
    The procession of my God, my King, into
    the sanctuary.
25 The singers went on, the musicians after
    them,
    In the midst of the young women beating
    tambourines.
26 Bless God in the congregations,
    Even the LORD, *you who are* of the
    fountain of Israel.
27 Benjamin, the youngest, is there, ruling
    them,
    The leaders of Judah *in* their company,
    The leaders of Zebulun, the leaders of
    Naphtali.
28¶ Your God has commanded your strength;
    Show Yourself strong, God, You who acted
    in our behalf.
29 Because of Your temple at Jerusalem
    Kings will bring gifts to You.
30 Rebuke the animals in the reeds,
    The herd of bulls with the calves of the
    peoples,
    Trampling the pieces of silver;
    He has scattered the peoples who delight
    in war.
31 [1]Messengers will come from Egypt;
    Cush will quickly stretch out her hands to
    God.
32¶ Sing to God, you kingdoms of the earth,
    Sing praises to the Lord,   *Selah*
33 To Him who rides upon the highest
    heavens, which are from ancient
    times;
    Behold, He speaks with His voice, a
    mighty voice.
34 Ascribe strength to God;
    His majesty is over Israel,
    And His strength is in the skies.
35 God, *You are* awesome from Your
    sanctuary.

The God of Israel Himself gives strength
    and power to the people.
Blessed be God!

PSALM 69

A Cry of Distress and a Curse on Adversaries.
For the music director; according to [†]Shoshannim.
A Psalm *of David.*

1 Save me, God,
    For the waters have threatened my life.
2 I have sunk in deep mud, and there is no
    foothold;
    I have come into deep waters, and a flood
    overflows me.
3 I am weary with my crying; my throat is
    parched;
    My eyes fail while I wait for my God.
4 Those who hate me without a cause are
    more than the hairs of my head;
    Those who would destroy me are
    powerful, those who oppose me with
    lies;
    What I did not steal, I then have to
    restore.
5¶ God, You know my foolishness,
    And my guilt is not hidden from You.
6 May those who wait for You not be
    ashamed because of me, Lord GOD of
    armies;
    May those who seek You not be dis-
    honored because of me, God of Israel,
7 Because for Your sake I have endured
    disgrace;
    Dishonor has covered my face.
8 I have become estranged from my
    brothers,
    And a stranger to my mother's sons.
9 For zeal for Your house has consumed
    me,
    And the taunts of those who taunt You
    have fallen on me.
10 When I wept in my soul with fasting,
    It became my disgrace.
11 When I made sackcloth my clothing,
    I became a proverb to them.
12 Those who sit in the gate talk about me,
    And songs of mockery by those habitually
    drunk *are about me.*
13¶ But as for me, my prayer is to You, LORD,
    at an acceptable time;
    God, in the greatness of Your mercy,
    Answer me with Your saving truth.
14 Rescue me from the mud and do not let
    me sink;
    May I be rescued from those who hate
    me, and from the depths of water.
15 May the flood of water not overflow me
    Nor the deep swallow me up,
    Nor the pit close its mouth on me.
16¶ Answer me, LORD, for Your mercy is good;
    According to the greatness of Your
    compassion, turn to me,
17 And do not hide Your face from Your
    servant,
    For I am in distress; answer me quickly.
18 Come near to my soul *and* redeem it;
    Ransom me because of my enemies!

68:31 [1]As in LXX; MT uncertain, possibly, Articles of *bronze;* or Articles of *red cloth*
69:1 [†]Or possibly Lilies

19 You know my disgrace, my shame, and my
   dishonor;
   All my enemies are ¹known to You.
20¶ Disgrace has broken my heart, and I am
   so sick.
   And I waited for sympathy, but there was
   none;
   And for comforters, but I found none.
21 They also gave me ¹a bitter herb in my
   food,
   And for my thirst they gave me vinegar to
   drink.
22¶ May their table before them become a
   snare;
   And when they are at peace, *may it
   become* a trap.
23 May their eyes grow dim so that they
   cannot see,
   And make their hips shake continually.
24 Pour out Your indignation on them,
   And may Your burning anger overtake
   them.
25 May their camp be desolated;
   May there be none living in their tents.
26 For they have persecuted him whom You
   Yourself struck,
   And they tell of the pain of those whom
   You have wounded.
27 Add guilt to their guilt,
   And may they not come into Your
   righteousness.
28 May they be wiped out of the book of life,
   And may they not be recorded with the
   righteous.
29¶ But I am afflicted and in pain;
   May Your salvation, God, set me *safely* on
   high.
30 I will praise the name of God with song,
   And exalt Him with thanksgiving.
31 And it will please the LORD better than an
   ox
   Or bull with horns and hoofs.
32 The humble have seen *it and* are glad;
   You who seek God, let your heart revive.
33 For the LORD hears the needy,
   And does not despise *those of* His *who are*
   prisoners.
34¶ Heaven and earth shall praise Him,
   The seas and everything that moves in
   them.
35 For God will save Zion and build the cities
   of Judah,
   So that they may live there and possess it.
36 The descendants of His servants will
   inherit it,
   And those who love His name will live
   in it.

PSALM 70

Prayer for Help against Persecutors.
For the music director. A Psalm *of David; for a
memorial.*
1 God, *hurry* to save me;
   LORD, hurry to help me!
2 May those who seek my life
   Be put to shame and humiliated;
   May those who delight in my harm
   Be turned back and dishonored.

3 May those who say, "Aha, aha!" be turned
   back
   Because of their shame.
4¶ May all who seek You rejoice and be glad
   in You;
   And may those who love Your salvation
   say continually,
   "May God be exalted!"
5 But I am afflicted and needy;
   Hurry to me, God!
   You are my help and my savior;
   LORD, do not delay.

PSALM 71

Prayer of an Old Man for Rescue.
1 In You, LORD, I have taken refuge;
   Let me never be put to shame.
2 In Your righteousness rescue me and save
   me;
   Extend Your ear to me and help me.
3 Be to me a rock of dwelling to which I
   may continually come;
   You have given the commandment to save
   me,
   For You are my rock and my fortress.
4 Save me, my God, from the hand of the
   wicked,
   From the grasp of the wrongdoer and the
   ruthless,
5 For You are my hope;
   Lord GOD, *You are* my confidence from
   my youth.
6 I have leaned on you since *my* birth;
   You are He who took me from my
   mother's womb;
   My praise is continually of You.
7¶ I have become a marvel to many,
   For You are my strong refuge.
8 My mouth is filled with Your praise
   And with Your glory all day long.
9 Do not cast me away at the time of *my* old
   age;
   Do not abandon me when my strength
   fails.
10 For my enemies have spoken against
   me;
   And those who watch for my life have
   consulted together,
11 Saying, "God has abandoned him;
   Pursue and seize him, for there is no one
   to save *him.*"
12¶ God, do not be far from me;
   My God, hurry to my aid!
13 May those who are enemies of my soul be
   put to shame *and* consumed;
   May they be covered with disgrace and
   dishonor, who seek to injure me.
14 But as for me, I will wait continually,
   And will praise You yet more and more.
15 My mouth shall tell of Your righteousness
   And of Your salvation all day long;
   For I do not know the art of writing.
16 I will come with the mighty deeds of the
   Lord GOD;
   I will make mention of Your righteousness, Yours alone.
17¶ God, You have taught me from my youth,
   And I still declare Your wondrous deeds.

---

18 And even when *I am* old and gray, God,
　do not abandon me,
Until I declare Your strength to *this*
　generation,
Your power to all who are to come.

19 For Your righteousness, God, *reaches* to
　the heavens,
You who have done great things;
God, who is like You?

20 You who have shown me many troubles
　and distresses
Will revive me again,
And will bring me up again from the
　depths of the earth.

21 May You increase my greatness
And turn *to* comfort me.

22¶ I will also praise You with a harp,
And Your truth, my God;
I will sing praises to You with the lyre,
Holy One of Israel.

23 My lips will shout for joy when I sing
　praises to You;
And my soul, which You have redeemed.

24 My tongue also will tell of Your righteous-
　ness all day long;
For they are put to shame, for they are
　humiliated who seek my harm.

PSALM 72

The Reign of the Righteous King.
A Psalm *of Solomon.*

1 Give the king Your judgments, God,
And Your righteousness to the king's
　son.

2 May he judge Your people with
　righteousness
And Your afflicted with justice.

3 May the mountains bring peace to the
　people,
And the hills, in righteousness.

4 May he vindicate the afflicted of the
　people,
Save the children of the needy,
And crush the oppressor.

5¶ May they fear You while the sun *shines,*
And as long as the moon *shines,*
　throughout all generations.

6 May he come down like rain upon the
　mown grass,
Like showers that water the earth.

7 May the righteous flourish in his days,
As well as an abundance of peace, until
　the moon is no more.

8¶ May he also rule from sea to sea,
And from the *Euphrates* River to the ends
　of the earth.

9 May the nomads of the desert bow before
　him,
And his enemies lick the dust.

10 May the kings of Tarshish and of the
　islands bring gifts;
May the kings of Sheba and Seba offer
　tributes.

11 And may all kings bow down before him,
All nations serve him.

12¶ For he will save the needy when he cries
　for help,
The afflicted also, and him who has no
　helper.

13 He will have compassion on the poor and
　needy,
And he will save the lives of the needy.

14 He will rescue their life from oppression
　and violence,
And their blood will be precious in his
　sight;

15 So may he live, and may the gold of Sheba
　be given to him;
And they are to pray for him continually;
They are to bless him all day long.

16¶ May there be abundance of grain on the
　earth on top of the mountains;
Its fruit will wave like *the cedars of*
　Lebanon;
And may those from the city flourish like
　the vegetation of the earth.

17 May his name endure forever;
May his name produce descendants as
　long as the sun *shines;*
And may *people* wish blessings on
　themselves by him;
May all nations call him blessed.

18¶ Blessed be the Lord God, the God of
　Israel,
Who alone works wonders.

19 And blessed be His glorious name
　forever;
And may the whole earth be filled with
　His glory.
Amen and Amen.

20¶ The prayers of David the son of Jesse are
　ended.

BOOK 3

PSALM 73

**The End of the Wicked Contrasted with That of
the Righteous.**
A Psalm *of Asaph.*

1 God certainly is good to Israel,
To those who are pure in heart!

2 But as for me, my feet came close to
　stumbling,
My steps had almost slipped.

3 For I was envious of the arrogant
As I saw the prosperity of the wicked.

4 For there are no pains in their death,
And their belly is fat.

5 They are not in trouble like other people,
Nor are they tormented together with *the
　rest of* mankind.

6 Therefore arrogance is their necklace;
The garment of violence covers them.

7 Their eye bulges from fatness;
The imaginations of *their* heart overflow.

8 They mock and wickedly speak of
　oppression;
They speak from on high.

9 They have set their mouth against the
　heavens,
And their tongue parades through the
　earth.

10¶ Therefore his people return here,
And abundant waters are drunk by them.

11 They say, "How does God know?
And is there knowledge with the Most
　High?"

12 Behold, these are the wicked;

And always at ease, they have increased
in wealth.

13 Surely in vain I have kept my heart pure
And washed my hands in innocence;

14 For I have been stricken all day long,
And punished every morning.

15¶ If I had said, "I will speak this way,"
Behold, I would have betrayed the
generation of Your children.

16 When I thought of understanding this,
It was troublesome in my sight

17 Until I entered the sanctuary of God;
Then I perceived their end.

18 You indeed put them on slippery
ground;
You dropped them into ruin.

19 How they are destroyed in a moment!
They are utterly swept away by sudden
terrors!

20 Like a dream when one awakes,
Lord, when stirred, You will despise their
image.

21¶ When my heart was embittered
And I was pierced within,

22 Then I was stupid and ignorant;
I was *like* an animal before You.

23 Nevertheless I am continually with
You;
You have taken hold of my right hand.

24 You will guide me with Your plan,
And afterward receive me to glory.

25¶ Whom do I have in heaven *but You?*
And with You, I desire nothing on earth.

26 My flesh and my heart *may* fail,
But God is the strength of my heart and
my portion forever.

27 For, behold, those who are far from You
will perish;
You have destroyed all those who are
unfaithful to You.

28 But as for me, the nearness of God is good
for me;
I have made the Lord God my refuge,
So that I may tell of all Your works.

PSALM 74

**An Appeal against the Devastation of the Land
by the Enemy.**
A Maskil of Asaph.

1 God, why have You rejected *us* forever?
Why does Your anger smoke against the
sheep of Your pasture?

2 Remember Your congregation, *which* You
purchased of old,
Which You have redeemed to be the tribe
of Your inheritance;
And this Mount Zion, where You have
dwelt.

3 Step toward the irreparable ruins;
The enemy has damaged everything in the
sanctuary.

4 Your adversaries have roared in the midst
of Your meeting place;
They have set up their own signs as
signs.

5 It seems like one bringing up
His axe into a forest of trees.

6 And now they break down all its carved
work

With axe and hammers.

7 They have burned Your sanctuary to the
ground;
They have defiled the dwelling place of
Your name.

8 They said in their heart, "Let's completely
subdue them."
They have burned all the meeting places
of God in the land.

9 We do not see our signs;
There is no longer any prophet,
Nor is there *anyone* among us who knows
how long.

10 How long, God, will the enemy taunt
You?
Shall the enemy treat Your name
disrespectfully forever?

11 Why do You withdraw Your hand, even
Your right hand?
Extend it from Your chest *and* destroy
them!

12¶ Yet God is my King from long ago,
Who performs acts of salvation in the
midst of the earth.

13 You divided the sea by Your strength;
You broke the heads of the sea monsters
in the waters.

14 You crushed the heads of Leviathan;
You gave him as food for the creatures of
the wilderness.

15 You broke open springs and torrents;
You dried up ever-flowing streams.

16 Yours is the day, Yours also is the night;
You have prepared the light and the
sun.

17 You have established all the boundaries of
the earth;
You have created summer and winter.

18¶ Remember this, Lord, that the enemy has
taunted *You,*
And a foolish people has treated Your
name disrespectfully.

19 Do not give the soul of Your turtledove to
the wild animal;
Do not forget the life of Your afflicted
forever.

20 Consider the covenant;
For the dark places of the land are full of
the places of violence.

21 May the oppressed person not return
dishonored;
May the afflicted and the needy praise
Your name.

22¶ Arise, God, *and* plead Your own cause;
Remember how the foolish person
taunts You all day long.

23 Do not forget the voice of Your
adversaries,
The uproar of those who rise against
You, which ascends continually.

PSALM 75

**God Humbles the Proud, but Exalts the
Righteous.**
For the music director; set to *Al-tashheth. A Psalm
of Asaph, a Song.*

1 We give thanks to You, God, we give
thanks,
For Your name is near;

People declare Your wondrous works.

2 "When I select an appointed time,
It is I who judge fairly.

3 "The earth and all who inhabit it are
unsteady;
It is I who have firmly set its pillars.
         Selah

4 "I said to the boastful, 'Do not boast,'
And to the wicked, 'Do not lift up the
horn;

5 Do not lift up your horn on high,
Do not speak with insolent pride.' "

6¶ For not from the east, nor from the
west,
Nor from the desert *comes* exaltation;

7 But God is the Judge;
He puts down one and exalts another.

8 For a cup is in the hand of the Lord, and
the wine foams;
It is well mixed, and He pours out of
this;
Certainly all the wicked of the earth must
drain *and* drink its dregs.

9¶ But as for me, I will declare *it* forever;
I will sing praises to the God of
Jacob.

10 And He will cut off all the horns of the
wicked,
But the horns of the righteous will be
lifted up.

PSALM 76

The Victorious Power of the God of Jacob.
For the music director; on stringed instruments.
A Psalm of Asaph, a Song.

1 God is known in Judah;
His name is great in Israel.

2 His tabernacle is in Salem;
His dwelling place also is in Zion.

3 There He broke the flaming arrows,
The shield, the sword, and the weapons of
war.   *Selah*

4¶ You are resplendent,
More majestic than the mountains of
prey.

5 .The stouthearted were plundered,
They sank into sleep;
And none of the warriors could use his
hands.

6 At Your rebuke, God of Jacob,
Both rider and horse were cast into a dead
sleep.

7 You, You *indeed* are to be feared,
And who may stand in Your presence,
once You are angry?

8¶ You caused judgment to be heard from
heaven;
The earth feared and was still

9 When God arose to judgment,
To save all the humble of the earth.
         Selah

10 For the wrath of mankind shall praise
You;
You will encircle Yourself with a remnant
of wrath.

11¶ Make vows to the Lord your God and
fulfill *them;*
All who are around Him are to bring gifts
to Him who is to be feared.

12 He will cut off the spirit of princes;
He is feared by the kings of the earth.

PSALM 77

**Comfort in Trouble from Recalling God's
Mighty Deeds.**
For the music director; according to Jeduthun.
A Psalm of Asaph.

1 My voice *rises* to God, and I will cry
aloud;
My voice *rises* to God, and He will listen
to me.

2 In the day of my trouble I sought the
Lord;
In the night my hand was stretched out
and did not grow weary;
My soul refused to be comforted.

3 *When* I remember God, then I am
restless;
When I sigh, then my spirit feels weak.
         Selah

4 You have held my eyelids *open;*
I am so troubled that I cannot speak.

5 I have considered the days of old,
The years of long ago.

6 I will remember my song in the night;
I will meditate with my heart,
And my spirit ponders:

7¶ Will the Lord reject forever?
And will He never be favorable again?

8 Has His favor ceased forever?
Has *His* promise come to an end
forever?

9 Has God forgotten to be gracious,
Or has He in anger withdrawn His
compassion?   *Selah*

10 Then I said, "It is my grief,
That the right hand of the Most High has
changed."

11¶ I shall remember the deeds of the
Lord;
I will certainly remember Your wonders of
old.

12 I will meditate on all Your work,
And on Your deeds with thanksgiving.

13 Your way, God, is holy;
What god is great like our God?

14 You are the God who works wonders;
You have made known Your strength
among the peoples.

15 By Your power You have redeemed Your
people,
The sons of Jacob and Joseph.   *Selah*

16¶ The waters saw You, God;
The waters saw You, they were in
anguish;
The ocean depths also trembled.

17 The clouds poured out water;
The skies sounded out;
Your arrows flashed here and there.

18 The sound of Your thunder was in the
whirlwind;
The lightning lit up the world;
The earth trembled and shook.

19 Your way was in the sea
And Your paths in the mighty waters,
And Your footprints were not known.

20 You led Your people like a flock
By the hand of Moses and Aaron.

PSALM 78

God's Guidance of His People in Spite of Their Unfaithfulness.

A Maskil of Asaph.

1 Listen, my people, to my instruction;
Incline your ears to the words of my mouth.
2 I will open my mouth in a parable;
I will tell riddles of old,
3 Which we have heard and known,
And our fathers have told us.
4 We will not conceal them from their children,
But we will tell the generation to come the praises of the LORD,
And His power and His wondrous works that He has done.
5¶ For He established a testimony in Jacob,
And appointed a law in Israel,
Which He commanded our fathers
That they were to teach them to their children,
6 So that the generation to come would know, the children yet to be born,
That they would arise and tell them to their children,
7 So that they would put their confidence in God
And not forget the works of God,
But comply with His commandments,
8 And not be like their fathers,
A stubborn and rebellious generation,
A generation that did not prepare its heart
And whose spirit was not faithful to God.
9¶ The sons of Ephraim were archers equipped with bows,
Yet they turned back on the day of battle.
10 They did not keep the covenant of God
And refused to walk in His Law;
11 They forgot His deeds
And His miracles that He had shown them.
12 He performed wonders before their fathers
In the land of Egypt, in the field of Zoan.
13 He divided the sea and caused them to pass through,
And He made the waters stand up like a heap.
14 Then He led them with the cloud by day
And all the night with a light of fire.
15 He split the rocks in the wilderness
And gave them plenty to drink like the ocean depths.
16 He brought forth streams from the rock
And made waters run down like rivers.
17¶ Yet they still continued to sin against Him,
To rebel against the Most High in the desert.
18 And in their heart they put God to the test
By asking for food that suited their taste.
19 Then they spoke against God;
They said, "Can God prepare a table in the wilderness?
20 "Behold, He struck the rock so that waters gushed out,
And streams were overflowing;
Can He also provide bread?

Will He prepare meat for His people?"
21¶ Therefore the LORD heard and was full of wrath;
And a fire was kindled against Jacob,
And anger also mounted against Israel,
22 Because they did not believe in God
And did not trust in His salvation.
23 Yet He commanded the clouds above
And opened the doors of heaven;
24 He rained down manna upon them to eat,
And gave them food from heaven.
25 Man ate the bread of angels;
He sent them food in abundance.
26 He made the east wind blow in the sky
And by His power He directed the south wind.
27 When He rained meat upon them like the dust,
Even winged fowl like the sand of the seas,
28 He let them fall in the midst of their camp,
All around their dwellings.
29 So they ate and were well filled,
And He satisfied their longing.
30 Yet before they had abandoned their longing,
While their food was in their mouths,
31 The anger of God rose against them
And killed some of their strongest ones,
And subdued the choice men of Israel.
32 In spite of all this they still sinned
And did not believe in His wonderful works.
33 So He brought their days to an end in futility,
And their years to an end in sudden terror.
34¶ When He killed them, then they sought Him,
And they returned and searched diligently for God;
35 And they remembered that God was their rock,
And the Most High God their Redeemer.
36 But they flattered Him with their mouth
And lied to Him with their tongue.
37 For their heart was not steadfast toward Him,
Nor were they faithful with His covenant.
38 But He, being compassionate, forgave their wrongdoing and did not destroy them;
And often He restrained His anger
And did not stir up all His wrath.
39 So He remembered that they were only flesh,
A wind that passes and does not return.
40¶ How often they rebelled against Him in the wilderness
And grieved Him in the desert!
41 Again and again they tempted God,
And pained the Holy One of Israel.
42 They did not remember His power,
The day when He redeemed them from the enemy,
43 When He performed His signs in Egypt
And His marvels in the field of Zoan,
44 And turned their rivers to blood,

And their streams, *so that* they could not
drink.
45 He sent swarms of flies among them that
devoured them,
And frogs that destroyed them.
46 He also gave their crops to the
grasshopper
And the product of their labor to the
locust.
47 He destroyed their vines with hailstones
And their sycamore trees with frost.
48 He also turned their cattle over to the
hailstones,
And their herds to bolts of lightning.
49 He sent His burning anger upon them,
Fury and indignation and trouble,
A band of destroying angels.
50 He leveled a path for His anger;
He did not spare their souls from death,
But turned their lives over to the plague,
51 And struck all the firstborn in Egypt,
The first and best of their vigor in the
tents of Ham.
52 But He led His own people out like sheep,
And guided them in the wilderness like a
flock;
53 He led them safely, so that they did not
fear;
But the sea engulfed their enemies.
54¶ So He brought them to His holy land,
To this hill country which His right hand
had gained.
55 He also drove out the nations from them
And apportioned them as an inheritance
by measurement,
And had the tribes of Israel dwell in their
tents.
56 Yet they tempted and rebelled against the
Most High God
And did not keep His testimonies,
57 But turned back and acted treacherously
like their fathers;
They turned aside like a treacherous bow.
58 For they provoked Him with their high
places
And moved Him to jealousy with their
carved images.
59 When God heard *them,* He was filled with
wrath
And He utterly rejected Israel;
60 So that He abandoned the dwelling place
at Shiloh,
The tent which He had pitched among
people,
61 And He gave up His strength to captivity
And His glory into the hand of the enemy.
62 He also turned His people over to the
sword,
And was filled with wrath at His inheritance.
63 Fire devoured His young men,
And His virgins had no wedding songs.
64 His priests fell by the sword,
And His widows could not weep.
65¶ Then the Lord awoke as *if from* sleep,
Like a warrior overcome by wine.
66 He drove His adversaries backward;
He put on them an everlasting disgrace.
67 He also rejected the tent of Joseph,
And did not choose the tribe of Ephraim,

68 But chose the tribe of Judah,
Mount Zion, which He loved.
69 And He built His sanctuary like the
heights,
Like the earth which He has established
forever.
70 He also chose His servant David
And took him from the sheepfolds;
71 From the care of the ewes with nursing
lambs He brought him
To shepherd Jacob His people,
And Israel His inheritance.
72 So he shepherded them according to the
integrity of his heart,
And guided them with his skillful hands.

PSALM 79

*Grieving over the Destruction of Jerusalem, and
Prayer for Help.*
A Psalm of Asaph.
1 God, the nations have invaded Your
inheritance;
They have defiled Your holy temple;
They have laid Jerusalem in ruins.
2 They have given the dead bodies of Your
servants to the birds of the sky as food,
The flesh of Your godly ones to the
animals of the earth.
3 They have poured out their blood like
water all around Jerusalem;
And there was no one to bury them.
4 We have become a disgrace before our
neighbors,
An *object of* derision and ridicule to those
around us.
5 How long, LORD? Will You be angry
forever?
Will Your jealousy burn like fire?
6 Pour out Your wrath upon the nations
which do not know You,
And upon the kingdoms which do not call
upon Your name.
7 For they have devoured Jacob
And laid waste his settlement.
8¶ Do not hold us responsible for the guilty
deeds of *our* forefathers;
Let Your compassion come quickly to
meet us,
For we have become very low.
9 Help us, God of our salvation, for the
glory of Your name;
And save us and forgive our sins for the
sake of Your name.
10 Why should the nations say, "Where is
their God?"
Let vengeance for the blood of Your
servants which has been shed
Be known among the nations in our sight.
11 Let the groaning of the prisoner come
before You;
According to the greatness of Your power,
let those who are doomed to die
remain.
12 And return to our neighbors seven times
as much into their lap
Their taunts with which they have
taunted You, Lord.
13 So we Your people and the sheep of Your
pasture

Will give thanks to You forever;
To all generations we will tell of Your
    praise.

PSALM 80

**God Implored to Rescue His People from Their
Calamities.**
*For the music director; set to El Shoshannim; Eduth.
A Psalm of Asaph.*
1   Listen, Shepherd of Israel,
    Who leads Joseph like a flock;
    You who are enthroned *above* the
        cherubim, shine forth!
2   Before Ephraim, Benjamin, and Manasseh,
        awaken Your power,
    And come to save us!
3   God, restore us
    And make Your face shine *upon us,* and
        we will be saved.
4¶ LORD God of armies,
    How long will You be angry with the
        prayer of Your people?
5   You have fed them with the bread of
        tears,
    And You have made them drink tears in
        large measure.
6   You make us an object of contention to
        our neighbors,
    And our enemies laugh among
        themselves.
7   God of armies, restore us
    And make Your face shine *upon us,* and
        we will be saved.
8¶ You removed a vine from Egypt;
    You drove out the nations and planted
        it.
9   You cleared *the ground* before it,
    And it took deep root and filled the land.
10 The mountains were covered with its
        shadow,
    And the cedars of God with its branches.
11 It was sending out its branches to the
        sea
    And its shoots to the *Euphrates* River.
12 Why have You broken down its hedges,
    So that all who pass *that* way pick its
        fruit?
13 A boar from the forest eats it away,
    And whatever moves in the field feeds on
        it.
14¶ God of armies, do turn back;
    Look down from heaven and see, and take
        care of this vine,
15 The shoot which Your right hand has
        planted,
    And of the son whom You have
        strengthened for Yourself.
16 It is burned with fire, it is cut down;
    They perish from the rebuke of Your face.
17 Let Your hand be upon the man of Your
        right hand,
    Upon the son of man whom You made
        strong for Yourself.
18 Then we will not turn back from You;
    Revive us, and we will call upon Your
        name.
19 LORD God of armies, restore us;
    Make Your face shine *upon us,* and we
        will be saved.

PSALM 81

God's Goodness and Israel's Waywardness.
*For the music director; on the Gittith. A Psalm
of Asaph.*
1   Sing for joy to God our strength;
    Shout joyfully to the God of Jacob.
2   Raise a song, strike the tambourine,
    The sweet sounding lyre with the harp.
3   Blow the trumpet at the new moon,
    At the full moon, on our feast day.
4   For it is a statute for Israel,
    An ordinance of the God of Jacob.
5   He established it as a testimony in Joseph
    When he went throughout the land of
        Egypt.
    I heard a language I did not know:
6¶ "I relieved his shoulder of the burden,
    His hands were freed from the basket.
7   "You called in trouble and I rescued you;
    I answered you in the hiding place of
        thunder;
    I put you to the test at the waters of
        Meribah.   *Selah*
8   "Hear, My people, and I will admonish you;
    Israel, if you would listen to Me!
9   "There shall be no strange god among
        you;
    Nor shall you worship a foreign god.
10 "I, the LORD, am your God,
    Who brought you up from the land of
        Egypt;
    Open your mouth wide and I will fill it.
11¶ "But My people did not listen to My voice,
    And Israel did not obey Me.
12 "So I gave them over to the stubbornness of
        their heart,
    To walk by their own plans.
13 "Oh that My people would listen to Me,
    That Israel would walk in My ways!
14 "I would quickly subdue their enemies
    And turn My hand against their
        adversaries.
15 "Those who hate the LORD would pretend
        to obey Him,
    And their time *of punishment* would be
        forever.
16 "But I would feed you with the finest of the
        wheat,
    And with honey from the rock I would
        satisfy you."

PSALM 82

Unjust Judgments Rebuked.
A Psalm of Asaph.
1   God takes His position in His assembly;
    He judges in the midst of the gods.
2   How long will you judge unjustly
    And show partiality to the wicked?
                                        Selah
3   Vindicate the weak and fatherless;
    Do justice to the afflicted and destitute.
4   Rescue the weak and needy;
    Save *them* from the hand of the wicked.
5¶ They do not know nor do they
        understand;
    They walk around in darkness;
    All the foundations of the earth are
        shaken.

6   I said, "You are gods,
And all of you are sons of the Most High.
7   "Nevertheless you will die like men,
And fall like one of the princes."
8   Arise, God, judge the earth!
For You possess all the nations.

PSALM 83

God Implored to Confound His Enemies.
A Song, a Psalm of Asaph.
1   God, do not remain quiet;
Do not be silent and, God, do not be
still.
2   For behold, Your enemies make an uproar,
And those who hate You have exalted
themselves.
3   They make shrewd plans against Your
people,
And conspire together against Your
treasured ones.
4   They have said, "Come, and let's wipe
them out as a nation,
So that the name of Israel will no longer
be remembered."
5   For they have conspired together with
one mind;
They make a covenant against You:
6   The tents of Edom and the Ishmaelites,
Moab and the Hagrites;
7   Gebal, Ammon, and Amalek,
Philistia with the inhabitants of Tyre;
8   Assyria also has joined them;
They have become a help to the children
of Lot.   *Selah*
9¶   Deal with them as with Midian,
As with Sisera *and* Jabin at the river of
Kishon,
10   Who were destroyed at En-dor,
Who became *like* dung for the ground.
11   Make their nobles like Oreb and Zeeb,
And all their leaders like Zebah and
Zalmunna,
12   Who said, "Let's possess for ourselves
The pastures of God."
13¶   My God, make them like the whirling
dust,
Like chaff before the wind.
14   Like fire that burns the forest,
And like a flame that sets the mountains
on fire,
15   So pursue them with Your heavy gale,
And terrify them with Your storm.
16   Fill their faces with dishonor,
So that they will seek Your name, Lord.
17   May they be ashamed and dismayed
forever,
And may they be humiliated and perish,
18   So that they will know that You alone,
whose name is the Lord,
Are the Most High over all the earth.

PSALM 84

Longing for the Temple Worship.
*For the music director; on the Gittith. A Psalm of the
sons of Korah.*
1   How lovely are Your dwelling places,
Lord of armies!

2   My soul longed and even yearned for the
courtyards of the Lord;
My heart and my flesh sing for joy to the
living God.
3   The bird also has found a house,
And the swallow a nest for herself, where
she may put her young:
Your altars, Lord of armies,
My King and my God.
4   Blessed are those who dwell in Your
house!
They are ever praising You.   *Selah*
5¶   Blessed is the person whose strength is in
You,
In whose heart are the roads *to Zion!*
6   Passing through the Valley of *¹Baca they
make it a spring;
The early rain also covers it with
blessings.
7   They go from strength to strength,
Every one of them appears before God in
Zion.
8¶   Lord God of armies, hear my prayer;
Listen, God of Jacob!   *Selah*
9   See our shield, God,
And look at the face of Your anointed.
10   For a day in Your courtyards is better than
a thousand *elsewhere.*
I would rather stand at the threshold of
the house of my God
Than live in the tents of wickedness.
11   For the Lord God is a sun and shield;
The Lord gives grace and glory;
He withholds no good thing from those
who walk with integrity.
12   Lord of armies,
Blessed is the person who trusts in You!

PSALM 85

Prayer for God's Mercy upon the Nation.
For the music director. A Psalm of the sons of Korah.
1   Lord, You showed favor to Your land;
You restored the fortunes of Jacob.
2   You forgave the guilt of Your people;
You covered all their sin.   *Selah*
3   You withdrew all Your fury;
You turned away from Your burning
anger.
4¶   Restore us, God of our salvation,
And cause Your indignation toward us to
cease.
5   Will You be angry with us forever?
Will You prolong Your anger to all
generations?
6   Will You not revive us again,
So that Your people may rejoice in You?
7   Show us Your mercy, Lord,
And grant us Your salvation.
8¶   I will hear what God the Lord will say;
For He will speak peace to His people, to
His godly ones;
And may they not turn back to
foolishness.
9   Certainly His salvation is near to those
who fear Him,
That glory may dwell in our land.
10   Graciousness and truth have met
together;

84:6 ¹Prob. *Weeping;* or *Balsam-shrubs*

Righteousness and peace have kissed each
other.
11 Truth sprouts from the earth,
And righteousness looks down from
heaven.
12 Indeed, the LORD will give what is good,
And our land will yield its produce.
13 Righteousness will go before Him
And will make His footsteps into a way.

PSALM 86

Pleading and Trust.
A Prayer of David.
1 Incline Your ear, LORD, *and* answer me;
For I am afflicted and needy.
2 Protect my soul, for I am godly;
You my God, save Your servant who trusts
in You.
3 Be gracious to me, Lord,
For I call upon You all day long.
4 Make the soul of Your servant joyful,
For to You, Lord, I lift up my soul.
5 For You, Lord, are good, and ready to
forgive,
And abundant in mercy to all who call
upon You.
6 Listen, LORD, to my prayer;
And give *Your* attention to the sound of
my pleading!
7 On the day of my trouble I will call upon
You,
For You will answer me.
8 There is no one like You among the gods,
Lord,
Nor are there any works like Yours.
9 All nations whom You have made will
come and worship before You, Lord,
And they will glorify Your name.
10 For You are great, and you do wondrous
deeds;
You alone are God.
11¶ Teach me Your way, LORD;
I will walk in Your truth;
Unite my heart to fear Your name.
12 I will give thanks to You, Lord my God,
with all my heart,
And I will glorify Your name forever.
13 For Your graciousness toward me is great,
And You have saved my soul from the
depths of ¹Sheol.
14¶ God, arrogant men have risen up against
me,
And a gang of violent men have sought
my life,
And they have not set You before them.
15 But You, Lord, are a compassionate and
gracious God,
Slow to anger and abundant in mercy and
truth.
16 Turn to me, and be gracious to me;
Grant Your strength to Your servant,
And save the son of Your maidservant.
17 Show me a sign of good,
That those who hate me may see *it* and be
ashamed,
Because You, LORD, have helped me and
comforted me.

PSALM 87

The Privileges of Citizenship in Zion.
A Psalm of the sons of Korah. A Song.
1 His foundation is in the holy mountains.
2 The LORD loves the gates of Zion
More than all the *other* dwelling places of
Jacob.
3 Glorious things are spoken of you,
City of God.   *Selah*
4 "I shall mention ¹Rahab and Babylon
among those who know Me;
Behold, Philistia and Tyre with Cush:
'This one was born there.'"
5 But of Zion it will be said, "This one and
that one were born in her";
And the Most High Himself will establish
her.
6 The LORD will count when He registers
the peoples,
"This one was born there."   *Selah*
7 Then those who sing as *well as* those who
play the flutes *will say,*
"All my springs *of joy* are in you."

PSALM 88

A Petition to Be Saved from Death.
*A Song. A Psalm of the sons of Korah. For the music
director; according to Mahalath Leannoth. A Maskil
of Heman the Ezrahite.*
1 LORD, the God of my salvation,
I have cried out by day and in the night
before You.
2 Let my prayer come before You;
Incline Your ear to my cry!
3 For my soul has had enough troubles,
And my life has approached ¹Sheol.
4 I am counted among those who go down
to the pit;
I have become like a man without
strength,
5 Abandoned among the dead,
Like the slain who lie in the grave,
Whom You no longer remember,
And they are cut off from Your hand.
6 You have put me in the lowest pit,
In dark places, in the depths.
7 Your wrath has rested upon me,
And You have afflicted me with all Your
waves.   *Selah*
8 You have removed my acquaintances far
from me;
You have made me an object of loathing to
them;
I am shut up and cannot go out.
9 My eye grows dim from misery;
I have called upon You every day, LORD;
I have spread out my hands to You.
10¶ Will You perform wonders for the
dead?
Or will the departed spirits rise *and* praise
You?   *Selah*
11 Will Your graciousness be declared in the
grave,
Your faithfulness in ¹Abaddon?
12 Will Your wonders be made known in the
darkness?

86:13 ¹I.e., the netherworld   **87:4** ¹I.e., Egypt, as a sea monster; not to be confused with Rahab
in Joshua 2   **88:3** ¹I.e., the netherworld   **88:11** ¹I.e., place of destruction

And Your righteousness in the land of
forgetfulness?
13¶ But I, Lord, have cried out to You for
help,
And in the morning my prayer comes
before You.
14 Lord, why do You reject my soul?
Why do You hide Your face from me?
15 I was miserable and about to die from my
youth on;
I suffer Your terrors; I grow weary.
16 Your burning anger has passed over
me;
Your terrors have destroyed me.
17 They have surrounded me like water all
day long;
They have encircled me altogether.
18 You have removed lover and friend far
from me;
My acquaintances are *in* a hiding place.

PSALM 89

**The Lord's Covenant with David and
Israel's Afflictions.**
A Maskil of Ethan the Ezrahite.
1 I will sing of the graciousness of the Lord
forever;
To all generations I will make Your
faithfulness known with my mouth.
2 For I have said, "Graciousness will be
built up forever;
In the heavens You will establish Your
faithfulness."
3 "I have made a covenant with My chosen;
I have sworn to My servant David,
4 I will establish your descendants forever
And build up your throne to all
generations." *Selah*
5¶ The heavens will praise Your wonders,
Lord;
Your faithfulness also in the assembly of
the holy ones.
6 For who in the skies is comparable to the
Lord?
Who among the sons of the mighty is like
the Lord,
7 A God greatly feared in the council of the
holy ones,
And awesome above all those who are
around Him?
8 Lord God of armies, who is like You,
mighty Lord?
Your faithfulness also surrounds You.
9 You rule the surging of the sea;
When its waves rise, You calm them.
10 You Yourself crushed ¹Rahab like one who
is slain;
You scattered Your enemies with Your
mighty arm.
11¶ The heavens are Yours, the earth also is
Yours;
The world and all it contains, You have
established them.
12 The north and the south, You have
created them;
Tabor and Hermon shout for joy at Your
name.
13 You have a strong arm;

Your hand is mighty, Your right hand is
exalted.
14 Righteousness and justice are the
foundation of Your throne;
Mercy and truth go before You.
15 Blessed are the people who know the
joyful sound!
Lord, they walk in the light of Your
face.
16 In Your name they rejoice all the day,
And by Your righteousness they are
exalted.
17 For You are the glory of their strength,
And by Your favor our horn is exalted.
18 For our shield belongs to the Lord,
And our king to the Holy One of Israel.
19¶ Once You spoke in vision to Your godly
ones,
And said, "I have given help to one who
is mighty;
I have exalted one chosen from the
people.
20 "I have found My servant David;
With My holy oil I have anointed him,
21 With whom My hand will be established;
My arm also will strengthen him.
22 "The enemy will not deceive him,
Nor will the son of wickedness afflict
him.
23 "But I will crush his adversaries before
him,
And strike those who hate him.
24 "My faithfulness and My favor *will be* with
him,
And in My name his horn will be exalted.
25 "I will also place his hand on the sea,
And his right hand on the rivers.
26 "He will call to Me, 'You are my Father,
My God, and the rock of my salvation.'
27 "I will also make him *My* firstborn,
The highest of the kings of the earth.
28 "I will maintain My favor for him forever,
And My covenant shall be confirmed to
him.
29 "So I will establish his descendants forever,
And his throne as the days of heaven.
30¶ "If his sons abandon My Law
And do not walk in My judgments,
31 If they violate My statutes
And do not keep My commandments,
32 Then I will punish their wrongdoing with
the rod,
And their guilt with afflictions.
33 "But I will not withhold My favor from
him,
Nor deal falsely in My faithfulness.
34 "I will not violate My covenant,
Nor will I alter the utterance of My lips.
35 "¹Once I have sworn by My holiness;
I will not lie to David.
36 "His descendants shall endure forever,
And his throne as the sun before Me.
37 "It shall be established forever like the
moon,
And a witness in the sky is faithful." *Selah*
38¶ But You have rejected and refused,
You have been full of wrath against Your
anointed.

39 You have ⸤repudiated the covenant of Your
servant;
You have profaned his crown in the dust.
40 You have broken down all his walls;
You have brought his strongholds to ruin.
41 All who pass along the way plunder him;
He has become a disgrace to his
neighbors.
42 You have exalted the right hand of his
adversaries;
You have made all his enemies rejoice.
43 You also turn back the edge of his sword,
And have not made him stand in battle.
44 You have put an end to his splendor
And cast his throne to the ground.
45 You have shortened the days of his youth;
You have covered him with shame.
Selah

46¶ How long, LORD?
Will You hide Yourself forever?
Will Your wrath burn like fire?
47 Remember what my lifespan is;
For what futility You have created all the
sons of mankind!
48 What man can live and not see death?
Can he save his soul from the power of
⸤Sheol?   *Selah*
49¶ Where are Your former acts of favor,
Lord,
Which You swore to David in Your
faithfulness?
50 Remember, Lord, the taunt against Your
servants;
How I carry in my heart *the taunts of* all
the many peoples,
51 With which Your enemies have taunted,
LORD,
With which they have taunted the
footsteps of Your anointed.
52¶ Blessed be the LORD forever!
Amen and Amen.

BOOK 4

PSALM 90

God's Eternity and the Brevity of Human Life.
A Prayer of Moses, the man of God.
1 Lord, You have been our dwelling place in
all generations.
2 Before the mountains were born
Or You gave birth to the earth and the
world,
Even from everlasting to everlasting, You
are God.
3¶ You turn mortals back into dust
And say, "Return, you sons of mankind."
4 For a thousand years in Your sight
Are like yesterday when it passes by,
Or *like* a watch in the night.
5 You have swept them away like a flood,
they fall asleep;
In the morning they are like grass that
sprouts anew.
6 In the morning it flourishes and sprouts
anew;
Toward evening it wilts and withers away.
7¶ For we have been consumed by Your
anger,

And we have been terrified by Your
wrath.
8 You have placed our guilty deeds before
You,
Our hidden *sins* in the light of Your
presence.
9 For all our days have dwindled away in
Your fury;
We have finished our years like a sigh.
10 As for the days of our life, they contain
seventy years,
Or if due to strength, eighty years,
Yet their pride is *only* trouble and tragedy;
For it quickly passes, and we disappear.
11 Who understands the power of Your
anger
And Your fury, according to the fear that is
due You?
12 So teach *us* to number our days,
That we may present *to You* a heart of
wisdom.
13¶ Do return, LORD; how long *will it be?*
And be sorry for Your servants.
14 Satisfy us in the morning with Your
graciousness,
That we may sing for joy and rejoice all
our days.
15 Make us glad according to the days You
have afflicted us,
And the years we have seen evil.
16 Let Your work appear to Your servants
And Your majesty to their children.
17 May the kindness of the Lord our God be
upon us;
And confirm for us the work of our hands;
Yes, confirm the work of our hands.

PSALM 91

Security of One Who Trusts in the LORD.
1 One who dwells in the shelter of the Most
High
Will lodge in the shadow of the Almighty.
2 I will say to the LORD, "My refuge and my
fortress,
My God, in whom I trust!"
3 For it is He who rescues you from the net
of the trapper
And from the deadly plague.
4 He will cover you with His pinions,
And under His wings you may take
refuge;
His faithfulness is a shield and wall.
5¶ You will not be afraid of the terror by
night,
Or of the arrow that flies by day;
6 Of the plague that stalks in darkness,
Or of the destruction that devastates at
noon.
7 A thousand may fall at your side
And ten thousand at your right hand,
But it shall not approach you.
8 You will only look on with your eyes
And see the retaliation *against* the
wicked.
9 For you have made the LORD, my refuge,
The Most High, your dwelling place.
10 No evil will happen to you,
Nor will any plague come near your tent.

89:39 ⸤I.e., scornfully rejected   89:48 ⸤I.e., the netherworld

11¶ For He will give His angels orders
concerning you,
To protect you in all your ways.
12 On their hands they will lift you up,
So that you do not strike your foot against
a stone.
13 You will walk upon the lion and cobra,
You will trample the young lion and the
serpent.
14¶ "Because he has loved Me, I will save him;
I will set him *securely* on high, because
he has known My name.
15 "He will call upon Me, and I will answer
him;
I will be with him in trouble;
I will rescue him and honor him.
16 "I will satisfy him with a long life,
And show him My salvation."

PSALM 92

Praise for the LORD's Goodness.
A Psalm, a Song for the Sabbath day.
1 It is good to give thanks to the LORD
And to sing praises to Your name, Most
High;
2 To declare Your goodness in the morning
And Your faithfulness by night,
3 With the ten-stringed lute and with the
harp,
With resounding music on the lyre.
4 For You, LORD, have made me joyful by
what You have done,
I will sing for joy over the works of Your
hands.
5¶ How great are Your works, LORD!
Your thoughts are very deep.
6 A stupid person has no knowledge,
Nor does a foolish person understand this:
7 When the wicked sprouted up like grass
And all who did injustice flourished,
It *was only* that they might be destroyed
forevermore.
8 But You, LORD, are on high forever.
9 For, behold, Your enemies, LORD,
For, behold, Your enemies will perish;
All who do injustice will be scattered.
10¶ But You have exalted my horn like *that of*
the wild ox;
I have been anointed with fresh oil.
11 And my eye has looked at my enemies,
My ears hear of the evildoers who rise up
against me.
12 The righteous person will flourish like the
palm tree,
He will grow like a cedar in Lebanon.
13 Planted in the house of the LORD,
They will flourish in the courtyards of our
God.
14 They will still yield fruit in advanced age;
They will be full of sap and very green,
15 To declare that the LORD is just;
He is my rock, and there is no malice in
Him.

PSALM 93

The Majesty of the LORD.
1 The LORD reigns, He is clothed with
majesty;

The LORD has clothed and encircled
Himself with strength.
Indeed, the world is *firmly* established; it
will not be moved.
2 Your throne is established from of old;
You are from eternity.
3¶ The floods have lifted up, LORD,
The floods have lifted up their voice,
The floods lift up their pounding waves.
4 More than the sounds of many waters,
Than the mighty breakers of the sea,
The LORD on high is mighty.
5 Your testimonies are fully confirmed;
Holiness is pleasing to Your house,
LORD, forevermore.

PSALM 94

The LORD Implored to Avenge His People.
1 LORD, God of vengeance,
God of vengeance, shine forth!
2 Rise up, Judge of the earth,
Pay back retribution to the proud.
3 How long, LORD, shall the wicked—
How long shall the wicked triumph?
4 They pour out *words,* they speak
arrogantly;
All who do injustice boast.
5 They crush Your people, LORD,
And afflict Your inheritance.
6 They kill the widow and the stranger
And murder the orphans.
7 They have said, "The LORD does not see,
Nor does the God of Jacob perceive."
8¶ Pay attention, you stupid ones among the
people;
And when will you understand, foolish
ones?
9 He who planted the ear, does He not
hear?
Or He who formed the eye, does He not
see?
10 He who disciplines the nations, will He
not rebuke,
He who teaches mankind knowledge?
11 The LORD knows human thoughts,
That they are *mere* breath.
12¶ Blessed is the man whom You discipline,
LORD,
And whom You teach from Your Law,
13 So that You may grant him relief from the
days of adversity,
Until a pit is dug for the wicked.
14 For the LORD will not abandon His people,
Nor will He abandon His inheritance.
15 For judgment will again be righteous,
And all the upright in heart will follow
it.
16 Who will stand up for me against
evildoers?
Who will take his stand for me against
those who do injustice?
17¶ If the LORD had not been my help,
My soul would soon have dwelt *in the
land of* silence.
18 If I should say, "My foot has slipped,"
Your faithfulness, LORD, will support me.
19 When my anxious thoughts multiply
within me,
Your comfort delights my soul.

20 Can a throne of destruction be allied with
You,
One which devises mischief by decree?
21 They band themselves together against
the life of the righteous
And condemn the innocent to death.
22 But the LORD has been my refuge,
And my God the rock of my refuge.
23 He has brought back their injustice upon
them,
And He will destroy them in their evil;
The LORD our God will destroy them.

PSALM 95

*Praise to the LORD and Warning against
Unbelief.*
1 Come, let's sing for joy to the LORD,
Let's shout joyfully to the rock of our
salvation.
2 Let's come before His presence with a
song of thanksgiving,
Let's shout joyfully to Him in songs *with
instruments.*
3 For the LORD is a great God
And a great King above all gods,
4 In whose hand are the depths of the
earth,
The peaks of the mountains are also His.
5 The sea is His, for it was He who made
it,
And His hands formed the dry land.
6¶ Come, let's worship and bow down,
Let's kneel before the LORD our Maker.
7 For He is our God,
And we are the people of His pasture and
the sheep of His hand.
Today, if you will hear His voice,
8 Do not harden your hearts as at Meribah,
As on the day of Massah in the
wilderness,
9 "When your fathers put Me to the test,
They tested Me, though they had seen My
work.
10 "For forty years I was disgusted with *that*
generation,
And said they are a people who err in
their heart,
And they do not know My ways.
11 "Therefore I swore in My anger,
They certainly shall not enter My rest."

PSALM 96

A Call to Worship the LORD the Righteous Judge.
1 Sing to the LORD a new song;
Sing to the LORD, all the earth.
2 Sing to the LORD, bless His name;
Proclaim the good news of His salvation
from day to day.
3 Tell of His glory among the nations,
His wonderful deeds among all the
peoples.
4 For great is the LORD, and greatly to be
praised;
He is to be feared above all gods.
5 For all the gods of the peoples are idols,
But the LORD made the heavens.
6 Splendor and majesty are before Him,
Strength and beauty are in His sanctuary.

7¶ Ascribe to the LORD, you families of the
peoples,
Ascribe to the LORD glory and strength.
8 Ascribe to the LORD the glory of His name;
Bring an offering and come into His
courtyards.
9 Worship the LORD in holy attire;
Tremble before Him, all the earth.
10 Say among the nations, "The LORD reigns;
Indeed, the world is *firmly* established, it
will not be moved;
He will judge the peoples fairly."
11¶ May the heavens be joyful, and may the
earth rejoice;
May the sea roar, and all it contains;
12 May the field be jubilant, and all that is in
it.
Then all the trees of the forest will sing
for joy
13 Before the LORD, for He is coming,
For He is coming to judge the earth.
He will judge the world in righteousness,
And the peoples in His faithfulness.

PSALM 97

The LORD's Power and Dominion.
1 The LORD reigns, may the earth rejoice;
May the many islands be joyful.
2 Clouds and thick darkness surround Him;
Righteousness and justice are the
foundation of His throne.
3 Fire goes before Him
And burns up His enemies all around.
4 His lightning lit up the world;
The earth saw *it* and trembled.
5 The mountains melted like wax at the
presence of the LORD,
At the presence of the Lord of the whole
earth.
6 The heavens declare His righteousness,
And all the peoples have seen His glory.
7¶ May all those be ashamed who serve
carved images,
Who boast in idols;
Worship Him, all you gods.
8 Zion heard *this* and was joyful,
And the daughters of Judah have rejoiced
Because of Your judgments, LORD.
9 For You are the LORD Most High over all
the earth;
You are exalted far above all gods.
10¶ Hate evil, you who love the LORD,
Who watches over the souls of His godly
ones;
He saves them from the hand of the
wicked.
11 Light is sown *like seed* for the righteous,
And gladness for the upright in heart.
12 Be joyful in the LORD, you righteous ones,
And praise the mention of His holy name.

PSALM 98

A Call to Praise the LORD for His Righteousness.
A Psalm.
1 Sing a new song to the LORD,
For He has done wonderful things,
His right hand and His holy arm have
gained the victory for Him.

2 The LORD has made His salvation known;
He has revealed His righteousness in the
sight of the nations.
3 He has remembered His graciousness and
His faithfulness to the house of Israel;
All the ends of the earth have seen the
salvation of our God.
4¶ Shout joyfully to the LORD, all the earth;
Be cheerful and sing for joy and sing
praises.
5 Sing praises to the LORD with the lyre,
With the lyre and the sound of melody.
6 With trumpets and the sound of the horn
Shout joyfully before the King, the LORD.
7¶ May the sea roar and all it contains,
The world and those who dwell in it.
8 May the rivers clap their hands,
May the mountains sing together for joy
9 Before the LORD, for He is coming to
judge the earth;
He will judge the world with
righteousness
And the peoples with fairness.

PSALM 99

Praise to the LORD for His Faithfulness to Israel.
1 The LORD reigns, the peoples tremble!
He sits *enthroned above* the cherubim,
the earth quakes!
2 The LORD is great in Zion,
And He is exalted above all the peoples.
3 May they praise Your great and awesome
name;
Holy is He.
4 The strength of the King loves justice;
You have established order;
You have executed justice and
righteousness in Jacob.
5 Exalt the LORD our God
And worship at His footstool;
Holy is He.
6¶ Moses and Aaron were among His priests,
And Samuel was among those who called
on His name;
They called upon the LORD and He
answered them.
7 He spoke to them in the pillar of cloud;
They kept His testimonies
And the statute that He gave them.
8 LORD our God, You answered them;
You were a forgiving God to them,
And *yet* an avenger of their *evil* deeds.
9 Exalt the LORD our God
And worship at His holy hill,
For the LORD our God is holy.

PSALM 100

All People Exhorted to Praise God.
A Psalm for Thanksgiving.
1 Shout joyfully to the LORD, all the earth.
2 Serve the LORD with jubilation;
Come before Him with rejoicing.
3 Know that the LORD Himself is God;
It is He who has made us, and ¹not we
ourselves;
We are His people and the sheep of His
pasture.

4¶ Enter His gates with thanksgiving,
And His courtyards with praise.
Give thanks to Him, bless His name.
5 For the LORD is good;
His mercy is everlasting
And His faithfulness is to all generations.

PSALM 101

The Psalmist's Profession of Uprightness.
A Psalm of David.
1 I will sing of mercy and justice;
To You, LORD, I will sing praises.
2 I will carefully attend to the blameless
way.
When will You come to me?
I will walk within my house in the
integrity of my heart.
3 I will set no worthless thing before my
eyes;
I hate the work of those who fall away;
It shall not cling to me.
4 A perverse heart shall leave me;
I will know no evil.
5 Whoever secretly slanders his neighbor,
him I will destroy;
I will not endure one who has a haughty
look and an arrogant heart.
6¶ My eyes shall be upon the faithful of the
land, that they may dwell with me;
One who walks in a blameless way is one
who will serve me.
7 One who practices deceit shall not dwell
within my house;
One who speaks lies shall not maintain
his position before me.
8 Every morning I will destroy all the
wicked of the land,
So as to eliminate from the city of the
LORD all those who do injustice.

PSALM 102

**Prayer of an Afflicted Man for Mercy on Himself
and on Zion.**
*A Prayer of the afflicted when he is weak and pours
out his complaint before the LORD.*
1 Hear my prayer, LORD!
And let my cry for help come to You.
2 Do not hide Your face from me on the day
of my distress;
Incline Your ear to me;
On the day when I call answer me
quickly.
3 For my days have ended in smoke,
And my bones have been scorched like a
hearth.
4 My heart has been struck like grass and
has withered,
Indeed, I forget to eat my bread.
5 Because of the loudness of my groaning
My bones cling to my flesh.
6 I resemble a pelican of the wilderness;
I have become like an owl of the ruins.
7 I lie awake,
I have become like a solitary bird on a
housetop.
8¶ My enemies have taunted me all day
long;

100:3 ¹Some mss *His we are*

Those who deride me have used my *name* as a curse.

9   For I have eaten ashes like bread,
And mixed my drink with weeping

10   Because of Your indignation and Your wrath;
For You have lifted me up and thrown me away.

11   My days are like a lengthened shadow,
And I wither away like grass.

12¶   But You, LORD, remain forever,
And Your name *remains* to all generations.

13   You will arise *and* have compassion on Zion;
For it is time to be gracious to her,
For the appointed time has come.

14   Surely Your servants take pleasure in her stones,
And feel pity for her dust.

15   So the nations will fear the name of the LORD,
And all the kings of the earth, Your glory.

16   For the LORD has built up Zion;
He has appeared in His glory.

17   He has turned His attention to the prayer of the destitute
And has not despised their prayer.

18¶   This will be written for the generation to come,
That a people yet to be created may praise the LORD:

19   For He looked down from His holy height;
From heaven the LORD looked upon the earth,

20   To hear the groaning of the prisoner,
To set free those who were doomed to death,

21   So that *people* may tell of the name of the LORD in Zion,
And His praise in Jerusalem,

22   When the peoples are gathered together,
And the kingdoms, to serve the LORD.

23¶   He has broken my strength in the way;
He has shortened my days.

24   I say, "My God, do not take me away in the middle of my days,
Your years are throughout all generations.

25   "In time of old You founded the earth,
And the heavens are the work of Your hands.

26   "Even they will perish, but You endure;
All of them will wear out like a garment;
Like clothing You will change them and they will pass away.

27   "But You are the same,
And Your years will not come to an end.

28   "The children of Your servants will continue,
And their descendants will be established before You."

PSALM 103

Praise for the LORD's Mercies.
A Psalm *of David.*

1   Bless the LORD, my soul,
And all that is within me, *bless* His holy name.

2   Bless the LORD, my soul,
And do not forget any of His benefits;

3   Who pardons all your guilt,
Who heals all your diseases;

4   Who redeems your life from the pit,
Who crowns you with favor and compassion;

5   Who satisfies your years with good things,
So that your youth is renewed like the eagle.

6¶   The LORD performs righteous deeds
And judgments for all who are oppressed.

7   He made known His ways to Moses,
His deeds to the sons of Israel.

8   The LORD is compassionate and gracious,
Slow to anger and abounding in mercy.

9   He will not always contend *with us,*
Nor will He keep *His anger* forever.

10   He has not dealt with us according to our sins,
Nor rewarded us according to our guilty deeds.

11   For as high as the heavens are above the earth,
So great is His mercy toward those who fear Him.

12   As far as the east is from the west,
So far has He removed our wrongdoings from us.

13   Just as a father has compassion on *his* children,
So the LORD has compassion on those who fear Him.

14   For He Himself knows ¹our form;
He is mindful that we are *nothing but* dust.

15¶   As for man, his days are like grass;
Like a flower of the field, so he flourishes.

16   When the wind has passed over it, it is no more,
And its place no longer knows about it.

17   But the mercy of the LORD is from everlasting to everlasting for those who fear Him,
And His justice to the children's children,

18   To those who keep His covenant
And remember His precepts, *so as* to do them.

19¶   The LORD has established His throne in the heavens,
And His sovereignty rules over all.

20   Bless the LORD, you His angels,
Mighty in strength, who perform His word,
Obeying the voice of His word!

21   Bless the LORD, all you His angels,
You who serve Him, doing His will.

22   Bless the LORD, all you works of His,
In all places of His dominion;
Bless the LORD, my soul!

PSALM 104

The LORD's Care over All His Works.

1   Bless the LORD, my soul!
LORD my God, You are very great;
You are clothed with splendor and majesty,

2   Covering Yourself with light as with a
cloak,
Stretching out heaven like a tent curtain.

3   He lays the beams of His upper chambers
in the waters;
He makes the clouds His chariot;
He walks on the wings of the wind;

4   He makes the winds His messengers,
Flaming fire His ministers.

5¶   He established the earth upon its
foundations,
So that it will not totter forever and ever.

6   You covered it with the deep sea as with a
garment;
The waters were standing above the
mountains.

7   They fled from Your rebuke,
At the sound of Your thunder they hurried
away.

8   The mountains rose; the valleys sank
down
To the place which You established for
them.

9   You set a boundary *so that* they will not
pass over,
So that they will not return to cover the
earth.

10¶   He sends forth springs in the valleys;
They flow between the mountains;

11   They give drink to every animal of the
field;
The wild donkeys quench their thirst.

12   The birds of the sky dwell beside them;
They lift up *their* voices from among the
branches.

13   He waters the mountains from His upper
chambers;
The earth is satisfied with the fruit of His
works.

14¶   He causes the grass to grow for the cattle,
And vegetation for the labor of mankind,
So that they may produce food from the
earth,

15   And wine, which makes a human heart
cheerful,
So that he makes *his* face gleam with oil,
And food, which sustains a human heart.

16   The trees of the LORD drink their fill,
The cedars of Lebanon which He planted,

17   Where the birds build their nests,
And the stork, whose home is the juniper
trees.

18¶   The high mountains are for the wild
goats;
The cliffs are a refuge for the rock hyrax.

19   He made the moon for the seasons;
The sun knows the place of its setting.

20   You appoint darkness and it becomes
night,
In which all the animals of the forest
prowl about.

21   The young lions roar for their prey
And seek their food from God.

22   *When* the sun rises they withdraw,
And they lie down in their dens.

23   A person goes out to his work
And to his labor until evening.

24¶   LORD, how many are Your works!
In wisdom You have made them all;
The earth is full of Your possessions.

25   There is the sea, great and broad,
In which are swarms without number,
Animals both small and great.

26   The ships move along there,
And Leviathan, which You have formed to
have fun in it.

27¶   They all wait for You
To give them their food in due season.

28   You give to them, they gather *it* up;
You open Your hand, they are satisfied
with good.

29   You hide Your face, they are terrified;
You take away their breath, they perish
And return to their dust.

30   You send forth Your Spirit, they are
created;
And You renew the face of the ground.

31¶   May the glory of the LORD endure forever;
May the LORD rejoice in His works;

32   He looks at the earth, and it trembles;
He touches the mountains, and they
smoke.

33   I will sing to the LORD as long as I live;
I will sing praise to my God while I have
my being.

34   May my praise be pleasing to Him;
As for me, I shall rejoice in the LORD.

35   May sinners be removed from the earth
And *may* the wicked be no more.
Bless the LORD, my soul.
Praise the LORD!

PSALM 105

The LORD's Wonderful Works in Behalf of Israel.

1   Give thanks to the LORD, call upon His
name;
Make His deeds known among the
peoples.

2   Sing to Him, sing praises to Him;
Tell of all His wonders.

3   Boast in His holy name;
May the heart of those who seek the LORD
be joyful.

4   Seek the LORD and His strength;
Seek His face continually.

5   Remember His wonders which He has
done,
His marvels and the judgments spoken by
His mouth,

6   You descendants of Abraham, His servant,
You sons of Jacob, His chosen ones!

7   He is the LORD our God;
His judgments are in all the earth.

8¶   He has remembered His covenant forever,
The word which He commanded to a
thousand generations,

9   *The covenant* which He made with
Abraham,
And His oath to Isaac.

10   Then He confirmed it to Jacob as a statute,
To Israel as an everlasting covenant,

11   Saying, "To you I will give the land of
Canaan
As the portion of your inheritance,"

12   When they were *only* a few people in
number,
Very few, and strangers in it.

13   And they wandered from nation to nation,
From *one* kingdom to another people,

14 He allowed no one to oppress them,
And He rebuked kings for their sakes,
saying,
15 "Do not touch My anointed ones,
And do not harm My prophets."
16¶ And He called for a famine upon the land;
He broke the whole staff of bread.
17 He sent a man before them,
Joseph, *who* was sold as a slave.
18 They forced his feet into shackles,
He was put in irons;
19 Until the time that his word came to pass,
The word of the LORD refined him.
20 The king sent and released him,
The ruler of peoples, and set him free.
21 He made him lord of his house,
And ruler over all his possessions,
22 To imprison his high officials at will,
That he might teach his elders wisdom.
23 Israel also came into Egypt;
So Jacob lived in the land of Ham.
24 And He made His people very fruitful,
And made them stronger than their
enemies.
25¶ He turned their heart to hate His people,
To deal cunningly with His servants.
26 He sent His servant Moses,
And Aaron, whom He had chosen.
27 They performed His wondrous acts among
them,
And miracles in the land of Ham.
28 He sent darkness and made *it* dark;
And they did not rebel against His words.
29 He turned their waters into blood,
And caused their fish to die.
30 Their land swarmed with frogs
Even in the chambers of their kings.
31 He spoke, and a swarm of flies
And gnats invaded all their territory.
32 He gave them hail for rain,
And flaming fire in their land.
33 He also struck their vines and their fig
trees,
And smashed the trees of their territory.
34 He spoke, and locusts came,
And creeping locusts, beyond number,
35 And they ate all the vegetation in their
land,
And ate the fruit of their ground.
36 He also fatally struck all the firstborn in
their land,
The first fruits of all their vigor.
37¶ Then He brought ¹the Israelites out with
silver and gold,
And among His tribes there was not one
who stumbled.
38 Egypt was glad when they departed,
For the dread of them had fallen upon
¹the Egyptians.
39 He spread out a cloud as a covering,
And fire to illumine by night.
40 They asked, and He brought quail,
And satisfied them with the bread of
heaven.
41 He opened the rock and water flowed out;
It ran in the dry places *like* a river.
42 For He remembered His holy word
With His servant Abraham;
43 And He led out His people with joy,

His chosen ones with a joyful shout.
44 He also gave them the lands of the
nations,
So that they might take possession of *the
fruit of* the peoples' labor,
45 *And* that they might keep His statutes
And comply with His laws;
Praise the LORD!

PSALM 106

Israel's Rebelliousness and the LORD's Help.
1 Praise the LORD!
Oh give thanks to the LORD, for He is
good;
For His mercy is everlasting.
2 Who can speak of the mighty deeds of the
LORD,
Or can proclaim all His praise?
3 How blessed are those who maintain
justice,
Who practice righteousness at all times!
4¶ Remember me, LORD, in *Your* favor
toward Your people.
Visit me with Your salvation,
5 So that I may see the prosperity of Your
chosen ones,
That I may rejoice in the joy of Your
nation,
That I may boast with Your ¹inheritance.
6¶ We have sinned like our fathers,
We have gone astray, we have behaved
wickedly.
7 Our fathers in Egypt did not understand
Your wonders;
They did not remember Your abundant
kindnesses,
But rebelled by the sea, at the Red Sea.
8 Nevertheless He saved them for the sake
of His name,
So that He might make His power known.
9 So He rebuked the Red Sea and it dried
up,
And He led them through the mighty
waters, as *through* the wilderness.
10 So He saved them from the hand of one
who hated *them,*
And redeemed them from the hand of the
enemy.
11 The waters covered their adversaries;
Not one of them was left.
12 Then they believed His words;
They sang His praise.
13¶ They quickly forgot His works;
They did not wait for His plan,
14 But became lustfully greedy in the
wilderness,
And put God to the test in the desert.
15 So He gave them their request,
But sent a wasting disease among them.
16¶ When they became envious of Moses in
the camp,
And of Aaron, the holy one of the LORD,
17 The earth opened and swallowed up
Dathan,
And engulfed the company of Abiram.
18 And a fire blazed up in their company;
The flame consumed the wicked.
19¶ They made a calf in Horeb,

20 And worshiped a cast metal image.
So they exchanged their glory
For the image of an ox that eats grass.
21 They forgot God their Savior,
Who had done great things in Egypt,
22 Wonders in the land of Ham,
And awesome things by the Red Sea.
23 Therefore He said that He would destroy
them,
If Moses, His chosen one, had not stood
in the gap before Him,
To turn away His wrath from destroying
them.
24 Then they rejected the pleasant land;
They did not believe His word,
25 But grumbled in their tents;
They did not listen to the voice of the
LORD.
26 Therefore He swore to them
That He would have them fall in the
wilderness,
27 And that He would bring down their
descendants among the nations,
And scatter them in the lands.
28¶ They also followed Baal-peor,
And ate sacrifices *offered to* the dead.
29 So they provoked *Him* to anger with their
deeds,
And a plague broke out among them.
30 Then Phinehas stood up and intervened,
And so the plague was brought to a halt.
31 And it was credited to him as righteousness,
To all generations forever.
32¶ They also provoked *Him* to wrath at the
waters of Meribah,
So that it went badly for Moses on their
account.
33 Because they were rebellious against His
Spirit,
He spoke rashly with his lips.
34¶ They did not destroy the peoples,
As the LORD had commanded them,
35 But they got involved with the nations
And learned their practices,
36 And served their idols,
Which became a snare to them.
37 They even sacrificed their sons and their
daughters to the demons,
38 And shed innocent blood,
The blood of their sons and their
daughters
Whom they sacrificed to the idols of
Canaan;
And the land was defiled with the blood.
39 So they became unclean in their practices,
And were unfaithful in their deeds.
40¶ Therefore the anger of the LORD was
kindled against His people,
And He loathed His inheritance.
41 So He handed them over to the nations,
And those who hated them ruled over
them.
42 Their enemies also oppressed them,
And they were subdued under their
power.
43 Many times He would rescue them;
They, however, were rebellious in their
plan,
And they sank down into their guilt.

44¶ Nevertheless He looked at their distress
When He heard their cry;
45 And He remembered His covenant for
their sake,
And relented according to the greatness of
His mercy.
46 He also made them *objects* of compassion
In the presence of all their captors.
47¶ Save us, LORD our God,
And gather us from the nations,
To give thanks to Your holy name
And glory in Your praise.
48 Blessed be the LORD, the God of Israel,
From everlasting to everlasting.
And all the people shall say, "Amen."
Praise the LORD!

BOOK 5

PSALM 107

The LORD Rescues People from Many Troubles.
1 Give thanks to the LORD, for He is good,
For His mercy is everlasting.
2 The redeemed of the LORD shall say *so,*
Those whom He has redeemed from the
hand of the enemy
3 And gathered from the lands,
From the east and from the west,
From the north and from the south.
4¶ They wandered in the wilderness in a
desert region;
They did not find a way to an inhabited
city.
5 *They were* hungry and thirsty;
Their souls felt weak within them.
6 Then they cried out to the LORD in their
trouble;
He saved them from their distresses.
7 He also had them walk on a straight way,
To go to an inhabited city.
8 They shall give thanks to the LORD for His
mercy,
And for His wonders to the sons of
mankind!
9 For He has satisfied the thirsty soul,
And He has filled the hungry soul with
what is good.
10¶ There were those who lived in darkness
and in the shadow of death,
Prisoners in misery and chains,
11 Because they had rebelled against the
words of God
And rejected the plan of the Most High.
12 Therefore He humbled their heart with
labor;
They stumbled and there was no one to
help.
13 Then they cried out to the LORD in their
trouble;
He saved them from their distresses.
14 He brought them out of darkness and the
shadow of death
And broke their bands apart.
15 They shall give thanks to the LORD for His
mercy,
And for His wonders to the sons of
mankind!
16 For He has shattered gates of bronze
And cut off bars of iron.

17¶ Fools, because of their rebellious way,
     And because of their guilty deeds, were
        afflicted.
18   Their souls loathed all kinds of food,
     And they came close to the gates of death.
19   Then they cried out to the LORD in their
        trouble;
     He saved them from their distresses.
20   He sent His word and healed them,
     And saved *them* from their destruction.
21   They shall give thanks to the LORD for His
        mercy,
     And for His wonders to the sons of
        mankind!
22   They shall also offer sacrifices of thanks-
        giving,
     And tell of His works with joyful singing.
23¶ Those who go down to the sea in ships,
     Who do business on great waters;
24   They have seen the works of the LORD,
     And His wonders in the deep.
25   For He spoke and raised a stormy wind,
     Which lifted the waves of the sea.
26   They rose up to the heavens, they went
        down to the depths;
     Their soul melted away in *their* misery.
27   They reeled and staggered like a drunken
        person,
     And were at their wits' end.
28   Then they cried out to the LORD in their
        trouble,
     And He brought them out of their dis-
        tresses.
29   He caused the storm to be still,
     So that the waves of the sea were hushed.
30   Then they were glad because they were
        quiet,
     So He guided them to their desired
        harbor.
31   They shall give thanks to the LORD for His
        mercy,
     And for His wonders to the sons of
        mankind!
32   They shall also exalt Him in the
        congregation of the people,
     And praise Him at the seat of the elders.
33¶ He turns rivers into a wilderness,
     And springs of water into a thirsty ground;
34   *And* a fruitful land into a salt waste,
     Because of the wickedness of those who
        dwell in it.
35   He turns a wilderness into a pool of water,
     And a dry land into springs of water;
36   And He has the hungry live there,
     So that they may establish an inhabited
        city,
37   And sow fields and plant vineyards,
     And gather a fruitful harvest.
38   He also blesses them and they multiply
        greatly,
     And He does not let their cattle decrease.
39¶ When they become few and lowly
     Because of oppression, misery, and
        sorrow,
40   He pours contempt upon noblemen
     And makes them wander in a pathless·
        wasteland.
41   But He sets the needy securely on high,
        away from affliction,
     And makes *his* families like a flock.

42   The upright see it and are glad;
     But all injustice shuts its mouth.
43   Who is wise? He is to pay attention to
        these things,
     And consider the mercy of the LORD.

PSALM 108

God Praised and Pleas to Give Victory.
A Song, a Psalm of David.
1   My heart is steadfast, God;
     I will sing, I will sing praises also with my
        soul.
2   Awake, harp and lyre;
     I will awaken the dawn!
3   I will give thanks to You, LORD, among the
        peoples,
     And I will sing praises to You among the
        nations.
4   For Your mercy is great above the
        heavens,
     And Your truth *reaches* to the skies.
5   Be exalted above the heavens, God,
     And *may* Your glory *be* above all the
        earth.
6   So that Your beloved may be rescued,
     Save with Your right hand, and answer
        me!
7¶   God has spoken in His holiness:
     "I will triumph, I will divide up Shechem,
     And measure out the Valley of Succoth.
8   "Gilead is Mine, Manasseh is Mine;
     Ephraim also is the helmet of My head;
     Judah is My scepter.
9   "Moab is My washbowl;
     I will throw My sandal over Edom;
     I will shout aloud over Philistia."
10¶ Who will bring me into the fortified city?
     Who will lead me to Edom?
11   God, have You Yourself not rejected us?
     And will You not go forth with our armies,
        God?
12   Give us help against the enemy,
     For deliverance by man is worthless.
13   Through God we will do valiantly,
     And it is He who will trample down our
        enemies.

PSALM 109

Vengeance Invoked upon Adversaries.
For the music director. A Psalm of David.
1   God of my praise,
     Do not be silent!
2   For they have opened a wicked and
        deceitful mouth against me;
     They have spoken against me with a lying
        tongue.
3   They have also surrounded me with
        words of hatred,
     And have fought against me without
        cause.
4   In return for my love they act as my
        accusers;
     But I am *in* prayer.
5   So they have repaid me evil for good,
     And hatred for my love.
6¶   Appoint a wicked person over him,
     And may an accuser stand at his right
        hand.

7 When he is judged, may he come out
guilty,
And may his prayer become sin.
8 May his days be few;
May another take his office.
9 May his children be fatherless,
And his wife a widow.
10 May his children wander about and beg;
And may they seek *sustenance* far from
their ruined homes.
11 May the creditor seize everything that he
has,
And may strangers plunder the product of
his labor.
12 May there be none to extend kindness to
him,
Nor any to be gracious to his fatherless
children.
13 May his descendants be eliminated;
May their name be wiped out in a
following generation.
14¶ May the guilt of his fathers be
remembered before the LORD,
And do not let the sin of his mother be
wiped out.
15 May they be before the LORD continually,
So that He may eliminate their memory
from the earth;
16 Because he did not remember to show
mercy,
But persecuted the afflicted and needy
person,
And the despondent in heart, to put *them*
to death.
17 He also loved cursing, so it came to him;
And he did not delight in blessing, so it
was far from him.
18 But he clothed himself with cursing as
with his garment,
And it entered his body like water,
And like oil into his bones.
19 May it be to him as a garment with which
he covers himself,
And as a belt which he constantly wears
around himself.
20 *May* this *be* the reward of my accusers
from the LORD,
And of those who speak evil against my
soul.
21¶ But You, GOD, the Lord, deal *kindly* with
me for the sake of Your name;
Because Your mercy is good, rescue me;
22 For I am afflicted and needy,
And my heart is wounded within me.
23 I am passing like a shadow when it
lengthens;
I am shaken off like the locust.
24 My knees are weak from fasting,
And my flesh has grown lean, without fatness.
25 I also have become a disgrace to them;
When they see me, they shake their head.
26¶ Help me, LORD my God;
Save me according to Your mercy.
27 And may they know that this is Your
hand;
You, LORD, have done it.
28 They will curse, but You bless;
When they arise, they will be ashamed,
But Your servant will be glad.

29 May my accusers be clothed with
dishonor,
And may they cover themselves with their
own shame as with a robe.
30¶ With my mouth I will give thanks
abundantly to the LORD;
And I will praise Him in the midst of
many.
31 For He stands at the right hand of the
needy,
To save him from those who judge his
soul.

PSALM 110

The LORD Gives Dominion to the King.
A Psalm of David.
1 The LORD says to my Lord:
"Sit at My right hand
Until I make Your enemies a footstool for
Your feet."
2 The LORD will stretch out Your strong
scepter from Zion, *saying,*
"Rule in the midst of Your enemies."
3 Your people will volunteer freely on the
day of Your power;
In holy splendor, from the womb of the
dawn,
Your youth are to You *as* the dew.
4¶ The LORD has sworn and will not change
His mind,
"You are a priest forever
According to the order of Melchizedek."
5 The Lord is at Your right hand;
He will shatter kings in the day of His
wrath.
6 He will judge among the nations,
He will fill *them* with corpses,
He will shatter the chief men over a broad
country.
7 He will drink from the brook by the
wayside;
Therefore He will lift up *His* head.

PSALM 111

The LORD Praised for His Goodness.
1 Praise the LORD!
I will give thanks to the LORD with all *my*
heart,
In the company of the upright and in the
assembly.
2 Great are the works of the LORD;
They are studied by all who delight in
them.
3 Splendid and majestic is His work,
And His righteousness endures forever.
4 He has caused His wonders to be
remembered;
The LORD is gracious and compassionate.
5 He has given food to those who fear Him;
He will remember His covenant forever.
6 He has made known to His people the
power of His works,
In giving them the inheritance of the
nations.
7¶ The works of His hands are truth and
justice;
All His precepts are trustworthy.
8 They are upheld forever and ever;

PSALM 112

They are performed in truth and
uprightness.
9 He has sent redemption to His people;
He has ordained His covenant forever;
Holy and awesome is His name.
10 The fear of the LORD is the beginning of
wisdom;
All those who follow His commandments
have a good understanding;
His praise endures forever.

PSALM 112

Prosperity of One Who Fears the LORD.
1 Praise the LORD!
Blessed is a person who fears the LORD,
Who greatly delights in His
commandments.
2 His descendants will be mighty on the
earth;
The generation of the upright will be
blessed.
3 Wealth and riches are in his house,
And his righteousness endures forever.
4 Light shines in the darkness for the
upright;
He is gracious, compassionate, and
righteous.
5 It *goes* well for a person who is gracious
and lends;
He will maintain his cause in judgment.
6 For he will never be shaken;
The righteous will be remembered
forever.
7¶ He will not fear bad news;
His heart is steadfast, trusting in the LORD.
8 His heart is firm, he will not fear,
But will look *with satisfaction* on his
enemies.
9 He has given freely to the poor,
His righteousness endures forever;
His horn will be exalted in honor.
10¶ The wicked will see it and be vexed,
He will gnash his teeth and melt away;
The desire of the wicked will perish.

PSALM 113

The LORD Exalts the Humble.
1 Praise the LORD!
Praise *Him,* you servants of the LORD,
Praise the name of the LORD.
2 Blessed be the name of the LORD
From this time *on* and forever.
3 From the rising of the sun to its setting,
The name of the LORD is to be praised.
4 The LORD is high above all nations;
His glory is above the heavens.
5¶ Who is like the LORD our God,
Who is enthroned on high,
6 Who looks far down to
The heavens and the earth?
7 He raises the poor from the dust,
He lifts the needy from the garbage heap,
8 To seat *them* with noblemen,
With the noblemen of His people.
9 He has the infertile woman live in the
house
As a joyful mother of children.
Praise the LORD!

PSALM 114

God's Rescue of Israel from Egypt.
1 When Israel went forth from Egypt,
The house of Jacob from a people of a
foreign language,
2 Judah became His sanctuary;
Israel, His dominion.
3¶ The sea looked and fled;
The Jordan turned back.
4 The mountains skipped like rams,
The hills, like lambs.
5 What ails you, sea, that you flee?
Jordan, that you turn back?
6 Mountains, that you skip like rams?
Hills, like lambs?
7¶ Tremble, earth, before the Lord,
Before the God of Jacob,
8 Who turned the rock into a pool of water,
The flint into a fountain of water.

PSALM 115

Heathen Idols Contrasted with the LORD.
1 Not to us, LORD, not to us,
But to Your name give glory,
Because of Your mercy, because of Your
truth.
2 Why should the nations say,
"Where, then, is their God?"
3 But our God is in the heavens;
He does whatever He pleases.
4 Their idols are silver and gold,
The work of human hands.
5 They have mouths, but they cannot
speak;
They have eyes, but they cannot see;
6 They have ears, but they cannot hear;
They have noses, but they cannot smell;
7 They have hands, but they cannot feel;
They have feet, but they cannot walk;
They cannot make a sound with their
throat.
8 Those who make them will become like
them,
Everyone who trusts in them.
9¶ Israel, trust in the LORD;
He is their help and their shield.
10 House of Aaron, trust in the LORD;
He is their help and their shield.
11 You who fear the LORD, trust in the LORD;
He is their help and their shield.
12 The LORD has been mindful of us; He will
bless *us.*
He will bless the house of Israel;
He will bless the house of Aaron.
13 He will bless those who fear the LORD,
The small together with the great.
14 May the LORD increase you,
You and your children.
15 May you be blessed of the LORD,
Maker of heaven and earth.
16¶ The heavens are the heavens of the LORD,
But the earth He has given to the sons of
mankind.
17 The dead do not praise the LORD,
Nor *do* any who go down into silence;
18 But as for us, we will bless the LORD
From this time and forever.
Praise the LORD!

PSALM 116

Thanksgiving for Rescue from Death.

1 I love the LORD, because He hears
My voice *and* my pleas.

2 Because He has inclined His ear to me,
Therefore I will call *upon Him* as long as I
live.

3 The snares of death encompassed me
And the terrors of ¹Sheol came upon me;
I found distress and sorrow.

4 Then I called upon the name of the LORD:
"Please, LORD, save my life!"

5¶ Gracious is the LORD, and righteous;
Yes, our God is compassionate.

6 The LORD watches over the simple;
I was brought low, and He saved me.

7 Return to your rest, my soul,
For the LORD has dealt *generously* with
you.

8 For You have rescued my soul from death,
My eyes from tears,
And my feet from stumbling.

9 I shall walk before the LORD
In the land of the living.

10 I believed when I said,
"I am greatly afflicted."

11 I said in my alarm,
"All people are liars."

12¶ What shall I repay to the LORD
For all His benefits to me?

13 I will lift up the cup of salvation,
And call upon the name of the LORD.

14 I will pay my vows to the LORD;
May it be in the presence of all His
people!

15 Precious in the sight of the LORD
Is the death of His godly ones.

16 O LORD, I surely am Your slave,
I am Your slave, the son of Your female
slave,
You have unfastened my restraints.

17 I will offer You a sacrifice of thanksgiving,
And call upon the name of the LORD.

18 I will pay my vows to the LORD,
May it be in the presence of all His
people,

19 In the courtyards of the LORD's house,
In the midst of you, Jerusalem!
Praise the LORD!

PSALM 117

A Psalm of Praise.

1 Praise the LORD, all nations;
Sing His praises, all peoples!

2 For His mercy toward us is great,
And the truth of the LORD is everlasting.
Praise the LORD!

PSALM 118

Thanksgiving for the LORD's Saving Goodness.

1 Give thanks to the LORD, for He is good;
For His mercy is everlasting.

2 Let Israel say,
"His mercy is everlasting."

3 Oh let the house of Aaron say,
"His mercy is everlasting."

4 Let those who fear the LORD say,
"His mercy is everlasting."

5¶ From *my* distress I called upon the LORD;
The LORD answered me *and put me* in an
open space.

6 The LORD is for me; I will not fear;
What can man do to me?

7 The LORD is for me among those who help
me;
Therefore I will look *with satisfaction* on
those who hate me.

8 It is better to take refuge in the LORD
Than to trust in people.

9 It is better to take refuge in the LORD
Than to trust in noblemen.

10¶ All nations surrounded me;
In the name of the LORD I will certainly
fend them off.

11 They surrounded me, yes, they
surrounded me;
In the name of the LORD I will certainly
fend them off.

12 They surrounded me like bees;
They were extinguished like a fire of
thorn bushes;
In the name of the LORD I will certainly
fend them off.

13 You pushed me violently so that I was
falling,
But the LORD helped me.

14 The LORD is my strength and song,
And He has become my salvation.

15¶ The sound of joyful shouting and salvation
is in the tents of the righteous;
The right hand of the LORD performs
valiantly.

16 The right hand of the LORD is exalted;
The right hand of the LORD performs
valiantly.

17 I will not die, but live,
And tell of the works of the LORD.

18 The LORD has disciplined me severely,
But He has not turned me over to death.

19¶ Open the gates of righteousness to me;
I will enter through them, I will give
thanks to the LORD.

20 This is the gate of the LORD;
The righteous will enter through it.

21 I will give thanks to You, for You have
answered me,
And You have become my salvation.

22¶ A stone which the builders rejected
Has become the chief cornerstone.

23 This came about from the LORD;
It is marvelous in our eyes.

24 This is the day which the LORD has made;
Let's rejoice and be glad in it.

25 Please, O LORD, do save *us;*
Please, O LORD, do send prosperity!

26 Blessed is the one who comes in the
name of the LORD;
We have blessed you from the house of
the LORD.

27 The LORD is God, and He has given us
light;
Bind the festival sacrifice to the horns of
the altar with cords.

28 You are my God, and I give thanks to You;
You are my God, I exalt You.

116:3 ¹I.e., the netherworld

29　Give thanks to the Lord, for He is good;
For His mercy is everlasting.

PSALM 119

Meditations and Prayers Relating to the
Law of God.

א　Aleph

1　Blessed are those whose way is blameless,
Who walk in the Law of the Lord.
2　Blessed are those who comply with His
testimonies,
And seek Him with all *their* heart.
3　They also do no injustice;
They walk in His ways.
4　You have ordained Your precepts,
That we are to keep *them* diligently.
5　Oh that my ways may be established
To keep Your statutes!
6　Then I will not be ashamed
When I look at all Your commandments.
7　I will give thanks to You with uprightness
of heart,
When I learn Your righteous judgments.
8　I will keep Your statutes;
Do not utterly abandon me!

ב　Beth

9¶　How can a young man keep his way
pure?
By keeping *it* according to Your word.
10　With all my heart I have sought You;
Do not let me wander from Your
commandments.
11　I have treasured Your word in my
heart,
So that I may not sin against You.
12　Blessed are You, Lord;
Teach me Your statutes.
13　With my lips I have told of
All the ordinances of Your mouth.
14　I have rejoiced in the way of Your
testimonies,
As much as in all riches.
15　I will meditate on Your precepts
And regard Your ways.
16　I shall delight in Your statutes;
I will not forget Your word.

ג　Gimel

17¶　Deal *generously* with Your servant,
That I may live and keep Your word.
18　Open my eyes, that I may behold
Wonderful things from Your Law.
19　I am a stranger on the earth;
Do not hide Your commandments from
me.
20　My soul is crushed with longing
For Your ordinances at all times.
21　You rebuke the arrogant, the cursed,
Who wander from Your commandments.
22　Take disgrace and contempt away from
me,
For I comply with Your testimonies.
23　Even though rulers sit *and* speak against
me,
Your servant meditates on Your statutes.
24　Your testimonies also are my delight;
They are my advisers.

ד　Daleth

25¶　My soul clings to the dust;
Revive me according to Your word.
26　I have told of my ways, and You have
answered me;
Teach me Your statutes.
27　Make me understand the way of Your
precepts,
And I will meditate on Your wonders.
28　My soul weeps because of grief;
Strengthen me according to Your word.
29　Remove the false way from me,
And graciously grant me Your Law.
30　I have chosen the faithful way;
I have placed Your judgments *before me.*
31　I cling to Your testimonies;
Lord, do not put me to shame!
32　I shall run the way of Your
commandments,
For You will enlarge my heart.

ה　He

33¶　Teach me, the way of Your statutes, Lord,
And I shall comply with it to the end.
34　Give me understanding, so that I may
comply with Your Law
And keep it with all *my* heart.
35　Make me walk in the path of Your
commandments,
For I delight in it.
36　Incline my heart to Your testimonies,
And not to *dishonest* gain.
37　Turn my eyes away from looking at what
is worthless,
And revive me in Your ways.
38　Establish Your word to Your servant
As that which produces reverence for You.
39　Take away my disgrace which I dread,
For Your judgments are good.
40　Behold, I long for Your precepts;
Revive me through Your righteousness.

ו　Vav

41¶　May Your favor also come to me, Lord,
Your salvation according to Your word;
42　So that I will have an answer for one who
taunts me,
For I trust in Your word.
43　And do not take the word of truth utterly
out of my mouth,
For I wait for Your judgments.
44　So I will keep Your Law continually,
Forever and ever.
45　And I will walk at liberty,
For I seek Your precepts.
46　I will also speak of Your testimonies
before kings
And shall not be ashamed.
47　I will delight in Your commandments,
Which I love.
48　And I shall lift up my hands to Your
commandments,
Which I love;
And I will meditate on Your statutes.

ז　Zayin

49¶　Remember the word to Your servant,
In which You have made me hope.
50　This is my comfort in my misery,
That Your word has revived me.

51 The arrogant utterly deride me,
Yet I do not turn aside from Your Law.
52 I have remembered Your judgments from
of old, LORD,
And comfort myself.
53 Burning indignation has seized me
because of the wicked,
Who abandon Your Law.
54 Your statutes are my songs
In the house of my pilgrimage.
55 LORD, I remember Your name in the night,
And keep Your Law.
56 This has become mine,
That I comply with Your precepts.

ח   Heth

57¶ The LORD is my portion;
I have promised to keep Your words.
58 I sought Your favor with all *my* heart;
Be gracious to me according to Your word.
59 I considered my ways
And turned my feet to Your testimonies.
60 I hurried and did not delay
To keep Your commandments.
61 The snares of the wicked have surrounded
me,
But I have not forgotten Your Law.
62 At midnight I will rise to give thanks to
You
Because of Your righteous judgments.
63 I am a companion to all those who fear
You,
And to those who keep Your precepts.
64 The earth is full of Your goodness, LORD;
Teach me Your statutes.

ט   Teth

65¶ You have treated Your servant well,
LORD, according to Your word.
66 Teach me good discernment and
knowledge,
For I believe in Your commandments.
67 Before I was afflicted I went astray,
But now I keep Your word.
68 You are good and You do good;
Teach me Your statutes.
69 The arrogant have forged a lie against
me;
With all *my* heart I will comply with Your
precepts.
70 Their heart is insensitive, like fat,
But I delight in Your Law.
71 It is good for me that I was afflicted,
So that I may learn Your statutes.
72 The Law of Your mouth is better to me
Than thousands of gold and silver *pieces.*

י   Yodh

73¶ Your hands made me and fashioned me;
Give me understanding, so that I may
learn Your commandments.
74 May those who fear You see me and be
glad,
Because I wait for Your word.
75 I know, LORD, that Your judgments are
righteous,
And that You have afflicted me in
faithfulness.
76 May Your favor comfort me,
According to Your word to Your servant.

77 May Your compassion come to me so that
I may live,
For Your Law is my delight.
78 May the arrogant be put to shame,
because they lead me astray with a lie;
But I shall meditate on Your precepts.
79 May those who fear You turn to me,
And those who know Your testimonies.
80 May my heart be blameless in Your
statutes,
So that I will not be ashamed.

כ   Kaph

81¶ My soul languishes for Your salvation;
I wait for Your word.
82 My eyes fail *with longing* for Your word,
While I say, "When will You comfort me?"
83 Though I have become like a wineskin in
the smoke,
I do not forget Your statutes.
84 How many are the days of Your servant?
When will You execute judgment on those
who persecute me?
85 The arrogant have dug pits for me,
People who are not in accord with Your
Law.
86 All Your commandments are faithful;
They have persecuted me with a lie; help
me!
87 They almost destroyed me on earth,
But as for me, I did not abandon Your
precepts.
88 Revive me according to Your faithfulness,
So that I may keep the testimony of Your
mouth.

ל   Lamedh

89¶ Forever, LORD,
Your word stands in heaven.
90 Your faithfulness *continues* throughout
generations;
You established the earth, and it stands.
91 They stand this day by Your ordinances,
For all things are Your servants.
92 If Your Law had not been my delight,
Then I would have perished in my misery.
93 I will never forget Your precepts,
For by them You have revived me.
94 I am Yours, save me;
For I have sought Your precepts.
95 The wicked wait for me to destroy me;
I will diligently consider Your testimonies.
96 I have seen a limit to all perfection;
Your commandment is exceedingly broad.

מ   Mem

97¶ How I love Your Law!
It is my meditation all the day.
98 Your commandments make me wiser than
my enemies,
For they are ever mine.
99 I have more insight than all my teachers,
For Your testimonies are my meditation.
100 I understand more than those who are
old,
Because I have complied with Your
precepts.
101 I have restrained my feet from every evil
way,
So that I may keep Your word.

102 I have not turned aside from Your
    judgments,
    For You Yourself have taught me.
103 How sweet are Your words to my taste!
    Yes, sweeter than honey to my mouth!
104 From Your precepts I get understanding;
    Therefore I hate every false way.

נ Nun

105¶ Your word is a lamp to my feet
    And a light to my path.
106 I have sworn and I will confirm it,
    That I will keep Your righteous judgments.
107 I am exceedingly afflicted;
    Revive me, LORD, according to Your word.
108 Be pleased to accept the voluntary
    offerings of my mouth, LORD,
    And teach me Your judgments.
109 My life is continually ¹in my hand,
    Yet I do not forget Your Law.
110 The wicked have set a trap for me,
    Yet I have not wandered from Your
    precepts.
111 I have inherited Your testimonies forever,
    For they are the joy of my heart.
112 I have inclined my heart to perform Your
    statutes
    Forever, *even* to the end.

ס Samekh

113¶ I hate those who are double-minded,
    But I love Your Law.
114 You are my hiding place and my shield;
    I wait for Your word.
115 Leave me, you evildoers,
    So that I may comply with the
    commandments of my God.
116 Sustain me according to Your word, that I
    may live;
    And do not let me be ashamed of my
    hope.
117 Sustain me so that I may be safe,
    That I may have regard for Your statutes
    continually.
118 You have rejected all those who stray from
    Your statutes,
    For their deceitfulness is useless.
119 You have removed all the wicked of the
    earth *like* impurities;
    Therefore I love Your testimonies.
120 My flesh trembles from the fear of You,
    And I am afraid of Your judgments.

ע Ayin

121¶ I have done justice and righteousness;
    Do not leave me to my oppressors.
122 Be a guarantor for Your servant for good;
    Do not let the arrogant oppress me.
123 My eyes fail *with longing* for Your
    salvation,
    And for Your righteous word.
124 Deal with Your servant according to Your
    graciousness,
    And teach me Your statutes.
125 I am Your servant; give me understanding,
    So that I may know Your testimonies.
126 It is time for the LORD to act,
    For they have broken Your Law.
127 Therefore I love Your commandments

128 Therefore I carefully follow all *Your*
    precepts concerning everything,
    I hate every false way.

פ Pe

129¶ Your testimonies are wonderful;
    Therefore my soul complies with them.
130 The unfolding of Your words gives light;
    It gives understanding to the simple.
131 I opened my mouth wide and panted,
    For I longed for Your commandments.
132 Turn to me and be gracious to me,
    As is right for those who love Your
    name.
133 Establish my footsteps in Your word,
    And do not let any wrongdoing have
    power over me.
134 Redeem me from oppression by man,
    So that I may keep Your precepts.
135 Make Your face shine upon Your servant,
    And teach me Your statutes.
136 My eyes shed streams of water,
    Because they do not keep Your Law.

צ Tsadhe

137¶ You are righteous, LORD,
    And Your judgments are right.
138 You have commanded Your testimonies in
    righteousness
    And great faithfulness.
139 My zeal has consumed me,
    Because my enemies have forgotten Your
    words.
140 Your word is very pure,
    Therefore Your servant loves it.
141 I am small and despised,
    Yet I do not forget Your precepts.
142 Your righteousness is an everlasting
    righteousness,
    And Your Law is truth.
143 Trouble and anguish have come upon
    me,
    Yet Your commandments are my delight.
144 Your testimonies are righteous forever;
    Give me understanding that I may live.

ק Qoph

145¶ I cried out with all my heart; answer me,
    LORD!
    I will comply with Your statutes.
146 I cried to You; save me
    And I shall keep Your testimonies.
147 I rise before dawn and cry for help;
    I wait for Your words.
148 My eyes anticipate the night watches,
    So that I may meditate on Your word.
149 Hear my voice according to Your
    faithfulness;
    Revive me, LORD, according to Your
    judgments.
150 Those who follow after wickedness
    approach;
    They are far from Your Law.
151 You are near, LORD,
    And all Your commandments are truth.
152 From long ago I have known from Your
    testimonies
    That You have founded them forever.

119:109 ¹ I.e., in danger

ר Resh

153¶ Look at my affliction and rescue me,
For I have not forgotten Your Law.
154 Plead my cause and redeem me;
Revive me according to Your word.
155 Salvation is far from the wicked,
For they do not seek Your statutes.
156 Great are Your mercies, LORD;
Revive me according to Your judgments.
157 Many are my persecutors and my
enemies,
Yet I do not turn aside from Your testimonies.
158 I see the treacherous and loathe *them,*
Because they do not keep Your word.
159 Consider how I love Your precepts;
Revive me, LORD, according to Your
faithfulness.
160 The sum of Your word is truth,
And every one of Your righteous
judgments is everlasting.

ש Shin

161¶ Rulers persecute me without cause,
But my heart stands in awe of Your
words.
162 I rejoice at Your word,
Like one who finds great plunder.
163 I hate and loathe falsehood,
But I love Your Law.
164 Seven times a day I praise You
Because of Your righteous judgments.
165 Those who love Your Law have great
peace,
And nothing causes them to stumble.
166 I hope for Your salvation, LORD,
And do Your commandments.
167 My soul keeps Your testimonies,
And I love them exceedingly.
168 I keep Your precepts and Your testimonies,
For all my ways are before You.

ת Tav

169¶ Let my cry come before You, LORD;
Give me understanding according to Your
word.
170 Let my pleading come before You;
Save me according to Your word.
171 Let my lips pour out praise,
For You teach me Your statutes.
172 Let my tongue sing about Your word,
For all Your commandments are
righteousness.
173 Let Your hand be ready to help me,
For I have chosen Your precepts.
174 I long for Your salvation, LORD,
And Your Law is my delight.
175 Let my soul live that it may praise You,
And let Your ordinances help me.
176 I have wandered about like a lost sheep;
search for Your servant,
For I do not forget Your commandments.

PSALM 120

Prayer for Rescue from the Treacherous.
A Song of Ascents.
1 I cried to the LORD in my trouble,
And He answered me.

2 Rescue my soul, LORD, from lying lips,
From a deceitful tongue.
3 What will *He* give to you, and what more
will *He* do to you,
You deceitful tongue?
4 Sharp arrows of the warrior,
With the *burning* coals of the broom
tree!
5¶ Woe to me, for I reside in Meshech,
For I have settled among the tents of
Kedar!
6 Too long has my soul had its dwelling
With those who hate peace.
7 I am *for* peace, but when I speak,
They are for war.

PSALM 121

The LORD, the Keeper of Israel.
A Song of Ascents.
1 I will raise my eyes to the mountains;
From where will my help come?
2 My help *comes* from the LORD,
Who made heaven and earth.
3 He will not allow your foot to slip;
He who watches over you will not
slumber.
4 Behold, He who watches over Israel
Will neither slumber nor sleep.
5¶ The LORD is your protector;
The LORD is your shade on your right
hand.
6 The sun will not beat down on you by
day,
Nor the moon by night.
7 The LORD will protect you from all
evil;
He will keep your soul.
8 The LORD will guard your going out and
your coming in
From this time and forever.

PSALM 122

Prayer for the Peace of Jerusalem.
A Song of Ascents, of David.
1 I was glad when they said to me,
"Let's go to the house of the LORD."
2 Our feet are standing
Within your gates, Jerusalem,
3 Jerusalem, that has been built
As a city that is firmly joined together;
4 To which the tribes go up, the tribes of
the LORD—
An ordinance for Israel—
To give thanks to the name of the
LORD.
5 For thrones were set there for judgment,
The thrones of the house of David.
6¶ Pray for the peace of Jerusalem:
"May they prosper who love you.
7 "May peace be within your walls,
And prosperity within your palaces."
8 For the sake of my brothers and my
friends,
I will now say, "May peace be within
you."
9 For the sake of the house of the LORD our
God,
I will seek your good.

PSALM 123

Prayer for the LORD's Help.
A Song of Ascents.

1   To You I have raised my eyes,
    You who are enthroned in the heavens!
2   Behold, as the eyes of servants *look* to the
    hand of their master,
    As the eyes of a female servant to the
    hand of her mistress,
    So our eyes *look* to the LORD our God,
    Until He is gracious to us.
3¶ Be gracious to us, LORD, be gracious to
    us,
    For we have had much more than enough
    of contempt.
4   Our soul has had much more than enough
    Of the scoffing of those who are at ease,
    And with the contempt of the proud.

PSALM 124

Praise for Rescue from Enemies.
A Song of Ascents, of David.

1   "Had it not been the LORD who was on our
    side,"
    Let Israel say,
2   "Had it not been the LORD who was on our
    side
    When people rose up against us,
3   Then they would have swallowed us alive,
    When their anger was kindled against
    us;
4   Then the waters would have flooded over
    us,
    The stream would have swept over our
    souls;
5   Then the raging waters would have swept
    over our souls."
6¶ Blessed be the LORD,
    Who has not given us to be torn by their
    teeth.
7   Our souls have escaped like a bird from
    the trapper's snare;
    The snare is broken and we have escaped.
8   Our help is in the name of the LORD,
    Who made heaven and earth.

PSALM 125

The LORD Surrounds His People.
A Song of Ascents.

1   Those who trust in the LORD
    Are like Mount Zion, *which* cannot be
    moved *but* remains forever.
2   *As* the mountains surround Jerusalem,
    So the LORD surrounds His people
    From this time and forever.
3   For the scepter of wickedness will not rest
    upon the land of the righteous,
    So that the righteous will not extend their
    hands to do wrong.
4¶ Do good, LORD, to those who are good
    And to those who are upright in their
    hearts.
5   But as for those who turn aside to their
    crooked ways,
    The LORD will lead them away with those
    who practice injustice.
    Peace be upon Israel.

PSALM 126

Thanksgiving for Return from Captivity.
A Song of Ascents.

1   When the LORD brought back the captives
    of Zion,
    We were like those who dream.
2   Then our mouth was filled with laughter
    And our tongue with joyful shouting;
    Then they said among the nations,
    "The LORD has done great things for
    them."
3   The LORD has done great things for us;
    We are joyful.
4¶ Restore our fortunes, LORD,
    As the streams in the South.
5   Those who sow in tears shall harvest with
    joyful shouting.
6   One who goes here and there weeping,
    carrying *his* bag of seed,
    Shall indeed come again with a shout of
    joy, bringing his sheaves *with him.*

PSALM 127

Prosperity Comes from the LORD.
A Song of Ascents, of Solomon.

1   Unless the LORD builds a house,
    They who build it labor in vain;
    Unless the LORD guards a city,
    The watchman stays awake in vain.
2   It is futile for you to rise up early,
    To stay up late,
    To eat the bread of painful labor;
    This is how He gives to His beloved
    sleep.
3¶ Behold, children are a gift of the
    LORD,
    The fruit of the womb is a reward.
4   Like arrows in the hand of a warrior,
    So are the children of one's youth.
5   Blessed is the man whose quiver is full of
    them;
    They will not be ashamed
    When they speak with their enemies in
    the gate.

PSALM 128

Blessedness of the Fear of the LORD.
A Song of Ascents.

1   Blessed is everyone who fears the
    LORD,
    Who walks in His ways.
2   When you eat the fruit of the labor of your
    hands,
    You will be happy and it will go well for
    you.
3   Your wife will be like a fruitful vine
    Within your house,
    Your children like olive plants
    Around your table.
4   Behold, for so shall a man
    Who fears the LORD be blessed.
5¶ The LORD bless you from Zion,
    And may you see the prosperity of
    Jerusalem all the days of your life.
6   Indeed, may you see your children's
    children.
    Peace be upon Israel!

PSALM 129

Prayer for the Overthrow of Zion's Enemies.
A Song of Ascents.

1 "Many times they have attacked me from
my youth up,"
Let Israel say,

2 "Many times they have attacked me from
my youth up;
Yet they have not prevailed against me.

3 "The plowers plowed upon my back;
They lengthened their furrows."

4 The LORD is righteous;
He has cut up the ropes of the wicked.

5¶ May all who hate Zion
Be put to shame and turned backward;

6 May they be like grass upon the
housetops,
Which withers before it grows up;

7 With which the harvester does not fill his
hand,
Or the binder of sheaves his arms;

8 Nor do those who pass by say,
"The blessing of the LORD be upon you;
We bless you in the name of the
LORD."

PSALM 130

Hope in the LORD's Forgiving Love.
A Song of Ascents.

1 Out of the depths I have cried to You,
LORD.

2 Lord, hear my voice!
Let Your ears be attentive
To the sound of my pleadings.

3 If You, LORD, were to keep *account of*
guilty deeds,
Lord, who could stand?

4 But there is forgiveness with You,
So that You may be revered.

5¶ I wait for the LORD, my soul waits,
And I wait for His word.

6 My soul *waits in hope* for the Lord
More than the watchmen for the
morning;
Yes, more than the watchmen for the
morning.

7 Israel, wait for the LORD;
For with the LORD there is mercy,
And with Him is abundant redemption.

8 And He will redeem Israel
From all his guilty deeds.

PSALM 131

Childlike Trust in the LORD.
A Song of Ascents, of David.

1 LORD, my heart is not proud, nor my eyes
arrogant;
Nor do I involve myself in great matters,
Or in things too difficult for me.

2 I have certainly soothed and quieted my
soul;
Like a weaned child *resting* against his
mother,
My soul within me is like a weaned
child.

3 Israel, wait for the LORD
From this time *on* and forever.

PSALM 132

***Prayer for the LORD's Blessing upon the
Sanctuary.***
A Song of Ascents.

1 Remember, LORD, in David's behalf,
All his affliction;

2 How he swore to the LORD
And vowed to the Mighty One of Jacob,

3 "I certainly will not enter my house,
Nor lie on my bed;

4 I will not give sleep to my eyes
Or slumber to my eyelids,

5 Until I find a place for the LORD,
A dwelling place for the Mighty One of
Jacob."

6¶ Behold, we heard *about* it in Ephrathah,
We found it in the field of Jaar.

7 Let's go into His dwelling place;
Let's worship at His footstool.

8 Arise, LORD, to Your resting place,
You and the ark of Your strength.

9 May Your priests be clothed with
righteousness,
And may Your godly ones sing for joy.

10¶ For the sake of Your servant David,
Do not turn away the face of Your
anointed.

11 The LORD has sworn to David
A truth from which He will not turn
back:
"I will set upon your throne *one* from the
fruit of your body.

12 "If your sons will keep My covenant
And My testimony which I will teach
them,
Their sons also will sit upon your throne
forever."

13¶ For the LORD has chosen Zion;
He has desired it as His dwelling place.

14 "This is My resting place forever;
Here I will dwell, for I have desired it.

15 "I will abundantly bless her food;
I will satisfy her needy with bread.

16 "I will also clothe her priests with
salvation,
And her godly ones will sing aloud for
joy.

17 "I will make the horn of David spring forth
there;
I have prepared a lamp for My anointed.

18 "I will clothe his enemies with shame,
But upon himself his crown will gleam."

PSALM 133

The Excellency of Brotherly Unity.
A Song of Ascents, of David.

1 Behold, how good and how pleasant it is
For brothers to live together in unity!

2 It is like the precious oil on the head,
Running down upon the beard,
As on Aaron's beard,
The oil which ran down upon the edge of
his robes.

3 It is like the dew of Hermon
Coming down upon the mountains of
Zion;
For the LORD commanded the blessing
there—life forever.

PSALM 134

Greetings of Night Watchers.
A Song of Ascents.
1 Behold, bless the LORD, all you servants of
the LORD,
Who serve by night in the house of the
LORD!
2 Lift up your hands to the sanctuary
And bless the LORD.
3 May the LORD bless you from Zion,
He who made heaven and earth.

PSALM 135

**Praise the LORD's Wonderful Works. Futility of
Idols.**
1 Praise the LORD!
Praise the name of the LORD;
Praise *Him,* you servants of the LORD,
2 You who stand in the house of the LORD,
In the courtyards of the house of our God!
3 Praise the LORD, for the LORD is good;
Sing praises to His name, for it is lovely.
4 For the LORD has chosen Jacob for
Himself,
Israel as His own possession.
5¶ For I know that the LORD is great
And that our Lord is above all gods.
6 Whatever the LORD pleases, He does,
In heaven and on earth, in the seas and in
all the ocean depths.
7 He causes the mist to ascend from the
ends of the earth,
He makes lightning for the rain;
He brings forth the wind from His treasuries.
8¶ He struck the firstborn of Egypt,
Both human *firstborn* and animal.
9 He sent signs and wonders into your
midst, Egypt,
Upon Pharaoh and all his servants.
10 He struck many nations
And brought death to mighty kings,
11 Sihon, king of the Amorites,
Og, king of Bashan,
And all the kingdoms of Canaan;
12 And He gave their land as an inheritance,
An inheritance to His people Israel.
13 Your name, LORD, is everlasting,
The mention of You, LORD, is throughout
all generations.
14 For the LORD will judge His people
And will have compassion on His
servants.
15 The idols of the nations are *nothing but*
silver and gold,
The work of human hands.
16 They have mouths, but they do not
speak;
They have eyes, but they do not see;
17 They have ears, but they do not hear,
Nor is there any breath at all in their
mouths.
18 Those who make them will become like
them,
Yes, everyone who trusts in them.
19¶ House of Israel, bless the LORD;
House of Aaron, bless the LORD;

20 House of Levi, bless the LORD;
You who revere the LORD, bless the LORD.
21 Blessed be the LORD from Zion,
Who dwells in Jerusalem.
Praise the LORD!

PSALM 136

Thanks for the LORD's Goodness to Israel.
1 Give thanks to the LORD, for He is good,
For His ¹faithfulness is everlasting.
2 Give thanks to the God of gods,
For His faithfulness is everlasting.
3 Give thanks to the Lord of lords,
For His faithfulness is everlasting.
4 To Him who alone does great wonders,
For His faithfulness is everlasting;
5 To Him who made the heavens with
skill,
For His faithfulness is everlasting;
6 To Him who spread out the earth above
the waters,
For His faithfulness is everlasting;
7 To Him who made *the* great lights,
For His faithfulness is everlasting:
8 The sun to rule by day,
For His faithfulness is everlasting,
9 The moon and stars to rule by night,
For His faithfulness is everlasting,
10¶ To Him who struck the Egyptians, that is,
their firstborn,
For His faithfulness is everlasting,
11 And brought Israel out from their midst,
For His faithfulness is everlasting,
12 With a strong hand and an outstretched
arm,
For His faithfulness is everlasting.
13 To Him who divided the Red Sea in
parts,
For His faithfulness is everlasting,
14 And allowed Israel to pass through the
midst of it,
For His faithfulness is everlasting;
15 But He overthrew Pharaoh and his army
in the Red Sea,
For His faithfulness is everlasting.
16 To Him who led His people through the
wilderness,
For His faithfulness is everlasting;
17 To Him who struck great kings,
For His faithfulness is everlasting,
18 And brought death to mighty kings,
For His faithfulness is everlasting:
19 Sihon, king of the Amorites,
For His faithfulness is everlasting,
20 And Og, king of Bashan,
For His faithfulness is everlasting,
21 And gave their land as an inheritance,
For His faithfulness is everlasting,
22 An inheritance to His servant Israel,
For His faithfulness is everlasting.
23¶ Who remembered us in our lowliness,
For His faithfulness is everlasting,
24 And has rescued us from our enemies,
For His faithfulness is everlasting;
25 Who gives food to all flesh,
For His faithfulness is everlasting.
26 Give thanks to the God of heaven,
For His faithfulness is everlasting.

136:1 ¹Or *mercy,* and so throughout the Psalm

PSALM 137

An Experience of the Captivity.
1 By the rivers of Babylon,
There we sat down and wept,
When we remembered Zion.
2 Upon the willows in the midst of it
We hung our harps.
3 For there our captors demanded of us
songs,
And our tormentors, jubilation, *saying,*
"Sing for us one of the songs of Zion!"
4¶ How can we sing the LORD's song
In a foreign land?
5 If I forget you, Jerusalem,
May my right hand forget *its skill.*
6 May my tongue cling to the roof of my
mouth
If I do not remember you,
If I do not exalt Jerusalem
Above my chief joy.
7¶ Remember, LORD, against the sons of
Edom
The day of Jerusalem,
Those who said, "Lay it bare, lay it bare
To its foundation!"
8 Daughter of Babylon, you devastated
one,
Blessed will be one who repays you
With the retribution with which you have
repaid us.
9 Blessed will be one who seizes and dashes
your children
Against the rock.

PSALM 138

Thanksgiving for the LORD's Favor.
A Psalm *of David.*
1 I will give You thanks with all my heart;
I will sing Your praises before the gods.
2 I will bow down toward Your holy
temple
And give thanks to Your name for Your
mercy and Your truth;
For You have made Your word great
according to all Your name.
3 On the day I called, You answered me;
You made me bold *with* strength in my
soul.
4¶ All the kings of the earth will give thanks
to You, LORD,
When they have heard the words of Your
mouth.
5 And they will sing of the ways of the
LORD,
For great is the glory of the LORD.
6 For the LORD is exalted,
Yet He looks after the lowly,
But He knows the haughty from afar.
7¶ Though I walk in the midst of trouble, You
will revive me;
You will reach out with Your hand against
the wrath of my enemies,
And Your right hand will save me.
8 The LORD will accomplish what concerns
me;
Your faithfulness, LORD, is everlasting;
Do not abandon the works of Your hands.

PSALM 139

God's Omnipresence and Omniscience.
For the music director. A Psalm of David.
1 LORD, You have searched me and known
me.
2 You know when I sit down and when I get
up;
You understand my thought from far away.
3 You scrutinize my path and my lying
down,
And are acquainted with all my ways.
4 Even before there is a word on my
tongue,
Behold, LORD, You know it all.
5 You have encircled me behind and in
front,
And placed Your hand upon me.
6 *Such* knowledge is too wonderful for me;
It is *too* high, I cannot comprehend it.
7¶ Where can I go from Your Spirit?
Or where can I flee from Your presence?
8 If I ascend to heaven, You are there;
If I make my bed in [1]Sheol, behold, You
are there.
9 *If* I take up the wings of the dawn,
If I dwell in the remotest part of the sea,
10 Even there Your hand will lead me,
And Your right hand will take hold
of me.
11 *If* I say, "Surely the darkness will
overwhelm me,
And the light around me will be night,"
12 Even darkness is not dark to You,
And the night is as bright as the day.
Darkness and light are alike *to You.*
13¶ For You created my innermost parts;
You wove me in my mother's womb.
14 I will give thanks to You, because [1]I am
awesomely and wonderfully *made;*
Wonderful are Your works,
And my soul knows it very well.
15 My frame was not hidden from You
When I was made in secret,
And skillfully formed in the depths of the
earth;
16 Your eyes have seen my formless
substance;
And in Your book were written
All the days that were ordained *for me,*
When as yet there was not one of them.
17¶ How precious also are Your thoughts for
me, God!
How vast is the sum of them!
18 Were I to count them, they would
outnumber the sand.
When I awake, I am still with You.
19¶ If only You would put the wicked to
death, God;
Leave me, you men of bloodshed.
20 For they speak against You wickedly,
And Your enemies take *Your name* in
vain.
21 Do I not hate those who hate You, LORD?
And do I not loathe those who rise up
against You?
22 I hate them with the utmost hatred;
They have become my enemies.
23¶ Search me, God, and know my heart;

139:8 [1] I.e., the netherworld   **139:14** [1] Some ancient versions *You are fearfully wonderful*

Put me to the test and know my anxious
thoughts;
24 And see if there is *any* hurtful way in
me,
And lead me in the everlasting way.

PSALM 140

Prayer for Protection against the Wicked.
For the music director. A Psalm of David.
1 Rescue me, LORD, from evil people;
Protect me from violent men
2 Who devise evil things in *their* hearts;
They continually stir up wars.
3 They sharpen their tongues like a snake;
The venom of a viper is under their lips.
                                          Selah
4¶ Keep me, LORD, from the hands of the
wicked;
Protect me from violent men
Who intend to trip up my feet.
5 The proud have hidden a trap for me, and
snares;
They have spread a net at the wayside;
They have set snares for me.   *Selah*
6¶ I said to the LORD, "You are my God;
Listen, LORD, to the sound of my
pleadings.
7 "GOD the Lord, the strength of my
salvation,
You have covered my head on the day of
battle.
8 "Do not grant, LORD, the desires of the
wicked;
Do not bring about his evil planning, *so
that* they *are not* exalted.   *Selah*
9¶ "As for the head of those who surround
me,
May the harm of their lips cover them.
10 "May burning coals fall upon them;
May they be cast into the fire,
Into bottomless pits from which they
cannot rise.
11 "May a slanderer not endure on the earth;
May evil hunt a violent person violently."
12¶ I know that the LORD will maintain the
cause of the afflicted,
And justice for the poor.
13 Certainly the righteous will give thanks to
Your name;
The upright will dwell in Your presence.

PSALM 141

*An Evening Prayer for Sanctification and
Protection.*
A Psalm of David.
1 LORD, I call upon You; hurry to me!
Listen to my voice when I call to You!
2 May my prayer be counted as incense
before You;
The raising of my hands as the evening
offering.
3 Set a guard, LORD, over my mouth;
Keep watch over the door of my lips.
4 Do not incline my heart to *any* evil thing,
To practice deeds of wickedness
With people who do wrong;
And may I not taste their delicacies.

5¶ May the righteous strike me with mercy
and discipline me;
It is oil for the head;
My head shall not refuse it,
For my prayer is still against their evil
deeds.
6 Their judges are thrown down by the
sides of the rock,
And they hear my words, for they are
pleasant.
7 As when one plows and breaks open the
earth,
Our bones have been scattered at the
mouth of [1]Sheol.
8¶ For my eyes are toward You, GOD, the
Lord;
In You I take refuge; do not leave me
defenseless.
9 Keep me from the jaws of the trap which
they have set for me,
And from the snares of those who do
wrong.
10 May the wicked fall into their own nets,
While I pass by safely.

PSALM 142

Prayer for Help in Trouble.
Maskil of David, when he was in the cave. A Prayer.
1 I cry out with my voice to the LORD;
With my voice I implore the LORD for
compassion.
2 I pour out my complaint before Him;
I declare my trouble before Him.
3 When my spirit felt weak within me,
You knew my path.
In the way where I walk
They have hidden a trap for me.
4 Look to the right and see;
For there is no one who regards me
favorably;
There is no escape for me;
No one cares for my soul.
5¶ I cried out to You, LORD;
I said, "You are my refuge,
My portion in the land of the living.
6 "Give *Your* attention to my cry,
For I have been brought very low;
Rescue me from my persecutors,
For they are too strong for me.
7 "Bring my soul out of prison,
So that I may give thanks to Your name;
The righteous will surround me,
For You will look after me."

PSALM 143

Prayer for Help and Guidance.
A Psalm of David.
1 Hear my prayer, LORD,
Listen to my pleadings!
Answer me in Your faithfulness, in Your
righteousness!
2 And do not enter into judgment with Your
servant,
For no person living is righteous in Your
sight.
3 For the enemy has persecuted my soul;
He has crushed my life to the ground;

141:7 [1]I.e., the netherworld

He has made me dwell in dark places, like
those who have long been dead.

4 Therefore my spirit feels weak within me;
My heart is appalled within me.

5¶ I remember the days of old;
I meditate on all Your accomplishments;
I reflect on the work of Your hands.

6 I spread out my hands to You;
My soul *longs* for You, like a weary land.
Selah

7¶ Answer me quickly, LORD, my spirit fails;
Do not hide Your face from me,
Or I will be the same as those who go
down to the pit.

8 Let me hear Your faithfulness in the
morning,
For I trust in You;
Teach me the way in which I should
walk;
For to You I lift up my soul.

9 Save me, LORD, from my enemies;
I take refuge in You.

10¶ Teach me to do Your will,
For You are my God;
Let Your good Spirit lead me on level
ground.

11 For the sake of Your name, LORD, revive
me.
In Your righteousness bring my soul out of
trouble.

12 And in Your faithfulness, destroy my
enemies,
And eliminate all those who attack my
soul,
For I am Your servant.

PSALM 144

Prayer for Rescue and Prosperity.
A Psalm *of David.*

1 Blessed be the LORD, my rock,
Who trains my hands for war,
And my fingers for battle;

2 My faithfulness and my fortress,
My stronghold and my savior,
My shield and He in whom I take refuge,
Who subdues my people under me.

3 LORD, what is man, that You look after
him?
Or a son of man, that You think of him?

4 Man is like the breath;
His days are like a passing shadow.

5¶ Bend down Your heavens, LORD, and
come down;
Touch the mountains, that they may
smoke.

6 Flash forth lightning and scatter them;
Send out Your arrows and confuse them.

7 Reach out with Your hand from on high;
Rescue me and save me from great
waters,
From the hand of foreigners

8 Whose mouths speak deceit,
And whose right hand is a right hand of
falsehood.

9¶ God, I will sing a new song to You;
On a harp of ten strings I will sing praises
to You,

10 Who gives salvation to kings,

Who rescues His servant David from the
evil sword.

11 Rescue me and save me from the hand of
foreigners,
Whose mouth speaks deceit
And whose right hand is a right hand of
falsehood.

12¶ When our sons in their youth *are* like
growing plants,
And our daughters like corner pillars
fashioned for a palace,

13 Our granaries *are* full, providing every
kind *of produce,*
And our flocks deliver thousands and ten
thousands in our fields;

14 *May* our cattle be bred
Without mishap and without ¹loss,
May there be no outcry in our streets!

15 Blessed are the people who are so situ-
ated;
Blessed are the people whose God is the
LORD!

PSALM 145

The LORD Exalted for His Goodness.
A Psalm *of Praise, of David.*

1 I will exalt You, my God, the King,
And I will bless Your name forever and
ever,

2 Every day I will bless You,
And I will praise Your name forever and
ever.

3 Great is the LORD, and highly to be
praised;
And His greatness is unsearchable.

4 One generation will praise Your works to
another,
And will declare Your mighty acts.

5 On the glorious splendor of Your majesty
And on Your wonderful works, I will
meditate.

6 People will speak of the power of Your
awesome acts,
And I will tell of Your greatness.

7 They will burst forth in speaking of
Your abundant goodness,
And will shout joyfully of Your
righteousness.

8¶ The LORD is gracious and compassionate;
Slow to anger and great in mercy.

9 The LORD is good to all,
And His mercies are over all His works.

10 All Your works will give thanks to You,
LORD,
And Your godly ones will bless You.

11 They will speak of the glory of Your
kingdom,
And talk of Your might,

12 To make known to the sons of mankind
Your mighty acts,
And the glory of the majesty of Your
kingdom.

13 Your kingdom is an everlasting kingdom,
And Your dominion *endures* throughout
all generations.
¹The LORD is faithful in His words,
And holy in all His works.

14¶ The LORD supports all who fall,

144:14 ¹Lit *going out;* i.e., miscarriage   **145:13** ¹ *The LORD...His works* in LXX (cf. DSS); not found in MT

And raises up all who are bowed down.
15 The eyes of all look to You,
And You give them their food in due time.
16 You open Your hand
And satisfy the desire of every living
thing.
17¶ The LORD is righteous in all His ways,
And kind in all His works.
18 The LORD is near to all who call on Him,
To all who call on Him in truth.
19 He will fulfill the desire of those who fear
Him;
He will also hear their cry for help and
save them.
20 The LORD watches over all who love Him,
But He will destroy all the wicked.
21 My mouth will speak the praise of the
LORD,
And all flesh will bless His holy name
forever and ever.

PSALM 146

The LORD, an Abundant Helper.
1 Praise the LORD!
Praise the LORD, my soul!
2 I will praise the LORD while I live;
I will sing praises to my God while I have
my being.
3 Do not trust in noblemen,
In mortal man, in whom there is no
salvation.
4 His spirit departs, he returns to the
earth;
On that *very* day his plans perish.
5 Blessed is he whose help is the God of
Jacob,
Whose hope is in the LORD his God,
6 Who made heaven and earth,
The sea and everything that is in them;
Who keeps faith forever;
7 Who executes justice for the oppressed;
Who gives food to the hungry.
The LORD frees the prisoners.
8¶ The LORD opens *the eyes of* those who are
blind;
The LORD raises up those who are bowed
down;
The LORD loves the righteous.
9 The LORD watches over strangers;
He supports the fatherless and the widow,
But He thwarts the way of the wicked.
10 The LORD will reign forever,
Your God, Zion, to all generations.
Praise the LORD!

PSALM 147

**Praise for Jerusalem's Restoration and
Prosperity.**
1 Praise the LORD!
For it is good to sing praises to our God;
For it is pleasant *and* praise is beautiful.
2 The LORD builds up Jerusalem;
He gathers the outcasts of Israel.
3 He heals the brokenhearted
And binds up their wounds.
4 He counts the number of the stars;
He gives names to all of them.

5 Great is our Lord and abundant in
strength;
His understanding is infinite.
6 The LORD supports the afflicted;
He brings the wicked down to the ground.
7¶ Sing to the LORD with thanksgiving;
Sing praises to our God on the lyre;
8 *It is* He who covers the heavens with
clouds,
Who provides rain for the earth,
Who makes grass sprout on the
mountains.
9 *It is* He who gives an animal its food,
And feeds young ravens that cry.
10 He does not delight in ¹the strength of the
horse;
He does not take pleasure in the ²legs of a
man.
11 The LORD favors those who fear Him,
Those who wait for His faithfulness.
12¶ Praise the LORD, Jerusalem!
Praise your God, Zion!
13 For He has strengthened the bars of your
gates;
He has blessed your sons among you.
14 He makes peace in your borders;
He satisfies you with the finest of the
wheat.
15 He sends His command to the earth;
His word runs very swiftly.
16 He showers snow like wool;
He scatters the frost like ashes.
17 He hurls His ice as fragments;
Who can stand before His cold?
18 He sends His word and makes them melt;
He makes His wind blow, and the waters
flow.
19 He declares His words to Jacob,
His statutes and His judgments to Israel.
20 He has not dealt this way with any *other*
nation;
And as for His judgments, they have not
known them.
Praise the LORD!

PSALM 148

The Whole Creation Invoked to Praise the LORD.
1 Praise the LORD!
Praise the LORD from the heavens;
Praise Him in the heights!
2 Praise Him, all His angels;
Praise Him, all His *heavenly* armies!
3 Praise Him, sun and moon;
Praise Him, all stars of light!
4 Praise Him, highest heavens,
And the waters that are above the
heavens!
5 They are to praise the name of the LORD,
For He commanded and they were
created.
6 He has also established them forever and
ever;
He has made a decree, and it will not pass
away.
7¶ Praise the LORD from the earth,
Sea monsters, and all the ocean depths;
8 Fire and hail, snow and clouds;
Stormy wind, fulfilling His word;

147:10 ¹I.e., as a military asset   ²I.e., as a military asset

9 Mountains and all hills;
Fruit trees and all cedars;
10 Animals and all cattle;
Crawling things and winged fowl;
11 Kings of the earth and all peoples;
Rulers and all judges of the earth;
12 Both young men and virgins;
Old men and children.
13¶ They are to praise the name of the LORD,
For His name alone is exalted;
His majesty is above earth and heaven.
14 And He has lifted up a horn for His
people,
Praise for all His godly ones,
For the sons of Israel, a people near to
Him.
Praise the LORD!

PSALM 149

Israel Invoked to Praise the LORD.
1 Praise the LORD!
Sing a new song to the LORD,
And His praise in the congregation of the
godly ones.
2 Israel shall be joyful in his Maker;
The sons of Zion shall rejoice in their
King.
3 They shall praise His name with dancing;
They shall sing praises to Him with
tambourine and lyre.
4 For the LORD takes pleasure in His people;
He will glorify the lowly with salvation.
5¶ The godly ones shall be jubilant in glory;

They shall sing for joy on their beds.
6 The high praises of God *shall be* in their
mouths,
And a two-edged sword in their hands,
7 To execute vengeance on the nations,
And punishment on the peoples,
8 To bind their kings with chains,
And their dignitaries with shackles of
iron,
9 To execute against them the judgment
written.
This is an honor for all His godly ones.
Praise the LORD!

PSALM 150

A Psalm of Praise.
1 Praise the LORD!
Praise God in His sanctuary;
Praise Him in His mighty expanse.
2 Praise Him for His mighty deeds;
Praise Him according to His excellent
greatness.
3¶ Praise Him with trumpet sound;
Praise Him with harp and lyre.
4 Praise Him with tambourine and
dancing;
Praise Him with stringed instruments and
flute.
5 Praise Him with loud cymbals;
Praise Him with resounding cymbals.
6 Everything that has breath shall praise the
LORD.
Praise the LORD!

THE PROVERBS

The Usefulness of Proverbs

1 The proverbs of Solomon the son of David, king of Israel:

2 To know wisdom and instruction,
To discern the sayings of understanding,

3 To receive instruction in wise behavior,
Righteousness, justice, and integrity;

4 To give prudence to the naive,
To the youth knowledge and discretion,

5 A wise person will hear and increase in learning,
And a person of understanding will acquire wise counsel,

6 To understand a proverb and a saying,
The words of the wise and their riddles.

7¶ The fear of the LORD is the beginning of knowledge;
Fools despise wisdom and instruction.

The Enticement of Sinners

8¶ Listen, my son, to your father's instruction,
And do not ignore your mother's teaching;

9 For they are a graceful wreath for your head
And necklaces for your neck.

10 My son, if sinners entice you,
Do not consent.

11 If they say, "Come with us,
Let's lie in wait for blood,
Let's ambush the innocent without cause;

12 Let's swallow them alive like Sheol,
Even whole, like those who go down to the pit;

13 We will find all *kinds* of precious wealth,
We will fill our houses with plunder;

14 Throw in your lot with us,
We will all have one money bag,"

15 My son, do not walk on the way with them.
Keep your feet from their path,

16 For their feet run to evil,
And they are quick to shed blood.

17 Indeed, it is useless to spread the *baited* net
In the sight of any bird;

18 But they lie in wait for their own blood;
They ambush their own lives.

19 Such are the ways of everyone who makes unjust gain;
It takes away the life of its possessors.

Wisdom Warns

20¶ Wisdom shouts in the street,
She raises her voice in the public square;

21 At the head of the noisy *streets* she cries out;
At the entrance of the gates in the city she declares her sayings:

22 "How long, you naive ones, will you love simplistic thinking?
And *how long will* scoffers delight themselves in scoffing
And fools hate knowledge?

23 "Turn to my rebuke,
Behold, I will pour out my spirit on you;
I will make my words known to you.

24 "Because I called and you refused,
I stretched out my hand and no one paid attention;

25 And you neglected all my advice
And did not want my rebuke;

26 I will also laugh at your disaster;
I will mock when your dread comes,

27 When your dread comes like a storm
And your disaster comes like a whirlwind,
When distress and anguish come upon you.

28 "Then they will call on me, but I will not answer;
They will seek me diligently but will not find me,

29 Because they hated knowledge
And did not choose the fear of the LORD.

30 "They did not accept my advice,
They disdainfully rejected every rebuke from me.

31 "So they shall eat of the fruit of their own way,
And be filled with their own schemes.

32 "For the faithlessness of the naive will kill them,
And the complacency of fools will destroy them.

33 "But whoever listens to me will live securely
And will be at ease from the dread of evil."

The Pursuit of Wisdom Brings Security

2 My son, if you will receive my words
And treasure my commandments within you,

2 Make your ear attentive to wisdom;
Incline your heart to understanding.

3 For if you cry out for insight,
And raise your voice for understanding;

4 If you seek her as silver
And search for her as for hidden treasures;

5 Then you will understand the fear of the LORD,
And discover the knowledge of God.

6 For the LORD gives wisdom;
From His mouth *come* knowledge and understanding.

7 He stores up sound wisdom for the upright;
He is a shield to those who walk in integrity,

8 Guarding the paths of justice,
And He watches over the way of His godly ones.

9 Then you will discern righteousness, justice,
And integrity, *and* every good path.

10 For wisdom will enter your heart,
And knowledge will be delightful to your soul;

11 Discretion will watch over you,

Understanding will guard you,
12 To rescue you from the way of evil,
From a person who speaks perverse
 things;
13 *From* those who leave the paths of
 uprightness
To walk in the ways of darkness;
14 Who delight in doing evil
And rejoice in the perversity of evil;
15 Whose paths are crooked,
And who are devious in their ways;
16 To rescue you from the strange woman,
From the foreign woman who flatters with
 her words,
17 Who leaves the companion of her youth
And forgets the covenant of her God;
18 For her house sinks down to death,
And her tracks *lead* to the dead;
19 None who go to her return,
Nor do they reach the paths of life.
20 So you will walk in the way of good
 people
And keep to the paths of the righteous.
21 For the upright will live in the land,
And the blameless will remain in it;
22 But the wicked will be eliminated from
 the land,
And the treacherous will be torn away
 from it.

The Rewards of Wisdom
3 My son, do not forget my teaching,
But have your heart comply with my
 commandments;
2 For length of days and years of life
And peace they will add to you.
3 Do not let kindness and truth leave you;
Bind them around your neck,
Write them on the tablet of your heart.
4 So you will find favor and a good reputation
In the sight of God and man.
5 Trust in the LORD with all your heart
And do not lean on your own understanding.
6 In all your ways acknowledge Him,
And He will make your paths straight.
7 Do not be wise in your own eyes;
Fear the LORD and turn away from evil.
8 It will be healing to your body
And refreshment to your bones.
9 Honor the LORD from your wealth,
And from the first of all your produce;
10 Then your barns will be filled with
 plenty,
And your vats will overflow with new
 wine.
11 My son, do not reject the discipline of the
 LORD
Or loathe His rebuke,
12 For whom the LORD loves He disciplines,
Just as a father *disciplines* the son in
 whom he delights.
13¶ Blessed is a person who finds wisdom,
And one who obtains understanding.
14 For *her* profit is better than the profit of
 silver,
And her produce better than gold.
15 She is more precious than jewels,

And nothing you desire compares with
 her.
16 Long life is in her right hand;
In her left hand are riches and honor.
17 Her ways are pleasant ways,
And all her paths are peace.
18 She is a tree of life to those who take hold
 of her,
And happy are those who hold on to her.
19 The LORD founded the earth by wisdom,
He established the heavens by understanding.
20 By His knowledge the ocean depths were
 burst open,
And the clouds drip with dew.
21 My son, *see that* they do not escape from
 your sight;
Comply with sound wisdom and
 discretion,
22 And they will be life to your soul
And adornment to your neck.
23 Then you will walk in your way securely,
And your foot will not stumble.
24 When you lie down, you will not be
 afraid;
When you lie down, your sleep will be
 sweet.
25 Do not be afraid of sudden danger,
Nor of trouble from the wicked when it
 comes;
26 For the LORD will be your confidence,
And will keep your foot from being
 caught.
27¶ Do not withhold good from those to
 whom it is due,
When it is in your power to do *it*.
28 Do not say to your neighbor, "Go, and
 come back,
And tomorrow I will give *it to you*,"
When you have it with you.
29 Do not devise harm against your neighbor,
While he lives securely beside you.
30 Do not contend with a person for no
 reason,
If he has done you no harm.
31 Do not envy a violent person,
And do not choose any of his ways.
32 For the devious are an abomination to the
 LORD;
But He is intimate with the upright.
33 The curse of the LORD is on the house of
 the wicked,
But He blesses the home of the righteous.
34 Though He scoffs at the scoffers,
Yet He gives grace to the needy.
35 The wise will inherit honor,
But fools increase dishonor.

A Father's Instruction
4 Listen, *my* sons, to the instruction
of a father,
And pay attention so that you may gain
 understanding,
2 For I give you good teaching;
Do not abandon my instruction.
3 When I was a son to my father,
Tender and the only son in the sight of my
 mother,
4 He taught me and said to me,

"Let your heart take hold of my words;
Keep my commandments and live;
5 Acquire wisdom! Acquire understanding!
Do not forget nor turn away from the
words of my mouth.
6 "Do not abandon her, and she will guard
you;
Love her, and she will watch over you.
7 "The beginning of wisdom *is:* Acquire
wisdom;
And with all your possessions, acquire
understanding.
8 "Prize her, and she will exalt you;
She will honor you if you embrace her.
9 "She will place on your head a garland of
grace;
She will present you with a crown of
beauty."
10¶ Listen, my son, and accept my sayings,
And the years of your life will be many.
11 I have instructed you in the way of
wisdom;
I have led you in upright paths.
12 When you walk, your steps will not be
hampered;
And if you run, you will not stumble.
13 Take hold of instruction; do not let go.
Guard her, for she is your life.
14 Do not enter the path of the wicked
And do not proceed in the way of evil
people.
15 Avoid it, do not pass by it;
Turn away from it and pass on.
16 For they cannot sleep unless they do evil;
And they are robbed of sleep unless they
make *someone* stumble.
17 For they eat the bread of wickedness,
And drink the wine of violence.
18 But the path of the righteous is like the
light of dawn
That shines brighter and brighter until the
full day.
19 The way of the wicked is like darkness;
They do not know over what they
stumble.
20¶ My son, pay attention to my words;
Incline your ear to my sayings.
21 They are not to escape from your sight;
Keep them in the midst of your heart.
22 For they are life to those who find them,
And healing to all their body.
23 Watch over your heart with all diligence,
For from it *flow* the springs of life.
24 Rid yourself of a deceitful mouth
And keep devious speech far from you.
25 Let your eyes look directly ahead
And let your gaze be fixed straight in front
of you.
26 Watch the path of your feet,
And all your ways will be established.
27 Do not turn to the right or to the left;
Turn your foot from evil.

Pitfalls of Immorality

5 My son, pay attention to my wisdom,
Incline your ear to my understanding,
2 So that you may maintain discretion
And your lips may comply with
knowledge.
3 For the lips of an adulteress drip honey,

And her speech is smoother than oil;
4 But in the end she is bitter as wormwood,
Sharp as a two-edged sword.
5 Her feet go down to death,
Her steps take hold of Sheol.
6 She does not ponder the path of life;
Her ways are unstable, she does not
know *it.*
7¶ Now then, *my* sons, listen to me
And do not turn away from the words of
my mouth.
8 Keep your way far from her,
And do not go near the door of her house,
9 Otherwise you will give your vigor to
others,
And your years to the cruel one;
10 And strangers will be filled with your
strength,
And your hard-earned possessions *will go*
to the house of a foreigner;
11 And you will groan in the end,
When your flesh and your body are
consumed;
12 And you say, "How I hated instruction!
And my heart disdainfully rejected
rebuke!
13 "I did not listen to the voice of my
teachers,
Nor incline my ear to my instructors!
14 "I was almost in total ruin
In the midst of the assembly and congregation."
15¶ Drink water from your own cistern,
And fresh water from your own well.
16 Should your springs overflow into the
street,
Streams of water in the public squares?
17 Let them be yours alone,
And not for strangers with you.
18 Let your fountain be blessed,
And rejoice in the wife of your youth.
19 *Like* a loving doe and a graceful mountain
goat,
Let her breasts satisfy you at all times;
Be exhilarated always with her love.
20 For why should you, my son, be
exhilarated with an adulteress,
And embrace the breasts of a foreigner?
21 For the ways of everyone are before the
eyes of the Lord,
And He observes all his paths.
22 His own wrongdoings will trap the
wicked,
And he will be held by the ropes of his
sin.
23 He will die for lack of instruction,
And in the greatness of his foolishness he
will go astray.

Parental Counsel

6 My son, if you have become a guarantor for
your neighbor,
Or have given a handshake for a
stranger,
2 *If* you have been ensnared by the words of
your mouth,
Or caught by the words of your mouth,
3 Then do this, my son, and save yourself:
Since you have come into the hand of
your neighbor,

Go, humble yourself, and be urgent with your neighbor *to free yourself.*

4 Give no sleep to your eyes,
Nor slumber to your eyelids;

5 Save yourself like a gazelle from *the hunter's* hand,
And like a bird from the hand of the fowler.

6¶ Go to the ant, you lazy one,
Observe its ways and be wise,

7 Which, having no chief,
Officer, or ruler,

8 Prepares its food in the summer
And gathers its provision in the harvest.

9 How long will you lie down, you lazy one?
When will you arise from your sleep?

10 "A little sleep, a little slumber,
A little folding of the hands to rest,"

11 Then your poverty will come in like a drifter,
And your need like an armed man.

12¶ A worthless person, a wicked man,
Is one who walks with a perverse mouth,

13 Who winks with his eyes, who signals with his feet,
Who points with his fingers;

14 Who, *with* perversion in his heart, continually devises evil,
Who spreads strife.

15 Therefore his disaster will come suddenly;
Instantly he will be broken and there will be no healing.

16¶ There are six things that the LORD hates,
Seven that are an abomination to Him:

17 Haughty eyes, a lying tongue,
And hands that shed innocent blood,

18 A heart that devises wicked plans,
Feet that run rapidly to evil,

19 A false witness *who* declares lies,
And one who spreads strife among brothers.

20¶ My son, comply with the commandment of your father,
And do not ignore the teaching of your mother;

21 Bind them continually on your heart;
Tie them around your neck.

22 When you walk, they will guide you;
When you sleep, they will watch over you;
And when you awake, they will talk to you.

23 For the commandment is a lamp and the teaching is light;
And rebukes for discipline are the way of life

24 To keep you from the evil woman,
From the smooth tongue of the foreign woman.

25 Do not desire her beauty in your heart,
Nor let her capture you with her eyelids.

26¶ For the price of a prostitute *reduces one* to a loaf of bread,
And an adulteress hunts for a precious life.

27 Can anyone take fire in his lap
And his clothes not be burned?

28 Or can a person walk on hot coals
And his feet not be scorched?

29 So is the one who goes in to his neighbor's wife;
Whoever touches her will not go unpunished.

30 *People* do not despise a thief if he steals
To satisfy himself when he is hungry;

31 But when he is found, he must repay seven times *as much;*
He must give up all the property of his house.

32 One who commits adultery with a woman is lacking sense;
He who would destroy himself commits it.

33 He will find wounds and disgrace,
And his shame will not be removed.

34 For jealousy enrages a man,
And he will not have compassion on the day of vengeance.

35 He will not accept any settlement,
Nor will he be satisfied though you make *it* a large gift.

The Lures of the Prostitute

7 My son, keep my words
And treasure my commandments within you.

2 Keep my commandments and live,
And my teaching as the ¹apple of your eye.

3 Bind them on your fingers;
Write them on the tablet of your heart.

4 Say to wisdom, "You are my sister,"
And call understanding *your* intimate friend,

5 So that they may keep you from an adulteress,
From the foreigner who flatters with her words.

6¶ For at the window of my house
I looked out through my lattice,

7 And I saw among the naive,
And discerned among the youths
A young man lacking sense,

8 Passing through the street near her corner;
And he walks along the way to her house,

9 In the twilight, in the evening,
In the middle of the night and the darkness.

10 And behold, a woman *comes* to meet him,
Dressed as a prostitute and cunning of heart.

11 She is boisterous and rebellious,
Her feet do not remain at home;

12 *She is* now in the streets, now in the public squares,
And lurks by every corner.

13 So she seizes him and kisses him,
And with a brazen face she says to him:

14 "I was due to offer peace offerings;
Today I have paid my vows.

15 "Therefore I have come out to meet you,
To seek your presence diligently, and I have found you.

16 "I have spread my couch with coverings,
With colored linens of Egypt.

17 "I have sprinkled my bed
With myrrh, aloes, and cinnamon.

7:2 ¹ Lit *pupil*

18 "Come, let's drink our fill of love until
        morning;
    Let's delight ourselves with caresses.
19 "For my husband is not at home;
    He has gone on a long journey.
20 "He has taken a bag of money with him.
    At the full moon he will come home."
21 With her many persuasions she entices
        him;
    With her flattering lips she seduces him.
22 Suddenly he follows her
    As an ox goes to the slaughter,
    Or as *one* walks in ankle bracelets to the
        discipline of a fool,
23 Until an arrow pierces through his liver;
    As a bird hurries to the snare,
    So he does not know that it *will cost him*
        his life.
24¶ Now therefore, *my* sons, listen to me,
    And pay attention to the words of my
        mouth.
25 Do not let your heart turn aside to her
        ways,
    Do not stray into her paths.
26 For many are the victims she has brought
        to ruin,
    And numerous are all those slaughtered
        by her.
27 Her house is the way to Sheol,
    Descending to the chambers of death.

The Commendation of Wisdom
8 Does not wisdom call,
    And understanding raise her voice?
2   On top of the heights beside the way,
    Where the paths meet, she takes her
        stand;
3   Beside the gates, at the opening to the
        city,
    At the entrance of the doors, she cries
        out:
4   "To you, people, I call,
    And my voice is to mankind.
5   "You naive ones, understand prudence;
    And, you fools, understand wisdom!
6   "Listen, for I will speak noble things;
    And the opening of my lips *will reveal*
        right things.
7   "For my mouth will proclaim truth;
    And wickedness is an abomination to my
        lips.
8   "All the words of my mouth are in
        righteousness;
    There is nothing crooked or perverted in
        them.
9   "They are all straightforward to him who
        understands,
    And right to those who find knowledge.
10 "Accept my instruction and not silver,
    And knowledge rather than choice gold.
11 "For wisdom is better than jewels;
    And all desirable things cannot compare
        with her.
12¶ "I, wisdom, dwell with prudence,
    And I find knowledge *and* discretion.
13 "The fear of the LORD is to hate evil;
    Pride, arrogance, the evil way,
    And the perverted mouth, I hate.
14 "Advice is mine and sound wisdom;
    I am understanding, power is mine.

15 "By me kings reign,
    And rulers decree justice.
16 "By me princes rule, and nobles,
    All who judge rightly.
17 "I love those who love me;
    And those who diligently seek me will
        find me.
18 "Riches and honor are with me,
    Enduring wealth and righteousness.
19 "My fruit is better than gold, even pure
        gold;
    And my yield *better* than choice silver.
20 "I walk in the way of righteousness,
    In the midst of the paths of justice,
21 To endow those who love me with
        wealth,
    That I may fill their treasuries.
22¶ "The LORD created me at the beginning of
        His way,
    Before His works of old.
23 "From eternity I was established,
    From the beginning, from the earliest
        times of the earth.
24 "When there were no ocean depths, I was
        born,
    When there were no springs abounding
        with water.
25 "Before the mountains were settled,
    Before the hills, I was born;
26 While He had not yet made the earth and
        the fields,
    Nor the first dust of the world.
27 "When He established the heavens, I was
        there;
    When He inscribed a circle on the face of
        the deep,
28 When He made firm the skies above,
    When the springs of the deep became
        fixed,
29 When He set a boundary for the sea
    So that the water would not violate His
        command,
    When He marked out the foundations of
        the earth;
30 Then I was beside Him, *as* a master
        workman;
    And I was *His* delight daily,
    Rejoicing always before Him,
31 Rejoicing in the world, His earth,
    And *having* my delight in the sons of
        mankind.
32¶ "Now then, sons, listen to me,
    For blessed are those who keep my ways.
33 "Listen to instruction and be wise,
    And do not neglect *it.*
34 "Blessed is the person who listens to me,
    Watching daily at my gates,
    Waiting at my doorposts.
35 "For one who finds me finds life,
    And obtains favor from the LORD.
36 "But one who sins against me injures
        himself;
    All those who hate me love death."

Wisdom's Invitation
9 Wisdom has built her house,
    She has carved out her seven pillars;
2   She has prepared her food, she has mixed
        her wine;
    She has also set her table;

3 She has sent out her attendants, she calls
out
From the tops of the heights of the city:
4 "Whoever is naive, let him turn in here!"
To him who lacks understanding she says,
5 "Come, eat of my food
And drink of the wine I have mixed.
6 "Abandon *your* foolishness and live,
And proceed in the way of understanding."
7¶ One who corrects a scoffer gets dishonor
for himself,
And one who rebukes a wicked person
gets insults for himself.
8 Do not rebuke a scoffer, or he will hate
you;
Rebuke a wise person and he will love
you.
9 Give *instruction* to a wise person and he
will become still wiser;
Teach a righteous person and he will
increase *his* insight.
10 The fear of the LORD is the beginning of
wisdom,
And the knowledge of the Holy One is
understanding.
11 For by me your days will be multiplied,
And years of life will be added to you.
12 If you are wise, you are wise for yourself,
And if you scoff, you alone will suffer *from
it.*
13¶ A woman of foolishness is boisterous,
She has a lack of understanding and
knows nothing.
14 She sits at the doorway of her house,
On a seat by the high places of the city,
15 Calling to those who pass by,
Who are going straight on their paths:
16 "Whoever is naive, let him turn in here,"
And to him who lacks understanding she
says,
17 "Stolen water is sweet;
And bread *eaten* in secret is pleasant."
18 But he does not know that the dead are
there,
That her guests are in the depths of Sheol.

Contrast of the Righteous and the Wicked

10 The proverbs of Solomon.
A wise son makes a father glad,
But a foolish son is a grief to his mother.
2 Ill-gotten gains do not benefit,
But righteousness rescues from death.
3 The LORD will not allow the righteous to
hunger,
But He will reject the craving of the
wicked.
4 Poor is one who works with a lazy hand,
But the hand of the diligent makes rich.
5 He who gathers in summer is a son who
acts wisely,
But he who sleeps in harvest is a son who
acts shamefully.
6 Blessings are on the head of the righteous,
But the mouth of the wicked conceals
violence.
7 The mentioning of the righteous is a
blessing,
But the name of the wicked will rot.
8 The wise of heart will receive commands,

9 But a babbling fool will come to ruin.
One who walks in integrity walks
securely,
But one who perverts his ways will be
found out.
10 He who winks the eye causes trouble,
And a babbling fool will come to ruin.
11 The mouth of the righteous is a fountain
of life,
But the mouth of the wicked conceals
violence.
12 Hatred stirs up strife,
But love covers all offenses.
13 On the lips of the discerning, wisdom is
found,
But a rod is for the back of him who has
no sense.
14 Wise people store up knowledge,
But with the mouth of the foolish, ruin is
at hand.
15 The rich person's wealth is his fortress,
The ruin of the poor is their poverty.
16 The wages of the righteous is life,
The income of the wicked, punishment.
17 One who is *on* the path of life follows
instruction,
But one who ignores a rebuke goes astray.
18 One who conceals hatred *has* lying lips,
And one who spreads slander is a fool.
19 When there are many words, wrongdoing
is unavoidable,
But one who restrains his lips is wise.
20 The tongue of the righteous is *like* choice
silver,
The heart of the wicked is *worth* little.
21 The lips of the righteous feed many,
But fools die for lack of understanding.
22 It is the blessing of the LORD that makes
rich,
And He adds no sorrow to it.
23 Doing wickedness is like sport to a fool,
And *so is* wisdom to a person of understanding.
24 What the wicked fears will come upon
him,
But the desire of the righteous will be
granted.
25 When the whirlwind passes, the wicked is
no more,
But the righteous *has* an everlasting
foundation.
26 Like vinegar to the teeth and smoke to the
eyes,
So is the lazy one to those who send him.
27 The fear of the LORD prolongs life,
But the years of the wicked will be
shortened.
28 The hope of the righteous is gladness,
But the expectation of the wicked
perishes.
29 The way of the LORD is a stronghold for
the upright,
But ruin to the workers of injustice.
30 The righteous will never be shaken,
But the wicked will not live in the land.
31 The mouth of the righteous flows with
wisdom,
But the perverted tongue will be cut out.
32 The lips of the righteous know what is
acceptable,

But the mouth of the wicked, what is
perverted.

Contrast of the Upright and the Wicked

11 A false balance is an abomination to
the LORD,
But a just weight is His delight.
2 When pride comes, then comes dishonor;
But with the humble there is wisdom.
3 The integrity of the upright will guide
them,
But the perversity of the treacherous will
destroy them.
4 Riches do not benefit on the day of
wrath,
But righteousness rescues from death.
5 The righteousness of the blameless will
smooth his way,
But the wicked will fall by his own
wickedness.
6 The righteousness of the upright will
rescue them,
But the treacherous will be caught by
their own greed.
7 When a wicked person dies, *his*
expectation will perish,
And the hope of strong people perishes.
8 The righteous is rescued from trouble,
But the wicked takes his place.
9 With *his* mouth the godless person
destroys his neighbor,
But through knowledge the righteous will
be rescued.
10 When things go well for the righteous, the
city rejoices,
And when the wicked perish, there is
joyful shouting.
11 By the blessing of the upright a city is
exalted,
But by the mouth of the wicked, it is torn
down.
12 One who despises his neighbor lacks
sense,
But a person of understanding keeps
silent.
13 One who goes about as a slanderer reveals
secrets,
But one who is trustworthy conceals a
matter.
14 Where there is no guidance the people
fall,
But in an abundance of counselors there is
victory.
15 One who is a guarantor for a stranger will
certainly suffer for it,
But one who hates being a guarantor is
secure.
16 A gracious woman attains honor,
And ruthless men attain riches.
17 A merciful person does himself *good,*
But the cruel person does himself harm.
18 A wicked person earns deceptive wages,
But one who sows righteousness *gets* a
true reward.
19 One who is steadfast in righteousness
attains life,
But one who pursues evil *attains* his own
death.
20 The perverse in heart are an abomination
to the LORD,

But the blameless in *their* walk are His
delight.
21 Be assured, the evil person will not go
unpunished,
But the descendants of the righteous will
be rescued.
22 *As* a ring of gold in a pig's snout
So is a beautiful woman who lacks
discretion.
23 The desire of the righteous is only good,
But the expectation of the wicked is
wrath.
24 There is one who scatters, and *yet*
increases all the more,
And there is one who withholds what is
justly due, *and yet it results* only in
poverty.
25 A generous person will be prosperous,
And one who gives *others* plenty of water
will himself be given plenty.
26 One who withholds grain, the people will
curse him,
But blessing will be on the head of him
who sells *it.*
27 One who diligently seeks good seeks
favor,
But one who seeks evil, evil will come to
him.
28 One who trusts in his riches will fall,
But the righteous will flourish like the
green leaf.
29 One who troubles his own house will
inherit wind,
And the foolish will be servant to the
wise-hearted.
30 The fruit of the righteous is a tree of life,
And one who is wise gains souls.
31 If the righteous will be repaid on the
earth,
How much more the wicked and the
sinner!

Contrast of the Upright and the Wicked

12 One who loves discipline loves
knowledge,
But one who hates rebuke is stupid.
2 A good person will obtain favor from the
LORD,
But He will condemn a person who
devises evil.
3 A person will not be established by
wickedness,
But the root of the righteous will not be
moved.
4 An excellent wife is the crown of her
husband,
But she who shames *him* is like
rottenness in his bones.
5 The thoughts of the righteous are just,
But the counsels of the wicked are
deceitful.
6 The words of the wicked wait in ambush
for blood,
But the mouth of the upright will rescue
them.
7 The wicked are overthrown and are no
more,
But the house of the righteous will stand.
8 A person will be praised according to his
insight,

But one of perverse mind will be despised.

9 Better is one who is lightly esteemed and has a servant,
Than one who honors himself and lacks bread.

10 A righteous person has regard for the life of his animal,
But *even* the compassion of the wicked is cruel.

11 One who works his land will have plenty of bread,
But one who pursues worthless *things* lacks sense.

12 The wicked person desires the plunder of evil people,
But the root of the righteous yields *fruit.*

13 An evil person is ensnared by the offense of his lips,
But the righteous will escape from trouble.

14 A person will be satisfied with good by the fruit of his words,
And the deeds of a person's hands will return to him.

15 The way of a fool is right in his own eyes,
But a person who listens to advice is wise.

16 A fool's anger is known at once,
But a prudent person conceals dishonor.

17 One *who* declares truth tells what is right,
But a false witness, deceit.

18 There is one who speaks rashly like the thrusts of a sword,
But the tongue of the wise brings healing.

19 Truthful lips will endure forever,
But a lying tongue is only for a moment.

20 Deceit is in the heart of those who devise evil,
But counselors of peace *have* joy.

21 No harm happens to the righteous,
But the wicked are filled with trouble.

22 Lying lips are an abomination to the LORD,
But those who deal faithfully are His delight.

23 A prudent person conceals knowledge,
But the heart of fools proclaims foolishness.

24 The hand of the diligent will rule,
But the lazy *hand* will be put to forced labor.

25 Anxiety in a person's heart weighs it down,
But a good word makes it glad.

26 The righteous person is a guide to his neighbor,
But the way of the wicked leads them astray.

27 A lazy person does not roast his prey,
But the precious possession of a person *is* diligence.

28 In the way of righteousness there is life,
And in *its* pathway there is no death.

Contrast of the Upright and the Wicked

13 A wise son *accepts his* father's discipline,
But a scoffer does not listen to rebuke.

2 From the fruit of a person's mouth he enjoys good,

But the desire of the treacherous is violence.

3 One who guards his mouth protects his life;
One who opens wide his lips comes to ruin.

4 The soul of the lazy one craves and *gets* nothing,
But the soul of the diligent is made prosperous.

5 A righteous person hates a false statement,
But a wicked person acts disgustingly and shamefully.

6 Righteousness guards the one whose way is blameless,
But wickedness brings the sinner to ruin.

7 There is one who pretends to be rich but has nothing;
Another pretends to be poor, but has great wealth.

8 The ransom of a person's life is his wealth,
But the poor hears no rebuke.

9 The light of the righteous 'rejoices,
But the lamp of the wicked goes out.

10 Through overconfidence comes nothing but strife,
But wisdom is with those who receive counsel.

11 Wealth *obtained* from 'nothing dwindles,
But one who gathers by labor increases *it.*

12 Hope deferred makes the heart sick,
But desire fulfilled is a tree of life.

13 One who despises the word will do badly,
But one who fears the commandment will be rewarded.

14 The teaching of the wise is a fountain of life,
To turn aside from the snares of death.

15 Good understanding produces favor,
But the way of the treacherous is their own disaster.

16 Every prudent person acts with knowledge,
But a fool displays foolishness.

17 A wicked messenger falls into adversity,
But a faithful messenger *brings* healing.

18 Poverty and shame *will come* to one who neglects discipline,
But one who complies with rebuke will be honored.

19 Desire realized is sweet to the soul,
But it is an abomination to fools to turn away from evil.

20 One who walks with wise people will be wise,
But a companion of fools will suffer harm.

21 Adversity pursues sinners,
But the righteous will be rewarded with prosperity.

22 A good person leaves an inheritance to his grandchildren,
And the wealth of a sinner is stored up for the righteous.

23 Abundant food *is in* the uncultivated ground of the poor,
But it is swept away by injustice.

24 He who withholds his rod hates his son,

But he who loves him disciplines him
diligently.

25 The righteous has enough to satisfy his
appetite,
But the stomach of the wicked is in need.

Contrast of the Upright and the Wicked

14 The wise woman builds her house,
But the foolish tears it down with her
own hands.

2 One who walks in his uprightness fears
the LORD,
But one who is devious in his ways
despises Him.

3 In the mouth of the foolish is a rod for *his*
back,
But the lips of the wise will protect them.

4 Where there are no oxen, the manger is
clean;
But much revenue *comes* by the strength
of the ox.

5 A trustworthy witness will not lie,
But a false witness declares lies.

6 A scoffer seeks wisdom and *finds* none,
But knowledge is easy for one who has
understanding.

7 Leave the presence of a fool,
Or you will not discern words of
knowledge.

8 The wisdom of the sensible is to
understand his way,
But the foolishness of fools is deceit.

9 Fools mock at sin,
But among the upright there is goodwill.

10 The heart knows its own bitterness,
And a stranger does not share its joy.

11 The house of the wicked will be
destroyed,
But the tent of the upright will flourish.

12 There is a way *which seems* right to a
person,
But its end is the way of death.

13 Even in laughter the heart may be in pain,
And the end of joy may be grief.

14 One with a wayward heart will have his
fill of his own ways,
But a good person will *be satisfied* with
his.

15 The naive believes everything,
But the sensible person considers his
steps.

16 A wise person is cautious and turns away
from evil,
But a fool is arrogant and careless.

17 A quick-tempered person acts foolishly,
And a person of evil devices is hated.

18 The naive inherit foolishness,
But the sensible are crowned with
knowledge.

19 The evil will bow down before the good,
And the wicked at the gates of the
righteous.

20 The poor is hated even by his neighbor,
But those who love the rich are many.

21 One who despises his neighbor sins,
But one who is gracious to the poor is
blessed.

22 Will they who devise evil not go astray?
But kindness and truth *will be to* those
who devise good.

23 In all labor there is profit,
But mere talk *leads* only to poverty.

24 The crown of the wise is their riches,
But the foolishness of fools is *simply*
foolishness.

25 A truthful witness saves lives,
But one *who* declares lies *is* deceitful.

26 In the fear of the LORD there is strong
confidence,
And his children will have refuge.

27 The fear of the LORD is a fountain of life,
By which one may avoid the snares of
death.

28 In a multitude of people is a king's glory,
But in the scarcity of people is a prince's
ruin.

29 One who is slow to anger has great
understanding;
But one who is quick-tempered exalts
foolishness.

30 A tranquil heart is life to the body,
But jealousy is rottenness to the bones.

31 One who oppresses the poor taunts his
Maker,
But one who is gracious to the needy
honors Him.

32 The wicked is thrust down by his own
wrongdoing,
But the righteous has a refuge when he
dies.

33 Wisdom rests in the heart of one who has
understanding,
But among fools it is made known.

34 Righteousness exalts a nation,
But sin is a disgrace to *any* people.

35 The king's favor is toward a servant who
acts wisely,
But his anger is toward him who acts
shamefully.

Contrast of the Upright and the Wicked

15 A gentle answer turns away wrath,
But a harsh word stirs up anger.

2 The tongue of the wise makes knowledge
pleasant,
But the mouth of fools spouts foolishness.

3 The eyes of the LORD are in every place,
Watching the evil and the good.

4 A soothing tongue is a tree of life,
But perversion in it crushes the spirit.

5 A fool rejects his father's discipline,
But he who complies with rebuke is
sensible.

6 Great wealth is *in* the house of the
righteous,
But trouble is in the income of the
wicked.

7 The lips of the wise spread knowledge,
But the hearts of fools are not so.

8 The sacrifice of the wicked is an
abomination to the LORD,
But the prayer of the upright is His
delight.

9 The way of the wicked is an abomination
to the LORD,
But He loves the one who pursues
righteousness.

10 There is severe punishment for one who
abandons the way;
One who hates a rebuke will die.

11 ¹Sheol and ²Abaddon *lie open* before the Lord,
How much more the hearts of mankind!

12 A scoffer does not love one who rebukes him;
He will not go to the wise.

13 A joyful heart makes a cheerful face,
But when the heart is sad, the spirit is broken.

14 The mind of the intelligent seeks knowledge,
But the mouth of fools feeds on foolishness.

15 All the days of the needy are bad,
But a cheerful heart *has* a continual feast.

16 Better is a little with the fear of the Lord
Than great treasure, and turmoil with the treasure.

17 Better is a portion of vegetables where there is love,
Than a fattened ox *served* with hatred.

18 A hot-tempered person stirs up strife,
But the slow to anger calms a dispute.

19 The way of the lazy one is like a hedge of thorns,
But the path of the upright is a highway.

20 A wise son makes a father glad,
But a foolish man despises his mother.

21 Foolishness is joy to one who lacks sense,
But a person of understanding walks straight.

22 Without consultation, plans are frustrated,
But with many counselors they succeed.

23 A person has joy in an apt answer,
And how delightful is a timely word!

24 The path of life *leads* upward for the wise,
So that he may keep away from ¹Sheol below.

25 The Lord will tear down the house of the proud,
But He will set the boundary of the widow.

26 Evil plans are an abomination to the Lord,
But pleasant words are pure.

27 He who profits illicitly troubles his own house,
But he who hates bribes will live.

28 The heart of the righteous ponders how to answer,
But the mouth of the wicked pours out evil things.

29 The Lord is far from the wicked,
But He hears the prayer of the righteous.

30 Bright eyes gladden the heart;
Good news refreshes the bones.

31 *One whose* ear listens to a life-giving rebuke
Will stay among the wise.

32 One who neglects discipline rejects himself,
But one who listens to a rebuke acquires understanding.

33 The fear of the Lord is the instruction for wisdom,
And before honor *comes* humility.

Contrast of the Upright and the Wicked

16 The plans of the heart belong to a person,
But the answer of the tongue is from the Lord.

2 All the ways of a person are clean in his own sight,
But the Lord examines the motives.

3 Commit your works to the Lord,
And your plans will be established.

4 The Lord has made everything for its own purpose,
Even the wicked for the day of evil.

5 Everyone who is proud in heart is an abomination to the Lord;
Be assured, he will not go unpunished.

6 By mercy and truth atonement is made for wrongdoing,
And by the fear of the Lord one keeps away from evil.

7 When a person's ways are pleasing to the Lord,
He causes even his enemies to make peace with him.

8 Better is a little with righteousness
Than great income with injustice.

9 The mind of a person plans his way,
But the Lord directs his steps.

10 A divine verdict is on the lips of the king;
His mouth should not err in judgment.

11 A just balance and scales belong to the Lord;
All the weights of the bag are His concern.

12 It is an abomination for kings to commit wicked acts,
Because a throne is established on righteousness.

13 Righteous lips are the delight of kings,
And one who speaks right is loved.

14 The fury of a king is *like* messengers of death;
But a wise person will appease it.

15 In the light of a king's face is life,
And his favor is like a cloud *with* the spring rain.

16 How much better it is to get wisdom than gold!
And to get understanding is to be chosen above silver.

17 The highway of the upright is to turn away from evil;
One who watches his way protects his life.

18 Pride *goes* before destruction,
And a haughty spirit before stumbling.

19 It is better to be humble in spirit with the needy
Than to divide the spoils with the proud.

20 One who pays attention to the word will find good,
And blessed is one who trusts in the Lord.

21 The wise in heart will be called understanding,
And sweetness of speech increases persuasiveness.

22 Understanding is a fountain of life to those who have it,
But the discipline of fools is foolishness.

23 The heart of the wise instructs his mouth
And adds persuasiveness to his lips.

24 Pleasant words are a honeycomb,
   Sweet to the soul and healing to the
   bones.
25 There is a way *which seems* right to a
   person,
   But its end is the way of death.
26 A worker's appetite works for him,
   For his hunger urges him *on.*
27 A worthless person digs up evil,
   While his words are like scorching
   fire.
28 A perverse person spreads strife,
   And a slanderer separates close friends.
29 A person of violence entices his neighbor
   And leads him in a way that is not good.
30 He who winks his eyes *does so* to devise
   perverse things;
   He who compresses his lips brings evil to
   pass.
31 A gray head is a crown of glory;
   It is found in the way of righteousness.
32 One who is slow to anger is better than
   the mighty,
   And one who rules his spirit, than one
   who captures a city.
33 The lot is cast into the lap,
   But its every decision is from the LORD.

Contrast of the Upright and the Wicked

17 Better is a dry morsel and quietness
   with it
   Than a house full of feasting with strife.
2 A servant who acts wisely will rule over a
   son who acts shamefully,
   And will share in the inheritance among
   brothers.
3 The refining pot is for silver and the
   furnace for gold,
   But the LORD tests hearts.
4 An evildoer listens to wicked lips;
   A liar pays attention to a destructive
   tongue.
5 One who mocks the poor taunts his
   Maker;
   One who rejoices at disaster will not go
   unpunished.
6 Grandchildren are the crown of the old,
   And the glory of sons is their fathers.
7 Excellent speech is not fitting for a fool,
   Much less are lying lips to a prince.
8 A bribe is a charm in the sight of its
   owner;
   Wherever he turns, he prospers.
9 One who conceals an offense seeks love,
   But one who repeats a matter separates
   close friends.
10 A rebuke goes deeper into one who has
   understanding
   Than a hundred blows into a fool.
11 A rebellious person seeks only evil,
   So a cruel messenger will be sent against
   him.
12 Let a person meet a bear robbed of her
   cubs,
   Rather than a fool in his foolishness.
13 One who returns evil for good,
   Evil will not depart from his house.
14 The beginning of strife is *like* letting out
   water,

So abandon the quarrel before it breaks
   out.
15 One who justifies the wicked and one
   who condemns the righteous,
   Both of them alike are an abomination to
   the LORD.
16 Why is there money in the hand of a fool
   to buy wisdom,
   When he has no sense?
17 A friend loves at all times,
   And a brother is born for adversity.
18 A person lacking in sense shakes hands
   And becomes guarantor in the presence of
   his neighbor.
19 One who loves wrongdoing loves strife;
   One who makes his doorway high seeks
   destruction.
20 One who has a crooked mind finds
   nothing good,
   And one who is corrupted in his language
   falls into evil.
21 He who fathers a fool *does so* to his
   sorrow,
   And the father of a fool has no joy.
22 A joyful heart is good medicine,
   But a broken spirit dries up the bones.
23 A wicked person accepts a bribe ᶠfrom an
   inside pocket
   To pervert the ways of justice.
24 Wisdom is in the presence of one who has
   understanding,
   But the eyes of a fool are on the ends of
   the earth.
25 A foolish son is a grief to his father,
   And bitterness to her who gave birth to
   him.
26 It is also not good to fine the righteous,
   Nor to strike the noble for *their*
   uprightness.
27 One who withholds his words has
   knowledge,
   And one who has a cool spirit is a person
   of understanding.
28 Even a fool, when he keeps silent, is
   considered wise;
   When he closes his lips, he is *considered*
   prudent.

Contrast of the Upright and the Wicked

18 One who separates himself seeks *his*
   own desire;
   He quarrels against all sound wisdom.
2 A fool does not delight in understanding,
   But in revealing his own mind.
3 When a wicked person comes, contempt
   also comes,
   And with dishonor *comes* taunting.
4 The words of a person's mouth are deep
   waters;
   The fountain of wisdom is a bubbling
   brook.
5 To show partiality to the wicked is not
   good,
   Nor to suppress the righteous in
   judgment.
6 A fool's lips bring strife,
   And his mouth invites beatings.
7 A fool's mouth is his ruin,
   And his lips are the snare of his soul.

17:23 ¹Lit *a fold in a robe;* i.e., secretly

8 The words of a gossiper are like dainty morsels,
And they go down into the innermost parts of the body.

9 He also who is lax in his work
Is a brother to him who destroys.

10 The name of the LORD is a strong tower;
The righteous runs into it and is safe.

11 A rich person's wealth is his strong city,
And like a high wall in his own imagination.

12 Before destruction the heart of a person is haughty,
But humility *goes* before honor.

13 One who gives an answer before he hears,
It is foolishness and shame to him.

14 The spirit of a person can endure his sickness,
But *as for* a broken spirit, who can endure it?

15 The mind of the discerning acquires knowledge,
And the ear of the wise seeks knowledge.

16 A person's gift makes room for him
And brings him before great people.

17 The first to plead his case *seems* right,
Until another comes and examines him.

18 The *cast* lot puts an end to quarrels,
And decides between the mighty ones.

19 A brother who is offended *is harder to be won* than a strong city,
And quarrels are like the bars of a citadel.

20 With the fruit of a person's mouth his stomach will be satisfied;
He will be satisfied *with* the product of his lips.

21 Death and life are in the power of the tongue,
And those who love it will eat its fruit.

22 He who finds a wife finds a good thing
And obtains favor from the LORD.

23 A poor person utters pleadings,
But a rich person answers defiantly.

24 A person of *too many* friends *comes* to ruin,
But there is a friend who sticks *closer* than a brother.

On Life and Conduct

19

Better is a poor person who walks in his integrity
Than a person who is perverse in speech and is a fool.

2 Also it is not good for a person to be without knowledge,
And one who hurries his footsteps errs.

3 The foolishness of a person ruins his way,
And his heart rages against the LORD.

4 Wealth adds many friends,
But a poor person is separated from his friend.

5 A false witness will not go unpunished,
And one *who* declares lies will not escape.

6 Many will seek the favor of a generous person,
And every person is a friend to him who *gives* gifts.

7 All the brothers of a poor person hate him;
How much more do his friends abandon him!
He pursues *them with* words, *but* they are gone.

8 One who gets wisdom loves his own soul;
One who keeps understanding will find good.

9 A false witness will not go unpunished,
And one *who* declares lies will perish.

10 Luxury is not fitting for a fool;
Much less for a slave to rule over princes.

11 A person's discretion makes him slow to anger,
And it is his glory to overlook an offense.

12 A king's wrath is like the roaring of a lion,
But his favor is like dew on the grass.

13 A foolish son is destruction to his father,
And the quarrels of a wife are a constant dripping.

14 House and wealth are an inheritance from fathers,
But a prudent wife is from the LORD.

15 Laziness casts *one* into a deep sleep,
And a lazy person will suffer hunger.

16 One who keeps the commandment keeps his soul,
But one who is careless of conduct will die.

17 One who is gracious to a poor person lends to the LORD,
And He will repay him for his good deed.

18 Discipline your son while there is hope,
And do not desire his death.

19 *A person of* great anger will suffer the penalty,
For if you rescue *him,* you will only have to do it again.

20 Listen to advice and accept discipline,
So that you may be wise the rest of your days.

21 Many plans are in a person's heart,
But the advice of the LORD will stand.

22 What is desirable in a person is his kindness,
And *it is* better to be a poor person than a liar.

23 The fear of the LORD *leads* to life,
So that one may sleep satisfied, untouched by evil.

24 The lazy one buries his hand in the dish,
But will not even bring it back to his mouth.

25 Strike a scoffer and the naive may become clever,
But rebuke one who has understanding,
and he will gain knowledge.

26 He who assaults *his* father *and* drives *his* mother away
Is a shameful and disgraceful son.

27 Stop listening, my son, to discipline,
And you will stray from the words of knowledge.

28 A worthless witness makes a mockery of justice,
And the mouth of the wicked swallows wrongdoing.

29 Judgments are prepared for scoffers,
And beatings for the backs of fools.

On Life and Conduct

20 Wine is a mocker, intoxicating drink a brawler,
And whoever is intoxicated by it is not wise.

2 The terror of a king is like the roaring of a lion;
One who provokes him to anger forfeits his own life.

3 Avoiding strife is an honor for a person,
But any fool will quarrel.

4 The lazy one does not plow after the autumn,
So he begs during the harvest and has nothing.

5 A plan in the heart of a person is *like* deep water,
But a person of understanding draws it out.

6 Many a person proclaims his own loyalty,
But who can find a trustworthy person?

7 A righteous person who walks in his integrity—
How blessed are his sons after him.

8 A king who sits on the throne of justice
Disperses all evil with his eyes.

9 Who can say, "I have cleansed my heart,
I am pure from my sin"?

10 Differing weights and differing measures,
Both of them are abominable to the LORD.

11 It is by his deeds that a boy distinguishes himself,
If his conduct is pure and right.

12 The hearing ear and the seeing eye,
The LORD has made both of them.

13 Do not love sleep, or you will become poor;
Open your eyes, *and you will* be satisfied with food.

14 "Bad, bad," says the buyer,
But when he goes his way, then he boasts.

15 There is gold, and an abundance of jewels;
But lips of knowledge are a *more* precious thing.

16 Take his garment when he becomes guarantor for a stranger;
And for foreigners, seize a pledge from him.

17 Bread *obtained by* a lie is sweet to a person,
But afterward his mouth will be filled with gravel.

18 Prepare plans by consultation,
And make war by wise guidance.

19 One who goes about as a slanderer reveals secrets;
Therefore do not associate with a gossip.

20 He who curses his father or his mother,
His lamp will go out in time of darkness.

21 An inheritance gained in a hurry at the beginning
Will not be blessed in the end.

22 Do not say, "I will repay evil";
Wait for the LORD, and He will save you.

23 Differing weights are an abomination to the LORD,
And a false scale is not good.

24 A man's steps are *ordained* by the LORD;

How then can a person understand his way?

25 It is a trap for a person to say carelessly, "It is holy!"
And after the vows to make inquiry.

26 A wise king scatters the wicked,
And drives a *threshing* wheel over them.

27 The spirit of a person is the lamp of the LORD,
Searching all the innermost parts of his being.

28 Loyalty and truth watch over the king,
And he upholds his throne by loyalty.

29 The glory of young men is their strength,
And the honor of old men is their gray hair.

30 Bruising wounds clean away evil,
And blows *cleanse* the innermost parts.

On Life and Conduct

21 The king's heart is *like* channels of water in the hand of the LORD;
He turns it wherever He pleases.

2 Every person's way is right in his own eyes,
But the LORD examines the hearts.

3 To do righteousness and justice
Is preferred by the LORD more than sacrifice.

4 Haughty eyes and a proud heart,
The lamp of the wicked, is sin.

5 The plans of the diligent certainly *lead* to advantage,
But everyone who is in a hurry certainly *comes* to poverty.

6 The acquisition of treasures by a lying tongue
Is a fleeting vapor, the pursuit of death.

7 The violence of the wicked will sweep them away,
Because they refuse to act with justice.

8 The way of a guilty person is crooked,
But as for the pure, his conduct is upright.

9 It is better to live on a corner of a roof
Than in a house shared with a contentious woman.

10 The soul of the wicked desires evil;
His neighbor is shown no compassion in his eyes.

11 When the scoffer is punished, the naive becomes wise;
But when the wise is instructed, he receives knowledge.

12 The righteous one considers the house of the wicked,
Bringing the wicked to ruin.

13 One who shuts his ear to the outcry of the poor
Will also call out himself, and not be answered.

14 A gift in secret subdues anger,
And a bribe [1]in an inside pocket, strong wrath.

15 The exercise of justice is joy for the righteous,
But terror to those who practice injustice.

16 A person who wanders from the way of understanding
Will rest in the assembly of the dead.

21:14 [1] Lit *a fold in a robe;* i.e., secretly

17 One who loves pleasure *will become* a
    poor person;
    One who loves wine and oil will not
    become rich.
18 The wicked is a ransom for the righteous,
    And the treacherous is in the place of the
    upright.
19 It is better to live in a desert land
    Than with a contentious and irritating
    woman.
20 There is precious treasure and oil in the
    home of the wise,
    But a foolish person swallows it up.
21 One who pursues righteousness and
    loyalty
    Finds life, righteousness, and honor.
22 A wise person scales the city of the
    mighty
    And brings down the stronghold in which
    they trust.
23 One who guards his mouth and his
    tongue,
    Guards his soul from troubles.
24 "Proud," "Arrogant," "Scoffer," are his
    names,
    One who acts with insolent pride.
25 The desire of the lazy one puts him to
    death,
    For his hands refuse to work;
26 All day long he is craving,
    While the righteous gives and does
    not hold back.
27 The sacrifice of the wicked is an
    abomination,
    How much more when he brings it
    with evil intent!
28 A false witness will perish,
    But a person who listens will speak
    forever.
29 A wicked person displays a bold face,
    But as for the upright, he makes his way
    sure.
30 There is no wisdom, no understanding,
    And no plan against the LORD.
31 The horse is prepared for the day of
    battle,
    But the victory belongs to the LORD.

On Life and Conduct
22 A *good* name is to be more desired than
    great wealth;
    Favor is better than silver and gold.
2   The rich and the poor have a common
    bond,
    The LORD is the Maker of them all.
3   A prudent person sees evil and hides
    himself,
    But the naive proceed, and pay the
    penalty.
4   The reward of humility *and* the fear of the
    LORD
    Are riches, honor, and life.
5   Thorns *and* snares are in the way of the
    perverse;
    One who guards himself will be far from
    them.
6   Train up a child in the way he should go,
    Even when he grows older he will not
    abandon it.
7   The rich rules over the poor,

And the borrower *becomes* the lender's
slave.
8   One who sows injustice will reap disaster,
    And the rod of his fury will perish.
9   One who is generous will be blessed,
    Because he gives some of his food to the
    poor.
10 Drive out the scoffer, and strife will leave,
    Even quarreling and dishonor will cease.
11 One who loves purity of heart
    And whose speech is gracious, the king is
    his friend.
12 The eyes of the LORD protect knowledge,
    But He overthrows the words of the
    treacherous person.
13 The lazy one says, "There is a lion out-
    side;
    I will be killed in the streets!"
14 The mouth of an adulteress is a deep pit;
    He who is cursed of the LORD will fall into
    it.
15 Foolishness is bound up in the heart of a
    child;
    The rod of discipline will remove it far
    from him.
16 One who oppresses the poor to make
    more for himself,
    Or gives to the rich, *will* only *come* to
    poverty.
17¶ Extend your ear and hear the words of the
    wise,
    And apply your mind to my knowledge;
18 For it will be pleasant if you keep them
    within you,
    So that they may be ready on your lips.
19 So that your trust may be in the LORD,
    I have taught you today, you indeed.
20 Have I not written to you excellent things
    Of counsels and knowledge,
21 To make you know the certainty of the
    words of truth,
    So that you may correctly answer him
    who sent you?
22¶ Do not rob the poor because he is poor,
    Nor crush the needy at the gate;
23 For the LORD will plead their case
    And take the life of those who rob them.
24¶ Do not make friends with a person *given*
    to anger,
    Or go with a hot-tempered person,
25 Or you will learn his ways
    And find a snare for yourself.
26¶ Do not be among those who shake hands,
    Among those who become guarantors for
    debts.
27 If you have nothing with which to repay,
    Why should he take your bed from under
    you?
28¶ Do not move the ancient boundary
    Which your fathers have set.
29¶ Do you see a person skilled in his work?
    He will stand before kings;
    He will not stand before obscure people.

On Life and Conduct
23 When you sit down to dine with a ruler,
    Consider carefully what is before you,
2   And put a knife to your throat
    If you are a person of *great* appetite.
3   Do not desire his delicacies,

For it is deceptive food.

4¶ Do not weary yourself to gain wealth;
Stop dwelling *on it.*

5 When you set your eyes on it, it is gone.
For *wealth* certainly makes itself wings
Like an eagle that flies *toward* the
heavens.

6¶ Do not eat the bread of a selfish person;
Or desire his delicacies;

7 For as he thinks within himself, so he is.
He says to you, "Eat and drink!"
But his heart is not with you.

8 You will vomit up the morsel you have
eaten
And waste your compliments.

9¶ Do not speak to be heard by a fool,
For he will despise the wisdom of your
words.

10¶ Do not move the ancient boundary
Or go into the fields of the fatherless,

11 For their Redeemer is strong;
He will plead their case against you.

12 Apply your heart to discipline,
And your ears to words of knowledge.

13¶ Do not withhold discipline from a child;
Though you strike him with the rod, he
will not die.

14 You shall strike him with the rod
And rescue his soul from Sheol.

15¶ My son, if your heart is wise,
My own heart also will be glad,

16 And my innermost being will rejoice
When your lips speak what is right.

17¶ Do not let your heart envy sinners,
But *live* in the fear of the LORD always.

18 Certainly there is a future,
And your hope will not be cut off.

19 Listen, my son, and be wise,
And direct your heart in the way.

20 Do not be with heavy drinkers of wine,
Or with gluttonous eaters of meat;

21 For the heavy drinker and the glutton will
come to poverty,
And drowsiness will clothe *one* with rags.

22¶ Listen to your father, who fathered you,
And do not despise your mother when
she is old.

23 Buy truth, and do not sell *it,*
Get wisdom, instruction, and
understanding.

24¶ The father of the righteous will greatly
rejoice,
And he who fathers a wise son will be
glad in him.

25 Let your father and your mother be glad,
And let her rejoice who gave birth to you.

26¶ Give me your heart, my son,
And let your eyes delight in my ways.

27 For a prostitute is a deep pit,
And a strange woman is a narrow well.

28 Certainly she lurks as a robber,
And increases the treacherous among
mankind.

29¶ Who has woe? Who has sorrow?
Who has contentions? Who has
complaining?
Who has wounds without cause?
Who has red eyes?

30 Those who linger long over wine,

Those who go to taste mixed wine.

31 Do not look at wine when it is red,
When it sparkles in the cup,
When it goes down smoothly;

32 In the end it bites like a snake
And stings like a viper.

33 Your eyes will see strange things
And your mind will say perverse things.

34 And you will be like one who lies down in
the middle of the sea,
Or like one who lies down on the top of
a ¹mast.

35 "They struck me, *but* I did not become ill;
They beat me, *but* I did not know *it.*
When will I awake?
I will seek another drink."

Precepts and Warnings

24 Do not be envious of evil people,
Nor desire to be with them;

2 For their minds plot violence,
And their lips talk of trouble.

3¶ By wisdom a house is built,
And by understanding it is established;

4 And by knowledge the rooms are filled
With all precious and pleasant riches.

5¶ A wise man is strong,
And a person of knowledge increases
power.

6 For by wise guidance you will wage
war,
And in an abundance of counselors there
is victory.

7¶ Wisdom is *too* exalted for a fool,
He does not open his mouth at the gate.

8¶ One who plans to do evil,
People will call a schemer.

9 The devising of foolishness is sin,
And the scoffer is an abomination to
humanity.

10¶ *If* you show yourself lacking courage on
the day of distress,
Your strength is meager.

11¶ Rescue those who are being taken away to
death,
And those who are staggering to the
slaughter, Oh hold *them* back!

12 If you say, "See, we did not know this,"
Does He who weighs the hearts not
consider *it?*
And does He who watches over your soul
not know *it?*
And will He not repay a person according
to his work?

13¶ My son, eat honey, for it is good;
Yes, the honey from the comb is sweet to
your taste;

14 Know *that* wisdom is the same for your
soul;
If you find *it,* then there will be a future,
And your hope will not be cut off.

15¶ Do not lie in ambush, you wicked person,
against the home of the righteous;
Do not destroy his resting place;

16 For a righteous person falls seven times
and rises again,
But the wicked stumble in *time of*
disaster.

17¶ Do not rejoice when your enemy falls,

And do not let your heart rejoice when he
stumbles,

18 Otherwise, the LORD will see and be displeased,
And turn His anger away from him.

19¶ Do not get upset because of evildoers
Or be envious of the wicked;

20 For there will be no future for the evil
person;
The lamp of the wicked will be put out.

21¶ My son, fear the LORD and the king;
Do not get involved with those of high
rank,

22 For their disaster will rise suddenly,
And who knows the ruin that can come
from both of them?

23¶ These also are sayings of the wise:
To show partiality in judgment is not
good.

24 One who says to the wicked, "You are
righteous,"
Peoples will curse him, nations will scold
him;

25 But for those who rebuke the wicked
there will be delight,
And a good blessing will come upon them.

26 One who gives a right answer
Kisses the lips.

27¶ Prepare your work outside,
And make it ready for yourself in the
field;
Afterward, then, build your house.

28¶ Do not be a witness against your neighbor
for no reason,
And do not deceive with your lips.

29 Do not say, "I shall do the same to him as
he has done to me;
I will repay the person according to his
work."

30¶ I passed by the field of a lazy one,
And by the vineyard of a person lacking
sense,

31 And behold, it was completely overgrown
with weeds;
Its surface was covered with weeds,
And its stone wall was broken down.

32 When I saw, I reflected upon it;
I looked, and received instruction.

33 "A little sleep, a little slumber,
A little folding of the hands to rest,"

34 Then your poverty will come like a drifter,
And your need like an armed man.

Similitudes and Instructions

25 These also are proverbs of Solomon
which the men of Hezekiah, king of
Judah, transcribed.

2¶ It is the glory of God to conceal a matter,
But the glory of kings is to search out a
matter.

3 As the heavens for height and the earth
for depth,
So the heart of kings is unsearchable.

4 Take away the impurities from the silver,
And there comes out a vessel for the
smith;

5 Take away the wicked before the king,
And his throne will be established in
righteousness.

6 Do not boast in the presence of the king,

And do not stand in the same place as
great people;

7 For it is better that it be said to you,
"Come up here,"
Than for you to be placed lower in the
presence of the prince,
Whom your eyes have seen.

8¶ Do not go out hastily to argue your case;
Otherwise, what will you do in the end,
When your neighbor humiliates you?

9 Argue your case with your neighbor,
And do not reveal the secret of another,

10 Or one who hears it will put you to
shame,
And the evil report about you will not
pass away.

11¶ Like apples of gold in settings of silver,
Is a word spoken at the proper time.

12 Like an earring of gold and a jewelry piece
of fine gold,
Is a wise person who offers rebukes to a
listening ear.

13 Like the cold of snow in the time of
harvest
Is a faithful messenger to those who send
him,
For he refreshes the soul of his masters.

14 Like clouds and wind without rain
Is a person who boasts of his gifts falsely.

15 Through patience a ruler may be
persuaded,
And a gentle tongue breaks bone.

16 Have you found honey? Eat only what you
need,
So that you do not have it in excess and
vomit it.

17 Let your foot rarely be in your neighbor's
house,
Or he will become weary of you and hate
you.

18 Like a club, a sword, and a sharp arrow
Is a person who gives false testimony
against his neighbor.

19 Like a bad tooth and an unsteady foot
Is confidence in a treacherous person in
time of trouble.

20 Like one who takes off a garment on a
cold day, or like vinegar on soda,
Is one who sings songs to a troubled
heart.

21 If your enemy is hungry, give him food to
eat;
And if he is thirsty, give him water to
drink;

22 For you will heap burning coals on his
head,
And the LORD will reward you.

23 The north wind brings rain,
And a gossiping tongue brings an angry
face.

24 It is better to live on a corner of the roof,
Than in a house shared with a
contentious woman.

25 Like cold water to a weary soul,
So is good news from a distant land.

26 Like a trampled spring and a polluted
well,
So is a righteous person who gives way
before the wicked.

27 It is not good to eat much honey,

Nor is it glory to search out one's own glory.

28 *Like* a city that is broken into *and* without walls
So is a person who has no self-control over his spirit.

Similitudes and Instructions

26 Like snow in summer and like rain in harvest,
So honor is not fitting for a fool.

2 Like a sparrow in *its* flitting, like a swallow in *its* flying,
So a curse without cause does not come *to rest.*

3 A whip is for the horse, a bridle for the donkey,
And a rod for the back of fools.

4 Do not answer a fool according to his foolishness,
Or you will also be like him.

5 Answer a fool as his foolishness *deserves,*
So that he will not be wise in his own eyes.

6 One who sends a message by the hand of a fool
Chops off *his own* feet *and* drinks violence.

7 *Like* useless legs to one who cannot walk,
So is a proverb in the mouths of fools.

8 Like one who binds a stone in a sling,
So is one who gives honor to a fool.

9 *Like* a thorn *that* sticks in the hand of a heavy drinker,
So is a proverb in the mouths of fools.

10 *Like* an archer who wounds everyone,
So is one who hires a fool or hires those who pass by.

11 Like a dog that returns to its vomit,
So is a fool who repeats his foolishness.

12 Do you see a person wise in his own eyes?
There is more hope for a fool than for him.

13 A lazy one says, "There is a lion on the road!
A lion is in the public square!"

14 *As* the door turns on its hinges,
So *does* a lazy one on his bed.

15 A lazy one buries his hand in the dish;
He is weary of bringing it to his mouth again.

16 A lazy one is wiser in his own eyes
Than seven *people* who can give a discreet answer.

17 *Like* one who takes a dog by the ears,
So is one who passes by *and* meddles with strife not belonging to him.

18 Like a maniac who shoots
Flaming arrows, arrows, and death,

19 So is a person who deceives his neighbor,
And says, "Was I not joking?"

20 For lack of wood the fire goes out,
And where there is no gossiper, quarreling quiets down.

21 *Like* charcoal to hot embers and wood to fire,
So is a contentious person to kindle strife.

22 The words of a gossiper are like dainty morsels,

And they go down into the innermost parts of the body.

23 *Like* an earthenware vessel overlaid with silver impurities
Are burning lips and a wicked heart.

24 One who hates disguises *it* with his lips,
But he harbors deceit in his heart.

25 When he speaks graciously, do not believe him,
Because there are seven abominations in his heart.

26 *Though his* hatred covers itself with deception,
His wickedness will be revealed in the assembly.

27 One who digs a pit will fall into it,
And one who rolls a stone, it will come back on him.

28 A lying tongue hates those it crushes,
And a flattering mouth works ruin.

Warnings and Instructions

27 Do not boast about tomorrow,
For you do not know what a day may bring.

2 Let another praise you, and not your own mouth;
A stranger, and not your own lips.

3 A stone is heavy and the sand weighty,
But the provocation of a fool is heavier than both of them.

4 Wrath is fierce and anger is a flood,
But who can stand before jealousy?

5 Better is open rebuke
Than love that is concealed.

6 Faithful are the wounds of a friend,
But deceitful are the kisses of an enemy.

7 A satisfied person despises honey,
But to a hungry person any bitter thing is sweet.

8 Like a bird that wanders from its nest,
So is a person who wanders from his home.

9 Oil and perfume make the heart glad,
And a person's advice is sweet to his friend.

10 Do not abandon your friend or your father's friend,
And do not go to your brother's house on the day of your disaster;
Better is a neighbor who is near than a brother far away.

11 Be wise, my son, and make my heart glad,
So that I may reply to one who taunts me.

12 A prudent person sees evil *and* hides himself;
But the naive proceed, *and* pay the penalty.

13 Take his garment when he becomes a guarantor for a stranger;
And for a foreign woman seize a pledge from him.

14 One who blesses his friend with a loud voice early in the morning,
It will be considered a curse to him.

15 A constant dripping on a day of steady rain
And a contentious woman are alike;

16 He who would restrain her restrains the wind,

And grasps oil with his right hand.

17 *As* iron sharpens iron,
So one person sharpens another.

18 One who tends the fig tree will eat its
fruit,
And one who cares for his master will be
honored.

19 As in water a face *reflects* the face,
So the heart of a person *reflects the*
person.

20 [1]Sheol and [2]Abaddon are never satisfied,
Nor are the eyes of a person ever satisfied.

21 The crucible is for silver and the furnace
for gold,
And each *is tested* by the praise accorded
him.

22 Though you pound the fool in a mortar
with a pestle along with crushed grain,
His foolishness *still* will not leave him.

23 ¶ Know well the condition of your flocks,
And pay attention to your herds;

24 For riches are not forever,
Nor does a crown *endure* to all
generations.

25 *When* the grass disappears, the new
growth is seen,
And the herbs of the mountains are
gathered in,

26 The lambs *will be* for your clothing,
And the goats *will bring* the price of a
field,

27 And *there will be* enough goats' milk for
your food,
For the food of your household,
And sustenance for your attendants.

Warnings and Instructions

28 The wicked flee when no one
is pursuing,
But the righteous are bold as a lion.

2 Due to a wrongdoing of a land its leaders
are many,
But by a person of understanding *and*
knowledge, so it endures.

3 A poor man who oppresses the helpless
Is *like* a driving rain which leaves no food.

4 Those who abandon the Law praise the
wicked,
But those who keep the Law strive against
them.

5 Evil people do not understand justice,
But those who seek the LORD understand
everything.

6 Better is a poor person who walks in his
integrity,
Than a person who is crooked, though he
is rich.

7 He who keeps the Law is a discerning
son,
But he who is a companion of gluttons
humiliates his father.

8 One who increases his wealth by [1]interest
of any kind,
Collects it for one who is gracious to the
poor.

9 One who turns his ear away from
listening to the Law,
Even his prayer is an abomination.

10 One who leads the upright astray in an
evil way
Will himself fall into his own pit,
But the blameless will inherit good.

11 The rich person is wise in his own eyes,
But the poor who has understanding sees
through him.

12 When the righteous triumph, there is
great glory,
But when the wicked rise, people hide
themselves.

13 One who conceals his wrongdoings will
not prosper,
But one who confesses and abandons
them will find compassion.

14 How blessed is the person who fears
always,
But one who hardens his heart will fall
into disaster.

15 *Like* a roaring lion and a rushing bear
Is a wicked ruler over a poor people.

16 A leader who is a great oppressor lacks
understanding,
But a person who hates unjust gain will
prolong *his* days.

17 A person who is burdened with the guilt
of human blood
Will be a fugitive until death; no one is to
support him!

18 One who walks blamelessly will receive
help,
But one who is crooked will fall all at
once.

19 One who works his land will have plenty
of food,
But one who follows empty *pursuits* will
have plenty of poverty.

20 A faithful person will abound with
blessings,
But one who hurries to be rich will not go
unpunished.

21 To show partiality is not good,
Because for a piece of bread a man will do
wrong.

22 A person with an evil eye hurries after
wealth
And does not know that poverty will
come upon him.

23 One who rebukes a person will afterward
find *more* favor
Than one who flatters with the tongue.

24 He who robs his father or his mother
And says, "There is no wrong done,"
Is the companion of a person who
destroys.

25 An arrogant person stirs up strife,
But one who trusts in the LORD will
prosper.

26 One who trusts in his own heart is a
fool,
But one who walks wisely will flee to
safety.

27 One who gives to the poor will never lack
anything,
But one who shuts his eyes will have
many curses.

28 When the wicked rise, people hide
themselves;

27:20 [1] I.e., The netherworld [2] I.e., the place of destruction **28:8** [1] Possibly interest on
money and food loans

But when they perish, the righteous increase.

Warnings and Instructions

29 A person often rebuked who becomes obstinate
Will suddenly be broken beyond remedy.
2 When the righteous increase, the people rejoice,
But when a wicked person rules, people groan.
3 A man who loves wisdom makes his father glad,
But he who involves himself with prostitutes wastes *his* wealth.
4 The king gives stability to the land by justice,
But a person who takes bribes ruins it.
5 A man who flatters his neighbor
Is spreading a net for his steps.
6 By wrongdoing an evil person is ensnared,
But the righteous sings and rejoices.
7 The righteous is concerned for the rights of the poor;
The wicked does not understand *such* concern.
8 Arrogant people inflame a city,
But wise people turn away anger.
9 When a wise person has a controversy with a foolish person,
The foolish person either rages or laughs, and there is no rest.
10 People of bloodshed hate the blameless person,
But the upright are concerned for his life.
11 A fool always loses his temper,
But a wise person holds it back.
12 If a ruler pays attention to falsehood,
All his ministers *become* wicked.
13 The poor person and the oppressor have this in common:
The LORD gives light to the eyes of both.
14 If a king judges the poor with truth,
His throne will be established forever.
15 The rod and a rebuke give wisdom,
But a child who gets his own way brings shame to his mother.
16 When the wicked increase, wrongdoing increases;
But the righteous will see their downfall.
17 Correct your son, and he will give you comfort;
He will also delight your soul.
18 Where there is no vision, the people are unrestrained,
But happy is one who keeps the Law.
19 A slave will not be instructed by words *alone;*
For *though* he understands, there will be no response.
20 Do you see a person who is hasty with his words?
There is more hope for a fool than for him.
21 One who pampers his slave from childhood
Will in the end *find* him to be rebellious.
22 An angry person stirs up strife,
And a hot-tempered person abounds in wrongdoing.

23 A person's pride will bring him low,
But a humble spirit will obtain honor.
24 One who is a partner with a thief hates his own life;
He hears the oath but tells nothing.
25 The fear of man brings a snare,
But one who trusts in the LORD will be protected.
26 Many seek the ruler's favor,
But justice for mankind *comes* from the LORD.
27 An unjust person is an abomination to the righteous,
And one who is upright in the way is an abomination to the wicked.

The Words of Agur

30 The words of Agur the son of Jakeh, the pronouncement.
The man declares to Ithiel, to Ithiel and Ucal:
2 I am certainly more stupid than any man,
And I do not have the understanding of a man;
3 Nor have I learned wisdom,
Nor do I have the knowledge of the Holy One.
4 Who has ascended into heaven and descended?
Who has gathered the wind in His fists?
Who has wrapped the waters in His garment?
Who has established all the ends of the earth?
What is His name or His Son's name?
Surely you know!
5¶ Every word of God is pure;
He is a shield to those who take refuge in Him.
6 Do not add to His words
Or He will rebuke you, and you will be proved a liar.
7¶ Two things I have asked of You;
Do not refuse me before I die:
8 Keep deception and lies far from me,
Give me neither poverty nor riches;
Feed me with the food that is my portion,
9 So that I will not be full and deny *You* and say, "Who is the LORD?"
And that I will not become impoverished and steal,
And profane the name of my God.
10¶ Do not slander a slave to his master,
Or he will curse you and you will be found guilty.
11¶ There is a kind *of person* who curses his father
And does not bless his mother.
12 There is a kind who is pure in his own eyes,
Yet is not washed from his filthiness.
13 There is a kind—oh how lofty are his eyes!
And his eyelids are raised *in arrogance.*
14 There is a kind *of person* whose teeth are *like* swords
And his jaw teeth *like* knives,
To devour the poor from the earth
And the needy from among mankind.
15¶ The leech has two daughters:

"Give" and "Give."
There are three things that will not be
satisfied,
Four that will not say, "Enough":
16 Sheol, the infertile womb,
Earth that is never satisfied with water,
And fire that never says, "Enough."
17 The eye that mocks a father
And scorns a mother,
The ravens of the valley will pick it out,
And the young eagles will eat it.
18¶ There are three things which are too
wonderful for me,
Four which I do not understand:
19 The way of the eagle in the sky,
The way of a snake on a rock,
The way of a ship in the middle of the
sea,
And the way of a man with a virgin.
20 This is the way of an adulterous woman:
She eats and wipes her mouth,
And says, "I have done no wrong."
21¶ Under three things the earth quakes,
And under four, it cannot endure:
22 Under a slave when he becomes king,
And a fool when he is satisfied with food,
23 Under an unloved woman when she gets
a husband,
And a female servant when she
dispossesses her mistress.
24¶ Four things are small on the earth,
But they are exceedingly wise:
25 The ants are not a strong people,
But they prepare their food in the
summer;
26 The rock hyraxes are not a mighty people,
Yet they make their houses in the rocks;
27 The locusts have no king,
Yet all of them go out in ranks;
28 The lizard you may grasp with the hands,
Yet it is in kings' palaces.
29¶ There are three things which are stately
in their march,
Even four which are stately when they
walk:
30 The lion, which is mighty among animals
And does not retreat from anything,
31 The strutting rooster or the male goat,
And a king when his army is with him.
32¶ If you have been foolish in exalting
yourself,
Or if you have plotted evil, put your hand
on your mouth.
33 For the churning of milk produces butter,
And pressing the nose produces blood;
So the churning of anger produces strife.

The Words of Lemuel

31 The words of King Lemuel, the
pronouncement which his mother taught
him:
2¶ What, my son?
And what, son of my womb?
And what, son of my vows?
3 Do not give your strength to women,
Or your ways to that which destroys
kings.
4 It is not for kings, Lemuel,
It is not for kings to drink wine,
Or for rulers to desire intoxicating drink,

5 Otherwise they will drink and forget what
is decreed,
And pervert the rights of all the needy.
6 Give intoxicating drink to one who is
perishing,
And wine to one whose life is bitter.
7 Let him drink and forget his poverty,
And remember his trouble no more.
8 Open your mouth for the people who
cannot speak,
For the rights of all the unfortunate.
9 Open your mouth, judge righteously,
And defend the rights of the poor and
needy.

Description of a Worthy Woman

10¶ An excellent wife, who can find her?
For her worth is far above jewels.
11 The heart of her husband trusts in her,
And he will have no lack of gain.
12 She does him good and not evil
All the days of her life.
13 She looks for wool and linen,
And works with her hands in delight.
14 She is like merchant ships;
She brings her food from afar.
15 And she rises while it is still night
And gives food to her household,
And portions to her attendants.
16 She considers a field and buys it;
From her earnings she plants a vineyard.
17 She surrounds her waist with strength
And makes her arms strong.
18 She senses that her profit is good;
Her lamp does not go out at night.
19 She stretches out her hands to the distaff,
And her hands grasp the spindle.
20 She extends her hand to the poor,
And she stretches out her hands to the
needy.
21 She is not afraid of the snow for her
household,
For all her household are clothed with
scarlet.
22 She makes coverings for herself;
Her clothing is fine linen and purple.
23 Her husband is known in the gates,
When he sits among the elders of the
land.
24 She makes linen garments and sells
them,
And supplies belts to the tradesmen.
25 Strength and dignity are her clothing,
And she smiles at the future.
26 She opens her mouth in wisdom,
And the teaching of kindness is on her
tongue.
27 She watches over the activities of her
household,
And does not eat the bread of idleness.
28 Her children rise up and bless her;
Her husband also, and he praises her,
saying:
29 "Many daughters have done nobly,
But you excel them all."
30 Charm is deceitful and beauty is vain,
But a woman who fears the LORD, she
shall be praised.
31 Give her the product of her hands,
And let her works praise her in the gates.

The Book of
ECCLESIASTES

The Futility of All Endeavors

1 The words of the Preacher, the son of David, king in Jerusalem.
2 "Futility of futilities," says the Preacher, "Futility of futilities! All is futility."
3 ¶ What advantage does a person have in all his work
Which he does under the sun?
4 A generation goes and a generation comes,
But the earth remains forever.
5 Also, the sun rises and the sun sets;
And hurrying to its place it rises there again.
6 Blowing toward the south,
Then turning toward the north,
The wind continues swirling along;
And on its circular courses the wind returns.
7 All the rivers flow into the sea,
Yet the sea is not full.
To the place where the rivers flow,
There they flow again.
8 All things are wearisome;
No one can tell it.
The eye is not satisfied with seeing,
Nor is the ear filled with hearing.
9 What has been, it is what will be,
And what has been done, it is what will be done.
So there is nothing new under the sun.
10 Is there anything of which one might say,
"See this, it is new"?
It has already existed for ages
Which were before us.
11 There is no remembrance of the earlier things,
And of the later things as well, which will occur,
There will be no remembrance of them
Among those who will come later still.

The Futility of Wisdom

12 I, the Preacher, have been king over Israel in Jerusalem. 13 And I set my mind to seek and explore by wisdom about everything that has been done under heaven. It is a sorry task with which God has given the sons of mankind to be troubled. 14 I have seen all the works which have been done under the sun, and behold, all is futility and striving after wind. 15 What is crooked cannot be straightened, and what is lacking cannot be counted.

16 I said to myself, "Behold, I have magnified and increased wisdom more than all who were over Jerusalem before me; and my mind has observed a wealth of wisdom and knowledge." 17 And I applied my mind to know wisdom and to know insanity and foolishness; I realized that this also is striving after wind. 18 Because in much wisdom there is much grief; and increasing knowledge results in increasing pain.

The Futility of Pleasure and Possessions

2 I said to myself, "Come now, I will test you with pleasure. So enjoy yourself." And behold, it too was futility. 2 I said of laughter, "It is senseless," and of pleasure, "What does this accomplish?" 3 I explored with my mind how to refresh my body with wine while my mind was guiding me wisely; and how to seize foolishness, until I could see what good there is for the sons of mankind to do under heaven for the few years of their lives. 4 I enlarged my works: I built houses for myself, I planted vineyards for myself; 5 I made gardens and parks for myself, and I planted in them all kinds of fruit trees; 6 I made ponds of water for myself from which to irrigate a forest of growing trees. 7 I bought male and female slaves, and I had slaves born at home. I also possessed flocks and herds larger than all who preceded me in Jerusalem. 8 I also amassed for myself silver and gold, and the treasure of kings and provinces. I provided for myself male and female singers, and the pleasures of the sons of mankind: many concubines.

9 Then I became great and increased more than all who preceded me in Jerusalem. My wisdom also stood by me. 10 All that my eyes desired, I did not refuse them. I did not restrain my heart from any pleasure, for my heart was pleased because of all my labor; and this was my reward for all my labor. 11 So I considered all my activities which my hands had done and the labor which I had exerted, and behold, all was futility and striving after wind, and there was no benefit under the sun.

Wisdom Surpasses Foolishness

12 So I turned to consider wisdom, insanity, and foolishness; for what will the man do who will come after the king, except what has already been done? 13 Then I saw that wisdom surpasses foolishness as light surpasses darkness. 14 The wise person's eyes are in his head, but the fool walks in darkness. And yet I know that one and the same fate happens to both of them. 15 Then I said to myself, "As is the fate of the fool, it will also happen to me. Why then have I been extremely wise?" So I said to myself, "This too is futility." 16 For there is no lasting remembrance of the wise, along with the fool, since in the coming days everything will soon be forgotten. And how the wise and the fool alike die! 17 So I hated life, for the work which had been done under the sun was unhappy to me; because everything is futility and striving after wind.

The Futility of Labor

18 So I hated all the fruit of my labor for which I had labored under the sun, because I must leave it to the man who will come after me. 19 And who knows whether he will be wise or a fool? Yet he will have control over all the

fruit of my labor for which I have labored by acting wisely under the sun. This too is futility. 20 Therefore I completely despaired over all the fruit of my labor for which I had labored under the sun. 21 When there is a person who has labored with wisdom, knowledge, and skill, and then gives his legacy to one who has not labored for it; this too is futility and a great evil. 22 For what does a person get in all his labor and in his striving with which he labors under the sun? 23 Because all his days his activity is painful and irritating; even at night his mind does not rest. This too is futility. 24 There is nothing better for a person than to eat and drink, and show himself some good in his trouble. This too I have seen, that it is from the hand of God. 25 For who can eat and who can have enjoyment without Him? 26 For to a person who is good in His sight, He has given wisdom and knowledge and joy, while to the sinner He has given the task of gathering and collecting so that he may give to one who is good in God's sight. This too is futility and striving after wind.

A Time for Everything

3 There is an appointed time for everything. And there is a time for every matter under heaven—

2 A time to give birth and a time to die;
   A time to plant and a time to uproot what is planted.
3 A time to kill and a time to heal;
   A time to tear down and a time to build up.
4 A time to weep and a time to laugh;
   A time to mourn and a time to dance.
5 A time to throw stones and a time to gather stones;
   A time to embrace and a time to shun embracing.
6 A time to search and a time to give up as lost;
   A time to keep and a time to throw away.
7 A time to tear apart and a time to sew together;
   A time to be silent and a time to speak.
8 A time to love and a time to hate;
   A time for war and a time for peace.

9 What benefit is there for the worker from that in which he labors? 10 I have seen the task which God has given the sons of mankind with which to occupy themselves.

God Set Eternity in the Heart of Mankind

11 He has made everything appropriate in its time. He has also set eternity in their heart, without the possibility that mankind will find out the work which God has done from the beginning even to the end. 12 I know that there is nothing better for them than to rejoice and to do good in one's lifetime; 13 moreover, that every person who eats and drinks sees good in all his labor—this is the gift of God. 14 I know that everything God does will remain forever; there is nothing to add to it and there is nothing to take from it. And God has so worked, that people will fear Him. 15 That which is, is what has already been, and that which will be has already been; and God seeks what has passed by.

16 Furthermore, I have seen under the sun that in the place of justice there is wickedness and in the place of righteousness there is wickedness. 17 I said to myself, "God will judge the righteous and the wicked," for a time for every matter and for every deed [1] is there. 18 I said to myself regarding the sons of mankind, "God is testing them in order for them to see that they are as animals, they to themselves." 19 For the fate of the sons of mankind and the fate of animals is the same. As one dies, so dies the other; indeed, they all have the same breath, and there is no advantage for mankind over animals, for all is futility. 20 All go to the same place. All came from the dust and all return to the dust. 21 Who knows that the spirit of the sons of mankind ascends upward and the spirit of the animal descends downward to the earth? 22 I have seen that nothing is better than when a person is happy in his activities, for that is his lot. For who will bring him to see what will occur after him?

The Evils of Oppression

4 Then I looked again at all the acts of oppression which were being done under the sun. And behold, I saw the tears of the oppressed and that they had no one to comfort them; and power was on the side of their oppressors, but they had no one to comfort them. 2 So I congratulated the dead who are already dead, more than the living who are still living. 3 But better off than both of them is the one who has never existed, who has never seen the evil activity that is done under the sun.

4 I have seen that every labor and every skill which is done is the result of rivalry between a person and his neighbor. This too is futility and striving after wind. 5 The fool folds his hands and consumes his own flesh. 6 One hand full of rest is better than two fists full of labor and striving after wind.

7 Then I looked again at futility under the sun. 8 There was a man without a dependent, having neither a son nor a brother, yet there was no end to all his labor. Indeed, his eyes were not satisfied with riches, and he never asked, "And for whom do I labor and deprive myself of pleasure?" This too is futility, and it is an unhappy task.

9 Two are better than one because they have a good return for their labor; 10 for if either of them falls, the one will lift up his companion. But woe to the one who falls when there is not another to lift him up! 11 Furthermore, if two lie down together they keep warm, but how can one be warm alone? 12 And if one can overpower him who is alone, two can resist him. A cord of three strands is not quickly torn apart.

13 A poor yet wise youth is better than an old and foolish king who no longer knows how to receive instruction— 14 for he has come out of prison to become king, even though he was born poor in his kingdom. 15 I have seen all those living under the sun move to the side of the second youth who replaces him. 16 There is no end to all the people, to all who were before

them. Even the ones who will come later will not be happy with him; for this too is futility and striving after wind.

Your Attitude toward God

5 Guard your steps as you go to the house of God, and approach to listen rather than to offer the sacrifice of fools; for they do not know that they are doing evil. 2 Do not be quick with your mouth or impulsive in thought to bring up a matter in the presence of God. For God is in heaven and you are on the earth; therefore let your words be few. 3 For the dream comes through much effort, and the voice of a fool through many words.

4 When you make a vow to God, do not be late in paying it; for *He takes* no delight in fools. Pay what you vow! 5 It is better that you not vow, than vow and not pay. 6 Do not let your speech cause you to sin, and do not say in the presence of the messenger *of God* that it was a mistake. Why should God be angry on account of your voice, and destroy the work of your hands? 7 For in many dreams and in many words there is futility. Rather, fear God.

8 If you see oppression of the poor and denial of justice and righteousness in the province, do not be shocked at the sight; for one official watches over another official, and there are higher officials over them. 9 After all, a king who cultivates the field is beneficial to the land.

The Foolishness of Riches

10 One who loves money will not be satisfied with money, nor one who loves abundance *with its* income. This too is futility. 11 When good things increase, those who consume them increase. So what is the advantage to their owners except to look *at them?* 12 The sleep of the laborer is sweet, whether he eats little or much; but the full stomach of the rich person does not allow him to sleep.

13 There is a sickening evil *which* I have seen under the sun: wealth being hoarded by its owner to his detriment. 14 When that wealth was lost through bad business and he had fathered a son, then there was nothing to support him. 15 As he came naked from his mother's womb, so he will return as he came. He will take nothing from the fruit of his labor that he can carry in his hand. 16 This also is a sickening evil: exactly as a person is born, so will he die. What then is the advantage for him who labors for the wind? 17 All his life *he* also eats in darkness with great irritation, sickness, and anger.

18 Here is what I have seen to be good and fitting: to eat, to drink, and enjoy oneself in all one's labor in which he labors under the sun *during* the few years of his life which God has given him; for this is his reward. 19 Furthermore, as for every person to whom God has given riches and wealth, He has also given him the opportunity to enjoy them and to receive his reward and rejoice in his labor; this is the gift of God. 20 For he will not often call to mind the years of his life, because God keeps him busy with the joy of his heart.

The Futility of Life

6 There is an evil which I have seen under the sun, and it is widespread among mankind: 2 a person to whom God has given riches, wealth, and honor, so that his soul lacks nothing of all that he desires, yet God has not given him the opportunity to enjoy these things, but a foreigner enjoys them. This is futility and a severe affliction. 3 If a man fathers a hundred *children* and lives many years, however many they may be, but his soul is not satisfied with good things and he does not even have a *proper* burial, *then* I say, "Better the miscarriage than he, 4 for *a miscarriage* comes in futility and goes into darkness; and its name is covered in darkness. 5 It has not even seen the sun nor does it know *it; yet* it is better off than that *man.* 6 Even if *the man* lives a thousand years twice, but does not see good things—do not all go to one *and the same* place?"

7 All a person's labor is for his mouth, and yet his appetite is not satisfied. 8 For what advantage does the wise person have over the fool? What does the poor person have, knowing *how* to walk before the living? 9 What the eyes see is better than what the soul desires. This too is futility and striving after wind.

10 Whatever exists has already been named, and it is known what man is; for he cannot dispute with the one who is mightier than he is. 11 For there are many words which increase futility. What *then* is the advantage to a person? 12 For who knows what is good for a person during *his* lifetime, *during* the few years of his futile life? He will spend them like a shadow. For who can tell a person what will happen after him under the sun?

Wisdom and Foolishness Contrasted

7 A good name is better than good [1] oil,
And the day of *one's* death *is better* than the day of one's birth.
2 It is better to go to a house of mourning
Than to go to a house of feasting,
Because [1] that is the end of every person,
And the living takes *it* to heart.
3 Sorrow is better than laughter,
For when a face is sad a heart may be happy.
4 The mind of the wise is in the house of mourning,
While the mind of fools is in the house of pleasure.
5 It is better to listen to the rebuke of a wise person
Than for one to listen to the song of fools.
6 For as the crackling of thorn bushes under a pot,
So is the laughter of the fool;
And this too is futility.
7 For oppression makes a wise person look foolish,
And a bribe corrupts the heart.
8 The end of a matter is better than its beginning;
Patience of spirit is better than arrogance of spirit.

7:1 1 I.e., olive oil   7:2 1 I.e., death

9 Do not be eager in your spirit to be angry,
For anger resides in the heart of fools.
10 Do not say, "Why is it that the former
days were better than these?"
For it is not from wisdom that you ask
about this.
11 Wisdom along with an inheritance is
good,
And an advantage to those who see the
sun.
12 For wisdom is protection *just as* money is
protection,
But the advantage of knowledge is that
wisdom keeps its possessors alive.
13 Consider the work of God,
For who is able to straighten what He has
bent?
14 On the day of prosperity be happy,
But on the day of adversity consider:
God has made the one as well as the other
So that a person will not discover
anything *that will come* after him.

15 I have seen everything during my lifetime of futility; there is a righteous person who perishes in his righteousness, and there is a wicked person who prolongs *his life* in his wickedness. 16 Do not be excessively righteous, and do not be overly wise. Why should you ruin yourself? 17 Do not be excessively wicked, and do not be foolish. Why should you die before your time? 18 It is good that you grasp one thing while not letting go of the other; for one who fears God comes out with both of them.

19 Wisdom strengthens a wise person more than ten rulers who are in a city. 20 Indeed, there is not a righteous person on earth who *always* does good and does not *ever* sin. 21 Also, do not take seriously all the words which are spoken, so that you do not hear your servant cursing you, 22 for you know that even you have cursed others many times as well.

23 I tested all this with wisdom, *and* I said, "I will be wise," but *wisdom* was far from me. 24 What has been is remote and very mysterious. Who can discover it? 25 I directed my mind to know and to investigate, and to seek wisdom and an explanation, and to know the evil of foolishness and the foolishness of insanity. 26 And I discovered as more bitter than death the woman whose heart is snares and nets, whose hands are chains. One who is pleasing to God will escape from her, but the sinner will be captured by her.

27 "Behold, I have discovered this," says the Preacher, "*by adding* one thing to another to find an explanation, 28 which I am still seeking but have not found. I have found one man among a thousand, but I have not found a woman among all these. 29 Behold, I have found only this, that God made people upright, but they have sought out many schemes."

Obey Rulers

8 Who is like the wise person and who knows the meaning of a matter? A person's wisdom illuminates his face and makes his stern face brighten up.
2 I say, "Keep the command of the king because of the oath before God. 3 Do not be in

a hurry to leave him. Do not join in an evil matter, for he will do whatever he pleases." 4 Since the word of the king is authoritative, who will say to him, "What are you doing?" 5 One who keeps a *royal* command experiences no trouble, for a wise heart knows the proper time and procedure. 6 For there is a proper time and procedure for every delight, though a person's trouble is heavy upon him. 7 If no one knows what will happen, who can tell him when it will happen? 8 No one has authority over the wind to restrain the wind, nor authority over the day of death; and there is no *military* discharge in the time of war, and evil will not save those who practice it. 9 All this I have seen, and have applied my mind to every deed that has been done under the sun at a time when one person has exercised authority over *another* person to his detriment.

10 So then, I have seen the wicked buried, those who used to go in and out of the holy place, and they are *soon* forgotten in the city where they did such things. This too is futility. 11 Because the sentence against an evil deed is not executed quickly, therefore the hearts of the sons of mankind among them are fully given to do evil. 12 Although a sinner does evil a hundred *times* and may lengthen his *life,* still I know that it will go well for those who fear God, who fear Him openly. 13 But it will not go well for the evil person and he will not lengthen his days like a shadow, because he does not fear God.

14 There is futility which is done on the earth, that is, there are righteous people to whom it happens according to the deeds of the wicked. On the other hand, there are evil people to whom it happens according to the deeds of the righteous. I say that this too is futility. 15 So I commended pleasure, for there is nothing good for a person under the sun except to eat, drink, and be joyful, and this will stand by him in his labor *throughout* the days of his life which God has given him under the sun.

16 When I devoted my mind to know wisdom and to see the business which has been done on the earth (even though one should never sleep day or night), 17 and I saw every work of God, *I concluded* that one cannot discover the work which has been done under the sun. Even though a person laboriously seeks, he will not discover; and even if the wise person claims to know, he cannot discover.

People Are in the Hand of God

9 For I have taken all this to my heart, even to examine it all, that righteous people, wise people, and their deeds are in the hand of God. People do not know whether *it will be* love or hatred; anything awaits them.
2 It is the same for all. There is one fate for the righteous and for the wicked; for the good, for the clean and the unclean; for the person who offers a sacrifice and for the one who does not sacrifice. As the good person is, so is the sinner; the one who swears *an oath* is just as the one who is afraid to swear an oath. 3 This is an evil in everything that is done under the sun, that there is one fate for everyone.

Furthermore, the hearts of the sons of mankind are full of evil, and insanity is in their hearts throughout their lives. Afterward *they go* to the dead. 4 For whoever is joined to all the living, there is hope; for better a live dog, than a dead lion. 5 For the living know that they will die; but the dead do not know anything, nor do they have a reward any longer, for their memory is forgotten. 6 Indeed their love, their hate, and their zeal have already perished, and they will no longer have a share in all that is done under the sun.

7 Go *then,* eat your bread in happiness, and drink your wine with a cheerful heart; for God has already approved your works. 8 See that your clothes are white all the time, and that there is no lack of oil on your head. 9 Enjoy life with the wife whom you love all the days of your futile life which He has given you under the sun, all the days of your futility; for this is your reward in life and in your work which you have labored under the sun.

Whatever Your Hand Finds to Do

10 Whatever your hand finds to do, do *it* with *all* your might; for there is no activity, planning, knowledge, or wisdom in Sheol where you are going.

11 I again saw under the sun that the race is not to the swift and the battle is not to the warriors, and neither is bread to the wise nor wealth to the discerning, nor favor to the skillful; for time and chance overtake them all. 12 For indeed, a person does not know his time: like fish that are caught in a treacherous net and birds caught in a snare, so the sons of mankind are ensnared at an evil time when it suddenly falls on them.

13 This too I saw as wisdom under the sun, and it impressed me: 14 there was a small city with few men in it, and a great king came to it, surrounded it, and constructed large siegeworks against it. 15 But there was found in it a poor wise man, and he saved the city by his wisdom. Yet no one remembered that poor man. 16 So I said, "Wisdom is better than strength." But the wisdom of the poor man is despised, and his words are ignored. 17 The words of the wise heard in calm are *better* than the shouting of a ruler among fools. 18 Wisdom is better than weapons of war, but one sinner destroys much good.

A Little Foolishness

10 Dead flies turn a perfumer's oil rancid, *so* a little foolishness is more potent than wisdom *and* honor. 2 A wise person's heart *directs him* toward the right, but the foolish person's heart *directs him* toward the left. 3 Even when the fool walks along the road, his sense is lacking, and he demonstrates to everyone *that* he is a fool. 4 If the ruler's temper rises against you, do not abandon your place, because composure puts great offenses to rest.

5 There is an evil I have seen under the sun, like a mistake that proceeds from the ruler: 6 foolishness is set in many exalted places while the rich sit in humble places. 7 I have seen slaves *riding* on horses and princes walking like slaves on the land.

8 One who digs a pit may fall into it, and a serpent may bite one who breaks through a wall. 9 One who quarries stones may be hurt by them, and one who splits logs may be endangered by them. 10 If the axe is dull and he does not sharpen *its* edge, then he must exert *more* strength. Wisdom *has* the advantage of bringing success. 11 If the serpent bites before being charmed, there is no benefit for the charmer. 12 Words from the mouth of a wise person are gracious, while the lips of a fool consume him; 13 the beginning of his talking is foolishness, and the end of it is evil insanity. 14 Yet the fool multiplies words. No person knows what will happen, and who can tell him what will come after him? 15 The labor of a fool makes him *so* weary that he does not *even* know how to go to a city. 16 Woe to you, land whose king is a boy, and whose princes feast in the morning. 17 Blessed are you, land whose king is of nobility, and whose princes eat at the appropriate time—for strength and not for drunkenness. 18 Through extreme laziness the rafters sag, and through idleness the house leaks. 19 *People* prepare a meal for enjoyment, wine makes life joyful, and money is the answer to everything. 20 Furthermore, in your bedroom do not curse a king, and in your sleeping rooms do not curse a rich person; for a bird of the sky will bring the sound, and the winged one will make *your* word known.

Cast Your Bread on the Waters

11 Cast your bread on the surface of the waters, for you will find it after many days. 2 Divide your portion to seven, or even to eight, for you do not know what misfortune may occur on the earth. 3 If the clouds are full, they pour out rain on the earth; and whether a tree falls toward the south or toward the north, wherever the tree falls, there it lies. 4 One who watches the wind will not sow and one who looks at the clouds will not harvest. 5 Just as you do not know the path of the wind, and how bones *are formed* in the womb of the pregnant woman, so you do not know the activity of God who makes everything.

6 Sow your seed in the morning and do not be idle in the evening, for you do not know whether one or the other will succeed, or whether both of them alike will be good. 7 The light is pleasant, and *it is* good for the eyes to see the sun. 8 Indeed, if a person lives many years, let him rejoice in them all; but let him remember the days of darkness, for they will be many. Everything that is to come *will be* futility.

9 Rejoice, young man, during your childhood, and let your heart be pleasant during the days of young manhood. And follow the impulses of your heart and the desires of your eyes. Yet know that God will bring you to judgment for all these things. 10 So remove sorrow from your heart and keep pain away from your body, because childhood and the prime of life are fleeting.

Remember God in Your Youth

12 Remember also your Creator in the days of your youth, before the evil days come

and the years approach when you will say, "I have no pleasure in them"; [2] before the sun and the light, the moon and the stars are darkened, and clouds return after the rain; [3] on the day that the watchmen of the house tremble, and strong men are bent over, the grinders stop working because they are few, and those who look through windows grow ʰdim; [4] and the doors on the street are shut as the sound of the grinding mill is low, and one will arise at the sound of the bird, and all the daughters of song will sing softly. [5] Furthermore, *people* are afraid of a high place and of terrors on the road; the almond tree blossoms, the grasshopper drags itself along, and the caper berry is ineffective. For man goes to his eternal home while the mourners move around in the street. [6] *Remember your Creator* before the silver cord is broken and the golden bowl is crushed, the pitcher by the spring is shattered and the wheel at the cistern is crushed; [7] then the dust will return to the earth as it was, and the spirit will return to God who gave it. [8] "Futility of futilities," says the Preacher, "all is futility!"

Purpose of the Preacher

[9] In addition to being wise, the Preacher also taught the people knowledge; and he pondered, searched out, and arranged many proverbs. [10] The Preacher sought to find delightful words and to write words of truth correctly.

[11] The words of the wise are like ʰgoads, and masters of *these* collections are like driven nails; they are given by one Shepherd. [12] But beyond this, my son, be warned: the writing of many books is endless, and excessive study is wearying to the body.

[13] The conclusion, when everything has been heard, *is:* fear God and keep His commandments, because this *applies to* every person. [14] For God will bring every act to judgment, everything which is hidden, whether it is good or evil.

12:3 [1] I.e., in their eyesight   **12:11** [1] I.e., spiked sticks for driving cattle

The Song of
SOLOMON

The Young Shulammite Bride and Jerusalem's Daughters

1 The [1]Song of Songs, which is Solomon's.

†The Bride

2¶ "May he kiss me with the kisses of his mouth!
For your love is sweeter than wine.
3 "Your oils have a pleasing fragrance,
Your name is *like* purified oil;
Therefore the young women love you.
4 "Draw me after you *and* let's run together!
The king has brought me into his chambers."

The Chorus

"We will rejoice in you and be joyful;
We will praise your love more than wine.
Rightly do they love you."

The Bride

5¶ "I am black and beautiful,
You daughters of Jerusalem,
Like the tents of Kedar,
Like the curtains of Solomon.
6 "Do not stare at me because I am dark,
For the sun has tanned me.
My mother's sons were angry with me;
They made me caretaker of the vineyards,
But I have not taken care of my own vineyard.
7 "Tell me, you whom my soul loves,
Where do you pasture *your flock,*
Where do you have *it* lie down at noon?
For why should I be like one who veils herself
Beside the flocks of your companions?"

Solomon, the Lover, Speaks

8¶ "If you yourself do not know,
Most beautiful among women,
Go out on the trail of the flock,
And pasture your young goats
By the tents of the shepherds.
9¶ "To me, my darling, you are like
My mare among the chariots of Pharaoh.
10 "Your cheeks are delightful with jewelry,
Your neck with strings of beads."

The Chorus

11¶ "We will make for you jewelry of gold
With beads of silver."

The Bride

12¶ "While the king was at his table,
My perfume gave forth its fragrance.
13 "My beloved is to me a pouch of myrrh
Which lies all night between my breasts.
14 "My beloved is to me a cluster of henna blossoms
In the vineyards of Engedi."

The Groom

15¶ "How beautiful you are, my darling,
How beautiful you are!
Your eyes are *like* doves."

The Bride

16¶ "How handsome you are, my beloved,
And so delightful!
Indeed, our bed is luxuriant!
17 "The beams of our house are cedars,
Our rafters, junipers.

The Bride's Admiration

2 "I am the rose of Sharon,
The lily of the valleys."

The Groom

2¶ "Like a lily among the thorns,
So is my darling among the young women."

The Bride

3¶ "Like an apple tree among the trees of the forest,
So is my beloved among the young men.
In his shade I took great delight and sat down,
And his fruit was sweet to my taste.
4 "He has brought me to *his* banquet hall,
And his banner over me is love.
5 "Refresh me with raisin cakes,
Sustain me with apples,
Because I am lovesick.
6 "His left hand is under my head,
And his right hand embraces me."

The Groom

7¶ "Swear to me, you daughters of Jerusalem,
By the gazelles or by the does of the field,
That you will not disturb or awaken *my* love
Until she pleases."

The Bride

8¶ "Listen! My beloved!
Behold, he is coming,
Leaping on the mountains,
Jumping on the hills!
9 "My beloved is like a gazelle or a young stag.
Behold, he is standing behind our wall,
He is looking through the windows,
He is peering through the lattice.
10¶ "My beloved responded and said to me,
'Arise, my darling, my beautiful one,
And come along.
11 'For behold, the winter is past,

1:1 [1]Or *Best of the Songs*   **1:2** † *The speaker identifications are not from the Hebrew text nor the Septuagint, but reflect an ancient tradition which appears in some manuscripts.*

The rain is over *and* gone.
12 'The blossoms have *already* appeared in
　　the land;
The time has arrived for pruning *the
　　vines,*
And the voice of the turtledove has been
　　heard in our land.
13 'The fig tree has ripened its fruit,
And the vines in blossom have given forth
　　their fragrance.
Arise, my darling, my beautiful one,
And come along!' "

The Groom

14¶ "My dove, in the clefts of the rock,
In the hiding place of the mountain
　　pathway,
Let me see how you look,
Let me hear your voice;
For your voice is pleasant,
And you look delightful."

The Chorus

15¶ "Catch the foxes for us,
The little foxes that are ruining the
　　vineyards,
While our vineyards are in blossom."

The Bride

16¶ "My beloved is mine, and I am his;
He pastures *his flock* among the lilies.
17 "Until the cool of the day, when the
　　shadows flee,
Turn, my beloved, and be like a gazelle
Or a young stag on the mountains of
　　Bether."

The Bride's Troubled Dream

3 "On my bed night after night I sought him
　Whom my soul loves;
I sought him but did not find him.
2 'I must arise now and go around in the
　　city;
In the streets and in the public squares
I must seek him whom my soul loves.'
I sought him but did not find him.
3 "The watchmen who make the rounds in
　　the city found me,
And I said, 'Have you seen him whom my
　　soul loves?'
4 "Hardly had I left them
When I found him whom my soul loves;
I held on to him and would not let him go
Until I had brought him to my mother's
　　house,
And into the room of her who conceived
　　me."

The Groom

5¶ "Swear to me, you daughters of Jerusalem,
By the gazelles or by the does of the field,
That you will not disturb or awaken *my*
　　love
Until she pleases."

Solomon's Wedding Day

The Bride

6¶ "What is this coming up from the
　　wilderness

Like columns of smoke,
Perfumed with myrrh and frankincense,
With all the scented powders of the
　　merchant?

The Chorus

7 "Behold, it is the *traveling* couch of
　　Solomon;
Sixty warriors around it,
Of the warriors of Israel.
8 "All of them are wielders of the sword,
Expert in war;
Each man has his sword at his side,
Guarding against the terrors of the night.
9 "King Solomon has made for himself a
　　sedan chair
From the timber of Lebanon.
10 "He made its posts of silver,
Its back of gold
And its seat of purple fabric,
With its interior lovingly inlaid
By the daughters of Jerusalem.
11 "Go out, you daughters of Zion,
And look at King Solomon with the crown
With which his mother has crowned him
On the day of his wedding,
And on the day of the joy of his heart."

Solomon's Love Expressed

4 "How beautiful you are, my darling,
How beautiful you are!
Your eyes are *like* doves behind your
　　veil;
Your hair is like a flock of goats
That have descended from Mount Gilead.
2 "Your teeth are like a flock of *newly* shorn
　　sheep
Which have come up from *their* watering
　　place,
All of which bear twins,
And not one among them has lost her
　　young.
3 "Your lips are like a scarlet thread,
And your mouth is beautiful.
Your temples are like a slice of a
　　pomegranate
Behind your veil.
4 "Your neck is like the tower of David,
Built with layers of stones
On which are hung a thousand shields,
All the round shields of the warriors.
5 "Your two breasts are like two fawns,
Twins of a gazelle
That graze among the lilies.
6 "Until the cool of the day
When the shadows flee,
I will go my way to the mountain of
　　myrrh
And to the hill of frankincense.
7¶ "You are altogether beautiful, my darling,
And there is no blemish on you.
8 "*Come* with me from Lebanon, *my* bride,
You shall come with me from Lebanon.
You shall come down from the summit of
　　Amana,
From the summit of Senir and Hermon,
From the dens of lions,
From the mountains of leopards.
9 "You have enchanted my heart, my sister,
my bride;

You have enchanted my heart with a
single *glance* of your eyes,
With a single strand of your necklace.
10 "How beautiful is your love, my sister, *my*
bride!
How much sweeter is your love than
wine,
And the fragrance of your oils
Than *that of* all *kinds of* balsam oils!
11 "Your lips drip honey, *my* bride;
Honey and milk are under your
tongue,
And the fragrance of your garments is like
the fragrance of Lebanon.
12 "A locked garden is my sister, *my* bride,
A locked spring, a sealed fountain.
13 "Your branches are an orchard of
pomegranates
With delicious fruits, henna with nard
plants,
14 Nard and saffron, spice reed and
cinnamon,
With all the trees of frankincense,
Myrrh, and aloes, along with all the finest
balsam oils.
15 "*You are* a garden spring,
A well of fresh water,
And flowing *streams* from Lebanon."

The Bride
16¶ "Awake, north *wind*,
And come, *wind of* the south;
Make my garden breathe out *fragrance*,
May its balsam oils flow.
May my beloved come into his garden
And eat its delicious fruits!"

The Torment of Separation

The Groom
5 "I have come into my garden, my sister,
my bride;
I have gathered my myrrh along with my
balsam.
I have eaten my honeycomb with my
honey;
I have drunk my wine with my milk.
Eat, friends;
Drink and drink deeply, lovers."

The Bride
2¶ "I was asleep but my heart was awake.
A voice! My beloved was knocking:
'Open to me, my sister, my darling,
My dove, my perfect one!
For my head is drenched with dew,
My locks with the dew drops of the
night.'
3 "I have taken off my dress,
How can I put it on *again?*
I have washed my feet,
How can I dirty them *again?*
4 "My beloved extended his hand through
the opening,
And my feelings were stirred for him.
5 "I arose to open to my beloved;
And my hands dripped with myrrh,
And my fingers with drops of myrrh,
On the handles of the bolt.
6 "I opened to my beloved,

But my beloved had turned away *and* had
gone!
My heart went out *to him* as he spoke.
I searched for him but I did not find him;
I called him but he did not answer me.
7 "The watchmen who make the rounds in
the city found me,
They struck me *and* wounded me;
The guards of the walls took my shawl
away from me.
8 "Swear to me, you daughters of Jerusalem,
If you find my beloved,
As to what you will tell him:
For I am lovesick."

The Chorus
9¶ "What kind of beloved is your beloved,
O most beautiful among women?
What kind of beloved is your beloved,
That you make us swear in this way?"

Admiration by the Bride

The Bride
10¶ "My beloved is dazzling and reddish,
Outstanding among ten thousand.
11 "His head is *like* gold, pure gold;
His locks are *like* clusters of dates
And black as a raven.
12 "His eyes are like doves
Beside streams of water,
Bathed in milk,
And perched in *their* setting.
13 "His cheeks are like a bed of balsam,
Banks of herbal spices;
His lips are lilies
Dripping with drops of myrrh.
14 "His hands are rods of gold
Set with topaz;
His abdomen is panels of ivory
Covered with sapphires.
15 "His thighs are pillars of alabaster
Set on pedestals of pure gold;
His appearance is like Lebanon,
Choice as the cedars.
16 "His mouth is *full of* sweetness.
And he is wholly desirable.
This is my beloved and this is my friend,
You daughters of Jerusalem."

Mutual Delight in Each Other

The Chorus
6 "Where has your beloved gone,
O most beautiful among women?
Where has your beloved turned,
That we may seek him with you?"

The Bride
2¶ "My beloved has gone down to his garden,
To the beds of balsam,
To pasture *his flock* in the gardens
And gather lilies.
3 "I am my beloved's and my beloved is
mine,
He who pastures *his flock* among the
lilies."

The Groom
4¶ "You are as beautiful as Tirzah, my darling,

As lovely as Jerusalem,
As awesome as an army with banners.
5 "Turn your eyes away from me,
For they have confused me;
Your hair is like a flock of goats
That have descended from Gilead.
6 "Your teeth are like a flock of ewes
That have come up from *their* watering
place,
All of which bear twins,
And not one among them has lost her
young.
7 "Your temples are like a slice of a
pomegranate
Behind your veil.
8 "There are sixty queens and eighty
concubines,
And young women without number;
9 *But* my dove, my perfect one, is unique:
She is her mother's only *daughter;*
She is the pure *child* of the one who gave
birth to her.
The young women saw her and called her
blessed,
The queens and the concubines *also,* and
they praised her, *saying,*
10¶ 'Who is this who looks down like the
dawn,
As beautiful as the full moon,
As pure as the sun,
As awesome as an army with banners?'
11 "I went down to the orchard of nut trees
To see the plants of the valley,
To see whether the vine had grown
Or the pomegranates had bloomed.
12 "Before I was aware, my soul set me
Over the chariots of my noble people."

The Chorus
13¶ "Come back, come back, O Shulammite;
Come back, come back, so that we may
look at you!"

The Groom
"Why should you look at the Shulammite,
As at the dance of the two armies?

Admiration by the Groom
7 "How beautiful are your feet in sandals,
Prince's daughter!
The curves of your hips are like jewels,
The work of the hands of an artist.
2 "Your navel is *like* a round goblet
That never lacks mixed wine;
Your belly is *like* a heap of wheat,
Surrounded with lilies.
3 "Your two breasts are like two fawns,
Twins of a gazelle.
4 "Your neck is like a tower of ivory,
Your eyes *like the* pools in Heshbon
By the gate of Bath-rabbim;
Your nose is like the tower of Lebanon,
Which looks toward Damascus.
5 "Your head crowns you like Carmel,
And the flowing hair of your head is like
purple threads;
The king is captivated by *your* tresses.
6 "How beautiful and how delightful you are,
My love, with *all* your delights!
7 "Your stature is like a palm tree,

And your breasts are *like its* clusters.
8 "I said, 'I will climb the palm tree,
I will grasp its fruit stalks.'
Oh, may your breasts be like clusters of
the vine,
And the fragrance of your breath like
apples,
9 And your mouth like the best wine!"

The Bride
"It goes *down* smoothly for my beloved,
Flowing gently *through* the lips of those
who are asleep.

The Union of Love
10¶ "I am my beloved's,
And his desire is for me.
11 "Come, my beloved, let's go out to the
country,
Let's spend the night in the villages.
12 "Let's rise early *and go* to the vineyards;
Let's see whether the vine has grown
And its buds have opened,
And whether the pomegranates have
bloomed.
There I will give you my love.
13 "The mandrakes have given forth
fragrance;
And over our doors are all delicious *fruits,*
New as well as old,
Which I have saved for you, my beloved.

The Lovers Speak
8 "Oh that you were like a brother to me
Who nursed at my mother's breasts.
If I found you outdoors, I would kiss
you;
No one would despise me, either.
2 "I would lead you *and* bring you
Into the house of my mother, who used to
instruct me;
I would give you spiced wine to drink
from the juice of my pomegranates.
3 "*Let* his left hand *be* under my head,
And his right hand embrace me."

The Groom
4¶ "Swear to me, you daughters of Jerusalem:
Do not disturb or awaken *my* love
Until she pleases."

The Chorus
5¶ "Who is this coming up from the
wilderness,
Leaning on her beloved?"

The Bride
"Beneath the apple tree I awakened you;
There your mother went into labor with
you,
There she was in labor *and* gave birth to
you.
6 "Put me like a seal over your heart,
Like a seal on your arm.
For love is as strong as death,
Jealousy is as severe as Sheol;
Its flames are flames of fire,
The flame of the LORD.
7 "Many waters cannot quench love,
Nor will rivers flood over it;

If a man were to give all the riches of his
house for love,
It would be utterly despised."

The Chorus
8¶ "We have a little sister,
And she has no breasts;
What shall we do for our sister
On the day when she is spoken for?
9   "If she is a wall,
We will build on her a battlement of
silver;
But if she is a door,
We will barricade her with planks of
cedar."

The Bride
10¶ "I was a wall, and my breasts were like
towers;
Then I became in his eyes as one who
finds peace.

11   "Solomon had a vineyard at Baal-hamon;
He entrusted the vineyard to caretakers.
Each one was to bring a thousand *shekels*
of silver for its fruit.
12   "My very own vineyard is at my
disposal;
The thousand *shekels* are for you,
Solomon,
And two hundred are for those who take
care of its fruit."

The Groom
13¶ "You who sit in the gardens:
My companions are listening for your
voice—
Let me hear it!"

The Bride
14¶ "Hurry, my beloved,
And be like a gazelle or a young stag
On the mountains of balsam trees!"

The Book of
ISAIAH

Rebellion of God's People

1 The vision of Isaiah the son of Amoz concerning Judah and Jerusalem, which he saw during the reigns of Uzziah, Jotham, Ahaz, *and* Hezekiah, kings of Judah.
2   Listen, heavens, and hear, earth;
    For the LORD has spoken:
    "Sons I have raised and brought up,
    But they have revolted against Me.
3   "An ox knows its owner,
    And a donkey its master's manger,
    But Israel does not know,
    My people do not understand."
4¶ Oh, sinful nation,
    People weighed down with guilt,
    Offspring of evildoers,
    Sons who act corruptly!
    They have abandoned the LORD,
    They have despised the Holy One of
        Israel,
    They have turned away from Him.
5¶ Where will you be stricken again,
    As you continue in *your* rebellion?
    The entire head is sick
    And the entire heart is faint.
6   From the sole of the foot even to the head
    There is nothing healthy in it,
    Only bruises, slashes, and raw wounds;
    Not pressed out nor bandaged,
    Nor softened with oil.
7¶ Your land is desolate,
    Your cities are burned with fire;
    As for your fields, strangers are devouring
        them in front of you;
    It is desolation, as overthrown by
        strangers.
8   The daughter of Zion is left like a shelter
        in a vineyard,
    Like a watchman's hut in a cucumber
        field, like a city under watch.
9   If the LORD of armies
    Had not left us a few survivors,
    We would be like Sodom,
    We would be like Gomorrah.

God Has Had Enough

10¶ Hear the word of the LORD,
    You rulers of Sodom;
    Listen to the instruction of our God,
    You people of Gomorrah!
11 "What are your many sacrifices to Me?"
    Says the LORD.
    "I have had enough of burnt offerings of
        rams
    And the fat of fattened cattle;
    And I take no pleasure in the blood of
        bulls, lambs, or goats.
12 "When you come to appear before Me,
    Who requires of you this trampling of My
        courtyards?
13 "Do not go on bringing your worthless
        offerings,
    Incense is an abomination to Me.

New moon and Sabbath, the proclamation
        of an assembly—
    I cannot endure wrongdoing and the
        festive assembly.
14 "I hate your new moon *festivals* and your
        appointed feasts,
    They have become a burden to Me;
    I am tired of bearing *them.*
15 "So when you spread out your hands *in
        prayer,*
    I will hide My eyes from you;
    Yes, even though you offer many prayers,
    I will not be listening.
    Your hands are covered with blood.
16¶ "Wash yourselves, make yourselves clean;
    Remove the evil of your deeds from My
        sight.
    Stop doing evil,
17 Learn to do good;
    Seek justice,
    Rebuke the oppressor,
    Obtain justice for the orphan,
    Plead for the widow's case.

Invitation to Debate

18¶ "Come now, and let us debate *your case,*"
    Says the LORD,
    "Though your sins are as scarlet,
    They shall become as white as snow;
    Though they are red like crimson,
    They shall be like wool.
19 "If you are willing and obedient,
    You will eat the best of the land;
20 But if you refuse and rebel,
    You will be devoured by the sword."
    For the mouth of the LORD has spoken.

Zion Corrupted; Will Be Redeemed

21¶ How the faithful city has become a
        prostitute,
    She *who* was full of justice!
    Righteousness *once* dwelt in her,
    But now murderers.
22 Your silver has become waste matter,
    Your drink diluted with water.
23 Your rulers are rebels
    And companions of thieves;
    Everyone loves a bribe
    And chases after gifts.
    They do not obtain justice for the orphan,
    Nor does the widow's case come before
        them.
24¶ Therefore the Lord GOD of armies,
    The Mighty One of Israel, declares,
    "Ah, I will have satisfaction against My
        adversaries,
    And avenge Myself on My enemies.
25 "I will also turn My hand against you,
    And smelt away your impurities as with
        lye;
    And I will remove all your slag.
26 "Then I will restore your judges as at first,
    And your counselors as at the beginning;

After that you will be called the city of
　righteousness,
A faithful city."
27¶ Zion will be redeemed with justice
　And her repentant ones with righteous-
　ness.
28 But wrongdoers and sinners together will
　be broken,
　And those who abandon the LORD will
　come to an end.
29 You certainly will be ashamed of the oaks
　which you have desired,
　And you will be embarrassed by the
　gardens which you have chosen.
30 For you will be like an oak whose leaf
　withers away,
　Or like a garden that has no water.
31 The strong man will become *like* flax
　fiber,
　And his work a spark.
　So they shall both burn together
　And there will be no one to extinguish
　them.

God's Universal Reign

2 The word which Isaiah the son of Amoz
　saw concerning Judah and Jerusalem.
2¶ Now it will come about that
　In the last days
　The mountain of the house of the LORD
　Will be established as the chief of the
　mountains,
　And will be raised above the hills;
　And all the nations will stream to it.
3 And many peoples will come and say,
　"Come, let's go up to the mountain of the
　LORD,
　To the house of the God of Jacob;
　So that He may teach us about His ways,
　And that we may walk in His paths."
　For the law will go out from Zion
　And the word of the LORD from Jerusalem.
4 And He will judge between the nations,
　And will mediate for many peoples;
　And they will beat their swords into
　plowshares, and their spears into
　pruning knives.
　Nation will not lift up a sword against
　nation,
　And never again will they learn war.
5¶ Come, house of Jacob, and let's walk in
　the light of the LORD.
6 For You have abandoned Your people, the
　house of Jacob,
　Because they are filled *with influences*
　from the east,
　And *they are* soothsayers like the
　Philistines.
　They also strike *bargains* with the
　children of foreigners.
7 Their land has also been filled with silver
　and gold
　And there is no end to their treasures;
　Their land has also been filled with
　horses,
　And there is no end to their chariots.
8 Their land has also been filled with idols;
　They worship the work of their hands,
　That which their fingers have made.
9 So *the common* person has been humbled

And *the* person *of importance* has been
　brought low,
　But do not forgive them.
10 Enter the rocky *place* and hide in the dust
　From the terror of the LORD and from the
　splendor of His majesty.
11 The proud look of humanity will be
　brought low,
　And the arrogance of people will be
　humbled;
　And the LORD alone will be exalted on
　that day.

A Day of Reckoning Coming

12¶ For the LORD of armies will have a day *of
　reckoning*
　Against everyone who is arrogant and
　haughty,
　And against everyone who is lifted up,
　That he may be brought low.
13 And *it will be* against all the cedars of
　Lebanon that are lofty and lifted up,
　Against all the oaks of Bashan,
14 Against all the lofty mountains,
　Against all the hills that are lifted up,
15 Against every high tower,
　Against every fortified wall,
16 Against all the ships of Tarshish
　And against all the delightful ships.
17 And the pride of humanity will be
　humbled
　And the arrogance of people will be
　brought low;
　And the LORD alone will be exalted on
　that day,
18 And the idols will completely vanish.
19 *People* will go into caves of the rocks
　And into holes in the ground
　Away from the terror of the LORD
　And the splendor of His majesty,
　When He arises to terrify the earth.
20 On that day people will throw away to the
　moles and the bats
　Their idols of silver and their idols of
　gold,
　Which they made for themselves to
　worship,
21 In order to go into the clefts of the rocks
　and the crannies of the cliffs
　Before the terror of the LORD and the
　splendor of His majesty,
　When He arises to terrify the earth.
22 Take no account of man, whose breath *of
　life* is in his nostrils;
　For why should he be esteemed?

God Will Remove the Leaders

3 For behold, the Lord GOD of armies is going
　to remove from Jerusalem and Judah
　Both supply and support, the entire supply
　of bread
　And the entire supply of water;
2 The mighty man and the warrior,
　The judge and the prophet,
　The diviner and the elder,
3 The captain of fifty and the esteemed
　person,
　The counselor and the expert artisan,
　And the skillful enchanter.
4 And I will make *mere* boys their leaders,

And mischievous *children* will rule over
them,
5   And the people will be oppressed,
Each one by another, and each one by his
neighbor;
The youth will assault the elder,
And the contemptible *person will assault*
the one honored.
6   When a man lays hold of his brother in
his father's house, *saying,*
"You have a cloak, you shall be our ruler!
And these ruins will be under your
authority,"
7   He will protest on that day, saying,
"I will not be *your* healer,
For in my house there is neither bread
nor cloak;
You should not appoint me ruler of the
people."
8   For Jerusalem has stumbled and Judah has
fallen,
Because their speech and their actions are
against the Lord,
To rebel against His glorious presence.
9   The expression of their faces testifies
against them,
And they display their sin like Sodom;
They do not *even* conceal *it.*
Woe to them!
For they have done evil to themselves.
10   Say to the righteous that *it will go* well *for
them,*
For they will eat the fruit of their actions.
11   Woe to the wicked! *It will go* badly *for
him,*
For what he deserves will be done to him.
12   My people! Their oppressors treat them
violently,
And women rule over them.
My people! Those who guide you lead *you*
astray
And confuse the direction of your paths.

God Will Judge
13¶   The Lord arises to contend,
And stands to judge the people.
14   The Lord enters into judgment with the
elders and leaders of His people,
"It is you who have devoured the vineyard;
The goods stolen from the poor are in
your houses.
15   "What do you mean by crushing My people
And oppressing the face of the poor?"
Declares the Lord God of armies.

Judah's Women Denounced
16¶   Moreover, the Lord said, "Because the
daughters of Zion are haughty
And walk with heads held high and
seductive eyes,
And go along with mincing steps
And jingle the anklets on their feet,
17   The Lord will afflict the scalp of the
daughters of Zion with scabs,
And the Lord will make their foreheads
bare."
18 On that day the Lord will take away the
beauty of *their* anklets, headbands, crescent
ornaments, 19 dangling earrings, bracelets,
veils, 20 headdresses, ankle chains, sashes,

perfume boxes, amulets, 21 finger rings, nose
rings, 22 festive robes, outer garments, shawls,
purses, 23 papyrus garments, undergarments,
headbands, and veils.
24   Now it will come about that instead of
balsam oil there will be a stench;
Instead of a belt, a rope;
Instead of well-set hair, a plucked-out
scalp;
Instead of fine clothes, a robe of sackcloth;
And branding instead of beauty.
25   Your men will fall by the sword
And your mighty ones in battle.
26   And her gates will lament and mourn,
And she will sit deserted on the ground.

A Remnant Prepared
4 For seven women will take hold of one man
on that day, saying, "We will eat our own
bread and wear our own clothes, only let us be
called by your name; take away our disgrace!"
2 On that day the Branch of the Lord will be
beautiful and glorious, and the fruit of the
earth *will be* the pride and the beauty of the
survivors of Israel. 3 And it will come about that
the one who is left in Zion and remains behind
in Jerusalem will be called holy—everyone
who is recorded for life in Jerusalem. 4 When
the Lord has washed away the filth of the
daughters of Zion and purged the bloodshed of
Jerusalem from her midst, by the spirit of judgment and the spirit of burning, 5 then the Lord
will create over the entire area of Mount Zion
and over her assemblies a cloud by day, and
smoke, and the brightness of a flaming fire by
night; for over all the glory will be a canopy.
6 And there will be a shelter to *give* shade from
the heat by day, and refuge and protection from
the storm and the rain.

Parable of the Vineyard
5 Let me sing now for my beloved
A song of my beloved about His vineyard.
My beloved had a vineyard on a fertile
hill.
2   He dug it all around, cleared it of stones,
And planted it with the choicest vine.
And He built a tower in the middle of it,
And also carved out a wine vat in it;
Then He expected *it* to produce *good*
grapes,
But it produced *only* worthless ones.
3¶   "And now, you inhabitants of Jerusalem
and people of Judah,
Judge between Me and My vineyard.
4   "What more was there to do for My
vineyard that I have not done in it?
Why, *when* I expected *it* to produce *good*
grapes did it produce worthless ones?
5   "So now let Me tell you what I am going to
do to My vineyard:
I will remove its hedge and it will be
consumed;
I will break down its wall and it will
become trampled ground.
6   "I will lay it waste;
It will not be pruned nor hoed,
But briars and thorns will come up.
I will also command the clouds not to rain
on it."

7¶ For the vineyard of the Lord of armies is
the house of Israel,
And the people of Judah are His delightful
plant.
So He waited for justice, but behold, *there
was* bloodshed;
For righteousness, but behold, a cry for
help.

Woes for the Wicked

8¶ Woe to those who attach house to house
and join field to field,
Until there is no more room,
And you alone are a landowner in the
midst of the land!
9 In my ears the Lord of armies *has sworn,*
"Many houses shall certainly become
desolate,
Even great and fine ones, without
occupants.
10 "For ten acres of vineyard will yield *only*
one ¹bath *of wine,*
And a ²homer of seed will yield *only* an
³ephah of grain."
11 Woe to those who rise early in the
morning so that they may pursue
intoxicating drink,
Who stay up late in the evening so that
wine may inflame them!
12 Their banquets are *accompanied by* lyre
and harp, *by* tambourine and flute, and
by wine;
But they do not pay attention to the deeds
of the Lord,
Nor do they consider the work of His
hands.
13¶ Therefore My people go into exile for
their lack of knowledge;
And their nobles are famished,
And their multitude is parched with
thirst.
14 Therefore Sheol has enlarged its throat
and opened its mouth beyond measure;
And Jerusalem's splendor, her multitude,
her noise *of revelry,* and the jubilant
within her, descend *into it.*
15 So *the common* people will be humbled
and *the* person *of importance* brought
low,
The eyes of the haughty also will be
brought low.
16 But the Lord of armies will be exalted in
judgment,
And the holy God will show Himself holy
in righteousness.
17 Then the lambs will graze as in their
pasture,
And strangers will eat in the ruins of the
wealthy.
18¶ Woe to those who drag wrongdoing with
the cords of deceit,
And sin as if with cart ropes;
19 Who say, "Let Him hurry, let Him do His
work quickly, so that we may see *it;*
And let the plan of the Holy One of Israel
approach
And come to pass, so that we may know
it!"

20 Woe to those who call evil good, and good
evil;
Who substitute darkness for light and light
for darkness;
Who substitute bitter for sweet and sweet
for bitter!
21 Woe to those who are wise in their own
eyes
And clever in their own sight!
22 Woe to those who are heroes in drinking
wine,
And valiant men in mixing intoxicating
drink,
23 Who declare the wicked innocent for a
bribe,
And take away the rights of the ones who
are in the right!
24¶ Therefore, as a tongue of fire consumes
stubble,
And dry grass collapses in the flame,
So their root will become like rot, and
their blossom blow away like dust;
For they have rejected the Law of the
Lord of armies,
And discarded the word of the Holy One
of Israel.
25 For this reason the anger of the Lord has
burned against His people,
And He has stretched out His hand
against them and struck them.
And the mountains quaked, and their
corpses lay like refuse in the middle of
the streets.
Despite all this, His anger is not spent,
But His hand is still stretched out.
26¶ He will also lift up a flag to the distant
nation,
And whistle for it from the ends of the
earth;
And behold, it will come with speed
swiftly.
27 No one in it is tired or stumbles,
No one slumbers or sleeps;
Nor is the undergarment at his waist
loosened,
Nor his sandal strap broken.
28 Its arrows are sharp and all its bows are
bent;
The hoofs of its horses seem like flint, and
its *chariot* wheels like a storm wind.
29 Its roaring is like a lioness, and it roars
like young lions;
It growls as it seizes the prey
And carries *it* off with no one to save *it.*
30 And it will roar against it on that day like
the roaring of the sea.
If one looks across to the land, behold,
there is darkness *and* distress;
Even the light is darkened by its
clouds.

Isaiah's Vision

6 In the year of King Uzziah's death I saw the
Lord sitting on a throne, lofty and exalted,
with the train of His robe filling the temple.
2 Seraphim were standing above Him, each
having six wings: with two *each* covered his
face, and with two *each* covered his feet, and

5:10 ¹About 6 gallons or 23 liters   ²About 7.7 cubic feet or 0.22 cubit meters or more   ³About 1 cubic
foot or 0.03 cubic meters

with two *each* flew. [3] And one called out to another and said,

"Holy, Holy, Holy, is the LORD of armies.
The whole earth is full of His glory."

[4] And the foundations of the thresholds trembled at the voice of him who called out, while the temple was filling with smoke. [5] Then I said,

"Woe to me, for I am ruined!
Because I am a man of unclean lips,
And I live among a people of unclean lips;
For my eyes have seen the King, the LORD of armies."

[6] Then one of the seraphim flew to me with a burning coal in his hand, which he had taken from the altar with tongs. [7] He touched my mouth *with it* and said, "Behold, this has touched your lips; and your guilt is taken away and atonement is made for your sin."

Isaiah's Commission

[8] Then I heard the voice of the Lord, saying, "Whom shall I send, and who will go for Us?" Then I said, "Here am I. Send me!" [9] And He said, "Go, and tell this people:

'Keep on listening, but do not understand;
And keep on looking, but do not gain knowledge.'
[10] "Make the hearts of this people insensitive,
Their ears dull,
And their eyes blind,
So that they will not see with their eyes,
Hear with their ears,
Understand with their hearts,
And return and be healed."

[11] Then I said, "Lord, how long?" And He answered,

"Until cities are devastated *and* without inhabitant,
Houses are without people
And the land is utterly desolate,
[12] The LORD has completely removed people,
And there are many forsaken places in the midst of the land.
[13] "Yet there will still be a tenth portion in it,
And it will again be *subject* to burning,
Like a terebinth or an oak
Whose stump remains when it is cut down.
The holy seed is its stump."

War against Jerusalem

7 Now it came about in the days of Ahaz, the son of Jotham, the son of Uzziah, king of Judah, that Rezin the king of Aram and Pekah the son of Remaliah, king of Israel, went up to Jerusalem to *wage* war against it, but could not conquer it. [2] When it was reported to the house of David, saying, "The Arameans have taken a stand by Ephraim," his heart and the hearts of his people shook as the trees of the forest shake from the wind.

[3] Then the LORD said to Isaiah, "Go out now to meet Ahaz, you and your son Shear-jashub, at the end of the conduit of the upper pool, on the road to the [1]fuller's field, [4] and say to him, 'Take care and be calm, have no fear and do

not be fainthearted because of these two stumps of smoldering logs, on account of the fierce anger of Rezin and Aram and the son of Remaliah. [5] Because Aram, *with* Ephraim and the son of Remaliah, has planned evil against you, saying, [6] "Let's go up against Judah and terrorize it, and take it for ourselves by assault and set up the son of Tabeel as king in the midst of it," [7] this is what the Lord GOD says:

"It shall not stand nor shall it come to pass.
[8] For the head of Aram is Damascus, and the head of Damascus is Rezin (now within another sixty-five years Ephraim will be broken to pieces, *so that it is* no longer a people), [9] and the head of Ephraim is Samaria, and the head of Samaria is the son of Remaliah. If you will not believe, you certainly shall not last."'"

The Child Immanuel

[10] Then the LORD spoke again to Ahaz, saying, [11] "Ask for a sign for yourself from the LORD your God; make *it* deep as Sheol or high as heaven." [12] But Ahaz said, "I will not ask, nor will I put the LORD to the test!" [13] Then he said, "Listen now, house of David! Is it too trivial a thing for you to try the patience of men, that you will try the patience of my God as well? [14] Therefore the Lord Himself will give you a sign: Behold, the [1]virgin will conceive and give birth to a son, and she will name Him [2]Immanuel. [15] He will eat curds and honey at the time He knows *enough* to refuse evil and choose good. [16] For before the boy knows *enough* to refuse evil and choose good, the land whose two kings you dread will be abandoned.

Trials to Come for Judah

[17] The LORD will bring on you, on your people, and on your father's house such days as have not come since the day that Ephraim separated from Judah—*the days of* the king of Assyria."

[18] On that day the LORD will whistle for the fly that is in the remotest part of the canals of Egypt and for the bee that is in the land of Assyria. [19] They will all come and settle on the steep ravines, on the ledges of the cliffs, on all the thorn bushes, and on all the watering places.

[20] On that day the Lord will shave with a razor, hired from regions beyond the *Euphrates* River (*that is,* with the king of Assyria), the head and the hair of the legs; and it will also remove the beard.

[21] Now on that day a person may keep alive *only* a heifer and a pair of sheep; [22] and because of the abundance of the milk produced he will eat curds, for everyone who is left within the land will eat curds and honey.

[23] And it will come about on that day, that every place where there used to be a thousand vines, *valued* at a thousand *shekels* of silver, will become briars and thorns. [24] *People* will come there with bows and arrows, because all the land will be briars and thorns. [25] As for all the hills which used to be cultivated with the plow, you will not go there for fear of briars and thorns; but they will become a place for pasturing oxen and for sheep to trample.

7:3 [1] I.e., launderer's   **7:14** [1] As in LXX; MT *young unmarried woman*   [2] I.e., God is with us

Damascus and Samaria Fall

8 Then the LORD said to me, "Take for yourself a large tablet and write on it in ordinary letters: [1]Maher-shalal-hash-baz. [2]And I will take to Myself faithful witnesses for testimony, Uriah the priest and Zechariah the son of Jeberechiah." [3]So I approached the prophetess, and she conceived and gave birth to a son. Then the LORD said to me, "Name him [1]Maher-shalal-hash-baz; [4]for before the boy knows how to cry out 'My father' or 'My mother,' the wealth of Damascus and the spoils of Samaria will be carried away before the king of Assyria."

[5]Again the LORD spoke to me further, saying,

6   "Inasmuch as these people have rejected
      the gently flowing waters of Shiloah
      And rejoice in Rezin and the son of
      Remaliah;
7   Now therefore, behold, the Lord is about
      to bring on them the strong and
      abundant waters of the *Euphrates*
      River,
      That is, the king of Assyria and all his
      glory;
      And it will rise over all its channels and
      go over all its banks.
8   "Then it will sweep on into Judah, it will
      overflow and pass through,
      It will reach as far as the neck;
      And the spread of its wings will fill the
      expanse of your land, Immanuel.

A Believing Remnant

9¶ "Be broken, you peoples, and be shattered;
      And listen, all remote places of the
      earth.
      Get ready, yet be shattered;
      Get ready, yet be shattered.
10   "Devise a plan, but it will fail;
      State a proposal, but it will not stand,
      For God is with us."

[11]For so the LORD spoke to me with mighty power and instructed me not to walk in the way of this people, saying,

12   "You are not to say, '*It is* a conspiracy!'
      Regarding everything that this people call
      a conspiracy,
      And you are not to fear what they fear or
      be in dread of *it.*
13   "It is the LORD of armies whom you are to
      regard as holy.
      And He shall be your fear,
      And He shall be your dread.
14   "Then He will become a sanctuary;
      But to both houses of Israel, *He will be* a
      stone of stumbling and a rock [1]of
      offense,
      And a snare and a trap for the inhabitants
      of Jerusalem.
15   "Many will stumble over them,
      Then they will fall and be broken;
      They will be snared and caught."

[16]Bind up the testimony, seal the Law among my disciples. [17]And I will wait for the LORD who is hiding His face from the house of Jacob; I will wait eagerly for Him. [18]Behold, I

and the children whom the LORD has given me are for signs and wonders in Israel from the LORD of armies, who dwells on Mount Zion.

[19]When they say to you, "Consult the mediums and the spiritists who whisper and mutter," should a people not consult their God? *Should they consult* the dead in behalf of the living? [20]To the Law and to the testimony! If they do not speak in accordance with this word, it is because they have no dawn. [21]They will pass through the land dejected and hungry, and it will turn out that when they are hungry, they will become enraged and curse their king and their God as they face upward. [22]Then they will look to the earth, and behold, distress and darkness, the gloom of anguish; and *they will be* driven away into darkness.

Birth and Reign of the Prince of Peace

9 But there will be no *more* gloom for her who was in anguish. In earlier times He treated the land of Zebulun and the land of Naphtali with contempt, but later on He will make *it* glorious, by the way of the sea, on the other side of the Jordan, Galilee of the Gentiles.

2   The people who walk in darkness
      Will see a great light;
      Those who live in a dark land,
      The light will shine on them.
3   You will multiply the nation,
      You will increase their joy;
      They will rejoice in Your presence
      As with the joy of harvest,
      As *people* rejoice when they divide the
      spoils.
4   For You will break the yoke of their
      burden and the staff on their
      shoulders,
      The rod of their oppressor, as at the battle
      of Midian.
5   For every boot of the marching warrior in
      the roar *of battle,*
      And cloak rolled in blood, will be for
      burning, fuel for the fire.
6   For a Child will be born to us, a Son will
      be given to us;
      And the government will rest on His
      shoulders;
      And His name will be called Wonderful
      Counselor, Mighty God,
      Eternal Father, Prince of Peace.
7   There will be no end to the increase of
      His government or of peace
      On the throne of David and over [1]his
      kingdom,
      To establish it and to uphold it with
      justice and righteousness
      From then on and forevermore.
      The zeal of the LORD of armies will
      accomplish this.

God's Anger with Israel's Arrogance

8¶   The Lord sends a message against Jacob,
      And it falls on Israel.
9   And all the people know *it,*
      That is, Ephraim and the inhabitants of
      Samaria,

8:1 [1]I.e., swift is the plunder, speedy is the prey
8:14 [1]Or *to trip on*   8:3 [1]I.e., swift is the plunder, speedy is the prey
9:7 [1]I.e., David's

Asserting in pride and in arrogance of heart:

10　"The bricks have fallen down,
But we will rebuild with smooth stones;
The sycamores have been cut down,
But we will replace *them* with cedars."

11　Therefore the LORD raises superior
adversaries against them from Rezin
And provokes their enemies,

12　The Arameans from the east and the
Philistines from the west;
And they devour Israel with gaping jaws.
In *spite of* all this, His anger does not turn away,
And His hand is still stretched out.

13¶　Yet the people do not turn back to Him
who struck them,
Nor do they seek the LORD of armies.

14　So the LORD cuts off head and tail from
Israel,
Both palm branch and bulrush in a single day.

15　The head is the elder and esteemed man,
And the prophet who teaches falsehood is
the tail.

16　For those who guide this people are
leading *them* astray;
And those who are guided by them are
confused.

17　Therefore the Lord does not rejoice over
their young men,
Nor does He have compassion on their
orphans or their widows;
For every one of them is godless and an
evildoer,
And every mouth is speaking foolishness.
In *spite of* all this, His anger does not turn away,
And His hand is still stretched out.

18¶　For wickedness burns like a fire;
It consumes briars and thorns;
It also sets the thickets of the forest
aflame
And they roll upward in a column of
smoke.

19　By the wrath of the LORD of armies the
land is burned,
And the people are like fuel for the fire;
No one spares his brother.

20　They devour *what is* on the right hand but
are *still* hungry,
And they eat *what is* on the left hand, but
they are not satisfied;
Each of them eats the flesh of his own
arm.

21　Manasseh *devours* Ephraim, and Ephraim
Manasseh,
And together they are against Judah.
In *spite of* all this, His anger does not turn away
And His hand is still stretched out.

Assyria Is God's Instrument

10 Woe to those who enact unjust
statutes
And to those who constantly record
harmful decisions,

2　So as to deprive the needy of justice
And rob the poor among My people of
their rights,

So that widows may be their spoil
And that they may plunder the orphans.

3　Now what will you do in the day of
punishment,
And in the devastation which will come
from afar?
To whom will you flee for help?
And where will you leave your wealth?

4　Nothing *remains* but to crouch among the
captives
Or fall among those killed.
In *spite of* all this, His anger does not turn
away
And His hand is still stretched out.

5¶　Woe to Assyria, the rod of My anger
And the staff in whose hands is My
indignation,

6　I send it against a godless nation
And commission it against the people of
My fury
To capture spoils and to seize plunder,
And to trample them down like mud in
the streets.

7　Yet it does not so intend,
Nor does it plan so in its heart,
But rather it is its purpose to destroy
And to eliminate many nations.

8　For it says, "Are not my officers all kings?

9　"Is not Calno like Carchemish,
Or Hamath like Arpad,
Or Samaria like Damascus?

10　"As my hand has reached to the kingdoms
of the idols;
Whose carved images *were greater* than
those of Jerusalem and Samaria,

11　Shall I not do the same to Jerusalem and
her images
Just as I have done to Samaria and her
idols?"

12 So it will be that when the Lord has
completed all His work on Mount Zion and on
Jerusalem, *He will say,* "I will punish the fruit
of the arrogant heart of the king of Assyria and
the arrogant pride of his eyes." 13 For he has
said,
"By the power of my hand and by my
wisdom I did *this,*
Because I have understanding;
And I removed the boundaries of the
peoples
And plundered their treasures,
And like a powerful man I brought down
their inhabitants,

14　And my hand reached to the riches of the
peoples like a nest,
And as one gathers abandoned eggs, I
gathered all the earth;
And there was not one that flapped its
wing, opened *its* beak, or chirped."

15¶　Is the axe to boast itself over the one who
chops with it?
Is the saw to exalt itself over the one who
wields it?
That would be like a club wielding those
who lift it,
Or like a rod lifting *the one who* is not
wood.

16　Therefore the Lord, the GOD of armies,
will send a wasting disease among his
stout warriors;

And under his glory a fire will be kindled
like a burning flame.

17 And the Light of Israel will become a fire
and Israel's Holy One a flame,
And it will burn and devour his thorns
and his briars in a single day.

18 And He will destroy the glory of his forest
and of his fruitful garden, both soul and
body,
And it will be as when a sick person
wastes away.

19 And the rest of the trees of his forest will
be so small in number
That a child could write them down.

A Remnant Will Return

20 Now on that day the remnant of Israel,
and those of the house of Jacob who have
escaped, will no longer rely on the one who
struck them, but will truly rely on the LORD,
the Holy One of Israel.

21 A remnant will return, the remnant of
Jacob, to the mighty God.

22 For though your people, Israel, may be
like the sand of the sea,
Only a remnant within them will return;
A destruction is determined, overflowing
with righteousness.

23 For a complete destruction, one that is determined, the Lord GOD of armies will execute in
the midst of the whole land.

24 Therefore this is what the Lord GOD of
armies says: "My people, you who dwell in
Zion, do not fear the Assyrian who strikes you
with the rod, and lifts up his staff against you
the way Egypt did. 25 For in a very little while
My indignation against you will be ended and
My anger will be directed toward their
destruction." 26 The LORD of armies will wield a
whip against him like the defeat of Midian at
the rock of Oreb; and His staff will be over the
sea, and He will lift it up the way He did in
Egypt. 27 So it will be on that day, that his
burden will be removed from your shoulders,
and his yoke from your neck; and the yoke will
be broken because of fatness.

28 ¶ He has come against Aiath,
He has passed through Migron;
At Michmash he deposited his baggage.

29 They have gone through the pass, saying,
"Geba will be our encampment for the
night."
Ramah is terrified, and Gibeah of Saul has
fled.

30 Cry aloud with your voice, daughter of
Gallim!
Pay attention, Laishah and wretched
Anathoth!

31 Madmenah has fled.
The inhabitants of Gebim have sought
refuge.

32 Yet today he will halt at Nob;
He shakes his fist at the mountain of the
daughter of Zion, the hill of Jerusalem.

33 ¶ Behold, the Lord, the GOD of armies, will
lop off the branches with terrifying
power;
Those also who are tall in stature will be
cut down,

And those who are lofty will be brought
low.

34 He will cut down the thickets of the forest
with an iron axe,
And Lebanon will fall by the Mighty One.

Righteous Reign of the Branch

11 Then a shoot will spring from the stem
of Jesse,
And a Branch from his roots will bear
fruit.

2 The Spirit of the LORD will rest on Him,
The spirit of wisdom and understanding,
The spirit of counsel and strength,
The spirit of knowledge and the fear of
the LORD.

3 And He will delight in the fear of the
LORD,
And He will not judge by what His eyes
see,
Nor make decisions by what His ears
hear;

4 But with righteousness He will judge the
poor,
And decide with fairness for the humble
of the earth;
And He will strike the earth with the rod
of His mouth,
And with the breath of His lips He will
slay the wicked.

5 Also righteousness will be the belt around
His hips,
And faithfulness the belt around His
waist.

6 ¶ And the wolf will dwell with the lamb,
And the leopard will lie down with the
young goat,
And the calf and the young lion ¹and the
fattened steer will be together;
And a little boy will lead them.

7 Also the cow and the bear will graze,
Their young will lie down together,
And the lion will eat straw like the ox.

8 The nursing child will play by the hole of
the cobra,
And the weaned child will put his hand
on the viper's den.

9 They will not hurt or destroy in all My
holy mountain,
For the earth will be full of the knowledge
of the LORD
As the waters cover the sea.

10 ¶ Then on that day
The nations will resort to the root of
Jesse,
Who will stand as a signal flag for the
peoples;
And His resting place will be glorious.

The Restored Remnant

11 ¶ Then it will happen on that day that the
Lord
Will again recover with His hand the
second time
The remnant of His people who will
remain,
From Assyria, Egypt, Pathros, Cush, Elam,
Shinar, Hamath,
And from the islands of the sea.

11:6 ¹ Some ancient versions will feed together

12 And He will lift up a flag for the nations
And assemble the banished ones of Israel,
And will gather the dispersed of Judah
From the four corners of the earth.
13 Then the jealousy of Ephraim will depart,
And those who harass Judah will be
eliminated;
Ephraim will not be jealous of Judah,
And Judah will not harass Ephraim.
14 They will swoop down on the slopes of
the Philistines on the west;
Together they will plunder the people of
the east;
They will possess Edom and Moab,
And the sons of Ammon will be subject to
them.
15 And the LORD will utterly destroy
The tongue of the Sea of Egypt;
And He will wave His hand over the
Euphrates River
With His scorching wind;
And He will strike it into seven streams
And make *people* walk over in *dry*
sandals.
16 And there will be a highway from Assyria
For the remnant of His people who will be
left,
Just as there was for Israel
On the day that they came up out of the
land of Egypt.

Thanksgiving Expressed

12 Then you will say on that day,
"I will give thanks to You, LORD;
For *although* You were angry with me,
Your anger is turned away,
And You comfort me.
2 "Behold, God is my salvation,
I will trust and not be afraid;
For the LORD GOD is my strength and
song,
And He has become my salvation."
3 Therefore you will joyously draw water
From the springs of salvation.
4 And on that day you will say,
"Give thanks to the LORD, call on His
name.
Make known His deeds among the
peoples;
Make *them* remember that His name is
exalted."
5 Praise the LORD in song, for He has done
glorious things;
Let this be known throughout the earth.
6 Rejoice and shout for joy, you inhabitant
of Zion,
For great in your midst is the Holy One of
Israel.

Prophecies about Babylon

13 The pronouncement concerning Babylon
which Isaiah the son of Amoz saw:
2 Lift up a flag on the bare hill,
Raise your voice to them,
Wave the hand that they may enter the
doors of the nobles.
3 I have commanded My consecrated ones,
I have also called for My warriors
Who boast in My eminence,
To *execute* My anger.

4 A sound of a roar on the mountains,
Like that of many people!
A sound of an uproar of kingdoms,
Of nations gathered together!
The LORD of armies is mustering the army
for battle.
5 They are coming from a distant country,
From the farthest horizons,
The LORD and the weapons of His
indignation,
To destroy the whole land.

Judgment on the Day of the LORD

6 Wail, for the day of the LORD is near!
It will come as destruction from the
Almighty.
7 Therefore all hands will fall limp,
And every human heart will melt.
8 They will be terrified,
Pains and anguish will take hold of
them;
They will writhe like a woman in labor,
They will look at one another in
astonishment,
Their faces aflame.
9 Behold, the day of the LORD is coming,
Cruel, with fury and burning anger,
To make the land a desolation;
And He will exterminate its sinners
from it.
10 For the stars of heaven and their
constellations
Will not flash their light;
The sun will be dark when it rises
And the moon will not shed its light.
11 So I will punish the world for its evil
And the wicked for their wrongdoing;
I will also put an end to the audacity of
the proud
And humiliate the arrogance of the
tyrants.
12 I will make mortal man scarcer than pure
gold
And mankind than the gold of Ophir.
13 Therefore I will make the heavens tremble,
And the earth will be shaken from its
place
At the fury of the LORD of armies
In the day of His burning anger.
14 And it will be that, like a hunted gazelle,
Or like sheep with no one to gather *them,*
Each of them will turn to his own people,
And each of them will flee to his own
land.
15 Anyone who is found will be thrust
through,
And anyone who is captured will fall by
the sword.
16 Their little ones also will be dashed to
pieces
Before their eyes;
Their houses will be plundered
And their wives raped.

Babylon Will Fall to the Medes

17 ¶ Behold, I am going to stir up the Medes
against them,
Who will not value silver or take pleasure
in gold.

18 And *their* bows will mow down the young
 men,
They will not even have compassion on
 the fruit of the womb,
Nor will their eye pity children.
19 And Babylon, the beauty of kingdoms, the
 glory of the Chaldeans' pride,
Will be as when God overthrew Sodom
 and Gomorrah.
20 It will never be inhabited or lived in from
 generation to generation;
Nor will the Arab pitch *his* tent there,
Nor will shepherds allow *their flocks* to
 lie down there.
21 But desert creatures will lie down there,
And their houses will be full of owls;
Ostriches also will live there, and shaggy
 goats will frolic there.
22 Hyenas will howl in their fortified towers
And jackals in their luxurious palaces.
Her *fateful* time also will soon come,
And her days will not be prolonged.

Israel's Taunt against Babylon

14 When the LORD has compassion on Jacob
and again chooses Israel, and settles
them on their own land, then strangers will
join them and attach themselves to the house
of Jacob. 2 The peoples will take them along and
bring them to their place, and the house of
Israel will make them their own possession in
the land of the LORD as male and female
servants; and they will take their captors
captive and will rule over their oppressors.

3 And it will be on the day when the LORD
gives you rest from your hardship, your
turmoil, and from the harsh service in which
you have been enslaved, 4 that you will take up
this taunt against the king of Babylon, and say,
 "How the oppressor has ceased,
 And how the onslaught has ceased!
5 "The LORD has broken the staff of the
 wicked,
The scepter of rulers,
6 Which used to strike the peoples in fury
 with unceasing strokes,
Which subdued the nations in anger with
 unrestrained persecution.
7 "The whole earth is at rest *and* is quiet;
They break forth into shouts of joy.
8 "Even the juniper trees rejoice over you,
 and the cedars of Lebanon, *saying,*
'Since you have been laid low, no *tree*
 cutter comes up against us.'
9 "Sheol below is excited about you, to meet
 you when you come;
It stirs the spirits of the dead for you, all
 the leaders of the earth;
It raises all the kings of the nations from
 their thrones.
10 "They will all respond and say to you,
 'Even you have become weak as we,
You have become like us.
11 'Your pride *and* the music of your harps
Have been brought down to Sheol;
Maggots are spread out *as your bed*
 beneath you
And worms are your covering.'
12 "How you have fallen from heaven,
You star of the morning, son of the dawn!

You have been cut down to the earth,
You who defeated the nations!
13 "But you said in your heart,
'I will ascend to heaven;
I will raise my throne above the stars of
 God,
And I will sit on the mount of assembly
In the recesses of the north.
14 'I will ascend above the heights of the
 clouds;
I will make myself like the Most High.'
15 "Nevertheless you will be brought down to
 Sheol,
To the recesses of the pit.
16 "Those who see you will stare at you,
They will closely examine you, *saying,*
'Is this the man who made the earth
 tremble,
Who shook kingdoms,
17 Who made the world like a wilderness
And overthrew its cities,
Who did not allow his prisoners to *go*
 home?'
18 "All the kings of the nations lie in glory,
Each in his own tomb.
19 "But you have been hurled out of your
 tomb
Like a rejected branch,
Clothed with those killed who have been
 pierced with a sword,
Who go down to the stones of the pit
Like a trampled corpse.
20 "You will not be united with them in
 burial,
Because you have ruined your country,
You have killed your people.
May the descendants of evildoers never
 be mentioned.
21 "Prepare a place of slaughter for his sons
Because of the wrongdoing of their
 fathers.
They must not arise and take possession
 of the earth,
And fill the surface of the world with
 cities."

22 "I will rise up against them," declares the
LORD of armies, "and eliminate from Babylon
name and survivors, offspring and descendants," declares the LORD. 23 "I will also make
it the property of the hedgehog and swamps of
water, and I will sweep it away with the broom
of destruction," declares the LORD of armies.

Judgment on Assyria

24 The LORD of armies has sworn, saying,
"Certainly, just as I have intended, so it has
happened, and just as I have planned, so it will
stand, 25 to break Assyria in My land, and I will
trample him on My mountains. Then his yoke
will be removed from them, and his burden
removed from their shoulders. 26 This is the
plan devised against the entire earth; and this
is the hand that is stretched out against all the
nations. 27 For the LORD of armies has planned,
and who can frustrate *it?* And as for His
stretched-out hand, who can turn it back?"

Judgment on Philistia

28 In the year that King Ahaz died, this
pronouncement came:

29 "Do not rejoice, Philistia, all of you,
Because the rod that struck you is broken;
For from the serpent's root a viper will
come out,
And its fruit will be a winged serpent.
30 "Those who are most helpless will eat,
And the poor will lie down in security;
I will kill your root with famine,
And it will kill your survivors.
31 "Wail, you gate; cry, you city;
Melt away, Philistia, all of you!
For smoke comes from the north,
And there is no straggler in his ranks.
32 "What answer will one give the
messengers of the nation?
That the LORD has founded Zion,
And the poor of His people will take
refuge in it."

Judgment on Moab

15 The pronouncement concerning
Moab:
Certainly in a night Ar of Moab is
devastated *and* ruined;
Certainly in a night Kir of Moab is
devastated *and* ruined.
2 The people have gone up to the temple
and *to* Dibon, to the high places to
weep.
Moab wails over Nebo and Medeba;
Everyone's head is bald *and* every beard
is cut off.
3 In their streets they have put on
sackcloth;
On their housetops and in their public
squares
Everyone is wailing, overcome with
weeping.
4 Heshbon and Elealeh also cry out,
Their voice is heard all the way to
Jahaz;
Therefore the armed men of Moab cry
aloud;
His soul trembles within him.
5 My heart cries out for Moab;
His fugitives are as far as Zoar *and*
Eglath-shelishiyah,
For they go up the ascent of Luhith
weeping;
Indeed, on the road to Horonaim they
raise a cry of distress over *their* col-
lapse.
6 For the waters of Nimrim are desolate.
Indeed, the grass is withered, the new
growth has died,
There is no greenery.
7 Therefore the abundance *which* they have
acquired and stored up,
They carry *it* off over the brook of
Arabim.
8 For the cry of distress has gone around
the territory of Moab,
Its wailing *goes* as far as Eglaim and its
howling to Beer-elim.
9 For the waters of Dimon are full of blood;
I will certainly bring added *woes* upon
Dimon,
A lion upon the fugitives of Moab and the
remnant of the land.

Prophecy of Moab's Devastation

16 Send the *tribute* lamb to the ruler of
the land,
From Sela by way of the wilderness to the
mountain of the daughter of Zion.
2 Then, like fluttering birds *or* scattered
nestlings,
The daughters of Moab will be at the
crossing places of the Arnon.
3 "Give *us* advice, make a decision;
Cast your shadow like night at high noon;
Hide the outcasts, do not betray the
fugitive.
4 "Let the outcasts of Moab stay with you;
Be a hiding place to them from the
destroyer."
For the oppressor has come to an end,
destruction has ceased,
Oppressors have been removed from
the land.
5 A throne will be established in faithfulness,
And a judge will sit on it in trustworthiness in the tent of David;
Moreover, he will seek justice,
And be prompt in righteousness.
6¶ We have heard of the pride of Moab, an
excessive pride;
Even of his arrogance, pride, and fury;
His idle boasts are false.
7 Therefore Moab will wail; everyone of
Moab will wail.
You will moan for the raisin cakes of
Kir-hareseth
As those who are utterly stricken.
8 For the fields of Heshbon have withered,
the vines of Sibmah *as well;*
The lords of the nations have trampled
down its choice clusters
Which reached as far as Jazer *and*
wandered to the deserts;
Its ¹tendrils spread themselves out *and*
passed over the sea.
9 Therefore I will weep bitterly for Jazer, for
the vine of Sibmah;
I will drench you with my tears, Heshbon
and Elealeh;
For the shouting over your summer fruits
and your harvest has fallen away.
10 Gladness and joy are taken away from the
fruitful field;
In the vineyards also there will be no
cries of joy or jubilant shouting,
No treader treads out wine in the presses,
For I have made the shouting to cease.
11 Therefore my inner being sounds like a
harp for Moab.
And my heart for Kir-hareseth.
12 So it will come about when Moab
presents himself,
When he tires himself upon *his* high
place
And comes to his sanctuary to pray,
That he will not prevail.
13 This is the word which the LORD spoke
earlier concerning Moab. 14 But now the LORD
has spoken, saying, "Within three years, as a
hired worker would count them, the glory of
Moab will become contemptible along with all

16:8 ¹ I.e., parts of a climbing plant that attach to its support

his great population, and *his* remnant will be
very small *and* impotent."

Prophecy about Damascus

17 The pronouncement concerning
Damascus:
"Behold, Damascus is about to be removed
from being a city
And will become a fallen ruin.
2   "The cities of Aroer are abandoned;
They will be for herds to lie down in,
And there will be no one to frighten
them.
3   "The fortified city will disappear from
Ephraim,
And sovereignty from Damascus
And the remnant of Aram;
They will be like the glory of the sons of
Israel,"
Declares the LORD of armies.
4¶   Now on that day the glory of Jacob will
fade,
And the fatness of his flesh will become
lean.
5   It will be like the reaper gathering the
standing grain,
As his arm harvests the ears,
Or it will be like one gleaning ears of
grain
In the Valley of Rephaim.
6   Yet gleanings will be left in it like the
shaking of an olive tree,
Two *or* three olives on the topmost
branch,
Four *or* five on the branches of a fruitful
tree,
Declares the LORD, the God of Israel.
7   On that day man will look to his
Maker
And his eyes will look to the Holy One of
Israel.
8   And he will not look to the altars, the
work of his hands,
Nor will he look to that which his fingers
have made,
Even the [1]Asherim and incense altars.
9   On that day their strong cities will be like
abandoned places in the forest,
Or like branches which they abandoned
before the sons of Israel;
And the land will be a desolation.
10   For you have forgotten the God of your
salvation
And have not remembered the rock of
your refuge.
Therefore you plant delightful plants
And set them with vine shoots of a
strange *god.*
11   On the day that you plant *it* you carefully
fence *it* in,
And in the morning you bring your seed
to blossom;
But the harvest will flee
On a day of illness and incurable pain.
12¶ Oh, the uproar of many peoples
Who roar like the roaring of the seas,
And the rumbling of nations
Who rush on like the rumbling of mighty
waters!

13   The nations rumble on like the rumbling
of many waters,
But He will rebuke them, and they will
flee far away,
And be chased like chaff on the
mountains before the wind,
Or like whirling dust before a gale.
14   At evening time, behold, *there is* terror!
Before morning they are gone.
This *will be* the fate of those who plunder
us
And the lot of those who pillage us.

Message to Ethiopia

18 Woe, land of whirring wings
Which lies beyond the rivers of [1]Cush,
2   Which sends messengers by the sea,
Even in papyrus vessels on the surface of
the waters.
Go, swift messengers, to a nation tall and
smooth,
To a people feared far and wide,
A powerful and oppressive nation
Whose land the rivers divide.
3   All you who inhabit the world, and live
on earth,
As soon as a flag is raised on the
mountains, you will see *it,*
And as soon as the trumpet is blown, you
will hear *it.*
4 For this is what the LORD has told me:
"I will quietly look from My dwelling place
Like dazzling heat in the sunshine,
Like a cloud of dew in the heat of
harvest."
5   For before the harvest, as soon as the bud
blossoms
And the flower becomes a ripening grape,
He will cut off the shoots with pruning
knives,
And remove *and* tear away the spreading
branches.
6   They will be left together for mountain
birds of prey,
And for the animals of the earth;
And the birds of prey will spend the
summer *feeding* on them,
And all the animals of the earth will
spend harvest time on them.
7   At that time a gift of tribute will be
brought to the LORD of armies
From a people tall and smooth,
From a people feared far and wide,
A powerful and oppressive nation,
Whose land the rivers divide—
To the place of the name of the LORD of
armies, *to* Mount Zion.

Message to Egypt

19 The pronouncement concerning
Egypt:
Behold, the LORD is riding on a swift cloud
and is about to come to Egypt;
The idols of Egypt will tremble at His
presence,
And the heart of the Egyptians will melt
within them.
2   "So I will incite Egyptians against
Egyptians;

17:8 [1] I.e., wooden symbols of a female deity (Asherah)   **18:1** [1] Or *Ethiopia*

And they will fight, each against his
brother and each against his neighbor,
City against city *and* kingdom against
kingdom.
3 "Then the spirit of the Egyptians will be
demoralized within them;
And I will confuse their strategy,
So that they will resort to idols and ghosts
of the dead,
And to mediums and spiritists.
4 "Furthermore, I will hand the Egyptians
over to a cruel master,
And a mighty king will rule over them,"
declares the Lord GOD of armies.
5¶ The waters from the sea will dry up,
And the river will be parched and dry.
6 The canals will emit a stench,
The streams of Egypt will thin out and dry
up;
The reeds and rushes will rot away.
7 The bulrushes by the Nile, by the edge of
the Nile
And all the sown fields by the Nile
Will become dry, be driven away, and be
no more.
8 And the fishermen will grieve,
And all those who cast a line into the Nile
will mourn,
And those who spread nets on the waters
will dwindle away.
9 Moreover, the manufacturers of linen
made from combed flax
And the weavers of white cloth will be
utterly dejected.
10 And the pillars *of Egypt* will be crushed;
All the hired laborers will be grieved in
soul.
11¶ The officials of Zoan are mere fools;
The advice of Pharaoh's wisest advisers
has become stupid.
How can you say to Pharaoh,
"I am a son of the wise, a son of ancient
kings"?
12 Well then, where are your wise men?
Please let them tell you,
And let them understand what the LORD
of armies
Has planned against Egypt.
13 The officials of Zoan have turned out to be
fools,
The officials of Memphis are deluded;
Those who are the cornerstone of her
tribes
Have led Egypt astray.
14 The LORD has mixed within her a spirit of
distortion;
They have led Egypt astray in all that it
does,
As a drunken person staggers in his
vomit.
15 There will be no work for Egypt
Which *its* head or tail, *its* palm branch or
bulrush, may do.
16 On that day the Egyptians will become
like women, and they will tremble and be in
great fear because of the waving of the hand of
the LORD of armies, which He is going to wave
over them. 17 The land of Judah will become a
cause of shame to Egypt; everyone to whom it

is mentioned will be in great fear because of
the plan of the LORD of armies which He is
making against them.
18 On that day five cities in the land of Egypt
will be speaking the language of Canaan and
swearing *allegiance* to the LORD of armies; one
will be called the City of ¹Destruction.
19 On that day there will be an altar to the
LORD in the midst of the land of Egypt, and a
memorial stone to the LORD beside its border.
20 And it will become a sign and a witness to
the LORD of armies in the land of Egypt; for
they will cry out to the LORD because of oppressors, and He will send them a Savior and a
Champion, and He will save them. 21 So the
LORD will make Himself known to Egypt, and
the Egyptians will know the LORD on that day.
They will even worship with sacrifice and
offering, and will make a vow to the LORD and
perform it. 22 And the LORD will strike Egypt,
striking but healing; so they will return to the
LORD, and He will respond to their pleas and
heal them.
23 On that day there will be a road from
Egypt to Assyria, and the Assyrians will come
into Egypt and the Egyptians into Assyria; and
the Egyptians will worship with the Assyrians.
24 On that day Israel will be the third *party*
to Egypt and Assyria, a blessing in the midst of
the earth, 25 whom the LORD of armies has
blessed, saying, "Blessed is Egypt My people,
and Assyria the work of My hands, and Israel
My inheritance."

Prophecy about Egypt and Ethiopia

20 In the year that the commander came to
Ashdod, when Sargon the king of Assyria
sent him and he fought against Ashdod and
captured it, 2 at that time the LORD spoke
through Isaiah the son of Amoz, saying, "Go
and loosen the sackcloth from your hips and
take your sandals off your feet." And he did so,
going naked and barefoot. 3 Then the LORD said,
"Even as My servant Isaiah has gone naked
and barefoot for three years as a sign and
symbol against Egypt and Cush, 4 so the king
of Assyria will lead away the captives of Egypt
and the exiles of Cush, young and old, naked
and barefoot with buttocks uncovered, to the
shame of Egypt. 5 Then they will be terrified
and ashamed because of Cush their hope and
Egypt their pride. 6 So the inhabitants of this
coastland will say on that day, 'Behold, such is
our hope, where we fled for help to be saved
from the king of Assyria; and how are we
ourselves to escape?' "

God Commands That Babylon Be Taken

21 The pronouncement concerning the
wilderness of the sea:
As windstorms in the Negev come in
turns,
It comes from the wilderness, from a
terrifying land.
2 A harsh vision has been shown to me;
The treacherous one *still* deals
treacherously, and the destroyer *still*
destroys.
Go up, Elam, lay siege, Media;

19:18 ¹Some mss and ancient versions *the Sun*

I have put an end to all the groaning she
  has caused.
3 For this reason my loins are full of
  anguish;
  Pains have seized me like the pains of a
  woman in labor.
  I am so bewildered I cannot hear, so
  terrified I cannot see.
4 My mind reels, horror overwhelms me;
  The twilight I longed for has been turned
  into trembling for me.
5 They set the table, they spread out the
  cloth, they eat, they drink;
  "Rise up, captains, oil the shields!"
6 For this is what the Lord says to me:
  "Go, station the lookout, have him report
  what he sees.
7 "When he sees a column of chariots,
  horsemen in pairs,
  A train of donkeys, a train of camels,
  He is to pay close attention, very close
  attention."
8 Then the lookout called,
  "Lord, I stand continually by day on the
  watchtower,
  And I am stationed every night at my
  guard post.
9 "Now behold, here comes a troop of riders,
  horsemen in pairs."
  And one said, "Fallen, fallen is Babylon;
  And all the images of her gods are
  shattered on the ground."
10 My downtrodden *people,* and my afflicted
  of the threshing floor!
  What I have heard from the Lord of
  armies,
  The God of Israel, I make known to you.

Pronouncements about Edom and Arabia
11 The pronouncement concerning Edom:
  One keeps calling to me from Seir,
  "Watchman, how far gone is the night?
  Watchman, how far gone is the night?"
12 The watchman says,
  "Morning comes but also night.
  If you would inquire, inquire;
  Come back again."
13 The pronouncement about Arabia:
  In the thickets of Arabia you must spend
  the night,
  You caravans of Dedanites.
14 Bring water for the thirsty,
  You inhabitants of the land of Tema;
  Meet the fugitive with bread.
15 For they have fled from the swords,
  From the drawn sword, and from the bent
  bow,
  And from the press of battle.
16 For this is what the Lord said to me: "In a
year, as a hired worker would count it, all the
splendor of Kedar will come to an end; 17 and
the remainder of the number of bowmen, the
warriors of the sons of Kedar, will be few; for
the Lord God of Israel has spoken."

The Valley of Vision
22 The pronouncement concerning the
  valley of vision:
  What is the matter with you now, that you
  have all gone up to the housetops?

2 You who were full of noise,
  You tumultuous town, you jubilant city;
  Your dead were not killed with the sword,
  Nor did they die in battle.
3 All your rulers have fled together,
  And have been captured without the bow;
  All of you who were found were taken
  captive together,
  Though they had fled far away.
4 Therefore I say, "Look away from me,
  Let me weep bitterly,
  Do not try to comfort me concerning the
  destruction of the daughter of my
  people."
5 For the Lord God of armies has a day of
  panic, subjugation, and confusion
  In the valley of vision,
  A breaking down of walls
  And a crying to the mountain.
6 Elam picked up the quiver,
  With the chariots, infantry, *and*
  horsemen;
  And Kir uncovered the shield.
7 Then your choicest valleys were full of
  chariots,
  And the horsemen took positions at the
  gate.
8 And He removed the defense of Judah.
  On that day you depended on the
  weapons of the house of the forest,
9 And you saw that the breaches
  In the *wall* of the city of David were
  many;
  And you collected the waters of the lower
  pool.
10 Then you counted the houses of Jerusalem
  And tore down houses to fortify the wall.
11 And you made a reservoir between the
  two walls
  For the waters of the old pool.
  But you did not depend on Him who
  made it,
  Nor did you take into consideration Him
  who planned it long ago.
12¶ Therefore on that day the Lord God of
  armies called *you* to weeping, to
  wailing,
  To shaving the head, and to wearing
  sackcloth.
13 Instead, there is joy and jubilation,
  Killing of cattle and slaughtering of
  sheep,
  Eating of meat and drinking of wine:
  "Let's eat and drink, for tomorrow we may
  die."
14 But the Lord of armies revealed Himself
  to me:
  "Certainly this wrongdoing will not be
  forgiven you
  Until you die," says the Lord God of
  armies.
15 This is what the Lord God of armies says:
  "Come, go to this steward,
  To Shebna who is in charge of the *royal*
  household,
16 'What right do you have here,
  And whom do you have here,
  That you have cut out a tomb for yourself
  here,
  You who cut out a tomb on the height,

You who carve a resting place for yourself
in the rock?

17 'Behold, the LORD is about to hurl you
violently, you strong man.
And He is about to grasp you firmly

18 *And* wrap you up tightly like a ball,
To be driven into a vast country;
There you will die,
And there your splendid chariots will be,
You shame of your master's house!'

19 "I will depose you from your office,
And I will pull you down from your
position.

20 "Then it will come about on that day,
That I will summon My servant Eliakim
the son of Hilkiah,

21 And I will clothe him with your tunic
And tie your sash securely around him.
I will hand your authority over to him,
And he will become a father to the
inhabitants of Jerusalem and to the
house of Judah.

22 "Then I will put the key of the house of
David on his shoulder;
When he opens, no one will shut,
When he shuts, no one will open.

23 "I will drive him *like* a peg in a firm place,
And he will become a throne of glory to
his father's house.

24 So they will hang on him all the glory of his
father's house, the offspring and the descendants, all the least of vessels, from bowls to all
the jars. 25 On that day," declares the LORD of
armies, "the peg driven into a firm place will
give way; it will even break off and fall, and the
load that is *hanging* on it will be cut off, for the
LORD has spoken."

The Fall of Tyre

23 The pronouncement concerning Tyre:
Wail, you ships of Tarshish,
For *Tyre* is destroyed, without house *or*
harbor;
It is reported to them from the land of
Cyprus.

2 Be silent, you inhabitants of the coastland,
You merchants of Sidon;
Your messengers crossed the sea

3 And *were* on many waters.
The grain of the Nile, the harvest of the
River was her revenue;
And she was the market of nations.

4 Be ashamed, Sidon,
For the sea speaks, the stronghold of the
sea, saying,
"I have neither been in labor nor given
birth,
I have neither brought up young men *nor*
raised virgins."

5 When the report *reaches* Egypt,
They will be in anguish over the report of
Tyre.

6 Pass over to Tarshish;
Wail, you inhabitants of the coastland.

7 Is this your jubilant *city*,
Whose origin is from antiquity,
Whose feet used to bring her to colonize
distant places?

8¶ Who has planned this against Tyre, the
bestower of crowns,

Whose merchants were princes, whose
traders were the honored of the earth?

9 The LORD of armies has planned it, to
defile the pride of all beauty,
To despise all the honored of the earth.

10 Overflow your land like the Nile, you
daughter of Tarshish,
There is no more restraint.

11 He has stretched His hand out over the
sea,
He has made the kingdoms tremble;
The LORD has given a command
concerning Canaan to demolish
its strongholds.

12¶ He has said, "You shall not be jubilant
anymore, you crushed virgin daughter
of Sidon.
Arise, pass over to Cyprus; even there you
will find no rest."

13 Behold, the land of the Chaldeans—this is
the people *that* did not exist; Assyria allocated
it for desert creatures—they erected their siege
towers, they stripped its palaces, they made it a
ruin.

14 Wail, you ships of Tarshish,
For your stronghold is destroyed.

15 Now on that day Tyre will be forgotten for
seventy years like the days of one king. At the
end of seventy years it will happen to Tyre as
in the song of the prostitute:

16 Take *your* harp, wander around the city,
You forgotten prostitute;
Pluck the strings skillfully, sing many
songs,
That you may be remembered.

17 It will come about at the end of seventy
years that the LORD will visit Tyre. Then she
will go back to her prostitute's wages and
commit prostitution with all the kingdoms
on the face of the earth. 18 Her profit and
her prostitute's wages will be sacred to the
LORD; it will not be stored up or hoarded, but
her profit will become sufficient food and
magnificent attire for those who dwell in the
presence of the LORD.

Judgment on the Earth

24 Behold, the LORD lays the earth waste,
devastates it, twists its surface, and
scatters its inhabitants. 2 And the people will
be like the priest, the servant like his master,
the female servant like her mistress, the buyer
like the seller, the lender like the borrower,
the creditor like the debtor. 3 The earth will
be completely laid waste and completely
plundered, for the LORD has spoken this word.
4 The earth dries up *and* crumbles away, the
mainland dries out *and* crumbles away, the
exalted of the people of the earth dwindle.
5 The earth is also defiled by its inhabitants,
for they violated laws, altered statutes, *and*
broke the everlasting covenant. 6 Therefore,
a curse devours the earth, and those who
live on it suffer for their guilt. Therefore, the
inhabitants of the earth decrease in number,
and few people are left.

7¶ The new wine mourns,
The vine decays,
All the joyful-hearted sigh.

8 The joy of tambourines ceases,

The noise of revelers stops,
The joy of the harp ceases.
9 They do not drink wine with song;
Intoxicating drink is bitter to those who
drink it.
10 The city of chaos is broken down;
Every house is shut up so that no one may
enter.
11 There is an outcry in the streets
concerning the wine;
All joy turns to gloom.
The joy of the earth is banished.
12 Desolation is left in the city
And the gate is battered to ruins.
13 For so it will be in the midst of the earth
among the peoples,
As the shaking of an olive tree,
As the gleanings when the grape harvest
is over.
14 They raise their voices, they shout for joy;
They cry out from the west concerning
the majesty of the LORD.
15 Therefore glorify the LORD in the east,
The name of the LORD, the God of Israel,
In the coastlands of the sea.
16 From the ends of the earth we hear songs:
"Glory to the Righteous One,"
But I say, "I am finished! I am finished!
Woe to me!
The treacherous deal treacherously,
And the treacherous deal very
treacherously."
17 Terror and pit and snare
Confront you, you inhabitant of the earth.
18 Then it will be that the one who flees the
sound of terror will fall into the pit,
And the one who climbs out of the pit will
be caught in the snare;
For the windows above are opened, and
the foundations of the earth shake.
19 The earth is broken apart,
The earth is split through,
The earth is shaken violently.
20 The earth trembles like a heavy drinker
And sways like a hut,
For its wrongdoing is heavy upon it,
And it will fall, never to rise again.
21 So it will happen on that day,
That the LORD will punish the *rebellious*
angels of heaven on high,
And the kings of the earth on earth.
22 They will be gathered together
Like prisoners in the dungeon,
And will be confined in prison;
And after many days they *will be*
punished.
23 Then the moon will be ashamed and the
sun be put to shame,
For the LORD of armies will reign on
Mount Zion and in Jerusalem,
And *His* glory will be before His elders.

Song of Praise for God's Favor

25 LORD, You are my God;
I will exalt You, I will give thanks to
Your name;
For You have worked wonders,
Plans *formed* long ago, with perfect
faithfulness.

2 For You have turned a city into a heap,
A fortified city into a ruin;
A palace of strangers is no longer a city,
It will never be rebuilt.
3 Therefore a strong people will glorify You;
Cities of ruthless nations will revere You.
4 For You have been a stronghold for the
helpless,
A stronghold for the poor in his distress,
A refuge from the storm, a shade from the
heat;
For the breath of the ruthless
Is like a *rain* storm *against* a wall.
5 Like heat in a dry land, You subdue the
uproar of foreigners;
Like heat by the shadow of a cloud, the
song of the ruthless is silenced.
6¶ Now the LORD of armies will prepare a
lavish banquet for all peoples on this
mountain;
A banquet of aged wine, choice pieces
with marrow,
And refined, aged wine.
7 And on this mountain He will destroy the
covering which is over all peoples,
The veil which is stretched over all
nations.
8 He will ¹swallow up death for all time,
And the Lord GOD will wipe tears away
from all faces,
And He will remove the disgrace of His
people from all the earth;
For the LORD has spoken.
9 And it will be said on that day,
"Behold, this is our God for whom we have
waited that He might save us.
This is the LORD for whom we have
waited;
Let's rejoice and be glad in His salvation."
10 For the hand of the LORD will rest on this
mountain,
And Moab will be trampled down in his
place
As straw is trampled down in the water of
a manure pile.
11 And he will spread out his hands in the
middle of it
As a swimmer spreads out *his hands* to
swim,
But *the Lord* will lay low his pride
together with the trickery of his
hands.
12 The unassailable fortifications of your
walls He will bring down,
Lay low, *and* throw to the ground, to the
dust.

Song of Trust in God's Protection

26 On that day this song will be sung in the
land of Judah:
"We have a strong city;
He sets up walls and ramparts for security.
2 "Open the gates, that the righteous nation
may enter,
The one that remains faithful.
3 "The steadfast of mind You will keep in
perfect peace,
Because he trusts in You.
4 "Trust in the LORD forever,

25:8 ¹I.e., destroy

For in GOD the LORD, *we have* an
everlasting Rock.
5 "For He has brought low those who dwell
on high, the unassailable city;
He lays it low, He lays it low to the
ground, He casts it to the dust.
6 "The foot will trample it,
The feet of the poor, the steps of the
helpless."
7¶ The way of the righteous is smooth;
O Upright One, make the path of the
righteous level.
8 Indeed, *while following* the way of Your
judgments, LORD,
We have waited for You eagerly;
Your name, and remembering You, is the
desire of *our* souls.
9 At night my soul longs for You,
Indeed, my spirit within me seeks You
diligently;
For when the earth experiences Your
judgments,
The inhabitants of the world learn
righteousness.
10 *Though* the wicked person is shown
compassion,
He does not learn righteousness;
He deals unjustly in the land of uprightness,
And does not perceive the majesty of the
LORD.
11¶ LORD, Your hand is lifted up, *yet* they do
not see it.
They see *Your* zeal for the people and are
put to shame;
Indeed, fire will devour Your enemies.
12 LORD, You will establish peace for us,
Since You have also performed for us all
our works.
13 LORD, our God, other masters besides You
have ruled us;
But through You alone we confess Your
name.
14 The dead will not live, the departed spirits
will not rise;
Therefore You have punished and
destroyed them,
And You have eliminated all remembrance
of them.
15 You have increased the nation, LORD,
You have increased the nation, You are
glorified;
You have extended all the borders of the
land.
16 LORD, they sought You in distress;
They could only whisper a prayer,
Your discipline was upon them.
17 As the pregnant woman approaches *the
time* to give birth,
She writhes *and* cries out in her labor
pains;
This is how we were before You, LORD.
18 We were pregnant, we writhed *in labor,*
We gave birth, as it seems, *only* to wind.
We could not accomplish deliverance for
the earth,
Nor were inhabitants of the world born.
19 Your dead will live;
Their corpses will rise.

You who lie in the dust, awake and shout
for joy,
For your dew *is as* the dew of the dawn,
And the earth will give birth to the
departed spirits.
20¶ Come, my people, enter your rooms
And close your doors behind you;
Hide for a little while
Until indignation runs *its* course.
21 For behold, the LORD is about to come out
from His place
To punish the inhabitants of the earth for
their wrongdoing;
And the earth will reveal her bloodshed
And will no longer cover her slain.

God's Blessings for Israel

27 On that day the LORD will punish
Leviathan the fleeing serpent,
With His fierce and great and mighty
sword,
Even Leviathan the twisted serpent;
And He will kill the dragon who *lives* in
the sea.
2¶ On that day,
"A vineyard of beauty, sing of it!
3 "I, the LORD, am its keeper;
I water it every moment.
So that no one will damage it,
I guard it night and day.
4 "I have no wrath.
Should someone give Me briars *and*
thorns in battle,
Then I would step on them, I would burn
them completely.
5 "Or let him rely on My protection,
Let him make peace with Me,
Let him make peace with Me."
6 In the days to come Jacob will take
root,
Israel will blossom and sprout,
And they will fill the whole world with
fruit.
7¶ Like the striking of Him who has struck
them, has He struck them?
Or like the slaughter of His slain, have
they been slain?
8 You contended with them by banishing
them, by driving them away.
With His fierce wind He has expelled
them on the day of the east wind.
9 Therefore through this Jacob's
wrongdoing will be forgiven;
And this will be the full price of the
pardoning of his sin:
When he makes all the altar stones like
pulverized chalk stones;
When ¹Asherim and incense altars will
not stand.
10 For the fortified city is isolated,
A homestead deserted and abandoned like
the desert;
There the calf will graze,
And there it will lie down and feed on its
branches.
11 When its limbs are dry, they are broken
off;
Women come *and* make a fire with them,
For they are not a people of discernment,

27:9 ¹I.e., wooden symbols of a female deity (Asherah)

Therefore their Maker will not have
compassion on them.
And their Creator will not be gracious to
them.

12 On that day the LORD will thresh from the
flowing stream of the *Euphrates* River to the
brook of Egypt, and you will be gathered up
one by one, you sons of Israel. 13 It will come
about also on that day that a great trumpet will
be blown, and those who were perishing in the
land of Assyria and who were scattered in the
land of Egypt will come and worship the LORD
on the holy mountain in Jerusalem.

Ephraim's Captivity Predicted

28 Woe to the proud crown of the
habitually drunk of Ephraim,
And to the fading flower of its glorious
beauty,
Which is at the head of the fertile valley
Of those who are overcome with wine!
2 Behold, the Lord has a strong and mighty
agent;
As a storm of hail, a tempest of
destruction,
Like a storm of mighty overflowing
waters,
He has thrown *it* down to the earth with
His hand.
3 The splendid crown of the habitually
drunk of Ephraim is trampled
underfoot.
4 And the fading flower of its glorious
beauty,
Which is at the head of the fertile valley,
Will be like the first-ripe fig prior to the
summer,
Which one sees,
And as soon as it is in his hand,
He swallows it.
5 On that day the LORD of armies will
become a beautiful crown
And a glorious wreath to the remnant of
His people;
6 A spirit of justice for him who sits in
judgment,
A strength to those who repel the
onslaught at the gate.
7 And these also reel with wine and stagger
from intoxicating drink:
The priest and the prophet reel with
intoxicating drink,
They are confused by wine, they stagger
from intoxicating drink;
They reel while having visions,
They stagger *when rendering* a verdict.
8 For all the tables are full of filthy vomit,
without a *single clean* place.
9 ¶ "To whom would He teach knowledge,
And to whom would He interpret the
message?
Those *just* weaned from milk?
Those *just* taken from the breast?
10 "For *He says,*
'Order on order, order on order,
Line on line, line on line,
A little here, a little there.' "
11 Indeed, He will speak to this people
Through stammering lips and a foreign
tongue,

12 He who said to them, "This is the place of
quiet, give rest to the weary,"
And, "This is the resting place," but they
would not listen.
13 So the word of the LORD to them will be,
"Order on order, order on order,
Line on line, line on line,
A little here, a little there,"
That they may go and stumble backward,
be broken, snared, and taken captive.

Judah Is Warned

14 Therefore, hear the word of the LORD, you
scoffers,
Who rule this people who are in
Jerusalem,
15 Because you have said, "We have made a
covenant with death,
And with Sheol we have made a pact.
The gushing flood will not reach us when
it passes by,
Because we have made falsehood our
refuge and we have concealed
ourselves with deception."
16 Therefore this is what the Lord GOD says:
"Behold, I am laying a stone in Zion, a
tested stone,
A precious cornerstone *for* the
foundation, firmly placed.
The one who believes *in it* will not be
disturbed.
17 "I will make justice the measuring line
And righteousness the level;
Then hail will sweep away the refuge of
lies,
And the waters will overflow the secret
place.
18 "Your covenant with death will be
canceled,
And your pact with Sheol will not stand;
When the gushing flood passes through,
Then you will become its trampling
ground.
19 "As often as it passes through, it will seize
you;
For morning after morning it will pass
through, *anytime* during the day or
night,
And it will be sheer terror to understand
what it means."
20 The bed is too short on which to stretch
out,
And the blanket is too small to wrap
oneself in.
21 For the LORD will rise up as *at* Mount
Perazim,
He will be stirred up as in the Valley of
Gibeon,
To do His task, His unusual task,
And to work His work, His extraordinary
work.
22 And now do not carry on as scoffers,
Or your shackles will be made stronger;
For I have heard from the Lord GOD of
armies
Of decisive destruction on all the earth.
23 ¶ Listen and hear my voice,
Pay attention and hear my words.
24 Does the farmer plow continually to plant
seed?

Does he *continually* turn and break up his ground?

25 Does he not level its surface
And sow dill and scatter cumin
And plant wheat in rows,
Barley in its place and rye within its area?

26 For his God instructs and teaches him properly.

27 For dill is not threshed with a threshing sledge,
Nor is the cartwheel driven over cumin;
But dill is beaten out with a rod, and cumin with a club.

28 *Grain for* bread is crushed,
Indeed, he does not continue to thresh it forever.
Because the wheel of *his* cart and his horses *eventually* damage *it,*
He does not thresh it *longer.*

29 This also comes from the LORD of armies,
Who has made *His* counsel wonderful and *His* wisdom great.

Jerusalem Is Warned

29 Woe, ¹Ariel, Ariel the city *where* David *once* camped!
Add year to year, keep *your* feasts on schedule.

2 I will bring distress to Ariel,
And she will be *a city of* grieving and mourning;
And she will be like an ¹Ariel to me.

3 I will camp against you encircling *you,*
And I will set up siegeworks against you,
And I will raise up battle towers against you.

4 Then you will be brought low;
From the earth you will speak,
And from the dust *where* you are prostrate
Your words *will come.*
Your voice will also be like that of a spirit from the ground,
And your speech will whisper from the dust.

5¶ But the multitude of your enemies will become like fine dust,
And the multitude of the ruthless ones like the chaff which blows away;
And it will happen instantly, suddenly.

6 From the LORD of armies you will be punished with thunder and earthquake and loud noise,
With whirlwind and tempest and the flame of a consuming fire.

7 And the multitude of all the nations who wage war against Ariel,
Even all who wage war against her and her stronghold, and who distress her,
Will be like a dream, a vision of the night.

8 It will be as when a hungry person dreams—
And behold, he is eating;
But when he awakens, his hunger is not satisfied,
Or as when a thirsty person dreams—
And behold, he is drinking,
But when he awakens, behold, he is faint

And his thirst is not quenched.
So will the multitude of all the nations be
Who wage war against Mount Zion.

9¶ Be delayed and horrified,
Blind yourselves and be blind;
They become drunk, but not with wine,
They stagger, but not with intoxicating drink.

10 For the LORD has poured over you a spirit of deep sleep,
He has shut your eyes—the prophets;
And He has covered your heads—the seers.

11 The entire vision will be to you like the words of a sealed book, which, when they give it to the one who is literate, saying, "Please read this," he will say, "I cannot, because it is sealed." 12 Then the book will be given to the one who is illiterate, saying, "Please read this." And he will say, "I cannot read."

13 Then the Lord said,
"Because this people approaches *Me* with their words
And honors Me with their lips,
But their heart is far away from Me,
And their reverence for Me consists of *the* commandment of men that is taught;

14 Therefore behold, I will once again deal marvelously with this people,
wondrously marvelous;
And the wisdom of their wise men will perish,
And the understanding of their men who have understanding will be concealed."

15¶ Woe to those who deeply hide their plans from the LORD,
And whose deeds are *done* in a dark place,
And they say, "Who sees us?" or "Who knows us?"

16 You turn *things* around!
Shall the potter be considered as equal with the clay,
That what is made would say to its maker, "He did not make me";
Or what is formed say to him who formed it, "He has no understanding"?

Blessing after Discipline

17¶ Is it not yet just a little while
Before Lebanon will be turned into a fertile field,
And the fertile field will be considered as a forest?

18 On that day those who are deaf will hear words of a book,
And out of *their* gloom and darkness the eyes of those who are blind will see.

19 The afflicted also will increase their joy in the LORD,
And the needy of mankind will rejoice in the Holy One of Israel.

20 For the ruthless will come to an end and the scorner will be finished,
Indeed all who are intent on doing evil will be eliminated,

21 Who cause a person to be indicted by a word,

29:1 ¹I.e., Lion of God, or Jerusalem   29:2 ¹Ariel (i.e., Jerusalem) is a Heb word for "altar hearth" where offerings were burned

And set a trap for the arbitrator at the
gate,
And defraud the one in the right with
meaningless arguments.

22 Therefore this is what the LORD, who
redeemed Abraham, says concerning the house
of Jacob:

"Jacob will not be ashamed now, nor will
his face turn pale now;
23   But when he sees his children, the work
of My hands, in his midst,
They will sanctify My name;
Indeed, they will sanctify the Holy One of
Jacob,
And will stand in awe of the God of Israel.
24   "Those who err in mind will know the
truth,
And those who criticize will accept
instruction.

Judah Warned against Egyptian Alliance

30 "Woe to the rebellious children,"
declares the LORD,
"Who execute a plan, but not Mine,
And make an alliance, but not of My
Spirit,
In order to add sin to sin;
2   Who proceed down to Egypt
Without consulting Me,
To take refuge in the safety of Pharaoh,
And to seek shelter in the shadow of
Egypt!
3   "Therefore the safety of Pharaoh will be
your shame,
And the shelter in the shadow of Egypt,
your humiliation.
4   "For their officials are at Zoan
And their ambassadors arrive at Hanes.
5   "Everyone will be ashamed because of a
people who do not benefit them,
Who are not a help or benefit, but a
source of shame and also disgrace."

6 The pronouncement concerning the
animals of the Negev:

Through a land of distress and anguish,
From where come lioness and lion, viper
and flying serpent,
They carry their riches on the backs of
young donkeys,
And their treasures on camels' humps,
To a people who will not benefit them;
7   Even Egypt, whose help is vain and
empty.
Therefore, I have called her
"¹Rahab who has been exterminated."
8   Now go, write it on a tablet in their
presence
And inscribe it on a scroll,
That it may serve in the time to come
As a witness forever.
9   For this is a rebellious people, false sons,
Sons who refuse to listen
To the instruction of the LORD;
10   Who say to the seers, "You must not see
visions";
And to the prophets, "You must not
prophesy the truth to us.
Speak to us pleasant words,
Prophesy illusions.

11   "Get out of the way, turn aside from the
path,
Stop speaking before us about the Holy
One of Israel!"

12 Therefore this is what the Holy One of Israel
says:

"Since you have rejected this word
And have put your trust in oppression and
crookedness, and have relied on them,
13   Therefore this wrongdoing will be to you
Like a breach about to fall,
A bulge in a high wall,
Whose collapse comes suddenly in an
instant,
14   Whose collapse is like the smashing of a
potter's jar,
So ruthlessly shattered
That a shard will not be found among its
pieces
To take fire from a hearth
Or to scoop water from a cistern."

15 For this is what the Lord GOD, the Holy One
of Israel, has said:

"In repentance and rest you will be saved,
In quietness and trust is your strength."
But you were not willing,
16   And you said, "No, for we will flee on
horses!"
Therefore you shall flee!
"And we will ride on swift horses!"
Therefore those who pursue you shall be
swift.
17   One thousand will flee at the threat of one
man;
You will flee at the threat of five,
Until you are left like a signal post on a
mountain top,
And like a flag on a hill.

God Is Gracious and Just

18¶ Therefore the LORD longs to be gracious to
you,
And therefore He waits on high to have
compassion on you.
For the LORD is a God of justice;
How blessed are all those who long for
Him.

19 For, you people in Zion, inhabitant in
Jerusalem, you will weep no longer. He will
certainly be gracious to you at the sound of
your cry; when He hears it, He will answer
you. 20 Although the Lord has given you bread
of deprivation and water of oppression, He,
your Teacher, will no longer hide Himself, but
your eyes will see your Teacher. 21 Your ears
will hear a word behind you, saying, "This is
the way, walk in it," whenever you turn to the
right or to the left. 22 And you will desecrate
your carved images plated with silver, and your
cast metal images plated with gold. You will
scatter them as a filthy thing, and say to them,
"Be gone!"
23 Then He will give you rain for your seed
which you will sow in the ground, and bread
from the yield of the ground, and it will be rich
and plentiful; on that day your livestock will
graze in a wide pasture. 24 Also the oxen and
the donkeys that work the ground will eat
seasoned feed, which has been winnowed with

30:7 ¹MT They are Rahab or arrogance, to remain; i.e., Egypt, as a sea monster; see note Job 26:12

shovel and pitchfork. 25 And on every lofty
mountain and every high hill there will be
streams running with water on the day of the
great slaughter, when the towers fall. 26 And
the light of the full moon will be like the light
of the sun, and the light of the sun will be
seven times *brighter,* like the light of seven
days, on the day the LORD binds up the fracture
of His people and heals the wound He has
inflicted.

27¶ Behold, the name of the LORD comes from
    a remote place;
    His anger is burning and dense with
      smoke;
    His lips are filled with indignation,
    And His tongue is like a consuming fire;
28 His breath is like an overflowing river,
    Which reaches to the neck,
    To shake the nations back and forth in a
      sieve,
    And to *put* in the jaws of the peoples the
      bridle which leads astray.
29 You will have songs as in the night when
    you keep the festival,
    And gladness of heart as when one
      marches to *the sound of* the flute,
    To go to the mountain of the LORD, to the
      Rock of Israel.
30 And the LORD will cause His voice of
    authority to be heard,
    And the descending of His arm to be seen
      in fierce anger,
    And *in* the flame of a consuming fire
    In cloudburst, downpour, and hailstones.
31 For at the voice of the LORD Assyria will
    be terrified,
    When He strikes with the rod.
32 And every blow of the rod of punishment,
    Which the LORD will lay on him,
    Will be with *the music of* tambourines
      and lyres;
    And in battles, brandishing weapons, He
      will fight them.
33 For [1]Topheth has long been ready,
    Indeed, it has been prepared for the king.
    He has made it deep and large,
    A pyre of fire with plenty of wood;
    The breath of the LORD, like a torrent of
      brimstone, sets it afire.

Help Not in Egypt but in God

31 Woe to those who go down to Egypt
    for help
    And rely on horses,
    And trust in chariots because they are
      many
    And in horsemen because they are very
      strong,
    But they do not look to the Holy One of
      Israel, nor seek the LORD!
2 Yet He also is wise and will bring disaster,
    And does not retract His words,
    But will arise against the house of
      evildoers,
    And against the help of the workers of
      injustice.
3 Now the Egyptians are human and not
    God,
    And their horses are flesh and not spirit;

So the LORD will stretch out His hand,
And *any* helper will stumble,
And one who is helped will fall.
And all of them will come to an end
    together.

4¶ For this is what the LORD says to me:
"As the lion or the young lion growls over
    his prey,
    Against which a band of shepherds is
      called out,
    And he will not be terrified at their voice
      nor disturbed at their noise,
    So will the LORD of armies come down to
      wage war on Mount Zion and on its
      hill."
5 Like flying birds so the LORD of armies
    will protect Jerusalem.
    He will protect and save *it;*
    He will pass over and rescue *it.*
    6 Return to Him against whom you have
been profoundly obstinate, you sons of Israel.
7 For on that day every person will reject his
silver idols and his gold idols, which your
hands have made for you as a sin.
8 And the Assyrian will fall by a sword not
    wielded by a man,
    And a sword not of man will devour him.
    So he will not escape the sword,
    And his young men will become forced
      laborers.
9 "His rock will pass away because of panic,
    And his officers will be terrified by the
      flag,"
    Declares the LORD, whose fire is in Zion
      and whose furnace is in Jerusalem.

The Glorious Future

32 Behold, a king will reign righteously,
    And officials will rule justly.
2 Each will be like a refuge from the wind
    And a shelter from the storm,
    Like streams of water in a dry country,
    Like the shade of a huge rock in an
      exhausted land.
3 Then the eyes of those who see will not
    be blinded,
    And the ears of those who hear will listen.
4 The mind of the rash will discern the
    truth,
    And the tongue of the stammerers will
      hurry to speak clearly.
5 No longer will the fool be called noble,
    Or the rogue be spoken of *as* generous.
6 For a fool speaks nonsense,
    And his heart inclines toward wickedness:
    To practice ungodliness and to speak error
      against the LORD,
    To keep the hungry person unsatisfied
    And to withhold drink from the thirsty.
7 As for a rogue, his weapons are evil;
    He devises wicked schemes
    To destroy *the* poor with slander,
    Even though *the* needy one speaks what is
      right.
8 But the noble person devises noble plans;
    And by noble plans he stands.
9¶ Rise up, you women who are at ease,
    And hear my voice;
    Listen to my word,

30:33 [1] I.e., the place of human sacrifice to Molech

You complacent daughters.
10 Within a year and *a few* days
You will be troubled, you complacent
daughters;
For the vintage is ended,
And the *fruit* gathering will not come.
11 Tremble, you *women* who are at ease;
Be troubled, you complacent *daughters;*
Strip, undress, and put *sackcloth* on *your*
waist,
12 Beat your breasts for the pleasant fields,
for the fruitful vine,
13 For the land of my people *in which* thorns
and briars will come up;
Indeed, for all the joyful houses *and for*
the jubilant city.
14 For the palace has been neglected, the
populated city abandoned.
Hill and watch-tower have become caves
forever,
A delight for wild donkeys, a pasture for
flocks,
15 Until the Spirit is poured out upon us
from on high,
And the wilderness becomes a fertile
field,
And the fertile field is considered as a
forest.
16 Then justice will dwell in the wilderness,
And righteousness will remain in the
fertile field.
17 And the work of righteousness will be
peace,
And the service of righteousness,
quietness and confidence forever.
18 Then my people will live in a peaceful
settlement,
In secure dwellings, and in undisturbed
resting places;
19 And it will hail when the forest comes
down,
And the city will be utterly laid low.
20 How blessed will you be, you who sow
beside all waters,
Who let the ox and the donkey out freely.

The Judgment of God

33 Woe to you, destroyer,
While you were not destroyed;
And he who is treacherous, while *others*
did not deal treacherously with him.
As soon as you finish destroying, you will
be destroyed;
As soon as you cease to deal
treacherously, *others* will deal
treacherously with you.
2 LORD, be gracious to us; we have waited
for You.
Be their strength every morning,
Our salvation also in the time of
distress.
3 At the sound of a roar, peoples flee;
At the lifting up of Yourself, nations
disperse.
4 Your plunder is gathered *as* the caterpillar
gathers;
Like an infestation of locusts, people
storm it.
5 The LORD is exalted, for He dwells on
high;

He has filled Zion with justice and
righteousness.
6 And He will be the stability of your times,
A wealth of salvation, wisdom, and
knowledge;
The fear of the LORD is his treasure.
7 Behold, their brave men cry out in the
streets,
The ambassadors of peace weep bitterly.
8 The highways are desolate, the traveler
has ceased,
He has broken the covenant, he has
despised the cities,
He has no regard for mankind.
9 The land mourns *and* wastes away,
Lebanon is shamed *and* withers;
Sharon is like a desert plain,
And Bashan and Carmel lose *their foliage.*
10 "Now I will arise," says the LORD,
"Now I will be exalted, now I will be lifted
up.
11 "You have conceived chaff, you will give
birth to stubble;
My breath will consume you like a fire.
12 "The peoples will be burned to lime,
Like cut thorns which are burned in the
fire.
13¶ "You who are far away, hear what I have
done;
And you who are near, acknowledge My
might."
14 Sinners in Zion are terrified;
Trembling has seized the godless.
"Who among us can live with the
consuming fire?
Who among us can live with everlasting
burning?"
15 One who walks righteously and speaks
with integrity,
One who rejects unjust gain
And shakes his hands so that they hold
no bribe;
One who stops his ears from hearing
about bloodshed
And shuts his eyes from looking at evil;
16 He will dwell on the heights,
His refuge will be the impregnable rock;
His bread will be given *him,*
His water will be sure.
17¶ Your eyes will see the King in His beauty;
They will see a distant land.
18 Your heart will meditate on terror:
"Where is one who counts?
Where is one who weighs?
Where is one who counts the towers?"
19 You will no longer see a fierce people,
A people of unintelligible speech which
no one comprehends,
Of a stammering tongue which no one
understands.
20 Look at Zion, the city of our appointed
feasts;
Your eyes will see Jerusalem, an
undisturbed settlement,
A tent which will not be folded;
Its stakes will never be pulled up,
Nor any of its ropes be torn apart.
21 But there the majestic *One,* the LORD,
will be for us
A place of rivers *and* wide canals

On which no boat with oars will go,
And on which no mighty ship will pass—
22 For the LORD is our judge,
The LORD is our lawgiver,
The LORD is our king;
He will save us—
23 Your *ship's* tackle hangs slack;
It cannot hold the base of its mast firmly,
Nor spread out the sail.
Then the prey of an abundant spoil will be
divided;
Those who limp will take the plunder.
24 And no resident will say, "I am sick";
The people who live there will be for-
given *their* wrongdoing.

God's Wrath against Nations

34 Come near, you nations, to hear; and
listen, you peoples!
Let the earth and all it contains hear, and
the world and all that springs from it.
2 For the LORD's anger is against all the
nations,
And *His* wrath against all their armies.
He has utterly destroyed them,
He has turned them over to slaughter.
3 So their slain will be thrown out,
And their corpses will give off their
stench,
And the mountains will be drenched with
their blood.
4 And all the heavenly 'lights will wear
away,
And the sky will be rolled up like a scroll;
All its lights will also wither away
As a leaf withers from the vine,
Or as *one* withers from the fig tree.
5 For My sword has drunk its fill in heaven;
Behold it shall descend for judgment upon
Edom,
And upon the people whom I have des
ignated for destruction.
6 The sword of the LORD is filled with
blood,
It drips with fat, with the blood of lambs
and goats,
With the fat of the kidneys of rams.
For the LORD has a sacrifice in Bozrah,
And a great slaughter in the land of Edom.
7 Wild oxen will also fall with them
And young bulls with strong ones;
So their land will be soaked with blood,
And their dust become greasy with fat.
8 For the LORD has a day of vengeance,
A year of retribution for the cause of Zion.
9 Its streams will be turned into pitch,
And its loose earth into brimstone,
And its land will become burning pitch.
10 It will not be extinguished night or day;
Its smoke will go up forever.
From generation to generation it will be
desolate;
None will pass through it forever and
ever.
11 But pelican and hedgehog will possess it,
And owl and raven will dwell in it;
And He will stretch over it the line of
desolation
And the plumb line of emptiness.

12 Its nobles—there is no one there
Whom they may proclaim king—
And all its officials will be nothing.
13 Thorns will come up in its fortified
towers,
Weeds and thistles in its fortified cities;
It will also be a haunt of jackals
And a habitat of ostriches.
14 The desert creatures will meet with the
wolves,
The goat also will cry to its kind.
Yes, the night-bird will settle there
And will find herself a resting place.
15 The tree snake will make its nest and lay
eggs there,
And it will hatch and gather *them* under
its protection.
Yes, the hawks will be gathered there,
Every one with its kind.
16 Seek from the book of the LORD, and read:
Not one of these will be missing;
None will lack its mate.
For His mouth has commanded,
And His Spirit has gathered them.
17 He has cast the lot for them,
And His hand has divided it to them by
the measuring line.
They shall possess it forever;
From generation to generation they will
dwell in it.

Zion's Happy Future

35 The wilderness and the desert will
rejoice,
And the desert will shout for joy and
blossom;
Like the crocus
2 It will blossom profusely
And rejoice with joy and jubilation.
The glory of Lebanon will be given to it,
The majesty of Carmel and Sharon.
They will see the glory of the LORD,
The majesty of our God.
3 Strengthen the exhausted, and make the
feeble strong.
4 Say to those with anxious heart,
"Take courage, fear not.
Behold, your God will come *with*
vengeance;
The retribution of God will come,
But He will save you."
5 Then the eyes of those who are blind will
be opened,
And the ears of those who are deaf will be
unstopped.
6 Then those who limp will leap like a deer,
And the tongue of those who cannot
speak will shout for joy.
For waters will burst forth in the
wilderness,
And streams in the desert.
7 The scorched land will become a pool
And the thirsty ground springs of water;
In the haunt of jackals, its resting place,
Grass *becomes* reeds and rushes.
8 A highway will be there, a roadway,
And it will be called the Highway of
Holiness.
The unclean will not travel on it,

34:4 [1] Lit *host;* i.e., sun, stars, etc.

But it *will* be for the one who walks *that*
    way,
And fools will not wander *on it*.
9 No lion will be there,
    Nor will any vicious animal go up on it;
    They will not be found there.
    But the redeemed will walk *there,*
10 And the redeemed of the LORD will return
    And come to Zion with joyful shouting,
    And everlasting joy will be on their heads.
    They will obtain gladness and joy,
    And sorrow and sighing will flee away.

Sennacherib Invades Judah

36 Now in the fourteenth year of King Hezekiah, Sennacherib king of Assyria marched against all the fortified cities of Judah and seized them. 2 And the king of Assyria sent Rabshakeh from Lachish to Jerusalem to King Hezekiah with a large army. And he stood by the conduit of the upper pool on the road to the ¹fuller's field. 3 Then Eliakim the son of Hilkiah, who was over the household, and Shebna the scribe, and Joah the son of Asaph, the secretary, went out to him.

4 And Rabshakeh said to them, "Say now to Hezekiah, 'This is what the great king, the king of Assyria says: "What is this confidence that you have? 5 I say, 'Your plan and strength for the war are only empty words.' Now on whom have you relied, that you have revolted against me? 6 Behold, you have relied on the staff of this broken reed, on Egypt, on which if a man leans, it will go into his hand and pierce it. So is Pharaoh king of Egypt to all who rely on him. 7 But if you say to me, 'We trust in the LORD our God,' is it not He whose high places and whose altars Hezekiah has taken away and has said to Judah and to Jerusalem, 'You shall worship before this altar'? 8 Now then, come make a wager with my master the king of Assyria: I will give you two thousand horses, if you are able on your part to put riders on them! 9 How then can you drive back *even* one official of the least of my master's servants and rely on Egypt for chariots and horsemen? 10 And have I now come up without the LORD's approval against this land to destroy it? The LORD said to me, 'Go up against this land and destroy it.' " ' "

11 Then Eliakim, Shebna, and Joah said to Rabshakeh, "Please speak to your servants in Aramaic, for we understand *it;* and do not speak to us in ¹Judean so that the people who are on the wall hear *you.*" 12 But Rabshakeh said, "Has my master sent me *only* to your master and to you to speak these words, *and* not to the men who sit on the wall, *doomed* to eat their own dung and drink their own urine with you?"

13 Then Rabshakeh stood and called out with a loud voice in Judean and said, "Hear the words of the great king, the king of Assyria! 14 This is what the king says: 'Do not let Hezekiah deceive you, for he will not be able to save you; 15 and do not let Hezekiah lead you to rely on the LORD, saying, "The LORD will certainly save us. This city will not be handed over to the king of Assyria!" 16 Do not listen to Hezekiah,' for this is what the king of Assyria

says: 'Surrender to me and come out to me, and eat, each one, of his vine and each of his fig tree, and each drink of the waters of his own cistern, 17 until I come and take you away to a land like your own land, a land of grain and new wine, a land of bread and vineyards. 18 *Beware* that Hezekiah does not mislead you, saying, "The LORD will save us." Has any one of the gods of the nations saved his land from the hand of the king of Assyria? 19 Where are the gods of Hamath and Arpad? Where are the gods of Sepharvaim? And when have they saved Samaria from my hand? 20 Who among all the gods of these lands have saved their land from my hand, that the LORD would save Jerusalem from my hand?' "

21 But they were silent and did not answer him *so much as* a word; for the king's command was, "Do not answer him." 22 Then Eliakim the son of Hilkiah, who was over the household, and Shebna the scribe, and Joah the son of Asaph, the secretary, came to Hezekiah with their clothes torn, and reported to him the words of Rabshakeh.

Hezekiah Seeks Isaiah's Help

37 Now when King Hezekiah heard *the report,* he tore his clothes, covered himself with sackcloth, and entered the house of the LORD. 2 Then he sent Eliakim, who was in charge of the household, with Shebna the scribe and the elders of the priests, covered with sackcloth, to Isaiah the prophet, the son of Amoz. 3 And they said to him, "This is what Hezekiah says: 'This day is a day of distress, rebuke, and humiliation; for children have come to the point of birth, and there is no strength to deliver *them.* 4 Perhaps the LORD your God will hear the words of Rabshakeh, whom his master the king of Assyria has sent to taunt the living God, and will avenge the words which the LORD your God has heard. Therefore, offer a prayer for the remnant that is left.' "

5 So the servants of King Hezekiah came to Isaiah. 6 And Isaiah said to them, "This is what you shall say to your master: 'This is what the LORD says: "Do not be afraid because of the words that you have heard, with which the servants of the king of Assyria have blasphemed Me. 7 Behold, I am going to put a spirit in him so that he will hear news and return to his own land. And I will make him fall by the sword in his own land." ' "

8 Then Rabshakeh returned and found the king of Assyria fighting against Libnah, for he had heard that the king had left Lachish. 9 Now he heard *them* say regarding Tirhakah king of Cush, "He has come out to fight against you," and when he heard *it* he sent messengers to Hezekiah, saying, 10 "This is what you shall say to Hezekiah king of Judah: 'Do not let your God in whom you trust deceive you by saying, "Jerusalem will not be handed over to the king of Assyria." 11 Behold, you yourself have heard what the kings of Assyria have done to all the lands, destroying them completely. So will you be saved? 12 Did the gods of the nations which my fathers destroyed save them: Gozan, Haran,

---

36:2 ¹I.e., launderer's   **36:11** ¹I.e., Hebrew

Rezeph, and the sons of Eden who *were* in Telassar? [13] Where is the king of Hamath, the king of Arpad, the king of the city of Sepharvaim, *and of* Hena and Ivvah?' "

Hezekiah's Prayer in the Temple

[14] Then Hezekiah took the letter from the hand of the messengers and read it, and he went up to the house of the LORD and spread it out before the LORD. [15] Hezekiah prayed to the LORD, saying, [16] "LORD of armies, God of Israel, who is enthroned *above* the cherubim, You are the God, You alone, of all the kingdoms of the earth. You made heaven and earth. [17] Incline Your ear, LORD, and hear; open Your eyes, LORD, and see; and listen to all the words of Sennacherib, who sent *them* to taunt the living God. [18] Truly, LORD, the kings of Assyria have laid waste all the countries and their lands, [19] and have thrown their gods into the fire, for they were not gods but *only* the work of human hands, wood and stone. So they have destroyed them. [20] But now LORD, our God, save us from his hand, so that all the kingdoms of the earth may know that You alone, LORD, are God."

God Answers through Isaiah

[21] Then Isaiah the son of Amoz sent *word* to Hezekiah, saying, "This is what the LORD, the God of Israel says: 'Because you have prayed to Me about Sennacherib king of Assyria, [22] this is the word that the LORD has spoken against him:

"She has shown contempt for you *and* derided you,
The virgin daughter of Zion;
The daughter of Jerusalem has shaken *her* head behind you!
[23] "Whom have you taunted and blasphemed? And against whom have you raised *your* voice
And haughtily raised your eyes?
Against the Holy One of Israel!
[24] "Through your servants you have taunted the Lord,
And you have said, 'With my many chariots I came up to the heights of the mountains,
To the remotest parts of Lebanon;
And I cut down its tall cedars *and* its choice junipers.
And I will come to its highest peak, its thickest forest.
[25] 'I dug *wells* and drank waters,
And with the sole of my feet I dried up All the canals of Egypt.'
[26] "Have you not heard?
Long ago I did it,
From ancient times I planned it.
Now I have brought it about
That you would turn fortified cities into ruined heaps.
[27] "Therefore their inhabitants were powerless,
They were shattered and put to shame;
They were *like* the vegetation of the field and the green grass,
Like grass on the housetops that is scorched before it has grown.

[28] "But I know your sitting down,
Your going out, your coming in,
And your raging against Me.
[29] "Because of your raging against Me
And because your complacency has come up to My ears,
I will put My hook in your nose
And My bridle in your lips,
And I will turn you back by the way that you came.

[30] "Then this shall be the sign for you: you will eat this year what grows of itself, in the second year what grows from the same, and in the third year sow, harvest, plant vineyards, and eat their fruit. [31] The survivors that are left of the house of Judah will again *take* root downward and bear fruit upward. [32] For out of Jerusalem a remnant will go, and out of Mount Zion survivors. The zeal of the LORD of armies will perform this." '

[33] "Therefore, this is what the LORD says about the king of Assyria: 'He will not come to this city nor shoot an arrow there; and he will not come before it with a shield, nor heap up an assault ramp against it. [34] By the way that he came, by the same he will return, and he will not come to this city,' declares the LORD. [35] 'For I will protect this city to save it for My own sake, and for My servant David's sake.' "

Assyrians Destroyed

[36] Then the angel of the LORD went out and struck 185,000 in the camp of the Assyrians; and when *the rest* got up early in the morning, behold, all of the 185,000 were dead. [37] So Sennacherib the king of Assyria departed and returned *home* and lived in Nineveh. [38] Then it came about, as he was worshiping in the house of Nisroch his god, that his sons Adrammelech and Sharezer killed him with the sword; and they escaped to the land of Ararat. And his son Esarhaddon became king in his place.

Hezekiah Healed

38 In those days Hezekiah became mortally ill. And Isaiah the prophet, the son of Amoz, came to him and said to him, "This is what the LORD says: 'Set your house in order, for you are going to die and not live.' " [2] Then Hezekiah turned his face to the wall and prayed to the LORD, [3] and said, "Please, LORD, just remember how I have walked before You wholeheartedly and in truth, and have done what is good in Your sight." And Hezekiah wept profusely.

[4] Then the word of the LORD came to Isaiah, saying, [5] "Go and say to Hezekiah, 'This is what the LORD, the God of your father David says: "I have heard your prayer, I have seen your tears; behold, I will add fifteen years to your life. [6] And I will save you and this city from the hand of the king of Assyria; and I will protect this city." '

[7] "And this shall be the sign to you from the LORD, that the LORD will perform this word that He has spoken: [8] Behold, I will make the shadow on the stairway, which has gone down with the sun on the stairway of Ahaz, go back ten steps." So the sun's *shadow* went back ten

steps on the stairway on which it had gone down.

9 *This is* a writing of Hezekiah king of Judah after his illness and recovery:

10 I said, "In the middle of my life
I am to enter the gates of Sheol;
I have been deprived of the rest of my years."

11 I said, "I will not see the Lord,
The Lord in the land of the living;
I will no longer look on mankind among the inhabitants of the world.

12 "Like a shepherd's tent my dwelling is pulled up and removed from me;
As a weaver I rolled up my life.
He cuts me off from the loom;
From day until night You make an end of me.

13 "I composed *my soul* until morning.
Like a lion—so He breaks all my bones,
From day until night You make an end of me.

14 "Like a swallow, *like* a crane, so I twitter;
I moan like a dove;
My eyes look wistfully to the heights;
Lord, I am oppressed, be my security.

15¶ "What shall I say?
For He has spoken to me, and He Himself has done it;
I will walk quietly all my years because of the bitterness of my soul.

16 "Lord, by *these* things *people* live,
And in all these is the life of my spirit;
Restore me to health and let me live!

17 "Behold, for *my own* welfare I had great bitterness;
But You have kept my soul from the pit of nothingness,
For You have hurled all my sins behind Your back.

18 "For Sheol cannot thank You,
Death cannot praise You;
Those who go down to the pit cannot hope for Your faithfulness.

19 "It is the living who give thanks to You, as I do today;
A father tells his sons about Your faithfulness.

20 "The Lord is *certain* to save me;
So we will play my songs on stringed instruments
All *the* days of our life at the house of the Lord."

21 Now Isaiah had said, "Have them take a cake of figs and apply it to the boil, so that he may recover." 22 Then Hezekiah had said, "What is the sign that I will go up to the house of the Lord?"

Hezekiah Shows His Treasures

39 At that time Merodach-baladan son of Baladan, king of Babylon, sent letters and a gift to Hezekiah, for he heard that he had been sick and had recovered. 2 Hezekiah was pleased, and let them see *all* his treasure house, the silver, the gold, the balsam oil, the excellent olive oil, his entire armory, and everything that was found in his treasuries. There was nothing in his house nor in all his realm that Hezekiah did not let them see.

3 Then Isaiah the prophet came to King Hezekiah and said to him, "What did these men say, and from where did they come to you?" And Hezekiah said, "They came to me from a far country, from Babylon." 4 Then he said, "What have they seen in your house?" So Hezekiah answered, "They have seen everything that is in my house; there is nothing among my treasuries that I have not let them see."

5 Isaiah then said to Hezekiah, "Hear the word of the Lord of armies, 6 'Behold, the days are coming when everything that is in your house, and what your fathers have stored up to this day, will be carried to Babylon; nothing will be left,' says the Lord. 7 'And some of your sons who will come from you, whom you will father, will be taken away, and they will become eunuchs in the palace of the king of Babylon.'" 8 Then Hezekiah said to Isaiah, "The word of the Lord which you have spoken is good." For he thought, "For there will be peace and truth in my days."

The Greatness of God

40 "Comfort, comfort My people," says your God.

2 "Speak kindly to Jerusalem;
And call out to her, that her warfare has ended,
That her guilt has been removed,
That she has received of the Lord's hand Double for all her sins."

3¶ The voice of one calling out,
"Clear the way for the Lord in the wilderness;
Make straight in the desert a highway for our God.

4 "Let every valley be lifted up,
And every mountain and hill be made low;
And let the uneven ground become a plain,
And the rugged terrain a broad valley;

5 Then the glory of the Lord will be revealed,
And all flesh will see *it* together;
For the mouth of the Lord has spoken."

6 A voice says, "Call out."
Then he answered, "What shall I call out?"
All flesh is grass, and all its loveliness is like the flower of the field.

7 The grass withers, the flower fades,
When the breath of the Lord blows upon it;
The people are indeed grass!

8 The grass withers, the flower fades,
But the word of our God stands forever.

9¶ Go up on a high mountain,
Zion, messenger of good news,
Raise your voice forcefully,
Jerusalem, messenger of good news;
Raise *it* up, do not fear.
Say to the cities of Judah,
"Here is your God!"

10 Behold, the Lord God will come with might,
With His arm ruling for Him.
Behold, His compensation is with Him,

And His reward before Him.

11 Like a shepherd He will tend His flock,
In His arm He will gather the lambs
And carry *them* in the fold of His robe;
He will gently lead the nursing *ewes.*

12¶ Who has measured the waters in the
hollow of His hand,
And measured the heavens with a span,
And calculated the dust of the earth with
a measure,
And weighed the mountains in a balance
And the hills in a pair of scales?

13 Who has directed the Spirit of the LORD,
Or as His counselor has informed Him?

14 With whom did He consult and *who* gave
Him understanding?
And *who* taught Him in the path of justice
and taught Him knowledge,
And informed Him of the way of
understanding?

15 Behold, the nations are like a drop from
a bucket,
And are regarded as a speck of dust on
the scales;
Behold, He lifts up the islands like fine
dust.

16 Even Lebanon is not enough to burn,
Nor its animals enough for a burnt
offering.

17 All the nations are as nothing before
Him,
They are regarded by Him as less than
nothing and meaningless.

18¶ To whom then will you liken God?
Or what likeness will you compare with
Him?

19 *As for* the idol, a craftsman casts it,
A goldsmith plates it with gold,
And a silversmith *fashions* chains of
silver.

20 He who is too impoverished for *such* an
offering
Selects a tree that does not rot;
He seeks out for himself a skillful
craftsman
To prepare an idol that will not totter.

21¶ Do you not know? Have you not heard?
Has it not been declared to you from the
beginning?
Have you not understood from the
foundations of the earth?

22 It is He who sits above the circle of the
earth,
And its inhabitants are like grasshoppers,
Who stretches out the heavens like a
curtain
And spreads them out like a tent to live
in.

23 *It is* He who reduces rulers to nothing,
Who makes the judges of the earth
meaningless.

24 Scarcely have they been planted,
Scarcely have they been sown,
Scarcely has their stock taken root in the
earth,
But He merely blows on them, and they
wither,
And the storm carries them away like
stubble.

25 "To whom then will you compare Me
That I would be *his* equal?" says the Holy
One.

26 Raise your eyes on high
And see who has created these *stars,*
The One who brings out their multitude
by number,
He calls them all by name;
Because of the greatness of His might and
the strength of *His* power,
Not one *of them* is missing.

27¶ Why do you say, Jacob, and you assert,
Israel,
"My way is hidden from the LORD,
And the justice due me escapes the notice
of my God"?

28 Do you not know? Have you not heard?
The Everlasting God, the LORD, the
Creator of the ends of the earth
Does not become weary or tired.
His understanding is unsearchable.

29 He gives strength to the weary,
And to *the one who* lacks might He
increases power.

30 Though youths grow weary and tired,
And vigorous young men stumble badly,

31 Yet those who wait for the LORD
Will gain new strength;
They will mount up *with* wings like
eagles,
They will run and not get tired,
They will walk and not become weary.

Israel Encouraged

41 "Listen to Me in silence, you coastlands,
And let the peoples gain new strength;
Let them come forward, then let them
speak;
Let's come together for judgment.

2 "Who has stirred one from the east
Whom He calls in righteousness to His
feet?
He turns nations over to him
And subdues kings.
He makes them like dust with his sword,
Like the wind-driven chaff with his bow.

3 "He pursues them, passing on in safety,
By a way he had not been traversing with
his feet.

4 "Who has performed and accomplished *it,*
Summoning the generations from the
beginning?
'I, the LORD, am the first, and with the last.
I am He.'"

5¶ The coastlands have seen and are afraid;
The ends of the earth tremble;
They have approached and have come.

6 Each one helps his neighbor
And says to his brother, "Be strong!"

7 So the craftsman encourages the smelter,
And he who smooths *metal* with the
hammer *encourages* him who beats
the anvil,
Saying of the soldering, "It is good";
And he fastens it with nails,
So that it will not totter.

8 "But you, Israel, My servant,
Jacob whom I have chosen,
Descendant of Abraham My friend,

9 You whom I have taken from the ends of
the earth

And called from its remotest parts,
And said to you, 'You are My servant,
I have chosen you and have not rejected
you.
10 'Do not fear, for I am with you;
Do not be afraid, for I am your God.
I will strengthen you, I will also help you,
I will also uphold you with My righteous
right hand.'
11 "Behold, all those who are angered at you
will be shamed and dishonored;
Those who contend with you will be as
nothing and will perish.
12 "You will seek those who quarrel with you,
but will not find them,
Those who war with you will be as
nothing and non-existent.
13 "For I am the LORD your God who takes
hold of your right hand,
Who says to you, 'Do not fear, I will help
you.'
14 "Do not fear, you worm Jacob, you people
of Israel;
I will help you," declares the LORD, "and
your Redeemer is the Holy One of
Israel.
15 "Behold, I turned you into a new, sharp
threshing sledge with double edges;
You will thresh the mountains and
pulverize *them,*
And make the hills like chaff.
16 "You will winnow them, and the wind will
carry them away,
And the storm will scatter them;
But you will rejoice in the LORD,
You will boast in the Holy One of Israel.
17¶ "The poor and needy are seeking water, but
there is none,
And their tongues are parched with thirst.
I, the LORD, will answer them Myself;
As the God of Israel I will not abandon
them.
18 "I will open rivers on the bare heights,
And springs in the midst of the valleys;
I will make the wilderness a pool of
water,
And the dry land fountains of water.
19 "I will put the cedar in the wilderness,
The acacia, the myrtle, and the olive tree;
I will place the juniper in the desert,
Together with the elm tree and the
cypress,
20 So that they may see and recognize,
And consider and gain insight as well,
That the hand of the LORD has done this,
And the Holy One of Israel has created it.
21¶ "Present your case," the LORD says.
"Bring forward your evidence,"
The King of Jacob says.
22 Let them bring *them* forward and declare
to us what is going to take place;
As for the former *events,* declare what
they *were,*
So that we may consider them and know
their outcome.
Or announce to us what is coming;
23 Declare the things that are going to come
afterward,
So that we may know that you are gods;

Indeed, do good or evil, that we may be
afraid and fear together.
24 Behold, you are less than nothing,
And your work is less than nothing!
He who chooses you is an abomination.
25¶ "I have put one from the north into
motion, and he has come;
From the rising of the sun he will call on
My name;
And he will come upon rulers as *upon*
mortar,
As the potter treads on clay."
26 Who has declared *this* from the begin-
ning, that we might know?
Or from former times, that we may say,
"*He is* right!"?
There was no one at all who declared,
There was no one at all who proclaimed,
There was no one at all who heard your
words.
27 "Previously *I said* to Zion, 'Behold, here
they are.'
And to Jerusalem, 'I will give a messenger
of good news.'
28 "But when I look, there is no one,
And there is no counselor among them
Who, if I ask, can give an answer.
29 "Behold, all of them are 'false;
Their works are nothing,
Their cast metal images are wind and
emptiness.

God's Promise concerning His Servant

42 "Behold, My Servant, whom I
uphold;
My chosen one *in whom* My soul delights.
I have put My Spirit upon Him;
He will bring forth justice to the nations.
2 "He will not cry out nor raise *His voice,*
Nor make His voice heard in the street.
3 "A bent reed He will not break *off*
And a dimly burning wick He will not
extinguish;
He will faithfully bring forth justice.
4 "He will not be disheartened or crushed
Until He has established justice on the
earth;
And the coastlands will wait expectantly
for His law."
5 This is what God the LORD says,
Who created the heavens and stretched
them out,
Who spread out the earth and its
offspring,
Who gives breath to the people on it
And spirit to those who walk in it:
6 "I am the LORD, I have called You in
righteousness,
I will also hold You by the hand and watch
over You,
And I will appoint You as a covenant to
the people,
As a light to the nations,
7 To open blind eyes,
To bring out prisoners from the dungeon
And those who dwell in darkness from
the prison.
8 "I am the LORD, that is My name;
I will not give My glory to another,

Nor My praise to idols.

9 "Behold, the former things have come to
pass,
Now I declare new things;
Before they sprout I proclaim *them* to
you."

10¶ Sing to the LORD a new song,
Sing His praise from the end of the earth!
You who go down to the sea, and all that
is in it;
You islands, and those who live on them.

11 Let the wilderness and its cities raise *their*
voices,
The settlements which Kedar inhabits.
Let the inhabitants of Sela sing aloud,
Let them shout for joy from the tops of
the mountains.

12 Let them give glory to the LORD
And declare His praise in the coastlands.

13 The LORD will go out like a warrior,
He will stir *His* zeal like a man of war.
He will shout, indeed, He will raise a war
cry.
He will prevail against His enemies.

The Blindness of the People

14¶ "I have kept silent for a long time,
I have kept still and restrained Myself.
Now like a woman in labor I will groan,
I will both gasp and pant.

15 "I will lay waste the mountains and hills
And wither all their vegetation;
I will turn the rivers into coastlands
And dry up the ponds.

16 "I will lead those who are blind by a way
they have not known,
In paths they have not known I will guide
them.
I will turn darkness into light before them
And uneven land into plains.
These are the things I will do,
And I will not leave them undone."

17 They will be turned back *and* be utterly
put to shame,
Who trust in idols,
Who say to cast metal images,
"You are our gods."

18¶ Hear, you who are deaf!
And look, you who are blind, so that you
may see.

19 Who is blind but My servant,
Or so deaf as My messenger whom I
send?
Who is so blind as one who is at peace
with Me,
Or so blind as the servant of the LORD?

20 You have seen many things, but you do
not retain *them;*
Your ears are open, but no one hears.

21 The LORD was pleased for His righteousness' sake
To make the Law great and glorious.

22 But this is a people plundered and
pillaged;
All of them are trapped in caves,
Or are hidden away in prisons;
They have become plunder, with no one
to save *them,*
And spoils with no one to say, "Give *them*
back!"

23¶ Who among you will listen to this?
Who will pay attention and listen in the
time to come?

24 Who gave Jacob up for spoils, and Israel to
plunderers?
Was it not the LORD, against whom we
have sinned,
And in whose ways they were not willing
to walk,
And whose Law they did not obey?

25 So He poured out on him the heat of His
anger
And the fierceness of battle;
And it set him aflame all around,
Yet he did not recognize *it;*
And it burned him, but he paid no
attention.

Israel Redeemed

43 But now, this is what the LORD says, *He
who is* your Creator, Jacob,
And He who formed you, Israel:
"Do not fear, for I have redeemed you;
I have called you by name; you are Mine!

2 "When you pass through the waters, I will
be with you;
And through the rivers, they will not
overflow you.
When you walk through the fire, you will
not be scorched,
Nor will the flame burn you.

3 "For I am the LORD your God,
The Holy One of Israel, your Savior;
I have given Egypt as your ransom,
Cush and Seba in exchange for you.

4 "Since you are precious in My sight,
Since you are honored and I love you,
I will give *other* people in your place and
other nations in exchange for your life.

5 "Do not fear, for I am with you;
I will bring your offspring from the east,
And gather you from the west.

6 "I will say to the north, 'Give *them* up!'
And to the south, 'Do not hold *them*
back.'
Bring My sons from afar
And My daughters from the ends of the
earth,

7 Everyone who is called by My name,
And whom I have created for My glory,
Whom I have formed, even whom I have
made."

Israel Is God's Witness

8¶ Bring out the people who are blind, even
though they have eyes,
And those who are deaf, even though they
have ears.

9 All the nations have gathered together
So that the peoples may be assembled.
Who among them can declare this
And proclaim to us the former things?
Let them present their witnesses so that
they may be justified,
Or let them hear and say, "It is true."

10 "You are My witnesses," declares the LORD,
"And My servant whom I have chosen,
So that you may know and believe Me
And understand that I am He.
Before Me there was no God formed,

And there will be none after Me.

11 "I, *only* I, am the LORD,
And there is no savior besides Me.

12 "It is I who have declared and saved and
proclaimed,
And there was no strange *god* among you;
So you are My witnesses," declares the
LORD,
"And I am God.

13 "Even from eternity I am He,
And there is no one who can rescue from
My hand;
I act, and who can reverse it?"

Babylon to Be Destroyed

14 This is what the LORD your Redeemer, the
Holy One of Israel says:
"For your sake I have sent to Babylon,
And will bring them all down as fugitives,
Even the Chaldeans, into the ships over
which they rejoice.

15 "I am the LORD, your Holy One,
The Creator of Israel, your King."

16 This is what the LORD says,
He who makes a way through the sea
And a path through the mighty waters,

17 Who brings out the chariot and the horse,
The army and the mighty man
(They will lie down together *and* not rise
again;
They have been extinguished, *and* have
gone out like a wick):

18 "Do not call to mind the former things,
Or consider things of the past.

19 "Behold, I am going to do something new,
Now it will spring up;
Will you not be aware of it?
I will even make a roadway in the
wilderness,
Rivers in the desert.

20 "The animals of the field will glorify Me,
The jackals and the ostriches,
Because I have given waters in the
wilderness
And rivers in the desert,
To give drink to My chosen people.

21 "The people whom I formed for Myself
Will declare My praise.

The Shortcomings of Israel

22 ¶ "Yet you have not called on Me, Jacob;
But you have become weary of Me, Israel.

23 "You have not brought to Me the sheep of
your burnt offerings,
Nor have you honored Me with your sac-
rifices.
I have not burdened you with offerings,
Nor wearied you with incense.

24 "You have not bought Me sweet cane with
money,
Nor have you satisfied Me with the fat of
your sacrifices;
Rather, you have burdened Me with your
sins,
You have wearied Me with your
wrongdoings.

25 ¶ "I, I *alone*, am the one who wipes out your
wrongdoings for My own sake,
And I will not remember your sins.

26 "Meet Me in court, let's argue our case
together;
State your *cause*, so that you may be
proved right.

27 "Your first forefather sinned,
And your spokesmen have rebelled
against Me.

28 "So I will profane the officials of the
sanctuary,
And I will turn Jacob over to destruction
and Israel to abuse.

The Blessings of Israel

44 "But now listen, Jacob, My servant,
And Israel, whom I have chosen:

2 This is what the LORD says, *He* who made
you
And formed you from the womb, who will
help you:
'Do not fear, Jacob My servant,
And 'Jeshurun, whom I have chosen.

3 'For I will pour water on the thirsty *land*
And streams on the dry ground;
I will pour out My Spirit on your
offspring,
And My blessing on your descendants;

4 And they will spring up among the grass
Like poplars by streams of water.'

5 "This one will say, 'I am the LORD's';
And that one will call on the name of
Jacob;
And another will write *on* his hand,
'Belonging to the LORD,'
And will give himself Israel's name with
honor.

6 "This is what the LORD says, *He who is* the
King of Israel and his Redeemer, the LORD of
armies:
'I am the first and I am the last,
And there is no God besides Me.

7 'Who is like Me? Let him proclaim and
declare it;
And, let him confront Me
Beginning with My establishing of the
ancient nation.
Then let them declare to them the things
that are coming
And *the events* that are going to take
place.

8 'Do not tremble and do not be afraid;
Have I not long since announced *it* to you
and declared *it?*
And you are My witnesses.
Is there any God besides Me,
Or is there any *other* Rock?
I know of none.'"

The Foolishness of Idolatry

9 Those who fashion an idol are all futile,
and their treasured things are of no benefit;
even their own witnesses fail to see or know,
so that they will be put to shame. 10 Who has
fashioned a god or cast an idol to no benefit?
11 Behold, all his companions will be put to
shame, for the craftsmen themselves are mere
men. Let them all assemble themselves, let
them stand up, let them tremble, let them be
put to shame together. 12 The craftsman of iron *shapes* a cutting

---

44:2 1 I.e., Israel

tool and does his work over the coals, fashioning it with hammers and working it with his strong arm. He also gets hungry and his strength fails; he drinks no water and becomes weary. **13** The craftsman of wood extends a measuring line; he outlines it with a marker. He works it with carving knives and outlines it with a compass, and makes it like the form of a man, like the beauty of mankind, so that it may sit in a house. **14** He will cut cedars for himself, and he takes a holm-oak or *another* oak and lets *it* grow strong for himself among the trees of the forest. He plants a laurel tree, and the rain makes it grow. **15** Then it becomes *something* for a person to burn, so he takes one of them and gets warm; he also makes a fire and bakes bread. He also makes a god and worships it; he makes it a carved image and bows down before it. **16** Half of it he burns in the fire; over *this* half he eats meat, he roasts a roast, and is satisfied. He also warms himself and says, "Aha! I am warm, I have seen the fire." **17** Yet the rest of it he makes into a god, his carved image. He bows down before it and worships; he also prays to it and says, "Save me, for you are my god."

18 They do not know, nor do they understand, for He has smeared over their eyes so that they cannot see, and their hearts so that they cannot comprehend. **19** No one remembers, nor is there knowledge or understanding to say, "I have burned half of it in the fire and also have baked bread over its coals. I roast meat and eat *it.* Then I make the rest of it into an abomination, I bow down before a block of wood!" **20** He feeds on ashes; a deceived heart has misled him. And he cannot save himself, nor say, "Is there not a lie in my right hand?"

God Forgives and Redeems

21 ¶ "Remember these things, Jacob,
And Israel, for you are My servant;
I have formed you, you are My servant,
Israel, you will not be forgotten by Me.
22 "I have wiped out your wrongdoings like a thick cloud
And your sins like a heavy mist.
Return to Me, for I have redeemed you."
23 Shout for joy, you heavens, for the LORD has done *it!*
Shout joyfully, you lower parts of the earth;
Break into a shout of jubilation, you mountains,
Forest, and every tree in it;
For the LORD has redeemed Jacob,
And in Israel He shows His glory.
24 This is what the LORD says, *He who is* your Redeemer, and the one who formed you from the womb:
"I, the LORD, am the maker of all things,
Stretching out the heavens by Myself
And spreading out the earth alone,
25 Causing the omens of diviners to fail,
Making fools of fortune-tellers;
Causing wise men to turn back
And making their knowledge ridiculous,
26 Confirming the word of His servant

And carrying out the purpose of His messengers.
It is I who says of Jerusalem, 'She shall be inhabited!'
And of the cities of Judah, 'They shall be built.'
And I will raise her ruins *again.*
27 "*I am* the One who says to the depth of the sea, 'Dry up!'
And I will make your rivers dry up.
28 "*It is I* who says of Cyrus, '*He is* My shepherd,
And he will carry out all My desire.'
And he says of Jerusalem, 'She will be built,'
And of the temple, 'Your foundation will be laid.'"

God Uses Cyrus

45 This is what the LORD says to Cyrus His anointed,
Whom I have taken by the right hand,
To subdue nations before him
And to undo *the weapons belt on* the waist of kings;
To open doors before him so that gates will not be shut:
2 "I will go before you and make the rough places smooth;
I will shatter the doors of bronze and cut through their iron bars.
3 "I will give you the treasures of darkness
And hidden wealth of secret places,
So that you may know that it is I,
The LORD, the God of Israel, who calls you by your name.
4 "For the sake of Jacob My servant,
And Israel My chosen *one,*
I have also called you by your name;
I have given you a title of honor
Though you have not known Me.
5 "I am the LORD, and there is no one else;
There is no God except Me.
I will ¹arm you, though you have not known Me,
6 So that *people* may know from the rising to the setting of the sun
That there is no one besides Me.
I am the LORD, and there is no one else,
7 The One forming light and creating darkness,
Causing well-being and creating disaster;
I am the LORD who does all these things.

God's Supreme Power

8 ¶ "Drip down, heavens, from above,
And let the clouds pour down righteousness;
Let the earth open up and salvation bear fruit,
And righteousness sprout with it.
I, the LORD, have created it.
9 ¶ "Woe to *the one* who quarrels with his Maker—
A piece of pottery among the *other* earthenware pottery pieces!
Will the clay say to the potter, 'What are you doing?'

45:5 ¹Or *embrace*

Or the thing you are making *say,* 'He has
no hands'?
10 "Woe to him who says to a father, 'What
are you fathering?'
Or to a woman, 'To what are you giving
birth?' "
11 This is what the LORD says, the Holy One
of Israel and his Maker:
"Ask Me about the things to come
concerning My sons,
And you shall commit to Me the work of
My hands.
12 "It is I who made the earth, and created
mankind upon it.
I stretched out the heavens with My
hands,
And I ordained all their ¹lights.
13 "I have stirred him in righteousness,
And I will make all his ways smooth.
He will build My city and let My exiles
go free,
Without any payment or reward," says
the LORD of armies.
14 This is what the LORD says:
"The products of Egypt and the
merchandise of Cush
And the Sabeans, men of stature,
Will come over to you and will be yours;
They will walk behind you, they will
come over in chains
And will bow down to you;
They will plead with you:
'God certainly is with you, and there is no
one else,
No other God.' "
15 Truly, You are a God who hides Himself,
God of Israel, Savior!
16 They will be put to shame and even
humiliated, all of them;
The manufacturers of idols will go away
together in humiliation.
17 Israel has been saved by the LORD
With an everlasting salvation;
You will not be put to shame or
humiliated
To all eternity.
18 For this is what the LORD says, *He* who
created the heavens (He is the God who
formed the earth and made it, He established it
and did not create it as a waste place, *but*
formed it to be inhabited):
"I am the LORD, and there is no one else.
19 "I have not spoken in secret,
In some dark land;
I did not say to the offspring of Jacob,
'Seek Me in a wasteland';
I, the LORD, speak righteousness,
Declaring things that are right.
20¶ "Gather yourselves and come;
Come together, you survivors of the
nations!
They have no knowledge,
Who carry around their wooden idol
And pray to a god who cannot save.
21 "Declare and present *your case;*
Indeed, let them consult together.
Who has announced this long ago?
Who has long since declared it?
Is it not I, the LORD?

And there is no other God besides Me,
A righteous God and a Savior;
There is none except Me.
22 "Turn to Me and be saved, all the ends of
the earth;
For I am God, and there is no other.
23 "I have sworn by Myself;
The word has gone out from My mouth in
righteousness
And will not turn back,
That to Me every knee will bow, every
tongue will swear *allegiance.*
24 "They will say of Me, 'Only in the LORD are
righteousness and strength.'
People will come to Him,
And all who were angry at Him will be
put to shame.
25 "In the LORD all the offspring of Israel
Will be justified and will boast."

Babylon's Idols and the True God

46 Bel has bowed down, Nebo stoops
over;
Their idols have become *loads* for the
animals and the cattle.
The things that you carry are
burdensome,
A load for the weary *animal.*
2 They stooped over, they have bowed
down together;
They could not rescue the burden,
But have themselves gone into captivity.
3¶ "Listen to Me, house of Jacob,
And all the remnant of the house of
Israel,
You who have been carried *by Me* from
birth
And have been carried from the womb;
4 Even to *your* old age I will be the same,
And even to *your* graying years I will carry
you!
I have done *it,* and I will bear *you;*
And I will carry *you* and I will save *you.*
5¶ "To whom would you liken Me
And make Me equal, and compare Me,
That we would be alike?
6 "Those who lavish gold from the bag
And weigh silver on the scale,
Hire a goldsmith, and he makes it *into* a
god;
They bow down, indeed they worship it.
7 "They lift it on the shoulder, carry it,
And set it in its place, and it stands *there.*
It does not move from its place.
Though one may shout to it, it cannot
answer;
It cannot save him from his distress.
8¶ "Remember this, and be assured;
Recall it to mind, you wrongdoers.
9 "Remember the former things long past,
For I am God, and there is no other;
I am God, and there is no one like Me,
10 Declaring the end from the beginning,
And from ancient times things which
have not been done,
Saying, 'My plan will be established,
And I will accomplish all My good
pleasure';
11 Calling a bird of prey from the east,

The man of My purpose from a distant
country.
Truly I have spoken; truly I will bring it to
pass.
I have planned *it,* I will certainly do it.
12¶ "Listen to Me, you stubborn-minded,
Who are far from righteousness.
13 "I bring near My righteousness, it is not far
off;
And My salvation will not delay.
And I will grant salvation in Zion,
And My glory for Israel.

Mourning for Babylon

47 "Come down and sit in the dust,
Virgin daughter of Babylon;
Sit on the ground without a throne,
Daughter of the Chaldeans!
For you will no longer be called tender
and delicate.
2   "Take the millstones and grind flour.
Remove your veil, strip off the skirt,
Uncover the leg, cross the rivers.
3   "Your nakedness will be uncovered,
Your shame will also be exposed;
I will take vengeance and will not spare
anyone."
4   Our Redeemer, the Lord of armies is His
name,
The Holy One of Israel.
5   "Sit silently, and go into darkness,
Daughter of the Chaldeans;
For you will no longer be called
The queen of kingdoms.
6   "I was angry with My people,
I profaned My heritage
And handed them over to you.
You did not show mercy to them,
On the aged you made your yoke very
heavy.
7   "Yet you said, 'I will be a queen forever.'
These things you did not consider
Nor remember the outcome of them.
8¶ "Now, then, hear this, you luxuriant one,
Who lives securely,
Who says in her heart,
'I am, and there is no one besides me.
I will not sit as a widow,
Nor know the loss of children.'
9   "But these two things will come on you
suddenly in one day:
Loss of children and widowhood.
They will come on you in full measure
In spite of your many sorceries,
In spite of the great power of your spells.
10 "You felt secure in your wickedness and
said,
'No one sees me,'
Your wisdom and your knowledge, they
have led you astray;
For you have said in your heart,
'I am, and there is no one besides me.'
11 "But evil will come on you
Which you will not know how to charm
away;
And disaster will fall on you
For which you cannot atone;
And destruction about which you do not
know
Will come on you suddenly.

12¶ "Persist now in your spells
And in your many sorceries
With which you have labored from your
youth;
Perhaps you will be able to benefit,
Perhaps you may cause trembling.
13 "You are wearied with your many counsels;
Let now the astrologers,
Those who prophesy by the stars,
Those who predict by the new moons,
Stand up and save you from what will
come upon you.
14 "Behold, they have become like stubble,
Fire burns them;
They cannot save themselves from the
power of the flame;
There will be no coal to warm by
Nor a fire to sit before!
15 "So have those become to you with whom
you have labored,
Those who have done business with you
from your youth;
Each has wandered in his own way;
There is no one to save you.

Israel's Obstinacy

48 "Hear this, house of Jacob, who are
named Israel
And who came from the waters of Judah,
Who swear by the name of the Lord
And invoke the God of Israel,
But not in truth nor in righteousness.
2   "For they name themselves after the holy
city,
And lean on the God of Israel;
The Lord of armies is His name.
3   "I declared the former things long ago,
And they went out of My mouth, and I
proclaimed them.
Suddenly I acted, and they came to pass.
4   "Because I know that you are obstinate,
And your neck is an iron tendon
And your forehead bronze,
5   Therefore I declared *them* to you long ago,
Before they took place I proclaimed *them*
to you,
So that you would not say, 'My idol has
done them,
And my carved image and my cast metal
image have commanded them.'
6   "You have heard; look at all this.
And you, will you not declare it?
I proclaim to you new things from this
time,
Hidden things which you have not
known.
7   "They are created now and not long ago;
And before today you have not heard
them,
So that you will not say, 'Behold, I knew
them.'
8   "You have not heard, you have not known.
Even from long ago your ear has not been
open,
Because I knew that you would deal very
treacherously;
And you have been called a rebel from
birth.
9   "For the sake of My name I delay My
wrath,

And *for* My praise I restrain *it* for you,
In order not to cut you off.
10 "Behold, I have refined you, but not as
silver;
I have tested you in the furnace of
affliction.
11 "For My own sake, for My own sake, I will
act;
For how can *My name* be profaned?
And I will not give My glory to another.

Rescue Promised

12¶ "Listen to Me, Jacob, Israel whom I called;
I am He, I am the first, I am also the last.
13 "Assuredly My hand founded the earth,
And My right hand spread out the
heavens;
When I call to them, they stand together.
14 "Assemble, all of you, and listen!
Who among them has declared these
things?
The LORD loves him; he will carry out His
good pleasure against Babylon,
And His arm *will be against* the
Chaldeans.
15 "I, *yes* I, have spoken; indeed I have called
him,
I have brought him, and He will make his
ways successful.
16 "Come near to Me, listen to this:
From the beginning I have not spoken in
secret,
From the time it took place, I was there.
And now the Lord GOD has sent Me, and
His Spirit."
17 This is what the LORD says, *He who is*
your Redeemer, the Holy One of Israel:
"I am the LORD your God, who teaches you
to benefit,
Who leads you in the way you should go.
18 "If only you had paid attention to My
commandments!
Then your well-being would have been
like a river,
And your righteousness like the waves of
the sea.
19 "Your descendants would have been like
the sand,
And your offspring like its grains;
Their name would never be eliminated or
destroyed from My presence."
20¶ Go out from Babylon! Flee from the
Chaldeans!
Declare with the sound of joyful shouting,
proclaim this,
Send it out to the end of the earth;
Say, "The LORD has redeemed His servant
Jacob."
21 They did not thirst when He led them
through the deserts.
He made the water flow out of the rock
for them;
He split the rock and the water gushed
out.
22 "There is no peace for the wicked," says
the LORD.

Salvation Reaches to the Ends of the Earth

49 Listen to Me, you islands,
And pay attention, you peoples from afar.

The LORD called Me from the womb;
From the body of My mother He named
Me.
2 He has made My mouth like a sharp
sword,
In the shadow of His hand He has
concealed Me;
And He has also made Me a sharpened
arrow,
He has hidden Me in His quiver.
3 He said to Me, "You are My Servant,
Israel,
In whom I will show My glory."
4 But I said, "I have labored in vain,
I have spent My strength for nothing and
futility;
Nevertheless, the justice *due* to Me is
with the LORD,
And My reward is with My God."
5¶ And now says the LORD, who formed Me
from the womb to be His Servant,
To bring Jacob back to Him, so that Israel
might be gathered to Him
(For I am honored in the sight of the
LORD,
And My God is My strength),
6 He says, "It is too small a thing that You
should be My Servant
To raise up the tribes of Jacob and to
restore the protected ones of Israel;
I will also make You a light of the
nations
So that My salvation may reach to the end
of the earth."
7 This is what the LORD, the Redeemer of
Israel *and* its Holy One,
Says to the despised One,
To the One abhorred by the nation,
To the Servant of rulers:
"Kings will see and arise,
Princes will also bow down,
Because of the LORD who is faithful, the
Holy One of Israel who has chosen
You."
8¶ This is what the LORD says:
"At a favorable time I answered You,
And on a day of salvation I helped You;
And I will watch over You and make You a
covenant of the people,
To restore the land, to give as inheritances
the deserted hereditary lands;
9 Saying to those who are bound, 'Go free,'
To those who are in darkness, 'Show
yourselves.'
They will feed along the roads,
And their pasture *will be* on all bare
heights.
10 "They will not hunger or thirst,
Nor will the scorching heat or sun strike
them down;
For He who has compassion on them will
lead them,
And He will guide them to springs of
water.
11 "I will make all My mountains a road,
And My highways will be raised up.
12 "Behold, these will come from afar;
And behold, these *will come* from the
north and from the west,
And these from the land of Aswan."

13 Shout for joy, you heavens! And rejoice,
you earth!
Break forth into joyful shouting,
mountains!
For the LORD has comforted His people
And will have compassion on His afflicted.

Promise to Zion

14¶ But Zion said, "The LORD has abandoned
me,
And the Lord has forgotten me."
15 "Can a woman forget her nursing child
And have no compassion on the son of
her womb?
Even these may forget, but I will not
forget you.
16 "Behold, I have inscribed you on the palms
of My hands;
Your walls are continually before Me.
17 "Your builders hurry;
Your destroyers and devastators
Will leave you.
18 "Raise your eyes and look around;
All of them gather together, they come to
you.
As I live," declares the LORD,
"You will certainly put them all on as
jewelry and bind them on as a bride.
19 "For your ruins and deserted places and
your destroyed land—
Now you will certainly be too cramped for
the inhabitants,
And those who swallowed you will be far
away.
20 "The children you lost will yet say in your
ears,
'The place is too cramped for me;
Make room for me that I may live here.'
21 "Then you will say in your heart,
'Who has fathered these for me,
Since I have been bereaved of my
children
And cannot conceive, and I am an exile,
and a wanderer?
And who has raised these?
Behold, I was left alone;
Where are these from?'"
22 This is what the Lord GOD says:
"Behold, I will lift up My hand to the
nations
And set up My flag to the peoples;
And they will bring your sons in their
arms,
And your daughters will be carried on
their shoulders.
23 "Kings will be your guardians,
And their princesses your nurses.
They will bow down to you with their
faces to the ground
And lick the dust from your feet;
And you will know that I am the LORD;
Those who hopefully wait for Me will not
be put to shame.
24¶ "Can the prey be taken from a mighty
man,
Or the captives of a tyrant be rescued?"
25 Indeed, this is what the LORD says:
"Even the captives of the mighty man will
be taken away,
And the prey of a tyrant will be rescued;

For I will contend with the one who
contends with you,
And I will save your sons.
26 "I will feed your oppressors with their own
flesh,
And they will become drunk with their
own blood as with sweet wine;
And humanity will know that I, the LORD,
am your Savior
And your Redeemer, the Mighty One of
Jacob."

God Helps His Servant

50 This is what the LORD says:
"Where is the certificate of divorce
By which I have sent your mother away?
Or to whom of My creditors did I sell you?
Behold, you were sold for your
wrongdoings,
And for your wrongful acts your mother
was sent away.
2 "Why was there no one when I came?
When I called, why was there no one to
answer?
Is My hand so short that it cannot
redeem?
Or do I have no power to rescue?
Behold, I dry up the sea with My rebuke,
I turn rivers into a wilderness;
Their fish stink for lack of water,
And die of thirst.
3 "I clothe the heavens with blackness,
And make sackcloth their covering."
4¶ The Lord GOD has given Me the tongue of
disciples,
So that I may know how to sustain the
weary one with a word.
He awakens Me morning by morning,
He awakens My ear to listen as a disciple.
5 The Lord GOD has opened My ear,
And I was not disobedient,
Nor did I turn back.
6 I gave My back to those who strike Me,
And My cheeks to those who pull out My
beard;
I did not hide My face from insults and
spitting.
7 For the Lord GOD helps Me,
Therefore, I am not disgraced;
Therefore, I have made My face like flint,
And I know that I will not be ashamed.
8 He who vindicates Me is near;
Who will contend with Me?
Let us stand up to each other.
Who has a case against Me?
Let him approach Me.
9 Behold, the Lord GOD helps Me;
Who is he who condemns Me?
Behold, they will all wear out like a
garment;
A moth will eat them.
10 Who is among you who fears the LORD,
Who obeys the voice of His servant,
Who walks in darkness and has no light?
Let him trust in the name of the LORD and
rely on his God.
11 Behold, all you who kindle a fire,
Who encircle yourselves with flaming
arrows,
Walk in the light of your fire

And among the flaming arrows you have
set ablaze.
This you will have from My hand:
You will lie down in torment.

Israel Exhorted

51 "Listen to Me, you who pursue
righteousness,
Who seek the LORD:
Look to the rock from which you were
cut,
And to the quarry from which you were
dug.
2 "Look to Abraham your father
And to Sarah who gave birth to you in
pain;
When *he was only* one I called him,
Then I blessed him and multiplied him."
3 Indeed, the LORD will comfort Zion;
He will comfort all her ruins.
And He will make her wilderness like
Eden,
And her desert like the garden of the
LORD.
Joy and gladness will be found in her,
Thanksgiving and the sound of a melody.
4¶ "Pay attention to Me, My people,
And listen to Me, My nation;
For a law will go out from Me,
And I will bring My justice as a light of
the peoples.
5 "My righteousness is near, My salvation has
gone forth,
And My arms will judge the peoples;
The coastlands will wait for Me,
And they will wait expectantly for My
arm.
6 "Raise your eyes to the sky,
Then look to the earth beneath;
For the sky will vanish like smoke,
And the earth will wear out like a
garment
And its inhabitants will die in the same
way.
But My salvation will be forever,
And My righteousness will not fail.
7 "Listen to Me, you who know
righteousness,
A people in whose heart is My Law;
Do not fear the taunting of people,
Nor be terrified of their abuses.
8 "For the moth will eat them like a garment;
Yes, the moth will eat them like wool.
But My righteousness will be forever,
And My salvation to all generations."
9¶ Awake, awake, put on strength, O arm of
the LORD;
Awake as in the days of old, the
generations of long ago.
Was it not You who cut ⁷Rahab in pieces,
Who pierced the dragon?
10 Was it not You who dried up the sea,
The waters of the great deep;
Who made the depths of the sea a
pathway
For the redeemed to cross over?
11 And the redeemed of the LORD will return
And come to Zion with joyful shouting,
And everlasting joy *will be* on their heads.

They will obtain gladness and joy,
And sorrow and sighing will flee away.
12¶ "I, I Myself, am He who comforts you.
Who are you that you are afraid of mortal
man,
And of a son of man *who* is made *like*
grass,
13 That you have forgotten the LORD your
Maker,
Who stretched out the heavens
And laid the foundations of the earth,
That you fear continually all day long
because of the fury of the oppressor,
As he makes ready to destroy?
And where is the rage of the oppressor?
14 The exile will soon be set free, and will not
die in the dungeon, nor will his bread be
lacking. 15 For I am the LORD your God, who
stirs up the sea so that its waves roar (the LORD
of armies is His name). 16 And I have put My
words in your mouth and have covered you
with the shadow of My hand, to establish the
heavens, to found the earth, and to say to Zion,
'You are My people.' "
17¶ Pull yourself up! Pull yourself up! Arise,
Jerusalem!
You who have drunk from the LORD's
hand the cup of His anger;
The chalice of staggering you have drunk
to the dregs.
18 There is no one to guide her among all
the sons *to whom* she has given
birth,
Nor is there anyone to take her by the
hand among all the sons she has raised.
19 These two things have happened to you;
Who will mourn for you?
The devastation and destruction, famine
and sword;
How shall I comfort you?
20 Your sons have fainted,
They lie *helpless* at the head of every
street,
Like an antelope in a net,
Full of the wrath of the LORD,
The rebuke of your God.
21¶ Therefore, listen to this, you afflicted,
Who are drunk, but not with wine:
22 This is what your Lord, the LORD, your
God
Who contends for His people says:
"Behold, I have taken from your hand the
cup of staggering,
The chalice of My anger;
You will never drink it again.
23 "I will put it into the hand of your
tormentors,
Who have said to you, 'Lie down so that
we may walk over *you.*'
You have also made your back like the
ground,
And like the street for those who walk
over *it.*"

Cheer for Prostrate Zion

52 Awake, awake,
Clothe yourself in your strength, Zion;
Clothe yourself with your beautiful
garments,

51:9 ⁷I.e., a sea monster, not to be confused with Rahab in Joshua 2

Jerusalem, the holy city;
For the uncircumcised and the unclean
    Will no longer come into you.
2   Shake yourself from the dust, rise up,
    Captive Jerusalem;
    Release yourself from the chains around
        your neck,
    Captive daughter of Zion.

3 For this is what the LORD says: "You were sold for nothing, and you will be redeemed without money." 4 For this is what the Lord GOD says: "My people went down to Egypt first to reside there; then the Assyrian oppressed them without reason. 5 And now, what do I have here," declares the LORD, "seeing that My people have been taken away without reason?" Again the LORD declares, "Those who rule over them howl, and My name is continually reviled all day long. 6 Therefore, My people shall know My name; therefore on that day I am the one who is speaking, 'Here I am.'"

7¶ How delightful on the mountains
    Are the feet of one who brings good
        news,
    Who announces peace
    And brings good news of happiness,
    Who announces salvation,
    And says to Zion, "Your God reigns!"
8   Listen! Your watchmen raise their
        voices,
    They shout joyfully together;
    For they will see with their own eyes
    When the LORD restores Zion.
9   Be cheerful, shout joyfully together,
    You ruins of Jerusalem;
    For the LORD has comforted His people,
    He has redeemed Jerusalem.
10 The LORD has bared His holy arm
    In the sight of all the nations,
    So that all the ends of the earth may
        see
    The salvation of our God.
11¶ Depart, depart, go out from there,
    Do not touch what is unclean;
    Go out of the midst of her, purify
        yourselves,
    You who carry the vessels of the LORD.
12 But you will not go out in a hurry,
    Nor will you go as fugitives;
    For the LORD will go before you,
    And the God of Israel will be your rear
        guard.

The Exalted Servant

13¶ Behold, My Servant will prosper,
    He will be high and lifted up and greatly
        exalted.
14 Just as many were appalled at you, My
        people,
    So His appearance was marred beyond
        that of a man,
    And His form beyond the sons of
        mankind.
15 So He will sprinkle many nations,
    Kings will shut their mouths on account
        of Him;
    For what they had not been told, they will
        see,
    And what they had not heard, they will
        understand.

The Suffering Servant

53 Who has believed our report?
    And to whom has the arm of the LORD
        been revealed?
2   For He grew up before Him like a tender
        shoot,
    And like a root out of dry ground;
    He has no stately form or majesty
    That we would look at Him,
    Nor an appearance that we would take
        pleasure in Him.
3   He was despised and abandoned by
        men,
    A man of great pain and familiar with
        sickness;
    And like one from whom people hide
        their faces,
    He was despised, and we had no regard
        for Him.
4¶ However, it was our sicknesses that He
        Himself bore,
    And our pains that He carried;
    Yet we ourselves assumed that He had
        been afflicted,
    Struck down by God, and humiliated.
5   But He was pierced for our offenses,
    He was crushed for our wrongdoings;
    The punishment for our well-being was
        laid upon Him,
    And by His wounds we are healed.
6   All of us, like sheep, have gone astray,
    Each of us has turned to his own way;
    But the LORD has caused the wrongdoing
        of us all
    To fall on Him.
7¶ He was oppressed and afflicted,
    Yet He did not open His mouth;
    Like a lamb that is led to slaughter,
    And like a sheep that is silent before its
        shearers,
    So He did not open His mouth.
8   By oppression and judgment He was
        taken away;
    And as for His generation, who
        considered
    That He was cut off from the land of
        the living
    For the wrongdoing of my people, to
        whom the blow was due?
9   And His grave was assigned with wicked
        men,
    Yet He was with a rich man in His death,
    Because He had done no violence,
    Nor was there any deceit in His mouth.
10¶ But the LORD desired
    To crush Him, causing Him grief;
    If He renders Himself as a guilt offering,
    He will see His offspring,
    He will prolong His days,
    And the good pleasure of the LORD will
        prosper in His hand.
11 As a result of the anguish of His soul,
    He will see it and be satisfied;
    By His knowledge the Righteous One,
    My Servant, will justify the many,
    For He will bear their wrongdoings.
12 Therefore, I will allot Him a portion with
        the great,
    And He will divide the plunder with the
        strong,

Because He poured out His life unto
death,
And was counted with wrongdoers;
Yet He Himself bore the sin of many,
And interceded for the wrongdoers.

The Fertility of Zion

54 "Shout for joy, infertile one, you who
have not given birth *to any child;*
Break forth into joyful shouting and cry
aloud, you who have not been in labor;
For the sons of the desolate one *will be*
more numerous
Than the sons of the married woman,"
says the LORD.
2 "Enlarge the place of your tent;
Stretch out the curtains of your dwellings,
do not spare *them;*
Lengthen your ropes
And strengthen your pegs.
3 "For you will spread out to the right and to
the left,
And your descendants will possess nations
And will resettle the desolate cities.
4¶ "Fear not, for you will not be put to shame;
And do not feel humiliated, for you will
not be disgraced;
But you will forget the shame of your
youth,
And no longer remember the disgrace of
your widowhood.
5 "For your husband is your Maker,
Whose name is the LORD of armies;
And your Redeemer is the Holy One of
Israel,
Who is called the God of all the earth.
6 "For the LORD has called you,
Like a wife forsaken and grieved in spirit,
Even like a wife of *one's* youth when she
is rejected,"
Says your God.
7 "For a brief moment I abandoned you,
But with great compassion I will gather
you.
8 "In an outburst of anger
I hid My face from you for a moment,
But with everlasting favor I will have
compassion on you,"
Says the LORD your Redeemer.
9¶ "For this is like the days of Noah to Me,
When I swore that the waters of Noah
Would not flood the earth again;
So I have sworn that I will not be angry
with you
Nor rebuke you.
10 "For the mountains may be removed and
the hills may shake,
But My favor will not be removed from
you,
Nor will My covenant of peace be
shaken,"
Says the LORD who has compassion on
you.
11¶ "Afflicted one, storm-tossed, *and* not
comforted,
Behold, I will set your stones in antimony,
And I will lay your foundations with
sapphires.
12 "Moreover, I will make your battlements of
rubies,

And your gates of crystal,
And your entire wall of precious stones.
13 "All your sons will be taught by the LORD;
And the well-being of your sons will be
great.
14 "In righteousness you will be established;
You will be far from oppression, for you
will not fear;
And from terror, for it will not come near
you.
15 "If anyone fiercely attacks *you,* it will not
be from Me.
Whoever attacks you will fall because of
you.
16 "Behold, I Myself have created the smith
who blows on the fire of coals
And produces a weapon for its work;
And I have created the destroyer to inflict
ruin.
17 "No weapon that is formed against you will
succeed;
And you will condemn every tongue that
accuses you in judgment.
This is the heritage of the servants of the
LORD,
And their vindication is from Me,"
declares the LORD.

The Free Offer of Mercy

55 "You there! Everyone who thirsts, come
to the waters;
And you who have no money come, buy
and eat.
Come, buy wine and milk
Without money and without cost.
2 "Why do you spend money for what is not
bread,
And your wages for what does not satisfy?
Listen carefully to Me, and eat what is
good,
And delight yourself in abundance.
3 "Incline your ear and come to Me.
Listen, that you may live;
And I will make an everlasting covenant
with you,
According to the faithful mercies shown
to David.
4 "Behold, I have made him a witness to the
peoples,
A leader and commander for the peoples.
5 "Behold, you will call a nation you do not
know,
And a nation which does not know you
will run to you,
Because of the LORD your God, the Holy
One of Israel;
For He has glorified you."
6¶ Seek the LORD while He may be found;
Call upon Him while He is near.
7 Let the wicked abandon his way,
And the unrighteous person his thoughts;
And let him return to the LORD,
And He will have compassion on him,
And to our God,
For He will abundantly pardon.
8 "For My thoughts are not your thoughts,
Nor are your ways My ways," declares the
LORD.
9 "For *as* the heavens are higher than the
earth,

So are My ways higher than your ways
And My thoughts than your thoughts.
10 "For as the rain and the snow come down
from heaven,
And do not return there without watering
the earth
And making it produce and sprout,
And providing seed to the sower and
bread to the eater;
11 So will My word be which goes out of My
mouth;
It will not return to Me empty,
Without accomplishing what I desire,
And without succeeding *in the purpose*
for which I sent it.
12 "For you will go out with joy
And be led in peace;
The mountains and the hills will break
into shouts of joy before you,
And all the trees of the field will clap *their*
hands.
13 "Instead of the thorn bush, the juniper will
come up,
And instead of the stinging nettle, the
myrtle will come up;
And it will be a memorial to the LORD,
An everlasting sign which will not be
eliminated."

Rewards for Obedience to God

56 This is what the LORD says:
"Guard justice and do righteousness,
For My salvation is about to come
And My righteousness to be revealed.
2 "Blessed is a man who does this,
And a son of man who takes hold of it;
Who keeps from profaning the Sabbath,
And keeps his hand from doing any evil."
3 Let not the foreigner who has joined
himself to the LORD say,
"The LORD will certainly separate me from
His people."
Nor let the eunuch say, "Behold, I am a
dry tree."
4 For this is what the LORD says:
"To the eunuchs who keep My Sabbaths,
And choose what pleases Me,
And hold firmly to My covenant,
5 To them I will give in My house and
within My walls a memorial,
And a name better than that of sons and
daughters;
I will give them an everlasting name
which will not be eliminated.
6¶ "Also the foreigners who join themselves to
the LORD,
To attend to His service and to love the
name of the LORD,
To be His servants, every one who keeps
the Sabbath so as not to profane it,
And holds firmly to My covenant;
7 Even those I will bring to My holy
mountain,
And make them joyful in My house of
prayer.
Their burnt offerings and their sacrifices
will be acceptable on My altar;
For My house will be called a house of
prayer for all the peoples."

8 The Lord GOD, who gathers the dispersed
of Israel, declares,
"I will yet gather *others* to them, to those
already gathered."
9¶ All you wild animals,
All you animals in the forest,
Come to eat.
10 His watchmen are blind,
All of them know nothing.
All of them are mute dogs unable to
bark,
Dreamers lying down, who love to
slumber;
11 And the dogs are greedy, they are never
satisfied.
And they are shepherds who have no
understanding;
They have all turned to their own way,
Each one to his unjust gain, without
exception.
12 "Come," *they say,* "let's get wine, and let's
drink heavily of intoxicating drink;
And tomorrow will be like today, only
more so."

Evil Leaders Rebuked

57 The righteous person perishes, and no
one takes it to heart;
And devout people are taken away, while
no one understands.
For the righteous person is taken away
from evil,
2 He enters into peace;
They rest in their [f]beds,
Each one who walked in his upright
way.
3 "But come here, you sons of a sorceress,
Offspring of an adulterer and a prostitute!
4 "Of whom do you make fun?
Against whom do you open wide your
mouth
And stick out your tongue?
Are you not children of rebellion,
Offspring of deceit,
5 Who inflame yourselves among the
oaks,
Under every luxuriant tree,
Who slaughter the children in the
ravines,
Under the clefts of the rocks?
6 "Among the [f]smooth *stones* of the ravine
Is your portion, they are your lot;
Even to them you have poured out a drink
offering,
You have made a grain offering.
Should I relent of these things?
7 "On a high and lofty mountain
You have made your bed.
You also went up there to offer sacrifice.
8 "Behind the door and the doorpost
You have set up your sign;
Indeed, far removed from Me, you have
uncovered yourself,
And have gone up and made your bed
wide.
And you have made an agreement for
yourself with them,
You have loved their bed,
You have looked at *their* manhood.

57:2 [f] I.e., graves   57:6 [f] I.e., symbols of fertility gods

9   "You have journeyed to the king with oil
      And increased your perfumes;
      You have sent your messengers a great
        distance
      And made *them* go down to ᵗSheol.
10 "You were tired out by the length of your
       road,
      Yet you did not say, 'It is hopeless!'
      You found renewed strength,
      Therefore you did not faint.
11¶ "Of whom were you worried and fearful
      When you lied, and did not remember Me
      Nor give *Me* a thought?
      Was I not silent, even for a long time,
      So you do not fear Me?
12 "I will declare your righteousness and your
       deeds,
      And they will not benefit you.
13 "When you cry out, let your collection *of*
      idols save you.
      But the wind will carry them all up,
      And a breath will take *them away.*
      But the one who takes refuge in Me will
       inherit the land
      And possess My holy mountain."
14¶ And it will be said,
     "Build up, build up, prepare the way,
     Remove *every* obstacle from the way of
      My people."
15 For this is what the high and exalted One
     Who lives forever, whose name is Holy,
     says:
     "I dwell *in* a high and holy place,
     And *also* with the contrite and lowly of
      spirit
     In order to revive the spirit of the lowly
     And to revive the heart of the contrite.
16 "For I will not contend forever,
     Nor will I always be angry;
     For the spirit would grow faint before Me,
     And the breath *of those whom* I have
      made.
17 "Because of the wrongful act of his unjust
      gain I was angry and struck him;
     I hid *My face* and was angry,
     And he went on turning away, in the way
      of his heart.
18 "I have seen his ways, but I will heal him;
     I will lead him and restore comfort to him
      and to his mourners,
19 Creating the praise of the lips.
     Peace, peace to him who is far away and
      to him who is near,"
     Says the LORD, "and I will heal him."
20 But the wicked are like the tossing sea,
     For it cannot be quiet,
     And its waters toss up refuse and mud.
21 "There is no peace," says my God, "for the
     wicked."

Observances of Fasts

58 "Cry loudly, do not hold back;
    Raise your voice like a trumpet,
    And declare to My people their
     wrongdoing,
    And to the house of Jacob their sins.
2   "Yet they seek Me day by day and delight to
     know My ways,
     As a nation that has done righteousness

     And has not forsaken the ordinance of
      their God.
     They ask Me *for* just decisions,
     They delight in the nearness of God.
3   'Why have we fasted and You do not see?
     Why have we humbled ourselves and You
      do not notice?'
     Behold, on the day of your fast you find
      your desire,
     And oppress all your workers.
4   "Behold, you fast for contention and strife,
      and to strike with a wicked fist.
     You do not fast like *you have done* today
      to make your voice heard on high!
5   "Is it a fast like this that I choose, a day for
      a person to humble himself?
     Is it for bowing one's head like a reed
     And for spreading out sackcloth and ashes
      as a bed?
     Will you call this a fast, even an accept-
      able day to the LORD?
6   "Is this not the fast that I choose:
     To release the bonds of wickedness,
     To undo the ropes of the yoke,
     And to let the oppressed go free,
     And break every yoke?
7   "Is it not to break your bread with the
      hungry
     And bring the homeless poor into the
      house;
     When you see the naked, to cover him;
     And not to hide yourself from your own
      flesh?
8   "Then your light will break out like the
      dawn,
     And your recovery will spring up quickly;
     And your righteousness will go before
      you;
     The glory of the LORD will be your rear
      guard.
9   "Then you will call, and the LORD will
      answer;
     You will cry for help, and He will say,
      'Here I am.'
     If you remove the yoke from your midst,
     The pointing of the finger and speaking
      wickedness,
10 And *if* you offer yourself to the hungry
     And satisfy the need of the afflicted,
     Then your light will rise in darkness,
     And your gloom *will become* like midday.
11 "And the LORD will continually guide you,
     And satisfy your desire in scorched places,
     And give strength to your bones;
     And you will be like a watered garden,
     And like a spring of water whose waters
      do not fail.
12 "Those from among you will rebuild the
      ancient ruins;
     You will raise up the age-old foundations;
     And you will be called the repairer of the
      breach,
     The restorer of the streets in which to
      dwell.

Keeping the Sabbath

13¶ "If, because of the Sabbath, you restrain
     your foot
     From doing as you wish on My holy day,

And call the Sabbath a pleasure, *and* the
holy *day* of the Lord honorable,
And honor it, desisting from your *own*
ways,
From seeking your *own* pleasure
And speaking *your own* word,
14 Then you will take delight in the Lord,
And I will make you ride on the heights of
the earth;
And I will feed you *with* the heritage of
Jacob your father,
For the mouth of the Lord has spoken."

Separation from God

59 Behold, the Lord's hand is not so short
That it cannot save;
Nor is His ear so dull
That it cannot hear.
2 But your wrongdoings have caused a sep-
aration between you and your God,
And your sins have hidden *His* face from
you so that He does not hear.
3 For your hands are defiled with blood,
And your fingers with wrongdoing;
Your lips have spoken deceit,
Your tongue mutters wickedness.
4 No one sues righteously and no one
pleads honestly.
They trust in confusion and speak lies;
They conceive trouble and give birth to
disaster.
5 They hatch vipers' eggs and weave the
spider's web;
The one who eats of their eggs dies,
And *from* what is crushed, a snake breaks
out.
6 Their webs will not become clothing,
Nor will they cover themselves with their
works;
Their works are works of wrongdoing,
And an act of violence is in their hands.
7 Their feet run to evil,
And they hurry to shed innocent blood;
Their thoughts are thoughts of
wrongdoing,
Devastation and destruction are in their
paths.
8 They do not know the way of peace,
And there is no justice in their tracks;
They have made their paths crooked,
Whoever walks on them does not know
peace.

A Confession of Wickedness

9¶ Therefore justice is far from us,
And righteousness does not reach us;
We hope for light, but there is darkness,
For brightness, but we walk in gloom.
10 We grope for the wall like people who are
blind,
We grope like those who have no eyes.
We stumble at midday as in the twilight;
Among those who are healthy *we are* like
the dead.
11 All of us growl like bears,
And moan sadly like doves;
We hope for justice, but there is none;
For salvation, *but* it is far from us.
12 For our wrongful acts have multiplied
before You,

And our sins have testified against us;
For our wrongful acts are with us,
And we know our wrongdoings:
13 Offending and denying the Lord,
And turning away from our God,
Speaking oppression and revolt,
Conceiving and uttering lying words from
the heart.
14 Justice is turned back,
And righteousness stands far away;
For truth has stumbled in the street,
And uprightness cannot enter.
15 Truth is lacking,
And one who turns aside from evil makes
himself a prey.
Now the Lord saw,
And it was displeasing in His sight that
there was no justice.
16 And He saw that there was no one,
And was amazed that there was not one
to intercede;
Then His own arm brought salvation to
Him,
And His righteousness upheld Him.
17 He put on righteousness like a breastplate,
And a helmet of salvation on His head;
And He put on garments of vengeance for
clothing
And wrapped Himself with zeal as a cloak.
18 According to *their* deeds, so will He
repay:
Wrath to His adversaries, retribution to
His enemies;
To the coastlands He will deal retribution.
19 So they will fear the name of the Lord
from the west
And His glory from the rising of the sun,
For He will come like a rushing stream
Which the wind of the Lord drives.
20 "A Redeemer will come to Zion,
And to those in Jacob who turn from
wrongdoing," declares the Lord.
21 "As for Me, this is My covenant with
them," says the Lord: "My Spirit who is upon
you, and My words which I have put in your
mouth shall not depart from your mouth, nor
from the mouth of your offspring, nor from the
mouth of your offspring's offspring," says the
Lord, "from now and forever."

A Glorified Zion

60 "Arise, shine; for your light has come,
And the glory of the Lord has risen upon
you.
2 "For behold, darkness will cover the earth
And deep darkness the peoples;
But the Lord will rise upon you
And His glory will appear upon you.
3 "Nations will come to your light,
And kings to the brightness of your rising.
4¶ "Raise your eyes all around and see;
They all gather together, they come to
you.
Your sons will come from afar,
And your daughters will be carried on the
hip.
5 "Then you will see and be radiant,
And your heart will thrill and rejoice;
Because the abundance of the sea will be
turned to you,

The wealth of the nations will come to you.

6 "A multitude of camels will cover you,
. The young camels of Midian and Ephah;
All those from Sheba will come;
They will bring gold and frankincense,
And proclaim good news of the praises of the LORD.

7 "All the flocks of Kedar will be gathered to you,
The rams of Nebaioth will serve you;
They will go up on My altar with acceptance,
And I will glorify My glorious house.

8 "Who are these who fly like a cloud
And like the doves to their windows?

9 "Certainly the coastlands will wait for Me;
And the ships of Tarshish *will come* first,
To bring your sons from afar,
Their silver and their gold with them,
For the name of the LORD your God,
And for the Holy One of Israel because He has glorified you.

10¶ "Foreigners will build up your walls,
And their kings will serve you;
For in My wrath I struck you,
And in My favor I have had compassion on you.

11 "Your gates will be open continually;
They will not be closed day or night,
So that *people* may bring you the wealth of the nations,
With their kings led in procession.

12 "For the nation and the kingdom which will not serve you will perish,
And the nations will be utterly ruined.

13 "The glory of Lebanon will come to you,
The juniper, the elm tree and the cedar together,
To beautify the place of My sanctuary;
And I will make the place of My feet glorious.

14 "The sons of those who afflicted you will come bowing to you,
And all those who despised you will bow down at the soles of your feet;
And they will call you the city of the LORD,
The Zion of the Holy One of Israel.

15¶ "Whereas you have been forsaken and hated
With no one passing through,
I will make you an object of pride forever,
A joy from generation to generation.

16 "You will also suck the milk of nations,
And suck the breast of kings;
Then you will know that I, the LORD, am your Savior
And your Redeemer, the Mighty One of Jacob.

17 "Instead of bronze I will bring gold,
And instead of iron I will bring silver,
And instead of wood, bronze,
And instead of stones, iron.
And I will make peace your administrators,
And righteousness your overseers.

18 "Violence will not be heard again in your land,

Nor devastation or destruction within your borders;
But you will call your walls salvation, and your gates praise.

19 "No longer will you have the sun for light by day,
Nor will the moon give you light for brightness;
But you will have the LORD as an everlasting light,
And your God as your glory.

20 "Your sun will no longer set,
Nor will your moon wane;
For you will have the LORD as an everlasting light,
And the days of your mourning will be over.

21 "Then all your people *will be* righteous;
They will possess the land forever,
The branch of My planting,
The work of My hands,
That I may be glorified.

22 "The smallest one will become a thousand,
And the least one a mighty nation.
I, the LORD, will bring it about quickly in its time."

Exaltation of the Afflicted

61 The Spirit of the Lord GOD is upon me,
Because the LORD anointed me
To bring good news to the humble;
He has sent me to bind up the broken-hearted,
To proclaim release to captives
And freedom to prisoners;

2 To proclaim the favorable year of the LORD
And the day of vengeance of our God;
To comfort all who mourn,

3 To grant those who mourn *in* Zion,
Giving them a garland instead of ashes,
The oil of gladness instead of mourning,
The cloak of praise instead of a disheartened spirit.
So they will be called oaks of righteousness,
The planting of the LORD, that He may be glorified.

4¶ Then they will rebuild the ancient ruins,
They will raise up the former devastations;
And they will repair the ruined cities,
The desolations of many generations.

5 Strangers will stand and pasture your flocks,
And foreigners will be your farmers and your vinedressers.

6 But you will be called the priests of the LORD;
You will be spoken of *as* ministers of our God.
You will eat the wealth of nations,
And you will boast in their riches.

7 Instead of your shame *you will have a* double *portion,*
And *instead of* humiliation they will shout for joy over their portion.
Therefore they will possess a double *portion* in their land,
Everlasting joy will be theirs.

8 For I, the LORD, love justice,

I hate robbery in the burnt offering;
And I will faithfully give them their
reward,
And make an everlasting covenant with
them.
9 Then their offspring will be known among
the nations,
And their descendants in the midst of the
peoples.
All who see them will recognize them
Because they are the offspring *whom* the
LORD has blessed.
10¶ I will rejoice greatly in the LORD,
My soul will be joyful in my God;
For He has clothed me with garments of
salvation,
He has wrapped me with a robe of
righteousness,
As a groom puts on a turban,
And as a bride adorns herself with her
jewels.
11 For as the earth produces its sprouts,
And as a garden causes the things sown in
it to spring up,
So the Lord GOD will cause righteousness
and praise
To spring up before all the nations.

Zion's Glory and New Name

62 For Zion's sake I will not keep silent,
And for Jerusalem's sake I will not keep
quiet,
Until her righteousness goes forth like
brightness,
And her salvation like a torch that is
burning.
2 The nations will see your righteousness,
And all kings your glory;
And you will be called by a new name
Which the mouth of the LORD will
designate.
3 You will also be a crown of beauty in the
hand of the LORD,
And a royal headband in the hand of
your God.
4 It will no longer be said to you,
"Forsaken,"
Nor to your land will it any longer be said,
"Desolate";
But you will be called, "My delight is in
her,"
And your land, "Married";
For the LORD delights in you,
And *to Him* your land will be married.
5 For *as* a young man marries a virgin,
So your sons will marry you;
And *as* the groom rejoices over the
bride,
So your God will rejoice over you.
6¶ On your walls, Jerusalem, I have
appointed watchmen;
All day and all night they will never keep
silent.
You who profess the LORD, take no rest for
yourselves;
7 And give Him no rest until He establishes
And makes Jerusalem an object of praise
on the earth.
8 The LORD has sworn by His right hand
and by His mighty arm:

"I will never again give your grain *as* food
for your enemies,
Nor will foreigners drink your new wine
for which you have labored."
9 But those who harvest it will eat it and
praise the LORD;
And those who gather it will drink it in
the courtyards of My sanctuary.
10¶ Go through, go through the gates,
Clear a way for the people!
Build up, build up the highway,
Remove the stones, lift up a flag over the
peoples.
11 Behold, the LORD has proclaimed to the
end of the earth:
Say to the daughter of Zion, "Behold, your
salvation is coming;
Behold His reward is with Him, and His
compensation before Him."
12 And they will call them, "The holy
people,
The redeemed of the LORD";
And you will be called, "Sought Out, A
City Not Abandoned."

God's Vengeance on the Nations

63 Who is this who comes from Edom,
With garments of glowing colors from
Bozrah,
This One who is majestic in His apparel,
Marching in the greatness of His strength?
"It is I, the One who speaks in righteous-
ness, mighty to save."
2 Why is Your apparel red,
And Your garments like one who treads in
the wine press?
3 "I have trodden the wine trough alone,
And from the peoples there was no one
with Me.
I also trod them in My anger
And trampled them in My wrath;
And their lifeblood is sprinkled on My
garments,
And I stained all My clothes.
4 "For the day of vengeance was in My heart,
And My year of redemption has come.
5 "I looked, but there was no one to help,
And I was astonished and there was no
one to uphold;
So My own arm brought salvation to Me,
And My wrath upheld Me.
6 "I trampled down the peoples in My anger
And made them drunk with My wrath,
And I poured out their lifeblood on the
earth."

God's Ancient Mercies Recalled

7¶ I will make mention of the mercies of the
LORD, *and* the praises of the LORD,
According to all that the LORD has granted
us,
And the great goodness toward the house
of Israel,
Which He has granted them according to
His compassion
And according to the abundance of His
mercies.
8 For He said, "Certainly they are My
people,
Sons who will not deal falsely."

So He became their Savior.

9 In all their distress He was distressed,
And the angel of His presence saved
them;
In His love and in His mercy He
redeemed them,
And He lifted them and carried them all
the days of old.

10 But they rebelled
And grieved His Holy Spirit;
Therefore He turned Himself to become
their enemy,
He fought against them.

11 Then His people remembered the days of
old, of Moses.
Where is He who brought them up out of
the sea with the shepherds of His
flock?
Where is He who put His Holy Spirit in
the midst of them;

12 Who caused His glorious arm to go at the
right hand of Moses,
Who divided the waters before them to
make for Himself an everlasting name,

13 Who led them through the depths?
Like the horse in the wilderness, they did
not stumble;

14 Like the cattle which go down into the
valley,
The Spirit of the LORD gave them rest.
So You led Your people,
To make for Yourself a glorious name.

You Are Our Father

15¶ Look down from heaven and see from
Your holy and glorious lofty habitation;
Where are Your zeal and Your mighty
deeds?
The stirrings of Your heart and Your
compassion are restrained toward me.

16 For You are our Father, though Abraham
does not know us
And Israel does not recognize us.
You, LORD, are our Father,
Our Redeemer from ancient times is Your
name.

17 Why, LORD, do You cause us to stray from
Your ways
And harden our heart from fearing You?
Return for the sake of Your servants, the
tribes of Your heritage.

18 Your holy people possessed Your sanctuary
for a little while,
Our adversaries have trampled *it* down.

19 We have become *like* those over whom
You have never ruled,
Like those who were not called by Your
name.

Prayer for Mercy and Help

64 Oh, that You would tear open the
heavens *and* come down,
That the mountains would quake at Your
presence—

2 As fire kindles brushwood, *as* fire causes
water to boil—
To make Your name known to Your
adversaries,
That the nations may tremble at Your
presence!

3 When You did awesome things which we
did not expect,
You came down, the mountains quaked at
Your presence.

4 For from days of old they have not heard
or perceived by ear,
Nor has the eye seen a God besides You,
Who acts in behalf of one who waits for
Him.

5 You meet him who rejoices in doing
righteousness,
Who remembers You in Your ways.
Behold, You were angry, for we sinned,
We continued in our sins for a long
time;
Yet shall we be saved?

6 For all of us have become like one who is
unclean,
And all our righteous deeds are like a
filthy garment;
And all of us wither like a leaf,
And our wrongdoings, like the wind, take
us away.

7 There is no one who calls on Your name,
Who stirs himself to take hold of You;
For You have hidden Your face from us
And have surrendered us to the power of
our wrongdoings.

8¶ But now, LORD, You are our Father;
We are the clay, and You our potter,
And all of us are the work of Your hand.

9 Do not be angry beyond measure, LORD,
Nor remember wrongdoing forever.
Behold, please look, all of us are Your
people.

10 Your holy cities have become a
wilderness,
Zion has become a wilderness,
Jerusalem a desolation.

11 Our holy and beautiful house,
Where our fathers praised You,
Has been burned *by* fire;
And all our precious things have become a
ruin.

12 Will You restrain Yourself at these things,
LORD?
Will You keep silent and afflict us beyond
measure?

A Rebellious People

65 "I permitted Myself to be sought by
those who did not ask *for Me;*
I permitted Myself to be found by those
who did not seek Me.
I said, 'Here am I, here am I,'
To a nation which did not call on My
name.

2 "I have spread out My hands all day long to
a rebellious people,
Who walk *in* the way which is not good,
following their own thoughts,

3 A people who continually provoke Me to
My face,
Offering sacrifices in gardens and burning
incense on bricks;

4 Who sit among graves and spend the
night in secret places;
Who eat pig's flesh,
And the broth of unclean meat is *in* their
pots.

5 "Who say, 'Keep to yourself, do not come
    near me,
For I am holier than you!'
These are smoke in My nostrils,
A fire that burns all the day.
6 "Behold, it is written before Me:
I will not keep silent, but I will repay;
I will even repay [f]into their laps,
7 Both your own wrongdoings and the
    wrongdoings of your fathers together,"
    says the LORD.
"Because they have burned incense on the
    mountains
And scorned Me on the hills,
Therefore I will measure their former
    work [f]into their laps."
8 This is what the LORD says:
"Just as the new wine is found in the
    cluster,
And one says, 'Do not destroy it, for there
    is benefit in it,'
So I will act in behalf of My servants
In order not to destroy all of them.
9 "I will bring forth offspring from Jacob,
And an heir of My mountains from Judah;
My chosen ones shall inherit it,
And My servants will live there.
10 "Sharon will be a pasture land for flocks,
And the Valley of Achor a resting place for
    herds,
For My people who seek Me.
11 "But as for you who abandon the LORD,
Who forget My holy mountain,
Who set a table for Fortune,
And fill a jug of mixed wine for Destiny,
12 I will destine you for the sword,
And all of you will bow down to the
    slaughter.
Because I called, but you did not answer;
I spoke, but you did not listen.
Instead, you did evil in My sight
And chose that in which I did not
    delight."
13 ¶ Therefore, this is what the Lord GOD
    says:
"Behold, My servants will eat, but you will
    be hungry.
Behold, My servants will drink, but you
    will be thirsty.
Behold, My servants will rejoice, but you
    will be put to shame.
14 "Behold, My servants will shout joyfully
    with a glad heart,
But you will cry out from a painful heart,
And you will wail from a broken spirit.
15 "You will leave your name as a curse to My
    chosen ones,
And the Lord GOD will put you to death.
But My servants will be called by another
    name.
16 "Because the one who is blessed on the
    earth
Will be blessed by the God of truth;
And the one who swears an oath on the
    earth
Will swear by the God of truth;
Because the former troubles are forgotten,
And because they are hidden from My
    sight!

New Heavens and a New Earth

17 ¶ "For behold, I create new heavens and a
    new earth;
And the former things will not be
    remembered or come to mind.
18 "But be glad and rejoice forever in what I
    create;
For behold, I create Jerusalem for
    rejoicing
And her people for gladness.
19 "I will also rejoice in Jerusalem and be glad
    in My people;
And there will no longer be heard in her
The voice of weeping and the sound of
    crying.
20 "No longer will there be in it an infant who
    lives only a few days,
Or an old person who does not live out
    his days;
For the youth will die at the age of a
    hundred,
And the one who does not reach the age
    of a hundred
Will be thought accursed.
21 "They will build houses and inhabit them;
They will also plant vineyards and eat
    their fruit.
22 "They will not build and another inhabit,
They will not plant and another eat;
For as the lifetime of a tree, so will be the
    days of My people,
And My chosen ones will fully enjoy the
    work of their hands.
23 "They will not labor in vain,
Or give birth to children for disaster;
For they are the descendants of those
    blessed by the LORD,
And their descendants with them.
24 It will also come to pass that before they call,
I will answer; while they are still speaking, I
will listen. 25 The wolf and the lamb will graze
together, and the lion will eat straw like the ox;
and dust will be the serpent's food. They will
do no evil or harm on all My holy mountain,"
says the LORD.

Heaven Is God's Throne

66 This is what the LORD says:
"Heaven is My throne and the earth is
    the footstool for My feet.
Where then is a house you could build for
    Me?
And where is a place that I may rest?
2 "For My hand made all these things,
So all these things came into being,"
    declares the LORD.
"But I will look to this one,
At one who is humble and contrite in
    spirit, and who trembles at My word.

Hypocrisy Rebuked

3 ¶ "But the one who slaughters an ox is like
    one who kills a person;
The one who sacrifices a lamb is like one
    who breaks a dog's neck;
One who offers a grain offering is like one
    who offers pig's blood;
One who burns incense is like one who
    blesses an idol.

65:6 [f] I.e., individually and fully   65:7 [f] I.e., individually and fully

As they have chosen their *own* ways,
And their souls delight in their abom-
    inations,
4   So I will choose their punishments
And bring on them what they dread.
Because I called, but no one answered;
I spoke, but they did not listen.
Instead, they did evil in My sight
And chose that in which I did not
    delight."
5   Hear the word of the LORD, you who
    tremble at His word:
"Your brothers who hate you, who exclude
    you on account of My name,
Have said, 'Let the LORD be glorified, so
    that we may see your joy.'
But they will be put to shame.
6   "A sound of uproar from the city, a voice
    from the temple,
The voice of the LORD who is dealing
    retribution to His enemies.
7¶ "Before she was in labor, she delivered;
Before her pain came, she gave birth to a
    boy.
8   "Who has heard such a thing? Who has
    seen such things?
Can a land be born in one day?
Can a nation be given birth all at once?
As soon as Zion was in labor, she also
    delivered her sons.
9   "Shall I bring to the point of birth but not
    give delivery?" says the LORD.
"Or shall I who gives delivery shut *the
    womb?*" says your God.

Joy in Jerusalem's Future
10 "Be joyful with Jerusalem and rejoice for
    her, all you who love her;
Be exceedingly glad with her, all you who
    mourn over her,
11 So that you may nurse and be satisfied
    with her comforting breasts,
So that you may drink fully and be
    delighted with her bountiful
    breasts."
12 For this is what the LORD says: "Behold, I
    extend peace to her like a river,
And the glory of the nations like an
    overflowing stream;
And you will be nursed, you will be
    carried on the hip and rocked back and
    forth on the knees.
13 "As one whom his mother comforts, so I
    will comfort you;
And you will be comforted in
    Jerusalem."
14 Then you will see *this,* and your heart will
    be glad,

And your bones will flourish like the new
    grass;
And the hand of the LORD will be made
    known to His servants,
But He will be indignant toward His
    enemies.
15 For behold, the LORD will come in fire,
And His chariots like the whirlwind,
To render His anger with fury,
And His rebuke with flames of fire.
16 For the LORD will execute judgment by
    fire
And by His sword on humanity,
And those put to death by the LORD will
    be many.
17 "Those who sanctify and purify themselves
    to go to the gardens,
Following one in the center,
Who eat pig's flesh, detestable things, and
    mice,
Will come to an end altogether," declares
    the LORD.

18 "For I know their works and their
thoughts; the time is coming to gather all the
nations and tongues. And they shall come and
see My glory. 19 And I will put a sign among
them and send survivors from them to the
nations: Tarshish, Put, Lud, Meshech, Tubal,
and Javan, to the distant coastlands that have
neither heard of My fame nor seen My glory.
And they will declare My glory among the
nations. 20 Then they shall bring all your countrymen from all the nations as a grain offering
to the LORD, on horses, in chariots, in litters,
on mules, and on camels, to My holy mountain
Jerusalem," says the LORD, "just as the sons of
Israel bring their grain offering in a clean
vessel to the house of the LORD. 21 I will also
take some of them as priests *and* Levites," says
the LORD.
22 "For just as the new heavens and the new
    earth,
Which I make, will endure before Me,"
    declares the LORD,
"So will your descendants and your name
    endure.
23 "And it shall be from new moon to new
    moon
And from Sabbath to Sabbath,
All mankind will come to bow down
    before Me," says the LORD.
24 "Then they will go out and look
At the corpses of the people
Who have rebelled against Me.
For their worm will not die
And their fire will not be extinguished;
And they will be an abhorrence to all
    mankind."

The Book of

JEREMIAH

Jeremiah's Call and Commission

1 The words of Jeremiah the son of Hilkiah, of the priests who were in Anathoth in the land of Benjamin, 2 to whom the word of the LORD came in the days of Josiah the son of Amon, king of Judah, in the thirteenth year of his reign. 3 It came also in the days of Jehoiakim the son of Josiah, king of Judah, until the end of the eleventh year of Zedekiah the son of Josiah, king of Judah, until the exile of Jerusalem in the fifth month.

4 Now the word of the LORD came to me, saying,
5 "Before I formed you in the womb I knew you,
And before you were born I consecrated you;
I have appointed you as a prophet to the nations."
6 Then I said, "Oh, Lord GOD!
Behold, I do not know how to speak,
Because I am a youth."
7 But the LORD said to me,
"Do not say, 'I am a youth,'
Because everywhere I send you, you shall go,
And all that I command you, you shall speak.
8 "Do not be afraid of them,
For I am with you to save you," declares the LORD.
9 Then the LORD stretched out His hand and touched my mouth, and the LORD said to me, "Behold, I have put My words in your mouth.
10 "See, I have appointed you this day over the nations and over the kingdoms,
To root out and to tear down,
To destroy and to overthrow,
To build and to plant."

The Almond Branch and Boiling Pot

11 And the word of the LORD came to me, saying, "What do you see, Jeremiah?" And I said, "I see a branch of an almond tree." 12 Then the LORD said to me, "You have seen well, for I am watching over My word to perform it."

13 And the word of the LORD came to me a second time, saying, "What do you see?" And I said, "I see a boiling pot, facing away from the north." 14 Then the LORD said to me, "Out of the north the evil will be unleashed on all the inhabitants of the land. 15 For, behold, I am calling all the families of the kingdoms of the north," declares the LORD; "and they will come and place, each one of them, his throne at the entrance of the gates of Jerusalem, and against all its walls around, and against all the cities of Judah. 16 And I will pronounce My judgments against them concerning all their wickedness, since they have abandoned Me and have offered sacrifices to other gods, and worshiped

the works of their own hands. 17 Now, belt your garment around your waist and arise, and speak to them all that I command you. Do not be dismayed before them, or I will make you dismayed before them. 18 Now behold, I have made you today like a fortified city and like a pillar of iron and walls of bronze against the whole land, to the kings of Judah, to its leaders, to its priests, and to the people of the land. 19 And they will fight against you but they will not overcome you, for I am with you to save you," declares the LORD.

Judah's Apostasy

2 Now the word of the LORD came to me, saying, 2 "Go and proclaim in the ears of Jerusalem, saying, 'This is what the LORD says:
"I remember regarding you the devotion of your youth,
Your love when you were a bride,
Your following after Me in the wilderness,
Through a land not sown.
3 "Israel was holy to the LORD,
The first of His harvest.
All who ate of it became guilty;
Evil came upon them," declares the LORD.'"
4 Hear the word of the LORD, house of Jacob, and all the families of the house of Israel. 5 This is what the LORD says:
"What injustice did your fathers find in Me,
That they went far from Me,
And walked after emptiness and became empty?
6 "They did not say, 'Where is the LORD
Who brought us up out of the land of Egypt,
Who led us through the wilderness,
Through a land of deserts and of pits,
Through a land of drought and of deep darkness,
Through a land that no one crossed
And where no person lived?'
7 "I brought you into the fruitful land
To eat its fruit and its good things.
But you came and defiled My land,
And you made My inheritance an abomination.
8 "The priests did not say, 'Where is the LORD?'
And those who handle the Law did not know Me;
The rulers also revolted against Me,
And the prophets prophesied by Baal
And walked after things that were of no benefit.
9¶ "Therefore I will still contend with you," declares the LORD,
"And I will contend with your sons' sons.
10 "For cross to the coastlands of Kittim and see,
And send to Kedar and observe closely,

And see if there has been *anything* like
this!

11 "Has a nation changed gods,
When they were not gods?
But My people have exchanged their glory
For that which is of no benefit.

12 "Be appalled at this, you heavens,
And shudder, be very desolate," declares
the LORD.

13 "For My people have committed two evils:
They have abandoned Me,
The fountain of living waters,
To carve out for themselves cisterns,
Broken cisterns
That do not hold water.

14¶ "Is Israel a slave? Or is he a servant born in
the home?
Why has he become plunder?

15 "The young lions have roared at him,
They have roared loudly.
And they have made his land a waste;
His cities have been destroyed, without
inhabitant.

16 "Also the men of Memphis and Tahpanhes
Have shaved your head.

17 "Have you not done this to yourself
By your abandoning the LORD your God
When He led you in the way?

18 "But now what are you doing on the road
to Egypt,
Except to drink the waters of the Nile?
Or what are you doing on the road to
Assyria,
Except to drink the waters of the
Euphrates River?

19 "Your own wickedness will correct you,
And your apostasies will punish you;
Know therefore and see that it is evil and
bitter
For you to abandon the LORD your God,
And the fear of Me is not in you,"
declares the Lord GOD of armies.

20¶ "For long ago I broke your yoke
And tore off your restraints;
But you said, 'I will not serve!'
For on every high hill
And under every leafy tree
You have lain down as a prostitute.

21 "Yet I planted you as a choice vine,
A completely faithful seed.
How then have you turned yourself before
Me
Into the degenerate shoots of a foreign
vine?

22 "Although you wash yourself with lye
And use much soap,
The stain of your guilt is before Me,"
declares the Lord GOD.

23 "How can you say, 'I am not defiled,
I have not gone after the Baals'?
Look at your way in the valley!
Know what you have done!
You are a swift young camel running
about senselessly on her ways,

24 A wild donkey accustomed to the wilder-
ness,
That sniffs the wind in her passion.
Who can turn her away *in* her mating
season?
None who seek her will grow weary;

In her month they will find her.

25 "Keep your feet from being bare,
And your throat from thirst;
But you said, 'It is hopeless!
No! For I have loved strangers,
And I will walk after them.'

26¶ "Like the shame of a thief when he is
discovered,
So the house of Israel is shamed;
They, their kings, their leaders,
Their priests, and their prophets,

27 Who say to a tree, 'You are my father,'
And to a stone, 'You gave me birth.'
For they have turned *their* backs to Me,
And not *their* faces;
But in the time of their trouble they will
say,
'Arise and save us!'

28 "But where are your gods
Which you made for yourself?
Let them arise, if they can save you
In the time of your trouble!
For *as many as* the number of your cities
Are your gods, Judah.

29¶ "Why do you contend with Me?
You have all revolted against Me,"
declares the LORD.

30 "In vain I have struck your sons;
They did not accept discipline.
Your sword has devoured your prophets
Like a destroying lion.

31 "You generation, look to the word of the
LORD.
Have I been a wilderness to Israel,
Or a land of thick darkness?
Why do My people say, 'We *are free to*
roam;
We will no longer come to You'?

32 "Can a virgin forget her jewelry,
Or a bride her attire?
Yet My people have forgotten Me
For days without number.

33 "How well you prepare your way
To seek love!
Therefore even to the wicked women
You have taught your ways.

34 "Also on your skirts is found
The lifeblood of the innocent poor;
You did not find them breaking in.
But in spite of all these things,

35 You said, 'I am innocent;
Surely His anger is turned away from me.'
Behold, I will enter into judgment with
you
Because you say, 'I have not sinned.'

36 "Why do you go around so much
Changing your way?
Also, you will be put to shame by Egypt,
Just as you were put to shame by Assyria.

37 "From this *place* as well you will go out
With your hands on your head;
For the LORD has rejected those in whom
you trust,
And you will not prosper with them."

The Defiled Land

3 *God* says, "If a husband divorces his wife
And she leaves him
And becomes another man's *wife,*
Will he return to her again?

Would that land not be completely defiled? But you are a prostitute *with* many lovers; Yet you turn to Me," declares the LORD.

2 "Raise your eyes to the bare heights and see;
Where have you not been violated?
You have sat for them by the roads
Like an Arab in the desert,
And you have defiled a land
With your prostitution and your wickedness.

3 "Therefore the showers have been withheld,
And there has been no spring rain.
Yet you had a prostitute's forehead;
You refused to be ashamed.

4 "Have you not just now called to Me,
'My Father, You are the friend of my youth?

5 'Will He be angry forever,
Or keep *His anger* to the end?'
Behold, you have spoken
And have done evil things,
And you have had your own way."

Faithless Israel

6 Then the LORD said to me in the days of King Josiah, "Have you seen what faithless Israel did? She went up on every high hill and under every leafy tree, and she prostituted herself there. 7 Yet I thought, 'After she has done all these things she will return to Me'; but she did not return, and her treacherous sister Judah saw it. 8 And I saw that for all the adulteries of faithless Israel, I had sent her away and given her a certificate of divorce, yet her treacherous sister Judah did not fear; but she went and prostituted herself also. 9 And because of the thoughtlessness of her prostitution, she defiled the land and committed adultery with stones and trees. 10 Yet in spite of all this her treacherous sister Judah did not return to Me with all her heart, but rather in deception," declares the LORD.

God Invites Repentance

11 And the LORD said to me, "Faithless Israel has proved herself to be more righteous than treacherous Judah. 12 Go and proclaim these words toward the north and say,

'Return, faithless Israel,' declares the LORD;
'I will not look at you in anger.
For I am gracious,' declares the LORD;
'I will not be angry forever.

13 'Only acknowledge your wrongdoing,
That you have revolted against the LORD your God,
And have scattered your favors to the strangers under every leafy tree,
And you have not obeyed My voice,' declares the LORD.

14 'Return, you faithless sons,' declares the LORD;
'For I am a master to you,
And I will take you, one from a city and two from a family,
And bring you to Zion.'

15 "Then I will give you shepherds after My own heart, who will feed you knowledge and understanding. 16 And it shall be in those days when you become numerous and are fruitful in the land," declares the LORD, "they will no longer say, 'The ark of the covenant of the LORD.' And it will not come to mind, nor will they remember it, nor miss *it*, nor will it be made again. 17 At that time they will call Jerusalem 'The Throne of the LORD,' and all the nations will assemble at it, at Jerusalem, for the name of the LORD; and they will no longer follow the stubbornness of their evil heart. 18 In those days the house of Judah will walk with the house of Israel, and they will come together from the land of the north to the land that I gave your fathers as an inheritance.

19 "Then I said,
'How I would set you among My sons
And give you a pleasant land,
The most beautiful inheritance of the nations!'
And I said, 'You shall call Me, My Father,
And not turn away from following Me.'

20 "However, *as* a woman treacherously leaves her lover,
So you have dealt treacherously with Me,
House of Israel," declares the LORD.

21 ¶ A voice is heard on the bare heights,
The weeping, the pleading of the sons of Israel.
Because they have perverted their way,
They have forgotten the LORD their God.

22 "Return, you faithless sons,
I will heal your faithlessness."
"Behold, we come to You;
For You are the LORD our God.

23 "Certainly the hills are a deception,
¹Commotion *on* the mountains.
Certainly in the LORD our God
Is the salvation of Israel.

24 "But the shame has consumed the product of our fathers' labor since our youth—their flocks and their herds, their sons and their daughters. 25 Let us lie down in our shame, and let our humiliation cover us; for we have sinned against the LORD our God, we and our fathers, from our youth even to this day. And we have not obeyed the voice of the LORD our God."

Judah Threatened with Invasion

4 "If you will return, Israel," declares the LORD,
"*Then* you should return to Me.
And if you will put away your detestable things from My presence,
And will not waver,

2 And *if* you will swear, 'As the LORD lives,'
In truth, in justice, and in righteousness;
Then the nations will bless themselves in Him,
And in Him they will boast."

3 For this is what the LORD says to the men of Judah and to Jerusalem:
"Break up your uncultivated ground,
And do not sow among thorns.

3:23 ¹ I.e., from idolatrous rituals

4 "Circumcise yourselves to the LORD
And remove the foreskins of your
hearts,
Men of Judah and inhabitants of
Jerusalem,
Or else My wrath will spread like fire
And burn with no one to quench it,
Because of the evil of your deeds."
5¶ Declare in Judah and proclaim in
Jerusalem, and say,
"Blow the trumpet in the land;
Cry aloud and say,
'Assemble, and let's go
Into the fortified cities.'
6 "Raise a flag toward Zion!
Take refuge, do not stand *still,*
For I am bringing evil from the north,
And great destruction.
7 "A lion has gone up from his thicket,
And a destroyer of nations has set out;
He has gone out from his place
To make your land a waste.
Your cities will be ruins,
Without an inhabitant.
8 "For this, put on sackcloth,
Mourn and wail;
For the fierce anger of the LORD
Has not turned away from us."
9 "And it shall come about on that day,"
declares the LORD, "that the heart of the king
and the hearts of the leaders will fail; and the
priests will tremble, and the prophets will be
astonished."
10 Then I said, "Oh, Lord GOD! Surely You
have utterly deceived this people and
Jerusalem, saying, 'You will have peace'; yet a
sword touches the throat."
11 At that time it will be said to this people
and to Jerusalem, "A scorching wind from the
bare heights in the wilderness, in the direction
of the daughter of My people—not to winnow
and not to cleanse, 12 a wind too strong for
this—will come at My command; now I will
also pronounce judgments against them."
13 "Behold, he goes up like clouds,
And his chariots like the whirlwind;
His horses are swifter than eagles.
Woe to us, for we are ruined!"
14¶ Wash your heart from evil, Jerusalem,
So that you may be saved.
How long will your wicked thoughts
Lodge within you?
15 For a voice declares from Dan,
And proclaims wickedness from Mount
Ephraim.
16 "Report *it* to the nations, now!
Proclaim to Jerusalem,
'¹Enemies are coming from a remote
country,
And they raise their voices against the
cities of Judah.
17 'Like watchmen of a field they are against
her all around,
Because she has rebelled against Me,'
declares the LORD.
18 "Your ways and your deeds
Have brought these things upon you.
This is your evil. How bitter!
How it has touched your heart!"

Grief over Judah's Devastation

19¶ My soul, my soul! I am in anguish! Oh,
my heart!
My heart is pounding in me;
I cannot keep silent,
Because, ¹my soul, you have heard
The sound of the trumpet,
The alarm of war.
20 Disaster upon disaster is proclaimed,
For the whole land is devastated;
Suddenly my tents are devastated,
And my curtains in an instant.
21 How long must I see the flag
And hear the sound of the trumpet?
22 "For My people are foolish,
They do not know Me;
They are foolish children
And have no understanding.
They are skillful at doing evil,
But they do not know how to do good."
23¶ I looked at the earth, and behold, *it was* a
¹formless and desolate emptiness;
And to the heavens, and they had no
light.
24 I looked on the mountains, and behold,
they were quaking,
And all the hills jolted back and forth.
25 I looked, and behold, there was no
human,
And all the birds of the sky had fled.
26 I looked, and behold, the fruitful land was
a wilderness,
And all its cities were pulled down
Before the LORD, before His fierce anger.
27¶ For this is what the LORD says:
"The whole land shall be a desolation,
Yet I will not execute a complete
destruction.
28 "For this the earth will mourn,
And the heavens above will become
dark,
Because I have spoken, I have purposed,
And I have not changed My mind, nor
will I turn from it."
29 At the sound of the horseman and archer
every city flees;
They go into the thickets and climb
among the rocks;
Every city is abandoned,
And no one lives in them.
30 And you, desolate one, what will you
do?
Although you dress in scarlet,
Although you adorn *yourself with* jewelry
of gold,
Although you enlarge your eyes with
makeup,
In vain you make yourself beautiful.
Your lovers despise you;
They seek your life.
31 For I heard a voice *cry* as of a woman in
labor,
The anguish as of one giving birth to her
first child.
The voice of the daughter of Zion gasping
for breath,
Stretching out her hands, *saying,*
"Ah, woe to me, for I faint before
murderers."

4:16 ¹As indicated in LXX; MT *watchmen* 4:19 ¹Another reading is *I have heard* 4:23 ¹Or *waste*

Jerusalem's Godlessness

5 "Roam about through the streets of Jerusalem,
And look and take notice.
And seek in her public squares,
If you can find a person,
If there is one who does justice, who seeks honesty,
Then I will forgive ¹her.

2 "And although they say, 'As the LORD lives,'
Certainly they swear falsely."

3 LORD, do Your eyes not *look* for honesty?
You have struck them,
But they did not weaken;
You have consumed them,
But they refused to accept discipline.
They have made their faces harder than rock;
They have refused to repent.

4¶ Then I said, "They are only the poor,
They are foolish;
For they do not know the way of the LORD
Or the judgment of their God.

5 "I will go to the great
And speak to them,
For they know the way of the LORD
And the judgment of their God."
But together they *too* have broken the yoke
And burst the restraints.

6 Therefore a lion from the forest will kill them,
A wolf of the deserts will destroy them,
A leopard is watching their cities.
Everyone who goes out of them will be torn in pieces,
Because their wrongdoings are many,
Their apostasies are numerous.

7¶ "Why should I forgive you?
Your sons have forsaken Me
And sworn by those who are not gods.
When I had fed them to the full,
They committed adultery
And stayed at the prostitute's house.

8 "They were well-fed lusty horses,
Each one neighing at his neighbor's wife.

9 "Shall I not punish *them* for these *things?*"
declares the LORD,
"And shall I not avenge Myself
On a nation such as this?

10¶ "Go up through her vine rows and destroy,
But do not execute a complete destruction;
Strip away her branches,
For they are not the LORD's.

11 "For the house of Israel and the house of Judah
Have dealt very treacherously with Me,"
declares the LORD.

12 They have lied about the LORD
And said, "Not He;
Misfortune will not come upon us,
Nor will we see sword or famine.

13 "The prophets are *as* wind,
And the word is not in them.
So it will be done to them!"

Judgment Proclaimed

14¶ Therefore, this is what the LORD, the God of armies says:
"Because you have spoken this word,
Behold, I am making My words fire in your mouth,
And this people wood, and it will consume them.

15 "Behold, I am bringing a nation against you from far away, you house of Israel,"
declares the LORD.
"It is an enduring nation,
It is an ancient nation,
A nation whose language you do not know,
Nor can you understand what they say.

16 "Their quiver is like an open grave,
All of them are warriors.

17 "They will devour your harvest and your food;
They will devour your sons and your daughters;
They will devour your flocks and your herds;
They will devour your vines and your fig trees;
They will demolish your fortified cities, in which you trust, with the sword.

18 "Yet even in those days," declares the LORD, "I will not make a complete destruction of you. **19** And it shall come about when they say, 'Why has the LORD our God done all these things to us?' then you shall say to them, 'Just as you have abandoned Me and served foreign gods in your land, so you will serve strangers in a land that is not yours.'

20¶ "Declare this in the house of Jacob
And proclaim it in Judah, saying,

21 'Now hear this, you foolish and senseless people,
Who have eyes but do not see,
Who have ears but do not hear.

22 'Do you not fear Me?' declares the LORD.
'Do you not tremble in My presence?
For I have placed the sand as a boundary for the sea,
An eternal limit, and it will not cross over it.
Though the waves toss, they cannot prevail;
Though they roar, they will not cross over it.

23 'But this people has a stubborn and rebellious heart;
They have turned aside and departed.

24 'They do not say in their heart,
"Let us now fear the LORD our God,
Who gives rain in its season,
Both the autumn rain and the spring rain,
Who keeps for us
The appointed weeks of the harvest."

25 'Your wrongdoings have turned these away,
And your sins have kept good away from you.

26 'For wicked people are found among My people,
They watch like fowlers lying in wait;
They set a trap,

They catch people.
27 'Like a cage full of birds,
So their houses are full of deceit;
Therefore they have become great and
rich.
28 'They are fat, they are sleek,
They also excel in deeds of wickedness;
They do not plead the cause,
The cause of the orphan, so that they may
be successful;
And they do not defend the rights of the
poor.
29 'Shall I not punish *them* for these *things?*'
declares the LORD,
'Or shall I not avenge Myself
On a nation such as this?'
30¶ "An appalling and horrible thing
Has happened in the land:
31 The prophets prophesy falsely,
And the priests rule on their *own*
authority;
And My people love it this way!
But what will you do when the end
comes?

The Coming Destruction of Jerusalem

6 "Flee to safety, you sons of Benjamin,
From the midst of Jerusalem!
Blow a trumpet in Tekoa
And raise a *warning* signal over
*¹Beth-haccerem;
For evil looks down from the north,
Along with a great destruction.
2 "The beautiful and delicate one, the
daughter of Zion, I will destroy.
3 "Shepherds and their flocks will come to
her,
They will pitch *their* tents around her,
They will pasture, each in his place.
4 'Prepare for war against her;
Arise, and let's attack at noon.
Woe to us, for the day declines,
For the shadows of the evening lengthen!
5 'Arise, and let's attack by night
And destroy her palaces!'"
6 For this is what the LORD of armies says:
"Cut down her trees
And pile up an assault ramp against
Jerusalem.
This is the city to be punished,
In whose midst there is only oppression.
7 "As a well keeps its waters fresh,
So she keeps fresh her wickedness.
Violence and destruction are heard in her;
Sickness and wounds are constantly
before Me.
8 "Be warned, Jerusalem,
Or I shall be alienated from you,
And make you a desolation,
An uninhabited land."
9¶ This is what the LORD of armies says:
"They will thoroughly glean the remnant of
Israel like the vine;
Pass your hand over the branches again
Like a grape gatherer."
10 To whom shall I speak and give warning,
That they may hear?
Behold, their ears are closed
And they cannot listen.

Behold, the word of the LORD has become
for them a rebuke;
They take no delight in it.
11 But I am full of the wrath of the LORD;
I am weary of holding *it* in.
"Pour *it* out on the children in the street
And on the gathering of young men
together;
For both husband and wife shall be taken,
The old and the very old.
12 "Their houses shall be turned over to
others,
Their fields and their wives together;
For I will stretch out My hand
Against the inhabitants of the land,"
declares the LORD.
13 "For from the least of them to the greatest
of them,
Everyone is greedy for gain,
And from the prophet to the priest
Everyone deals falsely.
14 "They have healed the brokenness of My
people superficially,
Saying, 'Peace, peace,'
But there is no peace.
15 "Were they ashamed because of the
abomination they had done?
They were not ashamed at all,
Nor did they know even how to be
ashamed.
Therefore they will fall among those who
fall;
At the time that I punish them,
They will collapse," says the LORD.
16¶ This is what the LORD says:
"Stand by the ways and see and ask for the
ancient paths,
Where the good way is, and walk in it;
Then you will find a resting place for your
souls.
But they said, 'We will not walk *in it.*'
17 "And I set watchmen over you, *saying,*
'Listen to the sound of the trumpet!'
But they said, 'We will not listen.'
18 "Therefore hear, you nations,
And know, you congregation, what is
among them.
19 "Hear, earth: behold, I am bringing disaster
on this people,
The fruit of their plans,
Because they have not listened to My
words,
And as for My Law, they have rejected it
also.
20 "For what purpose does frankincense come
to Me from Sheba,
And the sweet cane from a distant land?
Your burnt offerings are not acceptable
And your sacrifices are not pleasing to
Me."
21 Therefore, this is what the LORD says:
"Behold, I am placing stumbling blocks
before this people.
And they will stumble against them,
Fathers and sons together;
Neighbor and friend will perish."

The Enemy from the North
22¶ This is what the LORD says:

6:1 ¹I.e., house of the vineyard

"Behold, *there is* a people coming from the
 north land,
And a great nation will be stirred up from
 the remote parts of the earth.
23 "They seize bow and spear;
They are cruel and have no mercy;
Their voice roars like the sea,
And they ride on horses,
Lined up as a man for the battle
Against you, daughter of Zion!"
24 We have heard the report of it;
Our hands are limp.
Anguish has seized us,
Pain like *that of* a woman in childbirth.
25 Do not go out into the field,
And do not walk on the road;
For the enemy has a sword,
Terror is on every side.
26 Daughter of my people, put on sackcloth
And roll in ashes;
Mourn as for an only son,
A most bitter mourning.
For suddenly the destroyer
Will come against us.
27 ¶ "I have made you an assayer *and* an
 examiner among My people,
So that you may know and put their way
 to the test."
28 All of them are stubbornly rebellious,
Going about as a slanderer;
They are bronze and iron.
They are, all of them, corrupt.
29 The bellows blow fiercely,
The lead is consumed by the fire;
In vain the refining goes on,
But the wicked are not separated.
30 They call them rejected silver,
Because the LORD has rejected them.

Message at the Temple Gate

7 The word that came to Jeremiah from the
 LORD, saying, 2 "Stand at the gate of the
LORD's house and proclaim there this word,
and say, 'Hear the word of the LORD, all you of
Judah, who enter by these gates to worship the
LORD!' 3 This is what the LORD of armies, the
God of Israel says: "Amend your ways and your
deeds, and I will let you live in this place. 4 Do
not trust in deceptive words, saying, 'This
is the temple of the LORD, the temple of the
LORD, the temple of the LORD.' 5 For if you truly
amend your ways and your deeds, if you truly
practice justice between a person and his
neighbor, 6 *if* you do not oppress the stranger,
the orphan, or the widow, and do not shed
innocent blood in this place, nor follow other
gods to your own ruin, 7 then I will let you live
in this place, in the land that I gave to your
fathers forever and ever.

8 "Behold, you are trusting in deceptive
words to no avail. 9 Will you steal, murder,
commit adultery, swear falsely, offer sacrifices
to Baal, and follow other gods that you have
not known, 10 then come and stand before Me
in this house which is called by My name, and
say, 'We are saved!'—so that you may do all
these abominations? 11 Has this house, which is
called by My name, become a den of robbers in
your sight? Behold, I Myself have seen *it,*"
declares the LORD.

12 "But go now to My place which was in
Shiloh, where I made My name dwell at the
beginning, and see what I did to it because of
the wickedness of My people Israel. 13 And
now, because you have done all these things,"
declares the LORD, "and I spoke to you,
speaking again and again, but you did not
listen, and I called you but you did not answer,
14 therefore I will do to the house which is
called by My name, in which you trust, and to
the place which I gave you and your fathers,
just as I did to Shiloh. 15 I will hurl you out of
My sight, just as I have hurled out all your
brothers, all the descendants of Ephraim.

16 "As for you, do not pray for this people,
and do not lift up a cry or prayer for them,
and do not plead with Me; for I am not
listening to you. 17 Do you not see what they
are doing in the cities of Judah and in the
streets of Jerusalem? 18 The children gather
wood, the fathers kindle the fire, and the
women knead dough to make sacrificial cakes
for the queen of heaven; and *they* pour out
drink offerings to other gods in order to
provoke Me to anger. 19 Are they provoking
Me?" declares the LORD. "Is it not themselves
instead, to their own shame?" 20 Therefore this
is what the Lord GOD says: "Behold, My anger
and My wrath will be poured out on this place,
on human and animal *life,* and on the trees of
the field and the fruit of the ground; and it will
burn and not be quenched."

21 This is what the LORD of armies, the God
of Israel says: "Add your burnt offerings to your
sacrifices and eat flesh. 22 For I did not speak
to your fathers, or command them on the day
that I brought them out of the land of Egypt,
concerning burnt offerings and sacrifices. 23 But
this is what I commanded them, saying, 'Obey
My voice, and I will be your God, and you will
be My people; and you shall walk entirely in
the way which I command you, so that it may
go well for you.' 24 Yet they did not obey or
incline their ear, but walked by *their own*
advice *and* in the stubbornness of their evil
hearts, and they went backward and not forward. 25 Since the day that your fathers came
out of the land of Egypt until this day, I have
sent you all My servants the prophets, sending
them daily, again and again. 26 Yet they did not
listen to Me or incline their ear, but stiffened
their neck; they did more evil than their
fathers.

27 "So you shall speak all these words to
them, but they will not listen to you; and you
shall call to them, but they will not answer
you. 28 And you shall say to them, 'This is the
nation that did not obey the voice of the LORD
their God or accept discipline; trustworthiness
has perished and has been eliminated from
their mouth.

29 'Cut off your hair and throw *it* away,
And take up a song of mourning on the
 bare heights;
For the LORD has rejected and forsaken
The generation of His wrath.'
30 For the sons of Judah have done that which
is evil in My sight," declares the LORD. "They
have put their detestable things in the house
which is called by My name, to defile it.

31 They have built the high places of Topheth, which is in the Valley of Ben-hinnom, to burn their sons and their daughters in the fire, which I did not command, and it did not come into My mind.

32 "Therefore, behold, days are coming," declares the LORD, "when it will no longer be called Topheth, or the Valley of Ben-hinnom, but the Valley of the Slaughter; for they will bury in Topheth because there is no *other* place. **33** The dead bodies of this people will be food for the birds of the sky and for the animals of the earth; and no one will frighten *them away.* **34** Then I will eliminate from the cities of Judah and from the streets of Jerusalem the voice of joy and the voice of gladness, the voice of the groom and the voice of the bride; for the land will become a site of ruins.

The Sin and Treachery of Judah

8 "At that time," declares the LORD, "they will bring out the bones of the kings of Judah, the bones of its leaders, the bones of the priests, the bones of the prophets, and the bones of the inhabitants of Jerusalem from their graves. **2** They will spread them out to the sun, the moon, and to all the heavenly lights, which they have loved, which they have served, which they have followed, which they have sought, and which they have worshiped. They will not be gathered nor buried; they will be like dung on the face of the ground. **3** And death will be chosen rather than life by all the remnant that remains of this evil family, that remains in all the places to which I have driven them," declares the LORD of armies.

4 "You shall say to them, 'This is what the LORD says:

"Do *people* fall and not get up?
Does one turn away and not repent?
5 "Why has this people, Jerusalem,
Turned away in continual apostasy?
They hold on to deceit,
They refuse to return.
6 "I have listened and heard,
They have spoken what is not right;
No one repented of his wickedness,
Saying, 'What have I done?'
Everyone turned to his own course,
Like a horse charging into the battle.
7 "Even the stork in the sky
Knows her seasons;
And the turtledove, the swallow, and the crane
Keep to the time of their migration;
But My people do not know
The judgment of the LORD.
8¶ "How can you say, 'We are wise,
And the Law of the LORD is with us'?
But behold, the lying pen of the scribes
Has made *it* into a lie.
9 "The wise men are put to shame,
They are dismayed and caught;
Behold, they have rejected the word of the LORD,
So what *kind of* wisdom do they have?
10 "Therefore I will give their wives to others,
Their fields to *new* owners;
Because from the least even to the greatest

Everyone is greedy for gain;
From the prophet even to the priest,
Everyone practices deceit.
11 "They have healed the brokenness of the daughter of My people superficially,
Saying, 'Peace, peace,'
But there is no peace.
12 "Were they ashamed because of the abomination they had done?
They were not ashamed at all,
And they did not know how to be ashamed;
Therefore they will fall among those who fall;
At the time of their punishment they will collapse,"
Says the LORD.
13¶ "I will certainly snatch them away,"
declares the LORD.
"There will be no grapes on the vine
And no figs on the fig tree,
And the leaf will wither;
And what I have given them will pass away." ' "
14 Why are we sitting *still?*
Assemble yourselves, and let's go into the fortified cities
And perish there,
For the LORD our God has doomed us
And given us poisoned water to drink,
Because we have sinned against the LORD.
15 *We* waited for peace, but no good *came;*
For a time of healing, but behold, terror!
16 From Dan there is heard the snorting of his horses;
At the sound of the neighing of his stallions
The whole land quakes;
For they come and devour the land and its fullness,
The city and its inhabitants.
17 "For behold, I am sending serpents among you,
Vipers for which there is no charm;
And they will bite you," declares the LORD.
18¶ My sorrow is beyond healing,
My heart is faint within me!
19 Behold, listen! The cry of the daughter of my people from a distant land:
"Is the LORD not in Zion? Is her King not within her?"
"Why have they provoked Me with their carved images, with foreign idols?"
20 "Harvest is past, summer is over,
And we are not saved."
21 I am broken over the brokenness of the daughter of my people.
I mourn, dismay has taken hold of me.
22 Is there no balm in Gilead?
Is there no physician there?
Why then has not the health of the daughter of my people been restored?

Grief over Zion

9 Oh, that my head were waters
And my eyes a fountain of tears,
That I might weep day and night
For those slain of the daughter of my people!

2 Oh that I had in the desert
A travelers' lodging place;
So that I might leave my people
And go away from them!
For all of them are adulterers,
An assembly of treacherous people.
3 "They bend their tongues *like* their bows;
Lies and not truth prevail in the land;
For they proceed from evil to evil,
And they do not know Me," declares the
Lord.
4 "Let everyone be on guard against his
neighbor,
And do not trust any brother;
Because every brother utterly betrays,
And every neighbor goes about as a
slanderer.
5 "Everyone deceives his neighbor
And does not speak the truth.
They have taught their tongue to speak
lies;
They weary themselves committing
wrongdoing.
6 "Your dwelling is in the midst of deceit;
Through deceit they refuse to know Me,"
declares the Lord.
7 Therefore this is what the Lord of armies
says:
"Behold, I will refine them and put them to
the test;
For what *else* can I do, because of the
daughter of My people?
8 "Their tongue is a deadly arrow;
It speaks deceit;
With his mouth one speaks peace to his
neighbor,
But inwardly he sets an ambush for him.
9 "Shall I not punish them for these things?"
declares the Lord.
"Shall I not avenge Myself
On a nation such as this?
10¶ "I will take up a weeping and wailing for
the mountains,
And for the pastures of the wilderness a
song of mourning,
Because they are laid waste so that no one
passes through,
And the sound of the livestock is not
heard;
Both the birds of the sky and the animals
have fled; they are gone.
11 "I will make Jerusalem a heap of ruins,
A haunt of jackals;
And I will make the cities of Judah a
desolation without inhabitant."
12 Who is the wise person who may understand this? And *who is* he to whom the mouth
of the Lord has spoken, that he may declare it?
Why is the land destroyed, laid waste like the
desert, so that no one passes through? 13 The
Lord said, "Because they have abandoned My
Law which I put before them, and have not
obeyed My voice nor walked according to it,
14 but have followed the stubbornness of their
heart and the Baals, as their fathers taught
them," 15 therefore this is what the Lord of
armies, the God of Israel says: "Behold, I will
feed this people wormwood; and I will give
them poisoned water to drink. 16 I will also

scatter them among the nations, whom neither
they nor their fathers have known; and I will
send the sword after them until I have put an
end to them."
17 This is what the Lord of armies says:
"Consider and call for the mourning
women, that they may come;
And send for the 'skillful women, that
they may come!
18 "Have them hurry and take up a wailing for
us,
So that our eyes may shed tears,
And our eyelids flow with water.
19 "For a voice of wailing is heard from Zion:
'How devastated we are!
We are put to great shame,
For we have abandoned the land
Because they have torn down our
homes.'"
20 Now hear the word of the Lord, you
women,
And let your ears receive the word of His
mouth;
Teach your daughters wailing,
And *have every* woman *teach* her
neighbor a song of mourning.
21 For death has come up through our
windows;
It has entered our palaces
To eliminate the children from the streets,
The young men from the public squares.
22 Speak, "This is what the Lord says:
'The corpses of people will fall like dung
on the open field,
And like the sheaf after the reaper,
But no one will gather *them.*'"
23 This is what the Lord says: "Let no wise
man boast of his wisdom, nor let the mighty
man boast of his might, nor a rich man boast
of his riches; 24 but let the one who boasts
boast of this, that he understands and knows
Me, that I am the Lord who exercises mercy,
justice, and righteousness on the earth; for I
delight in these things," declares the Lord.
25 "Behold, the days are coming," declares
the Lord, "that I will punish all who are
circumcised and yet uncircumcised— 26 Egypt,
Judah, Edom, the sons of Ammon, Moab, and
all those inhabiting the desert who trim the
hair on their temples; for all the nations are
uncircumcised, and all the house of Israel are
uncircumcised of heart."

A Satire on Idolatry

10 Hear the word which the Lord speaks to
you, house of Israel. 2 This is what the
Lord says:
"Do not learn the way of the nations,
And do not be terrified by the signs of the
heavens,
Although the nations are terrified by
them;
3 For the customs of the peoples are futile;
For it is wood cut from the forest,
The work of the hands of a craftsman with
a cutting tool.
4 "They decorate *the idol* with silver and
gold;
They fasten it with nails and hammers

9:17 ¹ I.e., professional mourners

So that it will not totter.
5 "They are like a scarecrow in a cucumber
    field,
And they cannot speak;
They must be carried,
Because they cannot walk!
Do not fear them,
For they can do no harm,
Nor can they do any good."
6¶ There is none like You, LORD;
You are great, and Your name is great in
    might.
7 Who would not fear You, O King of the
    nations?
For it is Your due!
For among all the wise men of the nations
And in all their kingdoms,
There is none like You.
8 But they are altogether stupid and foolish;
The instruction *from* idols is *nothing but*
    wood!
9 Beaten silver is brought from Tarshish,
And gold from Uphaz,
The work of a craftsman and of the hands
    of a goldsmith;
Their clothing is of violet and purple;
They are all the work of skilled people.
10 But the LORD is the true God;
He is the living God and the everlasting
    King.
The earth quakes at His wrath,
And the nations cannot endure His
    indignation.
11 This is what you shall say to them: "The
gods that did not make the heavens and the
earth will perish from the earth and from
under these heavens."
12¶ *It is* He who made the earth by His power,
Who established the world by His
    wisdom;
And by His understanding He has
    stretched out the heavens.
13 When He utters His voice, *there is* a roar
    of waters in the heavens,
And He makes the clouds ascend from the
    end of the earth;
He makes lightning for the rain,
And brings out the wind from His
    storehouses.
14 Every person is stupid, devoid of
    knowledge;
Every goldsmith is put to shame by his
    idols,
For his cast metal images are deceitful,
And there is no breath in them.
15 They are worthless, a work of mockery;
At the time of their punishment they will
    perish.
16 The Portion of Jacob is not like these;
For He is the Maker of everything,
And Israel is the tribe of His inheritance;
The LORD of armies is His name.
17¶ Pick up your bundle from the ground,
You who live under siege!
18 For this is what the LORD says:
"Behold, I am slinging out the inhabitants
    of the land
At this time,
And I will cause them distress,
So that they may be found."

19¶ Woe to me, because of my injury!
My wound is incurable.
But I said, "This certainly is a sickness,
And I must endure it."
20 My tent is destroyed,
And all my ropes are broken.
My sons have gone from me and are no
    more.
There is no one to stretch out my tent
    again
Or to set up my curtains.
21 For the shepherds have become stupid
And have not sought the LORD.
Therefore they have not prospered,
And all their flock is scattered.
22 The sound of a report! Behold, it is
    coming—
A great roar from the land of the north—
To make the cities of Judah
A desolation, a haunt of jackals.
23¶ I know, LORD, that a person's way is not in
    himself,
Nor is it in a person who walks to direct
    his steps.
24 Correct me, LORD, but with justice;
Not with Your anger, or You will bring me
    to nothing.
25 Pour out Your wrath on the nations that
    do not know You,
And on the families who do not call upon
    Your name;
For they have devoured Jacob;
They have devoured him and consumed
    him,
And have laid waste his settlement.

The Broken Covenant

11 The word that came to Jeremiah from
the LORD, saying, 2 "Hear the words of
this covenant, and speak to the men of Judah
and to the inhabitants of Jerusalem; 3 and say to
them, 'This is what the LORD, the God of Israel
says: "Cursed is the one who does not obey the
words of this covenant 4 which I commanded
your forefathers on the day that I brought them
out of the land of Egypt, from the iron furnace,
saying, 'Listen to My voice, and do according
to all that I command you; so you shall be My
people, and I will be your God,' 5 in order to
confirm the oath which I swore to your forefathers, to give them a land flowing with milk
and honey, as *it is* this day." ' " Then I replied,
"Amen, LORD."

6 And the LORD said to me, "Proclaim all
these words in the cities of Judah and in the
streets of Jerusalem, saying, 'Hear the words of
this covenant and do them. 7 For I solemnly
warned your fathers on the day I brought them
up from the land of Egypt, even to this day,
warning *them* persistently, saying, "Listen to
My voice." 8 Yet they did not obey or incline
their ear, but walked in the stubbornness of
their evil heart, each one *of them;* therefore I
brought on them all the words of this covenant
which I commanded *them* to do, but they did
not.' "

9 Then the LORD said to me, "A conspiracy
has been found among the men of Judah and
among the inhabitants of Jerusalem. 10 They
have turned back to the wrongdoings of their

ancestors who refused to hear My words, and they have followed other gods to serve them. The house of Israel and the house of Judah have broken My covenant which I made with their fathers." 11 Therefore this is what the LORD says: "Behold, I am bringing disaster on them which they will not be able to escape; though they will cry out to Me, I will not listen to them. 12 Then the cities of Judah and the inhabitants of Jerusalem will go and cry out to the gods to whom they burn incense, but they certainly will not save them in the time of their disaster. 13 For your gods are as many as your cities, Judah; and as many as the streets of Jerusalem are the altars you have set up to the shameful thing, altars for burning incense to Baal.

14 "So as for you, do not pray for this people, nor lift up a cry or prayer for them; for I will not listen when they call to Me because of their disaster. 15 "What right has My beloved in My house When she has carried out many evil schemes? Can the sacrificial flesh take away from you your disaster, So that you can rejoice?"

16 The LORD named you "A green olive tree, beautiful in fruit and form"; With the noise of a great 1tumult He has set fire to it, And its branches are worthless. 17 The LORD of armies, who planted you, has pronounced evil against you because of the evil of the house of Israel and the house of Judah, which they have done to provoke Me by offering sacrifices to Baal.

Plots against Jeremiah

18¶ Moreover, the LORD made it known to me and I knew it; Then You showed me their deeds.

19 But I was like a gentle lamb led to the slaughter; And I did not know that they had devised plots against me, saying, "Let's destroy the tree with its fruit, And let's cut him off from the land of the living, So that his name will no longer be remembered."

20 But, LORD of armies, who judges righteously, Who puts the feelings and the heart to the test, Let me see Your vengeance on them, For to You I have committed my cause.

21 Therefore this is what the LORD says concerning the people of Anathoth, who are seeking your life, saying: "Do not prophesy in the name of the LORD, so that you do not die by our hand"; 22 therefore, this is what the LORD of armies says: "Behold, I am going to punish them! The young men will die by the sword, their sons and daughters will die by famine; 23 and a remnant will not be left to them, because I will bring disaster on the people of Anathoth—the year of their punishment."

Jeremiah's Prayer

12 Righteous are You, LORD, when I plead my case with You; Nevertheless I would discuss matters of justice with You: Why has the way of the wicked prospered? Why are all those who deal in treachery at ease?

2 You have planted them, they have also taken root; They grow, they have also produced fruit. You are near to their lips But far from their mind.

3 But You know me, LORD; You see me And examine my heart's attitude toward You. Drag them off like sheep for the slaughter, And set them apart for a day of slaughter!

4 How long is the land to mourn, And the vegetation of the countryside to dry up? Due to the wickedness of those who live in it, Animals and birds have been snatched away, Because people have said, "He will not see our final end."

5¶ "If you have run with infantrymen and they have tired you out, How can you compete with horses? If you fall down in a land of peace, How will you do in the thicket by the Jordan?

6 "For even your brothers and the household of your father, Even they have dealt treacherously with you, Even they have called aloud after you. Do not believe them, though they say nice things to you."

God's Answer

7¶ "I have forsaken My house, I have abandoned My inheritance; I have handed the beloved of My soul Over to her enemies.

8 "My inheritance has become to Me Like a lion in the forest; She has roared against Me; Therefore I have come to hate her.

9 "Is My inheritance like a speckled bird of prey to Me? Are the birds of prey against her on every side? Go, gather all the animals of the field, Bring them to devour!

10 "Many shepherds have ruined My vineyard, They have trampled down My field; They have made My pleasant field A desolate wilderness.

11 "It has been made a desolation; Desolate, it mourns before Me; The whole land has been made desolate, Because no one takes it to heart.

12 "On all the bare heights in the wilderness Destroyers have come,

---

11:16 1 I.e., confused noise

For the sword of the LORD is devouring
From one end of the land even to the other;
There is no peace for anyone.
13 "They have sown wheat but have harvested thorns,
They have strained themselves to no profit.
So be ashamed of your produce
Because of the fierce anger of the LORD."
14 This is what the LORD says concerning all My wicked neighbors who do harm to the inheritance with which I have endowed My people Israel: "Behold, I am going to drive them out of their land, and I will drive the house of Judah out from among them. 15 And it will come about that after I have driven them out, I will again have compassion on them; and I will bring them back, each one to his inheritance and each one to his land. 16 Then, if they will really learn the ways of My people, to swear by My name, 'As the LORD lives,' just as they taught My people to swear by Baal, they will be built up in the midst of My people. 17 But if they do not listen, then I will drive out that nation, drive it out and destroy it," declares the LORD.

The Ruined Undergarment

13 This is what the LORD said to me: "Go and buy yourself a linen undergarment and put it around your waist, but do not put it in water." 2 So I bought the undergarment in accordance with the word of the LORD, and put it around my waist. 3 Then the word of the LORD came to me a second time, saying, 4 "Take the undergarment that you bought, which is around your waist, and arise, go to the Euphrates and hide it there in a crevice of the rock." 5 So I went and hid it by the Euphrates, as the LORD had commanded me. 6 After many days the LORD said to me, "Arise, go to the Euphrates and take from there the undergarment which I commanded you to hide there." 7 Then I went to the Euphrates and dug, and I took the undergarment from the place where I had hidden it; and behold, the undergarment was ruined, it was completely useless.

8 Then the word of the LORD came to me, saying, 9 "This is what the LORD says: 'To the same extent I will destroy the pride of Judah and the great pride of Jerusalem. 10 This wicked people, who refuse to listen to My words, who walk in the stubbornness of their hearts and have followed other gods to serve them and to bow down to them, let them be just like this undergarment which is completely useless. 11 For as the undergarment clings to the waist of a man, so I made the entire household of Israel and the entire household of Judah cling to Me,' declares the LORD, 'so that they might be My people, for renown, for praise, and for glory; but they did not listen.'

Captivity Threatened

12 "Therefore you are to speak this word to them. 'This is what the LORD, the God of Israel says: "Every jug is to be filled with wine." ' And when they say to you, 'Do we not very well know that every jug is to be filled with wine?' 13 then say to them, 'This is what the LORD says: "Behold, I am going to fill all the inhabitants of this land—the kings who sit for David on his throne, the priests, the prophets, and all the inhabitants of Jerusalem—with drunkenness! 14 Then I will smash them against each other, both the fathers and the sons together," declares the LORD. "I will not have compassion nor be troubled nor take pity so as to keep from destroying them." ' "

15¶ Listen and pay attention, do not be haughty;
For the LORD has spoken.
16 Give glory to the LORD your God
Before He brings darkness
And before your feet stumble
On the mountains in the dark,
And while you are hoping for light
He makes it into gloom,
And turns it into thick darkness.
17 But if you do not listen to it,
My soul will weep in secret for such pride;
And my eyes will shed
And stream down tears,
Because the flock of the LORD has been taken captive.
18 Say to the king and the queen mother,
"Take a lowly seat,
For your beautiful crown
Has come down from your head."
19 The cities of the Negev have been locked up,
And there is no one to open them;
All Judah has been taken into exile,
Wholly taken into exile.
20¶ "Raise your eyes and see
Those coming from the north.
Where is the flock that was given you,
Your beautiful sheep?
21 "What will you say when He appoints over you—
And you yourself had taught them—
Former companions to be head over you?
Will sharp pains not take hold of you
Like a woman in childbirth?
22 "If you say in your heart,
'Why have these things happened to me?'
Because of the magnitude of your wrongdoing
Your skirts have been removed
And your ¹heels have suffered violence.
23 "Can the Ethiopian change his skin,
Or the leopard his spots?
Then you as well can do good
Who are accustomed to doing evil.
24 "Therefore I will scatter them like drifting straw
To the desert wind.
25 "This is your lot, the portion measured to you
From Me," declares the LORD,
"Because you have forgotten Me
And trusted in falsehood.
26 "So I Myself have stripped your skirts off over your face,
So that your shame will be seen.

13:22 ¹ I.e., a euphemism for private parts

27 "As for your adulteries and your *lustful*
  neighings,
  The outrageous sin of your prostitution
  On the hills in the field,
  I have seen your abominations.
  Woe to you, Jerusalem!
  How long will you remain unclean?"

Drought and a Prayer for Mercy

14 That which came as the word of the
  Lord to Jeremiah regarding the drought:
2 "Judah mourns
  And her gates languish;
  Her people sit on the ground in mourning
  garments,
  And the cry of Jerusalem has ascended.
3 "Their nobles have sent their servants for
  water;
  They have come to the cisterns and found
  no water.
  They have returned with their containers
  empty;
  They have been put to shame and
  humiliated,
  And they cover their heads,
4 Because the ground is cracked,
  For there has been no rain on the
  land.
  The farmers have been put to shame,
  They have covered their heads.
5 "For even the doe in the field has given
  birth only to abandon *her young,*
  Because there is no grass.
6 "The wild donkeys stand on the bare
  heights;
  They pant for air like jackals,
  Their eyes fail
  Because there is no vegetation.
7 "Though our wrongdoings testify against
  us,
  Lord, act for the sake of Your name!
  Our apostasies have indeed been many,
  We have sinned against You.
8 "Hope of Israel,
  Its Savior in time of distress,
  Why are You like a stranger in the land,
  Or like a traveler who has pitched *his tent*
  for the night?
9 "Why are You like a confused person,
  Like a warrior who cannot save?
  Yet You are in our midst, Lord,
  And we are called by Your name;
  Do not leave us!"

10 This is what the Lord says to this people:
"So much they have loved to wander; they
have not restrained their feet. Therefore the
Lord does not accept them; now He will
remember their wrongdoing and call their sins
to account." 11 So the Lord said to me, "Do
not pray for a good outcome on behalf of this
people. 12 When they fast, I am not going to
listen to their cry; and when they offer burnt
offering and grain offering, I am not going to
accept them. Rather, I am going to put an end
to them by the sword, famine, and plague."

False Prophets

13 But I said, "Oh, Lord God! Behold, the
prophets are telling them, 'You will not see
a sword, nor will you have famine; on the
contrary, I will give you lasting peace in this
place.' " 14 Then the Lord said to me, "The
prophets are prophesying falsehood in
My name. I have neither sent them nor
commanded them, nor spoken to them;
they are prophesying to you a false vision,
divination, futility, and the deception of their
own minds. 15 Therefore this is what the
Lord says concerning the prophets who are
prophesying in My name, although it was not
I who sent them—yet they keep saying: 'There
will be no sword or famine in this land'—by
sword and famine those prophets shall meet
their end! 16 And the people to whom they
are prophesying will be thrown out into the
streets of Jerusalem because of the famine and
the sword; and there will be no one to bury
them—*neither* them, *nor* their wives, nor
their sons, nor their daughters. For I will
pour out their *own* wickedness upon them.
17 "You will say this word to them,
  'Let my eyes stream down tears night and
  day,
  And let them not cease;
  For the virgin daughter of my people has
  been crushed with a mighty blow,
  With a sorely infected wound.
18 'If I go out to the country,
  There are those killed by the sword!
  Or if I enter the city,
  There are diseases from famine!
  For both prophet and priest
  Have wandered around in the land that
  they do not know.' "
19¶ Have You completely rejected Judah?
  Or have You loathed Zion?
  Why have You stricken us so that we are
  beyond healing?
  We waited for peace, but nothing good
  came;
  And for a time of healing, but behold,
  terror!
20 We know our wickedness, Lord,
  The wrongdoing of our fathers, for we
  have sinned against You.
21 Do not despise *us,* for the sake of Your
  own name;
  Do not disgrace the throne of Your glory.
  Remember *and* do not annul Your
  covenant with us.
22 Are there any among the idols of the
  nations who give rain?
  Or can the heavens grant showers?
  Is it not You, Lord our God?
  Therefore we wait for You,
  For You are the one who has done all
  these things.

Judgment Must Come

15 Then the Lord said to me, "*Even* if
  Moses and Samuel were to stand before
Me, My heart would not be with this people.
Send them away from My presence and have
them go! 2 And it shall be that when they say to
you, 'Where should we go?' then you are to tell
them, 'This is what the Lord says:
  "Those *destined* for death, to death;
  And those *destined* for the sword, to the
  sword;
  And those *destined* for famine, to famine;

And those *destined* for captivity, to captivity."'

3 And I will appoint over them four kinds *of doom,*" declares the LORD: "the sword to kill, the dogs to drag away, and the birds of the sky and the animals of the earth to devour and destroy. 4 I will make them an object of terror among all the kingdoms of the earth because of Manasseh, the son of Hezekiah, the king of Judah, for what he did in Jerusalem.

5 ¶ "Indeed, who will have pity on you,
Jerusalem,
Or who will mourn for you,
Or who will turn aside to ask about your welfare?
6 "You who have forsaken Me," declares the LORD,
"You keep going backward.
So I will stretch out My hand against you and destroy you;
I am tired of relenting!
7 "I will winnow them with a winnowing fork
At the gates of the land;
I will bereave *them* of children, I will destroy My people;
They did not repent of their ways.
8 "Their widows will be more numerous before Me
Than the sand of the seas;
I will bring against them, against the mother of a young man,
A destroyer at noon;
I will suddenly bring down on her
Shock and horror.
9 "She who gave birth to seven *sons* withers away;
Her breathing is labored.
Her sun has set while it was still day;
She has been shamed and humiliated.
So I will turn over their survivors to the sword
Before their enemies," declares the LORD.
10 ¶ Woe to me, my mother, that you have given birth to me
As a man of strife and a man of contention to all the land!
I have not lent, nor have people lent money to me,
Yet everyone curses me.
11 The LORD said, "I will certainly set you free for *purposes of* good;
I will certainly make the enemy plead with you
In a time of disaster and a time of distress.
12 ¶ "Can *anyone* smash iron,
Iron from the north, or bronze?
13 "I will give your wealth and your treasures
As plunder without cost,
For all your sins
And within all your borders.
14 "Then I will make your enemies bring *your possessions*
Into a land *that* you do not know;
For a fire has been kindled in My anger,
And it will burn upon you."

Jeremiah's Prayer and God's Answer

15 ¶ You know, LORD;
Remember me, take notice of me,
And take vengeance for me on my persecutors.
Do not, in view of Your patience, take me away;
Know that for Your sake I endure reproach.
16 Your words were found and I ate them,
And Your words became a joy to me and the delight of my heart;
For I have been called by Your name,
LORD God of armies.
17 I did not sit in a circle of revelers and celebrate.
Because of Your hand *upon me* I sat alone,
For You filled me with indignation.
18 Why has my pain been endless
And my wound incurable, refusing to be healed?
Will You indeed be to me like a deceptive *stream*
With water that is unreliable?
19 ¶ Therefore, this is what the LORD says:
"If you return, then I will restore you—
You will stand before Me;
And if you extract the precious from the worthless,
You will become My spokesman.
They, for their part, may turn to you,
But as for you, you are not to turn to them.
20 "Then I will make you to this people
A fortified wall of bronze;
And though they fight against you,
They will not prevail over you;
For I am with you to save you
And rescue you," declares the LORD.
21 "So I will rescue you from the hand of the wicked,
And I will redeem you from the grasp of the violent."

Distresses Foretold

16 The word of the LORD also came to me, saying, 2 "You shall not take a wife for yourself nor have sons or daughters in this place." 3 For this is what the LORD says concerning the sons and daughters born in this place, and concerning their mothers who give birth to them, and their fathers who father them in this land: 4 "They will die of deadly diseases, they will not be mourned or buried; they will be like dung on the surface of the ground. And they will perish by sword and famine, and their dead bodies will become food for the birds of the sky and for the animals of the earth."

5 For this is what the LORD says: "Do not enter a house of mourning, or go to mourn or to console them; for I have withdrawn My peace from this people," declares the LORD, "*and My* favor and compassion. 6 Both great people and small will die in this land; they will not be buried, *people* will not mourn for them, nor will anyone make cuts on himself or have his head shaved for them. 7 *People* will not break *bread* in mourning for them, to comfort anyone for the dead, nor give them a cup of consolation to drink for anyone's father or mother. 8 Moreover, you shall not go into a house of feasting to sit with them to eat and

drink." **9** For this is what the LORD of armies, the God of Israel says: "Behold, I am going to eliminate from this place, before your eyes and in your time, the voice of rejoicing and the voice of joy, the voice of the groom and the voice of the bride.

10 "Now it will happen that, when you tell this people all these words, they will say to you, 'For what reason has the LORD declared all this great disaster against us? And what is our wrongdoing, or what is our sin that we have committed against the LORD our God?' **11** Then you are to say to them, '*It is* because your forefathers have abandoned Me,' declares the LORD, 'and have followed other gods, and served and worshiped them; but they have abandoned Me and have not kept My Law. **12** You too have done evil, *even* more than your forefathers; for behold, each one of you is following the stubbornness of his own evil heart, without listening to Me. **13** So I will hurl you off this land to the land which you have not known, *neither* you nor your fathers; and there you will serve other gods day and night, because I will show you no compassion.'

God Will Restore Them

14 "Therefore behold, days are coming," declares the LORD, "when it will no longer be said, 'As the LORD lives, who brought up the sons of Israel out of the land of Egypt,' **15** but, 'As the LORD lives, who brought up the sons of Israel from the land of the north and from all the lands where He had banished them.' For I will restore them to their own land which I gave to their fathers.

16 "Behold, I am going to send for many fishermen," declares the LORD, "and they will fish for them; and afterward I will send for many hunters, and they will hunt them from every mountain and every hill and from the clefts of the rocks. **17** For My eyes are on all their ways; they are not hidden from My face, nor is their wrongdoing concealed from My eyes. **18** I will first repay them double for their wrongdoing and their sin, because they have defiled My land; they have filled My inheritance with the carcasses of their detestable idols and their abominations."

19¶ LORD, my strength and my stronghold,
And my refuge in the day of distress,
To You the nations will come
From the ends of the earth and say,
"Our fathers have inherited nothing but
  falsehood,
Futility, and things of no benefit."
20 Can a person make gods for himself?
But they are not gods!
21¶ "Therefore behold, I am going to make
  them know—
This time I will make them know
My power and My might;
And they will know that My name is the
  LORD."

The Deceitful Heart

17 The sin of Judah is written with an iron stylus;

With a diamond point it is engraved on
  the tablet of their hearts
And on the horns of their altars,
2 As they remember their children,
So they *remember* their altars and
  their ¹Asherim
By green trees on the high hills.
3 Mountain of Mine in the countryside,
I will turn over your wealth and all your
  treasures as plunder,
Your high places for sin throughout your
  borders.
4 And you will, even of yourself, let go of
  your inheritance
That I gave you;
And I will make you serve your enemies
In the land which you do not know;
For you have kindled a fire in My anger
Which will burn forever.
5¶ This is what the LORD says:
"Cursed is the man who trusts in mankind
And makes flesh his strength,
And whose heart turns away from the
  LORD.
6 "For he will be like a bush in the desert,
And will not see when prosperity comes,
But will live in stony wastes in the
  wilderness,
A land of salt that is not inhabited.
7 "Blessed is the man who trusts in the LORD,
And whose trust is the LORD.
8 "For he will be like a tree planted by the
  water
That extends its roots by a stream,
And does not fear when the heat comes;
But its leaves will be green,
And it will not be anxious in a year of
  drought,
Nor cease to yield fruit.
9¶ "The heart is more deceitful than all else
And is desperately sick;
Who can understand it?
10 "I, the LORD, search the heart,
I test the mind,
To give to each person according to his
  ways,
According to the results of his deeds.
11 "As a partridge that hatches eggs which it
  has not laid,
So is a person who makes a fortune, but
  unjustly;
In the middle of his days it will abandon
  him,
And in the end he will be a fool."
12¶ A glorious throne on high from the
  beginning
Is the place of our sanctuary.
13 LORD, the hope of Israel,
All who abandon You will be put to
  shame.
Those who turn away on earth will be
  written down,
Because they have forsaken the fountain
  of living water, *that is* the LORD.
14 Heal me, LORD, and I will be healed;
Save me and I will be saved,
For You are my praise.
15 Look, they keep saying to me,
"Where is the word of the LORD?

17:2 ¹ I.e., wooden symbols of a female deity (Asherah)

Let it come now!"
16 But as for me, I have not hurried away
from *being* a shepherd *following* after
You,.
Nor have I longed for the disastrous day;
You Yourself know that the utterance of
my lips
Was in Your presence.
17 Do not be a terror to me;
You are my refuge in a day of disaster.
18 Let those who persecute me be put to
shame, but as for me, let me not be put
to shame;
Let them be dismayed, but let me not be
dismayed.
Bring on them a day of disaster,
And crush them with double destruction!

The Sabbath Must Be Kept

19 This is what the LORD said to me: "Go and
stand at the public gate, through which the
kings of Judah come in and go out, as well as at
all the gates of Jerusalem; 20 and say to them,
'Listen to the word of the LORD, you kings of
Judah, and all Judah, and all inhabitants of
Jerusalem who come in through these gates.
21 This is what the LORD says: "Take care for
yourselves, and do not carry *any* load on the
Sabbath day or bring *anything* in through the
gates of Jerusalem. 22 You shall not bring a load
out of your houses on the Sabbath day nor do
any work, but keep the Sabbath day holy, just
as I commanded your forefathers. 23 Yet they
did not listen or incline their ears, but stiffened
their necks so as not to listen or accept discipline.
24 "But it will come about, if you give your
attention to Me," declares the LORD, "to bring
no load in through the gates of this city on the
Sabbath day, but to keep the Sabbath day holy
by doing no work on it, 25 then they will come
in through the gates of this city kings and
officials sitting on the throne of David, riding
in chariots and on horses, they and their
officials, the men of Judah and the inhabitants
of Jerusalem, and this city will be inhabited
forever. 26 They will come in from the cities
of Judah and from the areas surrounding
Jerusalem, from the land of Benjamin, from the
lowland, from the hill country, and from the
Negev, bringing burnt offerings, sacrifices,
grain offerings, and frankincense, and bringing
sacrifices of thanksgiving to the house of the
LORD. 27 But if you do not listen to Me, to keep
the Sabbath day holy by not carrying a load and
coming in through the gates of Jerusalem on
the Sabbath day, then I will set fire to its gates,
and it will devour the palaces of Jerusalem and
not go out." ' "

The Potter and the Clay

18 The word that came to Jeremiah from
the LORD, saying, 2 "Arise and go down to
the potter's house, and there I will announce
My words to you." 3 So I went down to the
potter's house, and there he was, making
something on the wheel. 4 But the vessel that
he was making of clay was spoiled in the hand
of the potter; so he remade it into another
vessel, as it pleased the potter to make.

5 Then the word of the LORD came to me,
saying, 6 "Am I not able, house of Israel, to deal
with you as this potter *does?*" declares the
LORD. "Behold, like the clay in the potter's
hand, so are you in My hand, house of Israel.
7 At one moment I might speak concerning a
nation or concerning a kingdom to uproot *it,* to
tear *it* down, or to destroy *it;* 8 if that nation
against which I have spoken turns from its evil,
I will relent of the disaster that I planned to
bring on it. 9 Or at *another* moment I might
speak concerning a nation or concerning a
kingdom to build up or to plant *it;* 10 if it does
evil in My sight by not obeying My voice, then
I will relent of the good with which I said that I
would bless it. 11 So now, speak to the men of
Judah and against the inhabitants of Jerusalem,
saying, 'This is what the LORD says: "Behold, I
am forming a disaster against you and devising
a plan against you. Now turn back, each of you
from his evil way, and correct your ways and
your deeds!" ' 12 But they will say, 'It's hopeless!
For we are going to follow our own plans, and
each of us will persist in the stubbornness of
his evil heart.'
13¶ "Therefore this is what the LORD says:
'Just ask among the nations,
Who *ever* heard *anything* like this?
The virgin of Israel
Has done a most appalling thing.
14 'Does the snow of Lebanon leave the rock
of the open country alone?
Or is the cold flowing water *from* a
foreign *land* ever dried up?
15 'For My people have forgotten Me,
They burn incense to worthless *gods.*
And they have stumbled in their ways,
In the ancient roads,
To walk on paths,
Not on a highway,
16 To make their land a desolation,
An object of perpetual hissing;
Everyone who passes by it will be
astonished
And shake his head.
17 'Like an east wind I will scatter them
Before the enemy;
I will show them My back and not *My*
face
In the day of their disaster.' "
18 Then they said, "Come and let's devise
plans against Jeremiah. Certainly the Law is
not going to be lost by the priest, nor advice by
the wise, nor *the divine* word by the prophet!
Come, and let's strike at him with *our* tongue,
and let's pay no attention to any of his words."
19¶ Give *Your* attention to me, LORD,
And listen to what my opponents are
saying!
20 Should good be repaid with evil?
For they have dug a pit for me.
Remember how I stood before You
To speak good in their behalf,
So as to turn Your wrath away from them.
21 Therefore, give their children over to
famine
And turn them over to the power of the
sword;
And let their wives become childless and
widowed.

Let their men also be slaughtered to
    death,
Their young men struck and killed by the
    sword in battle.
22 May a cry be heard from their houses
When You suddenly bring raiders upon
    them;
For they have dug a pit to capture me
And hidden snares for my feet.
23 But You, LORD, know
All their deadly schemes against me;
Do not forgive their wrongdoing
Or wipe out their sin from Your sight.
But may they be overthrown before You;
Deal with them in the time of Your
    anger!

The Broken Jar

19 This is what the LORD says: "Go and buy a potter's earthenware jar, and *take* some of the elders of the people and some of the senior priests. 2 Then go out to the Valley of Ben-hinnom, which is by the entrance of the ʹPotsherd Gate, and proclaim there the words that I tell you, 3 and say, 'Hear the word of the LORD, you kings of Judah and inhabitants of Jerusalem. This is what the LORD of armies, the God of Israel says: "Behold I am going to bring a disaster upon this place, at which the ears of everyone that hears of it will tingle. 4 Since they have abandoned Me and have made this place foreign, and have burned sacrifices in it to other gods that neither they nor their forefathers nor the kings of Judah had *ever* known, and *since* they have filled this place with the blood of the innocent 5 and have built the high places of Baal to burn their sons in the fire as burnt offerings to Baal, a *thing* which I did not command nor speak of, nor did it *ever* enter My mind; 6 therefore, behold, days are coming," declares the LORD, "when this place will no longer be called Topheth or the Valley of Ben-hinnom, but rather the Valley of Slaughter. 7 And I will frustrate the planning of Judah and Jerusalem in this place, and I will make them fall by the sword before their enemies and by the hand of those who seek their life; and I will make their carcasses food for the birds of the sky and the animals of the earth. 8 I will also turn this city into an object of horror and hissing; everyone who passes by it will be appalled and hiss because of all its disasters. 9 And I will make them eat the flesh of their sons and the flesh of their daughters, and they will eat one another's flesh during the siege and in the hardship with which their enemies and those who seek their life will torment them." '

10 "Then you are to break the jar in the sight of the men who accompany you, 11 and say to them, 'This is what the LORD of armies says: "To the same extent I will break this people and this city, just as one breaks a potter's vessel, which cannot again be repaired; and they will bury *their dead* in Topheth, because there is no *other* place for burial. 12 This is how I will treat this place and its inhabitants," declares the LORD, "so as to make this city like Topheth. 13 The houses of Jerusalem and the

houses of the kings of Judah will be defiled like the place Topheth, because of all the houses on whose rooftops they burned sacrifices to all the heavenly ʹlights and poured out drink offerings to other gods." ' "

14 Then Jeremiah came from Topheth, where the LORD had sent him to prophesy; and he stood in the courtyard of the LORD's house and said to all the people, 15 "This is what the LORD of armies, the God of Israel says: 'Behold, I am going to bring on this city and all its towns the entire disaster that I have declared against it, because they have stiffened their necks so as not to listen to My words.' "

Pashhur Persecutes Jeremiah

20 When Pashhur the priest, the son of Immer, who was chief overseer in the house of the LORD, heard Jeremiah prophesying these things, 2 Pashhur had Jeremiah the prophet beaten and put him in the stocks that were at the upper Benjamin Gate, which was by the house of the LORD. 3 Then on the next day, when Pashhur released Jeremiah from the stocks, Jeremiah said to him, "Pashhur is not the name the LORD has called you, but rather ʹMagor-missabib. 4 For this is what the LORD says: 'Behold, I am going to make you a horror to yourself and to all your friends; and while your eyes look on, they will fall by the sword of their enemies. So I will hand all Judah over to the king of Babylon, and he will take them away as exiles to Babylon and will kill them with the sword. 5 I will also give all the wealth of this city, all its produce and all its valuable things—even all the treasures of the kings of Judah I will hand over to their enemies, and they will plunder them, take them away, and bring them to Babylon. 6 And you, Pashhur, and all who live in your house will go into captivity; and you will enter Babylon, and there you will die and there you will be buried, you and all your friends to whom you have falsely prophesied.' "

Jeremiah's Complaint

7 ¶ LORD, You persuaded me and I let myself
        be persuaded;
You have overcome me and prevailed.
I have become a laughingstock all day
        long;
Everyone mocks me.
8   For each time I speak, I cry aloud;
I proclaim violence and destruction,
Because for me the word of the LORD has
        resulted
In taunting and derision all day long.
9   But *if* I say, "I will not remember Him
Nor speak anymore in His name,"
Then in my heart it becomes like a
        burning fire
Shut up in my bones;
And I am tired of holding *it* in,
And I cannot endure *it*.
10   For I have heard the whispering of many,
"Terror on every side!
Denounce *him*; let's denounce him!"
All my trusted friends,
Watching for my fall, say:

19:2 ¹ I.e., pottery fragment   **19:13** ¹ Lit *host;* i.e., sun, stars, etc.   **20:3** ¹ I.e., horror on every side

"Perhaps he will be persuaded, so that we
may prevail against him
And take our revenge on him."
11 But the LORD is with me like a powerful
champion;
Therefore my persecutors will stumble
and not prevail.
They will be put to great shame because
they have failed,
An everlasting disgrace that will not be
forgotten.
12 Yet, LORD of armies, who tests the
righteous,
Who sees the mind and the heart;
Let me see Your vengeance on them,
For to You I have disclosed my cause.
13 Sing to the LORD, praise the LORD!
For He has saved the soul of the needy
one
From the hand of evildoers.
14¶ Cursed be the day when I was born;
May the day when my mother gave birth
to me not be blessed!
15 Cursed be the man who brought the news
To my father, saying,
"A boy has been born to you!"
And made him very happy.
16 But may that man be like the cities
Which the LORD overthrew without
relenting,
And may he hear an outcry in the
morning
And an alarm for war at noon;
17 Because he did not kill me before birth,
So that my mother would have been my
grave,
And her womb forever pregnant.
18 Why did I ever come out of the womb
To look at trouble and sorrow,
So that my days have been spent in
shame?

Jeremiah's Message for Zedekiah

21 The word that came to Jeremiah from
the LORD when King Zedekiah sent
to him Pashhur the son of Malchijah and
Zephaniah the priest, the son of Maaseiah,
saying, 2 "Please inquire of the LORD in our
behalf, because Nebuchadnezzar king of
Babylon is making war against us; perhaps the
LORD will deal with us in accordance with all
His wonderful acts, so that *the enemy* will
withdraw from us."
3 But Jeremiah said to them, "You shall say
to Zedekiah as follows: 4 'This is what the LORD,
the God of Israel says: "Behold, I am going to
turn back the weapons of war that are in your
hands, with which you are making war against
the king of Babylon and the Chaldeans who
are besieging you outside the wall; and I will
gather them into the middle of this city. 5 And I
Myself will make war against you with an outstretched hand and a mighty arm, and in anger,
wrath, and great indignation. 6 I will also strike
the inhabitants of this city, both the people and
the animals; they will die of a great plague.
7 Then afterward," declares the LORD, "I will
hand Zedekiah king of Judah, his servants, and
the people, that is, those who survive in this
city from the plague, the sword, and the

famine, over to Nebuchadnezzar king of
Babylon, to their enemies, and to those who
seek their lives; and he will strike and kill
them with the edge of the sword. He will not
spare them nor have pity nor compassion." '
8 "You shall also say to this people, 'This is
what the LORD says: "Behold, I am setting
before you the way of life and the way of
death. 9 *Anyone* who stays in this city will die
by the sword, by famine, or by plague; but
anyone who leaves and goes over to the
Chaldeans who are besieging you will live,
and he will have his own life as plunder. 10 For
I have set My face against this city for harm
and not for good," declares the LORD. "It will
be handed over to the king of Babylon and he
will burn it with fire." '
11 "Then *say* to the household of the king of
Judah, 'Hear the word of the LORD, 12 house of
David, this is what the LORD says:
"Administer justice every morning;
And save the *person* who has been
robbed from the power of *his*
oppressor,
So that My wrath will not spread like
fire
And burn, with no one to extinguish *it*,
Because of the evil of their deeds.
13¶ "Behold, I am against you, you inhabitant
of the valley,
You rocky plain," declares the LORD,
"You who say, 'Who will come down
against us?
Or who will enter our dwellings?'
14 "But I will punish you according to the
results of your deeds," declares the
LORD,
"And I will kindle a fire in its forest
So that it may devour all its
surroundings." ' "

Warning of Jerusalem's Fall

22 This is what the LORD says: "Go down to
the house of the king of Judah and there
speak this word, 2 and say, 'Hear the word of
the LORD, O king of Judah, who sits on David's
throne, you and your servants and your people
who enter these gates. 3 This is what the LORD
says: "Do justice and righteousness, and save
one who has been robbed from the power
of *his* oppressor. And do not mistreat *or* do
violence to the stranger, the orphan, or the
widow; and do not shed innocent blood in this
place. 4 For if you will indeed perform this
instruction, then kings will enter the gates
of this house, sitting in David's place on his
throne, riding in chariots and on horses, *the
king* himself, his servants, and his people. 5 But
if you will not obey these words, I swear by
Myself," declares the LORD, "that this house
will become a place of ruins." ' " 6 For this is
what the LORD says concerning the house of
the king of Judah:
"You are *like* Gilead to Me,
Like the summit of Lebanon;
Yet most assuredly I will make you a
wilderness,
Cities that are not inhabited.
7 "For I will set apart destroyers against you,
Each with his weapons;

And they will cut down your choicest
cedars
And throw *them* on the fire.
8 "Many nations will pass by this city; and
they will say to one another, 'Why has the
LORD done this to this great city?' 9 Then they
will answer, 'Because they abandoned the
covenant of the LORD their God and bowed
down to other gods and served them.'"
10¶ Do not weep for the dead or mourn for
him,
But weep deeply for the one who goes
away;
For he will never return
Or see his native land.
11 For this is what the LORD says regarding
Shallum the son of Josiah, king of Judah, who
became king in the place of his father Josiah,
who went out from this place: "He will never
return there; 12 but in the place where they
took him into exile, there he will die and he
will not see this land again.

Messages about the Kings

13¶ "Woe to him who builds his house without
righteousness,
And his upstairs rooms without justice,
Who uses his neighbor's services without
pay
And does not give him his wages,
14 Who says, 'I will build myself a large
house
With spacious upstairs rooms,
And cut out its windows,
Paneling *it* with cedar and painting *it*
bright red.'
15 "Do you become a king because you are
competing in cedar?
Did your father not eat and drink
And do justice and righteousness?
Then it was well for him.
16 "He pled the cause of the afflicted and the
poor,
Then it was well.
Is that not *what it means* to know Me?"
Declares the LORD.
17 "But your eyes and your heart
Are *intent* only upon your own dishonest
gain,
And on shedding innocent blood,
And on practicing oppression and
extortion."
18 Therefore this is what the LORD says
regarding Jehoiakim the son of Josiah, king of
Judah:
"They will not mourn for him:
'Oh, my brother!' or, 'Oh, sister!'
They will not mourn for him:
'Oh, for the master!' or, 'Oh, for his
splendor!'
19 "He will be buried with a donkey's burial,
Dragged off and thrown out beyond the
gates of Jerusalem.
20 "Go up to Lebanon and cry out,
And raise your voice in Bashan;
Cry out also from Abarim,
For all your lovers have been crushed.
21 "I spoke to you in your prosperity;
But you said, 'I will not listen!'

This has been your way from your youth,
That you have not obeyed My voice.
22 "The wind will sweep away all your
shepherds,
And your lovers will go into captivity;
Then you will certainly be ashamed and
humiliated
Because of all your wickedness.
23 "You who live in Lebanon,
Nested in the cedars,
How you will groan when sharp pains
come on you,
Pain like a woman in childbirth!
24 "As I live," declares the LORD, "even
if ¹Coniah the son of Jehoiakim king of Judah
were a signet *ring* on My right hand, yet I
would pull you off; 25 and I will hand you over
to those who are seeking your life, yes, to
those of whom you are frightened, that is, to
Nebuchadnezzar king of Babylon and the
Chaldeans. 26 I will hurl you and your mother
who gave birth to you into another country
where you were not born, and there you will
die. 27 But as for the land to which they long to
return, they will not return to it.
28 "Is this man Coniah a despised, shattered
jar?
Or is he an undesirable vessel?
Why have he and his descendants been
hurled out
And cast into a land that they had not
known?
29 "O land, land, land,
Hear the word of the LORD!
30 This is what the LORD says:
'Write this man down *as* childless,
A man who will not prosper in his days;
For no man among his descendants will
prosper
Sitting on the throne of David
Or ruling again in Judah.'"

The Coming Messiah: the Righteous Branch

23 "Woe to the shepherds who are causing
the sheep of My pasture to perish and
are scattering *them!*" declares the LORD.
2 Therefore this is what the LORD, the God of
Israel says concerning the shepherds who are
tending My people: "You have scattered My
flock and driven them away, and have not been
concerned about them; behold, I am going to
call you to account for the evil of your deeds,"
declares the LORD. 3 "Then I Myself will gather
the remnant of My flock out of all the countries
where I have driven them, and bring them
back to their pasture, and they will be fruitful
and multiply. 4 I will also raise up shepherds
over them and they will tend them; and they
will not be afraid any longer, nor be terrified,
nor will any be missing," declares the LORD.
5¶ "Behold, *the* days are coming," declares the
LORD,
"When I will raise up for David a righteous
Branch;
And He will reign as king and act wisely
And do justice and righteousness in the
land.
6 "In His days Judah will be saved,
And Israel will live securely;

22:24 ¹ I.e., Jehoiachin

And this is His name by which He will be
called,
'The LORD Our Righteousness.'

7 "Therefore behold, *the* days are coming,"
declares the LORD, "when they will no longer
say, 'As the LORD lives, who brought the sons
of Israel up from the land of Egypt,' 8 but, 'As
the LORD lives, who brought up and led the
descendants of the household of Israel *back*
from *the* north land and from all the countries
where I had driven them.' Then they will live
on their own soil."

False Prophets Denounced

9¶   As for the prophets:
My heart is broken within me,
All my bones tremble;
I have become like a drunken man,
And like a man overcome by wine,
Because of the LORD
And because of His holy words.
10   For the land is full of adulterers;
For the land mourns because of the
curse.
The pastures of the wilderness have
dried up.
Their course is evil
And their might is not right.
11   "For both prophet and priest are defiled;
Even in My house I have found their
wickedness," declares the LORD.
12   "Therefore their way will be like slippery
paths to them,
They will be driven away into the gloom
and fall down in it;
For I will bring disaster upon them,
The year of their punishment," declares
the LORD.
13¶   "Moreover, among the prophets of Samaria
I saw an offensive thing:
They prophesied by Baal and led My
people Israel astray.
14   "Also among the prophets of Jerusalem I
have seen a horrible thing:
The committing of adultery and walking
in deceit;
And they strengthen the hands of
evildoers,
So that no one has turned back from his
wickedness.
All of them have become to Me like
Sodom,
And her inhabitants like Gomorrah.
15 Therefore this is what the LORD of armies
says concerning the prophets:
'Behold, I am going to feed them
wormwood
And make them drink poisonous water,
For from the prophets of Jerusalem
Ungodliness has spread into all the
land.'"
16¶   This is what the LORD of armies says:
"Do not listen to the words of the prophets
who are prophesying to you.
They are leading you into futility;
They tell a vision of their own
imagination,
Not from the mouth of the LORD.
17   "They keep saying to those who despise
Me,

'The LORD has said, "You will have
peace"';
And as for everyone who walks in the
stubbornness of his own heart,
They say, 'Disaster will not come on
you.'
18   "But who has stood in the council of the
LORD,
That he should see and hear His word?
Who has paid attention to His word and
listened?
19   "Behold, the storm of the LORD has gone
forth in wrath,
Even a whirling tempest;
It will swirl down on the head of the
wicked.
20   "The anger of the LORD will not turn
back
Until He has performed and carried
out the purposes of His heart;
In the last days you will clearly
understand it.
21   "I did not send *these* prophets,
But they ran.
I did not speak to them,
But they prophesied.
22   "But if they had stood in My council,
Then they would have announced My
words to My people,
And would have turned them back from
their evil way
And from the evil of their deeds.
23¶   "Am I a God who is near," declares the
LORD,
"And not a God far off?
24   "Can a person hide himself in hiding
places
So that I do not see him?" declares the
LORD.
"Do I not fill the heavens and the earth?"
declares the LORD.
25 "I have heard what the prophets have said
who prophesy falsely in My name, saying, 'I
had a dream, I had a dream!' 26 How long? Is
there *anything* in the hearts of the prophets
who prophesy falsehood, *these* prophets of the
deceitfulness of their own heart, 27 who intend
to make My people forget My name by their
dreams which they report to one another, just
as their fathers forgot My name because of
Baal? 28 The prophet who has a dream may
report *his* dream, but let him who has My
word speak My word truthfully. What does
straw have *in common* with grain?" declares
the LORD. 29 "Is My word not like fire?"
declares the LORD, "and like a hammer
which shatters a rock? 30 Therefore behold, I
am against the prophets," declares the LORD,
"who steal My words from each other.
31 Behold, I am against the prophets," declares
the LORD, "who use their tongues
and declare, 'The *Lord* declares!' 32 Behold, I
am against those who have prophesied false
dreams," declares the LORD, "and reported
them and led My people astray by their lies
and reckless boasting; yet I did not send them
nor command them, nor do they provide this
people the slightest benefit," declares the
LORD.
33 "Now when this people or the prophet or

a priest asks you, saying, 'What is the [1]pronouncement of the LORD?' then you shall say to them, 'What pronouncement?' The LORD declares, 'I will abandon you.' [34] Then as for the prophet or the priest or the people who say, 'The pronouncement of the LORD,' I will bring punishment upon that person and his household. [35] This is what each one of you will say to his neighbor and to his brother: 'What has the LORD answered?' or, 'What has the LORD spoken?' [36] For you will no longer remember the pronouncement of the LORD, because every person's own word will become the pronouncement, and you have perverted the words of the living God, the LORD of armies, our God. [37] This is what you will say to *that* prophet: 'What has the LORD answered you?' and, 'What has the LORD spoken?' [38] And if you say, 'The pronouncement of the LORD!' for that reason the LORD says this: 'Because you said this word, "The pronouncement of the LORD!" I have also sent *word* to you, saying, "You shall not say, 'The pronouncement of the LORD!'" ' [39] Therefore behold, I will certainly forget you and thrust you away from My presence, along with the city which I gave you and your fathers. [40] I will put an everlasting disgrace on you and an everlasting humiliation which will not be forgotten."

Baskets of Figs and the Returnees

24 After Nebuchadnezzar king of Babylon had taken into exile Jeconiah the son of Jehoiakim, king of Judah, and the officials of Judah with the craftsmen and metalworkers from Jerusalem and had brought them to Babylon, the LORD showed me: behold, two baskets of figs placed before the temple of the LORD. [2] One basket had very good figs, like first-ripe figs, and the other basket had very bad figs which could not be eaten due to rottenness. [3] Then the LORD said to me, "What do you see, Jeremiah?" And I said, "Figs: the good figs *are* very good, and the bad *ones,* very bad, which cannot be eaten due to rottenness."

[4] Then the word of the LORD came to me, saying, [5] "This is what the LORD, the God of Israel says: 'Like these good figs, so I will regard as good the captives of Judah, whom I have sent out of this place *into* the land of the Chaldeans. [6] For I will set My eyes on them for good, and I will bring them back to this land; and I will build them up and not overthrow them, and I will plant them and not uproot them. [7] I will also give them a heart to know Me, for I am the LORD; and they will be My people, and I will be their God, for they will return to Me wholeheartedly.

[8] 'But like the bad figs which cannot be eaten due to rottenness,' indeed, this is what the LORD says, 'so will I give up Zedekiah king of Judah and his officials, and the remnant of Jerusalem who remain in this land, and the ones who live in the land of Egypt. [9] I will make them an object of terror *and an* evil for all the kingdoms of the earth, as a disgrace and a proverb, a taunt and a curse in all the places where I will scatter them. [10] And I will send the sword, the famine, and the plague upon them until they are eliminated from the land which I gave to them and their forefathers.' "

Prophecy of the Captivity

25 The word that came to Jeremiah concerning all the people of Judah, in the fourth year of Jehoiakim the son of Josiah, king of Judah (that was the first year of Nebuchadnezzar king of Babylon), [2] *the word* which Jeremiah the prophet spoke to all the people of Judah and to all the inhabitants of Jerusalem, saying, [3] "From the thirteenth year of Josiah the son of Amon, king of Judah, even to this day, these twenty-three years the word of the LORD has come to me, and I have spoken to you again and again, but you have not listened. [4] And the LORD has sent to you all His servants the prophets again and again, but you have not listened nor inclined your ear to hear, [5] saying, 'Turn now, everyone from his evil way and from the evil of your deeds, and live on the land which the LORD has given to you and your forefathers forever and ever; [6] and do not follow other gods to serve them and to worship them, and do not provoke Me to anger with the work of your hands, then I will do you no harm.' [7] Yet you have not listened to Me," declares the LORD, "in order to provoke Me to anger with the work of your hands to your own harm.

[8] "Therefore this is what the LORD of armies says: 'Because you have not obeyed My words, [9] behold, I will send and take all the families of the north,' declares the LORD, 'and *I will send* to Nebuchadnezzar king of Babylon, My servant, and will bring them against this land and against its inhabitants and against all these surrounding nations; and I will completely destroy them and make them an object of horror and hissing, and an everlasting place of ruins. [10] Moreover, I will eliminate from them the voice of jubilation and the voice of joy, the voice of the groom and the voice of the bride, the sound of the millstones and the light of the lamp. [11] This entire land will be a place of ruins and an object of horror, and these nations will serve the king of Babylon for seventy years.

Babylon Will Be Judged

[12] 'Then it will be when seventy years are completed I will punish the king of Babylon and that nation,' declares the LORD, 'for their wrongdoing, and the land of the Chaldeans; and I will make it an everlasting desolation. [13] I will bring upon that land all My words which I have pronounced against it, all that is written in this book which Jeremiah has prophesied against all the nations. [14] (For many nations and great kings will make slaves of them, even them; and I will repay them according to their deeds and according to the work of their hands.)' "

[15] For this is what the LORD, the God of Israel, says to me: "Take this cup of the wine of wrath from My hand and give it to all the nations to whom I send you, to drink *from it.* [16] Then they will drink and loudly vomit and act insanely because of the sword that I am going to send among them."

[17] So I took the cup from the LORD's hand

23:33 [1] Or *burden,* and so throughout the ch

and gave it to all the nations to whom the LORD sent me, to drink *from it:* 18 *To* Jerusalem and the cities of Judah, and its kings *and* its officials, to make them places of ruins, objects of horror, hissing, and a curse, as it is this day; 19 *To* Pharaoh king of Egypt, his servants, his officials, and all his people; 20 and *to* all the foreign people, all the kings of the land of Uz, all the kings of the land of the Philistines (that is, Ashkelon, Gaza, Ekron, and the remnant of Ashdod); 21 *To* Edom, Moab, and the sons of Ammon; 22 and *to* all the kings of Tyre, all the kings of Sidon, and the kings of the coastlands which are beyond the sea; 23 and *to* Dedan, Tema, Buz, and all who trim the corners *of their hair;* 24 and *to* all the kings of Arabia and all the kings of the foreign people who live in the desert; 25 and *to* all the kings of Zimri, all the kings of Elam, and all the kings of Media; 26 and *to* all the kings of the north, near and far, one with another; and all the kingdoms of the earth which are on the face of the ground; and the king of Sheshach shall drink *it* after them.

27 "And you shall say to them, 'This is what the LORD of armies, the God of Israel says: "Drink, be drunk, vomit, fall down, and do not get up, because of the sword which I am sending among you." ' 28 And if they refuse to take the cup from your hand to drink, then you shall say to them, 'This is what the LORD of armies says: "You shall certainly drink! 29 For behold, I am beginning to inflict disaster on *this* city which is called by My name, so should you be completely free from punishment? You will not be free from punishment, for I am summoning a sword against all the inhabitants of the earth," declares the LORD of armies.'

30 "Therefore you shall prophesy against them all these words, and you shall say to them,

'The LORD will roar from on high
   And raise His voice from His holy
      dwelling;
   He will roar forcefully against His fold.
   He will shout like those who tread *the
      grapes,*
   Against all the inhabitants of the earth.
31   'A clamor has come to the end of the
      earth,
   Because the LORD has a controversy with
      the nations.
   He is entering into judgment with
      humanity;
   As for the wicked, He has turned them
      over to the sword,' declares the
      LORD."
32¶   This is what the LORD of armies says:
   "Behold, evil is going out
   From nation to nation,
   And a great storm is being stirred up
   From the remotest parts of the earth.
33 "Those put to death by the LORD on that day will be from one end of the earth to the other. They will not be mourned, gathered, or buried; they will be like dung on the face of the ground.
34   "Wail, you shepherds, and cry out;
   Wallow *in the dust,* you masters of the
      flock;

   For the days of your slaughter and your
      dispersions have come,
   And you will fall like a precious vessel.
35   "There will be no sanctuary for the
      shepherds,
   Nor escape for the masters of the flock.
36   "*Hear* the sound of the cry of the
      shepherds,
   And the wailing of the masters of the
      flock!
   For the LORD is destroying their pasture,
37   And the peaceful grazing places are
      devastated
   Because of the fierce anger of the LORD.
38   "He has left His hiding place like the lion;
   For their land has become a horror
   Because of the fierceness of the
      oppressing *sword*
   And because of His fierce anger."

Cities of Judah Warned

26 In the beginning of the reign of Jehoiakim the son of Josiah, king of Judah, this word came from the LORD, saying, 2 "This is what the LORD says: 'Stand in the courtyard of the LORD's house, and speak to all the cities of Judah who have come to worship *in* the LORD's house all the words that I have commanded you to speak to them. Do not omit a word! 3 Perhaps they will listen and everyone will turn from his evil way, and I will relent of the disaster which I am planning to inflict on them because of the evil of their deeds.' 4 And you shall say to them, 'This is what the LORD says: "If you do not listen to Me, to walk in My Law which I have set before you, 5 to listen to the words of My servants the prophets, whom I have been sending to you again and again, but you have not listened; 6 then I will make this house like Shiloh, and I will make this city a curse to all the nations of the earth." ' "

A Plot to Murder Jeremiah

7 The priests and the prophets and all the people heard Jeremiah speaking these words in the house of the LORD. 8 Yet when Jeremiah finished speaking everything that the LORD had commanded *him* to speak to all the people, *then* the priests and the prophets and all the people seized him, saying, "You must die! 9 Why have you prophesied in the name of the LORD, saying, 'This house will be like Shiloh and this city will be in ruins, without inhabitant'?" And all the people gathered to Jeremiah at the house of the LORD.

10 When the officials of Judah heard these things, they came up from the king's house to the house of the LORD and sat at the entrance of the New Gate of the LORD's *house.* 11 Then the priests and the prophets spoke to the officials and to all the people, saying, "A death sentence for this man! For he has prophesied against this city, just as you have heard with your own ears!"

12 Then Jeremiah spoke to all the officials and to all the people, saying, "The LORD sent me to prophesy against this house and against this city all the words that you have heard. 13 Now then, reform your ways and your deeds and obey the voice of the LORD your God; and

the LORD will relent of the disaster which He has pronounced against you. 14 But as for me, behold, I am in your hands; do with me as is good and right in your sight. 15 Only know for certain that if you put me to death, you will bring innocent blood on yourselves, and on this city and its inhabitants; for truly the LORD has sent me to you to speak all these words so that you hear them."

Jeremiah Is Spared

16 Then the officials and all the people said to the priests and the prophets, "No death sentence for this man! For he has spoken to us in the name of the LORD our God." 17 Then some of the elders of the land rose up and spoke to all the assembly of the people, saying, 18 "Micah of Moresheth used to prophesy in the days of Hezekiah king of Judah; and he spoke to all the people of Judah, saying, 'This is what the LORD of armies has said:

"Zion will be plowed *like* a field,
    And Jerusalem will become heaps of
        ruins,
    And the mountain of the house like the
        high places of a forest." '

19 Did Hezekiah king of Judah and all Judah actually put him to death? Did he not fear the LORD and plead for the favor of the LORD, and the LORD relented of the disaster which He had pronounced against them? But we are committing a great evil against our own lives!"

20 Indeed, *there was* also a man *who* used to prophesy in the name of the LORD, Uriah the son of Shemaiah from Kiriath-jearim; and he prophesied against this city and against this land words similar to all those of Jeremiah. 21 When King Jehoiakim and all his warriors and all the officials heard his words, then the king sought to put him to death; but Uriah heard *about it,* and he was afraid, so he fled and went to Egypt. 22 Then King Jehoiakim sent men to Egypt: Elnathan the son of Achbor and *certain* men with him, to Egypt. 23 And they brought Uriah from Egypt and led him to King Jehoiakim, who killed him with a sword and threw his dead body into the burial place of the common people.

24 But the hand of Ahikam the son of Shaphan was with Jeremiah, so that he was not handed over to the people to put him to death.

The Nations to Submit to Nebuchadnezzar

27 In the beginning of the reign of Zedekiah the son of Josiah, king of Judah, this word came to Jeremiah from the LORD, saying—2 this is what the LORD has said to me: "Make for yourself restraints and yokes and put them on your neck, 3 and send word to the king of Edom, the king of Moab, the king of the sons of Ammon, the king of Tyre, and to the king of Sidon by the messengers who come to Jerusalem to Zedekiah king of Judah. 4 Order them *to go* to their masters, saying, 'This is what the LORD of armies, the God of Israel says: "This is what you shall say to your masters: 5 'I have made the earth, mankind, and the animals which are on the face of the earth by My great power and by My outstretched arm, and I will give it to the one who

is pleasing in My sight. 6 And now I have handed all these lands over to Nebuchadnezzar king of Babylon, My servant, and I have also given him the animals of the field to serve him. 7 All the nations shall serve him and his son and his grandson until the time of his own land comes; then many nations and great kings will make him their servant.

8 'And it will be *that* the nation or the kingdom which will not serve him, Nebuchadnezzar king of Babylon, and will not put its neck under the yoke of the king of Babylon, I will punish that nation with the sword, with famine, and with plague,' declares the LORD, 'until I have eliminated it by his hand. 9 And as for you, do not listen to your prophets, your diviners, your dreamers, your soothsayers, or your sorcerers who talk to you, saying, "You will not serve the king of Babylon." 10 For they are prophesying a lie to you in order to remove you far from your land; and I will drive you away and you will perish. 11 But the nation that will bring its neck under the yoke of the king of Babylon and serve him, I will let remain on its land,' declares the LORD, 'and they will cultivate it and live in it.' " ' "

12 I spoke words like all these to Zedekiah king of Judah, saying, "Bring your necks under the yoke of the king of Babylon and serve him and his people, and live! 13 Why should you die, you and your people, by the sword, famine, and plague, as the LORD has spoken to the nation that will not serve the king of Babylon? 14 So do not listen to the words of the prophets who talk to you, saying, 'You will not serve the king of Babylon,' for they are prophesying a lie to you; 15 for I have not sent them," declares the LORD, "but they are prophesying falsely in My name, so that I will drive you away and that you will perish, you and the prophets who prophesy to you."

16 Then I spoke to the priests and to all this people, saying: "This is what the LORD says: 'Do not listen to the words of your prophets who prophesy to you, saying, "Behold, the vessels of the LORD's house will now shortly be brought back from Babylon"; for they are prophesying a lie to you. 17 Do not listen to them; serve the king of Babylon, and live! Why should this city become a place of ruins? 18 But if they are prophets, and if the word of the LORD is with them, have them now plead with the LORD of armies that the vessels which are left in the house of the LORD and the house of the king of Judah and in Jerusalem do not go to Babylon. 19 For this is what the LORD of armies says concerning the pillars, concerning the sea, concerning the kettle stands, and concerning the rest of the vessels that are left in this city, 20 which Nebuchadnezzar king of Babylon did not take when he led into exile Jeconiah the son of Jehoiakim, king of Judah, from Jerusalem to Babylon, and all the nobles of Judah and Jerusalem— 21 Yes, this is what the LORD of armies, the God of Israel, says concerning the vessels that are left in the house of the LORD and in the house of the king of Judah and in Jerusalem: 22 "They will be brought to Babylon and will be there until the day I visit them,"

declares the LORD. "Then I will bring them back and restore them to this place." ' "

Hananiah's False Prophecy

28 Now in the same year, in the beginning of the reign of Zedekiah king of Judah, in the fourth year, in the fifth month, Hananiah the prophet the son of Azzur, who was from Gibeon, spoke to me at the house of the LORD in the sight of the priests and all the people, saying, 2 "This is what the LORD of armies, the God of Israel says: 'I have broken the yoke of the king of Babylon. 3 Within two years I am going to bring back to this place all the vessels of the LORD's house, which Nebuchadnezzar king of Babylon took from this place and brought to Babylon. 4 I am also going to bring back to this place Jeconiah the son of Jehoiakim, king of Judah, and all the exiles of Judah who went to Babylon,' declares the LORD, 'for I will break the yoke of the king of Babylon.' "

5 Then Jeremiah the prophet spoke to the prophet Hananiah in the sight of the priests and in the sight of all the people who were standing at the house of the LORD, 6 and Jeremiah the prophet said, "Amen! May the LORD do so; may the LORD fulfill your words which you have prophesied, to bring back the vessels of the LORD's house and all the exiles, from Babylon to this place. 7 Yet hear now this word which I am going to speak so that you and all the people can hear it! 8 The prophets who were before me and before you from ancient times also prophesied against many lands and against great kingdoms regarding war, disaster, and plague. 9 As for the prophet who prophesies of peace, when the word of the prophet comes to pass, then that prophet will be known as one whom the LORD has truly sent."

10 Then Hananiah the prophet took the yoke from the neck of Jeremiah the prophet and broke it. 11 Hananiah spoke in the sight of all the people, saying, "This is what the LORD says: 'Even so within two full years I will break the yoke of Nebuchadnezzar king of Babylon from the neck of all the nations.' " Then Jeremiah the prophet went his way.

12 Then the word of the LORD came to Jeremiah after Hananiah the prophet had broken the yoke from the neck of Jeremiah the prophet, saying, 13 "Go and speak to Hananiah, saying, 'This is what the LORD says: "You have broken the yokes of wood, but in their place you have made yokes of iron." 14 For this is what the LORD of armies, the God of Israel says: "I have put a yoke of iron on the neck of all these nations, to serve Nebuchadnezzar king of Babylon; and they shall serve him. And I have also given him the animals of the field." ' " 15 Then Jeremiah the prophet said to Hananiah the prophet, "Listen now, Hananiah: the LORD has not sent you, and you have made this people trust in a lie. 16 Therefore, this is what the LORD says: 'Behold, I am going to remove you from the face of the earth. This year you are going to die, because you spoke falsely against the LORD.' "

17 So Hananiah the prophet died in the same year, in the seventh month.

Message to the Exiles

29 Now these are the words of the letter which Jeremiah the prophet sent from Jerusalem to the rest of the elders of the exile, the priests, the prophets, and all the people whom Nebuchadnezzar had taken into exile from Jerusalem to Babylon. 2 (This was after King Jeconiah and the queen mother, the high officials, the leaders of Judah and Jerusalem, the craftsmen, and the metalworkers had departed from Jerusalem.) 3 The letter was sent by the hand of Elasah the son of Shaphan and Gemariah the son of Hilkiah, whom Zedekiah king of Judah sent to Babylon to Nebuchadnezzar king of Babylon, saying, 4 "This is what the LORD of armies, the God of Israel, says to all the exiles whom I have sent into exile from Jerusalem to Babylon: 5 'Build houses and live in them; and plant gardens and eat their produce. 6 Take wives and father sons and daughters, and take wives for your sons and give your daughters to husbands, so that they may give birth to sons and daughters; and grow in numbers there and do not decrease. 7 Seek the prosperity of the city where I have sent you into exile, and pray to the LORD in its behalf; for in its prosperity will be your prosperity.' 8 For this is what the LORD of armies, the God of Israel says: 'Do not let your prophets who are in your midst or your diviners deceive you, and do not listen to their interpretations of your dreams which you dream. 9 For they prophesy falsely to you in My name; I have not sent them,' declares the LORD.

10 "For this is what the LORD says: 'When seventy years have been completed for Babylon, I will visit you and fulfill My good word to you, to bring you back to this place. 11 For I know the plans that I have for you,' declares the LORD, 'plans for prosperity and not for disaster, to give you a future and a hope. 12 Then you will call upon Me and come and pray to Me, and I will listen to you. 13 And you will seek Me and find Me when you search for Me with all your heart. 14 I will let Myself be found by you,' declares the LORD, 'and I will restore your fortunes and gather you from all the nations and all the places where I have driven you,' declares the LORD, 'and I will bring you back to the place from where I sent you into exile.'

15 "Because you have said, 'The LORD has raised up prophets for us in Babylon'—16 for this is what the LORD says concerning the king who sits on the throne of David, and concerning all the people who live in this city, your brothers who did not go with you into exile—17 this is what the LORD of armies says: 'Behold, I am sending upon them the sword, famine, and plague; and I will make them like rotten figs that cannot be eaten due to rottenness. 18 I will pursue them with the sword, with famine, and with plague; and I will make them an object of terror to all the kingdoms of the earth, to be a curse and an object of horror and hissing, and a disgrace among all the nations where I have driven them, 19 because they have not listened to My words,' declares the LORD, 'which I sent to them again and

again by My servants the prophets; but you did not listen,' declares the LORD. 20 'You, therefore, hear the word of the LORD, all you exiles, whom I have sent away from Jerusalem to Babylon.

21 'This is what the LORD of armies, the God of Israel says concerning Ahab the son of Kolaiah and concerning Zedekiah the son of Maaseiah, who are prophesying to you falsely in My name: "Behold, I am going to hand them over to Nebuchadnezzar king of Babylon, and he will kill them before your eyes. 22 Because of them a curse will be used by all the exiles from Judah who are in Babylon, saying, 'May the LORD make you like Zedekiah and Ahab, whom the king of Babylon roasted in the fire,' 23 because they acted foolishly in Israel, and committed adultery with their neighbors' wives, and falsely spoke words in My name which I did not command them. I am He who knows, and a witness," declares the LORD.' "

24 Now you shall speak to Shemaiah the Nehelamite, saying, 25 "This is what the LORD of armies, the God of Israel says: 'Because you have sent letters in your own name to all the people who are in Jerusalem, and to the priest Zephaniah the son of Maaseiah, and to all the priests, saying, 26 "The LORD has made you priest instead of Jehoiada the priest, to be the overseer of the house of the LORD for every insane person who prophesies, to put him in the stocks and in the iron collar. 27 So now, why have you not rebuked Jeremiah of Anathoth who prophesies to you, 28 seeing that he has sent *word* to us in Babylon, saying, 'The exile will be long; build houses and live *in them*, and plant gardens and eat their produce'?" ' "

29 Now Zephaniah the priest read this letter to Jeremiah the prophet. 30 Then the word of the LORD came to Jeremiah, saying, 31 "Send *word* to all the exiles, saying, 'This is what the LORD says concerning Shemaiah the Nehelamite: "Because Shemaiah has prophesied to you, although I did not send him, and he has made you trust in a lie," 32 therefore this is what the LORD says: "Behold, I am going to punish Shemaiah the Nehelamite and his descendants; he will not have anyone living among this people, and he will not see the good that I am going to do for My people," declares the LORD, "because he has spoken falsely against the LORD." ' "

Liberation from Captivity Promised

30 The word that came to Jeremiah from the LORD, saying, 2 "This is what the LORD, the God of Israel says: 'Write all the words which I have spoken to you in a book. 3 For behold, days are coming,' declares the LORD, 'when I will restore the fortunes of My people Israel and Judah.' The LORD says, 'I will also bring them back to the land that I gave to their forefathers, and they shall take possession of it.' "

4 Now these are the words which the LORD spoke concerning Israel and Judah:

5 "For this is what the LORD says:
'I have heard a sound of terror,
Of fear, and there is no peace.

6 'Ask now, and see
If a male can give birth.
Why do I see every man
With his hands on his waist, as a woman in childbirth?
And *why* have all faces turned pale?
7 'Woe, for that day is great,
There is none like it;
And it is the time of Jacob's distress,
Yet he will be saved from it.

8 'It shall come about on that day,' declares the LORD of armies, 'that I will break his yoke from their necks and will tear to pieces their restraints; and strangers will no longer make them their slaves. 9 But they shall serve the LORD their God and David their king, whom I will raise up for them.

10 'And do not fear, Jacob My servant,'
declares the LORD,
'And do not be dismayed, Israel;
For behold, I am going to save you from far away,
And your descendants from the land of their captivity.
And Jacob will return and be at peace, without anxiety,
And no one will make him afraid.
11 'For I am with you,' declares the LORD, 'to save you;
For I will completely destroy all the nations where I have scattered you,
Only I will not destroy you completely.
But I will discipline you fairly
And will by no means leave you unpunished.'

12 ¶ "For this is what the LORD says:
'Your broken *limb* is irreparable,
And your wound is incurable.
13 'There is no one to plead your cause;
No healing for *your* sore,
No recovery for you.
14 'All your lovers have forgotten you,
They do not seek you;
For I have wounded you with the wound of an enemy,
With the punishment of a cruel one,
Because your wrongdoing is great,
And your sins are numerous.
15 'Why do you cry out over your injury?
Your pain is incurable.
Because your wrongdoing is great
And your sins are numerous,
I have done these things to you.
16 'Therefore all who devour you will be devoured;
And all your adversaries, every one of them, will go into captivity;
And those who plunder you will become plunder,
And all who plunder you I will turn into plunder.
17 'For I will restore you to health
And I will heal you of your wounds,'
declares the LORD,
'Because they have called you an outcast, saying:
"It is Zion; no one cares for her." '

Restoration of Jacob

18 ¶ "This is what the LORD says:

'Behold, I will restore the fortunes of the
tents of Jacob
And have compassion on his dwellings;
And the city will be rebuilt on its ruins,
And the palace will stand on its rightful
place.

19 'From them will come a song of thanksgiving
And the voices of those who celebrate;
And I will multiply them and they will not
decrease;
I will honor them and they will not be
insignificant.

20 'Their children also will be as before,
And their congregation will be established
before Me;
And I will punish all their oppressors.

21 'Their leader shall be one of them,
And their ruler will come out from their
midst;
And I will bring him near and he shall
approach Me;
For who would dare to risk his life to
approach Me?' declares the LORD.

22 'You shall be My people,
And I will be your God.' "

23¶ Behold, the tempest of the LORD!
Wrath has gone forth,
A sweeping tempest;
It will whirl upon the head of the wicked.

24 The fierce anger of the LORD will not turn
back
Until He has performed and accomplished
The intent of His heart.
In the latter days you will understand this.

Israel's Mourning Turned to Joy

31 "At that time," declares the LORD, "I will
be the God of all the families of Israel,
and they shall be My people."

2¶ This is what the LORD says:
"The people who survived the sword
Found grace in the wilderness—
Israel, when it went to find its rest."

3 The LORD appeared to him long ago,
saying,
"I have loved you with an everlasting
love;
Therefore I have drawn you out with
kindness.

4 "I will build you again and you will be
rebuilt,
Virgin of Israel!
You will take up your tambourines again,
And go out to the dances of the revelers.

5 "Again you will plant vineyards
On the hills of Samaria;
The planters will plant
And will enjoy the fruit.

6 "For there will be a day when watchmen
On the hills of Ephraim call out,
'Arise, and let's go up to Zion,
To the LORD our God.' "

7¶ For this is what the LORD says:
"Sing aloud with joy for Jacob,
And be joyful with the chief of the
nations;
Proclaim, give praise, and say,
'LORD, save Your people,
The remnant of Israel!'

8 "Behold, I am bringing them from the
north country,
And I will gather them from the remote
parts of the earth,
Among them those who are blind and
those who limp,
The pregnant woman and she who is in
labor, together;
They will return here as a great assembly.

9 "They will come with weeping,
And by pleading I will bring them;
I will lead them by streams of waters,
On a straight path on which they will not
stumble;
For I am a father to Israel,
And Ephraim is My firstborn."

10¶ Hear the word of the LORD, you nations,
And declare it in the coastlands far away,
And say, "He who scattered Israel will
gather him,
And He will keep him as a shepherd
keeps his flock."

11 For the LORD has ransomed Jacob
And redeemed him from the hand of him
who was stronger than he.

12 "They will come and shout for joy on the
height of Zion,
And they will be radiant over the bounty
of the LORD—
Over the grain, the new wine, the oil,
And over the young of the flock and the
herd.
And their life will be like a watered
garden,
And they will never languish again.

13 "Then the virgin will rejoice in the
dance,
And the young men and the old together;
For I will turn their mourning into joy
And comfort them, and give them joy for
their sorrow.

14 "I will refresh the soul of the priests with
abundance,
And My people will be satisfied with My
goodness," declares the LORD.

15¶ This is what the LORD says:
"A voice is heard in Ramah,
Lamenting and bitter weeping.
Rachel is weeping for her children;
She refuses to be comforted for her
children,
Because they are no more."

16 This is what the LORD says:
"Restrain your voice from weeping
And your eyes from tears;
For your work will be rewarded," declares
the LORD,
"And they will return from the land of the
enemy.

17 "There is hope for your future," declares
the LORD,
"And your children will return to their own
territory.

18 "I have certainly heard Ephraim grieving,
'You have disciplined me, and I was
corrected,
Like an untrained calf;
Bring me back that I may be restored,
For You are the LORD my God.

19 'For after I turned back, I repented;

And after I was instructed, I 'slapped *my*
   thigh;
I was ashamed and also humiliated
Because I bore the shame of my youth.'
20 "Is Ephraim My dear son?
Is he a delightful child?
Indeed, as often as I have spoken against
   him,
I certainly *still* remember him;
Therefore My heart yearns for him;
I will certainly have mercy on him,"
   declares the LORD.
21¶ "Set up roadmarks for yourself,
Place guideposts for yourself;
Direct your mind to the highway,
The way by which you went.
Return, O virgin of Israel,
Return to these your cities.
22 "How long will you waver,
You rebellious daughter?
For the LORD has created a new thing on
   the earth:
A woman will shelter a man."
   23 This is what the LORD of armies, the God
of Israel says: "Once again they will speak this
word in the land of Judah and in its cities when
I restore their fortunes,
   'The LORD bless you, O place of
      righteousness,
   O holy hill!'
24 Judah and all its cities will live together in it,
the farmers and those who travel with flocks.
25 For I give plenty of water to the weary ones,
and refresh everyone who languishes." 26 At
this I awoke and looked, and my sleep had
been pleasant to me.

A New Covenant

27 "Behold, days are coming," declares the
LORD, "when I will sow the house of Israel and
the house of Judah with the seed of mankind
and the seed of animals. 28 And just as I have
watched over them to uproot *them,* tear *them*
down, ruin, destroy, and bring disaster *on
them,* so I will watch over them to build and
to plant *them,*" declares the LORD.
29 "In those days they will no longer say,
   'The fathers have eaten sour grapes,
   'But *it is* the children's teeth *that* have
      become blunt.'
30 But everyone will die for his own
wrongdoing; each person who eats the sour
grapes, his *own* teeth will become blunt.
31 "Behold, days are coming," declares the
LORD, "when I will make a new covenant with
the house of Israel and the house of Judah,
32 not like the covenant which I made with
their fathers on the day I took them by the
hand to bring them out of the land of Egypt,
My covenant which they broke, although I was
a husband to them," declares the LORD. 33 "For
this is the covenant which I will make with the
house of Israel after those days," declares the
LORD: "I will put My law within them and
write it on their heart; and I will be their God,
and they shall be My people. 34 They will not
teach again, each one his neighbor and each
one his brother, saying, 'Know the LORD,' for
they will all know Me, from the least of them

to the greatest of them," declares the LORD,
"for I will forgive their wrongdoing, and their
sin I will no longer remember."
35¶ This is what the LORD says,
   He who gives the sun for light by day
   And the fixed order of the moon and the
      stars for light by night,
   Who stirs up the sea so that its waves
      roar—
   The LORD of armies is His name:
36 "If this fixed order departs
   From Me," declares the LORD,
   "Then the descendants of Israel also will
      cease
   To be a nation before Me forever."
37 This is what the LORD says:
   "If the heavens above can be measured
   And the foundations of the earth searched
      out below,
   Then I will also reject all the descendants
      of Israel
   For everything that they have done,"
      declares the LORD.
   38 "Behold, days are coming," declares the
LORD, "when the city will be rebuilt for the
LORD from the Tower of Hananel to the Corner
Gate. 39 The measuring line will go out farther
straight ahead, to the hill Gareb; then it will
turn to Goah. 40 And the entire valley of the
dead bodies and of the ashes, and all the fields
as far as the brook Kidron to the corner of the
Horse Gate toward the east, shall be holy to
the LORD; it will not be uprooted or overthrown ever again."

Jeremiah Imprisoned

32 The word that came to Jeremiah from
the LORD in the tenth year of Zedekiah
king of Judah, which was the eighteenth year
of Nebuchadnezzar. 2 Now at that time the
army of the king of Babylon was besieging
Jerusalem, and Jeremiah the prophet was
imprisoned in the courtyard of the guard,
which *was at* the house of the king of
Judah, 3 because Zedekiah king of Judah
had imprisoned him, saying, "Why do you
prophesy, saying, 'This is what the LORD says:
"Behold, I am going to hand this city over to
the king of Babylon, and he will take it; 4 and
Zedekiah king of Judah will not escape from
the hand of the Chaldeans, but he will
certainly be handed over to the king of
Babylon, and he will speak with him face to
face and see him eye to eye. 5 Then he will
take Zedekiah to Babylon, and he will be there
until I visit him," declares the LORD. "If you
fight against the Chaldeans, you will not
succeed"'?"
   6 And Jeremiah said, "The word of the LORD
came to me, saying, 7 'Behold, Hanamel the
son of Shallum your uncle is coming to you,
saying, "Buy for yourself my field which is at
Anathoth, for you have the right of redemption
to buy *it.*"' 8 Then my uncle's son Hanamel
came to me in the courtyard of the guard in
accordance with the word of the LORD and
said to me, 'Buy my field, please, that is at
Anathoth, which is in the land of Benjamin;
for you have the right of possession and the

redemption is yours; buy *it* for yourself.' Then I knew that this was the word of the LORD.

9 "So I bought the field which was in Anathoth from Hanamel my uncle's son, and I weighed out the silver for him, seventeen shekels of silver. 10 And I signed and sealed the deed, and called in witnesses, and weighed out the silver on the scales. 11 Then I took the deeds of purchase, both the sealed *copy containing* the terms and conditions and the open *copy;* 12 and I gave the deed of purchase to Baruch the son of Neriah, the son of Mahseiah, in the sight of Hanamel my uncle's *son* and in the sight of the witnesses who signed the deed of purchase, in the sight of all the Jews who were sitting in the courtyard of the guard. 13 And I commanded Baruch in their sight, saying, 14 'This is what the LORD of armies, the God of Israel says: "Take these deeds, this sealed deed of purchase and this open deed, and put them in an earthenware jar, so that they may last a long time." 15 For this is what the LORD of armies, the God of Israel says: "Houses and fields and vineyards will again be purchased in this land."'

Jeremiah Prays and God Explains

16 "After giving the deed of purchase to Baruch the son of Neriah, I prayed to the LORD, saying, 17 'Oh, Lord GOD! Behold, You Yourself have made the heavens and the earth by Your great power and by Your outstretched arm! Nothing is too difficult for You, 18 who shows mercy to thousands, but repays the wrongdoing of fathers into the laps of their children after them, great and mighty God. The LORD of armies is His name; 19 great in counsel and mighty in deed, whose eyes are open to all the ways of the sons of mankind, giving to everyone according to his ways and according to the fruit of his deeds; 20 who has accomplished signs and wonders in the land of Egypt, *and* even to this day both in Israel and among mankind; and You have made a name for Yourself, as at this day. 21 You brought Your people Israel out of the land of Egypt with signs and wonders, and with a strong hand and an outstretched arm, and with great terror; 22 and You gave them this land, which You swore to their forefathers to give them, a land flowing with milk and honey. 23 They came in and took possession of it, but they did not obey Your voice or walk in Your Law; they did not do anything that You commanded them to do; therefore You have made all this disaster happen to them. 24 Behold, the assault ramps have reached the city to take it; and the city has been handed over to the Chaldeans who fight against it, because of the sword, the famine, and the plague; and what You have spoken has come to pass; and behold, You see *it.* 25 Yet You have said to me, Lord GOD, "Buy for yourself the field with money and call in witnesses"— although the city has been handed over to the Chaldeans.' "

26 Then the word of the LORD came to Jeremiah, saying, 27 "Behold, I am the LORD, the God of all flesh; is anything too difficult for

Me?" 28 Therefore this is what the LORD says: "Behold, I am going to hand this city over to the Chaldeans and to Nebuchadnezzar king of Babylon, and he will take it. 29 And the Chaldeans who are fighting against this city will enter and set this city on fire and burn it, with the houses where *people* have offered incense to Baal on their roofs and poured out drink offerings to other gods, to provoke Me to anger. 30 For the sons of Israel and the sons of Judah have been doing only evil in My sight since their youth; for the sons of Israel have been only provoking Me to anger by the work of their hands," declares the LORD. 31 "Indeed this city has been to Me a provocation of My anger and My wrath since the day that they built it, even to this day, so that it should be removed from My sight, 32 because of all the evil of the sons of Israel and the sons of Judah which they have done to provoke Me to anger—they, their kings, their leaders, their priests, their prophets, the men of Judah, and the inhabitants of Jerusalem. 33 They have turned *their* back to Me and not *their* face; though *I* taught them, teaching again and again, they would not listen to accept discipline. 34 But they put their detestable things in the house which is called by My name, to defile it. 35 They built the high places of Baal that are in the Valley of Ben-hinnom to make their sons and their daughters pass through *the fire* to Molech, which I had not commanded them, nor had it entered My mind that they should do this abomination, to mislead Judah to sin.

36 "Now therefore the LORD God of Israel says the following concerning this city of which you say, 'It has been handed over to the king of Babylon by sword, by famine, and by plague': 37 Behold, I am going to gather them out of all the lands to which I have driven them in My anger, in My wrath, and in great indignation; and I will bring them back to this place and have them live in safety. 38 They shall be My people, and I will be their God; 39 and I will give them one heart and one way, so that they will fear Me always, for their own good and for *the good of* their children after them. 40 I will make an everlasting covenant with them that I will not turn away from them, to do them good; and I will put the fear of Me in their hearts, so that they will not turn away from Me. 41 I will rejoice over them to do them good and will faithfully plant them in this land with all My heart and all My soul. 42 For this is what the LORD says: 'Just as I brought all this great disaster on this people, so I am going to bring on them all the good that I am promising them. 43 And fields will be purchased in this land of which you say, "It is a desolation, without man or animal; it has been handed over to the Chaldeans." 44 *People* will buy fields for money, sign and seal deeds, and call in witnesses in the land of Benjamin, in the areas surrounding Jerusalem, in the cities of Judah, in the cities of the hill country, in the cities of the lowland, and in the cities of the 'Negev; for I will restore their fortunes,' declares the LORD."

32:44 1 I.e., South country

Restoration Promised

33 Then the word of the LORD came to Jeremiah the second time, while he was still confined in the courtyard of the guard, saying, 2 "This is what the LORD says, *He* who made the earth, the LORD who formed it to create it, *He* whose name is the LORD: 3 'Call to Me and I will answer you, and I will tell you great and mighty things, which you do not know.' 4 For this is what the LORD, the God of Israel says concerning the houses of this city, and concerning the houses of the kings of Judah which have been torn down *to make a defense* against the assault ramps and the sword: 5 'While *they* are coming to fight the Chaldeans and to fill their houses with the bodies of people whom I have struck down in My anger and My wrath, and I have hidden My face from this city because of all their wickedness: 6 Behold, I am going to bring to it healing and a remedy, and I will heal them; and I will reveal to them an abundance of peace and truth. 7 And I will restore the fortunes of Judah and the fortunes of Israel, and will rebuild them as *they were* at first. 8 And I will cleanse them from all their wrongdoing by which they have sinned against Me, and I will forgive all their wrongdoings by which they have sinned against Me and revolted against Me. 9 'It will be to Me a name of joy, praise, and glory before all the nations of the earth, which will hear of all the good that I do for them, and they will be frightened and tremble because of all the good and all the peace that I make for it.'

10 "This is what the LORD says: 'Yet again there will be heard in this place, of which you say, "It is a waste, without man and without animal," *that is,* in the cities of Judah and in the streets of Jerusalem that are deserted, without man and without inhabitant and without animal, 11 the voice of joy and the voice of gladness, the voice of the groom and the voice of the bride, the voice of those who say,

"Give thanks to the LORD of armies,
 For the LORD is good,
 For His mercy is everlasting,"

as they bring a thanksgiving offering into the house of the LORD. For I will restore the fortunes of the land as *they were* at first,' says the LORD.

12 "This is what the LORD of armies says: 'There will again be in this place which is waste, without man or animal, and in all its cities, a pasture for shepherds who rest their flocks. 13 In the cities of the hill country, in the cities of the lowland, in the cities of the Negev, in the land of Benjamin, in the areas surrounding Jerusalem, and in the cities of Judah, the flocks will again pass under the hands of the one who counts them,' says the LORD.

The Davidic Kingdom

14 'Behold, days are coming,' declares the LORD, 'when I will fulfill the good word which I have spoken concerning the house of Israel and the house of Judah. 15 In those days and at that time I will make a righteous Branch of David sprout; and He shall execute justice and righteousness on the earth. 16 In those days Judah will be saved and Jerusalem will live in safety; and this is *the name* by which it will be called: the LORD is our righteousness.' 17 For this is what the LORD says: 'David shall not lack a man to sit on the throne of the house of Israel; 18 and the Levitical priests shall not lack a man before Me to offer burnt offerings, to burn grain offerings, and to prepare sacrifices continually.' "

19 And the word of the LORD came to Jeremiah, saying, 20 "This is what the LORD says: 'If you can break My covenant for the day and My covenant for the night, so that day and night do not occur at their proper time, 21 then My covenant with David My servant may also be broken, so that he will not have a son to reign on his throne, and with the Levitical priests, My ministers. 22 As the heavenly [1] lights cannot be counted, and the sand of the sea cannot be measured, so I will multiply the descendants of My servant David and the Levites who serve Me.' "

23 And the word of the LORD came to Jeremiah, saying, 24 "Have you not observed what these people have asserted, saying, 'The two families which the LORD chose, He has rejected them'? So they despise My people as no longer being a nation in their sight. 25 This is what the LORD says: 'If My covenant *for* day and night *does* not *continue, and* I have not established the fixed patterns of heaven and earth, 26 then I would reject the descendants of Jacob and David My servant, so as not to take from his descendants rulers over the descendants of Abraham, Isaac, and Jacob. But I will restore their fortunes and have mercy on them.' "

A Prophecy against Zedekiah

34 The word that came to Jeremiah from the LORD, when Nebuchadnezzar king of Babylon and all his army, with all the kingdoms of the earth that were *under* his control and all the peoples, were fighting against Jerusalem and all its cities, saying, 2 "This is what the LORD, the God of Israel says: 'Go and speak to Zedekiah king of Judah and say to him, "This is what the LORD says: 'Behold, I am handing this city over to the king of Babylon, and he will burn it with fire. 3 And as for you, you will not escape from his hand, for you will assuredly be caught and handed over to him; and you will see the king of Babylon eye to eye, and he will speak with you face to face, and you will go to Babylon.' " ' 4 Yet hear the word of the LORD, Zedekiah king of Judah! This is what the LORD says concerning you: 'You will not die by the sword. 5 You will die in peace; and as *spices* were burned for your fathers, the former kings who were before you, so they will burn *spices* for you; and they will mourn for you, *crying,* "Oh, *my* lord!" ' For I have spoken the word," declares the LORD.

6 Then Jeremiah the prophet spoke all these words to Zedekiah king of Judah in Jerusalem 7 when the army of the king of Babylon was fighting against Jerusalem and all the remaining cities of Judah, *that is,* Lachish and Azekah, for

---

33:9 1 I.e., This city   **33:22** 1 Lit *host;* i.e., sun, stars, etc.

they *alone* remained as fortified cities among the cities of Judah.

8 The word that came to Jeremiah from the LORD after King Zedekiah had made a covenant with all the people who were in Jerusalem, to proclaim release to them: 9 that each person was to set his male servant free and each his female servant, a Hebrew man or a Hebrew woman, so that no one would keep them, his Jewish brother *or sister,* in bondage. 10 And all the officials and all the people obeyed who had entered into the covenant that each person was to set his male servant free and each his female servant, so that no one would keep them in bondage any longer; they obeyed, and set *them free.* 11 But afterward they turned around and took back the male servants and the female servants whom they had set free, and brought them into subjection as male servants and as female servants.

12 Then the word of the LORD came to Jeremiah from the LORD, saying, 13 "This is what the LORD, the God of Israel says: 'I made a covenant with your forefathers on the day that I brought them out of the land of Egypt, from the house of bondage, saying, 14 "At the end of seven years each of you shall set free his Hebrew brother who has been sold to you and has served you for six years, and you shall send him out free from you." But your forefathers did not obey Me nor incline their ear to Me. 15 Although recently you *had* turned and done what is right in My sight, each one proclaiming release to his neighbor, and you had made a covenant before Me in the house which is called by My name. 16 Yet you turned and profaned My name, and each person took back his male servant and each his female servant whom you had set free according to their desire, and you brought them into subjection to be your male and female servants.'

17 "Therefore this is what the LORD says: 'You have not obeyed Me in proclaiming release, each one to his brother and each to his neighbor. Behold, I am proclaiming a release to you,' declares the LORD, 'to the sword, to the plague, and to the famine; and I will make you a terror to all the kingdoms of the earth. 18 I will give the people who have violated My covenant, who have not fulfilled the words of the covenant which they made before Me, *when* they cut the calf in two and passed between its parts— 19 the officials of Judah and the officials of Jerusalem, the high officials and the priests, and all the people of the land who passed between the parts of the calf— 20 I will hand them over to their enemies and to those who seek their lives. And their dead bodies will be food for the birds of the sky and the animals of the earth. 21 Zedekiah king of Judah and his officials I will also hand over to their enemies and to those who seek their lives, and to the army of the king of Babylon which has withdrawn from you. 22 Behold, I am going to give a command,' declares the LORD, 'and I will bring them back to this city, and they will fight against it and take it and burn it with fire; and I will make the cities of Judah a desolation without inhabitant.'"

The Rechabites' Obedience

35 The word that came to Jeremiah from the LORD in the days of Jehoiakim the son of Josiah, king of Judah, saying, 2 "Go to the house of the Rechabites and speak to them, and bring them into the house of the LORD, into one of the chambers, and give them wine to drink." 3 So I took Jaazaniah the son of Jeremiah, son of Habazziniah, and his brothers and all his sons, and all the household of the Rechabites, 4 and I brought them into the house of the LORD, into the chamber of the sons of Hanan the son of Igdaliah, the man of God, which was next to the chamber of the officials, which was above the chamber of Maaseiah the son of Shallum, the doorkeeper. 5 Then I set before the men of the house of the Rechabites pitchers full of wine, and cups; and I said to them, "Drink wine!" 6 But they said, "We will not drink wine, for Jonadab the son of Rechab, our father, commanded us, saying, 'You shall not drink wine, you or your sons, forever. 7 You shall not build a house, and you shall not sow seed nor plant a vineyard, nor own one; but you shall live in tents all your days, so that you may live many days in the land where you live as strangers.' 8 And we have obeyed the voice of Jonadab the son of Rechab, our father, in all that he commanded us, not to drink wine all our days, we, our wives, our sons, or our daughters, 9 nor to build ourselves houses to live in; and we do not have a vineyard, a field, or seed. 10 But we have lived *only* in tents, and have obeyed and have done according to all that our father Jonadab commanded us. 11 However, when Nebuchadnezzar king of Babylon came up against the land, we said, 'Come, and let's go to Jerusalem away from the army of the Chaldeans and the army of the Arameans.' So we have lived in Jerusalem."

Judah Rebuked

12 Then the word of the LORD came to Jeremiah, saying, 13 "This is what the LORD of armies, the God of Israel says: 'Go and say to the people of Judah and the inhabitants of Jerusalem, "Will you not accept instruction by listening to My words?" declares the LORD. 14 "The words of Jonadab the son of Rechab have been followed, which he commanded his sons: not to drink wine. And they do not drink *wine* to this day, for they have obeyed their father's command. But I have spoken to you again and again, yet you have not listened to Me. 15 Also I have sent to you all My servants the prophets, sending *them* again and again, saying: 'Turn now every person from his evil way and amend your deeds, and do not follow other gods to worship them. Then you will live in the land which I have given to you and to your forefathers; but you have not inclined your ear or listened to Me. 16 Indeed, the sons of Jonadab the son of Rechab have followed the command of their father which he commanded them, but this people has not listened to Me.'"' 17 Therefore this is what the LORD says, the God of armies, the God of Israel: 'Behold, I am bringing on Judah and on all the inhabitants of Jerusalem all the disaster that I have pronounced against them; because I

spoke to them but they did not listen, and I have called them but they did not answer.' "

18 Then Jeremiah said to the house of the Rechabites, "This is what the LORD of armies, the God of Israel says: 'Because you have obeyed the command of Jonadab your father, kept all his commands, and done according to all that he commanded you, 19 therefore this is what the LORD of armies, the God of Israel says: "Jonadab the son of Rechab will not lack a man to stand before Me always." ' "

Jeremiah's Scroll Read in the Temple

36 In the fourth year of Jehoiakim the son of Josiah, king of Judah, this word came to Jeremiah from the LORD, saying, 2 "Take a scroll and write on it all the words which I have spoken to you concerning Israel, Judah, and all the nations, from the day I *first* spoke to you, from the days of Josiah, even to this day. 3 Perhaps the house of Judah will listen to all the disaster which I plan to carry out against them, so that every person will turn from his evil way; then I will forgive their wrongdoing and their sin."

4 Then Jeremiah called Baruch the son of Neriah, and Baruch wrote on a scroll at the dictation of Jeremiah all the words of the LORD which He had spoken to him. 5 Jeremiah then commanded Baruch, saying, "I am restricted; I cannot go into the house of the LORD. 6 So you go and read from the scroll, which you have written at my dictation, the words of the LORD to the people at the LORD's house on a day of fasting. And you shall also read them to all *the people of* Judah who come from their cities. 7 Perhaps their pleading will come before the LORD, and everyone will turn from his evil way; for great is the anger and the wrath that the LORD has pronounced against this people." 8 So Baruch the son of Neriah acted in accordance with all that Jeremiah the prophet commanded him, reading from the book the words of the LORD in the LORD's house.

9 Now in the fifth year of Jehoiakim the son of Josiah, king of Judah, in the ninth month, all the people in Jerusalem and all the people who came from the cities of Judah to Jerusalem proclaimed a fast before the LORD. 10 Then Baruch read to all the people from the book the words of Jeremiah in the house of the LORD in the chamber of Gemariah the son of Shaphan the scribe, in the upper courtyard, at the entry of the New Gate of the LORD's house.

11 Now when Micaiah the son of Gemariah, the son of Shaphan, had heard all the words of the LORD from the book, 12 he went down to the king's house, into the scribe's chamber. And behold, all the officials were sitting there—Elishama the scribe, Delaiah the son of Shemaiah, Elnathan the son of Achbor, Gemariah the son of Shaphan, Zedekiah the son of Hananiah, and all the *other* officials. 13 And Micaiah declared to them all the words that he had heard when Baruch read from the book to the people. 14 Then all the officials sent Jehudi the son of Nethaniah, *who was* the son of Shelemiah, the son of Cushi, to Baruch, saying, "Take in your hand the scroll from which you have read to the people and come." So

Baruch the son of Neriah took the scroll in his hand and came to them. 15 And they said to him, "Sit down, please, and read it to us." So Baruch read it to them. 16 When they had heard all the words, they turned in fear one to another. And they said to Baruch, "We will certainly report all these words to the king." 17 Then they asked Baruch, saying, "Tell us, please, how did you write all these words? *Was it* at Jeremiah's dictation?" 18 And Baruch said to them, "He dictated all these words to me, and I wrote them with ink on the book." 19 Then the officials said to Baruch, "Go, hide yourself, you and Jeremiah, and do not let anyone know where you are."

The Scroll Is Burned

20 So they came to the king in the courtyard, but they had deposited the scroll in the chamber of Elishama the scribe; and they reported all the words to the king. 21 Then the king sent Jehudi to get the scroll, and he took it out of the chamber of Elishama the scribe. And Jehudi read it to the king as well as to all the officials who were standing beside the king. 22 Now the king was sitting in the winter house in the ninth month, with *a fire* burning in the brazier before him. 23 And when Jehudi had read three or four columns, *the king* cut it with a scribe's knife and threw *it* into the fire that was in the brazier, until all of the scroll was consumed in the fire that was in the brazier. 24 Yet the king and all his servants who heard all these words did not tremble in fear, nor did they tear their garments. 25 Even though Elnathan, Delaiah, and Gemariah urged the king not to burn the scroll, he would not listen to them. 26 And the king commanded Jerahmeel the king's son, Seraiah the son of Azriel, and Shelemiah the son of Abdeel to seize Baruch the scribe and Jeremiah the prophet, but the LORD hid them.

The Scroll Is Replaced

27 Then the word of the LORD came to Jeremiah after the king had burned the scroll and the words which Baruch had written at the dictation of Jeremiah, saying, 28 "Take again another scroll and write on it all the previous words that were on the first scroll, which Jehoiakim the king of Judah burned. 29 And concerning Jehoiakim king of Judah you shall say, 'This is what the LORD says: "You have burned this scroll, saying, 'Why have you written on it that the king of Babylon will certainly come and destroy this land, and will make mankind and animals disappear from it?' " 30 Therefore this is what the LORD says concerning Jehoiakim king of Judah: "He shall have no one to sit on the throne of David, and his dead body shall be thrown out to the heat of the day and the frost of the night. 31 I will also punish him, his descendants, and his servants for their wrongdoing, and I will bring on them and the inhabitants of Jerusalem and the people of Judah all the disaster that I have declared to them—but they did not listen." ' "

32 Then Jeremiah took another scroll and gave it to the scribe Baruch the son of Neriah, and he wrote on it at the dictation of Jeremiah

all the words of the book which Jehoiakim king of Judah had burned in the fire; and many similar words were added to them.

Jeremiah Warns against Trust in Pharaoh

37 Now Zedekiah the son of Josiah whom Nebuchadnezzar king of Babylon had made king in the land of Judah, reigned as king in place of Coniah the son of Jehoiakim. 2 But neither he nor his servants nor the people of the land listened to the words of the LORD which He spoke through Jeremiah the prophet.

3 Yet King Zedekiah sent Jehucal the son of Shelemiah, and the priest Zephaniah the son of Maaseiah, to Jeremiah the prophet, saying, "Please pray to the LORD our God in our behalf." 4 Now Jeremiah was *still* coming and going among the people, for they had not *yet* put him in prison. 5 Meanwhile, Pharaoh's army had set out from Egypt; and when the Chaldeans who had been besieging Jerusalem heard the report about them, they withdrew from Jerusalem.

6 Then the word of the LORD came to Jeremiah the prophet, saying, 7 "This is what the LORD, the God of Israel says: 'This is what you are to say to the king of Judah, who sent you to Me to inquire of Me: "Behold, Pharaoh's army, which has come out to help you, is going to return to its own land of Egypt. 8 Then the Chaldeans will return and fight against this city, and they will capture it and burn it with fire." 9 This is what the LORD says: 'Do not deceive yourselves, saying, "The Chaldeans will certainly go *away* from us," for they will not go. 10 For even if you had defeated the entire army of Chaldeans who were fighting against you, and there were *only* wounded men left among them, each man in his tent, they would rise up and burn this city with fire.' "

Jeremiah Imprisoned

11 Now it happened when the army of the Chaldeans had withdrawn from Jerusalem because of Pharaoh's army, 12 that Jeremiah left Jerusalem to go to the land of Benjamin in order to take possession of *some* property there among the people. 13 While he was at the Gate of Benjamin, a captain of the guard whose name was Irijah, the son of Shelemiah the son of Hananiah was there; and he arrested Jeremiah the prophet, saying, "You are deserting to the Chaldeans!" 14 But Jeremiah said, "A lie! I am not deserting to the Chaldeans"; yet he would not listen to him. So Irijah arrested Jeremiah and brought him to the officials. 15 Then the officials were angry at Jeremiah and they beat him, and put him in prison in the house of Jonathan the scribe, for they had made it into the prison. 16 For Jeremiah had come into the dungeon, that is, the vaulted cell; and Jeremiah stayed there many days.

17 Now King Zedekiah sent *men* and took him *out;* and in his palace the king secretly asked him and said, "Is there a word from the LORD?" And Jeremiah said, "There is!" Then he said, "You will be handed over to the king of Babylon!" 18 Moreover, Jeremiah said to King Zedekiah, "*In* what *way* have I sinned against you, or your servants, or this people, that you have put me in prison? 19 And where are your prophets who prophesied to you, saying, 'The king of Babylon will not come against you or against this land'? 20 But now, please listen, my lord the king; please let my plea come before you and do not make me return to the house of Jonathan the scribe, so that I will not die there." 21 Then King Zedekiah gave a command, and they placed Jeremiah in custody in the courtyard of the guardhouse, and gave him a loaf of bread daily from the bakers' street, until all the bread in the city was gone. So Jeremiah remained in the courtyard of the guardhouse.

Jeremiah Thrown into the Cistern

38 Now Shephatiah the son of Mattan, Gedaliah the son of Pashhur, Jucal the son of Shelemiah, and Pashhur the son of Malchijah heard the words that Jeremiah was speaking to all the people, saying, 2 "This is what the LORD says: '*Anyone* who stays in this city will die by the sword, by famine, or by plague; but *anyone* who surrenders to the Chaldeans will live and have his *own* life as plunder, and stay alive.' 3 This is what the LORD says: 'This city will certainly be handed over to the army of the king of Babylon and he will capture it.' " 4 Then the officials said to the king, "Please have this man put to death, since he is discouraging the men of war who are left in this city and all the people, by speaking words like these to them; for this man is not seeking the well-being of this people, but rather their harm." 5 And King Zedekiah said, "Behold, he is in your hands; for the king can *do* nothing against you." 6 So they took Jeremiah and threw him into the cistern *of* Malchijah the king's son, which was in the courtyard of the guardhouse; and they let Jeremiah down with ropes. Now in the cistern there was no water but *only* mud, and Jeremiah sank into the mud. 7 But Ebed-melech the Ethiopian, a eunuch, while he was in the king's palace, heard that they had put Jeremiah in the cistern. Now the king was sitting at the Gate of Benjamin; 8 and Ebed-melech went out from the king's palace and spoke to the king, saying, 9 "My lord the king, these men have acted wickedly in all that they have done to Jeremiah the prophet whom they have thrown into the cistern; and he will die right where he is because of the famine, for there is no more bread in the city." 10 Then the king commanded Ebed-melech the Ethiopian, saying, "Take thirty men from here under your authority and bring Jeremiah the prophet up from the cistern before he dies." 11 So Ebed-melech took the men under his authority and went into the king's palace to a *place* beneath the storeroom, and took from there worn-out clothes and worn-out rags, and let them down by ropes into the cistern to Jeremiah. 12 Then Ebed-melech the Ethiopian said to Jeremiah, "Now put these worn-out clothes and rags under your armpits under the ropes"; and Jeremiah did so. 13 So they pulled Jeremiah out with the ropes and lifted him out of the cistern, and Jeremiah stayed in the courtyard of the guardhouse.

Zedekiah Seeks an Answer from God

14 Then King Zedekiah sent *word* and had Jeremiah the prophet brought to him at the third entrance that is in the house of the LORD; and the king said to Jeremiah, "I am going to ask you something; do not hide anything from me." **15** And Jeremiah said to Zedekiah, "If I tell you, will you not certainly put me to death? Besides, if I give you advice, you will not listen to me." **16** But King Zedekiah swore to Jeremiah in secret, saying, "As the LORD lives, who made this life for us, I certainly will not put you to death, nor will I hand you over to these men who are seeking your life."

17 So Jeremiah said to Zedekiah, "This is what the LORD God of armies, the God of Israel says: 'If you will indeed surrender to the officers of the king of Babylon, then you will live, this city will not be burned with fire, and you and your household will survive. **18** But if you do not surrender to the officers of the king of Babylon, then this city will be handed over to the Chaldeans; and they will burn it with fire, and you yourself will not escape from their hands.' " **19** Then King Zedekiah said to Jeremiah, "I am in fear of the Jews who have deserted to the Chaldeans, for they may hand me over to them, and they will abuse me." **20** But Jeremiah said, "They will not turn you over. Please obey the LORD in what I am saying to you, so that it may go well for you and you may live. **21** But if you keep refusing to surrender, this is the word which the LORD has shown me: **22** 'Behold, all of the women who have been left in the palace of the king of Judah are going to be brought out to the officers of the king of Babylon; and those women will say,

"Your close friends
　Have misled and overpowered you;
　While your feet were sunk in the mire,
　They turned back."

23 They are also going to bring out all your wives and your sons to the Chaldeans, and you yourself will not escape from their hand, but will be seized by the hand of the king of Babylon, and this city will be burned with fire.' "

24 Then Zedekiah said to Jeremiah, "Let no one know about these words, and you will not die. **25** But if the officials hear that I have talked with you and come to you and say to you, 'Tell us now what you said to the king and what the king said to you; do not hide *it* from us and we will not put you to death,' **26** then you are to say to them, 'I was presenting my plea before the king, not to make me return to the house of Jonathan to die there.' " **27** Then all the officials came to Jeremiah and questioned him. So he reported to them in accordance with all these words which the king had commanded; and they stopped speaking with him, since the conversation had not been overheard. **28** So Jeremiah stayed in the courtyard of the guard until the day that Jerusalem was captured.

Jerusalem Captured

39 Now when Jerusalem was captured in the ninth year of Zedekiah king of Judah, in the tenth month, Nebuchadnezzar king of Babylon and all his army came to Jerusalem and laid siege to it; **2** in the eleventh year of Zedekiah, in the fourth month, in the ninth *day* of the month, the city *wall* was breached. **3** Then all the officials of the king of Babylon came in and sat down at the Middle Gate: Nergal-sar-ezer, Samgar-nebu, Sar-sekim the Rab-saris, Nergal-sar-ezer *the* Rab-mag, and all the rest of the officials of the king of Babylon. **4** And when Zedekiah the king of Judah and all the men of war saw them, they fled and left the city at night by way of the king's garden through the gate between the two walls; and he went out toward the ¹Arabah. **5** But the army of the Chaldeans pursued them and overtook Zedekiah in the plains of Jericho; and they took him and brought him up to Nebuchadnezzar king of Babylon at Riblah in the land of Hamath, and he passed sentence on him. **6** Then the king of Babylon slaughtered the sons of Zedekiah before his eyes at Riblah; the king of Babylon also slaughtered all the nobles of Judah. **7** He then blinded Zedekiah's eyes and bound him in shackles of bronze to bring him to Babylon. **8** The Chaldeans also burned the king's palace and the houses of the people with fire, and they tore down the walls of Jerusalem. **9** And as for the rest of the people who were left in the city, the deserters who had deserted to him and the rest of the people who remained, Nebuzaradan the captain of the bodyguard took *them* into exile in Babylon. **10** But some of the poorest people, who had nothing, Nebuzaradan the captain of the body-guard left behind in the land of Judah, and gave them vineyards and fields at that time.

Jeremiah Spared

11 Now Nebuchadnezzar king of Babylon gave orders regarding Jeremiah through Nebuzaradan the captain of the bodyguard, saying, **12** "Take him and look after him, and do not do anything harmful to him, but rather deal with him just as he tells you." **13** So Nebuzaradan the captain of the bodyguard sent *word,* along with Nebushazban the Rab-saris, Nergal-sar-ezer the Rab-mag, and all the leading officers of the king of Babylon; **14** they even sent *word* and took Jeremiah out of the courtyard of the guardhouse and entrusted him to Gedaliah, the son of Ahikam, the son of Shaphan, to take him home. So he stayed among the people.

15 Now the word of the LORD had come to Jeremiah while he was confined in the court-yard of the guardhouse, saying, **16** "Go and speak to Ebed-melech the Ethiopian, saying, 'This is what the LORD of armies, the God of Israel says: "Behold, I am going to bring My words on this city for disaster and not for prosperity; and they will take place before you on that day. **17** But I will save you on that day," declares the LORD, "and you will not be handed over to the men of whom you are afraid. **18** For I will assuredly rescue you, and you will not fall by the sword; but you will have your *own* life as plunder, because you have trusted in Me," declares the LORD.' "

Jeremiah Remains in Judah

40 The word that came to Jeremiah from the LORD after Nebuzaradan captain of the bodyguard had released him from Ramah, when he had taken him bound in chains among all the exiles of Jerusalem and Judah who were being exiled to Babylon. 2 Now the captain of the bodyguard had taken Jeremiah and said to him, "The LORD your God promised this disaster against this place; 3 and the LORD has brought *it* and done just as He promised. Because you *people* sinned against the LORD and did not listen to His voice, this thing has happened to you. 4 But now, behold, I am setting you free today from the chains that are on your hands. If you would prefer to come with me to Babylon, come *along,* and I will look after you; but if you would prefer not to come with me to Babylon, do not *come.* Look, the whole land is before you; go wherever it seems good and right for you to go." 5 As Jeremiah was still not going back, *¹he said,* "Go on back then to Gedaliah the son of Ahikam, the son of Shaphan, whom the king of Babylon has appointed over the cities of Judah, and stay with him among the people; or else go anywhere it seems right for you to go." So the captain of the bodyguard gave him a ration and a gift, and let him go. 6 Then Jeremiah went to Mizpah to Gedaliah the son of Ahikam and stayed with him among the people who were left in the land.

7 Now all the commanders of the forces that were in the field, they and their men, heard that the king of Babylon had appointed Gedaliah the son of Ahikam over the land, and that he had put him in charge of the men, women, and children, those of the poorest of the land who had not been exiled to Babylon. 8 So they came to Gedaliah at Mizpah, along with Ishmael the son of Nethaniah, Johanan and Jonathan the sons of Kareah, Seraiah the son of Tanhumeth, the sons of Ephai the Netophathite, and Jezaniah the son of the Maacathite, *both* they and their men. 9 Then Gedaliah the son of Ahikam, the son of Shaphan, swore to them and to their men, saying, "Do not be afraid of serving the Chaldeans; stay in the land and serve the king of Babylon, so that it may go well for you. 10 Now as for me, behold, I am going to stay in Mizpah to stand *for you* before the Chaldeans who come to us; but as for you, gather wine, summer fruit, and oil, and put *them* in your *storage* vessels, and live in your cities that you have taken over." 11 Likewise, also all the Jews who were in Moab and among the sons of Ammon and in Edom, and who were in all the *other* countries, heard that the king of Babylon had left a remnant for Judah, and that he had appointed over them Gedaliah the son of Ahikam, the son of Shaphan. 12 Then all the Jews returned from all the places to which they had been scattered and came to the land of Judah, to Gedaliah at Mizpah, and gathered wine and summer fruit in great abundance.

13 Now Johanan the son of Kareah and all the commanders of the forces that were in the field came to Gedaliah at Mizpah, 14 and said to him, "Are you well aware that Baalis the king of the sons of Ammon has sent Ishmael the son of Nethaniah to take your life?" But Gedaliah the son of Ahikam did not believe them. 15 Then Johanan the son of Kareah spoke secretly to Gedaliah in Mizpah, saying, "Let me go and kill Ishmael the son of Nethaniah, and no one will know! Why should he take your life, so that all the Jews who are gathered to you would be scattered and the remnant of Judah would perish?" 16 But Gedaliah the son of Ahikam said to Johanan the son of Kareah, "Do not do this thing, for you are telling a lie about Ishmael."

Gedaliah Is Murdered

41 Now in the seventh month Ishmael the son of Nethaniah, the son of Elishama, of the royal family and *one* of the chief officers of the king, along with ten men, came to Mizpah to Gedaliah the son of Ahikam. While they were eating bread together there in Mizpah, 2 Ishmael the son of Nethaniah and the ten men who were with him rose up, and struck and killed Gedaliah the son of Ahikam, the son of Shaphan, with the sword and put to death the one whom the king of Babylon had appointed over the land. 3 Ishmael also struck and killed all the Jews who were with him, *that is* with Gedaliah in Mizpah, and the Chaldeans who were found there, the men of war.

4 Now it happened on the next day after the killing of Gedaliah, when no one knew *about it,* 5 that eighty men came from Shechem, from Shiloh, and from Samaria with their beards shaved off, their clothes torn, and their bodies gashed, having grain offerings and incense in their hands to bring to the house of the LORD. 6 Then Ishmael the son of Nethaniah left Mizpah to meet them, weeping as he went; and as he met them, he said to them, "Come to Gedaliah the son of Ahikam!" 7 Yet it turned out that as soon as they came inside the city, Ishmael the son of Nethaniah and the men who were with him slaughtered them *and threw them* into the cistern. 8 But ten men who were found among them said to Ishmael, "Do not put us to death, for we have supplies of wheat, barley, oil, and honey hidden in the field." So he refrained and did not put them to death along with their companions.

9 Now as for the cistern where Ishmael had thrown all the bodies of the men whom he had struck and killed because of Gedaliah, it was the one that King Asa had constructed on account of Baasha, king of Israel; Ishmael the son of Nethaniah filled it with the dead. 10 Then Ishmael took captive all the remnant of the people who were in Mizpah, the king's daughters and all the people who were left in Mizpah, whom Nebuzaradan the captain of the bodyguard had put in the custody of Gedaliah the son of Ahikam. Ishmael the son of Nethaniah took them captive and proceeded to cross over to the sons of Ammon.

Johanan Rescues the People

11 But Johanan the son of Kareah and all the

commanders of the forces that were with him heard about all the evil that Ishmael the son of Nethaniah had done. [12] So they took all the men and went to fight with Ishmael the son of Nethaniah and they found him by the large pool that is in Gibeon. [13] Now as soon as all the people who were with Ishmael saw Johanan the son of Kareah and all the commanders of the forces that were with him, they were joyful. [14] So all the people whom Ishmael had taken captive from Mizpah turned around and came back, and went to Johanan the son of Kareah. [15] But Ishmael the son of Nethaniah escaped from Johanan with eight men, and went to the sons of Ammon. [16] Then Johanan the son of Kareah and all the commanders of the forces that were with him took from Mizpah all the remnant of the people whom he had recovered from Ishmael the son of Nethaniah, after he had struck and killed Gedaliah the son of Ahikam, *that is,* the men who were soldiers, *the* women, *the* children, and *the* high officials, whom he had brought back from Gibeon. [17] And they went and stayed in Geruth Chimham, which is beside Bethlehem, in order to proceed into Egypt [18] because of the Chaldeans; for they were afraid of them, since Ishmael the son of Nethaniah had struck and killed Gedaliah the son of Ahikam, whom the king of Babylon had appointed over the land.

Warning against Going to Egypt

42 Then all the commanders of the forces, Johanan the son of Kareah, Jezaniah the son of Hoshaiah, and all the people from the small to the great approached [2] and said to Jeremiah the prophet, "Please let our pleading come before you, and pray for us to the LORD your God for all this remnant—since we have been left *only* a few out of many, just as your own eyes *now* see us— [3] that the LORD your God will tell us the way in which we should walk, and the thing that we should do." [4] Then Jeremiah the prophet said to them, "I have heard *you.* Behold, I am going to pray to the LORD your God in accordance with your words; and I will tell you the whole message which the LORD gives you as an answer. I will not withhold a word from you." [5] Then they said to Jeremiah, "May the LORD be a true and faithful witness against us if we do not act in accordance with the whole message with which the LORD your God will send you to us. [6] Whether *it is* pleasant or unpleasant, we will listen to the voice of the LORD our God to whom we are sending you, so that it may go well for us when we listen to the voice of the LORD our God."

[7] Now at the end of ten days the word of the LORD came to Jeremiah. [8] Then he called for Johanan the son of Kareah and all the commanders of the forces that were with him, and for all the people from the small to the great, [9] and said to them, "This is what the LORD says, the God of Israel, to whom you sent me to present your plea before Him: [10] 'If you will indeed stay in this land, then I will build you up and not tear you down, and I will plant you and not uproot you; for I will relent of the

disaster that I have inflicted on you. [11] Do not be afraid of the king of Babylon, whom you are *now* fearing; do not be afraid of him,' declares the LORD, 'for I am with you to save you and rescue you from his hand. [12] I will also show you compassion, so that he will have compassion on you and restore you to your own soil. [13] But if you are going to say, "We will not stay in this land," so as not to listen to the voice of the LORD your God, [14] saying, "No, but we will go to the land of Egypt, where we will not see war, or hear the sound of a trumpet, or hunger for bread, and we will stay there"; [15] then in that case listen to the word of the LORD, you remnant of Judah. This is what the LORD of armies, the God of Israel says: "If you really set your minds to enter Egypt and go in to reside there, [16] then the sword, of which you are afraid, will overtake you there in the land of Egypt; and the famine, about which you are anxious, will follow closely after you there *in* Egypt, and you will die there. [17] So all the people who set their minds to go to Egypt to reside there will die by the sword, by famine, or by plague; and they will have no refugees or survivors from the disaster that I am going to bring on them."'"

[18] For this is what the LORD of armies, the God of Israel says: "As My anger and wrath have gushed out on the inhabitants of Jerusalem, so My wrath will gush out on you when you enter Egypt. And you will become a curse, an object of horror, [1] an imprecation, and a disgrace; and you will not see this place again." [19] The LORD has spoken to you, you remnant of Judah, "Do not go to Egypt!" You know for certain that I have admonished you today. [20] For you have *only* deceived yourselves; for it is you who sent me to the LORD your God, saying, "Pray for us to the LORD our God; and whatever the LORD our God says, tell us so, and we will do it." [21] So I have told you today, but you have not obeyed the LORD your God in whatever He has sent me to *tell* you. [22] And now you shall know for certain that you will die by the sword, by famine, or by plague in the place where you desire to go to reside.

In Egypt Jeremiah Warns of Judgment

43 But as soon as Jeremiah, whom the LORD their God had sent to them, had finished telling all the people all the words of the LORD their God—that is, all these words— [2] Azariah the son of Hoshaiah, Johanan the son of Kareah, and all the arrogant men said to Jeremiah, "You are telling a lie! The LORD our God has not sent you to say, 'You are not to enter Egypt to reside there'; [3] but Baruch the son of Neriah is inciting you against us in order to hand us over to the Chaldeans, so they will put us to death or exile us to Babylon!" [4] So Johanan the son of Kareah and all the commanders of the forces, and all the people, did not obey the voice of the LORD to stay in the land of Judah. [5] Instead, Johanan the son of Kareah and all the commanders of the forces took the entire remnant of Judah who had returned from all the nations to which they had been scattered, in order to reside in the

---

42:18 [1] Lit *a curse-formula*

land of Judah—6 the men, the women, the children, the king's daughters, and every person whom Nebuzaradan the captain of the bodyguard had left with Gedaliah the son of Ahikam and grandson of Shaphan, together with Jeremiah the prophet and Baruch the son of Neriah—7 and they entered the land of Egypt (for they did not obey the voice of the LORD) and went in as far as Tahpanhes.

8 Then the word of the LORD came to Jeremiah in Tahpanhes, saying, 9 "Take *some* large stones in your hands and hide them in the mortar in the brick *terrace* which is at the entrance of Pharaoh's palace in Tahpanhes, in the sight of some *of the* Jews; 10 and say to them, 'This is what the LORD of armies, the God of Israel says: "Behold, I am going to send *men* and get My servant Nebuchadnezzar the king of Babylon, and I am going to set his throne over these stones that I have hidden; and he will spread his canopy over them. 11 He will also come and strike the land of Egypt; those who are *meant* for death *will be given over* to death, and those for captivity to captivity, and those for the sword to the sword. 12 And I shall set fire to the temples of the gods of Egypt, and he will burn them and take them captive. So he will wrap himself with the land of Egypt as a shepherd wraps himself with his garment, and he will depart from there safely. 13 He will also smash to pieces the obelisks of Heliopolis, which is in the land of Egypt; and the temples of the gods of Egypt he will burn with fire." ' "

Conquest of Egypt Predicted

44 The word that came to Jeremiah for all the Jews living in the land of Egypt, those who were living in Migdol, Tahpanhes, Memphis, and the land of Pathros, saying, 2 "This is what the LORD of armies, the God of Israel says: 'You yourselves have seen all the disaster that I have brought on Jerusalem and all the cities of Judah; and behold, this day they are in ruins and no one lives in them, 3 because of their wickedness which they committed to provoke Me to anger by continuing to burn sacrifices *and* to serve other gods whom they had not known, *neither* they, you, nor your fathers. 4 Yet I sent you all My servants the prophets again and again, saying, "Oh, do not do this abominable thing which I hate." 5 But they did not listen or incline their ears to turn from their wickedness, so as not to burn sacrifices to other gods. 6 Therefore My wrath and My anger gushed out and burned in the cities of Judah and in the streets of Jerusalem, so they have become ruins and a desolation as *it is* this day. 7 Now then, this is what the LORD God of armies, the God of Israel says: "Why are you doing great harm to yourselves, to eliminate from yourselves man and woman, child and infant from among Judah, leaving yourselves without a remnant, 8 provoking Me to anger with the works of your hands, burning sacrifices to other gods in the land of Egypt where you are entering to reside, so that you may be eliminated and become a curse and a disgrace among all the nations of the earth?

9 Have you forgotten the wickedness of your fathers, the wickedness of the kings of Judah and the wickedness of their wives, your own wickedness and the wickedness of your wives, which they committed in the land of Judah and in the streets of Jerusalem? 10 Yet they have not become contrite *even* to this day, nor have they feared, nor walked in My Law or My statutes, which I placed before you and before your fathers." '

11 "Therefore this is what the LORD of armies, the God of Israel says: 'Behold, I am going to set My face against you for a disaster, even to eliminate all Judah. 12 And I will take away the remnant of Judah who have set their minds on entering the land of Egypt to reside there, and they will all meet their end in the land of Egypt; they will fall by the sword *or* meet their end by famine. From the small to the great, they will die by the sword and famine; and they will become a curse, an object of horror, 'an imprecation, and a disgrace. 13 And I will punish those who live in the land of Egypt, just as I have punished Jerusalem, with the sword, with famine, and with plague. 14 So there will be no survivor or refugee for the remnant of Judah who have entered the land of Egypt to reside there and *then* to return to the land of Judah, to which they are longing to return to live; for none will return except *a few* refugees.' "

15 Then all the men who were aware that their wives were burning sacrifices to other gods, along with all the women who were standing by, *as* a large assembly, including all the people who were living in Pathros in the land of Egypt, responded to Jeremiah, saying, 16 "As for the message that you have spoken to us in the name of the LORD, we are not going to listen to you! 17 But we will certainly carry out every word that has proceeded from our mouths, by burning sacrifices to the queen of heaven and pouring out drink offerings to her, just as we ourselves, our forefathers, our kings, and our leaders did in the cities of Judah and in the streets of Jerusalem; for *then* we had plenty of food and were well off and saw no misfortune. 18 But since we stopped burning sacrifices to the queen of heaven and pouring out drink offerings to her, we have lacked everything, and have met our end by the sword and by famine." 19 "And," *said the women,* "when we were burning sacrifices to the queen of heaven and pouring out drink offerings to her, was it without our husbands that we made for her sacrificial cakes in her image, and poured out drink offerings to her?"

Disaster for the Jews

20 Then Jeremiah said to all the people, to the men and women—even to all the people who were giving him *such* an answer—saying, 21 "As for the smoking sacrifices that you burned in the cities of Judah and in the streets of Jerusalem, you and your forefathers, your kings and your leaders, and the people of the land, did the LORD not remember them, and did *all of this* not come into His mind? 22 So the LORD was no longer able to endure *it,* because

---

44:12 1 Lit *a curse-formula*

of the evil of your deeds, because of the abominations which you have committed; so your land has become a place of ruins, an object of horror, and a curse, without an inhabitant, as *it is* this day. 23 Since you have burned sacrifices and have sinned against the LORD and not obeyed the voice of the LORD nor walked in His Law, His statutes, or His testimonies, therefore this disaster has happened to you, as *it has* this day."

24 Then Jeremiah said to all the people, including all the women, "Hear the word of the LORD, all Judah who are in the land of Egypt! 25 This is what the LORD of armies, the God of Israel says: 'As for you and your wives, you have spoken with your mouths and fulfilled *it* with your hands, saying, "We will certainly perform our vows that we have vowed, to burn sacrifices to the queen of heaven and pour out drink offerings to her." By all means fulfill your vows, and be sure to perform your vows!' 26 In return, hear the word of the LORD, all Judah who are living in the land of Egypt: 'Behold, I have sworn by My great name,' says the LORD, 'that My name shall never be invoked again by the mouth of anyone of Judah in all the land of Egypt, saying, "As the Lord GOD lives." 27 Behold, I am watching over them for harm and not for good, and all the people of Judah who are in the land of Egypt will meet their end by the sword or by famine until they are completely gone. 28 Those who escape the sword will return from the land of Egypt to the land of Judah few in number. Then all the remnant of Judah who have gone to the land of Egypt to reside there will know whose word will stand, Mine or theirs. 29 And this will be the sign to you,' declares the LORD, 'that I am going to punish you in this place, so that you may know that My words will assuredly stand against you for harm.' 30 This is what the LORD says: 'Behold, I am going to hand Pharaoh Hophra king of Egypt over to his enemies, to those who seek his life, just as I handed Zedekiah king of Judah over to Nebuchadnezzar king of Babylon, *who was* his enemy and was seeking his life.' "

Message to Baruch

45 *This is* the message which Jeremiah the prophet spoke to Baruch the son of Neriah, when he had written these words in a book at Jeremiah's dictation, in the fourth year of Jehoiakim the son of Josiah, king of Judah, saying: 2 "This is what the LORD, the God of Israel says to you, Baruch: 3 'You said, "Oh, woe to me! For the LORD has added grief to my pain; I am weary with my groaning and have found no rest." ' 4 This is what you are to say to him: 'This is what the LORD says: "Behold, what I have built I am going to tear down, and what I have planted I am going to uproot, that is, all *the people of* the land." 5 But as for you, are you seeking great things for yourself? Do not seek *them;* for behold, I am going to bring disaster on all flesh,' declares the LORD, 'but I will give your life to you as plunder in all the places where you may go.' "

Defeat of Pharaoh Foretold

46 That which came as the word of the LORD to Jeremiah the prophet concerning the nations.

2 To Egypt, concerning the army of Pharaoh Neco king of Egypt, which was by the river Euphrates at Carchemish, which Nebuchadnezzar king of Babylon defeated in the fourth year of Jehoiakim the son of Josiah, king of Judah:

3   "Set up the *buckler and shield,
     And advance to the battle!
4   "Harness the horses,
     And mount the steeds,
     Take your stand with helmets *on!*
     Polish the spears,
     Put on the coats of armor!
5   "Why have I seen *it?*
     They are terrified,
     They are retreating,
     And their warriors are defeated
     And have taken refuge in flight,
     Without facing back.
     Terror is on every side!"
     Declares the LORD.
6   Let not the swift man flee,
     Nor the warrior escape.
     In the north beside the river Euphrates
     They have stumbled and fallen.
7   Who is this that rises like the Nile,
     Like the rivers whose waters surge?
8   Egypt rises like the Nile,
     And like the rivers whose waters surge;
     And He has said, "I will rise and cover
       that land;
     I will destroy the city and its inhabitants."
9   Go up, you horses, and drive wildly, you
       chariots,
     So that the warriors may march forward:
     Cush and Put, who handle the shield,
     And the Lydians, who handle *and* bend
       the bow.
10   For that day belongs to the Lord GOD of
       armies,
     A day of vengeance, so as to avenge
       Himself on His foes;
     And the sword will devour and be
       satisfied,
     And drink its fill of their blood;
     For there will be a slaughter for the Lord
       GOD of armies,
     In the land of the north at the river
       Euphrates.
11   Go up to Gilead and obtain balm,
     Virgin daughter of Egypt!
     You have used many remedies in vain;
     There is no healing for you.
12   The nations have heard of your shame,
     And the earth is full of your cry *of
       distress;*
     For one warrior has stumbled over
       another,
     And both of them have fallen down
       together.

13 *This is* the message which the LORD spoke to Jeremiah the prophet about the coming of Nebuchadnezzar king of Babylon to strike the land of Egypt:

14 "Declare in Egypt and proclaim in Migdol,

Proclaim also in Memphis and Tahpanhes;
Say, 'Take your stand and get yourself
ready,
For the sword has devoured those around
you.'
15 "Why have your powerful ones been cut
down?
They do not stand because the LORD has
thrust them away.
16 "They have repeatedly stumbled;
Indeed, they have fallen, one against
another.
Then they said, 'Get up, and let's go
back
To our own people and our native land,
Away from the sword of the oppressor!'
17 "They shouted there, 'Pharaoh king of
Egypt *is nothing but* a big noise;
He has let the appointed time pass by!'
18 "As I live," declares the King,
Whose name is the LORD of armies,
"One certainly shall come *who is* like Tabor
among the mountains,
Or like Carmel by the sea.
19 "Make your baggage *ready for* exile,
Daughter living in Egypt,
For Memphis will become a desolation;
It will be destroyed *and* deprived of inhab-
itants.
20 "Egypt is a pretty heifer,
But a horsefly is coming from the north—
it is coming!
21 "Also her mercenaries in her midst
Are like fattened calves,
For they too have turned away *and* have
fled together;
They did not stand *their ground.*
For the day of their disaster has come
upon them,
The time of their punishment.
22 "Its sound moves along like a serpent;
For they move on like an army
And come to her as woodcutters with
axes.
23 "They have cut down her forest," declares
the LORD;
"Certainly it will no *longer* be found,
Even though they are more numerous
than locusts
And are without number.
24 "The daughter of Egypt has been put to
shame,
Turned over to the power of the people of
the north."
25 The LORD of armies, the God of Israel
says: "Behold, I am going to punish Amon of
Thebes, and Pharaoh, and Egypt along with her
gods and her kings, indeed, Pharaoh and those
who trust in him. 26 I shall hand them over to
those who are seeking their lives, that is, to
Nebuchadnezzar king of Babylon and to his
officers. Afterward, however, it will be inhabited as in the days of old," declares the LORD.
27 ¶ "But as for you, Jacob My servant, do not
fear,
Nor be dismayed, Israel!
For, see, I am going to save you from far
away,
And your descendants from the land of
their captivity;

And Jacob will return and be undisturbed
And secure, with no one making *him*
afraid.
28 "Jacob My servant, do not fear," declares
the LORD,
"For I am with you.
For I will make a complete destruction of
all the nations
Where I have driven you,
Yet I will not make a complete destruction
of you;
But I will correct you properly
And by no means leave you unpunished."

Prophecy against Philistia

47 The word of the LORD that came to
Jeremiah the prophet concerning the
Philistines, before Pharaoh conquered Gaza.
2 This is what the LORD says:
"Behold, waters are going to rise from the
north
And become an overflowing torrent,
And overflow the land and everything that
is in it,
The city and those who live in it;
And the people will cry out,
And every inhabitant of the land will
wail.
3 "Because of the noise of the galloping hoofs
of his stallions,
The roar of his chariots, *and* the rumbling
of his wheels,
The fathers have not turned back for *their*
children,
Because of the debility of *their* hands,
4 Because of the day that is coming
To destroy all the Philistines,
To eliminate from Tyre and Sidon
Every surviving ally;
For the LORD is going to destroy the
Philistines,
The remnant of the coastland of
Caphtor.
5 "Baldness has come upon Gaza;
Ashkelon has been destroyed.
Remnant of their valley,
How long will you gash yourself?
6 "Ah, sword of the LORD,
How long will you not be quiet?
Withdraw into your sheath;
Rest and stay still.
7 "How can it be quiet,
When the LORD has given it an order?
Against Ashkelon and against the sea
shore—
There He has summoned it."

Prophecy against Moab

48 Concerning Moab. This is what the LORD
of armies, the God of Israel says:
"Woe to Nebo, for it has been destroyed;
Kiriathaim has been put to shame, it has
been captured;
The high stronghold has been put to
shame and shattered.
2 "There is no longer praise for Moab;
In Heshbon they have devised disaster
against her:
'Come and let's cut her off from *being* a
nation!'

You too, ¹Madmen, will be silenced;
The sword will follow you.
3 "The sound of an outcry from Horonaim,
'Devastation and great destruction!'
4 "Moab is broken,
Her little ones have sounded out a cry *of distress.*
5 "For they will go up by the ascent of Luhith
With continual weeping;
For at the descent of Horonaim
They have heard the anguished cry of destruction.
6 "Flee, save yourselves,
So that you may be like a juniper in the wilderness.
7 "For because of your trust in your own achievements and treasures,
You yourself will also be captured;
And Chemosh will go off into exile
Together with his priests and his leaders.
8 "A destroyer will come to every city,
So that no city will escape;
The valley also will be ruined
And the plateau will be destroyed,
As the LORD has said.
9 "Give wings to Moab,
For she will flee away;
And her cities will become a desolation,
Without inhabitants in them.
10 "Cursed is the one who does the LORD'S work negligently,
And cursed is the one who restrains his sword from blood.
11¶ "Moab has been at ease since his youth;
He has also been peaceful, *like wine* on its dregs,
And he has not been poured from vessel to vessel,
Nor has he gone into exile.
Therefore he retains his flavor,
And his aroma has not changed.
12 Therefore behold, the days are coming," declares the LORD, "when I will send to him those who tip *vessels,* and they will tip him over, and they will pour out his vessels and smash his jars. 13 And Moab will be ashamed of Chemosh, just as the house of Israel was ashamed of Bethel, their confidence.
14 "How can you say, 'We are warriors,
And men competent for battle'?
15 "Moab has been destroyed and men have gone up to his cities;
His choicest young men have also gone down to the slaughter,"
Declares the King, whose name is the LORD of armies.
16 "The disaster of Moab will soon come,
And his catastrophe has hurried quickly.
17 "Mourn for him, all you who *live* around him,
And all of you who know his name;
Say, 'How the mighty scepter has been broken,
A staff of splendor!'
18 "Come down from your glory
And sit on the parched ground,
O daughter living in Dibon,
For the destroyer of Moab has come up against you,

He has ruined your strongholds.
19 "Stand by the road and keep watch,
You inhabitant of Aroer;
Ask him who flees and her who escapes
And say, 'What has happened?'
20 "Moab has been put to shame, for it has been shattered.
Wail and cry out;
Declare by the Arnon
That Moab has been destroyed.
21 "Judgment has also come upon the plain, upon Holon, Jahzah, and against Mephaath, 22 against Dibon, Nebo, and Beth-diblathaim, 23 against Kiriathaim, Beth-gamul, and Beth-meon, 24 against Kerioth, Bozrah, and all the cities of the land of Moab, far and near. 25 The horn of Moab has been cut off, and his arm broken," declares the LORD. 26 "Make him drunk, for he has become arrogant toward the LORD; so Moab will vomit, and he also will become a laughingstock. 27 Now was Israel not a laughingstock to you? Or was he caught among thieves? For whenever you speak about him you shake *your head in scorn.*
28 "Leave the cities and live among the rocky cliffs,
You inhabitants of Moab,
And be like a dove that nests
Beyond the mouth of the chasm.
29 "We have heard of the pride of Moab—he *is* very proud—
Of his haughtiness, his pride, his arrogance, and his self-exaltation.
30 "I know his fury," declares the LORD,
"But it is futile;
His idle boasts have accomplished nothing.
31 "Therefore I will wail for Moab,
For all of Moab I will cry out;
I will moan for the men of Kir-heres.
32 "More than the weeping for Jazer
I will weep for you, O vine of Sibmah!
Your tendrils stretched across the sea,
They reached to the sea of Jazer;
Upon your summer fruits and your grape harvest
The destroyer has fallen.
33 "So joy and rejoicing are removed
From the fruitful field, and from the land of Moab.
And I have eliminated the wine from the wine presses;
No one will tread *them* with shouting,
The shouting will not be shouts *of joy.*
34 From the outcry at Heshbon to Elealeh, to Jahaz they have raised their voice, from Zoar to Horonaim, *and to* Eglath-shelishiyah; for even the waters of Nimrim will become desolate. 35 And I will put an end to Moab," declares the LORD, "the one who offers *sacrifice* on the high place and the one who burns incense to his gods.
36 "Therefore My heart makes a sound like flutes for Moab; My heart also makes a sound like flutes for the men of Kir-heres. Therefore they have lost the abundance it produced. 37 For every head is *shaved* bald, and every beard cut short; there are gashes on all the

---

hands, and sackcloth around the waists. **38** On all the housetops of Moab and in its public squares there is mourning everywhere; for I have broken Moab like an undesirable vessel," declares the LORD. **39** "How shattered it is! *How* they have wailed! How Moab has turned his back—he is ashamed! So Moab will become a laughingstock and an object of terror to all around him."

40¶ For this is what the LORD says:
"Behold, one will fly swiftly like an eagle
And spread out his wings against Moab.

41 "Kerioth has been captured
And the strongholds have been seized,
So the hearts of the warriors of Moab on that day
Will be like the heart of a woman in labor.

42 "Moab will be destroyed from *being* a people
Because he has become arrogant toward the LORD.

43 "Terror, pit, and snare are *coming* upon you,
Inhabitant of Moab," declares the LORD.

44 "The one who flees from the terror
Will fall into the pit,
And the one who climbs up out of the pit
Will be caught in the snare;
For I will bring upon her, upon Moab,
The year of their punishment," declares the LORD.

45¶ "In the shadow of Heshbon
The fugitives stand without strength;
For a fire has spread out from Heshbon
And a flame from the midst of Sihon,
And it has devoured the forehead of Moab
And the scalps of the loud revelers.

46 "Woe to you, Moab!
The people of Chemosh have perished;
For your sons have been taken away captive,
And your daughters into captivity.

47 "Yet I will restore the fortunes of Moab
In the latter days," declares the LORD.
This is the extent of the judgment on Moab.

Prophecy against Ammon

49 Concerning the sons of Ammon. This is what the LORD says:
"Does Israel have no sons?
Or has he no heirs?
Why *then* has Malcam taken possession of Gad,
And his people settled in its cities?

2 "Therefore behold, the days are coming," declares the LORD,
"When I will cause an alarm of war to be heard
Against Rabbah of the sons of Ammon;
And it will become a desolate heap,
And her towns will be set on fire.
Then Israel will take possession of his possessors,"
Says the LORD.

3 "Wail, Heshbon, for Ai has been destroyed!
Cry out, daughters of Rabbah,
Put on sackcloth and mourn,
And move about inside the walls;
For Malcam will go into exile

Together with his priests and his leaders.

4 "How you boast about the valleys!
Your valley is flowing *away,*
You backsliding daughter
Who trusts in her treasures, *saying,*
'Who can come against me?'

5 "Behold, I am going to bring terror upon you,"
Declares the Lord GOD of armies,
"From all *directions* around you;
And you will be driven away one after another,
With no one to gather the fugitives together.

6 "But afterward I will restore
The fortunes of the sons of Ammon,"
Declares the LORD.

Prophecy against Edom

7¶ Concerning Edom.
This is what the LORD of armies says:
"Is there no longer *any* wisdom in Teman?
Has *good* advice been lost by the prudent?
Has their wisdom decayed?

8 "Flee away, turn back, dwell in the depths,
You inhabitants of Dedan,
For I will bring the disaster of Esau upon him
At the time I punish him.

9 "If grape pickers came to you,
Would they not leave gleanings?
If thieves *came* by night,
They would destroy *only* what was sufficient for them.

10 "But I have stripped Esau bare,
I have uncovered his hiding places
So that he will not be able to conceal himself;
His offspring have been destroyed along with his ⁷brothers
And his neighbors, and he no *longer* exists.

11 "Leave your orphans behind, I will keep *them* alive;
And let your widows trust in Me."

12 For this is what the LORD says: "Behold, those who were not sentenced to drink the cup will certainly drink *it,* so are you the one who will be held completely blameless? You will not be held blameless, but you will certainly drink it. **13** For I have sworn by Myself," declares the LORD, "that Bozrah will become an object of horror, a disgrace, a wasteland, and a curse; and all its cities will become permanent ruins."

14¶ I have heard a message from the LORD,
And a messenger is being sent among the nations, *saying,*
"Gather yourselves together and come against her,
And rise up for battle!"

15 "For behold, I have made you small among the nations,
Despised among people.

16 "As for the terror you cause,
The arrogance of your heart has deceived you,
You who live in the clefts of the rock,
Who occupy the height of the hill.

49:10 ¹ Or *relatives*

Though you make your nest as high as an
eagle's,
I will bring you down from there,"
declares the LORD.

17 "Edom will become an object of horror;
everyone who passes by it will be appalled
and will hiss at all its wounds. 18 Like the
overthrow of Sodom and Gomorrah with its
neighbors," says the LORD, "no one will live
there, nor will anyone of mankind reside in it.
19 Behold, one will come up like a lion from the
thicket of the Jordan to a perennially watered
pasture; for in an instant I will chase him away
from it, and I will appoint over it whoever is
chosen. For who is like Me, and who will
summon Me *into court?* And who then is the
shepherd who can stand against Me?"

20 Therefore hear the plan of the LORD
which He has planned against Edom, and His
purposes which He has in mind against the
inhabitants of Teman: they will certainly drag
them off, *even* the little ones of the flock; He
will certainly make their pasture desolate
because of them. 21 The earth has quaked at
the noise of their downfall. There is an outcry!
The noise of it has been heard at the Red Sea.
22 Behold, He will mount up and swoop like an
eagle, and spread out His wings against Bozrah;
and the hearts of the warriors of Edom on that
day will be like the heart of a woman in labor.

Prophecy against Damascus

23¶ Concerning Damascus:
"Hamath and Arpad are put to shame,
For they have heard bad news;
They despair.
There is anxiety at the sea,
It cannot be calmed.
24 "Damascus has become helpless;
She has turned away to flee,
And panic has gripped her;
Distress and labor pains have seized her
Like a woman in childbirth.
25 "How the city of praise has not been
deserted,
The town of My joy!
26 "Therefore, her young men will fall in her
streets,
And all the men of war will perish on that
day," declares the LORD of armies.
27 "I will set fire to the wall of Damascus,
And it will devour the fortified palace of
Ben-hadad."

Prophecy against Kedar and Hazor

28 Concerning Kedar and the kingdoms of
Hazor, which Nebuchadnezzar king of Babylon
defeated. This is what the LORD says:
"Arise, go up to Kedar
And devastate the people of the east.
29 "They will take away their tents and their
flocks;
They will carry off for themselves
Their tent curtains, all their goods and
their camels,
And they will call out to one another,
'Horror on every side!'
30 "Run away, flee! Dwell in the depths,
You inhabitants of Hazor," declares the
LORD;

"For Nebuchadnezzar king of Babylon has
formed a plan against you
And devised a scheme against you.
31 "Arise, go up against a nation which is at
ease,
Which lives securely," declares the LORD.
"It has no gates or bars;
They dwell alone.
32 "Their camels will become plunder,
And their many livestock for spoils,
And I will scatter to all the winds those
who cut the corners *of their hair;*
And I will bring their disaster from every
side," declares the LORD.
33 "Hazor will become a haunt of jackals,
A desolation forever;
No one will live there,
Nor will anyone of mankind reside in it."

Prophecy against Elam

34 The word of the LORD that came to Jere-
miah the prophet concerning Elam, at the
beginning of the reign of Zedekiah king of
Judah, saying:
35¶ "This is what the LORD of armies says:
'Behold, I am going to break the bow of
Elam,
The finest of their might.
36 'I will bring upon Elam the four winds
From the four ends of heaven,
And will scatter them to all these winds;
And there will be no nation
To which the outcasts of Elam will not go.
37 'So I will shatter Elam before their
enemies
And before those who seek their lives;
And I will bring disaster upon them,
Even My fierce anger,' declares the LORD,
'And I will send the sword after them
Until I have consumed them.
38 'Then I will set My throne in Elam,
And eliminate from there *the* king and
officials,'
Declares the LORD.
39 'But it will come about in the last days
That I will restore the fortunes of Elam,' "
Declares the LORD.

Prophecy against Babylon

50 The word which the LORD spoke concerning Babylon, the land of the
Chaldeans, through Jeremiah the prophet:
2 "Declare and proclaim among the nations.
Proclaim it and lift up a flag,
Do not conceal *it.* Say,
'Babylon has been captured,
Bel has been put to shame, Marduk has
been shattered;
Her idols have been put to shame, her
images have been shattered.'
3 For a nation has come up against her from the
north; it will make her land an object of horror,
and there will be no inhabitant in it. Whether
people or animals, they have wandered off,
they have gone!
4 "In those days and at that time," declares
the LORD, "the sons of Israel will come, they
and the sons of Judah as well; they will go
along weeping as they go, and *it will be* the
LORD their God *whom* they will seek. 5 They

will ask for the way to Zion, *turning* their faces
in its direction; they will come so that they
may join themselves to the LORD *in* an
everlasting covenant *that* will not be forgotten.

6¶ "My people have become lost sheep;
  Their shepherds have led them astray.
  They have made them turn aside *on* the
    mountains.
  They have gone from mountain to hill,
  They have forgotten their resting place.

7 "All who found them have devoured
    them;
  And their adversaries have said, 'We are
    not guilty,
  Since they have sinned against the LORD
    who is the habitation of righteousness,
  The LORD, the hope of their fathers.'

8¶ "Wander away from the midst of Babylon
  And go out from the land of the
    Chaldeans;
  Be like male goats at the head of the flock.

9 "For behold, I am going to rouse and bring
    up against Babylon
  A contingent of great nations from the
    land of the north,
  And they will draw up *their* battle lines
    against her;
  From there she will be taken captive.
  Their arrows will be like an expert
    warrior
  Who does not return empty-handed.

10 "Chaldea will become plunder;
  All who plunder her will have enough,"
    declares the LORD.

11¶ "Because you are glad, because you are
    jubilant,
  You who pillage My heritage,
  Because you skip about like a threshing
    heifer
  And neigh like stallions,

12 Your mother will be greatly ashamed,
  She who gave you birth will be
    humiliated.
  Behold, *she will be* the least of the
    nations,
  A wilderness, a dry land and a desert.

13 "Because of the wrath of the LORD she will
    not be inhabited,
  But she will be completely desolate;
  Everyone who passes by Babylon will be
    horrified
  And will hiss because of all her wounds.

14 "Draw up your battle lines against Babylon
    on every side,
  All of you who bend the bow;
  Shoot at her, do not spare *your* arrows,
  For she has sinned against the LORD.

15 "Raise your battle cry against her on every
    side!
  She has given herself up, her towers have
    fallen,
  Her walls have been torn down.
  For this is the vengeance of the LORD:
  Take vengeance on her;
  As she has done *to others, so* do to her.

16 "Eliminate the sower from Babylon
  And the one who wields the sickle at the
    time of harvest;
  From the sword of the oppressor

  Each of them will turn back to his own
    people
  And each of them will flee to his own
    land.

17 "Israel is a scattered flock, the lions have
driven *them* away. The first one *who* devoured
him was the king of Assyria, and this last one
who has gnawed his bones is Nebuchadnezzar
king of Babylon. 18 Therefore this is what the
LORD of armies, the God of Israel says: 'Behold,
I am going to punish the king of Babylon and
his land, just as I punished the king of Assyria.
19 And I will bring Israel back to his pasture
and he will graze on Carmel and Bashan, and
his desire will be satisfied in the hill country of
Ephraim and Gilead. 20 In those days and at that
time,' declares the LORD, 'search will be made
for the wrongdoing of Israel, but there will be
none; and for the sins of Judah, but they will
not be found; for I will forgive those whom I
leave as a remnant.'

21¶ "Against the land of ¹Merathaim, go up
    against it,
  And against the inhabitants of ²Pekod.
  Kill and completely destroy them,"
    declares the LORD,
  "And do according to everything that I
    have commanded you.

22 "The noise of battle is in the land,
  And great destruction.

23 "How the hammer of the whole earth
  Has been cut off and broken!
  How Babylon has become
  An object of horror among the nations!

24 "I set a trap for you and you were also
    caught, Babylon,
  While you yourself were not aware;
  You have been found and also seized
  Because you have engaged in conflict with
    the LORD."

25 The LORD has opened His armory
  And has brought out the weapons of His
    indignation,
  For it is a work of the Lord GOD of armies
  In the land of the Chaldeans.

26 Come to her from the farthest border;
  Open up her barns,
  Pile her up like heaps of grain
  And completely destroy her,
  Let nothing be left to her.

27 Put all her bulls to the sword;
  Let them go down to the slaughter!
  Woe be upon them, for their day has
    come,
  The time of their punishment.

28¶ There is a sound of fugitives and refugees
    from the land of Babylon,
  To declare in Zion the vengeance of the
    LORD our God,
  Vengeance for His temple.

29¶ "Summon ¹many against Babylon,
  All those who bend the bow;
  Encamp against her on every side,
  Let there be no escape.
  Repay her according to her work;
  According to all that she has done, *so* do
    to her;
  For she has become arrogant against the
    LORD,

50:21 ¹Or *double rebellion*   ²I.e., punishment (uncertain)   **50:29** ¹Another reading is *archers*

Against the Holy One of Israel.

30 "Therefore her young men will fall in her
  streets,
  And all her men of war will perish on that
  day," declares the LORD.
31 "Behold, I am against you, arrogant one,"
  Declares the Lord GOD of armies,
  "For your day has come,
  The time when I will punish you.
32 "The arrogant one will stumble and fall
  With no one to raise him up;
  And I will set fire to his cities,
  And it will devour all his surroundings."
33¶ This is what the LORD of armies says:
  "The sons of Israel are oppressed,
  And the sons of Judah as well;
  And all who took them captive have held
  them firmly,
  They have refused to let them go.
34 "Their Redeemer is strong, the LORD of
  armies is His name;
  He will vigorously plead their case
  So that He may bring rest to their land,
  But turmoil to the inhabitants of Babylon.
35 "A sword against the Chaldeans," declares
  the LORD,
  "And against the inhabitants of Babylon
  And against her leaders and her wise
  men!
36 "A sword against the oracle priests, and
  they will become fools!
  A sword against her warriors, and they
  will be shattered!
37 "A sword against their horses, against their
  chariots,
  And against all the foreigners who are in
  the midst of her,
  And they will become women!
  A sword against her treasures, and they
  will be plundered!
38 "A drought on her waters, and they will be
  dried up!
  For it is a land of idols,
  And they go insane at frightful images.
39¶ "Therefore the desert creatures will live
  there with the jackals;
  The ostriches also will live in it.
  It will never again be inhabited
  Nor lived in from generation to
  generation.
40 "As when God overthrew Sodom
  And Gomorrah with its neighbors,"
  declares the LORD,
  "No one will live there,
  Nor will anyone of mankind reside in it.
41¶ "Behold, a people is coming from the
  north,
  And a great nation and many kings
  Will be roused from the remote parts of
  the earth.
42 "They seize their bow and javelin;
  They are cruel and have no mercy.
  Their voice roars like the sea;
  And they ride on horses,
  Drawn up like a man for the battle
  Against you, daughter of Babylon.
43 "The king of Babylon has heard the report
  about them,
  And his hands hang limp;

Distress has gripped him,
  Agony like a woman in childbirth.
44 "Behold, one will come up like a lion from
  the thicket of the Jordan to a perennially
  watered pasture; for in an instant I will chase
  them away from it, and I will appoint over it
  whoever is chosen. For who is like Me, and
  who will summon Me into court? And who
  then is the shepherd who can stand against
  Me?" 45 Therefore hear the plan of the LORD
  which He has planned against Babylon, and His
  purposes which He has in mind against the
  land of the Chaldeans: they will certainly drag
  them off, even the little ones of the flock; He
  will certainly make their pasture desolate
  because of them. 46 At the shout, "Babylon has
  been conquered!" the earth quakes, and an
  outcry is heard among the nations.

Babylon Judged for Sins against Israel

51 This is what the LORD says:
  "Behold, I am going to stir up
  The spirit of a destroyer against Babylon
  And against the inhabitants of ᵗLeb-kamai.
2 "I will send foreigners to Babylon so that
  they may winnow her
  And devastate her land;
  For they will be opposed to her on every
  side
  On the day of her disaster.
3 "Let not him who bends his bow bend it,
  Nor let him rise up in his coat of armor.
  Do not spare her young men;
  Devote all her army to destruction.
4 "They will fall down dead in the land of the
  Chaldeans,
  And pierced through in their streets."
5¶ For neither Israel nor Judah has been
  forsaken
  By his God, the LORD of armies,
  Although their land is full of guilt
  Before the Holy One of Israel.
6 Flee from the midst of Babylon,
  And each of you save his life!
  Do not perish in her punishment,
  For this is the LORD's time of vengeance;
  He is going to repay to her what she
  deserves.
7 Babylon has been a golden cup in the
  hand of the LORD,
  Intoxicating all the earth.
  The nations have drunk of her wine;
  Therefore the nations are going insane.
8 Suddenly Babylon has fallen and been
  broken;
  Wail over her!
  Bring balm for her pain;
  Perhaps she may be healed.
9 We applied healing to Babylon, but she
  was not healed;
  Abandon her and let's each go to his own
  country,
  For her judgment has reached to heaven
  And it rises to the clouds.
10 The LORD has brought about our
  vindication;
  Come and let's recount in Zion
  The work of the LORD our God!
11¶ Sharpen the arrows, fill the quivers!

51:1 ᵗ Cryptic name for Chaldea; or the heart of those who rise up against Me

The Lord has stirred up the spirit of the
kings of the Medes,
Because His plan is against Babylon to
destroy it;
For it is the vengeance of the Lord,
vengeance for His temple.
12 Lift up a signal flag against the walls of
Babylon;
Post a strong guard,
Station sentries,
Set up an ambush!
For the Lord has both planned and
performed
What He spoke concerning the
inhabitants of Babylon.
13 You who live by many waters,
Abundant in treasures,
Your end has come,
The measure of your end.
14 The Lord of armies has sworn by Himself:
"I will certainly fill you with a population
like locusts,
And they will cry out with shouts of
victory over you."
15¶ It is He who made the earth by His
power,
Who established the world by His
wisdom,
And by His understanding He stretched
out the heavens.
16 When He utters His voice, there is a roar
of waters in the heavens,
And He makes the clouds ascend from the
end of the earth.
He makes lightning for the rain
And brings out wind from His
storehouses.
17 Every person is stupid, devoid of
knowledge;
Every goldsmith is put to shame by his
idols,
For his cast metal images are deceitful,
And there is no breath in them.
18 They are worthless, a work of mockery;
At the time of their punishment they will
perish.
19 The portion of Jacob is not like these;
For He is the Maker of everything,
And of the tribe of His inheritance;
The Lord of armies is His name.
20 He says, "You are My war-club, My
weapon of war;
And with you I shatter nations,
And with you I destroy kingdoms.
21 "With you I shatter the horse and his rider,
And with you I shatter the chariot and its
rider,
22 And with you I shatter man and woman,
And with you I shatter the old man and
youth,
And with you I shatter the young man and
virgin,
23 And with you I shatter the shepherd and
his flock,
And with you I shatter the farmer and his
team,
And with you I shatter governors and
officials.
24 "But I will repay Babylon and all the
inhabitants of Chaldea for all their evil that

they have done in Zion before your eyes,"
declares the Lord.
25 "Behold, I am against you, mountain of
destruction
That destroys the whole earth," declares
the Lord,
"And I will stretch out My hand against
you,
And roll you down from the rocky cliffs,
And I will make you a burnt out
mountain.
26 "They will not take from you even a stone
for a corner
Nor a stone for foundations,
But you will be desolate forever," declares
the Lord.
27¶ Lift up a signal flag in the land,
Blow a trumpet among the nations!
Consecrate the nations against her,
Summon against her the kingdoms of
Ararat, Minni, and Ashkenaz;
Appoint an officer against her,
Bring up the horses like bristly locusts.
28 Consecrate the nations against her,
The kings of the Medes,
Their governors and all their officials,
And every land under their control.
29 So the land quakes and writhes,
For the plans of the Lord against Babylon
stand,
To make the land of Babylon
A desolation without inhabitants.
30 The warriors of Babylon have ceased
fighting,
They stay in the strongholds;
Their strength is exhausted,
They are becoming like women;
Their homes are set on fire,
The bars of her gates are broken.
31 One courier runs to meet another,
And one messenger to meet another,
To tell the king of Babylon
That his city has been captured from end
to end;
32 The river crossing places have been
seized,
And they have burned the marshes with
fire,
And the men of war are terrified.
33¶ For this is what the Lord of armies, the
God of Israel says:
"The daughter of Babylon is like a
threshing floor
At the time that it is tread down;
In just a little while the time of harvest
will come for her."
34¶ "Nebuchadnezzar the king of Babylon has
devoured me, he has crushed me,
He has set me down like an empty vessel;
He has swallowed me like a monster,
He has filled his stomach with my
delicacies;
He has washed me away.
35 "May the violence done to me and to my
flesh be upon Babylon,"
The inhabitant of Zion will say;
And, "May my blood be upon the
inhabitants of Chaldea,"
Jerusalem will say.
36 Therefore this is what the Lord says:

"Behold, I am going to plead your case
And take vengeance for you;
And I will dry up her sea
And make her fountain dry.
37 "Babylon will become a heap *of ruins,* a
haunt of jackals,
An object of horror and hissing, without
inhabitants.
38 "They will roar together like young lions,
They will growl like lions' cubs.
39 "When they become heated up, I will serve
them their banquet
And make them drunk, so that they may
rejoice in triumph,
And may sleep a perpetual sleep
And not wake up," declares the LORD.
40 "I will bring them down like lambs to the
slaughter,
Like rams together with male goats.
41¶ "How ¹Sheshak has been captured,
And the praise of the whole earth has
been seized!
How Babylon has become an object of
horror among the nations!
42 "The sea has come up over Babylon;
She has been engulfed by its roaring
waves.
43 "Her cities have become an object of
horror,
A dry land and a desert,
A land in which no one lives
And through which no one of mankind
passes.
44 "I will punish Bel in Babylon,
And I will make what he has swallowed
come out of his mouth;
And the nations will no longer stream
toward him.
Even the wall of Babylon has fallen
down!
45¶ "Come out from her midst, My people,
And each of you save yourselves
From the fierce anger of the LORD.
46 "Now, so that your heart does not grow
faint,
And you are not afraid at the report that
will be heard in the land—
For the report will come in one year,
And after that another report in another
year,
And violence *will be* in the land
With ruler against ruler—
47 Therefore behold, days are coming
When I will punish the idols of Babylon;
And her whole land will be put to
shame.
And all her slain will fall in her midst.
48 "Then heaven and earth and everything
that is in them
Will shout for joy over Babylon,
Because the destroyers will come to her
from the north,"
Declares the LORD.
49¶ Indeed, Babylon is to fall *for* the slain of
Israel,
As the slain of all the earth have also
fallen for Babylon.
50 You who have escaped the sword,
Go! Do not stay!

Remember the LORD from far away,
And let Jerusalem come to your mind.
51 We are ashamed because we have heard
rebuke;
Disgrace has covered our faces,
Because strangers have entered
The holy places of the LORD's house.
52¶ "Therefore behold, the days are coming,"
declares the LORD,
"When I will punish her idols,
And the mortally wounded will groan
throughout her land.
53 "Though Babylon ascends to the heavens,
And though she fortifies her lofty
stronghold,
Destroyers will come from Me to her,"
declares the LORD.
54¶ The sound of an outcry from Babylon,
And of great destruction from the land of
the Chaldeans!
55 For the LORD is going to destroy Babylon,
And He will make *her* loud noise vanish
from her.
And their waves will roar like many
waters;
The clamor of their voices sounds forth.
56 For the destroyer is coming against her,
against Babylon,
And her warriors will be captured,
Their bows shattered;
For the LORD is a God of retribution,
He will fully repay.
57 "I will make her leaders and her wise men
drunk,
Her governors, her officials, and her
warriors,
So that they will sleep a perpetual sleep
and not wake up,"
Declares the King, whose name is the
LORD of armies.
58 This is what the LORD of armies says:
"The broad wall of Babylon will be
completely demolished,
And her high gates will be set on fire;
So the peoples will labor for nothing,
And the nations become exhausted *only*
for fire."
59 The command that Jeremiah the prophet
gave Seraiah the son of Neriah, the grandson of
Mahseiah, when he went with Zedekiah the
king of Judah to Babylon in the fourth year of
his reign. (And Seraiah was quartermaster.)
60 Jeremiah wrote on a single scroll all the disaster which would come against Babylon, *that
is,* all these words which have been written
concerning Babylon. 61 Then Jeremiah said to
Seraiah, "As soon as you come to Babylon, see
that you read all these words aloud, 62 and say,
'You, LORD, have promised concerning this
place to cut it off, so that there will be nothing
living in it, whether man or animal; but it will
be a permanent desolation.' 63 And as soon as
you finish reading this scroll, you shall tie a
stone to it and throw it into the middle of the
Euphrates, 64 and say, 'Just so shall Babylon
sink down and not rise *again,* because of the
disaster that I am going to bring upon her; and
they will become exhausted.'" To this point
are the words of Jeremiah.

51:41 ¹ Cryptic name for Babylon

The Fall of Jerusalem

52 Zedekiah was twenty-one years old when he became king, and he reigned for eleven years in Jerusalem; and his mother's name was Hamutal the daughter of Jeremiah of Libnah. [2] He did evil in the sight of the LORD, in accordance with everything that Jehoiakim had done. [3] For because of the anger of the LORD *this* came about in Jerusalem and Judah, until He drove them out from His presence. And Zedekiah revolted against the king of Babylon. [4] Now it came about in the ninth year of his reign, on the tenth *day* of the tenth month, that Nebuchadnezzar king of Babylon came, he and all his army, against Jerusalem, camped against it, and built a [1]bulwark all around it. [5] So the city was under siege until the eleventh year of King Zedekiah. [6] On the ninth *day* of the fourth month the famine was so severe in the city that there was no food for the people of the land. [7] Then the city was breached, and all the warriors fled and left the city at night by way of the gate between the two walls which *was* by the king's garden, though the Chaldeans were all around the city. And they went by way of the Arabah. [8] But the army of the Chaldeans pursued the king and overtook Zedekiah in the desert plains of Jericho, and all his army was scattered from him. [9] Then they captured the king and brought him up to the king of Babylon at Riblah in the land of Hamath, and he passed sentence on him. [10] And the king of Babylon slaughtered the sons of Zedekiah before his eyes, and he also slaughtered all the commanders of Judah in Riblah. [11] Then he blinded the eyes of Zedekiah; and the king of Babylon bound him with bronze shackles and brought him to Babylon and put him in prison until the day of his death.

[12] Now on the tenth *day* of the fifth month, which was the nineteenth year of King Nebuchadnezzar, king of Babylon, Nebuzaradan the captain of the bodyguard, who was in the service of the king of Babylon, came to Jerusalem. [13] And he burned the house of the LORD, the king's house, and all the houses of Jerusalem; even every large house he burned with fire. [14] So the entire army of the Chaldeans who *were* with the captain of the guard tore down all the walls around Jerusalem. [15] Then Nebuzaradan the captain of the guard took into exile some of the poorest of the people, the rest of the people who were left in the city, the deserters who had deserted to the king of Babylon, and the rest of the craftsmen. [16] But Nebuzaradan the captain of the guard left some of the poorest of the land to be vinedressers and farmers.

[17] Now the bronze pillars which belonged to the house of the LORD and the stands and the bronze sea, which were in the house of the LORD, the Chaldeans smashed to pieces and carried all their bronze to Babylon. [18] They also took the pots, the shovels, the snuffers, the basins, the pans, and all the bronze vessels which were used in temple service. [19] The captain of the guard also took the bowls, the firepans, the basins, the pots, the lampstands, the pans, and the 'drink offering bowls, whatever was fine gold, and whatever was fine silver. [20] The two pillars, the one sea, and the twelve bronze bulls that were under the sea, *and* the stands, which King Solomon had made for the house of the LORD—the bronze of all these vessels was beyond weight. [21] As for the pillars, the height of each pillar *was* [1]eighteen cubits, and it *was* twelve cubits in circumference and four fingers in thickness, *and* hollow. [22] Also, a capital of bronze was on top of it; and the height of each capital was [1]five cubits, with latticework and pomegranates on the capital all around, all of bronze. And the second pillar was like these, including pomegranates. [23] There were ninety-six exposed pomegranates; all the pomegranates *numbered* a hundred on the latticework all around.

[24] Then the captain of the guard took Seraiah the chief priest and Zephaniah the second priest, with the three officers of the temple. [25] He also took from the city one official who was overseer of the warriors, seven of the king's advisers who were found in the city, the scribe of the commander of the army who mustered the people of the land, and sixty men from the people of the land who were found inside the city. [26] Nebuzaradan the captain of the bodyguards took them and brought them to the king of Babylon at Riblah. [27] Then the king of Babylon struck them and put them to death in Riblah in the land of Hamath. So Judah was led into exile from its land.

[28] These are the people whom Nebuchadnezzar took into exile: in the seventh year 3,023 Jews; [29] in the eighteenth year of Nebuchadnezzar 832 persons from Jerusalem; [30] in the twenty-third year of Nebuchadnezzar, Nebuzaradan the captain of the guard took into exile 745 Jewish people; *there were* 4,600 people in all.

[31] Now it came about in the thirty-seventh year of the exile of Jehoiachin king of Judah, in the twelfth month, on the twenty-fifth of the month, that Evil-merodach king of Babylon, in the *first* year of his reign, showed favor to Jehoiachin king of Judah and brought him out of prison. [32] Then he spoke kindly to him and set his throne above the thrones of the kings who *were* with him in Babylon. [33] So Jehoiachin changed his prison clothes, and had his meals in the king's presence regularly all the days of his life. [34] And as his allowance, a regular allowance was given to him by the king of Babylon, a portion for each day, all the days of his life until the day of his death.

52:4 [1]I.e., a defensive wall　**52:21** [1]About 27 ft. high and 18 ft. in circumference or 8 m and 5.4 m
52:22 [1]About 7.5 ft. or 2.3 m

THE LAMENTATIONS
of Jeremiah

The Sorrows of Zion

1 How lonely sits the city
That *once* had many people!
She has become like a widow
Who was once great among the nations!
She who was a princess among the
provinces
Has become a forced laborer!

2 She weeps bitterly in the night,
And her tears are on her cheeks;
She has no one to comfort her
Among all her lovers.
All her friends have dealt treacherously
with her;
They have become her enemies.

3 Judah has gone into exile out of affliction
And harsh servitude;
She lives among the nations,
But she has not found a resting place;
All those who pursued her have overtaken
her
In the midst of distress.

4 The roads of Zion are in mourning
Because no one comes to an appointed
feast.
All her gates are deserted;
Her priests groan,
Her virgins are worried,
And as for *Zion* herself, it is bitter for her.

5 Her adversaries have become her masters,
Her enemies are secure;
For the LORD has caused her grief
Because of the multitude of her
wrongdoings;
Her little ones have gone away
As captives led by the enemy.

6 All of her splendor
Is gone from the daughter of Zion;
Her leaders have become like deer
That have found no pasture,
And they have fled without strength
From the pursuer.

7 *In* the days of her affliction and
homelessness
Jerusalem remembers all her treasures
That were *hers* since the days of old,
When her people fell into the hand of the
adversary
And no one helped her.
The adversaries saw her,
They laughed at her ruin.

8 Jerusalem sinned greatly,
Therefore she has become an object of
ridicule.
All who honored her despise her
Because they have seen her nakedness;
Even she herself groans and turns away.

9 Her uncleanness was in her *garment's*
seams;
She did not think of her future.
So she has fallen in an astonishing way;
She has no comforter.

"See, LORD, my affliction,
For the enemy has honored himself!"

10 The adversary has stretched out his hand
Over all her precious things,
For she has seen the nations enter her
sanctuary,
The ones whom You commanded
That they were not to enter Your con-
gregation.

11 All her people groan, seeking bread;
They have given their treasures for food
To restore their lives.
"See, LORD, and look,
For I am despised."

12 "*Is it* nothing to all you who pass *this* way?
Look and see if there is *any* pain like my
pain
Which was inflicted on me,
With which the LORD tormented *me* on
the day of His fierce anger.

13 "From ¹the height He sent fire into my
bones,
And it dominated *them*.
He has spread a net for my feet;
He has turned me back;
He has made me desolate,
Faint all day long.

14 "The yoke of my wrongdoings is bound;
By His hand they are woven together.
They have come upon my neck;
He has made my strength fail.
The Lord has handed me over
To *those against whom* I am not able to
stand.

15 "The Lord has thrown away all my strong
men
In my midst;
He has called an appointed time against
me
To crush my young men;
The Lord has trodden *as in* a wine press
The virgin daughter of Judah.

16 "For these things I weep;
My eyes run down with water;
Because far from me is a comforter,
One to restore my soul.
My children are desolate
Because the enemy has prevailed."

17 Zion stretches out with her hands;
There is no one to comfort her;
The LORD has commanded regarding
Jacob
That those around him become his
adversaries;
Jerusalem has become a filthy thing
among them.

18 "The LORD is righteous,
For I have rebelled against His command;
Hear now, all peoples,
And see my pain;
My virgins and my young men
Have gone into captivity.

19 "I called to my lovers, *but* they deserted
me;
My priests and my elders perished in the
city
While they sought food to restore their
strength themselves.

20 "See, LORD, for I am in distress;
My spirit is greatly troubled;
My heart is overturned within me,
For I have been very rebellious.
In the street the sword has made *women*
childless;
In the house it is like death.

21 "They have heard that I groan;
There is no one to comfort me,
All my enemies have heard of my disaster;
They are joyful that You have done *it*.
Oh, that You would bring the day which
You have proclaimed,
So that they will become like me.

22 "May all their wickedness come before
You;
And deal with them just as You have dealt
with me
For all my wrongdoings.
For my groans are many and my heart is
faint."

God's Anger over Israel

2 How the Lord has covered the daughter
of Zion
With a cloud in His anger!
He has hurled
The glory of Israel from heaven to earth,
And has not remembered His footstool
In the day of His anger.

2 The Lord has destroyed; He has not
spared
All the settlements of Jacob.
In His wrath He has overthrown
The strongholds of the daughter of Judah,
He has hurled *them* down to the ground;
He has profaned the kingdom and its
leaders.

3 In fierce anger He has cut off
All the strength of Israel;
He has pulled back His right hand
From the enemy.
And He has burned in Jacob like a flaming
fire
Consuming on all sides.

4 He has bent His bow like an enemy;
His right hand is positioned like an
adversary,
And He has killed everything that was
pleasant to the eye.
In the tent of the daughter of Zion
He has poured out His wrath like fire.

5 The Lord has become like an enemy.
He has engulfed Israel;
He has engulfed all its palaces,
He has destroyed its strongholds
And caused great mourning and grieving
in the daughter of Judah.

6 And He has treated His tabernacle
violently, like a *despised* garden;
He has destroyed His appointed meeting
place.
The LORD has caused

The appointed feast and Sabbath in Zion
to be forgotten,
And He has despised king and priest
In the indignation of His anger.

7 The Lord has rejected His altar,
He has ¹repudiated His sanctuary;
He has handed over
The walls of her palaces to the enemy.
They have made a noise in the house of
the LORD
As on the day of an appointed feast.

8 The LORD determined to destroy
The wall of the daughter of Zion.
He has stretched out a line,
He has not restrained His hand from
destroying,
And He has caused rampart and wall to
mourn;
They have languished together.

9 Her gates have sunk into the ground,
He has destroyed and broken her bars.
Her king and her leaders are among the
nations;
The Law is gone.
Her prophets, too, find
No vision from the LORD.

10 The elders of the daughter of Zion
Sit on the ground *and* ¹are silent.
They have thrown dust on their heads;
They have put on sackcloth.
The virgins of Jerusalem
Have bowed their heads to the ground.

11 My eyes fail because of tears,
My spirit is greatly troubled;
My heart is poured out on the earth
Because of the destruction of the daughter
of my people,
When little ones and infants languish
In the streets of the city.

12 They say to their mothers,
"Where is grain and wine?"
As they faint like a wounded person
In the streets of the city,
As their lives are poured out
In their mothers' arms.

13 How shall I admonish you?
What shall I compare to you,
Daughter of Jerusalem?
What shall I liken to you as I comfort you,
Virgin daughter of Zion?
For your collapse is as vast as the sea;
Who can heal you?

14 Your prophets have seen for you
Worthless and deceptive *visions;*
And they have not exposed your
wrongdoing
So as to restore you from captivity,
But they have seen for you worthless and
misleading pronouncements.

15 All who pass along the way
Clap their hands *in ridicule* at you;
They hiss and shake their heads
At the daughter of Jerusalem:
"Is this the city of which they said,
'Perfect in beauty,
A joy to all the earth'?"

16 All your enemies
Have opened their mouths wide against
you;

2:7 ¹I.e., scornfully rejected   2:10 ¹Another reading is *wail*

They hiss and gnash *their* teeth.
They say, "We have engulfed *her!*
This certainly is the day which we
    awaited;
We have reached *it,* we have seen *it!*"

17 The Lord has done what He determined;
He has accomplished His word
Which He commanded from days of old.
He has torn down without sparing,
And He has helped the enemy to rejoice
    over you;
He has exalted the might of your
    adversaries.

18 Their heart cried out to the Lord:
"You wall of the daughter of Zion,
Let *your* tears stream down like a river
    day and night;
Give yourself no relief,
Let your eyes have no rest.

19 "Arise, whimper in the night
At the beginning of the night watches;
Pour out your heart like water
Before the presence of the Lord;
Raise your hands to Him
For the life of your little ones
Who languish because of hunger
At the head of every street.

20 "See, Lord, and look!
With whom have You dealt this way?
Should women really eat their children,
The little ones who were born healthy?
Should priest and prophet really be killed
In the sanctuary of the Lord?

21 "On the ground in the streets
Lie young and old;
My virgins and my young men
Have fallen by the sword.
You have put *them* to death on the day of
    Your anger,
You have slaughtered, without sparing.

22 "You called as on the day of an appointed
    feast
My terrors on every side;
And there was no one who survived or
    escaped
On the day of the Lord's anger.
As for those whom I brought forth healthy
    and whom I raised,
My enemy annihilated them."

Jeremiah Shares Israel's Misery

3 I am the man who has seen misery
Because of the rod of His wrath.
2 He has driven me and made me walk
In darkness and not in light.
3 Indeed, He has turned His hand against
    me
Repeatedly all the day.
4 He has consumed my flesh and my skin,
He has broken my bones.
5 He has besieged and surrounded me with
    bitterness and hardship.
6 He has made me live in dark places,
Like those who have long been dead.
7 He has walled me in so that I cannot go
    out;
He has made my chain heavy.
8 Even when I cry out and call for help,
He shuts out my prayer.
9 He has blocked my ways with cut stone;

He has twisted my paths.
10 He is to me *like* a bear lying in wait,
Like a lion in secret places.
11 He has made my ways deviate, and torn
    me to pieces;
He has made me desolate.
12 He bent His bow
And took aim at me as a target for the
    arrow.
13 He made the arrows of His quiver
Enter my inward parts.
14 I have become a laughingstock to all my
    people,
Their song of ridicule all the day.
15 He has filled me with bitterness,
He has made me drink plenty of worm-
    wood.
16 He has also made my teeth grind with
    gravel;
He has made me cower in the dust.
17 My soul has been excluded from peace;
I have forgotten happiness.
18 So I say, "My strength has failed,
And *so has* my hope from the Lord."

Hope of Relief in God's Mercy

19¶ Remember my misery and my homeless-
    ness, the wormwood and bitterness.
20 My soul certainly remembers,
And is bent over within me.
21 I recall this to my mind,
Therefore I wait.
22 The Lord's acts of mercy indeed do not
    end,
For His compassions do not fail.
23 *They* are new every morning;
Great is Your faithfulness.
24 "The Lord is my portion," says my soul,
"Therefore I wait for Him."
25 The Lord is good to those who await Him,
To the person *who* seeks Him.
26 *It is* good that he waits silently
For the salvation of the Lord.
27 *It is* good for a man to bear
The yoke in his youth.
28 Let him sit alone and keep quiet,
Since He has laid *it* on him.
29 Let him put his mouth in the dust;
Perhaps there is hope.
30 Let him give *his* cheek to the one who is
    going to strike him;
Let him be filled with shame.
31 For the Lord will not reject forever,
32 For if He causes grief,
Then He will have compassion
In proportion to His abundant mercy.
33 For He does not afflict willingly
Or grieve the sons of mankind.
34 To crush under one's feet
All the prisoners of the land,
35 To deprive a man of justice
In the presence of the Most High,
36 To defraud someone in his lawsuit—
Of these things the Lord does not
    approve.
37 Who is there who speaks and it comes to
    pass,
Unless the Lord has commanded *it?*
38 *Is it* not from the mouth of the Most High
That both adversity and good proceed?

39 ¶ Of what can *any* living mortal, *or any* man,
Complain in view of his sins?

40 Let's examine and search out our ways,
And let's return to the LORD.

41 We raise our heart and hands
Toward God in heaven;

42 We have done wrong and rebelled;
You have not pardoned.

43 You have covered *Yourself* with anger
And pursued us;
You have slain *and* have not spared.

44 You have veiled Yourself with a cloud
So that no prayer can pass through.

45 You have made us *mere* refuse and rubbish
In the midst of the peoples.

46 All our enemies have opened their mouths against us.

47 Panic and pitfall have come upon us,
Devastation and destruction;

48 My eyes run down *with* streams of water
Because of the destruction of the daughter of my people.

49 My eyes flow unceasingly,
Without stopping,

50 Until the LORD looks down
And sees from heaven.

51 My eyes bring pain to my soul
Because of all the daughters of my city.

52 My enemies without reason
Hunted me down like a bird;

53 They have silenced me in the pit
And have thrown stones on me.

54 Waters flowed over my head;
I said, "I am cut off!"

55 I called on Your name, LORD,
Out of the lowest pit.

56 You have heard my voice,
"Do not cover Your ear from my *plea for* relief,
From my cry for help."

57 You came near on the day I called to You;
You said, "Do not fear!"

58 Lord, You have pleaded my soul's cause;
You have redeemed my life.

59 LORD, You have seen my oppression;
Judge my case.

60 You have seen all their vengeance,
All their schemes against me.

61 You have heard their reproach, LORD,
All their schemes against me.

62 The lips of my assailants and their talk
Are against me all day long.

63 Look at their sitting and their rising;
I am their mocking song.

64 You will repay them, LORD,
In accordance with the work of their hands.

65 You will give them shamelessness of heart,
Your curse will be on them.

66 You will pursue them in anger and eliminate them
From under the heavens of the LORD!

Distress of the Siege Described

4 How dark the gold has become,
How the pure gold has changed!
The sacred stones are spilled out
At the corner of every street.

2 The precious sons of Zion,
Weighed against pure gold,
How they are regarded as earthenware jars,
The work of a potter's hands!

3 Even jackals offer the breast,
They nurse their young;
But the daughter of my people has proved herself cruel,
Like ostriches in the wilderness.

4 The tongue of the infant clings
To the roof of its mouth because of thirst;
The children ask for bread,
But no one breaks *it* for them.

5 Those who used to eat delicacies
Are made to tremble in the streets;
Those who were raised in crimson *clothing*
Embrace garbage heaps.

6 For the wrongdoing of the daughter of my people
Is greater than the sin of Sodom,
Which was overthrown as in a moment,
And no hands were turned toward her.

7 Her consecrated ones were purer than snow,
They shined more than milk;
They were more ruddy *in* body than pearls of coral,
Their form *was like* lapis lazuli.

8 Their appearance is darker than soot,
They are not recognized in the streets;
Their skin is shriveled on their bones,
It is dry, it has become like wood.

9 Better *off* are those killed by the sword
Than those killed by hunger;
For they waste away, stricken
By the lack of the produce of the field.

10 The hands of compassionate women
Boiled their own children;
They became food for them
Due to the destruction of the daughter of my people.

11 The LORD has expended His wrath,
He has poured out His fierce anger;
And He has kindled a fire in Zion,
And it has consumed its foundations.

12 The kings of the earth did not believe,
Nor *did* any of the inhabitants of the world,
That the adversary and the enemy
Would enter the gates of Jerusalem.

13 Because of the sins of her prophets
And the wrongdoings of her priests,
Who have shed in her midst
The blood of the righteous,

14 They wandered, blind, in the streets;
They were defiled with blood,
Such that no one could touch their garments.

15 "Keep away! Unclean!" they cried out of themselves.
"Keep away, keep away, do not touch!"
For they distanced themselves as well as wandered;
People among the nations said,
"They shall not continue to reside *with us.*"

16 The presence of the LORD has scattered
them,
He will not continue to look at them;
They did not honor the priests,
They did not favor the elders.

17 Yet our eyes failed,
Looking for help was useless;
At our observation point we have watched
For a nation that could not save.

18 They hunted our steps
So that we could not walk in our streets;
Our end drew near,
Our days were finished
For our end had come.

19 Our pursuers were swifter
Than the eagles of the sky;
They chased us on the mountains,
They waited in ambush for us in the
wilderness.

20 The breath of our nostrils, the LORD's
anointed,
Was captured in their pits,
Of whom we had said, "In his shadow
We shall live among the nations."

21 Rejoice and be joyful, daughter of Edom,
Who lives in the land of Uz;
But the cup will pass to you as well,
You will become drunk and expose
yourself.

22 *The punishment* of your wrongdoing has
been completed, daughter of Zion;
He will no longer exile you.
But He will punish your wrongdoing,
daughter of Edom;
He will expose your sins!

A Prayer for Mercy

5 Remember, LORD, what has come upon us;
Look, and see our disgrace!

2 Our inheritance has been turned over to
strangers,
Our houses to foreigners.

3 We have become orphans, without a
father;
Our mothers are like widows.

4 We have to pay for our drinking water,
Our wood comes *to us* at a price.

5 Our pursuers are at our necks;
We are worn out, we are given no rest.

6 We have submitted to Egypt *and* Assyria
to get enough bread.

7 Our fathers sinned, *and* are gone;
It is we *who* have been burdened with
the punishment for their wrongdoings.

8 Slaves rule over us;
There is no one to rescue us from their
hand.

9 We get our bread at the risk of our lives
Because of the sword in the wilderness.

10 Our skin has become as hot as an oven,
Because of the ravages of hunger.

11 They violated the women in Zion,
The virgins in the cities of Judah.

12 Leaders were hung by their hands;
Elders were not respected.

13 Young men worked at the grinding mill,
And youths staggered under *loads* of
wood.

14 Elders are absent from the gate,
Young men from their music.

15 The joy of our hearts has ended;
Our dancing has been turned into
mourning.

16 The crown has fallen from our head;
Woe to us, for we have sinned!

17 Because of this our heart is faint,
Because of these things our eyes are dim;

18 Because of Mount Zion which lies
desolate,
Jackals prowl in it.

19¶ You, LORD, rule forever;
Your throne is from generation to
generation.

20 Why will You forget us forever?
Why do You abandon us for so long?

21 Restore us to You, LORD, so that we may
be restored;
Renew our days as of old,

22 Unless You have utterly rejected us
And are exceedingly angry with us.

The Book of
EZEKIEL

The Vision of Four Figures

1 Now it came about in the thirtieth year, on the fifth *day* of the fourth month, while I was by the river Chebar among the exiles, the heavens were opened and I saw visions of God. 2 (On the fifth of the month in the fifth year of King Jehoiachin's exile, 3 the word of the LORD came expressly to Ezekiel the priest, son of Buzi, in the land of the Chaldeans by the river Chebar; and there the hand of the LORD came upon him.)

4 As I looked, behold, a high wind was coming from the north, a great cloud with fire flashing intermittently and a bright light around it, and in its midst *something* like gleaming metal in the midst of the fire. 5 And within it there were figures resembling four living beings. And this was their appearance: they had human form. 6 Each of them had four faces and four wings. 7 Their legs were straight and their feet were like a calf's hoof, and they sparkled like polished bronze. 8 Under their wings on their four sides *were* human hands. As for the faces and wings of the four of them, 9 their wings touched one another; *their faces* did not turn when they moved, each went straight forward. 10 As for the form of their faces, *each had* a human face; all four had the face of a lion on the right and the face of a bull on the left, and all four had the face of an eagle. 11 Such were their faces. Their wings were spread out above; each had two touching another *being,* and two covering their bodies. 12 And each went straight forward; wherever the spirit was about to go, they would go, without turning as they went. 13 In the midst of the living beings there was something that looked like burning coals of fire, like torches moving among the living beings. The fire was bright, and lightning was flashing from the fire. 14 And the living beings ran back and forth like bolts of lightning.

15 Now as I looked at the living beings, behold, there was one wheel on the ground beside the living beings, for each of the four of them. 16 The appearance of the wheels and their workmanship *was* like sparkling topaz, and all four of them had the same form, their appearance and workmanship *being* as if one wheel were within another. 17 Whenever they moved, they moved in *any* of their four directions without turning as they moved. 18 As for their rims, they were high and awesome, and the rims of all four of them were covered with eyes all around. 19 Whenever the living beings moved, the wheels moved with them. And whenever the living beings rose from the earth, the wheels rose *also.* 20 Wherever the spirit was about to go, they would go in that direction. And the wheels rose just as they *did;* for the spirit of the living beings *was* in the wheels. 21 Whenever those went, they went; and whenever those stopped, they stopped.

And whenever those rose from the earth, the wheels rose just as they *did;* for the spirit of the living beings *was* in the wheels.

Vision of Divine Glory

22 Now over the heads of the living beings *there was* something like an expanse, like the awesome gleam of crystal, spread out over their heads. 23 Under the expanse their wings *were stretched out* straight, one toward the other; each one also had two *wings* covering its body on the one side and on the other. 24 And I also heard the sound of their wings, like the sound of abundant waters as they went, like the voice of the Almighty, a sound of a crowd like the sound of an army camp; whenever they stopped, they let down their wings. 25 And a voice came from above the expanse that was over their heads; whenever they stood still, they let down their wings.

26 Now above the expanse that was over their heads there was something resembling a throne, like lapis lazuli in appearance; and on that which resembled a throne, high up, *was* a figure with the appearance of a man. 27 Then I noticed from the appearance of His waist and upward *something* like gleaming metal that looked like fire all around within it, and from the appearance of His waist and downward I saw something like fire; and *there was* a radiance around Him. 28 Like the appearance of the rainbow in the clouds on a rainy day, so *was* the appearance of the surrounding radiance. Such *was* the appearance of the likeness of the glory of the LORD. And when I saw *it,* I fell on my face and heard a voice speaking.

The Prophet's Call

2 Then He said to me, "Son of man, stand on your feet, and I will speak with you." 2 And as He spoke to me the Spirit entered me and set me on my feet; and I heard *Him* speaking to me. 3 Then He said to me, "Son of man, I am sending you to the sons of Israel, to a rebellious people who have rebelled against Me; they and their fathers have revolted against Me to this very day. 4 So I am sending you to those who are impudent and obstinate children, and you shall say to them, 'This is what the Lord GOD says:' 5 As for them, whether they listen or not—for they are a rebellious house—they will know that a prophet has been among them. 6 And as for you, son of man, you are not to fear them nor fear their words, though thistles and thorns are with you and you sit on scorpions; you are not to fear their words nor be dismayed at their presence, since they are a rebellious house. 7 But you shall speak My words to them whether they listen or not, for they are rebellious. 8 "Now you, son of man, listen to what I am speaking to you; do not be rebellious like that

rebellious house. Open your mouth wide and eat what I am giving you." [9] Then I looked, and behold, a hand was extended to me; and behold, a scroll *was* in it. [10] When He spread it out before me, it was written on the front and back, and written on it were songs of mourning, sighing, and woe.

Ezekiel's Commission

3 Then He said to me, "Son of man, eat what you find; eat this scroll, and go, speak to the house of Israel." [2] So I opened my mouth, and He fed me this scroll. [3] And He said to me, "Son of man, feed your stomach and fill your body with this scroll which I am giving you." Then I ate it, and it was as sweet as honey in my mouth.

[4] Then He said to me, "Son of man, go to the house of Israel and speak with My words to them. [5] For you are not being sent to a people of unintelligible speech or difficult language, *but* to the house of Israel, [6] nor to many peoples of unintelligible speech or difficult language, whose words you cannot understand. But I have sent you to the people who understand you; [7] yet the house of Israel will not be willing to listen to you, since they are not willing to listen to Me. The entire house of Israel certainly is stubborn and obstinate. [8] Behold, I have made your face just as hard as their faces, and your forehead just as hard as their foreheads. [9] Like emery harder than flint I have made your forehead. Do not be afraid of them or be dismayed before them, since they are a rebellious house." [10] Moreover, He said to me, "Son of man, take into your heart all My words which I will speak to you and listen closely. [11] Go to the exiles, to the sons of your people, and speak to them and tell them, whether they listen or not, 'This is what the Lord GOD says.'"

[12] Then the Spirit lifted me up, and I heard a great rumbling sound behind me: "Blessed be the glory of the LORD from His place!" [13] And *I heard* the sound of the wings of the living beings touching one another and the sound of the wheels beside them, even a great rumbling sound. [14] So the Spirit lifted me up and took me away; and I went embittered in the rage of my spirit, and the hand of the LORD was strong on me. [15] Then I came to the exiles who lived beside the river Chebar *at* Tel-abib, and I sat there for seven days where they were living, causing consternation among them.

[16] Now at the end of seven days the word of the LORD came to me, saying, [17] "Son of man, I have appointed you as a watchman for the house of Israel; whenever you hear a word from My mouth, warn them from Me. [18] When I say to the wicked, 'You will certainly die,' and you do not warn him or speak out to warn the wicked from his wicked way so that he may live, that wicked person shall die for wrongdoing, but his blood I will require from your hand. [19] However if you have warned the wicked and he does not turn from his wickedness or from his wicked way, he shall die for wrongdoing, but you have saved yourself. [20] Again, when a righteous person turns away from his righteousness and commits sin, and I place an obstacle before him, he will die; since you have not warned him, he shall die in his sin, and his righteous deeds which he has done shall not be remembered; but his blood I will require from your hand. [21] However, if you have warned the righteous person that the righteous is not to sin, and he does not sin, he shall certainly live because he took warning; and you have saved yourself."

[22] Now the hand of the LORD was on me there, and He said to me, "Get up, go out to the plain, and there I will speak to you." [23] So I got up and went out to the plain; and behold, the glory of the LORD was standing there, like the glory that I saw by the river Chebar, and I fell on my face. [24] But the Spirit entered me and set me up on my feet; and He spoke with me and said to me, "Go, shut yourself inside your house. [25] And as for you, son of man, they will put ropes around you and bind you with them so that you do not go out among them. [26] Moreover, I will make your tongue stick to the roof of your mouth so that you will be unable to speak and will not be a man who reprimands them, since they are a rebellious house. [27] But when I speak to you, I will open your mouth and you will say to them, 'This is what the Lord GOD says:' The one who hears, let him hear; and the one who refuses, let him refuse; for they are a rebellious house.

Siege of Jerusalem Predicted

4 "Now you, son of man, get yourself a brick, place it before you, and inscribe a city on it—Jerusalem. [2] Then lay siege against it, build a siege wall, pile up an assault ramp, set up camps, and place battering rams against it all around. [3] Then get yourself an iron plate and set it up as an iron wall between yourself and the city, and direct your face toward it so that it is under siege, and besiege it. This *will be* a sign to the house of Israel.

[4] "Then you are to lie down on your left side and put the wrongdoing of the house of Israel on it; you shall bear their wrongdoing for the number of days that you lie on it. [5] For I have assigned you a number of days corresponding to the years of their wrongdoing, 390 days; so you shall bear the wrongdoing of the house of Israel. [6] When you have completed these *days,* you shall lie down a second time, *but* on your right side, and bear the wrongdoing of the house of Judah; I have assigned it to you for forty days, a day for each year. [7] Then you shall direct your face toward the siege of Jerusalem with your arm bared, and prophesy against it. [8] Now behold, I will put ropes around you so that you cannot turn from your one side to your other until you have completed the days of your siege.

Defiled Bread

[9] "But as for you, take wheat, barley, beans, lentils, millet, and spelt, and put them in one vessel and make them into bread for yourself; you shall eat it according to the number of the days that you lie on your side, 390 days. [10] Your food which you eat *shall be* twenty shekels a day by weight; you shall eat it from time to

time. [11] The water you drink shall be a ¹sixth of a hin by measure; you shall drink it from time to time. [12] You shall eat it as a barley cake, having baked *it* in their sight over human dung." [13] Then the LORD said, "In this way the sons of Israel will eat their bread unclean among the nations where I will scatter them." [14] But I said, "Oh, Lord GOD! Behold, I have never been defiled; for from my youth until now I have never eaten what died of itself or was torn by animals, nor has any unclean meat ever entered my mouth!" [15] Then He said to me, "See, I will give you cow's dung in place of human dung, so that you may prepare your bread over it." [16] Moreover, He said to me, "Son of man, behold, I am going to break the staff of bread in Jerusalem, and they will eat bread by weight and with anxiety, and drink water by measure and in horror, [17] because bread and water will be scarce; and they will tremble with one another and waste away in their guilt.

Jerusalem's Desolation Foretold

5 "As for you, son of man, take a sharp sword; take and use it *as* a barber's razor on your head and beard. Then take scales for weighing and divide the hair. [2] A third you shall burn in the fire at the center of the city, when the days of the siege are completed. Then you shall take a third and strike *it* with the sword all around the city, and a third you shall scatter to the wind; for I will unsheathe a sword behind them. [3] Take also a few *hairs* in number from them and bind them in the hems of your *robes*. [4] Take again some of them and throw them into the fire and burn them in the fire; from it a fire will spread to all the house of Israel.

[5] "This is what the Lord GOD says: 'This is Jerusalem; I have placed her at the center of the nations, with lands around her. [6] But she has rebelled against My ordinances more wickedly than the nations, and against My statutes more than the lands which surround her; for they have rejected My ordinances and have not walked in My statutes.' [7] Therefore, this is what the Lord GOD says: 'Because you have more turmoil than the nations that surround you *and* have not walked in My statutes, nor executed My ordinances, nor acted in accordance with the ordinances of the nations around you,' [8] therefore, this is what the Lord GOD says: 'Behold, I, even I, am against you, and I will execute judgments among you in the sight of the nations. [9] And because of all your abominations I will do among you what I have not done, and the like of which I will never do again. [10] Therefore, fathers will eat *their* sons among you, and sons will eat their fathers; for I will execute judgments on you and scatter all your remnant to every wind. [11] Therefore as I live,' declares the Lord GOD, 'Because you have defiled My sanctuary with all your detestable idols and with all your abominations, I definitely will also withdraw and My eye will have no pity, and I also will not spare. [12] A third of you will die by plague or perish by famine among you, a third will fall by the sword around you, and a third I will scatter to every

wind, and I will unsheathe a sword behind them. [13] 'Then My anger will be spent and I will satisfy My wrath on them, and I will be appeased; then they will know that I, the LORD, have spoken in My zeal, when I have spent My wrath upon them. [14] Moreover, I will make you a site of ruins and a disgrace among the nations that surround you, in the sight of everyone who passes by. [15] So it will be a disgrace, an *object of* abuse, a warning, and an object of horror to the nations that surround you when I execute judgments against you in anger, wrath, and raging reprimands. I, the LORD, have spoken. [16] When I send against them the deadly arrows of famine which were for the destruction of those whom I will send to destroy you, then I will also intensify the famine upon you and break off your provision of bread. [17] I will send on you famine and vicious animals, and they will bereave you of children; plague and bloodshed also will pass through you, and I will bring the sword on you. I, the LORD, have spoken.' "

Idolatrous Worship Denounced

6 Now the word of the LORD came to me, saying, [2] "Son of man, set your face toward the mountains of Israel, and prophesy against them [3] and say, 'Mountains of Israel, listen to the word of the Lord GOD! This is what the Lord GOD says to the mountains, the hills, the ravines, and the valleys: "Behold, I Myself am going to bring a sword against you, and I will destroy your high places. [4] So your altars will become deserted and your incense altars will be smashed; and I will make your slain fall in front of your idols. [5] I will also lay the dead bodies of the sons of Israel in front of their idols; and I will scatter your bones around your altars. [6] Everywhere you live, cities will be in ruins and the high places will be deserted, so that your altars will be in ruins and deserted, your idols will be broken and brought to an end, your incense altars will be cut down, and your works wiped out. [7] The slain will fall among you, and you will know that I am the LORD.

[8] "However, I will leave a remnant, in that you will have those who escaped the sword among the nations when you are scattered among the countries. [9] Then those of you who escape will remember Me among the nations to which they will be taken captive, how I have been hurt by their adulterous hearts which turned away from Me, and by their eyes which committed infidelity with their idols; and they will loathe themselves in their own sight for the evils which they have committed, for all their abominations. [10] Then they will know that I am the LORD; I have not said in vain that I would inflict this disaster on them." '

[11] "This is what the Lord GOD says: 'Clap your hands, stamp your foot and say, "Woe, because of all the evil abominations of the house of Israel, which will fall by the sword, famine, and plague! [12] *Anyone* who is far away will die by the plague, *anyone* who is near will

fall by the sword, and *anyone* who remains and is spared *from these* will die by the famine. So I will expend My wrath on them. [13] Then you will know that I am the LORD, when their dead are among their idols around their altars, on every high hill, on all the tops of the mountains, under every leafy tree and under every massive oak with thick branches—the places where they offered a soothing aroma to all their idols. [14] So through all their dwelling places I will stretch out My hand against them and make the land more desolate and waste than the wilderness toward Diblah; so they will know that I am the LORD." ' "

Punishment for Wickedness Foretold

7 Moreover, the word of the LORD came to me, saying, [2] "And you, son of man, this is what the Lord GOD says to the land of Israel: 'An end! The end is coming on the four corners of the land. [3] Now the end is upon you, for I will send My anger against you; I will judge you according to your ways and bring all your abominations upon you. [4] And My eye will have no pity on you, nor will I spare *you,* but I will bring your ways upon you, and your abominations will be among you; then you will know that I am the LORD!'

[5] "This is what the Lord GOD says: 'A disaster, a unique disaster, behold, it is coming! [6] An end is coming; the end has come! It has awakened against you; behold, it has come! [7] Your doom has come to you, you inhabitant of the land. The time has come, the day is near— panic rather than joyful shouting *on the* mountains. [8] Now I will shortly pour out My wrath on you and expend My anger against you; I will judge you according to your ways and bring on you all your abominations. [9] My eye will have no pity nor will I spare *you.* I will repay you according to your ways, while your abominations are in your midst; then you will know that I, the LORD, am striking.

[10] 'Behold, the day! Behold, it is coming! *Your* doom has gone forth; the rod has budded, arrogance has blossomed. [11] Violence has grown into a rod of wickedness. None of them *shall remain,* none of their people, none of their wealth, nor *anything* eminent among them. [12] The time has come, the day has arrived. Let neither the buyer rejoice nor the seller mourn; for wrath is against all their multitude. [13] Indeed, the seller will not regain what he sold as long as they *both* live; for the vision regarding all their multitude will not be averted, nor will any of them maintain his life by his wrongdoing.

[14] 'They have blown the trumpet and made everything ready, but no one is going to the battle, for My wrath is against all their multitude. [15] The sword is outside *the city* and the plague and the famine are within. *Anyone* who is in the field will die by the sword, while famine and the plague will consume those in the city. [16] Even when their survivors escape, they will be on the mountains like doves of the valleys, all of them moaning, each over his own wrongdoing. [17] All hands will hang limp, and all knees will drip with water. [18] They will put on

sackcloth and shuddering will overwhelm them; and shame *will be* on all faces, and a bald patch on all their heads. [19] They will fling their silver into the streets, and their gold will become an abhorrent thing; their silver and their gold will not be able to save them on the day of the wrath of the LORD. They cannot satisfy their appetite, nor can they fill their stomachs, because their wrongdoing has become a cause of stumbling.

The Temple Profaned

[20] Moreover, they transformed the splendor of His jewels into pride, and they made the images of their abominations *and* their detestable things with it; therefore I will make it an abhorrent thing to them. [21] And I will hand it over to the foreigners as plunder, and to the wicked of the earth as spoils; and they will profane it. [22] I will also turn My face away from them, and they will profane My treasure; then robbers will enter and profane it.

[23] 'Make the [1] chain, for the land is full of bloody crimes, and the city is full of violence. [24] Therefore, I will bring the worst of the nations, and they will take possession of their houses. I will also put an end to the pride of the strong ones, and their holy places will be profaned. [25] When anguish comes, they will seek peace, but there will be none. [26] Disaster will come upon disaster and rumor will be *added* to rumor; then they will seek a vision from a prophet, but the Law will be lost from the priest, and counsel from the elders. [27] The king will mourn, the prince will be clothed in horror, and the hands of the people of the land will tremble. I will deal with them because of their conduct, and by their judgments I will judge them. And they will know that I am the LORD.' "

Vision of Abominations in Jerusalem

8 Now it came about in the sixth year, on the fifth *day* of the sixth month, as I was sitting in my house with the elders of Judah sitting before me, that the hand of the Lord GOD fell upon me there. [2] Then I looked, and behold, something like the appearance of a man; from His waist and downward *there was* the appearance of fire, and from His waist and upward like the appearance of a glow, like gleaming metal. [3] And He extended the form of a hand and took me by the hair of my head; and the Spirit lifted me up between earth and heaven and brought me in the visions of God to Jerusalem, to the entrance of the north gate of the inner *courtyard,* where the seat of the idol of jealousy, which provokes to jealousy, *was located.* [4] And behold, the glory of the God of Israel *was* there, like the appearance which I saw in the plain.

[5] Then He said to me, "Son of man, raise your eyes now toward the north." So I raised my eyes toward the north, and behold, to the north of the altar gate *was* this idol of jealousy at the entrance. [6] And He said to me, "Son of man, do you see what they are doing, the great abominations which the house of Israel are committing here, so that I would be far from

---

7:23 [1] I.e., used for imprisonment

My sanctuary? But yet you will see still greater abominations!"

7 Then He brought me to the entrance of the courtyard, and when I looked, behold, a hole in the wall. 8 And He said to me, "Son of man, now dig through the wall." So I dug through the wall, and behold, an entrance. 9 Then He said to me, "Go in and see the wicked abominations that they are committing here." 10 So I entered and looked, and behold, every form of crawling things and animals *and* detestable things, with all the idols of the house of Israel, were carved on the wall all around. 11 And standing in front of them were seventy elders of the house of Israel, with Jaazaniah the son of Shaphan standing among them, each man *with* his censer in his hand; and the fragrance of the cloud of incense was rising. 12 Then He said to me, "Do you see, son of man, what the elders of the house of Israel are doing in the dark, each man in the rooms of his carved images? For they say, 'The LORD does not see us; the LORD has abandoned the land.'" 13 And He said to me, "Yet you will see still greater abominations which they are committing!"

14 Then He brought me to the entrance of the gate of the LORD's house which *was* toward the north; and behold, women were sitting there weeping for Tammuz. 15 And He said to me, "Do you see *this,* son of man? Yet you will see still greater abominations than these!"

16 Then He brought me into the inner courtyard of the LORD's house. And behold, at the entrance to the temple of the LORD, between the porch and the altar, *were* about twenty-five men *with* their backs to the temple of the LORD while their faces were toward the east; and they were [1]prostrating themselves eastward toward the sun. 17 And He said to me, "Do you see *this,* son of man? Is it a trivial thing for the house of Judah to commit the abominations which they have committed here, that they have filled the land with violence and provoked Me to anger repeatedly? Yet behold, they are putting the twig to their nose! 18 Therefore, I indeed will deal in wrath. My eye will have no pity nor will I spare; and though they cry out in My ears with a loud voice, yet I will not listen to them."

The Vision of Slaughter

9 Then He cried out in my presence with a loud voice, saying, "Come forward, you executioners of the city, each *with* his weapon of destruction in his hand." 2 And behold, six men came from the direction of the upper gate which faces north, each *with* his smashing weapon in his hand; and among them was one man clothed in linen with a scribe's kit at his waist. And they came in and stood beside the bronze altar.

3 Then the glory of the God of Israel ascended from the cherub on which it had been, to the threshold of the temple. And He called to the man clothed in linen at whose waist was the scribe's kit. 4 And the LORD said to him, "Go through the midst of the city, through the midst of Jerusalem, and make a mark on the foreheads of the people who groan and sigh over all the abominations which are being committed in its midst." 5 But to the others He said in my presence, "Go through the city after him and strike; do not let your eye have pity and do not spare. 6 Utterly kill old men, young men, *female* virgins, little children, and women, but do not touch any person on whom is the mark; and you shall start from My sanctuary." So they started with the elders who *were* before the temple. 7 He also said to them, "Defile the temple and fill the courtyards with the dead. Go out!" So they went out and struck and killed *the people* in the city. 8 And as they were striking *the people* and I *alone* was left, I fell on my face and cried out, saying, "Oh, Lord GOD! Are You going to destroy the entire remnant of Israel by pouring out Your wrath on Jerusalem?"

9 Then He said to me, "The guilt of the house of Israel and Judah is very, very great, and the land is filled with blood, and the city is full of perversion; for they say, 'The LORD has abandoned the land, and the LORD does not see!' 10 But as for Me, My eye will have no pity nor will I spare, but I will bring their conduct upon their heads."

11 Then behold, the man clothed in linen, at whose waist was the *scribe's* kit, reported, saying, "I have done just as You have commanded me."

Vision of God's Glory Departing from the Temple

10 Then I looked, and behold, in the [1]expanse that was over the heads of the cherubim *something* like a sapphire stone, in appearance resembling a throne, appeared above them. 2 And He spoke to the man clothed in linen and said, "Enter between the whirling wheels under the cherubim and fill your hands with coals of fire from between the cherubim, and scatter *them* over the city." And he entered in my sight.

3 Now the cherubim were standing on the right side of the temple when the man entered, and the cloud filled the inner courtyard. 4 Then the glory of the LORD went up from the cherub to the threshold of the temple, and the temple was filled with the cloud, and the courtyard was filled with the brightness of the glory of the LORD. 5 Moreover, the sound of the wings of the cherubim was heard as far as the outer courtyard, like the voice of God Almighty when He speaks.

6 And it came about when He commanded the man clothed in linen, saying, "Take fire from between the whirling wheels, from between the cherubim," he entered and stood beside a wheel. 7 Then the cherub reached out with his hand from between the cherubim to the fire which was between the cherubim, took *some coals* and put *them* into the hands of the one clothed in linen; and he took *them* and went out. 8 The cherubim appeared to have something like a human hand under their wings.

9 Then I looked, and behold, four wheels beside the cherubim, one wheel beside each cherub; and the appearance of the wheels *was*

8:16 [1] I.e., worshiping   10:1 [1] Or *firmament;* i.e., atmosphere and space

like the gleam of a Tarshish stone. 10 And as for their appearance, *all* four of them had the same likeness, as if one wheel were within another wheel. 11 When they moved, they went in *any of* their four directions without turning as they went; but they followed in the direction which they faced, without turning as they went. 12 And their whole body, their backs, their hands, their wings and the wheels were covered with eyes all around, the wheels belonging to *all* four of them. 13 The wheels were called, as I heard, the whirling wheels. 14 And each one had four faces. The first face *was* the face of a cherub, the second face *was* the face of a human, the third, the face of a lion, and the fourth, the face of an eagle.

15 Then the cherubim rose up. They are the living beings that I saw by the river Chebar. 16 Now when the cherubim moved, the wheels would move beside them; also when the cherubim lifted up their wings to rise from the ground, the wheels themselves would not turn away from beside them. 17 When the cherubim stood still, the wheels would stand still; and when they rose up, the wheels would rise with them, because the spirit of the living beings *was* in them.

18 Then the glory of the LORD departed from the threshold of the temple and stood over the cherubim. 19 When the cherubim departed, they lifted their wings and rose up from the ground in my sight with the wheels beside them; and they stood still at the entrance of the east gate of the LORD's house, and the glory of the God of Israel hovered over them. 20 These are the living beings that I saw beneath the God of Israel by the river Chebar; so I knew that they *were* cherubim. 21 Each one had four faces and each one four wings, and beneath their wings *was* the form of human hands. 22 As for the likeness of their faces, they were the same faces whose appearance I had seen by the river Chebar. Each one went straight ahead.

Evil Rulers to Be Judged

11 Now the Spirit lifted me up and brought me to the east gate of the LORD's house which faced eastward. And behold, *there were* twenty-five men at the entrance of the gate, and among them I saw Jaazaniah son of Azzur and Pelatiah son of Benaiah, leaders of the people. 2 Then He said to me, "Son of man, these are the men who devise wrongdoing and give evil advice in this city, 3 who say, '*The time* is not near to build houses. This *city* is the pot and we are the meat.' 4 Therefore, prophesy against them, prophesy, son of man!"

5 Then the Spirit of the LORD fell upon me, and He said to me, "Say, 'This is what the LORD says: "This is how you think, house of Israel, for I know your thoughts. 6 You have multiplied your slain in this city, and filled its streets with them." 7 Therefore, this is what the Lord GOD says: "Your slain whom you have laid in the midst of the city are the meat and this *city* is the pot; but I will bring you out of it. 8 You have feared a sword; so I will bring a sword upon you," the Lord GOD declares. 9 "And I will bring you out of the midst of the city, and hand you

over to strangers, and execute judgments against you. 10 You will fall by the sword. I will judge you to the border of Israel; so you shall know that I am the LORD. 11 This *city* will not be a pot for you, nor will you be meat in the midst of it; I will judge you to the border of Israel. 12 So you will know that I am the LORD; for you have not walked in My statutes, nor have you executed My ordinances, but you have acted in accordance with the ordinances of the nations around you." ' "

13 Now it came about, as I prophesied, that Pelatiah son of Benaiah died. Then I fell on my face and cried out with a loud voice, and said, "Oh, Lord GOD! Will You bring the remnant of Israel to a complete destruction?"

Promise of Restoration

14 Then the word of the LORD came to me, saying, 15 "Son of man, your brothers, your relatives, your fellow exiles, and the entire house of Israel, all of them, *are those* to whom the inhabitants of Jerusalem have said, 'Keep far from the LORD; this land has been given to us as a possession.' 16 Therefore say, 'This is what the Lord GOD says: "Though I had removed them far away among the nations, and though I had scattered them among the countries, yet I was a sanctuary for them for a little while in the countries where they had gone." ' 17 Therefore say, 'This is what the Lord GOD says. "I will gather you from the peoples and assemble you from the countries among which you have been scattered, and I will give you the land of Israel." ' 18 When they come there, they will remove all its detestable things and all its abominations from it. 19 And I will give them one heart, and put a new spirit within them. And I will remove the heart of stone from their flesh and give them a heart of flesh, 20 so that they may walk in My statutes, and keep My ordinances and do them. Then they will be My people, and I shall be their God. 21 But as for those whose hearts go after their detestable things and abominations, I will bring their conduct down on their heads," declares Lord GOD.

22 Then the cherubim lifted up their wings with the wheels beside them, and the glory of the God of Israel hovered over them. 23 The glory of the LORD went up from the midst of the city and stood over the mountain which is east of the city. 24 And the Spirit lifted me up and brought me in a vision by the Spirit of God to Chaldea, to the exiles. Then the vision that I had seen left me. 25 And I told the exiles all the things that the LORD had shown me.

Ezekiel Prepares for Exile

12 Then the word of the LORD came to me, saying, 2 "Son of man, you live in the midst of the rebellious house, who have eyes to see but do not see, ears to hear but do not hear; for they are a rebellious house. 3 So as for you, son of man, prepare for yourself baggage for exile and go into exile by day in their sight; that is, go into exile from your place to another place in their sight. Perhaps they will understand, though they are a rebellious house. 4 Bring your baggage out by day in their sight,

as baggage for exile. Then you shall go out at evening in their sight, as those who are going into exile. 5 Dig a hole through the wall in their sight and go out through it. 6 Load *the baggage* on *your* shoulder in their sight *and* carry *it* out in the dark. You shall cover your face so that you cannot see the land, for I have set you as a sign to the house of Israel."

7 Then I did so, just as I had been commanded. By day I brought out my baggage like the baggage of an exile. Then in the evening I dug through the wall with my hands; I went out in the dark *and* carried *the baggage* on *my* shoulder in their sight.

8 And in the morning the word of the LORD came to me, saying, 9 "Son of man, has the house of Israel, the rebellious house, not said to you, 'What are you doing?' 10 Say to them, 'This is what the Lord GOD says: "This pronouncement *concerns* the prince in Jerusalem as well as all the house of Israel who are in it." ' 11 Say, 'I am a sign to you. Just as I have done, so it will be done to them; they will go into exile, into captivity.' 12 The prince who is among them will load *his baggage* on *his* shoulder in the dark and go out. They will dig a hole through the wall to bring *it* out through it. He will cover his face so that he cannot see the land with *his* eyes. 13 I will also spread My net over him, and he will be caught in My net. And I will bring him to Babylon in the land of the Chaldeans; yet he will not see it, though he will die there. 14 And I will scatter to every wind all who are around him, his helpers and all his troops; and I will draw out a sword after them. 15 So they will know that I am the LORD, when I disperse them among the nations and scatter them among the countries. 16 But I will spare a few of them from the sword, the famine, and plague so that they may tell of all their abominations among the nations where they go, and may know that I am the LORD."

17 Moreover, the word of the LORD came to me, saying, 18 "Son of man, eat your bread with trembling, and drink your water with quivering and anxiety. 19 Then say to the people of the land, 'This is what the Lord GOD says concerning the inhabitants of Jerusalem in the land of Israel: "They will eat their bread with anxiety and drink their water with horror, because their land will be stripped of its fullness on account of the violence of all who live in it. 20 The inhabited cities will be in ruins, and the land will be a desolation. So you will know that I am the LORD." ' "

21 Then the word of the LORD came to me, saying, 22 "Son of man, what is this proverb you *people* have about the land of Israel, saying, 'The days are long, and every vision fails'? 23 Therefore say to them, 'This is what the Lord GOD says: "I will put an end to this proverb so that they will no longer use it as a proverb in Israel." But tell them, "The days are approaching as well as the fulfillment of every vision. 24 For there will no longer be any false vision or deceptive divination within the house of Israel. 25 For I the LORD will speak whatever word I speak, and it will be performed. It will no longer be delayed, for in your days, you

rebellious house, I will speak the word and perform it," declares the Lord GOD.' "

26 Furthermore, the word of the LORD came to me, saying, 27 "Son of man, behold, the house of Israel is saying, 'The vision that he sees is for many years *from now,* and he prophesies of times far off.' 28 Therefore say to them, 'This is what the Lord GOD says: "None of My words will be delayed any longer. Whatever word I speak will be performed," ' " declares the Lord GOD.

False Prophets Condemned

13 Then the word of the LORD came to me, saying, 2 "Son of man, prophesy against the prophets of Israel who prophesy, and say to those who prophesy from their own inspiration, 'Listen to the word of the LORD! 3 This is what the Lord GOD says: "Woe to the foolish prophets who are following their own spirit and have seen nothing! 4 Israel, your prophets have been like jackals among ruins. 5 You have not gone up into the breaches, nor did you build up a stone wall around the house of Israel to stand in the battle on the day of the LORD. 6 They see deceit and lying divination, those who are saying, 'The LORD declares,' when the LORD has not sent them; yet they wait for the fulfillment of *their* word! 7 Did you not see a false vision and tell a lying divination when you said, 'The LORD declares,' but it is not I who have spoken?" ' "

8 Therefore, this is what the Lord GOD says: "Because you have spoken deceit and have seen a lie, therefore behold, I am against you," declares the Lord GOD. 9 "So My hand will be against the prophets who see false visions and utter lying divinations. They will have no place in the council of My people, nor will they be written down in the register of the house of Israel, nor will they enter the land of Israel, so that you may know that I am the Lord GOD. 10 It is definitely because they have misled My people by saying, 'Peace!' when there is no peace. And when anyone builds a wall, behold, they plaster it over with whitewash; 11 so tell those who plaster *it* over with whitewash, that it will fall. A flooding rain will come, and you, hailstones, will fall, and a violent wind will break out. 12 Behold, *when* the wall has fallen, will you not be asked, 'Where is the plaster with which you plastered *it?* ' " 13 Therefore, this is what the Lord GOD says: "I will make a violent wind break out in My wrath. There will also be in My anger a flooding rain and hailstones to consume *it* in wrath. 14 So I will tear down the wall which you plastered over with whitewash and hurl it down to the ground, so that its foundation is exposed; and when it falls, you will perish in its midst. And you will know that I am the LORD. 15 So I will expend My wrath on the wall and on those who have plastered it over with whitewash; and I will say to you, 'The wall is gone and those who plastered it are gone, 16 *along with* the prophets of Israel who prophesy to Jerusalem, and who see a vision of peace for her when there is no peace,' declares the Lord GOD.

17 "Now you, son of man, set your face against the daughters of your people who are

talking like prophets from their own imagination. Prophesy against them [18] and say, 'This is what the Lord GOD says: "Woe to the women who sew *magic* bands on all wrists and make veils for the heads *of persons* of every stature to capture souls! Will you capture the souls of My people, but keep the souls *of others* alive for yourselves? [19] For handfuls of barley and pieces of bread, you have profaned Me to My people, to put to death some who should not die, and to keep others alive who should not live, by your lying to My people who listen to lies." ' "

[20] Therefore, this is what the Lord GOD says: "Behold, I am against your *magic* bands by which you capture souls there as birds, and I will tear them from your arms; and I will let them go, those souls whom you capture as birds. [21] I will also tear off your veils and save My people from your hands, and they will no longer be in your hands as prey; and you will know that I am the LORD. [22] Because you disheartened the righteous with falsehood when I did not cause him pain, but *you* have encouraged the wicked not to turn from his wicked way to keep him alive, [23] therefore you women will no longer see deceitful visions or practice divination, and I will save My people from your hands. So you will know that I am the LORD."

Idolatrous Elders Condemned

14 Then some elders of Israel came to me and sat down before me. [2] And the word of the LORD came to me, saying, [3] "Son of man, these men have set up their idols in their hearts and have put in front of their faces the stumbling block of their wrongdoing. Should I let Myself be consulted by them at all? [4] Therefore speak to them and tell them, 'This is what the Lord GOD says: "Anyone of the house of Israel who sets up his idols in his heart, puts in front of his face the stumbling block of his wrongdoing, and *then* comes to the prophet, I the LORD will let Myself answer him in the matter in view of the multitude of his idols, [5] in order to take hold of the hearts of the house of Israel who have turned away from Me due to all their idols." '

[6] "Therefore say to the house of Israel, 'This is what the Lord GOD says: "Repent and turn away from your idols, and turn your faces away from all your abominations. [7] For anyone of the house of Israel, or of the strangers who reside in Israel, who deserts Me, sets up his idols in his heart, puts in front of his face the stumbling block of his wrongdoing, and *then* comes to the prophet to request something of Me for himself, I the LORD will let Myself answer him Myself. [8] I will set My face against that person and make him a sign and a proverb, and I will eliminate him from among My people. So you will know that I am the LORD.

[9] "But if the prophet is persuaded so that he speaks a word, it is I, the LORD, who have persuaded that prophet; and I will stretch out My hand against him and eliminate him from among My people Israel. [10] And they will bear *the punishment for* their wrongdoing; as the wrongdoing of the inquirer is, so the wrongdoing of the prophet will be, [11] in order that the house of Israel may no longer stray from Me and no longer defile themselves with all their offenses. So they will be My people, and I shall be their God," ' declares the Lord GOD."

The City Will Not Be Spared

[12] Then the word of the LORD came to me, saying, [13] "Son of man, if a country sins against Me by being unfaithful, and I stretch out My hand against it, destroy its supply of bread, send famine against it, and eliminate from it *both* human and animal *life,* [14] even *though* these three men, Noah, Daniel, and Job were in its midst, by their *own* righteousness they could *only* save themselves," declares the Lord GOD. [15] "If I were to cause vicious animals to pass through the land and they depopulated it, and it became desolate so that no one would pass through it because of the animals, [16] *though* these three men were in its midst, as I live," declares the Lord GOD, "they could not save either *their* sons or *their* daughters. They alone would be saved, but the country would be desolate. [17] Or *if* I were to bring a sword on that country and say, 'A sword is to pass through the country,' and I eliminated human and animal *life* from it, [18] even *though* these three men were in its midst, as I live," declares the Lord GOD, "they could not save either *their* sons or *their* daughters, but they alone would be saved. [19] Or *if* I were to send a plague against that country and pour out My wrath on it in blood to eliminate man and animal from it, [20] even *though* Noah, Daniel, and Job were in its midst, as I live," declares the Lord GOD, "they could not save either *their* son or *their* daughter. They would save only themselves by their righteousness."

[21] For this is what the Lord GOD says: "How much more when I send My four severe judgments against Jerusalem: sword, famine, vicious animals, and plague to eliminate human and animal *life* from it! [22] Yet, behold, survivors will be left in it who will be brought out, *both* sons and daughters. Behold, they are going to come out to you, and you will see their conduct and actions; then you will be comforted for the disaster which I have brought against Jerusalem for everything which I have brought upon it. [23] Then they will comfort you when you see their conduct and actions, for you will know that I have not done without reason whatever I did to it," declares the Lord GOD.

Jerusalem like a Useless Vine

15 Then the word of the LORD came to me, saying, [2] "Son of man, how is the wood of the vine *better* than any wood of a branch which is among the trees of the forest? [3] Can wood be taken from it to make anything, or can *even* a peg be taken from it on which to hang any utensil? [4] If it has been put into the fire for fuel, *and* the fire has consumed both of its ends and its middle part has been charred, is it *then* good for anything? [5] Behold, while it is intact, it is not made into anything. How much less, when the fire has consumed it and it is charred, can it still be made into anything!

6 Therefore, this is what the Lord God says: 'As the wood of the vine among the trees of the forest, which I have given to the fire for fuel, so have I given up the inhabitants of Jerusalem; **7** and I set My face against them. *Though* they have come out of the fire, yet the fire will consume them. Then you will know that I am the Lord, when I set My face against them. **8** So I will make the land desolate, because they have acted unfaithfully,' " declares the Lord God.

God's Grace to Unfaithful Jerusalem

16 Then the word of the Lord came to me, saying, **2** "Son of man, make known to Jerusalem her abominations, **3** and say, 'This is what the Lord God says to Jerusalem: "Your origin and your birth are from the land of the Canaanite; your father was an Amorite and your mother a Hittite. **4** As for your birth, on the day you were born your navel cord was not cut, nor were you washed with water for cleansing; you were not rubbed with salt or even wrapped in cloths. **5** No eye looked with pity on you to do any of these things for you, to have compassion on you. Rather you were thrown out into the open field, for you were abhorred on the day you were born.

6 "When I passed by you and saw you squirming in your blood, I said to you *while you were* in your blood, 'Live!' Yes, I said to you *while you were* in your blood, 'Live!' **7** I made you very numerous, like plants of the field. Then you grew up, became tall and reached *the age* for fine jewelry; *your* breasts were formed and your hair had grown. Yet you were naked and bare.

8 "Then I passed by you and saw you, and behold, you were at the time for love; so I spread My garment over you and covered your nakedness. I also swore an oath to you and entered into a covenant with you so that you became Mine," declares the Lord God. **9** "Then I bathed you with water, washed off your blood from you, and anointed you with oil. **10** I also clothed you with colorfully woven cloth and put sandals of ¹fine leather on your feet; and I wrapped you with fine linen and covered you with silk. **11** I adorned you with jewelry, put bracelets on your wrists, and a necklace around your neck. **12** I also put a ring in your nose, earrings in your ears, and a beautiful crown on your head. **13** So you were adorned with gold and silver, and your dress was of fine linen, silk, and colorfully woven cloth. You ate fine flour, honey, and oil; so you were exceedingly beautiful and advanced to royalty. **14** Then your fame spread among the nations on account of your beauty, for it was perfect because of My splendor which I bestowed on you," declares the Lord God.

15 "But you trusted in your beauty and became unfaithful because of your fame, and you poured out your obscene practices on every passer-by to whom it might be *tempting*. **16** You took some of your clothes, made for yourself high places of various colors, and committed prostitution on them, *which* should not come about nor happen. **17** You also took your beautiful jewels *made* of My gold and of

My silver, which I had given you, and made for yourself male images so that you might commit prostitution with them. **18** Then you took your colorfully woven cloth and covered them, and offered My oil and My incense before them. **19** Also My bread which I gave you, fine flour, oil, and honey with which I fed you, you would offer before them for a soothing aroma; so it happened," declares the Lord God. **20** "Furthermore, you took your sons and daughters whom you had borne to Me and sacrificed them to idols to be devoured. Were your obscene practices a trivial matter? **21** You slaughtered My children and offered them to idols by making them pass through *the fire*. **22** And besides all your abominations and obscene practices, you did not remember the days of your youth, when you were naked and bare and squirming in your blood.

23 "Then it came about after all your wickedness ('Woe, woe to you!' declares the Lord God), **24** that you built yourself a shrine and made yourself a high place in every public square. **25** You built yourself a high place at the beginning of every street and made your beauty abominable, and you spread your legs to every passer-by and multiplied your obscene practice. **26** You also committed prostitution with the Egyptians, your lustful neighbors, and multiplied your obscene practice to provoke Me to anger. **27** So behold, I have stretched out My hand against you and cut back your rations. And I turned you over to the desire of those who hate you, the daughters of the Philistines, who are ashamed of your outrageous conduct. **28** Moreover, you committed prostitution with the Assyrians because you were not satisfied; you committed prostitution with them and still were not satisfied. **29** You also multiplied your obscene practice with the land of merchants, Chaldea; yet even with this you were not satisfied." '"

30 "How feverish is your heart," declares the Lord God, "while you do all these things, the action of a bold prostitute! **31** When you built your shrine at the beginning of every street and made your high place in every public square, in spurning a prostitute's fee, you were not like a prostitute. **32** You adulteress wife, who takes strangers instead of her husband! **33** *Men* give gifts to all prostitutes, but you give your gifts to all your lovers and lavish favors on them so that they will come to you from every direction for your obscene practices. **34** So it is the opposite for you from those women in your obscene practices, in that you are not approached for prostitution, and in *the fact* that you pay a prostitute's fee, and no fee is paid to you; so you are the opposite."

35 Therefore, you prostitute, hear the word of the Lord. **36** This is what the Lord God says: "Because your lewdness was poured out and your nakedness uncovered through your obscene practices with your lovers and with all your detestable idols, and because of the blood of your sons that you gave to idols, **37** therefore, behold, I am going to gather all your lovers whom you pleased, all those whom you loved as well as all those whom you hated. So I will

---

16:10 ¹ Meaning of the Heb uncertain

gather them against you from every direction and expose your nakedness to them so that they may see all your nakedness. **38** So I will judge you as women who commit adultery or shed blood are judged; and I will bring on you the blood of wrath and jealousy. **39** I will also hand you over to your lovers, and they will tear down your shrines, demolish your high places, strip you of your clothing, take away your jewels, and will leave you naked and bare. **40** They will incite a crowd against you, and they will stone you and cut you to pieces with their swords. **41** And they will burn your houses with fire and execute judgments against you in the sight of many women. Then I will put an end to your prostitution, and you will also no longer pay your lovers. **42** So I will satisfy My fury against you and My jealousy will leave you, and I will be pacified and no longer be angry. **43** Since you have not remembered the days of your youth but have caused Me unrest by all these things, behold, I in turn will bring your conduct *down* on your own head," declares the Lord GOD, "so that you will not commit this outrageous sin in addition to all your *other* abominations.

44 "Behold, everyone who quotes proverbs will quote *this* proverb about you, saying, 'Like mother, like daughter.' **45** You are the daughter of your mother, who loathed her husband and children. You are also the sister of your sisters, who loathed their husbands and children. Your mother was a Hittite and your father an Amorite. **46** Now your older sister is Samaria, who lives north of you with her daughters; and your younger sister, who lives south of you, is Sodom with her daughters. **47** Yet you have not *merely* walked in their ways and committed their abominations; *but*, as *if that were* too little, you also acted more corruptly in all your conduct than they. **48** As I live," declares the Lord GOD, "Sodom, your sister and her daughters have not done as you and your daughters have done! **49** Behold, this was the guilt of your sister Sodom: she and her daughters had arrogance, plenty of food, and carefree ease, but she did not help the poor and needy. **50** So they were haughty and committed abominations before Me. Therefore I removed them when I saw *it*. **51** Furthermore, Samaria did not commit half of your sins, for you have multiplied your abominations more than they. So you have made your sisters appear innocent by all your abominations which you have committed. **52** Also, bear your disgrace in that you have made judgment favorable for your sisters. Because of your sins in which you acted more abominably than they, they are more in the right than you. Yes, be also ashamed and bear your disgrace, in that you made your sisters appear innocent.

53 "Nevertheless, I will restore their fortunes, the fortunes of Sodom and her daughters, the fortunes of Samaria and her daughters, and along with them your own fortunes, **54** so that you will bear your disgrace and feel ashamed for all that you have done when you become a consolation to them. **55** Your sisters, Sodom with her daughters and Samaria with her daughters, will return to their former state,

and you with your daughters will *also* return to your former state. **56** As *the name of* your sister Sodom was not heard from your lips in your day of pride, **57** before your wickedness was uncovered, so now *you have become* the disgrace of the daughters of Edom and of all who are around her, of the daughters of the Philistines—those surrounding *you* who despise you. **58** You have suffered *the penalty of* your outrageous sin and abominations," the LORD declares. **59** For this is what the Lord GOD says: "I will also do with you as you have done, you who have despised the oath by breaking the covenant.

The Covenant Remembered

60 "Nevertheless, I will remember My covenant with you in the days of your youth, and I will establish an everlasting covenant with you. **61** Then you will remember your ways and be ashamed when you receive your sisters, *both* your older and your younger; and I will give them to you as daughters, but not because of your covenant. **62** So I will establish My covenant with you, and you shall know that I am the LORD, **63** so that you may remember and be ashamed, and not open your mouth again because of your disgrace, when I have forgiven you for all that you have done," the Lord GOD declares.

Parable of Two Eagles and a Vine

17 Now the word of the LORD came to me, saying, **2** "Son of man, ask a riddle and present a parable to the house of Israel, **3** saying, 'This is what the Lord GOD says: "A great eagle with great wings, long pinions, and a full plumage of many colors came to Lebanon and took away the top of the cedar. **4** He broke off the topmost of its young twigs and brought it to a land of merchants; he set it in a city of traders. **5** He also took from the seed of the land and planted it in fertile soil, a meadow beside abundant waters; he set it *like* a willow. **6** Then it sprouted and became a low, spreading vine with its branches turned toward him, but its roots remained under it. So it became a vine and produced shoots and sent out branches.

7 "But there was another great eagle with great wings and much plumage; and behold, this vine turned its roots toward him and sent out its branches toward him from the beds where it was planted, so that he might water it. **8** It was planted in good soil beside abundant waters, so that it would produce branches and bear fruit, *and* become a splendid vine." ' **9** Say, 'This is what the Lord GOD says: "Will it thrive? Will he not pull up its roots and cut off its fruit, so that it withers—so that all its sprouting shoots wither? And neither by great strength nor by many people can it be raised from its roots *again*. **10** Behold, though it is planted, will it thrive? Will it not completely wither as soon as the east wind strikes it— wither on the beds where it grew?" ' "

Zedekiah's Rebellion

11 Moreover, the word of the LORD came to me, saying, **12** "Say now to the rebellious house, 'Do you not know what these things *mean?*'

Say, 'Behold, the king of Babylon came to Jerusalem, took its king and leaders, and brought them to him in Babylon. **13** Then he took one of the royal family and made a covenant with him, putting him under oath. He also took away the mighty of the land, **14** so that the kingdom would be humbled, not exalting itself, *but* keeping his covenant so that it might continue. **15** But he revolted against him by sending his messengers to Egypt so that they might give him horses and many troops. Will he succeed? Will he who does these things escape? Can he indeed break the covenant and escape? **16** As I live,' declares the Lord GOD, 'In the country of the king who put him on the throne, whose oath he despised and whose covenant he broke, in Babylon he shall certainly die. **17** Pharaoh with *his* mighty army and great contingent will not help him in the war, when they pile up assault ramps and build siege walls to eliminate many lives. **18** Now he despised the oath by breaking the covenant, and behold, he pledged his allegiance, yet did all these things; he shall not escape.' " **19** Therefore, this is what the Lord GOD says: "As I live, My oath which he despised and My covenant which he broke, I will certainly inflict on his head. **20** And I will spread My net over him, and he will be caught in My net. Then I will bring him to Babylon and enter into judgment with him there *regarding* the unfaithful act which he has committed against Me. **21** All the choice men in all his troops will fall by the sword, and the survivors will be scattered to every wind; and you will know that I, the LORD, have spoken."

22 This is what the Lord GOD says: "I will also take *a sprig* from the lofty top of the cedar and set *it* out; I will break off from the topmost of its young twigs a tender one, and I will plant *it* on a high and lofty mountain. **23** On the high mountain of Israel I will plant it, so that it may bring forth branches and bear fruit, and become a stately cedar. And birds of every kind will nest under it; they will nest in the shade of its branches. **24** All the trees of the field will know that I am the LORD; I bring down the high tree, exalt the low tree, dry up the green tree, and make the dry tree flourish. I am the LORD; I have spoken, and I will perform *it.*"

God Deals Justly with Individuals

18 Then the word of the LORD came to me, saying, **2** "What do you *people* mean by using this proverb about the land of Israel, saying,

'The fathers eat sour grapes,
[1]But *it is* the children's teeth *that* have
become blunt'?

3 As I live," declares the Lord GOD, "you certainly are not going to use this proverb in Israel anymore. **4** Behold, all souls are Mine; the soul of the father as well as the soul of the son is Mine. The soul who sins will die.

5 "But if a man is righteous and practices justice and righteousness, **6** *if* he does not eat at the mountain *shrines*, or raise his eyes to the idols of the house of Israel, or defile his

neighbor's wife or approach a woman during her menstrual period— **7** and *if* a man does not oppress *anyone, but* restores to the debtor his pledge, does not commit robbery, *but* gives his bread to the hungry and covers the naked with clothing, **8** *and if* he does not lend *money* at interest or take [1]interest, *if* he keeps his hand from injustice *and* executes true justice between one person and another, **9** *if* he walks in My statutes and keeps My ordinances so as to deal faithfully—he is righteous *and* will certainly live," declares the Lord GOD.

10 "However, he may father a violent son who sheds blood, and does any one of these things to a brother **11** (though he himself did not do any of these things), that is, he even eats at the mountain *shrines,* and defiles his neighbor's wife, **12** oppresses the poor and needy, commits robbery, does not restore a pledge, but raises his eyes to the idols *and* commits abomination, **13** lends *money* at interest and takes [1]interest; will he live? He will not live! He has committed all these abominations, he shall certainly be put to death; his blood will be on himself.

14 "Now behold, he has fathered a son who saw all his father's sins which he committed, but he has seen *them* and does not do likewise. **15** He does not eat at the mountain *shrines* or raise his eyes to the idols of the house of Israel; he has not defiled his neighbor's wife, **16** nor oppressed anyone, nor retained a pledge, nor committed robbery; *instead,* he gives his bread to the hungry and covers the naked with clothing, **17** he keeps his hand from the poor, does not take *any kind of* interest *on loans, but* executes My ordinances, and walks in My statutes; he will not die for his father's guilt, he will certainly live. **18** As for his father, because he practiced extortion, robbed *his* brother, and did what was not good among his people, behold, he will die for his guilt.

19 "Yet you say, 'Why should the son not suffer *the punishment* for the father's guilt?' When the son has practiced justice and righteousness *and* has kept all My statutes and done them, he shall certainly live. **20** The person who sins will die. A son will not suffer *the punishment* for the father's guilt, nor will a father suffer *the punishment* for the son's guilt; the righteousness of the righteous will be upon himself, and the wickedness of the wicked will be upon himself.

21 "But if the wicked person turns from all his sins which he has committed and keeps all My statutes and practices justice and righteousness, he shall certainly live; he shall not die. **22** All his offenses which he has committed will not be remembered against him; because of his righteousness which he has practiced, he will live. **23** Do I take any pleasure in the death of the wicked," declares the Lord GOD, "rather than that he would turn from his ways and live?

24 "But when a righteous person turns away from his righteousness, commits injustice *and* does according to all the abominations that the wicked person does, will he live? All his

---

18:2 [1]Lit *I.e., the children suffer for the fathers' sins*   **18:8** [1]Or *usury,* and so throughout the ch; i.e., on other kinds of loans   **18:13** [1]I.e., on other kinds of loans

righteous deeds which he has done will not be remembered for his treachery which he has committed and his sin which he has committed; for them he will die. 25 Yet you say, 'The way of the Lord is not right.' Hear now, house of Israel! Is My way not right? Is it not your ways that are not right? 26 When a righteous person turns away from his righteousness, commits injustice and dies because of it, for his injustice which he has committed he dies. 27 But when a wicked person turns away from his wickedness which he has committed and practices justice and righteousness, he will save his life. 28 Since he understood and turned away from all his offenses which he had committed, he shall certainly live; he shall not die. 29 But the house of Israel says, 'The way of the Lord is not right.' Are My ways not right, house of Israel? Is it not your ways that are not right?

30 "Therefore I will judge you, house of Israel, each according to his conduct," declares the Lord GOD. "Repent and turn away from all your offenses, so that wrongdoing does not become a stumbling block to you. 31 Hurl away from you all your offenses which you have committed and make yourselves a new heart and a new spirit! For why should you die, house of Israel? 32 For I take no pleasure in the death of anyone who dies," declares the Lord GOD. "Therefore, repent and live!"

Song of Mourning for the Leaders of Israel

19 "As for you, take up a song of mourning for the leaders of Israel 2 and say, 'What was your mother? A lioness among lions! She lay down among young lions, She raised her cubs.
3 'When she brought up one of her cubs, He became a young lion, And he learned to tear *his* prey; He devoured people.
4 'Then nations heard about him; He was caught in their trap, And they brought him with hooks To the land of Egypt.
5 'When she saw, as she waited, *That* her hope was lost, She took another of her cubs *And* made him a young lion.
6 'And he walked about among the lions, He became a young lion; He learned to tear *his* prey; He devoured people.
7 'He destroyed their palaces And laid waste their cities; And the land and its fullness were appalled Because of the sound of his roaring.
8 'Then nations set against him On every side from *their* provinces, And they spread their net over him; He was caught in their trap.
9 'They put him in a wooden collar with hooks And brought him to the king of Babylon; They brought him in hunting nets So that his voice would no longer be heard

On the mountains of Israel.
10 'Your mother was like a vine in your vineyard, Planted by the waters; It was fruitful and thick with branches Because of abundant waters.
11 'And it had strong stems *fit* for scepters of rulers, And its height was raised above the clouds So that it was seen in its height with the mass of its branches.
12 'But it was uprooted in fury; It was thrown down to the ground; And the east wind dried up its fruit. Its strong stem was torn out So that it withered; The fire consumed it.
13 'And now it is planted in the wilderness, In a dry and thirsty land.
14 'And fire has gone out from *its* stem; It has consumed its shoots *and* fruit, So that there is no strong stem in it, A scepter to rule.' "
This is a song of mourning, and has become a song of mourning.

God's Dealings with Israel Rehearsed

20 Now in the seventh year, in the fifth *month*, on the tenth of the month, men from the elders of Israel came to inquire of the LORD, and they sat before me. 2 Then the word of the LORD came to me, saying, 3 "Son of man, speak to the elders of Israel and say to them, 'This is what the Lord GOD says: "Do you yourselves come to inquire of Me? As I live," declares the Lord GOD, "I certainly will not be inquired of by you." ' 4 Will you judge them, will you judge *them,* son of man? Make known to them the abominations of their fathers; 5 and say to them, 'This is what the Lord GOD says: "On the day when I chose Israel and swore to the descendants of the house of Jacob and made Myself known to them in the land of Egypt, when I swore to them, saying, I am the LORD your God, 6 on that day I swore to them, to bring them out from the land of Egypt into a land that I had selected for them, flowing with milk and honey, which is the glory of all the lands. 7 And I said to them, 'Throw away, each of you, the detestable things of his eyes, and do not defile yourselves with the idols of Egypt; I am the LORD your God.' 8 But they rebelled against Me and were not willing to listen to Me; they did not throw away, each of them, the detestable things of their eyes, nor did they abandon the idols of Egypt.

"Then I resolved to pour out My wrath on them, to use up My anger against them in the midst of the land of Egypt. 9 But I acted for the sake of My name, that it would not be defiled in the sight of the nations among whom they *lived,* in whose sight I made Myself known to them by bringing them out of the land of Egypt. 10 So I took them out of the land of Egypt and brought them into the wilderness. 11 I gave them My statutes and informed them of My ordinances, which, *if* a person follows them, then he will live by them. 12 Also I gave them My Sabbaths to be a sign between Me and

them, so that they might know that I am the LORD who sanctifies them. [13] But the house of Israel rebelled against Me in the wilderness. They did not walk in My statutes and they rejected My ordinances, which, *if* a person follows them, then he will live by them; and they greatly profaned My Sabbaths. Then I resolved to pour out My wrath on them in the wilderness, to annihilate them. [14] But I acted for the sake of My name, so that it would not be defiled before the eyes of the nations, before whose eyes I had brought them out. [15] Also I swore to them in the wilderness that I would not bring them into the land which I had given *them,* flowing with milk and honey, which is the glory of all the lands, [16] because they rejected My ordinances, and as for My statutes, they did not walk in them; they also profaned My Sabbaths, because their heart continually followed their idols. [17] Yet My eye spared them rather than destroying them, and I did not bring about their annihilation in the wilderness.

[18] "Instead, I said to their children in the wilderness, 'Do not walk in the statutes of your fathers or keep their ordinances or defile yourselves with their idols. [19] I am the LORD your God; walk in My statutes and keep My ordinances and follow them. [20] Sanctify My Sabbaths; and they shall be a sign between Me and you, so that you may know that I am the LORD your God.' [21] But the children rebelled against Me; they did not walk in My statutes, nor were they careful to follow My ordinances which, *if* a person follows them, then he will live by them; they profaned My Sabbaths. So I resolved to pour out My wrath on them, to use up My anger against them in the wilderness. [22] But I withdrew My hand and acted for the sake of My name, so that it would not be defiled in the sight of the nations in whose sight I had brought them out. [23] Also I swore to them in the wilderness that I would scatter them among the nations and disperse them among the lands, [24] because they had not complied with My ordinances, but had rejected My statutes and had profaned My Sabbaths, and their eyes were on the idols of their fathers. [25] I also gave them statutes that were not good, and ordinances by which they could not live; [26] and I pronounced them unclean because of their gifts, in that they made all their firstborn pass through *the fire* so that I might make them desolate, in order that they might know that I am the LORD.'

[27] "Therefore speak to the house of Israel, son of man, and say to them, 'This is what the Lord GOD says: "Again, in this your fathers have blasphemed Me by being disloyal to Me. [28] When I had brought them into the land which I swore to give to them, then they saw every high hill and every tree thick with branches, and there they offered their sacrifices and there they presented the provocation of their offering. There also they made their soothing aroma and there they poured out their drink offerings. [29] Then I said to them, 'What is the high place to which you go?' So its name is called 'Bamah to this day."' '

[30] Therefore, say to the house of Israel, 'This is what the Lord GOD says: "Will you defile yourselves in the way of your fathers and adulterously pursue their detestable things? [31] And when you offer your gifts, when you make your sons pass through the fire, you are defiling yourselves with all your idols to this day. So shall I be inquired of by you, house of Israel? As I live," declares the Lord GOD, "I certainly will not be inquired of by you. [32] And whatever comes into your mind certainly will not come about, when you say: 'We will be like the nations, like the families of the lands, serving wood and stone.'

God Will Restore Israel to Her Land

[33] "As I live," declares the Lord GOD, "with a mighty hand and with an outstretched arm and with wrath poured out, I assuredly shall be king over you. [34] I will bring you out from the peoples and gather you from the lands where you are scattered, with a mighty hand and with an outstretched arm and with wrath poured out; [35] and I will bring you into the wilderness of the peoples, and there I will enter into judgment with you face to face. [36] Just as I entered into judgment with your fathers in the wilderness of the land of Egypt, so I will enter into judgment with you," declares the Lord GOD. [37] "I will make you pass under the rod, and I will bring you into the bond of the covenant; [38] and I will purge from you the rebels and those who revolt against Me; I will bring them out of the land where they reside, but they will not enter the land of Israel. So you will know that I am the LORD.

[39] "As for you, house of Israel," this is what the Lord GOD says: "Go, serve, everyone *of you* his idols; but later you will certainly listen to Me, and My holy name you will no longer defile with your gifts and your idols. [40] For on My holy mountain, on the high mountain of Israel," declares the Lord GOD, "there the entire house of Israel, all of them, will serve Me in the land; there I will accept them and there I will demand your contributions and the choicest of your gifts, with all your holy things. [41] As a soothing aroma I will accept you when I bring you out from the peoples and gather you from the lands where you are scattered; and I will prove Myself to be holy among you in the sight of the nations. [42] And you will know that I am the LORD, when I bring you into the land of Israel, into the land which I swore to give to your forefathers. [43] And there you will remember your ways and all your deeds by which you have defiled yourselves; and you will loathe yourselves in your own sight for all the evil things that you have done. [44] Then you will know that I am the LORD, when I have dealt with you in behalf of My name, not according to your evil ways or according to your corrupt deeds, house of Israel," declares the Lord GOD.' "

[45] Now the word of the LORD came to me, saying, [46] "Son of man, set your face toward the south, and speak prophetically against the south and prophesy against the forest land of the Negev, [47] and say to the forest of the Negev,

'Hear the word of the Lord: this is what the Lord God says: "Behold, I am going to kindle a fire in you, and it will consume every green tree in you, as well as every dry tree; the blazing flame will not go out and the entire surface from south to north will be scorched by it. 48 And all mankind will see that I, the Lord, have kindled it; it will not go out." ' " 49 Then I said, "Oh, Lord God! They are saying of me, 'Is he not *just* speaking in riddles?' "

Parable of the Sword of the Lord

21 And the word of the Lord came to me, saying, 2 "Son of man, set your face against Jerusalem, and speak prophetically against the sanctuaries and prophesy against the land of Israel; 3 and say to the land of Israel, 'This is what the Lord says: "Behold, I am against you; and I will draw My sword from its sheath and cut off from you the righteous and the wicked. 4 Because I will cut off from you the righteous and the wicked, therefore My sword will go out from its sheath against humanity from south *to* north. 5 So humanity will know that I, the Lord, have drawn My sword from its sheath. It will not return *to its sheath* again." ' 6 As for you, son of man, groan with a breaking heart and bitter grief; you shall groan in their sight. 7 And when they say to you, 'Why are you groaning?' you shall say, 'Because of the news, for it is coming; and every heart will melt, all hands will go limp, every spirit will be disheartened, and all knees will drip with water. Behold, it is coming and it will happen,' declares the Lord God."

8 And the word of the Lord came to me, saying, 9 "Son of man, prophesy and say, 'This is what the Lord says:' Say,
'A sword, a sword sharpened
    And also polished!
10 'Sharpened to make a slaughter,
    Polished to flash like lightning!'
Or shall we rejoice, the rod of My son despising every tree? 11 And it is given to be polished, so that it may be handled; the sword is sharpened and polished, to hand it over to the slaughterer. 12 Cry out and wail, son of man; for it is against My people, it is against all the officials of Israel. They are turned over to the sword with My people, therefore slap *your* thigh. 13 For *there is* a testing; and what if even the rod which despises will cease to be?" declares the Lord God.

14 "You therefore, son of man, prophesy and clap *your* hands; and let the sword be doubled the third time, the sword for the slain. It is the sword for the great one slain, which surrounds them, 15 so that *their* hearts will waver, and many fall at all their gates. I have granted the slaughter of the sword. Oh! It is made for *striking like* lightning, it is sharpened *in readiness* for slaughter. 16 Prove yourself sharp, go to the right; set yourself; go to the left, wherever your edge is ordered. 17 I will also clap My hands, and I will satisfy My wrath; I, the Lord, have spoken."

The Instrument of God's Judgment

18 And the word of the Lord came to me, saying, 19 "Now as for you, son of man, make two ways for the sword of the king of Babylon to come; both of them will go out of one land. And make a signpost; make it at the head of the way to the city. 20 You shall mark a way for the sword to come to Rabbah of the sons of Ammon, and to Judah into fortified Jerusalem. 21 For the king of Babylon stands at the parting of the way, at the head of the two ways, to use divination; he shakes the arrows, he consults the household idols, he looks at the liver. 22 Into his right hand came the divination, 'Jerusalem,' to set up battering rams, to open the mouth for slaughter, to raise the voice with a battle cry, to set up battering rams against the gates, to pile up assault ramps, to build a siege wall. 23 And it will be to them like a false divination in their eyes; they have *sworn* solemn oaths. But he makes guilt known, so that they may be seized.

24 "Therefore, this is what the Lord God says: 'Because you have made your guilt known, in that your offenses are uncovered, so that in all your deeds your sins are seen— because you have come to mind, you will be seized by the hand. 25 And you, slain, wicked one, the prince of Israel, whose day has come, in the time of the punishment of the end,' 26 this is what the Lord God says: 'Remove the turban and take off the crown; this *will* no *longer be* the same. Exalt that which is low, and humble that which is high. 27 Ruins, ruins, ruins, I will make it! This also will be no *longer* until He comes whose right it is, and I will give it *to Him.*'

28 "And you, son of man, prophesy and say, 'This is what the Lord God says concerning the sons of Ammon and their taunting,' and say: 'A sword, a sword is drawn, sharpened for the slaughter, to make it consume, so that *it may be like* lightning— 29 while they see false visions for you, while they divine lies for you— to place you on the necks of the wicked who are killed, whose day has come, in the time of the punishment of the end. 30 Return *it* to its sheath. In the place where you were created, in the land of your origin, I will judge you. 31 I will pour out My indignation on you; I will blow on you with the fire of My wrath, and I will hand you over to brutal men, craftsmen of destruction. 32 You will be fuel for the fire; your blood will be in the midst of the land. You will not be remembered, for I, the Lord, have spoken.' "

The Sins of Israel

22 Then the word of the Lord came to me, saying, 2 "And you, son of man, will you judge, will you judge the bloody city? Then inform her of all her abominations. 3 And you shall say, 'This is what the Lord God says: "A city shedding blood in her midst, so that her time is coming; and a *city* that makes idols, contrary to her *own good,* for defilement! 4 You have become guilty by the blood which you have shed, and you have become defiled by your idols which you have made. So you have brought your days closer and have come to your years; therefore I have made you a disgrace to the nations, and an object of mocking to all the lands. 5 Those who are near and those

who are far from you will make fun of you, you of ill repute, full of turmoil.

6 "Behold, the rulers of Israel, each according to his power, have been among you for the purpose of shedding blood. 7 They have treated father and mother with contempt among you. They have oppressed the stranger in your midst; they have oppressed the orphan and the widow among you. 8 You have despised My holy things and profaned My Sabbaths. 9 Slanderous men have been among you for the purpose of shedding blood, and among you they have eaten at the mountain *shrines.* In your midst they have committed outrageous sin. 10 Among you they have uncovered *their* fathers' nakedness; among you they have abused her who was unclean in her menstruation. 11 And one has committed abomination with his neighbor's wife, another has outrageously defiled his daughter-in-law, and another among you has *sexually* abused his sister, his father's daughter. 12 Among you they have taken bribes to shed blood; you have taken interest, you have injured your neighbors by oppression, and you have forgotten Me," declares the Lord God.

13 "Behold, then, I strike with My hand your profit which you have made and the bloodshed which is among you. 14 Can your heart endure, or can your hands be strong for the days that I will deal with you? I, the Lord, have spoken and will act. 15 And I will scatter you among the nations and disperse you among the lands, and I will eliminate your uncleanness from you. 16 Then you will defile yourself in the sight of the nations, and you will know that I am the Lord." ' "

17 And the word of the Lord came to me, saying, 18 "Son of man, the house of Israel has become waste metal to Me; all of them are bronze, tin, iron, and lead in the smelting furnace; they are the waste metal of silver. 19 Therefore, this is what the Lord God says: 'Because all of you have become waste metal, therefore, behold, I am going to gather you into the midst of Jerusalem. 20 As they gather silver, bronze, iron, lead, and tin into the smelting furnace to blow fire on it in order to melt *it,* so I will gather *you* in My anger and in My wrath, and I will place you *there* and melt you. 21 And I will gather you and blow on you with the fire of My wrath, and you will be melted in the midst of it. 22 As silver is melted in the furnace, so you will be melted in the midst of it; and you will know that I, the Lord, have poured out My wrath on you.' "

23 And the word of the Lord came to me, saying, 24 "Son of man, say to her, 'You are a land that is not clean or rained on in the day of indignation.' 25 There is a conspiracy of her prophets in her midst like a roaring lion tearing the prey. They have devoured lives; they have taken treasure and precious things; they have made many widows in the midst of her. 26 Her priests have done violence to My Law and have profaned My holy things; they have made no distinction between the holy and the common, and they have not taught the difference between the unclean and the clean; and they have closed their eyes from My Sabbaths, and I am defiled among them. 27 Her

leaders within her are like wolves tearing the prey, by shedding blood *and* destroying lives in order to make dishonest profit. 28 And her prophets have coated with whitewash for them, seeing false visions and divining lies for them, saying, 'This is what the Lord God says,' when the Lord has not spoken. 29 The people of the land have practiced extortion and committed robbery, and they have oppressed the poor and needy, and have oppressed the stranger without justice. 30 I searched for a man among them who would build up a wall and stand in the gap before Me for the land, so that I would not destroy it; but I found no one. 31 So I have poured out My indignation on them; I have consumed them with the fire of My wrath; I have brought their way upon their heads," declares the Lord God.

Oholah and Oholibah's Sin and Its Consequences

23 The word of the Lord came to me again, saying, 2 "Son of man, there were two women, the daughters of one mother; 3 and they prostituted themselves in Egypt. They prostituted themselves in their youth; there their breasts were squeezed and there their virgin breasts were handled. 4 Their names were Oholah the elder and Oholibah her sister. And they became Mine, and they gave birth to sons and daughters. And *as for* their names, Samaria is Oholah and Jerusalem is Oholibah.

5 "Oholah prostituted herself while she was Mine; and she lusted after her lovers, after the Assyrians, *her* neighbors, 6 who were clothed in purple, governors and officials, all of them handsome young men, horsemen riding on horses. 7 She bestowed her obscene practices on them, all of whom *were* the choicest men of Assyria; and with all whom she lusted after, with all their idols she defiled herself. 8 She did not abandon her obscene practices from *the time in* Egypt; for in her youth men had slept with her, and they handled her virgin breasts and poured out their obscene practice on her. 9 Therefore, I handed her over to her lovers, to the Assyrians, after whom she lusted. 10 They uncovered her nakedness; they took her sons and her daughters, but they killed her with the sword. So she became a subject of gossip among women, and they executed judgments on her.

11 "Now her sister Oholibah saw *this,* yet she was more corrupt in her lust than she, and her obscene practices were more than the prostitution of her sister. 12 She lusted after the Assyrians, governors and officials, the ones near, opulently dressed, horsemen riding on horses, all of them handsome young men. 13 And I saw that she had defiled herself; they both took the same way. 14 So she increased her obscene practices. And she saw men carved on the wall, images of the Chaldeans drawn in bright red, 15 wearing belts around their waists, with flowing turbans on their heads, all of them looking like officers, like the Babylonians *in* Chaldea, the land of their birth. 16 And when she saw them she lusted after them and sent messengers to them in Chaldea. 17 And the Babylonians came to her to the bed of love and

defiled her with their obscene practice. And when she had been defiled by them, she turned away from them in disgust. 18 She exposed her obscene practices and exposed her nakedness; then I turned away from her in disgust, just as I had turned away from her sister in disgust. 19 Yet she multiplied her obscene practices, remembering the days of her youth, when she prostituted herself in the land of Egypt. 20 She lusted after their lovers, whose flesh is *like* the flesh of donkeys and whose discharge is *like* the discharge of horses. 21 So you longed for the outrageous sin of your youth, when the Egyptians handled your breasts because of the breasts of your youth.

22 "Therefore, Oholibah, this is what the Lord God says: 'Behold I am going to incite your lovers against you, from whom you turned away in disgust, and I will bring them against you from every side: 23 the Babylonians and all the Chaldeans, Pekod and Shoa and Koa, *and* all the Assyrians with them; handsome young men, governors and officials all of them, officers and men of renown, all of them riding on horses. 24 And they will come against you with weapons, chariots, and wagons, and with a contingent of peoples. They will attack you on every side with shield, [buckler, and helmet; and I will commit the judgment to them, and they will judge you according to their customs 25 I will set My jealousy against you, so that they may deal with you in wrath. They will remove your nose and your ears; and your survivors will fall by the sword. They will take your sons and your daughters; and your survivors will be consumed by the fire. 26 They will also strip you of your clothes and take away your beautiful jewelry. 27 So I will remove from you your outrageous sin and your prostitution *that you brought* from the land of Egypt, so that you will not raise your eyes to them or remember Egypt anymore.' 28 For this is what the Lord God says: 'Behold, I am going to hand you over to those whom you hate, to those from whom you turned away in disgust. 29 They will deal with you in hatred, take all your property, and leave you naked and bare. And the nakedness of your prostitution will be exposed, both your outrageous sin and your obscene practices. 30 These things will be done to you because you have adulterously pursued the nations, because you have defiled yourself with their idols. 31 You have walked in the way of your sister; therefore I will put her cup in your hand.' 32 This is what the Lord God says:

'You will drink your sister's cup,
  Which is deep and wide.
You will be laughed at and held in
  derision;
  Because it contains much.
33 'You will be filled with drunkenness and
  grief,
A cup of horror and desolation,
  The cup of your sister Samaria.
34 'And you will drink it and drain it.
Then you will gnaw on its fragments
  And tear your breasts;
for I have spoken,' declares the Lord God.
35 Therefore, this is what the Lord God says:

'Because you have forgotten Me and discarded Me behind your back, suffer on your own part *the punishment for* your outrageous sin and your obscene practices.' "

36 Moreover, the Lord said to me, "Son of man, will you judge Oholah and Oholibah? Then declare to them their abominations. 37 For they have committed adultery, and blood is on their hands. So they have committed adultery with their idols, and even made their sons, whom they bore to Me, pass through *the fire* to them as food. 38 Again, they have done this to Me: they have defiled My sanctuary on the same day, and have profaned My Sabbaths. 39 For when they slaughtered their children for their idols, they entered My sanctuary on the same day to profane it; and behold, this is what they did within My house.

40 "Furthermore, they have even sent for men who come from a great distance, to whom a messenger was sent; and behold, they came—for whom you bathed, put makeup on your eyes, and adorned yourselves with jewelry; 41 and you sat on a splendid couch with a table arranged in front of it on which you had set My incense and My oil. 42 And the sound of a carefree multitude was with her; and heavy drinkers were brought from the wilderness with people from the multitude of humanity. And they put bracelets on the wrists of the women and beautiful crowns on their heads. 43 "Then I said concerning her who was worn out by adulteries, 'Will they now commit adultery with her when she is *like this?*' 44 But they went in to her as they would go in to a prostitute. This is how they went in to Oholah and to Oholibah, the lewd women. 45 But they, righteous people, will judge them with the judgment of adulteresses and with the judgment of women who shed blood, because they are adulteresses and blood is on their hands.

46 "For this is what the Lord God says: 'Bring up a contingent against them and turn them over to terror and plunder. 47 The contingent will stone them with stones and cut them down with their swords; they will kill their sons and their daughters and burn their houses with fire. 48 So I will eliminate outrageous conduct from the land, so that all women will take warning and not commit outrageous sin as you have done. 49 Your outrageous conduct will be repaid to you, and you will bear the guilt for your idols; so you will know that I am the Lord God.' "

Parable of the Boiling Pot

24 Now the word of the Lord came to me in the ninth year, in the tenth month, on the tenth of the month, saying, 2 "Son of man, write the name of the day, this very day. The king of Babylon has laid siege to Jerusalem this very day. 3 Present a parable to the rebellious house and say to them, 'This is what the Lord God says:

"Put on the pot, put *it* on and also pour
  water into it;
4 Put in it the pieces of meat,
  Every good piece, the thigh and the
  shoulder;

23:24 1 I.e., small shield

Fill *it* with choice bones.
5 "Take the choicest of the flock,
And also stack wood under the pot.
Make it boil vigorously.
Also boil its bones in it."
6 'Therefore, this is what the Lord GOD says:
"Woe to the bloody city,
To the pot in which there is rust
And whose rust has not gone out of it!
Take out of it piece after piece,
Without making a choice.
7 "For her blood is in her midst;
She placed it on the bare rock;
She did not pour it on the ground
To cover it with dust.
8 "So that it may cause wrath to come up to take vengeance,
I have put her blood on the bare rock,
So that it will not be covered."
9 Therefore, this is what the Lord GOD says:
"Woe to the bloody city!
I also will make the wood pile great.
10 "Heap on the wood, kindle the fire,
Cook the meat thoroughly
And mix in the spices,
And let the bones be burned up.
11 "Then set it empty on its burning coals
So that it may be hot
And its bronze may glow,
And its filthiness may be melted in it,
Its rust eliminated.
12 "She has wearied *Me* with work,
Yet her great rust has not gone from her;
Let her rust *be* in the fire!
13 "In your filthiness is outrageous sin.
Because I *would* have cleansed you,
Yet you are not clean,
You will not be cleansed from your filthiness again
Until I have expended My wrath on you.
14 I, the LORD, have spoken; it is coming and I will act. I will not overlook, I will not pity, and I will not be sorry; according to your ways and according to your deeds I will judge you," declares the Lord GOD.' "

Death of Ezekiel's Wife Is a Sign

15 And the word of the LORD came to me, saying, 16 "Son of man, behold, I am about to take from you what is precious to your eyes with a fatal blow; but you shall not mourn and you shall not weep, and your tears shall not come. 17 Groan silently; do no mourning for the dead. Bind on your turban and put your sandals on your feet, and do not cover your mustache, and do not eat the bread of *other* people." 18 So I spoke to the people in the morning, and in the evening my wife died. And in the morning I did as I was commanded. 19 And the people said to me, "Will you not tell us what these things *mean* for us, that you are doing?" 20 Then I said to them, "The word of the LORD came to me, saying, 21 'Speak to the house of Israel, "This is what the Lord GOD says: 'Behold, I am about to profane My sanctuary, the pride of your power, that which is precious in your eyes and the longing of your soul; and your sons and your daughters whom you have left behind will fall by the sword. 22 And you will do just as I have done; you will

not cover *your* mustache, and you will not eat the bread of *other* people. 23 Your turbans will be on your heads, and your sandals on your feet. You will not mourn and you will not weep; but you will rot away in your guilty deeds, and you will groan to one another. 24 So Ezekiel will be a sign to you; according to all that he has done, you will do. When it comes, then you will know that I am the Lord GOD.' "

25 'As for you, son of man, will *it* not be on the day when I take from them their stronghold, the joy of their splendor, that which is precious in their eyes and their heart's longing, their sons and their daughters, 26 that on that day the one who escapes will come to you with information for *your* ears? 27 On that day your mouth will be opened to him who escaped, and you will speak and no longer be silenced. So you will be a sign to them, and they will know that I am the LORD.' "

Judgment on Gentile Nations—Ammon

25 And the word of the LORD came to me, saying, 2 "Son of man, set your face against the sons of Ammon and prophesy against them, 3 and say to the sons of Ammon, 'Hear the word of the Lord GOD! This is what the Lord GOD says: "Because you said, 'Aha!' against My sanctuary when it was profaned, and against the land of Israel when it was made desolate, and against the house of Judah when they went into exile, 4 therefore, behold, I am going to give you to the people of the east as a possession, and they will set up their encampments among you and make their dwellings among you; they will eat your fruit and drink your milk. 5 I will make Rabbah a pasture for camels, and the sons of Ammon a resting place for flocks. Then you will know that I am the LORD." 6 For this is what the Lord GOD says: "Because you have clapped your hands and stamped your feet, and have rejoiced with all the malice in your soul against the land of Israel, 7 therefore, behold, I have reached out with My hand against you and I will give you as plunder to the nations. And I will cut you off from the peoples and eliminate you from the lands. I will exterminate you. So you will know that I am the LORD."

Moab

8 'The Lord GOD says this: "Because Moab and Seir say, 'Behold, the house of Judah is like all the nations,' 9 therefore, behold, I am going to deprive the flank of Moab of *its* cities, of its cities which are on its frontiers, the glory of the land, Beth-jeshimoth, Baal-meon, and Kiriathaim; 10 and I will give it as a possession along with the sons of Ammon to the people of the east, so that the sons of Ammon will not be remembered among the nations. 11 So I will execute judgments on Moab, and they will know that I am the LORD."

Edom

12 'The Lord GOD says this: "Because Edom has acted against the house of Judah by taking vengeance, and has incurred great guilt, and avenged themselves upon them," 13 therefore this is what the Lord GOD says: "I will also

reach out with My hand against Edom and eliminate human and animal *life* from it. And I will turn it into ruins; from Teman even to Dedan they will fall by the sword. 14 And I will inflict My vengeance on Edom by the hand of My people Israel. Therefore, they will act in Edom in accordance with My anger and My wrath; so they will know My vengeance," declares the Lord GOD.

Philistia

15 'This is what the Lord GOD says: "Because the Philistines have acted in revenge, and have taken vengeance with malice in *their* souls to destroy with everlasting hostility," 16 therefore this is what the Lord GOD says: "Behold, I am going to reach out with My hand against the Philistines and eliminate the Cherethites; and I will destroy the remnant of the seacoast. 17 I will execute great vengeance on them with wrathful rebukes; and they will know that I am the LORD, when I inflict My vengeance on them." ' "

Judgment on Tyre

26 Now in the eleventh year, on the first of the month, the word of the LORD came to me, saying, 2 "Son of man, because Tyre has said in regard to Jerusalem, 'Aha! The gateway of the peoples is broken; it has opened to me. I shall be filled, *now that* she is laid waste,' 3 therefore this is what the Lord GOD says: 'Behold, I am against you, Tyre, and I will bring up many nations against you, as the sea brings up its waves. 4 They will destroy the walls of Tyre and tear down her towers; and I will sweep her debris away from her and make her a bare rock. 5 She will become a dry place for *the spreading of* nets in the midst of the sea, for I have spoken,' declares the Lord GOD; 'and she will become plunder for the nations. 6 Also her daughters who are on the mainland will be killed by the sword, and they will know that I am the LORD.' "

7 For the Lord GOD says this: "Behold, I am going to bring upon Tyre from the north Nebuchadnezzar king of Babylon, king of kings, with horses, chariots, cavalry, and a great army. 8 He will kill your daughters on the mainland with the sword; and he will make siege walls against you, pile up an assault ramp against you, and raise up a large shield against you. 9 And he will direct the blow of his battering rams against your walls, and he will tear down your towers with his axes. 10 Because of the multitude of his horses, the dust *raised by* them will cover you; your walls will shake from the noise of cavalry, wagons, and chariots when he enters your gates as *warriors* enter a city that is breached. 11 With the hoofs of his horses he will trample all your streets. He will kill your people with the sword, and your strong pillars will go down to the ground. 12 Also they will take your riches as spoils and plunder your merchandise, tear down your walls and destroy your delightful houses, and throw your stones, your timbers, and your debris into the water. 13 So I will put an end to the sound of your songs, and the sound of your harps will no longer be heard. 14 I will turn you

into a bare rock; you will become a dry place for *the spreading of* nets. You will not be rebuilt, for I the LORD have spoken," declares the Lord GOD.

15 The Lord GOD says this to Tyre: "Will the coastlands not shake from the sound of your downfall when the wounded groan, when the slaughter takes place in your midst? 16 Then all the princes of the sea will descend from their thrones, remove their robes, and strip off their colorfully woven garments. They will clothe themselves with trembling; they will sit on the ground, tremble again and again, and be appalled at you. 17 And they will take up a song of mourning over you and say to you,

'How you have perished, you inhabited one,
From the seas, you famous city,
Which was mighty on the sea,
She and her inhabitants,
Who imposed her terror
On all her inhabitants!
18 'Now the coastlands will tremble
On the day of your downfall;
Yes, the coastlands which are by the sea
Will be horrified at your passing.' "

19 For this is what the Lord GOD says: "When I make you a desolate city, like the cities which are not inhabited, when I bring up the deep over you and the great waters cover you, 20 then I will bring you down with those who go down to the pit, to the people of old, and I will make you remain in the lower parts of the earth, like the ancient ruins, with those who go down to the pit, so that you will not be inhabited; but I will put glory in the land of the living. 21 I will cause you sudden terrors and you will no longer exist; though you will be sought, you will never be found again," declares the Lord GOD.

Grief over Tyre

27 Moreover, the word of the LORD came to me, saying, 2 "And you, son of man, take up a song of mourning over Tyre; 3 and say to Tyre, who sits at the entrance to the sea, merchant of the peoples to many coastlands, 'This is what the Lord GOD says:

"Tyre, you have said, 'I am perfect in beauty.'
4 "Your borders are in the heart of the seas;
Your builders have perfected your beauty.
5 "They have made all *your* planks of juniper trees from Senir;
They have taken a cedar from Lebanon to make a mast for you.
6 "Of oaks from Bashan they have made your rudders;
With ivory they have inlaid your deck of boxwood from the coastlands of Cyprus.
7 "Your sail was of colorfully embroidered linen from Egypt
So that it became your flag;
Your awning was violet and purple from the coastlands of Elishah.
8 "The inhabitants of Sidon and Arvad were your rowers;
Your wise men, Tyre, were aboard; they were your sailors.

9 "The elders of Gebal and her wise men
were with you repairing your leaks;
All the ships of the sea and their sailors
were with you in order to deal in your
merchandise.
10 "Persia, Lud, and Put were in your army,
your men of war. They hung up shield and
helmet on you; they presented your splendor.
11 The sons of Arvad and your army were on
your walls, all around, and the Gammadim
were in your towers. They hung their shields
on your walls all around; they perfected your
beauty.
12 "Tarshish was your customer because of
the abundance of all kinds of wealth; with
silver, iron, tin, and lead they paid for your
merchandise. 13 Javan, Tubal, and Meshech,
they were your traders; with human lives and
vessels of bronze they paid for your merchandise. 14 Those from Beth-togarmah gave horses,
war horses, and mules for your merchandise.
15 The sons of Dedan were your traders. Many
coastlands were your market; they brought
ivory tusks and ebony as your payment. 16 Aram
was your customer because of the abundance
of your goods; they paid for your merchandise
with emeralds, purple, colorfully woven cloth,
fine linen, coral, and rubies. 17 Judah and the
land of Israel, they were your traders; with
the wheat of Minnith, cakes, honey, oil, and
balsam they paid for your merchandise.
18 Damascus was your customer because of
the abundance of your goods, because of the
abundance of all kinds of wealth, because of
the wine of Helbon and white wool. 19 Vedan
and Javan paid for your merchandise from
Uzal; wrought iron, cassia, and spice reed were
among your merchandise. 20 Dedan traded with
you in saddlecloths for riding. 21 Arabia and all
the princes of Kedar, they were your customers
for lambs, rams, and goats; for these they were
your customers. 22 The traders of Sheba and
Raamah, they traded with you; they paid for
your merchandise with the best of all balsam
oil, and with all kinds of precious stones, and
gold. 23 Haran, Canneh, Eden, the traders of
Sheba, Asshur, and Chilmad traded with you.
24 They traded with you in choice garments, in
clothes of violet and colorfully woven cloth,
and in blankets of two colors, and tightly
wound cords, which were among your merchandise. 25 The ships of Tarshish were the
carriers for your merchandise.
And you were filled and were very
glorious
In the heart of the seas.
26¶ "Your rowers have brought you
Into great waters;
The east wind has broken you
In the heart of the seas.
27 "Your wealth, your wares, your
merchandise,
Your seamen and your sailors,
Your repairers of leaks, your dealers in
merchandise,
And all your men of war who are in you,
With all your contingent that is in your
midst,
Will fall into the heart of the seas
On the day of your overthrow.

28 "At the sound of the cry of your sailors,
The pasture lands will shake.
29 "All who handle the oar,
The seamen and all the sailors of the sea
Will come down from their ships;
They will stand on the land,
30 And they will make their voice heard over
you
And cry out bitterly.
They will throw dust on their heads,
They will wallow in ashes.
31 "Also they will shave themselves bald for
you
And put on sackcloth;
And they will weep for you in bitterness
of soul
With bitter mourning.
32 "Moreover, in their wailing they will take
up a song of mourning for you
And sing a song of mourning over you:
'Who is like Tyre,
Like her who is silent in the midst of the
sea?
33 'When your merchandise went out from
the seas,
You satisfied many peoples;
With the abundance of your wealth and
your merchandise
You enriched the kings of the earth.
34 'Now that you are broken by the seas
In the depths of the waters,
Your merchandise and all your company
Have fallen in the midst of you.
35 'All the inhabitants of the coastlands
Are appalled at you,
And their kings are horribly afraid;
They have a troubled look.
36 'The merchants among the peoples hiss at
you;
You have become terrified
And you will cease to be forever.'"'"

Tyre's King Overthrown

28 The word of the LORD came again to me,
saying, 2 "Son of man, say to the leader of
Tyre, 'The Lord GOD says this:
"Because your heart is haughty
And you have said, 'I am a god,
I sit in the seat of gods
In the heart of the seas';
Yet you are a mortal and not God,
Although you make your heart like the
heart of God—
3   Behold, you are wiser than Daniel;
There is no secret that is a match for you!
4 "By your wisdom and understanding
You have acquired riches for yourself
And have acquired gold and silver for your
treasuries.
5 "By your great wisdom, by your trade
You have increased your riches,
And your heart is haughty because of your
riches—
6 Therefore this is what the Lord GOD says:
'Because you have made your heart
Like the heart of God,
7   Therefore, behold, I am going to bring
strangers against you,
The most ruthless of the nations.
And they will draw their swords

Against the beauty of your wisdom
And profane your splendor.
8 'They will bring you down to the pit,
And you will die the death of those who
 are killed
In the heart of the seas.
9 'Will you still say, "I am a god,"
In the presence of one who kills you,
Though you are a mortal and not God,
In the hands of those who wound you?
10 'You will die the death of the
 uncircumcised
By the hand of strangers,
For I have spoken!' declares the Lord
 GOD!" ' "

11 Again the word of the LORD came to me,
saying, 12 "Son of man, take up a song of
mourning over the king of Tyre and say to him,
'This is what the Lord GOD says:
"You had the seal of perfection,
 Full of wisdom and perfect in beauty.
13 "You were in Eden, the garden of God;
Every precious stone was your covering:
The ruby, the topaz and the diamond;
The beryl, the onyx and the jasper;
The lapis lazuli, the turquoise and the
 emerald;
And the gold, the workmanship of your
 settings and sockets,
Was in you.
On the day that you were created
They were prepared.
14 "You were the anointed cherub who
 covers,
And I placed you there.
You were on the holy mountain of
 God;
You walked in the midst of the stones of
 fire.
15 "You were blameless in your ways
From the day you were created
Until unrighteousness was found in you.
16 "By the abundance of your trade
You were internally filled with violence,
 And you sinned;
Therefore I have cast you as profane
From the mountain of God.
And I have destroyed you, you covering
 cherub,
From the midst of the stones of fire.
17 "Your heart was haughty because of your
 beauty;
You corrupted your wisdom by reason of
 your splendor.
I threw you to the ground;
I put you before kings,
That they may see you.
18 "By the multitude of your wrongdoings,
In the unrighteousness of your trade
You profaned your sanctuaries.
Therefore I have brought fire from the
 midst of you;
It has consumed you,
And I have turned you to ashes on the
 earth
In the eyes of all who see you.
19 "All who know you among the peoples
Are appalled at you;
You have become terrified
And you will cease to be forever." ' "

Judgment of Sidon

20 And the word of the LORD came to me,
saying, 21 "Son of man, set your face toward
Sidon, prophesy against her 22 and say, 'This is
what the Lord GOD says:
"Behold, I am against you, Sidon,
And I will appear in My glory in your
 midst.
Then they will know that I am the LORD,
 when I execute judgments against her,
And I will reveal Myself as holy in her.
23 "For I will send a plague to her
And blood to her streets,
And the wounded will fall in her midst
By the sword upon her on every side;
Then they will know that I am the LORD.
24 And there will no longer be for the house of
Israel a painful thorn or a hurtful thorn bush
from any surrounding them who despised
them; then they will know that I am the Lord
GOD."

Israel Regathered

25 'This is what the Lord GOD says: "When
I gather the house of Israel from the peoples
among whom they are scattered, and show
Myself holy among them in the sight of the
nations, then they will live on their land which
I gave to My servant Jacob. 26 They will live on
it securely; and they will build houses, plant
vineyards, and live securely when I execute
judgments upon all around them who despise
them. Then they will know that I am the LORD
their God." ' "

Judgment of Egypt

29 In the tenth year, in the tenth *month,* on
the twelfth of the month, the word of
the LORD came to me, saying, 2 "Son of man, set
your face against Pharaoh king of Egypt, and
prophesy against him and against all Egypt.
3 Speak and say, 'This is what the Lord GOD
says:
"Behold, I am against you, Pharaoh king of
 Egypt,
The great monster that lies in the midst of
 his canals,
That has said, 'My Nile is mine, and I
 myself have made it.'
4 "I will put hooks in your jaws
And make the fish of your canals cling to
 your scales.
And I will bring you up out of the midst of
 your canals,
And all the fish of your canals will cling to
 your scales.
5 "I will abandon you to the wilderness, you
 and all the fish of your canals;
You will fall on the open field; you will
 not be brought together or gathered.
I have given you for food to the animals of
 the earth and to the birds of the sky.
6 "Then all the inhabitants of Egypt will
 know that I am the LORD,
Because they have been only a staff made
 of reed to the house of Israel.
7 "When they took hold of you with the
 hand,
You broke and tore all their hands;
And when they leaned on you,

You broke and made all their hips shake."
8 'Therefore the Lord GOD says this:
"Behold, I am going to bring upon you a
sword, and I will cut off from you human and
animal *life*. **9** The land of Egypt will become a
desolation and place of ruins. Then they will
know that I am the LORD.

"Because you said, 'The Nile is mine, and
I have made *it*,' **10** therefore, behold, I am
against you and against your canals, and I will
make the land of Egypt an utter waste *and*
desolation, from Migdol *to* Syene and as far as
the border of Cush. **11** A human foot will not
pass through it, nor will the foot of an animal
pass through it, and it will not be inhabited for
forty years. **12** So I will make the land of Egypt a
desolation in the midst of deserted lands. And
her cities, in the midst of cities that are laid
waste, will be desolate for forty years; and I
will scatter the Egyptians among the nations
and disperse them among the lands."

13 'For this is what the Lord GOD says:
"At the end of forty years I will gather the
Egyptians from the peoples among whom they
were scattered. **14** And I will restore the fortunes of Egypt and bring them back to the land
of Pathros, to the land of their origin, and there
they will be a lowly kingdom. **15** It will be the
lowest of the kingdoms, and it will not raise
itself above the nations again. And I will make
them small so that they will not rule over the
nations. **16** And it will no longer be *a kingdom*
on which the house of Israel relies, bringing to
mind the guilt of their having turned to Egypt.
Then they will know that I am the Lord
GOD.'''

17 Now in the twenty-seventh year, in the
first *month,* on the first of the month, the word
of the LORD came to me, saying, **18** "Son of man,
Nebuchadnezzar king of Babylon made his
army labor hard against Tyre; every head had a
bald spot and every shoulder was rubbed raw.
But he and his army acquired no wages from
Tyre for the labor that he had performed
against it." **19** Therefore this is what the Lord
GOD says: "Behold, I am going to give the land
of Egypt to Nebuchadnezzar king of Babylon.
And he will carry off her wealth and capture
her spoils and seize her plunder; and it will be
wages for his army. **20** I have given him the land
of Egypt *for* his labor which he performed,
because they acted for Me," declares the Lord
GOD.

21 "On that day I will make a horn sprout for
the house of Israel, and I will open your mouth
among them. Then they will know that I am
the LORD."

Grief over Egypt

30 The word of the LORD came again to me,
saying, **2** "Son of man, prophesy and say,
'This is what the Lord GOD says:
    "Wail, 'Woe for the day!'
3 "For the day is near,
    Indeed, the day of the LORD is near;
    It will be a day of clouds,
    A time *of doom* for the nations.
4 "A sword will come upon Egypt,
    And there will be trembling in Cush;

When the slain fall in Egypt,
    They will take away her wealth,
    And her foundations will be torn down.
5 Cush, Put, Lud, all Arabia, Libya and the
people of the land that is in league will fall
with them by the sword."
6¶ 'This is what the LORD says:
    "Indeed, those who support Egypt will fall
    And the pride of her power will come
        down;
    From Migdol *to* Syene
    They will fall within her by the sword,"
    Declares the Lord GOD.
7 "They will be desolate
    In the midst of the desolated lands;
    And her cities will be
    In the midst of the devastated cities.
8 "And they will know that I am the LORD,
    When I set a fire in Egypt
    And all her helpers are broken.
9 On that day messengers will go out from Me
in ships to frighten carefree Cush; and trembling will come on them *as* on the day of
Egypt; for behold, it is coming!"
10 'This is what the Lord GOD says:
    "I will also make the hordes of Egypt cease
    By the hand of Nebuchadnezzar king of
        Babylon.
11 "He and his people with him,
    The most ruthless of the nations,
    Will be brought in to destroy the land;
    And they will draw their swords against
        Egypt
    And fill the land with the slain.
12 "Moreover, I will make the Nile canals dry
    And sell the land into the hands of evil
        men.
    And I will make the land desolate
    And all that is in it,
    By the hand of strangers; I the LORD have
        spoken."
13 'This is what the Lord GOD says:
    "I will also destroy the idols
    And make the images cease from
        Memphis.
    And there will no longer be a prince in
        the land of Egypt;
    And I will put fear in the land of Egypt.
14 "I will make Pathros desolate,
    Set a fire in Zoan
    And execute judgments on 'Thebes.
15 "I will pour out My wrath on 'Sin,
    The stronghold of Egypt;
    I will also eliminate the hordes of Thebes.
16 "I will set a fire in Egypt;
    Sin will writhe in anguish,
    Thebes will be breached
    And 'Memphis *will have* distresses daily.
17 "The young men of 'On and of Pi-beseth
    Will fall by the sword,
    And the women will go into captivity.
18 "In Tehaphnehes the day will be dark
    When I break there the yoke bars of
        Egypt.
    Then the pride of her power will cease in
        her;
    A cloud will cover her,
    And her daughters will go into captivity.
19 "So I will execute judgments on Egypt,

30:14 1 Or *No*   **30:15** 1 Or *Pelusium*   **30:16** 1 Or *Noph*   **30:17** 1 Or *Aven*

And they will know that I am the Lord.”’”

Victory for Babylon

20 In the eleventh year, in the first *month,* on the seventh of the month, the word of the Lord came to me, saying, 21 “Son of man, I have broken the arm of Pharaoh king of Egypt; and, behold, it has not been bound up for healing or wrapped with a bandage, so that it may be strong to wield the sword. 22 Therefore this is what the Lord God says: ‘Behold, I am against Pharaoh king of Egypt, and I will break his arms, both the strong and the broken; and I will make the sword fall from his hand. 23 And I will scatter the Egyptians among the nations and disperse them among the lands. 24 For I will strengthen the arms of the king of Babylon and put My sword in his hand; and I will break the arms of Pharaoh, so that he will groan before him with the groans of a wounded man. 25 So I will strengthen the arms of the king of Babylon, but the arms of Pharaoh will fail. Then they will know that I am the Lord, when I put My sword into the hand of the king of Babylon and he reaches out with it against the land of Egypt. 26 When I scatter the Egyptians among the nations and disperse them among the lands, then they will know that I am the Lord.’”

Pharaoh Warned of Assyria’s Fate

31 In the eleventh year, in the third *month,* on the first of the month, the word of the Lord came to me, saying, 2 “Son of man, say to Pharaoh king of Egypt and to his hordes,

‘Whom are you like in your greatness?
3 ‘Behold, Assyria *was* a cedar in Lebanon
   With beautiful branches and forest shade,
   And very high,
   And its top was among the clouds.
4 ‘The waters made it grow, the deep made
     it high.
   With its rivers it continually extended all
     around its planting place,
   And sent out its channels to all the trees
     of the field.
5 ‘Therefore its height was loftier than all
     the trees of the field
   And its boughs became many and its
     branches long
   Because of many waters as it spread them
     out.
6 ‘All the birds of the sky nested in its
     twigs,
   And under its branches all the animals of
     the field gave birth,
   And all great nations lived under its
     shade.
7 ‘So it was beautiful in its greatness, in the
     length of its branches;
   For its roots extended to many waters.
8 ‘The cedars in God’s garden could not
     match it;
   The junipers could not compare with its
     branches,
   And the plane trees could not match its
     branches.
   No tree in God’s garden could compare
     with it in its beauty.

9 ‘I made it beautiful with the multitude of
     its branches,
   And all the trees of Eden, which were in
     the garden of God, were jealous of it.
10 ‘Therefore this is what the Lord God says: “Because it is tall in stature and has put its top among the clouds, and its heart is haughty in its loftiness, 11 I will hand it over to a ruler of the nations; he will thoroughly deal with it. In accordance with its wickedness I have driven it out. 12 Foreign tyrants of the nations have cut it down and left it; on the mountains and in all the valleys its branches have fallen, and its branches have been broken in all the ravines of the land. And all the peoples of the earth have gone down from its shade and left it. 13 All the birds of the sky will nest on its fallen trunk, and all the animals of the field will rest on its *fallen* branches, 14 so that all the trees *by* the waters will not be exalted in their stature, nor put their tops among the clouds, nor will any of their well-watered mighty ones stand *straight* in their height. For they have all been turned over to death, to the earth beneath, among mankind, with those who go down to the pit.”

15 ‘This is what the Lord God says: “On the day when it went down to Sheol I caused mourning; I closed the deep over it and held back its rivers. And *its* many waters were stopped up, and I made Lebanon mourn for it, and all the trees of the field wilted away on account of it. 16 I made the nations quake from the sound of its fall when I made it go down to Sheol with those who go down to the pit; and all the well-watered trees of Eden, the choicest and best of Lebanon, were comforted in the earth beneath. 17 They also went down with it to Sheol to those who were slain by the sword; and *those who were* its strength lived in its shade among the nations.

18 “To which among the trees of Eden are you so alike in glory and greatness? Yet you will be brought down with the trees of Eden to the earth beneath; you will lie in the midst of the uncircumcised with those who were killed by the sword. This is Pharaoh and all his hordes!”’ declares the Lord God.”

Grief over Pharaoh and Egypt

32 In the twelfth year, in the twelfth month, on the first of the month, the word of the Lord came to me, saying, 2 “Son of man, take up a song of mourning over Pharaoh king of Egypt, and say to him,

‘You compared yourself to a young lion of
     the nations,
   Yet you are like the monster in the seas;
   And you burst forth in your rivers
   And muddied the waters with your feet
   And fouled their rivers.’”
3 This is what the Lord God says:
   “Now I will spread My net over you
   With a contingent of many peoples,
   And they will lift you up in My net.
4 “I will leave you on the land;
   I will hurl you on the open field.
   And I will cause all the birds of the sky to
     nest on you,
   And I will satisfy the animals of the whole
     earth with you.

5 "I will lay your flesh on the mountains
   And fill the valleys with your refuse.
6 "I will also make the land drink the dis-
   charge of your blood
   As far as the mountains,
   And the ravines will be full of you.
7 "And when *I* extinguish you,
   I will cover the heavens and darken their
   stars;
   I will cover the sun with a cloud
   And the moon will not give its light.
8 "All the shining lights in the heavens
   I will darken over you
   And will set darkness on your land,"
   Declares the Lord GOD.
9 "I will also trouble the hearts of many peoples
when I bring your destruction among the
nations, into lands which you have not known.
10 And I will make many peoples appalled at
you, and their kings will be horribly afraid of
you when I brandish My sword before them;
and they will tremble again and again, every
person for his own life, on the day of your
fall."

11 For the Lord GOD says this: "The sword of
the king of Babylon will attack you. **12** By the
swords of the warriors I will make your multitude fall; all of them are tyrants of the nations,
   And they will devastate the pride of
   Egypt,
   And all its multitude will be destroyed.
13 "I will also eliminate all its cattle from
   beside many waters;
   And a human foot will not muddy them
   anymore,
   And the hoofs of animals will not muddy
   them.
14 "Then I will make their waters settle,
   And make their rivers run like oil,"
   Declares the Lord GOD.
15 "When I make the land of Egypt a desolation,
   And the land is destitute of that which
   filled it,
   When I strike all those who live in it,
   Then they shall know that I am the LORD.
16 This is a song of mourning, and they shall
sing it. The daughters of the nations shall sing
it. Over Egypt and over all her hordes they
shall sing it," declares the Lord GOD.

17 In the twelfth year, on the fifteenth of the
month, the word of the LORD came to me, saying, **18** "Son of man, lament for the hordes of
Egypt and bring it down, her and the daughters
of the mighty nations, to the netherworld, with
those who go down to the pit;
19 'Whom do you surpass in beauty?
   Go down and make your bed with the
   uncircumcised.'
20 They shall fall in the midst of those who are
killed by the sword. She is turned over to the
sword; they have dragged her and all her
hordes away. **21** The strong among the mighty
ones shall speak of him *and* his helpers from
the midst of Sheol: 'They have gone down,
they lie still, the uncircumcised, killed by the
sword.'
22 "Assyria is there and all her company; her
graves are all around her. All of them killed,
fallen by the sword, **23** whose graves are set in

the remotest parts of the pit, and her company
is all around her grave. All of them killed,
fallen by the sword, who spread terror in the
land of the living.
24 "Elam is there and all her hordes around
her grave; all of them killed, fallen by the
sword, who went down uncircumcised to the
lower parts of the earth, who inflicted their
terror on the land of the living, and bore their
disgrace with those who go down to the pit.
25 They have made a bed for her among the
slain with all her hordes. Her graves are
around it, they are all uncircumcised, killed by
the sword (although their terror was inflicted
on the land of the living), and they bore their
disgrace with those who go down to the pit;
they were put in the midst of the slain.
26 "Meshech, Tubal, and all their hordes
are there; their graves surround them. All of
them were killed by the sword uncircumcised,
though they inflicted their terror on the land of
the living. **27** Nor do they lie beside the fallen
heroes of the uncircumcised, who went down
to Sheol with their weapons of war and whose
swords were placed under their heads; but the
punishment for their wrongdoing rested on
their bones, though the terror of *these* heroes
was once in the land of the living. **28** But in the
midst of the uncircumcised you will be broken
and lie with those killed by the sword.
29 "There *also is* Edom, its kings and all its
princes, who despite *all* their might are laid
with those killed by the sword; they will lie
with the uncircumcised and with those who go
down to the pit.
30 "There *also are* the chiefs of the north, all
of them, and all the Sidonians, who in *spite of*
the terror *resulting* from their might, in shame
went down with the slain. So they lay down
uncircumcised with those killed by the sword
and bore their disgrace with those who go
down to the pit.
31 "These Pharaoh will see, and he will find
consolation regarding all his hordes killed by
the sword, Pharaoh and all his army," declares
the Lord GOD. **32** "Though I inflicted the terror
of him on the land of the living, yet he will be
laid to rest among *the* uncircumcised *along*
with those killed by the sword, Pharaoh and all
his hordes," declares the Lord GOD.

The Watchman's Duty

33 Now the word of the LORD came to me,
saying, **2** "Son of man, speak to the sons
of your people and say to them, 'If I bring a
sword upon a land, and the people of the land
take one man from among them and make
him their watchman, **3** and he sees the sword
coming upon the land and blows the horn and
warns the people, **4** then someone who hears
the sound of the horn but does not take
warning, and a sword comes and takes him
away, his blood will be on his *own* head. **5** He
heard the sound of the horn but did not take
warning; his blood will be on himself. But had
he taken warning, he would have saved his
life. **6** But if the watchman sees the sword
coming and does not blow the horn and the
people are not warned, and a sword comes and
takes a person from them, he is taken away for

his wrongdoing; but I will require his blood from the watchman's hand.'

7 "Now as for you, son of man, I have appointed you as a watchman for the house of Israel; so you will hear a message from My mouth and give them a warning from Me. 8 When I say to the wicked, 'You wicked person, you will certainly die,' and you do not speak to warn the wicked about his way, that wicked person shall die for his wrongdoing, but I will require his blood from your hand. 9 But if you on your part warn a wicked person to turn from his way and he does not turn from his way, he will die for his wrongdoing, but you have saved your life.

10 "Now as for you, son of man, say to the house of Israel, 'This is what you have said: "Surely our offenses and our sins are upon us, and we are rotting away in them; how then can we survive?" '11 Say to them, 'As I live!' declares the Lord GOD, 'I take no pleasure at all in the death of the wicked, but rather that the wicked turn from his way and live. Turn back, turn back from your evil ways! Why then should you die, house of Israel?' 12 And you, son of man, say to your fellow citizens, 'The righteousness of a righteous one will not save him on the day of his offense, and as for the wickedness of a wicked one, he will not stumble because of it on the day when he turns from his wickedness; whereas a righteous one will not be able to live by his righteousness on the day when he commits sin.' 13 When I say to the righteous that he will certainly live, and he so trusts in his righteousness that he commits injustice, none of his righteous deeds will be remembered; but for that same injustice of his which he has committed he will die. 14 But when I say to the wicked, 'You will certainly die,' and he turns from his sin and practices justice and righteousness, 15 if a wicked person returns a pledge, pays back what he has taken by robbery, walks by the statutes which ensure life without committing injustice, he shall certainly live; he shall not die. 16 None of his sins that he has committed will be remembered against him. He has practiced justice and righteousness; he shall certainly live.

17 "Yet your fellow citizens say, 'The way of the Lord is not right,' when it is their own way that is not right. 18 When the righteous turns from his righteousness and commits injustice, then he shall die in it. 19 But when the wicked turns from his wickedness and practices justice and righteousness, he will live by them. 20 Yet you say, 'The way of the Lord is not right.' I will judge each of you according to his ways, house of Israel."

Word of Jerusalem's Capture

21 Now in the twelfth year of our exile, on the fifth of the tenth month, the survivor from Jerusalem came to me, saying, "The city has been taken." 22 Now the hand of the LORD had been upon me in the evening, before the survivors came. And He opened my mouth at the time they came to me in the morning; so my mouth was opened and I was no longer speechless.

23 Then the word of the LORD came to me, saying, 24 "Son of man, they who live in these ruins in the land of Israel are saying, 'Abraham was only one, yet he possessed the land; so to us who are many the land has been given as a possession.' 25 Therefore say to them, 'This is what the Lord GOD says: "You eat meat with the blood in it, raise your eyes to your idols as you shed blood. Should you then possess the land? 26 You rely on your sword, you commit abominations, and each of you defiles his neighbor's wife. Should you then possess the land?" '27 You shall say this to them: 'This is what the Lord GOD says: "As I live, those who are in the places of ruins certainly will fall by the sword, and whoever is in the open field I will give to the animals to be devoured, and those who are in the strongholds and in the caves will die of plague. 28 And I will make the land a desolation and a waste, and the pride of her power will be brought to an end; and the mountains of Israel will be deserted so that no one will pass through. 29 Then they will know that I am the LORD, when I make the land a desolation and a waste because of all their abominations which they have committed." '

30 "But as for you, son of man, your fellow citizens who talk with one another about you by the walls and in the doorways of the houses, speak one with another, each with his brother, saying, 'Come now and hear what the message is that comes from the LORD.' 31 And they come to you as people come, and sit before you as My people and hear your words, but they do not do them; for they do the lustful desires expressed by their mouth, and their heart follows their unlawful gain. 32 And behold, you are to them like a love song by one who has a beautiful voice and plays well on an instrument; for they hear your words but they do not practice them. 33 So when it comes—as it certainly will—then they will know that a prophet has been among them."

Prophecy against the Shepherds of Israel

34 Then the word of the LORD came to me, saying, 2 "Son of man, prophesy against the shepherds of Israel. Prophesy and say to those shepherds, 'This is what the Lord GOD says: "Woe, shepherds of Israel who have been feeding themselves! Should the shepherds not feed the flock? 3 You eat the fat and clothe yourselves with the wool, you slaughter the fat sheep without feeding the flock. 4 Those who are sickly you have not strengthened, the diseased you have not healed, the broken you have not bound up, the scattered you have not brought back, nor have you searched for the lost; but with force and with violence you have dominated them. 5 They scattered for lack of a shepherd, and they became food for every animal of the field and scattered. 6 My flock strayed through all the mountains and on every high hill; My flock was scattered over all the surface of the earth, and there was no one to search or seek for them." '"

7 Therefore, you shepherds, hear the word of the LORD: 8 "As I live," declares the Lord GOD, "certainly, because My flock has become plunder, and My flock has become food for all

the animals of the field for lack of a shepherd, and My shepherds did not search for My flock, but *rather* the shepherds fed themselves and did not feed My flock, 9 therefore, you shepherds, hear the word of the LORD: 10 'This is what the Lord GOD says: "Behold, I am against the shepherds, and I will demand My sheep from them and make them stop tending sheep. So the shepherds will not feed themselves anymore, but I will save My sheep from their mouth, so that they will not be food for them." ' "

The Restoration of Israel

11 For the Lord GOD says this: "Behold, I Myself will search for My sheep and look after them. 12 As a shepherd cares for his flock on a day when he is among his scattered sheep, so I will care for My sheep and will rescue them from all the places where they were scattered on a cloudy and gloomy day. 13 I will bring them out from the peoples and gather them from the countries and bring them to their own land; and I will feed them on the mountains of Israel, by the streams, and in all the inhabited places of the land. 14 I will feed them in a good pasture, and their grazing place will be on the mountain heights of Israel. There they will lie down in a good grazing place and feed in rich pasture on the mountains of Israel. 15 I Myself will feed My flock and I Myself will lead them to rest," declares the Lord GOD. 16 "I will seek the lost, bring back the scattered, bind up the broken, and strengthen the sick; but the fat and the strong I will eliminate. I will feed them with judgment.

17 "As for you, My flock, this is what the Lord GOD says: 'Behold, I am going to judge between one sheep and another, between the rams and the male goats. 18 Is it too little a thing for you to feed in the good pasture, that you must trample with your feet the rest of your pastures? Or *too little for you* to drink the clear waters, that you must muddy the rest with your feet? 19 But as for My flock, they must eat what you trample with your feet, and drink what you muddy with your feet!' "

20 Therefore, this is what the Lord GOD says to them: "Behold, I, I Myself will also judge between the fat sheep and the lean sheep. 21 Since you push away with *your* side and shoulder, and gore all the weak with your horns until you have scattered them abroad, 22 therefore, I will save My flock, and they will no longer be plunder; and I will judge between one sheep and another. 23 "Then I will appoint over them one shepherd, My servant David, and he will feed them; he will feed them himself and be their shepherd. 24 And I, the LORD, will be their God, and My servant David will be prince among them; I the LORD have spoken.

25 "And I will make a covenant of peace with them and eliminate harmful animals from the land, so that they may live securely in the wilderness and sleep in the woods. 26 I will make them and the places around My hill a blessing. And I will make showers fall in their season; they will be showers of blessing. 27 Also the tree of the field will yield its fruit and the earth will yield its produce, and they will be secure on their land. Then they will know that I am the LORD, when I have broken the bars of their yoke and have saved them from the hand of those who enslaved them. 28 They will no longer be plunder to the nations, and the animals of the earth will not devour them; but they will live securely, and no one will make *them* afraid. 29 I will establish for them a renowned planting place, and they will not again be victims of famine in the land, and they will not endure the insults of the nations anymore. 30 Then they will know that I, the LORD their God, am with them, and that they, the house of Israel, are My people," declares the Lord GOD. 31 "As for you, My sheep, the sheep of My pasture, you are mankind, *and* I am your God," declares the Lord GOD.

Prophecy against Mount Seir

35 Now the word of the LORD came to me, saying, 2 "Son of man, set your face against Mount Seir, and prophesy against it 3 and say to it, 'This is what the Lord GOD says:
"Behold, I am against you, Mount Seir,
    And I will reach out with My hand against
        you
    And make you a desolation and a waste.
4   "I will turn your cities to ruins,
    And you will become a desolation.
    Then you will know that I am the LORD.
5 Since you have had everlasting hostility and have turned over the sons of Israel to the power of the sword at the time of their disaster, at the time of the punishment of the end, 6 therefore as I live," declares the Lord GOD, "I will certainly doom you to bloodshed, and bloodshed will pursue you; since you have not hated bloodshed, therefore bloodshed will pursue you. 7 I will make Mount Seir a waste and a desolation and I will eliminate from it one who passes through and returns. 8 I will fill its mountains with its slain; those killed by the sword will fall on your hills, in your valleys, and in all your ravines. 9 I will make you a permanent desolation, and your cities will not be inhabited. Then you will know that I am the LORD.

10 "Since you have said, 'These two nations and these two lands will be mine, and we will possess them,' although the LORD was there, 11 therefore as I live," declares the Lord GOD, "I will deal *with you* according to your anger and according to your envy which you displayed because of your hatred for them; so I will make Myself known among them when I judge you. 12 Then you will know that I, the LORD, have heard all your insults which you have spoken against the mountains of Israel saying, 'They are desolate; they have been given to us as food.' 13 And you have spoken arrogantly against Me and have multiplied your words against Me; I Myself have heard *it.*"

14 This is what the Lord GOD says: "As all the earth rejoices, I will make you a desolation. 15 As you rejoiced over the inheritance of the house of Israel because it was desolate, so I will do to you. You will be a desolation, Mount Seir, and all Edom, all of it. Then they will know that I am the LORD." '

The Mountains of Israel to Be Blessed

36 "Now you, son of man, prophesy to the mountains of Israel and say, 'You mountains of Israel, hear the word of the LORD. 2 This is what the Lord GOD says: "Since the enemy has spoken against you, 'Aha!' and, 'The everlasting heights have become our possession,' 3 therefore prophesy and say, 'This is what the Lord GOD says: "For good reason they have made you desolate and harassed you from every side, so that you would become a possession of the rest of the nations; and you have been taken up in the talk and the rumor of the people." ' " 4 Therefore, you mountains of Israel, hear the word of the Lord GOD. This is what the Lord GOD says to the mountains and to the hills, to the ravines and to the valleys, to the desolate ruins and to the abandoned cities which have become plunder and an object of ridicule to the rest of the nations which are all around— 5 therefore the Lord GOD says this: "Certainly in the fire of My jealousy I have spoken against the rest of the nations, and against all Edom, who appropriated My land for themselves as a possession with wholehearted joy and with contempt of soul, in order to make its pastureland plunder." 6 Therefore prophesy in regard to the land of Israel and say to the mountains and to the hills, to the ravines and to the valleys, "This is what the Lord GOD says. 'Behold, I have spoken in My jealousy and in My wrath because you have endured the insults of the nations.' 7 Therefore the Lord GOD says this: 'I have sworn that the nations that are around you will certainly endure their insults themselves. 8 But as for you, mountains of Israel, you will grow your branches and bear fruit for My people Israel; for they are about to come. 9 For, behold, I am for you, and I will turn to you, and you will be cultivated and sown. 10 And I will multiply people on you, all the house of Israel, all of it; and the cities will be inhabited and the ruins will be rebuilt. 11 I will multiply on you people and animals, and they will increase and be fruitful; and I will populate you as you were previously, and treat you better than at the beginning. Then you will know that I am the LORD. 12 Yes, I will have people—My people Israel—walk on you and possess you, so that you will become their inheritance and never again bereave them of children.'

13 "The Lord GOD says this: 'Since they say to you, "You are a devourer of people and have bereaved your nation of children," 14 for that reason you will no longer devour people and no longer bereave your nation of children,' declares the Lord GOD. 15 I will not let you hear insults from the nations anymore, nor will you suffer disgrace from the peoples any longer, nor will you make your nation stumble any longer," declares the Lord GOD.' "

16 Then the word of the LORD came to me, saying, 17 "Son of man, when the house of Israel was living on their own land, they defiled it by their ways and their deeds; their way before Me was like the uncleanness of a woman in her impurity. 18 Therefore I poured out My wrath on them for the blood which they had shed on the land, because they had defiled it with their idols. 19 I also scattered them among the nations, and they were dispersed throughout the lands. According to their ways and their deeds I judged them. 20 When they came to the nations where they went, they profaned My holy name, because it was said of them, 'These are the people of the LORD, yet they have left His land.' 21 But I had concern for My holy name, which the house of Israel had profaned among the nations where they went.

Israel to Be Renewed for His Name's Sake

22 "Therefore say to the house of Israel, 'This is what the Lord GOD says: "It is not for your sake, house of Israel, that I am about to act, but for My holy name, which you have profaned among the nations where you went. 23 And I will vindicate the holiness of My great name which has been profaned among the nations, which you have profaned among them. Then the nations will know that I am the LORD," declares the Lord GOD, "when I show Myself holy among you in their sight. 24 For I will take you from the nations, and gather you from all the lands; and I will bring you into your own land. 25 Then I will sprinkle clean water on you, and you will be clean; I will cleanse you from all your filthiness and from all your idols. 26 Moreover, I will give you a new heart and put a new spirit within you; and I will remove the heart of stone from your flesh and give you a heart of flesh. 27 And I will put My Spirit within you and bring it about that you walk in My statutes, and are careful and follow My ordinances. 28 And you will live in the land that I gave to your forefathers; so you will be My people, and I will be your God. 29 Moreover, I will save you from all your uncleanness; and I will call for the grain and multiply it, and I will not bring a famine on you. 30 Instead, I will multiply the fruit of the tree and the produce of the field, so that you will not receive again the disgrace of famine among the nations. 31 Then you will remember your evil ways and your deeds that were not good, and you will loathe yourselves in your own sight for your wrongdoings and your abominations. 32 I am not doing this for your sake," declares the Lord GOD; "let that be known to you. Be ashamed and humiliated for your ways, house of Israel!"

33 'This is what the Lord GOD says: "On the day that I cleanse you from all your wrongdoings, I will populate the cities, and the places of ruins will be rebuilt. 34 The desolated land will be cultivated instead of being a desolation in the sight of everyone who passes by. 35 And they will say, 'This desolated land has become like the Garden of Eden; and the waste, desolated and ruined cities are fortified and inhabited.' 36 Then the nations around you that are left will know that I, the LORD, have rebuilt the ruined places and planted that which was desolated; I, the LORD, have spoken, and I will do it."

37 'This is what the Lord GOD says: "This too I will let the house of Israel ask Me to do for them: I will increase their people like a flock. 38 Like the flock for sacrifices, like the flock at

Jerusalem during her appointed feasts, so will the waste cities be filled with flocks of people. Then they will know that I am the LORD."'"

Vision of the Valley of Dry Bones

37 The hand of the LORD was upon me, and He brought me out by the Spirit of the LORD and set me down in the middle of the valley; and it was full of bones. [2] He had me pass among them all around, and behold, *there were* very many on the surface of the valley; and behold, *they were* very dry. [3] Then He said to me, "Son of man, can these bones live?" And I answered, "Lord GOD, You Yourself know." [4] Again He said to me, "Prophesy over these bones and say to them, 'You dry bones, hear the word of the LORD.' [5] This is what the Lord GOD says to these bones: 'Behold, I am going to make [1]breath enter you so that you may come to life. [6] And I will attach tendons to you, make flesh grow back on you, cover you with skin, and put breath in you so that you may come to life; and you will know that I am the LORD.'"

[7] So I prophesied as I was commanded; and as I prophesied, there was a *loud* noise, and behold, a rattling; and the bones came together, bone to its bone. [8] And I looked, and behold, tendons were on them, and flesh grew and skin covered them; but there was no breath in them. [9] Then He said to me, "Prophesy to the breath, prophesy, son of man, and say to the breath, 'The Lord GOD says this: "Come from the four winds, breath, and breathe on these slain, so that they come to life."'" [10] So I prophesied as He commanded me, and the breath entered them, and they came to life and stood on their feet, an exceedingly great army.

The Vision Explained

[11] Then He said to me, "Son of man, these bones are the entire house of Israel; behold, they say, 'Our bones are dried up and our hope has perished. We are completely cut off.' [12] Therefore prophesy and say to them, 'This is what the Lord GOD says: "Behold, I am going to open your graves and cause you to come up out of your graves, My people; and I will bring you into the land of Israel. [13] Then you will know that I am the LORD, when I have opened your graves and caused you to come up out of your graves, My people. [14] And I will put My [1]Spirit within you and you will come to life, and I will place you on your own land. Then you will know that I, the LORD, have spoken and done it," declares the LORD.'"

Reunion of Judah and Israel

[15] The word of the LORD came again to me, saying, [16] "Now you, son of man, take for yourself one stick and write on it, 'For Judah and for the sons of Israel, his companions'; then take another stick and write on it, 'For Joseph, the stick of Ephraim and all the house of Israel, his companions.' [17] Then put them together for yourself one to another into one stick, so that they may become one in your hand. [18] And when the sons of your people speak to you, saying, 'Will you not declare to us what you mean by these?' [19] say to them, 'This is what the Lord GOD says: "Behold, I am going to take the stick of Joseph, which is in the hand of Ephraim, and the tribes of Israel, his companions; and I will put them with it, with the stick of Judah, and make them one stick, and they will be one in My hand."' [20] The sticks on which you write will be in your hand before their eyes. [21] And say to them, 'This is what the Lord GOD says: "Behold, I am going to take the sons of Israel from among the nations where they have gone, and I will gather them from every side and bring them into their own land; [22] and I will make them one nation in the land, on the mountains of Israel; and one king will be king for all of them; and they will no longer be two nations, and no longer be divided into two kingdoms. [23] They will no longer defile themselves with their idols, or with their detestable things, or with any of their offenses; but I will rescue them from all their [1]dwelling places in which they have sinned, and will cleanse them. And they will be My people, and I will be their God.

The Davidic Kingdom

[24] "And My servant David will be king over them, and they will all have one shepherd; and they will walk in My ordinances, and keep My statutes and follow them. [25] And they will live on the land that I gave to My servant Jacob, in which your fathers lived; and they will live on it, they, and their sons and their sons' sons, forever; and My servant David will be their leader forever. [26] And I will make a covenant of peace with them; it will be an everlasting covenant with them. And I will place them and multiply them, and set My sanctuary in their midst forever. [27] My dwelling place also will be among them; and I will be their God, and they will be My people. [28] And the nations will know that I am the LORD who sanctifies Israel, when My sanctuary is in their midst forever."'"

Prophecy about Gog and Future Invasion of Israel

38 Now the word of the LORD came to me, saying, [2] "Son of man, set your face toward Gog of the land of Magog, the chief prince of Meshech and Tubal, and prophesy against him, [3] and say, 'This is what the Lord GOD says: "Behold, I am against you, Gog, chief prince of Meshech and Tubal. [4] So I will turn you around and put hooks into your jaws, and I will bring you out, and all your army, horses and horsemen, all of them magnificently dressed, a great contingent *with* shield and [1]buckler, all of them wielding swords; [5] Persia, Cush, and Put with them, all of them *with* buckler and helmet; [6] Gomer with all its troops; Beth-togarmah *from* the remote parts of the north with all its troops—many peoples with you.

[7] "Be ready, and be prepared, you and all your contingents that are assembled around

---

37:5 [1] Or *spirit,* and so throughout the ch   37:14 [1] Or *breath*   37:23 [1] Another reading is *offenses*
38:4 [1] I.e., small shield

you, and be a guard for them. [8] After many days you will be summoned; in the latter years you will come into the land that is restored from the sword, *whose inhabitants* have been gathered from many nations to the mountains of Israel which had been a continual place of ruins; but its people were brought out from the nations, and they are living securely, all of them. [9] And you will go up, you will come like a storm; you will be like a cloud covering the land, you and all your troops, and many peoples with you."

[10] 'This is what the Lord GOD says: "It will come about on that day, that thoughts will come into your mind and you will devise an evil plan, [11] and you will say, 'I will go up against the land of unwalled villages. I will go against those who are at rest, who live securely, all of them living without walls and having no bars or gates, [12] to capture spoils and to seize plunder, to turn your hand against the ruins that are *now* inhabited, and against the people who are gathered from the nations, who have acquired livestock and goods, who live at the center of the world.' [13] Sheba and Dedan and the merchants of Tarshish with all its villages will say to you, 'Have you come to capture spoils? Have you assembled your contingent to seize plunder, to carry away silver and gold, to take away livestock and goods, to capture great spoils?'" '

[14] "Therefore prophesy, son of man, and say to Gog, 'This is what the Lord GOD says: "On that day when My people Israel are living securely, will you not know *it?* [15] You will come from your place out of the remote parts of the north, you and many peoples with you, all of them riding horses, a large assembly and a mighty army; [16] and you will come up against My people Israel like a cloud to cover the land. It shall come about in the last days that I will bring you against My land, so that the nations may know Me when I show Myself holy through you before their eyes, Gog."

[17] 'This is what the Lord GOD says: "Are you the one of whom I spoke in former days through My servants the prophets of Israel, who prophesied in those days for *many* years that I would bring you against them? [18] It will come about on that day, when Gog comes against the land of Israel," declares the Lord GOD, "that My fury will mount up in My anger. [19] In My zeal and in My blazing wrath I declare *that* on that day there will certainly be a great earthquake in the land of Israel. [20] The fish of the sea, the birds of the sky, the animals of the field, all the crawling things that crawl on the earth, and all mankind who are on the face of the earth will shake at My presence; and the mountains will be thrown down, the steep pathways will collapse, and every wall will fall to the ground. [21] And I will call for a sword against 'him on all My mountains," declares the Lord GOD. "Every man's sword will be against his brother. [22] With plague and with blood I will enter into judgment with him; and I will rain on him and on his troops, and on the many peoples who are with him, a torrential rain, hailstones, fire, and brimstone. [23] So I will

prove Myself great, show Myself holy, and make Myself known in the sight of many nations; and they will know that I am the LORD." '

Prophecy against Gog—Invaders Destroyed

39 "And you, son of man, prophesy against Gog and say, 'This is what the Lord GOD says: "Behold, I am against you, Gog, chief prince of Meshech and Tubal; [2] and I will turn you around, lead you on a rope, take you up from the remotest parts of the north, and bring you against the mountains of Israel. [3] Then I will strike your bow from your left hand and make your arrows fall from your right hand. [4] You will fall on the mountains of Israel, you and all your troops, and the peoples who are with you; I will give you as food to every kind of predatory bird and animal of the field. [5] You will fall on the open field; for it is I who have spoken," declares the Lord GOD. [6] "And I will send fire upon Magog and those who inhabit the coastlands in safety; and they will know that I am the LORD.

[7] "And I will make My holy name known in the midst of My people Israel; and I will not allow My holy name to be profaned anymore. But the nations will know that I am the LORD, the Holy One in Israel. [8] Behold, it is coming and it shall be done," declares the Lord GOD. "That is the day of which I have spoken.

[9] "Then those who inhabit the cities of Israel will go out and make fires with the weapons and burn *them,* both 'bucklers and shields, bows and arrows, war clubs and spears, and for seven years they will make fires of them. [10] They will not take wood from the field or gather firewood from the forests, because they will make fires with the weapons; and they will take the spoils of those who plundered them and seize the plunder of those who plundered them," declares the Lord GOD.

[11] "On that day I will give Gog a burial place there in Israel, the valley of those who pass by east of the sea, and it will block the way of those who would pass by. So they will bury Gog there with all his horde, and they will call *it* the Valley of Hamon-gog. [12] For seven months the house of Israel will be burying them in order to cleanse the land. [13] And all the people of the land will bury *them;* and it will be to their renown *on* the day that I appear in My glory," declares the Lord GOD. [14] "They will also select men who will constantly pass through the land, burying those who were passing through, those left on the surface of the ground, in order to cleanse it. At the end of seven months they will conduct a search. [15] As those who pass through the land pass through and anyone sees a human bone, then he will set up a marker by it until the burial detail has buried it in the Valley of Hamon-gog. [16] And even *the* name of *the* city will be Hamonah. So they will cleanse the land." '

[17] "Now as for you, son of man, this is what the Lord GOD says: 'Say to every kind of bird and to every animal of the field: "Assemble and come, gather from every direction to My sacrifice, which I am going to sacrifice for you as a

great sacrifice on the mountains of Israel; and you will eat flesh and drink blood. **18** You will eat the flesh of warriors and drink the blood of the leaders of the earth, *as though they were* rams, lambs, goats, *and* bulls, all of them fattened livestock of Bashan. **19** So you will eat fat until you are full, and drink blood until you are drunk, from My sacrifice which I have sacrificed for you. **20** You will eat your fill at My table *with* horses and charioteers, *with* warriors and all the men of war," declares the Lord GOD.

21 "And I will place My glory among the nations; and all the nations will see My judgment which I have executed, and My hand which I have laid on them. **22** And the house of Israel will know that I am the LORD their God, from that day onward. **23** The nations will know that the house of Israel went into exile for their wrongdoing, because they were disloyal to Me, and I hid My face from them; so I handed them over to their adversaries, and all of them fell by the sword. **24** In accordance with their uncleanness and their offenses I dealt with them, and I hid My face from them." ' "

Israel Restored

25 Therefore this is what the Lord GOD says: "Now I will restore the fortunes of Jacob and have mercy on all the house of Israel; and I will be jealous for My holy name. **26** They will 'forget their disgrace and all their treachery which they perpetrated against Me, when they live securely on their *own* land with no one to make *them* afraid. **27** When I bring them back from the peoples and gather them from the lands of their enemies, then I shall show Myself holy through them in the sight of the many nations. **28** Then they will know that I am the LORD their God because I made them go into exile among the nations, and *then* I gathered them *again* to their own land; and I will leave none of them there any longer. **29** I will not hide My face from them any longer, for I will have poured out My Spirit on the house of Israel," declares the Lord GOD.

Vision of the Man with a Measuring Rod

40 In the twenty-fifth year of our exile, at the beginning of the year, on the tenth of the month, in the fourteenth year after the city was taken, on this very day the hand of the LORD was upon me and He brought me there. **2** In the visions of God He brought me into the land of Israel and set me on a very high mountain, and on it to the south *there was something* like a structure of a city. **3** So He brought me there; and behold, there was a man whose appearance was like the appearance of bronze, with a thread of flax and a measuring rod in his hand; and he was standing in the gateway. **4** And the man said to me, "Son of man, see with your eyes, hear with your ears, and pay attention to all that I am going to show you; for you have been brought here in order to show *it* to you. Declare to the house of Israel all that you see."

Measurements Relating to the Temple

5 And behold, there was a wall on the outside of the temple all around, and in the man's hand was a measuring rod of six 'cubits, each of which was a ²cubit and a hand width. So he measured the thickness of the wall, one rod; and the height, one rod. **6** Then he went to the gate which faced east, went up its steps, and measured the threshold of the gate, one rod in width; and the other threshold *was* one rod in width. **7** The guardroom *was* one rod long and one rod wide; and *there were* five cubits between the guardrooms. And the threshold of the gate by the porch of the gate facing inward *was* one rod. **8** Then he measured the porch of the gate facing inward, one rod. **9** And he measured the porch of the gate, eight cubits; and its side pillars, two cubits. And the porch of the gate was faced inward. **10** The guardrooms of the gate toward the east *numbered* three on each side; the three of them had the same measurement. The side pillars also had the same measurement on each side. **11** And he measured the width of the gateway, ten cubits, *and* the length of the gate, thirteen cubits. **12** *There was* a barrier *wall* one cubit *wide* in front of the guardrooms on each side; and the guardrooms *were* six cubits *square* on each side. **13** And he measured the gate from the roof of the one guardroom to the roof of the other, a width of twenty-five cubits, from *one* door to *the* door opposite. **14** He made the side pillars sixty cubits *high;* the gate *extended* all around to the side pillar of the courtyard. **15** And *from* the front of the entrance gate to the front of the inner porch of the gate *was* fifty cubits. **16** And *there were* shuttered windows *looking* toward the guardrooms, and toward their side pillars within the gate all around, and likewise for the porches. And *there were* windows all around inside; and on *each* side pillar *were* palm tree decorations.

17 Then he brought me into the outer courtyard, and behold, *there were* chambers and a stone pavement made for the courtyard all around; thirty chambers faced the pavement. **18** And the pavement (*that is,* the lower pavement) *was* by the side of the gates, corresponding to the length of the gates. **19** Then he measured the width from the front of the lower gate to the front of the exterior of the inner courtyard, a hundred cubits on the east and on the north.

20 And *as for* the gate of the outer courtyard which faced north, he measured its length and its width. **21** It had three guardrooms on each side; and its side pillars and its porches had the same measurement as the first gate. Its length *was* fifty cubits, and the width twenty-five cubits. **22** Its windows, its porches, and its palm tree decorations *had* the same measurements as the gate which faced east; and it was reached by seven steps, and its porch *was* in front of them. **23** The inner courtyard had a gate opposite the gate on the north as well as *the* gate on the east; and he measured a hundred cubits from gate to gate. **24** Then he led me toward the south, and

---

39:26 ¹ Another reading is *bear*   **40:5** ¹ I.e., "long" cubits, see note 2   ² A cubit and hand width equals about 21 in. or 53 cm

behold, there was a gate toward the south; and he measured its side pillars and its porches according to those same measurements. 25 The gate and its porches had windows all around like those other windows; the length was fifty cubits and the width, twenty-five cubits. 26 There were seven steps going up to it, and its porches were in front of them; and it had palm tree decorations on its side pillars, one on each side. 27 The inner courtyard had a gate toward the south; and he measured from gate to gate toward the south, a hundred cubits.

28 Then he brought me to the inner courtyard by the south gate; and he measured the south gate according to those same measurements. 29 Its guardrooms also, its side pillars, and its porches were according to those same measurements. And the gate and its porches had windows all around; it was fifty cubits long and twenty-five cubits wide. 30 There were porches all around, twenty-five cubits long and five cubits wide. 31 And its porches were toward the outer courtyard; and palm tree decorations were on its side pillars, and its stairway had eight steps.

32 Then he brought me into the inner courtyard toward the east. And he measured the gate according to those same measurements. 33 Its guardrooms also, its side pillars, and its porches were according to those same measurements. And the gate and its porches had windows all around; it was fifty cubits long and twenty-five cubits wide. 34 Its porches were toward the outer courtyard; and palm tree decorations were on its side pillars, on each side, and its stairway had eight steps.

35 Then he brought me to the north gate; and he measured it according to those same measurements, 36 with its guardrooms, its side pillars, and its porches. And the gate had windows all around; the length was fifty cubits' and the width twenty-five cubits. 37 And its side pillars were toward the outer courtyard; and palm tree decorations were on its side pillars, on each side, and its stairway had eight steps.

38 A chamber with its doorway was by the side pillars at the gates; there they rinse the burnt offering. 39 And in the porch of the gate were two tables on each side, on which to slaughter the burnt offering, the sin offering, and the guilt offering. 40 On the outer side, as one went up to the gateway toward the north, were two tables; and on the other side of the porch of the gate were two tables. 41 Four tables were on each side next to the gate; eight tables on which they slaughter sacrifices. 42 For the burnt offering there were four tables of cut stone, a cubit and a half long, a cubit and a half wide, and one cubit high, on which they set the utensils with which they slaughter the burnt offering and the sacrifice. 43 And the double hooks, 'one hand width in length, were installed in the house all around; and on the tables was the flesh of the offering.

44 From the outside to the inner gate were chambers for the singers in the inner courtyard, one of which was at the side of the north gate, with its front toward the south, and one at the side of the south gate facing north. 45 Then he said to me, "This is the chamber which faces south, intended for the priests who are responsible for the temple; 46 but the chamber which faces north is for the priests who are responsible for the altar. They are the sons of Zadok, who from the sons of Levi come near to the LORD to serve Him." 47 He measured the courtyard, a perfect square, a hundred cubits long and a hundred cubits wide; and the altar was in front of the temple.

48 Then he brought me to the porch of the temple and measured each side pillar of the porch, five cubits on each side; and the width of the gate was three cubits on each side. 49 The length of the porch was twenty cubits, and the width eleven cubits; and at the stairway by which it was ascended were columns belonging to the side pillars, one on each side.

The Inner Temple

41 Then he brought me to the sanctuary, and he measured the side pillars: six 'cubits wide on each side was the width of the side pillar. 2 The width of the entrance was ten cubits and the sides of the entrance were five cubits on each side. He also measured the length of the sanctuary, forty cubits, and the width, twenty cubits. 3 Then he went inside and measured each side pillar of the doorway, two cubits, and the doorway, six cubits high; and the width of the doorway, seven cubits. 4 And he measured its length, twenty cubits, and the width, twenty cubits, before the sanctuary; and he said to me, "This is the Most Holy Place."

5 Then he measured the wall of the temple, six cubits; and the width of the side chambers, four cubits, all around the house on every side. 6 The side chambers were in three stories, one above another, and thirty in each story; and the side chambers extended to the wall which stood on their inward side all around, so that they could be attached, but not be attached to the wall of the temple itself. 7 And the side chambers surrounding the temple were wider at each successive story. Because the structure surrounding the temple went upward by stages on all sides of the temple, for that reason the width of the temple increased as it went higher; and so one went up from the lowest story to the highest by way of the second story. 8 I saw also that the house had a raised platform all around; the foundations of the side chambers were a full rod of six long cubits in height. 9 The thickness of the outer wall of the side chambers was five cubits. But the free space between the side chambers belonging to the temple 10 and the outer chambers was twenty cubits in width around the temple on every side. 11 The doorways of the side chambers toward the free space consisted of one doorway toward the north, and another doorway toward the south; and the width of the free space was five cubits all around.

12 The building that was in front of the separate area at the side toward the west was seventy cubits wide; and the wall of the

---

building *was* five cubits thick all around, and its length *was* ninety cubits. ¹³ Then he measured the temple, a hundred cubits long; the separate area with the building and its walls *were* also a hundred cubits long. ¹⁴ Also the width of the front of the temple and *that of* the separate areas along the east *side* totaled a hundred cubits.

¹⁵ And he measured the length of the building along the front of the separate area behind it, with a gallery on each side, a hundred cubits; *he* also *measured* the inner sanctuary and the porches of the courtyard. ¹⁶ The thresholds, the latticed windows, and the galleries all around their three *stories,* opposite the threshold, were paneled with wood all around, and *from* the ground to the windows (but the windows were covered), ¹⁷ over the entrance, and to the inner house, and on the outside, and on all the wall all around inside and outside, *by* measurement. ¹⁸ It was carved with cherubim and palm trees; and a palm tree was between cherub and cherub, and *every* cherub had two faces: ¹⁹ a human face toward the palm tree on one side and a young lion's face toward the palm tree on the other side; they were carved on all the house all around. ²⁰ From the ground to above the entrance cherubim and palm trees were carved, as well as *on* the wall of the sanctuary.

²¹ The doorposts of the sanctuary were square; as for the front of the *inner* sanctuary, the appearance *of one doorpost was* like that *of the other.* ²² The altar *was* of wood, three cubits high, and its length two cubits; its corners, its base, and its sides *were* of wood. And he said to me, "This is the table that is before the LORD." ²³ The sanctuary and the *inner* sanctuary *each* had a double door. ²⁴ *Each of* the doors had two leaves, two swinging leaves; two *leaves* for one door and two leaves for the other. ²⁵ Also there were carved on them, on the doors of the main room, cherubim and palm trees like those carved on the walls; and *there was* a threshold of wood on the front of the porch outside. ²⁶ *And there were* latticed windows and palm trees on one side and on the other, on the sides of the porch; *the same were on* the side chambers of the house and the thresholds.

Chambers of the Temple

42 Then he brought me out into the outer courtyard, the way toward the north; and he brought me to the chamber which *was* opposite the separate area and opposite the building toward the north. ² Along the length, *which was* a hundred ¹cubits, *was* the north door; the width *was* fifty cubits. ³ Opposite the twenty *cubits* which *belonged* to the inner courtyard, and opposite the stone pavement which *belonged* to the outer courtyard, *was* gallery corresponding to gallery in three *stories.* ⁴ In front of the chambers *was* an inner passage ten cubits wide, a way of one *hundred* cubits; and their openings *were* on the north. ⁵ Now the upper chambers *were* smaller because the galleries took more *space* away from them than from the lower and middle

ones in the building. ⁶ For they *were* in three *stories* and had no pillars like the pillars of the courtyards; for that reason *the upper chambers* were set back from the ground *upward,* more than the lower and middle ones. ⁷ As for the outer wall by the side of the chambers, toward the outer courtyard facing the chambers, its length *was* fifty cubits. ⁸ For the length of the chambers which *were* in the outer courtyard *was* fifty cubits; and behold, *the length of those* facing the main room *was* a hundred cubits. ⁹ And below these chambers *was* the entrance on the east side, as one enters them from the outer courtyard.

¹⁰ In the thickness of the wall of the courtyard toward the east, facing the separate area and facing the building, *there were* chambers. ¹¹ And the way in front of them *was* like the appearance of the chambers which *were* on the north; according to their length, so was their width, and all their exits *were* according to their building plans and openings. ¹² Corresponding to the openings of the chambers which were toward the south was an opening at the head of the way, the way in front of the wall toward the east, as one enters them.

¹³ Then he said to me, "The north chambers *and* the south chambers, which are opposite the separate area, they are the holy chambers where the priests who are near to the LORD shall eat the most holy things. There they shall set the most holy things, the grain offering, the sin offering, and the guilt offering; for the place is holy. ¹⁴ When the priests enter, they shall not go out into the outer courtyard from the sanctuary without laying their garments there in which they minister, for they are holy. They shall put on other garments; then they shall approach that which is for the people."

¹⁵ Now when he had finished measuring the inner house, he brought me out by way of the gate which faced east, and measured it all around. ¹⁶ He measured on the east side with the measuring rod: five hundred rods by the measuring rod. ¹⁷ He measured on the north side: five hundred rods by the measuring rod. ¹⁸ On the south side he measured five hundred rods with the measuring rod. ¹⁹ He turned to the west side *and* measured five hundred rods with the measuring rod. ²⁰ He measured it on the four sides; it had a wall all around, the length five hundred *rods* and the width five hundred, to divide between the holy and the common.

Vision of the Glory of God Filling the Temple

43 Then he led me to the gate, the gate facing east; ² and behold, the glory of the God of Israel was coming from the way of the east. And His voice was like the sound of many waters; and the earth shone from His glory. ³ And *it was* like the appearance of the vision which I saw, like the vision which I saw when He came to destroy the city. And the visions *were* like the vision which I saw by the river Chebar; and I fell on my face. ⁴ And the glory of the LORD entered the house by way of the gate facing east. ⁵ And the Spirit lifted me up and

brought me into the inner courtyard; and behold, the glory of the LORD filled the house. 6 Then I heard *Him* speaking to me from the house, while a man was standing beside me. 7 And He said to me, "Son of man, *this is* the place of My throne and the place of the soles of My feet, where I will dwell among the sons of Israel forever. And the house of Israel will not again defile My holy name, neither they nor their kings, by their prostitution and by the corpses of their kings when they die, 8 by putting their threshold by My threshold, and their door post beside My door post, with *only* the wall between Me and them. And they have defiled My holy name by their abominations which they have committed. So I have consumed them in My anger. 9 Now let them remove their prostitution and the corpses of their kings far from Me, and I will dwell among them forever.

10 "As for you, son of man, inform the house of Israel of the temple, so that they will be ashamed of their wrongdoings; and have them measure the plan. 11 And if they are ashamed of everything that they have done, make known to them the plan of the house, its layout, its exits, its entrances, all its plans, all its statutes, and all its laws. And write *it* in their sight, so that they may observe its entire plan and all its statutes and execute them. 12 This is the law of the house: its entire area on the top of the mountain all around *shall be* most holy. Behold, this is the law of the house.

The Altar of Sacrifice

13 "And these are the measurements of the altar by cubits (the cubit *being* a 'cubit and a hand width): the base *shall be* a cubit and the width a cubit, and its border on its edge all around one span; and this *shall be the height of* the base of the altar. 14 And from the base on the ground to the lower ledge *shall be* two cubits, and the width one cubit; and from the smaller ledge to the larger ledge *shall be* four cubits, and the width one cubit. 15 The altar hearth *shall be* four cubits; and from the altar hearth *shall extend* upward four horns. 16 Now the altar hearth *shall be* twelve *cubits* long by twelve wide, square in its four sides. 17 And the ledge *shall be* fourteen *cubits* long by fourteen wide in its four sides, the border around it *shall be* half a cubit, and its base *shall be* a cubit all around; and its steps shall face east."

The Offerings

18 And He said to me, "Son of man, this is what the Lord GOD says: 'These are the statutes for the altar on the day it is built, to offer burnt offerings on it and to sprinkle blood on it. 19 You shall give to the Levitical priests who are from the descendants of Zadok, who come near to Me to serve Me,' declares the Lord GOD, 'a bull as a sin offering. 20 And you shall take some of its blood and put it on its four horns and on the four corners of the ledge, and on the border all around; so you shall cleanse it and make atonement for it. 21 You shall also take the bull as the sin offering, and it shall be burned in the appointed place of the house, outside the sanctuary.

22 'And on the second day you shall offer a male goat without blemish as a sin offering, and they shall cleanse the altar from sin as they cleansed *it* with the bull. 23 When you have finished cleansing *it,* you shall offer a bull without blemish and a ram without blemish from the flock. 24 You shall offer them before the LORD, and the priests shall throw salt on them, and they shall offer them up as a burnt offering to the LORD. 25 For seven days you shall prepare a goat as a sin offering daily; also a bull and a ram from the flock, *both* without blemish, shall be prepared. 26 For seven days they shall make atonement for the altar and purify it; so shall they consecrate it. 27 When they have completed the days, it shall be that on the eighth day and onward, the priests shall offer your burnt offerings on the altar, and your peace offerings; and I will accept you,' declares the Lord GOD."

Gate for the Prince

44 Then He brought me back by way of the outer gate of the sanctuary, which faces east; and it was shut. 2 And the LORD said to me, "This gate shall be shut; it shall not be opened, and no one shall enter by it, for the LORD God of Israel has entered by it; therefore it shall be shut. 3 As for the prince, he shall sit in it as prince to eat bread before the LORD; he shall enter by way of the porch of the gate and shall go out by the same way."

4 Then He brought me by way of the north gate to the front of the house; and I looked, and behold, the glory of the LORD filled the house of the LORD, and I fell on my face. 5 And the LORD said to me, "Son of man, pay attention, see with your eyes and hear with your ears everything that I say to you concerning all the statutes of the house of the LORD and all its laws; and pay attention to the entrance of the house, with all the exits of the sanctuary. 6 You shall say to the rebellious ones, to the house of Israel, 'This is what the Lord GOD says: "Enough of all your abominations, house of Israel, 7 when you brought in foreigners, uncircumcised in heart and uncircumcised in flesh, to be in My sanctuary to profane it, My house, when you offered My food, the fat, and the blood and they broke My covenant—*this* in addition to all your abominations. 8 And you have not taken responsibility for My holy things yourselves, but you have appointed *foreigners* to take responsibility for My sanctuary."

9 'This is what the Lord GOD says: "No foreigner uncircumcised in heart and uncircumcised in flesh, of all the foreigners who are among the sons of Israel, shall enter My sanctuary. 10 But the Levites who went far from Me when Israel went astray, who went astray from Me following their idols, shall suffer the punishment for their wrongdoing. 11 Yet they shall be ministers in My sanctuary, having oversight at the gates of the house and ministering *in* the house; they shall slaughter the burnt offering and the sacrifice for the

---

43:13 1 A cubit and hand width equals about 21 in. or 53 cm

people, and they shall stand before them to minister to them. [12] Since they ministered to them before their idols and became a stumbling block of wrongdoing to the house of Israel, for that reason I have sworn against them," declares the Lord GOD, "that they shall suffer the punishment for their wrongdoing. [13] And they shall not approach Me to serve as priests for Me, nor approach any of My holy things, to the things that are most holy; but they will bear their shame and their abominations which they have committed. [14] Nevertheless I will appoint them to take responsibility for the house, of all its service and of everything that shall be done in it.

Ordinances for the Levites

[15] "But the Levitical priests, the sons of Zadok, who took responsibility for My sanctuary when the sons of Israel went astray from Me, shall come near to Me to serve Me; and they shall stand before Me to offer Me the fat and the blood," declares the Lord GOD. [16] "They shall enter My sanctuary; they shall come near to My table to serve Me and assume the responsibility I give them. [17] And it shall be that when they enter at the gates of the inner courtyard, they shall be clothed with linen garments; and wool shall not be worn by them while they are ministering in the gates of the inner courtyard or in the house. [18] Linen turbans shall be on their heads and linen undergarments shall be around their waists; they shall not put on *anything that makes them* sweat. [19] And when they go out into the outer courtyard, into the outer courtyard to the people, they shall take off their garments in which they have been ministering and lay them in the holy chambers; then they shall put on other garments, so that they will not transfer holiness to the people with their garments. [20] Also they shall not shave their heads, yet they shall not let their locks grow long; they shall only trim *the hair of* their heads. [21] Nor shall any of the priests drink wine when they enter the inner courtyard. [22] And they shall not marry a widow or a divorced woman, but shall take virgins from the descendants of the house of Israel, or a widow who is the widow of a priest. [23] Moreover, they shall teach My people *the difference* between the holy and the common, and teach them to distinguish between the unclean and the clean. [24] In a dispute they shall take their stand to judge; they shall judge it according to My ordinances. They shall also keep My laws and My statutes in all My appointed feasts, and sanctify My Sabbaths. [25] They shall not go to a dead person to defile *themselves;* however, for father, for mother, for son, for daughter, for brother, or for a sister who has not had a husband, they may defile themselves. [26] And after he is cleansed, seven days [1]shall elapse for him. [27] On the day that he goes into the sanctuary, to the inner courtyard to minister in the sanctuary, he shall offer his sin offering," declares the Lord GOD.

[28] "And it shall be regarding an inheritance for them, *that* I am their inheritance; and you shall give them no property in Israel—I am their property. [29] They shall eat the grain offering, the sin offering, and the guilt offering; and everything banned from secular use in Israel shall be theirs. [30] And the first of all the first fruits of every kind and every contribution of every kind, from all your contributions, shall be for the priests; you shall also give to the priest the first of your dough, to make a blessing rest on your house. [31] The priests shall not eat any bird or animal that has died a natural death or has been torn to pieces by animals.

The LORD's Portion of the Land

45 "Now when you divide the land by lot for inheritance, you shall offer an allotment to the LORD, a holy portion of the land; the length shall be a length of twenty-five thousand [1]*cubits,* and the width shall be twenty thousand. It shall be holy within its entire surrounding boundary. [2] Out of this there shall be for the sanctuary a square encompassing five hundred by five hundred *cubits,* and fifty cubits for its open space round about. [3] From this area you shall measure a length of twenty-five thousand *cubits* and a width of ten thousand *cubits;* and in it shall be the sanctuary, the Most Holy Place. [4] It shall be the holy portion of the land; it shall be for the priests, the ministers of the sanctuary, who come near to serve the LORD, and it shall be a place for their houses and a holy place for the sanctuary. [5] *An area* twenty-five thousand *cubits* in length and ten thousand in width shall be for the Levites, the ministers of the house, *and* for their possession cities in which to live.

[6] "And you shall give the city possession of *an area* five thousand *cubits* wide and twenty-five thousand *cubits* long, alongside the allotment of the holy portion; it shall be for the entire house of Israel.

Portion for the Prince

[7] "And the prince shall have *land* on either side of the holy allotment and the property of the city, adjacent to the holy allotment and the property of the city, on the west side toward the west and on the east side toward the east, and in length comparable to one of the portions, from the west border to the east border. [8] *This* shall be his land as a possession in Israel; so My princes shall no longer oppress My people, but they shall give *the rest of* the land to the house of Israel according to their tribes."

[9] 'This is what the Lord GOD says: "Enough, you princes of Israel; get rid of violence and destruction, and practice justice and righteousness. Revoke your evictions of My people," declares the Lord GOD.

[10] "You shall have accurate balances, an accurate [1]ephah, and an accurate [2]bath. [11] The ephah and the bath shall be the same quantity, so that the bath will contain a tenth of a homer, and the ephah a tenth of a [1]homer; their standard shall be according to the homer.

44:26[1] Lit *they shall count*   **45:1**[1] Each of these cubits equals about 21 in. or 53 cm   **45:10**[1] I.e., a dry measure, about 1 cubic foot or 0.03 cubic meters   [2] I.e., a liquid measure, about 6 gallons or 23 liters   **45:11**[1] About 7.7 cubic feet or 0.22 cubic meters

12 And the shekel shall be twenty gerahs; twenty shekels, twenty-five shekels, *and* fifteen shekels shall be your mina.

13 "This is the offering that you shall offer: a sixth of an ephah from *each* homer of wheat; a sixth of an ephah from *each* homer of barley; 14 and the prescribed portion of oil (*namely,* the bath of oil), a tenth of a bath from *each* kor (*which is* ten baths *or* a homer, for ten baths are a homer); 15 and one sheep from *each* flock of two hundred from the watering places of Israel—for a grain offering, for a burnt offering, and for peace offerings, to make atonement for them," declares the Lord GOD. 16 "All the people of the land shall give to this offering for the prince in Israel. 17 And it shall be the prince's part *to provide* the burnt offerings, the grain offerings, and the drink offerings, at the feasts, on the new moons, and on the Sabbaths, at all the appointed feasts of the house of Israel; he shall provide the sin offering, the grain offering, the burnt offering, and the peace offerings, to make atonement for the house of Israel."

18 'This is what the Lord GOD says: "In the first *month,* on the first of the month, you shall take a bull without blemish and cleanse the sanctuary from sin. 19 And the priest shall take some of the blood from the sin offering and put *it* on the door posts of the house, on the four corners of the ledge of the altar, and on the posts of the gate of the inner courtyard. 20 And you shall do this on the seventh *day* of the month for everyone who does wrong inadvertently or is naive; so you shall make atonement for the house.

21 "In the first *month,* on the fourteenth day of the month, you shall have the Passover, a feast of seven days; unleavened bread shall be eaten. 22 On that day the prince shall provide for himself and all the people of the land a bull as a sin offering. 23 And *during* the seven days of the feast he shall provide as a burnt offering to the LORD seven bulls and seven rams without blemish on every day of the seven days, and a male goat daily as a sin offering. 24 And he shall provide as a grain offering an ¹ephah with a bull, an ephah with a ram, and a ²hin of oil with an ephah. 25 In the seventh *month,* on the fifteenth day of the month, at the feast, he shall provide like these, seven days for the sin offering, the burnt offering, the grain offering, and the oil."

The Prince's Offerings

46 'This is what the Lord GOD says: "The gate of the inner courtyard facing east shall be shut for the six working days; but it shall be opened on the Sabbath day and opened on the day of the new moon. 2 The prince shall enter by way of the porch of the gate from outside and stand by the post of the gate. Then the priests shall provide his burnt offering and his peace offerings, and he shall worship at the threshold of the gate and *then* go out; but the gate shall not be shut until the evening. 3 The people of the land shall also worship at the doorway of that gate before the LORD on the Sabbaths and on the new moons. 4 The burnt offering which the prince shall offer to the LORD on the Sabbath day shall be six lambs without blemish and a ram without blemish; 5 and the grain offering shall be an ¹ephah with the ram, and the grain offering with the lambs as much as he is able to give, and a ²hin of oil with an ephah. 6 On the day of the new moon *he shall offer* a bull without blemish, and six lambs and a ram, *which* shall be without blemish. 7 And he shall provide a grain offering, an ephah with the bull and an ephah with the ram, and with the lambs as much as he is able, and a hin of oil with an ephah. 8 When the prince enters, he shall go in by way of the porch of the gate, and go out by the same way. 9 But when the people of the land come before the LORD at the appointed feasts, one who enters by way of the north gate to worship shall go out by way of the south gate. And one who enters by way of the south gate shall go out by way of the north gate. No one shall return by way of the gate by which he entered, but shall go straight out. 10 And when they go in, the prince shall go in among them; and when they go out, he shall go out.

11 "At the festivals and the appointed feasts, the grain offering shall be an ephah with a bull and an ephah with a ram, and with the lambs as much as one is able to give, and a hin of oil with an ephah. 12 And when the prince provides a voluntary offering, a burnt offering, or peace offerings *as* a voluntary offering to the LORD, the gate facing east shall be opened for him. And he shall provide his burnt offering and his peace offerings as he does on the Sabbath day. Then he shall go out, and the gate shall be shut after he goes out.

13 "And you shall provide a lamb a year old without blemish as a burnt offering to the LORD daily; morning by morning you shall provide it. 14 You shall also provide a grain offering with it morning by morning, a sixth of an ephah and a third of a hin of oil to moisten the fine flour, a grain offering to the LORD continually by a permanent ordinance. 15 So they shall provide the lamb, the grain offering, and the oil, morning by morning, as a continual burnt offering."

16 'This is what the Lord GOD says: "If the prince gives a gift *from* his inheritance to any of his sons, it shall belong to his sons; it is their possession by inheritance. 17 But if he gives a gift from his inheritance to one of his servants, it shall be his until the year of release; then it shall return to the prince. His inheritance *shall be* only his sons'; it shall belong to them. 18 And the prince shall not take from the people's inheritance, depriving them of their property; he shall give his sons inheritance from his own property, so that My people will not be scattered, anyone from his property." ' "

The Boiling Places

19 Then he brought me through the entrance, which *was* at the side of the gate, into the holy chambers for the priests, which faced north; and behold, a place was there at the extreme rear toward the west. 20 And he

said to me, "This is the place where the priests shall boil the guilt offering and the sin offering, *and* where they shall bake the grain offering, so that they do not bring *them* out into the outer courtyard and transfer holiness to the people."

21 Then he brought me out into the outer courtyard and led me across to the four corners of the courtyard; and behold, in every corner of the courtyard *there was* a *small* courtyard. 22 In the four corners of the courtyard *there were* enclosed courtyards, forty ¹*cubits* long and thirty wide; these four in the corners *were* the same size. 23 And *there was* a row *of masonry* all around in them, around the four of them, and cooking hearths were made under the rows all around. 24 Then he said to me, "These are the cooking places where the ministers of the house shall cook the sacrifices of the people."

Water from the Temple

47 Then he brought me back to the door of the house; and behold, water was flowing from under the threshold of the house toward the east, for the house faced east. And the water was flowing down from under, from the right side of the house, from south of the altar. 2 And he brought me out by way of the north gate and led me around on the outside to the outer gate, by the way facing east. And behold, water was spurting out from the south side.

3 When the man went out toward the east with a line in his hand, he measured a thousand ¹cubits, and he led me through the water, water *reaching* the ankles. 4 Again he measured a thousand and led me through the water, water *reaching* the knees. Again he measured a thousand and led me through *the water,* water *reaching* the hips. 5 Again he measured a thousand; *and it was* a river that I could not wade across, because the water had risen, *enough* water to swim in, a river that could not be crossed *by wading.* 6 And he said to me, "Son of man, have you seen *this?*" Then he brought me back to the bank of the river. 7 Now when I had returned, behold, on the bank of the river *there were* very many trees on the one side and on the other. 8 Then he said to me, "These waters go out toward the eastern region and go down into the Arabah; then they go toward the sea, being made to flow into the sea, and the waters *of the sea* become fresh. 9 And it will come about that every living creature which swarms in every place where the river goes, will live. And there will be very many fish, for these waters go there and *the others* become fresh; so everything will live where the river goes. 10 And it will come about that fishermen will stand beside it; from Engedi to Eneglaim there will be a place for the spreading of nets. Their fish will be according to their kinds, like the fish of the Great Sea, very many. 11 But its swamps and marshes will not become fresh; they will be left for salt. 12 And by the river on its bank, on one side and on the other, will grow all *kinds of* trees for food. Their leaves will not wither and their fruit will not fail. They will bear fruit every month because their water flows from the sanctuary, and their fruit will be for food and their leaves for healing."

Boundaries and Division of the Land

13 This is what the Lord God says: "This *shall be* the boundary by which you shall divide the land for an inheritance among the twelve tribes of Israel; Joseph *shall have* two portions. 14 And you shall divide it for an inheritance, each one equally with the other; for I swore to give it to your forefathers, and this land shall fall to you as an inheritance.

15 "And this *shall be* the boundary of the land: on the north side, from the Great Sea *by* the way of Hethlon, to the entrance of Zedad; 16 Hamath, Berothah, Sibraim, which is between the border of Damascus and the border of Hamath; Hazer-hatticon, which is by the border of Hauran. 17 The boundary shall extend from the sea *to* Hazar-enan *at* the border of Damascus, and on the north toward the north is the border of Hamath. This is the north side.

18 "The east side, from between Hauran, Damascus, Gilead, and the land of Israel, *shall be* the Jordan; from the *north* border to the eastern sea you shall measure. This is the east side.

19 "The south side toward the south *shall extend* from Tamar as far as the waters of Meribath-kadesh, to the brook *of Egypt and* to the Great Sea. This is the south side toward the south.

20 "And the west side *shall be* the Great Sea, from the *south* border to a point opposite Lebo-hamath. This is the west side.

21 "So you shall divide this land among yourselves according to the tribes of Israel. 22 You shall divide it by lot for an inheritance among yourselves and among the strangers who stay in your midst, who bring forth sons in your midst. And they shall be to you as the native-born among the sons of Israel; they shall be allotted an inheritance with you among the tribes of Israel. 23 And in the tribe with which the stranger resides, there you shall give *him* his inheritance," declares the Lord God.

Division of the Land

48 "Now these are the names of the tribes: from the northern extremity, beside the way of Hethlon to Lebo-hamath, *as far as* Hazar-enan *at* the border of Damascus, toward the north beside Hamath, running from east to west, Dan, one *portion.* 2 Beside the border of Dan, from the east side to the west side, Asher, one *portion.* 3 Beside the border of Asher, from the east side to the west side, Naphtali, one *portion.* 4 Beside the border of Naphtali, from the east side to the west side, Manasseh, one *portion.* 5 Beside the border of Manasseh, from the east side to the west side, Ephraim, one *portion.* 6 Beside the border

---

46:22 ¹ Each of these cubits equals about 21 in. or 53 cm   47:3 ¹ Each of these cubits equals about 21 in. or 53 cm

of Ephraim, from the east side to the west side, Reuben, one *portion.* [7] Beside the border of Reuben, from the east side to the west side, Judah, one *portion.*

[8] "And beside the border of Judah, from the east side to the west side, shall be the allotment which you shall set apart, twenty-five thousand [1]*cubits* in width, and in length like one of the portions, from the east side to the west side; and the sanctuary shall be in the middle of it. [9] The allotment that you shall set apart to the LORD *shall be* twenty-five thousand *cubits* in length and ten thousand in width.

Portion for the Priests
[10] The holy allotment shall be for these, *namely* for the priests, toward the north twenty-five thousand *cubits in length,* toward the west ten thousand in width, toward the east ten thousand in width, and toward the south twenty-five thousand in length; and the sanctuary of the LORD shall be in its midst. [11] *It shall be* for the priests who are sanctified of the sons of Zadok, who have taken the responsibility I gave them, who did not go astray when the sons of Israel went astray as the Levites went astray. [12] It shall be an allotment to them from the allotment of the land, a most holy reserve, by the border of the Levites. [13] And alongside the border of the priests, the Levites *shall have* twenty-five thousand *cubits* in length and ten thousand in width. The entire length *shall be* twenty-five thousand *cubits* and the width ten thousand. [14] Moreover, they shall not sell or exchange any of it, or allow this choice *portion* of land to pass *to others;* for it is holy to the LORD.

[15] "The remainder, five thousand *cubits* in width *and* twenty-five thousand in length, shall be for common use for the city, for homes and for open spaces; and the city shall be in its midst. [16] And these *shall be* its measurements: the north side, 4,500 *cubits,* the south side 4,500 *cubits,* the east side 4,500 *cubits,* and the west side, 4,500 *cubits.* [17] The city shall have open spaces: on the north 250 *cubits,* on the south 250 *cubits,* on the east 250 *cubits,* and on the west 250 *cubits.* [18] The remainder of the length alongside the holy allotment shall be ten thousand *cubits* toward the east and ten thousand toward the west; and it shall be alongside the holy allotment. And its produce shall be food for the workers of the city. [19] And the workers of the city, out of all the tribes of Israel, shall cultivate it. [20] The whole allotment *shall be* twenty-five thousand by twenty-five thousand *cubits;* you shall set apart the holy

allotment, a square, with the property of the city.

Portion for the Prince
[21] "The remainder *shall be* for the prince, on the one side and on the other of the holy allotment and of the property of the city; in front of the twenty-five thousand *cubits* of the allotment toward the east border and westward in front of the twenty-five thousand toward the west border, alongside the portions, *it shall be* for the prince. And the holy allotment and the sanctuary of the house shall be in the middle of it. [22] And exclusive of the property of the Levites and the property of the city, *which are* in the middle of that which belongs to the prince, *everything* between the border of Judah and the border of Benjamin shall belong to the prince.

Portion for Other Tribes
[23] "As for the rest of the tribes: from the east side to the west side, Benjamin, one *portion.* [24] Beside the border of Benjamin, from the east side to the west side, Simeon, one *portion.* [25] Beside the border of Simeon, from the east side to the west side, Issachar, one *portion.* [26] Beside the border of Issachar, from the east side to the west side, Zebulun, one *portion.* [27] Beside the border of Zebulun, from the east side to the west side, Gad, one *portion.* [28] And beside the border of Gad, at the south side toward the south, the border shall be from Tamar to the waters of Meribath-kadesh, to the brook *of Egypt,* to the Great Sea. [29] This is the land which you shall divide by lot to the tribes of Israel for an inheritance, and these are their *several* portions," declares the Lord GOD.

The City Gates
[30] "Now these are the exits of the city: on the north side, 4,500 *cubits* by measurement, [31] shall be the gates of the city, named for the tribes of Israel, three gates toward the north: the gate of Reuben, one; the gate of Judah, one; *and* the gate of Levi, one. [32] On the east side, 4,500 *cubits,* shall be three gates: the gate of Joseph, one; the gate of Benjamin, one; *and* the gate of Dan, one. [33] On the south side, 4,500 *cubits* by measurement, shall be three gates: the gate of Simeon, one; the gate of Issachar, one; *and* the gate of Zebulun, one. [34] On the west side, 4,500 *cubits, shall be* three gates: the gate of Gad, one; the gate of Asher, one; *and* the gate of Naphtali, one. [35] *The city shall be* eighteen thousand *cubits* all around; and the name of the city from *that* day *shall be,* 'The LORD is there.' "

48:8 [1] Each of these cubits equals about 21 in. or 53 cm

The Book of
DANIEL

The Choice Young Men

1 In the third year of the reign of Jehoiakim king of Judah, Nebuchadnezzar king of Babylon came to Jerusalem and besieged it. 2 And the Lord handed Jehoiakim king of Judah over to him, along with some of the vessels of the house of God; and he brought them to the land of Shinar, to the house of his god, and he brought the vessels into the treasury of his god.

3 Then the king told Ashpenaz, the chief of his officials, to bring in some of the sons of Israel, including some of the royal family and of the nobles, 4 youths in whom there was no impairment, who were good-looking, suitable for instruction in every *kind of* expertise, endowed with understanding and discerning knowledge, and who had ability to serve in the king's court; and *he ordered Ashpenaz* to teach them the literature and language of the Chaldeans. 5 The king also allotted for them a daily ration from the king's choice food and from the wine which he drank, and *ordered* that they be educated for three years, at the end of which they were to enter the king's personal service. 6 Now among them from the sons of Judah were Daniel, Hananiah, Mishael, and Azariah. 7 Then the commander of the officials assigned *new* names to them; and to Daniel he assigned *the name* Belteshazzar, to Hananiah Shadrach, to Mishael Meshach, and to Azariah Abed-nego.

Daniel's Resolve

8 But Daniel made up his mind that he would not defile himself with the king's choice food or with the wine which he drank; so he sought *permission* from the commander of the officials that he might not defile himself. 9 Now God granted Daniel favor and compassion in the sight of the commander of the officials. 10 The commander of the officials said to Daniel, "I am afraid of my lord the king, who has allotted your food and your drink; for why should he see your faces looking gaunt in comparison to the youths who are your own age? Then you would make me forfeit my head to the king." 11 But Daniel said to the overseer whom the commander of the officials had appointed over Daniel, Hananiah, Mishael, and Azariah, 12 "Please put your servants to the test for ten days, and let us be given some vegetables to eat and water to drink. 13 Then let our appearance be examined in your presence and the appearance of the youths who are eating the king's choice food; and deal with your servants according to what you see." 14 So he listened to them in this matter, and put them to the test for ten days. 15 And at the end of ten days their appearance seemed better, and they were fatter than all the youths who had been eating the king's choice food. 16 So the overseer continued to withhold their choice food and the wine they were to drink, and kept giving them vegetables.

17 And as for these four youths, God gave them knowledge and intelligence in every *kind of* literature and expertise; Daniel even understood all *kinds of* visions and dreams. 18 Then at the end of the days which the king had specified for presenting them, the commander of the officials presented them before Nebuchadnezzar. 19 And the king talked with them, and out of them all not one was found like Daniel, Hananiah, Mishael, and Azariah; so they entered the king's personal service. 20 As for every matter of expertise and understanding about which the king consulted them, he found them ten times better than all the soothsayer priests *and* conjurers who *were* in all his realm. 21 And Daniel continued until the first year of Cyrus the king.

The King's Dream

2 Now in the second year of the reign of Nebuchadnezzar, Nebuchadnezzar had dreams; and his spirit was troubled and his sleep left him. 2 Then the king gave orders to call in the soothsayer priests, the conjurers, the sorcerers, and the *[1]*Chaldeans, to tell the king his dreams. So they came in and stood before the king. 3 The king said to them, "I had a dream, and my spirit is anxious to understand the dream."

4 Then the Chaldeans spoke to the king in Aramaic: "O king, live forever! Tell the dream to your servants, and we will declare the interpretation." 5 The king replied to the Chaldeans, "The command from me is firm: if you do not make known to me the dream and its interpretation, you will be torn limb from limb and your houses will be turned into a rubbish heap. 6 But if you declare the dream and its interpretation, you will receive from me gifts and a reward and great honor; therefore declare to me the dream and its interpretation." 7 They answered a second time and said, "Let the king tell the dream to his servants, and we will declare the interpretation." 8 The king replied, "I know for certain that you are trying to buy time, because you have perceived that the command from me is firm, 9 that if you do not make the dream known to me, there is only one decree for you. For you have agreed together to speak lying and corrupt words before me until the situation is changed; therefore tell me the dream, so that I may know that you can declare to me its interpretation." 10 The Chaldeans answered the king and said, "There is no person on earth who could declare the matter to the king, because no great king or ruler has *ever* asked anything like this of any soothsayer priest, sorcerer, or Chaldean. 11 Moreover, the thing which the king demands is difficult, and there is no one

2:2 1 Probably master astrologers, diviners, etc., and so throughout the ch

else who could declare it to the king except gods, whose dwelling place is not with *mortal flesh.*"

12 Because of this, the king became angry and extremely furious, and he gave orders to kill all the wise men of Babylon. **13** So the decree was issued that the wise men be killed; and they looked for Daniel and his friends, to kill *them.*

14 Then Daniel replied with discretion and discernment to Arioch, the captain of the king's bodyguard, who had gone out to kill the wise men of Babylon; **15** he said to Arioch, the king's officer, "For what reason is the decree from the king *so* harsh?" Then Arioch informed Daniel of the matter. **16** So Daniel went in and requested of the king that he would give him a grace period, so that he might declare the interpretation to the king.

17 Then Daniel went to his house and informed his friends, Hananiah, Mishael and Azariah, about the matter, **18** so that they might request compassion from the God of heaven concerning this secret, so that Daniel and his friends would not be killed with the rest of the wise men of Babylon.

The Secret Is Revealed to Daniel

19 Then the secret was revealed to Daniel in a night vision. Then Daniel blessed the God of heaven; **20** Daniel said,

"May the name of God be blessed forever and ever,
For wisdom and power belong to Him.
21 "It is He who changes the times and the periods;
He removes kings and appoints kings;
He gives wisdom to wise men,
And knowledge to people of understanding.
22 "It is He who reveals the profound and hidden things;
He knows what is in the darkness,
And the light dwells with Him.
23 "To You, God of my fathers, I give thanks and praise,
For You have given me wisdom and power;
Even now You have made known to me what we requested of You,
For You have made known to us the king's matter."

24 Thereupon, Daniel went to Arioch, whom the king had appointed to kill the wise men of Babylon; he went and said this to him: "Do not kill the wise men of Babylon! Take me into the king's presence, and I will declare the interpretation to the king."

25 Then Arioch hurriedly brought Daniel into the king's presence and spoke to him as follows: "I have found a man among the exiles from Judah who can make the interpretation known to the king!" **26** The king said to Daniel, whose name was Belteshazzar, "Are you able to make known to me the dream which I have seen and its interpretation?" **27** Daniel answered before the king and said, "As for the secret about which the king has inquired, neither wise men, sorcerers, soothsayer priests, *nor* diviners are able to declare *it* to the

king. **28** However, there is a God in heaven who reveals secrets, and He has made known to King Nebuchadnezzar what will take place in the latter days. This was your dream and the visions in your mind *while* on your bed. **29** As for you, O king, *while* on your bed your thoughts turned to what would take place in the future; and He who reveals secrets has made known to you what will take place. **30** But as for me, this secret has not been revealed to me for any wisdom residing in me more than *in* any *other* living person, but for the purpose of making the interpretation known to the king, and that you may understand the thoughts of your mind.

The King's Dream

31 "You, O king, were watching and behold, there was a single great statue; that statue, which was large and of extraordinary radiance, was standing in front of you, and its appearance was awesome. **32** The head of that statue *was made* of fine gold, its chest and its arms of silver, its belly and its thighs of bronze, **33** its legs of iron, *and* its feet partly of iron and partly of clay. **34** You continued watching until a stone was broken off without hands, and it struck the statue on its feet of iron and clay, and crushed them. **35** Then the iron, the clay, the bronze, the silver, and the gold were crushed to pieces all at the same time, and they were like chaff from the summer threshing floors; and the wind carried them away so that not a trace of them was found. But the stone that struck the statue became a great mountain and filled the entire earth.

The Interpretation—Babylon the First Kingdom

36 "This *was* the dream; and *now* we will tell its interpretation before the king. **37** You, O king, are the king of kings, to whom the God of heaven has given the kingdom, the power, the strength, and the honor; **38** and wherever the sons of mankind live, *or* the animals of the field, or the birds of the sky, He has handed *them* over to you and has made you ruler over them all. You are the head of gold.

Medo-Persia and Greece

39 And after you another kingdom will arise inferior to you, then another third kingdom of bronze, which will rule over all the earth.

Rome

40 Then there will be a fourth kingdom as strong as iron; just as iron smashes and crushes everything, so, like iron that crushes, it will smash and crush all these things. **41** And in that you saw the feet and toes, partly of potter's clay and partly of iron, it will be a divided kingdom; but it will have within it some of the toughness of iron, since you saw the iron mixed with common clay. **42** And *just as* the toes of the feet *were* partly of iron and partly of pottery, *so* some of the kingdom will be strong, and part of it will be fragile. **43** In that you saw the iron mixed with common clay, they will combine with one another in their descendants; but they will not adhere to one another, just as iron does not combine with pottery.

The Divine Kingdom

44 And in the days of those kings the God of heaven will set up a kingdom which will never be destroyed, and *that* kingdom will not be left for another people; it will crush and put an end to all these kingdoms, but it will itself endure forever. **45** Just as you saw that a stone was broken off from the mountain without hands, and that it crushed the iron, the bronze, the clay, the silver, and the gold, the great God has made known to the king what will take place in the future; so the dream is certain and its interpretation is trustworthy."

Daniel Promoted

46 Then King Nebuchadnezzar fell on his face and paid humble respect to Daniel, and gave orders to present to him an offering and incense. **47** The king responded to Daniel and said, "Your God truly is a God of gods and a Lord of kings and a revealer of secrets, since you have been able to reveal this secret." **48** Then the king promoted Daniel and gave him many great gifts, and he made him ruler over the entire province of Babylon, and chief prefect over all the wise men of Babylon. **49** And Daniel made a request of the king, and he appointed Shadrach, Meshach, and Abed-nego over the administration of the province of Babylon, while Daniel *was* at the king's court.

The King's Golden Image

3 Nebuchadnezzar the king made a statue of gold, the height of which *was* [1]sixty cubits, *and* its width six cubits; he set it up on the plain of Dura in the province of Babylon. **2** Nebuchadnezzar the king also sent *word* to assemble the satraps, the prefects and the governors, the counselors, the chief treasurers, the judges, the magistrates, and all the administrators of the provinces to come to the dedication of the statue that Nebuchadnezzar the king had set up. **3** Then the satraps, the prefects and the governors, the counselors, the chief treasurers, the judges, the magistrates, and all the administrators of the provinces were assembled for the dedication of the statue that Nebuchadnezzar the king had set up; and they stood before the statue that Nebuchadnezzar had set up. **4** Then the herald loudly proclaimed: "To you the command is given, you peoples, nations, and *populations of all* languages, **5** that at the moment you hear the sound of the horn, flute, lyre, trigon, psaltery, bagpipe, and all kinds of musical instruments, you are to fall down and worship the golden statue that Nebuchadnezzar the king has set up. **6** But whoever does not fall down and worship shall immediately be thrown into the middle of a furnace of blazing fire." **7** Therefore as soon as all the peoples heard the sound of the horn, flute, lyre, trigon, psaltery, bagpipe, and all kinds of musical instruments, all the peoples, nations, and *populations of all* languages fell down *and* worshiped the golden statue that Nebuchadnezzar the king had set up.

Worship of the Image Refused

8 For this reason at that time certain Chaldeans came forward and brought charges against the Jews. **9** They began to speak and said to Nebuchadnezzar the king: "O king, live forever! **10** You, O king, have made a decree that every person who hears the sound of the horn, flute, lyre, trigon, psaltery, and bagpipe, and all kinds of musical instruments, is to fall down and worship the golden statue. **11** But whoever does not fall down and worship shall be thrown into the middle of a furnace of blazing fire. **12** There are certain Jews whom you have appointed over the administration of the province of Babylon, *namely* Shadrach, Meshach, and Abed-nego. These men, O king, have disregarded you; they do not serve your gods, nor do they worship the golden statue which you have set up."

13 Then Nebuchadnezzar in rage and anger gave orders to bring Shadrach, Meshach, and Abed-nego; then these men were brought before the king. **14** Nebuchadnezzar began speaking and said to them, "Is it true, Shadrach, Meshach, and Abed-nego, that you do not serve my gods, nor worship the golden statue that I have set up? **15** Now if you are ready, at the moment you hear the sound of the horn, flute, lyre, trigon, psaltery and bagpipe, and all kinds of musical instruments, to fall down and worship the statue that I have made, *very well.* But if you do not worship, you will immediately be thrown into the midst of a furnace of blazing fire; and what god is there who can rescue you from my hands?"

16 Shadrach, Meshach, and Abed-nego replied to the king, "Nebuchadnezzar, we are not in need of an answer to give you concerning this matter. **17** If it be *so,* our God whom we serve is able to rescue us from the furnace of blazing fire; and He will rescue us from your hand, O king. **18** But *even* if He *does* not, let it be known to you, O king, that we are not going to serve your gods nor worship the golden statue that you have set up."

Daniel's Friends Protected

19 Then Nebuchadnezzar was filled with wrath, and his facial expression was changed toward Shadrach, Meshach, and Abed-nego. He answered by giving orders to heat the furnace seven times more than it was usually heated. **20** And he ordered certain valiant warriors who *were* in his army to tie up Shadrach, Meshach, and Abed-nego in order to throw *them* into the furnace of blazing fire. **21** Then these men were tied up in their trousers, their coats, their caps, and their *other* clothes, and were thrown into the middle of the furnace of blazing fire. **22** For this reason, because the king's command *was* harsh and the furnace had been made extremely hot, the flame of the fire killed those men who took up Shadrach, Meshach, and Abed-nego. **23** But these three men, Shadrach, Meshach, and Abed-nego, fell into the middle of the furnace of blazing fire *still* tied up.

24 Then Nebuchadnezzar the king was astounded and stood up quickly; he said to his counselors, "Was it not three men *that* we threw bound into the middle of the fire?" They replied to the king, "Absolutely, O king." **25** He

---

3:1 [1]About 90 ft. high and 9 ft. wide or 27 m and 2.7 m

responded, "Look! I see four men untied *and* walking about in the middle of the fire unharmed, and the appearance of the fourth is like a son of *the* gods!" 26 Then Nebuchadnezzar came near to the door of the furnace of blazing fire; he said, "Shadrach, Meshach, and Abed-nego, come out, you servants of the Most High God, and come here!" Then Shadrach, Meshach, and Abed-nego came out of the middle of the fire. 27 The satraps, the prefects, the governors, and the king's counselors gathered together *and* saw that the fire had no effect on the bodies of these men, nor was the hair of their heads singed, nor were their trousers damaged, nor had *even* the smell of fire touched them.

28 Nebuchadnezzar responded and said, "Blessed be the God of Shadrach, Meshach, and Abed-nego, who has sent His angel and rescued His servants who put their trust in Him, violating the king's command, and surrendered their bodies rather than serve or worship any god except their own God. 29 Therefore I make a decree that any people, nation, or *population of any* language that speaks anything offensive against the God of Shadrach, Meshach, and Abed-nego shall be torn limb from limb and their houses made a rubbish heap, because there is no other god who is able to save in this way." 30 Then the king made Shadrach, Meshach, and Abed-nego prosperous in the province of Babylon.

The King Acknowledges God

4 Nebuchadnezzar the king to all the peoples, nations, and *populations of all* languages who live in all the earth: "May your peace be great! 2 I am pleased to declare the signs and miracles that the Most High God has done for me.
3 "How great are His signs
And how mighty are His miracles!
His kingdom is an everlasting kingdom,
And His dominion is from generation to generation.

The Vision of a Great Tree

4 "I, Nebuchadnezzar, was at ease in my house and happy in my palace. 5 I saw a dream and it startled me; and *these* appearances *as I lay* on my bed and the visions in my mind kept alarming me. 6 So I gave orders to bring into my presence all the wise men of Babylon, so that they might make known to me the interpretation of the dream. 7 Then the soothsayer priests, the sorcerers, the 'Chaldeans, and the diviners came in and I related the dream to them, but they could not make its interpretation known to me. 8 But finally Daniel came in before me, whose name is Belteshazzar according to the name of my god, and in whom is 'a spirit of the holy gods; and I related the dream to him, *saying,* 9 'Belteshazzar, chief of the soothsayer priests, since I know that a spirit of the holy gods is in you and no secret baffles you, tell *me* the visions of my dream which I have seen, along with its interpretation.
10 'Now *these were* the visions in my mind

as I lay on my bed: I was looking, and behold, *there was* a tree in the middle of the earth and its height *was* great.
11 'The tree grew large and became strong,
And its height reached to the sky,
And it *was* visible to the end of the whole earth.
12 'Its foliage *was* beautiful and its fruit abundant,
And in it *was* food for all.
The animals of the field found shade under it,
And the birds of the sky lived in its branches,
And all living creatures fed from it.
13 'I was looking in the visions in my mind *as I lay* on my bed, and behold, an angelic watcher, a holy one, descended from heaven.
14 'He shouted out and spoke as follows:
"Chop down the tree and cut off its branches,
Shake off its foliage and scatter its fruit;
Let the animals flee from under it
And the birds from its branches.
15 "Yet leave the stump with its roots in the ground,
But with a band of iron and bronze *around it*
In the new grass of the field;
And let him be drenched with the dew of heaven,
And let him share with the animals in the grass of the earth.
16 "Let his mind change from *that of* a human
And let an animal's mind be given to him,
And let seven periods of time pass over him.
17 "This sentence is by the decree of the angelic watchers,
And the decision is a command of the holy ones,
In order that the living may know
That the Most High is ruler over the realm of mankind,
And He grants it to whomever He wishes
And sets over it the lowliest of people."
18 This is the dream *that* I, King Nebuchadnezzar, have seen. Now you, Belteshazzar, tell *me* its interpretation, since none of the wise men of my kingdom is able to make known to me the interpretation; but you are able, because a spirit of the holy gods is in you.'

Daniel Interprets the Vision

19 "Then Daniel, whose name is Belteshazzar, was appalled for a while as his thoughts alarmed him. The king responded and said, 'Belteshazzar, do not let the dream or its interpretation alarm you.' Belteshazzar replied, 'My lord, *if only* the dream *applied* to those who hate you, and its interpretation to your adversaries! 20 The tree that you saw, which became large and grew strong, whose height reached to the sky and was visible to all the earth, 21 and whose foliage *was* beautiful and its fruit abundant, and in which *was* food for all,

---

4:7 1 Probably master astrologers, diviners, etc.   4:8 1 Or possibly *the Spirit of the holy God,* and so throughout the ch

under which the animals of the field lived and in whose branches the birds of the sky settled—22 it is you, O king; for you have become great and grown strong, and your majesty has become great and reached to the sky, and your dominion to the end of the earth. 23 And in that the king saw an angelic watcher, a holy one, descending from heaven and saying, "Chop down the tree and destroy it; yet leave the stump with its roots in the ground, but with a band of iron and bronze *around it* in the new grass of the field, let him be drenched with the dew of heaven, and let him share with the animals of the field until seven periods of time pass over him," 24 this is the interpretation, O king, and this is the decree of the Most High, which has come upon my lord the king: 25 that you be driven away from mankind and your dwelling place be with the animals of the field, and you be given grass to eat like cattle and be drenched with the dew of heaven; and seven periods of time will pass over you, until you recognize that the Most High is ruler over the realm of mankind and bestows it on whomever He wishes. 26 And in that it was commanded to leave the stump with the roots of the tree, your kingdom will remain as yours after you recognize that *it is* Heaven *that* rules. 27 Therefore, O king, may my advice be pleasing to you: wipe away your sin by *doing* righteousness, and your wrongdoings by showing mercy to *the* poor, in case there may be a prolonging of your prosperity.'

The Vision Fulfilled

28 "All *of this* happened to Nebuchadnezzar the king. 29 Twelve months later he was walking on the *roof of* the royal palace of Babylon. 30 The king began speaking and was saying, 'Is this not Babylon the great, which I myself have built as a royal residence by the might of my power and for the honor of my majesty?' 31 *While* the word *was* still in the king's mouth, a voice came from heaven, *saying,* 'King Nebuchadnezzar, to you it is declared: sovereignty has been removed from you, 32 and you will be driven away from mankind, and your dwelling place *will be* with the animals of the field. You will be given grass to eat like cattle, and seven periods of time will pass over you until you recognize that the Most High is ruler over the realm of mankind and bestows it on whomever He wishes.' 33 Immediately the word concerning Nebuchadnezzar was fulfilled; and he was driven away from mankind and began eating grass like cattle, and his body was drenched with the dew of heaven until his hair had grown like eagles' *feathers* and his nails like birds' *claws.*

34 "But at the end of that period, I, Nebuchadnezzar, raised my eyes toward heaven and my reason returned to me, and I blessed the Most High and praised and honored Him who lives forever;

> For His dominion is an everlasting dominion,
> And His kingdom *endures* from generation to generation.

35 "All the inhabitants of the earth are of no account,
But He does according to His will among the army of heaven
And *among* the inhabitants of earth;
And no one can fend off His hand
Or say to Him, 'What have You done?'
36 At that time my reason returned to me. And my majesty and splendor were restored to me for the honor of my kingdom, and my state counselors and my nobles began seeking me out; so I was reestablished in my sovereignty, and surpassing greatness was added to me. 37 Now I, Nebuchadnezzar, praise, exalt, and honor the King of heaven, for all His works are true and His ways just; and He is able to humble those who walk in pride."

Belshazzar's Feast

5 Belshazzar the king held a great feast for a thousand of his nobles, and he was drinking wine in the presence of the thousand. 2 While he tasted the wine, Belshazzar gave orders to bring the gold and silver vessels which his father Nebuchadnezzar had taken out of the temple which *was* in Jerusalem, so that the king and his nobles, his wives, and his concubines could drink out of them. 3 Then they brought the gold vessels that had been taken out of the temple, the house of God which *was* in Jerusalem; and the king and his nobles, his wives, and his concubines drank out of them. 4 They drank the wine and praised the gods of gold and silver, of bronze, iron, wood, and stone.

5 Suddenly the fingers of a human hand emerged and began writing opposite the lampstand on the plaster of the wall of the king's palace, and the king saw the back of the hand that did the writing. 6 Then the king's face became pale and his thoughts alarmed him, and his hip joints loosened and his knees began knocking together. 7 The king called aloud to bring in the sorcerers, the ᶠChaldeans, and the diviners. The king began speaking and said to the wise men of Babylon, "Anyone who can read this inscription and explain its interpretation to me shall be clothed with purple and *have* a necklace of gold around his neck, and have authority as third *ruler* in the kingdom." 8 Then all the king's wise men came in, but they could not read the inscription or make known its interpretation to the king. 9 Then the King Belshazzar was greatly alarmed, his face grew *even more* pale, and his nobles were perplexed.

10 The queen entered the banquet hall because of the words of the king and his nobles; the queen began to speak and said, "O king, live forever! Do not let your thoughts alarm you or your face be pale. 11 There is a man in your kingdom in whom is a spirit of the holy gods; and in the days of your father, illumination, insight, and wisdom like the wisdom of the gods were found in him. And King Nebuchadnezzar, your father—your father the king—appointed him chief of the soothsayer priests, sorcerers, Chaldeans, *and* diviners. 12 *This was* because an extraordinary

---

5:7 ¹I.e., probably master astrologers, diviners, etc., and so throughout the ch.

spirit, knowledge and insight, interpretation of dreams, explanation of riddles, and solving of difficult problems were found in this Daniel, whom the king named Belteshazzar. Let Daniel now be summoned and he will declare the interpretation."

Daniel Interprets the Handwriting on the Wall

13 Then Daniel was brought in before the king. The king began speaking and said to Daniel, "Are you that Daniel who is one of the exiles from Judah, whom my father the king brought from Judah? 14 Now I have heard about you that a spirit of the gods is in you, and that illumination, insight, and extraordinary wisdom have been found in you. 15 Just now the wise men *and* the sorcerers were brought in before me to read this inscription and make its interpretation known to me, but they could not declare the interpretation of the message. 16 But I personally have heard about you, that you are able to give interpretations and solve difficult problems. Now if you are able to read the inscription and make its interpretation known to me, you will be clothed with purple and *wear* a necklace of gold around your neck, and you will have authority as the third *ruler* in the kingdom."

17 Then Daniel replied and said before the king, "Keep your gifts for yourself or give your rewards to someone else; however, I will read the inscription to the king and make the interpretation known to him. 18 O king, the Most High God granted sovereignty, greatness, honor, and majesty to Nebuchadnezzar your father. 19 Now because of the greatness which He granted him, all the peoples, nations, and *populations of all* languages trembled and feared in his presence; whomever he wished, he killed, and whomever he wished, he spared alive; and whomever he wished he elevated, and whomever he wished he humbled. 20 But when his heart was arrogant and his spirit became so overbearing that he behaved presumptuously, he was deposed from his royal throne, and *his* dignity was taken away from him. 21 He was also driven away from mankind, and his heart was made like *that of* animals, and his dwelling place *was* with the wild donkeys. He was given grass to eat like cattle, and his body was drenched with the dew of heaven, until he recognized that the Most High God is ruler over the realm of mankind, and *that* He sets over it whomever He wishes. 22 Yet you, his son, Belshazzar, have not humbled your heart, even though you knew all this, 23 but you have risen up against the Lord of heaven; and they have brought the vessels of His house before you, and you and your nobles, your wives, and your concubines have been drinking wine out of them; and you have praised the gods of silver and gold, of bronze, iron, wood, and stone, which do not see, nor hear, nor understand. But the God in whose hand are your life-breath and all your ways, you have not glorified. 24 Then the hand was sent from Him and this inscription was written out.

25 "Now this is the inscription that was written:

'1MENE, MENE, 2TEKEL, 3UPHARSIN.'

26 This is the interpretation of the message: 'MENE'—God has numbered your kingdom and put an end to it. 27 'TEKEL'—you have been weighed on the scales and found deficient. 28 '1PERĒS'—your kingdom has been divided and given to the Medes and Persians."

29 Then Belshazzar gave orders, and they clothed Daniel with purple and *put* a necklace of gold around his neck, and issued a proclamation concerning him that he *now* had authority as the third *ruler* in the kingdom.

30 That same night Belshazzar the Chaldean king was killed. 31 So Darius the Mede received the kingdom at about the age of sixty-two.

Daniel Serves Darius

6 It pleased Darius to appoint 120 satraps over the kingdom, to be in charge of the whole kingdom, 2 and over them, three commissioners (of whom Daniel was one), so that these satraps would be accountable to them, and that the king would not suffer loss. 3 Then this Daniel began distinguishing himself among the commissioners and satraps because he possessed an extraordinary spirit, and the king intended to appoint him over the entire kingdom. 4 Then the commissioners and satraps began trying to find a ground of accusation against Daniel regarding government affairs; but they could find no ground of accusation or *evidence of* corruption, because he was trustworthy, and no negligence or corruption was *to be* found in him. 5 Then these men said, "We will not find any ground of accusation against this Daniel unless we find *it* against him regarding the law of his God."

6 Then these commissioners and satraps came by agreement to the king and spoke to him as follows: "King Darius, live forever! 7 All the commissioners of the kingdom, the prefects and the satraps, the counselors and the governors, have consulted together that the king should establish a statute and enforce an injunction that anyone who offers a prayer to any god or person besides you, O king, for thirty days, shall be thrown into the lions' den. 8 Now, O king, establish the injunction and sign the document so that it will not be changed, according to the law of the Medes and Persians, which may not be revoked." 9 Thereupon, King Darius signed the document, that is, the injunction.

10 Now when Daniel learned that the document was signed, he entered his house (and in his roof chamber he had windows open toward Jerusalem); and he continued kneeling on his knees three times a day, praying and offering praise before his God, just as he had been doing previously. 11 Then these men came by agreement and found Daniel offering a prayer and imploring *favor* before his God. 12 Then they approached and spoke before the king about the king's injunction: "Did you not sign an injunction that any person who offers a prayer to any god or person besides

---

5:25 1 Or *a mina* (50 shekels) from verb "to count"   2 Or *a shekel* from verb "to weigh"   3 Or *and half-shekels* (singular: *peres*) from verb "to divide"   **5:28** 1 Or *half-shekel* from verb "to divide"

you, O king, for thirty days, is to be thrown into the lions' den?" The king replied, "The statement is true, according to the law of the Medes and Persians, which may not be revoked." 13 Then they responded and spoke before the king, "Daniel, who is one of the exiles from Judah, pays no attention to you, O king, or to the injunction which you signed, but keeps offering his prayer three times a day."

14 Then, as soon as the king heard this statement, he was deeply distressed, and set *his* mind on rescuing Daniel; and until sunset he kept exerting himself to save him. 15 Then these men came by agreement to the king and said to the king, "Recognize, O king, that it is a law of the Medes and Persians that no injunction or statute which the king establishes may be changed."

Daniel in the Lions' Den

16 Then the king gave orders, and Daniel was brought in and thrown into the lions' den. The king said to Daniel, "Your God whom you continually serve will Himself rescue you." 17 And a stone was brought and placed over the mouth of the den; and the king sealed it with his own signet ring and with the signet rings of his nobles, so that nothing would be changed regarding Daniel. 18 Then the king went to his palace and spent the night fasting, and no entertainment was brought before him; and his sleep fled from him.

19 Then the king got up at dawn, at the break of day, and went in a hurry to the lions' den. 20 And when he had come near the den to Daniel, he cried out with a troubled voice. The king began speaking and said to Daniel, "Daniel, servant of the living God, has your God, whom you continually serve, been able to rescue you from the lions?" 21 Then Daniel spoke to the king, "O king, live forever! 22 My God sent His angel and shut the lions' mouths, and they have not harmed me, since I was found innocent before Him; and also toward you, O king, I have committed no crime." 23 Then the king was very glad and gave orders for Daniel to be lifted up out of the den. So Daniel was lifted up out of the den, and no injury whatever was found on him, because he had trusted in his God. 24 The king then gave orders, and they brought those men who had maliciously accused Daniel, and they threw them, their children, and their wives into the lions' den; and they had not reached the bottom of the den before the lions overpowered them and crushed all their bones.

25 Then Darius the king wrote to all the peoples, nations, and *populations of all* languages who were living in all the land: "May your peace be great! 26 I issue a decree that in all the realm of my kingdom people are to tremble and fear before the God of Daniel;

For He is the living God and enduring forever,
And His kingdom is one which will not be destroyed,
And His dominion *will be* forever.
27 "He rescues, saves, and performs signs and miracles

In heaven and on earth,
He who has *also* rescued Daniel from the power of the lions."
28 So this Daniel enjoyed success in the reign of Darius, and in the reign of Cyrus the Persian.

Vision of the Four Beasts

7 In the first year of Belshazzar king of Babylon, Daniel saw a dream and visions in his mind *as he lay* on his bed; then he wrote the dream down *and* told the *following* summary of it. 2 Daniel said, "I was looking in my vision by night, and behold, the four winds of heaven were stirring up the great sea. 3 And four great beasts were coming up from the sea, different from one another. 4 The first *was* like a lion but had *the* wings of an eagle. I kept looking until its wings were plucked, and it was lifted up from the ground and set up on two feet like a man; a human mind also was given to it. 5 And behold, another beast, a second one, resembling a bear. And it was raised up on one side, and three ribs *were* in its mouth between its teeth; and they said this to it: 'Arise, devour much meat!' 6 After this I kept looking, and behold, another one, like a leopard, which had on its back four wings of a bird; the beast also had four heads, and dominion was given to it. 7 After this I kept looking in the night visions, and behold, a fourth beast, dreadful and terrible, and extremely strong; and it had large iron teeth. It devoured and crushed, and trampled down the remainder with its feet; and it was different from all the beasts that were before it, and it had ten horns. 8 While I was thinking about the horns, behold, another horn, a little one, came up among them, and three of the previous horns were plucked out before it; and behold, this horn possessed eyes like human eyes, and a mouth uttering great *boasts.*

The Ancient of Days Reigns

9¶ "I kept looking
Until thrones were set up,
And the Ancient of Days took *His* seat;
His garment *was* white as snow,
And the hair of His head like pure wool.
His throne *was* ablaze with flames,
Its wheels *were* a burning fire.
10 "A river of fire was flowing
And coming out from before Him;
Thousands upon thousands were serving Him,
And myriads upon myriads were standing before Him;
The court convened,
And the books were opened.
11 Then I kept looking because of the sound of the boastful words which the horn was speaking; I kept looking until the beast was killed, and its body was destroyed and given to the burning fire. 12 As for the rest of the beasts, their dominion was taken away, but an extension of life was granted to them for an appointed period of time.

The Son of Man Presented

13¶ "I kept looking in the night visions,

And behold, with the clouds of heaven
One like a son of man was coming,
And He came up to the Ancient of Days
And was presented before Him.
14 "And to Him was given dominion,
Honor, and a kingdom,
So that all the peoples, nations, and *pop-
ulations of all* languages
Might serve Him.
His dominion is an everlasting dominion
Which will not pass away;
And His kingdom is one
Which will not be destroyed.

The Vision Interpreted

15 "As for me, Daniel, my spirit was distressed within me, and the visions in my mind
kept alarming me. 16 I approached one of those
who were standing by and began requesting of
him the exact meaning of all this. So he told
me and made known to me the interpretation
of these things: 17 'These great beasts, which
are four *in number,* are four kings *who* will
arise from the earth. 18 But the 'saints of the
Highest One will receive the kingdom and take
possession of the kingdom forever, for all ages
to come.'
19 "Then I desired to know the exact
meaning of the fourth beast, which was different from all the others, exceedingly
dreadful, with its teeth of iron and its claws
of bronze, *and which* devoured, crushed, and
trampled down the remainder with its feet,
20 and *the meaning* of the ten horns that *were*
on its head, and the other *horn* which came
up, and before which three *of the horns* fell,
namely, that horn which had eyes and a mouth
uttering great *boasts,* and which was larger
in appearance than its associates. 21 I kept
looking, and that horn was waging war with
the saints and prevailing against them, 22 until
the Ancient of Days came and judgment was
passed in favor of the saints of the Highest
One, and the time arrived when the saints
took possession of the kingdom.
23 "This is what he said: 'The fourth beast
will be a fourth kingdom on the earth which
will be different from all the *other* kingdoms,
and will devour the whole earth and trample
it down and crush it. 24 As for the ten horns,
out of this kingdom ten kings will arise; and
another will arise after them, and he will be
different from the previous ones and will
humble three kings. 25 And he will speak
against the Most High and wear down the
saints of the Highest One, and he will intend to
make alterations in times and in law; and they
will be handed over to him for a time, times,
and half a time. 26 But the court will convene
for judgment, and his dominion will be taken
away, annihilated and destroyed forever.
27 Then the sovereignty, the dominion, and the
greatness of *all* the kingdoms under the whole
heaven will be given to the people of the saints
of the Highest One; His kingdom *will be* an
everlasting kingdom, and all the empires will
serve and obey Him.'
28 "At this point the revelation ended. As for
me, Daniel, my thoughts were greatly alarming

me and my face became pale, but I kept the
matter to myself."

Vision of the Ram and Goat

8 In the third year of the reign of Belshazzar
the king, a vision appeared to me, Daniel,
subsequent to the one which appeared to me
previously. 2 I looked in the vision, and while I
was looking, I was in the citadel of Susa, which
is in the province of Elam; and I looked in the
vision, and I myself was beside the Ulai
Canal. 3 Then I raised my eyes and looked, and
behold, a ram which had two horns was standing in front of the canal. Now the two horns
were long, but one *was* longer than the other,
with the longer one coming up last. 4 I saw
the ram butting westward, northward, and
southward, and no *other* beasts could stand
against him nor was there anyone to rescue
from his power, but he did as he pleased and
made himself great.
5 While I was observing, behold, a male goat
was coming from the west over the surface of
the entire earth without touching the ground;
and the goat *had* a prominent horn between
his eyes. 6 He came up to the ram that had the
two horns, which I had seen standing in front
of the canal, and rushed at him in his mighty
wrath. 7 And I saw him come up beside the
ram, and he was enraged at him; and he struck
the ram and smashed his two horns, and the
ram had no strength to withstand him. So he
hurled him to the ground and trampled on
him, and there was no one to rescue the ram
from his power. 8 Then the male goat made
himself exceedingly great. But once he became
powerful, the large horn was broken; and in its
place four prominent *horns* came up toward
the four winds of heaven.

The Little Horn

9 And out of one of them came a rather small
horn which grew exceedingly great toward
the south, toward the east, and toward the
'Beautiful *Land.* 10 It grew up to the heavenly
'lights, and some of the lights, that is, some of
the stars it threw down to the earth, and it
trampled them. 11 It even exalted itself to be
equal with the Commander of the army; and it
removed the regular sacrifice from Him, and
the place of His sanctuary was overthrown.
12 And because of an offense the army will
be given *to the horn* along with the regular
sacrifice; and it will hurl truth to the ground
and do *as it pleases* and be successful. 13 Then
I heard a holy one speaking, and another
holy one said to that particular one who was
speaking, "How long will the vision *about* the
regular sacrifice *apply,* while the offense causes
horror, so as to allow both the sanctuary and
the army to be trampled?" 14 And he said to
me, "For 2,300 evenings *and* mornings; then
the sanctuary will be properly restored."

Interpretation of the Vision

15 When I, Daniel, had seen the vision, I
sought to understand it; and behold, standing
before me was one who looked like a man.
16 And I heard the voice of a man between *the*

7:18 1 Lit *holy ones;* i.e., God's people   8:9 1 I.e., Israel   8:10 1 Lit *host*

banks of Ulai, and he called out and said, "Gabriel, explain the vision to this *man.*" 17 So he came near to where I was standing, and when he came I was frightened and fell on my face; and he said to me, "Son of man, understand that the vision *pertains* to the time of the end."

18 Now while he was talking with me, I was dazed with my face to the ground; but he touched me and made me stand at my place. 19 And he said, "Behold, I am going to inform you of what will occur at the final period of the indignation, because *it pertains* to the appointed time of the end.

The Ram's Identity

20 The ram which you saw with the two horns *represents* the kings of Media and Persia.

The Goat

21 The shaggy goat *represents* the kingdom of Greece, and the large horn that is between his eyes is the first king. 22 The broken *horn* and the four *horns that* came up in its place *represent* four kingdoms *which* will arise from *his* nation, although not with his power.

23 "And in the latter period of their dominion,
    When the wrongdoers have run *their course,*
    A king will arise,
    Insolent and skilled in intrigue.
24 "And his power will be mighty, but not by his *own* power,
    And he will destroy to an extraordinary degree
    And be successful and do *as he pleases;*
    He will destroy mighty men and the holy people.
25 "And through his shrewdness
    He will make deceit a success by his influence;
    And he will make himself great in his own mind,
    And he will destroy many while *they are* at ease.
    He will even oppose the Prince of princes,
    But he will be broken without human agency.
26 "And the vision of the evenings and mornings
    Which has been told is true;
    But as for you, keep the vision secret,
    Because *it pertains* to many days *in the future.*"

27 Then I, Daniel, was exhausted and sick for days. Then I got up and carried on the king's business; but I was astounded at the vision, and there was no one to explain *it.*

Daniel's Prayer for His People

9 In the first year of Darius the son of Ahasuerus, of Median descent, who was made king over the kingdom of the Chaldeans— 2 in the first year of his reign, I, Daniel, observed in the books the number of the years which was *revealed as* the word of the LORD to Jeremiah the prophet for the completion of the desolations of Jerusalem, *namely,* seventy years. 3 So I gave my attention to the

Lord God, to seek *Him by* prayer and pleading, with fasting, sackcloth, and ashes. 4 I prayed to the LORD my God and confessed, and said, "Oh, Lord, the great and awesome God, who keeps His covenant and faithfulness for those who love Him and keep His commandments, 5 we have sinned, we have done wrong, and acted wickedly and rebelled, even turning aside from Your commandments and ordinances. 6 Moreover, we have not listened to Your servants the prophets, who spoke in Your name to our kings, our leaders, our fathers, and all the people of the land.

7 "Righteousness *belongs* to You, Lord, but to us open shame, as *it is* this day—to the men of Judah, the inhabitants of Jerusalem, and all Israel, those who are nearby and those who are far away in all the countries to which You have driven them, because of their unfaithful deeds which they have committed against You. 8 Open shame *belongs* to us, LORD, to our kings, our leaders, and our fathers, because we have sinned against You. 9 To the Lord our God *belong* compassion and forgiveness, because we have rebelled against Him; 10 and we have not obeyed the voice of the LORD our God, to walk in His teachings which He set before us through His servants the prophets. 11 Indeed, all Israel has violated Your Law and turned aside, not obeying Your voice; so the curse has gushed forth on us, along with the oath which is written in the Law of Moses the servant of God, because we have sinned against Him. 12 So He has confirmed His words which He had spoken against us and against our rulers who ruled us, to bring on us great disaster; for under the entire heaven there has not been done *anything* like what was done in Jerusalem. 13 Just as it is written in the Law of Moses, all this disaster has come on us; yet we have not sought the favor of the LORD our God by turning from our wrongdoing and giving attention to Your truth. 14 So the LORD has kept the disaster in store and brought it on us; for the LORD our God is righteous with respect to all His deeds which He has done, but we have not obeyed His voice.

15 "And now, Lord, our God, *You* who brought Your people out of the land of Egypt with a mighty hand and made a name for Yourself, as *it is* this day—we have sinned, we have been wicked. 16 Lord, in accordance with all Your righteous acts, let now Your anger and Your wrath turn away from Your city Jerusalem, Your holy mountain; for because of our sins and the wrongdoings of our fathers, Jerusalem and Your people *have become* an object of taunting to all those around us. 17 So now, our God, listen to the prayer of Your servant and to his pleas, and for Your sake, Lord, let Your face shine on Your desolate sanctuary. 18 My God, incline Your ear and hear! Open Your eyes and see our desolations and the city which is called by Your name; for we are not presenting our pleas before You based on any merits of our own, but based on Your great compassion. 19 Lord, hear! Lord, forgive! Lord, listen and take action! For Your own sake, my God, do not delay, because Your city and Your people are called by Your name."

Gabriel Brings an Answer

20 While I was still speaking and praying, and confessing my sin and the sin of my people Israel, and presenting my plea before the LORD my God in behalf of the holy mountain of my God, **21** while I was still speaking in prayer, the man Gabriel, whom I had seen in the vision previously, came to me in *my* extreme weariness about the time of the evening offering. **22** And he instructed *me* and talked with me and said, "Daniel, I have come now to give you insight with understanding. **23** At the beginning of your pleas the command was issued, and I have come to tell *you*, because you are highly esteemed; so pay attention to the message and gain understanding of the vision.

Seventy Weeks and the Messiah

24 "Seventy weeks have been decreed for your people and your holy city, to finish the wrongdoing, to make an end of sin, to make atonement for guilt, to bring in everlasting righteousness, to seal up vision and prophecy, and to anoint the Most Holy Place. **25** So you are to know and understand *that* from the issuing of a decree to restore and rebuild Jerusalem, until Messiah the Prince, *there will be* seven weeks and sixty-two weeks; it will be built again, *with* streets and moat, even in times of distress. **26** Then after the sixty-two weeks, the Messiah will be cut off and have nothing, and the people of the prince who is to come will destroy the city and the sanctuary. And its end *will come* with a flood; even to the end there will be war; desolations are determined. **27** And he will confirm a covenant with the many for one week, but in the middle of the week he will put a stop to sacrifice and grain offering; and on the wing of abominations *will come* the one who makes desolate, until a complete destruction, one that is decreed, gushes forth on the one who makes desolate."

Daniel Is Terrified by a Vision

10 In the third year of Cyrus king of Persia, a message was revealed to Daniel, who was named Belteshazzar; and the message was true and *it concerned* great conflict, but he understood the message and had an understanding of the vision.

2 In those days, I, Daniel, had been mourning for three entire weeks. **3** I did not eat any tasty food, nor did meat or wine enter my mouth, nor did I use any ointment at all until the entire three weeks were completed. **4** On the twenty-fourth day of the first month, while I was by the bank of the great river, that is, the Tigris, **5** I raised my eyes and looked, and behold, there was a man dressed in linen, whose waist had a belt of pure gold of Uphaz. **6** His body also *was* like topaz, his face had the appearance of lightning, his eyes were like flaming torches, his arms and feet like the gleam of polished bronze, and the sound of his words like the sound of a multitude. **7** Now I, Daniel, alone saw the vision, while the men who were with me did not see the vision; nevertheless, a great fear fell on them, and they ran away to hide themselves. **8** So I was left alone and saw this great vision; yet no strength was left in me, for my complexion turned to a deathly pallor, and I retained no strength. **9** But I heard the sound of his words; and as soon as I heard the sound of his words, I fell into a deep sleep on my face, with my face to the ground.

Daniel Comforted

10 Then behold, a hand touched me and shook me on my hands and knees. **11** And he said to me, "Daniel, you who are treasured, understand the words that I am about to tell you and stand at your place, for I have now been sent to you." And when he had spoken this word to me, I stood up trembling. **12** Then he said to me, "Do not be afraid, Daniel, for from the first day that you set your heart on understanding *this* and on humbling yourself before your God, your words were heard, and I have come in *response to* your words. **13** But the prince of the kingdom of Persia was standing in my way for twenty-one days; then behold, Michael, one of the chief princes, came to help me, for I had been left there with the kings of Persia. **14** Now I have come to explain to you what will happen to your people in the latter days, because the vision *pertains* to the days still *future*."

15 When he had spoken to me according to these words, I turned my face toward the ground and became speechless. **16** And behold, one who resembled a human was touching my lips. Then I opened my mouth and spoke and said to him who was standing before me, "My lord, due to the vision anguish has come upon me, and I have retained no strength. **17** For how can such a servant of my lord talk with such as my lord? As for me, there remains just now no strength in me, nor has any breath been left in me."

18 Then *this* one with human appearance touched me again and strengthened me. **19** And he said, "You who are treasured, do not be afraid. Peace *be* to you; take courage and be courageous!" Now as soon as he spoke to me, I felt strengthened and said, "May my lord speak, for you have strengthened me." **20** Then he said, "Do you understand why I came to you? But I shall now return to fight against the prince of Persia; so I am leaving, and behold, the prince of Greece is about to come. **21** However, I will tell you what is recorded in the writing of truth. Yet there is no one who stands firmly with me against these *forces* except Michael your prince.

Conflicts to Come

11 "In the first year of Darius the Mede, I arose to be of assistance and a protection for him. **2** And now I will tell you the truth. Behold, three more kings are going to arise in Persia. Then a fourth will gain far more riches than all *of them*; as soon as he becomes strong through his riches, he will stir up the entire *empire* against the realm of Greece. **3** And a mighty king will arise, and he will rule with great authority and do as he pleases. **4** But as soon as he has arisen, his kingdom will be broken up and parceled out toward the four points of the compass, though not to his *own*

descendants, nor according to his authority which he wielded, because his sovereignty will be removed and *given* to others besides them.

5 "Then the king of the South will grow strong, along with *one* of his princes who will gain ascendancy over him and rule; his domain *will be* a great realm *indeed.* 6 And after *some* years they will form an alliance, and the daughter of the king of the South will come to the king of the North to reach an agreement. But she will not keep her position of power, nor will he remain with his power, but she will be given up, along with those who brought her in and the one who fathered her as well as he who supported her in *those* times. 7 But one of the descendants of her line will arise in his place, and he will come against *their* army and enter the fortress of the king of the North, and he will deal with them and prevail. 8 And he will also take into captivity to Egypt their gods with their cast metal images *and* their precious vessels of silver and gold, and he on his part will refrain from attacking the king of the North for *some* years. 9 Then the latter will enter the realm of the king of the South, but will return to his *own* land.

10 "And his sons will mobilize and assemble a multitude of great forces; and *one of them* will keep on coming and overflow and pass through, so that he may again wage war up to his fortress. 11 And the king of the South will be enraged and go out and fight with the king of the North. Then *the latter* will raise a great multitude, but *that* multitude will be handed over to the former. 12 When the multitude is carried away, his heart will be haughty, and he will cause tens of thousands to fall; yet he will not prevail. 13 For the king of the North will again raise a greater multitude than the former, and after an interval of some years he will press on with a great army and much equipment.

14 "Now in those times many will rise up against the king of the South; the violent ones among your people will also raise themselves up to fulfill the vision, but they will fall down. 15 Then the king of the North will come, pile up an assault ramp, and capture a well-fortified city; and the forces of the South will not stand *their ground,* not even their choicest troops, for there will be no strength to make a stand. 16 But he who comes against him will do as he pleases, and no one will *be able to* withstand him; he will also stay *for a time* in the 1Beautiful Land, with destruction in his hand. 17 And he will set his mind on coming with the power of his entire kingdom, bringing with him a proposal of peace which he will put into effect; he will also give him the daughter of women to ruin it. But she will not take a stand *for him* or be on his side. 18 Then he will turn his face to the coastlands and capture many. But a commander will put a stop to his taunting against him; moreover, he will repay him for his taunting. 19 So he will turn his face toward the fortresses of his own land, but he will stumble and fall and not be found.

20 "Then in his place one will arise who will allow an oppressor to pass through the 1Jewel of *his* kingdom; yet within a few days he will be broken, though not in anger nor in battle. 21 And in his place a despicable person will arise, on whom the majesty of kingship has not been conferred; but he will come in a *time of* tranquility and seize the kingdom by intrigue. 22 And the overflowing forces will be flooded away from him and smashed, and also the prince of the covenant. 23 After an alliance is made with him he will practice deception, and he will go up and gain power with a small *force of* people. 24 In a time of tranquility he will enter the richest *parts* of the realm, and he will accomplish what his fathers did not, nor his ancestors; he will distribute plunder, spoils, and possessions among them, and he will devise his schemes against strongholds, but *only* for a time. 25 And he will stir up his strength and courage against the king of the South with a large army; so the king of the South will mobilize an extremely large and mighty army for war; but he will not stand, because schemes will be devised against him. 26 Those who eat his choice food will destroy him, and his army will overflow, but many will fall down slain. 27 As for both kings, their hearts will be *intent* on evil, and they will speak lies *to each other* at the same table; but it will not succeed, because the end is still *to come* at the appointed time. 28 Then he will return to his land with much plunder; but his heart will be *set* against the holy covenant, and he will take action and *then* return to his *own* land.

29 "At the appointed time he will return and come into the South, but this last time it will not turn out the way it did before. 30 For ships of Kittim will come against him; therefore he will withdraw in fear and will return and curse the holy covenant and take action; so he will come back and pay attention to those who abandon the holy covenant. 31 Forces from him will arise, desecrate the sanctuary fortress, and do away with the regular sacrifice. And they will set up the abomination of desolation. 32 And by smooth *words* he will turn to godlessness those who act wickedly toward the covenant, but the people who know their God will be strong and take action. 33 And those who have insight among the people will give understanding to the many; yet they will fall by sword and by flame, by captivity and by plunder for *many* days. 34 Now when they fall they will be granted a little help, and many will join with them in hypocrisy. 35 And some of those who have insight will fall, to refine, purge, and cleanse them until the end time; because *it is* still *to come* at the appointed time.

36 "Then the king will do as he pleases, and he will exalt himself and boast against every god and will speak dreadful things against the God of gods; and he will be successful until the indignation is finished, because that which is determined will be done. 37 And he will show no regard for the gods of his fathers or for the desire of women, nor will he show regard for any *other* god; for he will boast against *them* all. 38 But instead he will honor a

---

11:16 1 I.e., Israel   **11:20** 1 Lit *splendor;* i.e., prob. Jerusalem and its temple

god of fortresses, a god whom his fathers did not know; he will honor *him* with gold, silver, precious stones, and treasures. **39** And he will take action against the strongest of fortresses with *the help of* a foreign god; he will give great honor to those who acknowledge *him* and will make them rulers over the many, and will parcel out land for a price.

40 "And at the end time the king of the South will wage war with him, and the king of the North will storm against him with chariots, horsemen, and with many ships; and he will enter countries, overflow *them*, and pass through. **41** He will also enter the Beautiful Land, and many *countries* will fall; but these will be rescued out of his hand: Edom, Moab, and the foremost of the sons of Ammon. **42** Then he will reach out with his hand against *other* countries, and the land of Egypt will not escape. **43** But he will gain control over the hidden treasures of gold and silver, and over all the precious things of Egypt; and Libyans and Ethiopians *will follow* at his heels. **44** But rumors from the East and from the North will terrify him, and he will go out with great wrath to eliminate and annihilate many. **45** And he will pitch the tents of his royal pavilion between the seas and the beautiful Holy Mountain; yet he will come to his end, and no one will help him.

The Time of the End

12 "Now at that time Michael, the great prince who stands *guard* over the sons of your people, will arise. And there will be a time of distress such as never occurred since there was a nation until that time; and at that time your people, everyone who is found written in the book, will be rescued. **2** And many of those who sleep in the dust of the ground will awake, these to everlasting life, but the others to disgrace *and* everlasting contempt. **3** And those who have insight will shine like the glow of the [1]expanse of heaven, and those who lead the many to righteousness, like the stars forever and ever. **4** But as for you, Daniel, keep these words secret and seal up the book until the end of time; many will roam about, and knowledge will increase."

5 Then I, Daniel, looked, and behold, two others were standing, one on this bank of the stream and the other on that bank of the stream. **6** And *someone* said to the man dressed in linen, "who was above the waters of the stream, "How long *will it be* until the end of *these* wonders?" **7** And I heard the man dressed in linen, who was above the waters of the stream, as he raised his right hand and his left toward heaven, and swore by Him who lives forever that *it would be* for a time, times, and half *a time;* and as soon as they finish smashing the power of the holy people, all these *events* will be completed. **8** But as for me, I heard but did not understand; so I said, "My lord, what *will be* the outcome of these *events?*" **9** And he said, "Go *your way,* Daniel, for *these* words *will be* kept secret and sealed up until the end time. **10** Many will be purged, cleansed, and refined, but the wicked will act wickedly; and none of the wicked will understand, but those who have insight will understand. **11** And from the time that the regular sacrifice is abolished and the abomination of desolation is set up, *there will be* 1,290 days. **12** Blessed is the one who is patient and attains to the 1,335 days! **13** But as for you, go *your way* to the end; then you will rest and rise for your allotted portion at the end of the age."

12:3 [1] Or *firmament;* i.e., atmosphere and space

The Book of
HOSEA

Hosea's Wife and Children

1 The word of the LORD which came to Hosea the son of Beeri, during the days of Uzziah, Jotham, Ahaz, and Hezekiah, kings of Judah, and during the days of Jeroboam the son of Joash, king of Israel.

2 When the LORD first spoke through Hosea, the LORD said to Hosea, "Go, take for yourself a wife inclined to infidelity, and children of infidelity; for the land commits flagrant infidelity, abandoning the LORD." 3 So he went and took Gomer the daughter of Diblaim, and she conceived and bore him a son. 4 And the LORD said to him, "Name him Jezreel; for in just a little while I will punish the house of Jehu for the bloodshed of Jezreel, and I will put an end to the kingdom of the house of Israel. 5 On that day I will break the bow of Israel in the Valley of Jezreel."

6 Then she conceived again and gave birth to a daughter. And the LORD said to him, "Name her 1Lo-ruhamah, for I will no longer take pity on the house of Israel, that I would ever forgive them. 7 But I will take pity on the house of Judah and save them by the LORD their God, and will not save them by bow, sword, battle, horses, or horsemen."

8 When she had weaned Lo-ruhamah, she conceived and gave birth to a son. 9 And the LORD said, "Name him 1Lo-ammi, because you are not My people, and I am not your God."

10¶ Yet the number of the sons of Israel
Will be like the sand of the sea,
Which cannot be measured or counted;
And in the place
Where it is said to them,
"You are not My people,"
It will be said to them,
"You are the sons of the living God."
11 And the sons of Judah and the sons of
Israel will be gathered together,
And they will appoint for themselves one
leader,
And they will go up from the land,
For the day of Jezreel will be great.

Israel's Unfaithfulness Condemned

2 Say to your brothers, "1Ammi," and to your
sisters, "2Ruhamah."
2 "Dispute with your mother, dispute,
Because she is not my wife, and I am not
her husband;
But she must remove her infidelity from
her face
And her adultery from between her
breasts,
3 Otherwise, I will strip her naked
And expose her as on the day she was
born.
I will also make her like a wilderness,
Make her like desert land,

And put her to death with thirst.
4 "Also, I will take no pity on her children,
Because they are children of infidelity.
5 "For their mother has committed
prostitution;
She who conceived them has acted
shamefully.
For she said, 'I will go after my lovers,
Who give me my bread and my water,
My wool and my flax, my oil and my
drink.'
6 "Therefore, behold, I will obstruct her way
with thorns,
And I will build a stone wall against her
so that she cannot find her paths.
7 "And she will pursue her lovers, but she
will not reach them;
And she will seek them, but will not find
them.
Then she will say, 'I will go back to my
first husband,
Because it was better for me then than
now!'
8¶ "Yet she does not know that it was I myself
who gave her the grain, the new wine,
and the oil,
And lavished on her silver and gold,
Which they used for Baal.
9 "Therefore, I will take back My grain at
harvest time
And My new wine in its season.
I will also take away My wool and My flax
That I gave to cover her nakedness.
10 "So now I will uncover her lewdness
Before the eyes of her lovers,
And no one will rescue her from My
hand.
11 "I will also put an end to all her joy,
Her feasts, her new moons, her Sabbaths,
And all her festivals.
12 "And I will destroy her vines and fig trees,
Of which she said, 'They are my wages for
prostitution
Which my lovers have given me.'
And I will turn them into a forest,
And the animals of the field will devour
them.
13 "I will punish her for the days of the Baals
When she used to offer sacrifices to them
And adorn herself with her nose ring and
jewelry,
And follow her lovers, so that she forgot
Me," declares the LORD.

Restoration of Israel

14¶ "Therefore, behold, I am going to persuade
her,
Bring her into the wilderness,
And speak kindly to her.
15 "Then I will give her her vineyards from
there,

1:6 1I.e., not having obtained mercy   1:9 1I.e., not my people   2:1 1I.e., my people   2I.e., she has
obtained compassion

And the Valley of Achor as a door of hope.
And she will respond there as in the days
of her youth,
As in the day when she went up from the
land of Egypt.
16 "And it will come about on that day,"
declares the LORD,
"That you will call Me ¹my husband
And no longer call Me my ²Baal.
17 "For I will remove the names of the Baals
from her mouth,
So that they will no longer be mentioned
by their names.
18 "On that day I will also make a covenant
for them
With the animals of the field,
The birds of the sky,
And the crawling things of the ground.
And I will eliminate the bow, the sword,
and war from the land,
And will let them lie down in safety.
19 "I will betroth you to Me forever;
Yes, I will betroth you to Me in righteousness and in justice,
In favor and in compassion,
20 And I will betroth you to Me in
faithfulness.
Then you will know the LORD.
21¶ "And it will come about on that day that I
will respond," declares the LORD.
"I will respond to the heavens, and they
will respond to the earth,
22 And the earth will respond to the grain, to
the new wine, and to the oil,
And they will respond to ¹Jezreel.
23 "I will sow her for Myself in the land.
I will also have compassion on her who
had not obtained compassion,
And I will say to those who were not My
people,
'You are My people!'
And they will say, 'You are my God!' "

Hosea's Redemption of Gomer

3 Then the LORD said to me, "Go again, love a
woman who is loved by her husband, yet is
committing adultery, as the LORD loves the sons
of Israel, though they turn to other gods and
love raisin cakes." ² So I purchased her for
myself for fifteen shekels of silver, and a
¹homer and a ²lethech of barley. ³ Then I said to
her, "You shall live with me for many days. You
shall not play the prostitute, nor shall you have
another man; so I will also be toward you."
⁴ For the sons of Israel will live for many days
without a king or leader, without sacrifice or
memorial stone, and without ephod or ¹household idols. ⁵ Afterward the sons of Israel will
return and seek the LORD their God and David
their king; and they will come trembling to the
LORD and to His goodness in the last days.

God's Controversy with Israel

4 Listen to the word of the LORD, you sons
of Israel,
Because the LORD has a case against the
inhabitants of the land,

For there is no faithfulness, nor loyalty,
Nor knowledge of God in the land.
2 There is oath-taking, denial, murder,
stealing, and adultery.
They employ violence, so that bloodshed
follows bloodshed.
3 Therefore the land mourns,
And everyone who lives in it languishes
Along with the animals of the field and
the birds of the sky,
And even the fish of the sea disappear.
4¶ Yet let no one find fault, and let no one
rebuke;
For your people are like those who
contend with a priest.
5 So you will stumble by day,
And the prophet also will stumble with
you by night;
And I will destroy your mother.
6 My people are destroyed for lack of
knowledge.
Since you have rejected knowledge,
I also will reject you from being My priest.
Since you have forgotten the Law of your
God,
I also will forget your children.
7¶ The more they multiplied, the more they
sinned against Me;
I will change their glory into shame.
8 They feed on the sin of My people,
And long for their wrongdoing.
9 And it will be, like people, like priest;
So I will punish them for their ways
And repay them for their deeds.
10 They will eat, but not have enough;
They will play the prostitute, but not
increase,
Because they gave up devoting themselves
to the LORD.
11¶ Infidelity, wine, and new wine take away
the understanding.
12 My people consult their wooden idol, and
their diviner's wand informs them;
For a spirit of infidelity has led them
astray,
And they have been unfaithful, departing
from their God.
13 They offer sacrifices on the tops of the
mountains
And burn incense on the hills,
Under oak, poplar, and terebinth,
Because their shade is pleasant.
Therefore your daughters play the
prostitute,
And your brides commit adultery.
14 I will not punish your daughters when
they play the prostitute,
Or your brides when they commit
adultery,
Because the men themselves slip away
with the prostitutes
And offer sacrifices with temple
prostitutes;
So the people without understanding are
ruined.
15¶ Though you, Israel, play the prostitute,
Judah must not become guilty;

2:16 ¹ Heb Ishi   ² Also meaning husband in Heb, besides a name for false gods   2:22 ¹ I.e., God sows
3:2 ¹ About 7.7 cubic feet or 0.22 cubic meters   ² About 3.8 cubic feet or 0.11 cubic meters
3:4 ¹ Heb teraphim

Also you are not to go to Gilgal,
Nor go up to Beth-aven
And take the oath:
"As the LORD lives!"
16 Since Israel is stubborn
Like a stubborn cow,
Will the LORD now pasture them
Like a lamb in a large field?
17 Ephraim is allied with idols;
Leave him alone.
18 Their liquor is gone,
They prostitute themselves continually;
Their rulers dearly love shame.
19 The wind wraps them in its wings,
And they will be put to shame because of
their sacrifices.

The People's Apostasy Rebuked

5 Hear this, you priests!
Pay attention, house of Israel!
Listen, *you of* the house of the king!
For the judgment *applies* to you,
Because you have been a trap at Mizpah,
And a net spread out on Tabor.
2 And the rebels have gone deep in
depravity,
But I will discipline all of them.
3 I know Ephraim, and Israel is not hidden
from Me;
Because now, Ephraim, you have been
unfaithful,
Israel has defiled itself.
4 Their deeds will not allow them
To return to their God.
For a spirit of infidelity is within them,
And they do not know the LORD.
5 Moreover, the pride of Israel testifies
against him,
And Israel and Ephraim stumble in their
wrongdoing;
Judah also has stumbled with them.
6 They will go with their flocks and
herds
To seek the LORD, but they will not find
Him;
He has withdrawn from them.
7 They have dealt treacherously with the
LORD,
For they have given birth to illegitimate
children.
Now the new moon will devour them
with their land.
8¶ Blow the horn in Gibeah,
And the trumpet in Ramah.
Sound an alarm at Beth-aven:
"Behind you, Benjamin!"
9 Ephraim will become a desolation in the
day of rebuke;
Among the tribes of Israel I make known
what is trustworthy.
10 The leaders of Judah have become like
those who displace a boundary
marker;
On them I will pour out My anger like
water.
11 Ephraim is oppressed, broken *by* judgment,
Because he was determined to follow
man's command.
12 Therefore I am like a moth to Ephraim,

And like rottenness to the house of Judah.
13 When Ephraim saw his sickness,
And Judah his sore,
Ephraim then went to Assyria
And sent *word* to King Jareb.
But he is unable to heal you,
Or to cure you of your sore.
14 For I *will be* like a lion to Ephraim
And like a young lion to the house of
Judah.
I, *yes* I, will tear to pieces and go away,
I will carry away, and there will be no one
to rescue.
15 I will go away *and* return to My place
Until they acknowledge their guilt and
seek My face;
In their distress they will search for Me.

The Response to God's Rebuke

6 "Come, let's return to the LORD.
For He has torn *us,* but He will heal us;
He has wounded *us,* but He will bandage
us.
2 "He will revive us after two days;
He will raise us up on the third day,
That we may live before Him.
3 "So let's learn, let's press on to know the
LORD.
His appearance is as sure as the dawn;
And He will come to us like the rain,
As the spring rain waters the earth."
4¶ What shall I do with you, Ephraim?
What shall I do with you, Judah?
For your loyalty is like a morning cloud,
And like the dew which goes away
early.
5 Therefore I have cut *them* in pieces by the
prophets;
I have slain them by the words of My
mouth;
And the judgments on you are *like* the
light *that* shines.
6 For I desire loyalty rather than sacrifice,
And the knowledge of God rather than
burnt offerings.
7 But like Adam they have violated the
covenant;
There they have dealt treacherously with
Me.
8 Gilead is a city of wrongdoers,
Tracked with bloody *footprints.*
9 And as a band of robbers lie in wait for a
person,
So a band of priests murder on the way to
Shechem;
Certainly they have committed an act of
infamy.
10 In the house of Israel I have seen a
horrible thing;
Ephraim's infidelity is there, Israel has
defiled itself.
11 Also, Judah, there is a harvest appointed
for you,
When I restore the fortunes of My
people.

Ephraim's Wrongdoing

7 When I would heal Israel,
The wrongdoing of Ephraim is uncovered,
And the evil deeds of Samaria,

For they practice deception;
The thief enters,
A band of robbers attack outside,
2   And they do not consider in their hearts
That I remember all their wickedness.
Now their deeds surround them;
They are before My face.
3   With their wickedness they make the king
happy,
And the officials with their lies.
4   They are all adulterers,
Like an oven heated by the baker,
Who stops stoking *the fire*
From *the time* the dough is kneaded until
it is leavened.
5   On the day of our king, the officials
became sick with the heat of wine;
He stretched out his hand with scoffers,
6   For their hearts are like an oven
As they approach their plotting;
Their anger smolders all night,
In the morning it burns like flaming fire.
7   All of them are hot like an oven,
And they consume their rulers;
All their kings have fallen.
None of them calls on Me.
8¶ Ephraim is himself thrown about with the
nations;
Ephraim has become a round loaf not
turned over.
9   Strangers devour his strength,
Yet he does not know *it;*
Gray hairs also are sprinkled on him,
Yet he does not know *it.*
10 Though the pride of Israel testifies against
him,
Yet they have not returned to the LORD
their God,
Nor have they sought Him, despite all
this.
11 So Ephraim has become like a gullible
dove, without sense;
They call to Egypt, they go to Assyria.
12 When they go, I will spread My net over
them;
I will bring them down like the birds of
the sky.
I will discipline them in accordance with
the proclamation to their assembly.
13 Woe to them, for they have strayed from
Me!
Destruction is theirs, for they have
rebelled against Me!
I would redeem them, but they have
spoken lies against Me.
14 And they do not cry to Me from their
heart
When they wail on their beds;
For the sake of grain and new wine they
assemble themselves,
They turn against Me.
15 Although I trained *and* strengthened their
arms,
Yet they devise evil against Me.
16 They turn, *but* not upward,
They are like a loose bow;
Their officials will fall by the sword
Because of the insolence of their tongue.
This *will be* their derision in the land of
Egypt.

Israel Reaps the Whirlwind

8   *Put* the trumpet to your lips!
Like an eagle *the enemy comes* against the
house of the LORD,
Because they have violated My covenant
And rebelled against My Law.
2   They cry out to Me,
"My God, we of Israel know You!"
3   Israel has rejected the good;
The enemy will pursue him.
4   They have set up kings, but not by Me;
They have appointed officials, but I did
not know *it.*
With their silver and gold they have made
idols for themselves,
So that they will be eliminated.
5   He has rejected your calf, Samaria,
saying,
"My anger burns against them!"
How long will they be incapable of
innocence?
6   For from Israel *comes* even this!
A craftsman made it, so it is not God;
Assuredly, the calf of Samaria will be
broken to pieces.
7   For they sow wind
And they harvest a storm.
The standing grain has no kernels;
It yields no grain.
If it were to yield, strangers would
swallow it.
8¶ Israel has been swallowed up;
They are now among the nations
Like a vessel in which no one delights.
9   For they have gone up to Assyria,
Like a wild donkey all alone;
Ephraim has paid fees for lovers.
10 Even though they pay *for allies* among the
nations,
I will gather them up now;
And they will begin to diminish
Because of the burden of the king of
officials.
11¶ Since Ephraim has multiplied altars for
sin,
They have become altars of sinning for
him.
12 Though I wrote for him ten thousand
precepts of My Law,
They are regarded as a strange thing.
13 As for My sacrificial gifts,
They sacrifice the flesh and eat *it,*
But the LORD has taken no delight in
them.
Now He will remember their guilt,
And punish *them* for their sins;
They will return to Egypt.
14 For Israel has forgotten his Maker and
built palaces;
And Judah has multiplied fortified cities,
But I will send a fire on its cities, and it
will consume its palatial buildings.

Ephraim Punished

9   Do not rejoice, Israel, with jubilation like
the nations!
For you have been unfaithful, abandoning
your God.
You have loved the earnings *of unfaithfulness* on every threshing floor.

2   Threshing floor and wine press will not
      feed them,
     And the new wine will fail them.
3   They will not remain in the LORD's land,
     But Ephraim will return to Egypt,
     And in Assyria they will eat unclean *food*.
4   They will not pour out drink offerings of
      wine to the LORD,
     Nor will their sacrifices please Him.
     Their bread will be to them like mourners'
      bread;
     All who eat it will be defiled,
     Because their bread will be for themselves
      alone;
     It will not enter the house of the LORD.
5   What will you do on the day of the
      appointed festival
     And on the day of the feast of the LORD?
6   For behold, they will be gone because of
      destruction;
     Egypt will gather them together, Memphis
      will bury them.
     Weeds will take possession of their
      treasures of silver;
     Thorns *will be* in their tents.
7¶   The days of punishment have come,
     The days of retribution have come;
     Let Israel know *this!*
     The prophet is a fool,
     The inspired person is insane,
     Because of the grossness of your
      wrongdoing,
     And *because your* hostility is *so* great.
8   Ephraim *was* a watchman with my God, a
      prophet;
     Yet the snare of a bird catcher is in all his
      ways,
     And there is *only* hostility in the house of
      his God.
9   They are deeply depraved
     As in the days of Gibeah;
     He will remember their guilt,
     He will punish their sins.
10¶ I found Israel like grapes in the wilder-
      ness;
     I saw your forefathers as the earliest fruit
      on the fig tree in its first *season*.
     But they came to Baal-peor and devoted
      themselves to ¹shame,
     And they became as detestable as that
      which they loved.
11   As for Ephraim, their glory will fly away
      like a bird—
     No birth, no pregnancy, and no
      conception!
12   Though they bring up their children,
     Yet I will bereave them of their children
      until not a person is left.
     Yes, woe to them indeed when I depart
      from them!
13   Ephraim, as I have seen,
     Is planted in a pasture like Tyre;
     But Ephraim is going to bring out his chil-
      dren for slaughter.
14   Give to them, LORD—what will You give?
     Give them a miscarrying womb and
      dried-up breasts.
15¶ All their evil is at Gilgal;
     Indeed, I came to hate them there!

     Because of the wickedness of their deeds
     I will drive them out of My house!
     I will no longer love them;
     All their leaders are rebels.
16   Ephraim is stricken, their root is dried
      up,
     They will produce no fruit.
     Even though they give birth to children,
     I will put to death the precious ones of
      their womb.
17   My God will reject them
     Because they have not listened to Him;
     And they will be wanderers among the
      nations.

Retribution for Israel's Sin

10 Israel is a luxuriant vine;
     He produces fruit for himself.
     The more his fruit,
     The more altars he made;
     The richer his land,
     The better he made the memorial stones.
2   Their heart is deceitful;
     Now they must suffer for their guilt.
     The LORD will break down their altars
     And destroy their memorial stones.
3¶   Certainly now they will say, "We have no
      king,
     For we do not revere the LORD.
     As for the king, what can he do for us?"
4   They speak *mere* words,
     With worthless oaths they make
      covenants;
     And judgment sprouts like poisonous
      weeds in the furrows of the field.
5   The inhabitants of Samaria will fear
     For the calf of Beth-aven.
     Indeed, its people will mourn for it,
     And its idolatrous priests will cry out
      over it,
     Over its glory, since it has left it.
6   The thing itself will be brought to
      Assyria
     As a gift of tribute to King Jareb;
     Ephraim will be seized with shame,
     And Israel will be ashamed of its own
      plan.
7   Samaria will be destroyed *with* her king,
     Like a twig on the surface of the water.
8   Also the high places of Aven, the sin of
      Israel, will be destroyed;
     Thorns and thistles will grow on their
      altars;
     Then they will say to the mountains,
     "Cover us!" And to the hills, "Fall on
      us!"
9   Since the days of Gibeah you have sinned,
      Israel;
     There they stand!
     Will the battle against the sons of injustice
      not overtake them in Gibeah?
10   When it is My desire, I will discipline
      them;
     And the peoples will be gathered against
      them
     When they are bound for their double
      guilt.
11¶ Ephraim is a trained heifer that loves to
      thresh,

9:10 ¹I.e., Baal

And I passed over her lovely neck;
I will harness Ephraim,
Judah will plow, Jacob will ʰharrow for
himself.
12 Sow for yourselves, *with a view* to
righteousness;
Harvest in accordance with kindness.
Break up your uncultivated ground,
For it is time to seek the LORD
Until He comes and rains righteousness
on you.
13 You have plowed wickedness, you have
harvested injustice,
You have eaten the fruit of lies.
Because you have trusted in your way, in
your many warriors,
14 An uproar will arise among your people,
And all your fortresses will be destroyed,
As Shalman destroyed Beth-arbel on the
day of battle,
When mothers were slaughtered with
their children.
15 So it will be done to you at Bethel because
of your great wickedness.
At dawn the king of Israel will be completely destroyed.

God Yearns over His People

11 When Israel *was* a youth I loved him,
And out of Egypt I called My son.
2 The more they called them,
The more they went away from them;
They kept sacrificing to the Baals
And burning incense to idols.
3 Yet it is I who taught Ephraim to walk,
I took them in My arms;
But they did not know that I healed them.
4 I pulled them along with cords of a man,
with ropes of love,
And I became to them as one who lifts the
yoke from their jaws;
And I bent down *and* fed them.
5¶ They will not return to the land of Egypt;
But Assyria—he will be their king
Because they refused to return *to Me.*
6 And the sword will whirl against their
cities,
And will destroy their oracle priests
And consume *them,* because of their
counsels.
7 So My people are determined to turn from
Me.
Though they call them to *the One* on
high,
None at all exalts *Him.*
8¶ How can I give you up, Ephraim?
How can I surrender you, Israel?
How can I make you like Admah?
How can I treat you like Zeboiim?
My heart is turned over within Me,
All My compassions are kindled.
9 I will not carry out My fierce anger;
I will not destroy Ephraim again.
For I am God and not a man, the Holy
One in your midst,
And I will not come in wrath.
10 They will walk after the LORD,
He will roar like a lion;
Indeed He will roar,

And *His* sons will come trembling from
the west.
11 They will come trembling like birds from
Egypt,
And like doves from the land of Assyria;
And I will settle them in their houses,
declares the LORD.
12¶ Ephraim surrounds Me with lies
And the house of Israel with deceit;
Judah is still unruly against God,
Even against the Holy One who is faithful.

Ephraim Reminded

12 Ephraim feeds on wind,
And pursues the east wind continually;
He multiplies lies and violence.
Moreover, he makes a covenant with
Assyria,
And oil is brought to Egypt.
2 The LORD also has a case against Judah,
And will punish Jacob according to his
ways;
He will repay him according to his deeds.
3 In the womb he took his brother by the
heel,
And in his mature strength he contended
with God.
4 Yes, he wrestled with the angel and pre-
vailed;
He wept and implored His favor.
He found Him at Bethel,
And there He spoke with us,
5 And the LORD, the God of armies,
The LORD is His name.
6 So as for you, return to your God,
Maintain kindness and justice,
And wait for your God continually.
7 A merchant, in whose hands are
fraudulent balances,
Loves to exploit.
8 And Ephraim said, "I have certainly
become rich,
I have found wealth for myself;
In all my labors they will find in me
No wrongdoing, which *would be* sin."
9 But I *have been* the LORD your God since
the land of Egypt;
I will make you live in tents again,
As in the days of the appointed festival.
10 I have also spoken to the prophets,
And I provided many visions,
And through the prophets I spoke in
parables.
11 Is there injustice *in* Gilead?
Certainly they are worthless.
In Gilgal they sacrifice bulls,
Yes, their altars are like stone heaps
Beside the furrows of a field.
12¶ Now Jacob fled to the land of Aram,
And Israel worked for a wife,
And for a wife he kept *sheep.*
13 But by a prophet the LORD brought Israel
up from Egypt,
And by a prophet he was protected.
14 Ephraim has provoked *God* to bitter
anger;
So his Lord will leave his guilt for
bloodshed on him
And bring his disgrace back to him.

10:11 ¹ I.e., pull a harrow, a farming device

Ephraim's Idolatry

13 When Ephraim spoke, *there was*
trembling.
He exalted himself in Israel,
But through Baal he incurred guilt and
died.

2 And now they sin more and more,
And make for themselves cast metal
images,
Idols skillfully made from their silver,
All of them the work of craftsmen.
They say of them, "Let the people who
sacrifice kiss the calves!"

3 Therefore they will be like the morning
cloud
And like dew which soon disappears,
Like chaff which is blown away from the
threshing floor,
And like smoke from a chimney.

4¶ Yet I *have been* the LORD your God
Since the land of Egypt;
And you were not to know any god except
Me,
For there is no savior besides Me.

5 I cared for you in the wilderness,
In the land of drought.

6 As *they had* their pasture, they became
satisfied,
And as they became satisfied, their heart
became proud;
Therefore they forgot Me.

7 So I will be like a lion to them;
Like a leopard I will lie in wait by the
wayside.

8 I will confront them like a bear deprived
of her cubs,
And I will tear open their chests;
I will also devour them there like a
lioness,
As a wild animal would tear them to
pieces.

9¶ It is to your own destruction, Israel,
That *you are* against Me, against your
help.

10 Where then is your king,
That he might save you in all your cities;
And your judges, to whom you said,
"Give me a king and princes"?

11 I gave you a king in My anger,
And took him away in My wrath.

12¶ The guilt of Ephraim is wrapped up;
His sin is stored up.

13 The pains of childbirth come on him;
He is not a wise son,
For it is not the time that he should delay
at the opening of the womb.

14 Shall I ransom them from the power of
Sheol?
Shall I redeem them from death?
Death, where are your thorns?

Sheol, where is your sting?
Compassion will be hidden from My sight.

15¶ Though he flourishes among the reeds,
An east wind will come,
The wind of the LORD coming up from the
wilderness;
And his fountain will become dry
And his spring will dry up;
It will plunder *his* treasury of every
precious article.

16 Samaria will pay the penalty for her guilt,
Because she has rebelled against her God.
They will fall by the sword,
Their children will be slaughtered,
And their pregnant women will be ripped
open.

Israel's Future Blessing

14 Return, Israel, to the LORD your God,
For you have stumbled because of your
wrongdoing.

2 Take words with you and return to the
LORD.
Say to Him, "Take away all guilt
And receive *us* graciously,
So that we may present the fruit of our
lips.

3 "Assyria will not save us,
We will not ride on horses;
Nor will we say again, 'Our god'
To the work of our hands;
For in You the orphan finds mercy."

4¶ I will heal their apostasy,
I will love them freely,
Because My anger has turned away from
them.

5 I will be like the dew to Israel;
He will blossom like the lily,
And he will take root like *the cedars of*
Lebanon.

6 His shoots will sprout,
His majesty will be like the olive tree,
And his fragrance like *the cedars of*
Lebanon.

7 Those who live in his shadow
Will again raise grain,
And they will blossom like the vine.
His fame *will be* like the wine of Lebanon.

8¶ Ephraim, what more have I to do with
idols?
It is I who answer and look after you.
I am like a luxuriant juniper;
From Me comes your fruit.

9¶ Whoever is wise, let him understand
these things;
Whoever is discerning, let him know
them.
For the ways of the LORD are right,
And the righteous will walk in them,
But wrongdoers will stumble in them.

The Book of
JOEL

The Devastation by Locusts

1 The word of the LORD that came to Joel, the son of Pethuel:

2 Hear this, you elders,
And listen, all inhabitants of the land.
Has *anything like* this happened in your days,
Or in your fathers' days?

3 Tell your sons about it,
And *have* your sons *tell* their sons,
And their sons the next generation.

4¶ What the gnawing locust has left, the swarming locust has eaten;
And what the swarming locust has left, the creeping locust has eaten;
And what the creeping locust has left, the stripping locust has eaten.

5 Awake, you heavy drinkers, and weep;
And wail, all you wine drinkers,
Because of the sweet wine,
For it has been eliminated from your mouth.

6 For a nation has invaded my land,
Mighty and without number;
Its teeth are the teeth of a lion,
And it has the jaws of a lioness.

7 It has made my vine a waste
And my fig tree a stump.
It has stripped them bare and hurled *them* away;
Their branches have become white.

8¶ Wail like a virgin clothed with sackcloth
For the groom of her youth.

9 The grain offering and the drink offering have been cut off
From the house of the LORD.
The priests mourn,
The ministers of the LORD.

10 The field is ruined,
The land mourns;
For the grain is ruined,
The new wine has dried up,
Fresh oil has failed.

11 Be ashamed, you farm workers,
Wail, you vinedressers,
For the wheat and the barley;
Because the harvest of the field is destroyed.

12 The vine has dried up
And the fig tree has withered;
The pomegranate, the palm also, and the apple tree,
All the trees of the field have dried up.
Indeed, joy has dried up
From the sons of mankind.

13¶ Put on *sackcloth*
And mourn, you priests;
Wail, you ministers of the altar!
Come, spend the night in sackcloth,
You ministers of my God,
For the grain offering and the drink offering

Have been withheld from the house of your God.

Starvation and Drought

14 Consecrate a fast,
Proclaim a solemn assembly;
Gather the elders
And all the inhabitants of the land
To the house of the LORD your God,
And cry out to the LORD.

15 Woe for the day!
For the day of the LORD is near,
And it will come as destruction from the Almighty.

16 Has food not been cut off before our eyes,
and
Joy and rejoicing from the house of our God?

17 The seeds have dried up under their shovels;
The storehouses have become desolate,
The grain silos are ruined,
Because the grain has dried up.

18 How the animals have groaned!
The herds of cattle have wandered aimlessly
Because there is no pasture for them;
Even the flocks of sheep have suffered.

19 To You, LORD, I cry out;
For fire has devoured the pastures of the wilderness,
And the flame has burned up all the trees of the field.

20 Even the animals of the field pant for You;
For the stream beds of water are dried up,
And fire has devoured the pastures of the wilderness.

The Terrible Visitation

2 Blow a trumpet in Zion,
And sound an alarm on My holy mountain!
Let all the inhabitants of the land tremble,
For the day of the LORD is coming;
Indeed, it is near,

2 A day of darkness and gloom,
A day of clouds and thick darkness.
As dawn is spread over the mountains,
So there is a great and mighty people;
There has never been *anything* like it,
Nor will there be again after it
To the years of many generations.

3 A fire consumes before them,
And behind them a flame devours.
The land is like the Garden of Eden before them,
But a desolate wilderness behind them,
And nothing at all escapes them.

4 Their appearance is like the appearance of horses;
And like war horses, so they run.

5 With a noise as of chariots
They leap about on the tops of the mountains,

Like the crackling of a flame of fire
consuming the stubble,
Like a mighty people drawn up for battle.
6 Before them the people are in anguish;
All faces turn pale.
7 They run like warriors,
They climb the wall like soldiers;
And each of them marches in line,
Nor do they lose their way.
8 They do not crowd each other,
Every warrior of them marches in his
path;
When they burst through the defenses,
They do not break ranks.
9 They storm the city,
They run on the wall;
They climb into the houses,
They enter through the windows like a
thief.
10 Before them the earth quakes,
The heavens tremble,
The sun and the moon become dark,
And the stars lose their brightness.
11 The LORD utters His voice before His
army;
His camp is indeed very great,
For mighty is one who carries out His
word.
The day of the LORD is indeed great and
very awesome,
And who can endure it?
12 "Yet even now," declares the LORD,
"Return to Me with all your heart,
And with fasting, weeping, and mourning;
13 And tear your heart and not *merely* your
garments."
Now return to the LORD your God,
For He is gracious and compassionate,
Slow to anger, abounding in mercy
And relenting of catastrophe.
14 Who knows, He might turn and relent,
And leave a blessing behind Him,
Resulting in a grain offering and a drink
offering
For the LORD your God.
15 Blow a trumpet in Zion,
Consecrate a fast, proclaim a solemn
assembly,
16 Gather the people, sanctify the
congregation,
Assemble the elders,
Gather the children and the nursing
infants.
Have the groom come out of his room
And the bride out of her bridal chamber.
17 Let the priests, the LORD's ministers,
Weep between the porch and the altar,
And let them say, "Spare Your people,
LORD,
And do not make Your inheritance a dis-
grace,
With the nations jeering at them.
Why should *those* among the peoples say,
'Where is their God?' "

Deliverance Promised

18¶ Then the LORD will be zealous for His
land,
And will have compassion for His people.

19 The LORD will answer and say to His
people,
"Behold, I am going to send you grain, new
wine, and oil,
And you will be satisfied *in full* with
them;
And I will never again make you a
disgrace among the nations.
20 "But I will remove the northern *army* far
from you,
And I will drive it into a dry and desolate
land,
Its advance guard into the eastern sea,
And its rear guard into the western sea.
And its stench will ascend and its odor of
decay will come up,
Because it has done great things."
21¶ Do not fear, land; shout for joy and
rejoice,
For the LORD has done great things.
22 Do not fear, animals of the field,
For the pastures of the wilderness have
turned green,
For the tree has produced its fruit,
The fig tree and the vine have yielded in
full.
23 So shout for joy, you sons of Zion,
And rejoice in the LORD your God;
For He has given you ¹the early rain for
your vindication.
And He has brought down for you the
rain,
The ²early and ³latter rain as before.
24 The threshing floors will be full of grain,
And the vats will overflow with the new
wine and oil.
25 "Then I will compensate you for the years
That the swarming locust has eaten,
The creeping locust, the stripping locust,
and the gnawing locust—
My great army which I sent among you.
26 "You will have plenty to eat and be
satisfied,
And you will praise the name of the LORD
your God,
Who has dealt wondrously with you;
Then My people will never be put to
shame.
27 "So you will know that I am in the midst of
Israel,
And that I am the LORD your God
And there is no other;
And My people will never be put to
shame.

The Promise of the Spirit

28¶ "It will come about after this
That I will pour out My Spirit on all
mankind;
And your sons and your daughters will
prophesy,
Your old men will have dreams,
Your young men will see visions.
29 "And even on the male and female servants
I will pour out My Spirit in those days.

The Day of the LORD

30 "I will display wonders in the sky and on
the earth,

2:23 ¹I.e., autumn; or possibly *the teacher for righteousness*   ²I.e., autumn   ³I.e., spring

Blood, fire, and columns of smoke.
31 "The sun will be turned into darkness,
And the moon into blood,
Before the great and awesome day of the
LORD comes.
32 "And it will come about *that* everyone who
calls on the name of the LORD
Will be saved;
For on Mount Zion and in Jerusalem
There will be those who escape,
Just as the LORD has said,
Even among the survivors whom the LORD
calls.

The Nations Will Be Judged

3 "For behold, in those days and at that time,
When I restore the fortunes of Judah and
Jerusalem,
2 I will gather all the nations
And bring them down to the Valley of
Jehoshaphat.
Then I will enter into judgment with
them there
On behalf of My people and My
inheritance, Israel,
Whom they have scattered among the
nations;
And they have divided up My land.
3 "They have also cast lots for My people,
Traded a boy for a prostitute,
And sold a girl for wine so that they may
drink.

4 Moreover, what are you to Me, Tyre, Sidon,
and all the regions of Philistia? Are you repaying Me with retribution? But if you are
showing Me *retribution,* swiftly and speedily I
will return your retribution on your head!
5 Since you have taken My silver and My gold,
brought My precious treasures to your temples,
6 and sold the sons of Judah and Jerusalem to
the Greeks in order to remove them far from
their territory, 7 behold, I am going to stir them
up from the place where you have sold them,
and return your retribution on your head. 8 I
will also sell your sons and your daughters into
the hand of the sons of Judah, and they will sell
them to the Sabeans, to a distant nation," for
the LORD has spoken.
9 ¶ Proclaim this among the nations:
Prepare for holy war; stir up the warriors!
Have all the soldiers come forward, have
them come up!
10 Beat your plowshares into swords,
And your pruning hooks into spears;

Let the weak *man* say, "I am a warrior."
11 Hurry and come, all you surrounding
nations,
And gather yourselves there.
Bring down, LORD, Your warriors.
12 Let the nations be awakened
And come up to the Valley of Jehoshaphat,
For there I will sit to judge
All the surrounding nations.
13 Put in the sickle, for the harvest is ripe.
Come, tread *the grapes,* for the wine
press is full;
The vats overflow, for their wickedness is
great.
14 Multitudes, multitudes in the valley of
decision!
For the day of the LORD is near in the
valley of decision.
15 The sun and moon have become dark,
And the stars have lost their brightness.
16 · The LORD roars from Zion
And utters His voice from Jerusalem,
And the heavens and the earth quake.
But the LORD is a refuge for His people,
And a stronghold for the sons of Israel.
17 Then you will know that I am the LORD
your God,
Dwelling on Zion, My holy mountain.
So Jerusalem will be holy,
And strangers will no longer pass through
it.

Judah Will Be Blessed

18 ¶ And on that day
The mountains will drip with sweet
wine,
And the hills will flow with milk,
And all the brooks of Judah will flow with
water;
And a spring will go out from the house of
the LORD
And water the Valley of Shittim.
19 Egypt will become a wasteland,
And Edom will become a desolate
wilderness,
Because of the violence done to the sons
of Judah,
In whose land they have shed innocent
blood.
20 But Judah will be inhabited forever,
And Jerusalem for all generations.
21 And I will avenge their blood *which* I
have not avenged,
For the LORD dwells in Zion.

The Book of
AMOS

Judgment on Neighbor Nations

1 The words of Amos, who was among the sheepherders from Tekoa, which he saw *in visions* concerning Israel in the days of Uzziah king of Judah, and in the days of Jeroboam son of Joash, king of Israel, two years before the earthquake.

2 And he said,
"The LORD roars from Zion,
And from Jerusalem He utters His voice;
And the shepherds' pasture grounds
    mourn,
And the summit of Carmel dries up."

3¶ This is what the LORD says:
"For three offenses of Damascus, and for
    four,
I will not revoke its *punishment,*
Because they threshed Gilead with iron
    sledges.

4 "So I will send fire upon the house of
    Hazael,
And it will consume the citadels of
    Ben-hadad.

5 "I will also break the *gate* bar of Damascus,
And eliminate *every* inhabitant from the
    Valley of Aven,
As well as him who holds the scepter,
    from Beth-eden;
So the people of Aram will be exiled to
    Kir,"
Says the LORD.

6¶ This is what the LORD says:
"For three offenses of Gaza, and for four,
I will not revoke its *punishment,*
Because they led into exile an entire
    population
To turn *them* over to Edom.

7 "So I will send fire on the wall of Gaza
And it will consume her citadels.

8 "I will also eliminate *every* inhabitant from
    Ashdod,
As well as him who holds the scepter,
    from Ashkelon;
And I will direct My power against Ekron,
And the remnant of the Philistines will
    perish,"
Says the Lord GOD.

9¶ This is what the LORD says:
"For three offenses of Tyre, and for four,
I will not revoke its *punishment,*
Because they turned an entire population
    over to Edom
And did not remember *the* covenant of
    brotherhood.

10 "So I will send fire on the wall of Tyre,
And it will consume her citadels."

11¶ This is what the LORD says:
"For three offenses of Edom, and for four,
I will not revoke its *punishment,*
Because he pursued his brother with the
    sword
And stifled his compassion;
His anger also tore continually,

And he maintained his fury forever.

12 "So I will send fire upon Teman
And it will consume the citadels of
    Bozrah."

13¶ This is what the LORD says:
"For three offenses of the sons of Ammon,
    and for four,
I will not revoke its *punishment,*
Because they ripped open the pregnant
    women of Gilead
In order to enlarge their borders.

14 "So I will kindle a fire on the wall of
    Rabbah,
And it will consume her citadels
Amid war cries on the day of battle,
And amid a storm on the day of tempest.

15 "Their king will go into exile,
He and his princes together," says the
    LORD.

Judgment on Moab

2 This is what the LORD says:
"For three offenses of Moab, and for four,
I will not revoke its *punishment,*
Because he burned the bones of the king
    of Edom to lime.

2 "So I will send fire upon Moab
And it will consume the citadels of
    Kerioth;
And Moab will die amid the panic *of bat-
    tle,*
Amid war cries and the sound of a
    trumpet.

3 "I will also eliminate the judge from her
    midst
And slay all her leaders with him," says
    the LORD.

Judgment on Judah

4¶ This is what the LORD says:
"For three offenses of Judah, and for four,
I will not revoke its *punishment,*
Because they rejected the Law of the
    LORD
And have not kept His statutes;
Their lies also have led them astray,
Those which their fathers followed.

5 "So I will send fire upon Judah,
And it will consume the citadels of
    Jerusalem."

Judgment on Israel

6¶ This is what the LORD says:
"For three offenses of Israel, and for four,
I will not revoke its *punishment,*
Because they sell the righteous for money,
And the needy for a pair of sandals.

7 "These who trample the head of the help-
    less to the dust of the earth
Also divert the way of the humble;
And a man and his father resort to the
    same girl
So as to profane My holy name.

8 "And on garments seized as pledges they
  stretch out beside every altar,
  And *in* the house of their God they drink
  the wine of those who have been
  fined.

9¶ "Yet it was I who destroyed the Amorite
  before them,
  Though his height *was* like the height of
  cedars
  And he *was as* strong as the oaks;
  I also destroyed his fruit above and his
  roots below.

10 "And it was I who brought you up from the
  land of Egypt,
  And led you in the wilderness for forty
  years
  So that you might take possession of the
  land of the Amorite.

11 "Then I raised up some of your sons to be
  prophets,
  And some of your young men to be
  Nazirites.
  Is this not so, you sons of Israel?" declares
  the LORD.

12 "But you made the Nazirites drink wine,
  And you commanded the prophets,
  saying, 'You shall not prophesy!'

13 "Behold, I am making a rut *in the ground*
  beneath you,
  Just as a wagon makes a rut when filled
  with sheaves.

14 "Refuge will be lost from the swift,
  And the strong will not strengthen his
  power,
  Nor the warrior save his life.

15 "The one who grasps the bow will not
  stand *his ground,*
  The swift of foot will not escape,
  Nor will the one who rides the horse save
  his life.

16 "Even the bravest among the warriors will
  flee naked on that day," declares the
  LORD.

All the Tribes Are Guilty

3 Hear this word which the LORD has spoken
  against you, sons of Israel, against the entire
family which He brought up from the land of
Egypt:

2 "You only have I known among all the
  families of the earth;
  Therefore I will punish you for all your
  wrongdoing."

3 Do two people walk together unless they
  have agreed to meet?

4 Does a lion roar in the forest when he has
  no prey?
  Does a young lion growl from his den
  unless he has captured *something?*

5 Does a bird fall into a trap on the ground
  when there is no device in it?
  Does a trap spring up from the earth
  when it captures nothing at all?

6 If a trumpet is blown in a city, will the
  people not tremble?
  If a disaster occurs in a city, has the LORD
  not brought it about?

7 Certainly the Lord GOD does nothing
  Unless He reveals His secret plan
  To His servants the prophets.

8 A lion has roared! Who will not fear?
  The Lord GOD has spoken! Who can *do*
  anything but prophesy?

9 Proclaim on the citadels in Ashdod and on
the citadels in the land of Egypt and say,
"Assemble yourselves on the mountains of
Samaria and see *the* great panic within her and
the oppressions in her midst. 10 But they do not
know how to do what is right," declares the
LORD, "these who store up violence and
devastation in their citadels."

11 Therefore, this is what the Lord GOD says:
"An enemy, one surrounding the land,
  Will take down your fortifications from
  you,
  And your citadels will be looted."

12 This is what the LORD says:
"Just as the shepherd snatches from the
  lion's mouth a couple of legs or a piece
  of an ear,
  So will the sons of Israel living in Samaria
  be snatched away—
  With *the* corner of a bed and *the* cover of
  a couch!

13 "Hear and testify against the house of
  Jacob,"
  Declares the Lord GOD, the God of armies.

14 "For on the day that I punish Israel's
  offenses,
  I will also punish the altars of Bethel;
  The horns of the altar will be cut off,
  And will fall to the ground.

15 "I will also strike the winter house together
  with the summer house;
  The houses of ivory will also perish,
  And the great houses will come to an
  end,"
  Declares the LORD.

"Yet You Have Not Returned to Me"

4 Hear this word, you cows of Bashan who
  are on the mountain of Samaria,
  Who exploit the poor, who oppress the
  needy,
  And say to their husbands, "Bring now,
  that we may drink!"

2 The Lord GOD has sworn by His holiness,
  "For behold, the days are coming upon you
  When they will take you away with *meat*
  hooks,
  And the last of you with fish hooks.

3 "You will go out *through* holes *in the walls,*
  One in front of the other,
  And you will be hurled to Harmon,"
  declares the LORD.

4¶ "Enter Bethel and do wrong;
  In Gilgal multiply wrongdoing!
  Bring your sacrifices every morning,
  Your tithes every three days.

5 "Offer a thanksgiving offering also from
  that which is leavened,
  And proclaim voluntary offerings, make
  them known.
  For so you love *to do,* you sons of Israel,"
  Declares the Lord GOD.

6¶ "But I gave you also cleanness of teeth in
  all your cities,
  And lack of bread in all your places;
  Yet you have not returned to Me,"
  declares the LORD.

7 "Furthermore, I withheld the rain from you
　　While *there were* still three months until
　　harvest.
　　Then I would send rain on one city,
　　But on another city I would not send rain;
　　One part would be rained on,
　　While the part not rained on would dry
　　up.
8 "So *the people of* two *or* three cities would
　　stagger to another city to drink water,
　　But would not be satisfied;
　　Yet you have not returned to Me,"
　　declares the LORD.
9 "I struck you with scorching *wind* and
　　mildew;
　　The caterpillar was devouring
　　Your many gardens and vineyards, fig
　　trees and olive trees;
　　Yet you have not returned to Me,"
　　declares the LORD.
10 "I sent a plague among you as in Egypt;
　　I killed your young men with the sword,
　　along with your captured horses,
　　And I made the stench of your camp rise
　　up in your nostrils;
　　Yet you have not returned to Me,"
　　declares the LORD.
11 "I overthrew you, as God overthrew Sodom
　　and Gomorrah,
　　And you were like a log snatched from a
　　fire;
　　Yet you have not returned to Me,"
　　declares the LORD.
12 "Therefore so I will do to you, Israel;
　　Because I will do this to you,
　　Prepare to meet your God, Israel."
13 For behold, He who forms mountains and
　　creates the wind,
　　And declares to a person what are His
　　thoughts,
　　He who makes dawn into darkness
　　And treads on the high places of the earth,
　　The LORD God of armies is His name.

"Seek Me So That You May Live"

5 Hear this word which I am taking up for
you as a song of mourning, house of Israel:
2　　She has fallen, she will not rise again—
　　The virgin Israel.
　　She lies unnoticed on her land;
　　There is no one to raise her up.
3 For this is what the Lord GOD says:
　　"The city which goes forth a thousand
　　strong
　　Will have a hundred left,
　　And the one which goes forth a hundred
　　strong
　　Will have ten left to the house of Israel."
4 For this is what the LORD says to the house
of Israel:
　　"Seek Me so that you may live.
5　　"But do not resort to Bethel
　　And do not come to Gilgal,
　　Nor cross over to Beersheba;
　　For Gilgal will certainly go into captivity
　　And Bethel will come to nothing.
6　　"Seek the LORD so that you may live,
　　Or He will break through like a fire,
　　house of Joseph,

And it will consume with no one to extin-
　　guish *it* for Bethel,
7　　*For* those who turn justice into worm-
　　wood,
　　And throw righteousness to the earth."
8¶ He who made the Pleiades and Orion,
　　And changes deep darkness into morning,
　　Who also darkens day *into* night,
　　Who calls for the waters of the sea
　　And pours them out on the surface of the
　　earth,
　　The LORD is His name.
9　　*It is* He who makes destruction flash upon
　　the strong,
　　So that destruction comes upon the for-
　　tress.
10¶ They hate him who rebukes in the ¹gate,
　　And they despise him who speaks *with*
　　integrity.
11　　Therefore because you impose heavy rent
　　on the poor
　　And take a tribute of grain from them,
　　Though you have built houses of cut
　　stone,
　　Yet you will not live in them;
　　You have planted beautiful vineyards, yet
　　you will not drink their wine.
12　　For I know your offenses are many and
　　your sins are great,
　　You who are hostile to the righteous *and*
　　accept bribes,
　　And turn away the poor *from justice* at
　　the gate.
13　　Therefore at such a time the prudent
　　person keeps quiet, because it is an
　　evil time.
14¶ Seek good and not evil, so that you may
　　live;
　　And so may the LORD God of armies be
　　with you,
　　Just as you have said!
15　　Hate evil, love good,
　　And establish justice in the gate!
　　Perhaps the LORD God of armies
　　Will be gracious to the remnant of
　　Joseph.
16 Therefore this is what the LORD God of
armies, the Lord says:
　　"There is mourning in all the public
　　squares,
　　And in all the streets they say, 'Oh no! Oh
　　no!'
　　They also call the farmer to mourning
　　And professional mourners to mourning
　　rites.
17　　"And in all the vineyards *there is*
　　mourning,
　　Because I will pass through the midst of
　　you," says the LORD.
18¶ Woe *to* you who are longing for the day of
　　the LORD,
　　For what purpose *will* the day of the LORD
　　be to you?
　　It *will be* darkness and not light;
19　　As when a man flees from a lion
　　And a bear confronts him,
　　Or he goes home, leans with his hand
　　against the wall,
　　And a snake bites him.

5:10 ¹I.e., the place where court was held

20 *Will* the day of the LORD not *be* darkness
instead of light,
Even gloom with no brightness in it?
21¶ "I hate, I reject your festivals,
Nor do I delight in your festive
assemblies.
22 "Even though you offer up to Me burnt
offerings and your grain offerings,
I will not accept *them;*
And I will not *even* look at the peace
offerings of your fattened oxen.
23 "Take away from Me the noise of your
songs;
I will not even listen to the sound of your
harps.
24 "But let justice roll out like waters,
And righteousness like an ever-flowing
stream.
25 "Did you present Me with sacrifices and
grain offerings in the wilderness for forty
years, house of Israel? 26 You also carried along
Sikkuth your king and Kiyyun, your images,
the star of your gods which you made for yourselves. 27 Therefore I will make you go into
exile beyond Damascus," says the LORD, whose
name is the God of armies.

"Carefree in Zion"

6 Woe to those who are carefree in Zion,
And to those who feel secure on the
mountain of Samaria,
The dignitaries of the foremost of nations,
To whom the house of Israel comes.
2 Go over to Calneh and look,
And go from there to Hamath the great,
Then go down to Gath of the Philistines.
Are they better than these kingdoms,
Or is their territory greater than yours?
3 Are you postponing the day of disaster,
And would you bring near the seat of
violence?
4¶ Those who lie on beds of ivory,
And lounge around on their couches,
And eat lambs from the flock,
And calves from the midst of the fattened
cattle,
5 Who improvise to the sound of the harp,
And like David have composed songs for
themselves,
6 Who drink wine from sacred bowls
While they anoint themselves with the
finest of oils—
Yet they have not grieved over the
collapse of Joseph.
7 Therefore, they will now go into exile at
the head of the exiles,
And the revelry of those who lounge
around will come to an end.
8¶ The Lord GOD has sworn by Himself, the
LORD God of armies has declared:
"I loathe the arrogance of Jacob,
And detest his citadels;
Therefore I will give up *the* city and all it
contains."
9 And it will be, if ten men are left in one
house, they will die. 10 Then one's uncle, or his
undertaker, will lift him up to carry out *his*
bones from the house, and he will say to the
one who is in the innermost part of the house,

"Is anyone else with you?" And that one will
say, "No one." Then he will answer, "Keep
quiet! For the name of the LORD is not to be
mentioned." 11 For behold, the LORD is going to
command that the great house be smashed to
pieces, and the small house to rubble.
12¶ Do horses run on rocks?
Or does one plow *them* with oxen?
Yet you have turned justice into poison,
And the fruit of righteousness
into ¹wormwood,
13 You who rejoice in ¹Lodebar,
And say, "Have we not by our *own*
strength taken ²Karnaim for
ourselves?"
14 "For behold, I am going to raise up a nation
against you,
House of Israel," declares the LORD God of
armies,
"And they will torment you from the
entrance of Hamath
To the brook of the Arabah."

Warning through Visions

7 This is what the Lord GOD showed me, and
behold, He was forming a swarm of locusts
when the spring crop began to sprout. And
behold, the spring crop *was* after the king's
mowing. 2 And it came about, when it had
finished eating the vegetation of the land, that
I said,
"Lord GOD, please pardon!
How can Jacob stand?
For he is small."
3 The LORD relented of this.
"It shall not be," said the LORD.
4 So the Lord GOD showed me, and behold,
the Lord GOD was calling to contend *with them*
by fire, and it consumed the great deep and
began to consume the farmland. 5 Then I said,
"Lord GOD, please stop!
How can Jacob stand?
For he is small."
6 The LORD relented of this.
"This too shall not be," said the Lord GOD.
7 So He showed me, and behold, the Lord
was standing by a vertical wall with a plumb
line in His hand. 8 And the LORD said to me,
"What do you see, Amos?" And I said, "A
plumb line." Then the Lord said,
"Behold I am about to put a plumb line
In the midst of My people Israel.
I will not spare them any longer.
9 "The high places of Isaac will become
deserted,
And the sanctuaries of Israel will be in
ruins.
Then I will rise up against the house of
Jeroboam with the sword."

Amos Accused; Gives an Answer

10 Then Amaziah, the priest of Bethel, sent
word to Jeroboam king of Israel, saying, "Amos
has conspired against you in the midst of the
house of Israel; the land is unable to endure
all his words. 11 For this is what Amos says:
'Jeroboam will die by the sword, and Israel will
certainly go from its land into exile.' " 12 Then
Amaziah said to Amos, "Go, you seer, flee to

6:12 ¹ I.e., bitterness   **6:13** ¹ Lit *nothing*   ² Lit *a pair of horns*

the land of Judah; and eat bread there and do your prophesying there! **13** But do not prophesy at Bethel any longer, for it is a sanctuary of the king and a royal residence."

14 Then Amos replied to Amaziah, "I am not a prophet, nor am I the son of a prophet; for I am a herdsman and a grower of sycamore figs. **15** But the LORD took me from following the flock, and the LORD said to me, 'Go prophesy to My people Israel.' **16** So now hear the word of the LORD: you are saying, 'You shall not prophesy against Israel nor shall you prophesy against the house of Isaac.' **17** Therefore, this is what the LORD says: 'Your wife will become a prostitute in the city, your sons and your daughters will fall by the sword, your land will be parceled up by a *measuring* line, and you yourself will die upon unclean soil. Furthermore Israel will certainly go from its land into exile.'"

Basket of Fruit and Israel's Captivity

8 This is what the Lord GOD showed me, and behold, *there was* a basket of summer fruit. **2** And He said, "What do you see, Amos?" And I said, "A basket of summer fruit." Then the LORD said to me, "The end has come for My people Israel. I will not spare them any longer. **3** The songs of the palace will turn to wailing on that day," declares the Lord GOD. "The corpses *will be* many; in every place they will throw them out. Hush!"

4 Hear this, you who trample the needy, to put an end to the humble of the land, **5** saying,
"When will the new moon be over,
  So that we may sell grain;
And the Sabbath, so that we may open the
  wheat *market,*
To make the ¹ephah smaller and the ·
  ²shekel bigger,
And to cheat with dishonest scales,
6 So as to buy the helpless for money,
  And the needy for a pair of sandals,
And *that* we may sell the refuse of the
  wheat?"
7¶ The LORD has sworn by the pride of
  Jacob,
"Indeed, I will never forget any of their
  deeds.
8 "Because of this will the land not quake,
And everyone who lives in it mourn?
Indeed, all of it will rise up like the Nile,
And it will be tossed about
And subside like the Nile of Egypt.
9 "And it will come about on that day,"
  declares the Lord GOD,
"That I will make the sun go down at noon,
And make the earth dark in broad day-
  light.
10 "Then I will turn your festivals into
  mourning,
And all your songs into songs of
  mourning;
And I will put sackcloth around
  everyone's waist,
And baldness on every head.
And I will make it like *a time of* mourning
  for an only son,
And the end of it will be like a bitter day.

11¶ "Behold, days are coming," declares the
  Lord GOD,
"When I will send a famine on the land,
Not a famine of bread or a thirst for water,
But rather for hearing the words of the
  LORD.
12 "People will stagger from sea to sea
And from the north even to the east;
They will roam about to seek the word of
  the LORD,
But they will not find *it.*
13 "On that day the beautiful virgins
And the young men will faint from thirst.
14 "*As for* those who swear by the guilt of
  Samaria,
And say, 'As your god lives, Dan,'
And, 'As the way of Beersheba lives,'
They will fall and not rise again."

God's Judgment Unavoidable

9 I saw the Lord standing beside the altar, and He said,
"Strike the pillar capitals so that the
  thresholds will shake,
And break them on the heads of them all!
Then I will put to death the rest of them
  with the sword;
They will not have a fugitive who will flee,
Nor a survivor who will escape.
2 "Though they dig into Sheol,
From there My hand will take them;
And though they ascend to heaven,
From there I will bring them down.
3 "And though they hide on the summit of
  Carmel,
I will track them down and take them
  from there;
And though they hide themselves from
  My sight on the bottom of the sea,
I will command the serpent from there,
  and it will bite them.
4 "And though they go into captivity before
  their enemies,
From there I will command the sword and
  it will kill them,
And I will set My eyes against them for
  harm and not for good."
5¶ The Lord GOD of armies,
The One who touches the land so that it
  quakes,
And all those who live in it mourn,
And all of it rises up like the Nile
And subsides like the Nile of Egypt;
6 The One who builds His upper chambers
  in the heavens
And has founded His vaulted dome over
  the earth,
He who calls for the waters of the sea
And pours them out on the face of the
  earth,
The LORD is His name.
7¶ "Are you not as the sons of Ethiopia to Me,
You sons of Israel?" declares the LORD.
"Have I not brought up Israel from the land
  of Egypt,
And the Philistines from Caphtor and the
  Arameans from Kir?
8 "Behold, the eyes of the Lord GOD are on
  the sinful kingdom,

8:5 ¹About 1 cubic foot or 0.03 cubic meters   ²About 0.5 oz. or 14 gm

And I will eliminate it from the face of the earth;
Nevertheless, I will not totally eliminate the house of Jacob,"
Declares the LORD.

9 "For behold, I am commanding,
And I will shake the house of Israel among all nations
As *grain* is shaken in a sieve,
But not a pebble will fall to the ground.

10 "All the sinners of My people will die by the sword,
Those who say, 'The catastrophe will not overtake or confront us.'

The Restoration of Israel

11¶ "On that day I will raise up the fallen shelter of David,
And wall up its gaps;
I will also raise up its ruins
And rebuild it as in the days of old;

12 So that they may possess the remnant of Edom

And all the nations who are called by My name,"
Declares the LORD who does this.

13¶ "Behold, days are coming," declares the LORD,
"When the plowman will overtake the reaper,
And the one who treads grapes *will overtake* him who sows the seed;
When the mountains will drip grape juice,
And all the hills will come apart.

14 "I will also restore the fortunes of My people Israel,
And they will rebuild the desolated cities and live *in them;*
They will also plant vineyards and drink their wine,
And make gardens and eat their fruit.

15 "I will also plant them on their land,
And they will not be uprooted again from their land
Which I have given them,"
Says the LORD your God.

The Book of
OBADIAH

Edom Will Be Humbled

1 The vision of Obadiah. This is what the Lord GOD says concerning Edom—
We have heard a report from the LORD,
And a messenger has been sent among the nations *saying,*
"Arise, and let's go up against her for battle"—

2 "Behold, I will make you small among the nations;
You are greatly despised.

3 "The arrogance of your heart has deceived you,
The one who lives in the clefts of the rock,
On the height of his dwelling place,
Who says in his heart,
'Who will bring me down to earth?'

4 "Though you make *your home* high like the eagle,
Though you set your nest among the stars,
From there I will bring you down,"
declares the LORD.

5 "If thieves came to you,
If robbers by night—
Oh how you will be ruined!—
Would they not steal *only* until they had enough?
If grape-pickers came to you,
Would they not leave *some* gleanings?

6 "Oh how Esau will be searched,
And his hidden treasures searched out!

7 "All the people allied with you
Will send you to the border,
And the people at peace with you
Will deceive you *and* overpower you.
They who eat your bread
Will set an ambush for you.
(There is no understanding in him.)

8 "Will I not on that day," declares the LORD,
"Eliminate wise men from Edom,
And understanding from the mountain of Esau?

9 "Then your warriors will be filled with terror, Teman,
So that everyone will be eliminated from the mountain of Esau by murder.

10¶ "Because of violence to your brother Jacob,
Shame will cover you,
And you will be eliminated forever.

11 "On the day that you stood aloof,
On the day that strangers carried off his wealth,
And foreigners entered his gate
And cast lots for Jerusalem—
You too were as one of them.

12 "Do not gloat over your brother's day,
The day of his misfortune,

And do not rejoice over the sons of Judah
On the day of their destruction;
Yes, do not boast
On the day of *their* distress.

13 "Do not enter the gate of My people
On the day of their disaster.
You indeed, do not gloat over their catastrophe
On the day of their disaster.
And do not lay *a hand* on their wealth
On the day of their disaster.

14 "Do not stand at the crossroads
To eliminate their survivors;
And do not hand over their refugees
On the day of their distress.

The Day of the LORD and the Future

15¶ "For the day of the LORD is near for all the nations.
Just as you have done, it will be done to you.
Your dealings will return on your own head.

16 "For just as you drank on My holy mountain,
All the nations will drink continually.
They will drink to the last drop,
And become as if they had never existed.

17 "But on Mount Zion there will be those who escape,
And it will be holy.
And the house of Jacob will possess their property.

18 "Then the house of Jacob will be a fire,
And the house of Joseph a flame;
But the house of Esau *will be* like stubble.
And they will set them on fire and consume them,
So that there will be no survivor of the house of Esau,"
For the LORD has spoken.

19 Then *those of* the ¹Negev will possess the mountain of Esau,
And *those of* the ²Shephelah the Philistine *plain;*
Also, they will possess the territory of Ephraim and the territory of Samaria,
And Benjamin *the territory of* Gilead.

20 And the exiles of this army of the sons of Israel,
Who are *among* the Canaanites as far as Zarephath,
And the exiles of Jerusalem who are in Sepharad,
Will possess the cities of the Negev.

21 ¹The deliverers will ascend Mount Zion
To judge the mountain of Esau,
And the kingdom will be the LORD'S.

1:19 ¹I.e., South country   ²I.e., the foothills   **1:21** ¹Or with ancient versions *Those who are rescued*

The Book of
JONAH

Jonah's Disobedience

1 The word of the LORD came to Jonah the son of Amittai, saying, **2** "Arise, go to Nineveh, the great city, and cry out against it, because their wickedness has come up before Me." **3** But Jonah got up to flee to Tarshish from the presence of the LORD. So he went down to Joppa, found a ship that was going to Tarshish, paid the fare, and boarded it to go with them to Tarshish away from the presence of the LORD.

4 However, the LORD hurled a great wind on the sea and there was a great storm on the sea, so that the ship was about to break up. **5** Then the sailors became afraid and every man cried out to his god, and they hurled the cargo which was in the ship into the sea to lighten *it* for them. But Jonah had gone below into the stern of the ship, had lain down, and fallen sound asleep. **6** So the captain approached him and said, "How is it that you are sleeping? Get up, call on your god! Perhaps *your* god will be concerned about us so that we will not perish."

7 And each man said to his mate, "Come, let's cast lots so that we may find out on whose account this catastrophe *has struck* us." So they cast lots, and the lot fell on Jonah. **8** Then they said to him, "Tell us, now! On whose account *has* this catastrophe *struck* us? What is your occupation, and where do you come from? What is your country, and from what people are you?" **9** So he said to them, "I am a Hebrew, and I fear the LORD God of heaven who made the sea and the dry land."

10 Then the men became extremely afraid, and they said to him, "How could you do this?" For the men knew that he was fleeing from the presence of the LORD, because he had told them. **11** So they said to him, "What should we do to you so that the sea will become calm for us?"—for the sea was becoming increasingly stormy. **12** And he said to them, "Pick me up and hurl me into the sea. Then the sea will become calm for you, because I know that on account of me this great storm *has come* upon you." **13** However, the men rowed *desperately* to return to land, but they could not, because the sea was becoming *even* stormier against them. **14** Then they cried out to the LORD and said, "We earnestly pray, O LORD, do not let us perish on account of this man's life, and do not put innocent blood on us; for You, LORD, have done as You pleased."

15 So they picked up Jonah and hurled him into the sea, and the sea stopped its raging. **16** Then the men became extremely afraid of the LORD, and they offered a sacrifice to the LORD and made vows.

17 And the LORD designated a great fish to swallow Jonah, and Jonah was in the stomach of the fish for three days and three nights.

Jonah's Prayer

2 Then Jonah prayed to the LORD his God from the stomach of the fish, **2** and he said,

"I called out of my distress to the LORD,
And He answered me.
I called for help from the depth of Sheol;
You heard my voice.
3 "For You threw me into the deep,
Into the heart of the seas,
And the current flowed around me.
All Your breakers and waves passed over me.
4 "So I said, 'I have been cast out of Your sight.
Nevertheless I will look again toward Your holy temple.'
5 "Water encompassed me to the point of death.
The deep flowed around me,
Seaweed was wrapped around my head.
6 "I descended to the base of the mountains.
The earth *with* its bars *was* around me forever,
But You have brought up my life from the pit, LORD my God.
7 "While I was fainting away,
I remembered the LORD,
And my prayer came to You,
Into Your holy temple.
8 "Those who are followers of worthless idols
Abandon their faithfulness,
9 But I will sacrifice to You
With a voice of thanksgiving.
That which I have vowed I will pay.
Salvation is from the LORD."

10 Then the LORD commanded the fish, and it vomited Jonah up onto the dry land.

Nineveh Repents

3 Now the word of the LORD came to Jonah the second time, saying, **2** "Arise, go to Nineveh, the great city, and proclaim to it the proclamation which I am going to tell you." **3** So Jonah got up and went to Nineveh according to the word of the LORD. Now Nineveh was [1]an exceedingly large city, a three days' walk. **4** Then Jonah began to go through the city one day's walk; and he cried out and said, "Forty more days, and Nineveh will be overthrown."

5 Then the people of Nineveh believed in God; and they called a fast and put on sackcloth, from the greatest to the least of them. **6** When the word reached the king of Nineveh, he got up from his throne, removed his robe from himself, covered *himself* with sackcloth, and sat on the [1]dust. **7** And he issued a proclamation, and it said, "In Nineveh by the decree of the king and his nobles: No person, animal, herd, or flock is to taste anything. They are not to eat, or drink water. **8** But *every* person and animal must be covered with sackcloth; and *people* are to call on God

vehemently, and they are to turn, each one from his evil way, and from the violence which is in their hands. 9 Who knows, God may turn and relent, and turn from His burning anger so that we will not perish."

10 When God saw their deeds, that they turned from their evil way, then God relented of the disaster which He had declared He would bring on them. So He did not do *it*.

Jonah's Displeasure Rebuked

4 But it greatly displeased Jonah, and he became angry. 2 Then he prayed to the LORD and said, "Please LORD, was this not what I said when I was still in my *own* country? Therefore in anticipation *of this* I fled to Tarshish, since I knew that You are a gracious and compassionate God, slow to anger and abundant in mercy, and One who relents of disaster. 3 So now, LORD, please take my life from me, for death is better to me than life." 4 But the LORD said, "Do you have a good reason to be angry?"

5 Then Jonah left the city and sat down east of it. There he made a shelter for himself and sat under it in the shade, until he could see what would happen in the city. 6 So the LORD God designated a plant, and it grew up over Jonah to be a shade over his head, to relieve him of his discomfort. And Jonah was overjoyed about the plant. 7 But God designated a worm when dawn came the next day, and it attacked the plant and it withered. 8 And when the sun came up God designated a scorching east wind, and the sun beat down on Jonah's head so that he became faint, and he begged with *all* his soul to die, saying, "Death is better to me than life!"

9 But God said to Jonah, "Do you have a good reason to be angry about the plant?" And he said, "I have good reason to be angry, *even* to the point of death!" 10 Then the LORD said, "You had compassion on the plant, for which you did not work and *which* you did not cause to grow, which came up overnight and perished overnight. 11 Should I not also have compassion on Nineveh, the great city in which there are more than 120,000 people, who do not know *the difference* between their right hand and their left, *as well as* many animals?"

The Book of
MICAH

Destruction in Israel and Judah

1 The word of the LORD which came to Micah of Moresheth in the days of Jotham, Ahaz, *and* Hezekiah, kings of Judah, *and* which he saw regarding Samaria and Jerusalem.

2 Hear, you peoples, all of you;
Listen carefully, earth and all it contains,
And may the Lord GOD be a witness against you,
The Lord from His holy temple.

3 For behold, the LORD is coming forth from His place.
He will come down and tread on the high places of the earth.

4 The mountains will melt under Him
And the valleys will be split,
Like wax before the fire,
Like water poured down a steep place.

5 All this is due to the wrongdoing of Jacob
And the sins of the house of Israel.
What is the wrongdoing of Jacob?
Is it not Samaria?
What is the high place of Judah?
Is it not Jerusalem?

6 For I will make Samaria a heap of ruins in the open country,
Planting places for a vineyard.
I will hurl her stones down into the valley,
And lay bare her foundations.

7 All of her idols will be crushed,
All of her earnings will be burned with fire,
And all of her images I will make desolate;
For she collected *them* from a prostitute's earnings,
And to the earnings of a prostitute they will return.

8¶ Because of this I must mourn and wail,
I must go barefoot and naked;
I must do mourning like the jackals,
And a mourning like the ostriches.

9 For her wound is incurable,
For it has come to Judah;
It has reached the gate of my people,
Even to Jerusalem.

10 Do not tell *it* in Gath,
Do not weep at all.
At ¹Beth-le-aphrah roll yourself in the dust in mourning.

11 Go on your way, inhabitant of ¹Shaphir, in shameful nakedness.
The inhabitant of ²Zaanan does not escape.
The mourning of ³Beth-ezel: "He will take from you its support."

12 For the inhabitant of ¹Maroth
Waits for *something* good,
Because a disaster has come down from the LORD
To the gate of Jerusalem.

13 Harness the chariot to the team of horses,

You inhabitant of Lachish—
She was the beginning of sin
To the daughter of Zion—
Because in you were found
The rebellious acts of Israel.

14 Therefore you will give parting gifts
In behalf of Moresheth-gath;
The houses of Achzib *will* become a deception
To the kings of Israel.

15 Moreover, I will bring on you
The one who takes possession,
You inhabitant of ¹Mareshah.
The glory of Israel will enter Adullam.

16 Shave yourself bald, yes, cut off your hair,
Because of the children of your delight;
Extend your baldness like the eagle,
For they will go from you into exile.

Woe to Oppressors

2 Woe to those who devise wrongdoing,
Who practice evil on their beds!
When morning comes, they do it,
Because it is in the power of their hands.

2 They covet fields, so they seize *them;*
And houses, so they take *them.*
They exploit a man and his house,
A person and his inheritance.

3 Therefore this is what the LORD says:
"Behold, I am planning against this family a catastrophe
From which you cannot remove your necks;
And you will not walk haughtily,
For it will be an evil time.

4 "On that day they will take up against you a song of mocking
And utter a song of mourning *and* say,
'We are completely destroyed!
He exchanges the share of my people;
How He removes it from me!
To the apostate He apportions our fields.'

5 "Therefore you will have no one applying a measuring line
For you by lot in the assembly of the LORD.

6¶ 'Do not prophesy,' *so* they prophesy.
But if they do not prophesy about these things,
Insults will not be turned back.

7 "Is it being said, house of Jacob:
'Is the Spirit of the LORD impatient?
Are these His works?'
Do My words not do good
For the one walking rightly?

8 "Recently My people have arisen as an enemy—
You strip the robe off the garment
From unsuspecting passers-by,
From those returned from war.

9 "You evict the women of My people,

1:10 ¹I.e., house of dust   **1:11** ¹I.e., pleasantness   ²I.e., going out   ³I.e., the house beside
1:12 ¹I.e., bitterness   **1:15** ¹I.e., possession

Each one from her pleasant house.
From her children you take My splendor
forever.
10 "Arise and go,
For this is no place of rest
Because of the uncleanness that brings on
destruction,
A painful destruction.
11 "If someone walking *after* wind and
falsehood
Had lied *and said,*
'I will prophesy to you about wine and
liquor,'
He would become a prophet to this
people.
12¶ "I will certainly assemble all of you, Jacob,
I will certainly gather the remnant of
Israel.
I will put them together like sheep in the
fold;
Like a flock in the midst of its pasture
They will be noisy with people.
13 "The one who breaks through goes up
before them;
They break through, pass through the
gate, and go out by it.
So their king passes on before them,
And the LORD at their head."

Rulers Denounced

3 And I said,
"Hear now, you leaders of Jacob
And rulers of the house of Israel:
Is it not for you to know justice?
2 "You who hate good and love evil,
Who tear off their skin from them
And their flesh from their bones,
3 Who eat the flesh of my people,
Strip off their skin from them,
Smash their bones,
And chop *them* up as for the pot,
And as meat in a cauldron!"
4 Then they will cry out to the LORD,
But He will not answer them.
Instead, He will hide His face from them
at that time
Because they have practiced evil deeds.
5 This is what the LORD says concerning the
prophets who lead my people astray:
When they have *something* to bite with
their teeth,
They cry out, "Peace!"
But against him who puts nothing in their
mouths
They declare holy war.
6 Therefore *it will be* night for you—with-
out vision,
And darkness for you—without
divination.
The sun will go down on the prophets,
And the day will become dark over
them.
7 The seers will be put to shame,
And the diviners will be ashamed.
Indeed, they will all cover *their* lips
Because there is no answer from God.
8 On the other hand, I am filled with
power—
With the Spirit of the LORD—
And with justice and courage

To make known to Jacob his rebellious
act,
And to Israel his sin.
9 Now hear this, you heads of the house of
Jacob
And rulers of the house of Israel,
Who despise justice
And twist everything that is straight,
10 Who build Zion with bloodshed,
And Jerusalem with malice.
11 Her leaders pronounce judgment for a
bribe,
Her priests teach for pay,
And her prophets divine for money.
Yet they lean on the LORD, saying,
"Is the LORD not in our midst?
Catastrophe will not come upon us."
12 Therefore on account of you,
Zion will be plowed *like* a field,
Jerusalem will become a heap of ruins,
And the mountain of the temple *will
become* high places of a forest.

Peaceful Latter Days

4 And it will come about in the last days
That the mountain of the house of the LORD
Will be established as the chief of the
mountains.
It will be raised above the hills,
And the peoples will stream to it.
2 Many nations will come and say,
"Come and let's go up to the mountain of
the LORD
And to the house of the God of Jacob,
So that He may teach us about His ways,
And that we may walk in His paths."
For from Zion will go forth the law,
And the word of the LORD from Jerusalem.
3 And He will judge between many peoples
And render decisions for mighty, distant
nations.
Then they will beat their swords into
plowshares,
And their spears into pruning hooks;
Nation will not lift a sword against nation,
And never again will they train for war.
4 Instead, each of them will sit under his
vine
And under his fig tree,
With no one to make *them* afraid,
Because the mouth of the LORD of armies
has spoken.
5 Though all the peoples walk,
Each in the name of his god,
As for us, we will walk
In the name of the LORD our God forever
and ever.
6¶ "On that day," declares the LORD,
"I will assemble those who limp
And gather the scattered,
Those whom I have afflicted.
7 "I will make those who limp a remnant,
And those who have strayed a mighty
nation,
And the LORD will reign over them on
Mount Zion
From now on and forever.
8 "As for you, tower of the flock,
Hill of the daughter of Zion,
To you it will come—

Yes, the former dominion will come,
The kingdom of the daughter of
Jerusalem.

9¶ "Now, why do you cry out loudly?
Is there no king among you,
Or has your counselor perished,
That agony has gripped you like a woman
in childbirth?

10 "Writhe and scream,
Daughter of Zion,
Like a woman in childbirth;
For now you will go out of the city,
Live in the field,
And go to Babylon.
There you will be rescued,
There the LORD will redeem you
From the hand of your enemies.

11 "And now many nations have been
assembled against you
Who say, 'Let her be defiled,
And let our eyes gloat over Zion!'

12 "But they do not know the thoughts of the
LORD,
And they do not understand His plan;
For He has gathered them like sheaves *to*
the threshing floor.

13 "Arise and thresh, daughter of Zion,
For I will make your horn iron,
And I will make your hoofs bronze,
So that you may pulverize many peoples,
And dedicate to the LORD their unjust
profit,
And their wealth to the Lord of all the
earth.

Birth of the King in Bethlehem

5 "Now muster yourselves in troops, daughter
of troops;
They have laid siege against us;
With a rod they will strike the judge of
Israel on the cheek.

2 "But as for you, Bethlehem Ephrathah,
Too little to be among the clans of Judah,
From you One will come forth for Me to
be ruler in Israel.
His times of coming forth are from long
ago,
From the days of eternity."

3 Therefore He will give them *up* until the
time
When she who is in labor has given birth.
Then the remainder of His kinsmen
Will return to the sons of Israel.

4 And He will arise and shepherd *His flock*
In the strength of the LORD,
In the majesty of the name of the LORD
His God.
And they will remain,
Because at that time He will be great
To the ends of the earth.

5 This One will be *our* peace.
When the Assyrian invades our land,
When he tramples on our citadels,
Then we will raise against him
Seven shepherds and eight leaders of
people.

6 They will shepherd the land of Assyria
with the sword,
The land of Nimrod at its entrances;

And He will rescue *us* from the Assyrian
When he invades our land,
And when he tramples our territory.

7¶ Then the remnant of Jacob
Will be among many peoples
Like dew from the LORD,
Like showers on vegetation
That do not wait for man,
Or delay for mankind.

8 The remnant of Jacob
Will be among the nations,
Among many peoples
Like a lion among the animals of the
forest,
Like a young lion among flocks of sheep,
Which, if he passes through,
Tramples and tears,
And there is no one who can rescue.

9 Your hand will be lifted up against your
adversaries,
And all your enemies will be eliminated.

10¶ "And it will be on that day," declares the
LORD,
"That I will eliminate your horses from
among you,
And destroy your chariots.

11 "I will also eliminate the cities of your
land,
And tear down all your fortifications.

12 "I will eliminate sorceries from your hand,
And you will have no fortune-tellers.

13 "I will eliminate your carved images
And your memorial stones from among
you,
So that you will no longer bow down
To the work of your hands.

14 "I will uproot your [1]Asherim from among
you,
And destroy your cities.

15 "And I will execute vengeance in anger and
wrath
On the nations which have not obeyed."

God's Indictment of His People

6 Hear now what the LORD is saying,
"Arise, plead your case before the
mountains,
And let the hills hear your voice.

2 "Listen, you mountains, to the indictment
by the LORD,
And you enduring foundations of the
earth,
Because the LORD has a case against His
people;
And He will dispute with Israel.

3 "My people, what have I done to you,
And how have I wearied you? Answer
Me.

4 "Indeed, I brought you up from the land of
Egypt,
I redeemed you from the house of slavery,
And I sent before you Moses, Aaron, and
Miriam.

5 "My people, remember now
What Balak king of Moab planned
And what Balaam son of Beor answered
him,
And what happened from Shittim to
Gilgal,

5:14 [1] I.e., wooden symbols of a female deity (Asherah)

So that you might know the righteous acts
of the LORD."

What God Requires of Mankind

6¶ With what shall I come to the LORD
And bow myself before the God on high?
Shall I come to Him with burnt offerings,
With yearling calves?
7 Does the LORD take pleasure in thousands
of rams,
In ten thousand rivers of oil?
Shall I give *Him* my firstborn *for* my
wrongdoings,
The fruit of my body for the sin of my
soul?
8 He has told you, mortal one, what is good;
And what does the LORD require of you
But to do justice, to love kindness,
And to walk humbly with your God?
9¶ The voice of the LORD will call to the
city—
And it is sound wisdom to fear Your
name:
"Hear, you tribe. Who has designated its
time?
10 "Is there still a person *in* the wicked house,
Along with treasures of wickedness,
And a short measure *that is* cursed?
11 "Can I justify dishonest balances,
And a bag of fraudulent weights?
12 "For the rich people of the city are full of
violence,
Her residents speak lies,
And their tongue is deceitful in their
mouth.
13 "So also I will make *you* sick, striking you
down,
Making *you* desolate because of your sins.
14 "You will eat, but you will not be satisfied,
And your filth *will be* in your midst.
You will *try to* remove *valuables for
safekeeping*,
But you will not save *it all*,
And what you do save I will turn over to
the sword.
15 "You will sow but you will not harvest.
You will tread the olive *press* but will not
anoint yourself with oil;
And *tread out* sweet wine, but you will
not drink *any* wine.
16 "The statutes of Omri
And every work of the house of Ahab are
maintained,
And you walk by their plans.
Therefore I will give you up for
destruction,
And your inhabitants for derision,
And you will suffer the taunting of My
people."

The Prophet Acknowledges Injustice

7 Woe to me! For I am
Like harvests of summer fruit, like gleanings
of grapes.
There is not a cluster of grapes *left* to eat,
Nor an early fig, *which* I crave.
2 The godly person has perished from the
land,
And there is no upright *person* among
mankind.

All of them lie in wait for bloodshed;
Each of them hunts the other *with* a net.
3 As for evil, both hands do it well.
The leader asks for a bribe, also the judge,
And the great one speaks the capricious
desire of his soul;
So they plot it together.
4 The best of them is like a thorn bush,
The most upright like a thorn hedge.
The day when you post your watchmen,
Your punishment is coming.
Then their confusion will occur.
5 Do not trust in a neighbor;
Do not have confidence in a close friend.
Guard your lips
From her who lies in your arms.
6 For son disavows father,
Daughter rises up against her mother,
Daughter-in-law against her mother-in-
law;
A person's enemies are the people of his
own household.

God Is the Source of Salvation and Light

7¶ But as for me, I will be on the watch for
the LORD;
I will wait for the God of my salvation.
My God will hear me.
8 Do not rejoice over me, enemy of mine.
Though I fall I will rise;
Though I live in darkness, the LORD is a
light for me.
9¶ I will endure the rage of the LORD
Because I have sinned against Him,
Until He pleads my case and executes
justice for me.
He will bring me out to the light,
And I will look at His righteousness.
10 Then my enemy will see,
And shame will cover her who said to me,
"Where is the LORD your God?"
My eyes will look at her;
At that time she will be trampled down
Like mud of the streets.
11 *It will be* a day for building your walls.
On that day *your* boundary will be
extended.
12 It *will be* a day when they will come to
you
From Assyria and the cities of Egypt,
From Egypt even to the *Euphrates* River,
Even from sea to sea and mountain to
mountain.
13 And the earth will become a wasteland
because of her inhabitants,
On account of the fruit of their deeds.
14¶ Shepherd Your people with Your scepter,
The flock of Your possession
Which lives by itself *in* the woodland,
In the midst of a fruitful field.
Let them feed *in* Bashan and Gilead
As in the days of old.
15 "As in the days when you went out from
the land of Egypt,
I will show you miracles."
16 Nations will see and be ashamed
Of all their might.
They will put *their* hand on *their* mouth,
Their ears will be deaf.
17 They will lick up dust like a snake,

Like reptiles of the earth.
They will come trembling out of their fortresses;
To the LORD our God they will come in trepidation,
And they will be afraid of You.

18 Who is a God like You, who pardons wrongdoing
And passes over a rebellious act of the remnant of His possession?
He does not retain His anger forever,
Because He delights in mercy.

19 He will again take pity on us;
He will trample on our wrongdoings.
Yes, You will cast all their sins
Into the depths of the sea.

20 You will give truth to Jacob
And favor to Abraham,
Which You swore to our forefathers
From the days of old.

The Book of
NAHUM

God Is Awesome

1 The pronouncement of Nineveh. The book of the vision of Nahum the Elkoshite:

2¶ A jealous and avenging God is the LORD;
The LORD is avenging and wrathful.
The LORD takes vengeance on His adversaries,
And He reserves wrath for His enemies.

3 The LORD is slow to anger and great in power,
And the LORD will by no means leave *the guilty* unpunished.
In *the* gale and *the* storm is His way,
And clouds are the dust *beneath* His feet.

4 He rebukes the sea and dries it up;
He dries up all the rivers.
Bashan and Carmel wither,
The blossoms of Lebanon wither.

5 Mountains quake because of Him,
And the hills come apart;
Indeed the earth is upheaved by His presence,
The world and all the inhabitants in it.

6 Who can stand before His indignation?
Who can endure the burning of His anger?
His wrath gushes forth like fire,
And the rocks are broken up by Him.

7 The LORD is good,
A stronghold in the day of trouble,
And He knows those who take refuge in Him.

8 But with an overflowing flood
He will make a complete end of its site,
And will pursue His enemies *into* darkness.

9¶ Whatever you devise against the LORD,
He will make a complete end of it.
Distress will not rise up twice.

10 Like tangled thorns,
And like those who are drunken with their drink,
They are consumed
Like stubble completely dried up.

11 From you has gone out
One who plotted evil against the LORD,
A wicked counselor.

12 This is what the LORD says:
"Though *they are at* full *strength* and so *they are* many,
So also they will be cut off and pass away.
Though I have afflicted you,
I will afflict you no longer.

13 "So now, I will break his yoke from upon you,
And I will tear your shackles to pieces."

14¶ The LORD has issued a command concerning you:
"Your name will no longer be perpetuated.
I will eliminate the carved image and the cast metal image
From the house of your gods.

I will prepare your grave,
For you are contemptible."

15¶ Behold, on the mountains, the feet of him who brings good news,
Who announces peace!
Celebrate your feasts, Judah,
Pay your vows.
For never again will the wicked one pass through you;
He is eliminated completely.

The Overthrow of Nineveh

2 The one who scatters has come up against you.
Keep watch over the fortress, watch the road;
Bind up your waist, summon all your strength.

2 For the LORD will restore the splendor of Jacob
Like the splendor of Israel,
Even though destroyers have laid waste to them
And ruined their vines.

3¶ The shields of his warriors are dyed red,
The warriors are dressed in scarlet,
The chariots are *fitted* with flashing steel
When he is prepared *to march,*
And the juniper spears are brandished.

4 The chariots drive wildly in the streets,
They rush around in the public squares;
Their appearance is like torches,
They drive back and forth like lightning flashes.

5 He remembers his officers;
They stumble in their advance,
They hurry to her wall,
And the ¹mantelet is set up.

6 The gates of the rivers are opened
And the palace sways back and forth.

7 It is set:
She is stripped, she is led away,
And her slave women are sobbing like the sound of doves,
Beating their breasts.

8¶ Though Nineveh *was* like a pool of water throughout her days,
Yet they are fleeing;
"Stop, stop,"
But no one turns back.

9 Plunder the silver,
Plunder the gold!
For there is no end to the treasure—
Wealth from every *kind of* desirable object.

10¶ She is emptied! Yes, she is desolate and waste!
Hearts are melting and knees wobbling!
Also trembling is in the entire body,
And all their faces have become pale!

11 Where is the den of the lions
And the feeding place of the young lions,

2:5 ¹ I.e., a shield used for stopping projectiles

Where the lion, lioness, *and* lion's cub
went
With nothing to disturb *them?*
12 The lion tore enough for his cubs,
Killed *enough prey* for his lionesses,
And filled his lairs with prey
And his dens with torn flesh.
13 "Behold, I am against you," declares the
LORD of armies. "I will burn up her chariots in
smoke, and a sword will devour your young
lions; I will eliminate your prey from the land,
and no longer will the voice of your
messengers be heard."

Nineveh's Complete Ruin

3 Woe to the bloody city, completely full of
lies *and* pillage;
Her prey does not leave.
2 The sound of the whip,
The sound of the roar of the wheel,
Galloping horses
And bounding chariots!
3 Horsemen charging,
Swords flashing, spears gleaming,
Many killed, a mass of corpses,
And there is no end to *the* dead bodies—
They stumble over the dead bodies!
4 *All* because of the many sexual acts of the
prostitute,
The charming one, the mistress of
sorceries,
Who sells nations by her sexual acts,
And families by her sorceries.
5 "Behold, I am against you," declares the
LORD of armies;
"And I will lift up your skirts over your
face,
And show the nations your nakedness,
And the kingdoms your shame.
6 "I will throw filth on you
And declare you worthless,
And set you up as a spectacle.
7 "And it will come about that all who see
you
Will shrink from you and say,
'Nineveh is devastated!
Who will have sympathy for her?'
Where shall I seek comforters for you?"
8¶ Are you better than 'No-amon,
Which was situated by the canals of the
Nile,
With water surrounding her,
Whose rampart *was* the sea,
Whose wall *consisted* of the sea?
9 Ethiopia was *her* might,
Egypt too, without limits.
Put and Lubim were among her helpers.

10 Yet she became an exile,
She went into captivity;
Also her small children were smashed to
pieces
At the head of every street;
They cast lots for her honorable men,
And all her great men were bound with
shackles.
11 You too will become drunk,
You will be hidden.
You too will search for a refuge from the
enemy.
12 All your fortifications are fig trees with
ripe fruit—
When shaken, they fall into the eater's
mouth.
13 Behold, your people are women in your
midst!
The gates of your land are opened wide to
your enemies;
Fire consumes your gate bars.
14 Draw for yourself water for a siege!
Strengthen your fortifications!
Go into the clay and tread the mortar!
Take hold of the brick mold!
15 There fire will consume you,
The sword will cut you down;
It will consume you as the creeping locust
consumes *a crop.*
Multiply yourself like the creeping
locust,
Multiply yourself like the migratory
locust.
16 You have made your traders more
numerous than the stars of heaven—
The creeping locust sheds its skin and
flies *away.*
17 Your courtiers are like the migratory
locust.
Your officials are like a swarm of locusts
Settling in the stone shelters on a cold
day.
The sun rises and they flee,
And the place where they are is not
known.
18 Your shepherds are sleeping, O king of
Assyria;
Your officers are lying down.
Your people are scattered on the
mountains
And there is no one to gather *them.*
19 There is no relief for your collapse,
Your wound is incurable.
All who hear about you
Will clap *their* hands over you,
For upon whom has your evil not come
continually?

3:8 ¹I.e., the city of Amon: Thebes

The Book of
HABAKKUK

Chaldeans Used to Punish Judah

1 The pronouncement which Habakkuk the prophet saw:

2¶ How long, LORD, have I called for help,
And You do not hear?
I cry out to You, "Violence!"
Yet You do not save.

3 Why do You make me see disaster,
And make *me* look at destitution?
Yes, devastation and violence are before me;
Strife exists and contention arises.

4 Therefore the Law is ignored,
And justice is never upheld.
For the wicked surround the righteous;
Therefore justice comes out confused.

5¶ "Look among the nations! Watch!
Be horrified! Be frightened speechless!
For *I am* accomplishing a work in your days—
You would not believe *it even* if you were told!

6 "For behold, I am raising up the Chaldeans,
That grim and impetuous people
Who march throughout the earth,
To take possession of dwelling places that are not theirs.

7 "They are terrifying and feared;
Their justice and authority originate with themselves.

8 "Their horses are faster than leopards,
And quicker than wolves in the evening.
Their horsemen charge along,
Their horsemen come from afar;
They fly like an eagle swooping down to devour.

9 "All of them come for violence.
Their horde of faces moves forward.
They gather captives like sand.

10 "They make fun of kings,
And dignitaries are *an object of* laughter to them.
They laugh at every fortress,
Then heap up dirt and capture it.

11 "Then they fly along *like* the wind and pass on.
But they will be held guilty,
They whose strength is their god."

12¶ Are You not from time everlasting,
LORD, my God, my Holy One?
We will not die.
You, LORD, have appointed them to *deliver* judgment;
And You, O Rock, have destined them to punish.

13 *Your* eyes are too pure to look at evil,
And You cannot look at harm *favorably.*
Why do You look *favorably*
At those who deal treacherously?
Why are You silent when the wicked swallow up
Those more righteous than they?

14 *Why* have You made people like the fish of the sea,
Like crawling things that have no ruler over them?

15 *The Chaldeans* bring all of them up with a hook,
Drag them away with their net,
And gather them together in their fishing net.
Therefore they rejoice and are joyful.

16 Therefore they offer a sacrifice to their net
And burn incense to their fishing net,
Because through these things their catch is large,
And their food is plentiful.

17 Will they therefore empty their net,
And continually slay nations without sparing?

God Answers the Prophet

2 I will stand at my guard post
And station myself on the watchtower;
And I will keep watch to see what He will say to me,
And how I may reply when I am reprimanded.

2 Then the LORD answered me and said,
"Write down the vision
And inscribe *it* clearly on tablets,
So that one who reads it may run.

3 "For the vision is yet for the appointed time;
It hurries toward the goal and it will not fail.
Though it delays, wait for it;
For it will certainly come, it will not delay *long.*

4¶ "Behold, as for the impudent one,
His soul is not right within him;
But the righteous one will live by his faith.

5 "Furthermore, wine betrays an arrogant man,
So that he does not achieve his objective.
He enlarges his appetite like Sheol,
And he is like death, never satisfied.
He also gathers to himself all the nations
And collects to himself all the peoples.

6¶ "Will all of these not take up a song of ridicule against him,
Even a saying *and* insinuations against him
And say, 'Woe to him who increases what is not his—
For how long—
And makes himself rich with debts!'

7 "Will your creditors not rise up suddenly,
And those who collect from you awaken?
Indeed, you will become plunder for them.

8 "Since you have looted many nations,
All the rest of the peoples will loot you—
Because of human bloodshed and violence done to the land,

To the town and all its inhabitants.

9 ¶ "Woe to him who makes evil profit for his
   household,
   To put his nest on high,
   To be saved from the hand of catastrophe!

10 "You have planned a shameful thing for
   your house
   By bringing many peoples to an end;
   So you are sinning against yourself.

11 "For the stone will cry out from the wall,
   And the rafter will answer it from the
   framework.

12 ¶ "Woe to him who builds a city with
   bloodshed,
   And founds a town with violence!

13 "Is it not indeed from the LORD of armies
   That peoples labor *merely* for fire,
   And nations become weary for nothing?

14 "For the earth will be filled
   With the knowledge of the glory of the
   LORD,
   As the waters cover the sea.

15 ¶ "Woe to him who makes his neighbor
   drink;
   To you who mix in your venom even to
   make *your neighbors* drunk,
   So as to look at their genitalia!

16 "You will be filled with disgrace rather than
   honor.
   Drink, you yourself, and expose your *own*
   foreskin!
   The cup in the LORD's right hand will
   come around to you,
   And utter disgrace *will come* upon your
   glory.

17 "For the violence done to Lebanon will
   overwhelm you,
   And the devastation of *its* animals by
   which you terrified them,
   Because of human bloodshed and violence
   done to the land,
   To the town and all its inhabitants.

18 ¶ "What benefit is a carved image when its
   maker has carved it,
   Or a cast metal image, a teacher of
   falsehood?
   For *its* maker trusts in his *own* handiwork
   When he fashions speechless idols.

19 "Woe to him who says to a *piece of* wood,
   'Awake!'
   To a mute stone, 'Arise!'
   That is *your* teacher?
   Behold, it is overlaid with gold and silver,
   Yet there is no breath at all inside it.

20 "But the LORD is in His holy temple.
   Let all the earth be silent before Him."

God's People Saved

3 A prayer of Habakkuk the prophet, according to ¹Shigionoth.

2 ¶ LORD, I have heard the report about You,
   and I was afraid.
   LORD, revive Your work in the midst of
   the years,
   In the midst of the years make *it* known.
   In anger remember mercy.

3 ¶ God comes from Teman,
   And the Holy One from Mount Paran.
                                        Selah

His splendor covers the heavens,
And the earth is full of His praise.

4 *His* radiance is like the sunlight;
   He has rays *flashing* from His hand,
   And the hiding of His might is there.

5 Before Him goes plague,
   And plague comes forth after Him.

6 He stood and caused the earth to shudder;
   He looked and caused the nations to
   jump.
   Yes, the everlasting mountains were
   shattered,
   The ancient hills collapsed.
   His paths are everlasting.

7 I saw the tents of Cushan under distress,
   The tent curtains of the land of Midian
   were trembling.

8 ¶ Did the LORD rage against the rivers,
   Or *was* Your anger against the rivers,
   Or *was* Your rage against the sea,
   That You rode on Your horses,
   On Your chariots of salvation?

9 You removed Your bow *from its holder,*
   The arrows of *Your* word were sworn.
                                        Selah
   You divided the earth with rivers.

10 The mountains saw You *and* quaked;
   The downpour of waters swept by.
   The deep raised its voice,
   It lifted high its hands.

11 Sun *and* moon stood in their lofty places;
   They went away at the light of Your
   arrows,
   At the radiance of Your flashing spear.

12 In indignation You marched through the
   earth;
   In anger You trampled the nations.

13 You went forth for the salvation of Your
   people,
   For the salvation of Your anointed.
   You smashed the head of the house of evil
   To uncover *him from* foot to neck.   *Selah*

14 You pierced with his own arrows
   The head of his leaders.
   They stormed in to scatter us;
   Their arrogance *was* like those
   Who devour the oppressed in secret.

15 You trampled on the sea with Your horses,
   On the foam of many waters.

16 ¶ I heard, and my inner parts trembled;
   At the sound, my lips quivered.
   Decay enters my bones,
   And in my place I tremble;
   Because I must wait quietly for the day of
   distress,
   For the people to arise *who* will attack us.

17 Even if the fig tree does not blossom,
   And there is no fruit on the vines,
   If the yield of the olive fails,
   And the fields produce no food,
   Even if the flock disappears from the fold,
   And there are no cattle in the stalls,

18 Yet I will triumph in the LORD,
   I will rejoice in the God of my salvation.

19 The Lord GOD is my strength,
   And He has made my feet like deer's *feet,*
   And has me walk on my high places.
   For the choir director, on my stringed
   instruments.

3:1 ¹Perhaps a highly emotional poetic form

The Book of
ZEPHANIAH

Day of Judgment on Judah

1 The word of the LORD which came to Zephaniah son of Cushi, son of Gedaliah, son of Amariah, son of Hezekiah, in the days of Josiah son of Amon, king of Judah:
2 ¶ "I will completely remove all *things* From the face of the earth," declares the LORD.
3 "I will remove human and animal *life;* I will remove the birds of the sky And the fish of the sea, And the ruins along with the wicked; And I will eliminate mankind from the face of the earth," declares the LORD.
4 "So I will stretch out My hand against Judah And against all the inhabitants of Jerusalem. And I will eliminate the remnant of Baal from this place, *And* the names of the idolatrous priests along with the *other* priests.
5 "And those who bow down on the house-tops to the heavenly 'lights, And those who bow down *and* swear to the LORD, but *also* swear by Milcom,
6 And those who have turned back from following the LORD, And those who have not sought the LORD nor inquired of Him."
7 ¶ Be silent before the Lord GOD! For the day of the LORD is near, Because the LORD has prepared a sacrifice, He has consecrated His guests.
8 "Then it will come about on the day of the LORD's sacrifice That I will punish the princes, the king's sons, And all who clothe themselves with foreign garments.
9 "And on that day I will punish all who leap on the *temple* threshold, Who fill the house of their lord with violence and deceit.
10 "And on that day," declares the LORD, "There will be the sound of a cry from the Fish Gate, Wailing from the 'Second Quarter, And a loud crash from the hills.
11 "Wail, you inhabitants of the 'Mortar, Because all the people of Canaan will be destroyed; All who weigh out silver will be eliminated.
12 "And it will come about at that time That I will search Jerusalem with lamps, And I will punish the people Who are stagnant in spirit, Who say in their hearts, 'The LORD will not do good nor harm!'
13 "Their wealth will become plunder,

And their houses desolate; Yes, they will build houses but not inhabit *them,* And plant vineyards but not drink their wine."
14 ¶ The great day of the LORD is near, Near and coming very quickly; Listen, the day of the LORD! In it the warrior cries out bitterly.
15 That day is a day of anger, A day of trouble and distress, A day of destruction and desolation, A day of darkness and gloom, A day of clouds and thick darkness,
16 A day of trumpet and battle cry Against the fortified cities And the high corner towers.
17 I will bring distress on mankind So that they will walk like those who are blind, Because they have sinned against the LORD; And their blood will be poured out like dust, And their flesh like dung.
18 Neither their silver nor their gold Will be able to save them On the day of the LORD's anger; And all the earth will be devoured By the fire of His jealousy, For He will make a complete end, Indeed a horrifying one, Of all the inhabitants of the earth.

Judgments on Judah's Enemies

2 Gather yourselves together, yes, join together, You nation without shame,
2 Before the decree takes effect— The day passes like chaff— Before the burning anger of the LORD comes upon you, Before the day of the LORD's anger comes upon you.
3 Seek the LORD, All you humble of the earth Who have practiced His ordinances; Seek righteousness, seek humility. Perhaps you will remain hidden On the day of the LORD's anger.
4 ¶ For Gaza will be abandoned, And Ashkelon *will become* a desolation; *The inhabitants of* Ashdod will be driven out at noon, And Ekron will be uprooted.
5 Woe to the inhabitants of the seacoast, The nation of the 'Cherethites! The word of the LORD is against you, Canaan, land of the Philistines; And I will eliminate you So that there will be no inhabitant.

1:5 ¹Lit *host;* i.e., sun, stars, etc.   1:10 ¹I.e., a district of Jerusalem   1:11 ¹I.e., a district of Jerusalem
2:5 ¹I.e., a segment of the Philistines with roots in Crete

6 So the seacoast will become grazing
places,
With pastures for shepherds and folds for
flocks.
7 And the coast will be
For the remnant of the house of Judah,
They will drive *sheep* to pasture on it.
In the houses of Ashkelon they will lie
down at evening;
For the LORD their God will care for them
And restore their fortunes.
8¶ "I have heard the taunting of Moab
And the abusive speech of the sons of
Ammon,
With which they have taunted My people
And boasted against their territory.
9 "Therefore, as I live," declares the LORD of
armies,
The God of Israel,
"Moab will assuredly be like Sodom,
And the sons of Ammon like Gomorrah—
Ground overgrown with weeds and *full of*
salt mines,
And a permanent desolation.
The remnant of My people will plunder
them,
And the remainder of My nation will
inherit them."
10 This they will have in return for their
arrogance, because they have taunted and
boasted against the people of the LORD of
armies. 11 The LORD will be terrifying to them,
for He will starve all the gods of the earth; and
all the coastlands of the nations will bow down
to Him, everyone from his *own* place.
12¶ "You also, Ethiopians, will be slain by My
sword."
13 And He will stretch out His hand against
the north
And eliminate Assyria,
And He will make Nineveh a desolation,
Parched like the wilderness.
14 Flocks will lie down in her midst,
All animals that range in herds;
Both the pelican and the hedgehog
Will spend their nights in the tops of her
pillars;
Birds will sing in the window,
Devastation *will be* on the threshold;
For He has uncovered the cedar work.
15 This is the presumptuous city
That dwells securely,
Who says in her heart,
"I am, and there is no one besides me."
How she has become a desolation,
A resting place for animals,
Everyone who passes by her will hiss
And wave his hand *in contempt.*

Woe to Jerusalem and the Nations

3 Woe to her who is rebellious and defiled,
The oppressive city!
2 She obeyed no voice,
She accepted no discipline.
She did not trust in the LORD,
She did not approach her God.
3 Her leaders within her are roaring lions,
Her judges are wolves at evening;
They have no bones to gnaw in the
morning.

4 Her prophets are insolent, treacherous
men;
Her priests have profaned the sanctuary.
They have done violence to the Law.
5 The LORD is righteous within her;
He will do no injustice.
Every morning He brings His justice to
light;
He does not fail.
But the criminal knows no shame.
6 "I have eliminated nations;
Their corner towers are deserted.
I have laid waste their streets,
With no one passing by;
Their cities have been laid waste,
Without a person, without an inhabitant.
7 "I said, 'You will certainly revere Me,
You will accept discipline.'
So her dwelling will not be eliminated
In accordance with everything that I have
stipulated for her.
Instead, they were eager to corrupt all
their deeds.
8¶ "Therefore wait for Me," declares the
LORD,
"For the day when I rise up as a witness,
Indeed, My decision *is* to gather nations,
To assemble kingdoms,
To pour out on them My indignation,
All My burning anger;
For all the earth will be devoured
By the fire of My zeal.
9 "For then I will restore to the peoples pure
lips,
So that all of them may call on the name
of the LORD,
To serve Him shoulder to shoulder.
10 "From beyond the rivers of Ethiopia
My worshipers, My dispersed ones,
Will bring My offerings.
11 "On that day you will feel no shame
Because of all your deeds
By which you have rebelled against Me;
For then I will remove from your midst
Your proud, arrogant ones,
And you will never again be haughty
On My holy mountain.

A Remnant of Israel

12 "But I will leave among you
A humble and lowly people,
And they will take refuge in the name of
the LORD.
13 "The remnant of Israel will do no wrong
And tell no lies,
Nor will a deceitful tongue
Be found in their mouths;
For they will feed and lie down
With no one to frighten *them.*"
14¶ Shout for joy, daughter of Zion!
Shout *in triumph,* Israel!
Rejoice and triumph with all *your* heart,
Daughter of Jerusalem!
15 The LORD has taken away *His* judgments
against you,
He has cleared away your enemies.
The King of Israel, the LORD, is in your
midst;
You will no longer fear disaster.
16 On that day it will be said to Jerusalem:

"Do not be afraid, Zion;
Do not let your hands fall limp.
17 "The LORD your God is in your midst,
A victorious warrior.
He will rejoice over you with joy,
He will be quiet in His love,
He will rejoice over you with shouts of
joy.
18 "I will gather those who are worried about
the appointed feasts—
They came from you, *Zion;*
The disgrace *of exile* is a burden on them.
19 "Behold, I am going to deal at that time
With all your oppressors;

I will save those who limp
And gather the scattered,
And I will turn their shame into praise
and fame
In all the earth.
20 "At that time I will bring you in,
Even at the time when I gather you
together;
Indeed, I will make you famous and
praiseworthy
Among all the peoples of the earth,
When I restore your fortunes before your
eyes,"
Says the LORD.

The Book of
HAGGAI

Haggai Begins Temple Building

1 In the second year of Darius the king, on the first day of the sixth month, the word of the LORD came by the prophet Haggai to Zerubbabel the son of Shealtiel, governor of Judah, and to Joshua the son of Jehozadak, the high priest, saying, 2 "This is what the LORD of armies says: 'This people says, "The time has not come, the time for the house of the LORD to be rebuilt." ' " 3 Then the word of the LORD came by Haggai the prophet, saying, 4 "Is it time for you yourselves to live in your paneled houses while this house *remains* desolate?" 5 Now then, the LORD of armies says this: "Consider your ways! 6 You have sown much, *only to* harvest little; *you* eat, but there is not *enough* to be satisfied; *you* drink, but there is not *enough* to become drunk; *you* put on clothing, but there is not *enough* for anyone to get warm; and the one who earns, earns wages *to put* into a money bag full of holes."

7 The LORD of armies says this: "Consider your ways! 8 Go up to the mountains, bring wood, and rebuild the temple, that I may be pleased with it and be honored," says the LORD. 9 "*You* start an ambitious project, but behold, *it comes* to little; when you bring *it* home, I blow it *away.* Why?" declares the LORD of armies. "*It is* because of My house which *remains* desolate, while each of you runs to his own house. 10 Therefore, because of you the sky has withheld its dew, and the earth has withheld its produce. 11 And I called for a drought on the land, on the mountains, on the grain, on the new wine, on the oil, on what the ground produces, on mankind, on cattle, and on all the products of the labor of your hands."

12 Then Zerubbabel the son of Shealtiel, and Joshua the son of Jehozadak, the high priest, with all the remnant of the people, obeyed the voice of the LORD their God and the words of Haggai the prophet, just as the LORD their God had sent him. And the people showed reverence for the LORD. 13 Then Haggai, the messenger of the LORD, spoke by the commission of the LORD to the people, saying, " 'I am with you,' declares the LORD." 14 So the LORD stirred up the spirit of Zerubbabel the son of Shealtiel, governor of Judah, and the spirit of Joshua the son of Jehozadak, the high priest, and the spirit of all the remnant of the people; and they came and worked on the house of the LORD of armies, their God, 15 on the twenty-fourth day of the sixth month in the second year of Darius the king.

The Builders Encouraged

2 On the twenty-first of the seventh month, the word of the LORD came by Haggai the prophet, saying, 2 "Speak now to Zerubbabel the son of Shealtiel, governor of Judah, and to Joshua the son of Jehozadak, the high priest, and to the remnant of the people, saying, 3 'Who is left among you who saw this temple in its former glory? And how do you see it now? Does it not seem to you like nothing in comparison? 4 But now take courage, Zerubbabel,' declares the LORD, 'take courage also, Joshua son of Jehozadak, the high priest, and all you people of the land take courage,' declares the LORD, 'and work; for I am with you,' declares the LORD of armies. 5 'As for the promise which I made you when you came out of Egypt, My Spirit remains in your midst; do not fear!' 6 For this is what the LORD of armies says: 'Once more in a little while, I am going to shake the heavens and the earth, the sea also and the dry land. 7 I will shake all the nations; and they will come *with* the wealth of all nations, and I will fill this house with glory,' says the LORD of armies. 8 'The silver is Mine and the gold is Mine,' declares the LORD of armies. 9 'The latter glory of this house will be greater than the former,' says the LORD of armies, 'and in this place I will give peace,' declares the LORD of armies."

10 On the twenty-fourth of the ninth *month,* in the second year of Darius, the word of the LORD came to Haggai the prophet, saying, 11 "The LORD of armies says this: 'Now ask the priests *for* a ruling: 12 If someone carries holy meat in the fold of his garment, and touches bread with this fold, or *touches* cooked food, wine, oil, or any *other* food, will it become holy?' " And the priests answered, "No." 13 Then Haggai said, "If one who is unclean from a corpse touches any of these *things,* will *the latter* become unclean?" And the priests answered, "It will become unclean." 14 Then Haggai responded and said, " 'So is this people. And so is this nation before Me,' declares the LORD, 'and so is every work of their hands; and what they offer there is unclean. 15 But now, do consider from this day onward: before one stone was placed on another in the temple of the LORD, 16 from that time *when* one came to a grain heap of twenty *measures,* there would be *only* ten; *and when* one came to the wine vat to draw fifty measures, there would be *only* twenty. 17 I struck you *and* every work of your hands with scorching wind, mildew, and hail; yet you did not come back to Me,' declares the LORD. 18 'Do consider from this day onward, from the twenty-fourth day of the ninth *month;* from the day when the temple of the LORD was founded, consider: 19 Is the seed still in the barn? Even including the vine, the fig tree, the pomegranate, and the olive tree, it has not produced *fruit. Yet* from this day on I will bless *you.* ' "

20 Then the word of the LORD came a second time to Haggai on the twenty-fourth *day* of the month, saying, 21 "Speak to Zerubbabel governor of Judah, saying, 'I am going to shake the heavens and the earth. 22 And I will overthrow

the thrones of kingdoms and destroy the power of the kingdoms of the nations; and I will overthrow the chariots and their riders, and the horses and their riders will go down, every one by the sword of another.' 23 'On that day,'

declares the LORD of armies, 'I will take you, Zerubbabel, son of Shealtiel, My servant,' declares the LORD, 'and I will make you like a signet ring, for I have chosen you,'" declares the LORD of armies.

The Book of
ZECHARIAH

A Call to Repentance

1 In the eighth month of the second year of Darius, the word of the LORD came to Zechariah the prophet, the son of Berechiah, the son of Iddo saying, 2 "The LORD was very angry with your fathers. 3 Therefore say to them, 'This is what the LORD of armies says: "Return to Me," declares the LORD of armies, "that I may return to you," says the LORD of armies. 4 "Do not be like your fathers, to whom the former prophets proclaimed, saying, 'This is what the LORD of armies says: "Return now from your evil ways and from your evil deeds." ' But they did not listen or pay attention to Me," declares the LORD. 5 "Your fathers, where are they? And the prophets, do they live forever? 6 But did My words and My statutes, which I commanded My servants the prophets, not overtake your fathers? Then they repented and said, 'Just as the LORD of armies planned to do to us in accordance with our ways and our deeds, so He has dealt with us.' " ' "

Patrol of the Earth

7 On the twenty-fourth day of the eleventh month, that is, the month Shebat, in the second year of Darius, the word of the LORD came to Zechariah the prophet, the son of Berechiah, the son of Iddo, as follows: 8 I saw at night, and behold, a man was riding on a red horse, and he was standing among the myrtle trees which were in the ravine, with red, 'sorrel, and white horses behind him. 9 Then I said, "What are these, my lord?" And the angel who was speaking with me said to me, "I will show you what these are." 10 And the man who was standing among the myrtle trees responded and said, "These are the ones whom the LORD has sent to patrol the earth." 11 So they responded to the angel of the LORD who was standing among the myrtle trees and said, "We have patrolled the earth, and behold, all the earth is still and quiet."

12 Then the angel of the LORD said, "LORD of armies, how long will You take no pity on Jerusalem and the cities of Judah, with which You have been indignant for these seventy years?" 13 And the LORD responded to the angel who was speaking with me with gracious words, comforting words. 14 So the angel who was speaking with me said to me, "Proclaim, saying, 'This is what the LORD of armies says: "I am exceedingly jealous for Jerusalem and Zion. 15 But I am very angry with the nations who are carefree; for while I was only a little angry, they furthered the disaster." 16 Therefore the LORD says this: "I will return to Jerusalem with compassion; My house will be built in it," declares the LORD of armies, "and a measuring line will be stretched over Jerusalem." ' 17 Again, proclaim, saying, 'This is what the LORD of armies says: "My cities will again overflow with prosperity, and the LORD will again comfort Zion and again choose Jerusalem." ' "

18 Then I raised my eyes and looked, and behold, there were four horns. 19 So I said to the angel who was speaking with me, "What are these?" And he said to me, "These are the horns that have scattered Judah, Israel, and Jerusalem." 20 Then the LORD showed me four craftsmen. 21 And I said, "What are these coming to do?" And he said, "These are the horns that have scattered Judah so that no one lifts up his head; but these *craftsmen* have come to frighten them, to throw down the horns of the nations who have lifted up *their* horns against the land of Judah in order to scatter it."

God's Favor to Zion

2 Then I raised my eyes and looked, and behold, *there was* a man with a measuring line in his hand. 2 So I said, "Where are you going?" And he said to me, "To measure Jerusalem, to see how wide it is and how long it is." 3 And behold, the angel who had been speaking with me was going out, and another angel was going out to meet him. 4 And he said to him, "Run, speak to that young man there, saying, 'Jerusalem will be inhabited as open country because of the multitude of people and cattle within it. 5 But I,' declares the LORD, 'will be a wall of fire to her on all sides, and I will be the glory in her midst.' "

6 "You there! Flee from the land of the north," declares the LORD, "because I have spread you out like the four winds of the heavens," declares the LORD. 7 "You, Zion! Escape, you who are living *with* the daughter of Babylon." 8 For the LORD of armies says this: "After glory He has sent me against the nations that plunder you, for the one who touches you, touches the apple of His eye. 9 For behold, I am going to wave My hand over them so that they will be plunder for their slaves. Then you will know that the LORD of armies has sent Me. 10 Shout for joy and rejoice, daughter of Zion; for behold I am coming and I will dwell in your midst," declares the LORD. 11 "And many nations will join themselves to the LORD on that day and will become My people. Then I will dwell in your midst, and you will know that the LORD of armies has sent Me to you. 12 And the LORD will possess Judah as His portion in the holy land, and will again choose Jerusalem.

13 "Be silent, all mankind, before the LORD; for He has roused Himself from His holy dwelling."

Joshua, the High Priest

3 Then he showed me Joshua the high priest standing before the angel of the LORD, and

---

1:8 1 I.e., light reddish-brown

Satan standing at his right to accuse him. ²And the Lord said to Satan, "The Lord rebuke you, Satan! Indeed, the Lord who has chosen Jerusalem rebuke you! Is this not a log snatched from the fire?" ³Now Joshua was clothed in filthy garments and was standing before the angel. ⁴And he responded and said to those who were standing before him, saying, "Remove the filthy garments from him." Again he said to him, "See, I have taken your guilt away from you and will clothe you with festive robes." ⁵Then I said, "Have them put a clean headband on his head." So they put the clean headband on his head and clothed him with garments, while the angel of the Lord was standing by.

⁶And the angel of the Lord admonished Joshua, saying, ⁷"The Lord of armies says this: 'If you walk in My ways and perform My service, then you will both govern My house and be in charge of My courtyards, and I will grant you free access among these who are standing *here.*

The Branch

⁸Now listen, Joshua, *you* high priest, you and your friends who are sitting in front of you— indeed they are men who are a sign: for behold, I am going to bring in My servant the Branch. ⁹For behold, the stone that I have put before Joshua; on one stone are seven eyes. Behold, I am going to engrave an inscription on it,' declares the Lord of armies, 'and I will remove the guilt of that land in one day. ¹⁰On that day,' declares the Lord of armies, 'every one *of you* will invite his neighbor to *sit* under *his* vine and under *his* fig tree.' "

The Golden Lampstand and the Olive Trees

4 Then the angel who had been speaking with me returned and woke me, like a person who is awakened from his sleep. ²And he said to me, "What do you see?" And I said, "I see, and behold, a lampstand all of gold with its bowl on the top of it, and its seven lamps on it with seven spouts *belonging* to *each of* the lamps which are on the top of it; ³also two olive trees by it, one on the right side of the bowl and the other on its left side." ⁴Then I said to the angel who was speaking with me, saying, "What are these, my lord?" ⁵So the angel who was speaking with me answered and said to me, "Do you not know what these are?" And I said, "No, my lord." ⁶Then he said to me, "This is the word of the Lord to Zerubbabel, saying, 'Not by might nor by power, but by My Spirit,' says the Lord of armies. ⁷'What are you, you great mountain? Before Zerubbabel *you will become* a plain; and he will bring out the top stone *with* shouts of "Grace, grace to it!" ' "

⁸Also the word of the Lord came to me, saying, ⁹"The hands of Zerubbabel have laid the foundation of this house, and his hands will finish *it.* Then you will know that the Lord of armies has sent me to you. ¹⁰For who has shown contempt for the day of small things? But these seven will rejoice when they see the plumb line in the hand of Zerubbabel—they

are the eyes of the Lord roaming throughout the earth."

¹¹Then I said to him, "What are these two olive trees on the right of the lampstand and on its left?" ¹²And I responded the second time and said to him, "What are the two olive branches which are beside the two golden pipes, which empty the golden *oil* from themselves?" ¹³So he answered me, saying, "Do you not know what these are?" And I said, "No, my lord." ¹⁴Then he said, "These are the two anointed ones, who are standing by the Lord of the whole earth."

The Flying Scroll

5 Then I raised my eyes again and looked, and behold, *there was* a flying scroll. ²And he said to me, "What do you see?" And I said, "I see a flying scroll; its length is †twenty cubits, and its width ten cubits." ³Then he said to me, "This is the curse that is going forth over the face of the entire land; everyone who steals certainly will be purged away according to the writing on one side, and everyone who swears *falsely* will be purged away according to the writing on the other side. ⁴I will make it go forth," declares the Lord of armies, "and it will enter the house of the thief and the house of the one who swears falsely by My name; and it will spend the night within that house and destroy it with its timber and stones."

⁵Then the angel who had been speaking with me went out and said to me, "Now raise your eyes and see what this is that is going forth." ⁶And I said, "What is it?" Then he said, "This is the ephah going forth." Again he said, "This is their †appearance in all the land. ⁷And behold, a lead cover was lifted up." *He continued,* "And this is a woman sitting inside the ephah." ⁸Then he said, "This is Wickedness!" And he thrust her into the middle of the ephah and threw the lead weight on its opening. ⁹Then I raised my eyes and looked, and there two women were coming out with the wind in their wings; and they had wings like the wings of the stork, and they lifted up the ephah between the earth and the heavens. ¹⁰So I said to the angel who was speaking with me, "Where are they taking the ephah?" ¹¹Then he said to me, "To build a temple for her in the land of Shinar; and when it is prepared, she will be set there on her own pedestal."

The Four Chariots

6 Now I raised my eyes again and looked, and behold, four chariots were going out from between the two mountains; and the mountains *were* bronze mountains. ²With the first chariot *were* red horses, with the second chariot black horses, ³with the third chariot white horses, and with the fourth chariot strong spotted horses. ⁴So I responded and said to the angel who was speaking with me, "What are these, my lord?" ⁵The angel replied to me, "These are the four spirits of heaven, going out after taking their stand before the Lord of all the earth, ⁶with one of which the black horses are going out to the north country; and the white ones are to go out after them, while

---

5:2 ¹About 30 ft. long and 15 ft. wide or 9 m and 4.5 m   **5:6** ¹Lit *eye;* some ancient versions *wrongdoing*

the spotted ones are to go out to the south country." 7 When the strong ones went out, they were eager to go to patrol the earth. And He said, "Go, patrol the earth." So they patrolled the earth. 8 Then He called out to me and spoke to me, saying, "See, those who are going to the land of the north have appeased My wrath in the land of the north."

9 The word of the LORD also came to me, saying, 10 "Take an offering from the exiles, from Heldai, Tobijah, and Jedaiah; and you shall go the same day and enter the house of Josiah the son of Zephaniah, where they have arrived from Babylon.

The Symbolic Crowns

11 Also take silver and gold, make an ornate crown, and set it on the head of Joshua the son of Jehozadak, the high priest. 12 Then say to him, 'The LORD of armies says this: "Behold, there is a Man whose name is Branch, for He will branch out from where He is; and He will build the temple of the LORD. 13 Yes, it is He who will build the temple of the LORD, and He who will bear the majesty and sit and rule on His throne. So He will be a priest on His throne, and the counsel of peace will be between the two offices." ' 14 Now the crown will become a reminder in the temple of the LORD to Helem, Tobijah, Jedaiah, and Hen the son of Zephaniah. 15 Those who are far away will come and build the temple of the LORD." Then you will know that the LORD of armies has sent me to you. And it will take place if you completely obey the LORD your God.

7 In the fourth year of King Darius, the word of the LORD came to Zechariah on the fourth day of the ninth month, which is Chislev. 2 Now the town of Bethel had sent Sharezer and Regemmelech and their men to seek the favor of the LORD, 3 speaking to the priests who belong to the house of the LORD of armies, and to the prophets, saying, "Shall I weep in the fifth month and fast, as I have done these many years?" 4 Then the word of the LORD of armies came to me, saying, 5 "Say to all the people of the land and to the priests, 'When you fasted and mourned in the fifth and seventh months these seventy years, was it actually for Me that you fasted? 6 And when you eat and drink, do you not eat for yourselves and drink for yourselves? 7 Are these not the words which the LORD proclaimed by the former prophets, when Jerusalem was inhabited and carefree along with its cities around it, and the Negev and the foothills were inhabited?' "

8 Then the word of the LORD came to Zechariah, saying, 9 "This is what the LORD of armies has said: 'Dispense true justice and practice kindness and compassion each to his brother; 10 and do not oppress the widow or the orphan, the stranger or the poor; and do not devise evil in your hearts against one another.' 11 But they refused to pay attention, and turned a stubborn shoulder and plugged their ears from hearing. 12 They also made their hearts as hard as a diamond so that they could not hear the Law and the words which the LORD of

armies had sent by His Spirit through the former prophets; therefore great wrath came from the LORD of armies. 13 And just as He called and they would not listen, so they called and I would not listen," says the LORD of armies; 14 "but I scattered them with a storm wind among all the nations whom they did not know. So the land was desolated behind them so that no one went back and forth, since they made the pleasant land desolate."

The Coming Peace and Prosperity of Zion

8 Then the word of the LORD of armies came, saying, 2 "The LORD of armies says this: 'I am exceedingly jealous for Zion, yes, with great wrath I am jealous for her.' 3 The LORD says this: 'I will return to Zion and dwell in the midst of Jerusalem. Then Jerusalem will be called the City of Truth, and the mountain of the LORD of armies will be called the Holy Mountain.' 4 The LORD of armies says this: 'Old men and old women will again sit in the public squares of Jerusalem, each person with his staff in his hand because of age. 5 And the public squares of the city will be filled with boys and girls playing in its squares.' 6 The LORD of armies says this: 'If it is too difficult in the sight of the remnant of this people in those days, will it also be too difficult in My sight?' declares the LORD of armies. 7 The LORD of armies says this: 'Behold, I am going to save My people from the land of the east and from the land of the west; 8 and I will bring them back and they will live in the midst of Jerusalem; and they shall be My people, and I will be their God in truth and righteousness.'

9 "The LORD of armies says this: 'Let your hands be strong, you who are listening in these days to these words from the mouth of the prophets, those who spoke in the day that the foundation of the house of the LORD of armies was laid, so that the temple might be built. 10 For before those days there was no wage for man nor any wage for animal; and for him who went out or came in there was no peace because of his enemies, and I sent all the people against one another. 11 But now I will not treat the remnant of this people as in the former days,' declares the LORD of armies. 12 'For there will be the seed of peace: the vine will yield its fruit, the land will yield its produce, and the heavens will provide their dew; and I will give to the remnant of this people all these things as an inheritance. 13 And it will come about that just as you were a curse among the nations, house of Judah and house of Israel, so I will save you that you may become a blessing. Do not fear; let your hands be strong.'

14 "For this is what the LORD of armies says: 'Just as I determined to do harm to you when your fathers provoked Me to anger,' says the LORD of armies, 'and I have not relented, 15 so I have again determined in these days to do good to Jerusalem and to the house of Judah. Do not fear! 16 These are the things which you shall do: speak the truth to one another; judge with truth and judgment for peace at your 1gates. 17 Also let none of you devise evil in your heart

---

8:16 1I.e., the place where court was held

against another, and do not love perjury; for all these *things* are what I hate,' declares the Lord."

18 Then the word of the Lord of armies came to me, saying, 19 "The Lord of armies says this: 'The fast of the fourth, the fast of the fifth, the fast of the seventh, and the fast of the tenth *months* will become joy, jubilation, and cheerful festivals for the house of Judah; so love truth and peace.'

20 "The Lord of armies says this: '*It will* yet *turn out* that peoples will come, that is, the inhabitants of many cities. 21 The inhabitants of one *city* will go to another, saying, "Let's go at once to plead for the favor of the Lord, and to seek the Lord of armies; I also will go." 22 So many peoples and mighty nations will come to seek the Lord of armies in Jerusalem, and to plead for the favor of the Lord.' 23 The Lord of armies says this: 'In those days ten people from all the nations will grasp the garment of a Jew, saying, "Let us go with you, for we have heard that God is with you." ' "

Prophecies against Neighboring Nations

9 The pronouncement of the word of the Lord is against the land of Hadrach, with Damascus as its resting place (for the eyes of mankind, especially of all the tribes of Israel, are toward the Lord),

2　And Hamath also, which borders on it;
　　Tyre and Sidon, though they are very wise.
3　For Tyre built herself a fortress,
　　And piled up silver like dust,
　　And gold like the mud of the streets.
4　Behold, the Lord will dispossess her
　　And throw her wealth into the sea;
　　And she will be consumed with fire.
5　Ashkelon will see *it* and be afraid.
　　Gaza too will writhe in great pain;
　　Also Ekron, because her hope has been ruined.
　　Moreover, the king will perish from Gaza,
　　And Ashkelon will not be inhabited.
6　And *a people of* mixed origins will live in Ashdod,
　　And I will eliminate the pride of the Philistines.
7　And I will remove their blood from their mouth
　　And their detestable things from between their teeth.
　　Then they also will be a remnant for our God,
　　And be like a clan in Judah,
　　And Ekron *will be* like a Jebusite.
8　But I will camp around My house because of an army,
　　Because of him who passes by and returns;
　　And no oppressor will pass over them anymore,
　　For now I have seen with My eyes.
9　Rejoice greatly, daughter of Zion!
　　Shout *in triumph,* daughter of Jerusalem!
　　Behold, your king is coming to you;
　　He is righteous and endowed with salvation,

　　Humble, and mounted on a donkey,
　　Even on a colt, the foal of a donkey.
10　And I will eliminate the chariot from Ephraim
　　And the horse from Jerusalem;
　　And the bow of war will be eliminated.
　　And He will speak peace to the nations;
　　And His dominion will be from sea to sea,
　　And from the *Euphrates* River to the ends of the earth.

Restoration of Judah and Ephraim

11¶　As for you also, because of the blood of *My* covenant with you,
　　I have set your prisoners free from the waterless pit.
12　Return to the stronghold, you prisoners who have the hope;
　　This very day I am declaring that I will restore double to you.
13　For I will bend Judah as My bow,
　　I will fill the bow with Ephraim.
　　And I will stir up your sons, Zion, against your sons, Greece;
　　And I will make you like a warrior's sword.
14　Then the Lord will appear over them,
　　And His arrow will go forth like lightning;
　　And the Lord God will blow the trumpet,
　　And march in the storm winds of the south.
15　The Lord of armies will protect them.
　　And they will devour and trample on the slingstones;
　　And they will drink *and* be boisterous as *with* wine;
　　And they will be filled like a *sacrificial* basin,
　　Drenched like the corners of the altar.
16　And the Lord their God will save them on that day
　　As the flock of His people;
　　For *they are like* the *precious* stones of a crown,
　　Sparkling on His land.
17　For how great *will* their loveliness and beauty *be!*
　　Grain will make the young men flourish, and new wine, the virgins.

God Will Bless Judah and Ephraim

10 Ask for rain from the Lord at the time of the spring rain—
　　The Lord who makes the storm winds;
　　And He will give them showers of rain, vegetation in the field to *each* person.
2　For the ʰhousehold idols speak deception,
　　And the diviners see an illusion
　　And tell deceitful dreams;
　　They comfort in vain.
　　Therefore *the people* wander like sheep,
　　They are wretched because there is no shepherd.
3　"My anger is kindled against the shepherds,
　　And I will punish the ʰmale goats;
　　For the Lord of armies has visited His flock, the house of Judah,

---

And will make them like His majestic
horse in battle.
4 "From them will come the cornerstone,
From them the tent peg,
From them the bow of battle,
From them every tyrant, all of them
together.
5 "And they will be like warriors,
Trampling down the enemy in the mud of
the streets in battle;
And they will fight, because the LORD will
be with them;
And the riders on horses will be put to
shame.
6 "And I will strengthen the house of Judah,
And I will save the house of Joseph,
And I will bring them back,
Because I have had compassion on them;
And they will be as though I had not
rejected them,
For I am the LORD their God and I will
answer them.
7 "Ephraim will be like a warrior,
And their heart will be joyful as if from
wine;
Indeed, their children will see it and be
joyful,
Their heart will rejoice in the LORD.
8 "I will whistle for them and gather them
together,
For I have redeemed them;
And they will be as numerous as they
were before.
9 "When I scatter them among the peoples,
They will remember Me in distant
countries,
And they with their children will live and
come back.
10 "I will bring them back from the land of
Egypt
And gather them from Assyria;
And I will bring them into the land of
Gilead and Lebanon
Until no room can be found for them.
11 "And they will pass through the sea of dis-
tress
And He will strike the waves in the sea,
So that all the depths of the Nile will dry
up;
And the pride of Assyria will be brought
down,
And the scepter of Egypt will depart.
12 "And I will strengthen them in the LORD,
And in His name they will walk," declares
the LORD.

The Doomed Flock

11 Open your doors, Lebanon,
So that a fire may feed on your cedars.
2 Wail, juniper, because the cedar has
fallen,
For the magnificent trees have been
destroyed;
Wail, oaks of Bashan,
Because the impenetrable forest has come
down.
3 There is a sound of the shepherds' wail,
For their splendor is ruined;
There is a sound of the young lions' roar,

For the pride of the Jordan is ruined.
4 This is what the LORD my God says:
"Pasture the flock doomed to slaughter. 5 Those
who buy them slaughter them and go unpunished, and each of those who sell them says,
'Blessed be the LORD, for I have become rich!'
And their own shepherds have no compassion
for them. 6 For I will no longer have compassion for the inhabitants of the land," declares
the LORD; "but behold, I will let the people fall,
each into another's power and into the power
of his king; and they will crush the land, and I
will not rescue them from their power."
7 So I pastured the flock doomed to
slaughter, therefore also the afflicted of the
flock. And I took for myself two staffs: the one
I called Favor, and the other I called Union; so I
pastured the flock. 8 Then I did away with the
three shepherds in one month, for my soul was
impatient with them, and their soul also was
tired of me. 9 Then I said, "I will not pasture
you. What is to die, let it die, and what is to
perish, let it perish; and let those who are
left eat one another's flesh." 10 And I took my
staff Favor and cut it in pieces, to break my
covenant which I had made with all the
peoples. 11 So it was broken on that day, and 1so
the afflicted of the flock who were watching
me realized that it was the word of the LORD.
12 And I said to them, "If it is good in your
sight, give me my wages; but if not, never
mind!" So they weighed out thirty shekels of
silver as my wages. 13 Then the LORD said to
me, "Throw it to the potter, that magnificent
price at which I was valued by them." So I took
the thirty shekels of silver and threw them to
the potter in the house of the LORD. 14 Then I
cut in pieces my second staff Union, to break
the brotherhood between Judah and Israel.
15 And the LORD said to me, "Take again for
yourself the equipment of a foolish shepherd.
16 For behold, I am going to raise up a
shepherd in the land who will not care for the
perishing, seek the scattered, heal the broken,
or provide for the one who is exhausted, but
will devour the flesh of the fat sheep and tear
off their hoofs.
17 "Woe to the worthless shepherd
Who abandons the flock!
A sword will be on his arm
And on his right eye!
His arm will be totally withered,
And his right eye will be blind."

Jerusalem to Be Attacked

12 The pronouncement of the word of the
LORD concerning Israel:
The LORD who stretches out the heavens,
lays the foundation of the earth, and forms
the spirit of a person within him, declares:
2 "Behold, I am going to make Jerusalem a
cup that causes staggering to all the peoples
around; and when the siege is against
Jerusalem, it will also be against Judah. 3 It
will come about on that day that I will make
Jerusalem a heavy stone for all the peoples; all
who lift it will injure themselves severely. And
all the nations of the earth will be gathered
against it. 4 On that day," declares the LORD,

11:11 1 Another reading is the sheep dealers who

"I will strike every horse with confusion and its rider with insanity. But I will watch over the house of Judah, while I strike every horse of the peoples with blindness. 5 Then the clans of Judah will say in their hearts, 'The inhabitants of Jerusalem are a strong support for us through the LORD of armies, their God.'

6 "On that day I will make the clans of Judah like a firepot among pieces of wood and a flaming torch among sheaves, so they will consume on the right and on the left all the surrounding peoples, while the inhabitants of Jerusalem again live on their own sites in Jerusalem. 7 The LORD also will save the tents of Judah first, so that the glory of the house of David and the glory of the inhabitants of Jerusalem will not be greater than Judah. 8 On that day the LORD will protect the inhabitants of Jerusalem, and the one who is feeble among them on that day will be like David, and the house of David *will be* like God, like the angel of the LORD before them. 9 And on that day I will seek to destroy all the nations that come against Jerusalem.

10 "And I will pour out on the house of David and on the inhabitants of Jerusalem the Spirit of grace and of pleading, so that they will look at Me whom they pierced; and they will mourn for Him, like one mourning for an only son, and they will weep bitterly over Him like the bitter weeping over a firstborn. 11 On that day the mourning in Jerusalem will be great, like the mourning of Hadadrimmon in the plain of Megiddo. 12 The land will mourn, every family by itself; the family of the house of David by itself and their wives by themselves; the family of the house of Nathan by itself and their wives by themselves; 13 the family of the house of Levi by itself and their wives by themselves; the family of the Shimeites by itself and their wives by themselves; 14 all the families that are left, every family by itself, and their wives by themselves.

False Prophets Ashamed

13 "On that day a fountain will be opened for the house of David and for the inhabitants of Jerusalem, for sin and for defilement.

2 "And it will come about on that day," declares the LORD of armies, "that I will eliminate the names of the idols from the land, and they will no longer be remembered; and I will also remove the prophets and the unclean spirit from the land. 3 And if anyone still prophesies, then his father and mother who gave birth to him will say to him, 'You shall not live, because you have spoken falsely in the name of the LORD'; and his father and mother who gave birth to him shall pierce him through when he prophesies. 4 Also it will come about on that day that the prophets will each be ashamed of his vision when he prophesies, and they will not put on a hairy robe in order to deceive; 5 but he will say, 'I am not a prophet; I am a cultivator of the ground, because a man sold me *as a slave* in my youth.' 6 And *someone* will say to him, 'What are these wounds between your arms?' Then he will say, '*Those* with which I was wounded at the house of my friends.'

7 ¶ "Awake, sword, against My Shepherd,
And against the Man, My Associate,"
Declares the LORD of armies.
"Strike the Shepherd and the sheep will be
scattered;
And I will turn My hand against the little
ones.

8 "And it will come about in all the land,"
Declares the LORD,
"That two parts in it will be cut off *and*
perish;
But the third will be left in it.

9 "And I will bring the third part through the
fire,
Refine them as silver is refined,
And test them as gold is tested.
They will call on My name,
And I will answer them;
I will say, 'They are My people,'
And they will say, 'The LORD is my God.'"

God Will Battle Jerusalem's Enemies

14 Behold, a day is coming for the LORD when the spoils *taken from* you will be divided among you. 2 For I will gather all the nations against Jerusalem to battle, and the city will be taken, the houses plundered, the women raped, and half of the city exiled, but the rest of the people will not be eliminated from the city. 3 Then the LORD will go forth and fight against those nations, as when He fights on a day of battle. 4 On that day His feet will stand on the Mount of Olives, which is in front of Jerusalem on the east; and the Mount of Olives will be split in its middle from east to west *forming* a very large valley. Half of the mountain will move toward the north, and the other half toward the south. 5 And you will flee by the valley of My mountains, for the valley of the mountains will reach to Azel; yes, you will flee just as you fled from the earthquake in the days of Uzziah king of Judah. Then the LORD, my God, will come, *and* all the holy ones with Him!

6 On that day there will be no light; the luminaries will die out. 7 For it will be a unique day which is known to the LORD, neither day nor night, but it will come about that at the time of evening there will be light.

8 And on that day living waters will flow out of Jerusalem, half of them toward the eastern sea and the other half toward the western sea; it will be in summer as well as in winter.

God Will Be King over All

9 And the LORD will be King over all the earth; on that day the LORD will be *the only* one, and His name *the only* one.

10 All the land will change into a plain from Geba to Rimmon south of Jerusalem; but Jerusalem will rise and remain on its site from Benjamin's Gate as far as the place of the First Gate to the Corner Gate, and from the Tower of Hananel to the king's wine presses. 11 *People* will live in it, and there will no longer be a curse, for Jerusalem will live in security.

12 Now this will be the plague with which the LORD will strike all the peoples who have gone to war against Jerusalem; their flesh will rot while they stand on their feet, and their

eyes will rot in their sockets, and their tongue will rot in their mouth. [13] And it will come about on that day that a great panic from the LORD will fall on them; and they will seize one another's hand, and the hand of one will be raised against the hand of another. [14] Judah also will fight at Jerusalem; and the wealth of all the surrounding nations will be gathered, gold, silver, and garments in great abundance. [15] And just like this plague, there will be a plague on the horse, the mule, the camel, the donkey, and all the cattle that will be in those camps.

[16] Then it will come about that any who are left of all the nations that came against Jerusalem will go up from year to year to worship the King, the LORD of armies, and to celebrate the Feast of Booths. [17] And it will be that whichever of the families of the earth does not go up to Jerusalem to worship the King, the LORD of armies, there will be no rain on them. [18] And if the family of Egypt does not go up or enter, then no *rain will fall* on them; it will be the plague with which the LORD strikes the nations that do not go up to celebrate the Feast of Booths. [19] This will be the punishment of Egypt, and the punishment of all the nations that do not go up to celebrate the Feast of Booths.

[20] On that day there will be *inscribed* on the bells of the horses, "HOLY TO THE LORD." And the cooking pots in the LORD's house will be like the bowls before the altar. [21] Every cooking pot in Jerusalem and in Judah will be holy to the LORD of armies; and all who sacrifice will come and take of them and boil in them. And there will no longer be a Canaanite in the house of the LORD of armies on that day.

God's Love for Jacob

1 The pronouncement of the word of the LORD to Israel through Malachi: **2** "I have loved you," says the LORD. But you say, "How have You loved us?" "*Was* Esau not Jacob's brother?" declares the LORD. "Yet I have loved Jacob; **3** but I have hated Esau, and I have made his mountains a desolation and *given* his inheritance to the jackals of the wilderness." **4** Though Edom says, "We have been beaten down, but we will return and build up the ruins"; this is what the LORD of armies says: "They may build, but I will tear down; and *people* will call them the territory of wickedness, and the people with whom the LORD is indignant forever." **5** And your eyes will see *this,* and you will say, "The LORD be exalted beyond the border of Israel!"

Sin of the Priests

6 " 'A son honors *his* father, and a servant his master. Then if I am a father, where is My honor? And if I am a master, where is My respect?' says the LORD of armies to you, the priests who despise My name! But you say, 'How have we despised Your name?' **7** *You are* presenting defiled food upon My altar. But you say, 'How have we defiled You?' In that you say, 'The table of the LORD is to be despised.' **8** And when you present a blind *animal* for sacrifice, is it not evil? Or when you present a lame or sick *animal,* is it not evil? So offer it to your governor! Would he be pleased with you, or would he receive you kindly?" says the LORD of armies. **9** "But now, do indeed plead for God's favor, so that He will be gracious to us. With such an offering on your part, will He receive any of you kindly?" says the LORD of armies. **10** "If only there were one among you who would shut the gates, so that you would not kindle *fire on* My altar for nothing! I am not pleased with you," says the LORD of armies, "nor will I accept an offering from your hand. **11** For from the rising of the sun even to its setting, My name *shall be* great among the nations, and in every place frankincense is going to be offered to My name, and a grain offering *that is* pure; for My name *shall be* great among the nations," says the LORD of armies. **12** "But you are profaning it by your saying, 'The table of the Lord is defiled, and as for its fruit, its food is to be despised.' **13** You also say, 'See, how tiresome it is!' And you view it as trivial," says the LORD of armies, "and you bring what was taken by robbery and *what is* lame or sick; so you bring the offering! Should I accept it from your hand?" says the LORD. **14** "But cursed be the swindler who has a male in his flock and vows *it,* but sacrifices a blemished *animal* to the Lord, for I am a great King," says the LORD of armies, "and My name is feared among the nations."

Priests to Be Disciplined

2 "And now, this commandment is for you, the priests. **2** If you do not listen, and if you do not take it to heart to give honor to My name," says the LORD of armies, "then I will send the curse upon you and I will curse your blessings; and indeed, I have cursed them *already,* because you are not taking *it* to heart. **3** Behold, I am going to rebuke your descendants, and I will spread dung on your faces, the dung of your feasts; and you will be taken away with it. **4** Then you will know that I have sent this commandment to you, so that My covenant may continue with Levi," says the LORD of armies. **5** "My covenant with him was *one of* life and peace, and I gave them to him *as an object of* reverence; so he revered Me and was in awe of My name. **6** True instruction was in his mouth and injustice was not found on his lips; he walked with Me in peace and justice, and he turned many back from wrongdoing. **7** For the lips of a priest should maintain knowledge, and *people* should seek instruction from his mouth; for he is the messenger of the LORD of armies. **8** But as for you, you have turned aside from the way; you have caused many to stumble by the instruction; you have ruined the covenant of Levi," says the LORD of armies. **9** "So I also have made you despised and of low reputation in the view of all the people, since you are not keeping My ways but are showing partiality in the instruction."

Sin in the Family

10 Do we not all have one Father? Is it not one God *who* has created us? Why do we deal treacherously, each against his brother so as to profane the covenant of our fathers? **11** Judah has dealt treacherously, and an abomination has been committed in Israel and in Jerusalem; for Judah has profaned the sanctuary of the LORD which He loves, and has married the daughter of a foreign god. **12** *As* for the man who does this, may the LORD eliminate from the tents of Jacob *everyone* who is awake and answers, or who presents an offering to the LORD of armies.

13 And this is another thing you do: you cover the altar of the LORD with tears, with weeping and sighing, because He no longer gives attention to the offering or accepts *it with* favor from your hand. **14** Yet you say, "For what reason?" Because the LORD has been a witness between you and the wife of your youth, against whom you have dealt treacherously, though she is your marriage companion and your wife by covenant. **15** But not one has done *so* who has a remnant of the Spirit. And why the one? He was seeking a godly offspring. Be careful then about your spirit, and *see that* none *of you* deals treacherously against the wife of your youth. **16** "For I hate divorce," says

the Lord, the God of Israel, "and him who covers his garment with violence," says the Lord of armies. "So be careful about your spirit, that you do not deal treacherously."

17 You have wearied the Lord with your words. Yet you say, "How have we wearied *Him?*" In that you say, "Everyone who does evil is good in the sight of the Lord, and He delights in them," or, "Where is the God of justice?"

The Purifier

3 "Behold, I am sending My messenger, and he will clear a way before Me. And the Lord, whom you are seeking, will suddenly come to His temple; and the messenger of the covenant, in whom you delight, behold, He is coming," says the Lord of armies. **2** "But who can endure the day of His coming? And who can stand when He appears? For He is like a refiner's fire, and like launderer's soap. **3** And He will sit as a smelter and purifier of silver, and He will purify the sons of Levi and refine them like gold and silver, so that they may present to the Lord offerings in righteousness. **4** Then the offering of Judah and Jerusalem will be pleasing to the Lord as in the days of old, and as in former years.

5 "Then I will come near to you for judgment; and I will be a swift witness against the sorcerers, the adulterers, against those who swear falsely, those who oppress the wage earner in his wages *or* the widow or the orphan, and those who turn away the stranger *from justice* and do not fear Me," says the Lord of armies. **6** "For I, the Lord, do not change; therefore you, the sons of Jacob, have not come to an end.

7 "From the days of your fathers you have turned away from My statutes and have not kept *them.* Return to Me, and I will return to you," says the Lord of armies. "But you say, 'How shall we return?'

You Have Robbed God

8 "Would anyone rob God? Yet you are robbing Me! But you say, 'How have we robbed You?' *In* tithes and offerings. **9** You are cursed with a curse, for you are robbing Me, the entire nation *of you!* **10** Bring the whole tithe into the storehouse, so that there may be food in My house, and put Me to the test now in this," says the Lord of armies, "if I do not open for you the windows of heaven and pour out for you a blessing until it overflows. **11** Then I

will rebuke the devourer for you, so that it will not destroy the fruit of your ground; nor will the vine in the field prove fruitless to you," says the Lord of armies. **12** "All the nations will call you blessed, for you will be a delightful land," says the Lord of armies.

13 "Your words have been arrogant against Me," says the Lord. "Yet you say, 'What have we spoken against You?' **14** You have said, 'It is pointless to serve God; and what benefit *is it for us* that we have done what He required, and that we have walked in mourning before the Lord of armies? **15** So now we call the arrogant blessed; not only are the doers of wickedness built up, but they also put God to the test and escape *punishment.*'"

The Book of Remembrance

16 Then those who feared the Lord spoke to one another, and the Lord listened attentively and heard *it,* and a book of remembrance was written before Him for those who fear Lord and esteem His name. **17** "And they will be Mine," says the Lord of armies, "on the day that I prepare *My* own possession, and I will have compassion for them just as a man has compassion for his own son who serves him." **18** So you will again distinguish between the righteous and the wicked, between one who serves God and one who does not serve Him.

Final Admonition

4 "For behold, the day is coming, burning like a furnace; and all the arrogant and every evildoer will be chaff; and the day that is coming will set them ablaze," says the Lord of armies, "so that it will leave them neither root nor branches. **2** But for you who fear My name, the sun of righteousness will rise with healing in its wings; and you will go forth and frolic like calves from the stall. **3** And you will crush the wicked underfoot, for they will be ashes under the soles of your feet on the day that I am preparing," says the Lord of armies.

4 "Remember the Law of Moses My servant, *the* statutes and ordinances which I commanded him in Horeb for all Israel.

5 "Behold, I am going to send you Elijah the prophet before the coming of the great and terrible day of the Lord. **6** He will turn the hearts of the fathers back to *their* children and the hearts of the children to their fathers, so that I will not come and strike the land with complete destruction."

THE NEW TESTAMENT

The Gospel According to
MATTHEW

The Genealogy of Jesus the Messiah

1 The record of the genealogy of Jesus the Messiah, the son of David, the son of Abraham:

2 Abraham fathered Isaac, Isaac fathered Jacob, and Jacob fathered [1]Judah and his brothers. 3 Judah fathered Perez and Zerah by Tamar, Perez fathered Hezron, and Hezron fathered Ram. 4 Ram fathered Amminadab, Amminadab fathered Nahshon, and Nahshon fathered Salmon. 5 Salmon fathered Boaz by Rahab, Boaz fathered Obed by Ruth, and Obed fathered Jesse. 6 Jesse fathered David the king.

David fathered Solomon by [1]her *who had been the wife* of Uriah. 7 Solomon fathered Rehoboam, Rehoboam fathered Abijah, and Abijah fathered Asa. 8 Asa fathered Jehoshaphat, Jehoshaphat fathered Joram, and Joram fathered Uzziah. 9 Uzziah fathered Jotham, Jotham fathered Ahaz, and Ahaz fathered Hezekiah. 10 Hezekiah fathered Manasseh, Manasseh fathered Amon, and Amon fathered Josiah. 11 Josiah fathered Jeconiah and his brothers, at the time of the deportation to Babylon.

12 After the deportation to Babylon: Jeconiah fathered Shealtiel, and Shealtiel fathered Zerubbabel. 13 Zerubbabel fathered Abihud, Abihud fathered Eliakim, and Eliakim fathered Azor. 14 Azor fathered Zadok, Zadok fathered Achim, and Achim fathered Eliud. 15 Eliud fathered Eleazar, Eleazar fathered Matthan, and Matthan fathered Jacob. 16 Jacob fathered Joseph the husband of Mary, by whom Jesus was born, who is called the Messiah.

17 So all the generations from Abraham to David are fourteen generations; from David to the deportation to Babylon, fourteen generations; and from the deportation to Babylon to the Messiah, fourteen generations.

Conception and Birth of Jesus

18 Now the birth of Jesus the Messiah was as follows: when His mother Mary had been [1]betrothed to Joseph, before they came together she was found to be pregnant by the Holy Spirit. 19 And her husband Joseph, since he was a righteous man and did not want to disgrace her, planned to [1]send her away secretly. 20 But when he had thought this over, behold, an angel of the Lord appeared to him in a dream, saying, "Joseph, son of David, do not be afraid to take Mary as your wife; for the Child who has been conceived in her is of the Holy Spirit. 21 She will give birth to a Son; and you shall name Him Jesus, for He will save His people from their sins." 22 Now all this took place so that what was spoken by the Lord through [1]the prophet would be fulfilled:

23 "BEHOLD, THE VIRGIN WILL CONCEIVE AND GIVE BIRTH TO A SON, AND THEY SHALL NAME HIM IMMANUEL," which translated means, "GOD WITH US." 24 And Joseph awoke from his sleep and did as the angel of the Lord commanded him, and took *Mary* as his wife, 25 but kept her a virgin until she gave birth to a Son; and he named Him Jesus.

The Visit of the Magi

2 Now after Jesus was born in Bethlehem of Judea in the days of Herod the king, behold, [1]magi from the east arrived in Jerusalem, saying, 2 "Where is He who has been born King of the Jews? For we saw His star in the east and have come to worship Him." 3 When Herod the king heard *this,* he was troubled, and all Jerusalem with him. 4 And gathering together all the chief priests and scribes of the people, he inquired of them where the Messiah was to be born. 5 They said to him, "In Bethlehem of Judea; for this is what has been written by [1]the prophet:

6 'AND YOU, BETHLEHEM, LAND OF JUDAH,
    ARE BY NO MEANS LEAST AMONG THE LEADERS
        OF JUDAH;
    FOR FROM YOU WILL COME FORTH A RULER
    WHO WILL SHEPHERD MY PEOPLE ISRAEL.' "

7 Then Herod secretly called for the magi and determined from them the exact time the star appeared. 8 And he sent them to Bethlehem and said, "Go and search carefully for the Child; and when you have found *Him,* report to me, so that I too may come and worship Him." 9 After hearing the king, they went on their way; and behold, the star, which they had seen in the east, went on ahead of them until it came to a stop over *the place* where the Child was *to be found.* 10 When they saw the star, they rejoiced exceedingly with great joy. 11 And after they came into the house, they saw the Child with His mother Mary; and they fell down and worshiped Him. Then they opened their treasures and presented to Him gifts of gold, frankincense, and myrrh. 12 And after being warned *by God* in a dream not to return to Herod, *the magi* left for their own country by another way.

The Escape to Egypt

13 Now when they had gone, behold, an angel of the Lord *appeared* to Joseph in a dream and said, "Get up! Take the Child and His mother and flee to Egypt, and stay there until I tell you; for Herod is going to search for the Child to kill Him." 14 So Joseph got up and took the Child and His mother while it was still night, and left for Egypt. 15 He stayed there until the death of

1:2 1 Gr *Judas;* a name of a person in the Old Testament is given in its Old Testament form 1:6 1 I.e., Bathsheba 1:18 1 Unlike engagement, a betrothed couple was considered married, but did not yet live together 1:19 1 Or *divorce her* 1:22 1 I.e., Isaiah 2:1 1 A caste of educated men specializing in astronomy, astrology, and natural science 2:5 1 I.e., Micah

Herod; *this happened* so that what had been spoken by the Lord through ¹the prophet would be fulfilled: "Out of Egypt I called My Son."

Herod Slaughters Babies

16 Then when Herod saw that he had been tricked by the magi, he became very enraged, and sent *men* and killed all the boys who were in Bethlehem and all its vicinity who were two years old or under, according to the time which he had determined from the magi. 17 Then what had been spoken through Jeremiah the prophet was fulfilled:
18 "A voice was heard in Ramah,
Weeping and great mourning,
Rachel weeping for her children;
And she refused to be comforted,
Because they were no more."
19 But when Herod died, behold, an angel of the Lord *appeared in a dream to Joseph in Egypt, and said, 20 "Get up, take the Child and His mother, and go to the land of Israel; for those who sought the Child's life are dead."
21 So Joseph got up, took the Child and His mother, and came into the land of Israel.
22 But when he heard that Archelaus was reigning over Judea in place of his father Herod, he was afraid to go there. Then after being warned *by God* in a dream, he left for the regions of Galilee, 23 and came and settled in a city called Nazareth. *This happened* so that what was spoken through the prophets would be fulfilled: "He will be called a Nazarene."

The Preaching of John the Baptist

3 Now in those days John the Baptist *came, preaching in the wilderness of Judea, saying, 2 "Repent, for the kingdom of heaven is at hand." 3 For this is the one referred to by Isaiah the prophet when he said,
"The voice of one calling ¹out in the wilderness,
'Prepare the way of the Lord,
Make His paths straight!'"
4 Now John himself had a garment of camel's hair and a leather belt around his waist; and his food was locusts and wild honey. 5 At that time Jerusalem was going out to him, and all Judea and all the region around the Jordan; 6 and they were being baptized by him in the Jordan River, as they confessed their sins.
7 But when he saw many of the Pharisees and Sadducees coming for baptism, he said to them, "You offspring of vipers, who warned you to flee from the wrath to come? 8 Therefore produce fruit consistent with repentance; 9 and do not assume that you can say to yourselves, 'We have Abraham *as our* father'; for I tell you that God is able, from these stones, to raise up children for Abraham. 10 And the axe is already laid at the root of the trees; therefore, every tree that does not bear good fruit is being cut down and thrown into the fire.
11 "As for me, I baptize you ¹with water for repentance, but He who is coming after me is mightier than I, and I am not fit to remove His

sandals; He will baptize you with the Holy Spirit and fire. 12 His winnowing fork is in His hand, and He will thoroughly clear His threshing floor; and He will gather His wheat into the barn, but He will burn up the chaff with unquenchable fire."

The Baptism of Jesus

13 Then Jesus *arrived from Galilee at the Jordan, *coming* to John to be baptized by him. 14 But John tried to prevent Him, saying, "I have *the* need to be baptized by You, and *yet* You are coming to me?" 15 But Jesus, answering, said to him, "Allow *it* at this time; for in this way it is fitting for us to fulfill all righteousness." Then he *allowed Him. 16 After He was baptized, Jesus came up immediately from the water; and behold, the heavens were opened, and he saw the Spirit of God descending as a dove *and* settling on Him, 17 and behold, a voice from the heavens said, "This is My beloved Son, with whom I am well pleased."

The Temptation of Jesus

4 Then Jesus was led up by the Spirit into the wilderness to be tempted by the devil. 2 And after He had fasted for forty days and forty nights, He then became hungry. 3 And the tempter came and said to Him, "If You are the Son of God, command that these stones become bread." 4 But He answered and said, "It is written: 'Man shall not live on bread alone, but on every word that comes out of the mouth of God.'"
5 Then the devil *took Him along into the holy city and had Him stand on the pinnacle of the temple, 6 and he *said to Him, "If You are the Son of God, throw Yourself down; for it is written:
'He will give His angels orders concerning You';
and
'On *their* hands they will lift You up,
So that You do not strike Your foot against a stone.'"
7 Jesus said to him, "On the other hand, it is written: 'You shall not put the Lord your God to the test.'"
8 Again, the devil *took Him along to a very high mountain and *showed Him all the kingdoms of the world and their glory; 9 and he said to Him, "All these things I will give You, if You fall down and worship me." 10 Then Jesus *said to him, "Go away, Satan! For it is written: 'You shall worship the Lord your God, and serve Him only.'" 11 Then the devil *left Him; and behold, angels came and *began to* serve Him.

Jesus Begins His Ministry

12 Now when Jesus heard that John had been taken into custody, He withdrew into Galilee; 13 and leaving Nazareth, He came and settled in Capernaum, which is by the sea, in the region of Zebulun and Naphtali. 14 *This happened* so that what was spoken through Isaiah the prophet would be fulfilled:

2:15 ¹I.e., Hosea   3:3 ¹Or *out, Prepare in the wilderness the way*   3:11 ¹The Gr here can be translated *in, with,* or *by*

15 "THE LAND OF ZEBULUN AND THE LAND OF
NAPHTALI,
BY THE WAY OF THE SEA, ON THE OTHER SIDE
OF THE JORDAN, GALILEE OF
THE [1]GENTILES—
16 THE PEOPLE WHO WERE SITTING IN DARKNESS
SAW A GREAT LIGHT,
AND THOSE WHO WERE SITTING IN THE LAND
AND SHADOW OF DEATH,
UPON THEM A LIGHT DAWNED."
17 From that time Jesus began to preach and
say, "Repent, for the kingdom of heaven is at
hand."

The First Disciples

18 Now as *Jesus* was walking by the Sea of
Galilee, He saw two brothers, Simon, who was
called Peter, and his brother Andrew, casting
a net into the sea; for they were fishermen.
19 And He *said to them, "Follow Me, and I
will make you fishers of people."
20 Immediately they left their nets and followed
Him. 21 Going on from there He saw two other
brothers, James the *son* of Zebedee, and his
brother John, in the boat with their father
Zebedee, mending their nets; and He called
them. 22 Immediately they left the boat and
their father, and followed Him.

Ministry in Galilee

23 Jesus was going about in all of Galilee,
teaching in their synagogues and proclaiming
the gospel of the kingdom, and healing every
disease and every sickness among the people.
24 And the news about Him spread throughout Syria; and they brought to Him all who
were ill, those suffering with various diseases
and severe pain, demon-possessed, people with
epilepsy, and people who were paralyzed; and
He healed them. 25 Large crowds followed Him
from Galilee and *the* Decapolis, and Jerusalem,
and Judea, and *from* beyond the Jordan.

The Sermon on the Mount; The Beatitudes

5 Now when Jesus saw the crowds, He went
up on the mountain; and after He sat down,
His disciples came to Him. 2 And He opened
His mouth and *began* to teach them, saying,
3 "Blessed are the poor in spirit, for theirs is
the kingdom of heaven.
4 "Blessed are those who mourn, for they
will be comforted.
5 "Blessed are the [1]gentle, for they will
inherit the earth.
6 "Blessed are those who hunger and thirst
for righteousness, for they will be satisfied.
7 "Blessed are the merciful, for they will
receive mercy.
8 "Blessed are the pure in heart, for they will
see God.
9 "Blessed are the peacemakers, for they will
be called sons of God.
10 "Blessed are those who have been
persecuted for the sake of righteousness, for
theirs is the kingdom of heaven.
11 "Blessed are you when *people* insult you
and persecute you, and falsely say all kinds of

evil against you because of Me. 12 Rejoice and
be glad, for your reward in heaven is great; for
in this same way they persecuted the prophets
who were before you.

Disciples and the World

13 "You are the salt of the earth; but if the
salt has become tasteless, how can it be made
salty *again?* It is no longer good for anything,
except to be thrown out and trampled underfoot by people.
14 "You are the light of the world. A city set
on a hill cannot be hidden; 15 nor do *people*
light a lamp and put it under a basket, but on
the lampstand, and it gives light to all who are
in the house. 16 Your light must shine before
people in such a way that they may see your
good works, and glorify your Father who is in
heaven.
17 "Do not presume that I came to abolish
the Law or the Prophets; I did not come to
abolish, but to fulfill. 18 For truly I say to you,
until heaven and earth pass away, not the
smallest letter or stroke of a letter shall pass
from the Law, until all is accomplished!
19 Therefore, whoever nullifies one of the
least of these commandments, and teaches
others *to do* the same, shall be called least in
the kingdom of heaven; but whoever keeps and
teaches *them,* he shall be called great in the
kingdom of heaven.
20 "For I say to you that unless your
righteousness far surpasses *that* of the scribes
and Pharisees, you will not enter the kingdom
of heaven.

Personal Relationships

21 "You have heard that the ancients were
told, 'YOU SHALL NOT MURDER,' and 'Whoever
commits murder shall be answerable to the
court.' 22 But I say to you that everyone who is
angry with his brother shall be answerable to
the court; and whoever says to his brother,
'[1]You good-for-nothing,' shall be answerable to
[2]the supreme court; and whoever says, 'You
fool,' shall be guilty *enough to go* into the
[3]fiery hell. 23 Therefore, if you are presenting
your offering at the altar, and there you
remember that your brother has something
against you, 24 leave your offering there before
the altar and go; first be reconciled to your
brother, and then come and present your
offering. 25 Come to good terms with your
accuser quickly, while you are with him on the
way *to court,* so that your accuser will not
hand you over to the judge, and the judge to
the officer, and you will not be thrown into
prison. 26 Truly I say to you, you will not come
out of there until you have paid up the last
[1]quadrans.
27 "You have heard that it was said, 'YOU
SHALL NOT COMMIT ADULTERY'; 28 but I say to you
that everyone who looks at a woman with lust
for her has already committed adultery with
her in his heart. 29 Now if your right eye is
causing you to sin, tear it out and throw it
away from you; for it is better for you to lose

4:15 [1] Lit *nations,* usually non-Jewish   5:5 [1] Or *humble, meek*   5:22 [1] Or *You empty-head;* Gr *Raka (Raca)*
from Aramaic *reqa*   [2] Lit *the Sanhedrin;* i.e., Jewish High Court   [3] Lit *Gehenna of fire*   5:26 [1] A small
Roman copper coin, worth about 1/64 of a laborer's daily wage

one of the parts of your *body,* than for your whole body to be thrown into hell. 30 And if your right hand is causing you to sin, cut it off and throw it away from you; for it is better for you to lose one of the parts of your *body,* than for your whole body to go into hell.

31 "Now it was said, 'WHOEVER SENDS HIS WIFE AWAY IS TO GIVE HER A CERTIFICATE OF DIVORCE'; 32 but I say to you that everyone who divorces his wife, except for *the* reason of sexual immorality, makes her commit adultery; and whoever marries a divorced woman commits adultery.

33 "Again, you have heard that the ancients were told, 'YOU SHALL NOT MAKE FALSE VOWS, BUT SHALL FULFILL YOUR VOWS TO THE LORD.' 34 But I say to you, take no oath at all, neither by heaven, for it is the throne of God, 35 nor by the earth, for it is the footstool of His feet, nor by Jerusalem, for it is THE CITY OF THE GREAT KING. 36 Nor shall you take an oath by your head, for you cannot make a single hair white or black. 37 But make sure your statement is, 'Yes, yes' *or* 'No, no'; anything beyond these is of evil *origin.*

38 "You have heard that it was said, 'EYE FOR EYE, and TOOTH FOR TOOTH.' 39 But I say to you, do not show opposition against an evil person; but whoever slaps you on your right cheek, turn the other toward him also. 40 And if anyone wants to sue you and take your ¹tunic, let him have your ²cloak also. 41 Whoever forces you to go one mile, go with him two. 42 Give to him who asks of you, and do not turn away from him who wants to borrow from you.

43 "You have heard that it was said, 'YOU SHALL LOVE YOUR NEIGHBOR and hate your enemy.' 44 But I say to you, love your enemies and pray for those who persecute you, 45 so that you may prove yourselves to be sons of your Father who is in heaven; for He causes His sun to rise on *the* evil and *the* good, and sends rain on *the* righteous and *the* unrighteous. 46 For if you love those who love you, what reward do you have? Even the tax collectors, do they not do the same? 47 And if you greet only your brothers *and sisters,* what more are you doing *than others?* Even the Gentiles, do they not do the same? 48 Therefore you shall be perfect, as your heavenly Father is perfect.

Charitable Giving to the Poor and Prayer

6 "Take care not to practice your righteousness in the sight of people, to be noticed by them; otherwise you have no reward with your Father who is in heaven.

2 "So when you give to the poor, do not sound a trumpet before you, as the hypocrites do in the synagogues and on the streets, so that they will be praised by people. Truly I say to you, they have their reward in full. 3 But when you give to the poor, do not let your left hand know what your right hand is doing, 4 so that your charitable giving will be in secret; and your Father who sees *what is done* in secret will reward you.

5 "And when you pray, you are not to be like the hypocrites; for they love to stand and pray in the synagogues and on the street corners so that they will be seen by people. Truly I say to you, they have their reward in full. 6 But as for you, when you pray, go into your inner room, close your door, and pray to your Father who is in secret; and your Father who sees *what is done* in secret will reward you.

7 "And when you are praying, do not use thoughtless repetition as the Gentiles do, for they think that they will be heard because of their many words. 8 So do not be like them; for your Father knows what you need before you ask Him.

The Lord's Prayer

9 "Pray, then, in this way:
'Our Father, who is in heaven,
Hallowed be Your name.
10 'Your kingdom come.
Your will be done,
On earth as it is in heaven.
11 'Give us this day our daily bread.
12 'And forgive us our debts, as we also have
forgiven our debtors.
13 'And do not lead us into temptation, but
deliver us from evil.'¹
14 For if you forgive *other* people for their offenses, your heavenly Father will also forgive you. 15 But if you do not forgive *other* people, then your Father will not forgive your offenses.

Fasting; The True Treasure; Wealth

16 "Now whenever you fast, do not make a gloomy face as the hypocrites *do,* for they distort their faces so that they will be noticed by people when they are fasting. Truly I say to you, they have their reward in full. 17 But as for you, when you fast, anoint your head and wash your face, 18 so that your fasting will not be noticed by people but by your Father who is in secret; and your Father who sees *what is done* in secret will reward you.

19 "Do not store up for yourselves treasures on earth, where moth and rust destroy, and where thieves break in and steal. 20 But store up for yourselves treasures in heaven, where neither moth nor rust destroys, and where thieves do not break in or steal; 21 for where your treasure is, there your heart will be also.

22 "The eye is the lamp of the body; so then, if your eye is clear, your whole body will be full of light. 23 But if your eye is bad, your whole body will be full of darkness. So if the light that is in you is darkness, how great is the darkness!

24 "No one can serve two masters; for either he will hate the one and love the other, or he will be devoted to one and despise the other. You cannot serve God and ¹wealth.

The Cure for Anxiety

25 "For this reason I say to you, do not be worried about your life, *as to* what you will eat or what you will drink; nor for your body, *as to* what you will put on. Is life not more than

---

5:40 ¹A long shirt worn next to the skin   ²Or *outer garment*   6:13 ¹Late mss add *For Yours is the kingdom and the power and the glory forever. Amen*   6:24 ¹Gr *mamonas,* for Aramaic *mamon* (mammon); i.e., wealth etc. personified as an object of worship

food, and the body more than clothing? 26 Look at the birds of the sky, that they do not sow, nor reap, nor gather *crops* into barns, and *yet* your heavenly Father feeds them. Are you not much more important than they? 27 And which of you by worrying can add a single day to his life's span? 28 And why are you worried about clothing? Notice how the lilies of the field grow; they do not labor nor do they spin *thread for cloth,* 29 yet I say to you that not even Solomon in all his glory clothed himself like one of these. 30 But if God so clothes the grass of the field, which is *alive* today and tomorrow is thrown into the furnace, *will He* not much more *clothe* you? You of little faith! 31 Do not worry then, saying, 'What are we to eat?' or 'What are we to drink?' or 'What are we to wear for clothing?' 32 For the Gentiles eagerly seek all these things; for your heavenly Father knows that you need all these things. 33 But seek first His kingdom and His righteousness, and all these things will be provided to you.

34 "So do not worry about tomorrow; for tomorrow will worry about itself. Each day has enough trouble of its own.

Judging Others

7 "Do not judge, so that you will not be judged. 2 For in the way you judge, you will be judged; and by your standard of measure, it will be measured to you. 3 Why do you look at the speck that is in your brother's eye, but do not notice the log that is in your own eye? 4 Or how can you say to your brother, 'Let me take the speck out of your eye,' and look, the log is in your own eye? 5 You hypocrite, first take the log out of your own eye, and then you will see clearly to take the speck out of your brother's eye!

6 "Do not give what is holy to dogs, and do not throw your pearls before pigs, or they will trample them under their feet, and turn and tear you to pieces.

Prayer and the Golden Rule

7 "Ask, and it will be given to you; seek, and you will find; knock, and it will be opened to you. 8 For everyone who asks receives, and the one who seeks finds, and to the one who knocks it will be opened. 9 Or what person is there among you who, when his son asks for a loaf of bread, will give him a stone? 10 Or if he asks for a fish, he will not give him a snake, will he? 11 So if you, *despite* being evil, know how to give good gifts to your children, how much more will your Father who is in heaven give good things to those who ask Him! 12 "In everything, therefore, treat people the same way you want them to treat you, for this is the Law and the Prophets.

The Narrow and Wide Gates

13 "Enter through the narrow gate; for the gate is wide and the way is broad that leads to destruction, and there are many who enter through it. 14 For the gate is narrow and the way is constricted that leads to life, and there are few who find it.

A Tree and Its Fruit

15 "Beware of the false prophets, who come to you in sheep's clothing, but inwardly are ravenous wolves. 16 You will know them by their fruits. Grapes are not gathered from thorn *bushes,* nor figs from thistles, are they? 17 So every good tree bears good fruit, but the bad tree bears bad fruit. 18 A good tree cannot bear bad fruit, nor can a bad tree bear good fruit. 19 Every tree that does not bear good fruit is cut down and thrown into the fire. 20 So then, you will know them by their fruits.

21 "Not everyone who says to Me, 'Lord, Lord,' will enter the kingdom of heaven, but the one who does the will of My Father who is in heaven *will enter.* 22 Many will say to Me on that day, 'Lord, Lord, did we not prophesy in Your name, and in Your name cast out demons, and in Your name perform many miracles?' 23 And then I will declare to them, 'I never knew you; LEAVE ME, YOU WHO PRACTICE LAW-LESSNESS.'

The Two Foundations

24 "Therefore, everyone who hears these words of Mine, and acts on them, will be like a wise man who built his house on the rock. 25 And the rain fell and the floods came, and the winds blew and slammed against that house; and *yet* it did not fall, for it had been founded on the rock. 26 And everyone who hears these words of Mine, and does not act on them, will be like a foolish man who built his house on the sand. 27 And the rain fell and the floods came, and the winds blew and slammed against that house; and it fell—and its collapse was great."

28 When Jesus had finished these words, the crowds were amazed at His teaching; 29 for He was teaching them as one who had authority, and not as their scribes.

Jesus Cleanses a Man with Leprosy

8 When Jesus came down from the mountain, large crowds followed Him. 2 And a man with *1*leprosy came to Him and bowed down before Him, and said, "Lord, if You are willing, You can make me clean." 3 Jesus reached out with His hand and touched him, saying, "I am willing; be cleansed." And immediately his leprosy was cleansed. 4 And Jesus *said to him, "See that you tell no one; but go, show yourself to the priest and present the offering that Moses commanded, as a testimony to them."

The Centurion's Faith

5 And when Jesus entered Capernaum, a centurion came to Him, begging Him, 6 and saying, "Lord, my servant is lying paralyzed at home, terribly tormented." 7 Jesus *said to him, "I will come and heal him." 8 But the centurion replied, "Lord, I am not worthy for You to come under my roof, but just say the word, and my servant will be healed. 9 For I also am a man under authority, with soldiers under me; and I say to this one, 'Go!' and he goes, and to another, 'Come!' and he comes, and to my slave, 'Do this!' and he does *it."* 10 Now when Jesus heard *this,* He was amazed and said to

---

8:2 1 I.e., leprosy or a serious, unspecified skin disease, and so throughout the ch; see Lev 13

those who were following, "Truly I say to you, I have not found such great faith with anyone in Israel. **11** And I say to you that many will come from east and west, and ¹recline *at the table* with Abraham, Isaac, and Jacob in the kingdom of heaven; **12** but the sons of the kingdom will be thrown out into the outer darkness; in that place there will be weeping and gnashing of teeth." **13** And Jesus said to the centurion, "Go; it shall be done for you as you have believed." And the servant was healed at that *very* moment.

Peter's Mother-in-law and Many Others Healed
14 When Jesus came into Peter's home, He saw his mother-in-law lying sick in bed with a fever. **15** And He touched her hand, and the fever left her; and she got up and waited on Him. **16** Now when evening came, they brought to Him many who were demon-possessed; and He cast out the spirits with a word, and healed all who were ill. **17** *This happened* so that what was spoken through Isaiah the prophet would be fulfilled: "HE HIMSELF TOOK OUR ILLNESSES AND CARRIED AWAY OUR DISEASES."

Discipleship Tested
18 Now when Jesus saw a crowd around Him, He gave orders to depart to the other side *of the sea*. **19** Then a scribe came and said to Him, "Teacher, I will follow You wherever You go." **20** And Jesus *said to him, "The foxes have holes and the birds of the sky *have* nests, but the Son of Man has nowhere to lay His head." **21** And another of the disciples said to Him, "Lord, allow me first to go and bury my father." **22** But Jesus *said to him, "Follow Me, and let the dead bury their own dead."

Jesus Calms the Storm
23 When He got into the boat, His disciples followed Him. **24** And behold, a violent storm developed on the sea, so that the boat was being covered by the waves; but *Jesus* Himself was asleep. **25** And they came to *Him* and woke Him, saying, "Save *us,* Lord; we are perishing!" **26** He *said to them, "Why are you afraid, you men of little faith?" Then He got up and rebuked the winds and the sea, and it became perfectly calm. **27** The men were amazed, and said, "What kind of a man is this, that even the winds and the sea obey Him?"

Jesus Sends Demons into Pigs
28 And when He came to the other side into the country of the Gadarenes, two demon-possessed men confronted Him as they were coming out of the tombs. *They were* so extremely violent that no one could pass by that way. **29** And they cried out, saying, "What business do You have with us, Son of God? Have You come here to torment us before the time?" **30** Now there was a herd of many pigs feeding at a distance from them. **31** And the demons begged Him, saying, "If You *are going to* cast us out, send us into the herd of pigs." **32** And He said to them, "Go!" And they came out and went into the pigs; and behold, the whole herd rushed down the steep bank into

the sea and drowned in the waters. **33** And the herdsmen ran away, and went to the city and reported everything, including what had happened to the demon-possessed men. **34** And behold, the whole city came out to meet Jesus; and when they saw Him, they pleaded with Him to leave their region.

A Paralyzed Man Healed
9 Getting into a boat, *Jesus* crossed over *the Sea of Galilee* and came to His own city. **2** And they brought to Him a paralyzed man lying on a stretcher. And seeing their faith, Jesus said to the man who was paralyzed, "Take courage, son; your sins are forgiven." **3** And some of the scribes said to themselves, "This man is blaspheming!" **4** And Jesus, perceiving their thoughts, said, "Why are you thinking evil in your hearts? **5** For which is easier, to say, 'Your sins are forgiven,' or to say, 'Get up and walk'? **6** But so that you may know that the Son of Man has authority on earth to forgive sins"—then He *said to the paralyzed man, "Get up, pick up your stretcher and go home." **7** And he got up and went home. **8** But when the crowds saw *this,* they were awe-struck, and they glorified God, who had given such authority to men.

Matthew Called
9 As Jesus went on from there, He saw a man called Matthew sitting in the tax collector's office; and He *said to him, "Follow Me!" And he got up and followed Him. **10** Then it happened that as Jesus was reclining *at the table* in the house, behold, many tax collectors and sinners came and *began* dining with Jesus and His disciples. **11** And when the Pharisees saw *this,* they said to His disciples, "Why is your Teacher eating with the tax collectors and sinners?" **12** But when *Jesus* heard *this,* He said, "*It is* not those who are healthy who need a physician, but those who are sick. **13** Now go and learn what this means: 'I DESIRE COMPASSION, RATHER THAN SACRIFICE,' for I did not come to call the righteous, but sinners."

The Question about Fasting
14 Then the disciples of John *came to Him, asking, "Why do we and the Pharisees fast, but Your disciples do not fast?" **15** And Jesus said to them, "The attendants of the groom cannot mourn as long as the groom is with them, can they? But the days will come when the groom is taken away from them, and then they will fast. **16** But no one puts a patch of unshrunk cloth on an old garment; for the patch pulls away from the garment, and a worse tear results. **17** Nor do *people* put new wine into old wineskins; otherwise the wineskins burst, and the wine pours out and the wineskins are ruined; but they put new wine into fresh wineskins, and both are preserved."

Miracles of Healing
18 While He was saying these things to them, behold, a *synagogue* official came and bowed down before Him, and said, "My

---

8:11 ¹ I.e., to dine

daughter has just died; but come and lay Your hand on her, and she will become alive again." **19** Jesus got up *from the table* and *began to* accompany him, along with His disciples.

20 And behold, a woman who had been suffering from a hemorrhage for twelve years came up behind Him, and touched the border of His cloak; **21** for she was saying to herself, "If I only touch His cloak, I will get well." **22** But Jesus, turning and seeing her, said, "Daughter, take courage; your faith has made you well." And at once the woman was made well.

23 When Jesus came into the official's house and saw the flute players and the crowd in noisy disorder, **24** He said, "Leave; for the girl has not died, but is asleep." And they *began* laughing at Him. **25** But when the crowd had been sent out, He entered and took her by the hand, and the girl got up. **26** And this news spread throughout that land.

27 As Jesus went on from there, two men who were blind followed Him, crying out, "Have mercy on us, Son of David!" **28** And after He entered the house, the men who were blind came up to Him, and Jesus *said to them, "Do you believe that I am able to do this?" They *said to Him, "Yes, Lord." **29** Then He touched their eyes, saying, "It shall be done for you according to your faith." **30** And their eyes were opened. And Jesus sternly warned them, saying, "See that no one knows *about this!*" **31** But they went out and spread the news about Him throughout that land.

32 And as they were going out, behold, a demon-possessed man who was unable to speak was brought to Him. **33** And after the demon was cast out, the man who was *previously* unable to speak talked; and the crowds were amazed, *and were* saying, "Nothing like this has ever been seen in Israel." **34** But the Pharisees were saying, "He casts out the demons by the ruler of the demons."

35 Jesus was going through all the cities and villages, teaching in their synagogues and proclaiming the gospel of the kingdom, and healing every disease and every sickness. **36** Seeing the crowds, He felt compassion for them, because they were distressed and downcast, like sheep without a shepherd. **37** Then He *said to His disciples, "The harvest is plentiful, but the workers are few. **38** Therefore, plead with the Lord of the harvest to send out workers into His harvest."

The Twelve Disciples; Instructions for Service

10 Jesus summoned His twelve disciples and gave them authority over unclean spirits, to cast them out, and to heal every disease and every sickness.

2 Now the names of the twelve apostles are these: The first, Simon, who is called Peter, and his brother Andrew; and James the son of Zebedee, and his brother John; **3** Philip and Bartholomew; Thomas and Matthew the tax collector; James the son of Alphaeus, and Thaddaeus; **4** Simon the Zealot, and Judas Iscariot, the one who also betrayed Him.

5 These twelve Jesus sent out after instructing them, saying, "Do not go on a road to Gentiles, and do not enter a city of Samaritans; **6** but rather go to the lost sheep of the house of Israel. **7** And as you go, preach, saying, 'The kingdom of heaven has come near.' **8** Heal *the* sick, raise *the* dead, cleanse those with leprosy, cast out demons. Freely you received, freely give. **9** Do not acquire gold, or silver, or copper for your money belts, **10** or a bag for *your* journey, or even two *tunics, or sandals, or a staff; for the worker is deserving of his support. **11** And whatever city or village you enter, inquire who is worthy in it, and stay at his house until you leave *that city.* **12** As you enter the house, give it your greeting. **13** If the house is worthy, *see that* your *blessing of* peace comes upon it. But if it is not worthy, take back your *blessing of* peace. **14** And whoever does not receive you nor listen to your words, as you leave that house or city, shake the dust off your feet. **15** Truly I say to you, it will be more tolerable for *the* land of Sodom and Gomorrah on the day of judgment, than for that city.

A Hard Road Ahead of Them

16 "Behold, I am sending you out as sheep in the midst of wolves; so be as wary as serpents, and as innocent as doves. **17** But be on guard against people, for they will hand you over to *the* courts and flog you in their synagogues; **18** and you will even be brought before governors and kings on My account, as a testimony to them and to the Gentiles. **19** But when they hand you over, do not worry about how or what you are to say; for what you are to say will be given you in that hour. **20** For it is not you who are speaking, but *It is* the Spirit of your Father who is speaking in you.

21 "Now brother will betray brother to death, and a father *his* child; and children will rise up against parents and cause them to be put to death. **22** And you will be hated by all because of My name, but it is the one who has endured to the end who will be saved. **23** "But whenever they persecute you in one city, flee to the next; for truly I say to you, you will not finish *going through* the cities of Israel until the Son of Man comes.

The Meaning of Discipleship

24 "A disciple is not above his teacher, nor a slave above his master. **25** It is enough for the disciple that he may become like his teacher, and the slave like his master. If they have called the head of the house Beelzebul, how much more *will they insult* the members of his household!

26 "So do not fear them, for there is nothing concealed that will not be revealed, or hidden that will not be known. **27** What I tell you in the darkness, tell in the light; and what you hear *whispered* in *your* ear, proclaim on the housetops. **28** And do not be afraid of those who kill the body but are unable to kill the soul; but rather fear Him who is able to destroy both soul and body in *hell. **29** Are two sparrows not sold for an *assarion? And *yet* not one of them

will fall to the ground apart from your Father. 30 But even the hairs of your head are all counted. 31 So do not fear; you are more valuable than a great number of sparrows.

32 "Therefore, everyone who confesses Me before people, I will also confess him before My Father who is in heaven. 33 But whoever denies Me before people, I will also deny him before My Father who is in heaven.

34 "Do not think that I came to bring peace on the earth; I did not come to bring peace, but a sword. 35 For I came to TURN A MAN AGAINST HIS FATHER, AND A DAUGHTER AGAINST HER MOTHER, AND A DAUGHTER-IN-LAW AGAINST HER MOTHER-IN-LAW; 36 and A PERSON'S ENEMIES WILL BE THE MEMBERS OF HIS HOUSEHOLD.

37 "The one who loves father or mother more than Me is not worthy of Me; and the one who loves son or daughter more than Me is not worthy of Me. 38 And the one who does not take his cross and follow after Me is not worthy of Me. 39 The one who has found his life will lose it, and the one who has lost his life on My account will find it.

The Reward for Service

40 "The one who receives you receives Me, and the one who receives Me receives Him who sent Me. 41 The one who receives a prophet in the name of a prophet shall receive a prophet's reward; and the one who receives a righteous person in the name of a righteous person shall receive a righteous person's reward. 42 And whoever gives one of these little ones just a cup of cold water to drink in the name of a disciple, truly I say to you, he shall by no means lose his reward."

John's Questions

11 When Jesus had finished giving instructions to His twelve disciples, He went on from there to teach and preach in their cities.

2 Now while in prison, John heard about the works of Christ, and he sent word by his disciples, 3 and said to Him, "Are You the Coming One, or are we to look for someone else?" 4 Jesus answered and said to them, "Go and report to John what you hear and see: 5 those who are BLIND RECEIVE SIGHT and those who limp walk, those with leprosy are cleansed and those who are deaf hear, the dead are raised, and the POOR HAVE THE GOSPEL PREACHED TO THEM. 6 And blessed is any person who does not take offense at Me."

Jesus' Tribute to John

7 As these disciples of John were going away, Jesus began speaking to the crowds about John: "What did you go out into the wilderness to see? A reed shaken by the wind? 8 But what did you go out to see? A man dressed in soft clothing? Those who wear soft clothing are in kings' palaces! 9 But what did you go out to see? A prophet? Yes, I tell you, and one who is more than a prophet. 10 This is the one about whom it is written:

'BEHOLD, I AM SENDING MY MESSENGER
AHEAD OF YOU,
WHO WILL PREPARE YOUR WAY BEFORE YOU.'

11 Truly I say to you, among those born of women there has not arisen anyone greater than John the Baptist! Yet the one who is least in the kingdom of heaven is greater than he. 12 And from the days of John the Baptist until now the kingdom of heaven has been treated violently, and violent men take it by force. 13 For all the Prophets and the Law prophesied until John. 14 And if you are willing to accept it, John himself is Elijah who was to come. 15 The one who has ears to hear, let him hear.

16 "But to what shall I compare this generation? It is like children sitting in the marketplaces, who call out to the other children, 17 and say, 'We played the flute for you, and you did not dance; we sang a song of mourning, and you did not mourn.' 18 For John came neither eating nor drinking, and they say, 'He has a demon!' 19 The Son of Man came eating and drinking, and they say, 'Behold, a gluttonous man and a heavy drinker, a friend of tax collectors and sinners!' And yet wisdom is vindicated by her deeds."

The Unrepenting Cities

20 Then He began to reprimand the cities in which most of His miracles were done, because they did not repent. 21 "Woe to you, Chorazin! Woe to you, Bethsaida! For if the miracles that occurred in you had occurred in Tyre and Sidon, they would have repented long ago in sackcloth and ashes. 22 Nevertheless I say to you, it will be more tolerable for Tyre and Sidon on the day of judgment than for you. 23 And you, Capernaum, will not be exalted to heaven, will you? You will be brought down to Hades! For if the miracles that occurred in you had occurred in Sodom, it would have remained to this day. 24 Nevertheless I say to you that it will be more tolerable for the land of Sodom on the day of judgment, than for you."

Come to Me

25 At that time Jesus said, "I praise You, Father, Lord of heaven and earth, that You have hidden these things from the wise and intelligent, and have revealed them to infants. 26 Yes, Father, for this way was well pleasing in Your sight. 27 All things have been handed over to Me by My Father; and no one knows the Son except the Father; nor does anyone know the Father except the Son, and anyone to whom the Son determines to reveal Him.

28 "Come to Me, all who are weary and burdened, and I will give you rest. 29 Take My yoke upon you and learn from Me, for I am gentle and humble in heart, and YOU WILL FIND REST FOR YOUR SOULS. 30 For My yoke is comfortable, and My burden is light."

Sabbath Questions

12 At that time Jesus went through the grainfields on the Sabbath, and His disciples became hungry and began to pick the heads of grain and eat. 2 Now when the Pharisees saw this, they said to Him, "Look, Your disciples are doing what is not lawful to do on a Sabbath!" 3 But He said to them, "Have

you not read what David did when he became hungry, he and his companions—⁴ how he entered the house of God, and they ate the consecrated bread, which was not lawful for him to eat nor for those with him, but for the priests alone? ⁵ Or have you not read in the Law that on the Sabbath the priests in the temple violate the Sabbath, and *yet* are innocent? ⁶ But I say to you that *something* greater than the temple is here. ⁷ But if you had known what this means: 'I DESIRE COMPASSION, RATHER THAN SACRIFICE,' you would not have condemned the innocent.

Lord of the Sabbath

⁸ For the Son of Man is Lord of the Sabbath."

⁹ Departing from there, He went into their synagogue. ¹⁰ And a man *was there* whose hand was withered. And they questioned Jesus, asking, "Is it lawful to heal on the Sabbath?"— so that they might bring charges against Him. ¹¹ But He said to them, "What man is there among you who has a sheep, and if it falls into a pit on the Sabbath, will he not take hold of it and lift it out? ¹² How much more valuable then is a person than a sheep! So then, it is lawful to do good on the Sabbath." ¹³ Then He *said to the man, "Stretch out your hand!" He stretched it out, and it was restored to normal, like the other. ¹⁴ But the Pharisees went out and conspired against Him, *as to* how they might destroy Him.

¹⁵ But Jesus, aware of *this,* withdrew from there. Many followed Him, and He healed them all, ¹⁶ and warned them not to tell who He was. ¹⁷ *This happened* so that what was spoken through Isaiah the prophet would be fulfilled:

¹⁸   "BEHOLD, MY SERVANT WHOM I HAVE
     CHOSEN;
     MY BELOVED IN WHOM MY SOUL DELIGHTS;
     I WILL PUT MY SPIRIT UPON HIM,
     AND HE WILL PROCLAIM JUSTICE TO THE
     GENTILES.
¹⁹   "HE WILL NOT QUARREL, NOR CRY OUT;
     NOR WILL ANYONE HEAR HIS VOICE IN THE
     STREETS.
²⁰   "A BENT REED HE WILL NOT BREAK *OFF,*
     AND A DIMLY BURNING WICK HE WILL NOT
     EXTINGUISH,
     UNTIL HE LEADS JUSTICE TO VICTORY.
²¹   "AND IN HIS NAME THE GENTILES WILL HOPE."

The Pharisees Rebuked

²² Then a demon-possessed man *who was* blind and unable to speak was brought to Jesus, and He healed him so that the man who was unable to speak talked and could see. ²³ And all the crowds were amazed and were saying, "This man cannot be the Son of David, can he?" ²⁴ But when the Pharisees heard *this,* they said, "This man casts out demons only by Beelzebul the ruler of the demons."

²⁵ And knowing their thoughts, *Jesus* said to them, "Every kingdom divided against itself is laid waste; and no city or house divided against itself will stand. ²⁶ And if Satan is casting out Satan, he has become divided against himself; how then will his kingdom stand? ²⁷ And if by Beelzebul I cast out the demons, by whom do your sons cast *them* out? Therefore, they will be your judges. ²⁸ But if I cast out the demons by the Spirit of God, then the kingdom of God has come upon you. ²⁹ Or, how can anyone enter the strong man's house and carry off his property, unless he first ties up the strong *man?* And then he will plunder his house.

The Unpardonable Sin

³⁰ The one who is not with Me is against Me; and the one who does not gather with Me scatters.

³¹ "Therefore I say to you, every sin and blasphemy shall be forgiven people, but blasphemy against the Spirit shall not be forgiven. ³² And whoever speaks a word against the Son of Man, it shall be forgiven him; but whoever speaks against the Holy Spirit, it shall not be forgiven him, either in this age or in the *age* to come.

Words Reveal Character

³³ "Either assume the tree *to be* good as well as its fruit good, or assume the tree *to be* bad as well as its fruit bad; for the tree is known by its fruit. ³⁴ You offspring of vipers, how can you, being evil, express *any* good things? For the mouth speaks from that which fills the heart. ³⁵ The good person brings out of *his* good treasure good things; and the evil person brings out of *his* evil treasure evil things. ³⁶ But I tell you that *for* every careless word that people speak, they will give an account of it on *the* day of judgment. ³⁷ For by your words you will be justified, and by your words you will be condemned."

The Desire for Signs

³⁸ Then some of the scribes and Pharisees said to Him, "Teacher, we want to see a sign from You." ³⁹ But He answered and said to them, "An evil and adulterous generation craves a sign; and *so* no sign will be given to it except the sign of Jonah the prophet; ⁴⁰ for just as JONAH WAS IN THE STOMACH OF THE SEA MONSTER FOR THREE DAYS AND THREE NIGHTS, so will the Son of Man be in the heart of the earth for three days and three nights. ⁴¹ The men of Nineveh will stand up with this generation at the judgment, and will condemn it because they repented at the preaching of Jonah; and behold, *something* greater than Jonah is here. ⁴² *The* Queen of *the* South will rise up with this generation at the judgment and will condemn it, because she came from the ends of the earth to hear the wisdom of Solomon; and behold, *something* greater than Solomon is here.

⁴³ "Now when the unclean spirit comes out of a person, it passes through waterless places seeking rest, and does not find *it.* ⁴⁴ Then it says, 'I will return to my house from which I came'; and when it comes, it finds *it* unoccupied, swept, and put in order. ⁴⁵ Then it goes and brings along with it seven other spirits more wicked than itself, and they come in and live there; and the last *condition* of that person becomes worse than the first. That is the way it will also be with this evil generation."

Changed Relationships

46 While He was still speaking to the crowds, behold, His mother and brothers were standing outside, seeking to speak to Him. **47** [¹Someone said to Him, "Look, Your mother and Your brothers are standing outside, seeking to speak to You."] **48** But Jesus replied to the one who was telling Him and said, "Who is My mother, and who are My brothers?" **49** And extending His hand toward His disciples, He said, "Behold: My mother and My brothers! **50** For whoever does the will of My Father who is in heaven, he is My brother, and sister, and mother."

Jesus Teaches in Parables

13 On that day Jesus had gone out of the house and was sitting by the sea. **2** And large crowds gathered to Him, so He got into a boat and sat down, and the whole crowd was standing on the beach.

3 And He told them many things in parables, saying, "Behold, the sower went out to sow; **4** and as he sowed, some *seeds* fell beside the road, and the birds came and ate them up. **5** Others fell on the rocky places, where they did not have much soil; and they sprang up immediately, because they had no depth of soil. **6** But after the sun rose, they were scorched; and because they had no root, they withered away. **7** Others fell among the thorns, and the thorns came up and choked them out. **8** But others fell on the good soil and yielded a crop, some a hundred, some sixty, and some thirty *times as much*. **9** The one who has ears, let him hear."

An Explanation for Parables

10 And the disciples came up and said to Him, "Why do You speak to them in parables?" **11** And Jesus answered them, "To you it has been granted to know the mysteries of the kingdom of heaven, but to them it has not been granted. **12** For whoever has, to him *more* shall be given, and he will have an abundance; but whoever does not have, even what he has shall be taken away from him. **13** Therefore I speak to them in parables; because while seeing they do not see, and while hearing they do not hear, nor do they understand. **14** And in their case the prophecy of Isaiah is being fulfilled, which says,

'YOU SHALL KEEP ON LISTENING, BUT SHALL
    NOT UNDERSTAND;
AND YOU SHALL KEEP ON LOOKING, BUT SHALL
    NOT PERCEIVE;
15 FOR THE HEART OF THIS PEOPLE HAS BECOME
    DULL,
WITH THEIR EARS THEY SCARCELY HEAR,
AND THEY HAVE CLOSED THEIR EYES,
OTHERWISE THEY MIGHT SEE WITH THEIR
    EYES,
HEAR WITH THEIR EARS,
UNDERSTAND WITH THEIR HEART, AND
    RETURN,
AND I WOULD HEAL THEM.'

16 But blessed are your eyes, because they see; and your ears, because they hear. **17** For truly I say to you that many prophets and righteous people longed to see what you see, and did not see *it*, and to hear what you hear, and did not hear *it*.

The Sower Explained

18 "Listen then to the parable of the sower. **19** When anyone hears the word of the kingdom and does not understand *it,* the evil *one* comes and snatches away what has been sown in his heart. This is the one sown *with seed* beside the road. **20** The one sown *with seed* on the rocky places, this is the one who hears the word and immediately receives it with joy; **21** yet he has no *firm* root in himself, but is *only* temporary, and when affliction or persecution occurs because of the word, immediately he falls away. **22** And the one sown *with seed* among the thorns, this is the one who hears the word, and the anxiety of the world and the deceitfulness of wealth choke the word, and it becomes unfruitful. **23** But the one sown *with seed* on the good soil, this is the one who hears the word and understands it, who indeed bears fruit and produces, some a hundred, some sixty, and some thirty *times as much*."

Weeds among Wheat

24 Jesus presented another parable to them, saying, "The kingdom of heaven is like a man who sowed good seed in his field. **25** But while his men were sleeping, his enemy came and sowed ¹weeds among the wheat, and left. **26** And when the wheat sprouted and produced grain, then the weeds also became evident. **27** And the slaves of the landowner came and said to him, 'Sir, did you not sow good seed in your field? How then does it have weeds?' **28** And he said to them, 'An enemy has done this!' The slaves *said to him, 'Do you want us, then, to go and gather them up?' **29** But he *said, 'No; while you are gathering up the weeds, you may uproot the wheat with them. **30** Allow both to grow together until the harvest; and at the time of the harvest I will say to the reapers, "First gather up the weeds and bind them in bundles to burn them; but gather the wheat into my barn." ' "

The Mustard Seed

31 He presented another parable to them, saying, "The kingdom of heaven is like a mustard seed, which a person took and sowed in his field; **32** and this is smaller than all the *other* seeds, but when it is *fully* grown, it is larger than the garden plants and becomes a tree, so that THE BIRDS OF THE SKY come and NEST IN ITS BRANCHES."

The Leaven

33 He spoke another parable to them: "The kingdom of heaven is like leaven, which a woman took and hid in three ¹sata of flour until it was all leavened." **34** All these things Jesus spoke to the crowds in parables, and He did not speak anything to them without a parable. **35** *This was* so that

---

12:47 ¹ This verse is not found in early mss **13:25** ¹ Prob. *darnel,* a weed resembling wheat
13:33 ¹ A Gr term for a Heb measure, totaling about 48 lb. or 22 kg of flour

what was spoken through the prophet would be fulfilled:

"I WILL OPEN MY MOUTH IN PARABLES;
I WILL PROCLAIM THINGS HIDDEN SINCE THE FOUNDATION OF THE WORLD."

The Weeds Explained

36 Then He left the crowds and went into the house. And His disciples came to Him and said, "Explain to us the parable of the weeds of the field." 37 And He said, "The one who sows the good seed is the Son of Man, 38 and the field is the world; and *as for* the good seed, these are the sons of the kingdom; and the weeds are the sons of the evil *one;* 39 and the enemy who sowed them is the devil, and the harvest is the end of the age; and the reapers are angels. 40 So just as the weeds are gathered up and burned with fire, so shall it be at the end of the age. 41 The Son of Man will send forth His angels, and they will gather out of His kingdom all stumbling blocks, and those who commit lawlessness, 42 and they will throw them into the furnace of fire; in that place there will be weeping and gnashing of teeth. 43 Then THE RIGHTEOUS WILL SHINE FORTH LIKE THE SUN in the kingdom of their Father. The one who has ears, let him hear.

Hidden Treasure

44 "The kingdom of heaven is like a treasure hidden in the field, which a man found and hid *again;* and from joy *over it* he goes and sells everything that he has, and buys that field.

A Costly Pearl

45 "Again, the kingdom of heaven is like a merchant seeking fine pearls, 46 and upon finding one pearl of great value, he went and sold everything that he had and bought it.

A Dragnet

47 "Again, the kingdom of heaven is like a dragnet that was cast into the sea and gathered *fish* of every kind; 48 and when it was filled, they pulled it up on the beach; and they sat down and gathered the good *fish* into containers, but the bad they threw away. 49 So it will be at the end of the age: the angels will come forth and remove the wicked from among the righteous, 50 and they will throw them into the furnace of fire; in that place there will be weeping and gnashing of teeth. 51 "Have you understood all these things?" They *said to Him, "Yes." 52 And Jesus said to them, "Therefore every scribe who has become a disciple of the kingdom of heaven is like a head of a household, who brings out of his treasure new things and old."

Jesus Revisits Nazareth

53 When Jesus had finished these parables, He departed from there. 54 And He came to His hometown and *began* teaching them in their synagogue, with the result that they were astonished, and said, "Where *did* this man *acquire* this wisdom and *these* miraculous powers? 55 Is this not the carpenter's son? Is His mother not called Mary, and His brothers, James, Joseph, Simon, and Judas? 56 And His

sisters, are they not all with us? Where then *did* this man *acquire* all these things?" 57 And they took offense at Him. But Jesus said to them, "A prophet is not dishonored except in his hometown and in his *own* household." 58 And He did not do many miracles there because of their unbelief.

John the Baptist Beheaded

14 At that time Herod the tetrarch heard the news about Jesus, 2 and said to his servants, "This is John the Baptist; he himself has been raised from the dead, and that is why miraculous powers are at work in him." 3 For when Herod had John arrested, he bound him and put him in prison because of Herodias, the wife of his brother Philip. 4 For John had been saying to him, "It is not lawful for you to have her." 5 Although Herod wanted to put him to death, he feared the crowd, because they regarded John as a prophet. 6 But when Herod's birthday came, the daughter of Herodias danced before *them* and pleased Herod, 7 so *much* that he promised with an oath to give her whatever she asked. 8 And after being prompted by her mother, she *said, "Give me the head of John the Baptist here on a platter." 9 And although he was grieved, the king commanded *it* to be given because of his oaths and his dinner guests. 10 He sent word and had John beheaded in the prison. 11 And his head was brought on a platter and given to the girl, and she brought *it* to her mother. 12 John's disciples came and took away the body and buried it; and they went and reported to Jesus.

Five Thousand Men Fed

13 Now when Jesus heard *about John,* He withdrew from there in a boat to a secluded place by Himself; and when the people heard *about this,* they followed Him on foot from the cities. 14 When He came ashore, He saw a large crowd, and felt compassion for them and healed their sick. 15 Now when it was evening, the disciples came to Him and said, "This place is secluded and the hour is already past *to eat;* send the crowds away, so that they may go into the villages and buy food for themselves." 16 But Jesus said to them, "They do not need to go; you give them *something* to eat!" 17 They *said to Him, "We have nothing here except five loaves and two fish." 18 And He said, "Bring them here to Me." 19 And ordering the crowds to sit down on the grass, He took the five loaves and the two fish, and looked up toward heaven. He blessed *the food* and breaking the loaves, He gave them to the disciples, and the disciples *gave them* to the crowds. 20 And they all ate and were satisfied, and they picked up what was left over of the broken pieces: twelve full baskets. 21 There were about five thousand men who ate, besides women and children.

Jesus Walks on the Water

22 Immediately *afterward* He compelled the disciples to get into the boat and to go ahead of Him to the other side, while He sent the crowds away. 23 After He had sent the crowds

away, He went up on the mountain by Himself to pray; and when it was evening, He was there alone. 24 But the boat was already 1a long distance from the land, battered by the waves; for the wind was contrary. 25 And in the 1fourth watch of the night He came to them, walking on the sea. 26 When the disciples saw Him walking on the sea, they were terrified, and said, "It is a ghost!" And they cried out in fear. 27 But immediately Jesus spoke to them, saying, "Take courage, it is I; do not be afraid."

28 Peter responded and said to Him, "Lord, if it is You, command me to come to You on the water." 29 And He said, "Come!" And Peter got out of the boat and walked on the water, and came toward Jesus. 30 But seeing the wind, he became frightened, and when he began to sink, he cried out, saying, "Lord, save me!" 31 Immediately Jesus reached out with His hand and took hold of him, and *said to him, "You of little faith, why did you doubt?" 32 When they got into the boat, the wind stopped. 33 And those who were in the boat worshiped Him, saying, "You are truly God's Son!"

34 When they had crossed over, they came to land at Gennesaret. 35 And when the men of that place recognized Him, they sent word into all that surrounding region and brought to Him all who were sick; 36 and they pleaded with Him that they might just touch the border of His cloak; and all who touched it were cured.

Tradition and Commandment

15 Then some Pharisees and scribes *came to Jesus from Jerusalem and said, 2 "Why do Your disciples break the tradition of the elders? For they do not wash their hands when they eat bread." 3 And He answered and said to them, "Why do you yourselves also break the commandment of God for the sake of your tradition? 4 For God said, 'HONOR YOUR FATHER AND MOTHER,' and, 'THE ONE WHO SPEAKS EVIL OF FATHER OR MOTHER IS TO BE PUT TO DEATH.' 5 But you say, 'Whoever says to his father or mother, "Whatever I have that would help you has been given to God," 6 he is not to 1honor his father or mother.' And by this you have invalidated the word of God for the sake of your tradition. 7 You hypocrites, rightly did Isaiah prophesy about you, by saying:

8   'THIS PEOPLE HONORS ME WITH THEIR LIPS,
     BUT THEIR HEART IS FAR AWAY FROM ME.
9   'AND IN VAIN DO THEY WORSHIP ME,
     TEACHING AS DOCTRINES THE
      COMMANDMENTS OF MEN.' "

10 After Jesus called the crowd to Him, He said to them, "Hear and understand! 11 It is not what enters the mouth that defiles the person, but what comes out of the mouth, this defiles the person."

12 Then the disciples came and *said to Him, "Do You know that the Pharisees were offended when they heard this statement?" 13 But He answered and said, "Every plant which My heavenly Father did not plant will be uprooted. 14 Leave them alone; they are

blind guides 1of blind people. And if a person who is blind guides another who is blind, both will fall into a pit."

The Heart of Man

15 Peter said to Him, "Explain the parable to us." 16 Jesus said, "Are you also still lacking in understanding? 17 Do you not understand that everything that goes into the mouth passes into the stomach, and is eliminated? 18 But the things that come out of the mouth come from the heart, and those things defile the person. 19 For out of the heart come evil thoughts, murders, acts of adultery, other immoral sexual acts, thefts, false testimonies, and slanderous statements. 20 These are the things that defile the person; but to eat with unwashed hands does not defile the person."

The Faith of a Canaanite Woman

21 Jesus went away from there, and withdrew into the region of Tyre and Sidon. 22 And a Canaanite woman from that region came out and began to cry out, saying, "Have mercy on me, Lord, Son of David; my daughter is severely demon-possessed." 23 But He did not answer her with even a word. And His disciples came up and urged Him, saying, "Send her away, because she keeps shouting at us!" 24 But He answered and said, "I was sent only to the lost sheep of the house of Israel." 25 But she came and began to bow down before Him, saying, "Lord, help me!" 26 Yet He answered and said, "It is not good to take the children's bread and throw it to the dogs." 27 And she said, "Yes, Lord; but please help, for even the dogs feed on the crumbs that fall from their masters' table." 28 Then Jesus said to her, "O woman, your faith is great; it shall be done for you as you desire." And her daughter was healed at once.

Healing Crowds

29 Departing from there, Jesus went along the Sea of Galilee, and after going up on the mountain, He was sitting there. 30 And large crowds came to Him bringing with them those who were limping, had impaired limbs, were blind, or were unable to speak, and many others, and they laid them down at His feet; and He healed them. 31 So the crowd was astonished as they saw those who were unable to speak talking, those with impaired limbs restored, those who were limping walking around, and those who were blind seeing; and they glorified the God of Israel.

Four Thousand Men Fed

32 Now Jesus called His disciples to Him and said, "I feel compassion for the people, because they have remained with Me now for three days and have nothing to eat; and I do not want to send them away hungry, for they might faint on the way." 33 The disciples *said to Him, "Where would we get so many loaves in this desolate place to satisfy such a large crowd?" 34 And Jesus *said to them, "How many loaves do you have?" And they said, "Seven, and a

---

14:24 1Lit many stadia from; a Roman stadion perhaps averaged 607 ft. or 185 m   14:25 1I.e., 3-6 a.m.   15:6 1I.e., by supporting them with it   15:14 1Later mss add of blind people

few small fish." 35 And He directed the people to sit down on the ground; 36 and He took the seven loaves and the fish; and after giving thanks, He broke them and started giving them to the disciples, and the disciples *gave them* to the crowds. 37 And they all ate and were satisfied, and they picked up what was left over of the broken pieces, seven large baskets full. 38 And those who ate were four thousand men, besides women and children.

39 And sending away the crowds, Jesus got into the boat and came to the region of Magadan.

Pharisees and Sadducees Test Jesus

16 The Pharisees and Sadducees came up, and putting *Jesus* to the test, they asked Him to show them a sign from heaven. 2 But He replied to them, "When it is evening, you say, '*It will be* fair weather, for the sky is red.' 3 And in the morning, '*There will be* a storm today, for the sky is red and threatening.' You know how to discern the appearance of the sky, but are you unable *to discern* the signs of the times? 4 An evil and adulterous generation wants a sign; and *so* a sign will not be given to it, except the sign of Jonah." And He left them and went away.

5 And the disciples came to the other side *of the sea*, but they had forgotten to bring *any* bread. 6 And Jesus said to them, "Watch out and beware of the leaven of the Pharisees and Sadducees." 7 They began to discuss *this* among themselves, saying, "*He said that* because we did not bring *any* bread." 8 But Jesus, aware *of this,* said, "You men of little faith, why are you discussing among yourselves *the fact* that you have no bread? 9 Do you not yet understand nor remember the five loaves of the five thousand, and how many baskets you picked up? 10 Nor the seven loaves of the four thousand, and how many large baskets you picked up? 11 How *is it that* you do not understand that I did not speak to you about bread? But beware of the leaven of the Pharisees and Sadducees." 12 Then they understood that He did not say to beware of the leaven of bread, but of the teaching of the Pharisees and Sadducees.

Peter's Confession of Christ

13 Now when Jesus came into the region of Caesarea Philippi, He was asking His disciples, "Who do people say that the Son of Man is?" 14 And they said, "Some *say* John the Baptist; and others, Elijah; and *still* others, Jeremiah, or one of the *other* prophets." 15 He *said to them, "But who do you yourselves say that I am?" 16 Simon Peter answered, "You are the Christ, the Son of the living God." 17 And Jesus said to him, "Blessed are you, Simon Barjona, because flesh and blood did not reveal *this* to you, but My Father who is in heaven. 18 And I also say to you that you are Peter, and upon this rock I will build My church; and the gates of Hades will not overpower it. 19 I will give you the keys of the kingdom of heaven; and whatever you bind on earth shall have been bound in heaven, and whatever you loose on earth shall have been loosed in heaven." 20 Then He gave the disciples strict orders

that they were to tell no one that He was the Christ.

Jesus Foretells His Death

21 From that time Jesus began to point out to His disciples that it was necessary for Him to go to Jerusalem and to suffer many things from the elders, chief priests, and scribes, and to be killed, and to be raised up on the third day. 22 And *yet* Peter took Him aside and began to rebuke Him, saying, "God forbid it, Lord! This shall never happen to You!" 23 But He turned and said to Peter, "Get behind Me, Satan! You are a stumbling block to Me; for you are not setting your mind on God's purposes, but men's."

Discipleship Is Costly

24 Then Jesus said to His disciples, "If anyone wants to come after Me, he must deny himself, take up his cross, and follow Me. 25 For whoever wants to save his life will lose it; but whoever loses his life for My sake will find it. 26 For what good will it do a person if he gains the whole world, but forfeits his soul? Or what will a person give in exchange for his soul? 27 For the Son of Man is going to come in the glory of His Father with His angels, and WILL THEN REPAY EVERY PERSON ACCORDING TO HIS DEEDS.

28 "Truly I say to you, there are some of those who are standing here who will not taste death until they see the Son of Man coming in His kingdom."

The Transfiguration

17 Six days later, Jesus *took with Him Peter and James, and his brother John, and *led them up on a high mountain by themselves. 2 And He was transfigured before them; and His face shone like the sun, and His garments became as white as light. 3 And behold, Moses and Elijah appeared to them, talking with Him. 4 Peter responded and said to Jesus, "Lord, it is good that we are here. If You want, I will make three tabernacles here: one for You, one for Moses, and one for Elijah." 5 While he was still speaking, a bright cloud overshadowed them, and behold, a voice from the cloud said, "This is My beloved Son, with whom I am well pleased; listen to Him!" 6 When the disciples heard *this,* they fell face down to the ground and were terrified. 7 And Jesus came to *them* and touched them and said, "Get up, and do not be afraid." 8 And raising their eyes, they saw no one except Jesus Himself alone.

9 When they were coming down from the mountain, Jesus commanded them, saying, "Tell the vision to no one until the Son of Man has risen from the dead." 10 And His disciples asked Him, "Why then do the scribes say that Elijah must come first?" 11 And He answered and said, "Elijah is coming and will restore all things; 12 but I say to you that Elijah already came, and they did not recognize him, but did to him whatever they wanted. So also the Son of Man is going to suffer at their hands." 13 Then the disciples understood that He had spoken to them about John the Baptist.

The Demon-possessed Boy

14 When they came to the crowd, a man came up to Jesus, falling on his knees before Him and saying, 15 "Lord, have mercy on my son, because he has seizures and suffers terribly; for he often falls into the fire and often into the water. 16 And I brought him to Your disciples, and they could not cure him." 17 And Jesus answered and said, "You unbelieving and perverse generation, how long shall I be with you? How long shall I put up with you? Bring him here to Me." 18 And Jesus rebuked him, and the demon came out of him, and the boy was healed at once.

19 Then the disciples came to Jesus privately and said, "Why could we not cast it out?" 20 And He *said to them, "Because of your meager faith; for truly I say to you, if you have faith the size of a mustard seed, you will say to this mountain, 'Move from here to there,' and it will move; and nothing will be impossible for you.1"

22 And while they were gathering together in Galilee, Jesus said to them, "The Son of Man is going to be handed over to men; 23 and they will kill Him, and He will be raised on the third day." And they were deeply grieved.

The Temple Tax

24 Now when they came to Capernaum, those who collected the 1two-drachma *tax* came to Peter and said, "Does your teacher not pay the two-drachma *tax?"* 25 He *said, "Yes." And when he came into the house, Jesus spoke to him first, saying, "What do you think, Simon? From whom do the kings of the earth collect customs or 1poll-tax, from their sons or from strangers?" 26 When *Peter* said, "From strangers," Jesus said to him, "Then the sons are exempt. 27 However, so that we do not offend them, go to the sea and throw in a hook, and take the first fish that comes up; and when you open its mouth, you will find a 1stater. Take that and give it to them for you and Me."

Rank in the Kingdom

18 At that time the disciples came to Jesus and said, "Who then is greatest in the kingdom of heaven?" 2 And He called a child to Himself and set him among them, 3 and said, "Truly I say to you, unless you change and become like children, you will not enter the kingdom of heaven. 4 So whoever will humble himself like this child, he is the greatest in the kingdom of heaven. 5 And whoever receives one such child in My name, receives Me; 6 but whoever causes one of these little ones who believe in Me to 1sin, it is better for him that a heavy millstone be hung around his neck, and that he be drowned in the depths of the sea.

Stumbling Blocks

7 "Woe to the world because of *its* stumbling blocks! For it is inevitable that stumbling blocks come; but woe to the person through whom the stumbling block comes!

8 "And if your hand or your foot is causing you to sin, cut it off and throw it away from you; it is better for you to enter life maimed or without a foot, than to have two hands or two feet and be thrown into the eternal fire. 9 And if your eye is causing you to sin, tear it out and throw it away from you. It is better for you to enter life with one eye, than to have two eyes and be thrown into the 1fiery hell.

10 "See that you do not look down on one of these little ones; for I say to you that their angels in heaven continually see the face of My Father who is in heaven.1

Ninety-nine Plus One

12 "What do you think? If any man has a hundred sheep, and one of them goes astray, will he not leave the ninety-nine on the mountains, and go and search for the one that is lost? 13 And if it turns out that he finds it, truly I say to you, he rejoices over it more than over the ninety-nine that have not gone astray. 14 So it is not *the* will of your Father who is in heaven for one of these little ones to perish.

Discipline and Prayer

15 "Now if your brother sins1, go and show him his fault in private; if he listens to you, you have gained your brother. 16 But if he does not listen *to you,* take one or two more with you, so that ON THE TESTIMONY OF TWO OR THREE WITNESSES EVERY MATTER MAY BE CONFIRMED. 17 And if he refuses to listen to them, tell it to the church; and if he refuses to listen even to the church, he is to be to you as a Gentile and a tax collector. 18 Truly I say to you, whatever you bind on earth shall have been bound in heaven; and whatever you loose on earth shall have been loosed in heaven.

19 "Again I say to you, that if two of you agree on earth about anything that they may ask, it shall be done for them by My Father who is in heaven. 20 For where two or three have gathered together in My name, I am there in their midst."

Forgiveness

21 Then Peter came up and said to Him, "Lord, how many times shall my brother sin against me and I *still* forgive him? Up to seven times?" 22 Jesus *said to him, "I do not say to you, up to seven times, but up to seventy-seven times.

23 "For this reason the kingdom of heaven is like a king who wanted to settle accounts with his slaves. 24 And when he had begun to settle *them,* one who owed him 1ten thousand talents was brought to him. 25 But since he did not have *the means* to repay, his master commanded that he be sold, along with his wife and children and all that he had, and

<hr>

17:20 1 Late mss add (traditionally v 21): *But this kind does not go out except by prayer and fasting*   17:24 1 Equivalent to about two denarii or two days' wages for a laborer, paid as a temple tax   17:25 1 I.e., a tax on each person in the census   17:27 1 A silver four-drachma Greek coin   18:6 1 Or *stumble,* and so throughout the ch   18:9 1 Lit *Gehenna of fire*   18:10 1 Late mss add (traditionally v 11): *For the Son of Man has come to save that which was lost*   18:15 1 Late mss add *against you*   18:24 1 By one estimate, a debt of 60 million working days for a laborer

repayment be made. 26 So the slave fell *to the ground* and prostrated himself before him, saying, 'Have patience with me and I will repay you everything.' 27 And the master of that slave felt compassion, and he released him and forgave him the debt. 28 But that slave went out and found one of his fellow slaves who owed him a hundred 1denarii; and he seized him and *began* to choke *him,* saying, 'Pay back what you owe!' 29 So his fellow slave fell *to the ground* and *began* to plead with him, saying, 'Have patience with me and I will repay you.' 30 But he was unwilling, and went and threw him in prison until he would pay back what was owed. 31 So when his fellow slaves saw what had happened, they were deeply grieved and came and reported to their master all that had happened. 32 Then summoning him, his master *said to him, 'You wicked slave, I forgave you all that debt because you pleaded with me. 33 Should you not also have had mercy on your fellow slave, in the same way that I had mercy on you?' 34 And his master, moved with anger, handed him over to the torturers until he would repay all that was owed him. 35 My heavenly Father will also do the same to you, if each of you does not forgive his brother from your heart."

Concerning Divorce

19 When Jesus had finished these words, He left Galilee and came into the region of Judea beyond the Jordan; 2 and large crowds followed Him, and He healed them there.

3 *Some* Pharisees came to Jesus, testing Him and asking, "Is it lawful *for a man* to divorce his wife for any reason *at all?*" 4 And He answered and said, "Have you not read that He who created *them* from the beginning MADE THEM MALE AND FEMALE, 5 and said, 'FOR THIS REASON A MAN SHALL LEAVE HIS FATHER AND HIS MOTHER AND BE JOINED TO HIS WIFE, AND THE TWO SHALL BECOME ONE FLESH'? 6 So they are no longer two, but one flesh. Therefore, what God has joined together, no person is to separate." 7 They *said to Him, "Why, then, did Moses command to GIVE *HER* A CERTIFICATE OF DIVORCE AND SEND HER AWAY?" 8 He *said to them, "Because of your hardness of heart Moses permitted you to divorce your wives; but from the beginning it has not been this way. 9 And I say to you, whoever divorces his wife, except for sexual immorality, and marries another woman 1commits adultery2."

10 The disciples *said to Him, "If the relationship of the man with his wife is like this, it is better not to marry." 11 But He said to them, "Not all men *can* accept this statement, but *only* those to whom it has been given. 12 For there are eunuchs who were born that way from their mother's womb; and there are eunuchs who were made eunuchs by people; and there are *also* eunuchs who made themselves eunuchs for the sake of the kingdom of heaven. The one who is able to accept *this,* let him accept *it.*"

Jesus Blesses Little Children

13 Then *some* children were brought to Him so that He would lay His hands on them and pray; and the disciples rebuked them. 14 But Jesus said, "Leave the children alone, and do not forbid them to come to Me; for the kingdom of heaven belongs to such as these." 15 After laying His hands on them, He departed from there.

The Rich Young Ruler

16 And someone came to Him and said, "Teacher, what good thing shall I do so that I may obtain eternal life?" 17 And He said to him, "Why are you asking Me about what is good? There is *only* One who is good; but if you want to enter life, keep the commandments." 18 *Then* he *said to Him, "Which ones?" And Jesus said, "YOU SHALL NOT COMMIT MURDER; YOU SHALL NOT COMMIT ADULTERY; YOU SHALL NOT STEAL; YOU SHALL NOT GIVE FALSE TESTIMONY; 19 HONOR YOUR FATHER AND MOTHER; and YOU SHALL LOVE YOUR NEIGHBOR AS YOURSELF." 20 The young man *said to Him, "All these I have kept; what am I still lacking?" 21 Jesus said to him, "If you want to be complete, go *and* sell your possessions and give to *the* poor, and you will have treasure in heaven; and come, follow Me." 22 But when the young man heard this statement, he went away grieving; for he was one who owned much property.

23 And Jesus said to His disciples, "Truly I say to you, it will be hard for a rich person to enter the kingdom of heaven. 24 And again I say to you, it is easier for a camel to go through the eye of a needle, than for a rich person to enter the kingdom of God." 25 When the disciples heard *this,* they were very astonished and said, "Then who can be saved?" 26 And looking at *them,* Jesus said to them, "With people this is impossible, but with God all things are possible."

The Disciples' Reward

27 Then Peter responded and said to Him, "Behold, we have left everything and followed You; what then will there be for us?" 28 And Jesus said to them, "Truly I say to you, that you who have followed Me, in the 1regeneration when the Son of Man will sit on His glorious throne, you also shall sit upon twelve thrones, judging the twelve tribes of Israel. 29 And everyone who has left houses or brothers or sisters or father or mother 1or children or farms on account of My name, will receive many times as much, and will inherit eternal life. 30 But many *who are* first will be last; and *the* last, first.

Laborers in the Vineyard

20 "For the kingdom of heaven is like a landowner who went out early in the morning to hire laborers for his vineyard. 2 When he had agreed with the laborers for a 1denarius for the day, he sent them into his vineyard. 3 And he went out about the 1third

---

18:28 1 The denarius was a day's wages for a laborer   19:9 1 One early ms *makes her commit adultery* 2 One early ms adds *and he who marries a divorced woman commits adultery*   19:28 1 Or *renewal;* i.e., the new world   19:29 1 One early ms adds *or wife*   20:2 1 The denarius was a day's wages for a laborer 20:3 1 I.e., 9 a.m.

hour and saw others standing idle in the marketplace; 4 and to those he said, 'You go into the vineyard also, and whatever is right, I will give you.' And *so* they went. 5 Again he went out about the 'sixth and the ninth hour, and did the same thing. 6 And about the 'eleventh *hour* he went out and found others standing *around;* and he *said to them, 'Why have you been standing here idle all day long?' 7 They *said to him, 'Because no one hired us.' He *said to them, 'You go into the vineyard too.'

8 "Now when evening came, the owner of the vineyard *said to his foreman, 'Call the laborers and pay them their wages, starting with the last *group* to the first.' 9 When those *hired* about the eleventh hour came, each one received a 'denarius. 10 And *so* when those *hired* first came, they thought that they would receive more; but each of them also received a denarius. 11 When they received it, they grumbled at the landowner, 12 saying, 'These who *were hired* last worked *only* one hour, and you have made them equal to us who have borne the burden of the day's *work* and the scorching heat.' 13 But he answered and said to one of them, 'Friend, I am doing you no wrong; did you not agree with me for a denarius? 14 Take what is yours and go; but I want to give to this last person the same as to you. 15 Is it not lawful for me to do what I want with what is my own? Or is your eye envious because I am generous?' 16 So the last shall be first, and the first, last."

Death, Resurrection Foretold

17 As Jesus was about to go up to Jerusalem, He took the twelve *disciples* aside by themselves, and on the road He said to them, 18 "Behold, we are going up to Jerusalem, and the Son of Man will be handed over to the chief priests and scribes, and they will condemn Him to death, 19 and they will hand Him over to the Gentiles to mock and flog and crucify, and on the third day He will be raised up."

Request for Preferred Treatment

20 Then the mother of the sons of Zebedee came to Jesus with her sons, bowing down and making a request of Him. 21 And He said to her, "What do you desire?" She *said to Him, "Say that in Your kingdom these two sons of mine shall sit, one at Your right, and one at Your left." 22 But Jesus replied, "You do not know what you are asking. Are you able to drink the cup that I am about to drink?" They *said to Him, "We are able." 23 He *said to them, "My cup you shall drink; but to sit at My right and at *My* left is not Mine to give, but *it is for those* for whom it has been prepared by My Father."

24 And after hearing *this,* the *other* ten *disciples* became indignant with the two brothers. 25 But Jesus called them to Himself and said, "You know that the rulers of the Gentiles domineer over them, and those in high position exercise authority over them. 26 It is not this way among you, but whoever wants to become prominent among you shall be your servant, 27 and whoever desires to be first among you shall be your slave; 28 just as the Son of Man did

not come to be served, but to serve, and to give His life as a ransom for many."

Sight for Those Who Are Blind

29 As they were leaving Jericho, a large crowd followed Him. 30 And two people who were blind, sitting by the road, hearing that Jesus was passing by, cried out, "Lord, have mercy on us, Son of David!" 31 But the crowd sternly warned them to be quiet; yet they cried out all the more, "Lord, Son of David, have mercy on us!" 32 And Jesus stopped and called them, and said, "What do you want Me to do for you?" 33 They *said to Him, "Lord, *we want* our eyes to be opened." 34 Moved with compassion, Jesus touched their eyes; and immediately they regained their sight and followed Him.

The Triumphal Entry

21 When they had approached Jerusalem and had come to Bethphage, at the Mount of Olives, Jesus then sent two disciples, 2 saying to them, "Go into the village opposite you, and immediately you will find a donkey tied *there* and a colt with it. Untie them and bring them to Me. 3 And if anyone says anything to you, you shall say, 'The Lord needs them,' and he will send them on immediately." 4 Now this took place so that what was spoken through the prophet would be fulfilled:

5   "SAY TO THE DAUGHTER OF ZION,
       'BEHOLD YOUR KING IS COMING TO YOU,
       HUMBLE, AND MOUNTED ON A DONKEY,
       EVEN ON A COLT, THE FOAL OF A DONKEY.'"

6 The disciples went and did just as Jesus had instructed them, 7 and brought the donkey and the colt, and laid their cloaks on them; and He sat on the cloaks. 8 Most of the crowd spread their cloaks on the road, and others were cutting branches from the trees and spreading them on the road. 9 Now the crowds going ahead of Him, and those who followed, were shouting,

       "Hosanna to the Son of David;
       BLESSED IS THE ONE WHO COMES IN THE NAME
       OF THE LORD;
       Hosanna in the highest!"

10 When He had entered Jerusalem, all the city was stirred, saying, "Who is this?" 11 And the crowds were saying, "This is Jesus the prophet, from Nazareth in Galilee."

Cleansing the Temple

12 And Jesus entered the temple *area* and drove out all those who were selling and buying on the temple *grounds,* and He overturned the tables of the money changers and the seats of those who were selling doves. 13 And He *said to them, "It is written: 'MY HOUSE WILL BE CALLED A HOUSE OF PRAYER'; but you are making it a DEN OF ROBBERS."

14 And *those who were* blind and *those who* limped came to Him in the temple *area,* and He healed them. 15 But when the chief priests and the scribes saw the wonderful things that He had done, and the children who were shouting in the temple *area,* "Hosanna to the Son of David," they became indignant, 16 and they said to Him, "Do You hear what these

children are saying?" And Jesus *said to them, "Yes. Have you never read, 'FROM THE MOUTHS OF INFANTS AND NURSING BABIES YOU HAVE PREPARED PRAISE FOR YOURSELF'?" 17 And He left them and went out of the city to Bethany, and spent the night there.

The Barren Fig Tree

18 Now in the early morning, when He was returning to the city, He became hungry. 19 And seeing a lone fig tree by the road, He came to it and found nothing on it except leaves alone; and He *said to it, "No longer shall there ever be *any* fruit from you." And at once the fig tree withered.

20 Seeing *this,* the disciples were amazed and asked, "How did the fig tree wither *all* at once?" 21 And Jesus answered and said to them, "Truly I say to you, if you have faith and do not doubt, you will not only do what *was done* to the fig tree, but even if you say to this mountain, 'Be taken up and cast into the sea,' it will happen. 22 And whatever you ask in prayer, believing, you will receive it all."

Authority Challenged

23 When He entered the temple *area,* the chief priests and the elders of the people came to Him while He was teaching, and said, "By what authority are You doing these things, and who gave You this authority?" 24 But Jesus responded and said to them, "I will also ask you one question, which, if you tell Me, I will also tell you by what authority I do these things. 25 The baptism of John was from what *source:* from heaven or from men?" And they began considering *the implications* among themselves, saying, "If we say, 'From heaven,' He will say to us, 'Then why did you not believe him?' 26 But if we say, 'From men,' we fear the people; for they all regard John as a prophet." 27 And answering Jesus, they said, "We do not know." He also said to them, "Neither am I telling you by what authority I do these things.

Parable of Two Sons

28 "But what do you think? A man had two sons, and he came to the first and said, 'Son, go work today in the vineyard.' 29 But he replied, 'I do not want to.' Yet afterward he regretted it and went. 30 And *the man* came to his second *son* and said the same thing; and he replied, 'I *will,* sir'; and *yet* he did not go. 31 Which of the two did the will of his father?" They *said, "The first." Jesus *said to them, "Truly I say to you that the tax collectors and prostitutes will get into the kingdom of God before you. 32 For John came to you in the way of righteousness and you did not believe him; but the tax collectors and prostitutes did believe him; and you, seeing *this,* did not even have second thoughts afterward so as to believe him.

Parable of the Landowner

33 "Listen to another parable. There was a landowner who PLANTED A VINEYARD AND PUT A FENCE AROUND IT, AND DUG A WINE PRESS IN IT, AND BUILT A TOWER, and he leased it to vine-growers and went on a journey. 34 And when the harvest time approached, he sent his slaves to the vine-growers to receive his fruit. 35 And the vine-growers took his slaves and beat one, killed another, and stoned another. 36 Again, he sent other slaves, more than the first; and they did the same things to them. 37 But afterward he sent his son to them, saying, 'They will respect my son.' 38 But when the vine-growers saw the son, they said among themselves, 'This is the heir; come, let's kill him and take possession of his inheritance!' 39 And they took him and threw him out of the vineyard, and killed him. 40 Therefore, when the owner of the vineyard comes, what will he do to those vine-growers?" 41 They *said to Him, "He will bring those wretches to a wretched end and lease the vineyard to other vine-growers, who will pay him the fruit in the *proper* seasons."

42 Jesus *said to them, "Did you never read in the Scriptures,

'A STONE WHICH THE BUILDERS REJECTED,
THIS HAS BECOME THE CHIEF CORNERSTONE;
THIS CAME ABOUT FROM THE LORD,
AND IT IS MARVELOUS IN OUR EYES'?

43 Therefore I say to you, the kingdom of God will be taken away from you and given to a people producing its fruit. 44 And the one who falls on this stone will be broken to pieces; and on whomever it falls, it will crush him."

45 When the chief priests and the Pharisees heard His parables, they understood that He was speaking about them. 46 And *although* they sought to arrest Him, they feared the crowds, since they considered Him to be a prophet.

Parable of the Marriage Feast

22 Jesus spoke to them again in parables, saying, 2 "The kingdom of heaven is like a king who held a wedding feast for his son. 3 And he sent his slaves to call those who had been invited to the wedding feast, and they were unwilling to come. 4 Again he sent other slaves, saying, 'Tell those who have been invited, "Behold, I have prepared my dinner; my oxen and my fattened cattle are *all* butchered and everything is ready. Come to the wedding feast!" ' 5 But they paid no attention and went their *separate* ways, one to his own farm, another to his business, 6 and the rest seized his slaves and treated them abusively, and *then* killed them. 7 Now the king was angry, and he sent his armies and destroyed those murderers and set their city on fire. 8 Then he *said to his slaves, 'The wedding feast is ready, but those who were invited were not worthy. 9 So go to the main roads, and invite whomever you find *there* to the wedding feast.' 10 Those slaves went out into the streets and gathered together all whom they found, both bad and good; and the wedding hall was filled with dinner guests.

11 "But when the king came in to look over the dinner guests, he saw a man there who was not dressed in wedding clothes, 12 and he *said to him, 'Friend, how did you get in here without wedding clothes?' And the man was speechless. 13 Then the king said to the servants, 'Tie his hands and feet, and throw

him into the outer darkness; there will be weeping and gnashing of teeth in that place.' **14** For many are called, but few *are* chosen."

Poll-tax to Caesar

15 Then the Pharisees went and plotted together how they might trap Him in what He said. **16** And they *sent their disciples to Him, along with the Herodians, saying, "Teacher, we know that You are truthful and teach the way of God in truth, and do not care what anyone thinks; for You are not partial to anyone. **17** Tell us then, what do You think? Is it permissible to pay a ¹poll-tax to Caesar, or not?" **18** But Jesus perceived their malice, and said, "Why are you testing Me, you hypocrites? **19** Show Me the coin *used* for the poll-tax." And they brought Him a denarius. **20** And He *said to them, "Whose image and inscription is this?" **21** They *said to Him, "Caesar's." Then He *said to them, "Then pay to Caesar the things that are Caesar's; and to God the things that are God's." **22** And hearing *this,* they were amazed; and they left Him and went away.

Jesus Answers the Sadducees

23 On that day *some* Sadducees (who say there is no resurrection) came to Jesus and questioned Him, **24** saying, "Teacher, Moses said, 'If a man dies having no children, his brother as next of kin shall marry his wife, and raise up children for his brother.' **25** Now there were seven brothers among us; and the first married and died, and having no children, he left his wife to his brother. **26** *It was* the same also *with* the second *brother;* and the third, down to the seventh. **27** Last of all, the woman died. **28** In the resurrection, therefore, whose wife of the seven will she be? For they all had her *in marriage.*"

29 But Jesus answered and said to them, "You are mistaken, since you do not understand the Scriptures nor the power of God. **30** For in the resurrection they neither marry nor are given in marriage, but are like angels in heaven. **31** But regarding the resurrection of the dead, have you not read what was spoken to you by God: **32** 'I AM THE GOD OF ABRAHAM, THE GOD OF ISAAC, AND THE GOD OF JACOB'? He is not the God of the dead, but of the living." **33** When the crowds heard *this,* they were astonished at His teaching.

34 But when the Pharisees heard that *Jesus* had silenced the Sadducees, they gathered together. **35** And one of them, ¹a lawyer, asked Him a question, testing Him: **36** "Teacher, which is the great commandment in the Law?" **37** And He said to him, " 'YOU SHALL LOVE THE LORD YOUR GOD WITH ALL YOUR HEART, AND WITH ALL YOUR SOUL, AND WITH ALL YOUR MIND.' **38** This is the great and foremost commandment. **39** The second is like it, 'YOU SHALL LOVE YOUR NEIGHBOR AS YOURSELF.' **40** Upon these two commandments hang the whole Law and the Prophets."

41 Now while the Pharisees were gathered together, Jesus asked them a question: **42** "What do you think about the Christ? Whose son is He?" They *said to Him, "*The son* of David." **43** He *said to them, "Then how does David in the Spirit call Him 'Lord,' saying,

44   'THE LORD SAID TO MY LORD,
        "SIT AT MY RIGHT HAND,
        UNTIL I PUT YOUR ENEMIES UNDER YOUR
            FEET" '?

45 Therefore, if David calls Him 'Lord,' how is He his son?" **46** No one was able to offer Him a word in answer, nor did anyone dare from that day *on* to ask Him any more questions.

Hypocrisy Exposed

23 Then Jesus spoke to the crowds and to His disciples, **2** saying: "The scribes and the Pharisees have seated themselves in the chair of Moses. **3** Therefore, whatever they tell you, do and comply with it all, but do not do as they do; for they say *things* and do not do *them.* **4** And they tie up heavy burdens and lay them on people's shoulders, but they themselves are unwilling to move them with *so much as* their finger. **5** And they do all their deeds to be noticed by *other* people; for they broaden their ¹phylacteries and lengthen the tassels *of their garments.* **6** And they love the place of honor at banquets, and the seats of honor in the synagogues, **7** and personal greetings in the marketplaces, and being called Rabbi by the people. **8** But as for you, do not be called Rabbi; for *only* One is your Teacher, and you are all brothers *and sisters.* **9** And do not call *anyone* on earth your father; for *only* One is your Father, He who is in heaven. **10** And do not be called leaders; for *only* One is your Leader, *that is,* Christ. **11** But the greatest of you shall be your servant. **12** Whoever exalts himself shall be humbled, and whoever humbles himself shall be exalted.

Eight Woes

13 "But woe to you, scribes and Pharisees, hypocrites, because you shut the kingdom of heaven in front of people; for you do not enter *it* yourselves, nor do you allow those who are entering to go in.¹

15 "Woe to you, scribes and Pharisees, hypocrites, because you travel around on sea and land to make one proselyte; and when he becomes *one,* you make him twice as much a son of ¹hell as yourselves.

16 "Woe to you, blind guides, who say, 'Whoever swears by the temple, *that* is nothing; but whoever swears by the gold of the temple is obligated.' **17** You fools and blind men! Which is more important, the gold or the temple that sanctified the gold? **18** And *you say,* 'Whoever swears by the altar, *that* is nothing; but whoever swears by the offering that is on it is obligated.' **19** You blind men, which is more important, the offering or the altar that sanctifies the offering? **20** Therefore, the one

---

22:17 ¹I.e., a tax on each person in the census   **22:35** ¹I.e., an expert in the Mosaic Law   **23:5** ¹I.e., small pouches containing Scripture texts, worn on the left forearm and forehead for religious purposes   **23:13** ¹Late mss add (traditionally v 14): *Woe to you, scribes and Pharisees, hypocrites, because you devour widows' houses even while for appearances' sake you make long prayers; therefore you will receive greater condemnation* (as v 14); cf. Mark 12:40; Luke 20:47   **23:15** ¹Gr Gehenna

who swears by the altar, swears *both* by the altar and by everything on it. 21 And the one who swears by the temple, swears *both* by the temple and by Him who dwells in it. 22 And the one who swears by heaven, swears *both* by the throne of God and by Him who sits upon it.

23 "Woe to you, scribes and Pharisees, hypocrites! For you tithe mint and dill and cumin, and have neglected the weightier provisions of the Law: justice and mercy and faithfulness; but these *are the things* you should have done without neglecting the others. 24 You blind guides, who strain out a gnat and swallow a camel!

25 "Woe to you, scribes and Pharisees, hypocrites! For you clean the outside of the cup and of the dish, but inside they are full of robbery and self-indulgence. 26 You blind Pharisee, first clean the inside of the cup and of the dish, so that the outside of it may also become clean.

27 "Woe to you, scribes and Pharisees, hypocrites! For you are like whitewashed tombs which on the outside appear beautiful, but inside they are full of dead men's bones and all uncleanness. 28 So you too, outwardly appear righteous to people, but inwardly you are full of hypocrisy and lawlessness.

29 "Woe to you, scribes and Pharisees, hypocrites! For you build the tombs for the prophets and decorate the monuments of the righteous, 30 and you say, 'If we had been *living* in the days of our fathers, we would not have been partners with them in *shedding* the blood of the prophets.' 31 So you testify against yourselves, that you are sons of those who murdered the prophets. 32 Fill up, then, the measure *of the guilt* of your fathers. 33 You snakes, you offspring of vipers, how will you escape the sentence of hell?

34 "Therefore, behold, I am sending you prophets and wise men and scribes; some of them you will kill and crucify, and some of them you will flog in your synagogues, and persecute from city to city, 35 so that upon you will fall *the guilt of* all the righteous blood shed on earth, from the blood of righteous Abel to the blood of Zechariah, the son of Berechiah, whom you murdered between the temple and the altar. 36 Truly I say to you, all these things will come upon this generation.

Grieving over Jerusalem

37 "Jerusalem, Jerusalem, who kills the prophets and stones those who have been sent to her! How often I wanted to gather your children together, the way a hen gathers her chicks under her wings, and you were unwilling. 38 Behold, your house is being left to you desolate! 39 For I say to you, from now on you will not see Me until you say, 'BLESSED IS THE ONE WHO COMES IN THE NAME OF THE LORD!'".

Signs of Christ's Return

24 Jesus left the temple *area* and was going *on His way* when His disciples came up to point out the temple buildings to Him. 2 But He responded and said to them, "Do you not see all these things? Truly I say to you, not *one*

stone here will be left upon another, which will not be torn down."

3 And as He was sitting on the Mount of Olives, the disciples came to Him privately, saying, "Tell us, when will these things happen, and what *will be* the sign of Your coming, and of the end of the age?"

4 And Jesus answered and said to them, "See to it that no one misleads you. 5 For many will come in My name, saying, 'I am the Christ,' and they will mislead many people. 6 And you will be hearing of wars and rumors of wars. See that you are not alarmed, for *those things* must take place, but *that* is not yet the end. 7 For nation will rise against nation, and kingdom against kingdom, and there will be famines and earthquakes in various places. 8 But all these things are *merely* the beginning of birth pains.

9 "Then they will hand you over to tribulation and kill you, and you will be hated by all nations because of My name. 10 And at that time many will fall away, and they will betray one another and hate one another. 11 And many false prophets will rise up and mislead many people. 12 And because lawlessness is increased, most people's love will become cold. 13 But the one who endures to the end is the one who will be saved. 14 This gospel of the kingdom shall be preached in the whole world as a testimony to all the nations, and then the end will come.

Perilous Times

15 "Therefore when you see the ABOMI-NATION OF DESOLATION which was spoken of through Daniel the prophet, standing in the holy place—let the [1]reader understand— 16 then those who are in Judea must flee to the mountains. 17 Whoever is on the housetop must not go down to get things out of his house. 18 And whoever is in the field must not turn back to get his cloak. 19 But woe to those women who are pregnant, and to those who are nursing babies in those days! 20 Moreover, pray that when you flee, it will not be in the winter, or on a Sabbath. 21 For then there will be a great tribulation, such as has not occurred since the beginning of the world until now, nor ever will *again*. 22 And if those days had not been cut short, no life would have been saved; but for the sake of the elect those days will be cut short. 23 Then if anyone says to you, 'Behold, here is the Christ,' or '*He is over* here,' do not believe *him*. 24 For false christs and false prophets will arise and will provide great signs and wonders, so as to mislead, if possible, even the elect. 25 Behold, I have told you in advance. 26 So if they say to you, 'Behold, He is in the wilderness,' do not go out; *or*, 'Behold, He is in the inner rooms,' do not believe *them*. 27 For just as the lightning comes from the east and flashes as far as the west, so will the coming of the Son of Man be. 28 Wherever the corpse is, there the vultures will gather.

The Glorious Return

29 "But immediately after the tribulation of

those days THE SUN WILL BE DARKENED, AND THE MOON WILL NOT GIVE ITS LIGHT, AND THE STARS WILL FALL from the sky, and the powers of the heavens will be shaken. 30 And then the sign of the Son of Man will appear in the sky, and then all the tribes of the earth will mourn, and they will see the SON OF MAN COMING ON THE CLOUDS OF THE SKY with power and great glory. 31 And He will send forth His angels with A GREAT TRUMPET BLAST, and THEY WILL GATHER TOGETHER His elect from the four winds, from one end of the sky to the other.

Parable of the Fig Tree

32 "Now learn the parable from the fig tree: as soon as its branch has become tender and sprouts its leaves, you know that summer is near; 33 so you too, when you see all these things, recognize that He is near, *right* at the door. 34 Truly I say to you, this generation will not pass away until all these things take place. 35 Heaven and earth will pass away, but My words will not pass away.

36 "But about that day and hour no one knows, not even the angels of heaven, nor the Son, but the Father alone. 37 For the coming of the Son of Man will be just like the days of Noah. 38 For as in those days before the flood they were eating and drinking, marrying and giving in marriage, until the day that Noah entered the ark, 39 and they did not understand until the flood came and took them all away; so will the coming of the Son of Man be. 40 At that time there will be two *men* in the field; one will be taken and one will be left. 41 Two *women* will be grinding at the mill; one will be taken and one will be left.

Be Ready for His Coming

42 "Therefore be on the alert, for you do not know which day your Lord is coming. 43 But be sure of this, that if the head of the house had known at what time of the night the thief was coming, he would have been on the alert and would not have allowed his house to be broken into. 44 For this reason you must be ready as well; for the Son of Man is coming at an hour when you do not think *He will.*

45 "Who then is the faithful and sensible slave whom his master put in charge of his household slaves, to give them their food at the proper time? 46 Blessed is that slave whom his master finds so doing when he comes. 47 Truly I say to you that he will put him in charge of all his possessions. 48 But if that evil slave says in his heart, 'My master is not coming for a long time,' 49 and he begins to beat his fellow slaves, and he eats and drinks with those habitually drunk; 50 *then* the master of that slave will come on a day that he does not expect, and at an hour that he does not know, 51 and he will cut him in two and assign him a place with the hypocrites; in that place there will be weeping and gnashing of teeth.

Parable of Ten Virgins

25 "Then the kingdom of heaven will be comparable to ten virgins, who took their lamps and went out to meet the groom. 2 Five of them were foolish, and five were prudent. 3 For when the foolish took their lamps, they did not take *extra* oil with them; 4 but the prudent ones took oil in flasks with their lamps. 5 Now while the groom was delaying, they all became drowsy and *began* to sleep. 6 But at midnight there finally was a shout: 'Behold, the groom! Come out to meet *him.*' 7 Then all those virgins got up and trimmed their lamps. 8 But the foolish *virgins* said to the prudent ones, 'Give us some of your oil, because our lamps are going out.' 9 However, the prudent ones answered, '*No,* there most certainly would not be enough for us and you *too;* go instead to the merchants and buy *some* for yourselves.' 10 But while they were on their way to buy *the oil,* the groom came, and those who were ready went in with him to the wedding feast; and the door was shut. 11 Yet later, the other virgins also came, saying, 'Lord, lord, open up for us.' 12 But he answered, 'Truly I say to you, I do not know you.' 13 Be on the alert then, because you do not know the day nor the hour.

Parable of the Talents

14 "For *it is* just like a man *about* to go on a journey, *who* called his own slaves and entrusted his possessions to them. 15 To one he gave five 'talents, to another, two, and to another, one, each according to his own ability; and he went on his journey. 16 The one who had received the five talents immediately went and did business with them, and earned five more *talents.* 17 In the same way the one who *had received* the two *talents* earned two more. 18 But he who received the one *talent* went away and dug *a hole in the* ground, and hid his master's money.

19 "Now after a long time the master of those slaves *came and *settled accounts with them. 20 The one who had received the five talents came up and brought five more talents, saying, 'Master, you entrusted five talents to me. See, I have earned five more talents.' 21 His master said to him, 'Well done, good and faithful slave. You were faithful with a few things, I will put you in charge of many things; enter the joy of your master.' 22 "Also the one who *had received* the two talents came up and said, 'Master, you entrusted two talents to me. See, I have earned two more talents.' 23 His master said to him, 'Well done, good and faithful slave. You were faithful with a few things, I will put you in charge of many things; enter the joy of your master.'

24 "Now the one who had received the one talent also came up and said, 'Master, I knew you to be a hard man, reaping where you did not sow, and gathering where you did not scatter *seed.* 25 And I was afraid, so I went away and hid your talent in the ground. See, you *still* have what is yours.'

26 "But his master answered and said to him, 'You worthless, lazy slave! Did you know that I reap where I did not sow, and gather where I did not scatter *seed?* 27 Then you ought to have put my money in the bank, and on my arrival

---

25:15 1 A talent was worth about fifteen years' wages for a laborer

I would have received my *money* back with interest. 28 Therefore: take the talent away from him, and give it to the one who has the ten talents.'

29 "For to everyone who has, *more* shall be given, and he will have an abundance; but from the one who does not have, even what he does have shall be taken away. 30 And throw the worthless slave into the outer darkness; in that place there will be weeping and gnashing of teeth.

The Judgment

31 "But when the Son of Man comes in His glory, and all the angels with Him, then He will sit on His glorious throne. 32 And all the nations will be gathered before Him; and He will separate them from one another, just as the shepherd separates the sheep from the goats; 33 and He will put the sheep on His right, but the goats on the left.

34 "Then the King will say to those on His right, 'Come, you who are blessed of My Father, inherit the kingdom prepared for you from the foundation of the world. 35 For I was hungry, and you gave Me *something* to eat; I was thirsty, and you gave Me *something* to drink; I was a stranger, and you invited Me in; 36 naked, and you clothed Me; I was sick, and you visited Me; I was in prison, and you came to Me.' 37 Then the righteous will answer Him, 'Lord, when did we see You hungry, and feed You, or thirsty, and give You *something* to drink? 38 And when did we see You *as* a stranger, and invite You in, or naked, and clothe You? 39 And when did we see You sick, or in prison, and come to You?' 40 And the King will answer and say to them, 'Truly I say to you, to the extent that you did *it* for one of the least of these brothers *or sisters* of Mine, you did *it* for Me.'

41 "Then He will also say to those on His left, 'Depart from Me, you accursed people, into the eternal fire which has been prepared for the devil and his angels; 42 for I was hungry, and you gave Me nothing to eat; I was thirsty, and you gave Me nothing to drink; 43 I was a stranger, and you did not invite Me in; naked, and you did not clothe Me; sick, and in prison, and you did not visit Me.' 44 Then they themselves also will answer, 'Lord, when did we see You hungry, or thirsty, or *as* a stranger, or naked, or sick, or in prison, and did not take care of You?' 45 Then He will answer them, 'Truly I say to you, to the extent that you did not do *it* for one of the least of these, you did not do *it* for Me, either.' 46 These will go away into eternal punishment, but the righteous into eternal life."

The Plot to Kill Jesus

26 When Jesus had finished all these words, He said to His disciples, 2 "You know that after two days the Passover is coming, and the Son of Man is *to be* handed over for crucifixion."

3 At that time the chief priests and the elders of the people were gathered together in the courtyard of the high priest named Caiaphas;

4 and they plotted together to arrest Jesus covertly and kill Him. 5 But they were saying, "Not during the festival, otherwise a riot might occur among the people."

The Precious Ointment

6 Now when Jesus was in Bethany, at the home of Simon 1the Leper, 7 a woman came to Him with an alabaster vial of very expensive perfume, and she poured it on His head as He was reclining *at the table*. 8 But the disciples were indignant when they saw *this*, and said, "Why this waste? 9 For this *perfume* could have been sold for a high price and *the money* given to the poor." 10 But Jesus, aware of this, said to them, "Why are you bothering the woman? For she has done a good deed for Me. 11 For you always have the poor with you; but you do not always have Me. 12 For when she poured this perfume on My body, she did it to prepare Me for burial. 13 Truly I say to you, wherever this gospel is preached in the whole world, what this woman has done will also be told in memory of her."

Judas' Bargain

14 Then one of the twelve, named Judas Iscariot, went to the chief priests 15 and said, "What are you willing to give me to betray Him to you?" And they set *out* for him thirty pieces of silver. 16 And from then on he looked for a good opportunity to betray Jesus.

17 Now on the first *day* of 1Unleavened Bread the disciples came to Jesus and asked, "Where do You want us to prepare for You to eat the Passover?" 18 And He said, "Go into the city to a certain man, and say to him, 'The Teacher says, "My time is near; I am keeping the Passover at your house with My disciples." ' " 19 The disciples did as Jesus had directed them; and they prepared the Passover.

The Last Passover

20 Now when evening came, Jesus was reclining *at the table* with the twelve. 21 And as they were eating, He said, "Truly I say to you that one of you will betray Me." 22 Being deeply grieved, they began saying to Him, each one: "Surely it is not I, Lord?" 23 And He answered, "He who dipped his hand with Me in the bowl is the one who will betray Me. 24 The Son of Man is going away just as it is written about Him; but woe to that man by whom the Son of Man is betrayed! It would have been good for that man if he had not been born." 25 And Judas, who was betraying Him, said, "Surely it is not I, Rabbi?" Jesus *said to him, "You have said it yourself."

The Lord's Supper Instituted

26 Now while they were eating, Jesus took *some* bread, and after a blessing, He broke *it* and gave *it* to the disciples, and said, "Take, eat; this is My body." 27 And when He had taken a cup and given thanks, He gave *it* to them, saying, "Drink from it, all of you; 28 for this is My blood of the covenant, which is being poured out for many for forgiveness of sins. 29 But I say to you, I will not drink of this

fruit of the vine from now on until that day when I drink it with you, new, in My Father's kingdom."

30 And after singing a hymn, they went out to the Mount of Olives.

31 Then Jesus *said to them, "You will all †fall away because of Me this night, for it is written: 'I WILL STRIKE THE SHEPHERD, AND THE SHEEP OF THE FLOCK WILL BE SCATTERED.' 32 But after I have been raised, I will go ahead of you to Galilee." 33 But Peter replied to Him, "*Even* if they all fall away because of You, I will never fall away!" 34 Jesus said to him, "Truly I say to you that this *very* night, before a rooster crows, you will deny Me three times." 35 Peter *said to Him, "Even if I have to die with You, I will not deny You!" All the disciples said the same thing as well.

The Garden of Gethsemane

36 Then Jesus *came with them to a place called Gethsemane, and *told His disciples, "Sit here while I go over there and pray." 37 And He took Peter and the two sons of Zebedee with Him, and began to be grieved and distressed. 38 Then He *said to them, "My soul is deeply grieved, to the point of death; remain here and keep watch with Me." 39 And He went a little beyond *them,* and fell on His face and prayed, saying, "My Father, if it is possible, let this cup pass from Me; yet not as I will, but as You *will.*" 40 And He *came to the disciples and *found them sleeping, and He *said to Peter, "So, you *men* could not keep watch with Me for one hour? 41 Keep watching and praying, so that you do not come into temptation; the spirit is willing, but the flesh is weak."

42 He went away again a second time and prayed, saying, "My Father, if this *cup* cannot pass away unless I drink *from* it, Your will be done." 43 Again He came and found them sleeping, for their eyes were heavy. 44 And He left them again, and went away and prayed a third time, saying the same thing once more. 45 Then He *came to the disciples and *said to them, "Are you still sleeping and resting? Behold, the hour is at hand and the Son of Man is being betrayed into the hands of sinners. 46 Get up, let's go; behold, the one who is betraying Me is near!"

Jesus' Betrayal and Arrest

47 And while He was still speaking, behold, Judas, one of the twelve, came accompanied by a large crowd with swords and clubs, *who* came from the chief priests and elders of the people. 48 Now he who was betraying Him gave them a sign *previously,* saying, "Whomever I kiss, He is *the one;* arrest Him." 49 And immediately *Judas* went up to Jesus and said, "Greetings, Rabbi!" and kissed Him. 50 But Jesus said to him, "Friend, *do* what you have come for." Then they came and laid hands on Jesus and arrested Him.

51 And behold, one of those who were with Jesus reached and drew his sword, and struck the slave of the high priest and cut off his ear. 52 Then Jesus *said to him, "Put your sword back into its place; for all those who take up the sword will perish by the sword. 53 Or do you think that I cannot appeal to My Father, and He will at once put at My disposal more than twelve †legions of angels? 54 How then would the Scriptures be fulfilled, *which say* that it must happen this way?"

55 At that time Jesus said to the crowds, "Have you come out with swords and clubs to arrest Me as *you would* against a man inciting a revolt? Every day I used to sit within the temple *grounds* teaching, and you did not arrest Me. 56 But all this has taken place so that the Scriptures of the prophets will be fulfilled." Then all the disciples left Him and fled.

Jesus before Caiaphas

57 Those who had arrested Jesus led Him away to Caiaphas, the high priest, where the scribes and the elders were gathered together. 58 But Peter was following Him at a distance, as far as the courtyard of the high priest, and he came inside and sat down with the officers to see the outcome. 59 Now the chief priests and the entire Council kept trying to obtain false testimony against Jesus, so that they might put Him to death. 60 They did not find *any,* even though many false witnesses came forward. But later on two came forward, 61 and said, "This man stated, 'I am able to destroy the temple of God and to rebuild it in three days.'" 62 The high priest stood up and said to Him, "Do You offer no answer for what these men are testifying against You?" 63 But Jesus kept silent. And the high priest said to Him, "I place You under oath by the living God, to tell us whether You are the Christ, the Son of God." 64 Jesus *said to him, "You have said *it* yourself. But I tell you, from now *on* you will see the Son of Man sitting at the right hand of power, and coming on the clouds of heaven."

65 Then the high priest tore his robes and said, "He has blasphemed! What further need do we have of witnesses? See, you have now heard the blasphemy; 66 what do you think?" They answered, "He deserves death!" 67 Then they spit in His face and beat Him with their fists; and others slapped Him, 68 and said, "Prophesy to us, You Christ; who is the one who hit You?"

Peter's Denials

69 Now Peter was sitting outside in the courtyard, and a slave woman came to him and said, "You too were with Jesus the Galilean." 70 But he denied *it* before them all, saying, "I do not know what you are talking about." 71 When he had gone out to the gateway, another *slave woman* saw him and *said to those who were there, "This man was with Jesus of Nazareth." 72 And again he denied *it,* with an oath: "I do not know the man." 73 A little later the bystanders came up and said to Peter, "You really are *one* of them as well, since even the way you talk gives you away." 74 Then he began to curse and swear, "I do not know the man!" And immediately a rooster crowed. 75 And Peter remembered the

---

26:31 1 I.e., have a lapse in faith   26:53 1 A legion equaled 6,000 troops

statement that Jesus had made: "Before a rooster crows, you will deny Me three times." And he went out and wept bitterly.

Judas' Remorse

27 Now when morning came, all the chief priests and the elders of the people conferred together against Jesus to put Him to death; 2 and they bound Him and led Him away, and handed Him over to Pilate the governor. 3 Then when Judas, who had betrayed Him, saw that He had been condemned, he felt remorse and returned the thirty pieces of silver to the chief priests and elders, 4 saying, "I have sinned by betraying innocent blood." But they said, "What *is that* to us? You shall see *to it* yourself!" 5 And he threw the pieces of silver into the temple sanctuary and left; and he went away and hanged himself. 6 The chief priests took the pieces of silver and said, "It is not lawful to put them in the temple treasury, since it is money paid for blood." 7 And they conferred together and with the money bought the Potter's Field as a burial place for strangers. 8 For this reason that field has been called the Field of Blood to this day. 9 Then that which was spoken through Jeremiah the prophet was fulfilled: "AND THEY TOOK THE THIRTY PIECES OF SILVER, THE PRICE OF THE ONE WHOSE PRICE HAD BEEN SET by the sons of Israel; 10 AND THEY GAVE THEM FOR THE POTTER'S FIELD, JUST AS THE LORD DIRECTED ME."

Jesus before Pilate

11 Now Jesus stood before the governor, and the governor questioned Him, saying, "*So* You are the King of the Jews?" And Jesus said to him, "*It is as* you say." 12 And while He was being accused by the chief priests and elders, He did not offer any answer. 13 Then Pilate *said to Him, "Do You not hear how many things they are testifying against You?" 14 And *still* He did not answer him in regard to even a single charge, so the governor was greatly amazed.

15 Now at *the Passover* Feast the governor was accustomed to release for the people *any* one prisoner whom they wanted. 16 And at that time they were holding a notorious prisoner called Barabbas. 17 So when the people gathered together, Pilate said to them, "Whom do you want me to release for you: Barabbas, or Jesus who is called Christ?" 18 For he knew that *it was* because of envy that 1 they had handed Him over.

19 And while he was sitting on the judgment seat, his wife sent him *a message,* saying, "*See that you have* nothing *to do* with that righteous Man; for last night I suffered greatly in a dream because of Him." 20 But the chief priests and the elders persuaded the crowds to ask for Barabbas, and to put Jesus to death. 21 And the governor said to them, "Which of the two do you want me to release for you?" And they said, "Barabbas." 22 Pilate *said to them, "Then what shall I do with Jesus who is called Christ?" They all *said, "Crucify Him!" 23 But

he said, "Why, what evil has He done?" Yet they kept shouting all the more, saying, "Crucify Him!"

24 Now when Pilate saw that he was accomplishing nothing, but rather that a riot was starting, he took water and washed his hands in front of the crowd, saying, "I am innocent of this Man's blood; you yourselves shall see." 25 And all the people replied, "His blood *shall be* on us and on our children!" 26 Then he released Barabbas for them; but after having Jesus flogged, he handed Him over to be crucified.

Jesus Is Mocked

27 Then the soldiers of the governor took Jesus into the 1 Praetorium and gathered the whole *Roman* 2 cohort to Him. 28 And they stripped Him and put a red cloak on Him. 29 And after twisting together a crown of thorns, they put it on His head, and *put* a 1 reed in His right hand; and they knelt down before Him and mocked Him, saying, "Hail, King of the Jews!" 30 And they spit on Him, and took the reed and beat Him on the head. 31 And after they had mocked Him, they took the cloak off Him and put His *own* garments back on Him, and led Him away to crucify *Him.*

32 As they were coming out, they found a man of Cyrene named Simon, whom they compelled to carry His 1 cross.

The Crucifixion

33 And when they came to a place called Golgotha, which means Place of a Skull, 34 they gave Him wine mixed with bile to drink; and after tasting *it,* He was unwilling to drink *it.*

35 And when they had crucified Him, they divided His garments among themselves by casting lots. 36 And sitting down, they *began* to keep watch over Him there. 37 And above His head they put up the charge against Him which read, "THIS IS JESUS THE KING OF THE JEWS."

38 At that time two 1 rebels *were being crucified with Him, one on the right and one on the left. 39 And those passing by were speaking abusively to Him, shaking their heads, 40 and saying, "You who *are going to* destroy the temple and rebuild *it* in three days, save Yourself! If You are the Son of God, come down from the cross." 41 In the same way the chief priests also, along with the scribes and elders, were mocking *Him* and saying, 42 "He saved others; He cannot save Himself! He is the King of Israel; let Him now come down from the cross, and we will believe in Him. 43 HE HAS TRUSTED IN GOD; LET GOD RESCUE HIM now, IF HE TAKES PLEASURE IN HIM; for He said, 'I am the Son of God.' " 44 And the 1 rebels who had been crucified with Him were also insulting Him in the same *way.*

45 Now from the 1 sixth hour darkness fell upon all the land until the 2 ninth hour. 46 And about the ninth hour Jesus cried out with a loud voice, saying, "ELI, ELI, LEMA SABAKTANEI?" that is, "MY GOD, MY GOD, WHY HAVE YOU

27:18 1 I.e., the Jewish leaders   27:27 1 I.e., the governor's official residence   2 Normally 600 men (the number varied)   27:29 1 Or *staff;* i.e., to mimic a king's scepter   27:32 1 I.e., the crossbeam for a cross   27:38 1 Or *robbers*   27:44 1 Or *robbers*   27:45 1 I.e., noon   2 I.e., 3 p.m.

FORSAKEN ME?" [47] And some of those who were standing there, when they heard it, said, "This man is calling for Elijah." [48] And immediately one of them ran, and taking a sponge, he filled it with sour wine and put it on a reed, and gave Him a drink. [49] But the rest *of them* said, "Let us see if Elijah comes to save Him[1]." [50] And Jesus cried out again with a loud voice, and gave up His spirit. [51] And behold, the veil of the temple was torn in two from top to bottom; and the earth shook and the rocks were split. [52] Also the tombs were opened, and many bodies of the saints who had fallen asleep were raised; [53] and coming out of the tombs after His resurrection, they entered the holy city and appeared to many. [54] Now as for the centurion and those who were with him keeping guard over Jesus, when they saw the earthquake and the *other* things that were happening, they became extremely frightened and said, "Truly this was the Son of God!"

[55] And many women were there watching from a distance, who had followed Jesus from Galilee while caring for Him. [56] Among them were Mary Magdalene, Mary the mother of James and Joseph, and the mother of the sons of Zebedee.

Jesus Is Buried

[57] Now when it was evening, a rich man from Arimathea came, named Joseph, who himself had also become a disciple of Jesus. [58] This man went to Pilate and asked for the body of Jesus. Then Pilate ordered it to be given *to him.* [59] And Joseph took the body and wrapped it in a clean linen cloth, [60] and laid it in his own new tomb, which he had cut out in the rock; and he rolled a large stone against the entrance of the tomb and went away. [61] And Mary Magdalene was there, and the other Mary, sitting opposite the tomb.

[62] Now on the next day, *that is, the day* which is after the preparation, the chief priests and the Pharisees gathered together with Pilate, [63] and they said, "Sir, we remember that when that deceiver was still alive, He said, 'After three days I am rising.' [64] Therefore, give orders for the tomb to be made secure until the third day; otherwise, His disciples may come and steal Him, and say to the people, 'He has risen from the dead,' and the last deception will be worse than the first." [65] Pilate said to them, "You have a guard; go, make it *as* secure as you know how." [66] And they went and made the tomb secure with the guard, sealing the stone.

Jesus Is Risen!

28 Now after the Sabbath, as it began to dawn toward the first *day* of the week, Mary Magdalene and the other Mary came to look at the tomb. [2] And behold, a severe earthquake had occurred, for an angel of the Lord descended from heaven and came and rolled away the stone, and sat upon it. [3] And his appearance was like lightning, and his clothing as white as snow. [4] The guards shook from fear of him and became like dead men. [5] And the angel said to the women, "Do not be afraid; for I know that you are looking for Jesus who has been crucified. [6] He is not here, for He has risen, just as He said. Come, see the place where He was lying. [7] And go quickly and tell His disciples that He has risen from the dead; and behold, He is going ahead of you to Galilee. There you will see Him; behold, I have told you."

[8] And they left the tomb quickly with fear and great joy, and ran to report to His disciples. [9] And behold, Jesus met them and said, "Rejoice!" And they came up and took hold of His feet, and worshiped Him. [10] Then Jesus *said to them, "Do not be afraid; go, bring word to My brothers to leave for Galilee, and there they will see Me."

[11] Now while they were on their way, some of the *men from the* guard came into the city and reported to the chief priests all that had happened. [12] And when they had assembled with the elders and consulted together, they gave a large sum of money to the soldiers, [13] and said, "You are to say, 'His disciples came at night and stole Him while we were asleep.' [14] And if this comes to the governor's ears, we will appease him and keep you out of trouble." [15] And they took the money and did as they had been instructed; and this story was widely spread among the Jews *and is* to this day.

The Great Commission

[16] But the eleven disciples proceeded to Galilee, to the mountain which Jesus had designated to them. [17] And when they saw Him, they worshiped *Him;* but some were doubtful. [18] And Jesus came up and spoke to them, saying, "All authority in heaven and on earth has been given to Me. [19] Go, therefore, and make disciples of all the nations, baptizing them in the name of the Father and the Son and the Holy Spirit, [20] teaching them to follow all that I commanded you; and behold, I am with you always, to the end of the age."

27:49 [1] Some early mss *And another took a spear and pierced His side, and there came out water and blood* (cf. John 19:34)

The Gospel According to

MARK

Preaching of John the Baptist

1 The beginning of the gospel of Jesus Christ, the Son of God, 2 just as it is written in Isaiah the prophet: "BEHOLD, I AM SENDING MY MESSENGER BEFORE YOU,

WHO WILL PREPARE YOUR WAY;

3   THE VOICE OF ONE CALLING ¹OUT IN THE WILDERNESS,

'PREPARE THE WAY OF THE LORD,

MAKE HIS PATHS STRAIGHT!' "

4 John the Baptist appeared in the wilderness, preaching a baptism of repentance for the forgiveness of sins. 5 And all the country of Judea was going out to him, and all the people of Jerusalem; and they were being baptized by him in the Jordan River, confessing their sins. 6 John was clothed with camel's hair and wore a leather belt around his waist, and his diet was locusts and wild honey. 7 And he was preaching, saying, "After me One is coming who is mightier than I, and I am not fit to bend down and untie the straps of His sandals. 8 I baptized you ¹with water; but He will baptize you ²with the Holy Spirit."

The Baptism of Jesus

9 In those days Jesus came from Nazareth in Galilee and was baptized by John in the Jordan. 10 And immediately coming up out of the water, He saw the heavens opening, and the Spirit, like a dove, descending upon Him; 11 and a voice came from the heavens: "You are My beloved Son; in You I am well pleased."

12 And immediately the Spirit *brought Him out into the wilderness. 13 And He was in the wilderness for forty days, being tempted by Satan; and He was with the wild animals, and the angels were serving Him.

Jesus Preaches in Galilee

14 Now after John was taken into custody, Jesus came into Galilee, preaching the gospel of God, 15 and saying, "The time is fulfilled, and the kingdom of God is at hand; repent and believe in the gospel."

16 As He was going along the Sea of Galilee, He saw Simon and Andrew, the brother of Simon, casting a net in the sea; for they were fishermen. 17 And Jesus said to them, "Follow Me, and I will have you become fishers of people." 18 Immediately they left their nets and followed Him. 19 And going on a little farther, He saw James the son of Zebedee, and his brother John, who were also in the boat mending the nets. 20 Immediately He called them; and they left their father Zebedee in the boat with the hired men, and went away to follow Him.

21 They *went into Capernaum; and immediately on the Sabbath Jesus entered the synagogue and began to teach. 22 And they were amazed at His teaching; for He was teaching them as one having authority, and not as the scribes. 23 Just then there was a man in their synagogue with an unclean spirit; and he cried out, 24 saying, "What business do you have with us, Jesus ¹of Nazareth? Have You come to destroy us? I know who You are: the Holy One of God!" 25 And Jesus rebuked him, saying, "Be quiet, and come out of him!" 26 After throwing him into convulsions and crying out with a loud voice, the unclean spirit came out of him. 27 And they were all amazed, so they debated among themselves, saying, "What is this? A new teaching with authority! He commands even the unclean spirits, and they obey Him." 28 Immediately the news about Him spread everywhere into all the surrounding region of Galilee.

Crowds Healed

29 And immediately after they left the synagogue, they entered the house of Simon and Andrew, with James and John. 30 Now Simon's mother-in-law was lying sick with a fever; and they immediately *spoke to Jesus about her. 31 And He came to her and raised her up, taking her by the hand, and the fever left her, and she served them.

32 Now when evening came, after the sun had set, they began bringing to Him all who were ill and those who were demon-possessed. 33 And the whole city had gathered at the door. 34 And He healed many who were ill with various diseases, and cast out many demons; and He would not permit the demons to speak, because they knew who He was.

35 And in the early morning, while it was still dark, Jesus got up, left the house, and went away to a secluded place, and prayed there for a time. 36 Simon and his companions eagerly searched for Him; 37 and they found Him and *said to Him, "Everyone is looking for You." 38 He *said to them, "Let's go somewhere else to the towns nearby, so that I may also preach there; for this is why I came." 39 And He went into their synagogues preaching throughout Galilee, and casting out the demons.

40 And a man with ¹leprosy *came to Jesus, imploring Him and kneeling down, and saying to Him, "If You are willing, You can make me clean." 41 Moved with compassion, Jesus reached out with His hand and touched him, and *said to him, "I am willing; be cleansed." 42 And immediately the leprosy left him, and he was cleansed. 43 And He sternly warned him and immediately sent him away, 44 and He *said to him, "See that you say nothing to

1:3 ¹Or out, Prepare in the wilderness the way   1:8 ¹The Gr here can be translated in, with, or by   2 The Gr here can be translated in, with, or by   1:24 ¹Or the Nazarene   1:40 ¹I.e., leprosy or a serious, unspecified disease, and so throughout the ch; see Lev 13

anyone; but go, show yourself to the priest and offer for your cleansing what Moses commanded, as a testimony to them." 45 But he went out and began to proclaim it freely and to spread the news around, to such an extent that Jesus could no longer publicly enter a city, but stayed out in unpopulated areas; and they were coming to Him from everywhere.

The Paralyzed Man Healed

2 When *Jesus* came back to Capernaum a few days later, it was heard that He was at home. 2 And many were gathered together, so that there was no longer space, not even near the door; and He was speaking the word to them. 3 And *some people* *came, bringing to Him a man who was paralyzed, carried by four *men*. 4 And when they were unable to get to Him because of the crowd, they removed the roof above Him; and after digging an opening, they let down the pallet on which the paralyzed man was lying. 5 And Jesus, seeing their faith, *said to the paralyzed man, "Son, your sins are forgiven." 6 But some of the scribes were sitting there and thinking *it* over in their hearts, 7 "Why does this man speak that way? He is blaspheming! Who can forgive sins except God alone?" 8 Immediately Jesus, aware in His spirit that they were thinking that way within themselves, *said to them, "Why are you thinking about these things in your hearts? 9 Which is easier, to say to the paralyzed man, 'Your sins are forgiven'; or to say, 'Get up, and pick up your pallet and walk'? 10 But so that you may know that the Son of Man has authority on earth to forgive sins"—He *said to the paralyzed man, 11 "I say to you, get up, pick up your pallet, and go home." 12 And he got up and immediately picked up the pallet and went out in the sight of everyone, so that they were all amazed and were glorifying God, saying, "We have never seen *anything* like this!"

13 And He went out again by the seashore; and all the people were coming to Him, and He was teaching them.

Levi (Matthew) Called

14 As He passed by, He saw Levi the *son* of Alphaeus sitting in the tax office, and He *said to him, "Follow Me!" And he got up and followed Him.

15 And it *happened that He was reclining *at the table* in his house, and many tax collectors and sinners were dining with Jesus and His disciples; for there were many *of them,* and they were following Him. 16 When the scribes of the Pharisees saw that He was eating with the sinners and tax collectors, they said to His disciples, "Why is He eating with tax collectors and sinners?" 17 And hearing *this,* Jesus *said to them, "*It is* not those who are healthy who need a physician, but those who are sick; I did not come to call the righteous, but sinners."

18 John's disciples and the Pharisees were fasting; and they *came and *said to Him, "Why do John's disciples and the disciples of the Pharisees fast, but Your disciples do not fast?" 19 And Jesus said to them, "While the groom is with them, the attendants of the groom cannot fast, can they? As long as they have the groom with them, they cannot fast. 20 But the days will come when the groom is taken away from them, and then they will fast, on that day.

21 "No one sews a patch of unshrunk cloth on an old garment; otherwise, the patch pulls away from it, the new from the old, and a worse tear results. 22 And no one puts new wine into old wineskins; otherwise the wine will burst the skins, and the wine is lost and the skins *as well;* but *one puts* new wine into fresh wineskins."

Question of the Sabbath

23 And it happened that He was passing through the grainfields on the Sabbath, and His disciples began to make their way *along* while picking the heads *of grain.* 24 The Pharisees were saying to Him, "Look, why are they doing what is not lawful on the Sabbath?" 25 And He *said to them, "Have you never read what David did when he was in need and he and his companions became hungry; 26 how he entered the house of God in the time of Abiathar *the* high priest, and ate the consecrated bread, which is not lawful for *anyone* to eat except the priests, and he also gave it to those who were with him?" 27 Jesus said to them, "The Sabbath was made for man, and not man for the Sabbath. 28 So the Son of Man is Lord, even of the Sabbath."

Jesus Heals on the Sabbath

3 He entered a synagogue again; and a man was there whose hand was withered. 2 And they were watching Him closely *to see* if He would heal him on the Sabbath, so that they might accuse Him. 3 He *said to the man with the withered hand, "Get up and come forward!" 4 And He *said to them, "Is it lawful to do good on the Sabbath or to do harm, to save a life or to kill?" But they kept silent. 5 After looking around at them with anger, grieved at their hardness of heart, He *said to the man, "Stretch out your hand." And he stretched it out, and his hand was restored. 6 The Pharisees went out and immediately *began* conspiring with the Herodians against Him, *as to* how they might put Him to death.

7 Jesus withdrew to the sea with His disciples; and a large multitude from Galilee followed, and *also* from Judea, 8 and from Jerusalem, and from Idumea, and beyond the Jordan, and the vicinity of Tyre and Sidon, a great number of people heard about everything that He was doing and came to Him. 9 And He told His disciples *to see* that a boat would be ready for Him because of the masses, so that they would not crowd Him; 10 for He had healed many, with the result that all those who had diseases pushed in around Him in order to touch Him. 11 And whenever the unclean spirits saw Him, they would fall down before Him and shout, "You are the Son of God!" 12 And He strongly warned them not to reveal who He was.

The Twelve Are Chosen

13 And He *went up on the mountain and *summoned those whom He Himself wanted,

and they came to Him. **14** And He appointed twelve, so that they would be with Him and that He *could* send them out to preach, **15** and to have authority to cast out the demons. **16** And He appointed the twelve: Simon (to whom He gave the name Peter), **17** James the *son* of Zebedee and John the brother of James (to them He gave the name Boanerges, which means, "Sons of Thunder"); **18** and Andrew, Philip, Bartholomew, Matthew, Thomas, James the son of Alphaeus, Thaddaeus, and Simon the Zealot; **19** and Judas Iscariot, who also betrayed Him.

20 And He *came home, and the crowd *gathered again, to such an extent that they could not even eat a meal. **21** And when His own people heard *about this,* they came out to take custody of Him; for they were saying, "He has lost His senses." **22** The scribes who came down from Jerusalem were saying, "He is possessed by Beelzebul," and "He casts out the demons by the ruler of the demons." **23** And *so* He called them to Himself and *began* speaking to them in parables: "How can Satan cast out Satan? **24** And if a kingdom is divided against itself, that kingdom cannot stand. **25** If a house is divided against itself, that house will not be able to stand. **26** And if Satan has risen up against himself and is divided, he cannot stand, but he is finished! **27** But no one can enter the strong man's house and plunder his property unless he first ties up the strong man, and then he will plunder his house.

28 "Truly I say to you, all sins will be forgiven the sons *and daughters* of men, and whatever blasphemies they commit; **29** but whoever blasphemes against the Holy Spirit never has forgiveness, but is guilty of an eternal sin"— **30** because they were saying, "He has an unclean spirit."

31 Then His mother and His brothers *came, and while standing outside they sent *word* to Him, calling *for* Him. **32** And a crowd was sitting around Him, and they *said to Him, "Behold, Your mother and Your brothers are outside looking for You." **33** Answering them, He *said, "Who are My mother and My brothers?" **34** And looking around at those who were sitting around Him, He *said, "Here are My mother and My brothers! **35** For whoever does the will of God, this is My brother, and sister, and mother."

Parable of the Sower and Soils

4 Again He began to teach by the sea. And such a very large crowd gathered to Him that He got into a boat on the sea and sat down; and the whole crowd was by the sea on the land. **2** And He was teaching them many things in parables, and was saying to them in His teaching, **3** "Listen *to this!* Behold, the sower went out to sow; **4** as he was sowing, some *seed* fell beside the road, and the birds came and ate it up. **5** Other *seed* fell on the rocky *ground* where it did not have much soil; and immediately it sprang up because it had no depth of soil. **6** And when the sun had risen, it was scorched; and because it had no root, it withered away. **7** Other *seed* fell among the thorns, and the thorns came up and choked it, and it yielded no crop. **8** Other *seeds* fell into the good soil, and as they grew up and increased, they yielded a crop and produced thirty, sixty, and a hundred *times as much.*" **9** And He was saying, "He who has ears to hear, let him hear."

10 As soon as He was alone, His followers, along with the twelve *disciples, began* asking Him *about* the parables. **11** And He was saying to them, "To you has been given the mystery of the kingdom of God, but for those who are outside, everything comes in parables, **12** so that WHILE SEEING THEY MAY SEE, AND NOT PERCEIVE, AND WHILE HEARING, THEY MAY HEAR, AND NOT UNDERSTAND, OTHERWISE THEY MIGHT RETURN AND IT WOULD BE FORGIVEN THEM."

Explanation of the Parable

13 And He *said to them, "Do you not understand this parable? How will you understand all the parables? **14** The sower sows the word. **15** These are the ones who are beside the road where the word is sown; and when they hear, immediately Satan comes and takes away the word which has been sown in them. **16** And in a similar way these are the ones sown *with seed* on the rocky *places,* who, when they hear the word, immediately receive it with joy; **17** and *yet* they have no *firm* root in themselves, but are *only* temporary; then, when affliction or persecution occurs because of the word, immediately they fall away. **18** And others are the ones sown *with seed* among the thorns; these are the ones who have heard the word, **19** but the worries of the world, and the deceitfulness of wealth, and the desires for other things enter and choke the word, and it becomes unfruitful. **20** And those are the ones sown *with seed* on the good soil; and they hear the word and accept *it* and bear fruit, thirty, sixty, and a hundred *times as much.*"

21 And He was saying to them, "A lamp is not brought to be put under a basket, or under a bed, is it? Is it not *brought* to be put on the lampstand? **22** For nothing is hidden, except to be revealed; nor has *anything* been secret, but that it would come to light. **23** If anyone has ears to hear, let him hear." **24** And He was saying to them, "Take care what you listen to. By your standard of measure it will be measured to you; and *more* will be given you besides. **25** For whoever has, to him *more* will be given; and whoever does not have, even what he has will be taken away from him."

Parable of the Seed

26 And He was saying, "The kingdom of God is like a man who casts seed upon the soil; **27** and he goes to bed at night and gets up daily, and the seed sprouts and grows—how, he himself does not know. **28** The soil produces crops by itself; first the stalk, then the head, then the mature grain in the head. **29** Now when the crop permits, he immediately puts in the sickle, because the harvest has come."

Parable of the Mustard Seed

30 And He was saying, "How shall we picture the kingdom of God, or by what parable shall we present it? **31** *It is* like a mustard seed,

which, when sown upon the soil, though it is the smallest of all the seeds that are upon the soil, 32 yet when it is sown, it grows up and becomes larger than all the garden plants, and forms large branches, with the result that THE BIRDS OF THE SKY can NEST UNDER its shade."

33 And with many such parables He was speaking the word to them, so far as they were able to understand it; 34 and He did not speak to them without a parable; but He was explaining everything privately to His own disciples.

Jesus Stills the Sea

35 On that day, when evening came, He *said to them, "Let's go over to the other side." 36 After dismissing the crowd, they *took Him along with them in the boat, just as He was; and other boats were with Him. 37 And a fierce gale of wind *developed, and the waves were breaking over the boat so much that the boat was already filling *with water. 38 And yet Jesus Himself was in the stern, asleep on the cushion; and they *woke Him and *said to Him, "Teacher, do You not care that we are perishing?" 39 And He got up and rebuked the wind and said to the sea, "Hush, be still." And the wind died down and it became perfectly calm. 40 And He said to them, "Why are you afraid? Do you still have no faith?" 41 They became very much afraid and said to one another, "Who, then, is this, that even the wind and the sea obey Him?"

The Demon-possessed Man Cured

5 They came to the other side of the sea, into the region of the Gerasenes. 2 When He got out of the boat, immediately a man from the tombs with an unclean spirit met Him. 3 He lived among the tombs; and no one was able to bind him anymore, not even with a chain, 4 because he had often been bound with shackles and chains; and the chains had been torn apart by him and the shackles broken in pieces; and no one was strong enough to subdue him. 5 Constantly, night and day, he was screaming among the tombs and in the mountains, and cutting himself with stones. 6 Seeing Jesus from a distance, he ran up and bowed down before Him; 7 and shouting with a loud voice, he *said, "What business do You have with me, Jesus, Son of the Most High God? I implore You by God, do not torment me!" 8 For He had already been saying to him, "Come out of the man, you unclean spirit!" 9 And He was asking him, "What is your name?" And he *said to Him, "My name is Legion, for we are many." 10 And he begged Him earnestly not to send them out of the region. 11 Now there was a large herd of pigs feeding nearby on the mountain. 12 And the demons begged Him, saying, "Send us into the pigs so that we may enter them." 13 Jesus gave them permission. And coming out, the unclean spirits entered the pigs; and the herd rushed down the steep bank into the sea, about two thousand of them; and they were drowned in the sea.

14 Their herdsmen ran away and reported it in the city and in the countryside. And the people came to see what it was that had happened. 15 And then they *came to Jesus and *saw the man who had been demon-possessed sitting down, clothed and in his right mind, the very man who had previously had the "legion"; and they became frightened. 16 Those who had seen it described to them how it had happened to the demon-possessed man, and all about the pigs. 17 And they began to beg Him to leave their region. 18 And as He was getting into the boat, the man who had been demon-possessed was begging Him that he might accompany Him. 19 And He did not let him, but He *said to him, "Go home to your people and report to them what great things the Lord has done for you, and how He had mercy on you." 20 And he went away and began to proclaim in Decapolis what great things Jesus had done for him; and everyone was amazed.

Miracles and Healing

21 When Jesus had crossed over again in the boat to the other side, a large crowd gathered around Him; and He stayed by the seashore. 22 And one of the synagogue officials, named Jairus, *came, and upon seeing Him, *fell at His feet 23 and *pleaded with Him earnestly, saying, "My little daughter is at the point of death; please come and lay Your hands on her, so that she will get well and live." 24 And He went off with him; and a large crowd was following Him and pressing in on Him.

25 A woman who had had a hemorrhage for twelve years, 26 and had endured much at the hands of many physicians, and had spent all that she had and was not helped at all, but instead had become worse—27 after hearing about Jesus, she came up in the crowd behind Him and touched His cloak. 28 For she had been saying to herself, "If I just touch His garments, I will get well." 29 And immediately the flow of her blood was dried up; and she felt in her body that she was healed of her disease. 30 And immediately Jesus, perceiving in Himself that power from Him had gone out, turned around in the crowd and said, "Who touched My garments?" 31 And His disciples said to Him, "You see the crowd pressing in on You, and You say, 'Who touched Me?'" 32 And He looked around to see the woman who had done this. 33 But the woman, fearing and trembling, aware of what had happened to her, came and fell down before Him and told Him the whole truth. 34 And He said to her, "Daughter, your faith has made you well; go in peace and be cured of your disease."

35 While He was still speaking, people *came from the house of the synagogue official, saying, "Your daughter has died; why bother the Teacher further?" 36 But Jesus, overhearing what was being spoken, *said to the synagogue official, "Do not be afraid, only believe." 37 And He allowed no one to accompany Him except Peter, James, and John the brother of James. 38 They *came to the house of the synagogue official, and He *saw a commotion, and people loudly weeping and wailing. 39 And after entering, He *said to them, "Why are you making a commotion and weeping? The child has not died, but is

asleep." **40** And they *began* laughing at Him. But putting them all outside, He *took along the child's father and mother and His own companions, and *entered *the room* where the child was *in bed.* **41** And taking the child by the hand, He *said to her, "Talitha, kum!" (which translated means, "Little girl, I say to you, get up!"). **42** And immediately the girl got up and *began* to walk, for she was twelve years old. And immediately they were completely astonished. **43** And He gave them strict orders that no one was to know about this, and He told *them* to have *something* given her to eat.

Teaching at Nazareth

6Jesus went out from there and *came into His hometown; and His disciples *followed Him. **2** And when the Sabbath came, He began to teach in the synagogue; and the many listeners were astonished, saying, "Where did this man *learn* these things, and what is *this* wisdom that has been given to Him, and such miracles as these performed by His hands? **3** Is this not the carpenter, the son of Mary and brother of James, Joses, Judas, and Simon? And are His sisters not here with us?" And they took offense at Him. **4** Jesus said to them, "A prophet is not dishonored except in his hometown and among his *own* relatives, and in his *own* household." **5** And He could not do any miracle there except that He laid His hands on a few sick people and healed *them.* **6** And He was amazed at their unbelief.

And He was going around the villages, teaching.

The Twelve Sent Out

7 And He *summoned the twelve and began to send them out in pairs, and gave them authority over the unclean spirits; **8** and He instructed them that they were to take nothing for *their* journey, except a mere staff—no bread, no bag, no money in their belt—**9** but *to* wear sandals; and He added, "Do not wear two ¹tunics." **10** And He said to them, "Wherever you enter a house, stay there until you leave town. **11** Any place that does not receive you or listen to you, as you go out from there, shake the dust off the soles of your feet as a testimony against them." **12** And they went out and preached that *people* are to repent. **13** And they were casting out many demons and were anointing with oil many sick people and healing them.

John's Fate Recalled

14 And King Herod heard *about it,* for His name had become well known; and *people* were saying, "John the Baptist has risen from the dead, and that is why these miraculous powers are at work in Him." **15** But others were saying, "He is Elijah." And others were saying, "*He is* a prophet, like one of the prophets *of old.*" **16** But when Herod heard *about it,* he kept saying, "John, whom I beheaded, has risen!" **17** For Herod himself had sent *men* and had John arrested and bound in prison on account of Herodias, the wife of his brother Philip, because he had married her. **18** For John had

been saying to Herod, "It is not lawful for you to have your brother's wife." **19** And Herodias held a grudge against him and wanted to put him to death, and could not *do so;* **20** for Herod was afraid of John, knowing that he was a righteous and holy man, and he had been protecting him. And when he heard him, he was very perplexed; and *yet* he used to enjoy listening to him. **21** An opportune day came when Herod, on his birthday, held a banquet for his nobles and military commanders, and the leading people of Galilee; **22** and when the daughter of Herodias herself came in and danced, she pleased Herod and his dinner guests; and the king said to the girl, "Ask me for whatever you want, and I will give it to you." **23** And he swore to her, "Whatever you ask of me, I will give *it* to you, up to half of my kingdom." **24** And she went out and said to her mother, "What shall I ask for?" And she said, "The head of John the Baptist." **25** Immediately she came in a hurry to the king and asked, saying, "I want you to give me at once the head of John the Baptist on a platter." **26** And although the king was very sorry, because of his oaths and his dinner guests, he was unwilling to refuse her. **27** Immediately the king sent an executioner and commanded *him* to bring *back* his head. And he went and beheaded him in the prison, **28** and brought his head on a platter, and gave it to the girl; and the girl gave it to her mother. **29** When his disciples heard *about this,* they came and carried away his body, and laid it in a tomb.

30 The apostles *gathered together with Jesus; and they reported to Him all that they had done and taught. **31** And He *said to them, "Come *away* by yourselves to a secluded place and rest a little while." (For there were many *people* coming and going, and they did not even have time to eat.) **32** And they went away in the boat to a secluded place by themselves.

Five Thousand Men Fed

33 *The people* saw them going, and many recognized *them* and ran there together on foot from all the cities, and got there ahead of them. **34** When Jesus went ashore, He saw a large crowd, and He felt compassion for them because they were like sheep without a shepherd; and He began to teach them many things. **35** And when it was already late, His disciples came up to Him and said, "This place is secluded and it is already late; **36** send them away so that they may go into the surrounding countryside and villages and buy themselves something to eat." **37** But He answered them, "You give them *something* to eat!" And they *said to Him, "Shall we go and spend two hundred ¹denarii on bread, and give *it* to them to eat?" **38** But He *said to them, "How many loaves do you have? Go look!" And when they found out, they *said, "Five, and two fish." **39** And He ordered them all to recline by groups on the green grass. **40** They reclined in groups of hundreds and fifties. **41** And He took the five loaves and the two fish, and looking up toward heaven, He blessed *the food* and broke the loaves and He gave *them* to the disciples

---

6:9 ¹A long shirt worn next to the skin   6:37 ¹The denarius was a day's wages for a laborer

again and again to set before them; and He divided the two fish among them all. 42 And they all ate and were satisfied; 43 and they picked up twelve full baskets of the broken pieces *of bread,* and of the fish. 44 There were five thousand [1]men who ate the loaves.

Jesus Walks on the Water

45 And immediately Jesus had His disciples get into the boat and go ahead of *Him* to the other side, to Bethsaida, while He Himself *dismissed the crowd. 46 And after saying goodbye to them, He left for the mountain to pray.

47 When it was evening, the boat was in the middle of the sea, and He was alone on the land. 48 Seeing them straining at the oars—for the wind was against them—at about the fourth watch of the night, He *came to them, walking on the sea; and He intended to pass by them. 49 But when they saw Him walking on the sea, they thought that it was a ghost, and they cried out; 50 for they all saw Him and were terrified. But immediately He spoke with them and *said to them, "Take courage; it is I, do not be afraid." 51 Then He got into the boat with them, and the wind stopped; and they were utterly astonished, 52 for they had not gained any insight from *the incident of* the loaves, but their hearts were hardened.

Healing at Gennesaret

53 When they had crossed over they came to land at Gennesaret, and moored at the shore. 54 And when they got out of the boat, immediately *the people* recognized Him, 55 and ran about that entire country and began carrying here and there on their pallets those who were sick, to wherever they heard He was. 56 And wherever He entered villages, or cities, or a countryside, they were laying the sick in the marketplaces and imploring Him that they might just touch the fringe of His cloak; and all who touched it were being healed.

Followers of Tradition

7 The Pharisees and some of the scribes *gathered to Him after they came from Jerusalem, 2 and saw that some of His disciples were eating their bread with unholy hands, that is, unwashed. 3 (For the Pharisees and all the *other* Jews do not eat unless they carefully wash their hands, *thereby* holding firmly to the tradition of the elders; 4 and *when they come* from the marketplace, they do not eat unless they completely cleanse themselves; and there are many other things which they have received *as traditions* to firmly hold, *such as* the washing of cups, pitchers, and copper pots.) 5 And the Pharisees and the scribes *asked Him, "Why do Your disciples not walk in accordance with the tradition of the elders, but eat their bread with unholy hands?" 6 But He said to them, "Rightly did Isaiah prophesy about you hypocrites, as it is written:

'THIS PEOPLE HONORS ME WITH THEIR LIPS,

BUT THEIR HEART IS FAR AWAY FROM ME.
7 'AND IN VAIN DO THEY WORSHIP ME,
TEACHING AS DOCTRINES THE
COMMANDMENTS OF MEN.'
8 Neglecting the commandment of God, you hold to the tradition of men."

9 He was also saying to them, "You are experts at setting aside the commandment of God in order to keep your tradition. 10 For Moses said, 'HONOR YOUR FATHER AND YOUR MOTHER'; and, 'THE ONE WHO SPEAKS EVIL OF FATHER OR MOTHER, IS CERTAINLY TO BE PUT TO DEATH'; 11 but you say, 'If a person says to his father or his mother, whatever I have that would help you is Corban (that is, [1]given *to God),'* 12 you no longer allow him to do anything for *his* father or *his* mother; 13 *thereby* invalidating the word of God by your tradition which you have handed down; and you do many things such as that."

The Heart of Man

14 After He called the crowd to Him again, He *began* saying to them, "Listen to Me, all of you, and understand: 15 there is nothing outside the person which can defile him if it goes into him; but the things which come out of the person are what defile the person[1]."

17 And when He *later* entered a house, away from the crowd, His disciples asked Him about the parable. 18 And He *said to them, "Are you so lacking in understanding as well? Do you not understand that whatever goes into the person from outside cannot defile him, 19 because it does not go into his heart, but into his stomach, and [1]is eliminated?" (*Thereby* He declared all foods clean.) 20 And He was saying, "That which comes out of the person, that *is what* defiles the person. 21 For from within, out of the hearts of people, come the evil thoughts, *acts of* sexual immorality, thefts, murders, *acts of* adultery, 22 deeds of greed, wickedness, deceit, indecent behavior, envy, slander, pride, *and* foolishness. 23 All these evil things come from within and defile the person."

The Syrophoenician Woman

24 Now Jesus got up and went from there to the region of Tyre[1]. And when He had entered a house, He wanted no one to know *about it;* and *yet* He could not escape notice. 25 But after hearing about Him, a woman whose little daughter had an unclean spirit immediately came and fell at His feet. 26 Now the woman was a [1]Gentile, of Syrophoenician descent. And she *repeatedly* asked Him to cast the demon out of her daughter. 27 And He was saying to her, "Let the children be satisfied first, for it is not good to take the children's bread and throw it to the dogs." 28 But she answered and *said to Him, "Yes, Lord, *but* even the dogs under the table feed on the children's crumbs." 29 And He said to her, "Because of this answer, go; the demon has gone out of your daughter." 30 And after going back to her home, she found the child lying on the bed, and the demon gone.

6:44 [1] I.e., 5,000 men plus women and children, cf. Matt 14:21   7:11 [1] Lit *a gift;* i.e., an offering   7:15 [1] Late mss add, as v 16: *If anyone has ears to hear, let him hear.*   7:19 [1] Lit *goes out into the latrine*   7:24 [1] Two early mss add *and Sidon*   7:26 [1] Lit *Greek*

31 Again He left the region of Tyre and came through Sidon to the Sea of Galilee, within the region of Decapolis. 32 And they *brought to Him one who was deaf and had difficulty speaking, and they *begged Him to lay His hand on him. 33 And *Jesus* took him aside from the crowd, by himself, and put His fingers in his ears, and after spitting, He touched his tongue *with the saliva;* 34 and looking up to heaven with a deep sigh, He *said to him, "Ephphatha!" that is, "Be opened!" 35 And his ears were opened, and the impediment of his tongue was removed, and he *began* speaking plainly. 36 And He gave them orders not to tell anyone; but the more He ordered them, the more widely they continued to proclaim *it.* 37 And they were utterly astonished, saying, "He has done all things well; He makes even those who are deaf hear, and those who are unable to talk, speak."

Four Thousand Men Fed

8 In those days, when there was again a large crowd and they had nothing to eat, *Jesus* summoned His disciples and *said to them, 2 "I feel compassion for the people because they have remained with Me for three days already and have nothing to eat. 3 And if I send them away hungry to their homes, they will faint on the way; and some of them have come from a great distance." 4 And His disciples replied to Him, "Where will anyone be able *to find enough* bread here in *this* desolate place to satisfy these people?" 5 And He was asking them, "How many loaves do you have?" And they said, "Seven." 6 And He *directed the people to recline on the ground; and taking the seven loaves, He gave thanks and broke them, and started giving them to His disciples to serve, and they served them to the people. 7 They also had a few small fish; and after He had blessed them, He told *the disciples* to serve these as well. 8 And they ate and were satisfied; and they picked up seven large baskets *full* of what was left over of the broken pieces. 9 About four thousand *men were *there;* and He dismissed them. 10 And immediately He got into the boat with His disciples and came to the region of Dalmanutha.

11 And the Pharisees came out and began to argue with Him, demanding from Him a sign from heaven, to test Him. 12 Sighing deeply in His spirit, He *said, "Why does this generation demand a sign? Truly I say to you, no sign will be given to this generation!" 13 And leaving them, He again embarked and went away to the other side.

14 And *the disciples* had forgotten to take bread, and did not have more than one loaf in the boat with them. 15 And He was giving orders to them, saying, "Watch out! Beware of the leaven of the Pharisees, and the leaven of Herod." 16 And they *began* to discuss with one another *the fact* that they had no bread. 17 And Jesus, aware of this, *said to them, "Why are you discussing *the fact* that you have no bread? Do you not yet comprehend or understand? Do you *still* have your heart hardened? 18 HAVING EYES, DO YOU NOT SEE? AND HAVING EARS, DO YOU

NOT HEAR? And do you not remember, 19 when I broke the five loaves for the five thousand, how many baskets full of broken pieces you picked up?" They *said to Him, "Twelve." 20 "When *I broke* the seven for the four thousand, how many large baskets full of broken pieces did you pick up?" And they *said to Him, "Seven." 21 And He was saying to them, "Do you not yet understand?"

22 And they *came to Bethsaida. And *some people *brought a man who was blind to Jesus and *begged Him to touch him. 23 Taking the man who was blind by the hand, He brought him out of the village; and after spitting in his eyes and laying His hands on him, He asked him, "Do you see anything?" 24 And he looked up and said, "I see people, for I see *them* like trees, walking around." 25 Then again He laid His hands on his eyes; and he looked intently and was restored, and *began* to see everything clearly. 26 And He sent him to his home, saying, "Do not even enter the village."

Peter's Confession of Christ

27 Jesus went out, along with His disciples, to the villages of Caesarea Philippi; and on the way He questioned His disciples, saying to them, "Who do people say that I am?" 28 They told Him, saying, "John the Baptist; and others *say* Elijah; and others, one of the prophets." 29 And He *continued* questioning them: "But who do you say that I am?" Peter answered and *said to Him, "You are the Christ." 30 And He warned them to tell no one about Him.

31 And He began to teach them that the Son of Man must suffer many things and be rejected by the elders and the chief priests and the scribes, and be killed, and after three days rise *from the dead.* 32 And He was stating the matter plainly. And Peter took Him aside and began to rebuke Him. 33 But turning around and seeing His disciples, He rebuked Peter and *said, "Get behind Me, Satan; for you are not setting your mind on God's purposes, but on man's."

34 And He summoned the crowd together with His disciples, and said to them, "If anyone wants to come after Me, he must deny himself, take up his cross, and follow Me. 35 For whoever wants to save his life will lose it, but whoever loses his life for My sake and the gospel's will save it. 36 For what does it benefit a person to gain the whole world, and forfeit his soul? 37 For what could a person give in exchange for his soul? 38 For whoever is ashamed of Me and My words in this adulterous and sinful generation, the Son of Man will also be ashamed of him when He comes in the glory of His Father with the holy angels."

The Transfiguration

9 And Jesus was saying to them, "Truly I say to you, there are some of those who are standing here who will not taste death until they see the kingdom of God when it has come with power."

2 And six days later Jesus *took with Him Peter, James, and John, and *brought them up

---

8:9 1 I.e., 4,000 men plus women and children, cf. Matt 15:38

on a high mountain by themselves. And He was transfigured before them; [3] and His garments became radiant and exceedingly white, as no launderer on earth can whiten them. [4] And Elijah appeared to them along with Moses; and they were talking with Jesus. [5] Peter responded and *said to Jesus, "Rabbi, it is good that we are here; let's make three tabernacles, one for You, one for Moses, and one for Elijah." [6] For he did not know how to reply; for they became terrified. [7] Then a cloud formed, overshadowing them, and a voice came out of the cloud: "This is My beloved Son; listen to Him!" [8] And suddenly they looked around and saw no one with them anymore, except Jesus alone.

[9] As they were coming down from the mountain, He gave them orders not to relate to anyone what they had seen, until the Son of Man rose from the dead. [10] They seized upon that statement, discussing with one another what rising from the dead meant. [11] And they asked Him, saying, "Why is it that the scribes say that Elijah must come first?" [12] And He said to them, "Elijah does come first and he restores all things. And yet how is it written of the Son of Man that He will suffer many things and be treated with contempt? [13] But I say to you that Elijah has indeed come, and they did to him whatever they wanted, just as it is written of him."

All Things Possible

[14] And when they came back to the other disciples, they saw a large crowd around them, and some scribes arguing with them. [15] Immediately, when the entire crowd saw Him, they were amazed and began running up to greet Him. [16] And He asked them, "What are you disputing with them?" [17] And one person from the crowd answered Him, "Teacher, I brought You my son, because he has a spirit that makes him unable to speak; [18] and whenever it seizes him, it slams him to the ground, and he foams at the mouth and grinds his teeth and becomes stiff. And I told Your disciples so that they would cast it out, but they could not do it." [19] And He answered them and *said, "O unbelieving generation, how long shall I be with you? How long shall I put up with you? Bring him to Me!" [20] And they brought the boy to Him. When he saw Him, the spirit immediately threw him into convulsions, and falling to the ground, he began rolling around and foaming at the mouth. [21] And He asked his father, "How long has this been happening to him?" And he said, "From childhood. [22] It has often thrown him both into the fire and into the water to kill him. But if You can do anything, take pity on us and help us!" [23] But Jesus said to him, " 'If You can?' All things are possible for the one who believes." [24] Immediately the boy's father cried out and said, "I do believe; help my unbelief!" [25] When Jesus saw that a crowd was rapidly gathering, He rebuked the unclean spirit, saying to it, "You mute and deaf spirit, I command you, come out of him and do not enter him

again!" [26] And after crying out and throwing him into terrible convulsions, it came out; and the boy became so much like a corpse that most of them said, "He is dead!" [27] But Jesus took him by the hand and raised him, and he got up. [28] When He came into the house, His disciples began asking Him privately, "Why is it that we could not cast it out?" [29] And He said to them, "This kind cannot come out by anything except prayer."

Death and Resurrection Foretold

[30] And from there they went out and began to go through Galilee, and He did not want anyone to know about it. [31] For He was teaching His disciples and telling them, "The Son of Man is to be handed over to men, and they will kill Him; and when He has been killed, He will rise three days later." [32] But they did not understand this statement, and they were afraid to ask Him.

[33] They came to Capernaum; and when He was in the house, He began to question them: "What were you discussing on the way?" [34] But they kept silent, for on the way they had discussed with one another which of them was the greatest. [35] And sitting down, He called the twelve and *said to them, "If anyone wants to be first, he shall be last of all and servant of all." [36] And He took a child and placed him among them, and taking him in His arms, He said to them, [37] "Whoever receives one child like this in My name receives Me; and whoever receives Me does not receive Me, but Him who sent Me."

Dire Warnings

[38] John said to Him, "Teacher, we saw someone casting out demons in Your name, and we tried to prevent him because he was not following us." [39] But Jesus said, "Do not hinder him, for there is no one who will perform a miracle in My name, and be able soon afterward to speak evil of Me. [40] For the one who is not against us is [1]for us. [41] For whoever gives you a cup of water to drink because of your name as followers of Christ, truly I say to you, he shall by no means lose his reward.

[42] "Whoever causes one of these little ones who believe in Me to sin, it is better for him if a heavy millstone is hung around his neck and he is thrown into the sea. [43] And if your hand causes you to sin, cut it off; it is better for you to enter life maimed, than, having your two hands, to go into [1]hell, into the unquenchable fire.[2] [45] And if your foot is causing you to sin, cut it off; it is better for you to enter life without a foot, than, having your two feet, to be thrown into hell.[1] [47] And if your eye is causing you to sin, throw it away; it is better for you to enter the kingdom of God with one eye, than, having two eyes, to be thrown into hell, [48] where THEIR WORM DOES NOT DIE, AND THE FIRE IS NOT EXTINGUISHED. [49] For everyone will be salted with fire. [50] Salt is good; but if the salt becomes unsalty, with what will you make it salty again? Have salt in yourselves, and be at peace with one another."

Jesus' Teaching about Divorce

10 Setting out from there, *Jesus* *went to the region of Judea and beyond the Jordan; crowds *gathered to Him again, and, as He was accustomed, He once more *began* to teach them.

2 And *some* Pharisees came up to Jesus, testing Him, and *began* questioning Him whether it was lawful for a man to divorce *his* wife. 3 And He answered and said to them, "What did Moses command you?" 4 They said, "Moses permitted *a man* to write a certificate of divorce and send *his wife* away." 5 But Jesus said to them, "Because of your hardness of heart he wrote you this commandment. 6 But from the beginning of creation, *God* CREATED THEM MALE AND FEMALE. 7 FOR THIS REASON A MAN SHALL LEAVE HIS FATHER AND MOTHER[1], 8 AND THE TWO SHALL BECOME ONE FLESH; so they are no longer two, but one flesh. 9 Therefore, what God has joined together, no person is to separate."

10 And in the house the disciples again *began* questioning Him about this. 11 And He *said to them, "Whoever divorces his wife and marries another woman commits adultery against her; 12 and if she herself divorces her husband and marries another man, she is committing adultery."

Jesus Blesses Little Children

13 And they were bringing children to Him so that He would touch them; but the disciples rebuked them. 14 But when Jesus saw *this*, He was indignant and said to them, "Allow the children to come to Me; do not forbid them, for the kingdom of God belongs to such as these. 15 Truly I say to you, whoever does not receive the kingdom of God like a child will not enter it at all." 16 And He took them in His arms and *began* blessing them, laying His hands on them.

The Rich Young Ruler

17 As He was setting out on a journey, a man ran up to Him and knelt before Him, and asked Him, "Good Teacher, what shall I do so that I may inherit eternal life?" 18 But Jesus said to him, "Why do you call Me good? No one is good except God alone. 19 You know the commandments: 'DO NOT MURDER, DO NOT COMMIT ADULTERY, DO NOT STEAL, DO NOT GIVE FALSE TESTIMONY, Do not defraud, HONOR YOUR FATHER AND MOTHER.'" 20 And he said to Him, "Teacher, I have kept all these things from my youth." 21 Looking at him, Jesus showed love to him and said to him, "One thing you lack: go and sell all you possess and give to the poor, and you will have treasure in heaven; and come, follow Me." 22 But he was deeply dismayed by these words, and he went away grieving; for he was one who owned much property.

23 And Jesus, looking around, *said to His disciples, "How hard it will be for those who are wealthy to enter the kingdom of God!" 24 And the disciples were amazed at His words. But Jesus responded again and *said to them, "Children, how hard it is to enter the kingdom

of God! 25 It is easier for a camel to go through the eye of a needle than for a rich person to enter the kingdom of God." 26 And they were even more astonished, and said to Him, "Then who can be saved?" 27 Looking at them, Jesus *said, "With people it is impossible, but not with God; for all things are possible with God."

28 Peter began to say to Him, "Behold, we have left everything and have followed You." 29 Jesus said, "Truly I say to you, there is no one who has left house or brothers or sisters or mother or father or children or farms, for My sake and for the gospel's sake, 30 but that he will receive a hundred times as much now in the present age, houses and brothers and sisters and mothers and children and farms, along with persecutions; and in the age to come, eternal life. 31 But many *who are* first will be last, and the last, first."

Jesus' Sufferings Foretold

32 Now they were on the road going up to Jerusalem, and Jesus was walking on ahead of them; and they were amazed, and those who followed were fearful. And again He took the twelve aside and began to tell them what was going to happen to Him, 33 *saying*, "Behold, we are going up to Jerusalem, and the Son of Man will be handed over to the chief priests and the scribes; and they will condemn Him to death and will hand Him over to the Gentiles. 34 And they will mock Him and spit on Him, and flog Him and kill *Him;* and three days later He will rise *from the dead.*"

35 James and John, the two sons of Zebedee, *came up to Jesus, saying to Him, "Teacher, we want You to do for us whatever we ask of You." 36 And He said to them, "What do you want Me to do for you?" 37 They said to Him, "Grant that we may sit, one on Your right and one on *Your* left, in Your glory." 38 But Jesus said to them, "You do not know what you are asking. Are you able to drink the cup that I drink, or to be baptized with the baptism with which I am baptized?" 39 They said to Him, "We are able." And Jesus said to them, "The cup that I drink you shall drink; and you shall be baptized with the baptism with which I am baptized. 40 But to sit on My right or on *My* left is not Mine to give; but *it is* for those for whom it has been prepared."

41 Hearing *this*, the *other* ten began to feel indignant with James and John. 42 Calling them to Himself, Jesus *said to them, "You know that those who are recognized as rulers of the Gentiles domineer over them; and their people in high position exercise authority over them. 43 But it is not this way among you; rather, whoever wants to become prominent among you shall be your servant; 44 and whoever wants to be first among you shall be slave of all. 45 For even the Son of Man did not come to be served, but to serve, and to give His life as a ransom for many."

Bartimaeus Receives His Sight

46 Then they *came to Jericho. And *later*, as He was leaving Jericho with His disciples and a large crowd, a beggar who was blind *named*

10:7 [1] Many late mss add *and shall cling to his wife*

Bartimaeus, the son of Timaeus, was sitting by the road. **47** And when he heard that it was Jesus the Nazarene, he began to cry out and say, "Jesus, Son of David, have mercy on me!" **48** Many were sternly telling him to be quiet, but he kept crying out all the more, "Son of David, have mercy on me!" **49** And Jesus stopped and said, "Call him *here.*" So they *called the man who was blind, saying to him, "Take courage, stand up! He is calling for you." **50** And throwing off his cloak, he jumped up and came to Jesus. **51** And replying to him, Jesus said, "What do you want Me to do for you?" And the man who was blind said to Him, "*¹Rabboni, *I want* to regain my sight!" **52** And Jesus said to him, "Go; your faith has made you well." And immediately he regained his sight and *began* following Him on the road.

The Triumphal Entry

11 And as they *approached Jerusalem, at Bethphage and Bethany, near the Mount of Olives, He *sent two of His disciples, **2** and *said to them, "Go into the village opposite you, and immediately as you enter it you will find a colt tied *there,* on which no one has ever sat; untie it and bring *it here.* **3** And if anyone says to you, 'Why are you doing this?' say, 'The Lord has need of it'; and immediately he will send it back here." **4** They went away and found a colt tied at the door, outside in the street; and they *untied it. **5** And some of the bystanders were saying to them, "What are you doing, untying the colt?" **6** And they told them just as Jesus had said, and they gave them permission. **7** They *brought the colt to Jesus and *put their cloaks on it; and He sat on it. **8** And many people spread their cloaks on the road, and others *spread* leafy branches which they had cut from the fields. **9** And those who went in front and those who followed were shouting:

"Hosanna!
BLESSED IS HE WHO COMES IN THE NAME OF
    THE LORD;
10   Blessed *is* the coming kingdom of our
    father David;
    Hosanna in the highest!"

11 And *Jesus* entered Jerusalem *and came* into the temple *area;* and after looking around at everything, He left for Bethany with the twelve, since it was already late.

12 On the next day, when they had left Bethany, He became hungry. **13** Seeing from a distance a fig tree in leaf, He went *to see* if perhaps He would find anything on it; and when He came to it, He found nothing but leaves, for it was not the season for figs. **14** And He said to it, "May no one ever eat fruit from you again!" And His disciples were listening.

Jesus Drives Money Changers from the Temple

15 Then they *came to Jerusalem. And He entered the temple *area* and began to drive out those who were selling and buying on the temple *grounds,* and He overturned the tables of the money changers and the seats of those who were selling doves; **16** and He would not allow anyone to carry merchandise through the

temple *grounds.* **17** And He *began* to teach and say to them, "Is it not written: 'MY HOUSE WILL BE CALLED A HOUSE OF PRAYER FOR ALL THE NATIONS'? But you have made it a DEN OF ROBBERS." **18** And the chief priests and the scribes heard *this,* and they *began* seeking how to put Him to death; for they were afraid of Him, because all the crowd was astonished at His teaching.

19 And whenever evening came, they would leave the city.

20 As they were passing by in the morning, they saw the fig tree withered from the roots up. **21** And being reminded, Peter *said to Him, "Rabbi, look, the fig tree that You cursed has withered." **22** And Jesus answered and *said to them, "Have faith in God. **23** Truly I say to you, whoever says to this mountain, 'Be taken up and thrown into the sea,' and does not doubt in his heart, but believes that what he says is going to happen, it will be *granted* to him. **24** Therefore, I say to you, all things for which you pray and ask, believe that you have received them, and they will be *granted* to you. **25** And whenever you stand praying, forgive, if you have anything against anyone, so that your Father who is in heaven will also forgive you for your offenses. **26** ['But if you do not forgive, neither will your Father who is in heaven forgive your offenses."]

Jesus' Authority Questioned

27 And they *came again to Jerusalem. And as He was walking in the temple *area,* the chief priests, the scribes, and the elders *came to Him, **28** and *began* saying to Him, "By what authority are You doing these things, or who gave You this authority to do these things?" **29** But Jesus said to them, "I will ask you one question, and you answer Me, and *then* I will tell you by what authority I do these things. **30** Was the baptism of John from heaven, or from men? Answer Me." **31** And they *began* considering *the implications* among themselves, saying, "If we say, 'From heaven,' He will say, 'Then why did you not believe him?' **32** But should we say, 'From men'?"—they were afraid of the people, for they all considered John to have been a real prophet. **33** Answering Jesus, they *said, "We do not know." And Jesus *said to them, "Neither am I telling you by what authority I do these things."

Parable of the Vine-growers

12 And He began to speak to them in parables: "A man planted a vineyard and put a fence around it, and dug a vat under the wine press and built a tower, and leased it to ¹vine-growers and went on a journey. **2** And at the *harvest* time he sent a slave to the vine-growers, in order to receive *his share* of the produce of the vineyard from the vine-growers. **3** And they took him, and beat him, and sent him away empty-handed. **4** And again he sent them another slave, and they wounded him in the head, and treated him shamefully. **5** And he sent another, and that one they killed; and *so with* many others, beating some and killing

others. 6 He had one more *man to send,* a beloved son; he sent him to them last *of all,* saying, 'They will respect my son.' 7 But those vine-growers said to one another, 'This is the heir; come, let's kill him, and the inheritance will be ours!' 8 And they took him and killed him, and threw him out of the vineyard. 9 What will the owner of the vineyard do? He will come and put the vine-growers to death, and give the vineyard to others. 10 Have you not even read this Scripture:

'A STONE WHICH THE BUILDERS REJECTED,
  THIS HAS BECOME THE CHIEF CORNERSTONE;
11 THIS CAME ABOUT FROM THE LORD,
  AND IT IS MARVELOUS IN OUR EYES'?"

12 And they were seeking to seize Him, and *yet* they feared the people, for they understood that He told the parable against them. And *so* they left Him and went away.

Jesus Answers the Pharisees, Sadducees, and Scribes

13 Then they *sent some of the Pharisees and Herodians to Him in order to trap Him in a statement. 14 They came and *said to Him, "Teacher, we know that You are truthful and do not care what anyone thinks; for You are not partial to anyone, but You teach the way of God in truth. Is it permissible to pay a 1poll-tax to Caesar, or not? 15 Are we to pay, or not pay?" But He, knowing their hypocrisy, said to them, "Why are you testing Me? Bring Me a 1denarius to look at." 16 And they brought *one.* And He *said to them, "Whose image and inscription is this?" And they said to Him, "Caesar's." 17 And Jesus said to them, "Pay to Caesar the things that are Caesar's, and to God the things that are God's." And they were utterly amazed at Him.

18 *Some* Sadducees (who say that there is no resurrection) *came to Jesus, and *began* questioning Him, saying, 19 "Teacher, Moses wrote for us that if a man's brother dies and leaves behind a wife and does not leave a child, his brother is to marry the wife and raise up children for his brother. 20 There were seven brothers; and the first took a wife, and died leaving no children. 21 The second one married her, and died leaving behind no children; and the third likewise; 22 and *so* the seven *together* left no children. Last of all the woman also died. 23 In the resurrection, which one's wife will she be? For *each of* the seven had her as *his* wife." 24 Jesus said to them, "Is this not the reason you are mistaken, that you do not understand the Scriptures nor the power of God? 25 For when they rise from the dead, they neither marry nor are given in marriage, but are like angels in heaven. 26 But regarding the fact that the dead rise, have you not read in the book of Moses, in *the passage about* the *burning* bush, how God spoke to him, saying, 'I AM THE GOD OF ABRAHAM, THE GOD OF ISAAC, AND THE GOD OF JACOB'? 27 He is not the God of the dead, but of the living; you are greatly mistaken."

28 One of the scribes came up and heard them arguing, and recognizing that He had answered them well, asked Him, "What commandment is the foremost of all?" 29 Jesus answered, "The foremost is, 'HEAR, ISRAEL! THE LORD IS OUR GOD, THE LORD IS ONE; 30 AND YOU SHALL LOVE THE LORD YOUR GOD WITH ALL YOUR HEART, AND WITH ALL YOUR SOUL, AND WITH ALL YOUR MIND, AND WITH ALL YOUR STRENGTH.' 31 The second is this: 'YOU SHALL LOVE YOUR NEIGHBOR AS YOURSELF.' There is no other commandment greater than these." 32 And the scribe said to Him, "Well *said,* Teacher; You have truly stated that HE IS ONE, AND THERE IS NO OTHER BESIDES HIM; 33 and to love Him with all the heart, and with all the understanding, and with all the strength, and to love one's neighbor as oneself, is much more than all the burnt offerings and sacrifices." 34 When Jesus saw that he had answered intelligently, He said to him, "You are not far from the kingdom of God." And *then,* no one dared any longer to question Him.

35 And Jesus responded and *began* saying, as He taught in the temple *area,* "How *is it that* the scribes say that the Christ is the son of David? 36 David himself said in the Holy Spirit,

'THE LORD SAID TO MY LORD,
  "SIT AT MY RIGHT HAND,
  UNTIL I PUT YOUR ENEMIES UNDER YOUR
    FEET."'

37 David himself calls Him 'Lord'; so in what sense is He his son?" And the large crowd enjoyed listening to Him.

38 And in His teaching He was saying: "Beware of the scribes who like to walk around in long robes, and *like* personal greetings in the marketplaces, 39 and seats of honor in the synagogues, and places of honor at banquets, 40 who devour widows' houses, and for appearance's sake offer long prayers. These will receive all the more condemnation."

The Widow's Coins

41 And *Jesus* sat down opposite the treasury, and *began* watching how the people were putting money into the treasury; and many rich people were putting in large amounts. 42 And a poor widow came and put in two 1lepta coins, which amount to a 2quadrans. 43 Calling His disciples to Him, He said to them, "Truly I say to you, this poor widow put in more than all the contributors to the treasury; 44 for they all put in out of their surplus, but she, out of her poverty, put in all she owned, all she had to live on."

Things to Come

13 As He was going out of the temple, one of His disciples *said to Him, "Teacher, look! What wonderful stones and what wonderful buildings!" 2 And Jesus said to him, "Do you see these great buildings? Not one stone will be left upon another, which will not be torn down."

3 As He was sitting on the Mount of Olives opposite the temple, Peter, James, John, and Andrew were questioning Him privately, 4 "Tell us, when will these things come about, and

---

12:14 1 I.e., a tax on each person in the census   12:15 1 The denarius was a day's wages for a laborer   12:42 1 The smallest Greek copper coin, about 1/128 of a laborer's daily wage   2 A small Roman copper coin, worth about 1/64 of a laborer's daily wage

what *will be* the sign when all these things are going to be fulfilled?" [5] And Jesus began to say to them, "See to it that no one misleads you. [6] Many will come in My name, saying, 'I am *He!*' and they will mislead many. [7] When you hear of wars and rumors of wars, do not be alarmed; *those things* must take place; but *that is* not yet the end. [8] For nation will rise up against nation, and kingdom against kingdom; there will be earthquakes in various places; there will *also* be famines. These things are *only* the beginning of birth pains.

[9] "But be on your guard; for they will hand you over to *the* courts, and you will be flogged in *the* synagogues, and you will stand before governors and kings for My sake, as a testimony to them. [10] And the gospel must first be preached to all the nations. [11] And when they arrest you and hand you over, do not worry beforehand about what you are to say, but say whatever is given you at that time; for you are not the ones speaking, but *it is* the Holy Spirit. [12] And brother will betray brother to death, and a father *his* child; and children will rise up against parents and have them put to death. [13] And you will be hated by everyone because of My name, but it is the one who has endured to the end who will be saved.

[14] "Now when you see the ABOMINATION OF DESOLATION standing where it should not be— let the [1]reader understand—then those who are in Judea must flee to the mountains. [15] Whoever is on the housetop must not go down, nor go in to get anything out of his house. [16] And whoever is in the field must not turn back to get his cloak. [17] But woe to those women who are pregnant, and to those who are nursing babies in those days! [18] Moreover, pray that it will not happen in winter. [19] For those days will be such a *time of* tribulation as has not occurred since the beginning of the creation which God created until now, and never will *again.* [20] And if the Lord had not shortened *those* days, no life would have been saved; but for the sake of the elect, whom He chose, He shortened the days. [21] And then if anyone says to you, 'Look, here is the Christ'; *or,* 'Look, there *He is*'; do not believe *it;* [22] for false christs and false prophets will arise, and will provide signs and wonders, in order to mislead, if possible, the elect. [23] But beware; I have told you everything in advance.

The Return of Christ

[24] "But in those days, after that tribulation, THE SUN WILL BE DARKENED AND THE MOON WILL NOT GIVE ITS LIGHT, [25] AND THE STARS WILL BE FALLING from heaven, and the powers that are in the heavens will be shaken. [26] And then they will see THE SON OF MAN COMING IN CLOUDS with great power and glory. [27] And then He will send forth the angels, and will gather together His elect from the four winds, from the end of the earth to the end of heaven.

[28] "Now learn the parable from the fig tree: as soon as its branch has become tender and sprouts its leaves, you know that summer is near. [29] So you too, when you see these things happening, recognize that He is near, *right* at the door. [30] Truly I say to you, this generation will not pass away until all these things take place. [31] Heaven and earth will pass away, but My words will not pass away. [32] But about that day or hour no one knows, not even the angels in heaven, nor the Son, but the Father *alone.*

[33] "Watch out, stay alert; for you do not know when the *appointed* time is. [34] *It is* like a man away on a journey, *who* upon leaving his house and putting his slaves in charge, *assigning* to each one his task, also commanded the doorkeeper to stay alert. [35] Therefore, stay alert—for you do not know when the master of the house is coming, whether in the evening, at midnight, or when the rooster crows, or in the morning— [36] so that he does not come suddenly and find you asleep. [37] What I say to you I say to all: 'Stay alert!' "

Death Plot and Anointing

14 Now the Passover and *Festival of Unleavened Bread* were two days away; and the chief priests and the scribes were seeking how to arrest Him covertly and kill *Him;* [2] for they were saying, "Not during the festival, otherwise there will be a riot of the people."

[3] While He was in Bethany at the home of Simon [1]the Leper, He was reclining *at the table,* and a woman came with an alabaster vial of very expensive perfume of pure [2]nard. She broke the vial and poured *the perfume* over His head. [4] But there were some indignantly *remarking* to one another, "Why has this perfume been wasted? [5] For this perfume could have been sold for over three hundred [1]denarii, and *the money* given to the poor." And they were scolding her. [6] But Jesus said, "Leave her alone! Why are you bothering her? She has done a good deed for Me. [7] For you always have the poor with you, and whenever you want, you can do good to them; but you do not always have Me. [8] She has done what she could; she has anointed My body beforehand for the burial. [9] Truly I say to you, wherever the gospel is preached in the entire world, what this woman has done will also be told in memory of her."

[10] Then Judas Iscariot, who was one of the twelve, went off to the chief priests in order to betray Him to them. [11] They were delighted when they heard *this,* and promised to give him money. And he *began* seeking how to betray Him at an opportune time.

The Last Passover

[12] On the first day of [1]Unleavened Bread, when the Passover *lamb* was being sacrificed, His disciples *said to Him, "Where do You want us to go and prepare for You to eat the Passover?" [13] And He *sent two of His disciples and *said to them, "Go into the city, and a man carrying a pitcher of water will meet you; follow him; [14] and wherever he enters, say to the owner of the house, 'The Teacher says,

---

13:14 [1] I.e., of the book of Daniel   **14:3** [1] I.e., a nickname; the man no doubt was cured   [2] An aromatic oil extracted from an East Indian plant   **14:5** [1] The denarius was a day's wages for a laborer   **14:12** [1] I.e., Passover week

"Where is My guest room in which I may eat the Passover with My disciples?' '15 And he himself will show you a large upstairs room furnished *and* ready; prepare for us there." 16 The disciples left and came to the city, and found *everything* just as He had told them; and they prepared the Passover.

17 When it was evening He *came with the twelve. 18 And as they were reclining *at the table* and eating, Jesus said, "Truly I say to you that one of you will betray Me—one who is eating with Me." 19 They began to be grieved and to say to Him one by one, "Surely not I?" 20 But He said to them, "*It is* one of the twelve, the one who dips *bread* with Me in the bowl. 21 For the Son of Man is going away just as it is written about Him; but woe to that man by whom the Son of Man is betrayed! *It would have been* good for that man if he had not been born."

The Lord's Supper

22 While they were eating, He took *some* bread, and after a blessing He broke *it,* and gave *it* to them, and said, "Take *it;* this is My body." 23 And when He had taken a cup *and* given thanks, He gave *it* to them, and they all drank from it. 24 And He said to them, "This is My blood of the covenant, which is being poured out for many. 25 Truly I say to you, I will not drink of the fruit of the vine again, until that day when I drink it, new, in the kingdom of God."

26 And after singing a hymn, they went out to the Mount of Olives.

27 And Jesus *said to them, "You will all ᶠfall away, because it is written: 'I WILL STRIKE THE SHEPHERD, AND THE SHEEP WILL BE SCATTERED.' 28 But after I am raised, I will go ahead of you to Galilee." 29 But Peter said to Him, "Even if they all fall away, yet I *will* not!" 30 And Jesus *said to him, "Truly I say to you, that this very night, before a rooster crows twice, you yourself will deny Me three times." 31 But Peter *repeatedly* said insistently, "*Even* if I have to die with You, I will not deny You!" And they all were saying the same thing as well.

Jesus in Gethsemane

32 They *came to a place named Gethsemane; and He *said to His disciples, "Sit here until I have prayed." 33 And He *took with Him Peter, James, and John, and began to be very distressed and troubled. 34 And He *said to them, "My soul is deeply grieved, to the point of death; remain here and keep watch." 35 And He went a little beyond *them,* and fell to the ground and *began* praying that if it were possible, the hour might pass Him by. 36 And He was saying, "Abba! Father! All things are possible for You; remove this cup from Me; yet not what I will, but what You *will.*" 37 And He *came and *found them sleeping, and *said to Peter, "Simon, are you asleep? Could you not keep watch for one hour? 38 Keep watching and praying, so that you will not come into temptation; the spirit is willing, but the flesh is weak." 39 And again He went away and prayed,

saying the same words. 40 And again He came and found them sleeping, for their eyes were heavy; and they did not know what to say in reply to Him. 41 And He *came the third time, and *said to them, "Are you still sleeping and resting? That is enough. The hour has come; behold, the Son of Man is being betrayed into the hands of sinners. 42 Get up, let's go; behold, the one who is betraying Me is near!"

Betrayal and Arrest

43 And immediately, while He was still speaking, Judas, one of the twelve, *came up, accompanied by a crowd with swords and clubs *who were* from the chief priests, the scribes, and the elders. 44 Now he who was betraying Him had given them a signal, saying, "Whomever I kiss, He is the one; arrest Him and lead Him away under guard." 45 And after coming, Judas immediately went to Him and *said, "Rabbi!" and kissed Him. 46 And they laid hands on Him and arrested Him. 47 But one of those who stood by drew his sword, and struck the slave of the high priest and cut off his ear. 48 And Jesus said to them, "Have you come out with swords and clubs to arrest Me, as *you would* against a man inciting a revolt? 49 Every day I was with you within the temple *grounds* teaching, and you did not arrest Me; but *this has taken place* so that the Scriptures will be fulfilled." 50 And His disciples all left Him and fled.

51 A young man was following Him, wearing *nothing but* a linen sheet over *his* naked *body;* and they *seized him. 52 But he pulled free of the linen sheet and escaped naked.

Jesus before His Accusers

53 They led Jesus away to the high priest; and all the chief priests, the elders, and the scribes *gathered together. 54 And Peter had followed Him at a distance, right into the courtyard of the high priest; and he was sitting with the officers and warming himself at the fire. 55 Now the chief priests and the entire ᶠCouncil were trying to obtain testimony against Jesus to put Him to death, and they were not finding any. 56 For many people were giving false testimony against Him, and *so* their testimonies were not consistent. 57 And *then* some stood up and *began* giving false testimony against Him, saying, 58 "We heard Him say, 'I will destroy this temple that was made by hands, and in three days I will build another, made without hands.' " 59 And not even in this respect was their testimony consistent. 60 And *then* the high priest stood up *and came* forward and questioned Jesus, saying, "Do You not offer any answer for what these men are testifying against You?" 61 But He kept silent and did not offer any answer. Again the high priest was questioning Him, and *said to Him, "Are You the Christ, the Son of ᶠthe Blessed *One?*" 62 And Jesus said, "I am; and you shall see the Son of Man sitting at the right hand of power, and coming with the clouds of heaven." 63 Tearing his clothes, the high priest *said, "What further need do we have of witnesses?

14:27 1 I.e., have a lapse in faith　**14:55** 1 Or *Sanhedrin*　**14:61** 1 A common way for the Jewish leaders to refer to God

64 You have heard the blasphemy; how does it seem to you?" And they all condemned Him as deserving of death. 65 And some began to spit on Him, and to blindfold Him, and to beat Him with their fists and say to Him, "Prophesy!" Then the officers took custody of Him and slapped Him *in the face.*

Peter's Denials

66 And while Peter was below in the courtyard, one of the slave women of the high priest *came, 67 and seeing Peter warming himself, she looked at him and *said, "You were with Jesus the Nazarene as well." 68 But he denied *it,* saying, "I neither know nor understand what you are talking about." And he went out onto the porch.[1] 69 The slave woman saw him, and began once more to say to the bystanders, "This man is *one* of them!" 70 But again he denied it. And after a little while the bystanders were again saying to Peter, "You really are *one* of them, for you are a Galilean as well." 71 But he began to curse *himself* and to swear, "I do not know this man of whom you speak!" 72 And immediately a rooster crowed a second time. And Peter remembered how Jesus had made the remark to him, "Before a rooster crows twice, you will deny Me three times." And he hurried on and *began to* weep.

Jesus before Pilate

15 Early in the morning the chief priests with the elders, scribes, and the entire [1]Council immediately held a consultation; and they bound Jesus and led Him away, and turned Him over to Pilate. 2 Pilate questioned Him: "*So* You are the King of the Jews?" And He answered him, "*It is as* you say." 3 And the chief priests *started* accusing Him of many things. 4 But Pilate questioned Him again, saying, "Do You offer nothing in answer? See how many charges they are bringing against You!" 5 But Jesus said nothing further in answer, so Pilate was amazed.

6 Now at *the Passover* Feast he used to release for them *any* one prisoner whom they requested. 7 And the one named Barabbas had been imprisoned with the rebels who had committed murder in the revolt. 8 And the crowd went up and began asking *Pilate to do* as he had been accustomed to do for them. 9 Pilate answered them, saying, "Do you want me to release for you the King of the Jews?" 10 For he was aware that the chief priests had handed Him over because of envy. 11 But the chief priests stirred up the crowd *to ask him* to release Barabbas for them instead. 12 And responding again, Pilate said to them, "Then what shall I do with Him whom you call the King of the Jews?" 13 They shouted back, "Crucify Him!" 14 But Pilate said to them, "Why, what evil has He done?" But they shouted all the more, "Crucify Him!" 15 Intent on satisfying the crowd, Pilate released

Barabbas for them, and after having Jesus flogged, he handed Him over to be crucified.

Jesus Is Mocked

16 Now the soldiers took Him away into the palace (that is, the Praetorium), and they *called together the whole *Roman* [1]cohort. 17 And they *dressed Him in purple, and after twisting together a crown of thorns, they put it on Him; 18 and they began saluting Him: "Hail, King of the Jews!" 19 And they *repeatedly* beat His head with a reed and spit on Him, and kneeling, they bowed down before Him. 20 And after they had mocked Him, they took the purple *cloak* off Him and put His *own* garments on Him. And they *led Him out to crucify Him.

21 And they *compelled a passer-by coming from the country, Simon of Cyrene (the father of Alexander and Rufus), to carry His cross.

The Crucifixion

22 Then they *brought Him to the place Golgotha, which is translated, Place of a Skull. 23 And they tried to give Him wine mixed with myrrh; but He did not take *it.* 24 And they *crucified Him, and *divided up His garments among themselves, casting lots for them *to decide* what each man would take. 25 Now it was the [1]third hour when they crucified Him. 26 The inscription of the charge against Him read, "THE KING OF THE JEWS."

27 And they *crucified two [1]rebels with Him, one on His right and one on His left. [2][29] Those passing by were hurling abuse at Him, shaking their heads and saying, "Ha! You who *are going to* destroy the temple and rebuild it in three days, 30 save Yourself by coming down from the cross!" 31 In the same way the chief priests also, along with the scribes, were mocking *Him* among themselves and saying, "He saved others; He cannot save Himself! 32 Let *this* Christ, the King of Israel, come down now from the cross, so that we may see and believe!" Those who were crucified with Him were also insulting Him.

33 When the [1]sixth hour came, darkness fell over the whole land until the [2]ninth hour. 34 At the [1]ninth hour Jesus cried out with a loud voice, "ELOI, ELOI, LEMA SABAKTANEI?" which is translated, "MY GOD, MY GOD, WHY HAVE YOU FORSAKEN ME?" 35 And when some of the bystanders heard *Him,* they *began* saying, "Look! He is calling for Elijah!" 36 And someone ran and filled a sponge with sour wine, put it on a reed, and gave Him a drink, saying, "Let us see if Elijah comes to take Him down." 37 But Jesus let out a loud cry, and died. 38 And the veil of the temple was torn in two from top to bottom. 39 And when the centurion, who was standing right in front of Him, saw that He died in this way, he said, "Truly this man was the Son of God!"

40 Now there were also *some* women watching from a distance, among whom *were* Mary Magdalene, Mary the mother of James the

---

14:68 [1] Later mss add *and a rooster crowed*   15:1 [1] Or *Sanhedrin*   15:16 [1] Normally 600 men (the number varied)   15:25 [1] I.e., 9 a.m.   15:27 [1] Or *robbers*   [2] Late mss add the following as v 28: *And the Scripture was fulfilled which says, "And He was counted with wrongdoers."*   15:33 [1] I.e., noon   [2] I.e., 3 p.m.   15:34 [1] I.e., 3 p.m.

Less and Joses, and Salome. **41** When He was in Galilee, they used to follow Him and serve Him; and *there were* many other women who came up with Him to Jerusalem.

Jesus Is Buried

42 When evening had already come, since it was the preparation day, that is, the day before the Sabbath, **43** Joseph of Arimathea came, a prominent member of the Council, who was himself also waiting for the kingdom of God; and he gathered up courage and went in before Pilate, and asked for the body of Jesus. **44** Now Pilate wondered if He was dead by this time, and summoning the centurion, he questioned him as to whether He was already dead. **45** And after learning this from the centurion, he granted the body to Joseph. **46** Joseph bought a linen cloth, took Him down, wrapped Him in the linen cloth, and laid Him in a tomb which had been cut out in the rock; and he rolled a stone against the entrance of the tomb. **47** Mary Magdalene and Mary the *mother* of Joses were watching *to see* where He was laid.

The Resurrection

16 When the Sabbath was over, Mary Magdalene, Mary the *mother* of James, and Salome bought spices so that they might come and anoint Him. **2** And very early on the first day of the week, they *came to the tomb when the sun had risen. **3** They were saying to one another, "Who will roll away the stone from the entrance of the tomb for us?" **4** And looking up, they *noticed that the stone had been rolled away; for it was extremely large. **5** And entering the tomb, they saw a young man sitting at the right, wearing a white robe; and they were amazed. **6** But he *said to them, "Do not be amazed; you are looking for Jesus the Nazarene, who has been crucified. He has risen; He is not here; see, *here is* the place where they laid Him. **7** But go, tell His disciples and Peter, 'He is going ahead of you to Galilee; there you will see Him, just as He told you.'" **8** And they went out and fled from the tomb,

for trembling and astonishment had gripped them; and they said nothing to anyone, for they were afraid.

9 [['Now after He had risen early on the first day of the week, He first appeared to Mary Magdalene, from whom He had cast out seven demons. **10** She went and reported to those who had been with Him, while they were mourning and weeping. **11** And when they heard that He was alive and had been seen by her, they refused to believe *it*.

12 Now after that, He appeared in a different form to two of them while they were walking along on their way to the country. **13** And they went away and reported it to the rest, but they did not believe them, either.

The Disciples Commissioned

14 Later He appeared to the eleven *disciples* themselves as they were reclining *at the table;* and He reprimanded them for their unbelief and hardness of heart, because they had not believed those who had seen Him after He had risen *from the dead*. **15** And He said to them, "Go into all the world and preach the gospel to all creation. **16** The one who has believed and has been baptized will be saved; but the one who has not believed will be condemned. **17** These signs will accompany those who have believed: in My name they will cast out demons, they will speak with new tongues; **18** they will pick up serpents, and if they drink any deadly *poison,* it will not harm them; they will lay hands on the sick, and they will recover."

19 So then, when the Lord Jesus had spoken to them, He was received up into heaven and sat down at the right hand of God. **20** And they went out and preached everywhere, while the Lord worked with *them,* and confirmed the word by the signs that followed.]]

[['*And they promptly reported all these instructions to Peter and his companions. And after that, Jesus Himself also sent out through them from east to west the sacred and imperishable proclamation of eternal salvation.*]]

16:9 [1] Later mss add vv 9-20   **16:20** [1] A few late mss and ancient versions contain this paragraph, usually after v 8; a few have it at the end of the ch

The Gospel According to
LUKE

Introduction

1 Since many have undertaken to compile an account of the things accomplished among us, 2 just as they were handed down to us by those who from the beginning were eyewitnesses and servants of the [1]word, 3 it seemed fitting to me as well, having investigated everything carefully from the beginning, to write *it out* for you in an orderly sequence, most excellent Theophilus; 4 so that you may know the exact truth about the things you have been taught.

John the Baptist's Birth Foretold

5 In the days of Herod, king of Judea, there was a priest named Zechariah, of the division of [1]Abijah; and he had a wife [2]from the daughters of Aaron, and her name was Elizabeth. 6 They were both righteous in the sight of God, walking blamelessly in all the commandments and requirements of the Lord. 7 And *yet* they had no child, because Elizabeth was infertile, and they were both advanced in years.

8 Now it happened *that* while he was performing his priestly service before God in the appointed order of his division, 9 according to the custom of the priestly office, he was chosen by lot to enter the temple of the Lord and burn incense. 10 And the whole multitude of the people were in prayer outside at the hour of the incense offering. 11 Now an angel of the Lord appeared to him, standing to the right of the altar of incense. 12 Zechariah was troubled when he saw *the angel,* and fear gripped him. 13 But the angel said to him, "Do not be afraid, Zechariah, for your prayer has been heard, and your wife Elizabeth will bear you a son, and you shall name him John. 14 You will have joy and gladness, and many will rejoice over his birth. 15 For he will be great in the sight of the Lord; and he will drink no wine or liquor, and he will be filled with the Holy Spirit while still in his mother's womb. 16 And he will turn many of the sons of Israel back to the Lord their God. 17 And *it is* he *who* will go *as a fore-runner* before Him in the spirit and power of Elijah, TO TURN THE HEARTS OF FATHERS BACK TO *THEIR* CHILDREN, and the disobedient to the attitude of the righteous, to make ready a people prepared for the Lord."

18 Zechariah said to the angel, "How will I know this? For I am an old man, and my wife is advanced in her years." 19 The angel answered and said to him, "I am Gabriel, who stands in the presence of God, and I was sent to speak to you and to bring you this good news. 20 And behold, you will be silent and unable to speak until the day when these things take place, because you did not believe my words, which will be fulfilled at their proper time."

21 And *meanwhile* the people were waiting for Zechariah, and were wondering at his delay in the temple. 22 But when he came out, he was unable to speak to them; and they realized that he had seen a vision in the temple, and he *repeatedly* made signs to them, and remained speechless. 23 When the days of his priestly service were concluded, he went back home.

24 Now after these days his wife Elizabeth became pregnant, and she kept herself in seclusion for five months, saying, 25 "This is the way the Lord has dealt with me in the days when He looked *with favor* upon *me,* to take away my disgrace among people."

Jesus' Birth Foretold

26 Now in the sixth month the angel Gabriel was sent from God to a city in Galilee named Nazareth, 27 to a virgin [1]betrothed to a man whose name was Joseph, of the descendants of David; and the virgin's name was Mary. 28 And coming in, he said to her, "Greetings, favored one! The Lord *is* with you." 29 But she was very perplexed at *this* statement, and was pondering what kind of greeting this was. 30 And the angel said to her, "Do not be afraid, Mary, for you have found favor with God. 31 And behold, you will conceive in your womb and give birth to a son, and you shall name Him Jesus. 32 He will be great and will be called the Son of the Most High; and the Lord God will give Him the throne of His father David; 33 and He will reign over the house of Jacob forever, and His kingdom will have no end." 34 But Mary said to the angel, "How will this be, since I am a virgin?" 35 The angel answered and said to her, "The Holy Spirit will come upon you, and the power of the Most High will overshadow you; for that reason also the holy Child will be called the Son of God. 36 And behold, even your relative Elizabeth herself has conceived a son in her old age, and she who was called infertile is now in her sixth month. 37 For nothing will be impossible with God." 38 And Mary said, "Behold, the Lord's bond-servant; may it be done to me according to your word." And the angel departed from her.

Mary Visits Elizabeth

39 Now at this time Mary set out and went in a hurry to the hill country, to a city of Judah, 40 and she entered the house of Zechariah and greeted Elizabeth. 41 When Elizabeth heard Mary's greeting, the baby leaped in her womb, and Elizabeth was filled with the Holy Spirit. 42 And she cried out with a loud voice and said, "Blessed *are* you among women, and blessed *is* the fruit of your womb! 43 And how has it happened to me that the mother of my Lord would come to me? 44 For behold, when the sound of your greeting reached my ears, the

---

1:2 [1] I.e., gospel   1:5 [1] Gr *Abia*   [2] I.e., of priestly descent   1:27 [1] Unlike engagement, a betrothed couple was considered married, but did not yet live together

baby leaped in my womb for joy. **45** And blessed *is* she who believed that there would be a fulfillment of what had been spoken to her by the Lord."

Mary's Song: The Magnificat

46 And Mary said:
"My soul exalts the Lord,
47 And my spirit has rejoiced in God my Savior.
48 "For He has had regard for the humble state of His bond-servant;
For behold, from now *on* all generations will call me blessed.
49 "For the Mighty One has done great things for me;
And holy is His name.
50 "And His mercy is to generation after generation
Toward those who fear Him.
51 "He has done mighty deeds with His arm;
He has scattered *those who were* proud in the thoughts of their hearts.
52 "He has brought down rulers from *their* thrones,
And has exalted those who were humble.
53 "He has filled the hungry with good things,
And sent the rich away empty-handed.
54 "He has given help to His servant Israel,
In remembrance of His mercy,
55 Just as He spoke to our fathers,
To Abraham and his descendants forever."
56 Mary stayed with her about three months, and *then* returned to her home.

John the Baptist Is Born

57 Now the time had come for Elizabeth to give birth, and she gave birth to a son. **58** Her neighbors and her relatives heard that the Lord had displayed His great mercy toward her; and they were rejoicing with her.
59 And it happened that on the eighth day they came to circumcise the child, and they were going to call him Zechariah, after his father. **60** And *yet* his mother responded and said, "No indeed; but he shall be called John." **61** And they said to her, "There is no one among your relatives who is called by this name." **62** And they ¹made signs to his father, as to what he wanted him called. **63** And he asked for a tablet and wrote as follows, "His name is John." And they were all amazed. **64** And at once his mouth was opened and his tongue *freed,* and he *began* speaking in praise of God. **65** And fear came on all those who lived around them; and all these matters were being talked about in the entire hill country of Judea. **66** All who heard *them* kept *them* in mind, saying, "What then will this child *turn out to* be?" For indeed the hand of the Lord was with him.

Zechariah's Prophecy

67 And his father Zechariah was filled with the Holy Spirit and prophesied, saying:
68 "Blessed *be* the Lord God of Israel,
For He has visited *us* and accomplished redemption for His people,

69 And has raised up a horn of salvation for us
In the house of His servant David—
70 Just as He spoke by the mouth of His holy prophets from ancient times—
71 Salvation from our enemies,
And from the hand of all who hate us;
72 To show mercy to our fathers,
And to remember His holy covenant,
73 *The* oath which He swore to our father Abraham,
74 To grant us that we, being rescued from the hand of *our* enemies,
Would serve Him without fear,
75 In holiness and righteousness before Him all our days.
76 "And you, child, also will be called the prophet of the Most High;
For you will go on before the Lord to prepare His ways;
77 To give His people *the* knowledge of salvation
By the forgiveness of their sins,
78 Because of the tender mercy of our God,
With which the Sunrise from on high will visit us,
79 To shine on those who sit in darkness and the shadow of death,
To guide our feet into the way of peace."
80 Now the child grew and was becoming strong in spirit, and he lived in the deserts until the day of his public appearance to Israel.

Jesus' Birth in Bethlehem

2 Now in those days a decree went out from Caesar Augustus, that a census be taken of all ¹the inhabited earth. **2** This was the first census taken while ¹Quirinius was governor of Syria. **3** And all *the people* were on their way to register for the census, each to his own city. **4** Now Joseph also went up from Galilee, from the city of Nazareth, to Judea, to the city of David which is called Bethlehem, because he was of the house and family of David, **5** in order to register along with Mary, who was ¹betrothed to him, and was pregnant. **6** While they were there, the time came for her to give birth. **7** And she gave birth to her firstborn son; and she wrapped Him in cloths, and laid Him in a manger, because there was no room for them in the inn.
8 In the same region there were *some* shepherds staying out in the fields and keeping watch over their flock at night. **9** And an angel of the Lord *suddenly* stood near them, and the glory of the Lord shone around them; and they were terribly frightened. **10** And *so* the angel said to them, "Do not be afraid; for behold, I bring you good news of great joy which will be for all the people; **11** for today in the city of David there has been born for you a Savior, who is Christ the Lord. **12** And this *will be* a sign for you: you will find a baby wrapped in cloths and lying in a manger." **13** And suddenly there appeared with the angel a multitude of the heavenly army *of angels* praising God and saying,

---

1:62 ¹I.e., gestured or nodded **2:1** ¹I.e., the Roman Empire **2:2** ¹Gr *Kyrenios* **2:5** ¹Unlike engagement, a betrothed couple was considered married, but did not yet live together

14 "Glory to God in the highest,
  And on earth peace among people with
    whom He is pleased."

15 When the angels had departed from them into heaven, the shepherds *began* saying to one another, "Let's go straight to Bethlehem, then, and see this thing that has happened, which the Lord has made known to us." **16** And they came in a hurry and found their way to Mary and Joseph, and the baby as He lay in the manger. **17** When they had seen *Him,* they made known the statement which had been told them about this Child. **18** And all who heard it were amazed about the things which were told them by the shepherds. **19** But Mary treasured all these things, pondering them in her heart. **20** And the shepherds went back, glorifying and praising God for all that they had heard and seen, just as had been told them.

Jesus Presented at the Temple

21 And when eight days were completed so that it was time for His circumcision, He was also named Jesus, the *name* given by the angel before He was conceived in the womb.

22 And when the days for their purification according to the Law of Moses were completed, they brought Him up to Jerusalem to present Him to the Lord **23** (as it is written in the Law of the Lord: "EVERY FIRSTBORN MALE THAT OPENS THE WOMB SHALL BE CALLED HOLY TO THE LORD"), **24** and to offer a sacrifice according to what has been stated in the Law of the Lord: "A PAIR OF TURTLEDOVES OR TWO YOUNG DOVES."

25 And there was a man in Jerusalem whose name was Simeon; and this man was righteous and devout, looking forward to the consolation of Israel; and the Holy Spirit was upon him. **26** And it had been revealed to him by the Holy Spirit that he would not see death before he had seen the Lord's Christ. **27** And he came by the Spirit into the temple; and when the parents brought in the child Jesus, to carry out for Him the custom of the Law, **28** then he took Him in his arms, and blessed God, and said,
29 "Now, Lord, You are letting Your
    bond-servant depart in peace,
    According to Your word;
30 For my eyes have seen Your salvation,
31 Which You have prepared in the presence
      of all the peoples:
32 A light for revelation for the Gentiles,
    And the glory of Your people Israel."

33 And His father and mother were amazed at the things which were being said about Him. **34** And Simeon blessed them and said to His mother Mary, "Behold, this *Child* is appointed for the fall and rise of many in Israel, and as a sign to be opposed— **35** and a sword will pierce your own soul—to the end that thoughts from many hearts may be revealed."

36 And there was a prophetess, Anna, the daughter of Phanuel, of the tribe of Asher. She was advanced in years and had lived with *her* husband for seven years after her marriage, **37** and *then* as a widow to the age of eighty-four. She did not leave the temple *grounds,* serving night and day with fasts and prayers. **38** And at that very moment she came up and *began* giving thanks to God, and continued to speak about Him to all those who were looking forward to the redemption of Jerusalem.

Return to Nazareth

39 And when *His parents* had completed everything in accordance with the Law of the Lord, they returned to Galilee, to their own city of Nazareth. **40** Now the Child continued to grow and to become strong, increasing in wisdom; and the favor of God was upon Him.

Visit to Jerusalem

41 His parents went to Jerusalem every year at the Feast of the Passover. **42** And when He was twelve years old, they went up *there* according to the custom of the feast; **43** and as they were returning, after spending the full number of days *required,* the boy Jesus stayed behind in Jerusalem, but His parents were unaware *of it.* **44** Instead, they thought that He was *somewhere* in the caravan, and they went a day's journey; and *then* they *began* looking for Him among their relatives and acquaintances. **45** And when they did not find Him, they returned to Jerusalem, looking for Him. **46** Then, after three days they found Him in the temple, sitting in the midst of the teachers, both listening to them and asking them questions. **47** And all who heard Him were amazed at His understanding and His answers. **48** When *Joseph and Mary* saw Him, they were bewildered; and His mother said to Him, "Son, why have You treated us this way? Behold, Your father and I have been anxiously looking for You!" **49** And He said to them, "Why *is it* that you were looking for Me? Did you not know that I had to be in My Father's *house?*" **50** And *yet* they on their part did not understand the statement which He had made to them. **51** And He went down with them and came to Nazareth, and He continued to be subject to them; and His mother treasured all *these* things in her heart.

52 And Jesus kept increasing in wisdom and stature, and in favor with God and people.

John the Baptist Preaches

3 Now in the fifteenth year of the reign of Tiberius Caesar, when Pontius Pilate was governor of Judea, and Herod was tetrarch of Galilee and his brother Philip was tetrarch of the region of Ituraea and Trachonitis, and Lysanias was tetrarch of Abilene, **2** in the high priesthood of Annas and Caiaphas, the word of God came to John, the son of Zechariah, in the wilderness. **3** And he came into all the region around the Jordan, preaching a baptism of repentance for the forgiveness of sins; **4** as it is written in the book of the words of Isaiah the prophet:
  "THE VOICE OF ONE CALLING ¹OUT IN THE
      WILDERNESS,
    'PREPARE THE WAY OF THE LORD,
    MAKE HIS PATHS STRAIGHT!
5 'EVERY RAVINE WILL BE FILLED,
    AND EVERY MOUNTAIN AND HILL WILL BE
      LOWERED;
    THE CROOKED WILL BECOME STRAIGHT,

3:4 ¹Or *out, Prepare in the wilderness the way*

AND THE ROUGH ROADS SMOOTH;
6 AND ALL FLESH WILL SEE THE SALVATION OF
GOD!' "

7 So he was saying to the crowds who were going out to be baptized by him, "You offspring of vipers, who warned you to flee from the wrath to come? 8 Therefore produce fruits that are consistent with repentance, and do not start saying to yourselves, 'We have Abraham *as our* father,' for I say to you that from these stones God is able to raise up children for Abraham. 9 But indeed the axe is already being laid at the root of the trees; so every tree that does not bear good fruit is cut down and thrown into the fire."

10 And the crowds were questioning him, saying, "Then what are we to do?" 11 And he would answer and say to them, "The one who has two ʰtunics is to share with the one who has none; and the one who has food is to do likewise." 12 Now even tax collectors came to be baptized, and they said to him, "Teacher, what are we to do?" 13 And he said to them, "Collect no more than what you have been ordered to." 14 And soldiers also were questioning him, saying, "What are we to do, we as well?" And he said to them, "Do not extort money from anyone, nor harass *anyone,* and be content with your wages."

15 Now while the people were in a state of expectation and they all were thinking carefully in their hearts about John, whether he himself perhaps was the Christ, 16 John responded to them all, saying, "As for me, I baptize you with water; but He is coming who is mightier than I, and I am not fit to untie the straps of His sandals; He will baptize you with the Holy Spirit and fire. 17 His winnowing fork is in His hand to thoroughly clear His threshing floor, and to gather the wheat into His barn; but He will burn up the chaff with unquenchable fire."

18 So with many other exhortations he preached the gospel to the people. 19 But when Herod the tetrarch was reprimanded by him regarding Herodias, his brother's wife, and regarding all the evil things which Herod had done, 20 *Herod* also added this to them all: he locked John up in prison.

Jesus Is Baptized

21 Now when all the people were baptized, Jesus also was baptized, and while He was praying, heaven was opened, 22 and the Holy Spirit descended upon Him in bodily form like a dove, and a voice came from heaven: "You are My beloved Son, in You I am well pleased."

Genealogy of Jesus

23 When He began *His ministry,* Jesus Himself was about thirty years old, being, as was commonly held, the son of Joseph, the son of Eli, 24 the son of Matthat, the son of Levi, the son of Melchi, the son of Jannai, the son of Joseph, 25 the son of Mattathias, the son of Amos, the son of Nahum, the son of Hesli, the son of Naggai, 26 the son of Maath, the son of Mattathias, the son of Semein, the son of Josech, the son of Joda, 27 the son of Joanan, the son of Rhesa, the son of Zerubbabel, the son of Shealtiel, the son of Neri, 28 the son of Melchi, the son of Addi, the son of Cosam, the son of Elmadam, the son of Er, 29 the son of Joshua, the son of Eliezer, the son of Jorim, the son of Matthat, the son of Levi, 30 the son of Simeon, the son of Judah, the son of Joseph, the son of Jonam, the son of Eliakim, 31 the son of Melea, the son of Menna, the son of Mattatha, the son of Nathan, the son of David, 32 the son of Jesse, the son of Obed, the son of Boaz, the son of Salmon, the son of Nahshon, 33 the son of Amminadab, the son of Admin, the son of Ram, the son of Hezron, the son of Perez, the son of Judah, 34 the son of Jacob, the son of Isaac, the son of Abraham, the son of Terah, the son of Nahor, 35 the son of Serug, the son of Reu, the son of Peleg, the son of Heber, the son of Shelah, 36 the son of Cainan, the son of Arphaxad, the son of Shem, the son of Noah, the son of Lamech, 37 the son of Methuselah, the son of Enoch, the son of Jared, the son of Mahalaleel, the son of Cainan, 38 the son of Enosh, the son of Seth, the son of Adam, the son of God.

The Temptation of Jesus

4 Now Jesus, full of the Holy Spirit, returned from the Jordan and was led *around* by the Spirit in the wilderness 2 for forty days, being tempted by the devil. And He ate nothing during those days, and when they had ended, He was hungry. 3 And the devil said to Him, "If You are the Son of God, tell this stone to become bread." 4 And Jesus answered him, "It is written: 'MAN SHALL NOT LIVE ON BREAD ALONE.' "

5 And he led Him up and showed Him all the kingdoms of the world in a moment of time. 6 And the devil said to Him, "I will give You all this domain and its glory, for it has been handed over to me, and I give it to whomever I want. 7 Therefore if You worship before me, it shall all be Yours." 8 Jesus replied to him, "It is written: 'YOU SHALL WORSHIP THE LORD YOUR GOD AND SERVE HIM ONLY.' "

9 And he brought Him into Jerusalem and had Him stand on the pinnacle of the temple, and said to Him, "If You are the Son of God, throw Yourself down from here; 10 for it is written:

'HE WILL GIVE HIS ANGELS ORDERS CON-
CERNING YOU, TO PROTECT YOU,'

11 and,

'ON *THEIR* HANDS THEY WILL LIFT YOU UP,
SO THAT YOU DO NOT STRIKE YOUR FOOT
AGAINST A STONE.' "

12 And Jesus answered and said to him, "It has been stated, 'YOU SHALL NOT PUT THE LORD YOUR GOD TO THE TEST.' "

13 And *so* when the devil had finished every temptation, he left Him until an opportune time.

Jesus' Public Ministry

14 And Jesus returned to Galilee in the power of the Spirit, and news about Him spread through all the surrounding region.

3:11 ¹A long shirt worn next to the skin

15 And He *began* teaching in their synagogues and was praised by all.

16 And He came to Nazareth, where He had been brought up; and as was His custom, He entered the synagogue on the Sabbath, and stood up to read. **17** And the scroll of Isaiah the prophet was handed to Him. And He unrolled the scroll and found the place where it was written:

18   "THE SPIRIT OF THE LORD IS UPON ME,
      BECAUSE HE ANOINTED ME TO BRING GOOD
      NEWS TO THE POOR.
      HE HAS SENT ME TO PROCLAIM RELEASE TO
      CAPTIVES,
      AND RECOVERY OF SIGHT TO THE BLIND,
      TO SET FREE THOSE WHO ARE OPPRESSED,
19   TO PROCLAIM THE FAVORABLE YEAR OF THE
      LORD."

20 And He rolled up the scroll, gave it back to the attendant, and sat down; and the eyes of all *the people* in the synagogue were intently directed at Him. **21** Now He began to say to them, "Today this Scripture has been fulfilled in your hearing." **22** And all *the people* were speaking well of Him, and admiring the gracious words which were coming from His lips; and *yet* they were saying, "Is this not Joseph's son?" **23** And He said to them, "No doubt you will quote this proverb to Me: 'Physician, heal yourself! All *the miracles that* we heard were done in Capernaum, do here in your hometown as well.' " **24** But He said, "Truly I say to you, no prophet is welcome in his hometown. **25** But I say to you in truth, there were many widows in Israel in the days of Elijah, when the sky was shut up for three years and six months, when a severe famine came over all the land; **26** and *yet* Elijah was sent to none of them, but *only* to Zarephath, *in the land* of Sidon, to a woman who was a widow. **27** And there were many with leprosy in Israel in the time of Elisha the prophet; and none of them was cleansed, but *only* Naaman the Syrian." **28** And all *the people* in the synagogue were filled with rage as they heard these things; **29** and they got up and drove Him out of the city, and brought Him to the crest of the hill on which their city had been built, so that they could throw Him down from the cliff. **30** But He passed through their midst and went on His way.

31 And He came down to Capernaum, a city of Galilee; and He was teaching them on the Sabbath; **32** and they were amazed at His teaching, because His message was *delivered* with authority. **33** In the synagogue there was a man possessed by the spirit of an unclean demon, and he cried out with a loud voice, **34** "Leave us alone! What business do You have with us, Jesus of Nazareth? Have You come to destroy us? I know who You are—the Holy One of God!" **35** But Jesus rebuked him, saying, "Be quiet and come out of him!" And when the demon had thrown him down in the midst *of the people,* it came out of him without doing him any harm. **36** And amazement came upon them all, and they *began* talking with one another, saying, "What is this message? For with authority and power He commands the unclean spirits, and they come out!" **37** And the news about Him was spreading into every locality of the surrounding region.

Many Are Healed

38 Then He got up and *left* the synagogue, and entered Simon's home. Now Simon's mother-in-law was suffering from a high fever, and they asked Him to help her. **39** And standing over her, He rebuked the fever, and it left her; and she immediately got up and served them.

40 Now while the sun was setting, all those who had *any who were* sick with various diseases brought them to Him; and He was laying His hands on each one of them and healing them. **41** Demons also were coming out of many, shouting, "You are the Son of God!" And *yet* He was rebuking them and would not allow them to speak, because they knew that He was the Christ.

42 Now when day came, Jesus left and went to a secluded place; and the crowds were searching for Him, and they came to Him and tried to keep Him from leaving them. **43** But He said to them, "I must also preach the kingdom of God to the other cities, because I was sent for this *purpose.* "

44 So He kept on preaching in the synagogues of [1] Judea.

The First Disciples

5 Now it happened that while the crowd was pressing around Him and listening to the word of God, He was standing by the lake of Gennesaret; **2** and He saw two boats lying at the edge of the lake; but the fishermen had gotten out of them and were washing their nets. **3** And He got into one of the boats, which was Simon's, and asked him to put out a little *distance* from the land. And He sat down and *continued* teaching the crowds from the boat. **4** Now when He had finished speaking, He said to Simon, "Put out into the deep water and let down your nets for a catch." **5** Simon responded and said, "Master, we worked hard all night and caught nothing, but I will do as You say *and* let down the nets." **6** And when they had done this, they caught a great quantity of fish, and their nets *began* to tear; **7** so they signaled to their partners in the other boat to come and help them. And they came and filled both of the boats, to the point that they were sinking. **8** But when Simon Peter saw *this,* he fell down at Jesus' knees, saying, "Go away from me, Lord, for I am a sinful man!" **9** For amazement had seized him and all his companions because of the catch of fish which they had taken; **10** and likewise also *were* James and John, sons of Zebedee, who were partners with Simon. And Jesus said to Simon, "Do not fear; from now on you will be catching people." **11** When they had brought their boats to land, they left everything and followed Him.

A Man with Leprosy Healed

12 While He was in one of the cities, behold, *there was* a man covered with leprosy; and when he saw Jesus, he fell on his face and

---

4:44 [1] I.e., the country of the Jews (including Galilee)

begged Him, saying, "Lord, if You are willing, You can make me clean." 13 And He reached out with His hand and touched him, saying, "I am willing; be cleansed." And immediately the leprosy left him. 14 And He ordered him to tell no one, *saying,* "But go and show yourself to the priest, and make an offering for your cleansing, just as Moses commanded, as a testimony to them." 15 But the news about Him was spreading *even* farther, and large crowds were gathering to hear *Him* and to be healed of their sicknesses. 16 But *Jesus* Himself would *often* slip away to the wilderness and pray.

A Man Lowered Through a Roof

17 One day He was teaching, and there were *some* Pharisees and teachers of the Law sitting *there* who had come from every village of Galilee and Judea, and *from* Jerusalem; and the power of the Lord was *present* for Him to perform healing. 18 And *some* men *were* carrying a man on a stretcher who was paralyzed; and they were trying to bring him in and to set him down in front of Him. 19 But when they did not find any *way* to bring him in because of the crowd, they went up on the roof and let him down through the tiles with his stretcher, into the middle *of the crowd,* in front of Jesus. 20 And seeing their faith, He said, "Friend, your sins are forgiven you." 21 The scribes and the Pharisees began thinking of the implications, saying, "Who is this *man* who speaks blasphemies? Who can forgive sins, except God alone?" 22 But Jesus, aware of their thoughts, responded and said to them, "Why are you thinking this way in your hearts? 23 Which is easier, to say: 'Your sins are forgiven you,' or to say, 'Get up and walk'? 24 But so that you may know that the Son of Man has authority on earth to forgive sins," He said to the man who was paralyzed, "I say to you, get up, and pick up your stretcher, and go home." 25 And immediately he got up before them, and picked up what he had been lying on, and went home glorifying God. 26 And they were all struck with astonishment and *began* glorifying God. They were also filled with fear, saying, "We have seen remarkable things today!"

Call of Levi (Matthew)

27 After that He went out and looked at a tax collector named Levi sitting in the tax office, and He said to him, "Follow Me." 28 And he left everything behind, and got up and *began* following Him.

29 And Levi gave a big reception for Him in his house; and there was a large crowd of tax collectors and other *people* who were reclining *at the table* with them. 30 The Pharisees and their scribes *began* grumbling to His disciples, saying, "Why do you eat and drink with the tax collectors and sinners?" 31 And Jesus answered and said to them, "*It is* not those who are healthy who need a physician, but those who are sick. 32 I have not come to call the righteous to repentance, but sinners."

33 And they said to Him, "The disciples of John often fast and offer prayers, the *disciples* of the Pharisees also do the same, but Yours eat and drink." 34 And Jesus said to them, "You cannot make the attendants of the groom fast while the groom is with them, can you? 35 But *the* days will come; and when the groom is taken away from them, then they will fast in those days." 36 And He was also telling them a parable: "No one tears a piece of cloth from a new garment and puts it on an old garment; otherwise he will both tear the new, and the patch from the new *garment* will not match the old. 37 And no one pours new wine into old wineskins; otherwise the new wine will burst the skins and it will be spilled out, and the skins will be ruined. 38 But new wine must be put into fresh wineskins. 39 And no one, after drinking old *wine* wants new; for he says, 'The old is fine.'"

Jesus Is Lord of the Sabbath

6 Now it happened that Jesus was passing through *some* grainfields on a Sabbath, and His disciples were picking the heads of grain, rubbing them in their hands, and eating *them.* 2 But some of the Pharisees said, "Why are you doing what is not lawful on the Sabbath?" 3 And Jesus, answering them, said, "Have you not even read what David did when he was hungry, he and those who were with him, 4 how he entered the house of God, and took and ate the ¹consecrated bread, which is not lawful *for anyone* to eat except the priests alone, and gave it to his companions?" 5 And He was saying to them, "The Son of Man is Lord of the Sabbath."

6 On another Sabbath He entered the synagogue and taught; and a man was there whose right hand was withered. 7 Now the scribes and the Pharisees were watching Him closely *to see* if He healed on the Sabbath, so that they might find *a reason* to accuse Him. 8 But He knew what they were thinking, and He said to the man with the withered hand, "Get up and come forward!" And he got up and came forward. 9 And Jesus said to them, "I ask you whether it is lawful to do good on the Sabbath or to do harm, to save a life or to destroy *it?*" 10 And after looking around at them all, He said to him, "Stretch out your hand!" And he did *so;* and his hand was restored. 11 But they themselves were filled with senseless rage, and *began* discussing together what they might do to Jesus.

Choosing the Twelve

12 Now it was at this time that He went off to the mountain to pray, and He spent the whole night in prayer with God. 13 And when day came, He called His disciples to Him and chose twelve of them, whom He also named as apostles: 14 Simon, whom He also named Peter, and his brother Andrew; and James and John; and Philip and Bartholomew; 15 and Matthew and Thomas; James *the son* of Alphaeus, and Simon who was called the Zealot; 16 Judas *the son* of James, and Judas Iscariot, who became a traitor.

17 And *then* Jesus came down with them and stood on a level place; and *there was* a large crowd of His disciples, and a great multitude of

---

6:4 ¹ Lit *loaves of presentation*

the people from all Judea and Jerusalem, and the coastal region of Tyre and Sidon, [18] who had come to hear Him and to be healed of their diseases; and those who were troubled by unclean spirits were being cured. [19] And all the people were trying to touch Him, because power was coming from Him and healing *them* all.

The Beatitudes

[20] And He raised His eyes toward His disciples and *began* saying, "Blessed *are* you who are poor, for yours is the kingdom of God. [21] Blessed *are* you who are hungry now, for you will be satisfied. Blessed *are* you who weep now, for you will laugh. [22] Blessed are you when the people hate you, and when they exclude you, and insult you, and scorn your name as evil, on account of the Son of Man. [23] Rejoice on that day and jump *for joy,* for behold, your reward is great in heaven. For their fathers used to treat the prophets the same way. [24] But woe to you who are rich, for you are receiving your comfort in full. [25] Woe to you who are well-fed now, for you will be hungry. Woe *to you* who laugh now, for you will mourn and weep. [26] Woe *to you* when all the people speak well of you; for their fathers used to treat the false prophets the same way.

[27] "But I say to you who hear, love your enemies, do good to those who hate you, [28] bless those who curse you, pray for those who are abusive to you. [29] Whoever hits you on the cheek, offer him the other also; and whoever takes away your cloak, do not withhold your [tunic] from him either. [30] Give to everyone who asks of you, and whoever takes away what is yours, do not demand *it* back. [31] Treat people the same way you want them to treat you. [32] If you love those who love you, what credit is *that* to you? For even sinners love those who love them. [33] And if you do good to those who do good to you, what credit is *that* to you? For even sinners do the same. [34] And if you lend to those from whom you expect to receive, what credit is *that* to you? Even sinners lend to sinners in order to receive back the same *amount.* [35] But love your enemies and do good, and lend, expecting nothing in return; and your reward will be great, and you will be sons of the Most High; for He Himself is kind to ungrateful and evil *people.* [36] Be merciful, just as your Father is merciful.

[37] "Do not judge, and you will not be judged; and do not condemn, and you will not be condemned; pardon, and you will be pardoned. [38] Give, and it will be given to you. They will pour into your lap a good measure—pressed down, shaken together, *and* running over. For by your standard of measure it will be measured to you in return."

[39] Now He also spoke a parable to them: "A person who is blind cannot guide *another* who is blind, can he? Will they not both fall into a pit? [40] A student is not above the teacher; but everyone, when he has been fully trained, will be like his teacher. [41] Why do you look at the speck that is in your brother's eye, but do not notice the log that is in your own eye? [42] How can you say to your brother, 'Brother, let me take out the speck that is in your eye,' when you yourself do not see the log that is in your own eye? You hypocrite, first take the log out of your own eye, and then you will see clearly to take out the speck that is in your brother's eye. [43] For there is no good tree that bears bad fruit, nor, on the other hand, a bad tree that bears good fruit. [44] For each tree is known by its own fruit. For *people* do not gather figs from thorns, nor do they pick grapes from a briar bush. [45] The good person out of the good treasure of his heart brings forth what is good; and the evil *person* out of the evil *treasure* brings forth what is evil; for his mouth speaks from that which fills *his* heart.

The Parable of the Builders

[46] "Now why do you call Me, 'Lord, Lord,' and do not do what I say? [47] Everyone who comes to Me and hears My words and acts on them, I will show you whom he is like: [48] he is like a man building a house, who dug deep and laid a foundation on the rock; and when there was a flood, the river burst against that house and *yet* it could not shake it, because it had been well built. [49] But the one who has heard and has not acted *accordingly* is like a man who built a house on the ground without a foundation; and the river burst against it and it immediately collapsed, and the ruin of that house was great."

Jesus Heals a Centurion's Slave

7 When He had completed all His teaching in the hearing of the people, He went to Capernaum. [2] Now a centurion's slave, who was highly regarded by him, was sick and about to die. [3] When he heard about Jesus, he sent some Jewish elders to Him, asking Him to come and save the life of his slave. [4] When they came to Jesus, they strongly urged Him, saying, "He is worthy for You to grant this to him; [5] for he loves our nation, and it was he who built us our synagogue." [6] Now Jesus *started* on His way with them; but already, when He was not *yet* far from the house, the centurion sent friends, saying to Him, "Lord, do not trouble Yourself *further,* for I am not worthy for You to enter under my roof; [7] for that reason I did not even consider myself worthy to come to You; but *just* say the word, and my servant shall be healed. [8] For I also am a man placed under authority, with soldiers under myself; and I say to this one, 'Go!' and he goes, and to another, 'Come!' and he comes, and to my slave, 'Do this!' and he does *it."* [9] Now when Jesus heard this, He was amazed at him, and turned and said to the crowd that was following Him, "I say to you, not even in Israel have I found such great faith." [10] And when those who had been sent returned to the house, they found the slave in good health.

[11] Soon afterward *Jesus* went to a city called Nain; and His disciples were going along with Him, accompanied by a large crowd. [12] Now as He approached the gate of the city, a dead man was being carried out, the only son of his

---

6:29 [1] A long shirt worn next to the skin

mother, and she was a widow; and a sizeable crowd from the city was with her. 13 When the Lord saw her, He felt compassion for her and said to her, "Do not go on weeping." 14 And He came up and touched the coffin; and the bearers came to a halt. And He said, "Young man, I say to you, arise!" 15 And the dead man sat up and began to speak. And *Jesus* gave him *back* to his mother. 16 Fear gripped them all, and they *began* glorifying God, saying, "A great prophet has appeared among us!" and, "God has visited His people!" 17 And this report about Him spread throughout Judea and in all the surrounding region.

The Messengers from John

18 The disciples of John also reported to him about all these things. 19 And after summoning two of his disciples, John sent them to the Lord, saying, "Are You the Coming One, or are we to look for another?" 20 When the men came to Him, they said, "John the Baptist has sent us to You, to ask, 'Are You the Coming One, or are we to look for another?'" 21 At that *very* time He cured many *people* of diseases and afflictions and evil spirits; and He gave sight to many *who were* blind. 22 And He answered and said to them, "Go and report to John what you have seen and heard: people who were blind receive sight, people who limped walk, people with leprosy are cleansed and people who were deaf hear, dead people are raised up, *and* people who are poor have the gospel preached to them. 23 And blessed is anyone who does not take offense at Me."

24 When the messengers of John had left, He began to speak to the crowds about John: "What did you go out into the wilderness to see? A reed shaken by the wind? 25 But what did you go out to see? A man dressed in soft clothing? Those who are splendidly clothed and live in luxury are *found* in royal palaces! 26 But what did you go out to see? A prophet? Yes, I tell you, and one who is more than a prophet. 27 This is the one about whom it is written:

'BEHOLD, I AM SENDING MY MESSENGER
AHEAD OF YOU,
WHO WILL PREPARE YOUR WAY BEFORE YOU.'

28 I say to you, among those born of women there is no one greater than John; yet the one who is least in the kingdom of God is greater than he." 29 When all the people and the tax collectors heard *this,* they acknowledged God's justice, having been baptized with the baptism of John. 30 But the Pharisees and the ¹lawyers rejected God's purpose for themselves, not having been baptized by John.

31 "To what then shall I compare the people of this generation, and what are they like? 32 They are like children who sit in the marketplace and call to one another, and say, 'We played the flute for you, and you did not dance; we sang a song of mourning, and you did not weep.' 33 For John the Baptist has come neither eating bread nor drinking wine, and you say, 'He has a demon!' 34 The Son of Man has come eating and drinking, and you say, 'Behold, a gluttonous man and a heavy drinker, a friend of tax collectors and sinners!' 35 And *yet* wisdom is vindicated by all her children."

The Anointing in Galilee

36 Now one of the Pharisees was requesting Him to eat with him, and He entered the Pharisee's house and reclined *at the table.* 37 And there was a woman in the city who was a sinner; and when she learned that He was reclining *at the table* in the Pharisee's house, she brought an alabaster vial of perfume, 38 and standing behind *Him* at His feet, weeping, she began to wet His feet with her tears, and she wiped them with the hair of her head, and *began* kissing His feet and anointing them with the perfume. 39 Now when the Pharisee who had invited Him saw *this,* he said to himself, "If this man were a prophet He would know who and what sort of person this woman *is* who is touching Him, that she is a sinner!"

Parable of Two Debtors

40 And Jesus responded and said to him, "Simon, I have something to say to you." And he replied, "Say it, Teacher." 41 "A moneylender had two debtors: the one owed five hundred ¹denarii, and the other, fifty. 42 When they were unable to repay, he canceled the debts of both. So which of them will love him more?" 43 Simon answered and said, "I assume the one for whom he canceled the greater debt." And He said to him, "You have judged correctly." 44 And turning toward the woman, He said to Simon, "Do you see this woman? I entered your house; you gave Me no water for My feet, but she has wet My feet with her tears and wiped them with her hair. 45 You gave Me no kiss; but she has not stopped kissing My feet since the time I came in. 46 You did not anoint My head with oil, but she anointed My feet with perfume. 47 For this reason I say to you, her sins, which are many, have been forgiven, for she loved much; but the one who is forgiven little, loves little." 48 And He said to her, "Your sins have been forgiven." 49 And *then* those who were reclining *at the table* with Him began saying to themselves, "Who is this *man* who even forgives sins?" 50 And He said to the woman, "Your faith has saved you; go in peace."

Women Support Jesus

8 Soon afterward, Jesus *began* going around from one city and village to another, proclaiming and preaching the kingdom of God. The twelve were with Him, 2 and *also* some women who had been healed of evil spirits and sicknesses: Mary who was called Magdalene, from whom seven demons had gone out, 3 and Joanna the wife of Chuza, Herod's steward, and Susanna, and many others who were contributing to their support out of their private means.

Parable of the Sower

4 Now when a large crowd was coming together, and those from the various cities were journeying to Him, He spoke by way of a parable: 5 "The sower went out to sow his seed;

7:30 ¹ I.e., experts in the Mosaic Law   7:41 ¹ The denarius was a day's wages for a laborer

and as he sowed, some fell beside the road, and it was trampled underfoot, and the birds of the sky ate it up. 6 Other *seed* fell on rocky *soil,* and when it came up, it withered away because it had no moisture. 7 Other *seed* fell among the thorns; and the thorns grew up with it and choked it out. 8 And *yet* other *seed* fell into the good soil, and grew up, and produced a crop a hundred times as much." As He said these things, He would call out, "The one who has ears to hear, let him hear."

9 Now His disciples *began* asking Him what this parable meant. 10 And He said, "To you it has been granted to know the mysteries of the kingdom of God, but to the rest *they are told* in parables, so that while seeing they may not see, and while hearing they may not understand.

11 "Now this is the parable: the seed is the word of God. 12 And those beside the road are the ones who have heard, then the devil comes and takes away the word from their heart, so that they will not believe and be saved. 13 Those on the rocky *soil are* the ones who, when they hear, receive the word with joy; and *yet* these do not have a *firm* root; they believe for a while, and in a time of temptation they fall away. 14 And the *seed* which fell among the thorns, these are the ones who have heard, and as they go on their way they are choked by worries, riches, and pleasures of *this* life, and they bring no fruit to maturity. 15 But the *seed* in the good soil, these are the ones who have heard the word with a good and virtuous heart, and hold it firmly, and produce fruit with perseverance.

Parable of the Lamp

16 "Now no one lights a lamp and covers it over with a container, or puts it under a bed; but he puts it on a lampstand so that those who come in may see the light. 17 For nothing is concealed that will not become evident, nor *anything* hidden that will not be known and come to light. 18 So take care how you listen; for whoever has, to him *more* will be given; and whoever does not have, even what he thinks he has will be taken away from him."

19 Now His mother and brothers came to Him, and they were unable to get to Him because of the crowd. 20 And it was reported to Him, "Your mother and Your brothers are standing outside, wishing to see You." 21 But He answered and said to them, "My mother and My brothers are these who hear the word of God and do *it.*"

Jesus Stills the Sea

22 Now on one of *those* days Jesus and His disciples got into a boat, and He said to them, "Let's cross over to the other side of the lake." So they launched out. 23 But as they were sailing along He fell asleep; and a fierce gale of wind descended on the lake, and they *began* to be swamped and to be in danger. 24 They came up to *Jesus* and woke Him, saying, "Master, Master, we are perishing!" And He got up and rebuked the wind and the surging waves, and they stopped, and it became calm. 25 And He said to them, "Where is your faith?" But

they were fearful and amazed, saying to one another, "Who then is this, that He commands even the winds and the water, and they obey Him?"

The Demon-possessed Man Cured

26 Then they sailed to the country of the Gerasenes, which is opposite Galilee. 27 And when He stepped out onto the land, a man from the city met Him who was possessed with demons; and he had not put on clothing for a long time and was not living in a house, but among the tombs. 28 And seeing Jesus, he cried out and fell down before Him, and said with a loud voice, "What business do You have with me, Jesus, Son of the Most High God? I beg You, do not torment me!" 29 For He *had already* commanded the unclean spirit to come out of the man. For it had seized him many times; and he was bound with chains and shackles and kept under guard, and *yet* he would break the restraints and be driven by the demon into the desert. 30 And Jesus asked him, "What is your name?" And he said, "Legion"; because many demons had entered him. 31 And they were begging Him not to command them to go away into the abyss.

32 Now there was a herd of many pigs feeding there on the mountain; and *the demons* begged Him to permit them to enter the pigs. And He gave them permission. 33 And the demons came out of the man and entered the pigs; and the herd rushed down the steep bank into the lake and was drowned.

34 Now when the herdsmen saw what had happened, they ran away and reported *everything* in the city, and in the country. 35 And *the people* came out to see what had happened; and they came to Jesus and found the man from whom the demons had gone out, sitting down at the feet of Jesus, clothed and in his right mind; and they became frightened. 36 Those who had seen *everything* reported to them how the man who had been demon-possessed had been made well. 37 And all the people of the territory of the Gerasenes and the surrounding region asked Him to leave them, because they were overwhelmed by great fear; and He got into a boat and returned. 38 But the man from whom the demons had gone out was begging Him that he might accompany Him; but *Jesus* sent him away, saying, 39 "Return to your home and describe what great things God has done for you." So he went away, proclaiming throughout the city what great things Jesus had done for him.

Miracles of Healing

40 And as Jesus was returning, the people welcomed Him, for they had all been waiting for Him. 41 And a man named Jairus came, and he was an official of the synagogue; and he fell at Jesus' feet, and *began* urging Him to come to his house; 42 for he had an only daughter, about twelve years old, and she was dying. But as He went, the crowds were pressing against Him.

43 And a woman who had suffered a *chronic* flow of blood for twelve years, and could not be healed by anyone, 44 came up behind Him and

touched the fringe of His cloak, and immediately her bleeding stopped. 45 And Jesus said, "Who is the one who touched Me?" And while they were all denying it, Peter said, "Master, the people are crowding and pressing in on You." 46 But Jesus said, "Someone did touch Me, for I was aware that power had left Me." 47 Now when the woman saw that she had not escaped notice, she came trembling and fell down before Him, and admitted in the presence of all the people the reason why she had touched Him, and how she had been immediately healed. 48 And He said to her, "Daughter, your faith has made you well; go in peace."

49 While He was still speaking, someone *came from the house of the synagogue official, saying, "Your daughter has died; do not trouble the Teacher anymore." 50 But when Jesus heard this, He responded to him, "Do not be afraid any longer; only believe, and she will be made well." 51 When He came to the house, He did not allow anyone to enter with Him except Peter, John, and James, and the girl's father and mother. 52 Now they were all weeping and mourning for her; but He said, "Stop weeping, for she has not died, but is asleep." 53 And they began laughing at Him, knowing that she had died. 54 He, however, took her by the hand and spoke forcefully, saying, "Child, arise!" 55 And her spirit returned, and she got up immediately; and He ordered that something be given her to eat. 56 Her parents were amazed; but He instructed them to tell no one what had happened.

Ministry of the Twelve

9 Now He called the twelve together and gave them power and authority over all the demons, and the power to heal diseases. 2 And He sent them out to proclaim the kingdom of God and to perform healing. 3 And He said to them, "Take nothing for your journey, neither a staff, nor a bag, nor bread, nor money; and do not even have two [1]tunics. 4 And whatever house you enter, stay there until you leave that city. 5 And as for all who do not receive you, when you leave that city, shake the dust off your feet as a testimony against them." 6 And as they were leaving, they began going throughout the villages, preaching the gospel and healing everywhere.

7 Now Herod the tetrarch heard about all that was happening; and he was greatly perplexed, because it was said by some that John had risen from the dead, 8 and by some that Elijah had appeared, and by others that one of the prophets of old had risen. 9 Herod said, "I myself had John beheaded; but who is this man about whom I hear such things?" And he kept trying to see Him.

10 When the apostles returned, they gave an account to Him of all that they had done. And taking them with Him, He withdrew privately to a city called Bethsaida. 11 But the crowds were aware of this and followed Him; and He welcomed them and began speaking to them about the kingdom of God, and curing those who had need of healing.

Five Thousand Men Fed

12 Now the day was ending, and the twelve came up and said to Him, "Dismiss the crowd, so that they may go into the surrounding villages and countryside and find lodging and get something to eat; because here, we are in a secluded place." 13 But He said to them, "You give them something to eat!" But they said, "We have no more than five loaves and two fish, unless perhaps we go and buy food for all these people." 14 (For there were about five thousand men.) But He said to His disciples, "Have them recline to eat in groups of about fifty each." 15 They did so, and had them all recline. 16 And He took the five loaves and the two fish, and, looking up to heaven, He blessed them and broke them, and gave them to the disciples again and again, to serve the crowd. 17 And they all ate and were satisfied; and the broken pieces which they had left over were picked up, twelve baskets full.

Peter Says Jesus is The Christ

18 And it happened that while He was praying alone, the disciples were with Him, and He questioned them, saying, "Who do the people say that I am?" 19 They answered and said, "John the Baptist, and others say Elijah; but others, that one of the prophets of old has risen." 20 And He said to them, "But who do you say that I am?" And Peter answered and said, "The Christ of God." 21 But He warned them and instructed them not to tell this to anyone, 22 saying, "The Son of Man must suffer many things and be rejected by the elders and chief priests and scribes, and be killed and be raised on the third day."

23 And He was saying to them all, "If anyone wants to come after Me, he must deny himself, take up his cross daily, and follow Me. 24 For whoever wants to save his life will lose it, but whoever loses his life for My sake, this is the one who will save it. 25 For what good does it do a person if he gains the whole world, but loses or forfeits himself? 26 For whoever is ashamed of Me and My words, the Son of Man will be ashamed of him when He comes in His glory and the glory of the Father and the holy angels. 27 But I say to you truthfully, there are some of those standing here who will not taste death until they see the kingdom of God."

The Transfiguration

28 About eight days after these sayings, He took along Peter, John, and James, and went up on the mountain to pray. 29 And while He was praying, the appearance of His face became different, and His clothing became white and gleaming. 30 And behold, two men were talking with Him; and they were Moses and Elijah, 31 who, appearing in glory, were speaking of His departure, which He was about to accomplish at Jerusalem. 32 Now Peter and his companions had been overcome with sleep; but when they were fully awake, they saw His glory and the two men who were standing with Him. 33 And as these two men were leaving Him, Peter said to Jesus, "Master, it is good that we are here; and let's make three

---

9:3 1 A long shirt worn next to the skin

tabernacles: one for You, one for Moses, and one for Elijah"—not realizing what he was saying. 34 But while he was saying this, a cloud formed and *began* to overshadow them; and they were afraid as they entered the cloud. 35 And *then* a voice came from the cloud, saying, "This is My Son, *My* Chosen One; listen to Him!" 36 And when the voice had spoken, Jesus was found alone. And they kept silent, and reported to no one in those days any of the things which they had seen.

37 On the next day, when they came down from the mountain, a large crowd met Him. 38 And a man from the crowd shouted, saying, "Teacher, I beg You to look at my son, because he is my only *son,* 39 and a spirit seizes him and he suddenly screams, and it throws him into a convulsion with foaming *at the mouth;* and only with difficulty does it leave him, mauling him *as it leaves.* 40 And I begged Your disciples to cast it out, and they could not." 41 And Jesus answered and said, "You unbelieving and perverse generation, how long shall I be with you and put up with you? Bring your son here." 42 Now while he was still approaching, the demon slammed him to the ground and threw him into a convulsion. But Jesus rebuked the unclean spirit, and healed the boy and gave him back to his father. 43 And they were all amazed at the greatness of God.

But while everyone was astonished at all that He was doing, He said to His disciples, 44 "As for you, let these words sink into your ears: for the Son of Man is going to be handed over to men." 45 But they did not understand this statement, and it was concealed from them so that they would not comprehend it; and they were afraid to ask Him about this statement.

The Test of Greatness

46 Now an argument started among them as to which of them might be the greatest. 47 But Jesus, knowing what they were thinking in their hearts, took a child and had him stand by His side, 48 and He said to them, "Whoever receives this child in My name receives Me, and whoever receives Me receives Him who sent Me; for the one who is least among all of you, this is the one who is great."

49 John answered and said, "Master, we saw someone casting out demons in Your name; and we *tried to* prevent him, because he does not follow along with us." 50 But Jesus said to him, "Do not hinder *him;* for the one who is not against you is for you."

51 When the days were approaching for His ascension, He was determined to go to Jerusalem; 52 and He sent messengers on ahead of Him, and they went and entered a village of the Samaritans to make arrangements for Him. 53 And they did not receive Him, because He was traveling toward Jerusalem. 54 When His disciples James and John saw *this,* they said, "Lord, do You want us to command fire to come down from heaven and consume them?" 55 But He turned and rebuked them.1 56 And they went on to another village.

Exacting Discipleship

57 As they were going on the road, someone said to Him, "I will follow You wherever You go." 58 And Jesus said to him, "The foxes have holes and the birds of the sky *have* nests, but the Son of Man has nowhere to lay His head." 59 And He said to another, "Follow Me." But he said, "Lord, permit me first to go and bury my father." 60 But He said to him, "Allow the dead to bury their own dead; but as for you, go and proclaim everywhere the kingdom of God." 61 Another also said, "I will follow You, Lord; but first permit me to say goodbye to those at my home." 62 But Jesus said to him, "No one, after putting his hand to the plow and looking back, is fit for the kingdom of God."

The Seventy-two Sent Out

10 Now after this the Lord appointed seventy-two others, and sent them in pairs ahead of Him to every city and place where He Himself was going to come. 2 And He was saying to them, "The harvest is plentiful, but the laborers are few; therefore plead with the Lord of the harvest to send out laborers into His harvest. 3 Go; behold, I am sending you out like lambs in the midst of wolves. 4 Carry no money belt, no bag, no sandals, and greet no one along the way. 5 And whatever house you enter, first say, 'Peace *be* to this house.' 6 And if a man of peace is there, your peace will rest upon him; but if not, it will return to you. 7 Stay in that house, eating and drinking what they provide; for the laborer is deserving of his wages. Do not move from house to house. 8 Whatever city you enter and they receive you, eat what is served to you; 9 and heal those in it who are sick, and say to them, 'The kingdom of God has come near to you.' 10 But whatever city you enter and they do not receive you, go out into its streets and say, 11 'Even the dust of your city which clings to our feet we wipe off *in protest* against you; yet be sure of this, that the kingdom of God has come near.' 12 I say to you, it will be more tolerable on that day for Sodom than for that city.

13 "Woe to you, Chorazin! Woe to you, Bethsaida! For if the miracles that occurred in you had occurred in Tyre and Sidon, they would have repented long ago, sitting in 'sackcloth and ashes. 14 But it will be more tolerable for Tyre and Sidon in the judgment than for you. 15 And you, Capernaum, will not be exalted to heaven, will you? You will be brought down to Hades!

16 "The one who listens to you listens to Me, and the one who rejects you rejects Me; but the one who rejects Me rejects the One who sent Me."

The Joyful Results

17 Now the seventy-two returned with joy, saying, "Lord, even the demons are subject to us in Your name!" 18 And He said to them, "I watched Satan fall from heaven like lightning. 19 Behold, I have given you authority to walk on snakes and scorpions, and *authority* over all the power of the enemy, and nothing will

injure you. **20** Nevertheless, do not rejoice in this, that the spirits are subject to you, but rejoice that your names are recorded in heaven."

21 At that very time He rejoiced greatly in the Holy Spirit, and said, "I praise You, Father, Lord of heaven and earth, that You have hidden these things from *the* wise and intelligent and have revealed them to infants. Yes, Father, for *doing* so was well pleasing in Your sight. **22** All things have been handed over to Me by My Father, and no one knows who the Son is except the Father, and who the Father is except the Son, and anyone to whom the Son determines to reveal *Him.*"

23 Turning to the disciples, He said privately, "Blessed *are* the eyes that see the things you see; **24** for I tell you that many prophets and kings wanted to see the things that you see, and did not see *them,* and to hear the things that you hear, and did not hear *them.*"

25 And behold, a lawyer stood up and put Him to the test, saying, "Teacher, what shall I do to inherit eternal life?" **26** And He said to him, "What is written in the Law? How does it read to you?" **27** And he answered, "YOU SHALL LOVE THE LORD YOUR GOD WITH ALL YOUR HEART, AND WITH ALL YOUR SOUL, AND WITH ALL YOUR STRENGTH, AND WITH ALL YOUR MIND; AND YOUR NEIGHBOR AS YOURSELF." **28** And He said to him, "You have answered correctly; do this and you will live." **29** But wanting to justify himself, he said to Jesus, "And who is my neighbor?".

The Good Samaritan

30 Jesus replied and said, "A man was going down from Jerusalem to Jericho, and he encountered robbers, and they stripped him and beat him, and went away leaving him half dead. **31** And by coincidence a priest was going down on that road, and when he saw him, he passed by on the other side. **32** Likewise a Levite also, when he came to the place and saw him, passed by on the other side. **33** But a Samaritan who was on a journey came upon him; and when he saw him, he felt compassion, **34** and came to him and bandaged up his wounds, pouring oil and wine on *them;* and he put him on his own animal, and brought him to an inn and took care of him. **35** On the next day he took out two *1*denarii and gave them to the innkeeper and said, 'Take care of him; and whatever more you spend, when I return, I will repay you.' **36** Which of these three do you think proved to be a neighbor to the man who fell into the robbers' *hands?*" **37** And he said, "The one who showed compassion to him." Then Jesus said to him, "Go and do the same."

Martha and Mary

38 Now as they were traveling along, He entered a village; and a woman named Martha welcomed Him into her home. **39** And she had a sister called Mary, who was also seated at the Lord's feet, and was listening to His word. **40** But Martha was distracted with all her preparations; and she came up *to Him* and said, "Lord, do You not care that my sister has left me to do the serving by myself? Then tell her to help me." **41** But the Lord answered and said to her, "Martha, Martha, you are worried and distracted by many things; **42** but *only* one thing is necessary; for Mary has chosen the good part, which shall not be taken away from her."

Instruction about Prayer

11 It happened that while Jesus was praying in a certain place, when He had finished, one of His disciples said to Him, "Lord, teach us to pray, just as John also taught his disciples." **2** And He said to them, "When you pray, say:

'*1*Father, hallowed be Your name.
Your kingdom come.
3 'Give us each day our daily bread.
4 'And forgive us our sins,
For we ourselves also forgive everyone who is indebted to us.
And do not lead us into temptation.'"

5 And He said to them, "Suppose one of you has a friend, and goes to him at midnight and says to him, 'Friend, lend me three loaves, **6** because a friend of mine has come to me from a journey and I have nothing to serve him'; **7** and from inside he answers and says, 'Do not bother me; the door has already been shut and my children and I are in bed; I cannot get up and give you *anything.*' **8** I tell you, even if he will not get up and give him *anything just* because he is his friend, yet because of his shamelessness he will get up and give him as much as he needs.

9 "So I say to you, ask, and it will be given to you; seek, and you will find; knock, and it will be opened to you. **10** For everyone who asks receives, and the one who seeks finds, and to the one who knocks, it will be opened. **11** Now which one of you fathers will his son ask for a fish, and instead of a fish, he will give him a snake? **12** Or he will even ask for an egg, *and his father* will give him a scorpion? **13** So if you, *despite* being evil, know how to give good gifts to your children, how much more will your heavenly Father give the Holy Spirit to those who ask Him?"

Pharisees' Blasphemy

14 And He was casting out a mute demon; when the demon had gone out, the man who was *previously* unable to speak talked, and the crowds were amazed. **15** But some of them said, "He casts out the demons by Beelzebul, the ruler of the demons." **16** Others, to test *Him,* were demanding of Him a sign from heaven. **17** But He knew their thoughts and said to them, "Every kingdom divided against itself is laid waste; and a house *divided* against itself falls. **18** And if Satan also has been divided against himself, how will his kingdom stand? For you claim that I cast out the demons by Beelzebul. **19** Yet if by Beelzebul I cast out the demons, by whom do your sons cast *them* out? Therefore, they will be your judges. **20** But if I cast out the demons by the finger of God, then the kingdom of God has come upon you.

21 When a strong *man,* fully armed, guards his own house, his possessions are secure. 22 But when *someone* stronger than he attacks him and overpowers him, *that man* takes away his armor on which he had relied and distributes his plunder. 23 The one who is not with Me is against Me; and the one who does not gather with Me scatters.

24 "When the unclean spirit comes out of a person, it passes through waterless places seeking rest, and not finding *any,* it then says, 'I will return to my house from which I came.' 25 And when it comes, it finds it swept and put in order. 26 Then it goes and brings along seven other spirits more evil than itself, and they come in and live there; and the last *condition* of that person becomes worse than the first."

27 While Jesus was saying these things, one of the women in the crowd raised her voice and said to Him, "Blessed is the womb that carried You, and the breasts at which You nursed!" 28 But He said, "On the contrary, blessed are those who hear the word of God and follow it."

The Sign of Jonah

29 Now as the crowds were increasing, He began to say, "This generation is a wicked generation; it demands a sign, and *so* no sign will be given to it except the sign of Jonah. 30 For just as Jonah became a sign to the Ninevites, so will the Son of Man be to this generation. 31 The Queen of the South will rise up with the men of this generation at the judgment and condemn them, because she came from the ends of the earth to listen to the wisdom of Solomon; and behold, *something* greater than Solomon is here. 32 The men of Nineveh will stand up with this generation at the judgment and condemn it, because they repented at the preaching of Jonah; and behold, *something* greater than Jonah is here.

33 "No one lights a lamp and puts *it away* in a cellar nor under a basket, but on the lampstand, so that those who enter may see the light. 34 Your eye is the lamp of your body; when your eye is clear, your whole body also is full of light; but when it is bad, your body also is full of darkness. 35 So watch out that the light in you is not darkness. 36 Therefore if your whole body is full of light, without any dark part, it will be wholly illuminated, as when the lamp illuminates you with its light."

Woes upon the Pharisees

37 Now when He had spoken, a Pharisee *asked Him to have lunch with him; and He went in and reclined *at the table.* 38 When the Pharisee saw *this,* he was surprised that *Jesus* had not first ceremonially washed before the meal. 39 But the Lord said to him, "Now you Pharisees clean the outside of the cup and of the dish; but your inside is full of greed and wickedness. 40 You foolish ones, did He who made the outside not make the inside also? 41 But give that which is within as a charitable gift, and then all things are clean for you. 42 "But woe to you Pharisees! For you pay

tithes of mint, rue, and every *kind of* garden herb, and *yet* you ignore justice and the love of God; but these are the things you should have done without neglecting the others. 43 Woe to you Pharisees! For you love the seat of honor in the synagogues and personal greetings in the marketplaces. 44 Woe to you! For you are like unseen tombs, and the people who walk over *them* are unaware *of it.*"

45 One of the [1]lawyers *said to Him in reply, "Teacher, when You say these things, You insult us too." 46 But He said, "Woe to you lawyers as well! For you load people with burdens that are hard to bear, while you yourselves will not even touch the burdens with one of your fingers. 47 Woe to you! For you build the tombs of the prophets, and *it was* your fathers *who* killed them. 48 So you are witnesses and you approve of the deeds of your fathers; because *it was* they *who* killed them, and you build *their tombs.* 49 For this reason also, the wisdom of God said, 'I will send them prophets and apostles, and *some* of them they will kill, and *some* they will persecute, 50 so that the blood of all the prophets, shed since the foundation of the world, may be charged against this generation, 51 from the blood of Abel to the blood of Zechariah, who was killed between the altar and the house *of God;* yes, I tell you, it shall be charged against this generation.' 52 Woe to you lawyers! For you have taken away the key of knowledge; you yourselves did not enter, and you hindered those who were entering."

53 When He left that place, the scribes and the Pharisees began to be very hostile and to interrogate Him about many *subjects,* 54 plotting against Him to catch Him in something He might say.

God Knows and Cares

12 Under these circumstances, after so many thousands of people had gathered together that they were stepping on one another, He began saying to His disciples first *of all,* "Beware of the leaven of the Pharisees, which is hypocrisy. 2 But there is nothing covered up that will not be revealed, and hidden that will not be known. 3 Accordingly, whatever you have said in the dark will be heard in the light, and what you have whispered in the inner rooms will be proclaimed on the housetops.

4 "Now I say to you, My friends, do not be afraid of those who kill the body, and after that have nothing more that they can do. 5 But I will warn you whom to fear: fear the One who, after He has killed *someone,* has *the* power to throw *that person* into [1]hell; yes, I tell you, fear Him! 6 Are five sparrows not sold for two [1]assaria? And *yet* not one of them has gone unnoticed in the sight of God. 7 But even the hairs of your head are all counted. Do not fear; you are more valuable than a great number of sparrows.

8 "Now I say to you, everyone who confesses Me before people, the Son of Man will also confess him before the angels of God; 9 but the

11:45 [1] I.e., experts in the Mosaic Law   12:5 [1] Gr *Gehenna*   12:6 [1] A Roman copper coin (singular *assarion*), about 1/16 of a laborer's daily wage

one who denies Me before people will be denied before the angels of God. **10** And everyone who speaks a word against the Son of Man, it will be forgiven him; but the one who blasphemes against the Holy Spirit, it will not be forgiven him. **11** Now when they bring you before the synagogues and the officials and the authorities, do not worry about how or what you are to speak in your defense, or what you are to say; **12** for the Holy Spirit will teach you in that very hour what you ought to say."

Greed Denounced

13 Now someone in the crowd said to Him, "Teacher, tell my brother to divide the *family* inheritance with me." **14** But He said to him, "You there—who appointed Me a judge or arbitrator over *the two of* you?" **15** But He said to them, "Beware, and be on your guard against every form of greed; for not *even* when one is affluent does his life consist of his possessions." **16** And He told them a parable, saying, "The land of a rich man was very productive. **17** And he began thinking to himself, saying, 'What shall I do, since I have no place to store my crops?' **18** And he said, 'This *is what* I will do: I will tear down my barns and build larger ones, and I will store all my grain and my goods there. **19** And I will say to myself, "You have many goods stored up for many years *to come;* relax, eat, drink, and enjoy yourself!" ' **20** But God said to him, 'You fool! This *very* night your soul is demanded of you; and *as for all* that you have prepared, who will own *it now?*' **21** Such is the one who stores up treasure for himself, and is not rich in relation to God."

22 And He said to His disciples, "For this reason I tell you, do not worry about *your* life, *as to* what you are to eat; nor for your body, *as to* what you are to wear. **23** For life is more than food, and the body *is more* than clothing. **24** Consider the ravens, that they neither sow nor reap; they have no storeroom nor barn, and *yet* God feeds them; how much more valuable you are than the birds! **25** And which of you by worrying can add a ¹day to his ²life's span? **26** Therefore if you cannot do even a very little thing, why do you worry about the other things? **27** Consider the lilies, how they grow: they neither labor nor spin; but I tell you, not even Solomon in all his glory clothed himself like one of these. **28** Now if God so clothes the grass in the field, which is *alive* today and tomorrow is thrown into the furnace, how much more *will He clothe* you? You of little faith! **29** And do not seek what you are to eat and what you are to drink, and do not keep worrying. **30** For all these things *are what* the nations of the world eagerly seek; and your Father knows that you need these things. **31** But seek His kingdom, and these things will be provided to you. **32** Do not be afraid, little flock, because your Father has chosen to give you the kingdom.

33 "Sell your possessions and give to charity; make yourselves money belts that do not wear out, an inexhaustible treasure in heaven, where no thief comes near nor does a moth destroy. **34** For where your treasure is, there your heart will be also.

Be in Readiness

35 "Be prepared, and *keep* your lamps lit. **36** You are also *to be* like people who are waiting for their master when he returns from the wedding feast, so that they may immediately open *the door* for him when he comes and knocks. **37** Blessed are those slaves whom the master will find on the alert when he comes; truly I say to you, that he will prepare himself *to serve,* and have them recline *at the table,* and he will come up and serve them. **38** Whether he comes in the ¹second watch, or even in the ²third, and finds *them* so, blessed are those *slaves.* **39** "But be sure of this, that if the head of the house had known at what hour the thief was coming, he would not have allowed his house to be broken into. **40** You too, be ready; because the Son of Man is coming at an hour that you do not think *He will.*"

41 Peter said, "Lord, are You telling this parable to us, or to everyone *else* as well?" **42** And the Lord said, "Who then is the faithful and sensible steward, whom his master will put in charge of his servants, to give them their rations at the proper time? **43** Blessed is that slave whom his master finds so doing when he comes. **44** Truly I say to you that he will put him in charge of all his possessions. **45** But if that slave says in his heart, 'My master will take a long time to come,' and he begins to beat the *other* slaves, *both* men and women, and to eat and drink and get drunk; **46** *then* the master of that slave will come on a day that he does not expect, and at an hour that he does not know, and will cut him in two, and assign him a place with the unbelievers. **47** And that slave who knew his master's will and did not get ready or act in accordance with his will, will receive many blows, **48** but the one who did not know *it,* and committed acts deserving of a beating, will receive *only* a few blows. From everyone who has been given much, much will be demanded; and to whom they entrusted much, of him they will ask all the more.

Christ Divides People

49 "I have come to cast fire upon the earth; and how I wish it were already kindled! **50** But I have a baptism to undergo, and how distressed I am until it is accomplished! **51** Do you think that I came to provide peace on earth? No, I tell you, but rather division; **52** for from now on five *members* in one household will be divided, three against two and two against three. **53** They will be divided, father against son and son against father, mother against daughter and daughter against mother, mother-in-law against daughter-in-law and daughter-in-law against mother-in-law."

54 And He was also saying to the crowds, "Whenever you see a cloud rising in the west, you immediately say, 'A shower is coming,' and so it turns out. **55** And whenever *you feel* a south wind blowing, you say, 'It will

---

12:25 ¹Lit *cubit* (about 18 in. or 45 cm) ²Or *height* **12:38** ¹I.e., 9 p.m. to midnight ²I.e., midnight to 3 a.m.

be a hot *day*,' and it turns out *that way.* ⁵⁶You hypocrites! You know how to analyze the appearance of the earth and the sky, but how *is it that* you do not know how to analyze this *present* time?

⁵⁷"And why do you not even judge by yourselves what is right? ⁵⁸For when you are going with your accuser *to appear* before the magistrate, on the way, make an effort to settle with him, so that he does not drag you before the judge, and the judge hand you over to the officer, and the officer throw you into prison. ⁵⁹I tell you, you will not get out of there until you have paid up the very last ¹lepton."

Call to Repent

13 Now on that very occasion there were some present who reported to Him about the Galileans whose blood Pilate had mixed with their sacrifices. ²And Jesus responded and said to them, "Do you think that these Galileans were *worse* sinners than all the *other* Galileans *just* because they have suffered this *fate?* ³No, I tell you, but unless you repent, you will all likewise perish. ⁴Or do you think that those eighteen on whom the tower in Siloam fell and killed them were *worse* offenders than all the *other* people who live in Jerusalem? ⁵No, I tell you, but unless you repent, you will all likewise perish."

⁶And He *began* telling this parable: "A man had a fig tree which had been planted in his vineyard; and he came looking for fruit on it and did not find *any.* ⁷And he said to the vineyard-keeper, 'Look! For three years I have come looking for fruit on this fig tree without finding any. Cut it down! Why does it even use up the ground?' ⁸But he answered and said to him, 'Sir, leave it alone for this year too, until I dig around it and put in fertilizer; ⁹and if it bears fruit next *year, fine;* but if not, cut it down.' "

Healing on the Sabbath

¹⁰Now *Jesus* was teaching in one of the synagogues on the Sabbath. ¹¹And there was a woman who for eighteen years had had a sickness caused by a spirit; and she was bent over double, and could not straighten up at all. ¹²When Jesus saw her, He called her over and said to her, "Woman, you are freed from your sickness." ¹³And He laid His hands on her; and immediately she stood up straight again, and *began* glorifying God. ¹⁴But the synagogue leader, indignant because Jesus had healed on the Sabbath, *began* saying to the crowd in response, "There are six days during which work should be done; so come during them and get healed, and not on the Sabbath day." ¹⁵But the Lord answered him and said, "You hypocrites, does each of you on the Sabbath not untie his ox or donkey from the stall and lead it away to water *it?* ¹⁶And this woman, a daughter of Abraham as she is, whom Satan has bound for eighteen long years, should she not have been released from this restraint on the Sabbath day?" ¹⁷And as He said this, all His opponents were being humiliated; and the entire crowd was rejoicing over all the glorious things being done by Him.

Parables of Mustard Seed and Leaven

¹⁸So He was saying, "What is the kingdom of God like, and to what shall I compare it? ¹⁹It is like a mustard seed, which a man took and threw into his own garden; and it grew and became a tree, and the birds of the sky nested in its branches."

²⁰And again He said, "To what shall I compare the kingdom of God? ²¹It is like leaven, which a woman took and hid in three sata of flour until it was all leavened."

Teaching in the Villages

²²And He was passing through one city and village after another, teaching, and proceeding on His way to Jerusalem. ²³And someone said to Him, "Lord, are there *just* a few who are being saved?" And He said to them, ²⁴"Strive to enter through the narrow door; for many, I tell you, will seek to enter and will not be able. ²⁵Once the head of the house gets up and shuts the door, and you begin standing outside and knocking on the door, saying, 'Lord, open up to us!' and He *then* will answer and say to you, 'I do not know where you are from.' ²⁶Then you will begin saying, 'We ate and drank in Your presence, and You taught in our streets!' ²⁷And *yet* He will say, 'I do not know where you are from; LEAVE ME, ALL YOU EVILDOERS.' ²⁸In that place there will be weeping and gnashing of teeth when you see Abraham, Isaac, Jacob, and all the prophets in the kingdom of God, but yourselves being thrown out. ²⁹And they will come from east and west, and from north and south, and will recline *at the table* in the kingdom of God. ³⁰And behold, *some* are last who will be first, and *some* are first who will be last."

³¹At that very time some Pharisees approached, saying to Him, "Go away and leave this place, because Herod wants to kill You." ³²And He said to them, "Go and tell that fox, 'Behold, I am casting out demons and performing healings today and tomorrow, and on the third *day* I reach My goal.' ³³Nevertheless I must go on My journey today and tomorrow and the next *day;* for it cannot be that a prophet would perish outside Jerusalem. ³⁴Jerusalem, Jerusalem, the *city* that kills the prophets and stones those who have been sent to her! How often I wanted to gather your children together, just as a hen *gathers* her young under her wings, and you were unwilling! ³⁵Behold, your house is left to you *desolate;* and I say to you, you will not see Me until you say, 'BLESSED IS THE ONE WHO COMES IN THE NAME OF THE LORD!' "

Jesus Heals on the Sabbath

14 It happened that when He went into the house of one of the leaders of the Pharisees on *the* Sabbath to eat bread, they were watching Him closely. ²And there in front of Him was a man suffering from ¹edema. ³And Jesus responded and said to the lawyers and

---

12:59 ¹The smallest Greek copper coin, about 1/128 of a laborer's daily wage
14:2 ¹I.e., extreme swelling

Pharisees, "Is it lawful to heal on the Sabbath, or not?" 4 But they kept silent. And He took hold of him and healed him, and sent him away. 5 And He said to them, "Which one of you will have a son or an ox fall into a well, and will not immediately pull him out on a Sabbath day?" 6 And they could offer no reply to this.

Parable of the Guests

7 Now He *began* telling a parable to the invited guests when He noticed how they had been picking out the places of honor *at the table,* saying to them, 8 "Whenever you are invited by someone to a wedding feast, do not take the place of honor, for someone more distinguished than you may have been invited by him, 9 and the one who invited you both will come and say to you, 'Give *your* place to this person,' and then in disgrace you will proceed to occupy the last place. 10 But whenever you are invited, go and take the last place, so that when the one who has invited you comes, he will say to you, 'Friend, move up higher'; then you will have honor in the sight of all who are dining at the table with you. 11 For everyone who exalts himself will be humbled, and the one who humbles himself will be exalted."

12 Now He also went on to say to the one who had invited Him, "Whenever you give a luncheon or a dinner, do not invite your friends, your brothers, your relatives, nor wealthy neighbors, otherwise they may also invite you *to a meal* in return, and *that* will be your repayment. 13 But whenever you give a banquet, invite people who are poor, who have disabilities, who are limping, *and* people who are blind; 14 and you will be blessed, since they do not have *the means* to repay you; for you will be repaid at the resurrection of the righteous."

15 Now when one of those who were reclining *at the table* with Him heard this, he said to Him, "Blessed is everyone who will eat bread in the kingdom of God!"

Parable of the Dinner

16 But He said to him, "A man was giving a big dinner, and he invited many; 17 and at the dinner hour he sent his slave to tell those who had been invited, 'Come, because everything is ready now.' 18 And *yet* they all alike began to make excuses. The first one said to him, 'I purchased a field and I need to go out to look at it; please consider me excused.' 19 And another one said, 'I bought five yoke of oxen, and I am going to try them out; please consider me excused.' 20 And another one said, 'I took a woman as my wife, and for that reason I cannot come.' 21 And the slave came *back* and reported this to his master. Then the head of the household became angry and said to his slave, 'Go out at once into the streets and lanes of the city and bring in here those who are poor, those with disabilities, those who are blind, and those who are limping.' 22 And *later* the slave said, 'Master, what you commanded has been done, and still there is room.' 23 And the master said to the slave, 'Go out into the roads and the hedges and press upon *them* to

come in, so that my house will be filled. 24 For I tell you, none of those men who were invited shall taste my dinner.' "

Discipleship Tested

25 Now large crowds were going along with Him, and He turned and said to them, 26 "If anyone comes to Me and does not 1 hate his own father, mother, wife, children, brothers, sisters, yes, and even his own life, he cannot be My disciple. 27 Whoever does not carry his own cross and come after Me cannot be My disciple. 28 For which one of you, when he wants to build a tower, does not first sit down and calculate the cost, *to see* if he has *enough* to complete *it?* 29 Otherwise, when he has laid a foundation and is not able to finish, all who are watching *it* will begin to ridicule him, 30 saying, 'This person began to build, and was not able to finish!' 31 Or what king, when he sets out to meet another king in battle, will not first sit down and consider whether he is strong *enough* with ten thousand *men* to face the one coming against him with twenty thousand? 32 Otherwise, while the other is still far away, he sends a delegation and requests terms of peace. 33 So then, none of you can be My disciple who does not give up all his own possessions.

34 "Therefore, salt is good; but if even salt has become tasteless, with what will it be seasoned? 35 It is useless either for the soil or the manure pile, *so* it is thrown out. The one who has ears to hear, let him hear."

The Lost Sheep

15 Now all the tax collectors and sinners were coming near Jesus to listen to Him. 2 And both the Pharisees and the scribes *began* to complain, saying, "This man receives sinners and eats with them."

3 And *so* He told them this parable, saying, 4 "What man among you, if he has a hundred sheep and has lost one of them, does not leave the *other* ninety-nine in the open pasture and go after the one that is lost, until he finds it? 5 And when he has found it, he puts it on his shoulders, rejoicing. 6 And when he comes home, he calls together his friends and his neighbors, saying to them, 'Rejoice with me, because I have found my sheep that was lost!' 7 I tell you that in the same way, there will be *more* joy in heaven over one sinner who repents than over ninety-nine righteous people who have no need of repentance.

The Lost Coin

8 "Or what woman, if she has ten silver coins and loses one coin, does not light a lamp and sweep the house and search carefully until she finds *it?* 9 And when she has found *it,* she calls together her friends and neighbors, saying, 'Rejoice with me, because I have found the coin which I had lost!' 10 In the same way, I tell you, there is joy in the presence of the angels of God over one sinner who repents."

The Prodigal Son

11 And He said, "A man had two sons. 12 The

14:26 1 I.e., in comparison to his love for Me

younger of them said to his father, 'Father, give me the share of the estate that is coming to me.' And *so* he divided his wealth between them. 13 And not many days later, the younger son gathered everything together and went on a journey to a distant country, and there he squandered his estate in wild living. 14 Now when he had spent everything, a severe famine occurred in that country, and he began doing without. 15 So he went and hired himself out to one of the citizens of that country, and he sent him into his fields to feed pigs. 16 And he longed to have his fill of the carob pods that the pigs were eating, and no one was giving him *anything*. 17 But when he came to his senses, he said, 'How many of my father's hired laborers have more than enough bread, but I am dying here from hunger! 18 I will set out and go to my father, and will say to him, "Father, I have sinned against heaven, and in your sight; 19 I am no longer worthy to be called your son; treat me as one of your hired laborers." ' 20 So he set out and came to his father. But when he was still a long way off, his father saw him and felt compassion *for him,* and ran and embraced him and kissed him. 21 And the son said to him, 'Father, I have sinned against heaven and in your sight; I am no longer worthy to be called your son.' 22 But the father said to his slaves, 'Quickly bring out the best robe and put it on him, and put a ring on his finger and sandals on his feet; 23 and bring the fattened calf, slaughter it, and let's eat and celebrate; 24 for this son of mine was dead and has come to life again; he was lost and has been found.' And they began to celebrate.

25 "Now his older son was in the field, and when he came and approached the house, he heard music and dancing. 26 And he summoned one of the servants and *began* inquiring what these things could be. 27 And he said to him, 'Your brother has come, and your father has slaughtered the fattened calf because he has received him back safe and sound.' 28 But he became angry and was not willing to go in; and his father came out and *began* pleading with him. 29 But he answered and said to his father, 'Look! For so many years I have been serving you and I have never neglected a command of yours; and *yet* you never gave me a young goat, so that I might celebrate with my friends; 30 but when this son of yours came, who has devoured your wealth with prostitutes, you slaughtered the fattened calf for him.' 31 And he said to him, 'Son, you have always been with me, and all that is mine is yours. 32 But we had to celebrate and rejoice, because this brother of yours was dead and *has begun* to live, and *was* lost and has been found.' "

The Unrighteous Manager

16 Now He was also saying to the disciples, "There was a rich man who had a manager, and this *manager* was reported to him as squandering his possessions. 2 And he summoned him and said to him, 'What is this I hear about you? Give an accounting of your management, for you can no longer be manager.' 3 And the manager said to himself, 'What am I to do, since my master is taking the management away from me? I am not strong enough to dig; I am ashamed to beg. 4 I know what I will do, so that when I am removed from the management *people* will welcome me into their homes.' 5 And he summoned each one of his master's debtors, and he *began* saying to the first, 'How much do you owe my master?' 6 And he said, 'A hundred jugs of oil.' And he said to him, 'Take your bill, and sit down quickly and write fifty.' 7 Then he said to another, 'And how much do you owe?' And he said, 'A hundred kors of wheat.' He *said to him, 'Take your bill, and write eighty.' 8 And his master complimented the unrighteous manager because he had acted shrewdly; for the sons of this age are more shrewd in relation to their own kind than the sons of light. 9 And I say to you, make friends for yourselves by means of the †wealth of unrighteousness, so that when it is all gone, they will receive you into the eternal dwellings.

10 "The one who is faithful in a very little thing is also faithful in much; and the one who is unrighteous in a very little thing is also unrighteous in much. 11 Therefore if you have not been faithful in the *use of* unrighteous wealth, who will entrust the true *wealth* to you? 12 And if you have not been faithful in *the use of* that which is another's, who will give you that which is your own? 13 No servant can serve two masters; for either he will hate the one and love the other, or he will be devoted to one and despise the other. You cannot serve God and wealth."

14 Now the Pharisees, who were lovers of money, were listening to all these things and were ridiculing Him. 15 And He said to them, "You are the ones who justify yourselves in the sight of people, but God knows your hearts; because that which is highly esteemed among people is detestable in the sight of God.

16 "The Law and the Prophets *were proclaimed* until John *came;* since that time the gospel of the kingdom of God has been preached, and everyone is forcing his way into it. 17 But it is easier for heaven and earth to pass away than for one stroke of a letter of the Law to fail.

18 "Everyone who divorces his wife and marries another commits adultery, and he who marries one who is divorced from a husband commits adultery.

The Rich Man and Lazarus

19 "Now there was a rich man, and he habitually dressed in purple and fine linen, enjoying himself in splendor every day. 20 And a poor man named Lazarus was laid at his gate, covered with sores, 21 and longing to be fed from the *scraps* which fell from the rich man's table; not only *that,* the dogs also were coming and licking his sores. 22 Now it happened that the poor man died and was carried away by the angels to †Abraham's arms; and the rich man also died and was buried. 23 And in Hades he

---

16:9 1 Gr *mamonas,* for Aramaic *mamon* (mammon); i.e., wealth, or money   16:22 1 Lit *Abraham's bosom;* or *lap;* ancient Jewish terminology for the place of the righteous dead

raised his eyes, being in torment, and *saw Abraham far away and Lazarus in his ¹arms. 24 And he cried out and said, 'Father Abraham, have mercy on me and send Lazarus, so that he may dip the tip of his finger in water and cool off my tongue, for I am in agony in this flame.' 25 But Abraham said, 'Child, remember that during your life you received your good things, and likewise Lazarus bad things; but now he is being comforted here, and you are in agony. 26 And besides all this, between us and you a great chasm has been set, so that those who want to go over from here to you will not be able, nor will *any people* cross over from there to us.' 27 And he said, 'Then I request of you, father, that you send him to my father's house—28 for I have five brothers—in order that he may warn them, so that they will not come to this place of torment as well.' 29 But Abraham *said, 'They have Moses and the Prophets; let them hear them.' 30 But he said, 'No, father Abraham, but if someone goes to them from the dead, they will repent!' 31 But he said to him, 'If they do not listen to Moses and the Prophets, they will not be persuaded even if someone rises from the dead.' "

Instructions

17 Now He said to His disciples, "It is inevitable that stumbling blocks come, but woe to one through whom they come! ²It is better for him if a millstone is hung around his neck and he is thrown into the sea, than that he may cause one of these little ones to sin. 3 Be on your guard! If your brother sins, rebuke him; and if he repents, forgive him. 4 And if he sins against you seven times a day, and returns to you seven times, saying, 'I repent,' you shall forgive him."

5 The apostles said to the Lord, "Increase our faith!" 6 But the Lord said, "If you had faith the size of a mustard seed, you could say to this mulberry tree, 'Be uprooted and be planted in the sea'; and it would obey you.

7 "Now which of you, having a slave plowing or tending sheep, will say to him after he comes in from the field, 'Come immediately and recline *at the table* to eat'? 8 On the contrary, will he not say to him, 'Prepare something for me to eat, and *properly* clothe yourself and serve me while I eat and drink; and afterward you may eat and drink'? 9 He does not thank the slave because he did the things which were commanded, does he? 10 So you too, when you do all the things which were commanded you, say, 'We are unworthy slaves; we have done *only* that which we ought to have done.' "

Ten Men with Leprosy Healed

11 While He was on the way to Jerusalem, He was passing between Samaria and Galilee. 12 And as He entered a village, ten men with leprosy who stood at a distance met Him; 13 and they raised their voices, saying, "Jesus, Master, have mercy on us!" 14 When He saw *them,* He said to them, "Go and show yourselves to the priests." And as they were going, they were cleansed. 15 Now one of them, when he saw

that he had been healed, turned back, glorifying God with a loud voice, 16 and he fell on his face at His feet, giving thanks to Him. And he was a Samaritan. 17 But Jesus responded and said, "Were there not ten cleansed? But the nine—where *are they?* 18 Was no one found who returned to give glory to God, except this foreigner?" 19 And He said to him, "Stand up and go; your faith has made you well."

Second Coming Foretold

20 Now He was questioned by the Pharisees as to when the kingdom of God was coming, and He answered them and said, "The kingdom of God is not coming with signs that can be observed; 21 nor will they say, 'Look, here *it is!*' or, 'There *it is!*' For behold, the kingdom of God is in your midst."

22 And He said to the disciples, "The days will come when you will long to see one of the days of the Son of Man, and you will not see *it.* 23 And they will say to you, 'Look there,' or, 'Look here!' Do not leave, and do not run after *them.* 24 For just like the lightning, when it flashes out of one part of the sky, shines to the other part of the sky, so will the Son of Man be in His day. 25 But first He must suffer many things and be rejected by this generation. 26 And just as it happened in the days of Noah, so will it also be in the days of the Son of Man: 27 people were eating, they were drinking, they were marrying, *and* they were being given in marriage, until the day that Noah entered the ark, and the flood came and destroyed them all. 28 It was the same as happened in the days of Lot: they were eating, they were drinking, they were buying, they were selling, they were planting, *and* they were building; 29 but on the day that Lot left Sodom, it rained fire and brimstone from heaven and destroyed them all. 30 It will be just the same on the day that the Son of Man is revealed. 31 On that day, the one who will be on the housetop, with his goods in the house, must not go down to take them out; and likewise the one in the field must not turn back. 32 Remember Lot's wife. 33 Whoever strives to save his life will lose it, and whoever loses *his life* will keep it. 34 I tell you, on that night there will be two in one bed; one will be taken and the other will be left. 35 There will be two women grinding at the same *place;* one will be taken and the other will be left. 36 [¹Two men will be in the field; one will be taken and the other will be left."] 37 And responding, they *said to Him, "Where, Lord?" And He said to them, "Where the body is, there also the vultures will be gathered."

Parables on Prayer

18 Now He was telling them a parable to show that at all times they ought to pray and not become discouraged, 2 saying, "In a certain city there was a judge who did not fear God and did not respect *any* person. 3 Now there was a widow in that city, and she kept coming to him, saying, 'Give me justice against my opponent.' 4 For a while he was unwilling; but later he said to himself, 'Even though I do not fear God nor respect *any* person, 5 yet

because this widow is bothering me, I will give her justice; otherwise by continually coming she will wear me out.'" [6] And the Lord said, "Listen to what the unrighteous judge *said; [7] now, will God not bring about justice for His elect who cry out to Him day and night, and will He delay long for them? [8] I tell you that He will bring about justice for them quickly. However, when the Son of Man comes, will He find faith on the earth?"

The Pharisee and the Tax Collector

[9] Now He also told this parable to some people who trusted in themselves that they were righteous, and viewed others with contempt: [10] "Two men went up into the temple to pray, one a Pharisee and the other a tax collector. [11] The Pharisee stood and *began* praying this in regard to himself: 'God, I thank You that I am not like other people: swindlers, crooked, adulterers, or even like this tax collector. [12] I fast twice a week; I pay tithes of all that I get.' [13] But the tax collector, standing some distance away, was even unwilling to raise his eyes toward heaven, but was beating his chest, saying, 'God, be merciful to me, the sinner!' [14] I tell you, this man went to his house justified rather than the other one; for everyone who exalts himself will be humbled, but the one who humbles himself will be exalted."

[15] Now they were bringing even their babies to Him so that He would touch them; but when the disciples saw *it,* they *began* rebuking them. [16] But Jesus called for the little ones, saying, "Allow the children to come to Me, and do not forbid such as these, for the kingdom of God belongs to such as these. [17] Truly I say to you, whoever does not receive the kingdom of God like a child will not enter it at all."

The Rich Young Ruler

[18] A ruler questioned Him, saying, "Good Teacher, what shall I do to inherit eternal life?" [19] But Jesus said to him, "Why do you call Me good? No one is good except God alone. [20] You know the commandments, 'DO NOT COMMIT ADULTERY, DO NOT MURDER, DO NOT STEAL, DO NOT GIVE FALSE TESTIMONY, HONOR YOUR FATHER AND MOTHER.'" [21] And he said, "All these things I have kept since *my* youth." [22] Now when Jesus heard *this,* He said to him, "One thing you still lack; sell all that you possess and distribute *the money* to the poor, and you will have treasure in heaven; and come, follow Me." [23] But when he had heard these things, he became very sad, for he was extremely wealthy. [24] And Jesus looked at him and said, "How hard it is for those who are wealthy to enter the kingdom of God! [25] For it is easier for a camel to go through the eye of a needle, than for a rich person to enter the kingdom of God!" [26] Those who heard *Him* said, "And *so* who can be saved?" [27] But He said, "The things that are impossible with people are possible with God."

[28] Peter said, "Behold, we have left our own homes and followed You." [29] And He said to them, "Truly I say to you, there is no one who has left house, or wife, or brothers, or parents,

or children for the sake of the kingdom of God, [30] who will not receive many times as much at this time, and in the age to come, eternal life."

[31] Now He took the twelve aside and said to them, "Behold, we are going up to Jerusalem, and all the things that have been written through the prophets about the Son of Man will be accomplished. [32] For He will be handed over to the Gentiles, and will be ridiculed, and abused, and spit upon, [33] and after they have flogged Him, they will kill Him; and on the third day He will rise." [34] The disciples understood none of these things, and *the meaning of* this statement was hidden from them, and they did not comprehend the things that were said.

Bartimaeus Receives Sight

[35] Now as Jesus was approaching Jericho, a man who was blind was sitting by the road, begging. [36] But when he heard a crowd going by, he *began* inquiring what this was. [37] They told him that Jesus of Nazareth was passing by. [38] And he called out, saying, "Jesus, Son of David, have mercy on me!" [39] Those who led the way were sternly telling him to be quiet; but he kept crying out all the more, "Son of David, have mercy on me!" [40] And Jesus stopped and commanded that he be brought to Him; and when he came near, He asked him, [41] "What do you want Me to do for you?" And he said, "Lord, *I want* to regain my sight!" [42] And Jesus said to him, "Regain your sight; your faith has made you well." [43] And immediately he regained his sight and *began* following Him, glorifying God; and when all the people saw *it,* they gave praise to God.

Zaccheus Converted

19 *Jesus* entered Jericho and was passing through. [2] And there was a man called by the name of Zaccheus; he was a chief tax collector and he was rich. [3] *Zaccheus* was trying to see who Jesus was, and he was unable due to the crowd, because he was short in stature. [4] So he ran on ahead and climbed up a sycamore tree in order to see Him, because He was about to pass through that *way.* [5] And when Jesus came to the place, He looked up and said to him, "Zaccheus, hurry and come down, for today I must stay at your house." [6] And he hurried and came down, and received Him joyfully. [7] When *the people* saw *this,* they all *began* to complain, saying, "He has gone in to be the guest of a man who is a sinner!" [8] But Zaccheus stopped and said to the Lord, "Behold, Lord, half of my possessions I am giving to the poor, and if I have extorted anything from anyone, I am giving back four times as much." [9] And Jesus said to him, "Today salvation has come to this house, because he, too, is a son of Abraham. [10] For the Son of Man has come to seek and to save that which was lost."

Parable of the Ten Minas

[11] Now while they were listening to these things, *Jesus* went on to tell a parable, because He was near Jerusalem and they thought that the kingdom of God was going to appear immediately. [12] So He said, "A nobleman went

to a distant country to receive a kingdom for himself, and *then* to return. 13 And he called ten of his own slaves and gave them ten *minas,* and said to them, 'Do business *with this money* until I come *back.'* 14 But his citizens hated him and sent a delegation after him, saying, 'We do not want this man to reign over us.' 15 When he returned after receiving the kingdom, he ordered that these slaves, to whom he had given the money, be summoned to him so that he would learn how much they had made by the business they had done. 16 The first *slave* appeared, saying, 'Master, your mina has made ten minas more.' 17 And he said to him, 'Well done, good slave; since you have been faithful in a very little thing, you are to have authority over ten cities.' 18 The second one came, saying, 'Your mina, master, has made five minas.' 19 And he said to him also, 'And you are to be over five cities.' 20 And *then* another came, saying, 'Master, here is your mina, which I kept tucked away in a handkerchief; 21 for I was afraid of you, because you are a demanding man; you take up what you did not lay down, and reap what you did not sow.' 22 He *said to him, 'From your own lips I will judge you, you worthless slave. Did you know that I am a demanding man, taking up what I did not lay down, and reaping what I did not sow? 23 And *so* why did you not put my money in the bank, and when I came back, I would have collected it with interest?' 24 And *then* he said to the *other slaves* who were present, 'Take the mina away from him and give it to the one who has the ten minas.' 25 And they said to him, 'Master, he *already* has ten minas.' 26 'I tell you that to everyone who has, *more* shall be given, but from the one who does not have, even what he does have shall be taken away. 27 But as for these enemies of mine who did not want me to reign over them, bring *them* here and slaughter them in my presence.' "

Triumphal Entry

28 After *Jesus* said these things, He was going on ahead, going up to Jerusalem.

29 When He approached Bethphage and Bethany, near the mountain that is called Olivet, He sent two of the disciples, 30 saying, "Go into the village ahead of *you;* there, as you enter, you will find a colt tied, on which no one yet has ever sat; untie it and bring it *here.* 31 And if anyone asks you, 'Why are you untying *it?'* you shall say this: 'The Lord has need of it.' " 32 So those who were sent left and found *it* just as He had told them. 33 And as they were untying the colt, its owners said to them, "Why are you untying the colt?" 34 They said, "The Lord has need of it." 35 And they brought it to Jesus, and they threw their cloaks on the colt and put Jesus *on it.* 36 Now as He was going, they were spreading their cloaks on the road. 37 And as soon as He was approaching, near the descent of the Mount of Olives, the whole crowd of the disciples began to praise God joyfully with a loud voice for all the miracles which they had seen, 38 shouting:

"BLESSED IS the King, THE ONE WHO COMES IN THE NAME OF THE LORD;

Peace in heaven and glory in the highest!" 39 And *yet* some of the Pharisees in the crowd said to Him, "Teacher, rebuke Your disciples!" 40 Jesus replied, "I tell you, if these stop speaking, the stones will cry out!"

41 When He approached *Jerusalem,* He saw the city and wept over it, 42 saying, "If you had known on this day, even you, the *conditions* for peace! But now they have been hidden from your eyes. 43 For the days will come upon you when your enemies will put up a barricade against you, and surround you and hem you in on every side, 44 and they will level you to the ground, and *throw down* your children within you, and they will not leave in you one stone upon another, because you did not recognize the time of your visitation."

Traders Driven from the Temple

45 And Jesus entered the temple *grounds* and began to drive out those who were selling, 46 saying to them, "It is written: 'AND MY HOUSE WILL BE A HOUSE OF PRAYER,' but you have made it a DEN OF ROBBERS."

47 And He was teaching daily in the temple; but the chief priests and the scribes and the leading men among the people were trying to put Him to death, 48 and *yet* they could not find anything that they might do, for all the people were hanging on to every word He said.

Jesus' Authority Questioned

20 On one of the days while He was teaching the people in the temple and preaching the gospel, the chief priests and the scribes with the elders confronted *Him,* 2 and they declared, saying to Him, "Tell us by what authority You are doing these things, or who is the one who gave You this authority?" 3 But He replied to them, "I will also ask you a question, and you tell Me: 4 Was the baptism of John from heaven or from men?" 5 They discussed among themselves, saying, "If we say, 'From heaven,' He will say, 'Why did you not believe him?' 6 But if we say, 'From men,' all the people will stone us to death, since they are convinced that John was a prophet." 7 And *so* they answered that they did not know where *it* came from. 8 And Jesus said to them, "Neither am I telling you by what authority I do these things."

Parable of the Vine-growers

9 But He began to tell the people this parable: "A man planted a vineyard and leased it to vine-growers, and went on a journey for a long time. 10 At *the harvest* time he sent a slave to the vine-growers, so that they would give him *his share* of the produce of the vineyard; but the vine-growers beat him and sent him away empty-handed. 11 And he proceeded to send another slave; but they beat him also and treated him shamefully, and sent him away empty-handed. 12 And he proceeded to send a third; but this one too they wounded and threw out. 13 Now the owner of the vineyard said, 'What am I to do? I will send my beloved son; perhaps they will respect him.' 14 But when the vine-growers saw him, they

---

19:13 1 A mina was equal to about 100 days' wages for a laborer

discussed with one another, saying, 'This is the heir; let's kill him so that the inheritance will be ours.' 15 And so they threw him out of the vineyard and killed him. What, then, will the owner of the vineyard do to them? 16 He will come and put these vine-growers to death, and will give the vineyard to others." However, when they heard *this,* they said, "May it never happen!" 17 But Jesus looked at them and said, "Then what is this *statement* that has been written:

'A STONE WHICH THE BUILDERS REJECTED,
THIS HAS BECOME THE CHIEF CORNERSTONE'?

18 Everyone who falls on that stone will be broken to pieces; but on whomever it falls, it will crush him."

Paying Taxes to Caesar

19 The scribes and the chief priests tried to lay hands on Him that very hour, and *yet* they feared the people; for they were aware that He had spoken this parable against them. 20 And so they watched Him closely, and sent spies who pretended to be righteous, in order that they might catch Him in *some* statement, so that they *could* hand Him over to the jurisdiction and authority of the governor. 21 And *the spies* questioned Him, saying, "Teacher, we know that You speak and teach correctly, and You are not partial to anyone, but You teach the way of God on the basis of truth. 22 Is it permissible for us to pay taxes to Caesar, or not?" 23 But He saw through their trickery and said to them, 24 "Show Me a *¹denarius.* Whose image and inscription does it have?" They said, "Caesar's." 25 And He said to them, "Then pay to Caesar the things that are Caesar's, and to God the things that are God's." 26 And they were unable to catch Him in a statement in the presence of the people; and they were amazed at His answer, and said nothing.

Is There a Resurrection?

27 Now some of the Sadducees (who maintain that there is no resurrection) came to Him, 28 and they questioned Him, saying, "Teacher, Moses wrote for us that if a man's brother dies, leaving a wife, and he is childless, that his brother is to marry the wife and raise up children for his brother. 29 So then, there were seven brothers; and the first took a wife and died childless; 30 and the second 31 and the third married her; and in the same way all seven died, leaving no children. 32 Finally the woman also died. 33 Therefore, in the resurrection, which one's wife does the woman become? For all seven married her."

34 Jesus said to them, "The sons of this age marry and *the women* are given in marriage, 35 but those who are considered worthy to attain to that age and the resurrection from the dead, neither marry nor are given in marriage; 36 for they cannot even die anymore, for they are like angels, and are sons of God, being sons of the resurrection. 37 But *as for* the fact that the dead are raised, even Moses revealed *this* in the *passage about the burning* bush, where he calls the Lord THE GOD OF ABRAHAM, THE

GOD OF ISAAC, AND THE GOD OF JACOB. 38 Now He is not the God of the dead, but of the living; for all live to Him." 39 Some of the scribes answered and said, "Teacher, You have spoken well." 40 For they did not have the courage to question Him any longer about anything.

41 But He said to them, "How *is it that* they say the Christ is David's son? 42 For David himself says in the book of Psalms,

'THE LORD SAID TO MY LORD,
"SIT AT MY RIGHT HAND,
43 UNTIL I MAKE YOUR ENEMIES A FOOTSTOOL
FOR YOUR FEET." '

44 Therefore David calls Him 'Lord,' and *so* how is He his son?"

45 And while all the people were listening, He said to the disciples, 46 "Beware of the scribes, who like to walk around in long robes, and love personal greetings in the market-places, and chief seats in the synagogues and places of honor at banquets, 47 who devour widows' houses, and for appearance's sake offer long prayers. These will receive all the more condemnation."

The Widow's Gift

21 Now He looked up and saw the wealthy putting their gifts into the *temple* treasury. 2 And He saw a poor widow putting in two ¹lepta coins. 3 And He said, "Truly I say to you, this poor widow put in more than all *of them;* 4 for they all contributed to the offering from their surplus; but she, from her poverty, put in all that she had to live on."

5 And while some were talking about the temple, that it was decorated with beautiful stones and ¹vowed gifts, He said, 6 "*As for* these things which you are observing, the days will come when there will not be left *one* stone upon another, which will not be torn down."

7 They asked Him questions, saying, "Teacher, when therefore will these things happen? And what *will be* the sign when these things are about to take place?" 8 And He said, "See to it that you are not misled; for many will come in My name, saying, 'I am *He,*' and, 'The time is near.' Do not go after them. 9 And when you hear of wars and revolts, do not be alarmed; for these things must take place first, but the end *will* not *follow* immediately."

Things to Come

10 Then He *continued by* saying to them, "Nation will rise against nation, and kingdom against kingdom, 11 and there will be massive earthquakes, and in various places plagues and famines; and there will be terrible sights and great signs from heaven.

12 "But before all these things, they will lay their hands on you and persecute you, turning you over to the synagogues and prisons, bringing you before kings and governors on account of My name. 13 It will lead to an opportunity for your testimony. 14 So make up your minds not to prepare beforehand to defend yourselves; 15 for I will provide you eloquence and wisdom which none of your adversaries will be able to oppose or refute.

20:24 ¹ The denarius was a day's wages for a laborer of a laborer's daily wage 21:5 ¹ I.e., gifts promised by vows 21:2 ¹ The smallest Greek copper coin, about 1/128

16 But you will be betrayed even by parents, brothers *and sisters, other* relatives, and friends, and they will put *some* of you to death, **17** and you will be hated by all people because of My name. **18** And *yet* not a hair of your head will perish. **19** By your endurance you will gain your lives.

20 "But when you see Jerusalem surrounded by armies, then recognize that her desolation is near. **21** Then those who are in Judea must flee to the mountains, and those who are inside the city must leave, and those who are in the country must not enter the city; **22** because these are days of punishment, so that all things which have been written will be fulfilled. **23** Woe to those women who are pregnant, and to those who are nursing babies in those days; for there will be great distress upon the land, and wrath to this people; **24** and they will fall by the edge of the sword, and will be led captive into all the nations; and Jerusalem will be trampled underfoot by the Gentiles until *the* times of the Gentiles are fulfilled.

The Return of Christ

25 "There will be signs in *the* sun and moon and stars, and on the earth distress among nations, in perplexity at the roaring of the sea and the waves, **26** people fainting from fear and the expectation of the things that are coming upon the world; for the powers of the heavens will be shaken. **27** And then they will see the Son of Man coming in a cloud with power and great glory. **28** But when these things begin to take place, straighten up and lift up your heads, because your redemption is drawing near."

29 And He told them a parable: "Look at the fig tree and all the trees: **30** as soon as they put forth *leaves,* you see for yourselves and know that summer is now near. **31** So you too, when you see these things happening, recognize that the kingdom of God is near. **32** Truly I say to you, this generation will not pass away until all things take place. **33** Heaven and earth will pass away, but My words will not pass away.

34 "But be on your guard, so that your hearts will not be weighed down with dissipation and drunkenness and the worries of life, and that this day will not come on you suddenly, like a trap; **35** for it will come upon all those who live on the face of all the earth. **36** But stay alert at all times, praying that you will have strength to escape all these things that are going to take place, and to stand before the Son of Man."

37 Now during the day He was teaching in the temple, but at evening He would go out and spend the night on the mountain that is called Olivet. **38** And all the people would get up very early in the morning *to come* to Him in the temple to listen to Him.

Preparing the Passover

22 Now the Feast of Unleavened Bread, which is called the Passover, was approaching. **2** And the chief priests and the scribes were trying to find a way to put Him to death, since they were afraid of the people.

3 And Satan entered Judas, the one called Iscariot, who belonged to the number of the twelve. **4** And he left and discussed with the chief priests and officers how he was to betray Him to them. **5** And they were delighted, and agreed to give him money. **6** And *so* he consented, and *began* looking for a good opportunity to betray Him to them away from the crowd.

7 Now the *first* day of Unleavened Bread came, on which the Passover *lamb* had to be sacrificed. **8** And *so Jesus* sent Peter and John, saying, "Go and prepare the Passover for us, so that we may eat *it.*" **9** They said to Him, "Where do You want us to prepare *it?*" **10** And He said to them, "When you have entered the city, a man carrying a pitcher of water will meet you; follow him into the house that he enters. **11** And you shall say to the owner of the house, 'The Teacher says to you, "Where is the guest room in which I may eat the Passover with My disciples?"' **12** And he will show you a large, furnished upstairs room; prepare *it* there." **13** And they left and found *everything* just as He had told them; and they prepared the Passover.

The Lord's Supper

14 When the hour came, He reclined *at the table,* and the apostles with Him. **15** And He said to them, "I have eagerly desired to eat this Passover with you before I suffer; **16** for I say to you, I shall not eat it *again* until it is fulfilled in the kingdom of God." **17** And when He had taken a cup *and* given thanks, He said, "Take this and share it among yourselves; **18** for I say to you, I will not drink of the fruit of the vine from now on until the kingdom of God comes." **19** And when He had taken *some* bread *and* given thanks, He broke it and gave it to them, saying, "This is My body, which is being given for you; do this in remembrance of Me." **20** And in the same way *He took* the cup after they had eaten, saying, "This cup, which is poured out for you, is the new covenant in My blood. **21** But behold, the hand of the one betraying Me is with Mine on the table. **22** For indeed, the Son of Man is going as it has been determined; but woe to that man by whom He is betrayed!" **23** And they began to debate among themselves which one of them it was who was going to do this.

Who Is Greatest

24 And a dispute also developed among them *as to* which one of them was regarded as being the greatest. **25** And He said to them, "The kings of the Gentiles domineer over them; and those who have authority over them are called 'Benefactors.' **26** But *it is* not this way for you; rather, the one who is the greatest among you must become like the youngest, and the leader like the servant. **27** For who is greater, the one who reclines *at the table* or the one who serves? Is it not the one who reclines *at the table?* But I am among you as the one who serves.

28 "You are the ones who have stood by Me in My trials; **29** and just as My Father has granted Me a kingdom, I grant you **30** that you may eat and drink at My table in My kingdom, and you will sit on thrones judging the twelve tribes of Israel.

31 "Simon, Simon, behold, Satan has demanded to sift you *men* like wheat; 32 but I have prayed for [1]you, that [2]your faith will not fail; and [3]you, when you have turned back, strengthen your brothers." 33 But he said to Him, "Lord, I am ready to go with You both to prison and to death!" 34 But He said, "I tell you, Peter, the rooster will not crow today until you have denied three times that you know Me."

35 And He said to them, "When I sent you out without money belt and bag and sandals, you did not lack anything, did you?" They said, "*No*, nothing." 36 And He said to them, "But now, whoever has a money belt is to take it along, likewise also a bag, and whoever has no sword is to sell his cloak and buy *one*. 37 For I tell you that this which is written must be fulfilled in Me: 'AND HE WAS COUNTED WITH WRONGDOERS'; for that which refers to Me has *its* fulfillment." 38 They said, "Lord, look, here are two swords." And He said to them, "It is enough."

The Garden of Gethsemane

39 And He came out and went, as was His habit, to the Mount of Olives; and the disciples also followed Him. 40 Now when He arrived at the place, He said to them, "Pray that you do not come into temptation." 41 And He withdrew from them about a stone's throw, and He knelt down and *began* to pray, 42 saying, "Father, if You are willing, remove this cup from Me; yet not My will, but Yours be done." 43 [1]Now an angel from heaven appeared to Him, strengthening Him. 44 And being in agony, He was praying very fervently; and His sweat became like drops of blood, falling down upon the ground]. 45 When He rose from prayer, He came to the disciples and found them sleeping from sorrow, 46 and He said to them, "Why are you sleeping? Get up and pray that you do not come into temptation."

Jesus Betrayed by Judas

47 While He was still speaking, behold, a crowd *came,* and the one called Judas, one of the twelve, was leading the way for them; and he approached Jesus to kiss Him. 48 But Jesus said to him, "Judas, are you betraying the Son of Man with a kiss?" 49 When those who were around Him saw what was going to happen, they said, "Lord, shall we strike with the sword?" 50 And one of them struck the slave of the high priest and cut off his right ear. 51 But Jesus responded and said, "Stop! No more of this." And He touched his ear and healed him. 52 And Jesus said to the chief priests and officers of the temple and elders who had come against Him, "Have you come out with swords and clubs as *you would* against a man inciting a revolt? 53 While I was with you daily in the temple, you did not lay hands on Me; but this hour and the power of darkness are yours."

Jesus' Arrest

54 Now they arrested Him and led *Him away,* and brought *Him* to the house of the high priest; but Peter was following at a distance.

55 After they kindled a fire in the middle of the courtyard and sat down together, Peter was sitting among them. 56 And a slave woman, seeing him as he sat in the firelight, and staring at him, said, "This man was with Him as well." 57 But he denied *it,* saying, "I do not know Him, woman!" 58 And a little later, another person saw him and said, "You are *one* of them too!" But Peter said, "Man, I am not!" 59 And after about an hour had passed, some other man *began* to insist, saying, "Certainly this man also was with Him, for he, too, is a Galilean." 60 But Peter said, "Man, I do not know what you are talking about!" And immediately, while he was still speaking, a rooster crowed. 61 And *then* the Lord turned and looked at Peter. And Peter remembered the word of the Lord, how He had told him, "Before a rooster crows today, you will deny Me three times." 62 And he went out and wept bitterly.

63 The men who were holding Jesus in custody *began* mocking Him and beating Him, 64 and they blindfolded Him and *repeatedly* asked Him, saying, "Prophesy, who is the one who hit You?" 65 And they were saying many other things against Him, blaspheming.

Jesus before the Sanhedrin

66 When it was day, the [1]Council of elders of the people assembled, both chief priests and scribes, and they led Him away to their council chamber, saying, 67 "If You are the Christ, tell us." But He said to them, "If I tell you, you will not believe; 68 and if I ask a question, you will not answer. 69 But from now on the Son of Man will be seated at the right hand of the power of God." 70 And they all said, "So You are the Son of God?" And He said to them, "You say *correctly* that I am." 71 And *then* they said, "What further need do we have of testimony? For we have heard *it* ourselves from His *own* mouth!"

Jesus before Pilate

23 Then the entire assembly of them set out and brought Him before Pilate. 2 And they began to bring charges against Him, saying, "We found this man misleading our nation and forbidding *us* to pay taxes to Caesar, and saying that He Himself is Christ, a King." 3 Now Pilate asked Him, saying, "*So* You are the King of the Jews?" And He answered him and said, "*It is as* you say." 4 But Pilate said to the chief priests and the crowds, "I find no grounds for charges in *the case of* this man." 5 But they kept on insisting, saying, "He is stirring up the people, teaching all over Judea, starting from Galilee, as far as this place!"

6 Now when Pilate heard *this,* he asked whether the man was a Galilean. 7 And when he learned that He belonged to Herod's jurisdiction, he sent Him to Herod, since he also was in Jerusalem at this time.

Jesus before Herod

8 Now Herod was overjoyed when he saw Jesus; for he had wanted to see Him for a long

---

22:32 [1] Gr singular, referring only to Peter   [2] Gr singular, referring only to Peter   [3] Gr singular, referring only to Peter   **22:43** [1] Most early mss do not contain vv 43 and 44   **22:66** [1] Or *Sanhedrin*

time, because he had been hearing about Him and was hoping to see some sign performed by Him. 9 And he questioned Him at some length; but He offered him no answer at all. 10 Now the chief priests and the scribes stood *there,* vehemently charging Him. 11 And Herod, together with his soldiers, treated Him with contempt and mocked Him, dressing Him in a brightly shining robe, and sent Him back to Pilate. 12 And *so* Herod and Pilate became friends with one another that very day; for previously, they had been enemies toward each other.

Pilate Seeks Jesus' Release

13 Now Pilate summoned to himself the chief priests, the ¹rulers, and the people, 14 and he said to them, "You brought this man to me on the ground that he is inciting the people to revolt; and behold, after examining *Him* before you, I have found no basis at all in *the case of* this man for the charges which you are bringing against Him. 15 No, nor has Herod, for he sent Him back to us; and behold, nothing deserving death has been done by Him. 16 Therefore I will punish Him and release Him." 17 [¹Now he was obligated to release to them at the feast one *prisoner.*]

18 But they cried out all together, saying, "Away with this man, and release to us Barabbas!" 19 (*He was* one who had been thrown into prison for a revolt that took place in the city, and for murder.) 20 But Pilate, wanting to release Jesus, addressed them again, 21 but they kept on crying out, saying, "Crucify, crucify Him!" 22 And he said to them a third time, "Why, what has this man done wrong? I have found in His case no grounds for *a sentence of* death; therefore I will punish Him and release Him." 23 But they were insistent, with loud voices, demanding that He be crucified. And their voices *began* to prevail. 24 And *so* Pilate decided to have their demand carried out. 25 And he released the man for whom they were asking, who had been thrown into prison for a revolt and murder; but he handed Jesus over to their will.

Simon Carries the Cross

26 And when they led Him away, they seized a man, Simon of Cyrene, as he was coming in from the country, and placed on him the cross to carry behind Jesus.

27 Now following Him was a large crowd of the people, and of women who were mourning and grieving for Him. 28 But Jesus turned to them and said, "Daughters of Jerusalem, stop weeping for Me, but weep for yourselves and for your children. 29 For behold, days are coming when they will say, 'Blessed are those who cannot bear, and the wombs that have not given birth, and the breasts that have not nursed.' 30 Then they will begin TO SAY TO THE MOUNTAINS, 'FALL ON US,' AND TO THE HILLS, 'COVER US.' 31 For if they do these things when the tree is green, what will happen when it is dry?"

32 Now two others, who were criminals, were also being led away to be put to death with Him.

The Crucifixion

33 And when they came to the place called The Skull, there they crucified Him and the criminals, one on the right and the other on the left. 34 [¹But Jesus was saying, "Father, forgive them; for they do not know what they are doing."] And they cast lots, dividing His garments among themselves. 35 And the people stood by, watching. And even the rulers were sneering at Him, saying, "He saved others; let Him save Himself if this is the Christ of God, His Chosen One." 36 The soldiers also ridiculed Him, coming up to Him, offering Him sour wine, 37 and saying, "If You are the King of the Jews, save Yourself!" 38 Now there was also an inscription above Him, "THIS IS THE KING OF THE JEWS."

39 One of the criminals who were hanged *there* was hurling abuse at Him, saying, "Are You not the Christ? Save Yourself and us!" 40 But the other responded, and rebuking him, said, "Do you not even fear God, since you are under the same sentence of condemnation? 41 And we indeed *are suffering* justly, for we are receiving what we deserve for our crimes; but this man has done nothing wrong." 42 And he was saying, "Jesus, remember me when You come into Your kingdom!" 43 And He said to him, "Truly I say to you, today you will be with Me in Paradise."

44 It was now about ¹the sixth hour, and darkness came over the entire land until ²the ninth hour, 45 because the sun stopped shining; and the veil of the temple was torn in two. 46 And Jesus, crying out with a loud voice, said, "Father, INTO YOUR HANDS I ENTRUST MY SPIRIT." And having said this, He died. 47 Now when the centurion saw what had happened, he *began* praising God, saying, "This man was in fact innocent." 48 And all the crowds who came together for this spectacle, after watching what had happened, *began* to return *home,* ¹beating their chests. 49 And all His acquaintances and the women who accompanied Him from Galilee were standing at a distance, seeing these things.

Jesus Is Buried

50 And a man named Joseph, who was a member of the Council, a good and righteous man 51 (he had not consented to their plan and action), *a man* from Arimathea, a city of the Jews, who was waiting for the kingdom of God— 52 this man went to Pilate and asked for the body of Jesus. 53 And he took it down and wrapped it in a linen cloth, and laid Him in a tomb cut into the rock, where no one had ever lain. 54 It was a preparation day, and a Sabbath was about to begin. 55 Now the women who had come with Him from Galilee followed, and they saw the tomb and how His body was laid. 56 And *then* they returned and prepared spices and perfumes.

23:13 ¹ I.e., other Jewish leaders   **23:17** ¹ Most early mss do not contain this v   **23:34** ¹ Most early mss do not contain *But Jesus was saying...doing*   **23:44** ¹ I.e., noon   ² I.e., 3 p.m.   **23:48** ¹ I.e., as a traditional sign of mourning or contrition

And on the Sabbath they rested according to the commandment.

The Resurrection

24 But on the first day of the week, at early dawn, they came to the tomb bringing the spices which they had prepared. 2 And they found the stone rolled away from the tomb, 3 but when they entered, they did not find the body of the Lord Jesus. 4 While they were perplexed about this, behold, two men *suddenly* stood near them in gleaming clothing; 5 and as the women were terrified and bowed their faces to the ground, *the men* said to them, "Why are you seeking the living One among the dead? 6 He is not here, but He has risen. Remember how He spoke to you while He was still in Galilee, 7 saying that the Son of Man must be handed over to sinful men, and be crucified, and on the third day rise *from the dead.*" 8 And they remembered His words, 9 and returned from the tomb and reported all these things to the eleven, and to all the rest. 10 Now *these women* were Mary Magdalene, Joanna, and Mary the *mother* of James; also the other women with them were telling these things to the apostles. 11 But these words appeared to them as nonsense, and they would not believe the women. 12 Nevertheless, Peter got up and ran to the tomb; and when he stooped and looked in, he *saw the linen wrappings only; and he went away to his home, marveling at what had happened.

The Road to Emmaus

13 And behold, on that very day two of them were going to a village named Emmaus, which was ¹sixty stadia from Jerusalem. 14 And they were talking with each other about all these things which had taken place. 15 While they were talking and discussing, Jesus Himself approached and *began* traveling with them. 16 But their eyes were kept from recognizing Him. 17 And He said to them, "What are these words that you are exchanging with one another as you are walking?" And they came to a stop, looking sad. 18 One *of them,* named Cleopas, answered and said to Him, "Are You *possibly* the only one living near Jerusalem who does not know about the things that happened here in these days?" 19 And He said to them, "What sort of things?" And they said to Him, "Those about Jesus the Nazarene, who proved to be a prophet mighty in deed and word in the sight of God and all the people, 20 and how the chief priests and our rulers handed Him over to be sentenced to death, and crucified Him. 21 But we were hoping that it was He who was going to redeem Israel. Indeed, besides all this, it is *now* the third day since these things happened. 22 But also some women among us left us bewildered. When they were at the tomb early in the morning, 23 and did not find His body, they came, saying that they had also seen a vision of angels who said that He was alive. 24 And *so* some of those who were with us went to the tomb, and found it just exactly as the women also had said; but Him they did not see." 25 And *then* He

said to them, "You foolish men and slow of heart to believe in all that the prophets have spoken! 26 Was it not necessary for the Christ to suffer these things and to come into His glory?" 27 Then beginning with Moses and with all the Prophets, He explained to them the things *written* about Himself in all the Scriptures.

28 And they approached the village where they were going, and He gave the impression that He was going farther. 29 And *so* they strongly urged Him, saying, "Stay with us, for it is *getting* toward evening, and the day is now nearly over." So He went in to stay with them. 30 And it came about, when He had reclined *at the table* with them, that He took the bread and blessed *it,* and He broke *it* and *began* giving *it* to them. 31 And *then* their eyes were opened and they recognized Him; and He vanished from their sight. 32 They said to one another, "Were our hearts not burning within us when He was speaking to us on the road, while He was explaining the Scriptures to us?" 33 And they got up that very hour and returned to Jerusalem, and found the eleven gathered together and those who were with them, 34 saying, "The Lord has really risen and has appeared to Simon!" 35 They *began* to relate their experiences on the road, and how He was recognized by them at the breaking of the bread.

Other Appearances

36 Now while they were telling these things, *Jesus* Himself *suddenly* stood in their midst and *said to them, "Peace *be* to you." 37 But they were startled and frightened, and thought that they were looking at a spirit. 38 And He said to them, "Why are you frightened, and why are doubts arising in your hearts? 39 See My hands and My feet, that it is I Myself; touch Me and see, because a spirit does not have flesh and bones as you *plainly* see that I have." 40 And when He had said this, He showed them His hands and His feet. 41 While they still could not believe *it* because of their joy and astonishment, He said to them, "Have you anything here to eat?" 42 They served Him a piece of broiled fish; 43 and He took it and ate *it* in front of them.

44 Now He said to them, "These are My words which I spoke to you while I was still with you, that all the things that are written about Me in the Law of Moses and the Prophets and the Psalms must be fulfilled." 45 Then He opened their minds to understand the Scriptures, 46 and He said to them, "So it is written, that the Christ would suffer and rise from the dead on the third day, 47 and that repentance for forgiveness of sins would be proclaimed in His name to all the nations, beginning from Jerusalem. 48 You are witnesses of these things. 49 And behold, I am sending the promise of My Father upon you; but you are to stay in the city until you are clothed with power from on high."

The Ascension

50 And He led them out as far as Bethany,

and He lifted up His hands and blessed them. [51] While He was blessing them, He parted from them and was carried up into heaven. [52] And

they, after worshiping Him, returned to Jerusalem with great joy, [53] and were continually in the temple praising God.

The Gospel According to
JOHN

The Deity of Jesus Christ

1 In the beginning was the Word, and the Word was with God, and the Word was God. 2 He was in the beginning with God. 3 All things came into being through Him, and apart from Him not even one thing came into being that has come into being. 4 In Him was life, and the life was the Light of mankind. 5 And the Light shines in the darkness, and the darkness did not grasp it.

The Witness John the Baptist

6 A man ¹came, one sent from God, and his name was John. 7 He came as a witness, to testify about the Light, so that all might believe through him. 8 ¹He was not the Light, but he came to testify about the Light.

9 ¹This was the true Light ²that, coming into the world, enlightens every person. 10 He was in the world, and the world came into being through Him, and yet the world did not know Him. 11 He came to His own, and His own people did not accept Him. 12 But as many as received Him, to them He gave the right to become children of God, to those who believe in His name, 13 who were born, not of blood, nor of the will of the flesh, nor of the will of a man, but of God.

The Word Made Flesh

14 And the Word became flesh, and dwelt among us; and we saw His glory, glory as of the only Son from the Father, full of grace and truth. 15 John *testified about Him and called out, saying, "This was He of whom I said, 'He who is coming after me has proved to be my superior, because He existed before me.' " 16 For of His fullness we have all received, and grace upon grace. 17 For the Law was given through Moses; grace and truth were realized through Jesus Christ. 18 No one has seen God at any time; God the only Son, who is in the arms of the Father, He has explained Him.

The Testimony of John the Baptist

19 This is the testimony of John, when the Jews sent priests and Levites to him from Jerusalem to ask him, "Who are you?" 20 And he confessed and did not deny; and this is what he confessed: "I am not the Christ." 21 And so they asked him, "What then? Are you Elijah?" And he *said, "I am not." "Are you the Prophet?" And he answered, "No." 22 Then they said to him, "Who are you? Tell us, so that we may give an answer to those who sent us. What do you say about yourself?" 23 He said, "I am THE VOICE OF ONE CALLING ¹OUT IN THE WILDERNESS, 'MAKE THE WAY OF THE LORD STRAIGHT,' as Isaiah the prophet said."

24 And the messengers had been sent from the Pharisees. 25 They asked him, and said to him, "Why then are you baptizing, if you are not the Christ, nor Elijah, nor the Prophet?" 26 John answered them, saying, "I baptize ¹in water, but among you stands One whom you do not know. 27 It is He who comes after me, of whom I am not worthy even to untie the strap of His sandal." 28 These things took place in Bethany beyond the Jordan, where John was baptizing people.

29 The next day he *saw Jesus coming to him, and *said, "Behold, the Lamb of God who takes away the sin of the world! 30 This is He in behalf of whom I said, 'After me is coming a Man who has proved to be my superior, because He existed before me.' 31 And I did not recognize Him, but so that He would be revealed to Israel, I came baptizing ¹in water." 32 And John testified, saying, "I have seen the Spirit descending as a dove out of heaven, and He remained upon Him. 33 And I did not recognize Him, but He who sent me to baptize ¹in water said to me, 'He upon whom you see the Spirit descending and remaining upon Him, this is the One who baptizes in the Holy Spirit.' 34 And I myself have seen, and have testified that this is the Son of God."

Jesus' Public Ministry; First Converts

35 Again the next day John was standing with two of his disciples, 36 and he looked at Jesus as He walked, and *said, "Behold, the Lamb of God!" 37 And the two disciples heard him speak, and they followed Jesus. 38 And Jesus turned and saw them following, and *said to them, "What are you seeking?" They said to Him, "Rabbi (which translated means Teacher), where are You staying?" 39 He *said to them, "Come, and you will see." So they came and saw where He was staying, and they stayed with Him that day; it was about the ¹tenth hour. 40 One of the two who heard John speak, and followed Him, was Andrew, Simon Peter's brother. 41 He first *found his own brother Simon and *said to him, "We have found the Messiah" (which translated means ¹Christ). 42 He brought him to Jesus. Jesus looked at him and said, "You are Simon the son of John; you shall be called Cephas" (which is translated Peter).

43 The next day He decided to go to Galilee, and He *found Philip. And Jesus *said to him, "Follow Me." 44 Now Philip was from Bethsaida, the city of Andrew and Peter. 45 Philip *found Nathanael and *said to him, "We have found Him of whom Moses wrote in the Law, and the prophets also wrote: Jesus the son of Joseph, from Nazareth!" 46 Nathanael

---

1:6 ¹Or came into being 1:8 ¹Lit That one; i.e., John 1:9 ¹I.e., the Word, Christ ²Or that enlightens every person coming into the world 1:23 ¹Or out, In the wilderness make the way 1:26 ¹The Gr here can be translated in, with, or by 1:31 ¹The Gr here can be translated in, with, or by 1:33 ¹The Gr here can be translated in, with, or by 1:39 ¹I.e., about 4 p.m. 1:41 ¹Gr Anointed One

said to him, "Can anything good be from Nazareth?" Philip *said to him, "Come and see." [47]Jesus saw Nathanael coming to Him, and *said of him, "Here is truly an Israelite, in whom there is no deceit!" [48]Nathanael *said to Him, "How do You know me?" Jesus answered and said to him, "Before Philip called you, when you were under the fig tree, I saw you." [49]Nathanael answered Him, "Rabbi, You are the Son of God; You are the King of Israel!" [50]Jesus answered and said to him, "Because I said to you that I saw you under the fig tree, do you believe? You will see greater things than these." [51]And He *said to him, "Truly, truly, I say to you, you will see heaven opened and the angels of God ascending and descending on the Son of Man."

Miracle at Cana

2 On the third day there was a wedding in Cana of Galilee, and the mother of Jesus was there; [2]and both Jesus and His disciples were invited to the wedding. [3]When the wine ran out, the mother of Jesus *said to Him, "They have no wine." [4]And Jesus *said to her, "What *business* do you have with Me, woman? My hour has not yet come." [5]His mother *said to the servants, "Whatever He tells you, do it." [6]Now there were six stone waterpots standing there for the Jewish custom of purification, containing ¹two or three measures each. [7]Jesus *said to them, "Fill the waterpots with water." So they filled them up to the brim. [8]And He *said to them, "Draw *some* out now and take *it* to the ¹headwaiter." And they took *it to him.* [9]Now when the headwaiter tasted the water which had become wine, and did not know where it came from (but the servants who had drawn the water knew), the headwaiter *called the groom, [10]and *said to him, "Every man serves the good wine first, and when *the guests* are drunk, *then he serves* the poorer *wine; but* you have kept the good wine until now." [11]This beginning of *His* signs Jesus did in Cana of Galilee, and revealed His glory; and His disciples believed in Him.

[12]After this He went down to Capernaum, He and His mother, and *His* brothers and His disciples; and they stayed there a few days.

First Passover—Cleansing the Temple

[13]The Passover of the Jews was near, and Jesus went up to Jerusalem. [14]And within the temple *grounds* He found those who were selling oxen, sheep, and doves, and the money changers seated *at their tables.* [15]And He made a whip of cords, and drove *them* all out of the temple *area,* with the sheep and the oxen; and He poured out the coins of the money changers and overturned their tables; [16]and to those who were selling the doves He said, "Take these things away from here; stop making My Father's house a place of business!" [17]His disciples remembered that it was written: "ZEAL FOR YOUR HOUSE WILL CONSUME ME." [18]The Jews then said to Him, "What sign do You show us as your authority for doing these things?" [19]Jesus answered them, "Destroy this temple, and in three days I will raise it up." [20]The Jews then said, "It took forty-six years to build this temple, and *yet* You will raise it up in three days?" [21]But He was speaking about the temple of His body. [22]So when He was raised from the dead, His disciples remembered that He said this; and they believed the Scripture and the word which Jesus had spoken.

[23]Now when He was in Jerusalem at the Passover, during the feast, many believed in His name as they observed His signs which He was doing. [24]But Jesus, on His part, was not entrusting Himself to them, because He knew all people, [25]and because He did not need anyone to testify about mankind, for He Himself knew what was in mankind.

The New Birth

3 Now there was a man of the Pharisees, named Nicodemus, a ruler of the Jews; [2]this man came to Jesus at night and said to Him, "Rabbi, we know that You have come from God *as* a teacher; for no one can do these signs that You do unless God is with him." [3]Jesus responded and said to him, "Truly, truly, I say to you, unless someone is born again he cannot see the kingdom of God." [4]Nicodemus *said to Him, "How can a person be born when he is old? He cannot enter his mother's womb a second time and be born, can he?" [5]Jesus answered, "Truly, truly, I say to you, unless someone is born of water and *the* Spirit, he cannot enter the kingdom of God. [6]That which has been born of the flesh is flesh, and that which has been born of the Spirit is spirit. [7]Do not be amazed that I said to you, 'You must be born again.' [8]The wind blows where it wishes, and you hear the sound of it, but you do not know where it is coming from and where it is going; so is everyone who has been born of the Spirit."

[9]Nicodemus responded and said to Him, "How can these things be?" [10]Jesus answered and said to him, "You are the teacher of Israel, and *yet* you do not understand these things? [11]Truly, truly, I say to you, we speak of what we know and testify of what we have seen, and you *people* do not accept our testimony. [12]If I told you earthly things and you do not believe, how will you believe if I tell you heavenly things? [13]No one has ascended into heaven, except He who descended from heaven: the Son of Man. [14]And just as Moses lifted up the serpent in the wilderness, so must the Son of Man be lifted up, [15]so that everyone who ¹believes will have eternal life in Him.

[16]"For God so loved the world, that He gave His only Son, so that everyone who believes in Him will not perish, but have eternal life. [17]For God did not send the Son into the world to judge the world, but so that the world might be saved through Him. [18]The one who believes in Him is not judged; the one who does not believe has been judged already, because he has not believed in the name of the only Son of God. [19]And this is the judgment, that the Light has come into the world, and people loved the darkness rather than the Light; for their deeds

---

2:6 ¹About 18 or 27 gallons each; or 68 or 102 liters   **2:8** ¹I.e., manager of the banquet   **3:15** ¹Or *believes in Him will have eternal life*

were evil. 20 For everyone who does evil hates the Light, and does not come to the Light, so that his deeds will not be exposed. 21 But the one who practices the truth comes to the Light, so that his deeds will be revealed as having been performed in God."

John the Baptist's Last Testimony

22 After these things Jesus and His disciples came into the land of Judea; and there He was spending time with them and baptizing. 23 Now John also was baptizing in Aenon, near Salim, because there was an abundance of water there; and *people* were coming and being baptized—24 for John had not yet been thrown into prison.

25 Then a matter of dispute developed on the part of John's disciples with a Jew about purification. 26 And they came to John and said to him, "Rabbi, He who was with you beyond the Jordan, to whom you have testified— behold, He is baptizing and all *the people* are coming to Him." 27 John replied, "A person can receive not even one thing unless it has been given to him from heaven. 28 You yourselves are my witnesses that I said, 'I am not the Christ,' but, 'I have been sent ahead of Him.' 29 He who has the bride is the groom; but the friend of the groom, who stands and listens to him, rejoices greatly because of the groom's voice. So this joy of mine has been made full. 30 He must increase, but I must decrease.

31 "He who comes from above is above all; the one who is *only* from the earth is of the earth and speaks of the earth. He who comes from heaven is above all. 32 What He has seen and heard, of this He testifies; and no one accepts His testimony. 33 The one who has accepted His testimony has certified that God is true. 34 For He whom God sent speaks the words of God; for He does not give the Spirit sparingly. 35 The Father loves the Son and has entrusted all things to His hand. 36 The one who believes in the Son has eternal life; but the one who does not obey the Son will not see life, but the wrath of God remains on him."

Jesus Goes to Galilee

4 So then, when the Lord knew that the Pharisees had heard that He was making and baptizing more disciples than John 2 (although Jesus Himself was not baptizing; rather, His disciples *were*), 3 He left Judea and went away again to Galilee. 4 And He had to pass through Samaria. 5 So He *came to a city of Samaria called Sychar, near the parcel of land that Jacob gave to his son Joseph; 6 and Jacob's well was there. So Jesus, tired from His journey, was just sitting by the well. It was about ꜟthe sixth hour.

The Woman of Samaria

7 A woman of Samaria *came to draw water. Jesus *said to her, "Give Me a drink." 8 For His disciples had gone away to the city to buy food. 9 So the Samaritan woman *said to Him, "How *is it that* You, *though* You are a Jew, are asking me for a drink, *though* I am a Samaritan woman?" (For Jews do not associate with Samaritans.) 10 Jesus replied to her, "If you knew the gift of God, and who it is who is saying to you, 'Give Me a drink,' you would have asked Him, and He would have given you living water." 11 She *said to Him, "Sir, You have no bucket and the well is deep; where then do You get *this* living water? 12 You are not greater than our father Jacob, are You, who gave us the well and drank of it himself, and his sons and his cattle?" 13 Jesus answered and said to her, "Everyone who drinks of this water will be thirsty again; 14 but whoever drinks of the water that I will give him shall never be thirsty; but the water that I will give him will become in him a fountain of water springing up to eternal life."

15 The woman *said to Him, "Sir, give me this water so that I will not be thirsty, nor come *all the way* here to draw *water.*" 16 He *said to her, "Go, call your husband and come here." 17 The woman answered and said to Him, "I have no husband." Jesus *said to her, "You have correctly said, 'I have no husband'; 18 for you have had five husbands, and the one whom you now have is not your husband; this *which* you have said *is* true." 19 The woman *said to Him, "Sir, I perceive that You are a prophet. 20 Our fathers worshiped on this mountain, and *yet* you *Jews* say that in Jerusalem is the place where one must worship." 21 Jesus *said to her, "Believe Me, woman, that a time is coming when you will worship the Father neither on this mountain nor in Jerusalem. 22 You *Samaritans* worship what you do not know; we worship what we do know, because salvation is from the Jews. 23 But a time is coming, and even now has arrived, when the true worshipers will worship the Father in spirit and truth; for such people the Father seeks *to be* His worshipers. 24 God is spirit, and those who worship Him must worship in spirit and truth." 25 The woman *said to Him, "I know that Messiah is coming (He who is called Christ); when that One comes, He will declare all things to us." 26 Jesus *said to her, "I am *He,* the One speaking to you."

27 And at this point His disciples came, and they were amazed that He had been speaking with a woman, yet no one said, "What are You seeking?" or, "Why are You speaking with her?" 28 So the woman left her waterpot and went into the city, and *said to the people, 29 "Come, see a man who told me all the things that I have done; this is not the Christ, is He?" 30 They left the city and were coming to Him.

31 Meanwhile the disciples were urging Him, saying, "Rabbi, eat *something.*" 32 But He said to them, "I have food to eat that you do not know about." 33 So the disciples were saying to one another, "No one brought Him *anything* to eat, did he?" 34 Jesus *said to them, "My food is to do the will of Him who sent Me, and to accomplish His work. 35 Do you not say, 'There are still four months, and *then* comes the harvest'? Behold, I tell you, raise your eyes and observe the fields, that they are white for harvest. 36 Already the one who reaps is receiving wages and is gathering fruit for eternal life, so that the one who sows and the

---

one who reaps may rejoice together. ³⁷ For in this *case* the saying is true: 'One sows and another reaps.' ³⁸ I sent you to reap that for which you have not labored; others have labored, and you have ¹come into their labor."

The Samaritans
³⁹ Now from that city many of the Samaritans believed in Him because of the word of the woman who testified, "He told me all the things that I have done." ⁴⁰ So when the Samaritans came to Jesus, they were asking Him to stay with them; and He stayed there two days. ⁴¹ Many more believed because of His word; ⁴² and they were saying to the woman, "*It is* no longer because of what you said *that* we believe, for we have heard for ourselves and know that this One truly is the Savior of the world."

⁴³ And after the two days, He departed from there for Galilee. ⁴⁴ For Jesus Himself testified that a prophet has no honor in his own country. ⁴⁵ So when He came to Galilee, the Galileans received Him, *only because* they had seen all the things that He did in Jerusalem at the feast; for they themselves also went to the feast.

Healing an Official's Son
⁴⁶ Therefore He came again to Cana of Galilee, where He had made the water into wine. And there was a royal official whose son was sick at Capernaum. ⁴⁷ When he heard that Jesus had come from Judea into Galilee, he went to Him and *began* asking *Him* to come down and heal his son; for he was at the point of death. ⁴⁸ Then Jesus said to him, "Unless you *people* see signs and wonders, you *simply* will not believe." ⁴⁹ The royal official *said to Him, "Sir, come down before my child dies." ⁵⁰ Jesus *said to him, "Go; your son is alive." The man believed the word that Jesus spoke to him and went *home.* ⁵¹ And as he was now going down, his slaves met him, saying that his son was alive. ⁵² So he inquired of them the hour when he began to get better. Then they said to him, "Yesterday at the ¹seventh hour the fever left him." ⁵³ So the father knew that *it was* at that hour in which Jesus said to him, "Your son is alive"; and he himself believed, and his entire household. ⁵⁴ This is again a second sign that Jesus performed when He had come from Judea into Galilee.

The Healing at Bethesda
5 After these things there was a feast of the Jews, and Jesus went up to Jerusalem. ² Now in Jerusalem, by the Sheep *Gate,* there is a pool which in Hebrew is called Bethesda, having five porticoes. ³ In these *porticoes* lay a multitude of those who were sick, blind, limping, *or* paralyzed.^{1 5} Now a man was there who had been ill for thirty-eight years. ⁶ Jesus, upon seeing this man lying *there* and knowing that he had already been *in that condition* for a long time, *said to him,

"Do you want to get well?" ⁷ The sick man answered Him, "Sir, I have no man to put me into the pool when the water is stirred up, but while I am coming, another steps down before me." ⁸ Jesus *said to him, "Get up, pick up your pallet and walk." ⁹ Immediately the man became well, and picked up his pallet and *began* to walk.

Now it was a Sabbath on that day. ¹⁰ So the Jews were saying to the man who was cured, "It is a Sabbath, and it is not permissible for you to carry your pallet." ¹¹ But he answered them, "He who made me well was the one who said to me, 'Pick up your pallet and walk.' " ¹² They asked him, "Who is the man who said to you, 'Pick *it* up and walk'?" ¹³ But the man who was healed did not know who it was, for Jesus had slipped away while there was a crowd in *that* place. ¹⁴ Afterward, Jesus *found him in the temple and said to him, "Behold, you have become well; do not sin anymore, so that nothing worse happens to you." ¹⁵ The man went away, and informed the Jews that it was Jesus who had made him well. ¹⁶ For this reason the Jews were persecuting Jesus, because He was doing these things on a Sabbath. ¹⁷ But He answered them, "My Father is working until now, and I Myself am working."

Jesus' Equality with God
¹⁸ For this reason therefore the Jews were seeking all the more to kill Him, because He not only was breaking the Sabbath, but also was calling God His own Father, making Himself equal with God.

¹⁹ Therefore Jesus answered and was saying to them, "Truly, truly, I say to you, the Son can do nothing of Himself, unless *it is* something He sees the Father doing; for whatever the Father does, these things the Son also does in the same way. ²⁰ For the Father loves the Son and shows Him all things that He Himself is doing; and *the Father* will show Him greater works than these, so that you will be amazed. ²¹ For just as the Father raises the dead and gives them life, so the Son also gives life to whom He wishes. ²² For not even the Father judges anyone, but He has given all judgment to the Son, ²³ so that all will honor the Son just as they honor the Father. The one who does not honor the Son does not honor the Father who sent Him.

²⁴ "Truly, truly, I say to you, the one who hears My word, and believes Him who sent Me, has eternal life, and does not come into judgment, but has passed out of death into life.

Two Resurrections
²⁵ Truly, truly, I say to you, a time is coming and even now has arrived, when the dead will hear the voice of the Son of God, and those who hear will live. ²⁶ For just as the Father has life in Himself, so He gave to the Son also to have life in Himself; ²⁷ and He gave Him authority to execute judgment, because He is

---

4:38 ¹ I.e., enjoyed the fruit of their labor   4:52 ¹ I.e., 1 p.m.   5:3 ¹ Late mss add the following as the remainder of v 3, and v 4: *paralyzed, waiting for the moving of the waters; for an angel of the Lord went down at certain seasons into the pool and stirred up the water; whoever then first stepped in after the stirring up of the water was made well from whatever disease with which he was afflicted*

the Son of Man. 28 Do not be amazed at this; for a time is coming when all who are in the tombs will hear His voice, 29 and will come out: those who did the good *deeds* to a resurrection of life, those who committed the bad *deeds* to a resurrection of judgment.

30 "I can do nothing on My own. As I hear, I judge; and My judgment is righteous, because I do not seek My own will but the will of Him who sent Me.

31 "If I *alone* testify about Myself, My testimony is not true. 32 There is another who testifies about Me, and I know that the testimony which He gives about Me is true.

Testimony of John the Baptist

33 You have sent *messengers* to John, and he has testified to the truth. 34 But the testimony I receive is not from man, but I say these things so that you may be saved. 35 He was the lamp that was burning and shining, and you were willing to rejoice for a while in his light.

Testimony of Works

36 But the testimony I have is greater than *the testimony of* John; for the works which the Father has given Me to accomplish—the very works that I do—testify about Me, that the Father has sent Me.

Testimony of the Father

37 And the Father who sent Me, He has testified about Me. You have neither heard His voice at any time, nor seen His form. 38 Also you do not have His word remaining in you, because you do not believe Him whom He sent.

Testimony of the Scripture

39 ⁱYou examine the Scriptures because you think that in them you have eternal life; and it is those ⁱScriptures that testify about Me; 40 and yet you are unwilling to come to Me so that you may have life. 41 I do not receive glory from people; 42 but I know you, that you do not have the love of God in yourselves. 43 I have come in My Father's name, and you do not receive Me; if another comes in his own name, you will receive him. 44 How can you believe, when you accept glory from one another and you do not seek the glory that is from the *one and* only God? 45 Do not think that I will accuse you before the Father; the one who accuses you is Moses, in whom you have put your hope. 46 For if you believed Moses, you would believe Me; for he wrote about Me. 47 But if you do not believe his writings, how will you believe My words?"

Five Thousand Men Fed

6 After these things Jesus went away to the other side of the Sea of Galilee (*or* Tiberias). 2 A large crowd was following Him, because they were watching the signs which He was performing on those who were sick. 3 But Jesus went up on the mountain, and there He sat with His disciples. 4 Now the Passover, the feast

of the Jews, was near. 5 So Jesus, after raising His eyes and seeing that a large crowd was coming to Him, *said to Philip, "Where are we to buy bread so that these *people* may eat?" 6 But He was saying this *only* to test him, for He Himself knew what He intended to do. 7 Philip answered Him, "Two hundred ⁱdenarii worth of bread is not enough for them, for each to receive *just* a little!" 8 One of His disciples, Andrew, Simon Peter's brother, *said to Him, 9 "There is a boy here who has five barley loaves and two fish; but what are these for so many *people?*" 10 Jesus said, "Have the people recline *to eat*." Now there was plenty of grass in the place. So the men reclined, about ⁱfive thousand in number. 11 Jesus then took the loaves, and after giving thanks He distributed *them* to those who were reclining; likewise also of the fish, as much as they wanted. 12 And when they had eaten their fill, He *said to His disciples, "Gather up the leftover pieces so that nothing will be lost." 13 So they gathered them up, and filled twelve baskets with pieces from the five barley loaves which were left over by those who had eaten. 14 Therefore when the people saw the sign which He had performed, they said, "This is truly the Prophet who is to come into the world."

Jesus Walks on the Water

15 So Jesus, aware that they intended to come and take Him by force to make Him king, withdrew again to the mountain by Himself, alone.

16 Now when evening came, His disciples went down to the sea, 17 and after getting into a boat, they *started to* cross the sea to Capernaum. It had already become dark, and Jesus had not yet come to them. 18 In addition, the sea *began* getting rough, because a strong wind was blowing. 19 Then, when they had rowed about ⁱtwenty-five or thirty stadia, they *saw Jesus walking on the sea and coming near the boat; and they were frightened. 20 But He *said to them, "It is I; do not be afraid." 21 So they were willing to take Him into the boat, and immediately the boat was at the land to which they were going.

22 The next day the crowd that stood on the other side of the sea saw that there was no other small boat there except one, and that Jesus had not gotten into the boat with His disciples, but *that* His disciples had departed alone. 23 Other small boats came from Tiberias near to the place where they ate the bread after the Lord had given thanks. 24 So when the crowd saw that Jesus was not there, nor His disciples, they themselves got into the small boats and came to Capernaum, looking for Jesus. 25 And when they found Him on the other side of the sea, they said to Him, "Rabbi, when did You get here?"

Words to the People

26 Jesus answered them and said, "Truly, truly, I say to you, you seek Me, not because you saw ⁱsigns, but because you ate some of

---

5:39 1 Or (a command) *Examine the Scriptures*   6:7 1 The denarius was a day's wages for a laborer
6:10 1 I.e., 5,000 men plus women and children, cf. Matt 14:21   6:19 1 Possibly 3-4 miles or 4.8-6.4 km; a Roman stadion perhaps averaged 607 ft. or 185 m   6:26 1 I.e., confirming miracles

the loaves and were filled. 27 Do not work for the food that perishes, but for the food that lasts for eternal life, which the Son of Man will give you, for on Him the Father, God, has set His seal." 28 Therefore they said to Him, "What are we to do, so that we may accomplish the works of God?" 29 Jesus answered and said to them, "This is the work of God, that you believe in Him whom He has sent." 30 So they said to Him, "What then are You doing as a sign, so that we may see, and believe You? What work are You performing? 31 Our fathers ate the manna in the wilderness; as it is written: 'HE GAVE THEM BREAD OUT OF HEAVEN TO EAT.' " 32 Jesus then said to them, "Truly, truly, I say to you, it is not Moses who has given you the bread out of heaven, but it is My Father who gives you the true bread out of heaven. 33 For the bread of God is that which comes down out of heaven and gives life to the world." 34 Then they said to Him, "Lord, always give us this bread."

35 Jesus said to them, "I am the bread of life; the one who comes to Me will not be hungry, and the one who believes in Me will never be thirsty. 36 But I said to you that you have indeed seen Me, and yet you do not believe. 37 Everything that the Father gives Me will come to Me, and the one who comes to Me I certainly will not cast out. 38 For I have come down from heaven, not to do My own will, but the will of Him who sent Me. 39 And this is the will of Him who sent Me, that of everything that He has given Me I will lose nothing, but will raise it up on the last day. 40 For this is the will of My Father, that everyone who sees the Son and believes in Him will have eternal life, and I Myself will raise him up on the last day."

Words to the Jews

41 So then the Jews were complaining about Him because He said, "I am the bread that came down out of heaven." 42 And they were saying, "Is this not Jesus, the son of Joseph, whose father and mother we know? How does He now say, 'I have come down out of heaven'?" 43 Jesus answered and said to them, "Stop complaining among yourselves. 44 No one can come to Me unless the Father who sent Me draws him; and I will raise him up on the last day. 45 It is written in the Prophets: 'AND THEY SHALL ALL BE TAUGHT OF GOD.' Everyone who has heard and learned from the Father, comes to Me. 46 Not that anyone has seen the Father, except the One who is from God; He has seen the Father. 47 Truly, truly, I say to you, the one who believes has eternal life. 48 I am the bread of life. 49 Your fathers ate the manna in the wilderness, and they died. 50 This is the bread that comes down out of heaven, so that anyone may eat from it and not die. 51 I am the living bread that came down out of heaven; if anyone eats from this bread, he will live forever; and the bread which I will give for the life of the world also is My flesh."

52 Then the Jews began to argue with one another, saying, "How can this man give us His flesh to eat?" 53 So Jesus said to them, "Truly, truly, I say to you, unless you eat the flesh of the Son of Man and drink His blood, you have no life in yourselves. 54 The one who eats My flesh and drinks My blood has eternal life, and I will raise him up on the last day. 55 For My flesh is true food, and My blood is true drink. 56 The one who eats My flesh and drinks My blood remains in Me, and I in him. 57 Just as the living Father sent Me, and I live because of the Father, the one who eats Me, he also will live because of Me. 58 This is the bread that came down out of heaven, not as the fathers ate and died; the one who eats this bread will live forever."

Words to the Disciples

59 These things He said in the synagogue as He taught in Capernaum.

60 So then many of His disciples, when they heard this, said, "This statement is very unpleasant; who can listen to it?" 61 But Jesus, aware that His disciples were complaining about this, said to them, "Is this offensive to you? 62 What then if you see the Son of Man ascending to where He was before? 63 It is the Spirit who gives life; the flesh provides no benefit; the words that I have spoken to you are spirit, and are life. 64 But there are some of you who do not believe." For Jesus knew from the beginning who they were who did not believe, and who it was who would betray Him. 65 And He was saying, "For this reason I have told you that no one can come to Me unless it has been granted him from the Father."

Peter's Confession of Faith

66 As a result of this many of His disciples left, and would no longer walk with Him. 67 So Jesus said to the twelve, "You do not want to leave also, do you?" 68 Simon Peter answered Him, "Lord, to whom shall we go? You have words of eternal life. 69 And we have already believed and have come to know that You are the Holy One of God." 70 Jesus answered them, "Did I Myself not choose you, the twelve? And yet one of you is a devil." 71 Now He meant Judas the son of Simon Iscariot; for he, one of the twelve, was going to betray Him.

Jesus Teaches at the Feast

7 After these things Jesus was walking in Galilee, for He was unwilling to walk in Judea because the Jews were seeking to kill Him. 2 Now the feast of the Jews, the Feast of Booths, was near. 3 So His brothers said to Him, "Move on from here and go into Judea, so that Your disciples also may see Your works which You are doing. 4 For no one does anything in secret when he himself is striving to be known publicly. If You are doing these things, show Yourself to the world." 5 For not even His brothers believed in Him. 6 So Jesus *said to them, "My time is not yet here, but your time is always ready. 7 The world cannot hate you, but it hates Me because I testify about it, that its deeds are evil. 8 Go up to the feast yourselves; I am not going up to this feast, because My time has not yet fully arrived." 9 Now having said these things to them, He stayed in Galilee.

10 But when His brothers had gone up to the

feast, then He Himself also went up, not publicly, but as *though* in secret. [11] So the Jews were looking for Him at the feast and saying, "Where is He?" [12] And there was a great deal of talk about Him in secret among the crowds: some were saying, "He is a good man"; others were saying, "No, on the contrary, He is misleading the people." [13] However, no one was speaking openly about Him, for fear of [1]the Jews.

[14] But when it was now the middle of the feast, Jesus went up into the temple *area,* and *began to* teach. [15] The Jews then were astonished, saying, "How has this man become learned, not having been educated?" [16] So Jesus answered them and said, "My teaching is not My own, but His who sent Me. [17] If anyone is willing to do His will, he will know about the teaching, whether it is of God, or I am speaking from Myself. [18] The one who speaks from himself seeks his own glory; but He who is seeking the glory of the One who sent Him, He is true, and there is no unrighteousness in Him.

[19] "Did Moses not give you the Law, and *yet* none of you carries out the Law? Why are you seeking to kill Me?" [20] The crowd answered, "You have a demon! Who is seeking to kill You?" [21] Jesus answered them, "I did one deed, and you all are astonished. [22] For this reason Moses has given you circumcision (not that it is from Moses, but from the fathers), and *even* on a Sabbath you circumcise a man. [23] If a man receives circumcision on a Sabbath so that the Law of Moses will not be broken, are you angry at Me because I made an entire man well on a Sabbath? [24] Do not judge by the outward appearance, but judge with righteous judgment."

[25] So some of the people of Jerusalem were saying, "Is this man not the one whom they are seeking to kill? [26] And *yet* look, He is speaking publicly, and they are saying nothing to Him. The rulers do not really know that this is the Christ, do they? [27] However, we know where this man is from; but when the Christ comes, no one knows where He is from." [28] Then Jesus cried out in the temple, teaching and saying, "You both know Me and you know where I am from; and I have not come of Myself, but He who sent Me is true, whom you do not know. [29] I do know Him, because I am from Him, and He sent Me." [30] So they were seeking to arrest Him; and *yet* no one laid a hand on Him, because His hour had not yet come. [31] But many of the crowd believed in Him; and they were saying, "When the Christ comes, He will not perform more signs than those which this man has done, will He?"

[32] The Pharisees heard the crowd whispering these things about Him, and the chief priests and the Pharisees sent officers to arrest Him. [33] Therefore Jesus said, "For a little while longer I am *going to be* with you, and *then* I am going to Him who sent Me. [34] You will seek Me, and will not find Me; and where I am, you cannot come." [35] The Jews then said to one another, "Where does this man intend to go that we will not find Him? He does not intend to go to the Dispersion among the Greeks, and teach the Greeks, does He? [36] What is this statement that He said, 'You will seek Me, and will not find Me; and where I am, you cannot come'?"

[37] Now on the last day, the great *day* of the feast, Jesus stood and cried out, saying, "If anyone is thirsty, let him come to Me and drink. [38] The one who believes in Me, as the Scripture said, 'From his innermost being will flow rivers of living water.'" [39] But this He said in reference to the Spirit, whom those who believed in Him were to receive; for the Spirit was not yet *given,* because Jesus was not yet glorified.

People's Division over Jesus

[40] Some of the people therefore, after they heard these words, were saying, "This truly is the Prophet." [41] Others were saying, "This is the Christ." But others were saying, "Surely the Christ is not coming from Galilee, is He? [42] Has the Scripture not said that the Christ comes from the descendants of David, and from Bethlehem, the village where David was?" [43] So a dissension occurred in the crowd because of Him. [44] And some of them wanted to arrest Him, but no one laid hands on Him.

[45] The officers then came to the chief priests and Pharisees, and they said to them, "Why did you not bring Him?" [46] The officers answered, "Never has a man spoken in this way!" [47] The Pharisees then replied to them, "You have not been led astray too, have you? [48] Not one of the rulers or Pharisees has believed in Him, has he? [49] But this crowd that does not know the Law is accursed!" [50] Nicodemus (the one who came to Him before, being one of them) *said to them, [51] "Our Law does not judge the person unless it first hears from him and knows what he is doing, does it?" [52] They answered and said to him, "You are not from Galilee as well, are you? Examine *the Scriptures,* and see that no prophet arises out of Galilee." [53] [[[1]And everyone went to his home.

The Adulterous Woman

8 But Jesus went to the Mount of Olives. [2] And early in the morning He came again into the temple *area,* and all the people were coming to Him; and He sat down and *began* teaching them. [3] Now the scribes and the Pharisees *brought a woman caught in the act of adultery, and after placing her in the center *of the courtyard,* [4] they *said to Him, "Teacher, this woman has been caught in the very act of committing adultery. [5] Now in the Law, Moses commanded us to stone such women; what then do You say?" [6] Now they were saying this to test Him, so that they might have *grounds for* accusing Him. But Jesus stooped down and with His finger wrote on the ground. [7] When they persisted in asking Him, He straightened up and said to them, "He who is without sin among you, let him *be the* first to throw a stone at her." [8] And again He stooped down and

---

7:13 [1] I.e., the Jewish leaders   **7:53** [1] Later mss add the story of the adulterous woman, numbering it as John 7:53-8:11

wrote on the ground. 9 Now when they heard *this,* they *began* leaving, one by one, beginning with the older ones, and He was left alone, and the woman *where she* was, in the center *of the courtyard.* 10 And straightening up, Jesus said to her, "Woman, where are they? Did no one condemn you?" 11 She said, "No one, Lord." And Jesus said, "I do not condemn you, either. Go. From now on do not sin any longer."]]

Jesus Is the Light of the World

12 Then Jesus again spoke to them, saying, "I am the Light of the world; the one who follows Me will not walk in the darkness, but will have the Light of life." 13 So the Pharisees said to Him, "You are testifying about Yourself; Your testimony is not true." 14 Jesus answered and said to them, "Even if I am testifying about Myself, My testimony is true, because I know where I came from and where I am going; but you do not know where I come from or where I am going. 15 You judge according to the flesh; I am not judging anyone. 16 But even if I do judge, My judgment is true; for I am not alone *in it,* but I and the Father who sent Me. 17 Even in your Law,it has been written that the testimony of two people is true. 18 I am He who testifies about Myself, and the Father who sent Me testifies about Me." 19 So they were saying to Him, "Where is Your Father?" Jesus answered, "You know neither Me nor My Father; if you knew Me, you would know My Father also." 20 These words He spoke in the treasury, as He taught in the temple *area;* and no one arrested Him, because His hour had not yet come.

21 Then He said again to them, "I am going away, and you will look for Me, and will die in your sin; where I am going, you cannot come." 22 So the Jews were saying, "Surely He will not kill Himself, will He, since He says, 'Where I am going, you cannot come'?" 23 And He was saying to them, "You are from below, I am from above; you are of this world, I am not of this world. 24 Therefore I said to you that you will die in your sins; for unless you believe that I am, you will die in your sins." 25 Then they were saying to Him, "Who are You?" Jesus said to them, "What have I even been saying to you *from* the beginning? 26 I have many things to say and to judge regarding you, but He who sent Me is true; and the things which I heard from Him, these I say to the world." 27 They did not realize that He was speaking to them *about* the Father. 28 So Jesus said, "When you lift up the Son of Man, then you will know that I am, and I do nothing on My own, but I say these things as the Father instructed Me. 29 And He who sent Me is with Me; He has not left Me alone, for I always do the things that are pleasing to Him." 30 As He said these things, many came to believe in Him.

The Truth Will Set You Free

31 So Jesus was saying to those Jews who had believed Him, "If you continue in My word, *then* you are truly My disciples; 32 and you will know the truth, and the truth will set you free." 33 They answered Him, "We are

Abraham's descendants and have never been enslaved to anyone; how *is it that* You say, 'You will become free'?"

34 Jesus answered them, "Truly, truly I say to you, everyone who commits sin is a slave of sin. 35 Now the slave does not remain in the house forever; the son does remain forever. 36 So if the Son sets you free, you really will be free. 37 I know that you are Abraham's descendants; yet you are seeking to kill Me, because My word has no place in you. 38 I speak of the things which I have seen with *My* Father; therefore you also do the things which you heard from *your* father."

39 They answered and said to Him, "Abraham is our father." Jesus *said to them, "If you are Abraham's children, do the deeds of Abraham. 40 But as it is, you are seeking to kill Me, a man who has told you the truth, which I heard from God; this Abraham did not do. 41 You are doing the deeds of your father." They said to Him, "We were not born as a result of sexual immorality; we have one Father: God." 42 Jesus said to them, "If God were your Father, you would love Me, for I came forth from God and am here; for I have not even come on My own, but He sent Me. 43 Why do you not understand what I am saying? *It is* because you cannot listen to My word. 44 You are of *your* father the devil, and you want to do the desires of your father. He was a murderer from the beginning, and does not stand in the truth because there is no truth in him. Whenever he tells a lie, he speaks from his own *nature,* because he is a liar and the father of lies. 45 But because I say the truth, you do not believe Me. 46 Which one of you convicts Me of sin? If I speak truth, why do you not believe Me? 47 The one who is of God hears the words of God; for this reason you do not hear *them,* because you are not of God."

48 The Jews answered and said to Him, "Do we not rightly say that You are a Samaritan, and You have a demon?" 49 Jesus answered, "I do not have a demon; on the contrary, I honor My Father, and you dishonor Me. 50 But I am not seeking My glory; there is One who seeks *it,* and judges. 51 Truly, truly I say to you, if anyone follows My word, he will never see death." 52 The Jews said to Him, "Now we know that You have a demon. Abraham died, and the prophets *as well;* and *yet* You say, 'If anyone follows My word, he will never taste of death.' 53 You are not greater than our father Abraham, who died, are You? The prophets died too. Whom do You make Yourself *out to be?*" 54 Jesus answered, "If I glorify Myself, My glory is nothing; it is My Father who glorifies Me, of whom you say, 'He is our God'; 55 and you have not come to know Him, but I know Him. And if I say that I do not know Him, I will be a liar like you; but I do know Him, and I follow His word. 56 Your father Abraham was overjoyed that he would see My day, and he saw *it* and rejoiced." 57 So the Jews said to Him, "You are not yet fifty years old, and You have seen Abraham?" 58 Jesus said to them, "Truly, truly I say to you, before Abraham was born, 'I am.'" 59 Therefore they picked up stones to throw at

---

8:58 1 Or *I AM;* Jesus may be referring to Ex 3:14, *I AM WHO I AM*

Him, but Jesus hid Himself and left the temple *grounds.*

Healing the Man Born Blind

9 As *Jesus* passed by, He saw a man *who had been* blind from birth. ² And His disciples asked Him, "Rabbi, who sinned, this man or his parents, that he would be born blind?" ³ Jesus answered, "*It was* neither *that* this man sinned, nor his parents; but *it was* so that the works of God might be displayed in him. ⁴ We must carry out the works of Him who sent Me as long as it is day; night is coming, when no one can work. ⁵ While I am in the world, I am the Light of the world." ⁶ When He had said this, He spit on the ground, and made mud from the saliva, and applied the mud to his eyes, ⁷ and said to him, "Go, wash in the pool of Siloam" (which is translated, Sent). So he left and washed, and came *back* seeing. ⁸ So the neighbors, and those who previously saw him as a beggar, were saying, "Is this not the one who used to sit and beg?" ⁹ Others were saying, "This is he," *still* others were saying, "No, but he is like him." The man himself kept saying, "I am *the one.*" ¹⁰ So they were saying to him, "How then were your eyes opened?" ¹¹ He answered, "The man who is called Jesus made mud, and spread *it* on my eyes, and said to me, 'Go to Siloam and wash'; so I went away and washed, and I received sight." ¹² And they said to him, "Where is He?" He *said, "I do not know."

Controversy over the Man

¹³ They *brought the man who was previously blind to the Pharisees. ¹⁴ Now it was a Sabbath on the day that Jesus made the mud and opened his eyes. ¹⁵ Then the Pharisees also were asking him again how he received his sight. And he said to them, "He applied mud to my eyes, and I washed, and I see." ¹⁶ Therefore some of the Pharisees were saying, "This man is not from God, because He does not keep the Sabbath." But others were saying, "How can a man who is a sinner perform such signs?" And there was dissension among them. ¹⁷ So they *said again to the man who was blind, "What do you say about Him, since He opened your eyes?" And he said, "He is a prophet." ¹⁸ The Jews then did not believe *it* about him, that he had been blind and had received sight, until they called the parents of the very one who had received his sight, ¹⁹ and they questioned them, saying, "Is this your son, who you say was born blind? Then how does he now see?" ²⁰ His parents then answered and said, "We know that this is our son, and that he was born blind; ²¹ but how he now sees, we do not know; or who opened his eyes, we do not know. Ask him; he is of age, he will speak for himself." ²² His parents said this because they were afraid of the ʲJews; for the Jews had already reached the decision that if anyone confessed Him to be Christ, he was to be excommunicated from the synagogue. ²³ *It was* for this reason *that* his parents said, "He is of age; ask him." ²⁴ So for a second time they summoned the

man who had been blind, and said to him, "Give glory to God; we know that this man is a sinner." ²⁵ He then answered, "Whether He is a sinner, I do not know; one thing I do know, that though I was blind, now I see." ²⁶ So they said to him, "What did He do to you? How did He open your eyes?" ²⁷ He answered them, "I told you already and you did not listen; why do you want to hear *it* again? You do not want to become His disciples too, do you?" ²⁸ They spoke abusively to him and said, "You are His disciple, but we are disciples of Moses. ²⁹ We know that God has spoken to Moses, but as for this man, we do not know where He is from." ³⁰ The man answered and said to them, "Well, here is the amazing thing, that you do not know where He is from, and *yet* He opened my eyes! ³¹ We know that God does not listen to sinners; but if someone is God-fearing and does His will, He listens to him. ³² Since the beginning of time it has never been heard that anyone opened the eyes of a person born blind. ³³ If this man were not from God, He could do nothing." ³⁴ They answered him, "You were born entirely in sins, and *yet* you are teaching us?" So they put him out.

Jesus Affirms His Deity

³⁵ Jesus heard that they had put him out, and upon finding him, He said, "Do you believe in the Son of Man?" ³⁶ He answered by saying, "And who is He, Sir, that I may believe in Him?" ³⁷ Jesus said to him, "You have both seen Him, and He is the one who is talking with you." ³⁸ And he said, "I believe, Lord." And he worshiped Him. ³⁹ And Jesus said, "For judgment I came into this world, so that those who do not see may see, and those who see may become blind." ⁴⁰ Those who were with Him from the Pharisees heard these things and said to Him, "We are not blind too, are we?" ⁴¹ Jesus said to them, "If you were blind, you would have no sin; but now *that* you maintain, 'We see,' your sin remains.

Parable of the Good Shepherd

10 "Truly, truly I say to you, the one who does not enter by the door into the fold of the sheep, but climbs up some other way, he is a thief and a robber. ² But the one who enters by the door is a shepherd of the sheep. ³ To him the doorkeeper opens, and the sheep listen to his voice, and he calls his own sheep by name and leads them out. ⁴ When he puts all his own *sheep* outside, he goes ahead of them, and the sheep follow him because they know his voice. ⁵ However, a stranger they simply will not follow, but will flee from him, because they do not know the voice of strangers." ⁶ Jesus told them this figure of speech, but they did not understand what the things which He was saying to them meant.

⁷ So Jesus said to them again, "Truly, truly I say to you, I am the door of the sheep. ⁸ All those who came before Me are thieves and robbers, but the sheep did not listen to them. ⁹ I am the door; if anyone enters through Me, he will be saved, and will go in and out and find pasture. ¹⁰ The thief comes only to steal

---

9:22 ¹ I.e., the Jewish leaders

and kill and destroy; I came so that they would have life, and have *it* abundantly. 11 "I am the good shepherd; the good shepherd lays down His life for the sheep. 12 He who is a hired hand, and not a shepherd, who is not the owner of the sheep, sees the wolf coming, and leaves the sheep and flees; and the wolf snatches them and scatters *the flock.* 13 *He flees* because he is a hired hand and does not care about the sheep. 14 I am the good shepherd, and I know My own, and My own know Me, 15 just as the Father knows Me and I know the Father; and I lay down My life for the sheep. 16 And I have other sheep that are not of this fold; I must bring them also, and they will listen to My voice; and they will become one flock, *with* one shepherd. 17 For this reason the Father loves Me, because I lay down My life so that I may take it back. 18 No one has taken it away from Me, but I lay it down on My own. I have authority to lay it down, and I have authority to take it back. This commandment I received from My Father."

19 Dissension occurred again among the Jews because of these words. 20 Many of them were saying, "He has a demon and is insane. Why do you listen to Him?" 21 Others were saying, "These are not the words of one who is demon-possessed. A demon cannot open the eyes of those who are blind, can it?"

Jesus Asserts His Deity

22 At that time the 1Feast of the Dedication took place in Jerusalem; 23 it was winter, and Jesus was walking in the temple *area,* in the portico of Solomon. 24 The Jews then surrounded Him and *began* saying to Him, "How long will You keep us in suspense? If You are the Christ, tell us plainly." 25 Jesus answered them, "I told you, and you do not believe; the works that I do in My Father's name, these testify of Me. 26 But you do not believe, because you are not of My sheep. 27 My sheep listen to My voice, and I know them, and they follow Me; 28 and I give them eternal life, and they will never perish; and no one will snatch them out of My hand. 29 1My Father, who has given *them* to Me, is greater than all; and no one is able to snatch *them* out of the Father's hand. 30 I and the Father are one."

31 The Jews picked up stones again to stone Him. 32 Jesus replied to them, "I showed you many good works from the Father; for which of them are you stoning Me?" 33 The Jews answered Him, "We are not stoning You for a good work, but for blasphemy; and because You, being a man, make Yourself *out to be* God." 34 Jesus answered them, "Has it not been written in your Law: 'I SAID, YOU ARE GODS'? 35 If he called them gods, to whom the word of God came (and the Scripture cannot be nullified), 36 are you saying of Him whom the Father sanctified and sent into the world, 'You are blaspheming,' because I said, 'I am the Son of God'? 37 If I do not do the works of My Father, do not believe Me; 38 but if I do *them,* even

though you do not believe Me, believe the works, so that you may know and understand that the Father is in Me, and I in the Father." 39 Therefore they were seeking again to arrest Him, and He eluded their grasp.

40 And He went away again beyond the Jordan to the place where John was first baptizing, and He stayed there. 41 Many came to Him and were saying, "While John performed no sign, yet everything John said about this man was true." 42 And many believed in Him there.

The Death and Resurrection of Lazarus

11 Now a certain man was sick: Lazarus of Bethany, the village of Mary and her sister Martha. 2 And it was the Mary who anointed the Lord with ointment, and wiped His feet with her hair, whose brother Lazarus was sick. 3 So the sisters sent *word* to Him, saying, "Lord, behold, he whom You love is sick." 4 But when Jesus heard *this,* He said, "This sickness is not meant for death, but *is* for the glory of God, so that the Son of God may be glorified by it." 5 (Now Jesus loved Martha and her sister, and Lazarus.) 6 So when He heard that he was sick, He then stayed two days *longer* in the place where He was. 7 Then after this He *said to the disciples, "Let's go to Judea again." 8 The disciples *said to Him, "Rabbi, the Jews were just now seeking to stone You, and *yet* You are going there again?" 9 Jesus replied, "Are there not twelve hours in the day? If anyone walks during the day, he does not stumble, because he sees the light of this world. 10 But if anyone walks during the night, he stumbles, because the light is not in him." 11 This He said, and after this He *said to them, "Our friend Lazarus has fallen asleep; but I am going so that I may awaken him from sleep." 12 The disciples then said to Him, "Lord, if he has fallen asleep, he will come out of it." 13 Now Jesus had spoken of his death, but they thought that He was speaking about actual sleep. 14 So Jesus then said to them plainly, "Lazarus died, 15 and I am glad for your sakes that I was not there, so that you may believe; but let's go to him." 16 Therefore Thomas, who was called Didymus, said to *his* fellow disciples, "Let's also go, so that we may die with Him!"

17 So when Jesus came, He found that he had already been in the tomb four days. 18 Now Bethany was near Jerusalem, about 1fifteen stadia away; 19 and many of the Jews had come to Martha and Mary, to console them about *their* brother. 20 So then Martha, when she heard that Jesus was coming, went to meet Him, but Mary stayed in the house. 21 Martha then said to Jesus, "Lord, if You had been here, my brother would not have died. 22 Even now I know that whatever You ask of God, God will give You." 23 Jesus *said to her, "Your brother will rise *from the dead.*" 24 Martha *said to Him, "I know that he will rise in the resurrection on the last day." 25 Jesus said to her, "I am the resurrection and the life; the one

---

10:22 1 Now known as Hanukkah, also the Feast of Lights   10:29 1 One early ms *What My Father has given Me is greater than all*   11:18 1 Possibly 2 miles or 3 km; a Roman stadion perhaps averaged 607 ft. or 185 m

who believes in Me will live, even if he dies,
26 and everyone who lives and believes in Me
will never die. Do you believe this?" 27 She
*said to Him, "Yes, Lord; I have come to
believe that You are the Christ, the Son of
God, *and* He who comes into the world."
28 When she had said this, she left and
called Mary her sister, saying secretly, "The
Teacher is here and is calling for you." 29 And
when she heard *this,* she *got up quickly and
came to Him.
30 Now Jesus had not yet come into the
village, but was still at the place where Martha
met Him. 31 Then the Jews who were with her
in the house and were consoling her, when
they saw that Mary had gotten up quickly and
left, they followed her, thinking that she was
going to the tomb to weep there. 32 So when
Mary came *to the place* where Jesus was, she
saw Him and fell at His feet, saying to Him,
"Lord, if You had been here, my brother would
not have died." 33 Therefore when Jesus saw
her weeping, and the Jews who came with her
also weeping, He was deeply moved in spirit
and was troubled, 34 and He said, "Where have
you laid him?" They *said to Him, "Lord, come
and see." 35 Jesus wept. 36 So the Jews were
saying, "See how He loved him!" 37 But some
of them said, "Could this man, who opened the
eyes of the man who was blind, not have also
kept this man from dying?"
38 So Jesus, again being deeply moved
within, *came to the tomb. Now it was a cave,
and a stone was lying against it. 39 Jesus *said,
"Remove the stone." Martha, the sister of the
deceased, *said to Him, "Lord, by this time
there will be a stench, for he has been *dead*
four days." 40 Jesus *said to her, "Did I not say
to you that if you believe, you will see the glory
of God?" 41 So they removed the stone. And
Jesus raised His eyes, and said, "Father, I thank
You that You have heard Me. 42 But I knew that
You always hear Me; nevertheless, because of
the people standing around I said *it,* so that
they may believe that You sent Me." 43 And
when He had said these things, He cried out
with a loud voice, "Lazarus, come out!" 44 Out
came the man who had died, bound hand and
foot with wrappings, and his face was wrapped
around with a cloth. Jesus *said to them,
"Unbind him, and let him go."
45 Therefore many of the Jews who came to
Mary, and saw what He had done, believed in
Him. 46 But some of them went to the Pharisees
and told them the things which Jesus had
done.

Conspiracy to Kill Jesus
47 Therefore the chief priests and the
Pharisees convened a council meeting, and
they were saying, "What are we doing in
regard to the fact that this man is performing
many signs? 48 If we let Him *go on* like this,
all *the people* will believe in Him, and the
Romans will come and take over both our place
and our nation." 49 But one of them, Caiaphas,
who was high priest that year, said to them,
"You know nothing at all, 50 nor are you taking
into account that it is in your best interest that

one man die for the people, and that the whole
nation not perish *instead.*" 51 Now he did not
say this on his own, but as he was high priest
that year, he prophesied that Jesus was going to
die for the nation; 52 and not for the nation
only, but in order that He might also gather
together into one the children of God who are
scattered abroad. 53 So from that day on they
planned together to kill Him.
54 Therefore Jesus no longer *continued to*
walk publicly among the Jews, but went away
from there to the region near the wilderness,
into a city called Ephraim; and there He stayed
with the disciples.
55 Now the Passover of the Jews was near,
and many went up to Jerusalem from the country prior to the Passover, in order to purify
themselves. 56 So they were looking for Jesus,
and saying to one another as they stood in the
temple *area,* "What do you think; that He will
not come to the feast at all?" 57 Now the chief
priests and the Pharisees had given orders that
if anyone knew where He was, he was to
report it, so that they might arrest Him.

Mary Anoints Jesus
12 Therefore, six days before the Passover,
Jesus came to Bethany where Lazarus
was, whom Jesus had raised from the dead.
2 So they made Him a dinner there, and
Martha was serving; and Lazarus was one of
those reclining *at the table* with Him. 3 Mary
then took a pound of very expensive perfume
of pure nard, and anointed the feet of Jesus
and wiped His feet with her hair; and the
house was filled with the fragrance of the
perfume. 4 But Judas Iscariot, one of His disciples, the one who intended to betray Him,
*said, 5 "Why was this perfume not sold for
three hundred 1denarii and *the proceeds*
given to poor *people?*" 6 Now he said this, not
because he cared about the poor, but because
he was a thief, and as he kept the money box,
he used to steal from what was put into it.
7 Therefore Jesus said, "Leave her alone, so
that she may keep it 1for the day of My burial.
8 For you always have the poor with you, but
you do not always have Me."
9 The large crowd of the Jews then learned
that He was there; and they came, not on
account of Jesus only, but so that they might
also see Lazarus, whom He raised from the
dead. 10 But the chief priests planned to put
Lazarus to death also, 11 because on account of
him many of the Jews were going away and
were believing in Jesus.

The Triumphal Entry
12 On the next day, when the large crowd
that had come to the feast heard that Jesus was
coming to Jerusalem, 13 they took the branches
of the palm trees and went out to meet Him,
and *began* shouting, "Hosanna! BLESSED IS HE
WHO COMES IN THE NAME OF THE LORD, indeed,
the King of Israel!" 14 Jesus, finding a young
donkey, sat on it; as it is written: 15 "DO NOT
FEAR, DAUGHTER OF ZION; BEHOLD, YOUR KING IS
COMING, SEATED ON A DONKEY'S COLT." 16 These
things His disciples did not understand at the

12:5 1 The denarius was a day's wages for a laborer   12:7 1 Or *in view of*

first; but when Jesus was glorified, then they remembered that these things were written of Him, and that they had done these things for Him. 17 So the people, who were with Him when He called Lazarus out of the tomb and raised him from the dead, continued to testify *about Him.* 18 For this reason also the people went to meet Him, because they heard that He had performed this sign. 19 So the Pharisees said to one another, "You see that you are not accomplishing anything; look, the world has gone after Him!"

Greeks Seek Jesus

20 Now there were some Greeks among those who were going up to worship at the feast; 21 these *people* then came to Philip, who was from Bethsaida of Galilee, and were making a request of him, saying, "Sir, we wish to see Jesus." 22 Philip *came and *told Andrew; *then* Andrew and Philip *came and *told Jesus. 23 But Jesus *answered them by saying, "The hour has come for the Son of Man to be glorified. 24 Truly, truly I say to you, unless a grain of wheat falls into the earth and dies, it remains alone; but if it dies, it bears much fruit. 25 The one who loves his life loses it, and the one who hates his life in this world will keep it to eternal life. 26 If anyone serves Me, he must follow Me; and where I am, there My servant will be also; if anyone serves Me, the Father will honor him.

Jesus Foretells His Death

27 "Now My soul has become troubled; and what am I to say? 'Father, save Me from this hour'? But for this purpose I came to this hour. 28 Father, glorify Your name." Then a voice came out of heaven: "I have both glorified *it,* and will glorify *it* again." 29 So the crowd who stood by and heard *it* were saying that it had thundered; others were saying, "An angel has spoken to Him!" 30 Jesus responded and said, "This voice has not come for My sake, but for yours. 31 Now judgment is *upon* this world; now the ruler of this world will be cast out. 32 And I, if I am lifted up from the earth, will draw all *people* to Myself." 33 Now He was saying this to indicate what kind of death He was going to die. 34 The crowd then answered Him, "We have heard from the Law that the Christ is to remain forever; and how *is it that* You say, 'The Son of Man must be lifted up'? Who is this Son of Man?" 35 So Jesus said to them, "For a little while longer the Light is among you. Walk while you have the Light, so that darkness will not overtake you; also, the one who walks in the darkness does not know where he is going. 36 While you have the Light, believe in the Light, so that you may become sons of Light."

These things Jesus proclaimed, and He went away and hid Himself from them. 37 But though He had performed so many signs in their sight, they *still* were not believing in Him. 38 *This happened* so that the word of Isaiah the prophet which he spoke would be fulfilled: "Lord, who has believed our report? And to whom has the arm of the Lord been revealed?" 39 For this reason they could not believe, for Isaiah said again, 40 "He has blinded their eyes and He hardened their heart, so that they will not see with their eyes and understand with their heart, and be converted, and *so* I will *not* heal them." 41 These things Isaiah said because he saw His glory, and he spoke about Him. 42 Nevertheless many, even of the rulers, believed in Him, but because of the Pharisees they were not confessing *Him,* so that they would not be excommunicated from the synagogue; 43 for they loved the approval of people rather than the approval of God.

44 Now Jesus cried out and said, "The one who believes in Me, does not believe *only* in Me, but *also* in Him who sent Me. 45 And the one who sees Me sees Him who sent Me. 46 I have come *as* Light into the world, so that no one who believes in Me will remain in darkness. 47 If anyone hears My teachings and does not keep them, I do not judge him; for I did not come to judge the world, but to save the world. 48 The one who rejects Me and does not accept My teachings has one who judges him: the word which I spoke. That will judge him on the last day. 49 For I did not speak on My own, but the Father Himself who sent Me has given Me a commandment *as to* what to say and what to speak. 50 And I know that His commandment is eternal life; therefore the things I speak, I speak just as the Father has told Me."

The Lord's Supper

13 Now before the Feast of the Passover, Jesus, knowing that His hour had come that He would depart from this world to the Father, having loved His own who were in the world, He loved them to the end. 2 And during supper, the devil having already put into the heart of Judas Iscariot, *the son* of Simon, to betray Him, 3 *Jesus,* knowing that the Father had handed all things over to Him, and that He had come forth from God and was going *back* to God, 4 *got up from supper and *laid His outer garments *aside;* and He took a towel and tied it around Himself.

Jesus Washes the Disciples' Feet

5 Then He *poured water into the basin, and began washing the disciples' feet and wiping them with the towel which He had tied around Himself. 6 So He *came to Simon Peter. He *said to Him, "Lord, You are washing my feet?" 7 Jesus answered and said to him, "What I am doing, you do not realize right now, but you will understand later." 8 Peter *said to Him, "Never shall You wash my feet!" Jesus answered him, "If I do not wash you, you have no place with Me." 9 Simon Peter *said to Him, "Lord, *then wash* not only my feet, but also my hands and my head!" 10 Jesus *said to him, "He who has bathed needs only to wash his feet; otherwise he is completely clean. And you are clean—but not all *of you.*" 11 For He knew the one who was betraying Him; *it was* for this reason *that* He said, "Not all *of you* are clean."

12 Then, when He had washed their feet, and taken His garments and reclined *at the table* again, He said to them, "Do you know what I have done for you? 13 You call Me

'Teacher' and 'Lord'; and you are correct, for so I am. 14 So if I, the Lord and the Teacher, washed your feet, you also ought to wash one another's feet. 15 For I gave you an example, so that you also would do just as I did for you. 16 Truly, truly I say to you, a slave is not greater than his master, nor *is* one who is sent greater than the one who sent him. 17 If you know these things, you are blessed if you do them. 18 I am not speaking about all of you. I know *the ones* whom I have chosen; but *this is happening* so that the Scripture may be fulfilled, 'HE WHO EATS MY BREAD HAS LIFTED UP HIS HEEL AGAINST ME.' 19 From now on I am telling you before *it* happens, so that when it does happen, you may believe that I am *He.* 20 Truly, truly I say to you, the one who receives anyone I send, receives Me; and the one who receives Me receives Him who sent Me."

Jesus Predicts His Betrayal

21 When Jesus had said these things, He became troubled in spirit, and testified and said, "Truly, truly I say to you that one of you will betray Me." 22 The disciples *began* looking at one another, at a loss *to know* of which one He was speaking. 23 Lying back on Jesus' chest was one of His disciples, whom Jesus loved. 24 So Simon Peter *nodded to this *disciple* and *said to him, "Tell *us* who it is of whom He is speaking." 25 He then simply leaned back on Jesus' chest and *said to Him, "Lord, who is it?" 26 Jesus then *answered, "That man is the one for whom I shall dip the piece *of bread* and give it to him." So when He had dipped the piece *of bread,* He *took and *gave *it* to Judas, *the son* of Simon Iscariot. 27 After this, Satan then entered him. Therefore Jesus *said to him, "What you are doing, do *it* quickly." 28 Now none of those reclining *at the table* knew for what purpose He had said this to him. 29 For some were assuming, since Judas kept the money box, that Jesus was saying to him, "Buy the things we need for the feast"; or else, that he was to give something to the poor. 30 So after receiving the piece *of bread,* he left immediately; and it was night.

31 Therefore when he had left, Jesus *said, "Now is the Son of Man glorified, and God is glorified in Him; 32 if God is glorified in Him, God will also glorify Him in Himself, and will glorify Him immediately. 33 Little children, I am *still* with you a little longer. You will look for Me; and just as I said to the Jews, now I also say to you: 'Where I am going, you cannot come.' 34 I am giving you a new commandment, that you love one another; just as I have loved you, that you also love one another. 35 By this all *people* will know that you are My disciples: if you have love for one another."

36 Simon Peter *said to Him, "Lord, where are You going?" Jesus answered, "Where I am going, you cannot follow Me now; but you will follow later." 37 Peter *said to Him, "Lord, why can I not follow You right now? I will lay down my life for You." 38 Jesus *replied, "Will you lay down your life for Me? Truly, truly I say to you,

a rooster will not crow until you deny Me three times.

Jesus Comforts His Disciples

14 "Do not let your heart be troubled; 1believe in God, believe also in Me. 2 In My Father's house are many rooms; if *that* were not so, I would have told you, because I am going *there* to prepare a place for you. 3 And if I go and prepare a place for you, I am coming again and will take you to Myself, so that where I am, *there* you also will be. 4 And you know the way where I am going." 5 Thomas *said to Him, "Lord, we do not know where You are going; how do we know the way?" 6 Jesus *said to him, "I am the way, and the truth, and the life; no one comes to the Father except through Me.

Oneness with the Father

7 If you had known Me, you would have known My Father also; from now on you know Him, and have seen Him."

8 Philip *said to Him, "Lord, show us the Father, and it is enough for us." 9 Jesus *said to him, "Have I been with you for so long a time, and *yet* you have not come to know Me, Philip? The one who has seen Me has seen the Father; how *can* you say, 'Show us the Father'? 10 Do you not believe that I am in the Father, and the Father is in Me? The words that I say to you I do not speak on My own, but the Father, as He remains in Me, does His works. 11 Believe Me that I am in the Father and the Father is in Me; otherwise believe because of the works themselves. 12 Truly, truly I say to you, the one who believes in Me, the works that I do, he will do also; and greater *works* than these he will do; because I am going to the Father. 13 And whatever you ask in My name, this I will do, so that the Father may be glorified in the Son. 14 If you ask Me anything in My name, I will do *it.*

15 "If you love Me, you will keep My commandments.

The Holy Spirit

16 I will ask the Father, and He will give you another Helper, so that He may be with you forever; 17 *the Helper is* the Spirit of truth, whom the world cannot receive, because it does not see Him or know *Him; but* you know Him because He remains with you and will be in you.

18 "I will not leave you as orphans; I am coming to you. 19 After a little while, the world no longer *is going to* see Me, but you *are going to* see Me; because I live, you also will live. 20 On that day you will know that I *am* in My Father, and you *are* in Me, and I in you. 21 The one who has My commandments and keeps them is the one who loves Me; and the one who loves Me will be loved by My Father, and I will love him and will reveal Myself to him." 22 Judas (not Iscariot) *said to Him, "Lord, what has happened that You are going to reveal Yourself to us and not to the world?" 23 Jesus answered and said to him, "If anyone loves Me, he will follow My word; and My Father

---

14:1 1 Or *you believe in God, believe also*

will love him, and We will come to him and make *Our* dwelling with him. **24** The one who does not love Me does not follow My words; and the word which you hear is not Mine, but the Father's who sent Me.

25 "These things I have spoken to you while remaining with you. **26** But the Helper, the Holy Spirit whom the Father will send in My name, He will teach you all things, and remind you of all that I said to you. **27** Peace I leave you, My peace I give you; not as the world gives, do I give to you. Do not let your hearts be troubled, nor fearful. **28** You heard that I said to you, 'I am going away, and I am coming to you.' If you loved Me, you would have rejoiced because I am going to the Father, for the Father is greater than I. **29** And now I have told you before it happens, so that when it happens, you may believe. **30** I will not speak much more with you, for the ruler of the world is coming, and he has ᶦnothing in *regard to* Me, **31** but so that the world may know that I love the Father, I do exactly as the Father commanded Me. Get up, let's go from here.

Jesus Is the Vine—Followers Are Branches

15 "I am the true vine, and My Father is the vinedresser. **2** Every branch in Me that does not bear fruit, He takes away; and every *branch* that bears fruit, He prunes it so that it may bear more fruit. **3** You are already clean because of the word which I have spoken to you. **4** Remain in Me, and I in you. Just as the branch cannot bear fruit of itself but must remain in the vine, so neither *can* you unless you remain in Me. **5** I am the vine, you are the branches; the one who remains in Me, and I in him bears much fruit, for apart from Me you can do nothing. **6** If anyone does not remain in Me, he is thrown away like a branch and dries up; and they gather them and throw them into the fire, and they are burned. **7** If you remain in Me, and My words remain in you, ask whatever you wish, and it will be done for you. **8** My Father is glorified by this, that you bear much fruit, and *so* prove to be My disciples. **9** Just as the Father has loved Me, I also have loved you; remain in My love. **10** If you keep My commandments, you will remain in My love; just as I have kept My Father's commandments and remain in His love. **11** These things I have spoken to you so that My joy may be in you, and *that* your joy may be made full.

Disciples' Relation to Each Other

12 "This is My commandment, that you love one another, just as I have loved you. **13** Greater love has no one than this, that a person will lay down his life for his friends. **14** You are My friends if you do what I command you. **15** No longer do I call you slaves, for the slave does not know what his master is doing; but I have called you friends, because all things that I have heard from My Father I have made known to you. **16** You did not choose Me but I chose you, and appointed you that you would go and bear fruit, and *that* your fruit would remain, so that whatever you ask of the Father in My name He may give to

you. **17** This I command you, that you love one another.

Disciples' Relation to the World

18 "If the world hates you, you know that it has hated Me before *it hated* you. **19** If you were of the world, the world would love *you as* its own; but because you are not of the world, but I chose you out of the world, because of this the world hates you. **20** Remember the word that I said to you, 'A slave is not greater than his master.' If they persecuted Me, they will persecute you as well; if they followed My word, they will follow yours also. **21** But all these things they will do to you on account of My name, because they do not know the One who sent Me. **22** If I had not come and spoken to them, they would not have sin; but now they have no excuse for their sin. **23** The one who hates Me hates My Father also. **24** If I had not done among them the works which no one else did, they would not have sin; but now they have both seen and hated Me and My Father as well. **25** But *this has happened* so that the word that is written in their Law will be fulfilled: 'THEY HATED ME FOR NO REASON.'

26 "When the Helper comes, whom I will send to you from the Father, *namely,* the Spirit of truth who comes from the Father, He will testify about Me, **27** and you are testifying as well, because you have been with Me from the beginning.

Jesus' Warning

16 "These things I have spoken to you so that you will not be led into sin. **2** They will ban you from the synagogue, yet an hour is coming for everyone who kills you to think that he is offering a service to God. **3** These things they will do because they have not known the Father nor Me. **4** But these things I have spoken to you, so that when their hour comes, you may remember that I told you of them. However, I did not say these things to you at the beginning, because I was with you.

The Holy Spirit Promised

5 "But now I am going to Him who sent Me; and none of you asks Me, 'Where are You going?' **6** But because I have said these things to you, grief has filled your heart. **7** But I tell you the truth: it is to your advantage that I am leaving; for if I do not leave, the Helper will not come to you; but if I go, I will send Him to you. **8** And He, when He comes, will convict the world regarding sin, and righteousness, and judgment: **9** regarding sin, because they do not believe in Me; **10** and regarding righteousness, because I am going to the Father and you no longer *are going to* see Me; **11** and regarding judgment, because the ruler of this world has been judged.

12 "I have many more things to say to you, but you cannot bear *them* at the present time. **13** But when He, the Spirit of truth, comes, He will guide you into all the truth; for He will not speak on His own, but whatever He hears, He will speak; and He will disclose to you what is to come. **14** He will glorify Me, for He will take

---

14:30 ᶦI.e., no grounds for any accusation

from Mine and will disclose *it* to you. 15 All things that the Father has are Mine; this is why I said that He takes from Mine and will disclose *it* to you.

Jesus' Death and Resurrection Foretold

16 "A little while, and you no longer *are going to* see Me; and again a little while, and you will see Me." 17 So some of His disciples said to one another, "What is this that He is telling us, 'A little while, and you are not *going to* see Me; and again a little while, and you will see Me'; and, 'because I am going to the Father'?" 18 So they were saying, "What is this that He says, 'A little while'? We do not know what He is talking *about.*" 19 Jesus knew that they wanted to question Him, and He said to them, "Are you deliberating together about this, that I said, 'A little while, and you are not *going to* see Me, and again a little while, and you will see Me'? 20 Truly, truly I say to you that you will weep and mourn, but the world will rejoice; you will grieve, but your grief will be turned into joy! 21 Whenever a woman is in labor she has pain, because her hour has come; but when she gives birth to the child, she no longer remembers the anguish because of the joy that a child has been born into the world. 22 Therefore you too have grief now; but I will see you again, and your heart will rejoice, and no one *is going to* take your joy away from you.

Prayer Promises

23 And on that day you will not question Me about anything. Truly, truly I say to you, if you ask the Father for anything in My name, He will give it to you. 24 Until now you have asked for nothing in My name; ask and you will receive, so that your joy may be made full. 25 "These things I have spoken to you in figures of speech; an hour is coming when I will no longer speak to you in figures of speech, but will tell you plainly about the Father. 26 On that day you will ask in My name, and I am not saying to you that I will request of the Father on your behalf; 27 for the Father Himself loves you, because you have loved Me and have believed that I came forth from the Father. 28 I came forth from the Father and have come into the world; again, I am leaving the world and going to the Father." 29 His disciples *said, "See, now You are speaking plainly and are not using any figure of speech. 30 Now we know that You know all things, and *that* You have no need for anyone to question You; this is why we believe that You came forth from God." 31 Jesus replied to them, "Do you now believe? 32 Behold, an hour is coming, and has *already* come, for you to be scattered, each to his own *home,* and to leave Me alone; and *yet* I am not alone, because the Father is with Me. 33 These things I have spoken to you so that in Me you may have peace. In the world you have tribulation, but take courage; I have overcome the world."

The High Priestly Prayer

17 Jesus spoke these things; and raising His eyes to heaven, He said, "Father, the hour has come; glorify Your Son, so that the Son may glorify You, 2 just as You gave Him authority over all mankind, so that to all whom You have given Him, He may give eternal life. 3 And this is eternal life, that they may know You, the only true God, and Jesus Christ whom You have sent. 4 I glorified You on the earth by accomplishing the work which You have given Me to do. 5 And now You, Father, glorify Me together with Yourself, with the glory which I had with You before the world existed.

6 "I have revealed Your name to the men whom You gave Me out of the world; they were Yours and You gave them to Me, and they have followed Your word. 7 Now they have come to know that everything which You have given Me is from You; 8 for the words which You gave Me I have given to them; and they received *them* and truly understood that I came forth from You, and they believed that You sent Me. 9 I ask on their behalf; I do not ask on behalf of the world, but on the behalf of those whom You have given Me, because they are Yours; 10 and all things that are Mine are Yours, and Yours are Mine; and I have been glorified in them. 11 I am no longer *going to be* in the world; and *yet* they themselves are in the world, and I am coming to You. Holy Father, keep them in Your name, *the name* which You have given Me, so that they may be one just as We *are.* 12 While I was with them, I was keeping them in Your name, which You have given Me; and I guarded them, and not one of them perished except the son of destruction, so that the Scripture would be fulfilled.

The Disciples in the World

13 But now I am coming to You; and these things I speak in the world so that they may have My joy made full in themselves. 14 I have given them Your word; and the world has hated them because they are not of the world, just as I am not of the world. 15 I am not asking You to take them out of the world, but to keep them away from the evil one. 16 They are not of the world, just as I am not of the world. 17 Sanctify them in the truth; Your word is truth. 18 Just as You sent Me into the world, I also sent them into the world. 19 And for their sakes I sanctify Myself, so that they themselves also may be sanctified in truth.

20 "I am not asking on behalf of these alone, but also for those who believe in Me through their word, 21 that they may all be one; just as You, Father, *are* in Me and I in You, that they also may be in Us, so that the world may believe that You sent Me.

Disciples' Future Glory

22 The glory which You have given Me I also have given to them, so that they may be one, just as We are one; 23 I in them and You in Me, that they may be perfected in unity, so that the world may know that You sent Me, and You loved them, just as You loved Me. 24 Father, I desire that they also, whom You have given Me, be with Me where I am, so that they may see My glory which You have given Me, for You loved Me before the foundation of the world.

25 "Righteous Father, although the world has

not known You, yet I have known You; and these have known that You sent Me; 26 and I have made Your name known to them, and will make it known, so that the love with which You loved Me may be in them, and I in them."

Judas Betrays Jesus

18 When Jesus had spoken these words, He went away with His disciples across the ravine of the Kidron, where there was a garden which He entered with His disciples. 2 Now Judas, who was betraying Him, also knew the place, because Jesus had often met there with His disciples. 3 So Judas, having obtained the *Roman* [1]cohort and officers from the chief priests and the Pharisees, *came there with lanterns, torches, and weapons. 4 Jesus therefore, knowing all the things that were coming upon Him, came out *into the open* and *said to them, "Whom are you seeking?" 5 They answered Him, "Jesus the Nazarene." He *said to them, "I am *He.*" And Judas also, who was betraying Him, was standing with them. 6 Now then, when He said to them, "I am *He,*" they drew back and fell to the ground. 7 He then asked them again, "Whom are you seeking?" And they said, "Jesus the Nazarene." 8 Jesus answered, "I told you that I am *He;* so if you are seeking Me, let these *men* go on their way." 9 *This took place* so that the word which He spoke would be fulfilled: "Of those whom You have given Me I lost not one." 10 Then Simon Peter, since he had a sword, drew it and struck the high priest's slave, and cut off his right ear; and the slave's name was Malchus. 11 So Jesus said to Peter, "Put the sword into the sheath; the cup which the Father has given Me, am I not to drink it?"

Jesus before the Priests

12 So the *Roman* [1]cohort, the commander, and the officers of the Jews arrested Jesus and bound Him, 13 and brought Him to Annas first; for he was the father-in-law of Caiaphas, who was high priest that year. 14 Now Caiaphas was the one who had advised the Jews that it was in their best interest for one man to die in behalf of the people.

15 Simon Peter was following Jesus, and *so was* another disciple. Now that disciple was known to the high priest, and he entered with Jesus into the courtyard of the high priest, 16 but Peter was standing at the door outside. So the other disciple, who was known to the high priest, went out and spoke to the doorkeeper, and brought Peter in. 17 Then the slave woman who was the doorkeeper *said to Peter, "You are not also *one* of this Man's disciples, are you?" He *said, "I am not." 18 Now the slaves and the officers were standing *there,* having made a charcoal fire, for it was cold and they were warming themselves; and Peter was also with them, standing and warming himself.

19 The high priest then questioned Jesus about His disciples, and about His teaching. 20 Jesus answered him, "I have spoken openly to the world; I always taught in synagogues and in the temple *area,* where all the Jews

congregate; and I said nothing in secret. 21 Why are you asking Me? Ask those who have heard what I spoke to them. Look: these people know what I said." 22 But when He said this, one of the officers, who was standing nearby, struck Jesus, saying, "Is that the way You answer the high priest?" 23 Jesus answered him, "If I have spoken wrongly, testify of the wrong; but if rightly, why do you strike Me?" 24 So Annas sent Him bound to Caiaphas the high priest.

Peter's Denial of Jesus

25 Now Simon Peter was *still* standing and warming himself. So they said to him, "You are not *one* of His disciples as well, are you?" He denied *it,* and said, "I am not." 26 One of the slaves of the high priest, who was related to the one whose ear Peter cut off, *said, "Did I not see you in the garden with Him?" 27 Peter then denied *it* again, and immediately a rooster crowed.

Jesus before Pilate

28 Then they *brought Jesus from Caiaphas into the [1]Praetorium, and it was early; and they themselves did not enter the Praetorium, so that they would not be defiled, but might eat the Passover. 29 Therefore Pilate came out to them and *said, "What accusation are you bringing against this Man?" 30 They answered and said to him, "If this Man were not a criminal, we would not have handed Him over to you." 31 So Pilate said to them, "Take Him yourselves, and judge Him according to your law." The Jews said to him, "We are not [1]permitted to put anyone to death." 32 *This happened* so that the word of Jesus which He said, indicating what kind of death He was going to die, would be fulfilled.

33 Therefore Pilate entered the Praetorium again, and summoned Jesus and said to Him, "You are the King of the Jews?" 34 Jesus answered, "Are you saying this on your own, or did others tell you about Me?" 35 Pilate answered, "I am not a Jew, am I? Your own nation and the chief priests handed You over to me; what have You done?" 36 Jesus answered, "My kingdom is not of this world. If My kingdom were of this world, My servants would be fighting so that I would not be handed over to the Jews; but as it is, My kingdom is not of this realm." 37 Therefore Pilate said to Him, "So You are a king?" Jesus answered, "You say *correctly* that I am a king. For this *purpose* I have been born, and for this I have come into the world: to testify to the truth. Everyone who is of the truth listens to My voice." 38 Pilate *said to Him, "What is truth?"

And after saying this, he came out again to the Jews and *said to them, "I find no grounds at all for charges in His case. 39 However, you have a custom that I release one *prisoner* for you at the Passover; therefore do you wish that I release for you the King of the Jews?" 40 So they shouted again, saying, "Not this Man, but Barabbas." Now Barabbas was a rebel.

18:3 1 Normally 600 men (the number varied)   **18:12** 1 Normally 600 men (the number varied)
18:28 1 I.e., governor's official residence   **18:31** 1 I.e., under Roman law

The Crown of Thorns

19 So Pilate then took Jesus and had Him flogged. 2 And the soldiers twisted together a crown of thorns and placed it on His head, and put a purple cloak on Him; 3 and they *repeatedly* came up to Him and said, "Hail, King of the Jews!" and slapped Him in the face *again and again.* 4 And *then* Pilate came out again and *said to them, "See, I am bringing Him out to you so that you will know that I find no grounds at all for charges in His case." 5 Jesus then came out, wearing the crown of thorns and the purple robe. And *Pilate* *said to them, "Behold, the Man!" 6 So when the chief priests and the officers saw Him, they shouted, saying, "Crucify, crucify!" Pilate *said to them, "Take Him yourselves and crucify *Him;* for I find no grounds for charges in His case!" 7 The Jews answered him, "We have a law, and by that law He ought to die, because He made Himself *out to be* the Son of God!"

8 Therefore when Pilate heard this statement, he was *even* more afraid; 9 and he entered the ⁱPraetorium again and *said to Jesus, "Where are You from?" But Jesus gave him no answer. 10 So Pilate *said to Him, "Are you not speaking to me? Do You not know that I have authority to release You, and I have authority to crucify You?" 11 Jesus answered him, "You would have no authority over Me at all, if it had not been given to you from above; for this reason the one who handed Me over to you has *the* greater sin." 12 As a result of this, Pilate made efforts to release Him; but the Jews shouted, saying, "If you release this Man, you are not a friend of Caesar; everyone who makes himself *out to be* a king opposes Caesar!"

13 Therefore when Pilate heard these words, he brought Jesus out, and sat down on the judgment seat at a place called The Pavement—but in Hebrew, Gabbatha. 14 Now it was the day of preparation for the Passover; it was about the ⁱsixth hour. And he *said to the Jews, "Look, your King!" 15 So they shouted, "Away with *Him,* away with *Him,* crucify Him!" Pilate *said to them, "Shall I crucify your King?" The chief priests answered, "We have no king except Caesar."

The Crucifixion

16 So he then handed Him over to them to be crucified.

17 They took Jesus, therefore, and He went out, carrying His own cross, to the *place* called the Place of a Skull, which in Hebrew is called, Golgotha. 18 There they crucified Him, and with Him two other men, one on either side, and Jesus in between. 19 Now Pilate also wrote an inscription and put it on the cross. It was written: "JESUS THE NAZARENE, THE KING OF THE JEWS." 20 Therefore many of the Jews read this inscription, because the place where Jesus was crucified was near the city; and it was written in Hebrew, Latin, *and* in Greek. 21 So the chief priests of the Jews were saying to Pilate, "Do not write, 'The King of the Jews'; rather, *write* that He said, 'I am King of

the Jews.' " 22 Pilate answered, "What I have written, I have written."

23 Then the soldiers, when they had crucified Jesus, took His outer garments and made four parts: a part to each soldier, and the ⁱtunic *also;* but the tunic was seamless, woven in one piece. 24 So they said to one another, "Let's not tear it, but cast lots for it, *to decide* whose it shall be." *This happened* so that the Scripture would be fulfilled: "THEY DIVIDED MY GARMENTS AMONG THEMSELVES, AND THEY CAST LOTS FOR MY CLOTHING." Therefore the soldiers did these things.

25 Now beside the cross of Jesus stood His mother, His mother's sister, Mary the *wife* of Clopas, and Mary Magdalene. 26 So when Jesus saw His mother, and the disciple whom He loved standing nearby, He *said to His mother, "Woman, behold, your son!" 27 Then He *said to the disciple, "Behold, your mother!" And from that hour the disciple took her into his own *household.*

28 After this, Jesus, knowing that all things had already been accomplished, in order that the Scripture would be fulfilled, *said, "I am thirsty." 29 A jar full of sour wine was standing *there;* so they put a sponge full of the sour wine on *a branch of* hyssop and brought it *up* to His mouth. 30 Therefore when Jesus had received the sour wine, He said, "It is finished!" And He bowed His head and gave up His spirit.

Care of the Body of Jesus

31 Now then, since it was the day of preparation, to prevent the bodies from remaining on the cross on the Sabbath (for that Sabbath was a high day), the Jews requested of Pilate that their legs be broken, and *the bodies* be taken away. 32 So the soldiers came and broke the legs of the first man, and of the other who was crucified with Him; 33 but after they came to Jesus, when they saw that He was already dead, they did not break His legs. 34 Yet one of the soldiers pierced His side with a spear, and immediately blood and water came out. 35 And he who has seen has testified, and his testimony is true; and he knows that he is telling the truth, so that you also may believe. 36 For these things took place so that the Scripture would be fulfilled: "NOT A BONE OF HIM SHALL BE BROKEN." 37 And again another Scripture says, "THEY WILL LOOK AT HIM WHOM THEY PIERCED."

38 Now after these things Joseph of Arimathea, being a disciple of Jesus, but a secret *one* for fear of the ⁱJews, requested of Pilate that he might take away the body of Jesus; and Pilate granted permission. So he came and took away His body. 39 Nicodemus, who had first come to Him by night, also came, bringing a mixture of myrrh and aloes, about a ⁱhundred litras *weight.* 40 So they took the body of Jesus and bound it in linen wrappings with the spices, as is the burial custom of the Jews. 41 Now in the place where He was crucified there was a garden, and in the garden *was* a new tomb in which no one had yet been laid.

19:9 ¹I.e., governor's official residence   19:14 ¹I.e., about noon   19:23 ¹A long shirt worn next to the skin   19:38 ¹I.e., the Jewish leaders   19:39 ¹I.e., Roman *libras* (about 75 lb. or 34 kg)

42 Therefore because of the Jewish day of preparation, since the tomb was nearby, they laid Jesus there.

The Empty Tomb

20 Now on the first *day* of the week Mary Magdalene *came early to the tomb, while it was still dark, and *saw the stone *already* removed from the tomb. **2** So she *ran and *came to Simon Peter and to the other disciple whom Jesus loved, and *said to them, "They have taken the Lord from the tomb, and we do not know where they have put Him." **3** So Peter and the other disciple left, and they were going to the tomb. **4** The two were running together; and the other disciple ran ahead, faster than Peter, and came to the tomb first; **5** and he stooped to look *in,* and *saw the linen wrappings lying *there;* however he did not go in. **6** So Simon Peter also *came, following him, and he entered the tomb; and he *looked at the linen wrappings lying *there,* **7** and the face-cloth which had been on His head, not lying with the linen wrappings but folded up in a place by itself. **8** So the other disciple who had first come to the tomb also entered then, and he saw and believed. **9** For they did not yet understand the Scripture, that He must rise from the dead. **10** So the disciples went away again to their own *homes.*

11 But Mary was standing outside the tomb, weeping; so as she wept, she stooped to look into the tomb; **12** and she *saw two angels in white sitting, one at the head and one at the feet, where the body of Jesus had been lying. **13** And they *said to her, "Woman, why are you weeping?" She *said to them, "Because they have taken away my Lord, and I do not know where they put Him." **14** When she had said this, she turned around and *saw Jesus standing *there,* and *yet* she did not know that it was Jesus. **15** Jesus *said to her, "Woman, why are you weeping? Whom are you seeking?" Thinking that He was the gardener, she *said to Him, "Sir, if you have carried Him away, tell me where you put Him, and I will take Him away." **16** Jesus *said to her, "Mary!" She turned and *said to Him in Hebrew, "Rabboni!" (which means, Teacher). **17** Jesus *said to her, "Stop clinging to Me, for I have not yet ascended to the Father; but go to My brothers and say to them, 'I am ascending to My Father and your Father, and My God and your God.'" **18** Mary Magdalene *came and announced to the disciples, "I have seen the Lord," and *that* He had said these things to her.

Jesus among His Disciples

19 Now when it was evening on that day, the first *day* of the week, and when the doors were shut where the disciples were *together* due to fear of the ¹Jews, Jesus came and stood in their midst, and *said to them, "Peace *be* to you." **20** And when He had said this, He showed them both His hands and His side. The disciples then rejoiced when they saw the Lord. **21** So Jesus said to them again, "Peace *be* to you; just as the Father has sent Me, I also send you." **22** And when He had said this, He breathed on them and *said to them, "Receive the Holy Spirit. **23** If you forgive the sins of any, *their sins* have been forgiven them; if you retain the *sins* of any, they have been retained."

24 But Thomas, one of the twelve, who was called Didymus, was not with them when Jesus came. **25** So the other disciples were saying to him, "We have seen the Lord!" But he said to them, "Unless I see in His hands the imprint of the nails, and put my finger into the place of the nails, and put my hand into His side, I will not believe."

26 Eight days later His disciples were again inside, and Thomas *was* with them. Jesus *came, the doors having been shut, and stood in their midst and said, "Peace *be* to you." **27** Then He *said to Thomas, "Place your finger here, and see My hands; and take your hand and put it into My side; and do not continue in disbelief, but *be* a believer." **28** Thomas answered and said to Him, "My Lord and my God!" **29** Jesus *said to him, "Because you have seen Me, have you *now* believed? Blessed *are* they who did not see, and *yet* believed."

Why This Gospel Was Written

30 So then, many other signs Jesus also performed in the presence of the disciples, which are not written in this book; **31** but these have been written so that you may believe that Jesus is the Christ, the Son of God; and that by believing you may have life in His name.

Jesus Appears at the Sea of Galilee

21 After these things Jesus revealed Himself again to the disciples at the Sea of Tiberias, and He revealed *Himself* in this way: **2** Simon Peter, Thomas who was called Didymus, Nathanael of Cana in Galilee, the *sons* of Zebedee, and two others of His disciples were together. **3** Simon Peter *said to them, "I am going fishing." They *said to him, "We are also coming with you." They went out and got into the boat; and that night they caught nothing.

4 But when the day was now breaking, Jesus stood on the beach; yet the disciples did not know that it was Jesus. **5** So Jesus *said to them, "Children, you do not have any fish to eat, do you?" They answered Him, "No." **6** And He said to them, "Cast the net on the right-hand side of the boat, and you will find *the fish.*" So they cast *it,* and then they were not able to haul it in because of the great quantity of fish. **7** Therefore that disciple whom Jesus loved *said to Peter, "It is the Lord!" So when Simon Peter heard that it was the Lord, he put on his outer garment (for he was stripped *for work),* and threw himself into the sea. **8** But the other disciples came in the little boat, for they were not far from the land, but about ¹two hundred cubits away, dragging the net *full* of fish.

9 So when they got out on the land, they *saw a charcoal fire *already* made and fish placed on it, and bread. **10** Jesus *said to them, "Bring some of the fish which you have now caught." **11** So Simon Peter went up and hauled

the net to land, full of large fish, 153; and although there were so many, the net was not torn.

Jesus Provides

12 Jesus *said to them, "Come *and* have breakfast." None of the disciples ventured to inquire of Him, "Who are You?" knowing that it was the Lord. 13 Jesus *came and *took the bread and *gave *it* to them, and the fish likewise. 14 This was now the third time that Jesus revealed Himself to the disciples, after He was raised from the dead.

The Love Question

15 Now when they had finished breakfast, Jesus *said to Simon Peter, "Simon, *son* of John, do you love Me more than these?" He *said to Him, "Yes, Lord; You know that I love You." He *said to him, "Tend My lambs." 16 He *said to him again, a second time, "Simon, *son* of John, do you love Me?" He *said to Him, "Yes, Lord; You know that I love You." He *said to him, "Shepherd My sheep." 17 He *said to him the third time, "Simon, *son* of John, do you love Me?" Peter was hurt because He said to him the third time, "Do you love Me?" And he said to Him, "Lord, You know all things; You know that I love You." Jesus *said to him, "Tend My sheep.

Our Times Are in His Hand

18 Truly, truly I tell you, when you were younger, you used to put on your belt and walk wherever you wanted; but when you grow old, you will stretch out your hands and someone else will put your belt on you, and bring *you* where you do not want *to go.*" 19 Now He said this, indicating by what kind of death he would glorify God. And when He had said this, He *said to him, "Follow Me!"

20 Peter turned around and *saw the disciple whom Jesus loved following *them*—the one who also had leaned back on His chest at the supper and said, "Lord, who is the one who is betraying You?" 21 So Peter, upon seeing him, *said to Jesus, "Lord, and what *about* this man?" 22 Jesus *said to him, "If I want him to remain until I come, what *is that* to you? You follow Me!" 23 Therefore this account went out among the brothers, that that disciple would not die; yet Jesus did not say to him that he would not die, but *only,* "If I want him to remain until I come, what *is that* to you?"

24 This is the disciple who is testifying about these things and wrote these things, and we know that his testimony is true.

25 But there are also many other things which Jesus did, which, if they were written in detail, I expect that even the world itself would not contain the books that would be written.

THE ACTS
of the Apostles

Introduction

1 The first account I composed, Theophilus, about all that Jesus began to do and teach, ² until the day when He was taken up *to heaven,* after He had given orders by the Holy Spirit to the apostles whom He had chosen. ³ To these He also presented Himself alive after His suffering, by many convincing proofs, appearing to them over *a period of* forty days and speaking of things regarding the kingdom of God. ⁴ Gathering them together, He commanded them not to leave Jerusalem, but to wait for what the Father had promised, "Which," *He said,* "you heard of from Me; ⁵ for John baptized with water, but you will be baptized with the Holy Spirit not many days from now."

⁶ So, when they had come together, they *began* asking Him, saying, "Lord, is it at this time that You are restoring the kingdom to Israel?" ⁷ But He said to them, "It is not for you to know periods of time or appointed times which the Father has set by His own authority; ⁸ but you will receive power when the Holy Spirit has come upon you; and you shall be My witnesses both in Jerusalem and in all Judea, and Samaria, and as far as the remotest part of the earth."

The Ascension

⁹ And after He had said these things, He was lifted up while they were watching, and a cloud took Him up, out of their sight. ¹⁰ And as they were gazing intently into the sky while He was going, then behold, two men in white clothing stood beside them, ¹¹ and they said, "Men of Galilee, why do you stand looking into the sky? This Jesus, who has been taken up from you into heaven, will come in the same way as you have watched Him go into heaven."

The Upper Room

¹² Then they returned to Jerusalem from the mountain called Olivet, which is near Jerusalem, a ¹Sabbath day's journey away. ¹³ When they had entered *the city,* they went up to the upstairs room where they were staying, that is, Peter, John, James, and Andrew, Philip and Thomas, Bartholomew and Matthew, James *the son* of Alphaeus, Simon the Zealot, and Judas *the son* of James. ¹⁴ All these were continually devoting themselves with one mind to prayer, along with *the* women, and Mary the mother of Jesus, and with His brothers.

¹⁵ At this time Peter stood up among the brothers *and sisters* (a group of about 120 people was there together), and said, ¹⁶ "Brothers, the Scripture had to be fulfilled, which the Holy Spirit foretold by the mouth of David concerning Judas, who became a guide to those who arrested Jesus. ¹⁷ For he was counted among us and received his share in this ministry." ¹⁸ (Now this man acquired a field with the price of his wickedness, and falling headlong, he burst open in the middle and all his intestines gushed out. ¹⁹ And it became known to all the residents of Jerusalem; as a result that field was called Hakeldama in their own language, that is, Field of Blood.) ²⁰ "For it is written in the book of Psalms:

'MAY HIS RESIDENCE BE MADE DESOLATE,
    AND MAY THERE BE NONE LIVING IN IT';

and,

'MAY ANOTHER TAKE HIS OFFICE.'

²¹ Therefore it is necessary that of the men who have accompanied us all the time that the Lord Jesus went in and out among us— ²² beginning with the baptism of John until the day that He was taken up from us—one of these *must* become a witness with us of His resurrection." ²³ So they put forward two men, Joseph called Barsabbas (who was also called Justus), and Matthias. ²⁴ And they prayed and said, "You, Lord, who know the hearts of all people, show which one of these two You have chosen ²⁵ to occupy this ministry and apostleship from which Judas turned aside to go to his own place." ²⁶ And they drew lots for them, and the lot fell to Matthias; and he was added to the eleven apostles.

The Day of Pentecost

2 When the day of Pentecost had come, they were all together in one place. ² And suddenly a noise like a violent rushing wind came from heaven, and it filled the whole house where they were sitting. ³ And tongues *that looked* like fire appeared to them, distributing themselves, and *a tongue* rested on each one of them. ⁴ And they were all filled with the Holy Spirit and began to speak with different tongues, as the Spirit was giving them *the ability* to speak out.

⁵ Now there were Jews residing in Jerusalem, devout men from every nation under heaven. ⁶ And when this sound occurred, the crowd came together and they were bewildered, because each one of them was hearing them speak in his own language. ⁷ They were amazed and astonished, saying, "Why, are not all these who are speaking Galileans? ⁸ And how *is it that* we each hear *them* in our own language to which we were born? ⁹ Parthians, Medes, and Elamites, and residents of Mesopotamia, Judea, and Cappadocia, Pontus and Asia, ¹⁰ Phrygia and Pamphylia, Egypt and the parts of Libya around Cyrene, and visitors from Rome, both Jews and ¹proselytes, ¹¹ Cretans and Arabs—we hear them speaking in our *own* tongues of the mighty deeds of God." ¹² And they all continued in amazement and great perplexity, saying to one another, "What does this mean?" ¹³ But others were

jeering and saying, "They are full of sweet wine!"

Peter's Sermon

14 But Peter, taking his stand with the *other* eleven, raised his voice and declared to them: "Men of Judea and all you who live in Jerusalem, know this, and pay attention to my words. 15 For these people are not drunk, as you assume, since it is *only* the ᵗthird hour of the day; 16 but this is what has been spoken through the prophet Joel:

17 'AND IT SHALL BE IN THE LAST DAYS,' God says,
    'THAT I WILL POUR OUT MY SPIRIT ON ALL
      MANKIND;
    AND YOUR SONS AND YOUR DAUGHTERS WILL
      PROPHESY,
    AND YOUR YOUNG MEN WILL SEE VISIONS,
    AND YOUR OLD MEN WILL HAVE DREAMS;
18   AND EVEN ON MY MALE AND FEMALE
      SERVANTS
    I WILL POUR OUT MY SPIRIT IN THOSE DAYS,
    And they will prophesy.
19   'AND I WILL DISPLAY WONDERS IN THE SKY
      ABOVE
    AND SIGNS ON THE EARTH BELOW,
    BLOOD, FIRE, AND VAPOR OF SMOKE.
20   'THE SUN WILL BE TURNED INTO DARKNESS
    AND THE MOON INTO BLOOD,
    BEFORE THE GREAT AND GLORIOUS DAY OF THE
      LORD COMES.
21   'AND IT SHALL BE *THAT* EVERYONE WHO CALLS
    ON THE NAME OF THE LORD WILL BE
    SAVED.'

22 "Men of Israel, listen to these words: Jesus the Nazarene, a Man attested to you by God with miracles and wonders and signs which God performed through Him in your midst, just as you yourselves know— 23 this *Man,* delivered over by the predetermined plan and foreknowledge of God, you nailed to a cross by the hands of godless men and put *Him* to death. 24 But God raised Him *from the dead,* putting an end to the agony of death, since it was impossible for Him to be held in its power. 25 For David says of Him,

    'I SAW THE LORD CONTINUALLY BEFORE ME,
    BECAUSE HE IS AT MY RIGHT HAND, SO THAT I
      WILL NOT BE SHAKEN.
26   'THEREFORE MY HEART WAS GLAD AND MY
      TONGUE WAS OVERJOYED;
    MOREOVER MY FLESH ALSO WILL LIVE IN HOPE;
27   FOR YOU WILL NOT ABANDON MY SOUL TO
      HADES,
    NOR WILL YOU ALLOW YOUR HOLY ONE TO
      UNDERGO DECAY.
28   'YOU HAVE MADE KNOWN TO ME THE WAYS OF
      LIFE;
    YOU WILL MAKE ME FULL OF GLADNESS WITH
      YOUR PRESENCE.'

29 "Brothers, I may confidently say to you regarding the patriarch David that he both died and was buried, and his tomb is with us to this day. 30 So because he was a prophet and knew that God had sworn to him with an oath to seat *one* of his descendants on his throne, 31 he looked ahead and spoke of the resurrection of the Christ, that He was neither abandoned to

Hades, nor did His flesh suffer decay. 32 *It is* this Jesus *whom* God raised up, *a fact* to which we are all witnesses. 33 Therefore, since He has been exalted at the right hand of God, and has received the promise of the Holy Spirit from the Father, He has poured out this which you both see and hear. 34 For it was not David who ascended into heaven, but he himself says:

    'THE LORD SAID TO MY LORD,
    "SIT AT MY RIGHT HAND,
35   UNTIL I MAKE YOUR ENEMIES A FOOTSTOOL
      FOR YOUR FEET."'

36 Therefore let all the house of Israel know for certain that God has made Him both Lord and Christ—this Jesus whom you crucified."

37 Now when they heard *this,* they were pierced to the heart, and said to Peter and the rest of the apostles, "Brothers, what are we to do?" 38 Peter *said* to them, "Repent, and each of you be baptized in the name of Jesus Christ for the forgiveness of your sins; and you will receive the gift of the Holy Spirit. 39 For the promise is for you and your children and for all who are far away, as many as the Lord our God will call to Himself." 40 And with many other words he solemnly testified and kept on urging them, saying, "Be saved from this perverse generation!" 41 So then, those who had received his word were baptized; and that day there were added about three thousand ᵗsouls. 42 They were continually devoting themselves to the apostles' teaching and to fellowship, to the breaking of bread and to ᵗprayer.

43 Everyone kept feeling a sense of awe; and many wonders and signs were taking place through the apostles. 44 And all the believers ᵗwere together and had all things in common; 45 and they would sell their property and possessions and share them with all, to the extent that anyone had need. 46 Day by day continuing with one mind in the temple, and breaking bread from house to house, they were taking their meals together with gladness and sincerity of heart, 47 praising God and having favor with all the people. And the Lord was adding to their number day by day those who were being saved.

Healing the Beggar Who Was Unable to Walk

3 Now Peter and John were going up to the temple at the ᵗninth *hour,* the hour of prayer. 2 And a man who had been unable to walk from birth was being carried, whom they used to set down every day at the gate of the temple which is called Beautiful, in order *for him* to beg for charitable gifts from those entering the temple *grounds.* 3 When he saw Peter and John about to go into the temple *grounds,* he *began* asking to receive a charitable gift. 4 But Peter, along with John, looked at him intently and said, "Look at us!" 5 And he gave them his attention, expecting to receive something from them. 6 But Peter said, "I do not have silver and gold, but what I do have I give to you: In the name of Jesus Christ the Nazarene, walk!" 7 And grasping him by the right hand, he raised him up; and immediately his feet and his ankles were strengthened.

2:15 1 I.e., 9 a.m.   2:41 1 I.e., persons   2:42 1 Lit *the prayers*   2:44 1 One early ms does not contain *were* and *and*   3:1 1 I.e., 3 p.m.

8 And leaping up, he stood and *began* to walk; and he entered the temple with them, walking and leaping and praising God. 9 And all the people saw him walking and praising God; 10 and they recognized him as being the very one who used to sit at the Beautiful Gate of the temple *to beg* for charitable gifts, and they were filled with wonder and amazement at what had happened to him.

Peter's Second Sermon

11 While he was clinging to Peter and John, all the people ran together to them at the portico named Solomon's, completely astonished. 12 But when Peter saw *this*, he replied to the people, "Men of Israel, why are you amazed at this, or why are you staring at us, as though by our own power or godliness we had made him walk? 13 The God of Abraham, Isaac, and Jacob, the God of our fathers, has glorified His servant Jesus, *the one* whom you handed over and disowned in the presence of Pilate, when he had decided to release *Him*. 14 But you disowned the Holy and Righteous One, and asked for a murderer to be granted to you, 15 but put to death the Prince of life, whom God raised from the dead, *a fact* to which we are witnesses. 16 And on the basis of faith in His name, *it is* the name of Jesus which has strengthened this man whom you see and know; and the faith which *comes* through Him has given him this perfect health in the presence of you all.

17 "And now, brothers, I know that you acted in ignorance, just as your rulers also did. 18 But the things which God previously announced by the mouths of all the prophets, that His Christ would suffer, He has fulfilled in this way. 19 Therefore repent and return, so that your sins may be wiped away, in order that times of refreshing may come from the presence of the Lord; 20 and that He may send Jesus, the Christ appointed for you, 21 whom heaven must receive until *the* period of restoration of all things, about which God spoke by the mouths of His holy prophets from ancient times. 22 Moses said, 'THE LORD GOD WILL RAISE UP FOR YOU A PROPHET LIKE ME FROM YOUR COUNTRYMEN; TO HIM YOU SHALL LISTEN regarding everything He says to you. 23 And it shall be that every soul that does not listen to that prophet shall be utterly destroyed from among the people.' 24 And likewise, all the prophets who have spoken from Samuel and *his* successors *onward,* have also announced these days. 25 It is you who are the sons of the prophets and of the covenant which God ordained with your fathers, saying to Abraham, 'AND IN YOUR SEED ALL THE FAMILIES OF THE EARTH SHALL BE BLESSED.' 26 God raised up His Servant for you first, and sent Him to bless you by turning every one *of you* from your wicked ways."

Peter and John Arrested

4 As they were speaking to the people, the priests and the captain of the temple *guard* and the Sadducees came up to them, 2 being greatly disturbed because they were teaching the people and proclaiming in Jesus the resurrection from the dead. 3 And they laid hands on them and put *them* in prison until the next day, for it was already evening. 4 But many of those who had heard the message believed; and the number of the men came to be about five thousand.

5 On the next day, their rulers and elders and scribes were gathered together in Jerusalem; 6 and Annas the high priest *was there,* and Caiaphas, John, and Alexander, and all who were of high-priestly descent. 7 When they had placed them in the center, they *began to* inquire, "By what power, or in what name, have you done this?" 8 Then Peter, filled with the Holy Spirit, said to them, "Rulers and elders of the people, 9 if we are on trial today for a benefit done to a sick man, as to how this man has been made well, 10 let it be known to all of you and to all the people of Israel, that by the name of Jesus Christ the Nazarene, whom you crucified, whom God raised from the dead—by this *name* this man stands here before you in good health. 11 He is the STONE WHICH WAS REJECTED by you, THE BUILDERS, *but* WHICH BECAME THE CHIEF CORNERSTONE. 12 And there is salvation in no one else; for there is no other name under heaven that has been given among mankind by which we must be saved."

Threat and Release

13 Now as they observed the confidence of Peter and John and understood that they were uneducated and untrained men, they were amazed, and *began* to recognize them as having been with Jesus. 14 And seeing the man who had been healed standing with them, they had nothing to say in reply. 15 But when they had ordered them to leave the Council, they *began* to confer with one another, 16 saying, "What are we to do with these men? For the fact that a noteworthy miracle has taken place through them is apparent to all who live in Jerusalem, and we cannot deny it. 17 But so that it will not spread any further among the people, let's warn them not to speak any longer to any person in this name." 18 And when they had summoned them, they commanded them not to speak or teach at all in the name of Jesus. 19 But Peter and John answered and said to them, "Whether it is right in the sight of God to listen to you rather than to God, make your *own* judgment; 20 for we cannot stop speaking about what we have seen and heard." 21 When they had threatened them further, they let them go (finding no basis on which to punish them) on account of the people, because they were all glorifying God for what had happened; 22 for the man on whom this miracle of healing had been performed was more than forty years old.

23 When they had been released, they went to their own *companions* and reported everything that the chief priests and the elders had said to them. 24 And when they heard *this,* they raised their voices to God with one mind and said, "Lord, it is You who MADE THE HEAVEN AND THE EARTH AND THE SEA, AND EVERYTHING THAT IS IN THEM, 25 who by the Holy Spirit, *through* the mouth of our father David Your servant, said,

'WHY WERE THE [1]NATIONS INSOLENT,
AND THE PEOPLES PLOTTING IN VAIN?
26 'THE KINGS OF THE EARTH TOOK THEIR STAND,
AND THE RULERS WERE GATHERED TOGETHER
AGAINST THE LORD AND AGAINST HIS
CHRIST.'
27 For truly in this city there were gathered together against Your holy servant Jesus, whom You anointed, both Herod and Pontius Pilate, along with the Gentiles and the peoples of Israel, 28 to do whatever Your hand and purpose predestined to occur. 29 And now, Lord, look at their threats, and grant *it* to Your bond-servants to speak Your word with all confidence, 30 while You extend Your hand to heal, and signs and wonders take place through the name of Your holy servant Jesus." 31 And when they had prayed, the place where they had gathered together was shaken, and they were all filled with the Holy Spirit and *began* to speak the word of God with boldness.

Sharing among Believers
32 And the congregation of those who believed were of one heart and soul; and not one *of them* claimed that anything belonging to him was his own, but all things were common property to them. 33 And with great power the apostles were giving testimony to the resurrection of the Lord Jesus, and abundant grace was upon them all. 34 For there was not a needy person among them, for all who were owners of land or houses would sell them and bring the proceeds of the sales 35 and lay *them* at the apostles' feet, and they would be distributed to each to the extent that any had need.
36 Now Joseph, a Levite of Cyprian birth, who was also called Barnabas by the apostles (which translated means Son of Encouragement), 37 owned a tract of land. So he sold it, and brought the money and laid it at the apostles' feet.

Fate of Ananias and Sapphira
5 But a man named Ananias, with his wife Sapphira, sold a piece of property, 2 and kept back *some* of the proceeds for himself, with his wife's full knowledge, and bringing a portion of it, he laid it at the apostles' feet. 3 But Peter said, "Ananias, why has Satan filled your heart to lie to the Holy Spirit and to keep back *some* of the proceeds of the land? 4 While it remained *unsold,* did it not remain your own? And after it was sold, was it not under your control? Why *is it* that you have conceived this deed in your heart? You have not lied to men, but to God." 5 And as he heard these words, Ananias collapsed and died; and great fear came over all who heard *about it.* 6 The young men got up and covered him up, and after carrying him out, they buried him.
7 Now an interval of about three hours elapsed, and his wife came in, not knowing what had happened. 8 And Peter responded to her, "Tell me whether you sold the land for this price?" And she said, "Yes, for that price." 9 Then Peter *said* to her, "Why *is it* that you have agreed together to put the Spirit of the

Lord to the test? Behold, the feet of those who have buried your husband are at the door, and they will carry you out *as well.*" 10 And immediately she collapsed at his feet and died; and the young men came in and found her dead, and they carried her out and buried her beside her husband. 11 And great fear came over the whole church, and over all who heard *about* these things.
12 At the hands of the apostles many signs and wonders were taking place among the people; and they were all together in Solomon's portico. 13 But none of the rest dared to associate with them; however, the people held them in high esteem. 14 And increasingly believers in the Lord, large numbers of men and women, were being added to *their number,* 15 to such an extent that they even carried the sick out into the streets and laid them on cots and pallets, so that when Peter came by at least his shadow might fall on any of them. 16 The people from the cities in the vicinity of Jerusalem were coming together as well, bringing people who were sick [1]or tormented with unclean spirits, and they were all being healed.

Imprisonment and Release
17 But the high priest stood up, along with all his associates (that is the sect of the Sadducees), and they were filled with jealousy. 18 They laid hands on the apostles and put them in a public prison. 19 But during the night an angel of the Lord opened the gates of the prison, and leading them out, he said, 20 "Go, stand and speak to the people in the temple *area* the whole message of this Life." 21 Upon hearing *this,* they entered into the temple *area* about daybreak and *began* to teach.
Now when the high priest and his associates came, they called the Council together, that is, all the Senate of the sons of Israel, and sent *orders* to the prison for them to be brought. 22 But the officers who came did not find them in the prison; and they returned and reported, 23 saying, "We found the prison locked quite securely and the guards standing at the doors; but when we opened *them,* we found no one inside." 24 Now when the captain of the temple *guard* and the chief priests heard these words, they were greatly perplexed about them as to what would come of this. 25 But someone came and reported to them, "The men whom you put in prison are standing in the temple *area* and teaching the people!" 26 Then the captain went along with the officers and *proceeded* to bring them *back* without violence (for they were afraid of the people, that they might be stoned).
27 When they had brought them, they had them stand before the Council. The high priest interrogated them, 28 saying, "We gave you strict orders not to continue teaching in this name, and yet, you have filled Jerusalem with your teaching and intend to bring this Man's blood upon us." 29 But Peter and the apostles answered, "We must obey God rather than men. 30 The God of our fathers raised up Jesus, whom you put to death by hanging Him

---

4:25 [1]Or Gentiles   5:16 [1]Lit and

on [7]a cross. [31] He is the one whom God exalted to His right hand as a Prince and a Savior, to grant repentance to Israel, and forgiveness of sins. [32] And we are witnesses [1]of these things; and *so is* the Holy Spirit, whom God has given to those who obey Him."

Gamaliel's Counsel

[33] But when they heard *this,* they became infuriated and *nearly* decided to execute them. [34] But a Pharisee named Gamaliel, a teacher of the Law, respected by all the people, stood up in the Council and gave orders to put the men outside for a short time. [35] And he said to them, "Men of Israel, be careful as to what you are about to do with these men. [36] For, some time ago Theudas appeared, claiming to be somebody, and a group of about four hundred men joined him. But he was killed, and all who followed him were dispersed and came to nothing. [37] After this man, Judas of Galilee appeared in the days of the census and drew away *some* people after him; he also perished, and all those who followed him were scattered. [38] And *so* in the present case, I say to you, stay away from these men and leave them alone, for if the source of this plan or movement is men, it will be overthrown; [39] but if the source is God, you will not be able to overthrow them; or else you may even be found fighting against God."

[40] They followed his advice; and after calling the apostles in, they flogged them and ordered them not to speak in the name of Jesus, and *then* released them. [41] So they went on their way from the presence of the Council, rejoicing that they had been considered worthy to suffer shame for *His* name. [42] And every day, in the temple and from house to house, they did not stop teaching and preaching the good news of Jesus *as* the Christ.

Choosing of the Seven

6 Now at this time, as the disciples were increasing in number, a complaint developed *on the part of* the [1]Hellenistic *Jews* against the *native* Hebrews, because their widows were being overlooked in the daily serving *of food.* [2] So the twelve summoned the congregation of the disciples and said, "It is not desirable for us to neglect the word of God in order to serve tables. [3] Instead, brothers *and sisters,* select from among you seven men of good reputation, full of the Spirit and of wisdom, whom we may put in charge of this task. [4] But we will devote ourselves to prayer and to the ministry of the word." [5] The announcement found approval with the whole congregation; and they chose Stephen, a man full of faith and of the Holy Spirit, and Philip, Prochorus, Nicanor, Timon, Parmenas, and Nicolas, a [1]proselyte from Antioch. [6] And they brought these men before the apostles; and after praying, they laid their hands on them.

[7] The word of God kept spreading; and the number of the disciples continued to increase greatly in Jerusalem, and a great many of the priests were becoming obedient to the faith.

[8] And Stephen, full of grace and power, was performing great wonders and signs among the people. [9] But some men from what was called the Synagogue of the Freedmen, *including* both Cyrenians and Alexandrians, and some from Cilicia and Asia, rose up and argued with Stephen. [10] But they were unable to cope with his wisdom and the Spirit by whom he was speaking. [11] Then they secretly induced men to say, "We have heard him speak blasphemous words against Moses and God." [12] And they stirred up the people, the elders, and the scribes, and they came up to him and dragged him away, and brought him before the Council. [13] They put forward false witnesses who said, "This man does not stop speaking against this holy place and the Law; [14] for we have heard him say that this Nazarene, Jesus, will destroy this place and change the customs which Moses handed down to us." [15] And all who were sitting in the Council stared at him, and they saw his face, *which was* like the face of an angel.

Stephen's Defense

7 Now the high priest said, "Are these things so?"

[2] And Stephen said, "Listen to me, brothers and fathers! The God of glory appeared to our father Abraham when he was in Mesopotamia, before he lived in Haran, [3] and He said to him, 'GO FROM YOUR COUNTRY AND YOUR RELATIVES, AND COME TO THE LAND WHICH I WILL SHOW YOU.' [4] Then he left the land of the Chaldeans and settled in Haran. And from there, after his father died, *God* had him move to this country in which you are now living. [5] But He gave him no inheritance in it, not even a foot of ground, and *yet,* He promised that He would give it to him as a possession, and to his descendants after him, *even* though he had no child. [6] But God spoke to this effect, that his DESCENDANTS WOULD BE STRANGERS IN A LAND THAT WAS NOT THEIRS, AND THEY WOULD ENSLAVE AND MISTREAT *THEM* FOR FOUR HUNDRED YEARS. [7] 'AND WHATEVER NATION TO WHICH THEY ARE ENSLAVED I MYSELF WILL JUDGE,' said God, 'AND AFTER THAT THEY WILL COME OUT AND SERVE ME IN THIS PLACE.' [8] And He gave him the covenant of circumcision; and so *Abraham* fathered Isaac, and circumcised him on the eighth day; and Isaac *fathered* Jacob, and Jacob, the twelve patriarchs.

[9] "The patriarchs became jealous of Joseph and sold him into Egypt. *Yet* God was with him, [10] and rescued him from all his afflictions, and granted him favor and wisdom in the sight of Pharaoh, king of Egypt, and he made him governor over Egypt and his entire household. [11] "Now a famine came over all Egypt and Canaan, and great affliction *with it,* and our fathers could find no food. [12] But when Jacob heard that there was grain in Egypt, he sent our fathers *there* the first time. [13] And on the second *visit,* Joseph made himself known to his brothers, and Joseph's family was revealed to Pharaoh. [14] Then Joseph sent *word* and invited his father Jacob and all his relatives to come to

---

5:30 [1] Lit *wood;* see Deut 21:23   5:32 [1] One early ms adds *in Him*   6:1 [1] Jews who adopted the Gr language and much of Gr culture through acculturation   6:5 [1] I.e., a Gentile convert to Judaism

him, seventy-five people *in all*. 15 And Jacob went down to Egypt, and he and our fathers died *there*. 16 And they were brought back *from there* to Shechem and laid in the tomb which Abraham had purchased for a sum of money from the sons of Hamor in Shechem.

17 "But as the time of the promise which God had assured to Abraham was approaching, the people increased and multiplied in Egypt, 18 until ANOTHER KING AROSE OVER EGYPT WHO DID NOT KNOW JOSEPH. 19 It was he who shrewdly took advantage of our nation and mistreated our fathers in order that they would abandon their infants *in the Nile,* so that they would not survive. 20 At this time Moses was born; and he was beautiful to God. He was nurtured for three months in his father's home. 21 And after he had been put outside, Pharaoh's daughter took him away and nurtured him as her own son. 22 Moses was educated in all the wisdom of the Egyptians, and he was proficient in speaking and action. 23 But when he was approaching the age of forty, it entered his mind to visit his countrymen, the sons of Israel. 24 And when he saw one *of them* being treated unjustly, he defended and took vengeance for the oppressed man by *fatally* striking the Egyptian. 25 And he thought that his brothers understood that God was granting them deliverance through him; but they did not understand. 26 And on the following day he appeared to them as they were fighting each other, and he tried to reconcile them to peace, by saying, 'Men, you are brothers, why are you injuring each other?' 27 But the one who was injuring his neighbor pushed him away, saying, 'WHO MADE YOU A RULER AND JUDGE OVER US? 28 YOU DO NOT INTEND TO KILL ME AS YOU KILLED THE EGYPTIAN YESTERDAY, DO YOU?' 29 At this remark, MOSES FLED AND BECAME A STRANGER IN THE LAND OF MIDIAN, where he fathered two sons.

30 "After forty years had passed, an angel appeared to him in the wilderness of Mount Sinai, in the flame of a burning thorn bush. 31 When Moses saw *it,* he was astonished at the sight; and as he approached to look *more* closely, the voice of the Lord came: 32 'I AM THE GOD OF YOUR FATHERS, THE GOD OF ABRAHAM, AND ISAAC, AND JACOB.' Moses shook with fear and did not dare to look closely. 33 But the LORD said to him, 'REMOVE YOUR SANDALS FROM YOUR FEET, FOR THE PLACE ON WHICH YOU ARE STANDING IS HOLY GROUND. 34 I HAVE CERTAINLY SEEN THE OPPRESSION OF MY PEOPLE WHO ARE IN EGYPT, AND HAVE HEARD THEIR GROANING, AND I HAVE COME DOWN TO RESCUE THEM; AND NOW COME, I WILL SEND YOU TO EGYPT.'

35 "This Moses whom they disowned, saying, 'WHO MADE YOU A RULER AND A JUDGE?' is the one whom God sent *to be* both a ruler and a deliverer with the help of the angel who appeared to him in the thorn bush. 36 This man led them out, performing wonders and signs in the land of Egypt and in the Red Sea, and in the wilderness for forty years. 37 This is the Moses who said to the sons of Israel, 'GOD WILL RAISE UP FOR YOU A PROPHET LIKE ME FROM YOUR COUNTRYMEN.' 38 This is the one who was in the

assembly in the wilderness together with the angel who spoke to him *at length* on Mount Sinai, and *who was with* our fathers; and he received living words to pass on to you. 39 Our fathers were unwilling to be obedient to him; on the contrary they rejected him and turned back to Egypt in their hearts, 40 saying to Aaron, 'MAKE US A GOD WHO WILL GO BEFORE US; FOR THIS MOSES WHO LED US OUT OF THE LAND OF EGYPT—WE DO NOT KNOW WHAT HAPPENED TO HIM.' 41 At that time they made a calf and brought a sacrifice to the idol, and were rejoicing in the works of their hands. 42 But God turned away and gave them over to serve the heavenly lights; as it is written in the book of the prophets: 'YOU DID NOT OFFER ME VICTIMS AND SACRIFICES FOR FORTY YEARS IN THE WILDERNESS, DID YOU, HOUSE OF ISRAEL? 43 YOU ALSO TOOK ALONG THE TABERNACLE OF MOLOCH AND THE STAR OF YOUR GOD ROMPHA, THE IMAGES WHICH YOU MADE TO WORSHIP. I ALSO WILL DEPORT YOU BEYOND BABYLON.'

44 "Our fathers had the tabernacle of testimony in the wilderness, just as He who spoke to Moses directed *him* to make it according to the pattern which he had seen. 45 Our fathers in turn received it, and they also brought it in with Joshua upon dispossessing the nations that God drove out from our fathers, until the time of David. 46 David found favor in God's sight, and asked that he might find a dwelling place for the ^1 house of Jacob. 47 But it was Solomon who built a house for Him. 48 However, the Most High does not dwell in *houses* made by *human* hands; as the prophet says:

49 'HEAVEN IS MY THRONE,
  AND THE EARTH IS THE FOOTSTOOL OF MY
   FEET;
  WHAT KIND OF HOUSE WILL YOU BUILD FOR
   ME?' says the Lord,
  'OR WHAT PLACE IS THERE FOR MY REST?
50 'WAS IT NOT MY HAND THAT MADE ALL THESE
   THINGS?'

51 "You men who are stiff-necked and uncircumcised in heart and ears are always resisting the Holy Spirit; you are doing just as your fathers did. 52 Which one of the prophets did your fathers not persecute? They killed those who had previously announced the coming of the Righteous One, and you have now become betrayers and murderers of Him; 53 you who received the Law as ordained by angels, and *yet* did not keep it."

Stephen Put to Death

54 Now when they heard this, they were infuriated, and they *began* gnashing their teeth at him. 55 But he, being full of the Holy Spirit, looked intently into heaven and saw the glory of God, and Jesus standing at the right hand of God; 56 and he said, "Behold, I see the heavens opened and the Son of Man standing at the right hand of God." 57 But they shouted with loud voices, and covered their ears and rushed at him with one mind. 58 When they had driven him out of the city, they *began* stoning *him;* and the witnesses laid aside their cloaks at the feet of a young man named Saul. 59 They *went*

7:46 1 I.e., the people of Israel

on stoning Stephen as he called on *the Lord* and said, "Lord Jesus, receive my spirit!" **60** Then he fell on his knees and cried out with a loud voice, "Lord, do not hold this sin against them!" Having said this, he fell asleep.

Saul Persecutes the Church
8 Now Saul approved of putting Stephen to death.

And on that day a great persecution began against the church in Jerusalem, and they were all scattered throughout the regions of Judea and Samaria, except for the apostles. **2** *Some* devout men buried Stephen, and mourned loudly for him. **3** But Saul *began* ravaging the church, entering house after house; and he would drag away men and women and put them in prison.

Philip in Samaria
4 Therefore, those who had been scattered went through *places* preaching the word. **5** Philip went down to the city of Samaria and *began* proclaiming the Christ to them. **6** The crowds were paying attention with one mind to what was being said by Philip, as they heard and saw the signs which he was performing. **7** For in *the case of* many who had unclean spirits, they were coming out *of them* shouting with a loud voice; and many who had been paralyzed or limped *on crutches* were healed. **8** So there was much rejoicing in that city.

9 Now a man named Simon had previously been practicing magic in the city and astonishing the people of Samaria, claiming to be someone great; **10** and all *the people,* from small to great, were paying attention to him, saying, "This man is the Power of God that is called Great." **11** And they were paying attention to him because for a long time he had astounded them with his magic arts. **12** But when they believed Philip as he was preaching the good news about the kingdom of God and the name of Jesus Christ, both men and women were being baptized. **13** Now even Simon himself believed; and after being baptized, he continued on with Philip, and as he observed signs and great miracles taking place, he was *repeatedly* amazed.

14 Now when the apostles in Jerusalem heard that Samaria had received the word of God, they sent them Peter and John, **15** who came down and prayed for them that they would receive the Holy Spirit. **16** (For He had not yet fallen upon any of them; they had simply been baptized in the name of the Lord Jesus.) **17** Then they *began* laying their hands on them, and they were receiving the Holy Spirit. **18** Now when Simon saw that the Spirit was given through the laying on of the apostles' hands, he offered them money, **19** saying, "Give this authority to me as well, so that everyone on whom I lay my hands may receive the Holy Spirit." **20** But Peter said to him, "May your silver perish with you, because you thought you could acquire the gift of God with money! **21** You have no part or share in this matter, for your heart is not right before God. **22** Therefore,

repent of this wickedness of yours, and pray to the Lord *that,* if possible, the intention of your heart will be forgiven you. **23** For I see that you are in the gall of bitterness and in the bondage of unrighteousness." **24** But Simon answered and said, "Pray to the Lord for me yourselves, so that nothing of what you have said may come upon me."

An Ethiopian Receives Christ
25 So, when they had solemnly testified and spoken the word of the Lord, they started back to Jerusalem, and were preaching the gospel to many villages of the Samaritans.

26 But an angel of the Lord spoke to Philip, saying, "Get ready and go south to the road that descends from Jerusalem to Gaza." (This is a desert *road.*) **27** So he got ready and went; and there was an Ethiopian eunuch, a court official of Candace, queen of the Ethiopians, who was in charge of all her treasure; and he had come to Jerusalem to worship, **28** and he was returning and sitting in his chariot, and was reading Isaiah the prophet. **29** Then the Spirit said to Philip, "Go up and join this chariot." **30** Philip ran up and heard him reading Isaiah the prophet, and said, "Do you understand what you are reading?" **31** And he said, "Well, how could I, unless someone guides me?" And he invited Philip to come up and sit with him. **32** Now the passage of Scripture which he was reading was this:

"He was led like a sheep to slaughter;
    And like a lamb that is silent before its
        shearer,
    So He does not open His mouth.
33   "In humiliation His justice was taken away;
    Who will describe His generation?
    For His life is taken away from the
        earth."

34 The eunuch answered Philip and said, "Please *tell me,* of whom does the prophet say this? Of himself, or of someone else?" **35** Then Philip opened his mouth, and beginning from this Scripture he preached Jesus to him. **36** As they went along the road they came to some water; and the eunuch *said, "Look! Water! What prevents me from being baptized?" *1* **38** And he ordered that the chariot stop; and they both went down into the water, Philip as well as the eunuch, and he baptized him. **39** When they came up out of the water, the Spirit of the Lord snatched Philip away; and the eunuch no longer saw him, but went on his way rejoicing. **40** But Philip found himself at Azotus, and as he passed through he kept preaching the gospel to all the cities, until he came to Caesarea.

The Conversion of Saul
9 Now Saul, still breathing threats and murder against the disciples of the Lord, went to the high priest, **2** and asked for letters from him to the synagogues in Damascus, so that if he found any belonging to *the Way, whether men or women, he might bring them in shackles to Jerusalem. **3** Now as he was traveling, it happened that he was approaching

---

8:36 1 Late mss add as v 37: *And Philip said, "If you believe with all your heart, you may." And he answered and said, "I believe that Jesus Christ is the Son of God."* **9:2** 1 See John 14:6

Damascus, and suddenly a light from heaven flashed around him; [4] and he fell to the ground and heard a voice saying to him, "Saul, Saul, why are you persecuting Me?" [5] And he said, "Who are You, Lord?" And He *said,* "I am Jesus whom you are persecuting, [6] but get up and enter the city, and it will be told to you what you must do." [7] The men who traveled with him stood speechless, hearing the voice but seeing no one. [8] Saul got up from the ground, and though his eyes were open, he could see nothing; and leading him by the hand, they brought him into Damascus. [9] And for three days he was without sight, and neither ate nor drank.

[10] Now there was a disciple in Damascus named Ananias; and the Lord said to him in a vision, "Ananias." And he said, "Here I am, Lord." [11] And the Lord *said* to him, "Get up and go to the street called Straight, and inquire at the house of Judas for a man from Tarsus named Saul, for he is praying, [12] and he has seen [1] in a vision a man named Ananias come in and lay his hands on him, so that he might regain his sight." [13] But Ananias answered, "Lord, I have heard from many people about this man, how much harm he did to Your saints in Jerusalem; [14] and here he has authority from the chief priests to arrest all who call on Your name." [15] But the Lord said to him, "Go, for he is a chosen instrument of Mine, to bear My name before the Gentiles and kings and the sons of Israel; [16] for I will show him how much he must suffer in behalf of My name." [17] So Ananias departed and entered the house, and after laying his hands on him said, "Brother Saul, the Lord Jesus, who appeared to you on the road by which you were coming, has sent me so that you may regain your sight and be filled with the Holy Spirit." [18] And immediately *something* like *fish* scales fell from his eyes, and he regained his sight, and he got up and was baptized; [19] and he took food and was strengthened.

Saul Begins to Preach Christ

Now for several days he was with the disciples who were in Damascus, [20] and immediately he *began* to proclaim Jesus in the synagogues, saying, "He is the Son of God." [21] All those hearing *him* continued to be amazed, and were saying, "Is this not the one who in Jerusalem destroyed those who called on this name, and had come here for the purpose of bringing them bound before the chief priests?" [22] But Saul kept increasing in strength and confounding Jews who lived in Damascus by proving that this *Jesus* is the Christ. [23] When many days had elapsed, the Jews plotted together to do away with him, [24] but their plot became known to Saul. They were also closely watching the gates day and night so that they might put him to death; [25] but his disciples took him at night and let him down through *an opening in* the wall, lowering him in a large basket.

[26] When he came to Jerusalem, he tried *repeatedly* to associate with the disciples; and

yet they were all afraid of him, as they did not believe that he was a disciple. [27] But Barnabas took hold of him and brought him to the apostles and described to them how he had seen the Lord on the road, and that He had talked to him, and how he had spoken out boldly in the name of Jesus at Damascus. [28] And he was with them, moving about freely in Jerusalem, speaking out boldly in the name of the Lord. [29] And he was talking and arguing with the Hellenistic *Jews;* but they were attempting to put him to death. [30] Now when the brothers learned *of it,* they brought him down to Caesarea and sent him away to Tarsus.

[31] So the church throughout Judea, Galilee, and Samaria enjoyed peace, as it was being built up; and as it continued in the fear of the Lord and in the comfort of the Holy Spirit, it kept increasing.

Peter's Ministry

[32] Now as Peter was traveling through all *those regions,* he also came down to the saints who lived at Lydda. [33] There he found a man named Aeneas who had been bedridden for eight years, because he was paralyzed. [34] Peter said to him, "Aeneas, Jesus Christ heals you; get up and make your own bed." Immediately he got up. [35] And all who lived at Lydda and Sharon saw him, and they turned to the Lord.

[36] Now in Joppa there was a disciple named Tabitha (which when translated means [1] Dorcas); this woman was excelling in acts of kindness and charity which she did *habitually.* [37] But it happened at that time that she became sick and died; and when they had washed *her body,* they laid *it* in an upstairs room. [38] Since Lydda was near Joppa, the disciples, having heard that Peter was there, sent two men to him, urging him, "Do not delay in coming to us." [39] So Peter got ready and went with them. When he arrived, they brought him into the room upstairs; and all the widows stood beside him, weeping and showing all the [1] tunics and garments that Dorcas used to make while she was with them. [40] But Peter sent them all out and knelt down and prayed, and turning to the body, he said, "Tabitha, arise." And she opened her eyes, and when she saw Peter, she sat up. [41] And he gave her his hand and raised her up; and calling the saints and widows, he presented her alive. [42] It became known all over Joppa, and many believed in the Lord. [43] And *Peter* stayed in Joppa many days with a tanner *named* Simon.

Cornelius' Vision

10 Now *there was* a man in Caesarea named Cornelius, a centurion of what was called the Italian [1] cohort, [2] a devout man and one who feared God with all his household, and made many charitable contributions to the *Jewish* people and prayed to God continually. [3] About the [1] ninth hour of the day he clearly saw in a vision an angel of God who had *just* come in and said to him, "Cornelius!" [4] And he looked at him intently and became terrified, and said, "What is it, lord?" And he

said to him, "Your prayers and charitable gifts have ascended as a memorial offering before God. 5 Now dispatch *some* men to Joppa and send for a man *named* Simon, who is also called Peter; 6 he is staying with a tanner *named* Simon, whose house is by the sea." 7 When the angel who *spoke to him left, he summoned two of his servants and a devout soldier from his personal attendants, 8 and after he had explained everything to them, he sent them to Joppa.

9 On the next day, as they were on their way and approaching the city, Peter went up on the housetop about 1the sixth hour to pray. 10 But he became hungry and wanted to eat; but while they were making preparations, he fell into a trance; 11 and he *saw the sky opened up, and an object like a great sheet coming down, lowered by four corners to the ground, 12 and on it were all *kinds of* four-footed animals and crawling creatures of the earth and birds of the sky. 13 A voice came to him, "Get up, Peter, kill and eat!" 14 But Peter said, "By no means, Lord, for I have never eaten anything unholy and unclean." 15 Again a voice *came to him a second time, "What God has cleansed, no *longer* consider unholy." 16 This happened three times, and immediately the object was taken up into the sky.

17 Now while Peter was greatly perplexed in mind as to what the vision which he had seen might mean, behold, the men who had been sent by Cornelius had asked directions to Simon's house, and they appeared at the gate; 18 and calling out, they were asking whether Simon, who was also called Peter, was staying there. 19 While Peter was reflecting on the vision, the Spirit said to him, "Behold, three men are looking for you. 20 But get up, go downstairs and accompany them without misgivings, for I have sent them Myself." 21 Peter went down to the men and said, "Behold, I am the one you are looking for; what is the reason for which you have come?" 22 They said, "Cornelius, a centurion, a righteous and God-fearing man well spoken of by the entire nation of the Jews, was *divinely* directed by a holy angel to send for you *to come* to his house and hear a message from you." 23 So he invited them in and gave them lodging.

Peter in Caesarea

Now on the next day he got ready and went away with them, and some of the brothers from Joppa accompanied him. 24 On the following day he entered Caesarea. Now Cornelius was expecting them and had called together his relatives and close friends. 25 When Peter entered, Cornelius met him, and fell at his feet and worshiped *him.* 26 But Peter helped him up, saying, "Stand up; I, too, am just a man." 27 As he talked with him, he entered and *found many people assembled. 28 And he said to them, "You yourselves know that it is forbidden for a Jewish man to associate with or visit a foreigner; and *yet* God has shown me that I am not to call any person

unholy or unclean. 29 That is why I came without even raising any objection when I was sent for. So I ask, for what reason did you send for me?"

30 Cornelius said, "Four days ago to this hour, I was praying in my house during the 1ninth hour; and behold, a man stood before me in shining clothing, 31 and he *said, 'Cornelius, your prayer has been heard and your charitable gifts have been remembered before God. 32 Therefore send *some men* to Joppa and invite Simon, who is also called Peter, to come to you; he is staying at the house of Simon *the* tanner, by the sea.' 33 So I sent *men* to you immediately, and you have been kind enough to come. Now then, we are all here present before God to hear everything that you have been commanded by the Lord."

Gentiles Hear Good News

34 Opening his mouth, Peter said: "I most certainly understand *now* that God is not one to show partiality, 35 but in every nation the one who fears Him and does what is right is acceptable to Him. 36 The word which He sent to the sons of Israel, preaching peace through Jesus Christ (He is Lord of all)—37 you yourselves know the thing that happened throughout Judea, starting from Galilee, after the baptism which John proclaimed. 38 *You know of* Jesus of Nazareth, how God anointed Him with the Holy Spirit and with power, and *how* He went about doing good and healing all who were oppressed by the devil, for God was with Him. 39 We are witnesses of all the things that He did both in the country of the Jews and in Jerusalem. They also put Him to death by hanging Him on 1a cross. 40 God raised Him up on the third day and granted that He be revealed, 41 not to all the people, but to witnesses who had been chosen beforehand by God, *that is,* to us who ate and drank with Him after He arose from the dead. 42 And He ordered us to preach to the people, and to testify solemnly that this is the One who has been appointed by God as Judge of the living and the dead. 43 All the prophets testify of Him, that through His name everyone who believes in Him receives forgiveness of sins."

44 While Peter was still speaking these words, the Holy Spirit fell upon all those who were listening to the message. 45 All the 1Jewish believers who came with Peter were amazed, because the gift of the Holy Spirit had also been poured out on the Gentiles. 46 For they were hearing them speaking with tongues and exalting God. Then Peter responded, 47 "Surely no one can refuse the water for these to be baptized, who have received the Holy Spirit just as we *did,* can he?" 48 And he ordered them to be baptized in the name of Jesus Christ. Then they asked him to stay on for a few days.

Peter Reports in Jerusalem

11 Now the apostles and the brothers *and sisters* who were throughout Judea heard that the Gentiles also had received the

---

10:9 1 I.e., noon   **10:30** 1 I.e., 3 to 4 p.m.   **10:39** 1 Lit *wood;* see Deut 21:23   **10:45** 1 Lit *believers from the circumcision*

word of God. 2 And when Peter came up to Jerusalem, 1the Jewish *believers* took issue with him, 3 saying, "You went to 1uncircumcised men and ate with them." 4 But Peter began and explained *at length* to them in an orderly sequence, saying, 5 "I was in the city of Joppa praying; and in a trance I saw a vision, an object coming down like a great sheet lowered by four corners from the sky; and it came to where I *was,* 6 and I stared at it and was thinking about it, and I saw the four-footed animals of the earth, the wild animals, the crawling creatures, and the birds of the sky. 7 I also heard a voice saying to me, 'Get up, Peter; kill and eat.' 8 But I said, 'By no means, Lord, for nothing unholy or unclean has ever entered my mouth.' 9 But a voice from heaven answered a second time, 'What God has cleansed, no longer consider unholy.' 10 This happened three times, and everything was drawn back up into the sky. 11 And behold, at that moment three men who had been sent to me from Caesarea came up to the house where we were *staying.* 12 And the Spirit told me to go with them without misgivings. These six brothers also went with me, and we entered the man's house. 13 And he reported to us how he had seen the angel standing in his house, and saying, 'Send *some men* to Joppa and have Simon, who is also called Peter, brought here; 14 and he will speak words to you by which you will be saved, you and all your household.' 15 And as I began to speak, the Holy Spirit fell upon them just as *He did* upon us at the beginning. 16 And I remembered the word of the Lord, how He used to say, 'John baptized with water, but you will be baptized with the Holy Spirit.' 17 Therefore, if God gave them the same gift as *He* also *gave* to us after believing in the Lord Jesus Christ, who was I that I could stand in God's way?" 18 When they heard this, they quieted down and glorified God, saying, "Well then, God has also granted to the Gentiles the repentance *that leads* to life."

The Church in Antioch

19 So then those who were scattered because of the persecution that occurred in connection with Stephen made their way to Phoenicia, Cyprus, and Antioch, speaking the word to no one except to Jews alone. 20 But there were some of them, men of Cyprus and Cyrene, who came to Antioch and *began* speaking to the 1Greeks as well, preaching the good news of the Lord Jesus. 21 And the hand of the Lord was with them, and a large number who believed turned to the Lord. 22 The news about them reached the ears of the church in Jerusalem, and they sent Barnabas off to Antioch. 23 Then when he arrived and witnessed the grace of God, he rejoiced and *began* to encourage them all with resolute heart to remain *true* to the Lord; 24 for he was a good man, and full of the Holy Spirit and faith. And considerable numbers were added to the Lord. 25 And he left for Tarsus to look for Saul; 26 and when he had found him, he brought him to Antioch. And for an entire year they met with the church and

taught considerable numbers of people; and the disciples were first called Christians in Antioch.
27 Now at this time *some* prophets came down from Jerusalem to Antioch. 28 One of them, named Agabus, stood up and indicated by the Spirit that there would definitely be a severe famine all over the world. And this took place in the *reign* of Claudius. 29 And to the extent that any of the disciples had means, each of them determined to send a *contribution* for the relief of the brothers *and sisters* living in Judea. 30 And they did this, sending it with Barnabas and Saul to the elders.

Peter's Arrest and Deliverance

12 Now about that time Herod the king laid hands on some who belonged to the church, to do them harm. 2 And he had James the brother of John executed with a sword. 3 When he saw that it pleased the Jews, he proceeded to arrest Peter as well. (Now *these* were 1the days of Unleavened Bread.) 4 When he had arrested him, he put him in prison, turning him over to four squads of soldiers to guard him, intending *only* after the Passover to bring him before the people. 5 So Peter was kept in the prison, but prayer for him was being made to God intensely by the church.
6 On the very night when Herod was about to bring him forward, Peter was sleeping between two soldiers, bound with two chains, and guards in front of the door were watching over the prison. 7 And behold, an angel of the Lord suddenly stood near *Peter,* and a light shone in the cell; and he struck Peter's side and woke him, saying, "Get up quickly." And his chains fell off his hands. 8 And the angel said to him, "Put on your belt and strap on your sandals." And he did so. And he *said to him, "Wrap your cloak around you and follow me." 9 And he went out and continued to follow, and *yet* he did not know that what was being done by the angel was real, but thought he was seeing a vision. 10 Now when they had passed the first and second guard, they came to the iron gate that leads into the city, which opened for them by itself; and they went out and went along one street, and immediately the angel departed from him. 11 When Peter came to himself, he said, "Now I know for sure that the Lord has sent forth His angel and rescued me from the hand of Herod and from all that the Jewish people were expecting." 12 And when he realized *this,* he went to the house of Mary, the mother of John, who was also called Mark, where many were gathered together and were praying. 13 When he knocked at the door of the gate, a slave woman named Rhoda came to answer. 14 When she recognized Peter's voice, because of her joy she did not open the gate, but ran in and announced that Peter was standing in front of the gate. 15 They said to her, "You are out of your mind!" But she kept insisting that it was so. They said, "It is his angel." 16 But Peter continued knocking; and when they had opened *the door,* they saw him and were amazed.

11:2 1 Lit *those from the circumcision*   11:3 1 I.e., Gentiles   11:20 1 Lit *Hellenists;* people who lived by Greek customs and culture   12:3 1 I.e., Passover week

17 But motioning to them with his hand to be silent, he described to them how the Lord had led him out of the prison. And he said, "Report these things to James and the brothers." Then he left and went to another place.

18 Now when day came, there was no small disturbance among the soldiers *as to* what could have become of Peter. 19 When Herod had searched for him and had not found him, he examined the guards and ordered that they be led away *to execution.* Then he went down from Judea to Caesarea and was spending time there.

Death of Herod

20 Now he was very angry with the people of Tyre and Sidon; and with one mind they came to him, and having won over Blastus the king's chamberlain, they were asking for peace, because their country was supported *with grain* from the king's country. 21 On an appointed day, after putting on his royal apparel, Herod took his seat on the rostrum and *began* delivering an address to them. 22 The people *repeatedly* cried out, "The voice of a god and not of a man!" 23 And immediately an angel of the Lord struck him because he did not give God the glory, and he was eaten by worms and died.

24 But the word of the Lord continued to grow and to be multiplied.

25 And Barnabas and Saul returned when they had fulfilled their mission to Jerusalem, taking along with *them* John, who was also called Mark.

First Missionary Journey

13 Now there were prophets and teachers at Antioch, in the church that was *there:* Barnabas, Simeon who was called Niger, Lucius of Cyrene, Manaen who had been brought up with Herod the tetrarch, and Saul. 2 While they were serving the Lord and fasting, the Holy Spirit said, "Set Barnabas and Saul apart for Me for the work to which I have called them." 3 Then, when they had fasted, prayed, and laid their hands on them, they sent them away.

4 So, being sent out by the Holy Spirit, they went down to Seleucia and from there they sailed to Cyprus. 5 When they reached Salamis, they *began* to proclaim the word of God in the synagogues of the Jews; and they also had John as their helper. 6 When they had gone through the whole island as far as Paphos, they found a magician, a Jewish false prophet whose name was Bar-Jesus, 7 who was with the proconsul, Sergius Paulus, a man of intelligence. This man summoned Barnabas and Saul and sought to hear the word of God. 8 But Elymas the magician (for so his name is translated) was opposing them, seeking to turn the proconsul away from the faith. 9 But Saul, who was also *known as* Paul, filled with the Holy Spirit, stared at him, 10 and said, "You who are full of all deceit and fraud, you son of the devil, you enemy of all righteousness, will you not stop making crooked the straight ways of the Lord? 11 Now, behold, the hand of the Lord is upon you, and you will be blind and not see the sun for a time." And immediately a mist and a darkness fell upon him, and he went about seeking those who would lead him by the hand. 12 Then the proconsul believed when he saw what had happened, being amazed at the teaching of the Lord.

13 Now Paul and his companions put out to sea from Paphos and came to Perga in Pamphylia; but John left them and returned to Jerusalem. 14 But going on from Perga, they arrived at Pisidian Antioch, and on the Sabbath day they went into the synagogue and sat down. 15 After the reading of the Law and the Prophets, the synagogue officials sent *word* to them, saying, "Brothers, if you have any word of exhortation for the people, say it." 16 Paul stood up, and motioning with his hand said,

"Men of Israel, and you who fear God, listen: 17 The God of this people Israel chose our fathers and made the people great during their stay in the land of Egypt, and with an uplifted arm He led them out from it. 18 For a period of about forty years He put up with them in the wilderness. 19 When He had destroyed seven nations in the land of Canaan, He distributed their land as an inheritance—*all of which took* about 450 years. 20 After these things He gave *them* judges until Samuel the prophet. 21 Then they asked for a king, and God gave them Saul the son of Kish, a man of the tribe of Benjamin, for forty years. 22 After He had removed him, He raised up David to be their king, concerning whom He also testified and said, 'I have found David, the son of Jesse, a man after My heart, who will do all My will.' 23 From the descendants of this man, according to promise, God has brought to Israel a Savior, Jesus, 24 after John had proclaimed, before His coming, a baptism of repentance to all the people of Israel. 25 And while John was completing his course, he kept saying, 'What do you suppose that I am? I am not *He.* But behold, one is coming after me, the sandals of whose feet I am not worthy to untie.'

26 "Brothers, sons of Abraham's family, and those among you who fear God, to us the message of this salvation has been sent. 27 For those who live in Jerusalem, and their rulers, recognizing neither Him nor the declarations of the prophets which are read every Sabbath, fulfilled *these* by condemning *Him.* 28 And though they found no grounds for *putting Him to* death, they asked Pilate that He be executed. 29 When they had carried out everything that was written concerning Him, they took Him down from the *1*cross and laid Him in a tomb. 30 But God raised Him from the dead; 31 and for many days He appeared to those who came up with Him from Galilee to Jerusalem, the very ones who are now His witnesses to the people. 32 And we preach to you the good news of the promise made to the fathers, 33 that God has fulfilled this *promise* to those of us *who are the* descendants by raising Jesus, as it is also written in the second Psalm: 'YOU ARE MY SON; TODAY I HAVE FATHERED YOU.' 34 *As for the fact* that He raised Him from the dead, never again to return to decay, He has spoken in this way: 'I WILL GIVE YOU THE HOLY AND FAITHFUL *MERCIES* OF DAVID.' 35 Therefore,

---

13:29 1 Lit *wood;* see Deut 21:23

He also says in another *Psalm:* 'YOU WILL NOT ALLOW YOUR HOLY ONE TO UNDERGO DECAY.' **36** For David, after he had served God's purpose in his own generation, fell asleep, and was buried among his fathers and underwent decay; **37** but He whom God raised did not undergo decay. **38** Therefore let it be known to you, brothers, that through Him forgiveness of sins is proclaimed to you, **39** and through Him everyone who believes is freed from all things, from which you could not be freed through the Law of Moses. **40** Therefore, see that the thing spoken of in the Prophets does not come upon *you:*

41   'LOOK, YOU SCOFFERS, AND BE ASTONISHED,
        AND PERISH;
    FOR I AM ACCOMPLISHING A WORK IN YOUR
        DAYS,
    A WORK WHICH YOU WILL NEVER BELIEVE,
        THOUGH SOMEONE SHOULD DESCRIBE IT TO
        YOU.' "

42 As Paul and Barnabas were going out, *the people repeatedly* begged to have these things spoken to them the next Sabbath. **43** Now when *the meeting of* the synagogue had broken up, many of the Jews and the God-fearing proselytes followed Paul and Barnabas, who were speaking to them and urging them to continue in the grace of God.

Paul Turns to the Gentiles

44 The next Sabbath nearly all the city assembled to hear the word of the Lord. **45** But when the Jews saw the crowds, they were filled with jealousy and *began* contradicting the things spoken by Paul, and were blaspheming. **46** Paul and Barnabas spoke out boldly and said, "It was necessary that the word of God be spoken to you first. Since you repudiate it and consider yourselves unworthy of eternal life, behold, we are turning to the Gentiles. **47** For so the Lord has commanded us,
    'I HAVE APPOINTED YOU AS A LIGHT TO THE
        GENTILES,
    THAT YOU MAY BRING SALVATION TO THE END
        OF THE EARTH.' "

48 When the Gentiles heard this, they *began* rejoicing and glorifying the word of the Lord; and all who had been appointed to eternal life believed. **49** And the word of the Lord was being spread through the whole region. **50** But the Jews incited the devout women of prominence and the leading men of the city, and instigated a persecution against Paul and Barnabas, and drove them out of their region. **51** But they shook off the dust *from* their feet *in protest* against them and went to Iconium. **52** And the disciples were continually filled with joy and with the Holy Spirit.

Acceptance and Opposition

14 In Iconium they entered the synagogue of the Jews together, and spoke in such a way that a large number of people believed, both of Jews and of Greeks. **2** But the unbelieving Jews stirred up the minds of the Gentiles and embittered them against the brothers. **3** Therefore they spent a long time *there* speaking boldly *with reliance* upon the

Lord, who was testifying to the word of His grace, granting that signs and wonders be performed by their hands. **4** But the people of the city were divided; and some sided with the Jews, while others, with the apostles. **5** And when an attempt was made by both the Gentiles and the Jews with their rulers, to treat them abusively and to stone them, **6** they became aware of it and fled to the cities of Lycaonia, Lystra and Derbe, and the surrounding region; **7** and there they continued to preach the gospel.

8 In Lystra a man was sitting whose feet were incapacitated. *He had been* disabled from his mother's womb, and had never walked. **9** This man was listening to Paul as he spoke. *Paul* looked at him intently and saw that he had faith to be made well, **10** and he said with a loud voice, "Stand upright on your feet!" And *the man* leaped up and *began* to walk. **11** When the crowds saw what Paul had done, they raised their voice, saying in the Lycaonian language, "The gods have become like men and have come down to us!" **12** And they *began* calling Barnabas, Zeus, and Paul, Hermes, since he was the chief speaker. **13** Moreover, the priest of Zeus, whose *temple* was just outside the city, brought oxen and garlands to the gates, and wanted to offer sacrifice with the crowds. **14** But when the apostles Barnabas and Paul heard *about it,* they tore their robes and rushed out into the crowd, crying out **15** and saying, "Men, why are you doing these things? We are also men, of the same nature as you, preaching the gospel to you, to turn from these ¹useless things to a living God, who MADE THE HEAVEN AND THE EARTH AND THE SEA, AND EVERYTHING THAT IS IN THEM. **16** In past generations He permitted all the nations to go their own ways; **17** yet He did not leave Himself without witness, in that He did good and gave you rains from heaven and fruitful seasons, satisfying your hearts with food and gladness." **18** And *even by* saying these things, *only with* difficulty did they restrain the crowds from offering sacrifices to them.

19 But Jews came from Antioch and Iconium, and having won over the crowds, they stoned Paul and dragged him out of the city, thinking that he was dead. **20** But while the disciples stood around him, he got up and entered the city. The next day he left with Barnabas for Derbe. **21** And after they had preached the gospel to that city and had made a good number of disciples, they returned to Lystra, to Iconium, and to Antioch, **22** strengthening the souls of the disciples, encouraging them to continue in the faith, and *saying,* "*It is* through many tribulations *that* we must enter the kingdom of God." **23** When they had appointed elders for them in every church, having prayed with fasting, they entrusted them to the Lord in whom they had believed.

24 They passed through Pisidia and came into Pamphylia. **25** When they had spoken the word in Perga, they went down to Attalia. **26** From there they sailed to Antioch, where they had been entrusted to the grace of God for the work that they had accomplished. **27** When

---

14:15 ¹ I.e., idols

they had arrived and gathered the church together, they *began* to report all the things that God had done with them and how He had opened a door of faith to the Gentiles. 28 And they spent a long time with the disciples.

The Council in Jerusalem

15 Some men came down from Judea and *began* teaching the brothers, "Unless you are circumcised according to the custom of Moses, you cannot be saved." 2 And after Paul and Barnabas had a heated argument and debate with them, *the brothers* determined that Paul and Barnabas and some others of them should go up to Jerusalem to the apostles and elders concerning this issue. 3 Therefore, after being sent on their way by the church, they were passing through both Phoenicia and Samaria, describing in detail the conversion of the Gentiles, and they were bringing great joy to all the brothers *and sisters.* 4 When they arrived in Jerusalem, they were received by the church, the apostles, and the elders, and they reported all that God had done with them. 5 But some of the sect of the Pharisees who had believed stood up, saying, "It is necessary to circumcise ¹them and to direct them to keep the Law of Moses."

6 The apostles and the elders came together to look into this matter. 7 After there had been much debate, Peter stood up and said to them, "Brothers, you know that in the early days God made a choice among you, that by my mouth the Gentiles would hear the word of the gospel and believe. 8 And God, who knows the heart, testified to them giving them the Holy Spirit, just as He also did to us; 9 and He made no distinction between us and them, cleansing their hearts by faith. 10 Since this *is the* case, why are you putting God to the test by placing upon the neck of the disciples a yoke which neither our forefathers nor we have been able to bear? 11 But we believe that we are saved through the grace of the Lord Jesus, in the same way as they also are."

12 All the people kept silent, and they were listening to Barnabas and Paul as they were relating all the signs and wonders that God had done through them among the Gentiles.

James' Judgment

13 After they stopped speaking, James responded, saying, "Brothers, listen to me. 14 Simeon has described how God first concerned Himself about taking a people for His name from among the Gentiles. 15 The words of the Prophets agree with this, just as it is written:
16 'AFTER THESE THINGS I will return,
    AND I WILL REBUILD THE FALLEN TABERNACLE
       OF DAVID,
    AND I WILL REBUILD ITS RUINS,
    AND I WILL RESTORE IT,
17 SO THAT THE REST OF MANKIND MAY SEEK THE
       LORD,
    AND ALL THE GENTILES WHO ARE CALLED BY
       MY NAME,'
18 SAYS THE LORD, WHO MAKES THESE THINGS
       known from long ago.

19 Therefore, it is my judgment that we do not cause trouble for those from the Gentiles who are turning to God, 20 but that we write to them that they abstain from things contaminated by idols, from *acts of* sexual immorality, from what has been strangled, and from blood. 21 For from ancient generations Moses has those who preach him in every city, since he is read in the synagogues every Sabbath."

22 Then it seemed good to the apostles and the elders, with the whole church, to choose men from among them to send to Antioch with Paul and Barnabas: Judas who was called Barsabbas, and Silas, leading men among the brothers, 23 and they sent this letter with them:

"The apostles and the brothers who are elders, to the brothers *and sisters* in Antioch, Syria, and Cilicia who are from the Gentiles: Greetings. 24 Since we have heard that some of our number to whom we gave no instruction have confused you by *their* teaching, upsetting your souls, 25 it seemed good to us, having become of one mind, to select men to send to you with our beloved Barnabas and Paul, 26 men who have risked their lives for the name of our Lord Jesus Christ. 27 Therefore, we have sent Judas and Silas, who themselves will also report the same things by word *of mouth.* 28 For it seemed good to the Holy Spirit and to us to lay upon you no greater burden than these essentials: 29 that you abstain from things sacrificed to idols, from blood, from things strangled, and from *acts of* sexual immorality; if you keep yourselves free from such things, you will do well. Farewell."

30 So when they were sent away, they went down to Antioch; and after gathering the congregation together, they delivered the letter. 31 When they had read it, they rejoiced because of its encouragement. 32 Judas and Silas, also being prophets themselves, encouraged and strengthened the brothers *and sisters* with a lengthy message. 33 After they had spent time *there,* they were sent away from the brothers *and sisters* in peace to those who had sent them out. ¹ 35 But Paul and Barnabas stayed in Antioch, teaching and preaching the word of the Lord, with many others also.

Second Missionary Journey

36 After some days Paul said to Barnabas, "Let's return and visit the brothers *and sisters* in every city in which we proclaimed the word of the Lord, *and see* how they are." 37 Barnabas wanted to take John, called Mark, along with them also. 38 But Paul was of the opinion that they should not take along with them this man who had deserted them in Pamphylia and had not gone with them to the work. 39 Now it turned into such a sharp disagreement that they separated from one another, and Barnabas took Mark with him and sailed away to Cyprus. 40 But Paul chose Silas, and left after being entrusted by the brothers to the grace of the Lord. 41 And he was traveling through Syria and Cilicia, strengthening the churches.

15:5 ¹ I.e., Gentile believers   15:33 ¹ Late mss add as v 34: *But it seemed good to Silas to remain there.*

The Macedonian Vision

16 Now *Paul* also came to Derbe and to Lystra. And a disciple was there, named Timothy, the son of a Jewish woman who was a believer, but his father was a Greek, 2 and he was well spoken of by the brothers *and sisters* who were in Lystra and Iconium. 3 Paul wanted this man to leave with him; and he took him and circumcised him because of the Jews who were in those parts, for they all knew that his father was a Greek. 4 Now while they were passing through the cities, they were delivering the ordinances for them to follow which had been determined by the apostles and elders in Jerusalem. 5 So the churches were being strengthened in the faith, and were increasing in number daily.

6 They passed through the Phrygian and Galatian region, after being forbidden by the Holy Spirit to speak the word in Asia; 7 and after they came to Mysia, they were trying to go into Bithynia, and the Spirit of Jesus did not allow them; 8 and passing by Mysia, they went down to Troas. 9 And a vision appeared to Paul in the night: a man of Macedonia was standing and pleading with him, and saying, "Come over to Macedonia and help us." 10 When he had seen the vision, we immediately sought to leave for Macedonia, concluding that God had called us to preach the gospel to them.

11 So after setting sail from Troas, we ran a straight course to Samothrace, and on the following *day* to Neapolis; 12 and from there to Philippi, which is a leading city of the district of Macedonia, a *Roman* colony; and we were spending some days in this city. 13 And on the Sabbath day we went outside the gate to a riverside, where we were thinking that there was a place of prayer; and we sat down and began speaking to the women who had assembled.

First Convert in Europe

14 A woman named Lydia was listening; *she was* a seller of purple fabrics from the city of Thyatira, *and* a worshiper of God. The Lord opened her heart to respond to the things spoken by Paul. 15 Now when she and her household had been baptized, she urged *us,* saying, "If you have judged me to be faithful to the Lord, come into my house and stay." And she prevailed upon us.

16 It happened that as we were going to the place of prayer, a slave woman who had a spirit of divination met us, who was bringing great profit to her masters by fortune-telling. 17 She followed Paul and us and cried out *repeatedly,* saying, "These men are bond-servants of the Most High God, who are proclaiming to you a way of salvation." 18 Now she continued doing this for many days. But Paul was greatly annoyed, and he turned and said to the spirit, "I command you in the name of Jesus Christ to come out of her!" And it came out at that very moment.

19 But when her masters saw that their hope of profit was *suddenly* gone, they seized Paul and Silas and dragged them into the marketplace before the authorities, 20 and when they had brought them to the chief magistrates, they

said, "These men, Jews as they are, are causing our city trouble, 21 and they are proclaiming customs that are not lawful for us to accept or to practice, *since* we are Romans."

Paul and Silas Imprisoned

22 The crowd joined in an attack against them, and the chief magistrates tore their robes off them and proceeded to order *them* to be beaten with rods. 23 When they had struck them with many blows, they threw them into prison, commanding the jailer to guard them securely; 24 and he, having received such a command, threw them into the inner prison and fastened their feet in the stocks.

25 Now about midnight Paul and Silas were praying and singing hymns of praise to God, and the prisoners were listening to them; 26 and suddenly there was a great earthquake, so that the foundations of the prison were shaken; and immediately all the doors were opened, and everyone's chains were unfastened. 27 When the jailer awoke and saw the prison doors opened, he drew *his* sword and was about to kill himself, thinking that the prisoners had escaped. 28 But Paul called out with a loud voice, saying, "Do not harm yourself, for we are all here!" 29 And *the jailer* asked for lights and rushed in, and trembling with fear, he fell down before Paul and Silas; 30 and after he brought them out, he said, "Sirs, what must I do to be saved?"

The Jailer Converted

31 They said, "Believe in the Lord Jesus, and you will be saved, you and your household." 32 And they spoke the word of God to him together with all who were in his house. 33 And he took them that *very* hour of the night and washed their wounds, and immediately he was baptized, he and all his *household.* 34 And he brought them into his house and set food before them, and was overjoyed, since he had become a believer in God together with his whole household.

35 Now when day came, the chief magistrates sent their officers, saying, "Release those men." 36 And the jailer reported these words to Paul, *saying,* "The chief magistrates have sent *word* that you be released. So come out now and go in peace." 37 But Paul said to them, "After beating us in public without due process—men *who* are Romans—they threw us into prison; and now they are releasing us secretly? No indeed! On the contrary, let them come in person and lead us out." 38 The officers reported these words to the chief magistrates. And they became fearful when they heard that they were Romans, 39 and they came and pleaded with them, and when they had led them out, they *repeatedly* asked them to leave the city. 40 They left the prison and entered *the house of* Lydia, and when they saw the brothers *and sisters,* they encouraged *them* and departed.

Paul in Thessalonica

17 Now when they had traveled through Amphipolis and Apollonia, they came to Thessalonica, where there was a synagogue of

the Jews. 2 And according to Paul's custom, he visited them, and for three Sabbaths reasoned with them from the Scriptures, 3 explaining and giving evidence that the Christ had to suffer and rise from the dead, and *saying,* "This Jesus whom I am proclaiming to you is the Christ." 4 And some of them were persuaded and joined Paul and Silas, along with a large number of the God-fearing Greeks and a significant number of the leading women. 5 But the Jews, becoming jealous and taking along some wicked men from the marketplace, formed a mob and set the city in an uproar; and they attacked the house of Jason and were seeking to bring them out to the people. 6 When they did not find them, they *began* dragging Jason and some brothers before the city authorities, shouting, "These men who have upset the world have come here also; 7 and Jason has welcomed them, and they all act contrary to the decrees of Caesar, saying that there is another king, Jesus." 8 They stirred up the crowd and the city authorities who heard these things. 9 And when they had received a pledge from Jason and the others, they released them.

Paul in Berea

10 The brothers immediately sent Paul and Silas away by night to Berea, and when they arrived, they went into the synagogue of the Jews. 11 Now these people were more noble-minded than those in Thessalonica, for they received the word with great eagerness, examining the Scriptures daily *to see* whether these things were so. 12 Therefore, many of them believed, along with a significant number of prominent Greek women and men. 13 But when the Jews of Thessalonica found out that the word of God had been proclaimed by Paul in Berea also, they came there as well, agitating and stirring up the crowds. 14 Then immediately the brothers sent Paul out to go as far as the sea; and Silas and Timothy remained there. 15 Now those who escorted Paul brought him as far as Athens; and receiving a command for Silas and Timothy to come to him as soon as possible, they left.

Paul in Athens

16 Now while Paul was waiting for them in Athens, his spirit was being provoked within him as he observed that the city was full of idols. 17 So he was reasoning in the synagogue with the Jews and the God-fearing *Gentiles,* and in the marketplace every day with those who happened to be present. 18 And some of the Epicurean and Stoic philosophers as well were conversing with him. Some were saying, "What could this scavenger of tidbits want to say?" Others, "He seems to be a proclaimer of strange deities,"—because he was preaching Jesus and the resurrection. 19 And they took him and brought him to the ¹Areopagus, saying, "May we know what this new teaching is which you are proclaiming? 20 For you are bringing some strange things to our ears; so we want to know what these things mean." 21 (Now all the Athenians and the strangers

visiting there used to spend their time in nothing other than telling or hearing something new.)

Sermon on Mars Hill

22 So Paul stood in the midst of the Areopagus and said, "Men of Athens, I see that you are very religious in all respects. 23 For while I was passing through and examining the objects of your worship, I also found an altar with this inscription, 'TO AN UNKNOWN GOD.' Therefore, what you worship in ignorance, this I proclaim to you. 24 The God who made the world and everything that is in it, since He is Lord of heaven and earth, does not dwell in temples made by hands; 25 nor is He served by human hands, as though He needed anything, since He Himself gives to all *people* life and breath and all things; 26 and He made from one *man* every nation of mankind to live on all the face of the earth, having determined *their* appointed times and the boundaries of their habitation, 27 that they would seek God, if perhaps they might feel around for Him and find *Him,* though He is not far from each one of us; 28 for in Him we live and move and exist, as even some of your own poets have said, 'For we also are His descendants.' 29 Therefore, since we are the descendants of God, we ought not to think that the Divine *Nature* is like gold or silver or stone, an image formed by human skill and thought. 30 So having overlooked the times of ignorance, God is now proclaiming to mankind that all people everywhere are to repent, 31 because He has set a day on which He will judge the world in righteousness through a Man whom He has appointed, having furnished proof to all people by raising Him from the dead."

32 Now when they heard of the resurrection of the dead, some *began* to scoff, but others said, "We shall hear from you again concerning this." 33 So Paul went out from among them. 34 But some men joined him and believed, among whom also were Dionysius the Areopagite and a woman named Damaris, and others with them.

Paul in Corinth

18 After these *events* Paul left Athens and went to Corinth. 2 And he found a Jew named Aquila, a native of Pontus having recently come from Italy with his wife Priscilla, because Claudius had commanded all the Jews to leave Rome. He came to them, 3 and because he was of the same trade he stayed with them, and they worked *together,* for they were tent-makers by trade. 4 And *Paul* was reasoning in the synagogue every Sabbath and trying to persuade Jews and Greeks.

5 But when Silas and Timothy came down from Macedonia, Paul *began* devoting himself completely to the word, testifying to the Jews that Jesus was the Christ. 6 But when they resisted and blasphemed, he shook out his garments and said to them, "Your blood *is* on your own heads! I am clean. From now on I will go to the Gentiles." 7 Then he left the

synagogue and went to the house of a man named Titius Justus, a worshiper of God, whose house was next door to the synagogue. 8 Crispus, the leader of the synagogue, believed in the Lord together with his entire household; and many of the Corinthians, as they listened *to Paul,* were believing and being baptized. 9 And the Lord said to Paul by a vision at night, "Do not be afraid *any longer,* but go on speaking and do not be silent; 10 for I am with you, and no one will attack you to harm you, for I have many people in this city." 11 And he settled *there* for a year and six months, teaching the word of God among them.

12 But while Gallio was proconsul of Achaia, the Jews rose up together against Paul and brought him before the judgment seat, 13 saying, "This man is inciting the people to worship God contrary to the *'*law." 14 But when Paul was about to open his mouth, Gallio said to the Jews, "If it were *a matter of* some crime or vicious, unscrupulous act, O Jews, it would be reasonable for me to put up with you; 15 but if there are questions about teaching and persons and your own law, see to it yourselves; I am unwilling to be a judge of these matters." 16 And he drove them away from the judgment seat. 17 But they all took hold of Sosthenes, the leader of the synagogue, and *began* beating him in front of the judgment seat. And *yet* Gallio was not concerned about any of these things.

18 Now Paul, when he had remained many days longer, took leave of the brothers *and sisters* and sailed away to Syria, and Priscilla and Aquila were with him. Paul *first* had his hair cut at Cenchrea, for he was keeping a vow. 19 They came to Ephesus, and he left them there. Now he himself entered the synagogue and reasoned with the Jews. 20 When they asked him to stay for a longer time, he did not consent, 21 but took leave of them and said, "I will return to you again if God wills," and he set sail from Ephesus.

22 When he had landed in Caesarea, he went up *to Jerusalem* and greeted the church, and went down to Antioch.

Third Missionary Journey

23 And after spending some time *there,* he left and passed successively through the Galatian region and Phrygia, strengthening all the disciples.

24 Now a Jew named Apollos, an Alexandrian by birth, an eloquent man, came to Ephesus; and he was proficient in the Scriptures. 25 This man had been instructed in the way of the Lord; and being fervent in spirit, he was accurately speaking and teaching things about Jesus, being acquainted only with the baptism of John; 26 and he began speaking boldly in the synagogue. But when Priscilla and Aquila heard him, they took him aside and explained the way of God more accurately to him. 27 And when he wanted to go across to Achaia, the brothers encouraged him and wrote to the disciples to welcome him; and when he had arrived, he greatly helped those who had believed through grace, 28 for he

powerfully refuted the Jews in public, demonstrating by the Scriptures that Jesus was the Christ.

Paul in Ephesus

19 Now it happened that while Apollos was in Corinth, Paul passed through the upper country and came to Ephesus, and found some disciples. 2 He said to them, "Did you receive the Holy Spirit when you believed?" And they *said* to him, "On the contrary, we have not even heard if there is a Holy Spirit." 3 And he said, "Into what then were you baptized?" And they said, "Into John's baptism." 4 Paul said, "John baptized with a baptism of repentance, telling the people to believe in Him who was coming after him, that is, in Jesus." 5 When they heard this, they were baptized in the name of the Lord Jesus. 6 And when Paul had laid hands upon them, the Holy Spirit came on them and they *began* speaking with tongues and prophesying. 7 There were about twelve men in all.

8 And he entered the synagogue and continued speaking out boldly for three months, having discussions and persuading *them* about the kingdom of God. 9 But when some were becoming hardened and disobedient, speaking evil of *'*the Way before the people, he withdrew from them and took the disciples away *with him,* and had discussions daily in the school of Tyrannus. 10 This took place for two years, so that all who lived in Asia heard the word of the Lord, both Jews and Greeks.

Miracles at Ephesus

11 God was performing extraordinary miracles by the hands of Paul, 12 so that handkerchiefs or aprons were even carried from his body to the sick, and the diseases left them and the evil spirits went out. 13 But also some of the Jewish exorcists, who went from place to place, attempted to use the name of the Lord Jesus over those who had the evil spirits, saying, "I order you in the name of Jesus whom Paul preaches!" 14 Now there were seven sons of Sceva, a Jewish chief priest, doing this. 15 But the evil spirit responded and said to them, "I recognize Jesus, and I know of Paul, but who are you?" 16 And the man in whom was the evil spirit, pounced on them and subdued all of them and overpowered them, so that they fled out of that house naked and wounded. 17 This became known to all who lived in Ephesus, both Jews and Greeks; and fear fell upon them all and the name of the Lord Jesus was being magnified. 18 Also many of those who had believed kept coming, confessing and disclosing their practices. 19 And many of those who practiced magic brought their books together and *began* burning *them* in the sight of everyone; and they added up the prices of the books and found *it to be* fifty thousand *pieces* of silver. 20 So the word of the Lord was growing and prevailing mightily.

21 Now after these things were finished, Paul resolved in the Spirit to go to Jerusalem after he had passed through Macedonia and Achaia, saying, "After I have been there, I

18:13 1 Or *Law*   19:9 1 See John 14:6

must also see Rome." **22** And after he sent into Macedonia two of those who assisted him, Timothy and Erastus, he himself stayed in Asia for a while.

23 About that time ¹a major disturbance occurred in regard to the Way. **24** For a man named Demetrius, a silversmith who made silver shrines of Artemis, was bringing considerable business to the craftsmen; **25** he gathered these men together with the workmen of similar *trades,* and said, "Men, you know that our prosperity depends upon this business. **26** You see and hear that not only in Ephesus, but in almost all of Asia, this Paul has persuaded and turned away a considerable number of people, saying that gods made by hands are not gods *at all.* **27** Not only is there danger that this trade of ours will fall into disrepute, but also that the temple of the great goddess Artemis will be regarded as worthless, and that she whom all of Asia and the world worship will even be dethroned from her magnificence."

28 When they heard *this* and were filled with rage, they *began* shouting, saying, "Great is Artemis of the Ephesians!" **29** The city was filled with the confusion, and they rushed together into the theater, dragging along Gaius and Aristarchus, Paul's Macedonian traveling companions. **30** And when Paul wanted to go into the assembly, the disciples would not let him. **31** Also some of the ¹Asiarchs who were friends of his sent *word* to him and *repeatedly* urged him not to venture into the theater. **32** So then, some were shouting one thing and some another, for the assembly was in confusion and the majority did not know for what reason they had come together. **33** Some of the crowd concluded *it was* Alexander, since the Jews had put him forward; and having motioned with his hand, Alexander was intending to make a defense to the assembly. **34** But when they recognized that he was a Jew, a single outcry arose from them all as they shouted for about two hours, "Great is Artemis of the Ephesians!"

35 After quieting the crowd, the town clerk *said, "Men of Ephesus, what person is there after all who does not know that the city of the Ephesians is guardian of the temple of the great Artemis and of the *image* which fell down from the sky? **36** So, since these are undeniable *facts,* you ought to keep calm and to do nothing rash. **37** For you have brought these men *here who are* neither temple robbers nor blasphemers of our goddess. **38** So then, if Demetrius and the craftsmen who are with him have a complaint against anyone, the courts are in session and proconsuls are *available;* have them bring charges against one another. **39** But if you want anything beyond this, it shall be settled in the lawful assembly. **40** For indeed, we are in danger of being accused of a riot in connection with today's *events,* since there is no *real* reason *for it,* and in this connection we will be unable to account for this disorderly gathering." **41** After saying this he dismissed the assembly.

Paul in Macedonia and Greece

20 After the uproar had ceased, Paul sent for the disciples, and when he had encouraged them and taken his leave of them, he left to go to Macedonia. **2** When he had gone through those regions and had given them much encouragement, he came to Greece. **3** And *there* he spent three months, and when a plot was formed against him by the Jews as he was about to set sail for Syria, he decided to return through Macedonia. **4** And he was accompanied by Sopater of Berea, *the son* of Pyrrhus, and by Aristarchus and Secundus of the Thessalonians, and Gaius of Derbe, and Timothy, and Tychicus and Trophimus of Asia. **5** Now these had gone on ahead and were waiting for us at Troas. **6** We sailed from Philippi after ¹the days of Unleavened Bread, and reached them at Troas within five days; and we stayed there for seven days.

7 On the first day of the week, when we were gathered together to break bread, Paul *began* talking to them, intending to leave the next day, and he prolonged his message until midnight. **8** There were many lamps in the upstairs room where we were gathered together. **9** And there was a young man named Eutychus sitting on the window sill, sinking into a deep sleep; and as Paul kept on talking, *Eutychus* was overcome by sleep and fell down from the third floor, and was picked up dead. **10** But Paul went down and fell upon him, and after embracing him, he said, "Do not be troubled, for he is still alive." **11** When *Paul* had gone *back* up and had broken the bread and eaten, he talked with them a long while until daybreak, and then left. **12** They took away the boy alive, and were greatly comforted.

Troas to Miletus

13 But we went ahead to the ship and set sail for Assos, intending from there to take Paul on board; for that was what he had arranged, intending himself to go by land. **14** And when he met us at Assos, we took him on board and came to Mitylene. **15** Sailing from there, we arrived the following day opposite Chios; and the next day we crossed over to Samos, and on the following day we came to Miletus. **16** For Paul had decided to sail past Ephesus so that he would not have to lose time in Asia; for he was hurrying, if it might be possible for him to be in Jerusalem the day of Pentecost.

Farewell to Ephesus

17 From Miletus he sent *word* to Ephesus and called to himself the elders of the church. **18** And when they came to him, he said to them,

"You yourselves know, from the first day that I set foot in Asia, how I was with you the whole time, **19** serving the Lord with all humility and with tears and trials which came upon me through the plots of the Jews; **20** how I did not shrink from declaring to you anything that was beneficial, and teaching you publicly and from house to house, **21** solemnly testifying to both Jews and Greeks of repentance toward

---

God and faith in our Lord Jesus Christ. 22 And now, behold, bound by the Spirit, I am on my way to Jerusalem, not knowing what will happen to me there, 23 except that the Holy Spirit solemnly testifies to me in every city, saying that chains and afflictions await me. 24 But I do not consider my life of any account as dear to myself, so that I may finish my course and the ministry which I received from the Lord Jesus, to testify solemnly of the gospel of God's grace.

25 "And now behold, I know that all of you, among whom I went about preaching the kingdom, will no longer see my face. 26 Therefore, I testify to you this day that I am innocent of the blood of all people. 27 For I did not shrink from declaring to you the whole purpose of God. 28 Be on guard for yourselves and for all the flock, among which the Holy Spirit has made you overseers, to shepherd the church of God which He purchased with His own blood. 29 I know that after my departure savage wolves will come in among you, not sparing the flock; 30 and from among your own selves men will arise, speaking perverse things to draw away the disciples after them. 31 Therefore, be on the alert, remembering that night and day for a period of three years I did not cease to admonish each one with tears. 32 And now I entrust you to God and to the word of His grace, which is able to build you up and to give you the inheritance among all those who are sanctified. 33 I have coveted no one's silver or gold or clothes. 34 You yourselves know that these hands served my own needs and the men who were with me. 35 In everything I showed you that by working hard in this way you must help the weak and remember the words of the Lord Jesus, that He Himself said, 'It is more blessed to give than to receive.' "

36 When he had said these things, he knelt down and prayed with them all. 37 And they all began to weep aloud and embraced Paul, and repeatedly kissed him, 38 grieving especially over the word which he had spoken, that they would not see his face again. And they were accompanying him to the ship.

Paul Sails from Miletus

21 Now when we had parted from them and had set sail, we ran a straight course to Cos, and on the next day to Rhodes, and from there to Patara; 2 and having found a ship crossing over to Phoenicia, we went aboard and set sail. 3 When we came in sight of Cyprus, leaving it on the left, we kept sailing to Syria and landed at Tyre; for the ship was to unload its cargo there. 4 After looking up the disciples, we stayed there for seven days; and they kept telling Paul, through the Spirit, not to set foot in Jerusalem. 5 When our days there were ended, we left and started on our journey, while they all, with wives and children, escorted us until we were out of the city. After kneeling down on the beach and praying, we said farewell to one another. 6 Then we boarded the ship, and they returned home.

7 When we had finished the voyage from Tyre, we arrived at Ptolemais, and after greeting the brothers and sisters, we stayed with them for a day. 8 On the next day we left and came to Caesarea, and we entered the house of Philip the evangelist, who was one of the seven, and stayed with him. 9 Now this man had four virgin daughters who were prophetesses. 10 As we were staying there for some days, a prophet named Agabus came down from Judea. 11 And he came to us and took Paul's belt and bound his own feet and hands, and said, "This is what the Holy Spirit says: 'In this way the Jews in Jerusalem will bind the man who owns this belt and hand him over to the Gentiles.' " 12 When we had heard this, we as well as the local residents began begging him not to go up to Jerusalem. 13 Then Paul replied, "What are you doing, weeping and breaking my heart? For I am ready not only to be bound, but even to die in Jerusalem for the name of the Lord Jesus." 14 And since he would not be persuaded, we became quiet, remarking, "The will of the Lord be done!"

Paul in Jerusalem

15 After these days we got ready and started on our way up to Jerusalem. 16 Some of the disciples from Caesarea also came with us, taking us to Mnason of Cyprus, a disciple of long standing with whom we were to stay.

17 After we arrived in Jerusalem, the brothers and sisters received us gladly. 18 And the following day Paul went in with us to James, and all the elders were present. 19 After he had greeted them, he began to relate one by one the things which God had done among the Gentiles through his ministry. 20 And when they heard about them, they began glorifying God; and they said to him, "You see, brother, how many thousands there are among the Jews of those who have believed, and they are all zealous for the Law; 21 and they have been told about you, that you are teaching all the Jews who are among the Gentiles to abandon Moses, telling them not to circumcise their children nor to walk according to the customs. 22 So what is to be done? They will certainly hear that you have come. 23 Therefore, do as we tell you: we have four men who have a vow upon themselves; 24 take them along and purify yourself together with them, and pay their expenses so that they may shave their heads; and then everyone will know that there is nothing to what they have been told about you, but that you yourself also conform, keeping the Law. 25 But regarding the Gentiles who have believed, we sent a letter, having decided that they should abstain from meat sacrificed to idols and from blood and what is strangled, and from sexual immorality." 26 Then Paul took along the men, and the next day, after purifying himself together with them, he went into the temple giving notice of the completion of the days of purification, until the sacrifice was offered for each one of them.

Paul Seized in the Temple

27 When the seven days were almost over, the Jews from Asia, upon seeing him in the temple, began to stir up all the crowd and laid hands on him, 28 crying out, "Men of Israel, help! This is the man who instructs everyone

everywhere against our people and the Law and this place; and besides, he has even brought Greeks into the temple and has defiled this holy place!" 29 For they had previously seen Trophimus the Ephesian in the city with him, and they thought that Paul had brought him into the temple. 30 Then the whole city was provoked and the people rushed together, and taking hold of Paul they dragged him out of the temple, and immediately the doors were shut. 31 While they were intent on killing him, a report came up to the commander of the Roman 1cohort that all Jerusalem was in confusion. 32 He immediately took along some soldiers and centurions and ran down to the crowd; and when they saw the commander and the soldiers, they stopped beating Paul. 33 Then the commander came up and took hold of him, and ordered that he be bound with two chains; and he began asking who he was and what he had done. 34 But among the crowd, some were shouting one thing and some another, and when he could not find out the facts because of the uproar, he ordered that Paul be brought into the barracks. 35 When Paul got to the stairs, it came about that he was carried by the soldiers because of the violence of the mob; 36 for the multitude of people kept following them, shouting, "Away with him!"

37 As Paul was about to be brought into the barracks, he *said to the commander, "May I say something to you?" And he said, "Do you know Greek? 38 Then you are not the Egyptian who some time ago stirred up a revolt and led the four thousand men of the Assassins out into the wilderness?" 39 But Paul said, "I am a Jew of Tarsus in Cilicia, a citizen of no insignificant city; and I beg you, allow me to speak to the people." 40 When he had given him permission, Paul, standing on the stairs, motioned to the people with his hand; and when there was a great silence, he spoke to them in the Hebrew dialect, saying,

Paul's Defense before the Jews

22 "Brothers and fathers, hear my defense which I now offer to you." 2 And when they heard that he was addressing them in the Hebrew dialect, they became even more quiet; and he *said,

3 "I am a Jew, born in Tarsus of Cilicia, but brought up in this city, educated under Gamaliel, strictly according to the Law of our fathers, being zealous for God just as you all are today. 4 I persecuted this Way to the death, binding and putting both men and women into prisons, 5 as also the high priest and all the Council of the elders can testify. From them I also received letters to the brothers, and started off for Damascus in order to bring even those who were there to Jerusalem as prisoners to be punished.

6 "But it happened that as I was on my way, approaching Damascus at about noon, a very bright light suddenly flashed from heaven all around me, 7 and I fell to the ground and heard a voice saying to me, 'Saul, Saul, why are you persecuting Me?' 8 And I answered, 'Who are

You, Lord?' And He said to me, 'I am Jesus the Nazarene, whom you are persecuting.' 9 And those who were with me saw the light, but did not understand the voice of the One who was speaking to me. 10 And I said, 'What shall I do, Lord?' And the Lord said to me, 'Get up and go on into Damascus, and there you will be told about everything that has been appointed for you to do.' 11 But since I could not see because of the brightness of that light, I came into Damascus being led by the hand by those who were with me.

12 "Now a certain Ananias, a man who was devout by the standard of the Law and well spoken of by all the Jews who lived there, 13 came to me, and standing nearby he said to me, 'Brother Saul, receive your sight!' And at that very moment I looked up at him. 14 And he said, 'The God of our fathers has appointed you to know His will and to see the Righteous One and to hear a message from His mouth. 15 For you will be a witness for Him to all people of what you have seen and heard. 16 Now why do you delay? Get up and be baptized, and wash away your sins by calling on His name.'

17 "It happened when I returned to Jerusalem and was praying in the temple, that I fell into a trance, 18 and I saw Him saying to me, 'Hurry and get out of Jerusalem quickly, because they will not accept your testimony about Me.' 19 And I said, 'Lord, they themselves understand that in one synagogue after another I used to imprison and beat those who believed in You. 20 And when the blood of Your witness Stephen was being shed, I also was standing nearby and approving, and watching over the cloaks of those who were killing him.' 21 And He said to me, 'Go! For I will send you far away to the Gentiles.'"

22 They listened to him up to this statement, and then they raised their voices and said, "Away with such a man from the earth, for he should not be allowed to live!" 23 And as they were shouting and throwing off their cloaks and tossing dust into the air, 24 the commander ordered that he be brought into the barracks, saying that he was to be interrogated by flogging so that he would find out the reason why they were shouting against him that way. 25 But when they stretched him out with straps, Paul said to the centurion who was standing by, "Is it lawful for you to flog a man who is a Roman and uncondemned?" 26 When the centurion heard this, he went to the commander and told him, saying, "What are you about to do? For this man is a Roman." 27 The commander came and said to Paul, "Tell me, are you a Roman?" And he said, "Yes." 28 The commander answered, "I acquired this citizenship for a large sum of money." And Paul said, "But I was actually born a citizen." 29 Therefore, those who were about to interrogate him immediately backed away from him; and the commander also was afraid when he found out that he was a Roman, and because he had put him in chains.

30 Now on the next day, wanting to know for certain why Paul had been accused by the Jews, he released him and ordered the chief

---

21:31 1 Normally 600 men (the number varied)

priests and all the Council to assemble, and he brought Paul down and placed him before them.

Paul before the Council

23 Now looking intently at the Council, Paul said, "Brothers, I have lived my life with an entirely good conscience before God up to this day." 2 But the high priest Ananias commanded those standing beside him to strike him on the mouth. 3 Then Paul said to him, "God is going to strike you, you whitewashed wall! Do you sit to try me according to the Law, and in violation of the Law, order me to be struck?" 4 But those present said, "Are you insulting God's high priest?" 5 And Paul said, "I was not aware, brothers, that he is high priest; for it is written: 'YOU SHALL NOT SPEAK EVIL OF A RULER OF YOUR PEOPLE.' "

6 But Paul, perceiving that one group were Sadducees and the other Pharisees, began crying out in the Council, "Brothers, I am a Pharisee, a son of Pharisees; I am on trial for the hope and resurrection of the dead!" 7 When he said this, a dissension occurred between the Pharisees and Sadducees, and the assembly was divided. 8 For the Sadducees say that there is no resurrection, nor an angel, nor a spirit, but the Pharisees acknowledge them all. 9 And a great uproar occurred; and some of the scribes of the Pharisaic party stood up and started arguing heatedly, saying, "We find nothing wrong with this man; suppose a spirit or an angel has spoken to him?" 10 And when a great dissension occurred, the commander was afraid that Paul would be torn to pieces by them, and he ordered the troops to go down and take him away from them by force, and bring him into the barracks.

11 But on the following night, the Lord stood near him and said, "Be courageous! For as you have testified to the truth about Me in Jerusalem, so you must testify in Rome also."

A Conspiracy to Kill Paul

12 When it was day, the Jews formed a conspiracy and put themselves under an oath, saying that they would neither eat nor drink until they had killed Paul. 13 There were more than forty who formed this plot. 14 They came to the chief priests and the elders and said, "We have put ourselves under an oath to taste nothing until we have killed Paul. 15 Now therefore, you and the Council notify the commander to bring him down to you, as though you were going to investigate his case more thoroughly; and as for us, we are ready to kill him before he comes near the place."

16 But the son of Paul's sister heard about their ambush, and he came and entered the barracks and told Paul. 17 Paul called one of the centurions to himself and said, "Take this young man to the commander, for he has something to report to him." 18 So he took him and led him to the commander and *said, "Paul the prisoner called me over to him and asked me to bring this young man to you because he has something to tell you." 19 The commander took him by the hand, and stepping aside, began to inquire of him privately, "What is it that you have to report to me?" 20 And he said, "The Jews have agreed to ask you to bring Paul down tomorrow to the Council, as though they were going to inquire somewhat more thoroughly about him. 21 So do not listen to them, for more than forty of them are in hiding to ambush him, and these men have put themselves under an oath not to eat or drink until they kill him; and now they are ready and waiting for assurance from you." 22 Then the commander let the young man go, instructing him, "Tell no one that you have notified me of these things."

Paul Moved to Caesarea

23 And he called to him two of the centurions and said, "Get two hundred soldiers ready by 'the third hour of the night to proceed to Caesarea, with seventy horsemen and two hundred spearmen." 24 They were also to provide mounts to put Paul on and bring him safely to Felix the governor. 25 And he wrote a letter with the following content:

26¶ "Claudius Lysias, to the most excellent governor Felix: Greetings.

27¶ When this man was seized by the Jews and was about to be killed by them, I came up to them with the troops and rescued him, after learning that he was a Roman. 28 And wanting to ascertain the basis for the charges they were bringing against him, I brought him down to their Council; 29 and I found that he was being accused regarding questions in their Law, but was not charged with anything deserving death or imprisonment.

30¶ When I was informed that there would be a plot against the man, I sent him to you at once, also instructing his accusers to bring charges against him before you."

31 So the soldiers, in accordance with their orders, took Paul and brought him by night to Antipatris. 32 But on the next day they let the horsemen go on with him, and they returned to the barracks. 33 When these horsemen had come to Caesarea and delivered the letter to the governor, they also presented Paul to him. 34 Now when he had read it, he also asked from what province Paul was, and when he learned that he was from Cilicia, 35 he said, "I will give you a hearing when your accusers arrive as well," giving orders for Paul to be kept in Herod's 'Praetorium.

Paul before Felix

24 Now after five days the high priest Ananias came down with some elders and an attorney named Tertullus, and they brought charges against Paul to the governor. 2 After Paul had been summoned, Tertullus began accusing him, saying to the governor,

"Since we have attained great peace through you, and since reforms are being carried out for this nation by your foresight, 3 we acknowledge this in every way and everywhere, most excellent Felix, with all thankfulness. 4 But,

---

23:23 1 l.e., 9 p.m.   23:35 1 l.e., governor's official residence

that I may not weary you further, I beg you to grant us a brief hearing, by your kindness. [5]For we have found this man a public menace and one who stirs up dissensions among all the Jews throughout the world, and a ringleader of the sect of the Nazarenes. [6]And he even tried to desecrate the temple, so indeed we arrested him.[7][8]By interrogating him yourself concerning all these matters, you will be able to ascertain the things of which we are accusing him." [9]The Jews also joined in the attack, asserting that these things were so.

[10]And when the governor had nodded for him to speak, Paul responded:

"Knowing that for many years you have been a judge to this nation, I cheerfully make my defense, [11]since you can take note of the fact that no more than twelve days ago I went up to Jerusalem to worship. [12]And neither in the temple did they find me carrying on a discussion with anyone or causing a riot, nor in the synagogues, nor in the city *itself*. [13]Nor can they prove to you *the things* of which they now accuse me. [14]But I confess this to you, that in accordance with [1]the Way, which they call a sect, I do serve the God of our fathers, believing everything that is in accordance with the Law and is written in the Prophets; [15]having a hope in God, which these men cherish themselves, that there shall certainly be a resurrection of both the righteous and the wicked. [16]In view of this I also do my best to maintain a blameless conscience *both* before God and before *other* people, always. [17]Now after several years I came to bring charitable gifts to my nation and to present offerings, [18]in which they found me *occupied* in the temple, having been purified, without *any* crowd or uproar. But *there were* some Jews from Asia— [19]who ought to have been present before you and to have been bringing charges, if they should have anything against me. [20]Or *else* have these men themselves declare what violation they discovered when I stood before the Council, [21]other than in regard to this one declaration which I shouted while standing among them, 'For the resurrection of the dead I am on trial before you today!' "

[22]But Felix, having quite accurate knowledge about [1]the Way, adjourned them, saying, "When Lysias the commander comes down, I will decide your case." [23]He gave orders to the centurion for Paul to be kept in custody and *yet* have *some* freedom, and not to prevent any of his friends from providing for his needs.

[24]Now some days later Felix arrived with Drusilla his wife, who was Jewish, and he sent for Paul and heard him *speak* about faith in Christ Jesus. [25]But as he was discussing righteousness, self-control, and the judgment to come, Felix became frightened and responded, "Go away for now, and when I have an opportunity, I will summon you." [26]At the same time he was also hoping that money would be given to him by Paul; therefore he also used to send for him quite often and talk with him. [27]But after two years had passed, Felix was succeeded by Porcius Festus; and Felix, wanting to do the Jews a favor, left Paul imprisoned.

Paul before Festus

25 Festus, then, after arriving in the province, went up to Jerusalem from Caesarea three days later. [2]And the chief priests and the leading men of the Jews brought charges against Paul, and they were pleading with Festus, [3]requesting a concession against Paul, that he might have him brought to Jerusalem (*at the same time,* setting an ambush to kill him on the way). [4]Festus then answered that Paul was being kept in custody in Caesarea, and that he himself was about to leave shortly. [5]"Therefore," he *said, "have the influential men among you go there with me, and if there is anything wrong about the man, have them bring charges against him."

[6]After *Festus* had spent no more than eight or ten days among them, he went down to Caesarea, and on the next day he took his seat on the tribunal and ordered that Paul be brought. [7]After Paul arrived, the Jews who had come down from Jerusalem stood around him, bringing many, and serious, charges against him which they could not prove, [8]while Paul said in his own defense, "I have not done anything wrong either against the Law of the Jews, or against the temple, or against Caesar." [9]But Festus, wanting to do the Jews a favor, replied to Paul and said, "Are you willing to go up to Jerusalem and stand trial before me on these *charges?*" [10]But Paul said, "I am standing before Caesar's tribunal, where I ought to be tried. I have done nothing wrong to *the* Jews, as you also very well know. [11]If, therefore, I am in the wrong and have committed something deserving death, I am not trying to avoid execution; but if there is nothing to the accusations which these men are bringing against me, no one can hand me over to them. I appeal to Caesar." [12]Then when Festus had conferred with his council, he answered, "You have appealed to Caesar; to Caesar you shall go."

[13]Now when several days had passed, King Agrippa and Bernice arrived in Caesarea, paying their respects to Festus. [14]And while they were spending many days there, Festus presented Paul's case to the king, saying, "There is a man who was left as a prisoner by Felix; [15]and when I was in Jerusalem, the chief priests and the elders of the Jews brought charges against him, asking for a sentence of condemnation against him. [16]I replied to them that it is not the custom of the Romans to hand over any person before the accused meets his accusers face to face, and has an opportunity to make his defense against the charges. [17]So after they had assembled here, I did not delay, but on the next day took my seat on the tribunal and ordered that the man be brought. [18]When the accusers stood up, they did not *begin* bringing any charges against him of crimes that I suspected, [19]but they *simply*

24:6 [1]Late mss add as the remainder of v 6: *We wanted to judge him according to our own Law.* v 7: *But Lysias the commander came along and took him out of our hands with much violence,* and the first part of v 8: *ordering his accusers to come before you.*   **24:14** [1]See John 14:6   **24:22** [1]See John 14:6

had some points of disagreement with him about their own religion and about a dead man, Jesus, whom Paul asserted to be alive. 20 And being at a loss how to investigate such matters, I asked whether he was willing to go to Jerusalem and stand trial there on these matters. 21 But when Paul appealed to be held in custody for 'the Emperor's decision, I ordered that he be kept in custody until I send him to Caesar." 22 Then Agrippa *said* to Festus, "I also would like to hear the man myself." "Tomorrow," he *said, "you shall hear him."

Paul before Agrippa

23 So, on the next day when Agrippa and Bernice came amid great pomp and entered the auditorium, accompanied by the commanders and the prominent men of the city, at the command of Festus, Paul was brought *before them*. 24 And Festus *said, "King Agrippa, and all you gentlemen present with us, you see this man about whom all the people of the Jews appealed to me, both in Jerusalem and here, shouting that he ought not to live any longer. 25 But I found that he had committed nothing deserving death; and since he himself appealed to the Emperor, I decided to send him. 26 Yet, I have nothing definite about him to write to my lord. Therefore, I have brought him before you *all* and especially before you, King Agrippa, so that after the investigation has taken place, I may have something to write. 27 For it seems absurd to me in sending a prisoner, not to indicate the charges against him as well."

Paul's Defense before Agrippa

26 Now Agrippa said to Paul, "You are permitted to speak for yourself." Then Paul extended his hand and *proceeded* to make his defense:

2 "Regarding all the things of which I am accused by the Jews, King Agrippa, I consider myself fortunate that I am about to make my defense before you today, 3 especially because you are an expert in all customs and questions among *the* Jews; therefore I beg you to listen to me patiently.

4 "So then, all Jews know my way of life since *my* youth, which from the beginning was spent among my *own* nation and in Jerusalem, 5 since they have known about me for a long time, if they are willing to testify, that I lived *as* a Pharisee according to the strictest sect of our religion. 6 And now I am standing trial for the hope of the promise made by God to our fathers; 7 *the promise* to which our twelve tribes hope to attain, as they earnestly serve *God* night and day. For this hope, O king, I am being accused by Jews. 8 Why is it considered incredible among you *people* if God raises the dead?

9 "So I thought to myself that I had to act in strong opposition to the name of Jesus of Nazareth. 10 And this is just what I did in Jerusalem; not only did I lock up many of the saints in prisons, after receiving authority from the chief priests, but I also cast my vote against them when they were being put to death. 11 And as I punished them often in all the synagogues, I tried to force them to blaspheme; and since I was extremely enraged at them, I kept pursuing them even to foreign cities.

12 "While so engaged, as I was journeying to Damascus with the authority and commission of the chief priests, 13 at midday, O king, I saw on the way a light from heaven, brighter than the sun, shining around me and those who were journeying with me. 14 And when we had all fallen to the ground, I heard a voice saying to me in the Hebrew dialect, 'Saul, Saul, why are you persecuting Me? 'It is hard for you to kick against the goads.' 15 And I said, 'Who are You, Lord?' And the Lord said, 'I am Jesus whom you are persecuting. 16 But get up and stand on your feet; for this *purpose* I have appeared to you, to appoint you as a servant and a witness not only to the things in which you have seen Me, but also to the things in which I will appear to you, 17 rescuing you from the *Jewish* people and from the Gentiles, to whom I am sending you, 18 to open their eyes so that they may turn from darkness to light, and from the power of Satan to God, that they may receive forgiveness of sins and an inheritance among those who have been sanctified by faith in Me.'

19 "For that reason, King Agrippa, I did not prove disobedient to the heavenly vision, 20 but *continually* proclaimed to those in Damascus first, and in Jerusalem, and *then* all the region of Judea, and *even* to the Gentiles, that they are to repent and turn to God, performing deeds consistent with repentance. 21 For these reasons *some* Jews seized me in the temple and tried to murder me. 22 So, having obtained help from God, I stand to this day testifying both to small and great, stating nothing but what the Prophets and Moses said was going to take place, 23 *as to* whether the Christ was to suffer, *and* whether, as first from the resurrection of the dead, He would proclaim light both to the *Jewish* people and to the Gentiles."

24 While Paul was stating these things in his defense, Festus *said in a loud voice, "Paul, you are out of your mind! *Your* great learning is driving you insane." 25 But Paul *said, "I am not insane, most excellent Festus; on the contrary, I am speaking out *with* truthful and rational words. 26 For the king knows about these matters, and I also speak to him with confidence, since I am persuaded that none of these things escape his notice; for this has not been done in a corner. 27 King Agrippa, do you believe the Prophets? I know that you believe." 28 Agrippa *replied* to Paul, "In a short *time* you are going to persuade me to make a Christian of myself." 29 And Paul *said,* "I would wish to God that even in a short or long *time* not only you, but also all who hear me this day would become such as I myself am, except for these chains."

30 The king stood up and the governor and Bernice, and those who were sitting with them, 31 and when they had gone out, they

began talking to one another, saying, "This man is not doing anything deserving death or imprisonment." [32] And Agrippa said to Festus, "This man could have been set free if he had not appealed to Caesar."

Paul Is Sent to Rome

27 Now when it was decided that we would sail for Italy, they proceeded to turn Paul and some other prisoners over to a centurion of the Augustan [1]cohort, named Julius. [2] And we boarded an Adramyttian ship that was about to sail to the regions along *the coast of* Asia, and put out to sea accompanied by Aristarchus, a Macedonian of Thessalonica. [3] The next day we put in at Sidon; and Julius treated Paul with consideration and allowed him to go to his friends and receive care. [4] From there we put out to sea and sailed under the shelter of Cyprus, because the winds were contrary. [5] When we had sailed through the sea along the coast of Cilicia and Pamphylia, we landed at Myra in Lycia. [6] There the centurion found an Alexandrian ship sailing for Italy, and he put us aboard it. [7] When we had sailed slowly for a good many days, and with difficulty had arrived off Cnidus, since the wind did not permit us *to go* farther, we sailed under the shelter of Crete, off Salmone; [8] and with difficulty sailing past it, we came to a place called Fair Havens, near which was the city of Lasea.

[9] When considerable time had passed and the voyage was now dangerous, since even the [1]fast was already over, Paul *started* admonishing *them*, [10] saying to them, "Men, I perceive that the voyage will certainly be with damage and great loss, not only of the cargo and the ship, but also of our lives." [11] But the centurion was more persuaded by the pilot and the captain of the ship than by what was being said by Paul. [12] The harbor was not suitable for wintering, so the majority reached a decision to put out to sea from there, if somehow they could reach Phoenix, a harbor of Crete facing southwest and northwest, and spend the winter *there*.

[13] When a moderate south wind came up, thinking that they had attained their purpose, they weighed anchor and *began* sailing along Crete, closer *to shore.*

Shipwreck

[14] But before very long a violent wind, called [1]Euraquilo, rushed down from the land; [15] and when the ship was caught *in it* and could not head up into the wind, we gave up and let ourselves be driven *by the wind*. [16] Running under the shelter of a small island called Cauda, we were able to get the *ship's* boat under control *only* with difficulty. [17] After they had hoisted it up, they used supporting cables in undergirding the ship; and fearing that they might run aground on *the shallows* of Syrtis, they let down the sea anchor and let themselves be driven along in this way. [18] The next day as we were being violently tossed by the storm, they began to jettison the cargo;

[19] and on the third day they threw the ship's tackle *overboard* with their own hands. [20] Since neither sun nor stars appeared for many days, and no small storm was assailing *us*, from then on all hope of our being saved was *slowly* abandoned.

[21] When many had lost their appetites, Paul then stood among them and said, "Men, you should have followed my advice and not have set sail from Crete, and *thereby* spared yourselves this damage and loss. [22] And *yet* now I urge you to keep up your courage, for there will be no loss of life among you, but *only* of the ship. [23] For this *very* night an angel of the God to whom I belong, whom I also serve, came to me, [24] saying, 'Do not be afraid, Paul; you must stand before Caesar; and behold, God has graciously granted you all those who are sailing with you.' [25] Therefore, keep up your courage, men, for I believe God that it will turn out exactly as I have been told. [26] But we must run aground on a certain island."

[27] But when the fourteenth night came, as we were being driven about in the Adriatic Sea, about midnight the sailors *began* to suspect that they were approaching some land. [28] And they took soundings and found *it to be* twenty fathoms; and a little farther on they took another sounding and found *it to be* fifteen fathoms. [29] Fearing that we might run aground somewhere on the rocks, they cast four anchors from the stern and prayed for daybreak. [30] But as the sailors were trying to escape from the ship and had let down the *ship's* boat into the sea, on the pretense that they were going to lay out anchors from the bow, [31] Paul said to the centurion and the soldiers, "Unless these men remain on the ship, you yourselves cannot be saved." [32] Then the soldiers cut away the ropes of the *ship's* boat and let it fall away.

[33] Until the day was about to dawn, Paul kept encouraging them all to take some food, saying, "Today is the fourteenth day that you have been constantly watching and going without eating, having taken in nothing. [34] Therefore, I encourage you to take some food, for this is for your survival, for not a hair from the head of any of you will perish." [35] Having said this, he took bread and gave thanks to God in the presence of them all, and he broke it and began to eat. [36] All of them were encouraged and they themselves also took food. [37] We were 276 people on the ship in all. [38] When they had eaten enough, they *began* lightening the ship by throwing the wheat out into the sea.

[39] Now when day came, they could not recognize the land; but they did notice a bay with a beach, and they resolved to run the ship onto it if they could. [40] And casting off the anchors, they left them in the sea while at the same time they were loosening the ropes of the rudders; and they hoisted the foresail to the wind and were heading for the beach. [41] But they struck a reef where two seas met and ran the ship aground; and the prow stuck firmly and remained immovable, while the stern *started to* break up due to the force *of the*

27:1 [1] Normally 600 men (the number varied)   **27:9** [1] I.e., Day of Atonement in September or October, which was a dangerous time of year for navigation   **27:14** [1] I.e., a northeaster

waves. **42** The soldiers' plan was to kill the prisoners, so that none *of them* would swim away and escape; **43** but the centurion, wanting to bring Paul safely through, kept them from *accomplishing* their intention, and commanded that those who could swim were to jump overboard first and get to land, **44** and the rest *were to follow,* some on planks, and others on various things from the ship. And so it happened that they all were brought safely to land.

Safe at Malta

28 When they had been brought safely through, then we found out that the island was called Malta. **2** The natives showed us extraordinary kindness, for they kindled a fire and took us all in because of the rain that had started and because of the cold. **3** But when Paul had gathered a bundle of sticks and laid them on the fire, a viper came out because of the heat and fastened itself on his hand. **4** When the natives saw the creature hanging from his hand, they *began* saying to one another, "Undoubtedly this man is a murderer, and though he has been saved from the sea, justice has not allowed him to live." **5** However, Paul shook the creature off into the fire and suffered no harm. **6** Now they were expecting that he was going to swell up or suddenly fall down dead. But after they had waited a long time and had seen nothing unusual happen to him, they changed their minds and *began* to say that he was a god.

7 Now in the neighboring parts of that place were lands belonging to the leading man of the island, named Publius, who welcomed us and entertained us warmly for three days. **8** And it happened that the father of Publius was lying *in bed* afflicted with a *recurring* fever and dysentery. Paul went in *to see* him, and after he prayed, he laid his hands on him and healed him. **9** After this happened, the rest of the people on the island who had diseases were coming to him and being cured. **10** They also showed us many honors, and when we were *about to* set sail, they supplied *us* with everything we needed.

Paul Arrives in Rome

11 After three months we set sail on an Alexandrian ship which had wintered at the island, and which had the Twin Brothers for its figurehead. **12** After we put in at Syracuse, we stayed there for three days. **13** From there we sailed around and arrived at Rhegium, and a day later a south wind came up, and on the second day we came to Puteoli. **14** There we found *some* brothers *and sisters,* and were invited to stay with them for seven days; and that is how we came to Rome. **15** And from there the brothers *and sisters,* when they heard about us, came as far as the Market of Appius and the Three Inns to meet us; and when Paul saw them, he thanked God and took courage.

16 When we entered Rome, Paul was allowed to stay by himself, with the soldier who was guarding him.

17 After three days Paul called together those who were the leading men of the Jews, and when they came together, he *began* saying to them, "Brothers, though I had done nothing against our people or the customs of our fathers, *yet* I was handed over to the Romans as a prisoner from Jerusalem. **18** And when they had examined me, they were willing to release me because there were no grounds for putting me to death. **19** But when the Jews objected, I was forced to appeal to Caesar, not that I had any accusation against my nation. **20** For this reason, therefore, I requested to see you and to speak with you, since I am wearing this chain for the sake of the hope of Israel." **21** They said to him, "We have neither received letters from Judea concerning you, nor has any of the brothers come here and reported or spoken anything bad about you. **22** But we desire to hear from you what your views are; for regarding this sect, it is known to us that it is spoken against everywhere."

23 When they had set a day for Paul, *people* came to him at his lodging in large numbers; and he was explaining to them by solemnly testifying about the kingdom of God and trying to persuade them concerning Jesus, from both the Law of Moses and from the Prophets, from morning until evening. **24** Some were being persuaded by the things said *by Paul,* but others would not believe. **25** And when they disagreed with one another, they *began* leaving after Paul said one *parting* statement: "The Holy Spirit rightly spoke through Isaiah the prophet to your fathers, **26** saying,

'Go to this people and say,
"You will keep on hearing, and will not
    understand;
And you will keep on seeing, and will not
    perceive;
27 For the hearts of this people have become
    insensitive,
And with their ears they hardly hear,
And they have closed their eyes;
Otherwise they might see with their eyes,
And hear with their ears,
And understand with their heart and
    return,
And I would heal them." '

28 Therefore, let it be known to you that this salvation of God has been sent to the Gentiles; they will also listen."[1]

30 Now Paul stayed two full years in his own rented lodging and welcomed all who came to him, **31** preaching the kingdom of God and teaching things about the Lord Jesus Christ with all openness, unhindered.

28:28 [1] Late mss add as v 29: *When he had spoken these words, the Jews departed, having a great dispute among themselves.*

The Letter of Paul to the
ROMANS

The Gospel Exalted

1 Paul, a bond-servant of Christ Jesus, called *as* an apostle, set apart for the gospel of God, 2 which He promised beforehand through His prophets in the holy Scriptures, 3 concerning His Son, who was born of a descendant of David according to the flesh, 4 who was declared the Son of God with power according to the Spirit of holiness by the resurrection from the dead, Jesus Christ our Lord, 5 through whom we have received grace and apostleship to bring about *the* obedience of faith among all the Gentiles in behalf of His name, 6 among whom you also are *the* called of Jesus Christ; 7 to all who are beloved of God in Rome, called *as* saints: Grace to you and peace from God our Father and the Lord Jesus Christ.

8 First, I thank my God through Jesus Christ for you all, because your faith is being proclaimed throughout the world. 9 For God, whom I serve in my spirit in the *preaching of the* gospel of His Son, is my witness *as to* how unceasingly I make mention of you, 10 always in my prayers requesting if perhaps now, at last by the will of God, I will succeed in coming to you. 11 For I long to see you so that I may impart some spiritual gift to you, that you may be established; 12 that is, that I may be encouraged together with you *while* among you, each of us by the other's faith, both yours and mine. 13 I do not want you to be unaware, brothers *and sisters,* that often I have planned to come to you (and have been prevented so far) so that I may obtain some fruit among you also just as among the rest of the Gentiles. 14 I am under obligation both to Greeks and to the ¹uncultured, both to the wise and to the foolish. 15 So, for my part, I am eager to preach the gospel to you also who are in Rome.

16 For I am not ashamed of the gospel, for it is the power of God for salvation to everyone who believes, to the Jew first and also to the Greek. 17 For in it *the* righteousness of God is revealed from faith to faith; as it is written: "BUT THE RIGHTEOUS *ONE* WILL LIVE BY FAITH."

Unbelief and Its Consequences

18 For the wrath of God is revealed from heaven against all ungodliness and unrighteousness of people who suppress the truth in unrighteousness, 19 because that which is known about God is evident within them; for God made it evident to them. 20 For since the creation of the world His invisible *attributes, that is,* His eternal power and divine nature, have been clearly perceived, being understood by what has been made, so that they are without excuse. 21 For even though they knew God, they did not honor Him as God or give thanks, but they became futile in their reasonings, and their senseless hearts were darkened. 22 Claiming to be wise, they

became fools, 23 and they exchanged the glory of the incorruptible God for an image in the form of corruptible mankind, of birds, four-footed animals, and crawling creatures.

24 Therefore God gave them up to vile impurity in the lusts of their hearts, so that their bodies would be dishonored among them. 25 For they exchanged the truth of God for falsehood, and worshiped and served the creature rather than the Creator, who is blessed forever. Amen.

26 For this reason God gave them over to degrading passions; for their women exchanged natural relations for that which is contrary to nature, 27 and likewise the men, too, abandoned natural relations with women and burned in their desire toward one another, males with males committing shameful acts and receiving in their own persons the due penalty of their error.

28 And just as they did not see fit to acknowledge God, God gave them up to a depraved mind, to do those things that are not proper, 29 *people* having been filled with all unrighteousness, wickedness, greed, *and* evil; full of envy, murder, strife, deceit, *and* malice; *they are* gossips, 30 slanderers, haters of God, insolent, arrogant, boastful, inventors of evil, disobedient to parents, 31 without understanding, untrustworthy, unfeeling, *and* unmerciful; 32 and although they know the ordinance of God, that those who practice such things are worthy of death, they not only do the same, but also approve of those who practice them.

The Impartiality of God

2 Therefore you have no excuse, you *foolish* person, everyone *of you* who passes judgment; for in that *matter in* which you judge someone else, you condemn yourself; for you who judge practice the same things. 2 And we know that the judgment of God rightly falls upon those who practice such things. 3 But do you suppose this, you *foolish* person who passes judgment on those who practice such things, and *yet* does them *as well,* that you will escape the judgment of God? 4 Or do you think lightly of the riches of His kindness and restraint and patience, not knowing that the kindness of God leads you to repentance? 5 But because of your stubbornness and unrepentant heart you are storing up wrath for yourself on the day of wrath and revelation of the righteous judgment of God, 6 who WILL REPAY EACH PERSON ACCORDING TO HIS DEEDS: 7 to those who by perseverance in doing good seek glory, honor, and immortality, *He will give* eternal life; 8 but to those who are self-serving and do not obey the truth, but obey unrighteousness, *He will give* wrath and indignation. 9 *There will be* tribulation and distress for every soul of mankind who does evil, for the Jew first and

---

1:14 ¹I.e., non-Hellenes

also for the Greek, **10** but glory, honor, and peace to everyone who does what is good, to the Jew first and also to the Greek. **11** For there is no partiality with God.

12 For all who have sinned without the Law will also perish without the Law, and all who have sinned under the Law will be judged by the Law; **13** for *it is* not the hearers of the Law *who* are righteous before God, but the doers of the Law *who* will be justified. **14** For when Gentiles who do not have the Law instinctively perform the *requirements* of the Law, these, though not having the Law, are a law to themselves, **15** in that they show the work of the Law written in their hearts, their conscience testifying and their thoughts alternately accusing or else defending them, **16** on the day when, according to my gospel, God will judge the secrets of mankind through Christ Jesus.

The Jews under the Law

17 But if you call yourself a Jew and rely upon the Law and boast in God, **18** and know *His* will and distinguish the things that matter, being instructed from the Law, **19** and are confident that you yourself are a guide to people who are blind, a light to those in darkness, **20** a corrector of the foolish, a teacher of the immature, possessing in the Law the embodiment of knowledge and of the truth— **21** *you*, therefore, who teach someone else, do you not teach yourself? *You* who preach that one is not to steal, do you steal? **22** *You* who say that one is not to commit adultery, do you commit adultery? *You* who loathe idols, do you rob temples? **23** You who boast in the Law, through your breaking the Law, do you dishonor God? **24** For "THE NAME OF GOD IS BLASPHEMED AMONG THE GENTILES BECAUSE OF YOU," just as it is written.

25 For indeed circumcision is of value if you practice the Law; but if you are a violator of the Law, your circumcision has turned into uncircumcision. **26** So if the uncircumcised man keeps the requirements of the Law, will his uncircumcision not be regarded as circumcision? **27** And he who is physically uncircumcised, if he keeps the Law, will he not judge you who though having the letter *of the Law* and circumcision are a violator of the Law? **28** For he is not a Jew who is one outwardly, nor is circumcision that which is outward in the flesh. **29** But he is a Jew who is one inwardly; and circumcision is of the heart, by the Spirit, not by the letter; and his praise is not from people, but from God.

All the World Guilty

3 Then what advantage does the Jew have? Or what is the benefit of circumcision? **2** Great in every respect. First, that they were entrusted with the actual words of God. **3** What then? If some did not believe, their unbelief will not nullify the faithfulness of God, will it? **4** ¹Far from it! Rather, God must prove to be true, though every person *be found* a liar, as it is written:

"SO THAT YOU ARE JUSTIFIED IN YOUR WORDS,

AND PREVAIL WHEN YOU ARE JUDGED."

5 But if our unrighteousness demonstrates the righteousness of God, what shall we say? The God who inflicts wrath is not unrighteous, is He? (I am speaking from a human viewpoint.) **6** Far from it! For *otherwise*, how will God judge the world? **7** But if through my lie the truth of God abounded to His glory, why am I also still being judged as a sinner? **8** And *why* not *say* (just as we are slanderously reported and as some claim that we say), "Let's do evil that good may come *of it*"? Their condemnation is deserved.

9 What then? Are we better *than they?* Not at all; for we have already charged that both Jews and Greeks are all under sin; **10** as it is written:

"THERE IS NO RIGHTEOUS PERSON, NOT EVEN ONE;

11 THERE IS NO ONE WHO UNDERSTANDS,
THERE IS NO ONE WHO SEEKS OUT GOD;

12 THEY HAVE ALL TURNED ASIDE, TOGETHER THEY HAVE BECOME CORRUPT;
THERE IS NO ONE WHO DOES GOOD,
THERE IS NOT EVEN ONE."

13 "THEIR THROAT IS AN OPEN GRAVE,
WITH THEIR TONGUES THEY KEEP DECEIVING,"
"THE VENOM OF ¹ASPS IS UNDER THEIR LIPS";

14 "THEIR MOUTH IS FULL OF CURSING AND BITTERNESS";

15 "THEIR FEET ARE SWIFT TO SHED BLOOD,

16 DESTRUCTION AND MISERY ARE IN THEIR PATHS,

17 AND THEY HAVE NOT KNOWN THE WAY OF PEACE."

18 "THERE IS NO FEAR OF GOD BEFORE THEIR EYES."

19 Now we know that whatever the Law says, it speaks to those who are under the Law, so that every mouth may be closed and all the world may become accountable to God; **20** because by the works of the Law none of mankind will be justified in His sight; for through the Law *comes* knowledge of sin.

Justification by Faith

21 But now apart from the Law *the* righteousness of God has been revealed, being witnessed by the Law and the Prophets, **22** but *it is the* righteousness of God through faith in Jesus Christ for all those who believe; for there is no distinction, **23** for all have sinned and fall short of the glory of God, **24** being justified as a gift by His grace through the redemption which is in Christ Jesus, **25** whom God displayed publicly as a ¹propitiation in His blood through faith. *This was* to demonstrate His righteousness, because in God's *merciful* restraint He let the sins previously committed go unpunished; **26** for the demonstration, *that is,* of His righteousness at the present time, so that He would be just and the justifier of the one who has faith in Jesus.

27 Where then is boasting? It has been excluded. By what kind of law? Of works? No, but by a law of faith. **28** For we maintain that a person is justified by faith apart from works of the Law. **29** Or is God *the God* of Jews only? Is He not *the God* of Gentiles also? Yes, of Gentiles also, **30** since indeed God who will

---

3:4 ¹Lit *May it never happen!* And so throughout the ch   3:13 ¹I.e., venomous snakes   3:25 ¹I.e., a means of reconciliation between God and mankind by paying the penalty for sin

justify the circumcised by faith and the uncircumcised through faith is one. · **31** Do we then nullify the Law through faith? Far from it! On the contrary, we establish the Law.

Abraham's Justification by Faith

4 What then shall we say that Abraham, our forefather according to the flesh, has found? **2** For if Abraham was justified by works, he has something to boast about; but not before God. **3** For what does the Scripture say? "ABRAHAM BELIEVED GOD, AND IT WAS CREDITED TO HIM AS RIGHTEOUSNESS." **4** Now to the one who works, the wages are not credited as a favor, but as what is due. **5** But to the one who does not work, but believes in Him who justifies the ungodly, his faith is credited as righteousness, **6** just as David also speaks of the blessing of the person to whom God credits righteousness apart from works:

7 "BLESSED ARE THOSE WHOSE LAWLESS DEEDS
    HAVE BEEN FORGIVEN,
    AND WHOSE SINS HAVE BEEN COVERED.
8 "BLESSED IS THE MAN WHOSE SIN THE LORD
    WILL NOT TAKE INTO ACCOUNT."

9 Is this blessing then on the circumcised, or on the uncircumcised also? For we say, "FAITH WAS CREDITED TO ABRAHAM AS RIGHTEOUSNESS." **10** How then was it credited? While he was circumcised, or uncircumcised? Not while circumcised, but while uncircumcised; **11** and he received the sign of circumcision, a seal of the righteousness of the faith which he had while uncircumcised, so that he might be the father of all who believe without being circumcised, that righteousness might be credited to them, **12** and the father of circumcision to those who not only are of the circumcision, but who also follow in the steps of the faith of our father Abraham which he had while uncircumcised.

13 For the promise to Abraham or to his descendants that he would be heir of the world was not through the Law, but through the righteousness of faith. **14** For if those who are of the Law are heirs, then faith is made void and the promise is nullified; **15** for the Law brings about wrath, but where there is no law, there also is no violation.

16 For this reason *it is* by faith, in order that *it may be* in accordance with grace, so that the promise will be guaranteed to all the descendants, not only to those who are of the Law, but also to those who are of the faith of Abraham, who is the father of us all, **17** (as it is written: "I HAVE MADE YOU A FATHER OF MANY NATIONS") in the presence of Him whom he believed, *that is,* God, who gives life to the dead and calls into being things that do not exist. **18** In hope against hope he believed, so that he might become a father of many nations according to that which had been spoken, "SO SHALL YOUR DESCENDANTS BE." **19** Without becoming weak in faith he contemplated his own body, now *as good as* dead since he was about a hundred years old, and the deadness of Sarah's womb; **20** yet, with respect to the promise of God, he did not waver in unbelief but

grew strong in faith, giving glory to God, **21** and being fully assured that what *God* had promised, He was able also to perform. **22** Therefore IT WAS ALSO CREDITED TO HIM AS RIGHTEOUSNESS. **23** Now not for his sake only was it written that it was credited to him, **24** but for our sake also, to whom it will be credited, to *us* who believe in Him who raised Jesus our Lord from the dead, **25** *He* who was delivered over because of our wrongdoings, and was raised because of our justification.

Results of Justification

5 Therefore, having been justified by faith, we have peace with God through our Lord Jesus Christ, **2** through whom we also have obtained our introduction by faith into this grace in which we stand; and we celebrate in hope of the glory of God. **3** And not only *this,* but we also celebrate in our tribulations, knowing that tribulation brings about perseverance; **4** and perseverance, proven character; and proven character, hope; **5** and hope does not disappoint, because the love of God has been poured out within our hearts through the Holy Spirit who was given to us.

6 For while we were still helpless, at *the* right time Christ died for the ungodly. **7** For one will hardly die for a righteous person; though perhaps for the good person someone would even dare to die. **8** But God demonstrates His own love toward us, in that while we were still sinners, Christ died for us. **9** Much more then, having now been justified by His blood, we shall be saved from the wrath *of God* through Him. **10** For if while we were enemies we were reconciled to God through the death of His Son, much more, having been reconciled, we shall be saved by His life. **11** And not only *this,* but we also celebrate in God through our Lord Jesus Christ, through whom we have now received the reconciliation.

12 Therefore, just as through one man sin entered into the world, and death through sin, and so death spread to all mankind, because all sinned— **13** for until the Law sin was in the world, but sin is not counted against *anyone* when there is no law. **14** Nevertheless death reigned from Adam until Moses, even over those who had not sinned in the likeness of the ¹violation *committed* by Adam, who is a ²type of Him who was to come.

15 But the gracious gift is not like the offense. For if by the offense of the one the many died, much more did the grace of God and the gift by the grace of the one Man, Jesus Christ, overflow to the many. **16** The gift is not like *that which came* through the one who sinned; for on the one hand the judgment *arose* from one *offense,* resulting in condemnation, but on the other hand the gracious gift *arose* from many offenses, resulting in justification. **17** For if by the offense of the one, death reigned through the one, much more will those who receive the abundance of grace and of the gift of righteousness reign in life through the One, Jesus Christ.

18 So then, as through one offense the result was condemnation to all mankind, so also

---

5:14 ¹ I.e., of God's command   ² Or *foreshadowing*

through one act of righteousness the result was justification of life to all mankind. **19** For as through the one man's disobedience the many were made sinners, so also through the obedience of the One the many will be made righteous. **20** The Law came in so that the offense would increase; but where sin increased, grace abounded all the more, **21** so that, as sin reigned in death, so also grace would reign through righteousness to eternal life through Jesus Christ our Lord.

Believers Are Dead to Sin, Alive to God

6 What shall we say then? Are we to continue in sin so that grace may increase? **2** [1]Far from it! How shall we who died to sin still live in it? **3** Or do you not know that all of us who have been baptized into Christ Jesus have been baptized into His death? **4** Therefore we have been buried with Him through baptism into death, so that, just as Christ was raised from the dead through the glory of the Father, so we too may walk in newness of life. **5** For if we have become united with *Him* in the likeness of His death, certainly we shall also be *in the likeness* of His resurrection, **6** knowing this, that our old self was crucified with *Him,* in order that our body of sin might be done away with, so that we would no longer be slaves to sin; **7** for the one who has died is freed from sin.

8 Now if we have died with Christ, we believe that we shall also live with Him, **9** knowing that Christ, having been raised from the dead, is never to die again; death no longer is master over Him. **10** For the death that He died, He died to sin once for all *time;* but the life that He lives, He lives to God. **11** So you too, consider yourselves to be dead to sin, but alive to God in Christ Jesus.

12 Therefore sin is not to reign in your mortal body so that you obey its lusts, **13** and do not go on presenting the parts of your body to sin *as* [1]instruments of unrighteousness; but present yourselves to God as those who are alive from the dead, and your body's parts *as* instruments of righteousness for God. **14** For sin shall not be master over you, for you are not under [1]the Law but under grace.

15 What then? Are we to sin because we are not under [1]the Law but under grace? [2]Far from it! **16** Do you not know that *the one* to whom you present yourselves *as* slaves for obedience, you are slaves of *that same one* whom you obey, either of sin resulting in death, or of obedience resulting in righteousness? **17** But thanks be to God that though you were slaves of sin, you became obedient from the heart to *that* form of teaching to which you were entrusted, **18** and after being freed from sin, you became slaves to righteousness. **19** I am speaking in human terms because of the weakness of your flesh. For just as you presented the parts of your body as slaves to impurity and to lawlessness, resulting in *further* lawlessness, so now present your body's parts as slaves to righteousness, resulting in sanctification. **20** For when you were slaves of sin, you

were free in relation to righteousness. **21** Therefore what benefit were you then deriving from the things of which you are now ashamed? For the outcome of those things is death. **22** But now having been freed from sin and enslaved to God, you derive your benefit, resulting in sanctification, and the outcome, eternal life. **23** For the wages of sin is death, but the gracious gift of God is eternal life in Christ Jesus our Lord.

Believers United to Christ

7 Or do you not know, brothers *and sisters* (for I am speaking to those who know the Law), that the Law has jurisdiction over a person as long as he lives? **2** For the married woman is bound by law to her husband as long as he is alive; but if her husband dies, she is released from the law concerning the husband. **3** So then, if while her husband is alive she gives herself to another man, she will be called an adulteress; but if her husband dies, she is free from the law, so that she is not an adulteress if she [1]gives herself to another man.

4 Therefore, my brothers *and sisters,* you also were put to death in regard to the Law through the body of Christ, so that you might belong to another, to Him who was raised from the dead, in order that we might bear fruit for God. **5** For while we were in the flesh, the sinful passions, which were *brought to light* by the Law, were at work in the parts of our body to bear fruit for death. **6** But now we have been released from the Law, having died to that by which we were bound, so that we serve in newness of the [1]Spirit and not in oldness of the letter.

7 What shall we say then? Is the Law sin? [1]Far from it! On the contrary, I would not have come to know sin except through the Law; for I would not have known about coveting if the Law had not said, "YOU SHALL NOT COVET." **8** But sin, taking an opportunity through the commandment, produced in me coveting of every kind; for apart from the Law sin *is* dead. **9** I was once alive apart from the Law; but when the commandment came, sin came to life, and I died; **10** and this commandment, which was to result in life, proved to result in death for me; **11** for sin, taking an opportunity through the commandment, deceived me, and through it, killed *me.* **12** So then, the Law is holy, and the commandment is holy and righteous and good.

13 Therefore did that which is good become *a cause of* death for me? Far from it! Rather *it was* sin, in order that it might be shown to be sin by bringing about my death through that which is good, so that through the commandment sin would become utterly sinful.

The Conflict of Serving Two Masters

14 For we know that the Law is spiritual, but I am fleshly, sold into bondage to sin. **15** For I do not understand what I am doing; for I am not practicing what I want *to do,* but I do the very thing I hate. **16** However, if I do the very thing I

6:2 [1]Lit *May it never happen!* **6:13** [1]Or *weapons* **6:14** [1]Or *law* **6:15** [1]Or *law* [2]Lit *May it never happen!* **7:3** [1]I.e., in marriage; lit *becomes another man's* **7:6** [1]Or *spirit* **7:7** [1]Lit *May it never happen!*

do not want *to do,* I agree with the Law, that *the Law is* good. [17] But now, no longer am I *the one* doing it, but sin that dwells in me. [18] For I know that good does not dwell in me, that is, in my flesh; for the willing is present in me, but the doing of the good *is* not. [19] For the good that I want, I do not do, but I practice the very evil that I do not want. [20] But if I do the very thing I do not want, I am no longer *the one* doing it, but sin that dwells in me. [21] I find then the principle that evil is present in me, the one who wants to do good. [22] For I joyfully agree with the law of God in the inner person, [23] but I see a different law in the parts of my body waging war against the law of my mind, and making me a prisoner of the law of sin, *the law* which is in my body's parts. [24] Wretched man that I am! Who will set me free from the body of this death? [25] Thanks be to God through Jesus Christ our Lord! So then, on the one hand I myself with my mind am serving the law of God, but on the other, with my flesh the law of sin.

Deliverance from Bondage

8 Therefore there is now no condemnation at all for those who are in Christ Jesus. [2] For the law of the Spirit of life in Christ Jesus has set you free from the law of sin and of death. [3] For what the Law could not do, weak as it was through the flesh, God did. sending His own Son in the likeness of sinful flesh and *as an offering* for sin, He condemned sin in the flesh, [4] so that the requirement of the Law might be fulfilled in us who do not walk according to the flesh but according to the Spirit. [5] For those who are in accord with the flesh set their minds on the things of the flesh, but those who are in accord with the Spirit, the things of the Spirit. [6] For the mind set on the flesh is death, but the mind set on the Spirit is life and peace, [7] because the mind set on the flesh is hostile toward God; for it does not subject itself to the law of God, for it is not even able *to do so,* [8] and those who are in the flesh cannot please God.

[9] However, you are not in the flesh but in the Spirit, if indeed the Spirit of God dwells in you. But if anyone does not have the Spirit of Christ, he does not belong to Him. [10] If Christ is in you, though the body is dead because of sin, yet the spirit is alive because of righteousness. [11] But if the Spirit of Him who raised Jesus from the dead dwells in you, He who raised Christ Jesus from the dead will also give life to your mortal bodies [1]through His Spirit who dwells in you.

[12] So then, brothers *and sisters,* we are under obligation, not to the flesh, to live according to the flesh— [13] for if you are living in accord with the flesh, you are going to die; but if by the Spirit you are putting to death the deeds of the body, you will live. [14] For all who are being led by the Spirit of God, these are sons *and daughters* of God. [15] For you have not received a spirit of slavery leading to fear again, but you have received a spirit of adoption as sons *and daughters* by which we cry out,

"Abba! Father!" [16] The Spirit Himself testifies with our spirit that we are children of God, [17] and if children, heirs also, heirs of God and fellow heirs with Christ, if indeed we suffer with *Him* so that we may also be glorified with *Him.*

[18] For I consider that the sufferings of this present time are not worthy *to be* compared with the glory that is to be revealed to us. [19] For the eagerly awaiting creation waits for the revealing of the sons *and daughters* of God. [20] For the creation was subjected to futility, not willingly, but because of Him who subjected *it,* in hope [21] that the creation itself also will be set free from its slavery to corruption into the freedom of the glory of the children of God. [22] For we know that the whole creation groans and suffers the pains of childbirth together until now. [23] And not only *that,* but also we ourselves, having the first fruits of the Spirit, even we ourselves groan within ourselves, waiting eagerly for *our* adoption as sons *and daughters,* the redemption of our body. [24] For in hope we have been saved, but hope that is seen is not hope; for who hopes for what he *already* sees? [25] But if we hope for what we do not see, through perseverance we wait eagerly *for it.*

Our Victory in Christ

[26] Now in the same way the Spirit also helps our weakness; for we do not know what to pray for as we should, but the Spirit Himself intercedes for *us* with groanings too deep for words; [27] and He who searches the hearts knows what the mind of the Spirit is, because He intercedes for the saints according to *the will of* God.

[28] And we know that [1]God causes all things to work together for good to those who love God, to those who are called according to *His* purpose. [29] For those whom He foreknew, He also predestined *to become* conformed to the image of His Son, so that He would be the firstborn among many brothers *and sisters;* [30] and these whom He predestined, He also called; and these whom He called, He also justified; and these whom He justified, He also glorified.

[31] What then shall we say to these things? If God *is* for us, who *is* against us? [32] He who did not spare His own Son, but delivered Him over for us all, how will He not also with Him freely give us all things? [33] Who will bring charges against God's elect? God is the one who justifies; [34] who is the one who condemns? Christ Jesus is He who died, but rather, was [1]raised, who is at the right hand of God, who also intercedes for us. [35] Who will separate us from the love of [1]Christ? *Will* tribulation, or trouble, or persecution, or famine, or nakedness, or danger, or sword? [36] Just as it is written:

> "For Your sake we are killed all day long;
> We were regarded as sheep to be
> slaughtered."

[37] But in all these things we overwhelmingly conquer through Him who loved us. [38] For I am convinced that neither death, nor life, nor

---

8:11 [1] One early ms *because of*   **8:28** [1] One early ms *He;* i.e., God   **8:34** [1] One early ms *raised from the dead*   **8:35** [1] Two early mss *God*

angels, nor principalities, nor things present, nor things to come, nor powers, **39** nor height, nor depth, nor any other created thing will be able to separate us from the love of God that is in Christ Jesus our Lord.

Deep Concern for Israel

9 I am telling the truth in Christ, I am not lying; my conscience testifies with me in the Holy Spirit, **2** that I have great sorrow and unceasing grief in my heart. **3** For I could wish that I myself were accursed, *separated* from Christ for the sake of my countrymen, my kinsmen according to the flesh, **4** who are Israelites, to whom belongs the adoption as sons *and daughters,* the glory, the covenants, the giving of the Law, the *temple* service, and the promises; **5** whose are the fathers, and from whom is the Christ according to the flesh, who is over all, God blessed forever. Amen.

6 But *it is* not as though the word of God has failed. For they are not all Israel who are *descended* from Israel; **7** nor are they all children because they are Abraham's descendants, but: "THROUGH ISAAC YOUR DESCENDANTS SHALL BE NAMED." **8** That is, it is not the children of the flesh who are children of God, but the children of the promise are regarded as descendants. **9** For this is the word of promise: "AT THIS TIME I WILL COME, AND SARAH WILL HAVE A SON." **10** And not only *that,* but there was also Rebekah, when she had conceived *twins* by one man, our father Isaac; **11** for though *the twins* were not yet born and had not done anything good or bad, so that God's purpose according to *His* choice would stand, not because of works but because of Him who calls, **12** it was said to her, "THE OLDER WILL SERVE THE YOUNGER." **13** Just as it is written: "JACOB I HAVE LOVED, BUT ESAU I HAVE HATED."

14 What shall we say then? There is no injustice with God, is there? ¹Far from it! **15** For He says to Moses, "I WILL HAVE MERCY ON WHOMEVER I HAVE MERCY, AND I WILL SHOW COMPASSION TO WHOMEVER I SHOW COMPASSION." **16** So then, *it does* not *depend* on the *person* who wants *it* nor the one who ¹runs, but on God who has mercy. **17** For the Scripture says to Pharaoh, "FOR THIS VERY REASON I RAISED YOU UP, IN ORDER TO DEMONSTRATE MY POWER IN YOU, AND THAT MY NAME MIGHT BE PROCLAIMED THROUGHOUT THE EARTH." **18** So then He has mercy on whom He desires, and He hardens whom He desires.

19 You will say to me then, "Why does He still find fault? For who has resisted His will?" **20** On the contrary, who are you, you *foolish* person, who answers back to God? The thing molded will not say to the molder, "Why did you make me like this," will it? **21** Or does the potter not have a right over the clay, to make from the same lump one object for honorable use, and another for common use? **22** What if God, although willing to demonstrate His wrath and to make His power known, endured with great patience objects of wrath prepared for destruction? **23** And *He did so* to make known the riches of His glory upon objects of mercy, which He prepared beforehand for

glory, **24** *namely* us, whom He also called, not only from among Jews, but also from among Gentiles, **25** as He also says in Hosea:
"I WILL CALL THOSE WHO WERE NOT MY
     PEOPLE, 'MY PEOPLE,'
AND HER WHO WAS NOT BELOVED,
     'BELOVED.' "
26 "AND IT SHALL BE THAT IN THE PLACE WHERE IT
     WAS SAID TO THEM, 'YOU ARE NOT MY
     PEOPLE,'
THERE THEY SHALL BE CALLED SONS OF THE
     LIVING GOD."
27 Isaiah cries out concerning Israel, "THOUGH THE NUMBER OF THE SONS OF ISRAEL MAY BE LIKE THE SAND OF THE SEA, *ONLY* THE REMNANT WILL BE SAVED; **28** FOR THE LORD WILL EXECUTE HIS WORD ON THE EARTH, THOROUGHLY AND QUICKLY." **29** And just as Isaiah foretold:
"IF THE LORD OF ARMIES HAD NOT LEFT US
     DESCENDANTS,
WE WOULD HAVE BECOME LIKE SODOM, AND
     WOULD HAVE BEEN LIKE GOMORRAH."
30 What shall we say then? That Gentiles, who did not pursue righteousness, attained righteousness, but the righteousness that is by faith; **31** however, Israel, pursuing a law of righteousness, did not arrive at *that* law. **32** Why? Because *they did* not *pursue it* by faith, but as though *they could* by works. They stumbled over the stumbling stone, **33** just as it is written:
"BEHOLD, I AM LAYING IN ZION A STONE OF
     STUMBLING AND A ROCK OF OFFENSE,
AND THE ONE WHO BELIEVES IN HIM WILL NOT
     BE PUT TO SHAME."

The Word of Faith Brings Salvation

10 Brothers *and sisters,* my heart's desire and my prayer to God for them is for *their* salvation. **2** For I testify about them that they have a zeal for God, but not in accordance with knowledge. **3** For not knowing about God's righteousness and seeking to establish their own, they did not subject themselves to the righteousness of God. **4** For Christ is the end of the Law for righteousness to everyone who believes.

5 For Moses writes of the righteousness that is based on the Law, that the person who performs them will live by them. **6** But the righteousness based on faith speaks as follows: "DO NOT SAY IN YOUR HEART, 'WHO WILL GO UP INTO HEAVEN?' (that is, to bring Christ down), **7** or 'Who will descend into the abyss?' (that is, to bring Christ up from the dead)." **8** But what does it say? "THE WORD IS NEAR YOU, IN YOUR MOUTH AND IN YOUR HEART"—that is, the word of faith which we are preaching, **9** that if you confess with your mouth Jesus *as* Lord, and believe in your heart that God raised Him from the dead, you will be saved; **10** for with the heart *a person* believes, resulting in righteousness, and with the mouth he confesses, resulting in salvation. **11** For the Scripture says, "WHOEVER BELIEVES IN HIM WILL NOT BE PUT TO SHAME." **12** For there is no distinction between Jew and Greek; for the same *Lord* is Lord of all, abounding in riches for all who call on Him; **13** for "EVERYONE WHO CALLS ON THE NAME OF THE LORD WILL BE SAVED."

9:14 ¹Lit *May it never happen!*   **9:16** ¹I.e., to win mercy or favor

14 How then are they to call on Him in whom they have not believed? How are they to believe in Him whom they have not heard? And how are they to hear without a preacher? 15 But how are they to preach unless they are sent? Just as it is written: "HOW BEAUTIFUL ARE THE FEET OF THOSE WHO BRING GOOD NEWS OF GOOD THINGS!"

16 However, they did not all heed the good news; for Isaiah says, "LORD, WHO HAS BELIEVED OUR REPORT?" 17 So faith comes from hearing, and hearing by the word of Christ.

18 But I say, surely they have never heard, have they? On the contrary:

"THEIR VOICE HAS GONE OUT INTO ALL THE
　　EARTH,
AND THEIR WORDS TO THE ENDS OF THE
　　WORLD."

19 But I say, surely Israel did not know, did they? First Moses says,

"I WILL MAKE YOU JEALOUS WITH THOSE WHO
　　ARE NOT A NATION,
WITH A FOOLISH NATION I WILL ANGER YOU."

20 And Isaiah is very bold and says,

"I WAS FOUND BY THOSE WHO DID NOT SEEK
　　ME,
I REVEALED MYSELF TO THOSE WHO DID NOT
　　ASK FOR ME."

21 But as for Israel, He says, "I HAVE SPREAD OUT MY HANDS ALL DAY LONG TO A DISOBEDIENT AND OBSTINATE PEOPLE."

Israel Has Not Been Rejected

11 I say then, God has not rejected His people, has He? 'Far from it! For I too am an Israelite, a descendant of Abraham, of the tribe of Benjamin. 2 God has not rejected His people whom He foreknew. Or do you not know what the Scripture says in the passage about Elijah, how he pleads with God against Israel? 3 "Lord, THEY HAVE KILLED YOUR PROPHETS, THEY HAVE TORN DOWN YOUR ALTARS, AND I ALONE AM LEFT, AND THEY ARE SEEKING MY LIFE." 4 But what is the divine response to him? "I HAVE KEPT for Myself SEVEN THOUSAND MEN WHO HAVE NOT BOWED THE KNEE TO BAAL." 5 In the same way then, there has also come to be at the present time a remnant according to God's gracious choice. 6 But if it is by grace, it is no longer on the basis of works, since otherwise grace is no longer grace.

7 What then? What Israel is seeking, it has not obtained, but those who were chosen obtained it, and the rest were hardened; 8 just as it is written:

"GOD GAVE THEM A SPIRIT OF STUPOR,
EYES TO SEE NOT AND EARS TO HEAR NOT,
DOWN TO THIS VERY DAY."

9 And David says,

"MAY THEIR TABLE BECOME A SNARE AND A
　　TRAP,
AND A STUMBLING BLOCK AND A RETRIBUTION
　　TO THEM.

10　"MAY THEIR EYES BE DARKENED TO SEE NOT,
AND BEND THEIR BACKS CONTINUALLY."

11 I say then, they did not stumble so as to fall, did they? Far from it! But by their wrongdoing salvation has come to the Gentiles, to make them jealous. 12 Now if

their wrongdoing proves to be riches for the world, and their failure, riches for the Gentiles, how much more will their fulfillment be! 13 But I am speaking to you who are Gentiles. Therefore insofar as I am an apostle of Gentiles, I magnify my ministry 14 if somehow I may move my own people to jealousy and save some of them. 15 For if their rejection proves to be the reconciliation of the world, what will their acceptance be but life from the dead? 16 If the first piece of dough is holy, the lump is also; and if the root is holy, the branches are as well.

17 But if some of the branches were broken off, and you, being a wild olive, were grafted in among them and became partaker with them of the rich root of the olive tree, 18 do not be arrogant toward the branches; but if you are arrogant, remember that it is not you who supports the root, but the root supports you. 19 You will say then, "Branches were broken off so that I might be grafted in." 20 Quite right, they were broken off for their unbelief, but you stand by your faith. Do not be conceited, but fear; 21 for if God did not spare the natural branches, He will not spare you, either. 22 See then the kindness and severity of God: to those who fell, severity, but to you, God's kindness, if you continue in His kindness; for otherwise you too will be cut off. 23 And they also, if they do not continue in their unbelief, will be grafted in; for God is able to graft them in again. 24 For if you were cut off from what is by nature a wild olive tree, and contrary to nature were grafted into a cultivated olive tree, how much more will these who are the natural branches be grafted into their own olive tree?

25 For I do not want you, brothers and sisters, to be uninformed of this mystery—so that you will not be wise in your own estimation—that a partial hardening has happened to Israel until the fullness of the Gentiles has come in; 26 and so all Israel will be saved; just as it is written:

"THE DELIVERER WILL COME FROM ZION,
HE WILL REMOVE UNGODLINESS FROM JACOB."
27　"THIS IS MY COVENANT WITH THEM,
WHEN I TAKE AWAY THEIR SINS."

28 In relation to the gospel they are enemies on your account, but in relation to God's choice they are beloved on account of the fathers; 29 for the gifts and the calling of God are irrevocable. 30 For just as you once were disobedient to God, but now have been shown mercy because of their disobedience, 31 so these also now have been disobedient, that because of the mercy shown to you they also may now be shown mercy. 32 For God has shut up all in disobedience, so that He may show mercy to all.

33 Oh, the depth of the riches, both of the wisdom and knowledge of God! How unsearchable are His judgments and unfathomable His ways! 34 For WHO HAS KNOWN THE MIND OF THE LORD, OR WHO BECAME HIS COUNSELOR? 35 Or WHO HAS FIRST GIVEN TO HIM, THAT IT WOULD BE PAID BACK TO HIM? 36 For from Him, and through Him, and to Him are all things. To Him be the glory forever. Amen.

11:1 1 Lit May it never happen!

Dedicated Service

12 Therefore I urge you, brothers *and sisters,* by the mercies of God, to present your bodies as a living and holy sacrifice, acceptable to God, *which is* your [1]spiritual service of worship. 2 And do not be conformed to this world, but be transformed by the renewing of your mind, so that you may prove what the will of God is, that which is good and acceptable and perfect.

3 For through the grace given to me I say to everyone among you not to think more highly of himself than he ought to think; but to think so as to have sound judgment, as God has allotted to each a measure of faith. 4 For just as we have many parts in one body and all the body's parts do not have the same function, 5 so we, who are many, are one body in Christ, and individually parts of one another. 6 However, since we have gifts that differ according to the grace given to us, *each of us is to use them properly:* if prophecy, in proportion to *one's* faith; 7 if service, in the *act of* serving; or the one who teaches, in the *act of* teaching; 8 or the one who [1]exhorts, in the *work of* [2]exhortation; the one who gives, with generosity; the one who is in leadership, with diligence; the one who shows mercy, with cheerfulness.

9 Love *must be* free of hypocrisy. Detest what is evil; cling to what is good. 10 *Be* devoted to one another in brotherly love; give preference to one another in honor, 11 not lagging behind in diligence, fervent in spirit, serving the Lord; 12 rejoicing in hope, persevering in tribulation, devoted to prayer, 13 contributing to the needs of the saints, practicing hospitality.

14 Bless those who persecute [1]you; bless and do not curse. 15 Rejoice with those who rejoice, and weep with those who weep. 16 Be of the same mind toward one another; do not be haughty in mind, but associate with the lowly. Do not be wise in your own estimation. 17 Never repay evil for evil to anyone. Respect what is right in the sight of all people. 18 If possible, so far as it depends on you, be at peace with all people. 19 Never take your own revenge, beloved, but leave room for the wrath *of God,* for it is written: "VENGEANCE IS MINE, I WILL REPAY," says the Lord. 20 "BUT IF YOUR ENEMY IS HUNGRY, FEED HIM; IF HE IS THIRSTY, GIVE HIM A DRINK; FOR IN SO DOING YOU WILL HEAP BURNING COALS ON HIS HEAD." 21 Do not be overcome by evil, but overcome evil with good.

Be Subject to Government

13 Every person is to be subject to the governing authorities. For there is no authority except from God, and those which exist are established by God. 2 Therefore whoever resists authority has opposed the ordinance of God; and they who have opposed will receive condemnation upon themselves. 3 For rulers are not a cause of fear for good behavior, but for evil. Do you want to have no fear of authority? Do what is good and you will have praise from the same; 4 for it is a servant

of God to you for good. But if you do what is evil, be afraid; for it does not bear the sword for nothing; for it is a servant of God, an avenger who brings wrath on the one who practices evil. 5 Therefore it is necessary to be in subjection, not only because of wrath, but also for the sake of conscience. 6 For because of this you also pay taxes, for *rulers* are servants of God, devoting themselves to this very thing. 7 Pay to all what is due them: tax to whom tax *is due;* custom to whom custom; respect to whom respect; honor to whom honor.

8 Owe nothing to anyone except to love one another; for the one who loves his neighbor has fulfilled *the* Law. 9 For this, "YOU SHALL NOT COMMIT ADULTERY, YOU SHALL NOT MURDER, YOU SHALL NOT STEAL, YOU SHALL NOT COVET," and if there is any other commandment, it is summed up in this saying, "YOU SHALL LOVE YOUR NEIGHBOR AS YOURSELF." 10 Love does no wrong to a neighbor; therefore love is the fulfillment of *the* Law.

11 *Do* this, knowing the time, that it is already the hour for you to awaken from sleep; for now salvation is nearer to us than when we *first* believed. 12 The night is almost gone, and the day is near. Therefore let's rid ourselves of the deeds of darkness and put on the armor of light. 13 Let's behave properly as in the day, not in carousing and drunkenness, not in sexual promiscuity and debauchery, not in strife and jealousy. 14 But put on the Lord Jesus Christ, and make no provision for the flesh in regard to *its* lusts.

Principles of Conscience

14 Now accept the one who is weak in faith, *but* not to have quarrels over opinions. 2 One person has faith that he may eat all things, but the one who is weak eats *only* vegetables. 3 The one who eats is not to regard with contempt the one who does not eat, and the one who does not eat is not to judge the one who eats, for God has accepted him. 4 Who are you to judge the servant of another? To his own master he stands or falls; and he will stand, for the Lord is able to make him stand.

5 One *person* values one day over another, another values every day *the same.* Each person must be fully convinced in his own mind. 6 The one who observes the day, observes it for the Lord, and the one who eats, does so with regard to the Lord, for he gives thanks to God; and the one who does not eat, *it is* for the Lord *that* he does not eat, and he gives thanks to God. 7 For not one of us lives for himself, and not one dies for himself; 8 for if we live, we live for the Lord, or if we die, we die for the Lord; therefore whether we live or die, we are the Lord's. 9 For to this *end* Christ died and lived *again,* that He might be Lord both of the dead and of the living.

10 But *as for* you, why do you judge your brother *or sister?* Or you as well, why do you regard your brother *or sister* with contempt? For we will all appear before the judgment seat of God. 11 For it is written:

12:1 [1] I.e., in contrast to offering a literal sacrifice   12:8 [1] Or *encourages*   [2] Or *encouragement*   12:14 [1] Two early mss do not contain *you*

"As I live, says the Lord, to Me every knee
    will bow,
And every tongue will give praise to
    God."
12 So then each one of us will give an account
of himself to God.

13 Therefore let's not judge one another
anymore, but rather determine this: not to put
an obstacle or a stumbling block in a brother's
or sister's way. 14 I know and am convinced
in the Lord Jesus that nothing is unclean in
itself; but to the one who thinks something is
unclean, to that *person it is* unclean. 15 For if
because of food your brother *or sister* is hurt,
you are no longer walking in accordance with
love. Do not destroy with your *choice* of food
that *person* for whom Christ died. 16 Therefore
do not let what is for you a good thing be
spoken of as evil; 17 for the kingdom of God is
not eating and drinking, but righteousness and
peace and joy in the Holy Spirit. 18 For the one
who serves Christ in this *way* is acceptable to
God and approved by *other* people. 19 So then
we pursue the things which make for peace
and the building up of one another. 20 Do not
tear down the work of God for the sake of food.
All things indeed are clean, but they are evil
for the person who eats and causes offense. 21 It
is good not to eat meat or to drink wine, or *to
do anything* by which your brother *or sister*
stumbles. 22 The faith which you have, have as
your own conviction before God. Happy is the
one who does not condemn himself in what he
approves. 23 But the one who doubts is condemned if he eats, because *his eating is* not
from faith; and whatever is not from faith is
sin.

Self-denial in behalf of Others

15 Now we who are strong ought to
bear the weaknesses of those without
strength, and not *just* please ourselves. 2 Each
of us is to please his neighbor for his good, to
his edification. 3 For even Christ did not please
Himself, but as it is written: "The taunts of
those who taunt You have fallen on Me."
4 For whatever was written in earlier times was
written for our instruction, so that through
perseverance and the encouragement of the
Scriptures we might have hope. 5 Now may the
God who gives perseverance and encouragement grant you to be of the same mind with
one another, according to Christ Jesus, 6 so that
with one purpose *and* one voice you may
glorify the God and Father of our Lord Jesus
Christ.
7 Therefore, accept one another, just as
Christ also accepted us, for the glory of God.
8 For I say that Christ has become a servant to
the circumcision in behalf of the truth of God,
to confirm the promises *given* to the fathers,
9 and for the Gentiles to glorify God for His
mercy; as it is written:
"Therefore I will give praise to You
    among the Gentiles,
And I will sing praises to Your name."
10 Again he says,
"Rejoice, you Gentiles, with His people."
11 And again,
"Praise the Lord all you Gentiles,

And let all the peoples praise Him."
12 Again Isaiah says,
"There shall come the root of Jesse,
And He who arises to rule over the
    Gentiles,
In Him will the Gentiles hope."
13 Now may the God of hope fill you with all
joy and peace in believing, so that you will
abound in hope by the power of the Holy
Spirit.

14 And concerning you, my brothers *and
sisters,* I myself also am convinced that you
yourselves are full of goodness, filled with all
knowledge and able also to admonish one
another. 15 But I have written very boldly to
you on some points so as to remind you again,
because of the grace that was given to me from
God, 16 to be a minister of Christ Jesus to the
Gentiles, ministering as a priest the gospel of
God, so that *my* offering of the Gentiles may
become acceptable, sanctified by the Holy
Spirit. 17 Therefore in Christ Jesus I have found
reason for boasting in things pertaining to God.
18 For I will not presume to speak of anything
except what Christ has accomplished through
me, resulting in the obedience of the Gentiles
by word and deed, 19 in the power of signs
and wonders, in the power of the Spirit; so
that from Jerusalem and all around as far as
Illyricum I have fully preached the gospel of
Christ. 20 And in this way I aspired to preach
the gospel, not where Christ was *already*
known by name, so that I would not build on
another person's foundation; 21 but just as it is
written:
"They who have not been told about Him
    will see,
And they who have not heard will
    understand."
22 For this reason I have often been prevented from coming to you; 23 but now, with no
further place for me in these regions, and since
I have had for many years a longing to come to
you 24 whenever I go to Spain—for I hope to
see you in passing, and to be helped on my
way there by you, when I have first enjoyed
your company for a while—25 but now, I am
going to Jerusalem, serving the saints. 26 For
Macedonia and Achaia have been pleased to
make a contribution for the poor among the
saints in Jerusalem. 27 For they were pleased
to do so, and they are indebted to them. For if
the Gentiles have shared in their spiritual
things, they are indebted to do them a service
also in material things. 28 Therefore, when I
have finished this, and have put my seal on
this fruit of theirs, I will go on by way of you
to Spain. 29 I know that when I come to you, I
will come in the fullness of the blessing of
Christ.
30 Now I urge you, brothers *and sisters,* by
our Lord Jesus Christ and by the love of the
Spirit, to strive together with me in your
prayers to God for me, 31 that I may be rescued
from those who are disobedient in Judea,
and *that* my service for Jerusalem may prove
acceptable to the saints; 32 so that I may come
to you in joy by the will of God and relax in
your company. 33 Now the God of peace *be*
with you all. Amen.

Greetings and Love Expressed

16 I recommend to you our sister Phoebe, who is a servant of the church which is at Cenchrea, [2] that you receive her in the Lord in a manner worthy of the saints, and that you help her in whatever matter she may have need of you; for she herself has also been a helper of many, and of myself as well.

[3] Greet Prisca and Aquila, my fellow workers in Christ Jesus, [4] who risked their own necks for my life, to whom not only do I give thanks, but also all the churches of the Gentiles; [5] also greet the church that is in their house. Greet Epaenetus, my beloved, who is the first convert to Christ from Asia. [6] Greet Mary, who has worked hard for you. [7] Greet Andronicus and Junia, my kinsfolk and my fellow prisoners, who are outstanding in the view of the apostles, who also were in Christ before me. [8] Greet Ampliatus, my beloved in the Lord. [9] Greet Urbanus, our fellow worker in Christ, and Stachys my beloved. [10] Greet Apelles, the approved in Christ. Greet those who are of the *household* of Aristobulus. [11] Greet Herodion, my kinsman. Greet those of the *household* of Narcissus, who are in the Lord. [12] Greet Tryphaena and Tryphosa, workers in the Lord. Greet Persis the beloved, who has worked hard in the Lord. [13] Greet Rufus, a choice man in the Lord, also his mother and mine. [14] Greet Asyncritus, Phlegon, Hermes, Patrobas, Hermas, and the brothers *and sisters* with them. [15] Greet Philologus and Julia, Nereus and his sister, and Olympas, and all the saints who are with them. [16] Greet one another with a holy kiss. All the churches of Christ greet you.

[17] Now I urge you, brothers *and sisters,* keep your eye on those who cause dissensions and hindrances contrary to the teaching which you learned, and turn away from them. [18] For such people are slaves, not of our Lord Christ but of their own appetites; and by their smooth and flattering speech they deceive the hearts of the unsuspecting. [19] For the report of your obedience has reached everyone; therefore I am rejoicing over you, but I want you to be wise in what is good, and innocent in what is evil. [20] The God of peace will soon crush Satan under your feet.

The grace of our Lord Jesus be with you.

[21] Timothy, my fellow worker, greets you, and *so do* Lucius, Jason, and Sosipater, my kinsmen.

[22] I, Tertius, who have written this letter, greet you in the Lord.

[23] Gaius, host to me and to the whole church, greets you. Erastus, the city treasurer, greets you, and Quartus, the brother.[1]

[25] Now to Him who is able to establish you according to my gospel and the preaching of Jesus Christ, according to the revelation of the mystery which has been kept secret for long ages past, [26] but now has been disclosed, and through the Scriptures of the prophets, in accordance with the commandment of the eternal God, has been made known to all the nations, *leading* to obedience of faith; [27] to the only wise God, through Jesus Christ, be the glory forever. Amen.

16:23 [1] Late mss add as v 24: *The grace of our Lord Jesus Christ be with you all. Amen.*

The First Letter of Paul to the
CORINTHIANS

Appeal to Unity

1 Paul, called *as* an apostle of Jesus Christ by the will of God, and our brother Sosthenes, 2 To the church of God which is in Corinth, to those who have been sanctified in Christ Jesus, saints by calling, with all who in every place call on the name of our Lord Jesus Christ, their *Lord* and ours: 3 Grace to you and peace from God our Father and the Lord Jesus Christ.

4 I thank *1*my God always concerning you for the grace of God which was given you in Christ Jesus, 5 that in everything you were enriched in Him, in all speech and all knowledge, 6 just as the testimony concerning Christ was confirmed in you, 7 so that you are not lacking in any gift, as you eagerly await the revelation of our Lord Jesus Christ, 8 who will also confirm you to the end, blameless on the day of our Lord Jesus Christ. 9 God is faithful, through whom you were called into fellowship with His Son, Jesus Christ our Lord.

10 Now I urge you, brothers *and sisters,* by the name of our Lord Jesus Christ, that you all agree and that there be no divisions among you, but that you be made complete in the same mind and in the same judgment. 11 For I have been informed concerning you, my brothers *and sisters,* by Chloe's *people,* that there are quarrels among you. 12 Now I mean this, that each one of you is saying, "I am with Paul," or "I *am* with Apollos," or "I *am* with Cephas," or "I *am* with Christ." 13 Has Christ been divided? Paul was not crucified for you, was he? Or were you baptized in the name of Paul? 14 I am thankful that I baptized none of you except Crispus and Gaius, 15 so that no one would say you were baptized in my name! 16 But I did baptize the household of Stephanas also; beyond that, I do not know if I baptized anyone else. 17 For Christ did not send me to baptize, but to preach the gospel, not with cleverness of speech, so that the cross of Christ would not be made of no effect.

The Wisdom of God

18 For the word of the cross is foolishness to those who are perishing, but to us who are being saved it is the power of God. 19 For it is written:

"I WILL DESTROY THE WISDOM OF THE WISE,
AND THE UNDERSTANDING OF THOSE WHO
    HAVE UNDERSTANDING, I WILL
    CONFOUND."

20 Where is the wise person? Where is the scribe? Where is the debater of this age? Has God not made foolish the wisdom of the world? 21 For since in the wisdom of God the world through its wisdom did not *come to* know God, God was pleased through the foolishness of the message preached to save those who believe. 22 For indeed Jews ask for signs and Greeks search for wisdom; 23 but we preach Christ crucified, to Jews a stumbling block, and to Gentiles foolishness, 24 but to those who are the called, both Jews and Greeks, Christ the power of God and the wisdom of God. 25 For the foolishness of God is wiser than mankind, and the weakness of God is stronger than mankind.

26 For consider your calling, brothers *and sisters,* that there were not many wise according to the flesh, not many mighty, not many noble; 27 but God has chosen the foolish things of the world to shame the wise, and God has chosen the weak things of the world to shame the things which are strong, 28 and the insignificant things of the world and the despised God has chosen, the things that are not, so that He may nullify the things that are, 29 so that no human may boast before God. 30 But *it is* due to Him *that* you are in Christ Jesus, who became to us wisdom from God, and righteousness and sanctification, and redemption, 31 so that, just as it is written: "LET THE ONE WHO BOASTS, BOAST IN THE LORD."

Paul's Reliance upon the Spirit

2 And when I came to you, brothers *and sisters,* I did not come as *someone* superior in speaking ability or wisdom, as I proclaimed to you the *1*testimony of God. 2 For I determined to know nothing among you except Jesus Christ, and Him crucified. 3 I also was with you in weakness and fear, and in great trembling, 4 and my message and my preaching were not in persuasive words of wisdom, but in demonstration of the Spirit and of power, 5 so that your faith would not rest on the wisdom of mankind, but on the power of God.

6 Yet we do speak wisdom among those who are mature; a wisdom, however, not of this age nor of the rulers of this age, who are passing away; 7 but we speak God's wisdom in a mystery, the hidden *wisdom* which God predestined before the ages to our glory; 8 *the wisdom* which none of the rulers of this age has understood; for if they had understood it, they would not have crucified the Lord of glory; 9 but just as it is written:

"THINGS WHICH EYE HAS NOT SEEN AND EAR HAS
    NOT HEARD,
AND *WHICH* HAVE NOT ENTERED THE HUMAN
    HEART,
ALL THAT GOD HAS PREPARED FOR THOSE WHO
    LOVE HIM."

10 *1*For to us God revealed *them* through the Spirit; for the Spirit searches all things, even the depths of God. 11 For who among people knows the *thoughts* of a person except the spirit of the person that is in him? So also the *thoughts* of God no one knows, except the Spirit of God. 12 Now we have not received the spirit of the world, but the Spirit who is from

God, so that we may know the things freely given to us by God. [13] We also speak these things, not in words taught by human wisdom, but in those taught by the Spirit, combining spiritual *thoughts* with spiritual *words.*

[14] But a natural person does not accept the things of the Spirit of God, for they are foolishness to him; and he cannot understand them, because they are spiritually discerned. [15] But the one who is spiritual discerns all things, yet he himself is discerned by no one. [16] For WHO HAS KNOWN THE MIND OF THE LORD, THAT HE WILL INSTRUCT HIM? But we have the mind of Christ.

Foundations for Living

3 And I, brothers *and sisters,* could not speak to you as spiritual people, but *only* as fleshly, as to infants in Christ. [2] I gave you milk to drink, not solid food; for you were not yet able *to consume it.* But even now you are not yet able, [3] for you are still fleshly. For since there is jealousy and strife among you, are you not fleshly, and are you not walking like *ordinary* people? [4] For when one person says, "I am with Paul," and another, "I *am* with Apollos," are you not *ordinary* people?

[5] What then is Apollos? And what is Paul? Servants through whom you believed, even as the Lord gave *opportunity* to each one. [6] I planted, Apollos watered, but God was causing the growth. [7] So then neither the one who plants nor the one who waters is anything, but God who causes the growth. [8] Now the one who plants and the one who waters are one; but each will receive his own reward according to his own labor. [9] For we are God's fellow workers; you are God's field, God's building.

[10] According to the grace of God which was given to me, like a wise master builder I laid a foundation, and another is building on it. But each person must be careful how he builds on it. [11] For no one can lay a foundation other than the one which is laid, which is Jesus Christ. [12] Now if anyone builds on the foundation with gold, silver, precious stones, wood, hay, *or* straw, [13] each one's work will become evident; for the day will show it because it is *to be* revealed with fire, and the fire itself will test the quality of each one's work. [14] If anyone's work which he has built on it remains, he will receive a reward. [15] If anyone's work is burned up, he will suffer loss; but he himself will be saved, yet *only* so as through fire.

[16] Do you not know that you are a temple of God and *that* the Spirit of God dwells in you? [17] If anyone destroys the temple of God, God will destroy that person; for the temple of God is holy, and that is what you are.

[18] *Take care that* no one deceives himself. If anyone among you thinks that he is wise in this age, he must become foolish, so that he may become wise. [19] For the wisdom of this world is foolishness in the sight of God. For it is written: "*He is* THE ONE WHO CATCHES THE WISE BY THEIR CRAFTINESS"; [20] and again, "THE LORD KNOWS THE THOUGHTS of the wise, THAT THEY ARE useless." [21] So then, no one is to be boasting in people. For all things belong to you, [22] whether Paul or Apollos or Cephas, or the world or life or death, or things present or things to come; all things belong to you, [23] and you belong to Christ, and Christ belongs to God.

Servants of Christ

4 This is the way *any* person is to regard us: as servants of Christ and stewards of the mysteries of God. [2] In this case, moreover, it is required of stewards that one be found trustworthy. [3] But to me it is an insignificant matter that I would be examined by you, or by *any* human court; in fact, I do not even examine myself. [4] For I am not aware of anything against myself; however I am not vindicated by this, but the one who examines me is the Lord. [5] Therefore do not go on passing judgment before [1]*the* time, *but wait* until the Lord comes, who will both bring to light the things hidden in the darkness and disclose the motives of *human* hearts; and then praise will come to each person from God.

[6] Now these things, brothers *and sisters,* I have figuratively applied to myself and Apollos on your account, so that in us you may learn not to exceed what is written, so that no one of you will become arrogant in behalf of one against the other. [7] For who considers you as superior? What do you have that you did not receive? And if you did receive it, why do you boast as if you had not received it?

[8] You are already filled, you have already become rich, you have become kings without us; and indeed, *I* wish that you had become kings so that we also might reign with you! [9] For I think, God has exhibited us, the apostles, last of all as men condemned to death, because we have become a spectacle to the world, both to angels and to mankind. [10] We are fools on account of Christ, but you are prudent in Christ! We are weak, but you are strong! You are distinguished, but we are without honor! [11] Up to this present hour we are both hungry and thirsty, and are poorly clothed and roughly treated and homeless; [12] and we labor, working with our own hands; when we are verbally abused, we bless; when we are persecuted, we endure *it;* [13] when we are slandered, we reply as friends; we have become as the scum of the world, the dregs of all things, *even* until now.

[14] I do not write these things to shame you, but to admonish you as my beloved children. [15] For if you were to have countless tutors in Christ, yet *you would* not *have* many fathers, for in Christ Jesus I became your father through the gospel. [16] Therefore I urge you, be imitators of me. [17] For this reason I have sent to you Timothy, who is my beloved and faithful child in the Lord, and he will remind you of my ways which are in Christ, just as I teach everywhere in every church. [18] Now some have become arrogant, as though I were not coming to you. [19] But I will come to you soon, if the Lord wills, and I shall find out, not the words of those who are arrogant, but their power. [20] For the kingdom of God is not in words, but in power. [21] What do you desire? That I come to you with a rod, or with love and a spirit of gentleness?

4:5 [1] I.e., the appointed time of judgment

Sexual Immorality Rebuked

5 It is actually reported that there is sexual immorality among you, and sexual immorality of such a kind as does not exist even among the Gentiles, *namely,* that someone has his father's wife. 2 You have become arrogant and have not mourned instead, so that the one who had done this deed would be removed from your midst.

3 For I, on my part, though absent in body but present in spirit, have already judged him who has so committed this, as though I were present. 4 In the name of our Lord Jesus, when you are assembled, and I with you in spirit, with the power of our Lord Jesus, 5 *I have decided* to turn such a person over to Satan for the destruction of his body, so that his spirit may be saved on the day of the *Lord.

6 Your boasting is not good. Do you not know that a little leaven leavens the whole lump *of dough?* 7 Clean out the old leaven so that you may be a new lump, just as you are *in fact* unleavened. For Christ our Passover also has been sacrificed. 8 Therefore let's celebrate the feast, not with old leaven, nor with the leaven of malice and wickedness, but with the unleavened bread of sincerity and truth.

9 I wrote to you in my letter not to associate with sexually immoral people; 10 I *did* not at all *mean* with the sexually immoral people of this world, or with the greedy and swindlers, or with idolaters, for then you would have to leave the world. 11 But actually, I wrote to you not to associate with any so-called brother if he is a sexually immoral person, or a greedy person, or an idolater, or is verbally abusive, or habitually drunk, or a swindler—not even to eat with such a person. 12 For what *business* of mine *is it* to judge outsiders? Do you not judge those who are within *the church?* 13 But those who are outside, God judges. REMOVE THE EVIL PERSON FROM AMONG YOURSELVES.

Lawsuits Discouraged

6 Does any one of you, when he has a case against his neighbor, dare to go to law before the unrighteous and not before the saints? 2 Or do you not know that the saints will judge the world? If the world is judged by you, are you not competent *to form* the smallest law courts? 3 Do you not know that we will judge angels? How much more matters of this life? 4 So if you have law courts dealing with matters of this life, do you appoint them *as judges* who are of no account in the church? 5 I say *this* to your shame. *Is it* so, *that* there is not among you anyone wise who will be able to decide between his brothers *and sisters,* 6 but brother goes to law with brother, and that before unbelievers?

7 Actually, then, it is already a defeat for you, that you have lawsuits with one another. Why not rather suffer the wrong? Why not rather be defrauded? 8 On the contrary, you yourselves do wrong and defraud. And this to *your* brothers *and sisters!*

9 Or do you not know that the unrighteous will not inherit the kingdom of God? Do not be deceived; neither the sexually immoral, nor idolaters, nor adulterers, nor *homosexuals, 10 nor thieves, nor *the* greedy, nor those habitually drunk, nor verbal abusers, nor swindlers, will inherit the kingdom of God. 11 Such were some of you; but you were washed, but you were sanctified, but you were justified in the name of the Lord Jesus Christ and in the Spirit of our God.

The Body Is the Lord's

12 All things are permitted for me, but not all things are of benefit. All things are permitted for me, but I will not be mastered by anything. 13 Food is for the stomach and the stomach is for food, however God will do away with both of them. But the body is not for sexual immorality, but for the Lord, and the Lord is for the body. 14 Now God has not only raised the Lord, but will also raise us up through His power. 15 Do you not know that your bodies are parts of Christ? Shall I then take away the parts of Christ and make them parts of a prostitute? *From it! 16 Or do you not know that the one who joins himself to a prostitute is one body *with her?* For He says, "THE TWO SHALL BECOME ONE FLESH." 17 But the one who joins himself to the Lord is one spirit *with Him.* 18 Flee sexual immorality. Every other sin that a person commits is outside the body, but the sexually immoral person sins against his own body. 19 Or do you not know that your body is a temple of the Holy Spirit within you, whom you have from God, and *that* you are not your own? 20 For you have been bought for a price: therefore glorify God in your body.

Teaching on Marriage

7 Now concerning the things about which you wrote, it is good for a man *not to touch a woman. 2 But because of sexual immoralities, each man is to have his own wife, and each woman is to have her own husband. 3 The husband must fulfill his duty to his wife, and likewise the wife also to her husband. 4 The wife does not have authority over her own body, but the husband *does;* and likewise the husband also does not have authority over his own body, but the wife *does.* 5 Stop depriving one another, except by agreement for a time so that you may devote yourselves to prayer, and come together again so that Satan will not tempt you because of your lack of self-control. 6 But this I say by way of concession, not of command. 7 *Yet I wish that all men were even as I myself am. However, each has his own gift from God, one in this way, and another in that.

8 But I say to the unmarried and to widows that it is good for them if they remain even as I. 9 But if they do not have self-control, let them marry; for it is better to marry than to burn *with passion.*

10 But to the married I give instructions, not I, but the Lord, that the wife is not to leave her husband 11 (but if she does leave, she must remain unmarried, or else be reconciled to her husband), and that the husband is not to divorce his wife.

12 But to the rest I say, not the Lord, that if any brother has an unbelieving wife, and she consents to live with him, he must not divorce her. 13 And if any woman has an unbelieving husband, and he consents to live with her, she must not divorce her husband. 14 For the unbelieving husband is sanctified through his wife, and the unbelieving wife is sanctified through her believing husband; for otherwise your children are unclean, but now they are holy. 15 Yet if the unbelieving one is leaving, let him leave; the brother or the sister is not under bondage in such *cases,* but God has called 1us in peace. 16 For how do you know, wife, whether you will save your husband? Or how do you know, husband, whether you will save your wife?

17 Only, as the Lord has assigned to each one, as God has called each, in this way let him walk. And so I direct in all the churches. 18 Was any man called *when he was already* circumcised? He is not to become uncircumcised. Has anyone been called in uncircumcision? He is not to be circumcised. 19 Circumcision is nothing, and uncircumcision is nothing, but *what matters is* the keeping of the commandments of God. 20 Each *person* is to remain in that state in which he was called.

21 Were you called as a slave? Do not let it concern you. But if you are also able to become free, take advantage of *that.* 22 For the one who was called in the Lord as a slave, is the Lord's freed person; likewise the one who was called as free, is Christ's slave. 23 You were bought for a price; do not become slaves of people. 24 Brothers *and sisters,* each one is to remain with God in that *condition* in which he was called.

25 Now concerning virgins, I have no command of the Lord, but I am offering direction as one who by the mercy of the Lord is trustworthy. 26 I think, then, that this is good in view of the present distress, that it is good for a man to remain as he is. 27 Are you bound to a wife? Do not seek to be released. Are you released from a wife? Do not seek a wife. 28 But if you marry, you have not sinned; and if a virgin marries, she has not sinned. Yet such people *as yourselves* will have trouble in this life, and I am *trying to* spare you. 29 But this I say, brothers, the time has been shortened, so that from now on those who have wives should be as though they had none; 30 and those who weep, as though they did not weep; and those who rejoice, as though they did not rejoice; and those who buy, as though they did not possess; 31 and those who use the world, as though they did not make full use of it; for the *present* form of this world is passing away.

32 But I want you to be free from concern. One who is unmarried is concerned about the things of the Lord, how he may please the Lord; 33 but one who is married is concerned about the things of the world, how he may please his wife, 34 and *his interests* are divided. The woman who is unmarried, and the virgin, is concerned about the things of the Lord, that she may be holy both in body and spirit; but

one who is married is concerned about the things of the world, how she may please her husband. 35 I say this for your own benefit, not to put a restraint on you, but to promote what is appropriate and *to secure* undistracted devotion to the Lord.

36 But if anyone thinks that he is acting dishonorably toward his virgin, if she is 1past her youth and it ought to be so, let him do what he wishes, he is not sinning; let 2them marry. 37 But the one who stands firm in his heart, if he is not under constraint, but has authority over his own will, and has decided this in his own heart, to keep his own virgin, he will do well. 38 So then, both the one who gives his own virgin in marriage does well, and the one who does not give *her* in marriage will do better.

39 A wife is bound as long as her husband lives; but if her husband dies, she is free to be married to whom she wishes, only in the Lord. 40 But in my opinion she is happier if she remains as she is; and I think that I also have the Spirit of God.

Take Care with Your Liberty

8 Now concerning food sacrificed to idols, we know that we all have knowledge. Knowledge makes *one* conceited, but love edifies *people.* 2 If anyone thinks that he knows anything, he has not yet known as he ought to know; 3 but if anyone loves God, he is known by Him.

4 Therefore, concerning the eating of food sacrificed to idols, we know that an idol is 1nothing at all in the world, and that there is no God but one. 5 For even if there are so-called gods whether in heaven or on earth, as indeed there are many gods and many lords, 6 yet for us there is *only* one God, the Father, from whom are all things, and we *exist* for Him; and one Lord, Jesus Christ, by whom are all things, and we *exist* through Him.

7 However, not all people have this knowledge; but some, being accustomed to the idol until now, eat *food* as if it were sacrificed to an idol; and their conscience, being weak, is defiled. 8 Now food will not bring us close to God; we are neither the worse if we do not eat, nor the better if we do eat. 9 But take care that this freedom of yours does not somehow become a stumbling block to the weak. 10 For if someone sees you, the one who has knowledge, dining in an idol's temple, will his conscience, if he is weak, not be strengthened to eat things sacrificed to idols? 11 For through your knowledge the one who is weak is ruined, the brother *or sister* for whose sake Christ died. 12 And so, by sinning against the brothers *and sisters* and wounding their conscience when it is weak, you sin against Christ. 13 Therefore, if food causes my brother to sin, I will never eat meat again, so that I will not cause my brother to sin.

Paul's Use of Freedom

9 Am I not free? Am I not an apostle? Have I not seen Jesus our Lord? Are you not my

7:15 1 One early ms *you*　7:36 1 Or *past puberty*　2 I.e., the woman and her betrothed or fiancé
8:4 1 I.e., what it represents does not exist

work in the Lord? 2 If I am not an apostle to others, at least I am to you; for you are the seal of my apostleship in the Lord.

3 My defense to those who examine me is this: 4 Do we not have a right to eat and drink? 5 Do we not have a right to take along a believing wife, even as the rest of the apostles and the brothers of the Lord, and Cephas? 6 Or do only Barnabas and I have no right to refrain from working? 7 Who at any time serves as a soldier at his own expense? Who plants a vineyard and does not eat its fruit? Or who tends a flock and does not consume some of the milk of the flock?

8 I am not *just* asserting these things according to human judgment, am I? Or does the Law not say these things as well? 9 For it is written in the Law of Moses: "YOU SHALL NOT MUZZLE THE OX WHILE IT IS THRESHING." God is not concerned about oxen, is He? 10 Or is He speaking entirely for our sake? Yes, it was written for our sake, because the plowman ought to plow in hope, and the thresher *to thresh* in hope of sharing *in the crops.* 11 If we sowed spiritual things in you, is it too much if we reap material things from you? 12 If others share the right over you, do we not more? Nevertheless, we did not use this right, but we endure all things so that we will cause no hindrance to the gospel of Christ. 13 Do you not know that those who perform sacred services eat *the food* of the temple, *and* those who attend regularly to the altar have their share from the altar? 14 So also the Lord directed those who proclaim the gospel to get their living from the gospel.

15 But I have used none of these things. And I have not written these things so that it will be done so in my case; for it would be better for me to die than *that.* No one shall make my boast an empty one! 16 For if I preach the gospel, I have nothing to boast *about,* for I am under compulsion; for woe to me if I do not preach the gospel. 17 For if I do this voluntarily, I have a reward; but if against my will, I have been entrusted with a commission *nonetheless.* 18 What, then, is my reward? That, when I preach the gospel, I may offer the gospel without charge, so as not to make full use of my right in the gospel.

19 For though I am free from all people, I have made myself a slave to all, so that I may gain more. 20 To the Jews I became as a Jew, so that I might gain Jews; to those who are under the Law, *I became* as *one* under the Law, though not being under the Law myself, so that I might gain those who are under the Law; 21 to those who are without the Law, *I became* as one without the Law, though not being without the law of God but under the law of Christ, so that I might gain those who are without the Law. 22 To the weak I became weak, that I might gain the weak; I have become all things to all people, so that I may by all means save some. 23 I do all things for the sake of the gospel, so that I may become a fellow partaker of it.

24 Do you not know that those who run in a race all run, but *only* one receives the prize? Run in such a way that you may win.

25 Everyone who competes in the games exercises self-control in all things. So they *do it* to obtain a perishable wreath, but we an imperishable. 26 Therefore I run in such a way as not *to run* aimlessly; I box in such a way, as to avoid hitting air; 27 but I strictly discipline my body and make it my slave, so that, after I have preached to others, I myself will not be disqualified.

Avoid Israel's Mistakes

10 For I do not want you to be unaware, brothers *and sisters,* that our fathers were all under the cloud and they all passed through the sea; 2 and they all were baptized into Moses in the cloud and in the sea; 3 and they all ate the same spiritual food, 4 and all drank the same spiritual drink, for they were drinking from a spiritual rock which followed them; and the rock was Christ. 5 Nevertheless, with most of them God was not pleased; for *their dead bodies* were spread out in the wilderness.

6 Now these things happened as examples for us, so that we would not crave evil things as they indeed craved *them.* 7 Do not be idolaters, as some of them were; as it is written: "THE PEOPLE SAT DOWN TO EAT AND TO DRINK, AND ROSE UP TO PLAY." 8 Nor are we to commit sexual immorality, as some of them did, and twenty-three thousand fell in one day. 9 Nor are we to put the Lord to the test, as some of them did, and were killed by the snakes. 10 Nor grumble, as some of them did, and were killed by the destroyer. 11 Now these things happened to them as an example, and they were written for our instruction, upon whom the ends of the ages have come. 12 Therefore let the one who thinks he stands watch out that he does not fall. 13 No temptation has overtaken you except *something* common to mankind; and God is faithful, so He will not allow you to be tempted beyond what you are able, but with the temptation will provide the way of escape also, so that you will be able to endure it.

14 Therefore, my beloved, flee from idolatry. 15 I speak as to wise people; you *then,* judge what I say. 16 Is the cup of blessing which we bless not a sharing in the blood of Christ? Is the bread which we break not a sharing in the body of Christ? 17 Since there is one loaf, we who are many are one body; for we all partake of the one loaf. 18 Look at the people of Israel; are those who eat the sacrifices not partners in the altar? 19 What do I mean then? That food sacrificed to idols is anything, or that an idol is anything? 20 *No,* but *I say* that things which *the Gentiles* sacrifice, they sacrifice to demons and not to God; and I do not want you to become partners with demons. 21 You cannot drink the cup of the Lord and the cup of demons; you cannot partake of the table of the Lord and the table of demons. 22 Or do we provoke the Lord to jealousy? We are not stronger than He, are we?

23 All things are permitted, but not all things are of benefit. All things are permitted, but not all things build *people* up. 24 No one is to seek his own *advantage,* but rather that of

his neighbor. 25 Eat anything that is sold in the meat market without asking questions, for the sake of conscience; 26 FOR THE EARTH IS THE LORD'S, AND ALL IT CONTAINS. 27 If one of the unbelievers invites you and you want to go, eat anything that is set before you without asking questions, for the sake of conscience. 28 But if anyone says to you, "This is meat sacrificed to idols," do not eat *it,* for the sake of that one who informed *you* and for the sake of conscience; 29 Now *by* "conscience" I do not mean your own, but the other person's; for why is my freedom judged by another's conscience? 30 If I partake with thankfulness, why am I slandered about that for which I give thanks?

31 Therefore, whether you eat or drink, or whatever you do, do all things for the glory of God. 32 Do not offend Jews or Greeks, or the church of God; 33 just as I also please everyone in all things, not seeking my own benefit but the *benefit* of the many, so that they may be saved.

Christian Order

11 Be imitators of me, just as I also am of Christ.

2 Now I praise you because you remember me in everything and hold firmly to the traditions, just as I handed them down to you. 3 But I want you to understand that Christ is the head of every man, and the man is the head of a woman, and God is the head of Christ. 4 Every man who has *something* on his head while praying or prophesying disgraces his head. 5 But every woman who has her head uncovered while praying or prophesying disgraces her head, for it is one and the same as the woman whose head is shaved. 6 For if a woman does not cover her head, have her also cut her hair off; however, if it is disgraceful for a woman to have her hair cut off or her head shaved, have her cover her head. 7 For a man should not have his head covered, since he is the image and glory of God; but the woman is the glory of man. 8 For man does not originate from woman, but woman from man; 9 for indeed man was not created for the woman's sake, but woman for the man's sake. 10 Therefore the woman should have *a symbol of* authority on her head, because of the angels. 11 However, in the Lord, neither is woman independent of man, nor is man independent of woman. 12 For as the woman *originated* from the man, so also the man *has his birth* through the woman; and all things *originate* from God. 13 Judge for yourselves: is it proper for a woman to pray to God *with her head* uncovered? 14 Does even nature itself not teach you that if a man has long hair, it is a dishonor to him, 15 but if a woman has long hair, it is a glory to her? For her hair is given to her as a covering. 16 But if anyone is inclined to be contentious, we have no such practice, nor have the churches of God.

17 Now in giving this *next* instruction I do not praise you, because you come together not for the better, but for the worse. 18 For, in the first place, when you come together as a church, I hear that divisions exist among you;

and in part I believe it. 19 For there also have to be factions among you, so that those who are approved may become evident among you. 20 Therefore when you come together it is not to eat the Lord's Supper, 21 for when you eat, each one takes his own supper first; and one goes hungry while another gets drunk. 22 What! Do you not have houses in which to eat and drink? Or do you despise the church of God and shame those who have nothing? What am I to say to you? Shall I praise you? In this I do not praise you.

The Lord's Supper

23 For I received from the Lord that which I also delivered to you, that the Lord Jesus, on the night when He was betrayed, took bread; 24 and when He had given thanks, He broke it and said, "This is My body, which is for you; do this in remembrance of Me." 25 In the same way *He* also *took* the cup after supper, saying, "This cup is the new covenant in My blood; do this, as often as you drink *it,* in remembrance of Me." 26 For as often as you eat this bread and drink the cup, you proclaim the Lord's death until He comes.

27 Therefore whoever eats the bread or drinks the cup of the Lord in an unworthy way, shall be guilty of the body and the blood of the Lord. 28 But a person must examine himself, and in so doing he is to eat of the bread and drink of the cup. 29 For the one who eats and drinks, eats and drinks judgment to himself if he does not *properly* recognize the body. 30 For this reason many among you are weak and sick, and a number are asleep. 31 But if we judged ourselves rightly, we would not be judged. 32 But when we are judged, we are disciplined by the Lord so that we will not be condemned along with the world.

33 So then, my brothers *and sisters,* when you come together to eat, wait for one another. 34 If anyone is hungry, have him eat at home, so that you do not come together for judgment. As to the remaining matters, I will give instructions when I come.

The Use of Spiritual Gifts

12 Now concerning spiritual *gifts,* brothers *and sisters,* I do not want you to be unaware. 2 You know that when you were pagans, *you were* led astray to the mute idols, however you were led. 3 Therefore I make known to you that no one speaking by the Spirit of God says, "Jesus is accursed"; and no one can say, "Jesus is Lord," except by the Holy Spirit.

4 Now there are varieties of gifts, but the same Spirit. 5 And there are varieties of ministries, and the same Lord. 6 There are varieties of effects, but the same God who works all things in all *persons.* 7 But to each one is given the manifestation of the Spirit for the common good. 8 For to one is given the word of wisdom through the Spirit, and to another the word of knowledge according to the same Spirit; 9 to another faith by the same Spirit, and to another gifts of healing by the one Spirit, 10 and to another the effecting of miracles, and to another prophecy, and to another the

distinguishing of spirits, to another *various* kinds of tongues, and to another the interpretation of tongues. [11] But one and the same Spirit works all these things, distributing to each one individually just as He wills.

[12] For just as the body is one and *yet* has many parts, and all the parts of the body, though they are many, are one body, so also is Christ. [13] For by one Spirit we were all baptized into one body, whether Jews or Greeks, whether slaves or free, and we were all made to drink of one Spirit.

[14] For the body is not one part, but many. [15] If the foot says, "Because I am not a hand, I am not *a part* of the body," it is not for this reason any less *a part* of the body. [16] And if the ear says, "Because I am not an eye, I am not *a part* of the body," it is not for this reason any less *a part* of the body. [17] If the whole body were an eye, where would the hearing be? If the whole *body* were hearing, where would the sense of smell be? [18] But now God has arranged the parts, each one of them in the body, just as He desired. [19] If they were all one part, where would the body be? [20] But now there are many parts, but one body. [21] And the eye cannot say to the hand, "I have no need of you"; or again, the head to the feet, "I have no need of you." [22] On the contrary, it is much truer that the parts of the body which seem to be weaker are necessary; [23] and those *parts* of the body which we consider less honorable, on these we bestow greater honor, and our less presentable parts become much more presentable, [24] whereas our more presentable parts have no need *of it.* But God has *so* composed the body, giving more abundant honor to that *part* which lacked, [25] so that there may be no division in the body, but *that* the parts may have the same care for one another. [26] And if one part *of the body* suffers, all the parts suffer with it; if a part is honored, all the parts rejoice with it.

[27] Now you are Christ's body, and individually parts of it. [28] And God has appointed in the church, first apostles, second prophets, third teachers, then miracles, then gifts of healings, helps, administrations, *and various* kinds of tongues. [29] All are not apostles, are they? All are not prophets, are they? All are not teachers, are they? All are not *workers of miracles,* are they? [30] All do not have gifts of healings, do they? All do not speak with tongues, do they? All do not interpret, do they? [31] But earnestly desire the greater gifts.

And yet, I *am going to* show you a far better way.

The Excellence of Love

13 If I speak with the tongues of mankind and of angels, but do not have love, I have become a noisy gong or a clanging cymbal. [2] If I have *the gift of* prophecy and know all mysteries and all knowledge, and if I have all faith so as to remove mountains, but do not have love, I am nothing. [3] And if I give away all my possessions *to charity,* and if I surrender my body so that I may [1]glory, but do not have love, it does me no good.

[4] Love is patient, love is kind, it is not jealous; love does not brag, it is not arrogant. [5] It does not act disgracefully, it does not seek its own *benefit;* it is not provoked, does not keep an account of a wrong *suffered,* [6] it does not rejoice in unrighteousness, but rejoices with the truth; [7] it keeps every confidence, it believes all things, hopes all things, endures all things.

[8] Love never fails; but if *there are gifts of* prophecy, they will be done away with; if *there are* tongues, they will cease; if *there is* knowledge, it will be done away with. [9] For we know in part and prophesy in part; [10] but when the perfect comes, the partial will be done away with. [11] When I was a child, I used to speak like a child, think like a child, reason like a child; when I became a man, I did away with childish things. [12] For now we see in a mirror dimly, but then face to face; now I know in part, but then I will know fully, just as I also have been fully known. [13] But now faith, hope, *and* love remain, these three; but the greatest of these is love.

Prophecy a Superior Gift

14 Pursue love, yet earnestly desire spiritual *gifts,* but especially that you may prophesy. [2] For the one who speaks in a tongue does not speak to people, but to God; for no one understands, but in *his* spirit he speaks mysteries. [3] But the one who prophesies speaks to people *for* edification, exhortation, and consolation. [4] The one who speaks in a tongue edifies himself; but the one who prophesies edifies the church. [5] Now I wish that you all spoke in tongues, but rather that you would prophesy; and greater is the one who prophesies than the one who speaks in tongues, unless he interprets, so that the church may receive edification.

[6] But now, brothers *and sisters,* if I come to you speaking in tongues, how will I benefit you unless I speak to you either by way of revelation, or of knowledge, or of prophecy, or of teaching? [7] Yet *even* lifeless *instruments,* whether flute or harp, in producing a sound, if they do not produce a distinction in the tones, how will it be known what is played on the flute or on the harp? [8] For if the trumpet produces an indistinct sound, who will prepare himself for battle? [9] So you too, unless you produce intelligible speech by the tongue, how will it be known what is spoken? For you will *just* be talking to the air. [10] There are, perhaps, a great many kinds of languages in the world, and none is incapable of meaning. [11] So if I do not know the meaning of the language, I will be unintelligible to the one who speaks, and the one who speaks will be unintelligible to me. [12] So you too, since you are eager to possess spiritual *gifts,* strive to excel for the edification of the church.

[13] Therefore, one who speaks in a tongue is to pray that he may interpret. [14] For if I pray in a tongue, my spirit prays, but my mind is unproductive. [15] What is *the outcome* then? I will pray with the spirit, but I will pray with the mind also; I will sing with the spirit, but I

13:3 [1]I.e., in martyrdom

will sing with the mind also. **16** For otherwise, if you bless *God* in the spirit *only,* how will the one who occupies the place of the outsider *know to* say the "Amen" at your giving of thanks, since he does not understand what you are saying? **17** For you are giving thanks well *enough,* but the other person is not edified. **18** I thank God, I speak in tongues more than you all; **19** nevertheless, in church I prefer to speak five words with my mind so that I may instruct others also, rather than ten thousand words in a tongue.

Instruction for the Church

20 Brothers *and sisters,* do not be children in your thinking; yet in evil be infants, but in your thinking be mature. **21** In the Law it is written: "BY MEN OF STRANGE TONGUES AND BY THE LIPS OF STRANGERS I WILL SPEAK TO THIS PEOPLE, AND EVEN SO THEY WILL NOT LISTEN TO ME," says the Lord. **22** So then, tongues are for a sign, not to those who believe but to unbelievers; but prophecy is not for unbelievers, but for those who believe. **23** Therefore if the whole church gathers together and all *the people* speak in tongues, and outsiders or unbelievers enter, will they not say that you are insane? **24** But if all prophesy, and an unbeliever or an outsider enters, he is convicted by all, he is called to account by all; **25** the secrets of his heart are disclosed; and so he will fall on his face and worship God, declaring that God is certainly among you.

26 What is *the outcome* then, brothers *and sisters?* When you assemble, each one has a psalm, has a teaching, has a revelation, has a tongue, has an interpretation. All things are to be done for edification. **27** If anyone speaks in a tongue, *it must be* by two or at the most three, and *each one* in turn, and one is to interpret; **28** but if there is no interpreter, he is to keep silent in church; and have him speak to himself and to God. **29** Have two or three prophets speak, and have the others pass judgment. **30** But if a revelation is made to another who is seated, then the first one is to keep silent. **31** For you can all prophesy one by one, so that all may learn and all may be exhorted; **32** and the spirits of prophets are subject to prophets; **33** for God is not a God of confusion, but of peace.

As in all the churches of the saints, **34** the women are to keep silent in the churches; for they are not permitted to speak, but are to subject themselves, just as the Law also says. **35** If they desire to learn anything, let them ask their own husbands at home; for it is improper for a woman to speak in church. **36** Or was it from you that the word of God *first* went out? Or has it come to you only?

37 If anyone thinks that he is a prophet or spiritual, let him recognize that the things which I write to you are the Lord's commandment. **38** But if anyone does not recognize *this,* 'he is not recognized.

39 Therefore, my brothers *and sisters,* earnestly desire to prophesy, and do not forbid speaking in tongues. **40** But all things must be done properly and in an orderly way.

The Fact of Christ's Resurrection

15 Now I make known to you, brothers *and sisters,* the gospel which I preached to you, which you also received, in which you also stand, **2** by which you also are saved, if you hold firmly to the word which I preached to you, unless you believed in vain.

3 For I handed down to you as of first importance what I also received, that Christ died for our sins according to the Scriptures, **4** and that He was buried, and that He was raised on the third day according to the Scriptures, **5** and that He appeared to Cephas, then to the twelve. **6** After that He appeared to more than five hundred brothers *and sisters* at one time, most of whom remain until now, but some have fallen asleep; **7** then He appeared to James, then to all the apostles; **8** and last of all, as to one untimely born, He appeared to me also. **9** For I am the least of the apostles, and not fit to be called an apostle, because I persecuted the church of God. **10** But by the grace of God I am what I am, and His grace toward me did not prove vain; but I labored even more than all of them, yet not I, but the grace of God with me. **11** Whether then *it was* I or they, so we preach and so you believed.

12 Now if Christ is preached, that He has been raised from the dead, how do some among you say that there is no resurrection of the dead? **13** But if there is no resurrection of the dead, then not even Christ has been raised; **14** and if Christ has not been raised, then our preaching is in vain, your faith also is in vain. **15** Moreover, we are even found *to be* false witnesses of God, because we testified against God that He raised ¹Christ, whom He did not raise, if in fact the dead are not raised. **16** For if the dead are not raised, then not even Christ has been raised; **17** and if Christ has not been raised, your faith is worthless; you are still in your sins. **18** Then also those who have fallen asleep in Christ have perished. **19** If we have hoped in Christ only in this life, we are of all people most to be pitied.

The Order of Resurrection

20 But the fact is, Christ has been raised from the dead, the first fruits of those who are asleep. **21** For since by a man death *came,* by a man also *came* the resurrection of the dead. **22** For as in Adam all die, so also in Christ all will be made alive. **23** But each in his own order: Christ the first fruits, after that those who are Christ's at His coming, **24** then *comes* the end, when He hands over the kingdom to *our* God and Father, when He has abolished all rule and all authority and power. **25** For He must reign until He has put all His enemies under His feet. **26** The last enemy that will be abolished is death. **27** For HE HAS PUT ALL THINGS IN SUBJECTION UNDER HIS FEET. But when He says, "All things are put in subjection," it is clear that this excludes the *Father* who put all things in subjection to Him. **28** When all things are subjected to Him, then the Son Himself will also be subjected to the One who subjected all things to Him, so that God may be all in all.

14:38 ¹ Two early mss *let him continue not to recognize* it   **15:15** ¹ I.e., the Messiah

29 For otherwise, what will those do who are baptized for the dead? If the dead are not raised at all, why then are they baptized for them? 30 Why are we also in danger every hour? 31 I affirm, brothers *and sisters,* by the boasting in you which I have in Christ Jesus our Lord, that I die daily. 32 If from human motives I fought with wild beasts at Ephesus, what good is it to me? If the dead are not raised, LET'S EAT AND DRINK, FOR TOMORROW WE DIE. 33 Do not be deceived: "Bad company corrupts good morals." 34 Sober up morally and stop sinning, for some have no knowledge of God. I say *this* to your shame.

35 But someone will say, "How are the dead raised? And with what kind of body do they come?" 36 You fool! That which you sow does not come to life unless it dies; 37 and that which you sow, you do not sow the body which is to be, but a bare grain, perhaps of wheat or of something else. 38 But God gives it a body just as He wished, and to each of the seeds a body of its own. 39 All flesh is not the same flesh, but there is one *flesh* of mankind, another flesh of animals, another flesh of birds, and another of fish. 40 There are also heavenly bodies and earthly bodies, but the glory of the heavenly is one, and the *glory* of the earthly is another. 41 There is one glory of the sun, another glory of the moon, and another glory of the stars; for star differs from star in glory.

42 So also is the resurrection of the dead. It is sown a perishable *body,* it is raised an imperishable *body;* 43 it is sown in dishonor, it is raised in glory; it is sown in weakness, it is raised in power; 44 it is sown a natural body, it is raised a spiritual body. If there is a natural body, there is also a spiritual *body.* 45 So also it is written: "The first MAN, Adam, BECAME A LIVING PERSON." The last Adam *was* a life-giving spirit. 46 However, the spiritual is not first, but the natural; then the spiritual. 47 The first man is from the earth, earthy; the second man is from heaven. 48 As is the earthy one, so also are those who are earthy; and as is the heavenly one, so also are those who are heavenly. 49 Just as we have borne the image of the earthy, *'we* will also bear the image of the heavenly.

The Mystery of Resurrection

50 Now I say this, brothers *and sisters,* that flesh and blood cannot inherit the kingdom of God; nor does the perishable inherit the imperishable. 51 Behold, I am telling you a mystery; we will not all sleep, but we will all be changed, 52 in a moment, in the twinkling of an eye, at the last trumpet; for the trumpet will sound, and the dead will be raised imperishable, and we will be changed. 53 For this perishable must put on the imperishable, and this mortal *must* put on immortality. 54 But when this perishable puts on the imperishable, and this mortal puts on immortality, then will come about the saying that is written: "DEATH HAS BEEN SWALLOWED UP in victory. 55 WHERE, O DEATH, IS YOUR VICTORY? WHERE, O DEATH, IS YOUR STING?" 56 The sting of death is sin, and the power of sin is the Law; 57 but thanks be to God, who gives us the victory through our Lord Jesus Christ.

58 Therefore, my beloved brothers *and sisters,* be firm, immovable, always excelling in the work of the Lord, knowing that your labor is not *in* vain in the Lord.

Instructions and Greetings

16 Now concerning the collection for the saints, as I directed the churches of Galatia, so you are to do as well. 2 On the first day of every week, each of you is to put aside and save as he may prosper, so that no collections *need to* be made when I come. 3 When I arrive, whomever you approve, I will send them with letters to take your gift to Jerusalem; 4 and if it is appropriate for me to go also, they will go with me.

5 But I will come to you after I go through Macedonia; for I am going through Macedonia, 6 and perhaps I will stay with you or even spend the winter, so that you may send me on my way wherever I go. 7 For I do not want to see you now *just* in passing; for I hope to remain with you for some time, if the Lord permits. 8 But I will remain in Ephesus until Pentecost; 9 for a wide door for effective *service* has opened to me, and there are many adversaries.

10 Now if Timothy comes, see that he has no reason to be afraid *while* among you, for he is doing the Lord's work, as I also am. 11 So do not look down on him, anyone. But send him on his way in peace, so that he may come to me; for I expect him with the brothers.

12 Now concerning our brother Apollos, I strongly encouraged him to come to you with the brothers; and it was not at all *his* desire to come now, but he will come when he has the opportunity.

13 Be on the alert, stand firm in the faith, act like men, be strong. 14 All that you do must be done in love.

15 Now I urge you, brothers *and sisters:* you know the household of Stephanas, that they are the first fruits of Achaia, and that they have devoted themselves to ministry to the saints; 16 I urge that you also be subject to such as these and to everyone who helps in the work and labors. 17 I rejoice over the coming of Stephanas, Fortunatus, and Achaicus, because they have supplied what was lacking on your part. 18 For they have refreshed my spirit and yours. Therefore acknowledge such men.

19 The churches of Asia greet you. Aquila and Prisca greet you heartily in the Lord, with the church that is in their house. 20 All the brothers *and sisters* greet you. Greet one another with a holy kiss.

21 The greeting is in my own hand—*that* of Paul. 22 If anyone does not love the Lord, he is to be accursed. *'Maranatha!* 23 The grace of the Lord Jesus be with you. 24 My love be with you all in Christ Jesus. Amen.

15:49 1 Two early mss *let's also*   16:22 1 Aramaic *[Our] Lord, come!*

CORINTHIANS

Introduction

1 Paul, an apostle of Christ Jesus by the will of God, and our brother Timothy,
To the church of God which is at Corinth with all the saints who are throughout Achaia:
2 Grace to you and peace from God our Father and the Lord Jesus Christ.
3 Blessed be the God and Father of our Lord Jesus Christ, the Father of mercies and God of all comfort, 4 who comforts us in all our affliction so that we will be able to comfort those who are in any affliction with the comfort with which we ourselves are comforted by God. 5 For just as the sufferings of Christ are ours in abundance, so also our comfort is abundant through Christ. 6 But if we are afflicted, it is for your comfort and salvation; or if we are comforted, it is for your comfort, which is effective in the patient enduring of the same sufferings which we also suffer; 7 and our hope for you is firmly grounded, knowing that as you are partners in our sufferings, so also you are in our comfort.
8 For we do not want you to be unaware, brothers and sisters, of our affliction which occurred in Asia, that we were burdened excessively, beyond our strength, so that we despaired even of life. 9 Indeed, we had the sentence of death within ourselves so that we would not trust in ourselves, but in God who raises the dead, 10 who rescued us from so great a danger of death, and will rescue us, He on whom we have set our hope. And He will yet deliver us, 11 if you also join in helping us through your prayers, so that thanks may be given by many persons in our behalf for the favor granted to us through the prayers of many.

Paul's Integrity

12 For our proud confidence is this: the testimony of our conscience, that in holiness and godly sincerity, not in fleshly wisdom but in the grace of God, we have conducted ourselves in the world, and especially toward you. 13 For we write nothing else to you than what you read and understand, and I hope you will understand until the end; 14 just as you also partially did understand us, that we are your reason to be proud as you also are ours, on the day of our Lord Jesus.
15 In this confidence I intended at first to come to you, so that you might twice receive a blessing; 16 that is, to pass your way into Macedonia, and again from Macedonia to come to you, and by you to be helped on my journey to Judea. 17 Therefore, I was not vacillating when I intended to do this, was I? Or what I decide, do I decide according to the flesh, so that with me there will be yes, yes and no, no at the same time? 18 But as God is faithful, our word to you is not yes and no. 19 For the Son of God, Christ Jesus, who was preached among you by us—by me and Silvanus and Timothy—was not yes and no, but has been yes in Him. 20 For as many as the promises of God are, in Him they are yes; therefore through Him also is our Amen to the glory of God through us. 21 Now He who establishes us with you in Christ and anointed us is God, 22 who also sealed us and gave us the Spirit in our hearts as a 1pledge.
23 But I call God as witness to my soul, that it was to spare you that I did not come again to Corinth. 24 Not that we domineer over your faith, but we are workers with you for your joy; for in your faith you are standing firm.

Reaffirm Your Love

2 But I decided this for my own sake, that I would not come to you in sorrow again. 2 For if I cause you sorrow, who then will be the one making me glad but the one who is made sorrowful by me? 3 This is the very thing I wrote you, so that when I came, I would not have sorrow from those who ought to make me rejoice; having confidence in you all that my joy was the joy of you all. 4 For out of much affliction and anguish of heart I wrote to you with many tears; not so that you would be made sorrowful, but that you might know the love which I have especially for you.
5 But if anyone has caused sorrow, he has caused sorrow not for me, but in some degree—not to say too much—for all of you. 6 Sufficient for such a person is this punishment which was imposed by the majority, 7 so that on the other hand, you should rather forgive and comfort him, otherwise such a person might be overwhelmed by excessive sorrow. 8 Therefore I urge you to reaffirm your love for him. 9 For to this end I also wrote, so that I might put you to the test, whether you are obedient in all things. 10 But one whom you forgive anything, I also forgive; for indeed what I have forgiven, if I have forgiven anything, I did so for your sakes in the presence of Christ, 11 so that no advantage would be taken of us by Satan, for we are not ignorant of his schemes.
12 Now when I came to Troas for the gospel of Christ and when a door was opened for me in the Lord, 13 I had no rest for my spirit, not finding Titus my brother; but saying goodbye to them, I went on to Macedonia.
14 But thanks be to God, who always leads us in triumph in Christ, and through us reveals the fragrance of the knowledge of Him in every place. 15 For we are a fragrance of Christ to God among those who are being saved and among those who are perishing: 16 to the one an aroma from death to death, to the other an aroma from life to life. And who is adequate for these things? 17 For we are not like the many, 1peddling the word of God, but as from sincerity,

---

1:22 1 Or first installment   2:17 1 Or diluting

but as from God, we speak in Christ in the sight of God.

Ministers of a New Covenant

3 Are we beginning to commend ourselves again? Or do we need, as some, letters of commendation to you or from you? 2 You are our letter, written in our hearts, known and read by all people, 3 revealing yourselves, that you are a letter of Christ, delivered by us, written not with ink but with the Spirit of the living God, not on tablets of stone but on tablets of human hearts.

4 Such *is the* confidence we have toward God through Christ. 5 Not that we are adequate in ourselves *so as* to consider anything as *having come* from ourselves, but our adequacy is from God, 6 who also made us adequate *as* servants of a new covenant, not of the letter but of the Spirit; for the letter kills, but the Spirit gives life.

7 But if the ministry of death, engraved in letters on stones, came with glory so that the sons of Israel could not look intently at the face of Moses because of the glory of his face, fading *as* it was, 8 how will the ministry of the Spirit fail to be *even* more with glory? 9 For if the ministry of condemnation has glory, much more does the ministry of righteousness excel in glory. 10 For indeed what had glory in this case has no glory, because of the glory that surpasses *it.* 11 For if that which fades away *was* with glory, much more that which remains *is* in glory.

12 Therefore, having such a hope, we use great boldness in *our* speech, 13 and *we are* not like Moses, *who* used to put a veil over his face so that the sons of Israel would not stare at the end of what was fading away. 14 But their minds were hardened; for until this very day at the reading of the old covenant the same veil remains unlifted, because it is removed in Christ. 15 But to this day whenever Moses is read, a veil lies over their hearts; 16 but whenever *someone* turns to the Lord, the veil is taken away. 17 Now the Lord is the Spirit, and where the Spirit of the Lord is, *there* is freedom. 18 But we all, with unveiled faces, looking as in a mirror at the glory of the Lord, are being transformed into the same image from glory to glory, just as from the Lord, the Spirit.

Paul's Apostolic Ministry

4 Therefore, since we have this ministry, as we received mercy, we do not lose heart, 2 but we have renounced the things hidden because of shame, not walking in trickery nor distorting the word of God, but by the open proclamation of the truth commending ourselves to every person's conscience in the sight of God. 3 And even if our gospel is veiled, it is veiled to those who are perishing, 4 in whose case the god of this world has blinded the minds of the unbelieving so that they will not see the light of the gospel of the glory of Christ, who is the image of God. 5 For we do not preach ourselves, but Christ Jesus as Lord, and ourselves as your bond-servants on account of Jesus. 6 For God, who said, "Light shall shine

out of darkness," is the One who has shone in our hearts to give the Light of the knowledge of the glory of God in the face of Christ.

7 But we have this treasure in earthen containers, so that the extraordinary *greatness* of the power will be of God and not from ourselves; 8 *we are* afflicted in every way, but not crushed; perplexed, but not despairing; 9 persecuted, but not abandoned; struck down, but not destroyed; 10 always carrying around in the body the dying of Jesus, so that the life of Jesus may also be revealed in our body. 11 For we who live are constantly being handed over to death because of Jesus, so that the life of Jesus may also be revealed in our mortal flesh. 12 So death works in us, but life in you.

13 But having the same spirit of faith, according to what is written: "I BELIEVED, THEREFORE I SPOKE," we also believe, therefore we also speak, 14 knowing that He who raised the Lord Jesus will also raise us with Jesus, and will present *us* with you. 15 For all things *are* for your sakes, so that grace, having spread to more and more people, will cause thanksgiving to overflow to the glory of God.

16 Therefore we do not lose heart, but though our outer person is decaying, yet our inner *person* is being renewed day by day. 17 For our momentary, light affliction is producing for us an eternal weight of glory far beyond all comparison, 18 while we look not at the things which are seen, but at the things which are not seen; for the things which are seen are temporal, but the things which are not seen are eternal.

The Temporal and Eternal

5 For we know that if our earthly tent which is our house is torn down, we have a building from God, a house not made by hands, eternal in the heavens. 2 For indeed, in this *tent* we groan, longing to be clothed with our ¹dwelling from heaven, 3 since in fact after putting it on, we will not be found naked. 4 For indeed, we who are in this tent groan, being burdened, because we do not want to be unclothed but to be clothed, so that what is mortal will be swallowed up by life. 5 Now He who prepared us for this very *purpose is* God, who gave us the Spirit as a ¹pledge.

6 Therefore, being always of good courage, and knowing that while we are at home in the body we are absent from the Lord— 7 for we walk by faith, not by sight— 8 but we are of good courage and prefer rather to be absent from the body and to be at home with the Lord. 9 Therefore we also have as our ambition, whether at home or absent, to be pleasing to Him. 10 For we must all appear before the judgment seat of Christ, so that each one may receive compensation for his deeds *done* through the body, in accordance with what he has done, whether good or bad.

11 Therefore, knowing the fear of the Lord, we persuade people, but we are well known to God; and I hope that we are also well known in your consciences. 12 We are not commending ourselves to you again, but *are* giving you an opportunity to be proud of us, so that you will

---

5:2 ¹ I.e., the resurrected body   5:5 ¹ Or first installment

have *an answer* for those who take pride in appearance and not in heart. [13] For if we have lost our minds, *it is* for God; if we are of sound mind, *it is* for you. [14] For the love of Christ controls us, having concluded this, that one died for all, therefore all died; [15] and He died for all, so that those who live would no longer live for themselves, but for Him who died and rose on their behalf.

[16] Therefore from now on we recognize no one by the flesh; even though we have known Christ by the flesh, yet now we know *Him in this way* no longer. [17] Therefore if anyone is in Christ, *this person is* a new creation; the old things passed away; behold, new things have come. [18] Now all *these* things are from God, who reconciled us to Himself through Christ and gave us the ministry of reconciliation, [19] namely, that God was in Christ reconciling the world to Himself, not counting their wrongdoings against them, and He has committed to us the word of reconciliation. [20] Therefore, we are ambassadors for Christ, as though God were making an appeal through us; we beg you on behalf of Christ, be reconciled to God. [21] He made Him who knew no sin *to be* [1]sin in our behalf, so that we might become the righteousness of God in Him.

Their Ministry Commended

6 And working together *with Him,* we also urge you not to receive the grace of God in vain—[2] for He says,

"AT A FAVORABLE TIME I LISTENED TO YOU,
  AND ON A DAY OF SALVATION I HELPED YOU."

Behold, now is "A FAVORABLE TIME," behold, now is "A DAY OF SALVATION"—[3] giving no reason for *taking* offense in anything, so that the ministry will not be discredited, [4] but in everything commending ourselves as servants of God, in much endurance, in afflictions, in hardships, in difficulties, [5] in beatings, in imprisonments, in mob attacks, in labors, in sleeplessness, in hunger, [6] in purity, in knowledge, in patience, in kindness, in the Holy Spirit, in genuine love, [7] in the word of truth, *and* in the power of God; by the weapons of righteousness for the right hand and the left, [8] by glory and dishonor, by evil report and good report; *regarded* as deceivers and yet true; [9] as unknown and *yet* well known, as dying and *yet* behold, we are alive; as punished and *yet* not put to death, [10] as sorrowful yet always rejoicing, as poor yet making many rich, as having nothing and *yet* possessing all things.

[11] Our mouth has spoken freely to you, you Corinthians, our heart is opened wide. [12] You are not restrained by us, but you are restrained in your own affections. [13] Now in the same way in exchange—I am speaking as to children— open wide *your hearts to us,* you as well.

[14] Do not be mismatched with unbelievers; for what do righteousness and lawlessness share together, or what does light have in common with darkness? [15] Or what harmony does Christ have with Belial, or what does a believer share with an unbeliever? [16] Or what agreement does the temple of God have with idols? For we are the temple of the living God; just as God said,

"I WILL DWELL AMONG THEM AND WALK
   AMONG THEM;
 AND I WILL BE THEIR GOD, AND THEY SHALL BE
   MY PEOPLE."

[17] "Therefore, COME OUT FROM THEIR MIDST AND
   BE SEPARATE," says the Lord.
 "AND DO NOT TOUCH WHAT IS UNCLEAN;
   And I will welcome you.
[18] "And I will be a father to you,
   And you shall be sons and daughters to
   Me,"
 Says the Lord Almighty.

Paul Reveals His Heart

7 Therefore, having these promises, beloved, let's cleanse ourselves from all defilement of flesh and spirit, perfecting holiness in the fear of God.

[2] Make room for us *in your hearts;* we have wronged no one, we corrupted no one, we have taken advantage of no one. [3] I do not speak to condemn *you,* for I have said before that you are in our hearts, to die together and to live together. [4] My confidence in you is great; my boasting in your behalf is great. I am filled with comfort; I am overflowing with joy in all our affliction.

[5] For even when we came into Macedonia our flesh had no rest, but we were afflicted on every side: conflicts on the outside, fears inside. [6] But God, who comforts the discouraged, comforted us by the arrival of Titus; [7] and not only by his arrival, but also by the comfort with which he was comforted among you, as he reported to us your longing, your mourning, your zeal for me; so that I rejoiced even more. [8] For though I caused you sorrow by my letter, I do not regret it; though I did regret it—*for* I see that that letter caused you sorrow, though only for a while—[9] I now rejoice, not that you were made sorrowful, but that you were made sorrowful to *the point of* repentance; for you were made sorrowful according to *the will of* God, so that you might not suffer loss in anything through us. [10] For the sorrow that is according to *the will of* God produces a repentance without regret, *leading* to salvation, but the sorrow of the world produces death. [11] For behold what earnestness this very thing, this godly sorrow, has produced in you: what vindication *of yourselves,* what indignation, what fear, what longing, what zeal, what punishment of wrong! In everything you demonstrated yourselves to be innocent in the matter. [12] So although I wrote to you, *it was* not for the sake of the offender nor for the sake of the one offended, but that your earnestness in our behalf might be made known to you in the sight of God. [13] Because of this, we have been comforted.

And besides our comfort, we rejoiced even much more for the joy of Titus, because his spirit has been refreshed by you all. [14] For if I have boasted to him about you regarding anything, I was not put to shame. But as we spoke all things to you in truth, so also our

---

5:21 [1] Or *a sin offering*

boasting before Titus proved to be *the* truth. **15** His affection abounds all the more toward you, as he remembers the obedience of you all, how you received him with fear and trembling. **16** I rejoice that in everything I have confidence in you.

Great Generosity

8 Now, brothers *and sisters,* we make known to you the grace of God which has been given in the churches of Macedonia, **2** that in a great ordeal of affliction their abundance of joy and their deep poverty overflowed in the wealth of their liberality. **3** For I testify that according to their ability, and beyond their ability, *they gave* voluntarily, **4** begging us with much urging for the favor of participation in the support of the saints, **5** and *this,* not as we had expected, but they first gave themselves to the Lord and to us by the will of God. **6** So we urged Titus that as he had previously made a beginning, so he would also complete in you this gracious work as well.

7 But just as you excel in everything, in faith, speaking, knowledge, and in all earnestness and in the love we inspired in you, *see* that you also excel in this gracious work. **8** I am not saying *this* as a command, but as proving, through the earnestness of others, the sincerity of your love as well. **9** For you know the grace of our Lord Jesus Christ, that though He was rich, yet for your sake He became poor, so that you through His poverty might become rich. **10** I give *my* opinion in this matter, for this is to your advantage, who were the first to begin a year ago not only to do *this,* but also to desire *to do it.* **11** But now finish doing it also, so that just as *there was* the willingness to desire it, so *there may be* also the completion of it by your ability. **12** For if the willingness is present, it is acceptable according to what *a person* has, not according to what he does not have. **13** For *this* is not for the relief of others *and* for your hardship, but by way of equality— **14** at this present time your abundance *will serve as assistance* for their need, so that their abundance also may serve as *assistance* for your need, so that there may be equality; **15** as it is written: "The one who *had gathered* much did not have too much, and the one who *had gathered* little did not have too little."

16 But thanks be to God who puts the same earnestness in your behalf in the heart of Titus. **17** For he not only accepted our appeal, but being himself very earnest, he has gone to you of his own accord. **18** We have sent along with him the brother whose fame in *the things of* the gospel *has spread* through all the churches; **19** and not only *that,* but he has also been appointed by the churches to travel with us in this gracious work, which is being administered by us for the glory of the Lord Himself, and *to show* our readiness, **20** taking precaution so that no one will discredit us in our administration of this generous gift; **21** for we have regard for what is honorable, not only in the sight of the Lord, but also in the sight of *other* people. **22** We have sent with them our brother, whom we have often tested and found diligent in many things, but now even more diligent because of *his* great confidence in you. **23** As for Titus, *he is* my partner and fellow worker among you; as for our brothers, *they are* messengers of the churches, a glory to Christ. **24** Therefore, openly before the churches, show them the proof of your love and of our reason for boasting about you.

God Gives Most

9 For it is superfluous for me to write to you about this ministry to the saints; **2** for I know your willingness, of which I boast about you to the Macedonians, *namely,* that Achaia has been prepared since last year, and your zeal has stirred up most of them. **3** But I have sent the brothers, in order that our boasting about you may not prove empty in this case, so that, as I was saying, you will be prepared; **4** otherwise, if *any* Macedonians come with me and find you unprepared, we—not to mention you—would be put to shame by this confidence. **5** So I considered it necessary to urge the brothers that they go on ahead to you and arrange in advance your previously promised generous gift, that the same would be ready as a generous gift, and not as *one grudgingly given due to* greediness.

6 Now *I say* this: the one who sows sparingly will also reap sparingly, and the one who sows generously will also reap generously. **7** Each one *must do* just as he has decided in his heart, not reluctantly or under compulsion, for God loves a cheerful giver. **8** And God is able to make all grace overflow to you, so that, always having all sufficiency in everything, you may have an abundance for every good deed; **9** as it is written:

"He scattered abroad, he gave to the
    poor,
His righteousness endures forever."

10 Now He who supplies seed to the sower and bread for food will supply and multiply your seed for sowing and increase the harvest of your righteousness; **11** you will be enriched in everything for all liberality, which through us is producing thanksgiving to God. **12** For the ministry of this service is not only fully supplying the needs of the saints, but is also overflowing through many thanksgivings to God. **13** Because of the proof given by this ministry, they will glorify God for *your* obedience to your confession of the gospel of Christ and for the liberality of your contribution to them and to all, **14** while they also, by prayer on your behalf, yearn for you because of the surpassing grace of God in you. **15** Thanks be to God for His indescribable gift!

Paul Confronts the Corinthians

10 Now I, Paul, myself urge you by the meekness and gentleness of Christ—I who am meek when face to face with you, but bold toward you when absent! **2** I ask that when I am present I *need* not be bold with the confidence with which I intend to be courageous against some, who regard us as if we walked according to the flesh. **3** For though we walk in the flesh, we do not wage battle according to the flesh, **4** for the weapons of our warfare are not of the flesh, but divinely powerful for the

destruction of fortresses. 5 We are destroying arguments and all arrogance raised against the knowledge of God, and we are taking every thought captive to the obedience of Christ, 6 and we are ready to punish all disobedience, whenever your obedience is complete.

7 You are looking at things as they are outwardly. If anyone is confident in himself that he is Christ's, have him consider this again within himself, that just as he is Christ's, so too are we. 8 For if I boast somewhat more about our authority, which the Lord gave for building you up and not for destroying you, I will not be put to shame, 9 for I do not want to seem as if I would terrify you by my letters. 10 For they say, "His letters are weighty and strong, but his personal presence is unimpressive and his speech contemptible." 11 Have such a person consider this, that what we are in word by letters when absent, such persons we are also in deed when present.

12 For we do not presume to rank or compare ourselves with some of those who commend themselves; but when they measure themselves by themselves and compare themselves with themselves, they have no understanding. 13 But we will not boast beyond our measure, but within the measure of the domain which God assigned to us as a measure, to reach even as far as you. 14 For we are not overextending ourselves, as if we did not reach to you, for we were the first to come even as far as you in the gospel of Christ; 15 not boasting beyond our measure, that is, in other people's labors, but with the hope that as your faith grows, we will be, within our domain, enlarged even more by you, 16 so as to preach the gospel even to the regions beyond you, and not to boast in what has been accomplished in the domain of another. 17 But THE ONE WHO BOASTS IS TO BOAST IN THE LORD. 18 For it is not the one who commends himself that is approved, but the one whom the Lord commends.

Paul Defends His Apostleship

11 I wish that you would bear with me in a little foolishness; but indeed you are bearing with me. 2 For I am jealous for you with a godly jealousy; for I betrothed you to one husband, to present you as a pure virgin to Christ. 3 But I am afraid that, as the serpent deceived Eve by his trickery, your minds will be led astray from sincere and pure devotion to Christ. 4 For if one comes and preaches another Jesus whom we have not preached, or you receive a different spirit which you have not received, or a different gospel which you have not accepted, this you tolerate very well! 5 For I consider myself not in the least inferior to the most eminent apostles. 6 But even if I am unskilled in speech, yet I am not so in knowledge; in fact, in every way we have made this evident to you in all things.

7 Or did I commit a sin by humbling myself so that you might be exalted, because I preached the gospel of God to you without charge? 8 I robbed other churches by taking wages from them to serve you; 9 and when I was present with you and was in need, I was not a burden to anyone; for when the brothers came from Macedonia they fully supplied my need, and in everything I kept myself from being a burden to you, and will continue to do so. 10 As the truth of Christ is in me, this boasting of mine will not be stopped in the regions of Achaia. 11 Why? Because I do not love you? God knows that I do!

12 But what I am doing I will also continue to do, so that I may eliminate the opportunity from those who want an opportunity to be regarded just as we are in the matter about which they are boasting. 13 For such men are false apostles, deceitful workers, disguising themselves as apostles of Christ. 14 No wonder, for even Satan disguises himself as an angel of light. 15 Therefore it is not surprising if his servants also disguise themselves as servants of righteousness, whose end will be according to their deeds.

16 Again I say, let no one think me foolish; but if you do, receive me even as foolish, so that I also may boast a little. 17 What I am saying, I am not saying as the Lord would, but as in foolishness, in this confidence of boasting. 18 Since many boast according to the flesh, I will boast also. 19 For you, being so wise, tolerate the foolish gladly. 20 For you tolerate it if anyone enslaves you, if anyone devours you, if anyone takes advantage of you, if anyone exalts himself, if anyone hits you in the face. 21 To my shame I must say that we have been weak by comparison.

But in whatever respect anyone else is bold—I am speaking in foolishness—I too am bold. 22 Are they Hebrews? So am I. Are they Israelites? So am I. Are they descendants of Abraham? So am I. 23 Are they servants of Christ?—I am speaking as if insane—I more so; in far more labors, in far more imprisonments, beaten times without number, often in danger of death. 24 Five times I received from the Jews thirty-nine lashes. 25 Three times I was beaten with rods, once I was stoned, three times I was shipwrecked, a night and a day I have spent adrift at sea. 26 I have been on frequent journeys, in dangers from rivers, dangers from robbers, dangers from my countrymen, dangers from the Gentiles, dangers in the city, dangers in the wilderness, dangers at sea, dangers among false brothers; 27 I have been in labor and hardship, through many sleepless nights, in hunger and thirst, often without food, in cold and exposure. 28 Apart from such external things, there is the daily pressure on me of concern for all the churches. 29 Who is weak without my being weak? Who is led into sin without my intense concern?

30 If I have to boast, I will boast of what pertains to my weakness. 31 The God and Father of the Lord Jesus, He who is blessed forever, knows that I am not lying. 32 In Damascus the ethnarch under Aretas the king was guarding the city of the Damascenes in order to seize me, 33 and I was let down in a basket through a window in the wall, and so escaped his hands.

Paul's Vision

12 Boasting is necessary, though it is not beneficial; but I will go on to visions and

revelations of the Lord. [2] I know a man in Christ, who fourteen years ago—whether in the body I do not know, or out of the body I do not know, God knows—such a man was caught up to the third heaven. [3] And I know how such a man—whether in the body or apart from the body I do not know, God knows— [4] was caught up into Paradise and heard inexpressible words, which a man is not permitted to speak. [5] In behalf of such a man I will boast; but in my own behalf I will not boast, except regarding *my* weaknesses. [6] For if I do wish to boast I will not be foolish, for I will be speaking the truth; but I refrain *from this,* so that no one will credit me with more than he sees *in* me or hears from me.

A Thorn in the Flesh

[7] Because of the extraordinary *greatness* of the revelations, for this reason, to keep me from exalting myself, there was given to me a thorn in the flesh, a messenger of Satan to torment me—to keep me from exalting myself! [8] Concerning this I pleaded with the Lord three times that it might leave me. [9] And He has said to me, "My grace is sufficient for you, for power is perfected in weakness." Most gladly, therefore, I will rather boast about my weaknesses, so that the power of Christ may dwell in me. [10] Therefore I delight in weaknesses, in insults, in distresses, in persecutions, in difficulties, in behalf of Christ; for when I am weak, then I am strong.

[11] I have become foolish; you yourselves compelled me. Actually I should have been commended by you, since I was in no respect inferior to the most eminent apostles, even though I am a nobody. [12] The distinguishing marks of a true apostle were performed among you with all perseverance, by signs, wonders, and miracles. [13] For in what respect were you treated as inferior to the rest of the churches, except that I myself did not become a burden to you? Forgive me this wrong!

[14] Here for this third time I am ready to come to you, and I will not be a burden to you; for I do not seek what is yours, but you; for children are not responsible to save up for *their* parents, but parents for *their* children. [15] I will most gladly spend and be expended for your souls. If I love you more, am I to be loved less? [16] But be that as it may, I did not burden you myself; nevertheless, devious person that I am, I took you in by deceit. [17] *Certainly* I have not taken advantage of you through any of those whom I have sent to you, have I? [18] I urged Titus *to go,* and I sent the brother with him. Titus did not take any advantage of you, did he? Did we not conduct ourselves in the same spirit *and walk* in the same steps?

[19] All this time you have been thinking that we are defending ourselves to you. *Actually,* it is in the sight of God that we have been speaking in Christ; and all for building you up, beloved. [20] For I am afraid that perhaps when I come I may find you to be not what I wish, and may be found by you to be not what you wish; that perhaps *there will be* strife, jealousy, angry tempers, selfishness, slanders, gossip, arrogance, disturbances; [21] *I am afraid* that when I come again my God may humiliate me before you, and I may mourn over many of those who have sinned in the past and not repented of the impurity, sexual immorality, and indecent behavior which they have practiced.

Examine Yourselves

13 This is the third time that I am coming to you. ON THE TESTIMONY OF TWO OR THREE WITNESSES EVERY MATTER SHALL BE CONFIRMED. [2] I have previously said when I was present the second time, and though now absent I say in advance to those who have sinned in the past and to all the rest *as well,* that if I come again I will not spare *anyone,* [3] since you are seeking proof of the Christ who speaks in me, who is not weak toward you, but mighty in you. [4] For indeed He was crucified because of weakness, yet He lives because of the power of God. For we too are weak 'in Him, yet we will live with Him because of the power of God *directed* toward you.

[5] Test yourselves *to see* if you are in the faith; examine yourselves! Or do you not recognize *this about* yourselves, that Jesus Christ is in you—unless indeed you fail the test? [6] But I expect that you will realize that we ourselves do not fail the test. [7] Now we pray to God that you do nothing wrong; not so that we ourselves may appear approved, but that you may do what is right, though we may appear unapproved. [8] For we cannot do anything against the truth, but *only* for the truth. [9] For we rejoice when we ourselves are weak, but you are strong; this we also pray for, that you become mature. [10] For this reason I am writing these things while absent, so that when present I *need* not use severity, in accordance with the authority which the Lord gave me for building up and not for tearing down.

[11] Finally, brothers *and sisters,* rejoice, mend your ways, be comforted, be like-minded, live in peace; and the God of love and peace will be with you. [12] Greet one another with a holy kiss. [13] All the saints greet you.

[14] The grace of the Lord Jesus Christ, and the love of God, and the fellowship of the Holy Spirit, be with you all.

13:4 [1] One early ms *with Him*

The Letter of Paul to the
GALATIANS

Introduction

1 Paul, an apostle (not *sent* from men nor through human agency, but through Jesus Christ and God the Father, who raised Him from the dead), 2 and all the brothers who are with me,
To the churches of Galatia:
3 Grace to you and peace from God the Father and our Lord Jesus Christ, 4 who gave Himself for our sins so that He might rescue us from this present evil age, according to the will of our God and Father, 5 to whom *be* the glory forevermore. Amen.

Distortion of the Gospel

6 I am amazed that you are so quickly deserting Him who called you by the grace of Christ, for a different gospel, 7 which is not *just* another *account;* but there are some who are disturbing you and want to distort the gospel of Christ. 8 But even if we, or an angel from heaven, should preach to you a gospel contrary to what we have preached to you, he is to be accursed! 9 As we have said before, even now I say again: if anyone is preaching to you a gospel contrary to what you received, he is to be accursed!
10 For am I now seeking the favor of people, or of God? Or am I striving to please people? If I were still trying to please people, I would not be a bond-servant of Christ.

Paul Defends His Ministry

11 For I would have you know, brothers *and sisters,* that the gospel which was preached by me is not of human invention. 12 For I neither received it from man, nor was I taught it, but *I received it* through a revelation of Jesus Christ. 13 For you have heard of my former way of life in Judaism, how I used to persecute the church of God beyond measure and tried to destroy it; 14 and I was advancing in Judaism beyond many of my contemporaries among my countrymen, being more extremely zealous for my ancestral traditions. 15 But when He who had set me apart *even* from my mother's womb and called *me* through His grace was pleased 16 to reveal His Son in me so that I might preach Him among the Gentiles, I did not immediately consult with flesh and blood, 17 nor did I go up to Jerusalem to those *who were* apostles before me; but I went away to Arabia, and returned once more to Damascus. 18 Then three years later I went up to Jerusalem to become acquainted with Cephas, and stayed with him for fifteen days. 19 But I did not see another one of the apostles except James, the Lord's brother. 20 (Now in what I am writing to you, I assure you before God that I am not lying.) 21 Then I went into the regions of Syria and Cilicia. 22 I was *still* unknown by sight to the churches of Judea which are in Christ; 23 but they only kept hearing, "The man who once persecuted us is now preaching the faith which he once tried to destroy." 24 And they were glorifying God because of me.

The Council at Jerusalem

2 Then after an interval of fourteen years I went up again to Jerusalem with Barnabas, taking Titus along also. 2 It was because of a revelation that I went up; and I submitted to them the gospel which I preach among the Gentiles, but *I did so* in private to those who were of reputation, for fear that somehow I might be running, or had run, in vain. 3 But not even Titus, who was with me, though he was a Greek, was compelled to be circumcised. 4 Yet *it was a concern* because of the false brothers secretly brought in, who had sneaked in to spy on our freedom which we have in Christ Jesus, in order to enslave us. 5 But we did not yield in subjection to them, even for an hour, so that the truth of the gospel would remain with you. 6 But from those who were of considerable repute (what they were makes no difference to me; God shows no favoritism)—well, those who were of repute contributed nothing to me. 7 But on the contrary, seeing that I had been entrusted with the gospel [1]to the uncircumcised, just as Peter *had been* [2]to the circumcised 8 (for He who was at work for Peter in *his* apostleship to the circumcised was at work for me also to the Gentiles), 9 and recognizing the grace that had been given to me, James and Cephas and John, who were reputed to be pillars, gave to me and Barnabas the right hand of fellowship, so that we *might go* to the Gentiles, and they to the circumcised. 10 *They* only *asked* us to remember the poor—the very thing I also was eager to do.

Peter (Cephas) Opposed by Paul

11 But when Cephas came to Antioch, I opposed him to his face, because he stood condemned. 12 For prior to the coming of some men from James, he used to eat with the Gentiles; but when they came, he *began* to withdraw and separate himself, fearing those from the circumcision. 13 The rest of the Jews joined him in hypocrisy, with the result that even Barnabas was carried away by their hypocrisy. 14 But when I saw that they were not straightforward about the truth of the gospel, I said to Cephas in the presence of all, "If you, being a Jew, live like the Gentiles and not like the Jews, how *is it that* you compel the Gentiles to live like Jews? 15 "We *are* Jews by nature and not sinners from the Gentiles; 16 nevertheless, knowing that a person is not justified by works of the Law but through faith in Christ Jesus, even we have believed in Christ Jesus, so that we may be justified by faith in Christ and not by works

---

2:7 1 Lit *of the uncircumcision;* i.e., to Gentiles   2 Lit *of the circumcision;* i.e., to Jews

of the Law; since by works of the Law no flesh will be justified. **17** But if, while seeking to be justified in Christ, we ourselves have also been found sinners, is Christ then a servant of sin? *¹Far from it!* **18** For if I rebuild what I have *once* destroyed, I prove myself to be a wrongdoer. **19** For through the Law I died to the Law, so that I might live for God. **20** I have been crucified with Christ; and it is no longer I who live, but Christ lives in me; and the *life* which I now live in the flesh I live by faith in the Son of God, who loved me and gave Himself up for me. **21** I do not nullify the grace of God, for if righteousness *comes* through the Law, then Christ died needlessly."

Faith Brings Righteousness

3 You foolish Galatians, who has bewitched you, before whose eyes Jesus Christ was publicly portrayed *as* crucified? **2** This is the only thing I want to find out from you: did you receive the Spirit by works of the Law, or by hearing with faith? **3** Are you so foolish? Having begun by the Spirit, are you now being perfected by the flesh? **4** Did you suffer so many things in vain—if indeed it was in vain? **5** So then, does He who provides you with the Spirit and works miracles among you, do it by works of the Law, or by hearing with faith? **6** Just as Abraham BELIEVED GOD, AND IT WAS CREDITED TO HIM AS RIGHTEOUSNESS. **7** Therefore, recognize that it is those who are of faith who are sons of Abraham. **8** The Scripture, foreseeing that God would justify the Gentiles by faith, preached the gospel beforehand to Abraham, *saying,* "ALL THE NATIONS WILL BE BLESSED IN YOU." **9** So then, those who are of faith are blessed with Abraham, the believer.

10 For all who are of works of the Law are under a curse; for it is written: "CURSED IS EVERYONE WHO DOES NOT ABIDE BY ALL THE THINGS WRITTEN IN THE BOOK OF THE LAW, TO DO THEM." **11** Now, that no one is justified by the Law before God is evident; for, "THE RIGHTEOUS ONE WILL LIVE BY FAITH." **12** However, the Law is not of faith; on the contrary, "THE PERSON WHO PERFORMS THEM WILL LIVE BY THEM." **13** Christ redeemed us from the curse of the Law, having become a curse for us—for it is written: "CURSED IS EVERYONE WHO HANGS ON A *¹TREE*"— **14** in order that in Christ Jesus the blessing of Abraham would come to the Gentiles, so that we would receive the promise of the Spirit through faith.

Intent of the Law

15 Brothers *and sisters,* I speak in terms of human relations: even though it is *only* a man's covenant, yet when it has been ratified, no one sets it aside or adds conditions to it. **16** Now the promises were spoken to Abraham and to his seed. He does not say, "And to seeds," as *one would in referring* to many, but *rather* as *in referring* to one, "And to your seed," that is, Christ. **17** What I am saying is this: the Law, which came 430 years later, does not invalidate a covenant previously ratified by God, so as to nullify the promise. **18** For if the inheritance is based on law, it is no longer

based on a promise; but God has granted it to Abraham by means of a promise.

19 Why the Law then? It was added on account of the *¹violations,* having been ordered through angels at the hand of a mediator, until the Seed would come to whom the promise had been made. **20** Now a mediator is not for one *party only;* but God is *only* one. **21** Is the Law then contrary to the promises of God? Far from it! For if a law had been given that was able to impart life, then righteousness would indeed have been based on law. **22** But the Scripture has confined everyone under sin, so that the promise by faith in Jesus Christ might be given to those who believe.

23 But before faith came, we were kept in custody under the Law, being confined for the faith that was destined to be revealed. **24** Therefore the Law has become our guardian *to lead us* to Christ, so that we may be justified by faith. **25** But now that faith has come, we are no longer under a guardian. **26** For you are all sons *and daughters* of God through faith in Christ Jesus. **27** For all of you who were baptized into Christ have clothed yourselves with Christ. **28** There is neither Jew nor Greek, there is neither slave nor free, there is neither male nor female; for you are all one in Christ Jesus. **29** And if you belong to Christ, then you are Abraham's descendants, heirs according to promise.

Sonship in Christ

4 Now I say, as long as the heir is a child, he does not differ at all from a slave, although he is owner of everything, **2** but he is under guardians and managers until the date set by the father. **3** So we too, when we were children, were held in bondage under the elementary principles of the world. **4** But when the fullness of the time came, God sent His Son, born of a woman, born under the Law, **5** so that He might redeem those who were under the Law, that we might receive the adoption as sons *and daughters.* **6** Because you are sons, God has sent the Spirit of His Son into our hearts, crying out, "Abba! Father!" **7** Therefore you are no longer a slave, but a son; and if a son, then an heir through God.

8 However at that time, when you did not know God, you were slaves to those which by nature are not gods. **9** But now that you have come to know God, or rather to be known by God, how is it that you turn back again to the weak and worthless elementary principles, to which you want to be enslaved all over again? **10** You meticulously observe days and months and seasons and years. **11** I fear for you, that perhaps I have labored over you in vain.

12 I beg of you, brothers *and sisters,* become as I *am,* for I also *have become* as you *are.* You have done me no wrong; **13** but you know that it was because of a bodily illness that I preached the gospel to you the first time; **14** and you did not despise that which was a trial to you in my bodily condition, nor express contempt, but you received me as an angel of God, as Christ Jesus *Himself.* **15** Where then is that sense of blessing you had? For I testify

---

2:17 ¹Lit *May it never happen!*   **3:13** ¹Or *cross;* lit *wood;* see Deut 21:23   **3:19** ¹I.e., of God's commands

about you that, if possible, you would have torn out your eyes and given them to me. [16] So have I become your enemy by telling you the truth? [17] They eagerly seek you, not in a commendable way, but they want to shut you out so that you will seek them. [18] But it is good always to be eagerly sought in a commendable way, and not only when I am present with you. [19] My children, with whom I am again in labor until Christ is formed in you— [20] but I could wish to be present with you now and to change my *tone of* voice, for I am at a loss about you!

Slave and Free

[21] Tell me, you who want to be under law, do you not listen to the Law? [22] For it is written that Abraham had two sons, one by the slave woman and one by the free woman. [23] But the son by the slave woman was born according to the flesh, and the son by the free woman through the promise. [24] This is speaking allegorically, for these *women* are two covenants: one *coming* from Mount Sinai giving birth to children who are to be slaves; she is Hagar. [25] Now this Hagar is Mount Sinai in Arabia and corresponds to the present Jerusalem, for she is enslaved with her children. [26] But the Jerusalem above is free; she is our mother. [27] For it is written:

"REJOICE, INFERTILE ONE, YOU WHO DO NOT
    GIVE BIRTH;
BREAK FORTH AND SHOUT, YOU WHO ARE NOT
    IN LABOR;
FOR THE CHILDREN OF THE DESOLATE ONE *ARE*
    MORE NUMEROUS
THAN *THOSE* OF THE ONE WHO HAS A
    HUSBAND."

[28] And you, brothers *and sisters,* like Isaac, are children of promise. [29] But as at that time the *son* who was born according to the flesh persecuted the one *who was born* according to the Spirit, so it is even now. [30] But what does the Scripture say?

"DRIVE OUT THE SLAVE WOMAN AND HER SON,
FOR THE SON OF THE SLAVE WOMAN SHALL
    NOT BE AN HEIR WITH THE SON OF THE FREE
    WOMAN."

[31] So then, brothers *and sisters,* we are not children of a slave woman, but of the free woman.

Follow the Spirit

5 It was for freedom that Christ set us free; therefore keep standing firm and do not be subject again to a yoke of slavery.

[2] Look! I, Paul, tell you that if you have yourselves circumcised, Christ will be of no benefit to you. [3] And I testify again to every man who has himself circumcised, that he is obligated to keep the whole Law. [4] You have been severed from Christ, you who are seeking to be justified by the [1]Law; you have fallen from grace. [5] For we, through the Spirit, by faith, are waiting for the hope of righteousness. [6] For in Christ Jesus neither circumcision nor uncircumcision means anything, but faith working through love.

[7] You were running well; who hindered you from obeying the truth? [8] This persuasion *did* not *come* from Him who calls you. [9] A little leaven leavens the whole lump *of dough.* [10] I have confidence in you in the Lord, that you will adopt no other view; but the one who is disturbing you will bear the punishment, whoever he is. [11] But as for me, brothers *and sisters,* if I still preach circumcision, why am I still persecuted? Then the stumbling block of the cross has been eliminated. [12] I wish that those who are troubling you would even emasculate themselves.

[13] For you were called to freedom, brothers *and sisters;* only *do* not *turn* your freedom into an opportunity for the flesh, but serve one another through love. [14] For the whole Law is fulfilled in one word, in the *statement,* "YOU SHALL LOVE YOUR NEIGHBOR AS YOURSELF." [15] But if you bite and devour one another, take care that you are not consumed by one another.

[16] But I say, walk by the Spirit, and you will not carry out the desire of the flesh. [17] For the desire of the flesh is against the Spirit, and the Spirit against the flesh; for these are in opposition to one another, in order to keep you from doing whatever you want. [18] But if you are led by the Spirit, you are not under the Law. [19] Now the deeds of the flesh are evident, which are: sexual immorality, impurity, indecent behavior, [20] idolatry, witchcraft, hostilities, strife, jealousy, outbursts of anger, selfish ambition, dissensions, factions, [21] envy, drunkenness, carousing, and things like these, of which I forewarn you, just as I have forewarned you, that those who practice such things will not inherit the kingdom of God. [22] But the fruit of the Spirit is love, joy, peace, patience, kindness, goodness, faithfulness, [23] gentleness, self-control; against such things there is no law. [24] Now those who belong to Christ Jesus crucified the flesh with its passions and desires.

[25] If we live by the Spirit, let's follow the Spirit as well. [26] Let's not become boastful, challenging one another, envying one another.

Bear One Another's Burdens

6 Brothers *and sisters,* even if a person is caught in any wrongdoing, you who are spiritual are to restore such a person in a spirit of gentleness; *each one* looking to yourself, so that you are not tempted as well. [2] Bear one another's burdens, and thereby fulfill the law of Christ. [3] For if anyone thinks that he is something when he is nothing, he deceives himself. [4] But each one must examine his own work, and then he will have *reason for* boasting, *but* to himself alone, and not to another. [5] For each one will bear his own load.

[6] The one who is taught the word is to share all good things with the one who teaches *him.* [7] Do not be deceived, God is not mocked; for whatever a person sows, this he will also reap. [8] For the one who sows to his own flesh will reap destruction from the flesh, but the one who sows to the Spirit will reap eternal life from the Spirit. [9] Let's not become discouraged in doing good, for in due time we will reap, if

we do not become weary. [10] So then, while we have opportunity, let's do good to all people, and especially to those who are of the household of the faith.

[11] See with what large letters I have written to you with my own hand! [12] All who want to make a good showing in the flesh try to compel you to be circumcised, simply so that they will not be persecuted for the cross of Christ. [13] For those who [1]are circumcised do not even keep the Law themselves, but they want to have you circumcised so that they may boast in your flesh. [14] But far be it from me to boast, except in the cross of our Lord Jesus Christ, through which the world has been crucified to me, and I to the world. [15] For neither is circumcision anything, nor uncircumcision, but a new creation. [16] And all who will follow this rule, peace and mercy *be* upon them, and upon the Israel of God.

[17] From now on let no one cause trouble for me, for I bear on my body the marks of Jesus.

[18] The grace of our Lord Jesus Christ be with your spirit, brothers *and sisters*. Amen.

6:13 [1] Two early mss *have been*

The Letter of Paul to the
EPHESIANS

The Blessings of Redemption

1 Paul, an apostle of Christ Jesus by the will of God,
To the saints who are [1]at Ephesus and *are* faithful in Christ Jesus: [2]Grace to you and peace from God our Father and the Lord Jesus Christ.

[3] Blessed *be* the God and Father of our Lord Jesus Christ, who has blessed us with every spiritual blessing in the heavenly *places* in Christ, [4]just as He chose us in Him before the foundation of the world, that we would be holy and blameless before [1]Him. In love [5]He predestined us to adoption as sons *and daughters* through Jesus Christ to Himself, according to the good pleasure of His will, [6]to the praise of the glory of His grace, with which He favored us in the Beloved. [7]In Him we have redemption through His blood, the forgiveness of our wrongdoings, according to the riches of His grace [8]which He lavished on us. In all wisdom and insight [9]He made known to us the mystery of His will, according to His good pleasure which He set forth in Him, [10]regarding *His* plan of the fullness of the times, to bring all things together in Christ, things in the heavens and things on the earth. [11]In Him we also have obtained an inheritance, having been predestined according to the purpose of Him who works all things in accordance with the plan of His will, [12]to the end that we who were the first to hope in the Christ would be to the praise of His glory. [13]In Him, you also, after listening to the message of truth, the gospel of your salvation—having also believed, you were sealed in Him with the Holy Spirit of the promise, [14]who is a first installment of our inheritance, in regard to the redemption of *God's own* possession, to the praise of His glory.

[15] For this reason I too, having heard of the faith in the Lord Jesus which *exists* among you and [1]your love for all the saints, [16]do not cease giving thanks for you, while making mention *of you* in my prayers; [17]that the God of our Lord Jesus Christ, the Father of glory, may give you a spirit of wisdom and of revelation in the knowledge of Him. [18]*I pray that* the eyes of your heart may be enlightened, so that you will know what is the hope of His calling, what are the riches of the glory of His inheritance in the saints, [19]and what is the boundless greatness of His power toward us who believe. *These are* in accordance with the working of the strength of His might [20]which He brought about in Christ, when He raised Him from the dead and seated Him at His right hand in the heavenly *places,* [21]far above all rule and authority and power and dominion, and every name that is named, not only in this age but also in the one

to come. [22]And He put all things in subjection under His feet, and made Him head over all things to the church, [23]which is His body, the fullness of Him who fills all in all.

Made Alive in Christ

2 And you were dead in your offenses and sins, [2]in which you previously walked according to the course of this world, according to the prince of the power of the air, of the spirit that is now working in the [1]sons of disobedience. [3]Among them we too all previously lived in the lusts of our flesh, indulging the desires of the flesh and of the mind, and were by nature children of wrath, just as the rest. [4]But God, being rich in mercy, because of His great love with which He loved us, [5]even when we were dead in our wrongdoings, made us alive together [1]with Christ (by grace you have been saved), [6]and raised us up with Him, and seated us with Him in the heavenly *places* in Christ Jesus, [7]so that in the ages to come He might show the boundless riches of His grace in kindness toward us in Christ Jesus. [8]For by grace you have been saved through faith; and [1]this *is* not of yourselves, *it is* the gift of God; [9]not a result of works, so that no one may boast. [10]For we are His workmanship, created in Christ Jesus for good works, which God prepared beforehand so that we would walk in them.

[11] Therefore remember that previously you, the Gentiles in the flesh, who are called "Uncircumcision" by the so-called "Circumcision" *which is* performed in the flesh by human hands— [12]*remember* that you were at that time separate from Christ, excluded from the people of Israel, and strangers to the covenants of the promise, having no hope and without God in the world. [13]But now in Christ Jesus you who previously were far away have been brought near by the blood of Christ. [14]For He Himself is our peace, who made both *groups into* one and broke down the barrier of the dividing wall, [15]by abolishing in His flesh the hostility, *which is* the Law *composed* of commandments *expressed* in ordinances, so that in Himself He might make the two one new person, *in this way* establishing peace; [16]and that He might reconcile them both in one body to God through the cross, by it having put to death the hostility. [17]And He came and preached peace to you who were far away, and peace to those who were near; [18]for through Him we both have our access in one Spirit to the Father. [19]So then you are no longer strangers and foreigners, but you are fellow citizens with the saints, and are of God's household, [20]having been built on the foundation of the apostles and prophets, Christ

1:1 1 Three early mss do not contain *at Ephesus*   **1:4** 1 Or *Him, in love. He*   **1:15** 1 Three early mss do not contain *your love*   **2:2** 1 I.e., people opposed to God   **2:5** 1 Two early mss *in Christ*   **2:8** 1 I.e., this salvation

Jesus Himself being the cornerstone, [21] in whom the whole building, being fitted together, is growing into a holy temple in the Lord, [22] in whom you also are being built together into a dwelling of God in the Spirit.

Paul's Stewardship

3 For this reason I, Paul, the prisoner of Christ Jesus for the sake of you Gentiles— [2] if indeed you have heard of the administration of God's grace which was given to me for you; [3] that by revelation there was made known to me the mystery, as I wrote before briefly. [4] By referring to this, when you read you can understand my insight into the mystery of Christ, [5] which in other generations was not made known to mankind, as it has now been revealed to His holy apostles and prophets in the Spirit; [6] to be specific, that the Gentiles are fellow heirs and fellow members of the body, and fellow partakers of the promise in Christ Jesus through the gospel, [7] of which I was made a minister, according to the gift of God's grace which was given to me according to the working of His power. [8] To me, the very least of all saints, this grace was given, to preach to the Gentiles the unfathomable riches of Christ, [9] and to enlighten all people as to what the plan of the mystery is which for ages has been hidden in God, who created all things; [10] so that the multifaceted wisdom of God might now be made known through the church to the rulers and the authorities in the heavenly places. [11] This was in accordance with the eternal purpose which He carried out in Christ Jesus our Lord, [12] in whom we have boldness and confident access through faith in Him. [13] Therefore I ask you not to become discouraged about my tribulations in your behalf, since they are your glory.

[14] For this reason I bend my knees before the Father, [15] from whom every family in heaven and on earth derives its name, [16] that He would grant you, according to the riches of His glory, to be strengthened with power through His Spirit in the inner self, [17] so that Christ may dwell in your hearts through faith; and that you, being rooted and grounded in love, [18] may be able to comprehend with all the saints what is the width and length and height and depth, [19] and to know the love of Christ which surpasses knowledge, that you may be filled to all the fullness of God.

[20] Now to Him who is able to do far more abundantly beyond all that we ask or think, according to the power that works within us, [21] to Him be the glory in the church and in Christ Jesus to all generations forever and ever. Amen.

Unity of the Spirit

4 Therefore I, the prisoner of the Lord, urge you to walk in a manner worthy of the calling with which you have been called, [2] with all humility and gentleness, with patience, bearing with one another in love, [3] being diligent to keep the unity of the Spirit in the bond of peace. [4] There is one body and one Spirit, just as you also were called in one hope

of your calling; [5] one Lord, one faith, one baptism, [6] one God and Father of all who is over all and through all and in all.

[7] But to each one of us grace was given according to the measure of Christ's gift. [8] Therefore it says,

"WHEN HE ASCENDED ON HIGH,
HE LED CAPTIVE THE CAPTIVES,
AND HE GAVE GIFTS TO PEOPLE."

[9] (Now this expression, "He ascended," what does it mean except that He also had descended into the lower parts of the earth? [10] He who descended is Himself also He who ascended far above all the heavens, so that He might fill all things.) [11] And He gave some as apostles, some as prophets, some as evangelists, some as [1]pastors and teachers, [12] for the equipping of the saints for the work of ministry, for the building up of the body of Christ; [13] until we all attain to the unity of the faith, and of the knowledge of the Son of God, to a mature man, to the measure of the stature which belongs to the fullness of Christ. [14] As a result, we are no longer to be children, tossed here and there by waves and carried about by every wind of doctrine, by the trickery of people, by craftiness in deceitful scheming; [15] but speaking the truth in love, we are to grow up in all aspects into Him who is the head, that is, Christ, [16] from whom the whole body, being fitted and held together by what every joint supplies, according to the proper working of each individual part, causes the growth of the body for the building up of itself in love.

The Christian's Walk

[17] So I say this, and affirm in the Lord, that you are to no longer walk just as the Gentiles also walk, in the futility of their minds, [18] being darkened in their understanding, excluded from the life of God because of the ignorance that is in them, because of the hardness of their heart; [19] and they, having become callous, have given themselves up to indecent behavior for the practice of every kind of impurity with greediness. [20] But you did not learn Christ in this way, [21] if indeed you have heard Him and have been taught in Him, just as truth is in Jesus, [22] that, in reference to your former way of life, you are to rid yourselves of the old self, which is being corrupted in accordance with the lusts of deceit, [23] and that you are to be renewed in the spirit of your minds, [24] and to put on the new self, which in the likeness of God has been created in righteousness and holiness of the truth.

[25] Therefore, ridding yourselves of falsehood, SPEAK TRUTH EACH ONE OF YOU WITH HIS NEIGHBOR, because we are parts of one another. [26] BE ANGRY, AND YET DO NOT SIN; do not let the sun go down on your anger, [27] and do not give the devil an opportunity. [28] The one who steals must no longer steal; but rather he must labor, producing with his own hands what is good, so that he will have something to share with the one who has need. [29] Let no unwholesome word come out of your mouth, but if there is any good word for edification according to the

---

4:11 [1] From Gr for shepherds

need *of the moment, say that,* so that it will give grace to those who hear. [30] Do not grieve the Holy Spirit of God, by whom you were sealed for the day of redemption. [31] All bitterness, wrath, anger, clamor, and slander must be removed from you, along with all malice. [32] Be kind to one another, compassionate, forgiving each other, just as God in Christ also has forgiven [1]you.

Be Imitators of God

5 Therefore be imitators of God, as beloved children; [2] and walk in love, just as Christ also loved [1]you and gave Himself up for us, an offering and a sacrifice to God as a fragrant aroma.

[3] But sexual immorality or any impurity or greed must not even be mentioned among you, as is proper among saints; [4] and *there must be no* filthiness or foolish talk, or vulgar joking, which are not fitting, but rather giving of thanks. [5] For this you know with certainty, that no sexually immoral or impure or greedy person, which amounts to an idolater, has an inheritance in the kingdom of Christ and God.

[6] *See that* no one deceives you with empty words, for because of these things the wrath of God comes upon the [1]sons of disobedience. [7] Therefore do not become partners with them; [8] for you were once darkness, but now you are light in the Lord; walk as children of light [9] (for the fruit of the light *consists* in all goodness, righteousness, and truth), [10] as you try to learn what is pleasing to the Lord. [11] Do not participate in the useless deeds of darkness, but instead even expose them; [12] for it is disgraceful even to speak of the things which are done by them in secret. [13] But all things become visible when they are exposed by the light, for everything that becomes visible is light. [14] For this reason it says,

"Awake, sleeper,
    And arise from the dead,
    And Christ will shine on you."

[15] So then, be careful how you walk, not as unwise people but as wise, [16] making the most of your time, because the days are evil. [17] Therefore do not be foolish, but understand what the will of the Lord *is*. [18] And do not get drunk with wine, in which there is debauchery, but be filled with the Spirit, [19] speaking to one another in psalms and hymns and spiritual songs, singing and making melody with your hearts to the Lord; [20] always giving thanks for all things in the name of our Lord Jesus Christ to *our* God and Father; [21] and subject yourselves to one another in the fear of Christ.

Marriage like Christ and the Church

[22] Wives, *subject yourselves* to your own husbands, as to the Lord. [23] For the husband is the head of the wife, as Christ also is the head of the church, He Himself *being* the Savior of the body. [24] But as the church is subject to Christ, so also the wives *ought to be* to their husbands in everything.

[25] Husbands, love your wives, just as Christ also loved the church and gave Himself up for

her, [26] so that He might sanctify her, having cleansed her by the washing of water with the word, [27] that He might present to Himself the church in all her glory, having no spot or wrinkle or any such thing; but that she would be holy and blameless. [28] So husbands also ought to love their own wives as their own bodies. He who loves his own wife loves himself; [29] for no one ever hated his own flesh, but nourishes and cherishes it, just as Christ also *does* the church, [30] because we are parts of His body. [31] FOR THIS REASON A MAN SHALL LEAVE HIS FATHER AND HIS MOTHER AND BE JOINED TO HIS WIFE, AND THE TWO SHALL BECOME ONE FLESH. [32] This mystery is great; but I am speaking with reference to Christ and the church. [33] Nevertheless, as for you individually, each *husband* is to love his own wife the same as himself, and the wife *must see to it* that she respects her husband.

Children and Parents

6 Children, obey your parents in the Lord, for this is right. [2] HONOR YOUR FATHER AND MOTHER (which is the first commandment with a promise), [3] SO THAT IT MAY TURN OUT WELL FOR YOU, AND THAT YOU MAY LIVE LONG ON THE EARTH.

[4] Fathers, do not provoke your children to anger, but bring them up in the discipline and instruction of the Lord.

Slaves and Masters

[5] Slaves, be obedient to those who are your masters according to the flesh, with fear and trembling, in the sincerity of your heart, as to Christ; [6] not by way of eye-service, as people-pleasers, but as slaves of Christ, doing the will of God from the heart. [7] With goodwill render service, as to the Lord, and not to people, [8] knowing that whatever good thing each one does, he will receive this back from the Lord, whether slave or free.

[9] And masters, do the same things to them, and give up threatening, knowing that both their Master and yours is in heaven, and there is no partiality with Him.

The Armor of God

[10] Finally, be strong in the Lord and in the strength of His might. [11] Put on the full armor of God, so that you will be able to stand firm against the schemes of the devil. [12] For our struggle is not against flesh and blood, but against the rulers, against the powers, against the world forces of this darkness, against the spiritual *forces* of wickedness in the heavenly *places*. [13] Therefore, take up the full armor of God, so that you will be able to resist on the evil day, and having done everything, to stand firm. [14] Stand firm therefore, having belted your waist with truth, and having put on the breastplate of righteousness, [15] and having strapped on your feet the preparation of the gospel of peace; [16] in addition to all, taking up the shield of faith with which you will be able to extinguish all the flaming arrows of the evil one. [17] And take the helmet of salvation and the sword of the Spirit, which is the word of God. [18] With every prayer and request, pray at all

---

4:32 [1] Two early mss *us*   5:2 [1] One early ms *us*   5:6 [1] I.e., people opposed to God

times in the Spirit, and with this in view, be alert with all perseverance and *every* request for all the saints, [19] and *pray* in my behalf, that speech may be given to me in the opening of my mouth, to make known with boldness the mystery of the gospel, [20] for which I am an ambassador in chains; that [1]in *proclaiming* it I may speak boldly, as I ought to speak.

[21] Now, so that you also may know about my circumstances *as to* what I am doing, Tychicus, the beloved brother and faithful servant in the Lord, will make everything known to you. [22] I have sent him to you for this very purpose, so that you may know about us, and that he may comfort your hearts.

[23] Peace be to the brothers *and sisters,* and love with faith, from God the Father and the Lord Jesus Christ. [24] Grace be with all those who love our Lord Jesus Christ with incorruptible *love.*

6:20 [1] Two early mss *I may speak it boldly*

The Letter of Paul to the
PHILIPPIANS

Thanksgiving

1 Paul and Timothy, bond-servants of Christ Jesus,

To all the saints in Christ Jesus who are in Philippi, including the overseers and deacons: **2** Grace to you and peace from God our Father and the Lord Jesus Christ.

3 I thank my God in all my remembrance of you, **4** always offering prayer with joy in my every prayer for you all, **5** in view of your participation in the gospel from the first day until now. **6** *For I am* confident of this very thing, that He who began a good work among you will complete it by the day of Christ Jesus. **7** For it is only right for me to feel this way about you all, because I have you in my heart, since both in my imprisonment and in the defense and confirmation of the gospel, you all are partakers of grace with me. **8** For God is my witness, how I long for you all with the affection of Christ Jesus. **9** And this I pray, that your love may overflow still more and more in real knowledge and all discernment, **10** so that you may discover the things that are excellent, that you may be sincere and blameless for the day of Christ; **11** having been filled with the fruit of righteousness which *comes* through Jesus Christ, for the glory and praise of God.

The Gospel Is Preached

12 Now I want you to know, brothers *and sisters,* that my circumstances have turned out for the greater progress of the gospel, **13** so that my imprisonment in *the cause of* Christ has become well known throughout the ¹praetorian guard and to everyone else, **14** and that most of the brothers *and sisters,* trusting in the Lord because of my imprisonment, have far more courage to speak the word of God without fear. **15** Some, to be sure, are preaching Christ even from envy and strife, but some also from goodwill; **16** the latter *do it* out of love, knowing that I am appointed for the defense of the gospel; **17** the former proclaim Christ out of selfish ambition rather than from pure motives, thinking that they are causing me distress in my imprisonment. **18** What then? Only that in every way, whether in pretense or in truth, Christ is proclaimed, and in this I rejoice.

But *not only that,* I also will rejoice, **19** for I know that this will turn out for my deliverance through your prayers and the provision of the Spirit of Jesus Christ, **20** according to my eager expectation and hope, that I will not be put to shame in anything, but *that* with all boldness, Christ will even now, as always, be exalted in my body, whether by life or by death.

To Live Is Christ

21 For to me, to live is Christ, and to die is gain. **22** But if *I am* to live *on* in the flesh, this *will mean* fruitful labor for me; and I do not

know which to choose. **23** But I am hard-pressed from both *directions,* having the desire to depart and be with Christ, for *that* is very much better; **24** yet to remain on in the flesh is more necessary for your sakes. **25** Convinced of this, I know that I will remain and continue with you all for your progress and joy in the faith, **26** so that your pride in Christ Jesus may be abundant because of me by my coming to you again.

27 Only conduct yourselves in a manner worthy of the gospel of Christ, so that whether I come and see you or remain absent, I will hear about you that you are standing firm in one spirit, with one mind striving together for the faith of the gospel; **28** and in no way alarmed by *your* opponents—which is a sign of destruction for them, but of salvation for you, and this *too,* from God. **29** For to you it has been granted for Christ's sake, not only to believe in Him, but also to suffer on His behalf, **30** experiencing the same conflict which you saw in me, and now hear *to be* in me.

Be like Christ

2 Therefore if there is any encouragement in Christ, if any consolation of love, if any fellowship of the Spirit, if any affection and compassion, **2** make my joy complete by being of the same mind, maintaining the same love, united in spirit, intent on one purpose. **3** Do nothing from selfishness or empty conceit, but with humility consider one another as more important than yourselves; **4** do not *merely* look out for your own personal *interests,* but also for the *interests* of others. **5** Have this attitude in yourselves which was also in Christ Jesus, **6** who, as He *already* existed in the form of God, did not consider equality with God something to be grasped, **7** but ¹emptied Himself *by* taking the form of a bond-servant *and* being born in the likeness of men. **8** And being found in appearance as a man, He humbled Himself by becoming obedient to the point of death: death on a cross. **9** For this reason also God highly exalted Him, and bestowed on Him the name which is above every name, **10** so that at the name of Jesus EVERY KNEE WILL BOW, of those who are in heaven and on earth and under the earth, **11** and *that* every tongue will confess that Jesus Christ is Lord, to the glory of God the Father.

12 So then, my beloved, just as you have always obeyed, not as in my presence only, but now much more in my absence, work out your own salvation with fear and trembling; **13** for it is God who is at work in you, both to desire and to work for *His* good pleasure.

14 Do all things without complaining or arguments; **15** so that you will prove yourselves to be blameless and innocent, children of God above reproach in the midst of a crooked and

---

1:13 ¹ Or *governor's palace*   **2:7** ¹ I.e., set aside His divine rights

perverse generation, among whom you appear as lights in the world, 16 holding firmly the word of life, so that on the day of Christ I can take pride because I did not run in vain nor labor in vain. 17 But even if I am being poured out as a drink offering upon the sacrifice and service of your faith, I rejoice and share my joy with you all. 18 You too, *I urge you,* rejoice in the same way and share your joy with me.

Timothy and Epaphroditus

19 But I hope, in the Lord Jesus, to send Timothy to you shortly, so that I also may be encouraged when I learn of your condition. 20 For I have no one *else* of kindred spirit who will genuinely be concerned for your welfare. 21 For they all seek after their own *interests,* not those of Christ Jesus. 22 But you know of his proven character, that he served with me in the furtherance of the gospel like a child *serving* his father. 23 Therefore I hope to send him immediately, as soon as I see how things *go* with me; 24 and I trust in the Lord that I myself will also be coming shortly. 25 But I thought it necessary to send to you Epaphroditus, my brother and fellow worker and fellow soldier, who is also your messenger and minister to my need, 26 because he was longing 'for you all and was distressed because you had heard that he was sick. 27 For indeed he was sick to the point of death, but God had mercy on him, and not only on him but also on me, so that I would not have sorrow upon sorrow. 28 Therefore I have sent him all the more eagerly, so that when you see him again you may rejoice and I may be less concerned *about you.* 29 Receive him then in the Lord with all joy, and hold people like him in high regard, 30 because he came close to death for the work of Christ, risking his life to compensate for your absence in your service to me.

The Goal of Life

3 Finally, my brothers *and sisters,* rejoice in the Lord. To write the same 'things *again* is no trouble for me, and it is a safeguard for you. 2 Beware of the dogs, beware of the evil workers, beware of the false circumcision; 3 for we are the *true* circumcision, who worship in the Spirit of God and take pride in Christ Jesus, and put no confidence in the flesh, 4 although I myself *could boast as* having confidence even in the flesh. If anyone else thinks he is confident in the flesh, I *have* more *reason:* 5 circumcised the eighth day, of the nation of Israel, of the tribe of Benjamin, a Hebrew of Hebrews; as to the Law, a Pharisee; 6 as to zeal, a persecutor of the church; as to the righteousness which is in the Law, found blameless. 7 But whatever things were gain to me, these things I have counted as loss because of Christ. 8 More than that, I count all things to be loss in view of the surpassing value of knowing Christ Jesus my Lord, for whom I have suffered the loss of all things, and count them *mere* rubbish, so that I may gain Christ, 9 and may be found in Him, not having a righteousness of my own derived from *the* Law, but that which is through faith in Christ, the righteousness

which *comes* from God on the basis of faith, 10 that I may know Him and the power of His resurrection and the fellowship of His sufferings, being conformed to His death; 11 if somehow I may attain to the resurrection from the dead.

12 Not that I have already grasped *it all* or have already become perfect, but I press on if I may also take hold of that for which I was even taken hold of by Christ Jesus. 13 Brothers *and sisters,* I do not regard myself as having taken hold of *it yet;* but one thing *I do:* forgetting what *lies* behind and reaching forward to what *lies* ahead, 14 I press on toward the goal for the prize of the upward call of God in Christ Jesus. 15 Therefore, all who are mature, let's have this attitude; and if in anything you have a different attitude, God will reveal that to you as well; 16 however, let's keep living by that same *standard* to which we have attained.

17 Brothers *and sisters,* join in following my example, and observe those who walk according to the pattern you have in us. 18 For many walk, of whom I often told you, and now tell you even as I weep, *that they are* the enemies of the cross of Christ, 19 whose end is destruction, whose god is *their* appetite, and *whose* glory is in their shame, who have their minds on earthly things. 20 For our citizenship is in heaven, from which we also eagerly wait for a Savior, the Lord Jesus Christ; 21 who will transform the body of our lowly condition into conformity with His glorious body, by the exertion of the power that He has even to subject all things to Himself.

Think of Excellence

4 Therefore, my beloved brothers *and sisters,* whom I long *to see,* my joy and crown, stand firm in the Lord in this way, my beloved. 2 I urge Euodia and I urge Syntyche to live in harmony in the Lord. 3 Indeed, true companion, I ask you also, help these women who have shared my struggle in *the cause of* the gospel, together with Clement as well as the rest of my fellow workers, whose names are in the book of life.

4 Rejoice in the Lord always; again I will say, rejoice! 5 Let your gentle *spirit* be known to all people. The Lord is near. 6 Do not be anxious about anything, but in everything by prayer and pleading with thanksgiving let your requests be made known to God. 7 And the peace of God, which surpasses all comprehension, will guard your hearts and minds in Christ Jesus.

8 Finally, brothers *and sisters,* whatever is true, whatever is honorable, whatever is right, whatever is pure, whatever is lovely, whatever is commendable, if there is any excellence and if anything worthy of praise, think about these things. 9 As for the things you have learned and received and heard and seen in me, practice these things, and the God of peace will be with you.

God's Provisions

10 But I rejoiced in the Lord greatly, that now at last you have revived your concern for me;

---

indeed, you were concerned *before,* but you lacked an opportunity *to act.* [11] Not that I speak from need, for I have learned to be content in whatever *circumstances* I am. [12] I know how to get along with little, and I also know how to live in prosperity; in any and every *circumstance* I have learned the secret of being filled and going hungry, both of having abundance and suffering need. [13] I can do all things through Him who strengthens me. [14] Nevertheless, you have done well to share *with me* in my difficulty.

[15] You yourselves also know, Philippians, that at the first *preaching* of the gospel, after I left Macedonia, no church shared with me in the matter of giving and receiving except you alone; [16] for even in Thessalonica you sent *a gift* more than once for my needs. [17] Not that I seek the gift *itself,* but I seek the profit which increases to your account. [18] But I have received everything in full and have an abundance; I am amply supplied, having received from Epaphroditus what you have sent, a fragrant aroma, an acceptable sacrifice, pleasing to God. [19] And my God will supply all your needs according to His riches in glory in Christ Jesus. [20] Now to our God and Father *be* the glory forever and ever. Amen.

[21] Greet every saint in Christ Jesus. The brothers who are with me greet you. [22] All the saints greet you, especially those of Caesar's household.

[23] The grace of the Lord Jesus Christ be with your spirit.

The Letter of Paul to the
COLOSSIANS

Thankfulness for Spiritual Attainments

1 Paul, an apostle of Christ Jesus by the will of God, and Timothy our brother, 2 To the saints and faithful brothers *and sisters* in Christ *who are* at Colossae: Grace to you and peace from God our Father.

3 We give thanks to God, the Father of our Lord Jesus Christ, praying always for you, 4 since we heard of your faith in Christ Jesus and the love which you have for all the saints; 5 because of the hope reserved for you in heaven, of which you previously heard in the word of truth, the gospel 6 which has come to you, just as in all the world also it is bearing fruit and increasing, even as *it has been doing* in you also since the day you heard *it* and understood the grace of God in truth; 7 just as you learned *it* from Epaphras, our beloved fellow bond-servant, who is a faithful servant of Christ on our behalf, 8 and he also informed us of your love in the Spirit.

9 For this reason we also, since the day we heard *about it,* have not ceased praying for you and asking that you may be filled with the knowledge of His will in all spiritual wisdom and understanding, 10 so that you will walk in a manner worthy of the Lord, to please *Him* in all respects, bearing fruit in every good work and increasing in the knowledge of God; 11 strengthened with all power, according to His glorious might, for the attaining of all perseverance and patience; joyously 12 giving thanks to the Father, who has qualified us to share in the inheritance of the saints in light.

The Incomparable Christ

13 For He rescued us from the domain of darkness, and transferred us to the kingdom of His beloved Son, 14 in whom we have redemption, the forgiveness of sins.

15 He is the image of the invisible God, the firstborn of all creation: 16 for by Him all things were created, *both* in the heavens and on earth, visible and invisible, whether thrones, or dominions, or rulers, or authorities—all things have been created through Him and for Him. 17 He is before all things, and in Him all things hold together. 18 He is also the head of the body, the church; and He is the beginning, the firstborn from the dead, so that He Himself will come to have first place in everything. 19 For it was the *Father's* good pleasure for all the fullness to dwell in Him, 20 and through Him to reconcile all things to Himself, whether things on earth or things in heaven, having made peace through the blood of His cross.

21 And although you were previously alienated and hostile in attitude, *engaged* in evil deeds, 22 yet He has now reconciled you in His body of flesh through death, in order to present you before Him holy and blameless and beyond reproach— 23 if indeed you continue in the faith firmly established and steadfast, and not shifting from the hope of the gospel that you have heard, which was proclaimed in all creation under heaven, and of which I, Paul, was made a minister.

24 Now I rejoice in my sufferings for your sake, and in my flesh I am supplementing what is lacking in Christ's afflictions in behalf of His body, which is the church. 25 I was made a minister of this *church* according to the commission from God granted to me for your benefit, so that I might fully carry out *the preaching of* the word of God, 26 *that is,* the mystery which had been hidden from the *past* ages and generations, but now has been revealed to His saints, 27 to whom God willed to make known what the wealth of the glory of this mystery among the Gentiles is, *the mystery* that is Christ in you, the hope of glory. 28 We proclaim Him, admonishing every person and teaching every person with all wisdom, so that we may present every person complete in Christ. 29 For this purpose I also labor, striving according to His power which works mightily within me.

You Are Built Up in Christ

2 For I want you to know how great a struggle I have in your behalf and for those who are at Laodicea, and for all those who have not personally seen my face, 2 that their hearts may be encouraged, having been knit together in love, and *that they would attain* to all the wealth that comes from the full assurance of understanding, *resulting* in a true knowledge of God's mystery, *that is,* Christ *Himself,* 3 in whom are hidden all the treasures of wisdom and knowledge. 4 I say this so that no one will deceive you with persuasive arguments. 5 For even though I am absent in body, I am nevertheless with you in spirit, rejoicing to see your orderly manner and the stability of your faith in Christ.

6 Therefore, as you have received Christ Jesus the Lord, *so* walk in Him, 7 having been firmly rooted and *now* being built up in Him and established ʸin your faith, just as you were instructed, *and* overflowing with gratitude.

8 See to it that there is no one who takes you captive through philosophy and empty deception in accordance with human tradition, in accordance with the elementary principles of the world, rather than in accordance with Christ. 9 For in Him all the fullness of Deity dwells in bodily form, 10 and in Him you have been made complete, and He is the head over every ruler and authority; 11 and in Him you were also circumcised with a circumcision performed without hands, in the removal of the body of the flesh by the circumcision of Christ, 12 having been buried with Him in baptism, in which you were also raised up with Him through faith in the working of God, who raised Him

from the dead. [13] And when you were dead in your wrongdoings and the uncircumcision of your flesh, He made you alive together with Him, having forgiven us all our wrongdoings, [14] having canceled the certificate of debt consisting of decrees against us, which was hostile to us; and He has taken it out of the way, having nailed it to the cross. [15] When He had disarmed the rulers and authorities, He made a public display of them, having triumphed over them through [1]Him.

[16] Therefore, no one is to act as your judge in regard to food and drink, or in respect to a festival or a new moon, or a Sabbath day— [17] things which are only a shadow of what is to come; but the substance belongs to Christ. [18] Take care that no one keeps defrauding you of your prize by delighting in humility and the worship of the angels, taking his stand on visions he has seen, inflated without cause by his fleshly mind, [19] and not holding firmly to the head, from whom the entire body, being supplied and held together by the joints and ligaments, grows with a growth which is from God.

[20] If you have died with Christ to the elementary principles of the world, why, as if you were living in the world, do you submit yourself to decrees, such as, [21] "Do not handle, do not taste, do not touch!" [22] (which all refer to things destined to perish with use)—in accordance with the commandments and teachings of man? [23] These are matters which do have the appearance of wisdom in self-made religion and humility and severe treatment of the body, but are of no value against fleshly indulgence.

Put On the New Self

3 Therefore, if you have been raised with Christ, keep seeking the things that are above, where Christ is, seated at the right hand of God. [2] Set your minds on the things that are above, not on the things that are on earth. [3] For you have died, and your life is hidden with Christ in God. [4] When Christ, who is our life, is revealed, then you also will be revealed with Him in glory.

[5] Therefore, treat the parts of your earthly body as dead to sexual immorality, impurity, passion, evil desire, and greed, which amounts to idolatry. [6] For it is because of these things that the wrath of God is coming [1]upon the [2]sons of disobedience, [7] and in them you also once walked, when you were living in them. [8] But now you also, rid yourselves of all of them: anger, wrath, malice, slander, and obscene speech from your mouth. [9] Do not lie to one another, since you stripped off the old self with its evil practices, [10] and have put on the new self, which is being renewed to a true knowledge according to the image of the One who created it— [11] a renewal in which there is no distinction between Greek and Jew, circumcised and uncircumcised, [1]barbarian, [2]Scythian, slave, and free, but Christ is all, and in all.

[12] So, as those who have been chosen of God, holy and beloved, put on a heart of compassion, kindness, humility, gentleness, and patience; [13] bearing with one another, and forgiving each other, whoever has a complaint against anyone; just as the Lord forgave you, so must you do also. [14] In addition to all these things put on love, which is the perfect bond of unity. [15] Let the peace of Christ, to which you were indeed called in one body, rule in your hearts; and be thankful. [16] Let the word of [1]Christ richly dwell within you, with all wisdom teaching and admonishing one another with psalms, hymns, and spiritual songs, singing with thankfulness in your hearts to God. [17] Whatever you do in word or deed, do everything in the name of the Lord Jesus, giving thanks through Him to God the Father.

Family Relations

[18] Wives, be subject to your husbands, as is fitting in the Lord. [19] Husbands, love your wives and do not become bitter against them. [20] Children, obey your parents in everything, for this is pleasing to the Lord. [21] Fathers, do not antagonize your children, so that they will not become discouraged.

[22] Slaves, obey those who are your human masters in everything, not with eye-service, as people-pleasers, but with sincerity of heart, fearing the Lord. [23] Whatever you do, do your work heartily, as for the Lord and not for people, [24] knowing that it is from the Lord that you will receive the reward of the inheritance. It is the Lord Christ whom you serve. [25] For the one who does wrong will receive the consequences of the wrong which he has done, and that without partiality.

4 Masters, grant your slaves justice and fairness, knowing that you also have a Master in heaven.

[2] Devote yourselves to prayer, keeping alert in it with an attitude of thanksgiving; [3] praying at the same time for us as well, that God will open up to us a door for the word, so that we may proclaim the mystery of Christ, for which I have also been imprisoned; [4] that I may make it clear in the way that I ought to proclaim it.

[5] Conduct yourselves with wisdom toward outsiders, making the most of the opportunity. [6] Your speech must always be with grace, as though seasoned with salt, so that you will know how you should respond to each person.

[7] As to all my affairs, Tychicus, our beloved brother and faithful servant and fellow bond-servant in the Lord, will bring you information. [8] For I have sent him to you for this very purpose, that you may know about our circumstances and that he may encourage your hearts; [9] and with him is Onesimus, our faithful and beloved brother, who is one of your own. They will inform you about the whole situation here.

[10] Aristarchus, my fellow prisoner, sends you his greetings; and also Barnabas' cousin Mark (about whom you received instructions; if he comes to you, welcome him); [11] and also Jesus

---

who is called Justus; these are the only fellow workers for the kingdom of God who are from the circumcision, and they have proved to be an encouragement to me. 12 Epaphras, who is one of your *own,* a bond-servant of Christ Jesus, sends you his greetings, always striving earnestly for you in his prayers, that you may stand mature and fully assured in all the will of God. 13 For I testify for him that he has a deep concern for you and for those who are in Laodicea and Hierapolis. 14 Luke, the beloved physician, sends you his greetings, and Demas *does also.* 15 Greet the brothers *and sisters* who are in Laodicea and also 'Nympha and the church that is in her house. 16 When this letter is read among you, have it also read in the church of the Laodiceans; and you, for your part, read my letter *that is coming* from Laodicea. 17 Tell Archippus, "See to the ministry which you have received in the Lord, so that you may fulfill it."

18 I, Paul, write this greeting with my own hand. Remember my imprisonment. Grace be with you.

4:15 1 Or *Nymphas* (masc)

The First Letter of Paul to the

THESSALONIANS

Giving Thanks for These Believers

1 Paul, Silvanus, and Timothy,
To the church of the Thessalonians in God the Father and the Lord Jesus Christ: Grace to you and peace.

2 We always give thanks to God for all of you, making mention *of you* in our prayers; 3 constantly keeping in mind your work of faith and labor of love and perseverance of hope in our Lord Jesus Christ in the presence of our God and Father, 4 knowing, brothers *and sisters,* beloved by God, *His* choice of you; 5 for our gospel did not come to you in word only, but also in power and in the Holy Spirit and with full conviction; just as you know what kind of men we proved to be among you for your sakes. 6 You also became imitators of us and of the Lord, having received the word during great affliction with the joy of the Holy Spirit, 7 so that you became an example to all the believers in Macedonia and Achaia. 8 For the word of the Lord has sounded forth from you, not only in Macedonia and Achaia, but in every place *the news of* your faith toward God has gone out, so that we have no need to say anything. 9 For they themselves report about us as to the kind of reception we had with you, and how you turned to God from idols to serve a living and true God, 10 and to wait for His Son from heaven, whom He raised from the dead, *that is,* Jesus who rescues us from the wrath to come.

Paul's Ministry

2 For you yourselves know, brothers *and sisters,* that our reception among you was not in vain, 2 but after we had already suffered and been treated abusively in Philippi, as you know, we had the boldness in our God to speak to you the gospel of God amid much opposition. 3 For our exhortation does not *come* from error or impurity or by way of deceit; 4 but just as we have been approved by God to be entrusted with the gospel, so we speak, not intending to please people, but *to please* God, who examines our hearts. 5 For we never came with flattering speech, as you know, nor with a pretext for greed—God is *our* witness— 6 nor did we seek honor from people, either from you or from others, though we could have asserted our authority as apostles of Christ. 7 But we proved to be *¹gentle* among you. As a nursing *mother* tenderly cares for her own children, 8 in the same way we had a fond affection for you and were delighted to share with you not only the gospel of God, but also our own lives, because you had become very dear to us. 9 For you recall, brothers *and sisters,* our labor and hardship: *it was by* working night and day so as not to be a burden to any of you, *that* we proclaimed to you the gospel of God. 10 You are witnesses, and *so is* God, *of* how

devoutly and rightly and blamelessly we behaved toward you believers; 11 just as you know how *we were* exhorting and encouraging and imploring each one of you as a father *would* his own children, 12 so that you would walk in a manner worthy of the God who calls you into His own kingdom and glory.

13 For this reason we also constantly thank God that when you received the word of God which you heard from us, you accepted *it* not *as* the word of *mere* men, but as what it really is, the word of God, which also is at work in you who believe. 14 For you, brothers *and sisters,* became imitators of the churches of God in Christ Jesus that are in Judea, for you also endured the same sufferings at the hands of your own countrymen, even as they *did* from the Jews, 15 who both killed the Lord Jesus and the prophets, and drove us out. They are not pleasing to God, but hostile to all people, 16 hindering us from speaking to the Gentiles so that they may be saved; with the result that they always reach the limit of their sins. But wrath has come upon them fully.

17 But we, brothers *and sisters,* having been orphaned from you *by absence* for a short while—in person, not in spirit—were all the more eager with great desire to see your face. 18 For we wanted to come to you—I, Paul, more than once—and Satan hindered us. 19 For who *is* our hope, or joy or crown of pride, in the presence of our Lord Jesus at His coming? Or *is it* not indeed you? 20 For you are our glory and joy.

Encouragement of Timothy's Visit

3 Therefore, when we could no longer endure *it,* we thought it best to be left behind, alone at Athens, 2 and we sent Timothy, our brother and God's fellow worker in the gospel of Christ, to strengthen and encourage you for the benefit of your faith, 3 so that no one would be disturbed by these afflictions. For you yourselves know that we have been destined for this. 4 For even when we were with you, we *kept* telling you in advance that we were going to suffer affliction; and so it happened, as you know. 5 For this reason, when I could no longer endure *it,* I also sent to find out about your faith, for fear that the tempter might have tempted you, and our labor would be for nothing.

6 But now that Timothy has come to us from you, and has brought us good news of your faith and love, and that you always think kindly of us, longing to see us just as we also *long to see* you, 7 for this reason, brothers *and sisters,* in all our distress and affliction we were comforted about you through your faith; 8 for now we *really* live, if you stand firm in the Lord. 9 For what thanks can we give to God for you in return for all the joy with which we rejoice

2:7 1 Three early mss *infants*

because of you before our God, [10] as we keep praying most earnestly night and day that we may see your faces, and may complete what is lacking in your faith?

[11] Now may our God and Father Himself, and our Lord Jesus, direct our way to you; [12] and may the Lord cause you to increase and overflow in love for one another, and for all people, just as we also *do* for you; [13] so that He may establish your hearts blameless in holiness before our God and Father at the coming of our Lord Jesus with all His saints.

Sanctification and Love

4 Finally then, brothers *and sisters,* we request and urge you in the Lord Jesus, that as you received *instruction* from us as to how you ought to walk and please God (just as you actually do walk), that you excel *even* more. [2] For you know what instructions we gave you by *the authority of* the Lord Jesus. [3] For this is the will of God, your sanctification; *that is,* that you abstain from sexual immorality; [4] that each of you know how to possess his own [1]vessel in sanctification and honor, [5] not in lustful passion, like the Gentiles who do not know God; [6] *and* that no one violate the rights and take advantage of his brother *or sister* in the matter, because the Lord is *the* avenger in all these things, just as we also told you previously and solemnly warned *you.* [7] For God has not called us for impurity, but in sanctification. [8] Therefore, the one who rejects *this* is not rejecting man, but the God who gives His Holy Spirit to you.

[9] Now as to the love of the brothers *and* sisters, you have no need for *anyone* to write to you, for you yourselves are taught by God to love one another; [10] for indeed you practice it toward all the brothers *and sisters* who are in all Macedonia. But we urge you, brothers *and sisters,* to excel *even* more, [11] and to make it your ambition to lead a quiet life and attend to your own *business* and work with your hands, just as we instructed you, [12] so that you will behave properly toward outsiders and not be in any need.

Those Who Died in Christ

[13] But we do not want you to be uninformed, brothers *and sisters,* about those who [1]are asleep, so that you will not grieve as indeed the rest *of mankind do,* who have no hope. [14] For if we believe that Jesus died and rose *from the dead,* so also God will bring with Him those who have fallen asleep [1]through Jesus. [15] For we say this to you by the word of the Lord, that we who are alive and remain until the coming of the Lord will not precede those who have fallen asleep. [16] For the Lord Himself will descend from heaven with a shout, with the voice of *the* archangel and with the trumpet of God, and the dead in Christ will rise first. [17] Then we who are alive, who

remain, will be caught up together with them in the clouds to meet the Lord in the air, and so we will always be with the Lord. [18] Therefore, comfort one another with these words.

The Day of the Lord

5 Now as to the periods and times, brothers *and sisters,* you have no need *of anything* to be written to you. [2] For you yourselves know full well that the day of the Lord is coming just like a thief in the night. [3] While they are saying, "Peace and safety!" then sudden destruction will come upon them like labor pains upon a pregnant woman, and they will not escape. [4] But you, brothers *and sisters,* are not in darkness, so that the day would overtake you like a thief; [5] for you are all sons of light and sons of day. We are not of night nor of darkness; [6] so then, let's not sleep as others do, but let's be alert and [1]sober. [7] For those who sleep, sleep at night, and those who are drunk, get drunk at night. [8] But since we are of *the* day, let's be [1]sober, having put on the breastplate of faith and love, and as a helmet, the hope of salvation. [9] For God has not destined us for wrath, but for obtaining salvation through our Lord Jesus Christ, [10] who died for us, so that whether we are awake or asleep, we will live together with Him. [11] Therefore, encourage one another and build one another up, just as you also are doing.

Christian Conduct

[12] But we ask you, brothers *and sisters,* to recognize those who diligently labor among you and are in leadership over you in the Lord, and give you instruction, [13] and that you regard them very highly in love because of their work. Live in peace with one another. [14] We urge you, brothers *and sisters,* admonish the unruly, encourage the fainthearted, help the weak, be patient with everyone. [15] See that no one repays another with evil for evil, but always seek what is good for one another and for all people. [16] Rejoice always, [17] pray without ceasing, [18] in everything give thanks; for this is the will of God for you in Christ Jesus. [19] Do not quench the Spirit, [20] do not utterly reject [1]prophecies, [21] but examine everything; hold firmly to that which is good, [22] abstain from every form of evil.

[23] Now may the God of peace Himself sanctify you entirely; and may your spirit and soul and body be kept complete, without blame at the coming of our Lord Jesus Christ. [24] Faithful is He who calls you, and He also will do it.

[25] Brothers *and sisters,* pray for us[1].

[26] Greet all the brothers *and sisters* with a holy kiss. [27] I put you under oath by the Lord to have this letter read to all the brothers *and sisters.*

[28] *May* the grace of our Lord Jesus Christ *be* with you.

4:4 [1] I.e., body; or wife 4:13 [1] I.e., have died 4:14 [1] I.e., as believers 5:6 [1] Or *self-controlled*
5:8 [1] Or *self-controlled* 5:20 [1] Or *prophetic gifts* 5:25 [1] Two early mss add *also*

The Second Letter of Paul to the
THESSALONIANS

Giving Thanks for Faith and Perseverance

1 Paul, Silvanus, and Timothy,
To the church of the Thessalonians in God our Father and the Lord Jesus Christ: 2 Grace to you and peace from God our Father and the Lord Jesus Christ.

3 We ought always to give thanks to God for you, brothers *and sisters,* as is *only* fitting, because your faith is increasing abundantly, and the love of each and every one of you toward one another grows *ever* greater. 4 As a result, we ourselves speak proudly of you among the churches of God for your perseverance and faith in the midst of all your persecutions and afflictions which you endure. 5 *This is* a plain indication of God's righteous judgment so that you will be considered worthy of the kingdom of God, for which you indeed are suffering. 6 For after all it is *only* right for God to repay with affliction those who afflict you, 7 and *to give* relief to you who are afflicted, *along* with us, when the Lord Jesus will be revealed from heaven with His mighty angels 8 in flaming fire, dealing out retribution to those who do not know God, and to those who do not obey the gospel of our Lord Jesus. 9 These people will pay the penalty of eternal destruction, away from the presence of the Lord and from the glory of His power, 10 when He comes to be glorified among His saints on that day, and to be marveled at among all who have believed—because our testimony to you was believed. 11 To this end also we pray for you always, that our God will consider you worthy of your calling, and fulfill every desire for goodness and the work of faith with power, 12 so that the name of our Lord Jesus will be glorified in you, and you in Him, in accordance with the grace of our God and *the* Lord Jesus Christ.

Man of Lawlessness

2 Now we ask you, brothers *and sisters,* regarding the coming of our Lord Jesus Christ and our gathering together to Him, 2 that you not be quickly shaken from your composure or be disturbed either by a spirit, or a message, or a letter as if from us, to the effect that the day of the Lord has come. 3 No one is to deceive you in any way! For *it will not come* unless the ¹apostasy comes first, and the man of lawlessness is revealed, the son of destruction, 4 who opposes and exalts himself above every so-called god or object of worship, so that he takes his seat in the temple of God, displaying himself as being God. 5 Do you not remember that while I was still with you, I was telling you these things? 6 And you know what restrains *him* now, so that he will be revealed in his time. 7 For the mystery of lawlessness is already at work; only ¹He who now restrains *will do so* until ²He is removed. 8 Then that lawless one

will be revealed, whom the Lord will eliminate with the breath of His mouth and bring to an end by the appearance of His coming; 9 *that is,* the one whose coming is in accord with the activity of Satan, with all power and false signs and wonders, 10 and with all the deception of wickedness for those who perish, because they did not accept the love of the truth so as to be saved. 11 For this reason God will send upon them a deluding influence so that they will believe what is false, 12 in order that they all may be judged who did not believe the truth, but took pleasure in wickedness.

Stand Firm

13 But we should always give thanks to God for you, brothers *and sisters* beloved by the Lord, because God has chosen you ¹from the beginning for salvation through sanctification by the Spirit and faith in the truth. 14 It was for this He called you through our gospel, that you may obtain the glory of our Lord Jesus Christ. 15 So then, brothers *and sisters,* stand firm and hold on to the traditions which you were taught, whether by word *of mouth* or by letter from us.

16 Now may our Lord Jesus Christ Himself and God our Father, who has loved us and given us eternal comfort and good hope by grace, 17 comfort and strengthen your hearts in every good work and word.

Request for Prayer

3 Finally, brothers *and sisters,* pray for us that the word of the Lord will spread rapidly and be glorified, just as *it was* also with you; 2 and that we will be rescued from troublesome and evil people; for not all have the faith. 3 But the Lord is faithful, and He will strengthen and protect you from the evil one. 4 We have confidence in the Lord concerning you, that you are doing, and will do, what we command. 5 May the Lord direct your hearts to the love of God and to the perseverance of Christ.

6 Now we command you, brothers *and sisters,* in the name of our Lord Jesus Christ, that you keep away from every brother *or sister* who leads a disorderly life and not *one* in accordance with the tradition which you received from us. 7 For you yourselves know how you ought to follow our example, because we did not act in an undisciplined way among you, 8 nor did we eat anyone's bread without paying for it, but with labor and hardship we *kept* working night and day so that we would not be a burden to any of you; 9 not because we do not have the right *to this,* but in order to offer ourselves as a role model for you, so that you would follow our example. 10 For even when we were with you, we used to give you this order: if anyone is not willing to work, then he is not to eat, either. 11 For we hear that

some among you are leading an undisciplined life, doing no work at all, but acting like busybodies. **12** Now we command and exhort such persons in the Lord Jesus Christ to work peacefully and eat their own bread. **13** But as for you, brothers *and sisters,* do not grow weary of doing good.

14 If anyone does not obey our instruction in this letter, take special note of that person *so as* not to associate with him, so that he will be put to shame. **15** And *yet* do not regard *that person* as an enemy, but admonish *that one* as a brother *or sister.*

16 Now may the Lord of peace Himself continually grant you peace in every circumstance. The Lord be with you all!

17 I, Paul, write this greeting with my own hand, and this is a distinguishing mark in every letter; this is the way I write. **18** The grace of our Lord Jesus Christ be with you all.

Correcting False Teaching

1 Paul, an apostle of Christ Jesus according to the commandment of God our Savior, and of Christ Jesus, *who is* our hope, 2 To Timothy, *my* true son in *the* faith: Grace, mercy, *and* peace from God the Father and Christ Jesus our Lord.

3 Just as I urged you upon my departure for Macedonia, to remain on at Ephesus so that you would instruct certain people not to teach strange doctrines, 4 nor to pay attention to myths and endless genealogies, which give rise to useless speculation rather than *advance* the plan of God, which is by faith, *so I urge you now.* 5 But the goal of our instruction is love from a pure heart, *from* a good conscience, and *from* a sincere faith. 6 Some people have strayed from these things and have turned aside to fruitless discussion, 7 wanting to be teachers of the Law, even though they do not understand either what they are saying or the matters about which they make confident assertions. 8 But we know that the Law is good, if one uses it lawfully, 9 realizing the fact that law is not made for a righteous person but for those who are lawless and rebellious, for the ungodly and sinners, for the unholy and worldly, for those who kill their fathers or mothers, for murderers, 10 for the sexually immoral, homosexuals, slave traders, liars, perjurers, and whatever else is contrary to sound teaching, 11 according to the glorious gospel of the blessed God, with which I have been entrusted.

Paul's Testimony

12 I thank Christ Jesus our Lord, who has strengthened me, because He considered me faithful, putting me into service, 13 even though I was previously a blasphemer and a persecutor and a violent aggressor. Yet I was shown mercy because I acted ignorantly in unbelief; 14 and the grace of our Lord was more than abundant, with the faith and love which are *found* in Christ Jesus. 15 It is a trustworthy statement, deserving full acceptance, that Christ Jesus came into the world to save sinners, among whom I am foremost. 16 Yet for this reason I found mercy, so that in me as the foremost *sinner* Jesus Christ might demonstrate His perfect patience as an example for those who would believe in Him for eternal life. 17 Now to the King eternal, immortal, invisible, the only God, *be* honor and glory forever and ever. Amen.

18 This command I entrust to you, Timothy, *my* son, in accordance with the prophecies previously made concerning you, that by them you fight the good fight, 19 keeping faith and a good conscience, which some have rejected and suffered shipwreck in regard to their faith. 20 Among these are Hymenaeus and Alexander, whom I have handed over to Satan, so that they will be taught not to blaspheme.

A Call to Prayer

2 First of all, then, I urge that requests, prayers, intercession, *and* thanksgiving be made in behalf of all people, 2 for kings and all who are in authority, so that we may lead a tranquil and quiet life in all godliness and dignity. 3 This is good and acceptable in the sight of God our Savior, 4 who wants all people to be saved and to come to the knowledge of the truth. 5 For there is one God, *and* one mediator also between God and mankind, *the* man Christ Jesus, 6 who gave Himself as a ransom for all, the testimony *given* at the proper time. 7 For this I was appointed as a preacher and an apostle (I am telling the truth, I am not lying), as a teacher of the Gentiles in faith and truth.

Instructions for Believers

8 Therefore I want the men in every place to pray, lifting up holy hands, without anger and dispute. 9 Likewise, *I want* women to adorn themselves with proper clothing, modestly and discreetly, not with braided hair and gold or pearls or expensive apparel, 10 but rather by means of good works, as is proper for women making a claim to godliness. 11 A woman must quietly receive instruction with entire submissiveness. 12 But I do not allow a woman to teach or to exercise authority over a man, but to remain quiet. 13 For *it was* Adam *who* was first created, *and* then Eve. 14 And *it was* not Adam *who* was deceived, but the woman was deceived and became a wrongdoer. 15 But women will be preserved through childbirth— if they continue in faith, love, and sanctity, with moderation.

Overseers and Deacons

3 It is a trustworthy statement: if any man aspires to the office of overseer, *it is* a fine work he desires *to do.* 2 An overseer, then, must be above reproach, the husband of one wife, 1 temperate, self-controlled, respectable, hospitable, skillful in teaching, 3 not over-indulging in wine, not a bully, but gentle, not contentious, free from the love of money. 4 *He must be* one who manages his own household well, keeping his children under control with all dignity 5 (but if a man does not know how to manage his own household, how will he take care of the church of God?), 6 and not a new convert, so that he will not become conceited and fall into condemnation incurred by the devil. 7 And he must have a good reputation with those outside *the church,* so that he will not fall into disgrace and the snare of the devil. 8 Deacons likewise *must be* men of dignity, not insincere, not prone to *drink* much wine,

not greedy for money, [9] *but* holding to the mystery of the faith with a clear conscience. [10] These men must also first be tested; then have them serve as deacons if they are beyond reproach. [11] †Women *must* likewise *be* dignified, not malicious gossips, but [2] temperate, faithful in all things. [12] Deacons must be husbands of one wife, *and* good managers of *their* children and their own households. [13] For those who have served well as deacons obtain for themselves a high standing and great confidence in the faith that is in Christ Jesus.

[14] I am writing these things to you, hoping to come to you before long; [15] but in case I am delayed, *I write* so that you will know how one should act in the household of God, which is the church of the living God, the pillar and support of the truth. [16] Beyond question, great is the mystery of godliness:

He who was revealed in the flesh,
Was vindicated in the Spirit,
Seen by angels,
Proclaimed among the nations,
Believed on in the world,
Taken up in glory.

Abandonment of Faith

[4] But the Spirit explicitly says that in later times some will fall away from the faith, paying attention to deceitful spirits and teachings of demons, [2] by means of the hypocrisy of liars seared in their own conscience as with a branding iron, [3] who forbid marriage *and advocate* abstaining from foods which God has created to be gratefully shared in by those who believe and know the truth. [4] For everything created by God is good, and nothing is to be rejected if it is received with gratitude; [5] for it is sanctified by means of the word of God and prayer.

A Good Minister's Discipline

[6] In pointing out these things to the brothers *and sisters,* you will be a good servant of Christ Jesus, *constantly* nourished on the words of the faith and of the good doctrine which you have been following. [7] But stay away from worthless stories that are typical of old women. Rather, discipline yourself for the purpose of godliness; [8] for bodily training is *just* slightly beneficial, but godliness is beneficial for all things, since it holds promise for the present life and *also* for the *life* to come. [9] It is a trustworthy statement deserving full acceptance. [10] For it is for this we labor and strive, because we have set our hope on the living God, who is the Savior of all mankind, especially of believers.

[11] Prescribe and teach these things. [12] Let no one look down on your youthfulness, but *rather* in speech, conduct, love, faith, *and* purity, show yourself an example of those who believe. [13] Until I come, give your attention to the *public* †reading, to exhortation, *and* teaching. [14] Do not neglect the spiritual gift within you, which was granted to you through *words of* prophecy with the laying on of hands by the council of elders. [15] Take pains with

these things; be *absorbed* in them, so that your progress will be evident to all. [16] Pay close attention to yourself and to the teaching; persevere in these things, for as you do this you will save both yourself and those who hear you.

Honor Widows

[5] Do not sharply rebuke an older man, but *rather* appeal to *him* as a father, *and to* the younger men as brothers, [2] to the older women as mothers, *and* to the younger women as sisters, in all purity.

[3] Honor widows who are actually widows; [4] but if any widow has children or grandchildren, they must first learn to show proper respect for their own family and to give back compensation to their parents; for this is acceptable in the sight of God. [5] Now she who is actually a widow and has been left alone has set her hope on God, and she continues in requests and prayers night and day. [6] But she who indulges herself in luxury is dead, *even* while she lives. [7] Give these instructions as well, so that they may be above reproach. [8] But if anyone does not provide for his own, and especially for those of his household, he has denied the faith and is worse than an unbeliever.

[9] A widow is to be put on the list only if she is not less than sixty years old, *having been* the wife of one man, [10] having a reputation for good works; *and* if she has brought up children, if she has shown hospitality to strangers, if she has washed the saints' feet, if she has assisted those in distress, *and* if she has devoted herself to every good work. [11] But refuse *to register* younger widows, for when they feel physical desires alienating them from Christ, they want to get married, [12] *thereby* incurring condemnation, because they have ignored their previous pledge. [13] At the same time they also learn *to be* idle, as they go around from house to house; and not merely idle, but also *they become* gossips and busybodies, talking about things not proper *to mention.* [14] Therefore, I want younger *widows* to get married, have children, manage their households, *and* give the enemy no opportunity for reproach; [15] for some have already turned away to follow Satan. [16] If any woman who is a believer has *dependent* widows, she must assist them and the church must not be burdened, so that it may assist those who are actually widows.

Concerning Elders

[17] The elders who lead well are to be considered worthy of double honor, especially those who work hard at preaching and teaching. [18] For the Scripture says, "YOU SHALL NOT MUZZLE THE OX WHILE IT IS THRESHING," and "The laborer is worthy of his wages." [19] Do not accept an accusation against an elder except on the basis of two or three witnesses. [20] Those who continue in sin, rebuke in the presence of all, so that the rest also will be fearful *of sinning.* [21] I solemnly exhort you in the presence of God and of Christ Jesus and of *His* chosen

angels, to maintain these *principles* without bias, doing nothing in a *spirit of* partiality. 22 Do not lay hands upon anyone too quickly and thereby share *responsibility for* the sins of others; keep yourself free from sin.

23 Do not go on drinking only water, but use a little wine for the sake of your stomach and your frequent ailments.

24 The sins of some people are quite evident, going before them to judgment; for others, their *sins* follow after. 25 Likewise also, deeds that are good are quite evident, and those which are otherwise cannot be concealed.

Instructions to Those Who Minister

6 All who are under the yoke as slaves are to regard their own masters as worthy of all honor so that the name of God and *our* doctrine will not be spoken against. 2 Those who have believers as their masters must not be disrespectful to them because they are brothers *or sisters,* but must serve them all the more, because those who partake of the benefit are believers and beloved. Teach and preach these *principles.*

3 If anyone advocates a different doctrine and does not agree with sound words, those of our Lord Jesus Christ, and with the doctrine conforming to godliness, 4 he is conceited *and* understands nothing; but he has a sick craving for controversial questions and disputes about words, from which come envy, strife, abusive language, evil suspicions, 5 and constant friction between people of depraved mind and deprived of the truth, who suppose that godliness is a means of gain. 6 But godliness *actually* is a means of great gain *when* accompanied by contentment. 7 For we have brought nothing into the world, so we cannot take anything out of it, either. 8 If we have food and covering, with these we shall be content.

9 But those who want to get rich fall into temptation and a trap, and many foolish and harmful desires which plunge people into ruin and destruction. 10 For the love of money is a root of all sorts of evil, and some by longing for it have wandered away from the faith and pierced themselves with many griefs.

11 But flee from these things, you man of God, and pursue righteousness, godliness, faith, love, perseverance, *and* gentleness. 12 Fight the good fight of faith; take hold of the eternal life to which you were called, and *for which* you made the good confession in the presence of many witnesses. 13 I direct you in the presence of God, who gives life to all things, and of Christ Jesus, who testified the good confession before Pontius Pilate, 14 that you keep the commandment without fault or reproach until the appearing of our Lord Jesus Christ, 15 which He will bring about at *the* proper time—He who is the blessed and only Sovereign, the King of kings and Lord of lords, 16 who alone possesses immortality and dwells in unapproachable light, whom no one has seen or can see. To Him *be* honor and eternal dominion! Amen.

17 Instruct those who are rich in this present world not to be conceited or to set their hope on the uncertainty of riches, but on God, who richly supplies us with all things to enjoy. 18 *Instruct them* to do good, to be rich in good works, to be generous and ready to share, 19 storing up for themselves the treasure of a good foundation for the future, so that they may take hold of that which is truly life.

20 Timothy, protect what has been entrusted to you, avoiding worldly, empty chatter and the opposing arguments of what is falsely called "knowledge"— 21 which some have professed and *thereby* have gone astray from the faith.

Grace be with you.

TIMOTHY

Timothy Charged to Guard His Trust

1 Paul, an apostle of Christ Jesus by the will of God, according to the promise of life in Christ Jesus,

2 To Timothy, my beloved son: Grace, mercy, and peace from God the Father and Christ Jesus our Lord.

3 I thank God, whom I serve with a clear conscience the way my forefathers did, as I constantly remember you in my prayers night and day, 4 longing to see you, even as I recall your tears, so that I may be filled with joy. 5 For I am mindful of the sincere faith within you, which first dwelled in your grandmother Lois and your mother Eunice, and I am sure that *it is* in you as well. 6 For this reason I remind you to kindle afresh the gift of God which is in you through the laying on of my hands. 7 For God has not given us a spirit of timidity, but of power and love and discipline.

8 Therefore do not be ashamed of the testimony of our Lord or of me His prisoner, but join with *me* in suffering for the gospel according to the power of God, 9 who saved us and called us with a holy calling, not according to our works, but according to His own purpose and grace, which was granted to us in Christ Jesus from all eternity, 10 but has now been revealed by the appearing of our Savior Christ Jesus, who abolished death and brought life and immortality to light through the gospel, 11 for which I was appointed a preacher, an apostle, and a teacher. 12 For this reason I also suffer these things; but I am not ashamed, for I know whom I have believed, and I am convinced that He is able to protect what I have entrusted to Him until that day. 13 Hold on to the example of sound words which you have heard from me, in *the* faith and love which are in Christ Jesus. 14 Protect, through the Holy Spirit who dwells in us, the treasure which has been entrusted to *you.*

15 You are aware of the fact that all who are in Asia turned away from me, among whom are Phygelus and Hermogenes. 16 The Lord grant mercy to the household of Onesiphorus, for he often refreshed me and was not ashamed of my chains; 17 but when he was in Rome, he eagerly searched for me and found me— 18 the Lord grant to him to find mercy from the Lord on that day—and you know very well what services he rendered at Ephesus.

Be Strong

2 You therefore, my son, be strong in the grace that is in Christ Jesus. 2 The things which you have heard from me in the presence of many witnesses, entrust these to faithful 1people who will be able to teach others also. 3 Suffer hardship with *me,* as a good soldier of Christ Jesus. 4 No soldier in active service entangles himself in the affairs of everyday life, so that he may please the one who enlisted *him.* 5 And if someone likewise competes as an athlete, he is not crowned *as victor* unless he competes according to the rules. 6 The hardworking farmer ought to be the first to receive his share of the crops. 7 Consider what I say, for the Lord will give you understanding in everything.

8 Remember Jesus Christ, risen from the dead, descendant of David, according to my gospel, 9 for which I suffer hardship even to imprisonment as a criminal; but the word of God is not imprisoned. 10 For this reason I endure all things for the sake of those who are chosen, so that they also may obtain the salvation which is in Christ Jesus *and* with *it* eternal glory. 11 The statement is trustworthy:

For if we died with Him, we will also live with Him;
12 If we endure, we will also reign with Him;
If we deny Him, He will also deny us;
13 If we are faithless, He remains faithful, for He cannot deny Himself.

An Unashamed Worker

14 Remind *them* of these things, and solemnly exhort *them* in the presence of God not to dispute about words, which is useless *and leads* to the ruin of the listeners. 15 Be diligent to present yourself approved to God as a worker who does not need to be ashamed, accurately handling the word of truth. 16 But avoid worldly *and* empty chatter, for it will lead to further ungodliness, 17 and their talk will spread like 1gangrene. Among them are Hymenaeus and Philetus, 18 *men* who have gone astray from the truth, claiming that the resurrection has already taken place; and they are jeopardizing the faith of some. 19 Nevertheless, the firm foundation of God stands, having this seal: "The Lord knows those who are His;" and, "Everyone who names the name of the Lord is to keep away from wickedness."

20 Now in a large house there are not only gold and silver implements, but also *implements* of wood and of earthenware, and some *are* for honor while others *are* for dishonor. 21 Therefore, if anyone cleanses himself from these *things,* he will be an implement for honor, sanctified, useful to the Master, prepared for every good work. 22 Now flee from youthful lusts and pursue righteousness, faith, love, *and* peace with those who call on the Lord from a pure heart. 23 But refuse foolish and ignorant speculations, knowing that they produce quarrels. 24 The Lord's bond-servant must not be quarrelsome, but be kind to all, skillful in teaching, patient when wronged, 25 with gentleness correcting those who are in opposition, if perhaps God may grant them

repentance leading to the knowledge of the truth, 26 and they may come to their senses and escape from the snare of the devil, having been held captive by him to do his will.

Difficult Times Will Come

3 But realize this, that in the last days difficult times will come. 2 For people will be lovers of self, lovers of money, boastful, arrogant, slanderers, disobedient to parents, ungrateful, unholy, 3 unloving, irreconcilable, malicious gossips, without self-control, brutal, haters of good, 4 treacherous, reckless, conceited, lovers of pleasure rather than lovers of God, 5 holding to a form of godliness although they have denied its power; avoid such people as these. 6 For among them are those who slip into households and captivate weak women weighed down with sins, led on by various impulses, 7 always learning and never able to come to the knowledge of the truth. 8 Just as Jannes and Jambres opposed Moses, so these men also oppose the truth, men of depraved mind, worthless in regard to the faith. 9 But they will not make further progress; for their foolishness will be obvious to all, just as was that also of Jannes and Jambres.

10 Now you followed my teaching, conduct, purpose, faith, patience, love, perseverance, 11 persecutions, and sufferings, such as happened to me at Antioch, at Iconium, and at Lystra; what persecutions I endured, and out of them all the Lord rescued me! 12 Indeed, all who want to live in a godly way in Christ Jesus will be persecuted. 13 But evil people and impostors will proceed from bad to worse, deceiving and being deceived. 14 You, however, continue in the things you have learned and become convinced of, knowing from whom you have learned them, 15 and that from childhood you have known the sacred writings which are able to give you the wisdom that leads to salvation through faith which is in Christ Jesus. 16 All Scripture is 1 inspired by God and beneficial for teaching, for rebuke, for correction, for training in righteousness; 17 so that the man or woman of God may be fully capable, equipped for every good work.

Preach the Word

4 I solemnly exhort you in the presence of God and of Christ Jesus, who is to judge the living and the dead, and by His appearing and His kingdom: 2 preach the word; be ready in season and out of season; correct, rebuke, and 1 exhort, with great patience and instruction. 3 For the time will come when they will not tolerate sound doctrine; but wanting to have their ears tickled, they will accumulate for themselves teachers in accordance with their own desires, 4 and they will turn their ears away from the truth and will turn aside to myths. 5 But as for you, use self-restraint in all things, endure hardship, do the work of an evangelist, fulfill your ministry.

6 For I am already being poured out as a drink offering, and the time of my departure has come. 7 I have fought the good fight, I have finished the course, I have kept the faith; 8 in the future there is reserved for me the crown of righteousness, which the Lord, the righteous Judge, will award to me on that day; and not only to me, but also to all who have loved His appearing.

Personal Concerns

9 Make every effort to come to me soon; 10 for Demas, having loved this present world, has deserted me and gone to Thessalonica; Crescens has gone to Galatia, Titus to Dalmatia. 11 Only Luke is with me. Take along Mark and bring him with you, for he is useful to me for service. 12 But I have sent Tychicus to Ephesus. 13 When you come, bring the overcoat which I left at Troas with Carpus, and the books, especially the parchments. 14 Alexander the coppersmith did me great harm; the Lord will repay him according to his deeds. 15 Be on guard against him yourself too, for he vigorously opposed our teaching. 16 At my first defense no one supported me, but all deserted me; may it not be counted against them. 17 But the Lord stood with me and strengthened me, so that through me the proclamation might be fully accomplished, and that all the Gentiles might hear; and I was rescued out of the lion's mouth. 18 The Lord will rescue me from every evil deed, and will bring me safely to His heavenly kingdom; to Him be the glory forever and ever. Amen.

19 Greet Prisca and Aquila, and the household of Onesiphorus. 20 Erastus remained at Corinth, but I left Trophimus sick at Miletus. 21 Make every effort to come before winter. Eubulus greets you, also Pudens, Linus, Claudia, and all the brothers and sisters. 22 The Lord be with your spirit. Grace be with you.

3:16 1 Lit God-breathed   4:2 1 Or encourage

The Letter of Paul to
TITUS

Salutation

1 Paul, a bond-servant of God and an apostle of Jesus Christ, for the faith of those chosen of God and the knowledge of the truth which is according to godliness, 2 in the hope of eternal life, which God, who cannot lie, promised long ages ago, 3 but at the proper time revealed His word in the proclamation with which I was entrusted according to the commandment of God our Savior;

4 To Titus, my true son in a common faith: Grace and peace from God the Father and Christ Jesus our Savior.

Qualifications of Elders

5 For this reason I left you in Crete, that you would set in order what remains and appoint elders in every city as I directed you, 6 namely, if any man is beyond reproach, the husband of one wife, having children who believe, not accused of indecent behavior or rebellion. 7 For the overseer must be beyond reproach as God's steward, not self-willed, not quick-tempered, not overindulging in wine, not a bully, not greedy for money, 8 but hospitable, loving what is good, self-controlled, righteous, holy, disciplined, 9 holding firmly the faithful word which is in accordance with the teaching, so that he will be able both to 1exhort in sound doctrine and to refute those who contradict it.

10 For there are many rebellious people, empty talkers and deceivers, especially those of the circumcision, 11 who must be silenced because they are upsetting whole families, teaching things they should not teach for the sake of dishonest gain. 12 One of them, a prophet of their own, said, "Cretans are always liars, evil beasts, lazy gluttons." 13 This testimony is true. For this reason reprimand them severely so that they may be sound in the faith, 14 not paying attention to Jewish myths and commandments of men who turn away from the truth. 15 To the pure, all things are pure; but to those who are defiled and unbelieving, nothing is pure, but both their mind and their conscience are defiled. 16 They profess to know God, but by their deeds they deny Him, being detestable and disobedient and worthless for any good deed.

Proclaim Sound Doctrine

2 But as for you, proclaim the things which are fitting for sound doctrine. 2 Older men are to be 1temperate, dignified, self-controlled, sound in faith, in love, in perseverance.

3 Older women likewise are to be reverent in their behavior, not malicious gossips nor enslaved to much wine, teaching what is good, 4 so that they may encourage the young women to love their husbands, to love their children, 5 to be sensible, pure, workers at home, kind, being subject to their own husbands, so that the word of God will not be dishonored.

6 Likewise urge the young men to be sensible; 7 in all things show yourself to be an example of good deeds, with purity in doctrine, dignified, 8 sound in speech which is beyond reproach, so that the opponent will be put to shame, having nothing bad to say about us.

9 Urge slaves to be subject to their own masters in everything, to be pleasing, not argumentative, 10 not stealing, but showing all good faith so that they will adorn the doctrine of God our Savior in every respect.

11 For the grace of God has appeared, bringing salvation to all people, 12 instructing us to deny ungodliness and worldly desires and to live sensibly, righteously, and in a godly manner in the present age, 13 looking for the blessed hope and the appearing of the glory of our great God and Savior, Christ Jesus, 14 who gave Himself for us to redeem us from every lawless deed, and to purify for Himself a people for His own possession, eager for good deeds.

15 These things speak and 1exhort, and rebuke with all authority. No one is to disregard you.

Godly Living

3 Remind them to be subject to rulers, to authorities, to be obedient, to be ready for every good deed, 2 to slander no one, not to be contentious, to be gentle, showing every consideration for all people. 3 For we too were once foolish, disobedient, deceived, enslaved to various lusts and pleasures, spending our life in malice and envy, hateful, hating one another. 4 But when the kindness of God our Savior and His love for mankind appeared, 5 He saved us, not on the basis of deeds which we did in righteousness, but in accordance with His mercy, by the washing of regeneration and renewing by the Holy Spirit, 6 whom He richly poured out upon us through Jesus Christ our Savior, 7 so that being justified by His grace we would be made heirs according to the hope of eternal life. 8 This statement is trustworthy; and concerning these things I want you to speak confidently, so that those who have believed God will be careful to engage in good deeds. These things are good and beneficial for people. 9 But avoid foolish controversies and genealogies and strife and disputes about the Law, for they are useless and worthless. 10 Reject a divisive person after a first and second warning, 11 knowing that such a person has deviated from what is right and is sinning, being self-condemned.

Personal Concerns

12 When I send Artemas or Tychicus to you,

1:9 1 Or encourage   2:2 1 Or level-headed   2:15 1 Or encourage

make every effort to come to me at Nicopolis, for I have decided to spend the winter there. [13] Diligently help Zenas the lawyer and Apollos on their way so that nothing is lacking for them. [14] Our people must also learn to engage in good deeds to meet pressing needs, so that they will not be unproductive.

[15] All who are with me greet you. Greet those who love us in the faith.

Grace be with you all.

The Letter of Paul to
PHILEMON

Salutation

1 Paul, a prisoner of Christ Jesus, and Timothy our brother,

To Philemon our beloved *brother* and fellow worker, 2 and to Apphia our sister, and to Archippus our fellow soldier, and to the church in your house: 3 Grace to you and peace from God our Father and the Lord Jesus Christ.

Philemon's Love and Faith

4 I thank my God always, making mention of you in my prayers, 5 because I hear of your love and of the faith which you have toward the Lord Jesus and toward all the saints; 6 *and I pray* that the fellowship of your faith may become effective *through the knowledge of every good thing which is in you for the sake of Christ. 7 For I have had great joy and comfort in your love, because the hearts of the saints have been refreshed through you, brother.

8 Therefore, though I have enough confidence in Christ to order you *to do* what is proper, 9 *yet* for love's sake I rather appeal *to you*—since I am such a person as Paul, an old man, and now also a prisoner of Christ Jesus—

Plea for Onesimus, a Free Man

10 I appeal to you for my son *Onesimus, whom I *fathered in my imprisonment, 11 who previously was useless to you, but now is useful both to you and to me. 12 I have sent him back to you in person, that is, *sending* my very heart, 13 whom I wanted to keep with me, so that in your behalf he might be at my service in my imprisonment for the gospel; 14 but I did not want to do anything without your consent, so that your goodness would not be, in effect, by compulsion, but of your own free will. 15 For perhaps *it was* for this reason *that* he was separated *from you* for a while, that you would have him back forever, 16 no longer as a slave, but more than a slave, a beloved brother, especially to me, but how much more to you, both in the flesh and in the Lord.

17 If then you regard me *as* a partner, accept him as *you would* me. 18 But if he has wronged you in any way or owes *you anything,* charge that to my account; 19 I, Paul, have written *this* with my own hand, I will repay *it* (not to mention to you that you owe to me even your own self as well). 20 Yes, brother, let me benefit from you in the Lord; refresh my heart in Christ.

21 Having confidence in your obedience, I write to you, since I know that you will do even more than what I say.

22 At the same time also prepare me a guest room, for I hope that through your prayers I will be given to you.

23 Epaphras, my fellow prisoner in Christ Jesus, greets you, 24 *as do* Mark, Aristarchus, Demas, *and* Luke, my fellow workers.

25 The grace of the Lord Jesus Christ be with your spirit.*

1:6 1 Or *in*   **1:10** 1 I.e., useful   2 I.e., led to the Lord   **1:25** 1 One early ms adds *Amen*

The Letter to the
HEBREWS

God's Final Word in His Son

1 God, after He spoke long ago to the fathers in the prophets in many portions and in many ways, 2 in these last days has spoken to us in *His* Son, whom He appointed heir of all things, through whom He also made the world. 3 And He is the radiance of His glory and the exact representation of His nature, and upholds all things by the word of His power. When He had made purification of sins, He sat down at the right hand of the Majesty on high, 4 having become so much better than the angels, to the extent that He has inherited a more excellent name than they.

5 For to which of the angels did He ever say,
"YOU ARE MY SON,
TODAY I HAVE FATHERED YOU"?
And again,
"I WILL BE A FATHER TO HIM
AND HE WILL BE A SON TO ME"?
6 And when He again brings the firstborn into the world, He says,
"AND LET ALL THE ANGELS OF GOD WORSHIP
HIM."
7 And regarding the angels He says,
"HE MAKES HIS ANGELS WINDS,
AND HIS MINISTERS A FLAME OF FIRE."
8 But regarding the Son *He says,*
"YOUR THRONE, GOD, IS FOREVER AND EVER,
AND THE SCEPTER OF RIGHTEOUSNESS IS THE
SCEPTER OF [1]HIS KINGDOM.
9 "YOU HAVE LOVED RIGHTEOUSNESS AND HATED
LAWLESSNESS;
THEREFORE GOD, YOUR GOD, HAS ANOINTED
YOU
WITH THE OIL OF JOY ABOVE YOUR
COMPANIONS."
10 And,
"YOU, LORD, IN THE BEGINNING LAID THE
FOUNDATION OF THE EARTH,
AND THE HEAVENS ARE THE WORKS OF YOUR
HANDS;
11 THEY WILL PERISH, BUT YOU REMAIN;
AND THEY ALL WILL WEAR OUT LIKE A GAR-
MENT,
12 AND LIKE A ROBE YOU WILL ROLL THEM UP;
LIKE A GARMENT THEY WILL ALSO BE
CHANGED.
BUT YOU ARE THE SAME,
AND YOUR YEARS WILL NOT COME TO AN
END."
13 But to which of the angels has He ever said,
"SIT AT MY RIGHT HAND,
UNTIL I MAKE YOUR ENEMIES
A FOOTSTOOL FOR YOUR FEET"?
14 Are they not all ministering spirits, sent out to *provide* service for the sake of those who will inherit salvation?

Pay Attention

2 For this reason we must pay much closer attention to what we have heard, so that we do not drift away *from it.* 2 For if the word spoken through angels proved unalterable, and every violation and act of disobedience received a just punishment, 3 how will we escape if we neglect so great a salvation? After it was at first spoken through the Lord, it was confirmed to us by those who heard, 4 God also testifying with them, both by signs and wonders, and by various miracles and by gifts of the Holy Spirit according to His own will.

Earth Subject to Man

5 For He did not subject to angels the world to come, about which we are speaking. 6 But someone has testified somewhere, saying,
"WHAT IS MAN, THAT YOU THINK OF HIM?
OR A SON OF MAN, THAT YOU ARE CONCERNED
ABOUT HIM?
7 "YOU HAVE MADE HIM FOR A LITTLE WHILE
LOWER THAN ANGELS;
YOU HAVE CROWNED HIM WITH GLORY AND
HONOR[1];
8 YOU HAVE PUT EVERYTHING IN SUBJECTION
UNDER HIS FEET."
For in subjecting all things to him, He left nothing that is not subject to him. But now we do not yet see all things subjected to him.

Jesus Briefly Humbled

9 But we do see Him who was made for a little while lower than the angels, *namely,* Jesus, because of His suffering death crowned with glory and honor, so that by the grace of God He might taste death for everyone. 10 For it was fitting for Him, for whom are all things, and through whom are all things, in bringing many sons to glory, to perfect the originator of their salvation through sufferings. 11 For both He who sanctifies and those who are sanctified are all from one *Father;* for this reason He is not ashamed to call them brothers *and sisters,* 12 saying,
"I WILL PROCLAIM YOUR NAME TO MY
BROTHERS,
IN THE MIDST OF THE ASSEMBLY I WILL SING
YOUR PRAISE."
13 And again,
"I WILL PUT MY TRUST IN HIM."
And again,
"BEHOLD, I AND THE CHILDREN WHOM GOD
HAS GIVEN ME."
14 Therefore, since the children share in flesh and blood, He Himself likewise also partook of the same, so that through death He might destroy the one who has the power of death, that is, the devil, 15 and free those who through fear of death were subject to slavery all their lives. 16 For clearly He does not give help to angels, but He gives help to the descendants of Abraham. 17 Therefore, in all things He had to be made like His brothers so that He might become a merciful and faithful high priest in

1:8 [1] Late mss *Your*   2:7 [1] One early ms continues, *and have appointed him over the works of Your hands*

things pertaining to God, to make ¹propitiation for the sins of the people. 18 For since He Himself was tempted in that which He has suffered, He is able to come to the aid of those who are tempted.

Jesus Our High Priest

3 Therefore, holy brothers and sisters, partakers of a heavenly calling, consider the Apostle and High Priest of our confession: Jesus; 2 He was faithful to Him who appointed Him, as Moses also was in all His house. 3 For He has been counted worthy of more glory than Moses, by just so much as the builder of the house has more honor than the house. 4 For every house is built by someone, but the builder of all things is God. 5 Now Moses was faithful in all God's house as a servant, for a testimony of those things which were to be spoken later; 6 but Christ was faithful as a Son over His house—whose house we are, if we hold firmly to our confidence and the boast of our hope.

7 Therefore, just as the Holy Spirit says,
"TODAY IF YOU HEAR HIS VOICE,
8　DO NOT HARDEN YOUR HEARTS AS WHEN THEY PROVOKED ME,
AS ON THE DAY OF TRIAL IN THE WILDERNESS,
9　WHERE YOUR FATHERS PUT ME TO THE TEST,
AND SAW MY WORKS FOR FORTY YEARS.
10　"THEREFORE I WAS ANGRY WITH THIS GENERATION,
AND SAID, 'THEY ALWAYS GO ASTRAY IN THEIR HEART,
AND THEY DID NOT KNOW MY WAYS';
11　AS I SWORE IN MY ANGER,
'THEY CERTAINLY SHALL NOT ENTER MY REST.'"

The Danger of Unbelief

12 Take care, brothers and sisters, that there will not be in any one of you an evil, unbelieving heart that falls away from the living God. 13 But encourage one another every day, as long as it is still called "today," so that none of you will be hardened by the deceitfulness of sin. 14 For we have become partakers of Christ if we keep the beginning of our commitment firm until the end, 15 while it is said,
"TODAY IF YOU HEAR HIS VOICE,
DO NOT HARDEN YOUR HEARTS, AS WHEN THEY PROVOKED ME."
16 For who provoked Him when they had heard? Indeed, did not all those who came out of Egypt led by Moses? 17 And with whom was He angry for forty years? Was it not with those who sinned, whose dead bodies fell in the wilderness? 18 And to whom did He swear that they would not enter His rest, but to those who were disobedient? 19 And so we see that they were not able to enter because of unbelief.

The Believer's Rest

4 Therefore, we must fear if, while a promise remains of entering His rest, any one of you may seem to have come short of it. 2 For indeed we have had good news preached to us, just as they also did; but the word they heard did not benefit them, because ¹they were not united

with those who listened with faith. 3 For we who have believed enter that rest, just as He has said,
"AS I SWORE IN MY ANGER,
THEY CERTAINLY SHALL NOT ENTER MY REST,"
although His works were finished from the foundation of the world. 4 For He has said somewhere concerning the seventh day: "AND GOD RESTED ON THE SEVENTH DAY FROM ALL HIS WORKS"; 5 and again in this passage, "THEY CERTAINLY SHALL NOT ENTER MY REST." 6 Therefore, since it remains for some to enter it, and those who previously had good news preached to them failed to enter because of disobedience, 7 He again sets a certain day, "Today," saying through David after so long a time just as has been said before,
"TODAY IF YOU HEAR HIS VOICE,
DO NOT HARDEN YOUR HEARTS."
8 For if Joshua had given them rest, He would not have spoken of another day after that. 9 Consequently, there remains a Sabbath rest for the people of God. 10 For the one who has entered His rest has himself also rested from his works, as God did from His. 11 Therefore let's make every effort to enter that rest, so that no one will fall by following the same example of disobedience. 12 For the word of God is living and active, and sharper than any two-edged sword, even penetrating as far as the division of soul and spirit, of both joints and marrow, and able to judge the thoughts and intentions of the heart. 13 And there is no creature hidden from His sight, but all things are open and laid bare to the eyes of Him to whom we must answer.

14 Therefore, since we have a great high priest who has passed through the heavens, Jesus the Son of God, let's hold firmly to our confession. 15 For we do not have a high priest who cannot sympathize with our weaknesses, but One who has been tempted in all things just as we are, yet without sin. 16 Therefore let's approach the throne of grace with confidence, so that we may receive mercy and find grace for help at the time of our need.

The Perfect High Priest

5 For every high priest taken from among men is appointed on behalf of people in things pertaining to God, in order to offer both gifts and sacrifices for sins; 2 he can deal gently with the ignorant and misguided, since he himself also is clothed in weakness; 3 and because of it he is obligated to offer sacrifices for sins for himself, as well as for the people. 4 And no one takes the honor for himself, but receives it when he is called by God, just as Aaron also was.

5 So too Christ did not glorify Himself in becoming a high priest, but it was He who said to Him,
"YOU ARE MY SON,
TODAY I HAVE FATHERED YOU";
6 just as He also says in another passage,
"YOU ARE A PRIEST FOREVER
ACCORDING TO THE ORDER OF
MELCHIZEDEK."

7 In the days of His humanity, He offered up both prayers and pleas with loud crying and tears to the One able to save Him from death, and He was heard because of His devout behavior. 8 Although He was a Son, He learned obedience from the things which He suffered. 9 And having been perfected, He became the source of eternal salvation for all those who obey Him, 10 being designated by God as High Priest according to the order of Melchizedek.

11 Concerning him we have much to say, and it is difficult to explain, since you have become poor listeners. 12 For though by this time you ought to be teachers, you have need again for someone to teach you the elementary principles of the actual words of God, and you have come to need milk and not solid food. 13 For everyone who partakes only of milk is unacquainted with the word of righteousness, for he is an infant. 14 But solid food is for the mature, who because of practice have their senses trained to distinguish between good and evil.

The Danger of Falling Away

6 Therefore leaving the elementary teaching about the Christ, let us press on to maturity, not laying again a foundation of repentance from dead works and of faith toward God, 2 of instruction about washings and laying on of hands, and about the resurrection of the dead and eternal judgment. 3 And this we will do, if God permits. 4 For it is impossible, in the case of those who have once been enlightened and have tasted of the heavenly gift and have been made partakers of the Holy Spirit, 5 and have tasted the good word of God and the powers of the age to come, 6 and then have 1fallen away, to restore them again to repentance, since they again crucify to themselves the Son of God and put Him to open shame. 7 For ground that drinks the rain which often falls on it and produces vegetation useful to those for whose sake it is also tilled, receives a blessing from God; 8 but if it yields thorns and thistles, it is worthless and close to being cursed, and it ends up being burned.

Better Things for You

9 But, beloved, we are convinced of better things regarding you, and things that accompany salvation, even though we are speaking in this way. 10 For God is not unjust so as to forget your work and the love which you have shown toward His name, by having served and by still serving the saints. 11 And we desire that each one of you demonstrate the same diligence so as to realize the full assurance of hope until the end, 12 so that you will not be sluggish, but imitators of those who through faith and endurance inherit the promises.

13 For when God made the promise to Abraham, since He could swear an oath by no one greater, He swore by Himself, 14 saying, "INDEED I WILL GREATLY BLESS YOU AND I WILL GREATLY MULTIPLY YOU." 15 And so, having patiently waited, he obtained the promise. 16 For people swear an oath by one greater than

themselves, and with them an oath serving as confirmation is an end of every dispute. 17 In the same way God, desiring even more to demonstrate to the heirs of the promise the fact that His purpose is unchangeable, confirmed it with an oath, 18 so that by two unchangeable things in which it is impossible for God to lie, we who have taken refuge would have strong encouragement to hold firmly to the hope set before us. 19 This hope we have as an anchor of the soul, a hope both sure and reliable and one which enters within the veil, 20 where Jesus has entered as a forerunner for us, having become a high priest forever according to the order of Melchizedek.

Melchizedek's Priesthood like Christ's

7 For this Melchizedek, king of Salem, priest of the Most High God, who met Abraham as he was returning from the slaughter of the kings and blessed him, 2 to whom also Abraham apportioned a tenth of all the spoils, was first of all, by the translation of his name, king of righteousness, and then also king of Salem, which is king of peace. 3 Without father, without mother, without genealogy, having neither beginning of days nor end of life, but made like the Son of God, he remains a priest perpetually.

4 Now observe how great this man was to whom Abraham, the patriarch, gave a tenth of the choicest spoils. 5 And those indeed of the sons of Levi who receive the priest's office have a commandment in the Law to collect a tenth from the people, that is, from their countrymen, although they are descended from Abraham. 6 But the one whose genealogy is not traced from them collected a tenth from Abraham and blessed the one who had the promises. 7 But without any dispute the lesser person is blessed by the greater. 8 In this case mortal men receive tithes, but in that case one receives them, of whom it is witnessed that he lives on. 9 And, so to speak, through Abraham even Levi, who received tithes, has paid tithes, 10 for he was still in the loins of his forefather when Melchizedek met him.

11 So if perfection was through the Levitical priesthood (for on the basis of it the people received the Law), what further need was there for another priest to arise according to the order of Melchizedek, and not be designated according to the order of Aaron? 12 For when the priesthood is changed, of necessity there takes place a change of law also. 13 For the one about whom these things are said belongs to another tribe, from which no one has officiated at the altar. 14 For it is evident that our Lord was descended from Judah, a tribe with reference to which Moses said nothing concerning priests. 15 And this is clearer still, if another priest arises according to the likeness of Melchizedek, 16 who has become a priest not on the basis of a law of physical requirement, but according to the power of an indestructible life. 17 For it is attested of Him,

"YOU ARE A PRIEST FOREVER
ACCORDING TO THE ORDER OF
MELCHIZEDEK."

6:6 1 Or committed apostasy; i.e., renounced the faith

18 For, on the one hand, there is *the* nullification of a former commandment because of its weakness and uselessness **19** (for the Law made nothing perfect); on the other hand, *there is the* introduction of a better hope, through which we come near to God. **20** And to the extent that *it was* not without an oath **21** (for they indeed became priests without an oath, but He with an oath through the One who said to Him,

"THE LORD HAS SWORN
AND WILL NOT CHANGE HIS MIND,
'YOU ARE A PRIEST FOREVER'");

22 by the same extent Jesus also has become the guarantee of a better covenant.

23 The *former* priests, on the one hand, existed in greater numbers because they were prevented by death from continuing; **24** Jesus, on the other hand, because He continues forever, holds His priesthood permanently. **25** Therefore He is also able to save forever those who come to God through Him, since He always lives to make intercession for them.

26 For it was fitting for us to have such a high priest, holy, innocent, undefiled, separated from sinners, and exalted above the heavens; **27** who has no daily need, like those high priests, to offer up sacrifices, first for His own sins and then for the *sins* of the people, because He did this once for all *time* when He offered up Himself. **28** For the Law appoints men as high priests who are weak, but the word of the oath, which came after the Law, *appoints* a Son, who has been made perfect forever.

A Better Ministry

8 Now the main point in what has been said *is this:* we have such a high priest, who has taken His seat at the right hand of the throne of the Majesty in the heavens, **2** a minister in the sanctuary and in the true tabernacle, which the Lord set up, not man. **3** For every high priest is appointed to offer both gifts and sacrifices; so it is necessary that this *high priest* also have something to offer. **4** Now if He were on earth, He would not be a priest at all, since there are those who offer the gifts according to the Law; **5** who serve a copy and shadow of the heavenly things, just as Moses was warned *by God* when he was about to erect the tabernacle; for, "SEE," He says, "THAT YOU MAKE all things BY THE PATTERN WHICH WAS SHOWN TO YOU ON THE MOUNTAIN." **6** But now He has obtained a more excellent ministry, to the extent that He is also the mediator of a better covenant, which has been enacted on better promises.

A New Covenant

7 For if that first *covenant* had been free of fault, no circumstances would have been sought for a second. **8** For in finding fault with the people, He says,

"BEHOLD, DAYS ARE COMING, SAYS THE LORD,
WHEN I WILL BRING ABOUT A NEW COVENANT
WITH THE HOUSE OF ISRAEL AND THE HOUSE
OF JUDAH,

9 NOT LIKE THE COVENANT WHICH I MADE WITH
THEIR FATHERS
ON THE DAY I TOOK THEM BY THE HAND
TO BRING THEM OUT OF THE LAND OF EGYPT;
FOR THEY DID NOT CONTINUE IN MY
COVENANT,
AND I DID NOT CARE ABOUT THEM, SAYS THE
LORD.

10 "FOR THIS IS THE COVENANT WHICH I WILL
MAKE WITH THE HOUSE OF ISRAEL
AFTER THOSE DAYS, DECLARES THE LORD:
I WILL PUT MY LAWS INTO THEIR MINDS,
AND WRITE THEM ON THEIR HEARTS.
AND I WILL BE THEIR GOD,
AND THEY SHALL BE MY PEOPLE.

11 "AND THEY WILL NOT TEACH, EACH ONE HIS
FELLOW CITIZEN,
AND EACH ONE HIS BROTHER, SAYING, 'KNOW
THE LORD,'
FOR THEY WILL ALL KNOW ME,
FROM THE LEAST TO THE GREATEST OF THEM.

12 "FOR I WILL BE MERCIFUL TOWARD THEIR
WRONGDOINGS,
AND THEIR SINS I WILL NO LONGER
REMEMBER."

13 When He said, "A new *covenant*," He has made the first obsolete. But whatever is becoming obsolete and growing old is about to disappear.

The Old and the New

9 Now even the first *covenant* had regulations for divine worship and the earthly sanctuary. **2** For a tabernacle was equipped, the outer *sanctuary,* in which *were* the lampstand, the table, and the sacred bread; this is called the Holy Place. **3** Behind the second veil there was a tabernacle which is called the Most Holy Place, **4** having a golden altar of incense and the ark of the covenant covered on all sides with gold, in which was a golden jar holding the manna, Aaron's staff which budded, and the tablets of the covenant; **5** and above it *were* the cherubim of glory overshadowing the [1] atoning cover; but about these things we cannot now speak in detail.

6 Now when these things have been so prepared, the priests are continually entering the outer tabernacle, performing the divine worship, **7** but into the second, only the high priest *enters* once a year, not without *taking* blood which he offers for himself and for the sins of the people committed in ignorance. **8** The Holy Spirit *is* signifying this, that the way into the holy place has not yet been disclosed while the outer tabernacle is still standing, **9** which *is* a symbol for the present time. Accordingly both gifts and sacrifices are offered which cannot make the worshiper perfect in conscience, **10** since they *relate* only to food, drink, and various washings, regulations for the body imposed until a time of reformation.

11 But when Christ appeared *as* a high priest of the good things [1] having come, *He entered* through the greater and more perfect tabernacle, not made by hands, that is, not of this creation; **12** and not through the blood of goats and calves, but through His own blood, He

---

9:5 [1] Also called *mercy seat;* i.e., where blood was sprinkled on the Day of Atonement   9:11 [1] One early ms *to come*

entered the holy place once for all *time,* having obtained eternal redemption. **13** For if the blood of goats and bulls, and the [1]ashes of a heifer sprinkling those who have been defiled, sanctify for the cleansing of the flesh, **14** how much more will the blood of Christ, who through the eternal Spirit offered Himself without blemish to God, cleanse your conscience from dead works to serve the living God? **15** For this reason He is the mediator of a new covenant, so that, since a death has taken place for the redemption of the violations that were *committed* under the first covenant, those who have been called may receive the promise of the eternal inheritance. **16** For where there is a covenant, there must of necessity be the death of the one who made it. **17** For a covenant is valid *only* when *people are* dead, [1]for it is never in force while the one who made it lives. **18** Therefore even the first *covenant* was not inaugurated without blood. **19** For when every commandment had been spoken by Moses to all the people according to the Law, he took the blood of the calves and the goats, with water and scarlet wool and hyssop, and sprinkled both the book itself and all the people, **20** saying, "THIS IS THE BLOOD OF THE COVENANT WHICH GOD COMMANDED YOU." **21** And in the same way he sprinkled both the tabernacle and all the vessels of the ministry with the blood. **22** And almost all things are cleansed with blood, according to the Law, and without the shedding of blood there is no forgiveness. **23** Therefore it was necessary for the copies of the things in the heavens to be cleansed with these things, but the heavenly things themselves with better sacrifices than these. **24** For Christ did not enter a holy place made by hands, a *mere* copy of the true one, but into heaven itself, now to appear in the presence of God for us; **25** nor was it that He would offer Himself often, as the high priest enters the Holy Place year by year with blood that is not his own. **26** Otherwise, He would have needed to suffer often since the foundation of the world; but now once at the consummation of the ages He has been revealed to put away sin by the sacrifice of Himself. **27** And just as it is destined for people to die once, and after this *comes* judgment, **28** so Christ also, having been offered once to bear the sins of many, will appear a second time for salvation without *reference to* sin, to those who eagerly await Him.

One Sacrifice of Christ Is Sufficient

10 For the Law, since it has *only* a shadow of the good things to come *and* not the form of those things itself, [1]can never, by the same sacrifices which they offer continually every year, make those who approach perfect. **2** Otherwise, would they not have ceased to be offered, because the worshipers, having once been cleansed, would no longer have had consciousness of sins? **3** But in those *sacrifices* there is a reminder of sins every year. **4** For it is impossible for the blood of bulls and goats to take away sins. **5** Therefore, when He comes into the world, He says,

"YOU HAVE NOT DESIRED SACRIFICE AND
  OFFERING,
BUT YOU HAVE PREPARED A BODY FOR ME;
6 YOU HAVE NOT TAKEN PLEASURE IN WHOLE
  BURNT OFFERINGS AND *OFFERINGS* FOR SIN.
7 "THEN I SAID, 'BEHOLD, I HAVE COME
  (IT IS WRITTEN OF ME IN THE SCROLL OF THE
  BOOK)
TO DO YOUR WILL, O GOD.' "
8 After saying above, "SACRIFICES AND OFFERINGS AND WHOLE BURNT OFFERINGS AND *OFFERINGS* FOR SIN YOU HAVE NOT DESIRED, NOR HAVE YOU TAKEN PLEASURE *IN THEM*" (which are offered according to the Law), **9** then He said, "BEHOLD, I HAVE COME TO DO YOUR WILL." He takes away the first in order to establish the second. **10** By this will, we have been sanctified through the offering of the body of Jesus Christ once for all *time.*

11 Every priest stands daily ministering and offering time after time the same sacrifices, which can never take away sins; **12** but He, having offered one sacrifice for sins for all time, SAT DOWN AT THE RIGHT HAND OF GOD, **13** waiting from that time onward UNTIL HIS ENEMIES ARE MADE A FOOTSTOOL FOR HIS FEET. **14** For by one offering He has perfected for all time those who are sanctified. **15** And the Holy Spirit also testifies to us; for after saying,

16 "THIS IS THE COVENANT WHICH I WILL MAKE
  WITH THEM
AFTER THOSE DAYS, DECLARES THE LORD:
I WILL PUT MY LAWS UPON THEIR HEARTS,
AND WRITE THEM ON THEIR MIND,"
He then says,
17 "AND THEIR SINS AND THEIR LAWLESS DEEDS
  I WILL NO LONGER REMEMBER."
18 Now where there is forgiveness of these things, an offering for sin is no longer *required.*

A New and Living Way

19 Therefore, brothers *and sisters,* since we have confidence to enter the holy place by the blood of Jesus, **20** by a new and living way which He inaugurated for us through the veil, that is, *through* His flesh, **21** and since *we have* a great priest over the house of God, **22** let's approach *God* with a sincere heart in full assurance of faith, having our hearts sprinkled *clean* from an evil conscience and our bodies washed with pure water. **23** Let's hold firmly to the confession of our hope without wavering, for He who promised is faithful; **24** and let's consider how to encourage one another in love and good deeds, **25** not abandoning our own meeting together, as is the habit of some people, but encouraging *one another;* and all the more as you see the day drawing near.

Christ or Judgment

26 For if we go on sinning willfully after receiving the knowledge of the truth, there no longer remains a sacrifice for sins, **27** but a terrifying expectation of judgment and THE FURY OF A FIRE WHICH WILL CONSUME THE ADVERSARIES. **28** Anyone who has ignored the Law of Moses is put to death without mercy on *the testimony of* two or three witnesses. **29** How much more severe punishment do you think he will deserve who has trampled underfoot the Son of

God, and has regarded as unclean the blood of the covenant by which he was sanctified, and has insulted the Spirit of grace? 30 For we know Him who said, "VENGEANCE IS MINE, I WILL REPAY." And again, "THE LORD WILL JUDGE HIS PEOPLE." 31 It is a terrifying thing to fall into the hands of the living God.

32 But remember the former days, when, after being enlightened, you endured a great conflict of sufferings, 33 partly by being made a public spectacle through insults and distress, and partly by becoming companions with those who were so treated. 34 For you showed sympathy to the prisoners and accepted joyfully the seizure of your property, knowing that you have for yourselves a better and lasting possession. 35 Therefore, do not throw away your confidence, which has a great reward. 36 For you have need of endurance, so that when you have done the will of God, you may receive what was promised.

37   FOR YET IN A VERY LITTLE WHILE,
        HE WHO IS COMING WILL COME, AND WILL NOT
            DELAY.
38   BUT MY RIGHTEOUS ONE WILL LIVE BY FAITH;
        AND IF HE SHRINKS BACK, MY SOUL HAS NO
            PLEASURE IN HIM.
39 But we are not among those who shrink back to destruction, but of those who have faith for the safekeeping of the soul.

The Triumphs of Faith

11 Now faith is the certainty of things hoped for, a proof of things not seen. 2 For by it the people of old gained approval.

3 By faith we understand that the world has been created by the word of God so that what is seen has not been made out of things that are visible. 4 By faith Abel offered to God a better sacrifice than Cain, through which he was attested to be righteous, God testifying about his gifts, and through faith, though he is dead, he still speaks. 5 By faith Enoch was taken up so that he would not see death; AND HE WAS NOT FOUND BECAUSE GOD TOOK HIM UP; for before he was taken up, he was attested to have been pleasing to God. 6 And without faith it is impossible to please Him, for the one who comes to God must believe that He exists, and that He proves to be One who rewards those who seek Him. 7 By faith Noah, being warned by God about things not yet seen, in reverence prepared an ark for the salvation of his household, by which he condemned the world, and became an heir of the righteousness which is according to faith.

8 By faith Abraham, when he was called, obeyed by going out to a place which he was to receive for an inheritance; and he left, not knowing where he was going. 9 By faith he lived as a stranger in the land of promise, as in a foreign land, living in tents with Isaac and Jacob, fellow heirs of the same promise; 10 for he was looking for the city which has foundations, whose architect and builder is God. 11 By faith even Sarah herself received ability to conceive, even beyond the proper time of life, since she considered Him faithful who had promised. 12 Therefore even from one

man, and one who was as good as dead at that, there were born descendants who were just as the stars of heaven in number, and as the innumerable grains of sand along the seashore.

13 All these died in faith, without receiving the promises, but having seen and welcomed them from a distance, and having confessed that they were strangers and exiles on the earth. 14 For those who say such things make it clear that they are seeking a country of their own. 15 And indeed if they had been thinking of that country which they left, they would have had opportunity to return. 16 But as it is, they desire a better country, that is, a heavenly one. Therefore God is not ashamed to be called their God; for He has prepared a city for them.

17 By faith Abraham, when he was tested, offered up Isaac, and the one who had received the promises was offering up his *only son;* 18 it was he to whom it was said, "THROUGH ISAAC YOUR DESCENDANTS SHALL BE NAMED." 19 He considered that God is able to raise people even from the dead, from which he also received him back as a type. 20 By faith Isaac blessed Jacob and Esau, even regarding things to come. 21 By faith Jacob, as he was dying, blessed each of the sons of Joseph, and worshiped, leaning on the top of his staff. 22 By faith Joseph, when he was dying, made mention of the exodus of the sons of Israel, and gave orders concerning his bones.

23 By faith Moses, when he was born, was hidden for three months by his parents, because they saw he was a beautiful child; and they were not afraid of the king's edict. 24 By faith Moses, when he had grown up, refused to be called the son of Pharaoh's daughter, 25 choosing rather to endure ill-treatment with the people of God than to enjoy the temporary pleasures of sin, 26 considering the reproach of Christ greater riches than the treasures of Egypt; for he was looking to the reward. 27 By faith he left Egypt, not fearing the wrath of the king; for he persevered, as though seeing Him who is unseen. 28 By faith he kept the Passover and the sprinkling of the blood, so that the destroyer of the firstborn would not touch them. 29 By faith they passed through the Red Sea as through dry land; and the Egyptians, when they attempted it, were drowned.

30 By faith the walls of Jericho fell down after the Israelites had marched around them for seven days. 31 By faith the prostitute Rahab did not perish along with those who were disobedient, after she had welcomed the spies in peace.

32 And what more shall I say? For time will fail me if I tell of Gideon, Barak, Samson, Jephthah, of David and Samuel and the prophets, 33 who by faith conquered kingdoms, performed acts of righteousness, obtained promises, shut the mouths of lions, 34 quenched the power of fire, escaped the edge of the sword, from weakness were made strong, became mighty in war, put foreign armies to flight. 35 Women received back their dead by resurrection; and others were tortured, not accepting their release, so that they might obtain a better resurrection; 36 and others

---

11:17 1 I.e., only son with Sarah

experienced mocking and flogging, and further, chains and imprisonment. [37] They were stoned, they were sawn in two, [¹]they were tempted, they were put to death with the sword; they went about in sheepskins, in goatskins, being destitute, afflicted, tormented [38] (*people* of whom the world was not worthy), wandering in deserts, *on* mountains, and *sheltering in* caves and holes in the ground.

[39] And all these, having gained approval through their faith, did not receive what was promised, [40] because God had provided something better for us, so that apart from us they would not be made perfect.

Jesus, the Example

12 Therefore, since we also have such a great cloud of witnesses surrounding us, let's rid ourselves of every obstacle and the sin which so easily entangles us, and let's run with endurance the race that is set before us, [2] looking only at Jesus, the originator and perfecter of the faith, who for the joy set before Him endured the cross, despising the shame, and has sat down at the right hand of the throne of God.

[3] For consider Him who has endured such hostility by sinners against Himself, so that you will not grow weary and lose heart.

A Father's Discipline

[4] You have not yet resisted to the point of shedding blood in your striving against sin; [5] and you have forgotten the exhortation which is addressed to you as sons,

"MY SON, DO NOT REGARD LIGHTLY THE
   DISCIPLINE OF THE LORD,
NOR FAINT WHEN YOU ARE PUNISHED BY HIM;
[6] FOR WHOM THE LORD LOVES HE DISCIPLINES,
AND HE PUNISHES EVERY SON WHOM HE
   ACCEPTS."

[7] It is for discipline that you endure; God deals with you as with sons; for what son is there whom *his* father does not discipline? [8] But if you are without discipline, of which all have become partakers, then you are illegitimate children and not sons. [9] Furthermore, we had earthly fathers to discipline us, and we respected *them;* shall we not much more be subject to the Father of spirits, and live? [10] For they disciplined *us* for a short time as seemed best to them, but He *disciplines us* for *our* good, so that we may share His holiness. [11] For the moment, all discipline seems not to be pleasant, but painful; yet to those who have been trained by it, afterward it yields the peaceful fruit of righteousness.

[12] Therefore, strengthen the hands that are weak and the knees that are feeble, [13] and make straight paths for your feet, so that *the limb* which is impaired may not be dislocated, but rather be healed.

[14] Pursue peace with all people, and the holiness without which no one will see the Lord. [15] See to it that no one comes short of the grace of God; that no root of bitterness springing up causes trouble, and by it many become defiled; [16] that *there be* no sexually immoral or godless person like Esau, who sold his own

birthright for a *single* meal. [17] For you know that even afterward, when he wanted to inherit the blessing, he was rejected, for he found no place for repentance, though he sought for it with tears.

Contrast of Sinai and Zion

[18] For you have not come to *a mountain* that can be touched and to a blazing fire, and to darkness and gloom and whirlwind, [19] and to the blast of a trumpet and the sound of words, which *sound was such that* those who heard begged that no further word be spoken to them. [20] For they could not cope with the command, "If even an animal touches the mountain, it shall be stoned." [21] And so terrible was the sight, *that* Moses said, "I am terrified and trembling." [22] But you have come to Mount Zion and to the city of the living God, the heavenly Jerusalem, and to myriads of angels, [23] to the general assembly and church of the firstborn who are enrolled in heaven, and to God, the Judge of all, and to the spirits of *the* righteous made perfect, [24] and to Jesus, the mediator of a new covenant, and to the sprinkled blood, which speaks better than *the blood* of Abel.

The Unshaken Kingdom

[25] See to it that you do not refuse Him who is speaking. For if those did not escape when they refused him who warned *them* on earth, much less *will* we *escape* who turn away from Him who *warns us* from heaven. [26] And His voice shook the earth then, but now He has promised, saying, "YET ONCE MORE I WILL SHAKE NOT ONLY THE EARTH, BUT ALSO THE HEAVEN." [27] This *expression,* "Yet once more," denotes the removing of those things which can be shaken, as of created things, so that those things which cannot be shaken may remain. [28] Therefore, since we receive a kingdom which cannot be shaken, let's show gratitude, by which we may offer to God an acceptable service with reverence and awe; [29] for our God is a consuming fire.

The Changeless Christ

13 Let love of the brothers *and* sisters continue. [2] Do not neglect hospitality to strangers, for by this some have entertained angels without knowing it. [3] Remember the prisoners, as though in prison with them, *and* those who are badly treated, since you yourselves also are in the body. [4] Marriage *is to be held* in honor among all, and the *marriage* bed *is to be* undefiled; for God will judge the sexually immoral and adulterers. [5] *Make sure that* your character is free from the love of money, being content with what you have; for He Himself has said, "I WILL NEVER DESERT YOU, NOR WILL I EVER ABANDON YOU," [6] so that we confidently say,

"THE LORD IS MY HELPER, I WILL NOT BE
   AFRAID.
WHAT WILL MAN DO TO ME?"

[7] Remember those who led you, who spoke the word of God to you; and considering the result of their way of life, imitate their faith.

11:37 [¹] One early ms does not contain *they were tempted*

8 Jesus Christ *is* the same yesterday and today, and forever. 9 Do not be misled by varied and strange teachings; for it is good for the heart to be strengthened by grace, not by foods, through which those who were so occupied were not benefited. 10 We have an altar from which those who serve the tabernacle have no right to eat. 11 For the bodies of those animals whose blood is brought into the Holy Place by the high priest *as an offering* for sin are burned outside the camp. 12 Therefore Jesus also suffered outside the gate, that He might sanctify the people through His own blood. 13 So then, let us go out to Him outside the camp, bearing His reproach. 14 For here we do not have a lasting city, but we are seeking *the city* which is to come.

God-pleasing Sacrifices

15 Through Him then, let's continually offer up a sacrifice of praise to God, that is, the fruit of lips praising His name. 16 And do not neglect doing good and sharing, for with such sacrifices God is pleased.

17 Obey your leaders and submit *to them*— for they keep watch over your souls as those who will give an account—so that they may do this with joy, not groaning; for this *would be* unhelpful for you.

18 Pray for us, for we are sure that we have a good conscience, desiring to conduct ourselves honorably in all things. 19 And I urge *you* all the more to do this, so that I may be restored to you more quickly.

Benediction

20 Now may the God of peace, who brought up from the dead the great Shepherd of the sheep through the blood of the eternal covenant, *that is,* Jesus our Lord, 21 equip you in every good thing to do His will, working in us that which is pleasing in His sight, through Jesus Christ, to whom *be* the glory forever and ever. Amen.

22 But I urge you, brothers *and sisters,* listen patiently to this word of exhortation, for I have written to you briefly. 23 Know that our brother Timothy has been released, with whom, if he comes soon, I will see you. 24 Greet all of your leaders and all the saints. Those from Italy greet you.

25 Grace be with you all.

The Letter of
JAMES

The Testing of Your Faith

1 James, a bond-servant of God and of the Lord Jesus Christ,
To the twelve tribes who are dispersed abroad: Greetings.

2 Consider it all joy, my brothers *and sisters,* when you encounter various trials, 3 knowing that the testing of your faith produces endurance. 4 And let endurance have *its* perfect result, so that you may be perfect and complete, lacking in nothing.

5 But if any of you lacks wisdom, let him ask of God, who gives to all generously and without reproach, and it will be given to him. 6 But he must ask in faith without any doubting, for the one who doubts is like the surf of the sea, driven and tossed by the wind. 7 For that person ought not to expect that he will receive anything from the Lord, 8 *being* a double-minded man, unstable in all his ways.

9 Now the brother *or sister* of humble *circumstances* is to glory in his high position; 10 but the rich person *is to glory* in his humiliation, because like flowering grass he will pass away. 11 For the sun rises with its scorching heat and withers the grass; and its flower falls off and the beauty of its appearance is destroyed; so also the rich person, in the midst of his pursuits, will die out.

12 Blessed is a man who perseveres under trial; for once he has been approved, he will receive the crown of life which *the Lord* has promised to those who love Him. 13 No one is to say when he is tempted, "I am being tempted by God"; for God cannot be tempted by evil, and He Himself does not tempt anyone. 14 But each one is tempted when he is carried away and enticed by his own lust. 15 Then when lust has conceived, it gives birth to sin; and sin, when it has run its course, brings forth death. 16 Do not be deceived, my beloved brothers *and sisters.* 17 Every good thing given and every perfect gift is from above, coming down from the Father of lights, with whom there is no variation or shifting shadow. 18 In the exercise of His will He gave us birth by the word of truth, so that we would be a kind of first fruits among His creatures.

19 You know *this,* my beloved brothers *and sisters.* Now everyone must be quick to hear, slow to speak, *and* slow to anger; 20 for a man's anger does not bring about the righteousness of God. 21 Therefore, ridding *yourselves* of all filthiness and *all* that remains of wickedness, in humility receive the word implanted, which is able to save your souls. 22 But prove yourselves doers of the word, and not just hearers who deceive themselves. 23 For if anyone is a hearer of the word and not a doer, he is like a man who looks at his natural face in a mirror; 24 for *once* he has looked at himself and gone away, he has immediately forgotten what kind of person he was. 25 But one who has looked intently at the perfect law, the *law* of freedom, and has continued *in it,* not having become a forgetful hearer but an active doer, this person will be blessed in what he does. 26 If anyone thinks himself to be religious, yet does not bridle his tongue but deceives his *own* heart, this person's religion is worthless. 27 Pure and undefiled religion in the sight of *our* God and Father is this: to visit orphans and widows in their distress, *and* to keep oneself unstained by the world.

The Sin of Partiality

2 My brothers *and sisters,* do not hold your faith in our glorious Lord Jesus Christ with *an attitude of* personal favoritism. 2 For if a man comes into your assembly with a gold ring *and is dressed* in bright clothes, and a poor man in dirty clothes also comes in, 3 and you pay special attention to the one who is wearing the bright clothes, and say, "You sit here in a good *place,*" and you say to the poor man, "You stand over there, or sit down by my footstool," 4 have you not made distinctions among yourselves, and become judges with evil motives? 5 Listen, my beloved brothers *and sisters:* did God not choose the poor of this world *to be* rich in faith and heirs of the kingdom which He promised to those who love Him? 6 But you have dishonored the poor man. Is it not the rich who oppress you and personally drag you into court? 7 Do they not blaspheme the good name by which you have been called?

8 If, however, you are fulfilling the royal law according to the Scripture, "You shall love your neighbor as yourself," you are doing well. 9 But if you show partiality, you are committing sin *and* are convicted by the Law as violators. 10 For whoever keeps the whole Law, yet stumbles in one *point,* has become guilty of all. 11 For He who said, "Do not commit adultery," also said, "Do not murder." Now if you do not commit adultery, but do murder, you have become a violator of the Law. 12 So speak, and so act, as those who are to be judged by *the* law of freedom. 13 For judgment *will be* merciless to one who has shown no mercy; mercy triumphs over judgment.

Faith and Works

14 What use is it, my brothers *and sisters,* if someone says he has faith, but he has no works? Can that faith save him? 15 If a brother or sister is without clothing and in need of daily food, 16 and one of you says to them, "Go in peace, be warmed and be filled," yet you do not give them what is necessary for *their* body, what use is that? 17 In the same way, faith also, if it has no works, is dead, *being* by itself.

18 But someone may *well* say, "You have faith and I have works; show me your faith without the works, and I will show you my

faith by my works." **19** You believe that ¹God is one. You do well; the demons also believe, and shudder. **20** But are you willing to acknowledge, you foolish person, that faith without works is useless? **21** Was our father Abraham not justified by works when he offered up his son Isaac on the altar? **22** You see that faith was working with his works, and as a result of the works, faith was perfected; **23** and the Scripture was fulfilled which says, "AND ABRAHAM BELIEVED GOD, AND IT WAS CREDITED TO HIM AS RIGHTEOUSNESS," and he was called a friend of God. **24** You see that a person is justified by works and not by faith alone. **25** In the same way, was Rahab the prostitute not justified by works also when she received the messengers and sent them out by another way? **26** For just as the body without *the* spirit is dead, so also faith without works is dead.

The Tongue Is a Fire

3 Do not become teachers in large numbers, my brothers, since you know that we *who are teachers* will incur a stricter judgment. **2** For we all stumble in many *ways*. If anyone does not stumble in what he says, he is a perfect man, able to rein in the whole body as well. **3** Now if we put the bits into the horses' . mouths so that they will obey us, we direct their whole body as well. **4** Look at the ships too: though they are so large and are driven by strong winds, they are *nevertheless* directed by a very small rudder wherever the inclination of the pilot determines. **5** So also the tongue is a small part *of the body,* and *yet* it boasts of great things.

See how great a forest is set aflame by such a small fire! **6** And the tongue is a fire, the *very* world of unrighteousness; the tongue is set among our body's parts as that which defiles the whole body and sets on fire the course of *our* life, and is set on fire by ²hell. **7** For every species of beasts and birds, of reptiles and creatures of the sea, is tamed and has been tamed by the human race. **8** But no one *among* mankind can tame the tongue; *it is* a restless evil, full of deadly poison. **9** With it we bless *our* Lord and Father, and with it we curse people, who have been made in the likeness of God; **10** from the same mouth come *both* blessing and cursing. My brothers *and sisters,* these things should not be this way. **11** Does a spring send out from the same opening *both* fresh and bitter *water?* **12** Can a fig tree, my brothers *and sisters,* bear olives, or a vine *bear* figs? Nor *can* salt water produce fresh.

Wisdom from Above

13 Who among you is wise and understanding? Let him show by his good behavior his deeds in the gentleness of wisdom. **14** But if you have bitter jealousy and selfish ambition in your heart, do not be arrogant and *so* lie against the truth. **15** This wisdom is not that which comes down from above, but is earthly, natural, demonic. **16** For where jealousy and selfish ambition exist, there is disorder and every evil thing. **17** But the wisdom from above

is first pure, then peace-loving, gentle, reasonable, full of mercy and good fruits, impartial, free of hypocrisy. **18** And the fruit of righteousness is sown in peace by those who make peace.

Things to Avoid

4 What is the source of quarrels and conflicts among you? Is the source not your pleasures that wage war in your body's parts? **2** You lust and do not have, *so* you commit murder. And you are envious and cannot obtain, *so* you fight and quarrel. You do not have because you do not ask. **3** You ask and do not receive, because you ask with the wrong motives, so that you may spend *what you request* on your pleasures. **4** You adulteresses, do you not know that friendship with the world is hostility toward God? Therefore whoever wants to be a friend of the world makes himself an enemy of God. **5** Or do you think that the Scripture says to no purpose, "¹He jealously desires the Spirit whom He has made to dwell in us"? **6** But He gives a greater grace. Therefore *it* says, "GOD IS OPPOSED TO THE PROUD, BUT GIVES GRACE TO THE HUMBLE." **7** Submit therefore to God. But resist the devil, and he will flee from you. **8** Come close to God and He will come close to you. Cleanse *your* hands, you sinners; and purify *your* hearts, you double-minded. **9** Be miserable, and mourn, and weep; let your laughter be turned into mourning, and your joy into gloom. **10** Humble yourselves in the presence of the Lord, and He will exalt you.

11 Do not speak against one another, brothers *and sisters.* The one who speaks against a brother *or sister,* or judges his brother *or sister,* speaks against the law and judges the law; but if you judge the law, you are not a doer of the law but a judge *of it.* **12** There is *only* one Lawgiver and Judge, the One who is able to save and to destroy; but who are you, judging your neighbor?

13 Come now, you who say, "Today or tomorrow we will go to such and such a city, and spend a year there and engage in business and make a profit." **14** Yet you do not know what your life will be like tomorrow. For you are *just* a vapor that appears for a little while, and then vanishes away. **15** Instead, *you ought* to say, "If the Lord wills, we will live and also do this or that." **16** But as it is, you boast in your arrogance; all such boasting is evil. **17** So for one who knows *the* right thing to do and does not do it, for him it is sin.

Misuse of Riches

5 Come now, you rich people, weep and howl for your miseries which are coming upon you. **2** Your riches have rotted and your garments have become moth-eaten. **3** Your gold and your silver have corroded, and their corrosion will serve as a testimony against you and will consume your flesh like fire. It is in the last days that you have stored up your treasure! **4** Behold, the pay of the laborers who mowed your fields, *and* which has been withheld by you, cries out *against you;* and the outcry of

---

2:19 ¹ One early ms *there is one God*   **3:6** ¹ Gr *Gehenna*   **4:5** ¹ Or *The spirit which He has made to dwell in us lusts with envy*

those who did the harvesting has reached the ears of the Lord of armies. [5] You have lived for pleasure on the earth and lived luxuriously; you have fattened your hearts in a day of slaughter. [6] You have condemned and put to death the righteous person; he offers you no resistance.

Exhortation

[7] Therefore be patient, brothers *and sisters,* until the coming of the Lord. The farmer waits for the precious produce of the soil, being patient about it, until it gets the early and late rains. [8] You too be patient; strengthen your hearts, for the coming of the Lord is near. [9] Do not complain, brothers *and sisters,* against one another, so that you may not be judged; behold, the Judge is standing right at the door. [10] As an example, brothers *and sisters,* of suffering and patience, take the prophets who spoke in the name of the Lord. [11] We count those blessed who endured. You have heard of the endurance of Job and have seen the outcome of the Lord's dealings, that the Lord is full of compassion and *is* merciful.

[12] But above all, my brothers *and sisters,* do not swear, either by heaven or by earth or with any other oath; but your yes is to be yes, and your no, no, so that you do not fall under judgment.

[13] Is anyone among you suffering? *Then* he must pray. Is anyone cheerful? He is to sing praises. [14] Is anyone among you sick? *Then* he must call for the elders of the church and they are to pray over him, anointing him with oil in the name of the Lord; [15] and the prayer of faith will [1]restore the one who is sick, and the Lord will raise him up, and if he has committed sins, they will be forgiven him. [16] Therefore, confess your sins to one another, and pray for one another so that you may be healed. A prayer of a righteous person, when it is [1]brought about, can accomplish much. [17] Elijah was a man with a nature like ours, and he prayed earnestly that it would not rain, and it did not rain on the earth for three years and six months. [18] Then he prayed again, and the sky poured rain and the earth produced its fruit.

[19] My brothers *and sisters,* if anyone among you strays from the truth and someone turns him back, [20] let him know that the one who has turned a sinner from the error of his way will save his soul from death and cover a multitude of sins.

5:15 [1] Lit *save*   5:16 [1] I.e., granted by God

The First Letter of
PETER

A Living Hope and a Sure Salvation

1 Peter, an apostle of Jesus Christ,
To those who reside as strangers, scattered throughout Pontus, Galatia, Cappadocia, Asia, and Bithynia, who are chosen 2 according to the foreknowledge of God the Father, by the sanctifying work of the Spirit, to obey Jesus Christ and be sprinkled with His blood: May grace and peace be multiplied to you.

3 Blessed be the God and Father of our Lord Jesus Christ, who according to His great mercy has caused us to be born again to a living hope through the resurrection of Jesus Christ from the dead, 4 to *obtain* an inheritance *which is* imperishable, undefiled, and will not fade away, reserved in heaven for you, 5 who are protected by the power of God through faith for a salvation ready to be revealed in *the* last time. 6 In this you greatly rejoice, even though now for a little while, if necessary, you have been distressed by various trials, 7 so that the proof of your faith, *being* more precious than gold which perishes though tested by fire, may be found to result in praise, glory, and honor at the revelation of Jesus Christ; 8 and though you have not seen Him, you love Him, and though you do not see Him now, but believe in Him, you greatly rejoice with joy inexpressible and full of glory, 9 obtaining as the outcome of your faith, the salvation of [1] your souls.

10 As to this salvation, the prophets who prophesied of the grace that *would come* to you made careful searches and inquiries, 11 seeking to know what person or time the Spirit of Christ within them was indicating as He predicted the sufferings of Christ and the glories to follow. 12 It was revealed to them that they were not serving themselves, but you, in these things which now have been announced to you through those who preached the gospel to you by the Holy Spirit sent from heaven— things into which angels long to look.

13 Therefore, prepare your minds for action, keep sober *in spirit,* set your hope completely on the grace to be brought to you at the revelation of Jesus Christ. 14 As obedient children, do not be conformed to the former lusts *which were yours* in your ignorance, 15 but like the Holy One who called you, be holy yourselves also in all *your* behavior; 16 because it is written: "YOU SHALL BE HOLY, FOR I AM HOLY."

17 If you address as Father the One who impartially judges according to each one's work, conduct yourselves in fear during the time of your stay *on earth;* 18 knowing that you were not redeemed with perishable things like silver or gold from your futile way of life inherited from your forefathers, 19 but with precious blood, as of a lamb unblemished and spotless, *the blood* of Christ. 20 For He was foreknown before the foundation of the world, but has appeared in these last times for the

sake of you 21 who through Him are believers in God, who raised Him from the dead and gave Him glory, so that your faith and hope are in God.

22 Since you have purified your souls in obedience to the truth for a sincere love of the brothers *and* sisters, fervently love one another from [1] the heart, 23 for you have been born again not of seed which is perishable, but imperishable, *that is,* through the living and enduring word of God. 24 For,

"ALL FLESH IS LIKE GRASS,
AND ALL ITS GLORY IS LIKE THE FLOWER OF GRASS.
THE GRASS WITHERS,
AND THE FLOWER FALLS OFF,
25 BUT THE WORD OF THE LORD ENDURES FOREVER."

And this is the word which was preached to you.

As Newborn Babes

2 Therefore, rid *yourselves* of all malice and all deceit and hypocrisy and envy and all slander, 2 and like newborn babies, long for the pure milk of the word, so that by it you may grow in respect to salvation, 3 if you have tasted the kindness of the Lord.

As Living Stones

4 And coming to Him as to a living stone which has been rejected by people, but is choice and precious in the sight of God, 5 you also, as living stones, are being built up as a spiritual house for a holy priesthood, to offer spiritual sacrifices that are acceptable to God through Jesus Christ. 6 For *this* is contained in Scripture:

"BEHOLD, I AM LAYING IN ZION A CHOICE STONE, A PRECIOUS CORNERSTONE,
AND THE ONE WHO BELIEVES IN HIM WILL NOT BE PUT TO SHAME."

7 This precious value, then, is for you who believe; but for unbelievers,

"A STONE WHICH THE BUILDERS REJECTED,
THIS BECAME THE CHIEF CORNERSTONE,"
8 and,
"A STONE OF STUMBLING AND A ROCK OF OFFENSE";

for they stumble because they are disobedient to the word, and to this they were also appointed.

9 But you are A CHOSEN PEOPLE, A royal PRIESTHOOD, A HOLY NATION, A PEOPLE FOR GOD'S OWN POSSESSION, so that you may proclaim the excellencies of Him who has called you out of darkness into His marvelous light; 10 for you once were NOT A PEOPLE, but now you are THE PEOPLE OF GOD; you had NOT RECEIVED MERCY, but now you have RECEIVED MERCY.

11 Beloved, I urge *you* as foreigners and strangers to abstain from fleshly lusts, which

wage war against the soul. 12 Keep your behavior excellent among the Gentiles, so that in the thing in which they slander you as evildoers, they may because of your good deeds, as they observe *them,* glorify God on the day of 1visitation.

Honor Authority

13 Submit yourselves for the Lord's sake to every human institution, whether to a king as the one in authority, 14 or to governors as sent by him for the punishment of evildoers and the praise of those who do right. 15 For such is the will of God, that by doing right you silence the ignorance of foolish people. 16 *Act* as free people, and do not use your freedom as a covering for evil, but *use it* as bond-servants of God. 17 Honor all people, love the brotherhood, fear God, honor the king.

18 Servants, be subject to your masters with all respect, not only to those who are good and gentle, but also to those who are harsh. 19 For this *finds* favor, if for the sake of conscience toward God a person endures grief when suffering unjustly. 20 For what credit is there if, when you sin and are harshly treated, you endure it with patience? But if when you do what is right and suffer *for it* you patiently endure it, this *finds* favor with God.

Christ Is Our Example

21 For you have been called for this purpose, because Christ also suffered for you, leaving you an example, so that you would follow in His steps, 22 *HE* WHO COMMITTED NO SIN, NOR WAS ANY DECEIT found IN HIS MOUTH; 23 and while being abusively insulted, He did not insult in return; while suffering, He did not threaten, but kept entrusting *Himself* to Him who judges righteously; 24 and He Himself brought our sins in His body up on the 1cross, so that we might die to sin and live for righteousness; by His wounds you were healed. 25 For you were continually straying like sheep, but now you have returned to the Shepherd and Guardian of your souls.

Godly Living

3 In the same way, you wives, be subject to your own husbands so that even if any *of them* are disobedient to the word, they may be won over without a word by the behavior of their wives, 2 as they observe your pure and respectful behavior. 3 Your adornment must not be *merely* the external—braiding the hair, wearing gold *jewelry,* or putting on apparel; 4 but *it should be* the hidden person of the heart, with the imperishable *quality* of a gentle and quiet spirit, which is precious in the sight of God. 5 For in this way the holy women of former times, who hoped in God, also used to adorn themselves, being subject to their own husbands, 6 just as Sarah obeyed Abraham, calling him lord; and you have proved to be her children if you do what is right without being frightened by any fear.

7 You husbands in the same way, live with *your wives* in an understanding way, as with

someone weaker, *since she is* a woman; and show her honor as a fellow heir of the grace of life, so that your prayers will not be hindered.

8 To sum up, all *of you* be harmonious, sympathetic, 1loving, compassionate, *and* humble; 9 not returning evil for evil or insult for insult, but giving a blessing instead; for you were called for the very purpose that you would inherit a blessing. 10 For,

"THE ONE WHO DESIRES LIFE, TO LOVE AND SEE GOOD DAYS,
MUST KEEP HIS TONGUE FROM EVIL AND HIS LIPS FROM SPEAKING DECEIT.
11 "HE MUST TURN AWAY FROM EVIL AND DO GOOD;
HE MUST SEEK PEACE AND PURSUE IT.
12 "FOR THE EYES OF THE LORD ARE TOWARD THE RIGHTEOUS,
AND HIS EARS ATTEND TO THEIR PRAYER,
BUT THE FACE OF THE LORD IS AGAINST EVILDOERS."

13 And who is there to harm you if you prove zealous for what is good? 14 But even if you should suffer for the sake of righteousness, you are blessed. AND DO NOT FEAR THEIR INTIMIDATION, AND DO NOT BE IN DREAD, 15 but 1sanctify Christ as Lord in your hearts, always *being* ready to make a defense to everyone who asks you to give an account for the hope that is in you, but with gentleness and respect; 16 and keep a good conscience so that in the thing in which you are slandered, those who disparage your good behavior in Christ will be put to shame. 17 For it is better, if God should will it *so,* that you suffer for doing what is right rather than for doing what is wrong. 18 For Christ also suffered for sins once for all *time, the* just for *the* unjust, so that He might bring us to God, having been put to death in the flesh, but made alive in the spirit; 19 in which He also went and made proclamation to the spirits in prison, 20 who once were disobedient when the patience of God kept waiting in the days of Noah, during the construction of the ark, in which a few, that is, eight persons, were brought safely through *the* water. 21 Corresponding to that, baptism now saves you—not the removal of dirt from the flesh, but an appeal to God for a good conscience— through the resurrection of Jesus Christ, 22 who is at the right hand of God, having gone into heaven, after angels and authorities and powers had been subjected to Him.

Keep Fervent in Your Love

4 Therefore, since Christ has 1suffered in the flesh, arm yourselves also with the same purpose, because the one who has suffered in the flesh has ceased from sin, 2 so as to live the rest of the time in the flesh no longer for human lusts, but for the will of God. 3 For the time already past is sufficient *for you* to have carried out the desire of the Gentiles, having pursued a course of indecent behavior, lusts, drunkenness, carousing, drinking parties, and wanton idolatries. 4 In *all* this, they are surprised that you do not run with *them* in the same excesses of debauchery, and they slander

---

2:12 1 I.e., Christ's coming again in judgment   2:24 1 Lit *wood;* see Deut 21:23   3:8 1 I.e., as brothers and sisters   3:15 1 I.e., set apart   4:1 1 I.e., suffered death

you; [5] but they will give an account to Him who is ready to judge the living and the dead. [6] For the gospel has for this purpose been preached even to those who are dead, that though they are judged in the flesh as people, they may live in the spirit according to *the will of* God.

[7] The end of all things is near; therefore, be of sound judgment and sober *spirit* for the purpose of prayer. [8] Above all, keep fervent in your love for one another, because love covers a multitude of sins. [9] Be hospitable to one another without complaint. [10] As each one has received a *special* gift, employ it in serving one another as good stewards of the multifaceted grace of God. [11] Whoever speaks *is to do so* as *one who is speaking* actual words of God; whoever serves *is to do so* as *one who is serving* by the strength which God supplies; so that in all things God may be glorified through Jesus Christ, to whom belongs the glory and dominion forever and ever. Amen.

Share the Sufferings of Christ

[12] Beloved, do not be surprised at the fiery ordeal among you, which comes upon you for your testing, as though *something* strange were happening to you; [13] but to the degree that you share the sufferings of Christ, keep on rejoicing, so that at the revelation of His glory you may also rejoice and be overjoyed. [14] If you are insulted for the name of Christ, you are blessed, because the Spirit of glory, and of God, rests upon you. [15] Make sure that none of you suffers as a murderer, or thief, or evildoer, or a troublesome meddler; [16] but if *anyone suffers* as a Christian, he is not to be ashamed, but is to glorify God in this name. [17] For *it is* time for judgment to begin with the household of God; and if *it begins* with us first, what *will be* the outcome for those who do not obey the gospel of God? [18] AND IF IT IS WITH DIFFICULTY THAT THE RIGHTEOUS IS SAVED, WHAT WILL BECOME OF THE GODLESS MAN AND THE SINNER? [19] Therefore, those also who suffer according to the will of God are to entrust their souls to a faithful Creator in doing what is right.

Serve God Willingly

5 Therefore, I urge elders among you, as *your* fellow elder and a witness of the sufferings of Christ, *and* one who is also a fellow partaker of the glory that is to be revealed: [2] shepherd the flock of God among you, exercising oversight, not under compulsion but voluntarily, according to *the will of* God; and not with greed but with eagerness; [3] nor yet as domineering over those assigned to your care, but by proving to be examples to the flock. [4] And when the Chief Shepherd appears, you will receive the unfading crown of glory. [5] You [1]younger men, likewise, be subject to *your* elders; and all of you, clothe yourselves with humility toward one another, because GOD IS OPPOSED TO THE PROUD, BUT HE GIVES GRACE TO THE HUMBLE.

[6] Therefore humble yourselves under the mighty hand of God, so that He may exalt you at the proper time, [7] having cast all your anxiety on Him, because He cares about you. [8] Be of sober *spirit,* be on the alert. Your adversary, the devil, prowls around like a roaring lion, seeking someone to devour. [9] So resist him, firm in *your* faith, knowing that the same experiences of suffering are being accomplished by your [1]brothers and sisters who are in the world. [10] After you have suffered for a little while, the God of all grace, who called you to His eternal glory in Christ, will Himself perfect, confirm, strengthen, *and* establish *you.* [11] To Him *be* dominion forever and ever. Amen.

[12] Through Silvanus, our faithful brother (for so I regard *him*), I have written to you briefly, [1]exhorting and testifying that this is the true grace of God. Stand firm in it! [13] She who is in Babylon, chosen together with *you,* sends you greetings, and *so does* my son, Mark. [14] Greet one another with a kiss of love.

Peace be to you all who are in Christ.

5:5 [1] Or *young people*   5:9 [1] Lit *fellowship*   5:12 [1] Or *encouraging*

The Second Letter of
PETER

Growth in Christian Virtue

1 Simon Peter, a bond-servant and apostle of Jesus Christ,

To those who have received a faith of the same kind as ours, by the righteousness of our God and Savior, Jesus Christ: 2 Grace and peace be multiplied to you in the knowledge of God and of Jesus our Lord, 3 for His divine power has granted to us everything pertaining to life and godliness, through the true knowledge of Him who called us by His own glory and excellence. 4 Through these He has granted to us His precious and magnificent promises, so that by them you may become partakers of *the* divine nature, having escaped the corruption that is in the world on account of lust. 5 Now for this very reason also, applying all diligence, in your faith supply moral *1*excellence, and in *your* moral excellence, knowledge, 6 and in *your* knowledge, self-control, and in *your* self-control, perseverance, and in *your* perseverance, godliness, 7 and in *your* godliness, brotherly kindness, and in *your* brotherly kindness, love. 8 For if these *qualities* are yours and are increasing, they do not make you useless nor unproductive in the true knowledge of our Lord Jesus Christ. 9 For the one who lacks these *qualities* is blind *or* short-sighted, having forgotten *his* purification from his former sins. 10 Therefore, brothers *and sisters,* be all the more diligent to make certain about His calling and choice of you; for as long as you practice these things, you will never stumble; 11 for in this way the entrance into the eternal kingdom of our Lord and Savior Jesus Christ will be abundantly supplied to you.

12 Therefore, I will always be ready to remind you of these things, even though you *already* know *them* and have been established in the truth which is present with *you.* 13 I consider it right, as long as I am in this *earthly* *1*dwelling, to stir you up by way of reminder, 14 knowing that the laying aside of my *earthly* dwelling is imminent, as also our Lord Jesus Christ has made clear to me. 15 And I will also be diligent that at any time after my departure you will be able to call these things to mind.

Eyewitnesses

16 For we did not follow cleverly devised tales when we made known to you the power and coming of our Lord Jesus Christ, but we were eyewitnesses of His majesty. 17 For when He received honor and glory from God the Father, such a declaration as this was made to Him by the Majestic Glory: "This is My beloved Son with whom I am well pleased"— 18 and we ourselves heard this declaration made from heaven when we were with Him on the holy mountain.

19 And *so* we have the prophetic word *made* more sure, to which you do well to pay attention as to a lamp shining in a dark place, until the day dawns and the morning star arises in your hearts. 20 *But* know this first *of all,* that no prophecy of Scripture becomes *a matter* of *someone's* own interpretation, 21 for no prophecy was ever made by an act of human will, but men moved by the Holy Spirit spoke from God.

The Appearance of False Prophets

2 But false prophets also appeared among the people, just as there will also be false teachers among you, who will secretly introduce destructive heresies, even denying the Master who bought them, bringing swift destruction upon themselves. 2 Many will follow their indecent behavior, and because of them the way of the truth will be maligned; 3 and in *their* greed they will exploit you with false words; their judgment from long ago is not idle, and their destruction is not asleep.

4 For if God did not spare angels when they sinned, but cast them into *1*hell and committed them to *2*pits of darkness, held for judgment; 5 and did not spare the ancient world, but protected Noah, a preacher of righteousness, with seven others, when He brought a flood upon the world of the ungodly; 6 and *if* He condemned the cities of Sodom and Gomorrah to destruction by reducing *them* to ashes, having made *them* an example of what is coming for the ungodly; 7 and *if* He rescued righteous Lot, *who was* oppressed by the perverted conduct of unscrupulous people 8 (for by what he saw and heard *that* righteous man, while living among them, felt *his* righteous soul tormented day after day by *their* lawless deeds), 9 *then* the Lord knows how to rescue the godly from a trial, and to keep the unrighteous under punishment for the day of judgment, 10 and especially those who indulge the flesh in *its* corrupt passion, and despise authority.

Reckless, self-centered, they speak abusively of *angelic* majesties without trembling, 11 whereas angels who are greater in might and power do not bring a demeaning judgment against them before the Lord. 12 But these, like unreasoning animals, born as creatures of instinct to be captured and killed, using abusive speech where they have no knowledge, will in the destruction of those creatures also be destroyed, 13 suffering wrong as the wages of doing wrong. They count it a pleasure to revel in the daytime. They are stains and blemishes, reveling in their *1*deceptions as they feast with you, 14 having eyes full of adultery that never cease from sin, enticing unstable souls, having hearts trained in greed, accursed children; 15 abandoning the right way, they have gone

---

1:5 1 Or *virtue*   1:13 1 I.e., human body   2:4 1 Gr *Tartarus,* a name used as a reference to the netherworld (hell)   2 One early ms *chains of darkness*   2:13 1 One early ms *love feasts*

astray, having followed the way of Balaam, the son of Beor, who loved the reward of unrighteousness; 16 but he received a rebuke for his own offense, *for* a mute donkey, speaking with a human voice, restrained the insanity of the prophet. 17 These are springs without water and mists driven by a storm, for whom the black darkness has been reserved. 18 For, while speaking out arrogant *words* of no value they entice by fleshly desires, by indecent behavior, those who barely escape from the ones who live in error, 19 promising them freedom while they themselves are slaves of corruption; for by what anyone is overcome, by this he is enslaved. 20 For if, after they have escaped the defilements of the world by the knowledge of the Lord and Savior Jesus Christ, they are again entangled in them and are overcome, the last state has become worse for them than the first. 21 For it would be better for them not to have known the way of righteousness, than having known it, to turn away from the holy commandment handed on to them. 22 It has happened to them according to the true proverb, "A DOG RETURNS TO ITS OWN VOMIT," and, "A sow, after washing, *returns* to wallowing in the mire."

Purpose of This Letter

3 Beloved, this is now the second letter I am writing to you in which I am stirring up your sincere mind by way of a reminder, 2 to remember the words spoken beforehand by the holy prophets and the commandment of the Lord and Savior *spoken* by your apostles.

The Coming Day of the Lord

3 Know this first *of all,* that in the last days mockers will come with *their* mocking, following after their own lusts, 4 and saying, "Where is the promise of His coming? For *ever* since the fathers 1 fell asleep, all things continue just as *they were* from the beginning of creation." 5 For when they maintain this, it escapes their notice that by the word of God *the* heavens existed long ago and *the* earth was

formed out of water and by water, 6 through which the world at that time was destroyed by being flooded with water. 7 But by His word the present heavens and earth are being reserved for fire, kept for the day of judgment and destruction of ungodly people.

8 But do not let this one *fact* escape your notice, beloved, that with the Lord one day is like a thousand years, and a thousand years like one day. 9 The Lord is not slow about His promise, as some count slowness, but is patient toward you, not willing for any to perish, but for all to come to repentance.

A New Heaven and Earth

10 But the day of the Lord will come like a thief, in which the heavens will pass away with a roar and the elements will be destroyed with intense heat, and the earth and its works will be 1 discovered. 11 Since all these things are to be destroyed in this way, what sort of people ought you to be in holy conduct and godliness, 12 looking for and hastening the coming of the day of God, because of which the heavens will be destroyed by burning, and the elements will melt with intense heat! 13 But according to His promise we are looking for new heavens and a new earth, in which righteousness dwells.

14 Therefore, beloved, since you look for these things, be diligent to be found spotless and blameless by Him, at peace, 15 and regard the patience of our Lord *as* salvation; just as also our beloved brother Paul, according to the wisdom given him, wrote to you, 16 as also in all *his* letters, speaking in them of these things, in which there are some things that are hard to understand, which the untaught and unstable distort, as *they do* also the rest of the Scriptures, to their own destruction. 17 You therefore, beloved, knowing this beforehand, be on your guard so that you are not carried away by the error of unscrupulous people and lose your own firm commitment, 18 but grow in the grace and knowledge of our Lord and Savior Jesus Christ. To Him *be* the glory, both now and to the day of eternity. Amen.

3:4 1 I.e., died   3:10 1 I.e., as worthless; late mss *burned up*

The First Letter of
JOHN

The Incarnate Word

1 What was from the beginning, what we have heard, what we have seen with our eyes, what we have looked at and touched with our hands, concerning the Word of Life—²and the life was revealed, and we have seen and testify and proclaim to you the eternal life, which was with the Father and was revealed to us—³what we have seen and heard we proclaim to you also, so that you too may have fellowship with us; and indeed our fellowship is with the Father, and with His Son Jesus Christ. ⁴These things we write, so that our joy may be made complete.

God Is Light

⁵This is the message we have heard from Him and announce to you, that God is Light, and in Him there is no darkness at all. ⁶If we say that we have fellowship with Him and yet walk in the darkness, we lie and do not practice the truth; ⁷but if we walk in the Light as He Himself is in the Light, we have fellowship with one another, and the blood of Jesus His Son cleanses us from all sin. ⁸If we say that we have no sin, we are deceiving ourselves and the truth is not in us. ⁹If we confess our sins, He is faithful and righteous, so that He will forgive us our sins and cleanse us from all unrighteousness. ¹⁰If we say that we have not sinned, we make Him a liar and His word is not in us.

Christ Is Our Advocate

2 My little children, I am writing these things to you so that you may not sin. And if anyone sins, we have an ¹Advocate with the Father, Jesus Christ the righteous; ²and He Himself is the ¹propitiation for our sins; and not for ours only, but also for the sins of the whole world. ³By this we know that we have come to know Him, if we keep His commandments. ⁴The one who says, "I have come to know Him," and does not keep His commandments, is a liar, and the truth is not in him; ⁵but whoever follows His word, in him the love of God has truly been perfected. By this we know that we are in Him: ⁶the one who says that he remains in Him ought, himself also, walk just as He walked.

⁷Beloved, I am not writing a new commandment to you, but an old commandment which you have had from the beginning; the old commandment is the word which you have heard. ⁸On the other hand, I am writing a new commandment to you, which is true in Him and in you, because the darkness is passing away and the true Light is already shining. ⁹The one who says that he is in the Light and yet hates his brother or sister is in the darkness until now. ¹⁰The one who loves his brother and sister remains in the Light, and there is nothing in him to cause stumbling. ¹¹But the one who hates his brother or sister is in the darkness and walks in the darkness, and does not know where he is going because the darkness has blinded his eyes.

¹²I am writing to you, little children, because your sins have been forgiven you on account of His name. ¹³I am writing to you, fathers, because you know Him who has been from the beginning. I am writing to you, young men, because you have overcome the evil one. I have written to you, children, because you know the Father. ¹⁴I have written to you, fathers, because you know Him who has been from the beginning. I have written to you, young men, because you are strong, and the word of God remains in you, and you have overcome the evil one.

Do Not Love the World

¹⁵Do not love the world nor the things in the world. If anyone loves the world, the love of the Father is not in him. ¹⁶For all that is in the world, the lust of the flesh and the lust of the eyes and the boastful pride of life, is not from the Father, but is from the world. ¹⁷The world is passing away and also its lusts; but the one who does the will of God continues to live forever.

¹⁸Children, it is the last hour; and just as you heard that antichrist is coming, even now many antichrists have appeared; from this we know that it is the last hour. ¹⁹They went out from us, but they were not really of us; for if they had been of us, they would have remained with us; but they went out, so that it would be evident that they all are not of us. ²⁰But you have an anointing from the Holy One, and you all know. ²¹I have not written to you because you do not know the truth, but because you do know it, and because no lie is of the truth. ²²Who is the liar except the one who denies that Jesus is the Christ? This is the antichrist, the one who denies the Father and the Son. ²³Whoever denies the Son does not have the Father; the one who confesses the Son has the Father also. ²⁴As for you, see that what you heard from the beginning remains in you. If what you heard from the beginning remains in you, you also will remain in the Son and in the Father.

The Promise Is Eternal Life

²⁵This is the promise which He Himself made to us: eternal life.

²⁶These things I have written to you concerning those who are trying to deceive you. ²⁷And as for you, the anointing which you received from Him remains in you, and you have no need for anyone to teach you; but as His anointing teaches you about all things, and

---

2:1 ¹Or *Intercessor* **2:2** ¹I.e., means of reconciliation with God by atoning for sins; or *sin-offering*

is true and is not a lie, and just as it has taught you, you remain in Him. 28 Now, little children, remain in Him, so that when He appears, we may have confidence and not draw back from Him in shame at His coming. 29 If you know that He is righteous, you know that everyone who practices righteousness also has been born of Him.

Children of God Love One Another

3 See how great a love the Father has given us, that we would be called children of God; and *in fact* we are. For this reason the world does not know us: because it did not know Him. 2 Beloved, now we are children of God, and it has not appeared as yet what we will be. We know that when He appears, we will be like Him, because we will see Him just as He is. 3 And everyone who has this hope *set* on Him purifies himself, just as He is pure.

4 Everyone who practices sin also practices lawlessness; and sin is lawlessness. 5 You know that He appeared in order to take away sins; and in Him there is no sin. 6 No one who remains in Him sins *continually;* no one who sins *continually* has seen Him or knows Him. 7 Little children, make sure no one deceives you; the one who practices righteousness is righteous, just as He is righteous; 8 the one who practices sin is of the devil; for the devil has been sinning from the beginning. The Son of God appeared for this purpose, to destroy the works of the devil. 9 No one who has been born of God practices sin, because His seed remains in him; and he cannot sin *continually,* because he has been born of God. 10 By this the children of God and the children of the devil are obvious: anyone who does not practice righteousness is not of God, nor the one who does not love his brother *and sister.*

11 For this is the message which you have heard from the beginning, that we are to love one another; 12 not as Cain, *who* was of the evil one and murdered his brother. And for what reason did he murder him? Because his *own* deeds were evil, but his brother's were righteous.

13 Do not be surprised, brothers *and sisters,* if the world hates you. 14 We know that we have passed out of death into life, because we love the brothers *and sisters.* The one who does not love remains in death. 15 Everyone who hates his brother *or sister* is a murderer, and you know that no murderer has eternal life remaining in him. 16 We know love by this, that He laid down His life for us; and we ought to lay down our lives for the brothers *and sisters.* 17 But whoever has worldly goods and sees his brother *or sister* in need, and closes his heart against him, how does the love of God remain in him? 18 Little children, let's not love with word or with tongue, but in deed and truth.

19 We will know by this that we are of the truth, and will set our heart at ease before Him, 20 that if our heart condemns us, that God is greater than our heart, and He knows all things. 21 Beloved, if our heart does not condemn us, we have confidence before God; 22 and whatever we ask, we receive from Him,

because we keep His commandments and do the things that are pleasing in His sight. 23 This is His commandment, that we believe in the name of His Son Jesus Christ, and love one another, just as He commanded us. 24 The one who keeps His commandments remains in Him, and He in him. We know by this that He remains in us, by the Spirit whom He has given us.

Testing the Spirits

4 Beloved, do not believe every spirit, but test the spirits to see whether they are from God, because many false prophets have gone out into the world. 2 By this you know the Spirit of God: every spirit that confesses that Jesus Christ has come in the flesh is from God; 3 and every spirit that does not confess Jesus is not from God; this is the *spirit* of the antichrist, which you have heard is coming, and now it is already in the world. 4 You are from God, little children, and have overcome them; because greater is He who is in you than he who is in the world. 5 They are from the world, therefore they speak *as* from the world, and the world listens to them. 6 We are from God. The one who knows God listens to us; the one who is not from God does not listen to us. By this we know the spirit of truth and the spirit of error.

God Is Love

7 Beloved, let's love one another; for love is from God, and everyone who loves has been born of God and knows God. 8 The one who does not love does not know God, because God is love. 9 By this the love of God was revealed in us, that God has sent His only Son into the world so that we may live through Him. 10 In this is love, not that we loved God, but that He loved us and sent His Son *to be* the [1]propitiation for our sins. 11 Beloved, if God so loved us, we also ought to love one another. 12 No one has ever seen God; if we love one another, God remains in us, and His love is perfected in us. 13 By this we know that we remain in Him and He in us, because He has given to us of His Spirit. 14 We have seen and testify that the Father has sent the Son *to be* the Savior of the world.

15 Whoever confesses that Jesus is the Son of God, God remains in him, and he in God. 16 We have come to know and have believed the love which God has for us. God is love, and the one who remains in love remains in God, and God remains in him. 17 By this, love is perfected with us, so that we may have confidence in the day of judgment; because as He is, we also are in this world. 18 There is no fear in love, but perfect love drives out fear, because fear involves punishment, and the one who fears is not perfected in love. 19 We love, because He first loved us. 20 If someone says, "I love God," and *yet* he hates his brother *or sister,* he is a liar; for the one who does not love his brother *and sister* whom he has seen, cannot love God, whom he has not seen. 21 And this commandment we have from Him, that the one who loves God must also love his brother *and sister.*

Overcoming the World

5 Everyone who believes that Jesus is the Christ has been born of God, and everyone who loves the Father loves the *child* born of Him. [2] By this we know that we love the children of God, when we love God and follow His commandments. [3] For this is the love of God, that we keep His commandments; and His commandments are not burdensome. [4] For whoever has been born of God overcomes the world; and this is the victory that has overcome the world: our faith.

[5] Who is the one who overcomes the world, but the one who believes that Jesus is the Son of God? [6] This is the One who came by water and blood, Jesus Christ; not with the water only, but with the water and with the blood. It is the Spirit who testifies, because the Spirit is the truth. [7] For there are three that testify: [8] the Spirit and the water and the blood; and the three are [1] in agreement. [9] If we receive the testimony of people, the testimony of God is greater; for the testimony of God is this, that He has testified concerning His Son. [10] The one who believes in the Son of God has the testimony in himself; the one who does not believe God has made Him a liar, because he has not believed in the testimony that God has given concerning His Son. [11] And the testimony is this, that God has given us eternal life, and this life is in His Son. [12] The one who has the Son has the life; the one who does not have the Son of God does not have the life.

This Is Written That You May Know

[13] These things I have written to you who believe in the name of the Son of God, so that you may know that you have eternal life. [14] This is the confidence which we have before Him, that, if we ask anything according to His will, He hears us. [15] And if we know that He hears us *in* whatever we ask, we know that we have the requests which we have asked from Him.

[16] If anyone sees his brother *or sister* committing a sin not *leading* to death, he shall ask and *God* will, for him, give life to those who commit sin not *leading* to death. There is sin *leading* to death; I am not saying that he should ask about that. [17] All unrighteousness is sin, and there is sin not *leading* to death.

[18] We know that no one who has been born of God sins; but He who was born of God keeps him, and the evil one does not touch him. [19] We know that we are of God, and that the whole world lies in *the power of* the evil one. [20] And we know that the Son of God has come, and has given us understanding so that we may know Him who is true; and we are in Him who is true, in His Son Jesus Christ. This is the true God and eternal life.

[21] Little children, guard yourselves from idols.

5:8 [1] Lit *for the one thing*

The Second Letter of
JOHN

Walk According to His Commandments

1 The elder to the chosen lady and her children, whom I love in truth; and not only I, but also all who know the truth, 2 because of the truth which remains in us and will be with us forever: 3 Grace, mercy, *and* peace will be with us, from God the Father and from Jesus Christ, the Son of the Father, in truth and love.

4 I was overjoyed to find *some* of your children walking in truth, just as we have received a commandment *to do* from the Father. 5 Now I ask you, lady, not as though *I were* writing to you a new commandment, but the one which we have had from the beginning, that we love one another. 6 And this is love, that we walk according to His commandments. This is the commandment, just as you have heard from the beginning, that you are to walk in it.

7 For many deceivers have gone out into the world, those who do not acknowledge Jesus Christ *as* coming in the flesh. This is the deceiver and the antichrist. 8 Watch yourselves, that you do not lose what we have accomplished, but *that* you may receive a full reward. 9 Anyone who goes too far and does not remain in the teaching of Christ, does not have God; the one who remains in the teaching has both the Father and the Son. 10 If anyone comes to you and does not bring this teaching, do not receive him into *your* house, and do not give him a greeting; 11 for the one who gives him a greeting participates in his evil deeds.

12 Though I have many things to write to you, I do not want to *do so* with paper and ink; but I hope to come to you and speak face to face, so that your joy may be made complete.

13 The children of your chosen sister greet you.

The Third Letter of
JOHN

A Good Report

1 The elder to the beloved Gaius, whom I love in truth. ²Beloved, I pray that in all respects you may prosper and be in good health, just as your soul prospers. ³For I was overjoyed when brothers came and testified to your truth, *that is,* how you are walking in truth. ⁴I have no greater joy than this, to hear of my children walking in the truth.

⁵Beloved, you are acting faithfully in whatever you accomplish for the brothers *and sisters,* and especially *when they are* strangers; ⁶and they have testified to your love before the church. You will do well to send them on their way in a manner worthy of God. ⁷For they went out for the sake of the Name, accepting nothing from the Gentiles. ⁸Therefore we ought to support such people, so that we may prove to be fellow workers with the truth.

⁹I wrote something to the church; but Diotrephes, who loves to be first among them, does not accept what we say. ¹⁰For this reason, if I come, I will call attention to his deeds which he does, unjustly accusing us with malicious words; and not satisfied with this, he himself does not receive the brothers either, and he forbids those who want *to do so* and puts *them* out of the church.

¹¹Beloved, do not imitate what is evil, but what is good. The one who does what is good is of God; the one who does what is evil has not seen God. ¹²Demetrius has received a *good* testimony from everyone, and from the truth itself; and we testify too, and you know that our testimony is true.

¹³I had many things to write to you, but I do not want to write to you with pen and ink; ¹⁴but I hope to see you shortly, and we will speak face to face.

¹⁵Peace *be* to you. The friends greet you. Greet the friends by name.

The Letter of
JUDE

The Warnings of History to the Ungodly

1 Jude, a bond-servant of Jesus Christ and brother of James,

To those who are the called, beloved in God the Father, and kept for Jesus Christ: 2 May mercy, peace, and love be multiplied to you.

3 Beloved, while I was making every effort to write you about our common salvation, I felt the necessity to write to you appealing that you contend earnestly for the faith that was once for all *time* handed down to the saints. 4 For certain people have crept in unnoticed, those who were long beforehand marked out for this condemnation, ungodly persons who turn the grace of our God into indecent behavior and deny our only Master and Lord, Jesus Christ.

5 Now I want to remind you, though you know everything once *and* for all, that 'the Lord, after saving a people out of the land of Egypt, subsequently destroyed those who did not believe. 6 And angels who did not keep their own domain but abandoned their proper dwelling place, *these* He has kept in eternal restraints under darkness for the judgment of the great day, 7 just as Sodom and Gomorrah and the cities around them, since they in the same way as these *angels* indulged in sexual perversion and went after strange flesh, are exhibited as an example in undergoing the punishment of eternal fire.

8 Yet in the same way these people also, dreaming, defile the flesh, reject authority, and speak abusively of *angelic* majesties. 9 But Michael the archangel, when he disputed with the devil and argued about the body of Moses, did not dare pronounce against him an abusive judgment, but said, "The Lord rebuke you!" 10 But these people disparage all the things that they do not understand; and all the things that they know by instinct, like unreasoning animals, by these things they are destroyed. 11 Woe to them! For they have gone the way of Cain, and for pay they have given themselves up to the error of Balaam, and perished in the rebellion of Korah. 12 These are the ones who are hidden reefs in your love feasts when they feast with you without fear, *like shepherds* caring *only* for themselves; clouds without water, carried along by winds; autumn trees without fruit, doubly dead, uprooted; 13 wild waves of the sea, churning up their own shameful deeds like *dirty* foam; wandering stars, for whom the gloom of darkness has been reserved forever.

14 *It was* also about these people *that* Enoch, *in the* seventh *generation* from Adam, prophesied, saying, "Behold, the Lord has come with many thousands of His holy ones, 15 to execute judgment upon all, and to convict all the ungodly of all their ungodly deeds which they have done in an ungodly way, and of all the harsh things which ungodly sinners have spoken against Him." 16 These are grumblers, finding fault, following after their *own* lusts; they speak arrogantly, flattering people for the sake of *gaining an* advantage.

Keep Yourselves in the Love of God

17 But you, beloved, ought to remember the words that were spoken beforehand by the apostles of our Lord Jesus Christ, 18 that they were saying to you, "In the last time there will be mockers, following after their own ungodly lusts." 19 These are the ones who cause divisions, worldly-minded, devoid of the Spirit. 20 But you, beloved, building yourselves up on your most holy faith, praying in the Holy Spirit, 21 keep yourselves in the love of God, looking forward to the mercy of our Lord Jesus Christ to eternal life. 22 And have mercy on some, who are doubting; 23 save others, snatching them out of the fire; and on some have mercy with fear, hating even the garment polluted by the flesh.

24 Now to Him who is able to protect you from stumbling, and to make you stand in the presence of His glory, blameless with great joy, 25 to the only God our Savior, through Jesus Christ our Lord, *be* glory, majesty, dominion, and authority before all time and now and forever. Amen.

1:5 1 One early ms *Jesus*

THE REVELATION
to John

The Revelation of Jesus Christ

1 The Revelation of Jesus Christ, which God gave Him to show to His bond-servants, the things which must soon take place; and He sent and communicated it by His angel to His bond-servant John, 2 who testified to the word of God and to the testimony of Jesus Christ, everything that he saw. 3 Blessed is the one who reads, and those who hear the words of the prophecy and keep the things which are written in it; for the time is near.

Message to the Seven Churches

4 John to the seven churches that are in Asia: Grace to you and peace from Him who is, and who was, and who is to come, and from the 'seven spirits who are before His throne, 5 and from Jesus Christ, the faithful witness, the firstborn of the dead, and the ruler of the kings of the earth. To Him who loves us and released us from our sins by His blood—6 and He made us into a kingdom, priests to His God and Father—to Him be the glory and the dominion forever and ever. Amen. 7 BEHOLD, HE IS COMING WITH THE CLOUDS, and every eye will see Him, even those who pierced Him; and all the tribes of the earth will mourn over Him. So it is to be. Amen.

8 "I am the Alpha and the Omega," says the Lord God, "who is and who was and who is to come, the Almighty."

The Patmos Vision

9 I, John, your brother and fellow participant in the tribulation and kingdom and persever- ance in Jesus, was on the island called Patmos because of the word of God and the testimony of Jesus. 10 I was in the 'Spirit on the Lord's day, and I heard behind me a loud voice like the sound of a trumpet, 11 saying, "Write on a scroll what you see, and send it to the seven churches: to Ephesus, Smyrna, Pergamum, Thyatira, Sardis, Philadelphia, and Laodicea." 12 Then I turned to see the voice that was speaking with me. And after turning I saw seven golden lampstands; 13 and in the middle of the lampstands I saw one like 'a son of man, clothed in a robe reaching to the feet, and wrapped around the chest with a golden sash. 14 His head and His hair were white like white wool, like snow; and His eyes were like a flame of fire. 15 His feet were like burnished bronze when it has been heated to a glow in a furnace, and His voice was like the sound of many waters. 16 In His right hand He held seven stars, and out of His mouth came a sharp two-edged sword; and His face was like the sun shining in its strength.

17 When I saw Him, I fell at His feet like a dead man. And He placed His right hand on me, saying, "Do not be afraid; I am the first and the last, 18 and the living One; and I was dead, and behold, I am alive forevermore, and I have the keys of death and of Hades. 19 There- fore write the things which you have seen, and the things which are, and the things which will take place after these things. 20 As for the mystery of the seven stars which you saw in My right hand, and the seven golden lamp- stands: the seven stars are the angels of the seven churches, and the seven lampstands are the seven churches.

Message to Ephesus

2 "To the angel of the church in Ephesus write:

The One who holds the seven stars in His right hand, the One who walks among the seven golden lampstands, says this:

2 'I know your deeds and your labor and perseverance, and that you cannot tolerate evil people, and you have put those who call themselves apostles to the test, and they are not, and you found them to be false; 3 and you have perseverance and have endured on account of My name, and have not become weary. 4 But I have this against you, that you have left your first love. 5 Therefore, remember from where you have fallen, and repent, and do the deeds you did at first; or else I am coming to you and I will remove your lamp- stand from its place—unless you repent. 6 But you have this, that you hate the deeds of the Nicolaitans, which I also hate. 7 The one who has an ear, let him hear what the Spirit says to the churches. To the one who overcomes, I will grant to eat from the tree of life, which is in the Paradise of God.'

Message to Smyrna

8 "And to the angel of the church in Smyrna write:

The first and the last, who was dead, and has come to life, says this:

9 'I know your tribulation and your poverty (but you are rich), and the slander by those who say they are Jews, and are not, but are a synagogue of Satan. 10 Do not fear what you are about to suffer. Behold, the devil is about to throw some of you into prison, so that you will be tested, and you will have tribulation for ten days. Be faithful until death, and I will give you the crown of life. 11 The one who has an ear, let him hear what the Spirit says to the churches. The one who overcomes will not be hurt by the second death.'

Message to Pergamum

12 "And to the angel of the church in Pergamum write:

The One who has the sharp two-edged sword says this:

1:4 1 Possibly a symbolic reference to the Holy Spirit in His fullness, or to seven key angels   1:10 1 Or spirit
1:13 1 Or the Son of Man

13 'I know where you dwell, where Satan's throne is; and you hold firmly to My name, and did not deny My faith even in the days of Antipas, My witness, My faithful one, who was killed among you, where Satan dwells. 14 But I have a few things against you, because you have *some* there who hold the teaching of Balaam, who kept teaching Balak to put a stumbling block before the sons of Israel, to eat things sacrificed to idols and to commit sexual immorality. 15 So you too, have some who in the same way hold to the teaching of the Nicolaitans. 16 Therefore repent; or else I am coming to you quickly, and I will wage war against them with the sword of My mouth. 17 The one who has an ear, let him hear what the Spirit says to the churches. To the one who overcomes, I will give *some* of the hidden manna, and I will give him a white stone, and a new name written on the stone which no one knows except the one who receives *it.'*

Message to Thyatira

18 "And to the angel of the church in Thyatira write:

The Son of God, who has eyes like a flame of fire, and feet like burnished bronze, says this:

19 'I know your deeds, and your love and faith, and service and perseverance, and that your deeds of late are greater than at first. 20 But I have *this* against you, that you tolerate the woman Jezebel, who calls herself a prophetess, and she teaches and leads My bond-servants astray so that they commit sexual immorality and eat things sacrificed to idols. 21 I gave her time to repent, and she does not want to repent of her sexual immorality. 22 Behold, I will throw her on a bed *of sickness,* and those who commit adultery with her into great tribulation, unless they repent of 1her deeds. 23 And I will kill her children with 1plague, and all the churches will know that I am He who searches the minds and hearts; and I will give to each one of you according to your deeds. 24 But I say to you, the rest who are in Thyatira, who do not hold this teaching, who have not known the deep things of Satan, as they call them— I place no other burden on you. 25 Nevertheless what you have, hold firmly until I come. 26 The one who overcomes, and the one who keeps My deeds until the end, I will give him authority over the nations; 27 AND HE SHALL RULE THEM WITH A ROD OF IRON, AS THE VESSELS OF THE POTTER ARE SHATTERED, as I also have received *authority* from My Father; 28 and I will give him the morning star. 29 The one who has an ear, let him hear what the Spirit says to the churches.'

Message to Sardis

3 "To the angel of the church in Sardis write: He who has the seven spirits of God and the seven stars, says this: 'I know your deeds, that you have a name that you are alive, and *yet* you are dead. 2 Be constantly alert, and strengthen the things that remain, which were about to die; for I have not found your deeds completed in the sight of My God. 3 So remember what you have received and heard; and keep *it,* and repent. Then if you are not alert, I will come

like a thief, and you will not know at what hour I will come to you. 4 But you have a few people in Sardis who have not soiled their garments; and they will walk with Me in white, for they are worthy. 5 The one who overcomes will be clothed the same way, in white garments; and I will not erase his name from the book of life, and I will confess his name before My Father and before His angels. 6 The one who has an ear, let him hear what the Spirit says to the churches.'

Message to Philadelphia

7 "And to the angel of the church in Philadelphia write:

He who is holy, who is true, who has the key of David, who opens and no one will shut, and who shuts and no one opens, says this:

8 'I know your deeds. Behold, I have put before you an open door which no one can shut, because you have a little power, and have followed My word, and have not denied My name. 9 Behold, I will make *those* of the synagogue of Satan, who say that they are Jews and are not, but lie—I will make them come and bow down before your feet, and *make them* know that I have loved you. 10 Because you have kept My word of perseverance, I also will keep you from the hour of the testing, that *hour* which is about to come upon the whole world, to test those who live on the earth. 11 I am coming quickly; hold firmly to what you have, so that no one will take your crown. 12 The one who overcomes, I will make him a pillar in the temple of My God, and he will not go out from it anymore; and I will write on him the name of My God, and the name of the city of My God, the new Jerusalem, which comes down out of heaven from My God, and My new name. 13 The one who has an ear, let him hear what the Spirit says to the churches.'

Message to Laodicea

14 "To the angel of the church in Laodicea write:

The Amen, the faithful and true Witness, the Origin of the creation of God, says this:

15 'I know your deeds, that you are neither cold nor hot; I wish that you were cold or hot. 16 So because you are lukewarm, and neither hot nor cold, I will vomit you out of My mouth. 17 Because you say, "I am rich, and have become wealthy, and have no need of anything," and you do not know that you are wretched, miserable, poor, blind, and naked, 18 I advise you to buy from Me gold refined by fire so that you may become rich, and white garments so that you may clothe yourself and the shame of your nakedness will not be revealed; and eye salve to apply to your eyes so that you may see. 19 Those whom I love, I rebuke and discipline; therefore be zealous and repent. 20 Behold, I stand at the door and knock; if anyone hears My voice and opens the door, I will come in to him and will dine with him, and he with Me. 21 The one who overcomes, I will grant to him to sit with Me on My throne, as I also overcame and sat with My Father on His throne. 22 The one who has an

---

2:22 1 One early ms *their*   **2:23** 1 Lit *death;* i.e., a particular kind of death

ear, let him hear what the Spirit says to the churches.' "

Scene in Heaven

4 After these things I looked, and behold, a door *standing* open in heaven, and the first voice which I had heard, like *the sound* of a trumpet speaking with me, said, "Come up here, and I will show you what must take place after these things." 2 Immediately I was in *the* [1]Spirit; and behold, a throne was standing in heaven, and *someone was* sitting on the throne. 3 And He who was sitting *was* like a jasper stone and a sardius in appearance; and *there was* a rainbow around the throne, like an emerald in appearance. 4 Around the throne *were* twenty-four thrones; and upon the thrones *I saw* twenty-four elders sitting, clothed in white garments, and golden crowns on their heads.

The Throne and Worship of the Creator

5 Out from the throne *came flashes of light-ning and sounds and peals of thunder. And *there were* seven lamps of fire burning before the throne, which are the seven spirits of God; 6 and before the throne *there was something* like a sea of glass, like crystal; and in the center and around the throne, four living creatures full of eyes in front and behind. 7 The first living creature *was* like a lion, the second creature like a calf, the third creature had a face like that of a man, and the fourth creature *was* like a flying eagle. 8 And the four living creatures, each one of them having six wings, are full of eyes around and within; and day and night they do not cease to say,

"Holy, holy, holy *is* the Lord God, the Almighty, who was and who is and who is to come."

9 And when the living creatures give glory, honor, and thanks to Him who sits on the throne, to Him who lives forever and ever, 10 the twenty-four elders will fall down before Him who sits on the throne, and they will wor-ship Him who lives forever and ever, and will cast their crowns before the throne, saying,

11 "Worthy are You, our Lord and our God, to receive glory and honor and power; for You created all things, and because of Your will they existed, and were created."

The Scroll with Seven Seals

5 I saw in the right hand of Him who sat on the throne a scroll written inside and on the back, sealed up with seven seals. 2 And I saw a strong angel proclaiming with a loud voice, "Who is worthy to open the scroll and to break its seals?" 3 And no one in heaven or on the earth or under the earth was able to open the scroll or to look into it. 4 Then I *began* to weep greatly because no one was found worthy to open the scroll or to look into it. 5 And one of the elders *said to me, "Stop weeping; behold, the Lion that is from the tribe of Judah, the Root of David, has overcome *so as to be able* to open the scroll and its seven seals."

6 And I saw [1]between the throne (with the four living creatures) and the elders a Lamb standing, as if slaughtered, having seven horns and seven eyes, which are the seven spirits of God sent out into all the earth. 7 And He came and took *the scroll* out of the right hand of Him who sat on the throne. 8 When He had taken the scroll, the four living creatures and the twenty-four elders fell down before the Lamb, each one holding a harp and golden bowls full of incense, which are the prayers of the saints. 9 And they *sang a new song, saying,

"Worthy are You to take the scroll and to break its seals; for You were slaughtered, and You purchased *people* for God with Your blood from every tribe, language, people, and nation. 10 You have made them *into* a kingdom and priests to our God, and they will reign upon the earth."

Angels Exalt the Lamb

11 Then I looked, and I heard the voices of many angels around the throne and the living creatures and the elders; and the number of them was [1]myriads of myriads, and thousands of thousands, 12 saying with a loud voice,

"Worthy is the Lamb that was slaughtered to receive power, wealth, wisdom, might, honor, glory, and blessing."

13 And I heard every created thing which is in heaven, or on the earth, or under the earth, or on the sea, and all the things in them, saying,

"To Him who sits on the throne and to the Lamb *be* the blessing, the honor, the glory, and the dominion forever and ever."

14 And the four living creatures were saying, "Amen." And the elders fell down and wor-shiped.

The First Seal: Conqueror on a White Horse

6 Then I saw when the Lamb broke one of the seven seals, and I heard one of the four living creatures saying *as with* a voice of thunder, "Come!" 2 I looked, and behold, a white horse, and the one who sat on it had a bow; and a crown was given to him, and he went out conquering and to conquer.

The Second Seal: War

3 When He broke the second seal, I heard the second living creature saying, "Come!" 4 And another, a red horse, went out; and to him who sat on it, it was granted to take peace from the earth, and that *people* would kill one another; and a large sword was given to him.

The Third Seal: Famine

5 When He broke the third seal, I heard the third living creature saying, "Come!" I looked, and behold, a black horse, and the one who sat on it had a pair of scales in his hand. 6 And I heard *something* like a voice in the center of the four living creatures saying, "A [1]quart of wheat for a [2]denarius, and three quarts of

---

4:2 [1] Or *spirit*   **5:6** [1] Lit *in the middle of the throne and of the four living creatures, and in the middle of the elders*   **5:11** [1] Gr for *10,000s of 10,000s*   **6:6** [1] Gr *choenix*; i.e., a dry measure almost equal to a qt.   [2] The denarius was a day's wages for a laborer

barley for a denarius; and do not damage the oil and the wine."

The Fourth Seal: Death

7 When *the Lamb* broke the fourth seal, I heard the voice of the fourth living creature saying, "Come!" 8 I looked, and behold, an ashen horse; and the one who sat on it had the name Death, and Hades was following with him. Authority was given to them over a fourth of the earth, to kill with sword, and famine, and *plague, and by the wild animals of the earth.

The Fifth Seal: Martyrs

9 When *the Lamb* broke the fifth seal, I saw underneath the altar the souls of those who had been killed because of the word of God, and because of the testimony which they had maintained; 10 and they cried out with a loud voice, saying, "How long, O Lord, holy and true, will You refrain from judging and avenging our blood on those who live on the earth?" 11 And a white robe was given to each of them; and they were told that they were to rest for a little while longer, until *the number of* their fellow servants and their brothers *and sisters* who were to be killed even as they *had been,* was completed also.

The Sixth Seal: Terror

12 And I looked when He broke the sixth seal, and there was a great earthquake; and the sun became as black as sackcloth made of hair, and the whole moon became like blood; 13 and the stars of the sky fell to the earth, as a fig tree drops its unripe figs when shaken by a great wind. 14 The sky was split apart like a scroll when it is rolled up, and every mountain and island was removed from its place. 15 Then the kings of the earth and the eminent people, and the commanders and the wealthy and the strong, and every slave and free person hid themselves in the caves and among the rocks of the mountains; 16 and they *said to the mountains and the rocks, "Fall on us and hide us from the sight of Him who sits on the throne, and from the wrath of the Lamb; 17 for the great day of Their wrath has come, and who is able to stand?"

An Interlude

7 After this I saw four angels standing at the four corners of the earth, holding back the four winds of the earth so that no wind would blow on the earth, or on the sea, or on any tree. 2 And I saw another angel ascending from the rising of the sun, holding the seal of the living God; and he called out with a loud voice to the four angels to whom it was granted to harm the earth and the sea, 3 saying, "Do not harm the earth, or the sea, or the trees until we have sealed the bond-servants of our God on their foreheads."

The 144,000

4 And I heard the number of those who were sealed: 144,000, sealed from every tribe of the sons of Israel:

5 from the tribe of Judah, twelve thousand *were* sealed, from the tribe of Reuben twelve thousand, from the tribe of Gad twelve thousand, 6 from the tribe of Asher twelve thousand, from the tribe of Naphtali twelve thousand, from the tribe of Manasseh twelve thousand, 7 from the tribe of Simeon twelve thousand, from the tribe of Levi twelve thousand, from the tribe of Issachar twelve thousand, 8 from the tribe of Zebulun twelve thousand, from the tribe of Joseph twelve thousand, *and* from the tribe of Benjamin, twelve thousand *were* sealed.

A Multitude from the Tribulation

9 After these things I looked, and behold, a great multitude which no one could count, from every nation and *all the* tribes, peoples, and languages, standing before the throne and before the Lamb, clothed in white robes, and palm branches *were* in their hands; 10 and they *cried out with a loud voice, saying,

"Salvation *belongs* to our God who sits on the throne, and to the Lamb."

11 And all the angels were standing around the throne and *around* the elders and the four living creatures; and they fell on their faces before the throne and worshiped God, 12 saying,

"Amen, blessing, glory, wisdom, thanksgiving, honor, power, and might *belong* to our God forever and ever. Amen."

13 Then one of the elders responded, saying to me, "These who are clothed in the white robes, who are they, and where have they come from?" 14 I said to him, "My lord, you know." And he said to me, "These are the ones who come out of the great tribulation, and they have washed their robes and made them white in the blood of the Lamb. 15 For this reason they are before the throne of God, and they serve Him day and night in His temple; and He who sits on the throne will spread His tabernacle over them. 16 They will no longer hunger nor thirst, nor will the sun beat down on them, nor any scorching heat; 17 for the Lamb in the center of the throne will be their shepherd, and will guide them to springs of the water of life; and God will wipe every tear from their eyes."

The Seventh Seal: Trumpets

8 When *the Lamb* broke the seventh seal, there was silence in heaven for about half an hour. 2 And I saw the seven angels who stand before God, and seven trumpets were given to them.

3 Another angel came and stood at the altar, holding a golden censer; and much incense was given to him, so that he might add it to the prayers of all the saints on the golden altar which was before the throne. 4 And the smoke of the incense ascended from the angel's hand with the prayers of the saints before God. 5 Then the angel took the *censer and filled it with the fire of the altar, and hurled it to the earth; and there were peals of thunder

---

6:8 1 Lit *death;* i.e., a particular kind of death   8:5 1 I.e., container to burn incense

and sounds, and flashes of lightning and an earthquake.

6 And the seven angels who had the seven trumpets prepared themselves to sound them.

7 The first sounded, and there was hail and fire mixed with blood, and it was hurled to the earth; and a third of the earth was burned up, and a third of the trees were burned up, and all the green grass was burned up.

8 The second angel sounded, and *something* like a great mountain burning with fire was hurled into the sea; and a third of the sea became blood, 9 and a third of the creatures which were in the sea and had life, died; and a third of the ships were destroyed.

10 The third angel sounded, and a great star fell from heaven, burning like a torch, and it fell on a third of the rivers and on the springs of waters. 11 The star is named Wormwood; and a third of the waters became wormwood, and many people died from the waters because they were made bitter.

12 The fourth angel sounded, and a third of the sun, a third of the moon, and a third of the stars were struck, so that a third of them would be darkened and the day would not shine for a third of it, and the night in the same way.

13 Then I looked, and I heard an eagle flying in midheaven, saying with a loud voice, "Woe, woe, woe to those who live on the earth, because of the remaining blasts of the trumpet of the three angels who are about to sound!"

The Fifth Trumpet: Shaft of the Abyss

9 Then the fifth angel sounded, and I saw a star from heaven which had fallen to the earth; and the key to the shaft of the abyss was given to him. 2 He opened the shaft of the abyss, and smoke ascended out of the shaft like the smoke of a great furnace; and the sun and the air were darkened from the smoke of the shaft. 3 Then out of the smoke came locusts upon the earth, and power was given them, as the scorpions of the earth have power. 4 They were told not to hurt the grass of the earth, nor any green thing, nor any tree, but only the people who do not have the seal of God on their foreheads. 5 And they were not permitted to kill anyone, but to torment for five months; and their torment was like the torment of a scorpion when it stings a person. 6 And in those days people will seek death and will not find it; they will long to die, and death will flee from them!

7 The appearance of the locusts was like horses prepared for battle; and on their heads appeared to be crowns like gold, and their faces were like human faces. 8 They had hair like the hair of women, and their teeth were like *the teeth* of lions. 9 They had breastplates like breastplates of iron; and the sound of their wings was like the sound of chariots, of many horses rushing to battle. 10 They have tails like scorpions, and stings; and in their tails is their power to hurt people for five months. 11 They have as king over them, the angel of the abyss; his name in Hebrew is ¹Abaddon, and in the Greek he has the name Apollyon.

12 The first woe has passed; behold, two woes are still coming after these things.

The Sixth Trumpet: Army from the East

13 Then the sixth angel sounded, and I heard a voice from the ¹four horns of the golden altar which is before God, 14 saying to the sixth angel who had the trumpet, "Release the four angels who are bound at the great river Euphrates." 15 And the four angels, who had been prepared for the hour and day and month and year, were released, so that they would kill a third of mankind. 16 The number of the armies of the horsemen was two hundred million; I heard the number of them. 17 And this is how I saw in my vision the horses and those who sat on them: *the riders* had breastplates *the color* of fire, of hyacinth, and of ¹brimstone; and the heads of the horses are like the heads of lions; and out of their mouths *came fire and smoke and ²brimstone. 18 A third of mankind was killed by these three plagues, by the fire, the smoke, and the brimstone which came out of their mouths. 19 For the power of the horses is in their mouths and in their tails; for their tails are like serpents and have heads, and with them they do harm.

20 The rest of mankind, who were not killed by these plagues, did not repent of the works of their hands so as not to worship demons and the idols of gold, silver, brass, stone, and wood, which can neither see nor hear nor walk; 21 and they did not repent of their murders, nor of their witchcraft, nor of their sexual immorality, nor of their thefts.

The Angel and the Little Scroll

10 I saw another strong angel coming down from heaven, clothed with a cloud; and the rainbow was on his head, and his face was like the sun, and his feet like pillars of fire; 2 and he had in his hand a little scroll, which was open. He placed his right foot on the sea and his left on the land; 3 and he cried out with a loud voice, as when a lion roars; and when he had cried out, the seven peals of thunder uttered their voices. 4 When the seven peals of thunder had spoken, I was about to write; and I heard a voice from heaven, saying, "Seal up the things which the seven peals of thunder have spoken, and do not write them." 5 Then the angel whom I saw standing on the sea and on the land raised his right hand to heaven, 6 and swore by Him who lives forever and ever, who created heaven and the things in it, and the earth and the things in it, and the sea and the things in it, that there will no longer be a delay, 7 but in the days of the voice of the seventh angel, when he is about to sound, then the mystery of God is finished, as He announced to His servants the prophets.

8 Then the voice which I heard from heaven, *I heard* again speaking with me, and saying, "Go, take the scroll which is open in the hand of the angel who stands on the sea and on the land." 9 And I went to the angel, telling him to give me the little scroll. And he *said to me, "Take it and eat it; it will make your stomach

---

9:11 ¹ I.e., destruction   9:13 ¹ Two early mss do not contain *four*   9:17 ¹ I.e., burning sulfur   ² I.e., burning sulfur

bitter, but in your mouth it will be sweet as honey." [10] I took the little scroll from the angel's hand and ate it, and in my mouth it was sweet as honey; and when I had eaten it, my stomach was made bitter. [11] And they *said to me, "You must prophesy again concerning many peoples, nations, languages, and kings."

The Two Witnesses

11 Then there was given to me a measuring rod like a staff; and someone said, "Get up and measure the temple of God and the altar, and those who worship in it. [2] Leave out the courtyard which is outside the temple and do not measure it, because it has been given to the nations; and they will trample the holy city for forty-two months. [3] And I will grant *authority* to my two witnesses, and they will prophesy for 1,260 days, clothed in sackcloth." [4] These are the two olive trees and the two lampstands that stand before the Lord of the earth. [5] And if anyone wants to harm them, fire flows out of their mouth and devours their enemies; and *so* if anyone wants to harm them, he must be killed in this way. [6] These have the power to shut up the sky, so that rain will not fall during the days of their prophesying; and they have power over the waters to turn them into blood, and to strike the earth with every plague, as often as they desire.

[7] When they have finished their testimony, the beast that comes up out of the abyss will make war with them, and overcome them and kill them. [8] And their dead bodies *will lie* on the street of the great city which ¹spiritually is called Sodom and Egypt, where also their Lord was crucified. [9] Those from the peoples, tribes, languages, and nations *will* look at their dead bodies for three and a half days, and will not allow their dead bodies to be laid in a tomb. [10] And those who live on the earth *will* rejoice over them and celebrate; and they will send gifts to one another, because these two prophets tormented those who live on the earth. [11] And after the three and a half days, the breath of life from God came into them, and they stood on their feet; and great fear fell upon those who were watching them. [12] And they heard a loud voice from heaven saying to them, "Come up here." And they went up into heaven in the cloud, and their enemies watched them. [13] And at that time there was a great earthquake, and a tenth of the city fell; seven thousand people were killed in the earthquake, and the rest were terrified and gave glory to the God of heaven.

[14] The second woe has passed; behold, the third woe is coming quickly.

The Seventh Trumpet: Christ's Reign Foreseen

[15] Then the seventh angel sounded; and there were loud voices in heaven, saying, "The kingdom of the world has become *the kingdom* of our Lord and of His Christ; and He will reign forever and ever." [16] And the twenty-four elders, who sit on their thrones before God, fell on their faces and worshiped God, [17] saying,

"We give You thanks, Lord God, the Almighty, the One who is and who was, because You have taken Your great power and have begun to reign. [18] And the nations were enraged, and Your wrath came, and the time *came* for the dead to be judged, and *the time* to reward Your bond-servants the prophets and the saints and those who fear Your name, the small and the great, and to destroy those who destroy the earth."

[19] And the temple of God which is in heaven was opened; and the ark of His covenant appeared in His temple, and there were flashes of lightning and sounds and peals of thunder, and an earthquake, and a great hailstorm.

The Woman, Israel

12 A great sign appeared in heaven: a woman clothed with the sun, and the moon under her feet, and on her head a crown of twelve stars; [2] and she was pregnant and she *cried out, being in labor and in pain to give birth.

The Red Dragon, Satan

[3] Then another sign appeared in heaven: and behold, a great red dragon having seven heads and ten horns, and on his heads *were* seven crowns. [4] And his tail *swept away a third of the stars of heaven and hurled them to the earth. And the dragon stood before the woman who was about to give birth, so that when she gave birth he might devour her Child.

The Male Child, Christ

[5] And she gave birth to a Son, a male, who is going to rule all the nations with a rod of iron; and her Child was caught up to God and to His throne. [6] Then the woman fled into the wilderness where she *had a place prepared by God, so that there she would be nourished for 1,260 days.

The Angel, Michael

[7] And there was war in heaven, Michael and his angels waging war with the dragon. The dragon and his angels waged war, [8] and they did not prevail, and there was no longer a place found for them in heaven. [9] And the great dragon was thrown down, the serpent of old who is called the devil and Satan, who deceives the whole world; he was thrown down to the earth, and his angels were thrown down with him. [10] Then I heard a loud voice in heaven, saying,

"Now the salvation, and the power, and the kingdom of our God and the authority of His Christ have come, for the accuser of our brothers *and sisters* has been thrown down, the one who accuses them before our God day and night. [11] And they overcame him because of the blood of the Lamb and because of the word of their testimony, and they did not love their life *even* when faced with death. [12] For this reason, rejoice, you heavens and you who dwell in them. Woe to the earth and the sea, because the devil has come down to you with great wrath, knowing that he has *only* a short time."

11:8 ¹ I.e., from the viewpoint of the Holy Spirit

13 And when the dragon saw that he was thrown down to the earth, he persecuted the woman who gave birth to the male *Child*. 14 But the two wings of the great eagle were given to the woman, so that she could fly into the wilderness to her place, where she *was nourished for a time, times, and half a time, away from the presence of the serpent. 15 And the serpent hurled water like a river out of his mouth after the woman, so that he might cause her to be swept away with the flood. 16 But the earth helped the woman, and the earth opened its mouth and drank up the river which the dragon had hurled out of his mouth. 17 So the dragon was enraged with the woman, and went off to make war with the rest of her children, who keep the commandments of God and hold to the testimony of Jesus.

The Beast from the Sea

13 And *the dragon* stood on the sand of the seashore.

Then I saw a beast coming up out of the sea, having ten horns and seven heads, and on his horns *were* ten crowns, and on his heads *were* blasphemous names. 2 And the beast that I saw was like a leopard, and his feet were like *those* of a bear, and his mouth like the mouth of a lion. And the dragon gave him his power and his throne, and great authority. 3 *I saw* one of his heads as if it had been fatally wounded, and his fatal wound was healed. And the whole earth was amazed *and followed* after the beast; 4 they worshiped the dragon because he gave his authority to the beast; and they worshiped the beast, saying, "Who is like the beast, and who is able to wage war with him?" 5 A mouth was given to him speaking arrogant words and blasphemies, and authority to act for forty-two months was given to him. 6 And he opened his mouth in blasphemies against God, to blaspheme His name and His tabernacle, *that is,* those who dwell in heaven.

7 It was also given to him to make war with the saints and to overcome them, and authority was given to him over every tribe, people, language, and nation. 8 All who live on the earth will worship him, *everyone* whose name has not been written since the foundation of the world in the book of life of the Lamb who has been slaughtered. 9 If anyone has an ear, let him hear. 10 If anyone *is destined* for captivity, to captivity he goes; if anyone kills with the sword, with the sword he must be killed. Here is the perseverance and the faith of the saints.

The Beast from the Earth

11 Then I saw another beast coming up out of the earth; and he had two horns like a lamb, and he spoke as a dragon. 12 He exercises all the authority of the first beast in his presence. And he makes the earth and those who live on it worship the first beast, whose fatal wound was healed. 13 He performs great signs, so that he even makes fire come down out of the sky to the earth in the presence of people. 14 And he deceives those who live on the earth because of the signs which it was given him

to perform in the presence of the beast, telling those who live on the earth to make an image to the beast who *had the wound of the sword and has come to life. 15 And it was given to him to give breath to the image of the beast, so that the image of the beast would even *speak and cause all who do not worship the image of the beast to be killed. 16 And he causes all, the small and the great, the rich and the poor, and the free and the slaves, to be given a mark on their right hands or on their foreheads, 17 and *he decrees* that no one will be able to buy or to sell, except the one who has the mark, *either* the name of the beast or the number of his name. 18 Here is wisdom. Let him who has understanding calculate the number of the beast, for the number is that of a *man; and his number is *six hundred and sixty-six.

The Lamb and the 144,000 on Mount Zion

14 Then I looked, and behold, the Lamb *was standing on Mount Zion, and with Him 144,000 who had His name and the name of His Father written on their foreheads. 2 And I heard a voice from heaven, like the sound of many waters and like the sound of loud thunder, and the voice which I heard *was* like *the sound* of harpists playing on their harps. 3 And they *sang a new song before the throne and before the four living creatures and the elders; and no one was able to learn the song except the 144,000 who had been purchased from the earth. 4 These are the ones who have not defiled themselves with women, for they are celibate. These *are* the ones who follow the Lamb wherever He goes. These have been purchased from mankind as first fruits to God and to the Lamb. 5 And no lie was found in their mouths; they are blameless.

Vision of the Angel with the Gospel

6 And I saw another angel flying in mid-heaven with an eternal gospel to preach to those who live on the earth, and to every nation, tribe, language, and people; 7 and he said with a loud voice, "Fear God and give Him glory, because the hour of His judgment has come; worship Him who made the heaven and the earth, and sea and springs of waters."

8 And another angel, a second one, followed, saying, "Fallen, fallen is Babylon the great, she who has made all the nations drink of the wine of the passion of her sexual immorality."

Doom for Worshipers of the Beast

9 Then another angel, a third one, followed them, saying with a loud voice, "If anyone worships the beast and his image, and receives a mark on his forehead or on his hand, 10 he also will drink of the wine of the wrath of God, which is mixed in full strength in the cup of His anger; and he will be tormented with fire and brimstone in the presence of the holy angels and in the presence of the Lamb. 11 And the smoke of their torment ascends forever and ever; they have no rest day and night, those who worship the beast and his image, and whoever receives the mark of his name."

13:15 1 One early ms *speak, and he will cause* **13:18** 1 Or *human* 2 I.e., spelled out in Gr as 600 + 60 + 6; one early ms has the letters for *616*

12 Here is the perseverance of the saints who keep the commandments of God and their faith in Jesus.

13 And I heard a voice from heaven, saying, "Write: 'Blessed are the dead who die in the Lord from now on!' " "Yes," says the Spirit, "so that they may rest from their labors, for their deeds follow with them."

The Harvest

14 Then I looked, and behold, a white cloud, and sitting on the cloud *was* one like [1]a son of man, with a golden crown on His head and a sharp sickle in His hand. **15** And another angel came out of the temple, calling out with a loud voice to Him who sat on the cloud, "Put in your sickle and reap, for the hour to reap has come, because the harvest of the earth is ripe." **16** Then He who sat on the cloud swung His sickle over the earth, and the earth was reaped.

17 And another angel came out of the temple which is in heaven, and he also had a sharp sickle. **18** Then another angel, the one who has power over fire, came out from the altar; and he called with a loud voice to him who had the sharp sickle, saying, "Put in your sharp sickle and gather the clusters from the vine of the earth, because her grapes are ripe." **19** So the angel swung his sickle to the earth and gathered *the clusters from* the vine of the earth, and threw *them* into the great wine press of the wrath of God. **20** And the wine press was trampled outside the city, and blood came out from the wine press, up to the horses' bridles, for a distance of [1]1,600 stadia.

A Scene of Heaven

15 Then I saw another sign in heaven, great and marvelous, seven angels who had seven plagues, *which are* the last, because in them the wrath of God is finished.

2 And I saw *something* like a sea of glass mixed with fire, and those who were victorious over the beast and his image and the number of his name, standing on the sea of glass, holding harps of God. **3** And they *sang the song of Moses, the bond-servant of God, and the song of the Lamb, saying,

"Great and marvelous are Your works,
Lord God, the Almighty;
Righteous and true are Your ways,
King of the [1]nations!
4 "Who will not fear You, Lord, and glorify Your name?
For You alone are holy;
For ALL THE NATIONS WILL COME AND WORSHIP BEFORE YOU,
For Your righteous acts have been revealed."

5 After these things I looked, and the temple of the tabernacle of testimony in heaven was opened, **6** and the seven angels who had the seven plagues came out of the temple, clothed in [1]linen, clean *and* bright, and their chests wrapped with golden sashes. **7** And one of the four living creatures gave the seven angels seven golden bowls full of the wrath of God,

who lives forever and ever. **8** And the temple was filled with smoke from the glory of God and from His power; and no one was able to enter the temple until the seven plagues of the seven angels were finished.

The Bowls of Wrath

16 Then I heard a loud voice from the temple, saying to the seven angels, "Go and pour out on the earth the seven bowls of the wrath of God."

2 So the first *angel* went and poured out his bowl on the earth; and a harmful and painful sore afflicted the people who had the mark of the beast and who worshiped his image.

3 The second *angel* poured out his bowl into the sea, and it became blood like *that* of a dead man; and every living [1]thing in the sea died.

4 Then the third *angel* poured out his bowl into the rivers and the springs of waters; and they became blood. **5** And I heard the angel of the waters saying, "Righteous are You, the One who is and who was, O Holy One, because You judged these things; **6** for they poured out the blood of saints and prophets, and You have given them blood to drink. They deserve it." **7** And I heard the altar saying, "Yes, Lord God, the Almighty, true and righteous are Your judgments."

8 And the fourth *angel* poured out his bowl upon the sun, and it was given *power* to scorch people with fire. **9** And the people were scorched with fierce heat; and they blasphemed the name of God who has the power over these plagues, and they did not repent so as to give Him glory.

10 And the fifth *angel* poured out his bowl on the throne of the beast, and his kingdom became darkened; and they gnawed their tongues because of pain, **11** and they blasphemed the God of heaven because of their pain and their sores; and they did not repent of their deeds.

12 The sixth *angel* poured out his bowl on the great river, the Euphrates; and its water was dried up, so that the way would be prepared for the kings from the east.

Har-Magedon (Armageddon)

13 And I saw *coming* out of the mouth of the dragon, and out of the mouth of the beast, and out of the mouth of the false prophet, three unclean spirits like frogs; **14** for they are spirits of demons, performing signs, which go out to the kings of the entire world, to gather them together for the war of the great day of God, the Almighty. **15** ("Behold, I am coming like a thief. Blessed is the one who stays awake and keeps his clothes, so that he will not walk about naked and *people* will not see his shame.") **16** And they gathered them together to the place which in Hebrew is called Har-Magedon.

The Seventh Bowl of Wrath

17 Then the seventh *angel* poured out his bowl upon the air, and a loud voice came out of the temple from the throne, saying, "It is

done." [18] And there were flashes of lightning and sounds and peals of thunder; and there was a great earthquake, such as there had not been since mankind came to be upon the earth, so great an earthquake *was it, and* so mighty. [19] The great city was split into three parts, and the cities of the nations fell. Babylon the great was remembered in the sight of God, to give her the cup of the wine of His fierce wrath. [20] And every island fled, and no mountains were found. [21] And huge hailstones, weighing about [1]a talent each, *came down from heaven upon people; and people blasphemed God because of the plague of the hail, because the hailstone plague *was extremely severe.

The Doom of Babylon

17 Then one of the seven angels who had the seven bowls came and spoke with me, saying, "Come here, I will show you the judgment of the great prostitute who sits on many waters, [2] with whom the kings of the earth committed *acts of* sexual immorality, and those who live on the earth became drunk with the wine of her sexual immorality." [3] And he carried me away [1]in the Spirit into a wilderness; and I saw a woman sitting on a scarlet beast, full of blasphemous names, having seven heads and ten horns. [4] The woman was clothed in purple and scarlet, and adorned with gold, precious stones, and pearls, holding in her hand a gold cup full of abominations and of the unclean things of her sexual immorality, [5] and on her forehead a name *was* written, a mystery: "BABYLON THE GREAT, THE MOTHER OF PROSTITUTES AND OF THE ABOMINATIONS OF THE EARTH." [6] And I saw the woman drunk with the blood of the saints, and with the blood of the witnesses of Jesus. When I saw her, I wondered greatly. [7] And the angel said to me, "Why do you wonder? I will tell you the mystery of the woman and of the beast that carries her, which has the seven heads and the ten horns. [8] "The beast that you saw was, and is not, and is about to come up out of the abyss and [1]go to destruction. And those who live on the earth, whose names have not been written in the book of life from the foundation of the world, will wonder when they see the beast, that he was, and is not, and will come. [9] Here is the mind which has wisdom. The seven heads are seven mountains upon which the woman sits, [10] and they are seven kings; five have fallen, one is, the other has not yet come; and when he comes, he must remain a little while. [11] The beast which was, and is not, is himself also an eighth and is *one* of the seven, and he goes to destruction. [12] The ten horns which you saw are ten kings who have not yet received a kingdom, but they receive authority as kings with the beast for one hour. [13] These have one purpose, and they give their power and authority to the beast.

Victory for the Lamb

[14] These will wage war against the Lamb, and the Lamb will overcome them because He is Lord of lords and King of kings; and those who are with Him *are the* called and chosen and faithful."

[15] And he *said to me, "The waters which you saw where the prostitute sits are peoples and multitudes, and nations and languages. [16] And the ten horns which you saw, and the beast, these will hate the prostitute and will make her desolate and naked, and will eat her flesh and will burn her up with fire. [17] For God has put it in their hearts to execute His purpose by having a common purpose, and by giving their kingdom to the beast, until the words of God will be fulfilled. [18] The woman whom you saw is the great city, which reigns over the kings of the earth."

Babylon Is Fallen

18 After these things I saw another angel coming down from heaven, having great authority, and the earth was illuminated from his glory. [2] And he cried out with a mighty voice, saying, "Fallen, fallen is Babylon the great! She has become a dwelling place of demons and a prison of every unclean spirit, and a prison of every unclean and hateful bird. [3] For all the nations have fallen because of the wine of the passion of her sexual immorality, and the kings of the earth have committed *acts of* sexual immorality with her, and the merchants of the earth have become rich from the excessive wealth of her luxury."

[4] I heard another voice from heaven, saying, "Come out of her, my people, so that you will not participate in her sins and receive *any* of her plagues; [5] for her sins have piled up as high as heaven, and God has remembered her offenses. [6] Pay her back even as she has paid, and give back *to her* double according to her deeds; in the cup which she has mixed, mix twice as much for her. [7] To the extent that she glorified herself and lived luxuriously, to the same extent give her torment and mourning; for she says in her heart, 'I sit *as* a queen and I am not a widow, and will never see mourning.' [8] For this reason in one day her plagues will come, [1]plague and mourning and famine, and she will be burned up with fire; for the Lord God who judges her is strong.

Grief over Babylon

[9] "And the kings of the earth, who committed *acts of* sexual immorality and lived luxuriously with her, will weep and mourn over her when they see the smoke of her burning, [10] standing at a distance because of the fear of her torment, saying, 'Woe, woe, the great city, Babylon, the strong city! For in one hour your judgment has come.'

[11] "And the merchants of the earth weep and mourn over her, because no one buys their cargo any more— [12] cargo of gold, silver, precious stones, and pearls; fine linen, purple, silk, and scarlet; every *kind of* citron wood, every article of ivory, and every article *made* from very valuable wood, bronze, iron, and marble; [13] cinnamon, spice, incense, perfume,

---

16:21 [1] I.e., as a measure of weight about 100 lb. or 45 kg　**17:3** [1] Or *in spirit*　**17:8** [1] One early ms *is going*
18:8 [1] Lit *death;* i.e., a particular kind of death

frankincense, wine, olive oil, fine flour, wheat, cattle, sheep, and *cargo* of horses, carriages, slaves, and human lives. 14 The fruit you long for has left you, and all things that were luxurious and splendid have passed away from you and *people* will no longer find them. 15 The merchants of these things, who became rich from her, will stand at a distance because of the fear of her torment, weeping and mourning, 16 saying, 'Woe, woe, the great city, she who was clothed in fine linen and purple and scarlet, and adorned with gold, precious stones, and pearls; 17 for in one hour such great wealth has been laid waste!' And every shipmaster and every passenger and sailor, and all who make their living by the sea, stood at a distance, 18 and were crying out as they saw the smoke of her burning, saying, 'What *city* is like the great city?' 19 And they threw dust on their heads and were crying out, weeping and mourning, saying, 'Woe, woe, the great city, in which all who had ships at sea became rich from her prosperity, for in one hour she has been laid waste!' 20 Rejoice over her, O heaven, and you saints and apostles and prophets, because God has pronounced judgment for you against her."

21 Then a strong angel picked up a stone like a great millstone and threw it into the sea, saying, "So will Babylon, the great city, be thrown down with violence, and will never be found again. 22 And the sound of harpists, musicians, flute players, and trumpeters will never be heard in you again; and no craftsman of any craft will ever be found in you again; and the sound of a mill will never be heard in you again; 23 and the light of a lamp will never shine in you again; and the voice of the groom and bride will never be heard in you again; for your merchants were the powerful people of the earth, because all the nations were deceived by your witchcraft. 24 And in her was found the blood of prophets and of saints, and of all who have been slaughtered on the earth."

The Fourfold Hallelujah

19 After these things I heard *something* like a loud voice of a great multitude in heaven, saying,

"Hallelujah! Salvation, glory, and power belong to our God, 2 BECAUSE HIS JUDGMENTS ARE TRUE AND RIGHTEOUS; for He has judged the great prostitute who was corrupting the earth with her sexual immorality, and HE HAS AVENGED THE BLOOD OF HIS BOND-SERVANTS ON HER." 3 And a second time they said, "Hallelujah! HER SMOKE RISES FOREVER AND EVER." 4 And the twenty-four elders and the four living creatures fell down and worshiped God who sits on the throne, saying, "Amen. Hallelujah!" 5 And a voice came from the throne, saying,

"Give praise to our God, all you His bond-servants, you who fear Him, the small and the great." 6 Then I heard *something* like the voice of a great multitude and like the sound of many waters, and like the sound of mighty peals of thunder, saying,

"Hallelujah! For the Lord our God, the Almighty, reigns.

Marriage of the Lamb

7 Let's rejoice and be glad and give the glory to Him, because the marriage of the Lamb has come, and His bride has prepared herself." 8 It was given to her to clothe herself in fine linen, bright *and* clean; for the fine linen is the righteous acts of the saints.

9 Then he *said to me, "Write: 'Blessed are those who are invited to the wedding feast of the Lamb.'" And he *said to me, "These are the true words of God." 10 Then I fell at his feet to worship him. But he *said to me, "Do not do that; I am a fellow servant of yours and your brothers *and sisters* who hold the testimony of Jesus; worship God! For the testimony of Jesus is the spirit of prophecy."

The Coming of Christ

11 And I saw heaven opened, and behold, a white horse, and He who sat on it *is* called Faithful and True, and in righteousness He judges and wages war. 12 His eyes *are* a flame of fire, and on His head *are* many crowns; and He has a name written *on Him* which no one knows except Himself. 13 *He is* clothed with a robe dipped in blood, and His name is called The Word of God. 14 And the armies which are in heaven, clothed in fine linen, white *and* clean, were following Him on white horses. 15 From His mouth comes a sharp sword, so that with it He may strike down the nations, and He will rule them with a rod of iron; and He treads the wine press of the fierce wrath of God, the Almighty. 16 And on His robe and on His thigh He has a name written: "KING OF KINGS, AND LORD OF LORDS."

17 Then I saw an angel standing in the sun, and he cried out with a loud voice, saying to all the birds that fly in midheaven, "Come, assemble for the great feast of God, 18 so that you may eat the flesh of kings and the flesh of commanders, the flesh of mighty men, the flesh of horses and of those who sit on them, and the flesh of all people, both free and slaves, and small and great."

19 And I saw the beast and the kings of the earth and their armies, assembled to make war against Him who sat on the horse, and against His army.

Doom of the Beast and False Prophet

20 And the beast was seized, and with him the false prophet who performed the signs in his presence, by which he deceived those who had received the mark of the beast and those who worshiped his image; these two were thrown alive into the lake of fire, which burns with brimstone. 21 And the rest were killed with the sword which came from the mouth of Him who sat on the horse, and all the birds were filled with their flesh.

Satan Bound

20 Then I saw an angel coming down from heaven, holding the key of the abyss and a great chain in his hand. 2 And he took hold of the dragon, the serpent of old, who is the devil and Satan, and bound him for a thousand years; 3 and he threw him into the abyss and shut *it* and sealed *it* over him, so that he would not

deceive the nations any longer, until the thousand years were completed; after these things he must be released for a short time.

4 Then I saw thrones, and they sat on them, and judgment was given to them. And *I saw* the souls of those who had been beheaded because of their testimony of Jesus and because of the word of God, and those who had not worshiped the beast or his image, and had not received the mark on their foreheads and on their hands; and they came to life and reigned with Christ for a thousand years. **5** The rest of the dead did not come to life until the thousand years were completed. This is the first resurrection. **6** Blessed and holy is the one who has a part in the first resurrection; over these the second death has no power, but they will be priests of God and of Christ, and will reign with Him for a thousand years.

Satan Freed and Doomed

7 When the thousand years are completed, Satan will be released from his prison, **8** and will come out to deceive the nations which are at the four corners of the earth, Gog and Magog, to gather them together for the war; the number of them is like the sand of the seashore. **9** And they came up on the broad plain of the earth and surrounded the camp of the saints and the beloved city, and fire came down from heaven and devoured them. **10** And the devil who deceived them was thrown into the lake of fire and ¹brimstone, where the beast and the false prophet *are* also; and they will be tormented day and night forever and ever.

Judgment at the Throne of God

11 Then I saw a great white throne and Him who sat upon it, from whose presence earth and heaven fled, and no place was found for them. **12** And I saw the dead, the great and the small, standing before the throne, and books were opened; and another book was opened, which is *the book* of life; and the dead were judged from the things which were written in the books, according to their deeds. **13** And the sea gave up the dead who were in it, and Death and Hades gave up the dead who were in them; and they were judged, each one *of them* according to their deeds. **14** Then Death and Hades were thrown into the lake of fire. This is the second death, the lake of fire. **15** And if anyone's name was not found written in the book of life, he was thrown into the lake of fire.

The New Heaven and Earth

21 Then I saw a new heaven and a new earth; for the first heaven and the first earth passed away, and there is no longer *any* sea. **2** And I saw the holy city, new Jerusalem, coming down out of heaven from God, prepared as a bride adorned for her husband. **3** And I heard a loud voice from the throne, saying, "Behold, the tabernacle of God is among the people, and He will dwell among them, and

they shall be His people, and God Himself will be among them¹, **4** and He will wipe away every tear from their eyes; and there will no longer be *any* death; there will no longer be *any* mourning, or crying, or pain; the first things have passed away."

5 And He who sits on the throne said, "Behold, I am making all things new." And He *said, "Write, for these words are faithful and true." **6** Then He said to me, "It is done. I am the Alpha and the Omega, the beginning and the end. I will give *water* to the one who thirsts from the spring of the water of life, without cost. **7** The one who overcomes will inherit these things, and I will be his God and he will be My son. **8** But for the cowardly, and unbelieving, and abominable, and murderers, and sexually immoral persons, and sorcerers, and idolaters, and all liars, their part *will be* in the lake that burns with fire and brimstone, which is the second death."

9 Then one of the seven angels who had the seven bowls, full of the seven last plagues, came and spoke with me, saying, "Come here, I will show you the bride, the wife of the Lamb."

The New Jerusalem

10 And he carried me away ¹in *the* Spirit to a great and high mountain, and showed me the holy city, Jerusalem, coming down out of heaven from God, **11** having the glory of God. Her brilliance was like a very valuable stone, like a stone of crystal-clear jasper. **12** It had a great and high wall, with twelve gates, and at the gates twelve angels; and names *were* written on *the gates,* which are *the names* of the twelve tribes of the sons of Israel. **13** *There were* three gates on the east, three gates on the north, three gates on the south, and three gates on the west. **14** And the wall of the city had twelve foundation stones, and on them *were the* twelve names of the twelve apostles of the Lamb.

15 The one who spoke with me had a gold measuring rod to measure the city, its gates, and its wall. **16** The city is laid out as a square, and its length is as great as the width; and he measured the city with the rod, ¹twelve thousand stadia; its length, width, and height are equal. **17** And he measured its wall, ¹144 cubits, *by* human measurements, which are *also* angelic *measurements.* **18** The material of the wall was jasper; and the city was pure gold, like clear glass. **19** The foundation stones of the city wall were decorated with every kind of precious stone. The first foundation stone was jasper; the second, sapphire; the third, chalcedony; the fourth, emerald; **20** the fifth, sardonyx; the sixth, sardius; the seventh, chrysolite; the eighth, beryl; the ninth, topaz; the tenth, chrysoprase; the eleventh, jacinth; the twelfth, amethyst. **21** And the twelve gates were twelve pearls; each one of the gates was a single pearl. And the street of the city was pure gold, like transparent glass.

22 I saw no temple in it, for the Lord God the

Almighty and the Lamb are its temple. 23 And the city has no need of the sun or of the moon to shine on it, for the glory of God has illuminated it, and its lamp *is* the Lamb. 24 The nations will walk by its light, and the kings of the earth will bring their glory into it. 25 In the daytime (for there will be no night there) its gates will never be closed; 26 and they will bring the glory and the honor of the nations into it; 27 and nothing unclean, and no one who practices abomination and lying, shall ever come into it, but only those whose names are written in the Lamb's book of life.

The River and the Tree of Life

22 And he showed me a river of the water of life, clear as crystal, coming from the throne of God and of †the Lamb, 2 in the middle of its street. On either side of the river *was* the tree of life, bearing twelve *kinds of* fruit, yielding its fruit every month; and the leaves of the tree *were* for the healing of the nations. 3 There will no longer be any curse; and the throne of God and of the Lamb will be in it, and His bond-servants will serve Him; 4 they will see His face, and His name *will be* on their foreheads. 5 And there will no longer be *any* night; and they will not have need of the light of a lamp nor the light of the sun, because the Lord God will illuminate them; and they will reign forever and ever.

6 And he said to me, "These words are faithful and true"; and the Lord, the God of the spirits of the prophets, sent His angel to show His bond-servants the things which must soon take place.

7 "And behold, I am coming quickly. Blessed is the one who keeps the words of the prophecy of this book."

8 I, John, am the one who heard and saw these things. And when I heard and saw *them,* I fell down to worship at the feet of the angel who showed me these things. 9 And he *said to me, "Do not do that; I am a fellow servant of yours and of your brothers the prophets, and of those who keep the words of this book. Worship God!"

The Final Message

10 And he *said to me, "Do not seal up the words of the prophecy of this book, for the time is near. 11 Let the one who does wrong still do wrong, and the one who is filthy still be filthy; and let the one who is righteous still practice righteousness, and the one who is holy still keep himself holy."

12 "Behold, I am coming quickly, and My reward *is* with Me, to reward each one as his work deserves. 13 I am the Alpha and the Omega, the first and the last, the beginning and the end."

14 Blessed are those who wash their robes, so that they will have the right to the tree of life, and may enter the city by the gates. 15 Outside are the dogs, the sorcerers, the sexually immoral persons, the murderers, the idolaters, and everyone who loves and practices lying.

16 "I, Jesus, have sent My angel to testify to you of these things for the churches. I am the root and the descendant of David, the bright morning star."

17 The Spirit and the bride say, "Come." And let the one who hears say, "Come." And let the one who is thirsty come; let the one who desires, take the water of life without cost.

18 I testify to everyone who hears the words of the prophecy of this book: if anyone adds to them, God will add to him the plagues that are written in this book; 19 and if anyone takes away from the words of the book of this prophecy, God will take away his part from the tree of life and from the holy city, which are written in this book.

20 He who testifies to these things says, "Yes, I am coming quickly." Amen. Come, Lord Jesus.

21 The grace of the Lord Jesus be with †all. Amen.

22:1 1 Or *the Lamb. In the middle of its street, and on either side of the river, was*
22:21 1 One early ms *the saints*

INTRODUCTIONS
to the
BOOKS OF THE BIBLE

GENESIS derives its title from a Greek word meaning "origin" or "beginning," which is appropriate for the first book of the Bible. Here is found the creation by God of the material universe and all its physical creatures, including the man and woman from whom all humanity descend. The book relates how evil came into the world and how God has dealt with succeeding generations in His plan to reconcile mankind to Himself through His grace, mercy, and lovingkindness, promising a Redeemer who would make reconciliation possible.

EXODUS derives its title from a Greek word which means "the way out" or "exit." The major part of the book tells of God's deliverance of the people of Israel from slavery in Egypt, and their subsequent journey toward the land which God had promised to Abraham. The principal person in the book is Moses, chosen by God to give the people His laws and commandments. Moses is also instructed in the building of the Tabernacle, in which the presence of God would dwell with His people during their journey.

LEVITICUS also derives its title from a Greek word, whose meaning is "pertaining to Levi." In accordance with God's instructions to Moses, the tribe of Levi was set aside for service in the Tabernacle, including the numerous types of offerings and sacrifices and the feast days to be observed. The emphasis of Leviticus is on the holiness of God and His desire that His people also be holy. The shedding of the blood of the sacrifices made peace with God possible.

NUMBERS received its title from the two "numberings" of the people: the first, of those who were delivered from Egypt, and the second, of those who entered Canaan thirty-nine years later. The life of the Israelites is described in their victories and defeats, as they either trust God or fail to trust Him, while wandering through the wilderness with the Tabernacle as their center. Finally God prepares a generation that is faithful to Him, and the people enter the Promised Land in spite of the problems they have faced.

DEUTERONOMY is another book whose title comes from the Greek, a word meaning "second Law" or "repeated Law." The Law needed to be repeated to Israel because: 1) there was a new generation of Israelites; 2) they were going into a settled life after being nomads; 3) they would be among idolatrous influences; and 4) they had to be convinced that the covenant which God made with Abraham was still valid for them. Deut 6:4-9 is an especially important statement and is still repeated in Jewish households today. Known as the Shema, it stresses the teaching of the Scriptures in the home.

JOSHUA derives its title from the name of the leader of the people after the death of Moses, who had been responsible for the first five books. Joshua became the principal aide to Moses, and as commander of the fighting men he led the people in the conquest of the Promised Land, and oversaw the allotment of the land to the various tribes. Before his death, Joshua reminds the people that God has kept all His promises, and he exhorts them to continue in obedience of the Law.

JUDGES is known by this title in the Hebrew Bible and in all the ancient versions. The "judge" was not only a judicial figure, but also a leader in military and administrative matters. The historical period of the book extends from the death of Joshua and the elders to the reign of Saul as king, a period of about 325 years. The book is mainly a repetition of: 1) "And the sons of Israel did evil in the sight of the Lord;" 2) "He sold them into the hands of...;" 3) "When the sons of Israel cried to the Lord;" and 4) "The Lord raised up a deliverer for them."

RUTH is the second of five books in the Hebrew Scriptures that are classified as the Megilloth ("Scrolls"), which are read on major holy days. Ruth is read each year at Pentecost. Ruth was the widowed daughter-in-law of Naomi who had left Bethlehem with her family during a famine, and went to Moab where her husband and two sons subsequently died. When Naomi decided to return to Bethlehem, Ruth insisted on going with her. There, she gleaned grain in the field of a near-kinsman, who later redeemed the property of Naomi and took Ruth as his wife. She had a son who became David's grandfather, and thus Ruth, a Gentile, figures in the ancestry of Jesus.

FIRST SAMUEL actually has been given several titles, but is best known by this Hebrew name which is used in most English translations. The initial subject of the book is the birth of Samuel, who was both a judge and a prophet. The book records the events leading to a major change in the government of Israel. The people clamor to have a king as the other nations of the world do, and God directs Samuel to anoint a king. As the last judge, Samuel follows the advice of God and anoints both Saul and David as kings, with David's becoming king after Saul's death.

SECOND SAMUEL originally formed one book with First Samuel, but the later division into two books seems proper. Second Samuel is

mainly the biography of King David. The events begin with David's becoming king over Judah at Hebron, and later becoming king over the entire nation. During this period David composed his Psalms, and the book of Psalms began to be collected. Second Samuel tells of sin and its consequences in the life of David, but it also shows that the plans of God go forward. The promise to David that a son of his will sit on the throne of Israel looks beyond Solomon to Jesus Christ, who will reign forever.

FIRST KINGS covers the period of the "Golden Age of Hebrew Wisdom Literature." During this time Solomon wrote The Song of Solomon, Proverbs, and Ecclesiastes. Solomon ruled over a united kingdom that was relatively strong until his death, which brought the division of the kingdom into Judah and Israel. In Israel, Jeroboam with ten tribes set up a regime with a new priesthood and places of idolatry. For more than 50 years there was constant conflict between Judah and Israel, until Ahab and Jehoshaphat formed an alliance which lasted about 40 years.

SECOND KINGS continues the history section of the Old Testament. In the early chapters, Elisha is the focus of the book as he gives spiritual guidance to the kingdom of Israel. The decline and fall of the Hebrew nation is given in detail. The judgment of God comes with the invasion of the northern kingdom by Assyria. The history of the southern kingdom ends with the conquest by the Babylonians and exile to Mesopotamia in 586 BC. The book covers about 290 years with 13 prophets writing their works during this period.

FIRST CHRONICLES is written from the perspective of a Jewish priest. The book does not name its author but it may have been Ezra. The main focus of the book is on the life of David. An account is given of his rise to power with his mighty men, the relocation of the Ark of the Covenant, the worship of the people, and the plans for the building of the Temple. One of the stirring passages in 1 Chronicles is the reaffirmation of God's covenant with David.

SECOND CHRONICLES is also written from the perspective of a priest, and it highlights the building of the Temple by Solomon. The southern kingdom of Judah followed God's will better than did the northern kingdom, Israel; thus Judah is the principal subject of Second Chronicles. Judah's history is one of intermittent revivals under some rulers, and rebellions under others. It teaches the fact that God's blessings and His judgments upon people depend upon their response to Him and His word. Nationally, Israel's golden age reached its zenith at the completion of the Temple by Solomon.

EZRA is entitled after an important man of God who served both as a priest and a scribe. His passions were the reinstitution of the worship of God, and the study and teaching of God's word. It is believed that Ezra was largely responsible for the Judaism practiced through New Testament times. The book gives an account of two phases of Judah's return from captivity in Mesopotamia. The first phase comes under Zerubbabel (538 BC), and the second under Ezra himself (458 BC). Most of the book was written in Hebrew, with some official decrees and letters in Aramaic.

NEHEMIAH is named for the Israelite who became the cupbearer to the king of Persia, Artaxerxes I. From this trusted position he was permitted to return to Judah as head of the third phase of Israel's restoration from exile (445 BC). Nehemiah organized the work of rebuilding in spite of strong opposition to the point that men were working with a tool in one hand, and a weapon in the other. He was assisted by Ezra in the reading of the Law to the people. Nehemiah was called back to the court of Persia, but after a time returned to Judah and carried on reforms.

ESTHER is entitled after its principal person, the woman who became queen of Persia. It relates the history of the Jewish people's being saved from extermination by the actions of two people, Esther and her older cousin Mordecai. Esther had become queen to Artaxerxes (Xerxes) after his wife Vashti refused to appear before the king and his court during a banquet of drinking. The name of God does not appear in this book, but there is no doubt that His will brings about the decree that saves the Jews and brings honor to Mordecai. The book of Esther is read during the Feast of Purim, when this victory is celebrated.

JOB is the first of five wisdom books in the Old Testament. The book describes the life of a man who suffers through many severe trials brought upon him by Satan. The central part of the book, written in poetic form, deals with friends of Job who engage in a dialogue over the reasons for Job's calamities. In the Scriptures Job is a historic person renowned for his patience and endurance. The events recorded in the book occur generally in the times of Abraham, Isaac and Jacob.

PSALMS is a treasury of poetry for reading and meditation that is loved by both Jews and Christians. Since many of the Psalms were written for public and private worship, the Hebrew title is "Praises," a word referring to poetic compositions accompanied by stringed instruments. The book is divided into five sections of unique characteristics, each closing with a doxology. Nearly half of the Psalms are credited to David, with the rest divided among several writers or written anonymously. Careful reading of the Psalms will serve to vitalize a believer's prayers and devotions.

PROVERBS derives its title from a Hebrew word meaning "to be like, similar, or parallel," which refers to the poetic style. A proverb is a profound idea in distilled form. These bits of truth are intended to give behavioral, moral,

and spiritual guidance. The most typical type of proverb in this book is the metaphor, which teaches truth by utilizing comparison or, more often, contrast. Many of the proverbs are meant to give instruction on how to act in certain situations. Over 500 of the 3,000 proverbs that Solomon spoke are preserved in this book.

ECCLESIASTES is entitled from a Greek word that means "preacher" or "one who calls an assembly together." The book is read at the annual Jewish Feast of Tabernacles, and is one of three books written by Solomon. It is probable that he wrote the Song of Solomon in his youth, Proverbs in his maturity, and Ecclesiastes in his old age. Two Hebrew expressions stand out in the book: "futility of futilities" and "under the sun." "Futility" occurs 37 times and indicates the fleeting, futile, and puzzling nature of life. "Under the sun" occurs 29 times and refers to the secular life. The ultimate answer to the meaning of life is to obey God and enjoy fellowship with Him.

SONG OF SOLOMON is a love song extolling faithfulness in marriage. It was written by Solomon in honor of his first marriage to a Shulamite girl (Eccl 9:9). Solomon wrote over 1,000 songs, and this one was God's choice to be preserved and handed down in the Scriptures. Read during Passover, it is the first of the five scrolls that are to be read by Jews at various annual feasts.

ISAIAH is a name meaning "Salvation of the LORD." Isaiah came from an aristocratic family in the kingdom of Judah. He is considered the greatest prophet, but he was also a great political advisor and voice for spiritual renewal. Isaiah gives the most varied picture of the Messiah of any Old Testament writer. Of special importance is his presentation of the Suffering Servant, which reaches its apex in Isaiah 52:13 through 53:12—the most detailed account of the sufferings of Christ to be found in the Old Testament. It is quoted or alluded to 85 times in the New Testament.

JEREMIAH is a name meaning "the Lord lifts up." He is the prophet of a New Covenant which will be written "on the heart." Jeremiah lived through a time of great change among the world powers with the fall of Assyria, the decline of Egypt and the rise of the Babylonian Empire. The kings of Judah were trusting more in international agreements than in God. The book of Jeremiah contains prophecies against Judah, oracles against the Gentiles, and historical and biographical information.

LAMENTATIONS is a poetic book mourning the fall of Jerusalem in 586 BC, one of the more tragic events in Old Testament history. The event is mentioned many times in God's word, and in Lamentations it receives its most poignant expression. The book consists of five poems artistically structured and filled with anguish. The first four poems are in an acrostic form of the Hebrew alphabet, each section

beginning with a successive letter of the 22 letters of the alphabet. Though this is the most mournful book of the Old Testament, in 3:22-26 there is an expression of hope in the Lord.

EZEKIEL was a priest taken into captivity in 597 BC during the second deportation, which was imposed on the Jewish leaders and aristocracy by Babylon. Ezekiel's house served as a meeting place for Hebrew elders as he ministered to the Israelites in exile. The fall of Jerusalem (586 BC) divides his ministry into two distinct parts. Before the fall he preaches repentance and a coming judgment on Jerusalem because of the sins of the people. After the fall, he preaches a message of consolation and reform which looks forward to an eventual restoration of Israel. The book of Ezekiel contains colorful prophecies like the vision of the valley of dry bones (Ezek 38) and other key prophecies for the end times, making it required reading for anyone who wants to know God's plans for the future.

DANIEL is the work of a lad of noble birth who rose to high positions of authority while in exile in Babylon. His ministry extended through the duration of the exile, covering the reigns of Nebuchadnezzar, Belshazzar, Darius, and Cyrus. The book details critical events during the reigns of these Babylonian kings. Throughout his experiences Daniel remained true to God and His leading in his life. Key passages in the book of Daniel include special revelations about the future of human empires in the world, and the promise of a Messiah who would bring lasting peace.

HOSEA was a younger contemporary of Amos in Israel, and of Isaiah and Micah in Judah. He saw the moral decline when sin dominated the social and spiritual life of the people. Through the experience of marriage to an unfaithful woman, a marriage ordered by God, Hosea comes to understand the love of God for His people, and the heartbreak of their unfaithfulness. The book is a reminder that sin is similar to infidelity in marriage, but there is hope for restoration because of God's great love.

JOEL is a name meaning "The Lord is God." Joel was from Judah, and he was acquainted with the Temple, to which he often refers. In his book he describes a plague of locusts and a severe drought, events which provide the basis for a message about God's judgment and the need to repent, pray, and fast. This judgment, "The Day of the Lord," does not refer to a single specific time but to a judgment that may come from God at any time. Joel's plea is summed up in 2:12-13, where the people are urged to return to a God of compassion and lovingkindness.

AMOS was a native of Tekoa, a town south of Jerusalem. He was a herdsman and grower of figs whom God called to proclaim His truth in Bethel, a town north of Jerusalem on the main road through the hill country. Here he examines the religious life of a self-satisfied

people whose worship and religious practices are abhorrent to God. The book is written in clear, forceful, and dramatic language in which the justice of God is prophesied to "roll out like waters and righteousness like an ever-flowing stream."

OBADIAH is the shortest book of the Old Testament, written by a prophet whose common Hebrew name means "Servant of the Lord." The occasion for the book is one of five invasions of Jerusalem, probably that of the Philistines and tribes of Arabia in 845 BC. The nation of Edom (descendants of Esau) revolted from Judah at this time, another episode in the long history of strife between Judah and Edom which hearkened back to the sibling rivalry between Esau and Jacob. The message against Edom in this book is fulfilled after 70 AD, when the nation disappears from history.

JONAH prophesied in the time of Jeroboam II, king of Israel. He predicted victory for the king, who was able to extend his realm and enjoy a time of peace and prosperity. At this time Jonah was called by God to go and preach repentance to an enemy nation trying to destroy his own people. He tries to flee from God, but after the experience of being swallowed by the "great fish" and other events, he finally resigns himself to the call and goes to give God's message to Nineveh.

MICAH is a name that means "who is like the Lord." Micah was a peasant farmer from a quiet village southwest of Jerusalem. He became a preacher of personal faith and ethics who tried to deter his countrymen from their evil course. At the time, the poor were oppressed to support the rich who could "buy" justice, and there were false prophets and corrupt priests. Micah predicted some events which have already occurred, such as the birth of the Messiah in Bethlehem, and some still in the future, like the regathering of Israel and the battle of Har-Magedon (Armageddon).

NAHUM was written by a native of Elkosh. Nahum prophesied at a time when Assyria was the dominant empire, and Nineveh was its most powerful city. The Assyrian king had conquered Egypt, and his son was a scholar-king who built libraries and palaces. It was at this time that God gave Nahum the message that Nineveh was to be destroyed. At the time, Nineveh was a strongly fortified city with walls 50 feet high and over 7 miles in circumference. The city was completely destroyed in 612 BC by the Babylonians, Medes, and Scythians.

HABAKKUK is a name that seems to have come from a Hebrew word meaning "to embrace." Habakkuk was a prominent citizen of Jerusalem. He prophesied after the fall of Nineveh in 612 BC and prior to the first invasion of Judah in 605 BC. It was a time of national trouble. King Josiah was killed at Megiddo, and his son ruled for only three months before being carried off to Egypt. God

gives Habakkuk the revelation that the "righteous will live by faith" and not by sight. He explains what will take place in five woes which will apply to Babylon and Judah.

ZEPHANIAH was a member of the royal house of Judah, and great-grandson of King Hezekiah. His name means "The Lord hides," which suggests that his parents gave him the name as a prayer for his safety. Zephaniah ministered during eventful times when King Josiah instituted his reforms, purging the country of Baal and restoring the worship of God. Zephaniah predicts the invasion of Judah and also judgment on the Gentile nations surrounding Judah. There is hope for all who "seek the Lord" (2:3).

HAGGAI is a name meaning "festal," and may indicate that this prophet was born during the time of a feast. He may have witnessed the destruction of Solomon's temple. Haggai preaches to those who have returned from captivity, encouraging them to rebuild the temple. He stresses the consequences of disobedience, as well as the blessings of obedience. When people give priority to God and His house, they are blessed for their obedience. For disobedience, they can expect to be cursed.

ZECHARIAH was a prophet of priestly lineage. He was born in Babylon, and was murdered in the temple compound in Jerusalem. His name means "The Lord remembers," and he records and interprets visions which he received from God. His messages were delivered to the Jews who had returned from exile. Some messages were directed to the high priest and to the governor. Zechariah makes prophecies about the first and second advents of the Messiah, and is a prophet of hope in the midst of despair.

MALACHI means "messenger," which may not be a name, but only a description. Little is known about him. He preached between the two terms of Nehemiah as governor of Judah, that is, from 432 to 420 BC. Malachi begins with the statement that the Lord "loved" Jacob and "hated" Esau. These words cover the whole range of relationships between God and people, from a non-relationship ("hate") to a strong, positive relationship. Malachi prophesies the coming of John the Baptist, and ends the book with the promise of judgment for the wicked, and hope for those who repent of sin and turn to the Lord.

THE GOSPELS, THE GOOD NEWS, contain divinely inspired accounts of the life of Jesus Christ, the Messiah, the eternal Son of God. The Gospels take us from Old Testament Law, given by Moses, to New Testament Grace through the message of the cross—the sacrifice of Jesus Christ, the spotless, perfect, sinless, blood offering.

MATTHEW, one of the twelve apostles, accepted Jesus as the Christ (Messiah), the eternal Son of God, and left his job in

Capernaum as a tax collector for the Romans to follow Him. Matthew records the birth and life of Jesus, His crucifixion, resurrection, and ascension. This Gospel sets forth the distinction between law and grace. Jesus is the eternal High Priest and gives Himself as the spotless, perfect blood sacrifice for all sinners, once for all time. Matthew tells us of conflicts between Jesus and the Jewish religious authorities, and he records five great discourses by Jesus, including the Sermon on the Mount.

MARK: The Gospel of Mark is a fast-moving narrative of the life of Jesus as the Servant King and His divine authority over illness, demon activity, and the created world as evidenced by twenty-one miracles! Mark gives us an account of God's Servant, Jesus Christ, atoning for our sins by His crucifixion, and His resurrection. Mark concludes with the great commandment of Jesus, the Christ, the Messiah, to His followers to be His witnesses throughout the world (16:15).

LUKE was a physician and a Gentile who recorded the birth, ministry, death, resurrection, and ascension of Christ. Luke tells us of Jesus the Messiah, who provides redemption for all believers. Prayer and praise dominate the Gospel of Luke, and twenty-seven parables spoken by Jesus are recorded. The Gospel of Luke is a constant source of joy to all who first learn, or are reminded of God's grace through His Messiah, the Redeemer— Jesus Christ who purchased salvation for all who trust Christ's shed blood and thereby become recipients of eternal life!

JOHN was an eye-witness of Jesus Christ throughout His earthly ministry, and he rejoiced to see the risen Christ the very day of the resurrection. The Gospel of John emphasizes Jesus Christ as God. Its purpose is to bring people to faith in Christ as Savior and Lord so that they will have eternal life. John records nine discourses given by Jesus and eight miracles. John wants us to know that Jesus is God, the Bread of Life, the Light of the world, the Door, the Good Shepherd, the Resurrection and the Life, the Way, the Truth and the Life, and the True Vine.

ACTS: The Book of Acts is the record by Luke the physician of the power of the Holy Spirit and His work through the apostles of Jesus. Luke was an eye-witness of many of the events, and he provides details about the activities of key leaders in the early church and emphasizes the supernatural character of the Christian faith. The Book of Acts provides the historic background for ten of Paul's letters and documents nine sermons each by Peter and Paul. It reveals God's leadership of His church through His chosen servants, the apostles.

ROMANS: The righteousness of God is revealed in Romans by the Apostle Paul, writing under the inspiration of the Holy Spirit. Romans is the key to understanding Paul's

teachings throughout the New Testament. The first man, Adam, sinned by disobeying God and the result is that all people are sinners, doomed to eternal death. But God provides salvation by His grace (unmerited favor) through faith alone; it cannot be earned by human effort of any kind. Justification and righteousness (right standing before God) are provided in and through Christ to all who accept Him as Lord and Savior. Paul emphasizes that salvation is directly available to all mankind, both Jews and Gentiles. He also discusses various responsibilities of those who accept and believe in Christ Jesus: they are to be subject to civil authorities, they are to serve one another, and in general are to become like Christ in their values and personal conduct.

FIRST CORINTHIANS: The Apostle Paul addresses divisions and dissension in the church, problems of immorality, unethical behavior, and more. The wisdom of God is contrasted with the wisdom of the world. Paul answers several questions about marriage and teaches the proper use of Christian liberty. He describes worship that honors the Lord, teaches the proper use of spiritual gifts, and gives instruction on the resurrection and the collection for needy believers in Jerusalem.

SECOND CORINTHIANS: The Apostle Paul again deals with the continuing tension, divisions, and strife in the Church at Corinth. False teachers had crept in, and some of the members were refusing to repent of sinful behavior. Also, Paul's personal integrity and authority as an apostle were being challenged by his opponents. He writes this letter in part to defend his apostleship, while at the same time showing his concern and love for the readers. Paul explains his ministry in detail, and describes his feelings, desires, obligations, and responsibilities to the church.

GALATIANS: The Apostle Paul again proclaims the gospel to the church at Galatia. Jewish Christians erroneously insisted that the Gentile converts to Christianity abide by certain Old Testament laws and rituals, especially circumcision. But Paul sternly corrects his readers and explains again that a person is saved solely by the grace of God (God's unmerited favor) through faith in Jesus Christ, the Messiah. Believers are to be led by the Holy Spirit, not by the law, and the leading of the Spirit will be evidenced by good attitudes and behavior toward others.

EPHESIANS: The Apostle Paul writes this letter to the church in Ephesus while imprisoned in Rome. Paul proclaims salvation by grace through faith in Jesus Christ, not by good deeds, not by being a good person. There is to be unity among believers, made possible by the Holy Spirit. The church is the body of Christ, and Christ is the head of the church. Believers are to be imitators of God and to live in love under control of the Holy Spirit. In that regard, Paul provides a number of admonitions and offers encouragement for setting a good

Christian example in a variety of challenging situations.

PHILIPPIANS: Paul speaks of unity among Christians and reminds them that God's abundant grace brings Christians joy even in the midst of adversity and suffering. The ultimate example of the joy of service is that of Christ's own humility and exaltation (2:1-11). Paul tells of salvation's joy for believers, cautions about those who advocate good works as a substitute for righteousness received through faith in Christ, and reveals the source of peace and serenity.

COLOSSIANS: Paul warns his readers of heresy and gives the Biblical view of the person and work of Christ as refutation of it. Paul teaches that understanding the grace of God motivates Christians to allow Christ first place in all things. He explains how this principle should be applied at home, work, prayer, and with unbelievers.

FIRST THESSALONIANS: In this book Paul offers his readers encouragement and hope for dealing with the loss of departed loved ones who have died believing in Christ. He also instructs them to practice moral purity, brotherly love, good work ethics, and to comfort those who have deceased loved ones. He assures believers of deliverance from the coming judgment of the Day of the Lord, and urges them to be watchful and orderly at all times.

SECOND THESSALONIANS: Paul reveals some of the signs and events leading to the Day of the Lord, the second coming of Jesus Christ, the Messiah. There will be persecution of believers, increased lawlessness, and apostasy (denunciation of the faith). The man of lawlessness, the Antichrist, will be revealed and worshiped; he will enter the temple of God and proclaim that he himself is God. But Christians need not fear—the Lord Jesus is in control and He will destroy the Antichrist. Paul encourages his readers not to get tired of doing good, and to discipline those among them who become rebellious.

FIRST TIMOTHY: Paul extols fighting the good fight (1:18), keeping faith, and maintaining a good conscience. He urges prayers, petitions to God, and giving thanks on behalf of all people. He gives instructions for public worship and sets forth qualifications for overseers and deacons. Paul warns against heretics and those who see ministry as a source of financial gain.

SECOND TIMOTHY: The Apostle Paul was awaiting his execution by the Romans when he wrote this letter to Timothy. In the letter, he tells Timothy to be strong in the grace that is in Christ Jesus, and to suffer hardship as a good soldier of Christ. He warns that difficult times will come and orders Timothy to "preach the word." In closing, Paul states, "I have fought the good fight, I have finished the course, I have kept the faith" (4:7).

TITUS: God desires that Christians be a credit to their faith in Christ in the church, at home, and in the world. Paul writes to Titus the Greek, who ministers on the island of Crete. Paul instructs him how to appoint the right kind of leaders in the church. He is to teach Christians, regardless of age or status, how to demonstrate their faith in the home and family. Titus is to warn the believers about those beliefs and behaviors that detract from their Christian testimony to the world.

PHILEMON: This brief letter is a masterpiece in Christian diplomacy, setting the example of how to deal with a serious conflict between brothers and sisters in Christ. During Paul's house arrest in Rome, Onesimus, a runaway slave, came into contact with Paul and was brought to faith in Christ by him. The two of them agreed that Onesimus should return to his master, Philemon. In the letter, Paul leaves it to Philemon to decide whether to retain Onesimus or to return him to Paul; he maintains that God's pardoning grace provides sufficient motive to forgive Onesimus and accept him into fellowship as a Christian brother. He does not address slavery as an issue, which indicates that Onesimus was in this position to make restitution for an unpaid debt, or a robbery or embezzlement committed against Philemon. Scripture does not record the result of Paul's request, but according to tradition, Onesimus was freed. There is a strong comparison to the New Covenant: the Master, the disobedience of people, and an everlasting guarantee (redemption and salvation from sin and eternal punishment).

HEBREWS: The people to whom Hebrews was written were steeped in Jewish law and tradition, but they had heard the gospel and had witnessed miracles. While they had grasped basic spiritual principles, their deficiencies included an unresponsive attitude to sound teaching and a reluctance to practice what they knew to be right. There were some committed Christians, including converted Jewish priests, who endured suffering for their faith. Others had been intellectually persuaded about Christianity but remained uncommitted in terms of their personal relationships with Christ, and some were not yet convinced of the truth of the gospel. This letter of exhortation reminds the Jewish converts and others of God's provision of a perfect priest and sacrifice for sin, in Jesus Christ.

JAMES: This letter by the half-brother of our Lord Jesus is a handbook of practical Christianity. It is a lesson in contrasts, like genuine and counterfeit wisdom, and true and false faith. The challenge to all Christians, is "If you possess genuine faith in Christ for salvation, demonstrate it!" Christians are to endure suffering with joy and to render service as a natural result of their faith. The best evidence of genuine faith is found in the way one lives.

FIRST PETER: The Apostle Peter describes people as living in spiritual ignorance and darkness until they accept Jesus as the Christ, High Priest, and Lord. God is the source of confidence to every believer who experiences trials and suffering. The proper conduct for a believer is illustrated by the suffering of Christ. Christians are to love and serve one another by using their spiritual gifts. Spiritual leaders are to edify those in their care, and all believers are to be vigilant in the fight against the devil.

SECOND PETER: In this letter the Apostle Peter is admonishing Christians who are being bombarded with false teaching in contrast to the truth. Peter warns them that false teachers promise counterfeit freedom and are motivated by personal gain. The antidote for false teaching is full and true spiritual knowledge. The divine realities of the Christian faith are highlighted for the instruction of the readers. Peter wishes for all his readers to continue growing both in grace and in the knowledge of the Lord Jesus.

FIRST JOHN: The Apostle John speaks to Christians as children in the family of God. John wants them to know that they really are in God's family, so he outlines several confirmations of the new birth. He also warns them that false prophets and opponents of Christ have joined forces to deceive Christians and draw them away from the truth. Love is an important aspect of John's teaching, and it is mentioned over fifty times in this short letter.

SECOND JOHN: In this letter, the Apostle John states the essentials of Christian conduct for the believer in Christ, and gives further warning about false teachers and heresies. As in John's day, believers always need to be wary of spiritual leaders who attempt to modify sound Biblical teaching.

THIRD JOHN: This letter condemns a man named Diotrephes, who had repudiated the Apostle John's authority by rejecting his letter to the church in which Diotrephes was a leader. Not only had he maligned John; he also refused to receive workers approved by John, and removed those who did receive them from the church. This brief letter encourages all believers to show hospitality to their fellow servants of Christ.

JUDE: The letter of Jude warns us about false teachers who creep in among those who truly believe in Jesus Christ. Jude characterizes ungodly leaders so that they can be identified and confronted. There is need for the renewal of spiritual fervor for the faith, and for rescue of those who are falling prey to ungodliness.

REVELATION: The apostle John was exiled to the island of Patmos in the Mediterranean (Aegean) Sea. While there, he received divine visions of things past, things present, and things future. Among other things, the book of Revelation tells us of the Second Coming of Jesus Christ (as King and Judge), the great tribulation, the millennium (a thousand years), the battle of Armageddon, the great white throne of judgment, and the New Jerusalem. Revelation was written in response to the direct command of the Lord, and there is a promise of blessing to all who read or hear its words.

Read Through the Bible In a Year

Jan.	Genesis	Matthew
1	1, 2, 3	1
2	4, 5, 6	2
3	7, 8, 9	3
4	10, 11, 12	4
5	13, 14, 15	5:1-26
6	16, 17	5:27-48
7	18, 19	6:1-18
8	20, 21, 22	6:19-34
9	23, 24	7
10	25, 26	8:1-17
11	27, 28	8:18-34
12	29, 30	9:1-17
13	31, 32	9:18-38
14	33, 34, 35	10:1-23
15	36, 37, 38	10:24-42
16	39, 40	11
17	41, 42	12:1-21
18	43, 44, 45	12:22-50
19	46, 47, 48	13:1-30
20	49, 50	13:31-58
21	Psalms 1-3	14:1-21
22	Exodus 1-3	14:22-36
23	4, 5, 6	15:1-20
24	7, 8	15:21-39
25	9, 10, 11	16
26	12, 13	17
27	14, 15	18:1-20
28	16, 17, 18	18:21-35
29	19, 20	19
30	21, 22	20:1-16
31	23, 24	20:17-34
Feb.	Exodus	Matthew
1	25, 26	21:1-22
2	27, 28	21:23-46
3	29, 30	22:1-22
4	31, 32, 33	22:23-46
5	34, 35	23:1-22
6	36, 37, 38	23:23-39
7	39, 40	24:1-28
8	Psalms 4-6	24:29-51
9	Leviticus 1-3	25:1-30
10	4, 5	25:31-46
11	6, 7	26:1-25
12	8, 9, 10	26:26-46
13	11, 12	26:47-75
14	13	27:1-26
15	14	27:27-50
16	15, 16	27:51-66
17	17, 18	28
18	19, 20	Psalms 7-9
19	21, 22	Mark 1:1-22

Feb.	Leviticus	Mark
20	23, 24	1:23-45
21	25	2
22	26, 27	3
23	Psalms 10-12	4:1-25
24	Numbers 1, 2	4:26-41
25	3, 4	5:1-20
26	5, 6, 7	5:21-43
27	8, 9, 10	6:1-29
28	11, 12, 13	6:30-56
March	Numbers	Mark
1	14, 15, 16	7:1-13
2	17, 18, 19	7:14-37
3	20, 21, 22	8:1-21
4	23, 24, 25	8:22-38
5	26, 27	9:1-29
6	28, 29, 30	9:30-50
7	31, 32, 33	10:1-31
8	34, 35, 36	10:32-52
9	Psalms 13-15	11:1-18
10	Deuteronomy 1, 2	11:19-33
11	3, 4	12:1-27
12	5, 6, 7	12:28-44
13	8, 9, 10	13:1-20
14	11, 12, 13	13:21-37
15	14, 15, 16	14:1-31
16	17, 18, 19	14:32-52
17	20, 21, 22	14:53-72
18	23, 24, 25	15:1-25
19	26, 27	15:26-47
20	28, 29	16
21	30, 31	Psalms 16, 17
22	32, 33, 34	Luke 1:1-20
23	Psalms 18, 19	1:21-38
24	Joshua 1-3	1:39-56
25	4, 5, 6	1:57-80
26	7, 8, 9	2:1-24
27	10, 11, 12	2:25-52
28	13, 14, 15	3
29	16, 17, 18	4:1-30
30	19, 20, 21	4:31-44
31	22, 23, 24	5:1-16
April	Psalms	Luke
1	20, 21, 22	5:17-39
2	Judges 1-3	6:1-26
3	4, 5, 6	6:27-49
4	7, 8	7:1-30
5	9, 10	7:31-50
6	11, 12	8:1-25
7	13, 14, 15	8:26-56
8	16, 17, 18	9:1-17
9	19, 20, 21	9:18-36

July	Job	Acts
24	32, 33	22
25	34, 35	23:1-15
26	36, 37	23:16-35
27	38, 39, 40	24
28	41, 42	25
29	Psalms 57-59	26
30	Proverbs 1, 2	27:1-26
31	3, 4, 5	27:27-44
Aug.	Proverbs	Acts
1	6, 7	28
2	8, 9	Psalms 60-62
3	10, 11, 12	Romans 1
4	13, 14, 15	2
5	16, 17, 18	3
6	19, 20, 21	4
7	22, 23, 24	5
8	25, 26	6
9	27, 28, 29	7
10	30, 31	8:1-21
11	Psalms 63-65	8:22-39
12	Ecclesiastes 1-3	9:1-15
13	4, 5, 6	9:16-33
14	7, 8, 9	10
15	10, 11, 12	11:1-18
16	Psalms 66, 67	11:19-36
17	Song of Sol. 1-3	12
18	4, 5	13
19	6, 7, 8	14
20	Psalms 68, 69	15:1-13
21	Isaiah 1, 2	15:14-33
22	3, 4	16
23	5, 6	Psalms 70, 71
24	7, 8	1 Corinthians 1
25	9, 10	2
26	11, 12, 13	3
27	14, 15, 16	4
28	17, 18, 19	5
29	20, 21, 22	6
30	23, 24, 25	7:1-19
31	26, 27	7:20-40
Sept.	Isaiah	1 Corinthians
1	28, 29	8
2	30, 31	9
3	32, 33	10:1-18
4	34, 35, 36	10:19-33
5	37, 38	11:1-16
6	39, 40	11:17-34
7	41, 42	12
8	43, 44	13
9	45, 46	14:1-20
10	47, 48, 49	14:21-40
11	50, 51, 52	15:1-28
12	53, 54, 55	15:29-58
13	56, 57, 58	16

Sept.	Isaiah	Psalms
14	59, 60, 61	72, 73
15	62, 63, 64	2 Corinthians 1
16	65, 66	2
17	Psalms 74-76	3
18	Jeremiah 1, 2	4
19	3, 4, 5	5
20	6, 7, 8	6
21	9, 10, 11	7
22	12, 13, 14	8
23	15, 16, 17	9
24	18, 19	10
25	20, 21	11
26	22, 23	12
27	24, 25, 26	13
28	27, 28, 29	Psalms 77, 78
29	30, 31	Galatians 1
30	32, 33	2
Oct.	Jeremiah	Galatians
1	34, 35, 36	3
2	37, 38, 39	4
3	40, 41, 42	5
4	43, 44, 45	6
5	46, 47	Psalms 79, 80
6	48, 49	Ephesians 1
7	50	2
8	51, 52	3
9	Psalms 81-83	4
10	Lamentations 1, 2	5
11	3, 4, 5	6
12	Psalms 84-86	Philippians 1
13	Ezekiel 1, 2	2
14	3, 4	3
15	5, 6, 7	4
16	8, 9, 10	Psalms 87, 88
17	11, 12, 13	Psalms 89, 90
18	14, 15	Colossians 1
19	16, 17	2
20	18, 19	3
21	20, 21	4
22	22, 23	Psalms 91-93
23	24, 25, 26	1 Thess 1
24	27, 28, 29	2
25	30, 31, 32	3
26	33, 34	4
27	35, 36	5
28	37, 38, 39	Psalms 94-96
29	40, 41	2 Thess 1
30	42, 43, 44	2
31	45, 46	3
Nov.	Ezekiel	Psalms
1	47, 48	97-99
2	Psalms 100-102	1 Timothy 1
3	Daniel 1, 2	2
4	3, 4	3

The Parables of Jesus

This list includes allegories, similes, and proverbs that have characteristics of parables.

	Matthew	Mark	Luke	John
New cloth on an old garment	9:16	2:21	5:36	
New wine into old wineskins	9:17	2:22	5:37	
Make friends with your opponent	5:25, 26		12:58, 59	
The blind guiding the blind			6:39	
The two foundations	7:24-27		6:48, 49	
Children in the marketplaces	11:16, 17		7:32	
Unclean spirit	12:43-45		11:24-26	
The sower	13:3-8	4:3-8	8:5-8	
Weeds among wheat	13:24-30			
The growth of the seed		4:26-29		
The mustard seed	13:31, 32	4:31, 32	13:18, 19	
The leaven	13:33		13:21	
The hidden treasure	13:44			
A costly pearl	13:45, 46			
A dragnet	13:47, 48			
The head of a household	13:52			
The lost sheep	18:12, 13		15:3-6	
The two debtors	18:23, 24		7:41, 42	
The good Samaritan			10:30-37	
Friend in need			11:5-8	
The foolish rich man			12:16-21	
The alert slaves			12:35-38	
The fruitless fig tree			13:6-9	
The great banquet			14:15-24	
The tower			14:28-30	
The king that sets out to battle			14:31, 32	
The lost coin			15:8, 9	
The prodigal son			15:11-32	
The unrighteous steward			16:1-8	
The rich man and Lazarus			16:19-31	
The master and his servant			17:7-10	
The widow and the unrighteous judge			18:2-8	
The Pharisee and the Publican			18:10-14	
The vine-growers			20:1-15	
Money usage			19:13-27	
The two sons	21:28-31			
The evil farmers	21:33-39	12:1-8	20:9-15	
The wedding feast	22:2-13			
The fig tree	24:32			
The man away on a journey		13:34		
The faithful and unfaithful slave	24:45-51		12:41-48	
The ten virgins	25:1-12			
The talents	25:14-30			
The vine and the branches				15:1-7

The Miracles of Jesus

	Matthew	Mark	Luke	John
Turning water into wine				2:1-12
Healing a nobleman's son				4:46-54
The first fish catch			5:1-11	
Healing a possessed man		1:21-28	4:33-35	
Healing Simon's mother-in-law	8:14-17	1:29-34	4:38-41	
Healing a man with leprosy	8:2-4	1:40-45	5:12-16	
Healing a paralyzed man	9:1-8	2:1-12	5:17-26	
The healing at Bethesda				5:1-9
Healing a man with a withered hand	12:9-14	3:1-6	6:6-11	
Healing the centurion's servant	8:5-13		7:1-10	
Resurrecting the widow's son at Nain			7:11-17	
Healing a demon possessed man	12:22-37		11:14	
Jesus calms the storm	8:23-27	4:35-41	8:22-25	
Jesus casts out demons	8:28-34	5:1-20	8:26-39	
Healing of a hemorrhaging woman	9:20-22	5:25-34	8:43-48	
Resurrecting Jairus's daughter	9:18, 19, 23-35	5:22-24, 35-43	8:40-42, 49-56	
Healing of two blind men and a mute	9:27-34			
Five thousand fed	14:15-21	6:35-44	9:12-17	6:5-14
Jesus walks on water	14:24-33	6:47-52		6:16-21
Healing of the Syrophoenician woman's daughter	15:21-28	7:24-30		
Healing of a deaf man		7:32-35		
Four thousand fed	15:32-38	8:1-9		
Healing a blind man in Bethsaida		8:22-26		
Healing a demon possessed boy	17:14-21	9:14-29	9:37-43	
The shekel in the fish	17:27			
Healing of a man unable to speak			11:14-26	
Healing of a sick woman			13:10-17	
Healing the man born blind				9:1-41
Healing of a man with edema			14:1-6	
Resurrecting Lazarus				11:38-44
Ten men with leprosy cleansed			17:12-19	
Bartimaeus receives sight	20:29-34	10:46-52	18:35-43	
The barren fig tree withers	21:18, 19	11:12-14		
Healing of the slave's right ear			22:50, 51	18:10
The second fish catch				21:4-6